INTERNATIONAL ENVIRONMENTAL LAW AND POLICY

SECOND EDITION

by

DAVID HUNTER
Senior Advisor, Center for International Environmental Law
Adjunct Professor of Law
Washington College of Law, American University

JAMES SALZMAN
Professor of Law
Washington College of Law, American University

DURWOOD ZAELKE
President, Center for International Environmental Law
Adjunct Professor of Law
Washington College of Law, American University

NEW YORK, NEW YORK
FOUNDATION PRESS
2002

COPYRIGHT © 1998 FOUNDATION PRESS

COPYRIGHT © 2002 By FOUNDATION PRESS

        395 Hudson Street

        New York, NY 10014

        Phone Toll Free 1–877–888–1330

        Fax (212) 367–6799

        fdpress.com

All Rights Reserved

Printed in the United States of America

ISBN 1–58778–084–4

TEXT IS PRINTED ON 10% POST CONSUMER RECYCLED PAPER

To Margaret, Dana and Sandy
D.H.

To Lisa and the Beans
J.S.

To Barbara, Cassidy and Hannah
D.Z.

*

INTRODUCTION

International environmental law and policy have come of age in the past decade, riveting the public's attention with news of ozone holes, climate change, and species extinctions. A young and dynamic field, international environmental law's importance cannot be underestimated for it involves, quite literally, the fate of future generations and that of the earth.

There are three basic reasons we wrote this book. First, all of us have practiced international environmental law and policy "in the field"—in government, business, and non-governmental organizations. While a theoretical foundation is essential in understanding international environmental law, so, too, is a sense of what really happens on the ground. We seek to impart a sophisticated understanding of the law as it is and, perhaps more important, as it could be.

Second, teaching materials in the field often present the field as a two-person play—focusing on the role of State actors (national governments) and international institutions to the exclusion of other key actors. In exploring the dynamics of the lawmaking process and implementation, we intentionally move beyond the traditional focus on State actors to assess the increasingly critical roles of transnational actors—citizens, nongovernmental organizations, scientists and business.

Finally, we believe that international environmental law and policy deserves treatment as an independent field, not as a subset of environmental law or public international law. To be sure, there are many areas of overlap; but international environmental law is fundamentally different in key respects.

The study of international environmental law is, initially, the study of facts, wild facts, that reflect our growing global environmental problems. These include climate change, ozone destruction, wildlife extinction and loss of biological diversity, and the contamination of air, land, and water throughout the world. These facts are the challenge international environmental lawyers—and ultimately our whole society—must address with a new and more powerful international environmental law. Any student who fully understands these facts should be motivated to learn what role the law can play in moving us toward a more sustainable future.

International environmental law also requires the study of human activity that lies at the root of each environmental problem, and how that activity has expanded due to our expanding population and consumption. Today, human economic activity threatens to surpass the ecological limits of the biosphere (if it has not already done so in certain instances). This is the challenge of discovering the limits of the biosphere through science, and determining the "scale" of economic activity that can be sustained within these limits—that is, what level of "development" is "sustainable."

International environmental law is the study of how we can and do use law to address the environmental challenges caused by our current level of economic development. This starts with the study of the process of making international law, including the study of a system described by one scholar/practitioner of the profession as "post-feudal society set in amber," a medieval system where only nation States can participate, and where citizens, industry, and environmental organizations have historically been excluded. The generally weak and exclusionary international system contrasts starkly with the robust and inclusive nature of many national law systems, and presents another challenge to international environmental lawyers.

Next is the study of the institutions that participate in the making, implementation and enforcement of international environmental law. In addition to nation States, this includes various United Nations organizations as well as other international and regional organizations. The role played by the corporate sector is critically important, especially the larger multinational corporations, as is the growing role played by the non-governmental sector, including such groups as Greenpeace, World Wildlife Fund, Sierra Club, World Conservation Union and the Center for International Environmental Law.

International environmental law is the study of relevant principles of law that may build upon traditional international law principles yet also are influenced by science, ethics, and political pragmatism. Principles such as the precautionary principle, the polluter pays principle, the principle of common but differentiated responsibilities, and the principle of subsidiarity all help provide an emerging framework for the development of international environmental law. They provide guidance for the negotiation and implementation of international environmental instruments and for resolving environmental disputes.

In sum, the study of international environmental law requires an understanding of the problems of environmental degradation and their causes, of the legal process for addressing the problems, including the process of law-making, compliance monitoring and dispute resolution, of the players who cause the problems and those who make the law to address the problems, and of the legal principles that form the foundation for the treaty law that now dominates the field. This comprises the first part of the book.

The second part of the book examines specific international environmental problems and the treaties and other legal mechanisms created in response. We begin with pollution of the air and atmosphere, including the specific regimes that address ozone depletion, climate change, and transndary air pollution. We then examine oceans, rivers and lakes, chemicals and hazardous wastes, wildlife, biodiversity, and the conservation of living natural resources and their habitats. These specific subjects are presented in the context of sustainable development. Cross-cutting themes include:

• the relation of our scientific understanding of the problem to the legal response;

• the relation of the problem to the global economy, e.g. fossil fuel emissions and oil;

• the evolution of the lawmaking process including the use of soft law, framework agreements, binding obligations, enforcement, and amendment procedures;

• the role of concepts and principles of international environmental law in the development of the field;

• the role of non-State actors, especially business and NGOs;

• the dynamic between the relatively rich and industrialized countries and the relatively poor and developing countries;

• the role of technology transfer, financial mechanisms and other steps for facilitating implementation of international environmental commitments;

• the domestic implementation and enforcement of international agreements.

We apply the knowledge learned in the first part on a problem-by-problem, and treaty-by-treaty basis, to learn what ecological constraints are being tested, and what the specific legal response has been. We also examine which factors were significant in building the consensus needed for nation States to agree to a specific treaty, including the role non-governmental organizations and corporations played, and the impacts on economic and technological development. We consider how the current response measures up to what the world could be doing.

The third section of the book examines the intersection of international environmental law with other fields, such as trade and international investment agreements, the law of war, human rights, and corporate codes of conduct. Since powerful protection of the international environment is provided by national laws, we also examine the extraterritorial application of domestic law. To a large extent the success of this integration process will determine our overall success in moving toward sustainable development.

This book is not intended to be taught from cover-to-cover in a one semester course. Rather, we encourage students and professors to select from among the subjects addressed, to tailor their courses to suit interests and concerns. The text's breadth of coverage is also intended to serve as a starting point for research seminars and specialty courses within the field, such as trade and environment or oceans law. The Teacher's Manual provides a number of syllabi and specific suggestions on teaching the material.

Beyond revisions describing developments in the field, our second edition of this book has been guided by comments from teachers over the last three years. In particular, we have added Working the Treaty sections for all the major agreements (questions that can only be answered by the students reading treaty text carefully), new Problem Exercises on Shipbreakers, the Balkans conflict, Forest Negotiations, Climate Negotiations, and POPs, and a completely revised chapter on Human Rights. Chapters 2 and 4 from the First edition have been combined into a new Chapter 2 – Root

Causes – and the history chapter has been moved up to Chapter 4, following the chapter on economics.

Such an undertaking would not have been possible without the assistance of many people. For the first edition, we thank our CIEL Law Fellows Carroll Muffett and Matthew Stilwell, CIEL Visiting Attorneys Vincenzo Franco, Eli Hillman, and Claudio Torres Nachon as well as our Dean's Fellows and other assistants at American University and CIEL: Natalie Bridgeman, Dr. Axel Bree, Ingrid Busson, Jackie Duobinis, Stephanie Feingold, James Freeman, Kris Genovese, Carolina Gonzalez, Nienke Grossman, Tiffany Gurnee, Eli Hillman, Tisha Illingworth, Matthew Lapin, Meredith McLean, Mark Noethen, Valeska Populoh, Marcos Pullman, Amy Rejent, Sarah Sung and Emily Yozell, Mark Williams, Mike Hsu, Elma Gates and Svetlana Zhekova. We are most grateful for the careful review of draft chapters by Paul Hagen, Lindy Johnson, Jon Van Dyke, Hays Parks, Andrew Herrup, Greg Block, Serena Wilson, Dr. Steven O. Anderson, Dr. Cathy Wessell, Dr. Dennis King, Hal Kane and Charlotte de Fontaubert. Additional background information was provided by David Caron, John Dernbach, Jeff Dunoff, Dan Esty, Tom Kane, Dr. Greg Maggio, Kenny Markowitz, Adil Najam, Chris Wold, Mike Walls and David Wirth. For the second edition, we also thank Jamie Abrams, Mary Stevens, Kathryn Walter, Emilie Thenard, Aaron Selverston, Jenifer Federico, Tom Higdon, Ana Maria Kleymeyer, Romina Picolotti, Daniel Taillant, Rick Herz, Eric Siever, Chris Bostic, Nienke Grossman, Meredith Reeves, Matthew Stillwell, Steve Charnovitz, Bella Sewall, Alejandra Goyenachea, Tatiana Tassoni, Patricia Svillick, Nathalie Bersconi, and Raj Shende, Tseming Yang, and Sean Murphy. All errors in the text are, however, our own. Our publisher, Steve Errick, has been a wry and helpful supporter of this book from the outset. Dean Claudio Grossman and American University's Washington College of Law were most generous in supporting our research.

Our students over the past decade directly contributed to this book, as well. They are working all over the world — creating environmental law organizations in Mexico, Ecuador, the Middle East, Portugal, and Brazil, bringing the very first environmental cases before the World Bank's Inspection Panel and NAFTA's Environmental Commission, and serving in government positions ranging from the UN and World Bank to South Africa and Chile. Most of all, though, we thank the support and patience of our wives: Margaret, Lisa and Barbara.

We welcome comments on the casebook, on both its strengths and areas for improvement. They may be sent to David Hunter (hunter202@earthlink.net), Jim Salzman (salzman@american.edu), or Durwood Zaelke (dzaelke@ciel.org).

DAVID HUNTER
JIM SALZMAN
DURWOOD ZAELKE

Washington, D.C.

NOTE ON THE INTERNET
AND *TREATY SUPPLEMENT*

In writing this book we have found the Internet to be a rich resource for materials on international environmental law and policy that would not have otherwise been accessible. The Internet's global reach and depth of data make it ideal for research and communication in the field. Every chapter lists relevant websites for students to explore. The casebook also has its own site on the World Wide Web at:

<http://www.wcl.american.edu/environment/IEL>

The site includes recent developments (essential in this fast-changing field) as well as hypertext links to treaty secretariats, relevant government, industry and NGO sites, and the agreements themselves.

While incorporating materials from the Internet for use in the book offers important advantages, it also has one serious disadvantage: the material or even the site containing the material may cease to exist after this book is published, making further reference impossible. While cognizant of this potential problem, we have decided to include Internet materials and references where particularly relevant. As of October, 2001, all the cited Internet material was present on the Web. Should readers come across a referenced site that no longer exists, it would be most helpful if they could contact us. We will post the news on the book web site and offer an alternative site.

The casebook contains relevant excerpts of all the international agreements covered, so it may be used as a stand-alone text. For those professors who wish students to refer to the full text of the agreements, an accompanying Treaty Supplement is also available from Foundation Press that contains 35 international environmental agreements and declarations.

*

FOREWORD
Paul Ehrlich

Aldo Leopold wrote, "One of the penalties of an ecological education is that one lives alone in a world of wounds... An ecologist must either harden his shell and make believe that the consequences of science are none of his business, or he must be the doctor who sees the marks of death in a community that believes itself well and does not want to be told otherwise." He could have been writing about an environmental lawyer.

The fabric of life is unraveling, but the vast majority of people are unaware of it. The economies and technologies of this century have provided us with standards of living that past kings could only have dreamt of, but they have come at the cost of natural capital—destroying and dispersing a one-time bonanza of fossil fuels, other minerals, soils, biological diversity, and fresh water. The impacts of the Earth's dominant animal now threaten the ecological life-support systems that underpin the human economy.

The loss of biodiversity is cresting toward the sixth wave of extinction, one that could rival the extinction episode in which the dinosaurs disappeared 65 million years ago. Over 40 percent of the Earth's terrestrial vegetated land surface has been degraded—that is, has a diminished capacity to supply civilization with benefits—because of the impacts of human land use. Human beings have been estimated to use, coopt, or destroy over 40 percent of terrestrial net primary productivity—the basic food supply of virtually all animals and microorganisms. Human appropriation of freshwater supplies is similarly extensive.

One does not need to be a scientist to appreciate the precariousness of our situation. Our survival depends upon the integrity of natural ecosystems, since they provide us with an array of indispensable services. These include: maintaining the gaseous quality of the atmosphere (in turn helping to stabilize the climate); running the hydrologic cycle that brings us freshwater; generating, preserving, and making fertile the soils upon which farming and forestry depend; controlling the vast majority of pests capable of destroying crops; and supplying us with fiber, timber, and food from land and sea. The human economy depends on natural ecosystems, but our cumulative actions are a direct threat to their, and thus our, continued well-being. We are busily sawing off the limb on which we are seated.

All of this must change, and I remain convinced we have the means to do so. That is why this casebook is so important. Lawyers and policy makers have central roles to play in healing our world of wounds. The core message of David Hunter, Jim Salzman and Durwood Zaelke throughout this book is that international environmental law is far more than treaty text. The litany of global threats is daunting and they cannot be addressed simply by passing a law. Complex issues such as population growth, ever-increasing consumption, gender inequity, the use of environmentally malign technologies, and the North-South economic divide all play their part in driving environmental degradation. Only by understanding the economics, science, and social forces driving specific environmental threats can effective legal and policy responses be developed.

When asked whether I am hopeful about the future of our species, I reply that I am optimistic about what we can do and guarded over what we will do. As you study the laws, policies, and case studies in this book, I urge you to consider what role you can play in promoting a sustainable society. Just as ecologists need to bring their insights and expertise to bear on environmental issues—to be objective and committed advocates—so, too, do lawyers and policy makers need to create legal frameworks that ensure quality of life for future generations. The stakes are too high, the consequences too important, to do any less. Human survival is intertwined with the survival of natural systems.

Paul R. Ehrlich

Stanford, California

ACKNOWLEDGMENTS

The authors gratefully acknowledge the permissions granted to reproduce the following materials.

"Comment: The Balance of Nature and Human Needs in Antarctica: The Legality of Mining," 9 Temp. Int'l & Comp. L.J. 387 (1995).

Allott, Philip, International Law and International Revolution: Reconceiving the World 7-16 (Hull University Press 1989).

Allott, Phillip, "Mare Nostrum: A New International Law of the Sea," in John Van Dyke et al., eds., Freedom for the Seas in the 21st Century: Ocean Governance and Environmental Harmony, © 1993. Published by Island Press, Washington, DC and Covelo, CA. For more information, contact Island Press directly at 1-800-828-1302, info@islandpress.org (E-mail), or www.islandpress.org (website).

Allott, Phillip, "State Responsibility and the Unmaking of International Law," 29 Harv. Int'l L.J. 102. Copyright © 1988 by the President and Fellows of Harvard College.

American Law Institute, Restatement (Third) of the Foreign Relations Law §601. Copyright 1988 by The American Law Institute. Reprinted with permission.

American National Standards Institute, ISO 14001. Copyright by the International Organization for Standardization (ISO). This material is reprinted from ISO 14001: 1996 with permission of the American Standards Institute (ANSI) on behalf of the International Organization for Standardization. No part of ISO 14001: 1996 may be copied or reproduced in any form, electronic system or otherwise or made available on the Internet, a public network, by satellite or otherwise without the prior written consent of the American Standards Institute, 11 West 42nd Street, New York, NY 10036.

Anand, Ram Prakash, "Changing Concepts of Freedom of the Seas: A Historical Perspective," in John Van Dyke et al., eds., Freedom for the Seas in the 21st Century: Ocean Governance and Environmental Harmony, © 1993. Published by Island Press, Washington, DC and Covelo, CA. For more information, contact Island Press directly at 1-800-828-1302, info@islandpress.org (E-mail), or www.islandpress.org (website).

Benedick, Richard Elliot, "Essay: A Case of Deja Vu," Scientific American (1992).

Benedick, Richard Elliot, Ozone Diplomacy (1991) from Ozone Diplomacy by Richard Elliot Benedick. Copyright © 1991 by the World Wildlife Fund, the Conservation Foundation and the Institute for the Study of Diplomacy. Reprinted by permission of Harvard University Press.

Benstein, Jeremy, "On Judiasm, Zionism and the Environment," Palestine-Israel Journal of Politics, Economics and Culture 69-70 (1998).

Biermann, Frank, "The Case for a World Environment Organization," 42 Environment 26-28 (2000). Reprinted with permission of the Helen Dwight Reid Educational Foundation. Published by Heldref Publications, 1319 Eighteenth St., NW, Washington, DC 20036-1802. Copyright © 2000.

Birnie, Patricia W. and Alan E. Boyle, International Law and the Environment (1992) by permission of Oxford University Press.

Blum, Jonathan, "The Deep Freeze: Torts, Choice of Law, and the Antarctic Treaty Regime," 8 Emory Int'l Law. Rev. 667, 668-69, 684 (1994).

Bodansky, Daniel, "Scientific Uncertainty and the Precautionary Principle," Environment 33:4 (1991). Reprinted with permission of the Helen Dwight Reid Educational Foundation. Published by Heldref Publications, 1319 Eighteenth St., N.W., Washington, D.C. 20036-1802. Copyright © 1991.

Bodansky, Daniel, "Customary (and not so Customary) International Environmental Law," 3 Indiana J. Global Leg. Stud. 105, 108-16 (1995).

Bodansky, Daniel, "Protecting the Marine Environment from Vessel-Source Pollution: UNCLOS III and Beyond," 18 Ecology Law Quarterly 719, 736-38 (1991). © 1991 by Ecology Law Quarterly. Reprinted from Ecology Law Quarterly, Vol. 18 No. 4, by permission.

Bostian, Ida L., "The Environmental Consequences of the Kosovo Conflict and the Nato Bombing of Serbia," Colo. J. Int'l Envtl. L. & Pol'y 1999 Y.B. 230, 232-35 (2000).

Bothe, M., "The Subsidiarity Principle," in E. Dommen, Fair Principles for Sustainable Development 123-36 (Edward Elgar Publishing Ltd. 1993).

Boyle, Alan E., "Marine Pollution Under the Law of the Sea Convention." Reproduced with permission from 79 AJIL 347 (1985), © The American Society of International Law.

Boyle, Alan and David Freestone, International Law and Sustainable Development: Past Achievements and Future Challenges 6-7 (1999). Reprinted with permission from Oxford University Press

Brown, Lester, et al., State of the World 24-26 (Worldwatch Institute 1997), at www.worldwatch.org.

Brown, Lester, "Eradicating Hunger: A Growing Challenge," in State of the World 43-62 (Worldwatch Institute 2001), at www.worldwatch.org.

Bruch, Carl and Jay E. Austin, "The 1999 Kosovo Conflict: Unresolved Issues in Addressing the Environmental Consequences of War," 30 Envtl. L. Rep. 10069, Copyright © 2000 Environmental Law Institute ®. Reprinted with permission from ELR - the Environmental Law Reporter ®. All rights reserved.

Burke, William T., "Unregulated High Seas Fishing and Ocean Governance," in John Van Dyke et al., eds., Freedom for the Seas in the 21st Century: Ocean Governance and Environmental Harmony, © 1993. Published by Island Press, Washington, DC and Covelo, CA. For more information, contact Island Press directly at 1-800-828-1302, info@islandpress.org (E-mail), or www.islandpress.org (website).

Burley, Anne-Marie Slaughter, "International Law and the International Relations Theory: A Dual Agenda." Reproduced with permission from 87 AJIL 205 (1993), © The American Society of International Law.

Burns, William C., "The International Convention to Combat Desertification: Drawing a Line in the Sand?" 16 Mich. J. Int'l L. 831, 849-50 (1995).

Caron, David D., "The International Whaling Commission and the North Atlantic Marine Mammal Commission: The Risks of Coercion in Consensual Structures." Reproduced with permission from 89 AJIL 154 (1995), © The American Society of International Law.

Caron, David, "International Sanctions, Ocean Management, and the Law of the Sea: A Study of Denial of Access to Fisheries," 16 Ecology Law Quarterly 311, 317-19 (1989). © 1989 by Ecology Law Quarterly. Reprinted from Ecology Law Quarterly, Vol. 16, by permission.

Carr, James and Matthew Gianni, "High Seas Fisheries, Large-Scale Drift Nets, and the Law of the Sea," in John Van Dyke et al., eds., Freedom for the Seas in the 21st Century: Ocean Governance and Environmental Harmony, © 1993. Published by Island Press, Washington, DC and Covelo, CA. For more information, contact Island Press directly at 1-800-828-1302, info@islandpress.org (E-mail), or www.islandpress.org (website).

Charney, Jonathan, "Universal International Law." Reproduced with permission from 87 AJIL. 529 (1993), © The American Society of International Law.

Charnovitz, Steve, "The NAFTA Environmental Side Agreement: Implications for Environmental Cooperation, Trade Policy, and American Treatymaking," 8 Temple Int'l & Comp. L.J. 257, 266-70 (1994).

Chayes, Abram and Antonia Handler Chayes, New Sovereignty 2-28. Reprinted by permission of the publisher from New Sovereignty by Abram Chayes and Antonia Handler Chayes, Cambridge, Mass.: Harvard University Press, Copyright © 1995 by Abram Chayes and Antonia Handler Chayes.

Clark, Dana and David Downes, "What Price Biodiversity?," Center for International Environmental Law.

Clarke, Robin, Water: The International Crisis (MIT Press 1993).

Coalition for Environmentally Responsible Economies, The CERES Principles (1989). Reprinted by permission.

Cobb, Clifford, Ted Halstead and Jonathan Rowe, "The Genuine Progress Indicator: Summary of Data and Methodology." Reprinted with permission, Copyright © 1995, Redefining Progress.

Colburn, Theo et al., Our Stolen Future (Dutton Publishing 1996).

Cousteau, Jacques-Yves and Bertrand Charrier, "The Antarctic: A Challenge to Global Environmental Policy," in Joe Verhoeven et al., eds., The Antarctic Environment and International Law 5-6 (1992)

Cusack, M. "International Law and the Transboundary Shipment of Hazaradous Waste to the Third World: Will the Basel Convention Make a Difference?" 5 Am. U. J. Int'l L. & Pol'y 393, 420-22 (1990).

Daily, Gretchen, "Introduction: What are Ecosystem Services?" in G. Daily, ed., Nature's Services: Societal Dependence on Natural Ecosystems, © 1996. Published by Island Press, Washington, DC and Covelo, CA. For more information, contact Island Press directly at 1-800-828-1302, info@islandpress.org (E-mail), or www.islandpress.org (website).

Daly, Herman E. and John B. Cobb, Jr., For the Common Good, Copyright © 1989, 1994 by Herman E. Daly and John B. Cobb, Jr. Reprinted by permission of Beacon Press, Boston.

Daly, Herman and Townsend, Kenneth, "Introduction to Essays Toward a Steady-State Economy," from Herman Daly and Kenneth Townsend, Valuing the Earth: Economics, Ecology, Ethics 29 (MIT Press 1992).

Daly, Herman, "Consumption and the Environment," 15 The Ethics of Consumption 5-8 (Report from the Institute for Philosophy and Public Policy 1995).

Devall, Bill and George Sessions, Deep Ecology: Living as if Nature Mattered (Peregrine Smith Books 1985). Used by permission.

Dobson, Andrew, Fairness and Futurity 23-30 (1999). Reprinted with permission of Oxford University Press.

Downes, David, "New Diplomacy for the Biodiversity Trade: Biodiversity, Biotechnology, and Intellectual Property in the Convention on Biological Diversity," 4 Touro J. Transnat'l L. 5-14, 2-24, 26-33 (1993). Permission granted by Touro International Law Review (Formerly Touro Journal of Transnational Law).

Dunn, Seth, "Decarbonizing the Energy Economy," in State of the World 96-99 (Worldwatch Institute 2001), at www.worldwatch.org.

Dupuy, Pierre-Marie, "Soft Law and the International Law of the Environment," 12 Mich. J. Int'l L. 420, 420-21, 424-28 (1991).

Ehrlich, Paul R., The Population Bomb © 1968, 1971 by Paul R. Ehrlich. Reprinted by permission of Ballantine Books, a Division of Random House, Inc.

Ehrlich, Paul and Anne Ehrlich, Betrayal of Science and Reason (Island Press 1996).

Ekins, Paul, "The Sustainable Consumer Society: A Contradiction in Terms?" Int'l Envtl. Affairs (University Press of New England 1991).

Elkington, John, Cannibals with Forks (Capstone Publishing Limited 1997).

Esty, Daniel, Greening the GATT, (Washington Institute for International Economics 1994).

Esty, Daniel, "Toward Data-Driven Environmentalism: The Environmental Sustainability Index," 31 Envtl. L. Rep. 10603, Copyright © 2000 Environmental Law Institute ®. Reprinted with permission from ELR - the Environmental Law Reporter ®. All rights reserved.

Europe Environment, "Shetland Oil Spill: EC Lawmakers Hesitant in the Face of Environmental Disasters," January 19, 1993. "Europe Environment," E.I.S., Brussels, Belgium (Fax: 32 2 732 66 51).

Fagin, Dan and Marianne Lavelle, and the Center for Public Integrity, from Toxic Deception: How the Chemical Industry Manipulates Science, Bends the Law, and Endangers your Health, © 1996. Published by arrangement with Kensington Publishing Corp., A Birch Lane Press Book.

Flavin, Chris, "The Legacy of Rio," in State of the World 6-7 (Worldwatch Institute 1997), at www.worldwatch.org.

Floit, Catherine, "Reconsidering Freedom of the High Seas: Protection of Living Marine Resources on the High Seas," in John Van Dyke et al., eds., Freedom for the Seas in the 21st Century: Ocean Governance and Environmental Harmony, © 1993. Published by Island Press, Washington, DC and Covelo, CA. For more information, contact Island Press directly at 1-800-828-1302, info@islandpress.org (E-mail), or www.islandpress.org (website).

Fowler, Robert J., "International Environmental Standards for Transnational Corporations," 25 Envt'l. L. 1 (1995).

Freese, C., "The Use It or Lose It Debate: Issues of a Conservation Paradox," in Harvesting Wild Species: Implications for Biodiversity Conservation (Johns Hopkins University Press 1997).

French, Hillary F., "Partnership for the Planet: An Environmental Agenda for the United Nations," Worldwatch Paper 32-34 (Worldwatch Institute 1995), at www.worldwatch.org.

French, Hillary F., "Assessing Private Capital Flows to Developing Countries," in State of the World 149-65 (Worldwatch Institute 1998), at www.worldwatch.org.

Gallopin, Gilberto, et al., Branch Points: Global Scenarios and Human Choice (Stockholm Environment Institute 1997).

Gleckman, Harris and Riva Krut, "Neither International nor Standard: The Limits of ISO 14001 as an Investment of Global Corporate Environmental Management," in Greener Management International (Greenleaf 1996).

Goldberg, Don, International Cooperative for Ozone Layer Protection (ICOLP) Study (Center for International Environmental Law 1994).

Goldberg, Donald, "As the World Burns: Negotiating the Framework Convention on Climate Change," 5 Georgetown Int'l Envt'l. L. Rev. 244 (1993). Reprinted with permission of the publisher, Georgetown University and the Georgetown International Environmental Law Review, © 1993.

Goodland, Robert and Herman Daly, "Environmental Sustainability: Universal and Non-Negotiable," 6 Ecological Applications 1002-17 (1996).

Greenpeace, "Money to Burn: The World Bank, Chemical Companies and Ozone Depletion" 1-4 (1994). Courtesy Greenpeace.

Greenpeace, "Insecticide Recently Banned in the U.S. - O.K. for Export," Greenpeace Toxic Trade Update, No. 7.1, pp. 22-23 (1994).

Greenpeace Antarctica Campaign excerpt at <http://www.greenoeace.org/_~comms/_vrml/rw/text/t09.html>. © Greenpeace International 1996.

Haas, Peter M., Robert O. Keohane, and Marc A. Levy, Institutions for the Earth: Sources of Effective International Environmental Protection (MIT Press 1993).

Handl, Gunther, "Compliance Control Mechanisms and International Environmental Obligations," 5 Tulane J. Int'l & Comp. L. 29 (1997).

Hardin, Garrett, "The Tragedy of the Commons." Reprinted with permission from Science 168: 243. Copyright 1968, American Association for the Advancement of Science.

Hart, H.L.A., The Concept of Law (1961). Reprinted with permission from Oxford University Press.

Heaton, Repetto, and Sobin, "Transforming Technology: An Agenda for Environmentally Sustainable Growth in the 21st Century," 6-7 (1991). Reprinted with permission by World Resources Institute, Washington, D.C.

Hempel, Lamont C., Environomental Governance: The Global Challenge © 1996. Published by Island Press, Washington, DC and Covelo, CA. For more information, contact Island Press directly at 1-800-828-1302, info@islandpress.org (E-mail), or www.islandpress.org (website).

Herblock Cartoon from Herblock at Large (New American Library, 1987).

Houck, Oliver A., "On the Law of Biodiversity and Ecosystem Management," 81 Minnesota L. Rev. 869, 945-48 (1997).

Housman, Robert, "Democratizing International Trade Decision-making," 27 Cornell Int'l L.J. 699 (1994). © Copyright 1994 by Cornell University. All rights reserved.

Housman, Robert, "The North American Free Trade Agreement's Lesson for Reconciling Trade and the Environment," 30 Stanford J. Int'l L. 379 (1994).

Hunter, Rod, "Standardization and the Environment," BNA International Environment Daily, March 29, 1993. Reprinted with permission from

International Environment Daily, March 29, 1993. Copyright 1993 by The Bureau of National Affairs, Inc. (800-372-1033) <http://www._bna.com>.

International Chamber of Commerce, Business Charter for Sustainable Development Principles for Environmental Management (1996). Reprinted with permission from Oxford University Press.

Jackson, Moana, "Indigenous Law and the Sea," in John Van Dyke et al., eds., Freedom for the Seas in the 21st Century: Ocean Governance and Environmental Harmony, © 1993. Published by Island Press, Washington, DC and Covelo, CA. For more information, contact Island Press directly at 1-800-828-1302, info@islandpress.org (E-mail), or www.islandpress.org (website).

Jacobsen, Judith, "Population, Consumption and Environmental Degradation: Problems and Solutions," 6 Colo. J. Int'l Envt'l. L. & Pol'y 255, 259-62 (1995). Originally published in the Colorado Journal of International Environmental Law & Policy, Copyright 1995. All rights reserved.

Johnson, Pierre Marc and Andre Beaulieu, The Environment & NAFTA, © 1996. Published by Island Press, Washington, DC and Covelo, CA. For more information, contact Island Press directly at 1-800-828-1302, info@islandpress.org (E-mail), or www.islandpress.org (website).

Joyner, Christopher, "Book Review: The Evolving Antarctic Legal Regime." Reproduced with permission from 83 AJIL 605 (1994), © The American Society of International Law.

Kane, Hal, The Truimph of the Mundane, © 2000. Published by Island Press, Washington, DC and Covelo, CA. For more information, contact Island Press directly at 1-800-828-1302, info@islandpress.org (E-mail), or www.islandpress.org (website).

Kingsbury, Benedict, "Indigenous Peoples as an International Legal Concept," in R.H. Barnes et al. eds., Indigenous Peoples of Asia 13, 15-16, 33 (1995). Reprinted with permission of the Association for Asian Studies.

Kitt, Jennifer, "Waste Exports to the Developing World: A Global Response," 7 Geo. Int'l Envtl. L. Rev. 485, 491-92 (1995). Reprinted with permission of the publisher, Georgetown University and Georgetown International Environmental Law Review. © 1995.

Knight, C. Foster, "Comment: Voluntary Environmental Standards vs. Mandatory Environmental Regulations and Enforcement in the NAFTA Market," 12 Ariz. J. Int'l & Comp. L. 619, 623-26 (1995).

Koh, Ambassador Tommy, "The Earth Summit's Negotiating Process: Some Reflections on the Art and Science of Negotiating," in N. Robinson, ed., Agenda 21 v-xiii (Oceana Publications Inc. 1993).

Krugman, Paul, Introduction to M. Jeff Hammond et al., Tax Waste, Not Work. Reprinted with permission, Copyright 1997, Redefining Progress.

Lamm, Richard, "Essay: The Heresy Trial of the Reverend Richard Lamm," 15 Envtl. L. 755 (1985).

Louka, Elli, "Bringing Polluters Before Transnational Courts: Why Industry Should Demand Strict and Unlimited Liability for the Transnational Movement of Hazardous and Radioactive Waste," 22 Denver J. Int'l L. & Pol'y 63, 78-81 (1993).

M2 Communications Ltd., "UK Introduces Measures to Reduce Marine Pollution," M2 Presswire, Aug. 15, 1996. (http://www.m2.com).

Mack, Julie, "International Fisheries Management: How the UN Conference on Straddling and Highly Migratory Fish Stocks Changes the Law of Fishing on the High Seas," 26 California Western Int'l L. J. 313, 319-20, 326-31 (1996).

Maggio, Gregory and Owen J. Lynch, "Human Rights, Environment, and Economic Development: Existing Standards in International Law and Global Society" (1996).

Makhijani, Arjun and Kevin Gurney, Mending the Ozone Hole 33, 286-87 (MIT Press 1995).

Miller, Bartlett P., "The Effect of the GATT and the NAFTA on Pesticide Regulation: A Hard Look at Harmonization," 6 Colo. J. Int'l Envt'l. L. & Pol'y 201, 203-05 (1995).

Miller, Ken, "A U.N. Occupation of American Parks?," Gannett News Serv., Sept. 12, 1996.

Mitchell, Ronald, "Compliance Theory: An Overview," in James Cameron, Improving Compliance with International Environmental Law (Kogan Page Publishers 1997).

"Multilateral Debt: The Human Costs, Oxfam International Position Paper," reproduced with permission of Oxfam Publishing, 274 Banbury Road, Oxford, OX2 7DZ.

Nanda, Ved P., International Environmental Law and Policy 274-75 (1995).

O'Connell, Mary Ellen, "Symposium: Enforcement and the Success of International Environmental Law," 3 Indiana J. Global Leg. Stud. 47, 56-64 (1995).

Ozone Action, "Deadly Complacency: U.S. CFC Production, the Black Market, and Ozone Depletion," (1995).

Palmer, Geoffrey, "New Ways to Make International Environmental Law." Reproduced with permission from 86 AJIL. 259 (1992), © The American Society of International Law.

Pennsylvania Department of Environmental Protection, "How Can I Endorse the CERES Principles?" at <http:\www.dep.state.pa.us/dep/_deputate/_pollprev/ceres/how.html>.

Peterson, M.J., Managing the Frozen South: The Creation and Evolution of the Antarctic Treaty System. © 1988 The Regents of the University of California.

Porter, Gareth, Global Environmental Politics. Copyright © 1991 by Westview Press. Reprinted by permission of Westview Press.

Randle, Russell V., "The Oil Pollution Act of 1990: Its Provisions, Intent, and Effects," 21 Envtl. L. Rep. 10119 (1991). Copyright © 1991 Environmental Law Institute ®. Reprinted with permission from ELR - the Environmental Law Reporter ®. All rights reserved.

Rawls, John, A Theory of Justice © 1971 by the President and Fellows of Harvard College. Reprinted by permission of Harvard University Press.

Rheingold, Paul quote in David Rubenstein, "Is There a Tort Case in the Air? Causal Connection is a Problem, But Never Underestimate the Plaintiffs' Bar," Corp. Leg. Times 1 (1992). © Corporate Legal Times. Reprinted with permission.

Rischitelli, Gary, "Developing a Global Right to Know," 2 ILSA J. Int'l & Comp. L. 99, 100-10 (1995).

Rosenne, Shabtai, Practice and Methods of International Law 69 (Oceana Publications Inc. 1984)

Sands, Phillipe J., Chernobyl: Law and Communication: Transboundary Nuclear Air Pollution - The Legal Materials 1-2, 51-52, 96 (1988). Reprinted with the permission of Cambridge University Press.

Sands, Phillipe, "Compliance with International Environmental Obligations: Existing International Legal Arrangements," in James Cameron, Improving Compliance with International Environmental Law (Kogan Page Publishers 1997).

Saylin, Gregory M., "The United Nations International Conference on Population and Development: Religion, Tradition, and Law in Latin America," 28 Vanderbilt J. Transnat'l L. 1245, 1255-56 (1995).

Salzman, James, "Labor Rights, Globalization and Institutions: The Role and Influence of the Organization for Economic Cooperation and Development," 21 Mich. L. Int'l L. 824-25 (2000).

Salzman, James, "Sustainable Consumption and the Law," 27 Envtl. L. 1243 (1998). This work appeared originally in 27 Envtl. L. 1243 (1998).

Schachter, Oscar, "United Nations Law," Reproduced with permission from 88 AJIL 1 (1994), © The American Society of International Law.

Schrijver, Nico, "Permanent Sovereignty Over Natural Resources Versus the Common Heritage of Mankind," in De Waart, Peters and Denters, eds., International Law and Development (1998). Excerpts reprinted with the kind permission from Kluwer Law International.

Seacor, Jessica E., "Environmental Terrorism: Lessons from the Oil Fires of Kuwait," 10 Am. U. J. Int'l L. & Pol'y 481 (1994).

Shabecoff, Philip, A New Name for Peace: International Environmentalism, Sustainable Development, and Democracy, 47-49, 73-77 (University Press of New England 1996).

Sharp, Major Walter G., "The Effective Deterrence of Environmental Damage During Armed Conflict: A Case Analysis of the Persian Gulf War," 137 Mil. L. Rev. 1 (1992). Portions of this article are reprinted from the Military Law Review, Department of the Army Pamphlet 27-100-137 (Summer 1992), at 1. The opinions and conclusions expressed herein are those of the individual author, and do not necessarily represent the views of The Judge Advocate General's School, United States Army, or any other governmental agency.

Sohn, Loius B., "The Stockholm Declaration on the Human Environment," 14 Harvard Int'l L. J. 423 (1973). Permission granted by the Harvard International Law Journal © 1973 by the President and Fellows of Harvard College.

Soroos, M., The Endangered Atmosphere: Preserving the Global Commons (University of South Carolina Press 1997).

Stauber, John and Sheldon Rampton, Toxic Sludge is Good for You (Common Courage Press 1995). 1-800-497-3207.

Stone, Christopher D., Earth and Other Ethics: The Case for Moral Plurism. Copyright © 1988 by Christopher D. Stone. Reprinted by permission of HarperCollins Publishers Inc.

Stone, Christopher D., The Gnat is Older than Man. Copyright © 1993 by Princeton University Press. Reprinted by permission of Princeton University Press.

Sumi, Kazuo, "The International Legal Issues Concerning the Use of Drift Nets, with Special Emphasis on Japanese Practices and Responses," in John Van Dyke et al., eds., Freedom for the Seas in the 21st Century: Ocean Governance and Environmental Harmony, © 1993. Published by Island Press, Washington, DC and Covelo, CA. For more information, contact Island Press directly at 1-800-828-1302, info@islandpress.org (E-mail), or www.islandpress.org (website).

Szasz, Paul, "International Norm-making," in E. Brown Weiss, ed., Environmental Changes and International Law: New Challenges and Dimensions (1992), © 1992 by the United Nations University. All rights reserved.

TRAFFIC Press Releases, "Yemeni Demand for Rhino Horn Dagger Continues" and "The First International Symposium on Endangered Species Used in Traditional East Asian Medicine: Substitutes for Tiger Bone and Musk." <http://www.traffic.org/brf_elephants_cites.html>.

Trimble, Philip, "International Law, World Order and Critical Legal Studies," 42 Stanford L. Rev. 811 (1990). © 1990 by the Board of Trustees of the Leland Stanford Junior University.

Tuchton, Jay, "The Citizen Petition Process Under NAFTA's Environmental Side Agreement: It's Easy to Use, But Does it Work?" 16 Env't L. Rep. 10018. Copyright © 1996 Environmental Law Institute®. Reprinted with permission from ELR - The Environmental Law Reporter ®.

Turley, Jonathan, "When in Rome: Multinational Misconduct and the Presumption Against Extraterritoriality," 84 Nw. U. L. Rev. 598 (YEAR). Reprinted by special permission of Northwestern University School of Law.

Tuxil, J. and C. Bright, "Losing Strands in the Web of Life," in State of the World 43-51 (Worldwatch Institute 1998), at www.worldwatch.org.

United Nations Environment Programme, Environmental Effects of Ozone Depletion 1 (UNEP 1991).

United Nations Environment Programme, The Impact of Ozone Layer Depletion 4-13 (UNEP 1994).

United States Arms Control and Disarmament Agency, Arms Control and Disarmament Agreements: Texts and Histories of the Negotiations 211-13 (1990). Reprinted by permission of U.S. Arms Control and Disarmament Agency (ACDA).

Uram, Charlotte, "International Regulation of the Sale and Use of Pesticides," 10 Nw. J. Int'l L. & Bus. 461 (1990). Reprinted by special permission of Northwestern University School of Law, Northwestern Journal of International Law & Business.

Vitousek, Peter M. et al., "Human Appropriation of the Products of Photosynthesis," Bioscience, Vol. 36(6) 368, 372-73. © 1991 American Institute of Biological Sciences.

Weiss, Edith Brown, in Fairness of Future Generations: International Law, Common Patrimony, and Intergenerational Equity (1996). Reprinted with permission of publisher, Transnational Publishers, Inc., Ardsley, New York.

Wirth, David A., "Trade Implications of the Basel Convention Amendment Banning North-South Trade in Hazardous Wastes," 19 Int'l Envtl. Rep. 976 (1996). Reprinted with permission from International Environment Reporter. Copyright 1996 by The Bureau of National Affairs, Inc. (800-372-1033) <http://www.bna.com>.

World Business Council on Sustainable Development, "Energy & Climate," at <http://www.wbcsd.ch/FocusAreas/Climateo/o20and o/o20Energy.html>.

World Commission on Environment and Development, Our Common Future (1988). Reprinted with permission from Oxford University Press.

World Development Report 1992: Development and the Environment (1992). Reprinted with permission from Oxford University Press.

World Resources Institute, Biodiversity Assessment Strategy. Reprinted with permission by World Resources Institute, Washington, D.C.

World Resources Institute, Global Biodiversity Strategy, 1992. Reprinted with permission by World Resources Institute, Washington, D.C.

World Resources Institute, World Resources Institute 1996-97, "Atmosphere and Climate," 315-25. Reprinted with permission by World Resources Institute, Washington, D.C.

"Is national sovereignty headed for extinction?" advertisements. Public Media Center and Sea Turtle Restoration Project, Earth Island Institute, PO Box 400, Forest Knolls, CA 94933, ph. 415-488-0370.

*

SUMMARY OF CONTENTS

III. International Environmental Law and Other Legal Regimes

TABLE OF CONTENTS

*

TABLE OF CASES

Principal cases are in bold type. Non-principal cases are in roman type. References are to Pages.

*

INTERNATIONAL ENVIRONMENTAL LAW AND POLICY

*

I. The Creation and Development of International Environmental Law

CHAPTER ONE

The Wild Environmental Facts

> *Words ought to be a little wild, for they are the assault of thoughts upon the unthinking.*
>
> John Maynard Keynes

Section I.   Global Environmental Challenges

This chapter presents an overview of some of the challenges facing our environment—the "wild facts" that our generation must confront through international environmental law and policy. At least four pressing global environmental problems demonstrate how we are currently reaching, and

1

perhaps have already exceeded, the "sustainable" limits of human activity—climate change, including global warming; stratospheric ozone depletion; species extinction and the loss of biodiversity; and the contamination of our air and water by hazardous chemicals and wastes. In addition, many local and regional environmental problems such as lack of access to fresh water, desertification, and air pollution now have a transboundary, if not global, dimension. The sections below present a brief overview of these environmental threats to place the development of international environmental law in its ecological context. We will study these threats as well as international efforts to address them in greater detail in Part II of the casebook.

———

A. CLIMATE CHANGE

Human activity is changing the global climate with unpredictable and potentially profound consequences for global weather patterns, ecosystems, and human health. Water vapor and gases such as carbon dioxide and methane cause the earth's atmosphere to act like a greenhouse, allowing warming energy from the sun to pass through the earth's surface and, subsequently, trapping a portion of that energy before it is radiated back into space. This "greenhouse effect" is a natural process; without it the energy from the sun would be lost in space, leaving the earth as cold and lifeless as Mars. It is also a homeostatic process, or a process tending toward equilibrium. The concentration of greenhouse gases in the atmosphere is kept relatively constant over time by complex natural cycles—carbon dioxide, for example, is absorbed by plants, released when the plants burn or decompose, and re-absorbed when new plants grow, only to be released again in an endless cycle.

Since the beginning of the Industrial Revolution in the early 19th century, human activity has interfered with these homeostatic processes, releasing carbon dioxide and other greenhouse gases into the atmosphere more quickly than are absorbed by natural "sinks," primarily oceans and forests. The result is that concentrations of these gases are increasing in the atmosphere. Due to the burning of fossil fuels, such as coal and oil, and the destruction of forests, the atmospheric concentration of carbon dioxide has increased by 31% since 1750, from 280 parts per million (ppm) to 370 ppm in 2000. (One part per million of CO_2 means there is one molecule of CO_2 to every million molecules of air.) Concentrations of methane, nitrous oxide, and other greenhouse gases are rising as well, with methane increasing over 150% from its 1750 level. As a result, an ever-greater proportion of the sun's energy is trapped within the atmosphere, and the planet is heating up.

According to the Third Assessment Report issued by the Intergovernmental Panel on Climate Change (IPCC) in 2001, the global average surface temperature has increased over the 20th century by approximately 1.1° Fahrenheit (0.6° Celsius). Globally, the 1990s was the warmest decade, and 1998 was the warmest year in the instrumental record. According to the IPCC report, "most of the warming observed over the last 50 years is attributable to human activities. Furthermore, it is very likely (90–99% chance) that the 20th century warming has contributed significantly to the observed sea level rise." Human influences will continue to change atmospheric composition throughout the 21st century. The global average surface temperature is projected to increase by 2.5 to 10.4° Fahrenheit (1.4 to 5.8° Celsius) by 2100 relative to 1990, with a corresponding rise in sea level of 0.30 to 2.9 feet (0.09 to 0.88 meters). The Intergovernmental Panel on Climate Change (IPCC), SUMMARY FOR POLICYMAKERS OF THE THIRD ASSESSMENT REPORT OF WORKING GROUP I OF THE IPCC (CLIMATE CHANGE 2001: THE SCIENTIFIC BASIS) 1–8 (2001).

The IPCC also concluded that "recent regional climate changes, particularly temperature increases, have already affected many physical and biological systems," in ways such as shrinkage of glaciers, thawing of permafrost, delayed freezing of ice on rivers and lakes, poleward shifts of plant and animal ranges, declining of some plant and animal populations, and earlier flowering of trees, emergence of insects, and egg-laying in birds. Regional changes in temperature of even a few degrees Fahrenheit have the potential to cause extreme losses in biodiversity. Many marine ecosystems, for example, highly productive areas like coral reefs, mangroves, and wetland areas, are extremely sensitive to variations in salinity, turbidity (the cloudiness of the water), and water depth and temperature, all of which can be initiated and/or strengthened by temperature change. The Intergovernmental Panel on Climate Change (IPCC), SUMMARY FOR POLICYMAKERS OF THE THIRD ASSESSMENT REPORT OF WORKING GROUP II OF THE IPCC (CLIMATE CHANGE 2001: IMPACTS, ADAPTATION, AND VULNERABILITY) 1–13 (2001) [hereinafter IPCC Impacts Report].

With a predicted sea level rise of as much as 2.9 feet by 2100, compounded by an increase in the frequency and severity of extreme weather events, large numbers of the world's human settlements would be in jeopardy, especially in less-developed areas with little capacity to adapt to climate change. Global temperature increases would likely have severe human health impacts, ranging from increased summer deaths from heat waves to increased risks of drowning, disease, and hunger from flooding. Many infectious diseases such as malaria and dengue, would likely increase in incidence and range. Small island states, such as the Maldives and the Seychelles, and highly urbanized low-lying coastal areas are particularly vulnerable to inundation and resulting population displacement. IPCC Impacts Report, *supra, at 1–13*.

To understand climate change, we must understand the difference between weather and climate. Climate change is not about the daily fluctuations in temperature and humidity we call weather; rather, it concerns long term shifts in weather patterns. While a temperature change of 6° F in a single day may be trivial, a permanent 6° F change in the average global temperature is not. The exact impacts of such a change are still uncertain, particularly with respect to differences within and among regions.

In this respect, "climate change" is perhaps a more useful descriptive term than "global warming." Thus instead of thinking of the earth "heating up," picture more energy being pumped into the earth's atmosphere. As a result, one would expect more extreme weather along with changing climates. Some regions of the world may experience a substantial cooling effect as a result of climate change. Other regions, of course, will experience increases in temperature. The impacts on human health, agriculture and natural ecosystems of such changes in temperatures could be dramatic. In addition, increased global temperatures are expected to increase the number and severity of floods, hurricanes, tornadoes, and other extreme weather events. Much of the insurance industry, for example, already believes that recent record-breaking payouts for natural disaster relief are related to human influences on the climate system.

A broad scientific consensus now exists that the climate is changing due to human activities, and failure to take measures to control the causes of climate change—primarily the burning of fossil fuels such as coal and oil—is becoming increasingly difficult to defend. Most countries of the world have signed the Framework Convention on Climate Change, and most industrialized countries made additional specific commitments in the 1997 Kyoto Protocol. As this edition goes to press, the likelihood of meaningful actions remains in doubt. Climate change is discussed further in Chapter 9, pages 588–653.

———

B.   OZONE DEPLETION

The stratospheric ozone layer is a blanket of diffuse gases encircling the earth at a distance of 12 to 50 kilometers above the surface. Named for the molecule of three weakly bound oxygen atoms (O_3 or ozone) that concentrate there, the stratospheric ozone layer shields the earth from high-energy ultraviolet (UV–B) radiation from the sun. UV–B radiation is extremely harmful to human health and the environment.

Like greenhouse gases, stratospheric concentrations of ozone have long been maintained at constant levels through natural, homeostatic processes. By interfering with these processes, synthetic chemicals are destroying stratospheric ozone more quickly than natural processes can replenish it. Chlorofluorocarbons (CFCs) and certain other widely used synthetic chemicals migrate into the upper atmosphere, where they are broken down by high-energy radiation. As these compounds break down, they release chlorine and bromine ions. These ions, in turn, catalyze a reaction that breaks down ozone molecules. The chlorine and bromine ions are not destroyed in this reaction, and each ion can destroy tens of thousands of ozone molecules. Beginning in the 1940s, global use of CFCs and other ozone depleting substances expanded dramatically, with a corresponding increase in atmospheric chlorine and bromine.

In Antarctica, where the greatest losses have occurred, up to 60% of stratospheric ozone is depleted each September, resulting in an "ozone hole" larger than the entire United States. A similar hole also exists above the Arctic. The ozone holes are increasing in size and duration. The thinning of the ozone layer is not confined to the poles, however. Unprecedented levels of ozone depletion have been measured over Europe, North

America, Australia, and New Zealand, with as much as a 10% decline over northern middle latitudes, and 35% over parts of Siberia. And the decline is continuing globally, at approximately 3% per decade.

The increased amounts of UV–B radiation striking the Earth's surface endanger human health, agriculture and the environment. Rates of skin cancer, for example, may increase by 2% for every 1% loss in ozone coverage. A 10% reduction of atmospheric ozone could result in an additional 300,000 cases of skin cancer and up to 1.75 million additional cases of cataracts *each year*. UV–B exposure also suppresses the body's immune response system, making it more vulnerable to certain diseases. Under laboratory conditions, increased radiation at the levels expected from ozone depletion inhibits the growth of many plants, including important commercial species such as soybeans, cotton, and certain trees. Not only could this impair crop production, but it may also alter the biodiversity of terrestrial ecosystems. UV–B radiation causes developmental abnormalities in fish, shellfish and amphibians, threatening hundred of species. The global decline of frogs, for example, has been attributed in part to increased UV–B exposure. Such exposure also reduces the productivity of phytoplankton, the base of the ocean's food web. Reductions in this fundamental food source could dramatically affect the biodiversity of the oceans, potentially threatening the entire marine food chain.

Beginning with a framework convention in 1985, the international community has taken a series of increasingly restrictive steps to reduce global production and consumption of ozone depleting substances. Known as the Montreal Protocol regime, these treaties have led to the nearly complete ban of CFCs and other ozone depleting substances. Despite dramatic reductions in the release of these substances, however, atmospheric concentrations of ozone-depleting substances will continue to rise until the middle of the next century, and stratospheric ozone levels will likely continue to fall. The long-term impacts of this "global experiment" with our ozone layer remain unknown. Global consumption of chlorofluorocarbons (CFCs), the most used ozone-depleting substance, has dropped from 1.1 million tons in 1986 to 160,000 tons in 1996. The United Nations Environment Program (UNEP) reports that the ozone layer is now expected to recover to its pre–1980 levels by 2050, and that without the Protocol, levels of ozone-depleting substances would have been five times higher than they are today and surface UV–B radiation levels would have doubled at mid-latitudes in the northern hemisphere. United Nations Environment Programme, GLOBAL ENVIRONMENT OUTLOOK 2000, at 26 (1999). For further discussion of ozone depletion and the Montreal Protocol regime, see Chapter 9, page 526.

C. SPECIES EXTINCTION AND LOSS OF BIODIVERSITY

Extinction is a natural consequence of evolutionary processes and a regular occurrence in the natural world. Species are driven extinct by predators that overhunt them, by competitors that co-opt their habitat or food sources, by diseases, and by natural disasters. Although extinction may be relatively common over geological time, mass extinction—the wide-spread and rapid die-off of thousands of species—is not. In the three billion year history of life on earth, scientists know of only five mass extinctions. The fifth mass extinction occurred 65 million years ago, most likely caused by a meteor striking the earth.

The world has now entered a sixth wave of mass extinction. By some estimates, the world is losing 27,000 species a year—that is 74 species every day, three every hour. This rate of extinction is at least a thousand times greater than the natural rate as determined through the fossil record. E.O. Wilson, THE DIVERSITY OF LIFE 280 (1992). Other estimates are even higher. World Bank ecologist Robert Goodland reports that the rate of species extinction may be as high as 150,000 species a year. *Tropical Deforestation: Solutions, Ethics and Religion*, Environmental Department Working Paper 43 (The World Bank, 1991). Unlike previous mass extinctions, the present mass extinction is the result of the day-to-day decisions of 6 billion human beings, one species among the 14 million or more species sharing the planet.

The underlying factors of human-caused species loss are complex and varied. Fundamentally, however, they boil down to the patterns and scale of human consumption. Humans overexploit other species directly for food, clothing, ornament, pets, and raw materials. We also harm them by destroying their habitat—through unsustainable logging, slash and burn agriculture, damming rivers, draining wetlands, and contaminating the air and water. Other global environmental threats such as climate change and ozone depletion also contribute to the loss of biodiversity.

The consequences of this wholesale destruction may be far more serious than most people realize. All life on earth is part of a dynamic, interdependent ecological system. As with every other species, humanity depends for its existence on the "ecosystem services" provided by the interactions of the earth's species with each other and with natural processes. Taken for granted, these services provided by the earth's biota—such as the cycling of oxygen, carbon, and nitrogen, decomposition of waste, stabilization of climate, maintenance of soil fertility, recycling of nutrients, pollination, water purification and many others—are essential to human survival and prosperity. Importantly, we lack the knowledge and ability to substitute for these services at the scales on which they operate. *See,* GRETCHEN DAILY, ED., NATURE'S SERVICES: SOCIETAL DEPENDENCE ON NATURAL ECOSYSTEMS (1997). Nor could we afford the substitutes, even if they did exist. A 1997 article in the journal *Nature* estimated that these ecosystem services are worth between $16 and $54 trillion every year. For comparison, the total output of all the world's economies is $18 trillion. Robert Costanza *et al., The Value of the World's Ecosystem Services and Natural Capital*, 387 NATURE 253 (1997). While the valuation methodologies of this study have been criticized, the importance of these services to our well-being are beyond dispute.

Moral and ethical reasons also justify the conservation of wildlife. The ongoing mass extinction is changing the planet's evolutionary processes. Ethicists can thoughtfully ask what right we have knowingly to imperil the future existence of other species. And for some the loss of wildlife means a little more of earth's magic is lost forever. Examples of species in danger of extinction due to human causes include all of the world's tiger species, most rhino species, both gorillas, two of the five freshwater dolphins, and all seven of the sea turtle species. Just as troubling are the scores of lesser-known species facing extinction or already extinct. Furthermore, it is worrisome to consider what will happen to the indigenous cultures dependent on specific species for their livelihoods once those species go extinct.

The current wave of extinctions presents major challenges for international environmental law and a number of different treaties address the conservation and sustainable use of wildlife and biodiversity. These include major global treaties such as the Convention on Biological Diversity, the Convention on International Trade in Endangered Species, and the Law of the Sea Convention, as well as numerous regional and bilateral wildlife treaties. See Chapter 13.

D. POLLUTION FROM TOXIC CHEMICALS AND HAZARDOUS WASTE

Beginning in the 1950s and 1960s, scientists discovered that DDT, PCBs, and many other synthetic chemicals have substantial impacts on human health and the environment. Many of these synthetic chemicals persist for decades or longer. They dissolve in fat, not water, and thus are absorbed and concentrated in the body fat and milk of animals that ingest them. And they stay there until the animal that first consumed the molecule passes it on to its offspring or is eaten itself. Each time one animal eats another, it adds to its own load of chemical baggage the load that was carried by its prey. Concentrations of persistent chemicals can thus increase by orders of magnitude until reaching the top of the food chain, which we and other predators occupy.

The impact of these chemicals on human health and wildlife is not altogether clear. Initially, concern focused on the acute poisoning of those who were most immediately exposed to high levels of specific chemicals. As our knowledge of cancer and other long-term diseases increased, however, our focus of concern broadened from the acute toxicity of hazardous substances to their ability to cause cancer or birth defects. Long-term exposure to even small amounts of DDT and related compounds, for example, have been shown to cause cancer under laboratory conditions. More recently, evidence is mounting that these same chemicals may have profound impacts on our endocrine systems, interfering with the chemical messages sent to and from our cells. Moreover, different substances can have cumulative effects—when combined, relatively safe doses of individual substances can have a harmful result. Still other combinations of chemicals have demonstrated synergistic effects, in which the harm caused by the interaction of two or more compounds far exceeds what would be expected by simply adding the effects of each chemical together. In other words, in the world of chemicals, $2+2$ sometimes equals 8 or 10 or 10,000.

Making matters still worse is the surprising lack of knowledge we have regarding the scale, movement, and impact of the chemicals that we are manufacturing. Each year, thousands of new synthetic chemicals are introduced into the global economy (and environment)—as pesticides, industrial feedstock, commercial chemicals, or industrial wastes. More than 100,000 synthetic chemicals are now on the market, and more than 250 are now also found in our bodies, regardless of where we live. Theo Colborn et al., Our Stolen Future 106 (1996). While some countries require limited testing of new chemicals, the number of new chemicals released each year far exceeds the testing capacity of even the most developed countries. As a result, we have a sophisticated understanding of the human health and environment impacts of only a small percentage of these chemicals. Furthermore, policymakers often ignore the physiological differences between adults and children, and men and women when setting standards for exposure to hazardous chemicals. In the U.S., for example, the Worker Protection Standard (WPS) for agricultural workers is based on a 154–lb male model. Although it is adjusted by weight for women workers, the WPS does not consider that women have significantly higher percentage body fat than their male counterparts. Since hazardous chemicals are often stored in body fat, this standard may be inadequate to protect women. Children and adolescents are often ignored altogether. Also, the multiple routes of exposure, via air, mouth, and skin, are not always factored in. In other words, when setting "safe" standards for occupational exposure, legislation may ignore ingestion of the same chemical through diet.

A related issue to the production and use of pesticides and other synthetic chemicals is the incidental production of hazardous waste. Worldwide generation of hazardous waste increased from approximately 5 million metric tons in 1945 to 400 million metric tons in the early 1990s, an eighty-fold increase since the end of World War II. Of the 400 million tons of hazardous wastes, 300 million tons were produced by OECD countries (Organization for Economic Cooperation and Development). United Nations Environment Programme (UNEP), Global Environment Outlook 2000 29 (1999).

The generation of such large amounts of waste has placed political and economic pressures on many countries to seek disposal sites outside of their own political boundaries. Disposal of hazardous waste may cost as much as $2,000 per ton in a developed country, versus $40 per ton in Africa. Many developing countries that receive hazardous wastes do not have the technical capacity to handle them safely, even when given full disclosure about the nature of the shipment. No one knows the exact volume of international trade in hazardous waste, and policing the trade has proven very difficult. Poland, for example, has intercepted over 1,300 deceptively labeled waste shipments from Germany. Perhaps with reason, countries have denounced such practices as "toxic colonialism." At the international level, shipments of transboundary hazardous waste are governed by the Basel Convention on the Control of Transboundary Movements of Hazardous Wastes and Their Disposal.

QUESTIONS AND DISCUSSION

1. The four environmental threats described above raise the concept of homeostasis—the ability of natural systems to maintain a state of equilibrium. Ecosystems are often remarkably resilient. This must be the case, for change is constant in any natural system. Species evolve and go extinct. Ice ages come and go. What distinguishes the current situation from geologic history is the *speed* and *scale* of change. Changes in the ozone layer, climate, species extinctions, and assimilation of chemicals are occurring not over millennia, but over decades, greatly outpacing the ability of natural systems to adapt.

2. Not surprisingly, as scientific understanding of climate change has improved, so too has scientists' confidence in warming estimates. The IPCC's Second Assessment Report on Climate Change, released in 1995, was equivocal in assessing the role of humans on climate change, stating:

> the balance of evidence suggests a discernible human influence on global climate.

Reflecting the increased confidence in modeling and understanding of the climate, the 2001 IPCC report states,

> the warming over the past 100 years is very unlikely to be due to internal variability alone [and] . . . in the light of new evidence and taking into account the remaining uncertainties, most of the observed warming over that last 50 years is likely to have been due to the increase in greenhouse gas concentrations.

The IPCC defines "very unlikely" as a 1–10% chance that the result is true and "likely" as having a 66–90% chance that the result is true. Do you think the increased certainty of the IPCC regarding the human causation of climate change would be sufficient to satisfy the causation element in a lawsuit?

3. Is it possible to imagine Montana's Glacier National Park without glaciers, or mountains such as the Himalayas and Mt. Kilamanjaro devoid of ice and snow? By the year 2050, there is a significant likelihood that these scenes will be reality. Vital Signs 2000, citing *Science*, the *State of the Arctic Report*, *Journal of Geophysical Research*, and the *Christian Science Monitor* reports that ice cover is melting worldwide.

> From the polar regions to high mountain glaciers, Earth's ice cover is melting at an astonishing rate. Global ice melt accelerated rapidly during the 1990s—the warmest decade on record. . . . The ice-covered polar regions are warming faster than the planet as a whole, and melting rapidly. The Arctic sea ice, covering an area roughly the size of the United States, has lost an average of 34,300 square kilometers—an area larger than the Netherlands—each year since 1978. But the ice has thinned even faster than it has shrunk. Between 1958–76 and the mid-1990s, the average thickness dropped from 3.1 meters to 1.8 meters, a decline of some 40 percent. The massive Antarctic ice cover, which averages 2.3 kilometers in thickness and represents 91 percent of the Earth's ice, is also melting—although there is disagreement over how quickly. . . . Outside the poles, most ice melt has occurred in mountain and subpolar glaciers, which respond much more rapidly to temperature change. As a whole, the world's glaciers are shrinking faster than they are growing, and losses in 1997–98 were "extreme," according to the World Glacier Monitoring Service. Scientists predict that up to a quarter of global mountain glacier mass could disappear by 2050, and up to half by 2100—leaving patches only in Alaska, Patagonia, and the Himalayas. Within the next thirty years, the Himalayan glacial area alone is expected to shrink by one fifth.

Lisa Mastny, *Ice Cover Melting Worldwide*, VITAL SIGNS 2000, at 126–27 (2000).

4. Do you consider the environmental problems of toxic chemicals and hazardous waste primarily global or more local problems? Does the distinction make a difference in terms of environmental law? Recall that chemicals circulate through the globe, and hazardous waste is often shipped across borders. Consider as well the persistence of certain pollutants. For example, the New York Times reports that contamination from lead smelting during the Roman Empire, from 366 B.C. to 36 A.D., has been found in ice samples extracted nearly 10,000 feet below the Greenland ice cap. Malcolm Brown, *Ice Cap Shows Ancient Mines Polluted the Globe*, New York Times, Dec. 9, 1997, at C7.

SECTION II.   LOCAL AND REGIONAL ENVIRONMENTAL CHALLENGES

In addition to global environmental threats, human activity causes serious environmental problems at the local and regional levels. Air pollution kills an estimated 300,000 to 700,000 people a year in developing countries, and a lack of access to freshwater and proper sanitation is linked to the death of 2 million children a year. Local and regional issues like these present profound challenges to national environmental and development policies, but they are also increasingly being addressed at the international level. International law can facilitate assistance and coordinate global efforts to respond to these local and regional challenges. Moreover, many of these issues, notably water and air pollution, can have significant transboundary impacts where the river or airshed is shared by more than one State.

––––––

A.   ACCESS TO FRESH WATER

Access to uncontaminated fresh water is one of the most pervasive environmental challenges facing the planet. Nearly one third of the world's population lacks access to proper sanitation facilities; more than one billion lack access to clean water. Lack of decent sanitation contributes to 900 million cases of diarrheal diseases every year. 200 million people are suffering from schistosomiasis or bilharzia and 900 million from hookworm. Epidemics such as cholera, typhoid and paratyphoid also thrive in areas with poor sanitation. The costs of this pollution, in terms of human suffering, lost productivity, health care, and foregone development, are staggering. The World Bank, 1992 WORLD DEVELOPMENT REPORT 5 (1992).

Access to fresh water is not only a supply problem but also a distributional problem. According to the UN, more than one quarter of the world's population lives in countries that face serious water shortages. In the coming decades as the population continues to grow and industry continues to expand, the increasing demand for water and its relative scarcity are expected to be major sources of conflict in much of the world. Because of the transboundary nature of many watersheds, these conflicts threaten international or regional security. Water has already emerged as a major issue in peace negotiations between nations such as Israel and Syria, Jordan, and the Palestinian Authority. The World Bank predicts increasing conflict due to water scarcity.

> Nearly all of the 3 billion increase in global population expected by 2025 will be in developing countries where water is already scarce. * * *
>
> One major outcome, with regional and even global consequences, is the greater likelihood of conflicts over water, in large part because of the imperatives of geography. Nearly 47 percent of the land area of the world, excluding Antarctica, falls within international water basins. And the number of rivers and lake basins shared by two or more countries are now more than 300.
>
> Water shortages will be especially adverse for agriculture, which takes 70–80 percent of all available fresh water in the world. Food security could be a casualty since the growth in food supply in recent decades has largely been fueled by irrigation—both the expansion in area and productivity increases.* * *

THE WORLD BANK, WORLD DEVELOPMENT REPORT 1999/2000, at 29 (2000).

Contaminated water has both human and natural causes. In many parts of the world, "clean" water does not occur naturally. Even in the absence of "pollution," rivers, streams, and lakes in Africa, South America, and elsewhere contain bacteria, parasites, and disease vectors dangerous to human and animal health. Human activity can make these waters even more hazardous. In the absence of proper sanitation, for example, human and livestock waste flow into these waterways, posing a direct threat to human health.

By clearing forests and farming or raising livestock on marginal lands, humans also increase soil erosion. Erosion leads not only to the loss of top soils vital for food production, but also to increased muddiness or "turbidity" of surface waters, threatening fish and other aquatic species, and further reducing the water's utility to humans. Runoff from agricultural lands also includes pesticides, fertilizers, and salts from depleted soil. As waterways flow through more heavily populated and industrialized areas, the water is further contaminated by industrial wastes and "non-point source" pollution from highways, streets, and municipal drainage systems. Although most natural contaminants may be removed by boiling water or allowing sediment to settle to the bottom, these anthropogenic contaminants usually cannot be removed without costly technological fixes, particularly in the case of ground water contamination. International responses to these and other freshwater issues are discussed in Chapter 11, page 769.

B.   AIR POLLUTION

The *1999/2000 World Development Report* describes the severe air pollution problems now facing many developing countries. "Air pollution, which is closely associated with urbanization and industrialization in developing countries, seriously impinges on the health of children and adults alike. Pollution particularly affects those already suffering from malnutrition and infectious disease.... For most children in the large cities of developing countries, breathing the air may be as harmful as smoking two packs of cigarettes a day." The World Bank, WORLD DEVELOPMENT REPORT 1999/2000 141 (2000). Even in developed countries, estimated deaths from air pollution are extremely high. In the U.S, for example, deaths related to air pollution number 50,000 to 100,000 annually. World Health Organization, FACT SHEET 187 (2000). To illustrate the significance of air pollution problems, consider the three examples below.

Indoor Air Pollution: Of the 3 million annual deaths from air pollution, 2.8 million are from indoor air pollution, and 67% of these are from rural developing countries. For hundreds of millions of the world's poorer citizens, smoke and fumes from indoor use of biomass fuel (such as wood, straw, and dung) pose much greater health risks than any outdoor pollution. Women and children suffer most from this form of pollution. World Health Organization, FACT SHEET 187 (2000).

Suspended Particulate Matter. In 2000, 1.1 billion people worldwide lived in urban areas that did not meet the standards for particulate matter (airborne dust and smoke) set by the World Health Organization (WHO), with cities such as Bangkok, Calcutta, and Delhi exceeding the WHO guidelines for suspended particulate matter by more than 100 percent. In China, smoke and small particles from burning coals cause more than 50,000 premature deaths and 400,000 new cases of chronic bronchitis a year. UNEP, GLOBAL ENVIRONMENT OUTLOOK 2000, at 90–91 (2000).

Lead: Exposure to lead emissions is primarily from cars that still use leaded fuel, industrial production especially paints and batteries, and contaminated food. In adults the consequences include risks of higher blood pressure and higher risks of heart attack and stroke. The consequences for children are even more disturbing. In Mexico City, lead exposure may contribute to as much as 20 percent of the incidence of hypertension. Estimates for Bangkok, as another example, suggest that the average child has lost four or more IQ points by the age of seven because of elevated exposure to lead, with enduring implications for adult productivity. The World Bank, WORLD DEVELOPMENT REPORT 1999/2000, at 141 (2000).

As with water distribution, clean air has also become a source of tension between nations. Countries with stringent air quality regulations downwind from countries with less restrictive policies often suffer despite their efforts at the national level. See Chapter 9.

———

QUESTIONS AND DISCUSSION

1. Given the interrelated nature of ecosystems, is there such a thing as a truly local environmental problem? Beyond the ethical reason of caring for the welfare of others, why should citizens of the developed world be concerned about problems of sanitation or health in cities in the developing world?

2. As we will see in Chapter Six, every nation-State is sovereign under international law. It has the right to decide for itself how to manage its own resources, how to govern its own people, how to deal with its own problems. When a State invites international assistance in addressing an internal environmental problem, the sovereignty issue is not raised. But what if the State does not want international assistance—or interference—in the management of its environment? Should the people of a country have the absolute right to refuse that interference, to address their own problems in their own way?

The 1987 forest fires in Indonesia provide a good example. The fires, which began in September 1997 as a result of slash and burn agriculture in an exceptionally dry year, destroyed hundreds of millions of acres. Not only did these fires pose a local threat to human health and the environment in Indonesia but also, they threatened the air quality of neighboring regions and the global climate. Smoke from the fires forced airports hundreds of miles away to close due to poor visibility and people to walk the street with handkerchiefs and masks over their mouths to help them breathe.

Indonesia is rich in biodiversity and natural resources. According to the World Conservation Monitoring Center, the fires in Indonesia threatened at least nineteen protected areas of international importance, including a World Heritage site (Ujung Kulon in Java), a wetland designated as internationally important under the Ramsar Convention (Berbak in Sumatra), and an international Biosphere Reserve (Tanjung Puting in Kalimantan). The fires threatened endangered species such as the orangutan, already at risk due to habitat loss.

Indonesian forests are critical as natural "sinks" for carbon dioxide, the most important greenhouse gas. When forests burn, they release their substantial stores of carbon dioxide into the atmosphere. The bogs have been accumulating biomass for up to 15,000 years, contain 10 percent of all the carbon locked in world soils, and some scientists estimate that Indonesia hosts one-fifth of the 600 billion tons of carbon stored in the world's peat bogs. Consequently, the peat fires in Indonesia caused widespread global concern that massive amounts of carbon dioxide could be released into the atmosphere, contributing to global warming and long-term climate change. Peat fires are underground fires that are hard to extinguish and burn for prolonged periods. An estimated 1.7 million hectares (4.2 million acres) burned, releasing more carbon dioxide into the atmosphere than an entire year's worth of fossil fuel burning in the entire European Community.

The forest fires in Indonesia began as "controlled" fires intended to open forestlands for agriculture and development, but quickly escaped, with significant transboundary and global effects. Assume for a moment that Indonesia preferred to let the fires burn themselves out, and use scarce government resources to deal with other problems. Should it have the right to do so? Or should Indonesia have a responsibility to the international community to fight the fires vigorously? What if the fires didn't contribute to global warming or cause transboundary air pollution, but still threatened species and ecosystems that had been designated as internationally important—as part of the world's cultural and biological heritage? Would this change your assessment? Would the international community have sufficient concern with environmental protection to justify providing international firefighting assistance efforts over Indonesia's objections? The issue of when, and if, local environmental problems become proper subjects of international law is a central and continuing concern of international environmental law and this book.

C. FOOD SECURITY AND AGRICULTURE

Food scarcity and the impact of agriculture on the environment are also "local" problems with global dimensions. More than 1 billion people are undernourished and the world's population is expected to increase up to 70 percent in the next 50 years. While population is constantly growing, our food sources may be nearing maximum production capacity. Between 1950 and 2000, the world production of grain nearly tripled, and reached an all-time per capita high in 1984 of 342 kilograms of grain per person. After 1984, production failed to match population growth, with 2000 per capita grain production 10 percent below 1984 level. Meanwhile, loss of topsoil, climate change, and desertification are reducing arable land. Up to 70% of the world's fisheries are depleted or under stress after years of over-exploitation; and fish catch per person has steadily declined in the last ten years. Lester Brown, *Eradicating Hunger: A Growing Challenge* in STATE OF THE WORLD 2001 at 45 (2001). To feed predicted population levels, food production will have to double at a time when 800 million people worldwide are already malnourished, 25 billion tons of topsoil are lost annually, and nearly three-quarters of the oceans' fish stocks are overexploited. The World Bank, WORLD DEVELOPMENT REPORT 1999/2000 28 (2000). In the absence of adequate food supplies from sustainable sources, people are forced into unsustainable uses of natural resources—over-hunting local species, farming on marginal lands subject to soil erosion, degradation and desertification, and migrating to urban areas where environmental pressures are magnified. The following reading describes these food security trends.

Lester Brown, *Eradicating Hunger: A Growing Challenge*
STATE OF THE WORLD, 2001, at 43–62 (2001)

1.1 billion people are undernourished and underweight as the new century begins. ... In its most basic form, hunger is a productivity problem. Typically people are hungry because they do not produce enough food to meet their needs or because they do not earn enough money to buy it. The only lasting solution is to raise the productivity of the hungry—a task complicated by the ongoing shrinkage in cropland per person in developing countries. * * *

Within agriculture, raising land productivity deserves even greater priority today than in the past. This means raising crop yields in biological terms wherever possible, including minor crops. It also means more multiple cropping, a potential not yet fully realized in all countries. * * *

Given the constraints on crop yields imposed by inadequate soil moisture, raising water productivity is a key to further gains in land productivity. Governments running the risk of an abrupt drop in food production as a result of aquifer depletion may be able to avoid such a situation by slowing population growth and raising water productivity in order to stabilize water tables.

Eradicating hunger also means getting more out of the existing harvest. It means increasing the efficiency with which the 35 percent of the world grain harvest that is fed to livestock, poultry, and fish is converted into animal protein. Simply put, it means eating less feedlot beef and less pork and more poultry and farmed fish or plant sources of protein. Within fish farming, it may also mean replacing fish monocultures with polycultures following the highly successful Chinese model. For the world's affluent, it means moving down the food chain by consuming less fat-rich livestock products, something they should be doing for health reasons anyway.

Stabilizing population is as essential as it is difficult. If rapid population growth continues in many developing countries, it will lead to further land fragmentation of holdings, as well as hydrological poverty on a scale now difficult to imagine. Literally hundreds of millions of people will not have enough water to meet their most basic needs, including food production. Addressing this challenge requires an effort ... [to raise] the educational level of women. As female education levels rise, fertility falls.... The nutrition of their children improves, even if incomes do not rise, apparently because more education brings a better understanding of nutrition. * * *

For sub-Saharan Africa, eradicating hunger depends on curbing the HIV/AIDS epidemic, which is depriving societies of healthy adults to work in the fields. If Africa continues to lose its adult breadwinners, it will further complicate efforts to eradicate hunger. * * *

Eradicating hunger ... will not be easy. It is difficult to eradicate for the same reasons it exists in the first place—rapid population growth, land hunger, and water scarcity. But there are also new forces that could complicate efforts to eliminate hunger. For example, Bangladesh, a country of 129 million people, has less than one tenth of a hectare of grainland per person—one of the smallest allotments in the world—and it is threatened by rising sea level. The World Bank projects that a 1–meter rise in sea level during this century, the upper range of the recent projections by the IPCC, would cost Bangladesh half its riceland. This, combined with the prospect of adding another 83 million people over the next half century, shows just how difficult it will be for Bangladesh, one of the world's hungriest countries, to feed its people. * * *

The war against hunger cannot be won with business as usual. Given the forces at work, it will no longer be possible to stand still. If societies do not take decisive steps, they face the possibility of being forced into involuntary retreat by continuing population growth, spreading land hunger, deepening hydrological poverty, increasing climate instability, and a shrinking backlog of unused agricultural technology. Eradicating hunger—never easy—will now take a superhuman effect ... dependent as much on the efforts of family planners as on farmers and as much on the decisions made in ministries of energy that shape future climate trends as on decisions made in ministries of agriculture.

Food security and the environmental impacts of agriculture are related to diet, which in turn is related to poverty and equity. It is the poor who must worry about their next meal; the rich eat what they want. A large scale change in the developed country diet from meat to vegetables and grains would be of far more significance than many people realize, as World Bank ecologist Robert Goodland explains in the excerpt below.

Robert Goodland, *Environmental Sustainability: Eat Better and Kill Less* 1, 5–7 (World Bank, 1996)

[T]he environmental impact of the agriculture sector probably exceeds the impacts of all other sectors, even manufacturing and industry in many countries. Agriculture has degraded more natural capital and caused more extinctions of species than any other sector. Agriculture uses more water than other sectors of the economy in many nations. Many aspects of agriculture can be heavy polluters (e.g., feedlot runoff, abattoirs, effluent from oil palm, rubber, coffee processing, irrigation and salination). The energy consumption of agriculture is one of the biggest, considering diesel (tractors, pumps), energy content of fertilizers and biocides, and transport infrastructure. * * *

Affluent people in OECD countries consume about 800 kg of grain indirectly, much of it inefficiently converted into animal flesh, with the balance as milk, cheese, eggs, ice cream and yogurt. Such diets are high in fats and protein, low in starch. In contrast, in low-consuming countries, annual consumption of grains averages 200 kg per person, practically all of it directly, with little inefficiency in conversion. Such diets are rich in starch and low in fats and protein. The grain consumption ratio between rich and poor countries is about four to one.

FAO [the UN Food and Agriculture Organization] calculates that almost 50% of global grains are fed to livestock. The two countries converting the most grain into meat are the United States and China—160 and 100 million tons respectively. Developing country's elites are eating increasingly high up the food chain. Developing countries' increased animal consumption between 1960 and 1990 was 48% for large ruminants, 53% for small ruminants, 200% for hogs and 280% for poultry. Little of this reaches the poor. Increased grain importation into developing countries is to feed "animals that are consumed by the minority higher-income sectors of society". The question becomes, would the world's more affluent be willing to simplify their diets for whatever reason—health, ethics, equity, environment, economics, religion? Would the grain thus freed-up be distributed to prevent famine and hunger where and when needed?

Not only are mammals inefficient converters, their production is environmentally costly in terms of water used and greenhouse gases [GHG] generated. The production of one pound of beef consumes over 2000 gallons of water, whereas grain production consumes 200 gallons, and vegetables about half that. Cattle contribute about 60 million tons of GHG per year, slightly less than rice paddies (70) but more than burning vegetation (55), gas drilling (45), termites (40) and landfills (40)....

One acre of cereals can produce twice to ten times as much protein as an acre devoted to beef production.... One acre of legumes can produce ten to twenty times more protein than an acre in beef production. The UN World Food Council calculates that "ten to fifteen percent of cereals now fed to livestock is enough to raise the world food supply to adequate levels." In summary, raising livestock is more destructive in depleting topsoil, groundwater and energy resources than all other human activities combined, as well as causing enormous environmental damage, such as clearing of forests, destruction of wildlife habitat, pollution of rivers and lakes.

QUESTIONS AND DISCUSSION

1. Environmental problems are often interrelated. As the Lester Brown reading suggests, food security is dependent on climate. Climate change is expected to shift growing zones and to produce more extreme weather events, such as hurricanes, tornadoes, and typhoons, with potentially major effects on food production. Goodland points out the significant contribution to greenhouse gases from cattle production, as compared to other forms of food production.

2. Diet is typically regarded as a fundamental personal choice. No one would seriously suggest criminalizing carnivorous habits. Short of shutting down steak houses and banning the Big Mac, what roles can national law play? For example, in 1996, the UN FAO World Food Summit suggested global implementation of national Food for All campaigns. Many governments offer significant subsidies to their agricultural sectors, but reducing these subsidies is politically difficult. Would negotiating an international agreement make it easier to reduce subsidies? To date, international law has been much more effective at reducing trade barriers than reducing agricultural subsidies. Why do you think this has been the case?

Do you think dietary choices could be changed by mandating an environmental label for food products? Note the poverty and equity issues that relate to diet, as well. As we approach limits to per capita grain production, how should we allocate the global grain supply? Does international law have a role to play in making such an allocation or would that be unwise interference with the market? Would it make a difference if dietary choices in developed countries were shown to decrease the food available to the world's very poor?

3. Genetically engineered crops and livestock, or biotech, are the most recent additions to the food safety and security debate. Although these may increase yields, they also present a variety of ethical, scientific, and policy challenges. What are the risks and advantages of using biotech? Is current environmental law equipped to address biotech concerns? Should biotech products be labeled as such? Should biotech crops allowed for animal consumption, but prohibited from human consumption be planted? What if they cross-pollinate with non-biotech crops? Also, what legal liabilities could potentially be created by cross-pollination?

SECTION III. POVERTY

Poverty has traditionally been thought of as wholly separate from environmental protection issues. Indeed, poverty alleviation and economic development are legitimate goals for international cooperation in their own right. Increasingly, however, alleviating poverty and environment protection have been recognized as interdependent goals and challenges. As Mahatma Gandhi reportedly said, "poverty is the greatest cause of environmental harm." The day-to-day challenges of life at poverty's edge may drive people to unsustainable uses of land and other resources. Environmental degradation, in turn, reduces the amount and quality of resources available, pushing the poor to use increasingly marginal resources and further perpetuating this destructive spiral.

In 1983, the United Nations appointed an independent commission of experts to examine in detail the relationship between development and the environment. The World Commission on Environment and Development— sometimes called the Brundtland Commission after its chairperson and former Norwegian Prime Minister, Gro Harlem Brundtland—released a comprehensive report in 1987 entitled *Our Common Future. Our Common Future*, discussed further in Chapter Four, has become a classic in international environmental policy for its role in arguing that economics and the environment should be integrated through the concept of sustainable development. The following excerpt from that report discusses the cyclical relationship between poverty and environmental degradation. As you read, consider how the facts presented may have changed in the decade since *Our Common Future* was released.

World Commission on Environment and Development
OUR COMMON FUTURE 29–31 (1987)

There are more hungry people in the world today than ever before in human history, and their numbers are growing. In 1980, there were 340 million people in 87 developing countries not getting enough calories to prevent stunted growth and serious health risks. This total was very slightly below the figure for 1970 in terms of share of the world population, but in terms of sheer numbers, it represented a 14 per cent increase. The World Bank predicts that these numbers are likely to go on growing.

The number of people living in slums and shanty towns is rising, not falling. A growing number lack access to clean water and sanitation and hence are prey to the diseases that arise from this lack. There is some progress, impressive in places. But, on balance, poverty persists and its victims multiply.

The pressure of poverty has to be seen in a broader context. At the international level there are large differences in per capita income, which ranged in 1984 from $190 in low-income countries (other than China and India) to $11,430 in the industrial market economies.

Such inequalities represent great differences not merely in the quality of life today, but also in the capacity of societies to improve their quality of life in the future. Most of the world's poorest countries depend for increasing export earnings on tropical agricultural products that are vulnerable to fluctuating or declining terms of trade. Expansion can often only be achieved at the price of ecological stress. Yet diversification in ways that will alleviate both poverty and ecological stress is hampered by disadvantageous terms of technology transfer, by protectionism, and by declining financial flows to those countries that most need international finance.

Within countries, poverty has been exacerbated by the unequal distribution of land and other assets. The rapid rise in population has compromised the ability to raise living standards. These factors, combined with growing demands for the commercial use of good land, often to grow crops for exports, have pushed many subsistence farmers onto poor land and robbed them of any hope of participating in their nations' economic lives. The same forces have meant that traditional shifting cultivators, who once cut forests, grew crops, and then gave the forest time to recover, now have neither land enough nor time to let forests re-establish. So forests are being destroyed, often only to create poor farmland that cannot support those who till it. Extending cultivation onto steep slopes is increasing soil erosion in many hilly sections of both developing and developed nations. In many river valleys, areas chronically liable to floods are now farmed.

These pressures are reflected in the rising incidence of disasters. During the 1970s, six times as many people died from "natural disasters" each year as in the 1960s, and twice as many suffered from such disasters. Droughts and floods, disasters among whose causes are widespread deforestation and overcultivation, increased most in terms of numbers affected. There were 18.5 million people affected by droughts annually in the 1960s, but 24.4 million in the 1970s; 5.2 million people were victims of floods yearly in the 1960s, compared with 15.4 million in the 1970s. The results are not in for the 1980s, but this disaster prone decade seems to be carrying forward the trend, with droughts in Africa, India, and Latin America, and floods throughout Asia, parts of Africa, and the Andean region of Latin America.

Such disasters claim most of their victims among the impoverished in poor nations, where subsistence farmers must make their land more liable to droughts and floods by clearing marginal areas, and where the poor make themselves more vulnerable to all disasters by living on steep slopes and unprotected shores—the only lands left for their shanties. Lacking food and foreign exchange reserves, their economically vulnerable governments are ill equipped to cope with such catastrophes.

The links between environmental stress and developmental disaster are most evident in sub-Saharan Africa. Per capita food production, declining since the 1960s, plummeted during the drought of the 1980s, and at the height of the food emergency some 35 million people were exposed to risk. Human overuse of land and prolonged drought threaten to turn the grasslands of Africa's Sahel region into desert. No other region more tragically suffers the vicious cycle of poverty leading to environmental degradation, which leads in turn to even greater poverty.

Five years after *Our Common Future*, the World Bank examined the complex interdependence of poverty, development, and environment protection in its 1992 *World Development Report*. Prepared in anticipation of the 1992 UN Conference on Environment and Development (UNCED or the Earth Summit), the World Development Report was the Bank's first major pronouncement on sustainable development.

THE WORLD BANK, WORLD DEVELOPMENT REPORT 1992, at 1–2 (1992)

The achievement of sustained and equitable development remains the greatest challenge facing the human race. Despite good progress over the past generation, more than 1 billion people still live in acute poverty and suffer grossly inadequate access to the resources—education, health services, infrastructure, land, and credit—required to give them a chance for a better life. The essential task of development is to provide opportunities so that these people, and the hundreds of millions not much better off, can reach their potential.

But although the desirability of development is universally recognized, recent years have witnessed rising concern about whether environmental constraints will limit development and whether development will cause serious environmental damage—in turn impairing the quality of life of this and future generations. * * *

[There is a] two-way relationship between development and the environment.... [E]nvironmental problems can and do undermine the goals of development. There are two ways in which this can happen. First, environmental quality—water that is safe and plentiful and air that is healthy—is itself part of the improvement in welfare that development attempts to bring. If the benefits from rising incomes are offset by the costs imposed on health and the quality of life by pollution, this cannot be called development. Second, environmental damage can undermine future productivity. Soils that are degraded, aquifers that are depleted, and ecosystems that are destroyed in the name of raising incomes today can jeopardize the prospects for earning income.

[The impact of economic growth on the environment is both good and bad. There are] conditions under which policies for efficient income growth can complement those for environmental protection [though there are also trade-offs].... There are strong "win-win" opportunities that remain unexploited. The most important of these relates to poverty reduction: not only is attacking poverty a moral imperative, but it is also essential for environmental stewardship. Moreover, policies that are justified on economic grounds alone can deliver substantial environmental benefits. Eliminating subsidies for the use of fossil fuels and water, giving poor farmers property rights on the land they farm, making heavily polluting state-owned companies more competitive, and eliminating rules that reward with property rights those who clear forests are examples of policies that improve both economic efficiency and the environment. Similarly, investing in better sanitation and water and in improved research and extension services can both improve the environment *and* raise incomes.

But these policies are not enough to ensure environmental quality; strong public institutions and policies for environmental protection are also essential. The world has learned over the past two decades to rely more on markets and less on governments to promote development. But environmental protection is one area in which government must maintain a central role. Private markets provide little or no incentive for curbing pollution. * * * The evidence indicates that the gains from protecting the environment are often high and that the costs in forgone income are modest if appropriate policies are adopted. Experience suggests that policies are most effective when they aim at underlying causes rather than symptoms, concentrate on addressing those problems for which the benefits for reform are greatest, use incentives rather than regulations where possible, and recognize administrative constraints.

Strong environmental policies complement and reinforce development. It is often the poorest who suffer most from the consequences of pollution and environmental degradation. Unlike the rich, the poor cannot afford to protect themselves from contaminated water; in cities they are more likely to spend much of their time on the streets, breathing polluted air; in rural areas they are more likely to cook on open fires of wood or dung, inhaling dangerous fumes; their lands are most likely to suffer from soil erosion. The poor may also draw a large part of their livelihood from unmarketed environmental resources: common grazing lands, for example, or forests where food, fuel, and building materials have traditionally been gathered. The loss of such resources may particularly harm the poorest. Sound environmental policies are thus likely to be powerfully redistributive.

A 2000 World Bank publication, *The Quality of Growth*, builds on the *1992 World Development Report* and re-states its main policy recommendations—removing environmentally damaging subsidies, clarifying property rights, accelerating the provision of sanitation, providing education, especially for women, and empowering local people, as well as using market-based instruments such as green taxes and taking collaborative approaches to pollution management.

QUESTIONS AND DISCUSSION

1. Tens of millions of poverty-stricken people each year abandon degraded rural areas for cities—either in their home countries or abroad—in the hope of finding work and a means of subsistence. These environmental refugees are flooding into already crowded urban areas that lack the infrastructure or the financial resources to support them. City boundaries are being pushed rapidly outward by shantytowns with poor or non-existent sanitation, few employment opportunities, and inadequate supplies of food and clean water. These mega-cities place tremendous pressure on their surrounding environments, further exacerbating existing environmental problems and extending the cycle of poverty. Because of soil erosion, urban expansion and other factors, China lost 3.87 million hectares of arable land between 1987 and

1992. Along with this land, China lost the capacity to produce 15 million tons of grain, enough to feed 45 million people. In its 1997 *State of the World* report, the WorldWatch Institute reports that China hopes to build as many as 600 new cities by 2010. The report notes that "[i]f this prompts cropland losses to industry, infrastructure, and housing at the rate experienced between 1987 and 1993, about 6.5 million hectares—another 5 percent of China's agricultural land—would be lost from production by 2010, even as population there rises by some 14 percent." Gary Gardner, *Preserving Global Cropland*, in LESTER BROWN ET AL., STATE OF THE WORLD 1997, at 46 (WorldWatch Institute, 1997). What would you expect the environmental consequences of China's policy to be?

2. Hal Kane, in a different WorldWatch report, notes that environmental degradation is a significant source of refugee flows. Indeed when poverty and environmental degradation occur within an already unstable political system, interacting forces can create refugee flows and political crises far greater than any of them would have created alone.

> Famine is sufficient to drive millions to relief camps and across borders. Often, however, famine combines with political extremism and armed conflict to force even more people to move. The fighting worsens famines because people cannot stay on their farms and because soldiers steal food; and the social disintegration that follows acute hunger and dislocation of people fuels violence because people's resistance against demagoguery weakens when their social networks are dispersed. * * *

> Thus, famine and conflict are tied together, and their combination produces far larger migrations than either would alone. Somalia, for instance, is a place where these problems have intersected, with disastrous consequences. Since early 1994, most fighting has occurred outside Mogadishu in the farm belt. And yet, according to some Somalia analysts, the U.S. and the U.N. paid little attention to one of the underlying causes of conflict, the struggle to control the nation's best farmland, which is coveted by the warlords. Actually, Somalia's conflict is the continuation of a 100-year-old movement of major Somali clans southward from nomadic grazing areas that have been becoming more and more overpopulated. Today, resident minority tribes such as the Gosha have been dispossessed of their land. Half a million Somalis were refugees in neighboring countries in 1993, and some 700,000 were internally displaced. Behind their wanderings lay not just fighting among clans but also long-term population growth and land scarcity.

> Poverty and environmental degradation often create scarcities that push people out of the regions where they live. Exhausted supplies of firewood and timber for heating and cooking and building, depleted wells, overcrowding in houses and schools, and a lack of electricity all plague poor regions. These scarcities often band together to form a cycle of inadequacy. Felled trees, for example, no longer anchor soil, which washes away and clogs rivers, and the disrupted flows of water cause further soil erosion and disrupt harvests of fish. In rural areas where people directly depend on the soil and water and forests for sustenance, poverty is essentially an environmental trend. These people are usually cash poor, yet so long as they are natural resource rich, they can remain home and prosper. But when people flee poverty they are often fleeing environmental impoverishment—after the topsoil blew away or the well ran dry—in places without a rural economy that can offer them alternative sources of livelihood.

Hal Kane, *The Hour of Departure: Forces that Create Refugees and Migrants*, WORLDWATCH PAPER 125, at 10–14 (1995).

The flow of environmental refugees can create further instability and conflict by creating new social pressures in the areas where refugees travel and settle. For example, four separate uprisings broke out in the cities of northern Nigeria between 1980 and 1985, all triggered by refugees who had been displaced by desertification and drought. Chapter 17 addresses these issues in the context of national security concerns. *See e.g.,* William C. Burns, *The International Convention to Combat Desertification: Drawing a Line in the Sand?,* 16 MICH. J. INT'L L. 831, 847–48 (1995); *Desertification and Migrations, in* DOWN TO EARTH—(CCD Newsletter No. 1, May 1996); NORMAN MYERS ET AL., ULTIMATE SECURITY: THE ENVIRONMENTAL BASIS OF POLITICAL STABILITY (1993).

3. For provocative discussions of potential ethical conflicts raised by poverty, *see* the excerpts in Chapter 2—and "The Singer Solution to World Poverty" at page 109.

SECTION IV. SYNERGIES AND CLIFFS: THE NON-LINEAR CONSEQUENCES OF LINEAR THINKING

A fundamental rule of classical toxicology is that "the dose makes the poison." The toxic amount of a substance might vary from person to person, depending upon variables such as body size and health, but the general rule is the same: the "biological response to a foreign substance increases [fairly steadily] as the dose becomes greater." THEO COLBORN ET AL., OUR STOLEN FUTURE 205 (1997). Policymakers and the public alike often assume that environmental problems develop in the same way, that the consequences of our actions keep fairly steady pace with the actions themselves. If a certain amount of a particular air pollutant is bad for the environment, a little more is a little worse, and a little less is a little better. If it holds true, this assumption of a linear relationship between cause and consequence allows policymakers to choose quite specifically the level of environmental protection they want. The problem, however, is that the assumption often does not hold: environmental degradation—and the impact on human health and society arising from that degradation—often does not progress in a linear fashion. Time and again, we have seen that a little bit more is not just a little bit worse, but a great deal worse. Our position is analogous to that of a blindfolded person walking toward the edge of a cliff: she is still on solid ground, and each step feels just like the last, until that one ... final ... step. Like her, we cannot know which step will be our last.

A. SYNERGISTIC INTERACTIONS OF TOXINS

One example of the non-linear relationship between cause and effect emerges from the study of toxins. A linear dose-response relationship appears to hold with respect to the toxic effects of many individual substances under laboratory conditions. But when substances are combined, they sometimes produce effects far greater than could be predicted by simply adding together their toxicities. As stated previously, two plus two does not necessarily equal four. Chemicals interacting this way are said to have "synergistic effects." The increased toxicity could not readily have been predicted from the characteristics of the substances considered separately. When substances interact synergistically, doses otherwise well below toxic levels can become extremely dangerous.

A classic case of synergy is asbestos and tobacco smoke. The combination of these two carcinogens produces a multiplicative increase in the rate of lung cancer mortality. Smokers exposed to asbestos are fifty times more likely to die of lung cancer than nonsmokers who are not exposed to asbestos, reflecting the five-fold increase in risk for asbestos exposure, times the ten-fold risk from smoking. A REPORT OF THE SURGEON GENERAL, U.S. DEPARTMENT OF HEALTH AND HUMAN SERVICES, PUBLIC HEALTH SERVICE, 1985 at 13.

In *Silent Spring*, Rachel Carson's historic exposé of the impact of chemical contamination on the environment (which many observers credit with launching the modern environmental movement), Dr. Carson illustrated synergies with the following example:

> The effect of a chemical of supposedly innocuous nature can be drastically changed by the action of another; one of the best examples is a close relative of DDT called methoxychlor. (Actually, methoxychlor may not be as free from dangerous qualities as it is generally said to be, for recent work on experimental animals shows a direct action on the uterus and a blocking effect on some of the powerful pituitary hormones—reminding us again that these are chemicals with enormous biologic effect. Other work shows that methoxychlor has a potential ability to damage the kidneys.) Because it is not stored to any great extent when given alone, we are told that methoxychlor is a safe chemical. But this is not necessarily true. If the liver has been damaged by another agent, methoxychlor is stored in the body at *100 times* its normal rate, and will then imitate the effects of DDT with long-lasting effects on the nervous system. Yet the liver damage that brings this about might be so slight as to pass unnoticed. It might have been the result of any of a number of commonplace situations— using another insecticide, using a cleaning fluid containing carbon tetrachloride, or taking one of the so-called tranquilizing drugs, a number (but not all) of which are chlorinated hydrocarbons and possess power to damage the liver.

RACHEL CARSON, SILENT SPRING 195–96 (1962).

Since the 1960s, such synergies among chemicals have been discovered in ever-greater numbers. Synergistic interactions have also been observed in mixtures of up to twenty or more chemicals. Combinations of substances have been discovered with synergistic effects 10,000 times more harmful than would be expected from simply adding the toxicities of the individual chemicals.

―――――

B. ENVIRONMENTAL CLIFFS

Non-linear responses are not restricted to the world of chemical interactions. The possibility of sudden, dramatic, and often unforeseen environmental changes—environmental cliffs—exists wherever there are multiple disturbances to complex systems. It is inherent in the very structure of the natural world.

Global Warming. The risk of crossing an unexpected critical line, of falling off an unseen cliff, or glacier in this case, can be seen in the possible relationship between global warming and the melting of polar ice. According to journalist Eugene Linden, like blindly walking toward a cliff, due to global warming we may be approaching the melting of the ice sheet without knowing it.

> If climate change brings about a large rise in sea level, the principal immediate cause will be the collapse of the West Antarctic ice sheet [WAIS]. WAIS is the world's last remaining marine ice sheet (meaning that it sits on the ocean floor rather than floats). It is so big that volcanic eruptions at its bottom only rarely cause a dimple on its surface. Marine ice sheets persist only as long as they have enough mass to squeeze out underlying seawater, which makes them inherently unstable. Should this ice sheet collapse or float free, as other marine ice sheets have done, global sea level would rise nearly 20 ft., which would inundate most of Florida and hundreds of low-lying cities from Jakarta to London.... As long as accumulation at the center offsets the amount of ice lost through sublimation (as ice turns directly into vapor) or the calving of icebergs, the great ice sheet remains stable. If it begins shedding ice rapidly, however, the sheet gets lighter, allowing warm seawater to intrude underneath, further speeding the flow of ice to the edges. At some point—no one knows when—the whole sheet begins to come apart. That is when sea level around the world would climb rapidly.

> Eugene Linden, *Antarctica: Warnings from the Ice*, Time, April 14, 1997, at 54.

Keystone species. Another non-linear environmental problem was demonstrated in a famous experiment by marine ecologist John Paine. In 1960, Paine removed all the individuals of the sea star *Pisaster* from tide pools off the Washington coast, in order to determine the effect of that removal on the surrounding ecosystem. He was astounded by the results. The tide pools are characterized by densely packed beds of mussels, barnacles, and seaweed, all attached to the rocky ocean floor, or to each other. *Pisaster* was the most important predator of one species of mussel, *Mytilus*. Once this predator was removed, the *Mytilus* population expanded unchecked, crowding out many other species. As a result, the entire nature of the ecosystem changed and seven of fifteen species disappeared. The system lost nearly half of its biodiversity because of the removal of a single species: it was pushed over our proverbial cliff.

This same experiment has been repeated time and again, unintentionally, by non-scientists. During the 19th and early 20th centuries, sea otters were heavily exploited all along the Pacific Coast of North America, both by indigenous hunters and by commercial operators. As a result of over hunting, sea otter populations eventually collapsed, with an unexpected result. Before the otters were over hunted, the waters off the Pacific coast were filled with thick forests of kelp, a type of blue-green algae that can grow as much as a hundred feet high. The kelp provided food and habitat for a rich variety of fish and invertebrate species. One of these species, the herbivorous sea urchin, feeds on kelp. Otters, in turn, feed on sea urchins. When the otters were removed from coastal ecosystems, the number of sea urchins increased dramatically. Uncontrolled, the sea urchins overgrazed the kelp, destroying the habitat it had provided for other species. As a result, once rich kelp beds were turned into vast "urchin barrens," inhospitable to most species. Fortunately, hunting of the sea otters ceased before the species was extinct. As sea otter populations have recovered, the kelp beds—and the ecosystems they support—have begun to return.

When an entire ecosystem is affected in this way, the economic and social consequences can be substantial. Rich fisheries can collapse; important food species can vanish; the entire natural order of a wide region can shift. Not all species extinctions lead to such significant ecosystem changes. Often, the loss of a single species is just that, the loss of one species. Take, for example, the extinction of England's large blue butterfly described below:

> In the simple grass-rabbits-foxes chain, a reduction in the rabbit population might be expected to result in an increase in the amount of grass (fewer consumers) and a decrease in the fox population (fewer prey). Some years ago, this happened in Britain, when large numbers of rabbits died from myxomatosis. Predator populations fell. In some places, stoat numbers were reduced to one-third of their pre-myxomatosis levels, rabbits being the principal prey of stoats [a predatorial animal similar to a weasel]. No longer nibbled, grasses also grew taller; and that was where the complications began. Being taller, they cast more shade on the ground, which suppressed the growth of many small herbs, including wild thyme (*Thymus drucei*), which until then grew in a few places in Devon and Cornwall. When they first hatch, larvae of the large blue butterfly (*Maculinea arion*) feed on wild thyme and enter into a symbiotic (interdependent) relationship with ants, living in ant nests until they pupate. As the grasses grew and the thyme disappeared from the sward, adult butterflies were unable to lay their eggs in appropriate places, and on 12 September 1979 the large blue butterfly was formally pronounced extinct in Britain, its last colony, in Devon, having died out.
>
> Michael Allaby, Basics of Environmental Science at 146 (Routledge Press, 1996).

The problem is, we cannot know in advance when such an extinction will be a quiet, lonely event and when it will trigger wholesale changes in the environment.

> Perhaps the greatest challenge of all lies in determining which characteristic species contribute most to their ecosystem, to productivity, to predictability. Are some species more essential than others from a functional, ecological point of view? In the present state of our ignorance, an attempt to answer this might lead to some nasty choices. Surely some species are more important to their ecosystems than are others, as indicators of ecological processes or as keystones that influence community structure. But which are these? We know pitifully few of them for coastal and ocean systems. So when some decision-maker asks which species might be sacrificed, we cannot say. The immense diversity of life seems simply redundant to many who are in the position of having to decide about environmental matters—and we might have to admit that some species may indeed be redundant. But when asked to identify such redundancies, we may react like the young Mozart when told by Emperor Josef II that his sonata contained too many notes. He replied that it contained "exactly the necessary number."

G. Carleton Ray, *Ecological Diversity in Coastal Zones and Oceans*, 36, 44–45 in Biodiversity (E.O. Wilson ed. 1988).

QUESTIONS AND DISCUSSION

1. In developing models of climate change, scientists have long assumed that the ability of the oceans to absorb CO_2, and thus slow global warming, would remain constant as global temperature increases. Studies, though, have called this assumption into question. Climate models developed by Jorge Sarmiento and Corinne Le Quere of Princeton University suggest that a global temperature increase of five degrees could slow the currents that carry CO_2 away from the ocean surface and into the depths. As these currents slow down, their ability to absorb CO_2 may be reduced by as much as 50%. The extra CO_2 will remain in the atmosphere, further exacerbating and speeding global climate change. This is one example of a positive "feedback loop"—a cyclical process triggered by environmental change that leads back to more change. Fred Pearce, *Will a Sea Change Turn Up the Heat?*, NEW SCIENTIST, November 30, 1996, at 16.

2. Synergistic effects emerge elsewhere in the environmental context. As with chemical toxins, the consequences of environmental degradation are usually evaluated in isolation. Just as chemicals can interact, environmental problems can also interact with each other. For example, ozone depletion causes increases in ultraviolet radiation, which in turn appears to suppress the human immune system. At the same time, our exposure to carcinogens and other chemicals is being increased due to the accumulation of persistent pollutants. Add this exposure to new disease vectors brought about by climate change, and humans and wildlife are faced with an often deadly "cocktail" of environmental synergisms. For an excellent discussion of environmental synergisms, see Andrew Dobson et. al., *Fatal Synergisms: Interactions Between Infectious Diseases, Human Population Growth, and Loss of Biodiversity*, in BIODIVERSITY AND HUMAN HEALTH 87 (Francesca Grifo & Joshua Rosenthal eds. 1997).

3. How can the law address the uncertainty and risk associated with synergies and cliffs? For example, should the law mandate an immediate halt to the production of new chemicals? Require people to avoid every action that might endanger a species? Require them to stop driving cars and burning fossil fuels now to hedge against the mere possibility that the West Antarctic ice sheet could collapse? Can the law compel such radical changes, or do we first have to undertake more fundamental changes in our economy, our culture and our ethical belief systems?

For the foreseeable future, at least, such a radical reversal of human habits may be impossible. How, then, do we determine which course of action to take? Is it wise to act as if environmental degradation always progresses at a steady pace, knowing that there are critical exceptions to this rule? On the other hand, how can we balance the identifiable costs and sacrifices of foregone development against the uncertain benefits of avoiding potential environmental cliffs? How do we deal with incomplete information in environmental decision-making? We will turn to these questions in Section VI.

SECTION V. HUMAN ACTIVITY AND THE ENVIRONMENT: THE PROBLEM OF SCALE

Further [economic] growth beyond the present scale is overwhelmingly likely to increase costs more rapidly than it increases benefits, thus ushering in a new era of "uneconomic growth" that impoverishes rather than enriches. This is the fundamental wild fact that so far has not found expression in words sufficiently feral to assault successfully the civil stupor of economic discourse.

Herman E. Daly & John B. Cobb, Jr., For the Common Good 2
(1989)

A. SCALE: THE RELATIVE SIZE OF HUMAN ACTIVITY WITHIN THE GLOBAL ECOSYSTEM

We have glimpsed an overview of the major environmental problems—global and local—facing the world. We have seen how these problems are often interrelated, in the sense that environmental degradation of one kind can often contribute to environmental degradation of another kind. More importantly, however, all of the environmental threats discussed so far, when considered together, suggest another underlying "wild fact"—the scale of human activity is growing too large to be indefinitely sustained by the Earth's environment.

Human activity, including the industrial economy, is a subsystem of the global ecological system. Its ability to grow is limited by the physical limits of the ecosystem. Scale refers to the scope or size of human activity relative to those ecosystem limits. In the past, the scale of human activity was so small relative to the limits, or "carrying capacity," of the global ecosystem that the planet's capacity to provide natural resources and absorb pollution seemed infinite. Because the "sources" of natural resources (such as oil, gas, timber, or fish) and the "sinks" that absorb and neutralize pollution (the atmosphere and oceans, for example) could be considered infinite, economists and lawmakers could justifiably assume a world without physical limits—a world in which limitless resources could support limitless growth.

This assumption has proven inadequate in the face of a new industrial economy. Over the past century, the scale of human activity has grown ever greater relative to the limits of what the earth can support. As ecological economist Robert Costanza explains, "It took all of human history to grow to the $600 billion/yr scale of the economy in 1900. Today, the world economy grows by this amount every two years. Unchecked, today's $16 trillion/yr global economy may be five times bigger only one generation or so hence." ROBERT COSTANZA ET AL., AN INTRODUCTION TO ECOLOGICAL ECONOMICS 7 (1997).

The human enterprise is now so large that humanity is drastically altering natural ecosystems and the processes they control. For millennia, human impacts were typically local, minor, and reversible. Today, human influence can be discerned in the most remote reaches of the biosphere; it is global in effect, rivaling or overshadowing natural biogeochemical and evolutionary processes; and many of the impacts are irreversible, certainly on a time scale of interest to society. Although much more by accident than by design, humanity now controls conditions over the entire biosphere.

To list just a few of many impacts, human activity has heavily transformed 40–50% of the ice-free land surface; coopted 50% of accessible, renewable fresh water; fully exploited or over exploited 65% of marine fisheries; increased the carbon dioxide concentration in the atmosphere by

30%; and driven 25% of bird species to extinction. Peter Vitousek et al., *Human domination of Earth's ecosystems*, 277 SCIENCE 494 (1997); John Holdren and Paul Ehrlich, *Human population and the global environment*, 62 AMERICAN SCIENTIST 282 (1974). As a result of fertilizer use and pollution, we have placed more nitrogen in circulation than by all natural sources (compared to about a 10% addition of carbon dioxide compared to natural sources). Tom Horton & Heather Dewar, *Nitrogen's Deadly Harvest*, THE BALTIMORE SUN, Sept. 24, 2000.

As human population and economic activity continue to expand, we are increasingly pushing up against the limits of what the biosphere can support. The degradation of the global environment—manifested in the collapse of ocean fisheries, ozone depletion, and climatic change—is the result. No one knows what exactly the limits are. Some of the predictions made in classic works such as the 1972 *Limits To Growth* have not come to pass, but this does not undermine the stubborn logic posed by ecological constraints. Consider the following passages written by Herman Daly and John Cobb, among the founders of a field now known as ecological economics.

Herman Daly & John Cobb, FOR THE COMMON GOOD 2–4, 21 (1989)

All of these [environmental] facts appear to us to be related in one way or another to one central underlying fact: the scale of human activity relative to the biosphere has grown too large. In the past 36 years (1950–86), population has doubled (from 2.5 to 5.0 billion). Over the same time period, gross world product and fossil fuel consumption have each roughly quadrupled. Further growth beyond the present scale is overwhelmingly likely to increase costs more rapidly than it increases benefits, thus ushering in a new era of "uneconomic growth" that impoverishes rather than enriches. This is the fundamental wild fact that so far has not found expression in words sufficiently feral to assault successfully the civil stupor of economic discourse. Indeed, contrary to Keynes, it seems that the wildness of either words or facts is nowadays taken as clear evidence of untruth. Moral concern is "unscientific." Statement of fact is "alarmist." * * *

The wild facts of today and their conflict with standard economic theory both have a well-known history. During the past two centuries, the economy has transformed the character of the planet and especially of human life. It has done so chiefly by industrialization. Industry has vastly increased the productivity of workers, so vastly that in spite of great population increases in industrialized nations, the goods and services available to each have increased still more. The standard of living has soared from bare subsistence to affluence for most people in the North Atlantic nations and Japan. Singapore, Hong Kong, Taiwan, and South Korea share in this prosperity. These are immense accomplishments.

During the same period, the study of the economy has matured, approaching the status of a science.... Public policy has been deeply affected by the ideas and proposals of economists.... But the industrial economy has consequences for the greater economy of life. * * *

Recently it has been ecologists especially and those whom they have aroused who have turned on the economy as the great villain. They see that the growth of the economy has meant the exponential increase of raw material inputs from the environment and waste outputs into the environment, and they see that little attention has been paid by economists either to the exhaustion of resources or to pollution. They complain that economists have not only ignored the source of inputs and the disposition of outputs, but also that they have encouraged the maximum of both, whereas living lightly in the world requires that throughput should be kept to the minimum sufficient to meet human needs. * * *

But at a deep level of our being we find it hard to suppress the cry of anguish, the scream of horror—the wild words required to express wild realities. We human beings are being led to a *dead* end—all too literally. We are ... killing the planet. Even the one great success of the program that has governed us, the attainment of material affluence, is now giving way to poverty. The United States is just now gaining a foretaste of the suffering that global economic policies, so enthusiastically embraced, have inflicted on hundreds of millions of others. If we continue on our present path, future generations, if there are to be any, are condemned to misery. The fact that many people of good will do not see this dead end is undeniably true, very regrettably, and it is our main reason for writing this book. [And for taking this course, we might add.]

Victor Furkiss describes our situation graphically: "Present-day society is locked into four positive feedback loops which need to be broken: economic growth which feeds on itself, population growth which feeds on itself, technological change which feeds on itself, and a pattern of income inequality which seems to be self sustaining and which tends to spur growth in the other three areas. Ecological humanism must create an economy in which economic and population growth is halted, technology is controlled, and gross inequalities of income are done away with." ... We believe that an economics for the common good is what ecological humanism calls for, and even more what stewardship of creation calls for.

The global system will change during the next forty years, because it will be physically forced to change. But if humanity waits until it is physically compelled to change, its options will be few indeed. None of them will be attractive. If it changes before it *has* to change, while it can still choose to change, it will not avoid suffering and crisis, but it can be drawn through them by a realistic hope for a better world.

In *For the Common Good*, Daly and Cobb describe the accomplishments of traditional growth economics, and then explain the need for a new paradigm to shift the world to a "steady state" economy. In a steady state economy, both human population and material wealth are maintained at constant levels, rather than continuing to grow unchecked. In order to be sustainable, human population and human economic activity must not only be stable, however, they must be maintained at a level that the Earth can support indefinitely. Human survival and comfort depend upon our use of resources from our environment; in fulfilling our collective needs and wants, we must take natural resources from our environment as raw material, use a portion of it, and return the rest to our environment as waste. This flow of materials into the human economy and out again is our economic "throughput." To be sustainable, Daly argues in another publication, we must keep this level of throughput low, otherwise we will exhaust our stock of natural resources and degrade our environment.

Since matter and energy cannot be created, production inputs must be taken from the environment, which leads to depletion. Since matter and energy cannot be destroyed, an equal amount of matter and energy in the form of waste must be returned to the environment, leading to pollution. Hence lower rates of throughput lead to less depletion and pollution, higher rates to more. The limits regarding what rates of depletion and pollution are tolerable must be supplied by ecology.

Herman E. Daly, *Introduction to Essays Toward a Steady—State Economy,* in Valuing the Earth: Economics, Ecology, Ethics 29 (Herman E. Daly & Kenneth N. Townsend eds. 1993).

———

QUESTIONS AND DISCUSSION

1. Daly and Townsend describe a "good scale" as "one that is at least sustainable, that does not erode environmental carrying capacity over time." They describe an "optimal scale" as one that is not only sustainable but also at a level "at which we have not yet sacrificed ecosystem services that are at present worth more at the margin than the production benefits derived from the growth in the scale of resource use." Herman E. Daly & Kenneth N. Townsend, *Introduction*, in Valuing the Earth, op. cit., at 2. In other words, the optimal scale is one at which the returns from increased production are not outweighed by corresponding losses in environmental services such as fresh air, clean water, and a stable climate system. What role can international environmental law play in helping the world determine the optimal scale? What role can it play in keeping our activity within the optimal limits?

2. Daly and Townsend also point out that in the future, sustainable advances in the human condition will be through "qualitative improvements rather than quantitative increases in throughput."

> [The steady state economy envisions] for the stock of wealth, a low rate of throughput (low production and equally low consumption) [which] means greater life expectancy or durability of goods and less time sacrificed to production. This means more "leisure" or nonjob time to be divided into consumption time, personal and household maintenance time, culture time, and idleness. This, too, seems socially desirable, at least within limits. * * *
>
> With constant physical stocks, economic growth must be in non-physical goods: service and leisure.... We [are now] goods-rich and time-poor ... the "harried leisure class".... Time-intensive activities (friendship, care of the aged and children, meditation, and reflection) are sacrificed in favor of commodity-intensive activities (consumption). At some point, people will feel rich enough to afford more time-intensive activities.... But advertising, by constantly extolling the value of material-intensive commodities, postpones this point. From an ecological point of view, of course, this is exactly the reverse of what is called for.

Valuing the Earth, op. cit., at 29, 36. What do you think such a no-growth economy might look like? How "global" would such an economy be? Does the idea of an economy based on qualitative rather than quantitative improvements in human life seem realistic or utopian? Would your support for a no-growth economy depend on whether you live in a developed or developing country, or on your socio-economic position within your own country?

3. What is the proper role of government and law in bringing about a shift toward a no-growth economy? Daly and Cobb argue that the "role of government is to set fair conditions within which the market can operate. It is also responsible for setting the overall size (scale) of the market." Herman E. Daly & John B. Cobb, For the Common Good at 14–15 (1989). Do you agree with Daly and Cobb on the role of government? If not, what should its primary role be? Does their model describe any countries today? What aspects of your country's governmental activities does it describe?

4. The shift away from traditional models of economic "growth" (more production and consumption of material goods or commodities) to "sustainable development" (reduced impacts of production and consumption, increased consumption of non-physical goods such as services and leisure) is a key theme underlying this book. We will explain the concept of sustainable development in more detail in Chapters 3 and 4, and we will return to it often throughout the book.

5. It is not only the scale of today's economy that threatens global ecology, but also the pace at which the global economy can introduce and mass-market new chemicals or other products potentially harmful to the environment. The rate of innovation and distribution can outstrip the institutional capacity to resolve such problems, or at the very least requires us to search for new and more effective ways to set global environmental policy.

————

B.   Physical Limits of the Ecosystem

Daly's work and others' is based on the physical limits of the biosphere. These limits may be described a number of different ways. In this section, we use the amount of available energy to illustrate physical limits. The general lesson of ecological constraints, however, is applicable to many resources and "ecosystem services", including for example a stable climate system or atmospheric protection from ultraviolet radiation.

Energy is neither created nor destroyed in a system. An important implication of thermodynamics is that our "stocks" of useful energy in the form of natural resources that can readily be converted to mechanical work (e.g. fossil fuels) are necessarily finite. When a piece of coal is burned, its useful energy dissipates in the form of heat. That heat cannot be put back into the coal without a greater amount of energy. That's why no one has developed the perpetual motion machine. Some stocks of energy, such as nuclear or geothermal, will last longer than others, but are nonetheless destroyed over time as they are used.

Paul R. Ehrlich et al., *Availability, Entropy, and the Laws of Thermodynamics*, 69–73 in Valuing the Earth, *op. cit.*

The essence of [energy] accounting is embodied in two concepts known as the first and second laws of thermodynamics. No exception to either one has ever been observed. The first law, also known as the law of conservation of energy, says that energy can neither be created nor destroyed. If energy in one form or one place disappears, the same amount must show up in another form or another place. In other words, although transformations can alter the *distribution* of amounts of energy among its different forms, the *total* amount of energy, when all forms are taken into account, remains the same.... The immediate relevance of the first law for human affairs is often stated succinctly as, "You can't get something for nothing." * * *

[The] fundamental point ... is that *different kinds of stored work are not equally convertible into useful, applied work....* * * *

With this background, one can state succinctly the subtle and overwhelmingly important message of the second law of thermodynamics: *all physical processes, natural and technological, proceed in such a way that the availability of the energy involved decreases....* What is consumed when we use energy, then, is not energy itself but its availability for doing useful work....

More generally, the laws of thermodynamics explain why we need a continuous input of energy to maintain ourselves, why we must eat much more than a pound of food in order to gain a pound of weight, and why the total energy flow through plants will always be much greater than that through plant-eaters, which in turn will be greater than that through flesh-eaters. They also make it clear that *all* the energy used on the face of the Earth, whether of solar or nuclear origin, will ultimately be degraded to heat. * * *

It is often asked whether a revolutionary development in physics ... might not open the way to circumvention of the laws of thermodynamics.... [T]o wait for the laws of thermodynamics to be overturned as descriptions of everyday experiences on this planet is, literally, to wait for the day when beer refrigerates itself in hot weather and squashed cats on the freeway spontaneously reassemble themselves and trot away.

Unlike fossil fuels or nuclear energy, solar energy is not a "stock" but a "flow." In human terms, the source of solar energy is inexhaustible. Our capacity to use this energy, though, remains quite small. Like all animals, humans have access to most solar energy only after it has been converted into biochemical energy by plants, through the process of photosynthesis. In this sense, the energy converted by photosynthesis serves as the ultimate limit of the biosphere. It provides the total food stock for all life.

Primary productivity is the amount of solar energy converted into biochemical energy through plant photosynthesis. Net primary productivity (NPP) is the energy yield of photosynthesis minus the energy needed by those plants for their own life processes. This is the amount of metabolized energy available for use by other species. In their 1986 article "Human Appropriation of the Products of Photosynthesis", Stanford University scientists calculated that "nearly 40% of potential terrestrial net primary productivity is used directly, co-opted, or foregone because of human activities." In other words, one species of the 14 million or more species on earth controls over one-third of the planet's energy flow, potentially "squeezing" the resources available for other species. The article is worth reading in full. An excerpt follows.

Peter Vitousek at el., *Human Appropriation of the Products of Photosynthesis*
BIOSCIENCE, Vol. 36, No. 6, at 368 (1986)

We examined human impact on the biosphere by calculating the fraction of net primary production (NPP) that humans have appropriated. NPP is the amount of energy left after subtracting the respiration of primary producers (mostly plants) from the total amount of energy (mostly solar) that is fixed biologically. NPP provides the basis for maintenance, growth, and reproduction of all heterotrophs (consumers and decomposers); it is the total food resource on Earth. We are interested in human use of this resource both for what it implies for other species, which must use the leftovers, and for what it could imply about limits to the number of people the earth can support.

Throughout this analysis, we treat NPP as the process responsible for input of organic matter and calculate human uses as output. In most cropland, input and use (harvesting) occur in the same year. In a given area of forest or other ecosystems dominated by perennials, however, human-caused output can temporarily exceed NPP input (in the same year a forest is harvested, for example). If the spatial scale is large enough, we can nevertheless calculate the fraction of forest NPP used by humans as the amount of organic material humans harvest or destroy by the total NPP of forests worldwide.

We calculated human influences in three ways. Our low estimate is simply the amount of NPP people use directly—as food, fuel, fiber, or timber. Our intermediate estimate includes all the productivity of lands devoted entirely to human activities (such as the NPP of croplands, as opposed to the proportion of crops actually eaten). We also include here the energy human activity consumes, such as in setting fires to clear land. Our high estimate further includes productivity capacity lost as a result of converting open land to cities and forests to pastures or because of desertification or overuse (overgrazing, excessive erosion). The high estimate seems a reasonable statement of human impact on the biosphere.

[W]e use a petagram (Pg) of organic matter, equivalent to 10^{15} grams or 10^9 metric tons, as our basic unit of measure. . . . We have . . . generally accepted intermediate or conservative (rather than extreme) estimates from the literature.

The low calculation of NPP used directly by people or domestic animals is "approximately 7.2 Pg of organic material directly each year—about three percent of the biosphere's total annual NPP." The intermediate calculation amounts to 42.6 Pg of NPP appropriated each year, which amounts to 19.0% of total NPP–30.7% on land and 2.2% in the seas.

The high estimate. This computation includes both the NPP humans have coopted and potential NPP lost as a consequence of human activities. . . . [While many effects on NPP must be considered, the] discussion is confined to four relatively well-defined changes in land use that can cause declines in NPP: replacement of natural ecosystems with agricultural systems, the permanent conversion of forests to pastures, desertification, and conversion of natural systems to areas of human habitation. [These] losses raise the calculated *potential* NPP of terrestrial ecosystems to 149.6 Pg. Thus, humans now appropriate nearly 40% . . . of potential terrestrial productivity, or 25% . . . of the potential global terrestrial and aquatic NPP. . . . Furthermore, humans also affect much of the other 60% of terrestrial NPP, often heavily.

[While the calculations are based on "inadequate data," the authors expect the data will improve as the international efforts to evaluate the status of food and agriculture continue.] Nonetheless, we believe that our calculations accurately reflect the magnitude of human appropriation of the products of photosynthesis, and we believe some reasonable conclusions can be drawn from these estimates. * * *

We estimate that organic material equivalent to about 40% of the present net primary production in terrestrial ecosystems is being co-opted by human beings each year.... People and associated organisms use this organic material largely, but not entirely, at human direction, and the vast majority of other species must subsist on the remainder. An equivalent concentration of resources into one species and its satellites has probably not occurred since land plants first diversified.

The co-option, diversion, and destruction of these terrestrial resources clearly contributes to human-caused extinctions of species and genetically distinct populations—extinctions that could cause a greater reduction in organic diversity than occurred at the Cretaceous—Tertiary boundary 65 million years ago. This decimation of biotic resources will foreclose numerous options for humanity because of the loss of potentially useful species and the genetic impoverishment of others that may survive.

The information presented here cannot be used directly to calculate Earth's long-term carrying capacity for human beings because, among other things, carrying capacity depends on both the affluence of the population being supported and the technologies supporting it. But our results do indicate that with *current* patterns of exploitation, distribution, and consumption, a substantially larger human population—half again its present size or more—could not be supported without co-opting well over half of terrestrial NPP. Demographic projections based on today's human population structures and growth rates point to at least that large an increase within a few decades and a considerable expansion beyond that. Observers who believe that limits to growth are so distant as to be of no consequence for today's decision makers appear unaware of these biological realities.

QUESTIONS AND DISCUSSION

1. Why does it matter that humans use 40% of terrestrial NPP? How would you explain the findings of this research in everyday terms? How reliable and useful for setting policy is the ecological limit imposed by NPP? In addition to giving three widely different estimates of NPP, the authors themselves note that "The information presented here cannot be used directly to calculate the earth's long-term carrying capacity for human beings, because, among other things, carrying capacity depends on both the affluence of the population being supported and the technologies supporting it...."

2. What amount of NPP do you think human activity appropriates today? Remember, the article was published in 1986, over fifteen years ago. How many people do you think we have added to the earth's population since then? How have the levels of human consumption changed? How many parking lots have we paved? Conversely, how many have we dug up and returned to grassland or forest? What do these measures indicate?

3. "Prior to human impacts, the earth's forests, grasslands, and other terrestrial ecosystems had the potential to produce a net total of some 150 billion tons of organic matter per year." Lester Brown et al., STATE OF THE WORLD 1994, at 8, *citing* Vitousek, *et al*. If we are only using 40% of NPP, how concerned should we be today that we are approaching the outer limit of the biosphere's carrying capacity? That limit must fall somewhere between 40% and 100%. How might we determine where? How likely is it that we will reach that limit? The *State of the World* report explains that we "have appropriated the 40 percent that was easiest to acquire. It may be impossible to double our share, yet theoretically that could happen in just 60 years if our share rose in tandem with population growth. And if average resource consumption per person continues to increase, that doubling would occur much sooner." *Id.*

4.   Our survival depends on the ecosystem services the earth's natural systems provide, which means we cannot directly appropriate 100% of NPP. Forests, for example, help regulate the hydrological cycle and wetlands filter pollutants. "As we destroy, alter, or appropriate more of these natural systems, for ourselves, these environmental services are compromised. At some point, the likely result is a chain reaction of environmental decline ... [that] could cause unprecedented human hardship, famine, and disease. Precisely when vital thresholds will be crossed, no one can say." STATE OF THE WORLD 1994 at 8. But we know we are getting closer and closer, the larger the scale of human activity becomes relative to the limits of the biosphere. What are the counter-arguments to these concerns? Is it reasonable to forego human development for fear that we might expand too far? How does the discussion of cliffs in the previous section affect your opinion?

5.   As an international environmental lawyer, how would you propose to regulate human activity to control the portion of NPP humans co-opt? How would you propose to allocate NPP? How much should humans be able to co-opt, compared to wild plants and animals? How would you regulate population, if at all? Consumption? Can technological advances overcome these problems? If so, how can the law promote technological development? We will explore consumption, population and technology in the next chapter.

6.   To what extent can market behavior compensate for the scarcity of terrestrial energy stocks? As terrestrial, high-grade energy stocks become increasingly scarce, the price will go up, and the search for substitutes will intensify. When high-grade energy gets scarce enough, and the price gets high enough, will the last amount of such energy ever be used? The importance of having the price of energy and other natural resources reflect the full environmental cost will be discussed in Chapter 3. Do you think the market alone will provide the incentives needed to develop solar substitutes? If you do not think the markets alone will provide the incentives, what role could the law play in ensuring the timely development of solar technology?

SECTION VI.   DECISION-MAKING IN THE FACE OF SCIENTIFIC UNCERTAINTY

A.   MANAGING UNCERTAINTY

Global environmental problems are plagued with uncertainty. How much more carbon dioxide can we emit before the Earth's climate system becomes so hot the polar ice melts and the sea rises? How will global warming interact with ozone depletion? And how close are we to the absolute limits of human activity imposed by other physical laws of the biosphere? The uncertainty underlying these issues can be addressed in two ways: by developing better information and by taking a precautionary approach.

Developing better information is the approach taken in the U.S. National Environmental Policy Act (NEPA), 42 U.S.C.A. §§ 4321–4370d. NEPA requires agencies of the U.S. government to prepare an environmental impact statement with respect to "major federal actions significantly affecting the quality of the human environment." 42 U.S.C.A. § 4332(C).

The implementing regulations establish what federal agencies must do when existing environmental information is inadequate.

> When an agency is evaluating reasonably foreseeable significant adverse effects on the human environment in an environmental impact statement and there is incomplete or unavailable information, the agency shall always make clear that such information is lacking.
>
> (a) If the incomplete information relevant to reasonably foreseeable significant adverse impacts is essential to a reasoned choice among alternatives and the overall costs of obtaining it are not exorbitant, the agency shall include the information in the environmental impact statement.
>
> (b) If the information ... cannot be obtained because the overall costs of obtaining it are exorbitant or the means to obtain it are not known, the agency shall include within the environmental impact statement:
>
> > (1) A statement that such information is incomplete or unavailable;
> >
> > (2) a statement of the relevance of the incomplete or unavailable information to evaluating reasonably foreseeable significant adverse impacts on the human environment;
> >
> > (3) a summary of existing credible scientific evidence which is relevant to evaluating the reasonably foreseeable significant adverse impacts on the human environment, and
> >
> > (4) the agency's evaluation of such impacts based upon theoretical approaches or research methods generally accepted in the scientific community.
>
> For the purposes of this section, "reasonably foreseeable" includes impacts which have catastrophic consequences, even if their probability of occurrence is low, provided that the analysis of the impacts is supported by credible scientific evidence, is not based on pure conjecture, and is within the rule of reason.

40 C.F.R. § 1502.22. NEPA has been a powerful model for similar laws throughout the world. Over 70% of the world's nations have now adopted environmental impact assessment requirements for certain types of governmental projects, and the concept of environmental impact assessment is now incorporated in many international treaties, declarations and resolutions. Kevin Gray, *International Environmental Impact Assessment*, 11 COLO. J. INT'L. ENVTL. L. & POL'Y 83, 89 (2000). *See* Chapter 7, page 432.

How would you apply the NEPA requirement relating to incomplete or unavailable information to the problem of global warming? Ozone depletion? Is it sufficient simply to acknowledge that uncertainty exists, and then proceed to act despite that uncertainty?

At least at the theoretical level, uncertainty is inherent in the scientific enterprise itself, and in the fundamental assumptions that underlie that enterprise. Modern science proceeds from the premise that no fact can be proven true beyond a shadow of a doubt. This premise finds expression in "Hume's Problem":

> [N]o matter how many times a phenomenon is observed, we cannot be sure that this represents a universal pattern or "law"—logically, even large numbers of past examples cannot guarantee that the same events and relationships will continue to be found in the future. Even when "laws" provide convincing and effective explanations for phenomena, we cannot be sure that such "laws" will

continue to hold true, nor that we have not imperfectly devised them and that new exceptions will not arise [under circumstances we have not foreseen.]

John M. Stonehouse & John D. Mumford, *Science, Risk Analysis and Environmental Policy Decisions*, UNEP ENVIRONMENT AND TRADE SERIES, No. 5, at 2 (1994). Because of Hume's Problem, science can never offer a definitive answer to a specific problem. The truth of a particular proposition can be disproved or "falsified," but never conclusively proven. The best that can be offered is that X or Y is *probably* the case, with the likelihood of its truth expressed as a probability.

The process of hypothesis-falsification-new hypothesis that constitutes scientific debate drives the expansion of human knowledge, but the inherent uncertainty associated with that debate can retard the development of law and policy. As a general rule, the law looks for proof of something before it takes action—the "smoking gun" or the "clear and convincing evidence." Law and policy ask science to provide answers in yes-or-no terms, yet science is uniquely designed not to give such answers. Those who oppose a particular action as against their own interests can thus always find scientists who are willing to emphasize the uncertainties—for example, as President George W. Bush explained in reversing his campaign pledge to limit carbon dioxide emissions, that the causal relationship between fossil fuel use and global climate change has not been conclusively proven. Indeed, given the adversarial nature of our legal system, the law often emphasizes science that is on one edge or the other, as lawyers marshal arguments for their respective positions.

What can be lost is an understanding of the broad consensus among scientists. Although some uncertainty will always exist no matter how much evidence is accumulated, the search for scientific consensus can help guide sound policy decisions. Moreover, as the complexity of a problem increases, the uncertainty associated with that problem—the possibility that some unforeseen factor or circumstance may affect the outcome— increases. Given that global environmental problems are among the most complex that society now faces, we can see why the interplay of science, uncertainty, and policy is so important to the development of international environmental law. It also implicates the importance of the press, which often presents two sides of a scientific issue (such as human activity contributing significantly to climate change) as possessing equal scientific support and merit, even if the vast majority of the world's scientists view one side as much more likely than the other. As climatologist Stephen Schneider has stated, "scientific fact can't be decided by consensus, but scientific policy can and should be."

The scientific and policy issues posed by global environmental threats simply involve too many variables and too much uncertainty to be completely resolved in a timeframe relevant for policy making. Yet the potential consequences of these threats are too high to defer policy choices in expectation of definitive scientific answers that may not come for decades, if at all. Scientists—with their command of the instruments and techniques for developing new knowledge—are playing an increasingly important role in environmental law and policy. In an essay entitled, *A New Scientific Methodology for Global Environmental Issues*, in ECOLOGICAL ECONOMICS

134–36 (Robert Costanza ed. 1991), Silvio Funtowicz and Jerome Ravetz argue that, in order to fulfill their role in a world where both uncertainty and the stakes of decisions are high, scientists must come to grips with the policy implications of their work and integrate their research on narrowly defined technical problems into the development of policy on broader issues. Moving from "objective" science into "subjective" policymaking, however, may carry a heavy price in terms of perceived credibility. We will return to the critical role science plays in environmental law and policy throughout the book. *See also* James Salzman, *Scientists as Advocates*, CONSERVATION BIOLOGY (June, 1989).

One way to respond to the uncertainty plaguing global environmental problems is to take a precautionary approach when deciding whether to proceed with activities that might harm the environment. The "precautionary principle" as it is known in international environmental law evolved from the recognition that scientific certainty often comes too late to design effective policy responses to environmental threats. In essence, the precautionary principle states that a lack of certainty is not an excuse for delaying cost-effective measures to prevent environmental harm, especially where the potential environmental effects may be irreversible, such as death or serious illness in the case of humans, or the extinction of species or disruption of global environmental systems. The precautionary principle is discussed further in Chapter 7, pages 405–411.

B.   SCENARIO FORMATION AS A POLICYMAKING TOOL

Because the global biosphere is a complex system, extrapolating current trends, however alarming they may be, will almost surely be inaccurate. As Murry Gell–Mann, Nobel physicist and professor at the Santa Fe Institute, explains, the only way to understand complex systems is to take "a crude look at the whole." An increasingly popular way to do so is through "scenario formation." Scenarios have been used by the military, by commercial entities, and by government planners. In a famous example, Royal Dutch Shell Group developed a range of scenarios to understand what a future rise in oil prices might look like. Not only did the scenarios prepare the company for the future rise in oil prices but also it broadened the strategic thinking of management by exposing the broader implications of oil price shocks and even led to the planners envisioning a future of fuel cells replacing internal combustion engines. Scenario planning does not claim to predict what *will* happen but, rather, identifies a range of consequences to inform planning today. Ideally, it avoids future policy makers saying, "Oh, if only we had considered that at the time!"

The Global Scenario Group, an international, interdisciplinary group of scholars has created a range of scenarios that describe likely future environments. Their study, known as *Branch Points*, developed three scenarios, each with two variants, to describe possible states of the world in the 21st century. "Great Transitions" is the best-case scenario—a smooth transition to environmental sustainability. "Barbarization," as the name suggests, is the worst-case scenario, and "Conventional Worlds" represents a business-as-usual approach, a continuation of current trends driven by the so-called "self-correcting logic of the market." As you read the following excerpt introducing the three scenarios, consider the role that law, and especially international environmental law, can play in determining which scenario our descendants will encounter.

Gilberto Gallopin et al., Branch Points: Global Scenarios and Human Choice vi-vii
(Stockholm Environment Institute 1997)

Today, globalization takes many forms—stresses on the biosphere, far-reaching cultural impacts of communications technology, expansion of worldwide commerce, and rise of new geo-political tensions. Driven by this powerful new constellation of forces, the world system is at an uncertain *branch point* from which a wide range of possible futures could unfold in the 21st century. The transformation of human civilization could be profound, perhaps as significant as the transition to settled agriculture and the industrial revolution. The aim of [the Branch Points] study is to explore scenarios of the future and to consider their implications.

The concept of sustainability implies the reconciliation of long-term development and environmental goals; it is concerned with the future. While the future is open and cannot be predicted, scenarios offer a powerful means for examining the forces shaping our world, the uncertainties that lie before us and the implications for tomorrow of our actions today. A scenario is a story, told in words and numbers, concerning the manner in which future events could unfold and offering lesions on how to direct the flow of events towards desirable pathways and way from undesirable ones. * * *

Three broad scenarios are depicted—*Conventional Worlds*, *Barbarization*, and *Great Transitions*—which are characterized by, respectively, essential continuity with current patterns, fundamental but undesirable social change, and fundamental and favorable social transformation. *Conventional Worlds* envision the global system of the 21st century evolving without major surprises, sharp discontinuities, or fundamental transformations in the basis for human civilization. The future is shaped by the continued evolution, expansion, and globalization of the dominant values and socio-economic relationships of industrial society. By contrast, the *Barbarization* and *Great Transition* scenario classes relax the notion of the long term continuity of dominant values and institutional arrangements.

Two variants are considered in detail for each class, for a total of six scenarios. Within *Conventional Worlds*, the *Reference* variant incorporates mid-range population and development projections, and typical technological change assumptions. The *Policy Reform* variant adds strong, comprehensive, and coordinated government action, as called for in many policy-oriented discussions of sustainability, to achieve greater social equity and environmental protection. In this scenario, the political will evolves for strengthening management systems and rapidly diffusing environmentally-friendly technology. Whatever their differences, *Conventional Worlds* variants share the premises of the continuity of institutions and values, the rapid growth of the world economy, and the convergence of global regions toward the norms set by highly industrial countries. In the business-as-usual *Reference* variant, the problem of resolving the social and environmental stress arising from global population and economic growth is left to the self-correcting logic of competitive markets. In the *Policy Reform* variant, sustainability is pursued as a proactive strategic priority.

Barbarization scenarios envision the grim possibility that the social, economic and moral underpinnings of civilization deteriorate, as emerging problems overwhelm the coping capacity of both markets and policy reforms. The *Breakdown* variant leads to unbridled conflict, institutional disintegration, and economic collapse. The *Fortress World* variant features an authoritarian response to the threat of breakdown. Ensconced in protected enclaves, elites safeguard their privilege by controlling an impoverished majority and managing critical natural resources, while outside the fortress there is repression, environmental destruction, and misery.

Great Transitions explore visionary solutions to the sustainability challenge, including new socio-economic arrangements and fundamental changes in values. These scenarios depict a transition to a society that preserves natural systems, provides high levels of welfare through material sufficiency and equitable distribution, and enjoys a strong sense of social solidarity. Population levels are stabilized at moderate levels and material flows through the economy are radically reduced through reduced consumerism and massive use of green technologies. The *Eco-communalism* variant incorporates a green vision of bio-regionalism, localism, face-to-face democracy, small technology, and economic autarky. The *New Sustainability Paradigm* variant shares some of these goals, but would seek to change the character of urban, industrial civilization rather than replaces it, to build a more humane and equitable global civilization rather than retreat into localism.

... At the branch point, a business-as-usual *Conventional Worlds–Reference* future could put severe social and environmental stress on the global system of the next century, and ... such stress would increase the peril of lurches towards *Barbarization*. A *Conventional World–Policy Reform* future would counter these risks, but due to limited political will and the sheer scale of the problem policy initiatives alone may be inadequate to the sustainability challenge. New values and institutions, a *Great Transition*, may be both needed for sustainability and desired as a new stage of civilization. Policy scenarios warrant our near term attention since they mitigate risk, while keeping open opportunities for the development of a new sustainability paradigm.

———

QUESTIONS AND DISCUSSION

1. Using climate change, biodiversity, or a topic of your choice, develop scenarios for the world in 2050 based on existing trends—a best-case scenario (incorporating, for example, the successful implementation of a global justice treaty, technological advances that improve the quality of life, and potential peace agreements), business-as-usual (e.g., the refusal of political leaders and industry groups to change their behavior towards more sustainable practices), and a worst-case scenario (such as increasing environmental harm and ethnic-based conflict over limited resources). Incorporate the wild facts of the global environment from Chapter 1 into the scenarios. What emerges as the most important variable—law, ethics, economic incentives, consumer choice or an unforeseen dynamic?

In many countries, the complexity of addressing environmental damage is compounded by political disagreements, while in other countries, where environmental hazards are a matter of life and death, the complexity is compounded by poverty, lack of governmental structures, war, and religious and ethnic conflict. What will be the magnitude of these challenges in 50 years? Which challenges should be addressed first? What is the interplay of the various forces? What tools most effectively address the problems?

2. Allen Hammond, one of the authors of *Branch Points* and World Resource Institute's chief information officer and senior scientist, wrote a book entitled *Which World? Scenarios for the 21st Century*. The book is the result of a five-year research project—the 2050 Project—organized by the Brookings Institute, the Santa Fe Institute, and the World Resources Institute. It adds to the scenario concepts presented in *Branch Points* by describing the critical trends that shape our future (demographic, ecological, social, and political) and by constructing three detailed scenarios ("Market World," "Fortress World," and "Transformed World") for specific regions of the world while considering the trends that are most applicable for each region. The book has a companion website that describes the different regional scenarios and has a "Build Your Own Scenario" feature. The site can be found at <http://mars3.gps.caltech.edu/whichworld//>.

3. To aid policymakers in gaining better understanding of the effects of human consumption on the biosphere as a whole, a coalition of scientists, corporations, foundations and international agencies announced the creation of a World Resource Survey on June 6, 2001. According to UN Secretary General Kofi Annan the project is "designed to bring the world's best science to bear on the present choices we face in managing the global environment." With up to 1,500 scientists volunteering their efforts, the project is expected to cost $21 million. Primarily funded by CNN founder Ted Turner's UN Foundation, it will "assess global environmental damage from the rapid consumption of natural resources." Another sponsor of the project, Timothy E. Wirth, president of the United Nations Foundation, called it "the first global report card on our environment."

> The project, set up and run by the United Nations Environment Program, will also benefit from 16,000 satellite images donated by NASA. Officials expect a final report to be published in 2005, with interim studies released occasionally.... Mr. Wirth, a former senator from Colorado and a former under secretary of state for global affairs, called the survey the first real assessment on the earth's life-support systems. * * *

> Calling the report crucial to understanding how to deal with growing human pressures on resources, Mr. Lash [President of World Resources Institute] said, "If it's successful, in a few years you will have a good statement of the state of the world's health in terms of its capacity to produce the goods and services that support all human well-being and prosperity—food, clean water, fiber, the materials that make our world possible."

Barbara Crossette, "Turner's UN Fund Plans World Resource Survey," *New York Times* (June 6, 2001).

4. Seeing the future is one of our key challenges to understanding human-ecosystem interactions, and to identifying ecosystem limits, from local wetlands, to coastal regions, to forests, as well as to the global systems such as the climate system. As technologists develop better tools for monitoring and measuring ecosystem interactions on a broad scale, and in real time, including through remote sensing, it becomes easier to visualize the human-ecosystem interactions and to take necessary corrective and preventive actions more confidently. The Environmental Legal Information Systems (ELIS), a partnership among CIEL, the University of Maryland, Baltimore, the Law Library of Congress, and Universities Space Research Association, is developing tools to assist legislators, policymakers, regulators and others stakeholders in improving the effectiveness of environmental laws and to make more knowledgeable and timely, ecosystem management decisions. ELIS is developing system architecture to link environmental laws with digital Earth Science information, initially through a geographic information interface, to enable these stakeholders to visualize the impacts of their actions and to educate new user communities. For further information *see* http://www.csee.umbc.edu/~elis/

Suggested Further Reading and Web Sites

Lester Brown et al., STATE OF THE WORLD

Lester Brown et al., VITAL SIGNS

> Annual publications from the Worldwatch Institute, an extremely influential NGO that documents important global trends. Both publications are indispensable reading for tracking issues. STATE OF THE WORLD provides readable analyses of selected issues while VITAL SIGNS monitors the earth's "vital signs" by tracking and graphing significant trends.

World Resources Institute, WORLD RESOURCES

> An annual publication by World Resources Institute which provides more raw data than the Worldwatch publications.

OECD ENVIRONMENTAL DATA, <HTTP://WWW.OECD.ORG/ENV/DATA>

> A compendium published every two years relating data on pollution and natural resources to such areas of economic activity as energy, transport, industry and agriculture. The data is approved by governments, so is as "official" as possible.

OECD, Sustainable Development: Critical Issues (2001)

UNEP GLOBAL ENVIRONMENTAL OUTLOOK (2000)

> UNEP's comprehensive integrated assessment of the global environment at the turn of the century.

THE WORLD BANK WORLD DEVELOPMENT REPORTS

> Annual publication issued by The World Bank reviewing a specific topic (e.g. "Entering the 21st Century," "Attacking Poverty," "Development and the Environment").

http://www.worldwatch.org/

> Homepage for the Worldwatch Institute.

http://www.wri.org/

> Homepage for World Resources Institute. Excellent links on specific environmental topics as well as WRI publications on a range of topics.

http://www.un.org/dpcsd/dsd/csd.htm

> Homepage of the U.N. Commission on Sustainable Development. The Country Profiles section of the site contains environmental information provided by countries to the Commission.

CHAPTER TWO

THE ROOT CAUSES

"We live in a material world, and I am a material girl."

– Madonna

SECTION I.   INTRODUCTION

The preceding chapter described the most pressing threats to the global environment—the wild environmental facts of ozone depletion, climate change, loss of biodiversity, crashing fisheries, etc. We know the immediate causes of these problems—ranging from CFCs and carbon emissions to changes in land use and destructive fishing practices. But, to assess proposed remedies of international environmental law and policy, we need to delve more deeply and consider what the driving forces are *behind these immediate causes.* In this chapter and the next we explore the underlying factors responsible for many of today's environmental problems. As we shall see, in addressing many of these drivers, law is neither the only option available to us nor necessarily the best one.

All things being equal, an increase in a society's population or consumption will increase its environmental impact for the simple reason that more resources will be consumed and more environmental impacts generated throughout the resource's life-cycle. But all things, of course, are not equal. The technology, cultural values, and institutions of the society must also enter into the equation, for they mediate the environmental impacts of consumption and population, sometimes for the better, sometimes for the worse.

Section II explores the influence of population, consumption, and technology on a population's environmental impact. We introduce the IPAT Identity, a simple but powerful formula explaining this dynamic. Section III turns to the role of cultural values and norms in shaping our behavior. First, we look at the culture of our current consumer society and introduce the philosophy of "deep ecology" as a possible counter-weight. Then we discuss what role ethics and organized religion have in molding our sense of moral responsibility to the natural world, and finally we consider the importance of education in teaching environmental values. Chapter 3 then addresses the same issue—what are the fundamental drivers underpinning many of our environmental problems—but does so through the perspective of ecological economics.

SECTION II.   CONSUMPTION, TECHNOLOGY AND POPULATION

To achieve sustainable development and a higher quality of life for all people, States should reduce and eliminate unsustainable patterns of production and consumption and promote appropriate demographic policies.

Rio Declaration on Environment and Development, Principle 8 (1992)

As mentioned above, all things being equal, an increase in population or consumption should increase environmental impact for the simple reason that more resources will be consumed and wastes generated. Much depends, however, on the role of technology. "Technology optimists" believe technology will allow us to expand population and consumption while stabilizing or reducing environmental impacts. On the other hand, as the "technology pessimists" point out, some technologies can accelerate environmental harm.

Whether we are "technology optimists" or not, it should be clear to all of us that the environmental health of the planet will not be assured over the long term unless we succeed in reducing the constant increases in population and consumption. The world's leading scientists are in consensus on this point. In 1992, for example, over 1,600 scientists signed *The World's Scientists' Warning to Humanity*. Among the signatories were over half the living Nobel laureates in the sciences. The *Warning* declared,

> The earth is finite. Its ability to provide for growing numbers of people is finite. And we are fast approaching many of the earth's limits. Current environmental practices which damage the environment, in both developed and underdeveloped nations, cannot be continued without the risk that vital global systems will be damaged beyond repair. Pressures resulting from unrestrained population growth put demands on the natural world that can overwhelm any efforts to achieve a sustainable future. If we are to halt the destruction of the environment, we must accept limits to that growth. * * *

> No more than one or a few decades remain before the chance to avert the threats we now confront will be lost and the prospects for humanity immeasurably diminished. * * *

The developed nations are the largest polluters in the world today. They must greatly reduce their over-consumption if we are to reduce pressures on resources and the global environment.... Acting on this recognition is not altruism, but enlightened self-interest: whether industrialized or not, we all have but one lifeboat. * * *

The 1993 *Statement on World Population*, issued by 58 national scientific academies, including the US National Academy of Sciences, the British Royal Society, the French, German, Swedish, Japanese, and Indian academies and others, expressed similar concerns over the environmental harms caused by continuing population growth, wasteful resource consumption, and poverty. One cannot lightly dismiss such warnings.

This chapter explores the relationships among population, consumption, and technology; the resulting environmental impact to the biosphere; and the role law should play in addressing these factors. It is worth keeping in mind several questions as you consider these issues:

- how many people can the earth support sustainably within the limits of the biosphere, and at what level of consumption?

- what role should international law play in bringing population and consumption within sustainable limits?

- what role can the law play, whether domestic or international, in influencing basic family and lifestyle choices?

- how much can technology reduce the environmental impact caused by a given population, consuming at a given level?

- how can law "direct" technology toward environmentally sustainable development?

————

A. CONSUMPTION—LIVING IN A MATERIAL WORLD

Americans are the fastest people who have ever lived. We have fast food, one-stop shopping, one-hour photo developing, microwave burritos, fifteen-second television commercials, and a legion of time saving devices.... Our speed comes in many varieties. In offices, the goal of going faster is met by even faster computers. On the roads, the desire for going faster is met by fast cars and straight highways. At factories, assembly lines are made more efficient and more prolific to produce more widgets in a year. What unifies these different kinds of speed is the common priority of more—making more, going more places, seeing more people, and doing more in a day or in a lifetime. * * *

It is a regime of speed. To serve it, Americans have changed almost every aspect of their lives, from the people they see to the places where they live. We have even changed the physical state of our country. To make fast motion possible, we put asphalt where once there was tall grass. We have strung wires across the entire country, reaching every little corner, to let instantaneous telephone communication reach all of us. We have also left graveyards of automobiles, and massive environmental damage, from polluted streams to tens of billions of tons of carbon dioxide in the atmosphere. * * *

While speed has many benefits, many of its burdens fall to the natural environment. It is nature that provides the raw materials for fast vehicles and fast assembly lines. In a sense, nature pays the bill for the pleasure and the power of people who travel at high speeds and build computers that do high-speed calculations.

Computers are an example of the trade-offs of high-speed technology and the environment. Computers allowed researchers to predict climate change and begin to promote policies to avoid it. Computers share information around the world that is crucial to environmental protection. They help many companies design manufacturing processes that reduce water and conserve resources. But Silicon Valley, where many computers are designed and built, has the highest concentration of hazardous-waste cleanup sites in the United States. Solvents commonly used in chip making, such as ethylene glycol ethers, are suspected of causing reproductive health problems. Trichloroethylene (TCE) and 1,1,1–trichloroethane, which are used to make and clean electronic components, are both linked to serious health problems. Worldwide, computers were already consuming about 240 billion kilowatt-hours of electricity a year by 1993, as much as the entire annual electricity use of Brazil.

Cars offer many trade-offs as well. People find them so desirable and valuable that they are a central part of most Americans' daily lives. Meanwhile, the area of the United States paved over by roads and parking lost is 153,730 square kilometers, a huge loss of nature. This is almost as much as the combined area of all US National Parks; 191,501 square kilometers.

Hal Kane, THE TRIUMPH OF THE MUNDANE 19–35 (2001).

––––––

1. THE CHALLENGES POSED BY CONSUMPTION

The issues surrounding consumption are enormously broad. Even the most austere human society necessarily consumes food, water, energy, land, and minerals, and each act of consumption has environmental consequences. As a result, the importance of maintaining levels of consumption within an environment's carrying capacity or natural limits to growth has long been recognized. The intellectual basis of this proposition was clearly laid out in eighteenth-century England by Thomas Malthus in his Essay On the Principle of Population. Its modern foundations were established in the late 1960s and early 1970s by a series of books including Schumacher's Small is Beautiful, the Club of Rome's report Limits to Growth, Ehrlich's "neo-Malthusian" warning in The Population Bomb, and Commoner's The Closing Circle. All of these works documented an inevitable confrontation between ever-expanding material demands and increasingly depleted finite resources, between growing pollution and the weakening ability of ecosystems to assimilate waste. At a basic level the messages challenged popular ideals of growth calling, for example, for simpler, local-based economies (Schumacher), population control (Ehrlich), and reduced consumption (Club of Rome).

The following excerpt from Paul Ekins provides a provocative perspective on the relationship between environmental impact and the interrelationships of population, consumption, and technology.

Paul Ekins, *The Sustainable Consumer Society: A Contradiction in Terms?* INT'L ENVT'L AFFAIRS, VOL. 3, NO. 4, AT 242–57 (Fall, 1991)

Introduction

My initial response to this title question is: "I hope not." For there is very little thinking being done on what might replace the consumer society if it is not sustainable. There are not even any mainstream alternative dreams or utopias to contrast with western consumerism.... The liberal-democratic consumer society, as epitomized by its paradigm, the United States, has seemingly become the ultimate to which humanity can aspire, destined to be embraced by–or imposed on–all the earth's people. This means that if the consumer society proves not to be sustainable, the transition to whatever comes after it will be extremely messy, for there will be no coherent conception of what it is one might be working towards.

Definitions

But this is to run ahead of my argument. The least an audience can expect in a lecture with "contradiction in terms" in its title is some definition of the terms in question. So I will spend some time exploring the two key concepts of "sustainability" and "consumer society."

- What is a "consumer society" and do we live in one?
- What is "sustainability" and is our society sustainable?

Definitions of "consume" as a verb in the Shorter Oxford Dictionary are three:

(1) to make away with or destroy; (2) to waste or squander; and (3) to use up. And a "consumer" is he who—or that which—consumes; that is, a maker away with, a destroyer, a wastrel or squanderer, or a user-up.

This does not seem a very flattering basis for the characterization of a whole society. The implications are made even more serious by the phrase often applied as an ideal to market-based economic systems: the phrase "consumer sovereignty." If a consumer society is one in which people's most notable function is as consumers, then "consumer sovereignty" indicates that those wastrels and destroyers have actually been enthroned.

A "consumer society," then, is one of which using up things (to use the least emotionally loaded term) is the principal characteristic; a consumer society based on free markets in which consumers are sovereign is one in which people's desire to use up things is given precedence over other desires and values.

Do we live in such a society? I believe that not only, to a very large extent, we do; but also that the creation of such a society has been absolutely deliberate and premeditated. Vance Packard's 1960 book *The Waste Makers* quotes a United States retailing analyst, Victor Lebow, issuing a trumpet call for consumerism shortly after the Second World War. He proclaimed:

> Our enormously productive economy ... demands that we make consumption our way of life, that we convert the buying and selling of goods into rituals.... We need things consumed, burned up, worn out, replaced and discarded at an ever increasing rate.

Mr. Lebow was a smart guy, and was giving an accurate description of the principal trajectory of life on the North American continent to the present day and of a lifestyle which practically every nation on earth now seeks to emulate.

The University of Maryland's Survey Research Center has done extensive time-use surveys in the United States to ascertain what this lifestyle consists of. Apart from working to afford the lifestyle; or studying so that they can later work to afford it; or engaging in such personal services as sleeping, eating, and washing—Americans now spend more time in the home watching TV than doing anything else. That is, they spend 15 hours a week or 40 percent of their free time watching TV as a primary activity, and keep it switched on for another five hours a week as accompaniment to other activities. In the United Kingdom, people admit to watching TV for about 45 percent of their free time. Out of the home, Americans spend more time shopping than doing anything else—about six hours a week.

TV and shopping in the United States are, of course, inseparably linked by advertisements. United States teenagers' weekly TV diet of 22 hours includes three to four hours of advertisements, amounting to more than 100,000 adverts watched before high school graduation. The shopping centers themselves are increasingly coming to express their importance as the sites of what a former director of New York's Metropolitan Museum of Art has called "America's chief cultural activity." ... The United States shopping mall in general has been called "the cathedral of post war culture" and "the culmination of all the American dreams, both decent and demented, the fulfillment, the model of the post-war paradise." There are 35,000 such malls in the United States, turning over two thirds of a trillion U.S. dollars (14 percent of the 1988 U.S. gross domestic product [GDP]) and 55 percent of non-automobile retail sales. To get Americans to buy from them and elsewhere, the U.S. media annually take $131 billion a year in advertising, more than $500 per U.S. citizen.

The most important point I want to make about this phenomenon is that it is propelled by a truly global impulse. Thus the *Wall Street Journal* crows over the new habits of the 100-million-strong Indian middle class: "The traditional conservative Indian who believes in modesty and savings is giving way to a new generation that thinks as freely as it spends." ...

This is what I mean by a consumer society. Pulling the foregoing threads together, it is one in which the possession and use of an increasing number and variety of goods and services is the principal cultural aspiration and the surest perceived route to personal happiness, social status, and national success. In discussing whether such a society is compatible with sustainability, it must always be borne in mind that it is a global consumer society that is at question. A consumerist North America might be sustainable, but adding in India and China's 40 percent of the world's population may yield a different picture. Consumerism is a virus that has spread globally, and the world has caught it, and that is how its effect must be evaluated.

Sustainability

The word "sustainability" ... [will be used] in its everyday meaning: sustainability is the capacity for continuation or prolongation into the foreseeable future. I shall also be concentrating on the environmental sustainability of economic activity and ducking the more difficult questions of social and cultural sustainability....

Practically everyone is now agreed that current human impacts on the biosphere, caused principally by economic activity, are not sustainable. They can not go on. Moreover, the timescale in which this unsustainability is expected to be manifested, with increasing disruption and unpleasantness, is decreasing. The 1990 *State of the World* from the Worldwatch Institute gives only 40 years, not just to turn around some of the key indicators of unsustainability, but actually to achieve a sustainable society. Given the magnitude of the task, that means reversing some of the current trends of destruction by the end of this decade. * * *

... Tropical deforestation rates increased by up to 90 percent over the 1980s; six of the ten warmest years on record have occurred since 1980, with records being set in 1988 and 1990. Five hundred to 1,000 new chemicals are released into the environment every year, and the U.S. National Research Council estimates that no information on toxic effects is available for 79 percent of the more than 48,500 chemicals listed by the Environmental Protection Agency. Twenty-four billion tons of topsoil are annually washed into the sea. Acid rain is seriously affecting 70,000 square kilometers of forest in fifteen European countries. World food production per head has fallen 7 percent from 1984 to 1989. The bad 1988 U.S. grain harvest severely depleted grain stocks. And irrigated land is coming under enormous pressure in the Third World from salinization. Water scarcity is increasing in North and East Africa, China, India, the Middle East, and parts of the United States. * * *

Economists are now fairly well agreed in general terms as to how the environment and economy interact. The environment:

- provides resources for the economy;
- absorbs, neutralizes, and recycles waste from the economy;
- provides survival services (climate, ozone layer), and amenity (wilderness, landscape) independently of, or in conjunction with, human activity.

In these terms, environmental unsustainability can be defined as excessive depletion of the economy's resources, and especially its bioresources; the emission of more wastes than the environment can neutralize, thus reducing the environment's ability to provide its services of survival or amenity.

There is no mystery as to how this situation has come about, as the Brundtland and the *State of the World* reports have made clear. It is caused by: the mass consumption of the rich; and the struggle of the very poor to stay alive.

The impact of mass consumption is obvious. One-quarter of the world's people in industrial countries who use between 60 and 80 percent of its fossil fuels and minerals are responsible for a similar proportion of resulting pollution problems (global warming, ozone depletion, acid rain, toxic wastes). When the sizable industrial sectors in many Third World countries are taken into account, industrial activity is responsible for close to 100 percent of these problems.

The destructive contribution of the very poor is more complex. Why do hundreds of millions of peasants in the Third World destroy today the resources which they will need tomorrow? It now seems clear that population pressure is only a small (though increasing) part of the answer. More important is that an increasing proportion of the resources *which the poor used to use sustainably for their survival* are being channeled into the consumer markets of the North or of the southern industrial elites. Thus tropical timber worth $8 billion and destroying 12 million acres of forest in its extraction is shipped annually from poor to rich countries. From 1974 to 1984 the land in Third World countries devoted to the major export crops rose by 11 percent. In Brazil, the percentage of land used for growing food for domestic consumption fell from 63 percent to 55 percent between 1967 and 1979. In Ecuador, where 1.2 percent of landowners own 66 percent of arable land, the area dedicated to the production of domestic staple crops declined by 26 percent.

Then there are the huge development projects—the dams, mines, factories, and power stations that destroy Third World natural resources. And the people who used to use those resources sustainably—in the main—are pushed into inhospitable forests or onto fragile soils in savannahs or up mountain slopes. * * *

I take pains to stress this point because as environmental constraints tighten and the struggle for resources intensifies, we can expect the poor to get an increasing share of the blame. It is important always to put on record the extent to which this is blaming the victims.

Sustainability and Consumerism

I hope that I have now established the point that the environmental crisis, the crisis of unsustainability, must be laid squarely at the door of northern industrial consumer lifestyles and their imitations now in nearly all countries of the Third World. The question on which I now wish to focus is that in the title of this lecture: can this unsustainability be converted to sustainability in the context of a consumer society as previously defined?

The writers Paul and Anne Ehrlich give a neat equation relating environmental impacts to three variables. One variable is population; and I take as given the desirability of stabilizing world population levels as soon as possible. The means of doing so are outside the scope of this paper. . . . The other two, more relevant to us here, are: degree of affluence, by which the Ehrlichs mean consumption per head, and technological sophistication, that is the environmental destructiveness of the technologies which generate the goods consumed [*note* that the Ehrlichs use A, Affluence, instead of C].

Thus Impact, I = (Population, P) x (Consumption, C) x (Technology, T).

We have established that I is currently much too high. Population is still increasing and, barring catastrophe, seems unlikely to stabilize much under twice today's level—that is, between 10 and 12 billion people. So the product of consumption and technology, in terms of environmental impact, has got to halve over the next 50 years simply to counteract population growth. In terms of the emissions of carbon dioxide in the United States, we have seen that a 90 percent decrease is called for to get within IPCC limits. In general, as a ballpark figure, it seems likely that all the key emissions or destructive activities will need to be reduced by not less than 50 percent.

Those who believe that the consumer society is compatible with sustainability—and this belief is formulated in a variety of different ways, such as through the popular phrases "sustainable growth," or "green growth," or a new era of economic growth (as in the Brundtland Report, p. xii)—presumably think that these sorts of reductions can not only be achieved by technology alone but that technology can so further reduce impacts that consumption can actually be allowed to grow as well. A 3 percent growth in economic output, green or otherwise, doubles consumption every 23 years. Third World countries want to catch up with the North and certainly want to exceed those rates; but let us be conservative and envisage a doubling of global consumption every 25 years. Now let us review the figures over a 50-year period:

$I = P \ x \ C \ x \ T$ [better known as I = P x A x T, where A stands for "affluence"]

I must be at least halved to achieve sustainability

P will double

C is set to quadruple (assuming 3 percent per-capita growth per annum).

That means that if sustainability is to be achieved by technology alone, in 50 years' time technology must have reduced the environmental impact of each unit of consumption to one sixteenth of its present level. That is more than a 93 percent reduction (this assumes that population growth does not change the average environmental impact per person). If population then stabilizes, technology will need to continue to reduce environmental impact per unit of consumption by half every 25 years to allow "green growth" to continue—so that by 2100, every unit of consumption would be making only 1.6 percent of its current environmental impact. We would then have a world with a far greater absolute gap between rich and poor countries, although the latter would have doubled their consumption every 25 years along with the rich. To achieve greater international equity would require still greater technological achievements if northern "green growth" were not to be reduced.

Now I got my first degree in electrical engineering and I have the greatest respect for technology; but I see nothing in prospect that portends those sorts of environmental technological achievements. Even today, when our economy is immensely environmentally inefficient and the scope for new environmental technologies is acknowledged to be colossal, some rich countries' governments are squealing, fudging, and mudging at the prospect even of stabilizing emissions over the next 15 years, let alone reducing them.

Recent figures on energy consumption amply bear out this skepticism on the green-ness of any production growth that is likely to be achieved. OECD countries are actually forecasting a 1 to 2 percent annual *increase* in the consumption of fossil fuels to the year 2000, which must increase emissions of carbon dioxide proportionately. The much-heralded decoupling of energy consumption from economic growth, which was the flagship of green growth, appears to have come to an abrupt halt. In 1987 and 1988, energy intensity (amount of energy per unit of GDP) actually increased slightly in the United States and several European countries. Another key indicator of continuing energy profligacy is the growth world wide in the number of vehicles—currently 5.1 percent for trucks and buses, and 4.7 percent for cars, with the United States and Europe having nearly 70 percent of the vehicle fleet. A 5 percent increase means a doubling time of less than 16 years, so that just to keep emissions from this source constant, the fuel efficiency of vehicles must double every two generations of vehicle (assuming an average vehicle life of eight years).

Of course, none of this means that there will be no economic sectors that grow strongly and greenly. Organic agriculture, solar energy, environmental services, and technologies of all sorts—all these will need to expand enormously to meet the challenge of sustainability. But the figures indicating the scale of the challenge show the extreme improbability of its being effectively met while industrial countries have continually growing aggregate levels of output.

Let us therefore acknowledge "green growth" for what it is: an essentially religious concept formulated by those who cannot bear—or, if they are politicians, think that their electorate cannot bear—the thought of an economy without growth. As with the existence of God, the possibility of green growth cannot be disapproved. Many will claim that they know how to find it and give directions to the promised land. And many others will wish to follow them there, for there is no more potent message than one that people want to hear. But for those who have looked the environmental crisis in the eye, who have done the sums, have seen the huge pent-up impulse towards western consumerism in the Third world, who have a realistic, rather than religious, assessment of technological potential, we must look beyond green growth for practical strategies for sustainability, with the outline of which I wish to end this piece.

Strategies for Sustainability

Returning to the $I = PCT$ [or I=PAT] equation, let us assume again that impacts must be halved over 50 years, that population will double, and that Third World consumption per head must quadruple. This time, however, let us say that rich countries experience no growth in consumption per head and that all population growth in the Third World will still be less than one fifth of per capita consumption in rich countries. Technology must then decrease the environmental impacts of each unit of consumption "only" by some 79 percent. This is still an ambitious target. It may just be achievable. Let the gung-ho technologists please concentrate on achieving it; let the rest of us in rich countries please help them by embracing green consumerism and green invest- ment with our hearts and wallets for all we are worth; but let us not also imagine that this will enable us sustainably to increase our consumption as well. It will not. How then will we cope with a no-growth economy?

The answer to this question has two parts, one economic and one human. The economic answer is the most difficult and least well-formulated. The smooth functioning of our economy depends on growth. Capitalists won't invest with- out the prospect of such growth. Productivity increases cause unemployment without growth in production. Redistribution to the less well-off becomes more difficult without overall growth in incomes. These are formidable problems. They explain the colossal ideological commitment to growth from capitalists and socialists alike. To solve them we will need to create an economy in which investment will continue to flow for constant, rather than ever-increasing, returns; in which technological progress is powered by considerations of envi- ronmental efficiency and job satisfaction, rather than increasing labor produc- tivity; in which a greater political commitment to equity, combined with greater incentives and access to resources allowing the poor to meet more of their needs directly rather than relying on state benefits, diminishes differentials of income and wealth.

There is no space here to explore these complex and profound issues, except to remark that there is no apparent way in which these conditions can be met through the unguided operation of the market mechanism. If private capital will not of itself invest in steady-state production, then it must be given social incentives to do so and must be supplemented by social investment. Turning to technology, the new objectives of quality of work, in terms of job satisfaction and human fulfillment, and environmental efficiency can only be pursued through the social assessment of technology and public policy. And redistrib- ution has always been a social, rather than a market, function.

There are legitimate doubts as whether current political forms and processes will allow such complex issues to be effectively and democratically addressed. Government failure through inflexible or self-serving bureaucracies, corrupt politicians, and the domination of entrenched private interests, is at least as common as market failure. It is the invention of appropriate political mecha- nisms to deal with these issues that I would identify as the historic challenge of sustainability. The objective of production growth has for a long time justified both alienating work and social injustice. Even without the environmental crisis, it could be argued that these are the really important issues facing industrial societies. Sustainability's rejection of indefinite aggregate growth has now brought them center-stage.

The human part of the answer about coping with a no-growth economy is where the good news lies, the silver lining to the looming environmental apocalypse which gives hope that it may yet be averted. To see this silver lining we will need to disabuse ourselves of one of the most powerful myths of human history: the myth that more money brings more happiness.

The fact that the myth is so deeply ingrained in folk wisdom and ideology means that it probably has some validity, and I would certainly agree that life in a market-based economy without a certain threshold of subsistence, as I have already mentioned. Below a certain threshold of subsistence, people need to be enabled to earn, spend, and consume more through growth in Third World countries and redistribution in First World countries, as I have already mentioned.

But for the rest, is it not true that the richer people are, the happier they are? The answer is no, not necessarily, because several other factors are greater determinants of our happiness and these may be in direct conflict with the objective of making more money.

The experimental Oxford psychologist Michael Argyle has published a detailed review of the literature on happiness, and reached conclusions which are, for the economist, most surprising—but, for a country facing a no-growth economy, most encouraging. "I believe," Argyle writes at the end of his book, "that the conditions of life which really make a difference to happiness are those covered by three sources—social relations, work, and leisure. And the establishment of a satisfying state of affairs in these spheres does not depend much on wealth, either absolute or relative, or on the material conditions of life." This is not uninformed gut feeling. Argyle reaches these conclusions on the basis of all the survey data on satisfaction and happiness that he could find. It is reinforced frequently through the book by such statements as:

- International differences in happiness are very small and are almost unrelated to economic prosperity.

- There is very little difference in satisfaction with income or material prosperity between rich and poor people and between those living in rich and poor countries.

- There is almost no relation between wealth and happiness between different countries. Rising prosperity in the United States since 1957 has been accompanied by a falling level of satisfaction.

- Three areas of life—other people, work, and leisure—are the three main domains of satisfaction. The most important "other people" relationships are overwhelmingly those of marriage and family.

Perhaps I ought to pause a little for the implications of those quotes to sink in. Here we have been, and still are, relentlessly rooting up communities, scattering families to the ends of the earth, squeezing family life to yield two full-time incomes, and damaging our health by stress and pollution—all to generate that extra percentage point or two of growth. Now Argyle tells us that the families, communities, health, and environment that we have sacrificed were far more important to our well-being than the income their sacrifice has yielded. It is as if as a society we are laboring under the delusions of a collective Midas— seeking to turn everything to gold, only to discover we have lost what we most value. It is an extraordinary and non-Marxian example of Marx's concept of false consciousness. If Argyle is right, the move to a no-growth society, if it can be smoothly executed, could not only yield sustainability but, through focusing attention on the "three main domains of happiness" above, instead of on commodities, make us happier as well.

Argyle makes another important point. Insofar as income increases satisfaction, it is not absolute but relative income that is important. "Satisfaction with income," he writes, "depends more on comparisons with incomes of others than on actual income—what people really want is to have more than other people." This is another bombshell for the economist. Wealth is a zero-sum good. If I get richer and you do not, then you get poorer because your relative position has worsened. If we both get richer by the same amount, neither of us is better off. At the individual level, such comparisons can be pushed too far. But at the social level they explain why, according to the National Opinion Research Center in Chicago, Americans are no more collectively satisfied now than they were in 1957, when their consumption was about a third of present levels. We can certainly all get richer through time. But we cannot all get richer than everybody else. In the relative wealth stakes, one person's gain is another's loss.

The public policy implications of this perspective on happiness are profound.... [P]ublic policy should seek to support families, reinforce communities, and increase the intrinsically satisfying quality of work and leisure, while enabling the creation and distribution of enough wealth to take everyone well over threshold to the point where income ceases to be a major determinant of happiness. At the same time, intrinsic achievements and satisfactions should be stressed to discourage the competitive beggar-my-neighbor attitudes of relative enrichment and impoverishment.

I do not underestimate the radical nature of the transformation of consciousness that snapping out of our Midas-delusion will entail. Nor, as an economist, am I unaware of the difficulties of restructuring our economy in accordance with this new consciousness. But I am convinced that this new consciousness is in our best individual—as well as our best collective—self-interest and that its realization is well within the possibilities of human nature. I hope that as the material facts of unsustainability begin to bite, they will shake us out of the Midas-dream and cut through the credulous fantasies of green growth and start us looking beyond consumption. If we do, and we keep hard heads, warm hearts, and moral principles through the difficult transition, then humanity will not only have a future, but a future far happier than the unsustainable present.

Ekins describes America's consumerism as "a virus that has spread globally." We are all consuming more on a per capita basis, in the U.S., Europe, and Asia, resulting in accelerated use of natural resources and associated environmental impacts both at home and abroad. Indeed, more goods and services have been consumed since 1950 than by all previous generations combined. From 1950 to 1990, per capita consumption of copper, steel, energy, timber and meat doubled; consumption of plastic increased five-fold and aluminum by seven-fold. While America has the highest per capita consumption levels in the world, the resource consumption in Western Europe and Japan is only slightly less. See Alan Durning, How Much Is Enough? 29, 38 (1992). The material consumption of the United States from 1900–1989 is displayed below in Figure 2–1. Interagency Working Group on Industrial Ecology, Material and Energy Flows (1998).

U.S. CONSUMPTION OF RAW MATERIALS

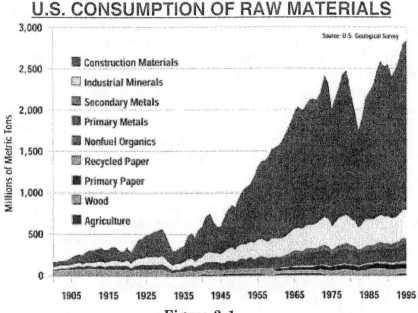

Figure 2–1

Consumption raises troubling equity issues. Until the mid-18th century, improvements in living standards worldwide were barely perceptible. Most societies were resigned to poverty as an inescapable fact of life. Since 1950 the richest 20% of humankind has doubled its per-capita consumption of energy, meat, timber, steel, and copper, and quadrupled its car ownership, greatly increasing global emissions of CFCs and greenhouse gases, accelerating tropical deforestation, and intensifying other environmental impacts. *Ibid.* In 1999, people living in the world's richest 20% of countries consumed 86% of the world's GDP. *Do the World Bank, IMF and WTO Help the Poor?*, 30 ECOLOGIST 6, Sept. 1, 2000; *For Richer, for Poorer,* 65 CAN. & WORLD BACKGROUNDER 6 May 1, 2000, at 4.

Contrast with that the fact that nearly half of the world's people (2.8 billion) live on less than $2 a day, and 1.5 billion—one-fourth—live on less than $1 a day. Worse, the rich-poor gap is growing. In 1960 the gap in per capita income between the richest people in the world and the poorest was 30:1. In 1999 it had more than doubled to 78:1. According to the World Bank, in rich countries, 1 child in 100 does not reach its fifth birthday, but in the poorest countries as many as 1 child in 5 does not. In poor countries, as many as 50 percent of the children under five are malnourished, while in the richer countries fewer than 5 percent are. THE WORLD BANK, WORLD DEVELOPMENT REPORT 2000/2001 at 3, 29, 141(2001).

The standard response to the equity issue from the international community has been to increase economic growth in the poorest countries. Indeed there is evidence indicating that economic growth and prosperity may also improve certain aspects of environmental degradation. Research based on "Kuznets curves" has demonstrated an association between an increase in per-capita wealth and a decrease in some types of pollution. When the amount of pollution is plotted against per-capita GNP, a curve shaped like an inverted "u" — ∩ — is produced.

As economic activity grows, air and water pollution first increase. Then, possibly because education increases along with income, which allows citizens to understand the environmental harms they suffer, pollution control is implemented and pollution decreases. This association has been relied on by the World Trade Organization and other advocates of trade liberalization to support a deregulatory approach to trade liberalization to spur economic growth.

It should be kept in mind, however, that the Kuznets curves only show an association between pollution and wealth, not necessarily causation. Further, the association is present only for some types of air and water pollution. Production of other important pollutants such as carbon dioxide and some persistent organic pollutants continue to increase with prosperity, as do some other types of environmental harms.

While most policy makers support the pressing need to reduce poverty and the equity gap in the developing world, the issue is what kind of development path these countries will follow—the model followed by developed countries that has caused most of our current environmental problems, or a more environmentally sustainable model. This, in turn, depends largely on what future international environmental law will require, including commitments of funding and technology transfer from industrialized to developing countries.

QUESTIONS AND DISCUSSION

1. Both Paul Ekins and Herman Daly reject the concept of "green growth"—i.e. that we can grow the economy indefinitely and still achieve sustainability. Do you agree? If one rejects the hope of traditional development as a means of growing out of poverty while avoiding global environmental threats, what other paths are available? As you read the excerpt below, compare it to Ekins' arguments on consumption. Herman Daly, *Consumption and the Environment*, in THE ETHICS OF CONSUMPTION, REPORT FROM THE INSTITUTE FOR PHILOSOPHY & PUBLIC POLICY, Vol. 15, No. 4, at 5–8 (Fall 1995).

> From a utility or demand perspective, value added by nature ought to be valued equally with value added by labor and capital. But from the supply or cost side, it is not, because value added by humans has a real cost in labor and an opportunity cost in both labor and capital use. We tend to treat natural value added as a subsidy, a free gift of nature. The greater the natural subsidy, the less the cost of labor and capital needed for further arrangement; the less the humanly added value, the lower the price, and the more rapid the use. * * *
>
> Thanks in part to natural subsidies, the economy has grown relative to the total ecosystem to such an extent that the basic pattern of scarcity has changed. It used to be that adding value was limited by the supply of agents of transformation, labor and capital. Now, value added is limited more by the availability of resources subsidized by nature to the point that they can receive value added. Mere knowledge means nothing to the economy unless it becomes incarnate in physical structure. * * *
>
> The physical growth of the subsystem is the transformation of natural capital into manmade capital. A tree is cut and turned into a table. We gain the service of the table; we lose the service of the tree. In a relatively empty world (small economic subsystem, ecosystem relatively empty of human beings and their artifacts), the service lost from fewer trees was nil, and the service gained from more tables was significant. In today's relatively fuller world, fewer trees means

loss of significant services, and more tables are not so important—at least not where most households already have several tables, as in much of the world they do. However, continued population growth will keep the demand for tables up, and we will incur ever greater sacrifices of natural services by cutting more and more trees, as long as population and the number of tables per capita keep growing.

There is both a cost and benefit to increasing total consumption, and thus the scale of the economic subsystem. The benefit is economic services gained (more tables); the cost is ecosystem services sacrificed (fewer trees to sequester carbon dioxide, prevent erosion, and so on). As scale increases, marginal costs tend to rise, marginal benefits tend to fall. The law of falling marginal benefits is simply a way of saying that, as rational beings, we satisfy our most pressing wants first; after that, we use resources to satisfy wants that are less pressing. The law of increasing marginal costs in like manner means that we first use the cheapest and most easily available resources; after that, we make use of less accessible and less concentrated resources, the intersection of falling marginal benefits and rising marginal costs defines the optimal scale, beyond which further growth would cost more than it is worth—would become anti-economic.

2. In *Sustainable Consumption*, Ekins argues that technology must achieve a 16–fold increase in efficiency. This conclusion is based in part on an assumption that current environmental impact (I) must be halved to reach sustainability. Given the environmental challenges presented in Chapter 1, do you agree? Are you persuaded by Ekins' analysis?

---

2. THE ROLE OF ADVERTISING AND PUBLIC RELATIONS IN CONSUMERISM

In the Ekins article, shopping is identified as "America's chief cultural activity" and the U.S. shopping mall as "the cathedral of post-war culture." To get us to the malls, advertising and public relations (PR) firms perpetually bombard us with the message that if you don't have the right car, insurance policy, soft drink, or television, you are somehow inadequate. You are not in "good hands" if you don't buy Allstate insurance. You'd better drink Pepsi if you want to belong in "generation next". And you are definitely in trouble if the person next to you possesses a "Sharper Image" than you.

In 2000, $218.9 billion was spent on advertising in the U.S., which among other things, supported the television programs that U.S. consumers spent 3 hours and 46 minutes a day watching (more than 52 days of nonstop watching per year). <http://www.mccann.com/html/coenreport.html#>; <http://www.oc-profam-net.org/media/tv_statistics.htm>. Procter & Gamble alone spent $3.7 billion on advertising in 2000, up from $2.6 billion in 1997. To put this in perspective, Procter & Gamble's advertising budget—aimed at promoting consumption—is 34 times greater than the entire budget of the United Nations Environment Program, the primary UN agency concerned with environmental protection (in 1998 numbers). Figures 2–2 and 2–3 below show the increase in total and per capita ad spending since 1950. Lester Brown et al., VITAL SIGNS 71 (1999). The growth of the internet has driven the average advertising budget up even further.

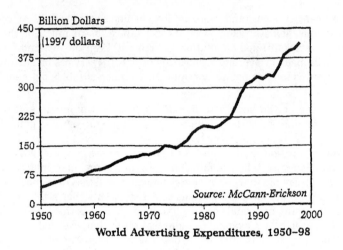

World Advertising Expenditures, 1950–98

Figure 2–2

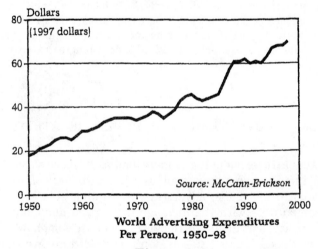

World Advertising Expenditures
Per Person, 1950–98

Figure 2–3

In addition to advertising, corporate PR firms also shape our consumer culture, and our perception of environmental problems. In *Toxic Sludge Is Good for You: Lies, Damn Lies and the Public Relations Industry* (Common Courage Press 1995) authors John Stauber and Sheldon Rampton examine the growing impact of public relations on the public's perception of environmental and other issues.

> PR has become a communications medium in its own right, an industry designed to alter perception, reshape reality and manufacture consent. It is run by a fraternity carefully organized so that only insiders can observe their peers at work. Veteran PR professionals can read the front page of almost any newspaper in the country, or watch a segment of broadcast news and identify which of their peers "placed," "handled" or "massaged" a specific story—even which executives arranged the "placement," managed the "spin" or wrote the CEO's quotes. But can you or I? Or do we assume, as we are supposed to, that some dogged reporter, trained and determined to be the objective "eyes and ears of the public," set out to research, investigate and report his or her findings as accurately as possible? * * *

Also disconcerting is the fact that the 150,000 PR practitioners in the U.S. outnumber the country's 130,000 reporters (and with the media downsizing its newsrooms, the gap is widening). Furthermore, some of the country's best journalism schools now send more than half their graduates directly into public relations. * * *

Examples of the power of PR to shape consumption and forestall regulation are provided in DAN FAGIN, MARIANNE LAVELLE, & THE CENTER FOR PUBLIC INTEGRITY, TOXIC DECEPTION: HOW THE CHEMICAL INDUSTRY MANIPULATES SCIENCE, BENDS THE LAW, AND ENDANGERS YOUR HEALTH at vii-viii (Birch Lane Press, 1996):

> On March 31, 1993, *Frontline*, a Public Broadcasting System television program, aired a provocative documentary, "In Our Children's Food," about the harmful effects of pesticides and the general inability of the federal government to regulate the widespread use of cancer-causing farm chemicals. * * *

> The morning after the program aired ..., however, a remarkable editorial appeared in the *Wall Street Journal*, titled " 'Frontline' Perpetuates Pesticide Myths," it was written by Dennis T. Avery, who was identified as a "fellow at the Hudson Institute" and "director of Hudson's Center on Global Food Issues." The author, an agriculture economist whose work is funded by agribusiness interests, charged in his opening paragraph that the *Frontline* documentary had "made recommendations that would increase our cancer and heart disease rates, increase the risk of world hunger, and plow down millions of square miles of wildlife habitat." Avery wrote about the "ignorance" of Rachel Carson, the respected author of the classic 1962 book *Silent Spring*, and also lamented the government's banning of the pesticide DDT, which, he said, was not "dangerous to people or birds."

> What most intrigued us was not the vitriol of Avery's editorial but its curious timing. No one places an op-ed article in a major newspaper the night before its publication; indeed, the *Frontline* program ended at 10 p.m., Eastern time. How did Avery do it?

> That question gnawed away at the producer [of the documentary Martin] Koughan so much that he telephoned Avery directly. Koughan discovered to his dismay that the editorial had been submitted to the *Wall Street Journal* a full *week* before the *Frontline* program was broadcast. He later ascertained that the pesticide industry had somehow obtained a copy of "In Our Children's Food" a *month* before the air date. An entire public-relations campaign had been waged against the show; individual PBS stations had been contacted, and the American Cancer Society had been persuaded to send out a nationwide bulletin to its members, advising them to disregard the information in the program. As Sheila Kaplan reported in *Legal Times*, the American Cancer Society instructed its branch offices how to respond to public inquiries, asserting that "the program makes unfounded suggestions that pesticide residues in food may be at hazardous levels."

> How did all of this happen? Porter/Novelli, a public relations and lobbying firm based in New York City—representing major chemical companies such as Rhone–Poulenc Ag Company, DuPont, and Hoechst–Roussel, in addition to the pesticide industry-financed Center for Produce Quality—had quietly been doing pro bono PR work for the American Cancer Society. When word became known that a major critical documentary was about to be telecast, the firm quickly sprang into damage-control action, orchestrating the American Cancer Society's "reaction" to the program. It was a public relations coup, one cited by critics of

"In Our Children's Food" as evidence that the dangers to children from pesticides had been overstated.

A postscript to this episode.... [A few weeks after the documentary, EPA and other federal agencies announced, in response to a National Academy of Sciences report on health risks to children from pesticide,] that they would initiate legislative and regulatory reforms to reduce pesticide use.... Nearly four years after this dramatic, heavily reported announcement, however, the EPA has not ordered a single pesticide removed from the market.

This kind of orchestrated and systematic advertising and PR campaign is increasingly common with respect to environmental issues and has been described as "Greenwash" or "Brownlash." In a similar vein, adolescents and children are often the targets of PR campaigns, as corporations seek and shape new, willing consumers in an almost completely unregulated manner. Today's market of 32 million American teenagers is larger than the baby boomers and spent more than $100 billion in the year 2000. Ron Wertheimer, *Television Review; Big Business, Ever Eager to Tap Into Teenage Wallets*, NEW YORK TIMES, February 26, 2001.

QUESTIONS AND DISCUSSION

1. Focusing on advertising as a key cause of increased consumption risks placing business as an environmental "villain," but the situation is more complicated. For one thing, an increasing number of environmentalists believe that the world's environmental problems cannot be solved *without* the resources and talent of business. Do you agree? If not, who will do the job? On the other hand, how far do you think businesses will move toward sustainable development without environmental law driving them in this direction? The type-casting of villains is problematic for another reason. Why are businesses any more the "villain" with respect to consumption than you and I—the "sovereign consumers" who buy the products? Consumers are not passive robots. You surely don't buy everything you see advertised. What role, then should consumers play in reducing consumption?

2. In the summer of 1997, shortly after President Clinton announced his intention to build public support for effective action under the Climate Change Convention, a coalition of automotive, electrical utility and gasoline companies announced a $13 million media campaign to oppose binding commitments to reduce greenhouse gas emissions. This sparked a six-month battle to persuade public opinion over the climate change issue. Nonetheless, according to a *New York Times* poll released just before the Climate Convention negotiations began in Kyoto in December 1997, nearly 65% of the U.S. public believed that the government should take action to cut greenhouse gases, and more than half said they would pay higher gas taxes. John Cushman, Jr., *Public Backs Tough Steps for a Treaty on Warming*, NEW YORK TIMES, Nov. 28, 1997, at A36. The Climate Change Coalition has continued its lobbying and PR activities since then, as well.

Many would argue that the public debate over the U.S. position on the climate change issue is a good thing. Information and opinions on important public issues are aired in the marketplace of ideas. Others, however, might argue that disinformation, not information, is being provided and that industry seeks to discredit the scientific consensus of the 2,500 scientists comprising the U.N.'s Intergovernmental Panel on Climate Change by obfuscating the issues. Do you think there is a proper balance between a company's ability to publicize its version of the facts and the public's right to unbiased information? This question is complicated, for few scientific studies can provide 100% certainty. How one distinguishes between genuine scientific criticism and groundless "criticism for hire" is problematic. For an excellent description of the "Brownlash" opposing environmental efforts, *see* Paul and Anne Ehrlich, BETRAYAL OF SCIENCE AND REASON (1996). For a fascinating history of the chemical industry's misinformation campaign in response to Rachel Carson's classic book, SILENT SPRING, *see* LINDA LEAR, RACHEL CARSON: WITNESS TO NATURE (1997).

In a similar vein, should PR firms be allowed to orchestrate the kind of response used to discredit the PBS documentary "In Our Children's Food"? Is this simply freedom of speech in action or is there some basis on which the law should intervene? For example, should the sources of information be disclosed so that the public knows what companies or other interests are paying for specific research papers or articles?

3.   The heart of the debate on advertising in U.S. society is consumer choice. On the one hand, industry claims that advertising does not force anyone to buy, that it increases consumers' knowledge, and that each individual is ultimately free to choose. Restrictions on advertising would thus hinder consumers' freedom of choice and the companies' freedom of commercial speech. On the other hand, the law already regulates some forms of advertising (tobacco, alcohol, prescription drugs) in order to protect consumers' health. If we accept regulations to protect health, would it be possible to regulate advertising to reduce consumption and protect the environment?

4.   Consider the idea of consumer sovereignty as described in the Ekins article. It implies that the consumer can have anything he or she wants. But how sovereign is the consumer when he or she does not have the means to distinguish between products that look alike but have very different environmental and social impacts?

Eco-labeling programs address this problem by establishing objective criteria to identify products that have lower environmental impacts than comparable products. Product manufacturers voluntarily apply for the label and, if they satisfy the criteria, may place the label on the product or package. These programs empower consumers with information, giving them a context to choose among products that appear identical but have very different environmental impacts. If consumers truly care about the environmental impact of their purchases, eco-labeled products will have a competitive edge, thus increasing the pressure for competitors to improve the environmental quality of their products, as well. This approach rewards industries that use environmentally sound production processes in a way all businesses understand—increased sales. As an example, the Canadian eco-labeling program's criteria for solvent-based paints require:

- volatile organic compound content below 380 grams per liter;
- no pigments of lead, cadmium, chromium VI or their oxides;
- no production or formulation with formaldehyde, mercury compounds or halogenated solvents;
- less than 10% aromatic hydrocarbons by weight.

The Forest Stewardship Council and Smartwood certify private timber from forests that are well managed to respect ecological values. Scientific Certification Systems and Green Seal are two U.S. labeling organizations that certify products such as paints and cleaners that have less impact on the environment. Scientific Certification Systems has developed an information disclosure label that shows the environmental profile of a product, based on an analysis of the environmental impact of the product throughout its life-cycle. Should the law promote programs such as these, or should they be treated as any other form of advertising? Similar product certification programs have been developed in the European Union and Japan. Note that eco-labeling proposals are looked upon with suspicion by developing countries, who believe eco-labelling requirements present non-tariff barriers to trade and limit their ability to export to the rich markets of developed countries. *See* James Salzman, *The Use and Abuse of Environmental Labels*, J. OF INDUSTRIAL ECOLOGY, Vol. 1, No. 2, at 11 (1997); James Salzman, ENVIRONMENTAL LABELLING IN OECD COUNTRIES (1991).

5. Given the difficulty in controlling advertising, perhaps a better approach is to provide more complete consumer information on the environmental impacts of products. Should the government, for instance, require environmental messages to accompany consumer advertising, such as requiring information on the danger of fossil fuel burning and global warming in car advertising, similar to the warning on cigarettes? The government might consider financing public service announcements that provide an environmental message. This was the strategy India's Supreme Court followed in the remarkable case of M.C. Mehta v. Union of India, JT 1991(4) SC 77, *discussed in* N. Nelivigi, M. Poojitha, & A. Rosencranz, *The Judiciary and the Environment; Recent Trends and Developments* 23 ENVTL. POL'Y & L. 102 (1993). In that case, the Court held that for Indian citizens to fulfill their Constitutional duty to protect and enhance the environment, they must be properly informed and educated about environmental issues. To the Court, this suggested that the government of India was obliged to take measures to increase environmental awareness. The Court specified several sweeping measures, including: every cinema, theater, touring cinema, and video parlor must show at least two environmental public service announcements or messages during every show; the Ministry of Environment must produce these materials for the shows; radio and television stations must program at least five minutes of environmental issues each day and more lengthy programs once a week; and all school curricula must include environmental issues in their curricula. Could the U.S. government take similar measures? Would this violate the First Amendment of the Constitution?

6. According to Claude Fussler and Peter James in *Driving Eco–Innovation* at 88–90 (1996) smart businesses are already developing new "marketing ethics" and new "sustainable marketing" strategies. These strategies start by asking "Is my product really necessary?" "Would it be sustainable in a world with 8–10 billion people?" "Is there a more sustainable way of providing the same function, or meeting the same need?" The authors point out that governments will be allies as they begin to intervene with green taxes and regulation to steer consumers to sustainable consumption. *See also* Elkington, Hailes, & Lye, *Who Needs It? Market Implications of Sustainable Lifestyles* (SustainAbility 1995); <http://www.sustainability.co.uk/>.

---

3.   THE NORTH–SOUTH DEBATE: OVER–CONSUMPTION vs. OVER–POPULATION

Much of the international debate over sustainable development, unfortunately, consists of mutual finger-pointing: developed countries blaming developing countries for over-population, and developing countries blaming developed countries for over-consumption. At its most extreme, sustainable development has been characterized as a means to deny developing countries the same lifestyle and levels of consumption enjoyed by developed countries. But focusing on the North–South debate misses the obvious point—we must address both over-population and over-consumption, if we are to reduce the scale of human activity to stay within the physical limits of the biosphere. The IPAT formula set out in the Ekins article describes this well.

> The consequences of the IPAT model are significant, for they suggest not only that lessening environmental impact depends upon both population *and* consumption, but that the location *where* population and consumption are reduced becomes critically important. In regard to the environmental impacts of commercial energy consumption, for example, the average African family would need to bear more than 90 children to equal the impact of an American couple with only two children. The scientific measure of "Ecological Footprints" illustrates the problem on a spatial scale. The Ecological Footprint is a calculation of the land needed to provide resources to satisfy a population's consumption needs. To provide its energy, food, and forestry needs, for example, the Netherlands Footprint requires an area over 17 times its size. Hence the Netherlands would need the land and resources of seventeen Netherlands to provide for its consumption demands.

> James Salzman, *Sustainable Consumption and the Law,* 27 Envt'l. L. 1243 (1998)

Gro Harlem Brundtland, former Prime Minister of Norway and chair of the World Commission on Environment & Development conveys the idea of ecological footprints even more powerfully:

> It is simply impossible for the world as a whole to sustain a Western level of consumption for all. In fact, if seven billion people were to consume as much energy and resources as we do in the West today we would need ten worlds, not one, to satisfy all our needs.

Quoted in Nick Robins et al., Rethinking Paper Consumption at 8 (1996).

Thus, viewing population and consumption strictly along North–South lines risks ignoring critical aspects of the problem. Population levels in the North may be too high precisely *because* of the current level of consumption. Adding to the North's population has a much greater marginal environmental impact than adding an equal amount to the South. The IPAT model makes this clear. The sustainable size of a population depends upon its overall environmental impact, which depends in turn on its consumption level and the technological efficiency of its production patterns. While the Earth may be able to support more people consuming at the level of an average person in China today, it cannot support the current population at the level of the average person in the United States. In fact, ecologists Gretchen Daily and Paul Ehrlich calculate that only 1.5 to 2 billion people could live sustainably at the current standard of Sweden or France—about one third of our global population. They calculate that if everyone were a vegetarian and the world's food supply were divided equally, giving everybody a diet of 2,350 calories a day, it could support 6 billion people. If the diet were equivalent to a good South American diet, with about 15 percent of calories from animal products, then it could support 4 billion people. A typical North American diet, with about 35 percent coming from animals, could feed only 2.5 billion. Gretchen Daily, *Visions,* Mother Jones, Nov. 1994, at 21.

Moreover, consumption patterns in the South are changing. Standards of living in many developing countries—at least in Asia and South America—are increasing. Rising middle classes in these countries aspire to consumption patterns that mirror those of the North. This level of consumption will certainly be no more sustainable in the South than in the North. There is, of course, an irreducible minimum level of human consumption. All people, whether in China, India, Bangladesh, or New York need a certain basic amount of material goods for food, clothing, and shelter. Much of the world's population still lives below this minimum. At some point consumption increases in the developing countries may have to be offset by consumption decreases in the developed countries, particularly as the developing world seeks to move beyond basic needs to a higher level of material consumption.

In the end, it is not a question of population *or* consumption being important. Both are critical for achieving sustainable development and both are critically interdependent. The countries of the world ultimately reached this same conclusion at the Rio Earth Summit in 1992. Endorsed by nearly every country in the world, Principle 8 of the *Rio Declaration* struck the following balance—"To achieve sustainable development and a higher quality of life for all people, States should reduce and eliminate unsustainable patterns of production and consumption and promote appropriate demographic policies."

What, then, is the environmental problem posed by population and consumption levels? The immediate answer might appear to be running out of materials, depleting finite natural resources. This was a central message of the influential 1972 book, *Limits to Growth*, and clearly is a concern for some resources, such as fossil fuels and precious metals. Can you think of other examples? Scarcity of resources may, however, be less of a threat than it appears. Consider pool balls for example. In the late 19th century, elephant ivory was the source of pool balls for billiards. As elephant tusks became scarcer, and ivory prices rose, a clever scientist figured out how to make pool balls using a material known as "bakelite" at a fraction of the cost. In many cases, resource substitution can overcome problems of resource scarcity.

A basic aspect of scarcity is cost. Since natural resources are finite, increasing consumption must inevitably lead to their scarcity. But when they will become "scarce" depends not simply on how much is in the ground, but also on the rates they are used, the amount societies can afford to pay (in standard economic or environmental terms) for their extraction and use, and the availability and cost of substitutes. There is an enormous amount of oil in shale, but the extraction costs for most of it exceed the price of oil on the commodities markets. By reducing economic costs, advances in extraction technology can "increase" the amount of natural resources economically available.

Thus the primary concern raised by population and consumption growth is not necessarily running out of materials. Instead, environmental scientists are most concerned over the environmental impacts caused by consumption and, in particular, the depletion and destruction of critical ecosystem services such as water purification, carbon sinks, climate stabilization, and atmospheric protection from ultraviolet radiation. *See* GRETCHEN DAILY ed., NATURE'S SERVICES (1997).

QUESTIONS AND DISCUSSION

1. *The Netherlands Fallacy.* A common response to concerns over population growth is to respond, "Look at the Netherlands. It is a very crowded country (over 1,000 people per square mile), with high levels of environmental protection and an enviable standard of living. Population growth isn't a problem there." This rejoinder is so common it has been called "The Netherlands Fallacy." After the above discussion of ecological footprints, do you see why this reference to the Netherlands is fallacious, and would be for Hong Kong, Singapore, and Tokyo, as well?

2. Although experts often recommend curbing population growth in developing countries in order to address their environmental problems, addressing consumption patterns in those countries, perhaps through improved technology transfers or policies, may have a far higher payoff over the short term. For different reasons, consumption is a major cause of environmental damage in both North and South. Consider the following example:

> A country has a serious problem with deforestation, which in turn exacerbates problems of species loss. For the sake of simplicity, imagine that this deforestation is caused solely by the expansion of cropland for food. As the forests of this country have shrunk over the past several decades, the country's population has grown rapidly. During that same time, food consumption per capita has not changed. People eat the same quantity and kinds of foods that they did before the spate of deforestation. Similarly, farming technology has not changed. Farmers get the same amount of food per acre, with the same tools and inputs, as they did before the deforestation began. Thus, population growth tracks with deforestation.

> It makes some sense to say, as many observers and analysts do, that slowing population growth is the remedy for the problem of deforestation in this country, because population growth is the only factor that has risen apace with deforestation. Yet we know that reducing fertility to slow and eventually stabilize population growth is a blunt tool that works only on very long time scales, and even then represents a rather abstract gain. In the meantime, forests and rare species can easily disappear entirely. Without intervening to affect how people use resources—specifically by farming, in our example—the environmental problems of deforestation and species loss will intensify.

> The most effective short-term response in our example would be policies that affect agricultural productivity: varieties of seeds, access to land and loans, and other facets of agricultural technology and policy. Family planning and other population policies, although essential for other reasons (particularly for human health) and on other time scales, are not the most appropriate short-term response to deforestation. Thus, a developing country with rapid population growth, rising deforestation, and no increase in food consumption per capita has, somewhat counter-intuitively, one version of a consumption problem.

> Where the consumption problem of wealthy, industrialized countries is about the massive production and use of energy and materials and the similarly massive generation of wastes, the consumption problem of poor countries is principally about technology and poverty [as inadequate technology and the everyday challenges of dealing with poverty often lead people to adopt unsustainable patterns of resource consumption simply to meet their basic needs]
> * * *

> Just as it is not customary to speak of a consumption problem in the South, it is not customary to speak of the need to improve the efficiency with which energy and materials are used in the South. It is well understood that when Northern countries use too much, they often use that amount inefficiently. Not

well understood is the corollary in the South: when poor countries use too little, they use the little that they have inefficiently. * * *

Consider that: The woman who cooks in an earthen pot over an open fire uses perhaps eight times more energy than her affluent neighbor with a gas stove and aluminum pans. The poor who light their homes with a wick dipped in a jar of kerosene get one fiftieth of the illumination of a 100-watt electric bulb, but use just as much energy.

Poverty presses the poor to be inefficient, "to use 'free' fuels and inefficient equipment because they do not have the cash or savings to purchase energy-efficient fuels and end-use devices."

Although the South and the North share some remedies for their respective consumption problems, the origins of those problems are vastly different. The industrialized world's consumption problem derives from excess. The Third World's consumption problem stems from poverty. It seems paradoxical that environmental damage could flow from dearth. But in fact environmental damage stems directly from poverty, the options that poverty excludes, and the low productivity that flows from it.

Judith Jacobsen, *Population, Consumption, and Environmental Degradation: Problems and Solutions*, 6 COLO. J. INT'L ENVTL. L. & POL'Y 255, 259–62 (1995).

Do you agree that developing countries have a "consumption" problem as described above, or would you describe it as a "technology problem"? *See also* Louis N. Camacho, *Consumption as a Theme in the North–South Dialogue*, THE ETHICS OF CONSUMPTION, REPORT FROM THE INSTITUTE FOR PHILOSOPHY & PUBLIC POLICY, Vol. 15, No. 4 at 32–34 (U. Md., 1995).

Jacobsen asserts that someone cooking over an open fire with earthenware pots consumes eight times more energy than a more affluent person cooking with aluminum pans and a gas stove. In reaching this conclusion, do you think Jacobsen took into account the energy involved in mining the gas? In building the infrastructure to refine and deliver the gas? In mining the materials and running the factories needed to produce the metal stove and the aluminum pans? In lighting the stores where the stove and pans were sold? It is important to recognize that, in industrialized nations, tremendous expenditures of energy and resources underlie even the most routine aspects of our lives.

---

4.   THE ROLE OF LAW IN CONSUMPTION

There is little international law in the field of consumption, although the issue is addressed directly in Chapter 4 of Agenda 21, the Earth Summit's program of action for achieving sustainable development.

4.3   ... [T]he major cause of the continued deterioration of the global environment is the unsustainable pattern of consumption and production, particularly in the industrialized countries, which aggravates poverty and imbalances. * * *

4.5   Although consumption patterns are very high in certain parts of the world, the basic consumer needs of a large section of humanity are not being met. This results in excessive demands and unsustainable lifestyles among the richer segments, which place immense stress on the environment. The poorer segments, meanwhile, are unable to meet food, health care, shelter and educational needs. * * *

4.8   ... (a) All countries should strive to promote sustainable consumption patterns;

(b) Developed countries should take the lead in achieving sustainable consumption patterns;

(c) Developing countries should seek to achieve sustainable consumption patterns in their development process, guaranteeing the provision of basic needs for the poor, while avoiding those unsustainable patterns, particularly in industrialized countries, generally recognized as unduly hazardous to the environment, inefficient and wasteful, in their development processes. This requires enhanced technological and other assistance from industrialized countries.

Report of the United National Conference on Environment and Development, Annex II, U.N. Doc. A/Conf.151.26, Para. 4.3, 4.5, 4.8. (June 3–14, 1992).

This language explaining the developed world's responsibility is noteworthy. Because Agenda 21 was adopted by consensus, the developed countries have for the first time acknowledged their primary responsibility to reduce the environmental impacts of consumption. Similar language has been included in subsequent international declarations, including the Istanbul Declaration on Human Settlements, Para. 10, United Nations Conference on Human Settlements (Habitat II), June 3–14, 1996, and the Programme of Action of the International Conference on Population and Development, U.N. Doc. A/CONF.171/13/Annex at 9, 15 (1994).

In general, there are four options for reducing the environmental impacts of consumption: sufficiency, pricing, awareness, and technological efficiency.

Sufficiency means directly reducing levels of consumption, and is clearly a difficult political choice. The option of government rationing, as we did in the United States during the Second World War and the "energy crisis" of the 1970s generally requires widespread public agreement that a sufficient crisis exists to justify such an interference with consumer autonomy. Indeed, government control of our consumption choices requires intervention far more coercive and intrusive than modern Western democracies will readily accept. As we will see in Chapter 4, more fundamental cultural changes may be necessary before such action by the government would be possible.

The next option for reducing the impacts of consumption is *pricing*— that is, to get the prices right for goods, services, and energy, by ensuring that prices reflect all environmental and social costs. More accurate pricing would reflect resource scarcity and environmental damage, driving up prices of certain goods and services. So long as the market subsidizes environmental degradation by keeping prices artificially low, consumers have no economic incentive to change their lifestyles to less environmentally harmful patterns and levels of consumption. If prices are corrected to reflect the full environmental life-cycle costs, then consumers will likely choose the forms of consumption least costly to the pocketbook and the environment. We will return to pricing in more detail in the next chapter.

To a certain extent it is also possible to reduce the impacts of consumption by *increasing consumer awareness* of the relative impacts of competing products, and promoting consumer preference for lower-impact consumption. This approach has a cultural element—effecting change by changing consumer preferences—which tends to run directly counter to the advertising-driven consumer society described by Ekins. Ecolabeling and green certification programs are examples of efforts to increase awareness.

The last option for reducing consumption impacts is to *improve resource efficiency* through technology, including better design and materials use. Efficiency means doing more with less, with no loss of convenience. This technological approach is the dominant policy in the United States today and is discussed in the final section of this Chapter.

QUESTIONS AND DISCUSSION

1. Given the difficulty of regulating consumption, how much of our effort to fashion appropriate international environmental law should we direct at this variable of the IPAT model? Consider this question after your read the section on technology, and again after you read the section on population.

2. Is consumption more suitable for international or domestic regulation? What strategies should the law take to promote more environmentally responsible consumption? How does the law regulate consumption today? Consider alcohol, tobacco, and other drugs. What about the ban on CFCs discussed in Chapter 9?

3. In fact, few domestic laws directly address the environmental impacts of consumption. Some domestic laws do mandate increased efficiency of products (such as those establishing minimum fuel efficiency for cars), and others have begun to internalize environmental costs (such as air pollution or waste). Taken together, these laws reduce the environmental impacts of some products and activities, but they are *ad hoc*, addressing only some products and some impacts. What other steps could the government take to reduce society's overall consumption?

Consider how government policies may actually *increase* consumption. For example, government subsidies of some products may lead to lower prices and thus to increased levels of consumption. Reducing subsidies on environmentally damaging products may be one way to change consumption patterns. Government subsidies for raising cattle and for logging timber on public lands are two often cited examples. Similarly, governments often promote consumption generally as a way to spur economic growth. Just read the business section of your daily newspaper. For example, the August 28, 1997 *New York Times* reported a story with the headline "Consumer Economic Confidence Is Up, Reaching a Six–Year High" specifically noting that the Consumer Confidence Index rose 2.4 points to 109.4 points! The government as well as many Wall Street analysts follow the Consumer Confidence Index as a major indicator for how the economy is doing. When the Index rises, spending increases, and the economy grows. Should the government be looking for better indicators of the long-term health of the economy? This is discussed further in the next chapter.

Another major way the government can affect consumption is not as a lawmaker, but as a consumer. The U.S. government is in fact the largest consumer in the world. By greening its procurement policies the government could reduce its overall environmental impact. President Clinton's Executive Order 12873, for example, seeks to create a stronger market for environmentally preferable goods by requiring federal agencies to increase their procurement of recycled materials. E.O. 12873, "Federal Acquisition, Recycling and Waste Prevention," Oct. 20, 1993. As a result, EPA is developing a host of "green" product specifications. Thirty-five states also offer procurement preferences for paper with recycled content. The nations of the world already cooperate with respect to the international trade aspects of government procurement. Could green procurement be added to these trade rules?

4. One new legal instrument that shows great promise in promoting sustainable consumption is Extended Producer Responsibility. Extended Producer Responsibility expands the responsibility of businesses to reduce their products' environmental impacts *throughout* the product's life-cycle. In the European Union, for example, producers are effectively required to take responsibility for their product packaging upon disposal. Today, such laws are being adopted around the world with significant consequences for product design and consumption patterns. Indeed, if the trend continues the market for many consumer products will be transformed into a *leasing* economy, with manufacturers mandated to recover and manage products at the end of their useful lives. *See* James Salzman, *Sustainable Consumption and the Law*, 27 Envt'l L. 101 (1998).

5. Chapter 1 discussed the concept of ecological limits, noting that the human species now appropriates about 40% of the earth's net primary productivity (NPP). How should we incorporate the concept of NPP and other biospheric limits into laws that address consumption? In the long term, do we have a choice about whether we reduce consumption? Isn't it inherent in the concept of limits that unbridled consumption can't go on forever?

B. TECHNOLOGY: PROMISES, PUSHES, AND PERILS

1. PROMISES OF TECHNOLOGY

Given the traditional reluctance to regulate consumption and population, it is critical to understand how far technology, the T variable in the IPAT formula, can take us towards sustainable development. The following excerpts suggest much promise from technology. As you read them, consider how we might be able to use law to develop, adopt and distribute new technologies more quickly, and how we might be able to use law to avoid the unintended negative side-effects of technology. Keep in mind, as well, any potential limits that might constrain the development of technology to solve our environmental problems.

Heaton, Repetto & Sobin, TRANSFORMING TECHNOLOGY: AN AGENDA FOR ENVIRONMENTALLY SUSTAINABLE GROWTH IN THE 21ST CENTURY (World Resources Institute 1994)

Today, the climate for innovation seems uniquely rich, poised between technological revolutions in progress and others just emerging. If environmental goals are integrated into these innovations, the transition to a sustainable future will happen faster, cost less, and have longer-lasting results.

The current moment offers an unmatched technical potential for environmental improvement, a fluid climate for technological advance, which badly needs to be exploited. The reservoir of available but unused technology is large. Developments on the horizon could yield major benefits if they are deployed and managed with an environmentally sustainable future in mind.

Enormous improvements in the quality of the global environment could be made with existing technologies, often at no, or small, additional cost. In agriculture, for example, alternative practices that exploit natural cycles and interrelations while decreasing reliance on such off-farm inputs as synthetic fertilizers can drastically reduce environmental damage. Increasingly, these practices are also being recognized as economically competitive with conventional input-intensive farming systems.

The examples of currently available energy saving technology are even more drastic. For example, Dow Chemical's Louisiana Division's returns of investments in energy efficiency average 198 percent for 167 audited projects carried out over seven years. . . . Enormous waste reduction is within reach. The Office of Technology Assessment estimates that about half of all environmentally harmful industrial wastes in the United States could be cut with available technology; with some R & D, another 25 percent could probably be eliminated. Even with current technology great gains are possible. Industry can make use of more recycled paper, metal, glass, waste oil, and plastics than it now does, and higher recycling rates would reduce the need to process virgin materials and the burden on waste-disposal facilities.

Revolutionary technological developments on the horizon could yield enormous environmental benefit, if developed appropriately. Biotechnology, still in its commercial infancy, could fuel a new and environmentally sounder "green revolution," freeing farming from heavy dependence on agri-chemicals. Although widely recognized for their pharmaceutical potential, biological tools are also likely to profoundly affect a wide variety of industrial activities. Enzymes used as industrial catalysts, microbial recovery of metals (biohydrometallurgy,) waste degradation, and biomass fuels and feedstocks are but a few examples. These applications could lower the energy-and pollution-intensity of production while decreasing dependence on fossil fuels. Like other new technologies, biotechnology may not represent an unequivocal environmental gain. Fears that poorly designed or poorly understood genetically-engineered organisms might become pests—a self-replicating environmental hazard—once released into the environment are reinforced by the limits to our understanding of ecology.

Materials technology, equally dynamic, shows even more immediate application. Products based on specially engineered materials probably now comprise more than a third of U.S. GNP—over $1 trillion yearly. Because composite materials typically perform better than conventional materials per unit of weight, they require less raw material and produce less waste. Perhaps most important, materials design has become so highly sophisticated that engineers can now incorporate environmental criteria rather than deal with them as an afterthought. Here too, though, potential environmental drawbacks need consideration. * * *

The term "information technology"—encompassing developments as diverse as real-time monitoring of effluent streams, computer-controlled manufacturing, software development, and chemical and biological sensors—undoubtedly covers the broadest range of potentially important new technologies. All these technologies could have an enormous impact on pollution prevention and control. The application of computers to manufacturing systems not only greatly increases their efficiency and flexibility but also makes possible real-time monitoring of reaction conditions and effluent streams. When coupled with sensors that recognize changes in such conditions, automated processes can both prevent pollution and use input materials and energy more efficiently.

The challenge is not only to encourage these revolutionary developments for their potential but also to ensure that environmental factors are designed at the earliest possible stage.

Dematerialization describes a technological shift away from economies based on enormous and increasing consumption of raw materials. Some modern societies seem to be dematerializing, and dematerialization is certainly a consequence of many of today's most creative technological changes.

One measure of dematerialization is the consumption of energy, steel, cement, and other materials in relation to changes in GNP. For instance, U.S. steel consumption per unit of GNP has dropped 30 percent since 1974; and while GNP has risen about 50 percent in western industrial countries over the same period, energy consumption grew by only 14 percent.

Technological change and new information make dematerialization possible. The obvious trend in industrial countries is away from resource-intensive (high-volume) production toward knowledge-intensive (high-value) production. In the United States, for example, the pattern of investment has shifted dramatically: information-related technology now comprises around 40 percent of all new capital investment. Indeed, because information can often substitute for material inputs, information is the fundamental agent of dematerialization.

Miniaturization and hyperminiaturization (nanotechnology) also promote the performance of countless industrial functions with vastly less energy and material expenditures. Many developments that were recently inconceivable are already on-line: turbo-chargers for automobile engines, fiber-optic cables one-fortieth of the weight of copper cables, or a 25000 rpm micropump implanted in a patient's heart.

————

QUESTIONS AND DISCUSSION

1. Are you persuaded by the preceding excerpt that technology is already showing us the route to sustainable development? The main claim found in the writings of many technological optimists proposes that as information rather than raw material becomes the critical input for wealth creation, the environment is better off.

The argument is that information acts as a complement to other factors of production, enabling cleaner and smarter manufacturing with less material throughput. Indeed, in some cases, intellectual capital and information may permit services to replace manufactured goods entirely. And, intuitively, the substitution of services for products makes sense. After all, at a basic level, people do not want products, they want the services that products provide. They do not want light bulbs, they want light; they do not want cars, they want physical access to other locations. Think of e-mail replacing letters, envelopes, and postal mail; telecommuting and subways replacing cars and traffic congestion; genetically engineered crops reducing the need for pesticides. More services and fewer smokestacks ought to mean less pollution and less environmental impact.

Indeed, a number of well-known scholars claim the economic changes underway provide a clear pathway toward sustainable development. For example, the UNESCO Professor of Economics at Columbia University, Graciela Chichilnisky, has argued that humans could achieve a new form of economic organization where the most important input of production is no longer machines, as in an industrialized society, but rather human knowledge. From the environmental perspective, instead of burning fossil fuels to power machines, the knowledge society "burns" information technology to power knowledge.... The data show that knowledge sectors [almost exclusively services] are becoming an increasingly important part of economic output. Furthermore, the data show that these sectors use progressively less materials, indirectly and directly, than the old industrial sectors.

These conclusions are both provocative and comforting, suggesting that the growing dominance of services and the prevalence of information technologies hold the solutions to many of the environmental challenges we face. While these conclusions are widely held, evidence to date indicates that they are also wrong. * * *

[As the text above noted, p. 55, absolute resource consumption has actually been increasing.] So what does it all mean? The data are both promising and troubling. They are promising because improvements in material intensity and pollution reductions are consistent with the theses that services are substituting for manufacturing and that knowledge is in certain instances replacing inputs of natural capital. The improvements in material intensity, though, may largely be due to other factors such as increased production efficiencies and input substitution. It is thus possible that the environmental bonus from the substitution of services and knowledge for material-intensive activities is not yet occurring to any significant degree—much as the information technology sector is yet to show increases in productivity—and will take decades to exhibit its potential.... At the same time, however, the data are quite disturbing because rising absolute consumption is offsetting improvements in resource use. In fact, the data raise the possibility of a counterthesis—that the information revolution and the rise of services have a net negative environmental impact because they increase overall economic activity and thus overall resource consumption and its impacts.

James Salzman, *Beyond the Smokestack: Environmental Protection in the Service Economy*, 47 UCLA L. Rev. 411, 427, 440–441 (1999)

2. The Heaton, Repetto and Sobin article discusses how globalization can help with technology:

Globalization means the removal of national barriers to information, investment, and trade. Despite debate about the extent of globalization and its desirability, science and technology have unquestionably become highly internationalized. In the 1960s, for example, two-thirds of the non-communist world's R & D was done in the United States; now, the United States is probably less than half. Foreign holders of U.S. patents have doubled, from about 20 percent in 1970 to more than 40 percent today. International trade has grown enormously, from about 7 percent of GNP in the United States in 1960 to around 15 percent today. The penetration of industrial markets by developing countries was one of the major economic phenomena of the 1970s. The growing speed with which technology can diffuse internationally means that environmental problems of global scope can call forth technological responses of equal scope.

The attractive benefits offered by foreign direct investment (FDI) to host developing countries are also undeniable. For the host country, FDI can provide needed capital, spur technology transfer, create jobs, and increase domestic competition and foreign exchange. Since the late 1970s, governments both within and outside the OECD have reversed their traditional opposition to liberalization of FDI, increasingly warming to the role of inward direct investment and creating legal structures to attract further investment. James Salzman, *Labor Rights, Globalization and Institutions:The Role and Influence of the Organization for Economic Cooperation and Development*, 21 Mich J. Int'l L. 769, 809 (2000). Globalization has its critics, of course, including many environmentalists, who are concerned that increasing globalization of trade and financial markets will lead to lower levels of environmental protection everywhere, as countries compete to provide investor-friendly regulatory environments. And environmentally harmful technologies can be diffused internationally as rapidly as environmentally friendly technologies. *See* Chapter 15. Labor groups, too, fear that globalized trade will lead to massive job losses in developed countries as industry races to developing countries in search of cheap, unorganized labor. Globalization is also opposed by more conservative interests, ranging from those who resent the possibility of increased immigration from developing to developed countries, to those who fear the specter of a "one-world government" operated by shadowy international bureaucrats. What impacts do you think economic globalization will have on the environment? What role can international law play in moderating or reducing the negative impacts of globalization?

3. Technological innovations in environmental protection emerge primarily in the industrialized countries with the infrastructure and resources to conduct the necessary research and development. The costs of purchasing and implementing these new technologies can be prohibitive for developing countries. As a result, international environmental treaties now commonly include provisions on technology transfer and technological assistance from developed to developing countries. The provisions generally obligate developed countries to transfer environmentally friendly technologies to developing countries on "fair and most favorable" terms. Because most technology is owned privately, transfers will be based on commercial rates. Should the developed countries have a responsibility to transfer new technologies at a reduced cost? If so, who should compensate the private owner of the technology? What international or domestic policies could be adopted to encourage technological innovation?

One approach to reducing the environmental impact of human consumption patterns is to increase energy and materials efficiency, thereby reducing the total amount of resources consumed for a given level of consumption. Technological innovation is at the heart of this approach and offers great potential for profit. The opportunities arise out of the critical role new technologies will play in reducing our impact on the global environment to sustainable levels while still allowing economic development. The market for environmental goods, services, and technologies is already substantial. The U.S. Environmental Technology (ET) industry (environmental technologies, goods and services) produced $196.5 billion in revenues in 1999 supporting more than 1.4 million U.S. jobs. ET is one of the fastest growing industry sectors worldwide. The global market for ET currently is estimated at about $500 billion and is expected to reach $545 billion by the year 2004. While the United States is a leading producer of ET, it exports only about 11 percent of its ET output while Japan, Germany, and Great Britain export over 20 percent of their ET output. US DEPARTMENT OF COMMERCE, ENVIRONMENTAL TECHNOLOGIES INDUSTRIES (2001).

There are different levels of optimism about how far we can move towards sustainability on the basis of technology alone. In FACTOR FOUR: DOUBLING WEALTH, HALVING RESOURCE USE, authors Ernst Von Weizsacker, Hunter Lovins, and Amory Lovins explain how, through technological innovation, "we can live twice as well—yet use half as much." They contend that such innovation is not merely possible, it is essential if widespread environmental destruction is to be avoided. FACTOR FOUR gives fifty examples of quadrupling resource productivity in energy and material use. For instance, the ultralight "hypercar" equipped with a hybrid-electric drive, could improve automobile fuel efficiency four-to-six fold, to approximately 110–190 miles per gallon.

The "Factor Ten Club" of prominent environmentalists believes that even greater cut-backs are needed, and feasible. In a declaration of principles announced in Carnoules, France in October 1994, the group asserted that technology can reduce our "material intensity" by a factor of ten in OECD countries. If achieved, the result would be a 50% worldwide reduction in resource consumption. In 1999, the OECD's Environment Policy Committee adopted the working goal of four to ten-fold reductions in material intensity.

Under reasonable assumptions about population growth and increases in consumption, especially in developing countries, the task left to technology may be even more daunting than presented in either FACTOR FOUR or the *Carnoules Declaration's* call for a factor ten reduction. Paul Ekins, for one, in *The Sustainable Consumer Society, op. cit.,* suggests that the technological efficiencies needed are far higher, and he is skeptical that we can achieve them. Based on UN projections from the early 1990s, Ekins estimates the product of consumption and technology must be cut in half over the next 50 years simply to keep up with population growth. If we assume a three percent growth rate in economic output in developing countries, consumption will double every 23 years. Ekins, extrapolating from this, determines that by the year 2050 compared to today, more than a 93 percent reduction of environmental impact per unit of consumption will be needed to achieve sustainability. If one is more optimistic and assumes rich countries experience no growth in per capita consumption, then Ekins estimates that the environmental impact of each unit of consumption must be reduced by "only" 79 percent. Still an ambitious target, but within the range of the "Factor Ten Club."

Ironically, increasing efficiency may only increase resource consumption. An example from over 130 years ago illustrates this point well. William Jevons, an observer of England's industrial revolution, recognized that over a short period of time the steam engine had become three times more efficient, i.e. it produced the same power with one-third the coal. In calculating the total coal consumption, however he did not find a similar decrease. In fact, there had been a ten-fold *increase* in coal consumption because the newly-efficient steam engine was now put to many more uses. William Rees, *More Jobs, Less Damage: a Framework for Sustainability, Growth and Employment,* ALTERNATIVES, Oct./Nov. 1995. Modern examples of this effect are easy to find. More efficient cars can be driven more, and their lower cost will make them more affordable to more consumers. The net result could be an overall increase in the cars produced, resources burned, and pollution emitted, even if relative efficiencies have increased. You may recall, with a chuckle, predictions by computer companies a decade ago of the paper-free office. Following the introduction of e-mail into an office, it turns out, paper consumption increases by 40%. Raju Narisetti, *Xerox Copiers Go Digital to Fight Off Printers,* WALL ST. J. EUROPE, May 13, 1998, at 5. Thus, unless efficiency gains offset increased levels of consumption, the net result can actually be an increase in total resource consumption.

———

QUESTIONS AND DISCUSSION

1. Achieving a factor ten improvement may be easier in materials than in energy, because of the physical stability of most materials. They can be used again and again. For those of you who have studied chemistry or physics, what do the laws of thermodynamics tell us about the limits of this efficiency gain?

2. Notwithstanding the examples of increased efficiency resulting in increased consumption, in many other cases improved technology reduces resource use. The substitution of photo-optic cables for copper wire provides a good example. At the same time, the observation of William Jevons gives cause for concern. How do you think technology optimists would respond to this concern?

3. In addition to increases in energy efficiency, fuel switching is also viewed as a way of reducing overall environmental impacts. Switching to renewable energy resources such as solar or wind do provide both economic and environmental promise for the future. Nuclear energy is also held out by some as the answer to global warming and other environmental problems caused by our reliance on fossil fuels. Nuclear fission can provide enormous amounts of energy with no release of carbon dioxide or other traditional air pollutants. However, ensuring the safe long-term operation of power plants and arranging for the long-term disposal of nuclear waste remain significant issues. Not surprisingly, few environmentalists support nuclear energy as a viable alternative.

4. Technology optimists (or "Cornucopians") contend that resource scarcity is simply an artificial construct and that humans will always find more efficient ways to extract resources and develop substitutes. They believe that technology ultimately will solve all of our environmental problems. On the other hand, technology pessimists (or "neo-Malthusians") point out the perils of technology, and the unintended environmental impacts whenever we try to solve our problems through this strategy. Which are you? How far do you think human ingenuity and market incentives will be able to push technology? Will it be able to reduce our environmental impact by the 16–fold factor Ekins argues is necessary for sustainable development? How can the law best guide future technological innovation? For a critique of the scientific errors propagated by some of the "technological optimist" arguments, *see* Paul Ehrlich et al., *No Middle Way on the Environment*, THE ATLANTIC MONTHLY, Dec. 1997, at 98.

5. In 1980, in an unusual dispute resolution process, academics Julian Simon and Paul Ehrlich made a bet. In a $1,000 wager, Simon asked Ehrlich to choose any five commodities whose price would increase in real terms over the coming decade. If their prices rose, Simon would pay $1,000. If they fell, Ehrlich would pay $1,000. The bet seemed a fair test since basic supply and demand would dictate that as resources become scarce their price will rise. Ehrlich and his colleagues chose copper, chrome, nickel, tin, and tungsten. In 1990, Ehrlich sent Simon a check in the mail. Three of the five metals had dropped in price since 1980. What did this bet prove? Are the Technology Pessimists/neo-Malthusians wrong? Was choosing the relative market price of commodities over a time period an accurate measure of resource depletion? What real costs would not be captured in the market price for a commodity?

Simon attempted to follow-up his wager with a bet for the 1990s, challenging Ehrlich to choose any trend pertaining to material human welfare that will get worse rather than improve by the year 2000. As examples, Simon suggested life expectancy, the price of a natural resource, some measure of air or water pollution, or the number of telephones per person. In response, Ehrlich and his colleagues offered to wager that within ten years ozone levels, global temperatures, the gap in wealth between the richest and poorest 10% of humanity and AIDS deaths will rise, while human sperm counts, the amount of fertile cropland, rain forest acreage, rice and wheat production and the fisheries harvest will fall. Simon rejected these trends as too indirectly related to human welfare. Do you agree? *The Sky's No Limit*, INTERNATIONAL HERALD TRIBUNE, July 2, 1996.

––––––

2. PUSHING TECHNOLOGY

Technological development presents a puzzle. If, as the FACTOR FOUR authors argue, many of the suggestions in their book are not complicated and could make dramatic environmental improvements now at small or negligible cost, why aren't they being adopted by businesses. We don't often find $20 bills lying on the sidewalk, so presumably if there is money to be made by these technologies there should be a line of people putting them in place. To a large extent, though, this isn't happening. Why is that? Cultural and institutional constraints have long limited the development, adoption, and distribution of new technologies. Some of the impediments include lack of information, risk-averse actors, lack of capital, and short-sighted or perverse public policies that slow improvement. Some of the other significant obstacles are described below.

Conventional ways of doing things hold practice in a vice-like grip. Most architects and engineers, too, are paid according to what they spend, not what they save, so efficiencies can directly reduce their profits by making them work harder for a smaller fee. * * * [Other impediments include:]

- the conventional education of nearly everybody dealing with natural resources, and the often insurmountable costs of replacing conventional personnel with the rare individuals who know better. This "human factor" may actually be the biggest obstacle and the biggest part of what economists usually call "transaction costs", the costs of overcoming inertia by taking action to change the way things are done;

- other transaction costs relate to the massive interests some capital owners have in preserving existing structures—and more inertia from customers who may simply be ignorant about what levels of resource efficiency they could demand;

- discriminatory financial criteria that often make efficiency jump over a tenfold higher hurdle than resource supply (for example, the very common insistence that an energy-saving measure should repay its investment in a year or two, while power plants are given 10–20 years to pay back); * * *

- obsolete regulations that specifically discourage or outlaw efficiency . . .; * * *

- the almost universal practice of regulating electric, gas, water and other utilities so that they are rewarded for increasing the use, and sometimes even penalized for increasing the efficiency, of resources.* * *

ERNST VON WEIZSÄCKER ET AL., FACTOR FOUR: DOUBLING WEALTH, HALVING RESOURCE USE, xxv-xxvi (1997)

In DRIVING ECO-INNOVATION: A BREAKTHROUGH DISCIPLINE FOR INNOVATION AND SUSTAINABILITY (1996), authors Claude Fussler and Peter James (Director of the Sustainable Business Center) see the post-Rio failure to move further towards sustainable development as the failure of innovation in business, which is the result of "innovation lethargy" and "corporate anorexia." They show technology adoption (and innovation) as an "S" curve, with a slow initial phase at the bottom of the "S" where early adopters start using the new technology, then a steep climb up the "S" as economies of scale kick in and management focuses on continuous improvement, cost cutting, and service improvements. At this stage the big players dominate. "They invest massively ahead of demand to maintain and strengthen market dominance." Finally the technology matures, the curve flattens out, and complacency and lethargy set in. Unfortunately, this is where the authors think most of today's established technology is—at the flat lethargy phase of innovation. *Id.* at 10–17.

If the market alone likely will not spur the massive campaign of research and development required to achieve significantly cleaner technologies (the 93% improvement Ekins argues is necessary), what can be done? One avenue worth exploring is the role law can play in developing, promoting, and distributing environmental technology at the level required to meet tomorrow's demands.

International law can always, of course, adopt an aspirational or hortatory approach to the issue of technology development, encouraging States and non-State actors to develop new technologies out of a sense of moral obligation. For example, Principle 9 of the *Rio Declaration* invites States to: "strengthen endogenous capacity-building for sustainable development ... by enhancing the development, adaptation and transfer of technologies, including new and innovative technologies."

Chapter 4 of *Agenda 21*, the global blueprint for sustainable development adopted in 1992, calls on States to take action to move toward sustainability by:

(a) Encouraging greater efficiency in the use of energy and resources

4.18 Reducing the amount of energy and materials used per unit in the production of goods and services can contribute both to the alleviation of environmental stress and to greater economic and industrial productivity and competitiveness. Governments, in cooperation with industry, should therefore intensify efforts to use energy and resources in an economically efficient and environmentally sound manner by:

> (a) Encouraging the dissemination of existing environmentally sound technologies;

> (b) Promoting research and development in environmentally sound technologies;

> (c) Assisting developing countries to use these technologies efficiently and to develop technologies suited to their particular circumstances;

> (d) Encouraging the environmentally sound use of new and renewable sources of energy;

(e) Encouraging the environmentally sound and sustainable use of renewable natural resources.

(b) Minimizing the generation of wastes

4.19　At the same time, society needs to develop effective ways of dealing with the problem of disposing of mounting levels of waste products and materials. Governments, together with industry, households and the public, should make a concerted effort to reduce the generation of wastes and waste products by:

(a) Encouraging recycling in industrial processes and at the consumer level;

(b) Reducing wasteful packaging of products; [and]

(c) Encouraging the introduction of more environmentally sound products.

Finally, Chapter 34 of Agenda 21 encourages States to transfer new technology and information to other States as it becomes available:

The availability of scientific and technological information and access to and transfer of environmentally sound technology are essential requirements for sustainable development.... The primary goal of improved access to technology information is to enable informed choices, leading to access to and transfer of such technologies and the strengthening of countries' own technological capabilities.

Technology transfer requirements are also a critical part of many specific international environmental treaties. Although it is not clear to what extent these provisions are enforceable, there is general agreement that technology transfer is a necessary concession from the industrialized North to gain developing country participation in and implementation of global environmental treaties.

Of course, through certain types of standards the law can also create strong incentives for technological innovation. By setting standards to be met and deadlines to meet them—without identifying the specific types of technology that must be adopted—the law can create greater flexibility and reward those entrepreneurs who discover less expensive technologies for meeting the standards. In some instances, the law can set "technology forcing" standards at a level beyond what current proven technologies can meet. In this way, every industry player is required to change technologies or production processes to achieve environmental goals.

This technology-forcing approach has been used only rarely at the international level—most notably in the Montreal Protocol regime, where certain ozone destroying substances were phased out before substitutes had been developed for all of the substances' uses. Technology-forcing has been more common at the national level. Technology-forcing regulation can spark a flurry of research and development activity as industry looks for profitable ways to meet the regulatory standard. For example, in the 1970 Amendments to the Clean Air Act, Congress imposed numerical standards for fuel efficiency and auto emissions that could not be met by existing technology, together with stiff penalties for failure to meet the standards. The 1970 Amendments covered critical pollutants such as hydrocarbons, carbon monoxide and nitrogen oxide. These standards were very stringent, requiring a 90% reduction in emissions in only five years. 42 U.S.C. 7521 (1970). Indeed, automakers proved unable to meet them—hydrocarbon emissions were reduced by only 25% between 1970 and 1975. By 1987, however, a 97% percent reduction in hydrocarbon emissions had been achieved. In the same period, emissions of carbon monoxide and other compounds were cut roughly in half. Although the initial targets in the Clean Air Act were not met, the law was nevertheless considered a success in reducing automobile air emissions. Other pollutants and stricter standards were added in subsequent amendments in 1977 and 1990.

In general, government has a key role in technology development and distribution, acting as a catalyst and amplifying the conditions that encourage innovation. Government also must develop strict environmental regulations, which "drive" the development of the technology market. A progressive regulatory approach to environmental problems can have long-term benefits for a country's economy. By stimulating public demand for environmentally friendly products, or raising standards for product performance and decreasing environmental impact, government standards can place domestic producers in a position of competitive advantage relative to their international competitors. As influential Harvard Business School Professor Michael Porter concludes, "When tough regulations anticipate standards that will spread internationally, they give a nation's companies a head start in developing products and services that will be valuable elsewhere." Michael Porter, *Competitive Advantage of Nations*, HARV. BUS. REV., Mar./Apr. 1990, at 73.

————

QUESTIONS AND DISCUSSION

1. The U.S. Congress was forced to adopt the technology-forcing approach in the 1970 U.S. Clean Air Act after automakers contended that technological fixes were unfeasible and entered into illegal cross-licensing agreements to eliminate commercial incentives for developing emissions control technologies. A 1968 memo from the Department of Justice set out the conspiracy:

> Following the publication and general acceptances of the Haagen–Smit theory, the automobile industry finally acknowledged that motor vehicles contributed to air pollution, which it had steadfastly denied prior thereto. The problem of how to control motor vehicle emissions was then turned over by the industry to the Automobile Manufacturers Association ... a trade association whose members manufacture 99 percent of the cars, trucks and buses produced annually in the United States.... From the very outset the industry realized that air pollution control devices do not help sell automobiles.

> The AMA Board ... formed the Vehicle Combustion Products Committee (VCP) to direct all industry efforts on a noncompetitive basis.... An AMA internal memorandum prepared for presentation at VCP and Engineering and Advisory Committee (EAC) meetings disclosed that ... dilatory tactics prevailed:

>> On the basis of the facts the industry is not convinced that exhaust emissions devices or systems are necessary for nationwide application to motor vehicles, but believes instead that they will be an economic and maintenance burden on motorists. It is therefore not prepared or desirous to initiate any voluntary program to impose these systems or devices....

The AMA cross-licensing agreement placed the automobile producers in a position where they did not have to fear that a competitor would develop an effective device or system for its exclusive use which might become required equipment and thus put the others at a competitive disadvantage. Justice found that the automakers had agreed not to purchase or utilize any device developed by a nonsignatory to the cross-licensing agreement.

Failure on the part of the manufacturers to purchase devices of independent companies, produced at costs of millions of dollars, discouraged such independents from further research, development, or manufacture of control devices to the great detriment of the American people, science and industry.

The Justice Department filed an antitrust suit, which was subsequently settled. It later turned out that the automakers had the technology for catalytic converters on the shelf, some of it dating back to the 1930s. Confidential Memorandum, U.S. Dept. Of Justice (undated) *reprinted in* U.S. Cong. Rec., H4063–4074 (May 18, 1971).

2. Technology-forcing legislation has not disappeared. Commercialization of the hydrogen fuel-cell vehicles is being driven by a California law requiring 10% of all cars sold in California to be "zero emission vehicles," originally by 1998, but since postponed until 2003. In January 2001, the states air-quality board reaffirmed this requirement and added a regulation requiring the top six automobile manufacturers to produce 3 million electric/low-polluting vehicle by 2012. The board mandated that manufacturers subdivide the 10% down into 2% of cars emitting no pollution, 2% hybrid, and 6% low-emission. This rule requires automobile manufacturers to produce 4,650 completely pollution-free cars by 2003 and 14,000 by 2012. If the external cost of pollution were included in the cost of gasoline-powered automobiles, which do you think would cost more? This is a critically important point. Unless there are market signals directly indicating environmental harm, there is, at best, a weak incentive for research and development of environmentally superior technologies absent legal requirements. We will discuss the concept of "externalities" in Chapter 3. Robert Salladay, *Air Quality Board Eases Mandate for Electric Cars*, S.F. CHRON. Jan. 26, 2001, at A1.

3. In the quest to replace high-emission vehicles that run on gasoline, hydrogen fuel cells have emerged as one of the most promising technologies for future energy production. Based on a theory dating back to 1839, fuel cells remained a curiosity until they were used in America's space program in the 1960s. Hydrogen fuel cells provide an efficient power source that produces neither air nor noise pollution. Hydrogen—which can be produced by running electric current through water—is passed through the membrane of a fuel cell, where a chemical reaction strips off electrons from hydrogen atoms, which in turn provide the power for the electric engine. The only emissions are water and some excess heat.

An infrastructure to support these technologies has begun to form over the last five years due to falling prices and new technological advances that are making fuel cell cars a reality. Because the main difficulty with introducing fuel-cell powered cars is resupplying the hydrogen, the current developments have focused on public transportation. *State of the World 2001* discusses the "Hydrogen Age."

Fuel cells are nearing the market for both stationary and transportation uses. Ballard Power Systems and FuelCell Energy plan to deliver their first commercial 250–kilowatt units in 2001. DaimlerChrysler, which is devoting $1.5 billion to fuel cell efforts over the next several years, aims to sell 20–30 of its fuel cell buses to transit systems in Europe by 2002, and to mass-produce 100,000 fuel cell cars and begin selling them by 2004. Toyota and Honda have set 2003 commercialization dates for their fuel cell vehicles.

An important stimulus of the fuel cell market has been the state of California's requirement that 2 percent of new cars sold in 2003 be zero-emission vehicles. The mandate has spurred new fuel cell investments and collaborations. The California Fuel Cell Partnership, composed of major car manufactures, energy companies, and government agencies, intends to test 70 fuel cell vehicles by 2003, with energy companies delivering hydrogen and other fuels to refueling stations. In November 2000, the partnership unveiled its headquarters, which includes a refueling station and public education center, and the first flee of vehicles in Sacramento.

Another region at the vanguard of the hydrogen transition is Iceland, where in February 1999 a $1–million joint venture to create the world's first hydrogen economy was launched by the government and other Icelandic institutions, DaimlerChrysler, Shell Hydrogen, and Norsk Hydro. The joint venture, Icelandic New Energy, emerged from a parliament-appointed study commission that recommended the initiative; it is now official government policy to promote the increased use of renewable resources—geothermal and hydroelectric resources provide 70 percent of the nation's energy—to produce hydrogen. The strategy is to begin with buses, followed by passenger cars and fishing vessels, with the goal of completing the transition between 2030 and 2040. * * *

The introduction of fuel cell cars faces three tough technical challenges: integrating small, inexpensive, and efficient fuel cells into the vehicles; designing tanks that can store hydrogen on board; and developing a hydrogen refueling infrastructure.... Wise decisions made in today's early hydrogen economy could yield enormous economic and environmental benefits. Wrong turns towards an interim infrastructure, on the other hand, could strand millions of dollars in financial assets, lock in fleets of obsolete fuel cell cars, and add millions of extra tons of carbon emission. There is an appropriate role for government to play in collaborating with transport and energy companies to develop a direct hydrogen infrastructure through greater research into storage technologies and the identification of barriers and strategies to surmount them.

Seth Dunn, *Decarbonizing the Energy Economy*, STATE OF THE WORLD 2001, AT 96–99 (Worldwatch Institute, 2001).

In February 2001, the United Nations' Global Environment Facility (GEF), an arm of the United Nations Development Program (UNDP), gave the go-ahead for a demonstration project that is expected to provide clean fuel cell city buses for five developing countries. Between 40 and 50 fuel cell buses will be delivered and deployed at a total cost of about $130 million between 2002 and 2003 to major cities and capitals with some of the world's worst air pollution levels in Brazil, Mexico, Egypt, India, and China. *United Nations Agency Launches Fuel Cell Bus Projects in Five Developing Countries*, Hydrogen & Fuel Cell Letter, February 2001.

4. The 35 million automobiles manufactured each year present an important opportunity for technology innovation since, as Figure 2–4 illustrates below, the world's automobile fleet continues to grow. Lester Brown et al., VITAL SIGNS 83 (1999). According to both FACTOR FOUR and DRIVING ECO-INNOVATION, only 2% of the fuel we put in our "car provides the final service of personal mobility while 75% is lost in waste heat (exhaust gases, radiation and cooling water)." While not as promising as fuel cells, hybrid vehicles combine the technical advantages of electric vehicles with the economical advantages of conventional vehicles. The result is an affordable, low emission, fuel-efficient vehicle with performance standards equal to or better than many conventional vehicles. Conventional vehicles with their internal combustion engines have benefited from decades of research and development and have evolved into very efficient and extremely popular modes of personal and public transportation.

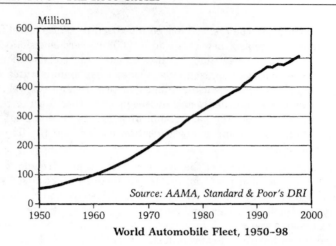

World Automobile Fleet, 1950–98

Figure 2–4

Electric vehicles are even more efficient and they have been around just as long as conventional vehicles. Yet, they still have not made it to mass markets. The technology to develop lightweight and long-range onboard batteries for electric vehicles is still too expensive to pass on to the average consumer.

5. How far can the law go in forcing technology? One difficulty in knowing how hard to push is that industry sometimes exaggerates the cost estimates for applying new technology. Former EPA Assistant Administrator William G. Rosenberg notes,

> Historically, annual costs are generally much lower than projections because of improved technology. For example, in 1971 the oil industry estimated that lead phase-out would cost 7 cents a gallon, or $7 billion a year. In 1990, with 99 percent of lead phaseout accomplished, actual costs are only $150 million to $500 million a year, 95 percent less than earlier estimates.

Rosenberg, *Clean Air Act Amendments*, 251 SCIENCE 1546, 1547 (1991). What can the law do to encourage more realistic cost estimates?

6. Is technology-forcing action like that in the Clean Air Act feasible at the international level? Although international bodies often establish voluntary standards that private organizations strive to meet, international law almost never imposes obligations directly on such organizations.

International law does have one technology-facilitating advantage over domestic law, however. By setting standards that apply throughout the world, international law can reduce some anti-competitive effects that may otherwise discourage the development and implementation of environmentally friendly technologies. The start-up costs for developing and implementing new technologies can be very high and, more important, new technologies can involve uncertainties over cost, product quality, and productivity. Corporations that pass these costs on to consumers through higher prices may lose consumers to the cheaper products of other manufacturers. Manufacturers may also be risk averse and prefer to avoid the uncertainty inherent in new technologies simply out of fear of losing market share to competitors. By harmonizing standards, international law can reduce these competitive pressures and help new technologies emerge. As we will see in Chapter 9 U.S. industry pushed for an international regime on CFCs for precisely these reasons. Faced with strict domestic CFC reductions, it was in their interest to ensure that their competitors in other countries were subject to the same constraints.

7.   Technology is often protected by intellectual property rights, including patents and copyright. The idea is to give inventors an economic incentive by promising them monopoly profits on the goods they invent for a fixed number of years—17 years in the United States. Can you think of ways intellectual property rights might inhibit the transfer of environmental technology from developed to developing countries? If an inventor does develop a key environmental technology, can government compel the owner to license the technology to the rest of the world? What if the owner demands too high a price? Can government compel a "fair" price?

8.   The free market responds to scarcity by increasing competition among buyers, causing the price of goods or services to increase, and the market ultimately to produce more of what is demanded or to provide substitutes to satisfy the demand. Following the logic of the market, as our environmental quality continues to decrease or become scarcer, the market should respond. For example, the air is so polluted in Tokyo that you can now buy a breath of oxygen on the street corner. Do you see any danger in leaving environmental quality to the market? Consider, for example, that the market will only sell us back environmental quality when it is profitable to do so. Will those with wealth be able to enjoy environmental quality and protect their health, while the poor will not? If a clean environment were established as a basic human right, how might this situation change? *See* Chapter 16 for discussion of rights to a clean and healthy environment.

––––––

3.   PERILS OF TECHNOLOGY

Although technology offers tremendous opportunities for decreasing the environmental impact of human population and consumption, it also presents many challenges. Often, technology merely transfers environmental risks or creates new risks to replace those it does eliminate. "Miracle technologies" long considered safe have had unintended and serious effects on human health and the environment. An obvious example, discussed in Chapter 1, is that of CFCs and related substances now implicated in ozone depletion. The reversal of CFCs' fate—from miracle chemical to ozone destroyer—is one of many examples where technological innovation has led to serious environmental problems. Three examples described below, provide useful guidance about why we should approach new technologies with caution and respect.

DDT. Dichloro-diphenyl-trichloroethane (DDT) was used widely as a pesticide from the early 1940s to the late 1960s. It was considered a vast improvement over the highly toxic copper-and arsenic-based pesticides that had long been in use. DDT promised to be the "miracle insecticide": it worked against a broad spectrum of insects, including mosquitoes, flies, fleas, lice, cockroaches and many agricultural pests. By the standards of the time, moreover, DDT was a remarkably safe product—it was stable, non-flammable, and demonstrated none of the characteristics associated at that time with toxicity. That is, it did not cause death or obvious disease in those exposed to high concentrations. The Swiss chemist who discovered DDT's insecticidal properties in 1938 was subsequently awarded the Nobel Prize for his work. Because it was believed both effective and safe, DDT use spread throughout U.S. gardens and suburbs, and indeed throughout the world.

Not until DDT had been in widespread use for more than two decades did its harmful effects begin to emerge. DDT is a persistent organic pollutant. It accumulates in the body fat of animals and people. This bio-accumulation has serious effects for animals throughout the food chain, with the most serious effects reserved for top-tier carnivores, whose concentrations of the toxin are orders of magnitude higher than in animals lower on the food chain. DDT caused die-offs in songbirds and fish; fragile eggshells in eagles and other birds of prey; and cancer and neurological effects in humans.

In 1972, the United States became the first country to ban the use of DDT. Other developed countries soon followed suit. DDT continues to be used in many developing countries, particularly for malaria control, and the recent treaty banning certain persistent organic pollutants explicitly did not ban DDT. For futher discussion of DDT, *see* Chapter 12, pp. 866–868; RACHEL CARSON, SILENT SPRING (1962); THEO COLBORN ET AL., OUR STOLEN FUTURE 199–200 (1996).

Genetic Engineering. In December 2000, the International Service for the Acquisition of Agri-biotech Applications (ISAAA) reported that, globally, 44.2 million hectares are tilled with genetically modified crops. Farmers bought and planted this 11% increase in engineered seeds because of "convenient and flexible crop management, higher productivity, and safer environment through decreased use of conventional pesticides." A December 2000 article in Science magazine noted the benefits associated with the increased use in genetically engineered crops. The potential benefits include increased crop yield and associated land preservation, reduced environmental impacts from pesticides as well as decreased production costs in money saved from not buying expensive chemicals, and soil conservation (some herbicides must be tilled in to the soil, leading to increased erosion potential. The modified crops may not require this type of herbicide.)

However, the potential risks of the use of genetically modified crops must be considered as well. The genetically modified crop may become invasive. It is difficult to predict the occurrence and extent of long-term environmental effects when nonnative organisms are introduced into an ecosystem. The crop may have direct effects on nontarget species, including beneficial insects. Plants engineered to produce proteins with pesticidal properties may affect populations of nontarget species. A highly publicized laboratory experiment, for example, suggested that monarch butterfly larvae could die from ingesting pollen from corn engineered to produce the *Bacillus thuringiensis* (Bt) toxin. Furthermore, pesticidal proteins produced by genetically engineered crops may bioaccumulate in predators. Finally, viruses with new biological characteristics could possibly arise in transgenic viral-resistant plants through recombination. While potential for beneficial uses of genetic engineering exist, meticulous care must be taken in developing, disseminating, implementing, and reporting on the technologies to avoid critical environmental harm. The Biosafety Protocol is discussed at page 953. *See generally,* L.L. Wolfenbarger and P.R. Phifer, *The Ecological Risks and Benefits of Genetically Engineered Plants*, SCIENCE Vol 290 15 Dec 2000.

Exotic Species. The introduction of an exotic species can wreak havoc on an ecosystem that has evolved independent of that species. In the absence of natural predators or competitors, exotic plants or animals can quickly deplete or displace native species, disrupting the natural systems of which those species are a part. The use of biological control strategies—for example, natural predators for insect pests, or waste-consuming bacteria—holds tremendous promise for reducing the environmental impact of human economic activity. These same strategies, however, can have profound environmental repercussions.

During the New Deal era, the United States Soil Conservation Service began encouraging farmers to plant kudzu, a vine introduced from Asia in the 1870s, to slow erosion (and prevent loss of topsoil) in Southern cotton lands. Farmers were paid up to $8 an acre to plant fields of the vine. By the end of World War II, a half million acres of land were covered in kudzu.

The hardiness and vitality that made kudzu an effective ground cover, however, turned it into a biological pest. Kudzu grows as much as a foot per day during the summer months—up to sixty feet per year—climbing trees, power poles, cars, anything in its path. Free of the insects that kept it in check in Asia, and resistant to most herbicides, the vines spread essentially unchecked, in spite of vigorous control efforts. Today, kudzu covers more than seven million acres in the Southeastern United States. As it spreads, kudzu chokes out native plants, killing entire forests by blocking the sunlight necessary to their survival.

————

QUESTIONS AND DISCUSSION

1. While technology has a critical role to play in the movement toward sustainable development, the lessons from the unintended consequences of technology teach that introducing synthetic or non-native entities into the environment must follow a precautionary strategy, and be done in moderation at first, with adequate controls. In addition to following the precautionary principle, proposed technology solutions also should be the subject of an environmental assessment. *See* Chapter 7, page 432.

2. An additional danger of chemical pesticides arises when the targeted pests develop resistance and even immunities to these compounds. Often, farmers respond by releasing higher doses of chemicals only to see the pests adapt again in a self-perpetuating cycle in which ever greater amounts of chemicals are released into the environment. Consider the chart in Chapter 12, page 882, showing this phenomenon. Can and should the law play a role in stopping this cycle? Or is the proper fix for this problem a technological one? Consider the solution of Monsanto, which bioengineered cotton seeds that can withstand higher concentrations of their pesticide "Roundup." Their argument is that the chemical can now be applied in higher concentrations, but less frequently, thus reducing the total amount used. Would it make more sense to bio-engineer seeds that were resistant to pests? Would it be as profitable? Allen Myerson, *Growing Seeds of Discontent*, N.Y. Times, Nov. 19, 1997, at D1.

3. How can the law require chemical manufacturers to develop chemicals responsibly, taking into consideration long-term effects on the environment, as well as human health? Consider that hydrochlorofluorocarbons (HCFCs) which were developed as a more ozone-friendly alternative to CFCs have since been proven to be significant greenhouse gases. What about requiring manufacturers to study continuously and report findings on the effects of their products? Consider that in 1991–92 the U.S. EPA offered amnesty from large fines to chemical manufacturers who submitted unpublished scientific studies that they should have submitted earlier. The agency received more than 10,000 studies "showing that chemicals already on the market could pose a 'substantial risk of injury to health or to the environment'—the kind of never-published data that the law says must be presented to the government immediately." Dan Fagin et al., TOXIC DECEPTION: HOW THE CHEMICAL INDUSTRY MANIPULATES SCIENCE, BENDS THE LAW, AND ENDANGERS YOUR HEALTH at 14–15 (Birch Lane Press, 1997).

4. What other examples come to mind of technology innovations that have unintended environmental effects? Consider the internal combustion engine and the pollution it causes, including carbon dioxide. Only in the last 20 years has the scientific community realized that carbon dioxide emissions are the number one greenhouse gas contributing to global warming.

C.   POPULATION GROWTH

1.   THE CHALLENGES POSED BY POPULATION

Population growth is, at its core, a simple numbers game—a problem based on the distinction between arithmetic and geometric growth. Arithmetic growth operates by the principle of simple addition. For example, a factory that produces two cars per hour will have produced two cars after the first hour, four cars after the second hour, six after the third hour, and so on. There is a steady rate of increase for each unit of time: $2+2+2$ ... Now imagine that instead of cars, our factory produces other factories, each capable of producing still more factories on its own. For the sake of simplicity, imagine as well that each of these factories can only produce for one hour—it has a limited lifespan. After one hour, our original factory has produced two new factories, at which point our original factory ceases production and the new factories start producing. After two hours, we have four factories, just as we had four cars in the original example. After three hours, however, we begin to see a difference. We now have eight factories, as compared to six cars. After four hours, the difference is greater still, sixteen factories and only eight cars. What about after ten hours? In the same time our auto factory has produced twenty new cars, our factory has produced 1024 new factories. This is the power of geometric growth, the force of the simple equation: $2 \times 2 \times 2$ ... Humans, like the factories in our hypothetical, are capable of geometric growth. We produce offspring that are themselves capable of reproducing: $2 \times 2 \times 2 \ldots$.

What if our hypothetical factory only produced one new factory in its hour-long lifetime? The equation would be changed, would it not? $1 \times 1 \times 1$ ... Assuming adequate resources, the factories could go on producing forever, with each new generation simply replacing the last. The factory factories have a replacement rate of 1. Humans also have a natural replacement rate—2.1 children per female—at which geometric population growth can be avoided. But when fertility rises above this replacement rate, even slightly, geometric population growth becomes inevitable. The more fertility exceeds the replacement rate, the faster the population will grow.

Stanford ecologist Paul Ehrlich first brought the issue of population growth to the public's eye in his 1968 book *The Population Bomb.* As Ehrlich explained, population numbers add up very quickly.

> It has been estimated that the human population of 6000 B.C. was about five million people, taking perhaps one million years to get there from two and a half million. The population did not reach 500 million until almost 8,000 years later—about 1650 A.D. This means it doubled roughly once every thousand years or so. It reached a billion people around 1850, doubling in some 200 years. It took only 80 years or so for the next doubling, as the population reached two billion around 1930. We have not completed the next doubling to four billion yet [in 1968], but we now have well over three billion people. The doubling time at present seems to be about 37 years. Quite a reduction in doubling time: 1,000,000 years, 1,000 years, 200 years, 80 years, 37 years. Perhaps the meaning of a 37 year doubling time is best brought home by a theoretical exercise. Let's examine what might happen on the absurd assumption that the population continued to double every 37 years into the indefinite future.

> If growth continued at that rate for about 900 years, there would be some 60,000,000,000,000,000 people on the face of the earth. Sixty million billion people. This is about 100 persons for every square yard of the Earth's surface, land and sea. * * *

Paul Ehrlich, THE POPULATION BOMB 18 (1968).

This passage was written over 30 years ago. Today's global population is over 6 billion. While the rate of population growth has slowed since 1968, the population is still growing at 1.2% annually, about 77 million people per year. <http://www.org/esa/population/wpp2000.htm>. Every second, three additional people are born. Although we are still a long way from Ehrlich's hypothetical 100 people per square yard of earth, how large will the world's population be when our grandchildren are growing up?

The United Nations recently estimated that the average woman in the developed world has 1.57 children during her lifespan, 3.1 in the developing world. This translates to 2.82 children for the average woman. Total fertility globally is projected to decline from 2.82 children per woman to 2.15 by 2050. As we noted earlier, the rate required for a stable population, for children to replace parents, is 2.1 children per woman. Thus we are currently experiencing population growth. An important fact, though often misunderstood, is that demographic changes take place over the period of several generations. Thus even if we reduced the global fertility rate *tomorrow* to 2.1 children per woman, the global population would *still grow* by at least three billion people before it stabilized. There are more young people alive today who have not yet begun to bear children than the older generation that is dying. This imbalance between young and old virtually guarantees that births will exceed deaths for several generation. This phenomenon of population growth despite low fertility rates is called "demographic momentum." In this sense, efforts today will only bring down the *rate* of population growth, not the absolute population. We are, in effect, running down the up escalator.

Figures 2–5 and 2–6 below show the current size and growth rate of the global population. Lester Brown et al., VITAL SIGNS 99 (2000).

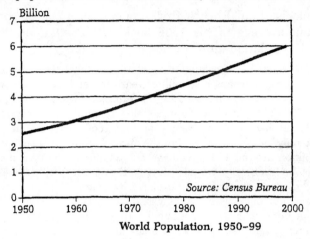

World Population, 1950–99

Figure 2–5

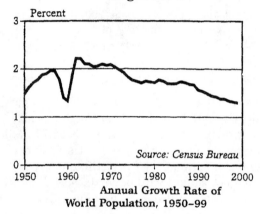

Annual Growth Rate of
World Population, 1950–99

Figure 2–6

Demographers estimate future rates of population growth based on assumptions of birth and death rates throughout the world. In the early 1990s, the United Nations summarized the demographers' best estimates as three long-term projections for population growth—"low," "medium," and "high."

Judith Jacobsen, *Population, Consumption, and Environmental Degradation: Problems and Solutions* 6 COLO. J. INT'L ENVTL. L. & POL'Y 255, 259–262 (1995).

United Nations demographers consider the "medium" projection the most probable. In it, modelers assume that average family size in the developing world outside China will fall gradually from its 1990 level of 4.4 children per woman to replacement level fertility by 2040. This trend would bring average world fertility to approximately replacement level and cause world population to rise from today's 5.6 billion to 10 billion in 2050, eventually stabilizing at 11.6 billion one hundred years later.

The "medium" projection assumes that fertility will fall to replacement level and no farther. In fact, however, fertility has fallen below 2.0 children per woman in much of Europe, East Asia, and in parts of the former Soviet Union and the Caribbean. The "low" projection is based on the idea that average world fertility could fall to 1.7 children per woman. Under this projection, world population would peak at about 8 billion in 2050 and decline thereafter, dropping below today's world population around the year 2100.

The "high" projection, in contrast, is based on the assumption that average world fertility never reaches exactly 2.1 children per woman but hovers above it at 2.2. This projection would produce a world population of 12.5 billion in 2050 and of 20 billion a century later, with no end to growth in sight. This calculation illustrates the enormous power of even the slightest exponential growth, an effect that lies behind much of the concern about world population growth among analysts and activists.

A closer look at the "medium" projection illustrates the long time scales on which demographic changes unfold. First, fertility is so high in some parts of the world that, realistically, a gradual decline to replacement level would take several decades. For example, the average number of children per woman exceeds 7.0 in several African countries, including Benin, Burkina Faso, Cote d'Ivoire, Mali, Niger, Somalia, Togo, and Uganda. Achieving replacement-level fertility in these nations would require more than a seventy percent reduction in birth rates. Singapore, under conditions of rapid economic growth and industrialization, a sophisticated health-care system, universal availability of family planning services, and a system of financial incentives and disincentives to encourage two-child families, achieved a seventy percent reduction in its fertility rate in about twenty years during the 1960s and 1970s—among the fastest fertility declines in the twentieth century. Slower reductions, however, are more common. Birth rate declines have begun in a few African countries only in the past few years. Thus it is entirely reasonable to expect the achievement of replacement-level fertility on a global scale to take several decades, at the very least.

Second, even after fertility reaches replacement level as a global average, it takes a century more for the world's population to stop growing, barring a dramatic change in mortality patterns. This is the result of demographic momentum.

Even the very optimistic assumptions about future fertility trends that are embodied in the United Nations' "low" projection would mean population growth until the middle of the twenty-first century. And world population would not fall below today's level until approximately 2100.

In 1996 and 1998, the United Nations revised its population growth projections—downward! In the *1998 Revision of the World Population Estimates and Projections*, the United Nations reported that the decline in overall fertility rates was greater than expected. From 1950 to 1955, the global average fertility rate was five births per woman. The current fertility rate is estimated to be 2.8 births per woman and falling. In Europe, the birth rate is now 1.4 children per woman—substantially lower than the replacement rate. Fertility rates in developing countries are generally higher, but nonetheless, on the decline overall. For example, in the past 25 years, the number of children per couple in Africa fell from 6.6 to 5.1, from

5.1 to 2.6 in Asia and from 5.0 to 2.7 in Latin American and the Caribbean. In 2000 the projections increased again, with the United Nations revising its population projections to 7.9 billion for the low case, 9.3 billion for the medium, and 10.9 billion people for the high. Part of this increase is due to the projected increase in life expectancy, with global averages moving from 65 years in 2000 to 76 in 2050. *See,* John Bongaarts, *Demographic Consequences of Declining Fertility,* 282 SCIENCE 419 (1998).

The causes of fertility decline are complex. A popular theory explaining declining fertility, known as the "demographic transition theory," posits three stages in a society's transition from rural to modern and industrialized states. In simple terms, the first stage of rural and developing societies exhibits high rates of fertility offset by high rates of mortality (particularly infant mortality). Having a large number of children is desirable to ensure an adequate number live to adulthood, provide labor for the family, and look after the parents in their old age.

The second stage of demographic transition is marked by a drop in mortality rates (most noticeably among infants) as sanitation, health care, and food quality are improved through modernization and development. During this stage populations rapidly increase because the traditionally high rates of fertility are no longer offset by high death rates. In the third stage, fertility rates decrease to a level commensurate with the death rates and the population stabilizes. What countries and regions today would you place in each stage of demographic transition?

A great deal of debate surrounds recent decreases in fertility. Economic development, low infant mortality, and education alone do not explain fertility rates in all countries. As an example, according to the demographic transition theory one would expect Egypt to have experienced a faster fertility decline than Morocco. Egypt enjoys more land, a stronger economy, a higher standard of living, better education (for men and women), and less child labor. Yet fertility in Egypt has remained fairly constant while Morocco's has decreased. Youssef Courbage, *Fertility Transition in the Mashriq and Maghrib,* in CARLA OBERMEYER, ED., FAMILY, GENDER AND POPULATION IN THE MIDDLE EAST (1995).

Certain factors clearly play a role in fertility rates, including whether children are essential to sustain the agricultural pattern of life or support elderly parents, whether they are more of an economic liability than an asset, the availability of education, birth control, and the status of women. The UN Population Fund's *State of the World Population 2000* report stated that two-thirds of the 300 million children lacking access to education are girls and, largely as a result, two-thirds of the 880 million illiterate adults are women.

Do declines in global average fertility rates mean that the population problem is solving itself? For the foreseeable future, the answer is no. As a result of demographic momentum, the human population will continue rising at least until the middle of this century. The direction population heads from there will depend on whether fertility rates stabilize above or below the replacement rate. In the interim, however, we will add between three and four billion new people to the world during that time, nearly all of them in the developing world. Recall the IPAT identity discussed earlier in the chapter. These people will increase the already severe pressures in developing countries on water supplies, food supplies, and the environment. International action on population can address and ease these pressures far more rapidly than can the invisible hand of demographic transition.

———

2.   THE ROLE OF LAW IN POPULATION

International law directed at population is entirely aspirational "soft" law, taking the form of declarations, programs of action, and resolutions. A key legal question in the area of population is whether a family's right to determine the number of children it bears is a basic human right protected under the U.N. Charter. The Charter commits member nations to promote "universal respect for, and observance of, human rights and fundamental freedoms for all without distinction as to race, sex, language or religion." U.N. Charter, Articles 55, 56 (1945). Article 16 of the 1948 Universal Declaration of Human Rights, G.A.Res. 217A, Article 16(1), (3), U.N.Doc. A/810 (1948), states:

> Men and women of full age, without any limitation due to race, nationality, or religion, have the right to marry and found a family. ... The family is the natural and fundamental group unit of society and is entitled to protection by society and the State.

The Universal Declaration is considered by many countries to be customary international law but its application to population control policies is disputed.

A number of other international declarations and UN General Assembly resolutions have endorsed the fundamental right of a family to determine its number of children. Both the Final Act of the UN International Conference on Human Rights at Teheran, 13 May 1988, Article 16, the Declaration on Social Progress and Development, Article 4, G.A. Res. 2542, U.N.Doc. A/7630 (1970), and other international instruments have pronounced that parents have the basic "right to determine freely and responsibly the number and spacing of their children." Yet the customary law status of these declarations is recognized by fewer nations than is the case with either the UN Charter or the Universal Declaration. Does the right to determine family size necessarily follow from the Universal Declaration? Article 29 of the Universal Declaration states:

> (1) Everyone has duties to the community in which alone the free and full development of personality is possible.

> (2) In the exercise of his rights and freedoms, everyone shall be subject only to such limitations as are determined by law solely for the purpose of securing due recognition of and respect for the rights and freedoms of others and of meeting the *just requirements* of morality, public order and the general welfare in a democratic society [emphasis added].

Countries such as China, which have laws and economic instruments promoting one-child families, have argued that international standards of human rights are aspirational and cannot supersede national cultural, economic and demographic conditions. China might also look to Article 29 of the Universal Declaration and contend that maintaining a low national birth rate is a "just requirement" of public order and general welfare that justifies limiting the choice of family size. A number of environmentalists endorse this position as well. But China's experience demonstrates that such coercive tactics may be ineffective.

Although Chinese officials were aware of the nation's looming overpopulation crisis from at least the 1950s, they did not take steps to address the problem for two decades. The Maoist government contended that China could always produce itself out of trouble because "every mouth is born with two hands attached." Beginning in 1971, China undertook efforts to slow the growth of a population that had already surpassed 850 million. The "later, longer, fewer" program urged Chinese to marry later, wait longer between children, and limit themselves to two children per family. The program met with significant success: average births per woman dropped from 5.8 in 1970 to 2.8 in 1977. Because China's population was already so high, however, even the lower birth rate translated into huge absolute increases. In 1979, the Chinese government imposed a one-child policy, enforced not only by political and economic pressure, but also allegedly by coerced abortions. Not surprisingly, the policy met with significant, often violent, resistance, particularly among the rural peasants that make up three-fourths of China's population. Within five years, the government was forced to relax the policy everywhere but in urban centers, where control is more easily maintained. Throughout rural China, families with two, three or more children are now common. The Chinese government claims that Chinese women now average two births each, but this figure may significantly under-represent the actual birth rate in the country. *See* Mark Hertsgaard, *Our Real China Problem*, ATLANTIC MONTHLY, Nov. 1997, at 97, 105–108; Nicholas Kristof, *China's Crackdown on Births: A Stunning, and Harsh, Success*, N.Y. TIMES, May 25, 1993, at 1.

QUESTIONS AND DISCUSSION

1. Pressure and coercion can take many forms, and a number of commentators have argued that few human rights are absolute. If the United States had four and a half times its current population, half as much land available for cultivation, fewer natural resources, and serious problems of deforestation and land degradation—that is, if the United States were in China's position today—do you think it would be so critical of China for its population control policies? China certainly has been criticized in the West for the alleged consequences of its one-child policy—infanticide of newborn daughters, forced sterilization, and other coercive actions. Some assert that families have an "inalienable right" to have as many children as they want, but rights also involve responsibilities. Because population size has an impact on local, regional and global ecosystem services, do others have legitimate interest in a family's size? At a certain level, in a society facing China's challenges, do certain individual rights have to become secondary to the society's greater interests? Recall Article 29(1) of the Universal Declaration: "Everyone has duties to the community . . . ."

2. As we have already noted, a number of international declarations state that the right to determine the size of one's family is a basic human right. Thus government measures to control family size, at a certain point, may become human rights abuses. Which of the following do you consider human rights abuses?

- payment of food or money for voluntary sterilization?

- denial of social benefits to couples who have more than one child?

- denial of tax deductions to couples who have more than two children?

- requiring (or prohibiting) abortions?

- requiring the use of contraceptive devices?

3. In 1994, 183 countries attended the Third International Conference on Population and Development in Cairo, Egypt. The Cairo Conference followed previous population conferences in Bucharest, 1974, and Mexico City, 1984. Recognizing that global population continues to grow at over 90 million people a year, the Cairo conferees developed a 20–year Program of Action to address population and development concerns, based on the premise that such action is an indispensable part of national and international efforts to achieve sustainable development. *See* Report of the International Conference on Population and Development, U.N. Doc. A/ CONF. 171/13 (Annex) (18 Oct. 1994).

> The Cairo Program's sixteen chapters address an array of issues affecting population growth and its impact on the environment, including gender issues, the role of the family in society, reproductive rights, population distribution and urbanization, international migration, education, and the role of technology. Although the Program encourages international cooperation in addressing population issues, it recognizes that individual states bear both ultimate responsibility and ultimate authority for controlling population growth within their territory. It calls for states to make population issues an integral element of development policies and programs. However, the Program also emphasizes human rights, including the right to reproductive freedom. Thus, it encourages states to base population programs on meeting human needs rather than demographic targets. Because of the recognized relationship between income, education levels, and fertility rates, the Program places particular emphasis on the need to empower women and eliminate all forms of gender bias and the need to secure equal and adequate educational opportunities for citizens of both sexes.

> Despite high hopes preceding the Conference, the Program of Action ran aground over the issues of birth control and abortion. The Vatican played a critical role in defeating consensus adoption of the Programme. Heading a coalition that included Latin American countries such as Argentina, Guatemala, and Ecuador, and Muslim countries such as Jordan, Egypt, and Iran, the Vatican opposed references in the Program to birth control and abortion. Among the complaints pressed by this coalition were charges that the Program of Action provided for abortion to be available on demand, that it promoted sexual immoralities, weakened the family, and advocated homosexual relationships.

Gregory M. Saylin, *The United Nations International Conference on Population and Development: Religion, Tradition, and Law in Latin America*, 28 Vand. J. Transnat'l L. 1245, 1255–56 (1995).

In the end, the Vatican and its supporters adopted the Program of Action in a "partial manner." The Vatican stated that it could not endorse the concept of "legal abortion" or the plans for reproductive rights and family planning, but it did approve nine of the Program's sixteen chapters, joining the Conference in its views on gender equality, migration, and the role of the family as the "basic unit of society.'' Report of the International Conference on Population and Development, at U.N. Doc. A/Conf/171/13 at 150 (1994).

4.   Because of the Vatican's strong policies on birth control, the Catholic Church is sometimes blamed for the high levels of population growth in heavily Catholic countries; however, the relationship between religion, culture, and population growth is more complex than this. The rate of population growth in a country bears a stronger relationship to a country's level of socio-economic development than to its dominant religion. Italy and Spain, both heavily Catholic countries, have among the lowest fertility rates in the world, 1.2 children per woman. Both are industrialized countries. Developing countries generally have experienced high birth rates, regardless of their dominant religion. Even this relationship, however, does not always hold. Brazil, which is both developing and predominantly Catholic, has a fertility rate only slightly above replacement. Nonetheless, the policies adopted by the Catholic Church, as with those of other religions, influence the opinions and conduct of hundreds of millions of people around the globe.

5.   One of the key messages to emerge out of the Cairo Conference was that the most effective ways to slow population growth are also important goals in their own rights—fighting poverty, improving nutrition, improving health care, increasing access to education, creating economic opportunity, and upholding human rights. In Chapter 1, we saw how the complex connections between social and natural systems create tremendous uncertainties and risks for policy makers; yet these connections also create opportunities. Resources dedicated to addressing one set of social problems may generate benefits relating to other social problems.

6.   Access to contraception is crucial to efforts to control population growth. Contraception provides couples, and particularly women, increased control over reproductive decisions. Allowing people the freedom to choose when and how often they will bear children is a necessary first step to bring population growth within sustainable limits. Many countries have legalized the sale of contraceptive devices, abortions, and family planning services. In the United States, as recently as 1971, the mailing or importation of contraceptive information was banned. Today, however, the law imposes few constraints on the sale or distribution of contraceptives. Issues of government approval and manufacturers' concerns over tort liability for injuries caused by contraceptive devices have limited the number of devices available on the market, particularly when compared to European countries. Nonetheless, Americans today have the legal right to contraceptive information and methods.

7.   An argument often heard in the United States is that the government does not, and should not, get involved with population policy. Upon reflection, though, it is obvious that the government is *already* intimately involved in population policy. In addition to issues raised in the previous note, consider the following discussion:

> Governments also regulate the number of spouses people may have (at least at one time), minimum age at marriage, and the availability of birth control methods, all of which have fairly direct effects on fertility. Laws against sexual assault, statutory rape (sex with minors), incest, extramarital sexual behavior, and even certain techniques of lovemaking are common regulations of reproductive behavior that may have some effect on birth rates, in part depending on enforcement. People who argue against national population policies because it would bring government into the bedroom conveniently ignore that it has always been there.

PAUL EHRLICH ET AL., THE STORK AND THE PLOW 107–108 (1995)

One could also mention laws concerning abortion, tax credits for children, welfare payments for families with dependent children, etc. There are credible independent arguments in favor of every one of these laws, but they clearly form a national population policy, whether they are described as such or not. *See* Mona Hyman, *The Population Crisis: Stork, the Plow, and the IRS*, 77 N.C.L. REV. 15 (1998).

----

3.   NEXT STEPS FOR POPULATION

Efforts to reduce population growth must be broad-based. No theory, including the demographic transition theory, fully explains why fertility decreases in some societies but not others. Some factors are clear, however. The dominant factor can be described as gender equity. Numerous studies have shown that women's education is closely correlated with fertility. For example, women with seven years of education have been shown to average three fewer children than women with no education. This is likely due to delayed marriage and childbirth until school is completed, greater knowledge of family planning, increased status, and the potential for employment that provides greater control of resources.

Yet currently women in developing countries attend school only half as long as men. Indeed the World Bank estimates that if the educational status of men and women had been equal 30 years ago, then fertility levels today would be close to stable. Other important equity factors include the status of women in society—whether they are able to exercise basic choices and personal mobility, and whether they are able to participate freely in society outside the home. Gender inequality is often reinforced through the legal system. In some countries, the husband legally controls marital property, and women are prohibited from owning property or exercising control over financial resources. Countries with more gender equity, where the status of women is higher than in comparably poor countries—Cuba, Sri Lanka, the state of Kerala in India—show reduced fertility rates. *See generally* Reed Boland, *The Environment, Population and Women's Human Rights*, 27 ENVTL. LAW 1166 (1997).

Other factors that have been shown to decrease fertility rates include provisions for old-age security (so children are not necessary to ensure their parents' economic well-being), improvements in basic health and nutrition, and the availability of family planning and contraceptive devices. As Malcom Potts, Professor of Population at the University of California, notes, "education and family size are correlated in countries with poor access to family planning (like the Philippines), but where people have unconstrained access to the means to control their family (like Thailand), educational differences in contraceptive use practically disappears." *Slower Population Growth Won't Last Forever*, N.Y. TIMES, Nov. 9, 1997, at D14.

What other role can international cooperation play? None of the steps for addressing population are easy for international law to mandate, particularly with any threat of sanctions against noncompliance. This helps explain why international law in this sphere has taken the form of declarations and programs of action. Development aid, though, is critical. If nothing else, demographic research has revealed that improving aspects of life not directly connected with fertility, such as education and the status of women, often leads to decreasing fertility rates. Hence many population control advocates endorse foreign aid programs directed at education, health, and nutrition, as well as family planning.

The funding of international family planning efforts in particular has been controversial, in large part because of the abortion debate. The U.S. Agency for International Development, the primary source of U.S. bilateral assistance to developing countries, supports a controversial but successful effort at promoting family planning in developing countries. The Foreign Assistance Act of 1961 provides the authority for the president to develop international policies on population planning. Since 1973, federal law has banned the use of government funds for abortions. At a UN population conference in 1984, the Reagan Administration declared it would not fund non-governmental organizations that provided abortion counseling, referral or other abortion-related services. This was known as the "Mexico City Policy" and was continued by the Bush Administration. Early in his first term President Clinton overturned this policy and restored funding to International Planned Parenthood and the UN Fund for Population Activities. Thomas Friedman, *The Reagan–Bush Era Is Left Behind in a Flurry of Executive Policy Moves*, N.Y. TIMES, Jan. 24, 1993, at 20. And one of President George W. Bush's very first acts as president was to overturn Clinton's policy.

In thinking about which forms of foreign aid are appropriate to confront the myriad problems of poverty and population growth, consider an appeal for "Reality Theology" proposed by former Colorado Governor Richard Lamm. Using the forum of a fictional heresy trial set in the near future, Lamm is intentionally provocative, indicting the shortcomings of traditional ethical values in the face of overpopulation and environmental degradation. As you read, consider whether Lamm is offering serious policy proposals, or using troubling proposals to suggest the moral and ethical dilemmas we will eventually face if we don't adopt a pro-active, rather than a reactive approach, to human population growth.

Richard D. Lamm, *Essay: The Heresy Trial of the Reverend Richard Lamm*, 15 ENVTL. L. 755 (1995)

Ladies and Gentlemen of the court, I come before you today to defend myself against your charges of heresy. Whether I speak truth or heresy is for you to decide. I shall defend myself with vigor and with solace based on Aldous Huxley's observation: "All great truths begin as heresy." * * *

All modern day curves—population, resource consumption, inflation, weapons—lead to disaster.

You object to how I have changed the Biblical quote from "love thy neighbor" to "love thy nearest neighbor." You ask how a church with a tradition of missionaries and universal caring could love only thy nearest neighbor. You object to my concept of "Toughlove" in which we simply accept the starvation in much of the Third World. You ask, "How can I ignore those pitiful scenes of megafamine that we see on our television sets every day?"

It is my sad and reluctant conclusion that the economy within the United States cannot keep up with all the problems outside of the United States and that we were foolish to try. It is my conclusion that "Toughlove" means that we let God's judgment take place in much of the Third World and that by trying to relieve this suffering all we do is postpone it. * * *

Reality Theology holds that it is not enough to "mean well." We must also "do good." It is not enough to keep starving people marginally alive so they procreate but do not establish their self-sufficiency. That is the sin of softheartedness—it is counter-productive generosity that merely expands the eventual die off. Reality Theology warns the world of the "Sin of Softheartedness." * * *

Reality Theology is a revolution in human thought. I do not claim it is the best scenario; far better had we listened to Schweitzer and learned to "foresee and forestall." But, alas, we did not and now we are left with no other practical alternatives. The stork has outflown the plow. Chaos is on the march. Triage ethics always stands by, dictated by nature, to push out all other ethical standards that fail. It is Theological Darwinism: if your ethics do not jibe with reality, my ethics will. * * *

We have thoughtlessly destroyed one million species in the last ten years, the products of twenty million centuries of evolution. We ethnocentrically thought the Earth belonged to us. But, alas, ecologically we belong to the Earth. And the Earth is now claiming its due from a myopic species called Man.

As we are clearly unable to alleviate all suffering and starvation, we have a Christian responsibility to use both our hearts and our heads to maximize the good we can do. But those answers—like in triage during war—are unorthodox and would require a change in policy for most of organized religion. But we cannot escape the task.

Write me a "happy" scenario for Bangladesh. Show me a happy outcome, a nice solution to a poverty-wracked country that has ninety million people crowded into a country the size of Iowa. An average Bangladeshi woman has fourteen pregnancies to produce 6.5 children who survive. More than sixty percent of all women have seven or more children. Many women are pregnant twenty-four times or more, and it is common to see a woman of thirty with eight living children and seven grandchildren. Please, my mind just does not see it. What is the happy ending?

Give me a scenario of social justice in Mexico City in the year 2000 with thirty million people in a cramped, polluted basin; or Calcutta with twenty million; or Cairo, Tehran, or Karachi with fourteen to sixteen million. Does God give a prize to the city with the largest number of deserving poor? Can we both liberate and maximize the poor? Paint me an acceptable picture when we have Third World populations with over forty percent under sixteen years of age packed into shantytowns and barrios without adequate health or housing. There are now fifty-eight cities with over five million people, compared to twenty-nine such cities in 1984, most of them filled with poor, uneducated, unskilled people in a pressure cooker of social and economic stress.

Write me a "Christian" scenario for these realities. There is none. That is why Reality Theology adopted its "Toughlove" philosophy. That is why Triage Ethics is, in the long run, the most compassionate. * * *

We all know the marvelous story of St. Martin of Tours who gave away half of his cloak to a naked beggar he met on the road. This has become a marvelous symbol of generosity and sharing, and it is part of our heritage. But the new analogy that we must consider is whether St. Martin, instead of meeting one starving beggar, had met twenty naked and starving beggars on his path. Would he have cut his cloak into twenty inadequate pieces? How would he have chosen among the twenty deserving and starving beggars? What standards and what values would he have brought to that decision? What happens when you have the resources to save a few but are confronted by many?

A story appeared a number of years ago that is a metaphor for Reality Theology. An American nun in Bangladesh, after a couple of days in the country, found a starving baby on her doorstep. She took in the baby, fed it and clothed it. The following morning there was another starving baby on her doorstep. She gave that one shelter and clothing also. On the third day, she was confronted with yet another starving baby. Finally, her Order told her to stop taking in the starving babies. The task was too immense, the numbers too gargantuan. "Leave them on the doorstep," ordered her superior.

Nothing in our Christian tradition can give us guidelines for these types of agonizing decisions. Our moral compasses gyrate wildly, but the issue will not disappear.

The intellectual civil war that goes on within my heart and my head is trying to reconcile the immense questions that my political training sees as unavoidable. I have neither a cloistered virtue nor a cloistered ethical standard. I am trying to reconcile ancient values with a new shattering and terrifying reality with which I am faced. Did we really think that we could solve all the world's problems?

You charge me with heresy having "Triage Ethics," and "Sins of Softheartedness." But what are the moral alternatives? * * *

Let me leave you with one final thought on my stand concerning these issues. I live in a world as I find it, not in a world as I wish it to be. I urge solutions not because I want to, but because I have no other choice. A world without vision leaves only tragic choices. Truly, where there is no vision, people perish.

Whether or not ethics are relative, it is clear that solutions are time specific. The house fire that initially can be put out with a garden hose or even a pitcher of water cannot be put out by the entire fire department ten minutes later.

We waited too long. We sowed the wind and we must now reap the whirlwind. I urge policies that will maximize the good—however harsh it may sound. These are agonizing decisions. * * *

You who say my solutions are too harsh should have done something back in the 1970's and 1980's. For we should have seen the shadow of starvation and chaos on the Earth and we should have acted to save Mother Earth. Alas, we did not. Hell is truly "truth seen too late."

QUESTIONS AND DISCUSSION

1. Many may find Governor Lamm's "sermon" troubling, or even offensive, but it clearly raises difficult moral issues. Lamm has said that one of the inspirations for writing his "sermon" was George Orwell's futuristic novel, 1984. Can you see why? How would you address his parable of St. Martin of Tours, when you have the resources to save few but are confronted by many? Have we waited too long to act? Should developed countries cut off foreign aid or channel it only to specific uses? Which would these be? An issue Lamm does not directly address is the interdependence of the global environment. As the previous chapters have shown, deforestation in the tropics and fossil fuel burning in China will have direct effects on distant countries. Thus, for the sake of self-preservation the developed countries cannot simply ignore what happens in the developing world. Do these interdependencies undermine Reality Theology? *See also,* Garrett Hardin, *Living on a Lifeboat,* 24 BIOSCIENCE 561 (1974).

2. In the United States, roughly one-quarter of population growth is due to immigration. While most advocates of restricting immigration have argued on economic grounds, there may also be an important environmental argument. Consider again the IPAT formula. Given U.S. consumption patterns, the average immigrant to the United States from a developing country will cause significantly higher environmental impacts than if they stayed in their native lands. Do you see why this is so? Should immigration into the United States from developing countries be limited because the world can't afford to have more people consuming at the levels at which we, ourselves, are consuming? Do you see a problem with this argument?

Needless to say, immigration policy is an extraordinarily divisive issue, particularly in a country like America, founded by immigrants. The Sierra Club had a very heated debate among its members over whether to adopt a policy on immigration, ultimately deciding not to. Few U.S. environmental groups have taken a position on immigration. Why do you think this is the case? Is it because environmental groups fear alienating their members by adopting a controversial anti-immigration policy? Or is it because strengthening immigration fence around the United States runs counter to the environmental view that the world's ecosystems are interconnected?

3. Some scholars have proposed more radical approaches to controlling human population growth. In his 1964 book THE MEANING OF THE TWENTIETH CENTURY, Kenneth Boulding proposed developing a system of marketable birth licenses. A nation facing unsustainable population growth would first set a goal for a stable population size. It could then issue birth licenses sufficient to offset the death rate and yield zero population growth. The licenses could then be bought and sold on the open market, thereby achieving an efficient allocation of child-bearing rights. Boulding, at 135–36. What is your response to such a proposal? Is it appropriate to allocate child-bearing rights on the basis of the willingness and ability to pay for them? Given the tremendous expense involved in raising a child in many industrialized nations, is it wrong to take into account the ability of potential parents to maintain and provide for the children they have? Is there anything wrong—as a practical, legal or ethical matter—with treating children as objects of commerce?

4. In light of current trends, some analysts are concerned that by the middle of this century there may be too *few* people. As noted above, the United Nations has reported that global fertility rates are falling. Some demographers and policy makers have become concerned over the rapidly dropping fertility rates in the wealthy countries of the world. Ben Wattenberg, for example, argues that in such a world:

> There is likely to be a lot more personal sadness ahead. There will be missing children and missing grandchildren. In an article in The Public Interest titled "World Population Implosion," the demographer Nicholas Eberstadt, of Harvard and the American Enterprise Institute, looks ahead and writes that "for many people, 'family' would be understood as a unit that does not include any biological contemporaries or peers" and that we may live in "a world in which the only biological relatives for many people—perhaps most people—will be their ancestors." Lots of people without brothers or sisters, uncles, aunts or cousins, children or grandchildren—lonelier people.

Ben Wattenberg, *The Population Explosion is Over,* N.Y. TIMES MAGAZINE, Nov. 23, 1997, at 60.

Others envision serious economic dislocation as fertility declines in developed nations. As the Director of the United Nations Population Division has argued,

These developed countries have a particularly important role because they provide a great deal of the economic leadership and social leadership. They are, basically, the producer nations, the consumer nations and the donor nations. China today is exporting to whom? Basically to the United States and Europe, and that's helping the Chinese economy. Europe alone consumes a great deal and produces a great deal. If they start shrinking there will be a readjustment, and it will be global in its impact. It will affect the entire world economy.

As quoted in Barbara Crossette, *Planet has room for improvement: Population experts are concerned about low growth in some nations,* THE DES MOINES REGISTER, November 2, 1997, at 12. Do you agree with this assessment? What are its policy implications?

SECTION III.   CULTURAL VALUES AND NORMS

The global environmental threats facing the earth demand that we learn how to make international environmental law a more powerful force for achieving environmental sustainability. But law is neither the only option available to us, nor always the best one. This section and those that follow examine other ways to change society's norms and redirect human behavior towards sustainable development. We start with the most basic issue—our relation to the natural environment.

We do not interact with our environment as purely biological organisms because we are not purely biological organisms. All human activity takes place within a cultural context. Everything about us—what we eat, what we "need," how we interact with one another, and how we interact with our environment—is influenced by the culture we live in. This section explores the role and potential of our societies' value systems in environmental protection. The categories we use to explore this issue—consumer culture, environmental ethics and religion are artificial since, of course, all three are interrelated and mutually reinforcing. As you read these sections, consider the role of law in this dynamic. Law surely reflects underlying cultural values and norms, but can it shape these as well?

A.   CONSUMER CULTURE AND DEEP ECOLOGY

Anthropologists characteristically explain that what separates humans from other animals is that humans adapt to their environments through culture rather than through information encoded in their genes. It is through culture that humans adapt to the biophysical environment as it is but also change—indeed, transform—this environment, both deliberately and accidentally.

Luther Gerlach, *Ecological Anthropology,* 1.2 (1994). In other words, human interaction with the environment is always filtered through the medium of culture. It is humanity's capacity for cultural evolution that has allowed us to spread across the face of the earth and co-opt an ever greater proportion of the earth's resources for our own purposes. It is this same capacity that can be redirected to achieve sustainable development. *See generally,* PAUL EHRLICH, HUMAN NATURES (2000).

We are not bound by our genes to continue expanding our economy until we have completely consumed our own environment. As cultural beings, we possess the capacity for radical change. The challenge is to recognize that cultural mores, just like laws and regulations, can be changed. An example of a broad cultural shift is the relatively recent change in social tolerance toward drunk driving; no longer is it socially acceptable to have a "drink for the road," and the incidence of drunk driving has been greatly reduced. This shift was due to far more than just stiffer legal punishments for drunk driving. Our attitude toward smoking is another example.

As we saw in Section I, the current culture in the United States and Western Europe is a culture of consumerism—a culture of consumption—and this culture is spreading throughout the world, driven in large part by advertising and the entertainment media. It is no exaggeration to claim that increasing numbers of the globe's 6 billion inhabitants want to wear the same pair of Nikes and designer jeans, while eating Le Big Mac and drinking Coke. These are global images of a global consumer society, and they symbolize a culture that must adapt to achieve sustainable development. Figure 2–7 shows this facet of globalization, charting the global explosion of fast-food chain restaurants. Lester Brown et al., VITAL SIGNS 151 (1999)

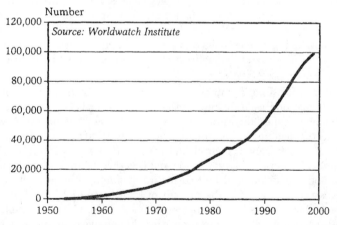

Estimated Number of Restaurants Worldwide of the Top 10 U.S. Fast-Food Chains with International Operations

Figure 2–7

Many environmental writers have offered alternative visions of a future culture more in line with the goal of sustainable development. The philosophy of "deep ecology" is among the more radical, founded on a rights-based biocentric perspective rather than anthropocentric or utilitarian worldview. Deep ecologists such as Bill Devall and George Sessions suggest in the excerpt below that we need to develop a more profound relationship with nature, a new ecological philosophy. They believe that such a relationship will provide greater human fulfillment and quality of life. They argue that deep ecology is the only effective way to reestablish our natural connections to the environment, and to protect it.

BILL DEVALL & GEORGE SESSIONS, DEEP ECOLOGY: LIVING AS IF NATURE MATTERED ix, 8, 65 (1985)

The environmental/ecology social movements of the twentieth century have been one response to the continuing crisis. These movements have addressed some of the problems and have tried to reform some of the laws and agencies which manage the land and to change some of the attitudes of the people in these societies. But more than just reform is needed. Many philosophers and theologians are calling for a new ecological philosophy for our time.

We believe, however, that we may not need something new, but need to reawaken something very old, to reawaken our understanding of Earth wisdom. In the broadest sense, we need to accept the invitation to the dance—the dance of unity of humans, plants, animals, the Earth. We need to cultivate an ecological consciousness. * * *

[Deep ecology also includes the cultivation of "ecological consciousness" or the knowledge that we are part of a greater whole.] This process involves becoming more aware of the actuality of rocks, wolves, trees, and rivers—the cultivation of the insight that everything is connected. Cultivating ecological consciousness is a process of learning to appreciate silence and solitude and rediscovering how to listen. It is learning how to be more receptive, trusting, holistic in perception, and is grounded in a vision of non-exploitative science and technology.

Deep ecology goes beyond a limited piecemeal shallow approach to environmental problems and attempts to articulate a comprehensive religious and philosophical worldview. The foundations of deep ecology are the basic intuitions and experiencing of ourselves and Nature which comprise ecological consciousness. Certain outlooks on politics and public policy flow naturally from this consciousness.

[Devall and Sessions argue that educational reform must occur if we wish to truly change our relationship to the environment.] The rise of academic and vocational overspecialization, together with the new "democratic" value relativism and the decline of the influence of the liberal arts, has thus played into the hands of certain governmental and corporate business interests. Liberal educational reformers, and even some radicals, are of the opinion that if we can disentangle governmental and corporate business influences from the schools, and if we can reestablish the pursuit of knowledge and liberal arts orientation at the center of the educational process once again, all will be well. While there is considerable merit to these proposals, this analysis only begins to scratch at the surface of our malaise. While the reestablishment of the centrality of the liberal arts may help overcome pervasive value relativism and reassert basic Western humanistic ideals, these same values are, in part, under attack from a different quarter. *That is, the humanistic anthropocentrism of the Western liberal arts orientation has been deeply implicated in the global environmental crisis.*

QUESTIONS AND DISCUSSION

1. How realistic is it to think that we can accomplish the profound cultural change necessary to solve our environmental problems? DEEP ECOLOGY was written in 1985, over a decade ago; has fundamental change really occurred? From the mainstream perspective, is Deep Ecology still viewed as a "tree-hugging," fringe movement?

Perhaps more important, how do cultural changes translate into changes in public policy? Will car drivers start riding their bicycles to work if they spend a couple of hours outside reading poetry or hiking on weekends? Even if Deep Ecology remains a very small movement, if it influences the right people it can have profound effects on policy and our environment. Although former Vice–President Al Gore, for example, bases his environmentalist views mostly on his religious tradition, he speaks frequently about "environmentalism of spirit" and the importance of "balance." *See* AL GORE, EARTH IN THE BALANCE 244 (1993).

2.   Where do we get a concern about nature—a connection with nature—if we live in a completely human-made landscape? If declines in frogs mean children no longer catch tadpoles, does it also mean a future decline in environmentalists? Consider writer Bill McKibben's thoughts on this subject:

> If nature were about to end, we might muster endless energy to stave it off; but if nature has already ended, what are we fighting for? Before any redwoods had been cloned or genetically improved, one could understand clearly what the fight against such tinkering was about. It was about the idea that a redwood was somehow sacred, that its fundamental identity should remain beyond our control. But once that barrier has been broken, what is the fight about, then? It's not like opposing nuclear reactors or toxic waste dumps, each one of which poses new risks to new areas. This damage is to an idea, the idea of nature, and all the ideas that descend from it. It is not cumulative. Wendell Berry once argued that without a "fascination" with the wonder of the natural world "the energy needed for its preservation will never be developed"—that "there must be a mystique of the rain if we are ever to restore the purity of the rainfall." This makes sense when the problem is transitory—sulfur from a smokestack drifting over the Adirondacks. But how can there be a mystique of the rain now that every drop—even the drops that fall as snow on the Arctic, even the drops that fall deep in the remaining forest primeval—bears the permanent stamp of man? Having lost its separateness, it loses its special power. Instead of being a category like God—something beyond our control—it is now a category like the defense budget or the minimum wage, a problem we must work out. This in itself changes its meaning completely, and changes our reaction to it.

> A few weeks ago, on the hill behind my house, I almost kicked the biggest rabbit I had ever seen. She had nearly finished turning white for the winter, and we stood there watching each other for a pleasant while, two creatures linked by curiosity. What will it mean to come across a rabbit in the woods once genetically engineered "rabbits" are widespread. Why would we have any more reverence or affection for such a rabbit than we would for a Coke bottle?

BILL MCKIBBEN, THE END OF NATURE 210–11 (1989).

Al Gore puts it another way.

> The more we rely on technology to mediate our relationship to nature, the more we encounter the same trade-off: we have more power to process what we need from nature more conveniently for more people, but the sense of awe and reverence that used to be present in our relationship to nature is often left behind. This is a primary reason that so many people now view the natural world merely as a collection of resources; indeed, to some people nature is like a giant data bank that they can manipulate at will. But the cost of such perceptions is high, and much of our success in rescuing the global ecological system will depend upon whether we can find a new reverence for the environment as a whole—not just its parts.

AL GORE, EARTH IN THE BALANCE 203–04 (1993).

To see how connected to the environment the next generation is, ask your daughter, son, cousin or other child the question, "where does milk come from?" Most children will, without hesitation, reply, "the supermarket." Linda C. Puig, *The udder side of education*, THE SAN DIEGO UNION-TRIB., Oct. 18, 1985, at B1.

3. Some other changes toward a green culture are already underway, including the "Voluntary Simplicity" movement in the United States, and the "Natural Step" in Sweden. Voluntary Simplicity started in 1981 with the publication of Duane Elgin's book by the same name. Recognizing that our efforts to make money and the material rewards we then buy are not necessarily making us happy, the Voluntary Simplicity movement advocates a return to a simpler and less stressful life, with more time spent with family, friends, and community. *See* <http://simpleliving.com/>. Note the difference between this voluntary movement and the involuntary simplicity being practiced by many in the developing world. See also the Center For A New American Dream, <www.NEWDREAM.ORG>.

4. Culture not only is an independent force for changing our behavior, it also has a profound influence on our laws, both domestic and international. Indeed, in a Separate Opinion in the Gabcikovo case decided by the International Court of Justice in 1997, Vice-President Weeramantry looked to the cultural practices of ancient civilizations to deduce legal principles of sustainable development, in particular reviewing the rich history of sustainable water development projects in Sri Lanka, formerly Ceylon, and many other cultures. Judge Weeramantry explained that:

> In drawing into international law the benefits of the insights available from other cultures, and in looking to the past for inspiration, international environmental law would not be departing from the traditional methods of international law, but would, in fact, be following in the path charted out by Grotius. * * *

> Because the Court is charged with "representation of the main forms of civilization and of the principal legal systems of the world," I see the Court as being charged with a duty to draw upon the wisdom of the world's several civilizations, where such a course can enrich its insights into the matter before it. In the context of environmental wisdom generally, there is much to be derived from ancient civilizations and traditional legal systems in Asia, the Middle East, Africa, Europe, the Americas, the Pacific, and Australia—in fact, the whole world. This is a rich source which modern environmental law has left largely untapped.

The case is discussed further in Chapter 6, page 338, on lawmaking.

5. In addition to hunting wild animals for food, and destroying critical habitat, humans use animals in a tremendous array of ways—as sources of food, clothing, and raw materials for furniture, jewelry, and other goods; as personal pets; as entertainment in zoos and circuses; and as human substitutes for medical experimentation, and products testing. For many of those who do recognize non-humans as moral subjects, these uses can be deeply troubling. One common response, of course, is vegetarianism. As Robert Goodland notes:

> The encouraging congruence of environmental impact with degree of sentience argues for promoting herbivory and demoting carnivory for those wanting to lessen both environmental and ethical damage.... The "higher" the animal is in evolutionary terms, the more people are reluctant to eat it. Few educated people would eat a primate for example; many more will eat an oyster.

Robert Goodland, *Environmental Sustainability: Eat Better and Kill Less* 9 (World Bank Environmental Department, May 8, 1996).

Some groups, such as People for the Ethical Treatment of Animals (PETA), go further, viewing many human uses of animals, particularly those associated with the manufacture of luxury goods like fur and jewelry, and the testing of commercial products, as acts of torture inflicted upon other sentient beings. To combat such acts, PETA and similar groups have employed not only consumer boycotts and political pressure, but also more drastic action, such as laboratory break-ins and destruction of stores and warehouses where furs are kept. Is such a position a necessary consequence of viewing animals as moral subjects? Does this view demand a moral absolutism? If you agree that we have duties to species or to ecosystems, how would you work to change the culture? How would you translate those duties into law? Would you allow trees to have standing to sue? Would you grant gorillas and other primates protection of international human rights law?

Another dilemma is highlighted in a recent report from the International Union for the Conservation of Nature, where their network of 10,000 scientists reports on "the intensifying clash between the hungry people and rare species." Of the world's 17,000 large nature preserves, nearly half are used by poor people for farming. According to the report's author, Jeff McNeely, an anthropologist, "Of the 900 million desperately poor earning less than $1 a day, 630 million live in rural areas with the most biodiversity. The very areas we're trying to conserve are where the poorest of the poor live." The report, done with another NGO, Future Harvest, recommends new farming methods that are more compatible with species conservation. "Hungry People vs. Rare Wildlife: A Call for New Farming Methods", New York Times, May 9, 2001.

6.   Our cultural attitudes toward animals and other non-human aspects of the environment also influence how we think about sustainable development more broadly. Throughout the history of the environmental movement, many philosophers have argued that the environment deserves our respect and protection for its own sake, independent of any benefit humans derive from it. In other words, other living things—and even the systems those living things are a part of—possess *intrinsic value*, which humans have a duty to respect. While this view has not received widespread acceptance in the law, it reflects views held by many aboriginal groups and by certain religions, and offers another potential foundation for the cultural re-organization essential to achieve a truly sustainable society. *See, e.g.,* Christopher Stone, *Should Trees Have Standing: Toward Legal Rights for Natural Objects*, 48 S. Cal. L. Rev. 371 (1974). The following section explores these important issues in more detail.

B.   ENVIRONMENTAL ETHICS

Ethical principles are important for two reasons. Together with principles of ecology, they can help build a better foundation for global environmental law to ensure the long-term survival of humanity. They also can, without any assistance from law, independently guide our behavior toward the common good, including sustainable development. The readings that follow consider what moral obligations we have to each other, to future generations, and to other living organisms. Theologian John Cobb notes that there are two elements fundamental to any ethical theory—first, judgment as to what is good or desirable, and second, principles of right action. As you read each excerpt, consider whether these two elements are explicit or implicit in the theory presented.

Ethical legitimacy plays a particularly important role in organizing action at the international level. As Professor Chris Stone explains in THE GNAT IS OLDER THAN MAN 242 (1993):

> [L]aw, where it is to be effective, has always to draw on morals ... [T]his ... is especially crucial in the area of international cooperation. In part, the special burden that morality must carry in the international field owes much to the absence of a strong central world government with powers, ultimately, of coercion. Treaties can and do raise the specter of sanctions. But in the near foreseeable future we cannot expect even the most muscular treaty-made law to be backed by the familiar threats that domestic law deploys against polluters, such as criminal fines, punitive damages, much less imprisonment of serious wrongdoers. In fact, as we saw, it is likely that the more effective and threatening the drafters of a proposed convention make its legal sanctions, the dimmer will be its prospects of widespread ratification.
>
> All this makes cooperation in the international arena all the more dependent on a feeling of rightness than on force. No world body has power to force a nation to protect its forests and wetlands.

To secure cooperation, the world often is left with only the threat of informal sanctions—of shining "the spotlight of shame" on the non-cooperator to show that he or she is a bad world citizen. In the next reading, Professor Stone elaborates on the importance of ethics for law generally, and for international law in particular.

CHRISTOPHER STONE, EARTH AND OTHER ETHICS 15–16, 26–27 (1987).

My concern is not with moral and legal philosophy for their own sake. Rather, the animating concern is worldly: What sort of planet will this be? ... [The different futures we might imagine creating] diverge in the number and variety of human, animal, and plant populations that will inhabit the earth. They diverge in the rate at which natural resources are depleted. In some there is more consumption in the near term, and more famine in the far. In some versions the oceans are dead; in others, the atmosphere is gone. There are differences in the world's wealth, both in the aggregate and in its distribution among peoples. There are differences, too, in the sorts of social institutions with which populations are governed: various shades of totalitarianism and democracy.

What futures we can realistically aim for—the range of potential hereafters—can be considered a question of *technology*, within the constraints, principally, of resources.

Which of these accessible futures we ought to select, why one ... might be considered morally preferable to any other: that is a question of *ethics*.

How we arrange our affairs so that the future we choose is the future that becomes the reality: that is the question of social institutions, of *law*. * * *

They are large questions, but they are real, and really upon us. Consider a basic: water. This nation's agriculture (and, indirectly, a portion of the world's food supply) depends upon vast underground water aquifers.... Yet, we are drawing them down, and poisoning them, at such a rate that by one estimate only 5 percent of the water that was available in 1800 will be available to the much larger population in 2100. This presents an inescapable moral dilemma. Ought we to restrict our own water usage, conserving it for the unborn? Ought we to invest capital into some mammoth public works project to desalinate seawater, even if the undertaking would infringe our own comforts ...? * * *

A sense of *limits* has always provided the drive for law and ethics. As Hume observed, if goods were in unlimited supply, questions of distributional justice, of allocating goods rightly, would not arise. The customs, etiquette, and property laws that grow up around a water hole in the desert reflect more elaborate consideration than those that develop in regions where water is plentiful. Today, however, it is not just a water hole, but the whole earth, that one fears is running dry of basic resources....

These [environmental] threats have intensified and extended the interest in distributional justice: what are the ethics of dividing a stable or even shrinking pie with others whose lives are spatially and temporally remote?

The questions of fairness and distributive justice raised by Professor Stone, and indeed by the ecosystem limits that characterize our global environmental problems, are the central challenge to modern moral philosophers. A reasoning process that may help us respond to this challenge is the "thought experiment" of philosopher John Rawls. In his landmark book *A Theory of Justice*, Rawls offers an approach to developing—or discovering—universal principles of law that addresses the critique that the principles each person might discover are necessarily influenced by that person's characteristics, such as her socio-economic status, politics, and religion. Rawls suggests that we might get around the problem of cultural, political, and economic differences—and free ourselves to choose rationally—by stepping behind a hypothetical "veil of ignorance." He argues that, in the absence of any knowledge of their own position in life, all rational actors would choose principles that ensured the fair and equitable allocation of rights, duties and opportunities among everyone in the society. In the following excerpt, Rawls explains the "veil of ignorance" and its implications for finding universal principles to govern society.

John Rawls, A THEORY OF JUSTICE 11–13 (1999)

In justice as fairness the original position of equality corresponds to the state of nature in the traditional theory of the social contract. This original position is not, of course, thought of as an actual historical state of affairs, much less as a primitive condition of culture. It is understood as a purely hypothetical situation characterized so as to lead to a certain conception of justice. Among the essential features of this situation is that no one knows his place in society, his class position or social status, nor does any one know his fortune in the distribution of natural assets and abilities, his intelligence, strength, and the like. I shall even assume that the parties do not know their conceptions of the good or their special psychological propensities. The principles of justice are chosen behind a veil of ignorance. This ensures that no one is advantaged or disadvantaged in the choice of principles by the outcome of natural chance or the contingency of social circumstances. Since all are similarly situated and no one is able to design principles to favor his particular condition, the principles of justice are the result of a fair agreement or bargain. For given the circumstances of the original position, the symmetry of everyone's relations to each other, this initial situation is fair between individuals as moral persons, that is, as rational beings with their own ends and capable, I shall assume, of a sense of justice. The original position is, one might say, the appropriate initial status quo, and thus the fundamental agreements reached in it are fair. This explains the propriety of the name "justice as fairness": it conveys the idea that the principles of justice are agreed to in an initial situation that is fair. The name does not mean that the concepts of justice and fairness are the same, any more than the phrase "poetry as metaphor" means that the concepts of poetry and metaphor are the same.

Justice as fairness begins, as I have said, with one of the most general of all choices which persons might make together, namely, with the choice of the first principles of a conception of justice which is to regulate all subsequent criticism and reform of institutions. Then, having chosen a conception of justice, we can suppose they are to choose a constitution and a legislature to enact laws, and so on, all in accordance with the principles of justice initially agreed upon. Our social situation is just if it is such that by this sequence of hypothetical agreements we would have contracted into the general system of rules which defines it. Moreover, assuming that the original position does determine a set of principles (that is, that a particular conception of justice would be chosen), it will then be true that whenever social institutions satisfy these principles those engaged in them can say to one another that they are cooperating on terms to which they would agree if they were free and equal persons whose relations with respect to one another were fair. They could all view their arrangements as meeting the stipulations which they would acknowledge in an initial situation that embodies widely accepted and reasonable constraints on the choice of principles. The general recognition of this fact would provide the basis for a public acceptance of the corresponding principles of justice. No society can, of course, be a scheme of cooperation which men enter voluntarily in a literal sense; each person finds himself placed at birth in some particular position in some particular society, and the nature of this position materially affects his life prospects. Yet a society satisfying the principles of justice as fairness comes as close as a society can to being a voluntary scheme, for it meets the principles which free and equal persons would assent to under circumstances that are fair. In this sense its members are autonomous and the obligations they recognize self-imposed.

One feature of justice as fairness is to think of the parties in the initial situation as rational and mutually disinterested. This does not mean that the parties are egoists, that is, individuals with only certain kinds of interests, say in wealth, prestige, and domination. But they are conceived as not taking an interest in one another's interests.

They are to presume that even their spiritual aims may be opposed, in the way that the aims of those of different religions may be opposed. Moreover, the concept of rationality must be interpreted as far as possible in the narrow sense, standard in economic theory, of taking the most effective means to given ends. I shall modify this concept to some extent, as explained later, but one must try to avoid introducing into it any controversial ethical elements. The initial situation must be characterized by stipulations that are widely accepted.

In working out the conception of justice as fairness, one main task clearly is to determine which principles of justice would be chosen in the original position. To do this, we must describe this situation in some detail and formulate with care the problem of choice which it presents. These matters I shall take up in the immediately succeeding chapters. It may be observed, however, that once the principles of justice are thought of as arising from an original agreement in a situation of equality, it is an open question whether the principle of utility would be acknowledged. Offhand it hardly seems likely that persons who view themselves as equals, entitled to press their claims upon one another, would agree to a principle which may require lesser life prospects for some simply for the sake of a greater sum of advantages enjoyed by others. Since each desires to protect his interests, his capacity to advance his conception of the good, no one has a reason to acquiesce in an enduring loss for himself in order to bring about a greater net balance of satisfaction. In the absence of strong and lasting benevolent impulses, a rational man would not accept a basic structure merely because it maximized the algebraic sum of advantages irrespective of its permanent effects on his own basic rights and interests. Thus it seems that the principle of utility is incompatible with the conception of social cooperation among equals for mutual advantage. It appears to be inconsistent with the idea of reciprocity implicit in the notion of a well-ordered society. Or at any rate, I shall argue.

I shall maintain instead that the persons in the initial situation would choose two rather different principles: the first requires equality in the assignment of basic rights and duties, while the second holds that social and economic inequalities, for example inequalities of wealth and authority, are just only if they result in compensating benefits for everyone, and in particular for the least advantaged members of society.

QUESTIONS AND DISCUSSION

1. Rawls's hypothetical thought experiment is performed under ideal conditions that do not exist in reality. Multiculturalists suggest that such an attempt to find universal principles can suppress differences and, as a result, cultural identities. Under this view, the "veil of ignorance" could then be just a way to impose one culture and one value system over others. Do you agree?

2. If we believe in human rights as inalienable rights inherent in human nature, is Rawls's thought experiment a way to identify them? Can we say the same thing for the right to an environment that protects life-supporting ecosystems? See Chapter 16, Human Rights and the Environment.

3. What do you think of Rawls's statement that "the concept of rationality must be interpreted as far as possible in the narrow sense, standard in economic theory, of taking the most effective means to given ends"?

In "The Singer Solution to World Poverty," the Australian philosopher Peter Singer uses his own thought experiment to argue that we have an ethical obligation to transfer our excess income to the poor who otherwise would likely die from easily preventable diseases, including those caused by pollution. He begins with the Brazilian film "Central Station," where Dora, a poor, retired school teacher is paid $1,000 to lead a nine year old boy to a rendezvous with allegedly wealthy people who want to adopt him. Dora buys a TV with some of the money and while watching it that night, is told by her neighbor that no wealthy couple would want to adopt a nine-year old street child and that she just led the boy to his death, as part of a scheme to harvest his organs for transplant. Her conscience gets the better of her, and the movie turns into her odyssey to rescue the young street boy. Singer states that we all know the woman has done something morally wrong, by, in essence, selling the boy to murderers for money.

Singer points out, though, that the average American spends about one-third of his or her income on goods and services that are no more critical to their health than Dora's new TV was to hers. Instead of eating at fancy restaurants or buying new clothes that are in style, by donating the money to charity we could make the difference between life and death for those who benefit from the charity's generosity. If this is the case, how can one draw an ethical distinction between Dora's sale of a homeless child for its organs and an American (or Briton, or German, or Japanese, etc.) who already enjoys material comfort yet spends money on further comforts, despite the knowledge that the money could be spent in ways that would save the lives of children in need? For a utilitarian philosopher like Singer, there is little difference at all, and certainly no justification for the hasty denunciation of Dora, on the one hand, and our glorification of the materialist culture, on the other.

Philosopher Peter Unger has posed similar moral conundrums. In one of his examples, Bill is approaching retirement and has invested most of his wealth in a unique and very expensive car that he cannot insure. While he loves owning the car, Bill also knows it is an asset and, once sold, will provide a comfortable retirement income. Out for a drive one day, Bill parks near a railroad track and goes for a walk. Looking up, he sees a runaway train that is heading directly toward a small child on the tracks that will surely be killed. While he cannot stop the train or get to the child in time, Bill can throw a switch and divert the train toward his car. If he does so, the child will live but his car will be destroyed and, with it, not only his joy in owning the car but his pension and financial security, as well. Bill does not divert the train and the child dies.

Bill's conduct surely strikes us as morally reprehensible but consider, as well, that perhaps we all make similar decisions every day. Most of us could donate far more money to groups like Unicef which, as a result, would likely save the lives of several (if not many) children. Unger tells us that a $200 donation, for example, would help ensure that an ill 2–year-old reaches a healthy age, beyond the dangerous early childhood years. Indeed, to make the example more practical, Unger provides the toll-free number for donating funds–(800) 367–5437–for Unicef. Both Singer and Unger's examples force us to consider whether our actions, in not contributing far more money to charity, are morally different than Dora's or Bill's. *See* Peter Singer, *The Singer Solution to World Poverty,* N.Y. TIMES MAG., September 5, 1999.

————

QUESTIONS AND DISCUSSION

1. Can you think of any differences between Bill's situation and the situation of students (and professors) with $200 they could spare, that would warrant a different moral conclusion about their behavior? One difference Singer notes is that only Bill can save the child on the tracks, while many millions of people can spare $200. But most of them are not doing it. Does this excuse you from not donating $200? Singer says no, this would be endorsing a follow-the-crowd ethic—the kind that led many Germans (and others) to look away when the Nazis were committing atrocities.

2. As noted in Chapter 1, millions of children die every year from disease that could be prevented with access to clean air and water. With these and the millions of other children at risk around the world, there will always be one more child to save with one more $200 contribution? Are we ethically obligated to give until we have nothing left? How much would we have to donate to equal Bill's sacrifice? Singer thinks $200,000 for most middle class Americans. Those who give 10% are far ahead of most in the United States. "Nevertheless, they should be doing much more, and they are in no position" to criticize Bill "for failing to make the much greater sacrifice" of his car. According to Singer:

> At this point various objections may crop up. Someone may say: "If every citizen living in the affluent nations contributed his or her share I wouldn't have to make such a drastic sacrifice, because long before such levels were reached, the resources would have been there to save the lives of all those children. . . . So why should I give more than my fair share?" Another, related, objection is that the Government ought to increase its overseas aid allocations, since that would spread the burden more equitably across all taxpayers.

> Yet the question of how much we ought to give is a matter to be decided in the real world—and that, sadly, is a world in which we know that most people do not, and in the immediate future will not, give substantial amounts to overseas aid agencies. We know, too, that the United States Government is not going to meet even the very modest United Nations-recommended target of 0.7 percent of gross national product; at the moment it lags far below that, at 0.09 percent, not even half of Japan's 0.22 percent or a tenth of Denmark's 0.97 percent. Thus, we know that the money we can give beyond the theoretical "fair share" is still going to save lives that would otherwise be lost. While the idea that no one need do more than his or her fair share is a powerful one, should it prevail if we know that others are not doing their fair share and that children will die preventable deaths unless we do more than our fair share? That would be taking fairness too far.

> Thus, this ground for limiting how much we ought to give also fails. In the world as it now is, I see no escape from the conclusion that each one of us with wealth surplus to his or her essential needs should be giving most of it to help people suffering from poverty so dire as to be life-threatening.

Singer calculates that an American household making $50,000 a year spends $30,000 on necessities, so ought to donate the other $20,000 to save the threatened children. A household making $100,000 a year ought to give away $70,000, and so on.

3. Even if we don't agree to give away our surplus income to Oxfam or Unicef, does Singer's analysis suggest that we have an independent duty to reduce our consumption? Or at least a duty to analyze our consumption and to begin to reduce the impacts it has on the environment, for example, by shifting from our 15 mpg SUV to a new hybrid vehicle getting 70 mpg? Would reducing our consumption save any lives? Is saving lives the only moral justification you can think of for reducing the impacts of our consumption? Would spending our surplus income to influence the political system to embrace sustainable development pass Singer's test of ethical correctness?

4. The notion of rights differs within the environmental and animal rights communities. How do you think the two communities would respond to the following assertions?

- An individual organism (such as a spotted owl) in nature has intrinsic value and rights independent of its usefulness to humans

- A species (such as spotted owls) has intrinsic value and rights independent of its usefulness to humans

- An ecosystem (such as an old-growth forest community) has intrinsic value and rights independent of its usefulness to humans

---

C.   ORGANIZED RELIGION

In January 1991, thirty-two eminent scientists led by Dr. Carl Sagan issued an open letter to the religious community discussing the critical role religion must play in environmental protection and calling on religious leaders to join the environmental effort. Two hundred and seventy-one spiritual leaders from eighty-three countries signed their names to the appeal. They included the Dalai Lama of Tibet, the Reverend Jesse Jackson, Mohammed Mehdi, Secretary General of the National Council on Islamic Affairs, and an array of other patriarchs, rabbis, tribal chiefs, cardinals, mullahs, archbishops, Zen abbots, and professors of theology.

In the wake of this letter, religious leaders have conducted several important summits on the relationship of environmental protection to religious faith. In February 1997, they released a joint statement on the role of the faithful in achieving environmental justice.

Care for God's Earth Requires Justice for the Poor
Statement by Senior Religious Leaders,
Feb. 5, 1997—Washington, DC

Americans are more clearly than ever committed to protection of the environment. For most, it is a moral issue which draws upon deep values and rises above partisan politics.

Over the past several years, major American faith groups, across a remarkably broad spectrum, have worked to establish a distinctively religious voice and comprehensive program. Scholars have prepared authoritative theological analyses. Program manuals have been sent to over 100,000 congregations. . . . Moral perspectives on public policy have been circulated through extensive legislative networks to federal, state, and local governments. * * *

We engage this challenge not so much as "environmentalists" but rather as people of faith seeking to better understand what it must mean to be religious, now and henceforth, as stewards of God's handiwork amidst a crisis in creation.

We come to the nation's capital, following the State of the Union address, to affirm that care for creation is now an irreversible priority for the American religious community. But we also wish to emphasize one perspective of fundamental importance to people of faith, and of particular urgency in this moment and political climate.

Some have called it "environmental justice". It springs from hundreds of years of teaching and struggle for social and economic freedom and opportunity, calling us now to the new challenge of distributing equitably the benefits and burdens of environmental protection. * * *

The biblical vision of the relation between human justice and ecological sustainability is vivid in present-day global conditions. God's creation is afflicted by unmoderated greed and unmet need. Over-consumption of natural resources by the wealthiest nations is the single greatest cause of global environmental degradation. Widespread poverty among developing nations, in turn, leads to the destruction of habitat and extinction of species.

Economic justice, therefore, is central to the our approach to such global environmental issues as sustainable development, climate change, biodiversity, deforestation, and pollution of land and water.

Here at home, in the very communities we serve, we see first-hand how low-income and vulnerable populations bear a disproportionate burden of environmental destruction. The health, homes, children, and communities of the poor are more likely to be poisoned environmentally. In turn, those who dwell in polluted conditions are likely, as a result, to suffer still greater economic burden.... The cycle is exacerbated by a political process which too often deprives communities of the right to know the sources and help shape the remedies of their afflictions—particularly when set against powerful, well-financed special interests.

When solutions are devised, they often come last and least to the poor—those whom we believe have a preferential claim on compassionate initiative.

As we speak, people in our congregations are in the midst of the immediate struggles for environmental justice. Harlem's Church of the Intercession, where John Audubon lies to rest, works to reduce bus emissions causing high rates of pediatric asthma. Minneapolis' Jewish Community Action is engaged in efforts to reclaim polluted urban land for job creation. West Dallas' New Waverly Baptist Church seeks adequate health services and financial settlements for congregants suffering from illness and disability caused by a nearby lead smelting plant. Parishioners in the diocese of Houma–Thibodaux, Louisiana have initiated an effort to prevent coastal erosion because loss of wetlands means loss of jobs and a way of life. The Interfaith Network for Earth Concerns in Portland, Oregon is helping provide citizen input to protect low-income neighborhoods from the effects of urban sprawl.

Air pollution, which contributes to thousands of deaths from lung disease, has greatest impact in congested, low-income urban areas. Three out of every five African-and Hispanic–Americans live in communities with dangerous abandoned toxic waste sites. One hundred thousand workers die annually from exposure to poisonous chemicals. Poor children suffer serious neurological damage and death from lead poisoning at twice the rate of others. These circumstances spring from degradations of God's creation, falling hardest upon the poorest of God's children, and this is not justice.

Since "God will champion the cause of the poor, the rights of the needy," (Ps 140:13) opportunities to do God's will lie before us here. We must protect our children's health. Stop toxic poisoning of poor communities. Save lives by cleaning our air and water. Renew urban environments. Assure communities the right to know the hazards which threaten their families, jobs, and neighborhoods. And guarantee racial justice within all such initiatives. * * *

Because the cause of environmental justice embraces the whole of God's creation, it would seem the perfect arena for all to work together for the common good. But only on a level playing field, where disproportionate power does not lie with special interests.

For our part, we are extending past efforts further forward through a three-year, $4 million campaign to allow individual partner groups to shape distinctive responses to ongoing issues of environmental sustainability and economic justice. This effort will help us enhance existing programs by integrating environmental initiatives directly into them.

The ultimate goal of this work, finally, is the renewal of religious imagination and devotion. So, when traditional liturgies resonate afresh with praise of divine handicraft ... when a theologian writes of a sacramental universe, and a parish priest reads that work and is stirred to his best sermon of the year ... when endangered species and habitats are included in the prayers of the people ... when clergy bring youth gangs to community gardens to broker peace agreements ... when a child suddenly remembers a religious school lesson during a walk in the woods: all these are occasions when care for creation brings life to faith, and draws all of us closer to God.

The careful preservation of our environment is a concern for every human being. For people of religious faith it is also a matter of reverence for the Creator. The pollution of the land, the air and the waters is a blasphemous insult to the one who gave us what was intended to be a bountiful and beautiful garden to provide generously for the human family.

Protecting the environment is not only a work which must be assumed by governments, industries and other coalitions, it is essentially a work which must be undertaken by individuals. And through our congregations, individuals and families can be challenged and empowered to lead the way by their own ecologically-sound lifestyles and their courageous advocacy. The redemption of the world and its people may be one of the highest priorities for the church in this age, and no church can be faithful in its mission if it does not intentionally seek to fulfill it.

––––––––

As the excerpt above indicates, organized religion is taking an increasingly active and important role in the pursuit of sustainable development. Groups such as the National Religious Partnership for the Environment—a federation comprised of the United States Catholic Conference, the Coalition on the Environment and Jewish Life, the National Council of Churches of Christ and the Evangelical Environmental Network—have adopted the position that environmental protection is now an essential part of the religious mission. "We act in faith to cherish and protect God's creation. Our goal is to integrate commitment to global sustainability and environmental justice permanently into all aspects of religious life." National Religious Partnership for the Environment. <www.NRPE.org/resources.html>. To commemorate the millennium, Pope John Paul II called for forgiveness of debts to developing countries. The Pope wrote,

> ... in the spirit of the Book of Leviticus (25:8–12), Christians will have to raise their voice on behalf of all the poor of the world, proposing the Jubilee as an appropriate time to give thought, among other things, to reducing substantially, if not canceling outright, the international debt which seriously threatens the future of many nations." called for debt forgiveness to developing countries.

Apostolic Letter, "As the Third Millennium Draws Near", Para 51, Nov. 14, 1994.

––––––––

QUESTIONS AND DISCUSSION

1. Does the Statement of Senior Religious Leaders' focusing on environmental justice and the poor bear direct application to international environmental politics? Does the more affluent North have a moral responsibility to assist the poorer South in achieving sustainable development? To reduce its own consumption in order to allow the South to consume a more equitable share of the Earth's natural resources? Does this moral basis underlie the concept of common but differentiated responsibilities as found in principle 7 of the Rio Declaration?

2. How does the discussion of religion and the environment contrast with the discussion of "deep ecology"? How does the position of humans differ in each?

3. Religion is also finding its way into the market, in the form of investment funds. There are now nearly 30 mutual funds with religious affiliations, with the oldest dating back to 1970. The funds screen investments to make sure they are not inconsistent with the religious beliefs of the investors. The return on investment has been respectable, but behind the overall market. Do you think these funds can be a positive force for environmental protection and sustainable development? There are other socially responsible investment funds that apply a "green" screen to their investments.

4. Jeremy Benstein argues below that understanding and sharing each other's various religious and cultural traditions can help us overcome conflict in the environmental arena. He also highlights aspects of the Jewish tradition's approach to environmental stewardship.

> First, political discourse too often ignores, or tries to sidestep, differences in worldviews and cultural values, in particular affairs of the spirit, in favor of technical details of policy-making. This is especially true regarding environmental issues. Yet it cannot be emphasized too strongly that the environmental crisis will not be solved with a technological quick-fix—that it is fundamentally a crisis of values, of how we see the world and our place in it. And these are precisely the questions that religion and culture have been asking since the dawn of human history.

> Not only have modernity, science and technology not obviated the need for clarifying these fundamental issues, they have made it an urgent necessity. Since religion and culture are the stuff of difference between us, conventional wisdom would have us avoid, or bracket, these explosive areas if we are to achieve peaceful coexistence. However, exactly the opposite is true: real coexistence can only come from confronting our differences openly, honestly, and generously. Moreover, it is my belief that not only do we have much to learn from one another, from our differences, but also that we will discover that we have much of importance in common, around which we can unite.

> For instance, in the context of the age-old religious history of the Middle East, Judaism, Christianity and Islam stand out against the pagan cultural background as the monotheistic traditions that have formed a foundational element in the development of the Western world. As religious traditions, we share the belief in a Supreme Creator, with us as creatures of God's Creation. Nature, therefore, is neither eternal (uncreated) nor divine in itself.

> This point alone has made Western monotheism the focus of severe criticism from environmental quarters. Space will not suffice for a thorough response to this charge, or a comprehensive survey of all the positive environmental insights of the biblical tradition, from Pentateuchal limitations on human exploitation of land, and animals, to Psalmic hymns, to the natural glories of Creation. In the Genesis stories alone, so maligned for the notorious verse (1:28) which allegedly mandates dominion over, and subjugation of the natural

world, we have on of the profoundest contributions of religion to Western environmental thought: the idea of stewardship. We are but caretakers—"serving" and "preserving" in the language of Genesis ch. 2—of a world that is emphatically not ours. Yes, human beings are unique, but it is precisely this unique status of the human—the nexus of the divine and the earthly—with our attendant rights and responsibilities, that allows us to address the environmental crisis at all, and reflect on our duties to the rest of Creation: how we can best wield the immense power that our unique creative faculties have endowed us with.

I would argue that Judaism, Christianity and Islam share this spiritual language that articulates appreciation of God's earth and the fullness thereof, aw and wonder at the daily miracles of the Creation, and fosters a sense of human responsibility for its continued well-being. Each tradition adds to that insight, or refracts it through its own prism of religious expression and cultural heritage. For instance, on the conceptual level, Jewish sources include a striking comment on the creation story of Genesis ch. 1, asking why humans, the crown of creation, were created last of all the created beings. The answer given is that if we become too arrogant as a species, we will remember that the lowly gnat preceded us in the order of Creation. Of God himself it is told, in another *midrash* (rabbinical literary homily or comment on the text): "When God created the first humans, God led them around the Garden of Eden and said: 'Look at my works! See how beautiful they are—how excellent! For your sake I created them all. See to it that you do not spoil and destroy My world; for if you do, there will be no one else to repair it after you.' "

Jeremy Benstein, *On Judaism, Zionism and the Environment*, Palestine–Israel Journal, Vol. V., No. 1, p. 69–70. *See also* Christopher Stone, *The Gnat is Older Than Man* (1993).

5. Arguments for environmental protection based on religious belief are a powerful mechanism for moving large sectors of the public to action. Many writers in the U.S. and Europe base their conceptions of faith on a Judeo-Christian tradition. Would their arguments convince members of African tribal religions, Buddhists, Muslims, or Hindus? How do you explain the spiritual importance of maintaining our environment to an atheist?

6. In his Separate Opinion in the Gabcikovo case decided by the International Court of Justice in 1997, Vice–President Weeramantry reviewed sustainable water development projects from ancient civilizations to give meaning to sustainable development. He notes that his "survey would not be complete without a reference also to the principles of Islamic law that inasmuch as all land belongs to God, and is never the subject of human ownership, but is only held in trust, with all the connotations that follow of due care, wise management, and custody for future generations. The first principle of modern environmental law—the principle of trusteeship of earth resources—is thus categorically formulated in this system." Judge Weeramantry then describes the early conservation laws of India, and traces the respect for nature in that country to the conversion of the king to Buddhism. The sermon that inspired the king's conversion explained:

O great King, the birds of the air and the beasts have as equal a right to live and move about in any part of the land as thou. The land belongs to the people and all living beings; thou art only the guardian of it.

According to the judge,

This sermon, which indeed contained the first principle of modern environmental law—the principle of trusteeship of earth resources—caused the king to start sanctuaries for wild animals—a concept which continued to be respected

for over twenty centuries. The traditional legal system's protection of fauna and flora, based on this Buddhist teaching, extended well into the 18th century.
* * *

The notion of not causing harm to others and hence *sic utere tuo ut alienum non laedas* was a central notion of Buddhism. It translated well into environmental attitudes. *"Alienum"* in this context would be extended by Buddhism to future generations as well, and to other component elements of the natural order beyond man himself, for the Buddhist concept of duty had an enormously long reach.

Why does Judge Weermantry use religion in an international legal opinion? If, as he contends, the concept of trusteeship is found in the world's major religious traditions, how would that strengthen his argument that there is a legal obligation of trusteeship?

7. The natural law tradition has, almost since the beginning of civilization, been closely intertwined with religious belief. Natural lawyers believe that principles can be discovered through reason which are both universal and provide us with the criteria to assess the validity of laws. These principles, according to natural lawyers such as Thomas Aquinas, exist whether or not we decide to have them embodied in written statutes or caselaw. The relationship of natural law to religion, and some of the difficulties associated with this are discussed in further depth in Chapter 6 (p. 325). There the question is asked whether natural law can assist us with developing international environmental law and policy in a more powerful and imaginative way.

8. According to Robert Fogel, recipient of the 1993 Nobel Prize in Economics:

It is not possible to deal with the future of egalitarianism in America without considering the role of religious movements, particularly those arising from evangelical Protestant churches or others that practice enthusiastic religion. We know from experience that black churches have played a key role in the continuing struggle for civil rights and that they received substantial support from many of the mainline white churches. The leadership role that churches played in the civil rights struggle was not an isolated incident. American churches and the lay movements they generated were in the forefront of earlier social reforms, such as the right of trade unions to strike, the use of state and federal fiscal policy to redistribute income from the rich to the poor, the right of women to vote, Prohibition, and the provision of universal primary education. The greatest of all the reform movement in American history, the abolition of slavery, was for decades almost exclusively a religious movement until a number of religiously inspired Northern politicians developed brilliant tactics and strategies necessary to create a winning antislavery coalition. * * *

Not only have American evangelical churches been independent of the state and represented the majority of Protestant churchgoers, but they have often served as critics of state policy and as advocates of individual rights. They played a leading role in ending aristocratic privilege in the United States and were principle vehicles through which the common people have been drawn into the process of shaping American society * * *

Political realignments are set in motion by the lag between new technologies and the human capacity to cope with the ethical and practical complexities that those new technologies entail. The response to profoundly disturbing problems ranging from the urban crisis and the domination of small business by large-scale industry to the numerous adjustments entailed by the Information Revolution has been both religious and political. The religious response has been more rapid because of the high degree of independence of specific evangelical congregations from hierarchical control and from the restraints imposed on political parties, which mist often trim their policies to maintain coalitions.

ROBERT WILLIAM FOGEL, THE FOURTH GREAT AWAKENING AND THE FUTURE OF EGALITARIANISM at 7–9 (2000).

Fogel argues that four "Great Awakenings" have occurred during American history. Each awakening has three sub-periods that can be seen as a bell curve: a phase of "religious revival," a phase of "rising political effect," and a phase of "challenge to the dominant political program." The First Great Awakening came in the 1730s and resulted in the American Revolution. The Second Great Awakening began around 1800 and led to the rise of the abolitionist and temperance movements, along with a push towards women's rights and produced a crusade against slavery that culminated in the Civil War. The Third Great Awakening began in 1890 and led to attacks on big business, the rise of the welfare state, and policies to promote diversity, but ended in the 1970s with attacks on liberal reform, the defeat of the Equal Rights Amendment, and the rise of the Religious Right. The Fourth Great Awakening began in the 1960s and led to attacks on materialist corruption and a rise in pro-life, pro-family, and media reform movements. The third phase of the Fourth Great Awakening has yet to occur.

9. What is the relationship between religion and the environment? The Judeo-Christian doctrine, for example, has long been accused of being a main root of today's ecological problems (Lynn White, Jr., *The Historical Roots of Our Ecologic Crisis* (1967)) starting with the declaration in Genesis of mankind's dominance over animals and the irreconcilable dualism of humanity and nature.

Do religious institutions have an obligation, or even a role, in addressing ecological problems? Do you agree with the statement by Steven Rockefeller below?

> The environmental crisis cannot be addressed without coming to terms with the spiritual dimension of the problem, and the spiritual problems of humanity cannot be worked out apart from a transformation of humanity's relation with nature.

Do you feel that your place of worship guides your community in its response to the environment? Would it have had more of a role during your parents' or grandparents' time?

SECTION IV.   EDUCATION

The importance of education to instilling cultural values and shaping views on our relation to the natural environment cannot be overestimated. Agenda 21 devotes an entire chapter to the issue of education and describes well its significance.

Agenda 21, Chapter 36
Education (1992)

36.3 Education, including formal education, public awareness and training should be recognized as a process by which human beings and societies can reach their fullest potential. Education is critical for promoting sustainable development and improving the capacity of the people to address environment and development issues. While basic education provides the underpinning for any environmental and development education, the latter needs to be incorporated as an essential part of learning. Both formal and non-formal education are indispensable to changing people's attitudes so that they have the capacity to assess and address their sustainable development concerns. It is also critical for achieving environmental and ethical awareness, values and attitudes, skills and behaviour consistent with sustainable development and for effective public participation in decision-making. To be effective, environment and development education should deal with the dynamics of both the physical/biological and socio-economic environment and human (which may include spiritual) development, should be integrated in all disciplines, and should employ formal and non-formal methods and effective means of communication. * * *

36.5. Recognizing that countries and regional and international organizations will develop their own priorities and schedules for implementation in accordance with their needs, policies and programmes, the following activities are proposed: * * *

(b) Governments should strive to update or prepare strategies aimed at integrating environment and development as a cross-cutting issue into education at all levels within the next three years. This should be done in cooperation with all sectors of society. The strategies should set out policies and activities, and identify needs, cost, means and schedules for their implementation, evaluation and review. A thorough review of curricula should be undertaken to ensure a multidisciplinary approach, with environment and development issues and their socio-cultural and demographic aspects and linkages. Due respect should be given to community-defined needs and diverse knowledge systems, including science, cultural and social sensitivities;

(c) Countries are encouraged to set up national advisory environmental education coordinating bodies or round tables representative of various environmental, developmental, educational, gender and other interests, including non-governmental organizations, to encourage partnerships, help mobilize resources, and provide a source of information and focal point for international ties. These bodies would help mobilize and facilitate different population groups and communities to assess their own needs and to develop the necessary skills to create and implement their own environment and development initiatives; * * *

(e) Relevant authorities should ensure that every school is assisted in designing environmental activity work plans, with the participation of students and staff. Schools should involve school children in local and regional studies on environmental health, including safe drinking water, sanitation and food and ecosystems and in relevant activities, linking these studies with services and research in national parks, wildlife reserves, ecological heritage sites etc.; * * *

Nongovernmental organizations also conduct major educational efforts. One example is the Earth Force Local Program, which addresses young people in grades five through nine both in schools and community-based organizations. The students identify a local environmental problem and come up with concrete steps leading to improvements. In doing so, they may identify and evaluate the condition of natural resources and habitats, review local demographics, and identify the composition and interests of the business, government and private actors involved in various issues. Based on their assessment, the students suggest measures they might take to influence either public policy or private practice to achieve a better environmental outcome. For example, students might host a town meeting about the problem, work to publicize existing conditions to prompt action, or propose a change to an existing policy or to local ordinances. Finally, they take civic action to implement their strategy and then evaluate the results of their efforts. The entire experience is designed not only to have a direct environmental benefit, but also to help students develop a heightened sense of personal responsibility for long-term care of the environment and continued involvement in their community.

Who controls the content of the education curriculum is a sensitive political issue. While NGOs have often been the first to prepare educational materials, corporate interests also have responded. Cutbacks in education funding are leading schools to rely more and more on free teaching materials supplied by corporations, many with poor environmental records. *Consumers or Citizens*, a report from the Center for Commercial–Free Public Education, notes that U.S. kids—exposed to an average of 40,000 TV commercials a year at home—now face commercials in the classroom. According to the Center, Shell Oil Co. provides a free video for schools called *Fueling America's Future* that teaches: "It takes gasoline to power the vehicles that take us to nature. And gasoline comes from nature!" American Nuclear Society's coloring book, *Let's Color and Do Activities with the Atoms Family*, instructs young students that, while "scientists" have known for years how to deal with nuclear "leftovers," Congress stubbornly refused to authorize a nuclear dump until 1982. The teaching aid recommends using "high radioactivity to 'sterilize' sewage sludge—turning waste into a benefit from our silent servant, the atom."

As might be expected in such a contentious area, however, others argue that environmental education at school has been taken over by environmental groups. The Nevada Policy Research Institute, for example, charges that

> Dr. Michael Sanera, a senior fellow at the Center for the New West, has done extensive studies on the content and quality of environmental education in the United States. His conclusion is that science textbooks "intentionally oversimplify and overemphasize information to get readers to take action on pro-environmental causes." ... Sanera has documented hundreds of instances of misinformation promoted as fact by the green alliance and adopted in textbooks. The powerful green coalition begins promoting its agenda by indoctrinating teachers in the colleges of education. Sanera says, "the materials in teacher textbooks mislead prospective teachers by mixing science with advocacy." * * *
>
> Nevada's children are learning environmental science presented by an education establishment trained by the green alliance. Using resources developed by the environmental movement, the science presented as fact is often myth or half-truths. Recently, parents in Elko and Spring Creek were outraged by Ranger Rick, a publication for schoolchildren distributed by the National Wildlife Federation. Found in most elementary school libraries, the publication presented the following as facts:
>
> - If people bought less gold and silver, there would be less need for mines, and that would be better for the environment.
>
> - Because of gold mining, thousands of miles of rivers and streams in the western United States have been killed.

Any data to support these statements is missing. In actuality the current mining industry has worked diligently to clean up after itself. But according to Dr. Sanera and others, this isn't about cleaning up the environment—it's about controlling huge tracts of land and water in order to keep the green alliance happy.

Web of Deception: Environmental Miseducation, Oct. 1, 1998, <http://www.npri.org/issues/issues98/i_b100198.htm>.

An interesting NGO education initiative aimed at corporations started in Sweden and increasingly adopted throughout the world is The Natural Step. The Natural Step was founded in 1989 by oncologist Karl–Heinrik Robért to educate the public about the urgent need to shift to a sustainable society. While working at one of Sweden's leading cancer research institutes, Dr. Robért became convinced that development of an effective response to environmental problems was being obstructed by disagreements on details, and that society was being prevented from addressing the issue of the human-environment relationship as a whole.

Dr. Robért's response was to ask 50 fellow scientists to help him outline the fundamental principles that should define a sustainable society. After going through 21 working drafts, the group identified the following fundamental conditions necessary for a sustainable society. Using these principles, set out below, Natural Step staff work with client companies to apply the principles to their business practices.

- **Substances from the Earth's crust cannot systematically increase in the biosphere**. (This means that fossil fuels, metals, and other minerals can not be extracted at a faster rate than their re-deposit back into the Earth's crust.)

- **Substances produced by society cannot systematically increase in the biosphere**. (This means that substances must not be produced at a faster rate than they can be broken down in nature. This requires a greatly decreased production of naturally occurring substances that are systematically accumulating beyond natural levels, and a phase-out of persistent human-made substances not found in nature.)

- **The physical basis for the productivity and diversity of nature must not be systematically deteriorated.** (This means that we cannot harvest or manipulate ecosystems in such a way as to diminish their productivity capacity, or threaten the natural diversity of life forms (biodiversity). This requires that we critically examine how we harvest renewable resources, and adjust our consumption and land-use practices to fall well within the regenerative capacities of our ecosystems.)

- **In order to meet the previous three system conditions, there must be a fair and efficient use of resources to meet human needs.** (This means that basic human needs must be met with the most resource-efficient methods possible, including just resource distribution.)

QUESTIONS AND DISCUSSION

1. How well do you think our educational institutions instill cultural values, such as tolerance and honesty? How well do you think they will teach "environmental literacy"? What is the role of law in this setting? Should we use the law to insist that environmental literacy be a mandatory subject in all public high schools? All schools from kindergarten through high school? What about older adults who are out of school?

Consider the approach of H.R. 2914, legislation introduced in 1997 by U.S. Representative Jim Saxton to establish a National Institute for the Environment, with the mission to improve the scientific basis for decision-making, to promote public environmental literacy, and education and training for scientists and other professionals. The "Sound Science for the Environment" Act (introduced Nov. 7, 1997, it was referred to the House Committee on Science, and subsequently, to the Subcommittees on Basic Research and on Energy and the Environment. It was not reintroduced in subsequent Congresses).

Sec. 2 Findings: The Congress finds the following:

(1) A healthy environment is essential to an enhanced quality of life, a competitive economy, and national security.

(2) The United States lacks an effective mechanism for providing and communicating a comprehensive, objective and credible scientific understanding of environmental issues in a timely manner to policy-makers and the public. * * *

(5) These scientific activities are best carried out through a neutral institution without regulatory responsibilities, where the public and private organizations and individuals can establish a shared understanding of the state of scientific knowledge on environmental issues, and support research, education, and information exchange to expand and spread the state of knowledge. * * *

Sec. 5. Duties and Functions; Sets the Duties of the Institute to:

(1) Initiate, facilitate, and where appropriate perform assessments of the current state of knowledge of environmental issues and their implications; * * *

(5) Establish a National Library for the Environment as a universally accessible, easy to use, electronic, state-of-the-art information system for scientists, decision-makers, and the public;

(6) Sponsor education and training of environmental scientists and professionals and improve public environmental literacy. * * *

Since most education decisions are made at the state and local level, do you think such a national institute would be useful? Should this legislation be reintroduced?

2. Although ideally each Earth Force project will result in a direct environmental benefit, the more important impact lies in the project's influence on the students themselves and on the communities where they live. What might the long-term impact of such programs be? Will the students' experience with Earth Force lead to a greater awareness of environmental issues throughout their lives? Will they be more willing to take action on those issues once they've seen that such action can have results? What if the project is not successful—could it have the opposite effect? How might these attitudes affect the larger community where the students live? The Earth Force website is <www.earthforce.org/caps/html>.

3. Given the division between corporate educational interests and the interests of environmental NGOs, should government legislate the content of the environmental curriculum?

4. The Natural Step/US is now bringing the framework to U.S. communities, educational institutions, and corporations. How successful do you think The Natural Step will be in the United States? Other countries forming Natural Step programs include the United Kingdom, New Zealand, Australia, France, Canada, and the Netherlands.

Suggested Further Reading and Web Sites

Gretchen Daily, ed., NATURE'S SERVICES (1997)

A readable and comprehensive review of the critical services ecosystems provide to humans. It provides the first rigorous effort to identify and, where possible, monetarily value ecosystem services. Clear message of why we need to be concerned over the impacts of consumption and population growth.

Gretchen Daily et al., THE STORK AND THE PLOW (1995)

Comprehensive discussion of population growth and food production issues.

Steven C. Rockefeller and John C. Elder, eds., SPIRIT AND NATURE: WHY THE ENVIRONMENT IS A RELIGIOUS ISSUE (1992)

A compilation of articles describing the role of the world's dominant religions in establishing ecological sustainability.

Ernst Von Weizsacker et al., FACTOR FOUR: DOUBLING WEALTH, HALVING RESOURCE USE (1997)

Describes some of the technological challenges in moving toward sustainable development and seeks to answer them.

Paul Hawken et al., NATURAL CAPITALISM (1999)

A provocative book by some of the leading thinkers on how business can contribute to environmental protection, reduce the impacts of consumption, and make a profit.

Alan Durning, HOW MUCH IS ENOUGH? (1992)

A well-researched and provocative analysis of the impacts and causes of consumption in the United States.

David Orr, ECOLOGICAL LITERACY: EDUCATION AND THE TRANSITION TO A POSTMODERN WORLD (1992)

This book focuses on how schools, colleges, and universities can answer the challenges presented by the recognition of the finite limits earth's resources. Chapter 7: *A Syllabus for Ecological Literacy* provides an excellent bibliography arranged by subject of the critical ecological books published over the past century.

http://www.zpg.org

Homepage for Zero Population Growth, the oldest NGO focusing on population issues.

http://www.unfpa.org

Homepage for the United Nations Population Fund; included in this page is information on the International Conference on Population and Development.

http://www.iisd.ca/linkages/cairo.html

The Cairo Conference home page containing all relevant documents and information on the UN International Conference on Population and Development.

http://www.nceet.snre.umich.edu/

Provides links to environmental education resources on the internet.

http://www.nrpe.org/

The National Religious Partnership for the Environment.

http://www.cep.unt.edu/novice.html

A short introduction to environmental ethics with lots of useful links to other sites.

CHAPTER THREE

ECONOMICS AND SUSTAINABLE DEVELOPMENT

SECTION I.   INTRODUCTION

As discussed in Chapter 1, solving global environmental problems such as climate change and ozone depletion requires that we keep economic activity within the ecological limits of the biosphere. It also requires that we alleviate poverty, as poverty itself is a cause of environmental degradation. In Chapter 2 we discussed how consumption, technology, and population interact to produce the environmental impacts that are already threatening to surpass biospheric limits. We also discussed the "technological optimists" and the "technological pessimists" and their different views of the future, which have as much to do with their beliefs about economics as they do with technology.

Chapter 3 reviews how our economic system can impede or promote environmental protection. Many of our current practices can be explained by "following the money," by understanding the particular circumstances (such as the "tragedy of the commons" and "externalities") that create incentives for environmentally harmful actions. We then consider specific instruments that can be used to correct these market failures. The last part of the chapter then introduces ecological economics, a multidisciplinary approach to economics that explicitly considers both the human and the natural economies.

The words "economics" and "ecology" are closely related, both deriving from the same Greek root. Economics is the science of managing a household, and is derived from the Greek word "oikonomos", meaning "house" (oikos) and "manager" (nomos). Ecology is the branch of science focusing on the interrelationships of organisms and their environment, and also is derived from oikos, meaning "house," and logos, meaning "the study of." But as you will see in this chapter, economics and ecology have evolved on different paths. Only recently have they begun to be put back together again.

Indeed this process can be marked with the date of June, 1992, when the leaders of more than 160 nations met in Rio de Janeiro, Brazil for the United Nations Conference on Environment and Development (UNCED or the Earth Summit). At UNCED's conclusion, the delegates adopted "sustainable development" as a political goal, accepting that "The right to development must be fulfilled so as to equitably meet developmental and environmental needs of present and future generations." This recognition of the need to address both environmental protection and poverty alleviation was a major advance, and underlines even more the importance of policies that make economic *and* environmental sense. The concept of sustainability is introduced at the end of this chapter, leading to the more detailed discussion of UNCED and sustainable development in Chapter 4.

Keep in mind the following questions as you read the chapter:

- What flaws in our current economic system are leading us down an unsustainable path? Recall the limits of the so-called "self-correcting logic" of the market in the Conventional Worlds scenario at the end of Chapter 1.

- Can the law "fix" economics to get us back on the path to environmental sustainability? To what extent does ecological economics provide the tools to do this?

- What else do we need to do in addition to "fixing" economics to achieve the goal of environmentally sustainable development? How much of the problem results from policymakers ignoring economists?

- Consider the difference between "market optimists" and "pessimists," and how they relate to the "technology optimists" and "pessimists."

SECTION II.   ECONOMICS AND ENVIRONMENTAL PROTECTION

To understand the fundamental challenges in moving toward sustainable development, it is important to recognize the inherent bias of our present economic system *against* environmental protection. Adam Smith, the father of modern economics, is credited with the theory of the "invisible hand," the notion that individuals pursuing wealth maximization will, through the mechanism of markets, maximize the common good. The key question, as John Elkington has suggested, is whether the common good created by the invisible hand of the market is undone by the environmental harm caused by its "invisible elbow."

While it is commonplace to speak of the "free market," a moment's reflection reveals that this is an empty phrase. Markets are not "free" for the simple reason that governments routinely regulate them—to prevent fraud and deception, insider trading, price fixing, coercive monopoly power, and so forth. Taxes, too, favor some activities in the market and penalize others. The question is thus not whether markets should be "free" from governmental regulation—they clearly never will be—but to what extent markets should be regulated for purposes of environmental protection. This section provides a primer on basic economic concepts, including market failures, that underlie the complex relationship between environmental degradation and market economics.

———

A.   PUBLIC GOODS AND THE TRAGEDY OF THE (MIS-MANAGED) COMMONS

> *There appears, then, to be some truth in the conservative dictum that everybody's property is nobody's property. Wealth that is free for all is valued by no one because he who is foolhardy enough to wait for its proper time of use will only find that it has been taken by another.... The fish in the sea are valueless to the fisherman, because there is no assurance that they will be there for him tomorrow if they are left behind today.*
>
> H. Scott Gordon, *The Economic Theory of Common Property Research: The Fishery* 62 J. POLITICAL ECON. 124, 124 (1954), *quoted in* ELINOR OSTROM, GOVERNING THE COMMONS 3 (1990).

On its face, one would think the market would automatically promote environmental protection. The most basic principle of economics, after all, is supply and demand. As the supply of a good becomes scarce, if it is in demand, its price will rise. Hence one would assume that as environmental goods such as clean air and clean water become scarce, their value would rise, it would become more expensive to pollute, and we would be provided with more clean air and public water. Why does this not happen?

Many environmental amenities, such as clean air and water, are "public goods" because their benefits are shared by all yet owned by no one. Because public goods are not exchanged in markets, because they are "free" in the eyes of the market, no price signals indicate scarcity and environmental degradation. No one owns clean air and therefore no one can prevent people from "using it," either to breathe or as a place to pollute. This type of market failure applies to "open access" resources, where there are no rules governing use; it is described as "the tragedy of the commons."

First popularized in a classic article of the same name by Garrett Hardin, the tragedy of the commons describes many causes of environmental degradation. 168 SCIENCE 243 (1968). Hardin asks us to imagine a common pasture shared by an entire village for grazing sheep. Everyone in the village has the right to unlimited use of the pasture. You have a flock of twenty sheep and bring them every day to graze beside all your neighbors' sheep. With each hour your flock spends in the pasture, the amount of future forage available for other flocks—and your own—is reduced. But, of course, the same rule holds with respect to your neighbors' flocks. The more the pasture is over-grazed now, the fewer sheep it will be able to support in the long term. If maximizing short term economic gain is your primary goal, are you going to let your sheep graze until they have eaten as much as they can or will you stop their feeding earlier?

The more they feed, the more they will weigh and be worth when it comes time to sell them. And if you stop your flock from feeding as much as it wants, of course, there is no guarantee your fellow shepherds will cut back on their flocks' grazing, as well. As a result, you will encourage your sheep to feed as much as possible, and your fellow shepherds will do the same. Soon, however, the grass on the village pasture will be nibbled down to the roots and not provide enough grazing for anyone's flock, including your own. While each shepherd's decision was individually rational in the short run, it was collectively foolish in the long run. It would have been far wiser for every shepherd to restrain his or her flock's grazing, but seeking to maximize short term economic gain ensured long term economic—and environmental—disaster. As Hardin wrote:

> In an approximate way, the logic of the [open-access, and rule-less] commons has been understood for a long time, perhaps since the discovery of agriculture or the invention of private property in real estate. But it is understood mostly only in special cases which are not sufficiently generalized. Even at this late date, cattlemen leasing national land on the western ranges demonstrate no more than an ambivalent understanding, in constantly pressuring federal authorities to increase the head count to the point where overgrazing produces erosion and weed-dominance. Likewise, the oceans of the world continue to suffer from the survival of the philosophy of the commons. Maritime nations still respond automatically to the shibboleth of the "freedom of the seas." Professing to believe in the "inexhaustible resources of the oceans," they bring species after species of fish and whales closer to extinction. * * *

> In a reverse way, the tragedy of the commons reappears in problems of pollution. Here it is not a question of taking something out of the commons, but of putting something in—sewage, or chemical, radioactive, and heat wastes into water; noxious and dangerous fumes into the air; and distracting and unpleasant advertising signs into the line of sight. The calculations of utility are much the same as before. The rational man finds that his share of the cost of the wastes he discharges into the commons is less than the cost of purifying his wastes before releasing them. Since this is true for everyone, we are locked into a system of "fouling our own nest," so long as we behave only as independent, rational, free-enterprisers. * * *

> The implication is that the free market will treat open-access resources or public goods as being free. If the primary objective of the market participants is individual wealth maximization, the market's failure to place limits on use of the resource will invariably result in the degradation of that resource.

There are two ways around the short-term wealth maximizing behavior that underlies the tragedy of the commons. The first is to eliminate the "commons" by assigning it to individuals as private property. The theory is that, if individuals have both the exclusive right to control and the exclusive right to benefit from a piece of property, they will manage that property so that its value is preserved over time. The second way to avoid the tragedy is to agree on a set of rules to manage the commons. Remember that in the sheep hypothetical, our shepherds had unrestricted access to the pastures. If the community as a whole—or government—imposes rules that limit use of the pasture, and enforces those limits, the quality of the pasture can be maintained indefinitely. Both of these approaches—privatization and regulation—have advantages and disadvantages. The challenge is determining which is appropriate under a particular set of circumstances.

B. EXTERNALITIES

How is it that someone polluting the air or water, as Hardin describes, is able to avoid paying the cost of the pollution caused? The answer is described in an economic concept known as "externalities." Assume you own a factory. You have to pay basic costs to operate (such as labor, materials, utilities, and so on), but absent government regulation you do not have to pay for the air and water resources that act as a sink for receiving your pollution (because air and water are public goods). As a result, in seeking to maximize short term economic gain, you will "overuse" the air and water and continue polluting. Make no mistake, your factory is causing real costs in the form of acid rain, smog, reduced air visibility, water that is undrinkable to humans and unlivable to wildlife, but all these costs are *external* to the costs you currently pay to operate. These costs are borne by the public in the form of damage to forests and streams, increased respiratory ailments, and reduced pleasure in clear vistas and safe beaches.

If, on the other hand, your factory has to pay for the external harm it causes, then it will reduce its pollution. The process for forcing the factory to recognize environmental and social costs is known as *internalizing externalities* and reflects a basic lesson of economics: when we have to pay more for something, we use less of it than if it is free. By internalizing externalities, we provide more accurate price signals to buyers. Thus, if environmental externalities were internalized, the more environmentally harmful products and processes would be relatively more costly. David Pearce explains externalities in the language of economists in the excerpt below.

David Pearce et al., Blueprint for a
Green Economy 154–57 (1989)

The most desirable feature of the price mechanism is that it signals to consumers what the cost of producing a particular product is, and to producers what consumers' relative valuations are. In a nutshell, this is the elegance and virtue of free markets which economists have (generally) found so attractive since the time of Adam Smith.* * *

[M]any environmental products, services and resources do not get represented in the price mechanism. This effectively amounts to them being treated as "free goods", i.e. they have zero prices. It follows that an *unfettered* price mechanism will use too much of the zero-priced good. Resources and environments will become degraded on this basis alone, i.e. because the price mechanism has wrongly recorded environmental goods as having zero prices when, in fact, they serve economic functions which should attract positive prices.

But economic goods and services themselves "use up" some of the environment. Trace gases "use" the atmosphere and troposphere as a waste sink; municipalities use rivers and coastal waters as cleansing agents for sewage, and so on. The cost of producing any good or service therefore tends to be a mixture of priced "inputs" (labour, capital, technology) and unpriced inputs (environmental services). The market price for goods and services does not therefore reflect the true value of the totality of the resources being used to produce them. Unfettered markets fail to allocate resources efficiently. Or, in the economists' language, there is a divergence between private and social cost. * * *

Once the divergence between private and social costs of production is accepted, it follows logically that the "proper" price for products and services is one that reflects the wider social costs of production, inclusive of any environmental services. Economists have shown that *if there is no divergence between private and social cost* then a free market works best-i.e., it achieves the most efficient allocation of resources-if prices reflect the cost of producing an extra unit of output, the so-called "marginal cost" (MC). In light of the discussion about the value of environmental services this rule needs to be modified to setting prices so that they reflect "marginal *social* cost" (MSC).

For any product that imposes pollution damage on a third party, this rule amounts to saying that the product being produced should have a price (P) in the market of :

$$P = MC + MEC = MSC$$

where MEC is the marginal pollution damage expressed in money terms, or the "marginal external cost". * * *

[A]s we have noted, there is no incentive for the market to reflect MEC in the price formula. Accordingly, actual prices will diverge from MSC by the amount MEC. Put another way, the prices of polluting products will be too low in the free market. There is a need to correct the market price by *making the polluter pay* the extra amount (MEC).

In international environmental law, the internalization of external costs is reflected in the Polluter Pays Principle, discussed in Chapter 7. *See also* Principle 16 of the *Rio Declaration, infra* page 197.

C.   Policy Options for Internalizing External Environmental Costs

Internalizing environmental externalities requires getting the price right for the environmental resource that is being over-used. Given the complexities of natural ecosystems, this is difficult if not impossible. Nevertheless, as the next section explains, there are a variety of policy tools for attempting this, including *inter alia*, regulatory controls, allocation of property rights, taxes and other economic instruments, and liability regimes. Some familiarity with these tools will help you understand the policy options available for addressing the international environmental problems discussed in Part II of the book.

———

1.   COMMAND AND CONTROL REGULATIONS

By far the most common way to internalize costs is indirectly, through "command-and-control" regulations aimed specifically at controlling pollution through emission, technology, or process standards. For example, the U.S. Clean Water Act has technology-based requirements to control discharges of water pollutants. *See, e.g.,* 33 U.S.C. 1316. In complying with the Clean Water Act requirements, companies must pay to clean their wastewater. The actual costs of the externalities are not included, but the costs of the environmental protection control measures (which serve as a surrogate for the externalities) are. Depending upon the *elasticity* of demand for the product, the added cost will be paid by the producer, the consumer, or both. Elasticity is a measure of how consumers react to a small change in the price of a product. If there are many potential substitutes for a product, then a small change in its price can lead to a large drop in consumer demand as consumers switch to substitute products. If few or no substitutes are available, and particularly if the product is considered a necessity, then consumer demand will be less elastic; it will remain relatively constant even as the price increases. If consumer demand is highly elastic, then producers will bear the additional costs of command-and-control regulations in the form of lost profits. If consumer demand is inelastic, however, the additional production costs created by the regulations can be passed on to the consumers, who will continue to buy the product even at the higher price.

Command-and-control regulations, while widespread, are criticized by economists and industry as inefficient and unwieldy in many circumstances. Most important, they are often prescriptive and provide little incentive for innovation because once the regulatory emission standard is met, the law creates no economic incentive to reduce pollution further. This supposedly encourages reliance on traditional, proven control technologies rather than pollution prevention strategies and new technologies.

———

2.   PROPERTY RIGHTS

An additional response to the tragedy of the commons is the creation or recognition of property rights in the environmental resource. These property rights can be vested in individuals or in communities (as is the case in many indigenous cultures). Once a resource is owned, the market can potentially be used to charge for access to the resource.

Theodore Panayotou, Economic Instruments for Environmental Management and Sustainable Development 17–23 (UNEP, 1994)

[The use of property rights to internalize externalities] is based on the recognition that excessive resource depletion and environmental degradation arise from misleading price signals which result from the absence (or thinness) of markets in resource and environmental assets. To the extent that the failure of markets to emerge is due to the lack of well-defined, secure, and transferable property rights over resources (as opposed to other reasons such as high transaction cost or failure to enforce contracts), establishment of secure property rights should lead to the emergence of markets and scarcity prices for the resource in question (assuming other barriers are absent). With exclusive and secure property rights, resource depletion is internal to the owners/users, while under open access it is external to the users. The consequence of this internalization is that the owner will not engage in resource extraction unless the price of the resource commodity covers not only the extraction cost but also the depletion or user cost, which is the foregone future benefit as a result of present use.

With secure property rights, the price of resource commodities such as minerals, oil, and timber would reflect the resource depletion cost and provide the right signals for efficient use and conservation in line with changing relative resource scarcities. This result is based on three assumptions: (a) that the resource markets that would emerge following the assignment of secure property rights would be competitive; (b) that there is no divergence between the private and the social rate of discount; and (c) that there are no significant externalities (such as environmental impacts) from resource extraction that have not been internalized through the established property rights. If these conditions are not met, secure property rights alone would not suffice to create the right incentives for socially optimal resource allocation: uncompetitive markets will lead to a distorted time path of resource use; higher private discount rates would lead to faster resource depletion than is socially optimal; and unaccounted, negative environmental externalities would have a similar effect....

Assignment of property rights as an instrument for the internalization of external cost has several advantages: (a) it goes to the root of the problem, the absence or malfunctioning of markets due to undefined property rights; (b) it relies on the government to do what it does best (i.e., to create the institutional infrastructure and legal framework for the efficient functioning of markets ...); (c) since the government does this only once, leaving future changes of property rights to the market, it has relatively low administrative costs and it minimizes distortionary interventions in the price system; (d) property rights can be easily attenuated (restricted in certain ways) to internalize other external costs or to pursue other social objectives, through liens, easements, and other restrictions of use and disposal; (e) unlike taxes and charges, property rights adjust automatically to changing circumstances ...; (f) regardless of how property rights are distributed, efficiency is ensured as long as the property rights have certain properties such as clarity, exclusivity, transferability and enforceability, and no other market failures are present.

The property rights approach to the internalization of external cost has a number of limitations.... One limitation is that the assignment of property rights is a politically contentious issue subject to rent seeking and corruption and can be used as an instrument to achieve political objectives (e.g., reward political supporters). A second limitation in how property rights are assigned (distributed) has momentous distributional implications: if granted free of charge, property right holders are given ownership to the entire present value of the infinite stream of rents flowing from the resource; if the rights are sold or auctioned, the issuing authority acquires the present value of rents which it can then expend or redistribute according to its own social, environmental, economic, or other objectives. The once-and-for-all distributional impact of property right assignment has a double-edged implication for social policy. On the one hand, it can be used as a means of improving wealth distribution; on the other hand, it creates strong pressures from politically powerful groups and organized interests who stake a claim to rights over natural resources in the public domain. While the assignment of secure property rights to open access resources is certain to improve efficiency, management and conservation, it may also deprive the poor of access to common resources important for survival, unless they are the recipients of the property rights.* * *

Property rights are particularly applicable to land and soils (land rights), water resources (water rights), minerals (mining rights), and other natural resources which can be parceled out and enclosed or their boundaries easily demarcated and defended, as the ability to exclude nonowners is critical to the effectiveness of property rights as an economic instrument that induces rational resource use. Property rights are less applicable to situations where the resource is mobile or fugacious, i.e., it moves across boundaries (e.g., marine fisheries).* * *

When externalities or public good aspects are pervasive as in the case of critical watersheds, forests with significant ecological functions, fisheries, wildlife, and biodiversity, the necessary restrictions and regulations of private use could be so many and their enforcement so costly that collective forms of ownership are a more efficient means of internalizing environmental costs. If externalities are local (e.g., local watershed, village forest, or local fishery), communal property rights combined with private use rights (regulated by the community) could internalize external costs with minimal management efficiency loss, especially when the community has a cohesive social organization and a tradition of collective resource management. It is important to stress here that the management responsibility for the communal resource (regulation of use, conservation, protection, and investment in productivity enforcement and sustainability) lies with the collective owner, the community, not the individual users. The community may exercise the management responsibility either directly through collective community institutions or internalize it into individual users through obligations, regulations, norms, taboos, and various social sanctions.* * *

Where externalities or public good aspects dominate (e.g., major national watersheds, offshore fisheries, biodiversity, and unique environmental assets), the most efficient means of internalization is likely to be state ownership with regulated individual use rights through concession and licensing. In this case the management responsibility lies with the state and could be exercised either directly through state agencies or indirectly through regulations and incentives. In the case of global public goods such as forests and biodiversity, where national sovereignty precludes global community property rights, internalization is effected through global conventions and international transfer mechanisms, internationally tradeable emission permits, or transferable development rights.

————

3.   TRADABLE PERMITS

A variant of creating property rights is the use of tradable emission permits (spelled "tradeable" permits by the British). Here, property rights are created in the form of marketable rights—for example, the right to emit a ton of sulfur dioxide, the right to catch a lobster, or the right to sell a pound of CFCs. Creating such a market requires the government to establish an overall level of activity and initially allocate the permits. After initial allocation, the market takes over and determines the most efficient allocation of resources (the situation where no party will be better off by trading or purchasing permits).

PANAYOTOU, *op. cit.*, at 24–27

Tradeable emission permits are a form of market creation. An aggregate level of allowable emissions is set for each airshed or watershed and allocated among polluters either according to the level of output or current level of emissions. Since the aggregate emissions quota is set at or below the current level of emissions, an artificial level of scarcity is created and permits acquire positive value (market price). Industrial producers with a deficit of permits or with expansion plans must secure emission permits by reducing emissions from existing plants. Alternatively, they may purchase permits from other polluters who are either able to reduce emissions at a lower cost than the industrial producers can or who find it more profitable to sell their permits than use them themselves. Thereby, the desired reduction of emissions (and hence the desired level of ambient environmental quality) is attained at the minimum possible cost to society and a strong incentive is provided for continued efforts to improve efficiency and to develop cleaner technologies. Even if the aggregate quota is set at the current level of emissions, the expansion of economic activity would create a scarcity of permits with all the desired incentives described above. Furthermore, government and non-government environmental organizations have always the option to purchase and retire pollution permits in order to speed up improvement in environmental quality.

Whether the emission permits are issued free of charge, sold at a fixed price or auctioned to the highest bidder makes no difference from the point of view of efficiency. As long as they are fixed in number and freely tradeable, the level of emissions reduction will be attained at the lowest possible cost to society. Distributionally, it matters a lot. Awarding pollution permits to polluters free of charge amounts to assigning property rights to them over the assimilative capacity of the environment, or at least a use right, up to the specified level described in the permit. Thus, the permit entitles the polluter to the present value of the stream of profits arising from free disposal of the allowable amount of emissions into the environment. If the permits are instead sold or auctioned, the state is the recipient of the revenue, which can then be passed on to the citizens either in the form of an increased supply of public goods or lower taxes.

Alternatively, emission permits could be allocated to the general public (say, one person one permit) with the total number of permits fixed at the socially acceptable level of emissions. Polluters would then have to buy their permits from the general public which has, under this allocation, the entitlement to the present value of benefits from the use of the assimilative capacity of the environment. In other words, the general public has the right to an unpolluted environment and should be compensated by the polluters for any reduction in environmental quality. (This, unlike the allocations discussed earlier, is consistent with the polluter pays principle.) Different combinations are also possible, e.g., 50% to polluters and 50% to the general public; or 30% to current polluters, 20% to future polluters, 20% to the public, 20% to the government (or the environmental protection agency) and 10% to environmental NGOs.

Whatever the allocation, efficiency and environmental quality is not compromised, only the distributional implications are different. Therefore, those who criticize pollution permits as a right to pollute are correct only in the case where the polluters are given the permit for free. If the polluter has paid a market price for the permit, the criticism could only be that the "price" of the permit is "too low," or the supply of permits is "too large," which is the equivalent to saying a higher level environmental quality is desired.

Establishing a system of emission permits has relatively high management costs: (a) it requires proper definition of airshed (trading permits across airsheds would create hot spots), which in turn requires knowledge of the sources and of the movement of pollutants under the local atmospheric conditions; (b) monitoring of ambient air quality in the airshed (or water quality in the watershed) and the relationship between emissions and ambient quality; (c) capacity to monitor or randomly inspect individual emission sources to ensure that the emissions limit specified in the permit is observed; and (d) a system of approving and recording credits, offsets, and trades among permit holders. Depending on the type of pollutant and the content of the permit, management requirements could be significantly reduced. For example, in the case of a global pollutant such as CO_2 there is no need to define the airshed since it makes no difference where in the world CO_2 is emitted or controlled. In the case of local pollutants, systems of self reporting, auditing, and random inspection with sanctions for violations may suffice to replace a formal system of approving and recording credits, offsets, and trades. Incentives for self-enforcement and group policing can be introduced to minimize monitoring and enforcement costs.

Tradeable emission permits are nothing but tradeable emission quotas, a concept that has wide applicability beyond air and water pollution and greenhouse gases. Consider the example of a mobile (or fugacious) resource such as an offshore fishery suffering from overfishing. Property rights cannot be assigned but a total allowable catch or aggregate catch quota can be set (at say the maximum sustainable economic yield) and allocated to existing fishermen in some equitable way (e.g., according to average historical catches). Potential entrants can be accommodated by reserving quotas for them or through the purchase of quotas from retiring fishermen. If trading is allowed, the individual tradeable quotas would gravitate towards the most efficient fishermen, ensuring that the allowable total catch is caught at the minimum possible cost. Thus overfishing is eliminated [assuming you have set the maximum total catch appropriately], the fishing resource is protected, economic efficiency is achieved (i.e., fishery rents are maximized), and fishermen who choose to leave the fishery, making all this possible, are fully compensated. New Zealand has successfully used this system to manage its marine fishery.

---

4. TAXES

As discussed in the previous reading, tradable permits are a hybrid of property rights and more traditional economic instruments. The traditional economic instruments include taxes, subsidies, and charges which can directly internalize externalities. To some extent, such instruments will always be necessary because some environmental functions cannot be privatized or allocated.

Taxes. One means of increasing environmental protection is by taxing environmentally destructive activities. Environmental taxes are a means of internalizing environmental externalities. By increasing the costs of polluting activities, environmental taxes discourage unnecessary pollution and waste.

Environmental taxes can ... be used to effect full-cost pricing (i.e. to bridge the gap between private and social costs). To do this, the tax should be set exactly equal to the marginal environmental damage corresponding to the socially optimal level of pollution. This tax, known as a Pigouvian tax, is the embodiment of full-cost pricing, adjusting the price of a good precisely by the amount of the reduction in social welfare caused by the externality associated with the good. The result is not a zero level of pollution externality but an optimal level: where the marginal benefit from the reduction of pollution equals its marginal cost; or alternatively the marginal damage (social costs) equals the marginal benefit from the production of the good....

Environmental taxes can be levied on (a) the pollutant itself (i.e., on effluents, emissions, or solid waste), or (b) on final products associated with environmental externalities. Taxes on pollutants, known also as pollution charges, are applied directly to the offending substances thereby providing the maximum incentive and flexibility for the polluter to reduce pollution; therefore pollution charges are more efficient than indirect taxes on inputs or final products. The latter does not provide an incentive to limit the pollutant itself, only to use less of the input or produce (consume) less of the final product.

Panayotou, *op. cit.*, at 31.

A number of economists in the United States and Europe have argued in favor of "green taxes" since at least the 1970s. In the monograph *Tax Waste, Not Work*, for example, M. Jeff Hammond and colleagues from the non-profit group Redefining Progress argue that the tax on individual earned income should be replaced by taxes on pollution and waste, at least in part. The group bases its argument on three propositions. First, society must take measures to protect the environment—some degree of environmental protection is essential. Second, taxes are among the most effective ways to implement environmental protection because they can transfer the cost of environmental damage directly to the person responsible for causing the damage. Third, by partially replacing current taxes with "green" taxes on pollution and waste, we could increase incentives to work, save, and invest, while at the same time creating strong disincentives against environmentally destructive behavior. In the following excerpt, Professor Paul Krugman explains the idea in greater depth.

Paul Krugman, *Introduction* to M. Jeff Hammond et al., Tax Waste, Not Work (1997), <http://www.rprogress.org/pubs/twnw/twnw_intro.html>

The proposition that it is important to protect the environment still has a few well-funded doubters. However, at this point the economic and human costs of pollution and other burdens on the environment, from the health effects of car exhausts to the collapse of overexploited fisheries, are by now too obvious for any but the most determined ideologue to ignore. And it is also obvious that our current system does not provide individuals incentive to act in an environmentally responsible manner. For example, I as an individual bear hardly any of the indirect costs that I impose on other people by driving my car or eating a fish dinner. Some form of public action to protect the environment against the consequences of the individual pursuit of self-interest is crucial.

Moreover, it has become clear in the last few years that the scope of such costs is wider than previously imagined. When environmentalism first became a powerful political force in the 1960s, most of the perceived problems were more or less local: They involved the quality of air in a given city, or the quality of water in a single river. As world population, production, and consumption grew and continue to grow, however, we see increasing evidence of human impacts on the global—as opposed to the local—environment. With the emergence of a scientific consensus on such issues as the adverse effect of manmade chemicals on the ozone layer or that of carbon dioxide and other greenhouse gases on global temperatures, we have reached a point at which decisions that made sense from an individual perspective may impose large costs not only on their neighbors but on humanity as a whole.

How can we best induce people to take the environmental consequences of their actions into account? There has long been an overwhelming consensus among economists that environmental problems should, in many if not all cases, be dealt with through a market mechanism—for example, that pollution should be limited either by taxing polluters or by auctioning off a limited quantity of pollution rights. Yet when America introduced national environmental regulation after 1970, this consensus was ignored: Environmental protection was based almost entirely on a top-down approach in which government agencies dictated specifics about production techniques, pollution control equipment, and so on, leaving little or no scope for individual initiative in meeting overall goals.

It was clear even at the time that this was a great missed opportunity—that although the environmental movement achieved significant successes, a market-based approach could have provided substantially more environmental protection at substantially less cost. With the shifting nature of our environmental problems, however, the case for a market-based approach has become much stronger. It is one thing to try to protect a river by regulating a small number of major point sources—say, by preventing chemical companies from dumping waste straight into the water or requiring municipalities to treat their sewage. It is quite another matter to try to limit the emissions of carbon dioxide, where such emissions are the result of hundreds of millions of individual decisions—whether to drive a small or a large car, to insulate a house or simply keep the heat up, to use coal or natural gas to generate electricity, and on and on. To figure out how these decisions should be modified is beyond the ability of any bureaucracy. However, a market-based incentive, such as a carbon tax, would put individual initiative to work on finding thousands of ways to reduce carbon dioxide emissions—purely as a matter of self-interest. And, in fact, the limited experience with market-based pollution controls to date suggests that, given flexibility, individual companies often find it surprisingly inexpensive to achieve pollution reductions that seemed very costly when imposed by rigid regulations.

Why has a market-based approach to the environment been rejected for so long? A generation ago, many influential people were simply hostile to markets in general; furthermore, there was a tendency on the part of some groups to regard environmental protection as a moral issue, and thus to reject any proposal that seemed to say that it was all right to pollute as long as you paid the price. Meanwhile, conservatives have tended to oppose any policy, such as pollution taxes or the auction of environmental licenses, which might yield revenue, fearing that it would simply be used to expand government. Today, however, appreciation of the virtues of the market mechanism is much more widespread, and some environmental groups have actually begun to take the lead in proposing market-based approaches. At the same time, ... fears about government expansion can be allayed by making the imposition of pollution taxes explicitly revenue neutral, by linking the new sources of revenue to reductions in other taxes.

And this linkage is a benefit in itself. Taxes drive a wedge between the interests of the individual and those of society similar to that created by environmental issues: if I choose to work or invest less because I will be allowed to keep only part of any increased earnings, I reduce the revenue of the government and thus impose either higher taxes or lower benefits on everyone else. Proposals for tax reform are based on the notion that restructuring the way taxes are collected can reduce the size of this wedge without reducing revenue. But what if extra revenue can be collected from new taxes that, rather than distorting incentives, actually serve to bring individual and social interests closer together—such as pollution taxes? This revenue will allow a reduction in existing tax rates, producing a secondary gain from a reduced wedge between earnings and take-home income. This "double dividend" may sound like magic, but it is in fact no more than basic economics.

It is probably important to make clear that while there has been extensive discussion and debate over the double dividend, the central principle is not really in dispute. There is no question that if we regard environmental protection as essential—as we surely do—the cost will be much less if we use a market mechanism to implement that protection, and the cost will be further reduced if the revenue from that market mechanism is used to reduce other, distorting, taxes. Some economists go even farther and argue that a pollution tax will produce economic gains even if the benefits from reduced pollution are ignored—that is, that the cost of environmental protection is actually negative. Others dispute this. However, you need not accept this strong form of the double dividend argument to accept that market-based, revenue-yielding environmental regulation will produce large net benefits—and that because it will cost so much less at the margin than our current system, it is in our interest not only to adopt such a system, but to use it to protect our environment much better than we do at present.* * *

---

5.   SUBSIDIES

In addition to internalizing the environmental costs that are now outside the market, getting the price right so that resources can be allocated efficiently also requires the elimination of price distortions, which typically occur in the form of government subsidies. Indeed, in terms of overall environmental impact, eliminating government subsidies is one of the most significant steps that can be taken. The following excerpt from the Business Council for Sustainable Development addresses the challenge of subsidies.

Roberto de Andraca & Ken F. McCready, INTERNALIZING ENVIRONMENTAL COSTS TO PROMOTE ECO-EFFICIENCY 42–45 (1994)

[S]ubsidies have generated heavy economic and environmental costs and created unsustainable dependencies, especially in the agriculture, transportation, and energy sectors.

In the agriculture sector in North America, Western Europe and Japan, "virtually the entire food chain attracts huge direct or indirect subsidies, as a cost to taxpayers and consumers of over $250 billion a year." Specifically, the World Resources Institute (WRI) estimates that U.S. irrigation farmers repay only 17 percent of full project costs; over $1 billion per year in water subsidies are directed to some six percent of farmers, encouraging production of commodities already in excess. Worse, this subsidy diverts scarce water in western states, leading to shortages for urban and industrial needs and creating considerable environmental damage: salinization of irrigated cropland, damage to wetlands and wildlife by contaminated irrigation drainage, and depletion of aquifers.

Agriculture is also heavily subsidized in developing countries. In Indonesia, for example, fertilizer, pesticide and irrigation subsidies have encouraged "wasteful and inefficient use" of these inputs; they act as a disincentive to conservation; and they are a burden on the government budget. Indonesia recently reformed its subsidy program, saving money and averting an infestation of pests that had developed resistance to the pesticides.

In a 1988 study of agriculture subsidies in developing countries, Robert Repetto argued that complementary policy reforms to correct such perverse incentives offer many benefits: lower fiscal burdens, reduced social inequities and improved resource conservation. Furthermore, unless these incentives are removed, the impact of remedial environmental projects will be "overwhelmed by the general pattern of unsustainable resource exploitation."

In the transportation sector, subsidies can lead to environmental problems. The WRI reports that the U.S. tax code encourages employers to offer employees free parking as a non-taxable fringe benefit. This benefit is valued at $85 billion annually and discourages the use of mass transit, car pooling and other alternatives to the private vehicle. This policy aggravates traffic congestion as well as air pollution.

The third major sector of concern is energy. Large-scale subsidization of the energy industry has created serious economic and environmental imbalances. A recent World Bank study estimated that overall global energy subsidies total $230 billion a year, mostly in the former Communist bloc, but also in China, Latin America (Brazil, Venezuela, Mexico) and Asia (India and Indonesia). If these subsidies were removed, global carbon dioxide emissions [the principal greenhouse gas] could be cut by nine percent. It would be in the interest of the OECD to help smooth the transition from energy subsidies in developing countries by assisting energy efficiency programs, allowing emission reductions at a lower cost.

The solutions in many developing countries are complex. In India, the Confederation of Indian Industries reports that farmers pay less than 10 percent of the costs of generation and delivering electricity, leading to wasteful consumption patterns. This has necessitated the construction of more fossil fuel plants while reducing income to the utilities and making investments in clean technologies more difficult. Many economists have suggested that direct payments to poor farmers would actually be a more "efficient" subsidy both in terms of overall cost and reduced environmental impact. * * *

At the same time it should be noted that some developed countries continue to subsidize certain energy sources, particularly coal: Germany, for example, provided in 1988 a combined subsidy and price support for coal of $67 per tonne of carbon emitted. [The United States also heavily subsidizes its energy industries.] Governments are just now beginning to take action on subsidies for sustainable development. Changing subsidies and inappropriate pricing policy is a difficult task, but it is an important part of making development sustainable.

———

6. LIABILITY REGIMES AND INSURANCE

The ultimate instrument to internalize externalities is legal liability, which at the international level is often referred to as State responsibility. One specific aspect, responsibility for transboundary environmental harm, is reflected in Principle 21 of the *Stockholm Declaration on the Human Environment,* and appears to be accepted as customary law. There is, however, little State practice in this area. Following the accident at the Chernobyl nuclear power plant, for example, despite demonstrable harm to downwind States, no nation brought a liability action against the Soviet Union. For further discussion of State responsibility, see Chapter 7, page 424. Insurance against liability also internalizes environmental costs.

The following reading explains that neither taxes nor any of the other economic instruments will work without the threat of legal sanction. Economic instruments only work within the framework of rules and boundaries established by law.

Liability Systems. This class of instruments aims to induce socially responsible behavior by establishing legal liability for (a) natural resource damage, (b) environmental damage, (c) property damage, (d) damage to human health or loss of life, (e) non-compliance to environmental laws and regulations, and (f) non-payment of due taxes, fees or charges. In a sense, all instruments have as an *ultimate* enforcement incentive, the threat of legal action and the use of the state's coercive powers (for example, if effluent taxes are not paid or an adequate number of emission permits to cover emissions are not purchased); administrative and ultimately legal measures are provided for to ensure compliance. The difference between liability systems from other instruments (except for enforcement incentives and non-compliance charges) is that the threat of legal action to recover damages is the economic instrument that internalizes the external cost in the first instance. Unlike taxes and charges, that are set at the level of marginal damage cost to alter the relative probability of environmentally harmful products and activities, and unlike environmental bonds and deposit refund systems that internalize *ex ante* the environmental risk, liability systems assess and recover damages *ex post*. Yet these systems do have the effect of preventive incentives as long as the expected (certainty equivalent) damage payments exceed the benefits from non-compliance. The frequency with which liability cases are brought to the courts and the magnitude of damages awarded influence *ex ante* behavior of potentially liable parties.

Liability insurance has emerged as an instrument for pooling and sharing liability risks among liable parties. The incentive effect of liability systems is not significantly dampened as long as the liability insurance premium varies with individual behavior or performance. For example, vehicle accident insurance may vary with the individual's driving habits and/or past accident record. Where potential damages are very large relative to the ability of the individual agent to pay a certain minimum level of damages, liability insurance is mandated by law.

Liability systems are not recommended for developing countries with poorly developed legal systems, or with cultures that very rarely use courts to resolve disputes or award damages (although "liability systems" are not unknown to traditional societies, where the tribal chief or the elders settle disputes and award damages).

Panayotou, *op. cit.* at 40–41.

————

7. INSTRUMENT CHOICE

Carol Rose has suggested that the choice of policy instrument should depend on the pressure on environmental resources. When there is little pressure on resources, such as clean air, the government need not step in. As pollution begins to affect the resource, a zoning approach that limits access or particular uses becomes relevant. As pressure continues and the resource begins to degrade, regulations that directly prescribe uses become necessary. And finally, if the resource falls under heavy pressure, Rose argues that creation of transferable property rights for use in environmental trading markets become necessary. Carol Rose, *Rethinking Environmental Controls: Management Strategies for Common Resources*, 1991 DUKE L.J. 1 (1991).

Similarly, Robert Costanza has argued that property rights are most relevant when pollution is well within the assimilative capacity of the environment. At the next level, when "emissions and concentrations have measurably damaged the environment and threatened the productivity of the system," Costanza argues for pollution charges linked to the degree of damage (i.e., Pigouvian taxes). The last level, what he calls "the regulatory zone," is reached when pollution threatens "to rise to the point that ecological criteria indicate irreversible, nonsustainable damage to the system." Here, direct regulation of pollution sources becomes necessary. ROBERT COSTANZA ET AL., AN INTRODUCTION TO ECOLOGICAL ECONOMICS 217–18 (1997).

————

QUESTIONS AND DISCUSSION

1. Why might a property rights approach not work in the context of climate change and ozone depletion? What policy instrument might work better? How does the analysis of property rights change when the "property" is owned in common by a community? By a state? By the entire planet?

2. Unregulated fisheries present a classic case of the tragedy of the commons. While it is in the common interest of all to conserve the fisheries, each fishing vessel's immediate interests are best served by catching as many fish as possible. The excerpts above suggest allocating property rights would provide a direct incentive for conserving the resource. This is effectively what happened under the UN Law of the Sea Convention. The Convention created "exclusive economic zones" that provided national jurisdiction over the living marine resources up to 200 nautical miles off the coast. This placed 90% of the world's fish catch within national jurisdictions. One would have expected that this would encourage strict national oversight to ensure conservation of domestic fish stocks, because countries now "owned" the fish within their exclusive economic zone. Yet exactly the opposite occurred. Nations eager to exploit their new national resources subsidized large fishing fleets that soon depleted local fisheries and moved on to foreign or high seas fisheries. Does this suggest that economists' solution to the tragedy of the commons is wrong? Or perhaps that States do not always follow the advice of economists?

How could the property rights have been allocated differently to encourage conservation?

3. Panayotou's paper makes several assumptions regarding property rights—including that competitive markets emerge after assigning the property rights, that private and social discount rates do not diverge, and that no significant externalities exist—and then explains that unless these assumptions are met, "secure property rights alone will not suffice." How do these assumptions influence your opinion about the effectiveness of using property rights to address environmental problems?

4. Panayotou's paper also notes that the property rights would be allocated by the political process, a process that can be corrupted. The paper also notes that how property rights are assigned has important distributional implications that "may deprive the poor of access to common resources important for survival, unless they are the recipients of the property rights." How realistic is it to think that the political process would give the poor property rights to common resources?

Property rights systems can have dramatically different effects on how a resource is treated depending upon how the property rights are initially assigned. In the discussion of tradable permits, Panayotou's paper proposes, as one alternative, that pollution emission permits might be distributed equally to the members of the general public, who could then keep or sell their permits at any price they believed fair. Do you think this approach would increase or decrease protection of the regulated resource?

How could a permit system be designed for a global, rather than a local or regional resource? Tradable permit systems have been proposed for greenhouse gases. From the readings above, how might these systems work? Assuming that each permit allowed emission of the equivalent of one ton of carbon dioxide, how would you go about establishing the total number of permits traded? What criteria would you use to determine initial allocation of permits?

5. Many environmental economists believe that sustainable development cannot be achieved without reform of the tax system to promote green taxes. Without changing the total of $7.5 trillion in tax revenue collected worldwide, taxes could be shifted from work to waste and other environmental problems. This would put the incentives in the right place, both for environmental protection, and for work—and may lead to increased job creation.

Many environmental economists also believe that we will not be able to achieve sustainable development without eliminating the estimated $500–$600 billion a year in environmentally harmful subsidies. *See* DAVID ROODMAN, PAYING THE PIPER: SUBSIDIES, POLITICS, AND THE ENVIRONMENT (Worldwatch Institute, 1996). In certain respects, subsidies cost us twice, first as we pay the initial tax to raise the funds needed for the subsidy, and second when we suffer the environmental damage encouraged by the subsidy. Recall the discussion of agricultural subsidies in developing countries in Andraca and McCready, excerpted above, and the complementary benefits resulting from removing subsides, including lower fiscal burdens, reduced social inequities and improved resource conservation. In view of these benefits, and in view of the fact that a number of subsidies clearly contradict the Polluter Pays Principle described *infra* in Chapter 7, page 412, why are they so difficult to remove? One theory argues that subsidies are difficult to remove because they provide a significant benefit to a small number of people while distributing the costs of providing that benefit over the population as a whole. Thus, those receiving the subsidy have a strong incentive to see it maintained, and a commonality of interest that promotes collective action. Because their numbers are relatively small, the transaction costs of pooling their resources and coordinating their activities are small compared to the benefits of cooperating. By comparison, each member of the general public shares an infinitesimal portion of the cost of the subsidy. The cost in time and resources of recouping this tiny loss far outweigh the actual return to the individual. Thus, individuals have little incentive to oppose the subsidy. As a result of general public inertia, then, the subsidy-seekers can maintain the subsidy indefinitely, to the disadvantage of society as a whole.

6. In addition to environmentally harmful subsidies, there are "green" subsidies as well. These include the Montreal Protocol Multilateral Fund, discussed in Chapter 9, page 569, which provides developing countries with the incremental cost of shifting away from production processes that use ozone-destroying chemicals. At the national level, Costa Rica provides a "transferable reforestation tax credit." Tax credits are awarded to landowners who conserve forest cover or native plant species on their property. The tax credit is transferable: small landholders who conserve forest cover can sell their tax credits to wealthy taxpayers (who need credits to offset against their high taxes).

Germany relies on a differential land use tax. Land uses are categorized from most environmentally beneficial (e.g., natural forest) to most environmentally destructive (e.g., industrial site). When the land owner changes the use of the land from a higher to a lower category, he or she must pay a charge depending on the degree of change. The greater the movement away from an environmentally beneficial use, the higher the charge. Panayotou, *op. cit.* at 35.

7. Environmentally destructive subsidies are generally provided by national governments. What role should international environmental law play in removing them? More generally, of the instruments you have just read about—property rights, market creation, taxes and liability instruments—which instruments do you think would be most suitable for national-level implementation, and which for the international level? Why?

8. Panayotou's paper on economic instruments discusses the use of liability insurance as a means of internalizing the costs of environmentally destructive behavior. The paper argues that, so long as insurance premiums vary with individual behavior, liability insurance schemes can create disincentives to environmentally irresponsible action, as well as paying for the environmental damage that may result from that behavior.

Because of the potentially huge payouts associated with many environmental problems, the insurance industry has become an important advocate of environmentally responsible behavior and, in some cases, of national and international action on environmental issues. For example, the insurance and re-insurance industries are among the more vocal business proponents of international action to control global warming. As we noted in Chapter 1, and as we will discuss at greater length in Chapter 9, one of the expected consequences of climate change is increased frequency and severity of natural disasters such as hurricanes, cyclones, droughts, floods and tornadoes. This has serious consequences for the insurance industry, which may bear the bulk of the expense for these disasters. While many insurers are reducing their exposure in coastal and island real estate, wildfire-prone regions, and floodplains, others are taking pro-active measures to prevent more drastic climate change in the future. Insurance companies are assisting government efforts in climate research and catastrophe modeling by providing support for such programs as the United States Global Climate Research Program and the Bermuda-based Risk Prediction Initiative. At the same time, the industry is lobbying governments to curb emissions of carbon dioxide and other greenhouse gases.

9. Do you think the analyses of Carol Rose and Robert Costanza are descriptive or prescriptive? Do you have confidence that we can accurately determine pressure on resources and ecological limits? Even if we can, and perhaps more important, do you think our political institutions can react intelligently to these findings?

D.   PROBLEMS OF VALUATION

As discussed, markets are efficient only when the prices for goods accurately reflect their full environmental and social cost. A key aspect in internalizing externalities, then, is valuation. If one agrees that externalities should be internalized—that polluters should pay—the obvious question is "how much"? This issue also arises in the context of cost-benefit analysis. In determining a course of action, expected gains are often compared with the expected losses to determine the action that appears to provide the maximum benefit. For ease of comparison, such cost-benefit analyses reduce all costs and benefits to a single unit—money.

——————

1.   VALUATION METHODS

Such valuation presents several challenges. Some harms may be estimated with a degree of confidence. The damage caused by acid rain to buildings may be determined by the price to repair the buildings. But what about the damage caused to a forest? Is the lost value determined by the decrease in the value of the forest's wood as timber? What about its loss for recreation? Its loss in providing important ecosystem services such as water retention in preventing floods and water purification? What about the loss of its aesthetic and recreational value? Economists use a number of methods to estimate these values, collectively known as "shadow pricing." Travel-cost methodology, for example, estimates the recreational value of a site by estimating the number of people who would visit the site and the average cost of their trip. Contingent valuation, also known as willingness-to-pay, asks people how much they would be willing to pay for a certain benefit, be it the existence of the Grand Canyon or clear skies. These estimates have obvious problems, and values may vary wildly depending upon the method employed. Under the U.S. Oil Pollution Act, Exxon was liable for the "natural resource damages" in Prince William Sound caused by the oil spill of the Exxon Valdez. How would you go about estimating the monetary value of these damages? For debates over the use of shadow pricing, and whether environmental amenities should be assigned monetary values at all, *see Note: "Ask a Silly Question ...": Contingent Valuation of Natural Resource Damages*, 105 HARV. L. REV. 1981 (1992); Brian Binger et al., *The Use of Contingent Valuation Methodology in Natural Resource Damage Assessments: Legal Fact and Economic Fiction*, 89 Nw. U.L. REV. 1029 (1995); Katherine Baker, *Consorting with Forests: Rethinking Our Relationship to Natural Resources and How We Should Value Their Loss*, 22 ECOLOGY L.Q. 677 (1995). Similar issues may arise in efforts to hold Iraq liable for environmental damage caused by their invasion of Kuwaiti oil fields and the subsequent Gulf War. *See* discussion in Problem Exercise in Chapter 17.

——————

2.   DISCOUNTING

Another aspect of valuation is discounting. What if an action taken today will have little effect in the present but will prove harmful and entail costs 50 or 100 years hence (such as emission of greenhouse gases in the last several decades)? Similarly, how does one compare the benefits of an action with clear costs today, such as not logging an old-growth forest, if the benefits will be accrued both today and into the future? These questions require assessing today the costs and benefits to future generations. Economists use discount rates to address this dilemma.

If you were offered $100 today or $110 a year from now, which would you accept? The answer would depend on what you would do with the money during the year. If you could place it in a bank account with 12% interest, presumably you would take the money now and invest it. In this manner, $100 today is the equivalent of $112 in a year. While this may seem an eminently reasonable way to take future costs and benefits into account, it poses serious problems over extended time periods. For instance, assume you want to grow a forest that will generate $1,000,000 in pleasure to recreationists in its 100th year. How much is that future $1,000,000 benefit worth today? If one uses the discount rate of 10% (which is the standard rate for these calculations used by the Office of Management and Budget), the answer is $73. Over long periods of time the choice of discount rates can significantly affect the interests of future generations. *See* FRANCES CAIRNCROSS, COSTING THE EARTH at 32 (1991).

SECTION III.   MEASURING THE ECONOMY: REDEFINING PROGRESS

What gets measured gets managed. The truth of this saying can be seen in how carefully we measure the performance of our economic systems. But our measurements do not consider the environment, and we miss a critical opportunity to manage the economy in an environmentally sustainable way. The standard macroeconomic measure of economic performance is Gross Domestic Product (GDP). It is an assumed goal of governments to raise the GDP because this leads to more jobs, prosperity, and happiness. Or does it? We need to consider what the GDP actually measures. The following excerpt was written by Redefining Progress, an NGO dedicated to stimulating public discourse on the type of future Americans desire, and how to achieve it. Its best known initiative is a proposal for an alternative to GDP known as GPI, the Genuine Progress Indicator. The web site for Redefining Progress is <http://www.rprogress.org>.

Redefining Progress, The Genuine Progress Indicator <http://www.cyberus.ca/choose.sustain/Question/GPI.html> (1997)

What is wrong with the GDP?

Since its introduction during World War II as a measure of wartime production capacity, the Gross National Product (since changed to Gross Domestic Product–GDP) has become the nation's foremost indicator of economic progress. It is now widely used by policy makers, economists, international agencies and the media as the primary scorecard of a nation's economic health and well-being.

Yet the GDP was never intended for this role. It is merely a gross tally of products and services bought and sold, with no distinctions between transactions that add to well-being, and those that diminish it. Instead of separating costs from benefits, and productive activities from destructive ones, the GDP assumes that every monetary transaction adds to well-being, by definition. It is as if a business tried to assess its financial condition by simply adding up all "business activity," thereby lumping together income and expenses, assets and liabilities.

On top of this, the GDP ignores everything that happens outside the realm of monetized exchange, regardless of its importance to well-being. The crucial economic functions performed in the household and volunteer sectors go entirely ignored. The contributions of the natural habitat in providing the resources that sustain us go unreckoned as well. As a result, the GDP not only masks the breakdown of the social structure and natural habitat; worse, it actually portrays such breakdown as economic gain.

GDP treats crime, divorce and natural disasters as economic gain. Since the GDP records every monetary transaction as positive, the costs of social decay and natural disasters are tallied as economic advance. Crime adds billions of dollars to the GDP due to the need for locks and other security measures, increased police protection, property damage, and medical costs. Divorce adds billions of dollars more through lawyer's fees, the need to establish second households and so forth. Hurricane Andrew was a disaster for Southern Florida. But the GDP recorded it as a boon to the economy of well over $15 billion.

GDP ignores the non-market economy of household and community. The crucial functions of childcare, elder care, other home-based tasks, and volunteer work in the community go completely unreckoned in the GDP because no money changes hands. As the non-market economy declines, and its functions shift to the monetized service sector, the GDP portrays this process as economic advance. The GDP also adds the cost of prisons, social work, drug abuse and psychological counseling that arise from the neglect of the non-market realm.

GDP treats the depletion of natural capital as income. The GDP violates basic accounting principles and common sense by treating the depletion of natural capital as income, rather than as the depreciation of an asset. The Bush Administration made this point in the 1992 report of the Council on Environmental Quality. "Accounting systems used to estimate GDP" the report said, "do not reflect depletion or degradation of the natural resources used to produce goods and services." As a result, the more the nation depletes its natural resources, the more the GDP goes up.

GDP increases with polluting activities and then again with clean-ups. Superfund clean-up of toxic sites is slated to cost hundreds of billions of dollars over the next thirty years, which gets added to the GDP. Since the GDP first added the economic activity that generated that waste, it creates the illusion that pollution is a double benefit for the economy. This is how the Exxon Valdez oil spill led to an increase in the GDP.

GDP takes no account of income distribution. By ignoring the distribution of income, the GDP hides the fact that a rising tide does not lift all boats. From 1973 to 1993, while GDP rose by over 50 percent, wages suffered a decline of almost 14 percent. Meanwhile, during the 1980s alone, the top 5 percent of households increased their real income by almost 20 percent. Yet the GDP presents this enormous gain at the top as a bounty to all. GDP ignores the drawbacks of living on foreign assets.

In recent years, consumers and government alike have increased their spending by borrowing from abroad. This raises the GDP temporarily, but the need to repay this debt becomes a growing burden on our national economy. To the extent that Americans borrow for consumption rather than for capital investment, they are living beyond their means and incurring a debt that eventually must be repaid. This downside of borrowing from abroad is completely ignored in the GDP. * * *

What is the Genuine Progress Indicator–GPI?

The Genuine Progress Indicator (GPI) is a new measure of the economic well-being of the nation from 1950 to present. It broadens the conventional accounting framework to include the economic contributions of the family and community realms, and of the natural habitat, along with conventionally measured economic production.

The GPI takes into account more than twenty aspects of our economic lives that the GDP ignores. It includes estimates of the economic contribution of numerous social and environmental factors which the GDP dismisses with an implicit and arbitrary value of zero. It also differentiates between economic transactions that add to well-being and those which diminish it.

The GPI then integrates these factors into a composite measure so that the benefits of economic activity can be weighed against the costs.

The GPI is intended to provide citizens and policy-makers with a more accurate barometer of the overall health of the economy, and of how our national condition is changing over time.

While per capita GDP has more than doubled from 1950 to present, the GPI shows a very different picture. It increased during the 1950s and 1960s, but has declined by roughly 45% since 1970. Further, the rate of decline in per capita GPI has increased from an average of 1% in the 1970s to 2% in the 1980s to 6% so far in the 1990s. This wide and growing divergence between the GDP and GPI is a warning that the economy is stuck on a path that imposes large—and as yet unreckoned—costs onto the present and the future.

Specifically, the GPI reveals that much of what economists now consider economic growth, as measured by GDP, is really one of three things: 1) fixing blunders and social decay from the past; 2) borrowing resources from the future; or 3) shifting functions from the community and household realm to that of the monetized economy. The GPI strongly suggests that the costs of the nation's current economic trajectory have begun to outweigh the benefits, leading to growth that is actually uneconomic.

If the mood of the public is any barometer at all, then it would seem that the GPI comes much closer than the GDP to the economy that Americans actually experience in their daily lives. It begins to explain why people feel increasingly gloomy despite official claims of economic progress and growth.

The GPI starts with the same personal consumption data the GDP is based on, but then makes some crucial distinctions. It adjusts for certain factors (such as income distribution), adds certain others (such as the value of household work and volunteer work), and subtracts yet others (such as the costs of crime and pollution). Because the GDP and the GPI are both measured in monetary terms, they can be compared on the same scale.* * * [The article then lists how the GPI treats specific categories of income, including the following.]

Resource depletion. If today's economic activity depletes the physical resource base available for tomorrow's, then it is not really creating well-being; rather, it is just borrowing it from future generations. The GDP counts such borrowing as current income. The GPI, by contrast, counts the depletion or degradation of wetlands, farmland, and non-renewable minerals (including oil) as a current cost.

Pollution. The GDP often counts pollution as a double gain; once when it's created, and then again when it is cleaned up. By contrast, the GPI subtracts the costs of air and water pollution as measured by actual damage to human health and the environment.

Long-term environmental damage. Climate change and the management of nuclear wastes are two long-term costs arising from the use of fossil fuels and atomic energy. These costs do not show up in ordinary economic accounts. The same is true of the depletion of stratospheric ozone arising from the use of chlorofluorocarbons. For this reason, the GPI treats as costs the consumption of certain forms of energy and of ozone-depleting chemicals.

QUESTIONS AND DISCUSSION

1. The GDP was developed in the early 1930s by the Commerce Department to provide a uniform set of national accounts to measure the condition of the economy. A Commerce economist, Simon Kuznets, later a Nobel Laureate, developed these measures. Ironically, Kuznets would become an influential critic of GDP. In 1962, he wrote that "distinctions must be kept in mind between quantity and quality of growth, between its costs and return, and between the short and the long run. Goals for 'more' growth should specify more growth *of what* and *for what*" (emphasis added). *See* Clifford Cobb et al., *If the GDP Is Up, Why Is America Down?*, Atlantic Monthly, Oct. 1995, at 3–11.

2. How do you think most people react to the news that GDP is up 3%? What might you tell them to place this statistic in perspective?

3. Research by Robert Repetto at the World Resources Institute notes the failure of GDP to capture depreciation of natural resources such as oil and timber; instead, the extraction of natural resources is counted as income and increases GDP. Repetto analyzed this issue in Indonesia, a "model" of rapid growth, with a 7% average increase of GDP from 1971–1984. He and his colleagues examined the depletion of oil, timber and productive land, the main sources of Indonesia's growth. Taking into account future losses of productivity (through erosion, loss of resources, and degradation of resources), the national income grew by only 4% over the same period (a measure Repetto calls "Net Domestic Product"). The conclusion? Almost half of Indonesia's future income was sacrificed to obtain its current economic growth. *See*, R. Repetto et al., Wasting Assets: Natural Resources in the National Income Accounts (World Resources Institute, 1989); F. Cairncross, Costing the Earth 36–39 (1992).

4. Initiatives to reform our national accounting system have also been advanced by national and international institutions.

In 1994, the U.S. Department of Commerce's Bureau of Economic Analysis released a limited "Green GDP" at the request of President Clinton. The new initiative created Integrated Economic and Environmental Satellite Accounts

(IEESAs), and extended the definition of capital to cover natural and environmental resources. It was designed to supplement, rather than replace, the existing system of national accounts.

The IEESAs focus on interactions between the economy and the environment that can be linked to market activities and valued in market prices. Unfortunately, the Green GDP was derailed after Congress refused to fund the program pending further study.

The United Nations Statistical Office has launched a similar initiative and released a handbook in 1993 describing a System of Environmental and Economic Accounting (SEEA). This system builds on and is designed to be used in combination with the System of National Accounts. The SEEA includes environmental functions and natural resources as assets of production similar to equipment and other physical assets. It also records the depletion of a particular resource as capital depreciation. The SEEA system is designed to give a more complete picture of assets and expenditures of a particular sector or business and can, therefore, provide a more sustainable model for decisionmaking.

Economists at the World Bank have proposed using SEEAs to develop an "Environmentally Adjusted Net Domestic Product." * * *

DANA CLARK & DAVID DOWNES, WHAT PRICE BIODIVERSITY?: ECONOMIC INCENTIVES AND BIODIVERSITY CONSERVATION IN THE UNITED STATES 8 (Center for International Environmental Law, 1995).

5. In the following excerpt, ecological economist Robert Costanza and his colleagues suggest that it would be better to directly measure how well basic human needs are being met, rather than just how much we consume:

> A completely different approach, however, would be to look directly at the actual well-being that is achieved—to separate the means (consumption) from the ends (well-being) without assuming that one is correlated with the other. * * * For example, Manfred Max–Neef has developed a matrix of human needs and has attempted to address well-being from this alternative perspective. While human needs can be classified according to many criteria, Max–Neef organized them into two categories: existential and axiological which he arranges as a matrix. He lists nine categories of axiological human needs which must be satisfied in order to achieve well-being: (1) subsistence, (2) protection, (3) affection, (4) understanding, (5) participation, (6) leisure, (7) creation, (8) identity, and (9) freedom. These are arrayed against existential needs of (1) having, as in consuming; (2) being, as in being a passive part of without necessarily having; (3) doing, as in actively participating in the work process; and (4) relating, as in interacting in social and organizational structures. The key idea here is that humans do not have primary needs for the products of the economy. The economy is only a means to an end. The end is the satisfaction of primary human needs. Food and shelter are ways of satisfying the need for subsistence. Insurance systems are ways to meet the need for protection. Religion is a way to meet the need for identity. And so on. Max–Neef summarizes as:
>
> > Having established a difference between the concepts of needs and satisfiers it is possible to state two postulates: first, fundamental human needs are finite, few and classifiable; second, fundamental human needs ... are the same in all cultures and in all historical periods. What changes, both over time and through cultures, is the way or the means by which the needs are satisfied.

This is a very different conceptual framework from conventional economics, which assumes that human desires are infinite and that, all else being equal, more is always better. According to this alternative conceptual framework, we should be measuring how well basic human needs are being satisfied if we want to assess well-being, not how much we are consuming, since the two are not necessarily correlated.

ROBERT COSTANZA ET AL., AN INTRODUCTION TO ECOLOGICAL ECONOMICS 132–38 (1997).

6. A new tool for measuring sustainability is the Environmental Sustainability Index (ESI). As you read, consider what steps could be taken to raise ESI to the importance of GDP in the eyes of policymakers. Also consider the components of the ESI and how easy or difficult it is to measure each. What are the importance of indexes such as these for measuring environmental change?

The ESI project seeks to gauge the ability of countries across the world to meet the environmental needs of their people and to achieve environmentally sustainable development. The ESI assesses environmental circumstances, results, and capacities across 22 core "indicators" based on 67 underlying variables, each supported by an independent database. The ESI, building on the widely used "pressure-state-response" environmental framework, reflects data and information on five broad components of environmental sustainability:

Environmental systems (describing the current condition of a nation's air, water, and terrestrial ecosystems);

Environmental stresses and risks (measuring the levels of pollution flows and resource exploitation);

Human vulnerability to environmental impacts (tracking human capacities to handle environmental exposures and risks);

Social and institutional capacity to respond to environmental challenges (describing a society's ability to address pollution an natural resource management challenges);

Contributions to global stewardship (reflecting both the transboundary harms a county emits and its contributions to collective efforts to address these harms).

Measuring performance and trying to provide a factual foundation for decision-making is, of course, nothing new in many segments of society. In the business world, companies have long had elaborate accounting procedures, which permit the tracking of various drivers of performance and long-term financial strength including the sales picture for each product line, cost trends, the liability of proposed capital expenditures, the success of marketing strategies, the results from advertising campaigns, and many other dimensions of corporate standing. Well-managed companies also use their data tracking systems to benchmark results and to set performance goals based on comparisons within the company (between individual business units and for the enterprise as whole over time)as well as against industry sector counterparts and the private sector in general. The ESI initiative reflects a belief that both the same capacity for data-driven analysis and comparative performance valuation can be established in three environmental domain, facilitating strategic decisionmaking and better long-term results. * * *

The value of distilling data into a single index as the ESI ranking, while controversial in some respects, has been demonstrated in many circumstances. Gross domestic product (GDP), for instance, has come to be viewed as a summary measure of economic results.... Governments around the world await the release each year of the new standings as a way of evaluating their performance.... The ESI seeks to provide a similar focal point for environmental conditions and trends—drawing top-level policymaker attention. Of course, the key to real and durable environmental progress is to get people (the public, the media, as well as business and governmental decisionmakers) to dig into the results and to try to understand the drivers of good (and bad) performance.

DANIEL C. ESTY, Toward Data–Driven Environmentalism: The Environmental Sustainability Index, 31 ELR 10603 (May 2001).

For more information on environmental indexes, *see* <http://alpha.ciesin.org/rivers/esi/> (an interactive map with global indicators based on sustainability practices, as well as links to over fifty papers on indicators of socioeconomic and environmental impacts).

SECTION IV. RECONCEIVING ECONOMICS AND ECOLOGY: ECOLOGICAL ECONOMICS

A. A TRANSDISCIPLINARY APPROACH TO SUSTAINABLE SOCIETIES

The goal of ecological economics is to re-integrate economics and ecology, and create a new "transdisciplinary" approach to making societies sustainable. It is based on re-conceiving the relationship between humans and the Earth, and determining how we can better manage our lives and our planet to ensure the long-term survival of both. Central to the goal of ecological economics is solving the problem of scale discussed in Chapter 1.

The early development of economics was interdisciplinary, with its pioneers including philosophers and scientists. Adam Smith was a moral philosopher. John Stuart Mill, who expanded the connection between individual behavior and the common good, was a social philosopher. W. Stanley Jevons, who pioneered the marginal utility theory of value, focused his early career on meteorology, logic, and statistics.

But by the end of the 19th century, science and economics were becoming more specialized, more professional, and more isolated from one another, and by the time the modern environmental movement began in the late 1960s, the separate disciplines were rarely speaking to one another.

Ecological economics was founded in the 1980s by a group of scholars from both disciplines in the United States and Sweden who realized the need to re-integrate their work to address more effectively the world's growing environmental problems. The International Society for Ecological Economics was formed in Barcelona in 1987, and the journal *Ecological Economics* was launched in 1989. The following reading introduces the concepts and fundamental principles of ecological economics. As you read, consider whether ecological economics offers a useful theoretical alternative to traditional economics.

Robert Costanza, *op. cit.*, at 78–83.

[Ecological economics ... advocates a fundamentally different, transdisciplinary vision of the scientific endeavor that emphasizes dialogue and cooperative problem solving.] The transdisciplinary view provides an overarching coherence that can tie disciplinary knowledge together and address the increasingly important problems that cannot be addressed within the disciplinary structure.

In this sense ecological economics is not an alternative to any of the existing disciplines. Rather it is a new way of looking at the problem that can add value to the existing approaches and address some of the deficiencies of the disciplinary approach. It is not a question of "conventional economics" versus "ecological economics"; it is rather conventional economics as one input (among many) to a broader transdisciplinary synthesis.

We believe that this transdisciplinary way of looking at the world is essential if we are to achieve the three interdependent goals of ecological economics discussed below: sustainable scale, fair distribution, and efficient allocation. This requires the integration of three elements: (1) a practical, shared vision of both the way the world works and of the sustainable society we wish to achieve; (2) methods of analysis and modeling that are relevant to the new questions and problems this vision embodies; and (3) new institutions and instruments that can effectively use the analyses to adequately implement the vision.

The importance of the integration of these three components cannot be overstated. Too often when discussing practical applications we focus only on the implementation element, forgetting that an adequate vision of the world and our goals is often the most practical device to achieving the vision, and that without appropriate methods of analysis even the best vision can be blinded. The importance of communication and education concerning all three elements can also not be overstated.

The basic points of consensus in the ecological economics vision are:

1. the vision of the earth as a thermodynamically closed and nonmaterially growing system, with the human economy as a subsystem of the global ecosystem. This implies that there are limits to biophysical throughput of resources from the ecosystem, through the economic subsystem, and back to the ecosystem as wastes;

2. the future vision of a sustainable planet with a high quality of life for all its citizens (both humans and other species) within the material constraints imposed by 1;

3. the recognition that in the analysis of complex systems like the earth at all space and time scales, fundamental uncertainty is large and irreducible and certain processes are irreversible, requiring a fundamentally precautionary stance; and

4. that institutions and management should be proactive rather than reactive and should result in simple, adaptive, and implementable policies based on a sophisticated understanding of the underlying systems which fully acknowledges the underlying uncertainties. This forms the basis for policy implementation which is itself sustainable.

Sustainable Scale, Fair Distribution, and Efficient Allocation. A complementary way of characterizing ecological economics is to list the basic problems and questions it addresses. We see three basic problems: allocation, distribution, and scale. Neoclassical economics deals extensively with allocation, secondarily with distribution, and not at all with scale. Ecological economics deals with all these, and accepts much of neoclassical theory regarding allocation. Our emphasis on the scale question is made necessary by its neglect in standard economics. Inclusion of scale is the biggest difference between ecological economics and neoclassical economics.

Allocation refers to the relative division of the resource flow among alternative product uses-how much goes to production of cars, to shoes, to plows, to teapots, and so on. A good allocation is one that is *efficient*, that is, that allocates resources among product end-uses in conformity with individual preferences as weighted by the ability of the individual to pay. The policy instrument that brings about an efficient allocation is relative prices determined by supply and demand in competitive markets.

Distribution refers to the relative division of the resource flow, as embodied in final goods and services, among alternative people. How much goes to you, to me, to others, to future generation. A good distribution is one that is *just* or *fair*, or at least one in which the degree of inequality is limited within some acceptable range. The policy instrument for bringing about a more just distribution is transfers, such as taxes and welfare payments.

Scale refers to the physical volume of the throughput, the flow of matter-energy from the environment as low-entropy raw materials and back to the environment as high-entropy wastes. It may be thought of as the product of population times per capita resource use. It is measured in absolute physical units, but its significance is relative to the natural capacities of the ecosystem to regenerate the inputs and absorb the waste outputs on a sustainable basis. ... For some purposes the scale of throughput might better be measured in terms of embodied energy.... [The authors explain scale further, similar to the presentation in Chapter 1.]

Priority of Problems. The problems of efficient allocation, fair distribution, and sustainable scale are highly interrelated but distinct; they are most effectively solved in a particular priority order, and they are best solved with independent policy instruments. There are an infinite number of efficient allocations, but only one for each distribution and scale. Allocative efficiency does not guarantee sustainability. It is clear that scale should not be determined by prices, but by a social decision reflecting ecological limits. Distribution should not be determined by prices, but by a social decision reflecting a just distribution of assets. Subject to these social decision, individualistic trading in the market is then able to allocate the scarce rights efficiently.

Distribution and scale involve relationships with the poor, future generations, and other species that are fundamentally social in nature rather than individual. *Homo economicus* as the self-contained atom of methodological individualism, or as the pure social being of collectivist theory, is a severe abstraction. Our concrete experience is that of "persons in community." We are individual persons, but our very individual identity is defined by the quality of our social relations. Our relations are not just external, they are also internal—that is, the nature of the related entities (ourselves in this case) changes when relations among them changes. We are related not only by a nexus of individual willingnesses-to-pay for different things, but also by relations of trusteeship for the poor, future generations, and other species. The attempt to abstract from these concrete relations of trusteeship and reduce everything to a question of individual willingness-to-pay is a distortion of our concrete experience as persons in community—an example of what A.N. Whitehead called "the fallacy of misplaced concreteness."

The prices that measure the opportunity costs of reallocation are unrelated to measures of the opportunity costs of redistribution or of a change in scale. Any trade-off among the three goals (e.g., an improvement in distribution in exchange for a worsening in scale or allocation, or more unequal distribution in exchange for sharper incentives seen as instrumental to more efficient allocation), involves an ethical judgment about the quality of our social relations rather than a willingness-to-pay calculation. The contrary view, that this choice among basic social goals and the quality of social relations that help to define us as persons should be made on the basis of individual willingness-to-pay, just as the trade-off between chewing gum and shoelaces is made, seems to be dominant in economics today, and is part of the retrograde modern reduction of all ethical choice to the level of personal tastes weighted by income. * * *

It seems clear, then, that we need to address the problems in the following order: first, establish the ecological limits of sustainable scale and establish policies that assure that the throughput of the economy stays within these limits. Second, establish a fair and just distribution of resources using systems of property rights and transfers. These property rights systems can cover the full spectrum from individual to government ownership, but intermediate systems of common ownership and systems for dividing the ownership of resources into ownership of particular services need much more attention. Third, once the scale and distribution problems are solved, market-based mechanisms can be used to allocate resources efficiently. This involves extending the existing market to internalize the many environmental goods and services that are currently outside the market. * * *

B.   ENVIRONMENTAL SUSTAINABILITY

The next reading by Goodland and Daly—two prominent ecological economists—presents "environmental sustainability" in greater detail to highlight the problem of scale. Environmental sustainability is presented as the priority goal, and is distinguished from economic sustainability, and social sustainability. Sustainable development is described as one of the means for reaching that goal. As you read the article, consider how the authors address the problems identified earlier in this chapter, including problems with the GDP, externalities, discounting, and public goods.

Robert Goodland & Herman Daly *Environmental Sustainability: Universal and Non–Negotiable,* ECOLOGICAL APPLICATIONS 6(4), at 1003–13 (1996)

The priorities of development are usually said to be the reduction of poverty, illiteracy, hunger, and disease. While these goals are fundamentally important, they are quite different from the goals of environmental sustainability, namely maintaining environmental sink and source capacities unimpaired. But "environmental sustainability" [ES] as a topic is legitimized by the [UN Secretary General] Boutros–Ghali pronouncement on economic development, and is the focus of this paper.

The tacit goal of economic development is to narrow the equity gap between the rich and the poor. Almost always this is taken to mean raising the bottom (i.e., enriching the poor), rather than lowering the top, or undertaking redistribution. Only very recently is it becoming admitted that bringing the low-income countries up to the affluence levels found in OECD (Organisation for Economic Cooperation and Development) countries, in 40 or even 100 years, is a totally unrealistic goal. We do not want to be accused of attacking a straw man—who ever claimed that global equality at current OECD levels was possible? However, most politicians and most citizens have not yet accepted the unrealistic nature of this goal. Most people would accept that it is *desirable* for low-income countries to be as rich as the North—and then leap to the false conclusion that it must therefore be *possible*! They are encouraged in this non sequitur by the realization that if greater equality cannot be attained by growth alone, then sharing and population stability will be necessary. Politicians find it easier to revert to wishful thinking than to face those two issues. Once we wake up to reality, however there is no further reason for dwelling on the impossible, and every reason to focus on what *is* possible.

One can make a persuasive case that achieving per capita income levels in low-income countries of U.S.$1500 to $2000 (rather than $21,000) is quite possible. Moreover, that level of income may provide 80% of the basic welfare provided by a $20,000 income—as measured by life expectancy, nutrition, education, and other measures of social welfare. This tremendously encouraging case remains largely unknown, even in development circles. It needs to be widely debated and accepted as the main goal of development. Its acceptance would greatly facilitate the transition to ES. But to accomplish the possible parts of the imperative of development, we must stop idolizing the impossible.* * *

Growth Compared with Development

Consider the dictionary distinction between growth and development: (1) *To grow* means to "increase in size (amount, degree) by assimilation": (2) *To develop* means to "expand, bring out potentialities, capabilities, to advance from a lower to a higher state." These definitions are useful in conceptualizing sustainability in that development is sustainable, and throughput growth is not.* * *

It is neither ethical nor helpful to the environment to expect poor countries to cut or arrest their development, which tends to be highly associated with throughput growth. Poor, small, developing economies need both growth and development. Therefore, the rich countries, which are responsible for most of today's global environmental damage ... must take the lead in this respect. Most local environmental damage (e.g., soil erosion, water pollution) occurs in developing countries. Poverty reduction will require considerable growth, as well as development in developing countries. But global environmental constraints are real, and more growth for the South must be balanced by negative throughput growth for the North if environmental sustainability is to be achieved. Future Northern growth should be sought from productivity increases in terms of throughput (e.g., reducing the energy intensity of production).

Development by the North must be used to free resources (source and sink functions of the environment) for growth and development so urgently needed by the poorer nations. Large-scale transfers to the poorer countries also will be required, especially as the impact of economic stability in the North countries may depress terms of trade and lower economic activity in developing countries. Higher prices for the exports of poorer countries, as well as debt relief will therefore be required. Most importantly, population stability is essential to reduce the need for growth everywhere, especially where population growth has the greatest impact (i.e., in Northern high-consuming nations: there the population growth has a doubling time of 162 yr.) as well as where population growth is the highest (i.e., in the poor, low-consuming countries, with a population doubling time of only 30 yr. exclusive of China).

Natural Capital and Sustainability

Intergenerational and intragenerational sustainability

Sustainability in economic terms can be described as the "maintenance of capital," sometimes phrased as "non-declining capital." Historically, at least as early as the Middle Ages the merchant traders used the word "capital" to refer to human-made capital. The merchants wanted to know how much of their trading ships' cargo sales receipts could be consumed by their families without depleting their capital. Economics Nobelist Sir John Hicks encapsuled the sustainability concept in 1946 when he defined income as the amount (whether natural or financial capital) one could consume during a period and still be as well off as at the end of the period. * * *

Today's OECD societies have already impoverished much of the world. Most people in the world today are already impoverished or barely above subsistence and can by no stretch of the imagination ever be as well off as the OECD average. Our successors or future generations seem to be more likely to be more numerous and poorer than today's generation. Sustainability indeed has an element of not harming the future (intergenerational equity), but only addressing the future element diverts attention from today's lack of sustainability (intragenerational equity). If the world cannot move towards intragenerational sustainability for this generation it will be greatly more difficult to achieve intergenerational sustainability in the future. . . .

Of the various forms of capital mentioned above, "environmental sustainability" refers to natural capital. So defining environmental sustainability includes at least two other terms, namely "natural capital" and "maintenance" or at least "non-declining". *Natural capital* is basically our natural environment, and is defined as the stock of environmentally-provided assets (such as soil and its microbes and fauna, atmosphere, forests, water, wetlands) that provides a useful flow of goods or services. The flow of useful goods and services from natural capital can be renewable or non-renewable, and marketed or non-marketed. Sustainability means maintaining environmental assets, or at least not depleting them. "Income" is sustainable by the generally accepted definition of Hicks: "the maximum value a person can consume during a week, and still expect to be as well off at the end of the week as at the beginning." Any consumption that is based on the depletion of natural capital should not be counted as income. Prevailing models of economic analysis tend to treat consumption of natural capital as income, and therefore tend to promote patterns of economic activity that are unsustainable. Consumption of natural capital is liquidation, the opposite of capital accumulation.

Natural capital is distinguished from manufactured and human or social capital. *Manufactured capital* includes houses, roads, factories, and ships. *Human or social capital* includes people, their capacity levels, institutions, cultural cohesion, education, information, and knowledge.

Human capital formation, by convention, is left out of the national accounts (the United Nations System of National Accounts, SNA) for various reasons, one of which is that if it is truly productive, it will eventually be reflected, through enhanced productivity, in a higher gross domestic product (GDP). Realization of the value of education and administration, for example, are lagged, and are conventionally assumed to be equal to their costs. The loss of natural capital, if not recorded—as is largely the case today—may take some time before it will reflect itself in income and productivity measurements.* * *

Now that the environment is so heavily used, the limiting factor for much economic development has become natural capital as much as man-made capital. In some cases, like marine fishing, it has become *the* limiting factor— fish have become limiting, rather than fishing boats. Timber is limited by remaining forests, not by saw mills; petroleum is limited by geological deposits and atmospheric capacity to absorb CO_2, not by refining capacity. As natural forests and fish populations become limiting we invest in plantation forests and fish ponds. This introduces a hybrid category that combines natural and human-made capital—a category we may call "cultivated natural capital". Thus, the subcategory of marketed natural capital, intermediate between human capital and natural capital, is *cultivated natural capital* such as agricultural products, pond-bred fish, cattle herds, and plantation forests. This category is vital to human well-being, accounting for most of the food we eat, and a good deal of the wood and fibers we use. The fact that humanity has the capacity to "cultivate" natural capital dramatically expands the capacity of natural capital to deliver services. But cultivated natural capital (agriculture) is decomposable into human-made capital (e.g .. tractors, diesel irrigation pumps, chemical fertilizers) and natural capital (e.g .. topsoil, sunlight, water). Eventually the natural capital proves limiting.

Natural capital is now scarce

In an era in which natural capital was considered infinite relative to the scale of human use, it was reasonable not to deduct natural-capital consumption from gross receipts in calculating income. That era is now past. The goal of environmental sustainability is thus the conservative effort to maintain the traditional meaning and measure of income in an era in which natural capital is no longer a free good, but is more and more the limiting factor in development. The difficulties in applying the concept arise mainly from operational problems of measurement and valuation of natural capital. . . .

Four degrees of environmental sustainability

Sustainability can be divided into four degrees—weak, intermediate, strong, and absurdly strong—depending on how much substitution one thinks there is among types of capital. We recognize that there are at least four kinds of capital. Human-made (the one usually considered in financial and economic accounts), natural capital (as defined previously, and leaving for the moment the case of cultivated natural capital), human capital (investments in education, health, and nutrition of individuals), and social capital (the institutional and cultural basis for a society to function).

Weak sustainability—This means maintaining total capital intact without regard to its composition from among the four different kinds of capital (natural, human-made, social, or human). This would imply that the different kinds of capital are perfect substitutes, at least within the boundaries of current levels of economic activity and resource endowment. Given current gross inefficiencies in resource use, weak sustainability would be a vast improvement as a welcome first step towards—but no means constitute—ES (environmental sustainability).

Weak sustainability means we could convert all or most of the world's natural capital into human-made capital or artifacts and still be as well off. . . . We disagree; society would be worse off (fewer choices) because natural and human-made capital are not perfect substitutes. On the contrary, they are compliments to a great extent.

Intermediate sustainability—This would require that in addition to maintaining the total level of capital intact, attention should be given to the composition of that capital from among natural, manufactured, and human. Thus oil may be depleted as long as the receipts are invested in other capital elsewhere (e.g., in human capital development, or in renewable energy resources), but, in addition, efforts should be made to define critical levels of each type of capital, beyond which concerns about sustainability could arise and these should be monitored to ensure that the patterns of development do not promote the total decimation of one kind of capital no matter what is being accumulated in the other forms of capital. This assumes that while manufactured and natural capital are substitutable over a sometimes significant but limited margin, they are complementary beyond that limited margin. The full functioning of the system requires at least a mix of the different kinds of capital. Since we do not know exactly where the boundaries of these critical limits for each type of capital lie, it behooves the sensible person to err on the side of caution in depleting resources (especially natural capital) at too fast a rate. Intermediate sustainability is a big improvement over weak sustainability and seems "sensible". Its great weakness is that it is difficult if not impossible to define critical levels of each type of capital, or rather each type of natural capital that is the limiting factor. We suspect that if the levels of the different types of natural capital become reliably defined, intermediate sustainability would approximate strong sustainability.

Strong sustainability—This requires maintaining different kinds of capital intact separately. Thus, for natural capital, receipts from depleting oil should be invested in ensuring that energy will be available to future generations at least as plentifully as enjoyed by the beneficiaries of today's oil consumption. This assumes that natural and human-made capital are not really substitutes but complements in most production functions. A sawmill (human-made capital) is worthless without the complementary natural capital of a forest. The same logic would argue that that if there are to be reductions in one kind of educational investments they should be offset by other kinds of education, not by investments in roads. Of the four degrees of sustainability, we prefer strong sustainability.

Absurdly strong sustainability—This would never deplete anything. Non-renewable resources—absurdly—could not be used at all: for renewables, only net annual growth rates could be harvested, in the form of the overmature portion of the stock.

The choice between intermediate and strong sustainability highlights the trade-offs between human-made capital and natural capital. Economic logic requires us to invest in the limiting factor, which now is often natural rather than manufactured capital.... Investing in natural capital (non-marketed) is essentially an infrastructure investment on a grand scale, that is the biophysical infrastructure of the human niche. Investment in such "infra-infrastructure" maintains the productivity of all previous economic economic investments in human-made capital, public or private, by rebuilding the natural capital stocks that have become limiting. Operationally, this translates into three concrete actions as follows:

1) Regeneration—Encouraging the growth of natural capital by reducing our level of current exploitation of it;

2) Relief of Pressure—Investing in projects to relieve pressure on natural capital stocks by expanding cultivated natural capital, such as tree plantations to relieve pressure on natural forests; and

3) Increase of Efficiency—Increasing the efficiency of (a) products (such as improved cookstoves, solar cookers, wind pumps, solar pumps, manure rather than chemical fertilizer), (b) infrastructure services (such as mulching toilets rather than conventional sewage treatment), and (c) lifestyle (such as less carnivorous diets).* * *

Criteria for Environmental Sustainability

The implications of implementing environmental sustainability are [thus] immense. We must learn how to manage the renewable resources for the long term: we have to reduce waste and pollution; we must learn how to use energy and materials with scrupulous efficiency; we must learn how to use solar energy economically; and we must invest in repairing the damage, as much as possible, done to Earth.... Environmental sustainability needs enabling conditions that are not themselves integral parts of environmental sustainability: ES needs not only economic and social sustainability, but also democracy, human resource development, empowerment of women, and much more investment in human capital than is common today (i.e., increased literacy, especially ecoliteracy).* * *

. . . The transition to environmental sustainability *will* inevitably occur. However, whether nations will have the wisdom and foresight to plan for an orderly and equitable transition to environmental sustainability, rather than allowing biophysical limits to dictate the timing and course of this transition, remains in doubt.

It is obvious that if pollution and environmental degradation were to grow at the same rate as economic activity, or even population growth, the damage to ecological and human health would be appalling, and the growth itself would be undermined and even self-defeating. Fortunately, this is not necessary. A transition to sustainability is possible, although it will require changes in policies and the ways humans value things. The key to the improvement of the well being of millions of people lies in the increase in added value of output after properly netting out all the environmental costs and benefits and after differentiating between the stock and flow aspects of the use of natural resources. In our view, this is the key to sustainable development. Without this needed adjustment in thinking and measurement, the pursuit of economic growth that does not account for natural capital and counts depletion of natural capital as an income stream will not lead to a sustainable development path.* * *

The Basic Conditions for Environmental Sustainability

The fundamental definition of environmental sustainability is contained in the input–output rule as follows:

Output Rule: Waste emissions from a project should be within the assimilative capacity of the local environment without unacceptable degradation of its future waste-absorptive capacity or other important services.

Input Rule: (a) *Renewables*: harvest rates of renewable resource inputs should be within the regenerative capacity of the natural system that generates them. (b) *Non-renewables*: depletion rates of non-renewable-resource inputs should be equal to the rate at which renewable substitutes are developed by human invention and investment. Part of the proceeds from liquidating non-renewables should be allocated to research in pursuit of sustainable substitutes.

Building on the economic definition of sustainability as "non-declining wealth per capita," and since wealth is so difficult to measure, environmental sustainability is now defined by the two fundamental environmental services—the source and sink functions—that must be maintained unimpaired during the period over which sustainability is required. While this general definition is robust—and irrespective of country, sector, or epoch—it can in turn be disaggregated.

The emphasis on maintenance is to be expected, first for intergenerational equity. Our descendants should have as much choice as we have. Second, as scale increases or matures, production is no longer for growth but for maintenance. "Production" is the maintenance cost of the stock and should be minimized. Sustainability demands that production and consumption be equal so that we maintain capital stocks. Efficiency demands that the maintenance cost (production equal to consumption) be minimized, given the capital stock.

The basic conditions for environmental sustainability can be summarized as follows:

A) Environmental sustainability requires four related conditions of economic sustainability:

1) Maintenance of per capita manufactured capital (e.g. artifacts, infrastructure), per capita.

2) Maintenance of renewable natural capital (e.g., healthy air and soils, natural forests, oceanic fish stocks), per capita.

3) Maintenance of per capita non-renewable substitutable natural capital, with capital values based on the value of services of the present stock of natural capital. For example, this means that if the cost of supplying energy substitutes rises, sufficient capital must be accumulated to maintain these services.

4) Maintenance of non-substitutable, non-renewable natural resources (e.g., waste absorption by environmental sink services). No depletion or deterioration of non-substitutable, non-renewable natural capital. This means no net increases in waste emissions beyond absorptive capacity.

B) All economic consumption should be priced to reflect full cost of all capital depletion, including waste creation, the cost of which is equal to the cost of reducing an equivalent amount of that particular waste.

C) Stating the conditions in per capita terms calls attention to the importance of stopping population growth. Theoretically, the per capita stock of all kinds of capital could remain constant as long as the stocks grew at the same rate as the population. But in actuality, the rate of growth of population and stocks of physical wealth must move towards zero.

To stop throughput of matter and energy from growing or hold throughput constant (we leave until later the need actually to reduce throughput) means stabilizing population on the demand side, and improving resource productivity or "dematerializing" the economy on the supply side. Sustainability does not imply optimality. Sustainability is a necessary but not sufficient condition of optimality. Resource productivity has increased already, although more progress is possible and needed. Such progress would include improvements in energy efficiency; more production with less energy and fewer materials; tight recycling; repair; re-use; and "decarbonization," another name of the transition to renewables such as wind, solar energy, and the hydrogen economy.* * *

A Dynamic Formulation: from Sustainability to Sustainable Development

[After discussing the IPAT formula presented in Chapter 2, the authors note that the] generalization can be nuanced. The inter-relationships among the three factors, and their links with shifts in the structure of the economy should be further disaggregated. Three trends need to be accelerated as we struggle towards sustainability.

First given the political unreality of a voluntary decline in the overall affluence of industrial countries how is the "pattern" of this affluence shifting? Specifically, is the economic structure of the economy shifting away from environmentally damaging activities (e.g., heavy and toxic industries) and towards less "natural capital-depleting" sectors (e.g., services)? This trend is to be encouraged, although some services deplete much natural capital (e.g., hospitals, hotels). Furthermore, while affluent Northern nations may be becoming less capital depleting by evolving into the service sector, at the same time much industry and other natural-capital-depleting activities are being transferred to developing countries. This is not a net gain for the sole global ecosystem, and may be a loss if developing countries' environmental standards are weaker than those whence the industries originated. Japan's huge success in using less input per unit of economic output, such as by de-linking energy and production, is based partly on the fact that most of Japan's aluminum, for example is smelted overseas. Similarly, Japan's forest natural capital is almost entirely intact; practically all timber is imported.* * *

Second, the clear trend in the consumption of natural resources per unit of output is improving in OECD and in places in developing countries. Two mechanisms need to be monitored here: improvements in economic efficiency (inputs per unit of output), and the degree of substitution away from environmentally critical inputs. Policy instruments, including taxes and user charges, can help promote such transitions, especially when the environmental costs are not captured in the workplace.

Third, the pollution impact per unit of economic activity is declining in places; less so in others. Here it is important to distinguish between the innovation of new technologies, and their dissemination and application. Many of the most profound forms of environmental damage in today's world (soil erosion, lack of clean water, municipal waste, etc.) do not require new technologies, but simply the application of existing ones. This in turn requires (a) that decision makers are persuaded that the benefits of using such technologies exceed the costs, and (b) that resources are available for putting them in place. Public policies can be targeted towards meeting both conditions.

The availability of resources to implement more sustainable strategies was a central argument in the findings of the Brundtland Commission's "Our Common Future", the United Nations Rio Earth Summit's "Agenda 21", and the World Bank's *World Development Report 1992*. These documents and Goodland and Daly argue strongly that the reduction of poverty (i.e., empowering the poor with human and fiscal resources) is a sine qua non of sustainability. The point here is a critical one: The clear goal of environmental sustainability needs the fuzzy process of environmentally sustainable development. The challenge is to distinguish between environmentally sustainable and unsustainable development.

Interactions among the driving factors—scale, structure, efficiency, technology, and investment in environmental protection—together with key feedback loops between economic activity and human behavior, such as the powerful impact of income on fertility, explain why in some situations economic growth and technological progress will sometimes cause increased environmental damage and sometimes less. For effective policymaking, it is essential that these various paths are disentangled so that policies may be targeted in a manner that induces changed behavior away from environmentally damaging and inequitable growth and towards accelerated sustainable poverty reduction.

———

QUESTIONS AND DISCUSSION

1. Is achieving environmental sustainability the goal of international environmental law? Or is the goal sustainable development? What difference does it make in evaluating the effectiveness of international environmental treaties?

2. The initial reading from *An Introduction to Ecological Economics* states that "It is clear that scale should not be determined by prices, but by a social decision reflecting ecological limits." Do you agree? According to economic theory, if the (generally externalized) costs of environmental degradation were internalized into a product's cost, the price of the product would reflect those costs. As the environment was increasingly degraded, product prices would rise, eventually stopping at a price point that balanced society's demand for a particular product with society's interest in a certain level of environmental protection. Do you think we have a sufficient understanding of the complexities of ecosystems to effectively identify all externalities? Even assuming all the externalities can be identified, is it possible to assign an accurate value to these externalities? How do you put a price on fresh air, wilderness, or an increased risk of cancer or birth defects? Are you confident that the market can determine an acceptable level of environmental quality?

Such profound social decisions generally would be made through the political process. Do you think the political process is up to the task? If not, how can we improve it, or how can we design another acceptable process for making this determination about the survival of human society? The ecological economists also argue that "Distribution should not be determined by prices, but by a social decision reflecting a just distribution of assets." Again, the political process is the one we would normally turn to for this type of determination. But how well suited is the political process for determining what constitutes fair distribution? How successful is the current U.S. tax code in ensuring just distribution of assets? Can you think of any alternatives? Consider this question after reading the excerpt from Rawls' *A Theory of Justice* in the next chapter.

3.   The ecological economists are re-conceiving economics and ecology to present a new vision for sustainable societies. "They present a historical narrative of how worldviews have evolved. This emphasizes how much worldviews *do* evolve and change." Robert Costanza, *op. cit.,* at xi. Must international environmental law also evolve and change to deal with the problem of scale, which is the problem of survival? In chapter 6, legal philosopher Philip Allott presents a vision for re-conceiving international society and international law.

4.   Goodland and Daly present environmental sustainability as an imperative that is "universal and non-negotiable." What do they mean? Are there legal principles that are universal and non-negotiable? Consider this question after rereading the section on ethics in the previous chapter , and the discussion of general principles in Chapter 5.

5.   Stuart L. Hart, writing in the Harvard Business Review, argues that the global economy is, in fact, three different but overlapping economies. We have been focusing on two of these economies, the *market economy* and *nature's economy*. The market economy is the economy that prevails in the developed nations and in the emerging economies of the developing world. It is the familiar economy of commerce, financial markets, industrial production and industrial pollution. *Nature's economy*, as we discussed in Chapter 1, consists of the natural systems and resources that sustain and constrain the human economies. The third economy Stuart Hart refers to—which is largely outside the formal economies discussed in this chapter—is the *survival economy*: the economy based on a traditional, community-based or tribal way of life that still predominates in the rural parts of most developing countries. In the *survival economy*, people satisfy their basic needs—food, clothing, shelter, fuel—more from nature than through a complex market system. Although three billion people live in the *survival economy*, more than half the human population, it is ignored by most economic theories and most environmentalists and policymakers. Yet the survival economy has a definite and direct impact on the human environment, an impact that is increasing as expansion of the market economy drives rural populations, which also are increasing, onto ever more marginal lands. *See* Stuart L. Hart, *Strategies for a Sustainable World*, HARVARD BUSINESS REV., Jan.-Feb. 1997, at 67–76. Does ecological economics provide a suitable framework for addressing the survival economy? If it does not, how might we address the relationships among the three economies?

C. COMMUNITY VS. GLOBALIZATION

In traditional economics, globalized trade is based on the "logic of exchange", which is designed to lower the price of goods and increase individual consumer choice. While the logic of exchange, or trade, works under its ideal assumptions—informed utility-maximizing parties with no externalities involved—this does not represent an accurate picture of the real world of real communities. The ecological economists present this fundamental problem of political economy within the context of individual choice versus collective choice, of "one of deciding when individuals, groups, communities, or the state should be entrusted with decision-making authority. . . ." Their views of community are discussed further in the final reading. We will return to this topic in Chapter 15 on International Trade, Investment, and the Environment.

> The difference between individual and community interest, of course, is intimately tied to the systemic character of environmental systems. Nature cannot readily be divided up and assigned to individuals. For this reason, collective management or collective limitations on individual choice are frequently appropriate. * * *

> Economics is founded on self interest. But this self that interests us so much is in reality not an isolated atom, but is constituted by its relations in community with others—the very identify of the self is social rather than atomistic. If the very self is constituted by relations of community, then self-interest can no longer be atomistically self-contained or defined independently of the community interest. . . . Distribution and scale involve relationships with the poor, future generations, and other species that are more social than individual in nature. *Homo economicus*, whether the self-contained atom of methodological individualism or the pure social automaton of collectivist ideology, is in neither case a severe abstraction. Our concrete experience is that of "persons in community." We are individual persons, but our very individual identity is defined by the quality of our social relations. . . . We are related not only by the external nexus of individual willingness-to-pay for different things, but also by relations of kinship, friendship, citizenship, and trusteeship for the poor, future generations, and for other species, not to mention our physical dependence on the same ecological life-support system. * * *

Robert Costanza et al., *op. cit.*, at 157–59.

————

QUESTIONS AND DISCUSSION

1. In *The Sustainable Consumer Society*, included in Chapter 2, Paul Ekins reports that our well-being depends more on our relations with others, especially family, than our wealth, at least above a certain minimum income level. The more elaborate Max–Neef matrix described above expands this view. Both help explain the concept of "person-in-community." What are the implications of this understanding of well-being for economics? For the environment? For international environmental law? Keep this "person-in-community" concept in mind when reading Philip Allott's essay in the next chapter, especially where he discusses the differences between the society humans form within their national political boundaries and the State-centered society beyond the borders.

2. The last reading notes that "we are related . . . by . . . our physical dependence on the same ecological life-support system." Consider how global environmental threats to the Earth's life-support system relate to Professor H.L.A. Hart's discussion in Chapter 5 of the minimum legal principles societies must have to ensure their survival.

3. Herman Daly argues that production should be local whenever possible:

> [[I]nternational trade] postpones the day when countries must face up to the discipline of living within natural regenerative and absorptive capacities, and by doing so probably serves on balance to increase throughput growth and environmental degradation. Free trade also introduces greater spatial separation between the production benefits and the environmental costs of throughput growth, making it more difficult for the latter to temper the growth of the former. Furthermore, as a result of the increased integration caused by trade, countries will face tightening environmental constraints more simultaneously and less sequentially than they would with less trade and integration. Therefore, there will be less opportunity to learn from other countries' prior experience with controlling throughput. In sum, by making supplies of resources and absorption capacities everywhere available to demands anywhere, free trade will tend to increase throughput growth and with it the rate of environmental degradation.

Herman Daly, *Problems with Free Trade: Neoclassical and Steady–State Perspectives*, in Zaelke, *et al.*, EDS. TRADE AND THE ENVIRONMENT: LAW, ECONOMICS, AND POLICY at 156 (Island Press, 1993).

Suggested Further Reading and Web Sites

Gretchen Daily, ed., NATURE'S SERVICES (1997)

A readable and comprehensive review of the critical services ecosystems provide to humans. Written by world-class scientists, it provides the first rigorous effort to identify and, where possible, monetarily value ecosystem services.

Herman Daly has written many of the basic works in ecological economics, including

BEYOND GROWTH: THE ECONOMICS OF SUSTAINABLE DEVELOPMENT (1996)

STEADY-STATE ECONOMICS (1991)

FOR THE COMMON GOOD : REDIRECTING THE ECONOMY TOWARD COMMUNITY, THE ENVIRONMENT, AND A SUSTAINABLE FUTURE (1989)

ECONOMICS, ECOLOGY, ETHICS : ESSAYS TOWARD A STEADY-STATE ECONOMY (1980)

Robert Costanza, ed., ECOLOGICAL ECONOMICS: THE SCIENCE AND MANAGEMENT OF SUSTAINABILITY (1991)

A comprehensive introduction to the field of ecological economics.

Frances Cairncross, COSTING THE EARTH (1991)

A readable and interesting treatment of how economics influences environmental protection. Provides a number of case studies to highlight problems and potential solutions.

Elinor Ostrom, GOVERNING THE COMMONS (1990).

A. Jansson et al., INVESTING IN NATURAL CAPITAL: THE ECOLOGICAL ECONOMICS OF SUSTAINABILITY (1994)

Journal of Environmental Economics & Management.

Marine Resource Economics (http:www.uri.edu/crd/enre/mrre)

Land Economics Resources (Publication of Resources for the Future).

Robert Repetto et al., *Green Fees: How a Tax Shift Can Work for the Environment and the Economy*, WRI Publications Brief 1 (Nov. 1992).

http://www.ecosystemvaluation.org

This site provides clear explanations of what ecosystem valuation is and how economists use these tools to measure environmental change. It includes examples of how indicators are used in the field and how they influence environmental decisionmaking.

http://www.neweconomics.org

Homepage of the New Economics Foundation, an NGO promoting practical and creative approaches for a just and sustainable economy. The Foundation hosts "The Other Economic Summit," an alternative to the G–7 summit that focuses on environmental and equity issues.

http://www.ecologicaleconomics.org

Homepage of the International Society for Ecological Economics, a not-for-profit organization with more than 1300 members in over 60 countries. The site contains an on-line forum, links to other sites, and an archive of curriculum and syllabi from courses.

http://iisd.ca/contents.htm

Extensive directory of information on sustainable development and economic issues.

http://www.aaea.org

Homepage of the American Association of Agricultural Economics.

CHAPTER FOUR

A BRIEF HISTORY FROM STOCKHOLM TO RIO

> *No place on the planet can remain an island of affluence in a sea of misery. We're either going to save the whole world or not one will be saved. . . . One part of the world cannot live in an orgy of unrestrained consumption while the rest destroys its environment just to survive.*
>
> Maurice Strong in his welcoming statement to the 1992 UN Conference on Environment and Development (the Earth Summit).

SECTION I.   INTRODUCTION

This Chapter presents a brief history of international environmental law, particularly as it relates to the concept of sustainable development. The history is organized around the two landmark conferences on environment and development issues: the 1972 UN Conference on the Human Environment (also known as the Stockholm Conference) and the 1992 UN Conference on Environment and Development (referred to as either UNCED, the Rio Conference, or the Earth Summit). The Chapter provides a chronological and geopolitical context for the rest of the book. The geopolitical context is critical to understanding both the past and the current status of international environmental law-making. At the global level, major differences in development patterns between industrialized and developing countries have led to generally different approaches to international environmental issues.

The industrialized countries include the United States and Canada, Europe, the former Soviet Union, Japan, Australia and New Zealand.

Although not all of these countries are located in the North, we will use the term "North", developed, or industrialized to refer to these countries. The North shares many characteristics that can be generalized in understanding the predominant North–South split in environmental affairs. The North is relatively wealthy, with a relatively high level of economic development. Corresponding social factors such as literacy rates and health indicators are strong. Environmental concerns have been on the national agendas of many industrialized countries for several decades. The North typically has a well-organized civil society, including successful and effective environmental organizations. The environmental sciences and related disciplines are often more advanced. The North is also the primary consumer of natural resources and the primary polluter. For these reasons and because it is generally more powerful in foreign affairs, the North typically sets the international agenda with respect to global environmental issues.

In contrast, the global South, or the developing countries, are less wealthy in economic terms. Many of these countries have large populations that are poor, barely surviving at or below the poverty level. Illiteracy, lower life expectancies, and occasional famine plague many countries in the South. Yet the South contains much of the world's natural wealth—for example, the largest standing tropical forests, most of the world's biodiversity, and the most valuable deposits of many of the world's most valuable minerals. Many countries in the South, at least those outside Africa, are rapidly industrializing and are beginning to face serious environmental pollution problems for the first time. Water shortages and contaminated water beset many large cities in the South, and many suffer severe air pollution, including Bangkok, Cairo, Mexico City and Santiago.

In international environmental negotiations the North's sense of urgency to solve global environmental problems is counterbalanced by the South's sense of urgency to redirect the global economy to overcome the cycle of poverty. To some in the South, environmental protection is a luxury to be addressed later, and thus viewed primarily as a potential drag on the engine of growth. Southern countries question whether environmental protection or natural resource exploitation issues should be addressed at all at the international level. In their view, these issues are inextricably linked to issues of economic development and should remain primarily internal matters. In general, many countries in the South believe that harmonizing environmental standards through global environmental agreements would slow their development and unreasonably limit their economic growth to respond to problems caused predominantly by the insatiable consumption of the North. Perhaps most importantly, many in the South view Northern environmental ambitions as an assault on the sovereignty of developing countries, aimed at controlling the development paths of the post-colonial South.

Emphasizing the substantial differences between North and South is not intended to belittle the significant differences within industrialized countries, for significant disagreements exist among these countries regarding specific environmental issues and will become readily apparent in the chapters in Part Two of the book. For example, the countries with economies in transition—i.e. those of central and eastern Europe and of the former Soviet Union—are frequently in significantly different positions in global environmental negotiations than are industrialized countries. Similarly, major differences can exist within developing countries. Small island states, for example are particularly vulnerable to many environmental threats. Some of the larger more economically powerful countries, such as China, India, Argentina, Brazil and Chile, may also have different approaches to the environment than poorer countries. Thus, neither the industrialized nor developing countries can be counted on as a bloc in an international environmental negotiation.

The challenge of international environmental diplomacy has been to accommodate these different perspectives. A marriage of sorts has emerged, in the words of the *Rio Declaration* in a "global partnership" between North and South to achieve sustainable development. The basis of this partnership includes mutual acceptance of the goals of environmental protection and development, a marriage between environmental protection and poverty alleviation, between the need to slow population growth and curb consumption, between obligations to protect the environment and obligations to provide financial assistance and technology transfers, and between the common responsibilities of all countries and a recognition that the North should bear different (and greater) responsibilities given their historical influence over the global economy.

The global partnership, which was elaborated at UNCED and subsequently reflected in many global environmental instruments, suggests a new relationship between North and South. The North must have the South's full cooperation to meet global environmental challenges, which gives the South potentially more leverage in international environmental affairs than in most other types of negotiations. The price demanded by the South for their cooperation is agreement to address environment *and* development. Understanding the differences in North–South priorities can help explain many of the compromises and decisions reflected in international environmental instruments.

Of course, not all countries in the North and South are created equally when it comes to their importance in resolving critical environmental issues. In recent years, the WorldWatch Institute has highlighted the growing importance of a relatively small group of countries to global environmental issues. Dubbed the "E–9", these eight countries plus the European Union can be expected to dominate global environmental politics and the development of international environmental law in the future. They include the country with the largest population—China; the one with the largest economy and carbon emissions—the United States; and the nation that arguably claims the richest array of biodiversity—Brazil. Together with the European Union, South Africa, Japan, India, Indonesia and Russia, the E–9 account for 59 percent of the world's population, 70 percent of its economic output, and 73 percent of all carbon emissions. Consider the following chart from Christopher Flavin, *Rich Planet, Poor Planet,* in LESTER BROWN, ET AL., EDS., STATE OF THE WORLD: 2001, at 1–20 (Worldwatch Institute, 2001)

	% of World Population	GNP /person (1998)	% Global CO_2 Emissions (1995)	Share of Flowering Plant Species (1990)	Infant Mortality Per Thousand Live Births
U.S.	4.6	29,240	23	8	4
Germany	1.3	26,570	4	1	5
Japan	2.1	32,350	5	2	7
Russia	2.4	2,260	7	9	17
South Africa	0.7	3,310	1	N.A.	31
Brazil	2.8	4,630	1	22	33
China	21	750	13	12	43
India	17	440	4	6	70
Indonesia	3.5	640	1	8	51

The industrial countries in the E–9 shape global trends in part because of their economic strength, their high levels of material consumption and social trend-setting, and their dominance of technology. The developing countries' influence, in contrast, is determined in part by their large populations, their rapid economic development, and their rich diversity of wildlife. Because these nine environmental heavyweights use such a large share of the world's resources and produce so much of its pollution, they have disproportionate responsibility and potential for resolving global environmental issues.

————

QUESTIONS AND DISCUSSION

1. The concept of the E–9 is useful for understanding what it takes to develop an effective international environmental regime. It may not be necessary to have every country participate in every treaty, but it is necessary to have those countries that have the most impact on specific issues involved in efforts to resolve the issue. How effective, for example, would an agreement such as the Kyoto Protocol that establishes clear targets and timetables for the reduction of carbon dioxide be if all of the countries except for the E–9 agreed to it?

The concept of the E–9 also highlights the relative power that is wielded by at least the larger developing countries in the environmental arena. The analogy drawn to the G–7 is useful in this regard, because the G–7 highlights the disproportionate power industrialized countries have had (compared to developing countries) in shaping the way the world conducts business. In the future, however, developing countries will wield much more power over the world's development in part because of their central role in solving global environmental issues.

2. What are the major differences between the North and South in their approaches to global environmental negotiations? What are the main differences among Northern countries? Among the Southern countries? What voting blocs could you foresee in specific negotiations?

3. The global partnership between North and South has grown increasingly tenuous since the 1992 UNCED. What signals can you identify in current affairs that suggest either this partnership is strengthening or disintegrating? In considering this question, consider as well the growing economic disparity between rich and poor countries. Among the E–9, for example, more than half of the population of China (53.7%), Indonesia (66.1%), and India (86.2%) earn less than $2 per day. In this respect, the E–9 also looks critical for the broader goals of sustainable development (discussed below in Section III).

SECTION II.   THE STOCKHOLM CONFERENCE ON THE HUMAN ENVIRONMENT

A.   THE ROAD TO STOCKHOLM

While some environmental treaties date back more than a century, the environment is a relatively new focus of international law. Many of the earliest environmental treaties relate to the conservation of migratory wildlife. For example, the Treaty for the Preservation and Protection of Fur Seals, July 7, 1911, 37 Stat. 1542, a convention between Russia, the United Kingdom, Japan and the United States, was aimed at curbing the slaughter of northern fur seals. Other early conventions addressed the allocation of shared watercourses. *See, e.g,* Convention on Certain Questions Relating to the Law on Watercourses, Swed–Nor., 120 L.N.T.S. 277 (May 11, 1929); Convention to Regulate the Hydro Electric Development and the International Section of the River Duno, Spain–Port., 82 L.N.T.S. 131 (Aug. 11, 1927); General Convention Relating to the Development of Hydraulic Power Affecting More than One State, 36 L.N.T.S. 76 (Dec. 9, 1923).

As countries industrialized in the first half of the century, environmental pollution issues became more prevalent. The *Trail Smelter Arbitration,* perhaps the most famous international environmental dispute, began in the 1930s when the United States complained that sulfur dioxide emissions from a smelter located across the border in Canada damaged U.S. crops. The 1941 arbitral panel's decision is still an important landmark in international environmental law. *See* discussion in Chapter 9.

Despite a few specific decisions and treaties, the field of international environmental law did not really take off until the early 1970s, when domestic law began to respond to the increasingly well-documented impacts of industrialization. In the United States, for example, the air was clearly dirty. White-collar workers in Pittsburgh would change their shirts at midday because they would be gray with soot. Ohio's Cuyahoga River actually caught fire on June 22, 1969. Birds dying from pesticide poisoning were common sights in suburbs. The 1962 publication of Rachel Carson's *Silent Spring* documented the impacts of decades of pesticide spraying on the global environment and galvanized public activism regarding environmental issues. Environmental concerns joined with the activism of the 1960s in major protests and political pressure, including most notably an enormous gathering on Earth Day in 1970. The 1969 passage of the National Environmental Protection Act and the ensuing passage of federal statutes addressing air pollution, water pollution, and solid wastes reflected the environmental transformation of American policies. Environmental law had become a legitimate issue for national policymaking. For a readable history of the U.S. environmental movement, *see* PHILIP SHABECOFF, A FIERCE GREEN FIRE (1995).

A similar transformation was occurring throughout the industrialized world as many countries passed national environmental laws and established environmental institutions in the late 1960s and early 1970s. Particularly in Europe where many environmental issues such as air and water pollution inherently present transboundary issues, the emerging environmentalism moved almost immediately to the international level. Motivated primarily by a concern over transboundary pollution, particularly in the form of acid rain, Sweden in 1968 suggested an international conference to address global environmental problems. Later Sweden would agree to host the 1972 UN Conference on the Human Environment in Stockholm.

During the years leading up to the Stockholm Conference, developing countries were, not surprisingly, facing a different set of issues and problems. Not having enjoyed the benefits of industrialization, developing countries were also not feeling the pressures from industrialized pollution. Many developing countries had only recently received their independence from the colonial powers, and were interested in defending their newly won independence and protecting the right to follow their own development paths. The numerical superiority of the South in the UN General Assembly emboldened them to sponsor a number of General Assembly Resolutions. The G–77 (named for the group of 77 developing countries, not aligned with either of the Cold War superpowers) flexed their electoral muscle, and over the space of ten years in the late 1960s and 1970s passed a series of resolutions affirming their right to development, their sovereignty over natural resources, and the need to handle environmental policies at the national level. This movement among developing countries was part of an effort to develop a "New International Economic Order" that they hoped would reverse the ongoing resource flows from the South to North and begin to introduce greater social equity in the global economy.

Six months prior to the Stockholm Conference, the developing countries sponsored and passed a resolution on development and environment specifically aimed at influencing the outcome of the Conference. The resolution emphasized the developing countries' strong sense that global concerns over environmental protection should not interfere with their development agenda and that environmental policy should be left to the individual States.

Development and Environment, UN General Assembly Resolution, A/RES/2849 (XXVI), 17 Jan. 1972

The General Assembly, * * *

Cognizant that, aside from environmental disturbances provoked by human settlements and ecological problems related to nature itself, pollution of world-wide impact is being caused primarily by some highly developed countries, as a consequence of their own high level of improperly planned and inadequately coordinated industrial activities, and that, therefore, the main responsibility for the financing of corrective measures falls upon those countries,

Convinced that most of the environmental problems existing in developing countries are caused by their lack of economic resources for dealing with such problems as the improvement of unfavourable natural areas or the rehabilitation of environmental conditions that have deteriorated through the application of improper methods and technologies,

Conscious that the main objective of developing countries is integrated and rational development, including industrial development based on advanced and adequate technologies, and that such development represents at the present stage the best possible solution for most of the environmental problems in the developing countries,

Conscious further that the quality of human life in the developing countries also depends, in large measure, on the solution of environmental problems which have their origin in nature and which are the product of under-development itself, within the general framework of development planning and the rational management of natural resources,

Emphasizing that, notwithstanding the general principles that might be agreed upon by the international community, criteria and minimal standards of preservation of the environment as a general rule will have to be defined at the national level and, in all cases, will have to reflect conditions and systems of values prevailing in each country, avoiding where necessary the use of norms valid in advanced countries, which may prove inadequate and of unwarranted social costs for the developing countries,

Stressing that each country has the right to formulate, in accordance with its own particular situation and in full enjoyment of its national sovereignty, its own national policies on the human environment, including criteria for the evaluation of projects,

Stressing further that in the exercise of such right and in the implementation of such policies due account must be taken of the need to avoid producing harmful effects on other countries, * * *

Bearing in mind the need for developed countries to provide additional technical assistance and financing, beyond the targets indicated in the International Development Strategy for the Second United Nations Development Decade [Gen. Assembly Res. 2626 (XXV)] and without affecting adversely their programmes of assistance in other spheres, to enable developing countries to enforce those new and additional measures that might be envisaged as a means of protecting and enhancing the environment, * * *

1. *Stresses* that both the action plan and the action proposals to be submitted to the Conference must, *inter alia*:

2. Respect fully the exercise of permanent sovereignty over natural resources, as well as the right of each country to exploit its own resources in accordance with its own priorities and needs and in such a manner as to avoid producing harmful effects on other countries;

3. Recognize that no environmental policy should adversely affect the present or future development possibilities of the developing countries;

4. Recognize further that the burden of the environmental policies of the developed countries cannot be transferred, directly or indirectly, to the developing countries;

5. Respect fully the sovereign right of each country to plan its own economy, to define its own priorities, to determine its own environmental standards and criteria, to evaluate its own social costs of production, and to formulate its own environmental policies, in the full understanding that environmental action must be defined basically at the national level, in accordance with locally prevailing conditions and in such a manner as to avoid producing harmful effects on other countries;

6. Avoid any adverse effects of environmental policies and measures on the economy of the developing countries in all spheres, including international

trade, international development assistance and the transfer of technology.
* * *

The vote in favor of the resolution was 85–2–34, with the United States and the United Kingdom opposing, and virtually all other developed countries abstaining. The resolution represents an early and clear statement of developing country perspective regarding international cooperation in the field of the environment.

B. AT STOCKHOLM

In announcing the Stockholm Conference, the UN General Assembly stated that the "main purpose" is to "serve as a practical means to encourage, and to provide guidelines for, action by Governments and international organizations designed to protect and improve the human environment, and to remedy and prevent its impairment, by means of international co-operation, bearing in mind the particular importance of enabling developing countries to forestall occurrence of such problems." U.N.G.A. 2581(XXIV) Jan. 8, 1970 (A/RES/2581(XXIV)) (unanimously adopted on Dec. 15, 1969); *see also* L. Sohn, *The Stockholm Declaration on the Human Environment,* HARV. INT'L L. J. 423 (1973).

In ONLY ONE EARTH, the background report commissioned for the Stockholm Conference, Rene Dubos and Barbara Ward described the challenge facing the Conference delegates in terms of stewardship for future generations.

> Now that mankind is in the process of completing the colonization of the planet, learning to manage it intelligently is an urgent imperative. Man must accept responsibility for the stewardship of the earth. The word *stewardship* implies, of course, management for the sake of someone else. Depending upon their scientific, social, philosophical, and religious attitudes, environmentalists have somewhat different views as to the nature of the party for whom they should act as stewards. But in practice the charge of the U.N. to the Conference was clearly to define what should be done to maintain the earth as a place suitable for human life not only now, but also for future generations.

BARBARA WARD & RENEE DUBOS, ONLY ONE EARTH: THE CARE AND MAINTENANCE OF A SMALL PLANET, at 9 (1972). *Only One Earth* is one of the earliest and most important efforts to place environmental issues in the context of development with current obligations to the future generations. It paved the way for the more famous *Our Common Future*, described below.

The Stockholm Conference was one of the most successful UN conferences ever held up to that time. One hundred and thirteen countries attended, although only India and the host country Sweden were represented by their head of state. The Conference occurred in the middle of the Cold War however, and East–West politics left their impact on it. The Soviet Bloc boycotted after East Germany was denied an invitation, although the Soviet Union and most other Soviet Bloc countries would ultimately support the conference decisions.

The Stockholm Conference had three major products: the Action Plan to protect the global environment; the United Nations Environment Program and the related Environment Fund; and the *Stockholm Declaration on the Human Environment*.

———

1.   THE STOCKHOLM ACTION PLAN

The *Stockholm Action Plan* was a comprehensive effort to identify those environmental issues requiring international action. It was comprised of 106 separate priority recommendations. These included relatively specific recommendations for international action in five major program areas, including:

- planning and managing human settlements for environmental quality;

- addressing the environmental aspects of natural resources management;

- identifying and controlling pollutants of broad international significance;

- exploring and strengthening the educational, informational, social and cultural aspects of environmental issues; and

- addressing the integration of development and environment.

The Action Plan launched a global environmental assessment program (known as Earthwatch), which continues to be vital for gaining information about the biosphere. The Action Plan also had a major impact on the development of subsequent international environmental agreements. For example, Recommendation 33 of the Action Plan "recommended that governments ... as a matter of urgency ... call for an international agreement, under the auspices of the International Whaling Commission (IWC) and involving all Governments concerned, for a ten year moratorium on commercial whaling." The IWC would subsequently adopt such a ban. *See* Chapter 13, page 984. The Action Plan gave similarly detailed advice concerning negotiations of the Convention on the International Trade in Endangered Species, the Bonn Convention on Migrating Species, and the Law of the Sea Convention.

2.   THE UNITED NATIONS ENVIRONMENT PROGRAMME (UNEP)

The Action Plan also helped to shape the agenda of the United Nations Environment Programme (UNEP), which was created at Stockholm. UNEP is still the primary UN organ with general authority over environmental issues. UNEP has played a critical role in the development and negotiation of major international environmental treaties, including most recently the global POPs treaty concluded in December, 2000, and discussed further in Chapter 13. UNEP also serves as the secretariat for several treaties and is generally responsible for gathering and distributing global environmental information. UNEP is discussed further in Chapter 5, page 219.

3.   THE STOCKHOLM DECLARATION

The following excerpt from Professor Louis Sohn, the rapporteur for the Declaration's negotiations, provides a brief summary of the comments made by countries as they signed the *Stockholm Declaration*. To what extent does this history help to explain the legal, political or moral status of the *Declaration?* Is it relevant to the interpretation of the *Declaration?*

Louis B. Sohn, *The Stockholm Declaration on the Human Environment* 14 Harv.Int'l L.J. 423, 431–33 (1973)

During the debate in the plenary session, the Indian representative said that "the Declaration represented an important milestone in the history of the human race," and that it was a "starting-point in the task of making the planet a fit place for future generations." He expressed the hope that the governments of countries not represented at the Conference—the Soviet Union, Cuba, and other Communist countries (with the exception of Romania and Yugoslavia)— would also subscribe to "the principles enshrined in the text." The representative of Chile felt that "the Declaration constituted a point of departure for a process which would continue well into the future," and emphasized that it was "a provisional document that might be improved in the future." The representative of Canada (J.A. Beesley), considered the Declaration "a first step toward the development of international environmental law." In his concluding speech, Maurice Strong, head of the UNCED, stated: "What many sceptics thought would only be a rhetorical statement has become a highly significant document reflecting community of interest among nations regardless of politics, ideologies or economic status."

The decisions of the Stockholm Conference were submitted to the General Assembly of the United Nations, which referred the matter to its Second Committee. The debate was opened by Mr. Strong who, even more forcefully than at Stockholm, hailed the Declaration as a major achievement. He noted that:

> It is the first acknowledgment by the community of nations of new principles of behaviour and responsibility which must govern their relationship in the environmental era. And it provides an indispensable basis for the establishment and elaboration of new codes of international law and conduct which will be required to give effect to the principles set out in the Declaration.

The representative of Kenya supported the Declaration's 26 principles, "for they were 'common convictions' which reinforced the Principles and Purposes of the Charter of the United Nations." The representative of Yugoslavia felt that the Declaration, despite its shortcomings, "was a well-balanced document, represented a moral and political commitment and provided a basis for launching joint international action." He also expressed the hope that the Declaration "would also stimulate countries to adopt a more positive approach to environmental problems." In a similar spirit, the representative of Ghana was hopeful that "the international community would regard itself as committed by the Declaration to resolve the problems of the planet", and noted the link in the Declaration between development and environment, which was of vital importance to the third world.

The representative of China pointed out that the Declaration was "a marked improvement on the original draft and reflected some of the reasonable demands of the developing countries," but his delegation continued to have reservation with regard to some of the principles it embodied. The representative of Chile considered that the text of the Declaration "lacked ideological balance ... and should be revised," as the United Nations should not attach "special priorities to a problem like that of the human environment, which was important only to a limited number of States." The Soviet representative, while complaining about the exclusion of the German Democratic Republic from the Stockholm Conference, and though his delegation rejected various decisions of the Conference, stated that in principle his delegation was "not opposed to the current session of the General Assembly taking note of the Declaration." He emphasized, however, that this "did not imply agreement with all its provisions." The representative of South Africa announced that his delegation could not accept the Declaration as it contained an unwarranted reference to South Africa's internal policies with respect to apartheid, and claimed that the Declaration could not be described as having been unanimously adopted.

After this discussion, the Committee adopted a widely sponsored draft resolution in which the General Assembly was asked to note with satisfaction the report of the Stockholm Conference, and to draw the attention of governments and of the newly established Governing Council for Environmental Programmes to the Declaration. This draft resolution was adopted by 103 votes to none, with 12 abstentions (the Soviet bloc and South Africa). The plenary session of the General Assembly adopted this text on December 15, 1972, as Resolution 2994, by 112 votes to none, with 10 abstentions.

Without using the term, the *Stockholm Declaration* helped to lay the groundwork for the subsequent acceptance of the concept of sustainable development. The *Declaration* emphasized the importance of integrating environment and development, of reducing or eliminating pollution, and of controlling the use of renewable and non-renewable resources. The *Declaration* seemed to suggest a human right to a healthy environment in several of its principles, and it had a heavy emphasis on development planning. In this way, the *Stockholm Declaration* is a visionary statement, particularly when compared with the *Rio Declaration* that would come twenty years later.

The *Stockholm Declaration* placed the primary responsibility for environmental protection on national and local governments, but the preamble nonetheless identified three areas where international cooperation and thus international law had a legitimate role to play: resources to support developing countries in carrying out their responsibilities, cooperation among nations, and action by international organizations in the common interest.

Principles 22 and 24 also emphasized the critical role of international cooperation. Principle 22 required States to cooperate in the further development of international law regarding liability and compensation for the victims of pollution and other environmental damage caused by activities within the jurisdiction or control of such States to areas beyond their jurisdiction. Principle 22 would appear almost verbatim in the *Rio Declara-*

tion twenty years later, testimony to the slow progress in developing an international law of liability and compensation. Principle 24 encouraged States to increase their efforts to protect the environment through international cooperation, which was viewed as "essential to effectively control, prevent, reduce, and eliminate adverse environmental effects...." Principle 24 emphasizes the equality of all states and the need to involve all States in international environmental protection. This Principle endorsed implicitly the legitimate role of international cooperation in addressing environmental issues.

Perhaps the most important principles of the *Stockholm Declaration* for the future development of international environmental law are Principles 1 and 21.

Principle 1 states:

> Man has the fundamental right to freedom, equality and adequate conditions of life, in an environment of a quality that permits a life of dignity and well-being, and he bears a solemn responsibility to protect and improve the environment for present and future generations.

This falls short of declaring a clear right to a healthy environment, nor has such a right yet been recognized in international law. Nonetheless, the *Stockholm Declaration* has had an important influence on the growth of environmental human rights in national constitutions. *See* discussion of human rights and the environment in Chapter 17.

Principle 21 states:

> States have, in accordance with the Charter of the United Nations and the principles of international law, the sovereign right to exploit their own resources pursuant to their own environmental policies, and the responsibility to ensure that activities within their jurisdiction or control do not cause damage to the environment of other States or of areas beyond the limits of national jurisdiction.

Principle 21, which would be repeated almost exactly as Principle 2 of the *Rio Declaration*, was fiercely debated at Stockholm. "Principle 21" as it is known to all international environmental lawyers continues today as an important statement of customary international environmental law.

———

QUESTIONS AND DISCUSSION

1. The entire *Stockholm Declaration* is included in the *Treaty Supplement* and at the casebook website at <http//:www.wcl.american.edu/environment/IEL>. Read the *Stockholm Declaration* carefully. Pay particular attention to the precise wording used throughout the document, as these words were the product of painstaking negotiations. Does anything surprise you in the Declaration? What would be different if the Declaration were to be revised today, thirty years later?

2. Stockholm legitimized the environment as an area of international concern, highlighted the scientific and ecological reasons why international cooperation was necessary, and promoted the linkage between environment and development issues. This latter point diffused the South's concern that environmental issues would simply be a backdoor way to slow Southern development and encouraged the South to participate further in international environmental cooperation.

Stockholm also spurred significant action at the national level. In part due to the Action Plan, many countries enacted environmental legislation and created environmental institutions either in anticipation of the conference or in response to it. A 1971 survey of environmental institutions in 138 countries found national environmental agencies or ministries in only eleven countries, of which two were developing countries. Five other developing countries had ministries for the integrated management of natural resources. Less than twenty years later, a 1989 UNEP survey of 158 countries showed that 120 developing countries (and presumably all industrialized countries) had national governmental institutions with environmental authority. Although over fifty of these countries had placed environmental authority in sub-divisions of other sectoral ministries, forty-four developing countries had created national environmental agencies. UNEP, NEW DIRECTIONS IN ENVIRONMENTAL LEGISLATION AND ADMINISTRATION PARTICULARLY IN DEVELOPING COUNTRIES (1989).

3. Stockholm Principle 16 reads:

> Demographic policies, which are without prejudice to basic human rights and which are deemed appropriate by Governments concerned, should be applied in those regions where the rate of population growth or excessive population concentrations are likely to have adverse effects on the environment or development, or where low population density may prevent improvement of the human environment and impede development.

No mention is made of consumption. After reading Chapter 2 of this book, do you find this surprising? Do you think the omission of consumption was intentional? Compare this Principle to Principle 8 of the *Rio Declaration*.

4. To what extent are developing country concerns, as expressed in the 1972 UNGA Resolution, (excerpted above), reflected in the *Stockholm Declaration*? Compare, for example, the formulation of Principle 21 and paragraph 5 of the UN General Assembly Resolution.

SECTION III.   FROM STOCKHOLM TO RIO: THE EMERGENCE OF SUSTAINABLE DEVELOPMENT

Sparked by the success of Stockholm, the remainder of the 1970s saw a proliferation of international environmental treaties addressing mostly conventional or "first generation" environmental issues such as air or water pollution. A wider variety of organizations became involved in treaty-making and a number of major conventions were negotiated. For example the International Maritime Organization facilitated several conventions addressing marine pollution (*e.g.,* MARPOL 73/78; London Convention, 1972). UNEP, newly created at the Stockholm Conference, affirmed its role in facilitating treaty negotiations by holding the negotiations for the 1974 Paris Convention for the Prevention of Marine Pollution from Land–Based Sources and initiating its Regional Seas Programme, which catalyzed international cooperation in the environmental management of the Mediterranean, the Caribbean and other regional seas.

The UN Economic Commission for Europe, a regional UN body including all of Europe and the United States, negotiated the Convention on Long–Range Transboundary Air Pollution. This framework convention was aimed primarily at curbing acid rain. Subsequent protocols would be passed throughout the 1980s and 1990s that would tighten the restrictions on emissions of sulfur dioxide, nitrous oxide, and volatile organic compounds.

Wildlife conservation and habitat protection also took a front seat in the 1970s. Global conventions included the 1973 Convention on the International Trade in Endangered Species (CITES); the Convention on Wetlands of International Importance (1971), often referred to as the "Ramsar Convention" after the city in Iran where it was negotiated; the Convention for the Protection of the World Cultural and Natural Heritage (1972) negotiated under the auspices of the UN Educational, Scientific and Cultural Organization (UNESCO); and the Convention on the Conservation of Migratory Species of Wild Animals negotiated in 1979 under the auspices of a non-governmental organization, the International Union for the Conservation of Nature (IUCN). Regional wildlife treaties were also adopted during this period, including the Convention on the Conservation of European Wildlife and Natural Habitats (1979).

As the 1980s approached, the conventional issues of air pollution gave way to what Professor Lynton Caldwell has called a "second generation" of environmental issues involving more complex and global processes inextricably connected with development issues. Examples include the Vienna Convention on Protection of the Ozone Layer, and the related Montreal Protocol and subsequent amendments. Also critical during the 1980s was negotiation of the UN Convention on the Law of the Sea, which set out a broad constitution for the oceans including critical provisions on protecting the ocean environment. The Basel Convention on control of the Transboundary Movements of Hazardous Wastes and Their Disposal (1989), the Framework Convention on Climate Change (1992) and the Convention on Biological Diversity (1992) are all further examples of the complicated and global approach now occupying much of international environmental treaty-making.

All this treaty-making clearly indicated that the field of international environmental law had come of age. But the field had (and still has) an *ad hoc* quality, consisting primarily of separate conventions?some global, some regional, some negotiated under UNEP, some negotiated under other arms of the UN system. As the number and scope of environmental treaties expanded, observers hoped to be able to superimpose some order on the emerging field, by placing international environmental law in the context of some broader organizing concept—to some extent at least, they found that organizing conceptual framework in the concept of sustainable development.

———

A. *Our Common Future* and Sustainable Development

Development has been one of the defining goals of international society since the end of World War II. Economic expansion has been considered fundamental to ending poverty in the developing world and raising standards of living worldwide. For decades, international institutions, foreign aid programs from developed countries, and non-profit organizations have expended tremendous resources to develop the energy, transportation, education, and institutional infrastructure necessary to fuel economic growth in the developing world. At the same time, most developed countries sought to maximize economic growth within their own borders. And why not? Ever-expanding global and national economies mean more wealth to go around, and ideally, ever higher standards of living for everyone, from the very poor to the very rich.

As discussed in Chapter 1, however, the current pace and manner of economic expansion may be incompatible with environmental sustainability. The development goal cannot, however, be abandoned. Poverty still must be reduced and standards of living raised throughout the developing world, as well as in the poorest sections of industrialized nations. Development cannot simply be subordinated to environmental protection. Instead, development and environmental protection must be integrated, and this process of integration lies at the core of the concept of "sustainable development."

Although sustainable development had been discussed among academics since at least the 1970s, it did not receive global attention among policy makers until publication of *Our Common Future*, a 1987 report by the World Commission on Environment and Development (also known as the "Brundtland Commission" after its chairperson, Norwegian Prime Minister Gro Harlem Brundtland). Established under the auspices of the UN General Assembly, the Brundtland Commission was charged with among other things "re-examin[ing] the critical issues of environment and development, and formulat[ing] innovative, concrete, and realistic action proposals to deal with them." OUR COMMON FUTURE, op. cit., at 356–57. The Brundtland Commission's Report, commonly known as *Our Common Future*, took an integrated approach to environment and development issues. Indeed, economic development was as central to the report as were environmental issues.

The Brundtland Commission did not invent the term sustainable development, but it did popularize the term and place it squarely in the center of international policymaking. The Commission's definition of sustainable development remains the most famous definition of the term: "development that meets the needs of the present without compromising the ability of future generations to meet their own needs." Partly because of its brilliant ambiguity, the concept of sustainable development has received nearly universal acceptance among every sector of international society.

World Commission on Environment and Development, Our Common Future ["The Brundtland Report"] 43–46, 364–66 (1987)

- sustainable development is development that meets the needs of the present without compromising the ability of future generations to meet their own needs. It contains within it two key concepts:

- the concept of "needs", in particular the essential needs of the world's poor, to which overriding priority should be given; and

- the idea of limitations imposed by the state of technology and social organization on the environment's ability to meet present and future needs.

Thus the goals of economic and social development must be defined in terms of sustainability in all countries—developed or developing. . . .

Development involves a progressive transformation of economy and society. But physical sustainability cannot be secured unless development policies pay attention to such considerations as changes in access to resources and in the distribution of costs and benefits. Even the narrow notion of physical sustainability implies a concern for social equity between generations, a concern that must logically be extended to equity within each generation.

The Concept of Sustainable Development

The satisfaction of human needs and aspirations is the major objective of development. The essential needs of vast numbers of people in developing countries—for food, clothing, shelter, jobs—are not being met, and beyond their basic needs these people have legitimate aspirations for an improved quality of life. A world in which poverty and inequity are endemic will always be prone to ecological and other crises. Sustainable development requires meeting the basic needs of all and extending to all the opportunity to satisfy their aspirations for a better life. * * *

Settled agriculture, the diversion of watercourses, the extraction of minerals, the emission of heat and noxious gases into the atmosphere, commercial forests, and genetic manipulation are all examples of human intervention in natural systems during the course of development. Until recently, such interventions were small in scale and their impact limited. Today's interventions are more drastic in scale and impact, and more threatening to life-support systems both locally and globally. This need not happen. At a minimum, sustainable development must not endanger the natural systems that support life on Earth: the atmosphere, the waters, the soils, and the living beings.

Growth has set no limits in terms of population or resource use beyond which lies ecological disaster. Different limits hold for the use of energy, materials, water, and land. Many of these will manifest themselves in the form of rising costs and diminishing returns, rather than in the form of any sudden loss of a resource base. But ultimate limits there are, and sustainability requires that long before these are reached, the world must ensure equitable access to the constrained resources and reorient technological efforts to relieve the pressure.

Economic growth and development obviously involve changes in the physical ecosystem. Every ecosystem everywhere cannot be preserved intact. A forest may be depleted in one part of a watershed and extended elsewhere, which is not a bad thing if the exploitation has been planned and the effects on soil erosion rates, water regimes, and genetic losses have been taken into account. In general, renewable resources like forests and fish stocks need not be depleted provided the rate of use is within the limits of regeneration and natural growth. But most renewable resources are part of a complex and interlinked ecosystem, and maximum sustainable yield must be defined after taking into account system-wide effects of exploitation.

As for non-renewable resources, like fossil fuels and minerals, their use reduces the stock available for future generations. But this does not mean that such resources should not be used. In general the rate of depletion should take into account the criticality of that resource, the availability of technologies for minimizing depletion, and the likelihood of substitutes being available. Thus land should not be degraded beyond reasonable recovery. . . . Sustainable development requires that the rate of depletion of non-renewable resources should foreclose as few future options as possible.

Development tends to simplify ecosystems and to reduce their diversity of species. And species, once extinct, are not renewable. The loss of plant and animal species can greatly limit the options of future generations; so sustainable development requires the conservation of plant and animal species.

So-called free goods like air and water are also resources. The raw materials and energy of production processes are only partly converted to useful products. The rest comes out as wastes. Sustainable development requires that the adverse impacts on the quality of air, water, and other natural elements are minimized so as to sustain the ecosystem's overall integrity.

In essence, sustainable development is a process of change in which the exploitation of resources, the direction of investments, the orientation of technological development, and institutional change are all in harmony and enhance both current and future potential to meet human needs and aspirations. * * *

[At the end of its report, the Brundtland Commission provided the following recommendations as its formula for moving toward sustainable development. These recommendations provide further insight into the Commission's views of the elements of sustainable development.]

1.   Revive Growth

Poverty is a major source of environmental degradation which not only affects a large number of people in developing countries but also undermines the sustainable development of the entire community of nations—both developing and industrialized. Economic growth must be stimulated, particularly in developing countries, while enhancing the environmental resource base. The industrialized countries can, and must contribute to reviving world economic growth. There must be urgent international action to resolve the debt crisis; a substantial increase in the flows of development finance; and stabilization of the foreign exchange earnings of low-income commodity exporters.

2.   Change the Quality of Growth

Revived growth must be of a new kind in which sustainability, equity, social justice, and security are firmly embedded as major social goals. A safe, environmentally sound energy pathway is an indispensable component of this. Education, communication, and international co-operation can all help to achieve those goals. Development planners should take account in their reckoning of national wealth not only of standard economic indicators, but also of the state of the stock of natural resources. Better income distribution, reduced vulnerability to natural disasters and technological risks, improved health, preservation of cultural heritage–all contribute to raising the quality of that growth.

3.   Conserve and Enhance the Resource Base

Sustainability requires the conservation of environmental resources such as clean air, water, forests, and soils; maintaining genetic diversity; and using energy, water and raw materials efficiently. Improvements in the efficiency of production must be accelerated to reduce per capita consumption of natural resources and encourage a shift to non-polluting products and technologies. All countries are called upon to prevent environmental pollution by rigorously enforcing environmental regulations, promoting low waste technologies, and anticipating the impact of new products, technologies and wastes.

4. Ensure a Sustainable Level of Population

Population policies should be formulated and integrated with other economic and social development programmes–education, health care, and the expansion of the livelihood base of the poor. Increased access to family planning services is itself a form of social development that allows couples, and women in particular, the right to self-determination.

5. Reorient Technology and Manage Risks

Technology creates risk, but it offers the means to manage them. The capacity for technological innovation needs to be greatly enhanced in developing countries. The orientation of technology development in all countries must also be changed to pay greater regard to environmental factors. National and international institutional mechanisms are needed to assess potential impacts of new technologies before they are widely used. Similar arrangements are required for major interventions in natural systems, such as river diversion or forest clearance. Liability for damages from unintended consequences must be strengthened and enforced. Greater public participation and free access to relevant information should be promoted in decision-making processes touching on environment and development issues.

6. Integrate Environment and Economics in Decision–Making

Environmental and economic goals can and must be made mutually reinforcing. Sustainability requires the enforcement of wider responsibilities for the impacts of policy decisions. Those making such policy decisions must be responsible for the impact of those decisions upon the environmental resource capital of their nations. They must focus on the sources of environmental damage rather than the symptoms. The ability to anticipate and prevent environmental damage will require that the ecological dimensions of policy be considered at the same time as the economic, trade, energy, agricultural, and other dimensions. They must be considered on the same agendas and in the same national and international institutions.

7. Reform International Economic Relations

Long term sustainable growth will require far-reaching changes to produce trade, capital, and technology flows that are more equitable and better synchronized to environmental imperatives. Fundamental improvements in market access, technology transfer, and international finance are necessary to help developing countries widen their opportunities by diversifying their economic and trade bases and building their self-reliance.

8. Strengthen International Co-operation

The introduction of an environmental dimension injects an additional element of urgency and mutual self-interest, since a failure to address the interaction between resource degradation and rising poverty will spill over and become a global ecological problem. Higher priorities must be assigned to environmental monitoring, assessment, research and development, and resource management in all fields of international development. This requires a high level of commitment by all countries to the satisfactory working of multilateral institutions; to the making and observance of international rules in fields such as trade and investment; and to constructive dialogue on the many issues where national interest do not immediately coincide but require negotiation to be reconciled. It requires also recognition of the essential importance of international peace and security. New dimensions of multilateralism are essential to sustainable human progress.

The Brundtland Report remains an important milestone in the UN's efforts to address global environmental problems. The Report catalogued the many interrelated environmental problems and highlighted their relationship to the global economy. The Report also had the good sense to mix the doom and gloom (i.e. the environmental threats) with some measure of optimism, calling for a concerted effort to resolve the problems of environment and development but reassuring us that we could make a better future if we took certain steps. By linking environmental protection and poverty alleviation to economic growth, the Report also diffused much of the resistance that would otherwise have come from the world's political leaders. Economic growth, after all is widely supported as a major policy goal of most countries.

Three specific challenges follow from accepting the goal of sustainable development: first is that of scale—how to keep economic activity within the limits of the biosphere, which we discussed in Chapter 1 and which is a central concern of ecological economics. Second is the challenge of equitable distribution—how to distribute the benefits of the economic system fairly between the rich and poor, the developed and developing countries, and between the present and future generations. Third is the challenge of efficient allocation—how to use scarce resources (labor, capital, and natural resources) in the most efficient manner. The issue of allocation is a primary focus of our current economic system, but the system has less to say about distribution; it generally accepts the initial distribution of resources as a given, and leaves the resolution of other distributive issues to the political process (for example, through a progressive income tax).

———

QUESTIONS AND DISCUSSION

1.   After reading the excerpt from *Our Common Future*, do you have a better sense of what "sustainable development" means? Or is the concept still ambiguous? In an annex to their 1989 *Blueprint for a Green Economy*, David Pearce and colleagues catalogued twenty-five definitions of sustainable development offered by various scholars, activists, and politicians between 1979 and 1988. Among them:

- "Sustainable development—development that is likely to achieve lasting satisfaction of human needs and improvement of the quality of life." ROBERT ALLEN, HOW TO SAVE THE WORLD (1980)

- "The concept of sustainable economic development as applied to the Third World . . . is therefore directly concerned with increasing the material standard of living of the poor at the 'grassroots' level, . . . and only indirectly concerned with economic growth at the aggregate, commonly national, level. In general terms, the primary objective is reducing the absolute poverty of the world's poor through providing lasting and secure livelihoods that minimize resource depletion, environmental degradation, cultural disruption and social instability." Edward Barbier,*The Concept of Sustainable Economic Development*, ENVTL. CONSERVATION, vol. 14(2), at 101, 103 (1987).

- "There are many dimensions to sustainability. First, it requires the elimination of poverty and deprivation. Second, it requires the conservation and enhancement of the resources base which alone can ensure that the elimination of the poverty is permanent. Third, it requires a broadening of the concept of development so that it covers not only economic growth but also social and cultural development. Fourth, and *most* important, it requires the unification of economics and ecology in decisionmaking at all levels." Prime Minister Gro Harlem Brundtland, Sir Peter Scott Lecture, 8 Oct. 1986.

- "[The] sustainable society is one that lives within the self-perpetuating limits of its environment. That society ... is not a 'no-growth' society.... It is, rather, a society that recognizes the limits of growth ... [and] looks for alternative ways of growing." James Coomer, *The Nature of the Quest for a Sustainable Society,* in QUEST FOR A SUSTAINABLE SOCIETY (J. Coomer ed., 1979).

- "The sustainability criterion suggests that, at a minimum, future generations should be left no worse off than current generations." TOM TIETENBERG, ENVIRONMENTAL AND NATURAL RESOURCE ECONOMICS (1984).

DAVID PEARCE, ET AL, BLUEPRINT FOR A GREEN ECONOMY, Annex (1989). Yet within these disparate definitions, Pearce discerns a common theme. Sustainable development is development measured not simply in terms of rising per capita income levels, but also in improved quality of life reflected in improved health, higher educational standards, and "general social wellbeing." Sustainable development is characterized by "a substantially increased emphasis on the value of natural, built and cultural environments, greater concern with the long-term consequences of economic activity, and an emphasis on improving equity both within (intragenerational) and across (intergenerational) generations." Pearce, *op. cit.,* at 1–2.

2. Recall the discussion of scientific uncertainty at the conclusion of Chapter 1. How, if at all, did the Brundtland Commission deal with the risk of catastrophic, non-linear environmental degradation? The Brundtland Commission asserted that "[g]rowth has set no limits in terms of population or resource use beyond which lies ecological disaster. Different limits hold for the use of energy, materials, water, and land. Many of these will manifest themselves in the form of rising costs and diminishing returns, rather than in the form of any sudden loss of a resource base." OUR COMMON FUTURE, op. cit., at 44. Does this reflect a linear or non-linear view of environmental degradation? What are the consequences of this view for the environment? For the economy?

3. In *Our Common Future,* the Brundtland Commission noted that "Meeting essential needs depends in part on achieving full growth potential, and sustainable development clearly requires economic growth in places where such needs are not being met. Elsewhere, it can be consistent with economic growth, provided the content of growth reflects the broad principles of sustainability and non-exploitation of others." *Id.* Thus, the Brundtland Commission emphasized economic growth, including economic growth in industrialized countries, as a primary means for solving global environmental problems. Given what we now know about ecological limitations, do you think the Brundtland Report's reliance on economic growth is defensible? Compare this to Herman Daly's approach introduced in Chapter 1, pages 28–30, that we cannot grow our way out of environmental problems. Does the Brundtland Commission reject the concept of limits to growth and thus Herman Daly's position? Should the Brundtland Report's recommendations be seen as a politically expedient way of making sure that the serious problems they outlined were not wholly ignored? In other words, would a report that called for limits to economic growth have received the attention and political support that *Our Common Future* received? How similar are the positions taken by Herman Daly, discussed in Chapter 1, and the Brundtland Commission? If they are different, which is more realistic politically? Which is more realistic ecologically?

4. The Brundtland Commission was not as highly regarded by all countries. The South, for example, was not completely enamored with *Our Common Future* and sustainable development. Consider the following critique.

While the WCED focused on environment and development as two faces of the same coin, subsequent debates have been on the basis that environment (protection) is something related to the North and sustainable development to the South.

The latter concept has now been pushed to the point of making it the burden of the South to ensure that it pursues policies that will not compromise the ability of future generations or worsen the burden on the environment with consequence for the North whose concerns have become identified as global environment issues.

The WCED report accepted the imperatives of growth for poverty eradication and development of the South. But since "political realism" seemed to rule out North–South income distribution and changes in consumption and lifestyles in the North, the commission interpolated existing models and argued for a continued 3 percent growth in the North to enable the South to grow, and showed great faith in the ability of technology to solve the problems.

A UNESCO publication released as part of the UNCED preparatory process, *Environmentally Sustainable Development,* differed from *Our Common Future* and said:

> "Ecological constraints are real and more growth for the poor must be balanced by negative throughput growth for the rich ... Large scale transfers to the poorer countries also will be required, especially as the impact of economic stability in rich countries may depress terms of trade and lower economic activity in developing countries. Higher prices for the exports of poorer countries therefore will be required. Most importantly population stability is essential to reduce the need for growth everywhere, but especially where population growth is highest, that is, in the poor countries."

> "Politically, it is very difficult to face up to the need for income redistribution and population stability. If the concept of sustainable development becomes a verbal formula for glossing over these harsh realities then it will have been a big step backwards." * * *

> The South Centre, in a report on "Environment and Development" (1991), pointed out that "sustainable development does not mean only that the needs of the present have to be met without prejudice to the satisfaction of future needs. It means also that the needs of the North should be met in ways that do not compromise the satisfaction of the present and future needs of the South."

C. Raghavan, *The Long March From Stockholm 72 to Rio 92*, TERRA VIVA, June 3, 1992, at 8–9. How would you respond to Mr. Raghavan's critique of sustainable development?

SECTION IV. UNCED AND THE RIO DECLARATION

A. THE CONTEXT OF RIO

Approaching the Earth Summit in early 1992, the world was facing neither a World War nor a Cold War. The alliances between countries that had developed through the prism of East–West politics no longer dominated international relations.

From the beginning, the Rio Conference was envisaged as a massive conference with an overly ambitious set of objectives. Indeed, the UN General Assembly identified over twenty different objectives for the Conference. As an example of their daunting breadth and complexity, four are listed below:

1. Examine the state of the environment and changes since Stockholm;

2. Identify regional and global strategies to address major environmental issues in the socio-economic development processes of all countries within a particular time-frame;

3. Recommend national and international measures to protect and enhance the environment, taking into account the specific needs of developing countries;

4. Promote the further development of international environmental law, taking into account the *Stockholm Declaration* as well as the special needs and concerns of the developing countries, and to examine in this context "the feasibility of elaborating general rights and obligations of States, as appropriate, in the field of the environment, and taking into account relevant existing international legal instruments".

See United Nations Conference on Environment and Development, UNGA Res. No. 44/228 (December 22, 1989). Ambassador Tommy Thong–Bee Koh, Chairman of the Preparatory Committee and Main Committee of UNCED, would later describe this resolution as the "Koran," a sacred text that guided the negotiators throughout their preparation for UNCED. Ambassador Koh would prove to be a critical personality in gaining final agreements on the Rio documents. Negotiations of the *Rio Declaration, Agenda 21,* and the *Forestry Principles* were under his direct oversight. The Biodiversity Convention and the Climate Change Conventions, which would also be opened for signature at UNCED, were negotiated under separate intergovernmental negotiating committees.

B.   At the Earth Summit

As the former N.Y. Times environment reporter, Phillip Shabecoff, wrote:

In terms of sheer magnitude, there had never been anything quite like the United Nations Conference on Environment and Development. With 115 heads of state and government attending, it was, as one participant quipped, "the mother of all summits." In all, 178 nations sent some seven thousand delegates to Rio. The meeting was covered by nearly nine thousand journalists, making it, according to the UN Department of Public Information, the most heavily reported single event in history. Over 1,400 nongovernmental organizations (NGOs) were represented at the conference, and virtually all of them participated in the Global Forum, the "parallel" NGO forum assembled in Flamengo Park on the ocean front in downtown Rio. An estimated twenty thousand environmentalists and representatives of women's, youth, indigenous peoples, business, labor, religious, and other independent groups attended the forum and many of them traveled to the official summit to speak, lobby, and brief reporters.

P. SHABECOFF, A NEW NAME FOR PEACE: INTERNATIONAL ENVIRONMENTALISM, SUSTAINABLE DEVELOPMENT AND DEMOCRACY 160 (1996)

All of the hooplah could not hide the serious divisions: between the rich and poor, the North and South, industrialized and developing countries. Although different perspectives and priorities had permeated all international environmental policymaking prior to UNCED, they had never been so explicitly on display or so central to decisions as they were at Rio. With the Cold War over, North–South issues would drive the agenda, freed for the first time from the distorting shadow of superpower conflict. These differences appeared at the very beginning with the basic question of whether UNCED was an environment or a development conference.

Environment v. Development. The South was concerned with promoting development and ensuring that any protection of the environment did not come at the expense of their right to develop. The South wanted to talk about access to fresh water and food security; some wanted to discuss desertification, an issue particularly acute in Africa. The South sought to clarify Northern responsibility for global environmental issues. They wanted to talk about funding for Southern cooperation on global problems that they had not caused. They wanted to talk about debt relief and open access to Northern markets.

The South wanted to talk about curbing consumption; the North about population growth. The South about *intra*generational equity; the North about *inter*generational equity and the need to protect future generations through sustainable development. The South was concerned that the term sustainable development might only apply to them, as the North was already developed.

The North brought an environmental agenda; they shaped the agenda to the extent that it covered climate change, forest conservation and biodiversity, all seen as being driven mainly by Northern interests in the global environment. The North realized they needed full cooperation from the South to address these global issues, but the North did not necessarily want to accept binding obligations as the price of gaining Southern cooperation. The North was also suffering from economic worries and did not feel generous; they brought little new money to the Earth Summit.

Funding. Perhaps the most controversial issues at Rio revolved around who was going to pay for the global effort to protect the environment and achieve sustainable development. The South had two related concerns, the amount of money and the mechanisms for delivering it. The South sought "new and additional funding" and lots of it—$70 billion to be precise. This was the estimated amount of new development assistance required for implementing *Agenda 21,* and the South wanted it added to the current $55 billion in official development assistance, bringing the total to $125 billion annually to achieve sustainable development. TerraVIVA, June 5, 1992, at 4. The G–77 nations (of which there were 128 at Rio) ultimately accepted a compromise where they called on the developed nations to reaffirm their commitment to meet the 0.7% of GNP in development assistance "as early as possible and not later than the year 2000 ... as a first step in the direction to providing adequate, new and additional funds." The North which had already agreed to a 0.7 percent level, did not want to commit to a specific date for reaching it. Only Denmark provided assistance at the

0.7% level at the time of Rio, and they sided strongly with the South in demanding a year 2000 target date. The South also wanted some initial pledges to be made at UNCED. The South was particularly upset because a $25 billion aid package had been put together for Russia very quickly right before UNCED. Why then could the industrialized countries not have brought a meaningful package to aid developing countries? The US offered $250 million, with most aimed at reforestation. As a step towards reaching consensus the G–77 suggested postponing the decision on the ultimate amount of new money until a pledging conference could be organized at the UN later in the year.

The second major issue related to the mechanism for providing funds to the South. The G–77 originally proposed a special and specific fund for implementing *Agenda 21*, separate from any existing mechanism. They rejected the North's view that the World Bank should monopolize the environmental aid flows through the Global Environmental Facility (GEF). *See* Chapter 21 (discussing the GEF). In mid-Conference, China indicated that they, and by implication others in the G–77, would drop their insistence on a separate mechanism in favor of a "restructured" GEF, as long as the criteria for restructuring were clear and led to a more equitable role for the South. Eventually both the biodiversity and climate change conventions would establish general criteria for their respective financial mechanisms and in the meantime adopted the GEF as their interim funding mechanism.

The U.S. Position. If the North–South divide was the grand drama of Rio, the subplot was surely the near isolation of the United States, as it lagged behind the rest of the industrialized countries on virtually every major issue. On May 29, just days before the Conference opened, for example, the United States announced it would not sign the Biodiversity Convention, even though it had provisionally adopted the draft convention at the end of the negotiating session only a week before. William Reilly, the EPA Administrator, spoke on the opening day to what was described as at best "tepid applause." He emphasized the need to conserve the world's forests, and reiterated the U.S. offer of $150 million of aid to protect forests in developing countries. This was labeled as "greenwash" by the South, which accused the United States of trying to deflect attention away from its failure to sign the Biodiversity Convention. Reilly explained that the United States would not sign unless the Convention clearly endorsed the GEF as the primary financial mechanism. The United States adamantly opposed any new financial mechanism specific to the convention.

The South viewed the U.S. support for forest conservation as a cynical effort to shift the obligation from the North's need to reduce greenhouse gas emissions to the South's responsibility to conserve forests as carbon sinks. Malaysia's Ambassador Ranji Sathia, in response to the U.S. proposal to provide $150 million for reforestation, stated "The amounts of money do not impress us. They are just trying to divert attention from their failings elsewhere for example, in the watering down of the climate change convention and their refusal to sign the biodiversity treaty." Despite intense and public international pressure, the United States ultimately refused to sign the Biodiversity Convention at UNCED. In response, other countries, for example India, threatened not to sign the Climate Convention in what was viewed as retaliation against the United States.

By the time President Bush appeared at the Summit, the United States had taken several steps to make itself seem more reasonable. For example, the United States would eventually put a total of $250 million in additional financing on the table. U.S. delegates also surprised observers by re-affirming a commitment to meeting the 0.7% level of foreign assistance by the year 2000. The U.S. spokesperson also said they did not oppose language in Principle 8 of the *Rio Declaration* calling for curbs on consumption.

Forests. The U.S. push for a global forests treaty was ultimately rejected by strong opposition from the South led by Malaysia. Eventually the governments would agree to negotiate a set of non-binding forest principles, which were mostly negotiated at the conference itself. The most difficult points of the forest principles had to do with the external debt issues, undervaluation of developing country forest products and the need for greater access to Northern markets. The South had an advantage in the forestry principles negotiations because the largest remaining forests are in the South (except for Siberia). One Southeast Asian representative to UNCED stated: "If the North persists in the view that the world's forests are a global inheritance, valued for their function as carbon 'sinks', then developing countries should be compensated so they can sustainably manage their forests while being allowed to develop." L. Makabenta, *Forests become the critical issue in Agenda XXI debates,* TERRAVIVA, June 10, 1992, at 10.

The South was concerned with the emphasis on forests as carbon sinks and reservoirs, instead of recognizing forests as the home of local people. They resented the concept that forests should be covered by international rules, when so many other resources located within national borders were not. As Anil Agarwal, a member of the Indian delegation to UNCED stated: "Its fascinating to see desert countries like Saudi Arabia and Kuwait, and Australia—one of the worst carbon dioxide polluters per capita—agree to consider forests as carbon sinks." A statement from Southern NGOs posed the following question: "If forest management is of global consequence, so is the management of the world's oil resources. Are we going to have a global oil convention for sustainable global production, management, and conservation of the world's oil resources?" *See* V. Menezes, *South outraged by North's forest convention ideology,* EARTH SUMMIT TIMES, June 11, 1992, at 4.

With this kind of serious disagreement among the delegates, it is easy to see how Ambassador Koh's leadership as head of the negotiating committee was critical. The following personal account of his efforts during the PrepCom meetings and during the last minute negotiations in the Main Committee before the actual heads of state arrived on June 12 reveals some of the drama and gamesmanship that can surround international negotiations.

Ambassador Tommy Koh, *The Earth Summit's Negotiating Process: Some Reflections on the Art and Science of Negotiating,* in N. ROBINSON, ED., AGENDA 21: EARTH'S ACTION PLAN (1993) p. vi et seq.

Size of Preparatory committee

In order to prepare for the Earth Summit, the UN decided to set up a Preparatory Committee. Because of the great interest in the Conference, the

Committee was enormous in size. It consisted of all the member states of the UN as well as non-member states such as Switzerland. *The size of the Committee made negotiation difficult. One of my challenges was how to gradually reduce the size of negotiating groups.* I will return to this later.

The PrepCom, as it came to be known, was mandated by our Koran to hold an organizational session in New York, from the 5th to the 16th of March 1990, and four substantive sessions in Nairobi, Geneva, Geneva and New York in 1991 and 1992. You may wonder why the four substantive sessions were held in three different cities on 3 continents. Was this an example of the UN diplomats awarding themselves junkets at the expense of their tax payers? It wasn't. It was an example of the kind of compromises that has to be struck in order to achieve consensus. The New York-based diplomats, who were the most politicized, wanted all the sessions to be held in New York. The Geneva-based diplomats argued that they should be held in Geneva, the home of the UNCED Secretariat. The supporters of UNEP, which is based in Nairobi, argued that they should be held in Nairobi.

The Organizational Session

The organizational session of the PrepCom was two weeks long. It was held in New York from the 5th to the 16th of March 1990. What were the objectives of the organizational session? It had five objectives. *First*, to elect its chairman. *Second*, to decide on the size of the Bureau and the distribution of the number agreed upon among the five regional groups. *Third*, to decide how many working groups to establish and which regional groups would provide candidates for their chairmanship. *Fourth*, to adopt a provisional agenda for the Earth Summit. Fifth, to adopt its rules of procedure.

Any reasonable person would think that you would need only one or two days, not two weeks, to agree on five such seemingly simple tasks. This was not the case and the two weeks were barely enough to complete our tasks. Of the five tasks, the only simple one was electing me. All the other candidates wisely withdrew when they realized the pain and suffering which the chairman would have to endure for the next two years and three months! The first thing I did on assuming the chair was to propose that we should refrain from polluting the air in our meeting rooms by prohibiting smoking at all our meetings. Before the nicotine addicts could rally their forces, I asked if there was any objection. Seeing none, I banged the gavel and pronounced that there was a consensus in favor of my proposal. The former Secretary–General of the UN, Javier Perez de Cuellar, watched in surprise because no UN chairman had succeeded in defeating the tobacco lobby at the UN before.

Any Objections?

The speed with which I used my gavel would give rise later to some unhappiness. As a result, I would count to five before banging my gavel. On one occasion, the chairman of the Group of 77, a wonderful man from Pakistan, Ambassador Jamshid Marker, remarked that my counting of 1,2,3,4,5 became faster and faster, the longer the meeting lasted.

Size of Bureau

I failed, however, to persuade my colleagues to accept a relatively small Bureau. For a Bureau to be efficient, it has to be representative but small. Many delegations wanted to be in the Bureau because they thought that it might become a negotiating forum. *A Bureau of 42 is too big to be useful. I will tell you later of the steps I took to invent a smaller but more efficient group to help me manage the negotiating process.* * * *

To return to my story. On the last day of the organizational session, 16th March 1990, there was still no agreement on the agenda. I was determined to get one. I instructed the Secretariat to arrange for interpreters to be available so that I could go through the night until 6.00 am the next morning. The Secretariat did not believe me and I had no interpreters after midnight. I had to persuade the non-Anglophones to work in English. This was by no means an easy task, especially with the Francophone group.

Maintain The Pressure

My strategy was to maintain the pressure on the delegates until they agreed to compromise. By 4.30 am, the delegates were so exhausted that they asked me to draft a compromise. I called for a short recess and, with the help of about a dozen colleagues representing the various interest groups, succeeded in crafting a compromise. I got my agenda. The meeting adjourned at 6.00 am on St. Patrick's Day. I felt exhausted but vindicated in my determination not to adjourn the meeting until I secured an agreement. If I had adjourned the meeting, the pressure would have eased and delegations would again dig in their heels. I also wanted to make the point to the Secretariat that when I set a deadline I meant to keep it. The Secretariat never doubted my resolve again. At all subsequent sessions of the PrepCom and the Main Committee, I had teams of interpreters ready to serve the meeting through the night and into the morning of the next day on the final day of each session. On two subsequent occasions I went through the night until 4.30 am on the last day of the 4th substantive session in New York and 6.00 am on the last day of the Main Committee at the Earth Summit in Rio. * * *

The Delegation of Power

The work of the PrepCom was carried out in four principal forums: the plenary of the PrepCom and the three working groups. The agenda of the plenary was long and complex. It included the difficult questions of financing sustainable development and the transfer of technology from developed to developing countries. It also included such questions as the relationship between the environment, on the one hand, and, poverty, population, the international economic order, and human settlements, on the other.

A good chairman must avoid the temptation of keeping everything under his wings. He must learn to delegate. He must also choose able men and women to delegate responsibility to. When it becomes clear that a delegate is unable to deliver, a chairman must do the very unpleasant job of replacing him with someone else. * * *

The Elephantine Bureau

The bureau of a committee or conference is supposed to act as its steering committee. The bureau of the PrepCom and the Earth Summit was unable to play this role effectively because of its size: 42 members. It was almost as difficult to reach a consensus among the 42 members of the bureau as among the 150–plus members of the PrepCom and the 170–plus members of the Summit. I had to invent another body to act as the steering committee.

De Facto Steering Committee

I convened twice weekly meetings of a group consisting of the chairmen of the five regional groups; the chairman of the Group of 77 (representing the developing countries); the chairman of the EC; the chairman of the Nordic Group; the chairman of CANZ (representing Canada, Australia and New Zealand); and the three countries which do not belong to any interest group: China, Japan and the USA. This group of 12 countries and the collegium functioned as the steering committee of the PrepCom and Summit. It proved to be a very effective body. During critical periods of the PrepCom and Summit, I would convene daily meetings of this group. In order to pacify the members of the bureau, who quite rightly felt bypassed, I would convene meetings of the bureau from time to time.

The Importance of Timing

In negotiation, timing is very important. A chairman who acts prematurely risks being rebuffed. A chairman who acts too slowly loses the opportunity to clinch a deal. I have observed that multilateral negotiations often pass through three phases: confrontation, crisis and resolution. A good chairman must not be unnerved by the phase of confrontation. He must wait for the period of crisis which often follows confrontation. It is at this maximum hour of danger and opportunity that he must strike and bring about a resolution.

Let me illustrate these general observations with the following concrete example. Working Group III, on law and institutions, was established at the beginning of the second substantive session in Geneva. It elected Dr. Bedrich Moldan of Czechoslovakia as its chairman. One of the items on its agenda was the drafting of the Rio Declaration on the Environment and Development, popularly referred to as the Earth Charter. At the beginning of the fourth substantive session, Dr. Moldan offered a compromise draft consisting of ten principles and three pre-requisites. He moved too soon. Also, his draft was viewed, rightly or wrongly, by the developing countries as favoring the viewpoint of the developed countries. Because of this, the developing countries refused to continue to negotiate under his chairmanship. Instead, an informal contact group was established under the co-chairmanship of Mr. Mukul Sanwal of India and Mr. Ole Holthe of Norway.

Going From 150 to 16

On the morning of 31st March 1992, three days before the end of that session, Mr. Sanwal and Mr. Holthe asked for permission to speak to our daily meeting at 9.00 am. They reported that they had gone as far as they could and were unable to make any further progress. They requested me to take over the negotiations. The meeting supported their request. I then convened a meeting of the de factor steering committee. I said I would be prepared to chair the negotiation provided they agreed to establish a small, closed, representative group of 16, eight to represent the North and eight to represent the South. The meeting agreed. The North was represented by USA; Portugal, Netherlands and Germany (EC); Australia (CANZ); Norway (alternating with Sweden); Japan and Russia. The South was represented by Pakistan, India, Iran, Brazil, Mexico, Nigeria, Tanzania and China.

Preparing A Negotiating Text

I made another request. I requested Mr. Sanwal and Mr. Holthe to produce a negotiating text by 6.30 pm on the 1st of April, 1992. They did so and the group of 16 began its work at 8.00 pm of the same evening. It adjourned before midnight and continued the next morning. A clean text, containing 27 principles, was agreed upon, ad referendum, at 6.15 pm on the 2nd of April, 1992. This text would eventually be adopted by the Earth Summit as the Rio Declaration Environment and Development.

The Negotiating Process in Rio

Apart from the clean text of the Rio Declaration, the other documents submitted to Rio contained 350 bracketed or disputed language. We had only one week in the Main Committee to remove these brackets and to find acceptable language. I was not at all sure that the job could be done.

Procedural Decisions

I persuaded the Committee to adopt a number of procedural decisions. *First*, that the negotiation would focus entirely on the bracketed language. I ruled out of order any delegate who tried to re-open discussion on unbracketed or agreed language. I also rebuffed the attempts by several delegations to insert new brackets on the ground that they had been inadvertently omitted by the Secretariat.

Fortunately, we had brought along the authoritative documents of the Prep-Com. Upon verification, we found no merit in any requests. *Second*, I refused to allow any delegation to make a new proposal if it met with a single objection. The reason is that any new proposal must advance the prospect of achieving consensus. *Third*, I asked the Committee to allow me to establish nine open-ended negotiating groups on the understanding that not more than three would meet concurrently. *Fourth*, I persuaded the Committee to work from Monday to Saturday and to meet morning, afternoon and evening. *Fifth*, I imposed a strict time-limit on the length of statements. *Sixth*, whenever the negotiation got stuck on a point, I would set up an ad hoc-open-ended negotiating group to deal with it and appoint an able colleague to chair the group. In this way, I was able to keep the negotiation moving at a steady pace.

A Long Day's Night

The final meeting of the Main Committee began at 9.00 pm on the 10th of June 1992. It continued through the night and ended at 6.00 am the next morning. I did take one short break. At 4.00 am, after eight hours in the chair, I was desperate to go to the toilet. I also sensed that there was a lot of tension in the room. I announced that we would recess the meeting for five minutes in order to enable me to make a discharge of a non-toxic waste. I promised to do it in an environmentally safe and sound manner. The delegates broke into laughter and the meeting resumed in a better mood. All bracketed language, excepting those relating to finance and forest, were resolved. Those two issues were referred to ministerial-level negotiations chaired by Brazil and Germany respectively. The Brazilians had consulted me on who to appoint to chair the difficult negotiation on forest. I recommended the German Minister for the Environment, Dr. Klaus Topfer. Consensus was achieved on those two issues on the 12th of June. The Summit was therefore able to adopt, on the 14th of June, the Rio Declaration, Agenda 21 and the Statement of Principles on Forests, by consensus. Thus ended the largest conference the UN has ever held.

Ultimately the Rio earth summit reached agreement on the following:

- the Rio Declaration on the Environment and Development;
- two binding conventions, the Biodiversity Convention and the Climate Change Convention;
- *Agenda 21,* an 800–page "blueprint" for sustainable development in the 21st century
- a set of non-binding forestry principles;
- agreements to develop subsequent legal instruments on the Convention on Desertification; a Convention on Straddling Fish Stocks; and on Land–Based Sources of Marine Pollution;

- an agreement to create the Commission on Sustainable Development to monitor implementation of the Rio Agreements and Agenda 21.

These are all discussed in this or subsequent chapters of this book.

QUESTIONS AND DISCUSSION

1. Comparisons between the Stockholm and Rio Conferences are inevitable. Both are part of a continual process of international diplomacy to improve global cooperation on environment and development issues. Rio came in a different era, however. The Cold War was over. Globalization of the economy, of the media and even of the environmental movement was more a reality in 1992 than in 1972. Perhaps most importantly, there was a far greater sense of urgency about environmental issues at Rio than at Stockholm. Moreover, the basic legitimacy of addressing the environment at the international level was no longer at issue, in large part because of the success of the Stockholm Conference. As a result, participation by government leaders, by the press and by NGOs was far greater at Rio. All of this led both to the "circus atmosphere" and the sense of expectation that surrounded Rio. On the eve of the Rio Conference, Lester Brown of the WorldWatch Institute compared the conferences in this way:

> At Stockholm, attendance totaled a few thousand. Here there may be close to 10,000 official delegates, perhaps 15,000 NGO representatives, and 6,000 or more journalists trying to cover the activities of both.

> Two national political leaders attended the Stockholm conference: Prime Minister Olaf Palme of Sweden, the host, and Indira Gandhi of India. At Rio, some 130 heads of state are expected to be present—one of the largest such gatherings on records.

> The issues also differ. At Stockholm, the focus was on industrial pollution of air and water. Although there were, even then, a few transboundary pollution issues, most of the concerns were locally focused.

> At Rio, the focus is much more on global issues: the need to stabilize climate and to protect the Earth's remaining plant and animal species. The issues at this conference are vastly more complex than those faced 20 years ago.

> There is another stark contrast. At Stockholm, the U.S. was playing a leadership role. Today, much to the dismay and even embarrassment of most Americans, the U.S. is no longer capable of leading. Indeed, it is widely viewed as a reactionary government whose positions have greatly weakened the prospects for a meaningful conference. * * *

> There is another sharp contrast with the Stockholm gathering. Here in Rio the poor countries have something that the rich countries now desperately need, namely, cooperation. Acting alone, no country, however wealthy, can stabilize the climate within its borders. No country can unilaterally protect the stratospheric ozone layer over its territory. If a single Third World country continues to use large quantities of CFCs, it will eventually deplete the stratospheric ozone layer over the entire Earth.

> At Rio, the two great issues of our time—environment and poverty—are converging. In poor countries, where the overwhelming concern is survival to the next harvest, it is difficult to elicit support for protecting the ozone layer or stabilizing climate. The bottom line may well be the realization that we can no longer separate the future habitability of the planet from the current international distribution of wealth.

> When we look back on this conference from the mid–21st century, we may well see it as a historical hinge point, an event that officially marked the end of the East–West ideological conflict and the shift to the new era, one where ecological issues predominate. In this new age, North–South ecological stresses, often entwined with economic issues, such as trade, investment, and aid, will dominate international affairs.

Lester Brown, *Time Is Running Out on the Planet,* EARTH SUMMIT TIMES, June 2, 1992, at 13. Looking at the impact of Rio, is it clear whether Lester Brown is right about the historical significance of Rio? Has Rio lived up to its expectations?

2. It is natural to speak of international affairs in terms of nations and treaty text, but the decisions are made by people. In this respect, the Tommy Koh excerpt provides insight into the role one person can play in shaping events of global importance (much the same could also be said of Maurice Strong, who oversaw both Stockholm *and* Rio). In reading Koh's account of the negotiations, identify the specific tricks and strategems he relied on to bring negotiators with very different positions together. How different do you think the outcome of UNCED would have been if a less talented diplomat had been chair?

3. One major difference between the Rio Conference and the Stockholm Conference was the greater involvement of civil society in the preparation for Rio. Hundreds of organizations participated in the alternative Eco–Forum. Diverse voices were heard in support of environmentally sustainable development. Civil society organizations had obtained over nine million signatures on an *Earth Pledge:*

> Recognizing that people's actions towards nature and each other are the source of growing damage to the environment and to resources needed to meet human needs and ensure survival, I pledge to act to the best of my ability to help make the Earth a secure and hospitable home for present and future generations.

————

C.   THE RIO DECLARATION

Initially, organizers hoped that a binding Earth Charter would emerge from UNCED based loosely on a recommendation of the Brundtland Commission. As negotiations progressed however, it became clear that an Earth Charter was not realistic. In place of an Earth Charter, the parties crafted a non-binding, but nonetheless important instrument, the *Rio Declaration on Environment and Development,* 31 I.L.M. 874 (1992).

The *Rio Declaration* may be understood as a bargain between the affluent North concerned with global environmental problems and the poor South concerned primarily with development questions. As you read it, you will see the elements of compromise between North and South in virtually every principle. In general, the compromise went like this: the North agreed to acknowledge it holds most of the responsibility for global environmental problems and thus that it should take more direct actions for protecting the environment; the North agreed to provide "new and additional" funding to assist the South in addressing global environmental issues; the North agreed to take the first steps to address environmental issues (for example by reducing greenhouse gases); and in return, the South agreed to cooperate in protecting the global environment.

In short, the North recognized that acting alone, it is unable to prevent climate change, conserve the planet's biological diversity, or otherwise

resolve global environmental threats. The North needed the full cooperation of the South. Beginning to understand the power they wield in these
negotiations, the South linked cooperation to its own priorities for development. In this way, the South potentially gained new leverage for influencing the international development agenda and the future development of
international environmental law, leverage it does not enjoy in other fields
of international law. Although the North did not put as much money on the
table at Rio as had been expected, the South still appears to have gained
the upper hand in the dialogue: the *Rio Declaration* seems to place
development issues above the environment, despite Rio being billed as an
environmental conference

The *Rio Declaration* can thus be read in several ways. First, it is a
political document reflecting the "grand bargain" between the North and
South. As Ileana Porras has noted:

> As an international statement of general principles and obligations, which was
> negotiated in detail by a large and representative number of delegations, it
> must be taken to reflect—to the extent any international instrument can do
> so—the current consensus of values and priorities in environment and develop-
> ment.

I. Porras, *The Rio Declaration: a New Basis for International Cooperation,*
in P. Sand, Ed., Greening International Law, p. 21 (1994).

The second way to read the *Rio Declaration* is from a legal perspective.
The *Rio Declaration* includes many emerging principles in the field of
environmental law. By confirming that a consensus exists among States on
the importance of these principles, the *Rio Declaration* may significantly
further the development of international environmental law, as well as the
possibility of incorporating specific principles in subsequent treaties, and
even the possibility of formal codification of an international binding
covenant on environment and development in the future. In this respect,
several of the individual principles (for example, Principles 2, 10, and 15) in
the Rio Declaration are particularly important. These and other principles
are discussed in more detail in Chapter 7.

Rio Declaration on Environment and Development

Preamble

The United Nations Conference on Environment and Development,

Having met at Rio de Janeiro from 3 to 14 June 1992,

Reaffirming the Declaration of the United Nations Conference on the Human
Environment, adopted at Stockholm on 16 June 1972, and seeking to build
upon it,

With the goal of establishing a new and equitable global partnership through
the creation of new levels of cooperation among States, key sectors of societies
and people,

Working towards international agreements which respect the interests of all to
protect the integrity of the global environmental and developmental system,

Recognizing the integral and interdependent nature of the Earth, our home,

Proclaims that:

Principle 1

Human beings are at the centre of concerns for sustainable development. They are entitled to a healthy and productive life in harmony with nature.

Principle 2

States have, in accordance with the Charter of the United Nations and the principles of international law, the sovereign right to exploit their own resources pursuant to their own environmental and developmental policies, and the responsibility to ensure that activities within their jurisdiction or control do not cause damage to the environment of other States or of areas beyond the limits of national jurisdiction.

Principle 3

The right to development must be fulfilled so as to equitably meet developmental and environmental needs of present and future generations.

Principle 4

In order to achieve sustainable development, environmental protection shall constitute an integral part of the development process and cannot be considered in isolation from it.

Principle 5

All States and all people shall cooperate in the essential task of eradicating poverty as an indispensable requirement for sustainable development, in order to decrease the disparities in standards of living and better meet the needs of the majority of the people of the world.

Principle 6

The special situation and needs of developing countries, particularly the least developed and those most environmentally vulnerable, shall be given special priority. International actions in the field of environment and development should also address the interests and needs of all countries.

Principle 7

States shall cooperate in a spirit of global partnership to conserve, protect and restore the health and integrity of the Earth's ecosystem. In view of the different contributions to global environmental degradation, States have common but differentiated responsibilities. The developed countries acknowledge the responsibility that they bear in the international pursuit of sustainable development in view of the pressures their societies place on the global environment and of the technologies and financial resources they command.

Principle 8

To achieve sustainable development and a higher quality of life for all people, States should reduce and eliminate unsustainable patterns of production and consumption and promote appropriate demographic policies.

Principle 9

States should cooperate to strengthen endogenous capacity-building for sustainable development by improving scientific understanding through exchanges of scientific and technological knowledge, and by enhancing the development, adaptation, diffusion and transfer of technologies, including new and innovative technologies.

Principle 10

Environmental issues are best handled with the participation of all concerned citizens, at the relevant level. At the national level, each individual shall have appropriate access to information concerning the environment that is held by public authorities, including information on hazardous materials and activities in their communities, and the opportunity to participate in decision-making processes. States shall facilitate and encourage public awareness and participation by making information widely available. Effective access to judicial and administrative proceedings, including redress and remedy, shall be provided.

Principle 11

States shall enact effective environmental legislation. Environmental standards, management objectives and priorities should reflect the environmental and developmental context to which they apply. Standards applied by some countries may be inappropriate and of unwarranted economic and social cost to other countries, in particular developing countries.

Principle 12

States should cooperate to promote a supportive and open international economic system that would lead to economic growth and sustainable development in all countries, to better address the problems of environmental degradation. Trade policy measures for environmental purposes should not constitute a means of arbitrary or unjustifiable discrimination or a disguised restriction on international trade. Unilateral actions to deal with environmental challenges outside the jurisdiction of the importing country should be avoided. Environmental measures addressing transboundary or global environmental problems should, as far as possible, be based on an international consensus.

Principle 13

States shall develop national law regarding liability and compensation for the victims of pollution and other environmental damage. States shall also cooperate in an expeditious and more determined manner to develop further international law regarding liability and compensation for adverse effects of environmental damage caused by activities within their jurisdiction or control to areas beyond their jurisdiction.

Principle 14

States should effectively cooperate to discourage or prevent the relocation and transfer to other States of any activities and substances that cause severe environmental degradation or are found to be harmful to human health.

Principle 15

In order to protect the environment, the precautionary approach shall be widely applied by States according to their capabilities. Where there are threats of serious or irreversible damage, lack of full scientific certainty shall not be used as a reason for postponing cost-effective measures to prevent environmental degradation.

Principle 16

National authorities should endeavour to promote the internalization of environmental costs and the use of economic instruments, taking into account the approach that the polluter should, in principle, bear the cost of pollution, with due regard to the public interest and without distorting international trade and investment.

Principle 17

Environmental impact assessment, as a national instrument, shall be undertaken for proposed activities that are likely to have a significant adverse impact on the environment and are subject to a decision of a competent national authority.

Principle 18

States shall immediately notify other States of any natural disasters or other emergencies that are likely to produce sudden harmful effects on the environment of those States. Every effort shall be made by the international community to help States so afflicted.

Principle 19

States shall provide prior and timely notification and relevant information to potentially affected States on activities that may have a significant adverse transboundary environmental effect and shall consult with those States at an early stage and in good faith.

Principle 20

Women have a vital role in environmental management and development. Their full participation is therefore essential to achieve sustainable development.

Principle 21

The creativity, ideals and courage of the youth of the world should be mobilized to forge a global partnership in order to achieve sustainable development and ensure a better future for all.

Principle 22

Indigenous people and their communities, and other local communities, have a vital role in environmental management and development because of their knowledge and traditional practices. States should recognize and duly support their identity, culture and interests and enable their effective participation in the achievement of sustainable development.

Principle 23

The environment and natural resources of people under oppression, domination and occupation shall be protected.

Principle 24

Warfare is inherently destructive of sustainable development. States shall therefore respect international law providing protection for the environment in times of armed conflict and cooperate in its further development, as necessary.

Principle 25

Peace, development and environmental protection are interdependent and indivisible.

Principle 26

States shall resolve all their environmental disputes peacefully and by appropriate means in accordance with the Charter of the United Nations.

Principle 27

States and people shall cooperate in good faith and in a spirit of partnership in the fulfillment of the principles embodies in this Declaration and in the further development of international law in the field of sustainable development.

QUESTIONS AND DISCUSSION

1. *Working with the Rio Declaration*. Re-read the *Rio Declaration* to answer the following questions:

- What specific rights or interests did the public receive in the *Rio Declaration*?

- How does the *Rio Declaration* address environmental impact assessment, and how does it differ from your understanding of domestic approaches to EIA?

- What principle reflects the polluter pays principle and how does it relate to your understand of ecological economics discussed in Chapter 3?;

- What are the specific elements of the precautionary principle as reflected in the *Rio Declaration*? To what decisions does the precautionary principle under the *Rio Declaration* apply?

2. How are the North–South issues reflected and/or resolved in the *Rio Declaration*? Can you tell how compromises were struck in many of the principles? An example is Principle 8's balanced approach to consumption (a problem primarily evident in the industrialized countries) and population (a problem primarily evident in developing countries). What do you think competing negotiating texts (referred to as bracketed text) might have been in earlier versions of Principles 1, 3, 7, and 11?

3. How does the *Rio Declaration* add to the definition or understanding of the concept of sustainable development? What elements of sustainable development appear to be highlighted explicitly in principles such as Principles 4 and 8? What elements are implicit in other principles? Do you agree with the following discussion of Principle 8 provided by Professor Ileana Porras:

> With its reference to patterns of production and consumption, Principle 8 addresses one of the most problematic inadequacies of the term sustainable development: because the term sustainable development refers to development as opposed to "growth" or "economy", it appears to apply exclusively to developing countries. Industrialized countries rarely refer to their activities as development activities, and, therefore, seem to be outside the scope of the term. The Rio Declaration provides a reminder that the intra-generational equity goal of sustainable development can only be achieved if industrialized countries cease to benefit, to the detriment of developing countries, from their ongoing unsustainable practices. With Principle 8, developed countries become full partners in the quest for sustainable development.

Ileana Porras, *The Rio Declaration: A New Basis for International Cooperation*, in PHILIPPE SANDS, GREENING INTERNATIONAL LAW 25 (1994). In this context, consider as well the discussion of the *Rio Declaration* and the right to development in Chapter 7, pages 383–389.

4. Both the *Stockholm* and *Rio Declarations* are examples of soft law instruments. What is the legal force of the *Rio Declaration*? To what extent can non-State actors assist in making the *Rio Declaration* more binding? What principles of the *Rio Declaration* seem more binding than others?

5. Compare the *Rio Declaration* to the 1972 UN General Assembly Resolution on Development and Environment introduced at the beginning of the chapter and the Stockholm Declaration. In what respects are they similar? How do they differ? Can you find examples of how principles of international environmental law develop over time?

D. *Agenda 21*

Agenda 21 is a remarkable document in many ways. With 40 chapters and over 800 pages, it is a comprehensive and detailed blueprint for the future implementation of sustainable development. It was intended to launch an ambitious "global partnership for sustainable development." *Agenda 21's* relatively brief preamble explains the structure and aspirations of the document:

Agenda 21, A/Conf.151/26 (1991)

PREAMBLE

1.1   Humanity stands at a defining moment in its history. We are confronted with a perpetuation of disparities between and within nations, a worsening of poverty, hunger, ill health and illiteracy, and the continuing deterioration of the ecosystems on which we depend for our well-being. However, integration of environment and development concerns, and greater attention to them will lead to the fulfilment of basic needs, improved living standards for all, better protected and managed ecosystems and a safer, more prosperous future. No nation can achieve this on its own; but together we can—in a global partnership for sustainable development.

1.2   This global partnership must build on the premises of General Assembly resolution 44/228 of 22 December 1989, which was adopted when the nations of the world called for the United Nations Conference on Environment and Development, and on the acceptance of the need to take a balanced and integrated approach to environment and development questions.

1.3   Agenda 21 addresses the pressing problems of today and also aims at preparing the world for the challenges of the next century. It reflects a global consensus and political commitment at the highest level on development is first and foremost the responsibility of Governments. National strategies, plans, policies and processes are crucial in achieving this. International cooperation should support and supplement such national efforts. In this context, the United Nations system has a key role to play. Other international, regional and sub-regional organizations are also called upon to contribute to this effort. The broadest public participation and the active involvement of the non-governmental organizations and other groups should also be encouraged.

1.4   The developmental and environmental objectives of Agenda 21 will require a substantial flow of new and additional financial resources to developing countries in order to cover the incremental costs for the actions they have to undertake to deal with global environmental problems and to accelerate sustainable development. Financial resources are also required for strengthening of Agenda 21. An indicative order-of-magnitude assessment will need to be examined and refined by the relevant implementing agencies and organizations.

1.5   In the implementation of the relevant program areas identified in Agenda 21, special attention should be given to the particular circumstances facing the economies in transition. It must also be recognized that these countries are facing unprecedented challenges in transforming their economies, in some cases in the midst of considerable social and political tension.

1.6   The program areas that constitute Agenda 21 are described in terms of the basis for action, objectives, activities and means of implementation. Agenda 21 is dynamic program. It will be carried out by the various actors according to the different situations, capacities and priorities of countries and regions in full respect of all the principles contained in the Rio Declaration on Environment and Development. It could evolve over time in the light of changing needs and circumstances. This process marks the beginning of a new global partnership for sustainable development.

In addition to the preamble, *Agenda 21* is divided into four major sections: (1) social and economic dimensions, (2) conservation and management of resources, (3) strengthening the role of major groups, and (4) the means of implementation. Each section is divided into a number of chapters, and each chapter addresses the basis of action, the objectives, activities, and means for implementation. Specific chapters of *Agenda 21* are discussed in subsequent chapters. The full text of *Agenda 21* can be found on the casebook website.

QUESTIONS AND DISCUSSION

1. *Agenda 21* provides a framework for evaluating the progress of different levels of government in achieving the integration of environment and development. *Agenda 21* is replete with specific calls for national and local efforts to achieve sustainable development. Chapter 28, for example, is entirely focused on strengthening the role and capacities of local authorities, particularly cities, to achieve sustainable development. It calls on all localities to develop by 1996 a consensus through consultation with the public about how to implement a "Local Agenda 21" for the community. Some states such as Virginia and Indiana have been particularly active in using *Agenda 21* as a policy framework. *Agenda 21* also called for the UN system to create opportunities for greater international cooperation among subnational and local governments. In 1994, the UN convened an international forum of local governments to discuss the environment, and the U.S. Agency for International Development launched a "sustainable cities" program to spread local lessons of sustainability.

2. *Agenda 21* is also interesting for what it does not include. It is silent, for example, regarding measures to control the environmental impacts of transnational corporations. And it provides much more coverage of traditional environmental problems than issues related to sustainable development, such as the integration of environmental concerns with poverty alleviation, social equity, or human rights. At the last minute, the delegates also rejected the South's push to include specific estimates of the cost of implementing each chapter. The North feared that such specific cost estimates would fuel demands for increased development assistance.

3. Ultimately the measure of *Agenda 21's* success is its implementation, and in this regard, *Agenda 21* has been disappointing. Many countries are not meeting the obligations established under various treaties, nor have they seriously implemented *Agenda 21's* blueprint of action. Economic growth in many parts of the world, including the United States, has in fact led to broad deterioration in most indicators of environmental health. Thus, we are further from the goal of sustainable development today than we were at the time of Rio. Writing in anticipation of Rio +5 in 1997, Professor John Dernbach concluded that "[d]espite all the promises and lofty rhetoric, the Earth Summit has had little discernible effect on U.S. law and policy."

> Five years after Rio, the United States still has no coherent or comprehensive commitment to sustainable development. There has been no concerted effort to progressively integrate governmental decisionmaking on environmental, social, and economic issues; no substantial improvement in our existing legal framework to better foster sustainable development; no implementation of satellite systems of social and environmental accounting; and no governmental use of sustainable development indicators. No agency or individual in the U.S. government even has government-wide responsibility for coordinating or implementing sustainable development policy. Although President Clinton appointed a blue ribbon panel [the President's council on sustainable development (PCSD)] that produced a sustainable development report with recommendations, there was little effort or interest in implementing those recommendations. * * *

> While the recommendations of the PCSD could provide part of the basis for a national strategy, the lack of governmental action to implement its recommendations reduces it to a discussion of some critical issues that the country must face if it is to move toward sustainability.... In early 1996, the PCSD issued its final report, Sustainable America: A New Consensus for Prosperity, Opportunity, and a Healthy Environment for the Future. The report, ... recommended 154 specific actions in 38 policy areas, including reform of pollution control laws, natural resources stewardship, education, international policy, and communities. More than 450 experts participated in the eight task forces that helped develop these recommendations.

> The PCSD operates outside of normal governmental decisionmaking processes, however, and it has no legal authority to make or implement decisions within the federal government. Regardless of the thoughtfulness of its proposals, they are only recommendations that must be implemented by others. Its report is not a plan of action, and few of its recommendations have even been implemented. Moreover, the report contains no recommendations concerning the major new issues raised in Rio.

John Dernbach, *U.S. Adherence to its Agenda 21 Commitments: A Five–Year Review*, 27 Envtl. L. Rep. 10504 (1997)

Section V.   The Post–Rio Era

By some measures, the post-Rio era has continued the momentum created by UNCED. Since UNCED, the Climate Change Convention, the Biodiversity Convention, the Law of the Sea Convention and the Convention to Combat Desertification have all entered into force. New agreements have also been negotiated on transboundary watercourses, biosafety, prior informed consent for chemical manufacturing, the global reduction of certain persistent organic chemicals, clear targets and timetables for industrialized countries to reduce greenhouse gases, and management of straddling fish stocks. Participation also increased in many of the global environmental agreements that now host more than 100 countries being parties.

Table 1. Parties to Global Environmental Agreements

Treaty	No. of Parties	Opened for Signature	Entered into Force
Convention on Biodiversity	176	1992	1993
CITES	152	1973	1987
Basel Convention	134	1989	1992
Montreal Protocol	172	1985	1988
Climate Change Convention	181	1992	1994
Desertification Convention	159	1994	1996
Ramsar Convention	123	1971	1975
UNESCO Heritage Convention	164	1972	1975
Law of the Sea Convention	132	1982	1994

A. SUSTAINABLE DEVELOPMENT AFTER RIO

More than anything perhaps, Rio marked the formal acceptance of sustainable development as the goal of a modern economy. Sustainable Development was the organizing conceptual framework for the entire North–South dialogue and is integrated throughout the various Rio texts. The *Rio Declaration* itself focused substantially on defining what was meant, or at least implied, by sustainable development. Thus, we can see both substantive aspects to sustainable development in Principles 3–8, and procedural aspects in Principles 10, and 15–18. Thus, according to the Rio Declaration, sustainable development involves: intergenerational equity (Principle 3); the integration of environmental protection into the development process (Principle 4); intragenerational equity and the alleviation of poverty (Principle 5); paying attention to countries with special development and environment needs (Principle 6); the reduction of unsustainable production and consumption (Principle 8); reductions in population (Principle 8); and effective environmental legislation (Principle 11). Sustainable development also reflects a commitment to certain procedural standards, including broad public participation and access to information and judicial review (Principle 10); use of the precautionary approach where there are threats of serious or irreversible environmental damage (Principle 15), the internalization of costs (Principle 16); environmental impact assessment (Principle 17), notification and consultation with affected States (Principles 18 and 19), and the involvement of all groups of people, including those frequently excluded from development processes such as women, the youth and indigenous peoples (Principles 20–22).

The concept of sustainable development was also discussed in major UN summits held annually in each of the three succeeding years after the

1992 UNCED. These summits included the 1993 Copenhagen Summit on Social Development, the 1994 Cairo Summit on Population, and the 1995 Beijing Conference on Women. Each of these summits sparked considerable interest and organized activities leading up to and during the meetings. They also each resulted in statements of principles and action plans, which help to define how we should integrate other issues into the definition of sustainable development. In this regard, they explicitly built on the framework of Rio.

Although Rio and the ensuing UN summits have added substantially to the understanding of sustainable development, it remains a broad and undefined concept. The following excerpt provides a useful approach to understanding the different approaches to defining sustainable development.

National Research Council Our Common Journey: A Transition Toward Sustainability 21–25 (1999)

Within this general [sustainable development] framework, an extraordinarily diverse set of groups and institutions have taken the concept of sustainable development and projected upon it their own hopes and goals. There have been extensive reviews of these diverse concepts and definitions. From these reviews, four types of key differences emerge. While sharing a common concern for the fate of the earth, proponents of sustainable development differ in their emphases on (1) what is to be sustained, (2) what is to be developed, (3) the types of links that should hold between the entities to be sustained and the entities to be developed, and (4) the extent of the future envisioned.

What Is To Be Sustained

The emphases on what is to be sustained fall within three major areas: nature, life support systems, and community. The most common emphases concern *life support systems*, where the life to be supported first is human. Subsumed within this group are emphases on the classic *natural resources*—which, while found in nature, are particularly useful for people. Classified as either renewable or nonrenewable, flow or stock, these resources have preoccupied many generations seeking to exploit, conserve or preserve them. In the last quarter of a century, the concept of natural resources has expanded, from a focus on primary products and production inputs to include the values of aesthetics, recreation, and the absorption and cleansing of pollution and waste. This extended view of natural resources becomes popularly associated with *environment* and the many features are defined by ecologists as *ecosystem services*. A recent study catalogued and valued 17 ecosystem services, ranging from atmospheric gas regulation to cultural opportunities.

A less anthropocentric view of life and values is found in the emphases on sustaining *nature* itself for its own intrinsic value. The earth's assemblages of life forms, whether described as *biodiversity* in general, or as species or ecosystems in particular, are to be sustained not only for their utilitarian service to humans, but also because of humanity's moral obligations. These obligations are characterized as "stewardship"—acknowledging the primacy of humans—or as the proper response to a form of "natural rights" in which earth and its other living things have equal claims to existence and sustenance. Additionally, not only are biological species seen as endangered, but cultural species are as well. Thus, the concept of *communities* to be sustained covers distinctive *cultures*, particular *groups* of people, and specific *places*.

WHAT IS TO BE SUSTAINED:	FOR HOW LONG? 25 years "Now and in the future" Forever	WHAT IS TO BE DEVELOPED:
NATURE Earth Biodiversity Ecosystems		**PEOPLE** Child Survival Life Expectancy Education Equity Equal Opportunity
LIFE SUPPORT Ecosystem Services Resources Environment	**LINKED BY** *Only* *Mostly* *But* *And* *Or*	**ECONOMY** Wealth Productive Sectors Consumption
COMMUNITY Cultures Groups Places		**SOCIETY** Institutions Social Capital States Regions

Figure 4-1

What Is To Be Developed

The emphases on what is to be developed also fall within three major areas: people, economy, and society. More often than not, when development is discussed, the emphasis is on the *economy*, with its *productive sectors* providing both employment and desired *consumption*, and *wealth* providing the incentives and the means for investment as well as funds for environmental maintenance and restoration. Yet another form of development stressed is human development. Such *people*-centered development focuses on the "quantity" of life as seen in the *survival of children* or increased *life expectancy*, and on the quality of life in terms of *education, equity,* and *equal* opportunity. Finally, some discussions of what is to be developed adopt a broader conception of *society,* emphasizing the well being and security of national *states, regions* and *institutions* and more recently, the valued social ties and community organizations known as *social capital.*

The Links Between

The concept of sustainable development links what is to be sustained and what is to be developed. The emphases differ according to whether the links are stated or implied. For example, the U.S. President's Council on Sustainable Development believes in "mutually reinforcing goals of economic growth, environmental protection, and social equity." It sees these goals as equal in importance and linked together. And is the operative conjunction between what is to be sustained, namely, the environment, and what is to be developed namely the economy and society.

But this is just one of many ways of envisioning the links between what is to be sustained and what is to be developed. Some views, while paying homage to sustainable development, focus almost entirely on just one of the two desiderata, the sustaining or the developing (thereby appearing to suggest "sustain *only*" or "develop *mostly*"). Others, while clearly emphasizing one or the other, subject this choice to a conditional constraint. For example, a Brundtland Commission member, noted "Sustainability is the nascent doctrine that economic growth and development must take place, and be maintained over time, *[but]* within the limits set by ecology in the broadest sense." Other views tend to leave to some set of public officials or decision makers with determining the exact nature of and tradeoffs between what is to be sustained or what is to be developed.

For How Long?

It is widely thought that sustainable development is meaningful only if it is intergenerational. Thus, there is general acceptance of the loosely stated time horizon of the World Conference on Environment and Development as *now and in the future.* The time horizons considered in specific contexts for figure sustainable development, however, range from a single generation of 25 years or so, to several generations, as in the Intergovernmental Panel on Climate Change (IPCC) assessments that extend until 2100, to an unstated, but implicit, *forever.* Each of these time periods presents very different prospects and obstacles for sustainable development. Over the space of a single generation, almost any development appears sustainable. Over forever, almost none do, as even the smallest growth in numbers, resource use, or economy extended indefinitely creates situations that seem surely unsustainable. Over the century encompassed by many energy-environment assessments (e.g., those of the IPCC), the large scale and the long-term dimensions of the future are both remote and uncertain. The sustainability of development in any usefully concrete sense is even more so.

Despite the various fault lines of disagreement over its precise definition, the concept of sustainable development has received nearly universal acceptance (at least rhetorically) among every sector of international society. Sustainable development has been incorporated in international declarations and treaties on the environment and, increasingly, in trade and investment treaties. It is a guiding concept for rethinking of development institutions such as the World Bank and the regional development banks. It is appearing in corporate charters and business strategies, and plans of action for governments at every level—from international institutions to city councils. It is being taught in schools, preached in churches, and discussed in civic organizations throughout the world. Ultimately, agreement over the precise definition of the term may be less important than the debate that is sparked by its brilliant ambiguity. Consider the next excerpt's description of the importance of sustainable development as a "contestable concept."

ANDREW DOBSON, FAIRNESS AND FUTURITY 23–30 (1999)

Outside the field of environmental economics, most of those now using the term "sustainable development" are content to adopt one or other of the two definitions in common use. These are the so-called "Brundtland definition" ("development which meets the needs of the present without compromising the ability of future generations to meet their own needs") and the *"Caring for the Earth* definition" ("improving the quality of life while living within the carrying capacity of supporting ecosystems"). These are generally deemed sufficient to express the concept; argument can then proceed as to what must be done to achieve it in practice.

This acquiescence in the concept of sustainable development makes many commentators and practitioners deeply uneasy, however. Such unease is particularly common among policy-makers and practitioners coming across the term for the first time. Partly because of the breadth of its endorsement—which suggests that it might have no meaning at all—there is a widespread desire to clarify more precisely the "meaning" of the concept.

This comes from two sources. First, there is a *technocratic* view that sustainable development can only be made "operational" in policy terms if a single and precise meaning can be agreed upon. For a start, the two common definitions are not the only ones available: of the "gallery" of definitions quoted by the Pearce report as long ago as 1989 (and many more have been added since [*see* page 184]), is it always clear which one we are talking about? Are they all the same? And what exactly do these vague definitions mean anyway? What is "development", what are "needs", what is it that must be "sustained", how is "quality of life" measured? Thus Harvey Brooks: "For the concept of sustainability ... to be operationally useful it must be more than just an expression of social values or political preferences disguised in scientific language. Ideally it should be defined so that one could specify a set of measurable criteria such that individuals and groups with widely differing values, political preferences or assumptions about human nature could agree whether the criteria are being met in a concrete development program."

Second, there is a *political* concern among some environmentalists that the lack of clarity of the definitions allows *anything* to be claimed as "sustainable" or as "promoting sustainable development". For example, does it allow economic growth or not? Does it mean a global redistribution of resources or not? At present the vagueness of the definitions, it is argued, allows business and "development" interests (and their government supporters) to claim they are in favour of sustainable development when actually they are the perpetrators of *un*sustainability. Sharachandra Lélé's conclusion is typical: "SD is in real danger of becoming a cliché ... a fashionable phrase that everyone pays homage to but nobody cares to define ... better articulation of the terms, concepts, analytical methods and policy-making principles ... is necessary to avoid either being dismissed as another development fad or co-opted by forces opposed to changes in the status quo."

Concepts, Conceptions, and Contestation

This search for a unitary and precise meaning of sustainable development is misguided. It rests on a mistaken view of the nature and function of political concepts. The crucial recognition here is that, like other political terms (democracy, liberty, social justice, and so on), sustainable development is a "contestable concept".

Contestable concepts are complex and normative, and they have two levels of "meaning". The first level is unitary but vague: it can often be expressed in a short definition (for example, "government of the people, by the people, for the people"). Often there will be a number of such definitions available; but neither this nor their vagueness makes such concepts meaningless or useless. At the first level contestable concepts are defined by a number of "core ideas". These are general, but substantive and non-redundant. Democracy, liberty, and social justice, for example, all have readily understood "first level" meanings. We know what the subject is when we use these terms, there are no other terms expressing the same set of core ideas, and even people holding widely different interpretations of them can agree on the evaluation of (necessarily extreme) situations in which democracy, liberty, and social justice are *not* present.

The interesting feature of contestable concepts comes in the second level of meaning. This is where the contest occurs: political argument over how the concept should be interpreted in practice. Is representative democracy sufficient, or should it be direct? Are positive freedoms necessary for liberty, or only negative ones? Is social justice about outcomes or only opportunity? Such questions reflect alternative *conceptions* of the concept: differing ways in which it can be understood. For common political concepts, the battle is neither over the first level of meaning nor indeed whether one accepts the normative goal. Almost everyone is in favour of democracy, liberty, and social justice; the debate is over alternative conceptions of what they mean, at the second level.

Sustainable development is a contestable concept of this kind. Its first level meaning is now given: for better or worse (and as a result of an interesting political evolution), the core ideas are fixed and cannot now be changed through rational argument. Rather, attention needs to focus on the second level. Here there *is* a battle for the "meaning" of sustainable development. But there is no point in trying to secure a universal "agreement" on a unitary meaning for the term. This will never happen, for those who use it have different interests and political values. Such agreement is only possible at the first level—and it now exists, coalesced around the Brundtland and *Caring for the Earth* definitions. At the second, there is contestation. This shouldn't be perceived as a remediable lack of precision over what sustainable development "means": rather, such contestation *constitutes* the political struggle over the direction of social and economic development. That is, disagreements over the "meaning of sustainable development" are not semantic disputations but *are* the substantive political arguments with which the term is concerned.

Core Ideas and the Political Agenda

Analysis of the discourse of sustainable development reveals six "core ideas" represented by the term. These are:

(1) Environment-economy integration: ensuring that economic development and environmental protection are integrated in planning and implementation.

(2) Futurity: an explicit concern about the impact of current activity on future generations.

(3) Environmental protection: a commitment to reducing pollution and environmental degradation and to the more efficient use of resources.

(4) Equity: a commitment to meeting at least the basic needs of the poor of the present generation (as well as equity between generations).

(5) Quality of life: a recognition that human well being is constituted by more than just income growth.

(6) Participation: the recognition that sustainable development requires the political involvement of all groups or "stakeholders" in society.

Three features of these core ideas are apparent. The first is that while individually most of them have been expressed and supported before, they have not previously been put together into a single phrase or concept. Each represents a substantive value or objective. In purely conceptual terms, therefore—at the first level—sustainable development is clearly neither meaningless not redundant.

The second feature is that sustainable development is evidently *not* the path of development which has been followed by the global economy, or by most individual nations, over the past fifty years; even less over the last twenty. Environmental concerns have not been integrated into economic planning and policy; the impact of current activity on future generations has been *assumed* to be benign, not explicitly considered. Argument could no doubt be had over the extent to which environmental protection, equity, participation and quality of life (*per se*, as opposed to income growth) have been serious goals of global or individual countries' policy; the first three have certainly not been generally achieved. But in any case the important point is that in signing *Agenda 21* the majority of countries have rhetorically accepted that sustainable development *does* represent a new trajectory for development.

And it is this that gives the term its political significance. The test is not whether the endorsement of sustainable development in international documents like *Agenda 21* and in national policies has actually (and already) changed the trajectory of development. Of course it hasn't (though some significant shifts are certainly apparent, such as international recognition of the importance of biodiversity, European carbon dioxide reduction policies and, in Britain, changes in transport policy). The question is whether the new discourse has changed the nature and salience of political activity and debate on these issues; and here there can be little question that it has.

In nearly every industrialized country, the period since the Brundtland Report, and then again since the Earth Summit, has seen much greater levels of activity and debate in the environmental policy field than before. In Britain, for example, we have had a White Paper, a national Sustainable Development Strategy, three accompanying strategies on climate change, forestry, and biodiversity, a forthcoming Environmental Bill setting up a new Environment Agency, a much-publicized Royal Commission report on transport and the environment, and so on. For local government, environmental management and now "Local Agenda 21" strategies have provided a major new field of initiative. The "greening of industry", while not as extensive as hoped for in some quarters, has seen a steady development of environmental management systems and practice. Meanwhile much of the most vibrant extra-institutional political activity has occurred over environmental issues, notably roadbuilding and animal welfare.

The relationship between this activity and the discourse of sustainable development has been three-fold. First, there can be little question that governments in democracies have felt obliged to do *something* in support of their public commitments. Once the policy arena has been opened up, particularly given the commitment to participation embedded within the sustainable development rhetoric, it has then been difficult to resist the further evolution of policy, as pressure groups and experts criticize initial proposals and demand stronger initiatives. The requirement to "do something" has infected local government and large businesses as well.

Second, government commitments to sustainable development have provided environmental pressure groups and the media with a valuable weapon, namely the apparent inconsistency between government rhetoric and action. The government's commitment to sustainable development—not least, in international agreements—is consistently used as a stick with which to beat the inadequacies of actual policy. This makes NGO and media pressure considerably more effective.

Third, the sustainable development discourse has set off a process of *institutional learning*. Throughout international agencies and national governments—and to a lesser extent, the business sector and other sectors—the sustainable development discourse is pushing institutions to reappraise their policies and policy-making processes. Sustainable development has provided new conceptual models for the relationship between environment and economy, and these have begun to shift the way policy-making is approached. This process is evident in all kinds of government institutions, from small district councils in England through national statutory bodies such as the Countryside Commission to international agencies like the World Bank. Of course, it has not shifted understanding or practice *enough:* a key problem (as we shall see below) is that the sustainable development "model" has had little to say about the deeper cultural presuppositions of the institutions themselves. But it would be difficult to deny that the new discourse—to put it at its weakest—has raised awareness, and placed environmental issues and the integration of environmental and economic concerns on the table of policy debate where they were not before.

It is of course the "not enough" claim which made by the ultra-greens, who see sustainable development as a way for government institutions and corporations to *pretend* to act on the environment while not in fact doing so. Ultra-greens claim, not just that sustainable development has been ineffectual, but that it is positively dangerous, since it ties the environmental movement to the interests of Northern governments and multinational corporations. Yet governments would not even be pretending if it had not been for the capacity of the sustainable development discourse to generate—and then to bind them to—new commitments. Given the long period from the mid–1970s to the 1980s in which the environment was off the political agenda, and the continued development of environmental policy now even after the initial media attention has gone, this should surely be counted as progress. The creation of a "discourse coalition" of otherwise disparate interests using the same vocabulary is a crucial component in the development of an environmental politics that has any hope of being successful. It is precisely the ability of sustainable development—a concept both substantive and challenging—to gather endorsements from states and large corporations as well as from the environmental movement, which is what makes it so important.

Indeed, the extraordinary thing about sustainable development in many ways is that it has acquired such widespread endorsement. For the third feature of the core ideas is that they are broad in scope. Sustainable development is not, for example, simply a commitment to protect the environment; though this is without doubt the central idea, it is by no means the only one. Other political concepts encompassing as broad a range of core ideas as this rarely gain such universal acceptance; such acceptance tends to be limited to rather more basic political ideas (such as democracy or liberty). Indeed, concepts as broad as sustainable development are generally ideological in character—such as, for example, socialism or conservatism.

———

QUESTIONS AND DISCUSSION

1. Do you agree with Dobson's assessment of the value of sustainable development? What counter arguments would you offer?

2. Part of the difficulty in pinpointing sustainable development's definition may stem from the fact that it touches on so many different disciplines, each with their own vocabulary and perspective. Sustainable development has an ethical dimension, an economic dimension, a governance dimension and a legal dimension. The impact of the concept of sustainable development on international law is somewhat less clear but no doubt still considerable. Consider the following passage from Professors Alan Boyle and David Freestone:

> The international community's strong commitment to the concept of sustainable development has had and will continue to have a considerable evolutionary impact on existing international environmental law and on the development of new law. Principle 27 of the Rio Declaration calls specifically for further development of international law "in the field of sustainable development", and at the request of the Commission on Sustainable Development, UNEP initiated a study in 1995 of the "the concept, requirements and implications of sustainable development and international law". Sustainable development also forms an important element in the elaboration of global environmental responsibility by the Rio instruments. Its most potentially revolutionary aspect, however, is that it makes a state's management of its own domestic environment and resources a matter of international concern for the first time in a systematic way. In both the global and the domestic context it may have acquired the character of an *erga omnes* principle. However, not all aspects of the law relating to sustainable development are necessarily relevant to the protection of the environment, nor do all aspects of international environmental law concern sustainable development. Animal rights, and the conservation of polar bears, pandas, and other "charismatic mega-fauna" may fall into this latter category, while transboundary environmental disputes also do not necessarily raise questions concerning sustainable development. * * *

> However, there remain fundamental uncertainties about the nature of sustainable development, which the Rio Declaration does not resolve, but which have a direct bearing on the question whether sustainable development is in any sense a legal principle. If it is a principle to be interpreted, applied, and achieved primarily at national level, by individual governments, there may be only a limited role for international definition and oversight. If, however, there is to be international accountability for achieving sustainability, whether globally or nationally, then it must be clear what the criteria for measuring this standard are, and what the evidential burden is in assessing the performance of individual states. Although the Commission on Sustainable Development does have a role in assessing national reports on implementation of Agenda 21, and in defining future policy, at present it is not the job of the Commission to answer the question whether any particular policy or development is or is not sustainable, although as its work evolves it may become clearer what are the parameters of the principle and the criteria for measuring it. Thus, although it is possible to identify the main elements of the concept, it is far from certain what

their specific normative implications are, or, indeed, how they relate to each other, or to human rights law and international economic law.

ALAN BOYLE & DAVID FREESTONE, INTERNATIONAL LAW AND SUSTAINABLE DEVELOPMENT: PAST ACHIEVEMENTS AND FUTURE CHALLENGES, 6–7 (1999). The legal dimension of sustainable development is discussed further in Chapter 6, page 338 (Judge Weeramantry's separate opinion filed in the Gabcikovo v. Nagymaros case), and again in Chapter 7's discussion of legal principles.

3. Does the concept of sustainable development help us in understanding how to divide the burdens of environmental protection between North and South, i.e. between developed and developing nations? What role should law play in ensuring that the goals of sustainable development are advanced, and what roles may be played by other social institutions and actors? By corporations? By individuals?

4. Has the discussion of sustainable development provided you a more useful means to frame the challenges facing the international community, or do you find it too vague a concept for practical use?

B.   RIO + . . . AND COUNTING

In June of 1997, the UN General Assembly held a Special Session, nicknamed "Rio +5," to assess how far we had come in achieving sustainable development in the five years since UNCED. The Special Session confirmed that most ecological indicators show little or no improvement since Rio.

> Five Years after UNCED, the state of the global environment has continued to deteriorate, as noted in the Global Environment Outlook of the United Nations Environment Programme (UNEP), and significant environmental problems remain deeply embedded in the socio-economic fabric of countries in all regions. Some progress has been made in terms of institutional development, international consensus-building, public participation and private sector actions and, as a result, a number of countries have succeeded in curbing pollution and slowing the rate of resource degradation. Overall, however, trends are worsening. Many polluting emissions, notably of toxic substances, greenhouse gases and waste volumes are continuing to increase although in some industrialized countries emissions are decreasing. Marginal progress has been made in addressing unsustainable production and consumption patterns. Insufficient progress has also been identified in the field of environmentally sound management and adequate control of adequate transboundary movements of hazardous and radioactive wastes. Many countries undergoing rapid economic growth and urbanization are also experiencing increasing levels of air and water pollution, with accumulating impacts on human health. Acid rain and transboundary air pollution, once considered a problem only in the industrialized countries, are increasingly becoming a problem in many developing regions. In many poorer regions of the world, persistent poverty is contributing to accelerated degradation of natural resources and desertification has spread. In countries seriously affected by drought and or desertification, especially those in Africa, their agricultural productivity, among other things, is uncertain and continues to decline, thereby hampering their efforts to achieve sustainable development. Inadequate and unsafe water supplies are affecting an increasing number of people worldwide, aggravating problems of ill health and food insecurity among the poor. Conditions in natural habitats and fragile ecosystems, including mountain ecosystems, are still deteriorating in all regions of the world, result-

ing in diminishing biological diversity. At the global level, renewable resources, in particular freshwater, forests, topsoil and marine fish stocks, continue to be used at rates beyond their viable rates of regeneration; without improved management, this situation is clearly unsustainable

While there has been progress in material and energy efficiency, particularly with reference to non-renewable resources, overall trends remain unsustainable. As a result, increasing levels of pollution threaten to exceed the capacity of the global environment to absorb them, increasing the potential obstacles to economic and social development in developing countries.

Programme for the Further Implementation of Agenda 21, paras. 9–10 *adopted by the Special Session of the UN General Assembly, June 23–27, 1997.*

In the face of these poor results, the delegates reconfirmed their commitment to the goals set forth in *Agenda 21* and the *Rio Declaration*, and called for greater leadership in the future. The United States, in particular, has been widely criticized for its lack of leadership since UNCED, particularly with respect to our approach to negotiations under the Climate Change Convention and our failure to ratify the Biodiversity Convention.

The UN's 1997 conclusions were affirmed again in UNEP's *Global Environmental Outlook 2000 Report* identified the following list of "fundamental global issues that threaten long-term sustainability" and which must be urgently addressed:

- The use of renewable resources—land, forests, fresh water, coastal areas, fisheries and urban air—is beyond their natural regeneration capacity and therefore is unsustainable.

- Greenhouse gases are still being emitted at levels higher than the stabilization target internationally agreed under the United Nations Framework Convention on Climate Change.

- Natural areas and the biodiversity they contain are diminishing due to the expansion of agricultural land and human settlements.

- The increasing, pervasive use and spread of chemicals to fuel economic development is causing major health risks, environmental contamination, and disposal problems.

- Global developments in the energy sector are unsustainable.

- Rapid, unplanned urbanization, particularly in coastal areas, is putting major stress on adjacent ecosystems.

- The complex and often little understood interactions among global biogeochemical cycles are leading to widespread acidification, climate variability, changes in the hydrological cycles, and the loss of biodiversity, biomass, and bioproductivity.

UNEP, GLOBAL ENVIRONMENT OUTLOOK 2000: UNEP'S MILLENIUM REPORT ON THE ENVIRONMENT 338 (Earthscan Publications Ltd.: London, 1999).

––––––

QUESTIONS AND DISCUSSION

1. Should the success of international environmental treaties or conferences be judged by the current state of the environment or by some guess of what the current state would be in the absence of the treaty or conference? While it is true that the environment has continued to deteriorate since Rio, do you think that the situation would be worse if there had not been an Earth Summit? How might you gather the evidence to support your position?

2. We are now approaching the 30th anniversary of the Stockholm Conference. How far do you think Barbara Ward and Rene Dubos—the authors of *Only One Earth*—would think we have come in fashioning a new "global loyalty" in the twenty-five years since they wrote that passage on page 173. Are there signs of hope that we are making progress toward their vision? Is Ward and Dubos' global loyalty reflected in the concept of Rio's "global partnership" for sustainable development? Are their visions still appropriate for the 21st century?

3. Review the January 17, 1972 UN General Assembly Resolution on Development and Environment, which is excerpted on page ___. To what extent have developing countries' perspectives changed since the time of Stockholm?

4. As this edition of the textbook goes to print, governments are preparing for the World Summit on Sustainable Development. Planned for 2002, the "Rio+10" summit is intended to evaluate progress in implementing the Rio promises and to re-confirm the global commitment to sustainable development. The United Nations is expecting over 100 heads of state and 50,000 other participants to attend the WSSD, making it of a similar scale to the original Rio conference. The agenda has yet be set, with proposals ranging from a focus on poverty alleviation to freshwater conservation to global governance.

5. To a large extent, the rest of this book could be called Rio + . . . And Counting. . . As you read on, consider whether the physical and legal developments we describe are moving us toward or further from the goal of sustainable development.

Suggested Further Reading

Lynton Caldwell, INTERNATIONAL ENVIRONMENTAL POLICY: FROM THE TWENTIETH TO THE TWENTY-FIRST CENTURY (1996)

A comprehensive history on the formation and implementation of international environmental policy.

Samuel Hays, CONSERVATION AND THE GOSPEL OF EFFICIENCY (1959)

A history of the American conservation movement from 1890–1920.

Philip Shabecoff, A FIERCE GREEN FIRE: THE AMERICAN ENVIRONMENTAL MOVEMENT (1993)

An engaging history of the U.S. environmental movement.

Philip Shabecoff, NEW NAME FOR PEACE: INTERNATIONAL ENVIRONMENTALISM, SUSTAINABLE DEVELOPMENT, AND DEMOCRACY (1996)

A history of the international environmental movement.

Mostafa Tolba & Iwona Rummel Bulska, GLOBAL ENVIRONMENTAL DIPLOMACY (1998)

CHAPTER FIVE

INTERNATIONAL INSTITUTIONS AND NON–STATE ACTORS

No single institution controls the management of global environmental issues. The UN Environment Programme (UNEP) is the principal international environmental organization, but it has limited authority and even more limited resources. The UN Development Programme (UNDP), much larger than UNEP, is charged with alleviating poverty and promoting economic development, a mandate that, as we have seen throughout the book, is intertwined with environmental protection. The UN Commission on Sustainable Development (CSD) was created twenty years after UNEP, in part to coordinate and integrate environmental issues with economic and other issues addressed within the UN system. Literally scores of other official, semi-official, and private organizations and agencies also work in areas relating to global environmental protection. These agencies sometimes work together, sometimes in competition, and often with little coordination.

The first section of this chapter presents an overview of the role of UNEP, UNDP and the CSD in international environmental law and policy. Other important public institutions are addressed in succeeding chapters of the book. Thus, for example, the World Trade Organization is discussed in Chapter 15 on International Trade and the World Bank and the Global Environmental Facility are discussed in Chapter 20 on International Finance. The European Union is discussed in Chapter 15 and, in greater detail in a self-contained chapter, on the casebook website. All of these institutions, as well as other public international organizations active in environmental protection, are on the casebook website.

The second section of the chapter addresses the role of conferences of the parties, secretariats and other permanent and semi-permanent bodies created by individual treaties. Reflecting the increasing calls by major political figures, Section three of the chapter presents several major proposals for reforming existing institutions or creating new ones to improve protection of the global environment. The final section addresses the role of non-state actors—nongovernmental organizations (NGOs) and corporations—in the creation and implementation of international environmental law.

International institutions play a particularly important role in international environmental law and policy, in large part because adjudicative institutions have not proven influential. While judicial bodies may establish generally applicable rules of State behavior, very few international environmental disputes have *ever* been resolved by courts or arbitration. Consider, for example, that the well-known *Trail Smelter* arbitration is over 50 years old and still cited as one of the few international environmental law cases. Moreover, inter-State proceedings based on State responsibility for environmental harm are designed to provide compensation *after* environmental harm has occurred. This judicial approach has limited utility for anticipating and avoiding environmental problems.

In the past twenty years, the nature of environmental problems addressed by international environmental law has also changed. To be sure, transboundary issues are still an important part of the field, but global environmental issues such as climate change, ozone depletion and biodiversity have begun to predominate. Transboundary pollution and environmental damage, in which one or more States brings claims based upon damage suffered in their territory because of actions taken (or not taken) within the territory of another State, fit fairly well within existing judicial and quasi-judicial dispute resolution processes. Global environmental issues, however, in which all or nearly all States may be both causing and suffering environmental damage, are ill-suited to judicial processes. Such issues need to be *managed* over time in ways that increase cooperation and coordination among a large number of stakeholders. This job falls to public international organizations both inside and outside the UN system, as well as bodies created under specific treaty regimes.

Public international organizations or inter-governmental organizations (IGOs or IOs), as they are often called, are neither States themselves nor purely non-State actors. The term "public international organization" typically refers to bodies that are created by international agreements among States. The agreement creating the organization establishes its goals, authority, and procedures. It also establishes (implicitly or explicitly) some form of commitment for participation and cooperation by the member States. IGOs are created by States and their governing bodies are generally, though not always, comprised of State delegates representing the interests of their respective States. At all but the highest levels, however, IGOs are staffed by professional civil servants from around the world who operate on behalf of the organization itself, rather than on behalf of particular States. Further, IGOs are often mission-oriented and develop agendas that differ from those of their constituent States, taking a more proactive role towards international issues than might any of their members (*see,* e.g., the discussion in Chapter 5 describing UNEP's active role in promoting international action to protect the ozone layer). Note, as well, that IGOs do not exist in a static world. Just as with agencies within national governments, IGOs compete for limited resources and political attention, seeking opportunities to expand their authority and resources, often at the expense at other IGOs.

SECTION I.   THE UNITED NATIONS

The United Nations and its subsidiary organs and specialized agencies have obviously played a critical role in international environmental law and policy. These institutions facilitate the creation of most new treaty law by sponsoring scientific deliberation on environmental issues, preparing draft conventions, and initiating and hosting negotiations of new international instruments for environmental protection. These same organizations also contribute to the development of customary international law by passing resolutions, declarations, model codes and guidelines on environmental issues. Perhaps the most important role of these organizations, however, is in the day-to-day implementation, monitoring and support of national efforts to protect the global environment.

————

A.   UNITED NATIONS ENVIRONMENT PROGRAMME (UNEP)
<http://www.unep.org>, <http://www.unep.net>

UNEP was conceived at the 1972 Stockholm Conference on the Human Environment and created by the UN General Assembly later that year. *See* U.N.G.A. Res. 2997 (1972). UNEP became the first UN agency with a specific environmental agenda. Its mission was to "facilitate international co-operation in the environmental field; to keep the world environmental situation under review so that problems of international significance receive appropriate consideration by Governments; and to promote the acquisition, assessment and exchange of environmental knowledge." UNITED NATIONS, EVERYONE'S UNITED NATIONS 168 (9th ed. 1978). From the outset, UNEP was conceived as a small coordinating body whose mission was to catalyze environmental cooperation within the UN system and member States, not to act directly as an executive agency. Its present work program focuses on five areas–(1) environmental information, assessment and research, including environmental emergency response capacity and strengthening of early warning and assessment functions; (2) enhanced coordination of environmental conventions and development of environmental policy instruments; (3) fresh water; (4) industry and technology transfer; and (5) support to Africa.

Structure. UNEP is governed by three bodies: a Governing Council, a Committee of Permanent Representatives and a High–Level Committee of Ministers and Officials. The Governing Council is comprised of the representatives of 58 States elected by the UN General Assembly to staggered terms of four years. The 58 States are selected geographically—sixteen seats are reserved for African nations, thirteen for Asian nations, six for Eastern European nations, ten for Latin America, and thirteen for Western European and other nations. The Governing Council is largely composed of State environment ministers and other representatives of national governments who have environmental or science expertise.

Since the Governing Council meets only once every two years, the day-to-day management of UNEP falls to the Executive Director, his staff, and the Committee of Permanent Representatives. UNEP's Executive Director is appointed by the UN Secretary–General in consultation with the member states. UNEP has about 300 professional and 500 general staff, sixty percent of whom are based at the headquarters in Nairobi. The remainder work in various Secretariats and regional offices located around the world.

The Committee of Permanent Representatives is comprised of representatives of all 187 UN members and reports to the Governing Council. Meeting quarterly, it serves as a communications link between UNEP and its member governments by providing advice on policy, program and financing. In the mid–1990s, the Committee of Permanent Representatives came under heavy criticism as a permanent and overpaid bureaucracy that tried to micro-manage UNEP. Indeed the Committee met a remarkable 50 additional times in 1996. At the same time, UNEP was suffering severe budget problems. In recent years, many States have reduced their voluntary contributions or earmarked the funds for specific projects because of the perception by donor governments that UNEP is not well managed. The United States, for example, gave $21 million in 1993 and 1994, but only $7 million in 1996. At the same time, the United Nations reduced its own support for UNEP due to budgetary shortfalls throughout the UN system. As a result, UNEP faced continuous cash crises throughout the 1990s and budgets fluctuated unpredictably. Over the same period of time, the importance of outside funding has increased. As a matter of comparison, in 1973 the United Nations' regular budget comprised 21.1 percent of UNEP's budget. In 1998–1999, the United Nations only provided 5.3 percent.

In part, UNEP's financial crisis reflected a broad lack of confidence in the organization. Many donor countries, particularly the United States and the United Kingdom, had for some time been dissatisfied with the way in which UNEP was run. In a United Nations reform paper in 1997, Secretary General Kofi Annan stated that UNEP should be reorganized, arguing that few of the goals UNEP was established to accomplish were being met and that scarce resources were being wasted by inefficient management. Annan explained that UNEP's focus should be on monitoring and assessment activities instead of project implementation, which could be better handled and funded by UNDP. See BNA–IED, *United Nations: Security General's Report on Reforms Gives New Support for Continuing UNEP*, July 22, 1997.

In the reorganization that followed, the High–Level Committee of Ministers and Officials was created. Composed of 36 members, the High–Level Committee is subsidiary to the Governing Council and has the same geographic composition as the Governing Council. Its mandate includes reviewing the effectiveness, efficiency and transparency of the secretariat's work, and preparing draft decisions for the Governing Council based on recommendations from the staff. As might be expected, many developing countries were hostile to this restructuring, claiming it would weaken their influence over UNEP decisions and relegate the Committee of Permanent Representatives of nothing more than a postman delivering news from Nairobi. Their opposition was unsuccessful, and the Committee of Permanent Representatives now is restricted to reviewing, monitoring and assessing the implementation of certain Governing Council decisions and meets only quarterly. *Decision Adopted by the Governing Council of the United Nations Environment Programme at Its Resumed Nineteenth Session*, UN Doc. UNEP/GC/19/1 B (1997).

Funding. The resources available to UNEP for the administration and implementation of its programs come from four distinct sources. <http://www.unep.org.rmn/funding.htm>

- the regular budget for the activities of the United Nations, which is funded by the United Nations members from assessed contributions and whose appropriations for the various departments are determined by the UN Controller;

- the Environment Fund (the main source of UNEP funding), which is voluntary and was established to provide additional financing for environmental programs under UNEP with the guidance of its Governing Council;

- Trust Funds, which are extra-budgetary resources whose programmes, apart from meeting the objectives of UNEP, are agreed and negotiated between UNEP and the donor (or several donors) and form separate accounts;

- Counterpart Contributions, which are also extra-budgetary resources, providing additional resources to the UNEP program of work or the program of work of trust funds administered by UNEP.

Voluntary contributions by governments to the Environment Fund are the main source of UNEP's finances but both the sum total of contributions and the number of contributing countries declined following the Earth Summit. As a Governing Council statement in 1997 described,

[O]ver ninety per cent of the total voluntary contribution to the Fund comes from only 15 countries. The decision of even a few of them to substantially reduce their contributions can have, and has had, a devastating effect on implementing the approved Programme, planning UNEP's work, and on its viability. Thus the Programme budget for 1996–97 will have to be reduced by over 30% in the light of such unforeseen drops in contributions. * * *

Governments pledge and make payments into the Environment Fund at their convenience. UNEP cannot commit, or spend, funds which have not been pledged or paid. The organization therefore needs to have measures in place which could cover the risk of a cash shortfall at any time.

The Environment Fund & Administrative & Other Budgetary Matters, UNEP/GC.19/INF.10 (Nov. 22, 1996).

Between 1973 and 1998, 142 countries made at least one donation to the UNEP's Environment Fund, with 11 countries contributing annually. UNEP's budget for 1998–99 was $75 million and, reflecting the vigor of the new Executive Director, Klaus Toepfer, the 2002–2003 work program and budget totaled almost $120 million. *See UNEP Aims For a Stronger Global Role*, February 9, 2001, ENVIRONMENT NEWS SERVICE. As a result of these chronic funding problems, UNEP's senior managers spend much of their time traveling to national capitals seeking support in the form of direct funding, personnel, or materiel. Ironically, as a result funding has been available for specific projects, but constantly lacking for core, administrative needs. *See* Judith Acheing, *Environment: Ministers Confront Global Environment Challenges*, INTER PRESS SERVICE, February 9, 2001, *available at* 2001 WL 4802665 (2001).

UNEP Programs. UNEP's Division of Programs, located in Nairobi, is responsible for implementation of its natural resource activities. The Division of Programs includes a specific unit dedicated to promoting environmental law. Among other things, the Environmental Law Unit prepares draft treaties to be reviewed and revised by ad hoc expert working groups convened by UNEP. Once the working group achieves consensus on non-binding language, the draft is submitted to the Governing Council for debate and adoption. Alternatively, if the draft concerns an instrument that is legally binding, then UNEP may convene a diplomatic conference to consider adoption. Both the Vienna Convention for the Protection of the Ozone Layer (Vienna Convention) and the Montreal Protocol on Substances that Deplete the Ozone Layer (Montreal Protocol) were adopted through this approach. *See* Chapter 9, p. 543. Over the last 25 years, more than 40 multilateral environmental treaties have been negotiated under UNEP's guidance, including for example the Convention on the International Trade of Endangered Species (CITES), the Basel Convention on the Control of Transboundary Movements of Hazardous Waste and Their Disposal (Basel Convention), the UN Convention to Combat Desertification, and several regional seas conventions. UNEP maintains the secretariats for many of these conventions, including CITES, the ozone treaties, the Basel Convention, the Biodiversity Convention and the Convention on the Conservation of Migratory Species of Wild Animals. (*See* the Secretariats discussion below.)

UNEP has also developed some important "soft law" instruments including the World Charter for Nature, as well as guidelines for management of shared resources, marine pollution from land-based sources and environmental impact statements.

Since 1982, UNEP has conducted its efforts to promote the development of international environmental law under a pair of ten-year work plans known as the first and second Montevideo Programmes. The First Montevideo Programme, which ended in 1991, led to the adoption, *inter alia*, of the Montreal Guidelines for the Protection of the Marine Environment against Pollution from Land-based Sources, the Vienna Convention for the Protection of the Ozone Layer and the Montreal Protocol to that convention, the Cairo Guidelines and Principles for the Environmentally Sound Management of Hazardous Wastes and the Basel Convention, and an array of other treaties and guidelines. The Second Montevideo Programme, which runs from 1992 to 2002, calls for action in eighteen areas, including: enhancing the capacity of States to implement their international environmental obligations; promoting widespread use of environmental impact assessment; "consider[ing] concepts or principles which may be applicable to the formation and development of international law in the field of environment and sustainable development"; and developing regimes for the conservation, management and sustainable development of soils and forests. *See* UNEP Gov. Council Dec. 17/25 Annex (21 May 1993) *reproduced in* UNEP, UNEP's NEW WAY FORWARD, App. III (1995). The Third Montevideo Programme, which has already been adopted, will start in 2003.

Although law has been an important focus of UNEP activity, UNEP conducts significant programmatic work in other areas, as well. For example, UNEP's division of Environmental Information and Assessment is responsible for monitoring, collecting, assessing and disseminating data regarding the Earth's environment. As part of this effort, UNEP established INFOTERRA, a global environmental information exchange system that provides scientific, technical and bibliographic environmental information. It operates through a system of 174 national focal points, generally located within the equivalent of the Ministry of the Environment (for example, the U.S. Environmental Protection Agency). The Global Resource Information Database (GRID) was created to acquire and disseminate environmental data to assist the African, Mediterranean and West Asia Environment Research and Information Networks. GRID Nairobi is now developing a strategy to assist developing countries to create and manage a database on biodiversity through a partnership between UNEP and the Global Environment Facility.

UNEP also maintains a global chemicals information clearinghouse as part of its chemicals program. The chemicals program is designed to increase awareness about hazards and best practices of chemicals production and use, as well as developing countries' capacity to implement those best practices. The flagship of the program is an International Register of Potentially Toxic Chemicals (*see* Chapter 12, p. 874). Similarly, UNEP is supporting the development of "cleaner production centers" in developing countries as part of its ongoing sustainable production and consumption program. Like the chemicals program, the sustainable production and consumption program includes the development and maintenance of an International Cleaner Production Information Clearinghouse. UNEP's sustainable production initiative has been among its most successful activities. It is managed through the Industry and Environment Centre located in Paris, France. The Centre serves as the focal point for disseminating information and promoting pollution prevention and more efficient use of raw materials. The Cleaner Production Program has been very effective in training and capacity building activities, particularly in developing countries, as well as in raising global awareness over the importance of a pollution prevention approach.

Assessing UNEP. From its inception, UNEP's potential responsibilities have extended to the whole of the human-environment relationship. The scope and severity of the threats to the environment on global, regional and local levels have proven far greater than was imagined just a quarter century ago. Yet both UNEP's authority and its capacity to address these threats is extremely limited. It lacks both the lawmaking authority and the human and financial resources necessary to fulfill its mandate effectively. Despite these limitations, UNEP has accomplished a great deal. In the following reading, former *New York Times* reporter Philip Shabecoff briefly reviews the successes and failures of UNEP's early years.

Philip Shabecoff, A NEW NAME FOR PEACE: INTERNATIONAL ENVIRONMENTALISM, SUSTAINABLE DEVELOPMENT, AND DEMOCRACY 47–49 (1996)

The UNEP was undoubtedly the single most positive and concrete product of the Stockholm conference on the international level. Despite its limited powers and resources and a variety of other handicaps, including the internal jealousies and power struggles within the UN system, UNEP proved to be of great service in its first decades to the effort to protect the global environment.

The UNEP mandate was confined chiefly to monitoring environmental developments, serving as a clearinghouse for environmental information, and acting as a catalyst and coordinator within the UN and among its member nations to carry out the agreements reached in Stockholm and to achieve other environmental objectives that transcended national boundaries. Under its first director, Maurice Strong, and his successor, the Egyptian microbiologist and government official Mostafa Kamal Tolba, who ran the agency for the better part of two decades UNEP achieved a number of significant successes.

Despite problems, UNEP's monitoring activities made substantial contributions to achieving a clearer vision of the state of the global environment and the threats confronting it. The Earthwatch system it set up included a Global Environmental Monitoring System (GEMS), which enlists thousands of scientists around the world to assess the health of ecosystems on a continuing basis; INFOTERRA, which disseminates information on a broad spectrum of environmental issues; and the International Register of Potential Toxic Chemicals.

Peter S. Thacher of the World Resources Institute, a former deputy director of the environmental program and a veteran environmental diplomat, concluded in 1991 that, "thanks in large part to progress made since Stockholm under UNEP's 'Earthwatch' activities, a basis now exists on which to assess risks and the likelihood of harmful impacts, and arrive at cooperative measures for reducing them or taking precautions." UNEP played an important role in developing scientific evidence of the threats of global warming and destruction of atmospheric ozone and in alerting the international public to those dangers.

[UNEP] also acted as a sponsor for a variety of multinational conferences, programs, plans and agreements covering such diverse agendas as human settlements, water resources management, transboundary movements of air pollution and hazardous waste, biological diversity, land degradation, desertification, environmental education and environmental law. One of the earliest and most successful UNEP initiatives was its Regional Seas program, particularly its Mediterranean Action Plan, with which the nations on the littoral of that fabled but troubled body of water joined forces to address its many pollution problems. Because of the initiative, normally hostile states such as Israel and Syria, Egypt and Libya, and Greece and Turkey sat peacefully at the same table to try to protect their shared resource and heritage. Stjepan Keckes, head of the program observed that a regional approach to problems enabled disparate nations to focus on problems they face in common. "Pollution is the unifying concept," he explained.

It was clear from the outset, however, that UNEP would not be the answer to the planet's environmental ills. Aside from the fact that it was deliberately given a limited role, with no real operational capacity, it labored under several handicaps that made it difficult to carry out even its assigned functions. One was the fact that it had no real authority within the UN system. Another was that, to accommodate a desire by Africans to have a UN agency on their continent, UNEP made its headquarters in Nairobi, Kenya, far from the diplomatic power centers of New York and Geneva. A number of critics contended that the autocratic, excessively centralized leadership style of Mostafa Tolba, who headed UNEP for seventeen years, seriously compromised its effectiveness. But an argument can also be made that, given its handicaps, UNEP would not have been able to accomplish as much as it did without his very firm leadership. Tolba's personal diplomacy certainly influenced several important environmental negotiations, including the decision at Montreal to phase out chemicals destroying the earth's protective ozone layer. UNEP's most onerous problem, however, was its lack of adequate funding. It was originally supposed to operate at a level of $100 million a year. But for many years it had a budget of only $30 million, less than some of the national non-profit environmental organizations in the United States.

But even without these handicaps UNEP, or indeed the UN system as a whole, was overmatched by the mounting complexity, scope, and seriousness of the threats to the global habitat. The UN system, divided into specific areas of responsibility and fiercely defended bureaucratic fiefdoms, was incapable of the kind of cross-sectoral approach demanded by these interwoven economic, ecological, and social dilemmas. Even more to the point, as Tolba noted, "the global problems are created and must be solved nationally within a global framework." But within national governments, he noted, environmental ministries have much less "clout" than do economic, finance, development, energy, industry, and agriculture ministries. And the framework itself–the UN–could not operate effectively without "Olympian leadership" from a national government or group of governments, said Brian Urquhart, the diplomat who served for decades as under-secretary-general of the UN. In recent years that leadership has been absent, he lamented, in large measure because the United States, which had led the world in the drive toward internationalism in the post-World War II era, no longer filled that role.

QUESTIONS AND DISCUSSION

1. Geoffrey Palmer agrees with Shabecoff's assessment. In *New Ways to Make International Environmental Law*, 86 AM.J. INT'L L. 259 (1992), Palmer notes:

> UNEP was established to act as a focal point for environmental action and coordination within the United Nations. It lacks any formal powers.... [I]t points out environmental problems to nations and suggests solutions. In fact, it does much more than its limited powers suggest. It has become an agency that sets out to produce concrete results in terms of treaties negotiated. In my opinion, without UNEP, the system to prevent ozone depletion now in place would not have been developed.

> UNEP can push states, probe their policies and plead with them; it cannot coerce them. UNEP lacks teeth. It has no executive authority. Partly for this reason, UNEP has made generous use of "soft law" instruments in the international consensus building that it engages in. All UNEP programs are financed by direct, voluntary contributions from member states. It has a

Governing Council composed of representatives of fifty-eight member states. UNEP has access to excellent scientific advice not filtered through nation-states. Given the nature of UNEP's constitution, its achievements are substantial, but it is not an adequate international organization for protecting the world's environment.

2. Reflecting the adoption of sustainable development at the Earth Summit as a guiding principle for environmental protection, UNEP has revised its mission statement to "provide leadership and encourage partnerships in caring for the environment by inspiring, informing and enabling nations and peoples to improve their quality of life without compromising that of future generations." <http://www.grid2.cr.usgs.gov/geo2000/pressrel/unep.htm>. Compare this to its mission statement on page 219. Do you think there is a practical difference between these two? How does the new statement reflect UNEP's turmoil over the past decade?

3. UNEP has been severely criticized for everything from simple management problems—e.g. the absence of top officials, including the Executive Director and deputy from UNEP headquarters for extended periods, an overpaid and top-heavy management structure, difficulties of different geographic operations—to a general lack of direction. *Review of the United Nations Environment Programme and the Administrative Practices of Its Secretariat, including the United Nations Office in Nairobi* (Report of the Office of Internal Oversight Services (OIOS)), 17 (Dec. 10, 1996). Much criticism during the crisis in 1996 and 1997 focused on the former Executive Director, Elizabeth Dowdeswell. But is blaming one person or, for that matter, UNEP for the poor coordination of international environmental policy appropriate? To what extent does making UNEP a scapegoat serve to excuse the failings of member countries? In this regard, consider the appropriate role for UNEP in light of the Commission on Sustainable Development, created after the Rio Conference and described below.

4. NGOs play an important role in UNEP's governance. While NGOs cannot vote, they regularly attend Governing Council sessions and other UNEP meetings as observers and may be invited by the Governing Council to make statements to the sessions. NGOs have significant access to the delegates at the Governing Council meetings. They are permitted to be on the floor during the session and their views on sectoral issues are given serious consideration by the Council.

B. COMMISSION ON SUSTAINABLE DEVELOPMENT
<http://www.un.org/dpcsd/dsd/csd.htm>

At the Rio Conference, participants called for the creation of a high-level UN commission to ensure and monitor the implementation of Agenda 21. Responding to that call, the UN General Assembly created the Commission on Sustainable Development (CSD) in January 1993. *See* G.A. Res. 47/191, GAOR, 47th Sess., UN Doc. A/RES/47/191 (1993).

The CSD is a functional commission within the Economic and Social Council, funded through the UN's regular budget. It has 53 member states elected for three-year terms with one-third elected annually. Memberships are allocated on a geographic basis, with 13 members from African nations, 11 from Asia, 10 from Latin America and the Caribbean, 6 from Eastern Europe and 13 from Western Europe and other countries. Only members may vote at the CSD's annual meetings, but other States, representatives of UN organizations and accredited inter-governmental and non-governmental organizations may attend the sessions as observers.

The tasks assigned to the CSD are staggering. A partial listing of these tasks is excerpted below. Daniel Esty has compared the CSD's mission to being told to "follow up on the Bible."

Resolution on Institutional Arrangement to Follow Up the United Nations Conference on Environment and Development, U.N.G.A. Res. 47/191 (Dec. 22,1992), *reprinted in* 32 I.L.M. 238 (1993)

[The General Assembly, in requesting that ECOSOC set up the CSD, recommended the following functions for the new commission:]

(a) To monitor progress in the implementation of Agenda 21 and activities related to the integration of environmental and developmental goals throughout the United Nations system through analysis and evaluation of reports from all relevant organs, organizations, programmes and institutions of the United Nations system dealing with various issues of environment and development, including those related to finance;

(b) To consider information provided by Governments, including, for example, in the form of periodic communications or national reports regarding the activities they undertake to implement Agenda 21, the problems they face, such as problems related to financial resources and technology transfer, and other environment and development issues they find relevant;

(c) To review the progress in the implementation of the commitments contained in Agenda 21, including those related to the provision of financial resources and transfer of technology; * * *

(f) To receive and analyse relevant input from competent non-governmental organizations, including the scientific and the private sector, in the context of the overall implementation of Agenda 21; * * *

(h) To consider, where appropriate, information regarding the progress made in the implementation of environmental conventions, which could be made available by the relevant Conferences of Parties;

(i) To provide appropriate recommendations to the General Assembly, through the Economic and Social Council, on the basis of an integrated consideration of the reports and issues related to the implementation of Agenda 21; * * *

5. Decides that the Commission, in the fulfillment of its functions, will, also:

(a) Monitor progress in promoting, facilitating and financing, as appropriate, the access to and transfer of environmentally sound technologies and corresponding know-how, in particular to developing countries, on favourable terms, including on concessional and preferential terms, as mutually agreed, taking into account the need to protect intellectual property rights as well as the special needs of developing countries for the implementation of Agenda 21; * * *

7. Also recommends that the Commission should:

(a) Provide for representatives of various parts of the United Nations system and other intergovernmental organizations, including international financial institutions, GATT, regional development banks, subregional financial institutions, relevant regional and subregional economic and technical cooperation organizations and regional economic integration organizations, to assist and advise the Commission in the performance of its functions, within their respective areas of expertise and mandates, and participate actively in its deliberations; and provide for the European Economic Community, within its areas of competence, to participate fully— as will be appropriately defined in the rules of procedure of the Commission—without the right to vote;

(b) Provide for non-governmental organizations, including those related to major groups as well as industry and the scientific and business communities, to participate effectively in its work and contribute within their areas of competence to its deliberations; * * *

12. ... [The CSD should] at its first substantive session, adopt a multi-year thematic programme of its work that will provide a framework to assess progress achieved in the implementation of Agenda 21 and ensure an integrated approach to all of its environment and development components as well as linkages between sectoral and cross-sectoral issues. This programme could be of clusters that would integrate in an effective manner related sectoral and cross-sectoral components of Agenda 21 in such a way as to allow the Commission to review the progress of the implementation of the entire Agenda 21 by 1997. This programme of work could be adjusted, as the need may arise, at the future sessions of the Commission; * * *

The tremendous responsibilities assigned the CSD far exceed the modest resources it has for implementing them. Thus, in monitoring the implementation of sustainable development around the world, it relies on voluntary self-reporting by States. Both the decision whether to report and the contents of any report submitted are left to the discretion of the States.

Many commentators suggest that the CSD's vast set of objectives and unrealistic expectations have required lowered expectations from the start. Consider the following comments from Hilary F. French of the Worldwatch Institute.

Hilary F. French, *Partnership for the Planet: An Environmental Agenda for the United Nations* WORLDWATCH PAPER 32–34 (July 1995)

[On the positive side, the CSD] has provided a forum where governments and nongovernmental participants can share information about successes and failures in implementing the Rio accords at the national and local levels. Agenda 21 called on all nations to devise national sustainable development strategies, and by June 1995, a total of 130 had created national organizations charged with implementing Agenda 21. However, only 17 countries have devised actual strategies based on their deliberations, though 17 more are in the process of doing so. There is also a growing movement worldwide to create sustainable cities and communities. The Toronto-based International Council for Local Environmental Initiatives is spearheading a campaign to promote the adoption of local Agenda 21s. An estimated 1,200 cities in 33 countries—including Buga, Colombia; Quito, Ecuador; and Lahti, Finland—already have such initiatives under way.

Governments are also using the CSD to exchange views on contentious issues that cut across traditional sectoral lines. For instance, the commission has taken up the role of trade in sustainable development as well as the question of changing unsustainable production and consumption patterns. It is also working to encourage governments to develop and use sustainable development indicators to supplement traditional reliance on the national income accounts. At the 1995 session, governments evaluated the adequacy of existing international actions to protect biodiversity, forest, and mountains, and to combat desertification and drought. This session led to the creation of an Inter–Governmental Panel on Forests to study whether or not a new international agreement is needed to protect this resource globally. It also launched an initiative to phase out the use of lead in gasoline around the world. * * *

Furthermore, the CSD has spurred cooperation among UN agencies, including the World Bank. These agencies now produce joint reports detailing their collective work in implementing the sections of Agenda 21 being reviewed in any particular year. This has proved to be a valuable coordinating mechanism.

Despite these useful initiatives, the CSD suffers from structural defects that impede substantive progress. First, its mandate is so broad that priorities are often difficult to discern. Second, the official reporting process has not worked well. Many governments do not submit the required reports on national action plans to implement Agenda 21. Those that do comply with this requirement tend to deliver documents that are long on self-congratulation and short on substantive analysis of remaining challenges. Finally, the CSD commands no resources of its own and has no coercive or regulatory powers, so it has no means of ensuring that its pronouncements are translated into actual policy changes at the national or local level.

The result of these deficiencies is that the CSD is acquiring a reputation in some quarters as a talk shop where not much of real significance happens. If the commission is to improve its standing, it will have to hone its agenda.

Despite recent similar critiques that the CSD "has been strong on generalities and good on phrases . . . [but] failed to find the link between what we know must be done and what governments are actually doing," the CSD has been useful in other ways. *Sustainable Development: Privately–Sponsored International Panel to Develop Action Plan for UN Commission* BNA–IED, May 11, 1999. The CSD has been effective in bringing to light some notable failures to comply with commitments made at the Earth Summit. Perhaps of most concern to developing countries was funding for implementation of Agenda 21. As Chapter 3 described, developed countries agreed to provide 0.7 percent of their GNP as official assistance to developing countries, but most have not adhered to the agreement. Denmark, Norway, Sweden and the Netherlands are the only four countries that have met, and in some cases, exceeded the 0.7 percent goal. The United States, in contrast, is the lowest contributor of all developed nations (in percentage terms). *See* Janine E. Dames, *An Examination of Mexico and the Unreasonable Goals of the United Nations Conference on Environment and Development (UNCED)*, 10 FORDHAM ENVTL. L.J. 71, 88–9 (1998). The CSD's stakeholder dialogue has also been praised by some groups, particularly NGOs, who claim that other UN bodies, such as the UNEP Governing Council, the forests panel, and the Secretariat for the UN Framework Convention on Climate Change should model their dialogues on CSD. See BNA–IED, May 10, 2000, Sustainable Development: U.N. Sustainable Development Body Planning "Earth Summit Plus 10" for 2002.

Preparations are underway for the tenth anniversary conference, "Earth Summit Plus 10," to be held in South Africa in 2002. The summit will examine the implementation of existing Rio agreements, assess progress that has occurred over the last decade under Agenda 21 and address new issues that have emerged. See BNA–IED, May 10, 2000, Sustainable Development: U.N. Sustainable Development Body Planning "Earth Summit Plus 10" for 2002.

———

C. UNITED NATIONS DEVELOPMENT PROGRAM

<http://www.undp.org/>

With a budget of US $750 million in the year 2000–more than six times that of UNEP—and over 6,000 employees worldwide, the United Nations Development Program (UNDP) is arguably the largest IGO working in the environmental field. UNDP was created in 1965 to administer and coordinate technical assistance for developing countries. As the relationship between environmental protection and social and economic development has been recognized, the UNDP has adjusted its priorities accordingly. It has incorporated principles of sustainable development throughout its development activities and is focussing its resources on "a series of objectives central to sustainable human development: poverty elimination, environmental regeneration, job creation, and advancement of women."

Many UNDP programs contribute indirectly to environmental protection by working to alleviate the underlying causes of environmental degradation such as poverty and gender inequity. For example, since 1976 UNDP has supported the political, social and economic empowerment of women through the United Nations Development Fund for Women (UNIFEM). By increasing economic and educational opportunities for women in the poorest countries, UNIFEM may lead to more sustainable resource use in those countries, as well as easing population pressures.

In addition to these indirect benefits, UNDP has taken a more direct approach to environmental protection in recent years. In response to Agenda 21 and the goal of sustainable development as articulated at the Earth Summit, UNDP created the Sustainable Energy and Environment Division (SEED). The creation of SEED consolidated into one office all of the operations at UNDP headquarters with responsibility for environmental issues. SEED's "mission is to help developing countries successfully design and carry out programmes which integrate the protection and regeneration of the environment and the use of natural resources to reduce poverty, generate sustainable livelihoods, and advance the status of women." To this end, SEED has been charged with ensuring that all aspects of UNDP's activities be considered from an environmental perspective. SEED is also charged with developing and integrating substantive strategies to guide UNDP's technical assistance in support of sustainable development. <http://www.undp.org/seed/>.

To make this more concrete, the following excerpt describes some of UNDP's more successful environmental protection efforts.

United Nations Development Programme
ACHIEVEMENTS IN PROTECTING AND REGENERATING THE ENVIRONMENT

UNDP helped many countries prepare for and participate in the 1992 UN Conference on Environment and Development (UNCED). Since then it has focused on assisting countries in realizing the goals of "Agenda 21," UNCED's blueprint for action. Agenda 21 states that poverty and environmental degradation are linked. Thus, UNDP helps countries adopt integrated approaches that focus on managing natural resources to improve the livelihoods of people living in poverty. Priority is given to "preventive" approaches. Care is taken to ensure that actions to cope with immediate crises do not interfere with the long-term sustainability of resources and development processes. Here are some examples.

AFRICA 2000

The Africa 2000 Network supports community-based projects that preserve the environment while promoting sustainable human development. It has provided grants of US$50,000 or less, along with technical assistance and training, to groups of women and men through some 530 grassroots projects designed, implemented and monitored by the beneficiaries. Areas covered include natural forest management, erosion control, range and watershed management, food preservation and storage, fish farming, livestock rearing and dairy farming, bee-keeping and management of accounts. Africa 2000 is currently operating in 12 countries; Burkina Faso, Burundi, Cameroon, Ghana, Kenya, Lesotho, Mauritania, Rwanda, Senegal, Tanzania, Uganda and Zimbabwe.

REPUBLIC OF KOREA: INTEGRATED PEST MANAGEMENT

Support for Integrated Pest Management (IPM) in the Republic of Korea (ROK) has had significant impact on environmental policy formulation. With a chemical-intensive strategy for food production, the country is one of Asia's heaviest users of pesticides but this is now changing rapidly. UNDP helped introduce IPM to policy-makers and farmers alike, training more than 2,000 farmers and over 80 guidance officers in 40 per cent of the counties nationwide in its use. Dissemination of the results of farmers' trials, and data on results in other countries, to local and national policy-makers encouraged the formulation of a strategy combining food security with environmental preservation. ROK became the first Asian nation to adopt a pesticide and fertilizer reduction policy. Current targets call for reducing the use of pesticides by 50 per cent and fertilizer by 40 per cent by the year 2004. Funds are now available for continued IPM research and education at both national and local levels.

KAZAKSTAN: ARAL SEASHORE REHABILITATION AND CAPACITY BUILDING PROGRAMME

In Central Asia, intensive cotton production with overuse of water and chemicals led to the drying up of half the surface of the Aral Sea, severe degradation of land and water resources and widespread ecological and economic disaster for some 30 million people. To help people living along the Kazakstan shore of the Aral Sea rehabilitate their environment and regain self-sufficiency, UNDP established three "Programme Support Centres" (PSCs) staffed by UN specialists. Opened in mid–1995, the Centres are responsible for 13 UNDP-supported projects that take a participatory approach to creating employment, improving health, rehabilitating the environment and strengthening the capacities of local communities and NGOs. The Centres have won the trust, not only of the local people, but of several donors to the region that use them to facilitate their work, including the World Bank, Egypt, Israel, Japan, Turkey and the United Kingdom.

PANAMA: IMPLEMENTING THE TROPICAL FOREST ACTION PLAN

Investments, incentives, participatory consultations and education are helping to slow the stripping of 70,000 hectares a year from the forests that cover 40 per cent of Panama's land mass. The capacity of the National Institute for Renewable Natural Resources was strengthened to help it identify and establish ways of mobilizing technical, economic and financial resources. New laws were approved providing environmental education and giving incentives for reforestation. National support for the Tropical Forest Action Plan is being promoted. Active participation of indigenous and farmer communities, NGOs, women's organizations and the private sector in formulating national resource policies has been encouraged by the formation of new groups. These include the National Advisory Board on Gender and Forest Development, the House of Forest Entrepreneurs of Panama, the Indigenous Technical Consultative Committee and the Committee of NGOs. Twelve new projects in the forest sector are being executed and another eight are in negotiation.

GLOBAL ENVIRONMENT PROGRAMMES

Among the global environment programmes in which UNDP plays an active role are: the US$2 billion Global Environment Facility (GEF), implemented by UNDP, the World Bank and UNEP, which provides grants to help developing countries reduce global warming, protect international waters, preserve biological diversity and prevent further depletion of the ozone layer. UNDP is also responsible for managing the Small Grants Programme, which supports community-based NGO projects related to the GEF's global concerns, and has thus far provided more than 1,300 grants of $50,000 or less to grassroots groups in 50 developing countries; the Office to Combat Desertification and Drought (UNSO), which spearheads UNDP's work to control desertification and prevent drought in all affected programme countries; and the Multilateral Fund of the Montreal Protocol (to protect the ozone layer), for which UNDP is one of four implementing agencies (with UNEP, UNIDO and the World Bank). Under this fund, as of 1998, UNDP has received $233.9 million for 905 projects in 64 countries. Upon completion these projects will have reduced emissions of 11,300 tonnes per year of ozone depleting substances to the world's atmosphere.

QUESTIONS AND DISCUSSION

1. The 178 nations attending the Rio Conference agreed that environmental protection and social and economic development should be integrated into the common goal of sustainable development. At the time of the Earth Summit, neither UNEP nor UNDP was prepared to coordinate global sustainable development efforts. Nonetheless, both agencies worked to ensure that they received a mandate to work on sustainable development or at least that their mandates were not weakened. Ultimately, the Rio delegates would create the CSD as the primary mechanism for coordinating environment and development issues at the UN level but UNEP and UNDP continued to try to position themselves for responding to the challenge presented by sustainable development. UNDP, with its far greater resources and political support, was able to take quicker and more positive action than UNEP. UNDP hired environmentalist James Speth, head of the World Resources Institute, to become its new director; it launched a new Capacity 21 program, aimed at building the capacity in developing countries to implement Agenda 21; and, as discussed above, it integrated its existing environmental activities into the SEED division. These proactive efforts to respond to the challenge of sustainable development are exactly what the delegates hoped would happen as a result of the Rio Conference.

Given the relative success of these programs at greening UNDP, is UNEP still necessary—particularly given its recent lack of funding and other problems? What about the CSD? The programs of UNEP, CSD and UNDP appear to overlap to some extent. Is this an efficient use of the United Nations' limited resources? Given the broad mandate of the CSD, the political battles within UNEP and its lack of a secure funding source, do you think the Commission could replace UNEP entirely? What might be lost and gained through such a restructuring? We will discuss this more in Section 3.

2. Both UNEP and UNDP along with the World Bank, are responsible for administering the Global Environment Facility (GEF). The GEF is the primary financial mechanism for providing environmental grants (as opposed to loans) to the developing world. The GEF provides grants in four focal areas–climate change, ozone depletion, loss of biodiversity, and conservation of international waters. The GEF is also the interim funding mechanism under a number of treaties, including the Biodiversity and Climate Change conventions.

The GEF is described further in Chapter 20, p. 1501.

3. In a stark illustration of the funding constraints imposed by Congress on funding for UN activities, while supporting the location of the Rio Plus 10 meeting outside the United States, U.S. delegates to the CSD refused to provide any financial support. Noting that a congressional funding compromise barred U.S. support for new global conferences within the UN system, the U.S. delegate stated that "the United States could not support the consensus for the 2002 meeting and would be unable to pay its share of funding for it, assuming that current statutory requirements stay in place." U.N. Body Asks New "Earth Summit" In 2002; U.S. Bound By Congressional Funding Accord, *BNA*, May 9, 2000.

SECTION II.   ADMINISTERING TREATIES: CoPs, SECRETARIATS AND SUBSIDIARY BODIES

In addition to establishing the specific obligations of State parties, most environmental treaties also create their own administrative and policymaking bureaucracy to help the parties fulfill treaty obligations, to help further the treaty's mission, and to provide fora for international environmental governance. These institutions may be permanent or intermittent, and include conferences of the parties, secretariats, and subsidiary bodies including technical or expert committees.

A.   CONFERENCES OF THE PARTIES

Much like a corporate board of directors, the conferences of the parties (CoPs) are the primary policy-making organs of most global environmental treaty regimes. The CoPs usually occur once every one or two years and conduct the major business of monitoring, updating, revising, and enforcing the conventions. The following article from the Climate Change Convention illustrates some of the responsibilities of a CoP.

U.N. Framework Convention on Climate Change, Article 7 (1992)

1. Conference of the Parties is hereby established.

2. The Conference of the Parties, as the supreme body of this Convention, shall keep under regular review the implementation of the Convention and any related legal instruments that the Conference of the Parties may adopt, and shall make, within its mandate, the decisions necessary to promote the effective implementation of the Convention. To this end, it shall:

(a) Periodically examine the obligations of the Parties and the institutional arrangements under the Convention, in the light of the objective of the Convention, the experience gained in its implementation and the evolution of scientific and technological knowledge;

(b) Promote and facilitate the exchange of information on measures adopted by the Parties to address climate change and its effects, taking into account the differing circumstances, responsibilities and capabilities of the Parties and their respective commitments under the Convention;

(c) Facilitate, at the request of two or more Parties, the coordination of measures adopted by them to address climate change and its effects, taking into account the differing circumstances, responsibilities and capabilities of the Parties and their respective commitments under the Convention.

(d) Promote and guide, in accordance with the objective and provisions of the Convention, the development and periodic refinement of comparable methodologies, to be agreed on by the Conference of the Parties, inter alia, for preparing inventories of greenhouse gas emissions by sources and removals by sinks, and for evaluating the effectiveness of measures to limit the emissions and enhance the removals of these gases;

(e) Assess, on the basis of all information made available to it in accordance with the provisions of the Convention, the implementation of the Convention by the Parties, the overall effects of the measures taken pursuant to the Convention, in particular environmental, economic and social effects as well as their cumulative impacts and the extent to which progress towards the objective of the Convention is being achieved;

(f) Consider and adopt regular reports on the implementation of the Convention and ensure their publication;

(g) Make recommendations on any matters necessary for the implementation of the Convention;

(h) Seek to mobilize financial resources in accordance with Article 4, paragraphs 3, 4 and 5, and Article 11;

(i) Establish such subsidiary bodies as are deemed necessary for the implementation of the Convention;

(j) Review reports submitted by its subsidiary bodies and provide guidance to them;

(k) Agree upon and adopt, by consensus, rules of procedure and financial rules for itself and for any subsidiary bodies;

(l) Seek and utilize, where appropriate, the services and cooperation of, and information provided by, competent international organizations and intergovernmental and non-governmental bodies; and

(m) Exercise such other functions as are required for the achievement of the objective of the Convention as well as all other functions assigned to it under the Convention.

3. The Conference of the Parties shall, at its first session, adopt its own rules of procedure as well as those of the subsidiary bodies established by the Convention, which shall include decision-making procedures for matters not already covered by decision-making procedures stipulated in the Convention. Such procedures may include specified majorities required for the adoption of particular decisions.

4. The first session of the Conference of the Parties shall be convened by the interim secretariat referred to in Article 21 and shall take place not later than one year after the date of entry into force of the Convention. Thereafter, ordinary sessions of the Conference of the Parties shall be held every year unless otherwise decided by the Conference of the Parties.

5. Extraordinary sessions of the Conference of the Parties shall be held at such other times as may be deemed necessary by the Conference, or at the written request of any Party, provided that, within six months of the request being communicated to the Parties by the secretariat, it is supported by at least one-third of the Parties.

6. The United Nations, its specialized agencies and the International Atomic Energy Agency, as well as any State member thereof or observers thereto not Party to the Convention, may be represented at sessions of the Conference of the Parties as observers. Any body or agency, whether national or international, governmental or non-governmental, which is qualified in matters covered by the Convention, and which has informed the secretariat of its wish to be represented at a session of the Conference of the Parties as an observer, may be so admitted unless at least one-third of the Parties present object. The admission and participation of observers shall be subject to the rules of procedure adopted by the Conference of the Parties.

Perhaps the most important function of the Climate Change Convention's CoP has been to periodically review the state of the science regarding climate change and to evaluate the ultimate effectiveness of the regime in meeting its objectives. For example, after determining that, in fact, the Convention would not meet its objective of stabilizing atmospheric greenhouse gas concentrations at safe levels, the CoP became the primary forum for the negotiation of binding targets and timetables under the 1997 Kyoto Protocol. Note, as well, Article 6's provision for participation, leaving the political decision of which observers to admit (if any) to future CoPs.

What is true of the Climate Change Convention is also true more generally: once an environmental regime has entered into force, the CoP provides the mechanism by which new protocols are adopted and amendments and modification made. Thus, the CoPs play a crucial role in the vitality and continuing development of environmental regimes, adapting those regimes to new information and changing circumstances as the need arises. Indeed, it is often through the CoP that the most stringent treaty obligations are created. For example, amendments and modifications adopted at a series of CoPs have extended both the scope and the extent of reductions in ozone depleting substances under the Montreal Protocol. At the same time, the CoPs increased the effectiveness of the ozone regime by establishing mechanisms for financing technology conversions in developing countries and for addressing non-compliance problems wherever they occur.

CoPs are also crucial to addressing environmental crises that cannot wait for the development and entry into force of entirely new conventions. For example, when elephant stocks plummeted in the 1980s and early 1990s, the CoP to CITES adopted a moratorium on trade in elephant ivory. Elephant populations have now begun to recover, largely as a result of the moratorium.

———

B.   SECRETARIATS

Secretariats are responsible for the day-to-day operations of the convention. The precise functions of the secretariat vary from one treaty to the next; among the more common functions are monitoring and reporting on treaty implementation, assisting implementation when necessary, promoting scientific research relevant to the treaty's objectives, and contributing to the further development of the law. In addition, virtually all secretariats serve as conduits for communications among the treaty parties. This role becomes increasingly important as the number of treaty parties increases. A treaty secretariat may be part of an existing institution–for example, UNEP administers the secretariats for CITES, the Basel Convention, and the Montreal Protocol–or it may be a stand-alone institution, like the Biodiversity and Climate Change secretariats. In either case, secretariats generally lack the authority and the resources to enforce a convention's obligations. People are often surprised to learn the size of treaty secretariats. A typical environmental secretariat has fewer than 20 employees and an annual budget of $1–3 million, yet the convention it oversees may involve activities in 100 or more countries. Thus, secretariats rely heavily on the parties' cooperation and veracity in monitoring compliance or gathering information under the treaty.

Gathering, Analyzing and Distributing Information. Secretariats are the information clearinghouses for most conventions. Environmental conventions often require that parties submit annual or biennial reports related to the specific convention goals. Thus, for example, under the Montreal Protocol parties must submit information regarding the quantity of ozone depleting substances they manufactured or used during the year. Under the Basel Convention, parties must submit reports regarding the amount of hazardous waste they exported or imported. The secretariats typically receive this information and compile it in uniform formats for the effective use of the conferences of the parties.

Maintaining Authoritative Convention Records. For some environmental regimes, the secretariat plays the critical role of maintaining the official, technical and other annexes that can be the heart of the convention. For example, the CITES Secretariat is charged with maintaining the different appendices to the convention, which list all species regulated under the convention. Similarly, the Bureau for the Convention on Wetlands of International Importance Especially as Waterfowl Habitat (known as the Ramsar Convention) maintains the list of designated wetlands as well as a list of "conservation targets."

Supporting the Conferences of the Parties. A routine but important function of treaty secretariats is to prepare and support the annual or biennial meetings of the parties. Each CoP requires staff to prepare, receive, translate, and circulate the official conference documents, as well as manage the logistics of the meeting itself. Preparation of the background papers for the CoP is particularly important for promoting the further development of the treaty regime.

Monitoring Compliance and Facilitating Implementation. Most treaty secretariats do not have actual enforcement authority, but some secretariats do have the "power of persuasion" to bring a violating party into compliance. Perhaps more importantly, secretariats often are responsible for identifying areas of noncompliance and bringing those issues to the Conference of the Parties or to the specific parties involved. Secretariats are also sometimes charged with providing or arranging for technical or other support to assist parties, particularly developing States, to improve their compliance with treaty obligations. Under the Montreal Protocol regime, for example, the Secretariat is involved in every stage of convention implementation–from organizing and arranging meetings that prompt action to compliance assistance. If a Party is not in compliance, it must follow a non-compliance procedure that urges Parties to write directly to the Secretariat with any knowledge about non-compliance either by another Party or by itself. The Secretariat then provides support to an Implementation Committee, which attempts to arrange for the support necessary for bringing the Party into compliance.

Coordinating with Other Treaty Regimes and Secretariats. With the recent proliferation of environmental treaties, as well as the growing interest in environmental protection at other international institutions, treaty secretariats are increasingly being asked to coordinate their activities with other secretariats or institutions. This is particularly important because environmental problems often are interconnected in ways not reflected by the ad hoc manner in which international environmental law develops. The Biodiversity Convention, for example, authorizes its Secretariat to "coordinate with other relevant international bodies and, in particular to enter into such administrative and contractual arrangements as may be required for the effective discharge of its functions." Interestingly, however, the Biodiversity Secretariat has not yet been granted observer status at the World Trade Organization. The Ramsar Bureau has been particularly proactive in coordinating with other international conventions and organizations, in part to try to enlarge Ramsar's role in addressing the interrelationship among conventions affecting wetlands. In particular, the Bureau is focusing on the relationship between water supply and aquatic ecosystem conservation (Biodiversity). In February, 1996, the Secretary–Generals from Ramsar and the Biodiversity Convention signed a Memorandum of Understanding that the Convention on Wetlands will assist the Biodiversity Convention on wetlands and inland water ecosystems issues.

The Convention on International Trade in Endangered Species (CITES) Secretariat provides a good example of a typical secretariat. The CITES Secretariat is a permanent secretariat, administered by UNEP and located in Geneva, Switzerland. The CITES Secretariat monitors the implementation of the convention, assists parties with compliance obligations, and makes recommendations to the biennial conference of the parties (CoP) on the enforcement and implementation of treaty provisions. The CITES Secretariat plays an integral role in monitoring and reporting on the trade of endangered species. Member States must submit annual reports documenting trade information, records of listed species, and the members' legislative, regulatory and administrative actions taken to protect the listed species. Because of its small staff, the CITES Secretariat relies on the Parties and various NGOs for the accuracy of these reports. The Secretariat also receives proposals from the Parties for amendments and revisions to the Convention and its appendices (listing endangered or threatened species of wildlife). Once the Secretariat receives these proposals, it considers them in light of the listing criteria and the needs of local communities. Following review, the secretariat makes its recommendations to the CoP. These recommendations are then considered by the CoP for final decision. The CITES Secretariat is bestowed with authority pursuant to Article XII of the Convention:

1. Upon entry into force of the present Convention, a Secretariat shall be provided by the Executive Director of the United Nations Environment Programme. . . .

2. The functions of the Secretariat shall be:

a) to arrange for and service meetings of the Parties;

b) to perform the functions entrusted to it under the provisions of Articles XV and XVI [regarding proposed amendments and revisions to the lists of species covered by the Convention] of the present Convention;

c) to undertake scientific and technical studies in accordance with programmes authorized by the Convention, including studies concerning standards for appropriate preparation and shipment of living specimens and the means of identifying specimens;

d) to study the reports of Parties and to request from Parties such further information with respect thereto as it deems necessary to ensure implementation of the present Convention;

e) to invite the attention of the Parties to any matter pertaining to the aims of the present Convention;

f) to publish periodically and distribute to the Parties current editions of Appendices I, II, and III together with any information which will facilitate identification of specimens of species included in those Appendices;

g) to prepare annual reports to the Parties on its work and on the implementation of the present Convention and such other reports as meetings of the Parties may request;

h) to make recommendations for the implementation of the aims and provisions of the present Convention, including the exchange of information of a scientific or technical nature; and

(i) to form any other function as may be entrusted to it by the Parties.

C. SUBSIDIARY BODIES AND COMMITTEES

In addition to secretariats, many environmental treaties also create subsidiary bodies or committees to address specific (and usually technical) issues arising under the treaty. The Biodiversity Convention's Subsidiary Body on Scientific, Technical and Technological Advice (SBSTTA) provides a good example of the role of these bodies. The SBSTTA's mission is to further scientific and technical cooperation among the appropriate conventions and institutions. Its members meet annually to draft proposals for consideration by the CoP. Article 25 of the Convention sets forth the SBSTTA's functions.

1. A subsidiary body for the provision of scientific, technical and technological advice is hereby established to provide the Conference of the Parties and, as appropriate, its other subsidiary bodies with timely advice relating to the implementation of this Convention. This body shall be open to participation by all Parties and shall be multidisciplinary. It shall comprise government representatives competent in the relevant field of expertise. It shall report regularly to the Conference of the Parties on all aspects of its work.

2. Under the authority of and in accordance with guidelines laid down by the Conference of the Parties, and upon its request, this body shall: (a) Provide scientific and technical assessments of the status of biological diversity; (b) Prepare scientific and technical assessments of the effects of types of measures taken in accordance with the provisions of this Convention; (c) Identify innovative, efficient and state-of-the-art technologies and know-how relating to the conservation and sustainable use of biological diversity and advise on the ways and means of promoting development and/or transferring such technologies; (d) Provide advice on scientific programmes and international cooperation in research and development related to conservation and sustainable use of biological diversity; and (e) Respond to scientific, technical, technological and methodological questions that the Conference of the Parties and its subsidiary bodies may put to the body.

3. The functions, terms of reference, organization and operation of this body may be further elaborated by the Conference of the Parties.

Similar to the SBSTTA, the Ramsar Convention has convened a Scientific and Technical Review Panel (STRP), consisting of a panel of individual volunteer experts that advises both the Ramsar Convention Bureau and Standing Committee on scientific matters. The STRP has addressed toxic chemicals, economic evaluation, the Ramsar Database, criteria for identification of wetlands of international importance, and an array of other issues. The STRP presents its reports at Standing Committee meetings, and its representatives may also participate in non-Ramsar technical and scientific meetings.

Another model used to address significant issues of treaty administration or implementation is the use of committees, typically authorized directly under the conferences of the parties. For example the biennial meetings of the CITES CoP are supplemented by the more frequent meetings of supplemental committees formed to address specific concerns.

The *standing committee* addresses issues relating to the budget, administrative concerns, and internal affairs. It consists of six representatives from
different regions, a representative from the depository government (Switzerland), and delegates from the host countries of the previous and upcoming CoPs. The *plant* and *animal committees* are responsible, among other
things, for reviewing trade data on Appendix II species to determine
whether more protection is necessary for those species. The *nomenclature
committee* works to develop and maintain standardized terminology and
descriptions for each species. The *identification committee* gathers information to help in identifying specimens and parts for customs officials.

———

D. CREATION OF EXPERT COMMUNITIES

Though often overlooked, an important role played by the secretariats
of UN agencies, the CSD, the OECD and other IGOs is the creation of
international communities of experts. Known as "epistemic communities,"
these provide "a network of professionals with recognized expertise and
competence in a particular domain and an authoritative claim to policy-
relevant knowledge within that domain or issue-area." Peter Haas, *Introduction: Epistemic Communities and International Policy Coordination*, 46
INTL'L ORGANIZATION 1, 3 (1992). Such communities play a fundamental role
in the development and implementation of international law and policy.
Consider the observations in two influential international relations articles.

> In articulating the cause-and-effect relationships of complex problems, helping
> states identify their interests, framing the issues for collective debate, propos-
> ing scientific policies, and identifying salient points for negotiation ... [m]em-
> bers of transnational epistemic communities can influence state interests either
> by directly identifying them for decision makers or by illuminating the salient
> dimensions of an issue from which the decision makers may then deduce their
> interests. The decision makers in one state may, in turn, influence the interests
> and behaviors of other states, thereby increasing the likelihood of convergent
> state behavior and international policy coordination, informed by the causal
> beliefs and policy preferences of the epistemic community.

Id. at 2, 4.

> When the same officials meet recurrently, they sometimes develop a sense of
> collegiality which may be reinforced by their membership in a common profes-
> sion, such as economics, physics, or meteorology. Individual officials may even
> define their roles partly in relation to their transnational reference group
> rather than in purely national terms.... Regularized patterns of policy coordi-
> nation can therefore create attitudes and relationships that will at least
> marginally change policy or affect its implementation....
>
> As such practices [i.e., patterns of regularized policy coordination] become
> widespread, transgovernmental elite networks are created, linking officials in
> various governments to one another by ties of common interest, professional
> orientation, and personal friendship. Even where attitudes are not fundamen-
> tally affected and no major deviations from central policy positions occur, the
> existence of a sense of collegiality may permit the development of flexible
> bargaining behavior in which concessions need not be required issue by issue or
> during each period.

Robert Keohane and Joseph Nye, *Transgovernmental Relations and International Organizations*, 27 WORLD POLITICS 39, 44–45 (1974)

In Part II of the book, we will see again and again how UNEP and other IGOs created experts groups to examine the extent of problems before commencing any type of negotiations. An obvious example of an epistemic community relevant today is the Intergovernmental Panel on Climate Change, created by the World Meteorological Organization and the United Nations Environment Program to assess the scientific, technical and socio-economic information relevant for understanding the risk of climate change. The Ozone Trends Panel played a critical role in the adoption of strict controls on ozone-depleting substances, and the IUCN's Red Book of Endangered and Threatened Species influences many national and international wildlife protection efforts.

Importantly, most of these groups' members (and others who work closely with the groups in an informal capacity) are not government officials but, rather, experts whose influence is both domestic and *transnational*. By providing a forum for government officials and nongovernmental experts to meet and share research and experiences on cutting edge policy issues, IGOs can frame the issues for future collective consideration, lay the groundwork for agreement and identify whose the influential voices in the policy debate shall be. Not all groups created by IGOs, of course, achieve such a level of authoritative expertise. But, at the very least, IGOs and their secretariats exercise potentially considerable power in creating influential international elites of like-minded officials and technocrats.

SECTION III. REFORMING THE UN FOR ENVIRONMENTAL PROTECTION

To many observers, the present UN institutional structure is clearly inadequate to meet the global environmental challenges we now face. For one thing, the concept of sustainable development, with its inherent requirement of integrating both environmental and developmental concerns, has meant that literally dozens of international institutions have laid some claim to a role in environmental protection. This in itself might not be so bad if there were a clear mechanism for coordination, cooperation and leadership, but the IGOs managing environmental issues "have been given narrow mandates, small budgets and limited support. No one organization has the authority or political strength to serve as a central clearinghouse or coordinator." DANIEL ESTY, GREENING THE GATT 78 (1993).

Sir Geoffrey Palmer argues that although UNEP's accomplishments have been significant, it is incapable of adequately addressing global environmental concerns.

Many of these problems are widely recognized, but the logical inference from the facts seems politically unpalatable; the only way to cure the problem is to create a proper international environmental agency within the United Nations system that has real power and authority. At the same time, other environmental components within the UN system should be restructured and reorganized. That restructuring needs to be rigorous if resources are to be saved and priorities redirected. With determination the task could be achieved without spending more resources in total than are expended now. * * *

The making and negotiation of the instruments themselves has to start anew each time. No organization commands clear power to coordinate international environmental negotiations. Each negotiation proceeds differently. The ozone negotiations were conducted in a different way and serviced by a different organization from those on climate change. Such an approach carries the grave risk that on each occasion the wheel must be reinvented. Common elements are not necessarily treated the same way.

There is no institutional machinery to evaluate gaps that may be found in the international framework of agreements or to develop means of assigning priorities among competing claims for attention. Nor is there any way of ensuring that environmental issues are effectively coordinated with and integrated into other activities that may be progressing at the international level. Scientific data and input, which are critical on the global issues, need to be assembled and tested before the political decisions are taken. Yet on each occasion the data are assembled in a different fashion. Institutional means need to be devised to channel scientific and technical expertise to the appropriate policy needs.

If an institutional home for the conduct of the negotiations themselves could be devised, it would cut the substantial costs of dealing with the global issues. Instead of having a new group of nations assemble to discuss each problem by holding a series of international meetings at different locations around the world in an effort to hammer out a consensus on the provisions of a multilateral convention, there could easily be a uniform method for bringing the nations together, conveying the relevant scientific information to them and conducting the negotiations. Such procedures offer the possibility of appreciably reducing the cost of all the present diplomatic activity, as well as increasing the coherence of the rules.

Geoffrey Palmer, *New Ways to Make International Environmental Law*, 86 AM. J. INT'L L. 259, 262–264 (1992).

Given the inherent nature of institutions to increase their resources and influence, forced centralization might offer real benefits through improved coordination among the fragmented convention secretariats and IGOs. As Dan Esty notes, "UNEP, CSD, UNDP, WMO, as well as the Organisation for Economic Cooperation and Development and the World Bank, have climate change programmes underway with little coordination and no sense of strategic division of labour. With entities stretched from Nairobi to Geneva, focus is dissipated, efforts splintered, responsibilities scattered, funding squandered, and accountability lost. Priorities are not set in a coordinated or systematic fashion nor are budgets rationalised." Daniel Esty, *The Value of Creating a Global Environmental Organization*, ENVIRONMENT MATTERS, June, 2000, at 13.

If one looks at the governance of international labor issues, by contrast, it's useful to note that "there are no functionally different secretariats for the many conventions on labor standards, which are administered instead by a single specialized organization, that is, the International Labour Organization (ILO)" Frank Biermann, *The Case for a World Environment Organization*, ENVIRONMENT, November, 2000, at 22, 24. Restructuring international environmental governance may offer additional benefits, as well. Economies of scale can improve the quality and size of financial and technology transfers to developing countries, a demand that will only grow over time. A centralized environmental body could also improve compliance through enhanced monitoring and establishing a "common comprehensive reporting system on the state of the environment and on the state of implementation in different countries as well as by stronger efforts in raising public awareness." *See* Biermann, *op cit.*, at 28.

These arguments have increasingly been taken up by influential political figures. In 1997, at the Earth Summit Plus 5, former German Chancellor Helmut Kohl endorsed the creation of a new global environmental organization. Denis Hayes, *Trade Organization Policies Threaten Global Environments Impact: The World*, SEATTLE POST-INTELLIGENCER, August 17, 1997. He argued that over the short term UNEP should be reformed and strengthened, but over the medium term a global environment umbrella organization created within the UN with UNEP as a major pillar. Kohl's proposal was supported by Brazil, Singapore and South Africa on the first day of the summit. In 1998, the President of France, Jacques Chirac, advocated the development of a world environmental organization, describing it as a "world authority . . . as an impartial and indisputable global center for the evaluation of our environment." *See* Biermann, *op cit.*, at 24. Even the WTO, often portrayed as inimical to environmental interests, has supported the idea. In March 1999, Renato Ruggiero, the Director General of the WTO, proposed that a World Environment Organization be created as a parallel organization of the WTO. Notably, he announced this at the first large-scale WTO meeting for civil society, with representatives from 26 intergovernmental organizations and 130 NGOs representing environmental, developmental, trade unions, consumer, academic and business interests. *WTO proposes a World Environment Organization,* THE GALLON ENVIRONMENT LETTER, March 19, 1999.

Calls for reform of environmental institutions have taken place against the backdrop of greater efforts for coordination among existing institutions. The increase in memoranda of agreement among various IGOs and treaty secretariats, for example, suggests this is happening. But many commentators have called for more. During the 2000 presidential campaign, in fact, three of Vice President Gore's senior advisors called for a new environmental IGO.

> A growing number of environmental problems—ozone depletion, global climate change, threats to biodiversity–are international in scope and require cross-border solutions. Industrial countries, including the United States, are disproportionately responsible for most of these environmental problems, but developing countries are also rapidly damaging common environmental resources. Solutions, therefore, require the participation of both developed and developing nations. But since the costs and benefits of addressing common environmental problems vary among countries, as do the available resources, global agreements must include effective transfer mechanisms and flexibility about the methods used by different countries to achieve environmental targets.

> No vehicle exists for nations to negotiate new multilateral pacts on environmental issues. That is one big reason why environmentalists have focused on the WTO. But using the WTO as the forum for multilateral environmental negotiations both endangers further trade liberalization and raises the risk that trade will be restricted in the name of environmentalism but in the service of

protectionism. To head off these risks, a new Democratic president should propose creating a new Global Environmental Organization to develop and enforce new international agreements on specific problems, using the successful Montreal Protocol on slowing ozone depletion as a model.

W. Bowman Cutter, Joan Spero, Laura D'Andrea Tyson, *New world,New deal,* 79 Foreign Affairs 80, 94 (March/April 2000)

While not lacking in aspiration, this proposal is rather sparse on helpful detail. A number of the more interesting and developed proposals for international environmental institutions are described below.

A. Environmental Protection Council

In 1989, New Zealand proposed creating an Environmental Protection Council, a type of international environmental legislature, within the UN. Sir Geoffrey Palmer, who presented the proposal as New Zealand's Ambassador to the UN, discusses it in the following excerpt.

Geoffrey Palmer, *op. cit.*, at 277–81 (1992)

New Zealand advanced a proposal in the 1989 General Assembly debate for a new United Nations institution, an Environmental Protection Council. The proposal was developed in the following way:

In New Zealand's judgment, the traditional response of international law, developing international legal standards in small incremental steps, each of which must be subsequently ratified by all countries, is no longer appropriate to deal with the highly complex environmental problems of the future.

The time has come for something more innovative, for a conceptual leap forward in institutional terms. And we see the need for the establishment of a new organ in the United Nations system–perhaps it would be called the "Environmental Protection Council," . . . I have no doubt that if the Charter were being drawn up today, there would be widespread support for including among the organs of the United Nations a body empowered to take binding decisions on global environmental issues. In our view, nothing less than an institution with this status will command the necessary respect and authority to achieve what is required.

Perhaps the most effective way to achieve this would be the inclusion in the United Nations Charter of a new Chapter dealing with the environment.

The missing institutional link, however, is the equivalent of a legislature. We would envisage the new Environmental Protection Council becoming the point in the United Nations system which links the streams of economic and environmental advice. It would perform the function that currently falls between the cracks in the mandates of all existing organizations. It would have responsibility for taking coordinated decisions on sustainable policies for global environmental protection. It would be empowered to take binding decisions. And if decisions are to be binding, the membership of the Council may need to be very wide—perhaps including all members of the United Nations. But the key thing is that it should have power to act—not just talk.

* * * What form should a new institution take? The most ambitious course is to create a new organ in the United Nations by amending the Charter. . . . But the procedures for changing the Charter are by no means easy, and the

permanent members of the Security Council have a veto. Although I favor creating a new UN organ, it is not the only option. An easier choice to achieve, and one that could provide a workable institutional framework, would be to create a new specialized UN agency.

Of course, it would be possible to expand and develop the United Nations Environment Programme, negotiate a charter for it, and charge it with some extra responsibilities. Or such bodies as the General Agreement on Tariffs and Trade and the International Monetary Fund could serve as models for a new environmental organization. But, to my mind, the most useful model is the one that has been developed over many years by the International Labour Organisation. * * *

The International Labour Organisation is the most advanced supertreaty system in terms of providing legislative outcomes of any of the international agencies. Borrowing loosely from the ILO Constitution, a new International Environment Organization could be established with the following features.

(1) A General Conference comprising all members, to be called together annually and more often if the Governing Council so decides. The conference shall consist of four representatives from each member; two shall be government delegates and the two others shall represent business and environmental organizations, respectively.

(2) A Governing Council of forty people–twenty representing governments, ten representing business organizations and ten representing environmental organizations.

(3) The ability of the conference to set international environmental regulations by a two-thirds majority of the votes cast by delegates present. The regulations would become binding without further action. There would also be provision for recommendations to be made to members.

(4) A Director–General and staff of the International Environment Office, to have explicit international responsibilities for educating people about the global environmental problems and what they can do to help.

(5) The office to have defined functions for gathering information and monitoring compliance, including verification of compliance with the regulations. There should be regular reviews of the environmental policies of member states and their compliance with the regulations.

(6) A thorough preparatory process, in which there are ample notice, thorough scientific and technical preparation, and consultation before regulations are made.

(7) Formal provision for authoritative and widely representative scientific advice and papers to be available to the organization.

(8) Detailed requirements for nations to report annually on action taken to implement agreed regulations. The environment and business representatives would be required to report separately from governments.

(9) Provision for any member to be able to submit complaints regarding nonobservance in respect of any other member to the International Environment Office.

(10) Discretion of the council to refer such complaints to a commission of inquiry for a full report. The commission shall consist of three appropriate experts of recognized impartiality and be chaired by a lawyer. The commission is to make findings of fact and rule on the steps to be taken to deal with the complaint and the time by which the steps must be taken.

Refusals by governments to accept these findings are to be referred to the full conference.

(11) Authority for the council to recommend measures to the conference to secure compliance when it is lacking. * * *

Many nations, particularly the most powerful and certainly the United States, are likely to be opposed to the creation of such an organization. There appears to be a broad consensus among governments that the creation of new institutions should be avoided when possible. In some quarters those sentiments derive from the ponderous nature of some UN structures and the impenetrable bureaucratic thickets surrounding them. Many nations reshape and reorganize their domestic agencies periodically. Such an effort ought to be made at the UN level. If the position is taken that the total outlay for bureaucratic resources must not exceed what it is now, great and beneficial restructuring could be achieved. It would involve cutting away existing overlaps in international agencies. Without a new institution, progress will be too slow and unsystematic. How much better it would be to have a coherent set of procedures and institutions for creating the norms. The ability to respond to the global challenges we face will be greatly reduced unless a new organization with clean lines of jurisdiction and new powers is created.

———————

B.   GLOBAL ENVIRONMENTAL ORGANIZATION

Daniel Esty suggests that environmentalists borrow from the experience of the World Trade Organization (WTO) and its predecessor, the General Agreement on Tariffs and Trade (GATT). In many respects, the WTO is an international success story. Its mandate and mission are almost universally accepted by the international community and, more importantly, member States have legally agreed to curtail their sovereignty in compliance with rules of the GATT and other WTO agreements. In Esty's view, the WTO serves as a powerful model for a new environmental institution he would call the Global Environmental Organization (GEO).

DANIEL ESTY, GREENING THE GATT 78–82, 85–86 (1993)

To make the best environmental policies politically feasible and to defend the long-term interests of all humankind in a healthy biosphere, the world needs GATT-like rules of mutual forbearance to protect the environment and a supporting international body to manage global environmental relations. Such a regime would contribute to international harmony. Specifically, it would help to ensure that environmental values are not overwhelmed by more established interests such as trade liberalization. It would respond to the "tragedy of the commons" problem and the difficulty of overcoming the collective-action problem to achieve mutually protective policies in the international environmental realm. And it would provide a bulwark against the tendency of governments to transfer environmental burdens to those who are outside their borders or politically weak.

From the perspective of economic theory, the case for a strong and comprehensive Global Environmental Organization (GEO) is overwhelming. The presence of global environmental externalities, the public goods nature of environmental programs, and the intergenerational tradeoffs inherent in environmental policy choices necessitate an overarching regulatory structure. Such a system is needed to limit self-serving (focused on local or national costs, not global consequences), irresponsible and destructive behavior and to ensure that all of the relevant environmental actors participate in a unified regulatory program. Without global cooperation and collective action, there is a serious, ongoing risk of "market failure" in environmental protection, as some countries and some companies free ride on the pollution control efforts of others.

An international environmental regime could help to alleviate both the market failure and the corresponding political failure that makes adoption of appropriate environmental policies on a national basis difficult, internalizing environmental regulations so that no one country would be competitively disadvantaged.... The presence of an institutional structure would help reward cooperation, discipline misbehavior, remind participants of the ongoing nature of the issue, and increase the chance of producing a "win-win" result.

Just as the GATT was built on a few central concepts such as nondiscrimination, negotiations to establish a Global Environmental Organization might initially focus on defining general environmental principles to guide the world community. For example, universal acceptance and application of the polluter pays principle—forcing governments, industry, and individuals alike to bear the full costs of the environmental burdens they impose on society—would create powerful incentives for pollution prevention and environmental care, consistent with the long term interest of the public in a healthy environment and ongoing economic growth. Other principles that might be developed include:

> –a commitment to good science and to life-cycle analysis of environmental issues so that policies are based on a comprehensive view of environmental effects from production through consumption to disposal of a product;

> –a "precautionary" approach to environmental regulation that skews policymaking errors toward protection of public health and ecology, especially in the face of potentially great environmental harms;

> –an emphasis on "pollution prevention" rather than end-of-pipe treatment.

Framing cardinal principles in the environmental realm that are also implementable as decision rules no doubt presents a more complicated challenge than the drafters of the GATT faced. In particular, an environmental regime entails a potentially more intrusive effort to prescribe certain behavior for governments (e.g., cost internalization) whereas the trade regime simply proscribes government actions that would disrupt the free flow of commerce. Moreover, cost internalization and the other environmental principles that might be advanced all have serious practical problems. Getting universal agreement on how to address uncertainties and to quantify incalculables would be no mean feat.

But the limits on our current knowledge and methodologies should not be crippling. A GEO need not begin life all-powerful. It would be appropriate for the new organization to have a sliding scale of authority depending on the global reach, severity, scientific certainty, and time urgency of the various environmental problems it took up (e.g., approaches to cleaning up toxic waste dumps). At the other end of the scale would be issues that demand compulsory international rules with clear sanctions for violators (e.g., ozone layer depletion). Such a structure would allow the GEO to grow into its job–with a mandate that expands (or contracts) as out understanding of environmental issues and analytic capacity evolves.

A GEO could also serve as a focal point for work to improve scientific understanding of ecological problems, gather data on environmental trends, refine analytic tools, and develop environmental "indicators" to track the success of different policies. In addition, the organization would be in a position to facilitate the exchange of environmental information and data and to promote the transfer of pollution control technologies, particularly to developing countries. It would also help broaden the link between different international policy spheres such as trade and development as well as trade and the environment. In doing so, the GEO would expand the scope for tradeoffs across a wider range of issues in pursuit of global environmental protection.

C.   WORLD ENVIRONMENTAL ORGANIZATION

In the excerpt below, Frank Biermann proposes an institution based on the WTO model, as well, but with different powers than Esty's.

Frank Biermann, *The Case for a World Environment Organization*, ENVIRONMENT, Nov., 2000, 28–29

UNEP would form the core of this new organization, which would, however, be empowered to coordinate other organizations and regimes. By large measure, a world environment organization of this type would follow the WTO model. This would require a basic Agreement on Establishing the World Environment Organization, which would contain a number of general principles–maybe building on the 1992 Rio Declaration on Environment and Development—as well as coordinating rules that govern the organization and its relationship with the issue—specific environmental regimes. The general principles will have to encompass more than purely environmental rules (e.g., the precautionary approach) but must also address, above all, the development concerns of the developing world. Hence, general principles, such as the right to development, the sovereign right over natural resources within a country's jurisdiction, or the principle of common but differentiated responsibilities and capabilities, need to be integrated into the constitutive instrument of a world environment organization.

Again following WTO usage, environmental regimes covered by the organization could be divided into multilateral and plurilateral environmental agreements. As for multilateral agreements, ratification would be compulsory for any new member of a world environment organization, but plurilateral agreements would still leave members the option to remain outside. The multilateral agreements would thus form the global environmental law code under the world environment organization, with the existing conferences of the parties— say, to the Montreal Protocol—being transformed into subcommittees under the ministerial conference of the organization.

This integration would enable the world environment organization to develop a common reporting system for all multilateral environmental agreements (e.g., an annual national report to the world environment organization); to develop a common dispute settlement system; to develop mutually agreed upon guidelines that may be followed—based on an interagency agreement—for the activities of the World Bank and the WTO dispute settlement system; and to develop a joint system of capacity building for developing countries along with financial and technological transfers.

The establishment of such an organization would create a number of welfare gains by increasing the overall efficiency in the system. For example, the sometimes minuscule secretariats of multilateral environmental agreements would be integrated into the world environment organization. Likewise, negotiations could be centralized geographically, which would especially benefit developing countries that are often not in a position to send diplomats with sufficient expertise to the various environmental treaty conferences around the world. A world environment organization at one specific seat—most likely in Africa—would allow especially the smaller developing countries to build up specialized environmental embassies with a highly qualified staff able to follow various complicated negotiations. The same could be said for nongovernmental organizations that could participate in global negotiations at lower costs.

For developed and developing countries, a centralizing and powerful world environment organization would hardly be acceptable if decisionmaking procedures did not grant them sufficient control over the outcome of negotiations and the organization's future evolution. Thus, a centralizing organization seems feasible only with a double-weighted majority system comparable to that of the Montreal Protocol as amended in 1990 or GEF as reformed in 1994. In both institutions, decisions require the assent of two-thirds of members that must include the simple majority of both developing and developed countries. In a sense, this system of developed-developing world parity in decisionmaking represents a new third path between the one-country, one-vote formula of the UN General Assembly, which grants developing countries a built-in majority, and the one-dollar, one-vote system of the World Bank and the International Monetary Fund (IMF), which favors the interests of the major industrialized countries.

Admittedly, decisionmaking procedures based on developed-developing world parity (veto rights for the developed and developing worlds as one group) are problematic, especially when it comes to the question of which country belongs to which group and who will decide. Singapore, for example, is still seen as a developing country even though its national per capita income is higher than that of many industrialized countries. The Montreal Protocol uses an issue-based classification scheme that draws a line between developing countries that consume less than 300 grams of chlorofluorocarbons (CFC) per person each year and all other countries (thus, for example, placing Kuwait in the group of industrialized countries). Such issue-based classification cannot be applied to a world environment organization meant to address all environmental issues. It seems that the second best option remains the self-definition of states, as done in the UN General Assembly, with the expectation that certain developing countries—especially those that wish to join the Organisation for Economic Cooperation and Development (OECD)—will also assume the respective additional responsibilities in international organizations.

———

D.   TRUSTEESHIP OF THE GLOBAL COMMONS

A number of scholars and public figures have called for the creation of trustees to advocate the interests of non-represented entities. Professor Christopher Stone supports the creation of an "Ocean Guardian," for example, and Professor Edith Brown Weiss has called for ombudsmen to represent the interests of future generations. *See* Christopher Stone, *Mending the Seas Through a Global Commons Trust Fund*, in FREEDOM FOR THE SEAS IN THE 21ST CENTURY at 171 (Jon M. Van Dyke, Durwood Zaelke & Grant Hewison eds. 1993); Edith Brown Weiss, IN FAIRNESS TO FUTURE GENERATIONS 109, 124–126 (1989). The Commission on Global Governance has similarly called for the environmental use of the existing UN Trustee-ship Council. Created to facilitate the transition of trust territories to independent self-government following decolonization after World War II, the Trusteeship Council defended the interests of territories without sover-eign status and ceased to operate in 1994 when the last trust territory became part of a national jurisdiction. In much the same way as trust territories have had no formal international representation, the global commons and future generations have no representation in international bodies.

Commission on Global Governance, Our Global Neighborhood 252–53 (1995)

We envisage the Trusteeship Council becoming the chief forum on global environmental and related matters. Its functions would include the administra-tion of environmental treaties in such fields as climate change, biodiversity, outer space, and the Law of the Sea. It would refer, as appropriate, any economic or security issues arising from these matters to the Economic Securi-ty Council or the Security Council.... [W]e suggest that the Commission on Sustainable Development (CSD), which now reports to ECOSOC, report to the proposed Economic Security Council. We would expect this new group to refer matters related to the global commons or other appropriate issues to the new Trusteeship Council.

The new role proposed for the Trusteeship Council would be fully in keeping with the important responsibilities assigned to it when it was established as a principal organ of the United Nations, with its own chamber at the UN in New York. The change in its role will require Chapters XII and XIII of the UN Charter to be revised. The new Council could be composed, as the Trusteeship Council was, of representatives of a number of member-states.... We suggest that the General Assembly determine the number and the criteria for selection.

The functions of the Council in this new role are such that it would benefit from contributions from civil society organizations. Governments, in consider-ing the reconstitution of the Trusteeship Council, should examine how best this could be secured. The Charter provided that "each member of the Trusteeship Council shall designate one specially qualified person to represent it." A similar provision would leave it open to governments to nominate a public official or someone with the required qualifications from civil society. Additionally, the procedures of the new Council could be drawn up to facilitate contributions by civil society organizations.

Many administrative and other matters will need to be considered if this proposal is to be implemented, but we believe they can all be satisfactorily handled. The most important step to be taken is the conceptual one that the time has come to acknowledge that the security of the planet is a universal need to which the UN system must cater.

E.   DEVELOPING COUNTRY CONCERNS

It is worth noting that all the reforms described above have come from developed country perspectives. What do developing countries want from international environmental governance? The excerpt below presents the perspective of Asian developing countries (ADC). The core argument is that a World Environmental Organization must be relevant to the environmental problems faced daily by the ADC, not the long term concerns focused on by the North such as climate change and loss of biodiversity but more mundane (and pressing) concerns such as crowded cities (where over half of the ADC population will reside by 2020), high levels of air pollution, severe traffic congestion, and increasing poverty. What can a new international environmental organization do to address these problems?

Raghbendra Jha, *An Asian Perspective on a World Environmental Organization*, MacArthur Foundation Project Working Paper, July 1999 <http://www.igidr.ac.in/?rjha/mfweo.html>

The existing institutions and global and regional environmental treaties have failed in (a) using side payment mechanisms for internalizing cross border externalities, (b) using issue linkage i.e. non-environmental incentives along with environmental negotiations, and (c) have not used global mechanisms to underpin and reinforce domestic policies on the environment. Any design of the WEO needs to address these deficiencies explicitly. * * *

A weak version of the WEO that merely acts as a clearing house for deals on (say) cash transfers from rich countries to ADC in exchange for the latter promising and delivering increased protection to their forests and biodiversity and other assets would be agreements between two willing partners and the WEO would do no more than facilitating them. Clearly, such an arrangement would not be objected to by the ADC. Given the scale of global environmental problems, and the fact that developing countries need strong incentives for exercising restraint in the environmental area, it might be the case that these types of environmental deals, by themselves, would not be able to make much of a dent on global environmental problems. In particular, issue-linkage and the internalizing of externalities from one such deal to another may not be optimally achieved within such arrangement. * * *

Public support for the notion of WEO within the ADC would be easier to obtain if it can be demonstrated that this organization is addressing not only global environmental problems but also (even indirectly) those that are of more immediate concern for the population of the ADC. This may be termed the "Southern Agenda" and as such shares commonalities with concerns of developing countries of Latin America and Africa as well... Most environmental problems of ADC would fall in the category of local, or at best, bilateral problems. These include urban congestion and air pollution from industrial effluents and vehicle emissions; soil erosion; overgrazing; desertification; water pollution from sewage runoff and agricultural pesticides since tap water is not potable in many countries; huge and rapidly growing population overstraining natural resources. Even in the relatively affluent East Asian economies, urban congestion and air pollution remain as pressing concerns. Thus global concerns such as CO_2, deforestation, ozone and biodiversity do not seem to have manifested themselves as much in these countries. Thus their enthusiasm about WEO purely focussed on global issues, seen as a primarily OECD concern is expected to be muted. If however some of the local concerns are also bundled in the WEO agenda, this agenda is likely to garner some support within ADC. * * *

Issue linkage in negotiations on the international environment can take various forms. These may include, for example, tariff concessions by developed countries in response to preservation of environmental assets by LDCs supplemented, when necessary, by cash side payments; the threat by the LDC to increase to increase their rate of deforestation unless tariff concessions are made and the rewarding of environmental protection by LDC by developed countries by tariff concessions, the reduction of non tariff barriers in developed countries in response to reduced carbon emission by LDC, writing off some international debt of LDC by developed countries, targeting FDI flows in response to environmental action taken by the LDC and so on. In each of these cases, there are two pertinent questions: first, what is the scale of inducement that is possible to developing countries; and, second, what is the room for action in these areas (within the aegis of a WEO) over and above what is already promised in the context of other international agreements such as the WTO?

* * *

Clearly a mild version of a WEO that, all environmental treaties under one umbrella, provides technical know-how and facilitates negotiations would be innocuous enough, therefore, acceptable. However, such a WEO would also not be very effective in controlling the problem of global externalities, assuming that this problem is of an emergent nature. Stronger versions of WEO would not be acceptable to ADC unless issue linkage of the sort discussed here becomes a reality.

———

QUESTIONS AND DISCUSSION

1. Answer the following for each of the proposals described above:

    (a) What advantages do they present over current international institutions?

    (b) To what extent do they require the surrender of state sovereignty to be effective?

    (c) Are their functions primarily executive or catalytic?

    (d) Would they have rule-making, enforcement, or adjudicatory powers?

    (e) Would they complement or replace UNEP and the Commission on Sustainable Development?

    Do you think the problems associated with UNEP are structural or political? That is, will a new organization with a different structure be any more successful than the present situation or will it face the same geopolitical dogfights and conflicts that UNEP faces?

2. If the goal of these new institutions is to achieve global adherence to and enforcement of environmental norms, how should these norms be substantively determined? Would these norms reflect the "common but differentiated responsibilities" of developed and less-developed nations under Agenda 21 and the "different ability to compete" under GATT and the World Trade Organization? *See* Rio Declaration on Environment and Development, Principle 7; Agreement Establishing the World Trade Organization, Article XI (2) and GATT 1994, Article XXXVI (8).

3. As Daniel Esty has argued, the WTO is an effective organization with significant power. Its power, however, derives directly from nations' willingness to subject themselves to the WTO's dispute resolution procedures. In a sense, the WTO reflects a "deal"—countries are assured of liberalized trade and reduction of trade barriers in exchange for relinquishing some aspects of sovereignty. Why would countries be willing to cede any sovereignty to a new environmental institution? Would they need to cede such sovereignty for the institution to be more effective than the current structure? Given the failure of nations to meet many of the goals established at the Rio Conference, is there the political will in the international community to create new international environmental regimes?

4. Why do you think the head of the WTO, Renato Ruggieri, called for the creation of a stronger environmental institution? Would such an institution likely ease or exacerbate the trade and environment conflict?

5. In considering the creation of a new international environmental organization, does Palmer's reliance on the International Labor Organization as a model provide a stronger or weaker place to begin than Esty's or Biermann's reliance on the WTO? Can you think of any other IGOs that present a useful model?

6. A theme emphasized by Palmer and the Commission on Global Governance is the importance of participation by individuals and NGOs. Much criticism of the current international governance system has been directed at a perceived lack of sensitivity to popular participation and the "top heavy" nature of the organizational structure. This has sometimes been described as the "democratic deficit" in international law and policy. Is there an inherent conflict between creating a more powerful institution, such as a GEO or an Environmental Protection Council, and increasing public participation?

7. Palmer recommends that the International Environment Organization take decisions based on a two-thirds majority of delegates present. Provided the requisite supermajority was achieved, these decisions would be binding on States even without their consent. Recall, moreover, that fully one half of the delegates would be non-State actors. Conceivably, then, the IEO could adopt binding decisions with the support of less than half of the member States. Given the reluctance of States to accept any international obligation without their consent, does this mechanism seem feasible? In what respects does the voting structure proposed by Biermann provide a better compromise?

8. The proposals suggested above would seem to provide greater and clearer environmental law-making authority to one institution. Would this also solve the problems of coordination and integration among current IGOs? In other words, would each of the reform proposals assist in increasing coordination among the many different institutions that today are active in the field of the environment? Would any of them assist in facilitating the integration of environmental protection with issues of economic development, human rights, or social equity? In this respect, would the creation of bodies with greater environmental powers promote sustainable development or *hinder* it? Should these proposals be modified to reflect a broader approach to sustainable development—one that does not separate environmental concerns from related issues?

9. Clearly, creating new international institutions with expanded powers will meet strong political opposition, particularly from existing institutions whose influence might be lessened. Television commentator and presidential candidate Pat Buchanan, for example, has condemned United States membership in the World Trade Organization as a "sweeping surrender of American sovereignty", which had "zero popular support" and has left the United States "horribly vulnerable to sudden devaluations by Third World regimes." According to Buchanan, to advocate membership in the WTO abdicates America's role in world affairs and is equivalent to "saying that America's sovereignty, independence are things of the past. They are gone forever. We must all accept our dependency upon the New World Order. . . . The battle for the future will be between the hired men of the Money Power who long ago abandoned as quaint but useless old ideas of nationhood—and populists, patriots and nationalists . . ." <http://www.iac.net/-davcam/survive.html>. If you were debating Buchanan on the creation of one of the new institutions described above, what responses would you prepare to his likely criticisms? How would your responses differ if you were debating an anti-globalization activist, fresh from protests at the World Bank?

SECTION IV.   THE ROLE OF NON-STATE ACTORS

A.   NGOs

Under traditional views of public international law, only States have rights and responsibilities. Nongovernmental actors, industry, and subnational governments are not allowed to participate in, nor are they subjects of, international law. As discussed in Chapter 6, this classical view of international lawmaking ignores the rich and dynamic role of non-State actors in modern international law generally and in international environmental law particularly. Information, capital and people (including activists) now circulate across national boundaries with little restriction by most States' authorities. Non–State actors, most notably multinational corporations and NGOs, now conduct their own foreign policy, gather their own information from informal sources, and increasingly expect to participate in international affairs.

In the environmental field, the number of NGOs has exploded in recent years, as has NGO capacity to build networks, gather and analyze technical information, and gain the attention of policymakers in many countries. The environmental movement has also "gone global." Virtually every country now has at least one environmental NGO, many of which are actively seeking partnerships and cooperative activities with their colleagues from other countries. The 2000 edition of the Yearbook of International Organizations, for example, contains entries on 29,495 organizations (in addition to 24,326 international NGOs). The United States certainly still has the richest assortment and diversity of environmental NGOs, but there are surprisingly sophisticated and effective organizations in all regions of the world. And as Philip Shabecoff, the former *New York Times* environmental writer, has noted, environmental NGOs are having an impact on international environmental governance. Philip Shabecoff, A NEW NAME FOR PEACE: INTERNATIONAL ENVIRONMENTALISM, SUSTAINABLE DEVELOPMENT, AND DEMOCRACY, 76–77 (1996).

> What is undeniable … is that environmentalists, far more than any other nongovernmental community except, perhaps, human rights activists, have forced their way into the previously closed rooms of international diplomacy. Even if their policies are not adopted, they are *there,* placing their position papers on the table and speaking out, not just in the corridors but in the once sacrosanct plenary halls and in the small, out-of-the-way chambers where deals are hammered out in secret meetings.

> While they have not yet created a new society, it may not be too far a reach to conclude that the civil sector activists may be the opening wedge of a new, more open system of international governance. Over the past quarter of a century they have eroded, if not broken, the monopoly of governments and their satraps in the international agencies in the process of reaching decisions affecting the relationships and joint activities of nation-states.

Of the thousands of environmental groups in the United States, relatively few have the capacity or interest to be involved in international issues—but the number is growing and includes most of the largest environmental organizations. According to the National Wildlife Federation's annual *Conservation Directory*, more than 100 NGOs describe themselves as involved in some aspect of international environmental protection.

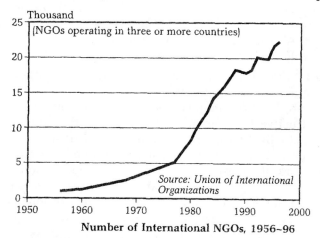

Number of International NGOs, 1956–96

For our general purposes, environmental NGOs participating in international issues can be divided into three categories. First are the large membership organizations, like the Natural Resources Defense Council, the Environmental Defense Fund, the National Audubon Society, the National Wildlife Federation, and the Sierra Club, which have the resources and technical expertise to work on a full range of environmental issues. Beginning in the late 1980s, almost all of these organizations added international departments to work on global and transnational issues. Their staffs often include lawyers, scientists and economists in an effort to bring an interdisciplinary approach to environmental issues. In addition, U.S. environmental law organizations like the Environmental Law Institute and EarthJustice (formerly the Sierra Club Legal Defense Fund) have in recent years expanded their interest to international issues.

The second group include organizations that are dedicated primarily, if not exclusively, to global and transnational environmental issues. These include organizations like WorldWatch, the World Resources Institute, and the Center for International Environmental Law (CIEL). Some of these organizations may be small and narrowly focused, but still very effective, like Earth Rights International (which works on the integration of human rights and environment with a staff of 20) or Bat Conservation International (which is dedicated to the global protection of bats and has a staff of thirty).

A third category of NGOs are those organizations that operate as parts of global networks. Most notable among these are the International Union for the Conservation of Nature (IUCN) (actually a network comprised of NGOs and government agencies concerned with nature conservation), Friends of the Earth–International (a network of 63 affiliate organizations), Greenpeace International (a federation of 26 national organizations with more than 3.3 million members), and the World Wide Fund for Nature (a federation of 27 national organizations boasting over 4.7 million members).

The Environmental Law Alliance Worldwide (ELAW) is a particularly interesting example of an international network of affiliated organizations. Comprised of over 300 public interest scientists and lawyers from 60 countries, ELAW is essentially the first global, virtual law firm dedicated to public interest environmental law. Advocates from over fifty countries access the ELAW network each year. Most of these NGOs have their own web page, easily found on the Internet.

Foreign NGOs display the same diversity found in the United States; some are professional organizations with expansive technical expertise, while many are local community-based, grassroots organizations. Regional and national networks of organizations improve the efficacy of individual organizations by facilitating coordination and exchanging information and expertise. For example, the European Environment Bureau (EEB) is a regional network of environmental NGOs in Europe, including much of the former Soviet Bloc. The EEB is located in Brussels, where it focuses on lobbying and influencing the European Union's institutions.

Environmental law NGOs are also thriving in the global South. South America boasts a number of the most sophisticated environmental law organizations anywhere in the world, including for example Sociedad Peruana Derecho Ambiental (Peru), Fundacion Ambiente y Recursos Naturales (Argentina), Centro Mexicano del Derecho Ambiental (Mexico), SEDERENA (Costa Rica), IDEADS (Guatemala), CEDHA (Argentina) and Fundepublico (Colombia). Nor is this limited to South America. Perhaps the most innovative environmental litigation in the world now emanates from Asia, and in particular from such public interest lawyers as India's M.C. Mehta and the Philippines' Tony Oposa. *See, e.g., Using Civil Litigation and the Judiciary to Protect the Environment in India,* in C. SALADIN, S. PORTER & D. HUNTER, EDS., USING LAW TO PROTECT THE ENVIRONMENT: CASE STUDIES FROM AROUND THE WORLD (CIEL: 1996). The Indonesian Environmental Law Center, Bangladesh Environmental Law Association and South Korean Environmental Law Association, are just a few examples of Asia's growing public interest environmental law movement. Likewise, Tanzania's Legal Environmental Action Team is an increasingly effective and influential organization in Africa.

Technology as the Glue. Although it is a common "world view" that ultimately binds environmental NGOs together, it is communication technology that turns this philosophy into action. The Internet, in particular, provides a vast opportunity for sharing experiences and mobilizing activists to push for stronger environmental policies. Not only do these electronic networks allow for effective lobbying on international issues such as the World Bank or the conservation of Antarctica, but they can also bring international pressure to bear on purely local issues. In 1996, for example, the Environmental Law Alliance Worldwide (ELAW) network, developed primarily to help environmental lawyers bring environmental cases in developing countries, banded together to oppose a Korean company's destruction of riparian habitat in Eugene, Oregon. Efforts like this suggest that the Internet and other communication advances will not only make it easier to "think globally", but also to "act locally."

As Jessica Tuchman Matthews observed in *Foreign Affairs:*

Technology is fundamental to NGOs' new clout. The nonprofit Association for Progressive Communications provides 50,000 NGOs in 133 countries access to the tens of millions of Internet users for the price of a local call. The dramatically lower costs of international communication have altered NGOs' goals and changed international outcomes. Within hours of the first gunshots of the Chiapas rebellion in southern Mexico in January 1994, for example, the Internet swarmed with messages from human rights activists. The worldwide media attention they and their groups focused on Chiapas, along with the influx of rights activists to the area, sharply limited the Mexican government's response. What in other times would have been a bloody insurgency turned out to be a largely nonviolent conflict. "The shots lasted ten days," Jose Angel Gurria, Mexico's foreign minister, later remarked, "and ever since, the war has been . . . a war on the Internet."

NGOs' easy reach behind other states' borders forces governments to consider domestic public opinion in countries with which they are dealing, even on matters that governments have traditionally handled strictly between themselves. At the same time, cross-border NGO networks offer citizens groups unprecedented channels of influence. Women's and human rights groups in many developing countries have linked up with more experienced, better funded, and more powerful groups in Europe and the United States. The latter work the global media and lobby their own governments to pressure leaders in developing countries, creating a circle of influence that is accelerating change in many parts of the world.

Jessica Tuchman Matthews, *Power Shift*, FOREIGN AFFAIRS 50 (1997). Examples like Chiapas abound, particularly in the environmental field. Many major controversies involving U.S. companies and their affiliates abroad have been widely broadcast over the Internet. For example, alleged environmental and human rights abuses surrounding Freeport McMoran's gold mining operations in Irian Jaya, Shell Oil's developments in Nigeria, and Texaco's drilling in Ecuador's Amazon have all been the focus of conferences and "action alerts" on the Internet.

The advent of broadcast faxing, express mail delivery services, electronic mail, and the Internet have dramatically increased the NGO community's ability to form and maintain networks, to share information, and to coordinate international lobbying efforts. The most important developments are not in the formation of permanent federations of groups or of formal networks, but rather the ability of networks and campaigns to form and dissolve readily. This dynamic process allows for concentrated efforts through new and changing alliances that focus on specific issues. Success often depends as much on internal diplomacy—the ability to attract and maintain the interest of a large number of NGOs—as it does on any one organization's ability to access official decisionmakers. These "virtual networks" allow coordinated action in many different countries around the same issue, with little need for expensive infrastructure or costly planning meetings.

To understand how this global environmental community works, consider recent efforts to convince the World Bank's Board of Executive Directors to support an independent investigation into a controversial South American dam. The investigation is based on a detailed letter drafted over the Internet by citizens living in the area affected by the project, with the help of U.S. lawyers. Two or three drafts of the thirty-page document are exchanged—at virtually no cost and virtually instantaneously. Copies of the final letter are posted on the Internet home page of both organizations. The letter is filed electronically with the World Bank Inspection Panel. Action alerts are immediately sent out to over fifty organizations and networks from over thirty countries, summarizing the facts, referring other NGOs to the homepage, and asking for support of the claim. Ultimately over ninety NGOs from over twenty countries would sign on to a letter of support sent to the Bank President. Fifteen more NGOs and NGO networks from different countries write their own letters. Ten of those fifteen call their government's representatives at the Bank and ask personally for their support. One European NGO begins circulating a video of the project, prepared two years earlier but still directly on point. If a significant new development occurs, the groups in the United States (home of the World Bank) or the groups in the project-affected area can send updates and briefings immediately over the Internet. More letters or phone calls, if necessary, are sent. Ultimately, the claimants board a plane and come to the World Bank headquarters, where they are hosted by their colleagues who have set up meetings with different executive directors, Bank staff, and the international press corps. The World Bank Executive Directors have felt the independent, but coordinated, pressure from groups in their home countries as well as elsewhere—and hopefully are convinced to support the investigation.

Another good illustration of NGO networking, is the network established specifically to provide NGO input into negotiations of the UN Economic Commission for Europe's Convention on Public Participation and Access to Environmental Information. The European Environment Bureau and Friends of the Earth (FoE)–Europe organized an electronic network, chaired by Jeremy Waites of FoE–Ireland, which provides periodic updates about the negotiations over the Web. Specific people or working groups, often separated by thousands of miles, agree to work on specific parts of the negotiating text to provide comments, background papers and proposed text. Working drafts of various documents are drafted, revised and revised again based on comments received over email. Prior to each negotiating session, an international meeting of NGOs is held to discuss the background papers and proposed text, and to discuss negotiating strategies. These discussions inform the Executive Committee, which presents the NGO position at the actual negotiations, where NGOs are provided official observer status.

Environmental NGOs are increasingly involved in all aspects of international environmental law. Often NGOs are in the background, for example providing analytical support for government officials and policymakers. More and more frequently, however, NGOs are taking an active and direct role in law development and implementation. The following examples are illustrative.

Direct Participation in International Negotiations. In recent years, NGOs have begun to participate directly in international negotiations as part of official delegations. For example, the U.S. delegations to international meetings now routinely include both environmental NGO and industry representatives as unofficial observers. CIEL attorneys, for example, have been on the official U.S. delegations to the Global Environmental Facility, OECD, the Intergovernmental Panel on Forests, and conferences of the parties of both the Climate Change Convention and the Biodiversity Convention.

Having NGO representatives on official delegations is mutually beneficial. The government benefits from the expertise, knowledge, and political "cover" of the NGO. The government also leverages resources to some extent, as NGO delegates typically pay their own expenses to travel and participate in the meetings. NGOs on the other hand gain from increased access to information and potentially more direct input into official positions.

In some instances, NGOs have more formally represented governments at international conferences. In these instances, NGOs actually speak for the government, in what is essentially a lawyer-client relationship. The Foundation for International Environmental Law and Development (FIELD), for example, represented Vanuatu and other island nations in the climate change negotiations and a CIEL attorney represented the Marshall Islands in negotiations over the Global Program of Action addressing land-based sources of marine pollution. Such representation can be very important, particularly for developing countries, because NGOs can often muster more resources and expertise with respect to these negotiations than many governments.

Shuttle Diplomacy, the Power to Convene. Located on the border of Russia and Estonia, Lake Peipsi or Lake Chudskoe, depending on which country you are from, is the fifth largest lake in Europe. The large, shallow lake suffers from many typical environmental problems, including pollution and overfishing. Mostly, however, the lake suffers from post-Soviet politics. Because of overriding issues relating to Estonia's separation from the Soviet Union, the federal governments have poor relations, and joint management of their transboundary lake is not one of their highest priorities.

Management of the lake *is* the highest priority, however, for the people, communities, and local governments living on its shores. Beginning in 1994, a small NGO named the Lake Peipsi/Chudskoe Project began its own form of "shuttle diplomacy." The Project strategically organized international conferences both to provide a neutral forum for informal discussions and to force the governments to commit publicly to protecting the lake. By inviting international experts on transboundary water management, for example from the Great Lakes, the NGOs also added credibility to their efforts and provided technical assistance to the governments. By including both Russians and Estonians, the Project was able to facilitate dialogue between the two countries' authorities. The dialogue now reaches all the way from local villages to the capitol cities and resulted in the negotiation of the Framework Agreement on Environmental Cooperation, signed on January 11, 1996, and on continued negotiations over specific management issues and joint projects involving the lake. *See* N. Desai & C. Abercrombie, ed. *Using Nongovernmental Intervention to Promote Transboundary Cooperation: the Case of Lake Peipsi/Chudskoe* (CIEL Case Study: 1996).

Promoting Accountability at International Institutions. Pushed by NGOs and donor governments the World Bank created the Inspection Panel in September 1993. The Panel's August 1994 opening marked the first time in the Bank's 50–year history that affected people harmed by Bank-funded projects could request independent reviews of Bank activities. With the Panel, the Bank also became the first international institution outside of the European Union to create a mechanism by which citizens could demand accountability without involving their government.

Project-affected people can file claims with the Panel, seeking an investigation into alleged violations of Bank policies and procedures. After receiving a claim, the Panel conducts a preliminary assessment, including a review of the claim and Management's response. Based on this assessment, the Panel recommends to the Executive Directors whether a full inspection is warranted. The Executive Directors retain sole power to authorize a full inspection. For inspections that go forward, the Panel enjoys broad investigatory powers including access to all Bank Management and staff. After the investigation, the Panel issues a fact-finding report with its recommendations to Bank Management and the Executive Directors.

Twenty-four claims have now been filed at the inspection panel. In the first claim filed with the Panel, for example, the Arun Concerned Group, a Nepalese human rights group, and several individuals living in the Arun Valley alleged that in reviewing a proposed 200–Megawatt hydroelectric dam for the region, the Bank failed to: (1) analyze adequately alternatives to the project and their comparative risks; (2) integrate demand-side planning into the country's energy strategy; (3) provide information in Nepal in compliance with the Bank's information policy; (4) complete an adequate environmental assessment when it changed designs for the access road; (5) provide adequate compensation for displaced families; or (6) prepare an indigenous peoples plan.

After reviewing the Bank Management's response and conducting a preliminary investigation in Nepal, the Panel issued its initial report on December 16, 1994. The Panel found reason to believe that each of the claimant's allegations were true, and requested from the Board of Executive Directors authority to conduct a more thorough investigation. The Board agreed to the inspection, and the Panel had just completed the inspection when World Bank President James Wolfensohn announced that the Bank was withdrawing its support for the project. Mr. Wolfensohn cited the work of the Inspection Panel as one of the reasons for his decision. For further discussion of the Inspection Panel, see Chapter 20, page 1488.

International Oversight of Domestic Law: Citizen Petitions Under the NAAEC. The North American Agreement on Environmental Cooperation (NAAEC) allows citizens to petition the North American Commission on Environmental Cooperation (CEC) regarding the enforcement of domestic environmental laws by the States party to the Agreement. Under the NAAEC, any NGO or person established or residing in the territory of a Party to the Agreement (i.e. Canada, the United States or Mexico) may make a submission to the CEC Secretariat asserting that a Party is failing to enforce an environmental law effectively. If the Secretariat determines that a submission merits a response and at least two of the three Parties agree to allow the inquiry to go forward, the Secretariat will prepare a final factual record containing: (1) a summary of the submission that initiated the process; (2) a summary of the response, if any, provided by the concerned Party; (3) a summary of any other relevant factual information; and (4) the facts as found by the Secretariat with respect to the matters raised in the submission. To date, 31 citizen petitions have been filed with the Commission, including 8 against the United States. The guidelines, and early citizen submission under them, are discussed in greater detail in Chapter 15, on NAFTA.

Expanded Role in Compliance and Implementation. NGOs have played a major role in monitoring compliance and improving implementation of environmental conventions. For example, NGOs such as WWF and TRAF-FIC provided well-publicized and important undercover operations that have helped to police CITES. Reports from Ozone Action highlight violations of the spirit, if not the substance, of the Montreal Protocol, and other NGOs such as the Natural Resources Defense Council have shifted their focus toward improving national implementation of international agreements. *See, e.g.,* Jim Vallette, *Deadly Complacency: US CFC Production, the Black Market and Ozone Depletion* (Ozone Action, Sept. 1995).

NGOs and convention secretariats sometimes develop symbiotic relationships, in which the NGO provides research or other services that the secretariat lacks the resources or authority to provide for itself and, in return, receives greater input into the decisions of the treaty secretariat and CoP. The CITES Secretariat has developed such relationships with two separate NGOs—the World Conservation Monitoring Centre (WCMC) and Traffic International. The WCMC was established jointly by the World Wide Fund for Nature (WWF), IUCN, and UNEP to provide information services on conservation and sustainable use issues to the international community. Since the early 1980s, the WCMC has been data manager for the CITES Secretariat, maintaining on the Secretariat's behalf all the trade records of species listed in the CITES Appendices. WCMC provides similar data management services for the World Heritage Convention, the Convention on Biological Diversity, the Convention on Migratory Species, and the Ramsar (Wetlands) Convention. Because conservation data has been centralized in this way, WCMC is working with the secretariats of the five major biodiversity-related treaties to seek ways to increase harmonisation in information management and reporting, thereby increasing resources available for implementing the agreements, increasing synergy in their application, and avoiding duplication of effort.

Traffic International is a decentralized network of national organizations created by WWF and IUCN to monitor international trade in endangered species. Traffic investigations and reports have been instrumental in tracking the growth of the illegal trade in wildlife. By identifying weaknesses in national customs enforcement in many countries, including the United States, identifying important trade routes for wildlife commodities, and investigating wildlife smuggling activities, Traffic has been instrumental to the effective implementation of CITES. In addition, Traffic provides the key communication medium for CITES parties through its bi-monthly Traffic Bulletin, thereby relieving the CITES Secretariat of this responsibility. The Traffic Bulletin provides news on enforcement activities throughout the world, changes in Annex III listings by parties, and discussions of emerging issues in the international wildlife trade. As a result of its activities, its policy recommendations receive close attention from both national governments and the CITES leadership. For example, Traffic has been instrumental in raising awareness among the CITES parties about the links between traditional medicine and unsustainable uses of tigers, rhinoceros, bears and other heavily traded species.

Sounding the Alarm: Bringing Science to the Attention of Policymakers. Perhaps the most important role of environmental NGOs in international environmental law is their role in bringing to the attention of international policymakers new potential threats to public health and the environment. NGOs often bring scientific expertise together or find other ways to disseminate new findings in the environmental sciences.

A clear example of this was the publication of the book, *Our Stolen Future,* which documents significant evidence that certain persistent organic pollutants (POPs) may present a previously unforeseen threat to human and animal health. These POPs are not (or not simply) toxic or carcinogenic—the classical measures of danger. Instead, they mimic hormones that control human and animal reproduction and development and other vital biological processes. T. COLBORN, D. DUMANOSKI, & J. P. MYERS, OUR STOLEN FUTURE (1995). Theo Colborn is a staff scientist at WWF and that organization supported her work into the effects of low doses of certain POPs such as DDT, PCBs, and dioxin on wildlife and possibly humans. *Our Stolen Future* triggered enormous debate in the press, particularly relating to allegations about the impact of these chemicals on human sperm counts. The book and surrounding press fueled ongoing efforts for international control over at least twelve of the POPs—the so-called "dirty dozen." The dirty dozen are the focus of several important international processes, including most notably work toward a global convention aimed at their control. NGOs such as Greenpeace and WWF have been major players in raising awareness about POPs and promoting such international action. For further discussion of the global effort to control POPs, *see* Chapter 12, or the web site for *Our Stolen Future* at <http:www.stolenfuture.org/>.

The ability to undertake cooperative endeavors, often on very short notice, has proven a central factor in increasing NGO impact on international processes. Environmental NGOs are diverse, however, and deep splits can divide them. Within the United States, for example, the environmental community split over the tuna/dolphin controversy between the United States and a number of Latin American countries. *See* Chapter 13, p. 995. It also fractured deeply over whether the North American Free Trade Agreement with Mexico would help build the capacity and political will within Mexico to improve the environment or whether it would lead to weaker environmental standards and further neglect of the border area by both countries. Like most differences within the NGO community, the NAFTA issue for the most part had no effect on the long-term unity of the environmental movement. More difficult and ultimately more important for the growth of an international environmental movement, however, is the North–South split among NGOs. Many officials from developing countries are deeply suspicious of NGOs, concerned that they are simply another means of advancing the interests of developed countries. In this regard, consider that at the Seattle WTO Ministerial meeting, 732 NGOs registered. An impressive showing by civil society, but realize that, of these, 52% (380) were from North America, roughly 30% were from Europe, and 10% were from Asia (including Australia, New Zealand, and Japan). Thus only 10% of the registered NGOs came from the Global South. <www.wto.org/english/forums_e/ngo_e/ngoinseattle_e.htm>

Philip Shabecoff, A NEW NAME FOR PEACE: INTERNATIONAL ENVIRONMENTALISM, SUSTAINABLE DEVELOPMENT, AND DEMOCRACY 73–77 (1996)

Given the astonishing diversity in philosophies, politics, goals, strategies, methods, membership, and resources of environmental groups and other NGOs engaged in issues of environment and development, not to mention their geographic dispersion, it would take a great leap of faith to speak of a coherent global movement. Indeed, one scholar employs chaos theory to explain environmentalism, noting that the theory enables meaning to be drawn from dynamic, "seemingly unrelated political, economic and environmental events." And in fact, the environmentalists and other NGOs are fragmented along many fault lines. Even within the industrialized nations, as we have seen among the German Greens, there are deep divisions over policies and tactics. But for many years the widest chasm was between the NGOs of North and South.

Unsurprisingly, perhaps, the differences between environmental groups from the industrialized countries and the developing countries mirror the differences between the countries themselves. Until fairly recently the northern NGOs were chiefly interested in actions to protect ecosystems such as tropical forests, to defend whales and other endangered species, and to reverse deterioration of the atmosphere, the land, and the oceans. To their southern counterparts, however, fighting poverty and achieving economic growth and an improved standard of living were the highest priorities. The demands of the northern environmentalists were viewed as, at best, indifference to the plight of [the] poor and, at worst, as complicity in the exploitation of the developing countries for the sake of continuing the high consumption patterns of the rich industrialized nations. Southern environmental organizations accused groups from the North of attempting to impose their own agendas.

This perspective was voiced in 1992 by Hira Jhamtani, an Indonesian environmentalist, who charged that "there is an imperialistic attitude between First and Third World NGOs." U.S. environmental groups, he contended, are more concerned with "projects and campaigns than with the actual needs of Third World NGOs and communities," for whom conservation issues can be "a matter of life and death." Northern environmentalists, Jhamtani wrote, must stop supporting projects "that maintain the status quo of oppression." * * *

Over the past few years, however, it has become apparent that even if diversity rather than unity is the hallmark of the global environmental movement, substantially increased cohesion and coordination are within the realm of the possible. Several trends point in this direction. One is the spread of coalitions among the environmentalists and other NGOs, not only within countries or among northern and southern organizations but across all the fissures that divide the movement. * * *

Most significant, the often antagonistic components of the global movement have, in recent years, started to listen to each other and even, on occasion, to hear each other. Much of this enhanced level of communication took place during preparations for the Earth Summit.... But even earlier, the policies of many groups had been changing to reflect a more expansive world view. Environmentalists in North American and Europe, whose interest in developing countries tended to focus exclusively on issues such as destruction of the rain forest or rising levels of fossil fuel use, began to take on a broader social perspective. The Northern Alliance, an ad hoc coalition of NGOs, adopted an agenda that gave high priority to "new economics and fair trade relations between North and South, East and West," as well as to solutions to the debt crisis and the prohibition on the export of socially and environmentally harmful products and technologies, including hazardous wastes, to developing nations. The alliance also called for a change in consumption patterns in the North that are now supported by "reckless exploitation of the earth."

For their part, activists in the developing countries, while continuing to insist that their problems originated in the North, began to acknowledge that they had as great a stake in addressing the ecological crisis as the rich industrialized nations had. S.M. Mohamed Idris of Malaysia, coordinator of the Third World Network, an alliance of southern NGOs, asserted that protecting the environment is not a luxury for the rich because "the destruction of the environment is going on perhaps even faster in the Third World and this ecological destruction is emerging as a major cause of poverty itself." He went on to say that environment and development issues are "parts of the same problem, the problem of the wrong model for development in both the North and the South."

In December 1991 hundreds of delegates of NGOs from around the globe gathered in Paris to plan a common strategy to take to the Earth Summit in Rio. It was not easy. The meeting was paid for by the French government, which also financed the trip for activists from the developing countries who could not otherwise afford it. Many of them were attending their first international conference. For much of the time the gathering sounded like a tenants meeting on the tower of Babel, with delegates shouting their slogans and proclaiming the primacy of their causes into the unhearing ears of the other delegates. By the end of the four-day meeting, however, a consensus on principles emerged, along with a sense of common purpose. It was stated in a draft "Citizens Action Plan for the 1990s," which began with the assertion that "a powerful common vision is emerging all over.... A planetary cultural ecology is being born, embodied in a full range of ethical principles."

QUESTIONS AND DISCUSSION

1. A recent example of NGOs' new-found power in shaping international legal developments was the ill-fated Multilateral Agreement on Investment (MAI) negotiated at the OECD. The MAI would have increased protections of foreign investors and, to its opponents, symbolized a worrying trend of globalization—international rules taking precedence over local protections. There's no doubt that NGO opposition doomed the MAI, forcing its initial major proponents—the United States and France—to move from support to opposition in a matter of months. The passage below describes the rapidity of the NGO opposition campaign.

Speaking to those involved in the campaign, many described the NGO opposition as a wildfire. Indeed, the rapidity and effectiveness of NGO opposition to the MAI was unprecedented. From the end of 1995, a small number of NGOs started to follow the negotiations and oppose both the goals and content of the MAI process. At the start, these were primarily environmental and social rather than labor groups. Labor groups were not far behind, however. The OECD held an informal meeting with interested NGOs in December of 1996. While the OECD was open in terms of announcing the process of the negotiations and their general status, in keeping with OECD procedures the internal documents were restricted. In February, 1997, however, the group Public Citizen, founded by Ralph Nader, got hold of the current Chairman's draft (i.e. the consolidated negotiating text up to that point) and posted it on the Internet. This posting provided the catalyst for widespread and hard line opposition of NGOs against the MAI. Just two months later, a more formal meeting for NGOs was hosted by members of the Negotiating Group and secreteriat officials. While the OECD's first consultative meeting with interested groups about the MAI had been in an empty room, the October briefing attracted over 70 representatives from 30 groups around the world. In a mere matter of months, through the internet and e-mail a global campaign against the MAI had come into being. Drafts and bulletins on the MAI were now regularly posted on a host of NGO websites. By 1998, anti-MAI campaigns were active in more than half of the OECD countries as well as many developing countries. The mood of these activities is well captured in the description of the Preamble Collaborative, an NGO with only three employees.

> The Preamble Collaborative was one of more than 600 organizations in nearly 70 countries expressing vehement opposition to the treaty, often in apocalyptic terms. The Collaborative's extensive World Wide Web site— featuring fact sheets, congressional testimony, position papers, and issue briefs—was part of a tidal wave of electronically amplified public opposition to the MAI... Suddenly, what had been a working document among 29 parties became available to anyone with a computer and a modem. And everyone with a computer and a modem got involved. OECD representatives quickly became the targets of unprecedented scrutiny. "If a negotiator says something to someone over a glass of wine, we'll have it on the Internet within an hour, all over the world," boasted the head of the Council of Canadians, a citizens' interest group claiming more than 100,-000 members. * * *

James Salzman, *Labor Rights, Globalization and Institutions: The Role and Influence of the Organization for Economic Cooperation and Development*, 21 MICH. J. INT'L L. 824–825 (2000).

2.   One of the standard responses rejecting greater NGO participation in international institutional activities is that NGOs "don't represent anybody." That is, a trade organization will likely represent a country's or industry sector's largest companies, a government obviously represents its citizens, but an NGO does not represent a formal constituency because it has not been given the right to "speak" on behalf of particular people or institutions. How would you respond to the following argument?

> No non-governmental organisation, whether speaking for business enterprises, trade unions or professional bodies, "public interest" concerns, or any other groups, has a valid claim in its own right to active participation in proceedings where the responsibility for decisions and outcome rests, and has to rest, with the governments of national sovereign states. A loose coalition of social lobby groups cannot legitimately claim to speak "for the people." In practice, NGOs stand for "no-go!" They will inevitably seek to block progress in favor of conserving the status quo.

Paraphrased from David Henderson, THE MAI AFFAIR: A STORY AND ITS LESSONS 1,2,70 (1999). Is there any way to ensure that NGO campaigns are based on fact rather than unfounded speculation, or is that an inevitable risk in the marketplace of ideas?

B.   CORPORATIONS

The role of corporations in the development and implementation of international environmental law is complicated, for business interests are often linked both to the cause and potential solution of most global environmental problems. Corporate influence in international environmental affairs is substantial, particularly in negotiations with direct impact on specific industrial sectors. Well-funded industry lobby groups, such as the Global Climate Coalition or the Coalition for Truth in Environmental Marketing Information, shape both public debate and treaty negotiations on issues from global warming to eco-labelling to forest management.

In some instances, corporate influence is difficult to assess because much of that influence takes place outside formal channels, thus avoiding measurement and control. It is important to note, however, that from a narrow perspective corporate interests are no different than any other "special interest," including environmental interests. They are trying to influence the political process. The agenda of corporate lobbyists is usually different from that of WWF and Greenpeace, but their end objective in influencing policy is little different. Nonetheless, environmental NGOs and corporate institutions do differ significantly in terms of the beneficiaries of lobbying, access to influential decisionmakers, and resources.

The common phrase, "what's good for General Motors is good for America," is not meant as a joke. Nor is the saying, "The business of America is business." If sustainable development means anything in practical terms, it means that environmental protection cannot destroy the economic foundation of a community. The world's businesses must be brought along a more sustainable path, not halted, but who has the responsibility to ensure this happens? Is it the businesses themselves, governments that regulate and enforce, consumers who create the market demand in the first place, or shareholders who, in legal terms, "own" the business? There is no simple answer to this question, and the issue is explored in more detail in Chapter 18 in the context of voluntary corporate codes of conduct. The following excerpt from Gareth Porter and Janet Welsh Brown describes the role business organizations played in the CFC negotiations and maritime pollution.

Gareth Porter & Janet Welsh Brown, GLOBAL ENVIRONMENTAL POLITICS 64–66 (1991)

Corporations as Actors

Although business firms function in national and international markets in which consumer demand is a major dynamic of economic growth—and of environmental degradation—businesses are more directly affected by environmental regulation and tend to resist national and international policies that they believe would impose significant new costs on them or otherwise reduce their expected profits. When businesses face stronger domestic regulations on an activity with a global environmental dimension, as did the U.S. chemical industry in the cases of CFC production, however, they are likely to support international action to impose similar standards on competitors abroad and may prefer an international agreement's standards to domestic ones because the former are weaker.

Business Actors and Veto Power

Business organizations enter into environmental politics with some significant assets: They need only to avert international action rather than to get consensus for it; they have good access to powerful bureaucratic sectors in most governments; and in some cases (marine oil pollution and ozone protection) they have the ability to put forward technical solutions that serve their own interests. In the past, certain business sectors have been able to use these assets to prevent the emergence, for example, of effective regimes for civil liability for oil pollution damage, for hazardous and noxious substances, for pollution from offshore oil operations, or for nuclear energy.

On some issues, such as whaling and tropical deforestation, business interests have been able to prevent or delay the formation of a global environmental regime by their close ties with a single government–in these cases, the Japanese government. Corporations have maximized their veto power by forming broad transnational coalitions to advance their goals. The best illustration of such power is the role of international shipping and oil in maritime pollution issues. In the 1950s and 1960s the International Chamber of Shipping, composed of thirty national associations of large shipowners, and the International Marine Forum, which represents the interests of major oil companies, effectively determined the shape of the international conventions on oil pollution prevention and liability. The international organization that had responsibility for deciding maritime pollution issues, the International Maritime Organization (IMO) ... was dominated by the states that controlled significant shipping, such as the United States, Japan, and Norway. Those states, in turn, were strongly influenced by the seven major oil companies, which owned a large percentage of world tanker tonnage directly or through dummy corporations. Oil and shipping interests were strongly represented in the delegations of maritime states, and the detailed technical papers submitted by both organizations defined the terms of the discussion.

Another case of business success in stalling international action is ozone protection in the 1970s and 1980s. The major chemical companies producing CFCs in several countries, along with the user industries, long exercised a veto over international efforts to control or phase out CFC production. Only nineteen chemical companies account for the world's entire production of CFCs, with most of it centered in the United States, the United Kingdom, France, and Japan. The U.S.-based firm DuPont produces one-fourth of the worldwide total annually, and the four major U.S. CFC producers (DuPont, Allied–Signal, ICI, and Great Lakes Chemical), along with the electronics industry, prevented the establishment of a global ozone protection policy for more than a decade after CFCs were first identified by scientists as the cause of ozone depletion.

In the late 1970s, as scientists and environmentalists began calling for controls on CFC use, the chemical industry lobbied successfully against a legislative ban on the use of CFCs in aerosol sprays as well as a Carter administration proposal to freeze CFC emissions. During the Reagan era, DuPont refused to develop safer substitutes unless the government provided economic incentives in the form of tax credits, and they discounted scientific evidence of damage to the ozone layer from CFCs.

Even as the CFC industry denied any imminent threat to the environment from CFC production and use, in 1986 it shifted to strong support for an international agreement to control emissions because it expected the protocol to be weaker than the most likely domestic U.S. regulations. Even after dramatic new evidence of a hole in the ozone layer over the Antarctic surfaced in early 1988, DuPont rejected the suggestion that it should discontinue the production of CFCs.

But when the Ozone Trends Panel issued its conclusive report in 1988 on the danger to the ozone layer from CFCs, major producers recognized that they could no longer resist phasing out CFCs. DuPont soon pledged a phaseout of the chemicals by 2000. A phaseout by 2000 would give the industry time to phase in its own preferred substitutes, the family of hydrochlorofluorocarbons or HCFCs, which have from one to ten percent of the ozone-destroying potential of CFCs and will be far more expensive than CFCs. In 1989 and 1990, DuPont and other producers turned their attention to ensuring that HCFCs would remain unregulated; they argued that safer substitutes may not emerge. U.S.-based producers were successful in getting the United States to oppose binding controls on HCFCs at the 1990 meeting of the Montreal Protocol, despite the danger that growth in the use of those chemicals could add significantly to ozone depletion. As a result, the amendments to the Montreal Protocol adopted in 1990 included only a non-binding declaration of intent to control HCFCs some thirty to fifty years into the future! [Subsequent amendments to the Montreal Protocol regime would tighten the phase-out of HCFCs, calling for stabilization of HCFC use by 1996, with an eventual ban by 2020.]

The above discussion reflects the traditional NGO view of industry as a procrastinator or enemy of environmental protection, and there are certainly continuing examples of this kind of corporate action. But more interesting is the growing environmental leadership emanating from some corporations, if for no other reason than to better position themselves in a more environmentally sensitive and conscious market place. For example, in the same example of ozone depletion, the high-tech users of CFCs have been proactive in transferring technology and taking other steps to promote the use of non-CFC technologies. *See* Chapter 9, page 580, discussing ICOLP.

The global leader in linking business initiatives with sustainable development is the World Business Council for Sustainable Development (WBCSD). Created by the 1995 merger of the Business Council for Sustainable Development and the International Chamber of Commerce's World Industrial Council for the Environment, the WBCSD represents 150 international companies from over 30 countries and 20 major industrial sectors. The WBCSD has assumed an important role in re-creating industry's relationship to the environment. It has undertaken joint projects with UNEP on industrial water issues and developed an on-going dialogue with the UN about environmental certification standards for forestry and other industries. In addition, the WBCSD has sponsored comprehensive reports on the "sustainable paper cycle", the responsibility of retailers in promoting sustainable consumption, and an array of other issues. It has also taken a lead in promoting Joint Implementation (JI) initiatives (i.e., allowing developed countries under the Kyoto Protocol to offset their own emissions of greenhouse gases by investing in emission-reduction projects in other countries) by holding JI seminars in Costa Rica, Bangkok, Singapore, Hong Kong, Tokyo, Prague and Estonia. The full range of its activities is described on its website at < http://www.wbcsd.ch/>. The role of corporations is discussed in greater detail in Chapter 18, addressing private environmental law. *See also* Chapter 2, addressing the role of technology in responding to global environmental problems.

QUESTIONS AND DISCUSSION

1. To guide your thinking about corporations, consider what, in the face of evidence concerning global warming, an environmentally responsible oil company should do. Stop selling oil? Cease exploration activities and cede the future market to competitors? Wait for a unified industry position? Question the science regarding climate change and launch a major advertising effort to sway public opinion against stricter controls? Who benefits and gains from these decisions? How would you justify to your CEO taking a pro-active position on climate change?

Remember, as well, that industry is not monolithic. Both Shell Oil and British Petroleum have resigned from the industry lobby group opposed to the Kyoto Protocol, the Global Climate Coalition, and joined the Business Environment Leadership Council of the Pew Center on Global Climate Change, a group supporting the Kyoto Protocol. <http://www.pewclimate.org/belc/index.cfm>. British Petroleum even announced in the Summer of 1997 that it supported stronger controls, including a global carbon tax, on the use of its products–and that it was implementing a long-term plan to shift from being primarily a hydrocarbon-based company to one that provided solar and other renewable energy. It has since created a greenhouse gas emissions trading scheme within its operations. Such actions by industry leaders send important messages to the smaller or more risk-averse business in the sector to follow their example.

2. The section on corporations identifies three significant differences between the political activities of environmental NGOs and corporate institutions: beneficiaries of lobbying, access to influential decisionmakers, and resources. Expand on these three categories by listing important differences for each category and giving examples. For instance, the meetings of the standard-setting body, the International Organization for Standardization, are held all over the world. Companies and trade associations have the resources to send representatives to every meeting while most NGOs do not, thus leading to the likelihood of stronger relative influence by corporate interests. Consider, too, the excerpt below, which compares corporate and NGO access to Codex, an important international standard-setting institution.

Robert Housman, *Democratizing International Trade Decision-making*, 27 CORNELL INT'L L.J. 699 (1994)

Unlike other international trade decision-making bodies that have been openly hostile to participatory decision-making, Codex has a history of openness. Codex is an intergovernmental organization within the United Nations system whose primary goals are to ensure food safety, and to protect against unfair trade practices in food trade. One of Codex's most important tasks is the harmonization of food safety standards. Codex standards are communicated to the GATT and receive substantial deference during both GATT negotiations and GATT dispute panel proceedings.

Although only states can be voting members of Codex, the Secretary General of Codex may invite NGOs to participate as observers. Observer status has been widely granted to a range of NGOs, including primary producer organizations, processor organizations, standards organizations, as well as to nations who are not Codex members. Observer status has also been granted to at least one consumer organization. Observers can receive Codex reports, take part in the preparatory work prior to meetings, and speak during meetings.

While Codex's procedures provide a participatory model for other international trade organizations, it is not without its own participatory flaws. Codex's principal participatory flaw is in the makeup of the individual country delegations—the actual Codex decision-makers. These country delegations commonly include a significant number of representatives from the agribusiness or pharmaceutical industry sectors. Consumer and food safety groups, which could offset the participation of the regulated community, are not generally found on Codex delegations or consulted on proposed standards. For example, a 1993 study by the National Food Alliance found that "over four-fifths of the nongovernmental participants on national delegations to Codex committees represented industry, while only one percent represented public interest organizations." The undesirable result is that food safety votes taken by Codex are heavily and disproportionately influenced by the regulated community. The need to correct this imbalance was recognized at the 1991 FAO/WHO Conference on Food Standards, Chemicals in Food and Food Trade. However, despite this recognition, an October 1993 report by the International Organization of Consumers Unions found that little progress has been made in addressing this problem.

Codex also suffers from another major participatory flaw in that while nongovernmental participation is allowed in many of its activities, its standard setting processes are closed to the public. For example, the public may not obtain or directly submit comments on the standards for pesticide residues developed within either the Codex Committee on Pesticide Residues or the Joint Meeting on Pesticide Residues; the public may only participate by commenting through their respective national delegation–the same delegations that are disproportionately industry oriented.

Assume you are the public relations officer for Codex. How would you respond to Housman's criticisms?

3. Of course, "talk is cheap." Many industry associations have been accused of talking about environmentally responsible behavior but not doing so in practice. Some trade associations have been accused of creating instant grassroots campaigns, so-called "astro-turf" campaigns. Misrepresentation is also a concern. In this regard, a major car company's ad several years ago claiming that its car was environmentally friendly because its air conditioner did not contain CFCs provides a case in point. But, equally, not all companies act in this manner. Perhaps the best advice for assessing corporations' claims of environmental leadership comes from the arms control field–"Trust, but verify." For an excellent discussion of environmental misinformation campaigns, *see* Paul and Anne Ehrlich, BETRAYAL OF SCIENCE AND REASON (1996). It is important to recognize as well, of course, that NGOs can be equally misleading in portraying environmental hazards or the actions of IGOs. The power of the web to disseminate widely "true" revelations that only later turn out to be false, after the damage has been done, makes this an even more serious issue.

For an example of NGO misinformation, *see* the Brent Spar problem exercise in Chapter 10, page 742.

Suggested Further Reading and Web Sites

UNITED NATIONS LEGAL ORDER (Oscar Schachter ed. 1996)

This comprehensive two-volume work addresses every aspect of the United Nations' role in the international system. It includes outstanding articles by Paul Szasz on lawmaking at the UN and Ved P. Nanda on the UN's role in international environmental law.

UNEP, UNEP'S NEW WAY FORWARD (1995)

Lee A. Kimball, TREATY IMPLEMENTATION: SCIENTIFIC AND TECHNICAL ADVICE ENTERS A NEW STAGE (1996)

Are International Institutions Doing their Job?, 90 AM.SOC.INT'L L. PROC. 224 (1996)

WORLD BANK, MAKING DEVELOPMENT SUSTAINABLE: THE WORLD BANK GROUP AND THE ENVIRONMENT (1994)

C.F. Amerasinghe, PRINCIPLES OF THE INSTITUTIONAL LAW OF INTERNATIONAL ORGANIZATIONS (1996)

Robert Keohane et al., INSTITUTIONS FOR THE EARTH (1993)

Barbara Bramble & Gareth Porter, *Non-Governmental Organizations and the Making of US International Environmental Policy*, in ANDREW HURRELL & BENEDICT KINGSBURY, THE INTERNATIONAL POLITICS OF THE ENVIRONMENT 314–53 (1991)

A. Dan Tarlock, *The Role of Non–Governmental Organizations in the Development of International Environmental Law*, 68 CHI.-KENT L. REV 61 (1992)

Philippe Sands, *The Role of Environmental NGOs in International Environmental Law*, DEVELOPMENT, No. 2, at 28 (1992)

Discussions of the role of U.S. NGOs in international environmental policy

http://www.wcl.american.edu/pub/iel/annex2.htm#6

Web sites for major environmental environmental players

CHAPTER SIX

INTERNATIONAL ENVIRONMENTAL LAWMAKING

> *Law constrains or it is a travesty to call it law. Law enters decisively into the willing of its subjects or it is a travesty to call it law.*
>
> *Law transcends the power of the powerful and transforms the situation of the weak or it is a travesty to call it law.*
>
> Philip Allott, EUNOMIA at xvii (1990)

SECTION I.   INTRODUCTION: THE CHANGING NATURE OF INTERNATIONAL LAW

Within the more sophisticated nation-States, there is a well-developed system for creating and enforcing law. In the most robust national systems, the legislative and executive powers are accountable under constitutions enforced by a judiciary with the power to issue authoritative and binding interpretations of existing law. National legislatures can create law of general applicability, which binds even those who may disagree with it. Increasingly throughout the world, citizens have the right to participate in national law-making—through referenda, legislative lobbying, and the election of representatives. Nation–States also have the power to implement and enforce the laws they create, and specific mechanisms often exist for citizens to participate here as well.

The international law-making system is far less developed. Under the principles of international law established by Hugo Grotius and his successors, each nation-State is independent and sovereign. No supra-national legislature exists with the power to create law applicable to the entire world. Moreover, States are the primary subjects of international law. Few international regimes allow the active participation of non-State actors in law-making. As a general rule, no State may be bound by any international obligation without its consent, although consent may sometimes be inferred. This chapter examines the processes by which that consent is created, formalized, and recognized, as well as the limited but growing number of examples when consent may not be necessary.

Two schools of thought have arisen to describe the characteristics and foundations of international law: natural law and positivism. Proponents of the former argue that law between states is based on truisms or self-evident principles, and therefore merely need to be discovered to be valid. Positivists, on the other hand, hold that international rules are valid only as a result of fixed, transparent political processes. Increasingly, scholars, NGOs, and governments themselves are recognizing that the existing international law-making system is inadequate for dealing with global environmental challenges. Critics contend that, without some means of norm-creation external to the political will of the States themselves, international law is not really law at all. The requirement of consensus retards the development of new law and frequently forces negotiators to accept the lowest common denominator in environmental protection. While rapid and aggressive legal responses to international environmental crises are not unknown, they remain rare. Too often, international law is the handmaiden of power, following rather than leading, facilitating rather than constraining. In the words of Philip Trimble:

> A quick look at the "rules" of international law shows why governments love international law. Contrary to the realist/idealist view of law as a restraint on unruly governments, international law confirms much more authority and power than it denies. For example, the basic rule of international law is that a state generally has exclusive authority to regulate conduct within its territory. International law thus confers authority to control entry and exit, to establish police control, to determine economic structure, to tax, to regulate, and to reinforce in many other ways the power and legitimacy of government. Public international law also grants government sovereignty over air space and control over the continental shelf and economic resources 200 miles into the sea. * * *
>
> Even the rules of public international law that expressly restrain government authority may at the same time give a government an excuse to impose its authority throughout its own society so that it can effectively discharge its

obligations under international law. International human rights law, for example, promotes national judicial review, general criminal law procedures, and a host of objectives that can best be met by assertions of national government power, especially against village or other traditional structures. * * *

The rules of international law accordingly are very congenial to governments. They mostly justify or legitimate the practical exercise of state power.

Phillip R. Trimble, *International Law, World Order and Critical Legal Studies*, 42 STAN L. REV. 811, 833–34 (1990).

In addition to lacking a general law-making institution, the international legal system remains remarkably exclusionary. The government of each State has an equal voice and an equal vote in most international fora (with some notable exceptions, such as the World Bank's weighted voting structure, which gives more power to the states contributing the most funding), providing the veneer of a democracy among the States. Nevertheless, the more powerful States still dominate. And even more troubling, individual citizens are generally denied both a voice and a vote. Non-participation is inherent in the very foundations of the international system. In the traditional view of international law, the international community is comprised of the States themselves, not of their constituent citizens. States possess international "personhood;" their citizens do not. Individuals, corporations, and other organizations recognized as juridical persons under the domestic law of individual States lack formal recognition before international courts or in other international fora.

To many observers, the non-participatory, consensus-based nature of the international law system hinders efforts to formulate an effective international response to our global environmental crisis, where States are held accountable under the rule of law. Increasingly, however, the limitations inherent in international law are being challenged. As non-State actors and new processes emerge in the international system, international law-making is slowly—and inevitably—developing some of the more robust characteristics of national systems. Moreover, a more accurate version of history suggests that citizens did have a more fundamental role in international law at one time.

In the following excerpt, Philip Allott discusses how national political and social systems have evolved since the Enlightenment, while the international system remained a "post-feudal society set in amber." The trends toward democratization and socialization that revolutionized human society within the nation-States remained vestigial at the international level. This difference is reflected in the systems of law that have developed at each level. While Allott decries the present state of international affairs, he argues that it is within our power to change the world by changing our own understanding of it—by "reconceiving" it.

Allott begins by examining the international system as it currently exists, and identifying the characteristics that, in his view, make that system intolerable. Among them: unequal social development, the proliferation of war and the materials of war, governmental oppression, degradation of the human environment, and degradation of the human spirit. For Allott, much of this human misery can be attributed to the fact that although we live in a world of ever-increasing economic, cultural and environmental interdependence, that world is divided, arbitrarily, into nation–States. The governments of those nation–States have seized for themselves a monopoly over governance of international society, raising barriers to citizens who could act internationally based on shared values and a shared sense of responsibility that should characterize our truly global society.

Having identified the flaws in the present State-centered system, Allott demonstrates that this system is neither natural nor inevitable, and indeed is itself the product of theory. He deconstructs the history of international theory and international community to show that it has not always been this way. By demonstrating the power theory has had in shaping the current system, Allott also demonstrates the power of theory to reshape the world. Allott shows us that international society need not, and indeed cannot, remain unchanged. He argues that we have both the capacity and the duty to replace the old theory and the old regime. To do so will require not a revolution of arms, but something more fundamental and more powerful: a revolution of the mind.

Philip Allott, International Law and International Revolution: Reconceiving the World 1–17 (1989)

I want to think aloud about a question which is easy to state but very difficult to answer.

Why do we put up with it all?

That question reflects a dull pain, an anguish, an anger even, that many people feel in considering the state of the world. It would be uttered as a sentimental question, not expecting an answer, at least not expecting a practical answer. But let us, for a while, treat it as a question to be answered in practical terms.

Why do we put up with it all? Obviously it is question which implies three other questions and it is those implied questions that give rise to all the difficulty.

What exactly is it that so troubles us in the state of the world? What is the cause or origin of the things that trouble us? What could and should we do to change those things?

Let us consider a practical example.

You will have heard of the country called Nowhere, but you may not know much about it in detail. Nowhere is an independent sovereign state with a President, a government, a single political party called the Nowhere People's Party, a population of 12 million people, consisting of two ethnic groups—the Noes and the Wheres. The ratio of Noes to Wheres is two-to-one. The Nowhere People's Party is dominated by the Wheres, the smaller ethnic group. The Wheres arrived in the country in the early nineteenth century and soon came to dominate the indigenous No people.

Nowhere's economy has been a two-product economy—copper and tourism. The copper-mining industry is controlled by a multinational company centred in a country called Superpower One. The tourism industry is controlled by Where businessmen in cooperation with various foreign interests. The menial labour in tourism is provided by the No people. In recent years Nowhere has been flourishing as an off shore financial centre, with foreign banks and holding companies establishing offices in the capital, Nowhere City. There has been a consumer boom, with great demand for imported video-tape recorders and cocaine. . . .

Nowhere's immediate neighbour is No-man's-land, whose population consists almost entirely of No people. No-mans-land is a multi-party state with a Westminster style parliament. It is a poorer country than Nowhere. It has a long-standing claim to the territory of Nowhere and supports a Nowenese Liberation Army which is seeking to overthrow the regime in Nowhere. The N.L.A. is also supported by a country called Superpower Two. A sum of money equivalent to one-third of its Gross Domestic Product is spent every year by each country on arms, which are obtained from Superpower One and Superpower Two and on the international arms market.

Nowhere has a written constitution containing a Declaration of Political and Social Rights. However, the President declared a State of Exception five years ago and the Declaration of Rights was suspended. The President's eldest son is the Chief Justice of the Supreme Court. His second son is Commander-in-Chief of the Nowhere Armed Forces. His youngest son is studying at Harford Business School.

I do not need to say much more. It is all very familiar. Nowhere is a member of many international organizations. It is also an object of interest to many international organizations, including the UN Security Council, the World Bank, the International Monetary Fund, leading international banks, Amnesty International, and the Church of Perpetual Healing, which has missionaries in Nowhere City, in the tourist resorts and in remote villages. . . .

You will not be surprised to hear that deforestation in the north of Nowhere has turned the fertile southern plain of No-man's-land into a virtual desert. Soil erosion in Nowhere is silting up the River Nouse which flows into No-man's-land. . . .

You react in two ways when you come across news items about Nowhere and No-man's-land. Either—so what? Or—so why?

Those who react with *so what?* believe that the world is as it is, human nature is as it is, and human beings are as they are, corrupt or corruptible, sometimes decent, always long-suffering, patient of the miseries and follies of the world. And societies are as they are, some progressive and some not progressive, some successful and some not successful. So it has always been through all human history, and so presumably, it will always be.

Those who react with *so why?* believe that *human beings are what they could be, not simply what they have been, and societies are systems made by human beings for human survival and human prospering, not for human oppression and human indignity.*

I suppose that, from now on, I will be speaking to so-why people but hoping to be overheard by so-what people.

Let us make an abstraction of the world-situation of which Nowhere and No-man's-land are one small part. And we may thereby begin to answer the first of the three subordinate questions—what exactly do we so object to in the present world situation?

Here is a possible short-list, containing five intolerable things.

(1) Unequal social development. That means that some human beings worry about the colour of the bed-sheets in their holiday-home in Provence or the Caribbean, while other human beings worry about their next meal or the leaking tin roof of the hut which is their home.

(2) War and armaments. From time to time, human beings murder and maim each other in the public interest, by the dozen and by the million, and bomb each other's villages and cities to rubble. And, all the time, human beings make

more and more machines for murdering and destroying in the public interest, and more and more machines to prevent other people from murdering and destroying in the public interest.

(3) Governmental oppression. In very many countries around the world, the ruling class are not servants of the people but enemies of the people, evil and corrupt and negligent and self-serving, torturing people, exploiting people, abusing people. And, in all countries, the people have to struggle to control the vanity and the obsessions of those who want to be their masters.

(4) Physical degradation. On the planet Earth are five billion human beings, one species of animal among countless other species of living things, a species which has taken over the planet, using the Earth's resources, irreversibly transforming the Earth as a physical structure and as a living system.

(5) Spiritual degradation. Human beings everywhere are being drawn into a single mass culture dominated by a crude form of capitalism, a mass culture which is stifling all competing values and all local cultures, a mass culture which is depraving human consciousness.

You may not like that list. You may worry about other things. You may want to challenge some items on my list, to defend something that I seem to be attacking.

You will have noticed that my list of five intolerable things consists of five clichés of so-called global anxiety. We have heard about them all until we are sick and tired of them. The mass media of communication exploit them at regular intervals, enriching their everyday fodder with an occasional healthy supplement of moral fibre—the emaciated survivor of the concentration camp, the family sleeping in the street, . . . riot police with batons and water-cannon, drug addicts killing themselves slowly, dead fish floating on a polluted river, the television set in the mud-hut.

Banal images of a reality made banal. So-why made as tedious as so-what.

And, then again, you may object that, surely, we are not simply putting up with such things. On the contrary, a lot of effort is being devoted to facing up to such things, to alleviating them, even to solving them. There are dozens of organizations and foundations and charities and conferences and good-hearted individuals worrying about each and every one of them. Surely some part of our taxes and some part of our voluntary giving is going to deal with precisely such world social problems.

I will add that as a sixth cause of our anger—perhaps the most painful of all.

(6) Social pragmatism. We treat the symptoms of worldwide disorder, because we cannot, or dare not, understand the disease. We see the effects because we cannot, or will not, see the cause.

So that brings us to the second question. What is the origin or cause of the things we find intolerable?

You will say, especially if you are a so-what person, that we cannot comment on the causes of the situation of Nowhere and No-man's land unless and until we know more of their territories and resources, their cultural characteristics, their history. Each is a sovereign independent state, with its own destiny to work out, its own possibilities, its own constraints. Who are we to know what is the best for them, let alone to do anything to bring about what is best for them?

I would ask you to notice three things about the two well known unknown countries I have described, three features of their structural situation.

The first is that they are not very independent. The market-price of Nowenese copper is determined in London, where demand is related very directly to the general state of world manufacturing industry at any particular time. Nowenese tourism depends on the international holiday companies which send their packaged tourists to fill the Nowenese hotels which have been built by foreign construction companies, using cement brought halfway round the world in ships controlled by foreign shipping lines. The off-shore companies established in Nowhere City are there because taxes are low, because few questions are asked, because the climate is pleasant. They may leave as suddenly as they arrived. And the territory of No-man's land, its physical environment, its climate even, depend on what is done in the territory of Nowhere. And even the minds of the Nowenese people are not their own. Their values and their wants are a function of forces far beyond their control—capitalism, foreign religions, international crime, world popular culture, militarism, materialism.

And, of course, Nowhere is not nowhere. It is everywhere. All the world is more or less Nowhere. Remember that the most economically successful countries in the world maintain their economies and their standard of living by selling goods and services to other countries.... And even the most successful countries depend on the value of their currency, which depends on international economic relativities, as well as on internal economic realities. And they depend on investment which, particularly if they have a substantial budget deficit, may be foreign investment, created and terminable through decisions made elsewhere. And they depend on technology which may be originated and controlled abroad. And they depend on cultural tides which sweep across the world, shaping human wants and human expectations and human anxieties. * * *

The second thing to notice about Nowhere and No-man's land is that their national identities do not coincide with their political identities. The No people in Nowhere feel more kinship with the No people in No man's-land than with the Where-dominated state of which they are said to be nationals. The No people in No-man's-land feel that Nowhere and its incoming Where people have usurped some part of the No birthright. * * *

We know that this problem of national identity has been one of the greatest social problems through all human history, giving rise to endless wars, endless struggle and suffering, endless oppression and exploitation. And, of course, it is very much with us today. It is hard to think of a single country in the world which is not significantly affected by one or more problems of national identity, including the United Kingdom of Great Britain and Northern Ireland.

The fact is that the political frontiers of the so-called nation-states have evolved under the pressure of forces other than merely those of national identity. And yet it is the political systems of the so-called nation-states which have, somehow, acquired the power to control the social development of all the peoples of the world, to determine the well-being of humanity, to determine the future of humanity.

The third thing to notice about the structural situation of Nowhere and No-man's-land is that their population consists of human beings. They share with us the species-characteristics of human beings. They think and want and hope and suffer and despair and laugh and weep as human beings. The mothers of their sons who are killed in their wars or their prisons or their hospitals have hearts as tender as the hearts of our mothers.... Whether we are so-what people or so-why people, we cannot stop ourselves from feeling *sympathy*.

And yet somehow we stop ourselves from feeling *responsibility* for them. They are aliens. As human beings, we know that we are *morally* responsible for all that we do, and do not do, to and for other human beings, a responsibility which we cannot think away, a responsibility which we owe to a billion human beings as we owe it to one human being. Every alien is also our neighbour. And yet as citizens, we have somehow been led to believe that we are not *socially* responsible for them—and that even our moral responsibility is qualified by their social alienation from us.

I have mentioned three structural features of the situation of two countries which are also structural features of the world situation. They are like geological fault-lines running through the world structure.

First, our single human destiny must nevertheless be pursued in isolated state-structures. Second, our national identity may be in conflict with our legal and political identity. Third, we are not able to take responsibility for human beings for whom we know we are responsible.

What I want to suggest to you is that there is a direct connection between the things which we find intolerable in the world situation and these three structural faults in the world system.

And that direct connection is located nowhere else than in our own minds. It is not a matter of physics or biology or physiology or geography or history. It is a matter of philosophy—that is to say, of human self-conceiving and human self-creating.

What we have to discover is not how the present world structure came about as a story of historical events, but how the present world structure came to seem natural and inevitable. The question of causation I am considering is the question of what causes certain social and legal situations to be accepted within human consciousness. In particular, what is the origin of the consciousness which makes possible, which legitimates, which naturalises, the way in which we conceive of international society and international law?

Why do we put up with it all? We put up with it all because our consciousness contains ideas which cause us to put up with it all. Who makes our consciousness? We make our consciousness. And so, if we can change our consciousness of the world, we can change the world. It is as simple as that.

That is the revolution I am proposing to you. A reconstruction of our understanding of the world in which we live, a reconceiving of the human world, and thereby a remaking of the human world.

Let us treat it as a mystery to be solved, how we got into our present state of consciousness about international society and international law. If we treat it as a whodunnit for a moment, I can name one of the guilty parties and I can explain the *modus operandi*.

Whodunnit? *It was Emmeric de Vattel in his study with an idea.*

That sounds unlikely. One particular Swiss writer, writing in 1758, making a certain use of certain words. Let me put the evidence before you.

I can express the same thing almost as briefly, but in a more abstract form.

Humanity, having been tempted for a while to conceive of itself as a society, chose instead to conceive of itself as a collection of states.

State-societies have undergone a long process of internal social change since the end of the Middle Ages. That process has been conducted on two planes—the plane of history and the plane of philosophy. There has been the plane of historical events, power-struggles, wars and civil wars, revolutions, institutional change, legislative reforms, everyday politics. And there has been the plane of philosophy, as human consciousness has sought ways to express what is and what might be in society, to legitimate what is, to bring about what might be.

On both planes—of history and philosophy—there have been two developments which have dominated all others in the evolving of the state-societies since the end of the Middle Ages: democratization and socialization. Democratization and socialization are words to describe two revolutions which have made the state societies we know today.

So, returning to the mystery of international society, I can now reformulate the story as follows.

International society, having chosen not to conceive of itself as a society, having chosen to conceive of itself as essentially different in kind from the state-societies in their internal aspect, has managed to avoid both forms of social revolution. The social world of humanity has been neither democratised nor socialised because humanity has chosen to regard its international world as an unsocial world.

What have democratisation and socialisation meant within the state-societies?

Democratisation has meant that societies became able to conceive of themselves as composed of the people, as governed by the people, and as serving the people. *Socialisation* has meant that societies acquired the capacity to form socially their social purposes.

The development of the idea of *democracy* was a response to the greatly increasing energy of national societies at the end of the Middle Ages, as their economies and the international economy developed dramatically, as humanity rediscovered the self-ordering capacity of the human mind, and hence the world-transforming possibilities not only of philosophy but also of natural science and technology. * * *

The response at the level of philosophy was to take up an old idea, the idea of sovereignty: the idea that a society is structurally a unity, and that that structure depends on an ultimate source of authority, an unwilled will, which is the ultimate source of social self-ordering, the source of law in society. The idea of sovereignty was structurally necessary to turn amorphous national societies into more and more complex self-organizing systems.

But there was obviously an inherent anti-social danger in sovereignty, an anti-systemic, self-disabling uncertainty. Who was to be the sovereign? How was the sovereign to be controlled? The difficulty was that the sovereign societies, as they developed, generated a particular sub-system which came to be known as *the state*.

The state came to be conceived as a public realm within society under the authority of the government. The public realm was loosely separated from the private realm, in which individuals remained, as it were, sovereign. But the state could determine for itself the limits of the public realm, by taking control of both physical power and law-making power.

The development of democracy at the level of *philosophy* took place primarily in the development of various theories of social contract and in their sub-theory of constitutionalism. Sovereignty could be retained to provide the systematic structure of society, with its public realm under the government. But sovereignty would be reconceived to contain the idea of self-government. A society was to be a structure of sovereignty, but also a structure of self-government. And that structure came to be expressed in the new-old form of the so called *constitution*. * * *

The new philosophy, of democratic constitutionalism, had the effect of increasing the actual power of those who controlled the power of government, who actually controlled the public realm. In other words, the constitution proved to be an excellent means of organizing democratic power but it proved incapable by itself of *determining social purpose*, of deciding how the great power of the state-society would be used. * * *

Especially in the nineteenth century, society developed as a system for generating value. The public realm came to be not merely a realm of power but a realm of value. Through the development of a professional bureaucracy, through the reform of the legal system, through the reform of parliaments, through the universalization of elementary education, ... through the development of mass communications ... , society became not merely a structure of political power but a system of shared social consciousness, a system for generating social values and social purposes. But communal values and social purposes would be generated not merely within the decision-making organs of government. They would be generated within the minds of the people....

The application of science and technology to agriculture and industry meant that the increase in social wealth was able to keep ahead of the increase in population, ... so that there was the possibility of social improvement ... of the living conditions and the opportunities of the mass of the people in a number of countries. Society became a means for human self creating, human self-perfecting through human interaction. And we have seen the wonderful results in the improvement of the living conditions and the opportunities of the mass of the people in a number of countries.

The question is—what happened to the organizing of the interaction between such societies, their international interaction, while all these developments were taking place internally?

What happened was that the sovereign was turned inside out, became the external manifestation of the society in question. What appeared on the international scene was not the totality of the evolved national societies. What appeared on the international scene was merely the internal *public realms* externalised. The internal public realms, the governments, were turned inside out like a glove.

Louis XIV is supposed to have said: *L'Etat, c'est moi—I am the state*, meaning that he was the embodiment of the French nation by being the embodiment of its public realm. He might have gone on to say: *Le monde, c'est nous, les etats*, meaning that the international system should be regarded as consisting of the governments meeting each other externally.

The result was that we came to have an international system which was, and is, post-feudal society set in amber. Undemocratised. Unsocialised. Capable only of generating so-called *international relations*, in which so-called *states* act in the name of so-called *national interests*, through the exercise of so-called *power*, carrying out so-called *foreign policy* conducted by means of so-called *diplomacy*, punctuated by medieval entertainments called *wars* or, in the miserable modern euphemism, *armed conflict*. That is the essence of the social process of the international non-society.

It is as if the external life of our societies were still a reflection of the internal life of centuries ago, a fitful struggle among Teutonic knights or European barons or Chinese feudal lords or Japanese shoguns.... It is as if there had never been Locke and Rousseau and Kant and Hegel and Marx, let alone Plato and Aristotle and Lao tzu and Confucius. It is as if the revolutions had never occurred—1789 and 1917 and all the other dramatic and undramatic social revolutions.

Nowadays people believe that such an international system is natural and inevitable. Far from it. It is not necessarily natural and it was not simply inevitable. And this is where we get back to Emmerich de Vattel in his study. It is not difficult to unravel the story by which the misconceiving of international society was perpetrated. I will present it as a drama in five acts.

Act One. In the sixteenth century, a critical question for theologians and philosophers was the question of how there could be a law applying both to the nations of Europe and to the peoples of the lands which had been newly visited or revisited. It was necessary to reconsider the question, which had been familiar to ancient Greece and Rome and medieval Christendom, of whether there could be said to be a universal legal system. The idea was proposed, particularly in Spain and not for the first time in human history, that all humanity formed a sort of society and that the law governing the whole of humanity reflected that fact.* * *

... [I]nternational law has not only the force of a pact and agreement among men, but also the force of a law; for the world as a whole, being in a way one single State, has the power to create laws that are just and fitting for all persons, as are the rules of the international law.

Francisco de Vitoria (1492–1546) took the view that the basis of a universal law for all human beings was found in natural reason, the rational character of human nature, which generated what he called a law of natural society and fellowship which binds together all human beings and which survives the establishment of civil power ... over particular peoples.... The rules of the law of nations were to be derived from natural law and from a "consensus of the greater part of the whole world, especially in behalf of the common good of all".

Francisco Suarez (1548–1617) conceived of a moral and political unity of the human race.

> The rational basis, moreover, of [the *jus gentium*, the law of nations] consists in the fact that the human race, into howsoever many different peoples and kingdoms it may be divided, always preserves a certain unity ... enjoined by the natural precept of mutual love and mercy; a precept which applies to all, even to strangers of every nation.

> Therefore, although a given sovereign state ... , commonwealth ... , or Kingdom ... may constitute a perfect community in itself, ... nevertheless each one of these states ... is also ... a member of that universal society [of the whole human race].

Act Two. In the seventeenth century, Hugo Grotius (1583–1645) began the process of separating the law of nations from the law of nature, but he did so precisely in order to make clear to the new sovereigns that their will was not the sole test of what is right even if it was the practical basis of what is lawful under the law of nations. The nations are sovereign and independent of each other. But they are all equally governed by the law of nations, which is the product of the common will of nations acting in the common interest of all nations. And they are governed by natural law, which is the product of human nature and hence indirectly is the work of God who made human nature to be as it is, including its sociability and its rationality. And they are governed by a moral order which comes directly from God.

> But just as the laws of each state ... have in view the advantage of that state, so by mutual consent it has become possible that certain laws should originate as between all states, or a great many states: and it is apparent that the laws thus originating had in view the advantage not of particular states, but of the great society of states.... And that is what is called the law of nations, whenever we distinguish that term from the law of nature.

Act Three. In the eighteenth century, an attempt was made by a German philosopher to construct a coherent and self-contained system of international law derived from natural law. That philosopher was Christian von Wolff (1679–1754). He proposed the view that the society of the whole human race continues to exist even after the creation of the nation-states.

> If we should consider that great society, which nature has established among men, to be done away with by the particular societies, which men enter into, when they united into a state, states would be established contrary to the law of nature, inasmuch as the universal obligation of all toward all would be terminated; which assuredly is absurd. Just as in the human body individual organs taken together constitute one organ; so likewise individual men do not cease to be members of that great society which is made up of the whole human race, because several have formed together a certain particular society. And in so far as these act together as associates, just as if they were all of one mind and will; even so are the members of that society united, which nature has established among men. After the human race was divided into nations, that society which before was between individuals continues between nations.
>
> ... The purpose of the society therefore, which nature has established among all nations, is to give mutual assistance in perfecting itself and its condition, consequently the promotion of the common good by its combined powers.

Act Four. And then a critical event occurred. The trouble with Wolff was that his book on international law was the last volume of a nine-volume work on natural law. And it was written in Latin. Only the learned read it, among whom was Emmerich de Vattel (1714–67). He decided to communicate Wolff's Volume Nine to the world. But he decided not simply to publish a translation. He wrote his own book, using Wolff's ideas so far as he approved of them. On Wolff's essential theoretical point, Vattel explicitly parted company with Wolff. * * *

> ... when men have agreed to act in common, and have given up their rights and submitted their will to the whole body as far as concerns the common good, it devolves henceforth upon that body, the State [*L'Etat*], and upon its rulers, to fulfil the duties of humanity towards outsiders in all matters in which individuals are no longer at liberty to act and it peculiarly rests with the state to fulfil these duties towards other States.

On Wolff's idea of a society of the nations, Vattel said:

> From the outset it will be seen that I differ entirely from M. Wolff in the foundation I lay for that division of the Law of Nations which he terms voluntary. M.Wolff deduces it from the idea of a sort of great republic ... set up by nature herself, of which all the Nations of the world are members. This does not satisfy me, and I find the fiction of such a republic neither reasonable nor well enough founded to deduce therefrom the rules of a Law of Nations at once universal in character and necessarily accepted by sovereign States. I recognise no other natural society among Nations than that which nature has set up among men in general. It is essential to every civil society ... that each member should yield certain of his rights to the general body and that there should be some authority capable of giving commands prescribing laws and compelling those who refuse to obey. Such an idea is not to be thought of between nations....

Those words have determined the course of history. They have made the world we know. Vattel has used the sovereignty theory of the state to disprove the possibility of a natural society among states. It is fascinating to see, through the course of his book, the word *state* coming to have its modern double meaning. It comes to refer both to the internal organization of the public realm of a society and to the whole of a society when seen externally.

Vattel's book was written in French, which was in those days the international language of the ruling class from London to St. Petersburg. The book was archetypally eighteenth-century—elegant, clear, rational, easy to understand, full of good sense and worldly wisdom. . . . And his book, unlike Wolff's, was read by everyone who mattered, was on the desk of every diplomat for a century or more. It was a book which formed the minds of those who formed international reality, the international reality which is still our reality today.

Act Five. In the nineteenth century, natural law ceased to have any hold on the mind of most philosophers, let alone diplomats and politicians. Natural law was swamped by utilitarianism, positivism and marxism. Natural law was dead beyond resurrection.

Throughout the nineteenth century social and legal philosophers continued to emit streams of discordant ideas about the true nature of international law. They might have saved themselves the mental effort. Vattel-minus-natural-law filled comfortably the busy minds of those whose job it was to act international-ly. And their seemingly rational reality became international society's actual reality.

The natural law framework of Vattel simply evaporated, leaving an internation-al society consisting of so-called states interacting with each other in a social wasteland, subject only to a vestigial law created by their actual or presumed or tacit consent. International society would be, and would remain, an unsocial interstatal system. * * *

Late in the nineteenth century there came to be newly unified and newly powerful state, bringing an immense increase of economic and political and military energy into an international system which was undeveloped, unsophis-ticated, unable to socialize the overwhelming volume of the new social energy. We have lived with the consequences in the twentieth century. We are living with the intolerable consequences today.

It is a speculation which is not only of intellectual interest. It is a might-have-been of history with a significance which is still practical. If Christian Wolff had written in simple lucid French like Vattel, or in excited and exciting French like . . . Rousseau, the world's conception of itself might have been fundamentally different, the history of the world might have been different, the story of the twentieth century might have been different.

Instead, we have the world as it is, a human world which human beings in general think is natural and inevitable but which requires each of us to be two people—with one set of moral judgments and social aspirations and legal expectations within our own national society, and another set . . . for every-thing that happens beyond the frontiers of our national society.

And the post-Vattel ethos which supports this wretched spiritual and psycho-logical dislocation has turned itself into an articulated system which is all-too-familiar. I will call it the *old regime* of the human world and its law. I will epitomise it in eight principles. And then, finally and equally briefly, I will put before you a *new view* of the human world and its law.

The old regime, which subtends everybody's everyday view of the human world and its law, can be stated as follows:

1. The human world consists of a collection of states, approximately one hundred and seventy-five of them, together with a number of ... international organizations.

2. International law is made by and for the states and international organizations, which are the only legislators and the only subjects of international law.

3. Individual human beings and non-governmental entities of all kinds, including industrial and commercial enterprises, are not subjects of international law.

4. International law organises the interaction of the states, that is to say the interaction of their public realms, the governmental aspect of their activity.

5. Other international transactions are a matter for international law only so far as they involve action by governments, either international action, or consequential internal action.

6. The internal realms of the state are independent of each other, protected by a formidable series of defensive concepts—sovereignty, the sovereign equality of states, sovereignty over territory, domestic jurisdiction, political independence and territorial integrity, non-intervention. From behind these conceptual barricades, each state is free to formulate its own policies and pursue its own interests.

7. States are thus, as Vattel proposed, inherently free and equal and independent sovereigns. International law is accordingly conceived as an act of sovereignty by which states choose to accept limits on the exercise of their natural freedom.

8. The only international responsibility for government activity is thus a form of legal responsibility, called state responsibility, for a breach by one state of another state's rights. And that breach takes one of three forms—a breach of territorial rights (property wrong), a breach of a general duty owed to another state (delictual wrong), a breach of a treaty (contractual wrong).

Beyond this, there is no systematic conception of an international society at all—no international social purposes, no international morality, no international moral responsibility, no international social accountability, no systematic international economy, no systematic international culture. And the people of the world do not govern themselves internationally. If anything, they have only a marginal effect on the international activity of their own government.

International social progress comes, if at all, as an incidental external consequence of internal activities, and as a more or less random outcome of so-called development assistance, and, especially, as a by-product of the wealth-creating and wealth distributing effects of international capitalism. . . .

What can we do about it? What should we do about it?

You will not be surprised to hear that the solution I propose is conceptual. I do not propose institutional change. . . . I do not propose that we take up arms to expropriate the expropriators. I do not propose that we use the power of the people to disempower the powerful.

What we will take up is not the power of arms but the power of ideas. We will let our best ideas of society and law flow into our imagining and our understanding of the human world. By *best ideas* I mean ideas that are philosophically fruitful, psychologically empowering, morally inspiring, practically effective.

Within ourselves we can find unrealised best ideas of society and law which are an inheritance secreted from more than five thousand years of intense social experience. We will, at last, take up our best ideas of society and law. We will make them into humanity's ideal. We will choose them as the programme of a revolution.

I will put a *new view of the human world and its law* also in the form of eight principles.

1. International society is the society of the whole human race and the society of all societies. In other words, everything human that happens in the world is part of the social process of international society. We, the people, are members of international society—as are all the countless subordinate societies that we form, including, among many others, the family, the ... corporation, the state-societies, and non-governmental and intergovernmental international organisations.

2. International society has a constitution like every other society, which carries the systematic structure of society from its past to its future, determining the way in which all social power is created and distributed throughout the world.

3. The state-societies and intergovernmental organisations are constitutional organs of international society, with special functions and powers in relation to the world public-realm, functions and powers delegated by international society under the international constitution and under international law.

4. International law is the law of international society, the true law of a true society. It is made, like all other law, through the total social process of international society, in which we all participate. . . .

5. The constitution of international society, like any other constitution, is not finally fixed. It is a dynamic thing, liable to unceasing change ... , constantly reformed by the ideas and aspirations of humanity. The era of unsocial interstatal society is ending—the era of international relations, state-power, foreign policy, ... war, the era of the old international law. The era of social international society has begun.

6. The responsibility of the state-societies, as organs of international society, is not merely a matter of property, delict, and contract. Nor is their responsibility merely legal responsibility. Their primary responsibility is for abuse of power. All governments everywhere are socially and legally responsible for the way in which they exercise the powers delegated to them by international society. And the same is true of all those individuals and societies, including industrial and commercial corporations, which exercise social power affecting human survival and prospering.

7. International law, like all law, is inherently dynamic—developing structurally and systematically, developing substantively, flowing into new areas, embodying and responding to social development of the world—human rights law, environmental law, natural resources law, sea law, space law, ... , economic law of all kinds, and international public law to control the use and abuse of public power.

8. International society and international law embody the social purposes which humanity chooses for itself and which are realised in the social power, legal and non-legal social power, which human beings exercise with a view to human survival and prospering.

Our consciousness extends throughout the world passing freely across political frontiers. Our sympathy extends to the whole of humanity. Our moral and social responsibility extends to the whole of humanity and to the whole of the physical world which we transform by our actions.

But our social ideals and our social possibilities are trapped and stifled within the mental structures which divide and disable the human world, structures which human consciousness has made and which human consciousness can remake.

The necessary revolution will free human consciousness from its self-subjection, from its self-disabling, from its self-destroying, allowing our ideas and our ideals, as well as our willing and our acting, to include the whole world, the physical world and the human world. The necessary revolution will leave us free to make and remake a human society which does not abolish our national societies but embraces and completes them.

The necessary revolution is a world revolution. The world revolution is a revolution not on the streets but in our minds.

QUESTIONS AND DISCUSSION

1.   In the absence of a global legislature or a universal set of norms, each State is left as the ultimate source of authority—and constraint—for its own actions, thus Allott's assertion that modern nation–States exist in an international non-society. As we will discuss throughout the chapter, this situation is growing increasingly unrealistic. When Grotius, Wolff and Vattel were writing, the single, universal human community was an abstraction, an ideal against which human relations could be measured. Today, the global human community is a reality. Since the end of World War II, the economies of the world have become increasingly interdependent. The rise of mass media created windows to see our neighbors on every corner of the globe. The transportation revolution and the emergence of the Internet have turned those windows into doors. Geography is no longer a serious constraint to the development of community: money, information and ideas now cross borders with the ease and speed of a telephone call or a modem link-up. Integration carries not only common opportunities, but also common risks.

As we have seen in Chapter 1, moreover, our shared community is not simply social, political, or economic. It is environmental. It is physical. The unrestrained use of fossil fuels in North America will lead to bigger storms and increased flooding in China. The unrestrained use of ozone depleting substances in China will raise skin cancer rates in North America.

When viewed in light of our shared economy, culture and environment, does Allott's call for a reconceptualization of human society seem unrealistic? Or essential? Can we expect to effectively address the threats to our global environment without first developing a sense of global community—a sense of personal responsibility for the common good of the globe? If such a sense of community does not emerge naturally, how might we promote its development? Consider how we might extend that community to generations yet unborn, as Edith Brown Weiss argues we must. *See infra at 398.*

2.   Allott's view that states alone are the subjects of international law has been the dominant view in the 20th Century and well supported by the authorities, including the RESTATEMENT OF FOREIGN RELATIONS LAW OF THE UNITED STATES, sec. 101 (3rd ed. 1987) ("The principal persons under international law are states.... [I]ndividuals ... can have any status ... given them by international law or agreement, and increasingly . . . have been accorded such aspects of personality in varying measures."), and concurring opinions of Judge Bork and Judge Edwards in *Tel-Oren, et al. v. Libyan Arab Republic, et al.,* 726 F.2d 774 (D.C.Cir.1984)(affirming dismissal of action by survivors and representatives of persons murdered in an attack on a civilian in Israel filed under the Alien Tort Claims Act of 1789, 28 U.S.C. § 1350 (1988)).

Judge Bork states in his concurring opinion that "the general rule that international law imposes duties only on states and on their agents or officials . . . [and] international law protections of persons [exists] solely in terms of state obligations. . . ." 726 F.2d at 805–06,817. Judge Edwards takes a broader view, noting that individuals are liable for war crimes under international law, when acting under color of state law, citing the Nuremberg precedent. He also recognizes that there is support even for "truly individual liability" under international law:

> That the individual's status in international law has been in flux since section 1350 [the Alien Tort Claims Act] was drafted [in 1789] explains in part the current mix of views about private party liability. Through the 18th century and into the 19th, writers and jurists believed that rules of international law bound individuals as well as states. In the 19th century, the view emerged that states alone were subjects of international law, and they alone were able to assert rights and be held to duties devolved from the law of nations. Under that view—which became firmly entrenched both in doctrine and in practice—individual rights existed only as rights of the state, and could be asserted, defended or withdrawn by the state. . . .
>
> In this century, once again writers have argued that both the rights and duties of international law should be applied to private parties. However, their discussions are more prescriptive than descriptive; they recognize shifts in firmly entrenched doctrine but are unable to define a clear new consensus. . . . 726 F.2d at 794.

According to Professor Paust, however, the "states alone" view is "simplistic and false," "ahistorical," and an "inhibiting myth":

> Interestingly, even some of the "supporting" material that [Judge Bork] used contains sufficient qualifying language to alert one to the fact that international law does address private rights and duties. Although Judge Edwards also argued that the "states alone" view became "firmly entrenched" by the early twentieth century, such a view was not correct, and was always challenged by other textwriters of that period, if not in relevant judicial decisions. Additionally, the inhibiting myth that Judge Bork would resurrect had rested on theories about the functioning of law at the state-to-state level, not the trends in actual decisions at the domestic level. In sum, it was, and is, simply not true that individuals could not benefit directly from international law or be subject either to civil or criminal sanctions for violations of international law.

Jordan J. Paust, INTERNATIONAL LAW AS LAW OF THE UNITED STATES 209–10, with supporting cites at 288–91 (1996). See Chapter 16 on human rights.

What are the implications for Allott's revolution of the mind that the relationship between the individual and the State has been in flux for the past several centuries and that the "states alone" view of international law may be a "myth"? Does it strengthen his position that the international legal system is a product of our conceptual thinking, and that it can be changed by "reconceiving" our conceptual framework? What does Professor Paust mean when he refers to the "inhibiting myth" of the "states alone" view? What is the myth inhibiting? What "myth" would you create to animate international environmental law?

3. Whatever the dominant theoretical view is today, non–State actors (whether NGOs, churches, corporations, educational institutions, or individuals) are still excluded as parties from most important international fora—including, for example, the International Court of Justice and the dispute resolution proceedings of the World Trade Organization, discussed in Chapter 15. They must generally rely on individual governments to represent their interests in international negotiations. Yet government delegations are often biased in favor of particular national interests, to the exclusion of others, who then have no voice in the international proceeding. Moreover, many interest groups have truly international interests and cannot be represented adequately by a single State.

Nevertheless, opportunities for the direct participation of non-State actors are increasing. Scientific unions identify environmental problems that need addressing and develop standards that often form the basis for international law-making. NGOs encourage new law-making by gathering and disseminating information to policy-makers and the general public, by monitoring the implementation of existing agreements and promoting change within individual States and institutions, and within the international community as a whole. Multinational corporations influence policy decisions at both national and international levels by lobbying decision-makers and by participating directly in international organizations. Indigenous groups have begun to assert their rights to territory, to cultural sovereignty, and to the value of their accumulated knowledge of the natural environment. And citizens are raising their voices by participating in the domestic political processes that shape international law and by bringing their own claims *as individuals* before international commissions, tribunals, and parliamentary bodies, particularly in human rights fora. Even international institutions that exclude non-State actors are increasingly subject to public pressure. Protesters are now a regular aspect of major meetings of the World Trade Organization and the International Monetary Fund.

For an optimistic view of the progress individuals are making in the international legal process, *see* Lung–Chu Chen, AN INTRODUCTION TO CONTEMPORARY INTERNATIONAL LAW, at 25 (2000).

> In recent decades, participation in the global constitutive process of authoritative decision has been greatly democratized. All participants—conveniently categorized as nation-states, international governmental organizations, nongovernmental organizations and associations, and individual human beings—now openly or recognizably play important roles and perform numerous functions. The role of nation-states has been, and continues to be, predominant at the international level. ... Multiplying hosts of private associations, dedicated to values other than power, are increasingly transnational in membership, goals, organizational structure, spheres of activity, and influence. Individuals, acting both alone and as representatives of groups, have ample opportunity to participate in all activities that comprise the making and application of law. Indeed, individuals are the ultimate participants in the international legal process and in each organization or association mentioned above. Such a realistic role has been recognized at various times but appears to be increasingly evident in the latter part of the twentieth century...

As you read the rest of this chapter, and the entire textbook, consider whether you agree with Lung–Chu Chen that individuals "are the ultimate participants in the international legal process" and have "ample opportunity" to participate in all aspects of the international lawmaking process. Is this theory or myth or a description of reality?

4. Direct democracy and representative democracy are different things. Individuals in the United States are denied a direct voice and a direct vote in Congress. Many nation States, however, do have national referenda on some issues, although not the

United States. (Even the U.S. election for President is not a national referenda, but a representative election, as shown by the election of President Bush in 2000, even though he lost the popular vote.)

Would it be better for the world to be governed by referendum? Is this what the critics of the World Trade Organization and the World Bank really are demanding? If so, do you think that the people who are able to travel to such protest events have values that are shared by the majority of the world's population? If we had global referenda and the protesters' values were to be swamped by billions of opposing votes, by those who wanted more trade, would they still want a direct international democracy? Or would they demand, not direct democracy, but a rational, expert based system of governance (which of course, we also do not now have)? Is the real issue how to open avenues of participation for all of society, and how to ensure accountability for abuses of power, as Allott suggests?

5. What is the role of the individual under a natural law theory of international law? Consider the following statement from Blackstone:

> The law of nations is a legal system of rules, deducible by natural reason, and established by universal consent among the civilized inhabitants of the world; in order to decide all disputes, to regulate all ceremonies and civilities, and to ensure the observance of justice and good faith, in that intercourse which must frequently occur between two or more independent states, and the individuals belonging to each.

4 WILLIAM BLACKSTONE COMMENTARIES ON THE LAWS OF ENGLAND 66 (1765–69). Is Blackstone suggesting that individuals are the ultimate source of power in international law? See also, *United States v. Von Leeb (The High Command Case)*, U.S. Military Tribunal, 1948, XI Trials of War Criminals 462, 487–90 (1950), cited in Paust, *supra*, at 25:

> Since international common law grows out of the common reactions and the composit thinking with respect to recurring situations by the various states composing the family of nations, it is pertinent to consider the general attitude of the citizens of states with respect to their military commanders and their obligations when their nations plan, prepare for and initiate or engage in war.
>
> While it is undoubtedly true that international common law in case of conflict with state law takes precedence over it and while it is equally true that absolute unanimity among all states in the family of nations is not required to bring an international common law into being, it is scarcely a tenable proposition that international common law will run counter to the consensus within any considerable number of nations. ... We may safely assume that the general and considered opinions of the people within states—the source from which international law springs....

Compare Blackstone and the excerpt from *The High Command Case* with the role of the individual as reflected in the RESTATEMENT section quoted above: "[I]ndividuals ... can have any status ... given them by international law or agreement...." Does the use of "international law or agreement" suggest that there may be common or customary law or general principles that address individuals?

6. Allott laments Vattel's expulsion of international law from the ambit of natural law theory. At the same time, he identifies a different process—the growth of constitutionalism within nation states, while feudalism remains in place between sovereign nations. Is there any good reason why constitutionalism has to stop at national boundaries? If natural law was considered insufficiently pragmatic, was that a reason in itself for constitutionalism to declare itself uninterested in international relations? What do you think of the idea of an international constitution? In a very real sense, there is a battle for constitutional supremacy between the

World Trade Organization and the climate change treaty regime still being negotiated. The World Trade Organization is one of the most powerful international organization in the world. The climate change treaty regime, however, must become equally or more powerful—to reach into the heart of the global industrial economy and regulate energy use—if it is to be successful in controlling climate change. We will return to natural law in the discussion of general principles later in the chapter.

SECTION II.   TRADITIONAL SOURCES OF LAW

Because the positivist approach predominates in the modern era, international lawyers generally must look for evidence of consent to prove that international law on a particular subject exists with respect to a particular State. As the primary judicial organ of the UN system, the International Court of Justice (ICJ) plays an important role in identifying and developing international law. The ICJ acts as both a legal advisory body to the UN system as well as a court for the settlement of disputes between States. Its fifteen judges are chosen to represent geographic regions and type of legal system. Article 38(1) of the ICJ Statute identifies the four traditional sources of law that the Court can employ to determine the applicable international law that is binding in a particular case:

> The Court, whose function is to decide in accordance with international law such disputes as are submitted to it, shall apply:
>
> (a) international conventions, whether general or particular, establishing rules expressly recognized by the contesting states;
>
> (b) international custom, as evidence of a general practice accepted as law;
>
> (c) the general principles of law recognized by civilized nations; and
>
> (d) . . . judicial decisions and the teachings of the most highly qualified publicists of the various nations, as subsidiary means for the determination of rules of law.

The first three sources—treaty, custom and general principles of international law—create binding legal obligations for States. By contrast, judicial decisions and the writings of publicists are subsidiary means for discovering what the law is, and thus do not create generally binding obligations for States. We examine each of these sources of international law in turn.

A.   TREATIES

Treaties play a dual role in the international system. Their primary function is to create specific legal obligations between the treaty parties. Treaties are the most easily discernible sources of international law because they derive their legitimacy directly from the express consent of States. They are the principle method for creating binding rules of international law, including international rules regarding the environment. Treaties can also contribute to the development of customary international law, as well as general principles.

This section examines the processes for initiating, negotiating, adopting, and ratifying treaties. As a framework for discussion, the section employs the Vienna Convention on the Law of Treaties. May 23, 1969, 1155 U.N.T.S. 331. For its parties, the Vienna Convention governs the major aspects of treaties, including negotiation, conclusion, interpretation, amendment, and termination. Even among non-parties, the Convention is widely accepted as a codification of customary international law. For example, although the United States has never ratified the Vienna Convention, the U.S. Department of State has declared that the principles expressed in the Convention are binding upon the United States. Because it codifies underlying customary law, the Vienna Convention binds non-parties as well as parties, and may apply to agreements concluded before as well as after 1980.

---

1. DEFINITION OF A TREATY

Article 2.1(a) of the Vienna Convention defines a "treaty" as "an international agreement concluded between States in written form and governed by international law, whether embodied in a single instrument or in two or more related instruments and whatever its particular designation." This definition, of course, is somewhat circular: a treaty is an instrument governed by international law. A more useful definition might be that a treaty is any instrument between two or more States that fulfills the requirements for valid treaties set out in the Vienna Convention itself. Note that the instrument need not be called a treaty; it can be called an agreement, convention, pact, covenant or virtually any other name. A treaty is a contract between States and, just as with commercial contracts, what is important is the manifest intent of the parties—in this case States—to be bound by their agreement. It is the obligatory character of the terms of a treaty, not its nominal designation, that determines whether a binding rule of international law has been created.

The only formal requirement is that there be a writing. While States may undertake binding international agreements without concluding a written instrument, the Vienna Convention does not govern such agreements, although they may be governed by general principles of international law. *See* Nuclear Test Cases (Australia v. France), 1974 ICJ Rep. 253, discussed *infra* page 905. Nor does it govern agreements between State and non-State actors, or agreements entirely among non-State actors. This limitation is made explicit in Article 1 of the Convention, which states that "The present Convention applies to treaties between States." This provision reflects the traditional view that non-State actors can be neither subjects nor authors of international law. Because the ICJ has now recognized the international personality of certain international organizations, a second Vienna Convention was negotiated to govern agreements among these organizations or between an international organization and a State. Vienna Convention on the Law of Treaties Between States and International Organizations or Between International Organizations, 25 I.L.M. 543 (March 21, 1986). Agreements between States and private individuals, organizations or corporations are not governed by international law, but by the law of contracts—either as applied in the territory of the contracting State or as otherwise specified in the contract itself. Aside from these requirements, however, the only limitation on the scope, form or subject matter of a treaty is that the terms of the treaty must not violate a peremptory norm of international law. This restriction is roughly analogous to domestic laws that prohibit contracts made for illegal purposes.

The Vienna Convention does not distinguish between the various forms that a treaty may take, such as multilateral or bilateral, nor the diverse legal functions that they perform. Thus:

> [I]f international society wishes to enact a fundamental, organic, constitutional law ... it employs the treaty. If two states wish to put on record their adherence to the principle of the three-mile limit of territorial waters ... they use a treaty. If further they wish to enter into a bargain which derogates from that principle, again they use a treaty. If Denmark wishes to sell to the United States of America her West Indian possessions ... they do so by treaty.... And if it is desired to create an international organization such as the International Union for the Protection of Works of Art and Literature, which resembles the corporation of private law, it is done by treaty.

Lord McNair, *The Functions and Differing Legal Character of Treaties*, 11 BRITISH Y.B. INT'L L. (1930) *reprinted in* MCNAIR, THE LAW OF TREATIES 739, 740 (1961).

Most treaties, particularly bilateral treaties, are much like contracts, creating legal obligations that are relatively narrow in scope and strictly limited to the parties involved in the negotiations. Some multilateral treaties, however, are considered to be "law-making" treaties in that they create general norms for future conduct. Almost like international legislation, these "law-making" treaties often are more broadly applicable and are open even to States that did not participate in the negotiations. Although in principle binding only on the parties, in some cases these treaties may codify and develop customary law or general principles. The Vienna Convention, as noted, is generally regarded as a partial codification of the customary international law governing international agreements between States. Similarly, the UN Convention on the Law of the Sea both codified existing customary international law and catalyzed the further development and "crystallization" of customary international law.

---

2. THE TREATY–MAKING PROCESS

Just as there is no prescribed form for treaties, neither is there a prescribed process for initiating the treaty-making process or for negotiating a treaty. Although States are still the predominant actors in the treaty-making process, international governmental organizations (IGOs), non-governmental organizations (NGOs), and other non-State actors are playing an increasingly significant role. This role is most pronounced in the early stages of the treaty-making process, where IGOs and NGOs have been instrumental in laying the groundwork for important multilateral environmental agreements. In a recent example, an NGO won the 1997 Nobel

Peace Prize in recognition of its role in catalyzing the negotiation of a treaty banning land mines.

Four basic steps are inherent in the conclusion of any international agreement: 1) identification of needs and goals; 2) negotiation; 3) adoption and signature; and 4) ratification. Even after these steps are completed, treaties must be implemented, monitored for compliance and, if necessary, modified or amended. For now, however, we will focus on treaty creation, using as a model the international response to ozone depletion described in *Ozone Diplomacy* by Richard Benedick. Ambassador Benedick led the United States negotiating team during the preparation of both the 1985 Vienna Convention for the Protection of the Ozone Layer and the 1987 Montreal Protocol on Substances that Deplete the Ozone Layer. In *Ozone Diplomacy*, Ambassador Benedick provides an exhaustive study of the background, issues, and processes of the ozone treaty negotiations.

———

a. Identification of Needs and Goals

Before an international agreement can be concluded, certain preliminary steps must be taken. The first step, of course, is that the need for action must be discovered—someone must conduct the research and synthesize the data that demonstrate, for example, that a particular substance harms the environment or a particular species is in danger of extinction. This seems an obvious point, yet it bears mention for two reasons. First, many important environmental problems have gone unaddressed for years or even decades before someone accumulated sufficient data to convince the international community to address them. Second, because there is neither a prescribed process for identifying treaty needs, nor any group of actors vested with primary responsibility for doing so, need identification has proven an important strategy for non-State actors to influence the international environmental law-making process. The following excerpt from Ambassador Benedick's account of the ozone depletion negotiations demonstrates the role of science in the early stages of treaty-making.

Richard Benedick, Ozone Diplomacy 9–19 (1998)

The Montreal Protocol was the result of research at the frontiers of science combined with a unique collaboration between scientists and policymakers. Unlike any previous diplomatic endeavor, it was based on continually evolving theories, on state-of-the-art computer models simulating the results of intricate chemical and physical reactions for decades into the future, and on satellite-, land-, and rocket-based monitoring of remote gases measured in parts per trillion. An international agreement of this nature could not, in fact, have occurred at any earlier point in history. * * *

In 1973, two University of Michigan scientists ... [discovered] that chlorine released in the stratosphere [from NASA rockets] could unleash a complicated chemical process that would continually destroy ozone for several decades. A single chlorine atom, through a catalytic chain reaction, could eliminate tens of thousands of the ozone molecules. * * *

In 1974, Mario Molina and Sherwood Rowland at the University of California, Irvine, became intrigued with some peculiar properties of a family of widely used anthropogenic chemicals, the chlorofluorocarbons. Molina and Rowland discovered that, unlike most other gases, CFCs are not chemically broken down or rained out quickly in the lower atmosphere but rather, because of their exceptionally stable chemical structure, persist and migrate slowly up to the stratosphere.... The two researchers concluded that CFCs are eventually broken down by solar radiation and in the process release large quantities of chlorine into the stratosphere.

The combined implications of these ... hypotheses were deeply disturbing. The researchers had not anticipated any link between CFCs and ozone depletion. There had been no prior suspicion that CFCs were harmful to the environment. Indeed, following their invention in the 1930s, CFCs had seemed an ideal chemical. They had been thoroughly tested by customary standards and found to be safe. The possibility that dangers could originate many miles above the Earth's surface was never considered. * * *

Initial Scientific Response

The U.S. scientific community reacted to the 1974 theories by mounting a major research campaign, involving the National Academy of Sciences and a growing number of prominent chemists, meteorologists, physicists, and space scientists from NASA, the National Oceanic and Atmospheric Administration (NOAA), and leading universities. The next several years were marked by intense professional and personal disputes within the scientific community. Although a series of laboratory and modeling studies resulting from these activities confirmed the validity of the chlorine—ozone linkage, they could not prove definitively that it described what was actually going on in the stratosphere. * * *

A Landmark International Report

In late 1984, in a conscious effort "to provide governments around the world with the best scientific information currently available on whether human activities represent a substantial threat to the ozone layer," a remarkable cooperative international scientific venture was launched. This integrative research was cosponsored by NASA, NOAA, the U.S. Federal Aviation Administration, the United Nations Environment Programme, the World Meteorological Organization (WMO), the West German Ministry for Research and Technology, and the Commission of the European Communities.

Coordinated by NASA, the work occupied approximately 150 scientists of various nations for over a year. The result, published by WMO and UNEP in 1986, was the most comprehensive study of the stratosphere ever undertaken....

A major finding of the WMO/UNEP report was that accumulations of CFCs 11 and 12 in the atmosphere had nearly doubled from 1975 through 1985. Since actual production of these chemicals had stagnated over this period, these measurements confirmed the existence of a potential for large future increases in stratospheric concentrations of these long-lived substances, particularly if the growth rate of their emissions were to resume.

The WMO/UNEP assessment predicted that continuing emissions of CFCs 11 and 12 at the 1980 rate could, through release of chlorine in the stratosphere, reduce the ozone layer by about 9 percent on a global average by the last half of the twenty-first century.... As a result, higher levels of biologically harmful ultraviolet radiation could reach heavily populated regions of the Northern Hemisphere. * * *

The study indicated, moreover, that the ozone layer was threatened not only by CFCs 11 and 12, which had been the original focus of international scientific concern, but also by [several related and chemically-similar compounds].* * *

[In 1985, prompted by the initial work of the WMO/UNEP group and other scientists, 43 nations, including the most important producers and consumers of CFCs, negotiated a framework treaty, the Vienna Convention for the Protection of the Ozone Layer, to encourage further scientific cooperation on the issue.]

The Antarctic Ozone Hole

Too late for analysis under the WMO/UNEP assessment, British scientists in 1985 published astonishing findings based on a review of land-based measurements of stratospheric ozone ... in the Antarctic. So unbelievable at first were these measurements that the scientists had delayed publication for nearly three years while they ... reviewed their data and the accuracy of their instruments. They finally concluded that ozone levels recorded during the Antarctic springtime (September–November) had fallen to about 50 percent lower than they had been in the 1960s.... The "ozone hole" (that is, a portion of the stratosphere in which greatly diminished ozone levels were measured) had also expanded by 1985 to cover an area greater in size than the United States.

[It is commonly asserted that the discovery of the Antarctic ozone hole provided the driving force behind the rapid negotiation of a substantive protocol to the Vienna Convention, the 1987 Montreal Protocol on Substances that Deplete the Ozone Layer. Benedick suggests that the data was, at that time, too uncertain to be a prime motivator for action. He notes, however, that stronger proof of the link between the ozone hole and chlorinated compounds that emerged shortly after the Protocol negotiations prompted the parties to negotiate more stringent reductions by amendment to the Protocol in 1989 and again in 1990. Throughout the history of the Protocol, the emergence of new scientific evidence has led the parties to increase the stringency of their reductions and to extend reductions to new groups of chemicals.]

---

b. Negotiation

In the case of a bilateral treaty, a State may initiate the treaty-making process simply by inviting another State to negotiate on a particular issue. Negotiations may then proceed, and a binding agreement be concluded. A simple exchange of diplomatic correspondence is sufficient—face-to-face negotiation between the parties is not required.

Nor is there a prescribed process for creating a multilateral treaty. Nonetheless, in recent decades, a somewhat standardized negotiating process has emerged. Negotiations may be initiated by individual States; more often, however, a State will recommend that an international organization, particularly the United Nations General Assembly (UNGA) or the UN Economic and Social Council (ECOSOC), establish a committee or convene an international conference to consider a particular issue. The host organization will then organize preparatory committees, working groups of technical and legal experts, scientific symposia and preliminary conferences. Increasingly, the organizing body will invite, or at least accept, comments from NGOs, scientific unions and other private groups. During these informal discussions, information is disseminated, the preliminary positions of interested States are established, the parameters of a possible agreement are narrowed, and the slow process of building international consensus begins.

This process of informal exchange may continue for years before a conference of plenipotentiaries (representatives with the authority to approve an international agreement on behalf of their respective governments) is convened. In the interim, the host government or organization, or some other qualified international body, will develop a draft convention to serve as the basis for discussions at the plenipotentiary conference. Generally, draft conventions are prepared with significant participation by the interested parties, and many disagreements among States are likely to be ironed out before the final conference convenes. At the plenipotentiary conference, delegates will seek to resolve their remaining disputes, and produce a final, authoritative version of the treaty, an "authentic text". For a good introduction to the negotiating process, *see* LYNTON K. CALDWELL, INTERNATIONAL ENVIRONMENTAL POLICY 119 (3RD ED.1996).

The following excerpt describes the negotiations that were undertaken for the 1987 Montreal Protocol on Substances that Deplete the Ozone layer (discussed further in Chapter 9). As you read this excerpt, pay attention to the roles of the various non-State actors in the negotiation process.

RICHARD BENEDICK, OZONE DIPLOMACY 68–76 (1998)

As the protocol negotiations began in December 1986, the only governments that had actually ratified the Vienna Convention [on the Protection of the Ozone Layer] were ... Canada, Finland, Norway, Sweden, ... the United States [and] the Soviet Union. Neither European Community countries nor Japan had yet ratified. This was not a propitious omen, since no regulatory protocol could become operational until the convention itself entered into force, and this required ratification by 20 governments. In a public statement in September 1986, the United Kingdom's Imperial Chemical Industries predicted that the ratification process for the Vienna Convention could take "several years."

The Lineup of Countries

The negotiating parties appeared to be divided into three major camps....

Officially, the European Community, negotiating as a bloc, followed the industry line.... The EC continued to advocate some form of production capacity cap. Because the scientific models indicated no significant ozone depletion for at least two decades, the EC Commission argued that there was time to delay actual production cuts and wait for more evidence.... This perspective was shared by Japan and the Soviet Union during most of the negotiations. * * *

In contrast, Canada, Finland, New Zealand, Norway, Sweden, Switzerland, and the United States publicly endorsed strong new controls. They argued that action had to be taken well before critical levels of chlorine accumulated. * * *

A third group of active participants, including Australia, Austria, and a number of developing countries, were initially uncommitted, but as the negotiations progressed they moved toward favoring stringent regulations. During the negotiations Argentina, Brazil, Egypt, Kenya, and Venezuela played increasingly important roles representing the perspectives of developing nations.

Geneva: A Slow Start

Against this background the United Nations Environment Programme convened the opening weeklong negotiating round in Geneva in December 1986. Although UNEP had hoped for attendance by more than 50 governments, only 25 showed up. * * *

The negotiations began chaotically, with general and unfocused debate. Canada, the Soviet Union, and the United States each proposed "illustrative" texts that were incompatible with one another. The U.S. text was the most comprehensive, covering not only control measures but also provisions for periodic assessments and adjustments, trade restrictions, and reporting. Three Nordic nations—Finland, Norway, and Sweden—jointly offered an amendment to the U.S. text, calling for immediate cuts rather than an initial freeze. The Canadians proposed complex national emissions quotas based on a formula incorporating gross national product and population. The Soviets seemed unfamiliar with, and sharply critical of, the scientific rationale for new controls. They suggested national allocations based rather vaguely on population and CFC production capacity, with a complete exemption for developing countries.

For its part, consistent with its "status quo" decision, the EC Commission declared that it had no mandate to negotiate anything other than a cap on production capacity. * * *

Vienna: A Few Steps Forward

The following weeks were marked by intensive U.S. diplomatic activity to promote a serious long-term control strategy. The second session convened, as planned, in Vienna in late February 1987. In order to focus the debate, the U.S. delegation proposed that four separate working groups be established to deal individually with the issues of science, trade, developing countries, and control measures.

At Vienna there was growing evidence of evolution in the attitudes of many participating governments. Canada and the Nordic nations quietly abandoned their separate concepts and supported the proposed U.S. text outline. This format also gained backing from other countries, including Egypt, Mexico, New Zealand, and Switzerland. Japan and the Soviet Union remained enigmatic.

Important gaps separated the United States and the EC, however, on virtually every substantive issue. The EC stated that even a small reduction beyond a freeze would be very difficult to accept, although it could at least be considered. An informal EC proposal would have postponed even minimal 10 or 20 percent reductions in CFC emissions by nearly a decade.* * *

An important step forward at Vienna, however, was the setting of a firm September date for the final plenipotentiaries' conference in Montreal. This both turned up the pressure and eradicated any lingering doubts or wishful thinking about the seriousness of the intent to push forward to a protocol.

Another significant result was the endorsement of a U.S. proposal to turn once more to the science. The scientists were asked to test on their models the future effects on ozone of alternative regulatory strategies that incorporated varying combinations of controlled substances and reduction schedules. A meeting of eight scientists from four countries ... was convened by UNEP in early April in Würzburg, West Germany. The results of this meeting had a decisive impact on the remainder of the negotiations.

Geneva Again: UNEP Takes a Stand

The number of participating governments rose to 33 at the third negotiating round, in Geneva in April 1987; of these, 11 were developing nations. UNEP

Executive Director Mostafa Tolba, attending for the first time ... unequivocally placed UNEP behind tough international regulations. From that point on, Tolba assumed a central role in the protocol negotiations, exerting his personal influence and his considerable authority as a scientist and head of a UN organization.

Tolba organized in Geneva for the first time small closed meetings of key delegation heads, away from the formality of the large plenary sessions and the swarms of interested-party observers, and primarily focused on the crucial control measures. Working in secrecy on an unofficial text enabled representatives to negotiate with more flexibility, since they did not in this process commit their governments to any particular formulation. * * *

This group was able to produce an unofficial draft, labeled Tolba's personal text, at the end of the Geneva session. The draft represented considerable progress and increasingly resembled the original U.S. proposal. When Tolba's text was presented to the plenary, many governments expressed interest. * * *

Final Maneuvers

In late June 1987 Tolba reconvened his group of key delegation heads in Brussels to consider the controls and other major provisions. In July a small number of legal experts met in The Hague to analyze the entire protocol text as it had emerged from various working groups, in order to produce a relatively uncluttered and internally consistent draft for the final negotiating session in Montreal. * * *

[D]uring contentious legal discussions in The Hague, the E.C. and U.K. representatives tried to alter many clauses in Tolba's "personal text" from the Brussels negotiation. It was mainly Tolba's own forceful personality, together with the strong will of a young State Department lawyer, Deborah Kennedy, that prevented a watered-down draft protocol from being presented at the final negotiating session in September.... Even so, the text contained numerous alternative formulations (in diplomatic parlance, "brackets") that required additional exhaustive negotiation in Montreal. * * *

It is difficult to imagine the degree of tension and suspense among participants and observers as the Montreal conference approached. There was a sense that governments were entering uncharted territory. But the number and extent of issues still to be resolved in the putative closing round of a complicated international negotiation were staggering. Conflicts and uncertainties marked virtually every paragraph of the proposed protocol.... Characteristic of the midsummer mood was a message to the State Department from Tokyo, only a few weeks before the scheduled final negotiating round, that the Japanese government did not expect an agreement to emerge from Montreal.

Montreal: Agreement at Last

The parties reconvened in Montreal on September 8, 1987. The number of participating governments had now grown to over 60, of which more than half were developing countries. Scores of observers included ... representatives of many environmental organizations; industrial firms and associations were, as usual, strongly in evidence. The international news media were well represented.

The first six days were devoted to attempts in various working groups to reach a greater convergence on the many bracketed portions of the protocol text. On September 14 the plenipotentiary conference was convened to complete the negotiations. * * *

Tolba and the conference chairman, Austrian diplomat Winfried Lang, worked tirelessly throughout the eight days in closed meetings with key participants to hammer out the necessary compromises. There were the perhaps inevitable midnight theatrics. And a precedent-setting international accord was finally unveiled on September 16.

Vignettes from that day in Montreal reveal many departures from the normally staid diplomatic style and reflect the sense of history making that prevailed. The atmosphere contrasted dramatically with the tentativeness and confusion that had marked the beginning of the negotiations, only nine months earlier.

In the early morning of September 16, the head of the Japanese delegation exultantly waved a last-minute cable that contained his authorization to sign the protocol.... A young Chinese scientist, who had single-handedly and with distinction represented his country for the first time, promised before the plenary to do his "personal best" to persuade his government to join later.... The representative of Senegal, attending the ozone negotiations for the first time, confided that he had signed the protocol before actually receiving instructions from Dakar, because "it was the right thing to do." The Venezuelan delegation, which all morning had been suffering through the lengthy roll call of nations while anxiously awaiting word from Caracas, broke into cheers when a breathless messenger finally arrived with the authorizing cable—just in the nick of alphabetical time. * * *

... Witnessing the fruition of 12 years of personal struggle, [Mostafa] Tolba declared that the agreement had shown "that the environment can be a bridge between the worlds of East and West, and of North and South. As a scientist, I salute you: for with this agreement the worlds of science and public affairs have taken a step closer together ... a union which must guide the affairs of the world into the next century." And he concluded, prophetically, "This Protocol is a point of departure ... the beginning of the real work to come."

QUESTIONS AND DISCUSSION

1. Although nation-States were the only formal participants in the protocol negotiations, the Benedick excerpt demonstrates the emerging role of the various non-State actors. In addition to being "strongly in evidence" at the final negotiations, industrial firms and associations played a significant role in defining the initial negotiating positions of the various States. This was as true for the European Community as for the United States. Indeed, U.S. insistence on strong international controls, including trade measures, was spurred largely by the demands of its own industries. Those industries feared that without international controls on ozone emissions the domestic controls they were already under would place them at a competitive disadvantage in international markets.

Scientists and scientific unions were also significant participants in the international process that led to the Montreal Protocol. Scientists, of course, discovered the link between CFCs and ozone depletion in the first place. But beyond this, notice how the diplomats turned to science when they reached a stalemate on potential regulatory measures. The development of international scientific consensus on the ozone problem was crucial to the development of international political consensus. Perhaps this is what prompted UNEP Executive Director Tolba to recognize the union of science and public affairs "which must guide the affairs of the world into the next century."

By the time NGOs arrived—as observers—at the plenary conference, the great majority of decisions about the Protocol regime had already been made. One pair of authors has attributed this non-involvement to a lack of NGO interest in the ozone issue before the Protocol was signed. At least one NGO, however, was interested. The Natural Resources Defense Council, a U.S. environmental group, attended an ozone workshop sponsored by the EPA and UNEP in 1986. At that workshop, NRDC learned from DuPont, the world's largest producer of CFCs, that DuPont could create CFC-substitutes less harmful to the ozone layer if offered the appropriate incentives. In response, NRDC advanced the first proposal anywhere in the world for a near-complete phase-out of all CFCs. *See* Barbara J. Bramble & Gareth Porter, *Nongovernmental Organizations and the Making of U.S. International Environmental Policy*, in INTERNATIONAL POLITICS OF THE ENVIRONMENT: ACTORS, INTERESTS AND INSTITUTIONS 313 (Andrew Hurrell & Benedict Kingsbury eds. 1992).

Finally, consider the role that individual personalities played in the negotiations. Had Mostafa Tolba been less charismatic, the Montreal Protocol might never have emerged or might have taken a very different form. Had Ambassador Lang not been an active and well-respected chairperson or had Deborah Kennedy been less assertive at The Hague, the Protocol might never have been completed on time. Benedick's description of the protocol negotiations gives them a particularly human face. Remember the Senegalese representative who signed the protocol—before receiving authorization—because "it was the right thing to do," and the Venezuelan delegate who "broke into cheers when a breathless messenger finally arrived with the authorizing cable." States can act only through the words and actions of human beings. This is a point easily forgotten in international law; yet its implications are critical, particularly for international lawyers.

2. Negotiations for an international agreement often drag on for years. For example, the "Uruguay Round" of international trade negotiations, which produced the World Trade Organization, lasted ten years. Negotiations on the UN Convention on the Law of the Sea lasted ten years. Although the Montreal Protocol negotiations recounted here took only nine months to complete, this seeming speed is somewhat deceptive. By the time the protocol negotiations began, the international community had been coming to grips with the problem of ozone depletion for more than a decade (thus Tolba's "12 years of personal struggle"). Moreover, the community had already reached agreement on the most difficult issue—whether to take international action in the first place. The international community committed itself to action when it concluded the general "framework" agreement on the ozone layer in 1985. *See* Vienna Convention for the Protection of the Ozone Layer, 22 Mar. 1985, *reprinted in* 26 I.L.M. 1516 (1987).

As the international community grows more skilled at concluding international environmental agreements, the length of negotiations may be shrinking. *See* Edith Brown Weiss, *International Environmental Law: Contemporary Issues and the Emergence of a New World Order*, 81 GEO. L.J. 675, 685–86 (1993). For example, the Framework Convention on Climate Change, the Environmental Protocol to the Antarctic Treaty, the Convention on Biological Diversity, and the United Nations Desertification Convention all were concluded in two years or less, though with many years of less formal preparatory work in each case.

3. The protocol negotiations continued for some time before a plenary conference was convened. One of the major purposes of those preliminary negotiations was the preparation of a draft text for the agreement. Often, a draft text is completed even before these early negotiations begin. Generally, States or international organizations have taken the lead in preparing draft conventions, but NGOs have also prepared draft texts for important environmental agreements, such as the draft

Convention on International Trade in Endangered Species prepared by the International Union for the Conservation of Nature.

4. Recall the role that NASA and the scientific community played in the formulation of policies to confront ozone depletion, particularly the modeling studies which confirmed the chlorine-ozone linkage. This approach has been followed in the climate treaty-making process, and institutionalized in the Intergovernmental Panel on Climate Change (IPCC), which assesses the scientific, technical and economic bases of international climate change policy. Unlike the early ozone debate, the global scientific community is in relative agreement on the reality of global warming, in part as a result of advances in computer modeling. Climate change is an example of scientific assessment driving the evolution of the international legal system. Forward-looking General Circulation Models, by showing a likely future, are a critical aspect of building the political will necessary for change. *See* discussion on climate change in Chapter 9. *See also* the discussion of scenarios in Chapter 1.

5. Environmental impact assessments (EIAs) are required under U.S. law for major Federal actions. Environmentalists hope to extend this practice, either through amendments or reinterpretation, to the negotiation of international treaties, and point particularly to Executive Order No. 12,114, "Environmental Effects Abroad of Major Federal Actions." Are treaties "major Federal actions?" How would U.S. insistence on an EIA affect negotiations?

In November 1999, President Clinton issued Executive Order 13,141, Environmental Review of Trade Agreements, which "committed [the U.S.] to a policy of careful assessment and consideration of the environmental impacts of trade agreements." The Order also highlighted the importance of the concept of sustainable development in international trade negotiations. The U.S. Trade Representative followed with guidelines for the environmental review of trade agreements. *See* Chapter 15. Note, however, that the U.S. has not joined the treaty on transboundary environmental impact assessment negotiated within the UN Economic Commission for Europe. *See* Chapter 7.

6. Even with scientific consensus on an environmental threat, science rarely offers complete answers. Is there a danger when law depends too much on science? If science does not yet understand every aspect of a threat, how should treaty negotiators deal with the unknown? Are negotiators and other lawmakers equipped to judge what science does not know? *See* discussion of the Precautionary Principle in Chapter 7. *See also* Wendy E. Wagner, *Congress, Science, and Environmental Policy*, 1999 U. Ill. L. Rev. 181 (1999).

---

c. *Adoption and Authentication*

Before the negotiation phase of the treaty-making process can be concluded, and the treaty "opened" for signature and ratification, the text must be adopted. Unless a State has specified otherwise, adoption of a treaty text does not make the treaty binding on that State. Adoption simply signifies the participants' agreement that the text of the treaty is acceptable in principle. Articles 9 and 10 of the Vienna Convention set out the procedures for adoption:

Vienna Convention, Article 9
Adoption of the Text

1. The adoption of the text of a treaty takes place by the consent of all the States participating in its drawing up except as provided in paragraph 2.

2. The adoption of the text of a treaty at an international conference takes place by the vote of two-thirds of the States present and voting, unless by the same majority they shall decide to apply a different rule.

Vienna Convention, Article 10
Authentication of the Text

The text of a treaty is established as authentic and definitive

(a) by such procedure as may be provided for in the text or agreed upon by the States participating in its drawing-up; or

(b) failing such procedure, by the signature, signature ad referendum or initialling by the representatives of those States of the text of the treaty or of the Final Act of a conference incorporating the text.

The conference delegates adopt a "Final Act" of the conference, which summarizes the history of the Conference and incorporates by reference all the documents and records produced there. The text of the treaty will be incorporated in or annexed to this Final Act. If the treaty negotiations occurred within an established international organization, such as the United Nations or one of its permanent organs or agencies, the treaty will be approved through the adoption of an appropriate resolution, in which the final text will be incorporated. Because it does not create binding obligations for any State, a treaty can be adopted at an international conference with less than full consensus. Nonetheless, many international conferences will still seek widespread agreement among participating States to ensure that States will sign and ratify the treaty once it is adopted.

When the final draft of the treaty has been adopted, it must be "authenticated" by a representative of each State, generally by signing the treaty. Authentication identifies the treaty text as the actual text the negotiating States agreed to and establishes that each signing State agrees in principle to its terms. Although there are exceptions, a State's signature on a treaty generally does not signify its consent to be bound by the treaty. By signing a treaty, however, a State does agree to refrain from acts "which would defeat the object and purpose of the treaty," until it has made clear its intention not to become a treaty party.

Vienna Convention, Article 18
Obligation not to defeat the object and purpose of a treaty
prior to its entry into force

A state is obliged to refrain from acts which would defeat the object and intent of the treaty when:

(a) it has signed the treaty or has exchanged instruments constituting this treaty subject to ratification, acceptance or approval, until it shall have made its intention clear not to become a party to the treaty; or

(b) it has expressed its consent to be bound by the treaty, pending the entry into force of the treaty and provided that such entry into force is not unduly delayed.

d. Ratification and accession

As should already be clear, a State will be bound by the terms of a treaty only if it takes affirmative steps to demonstrate its consent to be bound. Theoretically, there is no limit on the ways a State may express this consent. The means of expressing consent to a treaty include: "signature, exchange of instruments constituting a treaty, ratification, acceptance, approval or accession, or by any other means if so agreed." Vienna Convention, Article 11. With respect to multilateral agreements, the most common method of demonstrating consent is by ratification. Ratification is any authoritative act whereby a State declares to the international community that it considers itself bound by a treaty. Multilateral environmental treaties are typically ratified by depositing an "instrument of ratification" with the United Nations or another designated depositary organization. Only States that participated in the negotiation of, and subsequently signed, the treaty may bind themselves through ratification. Other States often may join by accession. Accession simply means that a State declares its intent to be bound by the treaty. The procedures for acceding often are specified in the treaty. Vienna Convention, Article 15. Most States also have domestic laws or constitutional rules that govern accession. MARK W. JANIS, AN INTRODUCTION TO INTERNATIONAL LAW 21–22 (3rd ed. 1999).

In many States, a treaty must be approved through domestic political processes before the treaty can be ratified. In the United States, for example, the Senate has not ratified the International Criminal Court, which was signed by President Clinton in 1998 and presented to the Senate for its consent. As long as the Senate refuses its consent, the United States cannot ratify the I.C.C. The Senate may also make its consent contingent on certain changes or exceptions. If these cannot be accommodated through reservations to the treaty (see below), the United States must renegotiate the treaty to incorporate the changes or the treaty cannot be ratified.

Because of the Senate ratification process in the United States, and similar processes in other States—which are a matter of domestic law, and not international law—months or even years may pass between the time a State signs a treaty and the time it ratifies. An extreme example concerns the United Nations Convention on the Prevention and Punishment of the Crime of Genocide, commonly known as the Genocide Convention. Nearly four decades passed between the time President Harry Truman signed the Genocide Convention in December 1948, and the time the Senate gave its "advice and consent" to ratification in 1986. Because of the need for an implementing statute, another two years passed before the United States could finally deposit its instrument of ratification. See FRANK NEWMAN & DAVID WEISSBRODT, INTERNATIONAL HUMAN RIGHTS: LAW, POLICY AND PROCESS 39 (1996).

Most treaties, of course, are ratified far more rapidly, but you should recognize that a State's signature on a treaty is only half the battle. Until the treaty is ratified and has entered into force, the State's obligations with respect to the treaty are very limited. This is particularly true with respect to the United States and environmental treaties, as the U.S. has yet to ratify (as of October, 2001) the Biodiversity Convention, the Basel Convention, and the Kyoto Protocol, to name a few.

————

e. *Limited Consent and Reservations*

A State may consent to be bound by only a portion of a treaty if the treaty permits or the other treaty parties agree to the limited consent. Vienna Convention, Article 17. Even when limited consent is not available, a party may enter reservations or objections to any part of a treaty so long as that reservation is not prohibited by the terms of the treaty, or incompatible with the treaty's object and purpose. Vienna Convention, Article 19. Any reservations must be entered at the time the State expresses its consent to be bound. The entry of a reservation affects the operation of the treaty as between the reserving State and other treaty parties. The nature of those effects depends upon whether other parties to the agreement accept or object to the reservation.

Vienna Convention, Article 21
Legal effects of reservations and of objections to reservations

1. A reservation established with regard to another party in accordance with articles 19, 20 and 23:

    (a) modifies for the reserving State in its relations with that other party the provisions of the treaty to which the reservation relates to the extent of the reservation; and

    (b) modifies those provisions to the same extent for that other party in its relations with the reserving State.

2. The reservation does not modify the provisions of the treaty for the other parties to the treaty *inter se*.

3. When a State objecting to a reservation has not opposed the entry into force of the treaty between itself and the reserving State, the provisions to which the reservation relates do not apply as between the two States to the extent of the reservation.

While reservations can be a tool for overcoming disagreements during negotiations, they are also a source of major exceptions to international environmental treaties. They may even threaten the ratification of the treaties themselves, since they can materially change the bargained-for rights and obligations of potential signatories. Because of the growing number of States and increasing public political pressure, the number of reservations in treaties has risen dramatically since the Vienna Treaty came into force. In evaluating the applicability of a specific treaty to a specific set of facts, lawyers must be certain to check for any applicable reservations. *See, e.g.*, discussion of reservations in the discussion of the Convention on International Trade in Endangered Species in Chapter 13. Because reservations can make implementation of treaties complex and difficult, and because an exhaustive negotiation process provides an opportunity for issues to be resolved, many recent multilateral environmental treaties simply provide that reservations are not permitted. To avoid formal reservations, where reservations are not authorized, States have begun adding interpretive notes to treaties, essentially pre-interpreting selected tenets.

————

f. Entry Into Force

The parties to a treaty are not bound by its terms until the treaty enters into force. No treaty enters into force for a specific State until that State ratifies the treaty according to its national law, deposits its instrument of ratification with the appropriate depository, and any conditions for the treaty's entry into force have been satisfied. If the treaty makes no special provision for entry into force, it enters into force as soon as all the negotiating States have ratified. More often, however, the treaty will provide for its entry into force after a certain minimum number of States have ratified, even if other States have not. Vienna Convention, Article 24. The treaty then becomes effective as between the ratifying States.

————

3. KEEPING TREATIES UP–TO–DATE

A treaty may be amended by agreement of the parties. In the case of multilateral treaties, every party to the treaty is entitled to participate in the amendment negotiations and to become a party to the new amendment. States are not required to do so, however, and a State can remain a treaty party without becoming party to the amendment. Vienna Convention, Article 40. States that adopt the amendment are bound by the terms of the original treaty with respect to States that do not become party to the amendment. Vienna Convention, Article 30, para. 4(b).

Two or more parties to a treaty may also modify the terms of the treaty as between themselves if the treaty so provides, or if the modification will not affect the treaty rights of other parties and the modification is not incompatible with the object and purpose of the treaty as a whole. Vienna Convention, Article 41.

Not surprisingly given the above discussion, the procedure for updating treaties (through, for example, amendments, protocols, and modifications) can be very cumbersome. In the following excerpt, Paul Szasz discusses ways States have begun to create more efficient and flexible means for amending treaties and circumventing strict application of consent.

Paul Szasz, *International Norm-making*
in Edith Brown Weiss, ed., Environmental Change in International Law **(1995)**

Traditionally, treaty law has been adjusted from time to time by additional treaty actions, either by amending existing instruments, by creating others to complement older texts, or by entirely superseding those that cannot easily be adapted to serve modern purposes. Generally, all these measures technically require full-scale treaty initiating,-formulating,-adopting, and entry-into-force procedures, with all the work and complications described [in the preceding sections].... Furthermore, because each such amendment or new treaty is subject to the same domestic treaty-acceptance procedures as the original instrument, and these procedures are accomplished with uneven speed and efficiency by different states, the pattern of ratifications becomes yet more complicated, creating an entirely uneven and ultimately unintelligible pattern of obligations among states that are parties to the same agreement but with different amendments, or that participate in different supplementary or superseding agreements. Instead of progressing towards a generally applicable international regime, the volume of international law may be growing at the cost of uniformity of coverage.

It is for this reason that a number of devices have been developed for simplifying the process of updating treaties, devices that concern one or both of the major phases of the legislative process described above. These devices include: the use of framework or umbrella conventions that merely state general obligations and establish the machinery for the further norm-formulating devices described under this heading; the supplementation of such conventions by individual protocols establishing particular substantive obligations in implementation of the general objectives of the convention; [or] the use of easily amendable technical annexes.

In respect of all these devices, the international phase of the treaty-making process—initiation, formulation, and adoption—can be simplified and accelerated by assigning them to specially designated, dedicated expert or representative organs that either meet periodically or that are easy to convene as the need for further legislative action arises, and that are serviced by a specialized secretariat thoroughly familiar with the regime in question as well as with other related regimes that must be taken into account. Thus the usual start-up time for these phases of the international legislative process can be largely eliminated, as well as much routine reporting and the repeated transfer of proposed texts among expert, restricted representative and plenary organs. Consequently texts ready for adoption by the states participating in the regime can be prepared in substantially shorter times—subject, of course, to the need to negotiate generally acceptable terms. Another important saving in time and effort can, however, be achieved in respect of the second, domestic, phase of the process. This may be done by providing in the basic convention that all or certain of these new instruments do not require ratification but enter into force in some simplified way.

(a) It may be provided that supplementary instruments require only signatures in order to bind states. While of course the constitutional requirements of certain of these parties will require that such signatures only be affixed after the completion of domestic procedures that correspond to those required for ratification, many other states will be able to take advantage of such provisions to achieve instant participation.

(b) It may be provided that once an amendment enters into force for a sufficient number of states, it automatically enters into force for all; this short-circuiting of the ratification process by those states that do not act early may, however, have to be purchased at the cost of providing in the basic treaty that a state on which an amendment is thus imposed can denounce the treaty in some simplified manner.

(c) It may be provided that certain amendments, especially to technical annexes, do not require any signatures and ratifications at all, but automatically enter into force for all parties to the basic treaty unless a sufficient number of them object within a stated time limit from the adoption of the amendment, or that such amendment enters into force for all treaty parties except those that object within a specified time period.

[Because states are reluctant to give up their authority to consent to or reject international obligations, these simplified procedures are usually limited to subordinate and technical matters. Further,] it is usually necessary to preserve some method for the state to opt out simply, either from the new legislative feature or, perhaps, from the entire regime. Although in a sense these are instances of an IGO organ "legislating" directly for states, the legal obligation of each state ultimately derives from its consent to the underlying treaty in which the particular empowerment of the IGO is set out, and consequently one might refer to a "derivative treaty obligation."

————

4. UNILATERAL TREATIES

In certain circumstances a State can create what is essentially a unilateral treaty with the international community. This was explored in the 1974 Nuclear Test Cases (New Zealand v. France). In the 1970s, Australia and New Zealand filed claims against France in the International Court of Justice seeking to halt French nuclear weapons testing in the South Pacific. The Court determined that the issue was moot because France had declared its intention to discontinue atmospheric testing. France had made a number of *consistent* and *public* statements concerning a future course of action. The statements were made by French officials of the highest rank. They were addressed to a party on the other side of an international dispute and were relevant to the subject matter of that dispute. And the statements were expressly not subject to any proviso. Because of the nature of its declarations, the Court held that France was bound to uphold them.

Nuclear Tests Cases (Australia v. France), 1974 ICJ Rep. 253

46. It is well recognized that declarations made by way of unilateral acts, concerning legal or factual situations, may have the effect of creating legal obligations. Declarations of this kind may be, and often are, very specific. When it is the intention of the State making the declaration that it should become bound according to its terms, that intention confers on the declaration the character of a legal undertaking, the State being thenceforth required to follow a course of conduct consistent with the declaration. An undertaking of this kind, if given publicly and with an intent to be bound, even though not made within the context of international negotiations, is binding. In these circumstances, nothing in the nature of a *quid pro quo*, nor any subsequent acceptance of the declaration, nor even any reply or reaction from other States, is required for the declaration to take effect, since such a requirement would be inconsistent with the strictly unilateral nature of the juridical act by which the pronouncement by the State was made.

47. Of course, not all unilateral acts imply obligation; but a State may choose to take up a certain position in relation to a particular matter with the intention of being bound—the intention is to be ascertained by interpretation of the act. When States make statements by which the freedom of their action is to be limited, a restrictive interpretation is called for.

48. With regard to the question of form, it should be observed that this is not a domain in which international law imposes any special or strict requirements. Whether a statement is made orally or in writing makes no essential difference,

for such statements made in particular circumstances may create commitments in international law, which does not require that they should be couched in written form. Thus the question of form is not decisive.... "[T]he sole relevant question is whether the language employed in any given declaration does reveal a clear intention." Temple of Preah Vihear, 1961 ICJ Rep. 52.

————

5. INTERPRETING A TREATY

The methodology for interpreting a treaty is outlined in Articles 31 and 32 of the Vienna Convention. Just as with a domestic U.S. statute, or a commercial contract, the Court must look first to the text itself in determining the intent of the treaty parties. Article 31(1) provides that "[a] treaty shall be interpreted in good faith in accordance with the ordinary meaning to be given to the terms of the treaty in their context and in the light of its object and purpose." The object and purpose are often stated clearly in a treaty, including in a preamble. Other times, they may have to be inferred from the overall structure of the treaty taken as a whole.

The "context" for interpreting a treaty includes the text itself, including the preamble and annexes, as well as:

(a) any agreement relating to the treaty which was made between all the parties in connection with the conclusion of the treaty;

(b) any instrument which was made by one or more parties in connection with the conclusion of the treaty and accepted by the other parties as an instrument related to the treaty;

(c) any relevant provision of international law applicable in the relations between the parties....

Vienna Convention, Article 31(2).

In addition, a court should consider the parties' own interpretation of the treaty as reflected in subsequent agreements regarding the treaty's interpretation and application and in the actual practice of the parties. Article 31(3). As a "supplementary means of interpretation," a court may consider the negotiating history or *travaux preparatoires* (literally "preparatory work") of the treaty. Article 32. This includes, for example, the Final Act of the Conference and any working papers or reports prepared during the treaty negotiations. However, reference to the *travaux* is generally limited to confirming an interpretation based on textual analysis or to resolving ambiguities or "manifestly absurd" results from the textual analysis.

In a recent ICJ case the Court suggested a supplementary basis of interpretation, noting that nothing in the Vienna Convention proscribes "the Court from taking into account the present-day state of scientific knowledge." *See* CASE CONCERNING KASIKILI/SEDUDU ISLAND (BOTSWANA V. NAMIBIA), 1999 I.C.J. 98, *REPRINTED IN* 39 I.L.M. 310 (2000).

————

B.   CUSTOM

In addition to treaty-making, international law is also created through the customary practice of States, where such practice is done under the belief that it is required by law. ICJ Art. 38(1)(B). Custom is in many ways harder than treaty law for practitioners, as it requires that you both articulate the rule of law, and then prove that the rule is accepted by States as law.

Daniel Bodansky *Customary (and Not So Customary) International Environmental Law*
3 IND. J. GLOBAL LEGAL STUD. 105, 108–09 (1995).

I.   The Orthodox Account of Customary International Law

In claiming that a norm, such as the duty to prevent transboundary harm or the precautionary principle, is part of customary law, what kind of claim is one making? According to the standard account of customary international law, claims about customary law are empirical claims about the ways that states (and other international actors) regularly behave. States, for example, generally grant immunity to foreign diplomats; refrain from exercising law enforcement functions in the territory of other states; and do not interfere with foreign vessels on the high seas. These represent significant regularities of behavior—apparently normatively based—amidst the extremely complex and often seemingly ad hoc interactions among states.

Anthony D'Amato, while departing in many respects from the standard account of customary international law, has forcefully captured its behavioral orientation:

> To approach the subject of custom from the simplest starting point, we look at the international scene. We could have expected to see nothing but chaos and anarchy, everybody fighting with each other all the time and nobody having any idea about what's going on—in other words, Hobbes' state of nature. But instead we see regularity. We see for the most part peace and peaceful accommodations....
>
> So we say to ourselves: "Aha! Something's going on here that's not explained." There is a systemic process here.... We are witnessing ordered behavior....
>
> Well, that's our customary-law problem: to figure out what laws account for these regularities. And so we start looking at what states do and what they claim. The laws could be anything. We don't dictate what international law is; we look for it and find it out there in the real world. International law is implicit in the interactions of these state units. Somehow they're interacting in ways that tell us that there is regularity there. If we were physicists we would say the same thing. If we saw a bunch of microbes, and they were acting in a certain orderly fashion, we would say that there must be some laws regulating their behavior.... So today we're looking at states, and we say the same thing—that there are certain laws that seem to account for their regular behavior. Anthony D'Amato, *Seminar on the Theory of Customary International Law*, in INTERNATIONAL LAW ANTHOLOGY 73, 74 (Anthony D'Amato ed. 1994)

In saying that customary rules represent regularities of behavior, several points should be noted. First, the approach is empirical rather than normative. It attempts to describe the existing norms that govern the relations among states, but does not advocate or prescribe new norms. Accordingly, it draws a clear distinction between *lex lata* (law as it is) and *lex ferenda* (law as it should be).

Second, customary rules are not equivalent to simple behavioral regularities.... Customary norms depend not only on state practice (that is, on observable regularities of behavior), but also on acceptance of these regularities as law by states [*opinio juris*].

Finally, customary rules represent regularities, but not necessarily uniformities, of behavior. The behavioral approach requires a general congruence between rules and behavior. If a purported rule says one thing and states generally do something else, one can no longer say that the rule "governs" behavior. Nevertheless, mistakes and violations of rules are possible.

Before the emergence of the modern multilateral law-making treaty at the end of the 19th century, customary law was a more important means of law-making for the international community. For example, both the law of the sea and the law of treaties were matters of customary international law until their codification in the latter part of this century. Today the role played by custom is changing, in part because the scope of treaty-made international law has grown so much. It is also more difficult to identify universal practice in a world where there are nearly 200 independent States of different cultures, interests, and legal systems. On the other hand, as the problems confronting the world grow increasingly urgent, international attitudes and international law are being forced to evolve more quickly. Telecommunications tools such as the Internet, together with other technological advances such as satellite-based observation, may ultimately make it easier to identify State practice and *opinio juris*.

---

1.   PROVING CUSTOM

As a general proposition, a customary rule of law is binding on all nations, "not because it was prescribed by any superior power, but because it has been generally accepted as a rule of conduct." *The Scotia*, 14 Wall. 170, 187 (1871) *quoted in The Paquete Habana*, 175 U.S. 677, 20 S.Ct. 290 (1900). To prove that a customary norm exists, a court must establish general acceptance of the rule: first, by demonstrating that State practice is consistent with the rule; and second, by demonstrating that States act in accordance with the rule from a sense of legal obligation to do so. This sense of legal obligation is known as *opinio juris*. Both State practice and *opinio juris* are required to prove the existence of a customary rule of international law.

---

a.   State Practice

While there is no precise definition of what constitutes State practice, the ICJ has required that practice be both extensive and virtually uniform and include those States that are particularly affected by the proposed norm. It is not necessary that State practice continue over a long period of time. Nor must State practice rigorously and consistently conform to the rule at issue. However, it must be clear that State conduct which is inconsistent with the customary practice has generally been treated as a breach of a rule. Whether State practice has been sufficiently consistent to establish a customary practice will generally depend on the facts of the case.

---

b. Opinio Juris

For a customary practice of States to be recognized as a rule of customary international law, it must appear that the practice follows from a sense of legal obligation (*opinio juris sive necessitatus*), rather than from a sense of moral obligation or political expediency. The existence of *opinio juris* is a factual matter that can be determined by consideration of a wide range of evidence, including *inter alia* diplomatic correspondence, government policy statements and press releases, opinions of official legal advisers, official manuals on legal questions, comments by governments on drafts produced by the International Law Commission, State legislation, international and national judicial decisions, legal briefs endorsed by the States, a pattern of treaties in the same form, resolutions and declarations by the United Nations, and other evidence.

---

c. The Persistent Objector

Once a custom is established it becomes binding on all States, regardless of whether those States contributed to the formation of the custom. Even those States that did not follow the practice or express a belief that the practice was law will be bound by the rule. However, under the traditional view a State may exclude itself from the obligations of a particular customary rule by persistent conduct exhibiting an unwillingness to be bound by the rule or a refusal to recognize it as law. RESTATEMENT OF FOREIGN RELATIONS LAW OF THE UNITED STATES, section 102, comment b. While the requirement for *opinio juris* is not the same as the consent required for treaty law, the failure to persistently object could be considered as implied consent to be bound by the custom. The ability of "persistent objectors" to opt-out of a customary rule illustrates the positivist influence on customary law.

---

2. CUSTOMARY LAW AND ENVIRONMENTAL PROTECTION

As the number of international treaties, declarations, and resolutions announcing principles of environmental protection has increased over time, scholars have begun to debate whether customary rules of international environmental law are emerging or have already emerged. Frequently mentioned examples of candidates for customary status include the principle that a State should not use its territory in a way that causes harm outside that territory (i.e. Principle 21 of the *Stockholm Declaration*), sustainable development, the precautionary principle, and the principle that State actions should be undertaken only after conducting an environmental impact assessment. These and other emerging concepts and principles of international environmental law are discussed in Chapter 7. These prospective customary norms face a particular difficulty when subjected to the standard test of customary norms (i.e., consistent State practice and the existence of *opinio juris*). Although their frequent reiteration in international documents of every kind provides strong evidence of possible *opinio juris*, State practice may be insufficiently uniform to satisfy the consistent State practice requirement. Nevertheless, these principles are increasingly being recognized in judicial opinions and elsewhere as customary law, perhaps reflecting changing notions of how customary law is made.

----

3. LAW–MAKING TREATIES AND THE CRYSTALLIZATION OF CUSTOM

In addition to creating specific obligations for their parties, treaties may contribute to the development of customary international law. An example is the UN Law of the Sea Convention, where negotiations took more than ten years and involved most of the world's nations. Even before workable rules for governing the world's oceans were developed, *opinio juris* developed around many new norms (for example, the existence of the 200–mile exclusive economic zone extending out from the coastline of each State). A treaty may also provide the basis for an entirely new rule of customary international law. In order for a treaty provision to bind States generally—that is, to become customary international law—it must "be of a fundamentally norm-creating character such as could be regarded as forming the basis of a general rule of law." North Sea Continental Shelf Case, 1969 ICJ Rep. 3, para. 72. Unless membership in the treaty were universal, it may still be necessary to demonstrate through a traditional analysis of State practice and *opinio juris*, that the international community actually regarded the rule as binding independent of the treaty obligation.

Even when a treaty does not immediately lead to the formation of a new customary rule, it can nonetheless contribute to the development of that rule. As the number of treaties and declarations that incorporate the rule increases, the argument becomes stronger that an international consensus is emerging. This approach supports the conclusion of many scholars and increasingly, jurists, that Principle 21 of the *Stockholm Declaration*, which prohibits States from acting within their own territory so as to cause harm outside their territory, is now a matter of customary international law.

----

4. PEREMPTORY NORMS OF GENERAL INTERNATIONAL LAW (*JUS COGENS*)

A peremptory norm is a norm accepted and recognized by the international community as one from which no derogation is permitted. No State can opt out of a peremptory norm, no matter how persistently they might object to it. Peremptory norms supercede all treaties, even those pre-dating the emergence of the norm, and invalidate any treaty in conflict with them. The international prohibitions of genocide and slavery are examples of this rare but important form of law.

Vienna Convention, Article 53

Treaties conflicting with a peremptory norm of general international law (jus cogens)

A treaty is void if, at the time of its conclusion, it conflicts with a peremptory norm of general international law. For the purposes of the present Convention, a peremptory norm of general international law is a norm accepted and recognized by the international community of States as a whole as a norm from which no derogation is permitted and which can be modified only by a subsequent norm of general international law having the same character. * * *

Article 64

Emergence of a new peremptory norm of general international law (jus cogens)

If a new peremptory norm of general international law emerges, any existing treaty which is in conflict with that norm becomes void and terminates. * * *

Article 71

Consequences of the invalidity of a treaty which conflicts with a peremptory norm of general international law

1. In the case of a treaty which is void under article 53 the parties shall:

    (a) eliminate as far as possible the consequences of any act performed in reliance on any provision which conflicts with the peremptory norm of general international law; and

    (b) bring their mutual relations into conformity with the peremptory norm of general international law.

Peremptory norms are universal; they are applicable to every State, regardless of whether it objects. A treaty that conflicts with a peremptory norm is void—even if the treaty comes later in time. A peremptory norm can be modified only by a subsequent norm of general international law having the same character. Does this strike you as surprising? If all States are sovereign, how can they be subjected to any international obligation without their—at least tacit—consent? Consider the discussion of general principles later in this chapter.

---

5. *ERGA OMNES* OBLIGATIONS

Ordinarily, when a State violates a treaty obligation or an obligation under customary international law, another State may only bring a complaint if it has been injured by the violation. However, there are certain norms of international law so important that a State owes a duty to obey those norms to the international community as a whole, rather than to individual States. The ICJ recognized this principle in dicta in *Barcelona Traction, Light and Power Co., Ltd.* (New Application 1962) (Belg. v. Spain), 1970 ICJ Rep. 3. When a State violates one of these obligations *erga omnes*—of all to all—any State may bring a complaint based on the violation, even if the complaining State has not been injured in a traditional sense.

Violation of such norms injures every State and, therefore, every State may bring a complaint. There is, as yet, no generally agreed list of international norms that create rights and obligations *erga omnes*. In enumerating an exemplary list in the *Barcelona Traction* case, the ICJ relied exclusively upon *jus cogens* norms: "Such obligations derive, for example, in contemporary international law, from the outlawing of acts of aggression, and of genocide, as also from the principles and rules concerning the basic rights of the human person, including protection from slavery and racial discrimination." *Id.* at para. 34. The Court went on to note that: "Some of the corresponding rights of protection have entered into the body of international law...; others are conferred by international instruments of a universal or quasi-universal character." *Id.*

The concept of *erga omnes* obligations creates interesting questions in the field of international environmental law. Consider, for example, the Montreal Protocol on Substances that Deplete the Ozone Layer. Participation in the Montreal Protocol is now nearly universal; it has been ratified by more than 160 states. Further, when a State violates its obligations under the Protocol, it contributes to depletion of the stratospheric ozone layer. This violation affects the long term interests of all States in the preservation of the ozone layer. Could a State that was not party to the Montreal Protocol bring a claim against a Protocol party for breaching its duties under the Protocol? More generally, what about environmental damage caused to the global commons such as the high seas or Antarctica? Should any State be able to bring a claim against another State for such damages or to prevent future damage?

––––––––

C. GENERAL PRINCIPLES

1. INTRODUCTION

"[G]eneral principles of law recognized by civilized nations" are another source of international law recognized by Article 38 of the ICJ Statute, although what is included within those principles is a matter of debate. Ian Brownlie, for one, states that "general principles" may refer to "rules accepted in the domestic law of all civilized states," or alternatively, to the general principles of private law used within all or most States, such as *res judicata* or *estoppel*, in so far as those principles are applicable to relations of States. General principles, then, fill in the gaps in international law that have not already been filled by treaty or custom. "What has happened is that international tribunals have employed elements of legal reasoning and private law analogies in order to make the law of nations a viable system for application in a judicial process." Ian Brownlie, Principles of Public International Law 16 (4th ed., 1990). Thus, "the most frequent use of general principles derives from the drawing of analogies with domestic law concerning rules of procedure, evidence, and jurisdiction." Patricia Birnie & Alan Boyle, International Law and the Environment 24 (1992). The Restatement of the Foreign Relations Law of the United States (3rd ed. 1987) suggests an even more restricted interpretation. Section 102(4) states that "General principles common to the major legal systems, even if not incorporated or reflected in customary law or international agreement, may be invoked as supplementary rules of international law where appropriate."

General principles, however, may be more powerful and may have greater evolutionary potential than suggested by the limited interpretations advanced by Brownlie, Birnie & Boyle, and the Restatement. At the least, general principles offer an alternate method of legal reasoning that is important to understand. The first excerpt from Shabtai Rosenne suggests the potential force of general principles, noting that they have an independent existence, that "their validity in international law does not derive from any consent of the parties or State practice as such," and that Article 38 "places this element on a footing of formal equality with the two positivist elements of custom and treaty, and thus is positivist recognition of the Grotian concept of the coexistence, implying no subordination, of positive law and the so-called natural law of nations." The second excerpt is from the 1996 ICJ advisory opinion on the *Legality of the Threat or Use of Nuclear Weapons,* and demonstrates the reliance on general principles in the absence of positive law.

Shabtai Rosenne, Practice and Methods of International Law 69 (1984)

[The reference to general principles of law in] Article 38, paragraph 1 c, does not refer to general principles of *international* law (really part of customary law) or of internal law, but is broader, embracing general principles of law as such. Some writers of extreme positivist leanings take the view that the general principles themselves must be reflected in one of the components of positive law, a treaty or customary law, but on the whole the practice of States and of most international courts and tribunals seems to prefer the first view. At the same time it is by now reasonably clear that, while shared concepts of internal law can be used as a fall-back, there are severe limits to that because of the characteristic differences between international law and internal law.... Both the International Court of Justice and the International Law Commission have run into difficulties when trying to apply abstract jurisprudential concepts unrelated to the basic features of the international community.

For this reason, the references to "general principles of law" seems to imply not generalizations reached by application of comparative law and abstract legal science (although that is not to be excluded entirely) so much as particularizations of an underlying sense of what is just in the circumstances. Having an independent existence, their validity in international law does not derive from any consent of the parties or State practice as such. As I have written elsewhere, that provision of the Statute "places this element on a footing of formal equality with the two positivist elements of custom and treaty, and thus is positivist recognition of the Grotian concept of the coexistence, implying no subordination, of positive law and the so-called natural law of nations (in the Grotian sense). The absence of subordination means that a norm of positive law cannot be invalidated by a general principle of law [now subject to the general recognition of the concept of *jus cogens*]—although a general principle of law will have to give way before a positive norm not because they are inherently in any hierarchial relationship, but because the positive norm, whether conventional or customary (in that order) will be *lex specialis* in relation to the general principle." 2 *The Law and Practice of the International Court* 610 (1965). * * *

[Equity is linked to "general principles of justice."] It is appropriate to conclude this section with the following extract from the judgment of the International Court of Justice in the *Tunisia/Libya Continental Shelf* case (ICJ Reports 1982, 18 at p. 60):

> 71.   Equity as a legal concept is a direct emanation of the idea of justice. The Court whose task is by definition to administer justice is bound to apply it. In the course of the history of legal systems the term "equity" has been used to define various legal concepts. It was often contrasted with the rigid rules of positive law, the severity of which had to be mitigated in order to do justice. In general, this contrast has no parallel in the development of international law; the legal concept of equity is a general principle directly applicable as law. Moreover, when applying positive international law, a court may choose among several possible interpretations of the law the one which appears, in the light of the circumstances of the case, to be closest to the requirements of justice. The task of the Court in the present case is to apply equitable principles as part of international law, and to balance up the various considerations to produce an equitable result. While it is clear that no rigid rules exist as to the exact weight to be attached to each element in the case, this is very far from being an exercise of discretion or conciliation; nor is it an operation of distributive justice.

In July 1996, the ICJ issued an advisory opinion on the *Legality of the Threat or Use of Nuclear Weapons* under international law, 35 I.L.M. 809 (1996). The Court ultimately decided that international law neither clearly allowed nor clearly prohibited the use of nuclear weapons, but that use of such weapons would generally not be allowed under principles of humanitarian law. The methods the Court used to reach its decision demonstrate that, in the absence of positive law, the international system can and will turn to more fundamental or general principles, suggesting the continuing viability and potential vitality of natural law as a source of international law.

The Court emphasized an interpretation of a provision in the 1899 Hague Convention Respecting the Laws and Customs of War on Land commonly referred to as the Martens Clause. The Martens Clause occurs at the end of a preambular passage:

> According to the views of the high contracting Parties, these provisions, the wording of which has been inspired by the desire to diminish the evils of war, so far as military requirements permit, are intended to serve as a general rule

of conduct for the belligerents in their mutual relations and in their relations with the inhabitants.

It has not, however, been found possible at present to concert regulations covering all the circumstances which arise in practice.

On the other hand, the high contracting Parties clearly do not intend that unforeseen cases should, in the absence of a written undertaking, be left to the arbitrary judgment of military commanders.

Until a more complete code of the laws of war has been issued, the High Contracting Parties deem it expedient to declare that, in cases not included in the Regulations adopted by them, *the inhabitants and the belligerents remain under the protection and the rule of the principles of the law of nations, as they result from the usages established among civilized peoples, from the laws of humanity, and the dictates of the public conscience.* [emphasis added]

In a dissenting opinion, Judge Shahabuddeen agreed with the Court's conclusion that the use of nuclear weapons is generally unlawful under principles of humanitarian law. Unlike the majority, he also believed that those principles made nuclear weapons use illegal even under "extreme circumstances." In the excerpt below, Judge Shahabuddeen analyzes the Martens Clause and points out that the source of principles embodied in the clause supercedes positive international law.

Advisory Opinion on the Use or Threat of Nuclear Weapons
Dissenting Opinion of Judge Shahabuddeen, 35 I.L.M. 871 (1996)

Some States argued that the Martens Clause depends on proof of the separate existence of a rule of customary international law prohibiting the use of a particular weapon, and that there is no such prohibitory rule in the case of nuclear weapons. The proposition is attractive.

However, an initial difficulty is this. As is recognized in paragraphs 78 and 84 of the Court's Advisory Opinion, it is accepted that the Martens Clause is a rule of customary international law. That means that it has a normative character— that it lays down some norm of State conduct. It is difficult to see what norm of State conduct it lays down if all it does is to remind States of norms of conduct which exist wholly dehors [outside] the Clause.* * *

[Judge Shahabuddeen then set out the portion of the Hague Convention containing the Martens Clause reproduced above.]

These statements support an impression that the Martens Clause was intended to fill gaps left by conventional international law and to do so in a practical way. How?

The Martens Clause bears the marks of its period; it is not easy of interpretation. One acknowledges the distinction between usages and law. However, as the word "remain" shows, the provision implied that there were already in existence certain principles of the law of nations which operated to provide practical protection to "the inhabitants and the belligerents" in the event of protection not being available under conventional texts.... Since "established custom" alone would suffice to identify a rule of customary international law, a cumulative reading is not probable. It should follow that "the principles of international law" (the new wording) could also be sufficiently derived "from the principles of humanity and from the dictates of public conscience"; as mentioned above, those "principles of international law" could be regarded as including principles of international law already derived "from the principles of humanity and from the dictates of public conscience".

In effect, the Martens Clause provided authority for treating the principles of humanity and the dictates of public conscience as principles of international law, leaving the precise content of the standard implied by these principles of international law to be ascertained in the light of changing conditions, inclusive of changes in the means and methods of warfare and the outlook and tolerance levels of the international community. The principles would remain constant, but their practical effect would vary from time to time: they could justify a method of warfare in one age and prohibit it in another. In this respect, M. Jean Pictet was right in emphasising, according to Mr. Sean McBride, "that the Declarations in the Hague Conventions ... by virtue of the Martens Clause, imported into humanitarian law principles that went much further than the written convention; it thus gave them a dynamic dimension that was not limited by time".

Nor should this be strange. Dealing with the subject of "Considerations of Humanity" as a source of law, Sir Gerald Fitzmaurice remarked that "all the implications of this view—i.e. in exactly what circumstances and to what extent considerations of humanity give rise in themselves to obligations of a legal character—remain to be worked out".... The substance of the proposition seems present in the judgment given in 1948 in Krupp's case, in which the United States Military Tribunal sitting at Nuremberg said:

> "The Preamble [of Hague Convention No. IV of 1907] is much more than a pious declaration. It is a general clause, making the usages established among civilized nations, the laws of humanity and the dictates of public conscience into the legal yardstick to be applied if and when the specific provisions of the Convention and the Regulations annexed to it do not cover specific cases occurring in warfare, or concomitant to warfare." (Annual Digest and Reports of Public International Law Cases, 1948, p. 622.)

A similar view of the role of considerations of humanity appears in the Corfu Channel case. There Judge Alvarez stated that the "characteristics of an international delinquency are that it is an act contrary to the sentiments of humanity" (ICJ Reports 1949, p. 45, separate opinion); and the Court itself said that Albania's "obligations are based, not on the Hague Convention of 1907, No. VIII, which is applicable in time of war, but on certain general and well-recognised principles, namely: elementary considerations of humanity, even more exacting in peace than in war; ..." (ICJ Reports 1949, p. 22).

Thus, Albania's obligations were "based ... on ... elementary considerations of humanity ...", with the necessary implication that those considerations can themselves exert legal force. In 1986 the Court considered that "the conduct of the United States may be judged according to the fundamental general principles of humanitarian law"; and it expressed the view that certain rules stated in common Article 3 of the 1949 Geneva Conventions were "rules which, in the Court's opinion, reflect what the Court in 1949 called 'elementary considerations of humanity' (Corfu Channel, Merits, ICJ Reports 1949, p. 22)" (Military and Paramilitary Activities in and against Nicaragua, Merits, ICJ Reports 1986, pp. 113–114, para. 218). * * *

I am not persuaded that the purpose of the Martens Clause was confined to supplying a humanitarian standard by which to interpret separately existing rules of conventional or customary international law on the subject of the conduct of hostilities; the Clause was not needed for that purpose.... It is also difficult to accept that all that the Martens Clause did was to remind States of their obligations under separately existing rules of customary international law.... The basic function of the Clause was to put beyond challenge the existence of principles of international law which residually served, with current effect, to govern military conduct by reference to "the principles of humanity and ... the dictates of public conscience." It was in this sense that "civilians and combatants (would) remain under the protection and authority of the principles of international law derived ... from the principles of humanity and from the dictates of public conscience." The word "remain" would be inappropriate in relation to "the principles of humanity and ... the dictates of public conscience" unless these were conceived of as presently capable of exerting normative force to control military conduct.

Thus, the Martens Clause provided its own self-sufficient and conclusive authority for the proposition that there were already in existence principles of international law under which considerations of humanity could themselves exert legal force to govern military conduct in cases in which no relevant rule was provided by conventional law. Accordingly, it was not necessary to locate elsewhere the independent existence of such principles of international law; the source of the principles lay in the Clause itself.

The majority opinion pointed to two fundamental principles of humanitarian law. The first principle is the protection of non-combatants, which requires that any method or instrument of warfare be able to distinguish between soldiers and civilians, and avoid causing harm to the latter. The second principle is proportionality: no method or instrument of warfare should cause suffering to combatants or other destruction greater than that necessary to achieve legitimate military purposes. The Court found that nuclear weapons are clearly unable to meet both requirements of humanitarian law and, therefore, should not be allowed. The Martens Clause identifies the sources of these principles in the "usages established among civilized peoples, the laws of humanity and the dictates of the public conscience." By referring to laws of humanity and dictates of public conscience, the Martens Clause arguably puts humanitarian law principles above positivist law and grounds them in general principles, and perhaps even natural law.

QUESTIONS AND DISCUSSION

1. The Martens Clause recognizes "laws of humanity" and "the dictates of public conscience" as sources of general international principles, at least in the context of the law of war. In Shahabuddeen's view, the substantive content of some general principles may not depend on the consent of States. Does this mean the principles of humanity referred to in the Martens Clause exist independently of the treaty it is expressed in? Independent of custom? Do you agree with Judge Shahabuddeen's analysis? If so, are there other general principles that exist independently of treaty or custom? Consider again our discussion of *jus cogens* norms. What possible origin might such norms have if not in "the dictates of public conscience" discoverable by the simple process of reason? What does Shahabuddeen's opinion suggest about the role of general principles in international law? Must we ultimately turn to transcendent principles to address extreme situations such as nuclear war? Or the collapse of the biosphere?

2.   The advisory opinion on the illegality of nuclear weapons may be the first time in history a global citizens initiative triggered an ICJ opinion. The questions addressed by the ICJ were first raised by the International Lawyers Against Nuclear Arms (ILANA), International Physicians for the Prevention of Nuclear War (IPPNW), and the International Peace Bureau (IPB) through a joint effort known as the World Court Project. The goal was to obtain an ICJ opinion on the legality of nuclear weapons as a step toward a total abolition of such weapons. The World Court Project ultimately convinced both the World Health Organization (WHO) and the United Nations General Assembly (UNGA) to ask for advisory opinions. The Court, however, accepted only UNGA's request, arguing that WHO's request was not related to the specific activity of the Agency.

The case attracted worldwide attention. Thirty-five States filed written statements and twenty-four made oral submissions. Four million people signed petitions condemning nuclear weapons; the World Court Project presented the petitions to the ICJ as evidence of public conscience on the issue. Can this be taken as evidence of the general public conscience about nuclear weapons? What is the significance of this impressive level of participation?

3.   According to Principle 1 of the *Stockholm Declaration* "Man has the fundamental right to freedom, equality and adequate conditions of life, in an environment of a quality that permits a life of dignity and well-being,"11 I.L.M. 1416 (1972). Principle 1 of the *Rio Declaration* says that "Human beings ... are entitled to a healthy and productive life in harmony with nature." 31 I.L.M. 874 (1992) Are these principles simply the product of State consent, or do they reflect something more fundamental? Would you consider them general principles of international law? Consider these questions again after reading chapters 7 and 16.

---

2.   SOURCES OF GENERAL PRINCIPLES

If general principles are to evolve, it is necessary to look for possible sources that may lead us to such principles. Rosenne mentions justice and equity as general principles, and the ICJ case discussed above relies on the "principles of the law of nations, as they result from the usages established among civilized peoples, from the laws of humanity, and the dictates of the public conscience."

In the following excerpts from Charney and Handl we look at the potential for lawmaking treaties to reflect or create general principles. We next look at the more fundamental sources of natural law, with excerpts from Vattel and H.L.A. Hart, and then we turn to ethics, with an excerpt from Professor Christopher Stone. Finally, we consider the separate opinion of Judge Weeramantry in the *Case Concerning the Gabcikovo–Nagymaros Project*, where the judge uses a natural law reasoning process to support the principle of sustainable development.

(a) *Lawmaking Treaties*

In the following excerpt, *Universal International Law*, Jonathan Charney maintains that multilateral forums like international organizations or ad hoc negotiating conferences represent a different way of creating international law, that gives more relevance to broad, multilateral consensus rather than to State practice and *opinio juris*. Charney argues that this new approach leads to "general international law" or "universal international law" which can bind non-parties even without their consent.

Jonathan Charney, *Universal International Law*, 87 Am.J.Int'l.L. 529, 543–48 (1993)

The relatively exclusive ways [of lawmaking] of the past are not suitable for contemporary circumstances. While customary law is still created in the traditional way, that process has increasingly given way in recent years to a more structured method, especially in the case of important normative developments.

Rather than state practice and *opinio juris*, multilateral forums often play a central role in the creation and shaping of contemporary international law. Those forums include the United Nations General Assembly and Security Council, regional organizations, and standing and ad hoc multilateral diplomatic conferences, as well as international organizations devoted to specialized subjects. Today, major developments in international law often get their start or substantial support from proposals, reports, resolutions, treaties or protocols debated in such forums. There, representatives of states and other interested groups come together to address important international problems of mutual concern. Sometimes these efforts result in a consensus on solving the problem and express it in normative terms of general application. At other times, the potential new law is developed through the medium of international relations or the practices of specialized international institutions and at later stages is addressed in international forums. That process draws attention to the rule and helps to shape and crystallize it.

The authoritativeness of the debates at these multilateral forums varies, depending upon many factors. Among the first is how clearly it is communicated to the participating states that the rule under consideration reflects a refinement, codification, crystallization or progressive development of international law. Of crucial importance is the amount of support given to the rule under consideration. Adoption of the rule by the forum in accordance with its procedures for decision making may not be necessary or even sufficient. On the other hand, unanimous support is not required. Consensus, defined as the lack of expressed objections to the rule by any participant, may often be sufficient.
* * *

How much, if any, evidence of state practice and/or *opinio juris* that is required outside the forum that considers the norm depends upon the facts of each case. . . . The clearer the norm debated, the clearer the intention to promote a norm of generally applicable international law, and the stronger the consensus in favor of the norm, the less need there will be for evidence from outside the forum. Similar attention over a period of time by the same or other forums may further strengthen the case for the norm. When these signals are weak, confirmation of the normative status of the rule may be sought in declarations of states outside the forum, the other evidence of *opinio juris*, and state practice before or after the meeting of the forum. In theory, however, one clearly phrased and strongly endorsed declaration at a near-universal diplomatic forum could be sufficient to establish new international law. Of course, reality may never be that unambiguous. Furthermore, any norm that attracts such definite and widespread support would necessarily be echoed in pronouncements and/or actions extrinsic to the forum. When that happens, precious little of such evidence should be needed, if any at all.

The process outlined above differs significantly from the traditional understanding of the customary lawmaking process as requiring general practice over time. It may thus be more accurate to call it *general* international law, as the International Court has done on numerous occasions.... Whatever its proper denomination, the lawmaking process is substantially advanced by the activity of these multilateral forums. * * *

I do not intend to suggest, however, that multilateral forums have independent legislative authority. ... Rather, the products of multilateral forums substantially advance and formalize the international lawmaking process. They make possible the rapid and unquestionable entry into force of normative rules if the support expressed in the forum is confirmed. Decisions taken at such a forum, support for the generally applicable rule, publication of the proposed rule in written form and notice to the international legal system call for an early response. If the response is affirmative (even if tacit), the rule may enter into law. This process avoids some of the mysteries of customary lawmaking. It also permits broader and more effective participation by all states and other interested groups and allows a tacit consent system to operate legitimately. While it is possible that the process may be abused, it is less open to abuse and miscommunication than classical customary lawmaking.... States are increasingly aware that the work of multilateral forums contributes to the development of general international law.

In the next excerpt, Professor Gunther Handl similarly argues that multilateral environmental lawmaking treaties with "general norm-creating provisions...of global applicability" create "general international law" that binds non-parties, including multilateral development banks (MDBs), even without their consent.

[G]eneral normative effects ... may flow from the nature of the MEA [multilateral environmental agreement], in particular, the fundamental importance to the international community of its normative contents, the process by which it has been adopted and the support it enjoys. A multilateral treaty that addresses fundamental concerns of the international community at large, and that as such is strongly supported by the vast majority of states, by international organizations and other transnational actors,—and this is, of course, precisely the case with the biodiversity, climate, and ozone regimes, amongst others— may indeed create expectations of general compliance, in short such a treaty may come to be seen as reflecting legal standards of general applicability. Whatever the short-hand explanatory labels for this extended normative reach—some refer to the treaty provisions concerned as representing a "law of higher normativity," others as giving expression to a general principle of law, still another as being the "product of a community consensus formed around the normative status of discrete decisions at international fora"—these treaties convey clear signals regarding the policy content and underpinnings of authority of the normative concepts involved, as well as the willingness of the international community to ensure their effectiveness, and as such must be deemed capable of creating rights and obligations both for third states and third organizations, including MDBs. * * *

It cannot be denied, first, that there exists today a growing and ever more specific body of norms of international law bearing on "sustainable development;" and second, that a large number of these concepts clearly represent affirmative duties incumbent upon states and international institutions, including MDBs, alike. The increase in such affirmative obligations testifies not only to the well-nigh universal endorsement of the fundamental importance of sustainable development. It also mirrors the on-going transition of the international legal system itself: from one imbued with the classical, voluntarist notion of international law—a system of limited restraints on the sovereign powers of states so as to ensure their mere coexistence—to one underpinning an emerging "international community" or, put differently, one of international cooperation toward achieving common objectives and goals.

Gunther Handl, *The Legal Mandate of Multilateral Development Banks as Agents for Change Toward Sustainable Development*, 92 AM.J.INT'L.L. 642, at 660–62 (1998).

A more cautious though broader view is taken in the following excerpt by Daniel Bodansky, *Customary (and Not So Customary) International Environmental Law*, 3 IND. J. GLOBAL LEGAL STUD. 105, 110–119 (1995). Bodansky notes that much of what is argued to be customary law is so often not supported by state practice, which in any event is a Herculean task to assess, that it is not really custom at all. He further notes that most international lawyers are better at assessing "verbal practice"—treaties and other legal texts, and so focus on this task. The result is "declarative law."

In my view, the focus by scholars on verbal practice is not merely methodological; it represents a fundamentally different ontology of international law—one that is discursive rather than behavioral in orientation. International environmental norms reflect not how states regularly behave, but how states speak to one another. They represent the evaluative standards used by states to justify their actions and to criticize the actions of others. Writers persist in characterizing these norms as "customary," the catch-all term generally applied to any non-treaty norm, but it would be more accurate to distinguish this type of norm from custom. Chodosh has suggested the term "declarative law". A more pointed characterization is "myth system", since these norms represent the collective ideals of the international community, which at present have the quality of fictions or half-truths.

While suggesting that most declarative law is not enforceable through independent third-party adjudication, Bodansky nonetheless concedes that "international environmental norms can play a significant role by setting the terms of the debate, providing evaluative standards, serving as a basis to criticize other states' actions, and establishing a framework of principles within which negotiations may take place to develop more specific norms, usually in treaties." He concludes with the suggestion that "our time and efforts would be better spent attempting to translate the general norms of international environmental relations into concrete treaties and actions."

QUESTIONS AND DISCUSSION

1. Do multilateral lawmaking treaties create general principles? Do they reflect them? What is the difference between the process for developing customary law through interaction with a treaty, and the process for developing general international law through a treaty? If general principles exist outside custom or treaties, where are they to be found? Is there a difference between "general international law" and "general principles"?

2. How does Bodansky's declarative law relate to the discussion of general international law in Charney and Handl? Is the verbal methodology described by Bodansky—how states talk to themselves—useful for the task of identifying general principles?

———

(b) *Natural Law*

Natural law and its method of legal reasoning also can assist in the creation or discovery of general principles. The expression "natural law" has been used since the time of the Roman jurists to denote:

> a system of rules and principles for the guidance of human conduct which, independently of enacted law or of the systems peculiar to any one people, might be discovered by the rational intelligence of man, and would be found to grow out of his *nature*, meaning ... his whole mental, moral, and physical constitution.

BLACK'S LAW DICTIONARY 1026 (6th ed. 1990). The rules of natural law are implicit in human nature and discoverable through the application of pure reason. Because natural law derives directly from human nature, it is universal—applicable to everyone, everywhere—and supersedes inconsistent human made laws. As described in Allott's essay, Vattel himself recognized this. For Vattel, people were not freed of their responsibility to all humanity simply because they joined together in separate States. Under Vattel's conception, while the duty to advance the common good of humanity continued to exist, that duty shifted from individual persons to the State as a whole.

> Such is man's nature that he is not sufficient unto himself and necessarily stands in need of the assistance and intercourse of his fellows, whether to preserve his life or to perfect himself and live as befits a rational animal....
> From this source we deduce a natural society existing among all men. The general law of the society is that each member should assist the others in all their needs, as far as he can do so without neglecting his duties to himself—a law which all men must obey if they are to live conformably to their nature ...;
> a law which our own welfare, our happiness, and our best interests should render sacred to each of us. Such is the general obligation we are under of performing our duties; let us fulfil them with care if we would work wisely for our greatest good. * * *
> Since the universal society of the human race is an institution of nature itself, that is, a necessary result of man's nature, all men of whatever condition are bound to advance its interests and to fulfil its duties. No convention or special agreement can release them from the obligation. When, therefore, men unite in civil society and form a separate State or Nation they may, indeed, make particular agreements with others of the same states, but their duties towards

the rest of the human race remain unchanged; but with this difference, that when men have agreed to act in common, and have given up their rights and submitted their will to the whole body as far as concerns the common good, it devolves henceforth upon that body, the state, and upon its rulers, to fulfil the duties of humanity towards outsiders in all matters in which individuals are no longer at liberty to act, and it peculiarly rests with the State to fulfil these duties toward other states. We have already seen that men, when united in society, remain subject to the Law of Nature. This society may be regarded as a moral person, since it has an understanding, a will, and a power peculiar to itself; and it is therefore obliged to live with other societies or States according to the laws of the natural society of the human race, just as individual men before the establishment of civil society lived according to them....

The end of the natural society established among men in general is that they should mutually assist one another to advance their own perfection and that of their condition; and Nations, too, since they may be regarded as so many persons living together in a state of nature, are bound mutually to advance this human society. Hence the end of the great society established by nature among all nations is likewise that of mutual assistance in order to perfect themselves and their condition.

Emmerich de Vattel, The Law of Nations or the Principles of Natural Law Applied to the Conduct and to the Affairs of Nations and Sovereigns 5–7 (1758) tr. C.G. Fenwick (Washington 1916) *quoted in* Allott, International Law and International Revolution: Reconceiving the World 22 n.6 (1989).

Despite acknowledging the universal applicability of natural law, however, Vattel believed that each State had a still higher responsibility to ensure its own welfare, and thereby, the welfare of its individual citizens. Vattel also believed that all States were, by nature, free and independent and that, as a consequence, "it is for each Nation to decide what its conscience demands of it, what it can or can not do" for the good of human society—it lies with each State "to judge the extent of its duty" to the human community, and other States may not interfere with that judgment.

By shifting the burdens of natural law from the shoulders of the individual to the shoulders of the State, then allowing each State to set for itself the bounds of its duty to the human community, Vattel laid the groundwork for the abandonment of universal natural law in international relations.

In the absence of natural law, two alternate theoretical foundations have been offered for international law. The first of these theories is "positivism." According to positivism, there are no principles outside of the human made law that can tell us what the law ought to be. In other words, the legitimacy of a given law cannot be measured against some underlying moral order or truth; laws are legitimate if they are made by an authoritative law-giver, such as the State. Under pure positivist theory, national laws instituting slavery, apartheid, or genocide would all be appropriate, so long as they were enacted through accepted lawmaking processes.

The second theoretical foundation is "contractarianism." Under contractarianism, the only legitimate basis for law-making is between parties who have contracted to coordinate their activities for mutual benefit. Contractarians like Hobbes and Locke reject the existence of any preexisting laws or principles—as these principles can only be formed through negotiation and contract based on self-interest. The result of the contract process is a settlement which reflects the aggregate effect of the parties' subjective desires.

Neither positivism nor contractarianism can provide international environmental lawyers with a justification for the strong international principles necessary to address today's wild environmental facts. One could argue that our environmental concerns, because they are so profound, require progress on two planes: *horizontally* they require a comprehensive environmental law that covers all important areas that have not yet been covered, and *vertically* they require a level of strength far greater than currently agreed upon among States.

Positivists are at pains to find reasons to improve international agreements that are short on substantive commitment, because laws are valid according to them provided there are no procedural defects in the way the laws are created. Positivists look at the facts as they are, and assert that the only meaningful analysis of the law is provided by a hard look at who has power in society. In the same way, contractarians cannot criticize laws reached through agreement between free, rational contractors.

Natural law is different. It suggests the possibility that there is an external and universal standard to which laws can be held and assessed. As universal principles, natural law principles apply everywhere, to everyone, at every time, and do not allow particular countries or legislatures to claim exceptions. This may be particularly helpful for international environmental law: here we have some basis, it would seem, for arguing for sufficiently strong and universal standards, as well as a basis for criticizing the generally lax standards in today's international environmental law. These universal principles, if recognized, would prevent any State from saying that they do not want such laws to be enacted—it is not what States want, or have power to get, but the principles that you ought to follow that matter.

Before exploring natural law theories further in the next readings from Hart, some difficulties with natural law need to be highlighted. One difficulty with natural law is that it assumes that humans, or indeed the whole of "creation", has some purpose, or end to which it is working toward, for example human perfection. This view is vulnerable to criticism as it too easily falls into one of two traps. On the one hand, natural law must be wary of any reliance on religious concepts. Much of natural law writing from Aquinas onwards is grounded on religious beliefs that are not shared by all today. On the other hand, international environmental lawyers also must be wary of the natural rights theorists from the Enlightenment era who believed that the laws of society are inseparable from the physical laws regulating plants, animals and planetary bodies. While the wild environmental facts demand that we strengthen international environmental law, we need to avoid confusing this with the pseudo-science of a deterministic approach.

In sum, if it is to help build a more muscular international environmental law, natural law may have to start with a thinner, more widely shared basis, while not disappearing into positivism or contractarianism. The difficulty remains as it has always: in the question of where we find or "discover" these universal principles of natural law. One possible source, discussed in Chapter 2, is Rawls' theory of justice. Rawls' veil-of-ignorance thought experiment might allow us, as Rawls intended, to arrive at some universal principles of justice.

H.L.A. Hart, a legal philosopher who is otherwise an avowed positivist, recognized a "minimum content" of natural law. According to Hart, natural law on a grand scale is impossible. As a positivist, he argues that the sole criterion for whether a law is valid or not is whether relevant institutions and common practice recognize the law as such. Only in one area does Hart allow the jump from description to prescription—survival. Hart submits that human society does pursue the goal of survival, and that this is also a valid purpose to which the law ought to aim. He describes the "minimum content of natural law" needed to regulate the society that must exist for humans to survive. Survival requires a legal system with a "specific content", according to Hart, including rules respecting persons, property, and promises, based on five "truisms."

H.L.A. Hart, The Concept of Law 193–99 (1961)

In considering the simple truisms which we set forth here, and their connection with law and morals, it is important to observe that in each case the facts mentioned afford a *reason* why, given survival as an aim, law and morals should include a specific content. The general form of the argument is simply that without such a content laws and morals could not forward the minimum purpose of survival which men have in associating with each other. In the absence of this content, men, as they are, would have no reason for obeying voluntarily any rules; and without a minimum of co-operation given voluntarily by those who find that it is in their interest to submit to and maintain the rules, coercion of others who would not voluntarily conform would be impossible. It is important to stress the distinctively rational connection between natural facts and the content of legal and moral rules in this approach, because it is both possible and important to inquire into quite different forms of connection between natural facts and legal or moral rules. Thus, the still young sciences of psychology and sociology may discover or may even have discovered that, unless certain physical, psychological, or economic conditions are satisfied, e.g. unless young children are fed and nurtured in certain ways within the family, no system of laws or code of morals can be established, or that only those laws can function successfully which conform to a certain type. Connections of this sort between natural conditions and systems of rules are not mediated by *reasons*; for they do not relate the existence of certain rules to the conscious aims or purpose of those whose rules they are. Being fed in infancy in a certain way may well be shown to be a necessary condition or even a *cause* of a population developing or maintaining a moral or legal code, but it is not a *reason* for their doing so. Such causal connections do not of course conflict with the connections which rest on purposes or conscious aims; they may indeed be considered more important or fundamental than the latter, since they may actually explain why human beings have those conscious aims or purposes which Natural Law takes as its starting-points. Causal explanations of this type do not rest on truisms nor are they mediated by conscious aims or purposes; they are for sociology or psychology like other sciences to establish by the methods of generalization and theory, resting on observation and, where possible, on experiment. Such connections therefore are of a different kind from those which relate the content of certain legal and moral rules to the facts stated in the following truisms.

(i) *Human vulnerability*. The common requirements of law and morality consist for the most part not of active services to be rendered but of forbearances, which are usually formulated in negative form as prohibitions. Of these the most important for social life are those that restrict the use of violence in killing or inflicting bodily harm. The basic character of such rules may be brought out in a question: If there were not these rules what point could there be for beings such as ourselves in having rules of *any* other kind? The force of this rhetorical question rests on the fact that men are both occasionally prone to, and normally vulnerable to, bodily attack. Yet though this is a truism it is not a necessary truth; for things might have been, and might one day be, otherwise. There are species of animals whose physical structure (including exoskeletons or a carapace) renders them virtually immune from attack by other members of their species and animals who have no organs enabling them to attack. If men were to lose their vulnerability to each other there would vanish one obvious reason for the most characteristic provision of law and morals: *Thou shalt not kill*.

(ii) *Approximate equality*. Men differ from each other in physical strength, agility, and even more in intellectual capacity. None the less it is a fact of quite major importance for the understanding of different forms of law and morality, that no individual is so much more powerful than others, that he is able, without co-operation, to dominate or subdue them for more than a short period. Even the strongest must sleep at times and, when asleep, loses temporarily his superiority. This fact of approximate equality, more than any other, makes obvious the necessity for a system of mutual forbearance and compromise which is the base of both legal and moral obligation. Social life with its rules requiring such forbearances is irksome at times; but it is at any rate less nasty, less brutish, and less short than unrestrained aggression for beings thus approximately equal. It is, of course, entirely consistent with this and an equal truism that when such a system of forbearance is established there will always be some who will wish to exploit it, by simultaneously living within its shelter and breaking its restrictions. This, indeed is, as we later show, one of the natural facts which makes the step from merely moral to organized, legal forms of control a necessary one. Again, things might have been otherwise. Instead of being approximately equal there might have been some men immensely stronger than others and better able to dispense with rest, either because some were in these ways far above the present average, or because most were far below it. Such exceptional men might have much to gain by aggression and little to gain from mutual forbearance or compromise with others. But we need not have recourse to the fantasy of giants among pygmies to see the cardinal importance of the fact of approximate equality: for it is illustrated better by the facts of international life, where there are (or were) vast disparities in strength and vulnerability between the states. This inequality, as we shall later see, between the units of international law is one of the things that has imparted to it a character so different from municipal law and limited the extent to which it is capable of operating as an organized coercive system.

(iii) *Limited Altruism*. Men are not devils dominated by a wish to exterminate each other, and the demonstration that, given only the modest aim of survival, the basic rules of law and morals are necessities, must not be identified with the false view that men are predominantly selfish and have no disinterested interest in the survival and welfare of their fellows. But if men are not devils, neither are they angels; and the fact that they are a mean between these two extremes is something which makes a system of mutual forbearance both necessary and possible. With angels, never tempted to harm others, rules requiring forbearances would not be necessary. With devils prepared to destroy, reckless of the cost to themselves, they would be impossible. As things are, human altruism is limited in range and intermittent, and the tendencies to aggression are frequent enough to be fatal to social life if not controlled.

(iv) *Limited Resources.* It is merely a contingent fact that human beings need food, clothes, and shelter; that these do not exist at hand in limitless abundance; but are scarce, have to be grown or won from nature, or have to be constructed by human toil. These facts alone make indispensable some minimal form of the institution of property (though not necessarily individual property), and the distinctive kind of rule which requires respect for it. The simplest forms of property are to be seen in rules excluding persons generally other than the "owner" from entry on, or the use of land, or from taking or using material things. If crops are to grow, land must be secure from indiscriminate entry, and food must, in the intervals between its growth or capture and consumption, be secure from being taken by others. At all times and places life itself depends on these minimal forbearances. Again, in this respect, things might have been otherwise than they are. The human organism might have been constructed like plants, capable of extracting food from air, or what it needs might have grown without cultivation in limitless abundance.

The rules which we have so far discussed are *static* rules, in the sense that the obligations they impose and the incidence of these obligations are not variable by individuals. But the division of labour, which all but the smallest groups must develop to obtain adequate supplies, brings with it the need for rules which are dynamic in the sense that they enable individuals to create obligations and to transfer, exchange, or sell their products; for these transactions involve the capacity to alter the incidence of those initial rights and obligations which define the simplest form of property. The same inescapable division of labour, and perennial need for co-operation, are also factors which make other forms of dynamic or obligation-creating rule necessary in social life. These secure the recognition of promises as a source of obligation. By this device individuals are enabled by words, spoken or written, to make themselves liable to blame or punishment for failure to act in certain stipulated ways. Where altruism is not unlimited, a standing procedure providing for such self-binding operations is required in order to create a minimum form of confidence in the future behaviour of others, and to ensure the predictability necessary for co-operation. This is most obviously needed where what is to be exchanged or jointly planned are mutual services, or wherever goods which are to be exchanged or sold are not simultaneously or immediately available.

(v) *Limited understanding and strength of will.* The facts that make rules respecting persons, property, and promises necessary in social life are simple and their mutual benefits are obvious. Most men are capable of seeing them and of sacrificing the immediate short-term interests which conformity to such rules demands. They may indeed obey, from a variety of motives: some from prudential calculation that the sacrifices are worth the gains, some from a disinterested interest in the welfare of others, and some because they look upon the rules as worthy of respect in themselves and find their ideals in devotion to them. On the other hand, neither understanding of long-term interest, nor the strength or goodness of will, upon which the efficacy of these different motives towards obedience depends, are shared by all men alike. All are tempted at times to prefer their own immediate interests and, in the absence of a special organization for their detection and punishment, many would succumb to the temptation.... "Sanctions" are therefore required not as the normal motive for obedience, but as a *guarantee* that those who would voluntarily obey shall not be sacrificed to those who would not. To obey, without this, would be to risk going to the wall. Given this standing danger, what reason demands is *voluntary* co-operation in a *coercive* system.

It is to be observed that the same natural fact of approximate equality between men is of crucial importance in the efficacy of organized sanctions. If some men were vastly more powerful than others, and not so dependent on their forbearance, the strength of the malefactors might exceed that of the supporters of law and order. Given such inequalities, the use of sanctions could not be successful and would involve dangers at least as great as those which they were designed to suppress. In these circumstances instead of social life being based on a system of mutual forbearances, with force used only intermittently against a minority of malefactors, the only viable system would be one in which the weak submitted to the strong on the best terms they could make and lived under their "protection". This, because of the scarcity of resources, would lead to a number of conflicting power centres, each grouped round its "strong man": these might intermittently war with each other, though the natural sanction, never negligible, of the risk of defeat might ensure an uneasy peace. Rules of a sort might then be accepted for the regulation of issues over which the "powers" were unwilling to fight. Again we need not think in fanciful terms of pygmies and giants in order to understand the simple logistics of approximate equality and its importance for law. The international scene, where the units concerned have differed vastly in strength, affords illustration enough. For centuries the disparities between states have resulted in a system where organized sanctions have been impossible, and law has been confined to matters which did not affect "vital" issues. How far atomic weapons, when available to all, will redress the balance of unequal power, and bring forms of control more closely resembling municipal criminal law, remains to be seen.

QUESTIONS AND DISCUSSION

1. From the above list of truisms, Hart derives his "universally recognized principles of conduct which ... may be considered the *minimum content* of Natural Law." Hart's theory is in no danger of falling in among religious, or "New Age" varieties of natural law. It has the advantage of relying only on issues of human survival. Hart, however, did not think that his "minimum content of natural law" applied to international society and law. He notes, for example, that pre-existing moral norms have little relevance to the field of international law, as international laws do not *in fact* correspond to moral claims but are valid nonetheless. Even a positivist such as Hart would authorize developing international laws using our reason to discover the ideals of global environmental legislation. According to Hart, it is not necessary to disapprove of natural law methodology *per se*, provided it is not used as a touchstone for the validity of law.

Allott's advice to Hart would no doubt be that if some, however minimal natural law principles apply to domestic law-making because of some fundamental understanding of humanity, there should be no reason for them not to apply at the international level. Do you agree? Recall Allott's injunction that a just international society means an increasing consciousness of our duties to assist the survival of people everywhere. It is no longer legitimate, to the extent that it ever was, for citizens of one country to disclaim responsibility for others in what should be a truly international society. Do you think that society on this level is necessitated by Hart's maxim of survival, in the same way society is at more local levels? Look again at the conditions that Hart says necessitate a minimum content of natural law. Which of them are applicable at the international level? With the possible exception of human equality, all of the conditions could apply as readily to nation-States as to individuals could they not? States, like people, are both capable of aggression and vulnerable to aggression; States are neither entirely good nor entirely evil; States exist in a world of limited resources; and States exist in a world of imperfect understanding and imperfect resolve. What about equality? Clearly, States are unequal in many respects: States differ widely in size and in economic, and military power. One argument for equality might be that States are equal because of their economic and ecological interdependence. To what extent do today's shared global environmental threats make all States approximately equal?

2. If Hart knew what we know today about the wild environmental facts, such as global warming, and the threat these facts pose for our survival, would he construe "survival" in a broader sense? In *The Concept of Law* he uses survival in the narrow sense that it only requires minimal laws against murder and theft, and minimal institutions such as courts, policing, and the concepts of property and contract. Do you think the survival maxim obliges us to take whatever legal measures are necessary to ensure the continuation of the human species? Can you argue that today's global environmental threats to human survival are even more fundamental than the threat of aggression from our fellow humans, for not even an aggressor can live without the life-support systems provided by the biosphere? Recall Hart's justification: "If there were not these rules what point could there be for beings such as ourselves in having rules of any other kind?"

3. Within the principle of survival there is a germ of an idea that could be used to argue for the survival of international society, though Hart himself probably would not extend his theory this far. Can you use Hart's principles and the structure of his argument to see how we might build a stronger foundation for international environmental law?

4. Hart provides principles that might be used in our quest for principles that do not share some of the infirmities of classic natural law. How far can the principle of survival take us in the search for general principles of international environmental law that are free from the bias of ideologies and beliefs, but respond to the common needs of humanity and the biosphere? We can look beyond people's desires, historically the limit-point of contractarian theory, and look at what measures *need* to be taken despite corporations or nation States not wanting them. We can take into account the very best current knowledge of the limits that the life-support systems on Earth place on economic activity, and elaborate legal principles that respond to these limits. As Phillip Allott points out, we should try to search for the "best ideas" about society and international relations, without being restricted to the "vestigial law created by . . . actual or presumed or tacit consent."

(c) Ethics

Reread the discussion of ethical principles in Chapter 2, in particular John Rawls' THEORY OF JUSTICE, and his "veil of ignorance" thought experiment, which was designed to force individuals to chose fairness in their own self interest. The implications Rawls's theory of justice has for global environment and development issues are considered in the next excerpt from Professor Stone.

Christopher Stone, THE GNAT IS OLDER THAN MAN 244–56 (1993)

International Environmental Ethics

[E]ven if we suppose there is some core of international morality, it does not take us very far. A moderate realist will grant that we can identify familiar moral principles which, by easy extension, condemn as evil the torture of prisoners or the rape of civilians. The problem at hand is much tougher because it lacks any well-chartered foundation in domestic moral literature: for example, in urging protection of the biosphere, to what moral principles can a global moralist refer? * * *

The most outspoken of the "reminders" have been the underdeveloped countries, most vocally the Group of 77 nations (G–77), 14 said collectively to represent 70 percent of the world's population but only 30 percent of its income. Their mood still finds its most authoritative expression in the U.N. General Assembly's 1974 Declaration on the Establishment of a New International Economic Order (NIEO). NIEO declared the principle of each nation's "full permanent sovereignty ... over its natural resources and economic activity." The phrase was originally understood as a denunciation of exploitation by others, but today the other side of the coin is considered equally significant and continues to cast a shadow over agreements on bio-diversity and forests: the sovereign right of each nation to exploit its own timberland and ecosystems without denunciation or interference by others. At the same time as the LDCs stress their sovereign independence, they insist that the developed states acknowledge a duty to reduce the material disparities in wealth. * * *

Distributive Justice

The distributive justice claims are appearing in the environmental context even more ubiquitously than those for corrective justice. That is because most of the controversy today focuses less on recrimination for past wrongs than on preventive measures to reduce degradation in the future. Unfortunately, the conflicts that arise over burden-sharing are particularly hard to mediate. The Law of the Sea negotiators had a tough enough time figuring out how to divide the anticipated (and one would now say, exaggerated) new wealth that was to be drawn from the oceans. In the pollution-oriented treaties, the negotiators are faced with offering everyone a smaller cut of the pie.

Most would agree that to cut the pie justly is to do so fairly. But what is "fair" in this context? One view of fairness is that it demands *equality of effort* to reduce pollution. But do we have equality of effort when each nation has expended the same sum on abatement efforts: $1 billion per nation? Or does fairness require the same percentage of each nation's GNP? Or installation by each nation of its "best available" technology?

On the other hand, the equality could be understood as an equality not of effort but *of outcome*. But outcome is ambiguous also. Some would say that the fair outcome is an equal reduction in units of emissions: every nation cuts back 100,000 tons. But if that is the process, the nation with the highest historical baselines will continue to out pollute the less developed nations—and maintain, "unfairly", their economic edge. Those who press for fair outcomes might therefore choose to aim for an all-things-considered outcome: each nation should put in so mush effort at pollution control until we all have not an equality of emissions, but an equality of wealth or of opportunity or at least some fundamental baseline index that assures a floor of adequate food, fuel, clothing, and the like.

The difficulties of sorting through these competing standards of "fairness" to find the morally right one is frustrating. And that frustration, in turn, provides a major boost for the various market solutions, which advertise the "unseen hand" of the market as rescuing the human mind from hard choices. Various schemes for marketable pollution allowances are a prime example. But most of the market-trading literature deals with the techniques and benefits of trading. It assumes someone else has provided an answer to the threshold question:

How shall we assign the original entitlements, the starting point from which the trading begins to operate? Is the right to pollute a personal right of each member of the human species, to be handed out per capita? Or is it a geopolitical right, to be allocated, like a vote in the U.N. General Assembly, evenly among nations? The snag with the first alternative is that it undermines incentives to control population and is theoretically obscure, anyway: Should each person on earth have a pro rata right to the globe's reserves of oil, fish, timber, and farmland? The problem with the second alternative is that to divide pollution entitlements evenly among nations would give the tiniest nation the right to pollute as much as the largest. Do we take the status quo as a starting point, so the rich can fortify the advantage they have gained over the poor, at the poor's expense? And so on.

These are not questions of economics, but unavoidably, of ethics. Indeed, in any social philosophy, the just distribution of entitlement—of power, wealth, office, opportunity—is among the hardest, most foundational issues. The stakes are all the more momentous when applied on a global scale, but all the more problem-ridden too. * * *

The Contemporary Philosophical Background

Defending the global environment will cost huge sums of money. The burdens, particularly of maintaining the commons areas, have to be somehow distributed. It is hoped that they can be apportioned according to some notion of justice. But what does justice demand? In what circumstances does it apply? And between whom—or what—do claims of transglobal justice run—nations or people?

The contemporary reference point for these questions has become John Rawls's monumental *A Theory of Justice*. But in our area of inquiry Rawls's ambitions were uncharacteristically bridled. He drew a sharp line between the principles of justice that prevail among persons within a society, about which he had much to say, and "justice between states," which he considered to be much thinner and less pregnant. The entire subject of international justice which I believe will be the great philosophical issue of the 1990s, Rawls touched upon in 1971 only indirectly in the course of illustrating conscientious refusals of citizens provoked by differences over foreign affairs; the entire treatment of international justice was thus disposed of in less than three pages too obscurely to rise to his indexer's attention. * * *

Rawls ... asks us to imagine ourselves as part of a hypothetical negotiation among all members of society at the time they came together into a social union. All the negotiants are assumed to be predominantly interested in their own welfare but are to imagine themselves hammering out the society's ground rules unaware of the particulars of how their lives will unfold. No one knows whether he or she will turn out to be a man or a woman, poor or rich, talented oboist or mentally retarded. The idea of laying down the framework from behind such a "veil of ignorance" is that, not knowing our gender, race, and so forth, we will vote for rules that are gender and race neutral—"fair" in the sense of not narrowly self-serving, and therefore "just."

Rawls maintains that, among other choices, the negotiants would agree on a set of rules reckoned to produce an equal distribution of primary goods. But there is a caveat that Rawls calls the Difference Principle. Unequal distributions are legitimate to the extent that the rules that permitted the inequalities to evolve make the least well off better off than they would have been without the rules. In other words, rules and institutions that make everyone better off are acceptable, even if some people emerge with more pie than others, as long as they maximize the welfare of the minimally well off.

The implications for international society could be weighty. To defend the rules of international trade or the concentration of carbon-belching industry in the industrialized North, an American might argue that although the underlying rules and practices that countenance them (those of international trade, banking, etc.) leave great disparities in wealth, they nonetheless operate to make even the least fortunate in Bangladesh better off than they would be otherwise—without those rules. That, at least, is how the argument goes. But can we really say with a straight face that if we were to surrender bits and pieces of our high technology opulence, the bottom would fall out of their jute and copper markets? The NIEO evidently thinks otherwise, that the practices which sustain existing disparities are simply stacked for the North, without any absolution measurable in long-term benefits to the least well off (or possibly even in the average welfare globally).

Who is right? If one is willing to accept that the international order is based upon sheer power, then the question of "right" does not enter and it is simply going to come down to our armies versus their terrorists. But for those who take morals seriously (who want the international order to be built on something beyond sheer power plays), the questions of justice are vital: Need the developed world defend existing practices by justifying them with some sort of Difference Principle defense?

Ironically, Rawls himself did not think so. He conceived his "veil-of-ignorance" thought experiment ... to apply only to persons engaged in "a cooperative venture for mutual advantage" in a "self-contained community." Rawls felt that the relations among people within each nation met the standards of cooperative interchange, but that the quality and extent of interaction among nations themselves did not.

In consequence, on Rawl's view the principles of justice that prevailed internally stopped at national boundaries. * * *

QUESTIONS AND DISCUSSION

1. Does the present international environmental lawmaking process satisfy Rawls's conception of "justice as fairness"? If not, what changes would you suggest? Do the efforts of the environmental movement to reform the international legal system to allow their full participation, including rights to information, to environmental assessment, to participation, and so on, reflect Rawls's focus on procedural fairness as an essential foundation for justice?

2. Does Rawls's "difference principle" justify the strategy of the World Trade Organization to improve the well-being of the world through economic globalization? Even if the vast majority of the economic benefits of globalization go to those who already have most of the economic wealth of the world?

3. What principles might emerge if, while our hypothetical legislators were behind the veil of ignorance, we presented them with the facts from Chapter 1 and all other scientific evidence about the human relationship to the environment—the principle of net primary productivity, the rate of human population growth, the rates of resource consumption and destruction, the risk of environmental cliffs and synergies? Not knowing whether they lived in an industrialized or developing country, on the edge of an ocean or the edge of a desert, in the present generation or a generation yet to be born? How would they respond in order that each might best protect his or her own interests? Would they formulate rules about the obligations the present generation owes to future generations? About the obligations the well-off citizens or States have to the less-well off? How would they strike the balance between the need to alleviate poverty and the need to protect the environment? Would they propose their own principles of sustainable development? Would you expect it to resemble the Rio Declaration? How might they balance the benefits of technology against the risks of environmental catastrophe?

4. Rawls' theory is also interesting to environmentalists with respect to how he treats "justice between generations." In A Theory of Justice the "original position" assumes a "present time of entry". This means that the only persons who are carrying out the thought experiment are those who exist at the present time. Rawls recognized, however, that nothing would prevent persons from making decisions that consumed all of society's resources in ways that would undermine future cultural and political institutions. Rawls thus required that persons in the "original position" not be individuals but be considered heads of families. In this way, they would have an incentive to accept a "principle of savings". By savings, Rawls meant setting aside some current income in order to consider the well-being of children and others in the extended future.

Rawls was not concerned with questions of environmental sustainability, but you can see how his concern with families does begin to introduce an important linkage to questions of sustainability. In 1977, in an article endorsed by Rawls, Jane English argued that Rawls' "veil of ignorance" experiment should also include an intergenerational element. That is, the persons in the original position would in addition to not knowing their race, gender, education, socioeconomic class, and so on, would also not know whether they were present in this generation or another generation. The power of this modification for environmental sustainability should be clear: persons would be far better stewards of the environment if there was a substantial risk that they could be "incarnated" into a world ruined by irresponsible previous generations. *See* Jane English, *Justice Between Generations,* Philosophical Studies 31 (1977) at 97–104. This concept of fairness between generations—or intergenerational equity—particularly as it applies to environment and development issues is discussed further in Chapter 7, page 398.

5. Stone tells us that "on Rawls' view the principles of justice that prevailed internally stopped at national boundaries." Is there any justification for treating ethics differently in the internal realm of a State and the external or international realm? Shouldn't the same ethical principles apply? The scientific rules of ecology remain the same internally and externally, and increasingly so do the rules governing economic activity. What about law?

6. Can science, in particular ecology, help us identify general principles of international environmental law? Is the Precautionary Principle an example of a general principle that is based on science? On ethics?

---

3. SUSTAINABLE DEVELOPMENT AS A GENERAL PRINCIPLE OF INTERNATIONAL LAW

In the 1997 decision, concerning the Gabcikovo—Nagymaros Project (Hungary v. Slovakia) Sept. 25 1997, the ICJ was directly confronted for the first time with the issue of how to balance environmental protection with the need for development. The *Gabcikovo* case revolved around a 1977 treaty between Hungary and Czechoslovakia (to which Slovakia was the successor) to build and jointly operate a system of locks on the Danube River. Once completed, the system was expected to contribute substantially to the economies of both parties—increasing shipping access to the region and powering two hydroelectric power plants with a combined output of nearly 900 megawatts. It also posed a serious threat to the surrounding environment. In an effort to minimize this threat, Article 15 of the treaty required the parties to ensure that water quality in the Danube would not be impaired by the project. In addition, Article 19 provided that "The Contracting Parties shall, through the means specified in the joint contractual plan, ensure compliance with the obligations for the protection of nature arising in connection with the construction and operation of the System of Locks."

Work on the project began in 1978. As new evidence emerged about the environmental consequences of the project, opposition to the project increased among the Hungarian public. After several years of delays and negotiations, Hungary suspended work on its part of the project in 1989. In 1992, Hungary notified Slovakia that it was terminating the treaty. When Hungary refused to resume work, Slovakia unilaterally constructed and eventually put into operation a modified system, known as Variant C. When Variant C became operational, it drastically reduced the flow of the Danube downstream from the project, thus affecting Hungary's interest in the river.

Slovakia and Hungary submitted their dispute to the ICJ. The Court's decisions were guided primarily by the law of treaties and by the customary law of international watercourses. The Court concluded that Hungary had breached the 1977 treaty by suspending work on the project and that this breach was not justified by a "state of ecological necessity." It also found that Slovakia's operation of Variant C, which substantially interfered with an international watercourse, constituted an internationally wrongful act. The Court determined that the 1977 treaty between the parties was still valid and directed them to undertake negotiations in good faith to address the concerns raised in the case.

In the course of its analysis the Court acknowledged the existence of environmental norms as part of the general corpus of international law. In reconciling the environmental and developmental conflicts of the situation, the Court directed the parties to consider the principle of sustainable development, a principle that both Hungary and Slovakia agreed was applicable to the situation. The ICJ's reference to sustainable development in this way, even in the absence of an applicable treaty provision expressly using the term, suggests that the Court may be ready to recognize new principles of international environmental law.

Case Concerning the Gabcíkovo–Nagymaros Project (Hungary v. Slovakia), 1997 I.C.J. 92

140. It is clear that the Project's impact upon, and its implications for, the environment are of necessity a key issue. The numerous scientific reports which have been presented to the Court by the Parties—even if their conclusions are often contradictory—provide abundant evidence that this impact and these implications are considerable.

In order to evaluate the environmental risks, current standards must be taken into consideration. This is not only allowed by the wording of Articles 15 and 19, but even prescribed, to the extent that these articles impose a continuing—

and thus necessarily evolving—obligation on the parties to maintain the quality of the water of the Danube and to protect nature.

The Court is mindful that, in the field of environmental protection, vigilance and prevention are required on account of the often irreversible character of damage to the environment and of the limitations inherent in the very mechanism of reparation of this type of damage.

Throughout the ages, mankind has, for economic and other reasons, constantly interfered with nature. In the past, this was often done without consideration of the effects upon the environment. Owing to new scientific insights and to a growing awareness of the risks for mankind—for present and future generations—of pursuit of such interventions at an unconsidered and unabated pace, new norms and standards have been developed, set forth in a great number of instruments during the last two decades. Such new norms have to be taken into consideration, and such new standards given proper weight, not only when States contemplate new activities but also when continuing with activities begun in the past. This need to reconcile economic development with protection of the environment is aptly expressed in the concept of sustainable development.

For the purposes of the present case, this means that the Parties together should look afresh at the effects on the environment of the operation of the Gabcíkovo power plant. In particular they must find a satisfactory solution for the volume of water to be released into the old bed of the Danube and into the side-arms on both sides of the river.

In a separate opinion, Judge Weeramantry, Vice–President of the ICJ, elaborated on the proper role of sustainable development in international law. As you read the following excerpt, keep in mind the following questions: What methods does Judge Weeramantry employ to show the legal status of sustainable development? Does he give the principle any more substance—any greater specificity—than it had before? If so, how? If not, what is the effect of his opinion? Does Judge Weeramantry consider sustainable development to be a customary norm or a general principle of international law? How does your answer affect the legal operation of the principle?

Case Concerning the Gabcíkovo–Nagymaros Project

Separate Opinion of Vice–President Weeramantry

This case raises a rich array of environmentally related legal issues. A discussion of some of them is essential to explain my reasons for voting as I have in this very difficult decision. Three issues on which I wish to make some observations, supplementary to those of the Court, are the role played by the principle of sustainable development in balancing the competing demands of development and environmental protection; the protection given to Hungary by what I would describe as the principle of continuing environmental impact assessment; and the appropriateness of the use of *inter partes* legal principles, such as estoppel, for the resolution of problems with an *erga omnes* connotation such as environmental damage.

A. The Concept of Sustainable Development

Had the possibility of environmental harm been the only consideration to be taken into account in this regard, the contentions of Hungary could well have proved conclusive.

Yet there are other factors to be taken into account—not the least important of which is the developmental aspect, for the Gabčíkovo scheme is important to Slovakia from the point of view of development. The Court must hold the balance even between the environmental considerations and the developmental considerations raised by the respective Parties. The principle that enables the Court to do so is the principle of sustainable development.

The Court has referred to it as a concept in paragraph 140 of its Judgment. However, I consider it to be more than a mere concept, but as a principle with normative value which is crucial to the determination of this case. Without the benefits of its insights, the issues involved in this case would have been difficult to resolve.

Since sustainable development is a principle fundamental to the determination of the competing considerations in this case, and since, although it has attracted attention only recently in the literature of international law, it is likely to play a major role in determining important environmental disputes of the future, it calls for consideration in some detail. Moreover, this is the first occasion on which it has received attention in the jurisprudence of this Court.

When a major scheme, such as that under consideration in the present case, is planned and implemented, there is always the need to weigh considerations of development against environmental considerations, as their underlying juristic bases—the right to development and the right to environmental protection— are important principles of current international law.

In the present case we have, on the one hand, a scheme which, even in the attenuated form in which it now remains, is important to the welfare of Slovakia and its people, who have already strained their own resources and those of their predecessor State to the extent of over two billion dollars to achieve these benefits.... Further, Slovakia has traditionally been short of electricity, and the power generated would be important to its economic development....

On the other hand, Hungary alleges that the project produces, or is likely to produce, ecological damage of many varieties, including harm to river bank fauna and flora, damage to fish breeding, damage to surface water quality, eutrophication, damage to the groundwater régime, agriculture, forestry and soil, deterioration of the quality of drinking water reserves, and sedimentation. Hungary alleges that many of these dangers have already occurred and more will manifest themselves, if the scheme continues in operation. In the material placed before the Court, each of these dangers is examined and explained in considerable detail.

How does one handle these considerations? Does one abandon the project altogether for fear that the latter consequences might emerge? Does one proceed with the scheme because of the national benefits it brings, regardless of the suggested environmental damage? Or does one steer a course between, with due regard to both considerations, but ensuring always a continuing vigilance in respect of environmental harm?

It is clear that a principle must be followed which pays due regard to both considerations. Is there such a principle, and does it command recognition in international law? I believe the answer to both questions is in the affirmative. The principle is the principle of sustainable development and, in my view, it is an integral part of modern international law. It is clearly of the utmost importance, both in this case and more generally.

I would observe, moreover, that both Parties in this case agree on the applicability to this dispute of the principle of sustainable development. Thus, Hungary states in its pleadings that:

"Hungary and Slovakia agree that the principle of sustainable development, as formulated in the Brundtland Report, the Rio Declaration and Agenda 21 is applicable to this dispute . . .

International law in the field of sustainable development is now sufficiently well established, and both Parties appear to accept this."

Slovakia states that "inherent in the concept of sustainable development is the principle that developmental needs are to be taken into account in interpreting and applying environmental obligations."

Their disagreement seems to be not as to the existence of the principle but, rather, as to the way in which it is to be applied to the facts of this case.

The problem of steering a course between the needs of development and the necessity to protect the environment is a problem alike of the law of development and of the law of the environment. Both these vital and developing areas of law require, and indeed assume, the existence of a principle which harmonizes both needs.

To hold that no such principle exists in the law is to hold that current law recognizes the juxtaposition of two principles which could operate in collision with each other, without providing the necessary basis of principle for their reconciliation. The untenability of the supposition that the law sanctions such a state of normative anarchy suffices to condemn a hypothesis that leads to so unsatisfactory a result.

Each principle cannot be given free rein, regardless of the other. The law necessarily contains within itself the principle of reconciliation. That principle is the principle of sustainable development.

This case offers a unique opportunity for the application of that principle, for it arises from a Treaty which had development as its objective, and has been brought to a standstill over arguments concerning environmental considerations.

The people of both Hungary and Slovakia are entitled to development for the furtherance of their happiness and welfare. They are likewise entitled to the preservation of their human right to the protection of their environment. . . .
The present case thus focuses attention, as no other case has done in the jurisprudence of this Court, on the question of the harmonization of developmental and environmental concepts. * * *

(c) Sustainable Development as a Principle of International Law

After the early formulations of the concept of development, it has been recognized that development cannot be pursued to such a point as to result in substantial damage to the environment within which it is to occur. Therefore development can only be prosecuted in harmony with the reasonable demands of environmental protection. Whether development is sustainable by reason of its impact on the environment will, of course, be a question to be answered in the context of the particular situation involved.

It is thus the correct formulation of the right to development that that right does not exist in the absolute sense, but is relative always to its tolerance by the environment. The right to development as thus refined is clearly part of modern international law. It is compendiously referred to as sustainable development.

The concept of sustainable development can be traced back, beyond the Stockholm Conference of 1972, to such events as the Founex meeting of experts in Switzerland in June 1971; the conference on environment and development in Canberra in 1971; and United Nations General Assembly resolution 2849 (XXVI). It received a powerful impetus from the Stockholm Declaration which, by Principle 11, stressed the essentiality of development as well as the essentiality of bearing environmental considerations in mind in the developmental process. Moreover, many other Principles of that Declaration provided a setting for the development of the concept of sustainable development and more than one-third of the Stockholm Declaration related to the harmonization of environment and development. * * *

The international community had thus been sensitized to this issue even as early as the early 1970s, and it is therefore no cause for surprise that the 1977 Treaty, in Articles 15 and 19, made special reference to environmental considerations. Both Parties to the Treaty recognized the need for the developmental process to be in harmony with the environment and introduced a dynamic element into the Treaty which enabled the Joint Project to be kept in harmony with developing principles of international law.

Since then, sustainable development has received considerable endorsement from all sections of the international community, and at all levels. Whether in the field of multilateral treaties,[1] international declarations,[2] the foundation documents of international organizations,[3] the practices of international financial institutions,[4] regional declarations and planning documents,[5] or State practice,[6] there is a wide and general recognition of the concept. The Bergen

---

1. For example, the United Nations Convention to Combat Desertification (The United Nations Convention to Combat Desertification in those Countries Experiencing Serious Droughts and/or Desertification, Particularly in Africa), 1994, Preamble, Art. 9(1); the United Nations Framework Convention on Climate Change, 1992, (XXXI ILM (1992) 849, Arts. 2 and 3); and the Convention on Biological Diversity (XXXI ILM (1992) 818, Preamble, Arts. 1 and 10.)

2. For example, the Rio Declaration on Environment and Development, 1992, emphasizes sustainable development in several of its Principles (e.g., Principles 4, 5, 7, 8, 9, 20, 21, 22, 24 and 27 refer expressly to "sustainable development" which can be described as the central concept of the entire document); and the Copenhagen Declaration, 1995 (paras. 6 & 8)....

3. For example, the North American Free Trade Agreement (Canada, Mexico, United States) (NAFTA, Preamble, XXXII ILM (1993), p. 289); the World Trade Organization (WTO) (paragraph 1 of the Preamble of the Marrakesh Agreement of 15 April 1994, establishing the World Trade Organization speaks of the "optimal use of the world's resources in accordance with the objective of sustainable development"—XXXIII ILM

(1994), pp. 1143–1144); and the European Union (Art. 2 of the ECT).

4. For example, the World Bank Group, the Asian Development Bank, the African Development Bank, the InterAmerican Development Bank, and the European Bank for Reconstruction and Development all subscribe to the principle of sustainable development. Indeed, since 1993, the World Bank has convened an annual conference related to advancing environmentally and socially sustainable development (ESSD).

5. For example, the Langkawi Declaration on the Environment, 1989, adopted by the "Heads of Government of the Commonwealth representing a quarter of the world's population" which adopted "sustainable development" as its central theme; Ministerial Declaration on Environmentally Sound and Sustainable Development in Asia and the Pacific, Bangkok, 1990 (Doc. 38a, p. 567); and Action Plan for the Protection and Management of the Marine and Coastal Environment of the South Asian Seas Region, 1983 (para. 10—"sustainable, environmentally sound development").

6. For example, in 1990, the Dublin Declaration by the European Council on the

ECE Ministerial Declaration on Sustainable Development of 15 May 1990, resulting from a meeting of Ministers from 34 countries in the ECE region, and the Commissioner for the Environment of the European Community, addressed "The challenge of sustainable development of humanity" (para. 6), and prepared a Bergen Agenda for Action which included a consideration of the Economics of Sustainability, Sustainable Energy Use, Sustainable Industrial Activities, and Awareness Raising and Public Participation. It sought to develop "sound national indicators for sustainable development" (para. 13 (b)) and sought to encourage investors to apply environmental standards required in their home country to investments abroad. It also sought to encourage UNEP, UNIDO, UNDP, IBRD, ILO, and appropriate international organizations to support member countries in ensuring environmentally sound industrial investment, observing that industry and government should co-operate for this purpose (para. 15 (f)). A Resolution of the Council of Europe, 1990, propounded a European Conservation Strategy to meet, *inter alia*, the legitimate needs and aspirations of all Europeans by seeking to base economic, social and cultural development on a rational and sustainable use of natural resources, and to suggest how sustainable development can be achieved.

The concept of sustainable development is thus a principle accepted not merely by the developing countries, but one which rests on a basis of worldwide acceptance.

In 1987, the Brundtland Report brought the concept of sustainable development to the forefront of international attention. In 1992, the Rio Conference made it a central feature of its Declaration, and it has been a focus of attention in all questions relating to development in the developing countries.

The principle of sustainable development is thus a part of modern international law by reason not only of its inescapable logical necessity, but also by reason of its wide and general acceptance by the global community.

The concept has a significant role to play in the resolution of environmentally related disputes. The components of the principle come from well-established areas of international law—human rights, State responsibility, environmental law, economic and industrial law, equity, territorial sovereignty, abuse of rights, good neighbourliness—to mention a few. It has also been expressly incorporated into a number of binding and far-reaching international agreements, thus giving it binding force in the context of those agreements. It offers an important principle for the resolution of tensions between two established rights. It reaffirms in the arena of international law that there must be both development and environmental protection, and that neither of these rights can be neglected.

The general support of the international community does not of course mean that each and every member of the community of nations has given its express and specific support to the principle—nor is this a requirement for the establishment of a principle of customary international law.

Environmental Imperative stated that there must be an acceleration of effort to ensure that economic development in the Community is "sustainable and environmentally sound" (Bulletin of the European Communities, 6–1990, Ann. II, p. 18). It urged the Community and Member States to play a major role to assist developing countries in their efforts to achieve "long-term sustainable development" (ibid. , p. 19).... It also expressly recited that: "As Heads of State or Government of the European Community, ... [w]e intend that action by the Community and its Member States will be developed ... on the principles of sustainable development and preventive and precautionary action" (ibid., Conclusions of the Presidency, Point 1.36, pp. 17–18).

As Brierly observes:

> It would hardly ever be practicable, and all but the strictest of positivists admit that it is not necessary, to show that every state has recognized a certain practice, just as in English law the existence of a valid local custom or custom of trade can be established without proof that every individual in the locality, or engaged in the trade, has practiced the custom. This test of *general* recognition is necessarily a vague one; but it is of the nature of customary law, whether national or international. . . .

J. BRIERLY, THE LAW OF NATIONS, 61 (6th ed., 1963).

Evidence appearing in international instruments and State practice (as in development assistance and the practice of international financial institutions) likewise amply supports a contemporary general acceptance of the concept.

Recognition of the concept could thus, fairly, be said to be worldwide.

(d) The Need for International Law to Draw upon the World's Diversity of Cultures in Harmonizing Development and Environmental Protection

This case, which deals with a major hydraulic project, is an opportunity to tap the wisdom of the past and draw from it some principles which can strengthen the concept of sustainable development, for every development project clearly produces an effect upon the environment, and humanity has lived with this problem for generations.

This is a legitimate source for the enrichment of international law, which source is perhaps not used to the extent which its importance warrants.

In drawing into international law the benefits of the insights available from other cultures, and in looking to the past for inspiration, international environmental law would not be departing from the traditional methods of international law, but would, in fact, be following in the path charted out by Grotius. Rather than laying down a set of principles *a priori* for the new discipline of international law, he sought them also *a posteriori* from the experience of the past, searching through the whole range of cultures available to him for this purpose. From them, he drew the durable principles which had weathered the ages, on which to build the new international order of the future. Environmental law is now in a formative stage, not unlike international law in its early stages. A wealth of past experience from a variety of cultures is available to it. It would be pity indeed if it were left untapped merely because of attitudes of formalism which see such approaches as not being entirely *de rigueur*. * * *

Moreover, especially at the frontiers of the discipline of international law, it needs to be multi-disciplinary, drawing from other disciplines such as history, sociology, anthropology, and psychology such wisdom as may be relevant for its purpose. * * *

Especially where this Court is concerned, "the essence of true universality" of the institution is captured in the language of Article 9 of the Statute of the International Court of Justice which requires the "representation of the *main forms of civilization* and of the principal legal systems of the world." (emphasis added) The struggle for the insertion of the italicized words in the Court's Statute was a hard one . . . and, since this concept has thus been integrated into the structure and the Statute of the Court, I see the Court as being charged with a duty to draw upon the wisdom of the world's several civilizations, where such a course can enrich its insights into the matter before it. The Court cannot afford to be monocultural, especially where it is entering newly developing areas of law.

This case touches an area where many such insights can be drawn to the enrichment of the developing principles of environmental law and to a clarification of the principles the Court should apply.

It is in this spirit that I approach a principle which, for the first time in its jurisprudence, the Court is called upon to apply—a principle which will assist in the delicate task of balancing two considerations of enormous importance to the contemporary international scene and, potentially, of even greater importance to the future.

(e) Some Wisdom from the Past Relating to Sustainable Development

There are some principles of traditional legal systems that can be woven into the fabric of modern environmental law. They are specially pertinent to the concept of sustainable development which was well recognized in those systems. Moreover, several of these systems have particular relevance to this case, in that they relate to the harnessing of streams and rivers and show a concern that these acts of human interference with the course of nature should always be conducted with due regard to the protection of the environment. In the context of environmental wisdom generally, there is much to be derived from ancient civilizations and traditional legal systems in Asia, the Middle East, Africa, Europe, the Americas, the Pacific, and Australia—in fact, the whole world. This is a rich source which modern environmental law has left largely untapped. * * *

[Judge Weeramantry next undertakes an extensive review of irrigation and water management systems in various cultures—the gigantic man-made lakes and reservoirs that have supplied human needs in Sri Lanka for twenty-five hundred years, the networks of irrigation furrows utilized by the Sonjo and Chagga tribes of Tanzania; the ancient system of *qanats*, which stretches more than 170,000 miles through Iran; and similar projects developed by the Chinese, the Inca, and Australian aborigines. With respect to each system, Judge Weeramantry highlights the relationship between its long-term sustainability and the protective attitude the builders harbored towards their environment. He places particular emphasis on the great number of cultures which have recognized that humans hold their environment in trust for future generations and which have acted accordingly.]

The ingrained values of any civilization are the source from which its legal concepts derive, and the ultimate yardstick and touchstone of their validity. This is so in international and domestic legal systems alike, save that international law would require a worldwide recognition of those values. It would not be wrong to state that the love of nature, the desire for its preservation, and the need for human activity to respect the requisites for its maintenance and continuance are among those pristine and universal values which command international recognition.

The formalism of modern legal systems may cause us to lose sight of such principles, but the time has come when they must once more be integrated into the corpus of the living law. As stated in the exhaustive study of *The Social and Environmental Effects of Large Dams*, already cited, "We should examine not only what has caused modern irrigation systems to fail; it is much more important to understand what has made traditional irrigation societies to succeed." . . . Observing that various societies have practiced sustainable irrigation agriculture over thousands of years, and that modern irrigation systems rarely last more than a few decades, the authors pose the question whether it was due to the achievement of a "congruence of fit" between their methods and "the nature of land, water and climate" . . . Modern environmental law needs to take note of the experience of the past in pursuing this "congruence of fit" between development and environmental imperatives.

By virtue of its representation of the main forms of civilization, this Court constitutes a unique forum for the reflection and the revitalization of those global legal traditions. There were principles ingrained in these civilizations as well as embodied in their legal systems, for legal systems include not merely written legal systems but traditional legal systems as well, which modern researchers have shown to be no less legal systems than their written cousins, and in some respects even more sophisticated and finely tuned than the latter.

Living law which is daily observed by members of the community, and compliance with which is so axiomatic that it is taken for granted, is not deprived of the character of law by the extraneous test and standard of reduction to writing. Writing is of course useful for establishing certainty, but when a duty such as the duty to protect the environment is so well accepted that all citizens act upon it, that duty is part of the legal system in question.

Moreover, when the Statute of the Court described the sources of international law as including the "general principles of law recognized by civilized nations", it expressly opened a door to the entry of such principles into modern international law.

(f) Traditional Principles that Can Assist in the Development of Modern Environmental Law

As modern environmental law develops, it can, with profit to itself, take account of the perspectives and principles of traditional systems, not merely in a general way, but with reference to specific principles, concepts, and aspirational standards.

Among those which may be extracted from the systems already referred to are such far-reaching principles as the principle of trusteeship of earth resources, the principle of intergenerational rights, and the principle that development and environmental conservation must go hand in hand. Land is to be respected as having a vitality of its own and being integrally linked to the welfare of the community. When it is used by humans, every opportunity should be afforded to it to replenish itself. Since flora and fauna have a niche in the ecological system, they must be expressly protected. There is a duty lying upon all members of the community to preserve the integrity and purity of the environment.

Natural resources are not individually, but collectively, owned, and a principle of their use is that they should be used for the maximum service of people. There should be no waste, and there should be a maximization of the use of plant and animal species, while preserving their regenerative powers. The purpose of development is the betterment of the condition of the people.

Most of them have relevance to the present case, and all of them can greatly enhance the ability of international environmental law to cope with problems such as these if and when they arise in the future.

There are many routes of entry by which they can be assimilated into the international legal system, and modern international law would only diminish itself were it to lose sight of them—embodying as they do the wisdom which enabled the works of man to function for centuries and millennia in a stable relationship with the principles of the environment. This approach assumes increasing importance at a time when such a harmony between humanity and its planetary inheritance is a prerequisite for human survival.

Sustainable development is thus not merely a principle of modern international law. It is one of the most ancient of ideas in the human heritage. Fortified by the rich insights that can be gained from millennia of human experience, it has an important part to play in the service of international law.

———

QUESTIONS AND DISCUSSION

1. Both the case itself and Judge Weeramantry's discussion leave open the question: how does the Court view sustainable development? Sustainable development may be too abstract to impose a specific rule on States, but as the Court suggests, and Weeramantry demonstrates, it may serve as a means for interpreting other international obligations. Is it, then, a general principle of law? Of natural law? Customary law?

According to natural law theorists, there are universal legal principles that exist independently of enacted laws and that can be discovered by our rational intelligence. Can you find the methodology of the natural law in Judge Weeramantry's opinion? For example, what role do the following statements play in the judge's argument: "sustainable development is . . . a part of modern international law by reason . . . of its inescapable logical necessity," and "the love of nature, the desire for its preservation, and the need for human activity to respect the requisites for its maintenance and continuance are among those pristine and universal values which command international recognition"?

2. Judge Weeramantry references principles *erga omnes*—or principles owed to the community of states—as opposed to any one specific state. He argues that environmental protection is an obligation owed to the international community as a whole. Do you agree?

3. For further discussion of general principles *see* BIN CHENG, GENERAL PRINCIPLES OF LAW AS APPLIED BY INTERNATIONAL COURTS AND TRIBUNALS (1953) (general principles can be derived from positive rules of law in even one state, provided such a principle is prescriptive under specific circumstances); 1 OPPENHEIM'S INTERNATIONAL LAW 36–40 (ROBERT JENNINGS & ARTHUR WATTS eds., 9th ed. 1992)(general principles may be derived from municipal law in an international context as well as relations among international organizations and private parties); OSCAR SCHACHTER, INTERNATIONAL LAW IN THEORY AND PRACTICE 50–55 (1991); MALCOLM N. SHAW, INTERNATIONAL LAW 81–84 (2ed. 1986)(domestic law and the general concept of equity included in the formulation of general principles).

———

D.   JUDICIAL DECISIONS AND THE WRITINGS OF EMINENT PUBLICISTS

In addition to treaties, customary norms, and general principles, Article 38 of the ICJ Statute lists judicial decisions and the writings of eminent publicists as subsidiary means for determining international law.

The writings of publicists may help States and courts discern what the law is, and may help decision-makers decide what the law should be, but they have no independent force. Similarly, international jurists may take guidance from the principles and reasoning employed by judges in national courts, even though those decisions are not, themselves, international law.

The Paquete Habana, 175 U.S. 677, 700–701 (1900)

International law is part of our law, and must be ascertained and administered by the courts of justice of appropriate jurisdiction, as often as questions of right depending upon it are duly presented for their determination. For this purpose, where there is no treaty, and no controlling executive or legislative act or judicial decision, resort must be had to the customs and usages of civilized nations; and, as evidence of these, to the works of jurists and commentators, who by years of labor, research and experience, have made themselves peculiarly well acquainted with the subjects of which they treat. Such works are resorted to by judicial tribunals, not for the speculations of their authors concerning what the law ought to be, but for trustworthy evidence of what the law really is. * * *

Chancellor Kent says: "In the absence of higher and more authoritative sanctions, the ordinances of foreign States, the opinions of eminent statesmen, and the writings of distinguished jurists, are regarded as of great consideration on questions not settled by conventional law. In cases where the principal jurists agree, the presumption will be very great in favor of the solidity of their maxims; and no civilized nation, that does not arrogantly set all ordinary law and justice at defiance, will venture to disregard the uniform sense of the established writers on international law." 1 Kent Com. 18.

One of the most persuasive publicists is the International Law Commission, the UN agency most responsible for the codification and progressive development of international law. The ILC prepared the draft text that eventually became the Vienna Convention on the Law of Treaties, for example. Among its most important work in the environmental context are its rules relating to non-navigational uses of international watercourses, which have been endorsed as a convention by the United Nations; its draft rules on state responsibility; and its draft rules on state responsibility for transboundary harms resulting from otherwise lawful activities.

Oscar Schachter, *United Nations Law*, 88 Am.J.Int'l.L. 1, 4–5 (1994)

The role of the International Law Commission in lawmaking is rather more complex than its statute suggests. At its inception its role was described as "scientific" in contrast to the political role of governments. Its members were to be experts of distinction, serving in their individual capacity, though nominated by UN member states and elected by the General Assembly. Their dual task in accordance with the relevant UN Charter article was to codify existing law and "progressively develop" the law. Almost from the very beginning, it was evident that codification involved a measure of progressive development. Inconsistencies in existing law often had to be dealt with and gaps filled. Questions of policy and expedience could not be avoided in these cases. Still, the major codifying conventions produced by the Commission and adopted by plenipotentiary conferences were in large part "restatements" of major areas of customary law. Some of these conventions were widely accepted as law even before they entered into legal effect. They have been treated as authoritative by nonparties as well as parties. As a practical matter, lawyers in or outside governments relying on the codification no longer search through diplomatic history or scattered case law for precedents. Practice thus follows the texts. Only rarely have some provisions been questioned on the ground that they went beyond codification and therefore bound only parties to the convention.

At the present time, several new factors raise questions as to the Commission's lawmaking role. For one thing, the major traditional subjects of customary law have been "codified" except for state responsibility. The Commission itself has changed. Observers see it as more "politicized," most of its members now diplomats or government officials. Only a few are comparable to the influential scholars on earlier commissions. A more basic problem is whether the Commission can be expected to carry out its main tasks satisfactorily through multilateral conventions that require general acceptance. The prevailing practice of seeking consensus or near-unanimity to adopt a convention has led to highly ambiguous or vacuous provisions. Another important, if less obvious, factor is the contradictory element in the lawmaking process. On the one hand, the rapidity of change creates the demand for new law; on the other hand, it leads to doubts about adopting new rules for an indefinite future. We may also discern dissonance resulting from the consciousness of interdependence and a sense (or fear) of loss of autonomy. The consequence is hesitation to move toward new treaty obligations of universal application.

The Commission's lawmaking may move in a different direction as suggested by its work on state responsibility. In that field the reports of the special rapporteurs (all eminent authorities) and the draft articles have become widely invoked evidence of general international law. In other fields, where the paucity of general practice makes it difficult to determine a clear line between *lex lata* and *de lege ferenda*, the Commission's studies and the comments of its members and governments provide authoritative material that can be invoked by governments and their legal advisers when concrete issues arise. True, this falls short of a definitive treaty or agreed codificatory text, but it is not without practical effect.

In the end, the "law" is determined by the subsequent conduct of the states and their views of the law (*opinio juris*). The Commission's role is not insignificant insofar as its draft articles provide systematization and generalization that give coherence to prior practice and diverse views. Even if this does not meet a positivist conception of law, it is undeniably a step toward the formation of legal order.

QUESTIONS AND DISCUSSION

1. In addition to the writings of publicists, the ICJ may also look for guidance to its prior decisions or those of other international tribunals. But the decisions of such tribunals, even of the ICJ itself, are binding only on the States whose dispute the court is deciding. For other States, such decisions may provide evidence of what the law is, but the decisions do not, themselves, create law. The principle of *stare decisis* thus does not exist in international law. In this respect, international law is much like the civil law tradition, where judicial opinions tend to be advisory, not binding, on non-parties. Having said this, note that ICJ opinions are cited as authority so frequently that the distinction between simply identifying the law and actually making it has been blurred. But consider again Judge Weeramantry's separate opinion in the *Gabcikovo* case. Was he simply restating what the law was at the time he wrote the decision, or was he taking a more active role in the development of the law? *See generally* H. Lauterpacht, The Development of International Law by the International Court of Justice (1958).

2. Because there are so few cases in the ICJ, common law-type evolution is severely limited in international law. In The Nature of the Common Law, Melvin A. Eisenberg argues that a purely text-based legal framework cannot be expected to address every conceivable dispute. He defines the content of the common law as "rules that would be generated at the present moment by application of the institutional principles of adjudication," which he calls "the generative conception of the common law." *See* M. Eisenberg, THE NATURE OF THE COMMON LAW (1987). How serious is the lack of adjudication, and the accompanying lack of the common law's "generative conception", for the evolution of international law?

SECTION III. INNOVATIONS IN INTERNATIONAL ENVIRONMENTAL LAWMAKING

A. INTERNATIONAL "SOFT" LAW

As described in the next reading, "soft law" is either "not yet law or not only law." Soft law is an important innovation in international lawmaking that describes a flexible process for States to develop and test new legal norms before they become binding upon the international community. The soft law process is more dynamic and democratic than traditional lawmaking, embracing a broader range of actors (including scientific organizations, academic specialists, NGOs and industry) and providing a more direct link with the larger society. It has become a critical part of the consensus-building that is ultimately needed to negotiate an environmental treaty. (Note that the distinction between "soft" and "hard" law is not precise; it is possible to have "soft" obligations in "hard" law form, for example in a framework treaty, such as the United Nations Framework Convention on Climate Change.)

Pierre-Marie Dupuy, *SOFT LAW AND THE INTERNATIONAL LAW OF THE ENVIRONMENT*
12 MICH. J. INT'L L. 420, 420–35 (1991)

INTRODUCTION

"Soft" law is a paradoxical term for defining an ambiguous phenomenon. Paradoxical because, from a general and classical point of view, the rule of law is usually considered "hard," i.e., compulsory, or it simply does not exist. Ambiguous because the reality thus designated, considering its legal effects as well as its manifestations, is often difficult to identify clearly.

Nevertheless, a new process of normative creation which jurists feel uncomfortable analyzing does exist and has been developing for more or less twenty years. "Soft" law certainly constitutes part of the contemporary law-making process but, as a social phenomenon, it evidently overflows the classical and familiar legal categories by which scholars usually describe and explain both the creation and the legal authority of international norms. In other words, "soft" law is a trouble maker because it is either not yet or not only law.

This heterogeneity requires that one first consider, without necessarily subscribing to any "sociological" school of thought, the social reasons for this phenomenon. There seem to be three:

The first reason is structural in nature: it is the existence and development of a ramified network of permanent institutions, both at the universal and regional levels, since the end of the Second World War. The "UN family" of organizations plays the leading role here. These institutions offer the world community a standing structure of cooperation which makes it possible to organize permanent and on-going political, economic and normative negotiations among the member States of this community. Furthermore, the increasingly important function of non-governmental organizations provides an efficient complement to the existing intergovernmental framework by assuring, in particular, a dynamic relationship between inter-State diplomacy and international public opinion.

The second reason is the diversification of the components of this world community. Since the late 1950s, the arrival of underdeveloped countries on the international stage has made it necessary to adapt and reconsider, by way of normative negotiation, a great number of international customary norms which had been elaborated at a time when these countries were not in existence as sovereign States. It is well known that these new States, having the weight of the majority without the power of the elder countries, have speculated on the utilization of "soft" instruments, such as resolutions and recommendations of international bodies, with a view toward modifying a number of the main rules and principles of the international legal order.

The last and most important element, closely linked to the previous one, is best characterized by the rapid evolution of the world economy and increasing State interdependence combined with the development of new fields of activity created by the unceasing progress of science and technology. This phenomenon requires the timely creation of new branches of international law that are adaptable and applicable to each new level of achievement reached as a result of technological advancement. Thus, international economic law and international law relating to the protection of the human environment are areas in which new "soft" regulations have emerged in predominant fashion.

The inter-relationship among these three elements, even if complex, is nonetheless quite evident: the steady evolution and adaptation of these new norms necessitate a constant renegotiation which usually takes place within the many organs of international organizations. One could say that the "soft" law "wave" reflects both, on the one hand, a desire for a new type of law rendered necessary by the previously enunciated factors and, on the other, a certain fear that existing law is too rigid—either too difficult to be rigorously applied by the poorest countries or incapable of adapting to the rapidly evolving areas which it is supposed to cover and regulate.

It would, however, be a mistake to believe that, given these considerations, "soft" law is solely an attribute of international law. For partly the same reasons, particularly given the rapid evolution of scientific advances, one can observe its appearance in certain domains of municipal law. For example, very few countries have yet adopted precise legislation providing for normative regulation of genetic research and its applications in "assisted procreation." The preference has instead been to define, through various institutions and procedures, a variety of "soft" ethical guidelines addressed to scientists and physicians without resorting to laws, decrees or other "hard" legal instruments. That this phenomenon is common nowadays is one of the many reasons why "soft" law should not be considered a "normative sickness" but rather a symbol of contemporary times and a product of necessity.

Because the existing body of international environmental law has, in part, emerged on the basis of "soft" norms, it provides a good field for observing the general sociological and juridical phenomenon termed "soft" law. The 1972 Stockholm Declaration adopted by the UN Conference on the Human Environment, for example, constitutes the normative program for the world community in this field. Although, from a formal point of view, the Declaration is only a non-binding resolution, many of its "principles," particularly Principle 21, have been relied upon by governments to justify their legal rights and duties. The subsequent State practice has been, no doubt, influenced by such provisions. It is in this context and with the benefit of these introductory remarks that we shall briefly and successively examine the creation (I), the forms and content (II), and the legal effects (III) of "soft" law in the field of international environmental law.

1. CREATION OF SOFT ENVIRONMENTAL LAW

a. *The Institutional Framework*

The primary function assumed by international institutions in the international "soft" law-making process has already been illustrated. In practice, the development of "soft" law norms with regard to the protection of the human environment began immediately after the Stockholm Conference, one of the consequences of which was the creation of a special subsidiary organ of the UN General Assembly devoted to the promotion of both universal and regional environmental law. This body, the United Nations Environment Program ("UNEP"), has played a leading role in the promotion of regional conventions aimed at, for example, protecting seas against pollution. Although it was not supposed to develop in such a manner, UNEP has also evolved into a standing structure for negotiating draft resolutions sent, after their elaboration, to the General Assembly, where their contents have been either passed as is or expressly referred to in resolutions. A prime example of this phenomenon is provided by the 1978 UNEP Draft Principles of Conduct in the Field of the Environment for the Guidance of States in the Conservation and Harmonious Utilization of Natural Resources Shared by Two or More States.

At the regional level in general and in Europe in particular, several international institutions have engaged in important activities related to environmental protection: the Organization for Economic Cooperation and Development ("OECD"), which, in particular, has adopted a series of recommendations conceived of as a follow-up to the Universal Stockholm Declaration regarding the prevention and abatement of transfrontier pollution; the EEC which has adopted Programmes of Action for the Environment, on the basis of which "hard" law is later established, mainly by way of "directive"; and the Council of Europe, which, even before the recent, intense international cooperation in this field, was perhaps the first international intergovernmental institution to bring to the attention of States the necessity of protecting the environment.

The action of non-governmental organizations ("NGOs") has also contributed to the enunciation of "soft" law principles regarding the environment. The International Law Association ("ILA"), for example, adopted an influential resolution in 1966 known as the Helsinki Rules on the Use of Waters of International Rivers which was expanded and enlarged by the same institution in 1982 with the adoption of the Montreal Rules of International Law Applicable to Transfrontier Pollution. The Institute of International Law ("IIL") has played an equally important role by promulgating resolutions on the Utilization of Non–Maritime International Waters; on the Pollution of Rivers and Lakes and International Law; and on Transboundary Air Pollution.

In this context, the regional commissions of the United Nations play a role that could become more important in the near future. This is reflected in the recent Bergen Declaration adopted on May 14, 1990, by thirty environment ministers at a meeting convened jointly by the United Nations Economic Commission for Europe and the government of Norway. One can find in the terms of this declaration different considerations, guidelines and principles which echo those of other contemporary declarations such as the Declaration on Human Responsibilities for Peace and Sustainable Development proposed a year earlier by

Costa Rica, or the Declaration of Environmental Interdependence adopted by the Interparliamentary Conference on the Global Environment in Washington, D.C. on May 2, 1990.

b. The Soft Lawmaking Process

As with other areas in which "soft" law plays a part, repetition is a very important factor in the international environmental "soft" lawmaking process. All of the international bodies referred to above should be viewed, as far as their recommendatory action in this field is concerned, as transmitting basically the same message. Cross-references from one institution to another, the recalling of guidelines adopted by other apparently concurrent international authorities, recurrent invocation of the same rules formulated in one way or another at the universal, regional and more restricted levels, all tend progressively to develop and establish a common international understanding. As a result of this process, conduct and behavior which would have been considered challenges to State sovereignty twenty years ago are now accepted within the mainstream.

Let us examine, by way of illustration, four substantial examples of this phenomenon in the context of international environmental "soft" law. The first example involves the principle of information and consultation. This principle usually manifests itself as an obligation whereby States must inform and consult one another, prior to engaging in any activity or initiative that is likely to cause transfrontier pollution, so that the country of origin of the potentially dangerous activity may take into consideration the interests of any potentially exposed country. From a more general point of view, the principle covers the additional duty to provide to these potentially exposed States all relevant and reasonably available information concerning transboundary natural resources and transfrontier environmental interference.

The principle of information and consultation has been reiterated for almost twenty years by the different organizations cited above as well as by others. It can be found in many recommendations or resolutions: the aforementioned 1978 UNEP Draft Principles of Conduct on Shared Natural Resources; UN General Assembly resolutions 3129 (XXVIII) of December 1973 and 3281 (the Charter of Economic Rights and Duties of States); OECD Council recommendations on Transfrontier Pollution and the Implementation of a Regime of Equal Right of Access and Non–Discrimination in Relation to Transfrontier Pollution. In the context of NGO activity, the same rule is contained in the already-mentioned ILA resolutions of 1966 and 1982, as well as in the IIL resolutions of 1961, 1979 and 1981.

The second example concerns, on a more specific level, environmental impact assessment procedures. These procedures are directly related to the principle of information and consultation since they make it possible to estimate the impact of a planned activity on the environment of a neighboring State. Adherence to such procedures has been recommended several times by various sources, such as the 1978 UNEP Draft Principles of Conduct on Shared Natural Resources and the 1981 UNEP Conclusions of the Study on the Legal Aspects Concerning the Environment Related to Off–Shore Mining and Drilling within the Limits of National Jurisdiction. These UNEP recommendations have both been endorsed by the UN General Assembly in its Resolution No. 37/27 of March 24, 1983, on International Co-operation in the Field of the Environment, as well as in its resolution No. 37/7 on the World Charter for Nature (Articles eleven and sixteen).

Support for the same procedures can be found in the 1974 OECD Declaration on Environmental Policy and other recommendations adopted by the same organization. A faithful echo of the same rule can also be found in a 1985 EEC Council Directive pertaining to the Assessment of the Effects of Certain Public and Private Projects on the Environment. It would be a mistake, however, to conclude that this type of rule has only been recognized by industrialized countries; it was, for instance, recognized and recommended by the Economic Commission for Africa Council of Ministers in 1984.

The third example of repetition in the international "soft" lawmaking process is provided by the principle of non-discrimination according to which States should not substantially differentiate between their own environment and those of other States as regards the elaboration and application of laws and regulations in the areas of prevention, reparation and repression of pollution. With regard to instances of transfrontier inland pollution, States must also allow persons concerned with such occurrences access to available administrative and judicial proceedings.

The principle of non-discrimination has been introduced quite systematically in OECD Council recommendations concerned with transfrontier pollution, in particular, recommendation C(77)28. One can also find this principle in the 1978 Draft Principles Relating to Shared Natural Resources and in several of the other recommendations already mentioned. It is interesting to note that, in this area and on the basis of those programmatory instruments, the same principle has been introduced in a "hard" instrument, namely the 1982 UN Convention on the Law of the Sea.

The final and most recent example of convergence between non-legally-binding texts of different natures and origins is to be found in contemporary approaches to the problems surrounding the protection of the global atmosphere. The number of "soft" instruments calling on the world community to strengthen international cooperation on the basis of a new "global" approach and the perception of the world atmosphere as part of the "common heritage of mankind" has been increasing in the past two to three years. If this phenomenon continues, it will likely have some legal consequence, particularly with regard to the environmental responsibility that the present generation has vis-à-vis future generations.

The contemporary "common heritage" approach is reflected, for example, in the UN General Assembly Resolution 43/53 of January 27, 1989, in which it is recognized "that climate change is a common concern of mankind...." A second reference can be found in the statement agreed to by the International Meeting of Legal and Policy Experts hosted by the Canadian government in Ottawa on February 20–22, 1989. This statement takes the form of a draft convention on the protection of the world climate and global atmosphere. It declares that "the atmosphere ... constitutes a common resource of vital interest to mankind." Another text which can be cited in this context is the Hague Declaration of March 11, 1989, signed by representatives of twenty-four States at the Hague at the initiative of France, the Netherlands and Norway. The Declaration states that it is the "duty of the community of nations vis-a-vis present and future generations to do all that can be done to preserve the quality of the atmosphere." Support for the same approach can also be found in the different reports of the Intergovernmental Panel on Climatic Change established in 1989 under the co-sponsorship of the World Meterological Organization and UNEP and in the Decision on Global Climate Change adopted by the UNEP Governing Council in May 1989.

These various texts appear to define a new trend which may eventually lead to the negotiation of a new general multilateral convention on the protection of the world climate. The adoption of such a convention has been called for, in particular, by the Noordwijk Declaration on Climate Change adopted at a ministerial conference of representatives of sixty-seven governments from every part of the world in November 1989.

[Such a convention addressing climate change, based on the principle that climate change was a "common concern" of humankind, was opened for signature at the 1992 Rio Conference on Environment and Development. A subsequent protocol was negotiated in Kyoto, Japan in December 1997.]

But these "soft" instruments, as is the case with others usually referred to in the general context of the "soft" law phenomenon, are in many respects rather heterogeneous in nature. Their substantial convergence does not create a new binding rule of international environmental law. This remark leads both to methodological problems, which will be dealt with later in this article, and necessitates a more thorough examination of the forms and content of "soft" environmental law.

2.   THE FORMS AND CONTENT OF SOFT ENVIRONMENTAL LAW

The examples provided earlier illustrate that much of "soft" law is incorporated within "soft" (i.e., non-binding) instruments such as recommendations and resolutions of international organizations, declarations and "final acts" published at the conclusion of international conferences and even draft proposals elaborated by groups of experts. It is thus generally understood that "soft" law creates and delineates goals to be achieved in the future rather than actual duties, programs rather than prescriptions, guidelines rather than strict obligations. It is true that in the majority of cases the "softness" of the instrument corresponds to the "softness" of its contents. After all, the very nature of "soft" law lies in the fact that it is not in itself legally binding.

Although this assertion is generally correct, it remains necessary both from a conceptual and, in certain situations, a practical point of view, to distinguish clearly between the substance and the instrument—they are not necessarily always in perfect accordance with one another. Two kinds of situations present themselves in which this type of potential incoherence can be observed. First, there are cases where the content of a formally non-binding instrument has been so precisely defined and formulated that, aside from the precaution of using "should" instead of "shall" to determine the proper behavior for concerned States, some of its provisions could be perfectly integrated into a treaty.

Moreover, it is extremely interesting to observe in practice, as the author has had the opportunity of doing in his capacity as legal advisor to the OECD Transfrontier Pollution Group (1974–80), that Member States' delegations approach the negotiation of those provisions with extreme care, just as if they were negotiating treaty provisions. Such behavior suggests that States do not view such "soft" recommendations as devoid of at least some political significance, if not, in the long term, any legal significance. In fact, for a few of these "soft" instruments, some States consider it necessary to formulate reservations to such texts, just as if they were creating formal legal obligations. The most famous example of this is the UN 1974 Charter on Economic Rights and Duties; this is also true for the OECD Council Recommendation C(74)224 on Some Principles Concerning Transfrontier Pollution [as well as for the Rio Declaration on Environment and Development].

Second, an increasing number of treaty provisions can be found in which the wording used is so "soft" that it seems impossible to consider them as creating a precise obligation or burden on States parties. The number of conventions in which such evasive prescriptions are enunciated appears to be increasing: for instance, many provisions of Part XII of the 1982 UN Convention on the Law of the Sea (e.g., Articles 204(1) and 217(2)); the majority of the articles of the 1979 Economic Commission for Europe Convention on Long–Range Transboundary Air Pollution; as well as the provisions of the 1985 Vienna Convention on the Protection of the Ozone Layer.

Such a situation can sometimes, if not often, be explained in light of the difficulties with which delegations have been confronted in trying to reach an agreement. This is certainly the case in the second of the last three cited examples. Another factor which explains the inclusion of "soft" provisions in the text of a treaty can, however, be identified: with regard to difficult and complex areas of concern, the protection of the ozone layer for example, States realize from the outset of negotiation that easy solutions do not exist and that too rigidly-defined obligations would only lead to inefficiency by deterring a significant number of concerned governments from ratifying the convention.

Thus, States prefer to define, by common agreement, programs of action which invite them to adopt, starting at the national level, adequate material and regulatory measures. One can assume that such a prudent strategy has been encouraged by the example furnished by the positive results often produced when States effectively take into account the guidelines proposed in some of the resolutions or recommendations defined within the framework of international organizations. One perceives, then, a sort of "soft" law "contagion" which affects the transformation of "soft" instruments into "hard" ones.

Even given the accuracy of this assertion, one must recognize that it does not simplify the task of defining the scope and nature of the "soft" law. It does, however, lead to the conclusion that the criteria used to identify "soft" law should no longer be formal, i.e., based on the compulsory or non-compulsory character of the instrument, but instead substantial, i.e., dependent on the nature and specificity of the behavior requested of the State, whether or not it is included in a legally binding instrument. To be more rigorous, if the norm is included in a non-binding instrument, it should be considered presumptive evidence of the "soft" nature of the norm; at the same time, the "hard" or "soft" nature of the obligation defined in a treaty provision should not necessarily be identified on the sole basis of the formally binding character of the legal instrument in which the concerned norm is integrated and articulated.

These observations lead to the conclusion that the identification of "soft" law, significant at least because it may potentially become "hard" law in the near or distant future, should derive from a systematic case-by-case examination in which a variety of factors are carefully considered. These factors would include, among others: the source and origin of the text (governmental or not); the conditions, both formal and political, of its adoption; its intrinsic aptitude to become a norm of international law; and the practical reaction of States to its statement. These criteria should be applied, for example, to the various texts mentioned earlier calling for a mankind-oriented and global approach to world climate protection. In other words, one must avoid grouping texts of remote origins and character in order to demonstrate the development of an emerging "soft" rule.

3. THE LEGAL EFFECT OF SOFT ENVIRONMENTAL LAW

Two different sets of problems must be considered with respect to a discussion of the legal impact of international environmental "soft" law. The first set of problems concerns the question of the influence of "soft" law on the general international law-making process. How and under what conditions do some "soft" norms become compulsory? The second set of problems is twofold: even before their evolution into "hard" laws, do existing "soft" regulations have any influence on the definition of the content of international law? If so, does this have any impact on the international responsibility of States for the commission of wrongful acts?

Again, it should be clearly noted that the international law of the environment is explored and used as an example here merely because it provides a fertile ground for analysis and not because it is a field in which "soft" law presents any particular theoretical or technical problems.

a. Soft Law and General International Law

The law-making process is a long-term process. This remains true even if the notion of "long-term" is a relative one—the prevailing conception of "long-term," as hinted by the International Court of Justice in the Continental Shelf case, is one which has tended to shorten over the last decades.

As early as Roman times, jurists spoke of *leges in statu nascendi* [law in process of forming, literally "in the state of being born."] (not to be confused with lex ferenda law as it should be). It is sufficiently clear that the creative process of customary rules enables different heterogeneous elements to participate in the crystallization of the new custom. It becomes equally obvious that the accumulation of recurrent resolutions can greatly contribute to the creation of such a new general customary rule. It should also be noted in this context that positive cross-references between *treaties* and *resolutions* (both types of instruments incorporating the same rule at the same time) are of real importance in this respect.

In the context of "soft" instruments, one could say, using the classical working of legal theory in regard to the creation of custom, that the cumulative enunciation of the same guideline by numerous nonbinding texts helps to express the *opinio juris* of the world community.

This last observation, although different in character, should be viewed in light of the one made in 1986 by the International Court of Justice with regard to several important resolutions adopted by the UN General Assembly: "The effect of consent to the text of such resolutions ... may be understood as an acceptance of the validity of the rule or set of rules declared by the resolution by themselves." Military and Paramilitary Activities in and Against Nicaragua (Nicar. v. U.S.), 1986 ICJ 4, 100 (Merits of June 27). One should certainly not systematically go that far in interpreting the frequent repetition of "soft" rules in different kinds of texts. However, taking into account the criteria outlined earlier at the end of Part I of this article, one should pay careful attention to indications of a new *opinio juris* likely to emerge among nations thanks to the frequent reiteration of certain identical principles.

This conclusion is somewhat problematic, however, if one takes into account the rather dogmatic concepts and legal categories presented by the classical theory identifying the "two elements" of customary law (practice and *opinio juris*) when analyzing the "soft" law phenomenon. This classical theory has been systematized by the positivist school to explain a law-making process in which the measure and conception of time was substantially different, and where the rule of law appeared as the end product of a long and careful ripening process.

Today, even given the heterogeneity of the contemporary law-making process, it would not be completely accurate to conclude that the relative importance of these two elements has been reversed so that the voicing of *opinio juris* takes precedence over the material element of State practice. It would be more consistent with the reality of this process to say that, through the channel of steadfast institutionalized negotiation, State practice is modified by the constant pressure of diplomacy. In this respect, general international law-making is no longer, if it has ever effectively been, a process characterized by the explicit recognition of "general practice accepted as law." As a result, "soft" law must also be viewed in light of the interaction of competing legal strategies pursued by different categories of States whose varied interests are not always considered by other States to be converging. In any event, it is evident that a substantial part of "soft" law today, in an impressionistic way, describes part of the "hard" law of tomorrow.

The normative emission of international institutions plays a catalytic role in this process. For example, one could argue convincingly that the information and consultation requirement has nearly reached the point beyond which it should be considered a customary norm. Evidence of this can be found in both the methodology and materials used by several groups of experts charged with the task of establishing draft codification articles describing the content of the general international law of the environment. Both the 1987 recommendations of the World Commission on Environment and Development Expert Group on Environmental Law and the ILC draft articles on the law of non-navigational uses of international watercourses provide major examples. Both drafts have been supported by reports and commentaries which both take into account and largely rely upon "soft" instruments emanating from international organizations, even if not necessarily consistently confirmed by actual and unanimous State practice.

This last element makes it difficult to identify among the codified principles the ones which already belong to *lex lata* and those which are still to be considered as *lex ferenda*. It does, however, sufficiently establish that the codifying bodies consider "soft" law at the very least to be a reliable indicator of actual trends in contemporary international environmental law-making. Rules and principles such as regular exchange of information, prior notification of planned activities capable of damaging the environment in a neighboring country, equal right of access to and non-discrimination between actual or potential victims of transfrontier pollution behind and across the frontiers, have been largely launched by "soft" instruments which are now explicitly cited and recalled as valuable materials in the codification process.

b.   Soft Law and International Responsibility

A "soft" norm can help to define the standards of good behavior corresponding to what is nowadays to be expected from a "well-governed State" without having been necessarily consecrated as an in force customary norm. Among those standards of good behavior which constitute the type of due diligence that can be expected from a State in the context of international cooperation are: prior consultation before enforcing a regulation or empowering a private person to undertake an activity which might create a significant risk of transfrontier pollution; early international notification of a polluting accident; due recourse to procedures of impact assessments; and nondiscrimination between and equality of access for victims of both national and transfrontier pollution. These and other standards of behavior were recognized in the context of a due diligence definition by the arbitrators in the famous Alabama Case.

Another indirect effect of international "soft" law regulations should not be underestimated: the impact of these "soft" norms on national legislatures and national legislation as reference models which anticipate internationally-grounded State obligations emerging in the near future.

When evaluating due diligence in the context of determining State responsibility under international law, one must consider the standards established by "soft" norms, although not (or not yet) compulsory in themselves. No single one of these standards by itself, it seems, should suffice in identifying illicit

State activity in instances where it is ignored. Such a deficiency should, however, create a presumption of illegality and, in instances where a number of such norms are violated, constitute evidence of an illicit act.

Of course, the evaluation of compliance with such standards of "good behavior" falls within the jurisdiction of international judges or arbitrators. From the point of view of international environmental law, it is disturbing to note the absence of recent arbitral or jurisdictional awards; States do not appear to be very keen on settling disputes in this area by entrusting them to independent third parties. Each State knows that rules of law and material situations are reversible and that a country victimized by transboundary pollution today could very well end up being the polluter of tomorrow.

Nevertheless, international standards based on "soft" law are not only available for use by international judges or arbitrators. They can also be of great help in every day inter-State diplomacy. They may also effectively be taken into account by municipal judges in evaluating the legality, with regard to international law, of any internal administrative action having had or able to have some damaging impact on the environment beyond national boundaries. Furthermore, municipal judges may take these international standards into account in order to give a correct interpretation to very generally formulated international obligations.

Albeit indirect, the legal effect of "soft" law is nevertheless real. "Soft" law is not merely a new term for an old (customary) process; it is both a sign and product of the permanent state of multilateral cooperation and competition among the heterogeneous members of the contemporary world community

The existence of "soft" law compels us to re-evaluate the general international law-making process and, in doing so, illuminates the difficulty of explaining this phenomenon by referring solely to the classical theory of formal sources of public international law.

QUESTIONS AND DISCUSSION

1. Some theorists have begun to question whether emerging principles of international environmental protection may represent either a new way to make customary soft law, or a new type of law altogether. See the earlier excerpt from Daniel Bodansky, *Customary (and Not So Customary) International Environmental Law*, *supra* at p. 310, where he argues that Principle 21 and similar environmental principles are not customary international law but a new kind of law—declarative international law—that may guide State behavior but has little normative force. What is the relation of Bodansky's declarative law to Dupuy's soft law?

2. The excerpts in this chapter from Charney, Handl, Dupuy, and Bodansky all argue that traditional ways of developing customary international law may not be appropriate for international environmental law. Whether it is the "soft law" of Dupuy, the "universal law" of Charney, the "general international law" of Handl, or the "declarative law" of Bodansky, the point is the same: States are creating generally applicable guidelines—if not always legally binding norms—in a variety of new and important ways, and they serve a variety of important functions.

3. How do voluntary standards fit into this scheme? Chapter 17 discusses the rapid growth of voluntary corporate standards of environmental conduct and environmental management being adopted by corporations around the world. Could nearly universal adoption of a management standard indicate the development of customary law? Consider this question, as well, in the treatment of international standards by trade agreements such as the Technical Barriers to Trade Agreement discussed in Chapter 15.

––––––––

B.   THE UNITED NATIONS AND LAW-MAKING

The United Nations is re-shaping how international law is made, both generally and with respect to environmental law. The following excerpt describes some of the law-making authority and practice of UN bodies.

Oscar Schachter, *United Nations Law*, 88 AM.J.INT'L. L. 1–6 (1994)

Neither the United Nations nor any of its specialized agencies was conceived as a legislative body. Their charters and governing instruments contemplated that their objectives would be carried out mainly through recommendations aimed at coordinating (or "harmonizing") the actions of their member states. The authority to impose mandatory rules was limited (with some exceptions) to the internal administration of the organization in question. Member states were free, of course, to create new law or repeal existing law through the traditional processes of treaty and customary law. What was not fully realized at first is that the UN political bodies–though denied legislative power–could act like legislatures by adopting lawmaking treaties and declarations of law. Their recommendations did not have to remain merely requests or wishes if the collective will of governments supported more authoritative outcomes. In retrospect, it is not surprising that the major intergovernmental bodies have utilized their recommendatory authority to achieve binding law where that served their aims and enjoyed the requisite political support. Although it has often been emphasized that they are not legislatures, most UN organs have acted much like parliamentary bodies in their proceedings. Moreover, member governments and international officials have often called for solutions to the world's problems through new law and legal regimes. Thus, demand stimulated supply and in various ways texts of legal import were produced. They have affected virtually every area of human life that cuts across national boundaries and even, in some important ways, matters entirely within states. * * *

The most obvious instrument of lawmaking in the UN system is the multilateral "norm-creating" treaty. Hundreds of such treaties have been concluded; they were initiated, negotiated and adopted by UN organs or by international conferences under the aegis of a UN body. Their subjects have been as diverse as the functions of the UN organizations. Many deal with problems that are technical and seemingly arcane. Others are addressed to problems affecting ordinary people: health, food, education, human rights, pollution, transportation, television. All, even the most technical, are the products of a political process, usually marked by conflicting interests and concerns over grants of power.

Their genesis in the UN system involves an apparent "democratization" of lawmaking markedly different from traditional treaty making and contemporary treaty negotiation by a few states. In the UN system the rule is that all member states have a right to participate in the negotiation and adoption process. They generally do so on the basis of "sovereign equality." Decisions are usually taken by simple or two-thirds majority vote. An obvious problem is that states are not, in fact, equal in population, capability, power or interest. Weighted voting is employed by a few institutions, especially financial bodies. Other solutions have also been found, for example, negotiating processes that take account of the uneven distribution of capability and impact. In many cases, voting has been dispensed with in efforts to achieve consensus. This solution is not always acceptable to majorities (as shown by the Law of the Sea Conference), and even the desirability of obtaining adherence to the treaty by important states may not overcome the weight of a firm majority.

A question of some consequence and subtlety is whether UN lawmaking treaties bind states that choose not to become parties and refrain from the acts that signify adherence. In a formal sense, those states are not bound by the treaty. However, some treaties such as codification conventions express preexisting customary law. Some "crystallize" emergent rules of law. Still others generate custom embodying the treaty rules, the treaty itself "attracting" practice. A much-cited example is the 1982 UN Convention on the Law of the Sea, which includes several important articles expressing "new custom" recognized during the period the treaty was being negotiated. The UN Covenants on Human Rights and other major human rights treaties have also been regarded by some jurists as new customary law or recognized general principles of law with respect to some of the rights expressed. To support that conclusion, it is argued that government statements in UN bodies and resolutions of UN organs are evidence of state practice and opinio juris. This position departs from the traditional view of custom as requiring uniformities of state practice revealed in behavior and the claims of states against other states. Some writers and occasionally governments have maintained that some general multilateral treaties adopted by a UN body constitute strong evidence of "generally accepted rules" binding on all. These varied arguments have led a critical French jurist to observe that the requirement of consent to treaties has not been "frontally assaulted but cunningly outflanked."

A related problem of lawmaking is raised by [UN General Assembly] resolutions that embody declarations of principles and rules of international law. They are regarded as especially significant when adopted without dissent. For example, the Declaration on Principles of International Law concerning Friendly Relations and Co-operation among States in Accordance with the Charter of the United Nations was adopted by consensus in 1970, after a decade of debate and negotiation. While its language is quite general, it elaborates the major principles of international law in the UN Charter, particularly on use of force, dispute settlement, nonintervention in domestic affairs, self-determination, duties of cooperation and observance of obligations, and "sovereign equality." Generally referred to as the "Friendly Relations Declaration," it has become the international lawyer's favorite example of an authoritative UN resolution.

The legal arguments that resolutions may be authoritative evidence of binding international law usually rest on characterizing them as (1) "authentic" interpretations of the UN Charter agreed by all the parties, (2) affirmations of recognized customary law, or (3) expressions of general principles of law accepted by states. These reasons fit into the three sources of international law contained in Article 38 of the Statute of the International Court of Justice. The Court itself has recognized the legal force of several UN declarations in some of its advisory opinions. But some caution is called for. Even a UN declaration adopted unanimously will have diminished authority as law if it is not observed by states particularly affected. Negative votes by a few concerned states to a declaratory resolution also cast doubt on its authority as presumptive evidence of existing law. We cannot apply a categorical rule to all cases; distinctions must be drawn that take into account the nature and importance of the legal rule in question. Declarations that affirm the prohibitions against aggression, genocide, torture or systematic racial discrimination would not be deprived of their legal value because they were not uniformly observed. On the other hand, declarations asserting or affirming legal rules of a less peremptory character would not prevail over evidence that such rules were not generally observed by affected states.

UN recourse to recommendatory authority to declare law is a reflection of the perceived need for more law in many fields. The traditional case-by-case process of customary law cannot meet the necessity for common action to deal with the numerous problems raised by technological developments, demographic and environmental impacts, changing attitudes as to social justice, or the many requirements of international business. While all of these matters could be dealt with by multilateral treaties, the treaty processes are often complicated and slow. In contrast, UN resolutions can be more readily attained. As we have noted, the curious result is that new law is often considered as "custom" or as based on already-recognized general principles. The law-declaring resolutions are not only a response to felt needs; they are also a consequence of the opportunity afforded by voting rules in the UN system. Weaker states, which constitute a majority in UN bodies, use their voting strength for lawmaking to improve their position vis-a-vis the more powerful states. However, these efforts are often limited by the realities of power and politics. It has come to be recognized that resolutions by majorities on economic matters are likely to remain "paper" declarations without much effect unless genuinely accepted by states with the requisite resources to carry them out. * * *

Taking the UN system as a whole, we can see that a large area of international regulation has been developed by the specialized agencies though this is not widely known. Many of these agencies use innovative techniques to extend the range of international regulation. The techniques are of particular interest since they significantly relax the traditional principle that no state is bound without its consent. An example is a provision for the amendment of treaties by treating silence as consent and allowing for "opting out." Another is an unusual provision that new decisions pursuant to a treaty may be binding on all members of the organization solely by virtue of their membership. Moreover, in practice, texts that are only recommendatory have as much effect as formal rules in channeling state conduct. "Codes" that lay down standards and prescribe action, but are not legally mandatory, may be incorporated into domestic law by states. An example is the Codex Alimentarius produced jointly by the Food and Agriculture Organization and the World Health Organization prescribing standards "for all principal foods." Many governments have incorporated the codex into their national regulations; others have explained why they could not accept the codex as such, but have nonetheless been influenced by its requirements, as have food growers and transporters. The codex is a notable example of a formally nonbinding instrument that has become effective law for many countries throughout the world on a matter of practical importance to all peoples.

A survey of UN lawmaking should not ignore the internal law of the international bodies. Rules of procedure, especially on rights of participation and voting, form an important part of internal law although they are based on the constituent treaties of the organizations. This is also true of the rules on financial responsibility. The international civil service has its own body of law, developed in part by the quasi-judicial administrative tribunals. Apart from these differentiated legal regimes are the special rules adopted by UN organs to govern the activities of various subsidiary bodies, including armed peace-keeping forces, humanitarian missions and regulatory bodies. These areas of internal law may have significant impact on the relations between UN organs and governmental agencies or private persons.

———

C. NON-CONSENSUS DECISION-MAKING

Geoffrey Palmer, *New Ways to Make International Environmental Law*

86 AM.J.INT'L.L. 259, 270–78 (1992)

Treaty Law and the Rule of Unanimous Consent

There are about 160 coequal sovereign states in the international community. At the moment, it is not possible to arrive at a system that includes legislation, enforcement and third-party adjudication unless all the nations agree. In their strongest form, arguments about sovereignty are used unhesitatingly by political decision makers to tell decision makers of other nations to keep out of matters that are not their business. What Brierly called the "incubus" of sovereignty still sits heavily upon the body of international law. As Brierly said, it stands "for something in the relations of states which is both true and very formidable." But it does not stand for everything. It is not an absolute. It cannot mean a state of international lawlessness, or a condition of permanent paralysis. * * *

Political decision makers in the international arena dwell little on theory and even less on jurisprudence. They want something practical that works. If they can be convinced that a broadly acceptable regime can be worked out that will offer the prospect of solving the problems, they will not quibble about the surrender of some sovereignty. The greater challenge is to design a regime that will satisfy them and meet their very real political needs.

The ordering of the affairs of nations in their relationships with one another has steadily eroded the power of nations to please themselves. The complexity of the modern world and the plethora of intricate treaties, sometimes on highly specialized subjects, that constitute the basis of most international obligations today have whittled away sovereignty. Political decision makers most assuredly do not think of themselves as inhabiting a world where they can take any actions they choose regardless of the consequences to other nations and people. They may choose to defend their actions on the basis of sovereignty, but they understand increasingly their mutual interdependence.... These conditions greatly affect the context in which the instruments of international law function. The formal rules tend to lag behind the contemporary reality. We need lawmaking methods that recognize the new reality.

Conventional international law takes time to develop. It is frequently cumbersome. Treaties have first to be negotiated, then ratified. This process can sometimes be so slow and time-consuming that events overtake the convention. * * *

The difficulties are greatly multiplied when virtually every country in the world is involved. Multilateral conventions will always be difficult to negotiate—they require extensive multilateral diplomacy. Nothing can change that. But the essential difficulty in making treaty law lies elsewhere. It is in the requirement of unanimous consent. * * *

[As Lord McNair, a leading writer on the law of treaties, once observed:]

> [W]e touch here one of the weakest spots in the now existing system of States, and it must be admitted that no national society which is not equipped with legislative and administrative machinery for effecting changes could hope to hold together for long. International society is clearly groping its way towards the creation of some escape from the present effect of the rule requiring the consent of all the parties affected by a change, and some of the attempts to mitigate that rule should be noted.
> * * *

Since he wrote, there have been developments in the way some international organizations create norms. In some cases, the world is well on the way toward having the international legislative process Lord McNair thought so necessary. Consequently, it is now possible for nations that do not agree with a particular norm to be bound by it. Unanimous consent is not required. * * *

Frederic Kirgis, Jr., has analyzed these "non-traditional" rule-making techniques of several international organizations, including the International Labour Organisation, the Universal Postal Union, the World Health Organization, the International Civil Aviation Organization and the International Maritime Organization. He finds that the use of such a supertreaty system is most advanced in the case of the ILO. But he also finds that "[t]he constituent instruments of most specialized agencies contain amendment procedures that bind all members if some fraction—often two-thirds—of the total membership adopts and ratifies the amendment." For example, for nonstate aircraft over the high seas, binding rules are made by a two-thirds majority in a representative ICAO body.

Another increasingly used procedure requires only tacit consent to the creation of new norms. Rules are adopted subject to being disallowed if a specified percentage of the membership blocks them. There is often an escape procedure for individual members as well. For example, the ICAO Council, which has thirty-three members, adopts international standards and recommended practices covering a wide range of matters relating to safety in the air. Standards become effective when adopted by two-thirds of the Council, unless in the meantime a majority of member states disapprove. While states that find it impracticable to comply may opt out, they will face considerable peer pressure to comply. The standards are in fact widely complied with.

Professor Kirgis's analysis points out just how far some of these agencies have moved from the traditional model and how effective these untraditional techniques are in developing new norms that change the conduct of the members. While it cannot be said these developments presage the imminent establishment of a world legislature, they do have clear applicability to global environmental problems. There is ample precedent for developing institutions with the power to make rules after following established procedures that are binding on the members of the organization. These developments are neither fresh nor novel. They have been going on for years and nations appear to feel comfortable with them. The organization whose constitution and procedures appear to have the most to offer for the environment is the ILO. * * *

The proleptic method of avoiding the rule of unanimous consent has already been employed in the environmental sphere in the Montreal Protocol on Substances that Deplete the Ozone Layer of 1987. Some little-noticed innovations were made that certainly go beyond the technical and change the rule of unanimous consent in dramatic ways. * * *

The Montreal Protocol requires an assessment and review of the control measures beginning in 1990 and "at least every four years thereafter." Parties must convene panels of experts and the secretariat must report the conclusions of these experts to the parties. On the basis of those assessments, the parties are to decide whether adjustments to the ozone-depleting potentials of the controlled substances should be made and "what the scope, amount and timing of any such adjustments and reductions should be." If adjustments are proposed, six months' notice must be given. All of that seems quite unexceptional until Article 2(9)(c) is reached:

> In taking such decisions, the Parties shall make every effort to reach agreement by consensus. If all efforts at consensus have been exhausted, and no agreement reached, such decisions shall, as a last resort, be adopted by a two-thirds majority vote of the Parties present and voting representing at least fifty per cent of the total consumption of the controlled substances of the Parties.

The next provision makes it explicit that the decisions taken are binding on all the parties. This provision, however, applies only to adjustments in ozone-depleting substances mentioned in the annex to the Montreal Protocol. To add new substances, as the London conference did, requires application of the ordinary rule.

This most instructive departure from the unanimous consent rule was further fine-tuned in the 1990 London Amendments to the Montreal Protocol. The developing countries objected to the weighting provisions, which gave power to those representing 50 percent of the combined total consumption of the substances (which meant that a few large chlorofluorocarbon-producing countries could block a new agreement). The final sixteen words of the provision above were deleted and the following words substituted: "a majority of the Parties operating under paragraph 1 of Article 5 present and voting and a majority of the Parties not so operating present and voting." In effect, this new provision gives a veto to both developed and developing countries. A two-thirds majority is required and it must include a simple majority of each group. Future adjustments should be easier to achieve than before.

The issue obviously arises as to what a nation will do if it does not agree with an adjustment made in accordance with the foregoing rule. The country is bound if it is a party to the Protocol. Withdrawal under the Vienna Convention itself is permitted at any time after four years from the date on which the Convention entered into force, which was September 22, 1988. Withdrawals can take effect one year after receipt of written notification. As amended in London in 1990, the Protocol now provides that any party may withdraw from it at any time after four years of assuming the obligations of reducing the consumption of controlled substances. The withdrawal takes effect one year after giving notice. Consequently, while there are fetters on the withdrawal of nations that do not get their own way, the system is nonetheless vulnerable to withdrawal.

On the other hand, there are provisions prohibiting nations that are parties to the treaty system from exporting controlled substances to nations that are not parties, or importing from them. These prohibitions may in time be extended to trade in products produced with controlled substances but not containing them. While these measures will certainly tend to discourage nations from trying to thwart the system, they are not certain to prevent it.

The ozone system is also vulnerable because of the nations that do not join.... The ozone example demonstrates that, while a framework treaty can be used to set standards later by means that do not involve unanimous consent, the consequences of the rule of consent cannot be avoided altogether.

The argument is strengthened by considering the record of ratification of the Montreal Protocol. As of September 1991, there were eighty countries that had ratified the Vienna Convention, seventy-three the Montreal Protocol, and only five the London Amendments. . . . Certainly, incentives should be provided for countries to sign, but what if the incentives do not work? Large countries with the capacity to frustrate the system of reductions may be inclined to do so. There are any number of reasons why nations may see an advantage in not complying with the general will.

The most persuasive analogy is with the power of acquisition the state has over land for public works in domestic law. If the power does not exist, the state must rely on private contracts. Large sums of money go to holdouts. Those who sell early may only get the market price. Those who hang on to the end will demand extraordinarily high prices for selling. That sort of behavior cannot be tolerated in the international sphere, where the future of the planet is in issue. * * *

There is more support for getting rid of the rule of unanimous consent than may be thought. That attitude was strikingly in evidence at the International Summit on the Protection of the Global Atmosphere, held at The Hague in March 1989. The twenty-four nations that signed the Hague Declaration laid down some new principles that would constitute a new approach to making international rules and enforcing them. Of course, the instrument that put them forward is of a soft law character.

For a document containing such far-reaching principles, the Hague Declaration was not difficult to negotiate, primarily because the drafters took care to stay at the level of general principle. Details on these issues could well have spawned substantial disagreement. Heads of government met to consider a draft that had been put together. I doubt that it took longer than five hours for the text to be amended and debated. As international negotiations go, it was a very easy one. * * *

The Hague Declaration calls for the "development of new principles of international law including new and more effective decision-making and enforcement mechanisms." Since the problems are planet-wide, solutions can only be devised on a global level. In designing the solutions, the different levels of development of nations must be taken into account. The declaration states that most of the emissions affecting the atmosphere originate in industrialized countries. Special obligations will have to be undertaken to assist developing countries. In concrete terms the nations that signed the declaration acknowledged several principles and undertook to promote them. What they undertook to do by a soft law method was to promote a new species of hard law. The first casualty was to be the rule of unanimous consent. They thus pledged themselves to promote

> [t]he principle of developing, within the framework of the United Nations, new institutional authority, either by strengthening existing institutions or by creating a new institution, which, in the context of the preservation of the earth's atmosphere, shall be responsible for combating any further global warming of the atmosphere and shall involve such decision-making procedures as may be effective even if, on occasion, unanimous agreement has not been achieved.

In terms of traditional international law, this statement is radical. It is the embryo of a legislative system for international environmental issues. Nations that do not agree with a rule and will not consent to its inclusion in a treaty may be obliged to follow the rule anyway. This principle opens up the opportunity for the creation of a new organization with the ability to create norms by special majorities. If state sovereignty is the foundation of international law, the Hague Declaration may be the first nail in its coffin. * * *

For twenty-four nations to accept a principle that involves the abolition of the unanimous consent rule is surely a significant and novel event in the life of international law. Some of the nations that espoused this principle are powerful and influential actors in international politics. France is a permanent member of the Security Council. Germany and Japan are among the foremost industrial powers on the planet. India is the most populous democracy.

Acceptance that nations can be bound without their consent opens the door to a quite different legal context from that in which international law has developed. It offers the prospect of fashioning an international legislative process for global environmental issues. It offers the practical means of securing the higher standards that may be required by an objective assessment of the scientific evidence, however politically inconvenient a particular measure may be for an individual country. The search for the lowest common denominator in environmental matters, as in others, can be a grinding and laborious diplomatic search that hungrily consumes energies and time—both of which are too scarce. Nations that do not want to change can sit tight and avoid change. A recurring theme at international conferences is the last-minute effort to persuade one country or another to go along. Language is softened, material is removed, and much of substance is lost. Herein lies a fundamental difference between the legislative and the diplomatic process. With legislation everyone is bound by the outcome, including those who do not agree. With treaties those who do not agree simply do not become bound.

————————

QUESTIONS AND DISCUSSION

1.   Do you agree with Palmer that the requirement of unanimous consent is at the root of international law's failure to address complex environmental issues effectively? How does Palmer's view compare with that of Allott in *Reconceiving the World*?

2.   Compare Palmer's suggestions with the earlier discussion of general principles. Which offers the best strategy for binding non-party states to environmental treaties?

3.   As Geoffrey Palmer points out, one of the biggest obstacles to developing strong international environmental treaties is the requirement for unanimous consent of States. This consent requirement often leads to a "lowest-common-denominator" approach to new multilateral environmental treaties. In an effort to achieve consensus among 100 or more negotiating States, negotiators must set the standards and goals of a new treaty at a level acceptable to the most recalcitrant participants. In the "Ottawa Process," which resulted in the conclusion of a multilateral treaty on landmines in less than a year, the Canadian government pioneered a new approach to multilateral treaty-making that avoids the problem of the "lowest-common-denominator."

Many States wanted to move the landmines issue to the UN Conference on Disarmament which operates by consensus and is notorious for slow negotiations. Fearing that this process would delay even modest action, Canada and a group of primarily Nordic countries decided to abandon the consensus approach and simply develop a treaty banning landmines among like-minded States.

Canada sponsored the first negotiating conference in Ottawa, Ontario in October 1996. At the conclusion of the conference, fifty governments pledged support for a rapid and complete ban on landmines. When the process resumed again in September 1997 at a conference in Oslo, Norway, more than 100 nations participated. At the conclusion of the Oslo Conference, the parties adopted a "Convention on the Prohibition of the Use, Stockpiling, Production and Transfer of Anti–Personnel Mines and on their Destruction." The treaty opened for signature on December 3, 1997. Over 120 nations have signed the treaty. Among those that have not yet agreed to sign are the United States, China, India, Pakistan, and North and South Korea.

Both before and during the "Ottawa Process," NGOs played an important role in developing international consensus around the landmine ban. Indeed one NGO, the International Campaign to Ban Landmines and its coordinator, Jody Williams, were awarded the 1997 Nobel Peace Prize for their work on the issue.

SECTION IV. BUILDING CONSENSUS

A recurring theme in this chapter has been the need to build consensus around new international environmental norms, whether in the course of negotiating a multilateral treaty, encouraging the development of new customary international law, or seeking support for a new norm of soft law. As we have seen, consensus among States is the critical determinant of international law, at least according to the dominant positivist view (even general principles—which do not depend on consent—nonetheless depend on some agreement as to which concepts have achieved this status.) In spite of the obstacles, non-State actors are now routinely playing a key role in the consensus-building process. This is particularly true in international environmental law. The following paragraphs briefly describe modern consensus-building processes.

International environmental issues are uniquely science driven. Science plays an indispensable role in identifying global environmental threats, in analyzing those threats, and in developing solutions. Science is also crucial to building consensus for action. Consider, for example, the comprehensive reports of the WMO/UNEP working group on ozone depletion, discussed with respect to treaty-making above. More than 150 scientists from around the world contributed to those reports. Before the first was completed, the international community could not even agree that there was a problem. The WMO/UNEP reports demonstrated not only that ozone depletion was occurring, but that it was occurring more rapidly and more dramatically than had been predicted. These reports convinced all but the most recalcitrant States that rapid and collective action was required and helped States establish the goals of that action. This example holds for most, if not all, international environmental issues, from climate change (see discussions of the 2,500 scientists on the International Panel on Climate Change in Chapter 9), to biodiversity loss, to persistent pollutants. One of the keys to building consensus, therefore, is developing a critical mass of scientific authority to show that an environmental problem is emerging, and also to help determine what preventive or corrective action is appropriate.

Another route to building consensus is through the promotion of soft law. Recall that in Judge Weeramantry's separate opinion in the *Gabcikovo* case he relied on dozens of soft law instruments and other sources to argue that sustainable development is a general principle of international law. Each soft law instrument, be it a conference declaration, a UN resolution, a statement of principles by an international organization, or a voluntary guideline adds to the critical mass of authority behind a new environmental norm. This increases the likelihood that *opinio juris* will emerge around the norm, or more modestly, that States will be prompted to incorporate the norm in future binding instruments. Thus, an important and effective way to strengthen international environmental law is to encourage international institutions, business groups, scientific organizations, NGOs, and individual States to acknowledge new principles, and to encourage States to behave consistently with them.

States themselves have been developing a new process for building consensus in the environmental field. Multilateral treaties are now routinely developed in a process that begins with a "framework" agreement, where the parties acknowledge the existence of a problem or threat, and commit to cooperative action, without undertaking substantive obligations. As knowledge and consensus grow within this framework, the agreement is supplemented by a series of protocols and amendments imposing progressively more specific and more stringent obligations on the treaty parties. The ozone regime is an important and successful model based on this approach, which is also being followed in the climate convention.

Judge Weeramantry's separate opinion in *Gabcikovo* suggests still another method for influencing the development of international environmental law: scholarship. Of course, the writings of well-respected publicists are themselves considered subsidiary means of demonstrating the law by the ICJ Statute. The comparative analysis of different legal systems and, more importantly, different cultures and traditions is also a legitimate route to the discovery of custom, and even general principles of international law. The discovery of custom and general principles can help build the common understanding essential for consent and consensus. General principles, in turn, can be influenced by natural law concepts, and this influence itself may grow in light of current environmental threats to human survival. In short, the importance of identifying universal principles as a foundation for consensus should not be underestimated.

Throughout all of these processes, there are growing opportunities for participation and influence by private citizens and NGOs. Recall, for example, that the UN General Assembly asked the ICJ for an advisory opinion on the legality of nuclear weapons because of the efforts of the World Court Project, a coalition of NGOs. And more than four million people signed a petition against nuclear weapons as evidence of the public conscience—of *public consensus*—on the desirability of banning nuclear weapons. Similar lessons can be learned from the experience of the International Campaign to Ban Landmines. The role of NGOs in international environmental law is discussed more thoroughly in Chapter 5.

As a final note, reconsider Philip Allott's article, where he proposes a re-conception of the world, a revolution where we as citizens re-conceive international law and our responsibility towards the whole of international society, as well as the biosphere. Among other things, Allott predicts that our re-conception of international society would lead to an international constitution, which would constrain abuses of power, and provide a firmer foundation for protecting the biosphere. Having read the materials in this chapter, do you agree with Allott's critique of the State-centered system of international law? More importantly, do you believe we can change that system simply by reconceiving it? Would it be *simple* to do so?

In Allott's vision of an international society where States do not monopolize international law-making—where international law does not merely reflect consent but instead more universal values of international society—what would be your role, as an international lawyer? In *State Responsibility and the Unmaking of International Law,* 29 HARV. INT'L L. J 1, 24–26, Allott "re-conceived" the international lawyer's role in this way:

> International lawyers are not the servants of governments but of international society. As lawyers they are servants not of power but of justice. It is thus the duty of international lawyers, even lawyers employed by governments, to consider not merely what is in the interest of this or that state but what is in the long-term interest of international society. More than any other kind of lawyer, international lawyers have a universalizing function. The rule which they perceive in one situation must be capable of conforming with a hypothetical rule for all situations. Customary international law has been a system of universalizing in the Rawlsian mode—universalized self-interest. [Rawls is discussed in Chapter 2].... It is the justice of capitalism.

> The future of international society—its survival and progress—will not be secured by abandoning even the limited concept of justice contained in customary international law....

> All government is a conspiracy. Good government is a conspiracy in favor of the people. Bad government is a conspiracy against the people. The modern government, seduced by Machiavelli and Hume, has made a Faustian bargain with the people under which the government has assumed power over all that science and technology make available and has taken the power over the human mind that modern mass communications make possible. Only law can have power over the government. * * *

> As governments further extend their Faustian ambitions into international society and international society becomes the main arena for the human struggle to survive and progress, the highest professional duty now rests on international lawyers to exert eternal vigilance on behalf of the people, because lawyers have power over the law, the only thing which can have power over the government. The task of the contemporary international lawyer is to redeem governments in the name of justice ... and in the name of humanity, whose interests transcend the interests of states and governments.

Do you agree with Allott about the proper role of the international lawyer and of justice? Are you up to the challenge?

Suggested Further Reading

Below are some of the major references on public international law and lawmaking

Ian Brownlie, PRINCIPLES OF PUBLIC INTERNATIONAL LAW (4th ed. 1990)

Shabtai Rosenne, PRACTICE AND METHODS OF INTERNATIONAL LAW (1984)

Christopher C. Joyner ed., THE UNITED NATIONS AND INTERNATIONAL LAW (1997)

J. Brierly, THE LAW OF NATIONS: AN INTRODUCTION TO THE INTERNATIONAL LAW OF PEACE (6th Ed. 1963)

Mark W. Janis, AN INTRODUCTION TO INTERNATIONAL LAW (3ed ed. 1999)

This is a very accessible text on international law, and students find it quite helpful.

J. BRIERLY, The Law of Nations: An Introduction to the International Law of Peace (6TH ED. 1963)

Edith Brown Weiss, ed., ENVIRONMENTAL CHANGE AND INTERNATIONAL LAW: NEW CHALLENGES AND DIMENSIONS (1992)

Collection of essays by leading scholars on various aspects of international environmental lawmaking and implementation.

INTERNATIONAL ENVIRONMENTAL TREATY-MAKING (L. Susskind, ed. 1992).

Jordan Paust, Joan Fitzpatrick, Jan Van Dyke, INTERNATIONAL LAW AND LITIGATION IN THE U.S. (2000)

CHAPTER SEVEN

PRINCIPLES AND CONCEPTS IN INTERNATIONAL ENVIRONMENTAL LAW

SECTION I.   INTRODUCTION

Despite the relatively ordered way we addressed the history of international environmental law from Stockholm to Rio in Chapter 4, the field of international environmental law for the most part has not developed in any systematic or strategic way. Rather, the field has developed *ad hoc* in response to specific environmental threats. As a result, the field consists of a large number of bilateral and multilateral treaties, each addressing a different global or regional environmental issue, and several general soft law instruments, such as the *Stockholm* and *Rio Declarations,* signed by most of the countries in the world but not intended to establish legally binding rules. A small but growing number of judicial or arbitral decisions have also addressed international environmental issues. But neither a universal declaration nor any generally applicable covenant currently establishes a binding set of principles or even a comprehensive framework for the field.

Despite the lack of any overarching instrument, a general framework for studying international environmental law exists based on concepts and principles that run through many international environmental instruments. This Chapter introduces a variety of principles and concepts, providing brief descriptions of how they may be applied in specific circumstances. For the purposes of learning international environmental law, these principles provide a measure of continuity to Parts II and III of the textbook, which address the international response to specific environmental threats and the relationship of environmental law to other international law fields, respectively. As you study each Chapter on specific environmental issues you should ask which concepts and principles are used as part of the legal response, and which are missing.

This chapter is probably best not read from beginning to end, but should be used instead as a reference for understanding the principles and concepts that appear in many of the ensuing chapters. Your understanding of these principles will also be enhanced by referring back to this chapter when addressing the problem exercises found in subsequent chapters, including for example the transboundary air pollution exercise on page 512.

A. CODIFICATION AND SOURCES OF INTERNATIONAL ENVIRONMENTAL PRINCIPLES

Beginning with the *Stockholm Declaration,* commentators have spent considerable effort identifying, elaborating and developing basic concepts and principles in international environmental law. These concepts and principles come from a wide variety of sources, including soft law instruments like the *Stockholm* and *Rio Declarations;* U.N. General Assembly Resolutions; arbitral decisions like the *Trail Smelter Arbitration,* discussed further in Chapter 9; judicial decisions of the International Court of Justice; the growing number of environmental treaties, many of which are described in Part II of the textbook; and expert commentary like that of the World Commission on Environment and Development's Legal Experts' Group, described below. Although the principles and concepts come from a wide range of sources, the following international environmental instruments are particularly important.

The 1972 *Stockholm Declaration.* The *Stockholm Declaration* was the first widely accepted effort to set forth basic concepts and principles, including the importance of integrating environment and development, of reducing or eliminating pollution, and of controlling the use of renewable and non-renewable resources. Without using the term, it helped lay the groundwork for the subsequent development of the concept of sustainable development. In many ways, the *Stockholm Declaration* is a more visionary environmental statement than the *Rio Declaration* that would come twenty years later.

Two specific elements of the *Stockholm Declaration* are worth noting with respect to the elaboration of international environmental law principles. First, Principle 1 of the *Declaration* at least implicitly suggested that there was a human right to a healthy environment. Second, Principle 21 strikes a balance between a state's sovereignty and its obligation not to cause harm to the environment of another State or of the global commons.

Principle 21 is widely viewed as reflecting customary international law, and is perhaps the most well known of all international environmental principles.

The 1982 *World Charter for Nature.* As the ten-year anniversary of Stockholm neared, many observers saw the need for a broad set of principles to reshape humanity's relationship to the natural environment. Zaire recommended to the UN General Assembly that they review a draft Charter previously developed by the IUCN, an international NGO that includes both environmental groups and wildlife agencies of governments. IUCN completed their draft in 1975, and worked to build support for it among governments. In 1982, the UN General Assembly adopted the *World Charter for Nature* with one dissenting vote (the United States). U.N.G.A. 37(VII) (1982), reprinted in the *Treaty Supplement.* Eighteen countries also abstained, including a group of Latin American nations who saw the *World Charter* as a violation of their permanent sovereignty over natural resources. The United States has never endorsed the *World Charter,* nor is it binding law even for those States that signed it. Nonetheless, the *Charter* remains an important soft law instrument in the further development of international environmental law principles, particularly as they relate to nature conservation. The *World Charter for Nature* is discussed further in Chapter 13.

The 1987 *WCED Experts Group on Environmental Law.* As part of its overall effort in reviewing development issues and the prospects for sustainable development, which culminated in the publication of *Our Common Future,* the World Commission on Environment and Development (WCED) established an Experts Group on Environmental Law. The main guidelines for the work of the Experts Group were:

1. to reinforce existing legal principles and to formulate new principles and rules of law which reflect and support the mainly anticipatory and preventive strategies which the Commission is committed to developing; * * *

2. to give special attention to *legal principles and rules which ought to be in place now or before the year 2000*; * * *

3. to consider not only principles regarding the obligations of States to reduce or avoid activities affecting the environment of other States, but also principles regarding the individual and collective responsibilities of States concerning future generations, other species and ecosystems of international significance and the global commons;

4. to prepare proposals for strengthening the legal and institutional framework for accelerating the development and application of international law in support of environmental protection and sustainable development within and among all States.

EXPERTS GROUP ON ENVIRONMENTAL LAW OF THE WORLD COMMISSION ON ENVIRONMENT AND DEVELOPMENT, ENVIRONMENTAL PROTECTION AND SUSTAINABLE DEVELOPMENT, Chairman's Introduction, at 1 (1987). The Experts Group's principles were annexed to the WCED's Report, *Our Common Future.* Among the principles were eight general principles, including for example a human right to a healthy environment as well as an obligation that States conserve the environment for the benefit of present and future generations, and twelve principles relating to transboundary natural resources and environmental interferences. These transboundary principles envisioned the reasonable and equitable use of shared resources and set forth a number of procedural principles for transboundary environmental cooperation. The principles identified by the WCED Legal Experts Group are included in the *Treaty Supplement*.

In addition to this set of principles elaborated as "Elements for a Draft Convention on Environmental Protection and Sustainable Development," the Experts Group also recommended that the United Nations prepare a new and legally-binding universal convention that "should consolidate existing and establish new legal principles, and set out the associated rights and responsibilities of States individually and collectively for securing environmental protection and sustainable development to the year 2000 and beyond." Writing in 1987, the WCED Experts Group recommended that such a convention be prepared in time to open for signature at the 1992 Rio Conference. The WCED's final report, *Our Common Future,* supported the Experts Group recommendation. *See* OUR COMMON FUTURE at 332–33. Although progress toward such a convention has been halting, the WCED Experts Group's thorough analysis and research supporting and explaining each principle has helped to build support for an eventual elaboration of a binding covenant regarding environmental law.

The 1992 *Rio Declaration.* Although not binding law, the *Rio Declaration* is recognized as an important reflection of the political consensus around international environmental principles as of 1992. As discussed in Chapter 3, the *Rio Declaration* is probably most remarkable for its integration of development concerns with environmental protection. From a strictly environmental perspective, some actually view it as a step backwards from both the *Stockholm Declaration* and the *World Charter for Nature.* On the other hand, by explicitly tackling the relationship between environment and development and particularly by reflecting the South's concerns over poverty alleviation and economic equity, the *Rio Declaration* is a more realistic articulation of the current consensus on international environmental protection and sustainable development. Because of the careful compromises found within so many of the *Rio Declaration's* principles, it is often viewed as the starting point for discussions concerning specific principles.

The 1995 *IUCN Draft Covenant on Environment and Development.* Taking a lead from the WCED's Legal Expert Group's recommendation, the IUCN Commission on Environmental Law began in 1989 to prepare a *Draft International Covenant on Environment and Development*, which they offered as a proposal for a universally binding treaty to cover environment and development issues. Although void of any official status, the *IUCN Draft Covenant* is an important elaboration of environment and development principles. The result of an intense, six-year negotiation by international environmental law experts from around the world, the draft covenant is a visionary proposal for a future treaty, and one that is being promoted by the IUCN and other international organizations and governments. The *IUCN Draft Covenant* can be found at the IUCN homepage: <http://www.iucn.org>.

QUESTIONS AND DISCUSSION

1. Many international policy makers recognize the need for further elaboration and clarification of basic principles in international environmental law, including the eventual codification of a set of binding international environmental principles. *See, e.g.,* UNEP, Position Paper on International Environmental Law Aiming at Sustainable Development, Annex I to the Final Report of the Expert Group Workshop on International Environmental Law Aiming at Sustainable Development, UNEP/IEL/WS/3/2 (Oct. 4, 1996); International Union for the Conservation of Nature's (IUCN's) Commission on Environmental Law, International Covenant on Environment and Development (March, 1995) [hereinafter IUCN Draft Covenant on Environment and Development]; Experts Group on Environmental Law of the World Commission on Environment and Development, Environmental Protection, and Sustainable Development: Legal Principles and Recommendations (1989); *see also* P. Sands, *International Law in the Field of Sustainable Development: Emerging Legal Principles,* in W. LANG, ED., SUSTAINABLE DEVELOPMENT AND INTERNATIONAL LAW (1995); D. Hunter, J. Sommer & S. Vaughan, *Concepts and Principles of International Environmental Law: An Introduction* (UNEP Environment and Trade Monograph No. 2, 1994). Nonetheless, the feasibility and desirability of codifying international environmental law into a general international environmental law covenant is hotly debated. Among the reasons given against codification are: that the process would take a long time, be contentious and result in a weak covenant, and that a general treaty would not assist in any specific context. Can you think of any specific problems that could be aided by a more settled body of international environmental law? How would the trade and environment debate be different if there were a well established set of environmental principles to weigh against the trade principles of nondiscrimination?

The *IUCN Draft Covenant's* foreword offers the following reasons in favor of a binding international agreement:

- to provide the legal framework to support the further integration of the various aspects of environment and development;

- to create an agreed single set of fundamental principles like a "code of conduct", as used in many civil law, socialist, and theocratic traditions, which may guide States, intergovernmental organizations, and individuals;

- to consolidate into a single juridical framework the vast body of widely accepted, but disparate, principles of "soft law" on environment and development (many of which are now declaratory of customary international law);

- to facilitate institutional and other linkages to be made between existing treaties and their implementation;

- to reinforce the consensus on basic legal norms, both internationally, where not all States are party to all environmental treaties, even though the principles embodied in them are universally subscribed to, and nationally, where administrative jurisdiction is often fragmented among diverse agencies and the legislation still has gaps;

- to fill in gaps in international law, by placing in a global context principles which only appear in certain places and by adding matters which are of fundamental importance but which are not in any universal treaty;

- to help level the playing field for international trade by minimizing the likelihood of non-tariff barriers based on vastly differing environmental and developmental policies;

- to save on scarce resources and diplomatic time by consolidating in one single instrument norms, which thereafter can be incorporated by reference into future agreements, thereby eliminating unnecessary reformulation and repetition, unless such reformulation is considered necessary; and

- to lay out a common basis upon which future lawmaking efforts might be developed.

IUCN Draft International Covenant on Environment & Development, (1995). Do you agree with the reasons set forth by the IUCN in defense of the need for an international binding covenant on environment and development? What other reasons might be offered in support of a binding covenant? The United States currently opposes negotiation of an international covenant. What reasons might the United States (or any other country) offer to oppose negotiation of a binding covenant?

B.   THE FUNCTIONS OF PRINCIPLES AND CONCEPTS IN INTERNATIONAL ENVIRONMENTAL LAW

Not surprisingly, given the wide range of sources for these principles and concepts and the relatively new and dynamic nature of international environmental law-making, the legal status of these concepts and principles varies. Some of them, for example the principles of good neighborliness and the obligation to resolve disputes peacefully, simply reflect the application of general international law principles to environmental issues. Others, most notably the obligation not to cause environmental harm to areas outside national jurisdiction, are now widely considered to be part of customary international environmental law, and thus binding for all states. Other concepts and principles, however, probably cannot yet be viewed as customary international law. Some of them are supported by considerable State practice, while others have just recently begun to be implemented at the national level. Some may be incorporated in legally binding instruments, including global environmental treaties, and thus may be binding on the Parties to those agreements. Virtually all of the environmental conventions negotiated since UNCED, for example, repeat many of the principles and concepts enunciated there.

Principles and concepts do not have to be binding, however, to have a significant impact on international environmental policy. The principles and concepts serve a number of other functions, as highlighted by the following hypothetical situations:

Principles provide a framework for negotiating and implementing new and existing agreements. Assume that you have been asked by Austria to represent them in negotiations over a global treaty to promote the conservation and sustainable use of the world's forests. Which international principles or concepts accepted in other contexts could help to reach consensus in the context of forests? General principles are frequently repeated in different settings. The principles apply substantively to many different international environmental issues, but their reappearance is also critical. Countries that have accepted a principle or an approach in one context may find it politically expedient to accept (or difficult not to accept) the principle in another context.

Some principles provide the rules of decision for resolving transboundary environmental disputes. Assume that you represent Austria in a dispute over the siting of a hazardous waste facility in the Czech Republic just five kilometers from the border. Your scientists tell you that both air emissions and waste discharges from the facility will harm Austria's environment. In the absence of any treaty, how would you argue Austria's case? Some of the principles outlined here place obligations on inter-State relations involving transboundary environmental disputes. In this respect, some of the principles described in this chapter may already be customary law, while others are undoubtedly still "emerging."

Some principles provide a framework for the development and convergence of national and subnational environmental laws. Assume you have been asked to provide comments on a draft environmental law of the Philippines. What internationally accepted principles, perhaps emanating from instruments signed by the Philippines, could you suggest be included in the national law? Even where principles or concepts have not yet become customary law, they can be used to put political pressure on States to apply these principles in domestic law. This process can also lead to greater harmonization of environmental norms and practices across various countries. Moreover, as described in Chapter 6 on lawmaking, customary law is formed by the consent of States as evidenced in part by State practice. The study of application of these principles in domestic law can thus further the development of customary international law.

Some principles assist in the integration of international environmental law with other fields such as international trade or human rights. Assume you must defend the United States' unilateral ban on the import of shrimp caught without turtle excluder devices (designed to protect endangered sea turtles) against a challenge in the World Trade Organization. What international environmental principles could you cite to show that your actions were consistent with international environmental law? To justify any technical violation of trade rules? What internationally recognized rights do individuals have in the environmental field?

Eventually some or all of these principles may be codified into a general covenant of international environmental law. Assume you have been asked to participate in negotiating a Universal Declaration on the Protection of the International Environment. These principles and concepts would provide a good starting point, as they are all rooted in existing international environmental instruments.

The following table (Table 1) presents an informal taxonomy of international environmental concepts and principles organized according to their different purpose and function in the field. Some of the principles serve more than one function. Note, too, that some of these principles are discussed in subsequent chapters.

TABLE 1: Functions of International Environmental Law Principles and Concepts

I. Principles Shaping Global Environmental and Developmental Instruments

1) Right to Life and a Healthy Environment*
2) State Sovereignty
3) Right to Development
4) Sustainable Development**
5) Common Heritage of Humankind
6) Common Concern
7) The Obligation Not to Cause Environmental Harm
8) Intergenerational and Intragenerational Equity
9) Common but Differentiated Responsibilities
10) Precautionary Principle
11) Duty to Assess Environmental Impacts
12) Principle of Subsidiarity
13) Right of Public Participation*

II. Principles Relating to Transboundary Environmental Disputes

1) Peaceful Resolution of Disputes***
2) Good Neighborliness and Duty to Cooperate
3) The Duty Not to Cause Environmental Harm
4) State Responsibility
5) Duty to Notify and Consult
6) Duty to Assess Environmental Impact Assessment
7) Equitable Utilization of Shared Resources****
8) Non–discrimination of Environmental Harms
9) Equal Right of Access to Justice*

III. Principles for Developing National Environmental Laws

1) Duty to Implement Effective Environmental Legislation***
2) Polluter and User Pays Principle
3) Pollution Prevention
4) Public Participation*
5) Access to Information*
6) Duty to Assess Environmental Impacts
7) Access to Justice

IV. Principles Governing International Institutions

1) Duty to Assess Environmental Impacts
2) Public Participation*
3) Access to Information*
4) Sustainable Development

---

* These principles are discussed in Chapter 16 (Human Rights and the Environment).

** This principle is discussed in Chapter 5 (History) and Chapter 6 (Lawmaking).

*** These principles are discussed in Chapter 8 (Implementation).

**** This principle is discussed in Chapter 11 (International Rivers and Lakes).

SECTION II. PRINCIPLES SHAPING INTERNATIONAL ENVIRONMENTAL LAW AND POLICY

A. STATE SOVEREIGNTY

Sovereign States are the primary subjects of international law, and as we saw in Chapter 6 on the lawmaking process, State sovereignty is important to international environmental law—indeed all international law—because of the fundamental tension between a State's interest in protecting its independence (i.e. its sovereignty) and the recognition that certain problems, in this case regional and global environmental problems, require international cooperation. Most international environmental treaties by their very nature constrain a State's sovereignty.

State sovereignty in the legal sense signifies independence—that is, the right to exercise, within a portion of the globe and to the exclusion of other States, the functions of a State such as the exercise of jurisdiction and enforcement of laws over persons therein. Sovereignty reflects the broad sweep of responsibilities, rights, authorities and powers that international law confers when it confers "Statehood."

Critical in the environmental context is the extent of territorial sovereignty. According to noted international scholar Ian Brownlie:

> In spatial terms the law knows four types of regime: territorial sovereignty, territory not subject to the sovereignty of any state or states and which possesses a status of its own (mandated and trust territories, for example), the *res nullius,* and the *res communis.* Territorial sovereignty extends principally over land territory, the territorial sea appurtenant to the land, and the seabed and subsoil of the territorial sea. The concept of territory includes islands, islets, rocks, and reefs. A *res nullius* consists of the same subject-matter legally susceptible to acquisition by states but not as yet placed under territorial sovereignty. The *res communis,* consisting of the high seas (which for present purposes include exclusive economic zones) and also outer space, is not capable of being placed under state sovereignty. In accordance with customary international law and the dictates of convenience, the airspace above and subsoil beneath state territory, the *res nullius,* and the *res communis* are included in each category.

IAN BROWNLIE, PRINCIPLES OF PUBLIC INTERNATIONAL LAW 107 (4th ed. 1990). Thus territorial sovereignty extends to the geographic borders of the country and to the underlying subsoil as well as the airspace overhead. States have sovereignty over inland waters, including groundwater, wholly within their boundaries and have substantial sovereign rights with respect to shared watercourses. Sovereignty over resources also extends outward through the Exclusive Economic Zone (EEZ) determined under the *Law of the Sea Convention* to be 200 nautical miles from the coast.

National sovereignty over the development of natural resources located within the State has been reaffirmed in many multilateral agreements, international declarations and resolutions. For example, the UNESCO Convention for the Protection of the World Cultural and Natural Heritage, while obliging contracting States to co-operate in the protection of certain components of cultural and natural heritage, emphasizes full respect for the sovereignty of States in which territory the cultural and natural heritage is situated. *UNESCO World Heritage Convention*, Article 6. Similarly, the 1992 *Biodiversity Convention* affirms that States have sovereign rights over their biological resources and the authority to regulate access to genetic resources through national legislation. *Biodiversity Convention*, Article 15; *see also Stockholm Declaration*, Principle 21; *Rio Declaration*, Principle 2.

Another manifestation of State sovereignty was the principle that all States enjoyed permanent sovereignty over the natural resources occurring within their territory. The principle emerged in the 1960s and 1970s in response to the concerns of former colonial States that most of the economic benefits received from the exploitation of natural resources in developing states were accruing to foreign corporations. Through the principle of permanent sovereignty over natural resources, the developing States reaffirmed their right to control the terms and conditions of how their resources would be exploited.

The contours of permanent sovereignty over natural resources are set forth in the following General Assembly Resolution:

G.A. Res. 2158 (XXI), U.N. GAOR, Twenty-first session (1966) (Sovereignty)

The General Assembly, * * *

Recognizing that the natural resources of the developing countries constitute a basis of their economic development in general and of their industrial progress in particular,

Bearing in mind that natural resources are limited and in many cases exhaustible and that their proper exploitation determines the conditions of the economic development of the developing countries both at present and in the future,

Considering that, in order to safeguard the exercise of permanent sovereignty over natural resources, it is essential that their exploitation and marketing should be aimed at securing the highest possible rate of growth of the developing countries,

Considering further that this aim can better be achieved if the developing countries are in a position to undertake themselves the exploitation and marketing of their natural resources so that they may exercise their freedom of choice in the various fields related to the utilization of natural resources under the most favourable conditions,

Taking into account the fact that foreign capital, whether public or private, forthcoming at the request of the developing countries, can play an important role inasmuch as it supplements the efforts undertaken by them in the exploitation and development of their natural resources, provided that there is government supervision over the activity of foreign capital to ensure that it is used in the interests of national development.

1. *Reaffirms* the inalienable right of all countries to exercise permanent sovereignty over their natural resources in the interest of their national development, in conformity with the spirit and principles of the Charter of the United Nations and as recognized in General Assembly resolution 1803 (XVII);

2. *Declares*, therefore, that the United Nations should undertake a maximum concerted effort to channel its activities so as to enable all countries to exercise that right fully;

3. *States* that such an effort should help in achieving the maximum possible development of the natural resources of the developing countries and in strengthening their ability to undertake this development themselves, so that they might effectively exercise their choice in deciding the manner in which the exploitation and marketing of their natural resources should be carried out;

4. *Confirms* that the exploitation of natural resources in each country shall always be conducted in accordance with its national laws and regulations;

5. *Recognizes* the right of all countries, and in particular of the developing countries, to secure and increase their share in the administration of enterprises which are fully or partly operated by foreign capital and to have a greater share in the advantages and profits derived therefrom on an equitable basis, with due regard to the development needs and objectives of the peoples concerned and to mutually acceptable contractual practices, and calls upon the countries from which such capital originates to refrain from any action which would hinder the exercise of that right;

6. *Considers* that, when natural resources of the developing countries are exploited by foreign investors, the latter should undertake proper and accelerated training of national personnel at all levels and in all fields connected with such exploitation;

7. *Calls upon* the developed countries to make available to the developing countries, at their request, assistance, including capital goods and know-how, for the exploitation and marketing of their natural resources in order to accelerate their economic development, and to refrain from placing on the world market non-commercial reserves of primary commodities which may have an adverse effect on the foreign exchange earnings of the developing countries.

This 1966 Resolution on Sovereignty was one of a series of General Assembly Resolutions extending through the 1960s and 1970s that developing countries promoted in an effort to create a New International Economic Order (NIEO). As was discussed in Chapter 5, UN General Assembly resolutions are viewed primarily as non-binding recommendations, but if widely accepted can reflect customary law. The NIEO resolutions, however, were typically opposed by the United States and other industrialized countries.

State sovereignty, including its manifestations as territorial sovereignty and permanent sovereignty over natural resources, is not absolute. It is in fact challenged all the time in international law. For example, most of the international law of human rights is intended to place certain minimum conditions on a State's behavior toward individuals. In the environmental context, State sovereignty is subject to the general duty, not to harm the interests, including environmental interests, of other States (discussed below in Section II.K. of this chapter). More broadly, the emergence of the concept of a common concern of humankind (discussed below in Section II.D.) may present a significant challenge to State sovereignty. As our knowledge of the ecological interrelatedness of the planet broadens, more activities or resources may qualify as "common concerns" of international society, which in turn provides conceptual justification for increasing international regulation. For example, some observers argue that a State's sovereign right to pursue its own development path may now be conditioned to reflect the goal of sustainable development. *See Rio Declaration*, Principle 3 (modifying the right to development to include intergenerational equity).

———

QUESTIONS AND DISCUSSION

1. Despite the increasing recognition of the need for international cooperation in resolving transnational and global environmental issues, the principle of sovereignty over environment and development issues has been reaffirmed in many international agreements, declarations and resolutions. In this regard, recall the developing countries' opposition to making environmental issues a focus of international cooperation, prior to the Stockholm Conference. Among other things, the State sovereignty principle should remind us of the paramount importance of national level actions for protecting the environment and achieving sustainable development, as well as the critical need to build environmental capacity within all countries.

2. Determining the extent and scope of a State's sovereignty is not quite as straightforward as one might expect. For example, sovereign air space is generally considered to reach to the altitude achievable by ordinary manned flight. The actual height of this altitude changes, however, as technology allows manned aircraft to achieve higher and higher altitudes. *See* U.N. Doc. A/AC.105/C.2/7 (1970)); C. Stone, The Gnat Is Older Than Man 35 (1993). This is not just an academic exercise, because the rights to air space are increasingly valuable. For example, the value of equatorial orbits led the equatorial nations to claim that their sovereignty included the space orbits over their territories. Their claim has never been recognized by other nations.

3. Among the rights that attach to statehood is that of sovereign equality; that is, that all States are treated equally as legal persons in international law. According to the *Declaration on Principles of International Law Concerning Friendly Relations and Co-operation Among States in Accordance With the Charter of the United Nations, Annex,* U.N.G.A. Resolution 2625 (XXV) (Oct. 24, 1970) [hereinafter 1970 *UN Declaration on International Law*]:

> All States enjoy sovereign equality. They have equal rights and duties and are equal members of the international community, notwithstanding differences of an economic, social, political or other nature.

> In particular, sovereign equality includes the following elements:

>   1. States are juridically equal;

>   2. Each State enjoys the rights inherent in full sovereignty;

>   3. Each State has the duty to respect the personality of other States;

>   4. The territorial integrity and political independence of the State are inviolable;

>   5. Each State has the right freely to choose and develop its political, social, economic and cultural systems.

The *1970 UN Declaration on International Law* provides evidence of a consensus within the United Nations on the meaning of certain principles in the UN Charter, and is thus widely considered to reflect customary international law.

4. Recall the discussion in Chapter 6 of Hart's "minimum content" of natural law that societies need for human survival. Which universal principles could you argue limit a State's sovereignty over its environment?

B.   RIGHT TO DEVELOPMENT

At different times, the concept of a right to development has reflected several different approaches: first, the interest of developing countries to control and enhance their own development; second, the right of all peoples to enjoy the right of self-determination, and third an individual's right to enjoy a minimum quality of life. Because of these different conceptions of the right to development, its application can be confusing. The right to development, like the related concept of permanent sovereignty over natural resources, is a manifestation of the developing countries' aspirations for achieving greater economic independence and forming a more equitable international economic order. Protecting the right of all countries and peoples to choose their own development path, even if that means exploiting or over-exploiting natural resources, is often a primary part of developing country agendas in international environmental negotiations. In addition, the right to a minimum level of development is tied closely to calls for economic justice and the need to alleviate poverty.

The UN General Assembly endorsed the right to development in its 1986 Declaration on the Right to Development, UNGA Res. 41/128, Annex (Dec. 4, 1986). Most countries endorsed the Declaration, with the exception of the United States. As you read the following excerpt, consider which of the different conceptions of a right to development seems to prevail in the Declaration.

Declaration on the Right to Development, A/RES/41/128, Annex (December 1986)

The General Assembly, . . .

Recognizing that development is a comprehensive economic, social, cultural and political process, which aims at the constant improvement of the well-being of the entire population and of all individuals on the basis of their active, free and meaningful participation in development and in the fair distribution of benefits resulting therefrom, . . .

Recalling the right of peoples to self-determination, by virtue of which they have the right freely to determine their political status and to pursue their economic, social and cultural development,

Recalling also the right of peoples to exercise, subject to the relevant provisions of both International Covenants on Human Rights, full and complete sovereignty over all their natural wealth and resources, . . .

Recognizing that the creation of conditions favourable to the development of peoples and individuals is the primary responsibility of their States,

Aware that efforts at the international level to promote and protect human rights should be accompanied by efforts to establish a new international economic order,

Confirming that the right to development is an inalienable human right and that equality of opportunity for development is a prerogative both of nations and of individuals who make up nations,

Proclaims the following Declaration on the Right to Development:

Article 1

1. The right to development is an inalienable human right by virtue of which every human person and all peoples are entitled to participate in, contribute to, and enjoy economic, social, cultural and political development, in which all human rights and fundamental freedoms can be fully realized.

2. The human right to development also implies the full realization of the right of peoples to self-determination, which includes, subject to the relevant provisions of both International Covenants on Human Rights, the exercise of their inalienable right to full sovereignty over all their natural wealth and resources.

Article 2

1. The human person is the central subject of development and should be the active participant and beneficiary of the right to development.

2. All human beings have a responsibility for development, individually and collectively, taking into account the need for full respect for their human rights and fundamental freedoms as well as their duties to the community, which alone can ensure the free and complete fulfilment of the human being, and they should therefore promote and protect an appropriate political, social and economic order for development.

3. States have the right and the duty to formulate appropriate national development policies that aim at the constant improvement of the well-being of the entire population and of all individuals, on the basis of their active, free and meaningful participation in development and in the fair distribution of the benefits resulting therefrom.

Article 3

1. States have the primary responsibility for the creation of national and international conditions favourable to the realization of the right to development.

2. The realization of the right to development requires full respect for the principles of international law concerning friendly relations and co-operation among States in accordance with the Charter of the United Nations.

3. States have the duty to co-operate with each other in ensuring development and eliminating obstacles to development. States should realize their rights and fulfil their duties in such a manner as to promote a new international economic order based on sovereign equality, interdependence, mutual interest and co-operation among all States, as well as to encourage the observance and realization of human rights.

Article 4

1. States have the duty to take steps, individually and collectively, to formulate international development policies with a view to facilitating the full realization of the right to development.

2. Sustained action is required to promote more rapid development of developing countries. As a complement to the efforts of developing countries, effective international co-operation is essential in providing these countries with appropriate means and facilities to foster their comprehensive development.

* * *

Article 6

* * *

3. States should take steps to eliminate obstacles to development resulting from failure to observe civil and political rights, as well as economic, social and cultural rights.

* * *

Article 8

1. States should undertake, at the national level, all necessary measures for the realization of the right to development and shall ensure, inter alia, equality of opportunity for all in their access to basic resources, education, health services, food, housing, employment and the fair distribution of income. Effective measures should be undertaken to ensure that women have an active role in the development process. Appropriate economic and social reforms should be carried out with a view to eradicating all social injustices.

2. States should encourage popular participation in all spheres as an important factor in development and in the full realization of all human rights.

The following excerpt from Ian Brownlie helps clarify the history of the right to development as well as some of the politics surrounding adoption of the 1986 Declaration.

IAN BROWNLIE, THE HUMAN RIGHT TO DEVELOPMENT, 1–2, 22–23 (1989)

2. The political and moral imperatives behind the value now described as the 'right to development' are twofold. The first is that the individual State should be able to control its own economy and thus to develop in its own way. The second is the idea that economic development as such is inadequate and the performance of an economic system should be related to qualitative criteria based upon human rights standards: excellence is not to be calculated exclusively in accordance with economic criteria. * * *

53. The original motivation behind the concept of the right to development was the need to enhance the implementation of existing human rights standards and to stress the interdependence of civil and political rights, on the one hand, and the economic and social rights on the other hand. The ethical quantities behind the thinking included the fundamental nature of development, the international duty of solidarity for development, moral interdependence, economic interdependence, the maintenance of peace, and the moral duty to make reparation to developing countries for the period of colonial exploitation (see the Report of the Secretary–General, Doc. E/CN.4/1334, 2 January 1979, pp. 20–28). * * *

55. The right to development, as presented in the Declaration of 1986 and elsewhere, reflects the idea of entitlement and the corresponding duties, particularly of States. This is of major significance. However, it fails, almost com-

pletely, to give structure and content to the concept of economic justice. The *modus operandi* offered is fairly obscure but, in so far as it can be discerned, it consists partly of the insistence on the implementation of existing human rights standards, and partly of the duty of States to cooperate with each other in order to create conditions favourable to the realisation of the right to development.

56.   Nothing is said about specific strategies for achieving levels of economic justice. No reference is made to the duty to provide development assistance as such. The Charter of Economic Rights and Duties of States is not mentioned once, and the establishment of a New International Economic Order receives but a single mention (in the preambular paragraphs). No doubt the relative absence of specificity was the political price to be paid for attracting a very low score of contrary votes and abstentions.

57.   The focus on human rights (as a sort of flag of convenience) has had the result that the *inter-State* connotations of economic equity have been weakened. Indeed, the focus on human rights may very well have increased the excuses for not giving economic aid, or for suspending existing programmes, as a form of non-forcible counter-measure on the basis that the potential recipient is not applying one or more human rights standards.

58.   The extent to which the economic aspect of development and development assistance has been played down in the Resolution of 1986 is evidenced by the relative absence of *"developing* States" from the cast of subjects and, or, beneficiaries of the right to development. The principal exception is to be found in Article 4(2) [of the 1986 UN Resolution], which provides that: 'Sustained action is required to promote more rapid development of developing countries. As a complement to the efforts of developing countries effective international co-operation is essential in providing these countries with appropriate means and facilities to foster their comprehensive development (and there is a reference also in Article 7). However, generally speaking, the emphasis is not on a polarity between developed and developing States, as it was in the resolutions of 1974 concerning the New International Economic Order and the Charter of Economic Rights and Duties of States.

In recent years, the United Nations has continued its efforts to promote the right to development, with a series of resolutions reaffirming the 1986 *Declaration*. The following UN General Assembly Resolution adopted in 2001 reflects the United Nations' current conception of the right to development.

The Right to Development, UNGA Res. No. 55/108, March 13, 2001

The General Assembly, * * *

Recalling that the Declaration on the Right to Development confirmed that the right to development is an inalienable human right and that equality of opportunity for development is a prerogative both of nations and of individuals who make up nations, * * *

1.   *Reaffirms* the importance of the right to development for every human person and all peoples in all countries, in particular the developing countries, as an integral part of their fundamental human rights, as well as the potential contribution that its realization could make to the full enjoyment of human rights and fundamental freedoms;

2. *Recognizes* that the passage of more than fifty years since the adoption of the Universal Declaration of Human Rights demands the strengthening of efforts to place all human rights and, in this context, the right to development in particular, at the top of the global agenda;

3. *Reiterates* that:

(a) The essence of the right to development is the principle that the human person is the central subject of development and that the right to life includes within it existence in human dignity with the minimum necessities of life;

(b) The existence of widespread absolute poverty inhibits the full and effective enjoyment of human rights and renders democracy and popular participation fragile;

(c) For peace and stability to endure, national action and international action and cooperation are required to promote a better life for all in larger freedom, a critical element of which is the eradication of poverty;

4. *Reaffirms* that democracy, development and respect for human rights and fundamental freedoms, including the right to development, are interdependent and mutually reinforcing, and in this context affirms that:

(a) The development experiences of countries reflect differences with regard to both progress and setbacks, and that the development spectrum has a wide range, not only between countries but also within countries;

(b) A number of developing countries have experienced rapid economic growth in the recent past and have become dynamic partners in the international economy;

(c) At the same time, the gap between developed and developing countries remains unacceptably wide and developing countries continue to face difficulties in participating in the globalization process, and many risk being marginalized and effectively excluded from its benefits;

(d) Democracy, which is spreading everywhere, has raised development expectations everywhere, that their non-fulfilment risks rekindling non-democratic forces, and that structural reforms that do not take social realities into account could destabilize democratization processes;

(e) Effective popular participation is an essential component of successful and lasting development;

(f) Democracy, respect for all human rights and fundamental freedoms, including the right to development, transparent and accountable governance and administration in all sectors of society, and effective participation by civil society are an essential part of the necessary foundations for the realization of social and people-centred sustainable development;

(g) The participation of developing countries in the international economic decision-making process needs to be broadened and strengthened. . . .

———

QUESTIONS AND DISCUSSION

1. Developing countries also brought their assertion of the right to development to UNCED and succeeded to a great extent in ensuring that the *Rio Declaration* gave the right to development equal or perhaps even greater recognition than any obligations to protect the environment. Principle 3 of the *Rio Declaration,* for example, reads: "The right to development must be fulfilled so as to equitably meet developmental and environmental needs of present and future generations." This is immediately followed by Principle 4, which reads: "In order to achieve sustainable development, environmental protection shall constitute an integral part of the development process and cannot be considered in isolation from it." Consider the following analysis from Professor Ileana Porras regarding these two principles:

> Many developed country delegates opposed the recognition of a right to development implied in Principle 3. There were two main lines of argument:
>
> (1) no such right existed (i.e. no such right had yet been recognized by the international community);
>
> (2) even if there were such a right, it was a limited right, constrained by natural limits (i.e. the limit of natural resources and that of the ecosystem to restore itself) and constrained by the principle of equity which required sustainable development.
>
> Finally, developed countries argued that Principles 3 and 4 should be combined. In insisting on their separation, developing country negotiators intended to ensure that the right to development would not be transformed into a right to "sustainable development."
>
> The meaning of these two principles is likely to be debated for years. On the one hand, Principle 4 provides that "environmental protection *shall* constitute an integral part of the development process" (emphasis added). On the other hand, this mandatory requirement is qualified by the preceding phrase "[i]n order to achieve sustainable development". Ambiguity remains as to whether the phrase "[i]n order to achieve sustainable development" is intended to be read as requiring States to pursue "sustainable development" or whether it simply sets up the definition of "sustainable development" in the mode of an aspiration. The juxtaposition of the two principles, however, suggests that not all development need be "sustainable" as the right to development set out in Principle 3 is unconditional, except to the extent that the purpose of the right to development is described as "to equitably meet the developmental and environmental needs of present and future generations". In considering the relationship between development and environment, the Rio Declaration thus appears to give pre-eminence to development. Environment and development are equal partners in "sustainable development" but the right to development comes before sustainable development.

Ileana Porras, *The Rio Declaration: a New Basis for International Cooperation,* in PHILIPPE SANDS, GREENING INTERNATIONAL LAW 25 (1994). Do you agree with Professor Porras' interpretation of the *Rio Declaration?* Does, for example, the conditioning of the right to development on meeting "environmental needs" in Principle 3 signal a more significant departure from the existing view of the right to development than recognized in the above passage? Do any other parts of the *Rio Declaration* shed light on the relationship or hierarchy between development and sustainable development? Has the right to development been transformed to a right to sustainable development?

3. The U.S. government persistently objects to the right to development. In signing Principle 3 of the *Rio Declaration*, the United States attached the following interpretative statement:

> The United States understands and accepts the thrust of principle 3 to be that economic development goals and objectives must be pursued in such a way that the development and environmental needs of present and future generations are taken into account. The United States cannot agree to, and would disassociate itself from, any interpretation of principle 3 that accepts a "right to development," or otherwise goes beyond that understanding. The United States

does not, by joining in consensus on the Rio Declaration, change its long-standing opposition to the so-called "right to development." Development is not a right. On the contrary, development is a goal we all hold, which depends for its realization in large part on the promotion and protection of human rights set out in the Universal Declaration of Human Rights.

A/Conf.151/26/Rev.1 (vol. II). Do you agree with the U.S. position? Since Rio, the U.S. position has been refined somewhat and the United States now appears to support an individual's right to develop to his or her full potential. The United States still resists the right of development as a right of States to demand a certain level of development or, for example, to demand foreign assistance or technology transfers. Perhaps this, too, is changing. When then-Vice President Al Gore spoke at the negotiations for the Kyoto Protocol to the Climate Change Convention, he said: "Developing countries understandably need strong economies to develop. That is their right." Does Gore's statement provide any support that the United States accepts the right to development as a legal principle?

4. The right to development (as well as the related principle of permanent sovereignty over natural resources, described above) are rooted in two different concerns of the United Nations: (a) the economic development of underdeveloped countries and (b) human rights and self-determination of peoples. These two concerns have sometimes led to uncertainty as to whether the principles apply to States or to peoples. Compare, for example, the 1986 UN Resolution on the Right to Development, primarily aimed at individual rights, to the 1966 Resolution on Permanent Sovereignty over Natural Resources, which seems to address primarily the rights of States.

Consider, too, Article 22.1 of the African Charter on Human and Peoples' Rights, which states that "All *peoples* shall have the right to their economic, social and cultural development with due regard to their freedom and identity and in the equal enjoyment of the common heritage of mankind." (Emphasis added.) Similarly, Article 25 of the UN Covenant on Economic, Social and Cultural Rights as well as Article 47 of the UN Covenant on Civil and Political Rights emphasize the right of all peoples to benefit from their natural resources: "Nothing in the present Covenant shall be interpreted as impairing the inherent right of all peoples to enjoy and utilize fully and freely their natural wealth and resources." What practical significance does it make whether the right to sovereignty over natural resources is a human right, a right of peoples or of States?

―――――――

C.   COMMON HERITAGE OF HUMANKIND

State sovereignty and the principles and rights that derive from it have historically been applied to the natural resources within a State. Yet, over half of the world's surface area lies outside the national borders of any one State. Those areas beyond the limits of national jurisdiction—the high seas, the sea-bed, Antarctica, outer space, and possibly the outer atmosphere, including the ozone layer—are frequently referred to as the "global commons." For resources in these areas outside the territorial reach of States, the concept of sovereignty does not readily apply. For many global commons resources, most notably the high seas fisheries, the general rule has been the right of capture—i.e. whoever captures a fish or other resource has the right to it. Concerned that this right of capture penalizes developing and land-locked states, participants in the Law of the Sea Convention and other negotiations perceived a need for a new conceptual framework to address resources in the global commons. This framework became known as the "common heritage of humankind". Although still important conceptually, the application of this principle today is largely limited to Antarctica, outer space and the moon, certain cultural landmarks, and possibly certain plant genetic resources.

An early expression of the common heritage of humankind addressed cultural and natural landmarks. The preamble of the *UNESCO Convention on World Heritage* states:

> Deterioration or disappearance of any ... cultural and natural heritage constitutes a harmful impoverishment of the heritage of all nations of the world, ... [P]arts of the cultural and natural heritage ... need to be preserved as part of the world heritage to mankind.

Later the concept of common heritage was applied to outer space, the moon and other celestial bodies. *See Treaty on Principles Governing the Activities of States in the Exploration and Use of Outer Space, Including the Moon and Other Celestial Bodies, done* January 27, 1967, 610 U.N.T.S. 205(1967), *reprinted in* 6 I.L.M. 386 (1967) [referred to as the *1967 Outer Space Treaty*]; *Agreement Governing the Activities of States on the Moon and Other Celestial Bodies, done* Dec. 5, 1979 [referred to as the *1979 Moon Treaty*]. The *Moon Treaty* provides that the peaceful exploration and exploitation of the Moon shall be carried out for the benefit of all humankind, including future generations. What general characteristics of the common heritage of humankind can be gleaned from the following passages of the *1979 Moon Treaty?*

Article 3

1. The moon shall be used by all States Parties exclusively for peaceful purposes. * * *

Article 4

1. The exploration and use of the moon shall be the province of all mankind and shall be carried out for the benefit and in the interests of all countries, irrespective of their degree of economic or scientific development. Due regard shall be paid to the interests of present and future generation as well as to the need to promote higher standards of living and conditions of economic and social progress and development.... * * *

Article 6

1. There shall be freedom of scientific investigation on the moon by all States Parties without discrimination of any kind, on the basis of equality and in accordance with international law.

2. In carrying out scientific investigations and in furtherance of the provisions of this Agreement, the States Parties shall have the right to collect on and remove from the moon samples of its mineral and other substances. Such samples shall remain at the disposal of those States Parties which caused them to be collected and may be used by them for scientific purposes. States Parties shall have regard to the desirability of making a portion of such samples available to other interested States Parties and the international scientific community for scientific investigation. States Parties may in the course of

scientific investigation also use mineral and other substances of the moon in quantities appropriate for the support of their missions. * * *

Article 7

1. In exploring and using the moon, States Parties shall take measures to prevent the disruption of the existing balance of its environment whether by introducing adverse changes in that environment, by its harmful contamination through the introduction of extra-environmental matter or otherwise. States Parties shall also take measures to avoid harmfully affecting the environment of the earth through the introduction of extraterrestrial matter or otherwise. * * *

Article 11

1. The moon and its natural resources are the common heritage of mankind, which finds its expression in the provisions of this Agreement and in particular in paragraph 5 of this article.

2. The moon is not subject to national appropriation by any claim of sovereignty, by means of use or occupation, or by any other means.

3. Neither the surface nor the subsurface of the moon, nor any part thereof of natural resources in place, shall become property of any State, international intergovernmental or non-governmental organization, national organization or non-governmental entity or of any natural person. The placement of personnel, space vehicles, equipment, facilities, stations and installations on or below the surface of the moon, including structures connected with its surface or the subsurface of the moon or any areas thereof. The foregoing provisions are without prejudice to the international regime referred to in paragraph 5 of this article.

4. States Parties have the right to exploration and use of the moon without discrimination of any kind, on a basis of equality and in accordance with international law and the terms of this Agreement.

5. States Parties to this Agreement hereby undertake to establish an international regime, including appropriate procedures, to govern the exploitation of the natural resources of the moon as such exploitation is about to become feasible. * * *

6. In order to facilitate the establishment of the international regime referred to in paragraph 5 of this article, State Parties shall inform the Secretary-General of the United Nations as well as the public and the international scientific community, to the greatest extent feasible and practicable, of any natural resources they may discover on the moon.

7. The main purposes of the international regime to be established shall include:

 (a) The orderly and safe development of the natural resources of the moon;

 (b) The rational management of those resources;

 (c) The expansion of opportunities in the use of those resources;

 (d) An equitable sharing by all States Parties in the benefits derived from those resources, whereby the interests and needs of the developing countries, as well as the efforts of those countries which have contributed either directly or indirectly to the exploration of the moon, shall be given special consideration.

The common heritage principle gained further prominence with the drafting of Part XI of the 1982 UN Law of the Sea Convention. Seeking to institute a common management regime for the deep sea bed, Articles 136, 137 and 140 of the Convention state:

> The Area and its resources are the common heritage of mankind.... No state shall claim or exercise sovereignty or sovereign rights over any part of the Area or its resources.... All rights in the resources of the Area are vested in mankind as a whole.... [T]he Authority shall provide for the equitable sharing of financial and other economic benefits derived from activities in the Area....

See Chapter 10, discussing the Law of the Sea Convention. More recently, the concept of common heritage of humankind has been applied in the protection of Antarctica and the decision to make that continent essentially the equivalent of a global park (with very limited rights for exploitation over the next fifty years). *See Antarctic Treaty*, December 1, 1959, 402 U.N.S.T. 71 (1959); Protocol on Environmental Protection, XI ATSCM/2 (June 21, 1991); *see also* Chapter 14, pages 1059–1066.

Since inclusion in the Antarctic Treaty, however, the role of the common heritage principle has been narrowed. The United States never fully accepted the principle's application to the deep sea-bed (at least with respect to benefit sharing). To get the United States to join the Law of the Sea Convention, the common heritage principle was removed from Part XI addressing the mining of the deep sea-bed. The principle was also not accepted in any of the UNCED agreements. As a result, the principle must be viewed as having only limited current application, but it remains an important principle conceptually and historically.

Where it does apply to a particular area or set of resources, the common heritage of humankind has at least four characteristics: non-appropriation; international management; shared benefits; and reservation for peaceful purposes.

Non-appropriation. Although areas under the common heritage of humankind are to be open for certain peaceful uses, including scientific research and even economic development, the areas are not open for appropriation by any one State. In this sense, the "ownership" of the global commons (or at least the deep sea-bed, the moon and to some extent Antarctica) can be said to remain with all of humanity. Claims by any State that it could assert territorial sovereignty over these areas are rejected by the international community. This concept of non-appropriation does not mean, however, that States are not allowed to "capture" natural resources and remove them from either the deep sea bed or the moon. *See, e.g.*, Law of the Sea Convention, Article 136; the Moon Treaty, Article 11; the Outer Space Treaty, Article II.

International Management. National management by one country of the areas covered by common heritage was viewed as undermining the concept that no country should be allowed to appropriate the commons. As a result, the Law of the Sea Convention initially established an elaborate system for the management of the deep sea-bed, including the creation of a Sea-bed Authority. The Moon Treaty also makes general reference to the desirability of an international management system once economic development of the moon is feasible. Antarctica, too, is managed cooperatively through an elaborate system of treaties and protocols.

Shared Benefits. In what is viewed as the most controversial aspect of the common heritage principle, benefits from the use and exploitation of natural resources in the deep sea-bed and the moon, for example, are to be shared among all countries. This is a critical provision for developing countries who realize that they do not command the technology to take advantage of resources in these hard-to-reach places. Rather than all benefits going to those who "capture" the resource first, some mechanism is required for making an equitable allocation of the benefits. In the Moon Treaty, for example, Article 11, para. 7(d) requires an "equitable sharing" by all States Parties in the benefits derived from the moon's resources.

As mentioned above, at least with respect to the deep sea-bed, the United States has never fully accepted the concept of shared benefits. Indeed, the United States agreed to sign the Law of the Sea Convention, only after the shared benefits provisions for deep seabed mining were eliminated.

Reserved for Peaceful Purposes. The original Outer Space Treaty as well as the subsequent Moon Treaty specified that these areas could only be used for peaceful purposes. As discussed in Chapter 8 (with respect to compliance with international law), the United States implicitly repudiated this concept when it started to develop the "Star Wars" Strategic Defense Initiative under President Reagan, but then subsequently reaffirmed its commitment to the demilitarization of space after the Cold War. The emphasis on peaceful uses of the sea-bed is not quite so clear, although the 1970 Sea–Bed Arms Control Treaty has outlawed implanting or placing nuclear weapons or weapons of mass destruction on the sea-bed.

———

QUESTIONS AND DISCUSSION

1. Nico Schrijver provides the following summary of the legal status of the common heritage of humankind (referred to as CHM). Note, however, that he is writing before Part XI of the Law of the Sea Convention was modified.

Nico Schrijver, *Permanent Sovereignty Over Natural Resources Versus the Common Heritage of Mankind*, 87, 95–99, in INTERNATIONAL LAW AND DEVELOPMENT (PETERS & DENTURE EDS. 1988)

The views of scholars vary considerably as to the legal status of the principle of CHM. Some argue that this principle is a new peremptory norm of general international law from which no derogation is permitted (a rule of *jus cogens*). They refer to the mandatory wording of Part XI of UNCLOS, especially Articles 136–145, and to Article 311, paragraph 6, which reads as follows:

States Parties agree that there shall be no amendments to the basic principle relating to the common heritage of mankind set forth in Article 136 and that they shall not be party to any agreement in derogation thereof.

At the opposite extreme, others deny any legal value to the principle and consider it to belong to the realm of politics and morality. Because of the many unresolved controversies about the contents and implications of the CHM, some authors even concluded that "the common heritage as a legal principle is dead". As so often, the truth is to be found somewhere in the middle. The principle is contained in several multilateral treaties, it has been introduced in Recommendations on the protection of the Antarctic environment and it is even referred to—albeit implicitly—in domestic deep sea-bed mining laws, including the US one. Attempts have been made to apply the principle to the field of transfer of technology. During the negotiations on UNCLOS and the Moon Treaty, the CHM principle was clarified, its basic constituent elements were specified and it was included as one of the main features of the new regimes. So the principle has at least some legal significance.

Furthermore, during these conferences almost all, if not all States accepted the principle as such. They only disagree on its modalities and implications. Its content is indeed not so elaborate as to allow for the derivation and identification of specific rights and obligations. Because exploitation of the sea-bed and moon is unlikely to take place in the near future no consensus on the CHM can be expected very soon.

Yet the principle of the CHM has gained currency in international law remarkably quickly as a new general principle of customary international law. This is not to say that it has (already) the status of *jus cogens*. The text of Part XI and Article 311(6) of UNCLOS cannot serve as a convincing argument for such a status. Apart from the fact that *jus cogens* can probably not be created by treaty, the *travaux preparatoires* [negotiating history] of Article 311(6) amount to the opposite. The present wording is a compromise text after a Chilean proposal to label the CHM explicitly as "a peremptory norm of general international law from which no derogation is permitted" proved to be unacceptable. Moreover, the specific fights and obligations to be derived from the principle of the CHM are not at all clear. While concluding that the CHM as a whole cannot be considered to be a norm of *jus cogens,* van Hoof has argued that its elements of non-appropriation and peaceful use are non-derogable norms of international law. In my view it is indeed still too early to appraise the exact legal value of the principle of CHM as such in the years to come it will depend on several factors, such as the following:

1.   Whether and when the Convention on the Law of the Sea will enter into force;

2.   Whether there will be "widespread and representative participation" of States which are engaged in exploration and exploitation of the moon and the deep sea-bed or not, or only in part;

3.   The way in which the future international regime for the exploitation of the moon's natural resources will be set up and the way the Preparatory Commission and later on the International Sea-bed Authority will elaborate Part XI of the Convention;

4.   The State practice of States whose interests are especially affected;

5.   Whether this principle will be applied in other areas of international law (e.g., Antarctic regime, Outer Space, environment) and will be clarified thereby.

Recall the discussion of peremptory norms and *jus cogens* in Chapter 6 on lawmaking. How would the factors identified by Nico Schrijver above help to clarify the status of the common heritage of humankind? The Law of the Sea Convention has entered into force, but the sections on the deep sea-bed were changed substantially. See Chapter 10, pages 759–767 on the deep sea-bed and consider whether the common heritage of humankind can still be considered a candidate for a peremptory norm of international law. Do the changes in the sea-bed regime reflect at all on the importance of the principle to the future exploitation and use of the moon?

2. The principles of common heritage of humankind and permanent sovereignty over natural resources are obviously related. To some extent, one starts where the other ends. Both principles derived from the New International Economic Order in the 1960s and 1970s, in which developing countries sought to assert their numerical superiority in the United Nations in ways that would reverse the era of colonialism. Thus in areas within State boundaries, the developing countries wanted to assert their independence to control the development, use and exploitation of those resources. At the same time, they wanted to avoid a colonial-like rush to exploit the global commons, knowing that industrialized countries commanded the technologies necessary to control most of the resources of the sea-bed, outer space, and Antarctica. Consider the common motivation of the two principles in reading the following from N. Schrijver, *op. cit.*, at 87, 99–101

> In the postwar era "permanent sovereignty over natural resources" and the "common heritage of mankind" evolved as two new main principles of international economic law. Both had a highly innovating impact on modern international law. At first glance these principles might look somewhat contradictory. For the principle of permanent sovereignty over natural resources basically purports to establish exclusive jurisdiction of States (or peoples) over natural resources in areas where they can exercise sovereign rights, while the principle of the common heritage of mankind basically aims at sharing the world's natural resources. Both principles form, however, underpinning pillars of the [New International Economic Order] ... and have, moreover, a firm status in international law. * * *

> In the context of their newly acquired independence, developing countries have deepened and broadened the extent of their permanent sovereignty over natural resources. They have deepened it by claiming as many rights as possible on the basis of permanent sovereignty over natural resources [PSNR], thereby "nationalizing" resource management. They have broadened the scope of PSNR by claiming exclusive rights over the natural resources of the sea in waters adjacent to their coast. To a considerable extent these claims have been accepted and recognized in the modern law of the sea.

> At the same time the principle of the CHM was claimed for the resources of the deep sea-bed and for geographically remote areas, such as Antarctica and even the Moon. It should be noted that the "Area", that is the sea-bed and ocean floor and the subsoil thereof to which the CHM principle applies, has been significantly reduced by the establishment of the 200 nm [nautical mile] Exclusive Economic Zone and by the extension of the Continental Shelf area under national economic jurisdiction. For this reason the Area has been popularly described as "the part of the sea-bed left over after the coastal States have grabbed whatever portions they think can be of value to them in the foreseeable future". This may be somewhat of an exaggeration, but it is a fact of life that the national and international resource regimes are in competition: the CHM regime can only start where it is agreed that the PSNR ends. * * *

> In recent decades it has become clear that the world is interdependent in many respects, in particular in the field of natural resources, including such issues as conservation, environmental protection, physical scarcity, secure supply and resources for development. Now that the principles of PSNR and the CHM have got a firm stand in international law and seem not to be contradictory, it might be relevant to conduct further research on the way they could complement each

other. For example, in [the] future, elements of the CHM could be a useful concept in the management of natural wealth and resources, now within the area of national economic jurisdiction, when their management significantly affects the "sovereign" territory of two or more States or even, in the case of the tropical rain forests (the "lungs of the earth"), the ecological balance of the whole planet. As the Brundtland Commission observed "legal regimes are being rapidly outdistanced by the accelerating pace and expanding scale of impacts on the environmental base of development". Therefore, the Commission appealed: "Human Laws must be reformulated to keep human activities in harmony with the unchanging and universal laws of nature". This would undoubtedly require a further evolution of international law from mainly inter-State oriented law delimiting national resource regimes towards an international law of mankind pursuing sustainable development, equitable sharing, management of the global commons and preservation for future generations. It might well be that such an evolution will not . . . grow spontaneously out of the "natural goodness" of man, but will finally be dictated by the "unnatural dirtiness" of our planet.

3.   Generally, developing countries have been the major supporters of the Common Heritage principle. This changed somewhat as the focus shifted to the genetic resources found in biodiversity. As Professor Christopher Stone writes in THE GNAT IS OLDER THAN MAN, 35 (1993):

> To declare the high seas and space to be part of the CHM is taken to mean they are at the least open to all users free of charge; there is an alternative, stronger sense to which the United States has never acceded: that designating them CHM means they are the common property of all nations and therefore their value, for example, extractable wealth like seabed minerals, has to be *divided* among nations, whoever does the extracting. In either view of CHM, calls to add biodiversity to common heritage is a threat to the biologically rich countries, many of which, such as Brazil and Colombia, are otherwise poor and inclined to resist loss of control over their own "internal" species and possibly patentable genetic resources.

Ultimately, the concept of common heritage was not applied generally to biodiversity; rather, in the Biodiversity Convention, the conservation of biodiversity is deemed to be the "common concern of humankind" discussed below.

D.   COMMON CONCERN OF HUMANKIND

The common heritage of humankind has been applied in attempts to develop an international regulatory regime for resources in global commons, but the concept has not been widely accepted when it comes to resources or activities located within countries. There, concepts of state sovereignty have historically dominated. At the same time, a growing consensus has emerged that because the planet is ecologically interdependent, humanity may have a collective interest in certain activities that take place, or resources that are located, wholly within State boundaries. What then provides the conceptual framework for international treaties that address these resources? The compromise reached with respect to the Biodiversity Convention and the Climate Change Convention is that these treaties address common "concerns" of humankind. Thus, for example, the Biodiversity Convention's preamble affirmed that "the conservation of biological diversity is a common concern of humankind," even though most terrestrial biodiversity is found within sovereign States. Likewise, the Climate Change Convention's preamble acknowledges that "change in the Earth's climate and its adverse effects are a common concern of humankind."

Although the principle of common concern was first used in the environmental context in the 1992 Biodiversity and Climate Change Conventions, all international environmental treaties and instruments arguably reflect a growing acceptance that protecting the environment and achieving sustainable development generally are "common concerns of humanity." Article 3 of the *IUCN Draft Covenant on Environment and Development,* states that the "global environment is a common concern of humanity." The commentary to the *Draft Covenant* offers the following explanation:

> Article 3 states the basis upon which the international community at all levels can and must take joint and separate action to protect the environment. It is based on the scientific reality that harm to the environment resulting from human activities (e.g., depletion of the stratospheric ozone layer, climate modification, and the erosion of biological diversity) adversely affect all humanity. World-wide cooperation to take concerted action is necessary to avoid environmental disaster. This implies acceptance of both the right and the duty of the international community as a whole to have concern for the global environment. * * *

> The conclusion that the global environment is a matter of "common concern" implies that it can no longer be considered as solely within the domestic jurisdiction of states due to its global importance and consequences for all. It also expresses a shift from classical treaty-making notions of reciprocity and material advantage, to action in the long-term interests of humanity.

> The concept of "common concern" is not new and has been applied in other fields. It forms the basis for international laws relating to human rights, humanitarian relief and international labour relations. Those obligations are now recognized as obligations *erga omnes,* owed by all States to the entire international community.

> The inter-dependence of the world's ecosystems and the severity of current environmental problems call for global solutions to most, if not all, environmental problems, thereby justifying designation of the global environment as a matter of "common concern". However, it is only recently that environmental protection has been seen in this way. Traces of the concept can be found in many multilateral environmental treaties, but to date the actual term has been applied only in texts concerning global climate change and the conservation of biological diversity.

IUCN, *Draft Covenant on Environment and Development,* 32 (1995). The principle of common concern can thus be seen in creative tension with the principle of State sovereignty. Prior to the negotiations of the Biodiversity Convention, for example, States were assumed to have complete control and discretion with respect to conservation of biodiversity found within their boundaries. Growing international concern in the widespread loss of biodiversity, however, led to pressure on all countries to agree jointly to its conservation and to find ways through international cooperation to facilitate such conservation. In this way, the conservation of biodiversity is no longer viewed as the province solely of individual States. The same can be said of the emission of fossil fuels that threatens the earth's climate system.

In general, the principle does not yet imply specific legal obligations beyond cooperation, but rather provides the conceptual framework for international lawmaking with respect to what would otherwise be activities or resources considered wholly within the sovereign control of individual States.

QUESTIONS AND DISCUSSION

1.   The concept of common concern should not be confused with common heritage. Common heritage was specifically considered and rejected by the negotiators of both the Climate Change and Biodiversity Conventions. Developing countries rejected application of the common heritage principle because they thought it would subject their natural resources to too much international control. Developed countries rejected common heritage because of the implication that benefits would have to be shared from these resources. Common concern was accepted in part because it did not carry with it any preconceived notions of benefit sharing or of joint management. In fact, the ambiguity of the concept of common concern is viewed positively in that it can provide the framework for international negotiations (and thus for the abdication of some aspects of State sovereignty), while still allowing flexibility in negotiating each specific regime.

2.   What significance should be placed on the fact that "common concern" is not mentioned as such in the *Rio Declaration?* Is it implied in the *Rio Declaration?*

3.   Do the ecological constraints on development and the recognition of the goal of sustainable development at Rio suggest that there is now a "common concern" that all States achieve sustainable development? Is this implicitly suggested by Principles 4 and 8 of the *Rio Declaration*, which seems to assume achieving sustainable development is the goal of international cooperation? Could such a finding eventually lead to a modification of the right to development to a right to *sustainable* development?

E.   INTERGENERATIONAL EQUITY

Protection of the global environment as well as sustainable development requires a long-term view. Indeed, the definition of sustainable development offered by the Brundtland Commission in *Our Common Future* refers to meeting the needs of present generations without sacrificing the needs of future generations. This focus on future generations as a rightful beneficiary of environmental protection has led to the principle of intergenerational equity. In essence, the principle is one of fairness, that present generations not leave future generations worse off by the choices we make today regarding development.

Intergenerational equity thus requires that we take into consideration the impact of our activities on future generations, giving them a "seat at the table" in making current decisions. At a minimum, implementing this principle requires using natural resources sustainably and avoiding irreversible environmental damage. It may also require modifications to our procedures for conducting environmental impact assessments and expansion of our concepts of judicial standing to future generations.

The importance of intergenerational equity can be seen, for example, in climate change. Because of the long lag-time between when greenhouse gas emissions occur and when they are naturally removed from the atmosphere (measured in decades to centuries, depending on the gas), decisions we make today to reduce our emissions will have profound impacts on the quality of life 100 years hence. Similarly, investments made today in researching and developing environmentally sustainable energy sources (as opposed to, for example, investing further in coal-fired power plants) also constrain the energy choices available to future generations.

Beginning with the *Stockholm Declaration,* international environmental instruments have emphasized the interests of future generations. The *Stockholm Declaration's* preamble notes that "To defend and improve the human environment for present *and* future generations has become an imperative goal of humankind...." Principle 1 states that "Man ... bears a solemn responsibility to protect and improve the environment for present and future generations," and Principle 2 requires the safeguarding of natural resources and ecosystems "for the benefit of present and future generations," Similarly, Principle 3 of the *Rio Declaration* states: "The right to development must be fulfilled so as to equitably meet developmental and environmental needs of present and future generations." *See also, e.g., United Nations General Assembly Resolution on the Historical Responsibility of States for the Protection of Nature for the Benefit of Present and Future Generations,* G.A. Res. 35/8 (Oct. 30, 1980); *Declaration of the Hague,* Mar. 11, 1989, 28 I.L.M. 1308 (1989).

Professor Edith Brown Weiss is the leading scholar on the principle of intergenerational equity. She describes intergenerational equity as the basis for the duty of the current generation to protect the natural system for future generations. Each generation has a right to use and enjoy the natural system, but must not allow that system to be destroyed or compromised in a way that diminishes the inheritance left for the next generation.

EDITH BROWN WEISS, IN FAIRNESS TO FUTURE GENERATIONS: INTERNATIONAL LAW, COMMON PATRIMONY, AND INTERGENERATIONAL EQUITY 37–39 (1996)

To derive the principles of intergenerational equity, it is necessary to return to the underlying purpose of our stewardship of the planet: to sustain the welfare and well-being of all generations. As indicated, this purpose has three aspects: to sustain the life-support systems of the planet; to sustain the ecological processes, environmental conditions and cultural resources necessary for the survival of the human species; and to sustain a healthy and decent human environment. This means passing on a robust planet to future generations. The theory of intergenerational justice says that each generation has an obligation to future generations to pass on the natural and cultural resources of the planet in no worse condition than received and to provide reasonable access to the legacy for the present generation. What then are the principles of intergenerational equity that will fulfill these purposes?

Four criteria should guide the development of principles of intergenerational equity. First, the principles should encourage equality among generations, neither authorizing the present generation to exploit resources to the exclusion of future generations, nor imposing unreasonable burdens on the present generation to meet indeterminate future needs. Second, they should not require one generation to predict the values of future generations. They must give future generations flexibility to achieve their goals according to their own values. Third, they should be reasonably clear in application to foreseeable situations. Fourth, they must be generally shared by different cultural traditions and be generally acceptable to different economic and political systems.

We propose three basic principles of intergenerational equity. First, each generation should be required to conserve the diversity of the natural and cultural resource base, so that it does not unduly restrict the options available to future generations in solving their problems and satisfying their own values, and should also be entitled to diversity comparable to that enjoyed by previous generations. This principle is called "conservation of options." Second, each generation should be required to maintain the quality of the planet so that it is passed on in no worse condition than that in which it was received, and should also be entitled to planetary quality comparable to that enjoyed by previous generations. This is the principle of "conservation of quality." Third, each generation should provide its members with equitable rights of access to the legacy of past generations and should conserve this access for future generations. This is the principle of "conservation of access."

These proposed principles constrain the actions of the present generation in developing and using the natural and cultural resources of our planet. They do not, however, dictate the details of how members of the present generation should manage their resources. The principles are reasonably clear in application and should, if respected, ensure the sustainability of the living environment and the cultural heritage. They appear to be shared generally by the world's major cultural traditions, and are consistent with different political and economic systems.

The principles can appropriately be viewed as implementing the poignant call of the World Commission on Environment and Development for "sustainable development," which the Commission defines as "development that meets the needs of the present without compromising the ability of future generations to meet their own needs." They are intended to ensure equitable access to our planetary natural and cultural environment and at the same time to recognize limits on how we use our environment so we can pass it to future generations in as good condition as we received it.

————

QUESTIONS AND DISCUSSION

1. Which, if any, of the generational principles Professor Edith Brown Weiss proposes are reflected in the *Rio Declaration* or the other materials on sustainable development?

2. The principle of intergenerational equity affirms the need to commit to the long-term protection of the environment and to give a voice to future generations, perhaps through the extension of judicial standing to future generations. Although a difficult concept for some civil law countries, particularly francophone countries, where the concept of equity does not translate well and is not a significant part of the legal tradition, the principle is beginning to appear in judicial decisions throughout the world. For example, in 1994, the Philippines Supreme Court allowed a case brought on behalf of present and future generations of children to stop deforestation in that country. The Court specifically endorsed the concept of intergenerational equity.

> Petitioners minors assert that they represent their generation as well as generations yet unborn. We find no difficulty in ruling that they can, for themselves, for others of their generation and for the succeeding generations, file a class suit. Their personality to sue in behalf of the succeeding generations can only be based on the concept of intergenerational responsibility insofar as the right to a balanced and healthful ecology is concerned. Nature means the created world in its entirety. Such rhythm and harmony indispensably include, *inter alia,* the judicious disposition, utilization, management, renewal and conservation of the country's forest, mineral, land, waters, fisheries, wildlife, off-shore areas and other natural resources to the end that their exploration, development and utilization be equitably accessible to the present as well as future generations. Needless to say, every generation has a responsibility to the next to preserve that rhythm and harmony for the full enjoyment of a balanced and healthful ecology. Put a little differently, the minors' assertion of their right to a sound environment constitutes, at the same time, the performance of their obligation to ensure the protection of that right for the generations to come.

Minors Oposa v. Secretary of the Department of Environment and Natural Resources, 33 I.L.M. 168, 185 n. 18 (1994). According to Tony Oposa, the lawyer who filed the case naming his children as the petitioners, the development of the principle of intergenerational equity in the international environmental literature was what convinced the court to allow standing on behalf of succeeding generations. In this way, the *Oposa Case* demonstrates how principles developed in international law can also assist in the progressive development of national law. Could future generations be granted standing in the United States?

3. In an economic sense, sustainable development recognizes each generation's responsibility to be fair to the next generation, by leaving an inheritance of wealth no less than they themselves had inherited. It may thus require changes in economic discount rates and other economic adjustments to ensure that future costs and benefits of current activities are adequately considered in current decision-making. In this regard, *see* Chapter 3, page 145, discussing discount rates.

4. The emphasis on intergenerational equity in international environmental law should not lead to neglect for equity within the current generation. Many observers believe that the principle of equity in international environmental law must also address current issues of social, economic and environmental justice. Thus, environmental costs and benefits should not be disproportionately placed on certain classes, races or ethnic groups. *Intra*generational equity is concerned with environmental justice within countries (as well as between countries) but without the temporal element of *inter*generational equity. It suggests a right not to be discriminated against in environmental terms (i.e. not to have to bear a disproportionate burden of environmental pollution or costs).

This principle of equity can be seen in different contexts in the *Rio Declaration,* for example in both the explicit statements emphasizing the indispensable role of poverty alleviation in achieving sustainable development (Principle 5) and principles that emphasized the specific role and plight of historically underrepresented groups, including women, youth, and indigenous peoples.

5. What concrete steps would be required in our national laws if we took seriously the rights of future generations? How do the principles of inter- and intragenerational equity relate to the environmental justice movement in the United States?

F. COMMON BUT DIFFERENTIATED RESPONSIBILITIES

All States have common responsibilities to protect the environment and promote sustainable development, but because of different social, economic, and ecological situations, countries must shoulder different responsibilities. This principle of "common but differentiated responsibilities" reflects core elements of equity, placing more responsibility on wealthier countries and those that are more responsible for causing specific global environmental problems. Differentiated responsibility also allows for ecological differences in countries—for example, the particular vulnerability of small island states to the flooding that may result from global warming. Perhaps most importantly, "common but differentiated responsibilities" presents a conceptual framework for compromise and cooperation in meeting future environmental challenges, because it allows countries that are in different positions with respect to specific environmental issues to be treated differently.

The principle is affirmed in various international instruments that recognize generally the different responsibilities and capabilities of industrialized and developing countries. The *Rio Declaration,* for example, offered the principle in the highly controversial Principle 7:

> In view of the different contributions to global environmental degradation, States have common but differentiated responsibilities. The developed countries acknowledge the responsibility that they bear in the international pursuit of sustainable development in view of the pressures their societies place on the global environment and of the technologies and financial resources they command.

As another example, the Climate Change Convention's guiding principles ask developed countries to take the lead in combating climate change and its effects, while giving full consideration to the needs and special circumstances of disproportionately burdened developing countries. *See Climate Change Convention,* Article 3; *see also, e.g., Montreal Protocol on Substances that Deplete the Ozone Layer,* Article 5.

The concept of common but differentiated responsibilities remains very controversial. The concept could arguably require industrialized countries to provide financial assistance, build developing-country capacity, transfer technologies or allow developing countries a less rigorous compliance regime in global environmental agreements. This latter issue—whether initially at least developing countries should be allowed less rigorous compliance requirements was one of the most difficult issues in negotiations over binding targets and timetables under the Kyoto Protocol. The differentiated responsibilities reflected in the Protocol fueled a widespread, industry-sponsored television advertisement in the United States charging that the agreement was "not global and won't work." The lack of binding commitments on developing countries was a major reason the United States pulled back from the Protocol in 2001. *See* Chapter 9, page 639.

––––––

QUESTIONS AND DISCUSSION

1.   Consider the following discussion of "differentiated responsibilities", offered by Ileana Porras, *op. cit.*, at 29:

> There are two distinct ways in which Principle 7 of the *Rio Declaration* begins to define "differentiated responsibility." First, it imputes differentiated responsibility to States in accordance with their different levels of responsibility for causing the harm. Second, it ties differentiated responsibility to the different capacities of States, by referring to the differentiated responsibility for sustainable development, acknowledged by developed countries in view of the "technologies and financial resources they command." Together, these two elements of differentiated responsibility provide the beginnings of a philosophical basis for international cooperation in the fields of environment and development. It is a basis that allows the characterization of the transfer of resources from developed to developing countries as "obligation" rather than as "aid" or assistance and provides a theoretical basis to justify different environmental standards, in view of the different capacities of States and their different contributions to environmental degradation.

What difference does it make to developing countries whether foreign assistance and different environmental standards are provided based on a sense of obligation as opposed to aid?

2.   In signing the Rio Declaration, the United States attached an interpretive statement to Article 7 clarifying that it entailed no legal responsibility for global environmental problems. What exactly do you think concerned the United States?

> The United States understands and accepts that principle 7 highlights the special leadership role of the developed countries, based on our industrial development, our experience with environmental protection policies and actions, and our wealth, technical expertise and capabilities.

> The United States does not accept any interpretation of principle 7 that would imply a recognition or acceptance by the United States of any international obligations or liabilities, or any diminution in the responsibilities of developing countries.

3.   Some economists argue that developing countries should be allowed to continue polluting as they develop their economies, and that this is a legitimate "comparative advantage" they should be able to exploit in international trade. *See* Chapter 15. Should this be considered as part of common but differentiated responsibilities? *See* GARETH PORTER, THE MYTH OF ENVIRONMENTAL ASSIMILATION CAPACITY (CIEL Discussion Paper, Dec. 1997).

4.   Review again the discussion of the nine environmental heavyweights, the E–9, in Chapter 4. Should the E–9 face common but differentiated responsibilities?

5.   Principle 7 of the *Rio Declaration*, which contains the principle of common but differentiated responsibilities, also affirmed the concept of a "global partnership" for protecting the environment: "States shall cooperate in a spirit of global partnership to conserve, protect and restore the health and integrity of the Earth's ecosystem." This principle of global partnership reflects the ecological interdependence of all states, and the need for broad North–South cooperation and compromise to resolve global environmental issues.

G. THE PRINCIPLE OF PREVENTION

Occasionally referred to in the pollution context as the pollution prevention principle, the principle of prevention generally reflects that protection of the environment is best achieved by *preventing* environmental harm in the first place rather than relying on remedies or compensation for such harm after it has occurred. Preventing environmental damage is almost always less costly than allowing the damage and incurring the environmental costs and other consequences later. As a guiding principle for international negotiations and national implementation, the prevention principle gives preference to environmental management policies that eliminate and reduce environmental damage before it occurs.

The principle is most developed at the international level with respect to pollution. Principle 6 of the Stockholm Declaration sets out the principle in sweeping terms:

> The discharge of toxic substances or of other substances and the release of heat, in such quantities or concentrations as to exceed the capacity of the environment to render them harmless, must be halted in order to ensure that serious or irreversible damage is not inflicted upon ecosystems.

The prevention principle can be implemented through pollution prevention or waste minimization policies, improved environmental management including periodic audits, environmental impact assessments, and policies reflecting life-cycle analyses and extended product responsibility. In this regard, the UNEP Governing Council urged countries to adopt:

> Alternative Clean Production methods (including raw material selection, product substitution, and clean production technologies and processes) as a means of implementing a precautionary principle in order to promote production systems which minimize or eliminate the generation of hazardous wastes....

UNEP Governing Council Decision, UNEP GC/SS.II/4B (August, 1990). This preference for clean production methods has appeared in international environmental treaties as well. For example, Article 4(3)(f) of the Bamako Convention on Transboundary Shipments of Hazardous Wastes requires that:

> Each Party shall strive to adopt and implement the preventive, precautionary approach to pollution problems which entails, *inter alia,* preventing the release into the environment of substances which may cause harm to humans or the environment without waiting for scientific proof regarding such harm. The Parties shall co-operate with each other in taking the appropriate measures to implement the precautionary principle to pollution prevention through application of Clean Production methods, rather than the pursuit of a permissible emissions approach based on assimilative capacity assumptions.

QUESTION AND DISCUSSION

1. Industry now recognizes that designing a product or process to minimize waste production is often more cost effective than relying on "end-of-pipe" technologies or disposal options. Beginning with the initial design of a product and of its production process and continuing all the way through the life-cycle of a product to disposal, many Fortune 500 companies now seek clean production methodologies and processes to reduce material inputs and waste discharges. For example, German automobile manufacturers design their automobiles to reduce the amount of waste when the car is scrapped. Each component of the automobile is designed to separate easily from the whole, and the components are individually coded to facilitate recycling and re-use. *See generally* BUSINESS COUNCIL FOR SUSTAINABLE DEVELOPMENT, CHANGING COURSE (1992).

2. To what extent does implementation of the prevention principle depend on availability of technology? Is the availability of cost-effective technologies for waste minimization more important for the application of the principle than, for example, the relative uncertainty of the environmental impacts (which is a critical aspect of the precautionary principle, discussed below)?

3. The prevention principle presupposes that policymakers will take an anticipatory approach, favoring the avoidance of environmental harm over compensation after it has occurred. This is particularly appropriate where environmental harm may be substantial and irreversible. Is the relationship between the prevention principle and the precautionary principle clear from the references in the UNEP Guidance above and in the Bamako Convention's discussion of Clean Production Methods?

Part of the argument for the Bamako Convention's approach is that we have learned enough about environmental pollution to know that we often underestimate its long-term impacts. In this respect, the precautionary principle suggests that we might want to control certain types of pollution, through waste minimization or pollution prevention, even where we do not have specific proof of specific types of harm. Should the precautionary and prevention principles apply differently to persistent chemicals that do not degrade in the environment as opposed to conventional pollutants where the environmental impacts are relatively well known and reversible?

———

H.   THE PRECAUTIONARY PRINCIPLE

Experience in the past decades with environmental problems such as ozone depletion, climate change and the accumulation of persistent chemicals in even the most remote parts of the earth have jolted policy makers to re-evaluate how we address potential environmental harm. At the center of that re-evaluation is the precautionary principle, which reflects the recognition that scientific certainty often comes too late to design effective legal and policy responses for preventing many potential environmental threats. Most environmental issues involve complex analyses of scientific, technical and economic factors. We rarely have anything approximating perfect knowledge when law-makers are asked to make decisions whether to respond to a specific threat.

The precautionary principle addresses how environmental decisions are made in the face of scientific uncertainty. The principle is closely related to the principle of prevention because both are concerned with taking anticipatory actions to avoid environmental harm *before* it occurs. Indeed, the precautionary principle can be viewed as the application of the principle of prevention where the scientific understanding of a specific environmental threat is not complete. Principle 15 of the 1992 Rio Declaration on Environment and Development is the most widely accepted elaboration of the precautionary principle:

> In order to protect the environment, the precautionary approach shall be widely applied by States according to their capabilities. Where there are threats of serious or irreversible damage, lack of scientific certainty shall not be used as a reason for postponing cost-effective measures to prevent environmental degradation.

Principle 15 thus forbids using scientific uncertainty as a reason for postponing cost-effective measures to prevent environmental harm. This focus on avoiding delay and on acting before environmental harm occurs illustrates the principle's emphasis on anticipating and avoiding harm. In this respect, the principle speaks more to *when* policy measures can be taken and on what basis, than to *what* type of measures should be taken. Although not clearly supported by the *Rio Declaration,* many commentators also argue that the precautionary principle acts to switch the burden of proof necessary for triggering policy responses from those who support prohibiting or reducing a potentially offending activity to those who want to continue the activity. Such a shift in the burden of proof can shorten the time period between when a potential threat to the environment is identified and when a legal response can be developed.

The precautionary principle does not prescribe what type of policy measures should be used in cases where the principle has been invoked. The primary condition placed by most (but not all) versions of the precautionary principle, including Principle 15, suggests that policy actions should be "cost-effective" in preventing environmental damage. Thus, the principle offers governments wide flexibility in selecting appropriate policy measures, once taking some measures is deemed appropriate. In most instances, the precautionary principle has been used to *allow* or *authorize*, but not to *require*, policy measures. In some instances, proposed activities are simply delayed until further scientific evidence can be gathered that demonstrates for example that the proposed activity will not cause any serious or irreversible damage or that a different policy measure is warranted either because it is more cost-effective or otherwise.

The precautionary principle thus provides a framework for governments to set preventative policies where existing science is incomplete or where no consensus exists regarding a particular threat. The principle is not intended to downgrade the role of science, and the fact that there is scientific uncertainty does not alleviate the need to take into account what ever science does exist. Existing science may, for example, identify the potential scale and seriousness of potential harm as well as the adequacy or effectiveness of policy measures, even where uncertainty remains regarding cause and effect. Moreover, as the state of scientific knowledge increases over time on a particular issue, policy measures adopted pursuant to the precautionary principle (or based on risk assessment, for that matter) may need to be revisited.

————

QUESTIONS AND DISCUSSION

1. In recent years, the precautionary principle has emerged as perhaps the most controversial of all international environmental principle. The strongest controversies have erupted as a result of the different approaches that Europe and the United States take to the precautionary principle in the context of international trade and environment issues. In fact, precaution has probably always been an element of both European and US environmental and health policy, but a strong World Trade Organization now provides for the first time an opportunity to challenge precaution-based policies as being trade-restrictive. The WTO's apparent preference for scientifically based environmental policies has provided opponents an opportunity to depict precaution as unscientific and protectionist.

Thus, for example, Europe invoked the precautionary principle as a justification for its decision to regulate genetically modified organisms (GMOs) in food, even in the admitted absence of scientific evidence that GMOs are harmful to human health or the environment. The US has argued that the EU's actions were not scientifically based as required under the WTO rules. The United States said the EU's position was protectionist and ran counter to all existing scientific evidence. The EU, in turn, argued that it had a right to set its own environmental and public health standards and noted that the treaty establishing the Community states that environmental policy should be "based on the precautionary principle". The controversy led among other things to the European Commission issuing a communication setting forth the proper use of the precautionary principle in the Community. The following excerpt from the paper's summary reveals the subtle ways the Commission is trying to defend and justify its use of the principle.

Communication from the Commission on the Precautionary Principle

3. The precautionary principle is not defined in the Treaty, which prescribes it only once—to protect the environment. But *in practice,* its scope is much wider, and specifically where preliminary objective scientific evaluation, indicates that there are reasonable grounds for concern that the potentially dangerous effects on the *environment, human, animal or plant health* may be inconsistent with the high level of protection chosen for the Community.

The Commission considers that the Community, like other WTO members, has the right to establish the level of protection—particularly of the environment, human, animal and plant health—that it deems appropriate. Applying the precautionary principle is a key tenet of its policy, and the choices it makes to this end will continue to affect the views it defends internationally, on how this principle should be applied.

4. The precautionary principle should be considered within a structured approach to the analysis of risk, which comprises three elements: risk assessment, risk management, risk communication. The precautionary principle is particularly relevant to the management of risk.

The precautionary principle, which is essentially used by decision-makers in the management of risk, should not be confused with the element of caution that scientists apply in their assessment of scientific data.

Recourse to the precautionary principle presupposes that potentially dangerous effects deriving from a phenomenon, product or process have been identified, and that scientific evaluation does not allow the risk to be determined with sufficient certainty.

The implementation of an approach based on the precautionary principle should start with a scientific evaluation, as complete as possible, and where possible, identifying at each stage the degree of scientific uncertainty.

5.   Decision-makers need to be aware of the degree of uncertainty attached to the results of the evaluation of the available scientific information. Judging what is an "acceptable" level of risk for society is an eminently *political* responsibility. Decision-makers faced with an unacceptable risk, scientific uncertainty and public concerns have a duty to find answers. Therefore, all these factors have to be taken into consideration.

In some cases, the right answer may be not to act or at least not to introduce a binding legal measure. A wide range of initiatives is available in the case of action, going from a legally binding measure to a research project or a recommendation.

The decision-making procedure should be transparent and should involve as early as possible and to extent reasonably possible all interested parties.

6.   Where action is deemed necessary, measures based on the precautionary principle should be, *inter alia*:

- *proportional* to the chosen level of protection,
- *non-discriminatory* in their application,
- *consistent* with similar measures already taken,
- *based on an examination of the potential benefits and costs* of action or lack of action (including, where appropriate and feasible, an economic cost/benefit analysis),
- *subject to review*, in the light of new scientific data, and
- *capable of assigning responsibility for producing the scientific evidence* necessary for a more comprehensive risk assessment.

The controversy has spilled over from the trade arena to recent international environmental negotiations. The role of precaution was one of the most difficult and contentious issues for negotiators in both the 2001 POPs Convention and the 2000 Biosafety Protocol. The POPs Convention provides the latest statement of precaution agreed to by a wide range of governments, including the United States. These issues as well as the controversy over precaution in international trade are discussed in Chapter 12 (POPs Convention), Chapter 13 (Biosafety Protocol); Chapter 15 (international trade), respectively.

2.   The current debate centers in part on the legal status of the principle. The European Union argues that the precautionary principle is a part of customary international law. The United States insists that the precautionary principle has no legal status, but is only an "approach" that can be used in certain narrow circumstances. Other countries, most notably Canada, have argued that the precautionary principle is an emerging general principle of international law, which thus should be viewed as subservient to the specific rules of the WTO.

3.   The controversy over the precautionary principle is not just about law, however; it is about the pace, methodology and extent of environmental regulation. Experi-

ence with environmental problems such as ozone depletion have taught us that current activities may have serious and irreversible environmental impacts in the distant future or in distant places on the earth. We also recognize that the increasing pace of the global economy provides shorter lead time for making key regulatory decisions over products, such as chemicals that may have unknown environmental impacts. This has led to the growing interest inside and outside governments for anticipating environmental damage and taking precautionary actions. On the other hand, industry supporters argue that the costs of such an approach in foregone economic opportunities would ultimately be too high for society. So intense is the controversy in the United States, that the precautionary principle may be the first and only international environmental principle to warrant its own advertisement in the *New York Times*. Exxon Mobil paid for an ad, entitled *Unbalanced Caution,* which after quoting Principle 15 of the *Rio Declaration* had the following to say about the precautionary principle:

> On the face of it, this is a reasonable principle. Business and government share a common goal to exercise appropriate caution to ensure that new products and business operations do not pose unwarranted risks to public health or the environment. Where risks to public health or the environment exist, cost-effective steps to manage and reduce these risks should be taken.

> Unfortunately, using highly speculative assertions of risk, some activists misuse the precautionary principle to justify product bans and to stop new developments, including those that hold enormous promise for improving human life. Despite the absence of meaningful scientific evidence, claims of serious potential harm are made, even in the face of experience with the safe use of targeted products. Some types of plastics, genetically modified grains, hormone-treated meat and even routine energy projects are opposed because they are seen as too risky. Trade protectionists also use the principle as an excuse to ban new products that compete with traditionally protected goods.

> Misuse of the precautionary principle should be cause for concern. In practice, advocates are now demanding the impossible by insisting on perfect certainty of no ill effects. A responsible approach to risk recognizes that all human activities include both benefits and risks. Electricity, air travel, and chemotherapy all entail risks, but on balance society recognizes that their benefits justify facing their associated risks (even while working to reduce these risks further).

> If the precautionary principle is used to block beneficial innovations, public welfare is damaged. An unbalanced and excessive caution can undermine economies, jobs, human aspirations, health and the environment. Unjustified fears can lead to counterproductive behavior (as, for example, when consumers avoid eating fruit because of the exaggerated fear of residual agricultural pesticides). Trade restrictions arising from the misuse of the principle strain international relations and hurt consumers and producers.

> Enormous benefits come from scientific research, innovative technology and new developments. That is why governments must avoid the utopian pursuit of a risk-free world and, instead, exercise common sense in applying the precautionary principle. Above all, we should rely on science-based risk assessment and management, recognize the potential benefits that new developments entail, and use the scientific tools society has to seek both greater safety and material progress.

About what is Exxon concerned? Are their fears justified?

4. A major point of debate is what level of scientific evidence is required to trigger application of the precautionary principle? Under the Rio Declaration's formulation, the threshold for triggering the principle appears to be the existence of identifiable threats of serious or irreversible damage. In some applications of the principle, the threshold has been one of "significant" damage. What is sufficiently "serious" or "significant" to trigger the principle is still unclear, but de minimis or negligible potential damage is probably not sufficient. Similarly, purely speculative threats to the environment probably are not sufficient to trigger the precautionary principle. On the other hand, in the *absence* of any scientific evidence one way or the other, should plausible and reasonable theories about serious or irreversible environmental threats be sufficient? In determining whether an identified threat is sufficiently reasonable or plausible, must governments consider all *existing* scientific evidence?

5. The precautionary principle in slightly different formulations has been included in many international environmental instruments. *See, e.g., World Charter for Nature,* Principle 11, G.A. Res. 37/7 (Oct. 28, 1982); *London Adjustments and Amendments to the Montreal Protocol on Substances that Deplete the Ozone Layer; and Non–Compliance Procedure,* at Annex II, Article I.A.1 (amendment to 6th preambular paragraph), Decision IV/18, Nov. 25, 1992, UNEP/Oz.L.Pro.4/15; *Treaty Establishing the European Economic Community,* Mar. 25, 1957, 294 U.N.T.S. 17, U.K.T.S. 15 (1979) *as amended by Treaty on European Union,* Title XVI, Article 130r, Feb. 7, 1992; *Biodiversity Convention,* Preamble; *Climate Change Convention,* Article 3.3; *Agenda 21,* para. 18.40(b)(iv) (1992); *Cartagena Protocol on Biosafety,* Article 10 (Jan. 28, 2000) (not yet in force); *Stockholm Convention on Persistent Organic Pollutants,* Articles 1, 8 (2001) (not yet in force). *See also* DAVID FREESTONE, THE PRECAUTIONARY PRINCIPLE IN INTERNATIONAL ENVIRONMENTAL LAW (1996); CAROLYN RAFFENSPERGER & JOEL TICKNER, PROTECTING PUBLIC HEALTH & THE ENVIRONMENT: IMPLEMENTING THE PRECAUTIONARY PRINCIPLE (1999); *See also* Chapter 1, page 35, discussing scientific uncertainty; Chapter 9, page 542, discussing the precautionary principle in the context of ozone depletion; Chapter 13, pages 953–964, discussing the Biosafety Protocol; Chapter 12, discussing the POPs Convention; and Chapter 15, discussing international trade.

6. The precautionary principle is increasingly being invoked at the national level either explicitly or implicitly. For example, Germany has adopted the precautionary principle as broad guidance for its environmental policy, stating that environmental protection policy should be preventative instead of reactive, employing avoidance and reduction of emissions technology at their source. The German position is that harm to the environment shall be avoided as far as possible. *Agenda 21* urges national implementation of the precautionary principle in several contexts. For example, all States, according to their capacity and available resources, are urged to introduce "the precautionary approach in water quality management, where appropriate, with a focus on pollution minimization and prevention through use of new technologies, product and process change, pollution reduction at source, effluent reuse, recycling and recovery, treatment and environmentally safe disposal." Para. 18.40(b)(iv).

The precautionary principle has also begun to appear in domestic judicial decisions. For example, in *611428 Ontario Ltd. v. Metropolitan Toronto and Region Conservation Authority (MTRCA),* [1996] OJ 1392 (Ontario Divisional Court), the Court upheld application of the precautionary principle to a case involving the proposed filling of a ravine with a small creek. The Ontario Mining and Lands Commissioner, denied the developers petition to be allowed to fill the creek. In setting forth her reasons the Commissioner made a series of findings as to the ecosystem function of first order streams such as the one that would be affected by placing fill in the valley. The Commissioner then noted that:

> No model was presented at the hearing to indicate a threshold for intrusion into the watershed beyond which development should not be allowed. In the

absence of such a model, *the tribunal finds that it is appropriate to apply a precautionary principle* to development involving first order and intermittent streams within headwaters of a watercourse, so that, in the absence of calculation of threshold or demonstration of no net impact, development within such a land should not proceed. *This precautionary principle is applied in recognition of the integral role of water in environmental and human health.*

The developer appealed, arguing among other things that the Commissioner had erred in applying the precautionary principle so as to place the burden of proof on the applicant (to show that the watercourse would *not* be affected). The Divisional Court unanimously upheld the Commissioner. In the view of the Court, some evidence supported the Commissioner's conclusion that the downstream waterbody *might* be degraded, and thus the Commissioner could essentially shift the burden of proof and require the applicant to show that the downstream watercourse would not be significantly altered. Given the procedural posture of the case, the decision suggests that the precautionary principle permits and justifies government action in the face of uncertainty, but does not necessarily require it.

See also, e.g., *Vellore Citizens Welfare Forum v. Union of India & ORS,* SCALE (PIL) 1981–97 (Kuldip Singh, J.) 703 (1996) (Indian Supreme Court adopted the precautionary principle as an essential element of sustainable development in addressing pollution caused by tanneries); *Shehla Zia v. WAPDA,* P L D 1994 Supreme Court 693 (Pakistan) (Pakistani Supreme Court invoking the precautionary principle to prevent the proposed construction of an electric grid station until its effects could be reviewed by an independent entity).

The principle is also gaining ground domestically in the United States, where many scientists and environmental activists are beginning to demand the United States take precautionary measures against GMOs and certain chemicals. These activists rely in part on the growing acceptance of the precautionary principle internationally to bolster their support. The precautionary approach may for example be reflected at least implicitly in such US environmental laws as the Endangered Species Act, National Environmental Policy Act, the Clean Air Act, the Comprehensive Environmental Response Compensation and Liability Act, and the Oil Pollution Act. Do you agree? Where has the precautionary principle been adopted and implemented in U.S. law? What about the Endangered Species Act, which has been described by the Supreme Court as the "institutionalization of caution"?

7. National implementation of the principle has proven difficult in all countries. Some commentators advocate the use of environmental bonds to provide funding in advance for any environmental damage that may occur from a specific activity. These performance bonds could be set at the level equal to the highest potential environmental harm. Because whatever is not used to respond to environmental damage will ultimately be returned to the project sponsor, environmental performance bonds would provide an incentive for avoiding potential harm. *See, e.g.,* L. Cornwell & R. Costanza, *Environmental Bonds: Implementing the Precautionary Principle in Environmental Policy,* in CAROLYN RAFFENSPERGER & JOEL TICKNER, EDS., PROTECTING PUBLIC HEALTH & THE ENVIRONMENT: IMPLEMENTING THE PRECAUTIONARY PRINCIPLE (1999). What are the advantages and disadvantages of using performance bonds to implement the precautionary principle? What other policy measures would be appropriate for implementing the precautionary principle?

I. THE POLLUTER AND USER PAYS PRINCIPLE

Under the polluter and user pays principle, States should take those actions necessary to ensure that polluters and users of natural resources bear the full environmental and social costs of their activities. The principle is thus designed to internalize environmental externalities, as discussed in Chapter 3, pages 130–143. The principle integrates environmental protection and economic activities, by ensuring that the full environmental and social costs (including costs associated with pollution, resource degradation, and environmental harm) are reflected in the ultimate market price for a good or service. Environmentally harmful or unsustainable goods will tend to cost more, and consumers will switch to less polluting substitutes. This will result in a more efficient and sustainable allocation of resources.

Originally recommended by the OECD Council in May 1972, the principle is still highly controversial, particularly in developing countries where the burden of internalizing environmental costs is perceived as being too high. Nonetheless, because of its role in harmonizing standards, the principle provides important guidance for formulating domestic environmental laws and policies. For example, under Principle 16 of the Rio Declaration: "National authorities should endeavour to promote the internalization of environmental costs and the use of economic instruments, taking into account the approach that the polluter should, in principle, bear the cost of pollution, with due regard to the public interest and without distorting international trade and investment."

Agenda 21 also endorses the polluter pays principle at least implicitly in Paragraph 30.3 by extolling governments to use "free market mechanisms in which the prices of goods and services should increasingly reflect the environmental costs" (para. 30.3) and by recommending that commodity prices should reflect environmental costs (para. 2.14). Implementation mechanisms for the principle include user fees or taxes, elimination of subsidies, environmental pollution standards, and greener accounting systems both at the national level and within the private sector.

The polluter pays principle was and still is seen as a critical principle for harmonizing environmental standards across all countries, thereby reducing the potential for countries to compete for investors by lowering their environmental standards or by subsidizing the costs of installing environmental technologies. The early OECD Council recommendations provide useful summaries of the original purpose of the principle, which has not changed significantly since.

Recommendation of the Council on Guiding Principles Concerning International Economic Aspects of Environmental Policies, Annex I, adopted at the Council's 239th meeting (May 26, 1972)

A. Guiding Principles

a) Cost Allocation: the Polluter–Pays Principle

1. Environmental resources are in general limited and their use may lead to their deterioration. When the cost of this deterioration is not adequately taken into account in the price system, the market fails to reflect the scarcity of such resources both at the national and international levels. Public measures are

thus necessary to reduce pollution and to reach a better allocation of resources by ensuring that prices of goods depending on the quality and/or quantity of environmental resources reflect more closely their relative scarcity and that economic agents concerned react accordingly.

2.   In many circumstances, in order to ensure that the environment is in an acceptable state, the reduction of pollution beyond a certain level will not be practical or even necessary in view of the costs involved.

3.   The principle to be used for allocating costs of pollution prevention and control measures to encourage rational use of scarce environmental resources and to avoid distortions in international trade and investment is the so-called "Polluter–Pays Principle." The Principle means that the polluter should bear the expenses of carrying out the above-mentioned measures decided by public authorities to ensure that the environment is in an acceptable state. In other words, the cost of these measures should be reflected in the cost of goods and services which cause pollution in production and/or consumption. Such measures should not be accompanied by subsidies that would create significant distortions in international trade and investment.

4.   This Principle should be an objective of Member countries; however, there may be exceptions or special arrangements, particularly for the transitional periods, provided that they do not lead to significant distortions in international trade and investment.

The OECD also issued a *Note on the Implementation of the Polluter–Pays Principle:*

1.   The Polluter–Pays Principle (applying to transitional periods with possible exceptions and in the long term) implies that in general it is for the polluter to meet the costs of pollution control and prevention measures, irrespective of whether these costs are incurred as the result of the imposition of some charge on pollution emission, or are debited through some other suitable economic mechanism, or are in response to some direct regulation leading to some enforced reduction in pollution.

2.   The Polluter–Pays Principle, as defined in paragraph 4 of the "Guiding Principles," states that the polluter should bear the expenses of preventing and controlling pollution "to ensure that the environment is in an acceptable state." The notion of an "acceptable state" decided by public authorities, implies that through a collective choice and with respect to the limited information available, the advantage of a further reduction in the residual social damage involved is considered as being smaller than the social cost of further prevention and control. In fact, the Polluter–Pays Principle is no more than an efficiency principle for allocating costs and does not involve bringing pollution down to an optimum level of any type, although it does not exclude the possibility of doing so.

3.   To reach a better allocation of resources in line with paragraph 2 of the Guiding Principles, it is desirable that the private costs of goods and services should reflect the relative scarcity of environmental resources used in their production. If this is the case, consumers and producers would adjust themselves to the total social costs for the goods and services they are buying and selling. The Polluter–Pays Principle is a means of moving towards this end. From the point of view of conformity with the Polluter–Pays Principle, it does not matter whether the polluter passes on to his prices some or all of the environmental costs or absorbs them.

The polluter and user pays principle has extended beyond the OECD countries to other fora, primarily those dominated by industrialized countries. Except for Principle 16 of the *Rio Declaration* and *Agenda 21* (quoted above), developing countries have for the most part not accepted the polluter and user pays principle. For more examples of the polluter pays principles, *see OECD Council Recommendation on Guiding Principles Concerning International Economic Aspects of Environmental Policies*, May 26, 1972, C(72)128 (1972); *OECD Council Recommendation on the Implementation of the Polluter–Pays Principle*, Nov. 14, 1974, C(74)223 (1974); *European Charter on the Environment and Health*, Principles for Public Policy, Article 11, Dec. 8, 1989, WHO Doc. ICP/RUD 113/Conf.Doc./1, *reprinted in* 20 ENVTL. POL. & LAW 57 (1990); *Convention on Transboundary Lakes and Watercourses*, Article 2(5)(b); *EEC Treaty, as amended by Single European Act*, Title VII, Article 130r, Para. 2, Feb. 17, 1982; *Agenda 21,* Para. 2.14, Para. 30.3 (1992).

QUESTIONS AND DISCUSSION

1. The Polluter Pays Principle speaks primarily to the allocation of costs between public authorities and private businesses. As formulated by the OECD, however, it does not require all environmental costs to be internalized. Rather, paragraph 1 of the *Note on Implementation* states that the polluter should bear the expense of preventing and controlling pollution "to ensure that the environment is in an acceptable state," as decided by public authorities. Can you see how *The Note on Implementation* essentially defines "acceptable state" as being a level of pollution control where the marginal benefits of more abatement would be equal to the marginal costs? *See* chapter 3, page 108, for discussion of cost internalization. In some circumstances, the problem of internalizing all environmental and social costs may be broader than the OECD's version of the Polluter Pays Principle and would require higher regulatory standards than those needed only for "an acceptable level of pollution." In this regard, consider the formulation of Principle 16, which does not seem to condition the principle on an "acceptable level" of pollution.

2. The OECD revisited the Polluter Pays Principle in 1974, just two years after the initial Council recommendation, in order to clarify exceptions to the principle—i.e. the circumstances under which governments could provide subsidies to support pollution control technologies. What circumstances would you think warrant subsidies from the public sector? *See Recommendation of the OECD Council on the Implementation of the Polluter–Pays Principle*, adopted at the 372nd Council Meeting (Nov. 14, 1974).

3. The polluter and user pays principle can be implemented through a variety of methods aimed generally at internalizing environmental costs, including for example the use of taxes or fees or the elimination of subsidies for pollution control. The different mechanisms for internalizing environmental costs were explored in Chapter 3, page 130.

The imposition of liability on the person who causes environmental damage is also a clear way of applying the polluter pays principle. The European Union recently recognized this in a paper on environmental liability presented by the European Commission:

These days, we are confronted with cases of severe damage to the environment resulting from human acts. The recent incident with the *Erika* resulted in large-scale contamination of the French coast and the suffering and painful death of several hundred thousands of sea birds and other animals. This was certainly not the first case of an oil spill at sea with terrible consequences for the environment. Some years ago, a catastrophe of a different kind happened near the Donana nature reserve, in the south of Spain, when the breach of a dam containing a large amount of toxic water caused enormous harm to the surrounding environment, including innumerable protected birds. These and other similar events raise the question of who should pay for the costs involved in the clean-up of the pollution and the restoration of the damage. Should the bill for this be paid by society at large, in other words, the taxpayer, or should it be the polluter who has to pay, in cases where he can be identified? * * *

One way to ensure that greater caution will be applied to avoid the occurrence of damage to the environment is indeed to impose liability on the party responsible for an activity that bears risks of causing such damage. This means that, when such an activity really results in damage, the party in control of the activity (the operator), who is the actual polluter, has to pay the costs of repair. * * *

The proposed regime should not only cover damage to persons and goods and contamination of sites but also damage to nature, especially to those natural resources that are important from a point of view of the conservation of biological diversity in the Community (namely the areas and species protected under the Natura 2000 network). So far, environmental liability regimes in EU Member States do not yet deal with that.

Liability for damage to nature is a prerequisite for making economic actors feel responsible for the possible negative effects of their operations on the environment as such. So far, operators seem to feel such responsibility for other people's health or property—for which environmental liability already exists, in different forms, at the national level—rather than for the environment. They tend to consider the environment "a public good" for which society as a whole should be responsible, rather than an individual actor who happened to cause damage to it. Liability is a certain way of making people realize that they are also responsible for possible consequences of their acts with regard to nature. This expected change of attitude should result in an increased level of prevention and precaution.

See White Paper on Environmental Liability, Com (2000) 66, final, 9 Feb. 2000. Can you see how the European Commission's approach to liability is tied closely to the polluter pays principle?

4. Originally developed with respect only to pollution, the economic and policy justifications for internalizing the environmental costs of natural resource use are similar, and have led several observers to suggest that the polluter pays principle should be renamed the polluter and user pays principle, and extended to cover the external costs of resource consumption. What are the potential criticisms of extending the principle to natural resources?

5. Given that the polluter pays principle has been developed primarily as a mechanism of allocating the costs of pollution control between public authorities and private parties, how does it relate to the issues of State responsibility? As currently constituted, the principle has not been invoked as a rule of decision for allocating costs between a polluting State and a State affected by the pollution. That situation is covered by Principle 21 of the *Stockholm Declaration* and the obligation not to cause environmental harm, discussed below. How would you argue that the Polluter Pays Principle should be extended to inter-State disputes?

J.   SUBSIDIARITY

The principle of subsidiarity reflects a preference for making decisions at the lowest level of government or social organization where the issue can be effectively managed. Subsidiarity thus does not tell us *what* the right decision is in any given context, but *where* in the hierarchy the decision should be made. Decisions made at the local level are often viewed as more likely to take account of local environmental conditions and the opinions of the local people who often bear the highest environmental costs of development decisions. On the other hand, many environmental issues inherently have national or international implications, for example transboundary or global air pollution. Decisionmakers thus must be in a position to balance local economic benefits and other concerns with international or national priorities. Finding the right level of decisionmaking is difficult. Because there is a natural tendency of bureaucracies to accrete more authority over more issues, the principle of subsidiarity places a presumption on decentralizing decisionmaking as far as is appropriate given the nature of the specific issue. All things being equal, therefore, the subsidiarity principle may work to reduce the body of international environmental law because more issues would tend to be addressed at lower levels of government.

M. Bothe, *The Subsidiarity Principle*, in E. DOMMEN, FAIR PRINCIPLES FOR SUSTAINABLE DEVELOPMENT 123–24, 135–36 (1993)

The Subsidiarity Principle is generally invoked where a case is made for decisions to be taken at the lowest possible level. In this sense, it is used as a principle of organization in both the social and political fields. Where possible, decisions should be taken by the individual and/or the family, not by society at large; by the local community, not by the state; and by the Member states of a federation, not by the federation.... [T]he principle can also be applied where a choice has to be made between national and international regulations.

The roots of and justification for the Subsidiarity Principle can be found in three different sources. Firstly, it is said that the principle was developed by catholic social philosophy ... but this is too narrow an explanation.... The old philosophical idea of personal autonomy is behind the principle and is transferred into social and political organization. A second source is political and constitutional theory: the principle of democracy requires decisions to be taken close to the citizen and with citizen participation. It is in this sense and for this reason that the principle appears in the council of Europe's European Charter of local self-government. Thirdly, on a practical level, it is argued that decision-making on a smaller scale is more efficient than decision-making in large units.

On these grounds, the Subsidiarity Principle is an element of argumentation in controversies about centralization versus decentralization in political systems. It is used to defend local autonomy against state power, or Member states of a federal state against the centre. It is used as a political weapon.

In controversies of this kind, where a central and a lower level of government compete for political power, the argument is often made that the Subsidiarity Principle is also part of positive law. It may be argued that it is inherent in the notion of federalism or in that of local autonomy. This is, to say at least, an inappropriate generalization. Subsidiarity means a preference for the lower level of decision-making. It means a burden of justification for centralization, or a kind of rebuttable presumption for decentralization.... In the history of federal states, the political and constitutional battle for the appropriate problem-solving level has shifted in one way or the other. It would be a distortion of constitutional history and constitutional law to say that a preference for the lower level of government is generally inherent in the notion of a federal system. The trend in the federal systems of Europe and North America during the 1930s and after the Second World War leaned more towards centralization.... In recent years, there has been a renaissance of decentralization, of a greater role for Member states in federal systems, and of regionalism and localism. There has been a rediscovery of subsidiarity.... The trend towards centralization was related to new concepts of state functions, in particular to the development of the welfare state. The rediscovery of subsidiarity is related to a more differentiated approach towards state regulation and towards the appropriate ways and means of solving the problems of modern society. * * *

The Subsidiarity Principle is related to sustainable development in many respects. One of the greatest mischiefs of past development policy has been mega-projects which have no actual roots in the environment where they happened to be planned by a centralized bureaucracy or, perhaps even worse, by a foreign enterprise. It is arguable that development would be better achieved by fostering smaller projects involving the self-interest and self-help of the local people. This is, indeed, a form of subsidiarity but only an example of the more general fundamental question of overcoming the center-periphery imbalance in developing countries. But whether this can be done by simply giving more powers to local governments and organizations or whether this does not rather require some kind of centrally-organized redistribution processes is a different and difficult problem.

As to the choice between the national and international levels of decision-making, it must be stressed that many international instruments proclaiming their adherence to the principle of sustainable development are reluctant to make national decisions as to how sustainable development is to be achieved a matter of international regulation.... The recent controversy, which will probably continue, on international norms for the preservation of forests is an example of the emphasis many developing countries place in this respect on the principle of national sovereignty. While some developing countries (or at least some political forces in these countries) stress the role of forests, mainly tropical rain forests, in affecting the world climate and as a treasure of biodiversity (which makes their preservation a matter of international concern), the countries where these forests are situated (or certain important political forces in those countries) regard them as a resource of a local character, which can legitimately be used for timber extraction or be converted to other uses (agriculture, mining, hydroelectric power generation) to increase the income of the population. Although sustainability (i.e., the enlightened self-interest of the forest countries) means restraints on those latter uses it still does not make forest preservation a matter of concern for others.

Insistence on national sovereignty is to a certain extent legitimate. It would be inappropriate if decisions on sustainable development were taken in international forums and not by the people concerned. As experience shows, decisions relating to sustainability rather than to development, which are imposed by international agencies, are difficult for some countries to accept and thus difficult to implement. In this connection subsidiarity is probably a better sword for sovereignty. It has an important role to play in relation to sustainable development. However, as already discussed in connection with many other environmental problems, some kind of control and possible corrective action regarding local decisions are appropriate and necessary. There are already some trends to internationalize decisions relating to sustainable development, thus diminishing the role of the Subsidiarity Principle.

In respect of the preservation of the environment, we are witnessing a development which took place (and was very controversial) in relation to human rights, i.e. that there are basic international values which the international community must protect. National sovereignty or subsidiarity must not be used as a shield against these legitimate common concerns.

———

QUESTIONS AND DISCUSSION

1.   Is there a fundamental conflict between the subsidiarity principle and the trend toward addressing global environmental problems through international law? Consider the following passage from M. Bothe, in which he discusses some of the factors for determining the "desirable division of tasks between national and international regulation":

> The fact that the environment of the globe is indivisible seems to suggest that any environmental problem must be dealt with at a global level, but this is far from being true. The protection of the atmosphere is certainly a global problem, but it could well be that the self-interest of each and every state would suffice to induce all states to take appropriate measures. Experience shows, however, that this is not the case. Within the European Communities, there are several cases where it is quite clear that without Community action, certain Member states would not have taken the measures deemed necessary for the protection of the environment.... It thus appears that the international regulation is an important means of overcoming political obstacles to good environmental policy which may exist at the national level in some states. It is not enough to rely on the states' well-informed self-interest if the goal is to preserve the world's environment. This is the basis of treaties that place an upper limit on certain emissions (air and water pollution), but also of the ... biodiversity convention. The controversy over a convention for forest conservation shows, however, that there are serious reservations about that concept, which are based on the idea of state sovereignty.

> In particular, the self-interest of states cannot be relied upon where it is physically possible for them to export environmental problems; for example, the classic case of the upstream state which pollutes a river without suffering the consequences. Where the sea is involved, every state is an upstream state, and thus pollution of the sea from land-based sources can be prevented only by international regulation. * * *

> [T]he concept of shared resources ... [also] requires international regulation. It is obvious that a resource which for physical reasons constitutes a unity, but which is subject to the territorial sovereignty of several states or is situated beyond the limits of national jurisdiction, can only be managed by an international agreement among the states concerned. The decisive practical and political questions are: to what extent management of a resource is needed and which are the states concerned. * * *

> Another important aspect which requires international regulation is a general interest in unrestricted trade. Where states, for environmental and similar reasons, impose requirements on products which are internationally traded, these requirements constitute so-called non-tariff barriers to international trade. Their restraining impact on international trade can be prevented by harmonizing those requirements. * * *

Another economic consideration which might suggest regulatory action at the international level is the regulation of competition. It is well known that environmental standards applicable to industrial production facilities may increase production costs and thus affect the competitive position of the enterprise in question. It is, thus, argued that a harmonization of environmental standards for production facilities is also needed in order to avoid environmental dumping or a distortion of competition.

M. Bothe, op. cit., at 128–31. What types of environmental issues generally might be better addressed at the international level? At the regional level? At the local level? What are the general reasons to ensure that environmental issues are addressed at the lowest possible level?

2.   The subsidiarity principle is probably most well known in Europe, where it is a fundamental principle for organizing the European Union. The principle can also be found in many sections of Agenda 21. The following passages from Agenda 21's Chapter 18, for example, reflects the subsidiarity principle with respect to implementing integrated water resource management.

18.12(*o*). Development and strengthening, as appropriate, of cooperation, including mechanisms where appropriate, at all levels concerned, namely:

1.   At the lowest appropriate level, delegation of water resources management, generally, to such a level, in accordance with national legislation, including decentralization of government services to local authorities, private enterprises and communities;

2.   At the national level, integrated water resources planning and management in the framework of the national planning process and, where appropriate, establishment of independent regulation and monitoring of freshwater, based on national legislation and economic measures;

3.   At the regional level, consideration, where appropriate, of the harmonization of national strategies and action programmes;

4.   At the global level, improved delineation of responsibilities, division of labour and coordination of international organizations and programmes, including facilitating discussions and sharing experiences in areas related to water resources management.

See also, e.g., Agenda 21, para. 12.28, 12.37.

3.   How does the U.S. Constitution reflect the subsidiarity principle? How do U.S. environmental laws?

4.   Is the subsidiarity principle in conflict with the principle of common concern? How does subsidiarity relate to the principle of state sovereignty over natural resources? Are they the same principle, albeit with different origins and objectives?

K.   OBLIGATION NOT TO CAUSE ENVIRONMENTAL HARM

A central principle in international environmental law is the obligation of States not to cause environmental harm. This principle has been elaborated in arbitral decisions, in Article 21 of the *Stockholm Declaration* and Article 2 of the *Rio Declaration*, and the ICJ advisory opinion regarding the legality of nuclear weapons. Moreover, the principle is generally considered a part of customary international law. The contours of this principle, probably more than any other, will determine the legal rights and responsibilities in most disputes regarding transnational environmental damage and can be considered a part of customary international law.

The obligation not to cause environmental harm has its roots in the common law principle of *sic utere tuo ut alienum non laedus* (i.e, do not use your property to harm another*)*. In the international law context, States are under a general obligation not to use their territory, or to allow others to use their territory, in a way that can harm the interests of another State. The obligation not to cause harm to other States was extended to environmental damage as early as 1941 in the well-known *Trail Smelter* arbitration.

In that case, fumes from a Canadian smelter were damaging U.S. citizens and property. After the two countries agreed to arbitration, the U.S.–Canada International Joint Commission issued the following opinion.

> The Tribunal, therefore, finds that the above decisions, taken as a whole, constitute an adequate basis for its conclusions, namely, that, under the principles of international law, as well as of the law of the United States, *no State has the right to use or permit the use of its territory in such a manner as to cause injury by fumes in or to the territory of another or the properties or persons therein, when the case is of serious consequence and the injury is established by clear and convincing evidence.*

United Nations, *Reports of International Arbitral Awards*, Vol. III, 1905–81 (emphasis added). For a more thorough treatment of the *Trail Smelter Arbitration, see* Chapter 9 (addressing transboundary air pollution). The *Trail Smelter Arbitration* technically provides little legal precedent (because the parties had agreed to a closely circumscribed arbitration proceeding), but the general obligation not to cause harm has been confirmed in several rulings by the International Court of Justice (ICJ), including for example in the *Corfu Channel* case, which concerned damage to British warships caused by mines placed in Albanian waters. In holding Albania responsible, the ICJ stated:

> From all the facts and observations mentioned above, the Court draws the conclusion that the laying of the minefield which caused the explosions on October 22nd, 1946, could not have been "accomplished without the knowledge of the Albanian Government." The obligations resulting for Albania from this knowledge are not disputed between the Parties. Counsel for the Albanian Government expressly recognized that [translation] "if Albania had been informed of the operation before the incidents of October 22nd, and in time to warn the British vessels and shipping in general of the existence of mines in the Corfu Channel, her responsibility would be involved. . . ."

> The obligations incumbent upon the Albanian authorities consisted in notifying, for the benefit of shipping in general, the existence of a mine field in Albanian territorial waters and in warning the approaching British warships of the imminent danger to which the minefield exposed them. Such obligations are based, not on the Hague Convention of 1907, No. VIII, which is applicable in time of war, but on certain general and well-recognized principles, namely: elementary considerations of humanity, even more exacting in peace than in war; the principle of the freedom of maritime communication; *and every State's obligation not to allow knowingly its territory to be used for acts contrary to the rights of other States* [emphasis added.]

In fact, Albania neither notified the existence of the minefield nor warned the British warships of the danger they were approaching.

But Albania's obligations to notify shipping of the existence of mines in her waters depends on her having obtained knowledge of that fact in sufficient time before October 22nd; and the duty of the Albanian coastal authorities to warn the British ships depends on the time that elapsed between the moment that these ships were reported and the moment of the first explosion.

On this subject, the Court makes the following observations. As has already been stated, the Parties agree that the mines were recently laid. It must be concluded that the minelaying, whatever may have been its exact date, was done at a time when there was a close Albanian surveillance over the Strait. If it be supposed that it took place at the last possible moment, i.e., in the night of October 21st–22nd, the only conclusion to be drawn would be that a general notification to the shipping of all States before the time of the explosions would have been difficult, perhaps even impossible. But this would certainly not have prevented the Albanian authorities from taking, as they should have done, *all* necessary steps immediately to warn ships near the danger zone, more especially those that were approaching that zone. When on October 22nd about 13.00 hours the British warships were reported by the look-out post at St. George's Monastery to the Commander of the Coastal Defences as approaching Cape Long. It was perfectly possible for the Albanian authorities to use the interval of almost two hours that elapsed before the explosion affecting *Saumarez* (14.53 hours or 14.55 hours) to warn the vessels of the danger into which they were running.

In fact, nothing was attempted by the Albanian authorities to prevent the disaster. These grave omissions involve the international responsibility of Albania. The Court therefore reaches the conclusion that Albania is responsible under international law for the explosions which occurred on October 22nd, 1946, in Albanian waters, and for the damage and loss of human life which resulted from them, and that there is a duty upon Albania to pay compensation to the United Kingdom.

Corfu Channel (U.K.v. Alb.), Merits, 1949 I.C.J. Rep. 4, 22–23 (Judgment of April 9). What general international obligations can be found in the above passage? How would these obligations be relevant to an international environmental dispute?

The principle not to cause environmental harm was elaborated as Principle 21 of the 1972 Stockholm Declaration:

> States have, in accordance with the Charter of the United Nations and the principles of international law, the sovereign right to exploit their own resources pursuant to their own environmental policies, and the responsibility to ensure that activities within their jurisdiction or control do not cause damage to the environment of other States or of areas beyond the limits of national jurisdiction.

The phrase "areas beyond the limits of national jurisdiction" includes for example, the oceans and Antarctica. The principle prohibits only the impacts from activities under a State's "jurisdiction or control." *See also Rio Declaration*, at Principle 2; *Lac Lanoux Arbitration*, (Spain v. Fr.) XII R.I.A.A. 281 (1957); *UNEP Principles for Shared Natural Resources*, Principle 3; *United Nations Convention on the Law of the Sea*, Part XII; *IUCN Draft Covenant*, at Principle 4; *IUCN Draft Covenant on Environment and Development*, at Article 11.

Most commentators assumed that Principle 21 reflected customary international law as supported by *Trail Smelter* and *Corfu Channel*. Until 1996, the ICJ, however, had never clearly confirmed that environmental interests were among those interests that should not be harmed by a State.

In a 1996 advisory opinion on the Legality of the Threat or Use of Nuclear Weapons, the International Court of Justice issued one of its only opinions addressing international environmental law. In a portion of the opinion garnering eleven of fourteen votes, the Court found that customary and conventional international law neither expressly authorize nor expressly prohibit the use of nuclear weapons. In reaching this conclusion, the Court considered whether such use might be prohibited by existing international environmental law. It determined that existing environmental treaties could not have been intended to "deprive a State of the exercise of its right to self-defense under international law," and that international environmental law did not constitute "an independent bar to the use of nuclear weapons." Paras. 30 and 33. While the Court's analysis focused primarily on treaties relating to the environment, it made the following observation:

> The Court recognizes that the environment is under daily threat and that use of nuclear weapons could constitute a catastrophe for the environment. The Court also recognizes that the environment is not an abstraction but represents the living space, the quality of life and the very health of human beings, including generations unborn. *The existence of the general obligation of States to ensure that activities within their jurisdiction and control respect the environment of other States or of areas beyond national control is now a part of the corpus of international law relating to the environment.*

Para. 29–30 (emphasis added). The Court's formulation is different from that of Principle 21, but it nonetheless seems to endorse the general obligation not to cause environmental harm.

QUESTIONS AND DISCUSSION

1. Because the obligation not to "harm" the environment of other States and to "respect" the environment of other States as noted by the ICJ reflects customary law, States will be held responsible for transgressions of the principle. To apply the principle, however, requires detailed answers to several significant issues, including, for example, what level of harm should trigger the obligation? To what standard of care should the State be held? What activities should be considered under the "jurisdiction and control" of a State? What remedies should be available to States who suffer such damage? These issues are discussed further in Section L, page 424 (discussing state responsibility).

2. Principle 21 clearly outlines the underlying tension between the principle of State sovereignty and the obligation not to cause damage to another State. How should this balance be struck? When should all damage be prohibited and when should one State be responsible for compensating another State for such damage?

3. How is the ICJ formulation of the principle different than that of Principle 21? How significant is this difference? The *Rio Declaration* also changed the wording of Principle 21. *Rio* appeared to elevate the importance of the principle not to cause harm (by moving it from Principle 21 to Principle 2), but it also changed the wording to confirm that states have "the sovereign right to exploit their own resources pursuant to their own environmental *and development* policies." Does this formulation seem to be stronger or weaker than the *Stockholm Declaration's* formulation? Do you agree with the following statement from Marc Pallemaerts:

> In the Stockholm Declaration, the sovereign right of States to exploit their natural resources was affirmed in the context of their national environmental policies, giving "a more ecological colour" to the principle of sovereignty over natural resources (which was originally established in a primarily economic context). This environmental colour is now neutralized by the parallel stress on national development policies. After Rio, a State's responsibility in the exercise of its sovereign right to exploit its natural resources will no longer be measured first and foremost in terms of its environmental policy obligations, which are now explicitly subordinated to the dictates of its economic development policy.

Marc Pallemaerts, *International Environmental Law From Stockholm to Rio: Back to the Future,*5–6, in P. SANDS, ED., GREENING INTERNATIONAL LAW (1994). Do you think, given the other principles of the Rio Declaration, that the term *development* in Principle 2 can be assumed to mean *sustainable development,* as we have come to understand that term?

4. The duty to prevent environmental harm is not absolute. In practice it appears to require States to use due diligence in taking all practicable steps. For example, Article 194 of the UN Convention on the Law of the Sea requires that:

> States shall take, individually or jointly as appropriate, all measures consistent with this Convention that are necessary to prevent, reduce and control pollution of the marine environment from any source, using for this purpose the best practicable means at their disposal and in accordance with their capabilities, and they shall endeavor to harmonize their policies in this connection.

See also Convention on Environmental Impact Assessment in a Transboundary Context, Article 2(1), *done* Feb. 25, 1991, 30 I.L.M. 800, 803 (providing that "[t]he Parties shall, either individually or jointly, take all appropriate and effective measures to prevent, reduce and control significant adverse transboundary environmental impact from proposed activities"). Other Conventions link the general principle to avoid harm to one that requires due diligence in environmental management. The Basel Convention, for example, requires the "environmentally sound management of hazardous wastes and other wastes," which is defined as: "taking all practicable steps to ensure that hazardous wastes or other wastes are managed in a manner which will protect human health and the environment against the adverse effects which may result from such wastes." Basel Convention, Article 2(8); *see also, e.g.,* London Convention, 1972. Does this suggest that a negligence standard should be the appropriate standard for holding a State responsible for environmental harm? Or should the focus of the inquiry simply be on the extent and nature—the "significance"—of the resulting harm, regardless of whether the acting State was at fault?

5. The growing understanding of our ecological interdependence presents a challenge to traditional notions of State sovereignty. A growing number of observers now argue that the traditional elaboration of the obligation not to harm the environment beyond a State's jurisdiction, as set forth in the *Stockholm* and *Rio Declarations,* may be too narrow to reflect the common concern of the international community in environmental protection and sustainable development. They argue that the principle should impose at least some obligations on a State not to cause substantial environmental damage to its *own* environment, as well. What arguments can you make to suggest that some international obligation exists that prohibits a State from harming its own environment? Consider this in light of the

concepts of "common concern" or "common heritage of humankind". *See, e.g.,* IUCN Draft Covenant on Environmental Development, Article II (1995).

6.   The general obligation not to cause environmental harm also informs the more specific principle of non-discrimination, which prohibits States from shifting the burden of environmental harms, particularly those caused by industrial pollution, on to the citizens of neighboring States who often have little political leverage in the country of origin. The OECD has been a leading forum in enunciating this principle, issuing for example the following recommendation:

> Countries should initially base their action on the principle of non-discrimination, whereby
>
> a) polluters causing transfrontier pollution should be subject to legal or statutory provisions no less severe than those which would apply for any equivalent pollution occurring within their country, under comparable conditions and in comparable zones, taking into account, when appropriate, the special nature and environmental needs of the zone affected;
>
> b) in particular, without prejudice to quality objectives or standards applying to transfrontier pollution mutually agreed upon by the countries concerned, the levels of transfrontier pollution entering into the zones liable to be affected by such pollution should not exceed those considered acceptable under comparable conditions and in comparable zones inside the country in which it originates, taking into account, when appropriate, the social state of the environment in the affected country;
>
> c) any country whenever it applies the Polluter–Pays Principle should apply it to all polluters within this country without making any difference according to whether pollution affects this country or another country. . . .

OECD Principles Concerning Transfrontier Pollution, Recommendation adopted on November 14th, 1974, (C(74)224) Annex: Some Principles Concerning Transfrontier Pollution, para. 4. Principle 14 of the *Rio Declaration* affirmed the principle of non-discrimination by concluding that "States should effectively cooperate to discourage or prevent the relocation and transfer to other States of any activities and substances that cause severe environmental degradation or are found to be harmful to human health."

L.   STATE RESPONSIBILITY

Under the principle of State responsibility, States are generally responsible for breaches of their obligations under international law. As Ian Brownlie puts it:

> Today one can regard responsibility as a general principle of international law, a concomitant of substantive rules and of the supposition that acts and omissions may be categorized as illegal by reference to the rules establishing rights and duties. Shortly, the law of responsibility is concerned with the incidence and consequences of illegal acts, and particularly the payment of compensation for loss caused. However, this, and many other generalizations offered on the subject, must not be treated as dogma, or allowed to prejudice the discussion which follows. Thus the law may prescribe the payment of compensation for the consequences of legal or "excusable" acts, and it is proper to consider this aspect in connection with responsibility in general. A scientific treatment of the subject is hindered by the relatively recent generalization of the notion of liability.

Brownlie, *op cit.*, at 433.

International tribunals have several times affirmed the role of State responsibility. In the *Chorzow Factory* case, for example, the Permanent Court of International Justice, the predecessor to the International Court of Justice, held:

> It is a principle of international law, and even a general conception of law, that any breach of an engagement involves an obligation to make reparation. In Judgment No. 8 . . . the Court has already said that reparation is the indispensable complement of a failure to apply a convention, and there is no necessity for this to be stated in the convention itself.

PCIJ (1928), Ser. A, no. 17, p. 29. The *Corfu Channel* case, discussed above, also affirmed the State responsibility principle. The Court found that in allowing its waters to be mined Albania had breached its international obligation to ensure that its territory was not used in a way that harmed others. Finding that Albania failed to take necessary steps to warn ships approaching the danger zone or to otherwise avoid the harm caused by exploding mines, the Court then concluded that Albania was "responsible under international law" for the explosions and was required to pay compensation for the loss of property and human life.

State responsibility extends to breaches of international environmental law, as well. Thus, for example, States are responsible for breaching the obligation not to cause environmental harm. As noted above, Principle 21 of the *Stockholm Declaration* and Principle 2 of the *Rio Declaration* refer to the "responsibility to ensure that activities within their jurisdiction or control do not cause damage to the environment. . . ." Many commentators thus refer to Stockholm Principle 21 and Rio Principle 2 as elaborating the principle of "State responsibility for environmental harm."

The U.S. *Restatement* (Third) *of the Law of Foreign Relations* sets forth a State's general obligations and resulting responsibility toward the environment in the following way:

601. State Obligations with Respect to Environment of Other States and the Common Environment

1. A state is obligated to take such measures as may be necessary, to the extent practicable under the circumstances, to ensure that activities within its jurisdiction or control

(a) conform to generally accepted international rules and standards for the prevention, reduction, and control of injury to the environment of another state or of areas beyond the limits of national jurisdiction; and

(b) are conducted so as not to cause significant injury to the environment of another state or of areas beyond the limits of national jurisdiction.

2. A state is responsible to all other states

(a) for any violation of its obligations under Subsection (1)(a), and

(b) for any significant injury, resulting from such violation, to the environment of areas beyond the limits of national jurisdiction.

3. A state is responsible for any significant injury, resulting from a violation of its obligations under Subsection (1), to the environment of another state or to

its property, or to persons or property within that state's territory or under its jurisdiction or control.

———

As noted in *Comment a* to Section 601, the Section "applies to environmental questions the general principles of international law relating to the responsibility of states for injury to another state or its property or to persons within its territory or their property, or for injury to interests common to all states." Despite the obviously close relationship between State responsibility and the obligation not to cause harm, it is nonetheless useful to think of the "obligation not to cause environmental harm" separately from the principle of "state responsibility." The latter is broader and applies to violations of all obligations under international law, for example breaches of the obligation to notify or consult, and not only for environmental harm.

———

QUESTIONS AND DISCUSSION

1. *Jurisdiction and Control.* A State is responsible (it must provide compensation) for harm caused by its own activities, but as set forth in Principle 21 a State is also responsible for harm caused by activities under a State's "jurisdiction and control." Under what circumstances is it also responsible for activities of the private sector? This is particularly important given that pollution and other types of environmental damage are often caused by private industry. Thus, for example, in the *Trail Smelter* arbitration Canada agreed to be held responsible for the injury caused by its private industry. *Comments c* and *d* to Section 601 of the *Restatement (Third) of Foreign Relations Law* state:

> *c.* *"Activities within its jurisdiction"* and *"significant injury."* An activity is considered to be within a state's jurisdiction under this section if the state may exercise jurisdiction to prescribe law with respect to that activity under sections 402–403. The phrase "activities within its jurisdiction or control" includes activities in a state's territory, on the coastal waters that are under its jurisdiction, Part V, as well as activities on ships flying its flag or on installations on the high seas operating under its authority.... International law does not address internal pollution, but a state is responsible under this section if pollution within its jurisdiction causes significant injuries beyond its borders. "Significant injury" is not defined but references to "significant" impact on the environment are common in both international law and United States law. The word "significant" excludes minor incidents causing minimal damage.... In special circumstances, the significance of injury to another state is balanced against the importance of the activity to the state causing the injury.

> *d.* *Conditions of responsibility.* A state is responsible under Subsections (2) and (3) for both its own activities and those of individuals or private or public corporations under its jurisdiction. The state may be responsible, for instance, for not enacting necessary legislation, for not enforcing its laws against persons acting in its territory or against its vessels, or for not preventing or terminating an illegal activity, or for not punishing the person responsible for it. In the case of ships flying its flags, a state is responsible for injury due to the state's own defaults under Subsection (1) but is not responsible for injury due to fault of the operators of the ship. In both cases, a state is responsible only if it has not

taken "such measures as may be necessary" to comply with applicable international standards and to avoid causing injury outside its territory, as required by Subsection (1). In general, the applicable international rules and standards do not hold a state responsible when it has taken the necessary and practicable measures; some international agreements provide also for responsibility regardless of fault in case of a discharge of highly dangerous (radioactive, toxic, etc.) substances, or an abnormally dangerous activity (e.g., launching of space satellites).... In all cases, however, some defenses may be available to the state; e.g., that it had acted pursuant to a binding decision of the Security Council of the United Nations, or that injury was due to the failure of the injured state to exercise reasonable care to avoid the threatened harm.... A state is not responsible for injury due to a natural disaster such as an eruption of a volcano, unless such disaster was triggered or aggravated by a human act, such as nuclear explosion in a volcano's vicinity. But a state is responsible if after a natural disaster has occurred it does not take necessary and practicable steps to prevent or reduce injury to other states.

Under Subsections (2)(b) and (3), responsibility of a state for a significant injury entails payment of appropriate damages if the complaining state proves the existence of a causal link between an activity within the jurisdiction of the responsible state and the injury to the complaining state. Determination of responsibility raises special difficulties in cases of long-range pollution where the link between multiple activities in some distant states and the pollution in the injured state might be difficult to prove. Where more than one state contributes to the pollution causing significant injury, the liability will be apportioned among the states, taking into account, where appropriate, the contribution to the injury of the injured state itself.

2. Given the above discussions, what would you consider to be the primary elements that must be demonstrated to bring a claim that a State is responsible for violating Principle 21's obligation not to cause environmental harm?

3. Is the United States responsible for harm caused to Mexico's environment from air pollution emanating from a coal-fired power plant located ten miles north of the U.S.-Mexico border? What if the company is incorporated in the United States, but the pollution that is harming Mexico is emanating from a company facility located ten miles south of the Border in Mexico? Would it change your analysis or strengthen the case for State responsibility if the electricity from the facility was all being exported to the United States? What if the power plant located in Mexico was built with financial support from the Overseas Private Investment Corporation, an export-promotion agency of the U.S. government?

4. State responsibility claims are rare in the environmental field, even though there are many examples of transboundary environmental harm. Consider the 1986 failure of the Chernobyl nuclear reactor, which spread radioactive air emissions over many European countries. No affected State brought a claim against the Soviet Union. Why? Does the failure to enforce State responsibility by bringing such claims affect the legal status of this principle. *See* Chapter 12, at page 897. Could private parties bring such claims?

5. *State Liability.* The International Law Commission and other observers separate "State responsibility" from "State liability". In their view State responsibility is the obligation to make restitution for damage caused by a violation of international law; State liability is the obligation to compensate for harm caused where there is no violation of law. In the environmental field, this distinction may have little practical significance at least when applied to transboundary environmental harm. In such cases, whether certain transboundary environmental harm is lawful or unlawful—i.e. whether it violates Principle 21 of the Stockholm Declaration—is dependent at least in part on the nature and significance of the harm as well as the reasonableness of the State's actions. Thus, for a State to be held responsible for violations of Principle 21, courts would make essentially the same inquiry as if they were trying to determine whether certain environmental harm is so significant as to require an obligation of State liability, even in the absence of any violation of an international legal standard.

For further discussion of State liability, *see* Eleventh Report on International Liability for Injurious Consequences Arising Out of Acts Not Prohibited by International Law, Doc. No. A/CN.4/468 (April 26, 1995). The International Law Commission has been working on the requirements for State liability for some time now, but they are yet to be completed. In fact, no international consensus exists regarding the details for when and how liability should be assessed for international environmental damage. Both the *Stockholm Declaration,* Principle 22, and *Rio Declaration,* Principle 13, urge the international community to "develop further international law regarding liability and compensation for adverse effects of environmental damage caused by activities within their jurisdiction or control." Several treaties including the 1989 Basel Convention contain an obligation for the Parties to:

> co-operate with the view to adopting, as soon as practicable, a protocol setting out appropriate rules and procedures in the field of liability and compensation for damage resulting from the transboundary movement and disposal of hazardous wastes and other wastes.

After many years of negotiations, the liability protocol under the Basel Convention was finally completed in 2000. See Chapter 12 (discussing liability under the Basel Convention), P. BIRNIE & A. BOYLE, INTERNATIONAL LAW OF THE ENVIRONMENT 139–60 (1992).

M.   GOOD NEIGHBORLINESS AND THE DUTY TO COOPERATE

The obligation for States to cooperate generally with their neighbors in addressing international issues is a binding principle of international law. It is reflected in part in Article 1.3 of the UN Charter, which includes among the purposes of the United Nations "to achieve international cooperation in solving international problems of an economic, social, cultural, or humanitarian character...." The *1970 UN Declaration of Principles on International Law* elaborated the general obligation to cooperate in the following way:

> States have the duty to co-operate with one another, irrespective of the differences in their political, economic and social systems, in the various spheres of international relations, in order to maintain international peace and security and to promote international economic stability and progress, the general welfare of nations and international co-operation free from discrimination based on such differences.

> To this end:

> a.   States shall co-operate with other States in the maintenance of international peace and security;

> b.   States shall co-operate in the promotion of universal respect for and observance of human rights and fundamental freedoms for all, and in the

elimination of all forms of racial discrimination and all forms of religious intolerance;

c.   States shall conduct their international relations in the economic, social, cultural, technical and trade fields in accordance with the principles of sovereign equality and non-intervention;

d.   States Members of the United Nations have the duty to take joint and separate action in co-operation with the United Nations in accordance with the relevant provisions of the Charter.

States should co-operate in the economic, social and cultural fields as well as in the field of science and technology and for the promotion of international cultural and educational progress. States should co-operate in the promotion of economic growth through-out the world, especially that of the developing countries.

Declaration of Principles on International Law Concerning Friendly Relations and Cooperation Among States in Accordance with the Charter of the United Nations, U.N.G.A. Res. 2625 (Oct. 24, 1970), *reprinted in* 9 I.L.M. 1292 (1972). No mention of environment is made in the UN Charter nor in the *1970 Declaration of Principles on International Law.* As discussed in Chapter 2 on the history of international environmental law, environmental issues did not emerge on the international agenda until the 1972 Stockholm Conference. One of Stockholm's most lasting legacies was to legitimize international cooperation in the field of the environment. Thus, after Stockholm the UN Charter's reference to the duty to cooperate in the "economic, social and cultural fields as well as in the field of science and technology" implicitly included cooperation regarding the global environment.

Principle 24 of the *Stockholm Declaration* stated the obligation in the following way:

International matters concerning the protection and improvement of the environment should be handled in a co-operative spirit by all countries, big or small, on an equal footing. Co-operation through multilateral or bilateral arrangements or other appropriate means is essential to effectively control, prevent, reduce and eliminate adverse environmental effects resulting from activities conducted in all spheres, in such a way that due account is taken of the sovereignty and interests of all States.

More generally, the *Stockholm Declaration* in its entirety as well as the *Rio Declaration* twenty years later set forth the need and obligation to cooperate. According to the final principle of the *Rio Declaration* (Principle 27), for example, "States and people shall cooperate in good faith and in a spirit of partnership in the fulfilment of the principles embodied in this Declaration and in the further development of international law in the field of sustainable development." Other principles in the *Rio Declaration* require or at least urge international cooperation to address a number of issues related to sustainable development, including *inter alia* poverty alleviation, capacity-building, the conservation, protection and restoration of the Earth's ecosystem, the relocation and transfer of pollution, and the maintenance of an open international economic system.

Much of international environmental law relates to fulfilling this general obligation to cooperate in investigating, identifying, and avoiding environmental harms. Over time the duty to cooperate in the environmental context has led to the development of more specific duties relating, for example, to the need to notify and consult with potentially affected States.

N. DUTIES TO PROVIDE PRIOR NOTIFICATION AND TO CONSULT IN GOOD FAITH

The principle of prior notification obliges States planning an activity to transmit to potentially affected States all necessary information sufficiently in advance so that the latter can prevent damage to its territory, and, if necessary, enter into consultation with the acting State. Under Article 19 of the *Rio Declaration,* for example: "States shall provide prior and timely notification and relevant information to potentially affected States on activities that may have a significant adverse transboundary environmental effect."

The requirement of prior notification is often closely connected to the obligation to consult in good faith, although conceptually at least the duty to notify could exist in situations where no duty to consult exists. Principle 6 of the *1978 UNEP Principles on Shared Natural Resources* illustrates this relationship:

> It is necessary for every State sharing a natural resource with one or more other States:
>
> 1. to notify in advance the other State or States of the pertinent details of plans to initiate, or make a change in, the conservation or utilization of the resources which can reasonably be expected to affect significantly the environment in the territory of the other State or States; and
>
> 2. upon request of the other State or States, to enter into consultations concerning the above mentioned plans.

The principle of consultation requires States to allow potentially affected parties an opportunity to review and discuss a planned activity that may have potentially damaging effects. The acting State is not necessarily obliged to conform to the interests of affected States, but should take them into account. The principle has been reiterated in various other declarations and conventions, frequently including a requirement that the consultation be "in good faith and over a reasonable period of time." *See, e.g., Rio Declaration*, Principle 19; *OECD Council Recommendation on Principles Concerning Transfrontier Pollution, reprinted in* 14 I.L.M. 242 (1975); *London Guidelines for the Exchange of Information on Chemicals in International Trade,* UNEP Governing Council Decision 15/30, at Article 11 (May 25, 1989); *Montreal Rules of International Law Applicable to Transfrontier Pollution,* Article 8 (International Law Association, 1982); *UNEP Governing Council Decision: Principles of Conduct in the Field of the Environment for the Guidance of States in the Conservation and Harmonious Utilization of Natural Resources Shared By Two or More States,* Principles 7 (1978); *Convention on the Protection of the Environment Between Denmark, Finland, Norway and Sweden, done* February 19, 1974, 1092 U.N.S.T. 279 (1974), *reprinted in* 13 I.L.M. 591 (1974); *see also* Lac

Lanoux Arbitration (Fr. v. Spain), 24 I.L.R. 101 (1957), discussed *infra* in Chapter 11, page 776.

———

QUESTIONS AND DISCUSSION

1. Under what circumstances might a State be obligated to provide prior notification to another State, but not be required to enter into good faith consultations?

2. *Problem Exercise.* Although the concept of prior notification and consultation seems relatively straightforward, implementing it can be difficult. Obstacles might include language differences between countries, differences between the legal, social or economic cultures of the countries, and a lack of institutional relations for exchanging information and conducting consultations. Design a notification and consultation regime for proposed projects affecting the U.S.-Mexico Border. Consider, for example, how the notification will be provided, to whom, and what it will contain. Consider, too, what forms of consultation will be required.

3. Consultation is often institutionalized through standing international bodies (for example, the U.S.-Canada International Joint Commission, the Nordic Council, or the European Council) and through new institutions created in the framework of a specific environmental convention. *See* Chapter 5, page 233 (discussing the authority of Conferences of the Parties and treaty secretariats). What advantages for notification and consultation do permanent institutions provide?

4. *Shared Resources.* The systems of notice and consultation are not only important for potential transboundary harm, but also for the exploitation of shared natural resources. For example, Article 3 of the 1974 *Charter of Economic Rights and Duties of States* (not in force) provides that:

> In the exploitation of natural resources shared by two or more countries, each State must co-operate on the basis of a system of information and prior consultation in order to achieve optimum use of such resources without causing damage to the legitimate interest of others.

> In the context of shared natural resources, notification and information exchange are seen as ways of increasing joint development of the resources. The motivation and the effect are not necessarily aimed at environmental protection.

5. *Prior Informed Consent.* Note that the obligation of notification and consultation does not typically require States to receive the consent of the affected State. Thus in a typical situation involving transboundary environmental harms, a country (State A) planning to build in its own territory a factory causing pollution or some other harm would be under an obligation to notify an affected State (State B) and to enter into good faith negotiations with State B, but there would be no requirement to gain State B's consent. If State A actually sought to act in the territory of State B, however, simple notification and consultation are typically not sufficient. Thus, for example, a party to the Basel Convention that seeks to dispose of hazardous wastes in another State must inform the importing State of the nature of the wastes and receive the written consent of the importing State. Other activities requiring prior informed consent include transporting hazardous wastes through a State, *Basel Convention*, Article 6 (4); lending emergency assistance after a nuclear accident, *International Atomic Energy Agency Convention on Assistance in the Case of a Nuclear Accident or Radiological Emergency*, Article 2; exporting domestically banned chemical substances, *London Guidelines for Chemical Information*, Article 7; and prospecting for genetic resources, *Biodiversity Convention*,

Article 15(5). *See also* Chapter 12, pages 873–880 (describing prior informed consent in the context of chemical regulation).

6. What practical difference is there between a general duty to cooperate and more specific obligations to consult in good faith or to receive prior informed consent? Is one just a subset of the other?

———

O. Duty to Assess Environmental Impacts

Environmental impact assessment (EIA) is the process for assessing the impact of proposed activities, policies or programs to integrate environmental issues into development planning. The EIA process should ensure that *before* granting approval (1) the appropriate government authorities have fully identified and considered the environmental effects of proposed activities under their jurisdiction and control and (2) affected citizens have an opportunity to understand the proposed project or policy and to express their views to decisionmakers.

Many international instruments, international institutions, and most countries now require some form of EIA. States are also increasingly recognized to be under a general obligation to assess the environmental impacts of their activities, regardless of where those impacts or activities are located. Thus, the duty to assess environmental impacts should be reviewed in several contexts: (1) global environmental issues; (2) transboundary environmental impacts; (3) the activities of international institutions and (4) national laws addressing national environmental impacts.

Global Environmental Issues. EIA is increasingly used as a specific mechanism to further the goals of global environmental treaties. For example, Article 14 of the Biodiversity Convention states that the signatories shall as far as possible and appropriate:

> Introduce appropriate procedures requiring environmental impact assessment of its proposed projects that are likely to have significant adverse effects on biological diversity with a view to avoiding or minimizing such effects and, where appropriate, allow for public participation in such procedures.

Part of the purpose in these global treaties is simply to ensure that specific environmental impacts are included and given full consideration in the normal course of implementing domestic EIA laws. By emphasizing the role of EIA, however, global treaties also heighten the profile of the specific environmental issue (say biodiversity conservation) at the national level, thus ensuring that national governments integrate these issues into their development planning. *See, e.g., Climate Convention,* Article 4(1)(f); *Law of the Sea Convention,* Art. 206; *World Charter for Nature,* Principle 11(c); *Wellington Convention on the Regulation of Antarctic Mineral Resources Activities,* Articles 37(7)(d)–(e), 39(2)(c), 54(3)(b), *reprinted in* 27 I.L.M. 868 (1988).

Transboundary Environmental Impacts. In the transboundary context, many commentators believe that the duty to conduct an EIA is probably now a requirement of customary law. It has also been recognized in numerous treaties, and an increasing number of States are assessing transboundary impacts as part of their EIA regime. As stated in Principle 4 of UNEP's Principles on Shared Natural Resources (1978):

> States should make environmental assessments before engaging in any activity with respect to a shared natural resource which may create a risk of significantly affecting the environment of another State or States sharing that resource.

The 1991 Espoo Convention on EIA in a Transboundary Context specifies a State's obligations related to transboundary environmental impact assessment for the members of the UN Economic Commission for Europe. The Convention is an important statement of consensus, at least among the members of the Economic Commission for Europe (not including the United States), about how transboundary EIA should be implemented.

EIAs at International Institutions. EIAs have also become common requirements for certain international institutions, particularly those that support development projects that could affect the environment. All of the multilateral development banks, for example, have environmental assessment policies that apply to their project activities. The World Bank's Operational Directive on Environmental Assessment, O.D. 4.01, explains the purpose of Environmental Assessment (EA) for the Bank's international lending activities:

> The purpose of EA is to improve decision making and to ensure that the project options under consideration are environmentally sound and sustainable. All environmental consequences should be recognized early in the project cycle and taken into account in project selection, siting, planning, and design. EAs identify ways of improving projects environmentally, by preventing, minimizing, mitigating, or compensating for adverse impacts. These steps help avoid costly remedial measures after the fact. By calling attention to environmental issues early, EAs (a) allow project designers, implementing agencies, and borrower and Bank staff to address environmental issues in a timely and cost-effective fashion; (b) reduce the need for project conditionality because appropriate steps can be taken in advance or incorporated into project design, or alternatives to the proposed project can be considered; and (c) help avoid costs and delays in implementation due to unanticipated environmental problems. EAs also provide a formal mechanism for interagency coordination on environmental issues and for addressing the concerns of affected groups and local nongovernmental organizations. In addition, the EA process plays an important role in building environmental management capability in the country.

World Bank, OD 4.01, para. 2 (Oct. 1991). The U.S. bilateral development and export credit agencies, such as the Agency for International Development, the Overseas Private Investment Corporation, and the Export–Import Bank, have also all adopted some form of EIA procedures. *See* Chapter 21 for further discussion of financial institutions.

International Obligation to Implement EIA at National Level. Less clear than the obligation to assess environmental impacts in the transboundary context is whether States are obligated to assess the impacts of planned activities that are expected to have impacts solely *within* their borders. Principle 17 of the *Rio Declaration* states: "Environmental impact assessment, as a national instrument, shall be undertaken for proposed activities that are likely to have a significant adverse impact on the environment and are subject to a decision of a competent national authority." Thus, the *Rio Declaration* suggests that EIA is required for public projects presenting significant environmental impacts regardless of where they are expected to occur. *See also UNEP Governing Council Decision: Goals and Principles of Environmental Impact Assessment*, UNEP/GC.14/17, Annex III, June 17, 1987; *EEC Council Directive: Assessment of the Effects of Certain Public and Private Projects on the Environment*, Dir. No. 85/337, June 27, 1985; WCED Legal Experts Group, Article 5.

QUESTIONS AND DISCUSSION

1.   EIA has been adopted in most countries, as well as many subnational jurisdictions. In 1987, UNEP issued a set of principles as a way to improve, harmonize and strengthen EIA. Although necessarily general and developed over ten years ago, the UNEP principles still provide a good framework for evaluating and implementing EIA. *See* UNEP, Goals and Principles of Environmental Impact Assessment (1987), *reprinted in* the *Treaty Supplement*.

2.   A number of critical issues in the national implementation of EIAs can be seen in the formulation of Principle 17 of the *Rio Declaration*. First EIAs only need be done for *significant adverse impacts*. Some country laws use "substantial" impacts as the threshold for triggering the EIA requirement. The Principle also only applies to decisions of a "competent national authority," which limits the application of the EIA to government decisions at the national level. An alternative approach might have encouraged countries to apply EIAs to subnational and local decisions, as well.

3.   Article 10.7 of the North American Agreement on Environmental Cooperation, the NAFTA Environmental Side Agreement, instructs the parties (Canada, Mexico and the U.S.) to negotiate an agreement on assessing the transboundary environmental impacts of proposed projects. As part of the effort under this Article, the U.S. Council on Environmental Quality issued a *Guidance on NEPA Analyses for Transboundary Impacts*.

> Neither the National Environmental Policy Act (NEPA), 42 U.S.C. secs. 4331–4344 nor the Council on Environmental Quality's (CEQ) regulations implementing NEPA define agencies' obligations to analyze effects of actions by administrative boundaries. Rather, the entire body of NEPA law directs federal agencies to analyze the effects of proposed actions to the extent they are reasonably foreseeable consequences of the proposed action, regardless of where those impacts might occur. Agencies must analyze indirect effects, which are caused by the action, are later in time or farther removed in distance, but are still reasonably foreseeable, including growth-inducing effects and related effects on the ecosystem, as well as cumulative effects. Case law interpreting NEPA has reinforced the need to analyze impacts regardless of geographic boundaries within the United States, and has also assumed that NEPA requires analysis of major federal actions that take place entirely outside of the United States that could have environmental effects within the United States.

> In sum, based on legal and policy considerations, CEQ has determined that agencies must include analysis of reasonably foreseeable transboundary effects of proposed actions in their analysis of proposed actions in the United States.

Council on Envtl. Quality, *Guidance on NEPA Analyses for Transboundary Impacts*, at 2–4 (July 1, 1997). What are the practical difficulties in implementing this guidance? How could acceptance of the UNECE Transboundary EIA Treaty or similar agreement help to facilitate implementation? Is this guidance useful as State practice for demonstrating that the obligation to study transboundary environmental impacts is part of customary law?

3. One of the primary reasons for conducting environmental assessments is to inform the public of proposed projects and to engage them in a meaningful dialogue about the potential benefits and environmental and social costs of a proposed activity. Public participation is included in almost all EIA regimes. The World Bank (as well as the other development banks), for example, includes the following consultation and public participation procedures as part of its environmental assessment (EA) process.

Public Consultation

15. For all Category A and B projects proposed for IBRD or IDA financing, during the EA process the borrower consults project-affected groups and local nongovernmental organizations (NGOs) about the project's environmental aspects and takes their views into account. The borrower initiates such consultations as early as possible. For Category A projects, the borrower consults these groups at least twice: (a) shortly after environmental screening and before the terms of reference for the EA are finalized; and (b) once a draft EA report is prepared. In addition, the borrower consults with such groups throughout project implementation as necessary to address EA-related issues that affect them.

Disclosure

16. For meaningful consultations between the borrower and project-affected groups and local NGOs on all Category A and B projects proposed for IBRD or IDA financing, the borrower provides relevant material in a timely manner prior to consultation and in a form and language that are understandable and accessible to the groups being consulted.

Int'l Bank for Reconstruction and Development, Operational Policy 4.01, at paras. 15–16 (January 1999). Are the Bank's requirements for consultation and participation sufficient? Does the Directive adequately explain why public participation is critical to the EA process? Under the Bank's policy the EA report is the borrower's property and the Bank must get permission to release it to the public. In what ways can the Bank influence borrowing countries to release environmental information and adopt broader public consultation? See Chapter 20, pages 1476–1501 regarding environmental issues at the World Bank. As suggested by the Bank's Assessment Policy, environmental assessment is closely linked to the principle of public participation, discussed next.

————

P. PUBLIC PARTICIPATION

The role of public participation in achieving environmental protection and sustainable development is becoming increasingly recognized among governments at both the domestic and international levels. Along with the exponential growth in non-governmental organizations interested in sustainable development issues, the trend toward recognizing the right of the public, particularly locally affected communities, to participate in the environment and development decisions that affect their lives is transforming the way international policy is made in the field of sustainable development.

Principle 10 of the Rio Declaration sets forth the general parameters of the principle of public participation, including the related principles of access to information and access to justice in environmental decisionmaking:

> Environmental issues are best handled with the participation of all concerned citizens, at the relevant level. At the national level, each individual shall have appropriate access to information concerning the environment that is held by public authorities, including information on hazardous materials and activities in their communities, and the opportunity to participate in decision-making processes. States shall facilitate and encourage public awareness and participation by making information widely available. Effective access to judicial and administrative proceedings, including redress and remedy, shall be provided.

The first legally binding global environmental instrument to include public participation explicitly was the 1996 Convention to Combat Desertification, Article 3 of which required Parties "to ensure that decisions on the design and implementation of programmes to combat desertification and/or mitigate the effects of drought are taken with the participation of populations and local communities. ..." Perhaps more important for promoting public participation has been developments at the regional level. The UN Economic Commission for Europe, for example, chose to implement Principle 10 through the Convention on Access to Information, Public Participation in Decisionmaking and Access to Justice in Environmental Matters, Doc. ECE–CEP–43 (June 25, 1998). The so-called "Aarhus Convention", named after the Danish town in which the Convention was signed, sets forth a number of minimum standards for national level decisionmaking in three areas, which some commentators believe are the pillars of environmental democracy: (1) public participation in environmental decisionmaking; (2) right to access information; and (3) equal access to justice (meaning to judicial review of environmental decisionmaking). The Aarhus Convention, although open for signature from any country, is primarily aimed at the integration of central and eastern European and former Soviet Union countries into the European Union and other western alliances. The Convention was pushed hard by NGOs, which had an unprecedented impact on the negotiations. The Aarhus Convention entered into force in 2001, but few western European countries have ratified it. The Organization of American States have chosen to implement Principle 10 through a non-binding action program, entitled the *Inter-American Strategy for the Promotion of Public Participation in Decision–Making for Sustainable Development.*

QUESTIONS AND DISCUSSION

1. Some Commentators have argued that the Aarhus Convention should be used as the basis for the negotiation of a global convention on environmental democracy. Do you agree that we need such a global convention? Based on what you know, would you think that the Aarhus Convention would be the place to start?

2. A critical corollary to the right of public participation (and a right of its own) is the right of the public to have access to environmental information. The Aarhus Convention sets forth minimal elements necessary for ensuring access to information as well as potential grounds for refusal of a request for information. What in your opinion would be reasonable grounds for refusing the public information regarding protection of the environment or public health? See Aarhus Convention, Article 4; *U.S. EU Directive on Freedom of Access to Information on the Enviorment (EEC/90/313).*

3. The Aarhus Convention primarily sets out standards for national policy making, with only a general exhortation to governments to "promote the application of the principles of this Convention in international environmental decision-making processes and within the framework of international organizations in matters relating to the environment." Article 3.7. Indeed, public participation procedures, including the equivalent of notice-and-comment rulemaking, are now common practice at international financial institutions and some multilateral environmental agreements. Some commentators have begun arguing that minimum standards for public participation should be developed at the international level, perhaps in the form of an administrative procedures treaty. Do you think such a treaty is a good idea? Do you think it is politically feasible? What incentives, for example, would developing countries have to enter into a general public participation instrument? See generally C. Saladin & B. Van Dyke, Implementing the principles of the Public Participation Convention in International Organizations (June, 1998) (available from the Center for International Environmental Law, www.ciel.org).

4. Equal Right of Access to Justice. An important international issue that arises in discussions of public participation is the extent to which citizens and affected communities in other countries have rights to participate in decisions across a political border that may have transboundary environmental impacts. The OECD took the lead in the late 1970s in promoting equal participatory rights of those affected by transfrontier pollution. In Article 4 of a 1977 OECD Recommendation on the Implementation of a Regime of Equal Right of Access and Non–Discrimination in Relation to Transfrontier Pollution, (17th May, 1977, (C(77)28)):

> 4. a) Countries of origin should ensure that any person who has suffered transfrontier pollution damage or is exposed to a significant risk of transfrontier pollution shall at least receive equivalent treatment to that afforded in the Country of origin in cases of domestic pollution and in comparable circumstances, to persons of equivalent condition or status;
>
> b) From a procedural standpoint, this treatment includes the right to take part in, or have resort to, all administrative and judicial procedures existing within the Country of origin in order to prevent domestic pollution, to have it abated and/or to obtain compensation for damage caused. * * *

Section 602(2) of the *Restatement (3rd) of the U.S. Foreign Relations Law* also addresses the duty to provide equal access to judicial and administrative proceedings:

> Where pollution originating in a state has caused significant injury to persons outside that state, or has created a significant risk of such injury, the state of origin is obligated to accord to the person injured or exposed to such risk access to the same judicial or administrative remedies as are available in similar circumstances to persons within the state.

Despite the number of pronouncements like the *Restatement* on the duty to provide equal access, State practice in this regard has lagged through much of the 1980s. Europe has taken the lead in ensuring access to transfrontier plaintiffs. In 1976, the European Court of Justice held that within the European Community the victim of transfrontier pollution may sue either in his or her own or in the polluter's country, and that a decision by either country's court can be executed in any Community country. *Bier v. Mines de Potasse d'Alsace,* 1976 Eur. Comm.

Ct.J.Rep. 1735. Previously, the Nordic Environmental Protection Convention of 1974 introduced a strong regime for citizens in the Nordic countries to assert their rights against transfrontier environmental nuisances. In addition to implementing the equal right of access principle, the convention also affirmed the principle of nondiscrimination of environmental harm and established an elaborate administrative structure, involving the designation of an agency in each State to institute lawsuits or otherwise safeguard the general environmental interests of the State against transfrontier environmental harm.

The right of equal access is less developed in the United States. The Boundary Waters Treaty between the United States and Canada provides in Article 2 that "any interference with or diversion from their natural channel of [waters flowing across the boundary or into boundary waters] on either side of the boundary, resulting in any injury on the other side of the boundary, shall give rise to the same rights and entitle the injured parties to the same legal remedies as if such injury took place in the country where such diversion or interference occurs." 36 Stat. 2448, T.S. No. 548, 12 Bevans 319. Article 4(2) relating to pollution contains no similar provision, however, and the United States has no other such agreement on remedies for pollution. Since negotiation of the North American Free Trade Agreement, however, the United States, Canada and Mexico have been examining their respective approaches to transfrontier access to justice with an eye toward expanding the rights of affected people living in the other countries. See also the discussion of forum non conveniens in Chapter 19, with regard to recent lawsuits aimed at holding companies accountable in US courts for their activities abroad.

CHAPTER EIGHT

MAKING INTERNATIONAL ENVIRONMENTAL LAW WORK: IMPROVING COMPLIANCE AND RESOLVING DISPUTES

SECTION I.   INTRODUCTION: EVALUATING EFFECTIVENESS

In Chapter 5, we examined international organizations that are helping to implement that law and to develop new law. In Chapter 6, we discussed the law-making processes for creating treaties, customary norms, and international soft law. And in Chapter 7, we reviewed emerging principles of international environmental law. At this point in the course, you will likely have already considered two basic but difficult questions — Does international environmental law make any difference? And is it, in fact, law at all?

The issue of whether international environmental law *works* and, if so, *how* it works, is of critical importance in developing new legal mechanisms for addressing environmental problems and in reforming existing structures. It is not sufficient simply to develop new law. The law must be translated into action and it must lead to real improvements in environmental quality—it must be effective.

In this chapter, we examine effectiveness. We consider what it means for international law to "work" and identify essential criteria of effectiveness. As several of the authors in this chapter note, an international environmental law may be considered effective if it contributes to improvements in environmental quality or slows or prevents further environmental degradation. Because many international environmental regimes are new, however, reliable data on the environmental impact of the activities they regulate are not readily available and, indeed, may not be available for years to come. In the absence of such data, many scholars have turned to implementation and compliance—the observable effects of a law on the actions of States, corporations, and individuals—as a proxy for measuring effectiveness as well as how the international community responds to instances of non-compliance. Because of the relative importance of treaties in international environmental law and because treaties generally establish more specific obligations than do customary norms of international environmental law, we emphasize implementation and compliance with treaty law.

It's worth noting at the outset that there is a large and growing body of scholarship by legal scholars, political scientists and social scientists on the effectiveness of international efforts to protect the environment. While this chapter presents a wide range of views, it only skims the surface of this rich field of study.

———

A. INTELLECTUAL HISTORY

The role of the law in shaping international relations and modifying national behavior has been intensely studied by both political scientists and international lawyers. By the end of the nineteenth century, at least four separate schools of thought had developed over the role law plays in governing international affairs. In simple terms, the first approach, based on the writings of Thomas Hobbes, was utilitarian, arguing that nations complied with international law only when it was in their self-interest to do so. Another approach relied on the philosophy of Immanuel Kant, contending that nations' compliance with international law is guided by moral imperatives that can be derived from principles of natural law and justice. The school based on Jeremy Bentham's writings was more process-based, suggesting that the formalized structure of relations among nations encouraged compliance. Finally, the writings of John Austin supported the theory that international law was not law at all for the simple reason that it could not be enforced. Rather, international law held sway out of its moral force and nations' fear of violating accepted maxims. Harold Hongju Koh, *Why Do Nations Obey International Law?*, 106 YALE L.J. 2599, 2608–11 (1997).

The inter-war period in the 1920s and 1930s had an enormous influence on scholars' views of international law. Disillusioned by President Wilson's inability to temper the punitive sanctions of the Treaty of Versailles, the failure of the League of Nations, and the rise of fascism, the most potent criticism of international law came from a school born after World War II known as "Political Realism." Political Realism's core message was one of "realpolitik," dismissing reliance on international law to control nations' activities as idealistic and naive. The exercise of national power (both military and economic) in the pursuit of selfish domestic interests governed international affairs, not law. Political Realism's greatest champion was George Kennan, a key architect of America's Cold War policy. According to Professor Anne–Marie Slaughter, Kennan argued that,

> Woodrow Wilson and his followers were the high priests of the "legalist-moralist" tradition in American foreign policy, a tradition naively projecting the ordered domestic existence of a liberal state onto the inherent anarchy of the international system. By trying to guarantee peace through an international organization [The League of Nations] dedicated to the high-minded ideals of Wilson's Fourteen Points, the Wilsonians disarmed themselves in the face of rising fascist power. More generally, wrote Kennan, they misunderstood the relative functions and capacities of law and diplomacy—
>
> > "History has shown that the will and the capacity of individual peoples to contribute to their world environment is constantly changing. It is only logical that the organizational forms (and what else are such things as borders and governments?) should change with them. The function of a system of international relationships is not to inhibit this process of change by imposing a legal straitjacket upon it but rather to facilitate it: to ease its transitions, to temper the asperities to which it often leads, to isolate and moderate the conflicts to which it gives rise, and to see that these conflicts do not assume forms too unsettling for international life in general. But this is a task for diplomacy, in the most old-fashioned sense of the term. For this, law is too abstract, too inflexible, too hard to adjust to the demands of the unpredictable and the unexpected."
>
> This, then, was the Realist challenge to international lawyers—a challenge to establish the "relevance" of international law. International legal theorists had long grappled with the theoretical conundrum of the sources of international legal obligation—of law being simultaneously "of" and "above" the state. Yet the endless debates on this question nevertheless assumed that international legal rules, however derived, had some effect on state behavior, that law and power interacted in some way, rather than marking opposite ends of the domestic-international spectrum. Political Realists, by contrast, gave no quarter. Their challenge struck at the heart of the discipline, claiming that international law was but a collection of evanescent maxims or a "repository of legal rationalizations."
>
> The Realist challenge was not merely academic posturing. It was mounted by one of the major architects of postwar foreign policy and formulated in terms of policy prescriptions that ignored law and lawyers. The efforts to answer it shaped the evolution of postwar international legal scholarship.

Anne–Marie Slaughter, *International Law and International Relations Theory: a Dual Agenda*, 87 AM.J.INT'L L. 205, 208–09 (1993).

The responses to the challenge of Political Realism form the basis of today's international relations and international legal theories. These responses shared two important traits in common. First, they sought to show that international law "mattered," that it was relevant to the practice of international relations. Second, they expanded their vision of the law's role, moving from a narrow focus on rules that dictate behavior and punish violations to the *process* of law, both its creation and implementation. This enlarged focus achieved two important results. It widened the breadth of international law to encompass the political process underpinning its creation and application (the "stuff" of international relations), and it breathed life into international law by conceiving of it as an evolving *process* rather than as static printed text on a page.

From today's vantage, the importance of international law may seem self-evident, for there has been an explosion of international institutions since World War II. And each institution's mandate and function has grown over time. The architects of the postwar world sought to bind nations closer together through institutions with clear legal mandates. Hence the United Nations system was based on a commitment to refrain from force in international relations, yet acknowledged force through the composition and veto powers of its Security Council. The Bretton Woods System and its triumvirate of economic institutions—the World Bank, the International Monetary Fund, and the GATT—would temper nations' faltering economies, the threat of currency fluctuations, and the dangers of escalating trade wars. To a lesser extent, natural resources were included in this international barn-raising, as well, through institutions such as the International Whaling Commission. At the regional level, this strategy of reduced conflict through closer economic and political ties was brought to life through the European Economic Community. The law was critical to the functioning of these new complex structures, determining the interrelations among these institutions, nations' rights and responsibilities toward these institutions and toward themselves, and the appropriate response to new, unforeseen situations as they developed, including, for example, the rise in influence of non-State transnational actors.

B.   Compliance vs. Effectiveness

An examination of the international relations theories developed over the last few decades, such as Regime Theory, the International Legal Process School, or the New Haven School, is beyond the scope of this casebook (those interested in further background should start with the excellent articles by Professors Slaughter and Koh cited above). Our intent in this section is more general, exploring what determines whether an international regime is effective or not, i.e., what makes the law "work"?

Keep in mind that compliance and effectiveness are not synonymous. Full compliance may not be sufficient to address an environmental problem or, equally, in another context may not even be necessary for effectiveness. Whether a treaty is ultimately effective will depend on a variety of factors in addition to implementation and compliance, including timeliness—is the treaty developed in time to respond to the problem?; membership—are all or most of the necessary States parties to the treaty?; and content—would the terms of the treaty, if properly implemented, fulfill the treaty's environmental purpose? Ronald Mitchell explores these issues in the following excerpt.

Ronald Mitchell, *Compliance Theory: An Overview,* in IMPROVING COMPLIANCE WITH INTERNATIONAL ENVIRONMENTAL LAW 3, 24–26. (JAMES CAMERON ET AL., EDS., 1996)

[A] word is in order regarding the relationship between compliance and effectiveness. While this chapter argues for better evaluation of whether and how treaties alter behaviour, such behavioural change is an important, but essentially intermediate goal. We are most interested in whether treaties produce the environmental improvements that motivate their negotiation in the first place. Compliance and behavioural change are valuable only if they lead to accomplishment of treaty goals. In Oran Young's terms, we are interested in a treaty's problem-solving, as well as behaviour-changing, impacts. Some recent scholars have proposed three indicators of effectiveness that go beyond compliance, namely, the degree to which

(1) parties achieved treaty goals,

(2) actual decisions corresponded with expert advice, and

(3) the environmental resource improved relative to what would have happened in the absence of the treaty.

Evaluating effectiveness defined as problem-solving requires making an often subjective choice among various possible definitions of the problem. First, "sharp statements of objectives seldom are achieved" in international environmental treaties, making it difficult to find the yardstick against which to measure effectiveness. Second, even if one defines effectiveness as the degree of environmental improvement, the multiple causes of most environmental phenomena and the generally poor quality of data make identification of causal links extremely tenuous.

Greater compliance is neither a necessary nor sufficient condition for effectiveness. First, high compliance is not necessary. Non-compliance with an ambitious goal may still produce considerable positive behavioral change that may significantly mitigate, if not solve, an environmental problem. Second, high compliance is not sufficient. High compliance levels with rules that merely codify existing behavior, or rules that reflect political rather than scientific realities, will prove inadequate to achieve the hoped-for environmental improvement. For example, compliance with the Montreal Protocol may prove perfect but too late to avoid irreversible harm from stratospheric ozone loss.

Even a treaty that can be empirically identified as the cause of compliance may fail to lead to the desired environmental improvement. Most environmental problems have three different types of sources–the regulated human behaviour, other non-regulated human behaviours, and non-human sources. A treaty that successfully brought a halt to an environmentally harmful behaviour might not preserve the environmental resource if other human behaviours and natural factors influencing environmental quality caused the resource to be depleted.

Having said that, however, compliance can provide a valuable proxy for effectiveness, since greater compliance will produce more environmental improvement so long as the rules do not have perverse effects, although the improvement may still be insufficient to mitigate the problem. In most cases negotiated rules have a positive relationship to better management, if not resolution, of the environmental problem. In these conditions, higher levels of compliance will lead to higher levels of effectiveness, *ceteris paribus....* In other cases ... determining whether a given rule will be more effective in solving an environmental problem will require evaluating the trade-offs between a rule that offers large nominal environmental benefits but is likely to elicit low compliance and another rule that offers smaller nominal environmental benefits but has a high likelihood of compliance. A particularly striking example of such trade-offs is involved in the current choice faced by the International Whaling Commission (IWC) regarding whether to maintain a moratorium on commercial whaling in a treaty to which fewer countries are willing to be parties or allow some commercial whaling to keep countries operating under treaty auspices.

C. EFFECTIVENESS OF INSTITUTIONAL PROCESS

In evaluating the effectiveness of an environmental treaty, it is also important to recognize that many environmental problems do not admit of short-term solutions. International action often begins slowly, with information exchange, cooperative scientific effort, the establishment of consultation procedures, or simply the announcement of shared principles. Such measures should not be deemed ineffective simply because they don't take immediate and dramatic action. Effectiveness is not a binary, "yes" or "no" question, much less at a fixed point in time. Evaluating the effectiveness of law and institutions requires that we understand how they combine to form a dynamic and on-going process that is capable of "learning" and improving.

In the following reading, Haas, Keohane and Levy discuss a basic framework for evaluating institutional effectiveness. They use the term "institutions" broadly to describe "persistent and connected sets of rules and practices that prescribe behavioral roles, constrain activity, and shape expectations." They include both treaties and international organizations within the term institutions because "clusters of rules are typically linked to organizations, and it is often difficult to disentangle their effects." The framework they present reflects the authors' understanding of the dynamic web of interactions that, over time, alters humanity's relationship with the environment. (Note that throughout this book, we use the term "institution" as synonymous with "organization.")

INSTITUTIONS FOR THE EARTH: SOURCES OF EFFECTIVE INTERNATIONAL ENVIRONMENTAL PROTECTION 3–24, (PETER M. HAAS, ROBERT O. KEOHANE, & MARC A. LEVY, EDS. 1993)

How can international institutions, which necessarily respect the principle of state sovereignty, contribute to the solution of difficult global problems? What are the sources of effectiveness for institutions which lack enforcement power?
* * *

Effective institutions can affect the political process at three key points in the sequence of environmental policy making and policy implementation: (1) They can contribute to more appropriate agendas, reflecting the convergence of political and technical consensus about the nature of environmental threats; (2) they can contribute to more comprehensive and specific international policies, agreed upon through a political process whose core is intergovernmental bargaining; and (3) they can contribute to national policy responses which directly control sources of environmental degradation. * * *

We are sensitive to the possibility that sometimes institutions will play meager roles ... by design. Environmental politics is replete with symbolic action, aimed at pacifying aroused publics and injured neighbors without imposing severe costs on domestic industrial or agricultural interests. Politics within international institutions are also often highly symbolic: governments can vote one way and act another. * * *

With these reservations in mind, we can nevertheless make some exploratory attempts to assess what factors may help to account for national policy change, and to ascertain degrees of, and conditions for, institutional effectiveness. * * *

We argue that, at the level of international society, effective management of environmental problems requires three fundamental conditions to be met. First, governmental concern must be sufficiently high to prompt states to devote scarce resources to solving the problem. Since concern is typically generated by political action within societies, it is unlikely to be sufficient without active networks of individuals and groups, linked to the political system, pointing out environmental hazards and demanding action on them.

Second, transboundary and commons problems cannot be effectively resolved without a hospitable contractual environment. By this phrase we mean that states must be able to make credible commitments, to enact joint rules with reasonable ease, and to monitor each other's behavior at moderate cost so that strategies of reciprocity can be followed. In short, it must be feasible for governments to make and keep agreements that incorporate jointly enacted rules, without debilitating fear of free-riding or cheating by others.

Finally, states must possess the political and administrative capacity to make the domestic adjustments necessary for the implementation of international norms, principles, or rules. By political and administrative capacity we refer not only to the ability of governments to make and enforce laws and regulations, but also to the broader ability of actors in civil society to play an effective role in policy making and implementation. On the side of the state, the issue is broadly political as well as administrative, since the legitimacy of governments, and the degree to which they receive loyalty from their subjects and honest service from their own officials, are often open to question. Civil society, for its part, must be capable of generating discussion and criticism of governmental action and inaction, and of participating in finding and carrying out policies that respond to environmental problems. Developing countries and the governments of Eastern Europe have typically lacked adequate capacity on both the governmental and societal dimensions—governments have often been unable either to understand or to regulate the impact of their citizens and industrial enterprises on the natural environment; and groups within civil society that could have been the source of information and criticism either do not exist or have been repressed.

* * * Any effective action of international institutions with respect to the global environment is likely to follow a path that increases concern or capacity, or improves the contractual environment. . . .

Institutions can offer rewards or punishments contingent on state policy in order to increase governmental concern, and government preferences may change in response to the resulting shifts in material incentives. . . . Institutions can also generate new information that alters states' perception of the consequences of their actions. * * *

Institutions can also heighten state concern by magnifying public pressure on recalcitrant states. . . . [For example,] public exposure in high-level meetings concerning the North Sea and acid rain . . . engendered political responses within the United Kingdom that contributed directly to policy changes there. . . . Institutions can shape domestic politics by providing information that is useful to particular domestic factions, by helping bureaucracies fight turf battles, and by generating salient public commitments around which political actors can focus domestic debates. International institutions can interact with nongovernmental organizations (NGOs) and environmental movements to increase public concern, either through cooperative programs or as a result of public criticism of the international institutions and national policies by NGOs leading environmental movements.... NGOs and environmental movements are often important sources of governmental concern about the natural environment.

In seeking to improve the contractual environment in order to enhance the ability to make and keep agreements, institutions have a variety of means at their disposal. They can reduce the costs of negotiating agreements by generating information about potential zones of agreement and providing a forum for bargaining. [Our research] finds that international institutions had this effect in the case of stratospheric ozone depletion, making it possible to advance negotiations in response to rapidly changing—and increasingly frightening—scientific findings. The monitoring activities of international institutions can also be vital to the ability of states to make and keep agreements. Wherever states have reason to fear the consequences of being cheated, monitoring can help reassure them that such cheating will be detected in time to make appropriate adjustments. Monitoring makes states' commitments more credible, thereby increasing the value of such commitments. * * *

Finally, in seeking to augment political and administrative capacity, institutions can foster the transfer of information, skills, and expertise necessary for effective domestic programs. This is the central goal for population institutions and the revised prior informed consent process governing the pesticide trade. In addition to these direct information-dissemination and training activities, institutions can build coalitions with development banks and foreign aid agencies in order to funnel major quantities of aid toward projects that will help weak states increase their administrative capacity. * * *

———

The focus by Haas et al. on national level behavioral change is significant–most international environmental agreements must be implemented through national laws. In this respect, international environmental law is unlike most areas of traditional international law. The laws of war, trade, diplomatic relations and human rights, for example, are concerned primarily with the actions of States, either with respect to other States or with respect to individuals. By contrast, international environmental law uses inter-State cooperation as a means of regulating the behavior of individuals and corporations. International environmental law is largely—but not exclusively—a system for coordinating national legal responses to unsustainable *private* behaviors.

This distinction creates both difficulties and advantages for international environmental law. International environmental law generally depends on national legislative and law enforcement systems. Implementation is not complete until the national implementing laws are enforced and complied with, and ultimately change the behavior of those businesses and other actors whose activities are harming the environment. Thus, if States lack the legislative capacity to create the appropriate laws, or the resources and infrastructure necessary to enforce those laws, international agreements will be ineffective. Adequate implementation will be contingent on mobilization of the often significant resources necessary to improve implementation and enforcement within each State. At the same time, the link to national law means that international environmental law may sometimes "borrow" domestic courts for its enforcement in a way that other types of international law cannot. We will return to both of these issues later in the chapter.

————

QUESTIONS AND DISCUSSION

1. Haas et al. argue that there are "three Cs" ensuring effectiveness—concern, contractual environment, and capacity. What specific examples can you provide of the three Cs? Do you think a treaty could be effective with only one or two of the Cs but not the third?

2. Haas et al. also refer to "leader" and "laggard" States. Leaders and laggards may be different with respect to different issues. While these positions may reflect different levels of environmental concern, they also may reflect different perceptions of State interests. Thus, Haas et al. note that "leaders are often motivated by being the first to suffer environmental damage." What factors might explain why the United States led the development of the Montreal Protocol and controls on marine oil pollution under the MARPOL Convention, but has been a laggard with respect to climate change and landmines, among others? While it may be appealing to categorize one group of States as pro-environment and another as anti-environment, such categorizations are not always accurate across issues.

This is an important insight for assessing the effectiveness of international institutions, as well. It is easy to blame UNEP or the OECD for inadequate actions, but these organizations only exist at the behest and direction of their member States. The "failure" of institutions to address adequately pressing problems is, in the final analysis, more a failure of their member States than the institutions. Do you agree?

3. Note the importance the authors attribute to NGO involvement in developing national and international policy responses to environmental problems—"If there is one key variable accounting for policy change, it is the degree of domestic environmental pressure in major industrialized democracies." The material in this chapter focuses primarily on efforts by States to ensure State compliance with international environmental obligations and the way States respond to instances of non-compliance. This action takes place, however, against a background of public pressure. NGOs promote the inclusion of enforcement and monitoring provisions in treaties, monitor State implementation of and compliance with agreements, call attention to non-compliance issues, and pressure their respective governments to take action with respect to non-compliance.

Considering the observations by Haas et al., how might the human rights situation in a country affect that country's acceptance and implementation of international obligations with respect to the environment? If a country's citizens are denied the right to organize and to speak openly against government policies, is there an increased likelihood that the country will more often be a laggard than a leader on environmental issues? Recall, in this respect, the authors' reference to political repression in Eastern Europe, a region with significant environmental problems. We examine the relationship between human rights and the environment in Chapter 16.

SECTION II.   IMPLEMENTATION AND COMPLIANCE

Do States comply with international environmental law? Do States—and ultimately individuals—adjust their behavior because of the explicit rules of environmental treaties and customary norms of international environmental law? Just as with respect to effectiveness generally, the question of whether a country complies with a treaty rarely admits of a binary—"yes" or "no" answer.

> Evaluating compliance against treaty provisions ... makes more sense than speaking of compliance with the treaty as a whole. Parties often comply with some treaty provisions while violating others. Within a nation, different actors—governments, industry and non-governmental organizations (NGOs)—may well be responsible for implementing different treaty provisions. To speak of "treaty compliance" therefore loses valuable empirical information by aggregating violation of one provision with compliance with another. It also deserves mention that measuring compliance by strict reference to legal standards suggests that compliance is binary, either one complies or one violates; in fact, treaties can induce considerable beneficial behavioral change that either falls short of actual compliance, *strictu sensu*, or goes beyond minimum treaty requirements.

Mitchell, *op. cit.* at 6.

> [T]he reality is that no country complies fully with all its international legal obligations. At best, countries substantially comply with their international commitments. They may comply fully with certain obligations in a treaty, such as reporting on activities by a certain date or reducing emissions of ozone depleting substances by a given date, but they may not fully comply with other obligations, such as providing financial assistance in the amount agreed upon or on a timely basis.

Edith Brown Weiss, *Understanding Compliance with International Environmental Agreements: The Baker's Dozen Myths*, 32 RICHMOND L. REV. 1555, 1560 (1999).

With respect to a specific treaty or treaty provision, compliance can only be reliably evaluated by determining whether and to what extent States and non-State actors altered their behavior to accord with the requirements of the provision, and then establishing a causal connection between the treaty provision and the observed change. As a general proposition it is widely accepted that States tend to comply with their obligations under international law. In his classic work, HOW NATIONS BEHAVE, Louis Henkin noted,

> It is probably the case that almost all nations observe almost all principles of international law and almost all of their obligations almost all of the time. Every day nations respect the borders of other nations, treat foreign diplomats and citizens and property as required by law, observe thousands of treaties with more than a hundred countries.

LOUIS HENKIN, HOW NATIONS BEHAVE 47 (1979). Harold Hongju Koh has stated the idea even more succinctly—"Like most laws, international rules are rarely enforced, but usually obeyed." Koh, *op. cit.*, at 2599.

Koh's version raises an important point. As we discussed in Chapter 6, there are few established mechanisms for enforcing international law. Unlike individuals, who suffer sanctions if they violate laws imposed by the sovereign authority of the State, States are themselves sovereign. No supranational authority exists to enforce international law against States that violate it. Why, then, do States comply with international law?

———

A. WHY DO STATES COMPLY WITH INTERNATIONAL LAW?

The following readings examine why States comply with international law in the absence of strong enforcement mechanisms. In the first excerpt, the late Abe Chayes and Antonia Handler Chayes (formerly Legal Advisor to the State Department and Undersecretary of the Air Force, respectively) offer a counter-intuitive thesis—that seemingly "weak" treaties without punitive sanctions are often as effective as treaties *with* sanctions. Because States are interconnected in a loose but broad fabric of international society and norms, States are motivated to comply with their international obligations not by fear of specific sanctions but by a more general interest in maintaining good standing in the international community. The challenge for the treaty regime is more about setting up procedures, institutions and norms that allow for the "management" of compliance problems than it is about the "enforcement" of specific and potentially narrow treaty requirements. In the second reading, Ronald Mitchell asserts the realist perspective that States tend to comply with international law because it is in their interest to do so.

ABRAM CHAYES & ANTONIA CHAYES, THE NEW SOVEREIGNTY 3–28 (1995)

If treaties are at the center of the cooperative regimes by which states and their citizens seek to regulate major common problems, there must be some means of assuring that the parties perform their obligations at an acceptable level. To provide this assurance, political leaders, academics, journalists, and ordinary citizens frequently seek treaties with "teeth"—that is, coercive enforcement measures. In part this reflects an easy but incorrect analogy to domestic legal systems, where the application of the coercive power of the state is thought to play an essential role in enforcing legal rules. Our first proposition is that, as a practical matter, coercive economic—let alone military—measures to sanction violations cannot be utilized for the routine enforcement of treaties in today's international system, or in any that is likely to emerge in the foreseeable future. The effort to devise and incorporate such sanctions in treaties is largely a waste of time. * * *

We identify three sorts of considerations that lend plausibility to the assumption of a propensity to comply: efficiency, interests, and norms. Of course these factors, singly or in combination, will not lead to compliance in every case or even in any particular case. But they support the assumption of a general propensity for states to comply with their treaty obligations, and they will lead to a better understanding of the real problems of noncompliance and how they can be addressed.

Efficiency

Decisions are not a free good. Governmental resources for policy analysis and decision making are costly and in short supply. Individuals and organizations seek to conserve these resources for the most urgent and pressing matters. In these circumstances, standard economic analysis argues against the continuous recalculation of costs and benefits in the absence of convincing evidence that circumstances have changed since the original decision. The alternative to recalculation is to follow the established treaty rule. Compliance saves transaction costs. In a different formulation, students of bureaucracy tell us that bureaucratic organizations operate according to routines and standard operating procedures, often specified by authoritative rules and regulations. The adoption of a treaty, like the enactment of any other law, establishes an authoritative rule system. Compliance is the normal organizational presumption. A heavy burden of persuasion rests on the proponent of deviation.

Interests

A treaty is a consensual instrument. It has no force unless the state has agreed to it. It is therefore a fair assumption that the parties' interests were served by entering into the treaty in the first place. Accordingly, the process by which international agreements are formulated and concluded is designed to ensure that the final result will represent, to some degree, an accommodation of the interests of the negotiating states. Modern treaty making, like legislation in a democratic polity, can be seen as a creative enterprise through which the parties not only weigh the benefits and burdens of commitment but also explore, redefine, and sometimes discover their interests. It is at its best a learning process in which not only national positions but also conceptions of national interest evolve and change. * * *

The same process may be seen in every major U.S. international negotiation. For example, at the end of what Ambassador Richard Benedick calls "the interagency minuet" in preparation for the Montreal Protocol to the Vienna Convention for the Protection of the Ozone Layer, the final U.S. position "was drafted by the State Department and was formally cleared by the Departments of Commerce and Energy, The Council on Environmental Quality, EPA, NASA, NOAA, OMB, USTR, and the Domestic Policy Council (representing all other interested agencies)." In addition to this formidable alphabet soup, the White House units, like the Office of Science and Technology Policy, the Office of Policy Development, and the Council of Economic Advisors, also got into the act.

In the United States in recent years, the increasing involvement of Congress and, with it, nongovernmental organizations and the broader public has introduced a new range of interests that must ultimately be reflected in the national position. Similar developments seem to be occurring in other democratic countries. Robert Putnam has described the process as a two-level game, in which the negotiations with the foreign parties must eventuate in a treaty that is acceptable to interested domestic constituencies.

For contemporary regulatory treaties, the internal analysis, negotiation, and calculation of benefits, burdens, and impacts are repeated at the international level. In anticipation of negotiations, the issues are reviewed in international forums long before formal negotiation begins. The negotiating process itself characteristically involves an intergovernmental debate that often lasts years, not only among national governments but also among international bureaucracies and nongovernmental organizations as well. The most notable case is the United Nations Conference on the Law of the Sea (UNCLOS III), which lasted for more than ten years and spawned innumerable committees, subcommittees, and working groups, only to be torpedoed by the United States, which, having sponsored the negotiations in the first place, refused to sign the agreement. Bilateral arms control negotiations between the United States and the Soviet Union were similarly extended, although only the two superpowers were directly involved. Environmental negotiations on ozone and global warming have followed very much the UNCLOS III pattern. The first conference on stratospheric ozone was convened by the United Nations Environment Program (UNEP) in 1977, eight years before the adoption of the Vienna Convention. The formal beginning of the climate-change negotiations in February 1991 was preceded by two years of work in the Intergovernmental Panel on Climate Change, convened by the World Meteorological Organization (WMO) and UNEP to consider scientific, technological, and policy response questions.

Especially in democracies, but to a certain extent elsewhere as well, this negotiating activity is open to some form of public scrutiny, triggering repeated rounds of national bureaucratic and political review and revision of tentative accommodations among affected interests. The two-level game gives some assurance that the treaty as finally signed and presented for ratification is based on considered and well-developed conceptions of national interest that have themselves been informed and shaped to some extent by the preparatory and negotiating process. * * *

It is true that a state's incentives at the treaty negotiating stage may be different from those it faces at the stage of performance. Parties on the giving end of the compromise, especially, might have reason to seek to escape the obligations they have undertaken. But the very act of making commitments entrenched in an international agreement changes the calculus at the compliance stage, if only because it generates expectations of compliance in others that must enter into the equation. Although states may know they can violate their treaty obligations if circumstances or their calculations go radically awry, they do not negotiate agreements with the idea that they can break them whenever the commitment becomes "inconvenient." * * *

Norms

Treaties are acknowledged to be legally binding on the states that ratify them. In common experience, people–whether as a result of socialization or otherwise–accept that they are obligated to obey the law. The existence of legal obligation, for most actors in most situations, translates into a presumption of compliance, in the absence of strong countervailing circumstances. So it is with states. It is often said that the fundamental norm of international law is *pacta sunt servanda*–treaties are to be obeyed. In the United States and many other countries, they become a part of the law of the land. Thus, a provision contained in an agreement to which a state has formally assented entails a legal obligation to obey and is presumptively a guide to action.

It seems almost superfluous to adduce evidence or authority for a proposition that is so deeply ingrained in common understanding and so often reflected in the speech of national leaders. Yet the realist argument that national actions are governed entirely by a calculation of interest is essentially a denial of the operation of normative obligation in international affairs. This position has held the field for some time in mainstream international relations theory (as have closely related postulates in other positivist social science disciplines). Nevertheless, it is increasingly being challenged by a growing body of empirical study and academic analysis. * * *

Jon Elster, often regarded as one of the most powerful scholars of the "rational act" school, says, "I have come to believe that social norms provide an important kind of motivation for action that is irreducible to rationality or indeed to any other form of optimizing mechanism." As applied to treaty obligations, this proposition seems almost self-evident. An example: in the absence of the Anti–Ballistic Missile (ABM) Treaty, the Soviet Union would have been legally free to build an ABM system. If they had exercised this freedom, it would surely have posed serious military and political issues for

U.S. analysts, diplomats, and intelligence officers. In due course the United States would have responded, either with its own ABM system or some other suitable military or political move. The same act, the construction of a Soviet ABM system, would be qualitatively different, however, if it were done in violation of the specific undertaking of the ABM Treaty. Transgression of such a fundamental engagement would trigger not a limited response but an anxious and hostile reaction across the board, jeopardizing the possibility of cooperative relations between the parties for a long time to come. Outrage when solemn commitments are treated as "scraps of paper" is rooted in U.S. history. It is unlikely that this kind of reaction is unique to the United States.

Even in the stark, high politics of the Cuban missile crisis, State Department lawyers argued that the United States could not lawfully react unilaterally, since the Soviet emplacement of missiles in Cuba did not amount to an "armed attack" sufficient to trigger the right of self-defense under Article 51 of the UN Charter. It followed that use of force in response to the missiles would be lawful only if approved by the Organization of American States (OAS). Though it would be foolish to contend that this legal position determined President Kennedy's decision, there is little doubt that the asserted need for advance OAS authorization for any use of force contributed to the mosaic of argumentation that led to the decision to respond initially by means of the quarantine rather than with an air strike. Robert Kennedy said later, "It was the vote of the Organization of American States that gave a legal basis for the quarantine ... and changed our position from that of an outlaw acting in violation of international law into a country acting in accordance with twenty allies legally protecting their position." * * *

In the next excerpt, Ronald Mitchell expands on the theme of self-interest discussed in the Chayes and Chayes piece. Mitchell focuses on the relationship of treaties to behavioural change in States; he argues that States often act in accordance with a treaty's provisions because those provisions tend to reflect national policy preferences. As you read the Mitchell piece, consider how his views differ from those of Abram and Antonia Chayes. Are they more pessimistic, more realistic, or neither? If Mitchell is correct, what does this suggest about the pace and degree of behavioural change in an international system dominated by nation-States?

Ronald Mitchell, *op. cit.*, at 7–11

The simplest explanation of why a government or other actor regulated by a treaty undertakes a given behaviour is because they believe it furthers their interest. Nations often negotiate treaties precisely "for the promotion of their national interests, and to evade legal obligations that might be harmful to them." As consensual agreements between nations, treaty provisions reflect the relative success of the different signatories in promoting their interests. Obviously, a key determinant of the willingness to comply is the degree of behavioural change the treaty requires. The degree of required change varies across treaties and across rules and actors within a single treaty.

Actors may comply because the treaty rules require no change in behaviour. Through successful negotiation a country may place all the burden for adjustment on other states. "Leader" states negotiating an environmental accord may already have established and implemented legislation that goes well beyond the requirements to which "laggard" states will agree. Industries already meeting a specified pollution standard may support treaties that require their foreign counterparts to do the same as a means of improving competitiveness without changing their behaviour. Especially when agreements reflect lowest common denominator policies, many states and companies will find themselves already in compliance. Some states may simply not be engaged, or only minimally engaged, in the activity regulated by the treaty, as is the case with Switzerland's membership in the oil pollution and whaling regimes.

Compliance is not surprising when agreements proscribe undesirable actions that no one currently has incentives to undertake, in hopes of restraining future economic, political or technological pressures for such actions. As in the Antarctic Treaty's constraints on mining, such agreements codify existing behaviours to "protect against changes in preferences." Compliance to date has been perfect because the availability of lower-cost sources elsewhere has meant that incentives to mine in Antarctica remain low.

States can also facilitate their own compliance by negotiating vague and ambiguous rules. Ambiguity may reflect agreements reached despite sincere differences about a specific rules content—"papering over"—or efforts to accrue environmental praise by agreeing to terms that appear to require behavioural change, but that prove sufficiently vague to allow business as usual. The absence of an international court to interpret such ambiguities authoritatively "naturally" leads states to interpret treaty rules so they can behave as their interests dictate while claiming their behaviour is in compliance. While excessively selfserving interpretations may well elicit international and domestic criticism, ambiguous treaty language makes charges of outright violation difficult.

When treaties require new behaviours, they may only require signatories to take actions they already know they want to take. Unilateral compliance may be a preferred option. In some such case, the state would have behaved as it did in any event, compliance being strictly coincidental. In others, the agreement provides international legitimacy which increases domestic political support enough to enable the government to implement a desired but otherwise unattainable policy. For example, a climate change agreement may provide some governments with the impetus necessary to adopt energy taxes. Treaties may also reflect "suasion" games where one or more powerful states benefit from unilateral compliance but benefit more if others also comply. While it will seek to get others to comply, such a state will comply whether or not those strategies succeed. DuPont's phase-out of CFCs and Conoco's installation of double-hull tankers before internationally required suggests these companies decided to comply independently of other companies' decisions, though they preferred that others comply.

The preceding sources of compliance show how actors may comply out of self-interest even if they define that interest myopically and independently of others' actions. However, the calculus leading a state to comply may involve more expanded notions of independent self-interest than realist scholars would concede. Institutionalists point to states adopting broader and longer-term views of self-interest, including joint gains and empathy, for example, that lead them to comply in a wider range of situations than realism would predict. States and corporations may fear the unknown and unintended side-effects of their current non-compliance on the future of the treaty and on a range of other relationships. They may fear adverse public opinion, domestically or internationally. Parties may comply with rules viewed as fair and legitimate even if costly at times. Even when dominant, powerful (hegemonic) states coerce weaker states to accept a treaty, legitimate social purposes and changes in perceived self-interest may cause nations to continue complying past the point that immediate self-interest can explain. These conceptions of self-interest veer away from strictly independent decision-making: rather than making worst case assumptions that no others will comply, the decision-maker forecasts compliance by others based on past experience to calculate the expected benefits of their own compliance. * * *

While compliance is calculated independently of other actors' behaviours, it is not a static decision. Over time, economic and technological changes can "cause national governments to change their minds about which rules or norms of behaviour should be reinforced and observed and which should be disregarded and changed." Reductions in the price of alternatives to chlorofluorocarbons (CFCs) have increased the likelihood that the Montreal Protocol's phase-out deadlines will be met. * * *

Powerful non-state actors, including multinational corporations, nongovernmental environmental groups and scientists, often influence international politics directly and by helping to define state interests. New scientific knowledge or greater environmental activism can cause increases in the perceived costs of an environmental externality and lead to greater compliance. Elections or larger social or political factors often change the bargaining positions of domestic bureaucratic and political groups, altering how a state assesses its interests in compliance. Domestic environmental groups may become increasingly powerful and concerned; treaties provide them with "a stronger case for constraint than would be possible in the absence of such obligations". * * *

At any given time, however, for those governments or non-state actors basing compliance decisions on self-interests independently defined, compliance proves robust and concerns over non-compliance are minimal. Indeed, the behaviour of these actors is not treaty-induced compliance. For these actors, treaty rules have been brought in line with existing or intended future behaviours, and not vice versa. When most parties to a treaty have such interests, the rule will exhibit high compliance even absent positive inducements or negative sanctions. * * *

Compliance as interdependent self-interest

* * * In coordination games, each actor prefers compliance so long as enough other actors comply. While "enough" varies from actor to actor, each assesses whether to comply based on the actions, or expected actions, of others. Realists see such complementarity of interests in compliance as explaining why most treaties require so little enforcement. * * *

Situations involving public goods can exhibit similar properties for some actors involved. If enough actors recognize that they can be better off collaborating to produce a public good and can trust each other enough to "jump" to this joint outcome, a subset of all actors can negotiate and comply with an agreement even though other nations continue to violate. Actors willing to tolerate non-compliance by others may achieve joint gains, even though those gains are less than they would be if all actors complied. * * *

Compliance in collaboration problems can arise from enforcement by a dominant or hegemonic state with system-wide concerns that sees what may be a collaboration problem for others as a suasion game. The dominant state manages the problem because it is capable of, and perceives sufficient benefits from, complying itself and/or enforcing compliance by others. Weak states are forced to comply with these "imposed orders" by "coercion, cooptation, and the manipulation of incentives." [For examples, *see* Chapter 19's discussion of extraterritorial applications of domestic law.]

Fears of free-riding can also be overcome if states view the benefits they derive in other existing and future international agreements as conditional upon a record of compliance. Such caution is fostered when states detect violations and either reciprocate with their own violation or "discount the value of agreements on the basis of past compliance." Even if compliance in a given instance may be costly when narrowly construed, the costs in other areas and on one's reputation can persuade a state to comply. Compliance under such conditions is possible but will be more fragile and more difficult to establish than when actors have independent interests in compliance.

Since such cooperation depends on some degree of international trust, decreases in underlying rivalries and competition, such as the end of the Cold War, will likely increase compliance levels. As with changes in power, such a change may produce changes to treaty rules as well as compliance levels, leading to spurious correlations. However, the regime itself can increase trust by improving knowledge and reducing misperceptions of other states. Over time, such trust, reputations, rule legitimacy, and habitual practice grow and can reinforce incentives for compliance.

In addition to the treaty-specific insights of the scholars excerpted above, recall, as well, that a dynamic system is at work. Treaties do not exist, nor are they negotiated, in isolation. They interact with one another and this has serious implications for compliance and effectiveness of *individual* treaties. Consider that over 240 international environmental agreements have now been signed, and more than two-thirds of these date from the Stockholm Conference in 1972. If one includes bilateral environmental agreements and agreements with at least one significant environmental provision, the number approaches 900. *See* Figure 8–1, below, from Lester Brown et al., VITAL SIGNS 134 (2000).

On the positive side, this growth provides powerful evidence of the international community's concern over environmental protection. On the negative side, however, this explosion of treaties and their accompanying commitments have created what some now call "treaty congestion." *Substantive treaty congestion* raises concerns because treaties' combined requirements may overlap and create inefficient redundancies, may leave gaps in coverage, or may even cause conflicting obligations. *Procedural treaty congestion* occurs by overextending the limited time and resources (especially in developing countries) necessary to ensure compliance with treaty obligations and to negotiate new agreements (so-called "negotiation fatigue"). Ironically, the growth of international environmental agreements, some have argued, may be a case where more is less. *See generally* Edith Brown Weiss, *Strengthening National Compliance with International Environmental Agreements*, 27 ENVTL. POL'Y & L. 297 (1997); Bethany Lukitsch Hicks, *Treaty Congestion In International Environmental Law: The Need For Greater International Coordination*, 32 U. RICH. L. REV. 1643 (1999).

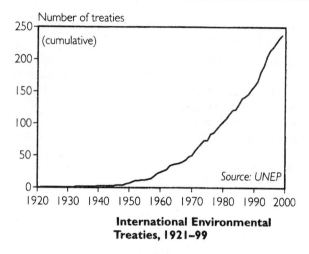

**International Environmental
Treaties, 1921–99**

Figure 8–1

QUESTIONS AND DISCUSSION

1. When "compliance is not caused by the treaty, but merely coincides with it," the treaty cannot logically be considered effective. Under certain circumstances, however, independent changes in State behavior may bear an indirect but still important relation to the existence of the treaty regime. A notable example is the Montreal Protocol on Substances that Deplete the Ozone Layer. Beginning in the mid–1970s, the United States, Canada, and the Nordic countries took dramatic unilateral action to reduce emissions of ozone-depleting CFCs. At the time the Montreal Protocol was negotiated, these countries maintained CFC reduction policies that were significantly more stringent than treaty requirements. The fact that these States maintained their policies following the Protocol's entry into force suggests that their compliance was only coincidental with the treaty. In fact, these States were leaders in negotiating stringent international controls precisely *because* they were opposed to bearing the significant burden of CFC reductions by themselves. By banning the use of aerosol CFCs, for example, the United States lost its global CFC markets to European countries that increased their own CFC production to feed global demand. If its economic competitors had not agreed to curb their own CFC production, the United States would have faced significant pressure from domestic industries to ease or abandon its own CFC controls. The conclusion of a global agreement allowed the United States to maintain an environmental policy it might otherwise have abandoned. As Mitchell notes, providing security against free riders and environmental "leakage"—in which environmental gains made by one country are undermined by actions in another—is a significant function of multilateral environmental agreements.

2. A number of international relations theorists have proposed factors to predict whether a State will comply with its international legal obligations. Which of the factors listed below do you think correlate closely with a State's compliance with its international environmental legal obligations? Why do you expect this is so?

- parliamentary ratification of treaties versus executive branch ratification
- high versus low per capita income
- high versus low percentage of women in political life
- high versus low number of pages of environmental laws

- high versus low amount of annual fines for environmental violations
- high versus low average level of formal education
- democracy versus dictatorship
- agricultural versus industrial economic base
- high versus low media reporting of environmental issues

3. Why might compliance and implementation in the context of international environmental law be different than in other areas of international law? For example, many international environmental problems have significant impacts that are difficult to reverse, except in the long-term (e.g. climate and ozone depletion). Moreover, enforcement of environmental treaties may be particularly difficult because there is little opportunity to take reciprocal actions as a form of sanction. When a country violates a trade agreement, for example, sanctions often take the form of a response in kind. If trade tariffs are judged illegal by the WTO, the injured country may raise countervailing tariffs. Environmental agreements do not present similar options because retaliation (equivalent countermeasures) in response to noncompliance would only exacerbate the overall environmental problem, to the detriment of all countries. Over-fishing, for example, would just lead to more over-fishing. With the range of potential sanctions reduced, reliance on innovative mechanisms for resolving compliance problems becomes important. Finally, the overall effectiveness and success of certain regimes in achieving their environmental goals may require the cooperation of every state. Thus, for example, a climate change convention that does not include the active participation of India and China will not be effective in preventing climate change.

4. In a provocative article, Professor Edith Brown Weiss proposes a dozen myths surrounding compliance with environmental agreements. As you read the list below, can you think of examples to prove her point? What about counter-examples?

One: All countries comply fully with their international commitments, or, countries never comply with their international commitments.

Two: Implementation, compliance, enforcement, and effectiveness are interchangeable terms that have the same meaning.

Three: Binding agreements are always preferable to nonbinding ones because countries comply with binding agreements better than they comply with nonbinding agreements.

Four: Secretariats for international agreements are like puppets on strings that governments control. They have little influence; their activities are minimal.

Five: The more precise the obligation, the better the compliance by parties.

Six: Regular country reports are critical for monitoring compliance. Full compliance by all states party to the agreement is essential.

Seven: Decentralizing implementation of the agreement and making local communities responsible improves compliance.

Eight: Democracy always promotes compliance. Democratic countries always comply better than nondemocratic countries.

Nine: The influence of nongovernmental organizations always leads to better state compliance.

Ten: Formal dispute resolution procedures are essential to achieving compliance with an international environmental agreement.

Eleven: Coercive measures in cases of noncompliance are essential to securing compliance with international environmental agreements.

Twelve: Markets create incentives for countries not to comply with agreements, or, free markets always promote compliance.

Edith Brown Weiss, *Understanding Compliance with International Environmental Agreements: The Baker's Dozen Myths,* 32 Richmond L. Rev. 1555, 1560 (1999). *See also,* Kal Raustiala, *Compliance and Effectiveness in International Regulatory Cooperation,* 32 Case Western Reserve J. Int'l. L. 387 (2000); Kal Raustiala et al., The Implementation and Effectiveness of International Environmental Commitments (1998).

———

B.   The View from Political Scientists

International environmental law and policy are, by their very nature, interdisciplinary fields, studied by lawyers, political scientists, ethicists, and natural scientists, among others. Many political scientists believe there are shortcomings to taking a law-based approach to resolving international environmental problems. In particular, political scientists' study of international environmental policy has been undergoing rapid change, with the early interest in problem definition and treaty making as problem solution rapidly giving way to skeptical questioning of environmental treaty regimes' effectiveness.

At our invitation, Kate O'Neill (University of California, Berkeley), William C.G. Burns (Pacific Institute for Studies in Development, Environment and Security), and Geoffrey Wandesforde–Smith (University of California, Davis) argue below that faith in law as an instrument of problem solving needs to be re-thought and bolstered as we get further and further from Rio. They briefly identify the problems associated with a narrow State-centered compliance approach to international environmental policy and argue that treaties are important because over time they also frame choices by non-State and sub-State actors that are crucial for treaty effectiveness. The full citations for their piece are available on the casebook website at (http://www.wcl.american.edu/environment/iel/teachmaterial.htm).

Kate O'Neill, William C.G. Burns, and Geoffrey Wandesforde–Smith

Working with the Limitations and Frustrations in a Treaty-Based Approach to International Environmental Problem Solving (2001)

There is now a substantial body of social science literature on environmental regimes that addresses the question of treaty effectiveness. In the last two or three years, partly in recognition of the methodological difficulties in proving treaties' actual and independent effectiveness, there has been a shift away from a focus on treaty compliance as a proxy measure for treaty effectiveness.

At the outset, we emphasize that we believe that treaties and treaty regimes do make a positive difference. However, it is increasingly clear that a meaningful assessment of the effectiveness of environmental treaties and treaty regimes takes longer to emerge, yields uneven results across States, and is much more heavily dependent on domestic political factors than most international legal scholars acknowledge.

Some commentators have taken the position that there should be a presumption against the effectiveness of legal responses to environmental maladies absent clear and convincing proof that the law changes State preferences. Moreover, they press for proof that legal approaches are more effective than other mechanisms for addressing environmental issues, such as relative price changes for environmental resources or the narrow but rational calculations of self-interest by a handful of rich and powerful States.

Others have argued that it is difficult, if not impossible, to adduce clear and convincing evidence that treaties change State preferences. Nonetheless, they view the establishment and enforcement of treaties as salutary, chiefly because their field of vision is more bottom up than top down and includes and considers the role of not only States but also non-State actors as powerful drivers of change. They also contend that a complex interplay of international law with domestic politics produces results that clearly influence choices by government actors. This goes beyond the conception of "law as evolving process" propounded in the first edition of this textbook. However, this ability of law to frame choices only comes into clear focus when specific agents of change are identified and when regime research employs substantially longer time frames than those in the early regime studies.

In this section, we briefly describe three strategies social scientists are currently pursuing in their effort to expand the conception of effectiveness beyond a narrow focus on compliance with international treaties. First, social scientists argue that greater attention to a wider range of policy mechanisms, such as emissions trading, would complement a legalistic approach to international regulation. Second, they stress that international policy effectiveness cannot be understood separately from domestic political factors and the active role of individuals and groups working in national politics. Third, there has been a shift in recent years towards examining the material factors that can improve countries' capacity to meet international commitments. Together, these strategies help facilitate an understanding of the limits of a treaty-based approach to international environmental problems, and significantly improve our understanding of the nuances and complexities of inducing nations to cooperate to confront global problems. They complement, rather than replace international law approaches, by demonstrating how international legal frameworks enable political action at the national level to redress environmental damage. For example, national environmental groups are able to use international legal commitments as a spur to prod their governments into action. Market-based policy mechanisms provide economic incentives to multinational corporations to change behavior. Finally, international legal frameworks have taken on a large capacity building role, in both developing and developed countries.

1. Acknowledging the Problem: Limits of a Positivist Approach to Treaty Compliance

Consider, first, political scientists and economists who are prepared to write off treaty-based approaches, essentially because of methodological problems in proving that regime processes are the most important factors affecting State preferences and because of a bias in favor of rival political economy theories about what drives change in the international system. Political economists assume State preferences are most directly determined and influenced by relative price changes for environmental goods and that States are impervious to the social processes of treaty compliance highlighted by Ronald Mitchell and by Abram and Antonia Chayes. Thus, the political economy challenge to the early compliance research on environmental regimes was to focus more directly on the determinants of effectiveness. However, it proved difficult to formulate an operational definition of effectiveness that researchers could easily recognize and which would facilitate inter-subjectively reliable measurements. Even more troubling difficulties arose when social scientists chose to extend the same demanding standards of analytical theory used previously in studies of security, trade, financial, and regional integration regimes to the new environmental regimes formed in the 1980s and 1990s.

The central claim in all these cases of regime formation is that international legal agreements can induce States to cooperate in accordance with the rules of international law. However, rigorous and systematic testing of this claim requires isolation of the causal link between the rules and the behaviors that embody compliance. Without proof of this nexus, it is impossible to distinguish the impact of legal rules from other variables that also plausibly influence State preferences and behavior, such as the influence of international institutions or domestic political considerations. In addition, the establishment of a causal connection between rules and compliance can be confounded by selection bias (some commentators contend that States only make treaties in issue areas where there are minimal problems of strategic cooperation) and by endogeneity (States may only enter into agreements with which they are likely to comply, rendering evidence of compliance uninteresting and inconsequential).

Given problems of research method in establishing that regime processes really *are* driving change, some regime analysts feel more comfortable in relying on traditional political economy variables, such as national interests or preferences in understanding regime impact. And they downplay, therefore, the role of other independent variables such as the political tactics and strategies of NGOs, the meetings of treaty parties, and all the other purportedly constitutive dimensions of State behavior on which so much regime research has concentrated. A recent review of the major effectiveness studies published in the last two years is trenchant.

> Despite ... variation across ... twenty-odd [environmental regime] cases ... in three books, the empirical picture of environmental cooperation and the role of environmental regimes in changing State preferences differs remarkably little—at least qualitatively—from that which has emerged in the security and trade literatures and from the expectations established by the political economy literature. Relative price changes, usually in the form of costly deterioration of environmental conditions and the development of improved environmental technologies, *have been by far the most important determinants of changes in State preferences.* Although these exogenous relative price changes may not be sufficient conditions for the establishment of effective regulation, it appears that without them nothing is likely to happen. Their primacy suggests that they set an important limit on the malleability of State preferences by institutions [such as environmental treaty regimes].

George W. Downs, *Constructing Effective Environmental Regimes*, 3 ANN. REV. POL. SCI. 25, 40–41 (2000) (emphasis added).

2. Mixing Law with Economic Policy Instruments

Another approach argues that if regimes are to be retained as primary tools of environmental problem-solving, they need very substantial restructuring to deal with the major political weaknesses of the international system, such as the lack of well-defined or enforced property rights. Works in this approach focus especially on the use of market-based economic policy tools, such as green taxes or emissions trading. A recent critique of the global climate change regime applies also to other instances where regimes seek to regulate global commons.

> Fundamental [to my critique] is the relationship between property rights and institutions, a central topic in economics and political science. Launching an emission trading system requires creating a new form of property right—the right to emit greenhouse gases—and institutions to monitor, enforce, and secure those new property rights. [T]he Kyoto Protocol fails principally because international law is a poor mechanism for securing property rights. This problem multiplies when the trading of these property rights must include the participation of countries that do not have strong and impartial national legal institutions, which is the case in most of the former Soviet Union and most developing countries. Yet these "illiberal" nations are exactly the ones whose inclusion is critical.... *Under international law, I argue, it is not possible to create the institutional conditions that are necessary for an international tradable emission permit system to operate effectively.* Kyoto's troubles indicate the need for clear thinking about the effectiveness of international treaties as devices for regulating behavior. The limited influence of international law requires careful design—to make the most of the levers that international law does offer. * * *

DAVID G. VICTOR, THE COLLAPSE OF THE KYOTO PROTOCOL AND THE STRUGGLE TO SLOW GLOBAL WARMING ix-xiii, 114–115, (2001) (emphasis added).

3.   Structure and Agency: International Law and Domestic Politics

Political scientists are also starting to look at how domestic politics, broadly defined, affects the way international environmental problems are addressed, and how international agreements are implemented. This brings into sharp focus the influence of national structures of environmental regulation and national political styles on implementation of international environmental agreements.

> The ... claim ... that institutional factors can significantly constrain the actions and choices of "free" political actors is by no means uncontested in the field of political science. * * *

> The emerging focus ... on how to evaluate the effectiveness, or success, of environmental regimes ... [has considered] factors located primarily ... at the international level ... [and this] has led to some clearly identifiable problems for studies of international environmental politics. First, ... [they] tend to ignore the political factors that may cause or contribute to international environmental degradation in the first place. Instead, questions of causality are left to natural scientists or economists. * * * Second, ... scholars have found it extremely difficult to derive and consistently maintain an operational definition of the concept of effectiveness ... [which is why] most of the literature ultimately relies [as a second best strategy] on the notion of State compliance, the degree to which States alter their behavior to comply with the terms of an agreement. * * *

> [So, we need] to move beyond the question of why States cooperate under anarchy by asking instead what political factors located at the domestic, or national, level of analysis determine distinctive national responses to issues of international environmental change and management. So far such factors have been used in this literature primarily to explain national interests toward regime formation. However, they also play an important role in understanding to a greater depth the processes and actors at the domestic level that may constrain or facilitate the process of regime

implementation and, more broadly, the fight against environmental degradation. They are absolutely critical in understanding different national responses to a national problem with transnational and international implications. * * *

The broader question of why States differ in their responses to similar international problems calls for an examination of countries' national level characteristics. I argue that the most important factors determining whether or not an advanced industrialized democracy imports waste are features of its system of environmental regulation. In the field of comparative politics, institutional explanations of political outcomes focus on the way interactions between governments and other societal actors are mediated by institutional structures and practices.... * * *

To that end, the key differences among countries with respect to the waste trade lie in two features of their regulatory systems. First, countries differ in terms of their structures of hazardous waste management and regulation—the allocation of responsibilities among different agencies and levels of government, as well as the structure of the hazardous waste disposal industry. The second set of differences concerns national styles of environmental regulation, which mediate government-industry-society (or, stakeholder) relations in the making and implementation of environmental policy. * * *

In each case, these rules and practices mediate the preferences of the actors involved, producing very different outcomes.

KATE O'NEILL, WASTE TRADING AMONG RICH NATIONS: BUILDING A NEW THEORY OF ENVIRONMENTAL REGULATION 1–2, 4–5, 8, 11–14 (2000).

The institutional focus on regulatory structure and political style can be complemented by careful attention to the roles played by the various agents, be they firms, social movements, or individuals, who influence environmental politics, and who have often used international law to enable their activities, within and across national borders. This is, fundamentally, a bottom-up understanding of international law's effectiveness.

Agency has been defined as the ability to choose among different courses of action, to learn from previous experience, and to transform difficult situations in constructive ways. Traditionally in international relations, State actors are the main wielders of agency when policy decisions are made. Some current approaches, by contrast, reflect a shift in the "center of gravity" to bring other sorts of actors and entrepreneurs into the picture as influential actors alongside States. Others are even prepared to say that agency in the international system has dispersed altogether to a variety of groups or even that States have abdicated agency in the face of the pushes and pulls of a global market economy. [So, students of treaties and regimes now] need to learn how to identify important actors who are not States. In addition, the idea of agency, or of what it means to be an actor in international politics and law, has to be rethought, because it can no longer easily be understood as if it were a fixed and undifferentiated property. This is no easy task.

The challenge is well worth taking up, however. The concept of agency and the identification of actual agents will provide a more dynamic and nuanced understanding of how environmental policy changes, both in comparative analyses of policy change across a set of countries, such as the member States of the EU, for example, and when the focus is on the way domestic actors and institutions interact with those at the sub-State, transnational, and international levels. In addition, understanding change in terms of agency encourages the depiction of the driving forces, or engines, of change in ways that allow for (human/social) choice, intentionality, mistakes and learning. These are more realistic bases for understanding change than those that rely on the vague and anonymous influence in international relations of the unseen pressures and invisible forces at work in global markets, and they allow for differentiated results as we move across cases of international environmental problem solving.

Our view, then, is that understanding agency, how it works, and how human actors, whether they be individuals or groups, exercise choice and learn within structural constraints are vital concerns for international law. We recognize, of course, that an interest in agents and structures is nothing new in social science and that there are unresolved academic debates about whether structure is more important than agency, or vice versa. One promising way to move forward is to specify the concept of agency more concretely and more elaborately than has been done so far. First, we need to identify where agency resides in the formation and implementation of environmental regimes and who exactly the influential agents are who shape regime dynamics. In place of the traditional assumption that the ability to change policy and policy processes is associated with official (State) actors we need to proceed on the modern assumption that agency is diffused—to sub-State, private and transnational actors—and that it is differentiated—different actors/agents have different functions in regimes. The question then becomes how to identify these actors and the influence they wield in a way that makes sense for empirical analysis. In addition, while it is relatively easy to draw up lists of groups involved in policy processes, especially as non-State actor proliferate, sorting out who or what is important in influencing outcomes is more complicated. Clearly, some categories of actors (usually lumped together as ''stakeholders'' in regime processes and politics) are important and they include government agencies, international organizations, social movement groups (environmental and non-environmental), industry actors and public opinion. However, ascribing agency and identifying more closely the relative importance of these specific agents are things we still have to do.

Adapted from KATE O'NEILL, AGENCY AND ENVIRONMENTAL POLICY CHANGE: COMPARING STRUCTURAL THEORIES IN A GLOBAL CONTEXT 4–5, 21 (June 2000) (unpublished manuscript). In the next excerpt, Michele Betsill provides an example of this agency approach, suggesting through a series of questions that effective international law, at least in the context of climate change, requires a focus on *local government*.

Municipal governments play a central role in mitigating global climate change. Although the political emphasis has primarily been on developing an international response to global warming through the negotiation of the United Nations Framework Convention on Climate Change and the Kyoto Protocol, countries will not be able to meet the commitments contained in these agreements without the assistance of city governments.... Furthermore, because city government is more closely linked to people's day-to-day lives, local officials may be more successful in prompting the behavioral changes necessary to abate the greenhouse gas (GHG) emissions that contribute to climate change.

Indeed, a growing number of municipal governments are joining global efforts to mitigate climate change through the control of GHG emissions. For example, 75 local governments in the U.S. currently participate in the

Cities for Climate Protection (CCP) campaign sponsored by the International Council for Local Environmental Initiatives (ICLEI). Officials in each of these cities have publicly recognized global climate change as a legitimate local concern and have committed to addressing that threat by controlling local GHG emissions. Many of these communities have successfully developed and implemented policies and programs to reduce emissions.

The CCP communities present an interesting empirical puzzle. While there may be multiple opportunities for cities to control their GHG emissions, there are a number of reasons why we would not expect municipal governments to take any such action. In the U.S., for example, there is no broader structure prompting local officials to control their emissions. There is no federal mandate for local action.... The U.S. Senate has prohibited the use of federal funds for activities that could be seen as implementing the Kyoto Protocol before it has been ratified, and some States (e.g. Colorado) have passed similar legislation. Why then have some U.S. cities chosen to become engaged on the issue of climate change in the face of these structural obstacles?

From a rational choice perspective, it makes little sense for a city government to expend resources to control its GHG emissions. In many ways, the choice of whether to control emissions presents local officials with a "Prisoner's Dilemma." First, it is not at all clear that local action to control emissions will have any measurable effect on the overall threat of global climate change.... Moreover, controlling local emissions will do little to protect a particular community from the potentially adverse effects of climate change.... In the absence of action by all cities to control local GHG emissions, there is little incentive for a particular municipal government to bear the economic burden of controlling its own emissions. Why have some cities decided that controlling GHG emissions is in their interest [given that climate change is generally framed as a global problem with future impacts]? ... What is going on in CCP communities—have officials successfully "localized" the threat of global climate change?

Michele M. Betsill, *Localizing Global Climate Change: Controlling Greenhouse Gas Emissions In U.S. Cities* 15–16 (Belfer Center for Science and International Affairs, Harvard University, September 2000).

4. Law Plus: It's Capacity, Stupid

This greater attention to domestic politics and to non-State actors, including international organizations, as well as to the interplay of environment and development issues, is also leading to much greater interest among social scientists with issues of capacity: how well countries are able, on different levels, to fulfill their international environmental commitments.

Political scientists now recognize that making treaties work takes much longer and is a process requiring more skillful and deliberate action by a wide variety of agents than early studies of treaties and regimes assumed. From this perspective, the compliance and effectiveness studies, while they understandably tried to ask necessary and hard-nosed questions about treaty regimes, were both premature and misconceived. They uncritically accepted the idea that treaties, once ratified, should immediately be able to compel compliance and deter cheating. Thus, they overlooked the necessity for someone to bring together the various material and non-material factors such as money, organization, training, and research needed to make compliance feasible, and not just among State institutions and in international arenas but at the sub-State level as well. The excerpt below makes this point in the context of regional seas.

In the early days of international environmental cooperation, States' *intentions* to protect the environment and to comply with their international environmental commitments were central concerns of environmental advocates. Today, State *abilities* (or capacity) to meet their commitments are receiving greater attention. States require minimum levels of scientific, legal and administrative capability to develop, enforce and reform domestic environmental law, regulation, research and monitoring. Even in the Baltic and Mediterranean regions, home of the oldest regional seas protection arrangements, serious gaps exist in administrative capacity and data gathering across States. After 25 years of European regional seas cooperation, it is time to take stock and draw lessons. * * *

Lesson One: Talk is cheap and essential. Environmental advocates often decry the "talk to action ratio" of policymakers, noting that talking about the environment is usually much cheaper than actually improving ecological quality. Yet, reaching agreement at the international level is difficult and time consuming. When one takes a longer view, the value of ongoing dialogue becomes clearer. It helps to expand the range of agreement on broad goals and specific policies. More importantly, international dialogue helps to build cooperative institutions and expand their scope and authority. Iterated exchange is required to build scientific agreement and common research agendas, as well as to construct shared monitoring and research protocols. All of this talk can also garner media attention and raise public environmental awareness.... [P]articipants and analysts should be more patient and appreciative of the "construction phase" in international environmental politics.

Lesson Two: Implementation costs money. While talk may be cheap and essential, it will not improve behavior or environmental quality on its own.... The lesson that implementation costs money may seem banal. Yet, most environmental cooperation arrangements dedicate few resources to assessing implementation or encouraging it.... International organizations played key roles in launching the regional environmental cooperation efforts around the Black, Caspian and Aral seas. Yet, relatively well-funded organizations like the World Bank and the EU failed to sustain even the small financial commitments needed to build phase one institutions and networks. Nor have the States in these regions dedicated additional resources to marine protection or tapped private sector sources such as the oil industry for support. Without cooperative implementation efforts and the dedication of greater resources toward implementation, policymakers will continue to "talk the talk" of environmental protection without "walking the walk."

Lesson Three: Capacity Building can work. State structure, law, and behavior do not change automatically to implement international agreements.... Minimum levels of State institutional and organizational capacity must exist in both science and environmental policy administration to achieve implementation. If State bodies and domestic NGOs are not functioning, new environmental policy norms and international commitments cannot be internalized and implemented. State capacity can not be assumed by international policymakers; it must be supported. Cooperation arrangements around European major seas have been successful in enhancing regional scientific cooperation and capacity.... However, enhancing national scientific and technical capacity does not automatically enhance science and technology-based policy advice or the capacity of policymakers and States to utilize such advice. These require institutionalized practices and States capable of administering and enforcing complex policy. * * *

International relations practitioners and analysts cannot assume that State environmental management capacity will expand over time within participant countries. Regional seas cooperation demonstrates that State environmental policy capacity can remain low or decline over time. Yet, regional seas cooperation also illustrates the benefits of international cooperative efforts to expand State capacity in such areas as environmental law, policy, administration, enforcement, and scientific monitoring. Additional research is warranted on the limits of State organizational capacity and on the design and effectiveness of initiatives intended to address these shortcomings. * * *

Stacy D. VanDeveer, *Protecting Europe's Seas: Lessons from the Last 25 Years,* 42 ENVIRONMENT 10, 12–13 and 24–25 (July/August 2000).

To conclude, international legal frameworks are not *per se* important in environmental problem solving because they cannot by themselves ensure that problems do get solved. Political economists would also like to believe, at least until someone conclusively proves otherwise, that treaties are unimportant because the processes they set in motion have less influence on State preferences than other factors. But as we have argued, here, this neo-Realist preoccupation with the impacts treaties have on States conceived as unitary, rational actors is both old fashioned and misguided. The value of treaties, we are slowly starting to learn, stems less from State compliance with their terms as negotiated than from the opportunity structures they offer to non-State and sub-State actors to become agents of change and powerful influences on international environmental policymaking in both domestic and international political arenas.

QUESTIONS AND DISCUSSION

1. This excerpt underlines an important, though often forgotten, insight—the law may frame or structure conflicts but it cannot, in and of itself, resolve conflicts. Law can only exist within the larger context of other legitimate, complementary social institutions. This is particularly the case for international law, since there are rarely credible enforcement authorities to make sanctions stick. The authors state that their view differs from the conception of "law as evolving process." Do you think it significantly differs or is this a case of different disciplines describing the same phenomenon, little different than the image of blind people describing different parts of an elephant?

2. The authors note that "social scientists argue that greater attention to a wider range of policy mechanisms, such as emissions trading, would complement a legalistic approach to international regulation." Such calls for greater emphasis on market instruments, such as those described in Chapter 3, are often contrasted with legal approaches such as prescriptive requirements (often called command-and-control). It is important to recognize, however, that trading markets cannot exist without such prescriptive requirements. The force that creates a market in the first place is regulatory proscription of a specific behavior, whether it be emitting sulfur dioxide or catching herring, followed by creation of property rights to carry out the prohibited behavior. These property rights are then traded among parties, e.g., in the acid rain trading program or individual transferable quotas (used in fisheries), for example. Given this, what makes trading any less "legalistic" than direct regulation?

3. *Problem Exercise* Assume you spent the summer working for the three authors. They have asked you to design a study to measure treaties' effectiveness. What would your study look like? What proxies or indicators would you use for effectiveness and how would you measure them?

C. MECHANISMS FOR IMPROVING IMPLEMENTATION AND COMPLIANCE

Implicit in Louis Henkin's observation that "almost all nations observe almost all principles of international law and almost all of their obligations almost all of the time" is the recognition that States do sometimes breach those obligations. In international environmental law, where both the costs of compliance and the consequences of non-compliance can be substantial, particular attention has been focused on the means for enabling States to comply with their international obligations. Before examining the methods for increasing compliance, however, it is important first to understand the reasons States fail to comply.

The reasons for non-compliance are varied, and not always resulting from bad will. As the Mitchell excerpt suggested, some States choose not to comply because the benefits of compliance simply do not outweigh its costs. States may consciously sign treaties in response to strong domestic and international pressures, but their internal cost-benefit analysis shows they will be better off through non-compliance, particularly if they can gain the benefits as a free rider on others' compliance efforts. Research indicates, however, that most non-compliance with international environmental law is due more to institutional incapacity than bad faith. Developing countries often lack the financial, administrative, or technical capacities for meaningful compliance. CITES restrictions on trade in endangered species, for example, are ineffective without strict and credible enforcement by customs officials. Non-compliance may result despite best efforts. A country may levy a stringent carbon tax to meet the Kyoto Protocol goals for greenhouse gas emissions, yet still fall short of the required emissions reductions. And finally, a country may comply with some treaty provisions while failing to comply with others.

A treaty regime's management of compliance problems may be broken into three components—a primary rule system, a compliance information system, and a non-compliance response system.

> The primary rule system consists of the actors, rules and processes related to the behaviour that is the substantive target of the regime. By its choice of who gets regulated and how, the primary rule system determines the degree and sources of pressures and incentives for compliance and violation. The compliance information system consists of the actors, rules and processes that collect, analyze and disseminate information regarding the instances of, and parties responsible for, violations and compliance. The self-reporting, independent monitoring, data analysis, and publishing activities that comprise the compliance information system determine the amount, quality, and uses made of data on compliance and enforcement. The non-compliance response system consists of the actors, rules, and processes governing the formal and informal responses

undertaken to induce those identified as in non-compliance to comply. The non-compliance response system determines the type, likelihood, magnitude, and appropriateness of responses to non-compliance.

Mitchell, *op. cit.*, at 16–19. In this section, we examine the first of the subsystems Mitchell identifies–the primary rules subsystem. We then review additional means for improving implementation and compliance–national capacity-building, financial assistance, technology transfers and technological assistance, and differential implementation schedules.

---

1. PARTICIPATION AND PRIMARY RULES

The first step in gaining compliance and facilitating implementation with international regimes is to establish a regime that is acceptable to most of the countries that are necessary to make the particular regime effective. This means at a minimum that the *process* of negotiation must include the effective participation of key countries. Through participation in the negotiation process, countries will be able to make necessary substantive changes to ensure subsequent compliance. More importantly, perhaps, they will become more committed to the goals and approaches adopted in the treaty.

In this respect, treaties to resolve global environmental issues require the active involvement and participation of both developed and developing countries. Gaining the effective participation of developing countries in the formation of the treaty cannot be taken for granted. In recent years, so many environmental treaties have been negotiated simultaneously that many developing countries could not participate effectively in all of the negotiations. For major conferences, the size of country delegations may vary greatly, with small countries sending only one official and large countries sending dozens. Covering disparate working groups or sub-meetings thus becomes impossible without greater organization among the smaller countries. As a result, many developing countries do not feel well represented in the agreement negotiations and may not be as willing to sign on as parties.

In the environmental field, several factors tend to strengthen the participation of developing countries. First, because developing countries are ultimately necessary for resolving many global environmental issues, they may in fact have substantial leverage in the environmental field that they do not enjoy in other fields of international law (such as international trade). Thus, for example, developing countries managed to gain significant financial promises from the North as part of the bargain for joining the Montreal Protocol regime to curb ozone depletion. Second, developing countries are beginning to organize themselves into more effective networks. The G–77 has held together on several major environmental issues, e.g., in opposing any agreement that they believe unreasonably impedes sovereign rights to exploit national forests or requiring developed countries to take the first major steps in responding to climate change. Smaller alliances have also been formed, allowing smaller countries to share the expense of participating in treaty negotiations and to multiply the political impact of participation. Thus, for example, the Association of Small Island States (AOSIS) has been an important player in the climate negotiations. Finally, other transnational actors such as environmental NGOs have at times provided technical assistance or even directly represented smaller developing countries in international negotiations. In this way, some elements of civil society are amplifying the voice of otherwise underrepresented countries.

Once all the necessary parties are participating, negotiators must conclude an agreement that establishes appropriate goals and appropriate mechanisms for achieving those goals. This involves a careful evaluation of whom to regulate, what activities to regulate, and how to regulate them. Another important aspect of primary rules is transparency. By making it easier to detect violations, other parties may be encouraged to comply by lessening their fear of free riders. Specificity in compliance goals also plays an important role. As the voluminous literature on rules versus standards makes clear, specific requirements remove uncertainty over actions to achieve compliance and reduce the likelihood of dispute over noncompliance. Ronald Mitchell, *op. cit.*, at 17–19.

---

2.   NATIONAL CAPACITY–BUILDING

International environmental law depends for its effectiveness on proper implementation and enforcement at the national level. International agreements must be translated into domestic laws and regulations and those regulations, in turn, must be translated into compliance by the regulated community. Additional administrative resources may need to be allocated for facilitating and monitoring compliance with the rules. And enforcement and judicial resources may be needed to sanction violations of the rules. For example, the Basel Convention requires the creation of a national body to administer requests for prior notification of waste shipments, and CITES requires parties to maintain an administrative authority to issue import and export permits and to monitor the populations of regulated wildlife. For these and other environmental treaties, then, the most important prerequisite of compliance is the existence at the national level of the legislative, administrative and executive infrastructures, called "institutional capacity," necessary for implementation and enforcement. Particularly in developing countries, such infrastructures may be inadequate to meet the new responsibilities. In these countries, the first step to improving compliance may be to help build the capacity to implement the treaty's obligations.

Because the active and effective participation of developing countries is essential in the shift to sustainable development, national capacity-building has become an important area of international cooperation. Chapter 37 of *Agenda 21* is dedicated to capacity-building in developing countries.

37.2 Building endogenous capacity to implement Agenda 21 will require the efforts of the countries themselves in partnership with relevant United Nations organizations, as well as with developed countries. The international community at the national, subregional and regional levels, municipalities, non-governmental organizations, universities and research centres, and business and other private institutions and organizations could also assist in these efforts. It is essential for individual countries to identify priorities and determine the means for building capacity and capability to implement Agenda 21, taking into account their environmental and economic needs. Skills, knowledge and technical know-how at the individual and institutional levels are necessary for institution-building, policy analysis and development management, including the assessment of alternative courses of action with a view to enhancing access to and transfer of technology and promoting economic development. Technical cooperation, including that related to technology transfer and know-how, encompasses the whole range of activities to develop or strengthen individual and group capacities and capabilities. It should serve the purpose of long-term capacity-building and needs to be managed and coordinated by the countries themselves. Technical cooperation, including that related to technology transfer and know-how, is effective only when it is derived from and related to a country's own strategies and priorities on environment and development and when development agencies and Governments define improved and consistent policies and procedures to support this process.

Capacity-building efforts are conducted both within and outside of specific treaty regimes. They involve the cooperation of international organizations and development institutions, national development agencies, such as the United States Agency for International Development (US–AID), NGOs, and, most importantly, the national governments of the developing nations themselves. As the excerpt from *Agenda 21* suggests, most of these programs focus on technical cooperation, technology transfer, and personnel training. The Montreal Protocol's ozone fund supports developing countries seeking alternatives to CFCs, the Food and Agriculture Organization (FAO) supports national pesticide registrars, and the International Maritime Organization's World Maritime University holds seminars for ship captains on relevant international and national environmental rules and standards. HAAS ET AL., *op. cit.*, at 404. Assistance may take an endless array of forms, from guidance on appropriate legislation to transfers of enforcement equipment to student and scholar exchange programs. The following excerpt from the United Nations Convention to Combat Desertification is indicative.

United Nations Convention to Combat Desertification, Article 19

Capacity building, education and public awareness

1. The Parties recognize the significance of capacity building—that is to say, institution building, training and development of relevant local and national capacities—in efforts to combat desertification and mitigate the effects of drought. They shall promote, as appropriate, capacity-building:

(a) through the full participation at all levels of local people, particularly at the local level, especially women and youth, with the cooperation of non-governmental and local organizations;

(b) by strengthening training and research capacity at the national level in the field of desertification and drought;

(c) by establishing and/or strengthening support and extension services to disseminate relevant technology methods and techniques more effectively, and by training field agents and members of rural organizations in participatory approaches for the conservation and sustainable use of natural resources;

(d) by fostering the use and dissemination of the knowledge, know-how and practices of local people in technical cooperation programmes, wherever possible;

(e) by adapting, where necessary, relevant environmentally sound technology and traditional methods of agriculture and pastoralism to modern socio-economic conditions;

(f) by providing appropriate training and technology in the use of alternative energy sources, particularly renewable energy resources, aimed particularly at reducing dependence on wood for fuel;

(g) through cooperation, as mutually agreed, to strengthen the capacity of affected developing country Parties to develop and implement programmes in the field of collection, analysis and exchange of information pursuant to article 16;

(h) through innovative ways of promoting alternative livelihoods, including training in new skills;

(i) by training of decision makers, managers, and personnel who are responsible for the collection and analysis of data for the dissemination and use of early warning information on drought conditions and for food production;

(j) through more effective operation of existing national institutions and legal frameworks and, where necessary, creation of new ones, along with strengthening of strategic planning and management; and

(k) by means of exchange visitor programmes to enhance capacity building in affected country Parties through a long-term, interactive process of learning and study.

2. Affected developing country Parties shall conduct, in cooperation with other Parties and competent intergovernmental and non-governmental organizations, as appropriate, an interdisciplinary review of available capacity and facilities at the local and national levels, and the potential for strengthening them.

----

3. POSITIVE COMPLIANCE MEASURES

A growing number of environmental treaties include provisions designed both to induce developing countries to participate in the treaty and to facilitate compliance by those that do participate. These measures can be grouped into three broad categories—financial cooperation; technology transfer; and differential implementation schedules and obligations. The inclusion of these "positive measures" stems from the recognition that for developing countries the burdens of implementing some international environmental agreements may be disproportionate to the corresponding benefit, particularly in the short term. By including positive measures within an agreement, the Parties may offset some of the economic and social costs associated with ratification and compliance, and spread the remaining costs more fairly among State parties. In so doing, the positive measures remove, or at least lower, political and economic barriers that might otherwise prevent some states from joining international efforts to protect the environment.

————

a.   Financial Cooperation

One critical element of national capacity, of course, is financial capacity. In implementing an international environmental agreement, countries can incur significant direct and indirect costs. The direct costs of implementation will include the expenditures necessary to administer and enforce new laws, and to develop or purchase any new technology necessary to comply with an agreement. The indirect costs will include the economic and social development foregone, or at least deferred, because of the policy changes. While generally a small percentage of total operating costs, implementation costs can fall heavily in some sectors and, overall, act as a considerable obstacle to compliance. As a result, financial assistance for both direct and indirect costs may be indispensable to the effective implementation of global environmental treaties.

Beginning with the 1990 London Amendments to the Montreal Protocol, most major environmental agreements have required developed country Parties to provide financial assistance to developing country Parties both to ensure adequate resources for implementation and to ease the socioeconomic burdens that implementation may create. Article 10 of the revised Montreal Protocol creates a Multilateral Fund, financed by developed country Parties, to facilitate technical cooperation and technology transfer and to cover the incremental implementation costs of the developing country Parties. Key developing countries, most notably China and India, insisted upon the inclusion of such a financial mechanism as a pre-requisite to their participation in the Protocol.

In 1991, the World Bank, UNEP and UNDP jointly launched the Global Environment Facility (GEF) to provide funding for developing countries on a grant or concessional basis to meet the incremental costs of measures to protect the global environment in four focal areas—climate change, biological diversity, international waters and ozone depletion. *See* Chapter 20, page 1501.

Financial assistance measures have been a constant point of contention between developed and developing countries. As the stance of China and India with respect to the Montreal Protocol suggests, developing countries consider financial assistance a critical prerequisite for their cooperation in global environmental agreements. They believe developed countries have a duty to provide financial assistance, both because of their greater contribution to global environmental problems and because of their greater resources. In some recent agreements, developing countries have demanded an explicit linkage between their specific substantive obligations and the donor countries' promises for financial and technical assistance. For example, Article 4.7. of the Climate Convention states that "The extent to which developing country Parties will effectively implement their commitments under the Convention will depend on the effective implementation by developed country Parties of their commitments ... related to financial resources and transfer of technology...."

For their part, developed countries have proven reluctant to "write a blank check" by committing to financial and technical aid with no specified limits, particularly without strong assurances that developing countries will comply with their obligations. Increasingly, specific conditions are being placed on assistance given to developing countries. As public financial resources tighten, donor countries seek greater confidence that their assistance dollars will be used efficiently and for the purposes identified. Thus donor countries are placing conditions on financial assistance and creating mechanisms for exercising greater oversight of how the money is used. This conditioning of financial assistance can by itself help in encouraging compliance with environmental treaties. For example, the World Bank requires that any project it finances, regardless of whether it has an environmental purpose, be consistent with the borrowing country's international environmental obligations (though whether this happens in practice is disputed).

Related to the issue of conditioning financial assistance is the issue of who controls the decisionmaking of the financial institutions. At the World Bank, for example, the donor countries control major policy decisions because voting is based on the amount of capital donated to the institution. The GEF, on the other hand, was realigned to provide developing countries with more equal control over policy decisions. Finding an acceptable middle ground remains one of the major challenges facing international environmental negotiators.

----

b. Technology Transfer

Technology transfer is, in many ways, analogous to financial assistance. Developing countries demand as part of the bargain to join global environmental agreements that developed countries share environmentally sustainable technologies. Access to these technologies is often essential to the successful implementation of a country's environmental treaty commitments but the costs of acquiring the new technologies can be prohibitive for developing countries. Thus, a growing number of agreements call on developed countries to transfer technologies to developing countries on fair or favorable terms. For example, Article 4.5 of the Framework Convention on Climate Change provides that,

> The developed country Parties ... shall take all practicable steps to promote, facilitate and finance, as appropriate, the transfer of, or access to, environmentally sound technologies and know-how to other Parties, particularly developing country Parties, to enable them to implement the provisions of the Convention. In this process, the developed country Parties shall support the development and enhancement of endogenous capacities and technologies of developing country Parties. Other Parties and organizations in a position to do so may also assist in facilitating the transfer of such technologies.

In exchange for such transfers, developed countries are interested in ensuring that the technologies provide real environmental benefits and do not provide developing countries with an unfair competitive advantage.

Technology transfer issues are complicated by the critical role of industry and other non-State actors. Many of the most important environmentally sustainable technologies are owned by the private companies that have invented them or who market them. Developed countries are thus greatly concerned that obligations to transfer technologies not interfere with the protection of intellectual property rights–and profits–of companies based in their territory. A major obstacle to U.S. adoption of the deep seabed provisions of the Law of the Sea Convention, for example, was the provision calling for "the transfer of technology ... to developing States ... under fair and reasonable terms and conditions." UNCLOS Article 144(2)(a). The issue is not only that developed countries might have to buy the property rights from the private sector in order to transfer them, but also that some developing countries provide inadequate protection to intellectual property. Once transferred, new technologies may be pirated and the competitive advantage of the company lost.

Chapter 34 of Agenda 21 devotes an entire chapter to the issue of technology transfer, reflecting its importance for achieving sustainable development. The general role of technology is discussed further in Chapter 2, page 69, and a successful technology transfer effort is discussed in Chapter 9, page 572, on ozone depletion.

---

c.   *Differential Implementation Schedules and Obligations*

The inclusion of financial cooperation and technology transfer requirements in environmental treaties is one manifestation of the principle of common but differentiated responsibilities. *See* Chapter 7, page 402. Another example is the inclusion of differential implementation schedules and obligations in many agreements.

Differential implementation schedules are justified for the same reasons as technology transfers, financial assistance, and other enabling mechanisms—to facilitate implementation of international environmental obligations by developing countries in ways that support sustainable development goals. Differential schedules, while initially slowing achievement of the agreement's objectives, are ultimately beneficial if the delay is unlikely to sacrifice the ultimate environmental protection goals and if additional time can avoid unnecessary economic hardship on the developing countries, thereby increasing the participation and support of those countries.

The Montreal Protocol, for instance, allows a ten-year grace period following ratification during which developing countries may increase their consumption of ozone-depleting substances during the same period that the developed countries are reducing or eliminating their own consumption. Developing countries were allowed to *increase* consumption levels to 0.3 Kg per capita in order to meet basic domestic needs. Following this period, developing countries would have ten more years to reduce their consumption by 50%. While this permissible growth may seem counterproductive, it provided a period for implementation that was viewed as acceptable and fair by developing countries.

Discussion over differential treaty obligations also dominated the 1997 negotiations regarding the Kyoto Protocol to the Climate Change Convention. Developing countries were not placed under any obligations to reduce greenhouse gas emissions and, even within developed countries, significant differences in baseline emissions, implementation capacity and other issues led to different targets and timetables. Thus, for example, the United States agreed to reduce greenhouse gas emissions by 7% from 1990 levels while Australia is allowed to *increase* its emissions by 8%.

Market-based instruments, such as tradable permit programs, may provide related means of implementation that facilitate treaty compliance. Under the proposed joint implementation strategy to reduce greenhouse gases, for example, a developing country with inefficient industries would be able to receive financing from a developed country to upgrade its technologies, in exchange for the developed country receiving the developing country's credit for reduced emissions. This exchange of money for reduced emission credits takes advantage of the differential marginal costs of reducing emissions in different countries. Such a market-based implementation mechanism could, it is argued, meet global and regional environmental goals at a lower cost than strict national reduction requirements.

QUESTIONS AND DISCUSSION

1. Positive measures are often justified in terms of equity as well as efficiency. Developed countries indisputedly control a disproportionate share of the world's wealth and historically have contributed disproportionately to global environmental problems. Should they thus be required to provide substantial additional resources for environmental protection? Consider in this regard the principle of common but differentiated responsibilities as set forth in Rio Principle 7:

> In view of the contributions to global environmental degradation, States have common but differentiated responsibilities. The developed countries acknowledge the responsibility that they bear in the international pursuit of sustainable development in view of the pressures their societies place on the global environment and of the technologies and financial resources they command.

Do you agree with this general approach? In addition to the approaches described above, what other steps might countries take consistent with the principle of common but differentiated responsibilities to facilitate full participation in and implementation of particular conventions?

2. International environmental agreements may require parties to take a number of specific, and easily verifiable, steps as part of the implementation of various agreements. For example, the Biodiversity Convention requires an inventory of existing biodiversity in a country. This is a necessary prerequisite for any further systematic steps at conservation. Such biodiversity assays require tremendous expenditures of time and resources, but are technically achievable by most developing countries if provided sufficient financial support. Another increasingly common mechanism is the use of regional or national action plans. Indeed the development and implementation of action plans has become a common mechanism for coordinating and catalyzing activities toward common international environmental goals. These plans help governments establish priorities and measure progress over time. *Agenda 21* itself is an action plan, and many international environmental agreements commit countries to develop implementation or action plans.

In the case of the Desertification Convention, for example, the focus is on the creation of national action plans to identify projects that are most effective in addressing the symptoms and causes of desertification. It provides detailed guidance on how the plans should be developed, both in terms of the subjects that must be addressed and the actors who should be involved. The Convention emphasizes a "bottom-up" approach, encouraging public participation. At the time, this was a strikingly novel approach for international environmental agreements. Why is the inclusion of civil society important for increasing the chances of effective implementation?

3. Given the growing emphasis and potentially wide variety of strategies to facilitate compliance, several conventions have adopted variations of an "implementation committee," particularly with respect to the more complicated and costly environmental problems such as atmospheric and air pollution. The basic objective of these implementation committees is to identify why specific countries may be having trouble implementing a convention and design a program of assistance, incentives or other strategies specifically tailored to assist that country to come into compliance. Implementation committees typically make their recommendations to the conference of the parties, placing the responsibility on all of the parties to help those who cannot currently comply. Thus, the implementation committee becomes a go-between of sorts between the convention parties and those countries facing compliance difficulties. *See* Chapter 5, page 239, discussing the subsidiary body for implementation under the Biodiversity Convention.

4. Because national governments—and consequently, national government officials—bear primary responsibility for implementing and enforcing most international environmental law, government corruption can be an important source of noncompliance. Although the potential for corruption exists in every government, that potential is greatly amplified in less developed countries and countries with economies in transition, where low government salaries may go unpaid for months at a time. Under these conditions, the incentive to accept bribes in exchange for "overlooking" enforcement problems may be immense. For those seeking to evade the law, these same conditions mean that the cost of bribery may be negligible relative to the costs of compliance.

In an effort to address this problem, the members of the OECD adopted a Convention on Combating Bribery of Foreign Public Officials in International Business Transactions. Parties to the Convention agree to take steps to make it a criminal offense under their domestic law for any person to bribe or offer to bribe a foreign public official to "act or refrain from acting in relation to the performance of official duties, in order to obtain or retain business or other improper advantage in the conduct of international business." Art. 1(1). Liability must extend not only to the individuals who offered the bribe, but also to any legal person–including a corporation–that incited, aided and abetted, or authorized the bribe. Violations should be punishable by seizure of the bribe and its proceeds, civil and administrative sanctions, and, with respect to natural persons, imprisonment. Art. 3. The Bribery Convention focuses on the businesses that offer bribes, rather than on the officials who accept them. Why? One likely reason is that most countries already prohibit their public officials from accepting bribes. Are there other reasons? Consider again the discussion of primary rules, which emphasized that the likelihood of compliance with a regime is influenced by the choice of who is regulated. What advantages might there be in punishing the businesses that offer the bribes rather than the officials that receive them?

d. Compliance Information Systems

While provisions to facilitate implementation can contribute to a culture of compliance, countries' progress in meeting treaty obligations must still be monitored. Without the means to ensure compliance, a perverse incentive may be created—one that rewards bad faith behavior in the form of strategic non-compliance. Countries could gain competitive advantage as well as take advantage of the financial assistance and other implementation mechanisms if there was not at least a credible threat of some monitoring to expose non-compliance.

The importance of compliance monitoring is not surprising. At the national level, laws are frequently not considered effective without the means to monitor compliance. Tax returns are audited, radar guns track speeding cars, and officials inspect factories to check emissions. Ensuring compliance with international agreements, however, is more problematic. Sovereign nations rarely consent to subject themselves to compliance procedures. At the international level, who plays the role of the tax auditors or traffic police?

The official responsibility for monitoring compliance with international environmental treaties generally lies with the individual treaty secretariats or similar bodies, with NGOs playing a critical though unofficial role. See Chapter 5, page 237 (discussing the role of secretariats as well as of NGOs in monitoring compliance). Mechanisms for compliance monitoring vary within treaties, although there is a heavy reliance on self-reporting. Other monitoring strategies, increasingly adopted in recent treaties, include independent verification by third parties and fact-finding missions.

Reporting. Most environmental treaties require countries to report on their activities implementing the treaty obligations. This includes reports on national efforts to curb trade in endangered wildlife, reduce greenhouse gas emissions, reduce levels of ozone destroying substances, conserve biological diversity, and many other activities. As an example, the Basel Convention requires the submission of information to UNEP, which acts as the convention's secretariat. Article 13 of the convention sets forth the detailed information requirements to be collected and transmitted to the secretariat. *See also*, CITES, Article VIII(7); Climate Change Convention, Article 12; Montreal Protocol, Article 7; Biodiversity Convention, Article 26.

Unfortunately, compliance with self-reporting requirements has often been poor. A 1995 report from UNEP, for example, indicated that only one-third to one-half of the parties had complied with the information reporting requirements of the Basel Convention. The Basel Convention is not unique in this regard; only about 60% of the parties to the 1972 London Dumping Convention comply with the reporting obligations imposed by that treaty. OECD, DISPUTE SETTLEMENT IN ENVIRONMENTAL CONVENTIONS, Sept. 26, 1994, at para. 37 (prepared for the Oct. 10–12, 1994 Joint Session of Trade and Environment Experts).

Verification. Verification activities, i.e. monitoring by a third party, have not been widely incorporated into international environmental law, except in a few treaties addressing marine resources. The International Whaling Commission, for example, has the authority to appoint observers to report on the activities of whaling vessels. Two recent developments suggest a potentially important shift toward stronger regional approaches to monitoring and verification. The Straddling Stocks Convention essentially "deputizes" parties in regional fishing agreements with powers to monitor the activities of other parties fishing in the region. Any member State may board and inspect fishing vessels flying the flag of other member States. Inspectors can look at the vessel, its license, gear, equipment, records, facilities, fish and fish products, and any relevant documents needed to verify compliance. Provisions for boarding and inspecting are clearly stated in the treaty, which also provides a specific penalty for refusal to let other member States board and inspect a vessel. *See* p. 694; *see also*, Convention for the Conservation of Anadromous Stocks in the North Pacific Ocean (1992) (authorizing any party to board, inspect and seize vessels violating the Convention).

Technological advances may also greatly improve verification activities. Remote sensing from satellites, for example, may provide the means to monitor national emissions of certain pollutants, forest resources, or even the activities of specific fishing vessels.

Fact-finding. The use of fact-finding missions to investigate alleged non-compliance, while common in the human rights field, is not common in international environmental law. This may be changing, however, with the emergence of regional institutions with authority to monitor and report on national environmental performance. For example, the OECD has been independently reviewing the environmental performance of each of its Member Countries, including their implementation of international treaties. After consultation with the country being examined, the OECD publishes its Country Report as well as recommendations for improvement. Regional trade blocs may also provide important regional fora for monitoring and reporting on environmental performance. For example, the NAFTA environmental side agreement created a trilateral commission (with representatives from Canada, the U.S. and Mexico) to investigate and report on allegations of a consistent pattern of lack of enforcement of environmental laws, including international environmental agreements. The inspection panels of the multilateral development banks have similar fact-finding authority. These panels can investigate alleged violations of the banks' environmental and social policies. It is also important to note that both the NAFTA side agreement and the inspection panels of multilateral development banks allow citizens or NGOs to trigger the fact-finding process. *See* Chapter 15, discussing NAFTA and Chapter 20, discussing financial institutions.

QUESTIONS AND DISCUSSION

1. How can overall compliance with reporting requirements be improved? As suggested in the preceding section, appropriate financial and technical assistance may need to be targeted towards improving reporting. Another possible strategy would be to try to streamline the reporting requirements that a country may face. If each of the growing number of multilateral environmental conventions require different reporting, the cumulative work load for understaffed and underbudgeted environmental agencies can be burdensome. As you read different environmental treaties, consider how their reporting requirements could be streamlined. Would it require greater cooperation between the different secretariats?

2.   Perhaps the most comprehensive study on compliance was undertaken by Edith Brown Weiss and Harold Jacobsen. They and their colleagues examined eight countries' and the European Union's implementation of five international environmental treaties (addressing both pollution and natural resources). In concluding that there has been a steady trend toward strengthened implementation and compliance, the study provides a wealth of empirical data and insights into compliance behavior and is a basic resource for more in-depth study of the issue. *See* HAROLD JACOBSEN AND EDITH BROWN WEISS, ENGAGING COUNTRIES: STRENGTHENING COMPLIANCE WITH INTERNATIONAL ENVIRONMENTAL ACCORDS (MIT PRESS 1998).

SECTION III.   RESPONDING TO NON-COMPLIANCE

In domestic law, the typical consequence for failure to comply with the law is an enforcement procedure and the imposition of sanctions on the offending party, whether that be a monetary fine, probation, or a prison term. Not surprisingly, this model does not translate well to international environmental agreements. Sovereign States do not generally subject themselves to sanctions. In practice, then, treaties' enforcement measures often are of less practical importance than positive measures to facilitate compliance.

Despite these caveats, enforcement measures and sanctions remain important. Not only do enforcement sanctions provide some recourse against the worst offenders of international environmental law, but the credible *threat* of potential sanctions is often what makes the *use* of sanctions unnecessary. Enforcement measures included in international environmental instruments include trade measures, membership sanctions, and liability.

———

A.   NON-COMPLIANCE PROCEDURES

Gunther Handl, *Compliance Control Mechanisms and International Environmental Obligations*
5 TUL. J. INT'L & COMP. L. 29 (1997)

Today, establishment of some form of "internal" compliance control procedure appears generally recognized as an indispensable element of MEAs [Multilateral Environmental Agreements]. Thus, most recent MEAs feature or are likely to feature a free-standing non-compliance procedure (NCP), administered by a special, dedicated institutional mechanism. The first such non-compliance procedure was established as part of the Montreal Protocol on Substances that Deplete the Ozone Layer. It has since served as a model for others, such as the 1994 Protocol to the 1979 UN ECE Convention on Long–Range Transboundary Air Pollution on Further Reduction of Sulphur Emissions (1994 Sulphur Protocol). It has also inspired agreement on, or calls for, the establishment of similar non-compliance mechanisms or procedures as part of the 1991 ECE

Protocol on Volatile Organic Compounds, the UN Framework Convention on Climate Change, the UN Convention to Combat Desertification, the Basel Convention on Transboundary Movement of Hazardous Wastes and Their Disposal, and the international convention on the mandatory application of the prior informed consent principle whose text is expected to be finalized in 1997.

The NCP offers a number of very significant advantages as regards the "management" of legal relations among the parties to the MEA. Typically, the NCP aims less at branding a state party as "defaulting on its obligations," and at imposing sanctions or providing remedies for past infractions, than at helping the incriminated party come into compliance and protecting the future integrity of the regime against would-be defectors. The NCP is hence forward- rather than backward-looking. It embodies a quintessentially collective ap- proach, rather than being steeped in the traditional paradigm of bilateralism– the relationship between the non-complying state and the directly injured other state or states.

These characteristics are of major importance, because normative provisions of an environmental regulatory regime undergo frequent adaptation and expan- sion in response to new scientific insights or technological developments. Compliance issues, therefore, can be expected to be relatively common and differ vastly in their individual significance for the regime as a whole. The routine invocation of traditional dispute settlement procedures to deal with such a range of issues of non-implementation and non-compliance thus will not be a realistic option either legally or politically. After all, the process of invoking principles of international state responsibility and liability is cumber- some and essentially confrontational, and, therefore, can be employed only occasionally and as an avenue of last resort. Indeed, invocation of state responsibility may be an inappropriate response because non-compliance might be as much due to a state's lack of capacity, as it might be the result of its intentional or negligent disregard of its obligations. Similarly, in the context of most international environmental treaties, the absence of appropriate reciproci- ty between injuring and injured state(s) will make reliance on traditional compliance strategies unworkable. For example, suspension of the operation of a multilateral agreement for the protection of the environment, as one of the permitted sanctions for a material breach of the treaty by a party, would make little sense, and indeed might be counterproductive. * * *

In the final analysis, the non-compliance procedure's major attraction lies in the fact that it enables the meeting of the parties to fine-tune "enforcement" of the various normative standards of the MEA. Such flexibility however, comes also at a price—A possible perception among parties that the details, if not the principle, of compliance with obligations arising under the MEA might be negotiable, a perception which could work at cross-purposes with compliance control efforts. However, in assessing costs and benefits, it should be remem- bered that while the NCP might well contribute to the "softening" of the international normativity of individual rules and regulations of the MEA, it keeps intact the regime as a whole. Indeed, the NCP might well be character- ized as "an effort at continued consensus building . . .;" or, in other words, "a process that straddles traditional law-making and law-enforcement functions." Moreover, it should be posited right away that a NCP would not supplant, but rather would complement traditional dispute settlement procedures. In this supplementary capacity, then, it is an indispensable mechanism of peer review for the vindication of the collective interest of state parties, provided the procedure is invocable informally, and is reasonably open and transparent.

Handl cites the non-compliance procedure of the Montreal Protocol as a model for subsequent treaties. Under the procedure, a Party that cannot meet its Protocol obligations may "self-report" its compliance problems to the Protocol's Implementation Committee. If the Committee finds that the Party will not be in compliance despite its best efforts, the Committee can prescribe measures to bring the Party back into compliance. The non-compliance procedure does not dictate a standard response to all cases of non-compliance, but instead allows the Parties to tailor their response to the specific circumstances and needs of the non-complying Party. This response may include assistance with collecting and reporting data, technical or financial assistance, technology transfer, or information transfer and personnel training. By avoiding the accusatory process, the Protocol eliminates a major disincentive to self-reporting by the Parties themselves, who are the best monitors of their own compliance.

If the Committee finds that a Party has not made a sufficient effort to meet its obligations, or if it is otherwise warranted by the circumstances, the Committee may recommend punitive action against the non-complying Party. If the non-complying Party is a developing country, the Committee may recommend suspending the Party's access to positive measures, such as the Multilateral Fund. The threat of such revocation has proven an effective incentive to comply. For example, when Mauritania failed to adequately report data on its consumption of controlled substances, the Implementation Committee proposed revoking the country's Article 5 status (as a developing country) and, thus, its access to technology and financial assistance. Before the next meeting of the parties at which the Committee's recommendation would have been considered, Mauritania submitted the required data, thereby avoiding the sanction. Similarly, when the Implementing Committee recommended reclassifying Kuwait and Lebanon as non-Article 5 Parties in 1995, both countries corrected their reporting problems under the Protocol and thus remained eligible for assistance from the Multilateral Fund.

B. ENFORCEMENT AND SANCTIONS

As the discussion of the Montreal Protocol non-compliance procedure suggests, the provision of additional assistance is not always the best response to party non-compliance. Particularly when a party's violation of its treaty obligations is the result of political preferences rather than incapacity, the other parties may turn to diplomatic and public pressure, withdrawal of membership benefits, trade measures, or other sanctions to enforce the treaty.

The most common means of responding to non-compliance is through diplomatic pressure. Conferences of the parties, treaty secretariats and less formal channels can be used to urge States to abide by their commitments. Informally, at least, a country's authority to participate as an equal partner in the development of treaty policies is significantly weakened if it is perpetually in non-compliance.

International environmental treaties often link compliance with the receipt of benefits arising from membership in the regime. As described above, parties to the Montreal Protocol may respond to instances of non-compliance by denying the non-complying party access to the Protocol's positive measures of financial cooperation and technology transfers. A party may also be designated as "not-in-compliance" with the Protocol by a Meeting of the parties to the Protocol, whereupon it is treated as a non-party to the agreement. Because trade in certain substances, products and technologies is sharply restricted between parties and non-parties, designating a party as not in compliance with the Protocol can be tantamount to the imposition of trade measures.

A number of environmental treaties explicitly provide for the use of trade measures as a sanction for non-compliance. Most environmental treaties with trade sanctions, however, also control movements of environmentally harmful substances or limit trade that is, itself, environmentally harmful. Examples include the Basel Convention (hazardous waste), CITES (endangered species and their parts), and the Montreal Protocol (ozone depleting substances). It remains a source of contention (though still untested) whether such provisions violate the GATT. *See* Chapter 15 on Trade and Environment.

QUESTIONS AND DISCUSSION

1. To some extent, compliance with international environmental agreements can be "enforced" through other mechanisms outside the formal treaty regime. Environmental NGOs have long called for multilateral financial institutions, such as the World Bank, to condition loans on compliance with international environmental obligations. Currently, the World Bank claims it will not finance any project that is inconsistent with the borrower's international environmental obligations, but in practice this has had limited impact on the Bank's loan portfolio or on the borrower's compliance with international environmental law. What other diplomatic and policy options are available for convincing parties to come into compliance?

2. *Unilateral Enforcement.* In some cases, non-compliance may be punished not by an international body, but by another country. The United States, for example, has on a number of occasions imposed trade restrictions on the activities of sovereign nations beyond U.S. borders. This extraterritorial application of domestic law is unpopular within the international community but, in many cases, effective. The well-known Tuna/Dolphin GATT dispute, for example, arose because the Marine Mammal Protection Act effectively forbade the import of tuna from countries whose fleets used purse seine nets in the Eastern Tropical Pacific (as well as from countries which imported tuna from these countries). This action, which was eventually found by a GATT dispute panel to violate international trade rules, led to adoption of much stronger dolphin conservation measures by a number of Latin American fleets.

Similarly, the U.S. Pelly and Packwood–Magnuson Amendments both impose trade sanctions on countries diminishing the effectiveness of international fisheries or wildlife conservation agreements. The threat of sanctions under those laws has been effective in convincing even non-member countries, such as Taiwan, to improve their compliance with CITES. In a problem exercise discussed in Chapter 10, page 690, Canada resorted to self-help in boarding and seizing a Spanish trawler in international waters. Canada was concerned that the Spanish fleet's harvesting of turbot, a straddling stock, would destroy conservation efforts in the adjoining Canadian waters. Chapter 19 specifically addresses the extraterritorial application of domestic laws.

3. For a helpful overview of research on why firms choose to comply with environmental law, *see* Mark Cohen's article, *Monitoring and Enforcement of Environmental Policy*, at <http://www.worldbank.org/nipr/work_paper/cohen/>.

C. LIABILITY FOR ENVIRONMENTAL DAMAGE

Many binding international environmental agreements, such as the Law of the Sea Convention, the Basel Convention, and the 1972 London Dumping Convention, explicitly call on parties to create and implement liability schemes for environmental damage caused by parties to the convention. Such schemes can provide an economic incentive to promote compliance, implement the polluter pays principle, and compensate those injured by environmentally harmful practices. These treaties can impose liability upon a State or, as is more frequently the case, create a civil liability system for imposing liability directly on the private actor that caused environmental harm.

In practice, treaty provisions for State liability have rarely been developed and *even less frequently applied*. The 1972 Convention on International Liability for Damage Caused by Space Objects, for example, imposes strict liability on a State that launches a space object that causes damage to aircraft in flight or to the earth's surface. The only claim made under the convention occurred in 1979 when the Soviet nuclear-powered satellite, Cosmos 954, disintegrated over Canada. While the USSR paid compensation to Canada of $3 million, this represented only half of the total claimed clean-up costs. *See also* Chapter 12, page 854, for discussion of the Basel Convention's lengthy negotiations to create a liability regime.

Countries have been more willing to create international legal obligations to impose civil liability directly on *private actors* to compensate for environmental harms they cause. A series of oil conventions, for example, are used to provide compensation for damage caused by oil spills. While not as comprehensive as the oil liability conventions, a set of conventions dating from 1960 imposes liability for damage resulting from the operation of nuclear power plants as well as the transportation and disposal of nuclear waste. Following the Chernobyl nuclear accident, these conventions were strengthened.

A third category of liability, in addition to liability conventions and conventions calling for the creation of liability schemes, arises from customary international law. Claims under customary law for environmental harms must address a number of basic questions—what threshold of damage triggers liability, to what standard of care should the liable party be held (negligence or strict liability), and what categories of damage should be compensable? Despite international consensus that States should not use their territories to harm other States, very few international disputes over environmental damage have led to claims for liability among

States. In 1941, the arbitral tribunal in the well-known Trail Smelter case ordered Canada to compensate the United States for damages caused by sulfur dioxide emissions. In another example, the United States paid Japan $2 million in 1955 as compensation for injuries caused by nuclear tests in the Marshall Islands. The compensation agreement, however, explicitly stated that the monies were paid "without reference to legal liability" and did not address whether they compensated for environmental damage as well as personal injuries.

In the following excerpt, Philippe Sands examines the use of judicial fora to enforce international environmental law and impose liability for environmental damages. The excerpt emphasizes both the State's role and the role of non-State actors.

Philippe Sands, COMPLIANCE WITH INTERNATIONAL ENVIRONMENTAL OBLI-GATIONS: EXISTING INTERNATIONAL LEGAL ARRANGEMENTS, IN IMPROVING COMPLIANCE WITH INTERNATIONAL ENVIRONMENTAL LAW 58 (James Cameron et al., eds., 1996)

Legal enforcement by states

As the principal subjects of international law, states have the primary role in enforcing rules of international environmental law. To be in a position to enforce a rule of international environmental law a state must have standing, and to have standing it must be able to prove that it is, in the words of the International Law Commission, an "injured state." This in turn means, according to Article 5 of the International Law Commission's Draft Articles on State Responsibility, that it is "a state a right of which is injured by the act of another state." Such rights could include those arising from a number of different sources, including: from a bilateral or multilateral treaty; from a binding decision of an act of an international organization; from a rule of customary international law; from the judgment of an international court or tribunal; from a treaty provision for a third state; or from a right created or established in favor of it as a particular state.

In cases involving environmental damage at least two situations need to be distinguished. The first is where one state is permitting activities which cause damage to the environment of another state, the second where one state is permitting or causing damage to the environment in an area beyond national jurisdiction.

Damage to the environment of a state

In situations involving damage to its environment, or consequential damage to its people or their property or other economic loss, a state will probably not find it difficult to claim that it is an "injured state" and that it may bring an international claim. In the Trail Smelter arbitration the United States invoked its right not to be subjected to the harmful consequences of transboundary air pollution from sulphur emissions in Canada, and to bring a claim against Canada for having violated its rights [*see* Chapter 9, page 504]. As a riparian state and a party to an international agreement with France, in the Lac Lanoux arbitration Spain relied upon prima facie rights to challenge France over proposed works which it alleged would violate its right to use the waters of the River Carol under certain conditions [*see* Chapter 11, page 776]. Similar considerations apply in respect of the Gabcikovo–Nagymaros dispute submitted by Hungary and Slovakia to the International Court for a determination of rights on the basis of a bilateral treaty between those two states and "principles of general international law" [*see* Chapter 11, page 780]. And Australia, in the Nuclear Tests Case, argued that French nuclear tests deposited radioactive fallout on Australian territory which violated its sovereignty and impaired its independent right to determine the acts which should take place within its territory [*see* Chapter 12, page 905].

Damage to the environment in areas beyond national jurisdiction

Not all cases will be as straightforward as the Trail Smelter Case, however. Both the Nuclear Tests Cases, brought by Australia and New Zealand against France calling on the latter to halt its atmospheric nuclear testing in the South Pacific region, and the Pacific Fur Seals case raise the issue of whether a state has standing to bring an environmental claim to prevent damage to an area beyond national jurisdiction, even if it has not suffered any material damage. This raises the possibility of bringing an action on the basis of obligations which are owed *erga omnes*, either on the basis of a treaty or on the basis of customary law. As a general matter, where one Party to a treaty or agreement believes that another Party is in violation of its obligations under that treaty or agreement, it will have the right, under the treaty or agreement, to seek to enforce the obligations of the Party alleged to be in violation, even if it has not suffered material damage. In most cases involving a violation of a treaty obligation, however, the applicant state is likely to have been induced into bringing a claim because it has suffered some form of material damage and not because it wishes to bring a claim to protect the interests of the international community. * * *

With respect to breaches of treaty obligations, the right of a state to enforce obligations will usually be settled by the terms of the treaty. Various human rights treaties permit any Party to enforce the obligations of any other Party by bringing a claim before the relevant treaty organs. * * *

The situation in general international law is less well developed, although there may be a move in the direction taken by the EC under some recent environmental treaties. Thus, a failure by one Party to the 1987 Montreal Protocol to fulfil its obligations under that treaty would entitle any other Party to the Protocol to seek to enforce the obligation by invoking the non-compliance or dispute settlement mechanisms under the Protocol, without having to show that it had suffered environmental damage as a result of the alleged failure. The 1989 Basel Convention similarly provides that any party "which has reason to believe that another Party is acting or has acted in breach of its obligations" under the Convention may inform the Secretariat and the Party against whom the allegations are made. Most other environmental treaties are less explicit, establishing dispute settlement mechanisms which will settle the question of enforcement rights in accordance with the provisions available under that treaty or related instruments. Some treaties specifically preclude their application to the global commons. The 1991 Espoo Convention, for example, precludes Parties from requesting an environmental impact assessment or other measures in respect to harm to the global commons.

Whether a state has, in the absence of a specific treaty right such as the Montreal Protocol, a general legal interest in the protection of the environment in areas beyond its national jurisdiction such as to allow it to exercise rights of legal protection on behalf of the international community as a whole (sometimes referred to as *actio popularis*) is a question which remains difficult to answer in the absence of state practice. This might be the situation, for example, where the activities of a state were alleged to be causing environmental damage to the global commons, such as the high seas, the sea-bed beyond national jurisdiction, outer space or perhaps the Antarctic, or to living resources found in or passing through those areas. In such cases, the question is which states, if any, have the right to enforce such international legal obligations as may exist to not cause environmental damage to an area of the global commons? * * *

The unwillingness of states to enforce obligations concerning the protection of the environment is, regrettably, supported by many examples. Perhaps the most notorious is the failure of any state to seek to enforce compliance by the former USSR with its international legal obligations arising out of the consequences of the accident at the Chernobyl nuclear power plant in 1986. This and other failures suggest that it is unlikely that the same states would seek to enforce obligations owed to the global commons, the violation of which may only lead to indirect harm to the state. * * *

Enforcement [by nongovernmental actors] in the national courts

* * * An enforcement role for individuals is envisaged by several treaties establishing international rules on civil liability. In relation to the jurisdiction of national courts, these fall into two categories: those treaties requiring victims to bring proceedings before the courts of the state in which the transboundary pollution originated, and those which allow victims to choose the courts of the state in which either the pollution originated or the damage was suffered. The nuclear liability conventions adopted in the 1960s fall into the former category. The requirement that victims of nuclear damage should have to make their claims before courts which may be several thousands of miles away from the area where damage occurred establishes an onerous burden. Moreover, they do not expressly allow for claims for environmental damage, although negotiations are currently underway to extend the definition of damage to include environmental damage. The oil pollution conventions adopted a decade or so later also provide support for the enforcement role of individuals, and are more accessible to individuals since they allow victims to claim before the courts of any contracting state or states where an incident has caused pollution damage. * * *

International enforcement [by nongovernmental actors]

At the international level the formal opportunities for non-governmental actors to play an enforcement role are extremely limited. Under some of the regional human rights treaties individual victims, including non-governmental organizations, may bring complaints directly to an international body. Thus, the European Convention on Human Rights allows the European Commission on Human Rights to receive petitions from any person, non-governmental organization or group of individuals claiming to be the victim of a violation by one of the Parties of the rights set forth in the Convention, provided that the Party against which the complaint has been lodged has accepted the competence of the Commission to receive such petitions. * * *

It is in their informal capacity as watchdogs that environmental organizations play an important role in the development, application and enforcement of international environmental law. Environmental organizations have long been active in monitoring and seeking to enforce compliance by states of international environmental laws and standards.

In discussing the role of NGOs in enforcing international environmental law, Sands described two classes of international environmental issues enforceable, under some circumstances, in domestic courts. First, international treaties governing transboundary pollution may allow victims to bring suit in the domestic courts of the country where the pollution originated, the country where the damage occurred, or both. Second, private international law treaties allocating jurisdiction to national courts in civil and commercial matters may provide a basis for environmental liability suits based on tort or other legal theories. In the following excerpt, Mary Ellen O'Connell expands on the potential role of national courts in enforcing international environmental law. O'Connell argues that similarities between international environmental law and domestic law make it possible to "borrow" domestic courts to enforce international environmental law in a wide range of cases. As you read the excerpt, consider what obstacles might be presented by national law doctrines, such as standing, sovereign immunity, and forum non conveniens (p. 1462).

> The use of domestic courts makes particular sense in the environmental area because domestic courts tend to focus on the most common polluters–individuals and corporations. The courts' clear authority over assets and persons is necessary for successful enforcement. Most courts can issue injunctions which may prevent environmental damage before it occurs. * * *
>
> Domestic courts may enforce international law in several different ways. The most common is in the form of enforcing domestic law that implements international law. A significant portion of international law, as adopted at the international level, can be realized only after it is implemented in domestic law. For example, the Convention on the International Trade in Endangered Species forbids the export and import of certain endangered species. Through domestic law, states that are parties to the convention control their citizens who wish to import or export endangered animals. Thus, after becoming a party to the treaty, many states, through their legislatures, adopt laws which apply to the state's citizens or territory, forbidding the export or import of certain animal species. A court enforcing such laws might not mention the treaty, but the treaty is implicitly being enforced. * * *
>
> Many domestic legal systems also allow the direct enforcement of international law, without prior implementation through the national legislature. Probably the most famous case in the United States demonstrating this principle is Paquette Habana. In Paquette Habana, U.S. Navy ships arrested Cuban fishing vessels during the Spanish–American War. The Navy then wanted to sell the vessels as prizes of war. The United States Supreme Court held that under international law, fishing vessels cannot be captured as prizes of war. Therefore, the Court ordered the vessels to be returned to their original owners.
>
> Given the available options, the question arises: Why is there any problem with enforcing international environmental law? Why is not all international law simply enforced by domestic courts? There are few serious difficulties in enforcing domestically implemented international law. However, direct enforcement of international law has proven problematic. Unfortunately, every country has erected barriers to the easy enforcement of international law through the courts.

Mary Ellen O'Connell, *Symposium: Enforcement and the Success of International Environmental Law* 3 IND. J. GLOBAL LEG. STUD. 47, 56–64 (1995).

———

QUESTIONS AND DISCUSSION

1. If formal enforcement of international environmental agreements is so rare and politically difficult, what informal mechanisms may a government employ for encouraging, persuading or convincing another country to comply with specific international environmental agreements? In this light, consider the excerpt by Abram and Antonia Chayes, and their contention that States now face a "new sovereignty" where their actions are constrained by the need to be a reasonable player in a global fabric of laws and institutions that require compliance of most international obligations most of the time.

2. What kind of informal enforcement can be achieved by NGOs? Consider in this respect the discussion of black-market CFCs described in Chapter 9, page 559, and illegal trade in species in Chapter 13, page 1005.

3. As support for O'Connell's argument that domestic legal doctrines pose obstacles to protection of the international environment, consider the discussion in Chapters 16 and 19 of the Alien Tort Claims Act and forum non conveniens at page 1338 and 1464.

SECTION IV.   DISPUTE AVOIDANCE AND DISPUTE RESOLUTION

The U.N. Charter places States under a general obligation to cooperate and resolve disputes peacefully. Most international environmental treaties provide for an array of increasingly formal dispute settlement mechanisms, ranging from informal consultation to formal arbitrations. In practice, however, the formal dispute settlement procedures are rarely used in most international environmental treaties. Several factors account for the lack of reliance on formal dispute mechanisms. First, the rules of decision in treaties often are not well-developed, thus involving great uncertainty for any parties to a specific dispute. No more than a handful of ICJ decisions, for example, touch on significant issues of international environmental law. Moreover, the jurisdiction or authority of the formal dispute resolution mechanisms may be inadequate to ensure a meaningful remedy. Formal dispute mechanisms can be slow and costly. Dispute settlement procedures may simply be inappropriate for reaching effective and practical solutions to the technical and difficult issues frequently posed by environmental treaties. It may be more efficient to resolve such disputes through informal negotiations between the parties, through the good offices of regional institutions, or at periodic conferences of the parties. The overriding reason, though, likely resides in a simple truism of international law—States are generally unwilling to cede their sovereignty by submitting to the jurisdiction of third-party arbitration or judicial settlement. Recent treaties, therefore, have focused as much on mechanisms to *avoid* disputes as on the procedures for settling them.

This shift to avoiding or preventing disputes is particularly important in the environmental field because it places the focus on avoiding or preventing environmental harm, as well. To the extent that problems of non-compliance can be detected and addressed early, the transaction costs (and environmental costs) of dispute avoidance will be lower than those of subsequent dispute settlement. Put another way, for many environmental issues, waiting until a dispute has ripened into one that requires formal dispute settlement may mean that irreversible environmental harm has already occurred. Dispute avoidance can thus be seen as closely linked to the concept of preventing environmental harm rather than compensating for it after the fact.

A. DISPUTE AVOIDANCE

Dispute avoidance mechanisms help ensure that parties comply with the obligations of the relevant agreement and, where a party is not in compliance, find non-confrontational means of bringing it into compliance. Implicit in this approach is the assumption that non-compliance is generally the result of incapacity or inadvertence, rather than of bad faith. Financial and technical provisions to facilitate compliance play a role in avoiding disputes, as do procedures that increase communication and build confidence between potential antagonists. Listed below are various practices to avoid disputes, many of which are employed in many environmental treaties.

Exchange of Information in General. Exchange of information provides all potentially concerned States with an opportunity to learn about environmental threats and responses. It builds confidence between States and allows them to come to informed decisions about complex and potentially politically charged issues. In addition, the exchange of information through specific, periodic reporting requirements is one of the most important tools for identifying environmental problems at early stages, when avoiding disputes is easier.

Notification. Prior notification to potentially affected States regarding activities that may have a significant adverse transboundary environmental effect is critical to prevent or minimize damage to their territory, including initiating consultations with the acting State. Emergency notification provisions are basic components of international approaches to oil spills, industrial accidents, and nuclear accidents, permitting affected parties the greatest possible opportunity to mitigate potential damage. *See, e.g.,* Chapter 12 on the Nuclear Treaties. Notification is often the first step to other dispute avoidance mechanisms, to consultations, prior informed consent procedures, and environmental impact assessments in the transboundary context.

Consultations. Because of the ecological interdependence of States, States planning to conduct activities that may harm the environment or natural resources of another state are often required by treaty to enter into good faith consultations over a reasonable time in an effort to minimize the environmental impacts. Consultation implies at least an opportunity to review and discuss a planned activity that may potentially cause damage. Increasingly, consultation is being institutionalized at the international level, either through existing international bodies (for example, the Nordic Council, the European Council and the U.N. system) or through new institutions created in the framework of specific environmental conventions. Such institutions are critical for building confidence over the long-term and for providing a mechanism for discussing and resolving potential disputes in the field of sustainable development.

Prior Informed Consent. States should receive the prior informed consent (PIC) of another State, before carrying out, or allowing one of its subjects to carry out, potentially harmful activities in that State. Activities that currently require prior informed consent include, e.g., exporting hazardous wastes into another State; transporting hazardous wastes through a State; lending emergency assistance after a nuclear accident; exporting domestically banned chemical substances; and prospecting for genetic resources. Ensuring that receiving States have the administrative capacity and necessary information to provide meaningful consent should be an important part of capacity-building efforts in the future. The ongoing elaboration of procedures for effective prior informed consent will also be critical. For a more thorough discussion of prior informed consent procedures, *see* Chapter 12 on PIC requirements for shipments of chemicals and hazardous waste.

Transboundary Environmental Impact Assessment. All States should undertake environmental impact assessment (EIA) before engaging in any activity that may create a risk of significantly affecting the environment of another State or States sharing a resource. EIA has been widely adopted for investigating and communicating potential transboundary impacts in many contexts, including for example when States plan activities that may cause substantial pollution or harm to the marine environment, or that are likely to have significant adverse effects on biological diversity. EIA has great potential for reducing conflicts in transboundary and global settings, because of its link to broad participation, consultation, notification and informed decisionmaking.

Joint Management Regimes and Institutions. States should cooperate in developing bilateral or regional regimes and institutions for managing shared transboundary resources. Establishing routine procedures for sharing information, setting environmental standards, allocating natural resources and discussing specific issues is an important means of building confidence, reducing overall transaction costs, and avoiding environmental disputes. By creating permanent institutions to address transboundary issues, countries will increase confidence and certainty in the long-term management and use of shared resources. Ultimately, such institutions can lead to cooperative development that enhances the value of the shared resource to all countries. One frequently cited example is the International Joint Commission between Canada and the United States, which is widely seen as providing a useful model for the long-term joint management of shared water and air sheds. For further discussion of the IJC, see Chapter 11, page 809 (regarding transboundary water issues).

B.   DISPUTE RESOLUTION

Most binding international environmental instruments contain one or more formal dispute settlement procedures. These range from vague calls for parties to resolve their differences to complex mechanisms involving lengthy and highly formalized procedures. The common approach in many international environmental instruments is to lay out a number of increasingly formal and binding options to the parties of a dispute. The following paper describes the manner in which dispute resolution typically progresses in international environmental agreements.

Stephen Porter & David Hunter

Dispute Resolution in the Context of Transboundary Environmental Impact Assessment: A Review of Selected Bilateral and Multilateral Agreements CIEL DISCUSSION PAPER **(March 1997)**

This paper is based on a survey of dispute avoidance and resolution approaches found in select environmental instruments.... For purposes of this paper, dispute avoidance mechanisms include those mechanisms such as information exchange, monitoring, and capacity building, that are designed to increase cooperation generally, identify potential conflicts as they are emerging, build confidence between parties, or otherwise assist in allowing the parties to avoid and prevent disputes before they arise. Dispute resolution generally speaking implies the informal and formal methods for settling or resolving disputes after such disputes have emerged. The terms "dispute resolution" and "dispute settlement" are used interchangeably in this paper. For obvious reasons, avoiding disputes can be more effective and less costly than resolving disputes after they have arisen. * * *

The obligation of States to settle disputes in a peaceful manner is well established in international law, and is enshrined in Article 33 of the United Nations Charter. Article 33 sets out a menu of dispute settlement mechanisms that are available to States including "negotiation, enquiry, mediation, conciliation, arbitration, judicial settlement, resort to regional agencies or arrangements, or other peaceful means of their own choice." These mechanisms and other closely related measures are familiar provisions of most international agreements, including those relating to the environment. Collectively, they represent the basic model for settling disputes between parties once they arise. The basic model involves a progressive process that facilitates dispute resolution by subjecting the dispute to gradually more intrusive and formal mechanisms. Initially, notification and information exchange requirements allow the parties to understand the factual basis for the other side's position. Consultation and negotiation requirements give the parties the opportunity to resolve the dispute among themselves in a mutually satisfactory way. Non-binding third party mechanisms (such as conciliation, fact-finding, use of good offices, or mediation) allow disputing parties to obtain an impartial perspective on the dispute. Finally, if all else fails, the parties may submit the dispute to binding procedures such as arbitration or judicial settlement.

This model of dispute resolution follows a logical progression and is included in many environmental and other agreements. In practice environmental disputes rarely, if ever, reach the point of binding settlement. Nonetheless, detailed dispute settlement procedures must lurk in the background to ensure the effectiveness of dispute avoidance mechanisms or less intrusive dispute settlement mechanisms. * * * [See Chapter 15, page 1225, on Article 14 of the NAAEC].

Measures Between Parties: Consultations and Negotiations

When a dispute arises and throughout the life of the dispute, the disputing parties are often in the best position to reach an accommodation. Most dispute settlement regimes reflect this dynamic by creating a clear preference in favor of negotiated settlement between the parties. The potential for subsequent binding arbitration or judicial settlement also puts pressure on the parties to settle their dispute before they lose some measure of control over the process.

The measures typically included in most international environmental instruments are consultation and/or negotiation. As a practical matter, consultation and negotiation tend to be closely linked. Generally consultation involves discussions between States that elaborate the positions and justifications of each side, whereas negotiations require a good faith effort to reach agreement based on a compromise between the positions elaborated during consultations. Many instruments may require that consultation or mediation be "in good faith and over a reasonable period of time." Otherwise, the mechanics of consultations and negotiations are frequently left up to the States, who typically conduct them in private, through diplomatic channels.

Non-binding Third–Party Measures: Good Offices, Fact–Finding, Conciliation, and Mediation

Where consultation and negotiation fail to produce a resolution of a dispute, many agreements refer the parties to one (or more) of several measures involving the participation of a third party. Under each of these methods, the third party attempts to assist the parties to reach an agreement that ends the dispute, although the level of involvement varies. Typically third party intervention attempts to clarify the facts underlying the dispute, facilitate communication between the disputants, encourage disputants to reevaluate their positions, and offer compromise suggestions or solutions. None of these methods can present a binding decision that would resolve the dispute, but they nonetheless can be very effective in moving entrenched disputants closer to a mutually acceptable resolution. Obviously the choice of the intervening third party is crucial. The third party could be another party to the agreement, one of any number of ad hoc or permanent bodies organized under the relevant agreement (ranging from a governing council to an ad hoc technical panel), an external body or organization, or even a professional mediator or conciliator. Some of these institutional issues are discussed further below.

Binding Third–Party Measures: Arbitral Tribunals and Judicial Bodies

The final step in most dispute settlement procedures is reference of the dispute to a binding arbitral or judicial process. Some environmental agreements, such as the Law of the Sea Convention or the Espoo Convention, contain detailed provisions for the constitution of an arbitral panel to resolve disputes. Typically, the parties select equal numbers of panelists from a roster and those panelists select another to serve as the head of the panel. The panels are typically empowered to establish their own rules of procedure, take whatever steps are necessary to gather all relevant information, and render a decision based on a majority vote. The decision is final and may or may not be made public.

Reference to the International Court of Justice (ICJ) is a common provision of last resort in many environmental agreements. Reliance on the ICJ is problematic, however, as ICJ jurisdiction will depend on agreement of the parties since relatively few countries have accepted compulsory ICJ jurisdiction. Parties may be wary accepting the jurisdiction of the ICJ for fear of establishing a negative precedent. Where the parties reach a settlement on their own, they will not necessarily be bound by that agreement in another circumstance in the future, whereas they might be if an ICJ decision were rendered. In addition, reference to the ICJ is likely to be costly and time consuming, and thus not suited to expeditious resolution of the dispute. Moreover, the confrontational model of judicial settlement may be better suited to cases where the parties are trying to assign liability and determine compensation for environmental damage than it is to cases involving prevention of future harm or steps necessary to achieve sustainable use of natural resources. * * *

DISPUTES INVOLVING NON–STATE ACTORS

As the Rio Declaration clarified, "environmental issues are best handled with the participation of all concerned citizens, at the relevant level." The UNEP working group recently highlighted the potential role for non-State actors to help avoid and resolve disputes and called for affected persons and their representatives to have "access to administrative and judicial proceedings in the country where the alleged harm originated without discrimination on the basis of their residence or nationality," particularly within the context of regional economic integration. * * *

The environmental agreements reviewed in the preparation of this report typically do not provide for public participation in dispute resolution processes—with two notable exceptions: the NAAEC (NAFTA Environmental Side Agreement), [*see* Chapter 15] and the Nordic Convention for the Protection of the Environment between Denmark, Finland, Norway, and Sweden. Typically dispute avoidance and settlement procedures apply only to States and the only recourse for individuals is to persuade their government to promote their claim before the relevant body. These two agreements could provide some guidance in designing a dispute avoidance and settlement procedure . . . that ensures some ability of the public to participate in dispute resolution and avoidance.

For example, the Montreal Protocol Implementation Committee permits issues of compliance to be raised by the secretariat, a party implicating another party, or a party admitting its own difficulties in complying. There is no provision for individuals or NGOs, however, who may be uniquely qualified to raise such issues, to trigger the compliance review and remediation process. It is not difficult to envision a mechanism, perhaps modeled on Article 14 of the NAAEC, that would allow the public to raise such issues with the secretariat which would then investigate and decide whether or not to refer the matter to the compliance committee. * * *

[The authors briefly review the CEC citizen submissions procedure discussed at length in chapter 15, on Trade and the Environment. They note the role citizens play in calling the CEC's attention to instances of party non-compliance with the terms of the NAAEC and also note that factual records prepared as a result of the process may be made available to the public.]

Nordic Convention Model: Reciprocal Access to National Remedies

The Nordic Convention provides another unique approach to ensure public participation in transboundary environmental matters. It provides reciprocal access to administrative and judicial authorities of each party for the citizens of each participating nation. The purpose is to provide affected individuals the ability to bring an action against the source of an environmental "nuisance" located in another State in that State's tribunals. Under the Nordic Convention, the complaining foreign national must be accorded the same treatment that a host country national would have under purely domestic circumstances. An affected individual may seek both to prevent environmental harm and to recover compensation for damages already suffered.

The Nordic Convention thus provides another model for improving the opportunities of non-State actors to bring directly actions to protect their interests.

QUESTIONS AND DISCUSSION

1. Recall the reading in Chapter 6 (page 328) by H.L.A. Hart about the minimum content of natural law. Hart states that sanctions are essential for ensuring the cooperation required for society to ensure its survival, at least in domestic society. For international society, however, he states that the inequality of power among States makes it impossible to have organized sanctions to punish those who violate the law. Having read the views on implementation, compliance, and sanctions expressed in this chapter, do you think Hart's view is true today for international environmental law?

2. The dispute settlement procedure established by the Law of the Sea Convention is one of the more sophisticated, with a compulsory judicial procedure for dispute resolution among parties. The process is flexible (parties may choose the means and fora to resolve disputes), comprehensive (most Law of the Sea disputes are ultimately subject to binding dispute resolution), and accommodating (certain vital national concerns are exempted from the dispute resolution procedures). A dispute between parties concerning the application or interpretation of the Law of the Sea Convention is first addressed informally, with an exchange of views through negotiation or other means. Since parties may jointly choose any dispute settlement process they wish, they can always decide to bypass the Convention procedure and use a bilateral, regional or other dispute settlement system. If informal negotiation fails to produce a mutually acceptable settlement, a party may request formal dispute resolution from among four fora—the International Court of Justice and three bodies created by the Law of the Sea Convention (the International Tribunal for the Law of the Sea, an arbitral tribunal, and a special technical arbitral tribunal). If the parties disagree over the appropriate forum, the dispute is submitted to a detailed process of compulsory arbitration.

3. Does it surprise you that so few international environmental disputes are resolved formally, e.g. adjudicated before the International Court of Justice? Does the paucity of formal cases suggest that traditional dispute resolution mechanisms are inadequate for international environmental law disputes or, on the contrary, does it show that they work by promoting informal resolution?

4. A small but increasingly important feature of dispute resolution is forum shopping. Just as litigants in the United States will often engage in extensive pretrial motions over venue (to stay in state or federal court, for example), States may engage in dispute resolution of the same matter in *different* fora. In a recent fisheries dispute between Chile and the European Union, for example, the EU challenged a Chilean conservation law forbidding the landing of swordfish in domestic ports. The EU argued that this violated the General Agreement on Tariffs and Trade (GATT) and requested dispute resolution at the WTO. Chile justified the law based on the overexploitation of the swordfish and sought formal arbitration under the UN Convention on the Law of the Sea. Which do you think is the more appropriate forum to decide this dispute? What factors should be considered and which do you think should be most important in resolving this type of forum shopping battle?

5. Under Principle 21 of the Stockholm Declaration, States are arguably responsible for harm they cause in other States. Yet State practice indicates the exact opposite. It is far more common for the State *injured* by pollution to pay the polluting State to halt its activities. Japan, for example, has offered to pay China to install scrubbers on its coal-burning power plants, in order to reduce the threat of acid deposition in Japan. Korea, which has not yet offered to pay, has failed to receive any relief from China in response to its pleas for reduced sulfur dioxide emissions. A. Dua and D. Esty, *APEC and Sustainable Development,* in WHITHER APEC: THE PROGRESS TO DATE AND AGENDA FOR THE FUTURE 151, 165 (1997). Sweden has given large amounts of foreign aid to the Baltic States to reduce their industrial emissions. The G–7 countries have signed a memorandum of understanding ensuring the closure of the Chernobyl nuclear plant. The agreement includes hundreds of millions of dollars in grants to complete nuclear and other energy projects in the Ukraine to make up for the lost energy from Chernobyl. GUNTHER HANDL, ED. 1995 YEARBOOK OF INTERNATIONAL ENVIRONMENTAL LAW 262–63 (1996). Do such actions undermine the polluter pays principle? Do they create a moral hazard by encouraging transfrontier pollution?

6. As this chapter describes, a country may fail to comply with its international environmental obligations for many reasons besides bad faith, such as lack of institutional and economic capacity. Should the reason for non-compliance matter in imposing sanctions and enforcement measures? If so, how could an agreement ensure that the level of enforcement varies in accordance with the cause of non-compliance?

7. One other rare type of sanction for environmental harms is UN-directed compensation. Passed during the Iraqi invasion of Kuwait, UN Security Council Resolution 687 declared,

> Iraq ... is liable under international law for any direct loss, damage, including environmental damage and the depletion of natural resources, or injury to foreign governments, nationals and corporations, as a result of Iraq's unlawful invasion and occupation of Kuwait.

U.N. Doc. S/RES/687 (1991). During its retreat from Kuwait, the Iraqi Army intentionally dynamited 732 oil wells in Kuwait. Over 650 of these oil wells caught fire and the other 82 that did not catch fire continuously poured oil into the countryside. At the peak of destruction, the damaged wells emitted more than half a million tons of aerial pollutants per day and poured 4 to 6 million million barrels of oil into the Persian Gulf, covering roughly 600 square miles of the Gulf and 300 miles of coastline. What categories of damage should be included within the UN Security Council resolution? Could damage to the global commons serve as the basis for a claim against Iraq under the resolution? Who could bring such a claim?

8. In April 1989, an international conference convened in Rome to discuss the possibility of creating an international environmental court. Since 1989, the foundation created to support this project, the International Court for the Environment Foundation, has participated in the 1992 Rio Conference, held three additional conferences and drafted a complete framework document for the creation of an international environmental court. This represents one of the most complete and structured proposals to date for a new international environmental system of adjudication and compensation.

Justice Amedeo Postiglione of the Italian Supreme Court, the director of the ICEF and leading voice in the call for an international environmental court, argues that,

> The human right to the environment must have, at the international level, a specific organ of protection for a fundamental legal and political reason: the environment is not a right of States but of individuals and cannot be effectively protected by the International Court of Justice in the Hague because the predominantly economic interests of States and existing institutions are often at loggerheads with the human right to the environment.

> [The Court would] decide any international environmental dispute involving the responsibility of States to the International Community which has not been settled through conciliation or arbitration within a period of 18 months; [and] decide any disputes concerning environmental damage, caused by private or public parties, including the State, where it is presumed that, due to its size,

characteristics and kind, this damage affects interests that are fundamental for safeguarding and protecting the human environment on earth.

Amedeo Postiglione, *The Global Environmental Crisis: The Need for an International Court of the Environment*, ICEF International Report at 33–36 (1996).

Standing would be granted to States, regional organizations, and international organizations. Standing would also be granted to an individual or NGO if the dispute has been tried by national courts and held inadmissible because there is no judicial remedy under national law, if the case has been dismissed on the merits, or if the dispute raises an issue of international importance.

Should environmental issues be handled differently than other international conflicts? The ICJ has created an "environmental chamber," presumably to highlight its interest and build expertise in environmental matters. In some U.S. environmental disputes, the courts appoint "special masters" to handle particularly complex or technical matters. Do such examples indicate the need for a special court as recommended by Justice Postiglione? Why does Justice Postiglione emphasize the need for an International Court for the Environment to recognize an individual right to a healthy environment? Note that UNCED did not explicitly recognize such a right under the Rio Declaration. What are the practical problems associated with the recognition of individual rights within the framework of international law? *See* Dinah Shelton, *What Happened to Human Rights at Rio?*, 3 Y.B. Int'l Envtl. L. 75 (1992); *see also*, Chapter 16, pages 1298–1301, on the human right to a healthy environment.

II. INTERNATIONAL ENVIRONMENTAL PROTECTION

CHAPTER NINE

THE LAW OF AIR AND ATMOSPHERE

> *[F]rom my house to the post office at the end of the road is a trip of six and a half miles. On a bicycle it takes about twenty-five minutes, in a car about eight or nine. I have walked it in an hour and a half. If you turned that trip on its end, the twenty-five minute pedal past Bateman's sand pit and the graveyard and the waterfall and Allen Hill would take me a mile beyond the height of Mt. Everest, past the point where the air is too thin to breathe without artificial assistance. Into that tight space, and the layer of ozone just above it, is crammed all that is life and all that maintains life.*

Bill McKibben, THE END OF NATURE 6 (1990)

SECTION I.   INTRODUCTION TO AIR POLLUTION ISSUES

We tend to take our air and atmosphere for granted. As discussed in Chapter 3, economists would say that we treat our air and atmosphere as a free good. We have, for example, used it as a major repository for wastes generated by industrialization. As industrialization has spread, air pollution has become a major problem throughout the world, particularly in urban centers. The public health consequences of air pollution are well known, and often much greater than other environmental issues, even in developing countries. For example, according to the World Bank, 1.3 billion people live in urban areas that do not meet World Health Organization air pollution standards, resulting in from 300,000 to 700,000 additional deaths each year. Death, of course, is not the only human health impact. Lead poisoning due to air pollution in Bangkok is estimated to have caused a decrease of four IQ points for the average child by the age of seven. Air pollution also causes significant damage to the environment, including buildings, materials and vegetation.

Air pollution has long been a concern of international law. Airsheds do not honor political boundaries. Transboundary air pollution has given rise to some of the most important international disputes, beginning in the 1940s with the well known *Trail Smelter Arbitration* between Canada and the United States. *Trail Smelter* involved the relatively simple case of a factory located wholly inside one country (Canada) but near and upwind of the border of another country (the United States). The straightforward factual questions concerned whether the polluting facility's plume of air pollution caused any damage to the neighboring State. The rule emanating from *Trail Smelter,* now widely accepted as customary international law, is that one State should not allow activities under its jurisdiction or control to harm the environment of a neighboring State or of areas beyond national jurisdiction. *Trail Smelter* and customary international law relating to transboundary air pollution are addressed in Part II of this Chapter.

Since the time of *Trail Smelter* we have learned much about the behavior of air pollutants in the atmosphere, how and where they travel and what impacts they can have even at great distances from the original source of the pollution. In cases where air pollutants travel long distances, the legal principle may be the same (i.e. that one State should not allow activities in its jurisdiction to harm the environment of another State), but questions of causation and proof are more difficult. Thus, for example, the Nordic countries tend to be downwind of many other European countries with many different air pollution sources. Trying to assign specific, detailed responsibility in an arbitration would be virtually impossible.

The nature of air pollutants and their impacts have also changed. Through the 1960s, air pollution was viewed as essentially a local problem, causing acute impacts on human health or the environment. The impact of long range pollutants came to the fore in the 1970s, particularly with respect to sulfur dioxide (SO_2) and nitrous oxide (NO_x) emissions and their contribution to acid rain (more properly called acid deposition, because it can occur both as snow and as dust in addition to rain).

Concern over acid deposition has led to significant international negotiations both in North America and in Europe. Europe, under the auspices of the U .N. Economic Commission for Europe, has adopted a complex and comprehensive regime for regulating long-range air pollution (known as the Convention on Long–Range Transboundary of Air Pollutants or LRTAP). After agreeing to a framework convention, the parties established a series of separate protocols to control NO_x, SO_2, volatile organic compounds (VOCs), and persistent organic pollutants (POPs). This treaty regime is important in its own right, but also as a model for the Montreal Protocol regime, the 1992 Climate Change Convention, and the 2001 POPs Convention.

In North America, acid deposition issues are relatively simple (at least when compared to Europe), because for the most part only two countries are involved—the United States and Canada—and most of the continent's sources of SO_2 and NO_x are located in the United States. Nonetheless, allocating responsibility among the many different private utilities on the continent is still difficult, and considerable debate exists over the extent of damage that can be ascribed to long-range acid deposition. Both the European and North American approach to regional air pollution generally (and acid deposition particularly) are discussed in Part III.

Beginning in the late 1970s and early 1980s, concern over national and regional air pollution problems like acid deposition gave way to concerns over global changes in the chemical composition of our atmosphere. We now understand that these changes in the atmosphere's composition, though measured only in small percentages, can have major impacts on the global environment and public health. These global threats include depletion of the stratospheric ozone layer caused by chlorofluorocarbons and other chemicals, discussed in Part IV of this Chapter, and changes in our climate, including global warming, caused by increased emissions of carbon dioxide and other greenhouse gases, discussed in Part V.

The remaining part of this Chapter will provide a basic introduction to the chemistry of our air and atmosphere as well as the causes and impacts of different air pollutants.

M. Soroos, The Endangered Atmosphere: Preserving a Global Commons 24–28 (1997)

The chemical composition of the atmosphere has been quite stable for the past 600 million years. Four gases comprise 99.99 percent of dry air: nitrogen (78.08 percent), oxygen (20.95 percent), argon (0.93 percent), and CO_2 (0.03 percent). The proportions of these gases are remarkably uniform up to an altitude of approximately 80 km. The atmosphere also contains minute proportions of forty naturally occurring trace gases, such as neon, helium, ozone, hydrogen, krypton, and methane. Despite their extremely low concentrations, some of these trace gases play a critical role in atmospheric and biological processes. Another important component is water vapor, which is present in amounts varying from 0 to 4 percent of the volume of the atmosphere. The lower levels of the atmosphere also contain varying amounts of minute liquid and solid particles known as aerosols, including such naturally occurring substances as soil dust, pollen, soot from forest fires, microorganisms, sea salt, and pollutants from human activities.

The atmosphere is comprised of several layers that are defined by the vertical profile of temperatures. . . . The lowest level, known as the troposphere, is a region in which temperatures decline sharply with altitude. The upper boundary of the troposphere is the tropopause, the altitude at which temperatures level off at minus 75–80C. before rising through the next layer, which is known as the stratosphere. The altitude of the tropopause ranges from an average of 10–12 km over the poles to 17 km over the equator and is generally highest during the summer and lowest in the winter. The upper boundary of the stratosphere is the stratopause, which is located at an altitude of approximately 50 km, where temperatures are a moderate minus 5_C at about 80 km, an altitude known as the mesopause. Beyond the mesopause is the thermosphere, which comprises only 0.0001 percent of the atmosphere's gases and extends upward to approximately 500 km. In the thermosphere temperatures again rise with altitude to as high as 1200_C due to heat released by the collision of highly energetic solar radiation with oxygen and nitrogen atoms and molecules. In the process electrically charged particles called ions are released, and thus much of the thermosphere is also known as the ionosphere. Beyond the thermosphere is the exosphere, which is comprised of thin interplanetary gases.

The troposphere, which contains approximately 85 percent of the atmosphere's gases, is not only the densest layer of the atmosphere but also the region in which most of the atmospheric phenomena known as weather takes place. The dynamic weather conditions occur because the air of the troposphere is subject to vertical mixing through the process of convection, which has been compared to a boiling pot of water heated from below. The air adjacent to the Earth's surface is warmed by heat given off by rocks, soil, and the seas after they absorb solar radiation. As the surface air is warmed, it expands and becomes less dense, which causes it to rise to higher altitudes where it mixes with cooler air. As the rising air is cooled, the water vapor it contains condenses to form clouds and precipitation. As the warm air rises, its place is taken by descending cooler, denser air from the higher altitudes, thus completing the convection current. The temperature inversion created by the relatively warm stratosphere acts like a ceiling that prevents the further ascent of the turbulent air of the troposphere into the stratosphere. The resulting circulation patterns within the troposphere redistribute heat and moisture, which is essential for maintaining the climates that have been so conducive to life on the planet. By contrast, the stratosphere is a region of relative calm and few clouds and is thus a preferable zone for jet traffic.

A basic understanding of the different components of the atmosphere is important for understanding the different types of environmental problems caused by air pollution. Some problems, such as urban smog, are local problems that occur due to increases in pollutants primarily in the lower atmosphere. Other problems such as the depletion of the ozone layer are due to changes in concentrations of different pollutants (e.g., chlorofluorocarbons) in the stratosphere. Box 9.1 provides a brief taxonomy of different air pollutants, what causes them, what damage that pollution causes, and what international legal regime, if any covers them.

Box 9.1: Air Pollutants and Impacts

Particulates refer to airborne particles larger than single molecules and smaller than 500 micrometers. They are emitted from most industrial sources and may take many forms. The most obvious effect of relatively high concentrations of particulate matter is reduced atmospheric visibility. More significantly, particulates exacerbate respiratory illnesses and over the long-term increase chronic bronchitis. According to the World Bank, reducing the levels of particulate emissions to meet World Health Organization standards would save 300,000 to 700,000 lives a year. Particulates can also cause direct chemical damage, such as corroding metallic surfaces and damaging vegetation. Particulates are for the most part a local or regional problem, although they are occasionally the focus of transboundary disputes.

Nitrous oxides (NO_x) are emitted from many industrial sources as well as automobiles. NO_x is also a precursor to photochemical smog, impairing respiratory function in asthmatics, increasing incidences of acute respiratory illness, and causing throat and eye irritation. NO_x, when mixed with water, causes acid rain. Acid rain has damaged rivers, lakes and forests in both eastern North America and Europe. NO_x is the subject of a protocol to the LRTAP Convention as well as the U.S.-Canada Bilateral Air Quality Agreement (BAQA).

Sulfur dioxide (SO_2) is also a primary cause of acid rain. The major sources of SO_2 are coal and oil combustion, i.e., stationary utility power plants, industrial boilers, and residential heaters. The effects of acid rain on the environment include acidification of natural water sources leading to adversely affected fish populations and the leaching of nutrients in the soil leading to loss in productivity of crops and forests and changes in the natural vegetation. SO_2 can cause respiratory tract problems, exacerbate respiratory illnesses, and over the long-term increase permanent harm to lung tissue and chronic bronchitis. Both the LRTAP regime and the U.S.-Canada BAQA address SO_2.

Volatile organic compounds (VOCs) are emitted from many industrial sources as well as automobile emissions. In the presence of sunlight, VOCs contribute to the creation of ozone and ''smog'' at the ground level. Such smog exacerbates asthma, causes eye and nose irritation, chest discomfort, headaches and nausea, worsens coughs, impairs pulmonary functions in people who are exercising, reduces the resistance to lung disease, and causes scarring of lungs over the long term. VOCs are covered by a protocol to the LRTAP Convention and are also the subject of international efforts to clean up urban air pollution in developing countries.

Persistent organic pollutants (POPs). Many industrial processes emit chemical byproducts in the form of organochlorides. These chemicals, which do not decompose easily and can travel great distances, bioaccumulate in plant and animal matter, resulting in abnormally high concentrations in animals at the top of the food chain. While the effects of POPs on animals and human health have been debated, many have linked the increase in the level of POPs to cancers, immune deficiencies, and decreases in fertility and reproductive stress. POPs are the subject of a protocol under the LRTAP Convention and the 2001 Stockholm POPs Convention.

Carbon Dioxide (CO_2) is the largest contributor to anthropogenic climate change and global warming. The economic, social, environmental and health impacts of climate change and global warming are hotly debated but are generally viewed to be substantial. CO_2 is emitted from the combustion of all fossil fuels. CO_2 emissions are now addressed under the 1992 Framework Convention on Climate Change and the 1997 Kyoto Protocol .

Chloroflourocarbons (CFCs) and a number of related chemicals lead to the depletion of the ozone layer, which in turn leads to increased levels of ultraviolet radiation striking the earth's surface. Such increased levels of ultraviolet radiation are expected to cause an estimated 300,000 additional cases of skin cancer and 1.7 million cases of cataracts worldwide, as well as significant harm to fish, wildlife and agricultural production. CFCs are covered by both the Montreal Protocol and climate change regimes.

D. ELSOM, ATMOSPHERIC POLLUTION: A GLOBAL PROBLEM 369–70 (2d ed. 1992); MARVIN SQUILLACE, ENVIRONMENTAL LAW: AIR POLLUTION 1–12 (2d ed. 1992).

QUESTIONS AND DISCUSSION

1. As you read the ensuing sections of this chapter, consider whether we should develop a law of atmosphere, perhaps in the form of an overarching convention.

What would be gained from such an approach as opposed to the *ad hoc* approach that we have adopted? We will return to this question after gaining a better understanding of the approach taken in developing an overarching Law of the Sea Convention.

What is the legal status of the atmosphere? Consider the following discussion presented by Patricia Birnie and Alan Boyle in *International Law & the Environment*, 390–91 (1992):

> The atmosphere is not a distinct category in international law. Because it consists of a fluctuating and dynamic air mass, it cannot be equated with airspace, which, above land, is simply a spatial dimension subject to the sovereignty of the subjacent states. But this overlap with territorial sovereignty also means that it cannot be treated as an area of common property beyond the jurisdiction of any state, comparable in this sense to the high seas. The alternative possibility of regarding it as a shared resource is relevant in situations of bilateral or regional transboundary air pollution, affecting other states or adjacent regional seas. The Executive Director of UNEP has referred to "airsheds" as examples of shared natural resources, and this status is consistent with regional approaches to the control and regulation of transboundary air pollution adopted in the [1979 LRTAP Convention] . . . and in regional seas agreements limiting air pollution of the marine environment. * * *
>
> The shared resources concept is of less use, however, in relation to global atmospheric issues such as ozone depletion or climate change. What is needed here is a legal concept which recognizes the unity of the global atmosphere and the common interest of all states in its protection. The traditional category of common property, is, as we have seen, an inadequate one for this purpose. The same objection applies to the use of "common heritage" in this context, with the additional difficulty that this concept has so far been applied only to mineral resources of the deep sea-bed and outer space and that its legal status remains controversial following rejection by the United States and a number of other countries opposed to the implications of the term. The atmosphere is clearly not outer space, despite the difficulty of defining the boundaries of that area. Moreover, Article 135 of the 1982 UNCLOS provides that the status of the sea-bed does not affect superjacent airspace, and thus offers no support for any wider use of the common heritage concept. Significantly, it was not employed in the 1985 Vienna Convention for the Protection of the Ozone Layer.
>
> That convention defines the "ozone layer" as "the layer of atmospheric ozone above the planetary boundary layer." This does not mean that the ozone layer is either legally or physically part of outer space. It remains part of the atmosphere, and falls partly into areas of common property, and partly into areas of national sovereignty. One purpose of the convention's definition is to indicate that it is concerned with stratospheric ozone, and not with low-level ozone, which . . . is an air pollutant. More importantly, however, the definition treats the whole stratospheric ozone layer as a global unity, without reference to legal concepts of sovereignty, shared resources or common property. It points to the emergence of a new status for the global atmosphere, which makes it appropriate to view the ozone layer as part of a common resource or common interest, regardless of who enjoys sovereignty over the airspace which it occupies.
>
> The same conclusion can also be drawn from UN General Assembly resolution 43/53, which declares that global climate change is "the common concern of mankind." This phraseology was the outcome of a political compromise over Malta's initial proposal to treat the global climate as the common heritage of mankind. . . . What it suggests is that the global climate should have a status

comparable to the ozone layer, and that the totality of the global atmosphere can now properly be regarded as the "common concern of mankind." By approaching the issues from this global perspective, the General Assembly has recognized both the artificiality of territorial boundaries in this context, and the inadequacy of treating global climate change in the same way as transboundary air pollution, for which regional or bilateral solutions remain more appropriate.

[T]he status of "common concern" is primarily significant in indicating the common legal interest of all states in protecting the global atmosphere, whether directly injured or not, and in enforcing rules concerning its protection.

Note that the above excerpt was written before the 1992 Framework Convention on Climate Change affirmed that the global climate system was a matter of "common concern." As you read that Convention, consider to what extent it has added meaning or conferred clearer legal status to the concept of common concern as applied to the atmosphere. *See also* Chapter 7, page 396, discussing the concept of common concern.

3.   Because many of the technologies, impacts and issues are the same no matter where local air pollution issues occur, urban air pollution has begun to gain the attention of international policymakers. Thus, for example, the U.S. Agency for International Development's Urban Program attempts to disseminate lessons from around the world on how to minimize urban air pollution. The globalization of these otherwise domestic and local issues is an important trend in international environmental law. The major focus of these efforts is not necessarily to establish uniform, minimum standards, but to marshal international development resources to respond to certain high-priority issues. What other issues relating to air pollution, or otherwise, can you think of that could benefit from international cooperation. What steps or policies could be adopted at the international level to have an impact on these issues? In this regard, consider some of the elements discussed in Chapter 8, pages 467–479, addressed in the context of facilitating implementation.

SECTION II.   CUSTOMARY INTERNATIONAL LAW AND TRANSBOUNDARY AIR POLLUTION

As industrialization has spread, the incidence of transboundary air pollution has increased. Stationary sources of air pollution such as factories and other industrial plants as well as mobile sources such as automobiles, when located or operated near borders, routinely lead to transboundary air pollution. Yet, only one international adjudication exists with respect to traditional air pollution issues (excluding the Nuclear Test Cases). That one case is the 1941 *Trail Smelter Arbitration*. After discussing this arbitration and exploring some of the reasons why other cases have not been brought, we present a problem exercise to highlight how the law has evolved since 1941 as well as the substantive customary law rules that may now apply to transboundary air pollution disputes. These rules are important, both because of possible future international litigation and because they provide the legal precedent for diplomatic solutions of such disputes.

A.   THE TRAIL SMELTER ARBITRATION

The Trail Smelter dispute is perhaps the most famous international environmental dispute. It involved transboundary SO_2 emissions emanating from a smelter located in British Columbia just a few miles north of the U.S.-Canada border. The facts of the case were presented by the Arbitral panel's 1941 final decision.

> In 1896, a smelter was started under American auspices near the locality known as Trail, B.C. In 1906, the Consolidated Mining and Smelting Company of Canada, Limited, obtained a charter of incorporation from the Canadian authorities, and that company acquired the smelter plant at Trail as it then existed. Since that time, the Canadian company, without interruption, has operated the Smelter, and from time to time has greatly added to the plant until it has become one of the best and largest equipped smelting plants on the American continent. In 1925 and 1927, two stacks of the plant were erected to 409 feet in height and the Smelter greatly increased its daily smelting of zinc and lead ores. This increased production resulted in more sulphur dioxide fumes and higher concentrations being emitted into the air. In 1916, about 5,000 tons of sulphur per month were emitted; in 1924, about 4,700 tons; in 1926, about 9,000 tons—an amount which rose near to 10,000 tons per month in 1930. In other words, about 300–350 tons of sulphur were being emitted daily in 1930. (It is to be noted that one ton of sulphur is substantially the equivalent of two tons of sulphur dioxide or SO_2.)

This plume of sulfur dioxide traveled across the U.S–Canada border and damaged the property of apple growers in Washington state. For a variety of reasons (discussed below), the Washington State residents could not bring a lawsuit either in Washington State or in British Colombia, so they asked the U.S. government to intervene on their behalf in 1927. This started a long and involved process that would take thirteen years. The initial procedural aspects of the case are described in the following article.

J. Read, *The Trail Smelter Dispute*,
THE CANADIAN YEARBOOK OF INT'L LAW 213–17 (1963)

The subject-matter of the dispute did not directly concern the two governments; nor did it involve claims by United States citizens against the Canadian government. It did not seem to come within any of the ordinary categories of arbitrable international disputes. It consisted rather of claims based on nuisance, alleged to have been committed by a Canadian corporation and to have caused damage to United States citizens and property in the State of Washington. Nevertheless, when the United States proposed to refer the questions at issue to the International Joint Commission, the Canadian government concurred; and, on August 7, 1928, it joined in a reference under Article 9 of the Boundary Waters Treaty of 1909. This Article provided for investigation and recommendation; but not for decision.* * *

The Commission made a unanimous report on February 28, 1931. It assessed the damage up to the year 1931 at $350,000 and made other recommendations covering the questions referred to it. The Consolidated Mining and Smelting Company had already commenced the construction of remedial works designed to lessen the output of sulphur from the smelter by about one-third. The works were to be completed in 1931, and the report was based on the expectation that they would bring about the cessation of damage.

The recommendations of the Commission were satisfactory to the Canadian government but they were rejected by the United States in February 1933. Negotiations which followed led to the submission of the dispute to a three-member tribunal by a Convention signed on April 15, 1935.

Without making a detailed examination of the Convention, consideration may be given to the following provisions:

Article I required the government of Canada to pay to the United States the sum of $350,000, to cover all damage which occurred prior to January 1, 1932.

Article II provided for the constitution of the Tribunal to consist of a neutral chairman and two national members.

Article III stated the questions:

(1) Whether damage caused by the Trail Smelter in the State of Washington has occurred since the first day of January, 1932, and, if so, what indemnity should be paid therefor?

(2) In the event of the answer to the first part of the preceding Question being in the affirmative, whether the Trail Smelter should be required to refrain from causing damage in the State of Washington in the future, and if so, to what extent?

(3) In the light of the answer to the preceding Question, what measures or regime, if any, should be adopted or maintained by the Trail Smelter?

(4) What indemnity or compensation, if any, should be paid on account of any decision or decisions rendered by the Tribunal pursuant to the next two preceding Questions?

Article IV stated the law to be applied by the Tribunal. . . . ["The Tribunal shall apply the law and practice followed in dealing with cognate questions in the United States of America as well as international law and practice, and shall give consideration to the desire of the high contracting parties to reach a solution just to all parties."] * * *

On April 16, 1938, the Tribunal reported its "final decision" on Question No. 1, as well as its temporary decisions on Questions No. 2 and No. 3, and provided for a temporary regime thereunder. There may be some confusion in terminology. The ultimate decision of the Tribunal was rendered on March 11, 1941, and it was very definitely *final*. The Tribunal there referred to the earlier decision as the "previous decision," an expression which is somewhat awkward. . . . Nevertheless, confusion can be avoided by using it and by putting the words "final" or "final decision" in quotation marks whenever it is necessary to discuss the finality of any part of the "previous decision."

As regards Question No. 1, the Agent for the government of the United States presented claims for damages of $1,849,156.16 with interest of $250,855.01, divided into seven categories: (a) cleared land and improvements; (b) uncleared land and improvements; (c) livestock; (d) property in the town of Northport; and (e) wrong done the United States in violation of sovereignty, measured by cost of investigation from January 1, 1932, to June 30, 1936; (f) interest on $350,000 accepted in satisfaction of damage to January 1, 1932, but not paid on that date; and (g) business enterprises.

The area claimed to be damaged contained more than 140,000 acres, including the town of Northport.

The Tribunal disallowed the claims of the United States under items (c), (d), (e), (f), and (g); but allowed them in part under the remaining items (a) and (b), that is, cleared and uncleared land and improvements.

In the conclusion of the "previous decision," the Tribunal reported, as its "final decision" regarding Question 1:

Damage caused by the Trail Smelter in the State of Washington has occurred since the first day of January, 1932, and up to October 1, 1937, and the indemnity to be paid therefor is seventy-eight thousand dollars ($78,000), and is to be complete and final indemnity and compensation for all damage which occurred between such dates. Interest at the rate of six per centum per year will be allowed on the above sum of seventy-eight thousand dollars ($78,000) from the date of the filing of this report and decision until date of payment. This decision is not subject to alteration or modification by the Tribunal hereafter.

The fact of existence of damage, if any, occurring after October 1, 1937, and the indemnity to be paid therefor, if any, the Tribunal will determine in its final decision.

As regards Questions Nos. 2 and 3, the Tribunal subjected the Trail Smelter to a temporary regime and provided for further and "more adequate and intensive study" under the supervision of two "Technical Consultants". . . .

For the best part of three years, and over three complete growing seasons, the Tribunal applied the temporary regime and conducted a comprehensive investigation of the behaviour of the smoke cloud wasted from the stacks of the smelter. The Tribunal, in its final decision, described this investigation in the following words:

The investigations made during the past three years on the application of meteorological observations to the solution of this problem at Trail have built up a fund of significant and important facts. This is probably the most thorough study ever made of any area subject to atmospheric pollution by industrial smoke. Some factors, such as atmospheric turbulence and the movement of the upper air currents have been applied for the first time to the question of smoke control. All factors of possible significance, including wind directions and velocity, atmospheric temperatures lapse rates, turbulence, geostrophic winds, barometric pressures, sunlight and humidity, along with atmospheric sulphur dioxide concentrations, have been studied. As said above, many observations have been made on the movements and sulphur dioxide concentrations of the air at higher levels by means of pilot and captive balloons and by airplane, by night and by day. Progress has been made in breaking up the long winter fumigations and in reducing their intensity. In carrying finally over to the non-growing season with a few minor modifications a regime of demonstrated efficiency for the growing season, there is a sound basis for confidence that the winter fumigations will be kept under control at a level well below the threshold of possible injury to vegetation. Likewise, for the growing season a regime has been formulated which should throttle at the source the expected diurnal fumigations to a point where they will not yield concentrations below the international boundary sufficient to cause injury to plant life. This is the goal which this Tribunal has set out to accomplish.

The Tribunal's reported its final decision to the governments on March 11, 1941. The most important part of the decision for international environmental law addressed whether the Trail Smelter should be enjoined from causing future damage to the State of Washington (i.e., the second question under Article III of the Tribunal's Convention).

Trail Smelter Case (United States v. Canada), Arbitral Tribunal, 1941, 3 UN Rep. Int'l Arb. Awards (1941)

Damage has occurred since January 1, 1932, as fully set forth in the previous decision. To that extent, the first part of the preceding question has thus been answered in the affirmative. * * *

The first problem which arises is whether the question should be answered on the basis of the law followed in the United States or on the basis of international law. The Tribunal, however, finds that this problem need not be solved here as the law followed in the United States in dealing with the quasi-sovereign rights of the States of the Union, in the matter of air pollution, whilst more definite, is in conformity with the general rules of international law.

Particularly in reaching its conclusions as regards this question as well as the next, the Tribunal has given consideration to the desire of the high contracting parties "to reach a solution just to all parties concerned".

As Professor Eagleton puts it: "A State owes at all times a duty to protect other States against injurious acts by individuals from within its jurisdiction." A great number of such general pronouncements by leading authorities concerning the duty of a State to respect other States and their territory have been presented to the Tribunal. These and many others have been carefully examined. International decisions, in various matters, from the Alabama case onward, and also earlier ones, are based on the same general principle, and, indeed, this principle, as such, has not been questioned by Canada. But the real difficulty often arises rather when it comes to determine what . . . is deemed to constitute an injurious act.

A case concerning, as the present one does, territorial relations, decided by the Federal Court of Switzerland between the Cantons of Soleure and Argovia, may serve to illustrate the relativity of the rule. Soleure brought a suit against her sister State to enjoin use of a shooting establishment which endangered her territory. The court, in granting the injunction, said: "This right (sovereignty) excludes . . . not only the usurpation and exercise of sovereign rights (of another State) . . . but also an actual encroachment which might prejudice the natural use of the territory and the free movement of its inhabitants." As a result of the decision, Argovia made plans for the improvement of the existing installations. These, however, were considered as insufficient protection by Soleure. The Canton of Argovia then moved the Federal Court to decree that the shooting be again permitted after completion of the projected improvements. This motion was granted. "The demand of the Government of Soleure", said the court, "that all endangerment be absolutely abolished apparently goes too far." The court found that all risk whatever had not been eliminated, as the region was flat and absolutely safe shooting ranges were only found in mountain valleys; that there was a federal duty for the communes to provide facilities for military target practice and that "no more precautions may be demanded for shooting ranges near the boundaries of two Cantons than are required for shooting ranges in the interior of a Canton". (R.O. 26, I, pp. 450, 451; 1t.O. 41, I, p. 137.)

No case of air pollution dealt with by an international tribunal has been brought to the attention of the Tribunal nor does the Tribunal know of any such case. The nearest analogy is that of water pollution. But, here also, no decision of an international tribunal has been cited or has been found.

There are, however, as regards both air pollution and water pollution, certain decisions of the Supreme Court of the United States which may legitimately be taken as a guide in this field of international law, for it is reasonable to follow by analogy, in international cases, precedents established by that court in dealing with controversies between States of the Union or with other controversies concerning the quasi-sovereign rights of such States, where no contrary rule prevails in international law and no reason for rejecting such precedents can be adduced from the limitations of sovereignty inherent in the Constitution of the United States.

In the suit of the *State of Missouri v. the State of Illinois,* 200 U.S. 496, 521, concerning the pollution, within the boundaries of Illinois, of the Illinois River, an affluent of the Mississippi flowing into the latter where it forms the boundary between that State and Missouri, an injunction was refused. "Before this court ought to intervene", said the court, "the case should be of serious magnitude, clearly and fully proved, and the principle to be applied should be one which the court is prepared deliberately to maintain against all considerations on the other side. (See Kansas v. Colorado, 185 U.S. 125.)" The court found that the practice complained of was general along the shores of the Mississippi River at that time, that it was followed by Missouri itself and that thus a standard was set up by the defendant which the claimant was entitled to invoke. * * *

In the matter of air pollution itself, the leading decisions are those of the Supreme Court in the State of Georgia v. Tennessee Copper Company and Ducktown Sulphur, Copper and Iron Company, Limited. Although dealing with a suit against private companies, the decisions were on questions cognate to those here at issue. Georgia stated that it had in vain sought relief from the State of Tennessee, on whose territory the smelters were located, and the court defined the nature of the suit by saying: "This is a suit by a State for an injury to it in its capacity of quasi-sovereign. In that capacity, the State has an interest independent of and behind the titles of its citizens, in all the earth and air within its domain."

On the question whether an injunction should be granted or not, the court said (206 U.S. 230):

> It (the State) has the last word as to whether its mountains shall be stripped of their forests and its inhabitants shall breathe pure air. ...It is not lightly to be presumed to give up quasi-sovereign rights for pay and ... if that be its choice, it may insist that an infraction of them shall be stopped. This court has not quite the same freedom to balance the harm that will be done by an injunction against that of which the plaintiff complains, that it would have in deciding between two subjects of a single political power. Without excluding the considerations that equity always takes into account ... it is a fair and reasonable demand on the part of a sovereign that the air over its territory should not be polluted on a great scale by sulphurous acid gas, that the forests on its mountains, be they better or worse, and whatever domestic destruction they may have suffered, should not be further destroyed or threatened by the act of persons beyond its control, that the crops and orchards on its hills should not be endangered from the same source. ...Whether Georgia, by insisting upon this claim, is doing more harm than good to her own citizens, is for her to determine. The possible disaster to those outside the State must be accepted as a consequence of her standing upon her extreme rights.

Later on, however, when the court actually framed an injunction, in the case of the Ducktown Company (237 U.S. 474, 477) (an agreement on the basis of an annual compensation was reached with the most important of the two smelters, the Tennessee Copper Company), they did not go beyond a decree "adequate to diminish materially the present probability of damage to its (Georgia's) citizens."

The Tribunal, therefore, finds that the above decisions, taken as a whole, constitute an adequate basis for its conclusions, namely, that, under the principles of international law, as well as of the law of the United States, no State has the right to use or permit the use of its territory in such a manner as to cause injury by fumes in or to the territory of another or the properties or persons therein, when the case is of serious consequence and the injury is established by clear and convincing evidence.

The decisions of the Supreme Court of the United States which are the basis of these conclusions are decisions in equity and a solution inspired by them, together with the regime hereinafter prescribed, will, in the opinion of the Tribunal, be "just to all parties concerned", as long, at least, as the present conditions in the Columbia River Valley continue to prevail.

Considering the circumstances of the case, the Tribunal holds that the Dominion of Canada is responsible in international law for the conduct of the Trail Smelter. Apart from the undertakings in the Convention, it is, therefore, the duty of the Government of the Dominion of Canada to see to it that this conduct should be in conformity with the obligation of the Dominion under international law as herein determined.

The Tribunal, therefore, answers Question No. 2 as follows:

(2) So long as the present conditions in the Columbia River Valley prevail, the Trail Smelter shall be required to refrain from causing any damage through fumes in the State of Washington; the damage herein referred to and its extent being such as would be recoverable under the decisions of the courts of the United States in suits between private individuals. The indemnity for such damage should be fixed in such manner as the Governments, acting under Article XI of the Convention, should agree upon.

The third question under Article III of the Convention is as follows: "In the light of the answer to the preceding question, what measures or regime, if any, should be adopted and maintained by the Trail Smelter?"

Answering this question in the light of the preceding one, since the Tribunal has, in its previous decision, found that damage caused by the Trail Smelter has occurred in the State of Washington since January 1, 1932, and since the Tribunal is of opinion that damage may occur in the future unless the operations of the Smelter shall be subject to some control, in order to avoid damage occurring, the Tribunal now decides that a regime or measure of control shall be applied to the operations of the Smelter and shall remain in full force unless and until modified in accordance with the provisions hereinafter set forth. [The regime ordered by the Tribunal was significant, costing the Trail smelter over $20 million in capital costs.]

QUESTIONS AND DISCUSSION

1. Based on the Trail Smelter opinion what legal advice could you give a State (or a private company operating in the State) that is responsible for bilateral air pollution? What legal standards appear to be provided by the opinion? Is all transboundary air pollution prohibited? Given the length and apparent expense of the arbitration, what practical advice might you give your client? Is there a strong incentive for settling such disputes in some other way?

2. Consider the Trail Smelter opinion in light of the sources of international law described in Chapter 6. Does the Tribunal's heavy reliance on national law surprise you? Is such reliance dependent on Article IV of the Convention establishing the arbitration, which highlighted the law of the United States, or do you think reliance on U.S. law would have been informative for the Tribunal, even without Article IV? In this regard, does the discussion of the Swiss case suggest that national level decisions regarding quasi-sovereigns is always a potential source of international law?

3. *The Trail Smelter Arbitration* does not technically provide much legal precedent for other disputes, given that it is the product of a fairly narrowly circumscribed arbitration based on a detailed agreement between the two parties. Nonetheless, the reasoning of Trail Smelter is still powerful today, not only in transboundary air pollution cases but also in international environmental law generally. As described in Chapter 7, pages 346–48, the *Trail Smelter Arbitration* was the genesis for Principle 21 of the *Stockholm Declaration*, a principle widely viewed to reflect customary international law: "States have . . . the sovereign right to exploit their own resources pursuant to their own environmental policies, and the responsibility to ensure that activities within their jurisdiction or control do not cause damage to the environment of other States or of areas beyond the limits of national jurisdiction."

4. So what has become of the Trail Smelter? The subject of the most famous international environmental law dispute has not disappeared. In fact, the Trail Smelter, now owned by Cominco, continues to operate causing major environmental problems both within British Colombia and across the border in Washington State. As of 1995, the *Trail Smelter* still emitted lead beyond the legal levels and was listed on the province's list of 85 worst polluters. L. Pynn, *Polluters' List Grows Faster than Prosecutions,* VANCOUVER SUN, March 3, 1995. To remedy this, Cominco updated the smelter in 1997, cutting emissions by an estimated 75%. As a result, blood lead levels in children dropped over 50% by 1999. Nonetheless blood lead levels are still higher in many children than the levels at which behavioral and other impacts have been observed (including the permanent loss of IQ levels). In 2001, a community-based task force set forth a series of recommendations, including calling for further reductions in emissions from the smelter, to try to continue to lower the level of lead in children's blood in and around the Trail Smelter. *See* T. Glavin, *Toxic Chemical Worries Straddle the Border,* VANCOUVER SUN, Nov. 19, 1991; *see also* the web page for the task force at http://mypage.direct.ca/t/tlp.

5. Transboundary air pollution cases such as *Trail Smelter* are not typically brought to a public international arbitration. At the time of the *Trail Smelter* dispute, the Washington state plaintiffs were barred from bringing the complaint in the courts of either the United States or Canada. The local action rule, a common law rule followed in both Canada and the United States, required that complaints relating to property be brought in the land where the harmed property was located (i.e. in Washington), but the Washington State rules of civil procedure would not permit the Court to have personal jurisdiction over the out-of-state smelter. At the time of the Trail Smelter Arbitration, for a court to have personal jurisdiction over a corporate defendant from outside of the state (including foreign corporations), the defendant had to have physical assets in the state or otherwise be subject to service of process in the state, *Pennoyer v. Neff,* 95 U.S. 714 (1877). In 1945, in *International Shoe Co. v. Washington,* 326 U.S. 310, the Supreme Court overruled *Pennoyer,* allowing personal jurisdiction where a "foreign" defendant had minimum contacts with a state sufficient for it to be reasonably brought before the state's courts. This lowered the barrier for bringing lawsuits against corporations not located in the specific state, including foreign defendant corporations.

Both because of the changing requirement for personal jurisdiction and the elimination of other barriers such as the local action rule, transboundary complaints are now easier to bring. *See, e.g., Michie, et al., v. Great Lakes Steel Division, National Steel Corp.,* 495 F.2d 213 (6th Cir.1974), *cert. den.* 419 U.S. 997 (1974). In that case, thirty-seven persons living in Ontario, Canada, filed a complaint against three corporations that operate seven plants in the United States immediately across the Detroit River from Canada. The Plaintiffs were allowed to file their lawsuit in Michigan under Michigan law.

Problem Exercise: Indonesia Fires.

The Trail Smelter case was decided over fifty years ago. Transboundary air pollution disputes today would be quite different, if for no other reason than international environmental law has developed significantly over the past five decades. Consider the following fact pattern, which is based in part on the actual situation in Indonesia in the fall of 1997. Fires in Indonesia set as part of a government agricultural promotion policy flared out of control and consumed somewhere between 250,000 and 4,000,000 acres. The thick smoke affected Malaysia, the Philippines, Singapore, Thailand, Brunei, and Papua New Guinea. The fires recurred in 2001, once again enveloping the region in thick smoke. As you work through the following exercise, consider how the legal arguments might change if it is the second time such fires spread. For a general discussion of forest fires in the region, see C. Barber & J. Schweithelm, Trial by Fire: Forest Fires and Forestry Policy in Indonesia's Era of Crisis and Reform (World Resources Institute, 2000).

In January of 2000, the government of Economia received a request by a private company, Monoculture, Inc., to develop a massive area of forests and peat bogs owned by the government. The request, which included a twenty-page environmental assessment, asked both for a concession to cut and sell all marketable timber on the lands and a permit to set fires on the land to clear it for agricultural development.

The tract of land was located six kilometers from one of the major tourist attractions in the neighboring State of Asphyxia, a world renowned canyon, listed as a World Heritage Site and boasting beautiful vistas over an expansive desert. Asphyxia referred to this area as "the Grand Canyon of the East." In addition to tourism, the area was home to the last remnant population of the canyon tortoise, an endangered species.

The environmental ministers of both Economia and Asphyxia had lunch together every month to discuss transboundary issues. At a lunch in February of 2000, the Economia environment minister informed the Asphyxia minister of the proposed project to sell the forest concession to Monoculture, Inc. The Asphyxia minister replied: "they're your forests, what difference does it make to us. Do what you want with them." Two days later, Economia approved of Monoculture, Inc.'s plans for developing the forest tract.

Monoculture, Inc. began immediately to cut the marketable timber from the forest tract. Over 60% of the timber was exported directly to nearby sawmills in Asphyxia, while the rest was processed inside Economia. Late in 2000, Monoculture began to set the forest fires to clear the land. Although their permit did not allow them to burn on windy days, Monoculture wanted to complete the fires before the monsoon rains came that would make burning the fires impossible. On December 5, 2000, the company lost control of the fires and they spread quickly throughout the heavily forested lands of Economia.

For three days, Economia hoped its efforts could contain the fires but on the fourth day several large peat bogs also caught fire. Peat bog fires can burn for months or even years. They are nearly impossible to put out, as the fires can burn underground. Peat bogs also hold large amounts of carbon and the resulting flames emit enormous amounts of thick dark smoke laden with carbon dioxide and other pollutants.

Although the fires never reached Asphyxia, the dense black smoke did on December 10. Economia did not alert Asphyxia about the run-away fires until December 11. It covered the region for three months, before the monsoon season finally came. The fires were exacerbated by the late monsoon season, which occurs like clockwork every seven years due to the El Niño weather patterns.

The thick smog caused serious economic, environmental and health problems in Asphyxia. The tourist areas were essentially shut down for three months, because the beautiful canyon vistas were virtually invisible. People with asthma and other lung disorders were encouraged to stay inside. Wildlife workers began to try to capture the Canyon tortoise on December 13, with the hopes of relocating them where the thick smoke would not affect them. Despite these efforts over half of the remaining population is believed to have suffocated in their burrows due to the smoke.

In February, 2001, Asphyxia informed Economia that it was bringing an action at the International Court of Justice for compensation of all the damages that occurred to property, the environment and people within its jurisdiction, as well as to the global atmosphere. Economia acceded to the jurisdiction of the Court.

Your professor will divide the class into two groups—one side will represent Asphyxia and the other will represent Economia. Consider the *Trail Smelter Arbitration,* the principles described in Chapter 7, as well as any international instruments found in the Treaty Supplement or provided you by your professor. Consider both procedural and substantive arguments that Asphyxia may be able to make against Economia.

SECTION III. LONG-RANGE TRANSBOUNDARY AIR POLLUTION

Beginning in the 1970s advances in our understanding of air currents and the regional transport of air pollutants led to increased calls for international control of air pollution, particularly in Europe. One of the first transboundary air pollution problems to gain widespread recognition was acid rain, caused primarily by emissions of sulfur dioxide (SO_2) and nitrogen oxides (NO_x). SO_2 and NO_x mix with water and are precipitated out of the atmosphere as acidic compounds. Acid deposition is primarily a regional issue, and given the close link between acid deposition and industrialization, the two regions that have had the longest problems with transboundary acid deposition are Europe and North America (although significant transboundary problems are now regularly occurring in Asia). The following excerpt succinctly describes the causes and effects of acid deposition, often incorrectly referred to as acid rain.

M. Soroos, The Endangered Atmosphere 38–42 (1997)

The human-generated pollutants principally responsible for increasing the presence of acids in the environment are sulfur dioxide (SO_2) and nitrogen oxides (NO_x). SO_2 emissions come primarily from the combustion of coal and petroleum and various smelting and industrial processes. Power generating plants burning high sulfur coal have been especially heavy emitters of SO_2 and NO_x, which accounts for a much smaller share of human-induced acid deposition, comes from many of the same sources as SO_2, but a far greater proportion is emitted from the tailpipes of automobiles and other motorized vehicles. Globally, sulfur and nitrogen emissions from human sources are on the same order of magnitude as those that occur naturally, although in certain regions the human component is much greater.

There are two basic types of processes through which acidic substances are formed from industrial pollutants and contaminate the environment. First, some of the oxides of sulfur and nitrogen fall out of the atmosphere in a dry form as gases or aerosols. They then combine with surface water to create acidic substances or are absorbed directly by plants to form acids. This dry type of deposition usually occurs within a few kilometers of where the pollutants are emitted. Second, much of the SO_2 and NO_x is transformed into sulfuric and nitric acids while in the atmosphere through a complex series of chemical reactions. The original pollutants are further oxidized in the presence of a photo-oxidant such as low-level ozone, which is created when pollutants such as hydrocarbons and NO_x are acted upon by sunlight. This process creates tiny droplets of sulfuric and nitric acid that dissolve in raindrops or clouds, resulting in acidic rain, snow, mist, or fog, or what is known as wet deposition. Wet deposition normally occurs farther from the pollution source than dry deposition because the process of oxidation occurs over an extended time during which the pollutants can be transported hundreds if not thousands of kilometers by wind currents. The extensive use of tall smokestacks at power plants, smelters, and factories has significantly added to the problem by causing sulfur and nitrogen oxides to be released at altitudes where they will remain in the atmosphere longer as they are carried by wind currents, increasing the likelihood that chemical reactions will take place that transform them to acids. * * *

There is no single threshold value below which precipitation is considered to be "acid rain," although most scientists regard pH readings below 4.5 to be highly acidic, which is ten times more than the acid content of normal rain. Extensive areas of Europe and eastern North America are regularly exposed to precipitation with a pH of 4.0 or lower, forty times the acidity of normal rain. Precipitation from specific storms can have much lower pH levels. Rain falling over Pitlockry, Scotland, in 1974 had a pH of 2.4; while precipitation tests at Wheeling, West Virginia, in 1979 had a pH of 1.5, the latter being 12,500 times normal acidity.

High levels of acid deposition can have severe consequences for the environment, especially for aquatic life and trees. Acidification first caused alarm when it was linked to the disappearance of fish in lakes and rivers in which the pH values of the water had dropped substantially. The problem was noticed early in the twentieth century in southern Norway and Sweden and later in eastern Canada, the northeastern United States, and the highland regions of the British Isles. The severity of the damage to aquatic life varies greatly from one place to another, even within the same region, depending upon the "buffering capacity" of the local soils and rocks. Areas rich in minerals that neutralize acids, such as those with limestone formations, display fewer manifestations of acid damage than those with other types of bedrock. The effects of acid deposition can be mitigated by spreading lime on the lakes and forest soils in affected regions, although this practice may have other undesirable effects.

Acid deposition also has significant impacts on many plant species. In relatively small doses it may have a fertilizing effect, thus stimulating the growth of agricultural crops. However, higher doses can have a harmful if not devastating impact on vegetation, especially forests. In the late 1970s scientists became concerned about unusual damage to Norwegian spruce trees in the forests of southern Germany, a condition that became known by the German term waldsterben (forest death) and later the more neutral term neuartige Waldschäeden (new forest decline). The phenomenon spread at an alarming rate through the forests of central Europe during the early 1980s. The proportion of German forests showing significant signs of disease grew from 8 percent in 1982 to 34 percent in 1983 and nearly 50 percent in 1984. By 1985 all major species of trees in central Europe were showing significant signs of disease. A forest damage assessment conducted in 1991 revealed that 18.5 percent of Europe's broadleaf trees and 24.4 percent of its conifers had lost at least one-quarter of their foliage. In the United Kingdom 56.7 percent of trees were at least moderately defoliated, and in Poland 45 percent were. Significant damage to forests, presumably linked to acid deposition, has also been noted in eastern North America and regions of Asia.

The processes through which these ecosystems are altered by acid deposition are complex and occur over extended periods. Species in aquatic environments can tolerate different levels of acidity. Numerous smaller species such as algae, zooplankton, phytoplankton, and aquatic insects cannot tolerate pH levels lower than 5.0 or even 5.5, which has serious implications because they are near the bottom of the food chain. As pH levels drop below 5.0, most fish and amphibian species disappear because of reproductive failures caused by the toxic effects of aluminum that acids release into the water. Loss of fish reduces the food supplies of species such as birds that feed upon them. The problem is most pronounced during "acid surges" that occur with spring runoffs or after droughts, when pH values are especially low. Scientists have had greater difficulty isolating the causes of forest decline in acidified regions because other factors such as extreme temperatures, droughts, diseases, insects, and other pollutants such as ozone may also be damaging trees. Moreover, trees weakened by natural causes may be more vulnerable to increased acidity of their environments or, alternatively, trees affected by acid deposition may be more susceptible to other environmental threats. It has also been difficult to determine the extent to which acids damage trees by coming into contact with their foliage or bark as opposed to their effects on soils. In the latter case, acids not only leach nutrients such as calcium and magnesium from the soil but also free toxic chemicals such as aluminum that enter trees through their roots.

These same pollutants can also adversely affect human health. Heavy concentrations of air pollutants such as SO_2, NO_x, particulates, and photochemical oxidants have been found to irritate the respiratory system, cause chronic lung disease, decrease pulmonary function, and increase heart stress, with the impact being the greatest among the young and elderly. Human health may be jeopardized in an indirect way if toxic metals, such as mercury and lead, are released into drinking water.

———

A.   THE NORTH AMERICAN APPROACH

Although acid deposition affects the U.S.-Mexico border to some extent, the primary transboundary acid deposition problem in North America is between the United States and Canada. No country on the planet receives as high a proportion of acidic deposition from another country as Canada receives from the United States—approximately one-half the total amount of acid deposition that falls on Canada comes from the United States. In return, Canada accounts for about 20% of the acid deposition in the United States. Negotiations between the two countries over how to address acid deposition began in the 1970s and continued throughout the 1980s. At times, these negotiations have been acrimonious, particularly during the Reagan Presidency when the United States would only agree to study the problem more. *See* Gregory Wetstone & Armin Rosencranz, *Transboundary Air Pollution: The Search for an International Response*, 8 HARV. ENVTL. L. REV. 89, 111–12 (1984). With passage of the 1990 U.S. Clean Air Act Amendments, however, the United States finally agreed to taking substantial steps toward reductions of SO_2 and NO_x, clearing the way for a bilateral agreement with Canada.

———

1.   THE 1991 U.S.–CANADA BILATERAL AIR QUALITY AGREEMENT

The 1991 U.S.–Canada Bilateral Air Quality Agreement, *reprinted in* 30 I.L.M. 676 (1991), outlines the joint efforts to control SO_2 and NO_x. The agreement requires each Party to accept specific emission reduction objectives and establishes several procedural and institutional mechanisms for future cooperation. Under Article IV: "Each Party shall establish specific objectives, which it undertakes to achieve, for emissions limitations or reductions of such air pollutants as the Parties agree to address." The United States agreed to the following commitments:

– to reduce annual SO_2 emissions by 10 million tons below 1980 levels by the year 2000, with some limited exceptions;

– to achieve a permanent national emission cap of 8.95 million tons of SO_2 per year for electric utilities by 2010;

– to promulgate additional standards if the EPA Administrator determines that annual SO_2 emissions from industrial sources may reasonably be expected to exceed 5.6 million tons; and

– to meet certain technology-based standards for the reduction of NO_x from both stationary and mobile sources.

In return, Canada agreed:

– to reduce SO_2 emissions in the seven easternmost provinces to 2.3 million tons per year by 1994;

– to maintain that cap until 1999;

– to achieve a permanent national cap of 3.2 million tons per year by 2000;

– to reduce NO_x emissions from stationary sources by 100,000 tons annually by 2000 and to develop further national emission targets; and

– to meet certain technology-based standards for reducing NO_x from mobile sources.

The 1991 agreement also built on the long history of cooperation between Canada and the United States, relying on the existing International Joint Commission (IJC) to provide an institutional structure for the active management of transboundary air issues. The IJC is a permanent bilateral commission originally established to address water quality issues along the U.S.-Canada border. Created under the 1909 Boundary Waters Treaty, the IJC consists of three members from both countries. As early as 1949 the IJC started to address select air pollution problems. In that year, the two governments asked the IJC to investigate the extent of air pollution caused by vessels on the Detroit River. In 1966, the governments expanded the role of the IJC, requesting it to identify and evaluate any major sources of transboundary air pollution and make recommendations for reducing air pollution in the Detroit–Windsor area. The resulting study sparked an elaborate and ongoing integration of the air pollution programs of Ontario and Michigan.

The 1991 Bilateral Air Quality Agreement charged the IJC with oversight of a permanent, bilateral Air Quality Committee, thus institutionalizing bilateral cooperation regarding air pollution. The critical role of the Air Quality Committee is to report on the progress of the parties in meeting specific objectives of the Agreement. The progress reports are to be completed at least every two years and submitted to the public and to the IJC. The IJC in turn is tasked with reviewing the Air Quality Committee's progress reports and soliciting public comments on the reports. The IJC then sends a summary of any comments along with recommendations to the parties. The parties then decide whether to modify the Agreement or any existing national policies, programs or measures. This institutional approach allows for the identification and avoidance of disputes before they become contentious. See BAQA, Articles 8–9.

The biannual progress reports are also made available to the public through the US Environmental Protection agency. See <*http://www.epa. gov/airmarkets*>. According to the last progress report issued in the year 2000, both Canada and the United States are on track to meet most of their commitments under the BAQA. Canada, for example, emitted less than 2.7 million tonnes of SO2 in 1998, which is well below the national cap of 3.2 million tonnes that had to be achieved by the year 2000. The United States, too, has had significant reductions in SO2 and were well below the 1999 allowable emissions limits. The report also projected that US emissions would "remain below the applicable caps for at least the next ten years [i.e. until 2010]." *See* US–Canada Air Quality Progress Report, 2–3 (2000)

QUESTIONS AND DISCUSSION

1. Canada and the United States also established notification and consultation requirements to facilitate bilateral cooperation with respect to air pollution. This provision is an example of how the notification and consultation principles described in Chapter 7 are applied to a specific bilateral issue.

Article V: Assessment, Notification, and Mitigation

1. Each Party shall, as appropriate and as required by its laws, regulations and policies, assess those proposed actions, activities and projects within the area under its jurisdiction that, if carried out, would be likely to cause significant transboundary air pollution, including consideration of appropriate mitigation measures.

2. Each Party shall notify the other Party concerning a proposed action, activity or project subject to assessment under paragraph 1 as early as practicable in advance of a decision concerning such action, activity or project and shall consult with the other Party at its request in accordance with Article XI.

3. In addition, each Party shall, at the request of the other Party, consult in accordance with Article XI concerning any continuing actions, activities or projects that may be causing significant transboundary air pollution, as well as concerning changes to its laws, regulations or policies that, if carried out, would be likely to affect significantly transboundary air pollution.

4. Consultations pursuant to paragraphs 2 and 3 concerning actions, activities or projects that would be likely to cause or may be causing significant transboundary air pollution shall include consideration of appropriate mitigation measures.

5. Each Party shall, as appropriate, take measures to avoid or mitigate the potential risk posed by actions, activities or projects that would be likely to cause or may be causing significant transboundary air pollution.

6. If either Party becomes aware of an air pollution problem that is of joint concern and requires an immediate response, it shall notify and consult the other Party forthwith.

Do these notification, consultation, and assessment provisions provide sufficient procedural safeguards to the Parties? To the public? How would you recommend improving these procedures? Does Article V meet the current standards for transboundary environmental assessment and/or principles of equal access to justice, as outlined in Chapter 7?

2. The United States agreed to the specific SO_2 goals in the 1991 Agreement, because in 1990 the United States Congress passed the Sulfur Dioxide Allowance Program as Title IV of the Clean Air Amendments, Pub. L. No. 101–549 (Nov. 15, 1990), 42 U.S.C. § 7651B. The Program was the first statutorily mandated, national, market-based tradable permit system in the United States. In addition to being aimed primarily at reducing acid deposition in Canada (and in the eastern United States), the SO_2 Allowance Program is an important model for future efforts to control certain types of pollutants, most notably carbon dioxide under the Climate Change Convention. In this regard, consider the following description of the program:

B. McLean, *The Evolution of Marketable Permits: The U.S. Experience With Sulphur Dioxide Allowance Trading*, 83–88 in D. ANDERSON & M. GRUBB, EDS., CONTROLLING CARBON AND SULPHUR: JOINT IMPLEMENTATION AND TRADING INITIATIVES (1997)

Although SO_2 emissions in the United States had declined from their peak of 33 million tons in 1973 to 25.9 million tons in 1980, the 1990 Clean Air Act set a goal of further reducing SO_2 by 10 million tons below the 1980 level to protect public health and the environment. It was expected that emissions other than those coming from the electric power sector would decline by 1.5 million tons (primarily from replacement of older, higher emitting facilities with new, lower emitting facilities) and that electric utility emissions would need to be reduce by 8.5 million tons. The reduction in utility emissions was to be accomplished as cost-effectively as possible through the application of a system of tradeable "allowances", where one allowance would be a limited authorization to emit one ton of SO_2. Emissions reductions were to begin in 1995 with full compliance expected by the year 2010. * * *

In 1995, ... 445 utility units reduced their SO_2 emissions to 5.3 million tons from their 1980 level of 10.9 million tons, with most of that reduction occurring in 1995. Since 8.7 million allowances were issued to these sources for 1995, they emitted 3.4 million tons (or 39 per cent) below their allowable emission level for that year. . . .

The expected costs of the programme have declined since it was debated in Congress. Early estimates of the cost ranged from $180 to $981 per ton of SO_2 removed during Phase I and from $374 to $981 per ton during Phase II. For the past year the cost of buying a ton of SO_2 reduction (for either Phase I or Phase II compliance) has been less than $100. . . . In 1990, total annualized costs were estimated by EPA to be $5 billion by the year 2010 if no trading were permitted, and $4 billion per year with unrestricted trading. These estimates were considered low by the utility industry. In 1994, the US General Accounting Office estimated the costs without trading to be $4.9 billion per year by 2010, but only $2.0 billion per year if full trading occurred.

There appear to be several explanations for the lower-than-expected compliance costs. First, the allowance system facilitates competition across all emission reduction options. Flue gas desulfurization, a major control technology option, costs 40 per cent less than before the 1990 Clean Air Act; removal efficiencies have also increased from 90 per cent to 95 per cent or more. Productivity at both low-and high-sulphur coal mines has continued to improve at rates exceeding 6 per cent per year, and rail transport tariffs, which had declined somewhat before the Clean Air Act, dropped by 40 per cent after the Act was passed.

Second, market systems with their competition and flexibility provide incentives for innovation. Companies are experimenting with fuels for which their boilers were not designed and blending fuels to minimize SO_2 emissions. Also, coal suppliers are "bundling" allowances with coal sales to increase their attractiveness. Market instruments such as options and swaps are being employed to reduce risks.

Third, in addition to trading, which allows the units with the lowest compliance costs to bear the burden of control, the banking provision has provided considerable flexibility in timing emissions reductions, minimizing operational disruptions and allowing capital expenditures to be delayed. Finally, a market system can reveal the true costs of compliance, informing the market participants, who, in turn, can make more cost-effective compliance choices.

The low cost being revealed only a few years after the high estimates were made raises other important questions. Why were the estimates of almost all economists and analysts so high? How can we do a better job of predicting costs for future programmes? And what weight should estimates by the regulated industry be given in debating and designing future programmes?

3.   The United States has two bilateral air quality agreements with Mexico, both of which are annexes to the Agreement on Cooperation for the Protection and Improvement of the Environment in the Border Area. Annex IV sets specific sulphur emission limits on new copper smelters and requires existing smelters to be controlled under local law. *See* Agreement Regarding Transboundary Air Pollution Caused by Copper Smelters, 26 I.L.M. 33 (1987). Annex V focuses on transboundary air pollution from major stationary sources. The agreement is designed to gather information about major pollution sources and possible efforts that could be undertaken to reduce air pollution from them. The agreement does not require either Party to take pollution control measures, but rather to identify what cost-effective measures should be undertaken. The concept is that by identifying and prioritizing appropriate steps, over time Mexico will be able to address them either with the help of foreign assistance from the United States or on their own. *See* Agreement of Cooperation Regarding International Transport of Urban Air Pollution, *reprinted in* 29 I.L.M. 29 (1990).

B.   THE CONVENTION ON LONG–RANGE TRANSBOUNDARY AIR POLLUTION

Because of the much larger number of countries sharing airspaces in Europe, a multilateral response to long-range air pollution has been virtually inevitable. In Europe, monitoring of SO_2 and NO_x has occurred since the late 1970s, and beginning in the 1980s Europe has been able to estimate the SO_2 and NO_x pollution budgets for most countries. Pollution budgets demonstrate whether and to what extent a country is a net importer or exporter of air pollution. According to Marvin Soroos,

> Several observations can be drawn from [Europe's pollution budgets] that help explain the conflicting positions that ECE members have taken on limiting air pollution. First, more than half of the emissions of SO_2 and NO_x of the European countries were deposited beyond the borders of the countries of their origin, either on the territory of other countries or in regional bodies of water, such as the North Atlantic and the Baltic and Mediterranean Seas. The proportion of "exported" pollutants has been especially great for the small, highly industrialized countries. Roughly 80 percent of the SO_2 emissions of Switzerland and the Netherlands drifted beyond their borders. More than 60 percent of sulfur pollution emitted in most of the other European countries was deposited outside their territories.

> Second, the emissions of acid-forming pollutants of several countries significantly exceeded the amount that was deposited on their territories, which indicates that substantial amounts of the pollution they generated flowed beyond their borders. The sulfur emissions of the United Kingdom, former East Germany, Spain, and Italy have been approximately three times as great as the sulfur deposition within their borders.

> Third, for some countries the amount of acid deposition has been considerably greater than the quantity of pollutants emitted within their borders, which means that significant amounts of the deposition in these countries came from foreign sources. Sulfur deposition in Norway was five times greater than the country's SO_2 emissions. The United Kingdom, Germany, Russia, and Poland each accounted for more of the sulfur deposition in Norway than did domestic sources. Austria, Switzerland, and Sweden received approximately 90 percent of

their sulfuric deposition from foreign sources; the Netherlands, France, and West Germany received more than half.

Soroos, *op. cit.*, 117–19. In response to the problem of acid deposition, the U.N. Economic Commission for Europe convened negotiations to develop the 1979 Convention on Long–Range Transboundary Air Pollution (the LRTAP Convention), 18 I.L.M. 1442 (1979) which entered into force on March 16, 1983. Parties to the agreement include most European countries, as well as Canada and the United States.

LRTAP was the first environmental treaty signed by both the East and West, and may even have assisted in reducing Cold War tensions in Europe. Through its definition of "air pollution," LRTAP was also one of the first pollution-related treaties that extended its protection beyond direct human health impacts to ecosystems. The LRTAP Convention applies to all "long-range transboundary air pollution" defined in part based on whether sources are so distant "that it is not generally possible to distinguish the contribution of individual emission sources or groups of sources." Article 1.

In the negotiations over the LRTAP, the United States argued for reliance on technology-based standards (i.e., standards requiring companies to use "best available technology") as opposed to across-the-board percentage cuts (i.e., targets and timetables for reducing emissions by a certain amount below a baseline year). The United States was afraid that they would be penalized for having already put substantial control technology in place by the time the LRTAP was being negotiated. To the extent that percentage reduction targets were to be used, the United States argued for an earlier baseline year so they would receive some credit for the percentage reductions already achieved under domestic law. Ultimately the LRTAP would require that countries develop "best available technology which is economically feasible and low- and non-waste technology." Article 6. The protocols to the LRTAP, however, adopt both technology-based standards and targets and timetables, as well as other policy responses. The LRTAP and its protocols thus provide a good vehicle for exploring different potential policy approaches to air pollution. These issues recur in all international negotiations regarding percentage reductions of pollution (see, e.g., the negotiations leading up to the Montreal Protocol and the Climate Change Convention, discussed *infra*).

If LRTAP were being negotiated today we would label it a "framework" convention. On its face it has relatively weak and general substantive standards, but it arranges for scientific cooperation and coordination; institutionalizes consultation and information exchange between Parties; and perhaps most importantly establishes a cooperative program for monitoring and evaluating air pollutants in Europe (EMEP). Due in large part to the ongoing advances in scientific understanding of air pollutants made through the EMEP program, the UNECE has returned continually to the LRTAP as a framework for the negotiations of specific protocols. The EMEP was established through Article 9, reprinted below.

CONVENTION ON LONG-RANGE TRANSBOUNDARY AIR POLLUTION
Article 1: Definitions

For the purpose of the present Convention:

a) "air pollution" means the introduction by man, directly or indirectly, of substances or energy into the air resulting in deleterious effects of such a nature as to endanger human health, harm living resources and ecosystems and material property and impair or interfere with amenities and other legitimate uses of the environment, and "air pollutants" shall be construed accordingly;

b) "long-range transboundary air pollution" means air pollution whose physical origin is situated wholly or in part within the area under the national jurisdiction of one State and which has adverse effects in the area under the jurisdiction of another State at such a distance that it is not generally possible to distinguish the contribution of individual emission sources or groups of sources.

Article 9: Implementation and Further Development of the Cooperative Programme for the Monitoring and Evaluation of the Long–Range Transmission of Air Pollutants in Europe

The Contracting Parties stress the need for the implementation of the existing "Co-operative programme for the monitoring and evaluation of the long-range transmission of air pollutants in Europe" (hereinafter referred to as EMEP) and with regard to the further development of this programme, agree to emphasize:

a) the desirability of Contracting Parties joining in and fully implementing EMEP which, as a first step, is based on the monitoring of sulphur dioxide and related substances;

b) the need to use comparable or standardized procedures for monitoring whenever possible;

c) the desirability of basing the monitoring programme on the framework of both national and international programmes. The establishment of monitoring stations and the collection of data shall be carried out under the national jurisdiction of the country in which the monitoring stations are located;

d) the desirability of establishing a framework for a co-operative environmental monitoring programme, based on and taking into account present and future national, subregional, regional and other international programmes;

e) the need to exchange data on emissions at periods of time to be agreed upon, of agreed air pollutants, starting with sulphur dioxide, coming from grid-units of agreed size; or on the fluxes of agreed air pollutants, starting with sulphur dioxide, across national borders, at distances and at periods of time to be agreed upon. The method including the model, used to determine the fluxes as well as the method, including the model, used to determine the transmission of air pollutants, based on the emissions per grid-unit, shall be made available and periodically reviewed, in order to improve the methods and the models;

f) their willingness to continue the exchange and periodic updating of national data on total emissions of agreed air pollutants, starting with sulphur dioxide;

g) the need to provide meteorological and physico-chemical data relating to processes during transmission;

h) the need to monitor chemical components in other media such as water, soil and vegetation, as well as a similar monitoring programme to record effects on health and environment;

i) the desirability of extending the national EMEP networks to make them operational for control and surveillance purposes.

————

QUESTION AND DISCUSSION

1. Consider the definitions from Article 1 of LRTAP, just excerpted. What do you think of the definition of long-range transboundary air pollution? Is it sufficiently specific to be able to determine whether a given air pollution problem should be considered under the Convention? Is reliance on the difficulty in determining the source of pollution the best approach to differentiating types of transboundary air pollution? Why or why not?

2. The Vienna Convention on the Protection of the Ozone Layer and the ensuing Montreal Protocol are often cited as the precedent for the "framework and protocol" approach to global environmental treatymaking. *See, e.g.,* Chapter 6, page 297. Yet the LRTAP Convention preceded the Vienna Convention by six years. To what extent is the LRTAP Convention a precedent for the Vienna Convention? Are there similarities in the approach?

3. In all, eight protocols have been negotiated under the LRTAP Convention. See Box 9.2. The first protocol, on long-term financing, entered into force on January 28, 1988. Subsequent protocols each address specific categories of pollutants, including SO_2 (two different protocols), NO_x, and VOCs. These protocols share a significant number of characteristics with one another, but they also have evolved over time to take increasingly sophisticated approaches to the control of air pollution. The protocols reflect a wide range of potential policy options for controlling air pollution, including for example technology-based standards, annual emission targets and timetables, ambient reduction targets in special management areas that allow greater flexibility in reaching net reductions, a science-based critical load concept that sets emission levels based on differences in environmental impacts throughout the continent, and joint implementation that allows two or more parties to meet their obligations together and thus more cost effectively.

For example, the NO_x Protocol, 28 I.L.M. 212 (1986), adopts a wide range of policy options for coping with transboundary emissions of NO_x. The Protocol institutes a clear target and timetable, by freezing emissions at 1987 levels. It also specifies certain technology-based standards, including, for example, a requirement to make unleaded gasoline available. Finally, the NO_x protocol requires parties to begin gathering information for a ¿critical loads" approach, which as of 1997 the parties were still negotiating. The critical loads approach is described below with respect to the Second SO_2 Protocol.

Other protocols have added their own innovations to the LRTAP regime. Under the VOC Protocol, for example, countries with different economic circumstances and varying potential to cause transboundary pollution can meet their emissions reduction requirement in alternative ways. It is the first agreement under LRTAP to provide this flexibility. All countries must meet their obligation under article 2, paragraph 2, by reducing VOC emissions by 30 percent between 1988 (the base year) and 1999. Moreover, countries may choose a different base year—any year between 1984 and 1990—from which the 30 percent reduction will be calculated. The U.S. insisted on allowing an earlier base year because it had already reduced VOC emissions substantially since passage of the 1970 Clean Air Act, while in many other countries emissions increased during that period. In addition to the United States, Switzerland and Liechtenstein chose 1984 as the base year; Denmark selected 1985.

Box 9.2: The LRTAP Convention and its Protocols (as of July 16, 2001)

Date	Instrument	Date Entered into Force	Number of Parties
1979	Convention on Long–Range Transboundary Air Pollution	1983	48
1984	Protocol on Long-term Financing of the EMEP	1988	38
1985	Protocol on the Reduction of Sulphur Emissions or their Transboundary Fluxes by at least 30 per cent	1987	22
1989	Protocol concerning the Control of Emissions of Nitrogen Oxides or their Transboundary Fluxes	1990	28
1991	Protocol concerning the Control of Emissions of Volatile Organic Compounds or their Transboundary Fluxes	1997	20
1994	Protocol on further Reduction of Sulphur Emissions	1998	23
1998	Protocol on Heavy Metals	—	10
1998	Protocol on Persistent Organic Pollutants	—	7
1999	Protocol to Abate Acidification, Eutrophication and Ground-level Ozone	—	0

The second alternative for meeting the emissions reduction requirement represents an innovative way to address transboundary pollution. Canada argued that it made no sense for it to decrease VOC emissions nationwide because emissions from only a small part of the country result in transboundary pollution to the U.S. It therefore proposed that countries that can trace transboundary flows to emissions from particular areas be able to designate such areas as tropospheric ozone management areas (TOMAs), and reduce emissions by 30 percent only in these areas. The protocol adopts this approach with two modifications: (1) all the signatories must agree to the designation of the TOMAs, which are delineated in Annex I; and (2) a country adopting the TOMA approach must ensure that total nationwide VOC emissions by 1999 do not exceed 1988 levels. Annex I lists TOMAs for Canada and Norway. In signing the protocol Ukraine also chose this option and listed the boundaries of a TOMA, even though the TOMA is not set forth in the annex.

4. *Sulfur Dioxide (SO₂).* Two protocols to LRTAP have addressed sulfur dioxide emissions: Protocol on the Reduction of Sulphur Emissions or their Transboundary Fluxes by at least 30 percent, 27 I.L.M. 698 (1988); Protocol on Further Reduction of Sulphur Emissions, 33 I.L.M. 1540 (1994). Parties to the first protocol committed to reducing their sulfur emissions 30% by 1993 from a 1980 baseline. The Parties were required to develop national programs for reaching this goal and to report on their progress. The Parties also agreed to report annually on their emissions. The United States did not ratify the first SO_2 protocol, as it preferred to address SO_2 emissions through bilateral discussions with Canada.

The Second Sulfur Protocol to the LRTAP Convention was opened for signature in 1994. A Second Sulfur Protocol was needed because the first Protocol did not sufficiently curb acid rain. The Second Sulfur Protocol adopts a "critical load" approach to controlling SO_2. A critical load is a quantitative estimate of an exposure to one or more pollutants below which significant harmful effects on specified sensitive elements of the environment do not occur according to present knowledge. To implement the critical loads approach, the Parties to the Second Sulfur Protocol cooperated in evaluating the tolerance of each country to acid deposition caused by sulfur dioxide. The entire continent was divided into a grid of 150 km x 150 km squares. The critical load for each square was determined based on soil characteristics and other factors. Then, relying on air pollutant transport models, the relative contribution of SO_2 emissions from each country to each square was measured. In most areas of the continent, SO_2 emissions far exceeded the critical load.

By running so-called "integrated assessment models" the Parties could compare the relative cost-effectiveness of different emission reductions. Although the critical loads analysis suggested that transboundary emissions would eventually have to be reduced by as much as 100% in some countries, the Parties decided on a goal of reducing the gap between current deposition and the critical loads by 60% over the 1980 levels. The Parties then determined the specific amounts of reduction each would have to make. The variation among Parties would depend on their relative contribution to exceedances of the critical levels throughout the continent. Some additional flexibility was also introduced by allowing different target dates for different countries and by allowing for joint implementation among the Parties. For example, Austria, Denmark and Sweden committed to reduce emissions by 80% as of the year 2000, and Spain agreed only to 35%. See Second Sulfur Protocol, Annex II.

The approach is difficult technically, because it depends on greater scientific knowledge than an approach based, for example, on best available technology. The critical load approach is worth studying, however, as it provides one of the most sophisticated and complex efforts at the international level to control pollution of any type. Compare the technology-based standard of Best Available Technology, the across-the-board targets and timetable approach (wherein every country agrees to the same percentage reduction) and the critical loads approach adopted in the Second Sulfur Protocol. What are the advantages and disadvantages of each approach? What characteristics of the problem of acid deposition in Europe suggest it is well-suited for a critical loads approach?

5. The Second Sulfur Protocol was negotiated in 1994, after the 1987 Montreal Protocol, the 1990 London Revisions to the Montreal Protocol, and the 1992 Climate Change Convention. After you study these conventions in the ensuing parts to this Chapter, return to the Second Sulfur Protocol, reprinted in the *Treaty Supplement,* and determine how lessons or approaches from those agreements may have affected the development of the Second Sulfur Protocol. For example, the concept of joint implementation is a major and controversial element of the Climate Change Convention, *see* Section V.F. of this Chapter, pages 665–71. *Compare, e.g.,* Article 2.7 of the Second Sulfur Protocol with Article 4.2(a) of the Climate Change Convention. Another example is the adoption of "Implementation Committees" under Annex V of the Montreal Protocol and Article 7 of the Second Sulfur Protocol. Under both regimes, the implementation committees are intended to investigate reasons for non-compliance and recommend specific measures, including assistance measures that other Parties can take, to facilitate compliance by all Parties. *See also* discussion of Implementation Committees in Chapter 8, page 493.

6. The United States' tradeable permits approach to the control of sulfur emissions is obviously quite different than the approach taken by Europe in the Second Sulfur Protocol. Can you see how the two approaches are based on somewhat different views of how sulfur pollution affects the environment? The critical loads approach taken by Europe assumes that sulfur emissions have different impacts in different locations and that *where* emissions are reduced matters to the overall health of the environment. The U.S. approach ignores this spatial differentiation between sulfur emissions, and implicitly assumes that a ton of sulfur emissions anywhere in the country provides an equal reduction in environmental impacts. (Although note that under the National Ambient Air Quality Standards (NAAQs), the United States has also placed a limit on ambient concentrations of SO_2, thus in theory at least avoiding any localized hotspots). Does the European approach reflect better science? Is the U.S. approach justified given the different political nature of the two continents? For example, the United States and Canada are only two countries so they do not face as difficult international negotiations as Europe faces. Moreover, the cost savings from the tradeable emissions system to the United States makes it worthwhile to ignore any differentiation that critical loads would allow among different U.S. polluters.

Suggested Further Reading and Web Sites

M. Soroos, The Endangered Atmosphere: Preserving a Global Commons (1997)

R. Somerville, The Forgiving Air: Understanding Environmental Change (1996)

J. Mackenzie & M. El–Ashry, Air Pollution's Toll on Forests & Crops (1989)

<http://gladstone.uoregon.edu/~rmitchel/iep/oldstudents/acid.htm>

This site provides links to full text down-loadable versions of the Convention, the Protocols, NGOs, as well as background information on acid rain and associated issues.

<http://www.unece.org>

This site provides an introduction to the UNECE, a calendar of meetings, press releases, links to UNECE treaties, publications, etc.

<http://www.gsf.de/UNEP/ijc.html>

This site provides basic information on the International Joint Commission, including contact information. No links.

Section IV. Ozone Depletion

"Politics is the art of taking good decisions on insufficient evidence"

Lord Kennett, during debate in House of Lords over the Montreal Protocol, (Oct. 20, 1988)

As of August 2000, the Montreal Protocol had been ratified by 175 countries, including virtually all industrialized countries and most developing countries. While the Protocol and its amendments have not eliminated the dangers of ozone depletion, they have established national commitments that will lessen the threat in years to come. The most important precedent in international law for the management of global environmental harms, the Montreal Protocol provides a useful model for other long-term environmental challenges such as global warming. The difficulties diplomats faced during the negotiation of the Protocol are much the same–

genuine scientific uncertainty over the scale of harm, a sharply divided international community, potentially high transition costs, and a global problem requiring a global solution.

The problems posed by ozone depletion were unlike anything international environmental law had ever addressed. With traditional air and water pollution, the harms are generally perceived to be localized and discrete. Even when pollution crosses national borders as acid rain or oil spills, the harm is still confined at worst to a region. The Protocol was thus the first treaty to address fully the global nature of a set of pollutants. Moreover, during the initial negotiations and ratification, there was genuine doubt whether ozone depletion had even occurred. As the chief American negotiator later commented, "the most extraordinary aspect of the treaty was its imposition of substantial short-term economic costs to protect human health and the environment against unproved future dangers.... At the time of the negotiations and signing, no measurable evidence of damage existed." RICHARD BENEDICK, OZONE DIPLOMACY 2 (1998). Thus the Protocol was also the first "precautionary treaty," instituting tough technology-forcing controls as a safeguard against uncertain future harms.

A.   THE SCIENCE AND ECONOMICS OF OZONE DEPLETION

The stratospheric ozone layer blankets the earth in a protective shield that effectively protects life on earth from the sun's harmful ultraviolet radiation (UV–B). Since 1974, scientists have suspected that an important group of man-made chemicals, including most notably chlorofluorocarbons (CFCs), could break down ozone molecules in the upper atmosphere. Over time, the role of CFCs and other ozone depleting substances (ODSs) in reducing the ozone layer has been confirmed. As a direct result of ozone layer depletion, increased UV–B strikes the earth's surface. This increase in UV–B has a potentially serious impact on human health and animals, including causing skin cancers and cataracts, damaging human immune systems, disrupting the food cycle of the ocean, and reducing the productivity of important agricultural crops and other plants.

As with other international environmental issues, the legal response to ozone depletion has been inextricably linked to our evolving understanding of the underlying science. The following section describes the current state of scientific knowledge regarding ozone depletion, as well as the economic and social ramifications of efforts to control ozone depleting substances.

---

1.   THE STRATOSPHERIC OZONE LAYER

The earth's atmosphere is divided into several different layers, defined by the variation of temperature with altitude. The lowest layer is the troposphere, extending to approximately 12 km above the earth. Immediately above the troposphere is the stratosphere, extending from 12 km to

50 km. The troposphere is very turbulent, affected strongly by the different characteristics of the earth's surface, whereas the stratosphere is relatively stable.

Ozone (O_3) is a simple molecule of three oxygen atoms. Ozone occurs naturally as a trace element of the atmosphere. According to a UNEP report, "If all the ozone in the atmosphere from ground level to a height of some 60 km could be assembled at the earth's surface, it would comprise a layer of gas only about 3 mm thick, weighing some 3000 million tonnes." Although ozone occurs throughout the troposphere and stratosphere, the highest concentration of ozone occurs in the middle of the stratosphere, in a region commonly called the "ozone layer." UNEP, Ozone Trends Panel Report 1 (1991).

Ozone, although a relatively small part of the atmosphere, performs a critical function. It absorbs certain frequencies of harmful UV–B radiation emitted from the sun. In the stratosphere, as ozone molecules absorb the incoming UV–B radiation, the energy blasts them apart. An equilibrium is maintained, however, by a series of chemical reactions that create ozone as a counterbalance to the ozone destroyed through absorption of UV–B radiation. It is this delicate balance that has been disrupted by the introduction of increased levels of CFCs and related substances, for now more ozone is destroyed than created. (For an in-depth treatment of the natural ozone balance in the atmosphere, *see* ARJUN MAKHIJANI & KEVIN GURNEY, MENDING THE OZONE HOLE 8–10 (1995)). Because of the long lag times involved in ozone atmospheric chemistry, ozone-layer depletion is now bound to continue throughout most of the 21st century.

---

2. THE DESTRUCTION OF ATMOSPHERIC OZONE

The role of chlorine, bromine, and several other chemicals in the destruction of ozone as part of the natural atmospheric balance was relatively well understood by the early 1970s. It was not until 1974, however, that F. Sherwood Rowland and Mario Molina published the first credible explanation of what happens to CFCs and their potential role in destruction of the ozone layer. The article, published in *Nature* under the rather difficult title of *Stratospheric Sink for Chlorofluoromethanes: Chlorine Atoms–Catalyzed Destruction of Ozone*, argued that the inert CFCs would be relatively stable in the lower atmosphere, in part because the ozone layer blocks UV–B from penetrating through the stratosphere. 239 NATURE 810 (1974). Even though CFCs are heavier than most atmospheric molecules, CFCs emitted on the earth's surface would eventually migrate to the stratosphere because of the constant mixing of the atmosphere. Once in the stratosphere, Rowland and Molina hypothesized that ultraviolet radiation would blast the CFCs apart, releasing highly reactive chlorine (Cl) and chlorine oxide (ClO) molecules. These molecules would then set off a chain-reaction, in which just one reactive chlorine atom could destroy thousands of stratospheric ozone molecules. Thus CFCs would act as a catalyst, upsetting the natural balance of ozone creation and destruction. There would not literally be a "hole" in the ozone layer, but a reduction in the concentration of ozone, and hence its ability to absorb radiation.

In the over twenty-five years since publication of the *Nature* article, Rowland and Molina's basic theory has never been seriously challenged, and in 1995 the two scientists shared the Nobel Prize for Chemistry. The mechanism for ozone layer destruction has since been more fully developed. Perhaps most important, a clear relationship between the concentrations of the intermediary compounds (for example, ClO) and ozone concentrations has been found over the Antarctic. This study, conducted by a high-flying plane and published in 1987, showed the first clear link between concentrations of chlorine compounds and ozone depletion. This and other evidence confirmed the role of CFCs and other man-made substances in ozone depletion, leading to a nearly universal consensus among the world's scientists regarding ozone depletion. *See, e.g.,* UNEP, Environmental Effects of Ozone Depletion 1 (1992).

Much of the early publicity over ozone depletion centered around the recurring Antarctic "ozone hole." Ozone depletion is worst in Antarctica because the ozone-destroying reaction catalyzed by ODSs occurs fastest on the surface of atmospheric micro-ice crystals. These ice crystals are most common in the coldest areas, for example on polar stratospheric clouds over Antarctica in the winter. Nonetheless, during the past decade, measurements of actual ozone loss have been made over all parts of the planet, with the exception of the equatorial regions. The following excerpts from a 1994 UNEP report provide a good review of typical findings.

> Over the past 10–15 years, there has been a large, rapid and unexpected loss of ozone in the stratosphere each spring above Antarctica. Every spring up to 95 percent of stratospheric ozone is destroyed at a height of 12–24 km above the earth's surface–the heart of the polar ozone layer. Satellite observations show that the ozone hole is sometimes larger than the area of the United States.

> The latest measurements show that throughout the entire stratosphere, from 12 to 50 km above the surface, half the ozone layer above Antarctica is destroyed each spring. Scientific theory did not predict this scale of destruction. The rate at which ozone in the stratosphere above mid-to high latitudes is now disappearing is much faster than was predicted.* * *

> The ozone layer is not only diminishing above Antarctica. In mid-December 1987, following what was, until 1991, the deepest Antarctic ozone hole ever, ground-based observations showed a sudden drop of about 10 percent in stratospheric ozone above southern Australia and New Zealand, which lasted for the rest of the month.

> Reduced ozone levels have now been measured year-round at latitudes much nearer the Equator, in both hemispheres, and the evidence suggests that these decreases are largely due to chlorine and bromine. Decreases in winter in the northern hemisphere have been recorded since the 1970s but there is now evidence of significant decreases in the spring and summer in both hemispheres at both middle and high latitudes (as much as 3.5 percent at 45° N in summer over the period 1979–91).

The rate of loss appears to be accelerating. The loss per decade was about 2 percentage points higher during the 1980s than during the 1970s... Ozone-layer depletion has also occurred in the northern hemisphere. In northern mid-latitudes, the ozone layer in the 38–43 km slice of the stratosphere thinned by 5–13 percent between 1979 and 1986. Ozone continues to thin during the winter at altitudes of 25 km and below. It is now thought inevitable that an Arctic ozone hole will form, though it is unlikely to be as deep or long-lived as its Antarctic counterpart.

UNEP, THE IMPACT OF OZONE LAYER DEPLETION 9, 12–13 (1994). The thinning trend has continued. The European Commission reported that the Arctic stratosphere may have lost up to 60% of its ozone during the 1999–2000 winter and that the average ozone concentrations over Europe were 15% less than those of the early 1970s. And NASA reported the ozone hole over Antarctic was three times the size of the United States, the largest it has ever been. G. Moulson, *Ozone Hole Over Antarctic Grows to Largest Ever,* BOSTON GLOBE, A–6 (Sept. 9, 2000); Joe Kirwin, *Ozone Depletion: Severe Stratospheric Ozone Losses in the Arctic Described by Europe*, NASA, BNA–IED, Apr. 6, 2000.

All other things being equal, scientists generally estimate that every 1% decline in the ozone layer produces a 2% increase in UV–B radiation at the earth's surface. Measurements in Australia, Argentina, and New Zealand, for example, have confirmed this relationship. Unfortunately, there are no long-term studies of surface-level UV–B to provide a baseline, and a number of potential variables could affect the actual amount of UV–B increase. For example, the amount of ultraviolet radiation reaching the Earth's surface can depend on local and regional air pollution and cloud cover, just to name a few.

---

3.   IMPACTS OF UV–B ON HUMAN HEALTH AND THE ENVIRONMENT

Increases in UV–B radiation, within the range currently predicted to result from ozone depletion, have serious impacts on human health. Just as disturbing are the potential impacts on agricultural crops, ocean resources and the general ecological balance of the biosphere. Much less is known about these impacts than is known about human health impacts.

Human Health

Increases in UV–B radiation lead to increased skin cancers, cataracts and sunburns. UNEP's 1998 Assessment predicts that, even if countries fully comply with the ozone agreements, incidences of skin cancer will continue to increase until 2060. Currently one in five Americans develops skin cancer during their lifetime, and one dies every hour. The incidence rate of basal cell carcinoma (the majority of non-malignant cancers) has increased recently among many white populations. In New Mexico, for example, one study found that between 1978 and 1991 there was an increase of 13% per year of basal cell carcinoma. Cataracts, too, are expected to increase as is other eye damage, including age-related near-sightedness and deformation of the lens capsule.

More recently, UV–B has been demonstrated to suppress the immune systems in humans with respect to some diseases. Unlike sunburns and skin cancers, the immuno-suppression impacts of UV–B affects humans of all skin color pigmentation. There is great uncertainty in quantifying the likely impacts of ozone depletion on immune systems, though recent studies have shown that the most sensitive 5% of individuals in a population of white Caucasians suffer significant inhibition of their cellular immunity against a bacterial infection when they are exposed to sunlight for 90 minutes around noon. For more detailed data on human health effects, *see* UNEP, Environmental Effects of Ozone Depletion: 1998 Assessment.

Plants

The growth and photosynthesis of certain plants, including strains of commercially valuable plants such as rice, corn, and soybeans, is reduced by relatively low increases in ultraviolet radiation. Some researchers have also linked ozone depletion to significant damage to commercial tree species such as white pine and loblolly pine. Charles Little, The Dying of the Trees: The Pandemic in America's Forests 186–88 (1995). The exact amount of damage caused by ozone depletion is difficult to estimate, both because most plant species have not been tested for sensitivity to UV–B and because many other variables can affect a plant's growth.

Aquatic Ecosystems and Wildlife

Increases in UV–B can reduce the growth of marine phytoplankton, which is the base of the ocean food chain and produces at least as much biomass as all terrestrial ecosystems combined. UV–B also damages midge larvae, the base of many fresh-water ecosystems. Amphibians and fish are also particularly vulnerable to UV–B. Controlled tests have demonstrated that excessive UV–B kills trout, and some researchers have linked increases in UV–B to the global decline in some frog species. Kathryn Phillips, Tracking the Vanishing Frogs 117–36 (1994).

Materials Damage

UV–B radiation will cause wood and plastic products to lose strength and color. Current research is insufficient to quantify the magnitude of economic loss from this impact.

—————

4.   THE ECONOMICS OF OZONE DEPLETING SUBSTANCES (ODS)

Many compounds containing chlorine are released into the environment, but most do not reach the stratosphere because they are water soluble and are "absorbed" into clouds. CFCs and the other human-made ODSs share two important qualities: they are chemically stable and insoluble in water. These qualities have made CFCs and other ODSs very valuable to industry for a wide range of uses, even as they make it possible to cause ozone depletion.

The Uses of ODSs. CFCs were developed in the 1920s by General Motors' chief chemist, Thomas Midgely. He had sought to develop a safe substitute for the ammonia and sulfur dioxide refrigerants then commonly in use. In place of these explosive and poisonous refrigerants, he synthesized a non-flammable, non-toxic substitute. His invention, CFC–12, was first announced at an American Chemical Society meeting. It is reported he demonstrated the compound's beneficial qualities by inhaling the gas and then exhaling over a fire to extinguish the flame. CFC–12 was quickly adapted to the Frigidaire line and soon became the refrigerant of choice. In a clever commercial strategy, General Motors did not patent the compound, thus speeding up its wide adoption. The use of CFCs in aerosol insecticides and as solvents during World War II greatly expanded the commercial applications of CFC–12 and CFC–113.

There are many kinds of CFCs, each with specific qualities and applications. Traditionally, major uses of CFCs have included air conditioning, refrigeration, foams, foam packaging, aerosol propellants, cleaning of electronics, and degreasing of parts. The Alliance for a Responsible CFC Policy, an industry group made up of ODS manufacturers, estimated in 1986 that CFC products were worth more than $20 billion and created over 250,000 jobs in the U.S. alone.

Other ODSs are also commercially valuable chemicals. Halons, for example, are widely used in fire extinguishers, carbon tetrachloride and methyl chloroform are used as cleaning agents, and methyl bromide is a popular agricultural pesticide used to control a wide variety of pests on over 100 crops. U.S. General Accounting Office, Pesticides: The Phaseout of Methyl Bromide in the United States 5 (1995).

In recent years, an estimated 75% of the consumption of CFCs and halons have been in Europe and North America. The fastest growing use of CFCs and other ODSs, however, has been in developing countries. For example, India and Thailand's use were both estimated to have increased 300% between 1985 and 1991. ODSs consumption worldwide peaked in 1988 at a level estimated at over 2.2 million tons per year.

Manufacture of ODSs. The manufacture of CFCs and other ODSs have always been concentrated in just a few multinational corporations. Worldwide the clear leaders have been Dupont and ICI, a British chemical company. The EPA's calculation of U.S. market shares in 1986, the year before the Montreal Protocol was negotiated, are shown below.

U.S. CFC Producers Market Share		U.S. Halon Producers Market Share	
DuPont	49%	DuPont	55%
Allied–Signal	25%	Great Lakes Chemical	34%
Pennwalt	13%	ICI Americas	11%
Kaiser Tech	9%		
Racon	4%		

Based on Weighted 1986 Average

Substitutes for ODSs. As will become apparent in the next section's discussion of the Montreal Protocol regime, the relative availability of substitutes for various uses of ODSs often helped to explain industry's positions toward the negotiations. As substitutes became available in industrialized countries, for example, their support for stronger controls on the specific ODS would increase. In addition, as the phase-out of different ODSs became more or less a certainty, the Montreal Protocol became 'technology forcing', supporting the development of new and inexpensive substitutes.

————

QUESTIONS AND DISCUSSION

1. CFCs and several other ODSs are known to be significant greenhouse gases. Their total impact on global warming is unclear, however, because of important indirect effects. For example, marine phytoplankton is one of the most important carbon sinks for removing carbon dioxide from the atmosphere. If ozone depletion reduces the productivity of phytoplankton, then all other things being equal we can expect the consequences of climate change to be worsened. Global warming also, paradoxically, is expected to make the stratosphere colder, which, in turn, increases ozone depletion. What are the policy implications of this relationship for the Montreal Protocol regime? Consider, too, that some of the chemical substitutes for ODSs (such as HFCs, discussed *infra*) are also powerful greenhouse gases. How would you coordinate international response to these two environmental threats?

2. Some confusion is created by the fact that too much ozone on the ground level (smog) is a serious health problem facing many urban areas. In essence, we have too much ground level ozone and not enough in the stratosphere. In addition, ground level ozone and other air pollutants may be masking the impacts of ozone depletion because they, too, can block UV–B. Ironically, smog has likely diminished the health impacts of ozone depletion in urban and industrialized areas. Indeed, the D.C. Circuit Court of Appeals struck down the EPA's proposed particulate standards, in part, because its cost-benefit analysis failed to consider the *beneficial* effects of smog through reduced ultraviolet radiation. American Trucking Associations v. EPA, 175 F.3d 1027 (1999). As countries tackle their local urban air pollution problems, however, the impact of UV–B will likely increase. In the meantime, policy makers may be lulled into a false sense of security because the anticipated impacts have been less than expected, at least in urban areas.

3. Although the ultimate impacts of ozone depletion are not known, the potential is frightening enough that some scientists have spent considerable energy trying to identify technological means to restore the ozone layer. Some have suggested exploding rockets into the stratosphere loaded with ozone. More realistically, scientists discovered a lowly bacteria living in the swamps along the Potomac River, among other places. The CFC-eating bacteria may offer a low-cost way of reducing the amount of CFCs released to the environment. *Bacteria Found to "Eat" Ozone–Damaging Chemicals*, WASH.POST, May 2, 1992 at 5. Consider this discovery in the light of the Biodiversity Convention's efforts to conserve all life forms for their potential benefit to humankind. More generally, how wise is it to consider technological fixes to global issues as enormous as ozone depletion? For some environmentalists, reliance on technology to save us from global environmental threats represents one of the major cultural impediments to taking more serious steps to avoid the threats in the first place. Do you agree?

4. One of the most disturbing aspects of ozone depletion is the lag time between when ODSs are released and when they stop depleting the ozone layer. The atmospheric lifetimes of some ODSs are hundreds of years. Others like methyl bromide may have life times of 2 years or less. This lag time means that we have in fact "banked" a considerable amount of ozone depletion into the next century. In addition, many ODSs are currently locked inside products such as automobile air conditioners or refrigerators. If not properly captured at the time of disposal, these banked ODSs represent another major source of ozone depletion. As a result, despite the strong efforts taken by the Montreal Protocol regime to phase out ODSs, the peak amount of ozone depletion is not expected to occur until at least 2005, assuming that all of the requirements in the Montreal Protocol regime are implemented. Moreover, even after the level of ozone depletion begins to fall, severe ozone depletion is expected to continue until after the year 2050. The long-term impacts of this level of ozone depletion are largely unknown.

5. Despite the virtual consensus by the world's atmospheric scientists of Rowlands' and Molina's theory of ozone depletion, the early 1990s witnessed a strong backlash against the theory, particularly in the United States. A standard charge of ozone depletion critics was that humans' emissions of CFCs and other chlorine compounds are insignificant compared to natural sources. Just one volcano, for instance, Mount Erebus, in Antarctica, emits 50 times more chlorine every year (as hydrochloric acid) than the global production of CFCs. Radio commentator Rush Limbaugh, summarizing the view of many ozone depletion skeptics, has therefore declared: "Conclusion: mankind can't possibly equal the output of even one eruption from Pinatubo [an erupting volcano similar to Erebus], much less a billion years' worth, so how can we destroy ozone?" Rush Limbaugh, The Way Things Ought to Be 156–57 (1992). How would you respond to Limbaugh's argument?

6. ODS production was for the most part concentrated in a relatively few large companies from a few countries. Why does the economic concentration of industry have implications for the negotiation of an international regime? If the manufacturers of ODSs were a large number of very small companies, would negotiations be easier or more difficult?

B. THE NEGOTIATIONS OVER THE MONTREAL PROTOCOL REGIME

This section presents a history of the diplomacy leading to international control of ODSs through the Montreal Protocol regime. Like many areas of international environmental law, the development of the Montreal Protocol regime has been a dynamic process over time. Table 9.3 shows the different instruments that together comprise the Montreal Protocol regime.

Table 9.3: The Montreal Protocol Treaty Regime	
1985	**Vienna Convention for the Protection of the Ozone Layer**
1987	**Montreal Protocol to the Vienna Convention**
1990	**London Amendments and Adjustments to the Montreal Protocol**
1992	**Copenhagen Amendments and Adjustments to the Montreal Protocol**
1994	**Vienna Adjustments to the Montreal Protocol**
1997	**Montreal Amendments and Adjustments to the Montreal Protocol**
1999	**Beijing Amendments and Adjustments to the Montreal Protocol**

The following chronological description of the Montreal Protocol regime's development provides a fuller understanding of the current challenges and effectiveness of the regime. It also allows us to draw important lessons for the resolution of similarly complex environmental challenges in the future.

————

1. PROLOGUE TO VIENNA

From today's perspective, gaining broad international support for the strict control of ODSs perhaps seems inevitable, but in the mid–1980s the likelihood of international controls on CFCs, much less on halons or other substances, appeared slim indeed. To make sense of the Protocol's development, one must keep clearly in mind how little was known with certainty at the time. As noted above, it was not until 1974 that Rowland and Molina first raised the potential role of CFCs in ozone depletion. While rejected by industry, their hypothesis was closely examined over the next three years in the United States by the National Academy of Sciences, National Aeronautic Space Administration (NASA), National Oceanographic and Atmospheric Administration (NOAA) and academic scientists. At this time, the United States accounted for over half of global CFC consumption, including a national market of $3 billion for aerosol propellants. CFCs were a strong growth industry, production having risen from 150,000 tons in 1960 to over 800,000 tons in 1974. BENEDICK, OZONE DIPLOMACY, 10–11 (1991).[1]

While research over CFCs' role in ozone depletion attracted some public attention, it was the unilateral public announcement in 1975 by the consumer products company, Johnson Wax, to replace CFCs in its brand-leading products such as Pledge and Glade that triggered a competitive race for CFC-free aerosols in the U.S. Without any government intervention, most companies' fear of losing sales to environmentally-conscious consumers drove them voluntarily away from CFCs to butane propellants. Indeed within two years the market for CFC aerosol propellants had fallen by two-thirds. The Clean Air Act Amendments of 1977 had granted the Administrator of EPA authority to regulate any substance that may reasonably be anticipated to affect the stratosphere, if such effect could reasonably be anticipated to endanger public health or welfare. In 1978, under this authority, EPA banned the use of CFC aerosol propellants for all but essential uses (i.e., military and medical uses). The U.S. action was followed soon after by CFC aerosol bans in Sweden, Canada, and Norway.

The United Nations Environment Program had focused on the role of CFCs in ozone depletion during the 1970s as well, funding a World Meteorological Organization study and producing policy documents on ozone layer protection. With the advent of national laws banning CFCs, in 1981 UNEP's Governing Council gave approval to develop an international

---

1. Much of the history in this section up through 1989 is drawn from Richard Benedick's excellent book, OZONE DIPLOMACY. Be-nedick was the chief ozone negotiator for the U.S. from 1985–1990.

agreement to protect the ozone layer. Over the next three years there were regular meetings of the Ad Hoc Working Group of Legal and Technical Experts for the Preparation of a Global Framework Convention for the Protection of the Ozone Layer. Despite the impressively long name and representatives from 24 nations, no substantive progress was made and few considered legal controls on CFCs very likely. The Group did, however, agree to convene an international negotiation in Vienna in 1985 to establish a framework convention. At this time, there was neither scientific consensus on the potential causes and mechanisms of ozone depletion nor data indicating whether any ozone depletion had even occurred.

———

2. THE VIENNA CONVENTION FOR THE PROTECTION OF THE OZONE LAYER (1985)

Attended by 43 nations (of which 16 were developing countries) and three industry groups, negotiations over the Vienna Convention produced the first international agreement to address CFCs. Expectations were low, with minimal public interest and no participation by any environmental organizations. From the outset, in a pattern that would follow for the next four years, U.S. and European Community (EC) negotiators were in conflict. The U.S. position, backed by Northern European countries, was to institute a ban on the use of CFC aerosol propellants. Broadening the ban already in place in a number of countries would lead to large, immediate reductions of CFCs. The EC argued against legal restrictions on consumption and favored limiting future CFC production levels through a ban on construction of new capacity. The major CFC-producers France and the United Kingdom strongly backed this position over the opposition of Germany, Denmark, the Netherlands and Belgium (all of whom supported a CFC aerosol ban). Since EC industry already had excess production capacity, over the longer term a ban on new growth would allow their production to increase while locking-in their competitive advantage over countries with nascent CFC industries.

With little environmental group interest in the negotiations, it was not surprising that industry groups strongly influenced national positions. The Alliance for a Responsible CFC Policy, a U.S. lobbying group with fifty companies, represented U.S. chemical industry interests during the negotiations. Opposing any controls, the multinationals Imperial Chemical Industries (ICI) and Atochem strongly lobbied the UK and French governments. The U.S. aerosol ban in 1978 had had immediate consequences on the competitive dynamic of worldwide CFC sales. American companies (led by DuPont) had traditionally dominated global production. From the 1978 aerosol ban to 1985, however, the U.S. chemical industry's share of global CFC sales dropped from 46% to 28%. Over the same period, European chemical companies increased their share from 38% to 45% (mostly from exports). Benedick, *op.cit.* at 26. From the American chemical industry's perspective, unilateral U.S. action had "given away markets" to their European competitors. Thus during the negotiations over the next few years, in an effort to achieve market parity, to level the playing field,

American industry groups consistently proved more willing to support international controls than their European counterparts.

Nonetheless, aside from the issue of banning CFC aerosol propellants, industry was united in its opposition to further controls. Until 1988, the CFC Alliance claimed that "current use of the compounds (CFCs) presents no significant risk to health or the environment." *Id.* at 26. Proposals for any reductions in the total use of CFCs were condemned as moving too far too fast. In the face of unproven harms, industry argued, it would be rash to limit the widespread use of inexpensive, non-toxic, non-flammable compounds. No affordable alternatives currently existed, phasing them in would be prohibitively expensive, and product performances would almost surely suffer.

The result of these initial negotiations, the Vienna Convention for the Protection of the Ozone Layer, was signed by 20 countries. UNEP Doc. IG.53/5, *reprinted in* 26 I.L.M. 1529 (1987). Rather than controls on CFC consumption or production, the Convention called for countries to take "appropriate measures" to protect the ozone layer and established an international mechanism for research, monitoring and exchange of information. With very little known about the scale of CFC production in Soviet bloc and developing countries, it was hoped this data would form the basis for establishing a global production baseline. No chemicals were identified as ozone-depleting substances. Instead, in a non-threatening description, the annex listed chemicals "thought to have the potential to modify the chemical and physical properties of the ozone layer." At the end of the meeting, despite objections by the EC, a non-binding resolution was passed calling for the next meeting to work toward a legally binding protocol addressing controls. Nonetheless, with the Vienna Convention's failure to establish controls on production or consumption, the future of CFCs still seemed bright.

Vienna Convention for the Protection of the Ozone Layer

Article 2

General Obligations

1. The Parties shall take appropriate measures in accordance with the provisions of this Convention and of those protocols in force to which they are party to protect human health and the environment against adverse effects resulting or likely to result from human activities which modify or are likely to modify the ozone layer.

2. To this end, the Parties shall, in accordance with the means at their disposal and their capabilities;

> (a) Co-operate by means of systematic observations, research and information exchange in order to better understand and assess the effects of human activities on the ozone layer and the effects on human health and the environment from modification of the ozone layer;

> (b) Adopt appropriate legislative or administrative measures and co-operate in harmonizing appropriate policies to control, limit, reduce or prevent human activities under their jurisdiction or control should it be found that these activities have or are likely to have adverse effects resulting from modification or likely modification of the ozone layer;

(c) Co-operate in the formulation of agreed measures, procedures and standards for the implementation of this Convention, with a view to the adoption of protocols and annexes;

(d) Co-operate with competent international bodies to implement effectively this Convention and protocols to which they are party.

3.   The provisions of this Convention shall in no way affect the right of Parties to adopt, in accordance with international law, domestic measures additional to those referred to in paragraphs 1 and 2 above, nor shall they affect additional domestic measures already taken by a Party, provided that these measures are not incompatible with their obligations under this Convention.

4.   The application of this article shall be based on relevant scientific and technical considerations.

Article 3

Research and Systematic Observations

1.   The Parties undertake, as appropriate, to initiate and co-operate in, directly or through competent international bodies, the conduct of research and scientific assessments on:

(a) The physical and chemical processes that may affect the ozone layer;

(b) The human health and other biological effects deriving from any modifications of the ozone layer, particularly those resulting from changes in ultra-violet solar radiation having biological effects. * * *

(c) Climatic effects deriving from any modifications of the ozone layer;

(d) Effects deriving from any modifications of the ozone layer and any consequent change in UV–B radiation on natural and synthetic materials useful to mankind;

(e) Substances, practices, processes and activities that may affect the ozone layer, and their cumulative effects;

(f) Alternative substances and technologies; * * *

2.   The Parties undertake to promote or establish, as appropriate, directly or through competent international bodies and taking fully into account national legislation and relevant ongoing activities at both the national and international levels, joint or complementary programmes for systematic observation of the state of the ozone layer and other relevant parameters, as elaborated in annex I.

3.   The Parties undertake to co-operate, directly or through competent international bodies, in ensuring the collection, validation and transmission of research and observational data through appropriate world data centres in a regular and timely fashion.

Article 4

Co-operation in the Legal Scientific and Technical Fields

1.   The Parties shall facilitate and encourage the exchange of scientific, technical, socio-economic, commercial and legal information relevant to this Convention as further elaborated in annex II. Such information shall be supplied to bodies agreed upon by the Parties. Any such body receiving information regarded as confidential by the supplying Party shall ensure that such information is not disclosed and shall aggregate it to protect its confidentiality before it is made available to all Parties.

2. The Parties shall co-operate, consistent with their national laws, regulations and practices and taking into account in particular the needs of the developing countries, in promoting, directly or through competent international bodies, the development and transfer of technology and knowledge. Such co-operation shall be carried out particularly through:

(a) Facilitation of the acquisition of alternative technologies by other Parties;

(b) Provision of information on alternative technologies and equipment . . .

(c) The supply of necessary equipment and facilities for research and systematic observations;

(d) Appropriate training of scientific and technical personnel. * * *

Article 6
Conference of the Parties

1. A Conference of the Parties is hereby established. The first meeting of the Conference of the Parties shall be convened by the secretariat . . . not later than one year after entry into force of the Convention. Thereafter, ordinary meetings of the Conference of the Parties shall be held at regular intervals to be determined by the Conference at its first meeting.* * *

Article 8
Adoption of Protocols

1. The Conference of the Parties may at a meeting adopt protocols pursuant to article 2.

2. The text of any proposed protocol shall be communicated to the Parties by the secretariat at least six months before such a meeting.

Article 9
Amendment of the Convention or Protocols

1. Any Party may propose amendments to this Convention or to any protocol. Such amendments shall take due account, inter alia, of relevant scientific and technical considerations.

2. Amendments to this Convention shall be adopted at a meeting of the Conference of the Parties. Amendments to any protocol shall be adopted at a meeting of the Parties to the protocol in question. The text of any proposed amendment of this Convention or to any protocol, except as may otherwise be provided in such protocol, shall be communicated to the Parties by the secretariat at least six months before the meeting at which it is proposed for adoption. The secretariat shall also communicate proposed amendments to the signatories to this Convention for information.

3. The Parties shall make every effort to reach agreement on any proposed amendment to this Convention by consensus. If all efforts at consensus have been exhausted, and no agreement reached, the amendment shall as a last resort be adopted by a three-fourth majority vote of the Parties present and voting at the meeting, and shall be submitted by the Depositary to all Parties for ratification, approval or acceptance.

4. The procedure mentioned in paragraph 3 above shall apply to amendments to any protocol, except that a two-thirds majority of the parties to that protocol present and voting at the meeting shall suffice for their adoption.

Article 10

Adoption and Amendment of Annexes

1. The annexes to this Convention or to any protocol shall form an integral part of this Convention or of such protocol, as the case may be, and, unless expressly provided otherwise, a reference to this Convention or its protocols constitutes at the same time a reference to any annexes thereto. Such annexes shall be restricted to scientific, technical and administrative matters.

2. Except as may be otherwise provided in any protocol with respect to its annexes, the following procedure shall apply to the proposal, adoption and entry into force of additional annexes to this Convention or of annexes to a protocol;

> (a) Annexes to this Convention shall be proposed and adopted according to the procedure laid down in article 9, paragraphs 2 and 3, while annexes to any protocol shall be proposed and adopted according to the procedure laid down in article 9, paragraphs 2 and 4;

> (b) Any party that is unable to approve an additional annex to this Convention or an annex to any protocol to which it is party shall so notify the Depositary, in writing, within six months from date of the communication of the adoption by the Depositary. The Depositary shall without delay notify all Parties of any such notification received. A party may at any time substitute an acceptance for a previous declaration of objection and the annexes shall thereupon enter into force for that Party;

> (c) On the expiry of six months from the date of the circulation of the communication by the Depositary, the annex shall become effective for all Parties to this Convention or to any protocol concerned which have not submitted a notification in accordance with the provision of subparagraph (b) above.

Article 11

Settlement of Disputes

1. In the event of a dispute between Parties concerning the interpretation or application of this Convention, the parties concerned shall seek solution by negotiation.

2. If the parties concerned cannot reach agreement by negotiation, they may jointly seek the good offices of, or request mediation by, a third party.

3. When ratifying, accepting, approving or acceding to this Convention, or any time thereafter, a State or regional economic integration organization may declare in writing to the Depositary that for a dispute not resolved in accordance with paragraph 1 or paragraph 2 above, it accepts one or both of the following means of dispute settlement as compulsory:

> (a) Arbitration in accordance with procedures to be adopted by the Conference of the Parties at its first ordinary meeting;

> (b) Submission of the dispute to the International Court of Justice.

4. If the parties have not, in accordance with paragraph 3 above, accepted the same or any procedure, the dispute shall be submitted to conciliation in accordance with paragraph 5 below unless the parties otherwise agree.

5. A conciliation commission shall be created upon the request of one of the parties to the dispute. The commission shall be composed of an equal number of members appointed by each party concerned and a chairman chosen jointly

by the members appointed by each party. The commission shall render a final and recommendatory award, which the parties shall consider in good faith.

6. The provisions of this article shall apply with respect to any protocol except as otherwise provided in the protocol concerned.

———

QUESTIONS AND DISCUSSION

1. *Working the Treaty*

   – Which obligations in the Convention are binding on the parties?

   – What concrete actions must a signatory take to comply with these obligations?

2. If you were the U.S. negotiator, how would you portray the Convention to journalists from the *New York Times* as a victory for American interests? If you were the EC negotiator, how would you present the Convention to the *Times of London* as a victory for European interests?

3. Why was collecting data to establish a baseline for global CFC production figures so important? Take a few minutes to outline the types or categories of information required to make informed policy decisions on something as complex as ozone depletion. Did the Vienna Convention ensure all of the relevant information would be available?

4. Although in retrospect the Vienna Convention did not adopt significant substantive provisions, it was nonetheless an important advance in international environmental law as it was one of the first international treaties recognizing and responding to a global environmental threat. Some analysts have said the treaty is the first to take an integrated, ecological approach to global environmental problems. What parts of the treaty reflect this approach?

5. The Vienna Convention is also considered one of the first international treaties to reflect the precautionary approach to environmental issues. This approach urges policy makers to take action in the face of scientific uncertainty. Is this interpretation of the Vienna Convention correct? Given the state of the scientific knowledge at the time of the convention, was the approach taken reasonable?

6. As you read the following sections regarding the Montreal Protocol, your view of the importance of the Vienna Convention may change. What was the legacy of the Vienna Convention? How effectively did it set the framework for the important steps taken at Montreal and subsequently?

7. NGOs were not represented in the Vienna Convention negotiations. Given the framework structure of the Convention and its few substantive obligations, do you think the outcome might have been any different if there had been civil society representation? If you had been chair of the negotiations and wished to incorporate some form of NGO participation, what models would you consider and how would the different models change the nature of NGOs' contributions?

———

3. PREPARATIONS FOR MONTREAL

In 1985, two months after negotiations ended over the Vienna Convention, British scientists announced an "ozone hole" in the Antarctic, triggering enormous public interest in ozone depletion. The scientists' data showed a 50% springtime reduction in the ozone layer compared to levels in the 1960s. Sharp decreases, however, had only begun in 1979, suggesting the reduction was non-linear. Ironically, because the data showed such a dramatic decline the British team had delayed publication of their findings for three years to confirm the accuracy of the data and U.S. satellites had automatically rejected accurate data of the depletion as clearly erroneous. While the ozone hole findings were startling and focused nations' attention on the negotiations, the discovery was of little help to diplomats because there was no proof of CFCs' role in creating the hole. Were CFCs to blame or was there another mechanism at work?

In 1984, one year before the Vienna Convention negotiations, an international scientific study had been launched by the U.S., Germany, WMO, and UNEP to determine the impact of human activities on the ozone layer. Published in 1986, the study provided governments their best information to date. The study concluded that atmospheric concentration of CFCs 11 and 12 had doubled from 1975 to 1985. Other important ozone depleting chemicals were also implicated, including more CFCs (CFC 113, 114, and 115), and a class of bromine compounds used as flame retardants called "halons." *See* WMO, ATMOSPHERE OZONE 1985: ASSESSMENT OF OUR UNDERSTANDING OF THE PROCESSES CONTROLLING ITS PRESENT DISTRIBUTION AND CHANGE (1986). Of more interest to the public were the estimated health effects. With current emission levels of ODSs, the study estimated an additional 150 million new cases of skin cancer in the U.S. by 2075, which would result in over 3 million deaths. The study further estimated that increased UV radiation would cause an additional 18 million eye cataracts in the U.S., many leading to blindness. Benedick, *op.cit.* at 21.

The model generating these estimates, however, was essentially informed guesswork. The springtime ozone hole could not be explained by current theories nor did surface measurements show any increase in UV–B radiation reaching the earth. Indeed, available records showed a *decrease* in radiation on the earth's surface. Nor was there a proven causal link between skin cancers and ozone depletion because it would take decades for carcinoma to develop. Qualifying its headline-grabbing predictions, the study concluded that taken as a whole there was "little overall support for the suggestion of a statistically significant trend" toward ozone depletion. *Id.* at 18.

Despite the study's cautionary conclusion, the ozone hole was linked in the public's mind to CFCs. Between Vienna and the next planned Meeting of the Parties in Montreal in 1987, UNEP held a number of informal workshops to review mechanisms for CFC reductions. These meetings proved helpful in establishing personal ties among the negotiators and gradually developing consensus.

Following the stalemate in Vienna, the U.S. position changed from merely advocating an aerosol propellant ban to a near-term freeze on consumption with the amount and date of future reductions open to negotiation. The U.S. supported its position with strong lobbying overseas. Sixty U.S. embassies were provided with talking points and directed to establish contact with relevant foreign ministries. Official U.S. delegations traveled to a number of capitals for face-to-face consultations and foreign media interviews. The talking points emphasized science rather than the

Antarctic ozone hole in case the hole was subsequently found to be unrelated to chlorine or simply disappeared. Benedick, *op.cit.*, at 56.

On the industry side, DuPont announced in 1986 that it could develop CFC substitutes within five years provided that regulatory requirements justified such a heavy investment in research and development (R & D). Without a legally-fixed phase-out goal to spur the market for CFC alternatives, DuPont feared developing more expensive substitutes for CFCs would prove a poor business decision. The U.S.-based CFC Alliance also broke from its previous position, calling for a cap on CFC growth. While this was still a tame recommendation compared to the U.S. government's call for reductions, it marked the first time an industry group had formally backed CFC controls. U.S. industry clearly preferred a strong international treaty to U.S. unilateral action.

4. THE MONTREAL PROTOCOL ON SUBSTANCES THAT DEPLETE THE OZONE LAYER (1987)

The negotiations in Montreal could not have shown a greater contrast to the small affair two years earlier in Vienna. With over 60 countries participating (more than half from developing countries), many industrial and environmental groups, and wide media coverage, the world's attention focused on Ozone depletion. The workshops and lobbying since Vienna paid off, for the Protocol was passed by consensus. *See* 26 I.L.M. 1550 (1987).

Coverage

In the Vienna Convention, no chemicals had been identified or regulated as ODSs. The Protocol, however, not only froze production and consumption levels of CFCs upon ratification (CFCs 11, 12, 113, 114, 115) and of halons three years later (Halons 1211, 1301, 2402), but also set in place a reduction schedule for CFCs. By 1998, a 50% reduction in CFC consumption was to be achieved. Because monitoring consumption of ODS was thought infeasible, a surrogate formula was adopted defining a country's consumption of CFCs or halons as:

$$consumption = production + imports - exports$$

Thus a major CFC producer could satisfy the reduction requirements by decreasing its domestic use but still continuing to export. An importing country would measure its consumption simply by adding domestic production and imports together.

In order to give countries flexibility in their reduction schedules, the Protocol developed a "basket" strategy. Each chemical's ozone-depleting potential (ODP) was compared to that of CFC 11 (arbitrarily given a value of 1). Since CFC 113 is less destructive of the ozone layer than CFC 11, its ODP is 0.8. Using the basket strategy, a country would achieve the same reduction in consumption levels either by using 8 tons less of CFC 11 or 10 tons less of CFC 113 (8 tons x ODP of 1 = 10 tons x ODP of 0.8). This arithmetic was important because CFC 113 was widely used as a solvent in the electronics industry. Countries like Japan, which had opposed CFC

113's inclusion in the Protocol, could now choose to reduce a greater percentage of other CFCs while conserving CFC 113's use.

The reduction schedules and basket strategy not only avoided chemical-by-chemical negotiations but provided clear signals for industrial development by removing uncertainty. CFC producers like DuPont and ICI could now justify heavy R & D spending in CFC alternatives. CFC users like IBM and Toshiba could justify investments for in-process recycling and recovery systems to reduce the need for additional, and certainly more expensive, CFC stocks. For companies in ratifying countries, long-term investments in CFC production or CFC consumption technologies suddenly seemed less attractive.

Trade Measures

If the Protocol's only teeth were scheduled phase-outs of controlled substances, countries would have a strong incentive not to sign in order to gain the newly-freed market share for themselves. To avoid this free rider behavior and as an incentive for countries to join, the Protocol provided tough trade measures.

Regarding imports, parties to the Protocol are prohibited from importing from non-parties either controlled substances or certain products *containing* controlled substances. These products include domestic, commercial and vehicle air conditioners, refrigerators, and portable fire extinguishers. The parties also decided to ban the import of products *produced* with controlled substances. While parties agreed on a list of products containing controlled substances, they had difficulty in drawing up a similar list for products produced with controlled substances and, as a result, left it to each party to draw up its own list of products. The country of origin can avoid these onerous restrictions only if it demonstrates full compliance with the Protocol's reduction schedules.

Regarding exports, parties must similarly ban the export of controlled substances to non-parties unless the country of destination can demonstrate full compliance with the Protocol's reduction schedules. Exports to non-parties that are in compliance are not counted as exports in the country's consumption calculation, so they must be offset by an equal reduction in production or imports.

As an example, if Country P is a party and Country N is a non-party and not in compliance with the Protocol, there can be no trade in controlled substances between the countries, and Country P cannot import products that are controlled substances, contain controlled substances, or were produced with controlled substances (depending on its list) from Country N. If Country N remains a non-Party but complies with the Protocol, Country P can export controlled substances to Country N but cannot subtract this amount from imports or production in calculating national consumption. Subject to the reduction schedules, parties may freely trade controlled substances amongst themselves. A more complete discussion of the relationship between the Montreal Protocol and the GATT is provided *infra*.

Technical and Financial Assistance

Article 5 of the Protocol addressed aid to developing countries. While developing countries' per capita consumption of CFCs in 1987 was much lower than in the developed world, their domestic requirements were steadily growing. Since the manufacture of CFCs is a low-cost, low-tech operation, no practical barriers prevented cottage CFC industries from sprouting around the globe. Thus in part to accept the responsibility for having created most of the ozone depleting substances and in part to encourage broad international participation, developed countries supported a ten-year grace period following ratification for developing countries before the control measures would apply. In other words, developing countries were permitted to increase their consumption to 0.3 Kg per capita in order to meet basic domestic needs. Following this period, developing countries would have ten more years to reduce their consumption by 50%. While this allowed growth may have seemed counterproductive, even if all the developing countries increased their use of ODS to 0.3 Kg per capita the total consumption would still only have been 25–30% of the 1986 U.S. and EC consumption. This is often cited as an example of the principle of common but differentiated responsibility (*see* page 402).

Moreover, negotiators thought it unlikely parties would reach their per capita limit because they believed CFC-based technologies would be largely dead within a decade. Rather, the growth limit provided a means to ease the transition away from ozone depleting substances. When it came to providing developing countries specific financial and technical assistance for alternative substances and new technologies, however, the Protocol provided only vague promises of facilitating access.

Ratification and Amendments

With clear restrictions negotiated, the problem remained of when the controls would enter into force. If parties were bound by the trade and reduction provisions as soon as they ratified, there would be a perverse incentive for countries to hold out and gain short-term competitive benefits by intransigence. To avoid this behavior, the Protocol entered into force only when at least 11 countries representing two-thirds of global production had ratified. This was yet another innovation in international law.

The most important innovation of the Protocol, however, was its flexibility. Parties were required to assess and review controls at least every four years. This would ensure that the Protocol's international controls reflected scientists' improved understanding of the mechanisms and causes of ozone depletion. If any of the controlled substances were found to be less harmful than thought or the schedules proved too stringent, the Protocol's reduction schedules could be canceled with a two-thirds majority of countries representing two-thirds of global consumption. Adding new control measures was relatively easier, requiring a two-thirds majority of countries representing half of global consumption.

With 24 nations signing in Montreal, the Protocol was universally hailed as a diplomatic triumph. Starting from low or no expectations in Vienna, within eighteen months strict international controls had been negotiated that would be refined and changed over time with the benefit of more knowledge. This structured evolution marked a new feature of international environmental law and showed great foresight. Not only have the parties met regularly since 1987, but every time parties have sought to tighten reduction schedules and bring new compounds under control.

Montreal Protocol on Substances That Deplete the Ozone Layer

The Parties to this Protocol,

Being Parties to the Vienna Convention for the Protection of the Ozone Layer * * *

Recognizing that world-wide emissions of certain substances can significantly deplete and otherwise modify the ozone layer in a manner that is likely to result in adverse effects on human health and the environment. * * *

Acknowledging that special provision is required to meet the needs of developing countries for these substances,

Noting the precautionary measures for controlling emissions of certain chlorofluorocarbons that have already been taken at national and regional levels,

Have Agreed As Follows: * * *

Article 2

Control Measures

1. Each Party shall ensure that [each year] its calculated level of consumption of the controlled substances in Group I of Annex A does not exceed its calculated level of consumption in 1986. By the end of the same period, each Party producing one or more of these substances shall ensure that its calculated level of production of the substances does not exceed its calculated level of production in 1986, except that such level may have increased by no more than ten per cent based on the 1986 level. Such increase shall be permitted only so as to satisfy the basic domestic needs of the Parties operating under Article 5 and for the purposes of industrial rationalization between Parties.

3. Each Party shall ensure that for the period 1 July 1993 to 30 June 1994 and in each twelve-month period thereafter, its calculated level of consumption of the controlled substances in Group I of Annex A does not exceed, annually, eighty per cent of its calculated level of consumption in 1986. * * *

4. Each Party shall ensure that for the period 1 July 1998 to 30 June 1999, and in each twelve-month period thereafter, its calculated level of consumption of the controlled substances in Group I of Annex A does not exceed, annually, fifty percent of its calculated level of consumption in 1986. * * *

9. (a) Based on the assessments made pursuant to Article 6, the Parties may decide whether:

> (i) adjustments to the ozone depleting potentials specified in Annex A should be made and, if so, what the adjustments should be; and

> > (ii) further adjustments and reductions of production or consumption of the controlled substances from 1986 levels should be undertaken and, if so, what the scope, amount and timing of any such reductions and adjustments should be.

(b) Proposals for such adjustments shall be communicated to the Parties by the secretariat at least six months before the meeting of the Parties at which they are proposed for adoption.

(c) In taking such decisions, the Parties shall make every effort to reach agreement by consensus. If all efforts at consensus have been exhausted, and no agreement reached, such decisions shall, as a last resort, be adopted by a two-thirds majority vote of the parties present and voting representing at least fifty per cent of the total consumption of the controlled substances of the Parties.

11.   Notwithstanding the provisions contained in this Article, Parties may take more stringent measures than those required by this Article.

Article 3
Calculation of Control Levels

For the purposes of Articles 2 and 5, each Party shall, for each Group of substances in Annex A, determine its calculated levels of:

(a) production by:

(i) multiplying its annual production of each controlled substance by the ozone depleting potential specified in respect of it in Annex A; and

(ii) adding together, for each such Group, the resulting figures;

(b) imports and exports, respectively, by following ... the procedure set out in subparagraph (a); and

(c) consumption by adding together its calculated levels of production and imports and subtracting its calculated level of exports as determined in accordance with subparagraphs (a) and (b). However, beginning on 1 January 1993, any export of controlled substances to non-Parties shall not be subtracted in calculating the consumption level of the exporting Party.

Article 4
Control of Trade with Non–Parties

1.   Within one year of the entry into force of this Protocol, each Party shall ban the import of controlled substances from any State not party to this Protocol.

2.   Beginning on 1 January 1993, no Party operating under paragraph 1 of Article 5 may export any controlled substance to any State not party to this Protocol.

3.   Within three years of the date of the entry into force of this Protocol, the Parties shall ... elaborate in an annex a list of products containing controlled substances. Parties that have not objected to the annex in accordance with those procedures shall ban, within one year of the annex having become effective, the import of those products from any State not party to this Protocol.

4.   Within five years of the entry into force of this Protocol, the Parties shall determine the feasibility of banning or restricting, from States not party to this Protocol, the import of products produced with, but not containing, controlled substances. If determined feasible, the Parties shall ... elaborate in an annex a list of such products. * * *

5.   Each Party shall discourage the export, to any State not party to this Protocol, of technology for producing and for utilizing controlled substances.

6.   Each Party shall refrain from providing new subsidies, aid, credits, guarantees or insurance programmes for the export to States not party to this Protocol of products, equipment, plants or technology that would facilitate the production of controlled substances.

Article 5
Special Situation of Developing Countries

1.   Any Party that is a developing country and whose annual calculated level of consumption of the controlled substances is less than 0.3 kilograms per capita on the date of the entry into force of the Protocol for it, or anytime thereafter within ten years of the date of entry into force of the Protocol shall, in order to meet its basic domestic needs, be entitled to delay its compliance with the control ... by ten years after that specified in those paragraphs. * * *

2.   The Parties undertake to facilitate access to environmentally safe alternative substances and technology for Parties that are developing countries and assist them to make expeditious use of such alternatives.

3.   The Parties undertake to facilitate bilaterally or multilaterally the provision of subsidies, aid, credits, guarantees or insurance programmes to Parties that are developing countries for the use of alternative technology and for substitute products.

Article 6
Assessment and Review of Control Measures

Beginning in 1990, and at least every four years thereafter, the Parties shall assess the control measures provided for in Article 2 on the basis of available scientific, environmental, technical and economic information. At least one year before each assessment, the Parties shall convene appropriate panels of experts qualified in the fields mentioned and determine the composition and terms of reference of any such panels. Within one year of being convened, the panels will report their conclusions, through the secretariat, to the Parties. * * *

Article 8
Non–Compliance

The Parties, at their first meeting, shall consider and approve procedures and institutional mechanisms for determining non-compliance with the provisions of this Protocol and for treatment of Parties found to be in non-compliance. * * *

Article 11
Meetings of the Parties

1.   The Parties shall hold meetings at regular intervals. The secretariat shall convene the first meeting of the Parties not later than one year after the date of the entry into force of this Protocol and in conjunction with a meeting of the Conference of the Parties to the Convention, if a meeting of the latter is scheduled within that period.

ANNEX A
CONTROLLED SUBSTANCES

Substance	Ozone Depleting Potential *
Group I	
$CFCl_3$ (CFC–11)	1.0
CF_2Cl_2 (CFC–12)	1.0
$C_2F_3Cl_3$ (CFC–113)	0.8
$C_2F_4Cl_2$ (CFC–114)	1.0
C_2F_5Cl (CFC–115)	0.6
Group II	
CF_2BrCl (halon–1211)	3.0
CF_3Br (halon–1301)	10.0
$C_2F_4Br_2$ (halon–2402)	(to be determined)

* These ozone depleting potentials are estimates based on existing knowledge and will be reviewed and revised periodically.

5.   THE LONDON ADJUSTMENTS AND AMENDMENTS TO THE MONTREAL PROTOCOL (1990)

Many issues had been glossed over at Montreal, including details of technical and financial assistance to developing countries, whether the 50% reduction in CFCs should become a complete phase-out and, most important, how to increase the number of signatories from the original twenty-four. To inform governments on the current state of science, an Ozone Trends Panel was formed with over 100 scientists from 10 countries. Their 1988 report concluded that ozone depletion had already occurred over populated areas of the Northern Hemisphere and that the ozone hole, a "large, sudden and unexpected" decrease in Antarctic ozone during Spring, had been regularly occurring over the last decade and could well be present in the Arctic as well. The study also presented the first solid data of chemical mechanisms linking halons and CFCs with ozone depletion. Perhaps most important, the scientific consensus underpinning the Montreal negotiations had estimated a 2% annual depletion of the ozone layer occurring by the year 2050 with no controls. New data, however, showed that a reduction of 2.3–6% was already occurring every spring. The problem was much more serious than had previously been appreciated. Benedick *op. cit.* at 110–11.

The media seized upon publication of the study, and Dupont surprisingly caused more headlines in announcing a voluntary halt to all CFC and halon production by the year 2000. This voluntary ban was followed soon after by pledges to halt the use of CFCs from other companies, including members of the CFC Alliance, plastic foam manufacturers, and car companies. Motorola and IBM pledged to stop using CFCs by 1992 and 1993, respectively. In Europe, the EC and UK governments flipped their earlier positions, calling for a ban on CFCs. The UK even offered to host the next Meeting of the Parties in 1990 where the London Amendments were adopted.

New Reduction Schedules

As Montreal had contrasted with Vienna, so, too, did the London Conference present a break from Montreal. With 123 countries present and over 200 media correspondents, the Protocol Meeting of the Parties was now a full-fledged international spectacle. In light of the new scientific data, there was now broad consensus for the eventual elimination of CFCs and halons; at issue was the scale and timing of reductions. Because the EC had not yet banned the use of CFC aerosol propellants, they could gain an easy 50% reduction with little cost or effort. The same percentage reduction for the United States, however, would be much harder because the easy reductions had already been taken. Agreeing to a complete phase-out would require developing alternatives for CFCs where none currently existed.

Because most countries had already exceeded the 1993 goal of a 20% reduction, a new goal of 50% reduction for 1995 was put in place with a total phase-out by 2000 for CFCs and halons.

Developing Countries

Montreal had glossed over the terms of assistance to developing countries. Some simple facts, however, illustrated the importance of bringing these countries on board. Industrialized countries, with less than 25% of the world's population, were consuming 88% of the CFCs, over twenty times the per capita consumption of developing countries. Benedick, *op. cit.*, at 148–49. China and India, representing approximately 37% of the global population, were not parties to the Protocol. These countries' large and growing domestic markets made the Protocol's trade restrictions moot. Huge local CFC industries could develop over time and never sell products outside the Chinese or Indian borders. Moreover, products containing CFCs, like refrigeration and air conditioning, were viewed as necessary to improve the standard of living in those countries and, indeed, essential in a number of their applications. The sale of CFC-chilled refrigerators in China, for example, had already grown from 2 per 1,000 households in 1981 to 423 per 1,000 in 1990. Robert Livernash, *The Future of Populous Economies: China and India Shape their Destinies*, ENVIRONMENT, July, 1995, at 6.

Developing countries showed keen interest in the emerging global scientific consensus over ozone layer depletion but rejected as unacceptable the options of either going without these products or paying more because of expensive substitutes and retrofitting existing equipment. Indeed, they charged it would be adding insult to injury to actually increase the profits of the multinational chemical industry that had produced the damaging substances in the first place. Article 5's ten-year growth allowance was helpful, but in light of the accelerated reduction schedules, developing country diplomats demanded firmer assurances of financial and technical assistance. If the Protocol would produce winners and losers, developing countries wanted guarantees they would not suffer as a result. Participation of non-parties such as China and India in negotiations prior to 1991, though without voting rights, was influential and paved the way for their later ratification.

Negotiations over a funding mechanism were tortuous in part because they took place in the shadow of the Earth Summit planned in Rio in 1992. There, the challenges of global warming and biodiversity would be addressed and any commitments made in the ozone context would loom large as binding precedents. For that reason, major donor countries opposed the creation of a new funding institution, and the United States opposed the concept of "additionality." Arguing that current development aid commitments should be diverted for ozone protection, the U.S. opposed granting any additional funds. After high-profile pressure and a White House cost-benefit analysis showing the benefit of reduced cancers far outweighing the costs of additional funds, the U.S. reversed its position and approved new funds with the proviso in the Annex that the funding was "without prejudice to any future arrangements that may be developed with respect to other environmental issues." Annex II, Art. 10; Benedick, *op. cit.*, at 184.

The North–South conflict was more heated over the sufficiency of aid. Developing countries sought assurance that if the aid proved insufficient they would be relieved from meeting their treaty obligations. From their perspective, they needed an exemption from obligations if the promised aid was inadequate through no fault of their own. They wanted to avoid writing their own check. The developed countries, however, wanted to avoid writing a blank check–providing financial and technical aid with the amounts determined by the recipient country. As a compromise, the Protocol acknowledged that "developing the capacity [of developing countries parties] to fulfill the obligations ... will depend upon the effective implementation" of adequate technology transfer and financial support. London Adjustments and Amendments to the Montreal Protocol, Annex II, Art. 5(5).

The parties approved an interim funding source that, in 1992, was permanently established as the Multilateral Fund with funding of $160 million from 1991–1993 and $510 million from 1994–1996. The Multilateral Fund is managed by an Executive Committee of seven developed and seven developing country parties. The parties oversee the Executive Committee and make majority decisions on the basis of one-country one-vote. UNEP serves as secretariat to the Executive Committee and treasurer of the Fund and, with UNDP and the World Bank, assist developing countries in making use of the Fund. Interestingly, the London Amendments did not mandate contributions. Rather, in a classic example of diplomatic compromise, countries committed themselves to "voluntary contributions on an assessed basis." Benedick, *op. cit.*, at 161. The first three-year budget was estimated at $160–240 million.

A new non-compliance procedure was also created. If a developing country party believes it cannot comply with the reduction schedules, it must notify the secretariat and its situation will be addressed at the next Meeting of Parties. In the meantime, no noncompliance actions (i.e. trade measures under Article 8) will be taken against the country. This "user-friendly" compliance procedure represents an important innovation in international environmental law and is detailed in the excerpts of the London Amendments below.

In the area of technology transfer, the issue at stake was patents and intellectual property rights (as would be the case with the Biodiversity Convention two years later, *see* Chapter 13). For the reasons discussed above, developing countries wanted guaranteed access to affordable and recent technologies. In opposition, the private sector sought assurance that its investments in developing ODS alternatives would produce a return on capital. Industry lobbied strongly against any weakening of patent protections, arguing that competition alone would ensure access at affordable prices. The final text required the parties to "take every practicable step" to transfer technology to developing countries "fairly and most favorably." Despite the lack of binding commitment, this marked the first treaty where developed countries had accepted their responsibility for protecting the environment by assisting developing countries with technology transfer. *Id.* at 198.

China and India, following establishment of the Multilateral Fund in 1991, have since both become parties to the Protocol. As of August, 2000, the Multilateral Fund had supported projects in China worth about $300 million and in India worth about $175 million.

Adjustments And Amendments To The Montreal Protocol On Substances That Deplete The Ozone Layer, UNEP/Oz.L.Pro 2/3 (Annex II) (London, 1990), reprinted in 30 I.L.M. 537 (1990)

Article 5 of the Protocol shall be replaced by the following:

1.   Any Party that is a developing country and whose annual calculated level of consumption of the controlled substances in Annex A is less than 0.3 kilograms per capita on the date of the entry into force of the Protocol for it, or any time thereafter until January 1, 1999, shall in order to meet its basic domestic needs, be entitled to delay for ten years its compliance with the control measures . . .
        * * *

4.   If a Party operating under paragraph 1 of this Article, at any time before the control measure obligations . . . become applicable to it, finds itself unable to obtain an adequate supply of controlled substances, it may notify this to the Secretariat. The Secretariat shall forthwith transmit a copy of such notification to the Parties, which shall consider the matter at their next Meeting, and decide upon appropriate action to be taken.

5.   Developing the capacity to fulfil the obligations of the Parties operating under paragraph 1 of this Article to comply with the control measures set out in Articles 2A to 2E and their implementation by those same Parties will depend upon the effective implementation of the financial co-operation as provided by Article 10 and transfer of technology as provided by Article 10A.

6.   Any Party operating under paragraph 1 of this Article may, at any time, notify the Secretariat in writing that, having taken all practicable steps it is unable to implement any or all of the obligations laid down in Articles 2A to 2E due to the inadequate implementation of Articles 10 and 10A. The Secretariat shall forthwith transmit a copy of the notification to the Parties, which shall consider the matter at their next Meeting, giving due recognition to paragraph 5 of this Article and shall decide upon appropriate action to be taken.

7.   During the period between notification and the Meeting of the Parties at which the appropriate action referred to in paragraph 6 above is to be decided, or for a further period if the Meeting of the Parties so decides, the non-compliance procedures referred to in Article 8 shall not be invoked against the notifying Party.

Article 10 of the Protocol shall be replaced by the following:

Article 10
Financial mechanism

1.   The Parties shall establish a mechanism for the purposes of providing financial and technical co-operation, including the transfer of technologies (to developing countries) . . . to enable their compliance with the control measures set out in Articles 2A to 2E of the Protocol. The mechanism . . . shall meet all agreed incremental costs of such Parties in order to enable their compliance with the control measures of the Protocol. An indicative list of the categories of incremental costs shall be decided by the meeting of the Parties.

2.   The mechanism established under paragraph 1 shall include a Multilateral Fund. It may also include other means of multilateral, regional and bilateral co-operation.

3.   The Multilateral Fund shall: * * *

(i) Assist Parties operating under paragraph 1 of Article 5, through country specific studies and other technical co-operation, to identify their needs for co-operation;

(ii) Facilitate technical co-operation to meet these identified needs;

(iii) Distribute, as provided for in Article 9, information and relevant materials, and hold workshops, training sessions, and other related activities, for the benefit of Parties that are developing countries. * * *

4.   The Multilateral Fund shall operate under the authority of the Parties who shall decide on its overall policies.

5.   The Parties shall establish an Executive Committee to develop and monitor the implementation of specific operational policies, guidelines and administrative arrangements,including the disbursement of resources, for the purpose of achieving the objectives of the Multilateral Fund. The Executive Committee shall discharge its tasks and responsibilities, specified in its terms of reference as agreed by the Parties, with the co-operation and assistance of the International Bank for Reconstruction and Development (World Bank), the United Nations Environment Programme, the United Nations Development Programme or other appropriate agencies depending on their respective areas of expertise. * * *

New Controlled Substances

In addition to the accelerated reduction schedules for CFCs and halons, the London Amendments instituted controls for new classes of ozone depleting substances. Chief among these was hydrochlorofluorocarbons (HCFCs). This class of compounds was significantly less harmful to the ozone layer and viewed by the major chemical companies as the primary replacement for CFCs. Dupont had already invested $250 million in R & D and spearheaded industry opposition to even mentioning HCFCs in the London Amendments, arguing that major investments in manufacturing equipment would require thirty to forty years for payback. If there was a strong likelihood HCFCs would be phased out, they contended, no one would make the necessary investments. The final compromise was two-fold: a requirement to report on production, import and export of HCFCs and a nonbinding resolution discouraging their use by a phase-out in 2040.

Beside HCFCs, the other broad class of CFC substitutes chemical companies pinned their hopes on were hydrofluorocarbons (HFCs). Because they were not ozone depleters there was little discussion of controlling their use in the Protocol. HFCs, however, are powerful greenhouse gases and environmental groups criticized the commercial substitution of greenhouse gases for ozone depleting substances as shortsighted.

The London Amendments also extended coverage to carbon tetrachloride and methyl chloroform. Together, these two compounds comprised 16% of industry's total stratospheric chlorine contribution, greater than that of CFCs or halons. Indeed, they had not been included in the Protocol because of their prevalence in so many applications (e.g. solvents, pesticides, dry cleaners). The London Amendments called for a scheduled phase-out of carbon tetrachloride by 2000 and of methyl chloroform by 2005.

Going beyond the Montreal control measures before it, the London Amendments provided for gradual phase-outs of the original five CFCs and three halons, added new phase-outs for ten more CFCs, carbon tetrachloride, and methyl chloroform, and required tracking and reporting of thirty-four HCFC "transitional substances."

6. ADJUSTMENTS AND AMENDMENTS

This rapid progress has continued at subsequent Meetings of the Parties. The Copenhagen Amendments in 1992 moved the CFC ban forward to 1996 and instituted a halon ban by 1994. 32 I.L.M. 874 (1993). Both the carbon tetrachloride and methyl chloroform bans were moved forward to 1996. The Seventh Meeting of the Parties in Vienna in 1995 followed suit by moving the HCFC ban forward from 2030 to 2020 and creating a new ban for the soil fumigant methyl bromide in 2010. Developing countries agreed to phase out HCFCs by 2040 and to freeze Methyl Bromide consumption by 2002. Subsequent meetings of the parties in Montreal, Cairo and Beijing have continued to accelerate phase outs while also expanding the number of compounds controlled, setting in place licensing systems for imports and exports, and limiting the use of feedstock ODSs for production processes. Table 9–4, on the following page, was created by UNEP's OzonAction Program and provides a brief summary of the amendments since the Montreal Protocol, showing how the requirements for phase out of ODSs have changed.

QUESTIONS AND DISCUSSION

1. *Working the Treaty*

   – What is the difference between an adjustment and a revision to the Protocol?

   – How does a country withdraw from the Protocol?

   – In what ways is the Protocol more protective than the Vienna Convention?

   – Reading the text of Article 5, are developed countries bound by the Protocol to assist developing countries with compliance? What should a developing country do if it could not meet the ten-year deadline?

   – Regarding the special situation of developing countries, does their ten-year grace period allow the trade of controlled substances?

2. The Montreal Protocol and subsequent revisions are considered important advances in international environmental law in part because they adopt specific, numerical standards and timetables for the complete elimination of a large number

Schedule of ODS Phase-outs
Table 9–4

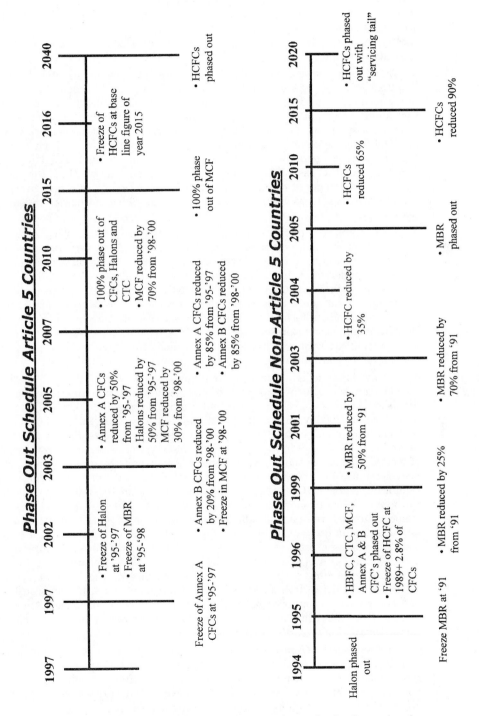

Phase Out Schedule Article 5 Countries

1997 | 1997 | 2002 | 2003 | 2005 | 2007 | 2010 | 2015 | 2016 | 2040

Freeze of Annex A CFCs at '95-'97

- Freeze of Halon at '95-'97
- Freeze of MBR at '95-'98

- Annex A CFCs reduced by 50% from '95-'97
- Halons reduced by 50% from '95-'97
- MCF reduced by 30% from '98-'00

- 100% phase out of CFCs, Halons and CTC
- MCF reduced by 70% from '98-'00

- Freeze of HCFCs at base line figure of year 2015

- HCFCs phased out

- Annex B CFCs reduced by 20% from '98-'00
- Freeze in MCF at '98-'00

- Annex A CFCs reduced by 85% from '95-'97
- Annex B CFCs reduced by 85% from '98-'00

- 100% phase out of MCF

Phase Out Schedule Non-Article 5 Countries

1994 | 1995 | 1996 | 1999 | 2001 | 2003 | 2004 | 2005 | 2010 | 2015 | 2020

Halon phased out

Freeze MBR at '91

- HBFC, CTC, MCF, Annex A & B CFC's phased out
- Freeze of HCFC at 1989+ 2.8% of CFCs

- MBR reduced by 25% from '91

- MBR reduced by 50% from '91

- MBR reduced by 70% from '91

- HCFC reduced by 35%

- MBR phased out

- HCFCs reduced 65%

- HCFCs reduced 90%

- HCFCs phased out with "servicing tail"

of commercially valuable chemical compounds. Numerical standards of any sort, let alone complete phase-outs, are rare in international law. To the extent they occur, in international environmental law they usually result from policies or guidelines issued by international institutions such as the WHO or the FAO. These are typically non-binding as they have not resulted from specific agreement by countries. To some extent, the unique accomplishments of the Montreal Protocol simply reflect the dire threat that ozone depletion presents to global environmental security. Consider this in light of the difficulty countries have had in reaching specific targets and timetables under the Climate Change Convention, described later in this chapter.

3. In providing special consideration to developing countries, Article 5 of the Montreal Protocol regime allows a grace period during which developing countries can continue to produce and consume the controlled substances provided their consumption does not exceed 0.3 kg per capita. Underlying this formulation appears to be an assumption that the capacity of the ozone layer to assimilate CFCs and other ODS should be shared among developing countries based on their population. Does this provision implicitly recognize the right of all humankind to a certain percentage of the assimilative capacity of the ozone layer? Does this provision support the concepts of common heritage of humankind or of a human right to a healthy environment as discussed in Chapter 7 page 389 and Chapter 16, page 1298, respectively?

4. Review Article 6 of the Montreal Protocol. Despite its simplicity, Article 6 has been enormously important in ensuring that the scientific understanding relating to ozone depletion is collected and presented in a relatively simple format for policy-makers to understand. Indeed, the facts of ozone depletion presented in Part I of this Section have been summarized from UNEP Panel reports issued under Article 6's mandate. Not only does the periodic review of scientific evidence assist in identifying trends, information gaps, and research priorities, but it also provides a significant platform to present the underlying science. This platform is important for rebutting contrarian or fringe science, which often demands a disproportionate amount of press attention.

5. Methyl bromide is a widely used fumigant and ODS. First addressed in the Copenhagen amendments, as part of the Vienna adjustments three years later developed countries agreed to phase out methyl bromide by 2010 and later moved up the date to 2005 with interim reductions of 25% by 1999, 50% by 2001, and 70% by 2003. Developing countries agreed to a freeze on consumption by 2002, a 20% reduction by 2005, and total ban by 2015. An exception was made, however, for use of methyl bromide in the quarantine and pre-shipment treatment of food. This use now accounts for up to a quarter of methyl bromide use and will remain a significant source of ODS. At the Eleventh Meeting of the Parties in Beijing, the European Union pushed to remove the exception but failed to gain sufficient support. Instead, the parties called for the provision of statistical data on methyl bromide used in quarantine and pre-shipment applications. The U.S. Clean Air Act bans the domestic production and importation of methyl bromide after January, 2001. China, however, has just opened up a new plant for the production of the substance, expanding a production capacity that already exceeds that of all other developing countries. Indeed, as of June, 1999, China, India, Russia, South Africa, and many smaller countries had not adopted the 1992 Copenhagen Amendments phasing out methyl bromide. *Parties To Montreal Protocol Discuss Restrictions on Use of Methyl Bromide*, BNA–IED, Dec. 6, 1999.

6. In *Mending the Ozone Hole: Science, Technology and Policy*, Arjun Makhijani and Kevin Gurney provide an in-depth look at current estimates of ozone depletion rates under different assumptions about ODS use. After a careful review, the two scientists conclude that additional steps beyond the current Montreal Protocol regime must be taken. Among these steps are the following:

> 6.   The use of leaded gasoline in the Third World should be eliminated as soon as possible, both because lead is toxic and because the ethylene dibromide in leaded gasoline is emitted in exhaust as methyl bromide.

7. Programs to examine the ozone-depleting potential of chloroform, methylene chloride, perchloroethylene, and dichloroethane should be instituted immediately.

8. A survey of all chlorine-and bromine-containing compounds with lifetimes estimated at more than 3 months and global emissions estimated at more than 200,000 tonnes per year should be undertaken in order to limit and eventually eliminate emissions of these compounds.

9. Policy-development studies as well as scientific studies of the contribution of biomass burning should be initiated as part of the Montreal Protocol process. Negotiations on ways to end the burning of tropical forests should be included in the Montreal Protocol process.

10. Third World subsidiaries of multinational corporations and joint ventures in which multinational corporations have more than 10 percent ownership should be required to follow the same phaseout schedule that applies to the industrialized countries. Laws mandating this will be needed in industrialized countries. This should also be made a part of the Montreal Protocol revision.

Makhijani & Gurney, *op. cit.*, at 286. Writing in 1995, Makhijani and Gurney argued that "adoption of these recommendations would end ozone depletion about 20–30 years earlier than might be expected with strict adherence to the compliance schedule of the Copenhagen Amendments to the Montreal Protocol." *Id.* at 287. How would you amend the Montreal Protocol to achieve these different results? Draft some prospective language. Which countries would be likely to oppose these changes? Based on the concepts and principles explicit in the Montreal Protocol regime as well as those discussed in Chapter 7, what are the strongest arguments for taking these proposed steps?

7. The treatment of HFCs and perfluorocarbons (PFCs) still remains contentious. These gases have long been recommended as ODS replacements. As mentioned previously, however, they are strong greenhouse gases. Indeed the 1997 Kyoto Protocol calls for reduction in emissions of six gases, including HFCs and PFCs as well as methane and CO2. Despite the fact that alternative compounds exist, the Multilateral Fund has spent millions of dollars financing the conversion of production processes in developing countries from CFCs to HFCs. Both the ozone and climate change secretariats have heeded these criticisms, and adopted resolutions calling for greater scientific cooperation among the treaty organizations.

How should the Montreal Protocol parties treat ODSs that contribute to climate change? There are currently no phase-out schedules for HFCs or PFCs. While NGOs have called for their control, industry has strongly resisted, arguing that this will frustrate the Kyoto Protocol's control strategy. Similar to the initial Montreal Protocol basket approach, the Kyoto Protocol allows countries to choose their emissions targets among the six restricted gases. Controlling HFCs and PFCs under the Montreal Protocol would limit Parties' flexibility to select among the gases, flexibility that was crucial in gaining support for Kyoto from some countries. The uncertainty surrounding HFCs could also prolong the use of CFCs in developing countries, industry has also argued, because without an accepted substitute they may be reluctant to invest in new technology. Do you think HFCs and PFCs should be regulated under the Montreal Protocol? If so, what are the implications for parties to the Kyoto Protocol? *See* Lawrence J. Speer, *Countries Agree on Need for Better Link Between Montreal Protocol, Climate Pact,* BNA–IED, Nov. 24, 1998.

8. *Problem Exercise:* You represent Pesticidios, a Brazilian subsidiary of Pesticide, Inc., a U.S. company. Pesticidios is planning to construct a new factory that manufactures a methyl bromide-based fumigant. The General Counsel of Pesticidios has asked you to write a memorandum detailing any international environmental obligations. What information do you need to know to be able to write the memorandum? What are the current obligations for developing countries under the Montreal Protocol and subsequent revisions with respect to methyl bromide? Does it make any difference that the actor is a private company and not a state? Does it make any difference that Pesticidios is a wholly owned subsidiary of a U.S. company?

When the General Counsel arrives in your office, she informs you that there has been a change in plans. Instead of building a manufacturing plant in Brazil, Pesticidios is planning to import the methyl bromide from Pesticide, Inc. How does this change the advice you would give the client? Would it be any different if Brazil was not a party to the Montreal Protocol for purposes of the regulation of methyl bromide?

———

C. CURRENT STATUS AND CROSS-CUTTING THEMES

1. COMPLIANCE MONITORING AND ENFORCEMENT

Assuming that all countries meet the Protocol's broad reductions in ODSs, scientists predict the ozone layer will stabilize by around 2050. In the meantime, however, because of ODSs still working their way up in the stratosphere, the situation continues to worsen with record low ozone layer concentrations reported annually over both the Arctic and Antarctic regions. The ozone hole over Antarctica, for example was larger and formed earlier than ever before in the year 2000, the last year for which we have records for writing this textbook. Although many scientists believe ozone depletion is close to bottoming out, we have not yet seen any reversal of the depletion trends.

With nearly universal ratification and coverage of over 90 ozone depleting compounds, the Protocol must be regarded as a triumph of international diplomacy. Based on data submitted by parties, UNEP claims that production and consumption of CFCs has decreased by over 86% since 1986, with one-third of developing countries stopping their consumption of halons and over half ending their consumption of carbon tetrachloride and methyl chloroform. <*http://www.unep.org/ozone/press-rel/Press–Rel–07–98–2.htm*>; Lawrence J. Speer, *New Controls on Process Agent Use Agreed To By Parties To Montreal Protocol*, BNA–IED, Nov. 25, 1998. Despite these impressive accomplishments, however, full implementation of the Protocol and subsequent amendments still faces significant obstacles. Russia and several former Soviet bloc countries requested, and were eventually granted, an extension to the 1996 ban on CFCs. Some of these countries, of course, were not sovereign nations at the time of the Montreal Protocol and London Amendments. Other industrial countries may yet have problems meeting the reduction schedules for methyl bromide and HCFC's. As many as 58 developing countries have announced their intention to phase out CFC's earlier than required, although notably absent from this list are such large countries as China, India, and the Philippines. Worldwatch Institute, VITAL SIGNS 1997, 102–03 (1997).

International Black Market CFCs

Due to a very high excise tax and reduced supply, CFC prices had shot up to $15 per pound in 1995 compared to just $1 per pound in 1989. Julie Halpert, *Freon Smugglers Find Big Market*, N.Y. Times, Apr. 30, 1995 at A1. The market for CFCs is still strong, however, in part because over 100 million older cars in the U.S. have CFC air conditioning units that need to be re-filled periodically. As a result, the smuggling market for CFC–12 has exploded. Some estimates place annual smuggling of CFCs as high as 30% of the total U.S. market and the effect has been felt by chemical companies. Both companies producing CFC alternatives and legitimate CFCs have seen their sales fall sharply. Because CFC–12 can be recycled, tracing the origin of the chemical is impossible. The Washington Post, Jan. 26, 1996 at D1.

An environmental group, Ozone Action, has been at the front of the ozone issue throughout the 1990s, spurring governmental action through its campaigning and research. The group published an investigative report on smuggling in 1995, the executive summary of which is excerpted below. What policy responses do the report's findings suggest?

Ozone Action, Deadly Complacency: US CFC Production, The Black Market, and Ozone Depletion, 4–6 (1995)

The United States government, prodded by US industry, is engaged in a global dragnet against one of the more popular commodities in the underground economy: chlorofluorocarbons (CFCs). The operation, known as Operation Cool Breeze involves the Federal Bureau of Investigation (FBI), Environmental Protection Agency (EPA), Customs Service, and even the Central Intelligence Agency (CIA) and Interpol. Since late 1994, government agents have targeted dozens of companies for investigation and impounded thousands of cylinders of CFCs. They have searched alleged smuggling centers in California, New York and Florida, and charged or implicated at least nine people with smuggling. Dozens of additional arrests may follow.

Among the findings of this report on the illegal CFC black market:

- Black market CFCs, according to government sources, are pouring into the United States at an estimated rate of 5 to 10 thousand tons a year, second only to cocaine as an illegal import at the Port of Miami.

- This report, the first of its kind, estimates the black market at a rate of 10 to 22 thousand tons per year. Ozone Action's analysis of shipping records reveals a potential black market in CFCs in 1994 of more than 22,000 tons, with suspicious shipment in 1995 of approximately 10,000 tons per year. These suspicious shipments may cost the U.S. government between $100 and $200 million a year in lost excise taxes and customs duties.

- The U.S. government's "Operation Cool Breeze" has confiscated 500 tons of CFCs. Rather than destroy this contraband, the U.S. government plans to either sell it or have the U.S. military use it. The Department of Defense is a major consumer of foreign CFCs and other ozone destroyers; in fact, DOD purchased 1,746 tons of CFCs from overseas in 1994.

Legal Production

Even more substantial threats, however, come from the shocking plans by Western corporations to continue production of hundreds of thousands of tons of CFCs well after the January 1, 1996 ban on the domestic production and importation of CFCs. If the United States and other Western countries prohibited the production and trade in CFCs after 1995–as most of the public assumes is the case and corporations were scrapping their production facilities, then Operation Cool Breeze would be a credible campaign for protecting the ozone layer.

This report reveals that the battle over "black market CFCs" is not an environmental one; rather, it is a strategic effort by Western corporations and governments to protect and enhance their market share of global CFC production. This bid for control over the ozone-destroying refrigerant market represents a "New Cold War," with the battle lines once again drawn between East and West.

Among the findings on the legal CFC market:

- Under U.S. law, companies may produce more than 200,000 tons of new CFCs in 1996, more than 100,000 tons a year from 1997 to 1999 and more than 50,000 tons per year from 2000 to 2005. Production is allowed for export to developing countries or "essential use" within the U.S.

- The West's concerns of a black market in CFCs are based in part on the truth, as demonstrated by arrests under Operation Cool Breeze. However, the real nature of the new East–West tensions was revealed in a recent note from India's Environment Ministry. In it, they accuse Western governments of waging a campaign for "eliminating competition from (developing) countries and handing over the developing countries' market for ozone depleting substances on a platter to multinational companies of developed countries."

- The U.S. contribution to the world's CFC trade is rising at an alarming rate. U.S. exports of CFC–11 and CFC–12 grew eightfold between 1990 and 1994, and imports nearly doubled from 1991 to 1994. An estimated 10 percent of the world's CFC production now flows in and out of US ports.

- A recent scientific assessment of CFC production allowed by current international rules projects global production of 2,189,000 tons of CFCs from 1995 to 2005. U.S. producers are allowed to produce 629,000 tons during this time period, with the estimated U.S. share of global production rising from 24 percent in 1995 to 31 percent in the years 1997 to 2005.

- Shipping records document that one small Caribbean territory, the Netherlands Antilles, imported CFCs from the U.S. in 1995 at a rate of more than 2,300 tons per year. These shipments vastly exceed the territory's maximum consumption allowed under the Montreal Protocol (about 90 tons per year) indicating that the Netherlands Antilles may serve as a major transshipment point for black market CFCs or as a false forwarding destination for CFCs smuggled into U.S. commerce.

———

The bulk of the black market CFCs are thought to come from Russia. At the Vienna Conference of the Parties in 1995, Russia conceded that it would not meet the phase-out date of 1996 for CFCs. Blaming its tardiness on the economic disarray caused by the break-up of the Soviet Union, Russia requested the same treatment as developing countries–a five-to-ten year extension on CFC production and use. This request was opposed by the EC and U.S., whose markets are awash in smuggled CFCs from Russia. In addition to Russia, other East European countries including Belarus, Poland, Bulgaria, and Ukraine all asked for an extension from the 1996 deadline. These extensions were eventually granted, but the large and growing size of the CFC black market poses a significant threat to protection of the ozone layer. Unless countries can monitor and control their domestic CFC production, the danger of the CFC black market will continue.

As mentioned in the Ozone Action excerpt, the U.S. enforcement initiative is called Operation Cool Breeze. As of February, 1998, the Department of Justice had prosecuted a total of 62 individuals and 7 businesses for CFC and halon smuggling violations. <http://www.ozone.org/doj.html>. Another interesting enforcement development has been the growth of regional initiatives. In May, 2000, for example, customs officers from countries in Central and Eastern Europe and the Baltic (Hungary, Poland, Slovakia, Slovenia, Latvia, Lithuania, Estonia, Romania, Bulgaria, Croatia) met at a UNEP-sponsored meeting to share policy initiatives to combat the growing illegal trade in ODSs. This was apparently the first time these countries had met to work jointly in preventing environmental crime. *See* UNEP News Release, *Evolving Role of Government Authorities to Prevent Environmental Crime*, May 18, 2000.

Reporting of Data

Under Article 7 of the Montreal Protocol, the Parties are now required to report a wide range of information to the secretariat. These data requirements include:

- statistical data on each Party's production, imports and exports of each of the controlled substances and, separately for each substance

  – amounts used for feedstocks,

  – amounts destroyed by technologies approved by the Parties, and

 – imports from and exports to Parties and non-Parties respectively.

- statistical data of each Party's annual imports and exports of each of the controlled substances that have been recycled.

- data shall be forwarded not later than nine months after the end of the year to which data relate.

Reporting is required both to aid scientists in their modeling and to monitor compliance. Nevertheless, the reporting requirements were quite controversial, due in part to industry's preference for treating all information as a trade secret. The EU insisted that its data be presented in aggregate only, as EU rules did not permit individual members to report trade information separately. Other countries and NGOs objected that country-specific information was essential to monitoring compliance. As a compromise, the EU must provide country-specific data on production, but is permitted to aggregate data on imports and exports.

Many countries have had difficulty implementing the requirements to report their consumption, import, and export of controlled substances and products containing controlled substances. Eight months after the reporting deadline for 1997 exports and imports of CFCs, for example, almost 25% of the parties had not submitted data.

In an effort both to improve enforcement and improve reporting, the 1997 Montreal Amendments created a licensing system for trade in ODSs. Each party must license ODS imports and exports. It is hoped that the ability to cross-check records between importing and exporting countries will better enable police and customs officials to track and identify illegal trading in new, used, recycled, and reclaimed controlled substances. Developing countries can request assistance from the Multilateral Fund to establish their licensing systems. The licensing system entered into force in November, 1999, after twenty Parties ratified the Montreal Amendment. Ozone Action has criticized the new system as merely adding a layer of bureaucracy to the existing trade of controlled substances, since smugglers can still forge the required documentation, while The Alliance For Responsible Atmospheric Policy, speaking for industry, supported the new system but claimed that effective control of illegal trade also requires the criminal prosecution of smugglers. Roland Blassnig, *Methyl Bromide Phaseout, CFC Export Licensing Only Gains at Montreal Meeting*, BNA–IED (Sept. 24, 1997).

To facilitate compliance, UNEP's OzonAction program has developed a training module and handbook for government officials to implement the licensing scheme. The World Bank has also proposed an international labeling system for products containing controlled substances. What other actions could be taken to improve the reporting record of Parties? Do either the licensing or labeling proposals raise any questions under GATT Article XI's prohibition against import licenses or GATT's restrictions on labeling requirements? *See* Chapter 15, on trade and the environment.

U.S. Implementation Measures

In addition to reduction schedules and enforcement initiatives, the United States has relied on economic instruments to speed up the phase-out of controlled substances. In 1988, the EPA created a marketable permit program. Using 1986 as a baseline, EPA issued allowances to five CFC producers, three halon producers, fourteen CFC importers and six halon importers. This small number of companies dominated the CFC and halon markets. Beside keeping down administrative costs, the program allowed companies to trade permits amongst themselves as they responded to market demands. Over time, allowances are "retired" in line with the overall reductions called for in the Protocol.

Complementing the permit program, an "ozone depleter tax" was introduced by Congress in 1989. The tax varies according to the controlled substance's ODP and has increased four-fold since 1990. The price signals not only capture some of industry's windfall profits and increase the cost of ODSs to consumers but have also provided a further incentive for research into alternatives. In its first five years, the tax raised $2.9 billion. Elizabeth Cook, *Making a Milestone in Ozone Protection: Learning from the CFC Phase–Out,* WRI Issues and Ideas 5 (1996). The government has also re-written many of its procurement specifications to promote CFC alternatives.

In addition to implementing the reductions called for in London, Subtitle VI of the 1990 Clean Air Act Amendments codified the marketable permit program for all controlled substances, banned the use of CFCs for "nonessential products," established a national program for the recapture and recycling of ODSs during the repair of appliances and vehicle air conditioners, and prohibited the knowing release of ODSs used as refrigerants. 42 U.S.C. §§ 7671f–7671i. In 1988, EPA had estimated the cost of halving CFC use by 2000 as $3.50 per kilogram. Thanks to the influence of government regulations and private initiatives, however, EPA significantly lowered its estimate down to $2.45 per kilogram for a total phase-out in 1996. Cook, *op. cit.* at 5. The following graph shows the effect of these measures on domestic CFC production. *Id.* at 3.

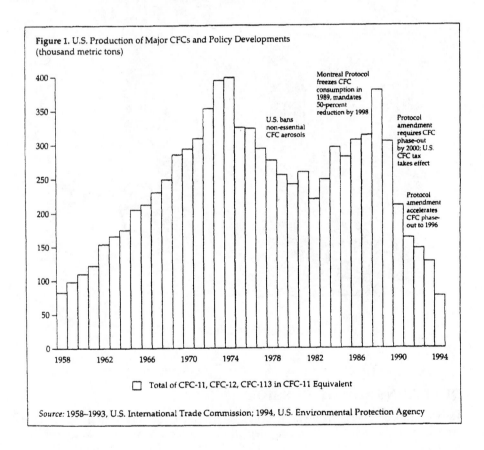

Figure 1. U.S. Production of Major CFCs and Policy Developments (thousand metric tons)

Total of CFC-11, CFC-12, CFC-113 in CFC-11 Equivalent

Source: 1958–1993, U.S. International Trade Commission; 1994, U.S. Environmental Protection Agency

THE WASHINGTON POST, JUNE 3, 1987 AT 17.

QUESTIONS AND DISCUSSION

1. Cultural or Social Behavioral Changes: In 1987, Secretary of Interior Hodel argued that the solution to ozone depletion was for everyone to wear hats and sunglasses. This comment was the subject of much ridicule, including the Herblock cartoon shown. THE WASHINGTON POST, June 3, 1987, at 17. As the impacts of ozone depletion worsen, however, we may have to consider ways to protect ourselves from the ultraviolet radiation. What role should the law or public policy play in facilitating changes in behavior? Some changes may be beyond the reach of the law, like de-emphasizing the beauty of a suntan. What about labeling requirements on suntan lotion that emphasize the danger from excessive exposure to the sun?

Although suntan lotions can protect against sunburn and other potential impacts of sun exposure by blocking some ultraviolet radiation, other impacts like suppression of immune systems are not prevented by suntan lotion. In fact, by enabling people to remain in the sun longer, suntan lotions can actually increase exposure and exacerbate the harms from damaging radiation in wavelengths not blocked by the sunscreen. Similar impacts can occur from sunglasses. The eye naturally responds to sunlight by squinting and reducing the pupil. This reduces the amount of UV that hits the retina. By blocking sunlight, sunglasses make the pupil stay open wider. Some sunglasses only block the visible part of the spectrum, however, and let ultraviolet radiation pass through to the eye. Because the pupil is dilated, increased radiation strikes the eye and cataracts are more likely. Should the law require warning requirements on sunglasses?

What other steps can be taken to reduce human exposure to the sun? One way may be to place playgrounds outside of the sun or to plant shady trees where children play. Children are particularly vulnerable to some impacts from ultraviolet radiation. Other vulnerable groups include farmers, fisherman and others who work outside. Should the Occupational Safety and Health Administration (OSHA) issue clothing standards for people exposed to sun while working?

2. One important development in recent years has been the adoption of daily UV–B reports by many weather stations around the country. Beginning in 1995, EPA started to release daily readings of UV–B in an effort to help people avoid the most dangerous times of the year as well as the most dangerous hours of the day (from 10:00 a.m. to 2:00 p.m.). These daily reports are already mandated in Australia and Canada.

————

2. NON–COMPLIANCE PROCEDURES

Article 8 of the Montreal Protocol requires the Parties to establish procedures and institutional mechanisms to determine non-compliance with the Protocol's provisions and treatment of Parties found to be in non-compliance. These procedures were developed in the Copenhagen Amendments (1992) and provide an innovative dispute resolution model.

Copenhagen Amendments, 32 I.L.M. 874 (1995)
Annex IV: Non–Compliance Procedure

The following procedure has been formulated pursuant to Article 8 of the Montreal Protocol. It shall apply without prejudice to the operation of the settlement of disputes procedure laid down in Article 11 of the Vienna Convention.

1. If one or more Parties have reservations regarding another Party's implementation of its obligations under the Protocol, those concerns may be addressed in writing to the Secretariat. Such a submission shall be supported by corroborating information.

2. The Secretariat shall, within two weeks of its receiving a submission, send a copy of that submission to the Party whose implementation of a particular provision of the Protocol is at issue. Any reply and information in support thereof are to be submitted to the Secretariat and to the Parties involved within three months of the date of the despatch or such longer period as the circumstances of any particular case may require. The Secretariat shall then transmit the submission, the reply and the information provided by the Parties to the Implementation Committee referred to in paragraph 5, which shall consider the matter as soon as possible.

3. Where the Secretariat, during the course of preparing its report, becomes aware of possible non-compliance by any Party with its obligations under the Protocol, it may request the Party concerned to furnish necessary information

about the matter. If there is no response from the Party concerned within three months or such longer period as the circumstances of the matter may require or the matter is not resolved through administrative action or through diplomatic contacts, the Secretariat shall include the matter in its report to the Meeting of the Parties pursuant to Article 12(c) of the Protocol and inform the Implementation Committee accordingly.

4. Where a party concludes that, despite having made its best, bona fide efforts, it is unable to comply fully with its obligations under the Protocol, it may address to the Secretariat a submission in writing, explaining, in particular, the specific circumstances that it considers to be the cause of its noncompliance. The Secretariat shall transmit such submission to the Implementation Committee which shall consider it as soon as practicable.

5. An Implementation Committee is hereby established. It shall consist of 10 Parties elected by the meeting of the Parties for two years, based on equitable geographical distribution. Outgoing Parties may be re-elected for one immediate consecutive term. The Committee shall elect its own President and Vice–President. Each shall serve for one year at a time. The Vice–President shall, in addition, serve as the rapporteur of the Committee.

6. The Implementation Committee shall, unless it decides otherwise, meet twice a year. The Secretariat shall arrange for and service its meetings.

7. The functions of the Implementation Committee shall be:

(a) To receive, consider and report on any submission in accordance with paragraphs 1, 2, and 4;

(b) To receive, consider and report on any information or observations forwarded by the Secretariat in connection with the preparation of the reports referred to in Article 12(c) of the Protocol and on any other information received and forwarded by the Secretariat concerning compliance with the provisions of the Protocol.

(c) To request, where it considers necessary, through the Secretariat, further information on matters under its consideration;

(d) To undertake, upon the invitation of the Party concerned, information-gathering in the territory of that Party for fulfilling the functions of the Committee;

(e) To maintain, in particular for the purposes of drawing up its recommendations, an exchange of information with the Executive Committee of the Multilateral Fund related to the provision of financial and technical cooperation, including the transfer of technologies to Parties operating under Article 5, paragraph 1, of the Protocol.

8. The Implementation Committee shall consider the submissions, information and observations referred to in paragraph 7 with a view to securing an amicable solution of the matter on the basis of respect for the provisions of the Protocol.

9. The Implementation Committee shall report to the Meeting of the Parties, including any recommendations it considers appropriate. The report shall be made available to the Parties not later than six weeks before their meeting. After receiving a report by the Committee the Parties may, taking into consideration the circumstances of the matter, decide upon and call for steps to bring about full compliance with the Protocol, and to further the Protocol's objectives.

10.   Where a Party that is not a member of the Implementation Committee is identified in a submission under paragraph 1, or itself makes such a submission, it shall be entitled to participate in the consideration by the Committee of that submission.

11.   No Party, whether or not a member of the Implementation Committee involved in a matter under consideration by the Implementation Committee, shall take part in the elaboration and adoption of recommendations on that matter to be included in the report of the Committee.

14.   The Meeting of the Parties may request the Implementation Committee to make recommendations to assist the Meeting's consideration of matters of possible non-compliance.

15.   The members of the Implementation Committee and any Party involved in its deliberations shall protect the confidentiality of information they receive in confidence.

16.   The report, which shall not contain any information received in confidence, shall be made available to any person upon request. All information exchanged by or with the Committee that is related to any recommendation by the Committee to the Meeting of the Parties shall be made available by the Secretariat to any Party upon its request; that Party shall ensure the confidentiality of the information it has received in confidence.

If requested by a party to conduct such a review, the Implementation Committee must make a report, including its recommendations, to the Meeting of the Parties, which then decides on the appropriate course of action. The parties agreed to an *Indicative List of Measures that Might Be Taken by Meeting of the Parties in Respect of Non–Compliance with the Protocol,* Annex IV, to the 1992 Copenhagen Revisions. Measures that might be taken by the Meeting of the Parties include providing assistance, issuing warnings, and suspending Protocol privileges concerning *inter alia* industrial rationalization, production, consumption, trade, transfer of technology, the Multilateral Fund, and other institutional arrangements.

QUESTIONS AND DISCUSSION

1.   The Montreal Protocol's Implementation Committee is an important innovation in international environmental law because it has both a dispute resolution element and an implementation element. It reflects an approach that facilitates compliance by encouraging Parties to self-police themselves. By coming to the Implementation Committee, Parties can ask for assistance from other parties. Facilitating compliance as opposed to mandating it through sanctions is a growing trend in international environmental law. It recognizes that issues like ozone depletion require all States working together. What advantages are there for States to initiate the non-compliance procedures themselves? Do you expect many parties to use this mechanism? Why or why not? UNEP's OzonAction program has compiled country data on ODS consumption and production on its website to provide visual trend analysis to show compliance. UNEP uses such trend analysis in discussions with government officials during regional network meetings to promote compliance facilitation.

2. As is often the case with multilateral environmental agreements, measures providing enforcement of the Protocol proved a difficult issue for negotiators. Countries are more willing to commit to burdensome standards if the sanctions and enforcement provisions are not particularly strong. Thus, for example, parties to disputes under the Vienna Convention are not required to submit to binding arbitration or adjudication; similarly, the Protocol's non-compliance procedures do not emphasize sanctions.

3. The last paragraph of the non-compliance procedure includes a provision for any "person" to obtain non-confidential information upon request. This is a potentially important innovation because it allows NGOs to monitor noncompliance disputes or activities by parties to an international agreement. Environmental groups also wanted a formal right to be able to raise issues of noncompliance to the Implementation Committee. Referring to the noncompliance procedures detailed above, how can non-State actors influence the process?

4. The excerpts below concerning Bulgaria provide a flavor of how the parties formally treat noncompliance. They are taken from the Report of the 23rd meeting of the Implementation Committee Under The Non–Compliance Procedure For The Montreal Protocol (1999). <http://www.unep.org/ozone/impcom–23–3.htm>

IV.A.   Presentations by countries

2. *Bulgaria*

12.   The representative of Bulgaria noted that her country was not in compliance with the Montreal Protocol in 1996 and 1997. She noted, however, that steps were being taken to bring Bulgaria into compliance and to phase-out ozone-depleting substances as soon as possible. In this regard she drew attention to conversion and recycling projects supported by the GEF as well as the recent development of a licensing system, increased training activity, expanded efforts to stop illegal traffic, and new public awareness activities.

13.   Representatives of GEF and the World Bank noted that the new report on GEF activities to assist ozone-depleting substance phase-out provided greater detail regarding ozone-depleting substance phase-out in Bulgaria including specific benchmarks as requested by the Implementation Committee at its last meeting.

IV.B.   Action by the Committee

23.   With regard to Bulgaria, the Committee decided to recommend to the Eleventh Meeting of the Parties:

1.   To note that Bulgaria acceded to the Vienna Convention and the Montreal Protocol on 20 November 1990 and acceded to the London and Copenhagen Amendments on 28 April 1999. The country is classified as a non-Article 5 Party under the Protocol and, for 1997, reported positive consumption of 1.6 ODP tonnes of Annex A Group II substances, none of which was for essential uses exempted by the Parties. As a consequence, in 1997 Bulgaria was in non-compliance with its control obligations under Articles 2A through 2E of the Montreal Protocol;

2.   To note with appreciation the work done by Bulgaria in coopera-tion with the Global Environment Facility to develop a country pro-gramme and establish a phase-out plan to bring Bulgaria into compli-ance with the Montreal Protocol by 1 January 2000;

3.   To monitor closely the progress of Bulgaria with regard to the phase-out of ozone-depleting substances, particularly towards meeting

the specific commitments noted above and in this regard, to request that Bulgaria submit a complete copy of its country programme when approved, including the specific benchmarks, to the Implementation Committee, through the Ozone Secretariat, for its consideration at its next meeting. To the degree that Bulgaria is working towards and meeting the specific time-based commitments noted above and continues to report data annually demonstrating a decrease in imports and consumption, Bulgaria should continue to be treated in the same manner as a Party in good standing. In this regard, Bulgaria should continue to receive international assistance to enable it to meet these commitments in accordance with item A of the indicative list of measures that might be taken by a Meeting of the Parties in respect of non-compliance. Through this decision, however, the Parties caution Bulgaria, in accordance with item B of the indicative list of measures, that in the event that the country fails to meet the commitments noted above in the times specified, the Parties shall consider measures, consistent with item C of the indicative list of measures. These measures could include the possibility of actions that may be available under Article 4, designed to ensure that the supply of CFCs and halons that is the subject of non-compliance is ceased and that exporting Parties are not contributing to a continuing situation of non-compliance.

How would you describe the Committee's message to Bulgaria in simple terms? Do you agree with the Committee's approach?

---

3. INTERNATIONAL FINANCE: THE MONTREAL PROTOCOL FUND

The parties established the Montreal Protocol Multilateral Fund ("Multilateral Fund") to provide financial and technical assistance, including the transfer of technologies, to developing countries. Article 10 of the London Amendments details the institutional arrangements.

The Executive Committee of the Fund is comprised of seven developed and seven developing countries. The chair rotates annually between developed and developing countries. The Executive Committee is charged generally with supervising and administering the fund, including, for example, reviewing all projects over $500,000, developing the plan and budget for the Fund, developing criteria for evaluating projects, monitoring the Fund's activities, and reporting annually to the Parties on the Fund's activities. A permanent Secretariat is responsible for assisting the daily operations of the Executive Committee.

The Executive Committee is authorized to call on UNDP, UNEP, and the World Bank to assist it in implementing the Fund. In the *Terms of Reference for the Multilateral Fund,* each agency's role is based on their comparative expertise. UNEP/OzL.Pro.4/15, Annex IX. UNEP is invited "to cooperate and assist in political promotion of the objectives of the Protocol, as well as in research, data gathering and the clearing-house functions;" UNDP and other agencies, within their areas of expertise, are invited "to cooperate and assist in feasibility and pre-investment studies and in other technical assistance measures;" and the World Bank is invited "to cooperate and assist in administering and managing the programme to finance the agreed incremental costs." UNIDO was later invited to assist with small and medium sized enterprises. To obtain assistance from the Fund, countries must prepare a Country Program study detailing their production and consumption of ODSs and a work program that details the planned steps for reducing ODSs (including technical assistance and pre-investment activities). These studies and program are typically conducted in cooperation with the implementing agencies.

The Fund was originally capitalized at $160 million, with an additional $80 million promised if India and China agreed to sign the Protocol. Contributions to the Fund are based on the U.N. scale of assessments. Countries can be credited up to 20 percent of their assessment for separate bilateral assistance. In some cases, countries can make in-kind contributions, in the form of expert personnel, technology, technology documentation, and training. By 2000 the Fund had disbursed over $1 billion supporting 3,300 projects and activities in 121 developing countries by 2000. <www.unmfs.org/general>.

––––––––

QUESTIONS AND DISCUSSION

1. Like the Global Environment Facility (*see* Chapter 20), the Multilateral Fund will only finance "incremental costs" (the additional costs to a developing country party of using ozone-safe, rather than ozone-depleting, technology). What is or is not an "incremental cost" has become one of the most important questions in interpreting the Montreal Protocol, as well as the Climate Change Convention, because it determines who pays (the individual country or the international society through the multilateral fund). Consider the following excerpts from the *Indicative List of Categories of Incremental Costs,* Annex VIII to the 1992 Copenhagen Revisions.

Reprinted in 32 I.L.M. 874 (1993)

The evaluation of requests for financing incremental costs of a given project shall take into account the following general principles:

(a) The most cost-effective and efficient option should be chosen, taking into account the national industrial strategy of the recipient party. It should be considered carefully to what extent the infrastructure at present used for production of the controlled substances could be put to alternative uses, thus resulting in decreased capital abandonment, and how to avoid deindustrialization and loss of export revenues;

(b) Consideration of project proposals for funding should involve the careful scrutiny of cost items listed in an effort to ensure that there is no double-counting;

(c) Savings or benefits that will be gained at both the strategic and project levels during the transition process should be taken into account on a case-by-case basis, according to criteria decided by the Parties and as elaborated in the guidelines of the Executive Committee;

(d) The funding of incremental costs is intended as an incentive for early adoption of ozone protecting technologies. In this respect the incremental costs are appropriate in each sector.

Examples of "incremental" costs include costs of converting existing production facilities, costs from premature retirement of production facilities, and costs of patents and designs for alternative technologies.

2. One of the most important developments at the Cairo Meeting of the Parties in 1998 was the decision to restrict the use of process agents–ODSs used as inert solvents in a wide range of chemical manufacturing processes. Although many process agents have been banned in industrialized countries since 1996, the Protocol allows continued production of controlled amounts of CFCs and carbon tetracholoride for use as "feedstocks" to make other substances. This use is significant, with U.S. consumption of process agents at about 2300 metric tons. It is estimated that 181 tons of this escape as emissions. The decision in Cairo establishes 25 applications in which CFCs and carbon tetracholoride may be used as process agents. The decision also creates country-by-country ceilings on replenishment of process agents and emissions of ODSs. Companies may use process agents as long as national emissions remain at an "insignificant" level, as defined in the decision. Beginning in 2002, countries that exceed their emissions ceilings will lose the feedstock exception for process agents, effectively banning their use. To address the concern that industry would take advantage of differential phase-out schedules by moving production processes to developing countries, beginning in June, 1999, all parties, developed and developing countries alike, agreed to ban new facilities using controlled substances as process agent.

A key issue during negotiation of the decision was how to structure financing. Developing countries would clearly seek assistance from the Multilateral Fund to finance measures such as process conversions and plant closures. But should funds be available for construction of new plants with efficient emissions control systems? India argued that funds should be available for construction of new and cleaner chlorinated rubber plants. Opponents countered that funding was intended to help developing countries eliminate the use of ODSs, not to subsidize ODS-dependent activities with reduced emissions. Is this approach consistent with the best available technology strategy prevalent in U.S. environmental law? Is it consistent with a tradable permit approach? So long as the net result is lower emissions of ODSs, why does it matter whether the process relies on non-ODS processes or better emissions control technology? It is interesting to note that French industry welcomed the decision since it brought the rest of the world in line with the 1995 EU ban on use of ODSs as process agents. Dupont, however, criticized the inflexibility of the new standards, claiming it disadvantaged companies that had already invested, at substantial expense. *See* Lawrence J. Speer, *New Controls on Process Agent Use Agreed To By Parties To Montreal Protocol*, BNA–IED, Nov. 25, 1998.

3. *The Multilateral Fund and the GATT.* Parties are not likely to challenge the Multilateral Fund's compatibility with GATT because a successful challenge could eliminate the Fund. But a non-party that believes its trade competitiveness has been impaired by financial assistance from the Fund to a party might challenge the grant as an unfair subsidy. A successful challenge would make the recipient country subject to countervailing duties under the GATT Subsidies Agreement. (*See* Chapter 15) To qualify as a subsidy, a financial contribution must confer a benefit on the receiving company. Does the fact that the Multilateral Fund only finances the incremental costs of compliance affect your consideration of this matter? Does it matter that these subsidies are pursuant to a multilateral agreement, as opposed to directly from a government to its domestic companies? Would it make a difference if most of the companies receiving subsidies, although operating in developing countries, actually were subsidiaries of companies from countries who are major donors to the Fund?

----

4.   TECHNOLOGY TRANSFER AND CAPACITY BUILDING

The issue of technology transfer is closely related to the funding mechanism. Initially, India, China, Brazil, and other developing countries proposed that substitute technologies should be made available on a "preferential and non-commercial basis." UNEP, REPORT OF THE OPEN-ENDED WORKING GROUP 3 (1990). When developed countries objected that they could not compel their industries to provide technology on other than commercial terms, India insisted they change their laws. But industry groups were adamant that technology could only be transferred to countries that respected intellectual property rights and that transfer should be handled through joint ventures and licensing arrangements. Ultimately the London Amendments in 1990 provided a compromise in the new Article 10A.

Article 10A: Transfer of technology

Each Party shall take every practicable step, consistent with the programmes supported by the financial mechanism, to ensure:

(a) That the best available, environmentally safe substitutes and related technologies are expeditiously transferred to Parties operating under paragraph 1 of Article 5; and

(b) That the transfers referred to in subparagraph (a) occur under fair and most favourable conditions.

Potential transferors of technology under the Protocol most likely will retain adequate protection of commercial intellectual property. The text of Article 10A, as well as its negotiating history, suggests that parties are not required to compel their industries to transfer technology under any circumstances, let alone to countries that do not provide adequate protection for intellectual property rights. What, then, does it mean that Parties must take "every practicable step, consistent with the programmes supported by the financial mechanism"?

The conflict between protection of intellectual property rights and the need to expedite the transfer of environmentally sound technologies is a recurring one in international environmental law. In the context of the Montreal Protocol, what remedies do developing countries have if they believe they are not receiving adequate access to substitute technologies? Under the Uruguay Round's Agreement on Trade–Related Aspects of Intellectual Property Rights (TRIPS agreement), countries are required to respect and protect intellectual property rights. Could strict enforcement of the TRIPs Agreement inhibit rapid phase-out of ODSs by developing country parties and discourage non-parties from joining the Protocol? Some analysts contend that strong protection of intellectual property rights could actually accelerate the transfer of technology, because transferers will be assured of a financial return and will have more confidence that their intellectual property will not be misappropriated. How would you recommend implementing the Montreal Protocol's technology transfer provisions so as to ensure rapid phase-out and full protection of intellectual property? To review some of UNEP's technology transfer activities, such as its Methyl Bromide Alternatives Discussion Forum, visit <http://www.uneptie.org/ozonaction/sector/mebr.html>.

In addition to meeting incremental costs incurred by developing countries, parties agreed that developing countries would require assistance in strengthening their institutional capacity to implement the Montreal Protocol. UNEP's OzonAction Program, for example, has been charged with developing activities such as an information clearinghouse, training, networking, refrigerant management plans, and other practical initiatives that promote technology transfer and adoption such as web-based discussion fora. Visiting OzonAction's website at <http://www.uneptie.org/ozonaction.html> gives a sense of the program's range and flexibility.

———

5. DEVELOPING COUNTRY PARTICIPATION

The negotiations over the Montreal Protocol regime, particularly in London, reflected a major conflict between the North and the South. Ozone depletion, unlike most international issues that had come before it, clearly could not be solved without the full cooperation of all countries, particularly the large developing countries such as India, China and Brazil. This fact gave those countries additional power in the negotiations requiring innovative compromises to meet their demands.

Among the compromises already mentioned were financial and technical assistance, including the technology transfer provisions described above. The establishment of the Multilateral Fund to finance the incremental costs of acquiring substitute technologies helped allay developing countries' fears that they might be charged exorbitant prices for new substitute technologies. Enticed by an offer from the developed countries to increase the Multilateral Fund by $80 million if they joined, India and China agreed to become parties. Without the Fund, and the resulting developing country participation, the Protocol would almost certainly be a failure because CFC use in developing countries would eventually have eclipsed use in developed countries.

Thus, this assistance was seen as an important part of the political bargain struck to obtain broader acceptance of the Protocol regime. Given the almost universal ratification of the Protocol in the few short years after the London negotiations, the compromises can be seen as a success. The developing countries did not want the bargain simply to be rhetorical, however, and they pressed for explicit linkage in the treaty between these assistance provisions and any developing countries obligations. Fulfillment of their commitment was made contingent upon the "effective implementation" by developed country parties of the provisions for technology transfer and for financial co-operation.

Under the Montreal Protocol regime, by 2000 developing countries were required to freeze CFC emissions at their 1995–97 average levels and, by 2005, reduce emissions by 50% and, by 2010, completely phase out CFCs. In reviewing progress by 1998, many developing countries were on target to meet these targets. Eight of the nine developing countries still producing CFCs, for example, had reduced production below baseline levels. China was the only country that had increased production levels but it, too, was in compliance with the Protocol. Daniel Pruzin, *EU Renews the Call for Accelerated Freeze on HCFC Production by Developing Countries*, BNA–IAD, July 17, 2000.

———

QUESTIONS AND DISCUSSION

1. Does the linkage of the North's financial responsibility to the South's performance have any legal status? How could a developing country use this argument in the context of the non-compliance procedures of the Protocol? What other statements or references in the Protocol regime strengthen the South's argument that the regime is a legally enforceable bargain with interlocked sets of responsibilities and rights? Reconsider Principles 6 and 7 of the Rio Declaration, at page 198. Do these principles strengthen the arguments of developing countries that their responsibility to comply with the substantive controls on ODSs depends on the industrialized countries fulfilling their obligation to provide funding and technology?

2. As suggested by Principle 7 of the Rio Declaration, States may have "common but differentiated" responsibilities in global environmental affairs. *See* Chapter 7, page 402. In addition to the financial and technological assistance provisions, the developing countries also received a differential timetable for compliance with the phase-out of ODS. Article 5.1 allows ten extra years for compliance with the Protocol control measures. By adopting this special treatment of developing countries, the Montreal Protocol was one of the first international environmental treaties to recognize the need to treat developing countries differently. This separate treatment has become the norm in subsequent conventions such as climate change, biodiversity and desertification.

3. Principle 6 of the Rio Declaration suggests that those countries "most environmentally susceptible" should be given special priority. As will be seen later in this Chapter, the small island states and other low-lying states formed an important and effective negotiating bloc in the climate change negotiations. This led to specific provisions addressing financing for the impact of climate change. No similar provision in the Montreal Protocol provides for special dispensation or funding for those countries expected to be hardest hit by the impacts of ozone depletion. As the impacts of ozone depletion become better understood, is it likely that such "ecological blocs" could emerge in future ozone debates? Would the types of provisions in the climate change convention, designed to assist in mitigating the impacts, be appropriate for the Montreal Protocol regime?

4. This discussion may bring to mind international liability claims. Southern countries like Chile or Argentina are most likely to feel the impacts of ozone depletion, yet they are relatively minor contributors to the problem. Is there any recourse for States that might be struck the hardest by ozone depletion? Refer to the discussion of the Trail Smelter arbitration dispute. What barriers would stand in the way of Chile or Argentina challenging the United States under a claim based on state responsibility?

———

6.   THE MONTREAL PROTOCOL AND INTERNATIONAL TRADE

The Montreal Protocol was one of the first multilateral environmental agreements to use trade measures to further its objectives. At the center of the trade controversy is the question whether the Protocol's trade provisions are consistent with the WTO agreements. Given the number of parties to the Protocol, a GATT dispute over implementation of the Protocol is unlikely. Nonetheless, the trade issues that faced the Protocol's negotiators, and the approaches they took to resolve those issues, provide useful lessons for future agreements and for understanding the complexities of the relationship between international trade and environmental protection. We will discuss the WTO regime in detail in Chapter 15.

The Protocol's primary trade restrictions are between parties and non-parties. Article 4 of the Protocol requires parties to prohibit:

- imports of controlled substances from non-parties;

- exports of controlled substances to non-parties unless the country of destination has submitted data showing it is in full compliance with the Protocol's phase-out provisions and a Meeting of the Parties has determined that it is in compliance.

- imports of products from non-parties of listed products that *contain* controlled substances unless the importing party has objected to the product list;

- imports of products from non-parties of products produced with, but not containing, controlled substances, unless the importing party has objected to the product list and assuming that such an import ban has been found feasible.

Under Article 4.5, Parties also "undertake to the fullest practicable extent to discourage" the export to any non-party of technology for producing or utilizing controlled substances and must refrain from providing new subsidies, aid, credits, guarantees, or insurance programs for the export to non-parties of products, equipment, plants, or technology for the production of "controlled substances." These restrictions do not apply, however, to products, plants, or technology for containment, recovery, recycling or destruction of controlled substances, for development of alternative substances, or for other emission reduction measures.

For purposes of trade restrictions, Article 4.9 of the Protocol defines non-parties as any "State or regional economic integration organization that has not agreed to be bound by the control measures in effect for [a particular] substance." These bans on imports do not apply, however, if the country of origin has submitted data showing it is in full compliance with the Protocol's phase-out provisions and if a Meeting of the Parties determines that it is in compliance. In practice, flexibility has been extended to non-parties that have submitted some, but not all, data required to demonstrate that they are in compliance with the Protocol's restrictions on controlled substances. UNEP, *Report of the Fifth Meeting of the Parties to the Montreal Protocol on Substances that Deplete the Ozone Layer,* UNEP/ Oz.L.Pro. 5/12, (Nov.19,1993).

The primary objective of the Protocol's measures restricting trade with non-parties is to encourage broad participation in the Protocol by preventing nonparticipating countries from enjoying a competitive advantage during the phase-out of ODSs and by discouraging the construction of ODSs production facilities in non-party countries. The ban on importing controlled substances from non-parties that do not comply with the Protocol's control provisions discourages expansion of production facilities in those countries. The ban on importing products *containing* or *produced with* controlled substances provides an incentive to countries that export such products to make their production methods and products ozone-safe, lest they lose their markets. The ban on exporting controlled substances gives non-parties an incentive to comply with the Protocol in order to maintain their supply of ODSs. The ban on exporting technologies or providing subsidies, aid, credits, etc. for the production of controlled substances by non-parties is intended to prevent them from building or expanding production facilities to meet new demand for controlled substances in emerging markets, particularly in developing countries.

Parties may trade controlled substances amongst themselves, but such trade is constrained by the phase-out schedules for production and consumption. Whether to place controls on consumption or production was one of the most difficult questions raised during the negotiations. The EC argued for production controls, since the relatively small number of producers could be easily monitored. But the United States and other countries pointed out that if production was limited, countries that depend on foreign producers might refuse to join the Protocol, fearful that as production was reduced they would be the first to lose their supply. The EC and U.S. also had more selfish reasons for preferring one or the other control regimes. The EC feared that if controls were placed on consumption, United States producers would soon have to look for export markets, which would put them in direct competition with EC producers. Conversely, the U.S. feared that production controls would permit EC producers to lock up the export market, since other countries would not be able to increase production to accommodate such markets.

In the end, controls were placed on both production and consumption. A party is allowed to increase its production by obtaining some or all of another party's allowed production. Why were parties permitted to transfer their allowances for production but not for consumption? In part production was made transferable to accommodate countries with small producers that might find, at some point, that their total production had become too small to be profitable. Such transfers, known as "industrial rationalization," permits parties with small producers to maintain economies of scale by combining their production with the production of other parties. Consumption transfers are not permitted because negotiators wanted to "lock in" any reductions that go beyond those required by the Protocol, and to make sure that every party, at a minimum, meets its required phase-out schedule.

Before they would agree to these controls, the EC insisted on obtaining an opinion on their compatibility with the GATT from a trade expert in the GATT secretariat, apparently expecting the expert to advise against such measures. On their face, the restrictions on trade with non-parties are quantitative restrictions, prohibited by article XI of the GATT. They also appear to conflict with the most favored nation ("MFN") principle of article I, because they discriminate between like products of parties and non-parties.

The GATT expert concluded, however, that trade measures *were* justifiable under the GATT article XX exceptions, which permit restrictive trade measures "necessary to protect human, animal or plant life or health" and "relating to conservation or exhaustion of exhaustible natural resources." *See*, UNEP, Report of the Ad Hoc Working Group on the Work of Its Third Session (1992). The legal expert stressed, however, that he was giving an opinion and that the formal decision as to whether the trade restrictions satisfied article XX's exceptions must come from the GATT contracting parties.

———

QUESTIONS AND DISCUSSION

1. Article XX's preamble prohibits measures that are "disguised restriction[s] on international trade." One might argue that the important environmental goals served by the Protocol, and the implicit linkage between realization of those goals and the use of trade measures, provide compelling evidence that the measures are not disguised restrictions. However, if the goal of the Protocol's trade measures is seen as increasing membership in the Protocol, and not minimizing ozone depletion *per se*, then do the measures meet Article XX(b)'s "necessary to" human health standard or Article XX(g)'s "relating to" conservation or exhaustion of exhaustible renewable resources standard?

K. Madhava Sarma, the head of the ozone secretariat, submitted a paper in 1999 to the WTO's Committee on Trade and Environment concluding that the Protocol's provisions are compatible with WTO rules. While acknowledging that the Article 4 trade restrictions might conflict with the national treatment and most favored nation principles, Sarma contended that the Article XX(b) exception applies because depletion of the ozone layer will have an adverse impact on human, animal and plant life, and the Article XX(g) exception applies because the ozone layer is an exhaustible natural resource. Moreover, because Article 4 of the Montreal Protocol exempts nonparties who comply with the control measures on ODSs from trade restrictions, Sarma argued, there is no discrimination among parties where the same conditions exist. *See* Daniel Pruzin, *Ozone Depletion: Trade Measures Under Montreal Pact Justified, Secretariat Tells Trade Body*, BNA–IED, June 30, 1999.

Recall that the Protocol bans the import of products from non-parties containing or produced with controlled substances. GATT Article XX exceptions may not be applied "in a manner which would constitute a means of arbitrary or unjustifiable discrimination between countries where the same conditions prevail." Do the same conditions prevail between parties and non-parties, both of which are in compliance with the Protocol's control measures? Consider the accounting requirements for parties that trade with nonparties. What apparent justification is there for discriminating between parties and non-parties who are in compliance other than to force non-parties to join the Protocol? *See also* Chapter 15, page 1177 (discussing the relationship of the GATT and multilateral environmental agreements).

2. Why are parties that do not fulfil their commitments under the Protocol not automatically subject to the same trade sanctions as non-parties? The Protocol's complicated non-compliance procedure, with its uncertain outcome, would seem to invite countries that do not choose to comply with the Protocol to become parties, thereby avoiding trade restrictions levied against non-Parties. This disparity of

treatment between parties and non-parties might be the kind of arbitrary or unjustifiable discrimination cautioned against by trade experts. These problems were recognized and at least two attempts made to amend the Protocol to apply the same treatment to parties as to non-parties with respect to compliance with the Protocol's control measures. *See* United States, *Proposal on Non–Compliance with the Montreal Protocol for the First Meeting of the Contracting Parties to the Protocol* (1988).

3.   Both the Montreal Protocol and the GATT have mechanisms that, in principle, could adjudicate disputes concerning the Protocol's trade-related measures arising between countries that are party to both agreements. Not only could this result in forum shopping (as the choice of forum well might dictate the outcome), but countries could easily be subject to conflicting requirements. The following examples illustrate some problems that could arise from adjudication of conflicts between the Montreal Protocol and GATT.

Example 1. Suppose Country MP–G, a party to both the Montreal Protocol and GATT, imposes trade restrictions on Country G, which is a party to GATT but is not a party to, nor in compliance with, the Protocol. In response, Country G brings a GATT challenge, and a dispute panel finds the trade restrictions violate GATT. To avoid sanctions under GATT, Country MP–G drops its trade restrictions against Country G. This prompts Country MP, a party to the Protocol but not to GATT, to bring a Protocol non-compliance action against Country MP–G. Country MP–G loses the action and is threatened with sanctions under the Protocol. Country MP–G is unable to reconcile its obligations under the two agreements so as to avoid being sanctioned by one of them.

Example 2. Suppose Country MP–G, a party to both the Montreal Protocol and GATT, is sanctioned with trade restrictions for not complying with the Protocol. Country MP–G challenges the trade restrictions under GATT, and a dispute panel finds that, indeed, the restrictions violate GATT. Other countries that are party to both agreements will then be unable to reconcile their respective obligations. If they enforce the Protocol trade sanctions against MP–G, they violate GATT; if they fail to enforce the Protocol, they violate the Protocol.

These conflicts remain, at the moment, hypothetical. Should the WTO need to become involved at all in this issue? What impact would it have if the Montreal Protocol parties decided that all trade disputes be subject only to the Protocol's dispute resolution procedures?

---

7.   THE ROLE OF NON–STATE ACTORS

The participation of non-state actors has been a significant factor in shaping the Montreal Protocol. Both industry and non-governmental environmental organizations have closely monitored the Protocol's development and provided the critically important impetus for rapid implementation.

Industry

Industry's response to ozone depletion has varied over time in reaction to mounting evidence of the impacts, the relative certainty of control measures being adopted, pressure from consumers, and cost-consciousness particularly among ODS users. Both ODS manufacturers and users quickly adapted to rapid marketplace and regulatory changes.

For ODS manufacturers, the products under threat of regulation were highly profitable. Any control measures reducing the demand for ODS would hurt their bottom line. Thus the earliest press releases and advertisements from DuPont and other ODS manufacturers argued forcefully for a "go-slow" approach. Later, however, seeking a competitive edge, certain ODS manufacturers actively led the effort to develop chemical alternatives. Indeed, chemical giants like DuPont had a distinct competitive advantage both because the 1978 U.S. aerosol ban had given them a head start in looking for alternatives and because of their expertise in fluorocarbon chemistry. The Montreal Protocol, for its part, established clear and certain timetables which gave companies confidence to invest in new chemicals.

As alternatives were brought to market by DuPont and others, the CFC Alliance became supportive of the Montreal Protocol efforts. Ironically, DuPont, the leading CFC producer, would come to be seen as a champion of CFC phase-outs and even make a well-publicized promise to halt the production of CFCs ahead of schedule. For DuPont, the advent of HCFCs made this public pronouncement possible. As CFCs were phased out, another chemical whose production DuPont dominated, HCFCs, were phased in. The acceptance of HCFCs diminished CFC manufacturers' opposition to the Montreal Protocol regime and helped to ensure a consensus could be reached over a CFC ban.

The experience of ODS users was similarly dramatic. ODSs were a costly raw material, thus the search for alternative substances and processes to eliminate the use of ODS often led to overall cost reductions. ODS users were not without major concerns, however, particularly where CFCs and other ODS were regarded as irreplaceable components of their products. The estimated costs of conversion varied wildly, depending on who did the estimates and assumptions over technology innovation. It was generally assumed that the greatest costs would fall on new products rather than on producers. The Society of Automotive Engineering, for example, predicted that retrofitting air conditioners to be non-CFC in all U.S. cars by 1997 would cost from $70–$140 billion. EPA estimated the costs at $3 billion. Benedick, *op. cit.* at 134.

Following the 1986 report of the WMO study confirming the seriousness of the Antarctic ozone hole, some industrial users of ODS began intensive research efforts into substitute processes and products and promised to expedite the termination of their use of ODS. Much sooner than expected, this research effort led many users, particularly in the electronics and aerospace industries, to develop and implement simple changes in cleaning processes and housekeeping procedures that drastically reduced ODS emissions. Faced with a common challenge, traditional competitors formed strategic alliances. Following Montreal, for instance, sixteen chemical companies from the United States, South Korea, Europe and Japan created a multimillion dollar cooperative toxicity testing program for CFC substitutes. *Id.* at 104.

Beyond providing certainty for capital expenditure planning, the tight deadlines forced rapid technological development. Despite many encouraging breakthroughs, however, the search for alternatives still proved especially costly for small and medium-sized companies who lacked adequate resources to research, develop, test and implement alternate technologies. This problem was even more acute in developing countries lacking the infrastructure and expertise to develop alternative technologies on their own.

In the fall of 1987, EPA organized small working groups of industry experts to appraise the technical feasibility of phasing out CFC solvent use and the problems posed by transferring technology and know-how. These workshops eventually led to the formation of the International Cooperative for Ozone Layer Protection (ICOLP), described in the following case study.

Don Goldberg, ICOLP Case Study, (Center for Int'l Envtl Law, 1994)

ICOLP is an association of international electronics and aerospace corporations created to find economically viable and effective alternatives to the use of ODS as solvents; to distribute information about these alternatives; and to encourage companies to use these alternatives. ICOLP essentially functions as an international clearinghouse to generate, gather, and distribute relevant information on alternatives. ICOLP's strategies included conducting research and development of alternative technologies; writing and publishing, usually with USEPA, manuals on alternative technologies; providing a database for open access to all pertinent information; sponsoring and conducting workshops that teach alternative production techniques; and assisting companies in developing countries to change to ozone-safe technologies.

Membership in ICOLP is open to all corporations that use ODS, related organizations or associations, and governments. Members include representatives from the electronics, computer, aerospace, and automobile industries ... ICOLP Members must commit themselves to eliminate ODS use and develop alternatives both for in-house use and for sharing with other companies. Most member companies phased out ODS use ahead of the impending regulatory requirements. Northern Telecom set the standard by phasing out the use of all CFC solvents from its worldwide operations in 1992 and eliminating the use of methyl chloroform in 1993. Although Northern Telecom incurred significant costs in changing over to ODS alternatives, these were more than offset by significant savings through the reduction of solvent costs, CFC taxes and waste disposal costs. IBM phased out its use of CFCs in 1993; AT & T completed its phase-out in 1994; and Matsushita and Toshiba in 1995. Digital Equipment Corporation went further, providing ICOLP with free and unrestricted access to new water-based cleaning technology it developed to replace ODS.

ICOLP first extended its efforts internationally by conducting several projects in Mexico designed to promote information exchange and spread alternative technologies. In many ways, Mexico was an ideal location for technology cooperation projects. Spurred by a desire to strengthen its position in the NAFTA negotiations, Mexico had recently embarked on an ambitious program to coordinate economic and environmental policy goals. Mexico was the first country to ratify the Montreal Protocol and had continued to be a leader among developing countries in implementation. However, Mexico's electronics industry-one of the fastest growing sectors of its economy-remained largely dependent on ODS. In fact, a 1987 study predicted that Mexico would be one of thirteen developing countries with the highest demand for CFCs by the year 2000.

The Mexico technology cooperation project began in 1991 by a partnership of the Mexican environmental agency (SEDUE), USEPA, ICOLP, and Northern

Telecom. The project was launched in Tijuana, where over 20 Mexican companies publicly committed to enlist in the program. Technology workshops provided a forum where specialists discussed new alternatives. For example, a 1993 joint ICOLP/World Bank workshop covered such topics as the background of the stratospheric ozone depletion issue, the economics of eliminating ODS, international and domestic legislation, available ODS substitutes and alternative technologies, and how to receive funding to support ODS phase-out. ICOLP members furnished *pro bono* experts for the project; alternative technology manuals; and access to the OZONET database. The Mexican government financed the project with funds from the Montreal Protocol Multilateral Fund. The government provided an office in Mexico City and expenses for technical experts, technology demonstrations, and implementation. While project approval and funding from the government and the World Bank have been somewhat slower than expected, many companies ultimately invested in new, ozone-safe technologies. Foreign companies, operating mainly in the Maquiladora trade zone for example, reduced total ODS use in Mexico by 60%.

ICOLP's efforts in other countries also led to significant reductions in ODS use. For example, ICOLP assisted Thai Airways in eliminating its uses of ODS. The Swedish EPA helped prepare a feasibility study for the phaseout, and British Aerospace helped to develop a technical manual to assist all airlines to harmonize aircraft maintenance with alternative substances and technologies. ODS use by multi national corporations in Thailand was almost completely eliminated. As with Mexico, however, the efforts to get small companies to reduce ODS use has been hampered somewhat by the slow delivery of financing. In another example, ICOLP members facilitated technology cooperation that allowed Turkey to reduce CFC–113 use from about 327 tons in 1990 to about 5 tons in 1993.

National and international governmental agencies played an important role in ICOLP. In addition to lending valuable technical assistance, EPA was an important facilitator in bringing together the industry partners and in creating fora and contacts to develop the concept and to spread it to other countries. EPA's participation lent an important "stamp of approval" and instant credibility to industry efforts. The same can also be said of SEDUE's support in the initial efforts to extend ICOLP to Mexico. Without such government involvement, ICOLP might be viewed as a self-serving industry group, not unlike many trade associations.

International agencies also lent their credibility and technical support. As noted above, UNEP ultimately assimilated the OZONET database on solvents into its larger database of OzonAction Information Clearinghouse that included all the sectors including solvents, thus relieving ICOLP of the expense of maintaining the database and giving it a potentially longer lifespan and larger audience. The success of the Mexico project prompted the World Bank to approach ICOLP to manage additional projects on technology cooperation in Brazil, China, India, Malaysia, Mexico, Thailand, and Turkey. The Bank was faced with increasing pressure to expedite distribution of the Multilateral Fund monies so as to assist in the phase-out of ozone-depleting substances. The combined total ODS consumption of these countries was almost 42,000 tons. ICOLP oversaw the projects, USEPA was an advisor, and Northern Telecom acted as technical advisor.

ICOLP member countries lend technical advisors and on-site project leaders. Co-financing for these projects comes from bilateral funds.

QUESTIONS AND DISCUSSION

1. In the search for a solution to the problem of stratospheric ozone depletion, one important objective has been to develop new, less adversarial models of interaction between international institutions, government regulators and interest groups. These models can also help in addressing potentially other complex and costly problems such as climate change and loss of biodiversity. ICOLP demonstrates that a new model of cooperation is possible between governments, environmentalists, and industry, emphasizing trust between parties and acknowledging the inextricable link between economic development and the environment.

The ICOLP case study also shows how sharing information and other forms of voluntary technology cooperation within industry can effectively address the environmental and economic consequences of stratospheric ozone depletion. What national or international policies can be introduced to encourage this type of voluntary technology sharing? In the United States, antitrust policies have long been a barrier to joint research, development and information sharing on technology cooperation. Recent changes in the U.S. antitrust laws protect the exchange of non-proprietary information between competitors, removing such ventures from the threat of antitrust sanctions and allowing companies to invest in longer-term, more costly research by pooling their resources. The National Productivity and Innovation Act of 1984 protects "innovative joint efforts necessary to help U.S. firms to compete internationally." *S. Rep. No. 427*, 98th Cong., 2d Sess. 4 (1984).

What incentives existed to encourage the ICOLP-member companies to become proactive? Some of ICOLP's activities demonstrate that protecting the environment can be good for both a corporation's public image and its profitability. In many cases, substitute processes and technologies proved more economical than the technologies they replaced. To what extent did the developments under the Montreal Protocol and subsequent revisions encourage ICOLP's approach to technology innovation and sharing? What role did the imminence of increased costs due to the proposed phase-outs play? Would ICOLP have worked without the technology-forcing aspects of the Montreal Protocol regime?

2. Multinational corporations, with their considerable financial and technical resources, can provide the substitute technologies necessary to eliminate ozone-depleting substances and processes. But multinational corporations cannot solve the problem of ozone depletion alone, for the use of ODS by smaller companies–particularly those in developing countries–is bound to grow rapidly unless they, too, have access to new substitute technologies and information. ICOLP's success has been based on environmental technology cooperation. This approach utilizes long-term business-to-business partnerships to promote innovation and entrepreneurship. Companies in industrialized countries work together with developing country companies to devise environmental strategies tailored to the particular needs of each company and region. ICOLP shared technology and know-how through a wide array of activities: conferences and workshops, technical manuals, an on-line database, and hands-on assistance. Can these strategies work for smaller companies? What other strategies are there for transferring this knowledge and technologies? *See* Stephen Schmidheiny, Changing Course 118–34 (1992).

3. ICOLP's OZONET was a computerized, on-line, international database that provided information on ODS alternative technologies for the solvent sector. Created by Northern Telecom, the OZONET database was designed to be a single, comprehensive source for pertinent information in an easily accessible format available to all interested parties. The ICOLP members provide the database with critical information on alternative processes and technologies. OZONET was assimilated into UNEP's more extensive database, "OzonAction Information Clearinghouse" for global use. How does the growth of the World Wide Web and other information technologies change how information sharing and technology transfer can be conducted?

4. One of the largest challenges facing implementation of the Montreal Protocol Fund has been finding willing companies in the South to adopt innovative technologies or processes. Even if all of the transitional costs are paid for by the Fund, what incentive is there for a company in Thailand, for example, to switch processes? They are probably used to their existing processes, the staff is well trained, and they are under no immediate obligation to eliminate use of the ODS. To change to an unknown technology, even one that is free, brings with it substantial uncertainty and no clear reward. How does that change with ICOLP's involvement? What other methods could be developed by the Fund and others to overcome the inertia of the "old way" of doing things and accelerate technology transfer? These same issues arise with respect to pollution prevention, generally, and efforts to implement the pollution prevention principle, as discussed in Chapter 7.

Non-Governmental Organizations (NGOs) and Citizens

Environmental organizations played an important role in the negotiations of the Montreal Protocol. Less well known are their ongoing efforts to monitor and facilitate the phase-out of ODS. The following are several examples of the range of NGO activity. How do these efforts help the overall global effort to implement the Montreal Protocol? How else can citizen groups help to hasten the end of ozone depletion?

(1) *Shareholders Liability Suit.* As part of an effort to keep pressure on the ODS manufacturers, Greenpeace and other NGOs organized a shareholder campaign against DuPont. Their goal was to place the phase-out of CFCs on the agenda at DuPont's annual meeting. DuPont rejected a shareholder's request to place the issue on the agenda, and the shareholder sued DuPont. In Roosevelt v. E.I. DuPont de Nemours & Co., 958 F.2d 416 (1992), the issue presented was whether the CFC phase-out was part of the routine, day-to-day operations of the company, and thus inappropriate for discussion by shareholders. If the plaintiffs could argue that the issue was one of broader corporate policy then it would be appropriate for the shareholders meeting. The shareholders lost the case. How would you argue that CFC phase-out was appropriate for shareholder's attention? What other steps can shareholders take?

(2) *The CFC labelling Case: Ozone Action v. Whirlpool.* In late 1995, Ozone Action, an NGO dedicated to restoring the ozone layer (not to be confused with the UNEP program, OzonAction), sued three manufacturers of refrigerators under a California state code that requires truth in advertising. Amana Refrigeration, Inc. et al., Cal. Civ. Act. No. 973286 (10/18/95). The refrigerator companies had labeled their products "CFC Free." The products did not contain CFCs, but they did contain HCFCs and were thus not completely ozone safe. The Federal Trade Commission had

long before ruled that "CFC Free" labels on HCFC equipment were misleading because most consumers would believe that the product was completely ozone safe. In the settlement, the companies agreed to change their labels. How does this type of policing of the ozone issue at the national and subnational level relate to the success of the Montreal Protocol?

(3) *Greenfreeze.* In an effort to spur the market for CFC-free products, Greenpeace has promoted the development of hydrocarbon refrigerators. Hydrocarbons, unlike CFCs, do not deplete the ozone layer and their effect on global warming is negligible. In 1992, Greenpeace provided substantial funding to a small East German refrigerator company producing an innovative hydrocarbon refrigerator. Sales of their hydrocarbon refrigerators rapidly increased to a significant market share. Spurred by potential loss of sales, major manufacturers followed their lead and hydrocarbon refrigerators soon accounted for more than 90% of all German sales. Greenpeace, No Excuses: A Report on Ozone and Climate Friendly Technologies That Documents Why CFCs/HCFCs/HFCs Are Obsolete 12–13 (1995).

Encouraged by this experience, Greenpeace has since successfully marketed the "green fridge" concept to five British refrigerator companies as well as many other manufacturers in developing countries, including India and China. Many refrigerator manufacturers, however, remain skeptical of hydrocarbon technology. Unlike CFCs, hydrocarbons are highly flammable. As a result, many manufacturers are concerned about the danger of explosion. Greenpeace remains convinced, however, that hydrocarbons are a safe and effective alternative to CFCs. *Sustainability Review* 9 (1996). Does this help explain Greenpeace's criticism of World Bank funding for CFC-alternatives excerpted earlier?

Problem Exercise: Torts, Tobacco and Ozone Depletion

> *Sooner or later, there will be litigation against the manufacturers. We talk about it all the time. If you had a bunch of melanoma cases and you could prove they came from depletion of the ozone, and you could make all the other things fall into place–it could happen. And if it happened, it would be as big as asbestos, or more so.*
>
> – Paul Rheingold, a leading toxic tort lawyer as quoted in David Rubenstein, *Is There a Tort Case in the Air?* CORP. LEGAL TIMES, June 1992, at 12.

Reconsider the broad potential impacts of ozone depletion. These harms are caused by the production of a relatively small number of chemicals by a relatively small number of companies. Are there public policy reasons for trying to hold the manufacturers of ozone depleting substances liable for damage they may cause? How far removed is the story of ozone depletion from the paradigm of a normal nuisance or toxic tort case? What are the major issues that arise in bringing such a case? Thinking through the elements of a tort claim, what are the major impediments?

Take the specific example of a soy bean farmer who believes his or her crop has been harmed by increased levels of ultraviolet radiation caused by ozone depletion. The basic mechanism for how CFCs and other ODS deplete the ozone layer is now accepted by all mainstream scientists. We know the quantities of ODS produced by the major manufacturers. We also know certain types of soy bean under laboratory conditions are stunted when exposed to increased levels of ultraviolet radiation. We are even beginning to measure increased levels of ultraviolet radiation over some locations that grow soy beans. Is this enough to establish liability in court?

One hurdle to the litigation in some jurisdictions would be causation: the requirement that a specific company's activities actually caused the specific damage. There is no way to differentiate the impact of CFCs produced by DuPont from those produced by any other company. In certain cases, for example, those involving the drug DES, some courts have adopted a market-share liability rule that allocates percentage of liability according to the percentage of market share held by each company. *See Sindell v. Abbott Laboratories*, 607 P.2d 924 (Cal.1980). Is Sindell applicable to ozone depletion?

Even assuming you are in a jurisdiction that accepts market-share liability theories, have you proven causation? To win, the soy bean farmer must show that his or her crop loss was more likely than not due to ozone depletion and not to some extraneous factor. Thus, for example, drought or cold weather might also affect productivity. Indeed, soy bean production naturally fluctuates from year to year based on a number of factors. Will demonstrating the physical harms of ozone depletion satisfy the "more likely than not" standard of civil liability? ·

In this context, what support does statistical information provide the prospective plaintiffs? Consider the case of increased skin cancers caused by ultraviolet radiation. Fairly good evidence shows that an increase in ultraviolet radiation leads to a statistical increase in skin cancers. Although a particular plaintiff cannot show that his or her skin cancer was caused by ozone depletion, the statistical increase in cancers may result in other claims. Consider the following Florida statute, which was passed primarily to allow the Florida Attorney General to sue cigarette manufacturers for increased expenditures under Medicaid:

> (9) In the event that medical assistance has been provided by Medicaid to more than one recipient, and the agency elects to seek recovery from liable third parties due to actions by the third parties or circumstances which involve common issues of fact or law, the agency may bring an action to recover sums paid to all such recipients in one proceeding. In any action brought under this subsection, the evidence code shall be liberally construed regarding the issues of causation and of aggregate damages. The issue of causation and damages in any such action may be proven by use of statistical analysis.

> (a) In any action under this subsection wherein the number of recipients for which medical assistance has been provided by Medicaid is so large as to cause it to be impracticable to join or identify each claim, the agency shall not be required to so identify the individual recipients for which payment has been made, but rather can proceed to seek recovery based upon payments made on behalf of an entire class of recipients.

> (b) In any action brought pursuant to this subsection wherein a third party is liable due to its manufacture, sale, or distribution of a product, the agency shall be allowed to proceed under a market share theory, provided that the products involved are substantially interchangeable among brands, and that

substantially similar factual or legal issues would be involved in seeking recovery against each liable third party individually.

30 Fla. State Code 409.910(9)(1994).

As a matter of public policy, is there any reason that these laws and some of the other efforts to hold cigarette manufacturers liable not be used to hold ODS manufacturers liable? Does it matter that in the case of cigarettes the victims were harmed when they chose to use the product whereas with ODS the victims only choice was exposure to sunlight?

Standard of Liability. Although causation may be the most difficult hurdle to overcome, to win a standard negligence claim against the ODS manufacturers, plaintiffs would also have to prove the companies acted unreasonably. The key to this inquiry is usually determining what the companies knew, when they knew it, and what they did about it. What factors in the history of the ozone depletion story weigh in favor of the companies? Does it matter that the companies have not violated any law, and may in fact have reduced their production of ODSs faster than required by the Montreal Protocol? On the other hand, is it relevant that the companies may have started, discontinued, and then started again research into ODS alternatives?

If your suit relies on what the companies knew and when, how can you get this information? Obviously you can sue and get discovery but you must have some non-frivolous claim to begin with. Without any additional knowledge do you think filing a tort action will violate Rule 11 of the Federal Rules of Civil Procedure? The Freedom of Information Act provides another avenue of gaining information, but that only includes information given to the government. One strategy might be to convince a Congressional committee to begin investigations and to issue a subpoena to the companies. Are there other ways to gain information?

Since no theory linking CFC's to ozone destruction existed until 1974, CFC production up to that point would likely be considered reasonable. At what point in the progress of our knowledge of the causes and impacts of ozone depletion can one argue that companies acted negligently by continuing production? Consider the discussion of the precautionary principle in Chapter 7, page 405. One possible application of the precautionary principle would require companies to act more conservatively in the face of scientific theories of environmental damage. How would this change the "reasonableness" standard?

What if the companies are still producing today? Companies clearly know that mass-marketing of HCFCs as the primary alternative to CFCs will continue to deplete the ozone layer (albeit at a lesser rate). In a tort action, under what standard would they be judged: negligence or strict liability? Is the manufacture of an ozone destroying substance today an ultrahazardous activity? Should it be?

D.   LESSONS FROM THE OZONE LAYER

This chapter has included a detailed history of ozone depletion because it teaches important lessons for the development of international environ-

mental law. While the Protocol has not proven a total success, its adoption and implementation do represent a diplomatic breakthrough. In no other treaty have so many disparate actors in international society successfully cooperated and compromised to address a global environmental threat.

At the heart of this success is the flexible nature of the Vienna Convention. Despite having only minimal substantive standards, the Vienna Convention provided a framework for the international community to respond through an evolving consensus to the urgency of ozone depletion. The Convention specifically helped to organize scientific reviews, to incorporate new scientific and economic developments, and to ensure that international policy makers had a forum for ongoing negotiation. In addition, the rules of decision set up by the Convention and the Protocol were a unique and powerful departure from the typical international rule requiring unanimous consent, moving the international response forward.

QUESTIONS AND DISCUSSION

1. The Precautionary Principle is one of the most important general environmental principles for avoiding environmental damage and achieving sustainable development. As set forth in Principle 15 in the *Rio Declaration*, the Precautionary Principle states that: "Where there are threats of serious or irreversible damage, lack of full scientific certainty shall not be used as a reason for postponing cost-effective measures to prevent environmental degradation."

Some analysts believe that the Montreal Protocol is one of the best examples of international implementation of the Precautionary Principle. Is this conclusion warranted? Despite the unprecedented international actions taken in combating ozone depletion, we certainly still are in the midst of a dangerous global experiment with respect to the impacts of increased ultraviolet radiation. In considering this further, review the chronology of events discussed above. Did the international community respond swiftly enough? Should other responses have been taken earlier?

2. Perhaps the most important question to ask is how can similar impacts from other chemicals or other human activities be avoided in the future? What standard would you apply to new chemicals? How can we implement the precautionary principle in a way that does not paralyze industry, yet holds out some hope for avoiding mistakes like those made in ozone depletion? Also consider these questions' relevance to endocrine disruptors, discussed in Chapter 12.

One possible way to implement the precautionary principle is to implement either on a national or international level a standard that chemicals must be proven safe before being mass marketed. Obviously, this places a heavier burden on the innovation and distribution of new chemicals, many of which provide important economic benefits. Is there some way to reduce this burden while still increasing the likelihood that threats like ozone depletion will be recognized early?

This could be done through an international or national agency that screens chemicals. One current example is the U.S. Food and Drug Administration, which requires that safety be ensured before mass marketing. Should we require a similar environmental screening for industrial chemicals? To reduce the burden on industry, perhaps this could be limited to persistent organic chemicals or chemicals that bioaccumulate. Companies could be required to explain where their chemicals go when their useful life is over. Do they break down into harmless by-products? Do

they end up in the food chain? Will the company take steps to ensure the chemicals are recycled or re-used? This latter step is consistent with new concepts of life-cycle analysis and extended producer responsibility. What role can international law or institutions play in promoting this type of policy response?

Suggested Further Reading and Web Sites

Richard Benedick, OZONE DIPLOMACY: NEW DIRECTIONS IN SAFEGUARDING THE PLANET (2nd ed., 1998).

UNEP, ENVIRONMENTAL EFFECTS OF OZONE DEPLETION: 1994 ASSESSMENT (1994).

Hilary F. French, *Learning From the Ozone Experience*, in Lester R. Brown et al., STATE OF THE WORLD (1997).

John Dewitt Horel, *Global Environmental Change: An Atmospheric Perspective* (1997).

Arjun Makhijani and Kevin Gurney, MENDING THE OZONE HOLE (1995).

John K. Setear, *Ozone, Iteration, and International Law,* 40 VA. J. INT'L L. 193 (1999).

http://www.unep.org/ozone/index.shtml

Home site of the Ozone Secretariat. Excellent site for treaty documents, details of control measures and dispute resolution procedures, meeting documents, contact addresses and phone numbers, frequently asked questions about ozone, and current issues.

www.uneptie.org/ozonaction.html

The homepage of UNEP's OzonAction Program.

http://www.unmfs.org/

Home page of the Multilateral Fund Secretariat.

http://www.ciesin.org/TG/OZ/oz-bib.html

Large bibliography on ozone publications.

http://www.epa.gov/docs/ozone/index.html

EPA database with technical and policy information on the phase-out of ozone-depleting substances, substitutes and new technologies.

http://www.acd.ucar.edu/

National Center for Atmospheric Research web site with specific information on U.S. efforts.

http://www.unep.org/ozone/ratif.shtml

Ozone secretariat's status of ratification by signatories of Montreal Protocol and subsequent amendments.

SECTION V. CLIMATE CHANGE

We have to be optimistic.
Global warming is so terrible for us.
For us, this treaty is survival.

—Penehuro LeFale, Cook Islands delegate,
Kyoto Conference

A. INTRODUCTION AND FACTS

Climate change looms as a defining issue of the 21st century, because it pits the potential disruption of our global climate system against the future of a fossil fuel-based economy. Policy-makers are the arbiters in this battle, attempting to negotiate between vastly different interests and challenged by significant uncertainties in science and computer modeling.

Climate change refers to the response of the planet's climate system to altered concentrations of "greenhouse gases" in the atmosphere. These gases earn their name because, like a glass greenhouse, these gases allow sunlight to pass through the atmosphere while trapping heat or infra-red radiation close to the earth's surface. If all else is held constant (e.g., cloud cover, capacity of the oceans to absorb carbon dioxide, etc.), increases in greenhouse gases will lead to "global warming"—an increase in global average temperatures—as well as other changes in the earth's climate patterns.

The major man-made (or "anthropogenic") greenhouse gases include carbon dioxide (CO_2), methane (CH_4), nitrous oxide (NOx), and chlorofluorocarbons (CFCs). These gases account for only 3% of the earth's atmosphere, but relatively small increases in their concentrations may alter the climate system. In addition, many land-use and agricultural practices directly influence the greenhouse effect or reduce the Earth's capacity to assimilate greenhouse gases. Thus, for example, forest loss often leads both to the release of carbon stored in the trees and reduces the ability of the remaining forest to absorb additional carbon from the atmosphere.

The expected impacts of climate change—increase in global temperature, a rise in the "energy" of storms, and the consequent sea level rise—could have significant environmental and social ramifications. Weather patterns could become more extreme and unpredictable and the intensity and frequency of floods, as well as the duration and severity of droughts, are expected to increase in many regimes. These conditions, coupled with warmer temperatures, could fan the spread of water and insect-borne diseases, such as typhoid, dengue and malaria. Areas currently facing food or water shortages could face increased shortages in the future. Forests and other ecosystems might not be able to adapt to the rate of change in temperature, leading to substantial loss of biodiversity and natural resources. The range of possible impacts is so broad and severe that many observers believe climate change to be the most significant environmental problem facing the planet.

Concern about climate change and calls for international action began in the 1970s and continued throughout the 1980s. In 1990, the United Nations authorized an Intergovernmental Negotiating Committee on Climate to begin discussions of a global treaty. These negotiations culminated in the 1992 Framework Convention on Climate Change ("the Climate Change Convention") signed at UNCED. The Climate Change Convention established a general framework, but delineated few specific and substantive obligations to curb climate change. Ongoing scientific research, however, continued to support the need for binding "targets and timetables" for the reduction of greenhouse gases. In December 1997, the Parties responded by negotiating the Kyoto Protocol to the Climate Change Convention, which established binding reduction targets for the United States and other developed countries.⊀Despite the growing scientific urgency, the potential economic costs of limiting fossil fuel use in both developing and developed countries have led to substantial opposition to the climate change regime.⊀ Indeed, in 2001 President George W. Bush unilaterally announced that the United States would not proceed with ratification of the Protocol. This announcement led to an acrimonious split with the European Union and indeed the rest of the world. As a result,⊀the climate regime remains a complex and controversial regime—a regime that will undoubtedly evolve substantially in the years to come.⊀

---

1. CLIMATE CHANGE SCIENCE

The basic mechanism of how CO_2 and other greenhouse gases warm the planet (i.e. the "greenhouse effect") has been well known for decades. Indeed, over a century ago, in 1896, the Swedish chemist Arrhenius first advanced the theory that carbon dioxide emissions from combustion of coal would lead to global warming. The debate regarding the science of climate change has not been over the proven warming potential of gases but, rather, over how much and at what rate the planet will warm, and how such warming will affect human health and the environment.

Although legitimate and important areas of uncertainty still exist with respect to the ultimate impacts of climate change, the range of uncertainty is narrowing over time. Perhaps most important, a global consensus now exists among the international scientific community that we are witnessing discernible impacts on our climate and natural systems due to human activities. In part, this conclusion reflects ongoing improvements in the accuracy of global climate models for predicting both global and regional impacts.

Anticipating the critical role that scientific consensus would play in building the political will to respond to climate change, UNEP and the World Meteorological Organization (WMO) created the Intergovernmental Panel on Climate Change (IPCC) in 1988. The IPCC was initially charged with assessing the scientific, technical and economic basis of climate change policy in preparation for the 1992 Earth Summit and the negotiations of the Climate Change Convention. After the Convention entered into force, the IPCC continued to provide technical reports to the Conference of the Parties and its scientific advisory body.

The IPCC is organized into three working groups: Working Group I concentrates on the science of the climate system, Working Group II on impacts of climate change and policy options for response, and Working Group III on the economic and social dimensions of climate change. The Working Groups' reports have been designed to inform the policy debate with thorough assessments every five years. The 1990 Assessments built momentum for the 1992 Framework Convention, and the 1995 Assessment's conclusion that climate change was already occurring helped to build the political commitment to establish clear targets and timetables at

Kyoto. The Third Assessment was released in 2001. They form the basis for much of the following summary of the facts. *See generally,* IPCC, Working Group I, THE SCIENCE OF CLIMATE CHANGE (Third Assessment Report, 2001); IPCC, Working Group II, IMPACTS, ADAPTATIONS & MITIGATION OF CLIMATE CHANGE (Third Assessment Report, 2001); IPCC, Working Group III, ECONOMIC AND SOCIAL DIMENSIONS OF CLIMATE CHANGE (Third Assessment Report, 2001).

To understand climate change, we must understand the global carbon cycle.

> The atmosphere is a critical part of two carbon cycles, which distribute a chemical raw material required by all living organisms. In the shorter cycle carbon is fixed in green plants and in certain microorganisms, such as algae, through the process of photosynthesis. This process takes place when sunlight is absorbed by chlorophyll, which powers a process that breaks down CO_2 from the atmosphere to form organic molecules, such as glucose and amino acids, that accumulate in the biomass of the plants. Animals, which are not capable of photosynthesis, obtain the carbon they need to produce energy for maintaining their bodily processes by eating plants or other animals that are primary or secondary consumers of plants. Carbon is returned to the atmosphere in the form of CO_2 through the cellular respiration of living plants and animals and their decomposition upon death. The carbon in vegetation is also released to the atmosphere when it's burned, as in forest and range fires or slash-and-burn farming. The oceans absorb and release vast quantities of CO_2 and thus serve as a buffer that keeps the level of CO_2 in the atmosphere relatively stable.

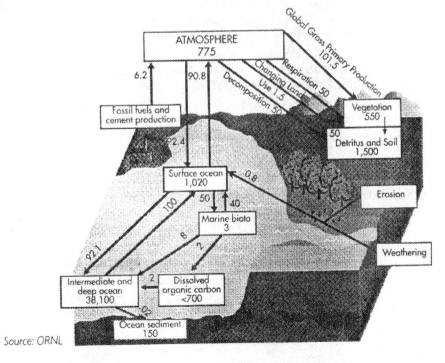

Global Carbon Cycle (in billion tons of carbon)

There is also a geological carbon cycle that takes place naturally on a much longer scale of time. The cycle begins when organic material from plants and animals slowly becomes locked into sedimentary deposits, where it may remain for hundreds of millions of years in the form of either carbonates containing the shells of marine organisms or organic fossils, such as coal, oil, and natural gas. Some of the carbon is eventually released when the geological formations in which it is locked are exposed to weathering and erosion. Human beings have greatly accelerated the release of this carbon by mining and drilling large quantities of fossil fuels and burning them to produce energy while in the process emitting CO_2.

M. SOROOS, THE ENDANGERED ATMOSPHERE 31 (1997).

LESTER BROWN ET AL., STATE OF THE WORLD 168 (2001).

In short, our use of fossil fuels is unlocking and releasing carbon dioxide taken out of the atmosphere in prehistoric times. In all, we are releasing an estimated 6.5 billion to 8.5 billion metric tons of carbon into the atmosphere every year. The planet's resiliency in adjusting to variations from the status quo is remarkable, as only about three billion tons of this amount remains in the atmosphere. The additional carbon is assimilated, either through plants and the soil or through increased absorption by the oceans. Nonetheless, the annual addition of three billion tons of carbon significantly increases atmospheric concentrations of CO_2. Ice core samples taken from the Antarctic and Greenland ice caps show that atmospheric concentrations of anthropogenic greenhouse gases—carbon dioxide, methane and nitrous oxide—have increased by about 30%, 145%, and 15%, respectively, in the industrial era. (*See* graphs below charting CO_2 concentrations and emissions over time and by economic region. Lester Brown et al., VITAL SIGNS 1999, at 58–61; Lester Brown, et al. VITAL SIGNS 2000, at 66.)

Carbon dioxide and NOx remain in the atmosphere and contribute to the greenhouse effect for many decades to centuries. This means that we have "banked" substantial amounts of greenhouse gases already, and any reductions taken today will not reduce the overall impact for some time. For example, the IPCC concluded that even if CO_2 emissions were maintained at 1994 levels, they would lead to a nearly constant rate of increase in atmospheric CO_2 concentrations for at least two centuries.

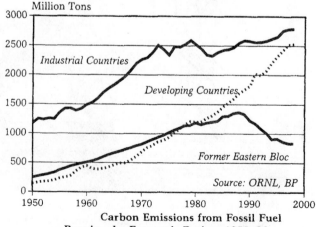

**Carbon Emissions from Fossil Fuel
Burning, by Economic Region, 1950–98**

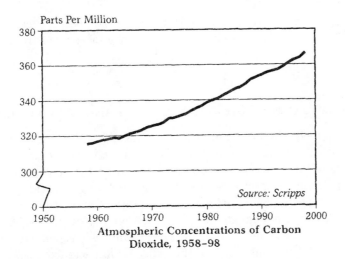

Parts Per Million

Source: Scripps

**Atmospheric Concentrations of Carbon
Dioxide, 1958–98**

Current Impact. The Earth's climate has changed over the past century, because of the increase in atmospheric concentrations of greenhouse gases. Despite variations in weather over the short-term, the long-term climate data suggest that the planet's average surface air temperature has increased by about 0.6° C since the late 19th century. In the Northern latitudes, temperatures have risen 0.8° C. *Northern Hemisphere Getting Greener,* N.Y.TIMES, Sept. 6, 2000. Nineteen ninety-eight was the hottest year on record. The 1990s were the warmest decade on record. Indeed, the seven warmest years on record occurred during the 1990s. *See* Lester Brown, et al., VITAL SIGNS 2000, at 64. Regional temperature changes are also evident. For example, the recent warming has been greatest over the mid-latitude continents in winter and spring, with a few areas of cooling, such as the North Atlantic ocean. Precipitation has increased over land in high latitudes of the Northern Hemisphere, especially during the winter.

Although some uncertainty remains over climate change, particularly regarding extreme weather conditions, the IPCC's Second Assessment could nonetheless conclude in 1995 that the observed warming trend was "unlikely to be entirely natural in origin" and that the balance of evidence suggested a "discernible human influence" on the Earth's climate. IPCC, WORKING GROUP I, THE SCIENCE OF CLIMATE CHANGE, 3–5 (Second Assessment Report, 1995). Given the conservative nature of the IPCC, this conclusion was critical for fueling the 1997 Kyoto negotiations. The IPCC has since compiled and released its Third Assessment, which concluded that "most of the warming observed over the last 50 years is likely to have been due to the increase in greenhouse gas concentrations" attributable to human activities.

According to the IPCC, failure to mitigate greenhouse gases will result in a projected increase of between 1.4 to 5.8° Celsius by the year 2100. Such a rate of warming is apparently without precedent for at least the last 10,000 years. Temperatures over land and particularly over the northern hemisphere are anticipated to be even more than these global averages. Temperatures are also expected to increase, even after concentrations of greenhouse gases are stabilized (although at a very slow rate). A general warming is expected to lead to an increase in the occurrence of extremely hot days and a decrease in the occurrence of extremely cold nights.

———

2. THE IMPACTS OF GLOBAL WARMING AND CLIMATE CHANGE

So what if climate changes? So what if the planet's temperature increases? The ultimate impact, if any, of these changes on human health and the environment is the source of much of the uncertainty that has clouded policymaking with respect to climate change. Working Group II of the IPCC was established "to review the state of knowledge concerning the impacts of climate change on physical and ecological systems, human health and socio-economic sectors." Over time their reports have helped to identify a scientific consensus on the expected impacts from climate change. Most significantly, the third IPCC Assessment released in 2001 found that climate change was *already* having a discernible impact on many different parameters in the environment.

> Available observational evidence indicates that regional changes in climate, particularly increases in temperature, have already affected a diverse set of physical and biological systems in many parts of the world. Examples of observed changes include shrinkage of glaciers, thawing of permafrost, later freezing and earlier break-up of ice on rivers and lakes, lengthening of mid-to high-latitude growing seasons, poleward and altitudinal shifts of plant and animal ranges, declines of some plant and animal populations, and earlier flowering of trees, emergence of insects, and egg-laying in birds. . . .

> In most cases, where changes in biological and physical systems were detected, the direction of change was that expected on the basis of known mechanisms. The probability that the observed changes in the expected direction (with no reference to magnitude) could occur by chance alone is negligible.

> Factors such as land-use change and pollution also act on these physical and biological systems, making it difficult to attribute changes to particular causes in some specific cases. However, taken together, the observed changes in these systems are consistent in direction and coherent across diverse localities and/or regions . . . with the expected effects of regional changes in temperature. Thus, from the collective evidence, there is *high confidence* [i.e. from 67%–90%] that recent regional changes in temperature have had discernible impacts on many physical and biological systems.

IPCC, Working Group II, Summary for Policymakers, Climate Change 2001: Impacts, Adaptation, and Vulnerability 3–4 (Third Assessment Review, 2001). The following is a summary of some of the expected impacts over the next century, most of which have been drawn from either the second or third assessment reports of the IPCC.

Oceans and Sea-level Rise. Global sea level has risen by between 10 and 20 cm over the past century, and this rise is very likely (i.e. between 90–99% likely) caused by this century's observed global warming. The IPCC estimates sea-level rise of between 9cm and 88 cm during the next century. The IPCC does not expect the rate of sea level rise to accelerate significantly, assuming that no cataclysmic shifts occur in for example the Greenland or West Antarctic Ice Sheets. IPCC, WORKING GROUP I, THE SCIENCE OF CLIMATE CHANGE, 17 (Third Assessment Report, 2001). Even if emissions stabilize, sea levels will rise for centuries to come due to thermal expansion of the ocean.

The primary variable in modeling future sea level rise, at least over the long term, remains the stability of the ice sheets. The Antarctic ice sheet is likely to gain mass because of greater precipitation over the next century, while the Greenland ice sheet is likely to lose mass. In fact, local warming over Greenland is likely to be one to three times the global average. Ice sheet models project that a local warming of larger than 3°C, if sustained for millennia, would lead to virtually a complete melting of the Greenland ice sheet with a resulting sea level rise of about 7 meters! A local warming of 5.5°, if sustained for 1000 years, would be likely to result in a contribution from Greenland of about 3 meters to sea level rise. Some, but not all models also predict that melting from the West Antarctic Ice Sheet could contribute up to 3 meters to sea level rise as well over the next 1000 years. The cataclysmic release of the West Antarctic Ice Sheet from where it is grounded under the sea, is thought to be "very unlikely" (i.e. between 1 and 10% likely). IPCC, WORKING GROUP I at 16–17.

Coastal and Marine Ecosystems. Coastal systems are expected to vary widely in their response to changes in climate and sea level. Climate change and sea level rise or changes in storms or storm surges could result in the erosion of shores and associated habitat, increased salinity of estuaries and freshwater aquifers, altered tidal ranges in rivers and bays, changes in sediment and nutrient transport, a change in the pattern of chemical and microbiological contamination in coastal areas, and increased coastal flooding. Changes in coastal ecosystems, such as saltwater marshes, mangroves, coral reefs, and river deltas, would harm tourism, freshwater supplies, fisheries and biodiversity.

Under different estimates of sea-level rise, the impacts on low-lying areas could, of course, be severe. For example, several countries could be submerged, including the Maldives and the Cook Islands. Louisiana has already lost significant amounts of coastal land because of a recent rise in the Gulf of Mexico. Under some of the more dire predictions, the entire city of New Orleans could be inundated. Florida might fare even worse. The coastal development on both shores would be threatened and most of the Florida Keys and the Everglades will be flooded according to some predictions.

In addition to sea-level rise, climate change may also alter ocean circulation and vertical mixing, as well as reductions in sea-ice cover. As a result, nutrient availability, biological productivity, the structure and functions of marine ecosystems, and heat and carbon storage capacity may be affected. Reductions in ice cover are inhibiting the migratory patterns of arctic species, such as polar bears, impeding their foraging and hunting, and disrupting the region's food chain. Coastal areas will suffer from increased and stronger flooding, sea water intrusion into fresh water and accelerated erosion. Increased ocean temperatures are a known cause of coral bleaching and other stresses on coral reefs.

Weather Intensity. Warmer temperatures are very likely to lead to a more vigorous hydrological cycle; this translates into prospects for more severe droughts, floods and heat waves in some places. Several models indicate an increase in precipitation intensity, suggesting a possibility for more extreme storms. According to the IPCC, changes in the occurrence or geographical distribution of hurricanes and other tropical storms are possible, but still not certain. Summer monsoons in Asia are expected to dump more rain, and cyclones and hurricanes are expected to have greater average wind and precipitation. The impacts on tornadoes, thunderstorms and other more localized weather patterns cannot currently be estimated. IPCC, Working Group I, at 15–16.

Public Health Impacts. The increase in global temperatures may have significant impacts on public health, particularly in developing countries. The World Health Organization identified such health impacts of global warming as increased illnesses and deaths from heat waves and air pollution; increased outbreaks of some insect-borne infectious diseases; and increased cases of diarrhea and other water-borne diseases that are particularly dangerous in developing countries. The IPCC suggests that under most scenarios both malaria and dengue will expand their geographical and seasonal ranges. In some northern countries on the other hand, the reduced cold may result in fewer total deaths even including those in countries by the increased heat.

Agriculture and Food Security. Existing studies suggest that global agricultural production could remain relatively stable in the face of anticipated climate change, but crop yields and changes in productivity could vary considerably across regions and among localities. Productivity is projected to increase in some areas and decrease in others, especially the tropics and subtropics. Many of the world's poorest people—particularly those living in subtropical and tropical areas and semi-arid and arid regions—may face the greatest risk of increased hunger. Most at risk will probably be populations in sub-Saharan Africa; south, east and southeast Asia; tropical areas of Latin America; as well as some Pacific island nations. Some of these countries also have little capacity to improve farming practices or water management in response to climate change.

Forest Loss and Impacts. Sustained climate change is expected to lead to substantial regional changes in the extent and type of forest cover, with some regions gaining and some losing forest productivity. With appropriate land-use management and product management, timber production may actually increase modestly if there is a small amount of climate change. Natural forest ecosystems, however, will suffer as migration of ecosystems is "unlikely to occur". Possible changes in water availability could also force major changes in vegetation types in roughly one-third of the world's existing forested areas—with the greatest changes occurring in high latitudes and the least in the tropics. The United States would not escape these impacts, as some scientists predict that the beech and sugar maple may disappear from the eastern seaboard of the United States, incapable of reproducing under altered weather and climate conditions.

In the short-term at least, net primary productivity could increase. Some changes in northern latitude forests are already being measured. Forests from central Europe to Siberia and to a lesser extent in North America have been growing more vigorously during the past two decades, presumably because warmer temperatures have lengthened the growing season by nearly three weeks. *Northern Hemisphere Getting Greener*, N.Y. TIMES (Sept 6, 2001). Forests and their impact on climate are discussed further, *infra* at page 645.

Deserts and Desertification. Deserts are likely to become more extreme; with few exceptions, they are projected to become hotter but not significantly wetter. Desertification, which is the degradation of land in arid regions, would increase and more likely be irreversible if the environment became drier and the soil further degraded. Shifts in temperature and precipitation in temperate rangelands may result in altered growing seasons and boundary shifts between grasslands, forests and shrublands.

Water and Ice Resources. Climate change will intensify the global hydrological cycle, which could have major impacts on regional water resources. Changes in the total amount and frequency of precipitation directly affect the magnitude and timing of floods and droughts. Relatively small changes in temperature and precipitation can result in relatively large changes in runoff, especially in arid and semi-arid regions. More intense rainfall would tend to increase runoff and the risk of flooding. A warmer climate could decrease the proportion of precipitation falling as snow, leading to reductions in spring runoff and increases in winter runoff.

Satellite data show an estimated 10% loss in the extent of snow cover since the 1960s, as well as a reduction of about two weeks in the annual duration of lake and river ice cover in the mid and high latitudes of the Northern hemisphere during the last century. Glaciers have also been retreating during the last century, and between one-third to one-half of existing mountain glacier mass is predicted to disappear over the next 100 years. The glaciers of Glacier National Park are expected to have completely disappeared by 2050. Spring and summer sea-ice in the Northern hemisphere has decreased from 10–15% since the 1950s, with late summer sea-ice in the Arctic ocean declining an estimated 40%!

Access to adequate water supplies already is a serious problem in many regions, including some low-lying coastal areas, deltas and small islands, making countries in these regions particularly vulnerable to any additional reduction in indigenous water supplies. Although uncertainty remains with respect to how precipitation will be affected by global warming, most climate change scenarios predict that annual mean streamflows will decline in central Asia, the area around the Mediterranean, southern Africa and Australia. Many of these regions are already water stressed. The reduced extent of glaciers and depth of snow cover also would affect the seasonal distribution of river flow and water supply in many regions. Ultimately, the impacts of climate change will depend in part on the ability of water resource managers to respond not only to climate change but also to population growth and changes in demands, technology, and economic and social conditions.

Biodiversity Loss. As suggested by the above discussion of impacts on forests, freshwater, and oceans, climate change could cause quite substantial harm to biodiversity. The IPCC concluded that:

> Distributions, population sizes, population density, and behavior of wildlife have been, and will continue to be, affected directly by changes in global or regional climate and indirectly through changes in vegetation. Climate change will lead to poleward movement of the boundaries of freshwater fish distributions along with loss of habitat for cold-and cool-water fishes and gain in habitat for warm-water fishes.... Many species and populations are already at high risk, and are expected to be placed at greater risk by the synergy between climate change rendering portions of current habitat unsuitable for many species, and land-use change fragmenting habitats and raising obstacles to species migration. Without appropriate management, these pressures will cause some species currently classified as "critically endangered" to become extinct and the majority of those labeled "endangered or vulnerable" to become rarer, and thereby closer to extinction, in the 21st century.

IPCC Working Group II, at 11 (2001). Negative synergies that reduce the resilience of nature to climatic changes and thus put biodiversity at even greater risk are described further below.

> Rapid global climate change could not be happening at a worse time. Massive changes ... would have been less disastrous for biological diversity and integrity if they had occurred in the past. A century ago—in a world less transformed by humans—organisms would have had a better chance of adapting to rapidly increasing temperatures, rising sea levels, and unpredictable changes in precipitation. * * *

> Now, imagine that the predictions for climate alteration had been borne out a century ago or more, before the explosion of human numbers and technology. It is likely that the expected increases in temperature and severe and unpredictable changes in precipitation would have led to ecological transformation on a vast scale (as did the glaciations some thousands of years before). Nevertheless, the situation would not be nearly as bleak for the organisms or for the humans trying to save them.

> For one thing, engineered physical barriers were much less ubiquitous. A century ago, few dams would have prevented the movement of aquatic organisms up and down river. Humans had cleared few low and tropical areas, so animals could move freely over coastal plains and between mountain ranges. Such places as Central America, eastern Brazil, the foothills of the Andes, central and southern Africa, most of Madagascar, the Philippines, Indonesia, and Southeast Asia—areas with significant topographic relief—were sparsely settled. Today humans have usurped these arable and loggable lands. A century ago, therefore, the distributions of species were much larger and more continuous, particularly in the lowlands and in coastal areas.

> If rapid climate change had occurred under these relatively benign conditions, many species could have adjusted, especially those in regions with considerable topographic relief. Much of the lowland biota could still have found safety in the cooler and more diverse climates of mountainous areas. Now, however, many wild areas have disappeared, and much of the lowland flora and fauna, if they still persist, are prevented from reaching the mountains or find the lower

slopes already occupied by reservoirs, highways, farms and plantation, not to mention armed humans.

R. PETERS AND T. LOVEJOY, GLOBAL WARMING AND BIOLOGICAL DIVERSITY xiii–xiv (1993).

————

3.   CAUSES OF CLIMATE CHANGE

To design a set of policy responses to minimize the impacts of climate change requires an understanding of the major causes of that change.

GHG Emissions. The primary cause of climate change, of course, is the increased emissions of greenhouse gases from fossil fuel burning and other industrial processes. Each of the major greenhouse gases has different sources. *Carbon dioxide,* comprising nearly 50% of all anthropogenic greenhouse gases is by far the most important. Eighty percent of all carbon dioxide is emitted by fossil fuel burning, in everything from large power plants to automobiles. Much of the remaining 20% of CO_2 emissions comes from cement manufacturing and deforestation. *Methane* is produced by waste decomposition, the decay of plants and from certain agricultural practices such as cattle production and the flooding of fields to grow rice. *Nitrous oxides* are typically produced from automobile exhaust and other industrial processes. *Chlorofluorocarbons* (CFCs) were used in refrigerants, air conditioners and other products, until their phase-out under the Montreal Protocol regime, discussed *supra.* Unfortunately, among the most potent greenhouse gases are the common alternatives to CFCs, including hydrofluorocarbons (HFCs), perfluorocarbons (PFCs), and sulphur hexafluoride (SF_6), all of which are now covered by the Kyoto Protocol.

Not all greenhouse gases are created equal; different gases have different "global warming potentials" (GWPs). The technical definition of global warming potential is the cumulative radiative forcing between the present and some chosen time horizon caused by a unit mass of gas emitted now, expressed relative to that for some reference gas, typically CO_2. Thus, for example, the global warming potential of methane is 56 times that of CO_2 or, put another way, methane is 56 times more potent in causing global warming than is CO_2 in a century. The global warming potential for nitrous oxide is 280 and the global warming potential is in the thousands for many of the HFCs, PFCs and SF_6. Thus emitting one ton of these compounds into the atmosphere has dramatically higher impacts than emitting one ton of CO_2 or even methane.

Most greenhouse gas emissions come from industrial activity and thus, not surprisingly, the United States and other industrialized countries are the primary contributors to the increase in atmospheric concentrations of greenhouse gases over the past century. As shown in Table 10.5, with over 30% of historic carbon dioxide emissions, the United States is by far the largest contributor to atmospheric levels of carbon dioxide.

Table 10.5: Cumulative Carbon Dioxide emissions (1900–1990)[1]

Country	Percent Cumulative CO_2 Emissions	Country	Percent Cumulative CO_2 Emissions
United States	30.3%	Japan	3.7%
Europe(including CEE)	27.7%	Middle East	2.7%
Former Soviet Union	13.7%	Africa	2.5%
China, India and Developing Asia	12.2%	Canada	2.3%
South and Central America	3.8%	Australia	1.1%

The United State is also the world's leader in current emissions as well. With only 4% of the world's population, we now emit an estimated 25% of the world's greenhouse gases each year. China is next at approximately 12%. Although China's emissions grew significantly over most of the last decade, in the past two years there carbon dioxide emissions have been reduced significantly, in part as they have shifted away from a major emphasis on coal.

National totals, however, represent only part of the picture, because they depend on both population size and the level of industrial activity. Per capita emissions may provide a better measure for comparing a region's contribution to climate change. Again, the United States had the highest per capita emissions—19.4 metric tons per person per year—among the nations that were the major sources of global emissions in 1995 (the oil-rich middle eastern countries generally lead in per capita emissions). By contrast, per capita emissions in India and China were 1.1 and 2.6 metric tons per year. A representative review of other countries also demonstrates the significantly disproportionate amount of CO_2 emitted by the United States—Germany 10.3 metric tons, Japan 9.2, Canada 14.7, Indonesia 1.5, and Brazil 1.5. *See* Eileen Claussen & Lisa McNeilly, *Equity & Global Climate Change: The Complex Elements of Global Fairness* (Pew Center on Global Climate Change, Oct. 29, 1998).

Carbon Reservoirs and Sinks. Complicating matters even more is that processes other than emissions of greenhouse gases are influencing the climate system. Many forestry, land-use and agricultural practices are eliminating important natural sinks and reservoirs for atmospheric carbons. "Carbon sinks" refer to processes that remove a net amount of carbon from the atmosphere (e.g. photosynthesis). Thus, carbon sinks present important opportunities for reducing the overall increase in atmospheric concentrations of greenhouse gases. The critical importance of sinks can be understood by recognizing that only 40% of the estimated man-made emissions of CO2 over the last century is showing up in the atmosphere; the remaining 60% has been absorbed either by the oceans, forests or other sinks. "Carbon reservoirs" currently store carbon previously removed from the atmosphere. Carbon reservoirs are in equilibrium with

---

1. Adopted from World Resources Institute, Historic CO_2 Emissions by Fossil Fuels,   http//www.wri.org (September, 2001).

the atmosphere unless disturbed, in which case they can release carbon and add to the concentrations of greenhouse gases in the atmosphere.

Forests are perhaps the most well known carbon reservoirs and sinks. Mature forests tend to be carbon reservoirs. The relationship of forests to the global climate system is complex and not completely understood. As the IPCC has concluded:

> A sustainably managed forest comprising all stages of a stand life cycle operates as a functional system that maintains an overall carbon balance, retaining a part in the growing trees, transferring another part into the soils, and exporting carbon as forest products. Recently disturbed and regenerating areas lose carbon; young stands gain carbon rapidly, mature stands less so; and overmature stands may lose carbon... During the early years of the life cycle, when trees are small, the areas is likely to be a source of carbon; it becomes a sink when carbon assimilation exceeds soil respiration. * * *

> Human activities modify carbon flows between the atmosphere, the land, and the oceans. Land use and land-use change are the main factors that affect terrestrial sources and sinks of carbon. Clearing of forests has resulted in a reduction of the global area of forests by almost 20 percent during the past 140 years. Management practices can restore, maintain, and enlarge vegetation and soil carbon stocks, however.

> Expansion of agriculture through conversion of forests and grassland during the past 240 years has led to a net release of about 121 Gigatons of carbon, of which about 60 percent has been emitted in the tropics (primarily during the past half-century) and about 40 percent in middle and high latitudes (primarily before the middle of the 20th century). During the 1980s, more than 90 percent of the net release of carbon to the atmosphere was the result of land-use changes in the tropics.

> Reducing the rate of forest clearing can reduce carbon losses from terrestrial ecosystems. Establishing forests on previously cleared land provides an opportunity to sequester carbon in tree biomass and forest soils, but it will take decades to centuries to restore carbon stocks that have been lost as a result of land-use change in the past. * * *

> Global emissions of the greenhouse gases methane and nitrogen oxide from land use-related activities [expressed as CO_2–equivalents] exceed net CO_2 from land-use change.

Intergovernmental Panel on Climate Change, LAND USE, LAND-USE CHANGE, AND FORESTRY, at 26–27 [hereinafter IPCC SPECIAL REPORT ON LAND USE AND FORESTRY]. Thus, forests can act as reservoirs (storing carbon), sinks (sequestering carbon) or sources (emitting carbon) depending on the relative maturity of the forest as well as the human-caused interferences and uses of the land. Over time, changes in forest cover, for example through deforestation and conversion to agriculture, have contributed significantly to the level of carbon in the atmosphere. From 1850 to 1998, approximately one-third of man-made CO_2 emissions into the atmosphere have come from releases due to land-use changes, mostly through deforestation. On the other hand, wise management of forests provide substantial opportunities for significantly mitigating the climate impacts of forest changes. Moreover, ongoing global warming and increased concentrations of CO_2 are supporting more forest growth at least in the short to mid term, thus producing an important positive feedback loop to reduce the impacts of climate change.

During the past decade, the IPCC found that forests and other terrestrial sinks have resulted in a net sequestration of between 0.7–1.0 Gigatons of carbon per year. IPCC Special Report on Land–Use and Forests, at 25.

The impacts from climate are expected to be significantly different across regions. Not all regions will face the same extent of warming for example. Perhaps more important, some regions particularly developing countries do not have the capacity to adapt well to the changes and impacts that are coming. In this respect, consider the Table 10:6, adopted from the IPCC's Working Group II, Climate Change 2001: Impacts, Adaptation, and Vulnerability 14–15 (Third Assessment 2001), which identifies some of the major issues relating to three regions: North America, Africa and Small Island States.

Table 10.6: Adaptive Capacity, Vulnerability, and Key Concerns

North America

- Adaptive capacity of human systems is generally high and vulnerability low in North America, but some communities (e.g., indigenous peoples and those dependent on climate-sensitive resources) are more vulnerable; social, economic, and demographic trends are changing vulnerabilities in subregions.

- Some crops would benefit from modest warming accompanied by increasing CO_2, but effects would vary among crops and regions (*high confidence*), including declines due to drought in some areas of Canada's Prairies and the U.S. Great Plains, potential increased food production in areas of Canada north of current production areas, and increased warm-temperate mixed forest production (*medium confidence*). However, benefits for crops would decline at an increasing rate and possibly become a net loss with further warming (*medium confidence*).

- Snowmelt-dominated watersheds in western North America will experience earlier spring peak flows (*high confidence*), reductions in summer flows (*medium confidence*), and reduced lake levels and outflows for the Great Lakes-St. Lawrence under most scenarios (*medium confidence*); adaptive responses would offset some, but not all, of the impacts on water users and on aquatic ecosystems (*medium confidence*).

- Unique natural ecosystems such as prairie wetlands, alpine tundra, and cold-water ecosystems will be at risk and effective adaptation is unlikely (*medium confidence*).

- Sea-level rise would result in enhanced coastal erosion, coastal flooding, loss of coastal wetlands, and increased risk from storm surges, particularly in Florida and much of the U.S. Atlantic coast (*high confidence*).

- Weather-related insured losses and public sector disaster relief payments in North America have been increasing; insurance sector planning has not yet systematically included climate change information, so there is potential for surprise (*high confidence*).

- Vector-borne diseases—including malaria, dengue fever, and Lyme disease—may expand their ranges in North America; exacerbated air quality and heat stress morbidity and mortality would occur (*medium confi-*

dence); socioeconomic factors and public health measures would play a large role in determining the incidence and extent of health effects.

Africa

- Adaptive capacity of human systems in Africa is low due to lack of economic resources and technology, and vulnerability high as a result of heavy reliance on rain-fed agriculture, frequent droughts and floods, and poverty.

- Grain yields are projected to decrease for many scenarios, diminishing food security, particularly in small food-importing countries (*medium to high confidence*).

- Major rivers of Africa are highly sensitive to climate variation; average runoff and water availability would decrease in Mediterranean and southern countries of Africa (*medium confidence*).

- Desertification would be exacerbated by reductions in average annual rainfall, runoff, and soil moisture, especially in southern, North, and West Africa (*medium confidence*).

- Increases in droughts, floods, and other extreme events would add to stresses on water resources, food security, human health, and infrastructures, and would constrain development in Africa (*high confidence*).

- Significant extinctions of plant and animal species are projected and would impact rural livelihoods, tourism, and genetic resources (*medium confidence*).

- Coastal settlements in, for example, the Gulf of Guinea, Senegal, Gambia, Egypt, and along the East–Southern African coast would be adversely impacted by sea-level rise through inundation and coastal erosion (*high confidence*).

Small Island States

- Adaptive capacity of human systems is generally low in small island states, and vulnerability high; small island states are likely to be among the countries most seriously impacted by climate change.

- The projected sea-level rise of 5 mm/yr for the next 100 years would cause enhanced coastal erosion, loss of land and property, dislocation of people, increased risk from storm surges, reduced resilience of coastal ecosystems, saltwater intrusion into freshwater resources, and high resource costs to respond to and adapt to these changes (*high confidence*).

- Islands with very limited water supplies are highly vulnerable to the impacts of climate change on the water balance (*high confidence*).

- Coral reefs would be negatively affected by bleaching and by reduced calcification rates due to higher CO_2 levels (*medium confidence*); mangrove, sea grass bed, and other coastal ecosystems and the associated biodiversity would be adversely affected by rising temperatures and accelerated sea-level rise (*medium confidence*).

- Limited arable land and soil salinization makes agriculture of small island states, both for domestic food production and cash crop exports, highly vulnerable to climate change (*high confidence*).

- Tourism, an important source of income and foreign exchange for many islands, would face severe disruption from climate change and sea-level rise (*high confidence*).

QUESTIONS AND DISCUSSION

1. Any discussions of the impacts of climate change have to consider the significant uncertainty that persists in predicting with any precision the types and extent of impacts from a change in our climate. This is particularly true with respect to the impact of changes in precipitation (as opposed to changes in temperature). The existing models do not yet appear to be very predictive with respect to the impacts of changes in precipitation, even as we are gaining more clarity with respect to the impact from the general warming of the planet. In addition, the potential that we are approaching an "environmental cliff" where climate change may trigger non-linear and more catastrophic results is possible, albeit uncertain. Take for example the following excerpt from the IPCC.

> Projected climate changes during the 21st century have the potential to lead to future large-scale and possibly irreversible changes in Earth systems resulting in impacts at continental and global scales. These possibilities are very climate scenario-dependent and a full range of plausible scenarios has not yet been evaluated. Examples include significant slowing of the ocean circulation that transports warm water to the North Atlantic, large reductions in the Greenland and West Antarctic Ice Sheets, accelerated global warming due to carbon cycle feedbacks in the terrestrial biosphere, and releases of terrestrial carbon from permafrost regions and methane from hydrates in coastal sediments. The likelihood of many of these changes in Earth systems is not well-known, but is probably very low; however, their likelihood is expected to increase with the rate, magnitude, and duration of climate change.

> If these changes in Earth systems were to occur, their impacts would be widespread and sustained. For example, significant slowing of the oceanic thermohaline circulation would impact deep-water oxygen levels and carbon uptake by oceans and marine ecosystems, and would reduce warming over parts of Europe. Disintegration of the West Antarctic Ice Sheet or melting of the Greenland Ice Sheet could raise global sea level up to 3 m each over the next 1,000 years, submerge many islands, and inundate extensive coastal areas. Depending on the rate of ice loss, the rate and magnitude of sea-level rise could greatly exceed the capacity of human and natural systems to adapt without substantial impacts. Releases of terrestrial carbon from permafrost regions and methane from hydrates in coastal sediments, induced by warming, would further increase greenhouse gas concentrations in the atmosphere and amplify climate change.

2. *Sulfates and Global Cooling.* Some of the greatest confusion regarding climate change, among both scientists and policymakers, has been the role of sulfate particulate emissions in the global climate system. Sulfate particulates (also called sulfate aerosols) are emitted from the combustion of fossil fuels and biomass. Unlike CO_2, however, sulfate particulates have a cooling effect on the planet, essentially because they reflect sunlight away from the earth's surface. The relative magnitude of this cooling effect was not well understood until recently. Indeed, in the 1970s the relative effect of aerosol cooling was thought by some scientists to be greater than the global warming effect of the same emissions. As a result, some scientists were for a short time worried about a global cooling! Indeed, global cooling was one of the major concerns at the 1972 Stockholm Conference.

Since then, our understanding of the effect of aerosols has increased. The net effect of sulfate aerosols is now recognized to be less than the warming effect of CO_2, although locally the cooling from aerosol emissions can completely mask or offset the warming effect due to greenhouse gases. While the cooling is typically focused in particular regions, it can have impacts on a continent's or hemisphere's overall climate patterns. This means some areas of the globe may be experiencing cooling as a result of fossil fuel combustion. Moreover, anthropogenic sulfate aerosols are short-lived in the atmosphere (a matter of weeks as compared to decades for CO_2 and NOx). As a result, the cooling effect of sulfate aerosols on climate adjusts rapidly to increases or decreases in emissions. Thus, as we reduce fossil fuel emissions, the masking effect of the aerosols will end sooner than the warming affects of the greenhouse gases.

3.   *Feedback Loops.* Among the important remaining uncertainties for predicting the ultimate ramifications of climate change are the series of "feedback loops" in the planet's climate system. Some of these feedback loops may intensify the global warming impact of climate change (positive feedback loops), while others may tend to minimize the impacts of global warming (negative feedback loops). For example, as the atmosphere warms, it should hold more water vapor, which in turn will cause an increase in temperature. More clouds are also expected to form, but their effect on temperature will depend on whether they are low cumulus clouds, which tend to reflect sunlight, or high cirrus clouds, which tend to trap heat. The reduction in ice and snowcover because of an increase in temperature will provide a positive feedback, as the so-called albedo effect (the earth's reflectivity) will decrease, reflecting less sunlight away from the earth's surface. On the other hand, CO_2 can spur the growth of plants (all other factors being equal), which in turn increases the amount of carbon removed from the atmosphere by photosynthesis. This latter negative feedback loop is often emphasized by those who argue that climate change will not be substantial.

4.   Unfortunately, it appears that the developing countries may be the hardest hit by the impacts of climate change and in any event have limited resources with which to adapt to the changes that are coming.

The ability of human systems to adapt to and cope with climate change depends on such factors as wealth, technology, education, information, skills, infrastructure, access to resources, and management capabilities. There is potential for developed and developing countries to enhance and/or acquire adaptive capabilities. Populations and communities are highly variable in their endowments with these attributes, and the developing countries, particularly the least developed countries, are generally poorest in this regard. As a result, they have lesser capacity to adapt and are more vulnerable to climate change damages, just as they are more vulnerable to other stresses. This condition is most extreme among the poorest people. * * *

The projected distribution of economic impacts is such that it would increase the disparity in well-being between developed countries and developing countries, with disparity growing for higher projected temperature increases....* * *

The effects of climate change are expected to be greatest in developing countries in terms of loss of life and relative effects on investment and the economy. For example, the relative percentage damages to GDP from climate extremes have been substantially greater in developing countries than in developed countries.

IPPC Working Group II, at 8.

5.   Often the media and others confuse weather with climate. Weather refers to meteorological conditions at a specific place and time, including temperature, humidity, wind, precipitation, and barometric pressure. Climate refers to weather patterns that prevail over extended periods of time, including both average and extreme weather. Climate change often receives front-page media coverage only during droughts or floods. Unfortunately, this means that as soon as the weather breaks or appears to go back to normal, media coverage wanes and many people are left believing that the climate change stories were a false alarm.

The variability that is inherent in weather masks the long-term trends of climate, making it even more difficult to actually measure changes in climate. In 1997, when President Clinton was hoping to build political support for a stronger U.S. position on the reduction of greenhouse gases, he invited many of the nation's weather reporters to the White House for a briefing on climate change. He then asked them to return home and educate people about what was happening to the global climate. Does this seem like a good tactic for building political support for an international agreement?

B.   RESPONDING TO CLIMATE CHANGE

The scientific understanding of climate change is fundamental to determining the appropriate policy response. The potential economic, environmental and social impacts of climate change are hard to ignore, and many of these impacts are beginning to be observed. At the same time, many of the impacts are still uncertain or poorly understood. Moreover, forgoing development now to avoid uncertain climate impacts in the future does not resonate well with countries of the Global South grappling with poverty and underdevelopment. These arguments are often supported by countries (and industries) with vested interests in the continued production and consumption of fossil fuels that have tried to drive the scientific debate through a well-funded, but small, group of self-proclaimed "global warming skeptics."

----

1.   MITIGATION AND ADAPTATION STRATEGIES

A wide range of policy options are available for curbing the impacts of greenhouse gases, although many of them require significant restructuring of our economies, particularly the energy and transportation sectors. The international negotiations have focused on imposing clear national targets and timetables for overall reduction of greenhouse gases, but ultimately left the policy mix of how to achieve the targets and timetables largely to the national governments.

In 1995, Working Group III of the IPCC succinctly listed the difficult problems facing decisionmakers in designing policies to curb climate change:

a considerable number of remaining uncertainties (which are inherent in the complexity of the problem), the potential for irreversible damages or costs, a very long planning horizon, long time lags between emissions and effects, wide regional variation in causes and effects, the irreducibly global scope of the problem, and the need to consider multiple greenhouse gases and aerosols. Yet another complication arises from the fact that effective protection of the climate system requires global cooperation.

IPCC Working Group III, *Summary for Policymakers: The Economic and Social Dimensions of Climate Change* (1995). The IPCC then made several general recommendations for responding to climate change. They recommend a portfolio of actions aimed at mitigation, adaptation and research—a portfolio that varies over time and between countries. Earlier mitigation will increase the flexibility and reduce the costs of necessary responses later. The choice of abatement paths involved balancing the economic risks of rapid abatement now (risks that capital stock will be retired prematurely and unnecessarily) against the corresponding risk of delay (risks that more rapid emissions reductions will then be required, necessitating premature retirement of future capital stock).

Generally, policymakers have focused on the "no-regrets" approach to climate change policy, undertaking measures such as improvements in energy efficiency, forest management, and air pollution control, that provide economic and environmental benefits additional to any climate benefits that may be achieved. Increased energy efficiency technologies often pay for themselves through lower energy costs. Reducing air emissions may improve local public health conditions more than the cost of the technologies. Thus, these "no-regrets" policies make good sense, and can be pursued even while the extent of harm from climate change remains uncertain.

Increasing Energy Efficiency. One major policy goal is to increase energy efficiency, so that we get the same amount of "work" from burning less fossil fuels. Energy efficiency technologies provide a growing opportunity for protecting the environment and saving energy costs. Innovations like high-efficiency light-bulbs, refrigerators and other household appliances can greatly reduce the amounts of energy use and reduce overall operating costs. They also offer every individual an opportunity to participate in responding to climate change.

Fuel Switching. Another major strategy is fuel switching, moving the economy away from fossil fuels and towards cleaner technologies. Best among these alternatives are solar and wind power, and hydrogen fuel cells, which have limited environmental impacts—but hydroelectric, geothermal and nuclear sources of energy also result in lower GHG emissions than traditional fossil-fuel sources. Even switching from coal and oil to natural gas, which is far more efficient, can result in significantly lower emissions.

Restructuring Transportation. Transportation accounts for a significant percentage of greenhouse gas emissions. New technologies such as fuel cell, electric or super-efficient cars will likely soon be mass-produced, offering a major opportunity for reduced greenhouse gas emissions from automobile travel. Additionally, enhanced public transportation policies and improved land-use patterns could significantly reduce the use of automobiles and thus the resulting GHG emissions.

Expanding Sinks and Reservoirs. CO_2 emissions may be offset if the carbon sequestration impacts of forests and other carbon sinks are enhanced. Reforestation and improved control of forest fires are important strategies for responding to climate change.

Carbon Taxes. Many analysts have recommended the use of carbon taxes as a way to establish appropriate market incentives for increasing the conservation of energy and encouraging switches away from more polluting fuels. A carbon tax on the order of $100 per ton of carbon (approximately 30 cents per gallon of gasoline) is the common estimate of what it would take to change consumption significantly. The carbon tax has proven to be very controversial in the United States, where energy prices are the lowest in the world, but the European Union has endorsed such a tax subject to U.S. adoption.

Other greenhouse gases offer similar opportunities for control without significant costs. Methane emissions from solid waste landfills, for example, can be recovered and used to produce energy. Emissions from leaky oil and gas pipelines can also pay for themselves through increased efficiency. Other sources are more difficult. Scientists have experimented with different cattle feeds that can actually reduce the amount of methane "emitted" from the digestive tracts of cattle. New agricultural practices for the production of rice are also being explored.

Obviously, the key to many of these options is technological innovation. In its 2001 report, the IPCC provided the following conclusion with respect to advances in technology.

> Significant technical progress relevant to greenhouse gas emissions reduction has been made since the SAR in 1995 and has been faster than anticipated. Advances are taking place in a wide range of technologies at different stages of development, e.g., the market introduction of wind turbines, the rapid elimination of industrial by-product gases such as N20 from adipic acid production and perfluorocarbons from aluminum production, efficient hybrid engine cars, the advancement of fuel cell technology, and the demonstration of underground carbon dioxide storage. Technological options for emissions reduction include improved efficiency of end use devices and energy conversion technologies, shift to low-carbon and renewable biomass fuels, zero-emissions technologies, improved energy management, reduction of industrial by-product and process gas emissions, and carbon removal and storage.

Intergovernmental Panel on Climate Change, Working Group III, Summary for Policymakers, CLIMATE CHANGE 2001: MITIGATION, at 5 (Third Assessment Report, 2001).

———————

2. UNDERSTANDING THE COSTS AND BENEFITS OF PREVENTING CLIMATE CHANGE

Much of the current debate regarding the appropriate response to climate change is related to an evaluation of the benefits and costs of different strategies. Of course, given the enormous range and complexity of the potential impacts from climate change (described above), it is no surprise to find that estimates of costs and benefits vary considerably and are shrouded with significant levels of uncertainty.

Relatively crude yet nonetheless informative efforts have been made to quantify the costs of reducing greenhouse gas emissions to 1990 levels or below. Different models running different assumptions can arrive at vastly different estimates of the costs. Defensible predictions have placed the cost of controlling greenhouse gas emissions at between $20 per ton and $400 per ton. The IPCC concluded after reviewing a number of different scenarios, that at least half of the necessary emissions reductions would pay for themselves through lower energy costs and the other half would settle out at around $100 per ton. The United States, at least under President Clinton, settled on an estimate closer to the $20. Its estimate assumed the United States would gain much of its reductions under emissions trading and other flexibility mechanisms. Consider as well the following discussion of costs and benefits.

World Resources Institute, *Atmosphere and Climate*, in WORLD RESOURCES 1996–97, at 320–24 (1997)

Economic Costs of Controlling Emissions

Economic analysis of the costs and benefits of reducing carbon dioxide emissions can help policymakers decide whether emissions should be curtailed and, if so, how much and on what kind of schedule. However, assigning realistic dollar values to these various costs and benefits has proved extremely difficult. In spite of much effort, analyses are still somewhat rudimentary, with results varying from study to study because of differences in background assumptions such as the availability and cost of new energy-efficient technologies or the projected growth in the global economy (and thus the growth in emissions). . . . Nonetheless, IPCC has drawn a number of tentative conclusions from a recent review of these studies.

In general, estimates of the annual costs of holding national CO_2 emissions at their 1990 levels run at about 1 to 2 percent of the gross domestic product (GDP) in OECD countries over the long term. Reducing emissions substantially below 1990 levels could cost as much as 3 percent of GDP. Bottom-up studies are more optimistic, suggesting that the costs of reducing emissions 20 percent below 1990 levels within several decades are negligible to negative. In the long term, similar studies suggest, 50 percent reductions in emissions may be possible without increasing the costs of the total energy system. Such conclusions are possible, the studies assert, because many energy-efficiency improvements pay for themselves with the savings on energy costs. As much as 10 to 30 percent of current energy demand could be eliminated with off-the-shelf and soon-to-be-available technologies, such as better electric motors, more fuel-efficient cars, and better insulation of dwellings. Realizing these potential savings, however, relies on adopting policy measures such as energy or fuel-efficiency standards for appliances and cars and eliminating market distortions such as low, subsidized energy prices that reduce the economic benefit to the consumer of saving energy. * * *

The timing of emission reductions can have a large effect on abatement costs. Under certain circumstances, deferring emission reductions somewhat may save money because the cost per ton of reducing emissions is expected to decline with time. This is because the costs of renewable energy sources such as solar or wind energy are expected to go down. At the same time, new, more efficient industrial processes and consumer products will be coming on line. In addition, when emissions are deferred, capital equipment such as industrial boilers, vehicles, or air-conditioning systems can be turned over naturally at the end of their life cycles rather than being replaced sooner with more efficient, but more expensive, models. The trade-off, of course, is that delaying emissions in the beginning necessitates steeper cuts later on or, alternatively, accepting a higher rate of global warming. A key finding from many economic analyses is the important role that research and development can play in lowering the costs of reducing emissions. Vigorous promotion of research and development that focuses on renewable energy sources and energy-efficient technologies can cut the eventual costs of abatement significantly, and is therefore considered a prudent investment even in the near term, particularly if emission cuts are delayed and new technologies are being relied upon to drastically reduce emissions in the future. * * *

Economic Benefits of Reducing Emissions

If setting a price tag on the costs of cutting greenhouse gas emissions is difficult, determining the dollar value of the benefits is even more problematic. The primary benefit of abatement is avoiding the damages associated with global warming, which include coastal inundation from rising sea levels, disruption of rainfall and therefore water use patterns, agricultural effects due to heat stress, and ecosystem damage such as loss of biodiversity and habitat disruption. Other important potential benefits also come from cutting energy-related emissions, however such as cleaner air, reduced damage to crops and forests, and less environmental disruption from fossil fuel extraction. These not only have an economic value but are widely accorded a higher and more urgent priority by many countries and communities.

Pricing the damages from additional global warming involves many unknowns, since the actual extent and regional distribution of the effects are uncertain. Also, although some effects such as property loss or crop damage are relatively easy to quantify, quantification of damage to environmental amenities such as clean functioning ecosystems, or biodiversity has always been troublesome for economists because these are intangibles not traded in the market and their value to human welfare has not been quantified. The long-term and uncertain nature of climate change also complicates the pricing of damages, since many of these damages occur in the future and standard economic practice involves discounting these to some lesser, present-day value so that they are comparable to benefits and costs today. The choice of the "discount rate"—the interest rate used to discount the damages—then becomes crucial in estimating the monetary value of the effects from global warming that future generations will suffer.

Despite these difficulties, a number of studies have tried to price the damages expected from global warming. These studies generally assume a doubling of the atmospheric carbon dioxide concentration from pre-industrial levels, leading to an average 2.5 C warming. Under these conditions, a very limited set of damages has been estimated at 1 to 1.5 percent of GDP per year in developed countries and 2 to 9 percent of GDP per year in developing countries, with island nations potentially suffering much higher damages. Of course, carbon dioxide concentrations may not stop at a doubling, and warming may continue, in which case additional damage will occur. In fact, they may rise geometrically as warming proceeds. For example, damages from a 10_ C rise might reach 6 percent of GDP or more. There is also the risk of a climate catastrophe in which the global climate regime changes quickly in unforeseen and deleterious ways. In this case, the damage could escalate rapidly.

Other benefits—both local and regional—of emissions abatement, including air quality improvements can be quite high. For example, one study estimated that the value of air quality benefits in India from freezing emissions at 1990 levels would actually exceed the costs of the freeze. Likewise, studies in Europe and the United States indicate that such non-climate-related benefits could offset 30 to 100 percent of abatement costs. At least some economists who have studied the matter believe that taking into account both climate and other benefits of cutting carbon dioxide and the need to avoid the risk of a climate disaster provide a plausible economic justification for making substantial investments in emissions abatement.

_____

QUESTIONS AND DISCUSSION

1. Are traditional cost-benefit analyses like the above useful in addressing an issue as complex and unpredictable as climate change? Some economic reviews of climate change suggest that no action should be taken. In 1995, the *Economist* magazine, for example, argued that the uncertainty over both the costs and benefits of global warming (because some areas of the world might benefit from a warmer climate) and the affect of discounting future costs counsel against taking extreme action today. The pessimistic prediction that global warming would reduce the world's income by 20% a century hence, it is argued, simply means that "the world economy expands a little more slowly than otherwise," since "the world economy could, if recent growth continues, be over 300% bigger in 2095 than today—and so that much better able to bear the costs of coping with climate change." Asking the hard question—why should people sacrifice today for a problem whose extent and cost remain uncertain?—the *Economist* argues that "There are more pressing environmental concerns such as urban smog, the spread of disease and inadequate sanitation in poor countries. Unlike global warming, these cause enormous suffering for millions of people now. And it would cost less to alleviate or even eliminate them than to reduce sharply the world's output of greenhouse gases." *Stay Cool,* THE ECONOMIST, Apr. 1, 1995, at 11.

Does this approach suggest that we should take no steps to curb climate change? Or does it argue more for taking the "no regrets" steps? How do these economic arguments reflect the risk of an all-out climate catastrophe from climate change? Even if this risk is low, do traditional economic-based arguments reflect our risk-aversion to major damage? Also, how confident are we that any estimate of costs adequately reflect harm to natural ecosystems on the scale presented by climate change?

2. Much of this chapter has emphasized the costs that will occur from climate change. While these costs will clearly and significantly outweigh any benefits from climate change, some beneficial impacts can nonetheless be identified. The IPPC, for example, identified the following benefits:

- Increased potential crop yields in some regions at mid-latitudes for increases in temperature of less than a few ËC.

- A potential increase in global timber supply from appropriately managed forests.

- Increased water availability for populations in some water-scarce regions-for example, in parts of southeast Asia.

- Reduced winter mortality in mid-and high-latitudes. Reduced energy demand for space heating due to higher winter temperatures.

IPCC Working Group I, at 5–6

3.   Some observers have been pushing for global technological fixes to the climate change problem. Most commonly discussed is massive fertilization of the ocean with iron to stimulate the growth of algae and plankton, which in turn would sequester more carbon from the atmosphere. Initial experiments in such ocean fertilization have already begun. In 1999, an international research team dumped over 8600 kilograms of iron into the ocean off the coast of Tasmania. One month later, the algae bloom could be seen from satellites and an estimated 3000 tons of carbon were removed from the atmosphere to the sea. Margaret Munro, *Ironing Out Global Warming,* THE NATIONAL POST, A18 (Oct. 17, 2000); Phillip Boyd, et al, *A Mesoscale Phytoplankton Bloom in the Polar Southern Ocean Stimulated by Iron Fertilization,* NATURE 695–702 (Oct. 12, 2000). Do you see any potential problems with massive fertilization of the oceans? Does this seem like an acceptable method to reduce concentrations of carbon in the atmosphere?

C.   THE GLOBAL POLITICS OF CLIMATE CHANGE

At times, divisions between blocs of countries over the negotiations of the climate change regime have been as intense as virtually any issues outside the realm of war and national defense. The most consistent divisions have included a split between the North and South; between various countries within the G–77, for example differences between low-lying states (the victims of climate change) and the oil-producing states (primary beneficiaries of fossil fuel dependence); and between the European Union and the United States. Although these divisions ebb and flow, most of these tensions have persisted throughout the negotiation of the climate regime beginning before the 1992 Earth Summit.

1.   *The North–South split*

The split in negotiations between the industrialized and developing countries is particularly intense because consumption of fossil fuels (and thus the release of greenhouse gases) is viewed as inextricably linked to economic development. Developing countries do not want to accept any requirement through the climate change negotiations that will slow their economic growth. The international concern with climate change arguably distracts attention from the more pressing concerns of urban air pollution and lack of safe drinking water. Moreover, by most measures, industrialized countries are primarily responsible for the current composition of the atmosphere. Although China now ranks as the second largest emitter of greenhouse gases behind the United States, its *per capita* emissions are less than 1/8th that of the United States. India's emissions are less than 1/20th of the United States. Furthermore, given that CO_2 and other greenhouse gases remain in the atmosphere for decades or more, the industrialized countries have "banked" an even greater percentage of the total responsibility for global warming. To developing countries, this is compelling justification for requiring industrialized countries to make significant reductions in greenhouse gas emissions first. On the other hand, emissions are growing fastest in the global South, and no effort to curb climate change solely by reducing emissions in industrialized countries will be successful. In this light, consider the following analysis of the global production of carbon dioxide.

2. Divisions within the G–77

More than with many environmental issues, the G–77 (developing countries) are far from unified in their positions on climate change. Deep differences make the global negotiations even more difficult than most. The following examples highlight the different priorities for developing countries in approaching the climate change negotiations.

Impacts on the Small Island States. Not surprisingly, the group of countries taking the strongest position on climate change are those countries that have the most to lose—small island States and those States like Bangladesh that are barely above sea level. About thirty small island states have joined the Alliance of Small Island States (AOSIS), which promotes the interests of island nations in the climate change negotiations. According to the current best estimates of sea level rise, some island States like the Maldives will be totally inundated by the middle part of the next century. AOSIS has supported a 20% cut in GHG emissions from 1990 levels for all industrialized countries by the year 2005. AOSIS is also seeking a funding mechanism for countries most vulnerable to climate change. Countries would have access to these funds as compensation for damages incurred due to sea-level rise and increased storm activity, as well as to finance climate change adaptation strategies, such as the construction of sea-walls.

OPEC. At the opposite extreme are the oil-producing nations, which have not supported any specific measures to curb global warming. Some delegates believe the OPEC nations joined the Climate Convention simply to block any international agreement that would reduce global oil demand. At recent negotiations, the OPEC countries also articulated their interest in a compensation fund. In their version of the fund, the money would be used to reimburse oil-producing states for any financial loss incurred due to reduced oil demand (and prices), which might be a consequence of binding emissions reductions under the climate change regime.

Brazil and the Amazon Basin. Brazil and the countries of the Amazon Basin bring an additional concern to discussions regarding climate change. They saw the focus of the United States and other industrialized countries on forest conservation and climate sinks as a cynical effort to shift the responsibility for climate change to developing countries. Brazil objects to the "internationalization" of the Amazon, whether under a global forestry policy, under the Biodiversity Convention, or under the Climate Change Convention. They particularly object to OPEC countries (mostly deserts) and large oil-consuming countries arguing that forest conservation should be permitted as a way to offset industrial GHG emissions. At the same time, some forested countries, for example Costa Rica and Colombia, supported the creation under the climate change regime of any mechanisms that could result in significant financial investments in the conservation of forests inside their country.

3.   The Persistent EU–US Division

Serious differences also exist within the industrialized world. The publicly articulated position of the United States has always been significantly weaker than that of the European Union. In addition, differences between the industrial sectors of Europe and the United States led to conflicts over which gases should be included and to what extent production of these gases should be restricted. The United States has always sought unlimited carbon trading and unrestricted credits for its substantial and growing forests, while Europe has always sought the flexibility and cost-savings that would come from having a regional target, thus allowing trading between countries within the European Union, but has sought limits to trading outside such regional blocs. These differences came to a head in 2001, when the United States under newly elected President George W. Bush announced its unilateral renunciation of the Kyoto Protocol. As discussed below, this announcement led the European Union to push for Kyoto ratification over US objections.

QUESTIONS AND DISCUSSION

1.   At first glance, the demand by OPEC nations to be compensated for declines in demand of their oil products seems to turn the concept of compensation for damages on its head. We do not typically think about the need to compensate States for stopping production of something that international society has decided causes widespread harm. Nonetheless, some precedent exists for their position. Developing countries supported the concept of the common heritage of mankind under the Law of the Sea Convention in part to ensure that revenues from deep seabed mining would compensate those countries (mostly developing countries) whose land-based mining industries could be harmed. Some of these developing economies were very dependent on their mineral deposits, and they feared a collapse of their economies from the production of low-cost deep seabed minerals. Of course, deep sea-bed minerals have yet to be commercially exploited, but is there any other difference in the position of the OPEC nations, given that their economies, too, will suffer from a decline in demand for oil?

2.   The climate change negotiations place developing countries in an unusually powerful position. Unlike most other fields of international law, the cooperation of key developing countries is required for a successful climate change regime. For example, the World Trade Organization managed to operate successfully for many years without China's participation; the climate regime will clearly not be a success without China. Although the industrialized countries are currently the primary sources of greenhouse gas emissions, this is expected to change in the middle of the next century. Without the cooperation of the developing countries, greenhouse gas reductions made in the North would not make a significant difference in the overall warming trend if the South does not eventually agree to some limitations as well. How should the South use this leverage? Should they use it with respect to issues of development?

3.   A major issue since the Kyoto Protocol has been on what terms developing countries should accept emission reduction targets and timetables. Put another way, assuming that we have decided that to avoid certain types of damage we must place a limit on annual global emissions of greenhouse gases, how would you propose allocating among countries the right to pollute a certain amount? Should this allocation be based on current or past emissions? Should it be tied to per capita income levels, allowing for greater growth in poorer countries? Should each person be given an equal right to emit a certain amount of greenhouse gases—for example by allocating a country's emissions levels based on population? Should we consider the greenhouse gas emissions per dollar value of production (thus giving a priority to those who use the energy most efficiently)? How can we include carbon sinks and reservoirs in a system based on per capita rights to emit? *See, e.g.,* Eileen Claussen & Lisa McNeilly, *Equity & Global Climate Change: The Complex Elements of Global Fairness* (Pew Center on Global Climate Change, October 29, 1998).

4. *Countries in Economic Transition.* The industrialized countries of the former Soviet bloc bring slightly different concerns to the table than most other industrialized countries. Their economies, which had been among the most inefficient in the world, have undergone significant restructuring and transition since the collapse of the Soviet system. Production at many of the largest polluting factories has come to a standstill due to severe economic conditions. Their current rates of GHG emissions are frequently well below their past rates, including the 1990 baseline year. As a result, these countries insisted on receiving sellable allowances for the difference between their actual emissions and the amount they are allowed to emit under the Protocol. Their position was ultimately accepted because countries like the United States saw this as a convenient mechanism for helping meet their own commitments through trading carbon allowances (discussed below). What are the policy arguments for and against allowing the former Soviet countries to sell these "carbon credits"?

Box 10.7: Development of the Climate Change Regime

1979	WMO convenes First World Climate Conference
1988	First IPCC Session
1990	2nd World Climate Conference recommends a framework climate change convention
1990	First Session of the Intergovernmental Negotiating Committee for a Framework Convention on Climate Change (FCCC)
1992	UN FCCC Signed at the Rio Earth Summit
1994	UN FCCC enters into force
1995	Berlin Mandate Agreed by the First Conference of Parties to the UN FCCC
1995	IPCC's Second Assessment concludes that human activities are changing the climate
1997	Kyoto Protocol is concluded
1999	Buenos Aires Mandate
2000	IPCC's Third Assessment identifies discernible man-made effect on the environment
2000	The parties fail to reach agreement at the Sixth Conference of the Parties at the Hague
2001	President George W. Bush takes office and unilaterally repudiates the Kyoto Protocol
2001	Europe, Japan, and the rest of the world reach agreement on the Kyoto Protocol in Bonn, and agree to seek ratification and entry into force without the United States
2002	World Summit on Sustainable Development (Entry into force of the Kyoto Protocol?)

Given the high stakes involved in the climate negotiations and the various different approaches taken by different countries, it is no wonder that the climate regime is taking years to develop. Although at times the pace is maddeningly slow with significant backward steps (for example, the US withdrawal of support for the Kyoto Protocol), international cooperation with respect to climate change has continued to march forward and promises to be significant in years to come as well. The chronology provided in Box 10.7, should help you to understand the development of the climate regime.

―――――

D. THE FRAMEWORK CONVENTION ON CLIMATE CHANGE

The following is a summary of the negotiations leading up to the 1992 Framework Convention on Climate Change, written by Donald Goldberg of the Center for International Environmental Law, the first NGO observer on the U.S. delegation to the climate negotiations.

D. Goldberg, *As the World Burns: Negotiating the Framework Convention on Climate Change*, 5 GEO. INT'L ENVTL. L. REV. 239, 244–51 (1993)

[In 1990, the IPCC] recommended a framework climate change convention following the format of the Vienna Convention [on depletion of the ozone layer], framed so as to gain the largest possible number of adherents, with provisions for separate annexes and protocols to deal with specific obligations. The Vienna Convention became the accepted model after the IPCC report, although it was not clear until the last round of negotiations whether the climate treaty, unlike the Vienna Convention, would contain specific binding obligations to reduce GHG emissions (it does not). * * *

Shortly after the Second World Climate Conference [held in November 1990], the U.N. General Assembly established the Intergovernmental Negotiating Committee for a Framework Climate Convention (INC). Charged by the General Assembly with producing an agreement to be signed at the Rio Earth Summit in June 1992, the INC began its deliberations in Chantilly, Virginia, in February 1991, in the midst of a record heat wave.

Convention Negotiations

By the time of the opening session of the Climate Convention negotiations, a number of countries had already committed to reducing GHG emissions. The European Community (EC) had committed to returning its joint CO_2 emissions to 1990 levels by the year 2000. The EC reaffirmed this commitment in Chantilly and also promised to provide financial assistance to help developing countries respond to climate change. Its position was based on individual country commitments by Germany, Denmark, Switzerland, Sweden, Australia, Austria, Norway, and Canada. Many of these commitments went beyond stabilization at 1990 levels or promised deeper CO2 cuts in later years.

Japan had previously stated that its "emissions of CO2 should be stabilized on a per capita basis in the year 2000 and beyond at about the same level as in 1990," and "the emission of methane should not exceed the present [1990] level." In the opening round, Japan called for negotiation first of a basic framework, but suggested the convention might also contain concrete measures to be taken by the parties.

The Group of 77 developing countries (actually composed of 127 developing countries) made a point of the fact that 75% of energy-related CO2 emissions are attributable to industrialized countries, but acknowledged, nevertheless, that developing countries have a responsibility not to follow the same path. They called for industrialized countries to transfer environmentally sound technologies to developing countries on preferential and non-commercial terms to help developing countries avoid the environmentally destructive aspects of development. They also called for the creation of a differentiated regime under the climate convention for developing countries, along the lines of the Montreal Protocol.

The United States, as expected, rejected targets and timetables, instead advocating a "no regrets" policy of actions that would be taken only insofar as they produced benefits having nothing to do with global warming. For example, the U.S. might promote the use of a new energy technology that would have global warming benefits if it could be shown to be more cost-effective, or to reduce urban pollution, but not merely for the purpose of reducing GHG emissions. The U.S. also supported further research to resolve uncertainties and a "comprehensive approach" to reducing emissions, which would take into account not just CO2, but all Greenhouse gases.

The United States attempted to deflect some of the criticism aimed at it during the first negotiating round by releasing a White House "Action Agenda," intended to demonstrate that the U.S. was acting responsibly with regard to its GHG emissions. The Action Agenda purported to show that U.S. policies would result in GHG emissions in the year 2000 at or below 1987 levels. Unlike the European plan, however, the U.S. approach contemplated significant increases in domestic CO2 emissions. To achieve its year 2000 target, the U.S. plan relied heavily on the phase-out of CFCs, then thought to account for approximately 11% of radiative forcing. Both the Europeans and environmentalists objected that the U.S. plan was disingenuous, since CFCs were already scheduled to be phased out under the Montreal Protocol on Substances That Deplete the Ozone Layer, and were not included in other countries' emissions reduction plans.* * *

The first round ended with the U.S. and the EC deadlocked on the question of whether the agreement should include firm commitments to reduce Greenhouse gases. To break the deadlock, the U.K. Environment Secretary, Michael Heseltine, traveled to the United States shortly before the start of the second round with an offer of compromise. The EC would accept the U.S.'s comprehensive approach—excluding gases already controlled by the Montreal Protocol—if the U.S. would accept targets and timetables. The U.S. declined, and little additional progress was made in the second round. In hopes of moving the process incrementally forward, Japan, with the support of the U.K. and France, floated an informal paper proposing a "pledge and review" approach, under which parties would pledge to undertake actions to reduce emissions, and an international body would review the implementation of those pledges. Environmentalists were quick to lampoon this approach as "hedge and retreat."

Supporters of pledge and review—stung by environmentalists' criticism—backed away from the proposal at the next negotiating round, in Nairobi in September 1991, and reaffirmed their support for stabilization of CO2 emissions at 1990 levels by 2000. The EC also called for a treaty objective to stabilize Greenhouse gases at levels that would "prevent dangerous anthropogenic interference with climate" within a timeframe that would "allow ecosystems to adapt naturally." The U.S. continued to resist any binding commitments on targets and timetables.

But cracks in the U.S. position were beginning to appear. In December 1991, when White House Chief-of-Staff John Sununu—the Administration's strongest opponent of greenhouse gas controls—resigned, the White House began to review its position. EPA Director William Reilly argued that stabilization tied to population growth was achievable, based on EPA's innovative "Green" Programs. By the start of the last negotiating round, in February 1992, Administration officials were reporting that a change in U.S. policy was in the making. The first complete draft text was introduced at the fourth negotiation, held in Geneva in December 1991. The draft was over 110 pages long, and most of the text was bracketed, indicating that the text was controversial and had not yet been approved by the full Committee. Nevertheless, its introduction signaled that the Committee might yet complete its work in time for the Rio Earth Summit in June. * * *

Meanwhile, it was becoming clear that negotiators would never resolve all the issues under discussion in time for Rio, and a wholesale jettisoning of bracketed provisions began. As time grew short, negotiators agreed to return to the UN at the end of April, to try to finish their work. During the interim the INC Chairman, in consultation with a number of countries, substantially revised the text, paring it down to a third of its previous size.

The Chairman's text was in many respects a fait accompli—there was simply not enough time to make large-scale revisions. Ground-breaking approaches to dispute settlement, a financial mechanism, technology transfer, amendments, annexes, protocols, and entry into force provisions contained in earlier drafts were dropped in favor of formulations that in some respects actually marked a retreat from previous international environmental agreements.

The commitment section of the Chairman's text acknowledged the fact that a legally binding commitment to reduce Greenhouse gases was beyond reach, if the U.S. was to be a signatory. It reflected a consensus of the other industrial countries that an agreement would not be meaningful without the participation of the U.S. The EC and Japan mildly protested the weak commitment section, but made clear they would not hold out for stronger language. The Chairman blamed the weak and ambiguous GHG commitment language squarely on the U.S.

Had the U.S. not taken such a hard line on commitments, the Convention would no doubt have been stronger. But the difference a more constructive U.S. approach might have made should not be overstated. Not every industrialized country other than the U.S. was prepared to make commitments to deep cuts in CO2 or other GHG emissions. Indeed, the best the EC could offer was to stabilize its emissions at 1990 levels by the year 2000. Japan's commitment was even weaker, though it probably would have accepted the EC target. Nevertheless, a firm commitment to any targets and timetables would have been a significant improvement, and might have accelerated the entire process of negotiating an effective global warming agreement by a year or more.

The resulting Framework Convention on Climate Change was in many ways disappointing to environmentalists, but was nonetheless a positive step in the control of greenhouse gases. Central to the Convention is the objective found in Article 2. That objective requires the Parties to achieve "stabilization of greenhouse gas concentrations in the atmosphere at a level that would prevent dangerous anthropogenic interference with the climate system." This objective is the standard by which the Parties' commitments under the climate regime are to be measured. Under Articles 4(2)(d) and 7(2)(a), the Conference of the Parties is charged with periodically evaluating implementation of the Convention to ensure that commitments are adequate to meet this overall objective. It was just such an evaluation that would ultimately lead to the recognition that binding targets were necessary in the Kyoto Protocol.

Perhaps the most controversial provisions were those that addressed the specific commitments of the Parties. The Parties are essentially divided into three categories: all Parties; "Annex I," which include all industrialized country Parties; and "Annex II," which includes all industrialized country Parties except those from the former Soviet bloc in a process of economic transition. Article 4(1) places certain information and data collecting requirements on all Parties. Article 4(2) subjects the Annex I countries to additional requirements, including most notably the obligation to "adopt national polices and take corresponding measures on the mitigation of climate change, by limiting anthropogenic emissions of greenhouse gases and protecting and enhancing greenhouse gas sinks and reservoirs." This requirement to adopt a national policy is not tied legally to any specific target, but Article 4(2)(b) requires the developed countries to provide detailed information on their policies as well as on their emissions *"with the aim of* returning individually or jointly to their 1990 levels.... " Environmentalists argued that these provisions reflected a commitment, albeit a non-binding one, by developed countries to stabilize their emissions at 1990 levels by the year 2000.

Just as important as the substantive standards in the Climate Change Convention is the institutional framework established for the continued implementation of the Convention and the progressive development of the regime through protocols or amendments. As with the Montreal Protocol regime, the Convention vests important policymaking authority in the Conference of the Parties, day-to-day monitoring of implementation in the Secretariat, and advisory obligations in a scientific and technical subsidiary body. The Convention selected the Global Environment Facility as the interim financial mechanism (*see* Chapter 20) and established a relatively unique subsidiary body and procedures for facilitating implementation.

UNITED NATIONS FRAMEWORK CONVENTION ON CLIMATE CHANGE

The Parties to this Convention,

Acknowledging that change in the Earth's climate and its adverse effects are a common concern of humankind,* * *

Noting that the largest share of historical and current global emissions of greenhouse gases has originated in developed countries, that per capita emissions in developing countries are still relatively low and that the share of global emissions originating in developing countries will grow to meet their social and development needs,* * *

Have agreed as follows:

ARTICLE 1: DEFINITIONS

For the purposes of this Convention: * * *

4. "Emissions" means the release of greenhouse gases and/or their precursors into the atmosphere over a specified area and period of time.

5. "Greenhouse gases" means those gaseous constituents of the atmosphere, both natural and anthropogenic, that absorb and re-emit infra-red radiation. * * *

7. "Reservoir" means a component or components of the climate system where a greenhouse gas or a precursor of a greenhouse gas is stored.

8. "Sink" means any process, activity or mechanism which removes a greenhouse gas, an aerosol or a precursor of a greenhouse gas from the atmosphere.

9. "Source" means any process or activity which releases a greenhouse gas, an aerosol or a precursor of a greenhouse gas into the atmosphere.

ARTICLE 2: OBJECTIVE

The ultimate objective of this Convention and any related legal instruments that the Conference of the Parties may adopt is to achieve, in accordance with the relevant provisions of the Convention, stabilization of greenhouse gas concentrations in the atmosphere at a level that would prevent dangerous anthropogenic interference with the climate system. Such a level should be achieved within a time frame sufficient to allow ecosystems to adapt naturally to climate change, to ensure that food production is not threatened and to enable economic development to proceed in a sustainable manner.

ARTICLE 3: PRINCIPLES

In their actions to achieve the objective of the Convention and to implement its provisions, the Parties shall be guided, inter alia, by the following:

1. The Parties should protect the climate system for the benefit of present and future generations of humankind, on the basis of equity and in accordance with their common but differentiated responsibilities and respective capabilities. Accordingly, the developed country Parties should take the lead in combating climate change and the adverse effects thereof.

2. The specific needs and special circumstances of developing country Parties, especially those that are particularly vulnerable to the adverse effects of climate change, and of those Parties, especially developing country Parties, that would have to bear a disproportionate or abnormal burden under the Convention, should be given full consideration.

3. The Parties should take precautionary measures to anticipate, prevent or minimize the causes of climate change and mitigate its adverse effects. Where there are threats of serious or irreversible damage, lack of full scientific certainty should not be used as a reason for postponing such measures, taking into account that policies and measures to deal with climate change should be cost-effective so as to ensure global benefits at the lowest possible cost. To achieve this, such policies and measures should take into account different socio-economic contexts, be comprehensive, cover all relevant sources, sinks and reservoirs of greenhouse gases and adaptation, and comprise all economic sectors. Efforts to address climate change may be carried out cooperatively by interested Parties.

4. The Parties have a right to, and should, promote sustainable development. Policies and measures to protect the climate system against human-induced change should be appropriate for the specific conditions of each Party and should be integrated with national development programmes, taking into account that economic development is essential for adopting measures to address climate change.* * *

ARTICLE 4: COMMITMENTS

1. All Parties, taking into account their common but differentiated responsibilities and their specific national and regional development priorities, objectives and circumstances, shall:

(a) Develop, periodically update, publish and make available to the Conference of the Parties, in accordance with Article 12, national inventories of anthropogenic emissions by sources and removals by sinks of all greenhouse gases not controlled by the Montreal Protocol, using comparable methodologies to be agreed upon by the Conference of the Parties;

(b) Formulate, implement, publish and regularly update national and, where appropriate, regional programmes containing measures to mitigate climate change by addressing anthropogenic emissions by sources and removals by sinks of all greenhouse gases not controlled by the Montreal Protocol, and measures to facilitate adequate adaptation to climate change;

(c) Promote and cooperate in the development, application and diffusion, including transfer, of technologies, practices and processes that control, reduce or prevent anthropogenic emissions of greenhouse gases not controlled by the Montreal Protocol in all relevant sectors, including the energy, transport, industry, agriculture, forestry and waste management sectors;

(d) Promote sustainable management, and promote and cooperate in the conservation and enhancement, as appropriate, of sinks and reservoirs of all greenhouse gases not controlled by the Montreal Protocol, including biomass, forests and oceans as well as other terrestrial, coastal and marine ecosystems;

(e) Cooperate in preparing for adaptation to the impacts of climate change; develop and elaborate appropriate and integrated plans for coastal zone management, water resources and agriculture, and for the protection and rehabilitation of areas, particularly in Africa, affected by drought and desertification, as well as floods;

(f) Take climate change considerations into account, to the extent feasible, in their relevant social, economic and environmental policies and actions, and employ appropriate methods, for example impact assessments, formulated and determined nationally, with a view to minimizing adverse effects on the economy, on public health and on the quality of the environment, of projects or measures undertaken by them to mitigate or adapt to climate change;

(g) Promote and cooperate in scientific, technological, technical, socio-economic and other research, systematic observation and development of data archives related to the climate system and intended to further the understanding and to reduce or eliminate the remaining uncertainties regarding the causes, effects, magnitude and timing of climate change and the economic and social consequences of various response strategies;

(h) Promote and cooperate in the full, open and prompt exchange of relevant scientific, technological, technical, socio-economic and legal information related to the climate system and climate change, and to the economic and social consequences of various response strategies;

(i) Promote and cooperate in education, training and public awareness related to climate change and encourage the widest participation in this process, including that of non-governmental organizations; and

(j) Communicate to the Conference of the Parties information related to implementation, in accordance with Article 12.

2.   The developed country Parties and other Parties included in annex I commit themselves specifically as provided for in the following:

(a) Each of these Parties shall adopt national policies and take corresponding measures on the mitigation of climate change, by limiting its anthropogenic emissions of greenhouse gases and protecting and enhancing its greenhouse gas sinks and reservoirs. These policies and measures will demonstrate that developed countries are taking the lead in modifying longer-term trends in anthropogenic emissions consistent with the objective of the Convention, recognizing that the return by the end of the present decade to earlier levels of anthropogenic emissions of carbon dioxide and other greenhouse gases not controlled by the Montreal Protocol would contribute to such modification, and taking into account the differences in these Parties' starting points and approaches, economic structures and resource bases, the need to maintain strong and sustainable economic growth, available technologies and other individual circumstances, as well as the need for equitable and appropriate contributions by each of these Parties to the global effort regarding that objective. These Parties may implement such policies and measures jointly with other Parties and may assist other Parties in contributing to the achievement of the objective of the Convention and, in particular, that of this subparagraph;

(b) In order to promote progress to this end, each of these Parties shall communicate, within six months of the entry into force of the Convention for it and periodically thereafter, and in accordance with Article 12, detailed information on its policies and measures referred to in subparagraph (a) above, as well as on its resulting projected anthropogenic emissions by sources and removals by sinks of greenhouse gases not controlled by the Montreal Protocol for the period referred to in subparagraph (a), with the aim of returning individually or jointly to their 1990 levels of these anthropogenic emissions of carbon dioxide and other greenhouse gases not controlled by the Montreal Protocol. This information will be reviewed by the Conference of the Parties, at its first session and periodically thereafter, in accordance with Article 7;

(c) Calculations of emissions by sources and removals by sinks of greenhouse gases for the purposes of subparagraph (b) above should take into account the best available scientific knowledge, including of the effective capacity of sinks and the respective contributions of such gases to climate change. The Conference of the Parties shall consider and agree on methodologies for these calculations at its first session and review them regularly thereafter;

(d) The Conference of the Parties shall, at its first session, review the adequacy of subparagraphs (a) and (b) above. Such review shall be carried out in the light of the best available scientific information and assessment on climate change and its impacts, as well as relevant technical, social and economic information. Based on this review, the Conference of the Parties shall take appropriate action, which may include the adoption of amendments to the commitments in subparagraphs (a) and (b) above. The Conference of the Parties, at its first session, shall also take decisions regarding criteria for joint implementation as indicated in subparagraph (a) above. A second review of subparagraphs (a) and (b) shall take place not later than 31 December 1998, and thereafter at regular intervals determined by the Conference of the Parties, until the objective of the Convention is met;

(e) Each of these Parties shall:

(i) coordinate as appropriate with other such Parties, relevant economic and administrative instruments developed to achieve the objective of the Convention; and

(ii) identify and periodically review its own policies and practices which encourage activities that lead to greater levels of anthropogenic emissions of greenhouse gases not controlled by the Montreal Protocol than would otherwise occur;

(f) The Conference of the Parties shall review, not later than 31 December 1998, available information with a view to taking decisions regarding such amendments to the lists in annexes I and II as may be appropriate, with the approval of the Party concerned;

(g) Any Party not included in annex I may, in its instrument of ratification, acceptance, approval or accession, or at any time thereafter, notify the Depositary that it intends to be bound by subparagraphs (a) and (b) above. The Depositary shall inform the other signatories and Parties of any such notification.

3. The developed country Parties and other developed Parties included in annex II shall provide new and additional financial resources to meet the agreed full costs incurred by developing country Parties in complying with their obligations under Article 12, paragraph 1. They shall also provide such financial resources, including for the transfer of technology, needed by the developing country Parties to meet the agreed full incremental costs of implementing measures that are covered by paragraph 1 of this Article and that are agreed between a developing country Party and the international entity or entities referred to in Article 11, in accordance with that Article. The implementation of these commitments shall take into account the need for adequacy and predictability in the flow of funds and the importance of appropriate burden sharing among the developed country Parties.

4. The developed country Parties and other developed Parties included in annex II shall also assist the developing country Parties that are particularly vulnerable to the adverse effects of climate change in meeting costs of adaptation to those adverse effects.

5. The developed country Parties and other developed Parties included in annex II shall take all practicable steps to promote, facilitate and finance, as appropriate, the transfer of, or access to, environmentally sound technologies and know-how to other Parties, particularly developing country Parties, to enable them to implement the provisions of the Convention. In this process, the developed country Parties shall support the development and enhancement of endogenous capacities and technologies of developing country Parties. Other Parties and organizations in a position to do so may also assist in facilitating the transfer of such technologies.

6. In the implementation of their commitments under paragraph 2 above, a certain degree of flexibility shall be allowed by the Conference of the Parties to the Parties included in annex I undergoing the process of transition to a market economy, in order to enhance the ability of these Parties to address climate change, including with regard to the historical level of anthropogenic emissions of greenhouse gases not controlled by the Montreal Protocol chosen as a reference.

7.   The extent to which developing country Parties will effectively implement their commitments under the Convention will depend on the effective implementation by developed country Parties of their commitments under the Convention related to financial resources and transfer of technology and will take fully into account that economic and social development and poverty eradication are the first and overriding priorities of the developing country Parties. * * *

QUESTIONS AND DISCUSSION

1.   *Working the Treaty.* How does the Climate Change Convention apply the following principles described generally in Chapter 7? What are the implications of these principles with respect to climate change?

- common concern of humankind;

- common but differentiated responsibility;

- the precautionary principle;

- intergenerational equity;

- the right to development.

What other general concepts or principles of international environmental law are found in the Climate Change Convention?

2.   After the United States repudiated the Kyoto Protocol in 2001, many observers argued the United States was out of compliance with the framework convention. Is this possible? What binding commitments did Parties to the Climate Change Convention make? Can you make an argument that a Party to the Climate Change Convention is legally obligated to meet 1990 levels by the year 2000? What commitments are imposed by the Convention after the year 2000?

3.   Re-read the obligations found in Article 4 regarding Annex I countries (i.e., industrialized countries). Does this provision reflect a compromise between those wanting a clear target and timetable, and those countries wanting no target? Is there a clear winner? Does the requirement that the Conference of the Parties review the adequacy of these commitments tip the balance one way or the other?

4.   One of the major issues heading into the climate change negotiations was the extent to which the Convention would single out CO_2 emissions as the major cause of climate change. The United States supported a broader approach that would deal with all greenhouse gas emissions, primarily because it wanted greater flexibility in designing policy responses. To what extent does the Convention address CO_2 specifically? Does the Convention adopt the "basket-of-gases" approach promoted by the United States? A related issue was the extent to which the Convention would focus solely on emission reductions or whether it would also emphasize activities that enhance the sequestration of greenhouse gases (i.e. by creating or maintaining carbon sinks and reservoirs). What approach did the Convention take to this issue?

5.   How does the Climate Change Convention compare to the Vienna Convention on Substances that Deplete the Ozone Layer? Coming as it does on the heels of the ozone regime's successful adaptation to advances in scientific knowledge and technological innovation, the Climate Convention is clearly more self-conscious about its role as a framework convention. What aspects of the Convention suggest that the parties will be able to respond adequately to scientific developments with respect to climate change?

---

1. THE FIRST COP AND THE BERLIN MANDATE

The Convention required the first Conference of the Parties (CoP) to "review the adequacy" of the developed countries' commitments, "in light of the best available scientific information and assessment on climate change and its impacts...." Although the Convention did not include a legally binding obligation to meet 1990 levels of GHG emissions by the year 2000, Article 4 required at least that developed country Parties try to meet that target. To outside observers, two things were clear: first, the original target of freezing emissions at 1990 levels for Annex I countries was not going to be sufficient to meet the Convention's Article 2 objective—i.e., to achieve stabilization of greenhouse gas concentrations at a safe level. Even if it was sufficient, the second obvious development was that few developed countries were even going to come close to meeting the 1990–level freeze.

Environmentalists and most developing countries thus came to Berlin hoping to persuade the Annex I countries to step up their level of commitment, both financially and politically. A group of developing countries offered a first draft of what became known as the "Berlin Mandate," which would establish a timetable for developed countries to negotiate a protocol with clear "quantifiable emissions limitation and reduction objectives" (QELROs)—a new term for "targets and timetables." The Berlin Mandate set the Parties on a path to negotiate targets and timetables by the third session of the CoP, which was scheduled for December, 1997 in Kyoto, Japan. The Ad hoc Working Group on the Berlin Mandate (AGBM) was tasked with the negotiations.

Conclusion of Outstanding Issues and Adoption of Decisions (The Berlin Mandate) FCCC/CP/1995/L.14 (April 7, 1995)

The Conference of the Parties, at its first session, having reviewed Article 4, paragraph 2 (a) and (b) and concluded that these are not adequate, agrees to begin a process to enable it to take appropriate action for the period beyond 2000, including the strengthening of the commitments of Annex I Parties in Article 4, paragraph 2 (a) and (b) through the adoption of a protocol or another legal instrument.* * *

2. The process will, *inter alia*:

(a) Aim, as the priority in the process of strengthening the commitments in Article 4.2 (a) and (b) of the Convention, for developed country/other Parties included in Annex I, both to elaborate policies and measures, as well as to set quantified limitation and reduction objectives within specified time-frames, such as 2005, 2010 and 2020, for their anthropogenic emissions by sources and removals by sinks of greenhouse gases not controlled by the Montreal Protocol taking into account the differences in starting points and approaches, economic structures and resource bases, the need to maintain strong and sustainable economic growth, available technologies and other individual circumstances, as well as the need for equitable and appropriate contributions by each of these

Parties to the global effort, and also the process of assessment and analysis referred to in section III, paragraph 4, below;

(b) Not introduce any new commitments for [developing country] Parties . . ., but reaffirm existing commitments in Article 4.1 and continue to advance the implementation of these commitments in order to achieve sustainable development, taking into account Article 4.3, 4.5 and 4.7;* * *

6.   The process should begin without delay and be conducted as a matter of urgency, in an open-ended ad hoc group of Parties hereby established, which will report to the second session of the Conference of the Parties on the status of this process. The sessions of this group should be scheduled to ensure completion of the work as early as possible in 1997 with a view to adopting the results at the third session of the Conference of the Parties.

---

2.   PRELUDE TO KYOTO

In 1995, the IPCC released a report that was one of the most significant milestones in the development of the climate change regime. For the first time, the IPCC formally reported a consensus among scientists that "the balance of evidence suggests that there is a discernible human influence on global climate." This conclusion sparked considerable debate, pitting the great majority of atmospheric scientists and environmentalists who endorsed the IPCC report, against a small but vocal group of "greenhouse skeptics" funded substantially by the fossil fuel industry. *See* Ozone Action, TIES THAT BLIND (1996).

Despite the initial controversy, the IPCC Report provided one of the most important catalysts for the negotiation of the Kyoto Protocol. The scientific consensus that climate change was not only a serious long-term problem but was actually occurring now provided the political leaders with critical support for adopting targets and timetables. On the other hand, global emissions of greenhouse gases had increased in the years since Rio, making efforts based on a 1990 baseline even more difficult for some countries, including the United States.

At Berlin, the United States continued its lack of clear commitment to any target or timetable, although this position was an increasingly isolated one. Finally, in part because of the findings in the 1995 IPCC Report and because of growing public pressure, the United States surprised climate negotiators by announcing for the first time that it would support binding targets and timetables for greenhouse gas emissions. The U.S. was silent, however, on what specific levels it would support. Nonetheless, the public announcement gave a shot in the arm to the negotiations and offered the first promise that a meaningful regime might be negotiated at Kyoto.

Through the next year the United States remained silent about specific targets and timetables. Increasing pressure built from Europe as well as the developing countries for the United States to show leadership on this issue. Instead, President Clinton announced at the five-year anniversary of the Earth Summit (June 1997) that he would use the six months remaining before Kyoto to educate the American public about the need for greenhouse gas reductions.

The Europeans and others were not pleased with the U.S. position. Perhaps the loudest cheers during the entire session greeted British Prime Minister Tony Blair when he indirectly criticized the United States by saying "some of the greatest industrialized nations" have not lived up to their promises. He stated further that: "The biggest responsibility falls on those countries with the biggest emissions. . . . We in Europe have put our cards on the table. It is time for the special pleading to stop and for others to follow suit." The G–77 Chairman, Daudi Mwakawago was even clearer: "[President Clinton] articulated the problems very clearly, but when it came to global action, joining the rest of humanity to address them, there wasn't very much there."

Clinton's announcement that he would build political will over the next six months catalyzed both sides of the climate debate to rally their troops and build political support for either a stronger or weaker convention. Just a few months after Clinton's June speech, industry announced a $13 million dollar campaign under the ambiguous name of the "Global Climate Information Project." Amid a refrain of "It's not global, and it won't work," industry first attacked the Climate Change Convention as being unfair to U.S. industry because it let developing countries off-the-hook. Other ads in the campaign claimed that energy prices would rise more than 20%. Over 1500 utilities, trade associations, labor unions and other corporations signed on to an advertisement asking the President not to "rush into an unwise and unfair United Nations Agreement that's bad for America." WASHINGTON POST, Oct. 6, 1997, at A9. The U.S. Senate added their support to this position passing a resolution urging the President not to agree to any convention that did not include binding targets on developing countries. The Byrd–Hagel Resolution, as it has since been referred to, strongly influenced both the Kyoto negotiations and the ensuing national dialogue over whether to support the Kyoto Protocol. When the Bush Administration repudiated the Protocol in 1992, it cited the same two reasons highlighted in the Byrd–Hagel Resolution—i.e. that the Protocol did not include developing countries and that the costs would be too high on the US economy.

Environmental groups countered by launching media and public information campaigns, and grass roots actions to raise awareness and garner support for US commitments to cut greenhouse gases. Some environmental groups attacked Vice President Gore, quoting passages from his book *Earth in the Balance* and running advertisements with the words "Withdrawn by the author" superimposed over a copy of the book's cover. A scientist's statement signed by over 2600 leading scientists was handed to the President on June 18, 1997, endorsing strong and clear commitments at Kyoto. A similar statement from over 1000 leading economists argued that the United States could meet the objectives of the climate convention without harming the national economy.

The Administration engaged in a flurry of public relations actions, including Vice President Gore hiking five miles to the base of the shrinking Grinnel Glacier in Glacier National Park, to dramatize the current impacts of climate change. Inside the White House, however, infighting continued between those pushing the Administration to come as close as possible to the European position and others cautioning that dramatic steps could harm the robust U.S. economy. Even a Department of Energy study, which concluded that energy efficiency technologies could allow the United States to reach 1990 levels by the year 2010 with little or no overall costs to the economy, could not soften the Administration's position.

The Clinton Administration announced its long-awaited policy on October 22, 1997. The U.S. position proposed a binding target of stabilizing emissions at 1990 levels by the year 2008 to 2012, and further unspecified reductions by the year 2017. To meet these targets, the President outlined a program of $5 billion in tax and other incentives to spur energy efficiency technologies; endorsed the concept of an international pollution trading system that would allow for reduced costs of compliance; and emphasized the restructuring of the electric industry concurrent to deregulation (a process that was already beginning). The Administration's position drew immediate criticism from both U.S. environmentalists and industry groups, and by governments around the world, especially European, who believed the United States' dominant role in the international political system warranted stronger leadership.

With the U.S. position finally publicized, the major proposals for targets and timetables leading up to Kyoto could be identified. See Box 10–8.

Box 10–8: Kyoto Negotiating Positions on GHG reductions

Country/Bloc	Position
AOSIS	20% below 1990 levels by 2005
G–77	35% below 1990 levels by 2020
European Union	7.5 ≠low 1990 levels by 2005; 15% below by 2010
Russia	1990 levels by 2010
Czech Republic	5% below 1990 levels by 2005; 15% below by 2010
Eastern Europe	1990 levels by 2005
Peru	15% below 1990 levels by 2005
Brazil	30% below 1990 levels by 2020
Switzerland	10% below 1990 levels by 2010 based on per capita consumption
Japan	0–5% below 1990 levels by 2008–2012, depending on economic factors
United States	1990 levels by 2008 to 2012; further, unspecified cuts by 2017

QUESTIONS AND DISCUSSION

1. The Berlin Mandate set out certain parameters for the negotiation of the Kyoto Protocol. For example, the mandate states that the Kyoto negotiations should "not introduce any new commitments" on developing countries. During the Kyoto negotiations, this aspect of the Berlin Mandate would come under intense criticism in the United States, particularly from industry. What justification is there for treating developing countries differently?

2. President Clinton quite explicitly made the run-up to Kyoto an exercise in building political support. He challenged environmentalists to show that the U.S. population would support strong action on climate change. On one hand, this seems a fair role for environmental groups to play—but what does it say about the President's own willingness to take a bold leadership position? How would you build political will for strong and controversial international action?

———

E. THE KYOTO PROTOCOL

Not since the 1992 Earth Summit had so much press and attention been paid to an international environmental negotiation as was paid to the Kyoto negotiations. Kyoto teemed with thousands of official delegates, reporters, scientists, activists, industry officials—and not one of them went to Kyoto knowing how the Protocol would turn out, or indeed even if there would be a Protocol. The various positions of the key parties—the European Community, the United States, the G–77—seemed too distant for any meaningful agreement to be reached. Virtually the entire text of the Kyoto Protocol was heavily bracketed, often with more than two alternative provisions elaborated. Yet, the public scrutiny was such that failure to reach an agreement would have been deemed an embarrassing failure to many of the governments. And no one wanted to be blamed for "killing Kyoto."

One turning point came when Vice President Al Gore agreed to attend the conference. Although he did not make any specific commitments, he did publicly instruct the U.S. delegation to be "flexible" in order to reach an agreement. More important than what he said was that he was there at all—his presence in Kyoto raised the political stakes of failure. Within a few days, the United States announced that it would consider flexible targets and timetables, meaning that all the industrialized parties did not have to agree to the same emission reductions and the same baseline year. Japan immediately tabled a new proposal that had the EU reducing emissions more than either the U.S. or Japan.

Not surprisingly, the European Union criticized the Japanese position, claiming that they were failing to play the appropriate role of the host of a negotiation—i.e. to facilitate consensus. The European Union insisted on being able to use a bubble concept, by which it could meet the emissions reductions through a system of trading between member countries. The overall costs of compliance would be less as, for example, emission credits would be traded between Italy or Spain and the United Kingdom or Germany. The United States, complaining that the Europeans had an unfair economic advantage in complying with any emission standards, announced that it was considering creating its own emissions trading bloc that included Japan, Russia, the United States, Canada, Australia and New Zealand (collectively referred to as the Umbrella Group).

With two days left to go, the United States had finally agreed to a 3% reduction in emissions from 1990 levels and deals were starting to be made.

The final negotiating session went essentially non-stop for forty-eight hours and the end of the session had to be extended for several hours. Even so, only the heavy-handed work of the negotiation's Argentinian Chairperson Raul Estrada averted last minute disputes between the G–77 and the industrialized countries that could have derailed the entire agreement. A hastily crafted compromise put off for one year any further discussions about developing country commitments, thus paving the way for final adoption of the Protocol.

The core of the Kyoto Protocol is targets and timetables, or "quantified emissions limitation and reduction objectives" (QELROs), for industrialized (Annex I) Parties to reduce their net emissions of greenhouse gases. Most European countries agreed to lower their emission 8% below 1990 levels, while the United States agreed to a 7% reduction. See Annex B to the Protocol for the full listing of commitments (reprinted *infra* p. 636). Countries in economic transition were allowed to select an alternative baseline year other than 1990, and several countries did so. In addition, all countries had the option of choosing 1995 as the baseline year for three relatively minor but potent greenhouse gases (hydrofluorocarbons, perfluorocarbons and sulphur hexafluoride). All of the reduction targets must be met over a five-year commitment period—from 2008 to 2012—which is to be followed by subsequent commitment periods and presumably stricter emission targets. For a further summary of the Kyoto Protocol, see D. Goldberg, A Legal Analysis of the Kyoto Protocol (CIEL, 1998).

In addition to the targets and timetables, the Kyoto Protocol also set forth broad and general guidance for four different flexibility mechanisms, including emissions trading, joint implementation, the EO's bubble, and a new initiative called the "Clean Development Mechanism." Parameters were also set for a compliance and monitoring system and for the accounting of at least certain land-use and forestry activities that could alter carbon reservoirs or sinks. Many of these provisions raised as many questions as they answered, and set the stage for further negotiations after Kyoto.

KYOTO PROTOCOL TO THE UNITED NATIONS FRAMEWORK CONVENTION ON CLIMATE CHANGE

Article 2

1. Each Party included in Annex I in achieving its quantified emission limitation and reduction commitments under Article 3, in order to promote sustainable development, shall:

(a) Implement and/or further elaborate policies and measures in accordance with its national circumstances, such as:

(i) Enhancement of energy efficiency in relevant sectors of the national economy;

(ii) Protection and enhancement of sinks and reservoirs of greenhouse gases not controlled by the Montreal Protocol, taking into account its commitments under relevant international environmental agreements; promotion of sustainable forest management practices, afforestation and reforestation;

(iii) Promotion of sustainable forms of agriculture in light of climate change considerations;

(iv) Promotion, research, development and increased use of new and renewable forms of energy, of carbon dioxide sequestration technologies and of advanced and innovative environmentally sound technologies;

(v) Progressive reduction or phasing out of market imperfections, fiscal incentives, tax and duty exemptions and subsidies in all greenhouse gas emitting sectors that run counter to the objective of the Convention and application of market instruments;

(vi) Encouragement of appropriate reforms in relevant sectors aimed at promoting policies and measures which limit or reduce emissions of greenhouse gases not controlled by the Montreal Protocol;

(vii) Measures to limit and/or reduce emissions of greenhouse gases not controlled by the Montreal Protocol in the transport sector;

(viii) Limitation and/or reduction of methane through recovery and use in waste management, as well as in the production, transport and distribution of energy;

(b) Cooperate with other such Parties to enhance the individual and combined effectiveness of their policies and measures adopted under this Article, pursuant to Article 4, paragraph 2(e)(i), of the Convention. To this end, these Parties shall take steps to share their experience and exchange information on such policies and measures, including developing ways of improving their comparability, transparency and effectiveness. * * *

Article 3

1. The Parties included in Annex I shall, individually or jointly, ensure that their aggregate anthropogenic carbon dioxide equivalent emissions of the greenhouse gases listed in Annex A do not exceed their assigned amounts, calculated pursuant to their quantified emission limitation and reduction commitments inscribed in Annex B and in accordance with the provisions of this Article, with a view to reducing their overall emissions of such gases by at least 5 per cent below 1990 levels in the commitment period 2008 to 2012.

2. Each Party included in Annex I shall, by 2005, have made demonstrable progress in achieving its commitments under this Protocol.

3. The net changes in greenhouse gas emissions from sources and removals by sinks resulting from direct human-induced land use change and forestry activities, limited to afforestation, reforestation, and deforestation since 1990, measured as verifiable changes in carbon stocks in each commitment period, shall be used to meet the commitments in this Article of each Party included in Annex I. The greenhouse gas emissions by sources and removals by sinks associated with those activities shall be reported in a transparent and verifiable manner and reviewed in accordance with Articles 7 and 8.

4. Prior to the first session of the Conference of the Parties serving as the meeting of the Parties to this Protocol, each Party included in Annex I shall provide for consideration by the Subsidiary Body for Scientific and Technological Advice data to establish its level of carbon stocks in 1990 and to enable an estimate to be made of its changes in carbon stocks in subsequent years. The Conference of the Parties serving as the meeting of the Parties to this Protocol shall, at its first session or as soon as practicable thereafter, decide upon modalities, rules and guidelines as to how and which additional human-induced activities related to changes in greenhouse gas emissions by sources and

removals by sinks in the agricultural soil and land use change and forestry categories, shall be added to, or subtracted from, the assigned amount for Parties included in Annex I, taking into account uncertainties, transparency in reporting, verifiability, the methodological work of the Intergovernmental Panel on Climate Change, the advice provided by the Subsidiary Body for Scientific and Technological Advice in accordance with Article 5 and the decisions of the Conference of the Parties. Such a decision shall apply in the second and subsequent commitment periods. A Party may choose to apply such a decision on these additional human-induced activities for its first commitment period, provided that these activities have taken place since 1990.

5.   The Parties included in Annex I undergoing the process of transition to a market economy whose base year or period was established pursuant to decision 9/CP.2 of the Conference of the Parties at its second session, shall use that base year or period for the implementation of their commitments under this Article. Any other Party included in Annex I undergoing the process of transition to a market economy which has not yet submitted its first national communication under Article 12 of the Convention may also notify the Conference of the Parties serving as the meeting of the Parties to this Protocol that it intends to use a historical base year or period other than 1990 for the implementation of its commitments under this Article. The Conference of the Parties serving as the meeting of the Parties to this Protocol shall decide on the acceptance of such notification.

6.   Taking into account Article 4, paragraph 6, of the Convention, in the implementation of their commitments under this Protocol other than those in this Article, a certain degree of flexibility shall be allowed by the Conference of the Parties serving as the meeting of the Parties to this Protocol to the Parties included in Annex I undergoing the process of transition to a market economy.

7.   In the first quantified emission limitation and reduction commitment period, from 2008 to 2012, the assigned amount for each Party included in Annex I shall be equal to the percentage inscribed for it in Annex B of its aggregate anthropogenic carbon dioxide equivalent emissions of the greenhouse gases listed in Annex A in 1990, or the base year or period determined in accordance with paragraph 5 above, multiplied by five. Those Parties included in Annex I for whom land-use change and forestry constituted a net source of greenhouse gas emissions in 1990 shall include in their 1990 emissions base year or period the aggregate anthropogenic carbon dioxide equivalent emissions by sources minus removals by sinks in 1990 from land use change for the purposes of calculating their assigned amount.

8.   Any Party included in Annex I may use 1995 as its base year for hydrofluorocarbons, perfluorocarbons and sulphur hexafluoride, for the purposes of the calculation referred to in paragraph 7 above.

9.   Commitments for subsequent periods for Parties included in Annex I shall be established in amendments to Annex B to this Protocol, which shall be adopted in accordance with the provisions of Article 21, paragraph 7. The Conference of the Parties serving as the meeting of the Parties to this Protocol shall initiate the consideration of such commitments at least seven years before the end of the first commitment period mentioned in paragraph 1 above. * * *

10.   Any emission reduction units, or any part of an assigned amount, which a Party acquires from another Party in accordance with the provisions of Article 6 or of Article 17 shall be added to the assigned amount for the acquiring Party.

11.   Any emission reduction units, or any part of an assigned amount, which a Party transfers to another Party in accordance with the provisions of Article 6

or of Article 16 bis shall be subtracted from the assigned amount for the transferring Party.

12. Any certified emission reductions which a Party acquires from another Party in accordance with the provisions of Article 12 shall be added to the assigned amount for the acquiring Party.

13. If the emissions of a Party included in Annex I during a commitment period are less than its assigned amount under this Article, this difference shall, on request of that Party, be added to the assigned amount for that Party for subsequent commitment periods.

14. Each Party included in Annex I shall strive to implement the commitments mentioned in paragraph 1 above in such a way as to minimize adverse social, environmental and economic impacts on developing country Parties, particularly those identified in Article 4, paragraphs 8 and 9, of the Convention. In line with relevant decisions of the Conference of the Parties on the implementation of those paragraphs, the Conference of the Parties serving as the meeting of the Parties to this Protocol shall, at its first session, consider what actions are necessary to minimize the adverse effects of climate change and/or the impacts of response measures on Parties referred to in those paragraphs. Among the issues to be considered shall be the establishment of funding, insurance and transfer of technology.

Article 4

1. Any Parties included in Annex I that have agreed to jointly fulfil their commitments under Article 3 shall jointly be deemed to have met those commitments provided that their total combined aggregate anthropogenic carbon dioxide equivalent emissions of the greenhouse gases listed in Annex A do not exceed their assigned amounts calculated pursuant to their quantified emission limitation and reduction commitments inscribed in Annex B and in accordance with the provisions of Article 3. The respective emission level allocated to each of the Parties to the agreement shall be set out in that agreement.* * *

4. If Parties acting jointly do so in the framework of, and together with, a regional economic integration organization, any alteration in the composition of the organization after adoption of this Protocol shall not affect existing commitments under this Protocol. Any alteration in the composition of the organization shall only apply for the purposes of those commitments under Article 3 that are adopted subsequent to that alteration.

5. In the event of failure by the Parties to such an agreement to achieve their total combined level of emission reductions, each Party to that agreement shall be responsible for its own level of emissions set out in the agreement.

6. If Parties acting jointly do so in the framework of, and together with, a regional economic integration organization which is itself a Party to this Protocol, each member State of that regional economic integration organization individually, and together with the regional economic integration organization acting in accordance with Article 24, shall, in the event of failure to achieve the total combined level of emission reductions, be responsible for its level of emissions as notified in accordance with this Article. * * *

Article 6

1. For the purpose of meeting its commitments under Article 3, any Party included in Annex I may transfer to, or acquire from, any other such Party emission reduction units resulting from projects aimed at reducing anthropo-

genic emissions by sources or enhancing anthropogenic removals by sinks of greenhouse gases in any sector of the economy, provided that:

(a) Any such project has the approval of the Parties involved;

(b) Any such project provides a reduction in emissions by sources, or an enhancement of removals by sinks, that is additional to any that would otherwise occur;

(c) It does not acquire any emission reduction units if it is not in compliance with its obligations under Articles 5 and 7; and

(d) The acquisition of emission reduction units shall be supplemental to domestic actions for the purposes of meeting commitments under Article 3. * * *

Article 7

1. Each Party included in Annex I shall incorporate in its annual inventory of anthropogenic emissions by sources and removals by sinks of greenhouse gases not controlled by the Montreal Protocol, submitted in accordance with the relevant decisions of the Conference of the Parties, the necessary supplementary information for the purposes of ensuring compliance with Article 3, to be determined in accordance with paragraph 4 below.

2. Each Party included in Annex I shall incorporate in its national communication, submitted under Article 12 of the Convention, the supplementary information necessary to demonstrate compliance with its commitments under this Protocol, to be determined in accordance with paragraph 4 below. * * *

Article 8

1. The information submitted under Article 7 by each Party included in Annex I shall be reviewed by expert review teams pursuant to the relevant decisions of the Conference of the Parties and in accordance with guidelines adopted for this purpose by the Conference of the Parties serving as the meeting of the Parties to this Protocol under paragraph 4 below. The information submitted under Article 7, paragraph 1, by each Party included in Annex I shall be reviewed as part of the annual compilation and accounting of emissions inventories and assigned amounts. Additionally, the information submitted under Article 7, paragraph 2, by each Party included in Annex I shall be reviewed as part of the review of communications.* * *

3. ... The expert review teams shall prepare a report to the Conference of the Parties serving as the meeting of the Parties to this Protocol, assessing the implementation of the commitments of the Party and identifying any potential problems in, and factors influencing, the fulfilment of commitments. Such reports shall be circulated by the secretariat to all Parties to the Convention. The secretariat shall list those questions of implementation indicated in such reports for further consideration by the Conference of the Parties serving as the meeting of the Parties to this Protocol. * * *

Article 10

All Parties, taking into account their common but differentiated responsibilities and their specific national and regional development priorities, objectives and circumstances, without introducing any new commitments for Parties not included in Annex I, but reaffirming existing commitments under Article 4, paragraph 1, of the Convention, and continuing to advance the implementation of these commitments in order to achieve sustainable development, taking into account Article 4, paragraphs 3, 5 and 7, of the Convention, shall:

(a) Formulate, where relevant and to the extent possible, cost-effective national, and where appropriate, regional programmes to improve the quality of local emission factors, activity data and/or models which reflect the socio-economic conditions of each Party for the preparation and periodic updating of national inventories of anthropogenic emissions by sources and removals by sinks of all greenhouse gases not controlled by the Montreal Protocol, using comparable methodologies to be agreed upon by the Conference of the Parties, and consistent with the guidelines for the preparation of national communications adopted by the Conference of the Parties;

(b) Formulate, implement, publish and regularly update national and, where appropriate, regional programmes containing measures to mitigate climate change and measures to facilitate adequate adaptation to climate change:

(i) Such programmes would, *inter alia*, concern the energy, transport and industry sectors as well as agriculture, forestry and waste management. Furthermore, adaptation technologies and methods for improving spatial planning would improve adaptation to climate change; and

(ii) Parties included in Annex I shall submit information on action under this Protocol, including national programmes, in accordance with Article 7; and other Parties shall seek to include in their national communications, as appropriate, information on programmes which contain measures that the Party believes contribute to addressing climate change and its adverse impacts, including the abatement of increases in greenhouse gas emissions, and enhancement of and removals by sinks, capacity building and adaptation measures.

(c) Cooperate in the promotion of effective modalities for the development, application and diffusion of, and take all practicable steps to promote, facilitate and finance, as appropriate, the transfer of, or access to, environmentally sound technologies, know-how, practices and processes pertinent to climate change, in particular to developing countries, including the formulation of policies and programmes for the effective transfer of environmentally sound technologies that are publicly owned or in the public domain and the creation of an enabling environment for the private sector, to promote and enhance access to, and transfer of, environmentally sound technologies. * * *

Article 12

1. A clean development mechanism is hereby defined.

2. The purpose of the clean development mechanism shall be to assist Parties not included in Annex I in achieving sustainable development and in contributing to the ultimate objective of the Convention, and to assist Parties included in Annex I in achieving compliance with their quantified emission limitation and reduction commitments under Article 3.

3. Under the clean development mechanism:

(a) Parties not included in Annex I will benefit from project activities resulting in certified emission reductions; and

(b) Parties included in Annex I may use the certified emission reductions accruing from such project activities to contribute to compliance with part of their quantified emission limitation and reduction commitments under Article 3, as determined by the Conference of the Parties serving as the meeting of the Parties to this Protocol.

4. The clean development mechanism shall be subject to the authority and guidance of the Conference of the Parties serving as the meeting of the Parties

to this Protocol and be supervised by an executive board of the clean development mechanism.

5.   Emission reductions resulting from each project activity shall be certified by operational entities to be designated by the Conference of the Parties serving as the meeting of the Parties to this Protocol, on the basis of:

(a) Voluntary participation approved by each Party involved;

(b) Real, measurable, and long-term benefits related to the mitigation of climate change; and

(c) Reductions in emissions that are additional to any that would occur in the absence of the certified project activity.

6.   The clean development mechanism shall assist in arranging funding of certified project activities as necessary.* * *

8.   The Conference of the Parties serving as the meeting of the Parties to this Protocol shall ensure that a share of the proceeds from certified project activities is used to cover administrative expenses as well as to assist developing country Parties that are particularly vulnerable to the adverse effects of climate change to meet the costs of adaptation.

9.   Participation under the clean development mechanism, including in activities mentioned in paragraph 3(a) above and acquisition of certified emission reductions, may involve private and/or public entities, and is to be subject to whatever guidance may be provided by the executive board of the clean development mechanism.

10.   Certified emission reductions obtained during the period from the year 2000 up to the beginning of the first commitment period can be used to assist in achieving compliance in the first commitment period. * * *

Article 17

The Conference of the Parties shall define the relevant principles, modalities, rules and guidelines, in particular for verification, reporting and accountability for emissions trading. The Parties included in Annex B may participate in emissions trading for the purposes of fulfilling their commitments under Article 3 of this Protocol. Any such trading shall be supplemental to domestic actions for the purpose of meeting quantified emission limitation and reduction commitments under that Article.

Annex A

Greenhouse Gases
Carbon dioxide
Methane
Nitrous Oxide
Hydrofluorocarbons
Perfluorocarbons
Sulphur hexafluoride * * *

Annex B: Reduction Commitments as Percentage from Base Year

Australia	108	Austria	92
Belgium	92	Bulgaria	92
Canada	94	Croatia	95
Czech Republic	92	Denmark	92
Estonia	92	European Community	92

Finland	92	France	92
Germany	92	Greece	92
Hungary	94	Iceland	110
Italy	92	Japan	94
Latvia	92	Liechtenstein	92
Lithuania	92	Luxembourg	92
Monaco	92	Netherlands	92
New Zealand	100	Norway	101
Poland	94	Portugal	92
Romania	92	Russian Federation	100
Slovakia	92	Slovenia	92
Spain	92	Sweden	92
Switzerland	92	Ukraine	100
United Kingdom	92	USA	93

QUESTIONS AND DISCUSSION

1. *Working the Treaty.* Answer the following questions from the Kyoto Protocol.

   - By what year must Annex I countries show demonstrable progress toward their target emissions level?
   - What are the conditions placed on trading emissions reduction units?
   - What is the purpose of the clean development mechanism?
   - What number of Parties is necessary for the Protocol to enter into force?
   - Does the Protocol penalize non-Parties?

2. *Policies and Measures.* From the start of negotiations, the United States and Europe disagreed on whether to adopt, in addition to targets and timetables, a list of mandatory 'policies and measures' that countries would have to adopt to lower greenhouse gas emissions. The European Union supported harmonized policies and measures, because they would be required to harmonize their measures inside the Union anyway. Enshrining these policies and measures in the Protocol, itself, would eliminate any competitive disadvantage Europe's industries might face compared to the United States and Japan. The United States adamantly opposed this approach, however, insisting that it must retain flexibility to choose policies and measures that would minimize domestic costs. The Protocol's ultimate language on policies and measures is not mandatory, and the measures listed in Article 2—for example, enhancement of energy efficiency, protection of sinks and reservoirs, promotion of sustainable agriculture, and promotion of renewable energy—are fairly general and, by-and-large, uncontroversial.

3. Because countries in economic transition currently emit at levels far below their levels in the baseline period from 1985–90, many of these countries will not emit their assigned amounts under the Kyoto Protocol even assuming they take no steps to reduce Greenhouse gases. Under the Protocol, these countries may be permitted to sell this so-called "hot air" to other Annex I countries. The amount of hot air from economies in transition, notably Russia and Ukraine, is difficult to determine. Estimates vary, but a reasonable guess is that under business-as-usual their emissions would rise to 10% below 1990 levels during the first budget period, suggesting that they will have 305.7 million megatonnes of CO_2 to sell to Annex I countries, which represents 1.7% of the Annex I emission reduction targets. Elimination of this "loophole" would have increased the amount of emissions reduction actually needed to reach the target level, but it is likely that, without the availability of hot air, the United States and several other countries would have adopted less stringent targets.

4. As a "regional economic integration organization" under the Climate Change Convention, the European Union anticipated that under the Kyoto Protocol it would be allowed to adopt an EU-wide target or "bubble," which could then be apportioned among EU members in any manner the members chose. Consequently, the European Union developed a burden-sharing arrangement that required Germany to reduce its emissions by 30% from 1990 levels by 2010, while permitting Portugal to increase its emissions by 40%. The United States and other Umbrella Group countries objected to this arrangement because it gave EU countries a competitive advantage over those countries that had to go it alone. U.S. representatives also believed that EU compliance would be achieved largely through Germany taking advantage of reduced emissions from eastern Germany's economic restructuring. For its part, the United States wanted full emissions trading between Annex I countries, which Europe opposed. As a negotiating ploy, U.S. negotiator Stuart Eisenstat said informally that a number of countries had agreed to be under a single "umbrella," analogous to the EU bubble. A panicked Europe, concerned that the Umbrella Group countries might gain a monopoly on access to Russian "hot air" credits, agreed to full emissions trading between Annex I countries.

5. The Protocol has its flaws and is clearly only a first step toward a global resolution of climate change. Yet one should not underestimate the potentially profound impact of the industrialized countries agreeing to *limit* their emissions of greenhouse gases. Why did they do it? What factors influenced their decision to complete an agreement at all in Kyoto? What pressures drove governments to negotiate for forty-eight hours and to continue the negotiations a full day longer than was scheduled? Does the Kyoto process provide lessons about how international law, or at least international treaties, is made?

F.   THE POST-KYOTO NEGOTIATIONS

No sooner had the ink dried on the Kyoto Protocol than it became clear that significant ambiguities existed in the text of the Protocol that could lead to vastly different reduction requirements for the United States and other Annex I countries. Several provisions of the protocol were deliberately left ambiguous allowing countries to make their own interpretations and thus their own calculations of the costs they faced in meeting their emission reduction targets. With the clock already ticking toward the first reporting period of 2008, however, all of the Parties recognized some urgency in clarifying a unified interpretation of the Protocol. At the very least the institutional, procedural and reporting requirements for the first reporting period needed to be established.

In order to build the political momentum for an agreement and given the lesson of the Berlin Mandate, the Parties meeting in Buenos Aires in 1999 agreed to a 'Buenos Aires Workplan', which among other things set forth a negotiating schedule that would clarify all major ambiguities in the Kyoto Protocol by the Sixth Conference of the Parties (CoP–6), scheduled in late 2000 for the Hague. All negotiations then began to aim at CoP–6 as the determinative meeting for the Kyoto Protocol. Whether signatories to the Protocol would be willing to ratify the agreement would depend on whether and how agreement was reached in clarifying the Protocol's approach.

The run-up to CoP–6 was also intertwined with US politics, because the meeting was scheduled for just a few weeks after the US Presidential elections. Because the 2000 election was shrouded with confusion, the US delegation actually went to the Hague not knowing for sure whether Al Gore, a self-proclaimed friend to the environment, or George W. Bush, a self-avowed oil and gas man, would be the next President. US and European NGOs also targeted the Hague talks as being crucial. Environmental activists sandbagged the entire building where the negotiations were being held to underscore the perils of sea level rise. Even the chair of the negotiations, Jan Pronk, came outside to lay a sandbag. The United States was widely seen as slowing progress at the negotiations and indeed some of the nearly 200 students brought over to the negotiations by Greenpeace USA, feigned sleep at a table under the banner "US delegation Hard at Work on Negotiations."

Despite all of the pressure that had targeted the Hague negotiations and despite postponing closure of the meeting for more than a day, the United States and European Union could not bridge their remaining differences. Rather than closing the meeting, the Chairman suspended discussions until an unspecified later date. Subsequently, what would become known as CoP6–bis was scheduled for Bonn in July of 2001. The failure to reach consensus at the Hague was particularly important, because with the new year (2001) came a new US Presidency. It was clear that US policy toward climate change would change dramatically. In February 2001, everyone learned just how dramatically when President Bush unilaterally announced that the United States would not honor its commitment to support the Kyoto Protocol.

The Bush Administration offered neither an apology nor an alternative, leaving Europeans and others furious at the unilateral and unexplained shift. Protests occurred at US Embassies around the world, and Bush was widely decried as a 'climate criminal'. Europe quickly called for other countries to join it in negotiating the outstanding issues under the Protocol and pushing for ratification without the United States.

This split between Europe and the United States left Japan in the middle. The Kyoto Protocol could theoretically enter into force without the United States, but only if Europe, Japan and Russia all agreed to ratify it. Japan's Prime Minister would ultimately milk this position first for support from the US in propping up Japan's ailing banking industry and then subsequently gaining concessions from Europe in the climate negotiations before announcing that it would indeed sign the Kyoto Protocol. Aiding the effort to woo Japan was the fact that the Protocol bore the name of one of Japan's most important cities. Buttons at subsequent climate negotiations were passed out with the flag of Japan, saying "Honour Kyoto"—a clear effort to remind the Japanese that as the hosts of the Protocol negotiations they had a special interest in ensuring its success.

Given the US position toward the Protocol and that it was actively lobbying others to reject the Protocol as well, most observers thought little progress would be made at the Bonn CoP6–bis meeting. Europe nonetheless kept pushing hard for an agreement, hoping that Japan and the other industrialized countries would join them in responding to the climate change threat and in isolating the United States. The Chairperson of the negotiations, Dutch Environment Minister Jan Pronk, issued a paper (known as the Second Pronk Paper) that essentially outlined a proposed set of policies that he believed could and should be accepted by all the countries of the world except the United States.

In part because of Pronk's effort, European resolve more generally and the United States' own unilateral bungling, the Parties other than the United States surprised most observers by reaching an agreement on the key elements of the Protocol. The United States had undermined its own position by promising to offer an alternative policy approach to the Protocol and then delivering nothing but a commitment to research the causes and impacts of climate change. The July agreement clarifying the details of the Protocol sets the stage for all of the countries in the world (except the United States) to ratify the Kyoto Protocol and begin to meet their obligations under the first reporting period. Substantial uncertainty remains at the time of writing this textbook, however, because the United States may yet offer an alternative approach to attract enough Parties to prevent the Protocol from coming into force.

The following discussions address the major issues that have dominated negotiations since the Kyoto Protocol and describe the conclusions that were reached in the July 2001 negotiations. These issues may continue to plague negotiations into the near future, particularly because further negotiations will undoubtedly have to take place to bring the United States back into the regime. The issues discussed below include: (1) the scope and role of emissions trading and other 'flexibility mechanisms'; (2) the extent of land-use and forest changes that would be allowed in the calculations for the first reporting commitment; (3) the parameters of a compliance monitoring and enforcement mechanism; and (4) funding and financing issues.

----

1. THE FLEXIBILITY MECHANISMS: TRADING, JOINT IMPLEMENTATION AND THE CLEAN DEVELOPMENT MECHANISM

One of the most controversial and complicated issues in the climate change negotiations has been the extent to which industrialized (Annex I) countries will be allowed to meet their own obligations by financing or undertaking activities in other countries. For example, would the United States be allowed to meet its obligations under the Convention by investing in energy efficiency in China? In some respects, the nature of climate change is ideal for establishing global trading markets in pollution; the reduction of one ton of carbon dioxide emissions anywhere in the world reduces climate change as much as any other ton of reduction. This has led many observers to develop different trading schemes to allow greater flexibility in meeting climate change targets. In theory, at least, such trading schemes can result in lowering the costs of compliance.

The Protocol contains four mechanisms (collectively know as 'flexibility mechanisms') that allow parties to meet their commitments jointly. Emissions trading under Article 17 allows one Annex I party to purchase or otherwise transfer part of its assigned amount to another Annex I party.

Like emissions trading, joint implementation (JI) under Article 6 may take place only between Annex I countries. JI involves the sale of "reduction units" from one Annex I party, or private enterprise, to another Annex I party or enterprise. Reduction units are generated by specific projects that reduce emissions or increase removals in the selling country. JI may be distinguished from emissions trading in that emissions trading is program-based, while JI is project-based. Emissions trading may also occur before associated emissions reductions are achieved, while JI reduction units can be transferred only after they have accrued. Emissions trading may be government-to-government, while JI may be initiated and undertaken by private sector entities. But in the final analysis, emissions trading and JI are closely linked; indeed, JI cannot occur without a concurrent emissions trade (or its equivalent). The third approach, joint fulfillment of commitments under Article 4 allows an agreement between two or more parties to meet their combined commitments by reducing their aggregated emissions. Article 4 essentially allows parties to create a bubble around one or more of them to create their own targets and timetables, as long as the aggregate emissions from the parties do not exceed the aggregate allowances under the Protocol. Article 4 allows the European Union, for example, to operate essentially as one entity within the Protocol. Finally, the Clean Development ment Mechanism (CDM), which is defined in Article 12, replaces JI with respect to non-Annex I countries (i.e. developing countries). Article 12 provides that Annex I parties, or their private entities, may fund activities in non-Annex I countries that result in emissions reductions and, after they are certified, use those reductions to contribute to their own compliance.

Many controversies continued beyond Kyoto regarding how the flexibility mechanisms would operate. Among the controversies was whether the use of emissions trading under Article 17 and the other flexibility mechanisms should be capped or not. In other words, would countries be forced to meet most or at least some amount of their emission reduction targets by reducing emissions *at home,* or could they simply purchase all of their needed emissions from Russia or other countries that had emission reduction units to sell.

The European Union sought a cap on emissions trading of 50% of the total reductions required, relying on the following language in Article 17 of the Protocol: "Any such trading shall be *supplemental* to domestic actions for the purpose of meeting quantified emission limitation and reduction commitments under [Article 3]." The United States wanted unlimited trading because they believed they could buy emission reduction units from the former Soviet Bloc very cheaply. Legitimate concerns existed over how to monitor, verify and ensure the validity of any trade and strong policy reasons also argued for forcing the United States to take some domestic measures.

Europe's position was somewhat disingenuous, however, because the supplementarity condition would not apply to their emissions trading within the European Union. The supplementarity condition is not included in Article 4, which allows the European Union to meet its climate obligations as a bloc. This 'bubble concept' allows investments from countries like France or Austria that have high greenhouse gas emissions but relatively efficient production processes to flow to countries like Spain, Portugal or Greece, which have less efficient factories in which the reduction of greenhouse gases will cost less.

Ultimately, the Parties could not agree to any numerical cap on emissions trading under Article 17, deciding instead on general language requesting that countries through their actions move toward narrowing per capita emissions. Section VI of the July 2001 Bonn Agreement concluded:

> That the Parties included in Annex I shall implement domestic action in accordance with national circumstances and with a view to reducing emissions in a manner conducive to narrowing per capita differences between developed and developing country Parties while working towards achievement of the ultimate objective of the Convention.

> That the use of the mechanisms shall be supplemental to domestic action and domestic action shall thus constitute a significant element of the effort made by each Party included in Annex I to meet its quantified emission limitation and reduction commitments under Article 3, paragraph 1.

Review of the Implementation of Commitments and of Other Provisions of the Convention, Decision 5/CP.6, FCCC/CP/2001/L.7 (July 24, 2001) [hereinafter July 2001 Bonn Agreement].

More complicated, if not more politically contentious, was the debate over the technical rules to ensure the flexibility mechanisms are in fact leading to additional reductions (i.e. reductions over and above what would have occurred without the trade or investment). For example, trading with Russia and other former Soviet bloc countries—i.e. purchasing so-called "hot air"—was clearly not going to lead to further reductions, because those countries were not going to emit their allowed levels in any event. These issues are even more complex when it comes to those mechanisms that allow Annex I countries to invest in or trade with developing countries, which have no quantified targets on emissions under the Protocol. Most prominent among these mechanisms is the CDM, established by Article 12 of the Kyoto Protocol.

The Protocol provided little guidance as to what the CDM would be; it was virtually undefined. The CDM was potentially a funding mechanism, a clearinghouse, or merely a mechanism for accreditation and oversight. Although the G77 as a bloc opposed joint implementation, they readily accepted the CDM. One possible explanation is that developing countries feared that joint implementation would go the way of previous "commodity" agreements, which yielded little profit for sellers. The CDM on the other hand might allow them to coordinate prices–in effect, to create a carbon cartel. Of course, purchasing countries, particularly the United States, worked to oppose such an outcome.

The July 2001 Bonn Agreement did help to clarify some elements of the CDM. First, the CDM is intended to allow Annex I countries to invest in projects in developing countries and thereby receive credit for certified emission reductions achieved through the investment. Among the decisions taken by the Parties:

• The CDM would not support projects involving nuclear facilities;

- Public funding for CDM projects from Annex I parties should not result in the diversion of official development assistance and should be separate from financial obligations of Annex I parties under the convention.

- Small-scale projects that would be eligible include renewable energy projects under 15 megawatts, energy efficiency projects that reduce consumption by at least 15 Gigawatt-hours per year.

- Afforestation and reforestation projects shall be the only eligible land-use, land-use change and forestry projects under the CDM during the first commitment period. The framework for accepting these projects must address issues relating to "non-permanence, additionality, leakage, scale, uncertainties, socio-economic and environmental impacts (including impacts on bio-diversity and natural ecosystems)."

_____

QUESTIONS AND DISCUSSION

1. The flexibility mechanisms intended to operate in developing countries—i.e. joint implementation and the CDM—raise additional questions for ensuring that any emission reduction credits are indeed additional to "business as usual" over the long-term. Consider the following discussion of joint implementation. Although written before the Kyoto Protocol was negotiated, its discussion of the technical issues of JI are relevant as well to the Clean Development Mechanism.

Goldberg, *Twelve Principles for Joint Implementation* (CIEL, 1997)

Problems with the JI Methodology

An equally important set of objections focus on the technical difficulty of assessing the climate benefits resulting from JI. Quantifying these benefits requires an estimation of GHG emissions that would have occurred if a given JI project had *not* been undertaken (what would be the emissions "but for" the project?). JI opponents argue that accurately measuring, monitoring and verifying these benefits will be impossible. Part of the difficulty is due to the wide variance in methodologies used by project developers and country programs to compute such benefits. The methodological and technical challenges of JI projects include, among other things, guaranteeing financial and environmental additionality, determining baselines, monitoring and verifying reduced or sequestered emissions, guarding against leakage, and assuring durability of emissions offsets.

Financial additionality refers to the need for funds for JI pilot projects to be "new and additional" to the financial obligations of Annex II Parties (mainly OECD countries) within the framework of the financial mechanism of the FCCC as well as to current official development assistance flows. Although future JI funding is expected to come primarily from the private sector, some countries (e.g., the Netherlands and Switzerland) are currently using government funds to finance projects. While such government involvement may be essential to initiate projects during the pilot phase (and possibly even beyond), it may conflict with the requirement that JI funding "be additional" to pre-existing international development assistance. The possibility that some JI projects may be linked to, or be components of, projects financed by the World Bank, the Global Environment Facility, or other international financial institutions, makes determining financial additionality much more difficult.

Environmental or *emissions additionality* currently requires JI pilot projects to bring about real, measurable and long-term environmental benefits related to the mitigation of climate change that would not have occurred in the absence of such activities. This requirement is essential if JI is to become an acceptable tool for controlling global warming, yet its execution has turned out to be extremely complicated (some would say impossible, since it can never be known with certainty what would have happened had the project not been implemented). First, an emissions baseline must be selected, against which any carbon benefits obtained by mitigation efforts may be measured. For project baselines, as opposed to sectoral or national baselines, the project developer must determine a reference case, which is the amount of GHG emissions that would be produced or sequestered on the project site in the absence of the JI project. This requires identifying all of the carbon sources and sinks located on the project site. The reference case will be "static" if it includes only existing sources and sinks, or it could be "dynamic," taking into account subsequent changes in the local economy, population, or environment. The project developer then computes a project case that measures the emissions effects of the project for the same time period as the reference case and from which net project GHG benefits can be derived.

Leakage presents a further JI challenge. Leakage is the phenomenon by which reducing or sequestering emissions in a specific place simply shifts the pollution-causing activity somewhere else. Theoretically, leakage may be controlled on the local and national level if the host country has a comprehensive sector-wide or nation-wide GHG mitigation plan and the political will and capacity to enforce it. Even so, the country may not be able unilaterally to control international leakage if, for example, companies faced with increased environmental restrictions simply move their operations to other countries where rules are more lax.

Project duration is a key element of full carbon accounting. Net GHG offsets must be calculated not only for the present time, but also must be monitored, verified, and guaranteed for the life of the project. Therefore, provisions must be made to ensure against loss due to project failure. This is particularly important in forestry projects, where credits produced by carbon sequestration will likely be used to offset fossil fuel emissions. Those emissions are believed to retain their radiative forcing qualities in the atmosphere for 100 years or more. Forest projects thus must be sufficiently durable to account for the long atmospheric residency of the CO_2 emissions they offset, and must anticipate and account for possible loss of trees from insect infestation, disease, fire, or accident (here it may be important to distinguish between natural and anthropogenic causes).

Monitoring and Verification, preferably by third parties, is another essential element of JI accounting. JI presents a moral hazard that, intentionally or not, project sponsors and hosts will exaggerate the carbon emissions of the baseline case as well as the mitigation or reduction achieved by the project case. Both parties benefit from calculating the maximum number of carbon credits obtained from the project. Rigorous monitoring and verification is needed to counteract the moral hazard dilemma and ensure that reported carbon mitigation represents genuine reductions. Monitoring entails measuring and calculating the carbon benefits obtained by the project. Currently, it is usually done by the project developer rather than an independent, third party. Due to the wide range of potential JI project types, no monitoring methodologies have yet been developed that can be universally employed. Carbon benefits claimed by the developer must subsequently be verified by a qualified third party—which itself should be certified or licensed by a reputable entity. Verified project results are then reported to the project host and home countries, to be integrated into their GHG tracking records and in turn reported to the FCCC via their respective submissions to the SBSTA. Monitoring and verification may thus add significant cost to JI projects. Some NGOs argue that the costs of monitoring and verification will outweigh the other benefits of JI. Other NGOs add that even if JI project results can be monitored and verified, it will be impossible to police potentially thousands of deals, and to provide enforcement of those which do not comply with agreed requirements. * * *

Despite the potential offered by JI as a tool to address climate change, significant questions remain unanswered. The controversy surrounding JI, as voiced by concerned developing countries and environmental NGOs, and the unresolved methodological problems involved in the implementation, monitoring and enforcement of JI suggest that serious consideration must be given before deciding to proceed to full JI. Any decision about the future of JI must be guided by the following principles.

Some developing countries, particularly Costa Rica, have jumped on the JI bandwagon, creating national programs to solicit projects actively from developed countries. Why would developing countries want to proactively support JI projects? Are there any reasons arguing against such an approach?

---

2. THE ROLE OF FORESTS AND LAND–USE CHANGES IN THE KYOTO PROTOCOL

Both the Framework Convention and the Kyoto Protocol clearly contemplate that sinks such as forests would be within the ambit of the climate regime. Most significantly, Article 3.3 of the Kyoto Protocol allows for Parties to meet their target level by counting the net changes in greenhouse gas emissions resulting from human-induced "afforestation, reforestation, and deforestation" since 1990. This provision was especially unclear and open to interpretation, and thus generated enormous debate during the post-Kyoto negotiations.

Uncertainty relating to land-use and forestry practices to a country's carbon stock led negotiators to limit Article 3.3.'s coverage to afforestation, reforestation and deforestation. Article 3.4 provided that additional activities, presumably including for example conservation, forest management and harvesting, could be considered in meeting targets and timetables in subsequent commitment periods. Article 3.4 also required countries to provide the data necessary to establish a 1990 baseline for its carbon stock (i.e. the amount of carbon held in forests and other terrestrial sinks and reservoirs).

The Kyoto Protocol's coverage of forests raised many difficult and controversial issues. Afforestation, reforestation and deforestation were not defined in the Protocol, leaving them open for a wide range of definitions that could fundamentally change the effect of the Protocol in reducing greenhouse gas emissions. With large areas of growing forests, the United States in particular argued for liberal and expansive application of Article 3.3. For example, although harvesting was specifically rejected as an activity that must be counted in the first commitment period, the United States at one point suggested that restocking of harvested areas could be counted as reforestation. The impact of such an interpretation could be huge. In 1995, some 1.6 billion seedlings were planted in the United States, according to the American Forest and Paper Association. A tree sequesters roughly a ton of CO_2 and takes 40 or so years to mature. Assuming a steady rate of planting and growth from 1990 on, in 2010 the carbon sequestered in trees planted in the United States since 1990 would be roughly 800 million tons, or about 16% of U.S. 1990 emissions. In other words, simply by defining reforestation to include restocking after harvesting, the United States may be able to meet the commitments it made at the Kyoto Protocol and be having a greater impact on the climate system in the year 2008! Similarly, despite rejection of forest management as a creditable activity under Article 3.3, the United States also considered taking credit for reforestation and afforestation initiated before 1990 but that require some form of post–1990 management.

Article 3.3 could also have been read to require Annex I parties only to report emissions and removals that occur during commitment periods. Such an interpretation, however, would have created a perverse incentive to deforest areas before the year 2008 (i.e. the beginning of the first commitment period), thus creating more land for afforestation activities. Consider, too, that under IPCC Guidelines, emissions from deforestation are all counted in the year the activity takes place, while removals from reforestation are counted over decades, as the carbon accrues. Parties that follow such a strategy would have reported no emissions from the deforestation, but most or all of the removals from subsequent reforestation.

The widely varying interpretations of Articles 3.3 and 3.4 made forest issues central to the post-Kyoto negotiations. Ultimately, the decision reached at the Bonn meeting rejected the most extreme positions, thus reducing the potential of accounting for forests in lessening the Annex I country's commitments.

July 2001 Bonn Agreement, Part VII: Land–Use, Land–Use Change and Forestry

The Conference of the Parties:

1.Affirms that the following principles govern the treatment of land-use, land-use change and forestry (LULUCF) activities:

(a) That the treatment of these activities be based on sound science,

(b) Consistent methodologies be used over time for the estimation and reporting of these activities,

(c) The aim stated in Article 3, paragraph 1, of the Kyoto Protocol not be changed by accounting for LULUCF activities,

(d) That the mere presence of carbon stocks be excluded from accounting,

(e) That the implementation of LUCLUCF activities contributes to the conservation of biodiversity an sustainable use of natural resources,

(f) That accounting for LULUCF does not imply a transfer of commitments to a future commitment period,

(g) That reversal of any removal due to LULUCF activities be accounted for at the appropriate point in time,

(h) That accounting excludes removals resulting from (a) elevated carbon dioxide concentrations above their pre-industrial level; (b) indirect nitrogen deposition and (c) the dynamic effects of age structure resulting from activities and practices before the reference year.

The Conference of the Parties agrees:

2. On a definition of "forest" and on definitions of the activities "afforestation", "reforestation" and "deforestation" for the purpose of implementing Article 3.3. These activities shall be defined on the basis of a change in land use.

3. That debits from harvesting during the first commitment period following afforestation and reforestation since 1990 shall not be greater than credits earned on that unit of land.

4. That "forest management", "cropland management", "grazing land management" and "revegetation" are eligible land-use, land-use change and forestry activities under Article 3, paragraph 4, of the Kyoto Protocol. A Party may choose to apply any or all of these activities during the first commitment period. A Party shall fix its choice of eligible activities prior to the start of the first commitment period.

5. That, during the first commitment period, a Party that selects any or all of the activities mentioned in paragraph 4 above shall demonstrate that such activities have occurred since 1990, and are human-induced. Such activities should not account for emissions and removals resulting from afforestation, reforestation and deforestation as determined under Article 3, paragraph 3.

6. That the following accounting rules are applicable in the first commitment period. They aim to pragmatically implement the guiding principles in the preamble:

   (a) Application of net-net accounting (net emissions or removals over the commitment period less net removals in the base year, times five) for agricultural activities (cropland management, grazing land management and revegetation);

   (b) Accounting for forest management up to the level of any possible Article 3.3 debits, if the total carbon stock change in the managed forests since 1990 is equal to or larger than this Article 3.3 debit (up to 8.2 megatons of carbon per Party per year; no discounting);

   (c) Additions to and subtractions from the assigned amount of a Party, resulting from forest management under Article 3.4 after the application of the Article 3.3 debit compensation described in subparagraph (b) above, and resulting from forest management undertaken under Article 6, shall note exceed the value inscribed in Appendix Z to this decision.

7. That the eligibility of LULUCF activities under Article 12 [addressing the Clean Development Mechanism] is limited to afforestation and reforestation. . . .

———————

At the very least, the Parties agreement in Bonn clarifies the amount to which forests will be allowed to provide a "loophole" to the targets agreed in the Protocol. Appendix Z to the agreement (not reproduced above) limits the amount of credits that parties can take for forest management activities to a total of 54 megatons of carbon, a little more than 2% of Annex I emissions (excluding the United States, which did not participate in the Post–Kyoto agreement). Much of these reductions from forest management activities probably would have occurred anyway even without the agreement (i.e. they do not reflect any additional reductions over "business-as-usual"). The impact of including cropland and grazing land management and revegetation under Article 3.4 remains unclear. These activities are counted on a "net/net" basis, which means that only improvements in reductions measured against a 1990 baseline give rise to credits. Further analysis is required to determine how much of the resulting credit may reflect "business as usual", but it is reasonable to assume that significant improvements over the 1990 baseline will be mainly the result of real efforts to improve soil and sequester carbon.

QUESTIONS AND DISCUSSION

1. Perhaps most troubling, the sinks text is noticeably lacking in any environmental standards or criteria. It contains some general principles (e.g., sinks activities must "contribute to the conservation of biodiversity and sustainable use of natural forests)." Further, the SBSTA is tasked with developing definitions and modalities that take into account, *inter alia*, socio-economic impacts, including impacts on biodiversity and natural systems. Nonetheless, reforestation through plantation forests even with substantial losses in biodiversity may result in valid credits.

2. The climate change regime may turn out to be the most important international agreement on forest conservation as well, given that governments have not been able to reach consensus on a binding instrument on the sustainable management of forests. For further discussion of international forest policy, see Chapter 14. *See also* IPCC, SPECIAL REPORT ON LAND USE, LAND-USE CHANGE, AND FORESTRY (2000).

-----

3.   COMPLIANCE MONITORING AND ENFORCEMENT

Compliance was the last area that kept Parties apart throughout the marathon negotiating session in the Bonn Cop 6–bis meeting. Article 18 of the Kyoto Protocol provides that the parties:

> shall approve appropriate and effective procedures and mechanisms to determine and to address cases of non-compliance with the provisions of the Protocol, including through the development of an indicative list of consequences, taking into account the cause, type, degree and frequency of non-compliance. Any procedures and mechanisms under this Article entailing binding consequences shall be adopted by means of an amendment to this Protocol.

The United States and Europe generally supported a strong and clear compliance system. At issue was how to penalize or otherwise ensure that Parties do not miss their targets during the commitment period. The resulting agreement created a complex and innovative compliance system. The agreement establishes that:

- There will be a **compliance committee** comprised of two "branches." The **facilitative branch** will be available to assist all Parties—both developed (Annex I) and developing (non-Annex I)—in their implementation of the Protocol. Importantly, it will serve as an "early warning system" for Annex I Parties that may have trouble meeting their emissions targets.

- The **enforcement branch** will serve as a judicial-like forum for determining whether an Annex I Party has (1) met its target, (2) complied with its monitoring and reporting requirements and (3) met the eligibility tests for participating in the flexibility mechanisms. When the enforcement branch finds that a Party has failed to comply with one of these obligations, the enforcement branch will decide upon the appropriate consequence(s) for the Party.

- The **membership** of both the facilitative and enforcement branches will be based upon equitable geographical representation. This was a dramatic victory for the G–77 and China. "Composition" of the enforcement branch was the final, seemingly most intractable issue for negotiators to agree upon. Because only industrialized countries are facing targets and timetables under the Protocol, many Annex I countries believed that they should comprise the clear majority of the compliance bodies.

- There will be specific **consequences** when an Annex I Party fails to comply with its emissions target: (1) For every ton of emissions by which a Party exceeds its target, 1.3 tons will be deducted from its assigned amount for the subsequent commitment period. That rate may be increased for future commitment periods. (2) The Party will prepare a detailed plan explaining how it will meet its reduced target for the subsequent commitment period. The enforcement branch will have the power to review the plan and assess whether or not it is likely to work. (3) The Party will not be able to use Article 17 emissions trading to sell parts of its emissions allocation ("assigned amount") in the next commitment period.

- After the enforcement branch determines that a Party has exceeded its target, the Party will have the right to **appeal** the decision to the supreme body of the Protocol, the Conference of the Parties serving as the meeting of the protocol (the COP/MOP). The branch's decision will stand unless a three-quarters majority of the COP/MOP votes to overturn it. The appeals provision was a significant concession to the G–77 and China, who wanted assurances that decisions of the enforcement branch could not be made completely independently from COP/MOP oversight.

QUESTIONS AND DISCUSSION

1. The last sentence of Article 18 of the Kyoto Protocol provides that "binding consequences" of non-compliance may be adopted only by a Protocol amendment. That requirement reflects the inability of the Parties to agree at Kyoto upon the issue of non-compliance consequences. Japan, Russia and Australia have long resisted the desires of most other Parties to adopt "legally binding" consequences. In order to win agreement on the compromise summarized above, the parties deleted a political commitment to adopt an instrument that would have established the "legally binding" character of the consequences. Yet the text that was agreed upon appears to establish what the consequences will be (see above) and gives the enforcement branch the power to apply them. What is the difference, if any, between non-compliance consequences that are "legally binding" in the Article 18 sense or in fact binding in a political sense?

G. CROSS-CUTTING ISSUES

1. OZONE DEPLETION AND CLIMATE CHANGE

Ozone depletion and climate change are frequently confused. For most purposes they should be considered two completely separate environmental issues. They involve different chemical processes, have mostly different causes, and result in different threats to human health and the environment.

Yet, climate change and ozone depletion do overlap somewhat. Both CFCs, the main cause of ozone depletion, and ozone itself are greenhouse gases. Thus, the addition of CFCs to the atmosphere adds directly to global warming, but in destroying ozone it leads to global cooling. The two effects come close to canceling each other out. Moreover global warming at the earth's surface by trapping heat means the stratospheric ozone layer is actually colder. This allows more ice crystals to form, which act as a catalyst, increasing the chemical reaction that depletes the ozone layer. Thus as climate change worsens, so too will ozone depletion. The situation is complicated further, however, because most of the substitutes allowed for CFCs under the Montreal Protocol regime are more potent greenhouse gases than CFCs. Despite the overall ambiguity, the United States argued that countries should get some credit under the climate regime for eliminating CFCs, but the Kyoto Protocol clearly rejected the U.S. "all gases" position and excluded substances covered by the Montreal Protocol regime.

More important for our purposes is the relationship between climate change and ozone depletion with respect to international treaty making. As early as 1989, IPCC Working Group III, charged with developing the elements of a climate convention, turned to the Framework/Protocol model of the ozone regime. Since that time, the experience with the Montreal Protocol regime, particularly the flexibility with which it has adjusted to advances in science and technology, strengthens the arguments for using the Framework/Protocol mechanism to address complex issues such as climate change.

The Montreal Protocol regime is thus widely thought of as a successful and appropriate response to the threats posed by ozone depletion. In this respect, our experience there should embolden policymakers to take significant and meaningful steps with respect to climate change. Consider the following comments from U.S. ozone negotiator Richard Benedick, written on the eve of UNCED in 1992.

> The current debate about greenhouse warming conveys a distinct sense of deja vu. The world again confronts a classic situation: weighing the risks of action and inaction in the face of uncertainties. Short-term costs loom large; long-term dangers seem remote... The Antarctic ozone hole is an example of what scientists call a nonlinear response; that is, the ozone layer kept absorbing ever more chlorine from man-made sources without revealing any problem, until the concentrations reached a breaking point, and collapse ensued. With respect to greenhouse warming, scientists warn that the billions of tons of carbon dioxide and other gases being emitted by modem industrial economies constitute an unpredictable experiment on the atmosphere. Are we approaching other unknown thresholds?...

Had CFCs been permitted to continue growing, they would have wrought irreparable damage on the ozone layer. And yet at the time, powerful voices in government and industry strongly opposed regulations, on the grounds of incomplete scientific evidence. Under these circumstances, the lesson for the policymaker seems clear: if we are to err, let us err on the side of caution. The very existence of scientific uncertainty about global warming should lead us to action rather than delay, especially when most of the international scientific community persistently warns of the risks... Significantly, the Montreal Protocol on Substances that Deplete the Ozone Layer departed from the customary accommodation of environmental regulation to commercial convenience. It did not merely prescribe "best available technology" to replace CFCs. Rather the designers of the treaty mandated a timetable for deep cuts in consumption of these useful chemicals with full knowledge that the technology "did not yet exist to achieve those cuts." The treaty furnished an unmistakable market signal that made it worthwhile for companies to invest in research into new chemicals and processes they had previously eschewed... I suspect we would find the same forces at work if we would focus on reducing dependence on fossil fuels in the current international negotiations on a climate treaty.

Richard Benedick, *Essay: A Case of Deja Vu,* SCIENTIFIC AMERICAN, April, 1992, at 160

Benedick's comments continue to be relevant today, given the relatively weak approach taken in Kyoto. Benedick is obviously calling for a precautionary approach to addressing serious, long-term environmental problems. Does the experience with the climate change convention suggest we have learned the lessons of ozone depletion well? How would application of the precautionary principle apply to the climate change issue? Does the Montreal Protocol still seem like an appropriate model?

Do you agree with the view that clear standards like those in the Montreal Protocol create a strong market signal for technological innovation? If clear legal standards, including prohibitions, provide market incentives and economic opportunities, why is the trend in environmental policymaking toward adopting so-called economic instruments? What is the major difference between so-called economic instruments, such as taxes, and clear legal standards like those in Montreal Protocol when it comes to forcing technological innovations? Why might "technological optimists" (i.e. those who believe technology will solve our environmental problems) nonetheless favor a precautionary approach in setting clear targets and timetables regarding GHG emissions?

---

2. ENERGY PLANNING AND CLIMATE POLICY

A number of leading scientists have recommended that increased research efforts be dedicated to nuclear energy. Indeed nuclear fission is "clean" in the sense that it does not create greenhouse gases. Not surprisingly, many environmentalists are opposed to nuclear energy because of the threat of radioactive leaks, the problems in disposing of spent fuel, and the danger in transporting fuels for reprocessing (*see* Chapter 9, page 671, for a problem exercise on ocean shipments of radioactive waste). Similarly, many reputable scientists and policy analysts support increased use of hydropower, another "clean" source of energy. This, too, is opposed by many environmentalists because of the environmental and human rights problems associated with dam construction. Are environmentalists trying to have it both ways? Is it responsible to argue strongly in favor of reducing greenhouse gases while at the same time opposing development of energy sources that do not produce greenhouse gases? If you were the Secretary of Energy in the United States, how would you allocate research funds among the following areas: solar energy, wind power, geothermal energy, nuclear energy, hydrogen fuel cells, hydropower, biomass, coal-fired and oil-fired power plants? Which of these do you think could provide a significant amount of energy within the next decade?

3.   CLIMATE LITIGATION, LIABILITY AND COMPENSATION

The victims of climate change are not the same States that have caused most of the problem. Take for example, the plight of the island States that will suffer most from sea-level rise. Most of them have added negligible contributions to greenhouse concentrations in the atmosphere. The island of Tuvalu, for example is predicted to be uninhabitable due to sea level rise by 2050. Its 10,000 inhabitants have already begun looking for a new home. Neither the Climate Change Convention nor the Kyoto Protocol meaningfully addressed the issue of legal liability, although several provisions did address the plight of particularly vulnerable countries. If you were the general counsel for Tuvalu, what advice would you give him? What legal remedies might the island States have against those countries that have contributed the most to the problem? Prepare an outline of the cases, principles and treaty precedents you would use to make your argument for compensation from industrialized countries. Now change your perspective to that of the industrialized countries. *See* Durwood Zaelke & James Cameron, *Global Warming and Climate Change—An Overview of the International Legal Process*, 5 Am U. J.Int'l L. & Pol'y 249 (1990).

In addition to island states suing industrialized states, environmental groups and trial lawyers are now considering climate-based litigation. What hurdles will they face? To what extent does the IPCC's Third Assessment Report demonstrate sufficient causation to support a claim in US Court? What legal theories or causes of action would you think are the strongest for the plaintiffs? *Global Warming May Bring New Variety of Class Action*, N.Y.Times (Sept. 6, 2001).

The victims of climate change are not the only ones looking at the courts. In 1999, the Western Fuel Association, a trade group comprised of coal companies, sued several environmental groups including Friends of the Earth and Rainforest Action Network, claiming that an advertisement linking coal to climate change was libelous and improperly disadvantage coal vis-à-vis renewables and solar energy. The case was dismissed without prejudice on venue grounds, as several of the organizations did not have minimum contacts with the chosen forum (Wyoming). Why do you think the defendants chose to bring the case in Wyoming?

4.   THE FUTURE OF THE CLIMATE REGIME

The Protocol enters into force after 55 parties, representing at least 55 percent of global carbon emissions, have ratified it. Early after taking office in 2001, President George W. Bush repudiated the Protocol and announced that he would not present it to the Senate for ratification. The European Union, Japan and most other countries in the world have announced their intention to seek ratification of the Protocol without the United States. This split among the countries most responsible for climate change, and particularly the US recalcitrance in addressing climate change, undoubtedly cannot last. What do you think will happen next? Can the Protocol be effective without the United States? Can the United States continue to be isolated on this issue internationally? These issues are not answered as this book goes to print, making the future of the climate regime very uncertain.

Suggested Further Reading and Web Sites

National Assessment Synthesis Team, CLIMATE CHANGE IMPACTS OF CLIMATE VARIABILITY AND CHANGE (Cambridge Press, 2000)

Ross Gelbspan, THE HEAT IS ON: THE HIGH STAKES BATTLE OVER EARTH'S THREATENED CLIMATE (1997). Gelbspan focuses on the energy industry and shows how it has willfully created an appearance of uncertainty within the scientific community in order to slow down policy response to climate change.

Stephen H. Schneider, LABORATORY EARTH: THE PLANETARY GAMBLE WE CAN'T AFFORD TO LOSE (1997). Stanford climatologist Stephen Schneider writes of the United States' position in dealing with the shift in the planet's climate.

R. Peters and T. Lovejoy, GLOBAL WARMING AND BIOLOGICAL DIVERSITY (1993)

http://www.ipcc.ch/
    The website for the intergovernmental panel on climate change, with copies of all of their reports.

http://www.unfccc.de
    The official site of the United Nations Framework Convention on Climate Change. This homepage provides full text versions of all documentation from Kyoto and all past and present UN press releases. This site also links to the Third Conference of the Parties (CoP) (http://www.cop3.de).

http://www.safeclimate.net
    A website maintained by the World Resources Institute that allows you to calculate your own individual contribution to climate change.

http://www.pewclimate.org/
    An independent policy organization with a variety of reports and recommendations on climate policy.

CHAPTER TEN

Oceans and Seas

SECTION I.   HISTORY AND BACKGROUND

Our planet should not be called Earth but Ocean–at least seven-tenths is covered with seas.

We know little about this water planet. Although the oceans are just as diverse as the land, and interwoven with human history, we tend to see them as barriers, as alien spaces. In reality, however, ocean ecosystems are continuous–or rather, a single ecosystem, a world ocean with land masses as the true barriers, though gradients of temperature and salinity separate the oceans into a multiple series of discrete regions.

It takes a leap of the imagination to perceive the integral role of the ocean in our planet's workings. The interdependent circulatory systems of ocean and atmosphere determine climatic flows right around the globe. At the same time, the great accumulations of seawater, almost entirely placid beneath the surface, exert a major stabilizing influence on climate. * * *

The oceans give no more of a liquid covering to the globe than a film of moisture on a football, yet their depth and grandeur are remarkable–Mount Everest could be readily lost in the Mariana Trench. Underwater landscapes are extraordinarily varied, with spectacular geologic features. Along the edges of land masses are barely sloping continental shelves, accounting for about eight percent of the ocean's expanse. Fed by sediments washed off the land, these shelves are often very fertile, and support abundant fisheries. Twice as extensive are the continental slopes, with gradients 4–10 times steeper, reaching down as far as 500 metres. Eventually these drop away to 3,000 metres or more, until they meet the "foothills" of the abyssal floor.

NORMAN MYERS ed., GAIA: AN ATLAS OF PLANET MANAGEMENT 64–93 (1993)

————

A.   THE OCEANS

The importance of the world's oceans cannot be overestimated. Life began in the oceans and it remains our link to life through its control of climate, provision of food and minerals, sequestration of carbon, assimilation of wastes, and other irreplaceable services. Yet the oceans' ecosystems are under unprecedented stress.

Overfishing—The marine fish catch has increased over fourfold since 1950. This catch now satisfies ever-increasing global demands of fish for human consumption, animal feed supplements and fertilizer (one-third of the fish market), and fish oil. The use of government subsidies to build fleets with modern fishing technology (that now bears more resemblance to a vacuum cleaner than a fishing rod) has created a situation where too many boats are chasing too few fish. Indeed the fishery catch as measured by catch per unit of effort has markedly declined in recent years. The environmental consequences have been a series of spectacular fishery collapses, decimating entire fishing communities. The commercial cod fishery off New England, for example, once described as inexhaustible no longer exists. The UN Food and Agriculture Organization (FAO) estimates that two-thirds of the world's fisheries are currently under threat from overfishing. Beyond depleting commercial fish stocks, the by-catch (discarded fish) and other environmental damage to seabed organisms caused by fishing threatens the marine ecosystem.

Ocean Pollution—The seas have always been a dumping ground for garbage. But modern technology has tremendously increased the amount of direct discharges from ships into the sea–ranging from operational discharges of oil and sewage dumping to incineration. Unintentional discharges have greatly increased as well, most notoriously from oil spills.

Land-Based Marine Pollution—Pollution of the oceans from land-based sources is in many ways the most pernicious threat, for it comprises 70% of marine pollution. The waste soup discharged into the ocean comes from many sources—agricultural run-off, urban drainage systems, sewage treatment plants, deposition from air pollution and industrial effluent.

Because fishing and dumping in the seas are "free," since there are no fees to pay, the externalities of overfishing and dumping are borne by all. The seas have enormous capacities to assimilate wastes and support productive ecosystems, but these capacities have limits. Beyond the collapse of several major fisheries around the globe, what are some of the most telling signs that our activities are exceeding the limits of healthy marine ecosystems?

- A number of dead whales washed up on beaches have been transported to incinerators for disposal. The levels of toxic compounds in their bodies were so high their corpses were legally classified as hazardous waste;

- A "dead zone" of low oxygen has started appearing regularly in the Gulf of Mexico off the U.S. coast, the Adriatic, the Black Sea, the Inland Sea of Japan, and other bays and bodies of water;

- "red tides" and phytoplanktonic blooms have been appearing regularly off the coasts of Brazil, Sri Lanka, Japan, Spain and the U.S., choking much of the life in their wake.

This chapter explores the legal agreements and instruments that govern our relations with the ocean environment. The legal framework known as the law of the sea is a complicated structure of overlapping and occasionally conflicting duties and interests among flag States, coastal States and port States, regulated by regional and global organizations (both public and private). While a major chapter in this casebook, our treatment of the law of the sea can only begin to explore this immensely rich area of international law.

The remainder of this Section lays out the history of the law of the sea and the basic rights and obligations created by the dominant legal text, the UN Convention on the Law of the Sea. Section II addresses the law of the sea's protections for fisheries, examining highly migratory species, straddling stocks, and driftnets. Section III examines marine pollution caused by ships. The MARPOL 73/78 convention governs operational discharges. Its sophisticated compliance and enforcement mechanisms provide an important model for other international environmental law agreements. The London Convention, 1972, provides an instructive example of how international agreements evolve banning activities they were created to regulate. Section IV addresses land-based marine pollution, an immensely important yet difficult area to control because of the wide range of sources. The last section, Section V, presents a problem exercise describing the environmental controls on deep seabed mining. The Law of the Sea Convention's recognition of the deep seabed as the common heritage of mankind and its sharing of the deep sea mining profits among nations delayed U.S. acceptance of the Convention for more than a decade.

B.   HISTORY OF LAW OF THE SEA

The law of the sea extends back to Roman times and perhaps earlier. These laws, driven by commercial and military concerns, have regulated the use of and passage on the seas. With the exception of a small number of fisheries agreements, environmental matters were not a concern of oceans law until after World War II, primarily because the seas' bounty appeared inexhaustible and pollution remained small-scale and local.

The modern law of the seas is built upon a small number of basic principles. The most important of these is the "freedom of the seas"—the oceans' status as a global commons upon which nations' freedom to travel and extract resources is unimpeded. Although originally a part of Roman law, freedom of the seas was not re-introduced as a legal doctrine until 1609 through the writings of the Dutch scholar, Hugo Grotius. Published anonymously, Grotius' book, MARE LIBERUM, defended the Netherlands' right to sail in the Indian Ocean and Eastern Seas in order to trade with India and the East Indies. Spain and Portugal exercised both commercial and political dominion over this region, and sought to exclude competitor mercantile nations. Grotius argued that peaceful navigation and fishing on the high seas was a basic right of all nations. As he concluded, "the sea is common to all because it is so limitless that it cannot become a possession of one, and because it is adapted for the use of all, whether we consider it from the point of view of navigation or of fisheries." *See,* R.P. Anand, *Changing Concepts of Freedom of the Seas: A Historical Perspective,* in Jon Van Dyke et al., eds., FREEDOM FOR THE SEAS IN THE 21ST CENTURY 74–75 (1993). By the early 1800s this legal principle was universally accepted by major powers, largely as a result of State practice and the powerful Dutch and British fleets' establishment of naval dominance around the globe to protect their commerce and colonies.

Grotius' principle is straightforward. One nation's use of a sea-lane for passage does not impede any other nation's right to travel on the sea-lane, nor does one nation's fishing in an area impede other nations from fishing there, either. In terms of fisheries, this principle allocates property rights on the basis of the law of capture. Yet such an arrangement provides a perfect setting for the tragedy of the commons, where individual actors' interests to exploit a resource for short-term benefits are stronger than the common interest to restrict short-term exploitation and conserve the resource. *See* Chapter 3, p. 127. With rights come duties, yet the right of unimpeded resource extraction granted by the traditional freedom of the seas doctrine did not impose a parallel responsibility to work collectively to conserve ocean resources. If every nation can fish unimpeded on the high seas, no nation can effectively manage the resource for the benefit of all. Since the oceans' resources were thought inexhaustible, though, this lack of parallel obligations was not a concern.

The freedom of the seas has always been limited by a customary law of "territorial seas," permitting exclusive national jurisdiction over a narrow marine zone off the coast (generally three miles). This was known popularly as the "cannon shot rule," reflecting the fact that shore-based cannons could not fire farther than three miles out to sea. It was not until the 1930s that an initial attempt was made by the League of Nations to codify the law of the seas. Following World War II, the United States, the new world superpower, dramatically challenged the traditional freedom of the seas doctrine. The Truman Proclamations extended American coastal jurisdiction and control to the natural resources and seabed of its contiguous continental shelf as well as to the fisheries in its coastal waters. 10 FED. REG. 12304, 12305, Sept. 28, 1945. The claim of sovereign authority over high seas resources directly off the coast eliminated the traditional three mile limit of the territorial sea. This precedent was quickly adopted by other nations laying similar claims, led by Latin American countries, and by 1958 almost 20 countries had declared legal control of their continental shelves. Anand, *op. cit.* at 78–79. This "creeping jurisdiction" continued for the next 30 years, greatly weakening the freedom of the seas doctrine and causing international conflicts between coastal States and fishing nations.

The UN held its first Conference on the Law of the Sea (UNCLOS I) in 1958. Four conventions were adopted: the Convention on the Territorial Sea and Contiguous Zone, Convention on the High Seas, Convention on Fishing and Conservation of Living Resources of the High Seas, and Convention on the Continental Shelf. The environment was not forgotten, as the Geneva Convention on the High Seas addressed specific sources of pollution, such as oil pollution from vessels and pollution from radioactive substances. Article 24, 25. But the environmental protections granted by the conventions were weak, neither establishing a comprehensive duty to protect the marine environment nor assigning respective duties and responsibilities of States to address marine pollution. While indicative of emerging customary international law, none of the conventions came into force. The second UN Conference on the Law of the Sea (UNCLOS II), held in 1960, failed to reach agreement on the extent of the territorial sea.

Indeed the fundamental conflict during UNCLOS I and UNCLOS II and, as we shall see, the central conflict in most law of the sea disputes was the tension between the interests of maritime nations who rely on the seas for commerce and navigation and the interests of coastal States who rely on the natural resources of the adjacent sea. Maritime nations favor expansive freedom of the seas and limited national jurisdiction over coastal waters while coastal States champion, in both word and deed, enlarged national jurisdiction over adjacent waters. This conflict has important implications not only for control of resources but for compliance and enforcement of pollution laws, as well. By the end of 1973, over one-third of the ocean, equal in surface area to the land mass of the earth, had been claimed by coastal States as subject to national jurisdiction.

―――――

C.   UN CONVENTION ON THE LAW OF THE SEA

The combined momentum of the Stockholm Conference on the Human Environment in 1972, calls from the UN General Assembly for a comprehensive law of the sea, and increasing national concern over creeping jurisdiction provided the opportunity for international negotiations to recommence on governance of the sea. The UN Third Conference on the Law of the Sea (UNCLOS III) began in 1973 and concluded in 1982. Over almost a decade, nations cajoled, bickered, and negotiated a remarkably comprehensive document. The complexity of the negotiations is hard to imagine. Consensus was sought on virtually every issue governing humans' relationship with the sea, from fisheries, pollution, and conservation to mining, laying of sea cables, navigation, and jurisdictional authority. If widely adopted, the result would have an immediate impact on nations' political, economic and scientific interests. Alliances of nations with similar interests on one issue would splinter on other issues. Indeed one of the surprising developments during the Conference negotiations was the influence of land-locked States (with unusual allies such as Uganda, Switzerland, Nepal, and Bolivia) who acted as a strategically important caucus. Why do you think land-locked States were greatly concerned over the Law of the Sea negotiations?

The resulting document, known as the UN Convention on the Law of the Sea (UNCLOS) was signed in 1982 and came into force in 1994. U.N.Doc. A/CONF.62/122, *reprinted in* 21 I.L.M. 1261 (1982). It provides the first global framework on all aspects of the law of the sea and may be thought of as "the constitution for ocean governance," providing broad rules and direction to guide general behavior but often requiring issue-specific agreements to give its provisions concrete meaning (just as agency regulations are needed to implement framework statutes). Like no other international negotiation, by the time UNCLOS was signed its provisions *already* constituted customary international law in the eyes of most countries. As of January 2001, 135 States had ratified UNCLOS. The UNCLOS Secretariat's Web site contains a great deal of useful current information and is located at: <http://www.un.org/Depts/los/>. To avoid confusion, it is worth noting that we refer to the Convention as "UNCLOS" (as do many others) but the Convention is also known as the LOS Convention, LOSC, the 1982 Convention, or UNCLOS 1982.

UNCLOS is a massive document, consisting of 320 articles and nine annexes. It is organized as shown on the next page.

In terms of environmental protection, UNCLOS' major accomplishments lie in its treatment of jurisdictional authority, the establishment of obligations to protect and preserve the marine environment, and comprehensive coverage of specific environmental threats posed by pollution and overfishing.

1.   JURISDICTIONAL ZONES

In striking a balance between the interests of coastal States, land-locked States and maritime powers, UNCLOS established an unprecedented series of jurisdictional zones, varying in degrees of national control. The ports of a coastal State are regarded as internal waters and, with few exceptions relating to inspections and enforcement that will be discussed in Section III.A., ships in port are subject to the full range of the coastal State's national authority. Article 11. From the baseline (usually the coast and harbor walls) to 12 nautical miles offshore is the *territorial sea*. Article 3. Subject to the right of innocent passage, discussed below, the coastal State exercises almost complete authority in the territorial sea. From 12 to 24 miles is the *contiguous zone*. Article 33. Here the coastal State's sovereignty is more limited, though it may act to prevent infringement of its customs, fiscal, immigration or sanitary laws and regulations. From the boundary of the territorial sea (generally 12 miles) out to 200 nautical miles is the *exclusive economic zone* (EEZ). Article 57. Beyond the EEZ, more than 200 nautical miles off the coast, lie the *high seas*, an area beyond national jurisdictions that are part of the global commons. The special cases of archipelagic waters, straits and continental shelves are dealt with separately. Articles 37–45, 46–54, 76–83. The jurisdictional authority granted over the territorial sea, contiguous and exclusive economic zones extends both to the air space above and subsoil beneath the waters.

Each jurisdictional zone established by UNCLOS is subject to the right of passage of vessels on the sea. Each zone has its own designated form of passage and the rights and duties of the coastal and navigational State vary accordingly. The right of passage through an international strait is known as transit passage (Article 38), through archipelagic waters as archipelagic sea lane passage (Articles 52, 54), through the territorial sea as innocent passage (Article 17) and as navigational freedoms for the EEZ and high seas. D.G. Stephens , *The Impact of the 1982 Law of the Sea Convention on the Conduct of Peacetime Naval/Military Operations,* 29 Cal. W. Int'l L.J. 283 (1999).

A coastal State may not deny, hamper or impair a vessel's innocent passage (Article 24), but this prohibition is qualified in two ways. Rights of passage explicitly do not protect a vessel conducting "any act of willful and serious pollution in contravention of international law" or "any fishing activities." Article 19(2)(h), (i). Moreover, a coastal State is granted the authority to adopt laws and regulations limiting the right of innocent passage in regard to conservation of living marine resources, preservation of the environment, and the control and reduction of pollution. Article 21(1). It may not, however, limit the right of innocent passage based on a foreign ship's design, construction, crew or equipment unless the minimum regulations are based on generally accepted international rules or standards. Article 21(2). As we shall see, some countries have charged that the U.S. Oil Pollution Act violates this requirement. The balance between preserving the right of innocent passage and environmental protection provides a permanent source of tension between coastal and maritime States.

The exclusive economic zone, known as the "EEZ," was another important innovation of UNCLOS. Articles 55–75. Together, national EEZs cover over 30% of the world's seas, approximately 90% of the commercial fisheries, and almost all the presently exploitable mineral resources. Barbara Kwiatkowska, The 200 mile exclusive economic zone in the new Law of the Sea at xxiii (1989). By bringing such an important part of the ocean's resources under national jurisdiction, the EEZ dramatically weakened the impact of the traditional freedom of the seas doctrine. Within the EEZ, coastal States have the sovereign right to explore, exploit, conserve and manage the natural resources, both mineral and living. Article 56. Coastal States may pass relevant laws exercising these rights and are granted the authority to board, inspect, and arrest crews in the EEZ violating the laws. Article 73. Other States passing through the EEZ must have "due regard" to the coastal State's rights and duties. Article 58.

The creation of a 200–mile EEZ greatly increased coastal States' ability to manage fisheries. It was thought at the time that this would provide a classic resolution of the tragedy of the commons by allocating property rights to common resources (Section II discusses the fisheries crisis). With this increased right to exploit resources, however, UNCLOS also imposes increased environmental responsibility. The coastal State exercises authority to protect and preserve the marine environment in its EEZ and *"shall"* ensure the conservation and utilization of its living marine resources. Articles 56, 61, 62.

2. ENVIRONMENTAL STANDARDS AND DUTIES

The law of the sea conventions prior to UNCLOS did not require nations to regulate ocean pollution and only in a few cases did it give them the power to do so. What state of affairs did negotiators to the UN Law of the Sea Convention confront in 1974, with respect to environmental protection of the oceans?

Some important flag states [,i.e. States where ships are registered,] were not parties to these [law of the sea conventions] and adopted their own national regulations of a rather lower standard, while others, though accepting international standards, were lax in inspecting, prosecuting violations or following up reports from coastal states. Nor, for the most part, were there any international standards regulating pollution from pipelines and seabed operations, although rigs and platforms were generally treated as ships for the purposes of conventions on vessel pollution and dumping. Regulation of other sources of pollution, such as dumping or land-based pollution, was simply not covered by the Geneva Conventions. The net result was to leave states largely free to adopt their own regulations on marine pollution, subject only to the few limitations imposed by international law, and the application of internationally accepted standards was in effect permissive rather than obligatory.

These deficiencies could not be made good by coastal states alone, which had power to prescribe rules for the operation of ships only within the territorial sea and for seabed operations on the continental shelf. Beyond those limited zones of authority, the flag state or state of nationality retained sole jurisdiction and the narrow concept of the contiguous zone did not materially alter this position in respect of pollution. A dominant theme of the Law of the Sea Conference was the failure of this traditional structure of prescriptive jurisdiction to protect the interests of coastal states. On the one hand, the power of the coastal state to regulate shipping and activities off its coast was too limited; on the other, the duty of the flag state to adopt and enforce appropriate regulations was too imperfectly defined and observed. But more important was the realization that it could not be conducive to the protection and preservation of the marine environment to continue with a legal regime.

The approach of the Convention to these problems is threefold. It attempts firstly to create a general duty to regulate all sources of marine pollution. Secondly, there is a redistribution and redefinition of the balance of prescriptive powers and duties between coastal and flag states, to some extent enhancing the power of the former at the expense of the latter's traditional primacy in the regulation of shipping. Finally, the Convention not only determines who may or should regulate pollution; it tries for the first time to control the content and standard of those regulations through a preference, in most cases, for internationally agreed rules. This approach serves a limiting function in two alternative senses. When specifying international rules as a maximum standard of regulation, it seeks to prevent abuse and the imposition of excessively onerous burdens on foreign vessels; when specifying them as a minimum standard, it gives content and effectiveness to the state's duty to regulate. A measure of uniformity is thus also achieved.

Alan Boyle, *Marine Pollution Under the Law of the Sea Convention*, 79 AM. J. INT'L
L. 347, 351–53 (1985).

Alan Boyle alludes to the problem of flag States adopting lower
national standards than accepted international standards. These nations
are collectively known as "flag of convenience" States and present an
important challenge for effective marine environmental protection. This
issue is addressed further in Section III.

While provisions concerning environmental protection appear throughout UNCLOS, they are concentrated in Part XII, Articles 192–236. In
particular, the principle of freedom of the seas is qualified by a duty to
preserve the marine environment. This duty limits the actions of *both*
coastal and high seas States, dramatically departing from the unimpeded
laissez-faire of freedom of the seas. It also provides the authority for
development of further international legal instruments. In reading the
relevant Articles excerpted below, consider to what extent they departed
from the traditional law of the sea prior to 1981.

U.N. Convention on the Law of the Seas

Article 192

General obligation

States have the obligation to protect and preserve the marine environment.

Article 193

Sovereign right of States to exploit their natural resources

States have the sovereign right to exploit their natural resources pursuant to
their environmental policies and in accordance with their duty to protect and
preserve the marine environment.

Article 194

Measures to prevent, reduce and control
pollution of the marine environment

1. States shall take, individually or jointly as appropriate, all measures consistent with this Convention that are necessary to prevent, reduce and control
pollution of the marine environment from any source, using for this purpose
the best practicable means at their disposal and in accordance with their
capabilities, and they shall endeavour to harmonize their policies in this
connection.

2. States shall take all measures necessary to ensure that activities under
their jurisdiction or control are so conducted as not to cause damage by
pollution to other States and their environment, and that pollution arising from
incidents or activities under their jurisdiction or control does not spread beyond
the areas where they exercise sovereign rights in accordance with this Convention.

3. The measures taken pursuant to this Part shall deal with all sources of
pollution of the marine environment. These measures shall include, *inter alia*,
those designed to minimize to the fullest possible extent:

> (a) the release of toxic, harmful or noxious substances, especially those
> which are persistent, from land-based sources, from or through the atmo-
> sphere or by dumping;

(b) pollution from vessels, in particular measures for preventing accidents and dealing with emergencies, ensuring the safety of operations at sea, preventing intentional and unintentional discharges, and regulating the design, construction, equipment, operation and manning of vessels;

(c) pollution from installations and devices used in exploration or exploitation of the natural resources of the sea-bed and subsoil, in particular measures for preventing accidents and dealing with emergencies, ensuring the safety of operations at sea, and regulating the design, construction, equipment, operation and manning of such installations or devices;* * *

4. In taking measures to prevent, reduce or control pollution of the marine environment, States shall refrain from unjustifiable interference with activities carried out by other States in the exercise of their rights and in pursuance of their duties in conformity with this Convention.

5. The measures taken in accordance with this Part shall include those necessary to protect and preserve rare or fragile ecosystems as well as the habitat of depleted, threatened or endangered species and other forms of marine life.

Article 195

Duty not to transfer damage or hazards or transform one type of pollution into another

In taking measures to prevent, reduce and control pollution of the marine environment, States shall act so as not to transfer, directly or indirectly, damage or hazards from one area to another or transform one type of pollution into another.

Article 196

Use of technologies or introduction of alien or new species

1. States shall take all measures necessary to prevent, reduce and control pollution of the marine environment resulting from the use of technologies under their jurisdiction or control, or the intentional or accidental introduction of species, alien or new, to a particular part of the marine environment, which may cause significant and harmful changes thereto.

2. This article does not affect the application of this Convention regarding the prevention, reduction and control of pollution of the marine environment.* * *

Article 204

Monitoring of the risks or effects of pollution

1. States shall, consistent with the rights of other States, endeavour, as far as practicable, directly or through the competent international organizations, to observe, measure, evaluate and analyse, by recognized scientific methods, the risks or effects of pollution of the marine environment.

2. In particular, States shall keep under surveillance the effects of any activities which they permit or in which they engage in order to determine whether these activities are likely to pollute the marine environment.

Article 205

Publication of reports

States shall publish reports of the results obtained pursuant to article 204 or provide such reports at appropriate intervals to the competent international organizations, which should make them available to all States.

Article 206
Assessment of potential effects of activities

When States have reasonable grounds for believing that planned activities under their jurisdiction or control may cause substantial pollution of or significant and harmful changes to the marine environment, they shall, as far as practicable, assess the potential effects of such activities on the marine environment and shall communicate reports of the results of such assessments in the manner provided in article 205.

Taken together, these articles represent a fundamental shift in the law of the sea–away from maritime power and toward shared duties as the basis for international relations. As Professor Boyle has noted, this shift means that "it is no longer a power to control, still less a freedom to pollute, that characterizes the legal regime of the marine environment, but a new framework based on obligations of control, regulation, enforcement, cooperation and responsibility." Boyle, *op. cit.*, at 351. Indeed, the language of these articles is strong, using the non-discretionary "shall" rather than the hortatory "should" or "make best efforts." The articles are not, however, detailed enough to provide practical guidance in specific situations. Would they, for example, allow the sinking of a decommissioned oil rig in the North Atlantic (the cause of a conflict between Shell Oil and Greenpeace addressed in a problem exercise in Section III)? For this reason, supplemented agreements have been necessary to give specific meaning to UNCLOS mandates.

3. DISPUTE RESOLUTION

Another important innovation of UNCLOS is its compulsory procedure for dispute resolution among parties. Such a procedure ensures respect for and compliance with the UNCLOS provisions and clarifies provisions that may be ambiguous or conflicting. The dispute settlement provisions are complex, addressed in more than 100 articles in UNCLOS. The process is flexible (parties may choose the means and fora to resolve disputes), comprehensive (most UNCLOS disputes are ultimately subject to binding dispute resolution), and accommodating (certain vital national concerns are exempted from the dispute resolution procedures). The basic provisions of the scheme are described below.

All parties accept the obligation to settle disputes by peaceful means. A dispute between parties concerning the application or interpretation of UNCLOS is first addressed informally by exchanging views through negotiation. In a sense, the dispute resolution process is either simple or complex, depending upon the will of the parties. Since parties may jointly choose any dispute settlement process they wish, they can always decide to bypass the UNCLOS procedure entirely by deciding to use a bilateral, regional or other dispute settlement system. If informal negotiation fails to produce a mutually acceptable settlement, a party may request formal dispute resolution. There are four fora for States to choose from (and note that only States may be parties to a dispute)–the International Court of Justice and three bodies created by UNCLOS (the International Tribunal for the Law of the Sea, an arbitral tribunal, and a special technical arbitral tribunal). The parties to the dispute may agree to choose any one of the fora. If they disagree over the appropriate forum, the dispute is submitted to compulsory arbitration as provided for in Annex VII. Articles 280–287. The International Tribunal for the Law of the Sea is composed of twenty-one independent members elected by UNCLOS Parties. Since the United States is not yet a Party to UNCLOS, the United States was granted provisional membership until 1998. Since then, they have had no voice in the tribunal.

There are a number of limitations and exceptions to the dispute resolution procedures. The most relevant to environmental concerns is the exclusion of a coastal State's fisheries management within its EEZ and certain aspects of marine research within the EEZ. Article 297. If, however, a coastal State manifestly fails to conserve its marine resources or arbitrarily refuses to determine the allowable catch for another State, then the dispute is submitted to a non-binding conciliation procedure. Disputes under Part XI of UNCLOS concerning the deep seabed fall under the jurisdiction of the Seabed Disputes Chamber of the International Tribunal for the Law of the Sea (described in Section V).

4.   REGIONAL SEAS

Many regional seas, including enclosed or semi-enclosed ocean areas, are of immense importance to nations' livelihoods. Regional seas include the Mediterranean, Black Sea, Caspian Sea, Baltic Sea, South Pacific and others. The most effective marine protection is often local, and a number of UNCLOS articles call on States to cooperate in regional organizations. These organizations can be more responsive to local problems and concerns, and more efficient in providing appropriate solutions tailored to local ecological, economic and political conditions. For example, UNCLOS Article 197 declares:

Article 197

Co-operation on a global or regional basis

States shall co-operate on a global basis and, as appropriate, on a regional basis, directly or through competent international organizations, in formulating and elaborating international rules, standards and recommended practices and procedures consistent with this Convention, for the protection and preservation of the marine environment, taking into account characteristic regional features.

At least twenty oceans treaties may be considered regional, generally focusing on enclosed or semi-enclosed seas. As the map below illustrates, regional conventions cover much of the world's oceans and most of its coastlines. JON VAN DYKE ET AL. EDS., FREEDOM FOR THE SEAS IN THE 21ST CENTURY 161 (1993). UNEP's Regional Seas Program has sponsored regional treaties in thirteen areas. These treaties promote environmental assessments, management, and institutional arrangements. They are generally regarded as having been successful in facilitating cooperation, technical training and assistance, institutional capacity building, and raising awareness. Regional treaties are not without their failings and critics, however, particularly in regard to ocean pollution. See PATRICIA BIRNIE AND ALAN BOYLE, INTERNATIONAL LAW AND THE ENVIRONMENT 260, 262 (1992).

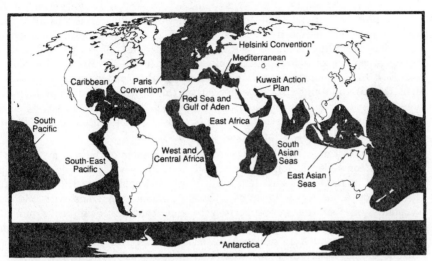

FIGURE 12.10 GLOBAL MAP SHOWING REGIONS OF THE WORLD'S OCEANS REGULATED BY REGIONAL CONVENTIONS OR TREATIES *Asterisks designate conventions formed outside of the UNEP Regional Seas Programme.*

QUESTIONS AND DISCUSSION

1. *Working the treaty*

    – What sources of pollution, if any, are excluded from the UNCLOS general obligations?

    – Are States required to act to prevent, reduce and control *indirect* sources of pollution?

    – Does UNCLOS create general obligations to assess the effectiveness of efforts to control marine pollution?

    – If a nation plans to undertake an activity that may cause significant environmental impact, does UNCLOS require it to consult with affected States?

2. If UNCLOS negotiations ended officially in 1982, why did the Convention only come into force for some countries in 1994? As will be discussed in detail in Section V, the United States actively participated in the negotiations of UNCLOS but did not sign the Convention in 1982 out of concerns over Part XI, the deep seabed mining provisions. A new agreement was finally reached in 1994 addressing deep seabed concerns and the U.S. and a number of other hold-out countries signed that agreement and UNCLOS. During the decade of negotiations, the U.S. regarded the other sections of UNCLOS as customary law and complied with its provisions. PRESIDENTIAL PROCLAMATION 5030, March 10, 1983. As of October, 2001, the Senate had not yet ratified UNCLOS, hence the United States still was not a party to the Convention (though it has signed the 1994 Agreement relating to the implementation of Part XI of the Convention). As a result, and despite the fact that it complies with UNCLOS provisions, the U.S. is not represented in any UNCLOS decisionmaking posts.

3. To some historians, the doctrine of freedom of the seas was an inevitable development. Because the major seventeenth century maritime powers—Britain, the Netherlands, Spain, Portugal—were unable to assert sovereignty over the high seas, the next best commercial alternative was unimpeded access to all. Indeed, Hugo Grotius first developed his doctrine of freedom of the seas in a brief written for the major trading business, the Dutch East India Company, to defend the company's capture of a Portuguese ship in 1604 in the Straits of Malacca. The Dutch East India Company was trying to challenge the Portuguese monopoly in the Indian Ocean trade and Grotius argued that the Portuguese attempt to exclude others from the lucrative East Indian trade was a belligerent act, justifying seizure of ships and property. Interestingly, given Grotius' fame as a proponent of freedom of the seas, he occasionally argued against the doctrine.

> [N]either Grotius nor Holland was in favor of freedom of the seas as a principle. Grotius conveniently forgot the "freedom of the sea" principle he had propounded in 1609 with such fervor and went to England in 1613 with a Dutch delegation to argue in favor of a Dutch monopoly of trade with the Spice Islands. In fact, he was surprised to find that his own book, published anonymously, was being quoted by the British against him. Successive attempts by each European state to demand freedom of the seas for the lucrative spice trade of the East Indies, and later attempts by each state to try to create a monopoly for itself, led to a spate of books by numerous scholars in Europe. In this battle of books and wits, it was not Grotius, as is generally assumed, who won. The real victor was John Selden, a brilliant British scholar and statesman, whose *Mare Clausum, sen de Domino Maris Libri Duo (The Closed Sea; or, Two Books Concerning the Rule Over the Sea)*, written at the behest of the English Crown, remained the most authoritative work on maritime law in Europe for the next 200 years. Although several other publicists countered Selden's arguments, all of the European countries continued to follow his prescription in controlling as much ocean as their power would permit. Selden won this protracted battle not by the brilliance of his arguments but by the "louder language" of the powerful British navy.

R.P. Anand, *Changing Concepts of Freedom of the Seas: a Historical Perspective*, in Jon Van Dyke et al., eds., Freedom for the Seas in the 21st Century 75–76 (1993).

4. The worldview expressed by the freedom of the seas doctrine is not universally shared. Indeed many indigenous cultures have long viewed the ocean as a common heritage deserving much greater protection than the freedom of the seas provides. The law of the sea of the Maori (indigenous peoples of New Zealand) is described below.

> For the Maori people, *te tikanga o te moana*, or the law of the sea, is predicated on four basic concepts deeply rooted in Maori cultural values. First, the sea is part of a global environment in which all parts are interlinked. Second, the sea, as one of the *taonga*, or treasures of Mother Earth, must be nurtured and protected. Third, the protected sea is a *koha*, or gift, which humans may use. Fourth, that use is to be controlled in a way that will sustain its bounty.

> From this cultural and divinely ordained matrix the actual *tikanga*, or law, is developed. Thus, for example, *te tikanga o nga kaitaki* aims to stop pollution of coastal water not by seeking more effective methods of waste disposal, as is often advocated today, but by ensuring that any activity produces as little waste as possible at its source. Such laws were rigidly enforced by various sanctions and through *korero tunhonohono*, or agreements among the various tribal nations that make up the Maori people.

> It is impossible to detail here all of the various laws of *te tai ao*, the environment. It is submitted, however, that within the values and norms that

shaped those laws are the seeds of understanding that could transform current international thinking on protection of the global marine environment.

Two of the many claims laid by Iwi Maori before the Waitangi Tribunal give an indication of the interrelated view of the environment encapsulated within indigenous Maori law. In the Kaituna claim, the people of Te Arawa objected to the discharge of sewage into the Kaituna River. For the Maori, the river was part of an interconnected water system involving Lake Rotorua, Lake Rotoiti, and the Maketsu Estuary. Each body of water is important to the people of Te Arawa as a source of food, as the site of important historical events, and as the base of spiritual sustenance. To discharge sewage into such waterways not only would be a *hara*, or wrongful act that breached the laws protecting tangible food sources, but would also breach the laws protecting the intangible spiritual sources of the Iwi's well-being. *Nga tikanga o te tai ao*—the laws of the environment—sought to protect both the tangible and intangible, since together they strengthen *te korowai a Papatuanukau*—the cloak of Mother Earth.

Moana Jackson, *Indigenous Law and the Sea*, in JON VAN DYKE ET AL. EDS., FREEDOM FOR THE SEAS IN THE 21ST CENTURY 46 (1993). Assume that *te tikanga o te moana* rather than the freedom of the seas doctrine formed the basis for the modern law of the sea. How might the law of the sea's treatment of jurisdictional zones and allocation of rights and obligations be different? Note that the basis of *te tikanga o te moana's* effectiveness as a common property regime is the shared set of norms among the Maori. Are there any similar norms shared by the global community?

5. The phenomenon of "creeping jurisdiction," triggered by the Truman Proclamations, was a serious concern during negotiations over UNCLOS. The Canadian Arctic Waters Pollution Prevention Act provides a good example of how environmental, as well as commercial, motivations drove efforts to extend national authority. In 1970, out of concern for the potentially devastating impact of an oil spill on the fragile Arctic ecosystem, Canada passed a law creating a "special prevention" zone of 100 miles extending around its northern archipelago. Its jurisdictional claim was not absolute. Rather, the law mandated certain safety requirements for ships travelling in these waters such as hull and fuel tank construction, the use of double hulls, certain navigational aids and equipment, maximum quantities of cargo carried, etc. If a foreign nation's vessel did not comply with the law, Canada proclaimed the right to prohibit access to its special prevention zone. The U.S. vigorously opposed Canada's unilateral extension of its national authority to international waters and refused to recognize the law. Responding to the U.S. criticisms of its law, Canada responded that the U.S. had a rich history of unilateral extensions of limited maritime jurisdiction dating back to 1790. J. Beesley, *The Canadian Approach to International Environmental Law*, 11 CAN. YEARBOOK INT'L. 3 (1973). Ultimately Canada's actions provided a model for development of the EEZ during the UNCLOS negotiations.

Notwithstanding its role in setting off the rush of creeping jurisdiction, U.S. concerns over enlarged jurisdictional claims were very real. During the 1970s, the extension of jurisdictional zones beyond 200 miles and the claims by archipelagic States to treat all waters embraced by their islands as territorial waters held out the possibility of closing sea lanes to foreign vessels. The commercial and military implications of such actions proved a strong impetus to negotiate UNCLOS.

Despite the creation of EEZs, creeping jurisdiction continues today. A number of Latin American countries have made legal claims to limited jurisdictional authority beyond those granted by UNCLOS. In 1991, for instance, Chile introduced the idea of a "Presential Sea," extending conservation measures similar to those taken within Chile's EEZ to the adjacent high seas. The Presential Sea would allow increased surveillance and monitoring of fishing vessels. Chile argued that these activities were necessary to ensure that fisheries conservation efforts in its EEZ were not undermined. The Presential Sea is now part of Chilean Law. Law No. 19.079 (Chile), Official Journal, Sept. 6, 1991. The problem exercise in Section II addresses a similar action by Canada in 1995 to promote the conservation of halibut.

6. As described in the text, the UNCLOS conservation duties spelled out in Section XII are strict. Article 194, for example, states that parties shall take all measures consistent with UNCLOS that are necessary to prevent, reduce and control marine pollution from any source. The use of the word "shall" as the operative requirement for taking conservation actions makes it binding, but Article 194 does make some accommodation for developing countries. The requirement to address pollution is further qualified by the proviso that States shall take these efforts "in accordance with their abilities." Article 194(1). Is this an example of the "common but differentiated responsibility" principle? See Chapter 7, page 402. It is important to note that unlike many other international agreements, UNCLOS does not allow parties to make reservations in respect to certain provisions. Acceptance of UNCLOS is a package all-or-nothing deal, which explains why the U.S. did not ratify the treaty in 1982.

7. The classic conflict over high seas freedoms between maritime States and coastal States also occurs *within* governments of countries with large coast lines and extensive naval interests, such as the United States. Hence the United States has argued for limited jurisdiction by other countries over U.S. ships yet broad jurisdiction over foreign vessels in U.S. waters. Which interests do you think the following U.S. government departments and agencies generally defend, maritime State or coastal State–Environmental Protection Agency, Department of Justice, National Oceanographic and Atmospheric Administration, Department of Defense, Department of State?

8. The coastal State is granted regulatory jurisdiction over all sources of pollution in its waters, including vessel pollution. Within the EEZ, though, these pollution regulations must comport with generally accepted international standards. Articles 211, 220, 221. As a result, this grant of authority may not be as sweeping a power as it seems, for the maritime powers still exercise considerable influence in determining the international standards for shipping. Most international maritime standards are established by a UN agency known as the International Maritime Organization (IMO). Based in London, the IMO was created in 1958 and has expanded its authority to include most aspects of vessel pollution. It serves as the secretariat for the conventions we will examine in Section III, including MARPOL 73/78, the London Convention, and the civil liability conventions.

As an example of the potential conflict between national and international standards, the U.S. Clean Water Act uses a "sheen test" to determine if a discharge of oil violates the statute while MARPOL, the international agreement covering oil discharges, uses a numerical parts per million standard to determine if a discharge violates its requirements. The U.S. law relies on a visual test while MARPOL relies on a physical measurement of oil concentration. As a result, an oil discharge by a vessel could fail the Clean Water Act's sheen test but pass MARPOL's concentration test. Within U.S. territorial waters, then, the vessel would be found in violation of the Clean Water Act, but it would *not* be in violation within the EEZ. There, the generally accepted standard established by MARPOL, oil concentration, operates. The interplay of coastal and flag State rights in enforcement activities—monitoring compliance, trying alleged violations, and punishing guilty parties—is complex and is discussed in detail in Section III.A.

9. Some scholars have argued that the freedom of the seas works against the interests of developing countries. The right to fish in distant waters favors those nations with the technology to support such fishing fleets. Similarly, only developed nations have the economic and technical capacity to mine the deep seabed. These comparative advantages among nations may alter over time. But absent restraints on the current exploitation of ocean resources, i.e., unless there are limits on the freedom of the seas, there is no guarantee that other less developed nations will, as they obtain greater economic and technological capacity, share on equal terms the ocean's bounty if it is already degraded. What are the implications of this argument? Do you agree with them?

Problem Exercise: Shipments of Plutonium

As part of a national long-term strategy to reduce its dependence on foreign oil imports, Japan has committed to dependence on nuclear power. To maintain its fuel source, Japan periodically ships spent nuclear waste to France and England for reprocessing. This waste is, in fact, plutonium, an extraordinarily harmful material that can cause cancer even in minute amounts. Over a period of 20 years, Japan intends to send by sea up to 45 shipments of plutonium for reprocessing. Serious concern has been expressed both by environmental groups and most countries along the shipment route over the human health and environmental risks posed by this practice. Possible threats to the shipment could come from attacks at port, attacks on the seas, sabotage or terrorist actions, and the ship sinking due to navigational error or inclement weather. In any of these cases, significant amounts of plutonium might be released into the environment or obtained by potentially hostile groups.

The first shipment, one ton of plutonium, was sent on a refitted freighter, the *Akatsuki Maru*. It was accompanied on its long voyage by a Japanese Coast Guard cutter fitted with light arms. Citing security concerns, Japan did not reveal the ship's intended route. Japan did declare that the ship would not pass through the territorial waters or EEZs of coastal States unless circumstances and prudence made this unavoidable. While Japan provided the U.S. and French governments more detailed information concerning the shipments, no environmental impact assessments were made public (if, indeed, they even had been conducted).

Assume you are legal counsel to the South African Ministry of Foreign Affairs. Barred from the Suez Canal, Japan's plutonium shipments will almost certainly round the Cape of Good Hope, likely passing through South Africa's territorial sea or EEZ to avoid the worst of the gales and winds ripping through the Southern Ocean. *See* the advertisement published by environmentalists opposing the shipment. Your Foreign Minister wishes to know whether international law would permit South Africa or the other nations along the shipment route to take the following actions against plutonium bearing ships:

- prohibit the *Akatsuki Maru* from entering South Africa's EEZ;
- prohibit the *Akatsuki Maru* from entering South Africa's territorial sea;
- demand that Japan prepare and publish an environmental impact statement concerning the proposed shipment;

- demand that Japan conduct research, develop alternative techniques to foreign shipment, and mitigate all reasonably foreseeable damage;

- demand that Japan notify and consult with nations along the shipment route?

The Foreign Minister, a former law of the sea practitioner, suggests that you consider the application of three bodies of law: UNCLOS, the precautionary principle and other principles of international environmental law, and International Court of Justice cases described earlier in the casebook. In addition to the UNCLOS Articles excerpted in Section I of this chapter, consider the applicability of these below:

Article 25

Rights of protection of the coastal State

1. The coastal State may take the necessary steps in its territorial sea to prevent passage which is not innocent.* * *

3. The coastal State may, without discrimination in form or in fact among foreign ships, suspend temporarily in specified areas of its territorial sea the innocent passage of foreign ships if such suspension is essential for the protection of its security, including weapons exercises. Such suspension shall take effect only after having been duly published.

Article 211

Pollution from vessels

* * * 4. Coastal States may, in the exercise of their sovereignty within their territorial sea, adopt laws and regulations for the prevention, reduction and control of marine pollution from foreign vessels, including vessels exercising the right of innocent passage. Such laws and regulations shall, in accordance with Part II, section 3, not hamper innocent passage of foreign vessels.

SECTION II. CONSERVATION OF LIVING MARINE RESOURCES

A. STATE OF THE WORLD'S FISHERIES

In 1998, global fish production reached 117 million tons (86 million from oceanic catch and 31 million from aquaculture). This represents a more than six-fold increase over the catch in 1950. But this massive increase in fishing activity has come at a high cost, driving many of the world's fisheries to the point of collapse. The FAO has estimated that about 10% of the world's major fisheries are depleted, 15%–18% are overexploited, and 47%–50% are fully exploited, leaving just one-quarter of the world's marine fish populations underexploited or moderately exploited. Following the collapse of the fisheries of George's Banks and the Grand Banks in the Northwest Atlantic, in 1994 the U.S. federal government ordered an emergency closure of more than 6,000 square miles off the Massachusetts coast, effectively shutting down an industry generating $200 million per year. The fishing industry in Labrador, Canada, was similarly shut down with 30,000 people losing jobs. Such collapses, unthinkable in the past, have now become a terrible prospect in many countries. The graph below shows the world's fish catch from 1950–1998 (note the increasing importance of aquaculture). *See* LESTER BROWN ET AL., VITAL SIGNS 2000 at 40–41 (2000); FAO, THE STATE OF THE WORLD'S FISHERIES AND AQUACULTURE 2000 (2000); J.R. McGOODWIN, CRISIS IN THE WORLD'S FISHERIES: PEOPLE, PROBLEMS AND POLICIES 51 (1990).

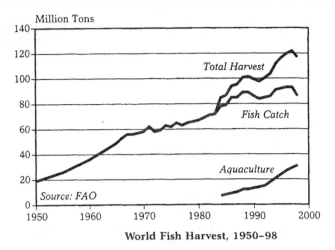

World Fish Harvest, 1950–98

Over the last decade, the total marine fish catch has remained roughly constant. Because fishing fleet capacity has doubled since 1970, however, the global catch as measured by catch per unit of effort has markedly decreased. This suggests that harvested fish have become smaller, harder to locate and catch, or both. Surpassing the levels of sustainable fisheries has grave potential consequences, particularly for developing countries. It is estimated that developing countries take in a fishery trade surplus of $16.8 billion a year—exceeding income from coffee, tea, and rubber—and are responsible for almost 50% of the world's total fish exports. Twenty percent of the world's population obtains 20% of its protein consumption from fish. In Asia, as much as 50% of the population's protein source is from fish. All but four of the 30 countries most dependent on fish as a primary source of protein are developing countries. Moreover, over a hundred million of the globe's poorest people depend on fisheries for jobs. While such figures are inexact, the importance of fisheries to the economies of developing countries and to the diet and employment of its inhabitants can scarcely be overestimated. Arguably this and access to freshwater are the most significant immediate threats facing the global environment. As we shall see in this section, international law has played a role in creating this crisis and must play role in any possible resolution. THE STATE OF WORLD FISHERIES AND AQUACULTURE 2000, *available at* <http://www.fao.org/fi/default.asp>; Polly Ghazi et al., *Our plundered seas,* THE OBSERVER, April 2, 1995.

The need for international cooperation to address fisheries conservation is obvious. Many species of commercially important fish travel both in the open ocean and in national waters, paying no heed to jurisdictional boundaries. Two recent developments have accelerated the depletion of the world's fisheries. The first is government subsidies. Following UNCLOS' 1982 extension of exclusive national jurisdiction over marine resources out to 200 nautical miles (the EEZ), many nations granted subsidies to encourage the development of their domestic fishing industries. As fish stocks within the EEZ dwindled under intense fishing pressure, these fleets moved to international waters in search of new fish.

Second, advances in technology have transformed fishing from a trade to a science. The introduction of nylon nets, outboard motors, sophisticated sonar, tracking buoys and satellite data now allow astonishingly effective harvesting. Advertisements in the trade magazines are not exaggerating when they boast: "Now, fish have nowhere to hide!" At the same time, the growth of factory ships with flash-freezers has greatly increased the amount of fish a ship can store. The net effects have been too many boats seeking too few fish, increased international tensions, high seas rammings, and net-cutting incidents. The common practices of "by-catch" (discarding of non-target species, such as dolphins in the tuna fishery) and "high-grading" (discarding of small or otherwise unfit target species) have also significantly exacerbated pressures on the ocean's living marine resources.

> FAO estimates that for every three tons of fish landed at the dock, another ton of unwanted creatures is thrown overboard dead or dying. That works out to 27 million tons of so-called bycatch killed each year. The annual death toll includes eighty thousand albatross drowned after taking bait on floating hooks trailed on miles of line behind "longliner" fishing vessels; one hundred thousand sea turtles ensnared in shrimp trawls; hundreds of thousands of seabirds ensnared in enormous open ocean drifnets; so many thousands of dolphins and porpoises drowned in traps and gill nets as to decimate seven stocks and threaten forty-six others; untold billions of juvenile cod, redfish, pollock, and other valuable fish; and countless sharks, squids, crab, starfish, sponges, anemones, and other creatures... Some fisheries are more damaging than others. Because their nets must be fine enough to catch tiny prey, shrimp trawls have enormous bycatch. Eight to nine pounds of unwanted creatures die every pound of shrimp harvested in the Gulf of Mexico [not to mention the damage to the sea floor communities as shrimp trawls drag along the bottom]... A particularly disturbing development is the advent of "biomass fishing." Huge trawls with extremely fine mesh gather anything larger than an American quarter. Most of the net's contents are ground into meal and fed to farmed shrimp, fish, and poultry or simply spread on fields. The ecological effects can only be guessed at.

COLIN WOODARD, OCEAN'S END 43–44 (2000).

The depletion of fisheries and improved fishing technology have necessarily led to reduced quotas for boats with results that in less dire circumstances would be laughable. Trawlers in British Columbia fished their annual quota of 847 tons of roe herring after eight minutes. Polly Ghazi et al., *Our plundered seas*, THE OBSERVER, April 2, 1995. And the pressure to overfish continues, even as scientists and economists try to calculate the costs.

John Tibbetts, *Ocean Commotion*, ENVIRONMENTAL HEALTH PERSPECTIVES, APR. 1996

A story about the sea and its fading riches is told in various ways in coastal communities around the world. It is the story of people who ruin the natural wealth that sustained them for generations. Nowhere is this tale more tragic than in some impoverished nations of the South Pacific and eastern Caribbean, where local people have killed off their fisheries by blowing up coral reefs. "People in very poor, remote areas use dynamite to kill fish, destroying entire reefs," says William Fenical, an oceanographer at the University of California, San Diego. "In Martinique, they have become so effective in removing resources from reefs that there are no sizable fish left. People are reduced to trapping fish two inches long."

Similar exploitation of fisheries has occurred from Asia to North America, from Africa to Australia. Once-vast populations of herring, salmon, menhaden, pollock, cod, several species of tuna, flounder, weakfish, snapper, and redfish have been depleted by overfishing... Meanwhile, sprawling coastal cities continue to experience rapid growth, polluting and destroying marine habitats. Fourteen of the world's 15 largest metropolitan areas—with 10 million people or more—are near coastal waters. These urban settlements, along with modern agriculture, send huge amounts of pollutants into coastal waters, including sewage, persistent organic pollutants, radioactive substances, heavy metals, oils, sediments, and nutrients. Other major threats to the ocean are introductions of alien species, declining species diversity, and climate change.

These threats, moreover, are coalescing, with dangerous results for both ecosystem and human health. "We are starting to see the effects of multiple assaults on ecosystems, and synergies among these multiple assaults," says Paul Epstein of the Harvard University School of Public Health. Numerous coastal bays and sounds, pummeled by overfishing, pollution, and habitat destruction, have become breeding grounds for toxic algal blooms and water-borne disease. * * *

Fishing is still the mainstay of thousands of coastal communities ... But since the early 1990s, more than 100,000 fishermen have lost jobs. In particular, small coastal towns and villages rely on fishing, but as fish populations continue to stagnate or decline, so will many local economies and cultures. * * *

Numerous nations, including the United States, the former Soviet Union, most European countries, and Japan, have subsidized their fishing industries through low-or no-interest loans and payments. The FAO estimates that in 1993, government subsidies were $54 billion a year; and to rehabilitate fishery stocks to 1970 levels, nations would have to remove 23% of the world's fishing fleet at a cost of $73 billion.

Furthermore, fishing on the high seas—international waters outside nations' Exclusive Economic Zones (EEZs), which extend 200 nautical miles (230 miles) from coastlines—is lightly regulated. "Few states have implemented legislation governing the rights and obligations of their vessels fishing on the high seas," states the FAO. In addition, of the governing bodies that regulate fisheries, "international institutions are generally weak compared with national and local governments," states the report Global Marine Biological Diversity: A Strategy for Building Conservation into Decision Making, a 1993 plan sponsored by the Center for Marine Conservation, the World Bank, the UN Environment Programme, and others.

But even within nations' EEZs, catch quotas are often guided by economic interests rather than scientific recommendations. Many governments are unwilling to take measures that would drive fishermen into bankruptcy and unemployment lines. For example, to prevent overfishing by foreign trawlers in the American EEZ, the U.S. Congress passed the Magnuson Fishery Conservation and Management Act in 1975, which created eight regional management councils composed primarily of state officials and commercial and recreational fishermen. The councils recommend limits on fishing and allocate catches among competing fishermen. Then, the councils offer their recommendations to the National Marine Fisheries Service and the Secretary of Commerce, who make the final determinations on fishing regulations.

Because fisheries biology is imprecise, scientists usually give resource managers a range of fish population estimates, which are used to recommend catch quotas. Some managers take an optimistic approach, choosing the high range in the population estimate when recommending a catch quota, and as a result too many fish may be caught, says Eugene H. Buck, Congressional Research Service (CRS) senior analyst. Fishermen are "worried about paying their bills. So managers want to maximize the economic benefit of the resource, but it's a short-term view," he said. * * *

"For a long time, we have understood the short-term consequences of stopping overfishing," says Charlotte de Fontaubert, marine specialist at the Center for

International Environmental Law in Washington, DC. "It would mean the loss of 20–40% of the nation's fishing fleet and the destruction of coastal communities. But we haven't been willing to face the social impacts and costs of what we need to do. This is not just a problem in the United States; you see the same problem elsewhere, including Europe."

Overfishing has major impacts on the equilibrium of marine areas, scientists say. The fish species most favored by consumers are carnivores—predators such as tuna and swordfish that are comparable to a lion or an eagle in a terrestrial system. "When you take a top-level predator from an ecosystem, you harm its balance because lower predators abound and overconsume the next group down the food chain," says Fenical. "Overfishing can have an amazingly negative impact on the ocean."

Unregulated fisheries is the classic case of the tragedy of the commons. While it is in the common interest of all to conserve the fisheries, each fishing vessel's immediate interests are best served by catching as many fish as possible. A traditional solution to the tragedy is to allocate property rights in order to provide a direct incentive for conserving the resource. As an example, in 1974 New England fishermen were harvesting only 12% of the fish caught in their waters. Most were caught by boats from the Soviet Union, Poland and elsewhere. Thus when the exclusive economic zones were created in UNCLOS, placing 90% of the world's fish catch within national jurisdictions, it was thought that this would encourage strict national oversight to ensure conservation of domestic fish stocks.

Yet exactly the opposite has occurred. Nations eager to exploit their new national resources subsidized large fishing fleets. Between 1970 and 1990, the global fishing fleet doubled from 585,000 to 1.2 million commercial boats, in addition to the millions of small fishing boats. In the United States, the Arctic Alaska Fisheries Corporation received about $100 million in federal loan guarantees. The European Union increased subsidies to the fishing industry from $80 million in 1983 to $580 million by 1990. Twenty percent of the subsidy went to build new boats or improve old ones. Once the EEZ fisheries were depleted, vessels moved on to foreign or high seas fisheries (a practice known as "pulse fishing"). In 1994 Indonesia announced its intention to purchase over 81,000 new fishing vessels, with foreign sources providing most of the $4 billion investment. Though the official European Union position has been to decommission 40 percent of its fishing capacity, it actively provided "exit grants" so companies could relocate their boats outside European waters. Dick Russell, *Vacuuming the Seas; Where Countries Collide*, E MAGAZINE, July, 1996, p. 28.

Where are these boats "relocated" to? Often to developing countries, who are increasingly selling permits to foreign vessels to fish their waters. Senegal, for example, has been paid to allow intensive fishing of its waters by EU fleets. Thus much of the responsibility for overfishing lies with coastal States who, under UNCLOS, also bear the chief responsibility of conserving the fish stocks and managing their recovery. What steps would you recommend coastal states take to address the problem of overfishing in the EEZ? Why do you think these steps have largely been ineffective?

———

QUESTIONS AND DISCUSSION

1. The image of too many boats chasing too few fish is more than a quaint description. The number of violent incidents between fishing boats has dramatically increased. International fisheries conflicts are now taking place literally all over the world, from the Bering Sea (pollock, herring and cod), the Grand Banks (northern cod, plaice and redfish) and the Sea of Okhotsk (pollock, herring and sole) to the Southeast Pacific (jack mackerel, blue whiting and horse mackerel), the Patagonian Shelf (squid, krill and hake), and between Australia and New Zealand (orange roughy). Consider the image below. Dick Russell, *Vacuuming the Seas; Where Countries Collide,* E MAGAZINE, July, 1996, p. 28.

> At sea 200 miles southwest of Iceland last summer, the crew of a super-trawler big enough to contain a dozen Boeing 747 jumbo jets unloaded a staggering 50 tons of oceanic redfish into flash-freezers down below, as the Icelandic ship's captain began maneuvering against nearby Russian and Japanese vessels for the next set. Emotions were running high, as there was a lot at stake. Each ship was trawling nets with opening circumferences of almost two miles; that's the equivalent of 10 New York City blocks wide by two Empire State Buildings high. Soon the Russian boat steamed over the Icelander's net, and the Japanese trawler ripped loose the Russian's lines.

2. Based on 1989 data, the FAO estimated in 1992 that $54 billion dollars were spent on global subsidies to the fishing industry, yet the industry lost $50 billion. Fleets spent approximately 46% of their revenue paying back capital investment in their high-tech boats. This regularly cited statistic, like many other subsidy statistics, is necessarily inexact because money is distributed in both direct and indirect ways. Subsidies have "taken the form of grants, low-cost loans and loan guarantees for new vessel construction and repair; subsidies to the purchase of new gear; support for construction of cold storage and processing plants; support for fish prices and fishermen's wages; and the provision of marine insurance, harbor maintenance, and fuel discounts." Christopher D. Stone, *The Maladies in Global Fisheries: Are Trade Laws Part of the Treatment?*, U.S.C. Law School Working Paper Series, No. 97–12, at 35; <http://www.worldbank.org/html/extpb/abshtml/14216.htm>. Regardless of the exact figure, the long-term ramifications of such large government subsidies pose harmful threats to both fish stocks and the economies of fishing communities.

Opponents of fisheries subsidies believe such aid reduces fishing costs, which leads to overexploitation and places a downward pressure on the price of fish. For a period of time, the government is able to maintain the economic well-being of the fishing industry, but overfishing continues to add to the decline in fish stocks. As Christopher Stone has described, "the disease feeds on itself: the more subsidies, the more capacity; the more capacity; the fewer fish per unit effort; the lower the fishers' returns, the more intense the pressure for government relief." Stone, *op. cit.* Subsidies also pose problems for developing countries. "Subsidized fishing by wealthier nations limits the ability of developing countries to develop their own sustainable fishing industries with the benefit of full access to markets and true market prices." World Trade Organization, Committee on Trade and Environment WT/CTE/W/121 June 28, 1999.

In calculating total social costs, consider, as well, the payments that follow failed fisheries. The Marine Fish Conservation Network reports that American taxpayers have spent more than $160 million since 1994 to "mitigate the economic and ecological impacts of fishery management failures in New England, Alaska and along the West Coast." Cat Lazaroff, *New Law Could Save Millions Spent on Facilities Mismanagement*, March 10, 2000, <http://www.ens.lycos.com/ ens/ mar2000/2000L–03–10–06/html>.

3. Fishery issues are increasingly arising at the WTO. Peru, Australia, Iceland, New Zealand, the Philippines, Norway, and the United States have called for a WTO agreement to reduce fishery subsidies. Ideally, this would both reduce barriers to trade and protect the environment. Reducing overcapacity would arguably lead to higher seafood prices and less pressure on already stressed fisheries. In one of the rare instances of free trade clearly supporting environmental protection, a Communication from the United States to the WTO Committee on Trade and Environment argued that "subsidies in fisheries tend to promote harvesting operations and capitalization by reducing fixed and variable costs and supporting prices and incomes. Only rarely do they directly promote exports. Further it seems that cost reducing subsidies far outweigh subsidies that support incomes and prices, so their aggregate trade effect is usually to suppress prices." World Trade Organization, Committee on Trade Environment, WT/CTE/W/154, July 4, 2000, at 2. A proposal to address (and presumably remove) subsidies received strong support at the Seattle WTO Ministerial and may well have been adopted had talks not broken down over agriculture. *See* Thorir Ibsen (Iceland Ministry for Foreign Affairs), *Sustainable Fisheries: The Linkages With Trade And Environment.* <http://www.iisd.ca/linkages/journal/ibsen.html >.

4. A fisheries dispute between the EU and Chile has also arisen at the WTO. The EU has traditionally caught swordfish and processed them in Chile prior to export to the U.S. A recent Chilean conservation law, however, forbade the landing of swordfish in domestic ports. The EU argues that this violates Article 5 of the General Agreement on Tariffs and Trade (GATT)—establishing the free transit of goods when merely passing through a country as part of a larger journey. Chile justifies the law based on the overexploitation of the swordfish and on the grounds that such measures are necessary under GATT Articles 20(b) and 20(g). The EU has requested dispute resolution at the WTO. In response, Chile has sought formal arbitration under UNCLOS. Which do you think is the more appropriate forum to decide this dispute? What factors should be considered and which do you think should be most important in resolving this forum shopping battle? *See, Fisheries Dispute with EU Escalates; Primacy of Conservation Over Trade is at Stake*, LATIN AMERICA WEEKLY REPORT, August 8, 2000 at 368.

The EU and Chile later agreed to drop their respective challenges, reaching a compromise that permits four EU vessels to trans-ship or land up to 1,000 tons of swordfish at three Chilean ports and also puts in place an intensive data collection program to evaluate swordfish stocks. In exchange, they also settled their dispute over Chilean liquor taxes. *EU and Chile Resolve Squabbles on Swordfish and Liquor*, EUROPEAN REPORT, Jan. 27, 2001.

5. A growing source of fish and, some argue, a potential relief from pressure on fisheries, has been the growth of aquaculture, also known as fish farming or mariculture. Aquaculture has become one of the world's fastest-growing food industries. Total sales around the globe of seafood "grown" for consumption amounted to almost 20% of the seafood eaten in 1994 and accounted for over 25% in 2000. While over half of the world's aquaculture is carp raised in China for local consumption, salmon and shrimp farms have become multi-billion dollar businesses providing important export earnings for countries such as Thailand and Ecuador.

The World Bank reports that by 2010 aquaculture could provide 40% of the global fish consumed and over 50% of the commercial fish value.

Aquaculture raises environmental concerns of its own, however, and has the potential to increase pressure on wild stocks for three reasons. The first is destruction of mangrove wetlands, the nurseries for many species, to create ponds for shrimp aquaculture. Some environmentalists have called this practice as destructive as "slash-and-burn" deforestation. *Oceans and the Law of the Seas: Report of the Secretary–General*, U.N. GA, 55th Sess., at 26, U.N. Dov. A/55/61 (2000). Second, farmed fish take more out of the oceans than they keep in because their processed food is largely made up of ground fish taken from the oceans. The economist, Rosamond Naylor, estimates that almost two pounds of wild fish are needed for every pound of farmed fish. And last, disease and pollution can spread from farms (really, enclosed cages) and harm wild fish populations. <http://www.stanford.edu/dept/news/report/news/february28/aaasnaylor–228.html>.

6. The impacts of climate change on fisheries are still unclear, but could be significant. Increasing ocean temperature will influence the ranges of marine organisms, likely reducing the habitat for species sensitive to temperatures at the ocean surface layers (the area where most marine life lives).

> In the northwestern Pacific, the enormous swath of ocean bordering California and southern Alaska, average surface temperatures jumped by two degrees F in 1977 and have remained at these levels every since. John McGowan of the Scripps Institution of Oceanography found that over the period there has been a 70 percent decline in zooplankton, the tiny animals that, directly or indirectly, feed virtually all higher life... A once-common seabird, the sooty shearwater, declined by 90 percent. Most fish populations have fallen by 5 percent per year since 1986, and near shore species like kelp, urchins, and abalone have collapsed while warmer water species have moved in. The short-beaked dolphin, a species that prefers warm water, has undergone a twenty-five-fold increase in the waters off California, while Alaska's cold-water fur seals and sea lions have been dwindling.

COLIN WOODARD, OCEAN'S END 51 (2000).

B.   FISHERIES LAW

In the past, fisheries law has closely resembled property law. Living marine resources within a nation's territory belonged exclusively to the nation just as did its oil and coal. Fisheries beyond national jurisdiction—in the high seas—were common resources subject to the law of capture. Resources belonged to whomever took the property into possession first. Thus in an international arbitration between the United States and Great Britain in 1898, British ships were held to be exercising a legitimate freedom of the sea when they caught fur seals more than three miles off the U.S. coast. *Bering Sea Fur Seals Arbitration* (Gr. Brit. v. U.S.), *reprinted in* J. MOORE, INTERNATIONAL ARBITRATIONS 755 (1893). This simple regime has evolved since the 1950s, however, into an international framework of living marine resource law with three guiding principles–harvest levels based on scientific data, regulation of the species through its whole range, and broad consideration of the relevant ecological factors affecting conservation of the species and its habitat. Birnie & Boyle, INTERNATIONAL LAW AND THE ENVIRONMENT 425 (1993).

1. COD WARS

The main conflict in international regulation of fisheries has been the tension between coastal states and high seas vessels. In the 1970s, Iceland unilaterally declared it was extending its exclusive fishing zone from 12 miles to 200 miles. British vessels, who had traditionally fished well within the 200–mile zone, refused to recognize Iceland's claim. A series of violent "cod wars" took place in the North Atlantic, with Iceland's coast guard chasing British fishing trawlers and, in turn, being rammed by British warships. In 1976, alone, there were over four dozen rammings. The dispute was placed before the International Court of Justice, which ruled that in the case of a conflict between a coastal State's rights to manage its living marine resources and another State's high seas freedom of fishing, neither party's fishing rights were absolute—coastal and high seas States share responsibility in the conservation of living marine resources. Icelandic Fisheries Case (United Kingdom v. Iceland), 1974 I.C.J. 3 (1974). The Court declared:

> [B]oth states have an obligation to take full account of each other's rights and of any fishery conservation measures the necessity of which is shown to exist in those waters. It is one of the advances of maritime international law, resulting from the intensification of fishing, that the former laissez-faire treatment of the living resources of the high seas has been replaced by a recognition of a duty to have due regard to the rights of other states and the needs of conservation for the benefit of all. Consequently, both Parties have the obligation to keep under review the fishery resources in the disputed waters and to examine together, in the light of scientific and other available information, the measures required for conservation and development of equitable exploitation of those resources.

---

2. UNCLOS

Soon after this decision, UNCLOS addressed directly these inherent tensions between ownership and exploitation of living marine resources. Within its territorial sea (up to 12 nautical miles off the coast), a coastal state has exclusive sovereignty to regulate fisheries. Article 2. Out to the limits of the EEZ (up to 200 nautical miles off the coast), a coastal state retains the rights to explore, exploit, and manage the living and non-living natural resources. Article 56. These rights, though, are limited by the responsibility to manage and conserve the living marine resources. Article 61. Coastal nations are also required to enter into agreements with other State to fish in the EEZ if the coastal nation lacks capacity to harvest the optimum yield, giving preference to landlocked and geographically disadvantaged states. Article 62. Together, territorial waters and the EEZ comprise roughly 40% of the world's oceans and 90% of its living marine resources.

UNCLOS also addressed four categories of fish that historically have provided serious challenges to the rule of international law: straddling stocks, highly migratory species, anadromous species, and catadromous species. "Straddling stocks" are fish whose habitat straddles the EEZ and the high seas. Highly migratory species may traverse the waters of several nations as well as the high seas. Anadromous species, such as salmon, are born in fresh water, spend most of their life in the sea, and return to fresh water to spawn. Catadromous species, such as eels, live in fresh water and enter salt water to spawn.

As you read the UNCLOS provisions below, consider whether they expand or limit the high seas freedom to fish. How are rights to exploit living marine resources conditioned on obligations to conserve them? Does UNCLOS provide solutions to the problems posed by straddling stocks, highly migratory species, anadromous species, and catadromous species, or simply call on the Parties to resolve the issues themselves?

UN Convention on the Law of the Sea

Article 56

Rights, jurisdiction and duties of the coastal State in the exclusive economic zone

1. In the exclusive economic zone, the coastal State has:

(a) sovereign rights for the purpose of exploring and exploiting, conserving and managing the natural resources, whether living or non-living, of the waters superjacent to the sea-bed and of the sea-bed and its subsoil, and with regard to other activities for the economic exploitation and exploration of the zone, such as the production of energy from the water, currents and winds; * * *

2. In exercising its rights and performing its duties under this Convention in the exclusive economic zone, the coastal State shall have due regard to the rights and duties of other States and shall act in a manner compatible with the provisions of this Convention. * * *

Article 61

Conservation of the living resources

1. The coastal State shall determine the allowable catch of the living resources in its exclusive economic zone.

2. The coastal State, taking into account the best scientific evidence available to it, shall ensure through proper conservation and management measures that the maintenance of the living resources in the exclusive economic zone is not endangered by over-exploitation. As appropriate, the coastal State and competent international organizations, whether subregional, regional or global, shall co-operate to this end.

3. Such measures shall also be designed to maintain or restore populations of harvested species at levels which can produce the maximum sustainable yield, as qualified by relevant environmental and economic factors, including the economic needs of coastal fishing communities and the special requirements of developing States, and taking into account fishing patterns, the interdependence of stocks and any generally recommended international minimum standards, whether subregional, regional or global.

4. In taking such measures the coastal State shall take into consideration the effects on species associated with or dependent upon harvested species with a view to maintaining or restoring populations of such associated or dependent species above levels at which their reproduction may become seriously threatened.

5. Available scientific information, catch and fishing effort statistics, and other data relevant to the conservation of fish stocks shall be contributed and

exchanged on a regular basis through competent international organizations, whether subregional, regional or global, where appropriate and with participation by all States concerned, including States whose nationals are allowed to fish in the exclusive economic zone.

Article 62
Utilization of the living resources

1. The coastal State shall promote the objective of optimum utilization of the living resources in the exclusive economic zone without prejudice to article 61.

2. The coastal State shall determine its capacity to harvest the living resources of the exclusive economic zone. Where the coastal State does not have the capacity to harvest the entire allowable catch, it shall, through agreements or other arrangements and pursuant to the terms, conditions, laws and regulations referred to in paragraph 4, give other States access to the surplus of the allowable catch. * * *

4. Nationals of other States fishing in the exclusive economic zone shall comply with the conservation measures and with the other terms and conditions established in the laws and regulations of the coastal State. These laws and regulations shall be consistent with this Convention. * * *

Article 63
Stocks occurring within the exclusive economic zones of two or more coastal States or both within the exclusive economic zone and in an area beyond and adjacent to it

1. Where the same stock or stocks of associated species occur within the exclusive economic zones of two or more coastal States, these States shall seek, either directly or through appropriate subregional or regional organizations, to agree upon the measures necessary to co-ordinate and ensure the conservation and development of such stocks without prejudice to the other provisions of this Part.

2. Where the same stock or stocks of associated species occur both within the exclusive economic zone and in an area beyond and adjacent to the zone, the coastal State and the States fishing for such stocks in the adjacent area shall seek, either directly or through appropriate subregional or regional organizations, to agree upon the measures necessary for the conservation of these stocks in the adjacent area.

Article 64
Highly migratory species

1. The coastal State and other States whose nationals fish in the region for the highly migratory species listed in Annex I shall co-operate directly or through appropriate international organizations with a view to ensuring conservation and promoting the objective of optimum utilization of such species throughout the region, both within and beyond the exclusive economic zone. In regions for which no appropriate international organization exists, the coastal State and other States whose nationals harvest these species in the region shall co-operate to establish such an organization and participate in its work. * * *

Article 65
Marine mammals

Nothing in this Part restricts the right of a coastal State or the competence of an international organization, as appropriate, to prohibit, limit or regulate the exploitation of marine mammals more strictly than provided for in this Part. States shall co-operate with a view to the conservation of marine mammals and in the case of cetaceans shall in particular work through the appropriate international organizations for their conservation, management and study.

Article 66
Anadromous stocks

1. States in whose rivers anadromous stocks originate shall have the primary interest in and responsibility for such stocks.

2. The State of origin of anadromous stocks shall ensure their conservation by the establishment of appropriate regulatory measures for fishing in all waters landward of the outer limits of its exclusive economic zone.... The State of origin may, after consultations with the other States referred to in paragraphs 3 and 4 fishing these stocks, establish total allowable catches for stocks originating in its rivers.

3. (a) Fisheries for anadromous stocks shall be conducted only in waters landward of the outer limits of exclusive economic zones, except in cases where this provision would result in economic dislocation for a State other than the State of origin. With respect to such fishing beyond the outer limits of the exclusive economic zone, States concerned shall maintain consultations with a view to achieving agreement on terms and conditions of such fishing giving due regard to the conservation requirements and the needs of the State of origin in respect of these stocks. * * *

4. In cases where anadromous stocks migrate into or through the waters landward of the outer limits of the exclusive economic zone of a State other than the State of origin, such State shall co-operate with the State of origin with regard to the conservation and management of such stocks. * * *

Article 67
Catadromous species

1. A coastal State in whose waters catadromous species spend the greater part of their life cycle shall have responsibility for the management of these species and shall ensure the ingress and egress of migrating fish. * * *

3. In cases where catadromous fish migrate through the exclusive economic zone of another State, whether as juvenile or maturing fish, the management, including harvesting, of such fish shall be regulated by agreement between the State mentioned in paragraph 1 and the other State concerned. Such agreement shall ensure the rational management of the species and take into account the responsibilities of the State mentioned in paragraph 1 for the maintenance of these species.

* * *

Article 87
Freedom of the high seas

1. The high seas are open to all States, whether coastal or land-locked. Freedom of the high seas is exercised under the conditions laid down by this Convention and by other rules of international law. It comprises, *inter alia*, both for coastal and land-locked States:

(a) freedom of navigation; * * *

(e) freedom of fishing, subject to the conditions laid down in section 2; [Articles 116–120] * * *

2. These freedoms shall be exercised by all States with due regard for the interests of other States in their exercise of the freedom of the high seas, and also with due regard for the rights under this Convention with respect to activities in the Area.

* * *

Article 116

Right to fish on the high seas

All States have the right for their nationals to engage in fishing on the high seas subject to:

(a) their treaty obligations;

(b) the rights and duties as well as the interests of coastal States provided for, *inter alia*, in article 63, paragraph 2, and articles 64 to 67; and

(c) the provisions of this section.

Article 117

Duty of States to adopt with respect to their nationals measures for the conservation of the living resources of the high seas

All States have the duty to take, or to co-operate with other States in taking, such measures for their respective nationals as may be necessary for the conservation of the living resources of the high seas.

Article 118

Co-operation of States in the conservation and management of living resources

States shall co-operate with each other in the conservation and management of living resources in the areas of the high seas. States whose nationals exploit identical living resources, or different living resources in the same area, shall enter into negotiations with a view to taking the measures necessary for the conservation of the living resources concerned. They shall, as appropriate, co-operate to establish subregional or regional fisheries organizations to this end.

Article 119

Conservation of the living resources of the high seas

1. In determining the allowable catch and establishing other conservation measures for the living resources in the high seas, States shall:

(a) take measures which are designed, on the best scientific evidence available to the States concerned, to maintain or restore populations of harvested species at levels which can produce the maximum sustainable yield, as qualified by relevant environmental and economic factors, including the special requirements of developing States. * * *

(b) take into consideration the effects on species associated with or dependent upon harvested species with a view to maintaining or restoring populations of such associated or dependent species above levels at which their reproduction may become seriously threatened.

2. Available scientific information, catch and fishing effort statistics, and other data relevant to the conservation of fish stocks shall be contributed and

exchanged on a regular basis through competent international organizations.
* * *

---

3. THE INTERNATIONAL TRIBUNAL FOR THE LAW OF THE SEA

The International Tribunal for the Law of the Sea (ITLOS) had issued decisions in four cases by January, 2001, three of which involved allegedly illegal fishing practices. In the Southern Bluefin Tuna cases, New Zealand and Australia brought an action challenging Japan's experimental catch program. A highly prized meat for sushi (now more valuable per pound than gold), Southern Bluefin Tuna (SBT) populations have come under heavy pressure in recent decades. In 1993, the Convention for the Conservation of Southern Bluefin Tuna was created to manage stocks (and to which Australia, Japan and New Zealand are all parties). With the assistance of its Scientific Committee, the Commission set a total allowable catch (TAC) for tuna. Starting in 1995, Japan proposed increasing the TAC, but no agreement has been reached to do so. In 1998, Japan increased its harvest of tuna by 2,000 tons in a program it described as experimental fishing, deemed as necessary to collect more scientific data for establishing TACs (*see* similar actions by Japan for whaling, p. 976). Australia and New Zealand claimed that this was a sham commercial operation, and alleged that Japan had breached its UNCLOS obligations to conserve and manage the tuna by failing to restore population levels to maximum sustainable yield or cooperate with New Zealand and Australia in good faith.

The dispute went first to the ITLOS on a request by Australia and New Zealand for provisional measures of protection in advance of a final resolution of the matter. On August 27, 1999, the ITLOS issued an interim order granting certain provisional measures. ITLOS concluded that Japan had breached its UNCLOS obligations by:

(a) failing to adopt necessary conservation measures for its nationals fishing on the high seas so as to maintain or restore the SBT stock to levels which can produce the maximum sustainable yield, as required by Article 119 and contrary to the obligation in Article 117 to take necessary conservation measures for its nationals;

(b) carrying out unilateral experimental fishing in 1998 and 1999 which has or will result in SBT being taken by Japan over and above previously agreed Commission [Commission for the Conservation of Southern Bluefin Tuna] national allocations;

(c) taking unilateral action contrary to the rights and interests of New Zealand as a coastal State as recognised in Article 116(b) and allowing its nationals to catch additional SBT in the course of experimental fishing in a way which discriminates against New Zealand fishermen contrary to Article 119 (3);

(d) failing in good faith to co-operate with New Zealand with a view to ensuring the conservation of SBT, as required by Article 64 of UNCLOS;

(e) otherwise failing in its obligations under UNCLOS in respect of the conservation and management of SBT, having regard to the requirements of the precautionary principle.

ITLOS ordered Japan to refrain immediately from authorizing or conducting any further experimental fishing for SBT without the agreement of New Zealand and Australia, negotiate and cooperate in good faith with New Zealand in setting future conservation measures to restore the SBT stock to maximum sustainable yield levels, and not to exceed the existing TAC until a new one is set.

For a final resolution of the dispute, Australia and New Zealand invoked the UNCLOS dispute resolution procedures to create a five-member Arbitral Tribunal specially appointed to address the Southern Bluefin Tuna case. The members of the Arbitral Tribunal were selected by the agreement of Australia, New Zealand and Japan and administered by the World Bank's International Centre for Settlement of Investment Disputes. Japan argued that the dispute was not within the ambit of the UNCLOS, that the Arbitral Tribunal therefore lacked jurisdiction, and that the proper mechanism for dispute resolution was the 1993 Convention signed by Japan, Australia, and New Zealand. The Arbitral Tribunal issued its decision on August 4, 2000, agreeing with Japan, in part. The Tribunal found that the claim appropriately fell under both UNCLOS and the 1993 Convention. However, by a vote of 4 to 1, it sustained Japan's contention that a provision of the 1993 Convention excluded compulsory jurisdiction over disputes arising both under it and UNCLOS, effectively preempting the UNCLOS dispute process. Accordingly, the Arbitral Tribunal unanimously revoked the one-year old ITLOS provisional ruling that enjoined Japan from conducting an experimental fishing program for southern bluefin tuna. At the same time, the Tribunal declared that revocation of provisional measures did *not* mean that the parties may disregard the effects of those measures. It noted that the ongoing negotiations among the parties had narrowed the gap between them, and that Japan had offered mediation or arbitration under the 1993 Convention. It encouraged all parties, in the interest of achieving a successful settlement to abstain from engaging in any act that may aggravate the proceedings.

<http://www.worldbank.org/icsid/bluefintuna/pressrelease2.htm>.

In the Camouco case, a fishing vessel (the Camouco) registered in Panama was found using longline fishing gear in the EEZ of the Crozet Islands (French territory). As the French coast guard attempted to halt the vessel, crew members threw 48 bags overboard. One bag was retrieved and revealed 34 kilograms of fresh toothfish. France alleged the Camouco had engaged in unlawful fishing in its EEZ, failed to declare entry while having fish aboard the vessel, concealed the vessel's foreign flag, and attempted flight. Panama requested the Tribunal to order the prompt release of the Camouco and its Master, while France opposed the request and, in case it were granted, asked for deposit of bond no less than FF20 million. The Tribunal ordered the release of the master and Camouco, but also required an FF8 million bank guarantee as security.

———

QUESTIONS AND DISCUSSION

1. In the swordfish dispute between the EU and Chile (described above at page 679), the EU threatened to submit the dispute before a WTO dispute panel while

Chile countered with a threat to submit it before ITLOS. With the growth of multilateral environmental agreements, disputes over the primacy of competing dispute resolution fora will become increasingly important. If parties to the dispute are parties both to relevant agreements with dispute resolution mechanisms and to UNCLOS, how do you think the proper dispute resolution forum should be determined?

2.   Japan, New Zealand and Australia all alleged the failure of good faith negotiations on behalf of the other party. Which party is better suited to bear the burden of conducting negotiations in good faith or should both parties bear the burden? How could the precautionary principle help in deciding this?

3.   At the end of 1999, the Tribunal was in a state of dire financial need with an unpaid balance of $1,473,290 and issued an appeal for all parties to pay assessed contributions. From the Tribunal's creation through 2001, however, it had decided only four cases. Do the frequency of use and failure to pay dues represent a lack of support on behalf of the parties? Is it time to consider the Tribunal a failed experiment, or is case volume an inappropriate measure of success? *Report of the Tenth Meeting of the States Parties*, June 22, 2000, <http://www.un.org/Depts/los/Docs/SPLOS/SPLOS_60.htm>.

4.   Fishery conservation depends critically on accurate scientific data concerning population size and age distribution in order to determine the status of a fish population, i.e. whether it needs protection or not. Otherwise setting quotas is reduced to guesswork. Yet this data is difficult to gather. Indeed, while advances have been made in the field, one scientist described the process to the authors as the equivalent of flying over the Serengeti at night in a helicopter, dropping a net, and estimating the total zebra population from those caught in the net.

UNCLOS contains both direct and indirect provisions requiring collection and sharing of data. Article 117, for example, declares that States have the duty to cooperate with other States in taking steps to conserve living marine resources. While not explicitly stated, this Article has been interpreted to require data collection because one cannot develop effective conservation measures without population data. Article 119 is more explicit, calling on States to take measures to conserve high seas species based on "the best scientific evidence available to the States concerned." Article 119 also requires contribution and exchange of available scientific information of fishing statistics on a regular basis. Clearly the best source for fishing statistics are the fishing boats, themselves. Why might reliance on this source of information be problematic? Do you think independently paid observers could provide a solution?

A number of environmental groups, notably Greenpeace and Earth Island Institute, have sneaked video cameras on board fishing boats to publicize the problems of by-catch and high-grading (discarding target fish because they are too small or injured). Videos of dead dolphins in tuna nets proved particularly effective in generating support for amendments to the U.S. Marine Mammal Protection Act that linked restrictions on tuna imports to dolphin mortality in the Eastern Tropical Pacific (*see* p. 995).

5.   Article 117 requires States to take measures "as may be necessary for the conservation of the living resources of the high seas." Historically, however, "conservation" in the context of fisheries management has meant conserving stocks in order to maintain a commercial fishery and maximize its yield, not conservation for its own sake. Indeed, the 1958 Geneva Convention on Fishing and Conservation of Living Resources of the High Seas defines conservation of the high seas living marine resources as "the aggregate of the measures rendering possible the optimum sustainable yield for these resources so as to secure a maximum supply of food and other marine products." Birnie & Boyle, *op. cit.,* at 436

Article 119 of UNCLOS introduced an important innovation. Similar to the earlier Geneva Convention provision just quoted, it requires States to manage species at levels that can produce the "maximum sustainable yield" (*see also* Article 61(3)). This goal, however, is not absolute, for it is "qualified by relevant environmental and economic factors." The fisheries quota resulting from qualifying the maximum sustainable yield on environmental and economic considerations is known as the "optimum yield." Conditioning sustainable yield on environmental factors was a significant innovation of UNCLOS and, in practice, would enable adoption of a lower annual catch than might be maintained if the management goal were simply maximum sustainable yield. Under what circumstances might one manage a fishery at a level below its maximum sustainable yield?

6. While Article 62 requires coastal States to allow other nations to fish in its EEZ if it cannot harvest an optimum yield, the practice is more complicated. If a country does not want to open its EEZ to other flag State's ships, it can either (a) play with its stock assessments to show a low optimum yield, or (b) adjust its optimum yield down for "economic or environmental" reasons (Article 61(3)). In practice, not surprisingly, developed countries have no problem creating capacity to take their optimum yield. Many developing countries, on the other hand, employ "joint ventures" to sell access to their EEZs to distant water fishing nations such as Japan, Korea, and Taiwan. A recurring problem with this practice, however, has been corruption and poor management. Agreements have been criticized for allowing access for too little money and for not reflecting scientific management practices. This trend, particularly in Africa, has depleted fisheries that supported coastal, artisanal fisheries.

7. As with all international environmental agreements, the success of UNCLOS rests with national implementation. Even the most sophisticated international environmental laws have limited impact if not reinforced effectively at the national level. The following excerpt presents an accurate, though discouraging, history of the U.S. management of its fisheries. Oliver A. Houck, *On the Law of Biodiversity and Ecosystem Management,* 81 MINN. L. REV. 869, 945–48 (1997).

> Beyond public forests and rangelands, beyond the reach of piers and offshore oil platforms, lies one of the world's oldest economies: commercial fisheries. Since 1976, the United States has exercised an extended fisheries jurisdiction stretching 200 miles from the shoreline. This jurisdiction covers more than 100,000 miles of U.S. coastline, and more than 2.2 million nautical square miles of ocean—an area roughly doubling the size of the United States and encompassing nearly 20% of the world's maritime fisheries. As a matter of simple geography, the management responsibility is awesome. Only this decade have statistics revealed how poorly the United States has exercised this responsibility. Much of the New England fishing fleet, once the pride of the region, now sits grounded in port; the federal government is now trying to buy out the boats. Salmon fishing has been banned off the coast of Washington, and severely restricted down the western seaboard. Chesapeake Bay oysters are at 1% of historical levels; swordfish are landing at 60 pounds instead of 1000 pounds and more; bluefin tuna are down 90% since 1975; haddock are down 94% since 1960; and harvestable cod and yellowtail flounder are at their lowest levels on record. Between 1990 and 1992, the chief groundfish species of New England dropped 30% from historic averages. The biomass of bottomfish in the Gulf of Mexico has dropped 85% since 1973, largely due to shrimp trawling.

> These declines have economic consequences. In 1990, near the onset of the current crashes, U.S. fishermen landed a record 4.4 million metric tons, valued at $3.6 billion. In that year, U.S. consumers spent $26.7 billion for fishery products; an estimated 17 million recreational fishermen caught 230.9 million

fish on 39.8 million trips into just the Atlantic Ocean and the Gulf of Mexico. U.S. fisheries generate an estimated $111 billion a year, and employ 1.5 million working Americans. The collapse of the New England fishing industry alone cost 14,000 jobs and $350 million in annual revenues. Something went very wrong.

Fisheries management will never be a simple business. Managers often lack basic information on fish populations, and even healthy stocks fluctuate widely in nature, often undermined by natural or human events over which managers have no control. Managers also face the balkanization of law enforcement jurisdictions, with state, federal, and international authorities often exercising control over the same stocks and species. Add to this palette the growing conflicts among fisheries users and fishery-dependent communities: recreational fishers versus commercial, seiners versus longliners, large boats versus small, wild culture versus mariculture, and the ultimate enigma of whether the objective of management is to increase production, or biomass, or dollar value, or to lower consumer prices, or to preserve coastal traditions and ways of life. In all of this tug of war, we have never attempted to manage the ecosystem as a whole—assuming that such a thing is even possible—or to preserve ecosystem diversity. More disappointing, we have been unable to maintain even the best-known and most commercially-important fish stocks at sustainable levels, despite an elaborate statutory framework requiring just that. These failures reveal the imprint of both consensus-based politics and a poorly articulated standard of law.

If the passage and implementation of domestic laws have failed to manage fisheries effectively, is there any reason to think that international fisheries laws will prove more successful?

8. Concern with overfishing in U.S. waters led to passage of the Magnuson Fishery Conservation and Management Act in 1976 (the "Magnuson Act"). 16 U.S.C. 1801–1882. The Magnuson Act asserts U.S. sovereignty over fisheries and other living marine resources throughout the 200–mile EEZ.

The Magnuson Act established ten regional fishery councils charged with preparing Fishery Management Plans (FMPs) for all fisheries in need of management or conservation. The Secretary of Commerce reviews every FMP for compliance with eight specific national standards for conservation, equity, and efficiency. There are now more than 30 approved FMPs for U.S. fisheries. Most FMPs include open access management tools, with no restriction placed on the number of fishing vessels (although there may be restrictions on equipment, length of season, size of fish, or total catch). Because these tools have failed to reverse the decline in fisheries, a few fisheries have begun to experiment with limiting access to a certain category of fishing vessels. All limited access plans must be aimed at achieving optimum yield from a fishery and can be approved only after the regional council and the Secretary of Commerce have considered several factors, including past and present participation in the fishery, the economics of the fishery, the ability of fishing vessels to switch to other fisheries, the cultural and social framework relevant to the fishery, and any other relevant considerations. 16 U.S.C. 1853(b)(6).

---

4. STRADDLING STOCKS

a. Problem Exercise: The Seizure of the Estai

Many UNCLOS provisions, including Article 63, emphasize the importance of States cooperating in regional fisheries organizations to manage, utilize, and conserve living marine resources. NAFO, the Northwest Atlantic Fisheries Organization, is a regional organization established in 1979 to regulate the fishing grounds in the high seas of the Northwest Atlantic. Its stated purpose is to "promote the conservation and optimum utilization of the fishery resources of the Northwest Atlantic area within a framework appropriate to the regime of extended coastal State jurisdiction over fisheries." NAFO has fifteen Member States who meet annually to agree on the Total Allowable Catch (TAC) for commercially important species and to allocate quotas to each Member State's fishing fleet. The TAC are based upon the recommendations of NAFO's scientific board. The board draws upon fisheries research, such as whether harvests are increasing or decreasing and the size of fish caught, to determine whether fish stocks need protection.

The country quotas are a political decision, agreed by majority vote among the Member States and largely based on previous national activity in the fishery. The fishing fleets of Spain and Portugal are represented by the single delegate of the European Union (EU). All other NAFO member countries (Canada, Iceland, Japan, Poland, Estonia, Cuba, etc.) have one delegate each, though most have much smaller fleets than Spain's. The U.S. is not a member of NAFO, but it attends meetings as an observer.

NAFO's powers are limited. For example, the TACs and quotas are not binding. Once quotas have been allocated, if a member state disagrees with the decision it may use the Objection Procedure within 60 days and declare its own quota. In 1986, for example, NAFO set a TAC for American Plaice (a flounder) of 700 tons. The EU formally objected to this TAC and set itself a quota of 21,161 tons.

NAFO does not have rules limiting the size of fish that can be caught, though it does set minimum widths for net mesh size. The mesh regulations are set so that juvenile fish can swim through the nets. NAFO has no powers of independent enforcement. Violations are reported to Member States who are expected to police the ships flying under their flag.

Following the collapse of the Atlantic Cod fishery in 1990, NAFO banned the harvest of major commercial groundfish species. Looking for new sources of income, the Spanish and Portuguese fleets turned to the Greenland Halibut (better known as turbot). In the 1980s, only Canada had commercially fished for turbot in the North Atlantic. Heavy international fishing began in 1990 and following the harvest in 1993, when the EU fished 45,000 tons of turbot, the NAFO scientific board warned that conservation measures were needed and recommended a TAC of 40,000 tons. Thus in 1994, for the first time, NAFO set in place a TAC for turbot. After debate among the NAFO members, a TAC was set of 27,000 tons. Canada was allotted a quota of 16,300 tons and the EU 3,400 tons. Unhappy with the 90% reduction from its 1993 catch, the EU formally objected to the TAC and set itself a quota at 18,630 tons.

Most of the turbot's habitat is on the Grand Banks of Newfoundland, the richest fishing ground in the Northwest Atlantic. While most of the Grand Banks lie within Canada's EEZ, parts of the Grand Banks extend more than 200 miles off Canada's coast (the so-called "nose" and "tail" of the Grand Banks). The annual catch of turbot and a map of the Grand

Banks are shown on the next page (note that this information was provided in a press kit distributed free of charge by Canadian embassies).

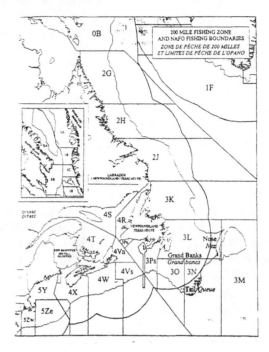

COMPARISON OF GREENLAND HALIBUT CATCHES INSIDE AND OUTSIDE THE CANADIAN 200-MILE FISHING ZONE

COMPARAISON DES PRISES DE FLÉTAN DU GROËNLAND À L'INTÉRIEUR ET À L'EXTÉRIEUR DE LA ZONE DE PÊCHE CANADIENNE DE 200 MILLES

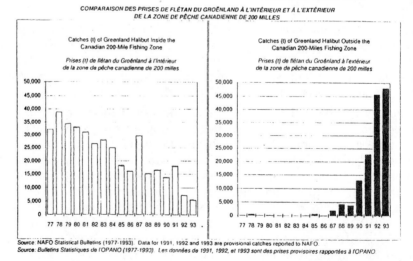

Source: NAFO Statistical Bulletins (1977-1993). Data for 1991, 1992 and 1993 are provisional catches reported to NAFO.
Source: Bulletins Statistiques de l'OPANO (1977-1993). Les données de 1991, 1992, et 1993 sont des prises provisoires rapportées à l'OPANO.

Ignorant of national jurisdictions, fish stocks in the Grand Banks move freely in and out of Canadian waters. Following the collapse of the cod fishery in the early 1990s, Newfoundland shut down most of its fishery industry, placing over 30,000 fishermen on unemployment lines, in the hope that the fishery would revive once free of overfishing pressures. In the case of cod this has proven optimistic. The cod population has continued its decline since the moratorium was announced.

Concerned that overfishing of halibut would lead to a similar situation, Canada established strict quotas for turbot caught within its EEZ (open only to Canadian boats). To ensure the effectiveness of its conservation measures, to ensure these "straddling stocks" were not depleted by over-fishing in international waters, the Canadian Parliament amended the Coastal Fisheries Protection Act in May, 1994. The amendments extended Canada's enforcement jurisdiction to all areas regulated by NAFO, provided for inspection of vessels to ensure compliance, and permitted arrests for violations of the Act. The relevant provisions were:

> Section 5.2: [N]o person, being aboard a foreign fishing vessel of a prescribed class, shall, in the NAFO Regulatory Area, fish or prepare to fish for a straddling stock in contravention of any of the prescribed conservation and management measures. [i.e. NAFO quotas]

> Section 7: [A] protection officer may . . . for the purpose of ensuring compliance with this Act and the regulations, board and inspect any fishing vessel found within Canadian fisheries waters or the NAFO Regulatory Area.

> Section 8: [A] protection officer may arrest without warrant any person who the officer suspects on reasonable grounds has committed an offense under this Act.

In simple terms, the law authorized Canadian warships to board fishing vessels both within and outside the 200 mile zone and enforce NAFO conservation measures. Following the EU's objection to the turbot TAC, the law was amended in 1995 to include enforcement authority over Spanish and Portuguese vessels.

On March 9th, 1995, Canadian warships boarded and seized the Spanish trawler, the Estai. When finally boarded, the Estai was in interna-tional waters, 12 miles outside Canada's 200 mile zone. The Estai was towed back to port in Newfoundland, its crew arrested, and its catch inspected and measured by Canadian authorities. Canada announced that the Estai had falsified its logbook records, used double nets with illegally small mesh, and caught large numbers of juvenile turbot.

The incident caused an international uproar. Spain denounced the Estai's seizure as "piracy." Canada declared it a rational, necessary act of conservation entirely consistent with international environmental law. Spain brought a challenge against Canada's actions to the International Court of Justice. Referring to the UNCLOS provisions excerpted previously in this chapter and those cited below, as well as principles of international environmental law discussed in Chapter 7, craft legal arguments both for Spain and Canada. Given that an ICJ case can take several years before resolution, what practical actions would you advise Spain and Canada to consider in resolving the conflict? Do you think the EU would support sanctions against Canada? Why might it not?

UNCLOS, Article 101

Piracy consists of any of the following acts:

(a) any illegal acts of violence or detention, or any act of depredation, committed for private ends by the crew or the passengers of a private ship or a private aircraft * * *

(b) any act of voluntary participation in the operation of a ship or of an aircraft with knowledge of facts making it a pirate ship or aircraft; * * *

UNCLOS, Article 110

... a warship which encounters on the high seas a foreign ship ... is not justified in boarding it unless there is reasonable ground for suspecting that:

(a) the ship is engaged in piracy; [matters involving fisheries are not listed as reasonable grounds for boarding]. * * *

UNCLOS, Article 279

States Parties shall settle any dispute between them concerning the interpretation or application of this Convention by peaceful means in accordance with Article 2, paragraph 3, of the Charter of the United Nations and, to this end, shall seek a solution by the means indicated in Article 33, paragraph 1, of the Charter.

U.N. Charter, Article 2, Paragraph 3

All Members shall settle their international disputes by peaceful means in such a manner that international peace and security, and justice, are not endangered.

U.N. Charter, Article 33, Paragraph 1

The parties to any dispute, the continuance of which is likely to endanger the maintenance of international peace and security, shall, first of all, seek a solution by negotiation, enquiry, mediation, conciliation, arbitration, judicial settlement, resort to regional agencies or arrangements, or other peaceful means of their own choice.

Webster's Third New International Dictionary defines piracy as "robbery on the high seas." Relevant excerpts from additional treaties may be found on the casebook web site at <http://www.wcl.american.edu/environment/iel/teachmaterial.html>.

————

b. The Straddling Stocks Treaty.

The problem of straddling stocks is not unique to George's Bank. Indeed, it would be a remarkable coincidence if ecosystems and habitats fit easily into jurisdictional lines determined by political negotiation. The "Donut Hole" in the Bering Sea, for example, is an area of high seas completely surrounded by the EEZ of the United States and Russia. Although the United States and Russia control most of the area where straddling stocks are found, other nations heavily fish the Donut Hole, frustrating national conservation efforts. Not until fish stocks collapsed (annual catch down from 1.4 million tons in 1989 to 10,000 tons in 1994) did States cooperate and agree to suspend fishing and negotiate a conservation agreement. Convention on the Conservation and Management of Pollack Resources in the Central Bering Sea, June 16, 1994, 34 I.L.M. 67

(1995). A similar situation arises in the "Peanut Hole" in the Sea of Okhotsk. Russia's EEZ covers 97% of the Sea but the remaining 3% is heavily fished by other nations.

Straddling stocks and highly migratory fish were the subject of negotiation at the Earth Summit in 1992, but proved too contentious to resolve. As a compromise, States agreed to hold an international conference under direction of the UN. It was left open whether the final product would be binding rules or simply recommendations. The primary conflict during negotiations, not surprisingly, involved balancing the traditional high seas freedom of fishing with coastal States' responsibility for conservation of living marine resources. It was clear to all, though, that the status quo of UNCLOS was inadequate.

The Canada–Spain dispute over turbot took place just prior to the final negotiating session (not, as it later emerged, by coincidence). Partly as a result of international media attention, negotiations resulted in a binding treaty–the Agreement for the Implementation of the Provisions of the United Nations Convention on the Law of the Sea of December 10, 1982 Relating to the Conservation and Management of Straddling Fish Stocks and Highly Migratory Fish Stocks, was opened for signature on December 4, 1995. U.N. Doc. A/CONF.164/37 (1995). Every provision of the treaty, known as the "Straddling Stocks Convention" or "Fish Stocks Treaty," was passed by consensus. A significant achievement, the treaty directly limits the high seas freedom of fishing, subjecting it to the conservation mandates of regional organizations, as well as enhancing states' investigation and enforcement authorities on the high seas. The Treaty gives meaning to a number of international environmental principles and duties, including the precautionary principle, the duty to consult, and the duty to cooperate.

Julie Mack, *International Fisheries Management: How the U.N. Conference on Straddling and Highly Migratory Fish Stocks Changes the Law of Fishing on the High Seas*
26 CAL. W. INT'L L.J. 313, 326–31 (1996)

Although the [Straddling and Migratory Fish Stocks Treaty's] regulations are international in scope, most of its provisions will be implemented by regional management organizations. Such organizations may be newly established in furtherance of the Fish Stock Treaty or pre-existing organizations that are re-arranged or strengthened by it. The Fish Stock Treaty sets out general and specific standards for the development of regional organizations. In recognition of the problems of cooperation faced by existing organizations, the Fish Stock Treaty strengthens the duty to cooperate and makes it clearer than it was under UNCLOS.

Under the Fish Stock Treaty, all states with a real interest in the fisheries concerned must become members of these organizations or agree to comply with organization regulations.[1] Most importantly, if states refuse either to comply or become members, they will have no access to that fishery's resources. This provision

---

1. Article 8(3). A state with a real interest is one which is fishing for the particular straddling or migratory fish stock regulated by the organization, or fishing generally in the region in question. Article 8 ensures that regional organizations will be open to all states without discrimination.

drastically alters the traditional idea of freedom of the high seas. For the first time, international law will limit access to high sea fisheries. If states do not cooperate, they will be barred from fishing the region in question. * * *

Because of the stronger duty to cooperate and the right of organizations to exclude non-members, DWFNs [distant water fishing nations] voiced concern about being denied entry into organizations. This remained a controversial point because coastal states wanted to ensure that only states with a real interest in the fishery would become members. The Fish Stock Treaty attempts to address this issue by setting out the rights of new members to ensure that DWFN interests are balanced with those of the coastal state. It mandates that needs of coastal states, the existing level of fishing, and new member contributions to conservation must be considered when deciding upon new entrants. Nongovernmental organizations also reserved the right to participate in organizational meetings as observers and receive records from meetings. * * *

The Fish Stock Treaty will increase the effectiveness of regional organizations. They will be made stronger by the ability to exclude nonmembers thereby limiting the problem of exploitation by non-party states. Even though regional management organizations will become more effective, their ultimate success will depend on stronger enforcement provisions for both coastal and flag states.

The Fish Stock Treaty addresses many of the problems of compliance and enforcement under UNCLOS. These were topics of intense debate between coastal states and DWFNs. Coastal states wanted stronger enforcement powers under the regional organizations, while DWFNs wanted to keep accountability with the flag state alone. The final draft attempts to balance these interests while making enforcement efforts within regional organizations more effective.

The problem of non-member states fishing in organization territory was a substantial concern under UNCLOS. The ability to exclude the vessels of non-member states from fishing the regulated high seas will give states the enforcement power they need to successfully deter unregulated fishing. Member states will be able to investigate and possibly even seize those vessels fishing illegally. Likewise, flag states have a stronger obligation to ensure that vessels flying their flags comply with organization regulations.

The Fish Stock Treaty also provides stronger enforcement measures against the member states of each organization. States must cooperate through regional organizations to ensure compliance with and enforcement of, the organization's management measures. Member states or flag states may undertake investigations directly or in cooperation with other interested states. If a member state alleges a violation, the flag state has a duty to investigate. All states have the duty to cooperate with concerned state authorities to make sure all alleged violations are investigated and sanctioned if violations are found.

Furthermore, any member state may board and inspect fishing vessels flying the flag of other member states. Inspectors can look at the vessel, its license, gear, equipment, records, facilities, fish and fish products, and any relevant documents needed to verify compliance. Provisions for boarding and inspecting are clearly stated in the treaty, but organizations may choose to establish stronger provisions. Unfortunately, they may also choose to limit these provisions. The treaty also provides a specific penalty for refusal to let other member states board and inspect a vessel. If violations are found during these inspections, the flag state must be immediately notified. The flag state must order the vessel to submit to investigation and suspend its authorization to fish if it does not comply. * * *

The Fish Stock Treaty does provide some further enforcement rights for coastal and member states. It states that when a vessel engages in prohibited activities, other member states may take action to keep it from fishing that region until the flag state investigates. [If the inspection indicates the vessel has committed a "serious violation," it can be towed to the nearest appropriate port for further inspection. "Serious violation" is defined to include the use of prohibited fishing gear or violation of an established quota.] This action must be in accordance with international law or regional procedures established for this purpose. Port states are also given a role in supporting conservation efforts. They may board and inspect documents, fishing gear and catch when vessels are voluntarily in their ports or offshore terminals. If a port state finds a violation, it may prohibit landings in its ports or prohibit transfer of the catch for shipping. So, although flag states still have primary authority, other states can take some limited action against vessels who fish illegally. * * *

Overall, the Fish Stock Treaty provides for better enforcement among the regional management organizations. It gives member states more authority to monitor and conduct investigations. But because flag states still have primary authority over the investigation and sanctioning process, there will always be a risk that investigations will not be thorough or that penalties will not be strong enough. It is hoped that the clearer delineation of enforcement duties of flag states and the chance of losing access to fisheries will minimize this risk and make the conservation efforts of regional groups much more effective.

QUESTIONS AND DISCUSSION

1. It later emerged that Canada's seizure of the Estai was part of a larger diplomatic strategy to strengthen the enforcement provisions of the straddling stocks treaty, then under negotiation. The Canadian Fisheries Minister, Brian Tobin, was a former radio disc jockey and understood well the power of public relations. Immediately following the seizure, he held regular press conferences and Canada's embassies were provided with slick press packs presenting its version of the story. The seized nets from the Estai, retrieved from the bottom of the ocean, were flown to New York and displayed outside the building where straddling stock negotiations were underway, providing a terrific photo opportunity that many newspapers used. The story of the Estai, then, provides two important lessons—(1) the crises that often drive public demands for environmental protection can be both natural and manufactured, and (2) the court of public opinion may prove more effective (and rapid) than the court of law.

2. *Problem Exercise*—If the Canada–Spain turbot conflict had occurred after adoption of the Straddling and Migratory Fish Stocks Treaty, how would the events have likely played out? Would the boarding, inspection and seizure of the Estai have constituted a violation of international law? *See* Jon Van Dyke, *The Straddling and Migratory Stocks Agreement and the Pacific*, 11 INT'L J. OF MARINE & COASTAL L. 406 (1996).

3. *Problem Exercise*—The Russian Minister of Fisheries has asked your advice on how to address the problems of the Peanut Hole following adoption of the Straddling and Migratory Fish Stocks Treaty. The Minister wants to reduce the amount of fishing in the hole to keep it in line with conservation efforts within the EEZ, but also wants to use the opportunity to exclude as many distant water fishing nations as possible. What steps would you advise Russia to take? Should it create a regional fisheries organization? How does Article 11 of the Treaty, below, affect the decision?

Straddling and Migratory Fish Stocks Treaty

Article 11

New members or participants

In determining the nature and extent of participatory rights for new members of a subregional or regional fisheries management organization, or for new participants in a subregional or regional fisheries management arrangement, States shall take into account, inter alia:

(a) the status of the straddling fish stocks and highly migratory fish stocks and the existing level of fishing effort in the fishery;

(b) the respective interests, fishing patterns and fishing practices of new and existing members or participants;

(c) the respective contributions of new and existing members or participants to conservation and management of the stocks, to the collection and provision of accurate data and to the conduct of scientific research on the stocks;

(d) the needs of coastal fishing communities which are dependent mainly on fishing for the stocks;

(e) the needs of coastal States whose economies are overwhelmingly dependent on the exploitation of living marine resources; and

(f) the interests of developing States from the subregion or region in whose areas of national jurisdiction the stocks also occur.

4. UNCLOS Article 63 calls on coastal and other relevant fishing states to seek, either directly or through appropriate regional organizations, measures to conserve straddling stocks. There are a number of regional organizations similar to NAFO and the Convention for the Conservation of Southern Bluefin Tuna. These include, for example, the International Convention for the Conservation of Atlantic Tunas (May 14, 1966, 20 U.S.T. 2887, 673 U.N.T.S. 63), the Convention for the Prohibition of Fishing with Long Driftnets in the South Pacific (May 17, 1991, S. Treaty Doc. 102–7 (1991)), the Convention for the Establishment of an Inter–American Tropical Tuna Commission (1949, 1 U.S.T. 230, T.I.A.S. 2044), the Convention Concerning Fishing in the Black Sea (March 21, 1960, 377 U.N.T.S. 220), the Convention for the Future Multilateral Cooperation in the North–East Atlantic Fisheries (March 17, 1982, 1285 U.N.T.S. 130), the FAO Code of Conduct for Responsible Fisheries, and others.

The International Convention for the Conservation of Atlantic Tunas (ICCAT), established in 1966 to conserve tuna species in the Atlantic Ocean, illustrates well the limitations of many such organizations. Its jurisdiction covers the entire migratory range of tunas and is open to all United Nations members and its specialized agencies. The Convention coordinates the scientific research by its members' national institutions. The Convention's governing body, the International Commission for the Conservation of Atlantic Tunas (ICCAT), meets annually. Based on the scientific information gathered from its Member States, the Commission recommends regulatory measures to maintain populations of tunas and tuna-like fish at levels that permit the maximum sustainable yield.

In practice, the Commission's influence has been limited by a lack of consensus among its members on management measures and allocation levels. Gathering reliable fishing statistics has also proven difficult, because not all nations provide catch data and the activities of non-contracting parties go unreported. Finally, the most significant practical constraint on effective conservation has been the ICCAT's inability to allocate allowable catches once it has determined the maximum sustainable yield of fish stocks. ICCAT has no direct enforcement authority, nor the ability to control the fishing activities of non-contracting parties. It does, however, have a unique ability among fishery organization to impose trade sanctions. In the case of swordfish, for example, ICCAT parties passed a resolution in 1995 calling on the ICCAT Commission to notify all non-Contracting parties whose vessels fished for Atlantic swordfish of ICCAT's conservation programs. The Commission must annually identify the vessels of non-Contracting parties whose actions diminish the effectiveness of the ICCAT conservation recommendations. If, after notification, the non-Contracting flag States do not rectify their vessels' behavior, the Commission "will recommend that Contracting parties take non-discriminatory trade restrictive measures, consistent with their international obligations, with respect to Atlantic swordfish products in any form from those non-Contracting parties." ICCAT Resolution 95–13, *Action plan to ensure the effectiveness of the conservation program for the Atlantic swordfish.* A similar resolution was passed for the Atlantic bluefin tuna. ICCAT Resolution 94–3, *Action plan to ensure the effectiveness of the conservation program for Atlantic bluefin tuna.* To date, sanctions have been authorized against Belize and Honduras (non-contracting) and Equatorial Guinea (contracting). If you have studied Chapter 15 on trade, do you think these sanctions would be permissible under the GATT?

———

5. DRIFTNETS

Driftnets range up to 40 miles in length and between 25 and 50 feet in depth. These fine monofilament or multifilament nylon mesh nets hang in the water like large curtains from floats on the surface; weighted lead lines keep the nets hanging straight. Driftnets may be anchored to fish in place or may be left to drift with the winds and currents. Their depth can be controlled by adjusting their buoyancy. Fishing passively, the nets are transparent and almost invisible to the eye as well as acoustically invisible to the echo-locating frequencies of some cetaceans. Mesh size may vary, depending on the area and target species. Marine life is vulnerable to high seas driftnet fishing for a number of reasons. First, a high percentage of marine life is concentrated in the thin upper layer of the ocean. Second, many marine species, including marine mammals, feed on driftnet target species such as squid. Third, migration routes often cross areas where driftnet fishing is conducted.

Called "curtains of death" by their critics, driftnets have proven an inexpensive and effective gear to catch fish. Manufactured for durability, synthetic plastic driftnets are not detected by fish who cross their path. The driftnets are indiscriminate, though, and trap whatever becomes entangled in their mesh. Often this includes marine mammals, seabirds, and other species of non-target fish. This catch is referred to as "incidental take" or "by-catch." Marine mammals such as dolphins are at extreme risk because after swimming into the driftnet they twist and turn in attempts to get to the surface for air and eventually drown. Hundreds of tons of commercially valuable species relied on by other fishers for their livelihood are also discarded. It is reported that as much as 80% of the catch taken by the Italian driftnet swordfish fishery is by-catch. Only one in five fish is used as food, the rest discarded, often dead. EUROPE ENV'T (Nov. 9, 1993). Those fish not killed in the nets may be maimed and die soon after. Lost or broken driftnets continue to trap living marine resources. It is a matter of dispute how long it takes these "ghost nets" to tangle themselves up into harmless balls of plastic, but until that point they remain hazardous.

Despite these environmental harms, international concern over driftnets did not mobilize until the late 1980s when driftnets were extensively used in the South Pacific region for albacore tuna. From 1987–1989, the number of boats using driftnets in the fishery increased from around 30 to over 170. These are some of the richest fishing grounds in the world and coastal states feared the destruction of their local living marine resources by distant water fishing nations such as Japan, Taiwan and Korea. Hence, the South Pacific nations led the international diplomatic efforts to outlaw driftnets.

Government leaders from South Pacific island states declared their intention at the South Pacific Forum in 1989 to create a "driftnet free zone" and started earnestly mobilizing international efforts to draft laws. Tarawa Declaration (1989). Soon after, the UN General Assembly adopted Resolution 44/225, U.N. Doc. A/RES/44/225 (1990). The resolution expressed concern that over 1,000 fishing vessels were using large scale driftnets around the world, causing heavy environmental damage. The resolution recommended that members of the international community agree on a moratorium for:

> all large-scale pelagic driftnet fishing by 30 June, 1992, with the understanding that such a measure will not be imposed in a region or, if implemented, can be lifted, should effective conservation and management measures be taken based upon statistically sound analysis to be jointly made by concerned parties of the international community with an interest in the fishery resources of the region, to prevent unacceptable impact of such fishing practices on that region and to ensure the conservation of the living marine resources of that region.

The first multilateral agreement regulating driftnetting was the Convention for the Prohibition of Fishing with Long Driftnets in the South Pacific, known as the Wellington Convention. 29 I.L.M. 1454 (1990). The core provision of the Wellington Convention is its prohibition of member States' nationals and the vessels documented under its laws from engaging in driftnet fishing activities within the Convention Area. The parties also agree to take a range of additional measures against driftnet fishing activities. The Convention entered into force May 17, 1991, and has nine parties, including Australia, New Zealand and the United States. Its two most significant provisions are excerpted below.

Article 2

Measures Regarding Nationals and Vessels

Each Party undertakes to prohibit its nationals and vessels documented under its laws from engaging in driftnet fishing activities within the Convention Area.

Article 3

Measures Against Driftnet Fishing Activities

(1) Each Party undertakes:

(a) not to assist or encourage the use of driftnets within the Convention Area; and

(b) to take measures consistent with international law to restrict driftnet fishing activities within the Convention Area, including but not limited to:

(i) prohibiting the use of driftnets within areas under its fisheries jurisdiction; and

(ii) prohibiting the transhipment of driftnet catches within areas under its jurisdiction.

(2) Each Party may also take measures consistent with international law to:

(a) prohibit the landing of driftnet catches within its territory;

(b) prohibit the processing of driftnet catches in facilities under its jurisdiction;

(c) prohibit the importation of any fish or fish product, whether processed or not, which was caught using a driftnet;

(d) restrict port access and port servicing facilities for driftnet fishing vessels; and

(e) prohibit the possession of driftnets on board any fishing vessel within areas under its fisheries jurisdiction.* * *

In response to the UN General Assembly resolution and Wellington Convention, Japan and later Taiwan announced their intention to stop driftnet fishing in the South Pacific. In 1991, the General Assembly adopted a second driftnet resolution. This resolution was much more forceful than its predecessor, however, and called upon states to *ban* driftnet fishing entirely by December 31, 1992. U.N.Doc. A/RES/46/215 (1991). This ban has taken effect and, in general, been complied with. A number of commentators, however, have criticized the total ban approach. Consider the following critiques from Japanese and American fishery law experts and a reply from Greenpeace.

Kazuo Sumi, *The International Legal Issues Concerning the use of Drift Nets, with Special Emphasis on Japanese Practices and Responses*, in JON VAN DYKE ET AL., *op. cit.*, at 293–94, 300–01

Environmentalists denouncing the use of drift nets have directed their attacks on large-scale high seas fishing. They have not expressed concern over the use of small-scale coastal drift nets. The sole basis for making this distinction is that drift nets used on the high seas are larger than those used in coastal waters. From the viewpoint of conservation of living marine resources, however, is discrimination between drift nets on the high seas and those in coastal waters justifiable?

Living marine resources, including marine mammals, seabirds, and turtles, are far more abundant in coastal waters than on the high seas. Furthermore, although the length of net deployed per fishing vessel is shorter in coastal drift net fisheries, the number of fishing vessels is far greater in coastal waters than on the high seas. The use of drift nets may actually be more destructive in coastal waters than on the high seas.

Despite suggestions that coastal fisheries may be better managed, it is doubtful whether drift nets in coastal waters have been better managed than those on the high seas and whether more information and data concerning coastal fisheries have been accumulated than those concerning the high seas.

It seems that the UN Driftnet Resolution has assumed that although large-scale high seas drift nets have adverse impacts on marine resources, smaller-scale coastal drift nets do not, though entanglement problems may also occur in coastal drift net fisheries.

In preambular paragraph 2 of the UN Driftnet Resolution, drift net fishing is denounced as "a highly indiscriminate and wasteful fishing method." Is this denunciation based on valid reasoning?

All types of fishing gear take species other than those targeted. As long as fishing activities are carried out in a natural milieu, their impact on nontarget species is more or less inevitable. In the trawl fishery, for example, both target and nontarget species are caught without discrimination. At present, no persuasive evidence exists showing drift net fishing to be more environmentally destructive than any other commercial fishing method. Comparative studies about the effects of various types of fishing gear should precede political decisions limiting their use.

The National Oceanic and Atmospheric Administration (NOAA) of the U.S. Department of Commerce has condemned high seas drift netting. Its condemnation, however, contains no reference to incidental take by coastal drift netting. According to NOAA, "approximately 1,000 marine mammals were entangled or killed in the Prince William Sound/Copper River Delta salmon drift gillnet fishery during the 1978 season," and an "estimated 335 harbor seals and 45 California sea lions were killed annually incidental to gillnetting in the Columbia River, Willapa Bay and Grays Harbor fisheries." The agency contradicts itself, demanding a total ban on high seas drift net fishing on the grounds of by-catch while keeping silent about the use of drift nets in coastal waters.

The U.S. government also seeks to transform a moratorium recommendation embodied in the UN Drift Resolution into a binding legal principle. The U.S. policy statement on the UN resolution reads:

> Unless joint assessment by all concerned members of the international community of scientifically sound data from a specific large scale pelagic driftnet fishery concludes there is no reasonable expectation of unacceptable impacts by that fishery, the conditions of relief from the moratorium recommended in UNGA 44/225 are not met.

The notion of "unacceptable impacts" will inevitably bring an unnecessary interpretative problem into high seas fisheries, particularly since the question of whether the impacts will be unacceptable must be determined by "all concerned members of the international community," not by a single state. In addition, the doctrine of unacceptable impacts will have a significant impact on coastal fisheries. If this doctrine is applied to coastal fishing, a number of fishers who use small-scale drift nets or other gear will be deprived of a means of living. * * *

[In response to criticisms that driftnet fishing harms ecosystems, Professor Sumi replies that] Removal of a few selected species may result in the remaining undesirable fish becoming dominant in the specific fishing ground; the undesirable species may then suppress the recovery of the more desirable species. When a full cross-section of species is taken so as to avoid overfishing of each species, the original ecosystem balance is likely to be restored. Accordingly, fishing that removes a full cross-section of marine life in a specific fishing ground may be ecologically healthier than fishing that removes only a few selected species.

Moreover, environmental groups' estimates of incidental takes are exaggerated. The research results of the 1989 cooperative observer program among Japan, Canada, and the United States demonstrate that the by-catch proportion is less than expected. Tens of millions of dolphins and hundreds of millions, perhaps billions, of seabirds live in and around the Pacific. Available food supplies and environmental conditions have a greater effect on the population size of these animals than does entrapment by drift nets.

Efforts should, of course, be made to avoid unnecessary by-catch. It is not rational, however, to claim that there should be no incidental take of even a single animal. The key question is the measurement of the population stock from which a marine mammal is taken and the determination of the allowable level of accidental take so that the marine mammal stock will not be disadvantaged.

William T. Burke, *Unregulated High Seas Fishing and Ocean Governance*, in VAN DYKE ET AL., *op. cit.*, at 237, 259

Whether drift nets are more destructive to nontarget species than other gear seems mostly irrelevant if drift nets take significant by-catches. Such a problem needs to be resolved, whatever the gear. On the other hand, if all large-scale gear is similarly destructive unless regulated adequately, it is difficult to argue for or justify unusually drastic remedies for drift nets alone. One remedy currently recommended by the UN General Assembly would reverse the traditional burden, requiring those who seek to restrict fishing activity to establish the basis for restriction. The notion of reversing the burden of proof to require that the fishing operation be shown not to have "unacceptable impacts" would surely be more difficult to justify if this gear did not differ from other gear in its incidental destructiveness. In this event, the remedy proposed needs to be assessed in terms of all gear having similar effects. This might mean that reversing the burden of proof has a different calculus of costs and benefits. * * *

If these sound conservation and management principles require termination of the use of drift nets on the high seas, it is difficult to understand why the reasoning involved and similar considerations would not apply to other gear on the high seas, such as tuna purse seines or longlines, or to this and all other gear taking fish within 200 miles. At the very least, if purse seines have effects on dolphins, as is known to be the case, their use might be considered to be unacceptable to other states when the fishing states are unable to establish that purse seining does not lead to declines in the dolphin population. Again, the fishery would be required to terminate because of the lack of information. * * *

For fisheries within 200 miles, presumably the coastal state has sovereign rights that it may use to control their harvest. But these fisheries unquestionably have affects on marine mammals that also are found on the high seas. If high seas fisheries can be stopped because of unacceptable impacts, defined in biological terms, the same principle should be considered to burden the coastal state whose vessels also inflict mortality on the same species within national jurisdiction.

James Carr and Matthew Gianni, *High Seas Fisheries, Large–Scale Drift Nets, and the Law of the Sea*, in VAN DYKE ET AL., *op. cit.*, at 274–76

Small-scale coastal gill nets are among the most widely used gear type in the world. Although numerous examples exist of this method being responsible for significant incidental takes of marine animals, small-scale gill net fishing can be, if conducted in an appropriate fashion, one of the more selective forms of fishing. In any case, several important distinctions exist between large-scale drift nets used on the high seas and small-scale gill nets used in coastal areas within EEZs, especially concerning the potential to prevent negative impacts on the ecosystem through the use of regulatory measures.

Large-scale pelagic drift nets on the high seas are generally used in areas where stocks are widely dispersed and where the migratory patterns, distribution, and abundance of populations of targeted species are poorly understood. Large quantities of netting must be deployed on the high seas to ensure adequate catches. Because information on the distribution and abundance of target populations is rarely available, even less is likely to be known of nontarget species of fish, birds, and marine mammals on the vast expanses of the high seas, and therefore they cannot be easily avoided as by-catch.

On the other hand, small-scale gear is often deployed in areas where the distribution of target species is relatively concentrated and better known. Also better known are the locations and migration routes of potential by-catch species, including nontarget species of fish, whales, dolphins, seals, and other marine animals. This information affords much greater opportunity to avoid potentially harmful incidental takes. * * *

Large-scale drift nets are more apt to be lost or cut loose by vessels under adverse conditions. Lost nets are known to pose a hazard to navigation. Furthermore, vessels passing over these nets are likely to sever sections, adding to the problem of lost gear, referred to as "ghost nets." The Japanese government has estimated conservatively that 0.05 percent of the nets set every night by Japanese vessels are not recovered, which means that 10 miles of netting is lost *each night* in the North Pacific from Asian vessels alone. These estimates do not take into consideration the amount of net that may be discarded at sea during the course of fishing operations as the netting material becomes progressively more damaged and less effective. Japanese sources report that as much as one-third of the net material becomes unusable in an average trip by a squid drift net vessel.

The information available on the effects of lost or discarded large-scale drift net gear certainly gives cause for concern. Contrary to the claims of proponents of high seas drift net fishing that these nets simply ball up and sink, and therefore do not pose a threat of "ghost fishing," many scientists believe that lost or discarded nets may continue "passively" to ensnare and kill marine creatures indefinitely.

Small-scale gear, in contrast, can be much more effectively tended and monitored. In coastal gill net fisheries, vessels often will remain attached to the nets while fishing. Small-scale gear can more readily be retrieved under adverse weather conditions or in the presence of migrating marine mammals and birds, approaching vessels, or other potential obstacles. Therefore, lost netting and consequent ghost fishing is likely to be much less of a problem in small-scale gill net fisheries than it is with high seas drift netting.

According to the 1990 report of the secretary general to the UN General Assembly, as much as 40 percent of the catch is discarded or lost as "drop-out" when large-scale pelagic drift nets are retrieved. "High grading," the practice of discarding all but the largest or most valuable fish in a catch, is commonly done in high seas drift net fisheries to maximize the limited hold space of the vessels.

By contrast, in coastal fisheries much of the nontarget catch may be retained on board to be sold to local markets or sold "over the side" to vessels that deliver to the markets. Thus, at least the potential exists for reducing much of the waste associated with discards. There is also, of course, much greater opportunity for enforcement of any regulations against discarding within national waters, as opposed to the high seas. Moreover, many of the fish and other marine animals that survive an encounter with high seas drift nets suffer considerable damage in terms of skin and scale loss, effects that have been documented in the South Pacific. In addition to drop-out of dead fish and wildlife, this may represent a considerable source of eventual mortality.

QUESTIONS AND DISCUSSION

1. The development of the driftnet ban provides a common model of international environmental law's evolution. The original regional agreement, the Tarawa Declaration, led to a General Assembly Resolution calling for a moratorium, to the Wellington Convention and finally to the General Assembly Resolution banning driftnet fishing. It is common to think that the great economic and military powers effectively "make" international law. None of the Tarawa signatories are major international powers, yet their initiative and persistence led to a worldwide ban affecting nations with much larger commercial and political influence. Why do you think the Tarawa Declaration ended up being so influential?

2. After reading these excerpts, do you believe the total ban on driftnets is warranted or are alternatives such as managed fisheries, seasonal closures, and additional information gathering more appropriate? On what basis should the international community consider banning other types of fishing gear such as small-scale driftnets and trawls that may have a high rate of bycatch? The last excerpt, written by Greenpeace representatives, argues that banning high seas driftnets is a valid application of the precautionary principle. Do you agree? What if it were shown that the environmental impacts of driftnets are no different than other common types of fishing gear? Do you find Greenpeace's distinction between the impacts of driftnets in coastal and high seas fisheries persuasive? Would it matter whether the fishery was in a developed or developing country?

3. Analyze the legality of large-scale driftnet fishing under the UNCLOS articles excerpted earlier. Do their provisions suggest high seas driftnet fishing should be continued or do they support the ban?

4. In arriving at the unprecedented recommendation of a ban on driftnet fishing, General Assembly Resolution 46/215 provided the following justification:

> ... members of the international community have reviewed the best available scientific data on the impact of large-scale pelagic drift-net fishing and have failed to conclude that this practice has no adverse impact which threatens the conservation and sustainable management of living marine resources, * * *

> ... the grounds for concerns expressed about the unacceptable impact of large scale-pelagic drift-net fishing in resolutions 44/225 and 45/197 [a General Assembly resolution reinforcing support for resolution 44/225] have been confirmed and ... evidence has not demonstrated that the impact can be fully prevented.

Reading through the double negative grammar, how is the burden of proof allocated and what is the legal standard? What evidence could satisfy this standard, or is driftnet fishing inherently unacceptable?

5. Refer back to the Convention for the Prohibition of Fishing With Long Driftnets in the South Pacific. Article 3(1)(b)(ii) contains prohibitions on the transhipment of driftnet catches within areas under its jurisdiction. This would include the EEZ. Does this interfere with the rights of passage guaranteed by UNCLOS (*see* p. 661)? Article 3(2)(c) prohibits the importation of any fish or fish product caught using a driftnet. Does this violate the GATT? How is this different from the U.S. practice found to violate the GATT in the Tuna/Dolphin cases (*see* p. 1160)?

6. Fishing nets have been used for thousands of years, but only recently have they been so destructive to fisheries. Why is the harm so recent? The answer is technology. Modern fishing vessels are capable of laying much longer nets than before and storing the catch in flash freezers. More important, though, are the advances in synthetic organic chemistry since World War II. Before the advent of plastic, fishing nets were made of natural fibers such as cotton, flax, or hemp. The nets could often both be seen and "heard" by fish. When nets became lost or discarded they would sink and disintegrate rapidly. With the advent of plastic monofilament fishing nets and their adoption by many developing countries, largely underwritten by the FAO, driftnets were widely used by the mid–1970s. Today, only a few subsistence fisheries around the globe still use natural fibers for their nets.

7. The European Union prohibited the use of driftnets longer than 2.5 kilometers in December, 1991, but included a derogation until December 1993 for vessels that had previously used longer nets to fish for albacore tuna in the Atlantic, on the condition the net length did not exceed 5 km. Driftnets were to be prohibited altogether as of January 1, 1998. The EU has faced significant violations of its prohibition, particularly from the Italian fleet. In May 1995, six environmental and animal protection organizations filed suit in the U.S. Court of International Trade seeking to compel the U.S. to identify Italy in violation of the U.N. ban on driftnets—a designation that would result in a ban of more than $2 million dollars in Italian fish imports. The groups alleged that Italian fishing vessels continue to use driftnets longer than 2.5 kilometers (reportedly 6 to 7 miles long) in the Mediterranean to fish for swordfish, and that thousands of whales, dolphins, and sharks were being caught inadvertently in the process.

In February, 1996, the Court ruled that the Commerce and State Departments must declare officially that Italy was violating the driftnet ban. Under the ruling, failure of Italy to prove it had complied with the driftnet ban would result in a ban on U.S. imports of Italian fish and fish products. Additional sanctions could be expected if the import ban failed to force Italy into compliance. In defense of its actions, Italy has claimed that much of its 600–vessel driftnet fleet is controlled by the Mafia and is beyond the reach of government enforcement. A full embargo could reportedly cost Italy $1 billion a year. Thomas W. Lippman, *Italy Faces Cutoff of Exports to U.S.; Federal Court Rules Worldwide Ban on Driftnets is Being Defied*, WASHINGTON POST, March 14, 1996. The EU has since announced a total ban on driftnets for major migratory fish species by 2002. *EU Report Points up Uneven Observance of Driftnet Legislation*, EUROPEAN REPORT, June 28, 2000. For a case study of the resolution of drift net controversy along the California coast, *see* James Salzman, *Scientists as Advocates,* 3 CONSERVATION BIOLOGY 170 (1989).

8. The March 2000 Report of the Secretary General on Oceans and the Law of the Sea to the United Nations General Assembly cites illegal, unregulated and unreported ("IUU") fishing as one of the most severe problems facing global fisheries. *Oceans and the Law of the Seas: Report of the Secretary–General*, U.N. GA, 55th Sess., at 26, U.N. Dov. A/55/61 (2000). The FAO has been requested to provide "statistics and data of fishing vessels in general, and in particular, of fishing vessels engaged in IUU fishing" and is hosting negotiations on a draft International Plan of Action on Illegal, Unregulated and Unreported Fishing.

In some cases IUU is simply the result of local vessels violating the law. There exist, however, ships that rely on dummy companies to hide their owners' identities, fly flags of convenience, or fly no flags at all as they move from one fishery to another, catching as many fish as possible through use of driftnets or other prohibited gear. This problem is most severe in the Patagonian toothfish fishery (also known as Chilean Sea Bass) in Antarctica's Southern Ocean.

In a fascinating use of the web to attack IUU fishing, an NGO campaign against IUU fishing in the Patagonian toothfish fishery (directed by a group known as "Isofish") seeks to report on the activities of unlicensed longline fishing vessels operating within the fishery area. The site, <http://www.isofish.org.au/boats/index.htm>, contains available information on all the boats operating in the fishery— their Lloyds number, ownership, flag State, and fishing history. The entry for the Alida Glacial, for example, reports:

10 January 1998—East London, South Africa—The captain of the Alida Glacial is found guilty of carrying illegal equipment for longline fishing and for carrying out longlining operations without a permit to fish in South African waters. Consequently the Norwegian skipper is fined R1000. GB/Alida Glacial/Fax :10–March–98.

27 December 1997—East London, South Africa—The captain of the Alida Glacial is arrested when the vessel arrives in Port. GB /Alida Glacial /Fax : 10–Mar–98.

29 August 97—French Territory (near Crozet Islands)—A crewperson on board the Kerguelen de Tremarec reports the Alida Glacial hauling in two long lines—she is undistinguishable by name which is reported to be physically masked. (Gautier & Duhamel 1997)

13 May 97—Alida Glacial is recorded on video, by an Australian cameraman, fishing illegally in the Australian EEZ off Heard Island. (Purves & Wissema 1997)

Why is Isofish collecting this type of information? Assume you were your country's top fisheries official and you have a meeting scheduled with the head of the customs and port authorities. How would you suggest using this website? For more information on the patagonian toothfish fishery, *see* page 1057.

Section III.   Marine Pollution From Ships

The operational discharges, spills and intentional dumping from ships are an important source of pollution to the marine environment. At least eight international agreements address threats posed by vessel pollution and dumping. This section focuses on two of these. MARPOL 73/78 regulates both the operational discharge and unintentional release of pollutants such as oil, garbage, plastics and sewage from ships. It has a sophisticated framework for compliance and enforcement, providing an important model for international environmental law. The London Convention, 1972, controls the intentional dumping and incineration of wastes at sea. Thanks to the success of this Convention, the practice of waste disposal through ocean dumping has greatly declined.

A.   Marpol 73/78

1.   INTRODUCTION

Shortly after midnight, on March 24, 1989, the Exxon Valdez steamed out of Prince William Sound in Alaska. The supertanker, longer than three football fields laid end-to-end, had just left the Alyeska pipeline terminal in the city of Valdez and carried 53 million gallons of crude oil. Disaster struck soon after leaving the terminal when the ship ran aground on the Bligh Reef, ripping open the hull and puncturing 11 of the 17 cargo tanks. Over 10 million gallons of oil spilled into the Sound's pristine waters. Oil soon inundated the 1,100 miles of shoreline creating a 3,000 square mile oil slick with dead sea birds, otters and other marine life in its wake. In all, the clean-up of the oil spill involved more than 11,000 people, 1,200 vessels and 80 aircraft, costing over $2 billion. While the best known oil spill, the Exxon Valdez was hardly the first, or the biggest. The Torrey Canyon, Argo

Merchant, Aegean Captain, Braer and Amoco Cadiz spills, to name just a few, are equally notorious along certain ocean coastlines. Indeed in U.S. waters alone over 10,000 oil spills are reported annually. While the vast majority of these spills are minor they, too, pose environment threats. While not often viewed as a serious problem, oil released from operational discharges causes as great if not greater environmental harm than the well-publicized spills.

The direct response of the international community to the problem of oil spills and other vessel pollution is the International Convention for the Prevention of Pollution from Ships, negotiated in London in 1973. Following a series of tanker spills in 1976 and 1977, a separate Protocol was negotiated in 1978. The Protocol provided that it and the 1973 Convention would be read as a single document, known as MARPOL 73/78 (short for MARine POLlution). 17 I.L.M. 546 (1978). The negotiations were supervised by the International Maritime Organization (IMO), a UN agency created in 1958 to regulate the shipping industry. The IMO's mandate extends to ship pollution and it serves as MARPOL's secretariat. The convention applies to all ships operating in the marine environment under the flag of a State party (i.e. a ship registered under a party's nationality) or ships operating under a party's authority (within its ports and coastal waters).

The overarching goal of MARPOL is to create a verifiable, enforceable regime to prevent pollution discharges from ships. MARPOL consists of six annexes, each with regulations controlling specific types of pollution. Regulations covering oil pollution (Annex I) and noxious liquid substances in bulk (Annex II) are mandatory for all parties. The other annexes are optional, and parties may choose whether or not to adopt the annexes regulating pollution from harmful substances carried in packaged forms (Annex III), sewage (Annex IV, not yet in force), garbage (Annex V), or air pollution (Annex VI, not yet in force). Annex VI, adopted in 1997, sets a global cap on sulphur oxide and nitrogen oxide emissions from ship exhaust systems and would create regional "SOx Emission Control Areas" to reduce sulfur emissions. This presents a different focus from the other annexes, since the main impact of sulfur dioxide emissions is acid rain falling on land, not waste discharges into the marine environment.

MARPOL's focus is on operational discharges and exempts from its coverage the intentional dumping of wastes (covered by the London Convention, 1972) or the release of substances directly arising from deep seabed activities. In the sections below, Annex I's provisions for oil discharges are discussed in detail in order to illustrate its sophisticated and innovative compliance procedures. The policy conflict inherent in addressing vessel source pollution is similar to that found in other areas of ocean law—tension between the right of coastal States to control, conserve and protect marine resources, on the one hand, and flag States' rights of navigation and innocent passage on the other. The parameters of international vessel pollution treaties, such as MARPOL, are established by Article 211 of UNCLOS.

UNCLOS, Article 211
Pollution from vessels

1. States, acting through the competent international organization or general diplomatic conference, shall establish international rules and standards to prevent, reduce and control pollution of the marine environment from vessels and promote the adoption, in the same manner, wherever appropriate, of routing systems designed to minimize the threat of accidents which might cause pollution of the marine environment, including the coastline, and pollution damage to the related interests of coastal states. Such rules and standards shall, in the same manner, be re-examined from time to time as necessary.

2. States shall adopt laws and regulations for the prevention, reduction and control of pollution of the marine environment from vessels flying their flag or of their registry. Such laws and regulations shall at least have the same effect as that of generally accepted international rules and standards established through the competent international organization or general diplomatic conference. * * *

4. Coastal states may, in the exercise of their sovereignty within their territorial sea, adopt laws and regulations for the prevention, reduction and control of marine pollution from foreign vessels, including vessels exercising the right of innocent passage. Such laws and regulations shall ... not hamper innocent passage of foreign vessels.

————

2. ANNEX I: OIL POLLUTION

Oil is the most pervasive pollutant discharged from ships. Transporting almost half the world's oil, over 3,200 tankers cross the world's oceans every day. Dwarfing other sea-going vessels, the largest supertanker, the Jahre Viking, carries more than 600,000 tons of oil, enough to fill a line of fuel trucks 200 miles long. Haveman, *Why Oil Spills Are Increasing*, L.A. TIMES, March 26, 1993, at A1. Notorious oil tanker spills have caused large and immediate environmental harms. Smaller deliberate discharges from ships, however, are more commonplace and can be more harmful. After a tanker discharges its cargo, oil remains on the tank walls much as a residue is visible on the walls of a glass of milk after it has been drunk. Traditionally, ships have loaded empty cargo tanks with sea water to provide ballast and then discharged the polluted water when loading up with oil. Residue oil only accounts for 0.4% of total cargo, but this means 400 tons of discharged oil for every voyage of a typical tanker. Ronald B. Mitchell, *Intentional Oil Pollution*, ENVIRONMENT, May 1995. Bilge water, collected at the bottom of a ship, is also contaminated by oil, solvents and other contaminants and is routinely discharged to ensure a ship remains stable.

The environmental impacts of oil discharges vary considerably. The oil carried by tankers is actually a mixture of many different chemical compounds (known as hydrocarbons). Some of these compounds are heavy and long-lived, others light and break down quickly in the environment. The biological impacts of different hydrocarbons vary, as well, in terms of toxicity and carcinogenicity. Beyond the chemical composition of the released oil, the environmental impacts of oil spills and discharges will vary depending upon whether the spill is in the open ocean or a more enclosed body of water, the dispersion of oil through wind, waves and current, the temperature of the water and, most important, the local species exposed to the spill. In the right setting, small spills from operational discharges naturally degrade quickly and cause little harm. At the other extreme, large oil spills can be haunting–piles of dead birds and marine mammals washed up on beaches. While volunteers and governments struggle to rescue and clean oiled birds, chemically disperse the slicks, and use mechanical booms to arrest the flow of oil, these measures have for the most part proven ineffective and occasionally more harmful than the spill, itself. DOUGLAS BRUBAKER, MARINE POLLUTION AND INTERNATIONAL LAW 12–30 (1993). The lethal impacts of spills can continue for years as the oil works its way through the food chain, from the plankton and invertebrates at the base through shellfish, fish, birds and mammals. Fred Pearce, *What turns an oil spill into a disaster?*, NEW SCIENTIST, January 30, 1993.

Oil is the marine pollutant with the oldest history of international attention, dating from an international agreement among seven nations in 1926. Almost three decades later, in 1954, in response to the huge increase in the ocean transport of oil and subsequent pollution, thirty-two countries met to draft the International Convention for the Prevention of Pollution of the Sea by Oil (OILPOL). 327 U.N.T.S. 3, U.K.T.S. 54 (1958).

Representing 95% of the world's shipping tonnage, the parties prohibited discharges of oil within 50 miles of the coast. Countries were required to impose fines large enough to deter violations and ensure their ports provided facilities for receiving waste oil. While an important precedent as the first binding treaty on oil pollution, the results were weak. By the terms of the treaty, ships need only sit fifty miles off the coast discharging dirty water from ballast and tanks before entering port. The oil still drifted onshore after its unsupervised legal discharge at sea.

Amendments in 1962 and 1969 strengthened OILPOL's requirements. In particular, the 1969 amendments forbade ship discharges unless they met the following conditions:

- the tanker is proceeding en route;
- the total quantity of discharged oil is less than 1/15,000 of the ship's capacity;
- the instantaneous rate of discharge does not exceed 60 liters per mile;
- the tanker is not within fifty miles of land.

1969 Amendments to the International Convention for the Prevention of Pollution of the Sea by Oil, 21 October 1969, reprinted in 1 I.P.E. 366.

In the early 1970s, however, a number of nations began to question the effectiveness of OILPOL. In 1972, the U.S. passed the Port and Waterways Act, requiring all new tankers to have a segregated ballast tank system in order to sail through U.S. waters. Pub. L. No. 92–340, as amended by the *Ports and Tanker Safety Act of 1978,* 46 U.S.C. 391(a) This unilateral action, coupled with widespread recognition of the failings of OILPOL led to calls for a more comprehensive, enforceable international convention— MARPOL.

MARPOL relies on three very different approaches to prevent pollution: *mandatory discharge standards* that ships must observe when discharging oily water and other wastes, *construction, design, equipment, and manning* (CDEM) *specifications* that eliminate or reduce specific types of pollution, and *navigation standards* that limit ships' activities in ecologically sensitive areas.

a. Mandatory Discharge Standards

MARPOL largely retained the controls on discharges of oil and operating procedures for washing tanks and ballast water in the OILPOL agreements. But MARPOL parties recognized that requiring ships to follow specific procedures, such as discharging beyond fifty miles of the coast, was vulnerable to the human element—wilful noncompliance by the captain and crew. Widespread enforcement proved nearly impossible. Indeed, how could a nation effectively police the ocean, monitoring whether a ship discharged oily water on the high seas day and night, much less the quantity and concentration discharged? The restriction on discharge of oily water by vessels is matched by an obligation on port States to provide reception facilities for disposal of the discharge.

b. Construction, Design, Equipment, and Manning Specifications

In addition to its discharge requirements, MARPOL set in place a series of detailed technical specifications to reduce the opportunity for noncompliance. Following the initiative of the U.S. in its Port and Waterways Act, MARPOL required that all new ships be built with segregated ballast tanks. In practice, this required dedicating approximately 30% of the total cargo volume for tanks that would carry only ballast, never oil. MARPOL included other technical design specifications such as special tanks for holding oily residues, oil-water separating equipment and filters, and limits on the size and arrangement of cargo tanks. Subsequent amendments in the 1990s adopted in the wake of the Exxon Valdez oil spill required that new tankers be built with double hulls and wing tanks extending the full depth of the ship's sides. *IMO Provisions Requiring Double Hulls on New Ships Takes Effect, Agency Announces*, 16 INTL. ENVTL. REP. 514 (1993).

c. Navigation Standards

Finally, recognizing that some sea regions were particularly vulnerable to oil pollution, MARPOL introduced restrictions for ships passing through Special Areas, defined as "an area where for recognized technical reasons in relation to its oceanographical and ecological condition and to the particular character of its traffic, the adoption of special mandatory methods for the prevention of sea pollution by oil is required." MARPOL Annex I, Regulation 1(10). For oil discharges, the Mediterranean Sea, Baltic Sea, Black Sea, Red Sea, Gulf waters and North West European Waters have been defined as Special Areas. Within these waters, tankers and ships of 400 tons gross tonnage and above are prohibited from any discharge of oil at all. In return, governments with coastlines along the special areas undertake to ensure that all oil loading terminals will have adequate facilities for reception and treatment of oily water. The stricter provisions regarding discharges in a special area, however, do not come into force unless there are adequate reception facilities provided in port.

----

3. COMPLIANCE

MARPOL's most important innovation was its treatment of compliance issues. Catching most ships in the act of illegally discharging oil was neither realistic nor did it provide a credible threat of enforcement. In addition to its emphasis on easily verified technical requirements, i.e. mandatory tanker design standards, MARPOL also provided the means to ensure compliance through innovative documentation requirements: record books, oil discharge data and certificates to operate.

Compliance with design standards was ensured through the requirement that all tankers over 150 tons and all other ships over 400 tons hold an International Oil Pollution Prevention (IOPP) Certificate. As detailed below, the IOPP Certificate provides evidence that MARPOL's technical standards are satisfied. The Certificates are issued not by governments but, rather, by a small number of authorized "classification societies." MARPOL's use of private sector bodies has proven generally effective and is an important example of the role *non-State actors* play in international environmental law. Insurance companies often require an IOPP Certificate for coverage.

MARPOL, Annex I, Regulation 4

Surveys and Inspections

(1) Every oil tanker of 150 tons gross tonnage and above, and every other ship of 400 tons gross tonnage and above, shall be subject to the surveys specified below:

(a) An initial survey before the ship is put in service or before the Certificate required under Regulation 5 of this Annex is issued for the first time, which shall include a complete survey of its structure, equipment, fittings, arrangements and material in so far as the ship is covered by this Annex. This survey shall be such as to ensure that the structure, equipment, systems, fittings arrangements and material fully comply with the requirements of this Annex.

(b) Periodical surveys at intervals specified by the Administration, but not exceeding five years, which shall be such as to ensure that the structure, equipment, systems, fittings arrangements and material fully comply with the applicable requirements of this Annex.

(c) A minimum of one intermediate survey during the period of validity of the Certificate which shall be such as to ensure that the equipment and associated pump and piping systems, including oil discharge monitoring and control systems, crude oil washing systems, oily-water separating equipment and oil filtering systems, fully comply with the applicable requirements of this Annex and are in good working order. * * *

(3) (d) When a nominated surveyor or recognized organization determines that the condition of the ship or its equipment does not correspond substantially

with the particulars of the Certificate or is such that the ship is not fit to proceed to sea without presenting an unreasonable threat of harm to the marine environment, such surveyor organization shall immediately ensure that corrective action is taken and shall in due course notify the Administration. If such corrective action is not taken, the Certificate should be withdrawn ... and if the ship is in the port of another Party, the appropriate authorities of the Port State shall also be notified immediately.

(4) (a) The condition of the ship and its equipment shall be maintained to conform with the provisions of the present Protocol to ensure that the ship in all respects will remain fit to proceed to sea without presenting an unreasonable threat of harm to the marine environment. * * *

MARPOL, Annex I, Regulation 5,
Issue of Certificate

(1) An International Oil Pollution Prevention Certificate shall be issued after survey in accordance with Regulation 4 of this Annex. * * *

(2) Such Certificate shall be issued either by the Administration [i.e., the flag state] or by any persons or organizations duly authorized by it. In every case the Administration assumes full responsibility for the Certificate.

MARPOL, Annex I, Regulation 8
Duration of Certificate

(1) An International Oil Pollution Prevention Certificate shall be issued for a period specified by the Administration, which shall not exceed five years from the date of issue. * * *

(2) A Certificate shall cease to be valid if significant alterations have taken place in the construction, equipment, systems, fittings, arrangements or material required without the sanction of the Administration. * * *

(3) A Certificate issued to a ship shall also cease to be valid upon transfer of the ship to the flag of another State. * * *

MARPOL's compliance provisions also extended to vessel operations. The primary means to verify compliance with MARPOL is the requirement of an Oil Record Book to record *all* operations involving oil on the vessel.

MARPOL, Annex I, Regulation 20
Oil Record Book

(2) The Oil Record Book shall be completed on each occasion, on a tank to tank basis if appropriate, whenever any of the following operations take place in the ship:

(a) for machinery space operations (all ships):

    (i) ballasting or cleaning of oil fuel tanks

    (ii) discharge of dirty ballast or cleaning water * * *

    (iii) disposal of oily residues (sludge)

    (iv) discharge overboard or disposal otherwise of bilge water* * *

(b) for cargo/ballast operations (oil tankers):

(i) loading of oil cargo

(ii) internal transfer of oil cargo during voyage

(iii) unloading of oil cargo * * *

(x) disposal of residues

(4) Each operation described [above] * * * shall be fully recorded without delay in the Oil Record Book so that all the entries in the book appropriate to that operation are completed. Each completed operation shall be signed by the officer or officers in charge of the operations concerned and each completed page shall be signed by the master of the ship. * * *

Because Oil Record Books can be falsified, as objective verification all tankers above 150 tons were also required to operate an oil discharge monitoring and control system, the equivalent of an airplane's "black box." The system provides a continuous record. Thus whenever there is a discharge of oil residues, the system monitors the instantaneous rate of discharge (MARPOL limits discharges to 60 liters per nautical mile for tankers) and the total quantity discharged. Records must be kept for three years.

QUESTIONS AND DISCUSSION

1. Assume you are the port inspector and a tanker has just arrived that the Coast Guard suspects has been illegally discharging oil within the EEZ. Describe the search you would conduct to ensure compliance with MARPOL. What questions would you ask the crew?

2. The U.S. has implemented MARPOL through the Act to Prevent Pollution From Ships (APPS). 33 U.S.C. 1901, et seq. The law makes it:

unlawful to act in violation of the MARPOL Protocol ... or the regulations issued thereunder. The Secretary shall cooperate with other parties to the MARPOL Protocol ... in the detection of violations and in enforcement of the MARPOL Protocol. * * *

33 U.S.C.A. 1907 (a) (1997)

While catching a ship in the act of discharging garbage is difficult, a number of APPS enforcement cases have been successful. In United States v. Princess Cruises, 93 CR 6058, S.D. Fla. (April 26, 1993), Princess Cruises pled guilty to a felony violation of the APPS and was fined $500,000. Two resourceful passengers had filmed the discharge of 20 plastic bags of garbage five miles off the Florida coast. The passengers received $250,000 from the government as a bounty for their assistance in obtaining a conviction. In United States v. Regency Cruises, Case No. 94–245–Cr–T–21(c) (Mp. Fla. Oct. 25, 1994), defendants pled guilty to two felony violations and were levied a $250,000 fine for discharging plastic bags filled with garbage. Local fishermen saw the bags in the ocean and reported them to the Coast Guard. When opened, the bags contained garbage that identified the specific ship and voyage. Using a bounty system to improve enforcement efforts can be particularly effective when monitoring is practically difficult, as is the case with MARPOL. What are the disadvantages of such a reward system for information leading to prosecutions?

3. MARPOL's unique compliance approach is based on two complementary strategies: technical specifications and certification by private parties. While the text above has described the advantage of these strategies, they also have shortcomings. What might they be?

Despite the general guidance on technical standards provided in the MARPOL regulations, each classification society has its own rules governing inspections. While an IOPP survey examines the essential parts of the ship and factors governing strength and dependability, different societies conduct different kinds of surveys and the intervals between surveys vary. As a result, evaluating certificates is difficult for port authorities. Moreover, safety aspects are often left out entirely by classification society inspections (e.g. radio equipment) because they are the responsibility of the flag State. And carrying out a thorough inspection has physical limits, as well. Examining a typical large ship requires climbing 10 kilometers of ladders while checking 1,000 kilometers of welds and 100,000 structural elements. *Why Inspection Systems Must be Simplified*, LLOYD'S LIST, Oct. 11, 1995.

4.   Authorizing private bodies to conduct inspections is cost-effective for governments but ultimately the certificate is only as good as the body authorizing it. Who are these classification societies?

> Originally, ship classification societies such as Lloyd's of London or Veritas of France inspected vessels on behalf of shipowners who wanted to know what sort of boat they were getting. Then with the introduction of an international law imposing ship safety standards, governments turned to the few existing classification companies, as they had the engineers and know-how required to establish certificates of conformity authorizing vessels to add their names to national registers. Over the last 25 years, classification companies have been springing up all over the world and they have been making out certificates even though they do not necessarily have the expertise to do so. Twelve classification companies are represented by an international association which is covered by the IMO umbrella, but there are 40 or so companies about which virtually nothing is known, say IMO sources. They nevertheless allow vessels to register and then sail under a so-called flag-of-convenience. Irrespective of the suspicions that such a flag tends to evoke, no government has the right to turn down certificates issued by another government.

Shetland Oil Spill: EC Lawmakers Hesitant in the Face of Environmental Disasters, EUROPE ENVIRONMENT, Jan. 19, 1993.

These 40 classification societies' certificates, known as "pseudo-IOPP" Certificates, are used by ships which are registered in a foreign country to avoid stringent standards or high costs. This practice of foreign registration is known as "flying a flag of convenience," and discussed later in this section. Because these classification societies are neither monitored nor authorized by MARPOL member countries, their standards are suspect and likely lax. To address this issue, France supported a proposal by Greenpeace to the IMO's Flag State Implementation Subcommittee in 1994. Complaining that ships are "routinely permitted to enter ports of MARPOL parties and to freely operate in coastal waters, as long as they carry pseudo-IOPP Certificates issued by a classification society," the proposal recommended that MARPOL member States set a date after which pseudo-IOPP Certificates would no longer be accepted as evidence of compliance with MARPOL. *Authority of Port State Inspectors Debated at IMO FSI Subcommittee Meeting*, OIL SPILL INTELLIGENCE REPORT, Feb. 17, 1994. The proposal was not adopted after some countries contended that the Subcommittee should focus more on why countries have not yet ratified MARPOL rather than punishing pseudo-Certificates. What was the point of these countries' argument? How should certificates from non-MARPOL States be regarded by MARPOL parties?

You will recall the previous chapter's discussion of the Montreal Protocol's treatment of non-parties. To provide an incentive for non-parties to ratify the

Protocol, trade in ozone-depleting substances is banned between parties and non-parties. The Basel Convention on the Transfrontier Movement of Hazardous Wastes (*see* Chapter 12) provides a similar mechanism, banning trade in hazardous wastes between parties and non-parties. How could these treaties serve as a model for pseudo-IOPP Certificates? What might the consequences be for international shipping commerce?

5. Because most marine animals cannot distinguish debris from food, marine debris has become a major source of injury and death to the wildlife eating it or becoming entangled. The debris most threatening to wildlife include net fragments, fishing line, plastic bags, balloons, and other pieces of plastic. To publicize this environmental threat, an environmental group, the Center for Marine Conservation, sponsored its first Coastal Cleanup in 1986. Over 2,800 volunteers collected 124 tons of garbage along the Texas coastline.

By 1998, the cleanup had become global, with over 509,000 volunteers participating from 79 countries. The cleanup resulted in the removal of over 5.3 million pounds of trash at 3,000 sites, covering approximately 12,000 miles of waterways and beaches. The most prevalent kind of debris found was plastic, followed by paper, metal and glass. Ironically, all of these substances are recyclable. The Coastal Cleanup has created a greater public awareness of the issue of marine pollution in an attempt to discourage the dumping of debris in the marine environment. Although marine debris still remains a problem, the success of the Cleanup campaign provides an example of how creating public awareness of an environmental issue can combat the problem.

The problem of marine debris is not limited to populated areas. The uninhabited Ducie Atoll in the South Pacific is an important breeding area for seabirds. It is 300 miles from the nearest inhabited island and over 3,000 miles from the nearest continent, yet a beachwalk revealed over 950 pieces of trash along a 1.5 mile stretch of beach. As you read over the remarkable variety of trash items listed in Table 11–2 below, how do you think they ended up on the atoll beaches?

Table 11–2: Debris Found on Ducie Atoll

Buoys: large	46	Gloves (1 pair)	2
small	67	Canned meat (leaking but intact)	1
Crates (bread, bottle)	14	Cigarette lighters (not working)	3
Plastic bottles (drinks, toiletries)	71	Doll's heads (1 male, 1 female)	2
Glass bottles (from 15 countries)	171	Copper sheeting from shipwrecks	8
Jars	18	Truck tire	1
Broken plastic pieces	268	Plastic ninepin	1
Bottle tops	74	Glue syringe	1
Pieces of plastic pipe	29	Small gas cylinder	1
Pieces of rope	44	Construction worker's hat	1
Shoes	25	Plastic coat hanger	1
Fluorescent tubes	6	Toy soldier	1
Light bulbs	6	Half a toy airplane	1
Aerosol cans	7	Tea strainer	1
Food/drink cans	7	Football (punctured)	1
Pop tops	2	Car floormat	1
Gasoline cans	4	Asthma inhaler	1

<http://seawifs.gsfc.nasa.gov/OCEAN_PLANET/HTML/peril_marine_debris.html>

4. MARPOL ANNEXES II, III, IV AND V

In addition to Annex I addressing oil pollution, all parties to MARPOL must comply with Annex II while Annexes III, IV and V are optional. The basic structure of each annex is the same as Annex I, described above.

Table 11–3: MARPOL Annexes

MARPOL Annex	Coverage	Provisions	Status
I	Oil	Mandatory	In Force
II	Noxious Liquid Substances	Mandatory	In Force
III	Packaged Hazardous Substances	Optional	In Force
IV	Sewage	Optional	Not yet in Force
V	Garbage & Plastics	Optional	In Force
VI	Air Pollution		Not yet in Force

Annex II regulates pollution from noxious liquid substances in bulk and its provisions are mandatory. Noxious liquids are divided into four categories (A, B, C, D) depending on the degree of hazard to marine resources or human health. Category A discharges present "a major hazard" while Category D discharges present only "a recognizable hazard." Similarly, the requirements are most stringent for Category A liquids, where discharges are prohibited, and progressively less stringent for Categories B, C, and D liquids. In special areas such as the Black Sea and the Mediterranean Sea, discharge requirements are even more stringent for each category of liquid.

Annex II, similar to Annex I, requires that parties ensure reception facilities in their ports for disposal of noxious liquid substances but compliance with this requirement is poor and many ports do not have such facilities. To assist in compliance monitoring, ships must carry a Cargo Record Book for recording discharges, and special procedures are mandated for washing down cargo tanks. Finally, a survey system similar to the IOPP Certification system is mandated. The document is called an International Pollution Prevention Certificate for the Carriage of Noxious Liquid Substances in Bulk. Certification societies are authorized by the State to inspect the ship at least every five years. If it is determined that the ship does not correspond substantially with its Certificate, it may be detained in port until it no longer presents an unreasonable threat of harm to the marine environment.

Annex III regulates marine pollution by harmful substances carried in packaged forms, freight containers, portable tanks or road and rail tank wagons. Annex IV regulates marine pollution by discharge of sewage from ships but is not yet in force. Annex V regulates pollution by discharge of garbage from ships. Throwing any plastic overboard is prohibited entirely. In the past it has been common practice to throw tangled drift nets overboard where they would continue to ensnare fish, birds and marine mammals before knotting into a ball. Because plastic fishing nets are regarded as "garbage," MARPOL prohibits this practice. Packaging and lining materials that float may not be discarded within 25 miles of the coast. Disposal of other garbage wastes, such as food, paper products, glass, metal, bottles and similar refuse is prohibited within 12 miles of the coast. In special areas, defined as the Persian Gulf, the Mediterranean, Baltic, Black and Red Seas, disposal of all garbage except food waste is prohibited. Since there are no recording requirements, short of seeing a ship discharge garbage illegally, enforcement of Annex V has proven difficult. In 1997, Annex VI was adopted, addressing marine air pollution. Annex VI is expected to be in force by January 1, 2004. *Air and Sewage Rules Tightened,* LLOYDS LIST 5, Mar. 17, 2000; Hugh O' Mahoney, *Owners Must Heed Impending Emissions Rules,* LLOYDS LIST, Dec. 7, 2000.

---

5.   ENFORCEMENT

MARPOL parties represent over 90% of the world merchant fleet's gross registered tonnage. Given what you have read to this point, how effective do you think MARPOL's compliance regime actually is? In what circumstances might it be ineffective? In particular, how could MARPOL's goals be frustrated even if compliance monitoring is effective? Consider the true story described below.

A Dutch pilot in the port of Rotterdam guides a small, Greek-owned tanker to its dock. The mostly Filippino crew can barely understand their Greek captain, and it takes 10 minutes to respond to his orders. There are no lifeboats. The main fire pump cannot be located. The emergency fire pump does not work. The emergency generator, supposed to start up if the main engine fails, is out of commission. The pilot concludes, "everything that should have been there either wasn't there or didn't work." Haveman, *Why Oil Spills Are Increasing,* L.A. TIMES, March 26, 1993, at A1.

Incidents of this type are not uncommon in major ports. While the pilot was most concerned with safety equipment failings, it is likely that this ship's pollution control equipment was in comparably poor, if not even worse shape. Indeed, keeping vessels "ship-shape" is a widespread problem. Shell Oil claims that 20% of the world's tankers fail to satisfy international safety standards. British Petroleum failed 299 of the 960 ships it inspected to carry its cargo. *Ibid.*

There are treaties in place requiring proper equipment and maintenance, but inspection, enforcement and punishment of violations remain major challenges, due in large part to the separation of authority among flag States, coastal States, and port States. In basic terms, the port/coastal State plays the role of police and the flag State as judge and jailer. Professor Bodansky describes this division of authority in the excerpt below.

Daniel Bodansky, *Protecting the Marine Environment From Vessel–Source Pollution: UNCLOS III and Beyond*
18 Ecology L.Q. 719, 736–38

Vessel-source pollution often has international dimensions. Who may exercise jurisdiction when a vessel flies a foreign flag or causes pollution on the high seas? Which State or States may impose standards and exercise criminal or civil jurisdiction when international standards are violated? On the one hand, since vessel-source pollution often occurs in or affects the waters or territory of coastal States, coastal States have a strong interest in prescribing and enforcing standards. On the other hand, the traditional principle of freedom of navigation implies that flag States should have primary jurisdiction over vessels. Reconciling these competing coastal and maritime interests has been one of the central problems for the law of the sea.

1.   *Flag State Jurisdiction*

Flag State jurisdiction at sea, like territorial jurisdiction on land, has traditionally been the core form of jurisdiction and as such, has not required special justification. Flag State jurisdiction is necessary, given the principle of the high seas since on the high seas a vessel must be subject to the authority of some State to preserve order.

Perhaps because of its unquestioned status, the exact juridical basis of flag State jurisdiction has always been somewhat murky. According to one theory, a vessel is a floating part of a flag State's territory, and therefore flag State jurisdiction is a type of territorial jurisdiction. Others view flag State jurisdiction as an exercise of nationality jurisdiction, since a vessel possesses the nationality of its flag. Still others justify State flag jurisdiction on pragmatic grounds. In any event, the only limitation placed by customary international law on flag State jurisdiction is the principle that States have exclusive enforcement jurisdiction within their territory. For this reason a flag State may not ordinarily take enforcement measures against its vessels in another State's territorial sea or internal waters, since this would infringe on the coastal State's sovereignty.

In discussions concerning flag State jurisdiction, the question has not been its permissibility but rather its adequacy. Critics argue that since pollution on the high seas or in another's coastal waters normally does not affect the flag State, the flag State has little incentive to prescribe environmental standards or take adequate enforcement measures. Moreover, since shipowners have wide latitude in choosing where to register their vessels, they can choose a ''flag of convenience'' with comparatively lax environmental regulation or enforcement.

2.   *Coastal State Jurisdiction*

Coastal States suffer most directly from marine pollution and therefore have the greatest interest in preventing vessel-source pollution. As a result of this interest as well as their general concern with the adequacy of flag-State jurisdiction, coastal States have claimed the right to exercise prescriptive and enforcement jurisdiction over vessel-source pollution. This claim is largely based on the territoriality principle, since coastal States have sovereignty over their internal waters and territorial sea. But broader coastal State jurisdiction has on occasion been asserted on the grounds that pollution beyond the territorial sea may affect the coastal State or threaten its security.

Since coastal State jurisdiction may impinge on the ability of vessels to navigate freely, rules pertaining to coastal State jurisdiction must balance coastal States' interest in controlling pollution against maritime States' interest—and the interest of the world at large—in free navigation.

In general, the balancing of coastal and maritime interests has been undertaken in broad geographic terms, by dividing the oceans into different zones: internal waters; the territorial sea; the contiguous zone; and now, in UNCLOS, the exclusive economic zone (the EEZ). Each zone has its own allocation of jurisdiction between coastal and flag States. As one goes further out to sea, the balance of interests between coastal and maritime States changes: the coastal State's interest in protecting the environment weakens and the maritime State's interest in freedom of navigation grows. For both reasons, coastal State jurisdiction diminishes. Thus, in their internal waters, States have plenary powers in their territorial sea, their authority is limited by the regime of innocent passage; and beyond the territorial sea, vessels have high seas navigation rights.

3. Port State Jurisdiction

Port State jurisdiction is generally defined as jurisdiction based solely on the presence of the vessel in port. If a pollution incident occurs in or affects a State's coastal waters, the State may exercise jurisdiction as a coastal State. It acts as a port State if its State if its sole connection with the incident is the delinquent vessel's presence.

From a policy standpoint, port enforcement represents a compromise between coastal and flag State enforcement. On the one hand, port States may be more inclined than flag States to enforce environmental norms, since port States are themselves coastal and, as such are at risk from substandard and delinquent vessels. Port State jurisdiction therefore serves as a useful corrective to inadequate flag State enforcement. On the other hand, port State enforcement is preferable to coastal State enforcement since it interferes much less with freedom of navigation and can generally be performed more safely. Stopping and boarding a vessel in transit at sea for inspection purposes directly interferes with the vessel's movement and can be hazardous, depending on the weather and location. In contrast inspecting a vessel while in port imposes little if any burden on navigation and can be performed safely. Even bringing a proceeding against a vessel does not hinder navigation so long as the vessel is able to go free upon posting bond. Only if the port State actually detains the vessel to carry out the investigation or proceeding is there an interference with the vessel's freedom of movement. Moreover, port States have a direct economic interest in shipping and receiving goods, and therefore they are more likely than coastal States to balance environmental measures against maritime commerce.

Since by definition a port State has no connection with a pollution offense other than the vessel's presence in port, it cannot prescribe standards on the basis of territoriality, nationality, protective, or passive personality principles. The only basis for port State prescriptive jurisdiction would be if the universality principle extended to vessel-source pollution, that is, if vessel-source pollution were a universal crime that any State could proscribe.

Because there is little support for this proposition, port State jurisdiction is usually limited to enforcement where the location of the vessel at the time of enforcement (in port) is the key variable. It should be noted, however, that when a port State takes an enforcement measure such as inspecting a vessel to determine whether the vessel has committed a discharge violation on the high seas, the port State is investigating a violation of another State's law, not its own, which it lacks jurisdiction to prescribe.

----

a. Port and Coastal States

Under MARPOL, port and coastal States have the primary responsibility of detecting violations. They have the right to inspect vessels in their ports and offshore terminals and, in particular circumstances, detain them. Annex I permits inspection of the Oil Record Book and discharge monitoring equipment records, and observation of whether "normal" amounts of oily discharge are in the ballast tanks or slop tanks. Annex I, Regulation 20. The ability for further inspection of ships with IOPP Certificates, however, is limited.

MARPOL, Article 5

Certificates and Special Rules on Inspection of Ships

(2) A ship required to hold a certificate in accordance with the provisions of the Regulations is subject, while in the ports or off-shore terminals under the jurisdiction of a Party, to inspection by officers duly authorized by that Party. Any such inspection shall be limited to verifying that there is on board a valid [IOPP] certificate, unless there are clear grounds for believing that the condition of the ship or its equipment does not correspond substantially with the particulars of that certificate. In that case, or if the ship does not carry a valid certificate, the Party carrying out the inspection shall take such steps as will ensure that the ship shall not sail until it can proceed to sea without presenting an unreasonable threat of harm to the marine environment. * * *

(4) With respect to the ships of non-Parties to the Convention, Parties shall apply the requirements of the present Convention as may be necessary to ensure that no more favorable treatment is given to such ships.

MARPOL 1994

Amendments to Article 5

(1) A ship when in a port or an offshore terminal of another party is subject to inspection by officers duly authorized by such party concerning operations requirements, where there are clear grounds for believing that the master or crew is not familiar with essential shipboard procedures relating to the prevention of pollution by oil;

(2) under the above circumstances, the party shall take steps to ensure that the ship shall not sail until the situation has been brought to order in accordance with the requirements of this annex. * * *

Thus a port State (and coastal State at an offshore terminal) may carry out intensive inspections of all ships without IOPP Certificates and, with cause, of ships with IOPP Certificates. If a ship inspection reveals significant violations such as those described in the passage introducing this section, then the ship may be held in port until the repairs are made. This enforcement tool, however, is not always exercised. Often the ship's owner promises to make the necessary repairs elsewhere and the ship leaves, its seaworthiness as sound as its owner's promise.

UNCLOS Article 220(6) also provides authority for a coastal State to detain foreign ships and institute legal proceedings if their violation of applicable international rules for the prevention, reduction and control of pollution from vessels causes "major damage or threat of major damage to the coastline or related interests of the coastal State," or to any resources of its territorial sea or exclusive economic zone. Do you think a coastal State may carry out inspections when a ship of a foreign flag State is in its waters but neither in port nor at an offshore terminal? *See* Cheng–Pang

Wang, *A Review of Enforcement Regime for Vessel–Source Oil Pollution Control*, 16 OCEAN DEV. & INT'L L. at 319 (1986).

The separate authorities to detect a violation (prescriptive jurisdiction), try the accused (adjudicative jurisdiction), and punish the offender (enforcement jurisdiction), while combined together in national legal systems, are not vested in the same State under MARPOL and UNCLOS. Upon finding a violation, the port or coastal authority is required to pass along its findings to the flag State for enforcement proceedings unless the violation occurs within its territorial waters. (The term "Administration" in the text that follows refers to the flag State authority).

MARPOL, Article 4
Violation

(1) Any violation of the requirements of the present Convention shall be prohibited and sanctions shall be established therefor under the law of the Administration of the ship concerned [i.e. the flag State] wherever the violation occurs. * * *

(2) Any violation of the requirements of the present Convention within the jurisdiction of any Party to the Convention shall be prohibited and sanctions shall be established therefor under the law of that Party. Whenever such a violation occurs, that Party shall either:

(a) cause proceedings to be taken in accordance with its law; or

(b) furnish to the Administrator of the ship such information and evidence as may be in its possession that a violation has occurred.

MARPOL, Article 6
Detection of Violations and Enforcement of this Convention

(1) Parties to the Convention shall co-operate in the detection of violations and the enforcement of the provisions of the present Convention, using all appropriate and practicable measures of detection and environmental monitoring, adequate procedures for reporting and accumulation of evidence.

(2) A ship to which the present Convention applies may, in any port or offshore terminal of a Party, be subject to inspection by officers appointed or authorized by that Party for the purpose of verifying whether the ship has discharged any harmful substances in violation of the provisions of the Regulations. If an inspection indicates a violation of the Convention, a report shall be forwarded to the Administration [i.e., the flag State] for any appropriate action. * * *

(4) Upon receiving such evidence, the Administration so informed shall investigate the matter, and may request the other party to furnish further or better evidence of the alleged contravention. If the Administration is satisfied that sufficient evidence is available to enable proceedings to be brought in respect of the alleged violation, it shall cause proceedings to be taken in accordance with its law as soon as possible. * * *

---

b.   *Flag States*

The flag State exercises ultimate enforcement authority. In addition to regulating ships under its registry for safety at sea, manning and training of crews, enforcing construction and design standards, as well as proper equipment and general seaworthiness, a flag State has the duty to ensure that ships flying its flag comply with MARPOL and that tankers over 150 tons and other ships over 400 tons carry an IOPP Certificate. In its judicial proceedings, a flag State may find a vessel not guilty, take no action because of "insufficient evidence," take no action for "other and unspecified reason," give a warning, levy a fine, or take other "unspecified actions." Gerard Peet, *The MARPOL Convention: Implementation and Effectiveness*, 7 JOURNAL OF ESTUARINE & COASTAL L. 290 (1992).

Under most circumstances, even if the violation occurred *outside* the flag State's waters, enforcement proceedings in the flag State *pre-empt and suspend* enforcement proceedings commenced in the port or coastal State. The enforcement proceeding changes venue to the flag State authorities. There are, however, two important exceptions to this practice of flag State enforcement. The flag State does not have the right to suspend the proceedings and bring charges in its own courts (1) when the discharge causes major damage to a coastal State, or (2) when the flag State has a history of non-enforcement. Proving a history of non-enforcement, however, is difficult to do without open access to the flag State's enforcement proceedings.

UNCLOS, Article 228
Suspension and restrictions on institution of proceedings

1. Proceedings to impose penalties in respect of any violation of applicable laws and regulations or international rules and standards relating to the prevention, reduction and control of pollution from vessels committed by a foreign vessel beyond the territorial sea of the State instituting proceedings shall be suspended upon the taking of proceedings to impose penalties in respect of corresponding charges by the flag state within six months of the date on which proceedings were first instituted, *unless those proceedings relate to a case of major damage to the coastal state or the flag state in question has repeatedly disregarded its obligation to enforce effectively the applicable international rules and standards in respect of violations committed by its vessels.* The flag state shall in due course make available to the State previously instituting proceedings a full dossier of the case and the records of the proceedings, whenever the flag state has requested the suspension of proceedings in accordance with this article. When proceedings instituted by the flag state have been brought to a conclusion, the suspended proceedings shall be terminated. [emphasis added]

QUESTIONS AND DISCUSSION

1. A study in 1990 examined reported violations to the IMO since 1983. Over 1,000 alleged discharges had been reported. Roughly half the flag States had not submitted reports detailing the actions taken against the alleged violators (in violation of Article 6's reporting requirements). In only 206 cases did flag States report taking action, which resulted in 77 fines. From the data, over a 7–year period fewer than 8% of reported discharge violations resulted in punishment. Peet, *op. cit.* at 290–92. A fundamental reason for this poor record is the role of flag States as flags of convenience. A 1997 Freedom of Information Act request to the State Department examined the fate of 45 U.S. referrals of MARPOL violations to flag States. Only about 7% of the referrals led to convictions and roughly 40% of the flag States never replied at all. What steps could be taken to improve the reporting of flag States?

2. *Problem Exercise* Assume a ship registered in Country X is boarded for inspection while in port in Country Y. Country Y authorities uncover a discrepancy between the ship's Oil Record Book and the data on its discharge monitoring and control system (its "black box"). The authorities believe the ship illegally discharged oil 80 miles off the coast based on the report of a passing yacht and the ship's captain is now being held without bail for a criminal violation of Country Y's Clean Water Act. You have been retained as local defense counsel by the ship's owner. What motions would you consider making prior to trial? What additional facts would you need to know to assess your chances of success?

----

6.   FLAGS OF CONVENIENCE

An oil tanker spills 420,000 gallons of oil into Narragansett Bay off Rhode Island. Subsequent research uncovers that the vessel had been registered in Liberia, insured by a Bermuda company managed from London, and owned by a Greek. This dizzying multinational mix is common in the shipping industry. Lohr, *Tanker in Big Spill Typifies Freewheeling Industry*, NEW YORK TIMES, July 3, 1989, at 1. A potentially weak spot in MARPOL (as well as most law of the sea conventions) is its dependence on flag States to enforce their measures and punish violations. As described in the last section, in most cases the "law of the flag" takes precedence over the "law of the port of call." Shipowners are well aware of this potential weakness and often register their ships in countries with weak enforcement regimes or which are not parties to law of the sea agreements. These countries are known as "flag of convenience" States and, in exchange for registration and annual tonnage fees, allow ownership and control of their flag ships by non-citizens. Usually small countries, flag of convenience States as a rule levy low or no income taxes and have neither the laws nor the administration effectively to impose international regulations or to control their registered ships. Indeed the ships may actually *never* visit their flag State.

In 1995, 1,263 tankers were registered in Liberia. Liberia is now the second largest ship registry with 60.5 million gross tons compared to Panama with 98.2 million gross tons (the United States is 15th, with less then 5% of the total tonnage). Ann Toh, *Cambodia Ship Registry Eyes Top 20 Position*, BUS. TIMES (Sing.), Aug. 16, 2000; John V. Berry, *The Diminuation of the Merchant Marine: A National Security Risk*, 74 U. DET. MERCY L. REV. 465, 473 (1997). Roughly 30% of the world's shipping tonnage is carried by ships operating under flags of convenience. FINANCIAL TIMES, June 30, 1995. In addition to their historically lax enforcement of MARPOL and other maintenance and safety standards, flag of convenience States permit shipowners to economize by employing non-national crews. A U.S. registered ship, for instance, with few exceptions must carry American crew. In 1993, the basic monthly wage for a seaman in the International Transport Workers' Federation, comprised primarily of developing country unions, was $821, a good deal less than the wages of a U.S. or British seaman. The going rate for Filippino seamen, however, was even lower at $276 a month and for Chinese seamen only $50 a month. Lohr, *op. cit.*; Hamer, *Time to run tighter ships on the high seas,* NEW SCIENTIST, January 16, 1993, at 4.

The corporate laws of flag of convenience States further complicate enforcement efforts. Liberia, for instance, provides anonymity for corporate ownership. Moreover, many shipowners use shell corporations to hold title to their fleets, attempting to shield themselves from liability. When the Amoco Cadiz ran aground, it took almost three weeks to identify and contact the ship's owners. The ability to transfer registrations also encourages a race to the bottom. When, under intense international pressure, Liberia imposed a more stringent inspection system, over 70 ships simply transferred their registrations to other flag States with less stringent requirements. Wang, *op. cit.* at 332–33. Yet the link between seaworthiness and registration flag is clear. Liberia's vessel casualty rate is five times higher than Britain's, and some flags of convenience casualty rates are ten times higher or worse. Hamer, *Time to run tighter ships on the high seas,* NEW SCIENTIST, January 16, 1993, at 4.

In the face of lax or non-existent enforcement by flags of convenience, the most effective international response has been through increased port State controls. As mentioned above, a port State may detain foreign ships if they fail inspections, or have caused, or threaten to cause, major pollution damage to its coast or waters. Port State controls have been significantly strengthened by regional initiatives. In particular, the Paris Memorandum of Understanding (Paris MOU) has proven quite effective. The Paris MOU provides a uniform inspection system among 19 Western European countries to ensure compliance with MARPOL and other relevant safety conventions. Results of Paris MOU member countries' port inspections are entered in a common database in France. Port authorities are put on notice of ships with a history of compliance violations. If a ship passes the port inspection by a Paris MOU party, it is given a certificate which shields it from further Paris MOU party inspections for a period of six months unless there is evidence of substandard conditions. If, upon inspection, a vessel is found out of compliance then repairs are required before the ship can leave port. Over 70% of ships sailing to Western Europe are inspected for compliance with MARPOL and other IMO conventions. Birnie & Boyle, *op. cit.* at 270–71. For a similar NGO effort to address illegal fishing for Patagonian Toothfish, *see* page 706.

Recall the MARPOL provisions under Article 5(4)establishing that parties shall apply the requirements of the Convention as may be necessary to ensure that non-party ships receive "no more favorable treatment" than MARPOL party ships. This text provides support for these tough inspection programs for non-MARPOL party ships. Do you see why? While these provisions add nothing to MARPOL's requirements, the Paris MOU's database provides a record of problem ships and, more important, the Paris MOU represents an agreement that enforcement will be pursued vigorously. In the U.S., a similar list of countries operating substandard ships is kept by the Coast Guard. When in U.S. ports, these ships are subject to close scrutiny by local authorities. Similarly high levels of inspections take place in Canadian, Japanese and other ports. Kasoulides, *Paris Memoran-*

dum of Understanding: A Regional Regime of Enforcement, 5 J. Estuarine
& Coastal L. 180, 185 (1990); Birnie and Boyle, *op. cit.* at 270–71. Since the
Paris MOU, the IMO has been working to extend these strategies for port
State control. Four agreements have since been drafted covering Latin
America, Asia and the Pacific, the Caribbean and the Mediterranean.
Agreements for the Indian Ocean and West and Central Africa have been
signed and preliminary draft MOUs are in progress for the Black Sea and
Persian Gulf. Report of the Secretary–General, March 2000, UN A/55/61.
Such initiatives play an important role in developing adequate administra-
tive infrastructures and prompting strong national legislation.

QUESTIONS AND DISCUSSION

1. Many observers of MARPOL believe it has been an overall success, with over
90% of the world's shipping tonnage flying MARPOL party flags. Estimates are
obviously approximate, but since 1973 one study claims tanker operational pollution
has dropped by 85%. At the same time, however, MARPOL has important shortcomings. Despite requirements since 1983, over 70% of parties' oil ports have inadequate reception facilities for oily wastes from ships. Overall enforcement around the
world is spotty, as well. Andrew Griffin, *Marpol 73/78 and Vessel Pollution: A Glass
Half Full or Half Empty?*, 1 IND. J. GLOBAL LEGAL STUD. 489, 505 (1994); *Intertanko
Hits Out at Ports' lack of Waste Oil Reception Facilities*, SHIPPING TIMES, Apr. 26,
1995, at 1.

Assuming these assessments are accurate, what amendments to MARPOL
might ensure better enforcement of detected violations? How might they take into
account the costs of compliance, the primacy of flag State enforcement authority,
and the flag of convenience issues? Why have the MARPOL parties not already met
and amended the treaty with such measures?

2. The FAO has proposed a Compliance Agreement to address flag State responsibilities. The Agreement set forth three general rules:

- Each State must ensure that its vessels do not engage in any activity that
  undermines the effectiveness of international fishery conservation and management measures, whether or not the Flag State is a member of the regional
  fishery organization that adopted such measures.

- No Flag State shall allow any of its vessels to be used for fishing on the high
  seas unless the Flag State has specifically authorized it to do so.

- No Flag State shall grant such authority to a vessel unless the Flag State is
  able to control the fishing activities of that vessel.

These requirements are similar to those in the Straddling Stocks Agreement (p.
694). How would you modify these to address the responsibility of a flag state for
pollution by its vessels? Recall that one of the spurs for the Straddling Stocks
Agreement was Canada's seizure of the Spanish fishing vessel, the Estai. Do you
think a similar high-profile action taken against a polluting flag of convenience
vessel would lead to international pressure for stronger rules?

3. MARPOL is not a preemptive treaty and understanding the complex interplay
of MARPOL, UNCLOS, and national laws is critical in establishing respective
adjudicative and enforcement authority for MARPOL violations. A MARPOL party
retains the unilateral right to enforce its national laws and regulations pertaining to
the passage of vessels, conservation of living resources and environmental protec-

tion within its territorial waters (generally up to twelve nautical miles provided this does not impair or deny innocent passage. UNCLOS, Article 211(4)). These laws need not conform to generally accepted international standards such as MARPOL. Thus within the territorial waters of the U.S., foreign ships must pay special attention to provisions of the Clean Water Act and the U.S. legislation implementing MARPOL, the Act to Prevent Pollution From Ships. 33 U.S.C. 1901, 1908(a). When passing within the EEZ (between 12 and 200 nautical miles off the coast), the State may enforce its laws so long as they conform to generally accepted international standards. UNCLOS Article 58.

The jurisdictional reach of the Act to Prevent Pollution from Ships and the Clean Water Act to foreign-flagged vessels varies depending upon the nationality of the vessel and the discharge. For U.S.-flagged ships, the Act to Prevent Pollution from Ships applies in all waters. For foreign-flagged ships, with respect to MARPOL Annexes I and II (oil and liquid substances), the Act applies to the "navigable waters" of the U.S. (which include the territorial sea under UNCLOS). In 1988, President Reagan extended U.S. navigable waters from 3 miles to 12 nautical miles but did *not* apply this extension to pre-existing Federal or State law. Proclamation No. 5928, 54 Fed. Reg. 777 (Dec. 27, 1988). Since the Act to Prevent Pollution from Ships pre-dates the Proclamation, its jurisdiction over foreign-flagged vessels violating MARPOL Annexes I and II is thus limited to 3 miles. For foreign-flagged ships violating MARPOL Annex V (garbage), the APPS has a broader reach and applies within the territorial waters and the exclusive economic zone. 33 U.S.C. 1902(a). Under the Clean Water Act, discharges of pollutants are prohibited in U.S. navigable waters. Since the Clean Water Act pre-dates President Reagan's proclamation, this prohibition extends three miles to sea. For oil and hazardous substances which may affect natural resources, however, discharges are prohibited 12 miles out to sea.

If a foreign ship spills oil 2 miles off the U.S. coast, can the U.S. enforce the Clean Water Act provisions if they are more stringent than MARPOL? What about if the ship dumps garbage and oil more than 15 miles off the coast?

4. How far does a State's adjudicative authority extend? UNCLOS Article 220(1) allows a *coastal* State to bring proceedings against a ship in its port or offshore terminal for violations of international rules or laws adopted in accordance with UNCLOS that occur within the State's territorial waters or EEZ. UNCLOS Article 218 allows a *port* State to bring proceedings against a ship for such violations occurring *outside* the EEZ. Thus a port State has independent jurisdiction over discharges not only within its territorial seas, but also for discharges on the high seas. This important innovation is known as the "universal enforcement jurisdiction" of a port State and effectively allows for a port State to compensate for ineffective enforcement by flag States. BARBARA KWAITKOWSKA, THE 200 MILE EXCLUSIVE ECONOMIC ZONE IN THE NEW LAW OF THE SEA 180 (1989); Birnie & Boyle, *op. cit.* at 282. Since MARPOL Article 9(2) declares that the Convention is without prejudice to the codification and development of UNCLOS, UNCLOS Article 218 provides a significant enlargement of MARPOL's provision merely for inspection by a port State for discharge violations occurring within the port State's jurisdiction. *Id.* at 181. Why is the distinction between port States and coastal States important? In what situations would a port State not be a coastal State?

5. Invasive species have recently emerged as a MARPOL issue with important environmental consequences. It is generally accepted that the zebra mussels overwhelming the Great Lakes in the U.S. were brought there in ship's ballast water. The disruption of ecosystems by the introduction of exotic organisms has important consequences for fisheries (through predation) and civil engineering (through, e.g., clogging pipes). As Colin Woodard describes,

San Francisco Bay, a busy shipping port, is home to at least 212 exotic species. The fish population is now a bizarre mix of Mississippi catfish, East Asian gobies, Japanese carp, and aquarium goldfish. The bottom is controlled by Chinese mitten crabs (which can harbor human parasites and whose burrowing causes levees to collapse) and Asian clams (which filter out virtually all plankton, starving out native fish). A new species takes hold in the Bay every twelve weeks on average. Exotic invaders tend to wreak the most havoc in ecosystems already damaged by other stresses. A North American bristle worm now dominates the bottom of Poland's highly polluted Vistula lagoon. Mnemiopsis leidyi snuffed out most other life in the Black Sea after massive algae blooms, overfishing, and pollution weakened native communities.

COLIN WOODARD, OCEAN'S END 49 (2000).

In 1991, the IMO adopted the International Guidelines for Preventing the Introduction of Unwanted Aquatic Organisms and Pathogens from Ships' Ballast Water and Sediment Discharges. They were used soon after when the U.S. notified the IMO that U.S. inspectors found three ships' ballast water contained strains of cholera. A team from the Smithsonian Environmental Research Center examined 15 ships coming into the Chesapeake Bay and found that 830 million bacteria and 7,400 million viruses could be found in the average liter of ballast water tested. The tests revealed vibrio cholerae, a bacteria that causes cholera, in the ballast water of all 15 ships. David Derbyshire, *Ship Water Spreading Disease,* DAILY TELEGRAPH, Nov. 2. 2000. The IMO's Marine Environment Protection Committee (MEPC) plans to adopt new regulations for the management of ballast water by 2003. This proposed annex would establish a two-tier system. Tier 1 would require all ships to phase-in management procedures. Tier 2 would allow for the designation of certain areas where further controls may be placed on the discharge or uptake of ballast water. *After Erika,* MARINE LOG, vol. 105, iss. 11, Nov. 1, 2000. Do you think requiring certain types of equipment, following MARPOL's CDEM approach, would be a better approach?

6. Below is a description of a typical enforcement problem involving ships flying flags of convenience. In this case, British authorities sought to bring an action against a ship registered in Panama.

The first report of the alleged pollution offence was made at 1231 on 13 May 1996 by an RAF Tornado. It observed the vessel MV VACY ASH discharging a substance into the sea some 50 miles from the entrance to the river Tyne.

The Marine Pollution Control Unit (MPCU) immediately scrambled one of its contracted surveillance aircraft to overfly the area. The report received at 1302 confirmed a slick from the MV VACY ASH, which appeared to be stopped and to be pumping overboard from the port side amidships. A number of photographs were taken.

The discharge was also observed by the Ministry of Agriculture, Fisheries and Food research vessel, RV CORYSTES. The scientist in charge reported that the slick consisted of a mixture of discrete small particles and glutinous masses up to 30mm or more in size. A sample was taken.

The Panamanian registered vessel underwent a port state control inspection on arrival in the river Tyne. It was found that the previous cargo had been palm oil, loaded in Brazil and discharged in Hull. In accordance with MARPOL, tank washings of a category D substance such as palm oil may be discharged at sea only if the vessel maintains a minimum speed of 7 knots.

An examination of the logbooks revealed that entries for the date of the discharge had not been correctly made. No entry had been made in the Cargo

Record Book since 11 May, in apparent contravention of the MARPOL regulations.

It was not possible for the UK to take prosecution action in this instance because the alleged offence occurred outside territorial waters. The MPCU has reported the incident to the flag state, via the Foreign and Commonwealth Office, for investigation.

UK introduces measures to reduce marine pollution, M2 Presswire, Aug. 15, 1996.

In response, the UK government announced its intention to create a "pollution zone" extending from 12 to 200 miles off the coast. Any ship committing a pollution offense within the zone would be liable to prosecution in UK courts. In reference to the pollution incident described above and the proposed zone, the Minister for Aviation and Shipping explained, "I am determined that we should take all reasonable measures to prevent illegal discharges. We will provide incentives to encourage ships to dispose of waste responsibly but we will also increase deterrents–by making it clear to potential polluters that they risk having their actions publicised as well as facing stiff fines if successfully prosecuted. This incident has been reported to the ship's flag State. In general, experience has shown that this is rarely effective in bringing sanctions against polluters. The establishment of a UK pollution zone will greatly increase our ability to prosecute any ship suspected of committing a pollution offence." *Ibid*.

Does creation of a "pollution zone" or enforcement actions against foreign ships violate UNCLOS? If the British refused to suspend proceedings against the MV Vacy Ash, what steps could Panama take?

7.   Detention of a ship by the coastal State is the most powerful enforcement tool against ship owners. UNCLOS Article 229 provides that coastal States may bring civil claims for money damages "in respect of any claim for loss or damage resulting from pollution of the marine environment." The best way to ensure damages are actually paid is to hold the ship until the money is received or to require a bond. MARPOL Article 7 provides a counterbalance to this threat of detention, however, by providing compensation for ship owners whose vessels are "unduly" detained.

MARPOL Article 7

Undue Delay to Ships

(1) All possible efforts shall be made to avoid a ship being unduly detained or delayed under Articles 4, 5, or 6 of the present Convention. [i.e., certification and inspection of ships, detection of violations, and enforcement]

(2) When a ship is unduly detained or delayed under Articles 4, 5, or 6 of the present Convention, it shall be entitled to compensation for any loss or damaged suffered.

8.   *Problem Exercise* The owner of the tanker, The Oilspot, contacts your law firm. The Oilspot is registered in the country of Convenience. While stopping for supplies in a port in the country of Clean, The Oilspot was inspected by the port authorities and the ship has been detained. The port authorities are now bringing suit against the Oilspot's captain, crew, and owner for the following alleged actions:

– three counts of illegal pollution of oily bilge water for discharges 250 miles, 150 miles, and 5 miles off the coast;

– the unseaworthiness of the vessel despite a valid IOPP certificate issued by the Convenience Classification Society;

– a claim for $100,000 for natural resource damage to local fish stocks from the illegal discharges;

The Oilspot captain has told the owner that any discharges were negligible and that the ship is "in fine condition." What legal advice would you give the captain in regard to each allegation? What additional information do you need to determine the likely outcome of your advised actions?

9. While registration under flags of convenience allows corporations to avoid many of the restrictions of MARPOL and other maritime treaties, this does not provide a complete shield from liability. The *Amoco Cadiz* spill occurred on the night of March 16, 1978, when the tanker ran aground on the rocks off Portsall on the Brittany coast of France. She was flying the Liberian flag, manned by an Italian crew, and was carrying cargo of 220,000 tons of crude oil. Over the eleven days following the grounding more than 125 miles of coastline were smothered with oil. Following the spill, Standard Oil set up a fund in France of $16.7 million and made an additional $13.3 million available in accordance with the international agreements governing liability for oil spills (discussed in the next section). In addition to these funds, however, the nation of France and French private parties sued Standard Oil and Amoco in U.S. courts. This suit was seen as a direct challenge to international oil spill liability agreements and their role in providing the exclusive avenue for liability following oil spills. Under their provisions, suit should have been brought in French court (where the spill occurred) or in a Liberian court (the flag State).

In the case, In re Oil Spill by Amoco Cadiz off the Coast of France on March 16, 1978, 699 F.2d 909 (7th Cir.1983), a U.S. court upheld jurisdiction over a claim based upon negligent operation of the foreign-owned Amoco Cadiz. The case was filed by French citizens against affiliates of Standard Oil Company (Indiana), including Amoco Transport Company, the Liberian company which owned the tanker. The French plaintiffs argued that U.S. law, not French law or the international oil spill liability agreement provisions, was applicable. Piercing the flag of convenience shield, plaintiffs argued the true ship owner to be the U.S. parent corporation because of the absence of significant links between the tanker and the flag State. The Court agreed, holding that there did not "appear to be any real Liberians in the picture–Liberian registry having been obtained no doubt for the none too credible purpose of avoiding liability, rather than to conduct business in or from Liberia. The real purchaser of the Amoco Cadiz was Standard Oil Company (Indiana)." As a result, the court applied the Illinois long-arm statute to hold the parent company, Standard Oil, liable for damages of the spill. Id at 914. The French plaintiffs were granted judgment in 1978. Walter Keichel III, *The Admiralty Case of the Century*, FORTUNE, April 23, 1979.

10. Most international agreements employ an "explicit acceptance" procedure for adoption of amendments. Amendments enter into force a set period of time after a specified number of parties have accepted the amendment. If acceptance requires a simple majority or two-thirds majority of the parties, as many as 50 nations have to act and it is often many years before the amendment enters into force. To avoid this delay, a number of IMO agreements allow for amendments through a process known as the "tacit acceptance procedure." In this process, an amendment enters into force on a set date unless it is rejected by a specified number of countries. This ensures speed of acceptance and clarity of when an amendment will likely become effective. Does this undermine the concept of "State consent" as the basis for obligation under international law? Would this be useful in other areas of international environmental law?

11. A large number of international agreements address potential pollution from ships. The International Convention on Liability and Compensation of the Carriage by Sea of Hazardous and Noxious Substances was adopted in 1996. The Convention imposes strict liability on shipowners for damage to people, property or the environment caused by discharges of certain hazardous and noxious substances (radioactive substances are excluded). The ship owner's liability is limited and if damages exceed this amount the Convention provides the remaining compensation (from a general international fund) up to 250 million British pounds. Lindy Johnson, *Vessel Source Pollution*, in G. HANDL, ED., YEARBOOK OF INTERNATIONAL ENVIRONMENTAL LAW, 1996.

Human error is estimated to contribute to 60%–85% of tanker accidents. The Safety of Life at Sea Convention (SOLAS) is directed at the seaworthiness and safety aspects of vessel operation and provides indirect assurance of environmental protection. Amendments in 1996 provided port States the authority to conduct more detailed inspections of tankers and bulk carriers—with special attention to corrosion, mandatory ship reporting systems, and enhanced vessel inspections—if there is reason to believe the master or crew are unfamiliar with safety or anti-pollution procedures. In practice, port authorities may request crews to perform certain drills to test their competence. The International Convention on Standards of Training, Certification and Watchkeeping for Seafarers (1978) and the International Regulations for Preventing Collisions at Sea (1972) are two other IMO agreements that ensure safe operation of tankers while the International Convention on Oil Pollution Preparedness Response and Cooperation (1990) facilitates international cooperation in preparing for and responding to major oil spills. For a description of these agreements and others, see <http://www.IMO.ORG/imo/convent/liabilit.htm>.

B.   CASE STUDY: THE OIL POLLUTION ACT OF 1990

The case study from the First Edition has been moved to the casebook website at <http://www.wcl.american.edu/pub/environment/teachmaterial.htm>. It describes the liability regime for oil spills (the International Convention on Civil Liability for Oil Pollution Damage and the International Oil Pollution Compensation Fund Convention). In the wake of the Exxon Valdez oil spill in Alaska, the United States Congress felt that liability levels of the existing conventions were too low and passed the Oil Pollution Act of 1990 (OPA). OPA effectively removed the liability limit for oil spills and required tankers transporting oil to the United States to have double hull construction. Despite strong protests from some countries that OPA was a unilateral imposition of America's shipping standards on the rest of the world and therefore a violation of UNCLOS, OPA remained in force. As a result, MARPOL was amended in 1992 to require double hulls or alternative designs with the same level of protection in tankers and a new protocol for oil pollution was adopted that significantly raised the upper limit on liability. The case provides a clear example of national law driving international law.

C.   THE LONDON CONVENTION, 1972

1.   BACKGROUND

Today, deliberate and direct disposal of waste at sea accounts for an estimated ten percent of the pollution that enters the oceans every year.

Often, this waste contains toxic and environmentally harmful materials. Ocean dumping presents a classic case of externalities–unrestricted ocean dumping is "free" to individual countries, but the pollution imposes a cost on the international community through damage to marine resources and contamination of the food chain, both today and in the future. The legal treatment of ocean dumping is controlled by The Convention on the Prevention of Marine Pollution by Dumping of Wastes and Other Matter. 11 I.L.M. 129. This Convention is better known as the London Convention, 1972, or by its earlier name, the London Dumping Convention.

The London Convention established international controls regulating the dumping and incineration of wastes at sea. The term, "dumping," is defined in Article III as the deliberate disposal of wastes and other matter at sea by ships, aircraft, and man-made structures at sea. The Convention's coverage is vast, including sewage sludge, dredged materials, construction and demolition debris, explosives, chemical munitions, radioactive wastes, and other materials loaded on a vessel for the purpose of dumping. The London Convention is widely regarded as one of the most successful treaties addressing marine pollution. Periodic resolutions and amendments since 1978 have both strengthened its controls and extended its breadth of coverage considerably.

MARPOL and the London Convention are sometimes confused with one another but cover very different activities. MARPOL controls the *operational* pollution from ships as well as *unintentional* releases of pollution. The London Convention covers the *intentional* dumping of wastes from ships. To ensure this delineation, MARPOL Article 2 excludes from its definition of "discharge" any dumping within the meaning of the London Convention and, similarly, the London Convention's definition of dumping excludes wastes incidental to the normal operation of vessels, aircraft, and man-made structures (covered by MARPOL).

Brennan van Dyke, *The London Convention, 1972* in Housman et al., THE USE OF TRADE MEASURES IN SELECT MULTILATERAL ENVIRONMENTAL AGREEMENTS 254–59 (UNEP, 1995)

Ocean dumping of dredged and other contaminated material seriously risks poisoning animal and plant life, and contaminating our dwindling marine food supply. In the beginning of this decade, about 80–90% of the waste deliberately dumped at sea was sediment that had been dredged from harbors; other pollution sources were industrial wastes, sewage sludge, radioactive wastes and fallout from incineration at sea. Roughly 10% of dredged material was severely contaminated by heavy metals that entered the water through land run-off and discharges from vessel, industrial, and municipal sources. Even disposal of uncontaminated materials has the potential to adversely harm the marine ecosystem, for example, by burying benthic organisms or otherwise significantly altering habitats. Careful consideration of the location for a discharge can mitigate some of these negative impacts, though many substances simply cannot safely be dumped at sea.

When the Inter–Governmental Working Group on Marine Pollution first convened in June of 1971, in preparation for the Stockholm Conference on the Human Environment, it decided to draft an international agreement to regulate dumping at sea. In November of 1972, after 18 months of difficult negotiations, the countries finally completed the London Convention. The task assumed by the drafters was daunting; it required achieving consensus among many countries to adopt comprehensive and often expensive solutions to the complex problem of marine dumping. It is a testimony to the seriousness of marine pollution that these countries carried the project through to completion.

Given the dissension and friction that the negotiators had to overcome, it is perhaps not surprising that the initial Convention, like so many multilateral environmental agreements, soon proved too weak to fully achieve its goals. Consequently, after the Convention entered into force on 30 August, 1975, the contracting parties continually discovered that threats to the marine environment from dumping were more serious than had been believed and that they needed to take even more stringent measures to sufficiently protect the oceans from pollution by dumping. The concerns that the Convention addresses are so vital that the contracting parties continued, and still continue, to alter and refine their obligations and responsibilities, despite the difficulty and cost of doing so. Over the years, the Convention has become increasingly restrictive in the regulation of ocean dumping, so that presently it prohibits outright many kinds of marine dumping. * * *

From its inception, the Convention's core protective strategy has been to require all ships intending to dump wastes of any kind at sea to first obtain a permit from the authorized national authority. The kind of permit required depends on the category of waste to be disposed. The Annexes to the Convention categorize wastes from those that may not be dumped at sea to those that may be dumped under regulated conditions.

The parties convene regularly in Consultative Meetings. One purpose is to improve the effectiveness of the Convention, if warranted, through resolutions of the parties. Resolutions that amend the Annexes to the Convention must be founded on scientific or technical considerations and must be approved by two-thirds of the parties present at a consultative or scientific meeting of the contracting parties. The parties have a 100 day period before such an amendment automatically enters into force, during which time any party may submit a declaration stating its decision not to accept the amendment. [this is known as the tacit amendment of instruments]. Such declaration may be revoked at any time, whereupon the amendment will enter into force for the revoking party. The parties also adopt resolutions that are non-binding, even between the parties that have adopted them. Yet, despite their voluntary nature, the parties have a history of complying with them. Moreover, such resolutions reflect the views of the nations that voted for them and, consequently, may provide evidence of emerging customary international law.

The Convention's controls on ocean dumping have now extended to incineration of sewage sludge and industrial waste as well as disposal of low level radioactive wastes. To reflect this enlarged coverage, during the Fifteenth Consultative Meeting in 1992 the parties changed the name "London Dumping Convention" to "London Convention, 1972," in order to reinforce that the member States' objective is protection of the marine environment, not just ocean dumping.

The transformation of the London Convention came full circle in 1996, when a new Protocol all but replaced the original 1972 agreement. Indeed, the 1996 Protocol virtually re-writes the London Convention.

2.   THE PERMITTING PROCESS, COMPLIANCE AND ENFORCEMENT

Reflecting the incremental changes brought about by amendments over the years to the London Convention, the 1996 Protocol bans the incineration at sea of wastes or other matter. Protocol, Article 5. Rejecting the progressively stricter "Black" and "Grey" lists of the original agreement, the Protocol employs a "reverse list" strategy. The dumping of *any* waste or other matter is prohibited *unless* it is listed in Annex I. These materials, e.g. dredged material, sewage sludge, vessels and platforms or other man-made structures at sea, may not be dumped without a permit. This approach had already been employed in regional agreements such as the Oslo, Paris and Helsinki Conventions (discussed *infra*). The provisions for issuance of permits, set out in Annex II of the Protocol, are demanding. Those requesting permits to dump must undertake assessments to identify opportunities for waste prevention at source, consideration of alternative waste management options, dump-site selection, and assessment of potential effects. This strategy effectively incorporates the precautionary approach. Indeed, the precautionary approach and polluter pays principles are established as general obligations of the parties. Article 6 reinforces the duty to manage wastes locally by prohibiting the export of wastes to other countries for dumping or incineration at sea.

There are several exceptions to the London Convention dumping provisions. For example, vessels and aircraft entitled to sovereign immunity under international law are exempt from the Convention's provisions (in practice this usually means navy ships). This exemption is less sweeping than it may appear, though, because Parties must ensure all their vessels "act in a manner consistent with the object and purpose" of the Protocol, Article 10. Nations may also express their consent to be bound.

The London Convention's compliance provisions require parties to keep records showing the nature and quantities of permitted dumping as well as the location, time and method used. Perhaps surprisingly, there are no provisions for sanctions for failure to enforce the London Convention requirements. Despite the lack of sanctions, however, voluntary compliance with the London Convention is high. Annex 3 of the Protocol establishes a dispute resolution process that was agreed to in 1978 but never adopted. Despite the lack of a formal noncompliance procedure prior to the Protocol, regular Consultative Meetings have provided a forum to work out disputes informally. In stark contrast to the enforcement problems plaguing MARPOL and the weak international response to land-based marine pollution, "there is no evidence, unusually, of any non-party dumping significant wastes at sea, or asserting a freedom to do so beyond that implied by the 1982 UNCLOS and the various global and regional instruments." Birnie & Boyle, *op. cit.*, at 332.

----

3.   INCINERATION, INDUSTRIAL WASTES, AND RADIOACTIVE WASTES

If one tracks the amendments to the London Convention since its inception, two trends are apparent. First, the Convention has increasingly restricted ocean dumping, now prohibiting completely certain practices that were commonplace twenty years ago. Second, the precautionary approach has shifted the burden from the government to the dumping party, i.e. a shift from (1) dumping unless it were proven harmful to (2) no dumping unless it is shown there are no alternatives.

This trend is most apparent in the case of incineration and the dumping of industrial and radioactive wastes. At the time the London Convention was drafted, little incineration occurred at sea and the Convention did not address the issue. In 1978, responding to increased marine incineration the parties amended the annexes to allow waste incineration at sea, subject to compliance with permits for certain materials. Throughout the 1980s, incineration was commonplace in the North Sea where huge, specially designed incinerator ships burned over 100,000 tons of waste every year. Scientists expressed concern that the toxic ash from this incineration was poisoning marine life in the North Sea. In response, in 1991 the parties adopted a resolution to minimize marine incineration of noxious liquid wastes and to prohibit incineration of industrial wastes and sewage sludge altogether by the end of 1994. A November 1993 amendment formalized the ban. A similarly incremental process led to the prohibition on dumping of industrial wastes by January 1, 1996.

Prohibiting the dumping of radioactive wastes has proven more complicated. Originally, the Convention distinguished between high-level and low-level radioactive wastes (as defined by the International Atomic Energy Agency, IAEA). The ocean dumping of high-level radioactive wastes was prohibited. With appropriate permits granted by national authorities, ocean dumping of low-level radioactive wastes was allowed. During the Seventh Consultative Meeting in 1983, parties adopted a non-binding resolution establishing a moratorium on all dumping at sea of radioactive materials while scientific studies were undertaken. This moratorium was not legally binding, though a number of nations nonetheless opted out (including The Russian Federation, China, Belgium, France, the U.K., and the U.S.). Britain finally joined the moratorium after its seamen's union refused to handle the loading of nuclear waste. *Nuclear Dumping*, Reuters, Sept. 20, 1985. At the time of formal implementation of the ban in 1994, only Russia opted out.

The Protocol's prohibition on dumping of low-level radioactive wastes is subject to the findings of a periodic 25–year scientific review. The dumping of these wastes used to be permitted under the Convention but the IAEA had not defined the level of "de minimis." This left countries with the authority to dump radioactive wastes if they determined to their own satisfaction that the level of radioactivity was de minimis. The 21st Consultative Meeting of the London Convention finally resolved this issue by establishing an evaluation procedure to determine de minimis levels. Report of the Secretary–General, March 2000, UN A/55/61.

---

4.   DEVELOPING COUNTRY PROVISIONS

The Protocol contains a number of provisions designed to encourage developing countries to become parties. New parties to the Protocol are given a five-year period to achieve full compliance with its provisions, based on established needs. Protocol, Article 26. If a developing country still cannot comply fully, it may apply for up to five more years of a "Transitional Period" for coming into compliance. Why do you think a country would want to become a party if it knows it cannot comply with the Convention's requirements? In contrast to the original Convention text, the Protocol provides a detailed Technical Cooperation and Assistance Program that promotes bilateral and multilateral support for the prevention, reduction and elimination of ocean dumping. Protocol, Article 13. For the period 1997–1998, for example, seven projects were developed and planned by the IMO. Technical Co-operation and Assistance Activities Related to the London Convention, 1972, IMO Resolution LC.55(SM). In 1999, the program focused on training seafaring workers, implementing and strengthening the revised International Convention on Standards of Timing, Certification and Watchkeeping for Seafareres, and working towards the ratification of marine environment conventions. Technical Co-operation Committee, 44th Sess. June 26, 1997.

1996 Protocol to the Convention on the Prevention of Marine Pollution by Dumping of Wastes and Other Matter, 1972

Article 1
Definitions

* * * 4.1 "Dumping" means:

.1   any deliberate disposal at sea of wastes or other matter from vessels, aircraft, platforms or other man-made structures at sea;

.2   any deliberate disposal at sea of vessels, aircraft, platforms or other man-made structures at sea; * * *

.7   "Sea" means all marine waters other than the internal waters of States, as well as the seabed and the subsoil thereof; it does not include sub-seabed repositories accessed only from land.

Article 3
General Obligations

1.   In implementing this Protocol, Contracting Parties shall apply a precautionary approach to environmental protection from dumping of wastes or other matter whereby appropriate preventative measures are taken when there is reason to believe that wastes of other matter introduced into the marine environment are likely to cause harm even when there is no conclusive evidence to prove a causal relation between inputs and their effects.

2.   Taking into account the approach that the polluter should, in principle, bear the cost of pollution, each Contracting Party shall endeavor to promote practices whereby those it has authorized to engage in dumping or incineration at sea bear the cost of meeting the pollution prevention and control requirements for the authorized activities, having due regard to the public interest. * * *

Article 4
Dumping of Wastes or Other Matters

1.   Contracting Parties Shall Prohibit the Dumping of Any Wastes or Other Matter With the exception of those listed in Annex 1.

.2 The dumping of wastes or other matter listed in Annex 1 shall require a permit. Contracting Parties shall adopt administrative or legislative measures to ensure that issuance of permits and permit conditions comply with provisions of Annex 2. Particular attention shall be paid to opportunities to avoid dumping in favor of environmentally preferable alternatives. * * *

Article 5

Incineration at Sea

Contracting Parties shall prohibit incineration at sea of wastes or other matter.

Article 6

Export of Wastes or Other Matters

Contracting Parties shall not allow the export of wastes or other matter to other countries for dumping or incineration at sea.

* * *

Article 9

Issuance of Permits and Reporting

1. Each Contracting Party shall designate an appropriate authority or authorities to:

.1 issue permits in accordance with this Protocol;

.2 keep records of the nature and quantities of all wastes or other matter for which dumping permits have been issued and where practicable the quantities actually dumped and the location, time and method of dumping; and

.3 Monitor individually, or in collaboration with other Contracting Parties and competent international organizations, the condition of the sea for the purposes of this Protocol.

2. The appropriate authority or authorities of a Contracting Party shall issue permits in accordance with this Protocol in respect of wastes or other matter intended for dumping or, as provided for in article 8.2, incineration at sea.

.1 loaded in its territory; and

.2 loaded onto a vessel or aircraft registered in its territory or flying its flag, when the loading occurs in the territory of a State not a Contracting Party to this Protocol. * * *

Article 10

Application and Enforcement

1. Each Contracting Party shall apply the measures required to implement this Protocol to all:

.1 vessels and aircraft loading in its territory or flying its flag;

.2 vessels and aircraft loading in its territory the wastes or other matter which are to be dumped or incinerated at sea; and

.3 Vessels, aircraft and platforms or other man-made structures believed to be engaged in dumping or incineration at sea in areas within which it is entitled to exercise jurisdiction in accordance with international law.

2. Each Contracting Party shall take appropriate measures in accordance with international law to prevent and if necessary punish acts contrary to the provisions of this Protocol.

3. Contracting Parties agree to co-operate in the development of procedures for the effective application of this Protocol in areas beyond the jurisdiction of any State, including procedures for the reporting of vessels and aircraft observed dumping or incinerating at sea at contravention of this Protocol.

4. This Protocol shall not apply to those vessels and aircraft entitled to sovereign immunity under international law. However each Contracting Party shall ensure by the adoption of appropriate measures that such vessels and aircraft owned or operated by it act in a manner consistent with the object and purpose of this Protocol and shall inform the Organization accordingly.

5. A State may, at the time it expresses its consent to be bound by this Protocol, or at any time thereafter, declare that it shall apply the provisions of this Protocol to its vessels and aircraft referred to in paragraph 4, recognizing that only that State may enforce those provisions against such vessels and aircraft.

* * *

Article 15

Responsibility and Liability

In accordance with the principles of international low regarding State responsibility for damage to the environment of other States or to any other area of the environment, the Contracting Parties undertake to develop procedures regarding liability arising from the dumping or incineration at sea of wastes or other matter.

* * *

Annex 1

Wastes or Other Matter That May Be Considered for Dumping

1. The following wastes or other matter are those that may be considered for dumping being mindful of the Objectives and General Obligations of this Protocol set out in articles 2 and 3:

> .1   dredged material;
>
> .2   sewage sludge;
>
> .3   fish waste, or material resulting from industrial fish processing operations;
>
> .4   vessels and platforms or other man-made structures at sea;
>
> .5   inert, inorganic geological material;
>
> .6   organic material of natural origin; and
>
> .7   bulky items primarily comprising iron, steel, concrete and similarly unharmful materials for which the concern is physical impact, and limited to those circumstances where such wastes are generated at locations, such as small islands with isolated communities, having no practicable access to disposal options other than dumping.

2. The wastes or other matter listed in paragraphs 1.4 and 1.7 may be considered for dumping, provided that material capable of creating floating debris or otherwise contributing to pollution of the marine environment has

been removed to the maximum extent and provided that the material dumped poses no serious obstacle to fishing or navigation.

3.   Notwithstanding the above, materials listed in paragraphs 1.1 to 1.7 containing levels of radioactivity greater than *de minimis* (exempt) concentrations as defined by the IAEA and adopted by Contracting Parties, shall not be considered eligible for dumping: provided further that within 25 years of 20 February 1994, and at each 25 year interval thereafter. Contracting Parties shall complete a scientific study relating to all radioactive wastes and other radioactive matter other than high level wastes or matter, taking into account such other factors as Contracting Parties consider appropriate and shall review the prohibition on dumping of such substances in accordance with the procedures set forth in article 22.

---

5.   REGIONAL AGREEMENTS

As with MARPOL and the Paris Memorandum of Understanding, regional agreements play an important role in strengthening the implementation and effectiveness of the London Convention. By adding a level of institutional supervision closer to the implementation level, regional agreements effectively reinforce the baseline requirements of the Convention by ensuring compliance with its provisions.

For example, the Convention for the Prevention of Marine Pollution by Dumping from Ships and Aircraft, known as the Oslo Convention, was adopted in 1972. 11 I.L.M. 262 (1972). This is a regional convention for 13 Northeast Atlantic Ocean countries regulating the dumping of wastes along the coastline from Portugal to Norway—excluding the Mediterranean and Baltic. Under the Oslo Convention, "dumping" means "any deliberate disposal of substances and materials into the sea by or from ships or aircraft." The Convention uses "black lists" to prohibit the dumping of certain substances (as the London Convention did prior to the 1996 Protocol). It does not cover radioactive wastes.

Under the auspices of the 1992 Convention for the Protection of the Marine Environment in the North East Atlantic (OSPAR), the Oslo Convention has been merged with the Paris Convention for the Prevention of Marine Pollution from Land Based Sources (1974) to address dumping in Europe and the North Atlantic. All the European nations bordering the northeast Atlantic are signatories. OSPAR entered into force March 25, 1998. OSPAR contains annexes covering the prevention of pollution caused by immersion or incineration of wastes, prevention and elimination of offshore pollution, and evaluation of the quality of the marine environment. Hence it covers pollution from offshore, land-based, ocean dumping and ocean incineration sources. *EC Signs Convention on Protection of North East Atlantic*, EUROPE ENVIRONMENT, Oct. 6, 1992. In July, 1995, for example, the OSPAR Commission adopted a binding decision to phase out the use and marketing of short-chained chlorinated paraffins. The OSPAR Parties can adopt decisions with a two-thirds majority vote, but nations may choose not to regard the decision as binding. While OSPAR replaced the Oslo and Paris Convention, any prior decisions, agreements or recommendations issued under those conventions are still applicable unless the OSPAR parties decide otherwise. *See* <www.ospar.org>.

Putting the precautionary principle into practice, OSPAR requires that parties wishing to dump waste in the North Sea establish both that no harm to the marine environment will result and that no adequate disposal alternative exists. The regulation of ocean dumping is based on a reverse list similar to that of the 1996 Protocol to the London Convention. Thus OSPAR's Annex II lists the only wastes that may be dumped, subject to a permit, in the North Atlantic and Arctic seas. With the exception of the United Kingdom, all North Sea countries have halted ocean dumping of industrial waste. Birnie & Boyle, *op. cit.*, at 330. Incineration within the Convention's area is also prohibited.

Although many of the controls under OSPAR and the London Convention are redundant, mechanisms for the control of marine pollution at a regional level provide credible enforcement of the Convention's provisions (recall how the Paris MOU ensures that port State inspections of vessels required under MARPOL really take place). The OSPAR Commission assesses Parties' compliance based on submitted implementation reports. The Commission has the authority to call for steps to bring about the full compliance of a Party. OSPAR, Article 23. OSPAR has been a leader in creating agreements to address the dumping of radioactive waste at sea, the disposal of used oil rigs and other offshore installations, and limits on emissions and discharges in the vinyl chloride sector. Most notably, OSPAR has been been at the vanguard of efforts to eliminate or reduce discharge of radioactive substances. *NEA Examines Option for Spent Fuel*, BNA IED, Aug. 24, 2000.

QUESTIONS AND DISCUSSION

1. As of February 2001, 79 nations had ratified or acceded to the London Convention, approximately half from industrialized Europe and North America. The 1996 Protocol is halfway to ratification with thirteen contracting parties. How would you describe the customary law status of the London Convention and the 1996 Protocol? UNCLOS Article 210(6) states that national laws and regulations preventing and controlling dumping shall be no less effective than relevant global rules and standards. In a non-binding communication to the Contracting Parties of the London Convention, the Division for Ocean Affairs of the United Nations Office of Legal Affairs has declared that the rules of the London Convention should be regarded as global and therefore are binding upon *all* UNCLOS members, regardless of whether they have ratified the London Convention. Brennan van Dyke, *op. cit.*, at 256–57.

Do you find the argument that the provisions of the London Convention should be binding on all parties to UNCLOS persuasive? How would you argue the provisions of the Convention represent customary international law? What about the provisions of the 1996 Protocol?

2. Under the London Convention, jurisdiction over ocean dumping rests with flag States (States whose ships fly their flags), loading States (States where the wastes are loaded), and coastal States (States in whose waters the wastes are dumped). Primary responsibility for issuing permits rests with the loading State, regardless of the nationality of the ship or aircraft, or where the dumping is to take place. 1996 Protocol, Article 9. Vessels of parties to the Convention cannot escape this provision by loading in non-party States; in this case, the flag State is required to act as a licensing authority. Similarly, there are no Convention provisions forbidding the authority from granting a permit to a ship from a non-party, provided that the ship complies with the relevant rules of the Convention. Coastal States have jurisdiction to issue licenses and to regulate or prohibit all dumping within their Exclusive Economic Zone (200 nautical miles off their coast). Thus, while UNCLOS ensures ships navigation freedoms, this right does not protect them from coastal State action if the State has claimed its EEZ and dumping is taking place in its waters without consent.

Two articles in UNCLOS reinforce the London Convention's provisions. UNCLOS Article 210 requires States to adopt laws and regulations that reduce, prevent and control pollution from marine dumping. The coastal State is given the primary authority to control dumping within its territorial seas, the EEZ and its continental shelf. UNCLOS Article 216 provides that laws regulating marine dumping shall be enforced by the coastal State within its waters, by the flag State for ships flying its flag, and by any State where loading occurs within its waters. In effect, these articles provide a framework for the international regulation of dumping without detailing the treatment of specific substances.

3.   To assess the impacts of a ban on ocean dumping of industrial waste, in 1991 IMO commissioned a Global Waste Survey. The Survey found an enormous difference between waste management practices in developed and developing countries, discussed in detail in Chapter 12. In particular, the Survey found that the ban on ocean dumping would likely increase the occurrence of illegal ocean dumping over the short to medium term. Of the 101 countries surveyed, 64 stated that they did *not* have land-based facilities to manage the disposal of hazardous wastes. *Industrial Waste Dumping "Catastrophic" Says Report,* IMO News, No. 1:1996, at 18. Where will the hazardous waste in the countries be disposed of if they are banned from ocean dumping and have no adequate land-based sites? How do the prohibitions of the Bamako and Lomé Conventions affect this situation? (*See* Chapter 12, pages 852–854).

4.   The requirement that London Convention parties meet regularly, as called for in the Vienna Convention for the Protection of the Ozone Layer and other agreements, has enabled the London Convention parties to respond rapidly to improved understanding of the harms caused by ocean dumping. In practice, the parties typically meet every year to review the status of the London Convention and new information. Occasionally this leads to adoption of resolutions and amendments to the Convention's provisions. While the resolutions are non-binding and hence voluntary, parties have largely complied with them and laid the foundation for emerging customary international law. Amendments to the 1996 Protocol require a two-thirds majority of Contracting Parties present.

5.   As with many other international environmental agreements, NGOs are active in complementing (and sometimes challenging) State enforcement efforts. In September 2000, for example, Greenpeace filed a complaint against Hong Kong for the dumping of toxic waste, alleging that more then 300,000 cubic metres of toxic waste, in the form of mud, had been dumped. In the public spotlight, the Beijing delegates at the London Convention agreed to look into these allegations. Jennifer Ehrlick, *International Scrutiny Over Marine Dumping,* SOUTH CHINA MORNING POST, Sept. 23, 2000.

6.   While compliance with the London Convention has been very high, there is at least one notable exception. Russia and Japan have publicly exchanged accusations over disposing large amounts of radioactive waste at sea. Japan first accused the

Russian navy of dumping low-level radioactive waste water in the Sea of Japan. The Russian Atomic Energy Minister, on a visit to Japan in October 1993, countered that Japanese nuclear power plants were discharging 10 times as much radioactivity into the sea. Japan responded by claiming that it was not the level of radioactivity that mattered, but more importantly that Russia had dumped high-level radioactive wastes in international waters in violation of the London Convention. Indeed, despite assurances by the Soviet Union in 1989 that it had never dumped radioactive waste, it now appears that the Soviet Union has dumped into the ocean double the amount of radioactive material of all 12 other nuclear countries *combined*. This includes 18 nuclear reactors. W. Broad, *Russians Describe Extensive Dumping of Nuclear Waste,* New York Times, April 27, 1993, at A1; *Nuclear material dumped off Japan,* New York Times, Oct. 19, 1993, at A1; *Russia, Japan accuse each other of dumping,* Nuclear News, Dec. 1993, at 59.

The Convention also been criticized for a big exception—its lack of regulation of radioactive wastes from a land-based pipeline. Critics argue that this source of pollution creates significant risks as the radioactive material builds in seafood and seaweed, enters rivers, and accumulates on beaches. Greenpeace claims that more than "one million litres of liquid radioactive waste pours into the sea a day." *Delegates Get Big Picture of Radioactive Nuclear Waste Dumping*, Environment News Service June 27, 2000. Why do you think this obvious source of marine pollution is not covered by the London Convention?

7. Why do you think the OSPAR parties, all of whom participate in the IMO, have been so much more successful in addressing marine pollution issues working through OSPAR rather than MARPOL or the London Convention?

———

Problem Exercise: The Brent Spar

The North Sea has become one of the most productive oil fields in the world. Hundreds of platforms have been erected in this part of the Atlantic Ocean to support oil exploration and drilling. In September 1991, the British subsidiary of Shell Oil, Shell UK, stopped operating a North Sea oil installation known as the Brent Spar. From 1991–1995, Shell UK carried out studies to determine the most appropriate means to "decommission," i.e. to dismantle and dispose of, the Brent Spar.

The Brent Spar is a large metal structure weighing 14,500 tons. It consists of six storage tanks that lie beneath the water. Its size made disposal a challenge. Lifting it out of the water or rotating it to a horizontal position for dismantling was likely to compromise its structural integrity, risking buckling and imploding of the tanks. Shell argued that land disposal would pose undue risk to people and the environment. Thus in its formal request for a disposal permit from the UK government, Shell UK contended that analysis of the environmental, safety, occupational health, and economic considerations all favored deep water disposal of the Brent Spar. In February 1995, the UK government announced its intention to approve deep water disposal of the Spar at a site in the Atlantic. The Government proceeded to notify the other parties to the Oslo Convention, none of whom made any objections to the plan.

Soon after the UK government's approval had been granted, the environmental group, Greenpeace, learned of the disposal plans and quickly organized a direct action campaign. On April 30, 1995, a small group of Greenpeace activists landed on the Brent Spar and occupied it in protest of the disposal plans. Greenpeace scientists had concluded that deep water disposal was environmentally irresponsible. In its public statements, Greenpeace claimed that the Brent Spar contained 5,550 tons of oil and "over 100 tons of toxic sludge—including oil, arsenic, cadmium, PCBs and lead—and more than thirty tonnes of radioactive waste." Disposal in deep water, they argued, would eventually release these harmful pollutants. Shell denied these assertions, claiming the pollutant concentrations in the Brent Spar were minimal. Greenpeace also argued that the issue went beyond the specific case of the Brent Spar, since dumping the platform at sea would set an important precedent for the future disposal of some 400 other oil installations in the North Sea.

The Greenpeace activists were finally removed from the Brent Spar on May 23, 1995, but their departure was accompanied by heavy media coverage. Environmentalists in Europe were loudly pressing for a boycott of Shell Oil. These threats grew ugly in a few instances. In June 1995, protesters in Germany threatened to damage 200 Shell service stations. Fifty were subsequently damaged, two fire-bombed, and one raked with bullets. Towards the end of June, the German government and several other European governments publicly declared their opposition to deep sea disposal of the Brent Spar.

Drawing on the sources in this chapter, the Treaty Supplement and other material you have studied thus far (including, for example, the principles in Chapter 7), craft the best legal arguments in favor and against the UK government's approval of deep water disposal for the Brent Spar. What are the strongest *policy* arguments in favor and against deep water disposal? Additional materials are on the Teaching Materials page of the casebook website.

Postscript Shortly after several European countries, led by Germany, indicated their official opposition to deep water disposal of the Brent Spar, Shell UK was instructed by its parent company to cancel the planned disposal and find another solution. This posed two problems. First, the British government was furious with its European partners in OSPAR for their policy reversal. They had been given the opportunity to oppose deep sea disposal of the Brent Spar and had not objected. Only when public opinion had been aroused, after the permit had been granted, did these governments oppose the UK.

Second, Shell UK now needed a permit from the government for the new disposal scheme. But in obtaining its original permit Shell UK had made a convincing case that deep water disposal was the "Best Practicable Environmental Option"—a legal requirement to obtain the dumping permit. Shell UK now had to explain why it was incorrect before, why its analysis of the environmental, safety, occupational health, and economic considerations no longer favored deep water disposal of the Brent Spar. The UK Government has made clear its stance that the original deep water disposal option remained the standard against which any other disposal solution must be compared. As Shell UK attempted to unsnarl this problem, the Brent Spar was towed and sat anchored in the deep waters of Erfjord, a Norwegian fjord. Shell winnowed a series of 30 disposal proposals down to 11, ranging from land disposal to a floating aquarium. Shell finally decided to re-use much of the main steel structure in the construction of new harbor facilities near Stavanger, Norway.

Greenpeace's ability to raise public awareness and prevent the deep water disposal of the Brent Spar was widely regarded as an NGO triumph. Shortly after the about-face by Shell, Peter Melchett, the Executive Director of Greenpeace–UK, sent a letter of apology to the Chairman of Shell UK. It turned out that some of Greenpeace's dire warnings over the Brent Spar's toxic contents had been incorrect. Shell's public statements about the Brent Spar's contents had, after all, been accurate. The Greenpeace scientists who analyzed samples from the Brent Spar containers had believed, incorrectly, they were taken from the top of the storage tanks rather than from access vent pipes. As a result, their extrapolation of total oil content was incorrect. As Melchett explained in his public letter, however, these calculations were not central to Greenpeace's position.

> In any event, as you know, the basic argument between Greenpeace and the European governments that supported our position on the one hand, and Shell UK and the UK Government on the other, was not about the contents of the Brent Spar, nor the physical characteristics of the proposed dump site. The argument was about whether it was right to dump industrial waste of any sort in the deep oceans, whether dumping the Brent Spar would be a precedent for dumping other oil installations, and indeed other waste in the oceans, and, fundamentally, over whether we should dump wastes into any part of the environment, as opposed to reducing waste, and recycling, treating or containing harmful materials. Our view remains that the division between us on the Brent Spar depends on how deeply we value our environment, and what damage and precedents we find unacceptable.

<http://www.greenpeace.org/comms/brent/sep04.html>

A number of commentators have since denounced Greenpeace's actions as "typical" of irresponsible environmental organizations, inaccurately over-stating the threats posed by industrial activities to scare the public. Do you think the public outrage that forced Shell's hand would have resulted if Greenpeace had learned of its calculation error earlier and not discussed the Brent Spar's contents?

Who do you think was "right" in this dispute? How should the balance be made between the potential environmental and safety harms from onshore disposal of a massive oil platform and the potential pollution consequences of deep water disposal? Can any "scientific" decision be made to determine the best disposal option or is this ultimately a subjective policy choice among unattractive options? Despite criticism, Greenpeace declared their efforts a success after the OSPAR Commission banned the dumping of decommissioned platforms at sea. Alan Dickey, *Greenpeace Claims Victory Over Platform Dumping,* LLOYDS LIST, Aug. 18, 1999.

Problem Exercise: Decommissioning Nuclear Submarines

While there has been a great deal of publicity over the problems inherent in decommissioning nuclear weapons, an equally pressing (and perhaps more difficult) problem arises in the decommissioning of nuclear submarines. As of 1986, there were approximately 400 submarines powered by nuclear reactors. The working life of a nuclear sub is from 15–20 years, after which the nuclear reactor must be decommissioned and disposed of. As with land-based nuclear reactors, the contents of submarine nuclear reactors include highly radioactive materials some of which may remain dangerously "hot" for hundreds of thousands of years. While there is genuine scientific uncertainty over the extent of the threat posed by ocean dumping of radioactive materials, the potential harms to human health and living marine resources could be considerable. While the U.S. Navy has chosen land-disposal for its subs' reactors, many other nations regard deep sea disposal as a viable alternative. At the current rate of decommissioning, this could lead to approximately 15 nuclear subs dumped in the deep sea every year for the foreseeable future. The legal status of this disposal alternative, however, is strongly disputed.

Assume you are legal counsel to the British Royal Navy. Your commanding officer has asked for a legal opinion on whether ocean dumping of decommissioned British subs violates the London Convention, the Law of the Sea Convention, or customary international law. Your officer, a former law of the sea practitioner, has provided you some background research and pertinent questions to guide your research. Provide the strongest legal and policy arguments in favor and against ocean dumping. *See,* W. Jackson Davis and Jon Van Dyke, *Dumping of decommissioned nuclear submarines at sea: a technical and legal analysis,* 14 MARINE POLICY 467 (1990); Jon Van Dyke, *Ocean disposal of nuclear wastes,* 12 MARINE POLICY 82 (1988).

London Convention

Is ocean disposal of a decommissioned, empty nuclear submarine in Her Majesty's Navy "dumping" as defined by the LC?

Does the 25–year moratorium on dumping of low-level radioactive waste and the ban on dumping of high-level radioactive waste apply to the ocean disposal of submarines?

Does the status of the submarines as naval vessels affect their status under the LC? What is the policy reason for such an exemption, if it exists?

Law of the Sea Convention

Do Articles 87 and 192 (see pages 663 and 684) of the Law of the Sea Convention permit ocean dumping of nuclear reactors?

Article 236 qualifies the sovereign immunity exclusion for certain vessels and Article 29 defines types of navy vessels. What is their significance in this situation?

UNCLOS Article 236

The provisions of this Convention regarding the protection and preservation of the marine environment do not apply to any warship, naval auxiliary, other vessels of aircraft owned or operated by a State and used, for the time being, only on government non-commercial service. However, each state shall ensure by the adoption of appropriate measures not impairing operations of operational capabilities of such vessels or aircraft owned or operated by it, that such vessels or aircraft act in a manner consistent, so far as is reasonable and practicable, with this Convention.

Article 29

For purposes of this Convention, "warship" means a ship belonging to the armed forces of a State bearing the external marks distinguishing such ships of its nationality, under the command of an officer duly commissioned by the government of the State and whose name appears in the appropriate service list or its equivalent, and manned by a crew which is under regular armed forces discipline.

Postscript While the British continue to maintain that deep sea disposal remains the best environmental option for certain types of radioactive waste, they did adopt the 25–year moratorium on disposal of low-level radioactive waste. Russia did not adopt the moratorium and has asked for international help to decommission and dispose safely its aging submarines. Russia has claimed that without substantial financial and technical assistance it cannot construct adequate land-based disposal facilities. The problem is pressing and serious. As recently as April, 1996, a Western scientist advising the Russian Federation claimed that Russia was preparing to dump 20 nuclear submarines at sea. He described a number of these as, "floating Chernobyls." Mike Merrit and Julie Kirkbride, *Russians set to sink rotting N-sub fleet*, SUNDAY TELEGRAPH, April 28, 1996; Michael Binyon, *Moscow seeks help over nuclear waste*, TIMES OF LONDON, Jan. 25, 1995; James R. McCullagh, *Comment, Russian Dumping of Radioactive Wastes in the Sea of Japan: An Opportunity to Evaluate the Effectiveness of the London Convention 1972*, 5 PAC. RIM. L. & POL'Y 399 (1996).

Norway, Russia and the U.S. created a program in September, 1996, to cooperate in the disposal of radioactive waste from de-commissioned Russian nuclear submarines and other military waste in the Arctic. Called the Arctic Military Environmental Cooperation (AMEC), it is a three-million dollar program establishing a forum among the three countries to undertake joint projects and exchange information. In 1999, AMEC worked with the Russian military to combat the environmental effects of radioactive and nonradioactive nuclear waste. This trilateral agreement integrates environmental techniques, which also helps build trust among the three nations. *See* Department of Defense Annual Report to the President and the Congress, chapter 17 (1999).

Other proposals include burying nuclear waste beneath the seabed of France and South Africa inside torpedo-shaped steel and lead containers. However, sub-seabed disposal may violate the IMO and the London Convention's moratorium on sub-seabed disposal of radioactive wastes. Sweden has proposed disposing of radioactive waste beneath the seabed via a tunnel from the coast. Would this violate the moratorium or could this be considered terrestrial rather than sub-seabed disposal? *Nuclear plots for sale in seabed graveyard proposes sub-seabed nuclear waste disposal inside torpedo-shaped steel and lead containers*, NEW SCIENTIST, Dec. 9, 1995.

SECTION IV. LAND–BASED MARINE POLLUTION

(W)e have had one global convention, namely the 1982 Law of the Sea Convention, several regional framework conventions, and four regional agreements that contain provisions relevant to land-based marine pollution. There has not been a single case relating to land-based marine pollution heard by an international tribunal and not one incident of transfrontier land-based marine pollution has been reported. There have been few writings by publicists on the topic. There is little evidence of state practice or of incontestable rules of customary international law specifically on land-based marine pollution. At this stage, specific rules in this field exist only in the form of conventional law.

MENG QING–NAN, LAND-BASED MARINE POLLUTION 63–64 (1987)

————

A. SCOPE OF THE PROBLEM

While the passage above was written over a decade ago, little has happened to change Meng Qing–Nan's depressing observations. This lack of progress might seem surprising because land-based marine pollution (LBMP) is the single most important source of pollution to the marine environment, contributing over 70% of total contaminants. LBMP is, however, exceedingly difficult to regulate and at its broadest includes any substance or energy from a land-based activity that pollutes the seas. In practice, this covers most activities in modern industrialized society and encompasses a vast range of substances and sources. These include garbage and sewage from municipalities, water effluent and air emissions from factories, pulp and paper mills, refineries and chemical plants, fertilizer and pesticides from farms, hot water from power stations, stormwater run-off, soil eroded from farms and logging, and atmospheric emissions from vehicles, utilities, and incinerators. Some of these pollutants are piped directly into the sea while others enter through run-off into rivers or are washed out of the atmosphere by rain or dry deposition. The most environmentally harmful LBMP pollutants are persistent organic pollutants, heavy metals, hydrocarbons, and nutrients. It has been estimated that at least 150,000 different chemicals are dumped into the oceans every year. *World Environment Report*, Oct. 25, 1995; Polly Ghazi, *Nine Lives 8 Poisoned Waters: Life–and slow death–in the world's cruel seas*, THE GUARDIAN, Oct. 1, 1995.

Given current demographic trends, LBMP will likely worsen in the future. Today, over half the world's population lives within a 120–mile coastal strip representing only 10% of the entire land surface of the earth, and two-thirds of the population lives within 240 miles of a coast. *The Global Challenge*, POPULATION REP. vol. 28, iss. 3, Sept. 22, 2000. In the U.S., more than 50% of the people live within 50 miles of the ocean or the

Great Lakes. Don Walsh, *America's Marine Sanctuaries*, U.S. NAVAL INST. PROC. vol. 126, iss. 6, at 89, June 1, 2000. Even the inland population contributes significantly to LBMP through drainage systems and rivers. In fact 41% of the continental U.S. drains into the Gulf of Mexico through the Mississippi River. Mike Dunne, *"Dead Zone" Cure Not Up to Farmers Alone*, BATON ROUGE ADVOC. Nov. 8, 2000, at 11B. The combined run-off of fertilizer, sewage and other nutrients into the sea has provided ideal conditions for explosive growth of algae. As the dead algae are decomposed by bacteria, the bacteria consume so much oxygen that other sea life that cannot swim away literally suffocates. This condition, known as "hypoxia," is the reason for the seven thousand square mile "dead zone" that regularly appears in the Gulf of Mexico, and smaller sterile zones in "America's Chesapeake Bay and New York Bight, the Adriatic, North, and Baltic Seas, the Inland Sea of Japan, the Yellow Sea, the Persian Gulf, and bays and harbors the world over." COLIN WOODARD, OCEAN'S END 46–47 (2000).

The cumulative environmental impacts of these pollutants is considerable. In addition to algal blooms and coral bleaching, a more frightening consequence that still is not well understood concerns damage to the immune system of mammals. In particular, the persistence of toxic chemicals in body tissues leads to increasingly greater concentrations in organisms as they move up the food chain, reaching their highest concentrations in top predators like seals and dolphins. In graphic demonstration of this "bio-accumulation," a number of dead whales washed ashore have been disposed of as hazardous waste because of the concentrations of contaminants in their bodies. Indeed beluga whales from the St. Lawrence River in Canada have been called the most polluted animals on earth.

In one case, autopsies of dead beluga whales revealed high concentrations of a pesticide called Mirex. This was difficult to explain, though, because no Mirex was used in the vicinity of the whales' habitat. How did it get in their bodies? Careful research showed that Mirex had accumulated in the tissues of migrating eels from Lake Ontario, more than 600 miles away. When the whales fed on the eels, the Mirex bio-accumulated in the whale's tissue. Ghazi, *op. cit.* Such contaminants in living marine resources are all the more worrying when one realizes that humans stand atop the food chain and many indigenous communities, such as the Inuit and the inhabitants of the Faroe Islands, depend almost entirely on marine mammals as a protein and fat source. How widespread are the potential impacts of LBMP?

In 1988, a plague struck every seal colony in the North Sea. When the outbreak ended six months later, more than half the population—20,000 harbor seals—had perished. In 1987, as much as half of the near-shore population of bottlenose dolphins along the U.S. east coast died. In 1990, a similar plague struck the Mediterranean shorelines of Spain, France and Greece, where more than 1,000 striped dolphins washed ashore dead. While scientists have been unable to prove conclusively that these die-offs are due to toxic, land-based marine pollutants, to many they are regarded as the likely culprit. Peter Jaret, *Defense Systems Under Fire*, NAT'L WILDLIFE vol. 38, iss. 6, at 36, Oct. 1, 2000. All the bodies of the washed-up marine mammals contained high amounts of industrial compounds, especially PCBs. The most effective immune-suppressor has been shown to be PCBs, followed in toxicity by mercury, lead, dioxins and pesticides such as DDT. Marla Cone, *Destroying the Balance of Nature,* L.A. TIMES, May 12, 1996, at 1.

The most convincing evidence of these compounds' impact was shown in a study of harbor seals. Seal pups from the relatively unpolluted Scottish waters were kept in two separate groups. The first group was fed herring from the Baltic Sea, the site of extensive industrial pollution. The second group was fed herring from the less polluted Atlantic. The bodies of the Baltic herring contained 10 times more PCBs than the Atlantic herring. Two years later, assays showed that seals fed the Baltic fish had developed one-quarter fewer "natural killer" cells—the body's defense against viruses—and 35% fewer T cells, white blood cells necessary to clear infections and produce antibodies. The researchers described these results as comparable to the conditions of AIDS patients. Put simply, they were much more vulnerable to disease. *Id.* This is just one example of the potential consequences of LBMP. In 1997, newspapers on the East coast of the U.S. were filled with reports of a "dead zone" annually appearing in the Gulf of Mexico and outbreaks of the Pfisteria bacteria contaminating fisheries in the Chesapeake Bay. The Gulf of Mexico's "dead zone" is likely the result of urban and agricultural runoff from all states along the Mississippi. The amount of pollution is considerable since, for example, industrialized hog farms in Missouri produce more waste than is produced by the city of St. Louis. *Hog Waste: A Dirty Job for the EPA*, ST. LOUIS POST-DISPATCH, Oct. 17, 1997, at 6B. Scientists suspect the waste from 625 million chickens on the peninsula of the Chesapeake Bay is the main culprit of the Pfisteria outbreak. David Lawuter, *Farm Runoff Suspected in Fish Disease*, L.A. TIMES, Sept. 21, 1997, at A18.

> The seas are a sump. They continuously absorb vast quantities of silt and minerals washed down from the land. Now, however, we are asking them to accept growing amounts of human-generated materials as well, from sewage sludge, industrial effluent, and agricultural run-off, all with their chemical contaminants, to radioactive wastes.

> The oceans can do a good job for us as a gigantic "waste treatment works." The question is, how much waste can they safely handle? That is to say, what sorts of waste are they fitted to absorb, where can they best accommodate it, how long will they take to degrade it through natural processes—and what level of adverse consequences are we prepared to accept?

> These critical factors are not receiving nearly enough attention. Each year we dump hundreds of new chemicals into the seas, to go with the thousands already there, and with next to no idea of their potential impact. Human-made toxic substances are being detected in deep ocean trenches, even as far as Antarctica. This phenomenon is the result of global circulatory systems, processes of which we have hardly any understanding.

> Chemical run-off caused by humans into the oceans is much greater than Nature's contribution—mercury two-and-a-half times the natural rate, manganese four times, zinc, copper, and lead about 12 times, antimony 30 times, and phosphorus 80 times. As for oil, human-caused pollution—often by wanton carelessness, or even deliberate discharge accounts for four-fifths or more of the

total volume entering the seas—some 3.2 million tons a year. We hear much about oil-killed birds and other marine creatures. Fortunately they generally recover their numbers within a few years. The worst damage is more insidious: certain components of oil are toxic, others are carcinogenic, and they tend to persist for extended periods of time.

Heavy metals such as mercury, lead, cadmium, and arsenic, and chemicals such as DDT and PCBs must rank high on the list of harmful pollutants. We have learned to our cost of the effects of mercury through the Minamata episode in Japan and more recent deaths in Indonesia; and we have discovered too late the impact of DDT and PCBs, through reproductive failures among birds of prey and other wildlife.

The most significant factor of all is that at least 85% of ocean pollution arises from human activities on land, rather than at sea, and that 90 percent of these pollutants remain in coastal waters—by far the most biologically productive sector of the oceans.

NORMAN MYERS, ED., GAIA: AN ATLAS OF PLANET MANAGEMENT 78–80 (1993)

The challenges to effective regulation of LBMP are daunting. In addition to the many pathways of LBMP into the ocean—coastal pipes, coastal dumping, rivers, canals, underground watercourses, run-off, and atmospheric deposition—the types and concentration of pollutants vary from country to country, as does the marine environment and the economic capacity to control discharges. Poverty, public health, and management of human settlements also play an important contributing role.

Moreover, LBMP regulation poses greater potential conflict with State sovereignty than regulation of other marine pollutant sources, such as pollution from ships. By definition, LBMP occurs within a State's borders so regulation of LBMP relates immediately to national self-interest. Indeed, full control of LBMP would require controlling pollutants from nearly every major economic activity, including manufacturing, agriculture, energy production, and transport. Thus international agreement to a strong treaty controlling LBMP would have direct consequences for entirely domestic activities underpinning the economy. Put simply, any attempt to regulate LBMP directly impacts national economic goals and priorities. Hence governments fear that national acceptance of international rules and standards on LBMP will bind the hands of the sovereign State.

————

QUESTIONS AND DISCUSSION

1. The harmful impacts of LBMP are so clear that nations already have ample reason to regulate discharges. Given that, why would creating an international agreement provide any additional impetus for nations to act if they have not already done so? How would you respond to the argument that LBMP should not be addressed by international law, at all, since it is first and foremost an issue of domestic concern? Do you think a regional approach to LBMP would be more effective than a global initiative or can the problems only be practically addressed at the national and local level? How do the economic theories of free riders and the global commons relate to LBMP?

2. What is the proper treaty structure for addressing LBMP? Will international law be most effective in reducing pollution through lists and restrictions found in treaties such as MARPOL and the London Convention? Or do you think viewing LBMP as a challenge of integrated coastal management is more useful, in which case the capacity-building approach found in the Convention to Combat Desertification (Chapter 14, p. 1109) is more appropriate?

3. International initiatives to address LBMP also raise the issue of fairness. Most of the LBMP pollution in the marine environment has accumulated from years of discharged waste by developed industrialized countries (e.g., PCBs). Dumping their wastes into the seas for no price certainly assisted in the developed countries' economic development. Yet from the developing countries' perspective, international commitments to control LBMP could limit their national economic development even though they contributed little to the current problem. They will, it has been argued, be paying for developed countries' earlier land-based pollution. The issue of developed country responsibility for existing LBMP is a serious obstacle to the adoption of uniform international rules and standards or climate change. Is this argument similar to those raised during the Montreal Protocol or climate change negotiations (with respect to the historical contribution of industrialized countries to CFCs or greenhouse gases, respectively)? What facts might be critical for determining whether developed countries should be held responsible for their historical contribution of pollutants to the environment?

4. For students of U.S. environmental law, consider the experience of the Clean Water Act in controlling nonpoint source pollution (pollution from run-off). What does this suggest for the likely success of international controls?

B. LEGAL CONTROLS

While most states would agree that the prevention and control of LBMP is a legitimate subject of international action, the complexity of the issues and strong concern over protecting national interests has led to very limited progress at the international level. As one commentator has noted, "Compared with the history of international agreements on vessel-source marine pollution, the development of the international law on LBMP is ... at a pioneer stage." Qing–Nan, *op. cit.* at 92. This remark is equally true in comparison to fisheries law, as well. In contrast to other law of the sea issues, legal efforts to address LBMP's environmental impacts have led to the development of a framework of non-binding standards rather than concrete rules and regulations. Agenda 21, Chapter 17.18.

The starting point, as with all marine pollution issues, is at UNCLOS. UNCLOS addresses issues relevant to LBMP throughout the Convention, but it specifically addresses LBMP in Articles 207 and 213. Article 207 requires all countries, both coastal and land-locked, to take domestic measures to prevent pollution of the marine environment from land-based sources by adopting laws and regulations to minimize the release of toxic, harmful, or noxious substances. States should work to develop internationally agreed-upon rules and standards, but States need only take these "into account" in setting national standards. In seeking a proper balance between economic development and protection of the marine environment, states need only act to the best means at their disposal, taking into account their capacities and need for economic development. Article 213 calls for enforcement of LBMP laws and regulations adopted in accordance with article 207.

UNCLOS Article 207
Pollution from land-based sources

1. States shall adopt laws and regulations to prevent, reduce and control pollution of the marine environment from land-based sources, including rivers, estuaries, pipelines and outfall structures, taking into account internationally agreed rules, standards and recommended practices and procedures.

2. States shall take other measures as may be necessary to prevent, reduce and control such pollution.

3. States shall endeavour to harmonize their policies in this connection at the appropriate regional level.

4. States, acting especially through competent international organizations or diplomatic conference, shall endeavour to establish global and regional rules, standards and recommended practices and procedures to prevent, reduce and control pollution of the marine environment from land-based sources, taking into account characteristic regional features, the economic capacity of developing States and their need for economic development. Such rules, standards and recommended practices and procedures shall be re-examined from time to time as necessary.

5. Laws, regulations, measures, rules, standards and recommended practices and procedures referred to in paragraphs 1, 2 and 4 shall include those designed to minimize, to the fullest extent possible, the release of toxic, harmful or noxious substances, especially those which are persistent, into the marine environment.

UNCLOS Article 213
Enforcement with respect to pollution from land-based sources

States shall enforce their laws and regulations adopted in accordance with article 207 and shall adopt laws and regulations and take other measures necessary to implement applicable international rules and standards established through competent international organizations or diplomatic conference to prevent, reduce and control pollution of the marine environment from land-based sources.

––––––––––

1. MONTREAL GUIDELINES

Seeking to translate UNCLOS' treatment of LBMP into applicable standards, UNEP established a Group of Experts which, between 1983 and 1985, developed and adopted the Montreal Guidelines for the Protection of the Marine Environment against Pollution from Land–Based Sources. UNEP/WG.120/3. The Montreal Guidelines provided broad guidance for the control of LBMP. Its provisions addressed the establishment of control strategies, rules, criteria, standards, and procedures for pollution reduction, technical assistance and co-operation, monitoring and compliance management, and creation of special protected areas. In all, there were 19 guidelines and three annexes. Their coverage was broader than any other international LBMP instruments, encompassing both fixed and mobile municipal, industrial and agricultural sources whose pollution reaches the marine environment. These detailed prescriptions came at a cost, however, for the guidelines had no teeth. They were recommendations, written in broad language, and presented as a checklist of basic provisions from which governments may select to meet the needs of specific regions.

————

2.   GLOBAL PROGRAM OF ACTION FOR THE PROTECTION OF THE MARINE ENVIRONMENT FROM LAND–BASED ACTIVITIES

While far-reaching in coverage, the Montreal Guidelines were not widely implemented. Recognizing this, the Earth Summit called for a new initiative involving a host of protective measures ranging from the precautionary approach and impact assessments to economic incentives and improved living standards of coastal populations. Agenda 21, Chapter 17.24, 17.25.

To promote Agenda 21's proposals and remedy the Montreal Guidelines' failure, a UNEP conference was held in Washington in 1995. Delegates adopted two documents: the Global Program of Action for the Protection of the Marine Environment from Land–Based Activities, and The Washington Declaration on Protection of Marine Resources from Land–Based Activities. Much more detailed and practical than the Montreal Guidelines, The Global Program of Action's 60 pages of recommendations provide concrete guidance for nations to establish priorities, participate in regional and sub-regional arrangements, manage source-specific pollutant reductions, address physical destruction of habitats, and locate funding sources. UNEPO(OCA)/LBA/IG.2/7. The strategies deal specifically with nutrients, sewage, oils, and five other pollutants. The Global Program of Action focuses, as well, on international cooperation, financing, and capacity-building and provides practical guidance to assist nations in meeting their existing commitments under other agreements such as UNCLOS, the UNEP Regional Seas Program, the London Convention, MARPOL 73/78 and the Basel Convention. The Global Program of Action is non-binding.

The Washington Declaration summarizes well the objectives of the Global Program of Action and expresses the intention of the international community to take effective action.

Washington Declaration on Protection of the Marine Environment from Land-based Activities

Recognizing the interdependence of human populations and the coastal and marine environment, and the growing and serious threat from land-based activities, to both human health and well-being and the integrity of coastal and marine ecosystems and biodiversity, * * *

Noting that there are major differences among the different regions of the world and the States which they comprise in terms of environmental, economic and social conditions and level of development which will lead to different judgments on priorities in addressing problems related to the degradation of the marine environment by land-based activities, * * *

Hereby declare their commitment to protect and preserve the marine environment from the impacts of land-based activities, and

Declare their intention to do so by:

1.   Setting as their common goal sustained and effective action to deal with all land-based impacts upon the marine environment, specifically those resulting from sewage, persistent organic pollutants, radioactive substances, heavy metals, oils (hydrocarbons), nutrients, sediment mobilization, litter, and physical alteration and destruction of habitat;

2.   Developing or reviewing national action programs within a few years on the basis of national priorities and strategies;

3.   Taking forward action to implement these programs in accordance with national capacities and priorities;

4.   Cooperating to build capacities and mobilize resources for the development and implementation of such programs, in particular for developing countries, especially the least developed countries, countries with economies in transition and small island developing States (hereinafter referred to as "countries in need of assistance");

5.   Taking immediate preventive and remedial action, wherever possible, using existing knowledge, resources, plans and processes;

6.   Promoting access to cleaner technologies, knowledge and expertise to address land-based activities that degrade the marine environment, in particular for countries in need of assistance;

7.   Cooperating on a regional basis to coordinate efforts for maximum efficiency and to facilitate action at the national level, including, where appropriate, becoming parties to and strengthening regional cooperative agreements and creating new agreements where necessary;* * *

13.   According priority to implementation of the Global Program of Action within the United Nations system, as well as in other global and regional institutions and organizations with responsibilities and capabilities for addressing marine degradation from land-based activities, and specifically:

(a) Securing formal endorsement of those parts of the Global Program of Action that are relevant to such institutions and organizations and incorporating the relevant provisions into their work programs;

(b) Establishing a clearing-house mechanism to provide decision makers in all States with direct access to relevant sources of information, practical experience and scientific and technical expertise and to facilitate effective scientific, technical and financial cooperation as well as capacity-building; and

(c) Providing for periodic intergovernmental review of the Global Program of Action, taking into account regular assessments of the state of the marine environment; * * *

17.   Acting to develop, in accordance with the provisions of the Global Program of Action, a global, legally binding instrument for the reduction and/or elimination of emissions, discharges and, where appropriate, the elimination of the manufacture and use of the persistent organic pollutants identified in decision 18/32 of the Governing Council of the United Nations Environment Program. The nature of the obligations undertaken must be developed recognizing the special circumstances of countries in need of assistance. Particular attention should be devoted to the potential need for the continued use of certain persistent organic pollutants to safeguard human health, sustain food produc-

tion and to alleviate poverty in the absence of alternatives and the difficulty of acquiring substitutes and transferring of technology for the development and/or production of those substitutes; * * *

QUESTIONS AND DISCUSSION

1. Point 17 of the Declaration may seem out of place. It reflects the decision of the delegates to work toward negotiation of a binding treaty to limit or ban the worst persistent organic pollutants (POPs), but what is it doing in a plan of action for LBMP? The negotiation of the Washington Declaration occurred soon after the UNEP Governing Council adopted decision 18/32 (referenced in Point 17). This decision created an experts panel to gather information on POPs—their exposure pathways, transport, risks and benefits—and policies for eliminating emissions, discharges and losses of persistent organic pollutants. Their report led to negotiations that culminated in the The Stockholm Convention on Implementing International Action on Certain Persistent Organic Pollutants (See page 885). If decision 18/32 had already been adopted, why do you think negotiators of the Washington Declaration included Point 17 in the text?

2. In describing UNCLOS Article 207's treatment of LBMP, Professors Patricia Birnie and Alan Boyle have observed that the loose nature of obligations "leaves little doubt that states did not wish to commit themselves to the same level of international control as is imposed on other sources of marine pollution. The social and economic costs of such measures were seen as unacceptably high, and the preferred solution was thus a weaker level of international regulation, a greater latitude for giving preference to other national priorities, and resort to regional cooperation as the primary level at which international action should occur." PATRICIA W. BIRNIE & ALAN E. BOYLE, INTERNATIONAL LAW & THE ENVIRONMENT 308 (1992). Do you think it aptly describes the Global Program of Action, as well? How would you characterize the Global Program of Action's failure to address sanctions or enforcement of non-compliance with LBMP control measures? What incentives exist for states to make good faith efforts to implement the Global Program of Action?

3. An additional complication to controlling LBMP is the definition of pollution. Article 1 of UNCLOS defines "pollution of the marine environment" as:

> the introduction by man, directly or indirectly, of substances or energy into the marine environment, including estuaries, which results or is likely to result in such deleterious effects as harm to living resources and marine life, hazards to human health, hindrance to marine activities, including fishing and other legitimate uses of the sea, impairment of quality for use of sea water and reduction of amenities.

But whether or not a discharge harms the environment depends on a number of factors. At one extreme, any waste discharge could result in a theoretical reduction of the assimilative capacity of the environment. Does that mean all waste discharges should be regulated as "pollution"? Or, should governments seek to identify pollution which measurably harms the environment, i.e. pollution which "detectably," "significantly" or "meaningfully" harms the environment? If past experience is any guide, our scientific understanding of toxicology and ecology will determine this answer. As we learn more about the causal links between even trace amounts of certain contaminants and marine life, how does our working definition of "pollution" change? What factors would you consider in determining whether a discharge "harms" the environment? What indicators would you want to have periodically measured?

4. *Problem Exercise* No cases relating to LBMP have been heard by an international tribunal. This is due in part to the paucity of international law on the subject and in part to the tremendous difficulty in establishing causation against individual parties. Assume you are advising a tour company in Denmark that organizes seal watching cruises. The seal populations that passengers pay to view are dying rapidly, sending the company into bankruptcy. Research indicates that LBMP is the most likely culprit; the company has suffered a legally cognizable harm but whom can it sue? Since the deadly toxins bio-accumulate, many of the compounds may have been dumped in the ocean by companies in Belgium, the Netherlands, Denmark, Norway or the UK years ago. Even if you can identify a small number of factories that discharge toxics, the link between their discharges and the seal deaths is unclear. What additional information would you need to build a compelling case? What if you were retained by a client who conducts whale-watching cruises of beluga whales in the St. Lawrence River? Would this case be any easier to win?

C. REGIONAL SEAS AGREEMENTS

The absence of binding global commitments on LBMP illustrates well the limits of effective international response to certain environmental problems. UNEP's Regional Seas Program also addresses the assessment and control of land-based sources of marine pollution. Since the Stockholm Conference in 1972, the regional approach to marine pollution control has consistently been endorsed by the UNEP governing council. UNEP's regional control strategy has four components:

–action plans for research, assessment and monitoring,

–legally binding conventions

–technical protocols and annexes focused on specific threats (such as LBMP)

–financial and institutional provisions supporting these activities.

Qing–Nan, op. cit. at 113–14.

By the end of 1983, conventions under the UNEP framework had been adopted in six regions: the Mediterranean (1976), the Kuwait region (1978), the West and Central Africa Region (1981), the South–East Pacific Region (1981), the Red Sea and Gulf of Aden Region (1982), and the Wider Caribbean Region (1983). These regional framework conventions generally contain only one provision on LBMP, calling for contracting Parties to take all appropriate measures to prevent, abate and combat pollution of the regional seas caused by discharges from rivers, coastal establishments or outfalls, or emanating from any other land-based sources within their territories. Qing–Nan, *op. cit.* at 114–17. Concrete, source-specific limits for LBMP, however, remained the exception rather than the rule at the international level.

Four other regional conventions contain specific and detailed rules on LBMP. They are the Convention for the Prevention of Marine Pollution from Land–Based Sources (the Paris Convention); the Convention on the Protection of the Marine Environment of the Baltic Sea Area (the Helsinki Convention); the Protocol for the Protection of the Mediterranean Sea against Pollution from Land-based Sources (the Med Protocol on LBMP); and the Protocol for the Protection of the South–East Pacific against

Pollution from Land–Based Sources (the Lima Protocol on LBMP). These regional conventions, in contrast to international treaties on marine pollution, also generally cover internal waters of the contracting state.

Adopted in 1983, the Cartagena Agreement is a UNEP Regional Seas agreement that applies to the wider Caribbean region. The *Protocol to the Cartagena Agreement*, adopted in 1999, represents a break from past approaches and provides a new model of tough LBMP controls for regional conventions. Protocol Concerning Pollution From Land–Based Sources and Activities to the Convention for the Protection and Development of the Marine Environment of the Wider Caribbean Region. The Protocol contains a series of annexes that together provide a detailed and source-specific control program for significant sources of LBMP. Its general obligations require each contracting party to take appropriate measures to prevent, reduce and control LBMP in the Convention Area. In this respect, the draft Protocol is little different than most regional conventions. In two areas, however, the Protocol marks a radical departure.

First, it represents the first significant application of the Global Program of Action, providing concrete and detailed provisions for monitoring and impact assessment, reporting mechanisms, and institutional structures to ensure there is follow-through. Second, the draft Protocol contains annexes with *detailed* emission and effluent limits for important LBMP sources. These limits closely resemble national water pollution regulations, setting maximum numeric levels for BOD, pH, temperature, and other measures of pollution. Strict timetables are set for coming into compliance. Such strict numeric requirements in LBMP agreements are unprecedented, leaving no doubt whether or not countries are in compliance. This marks the first agreement creating regional standards for domestic wastewater. Report of the Secretary–General, UN A/55/61, March 2000. For a description of the Protocol and its text, *see* <http://grid2.cr.usgs.gov/cep-net/law/cartnut.html>.

QUESTIONS AND DISCUSSION

1. While regional seas agreements provide the strongest international response to LBMP, they have not been terribly effective in reversing present levels of overall pollution. States have been much more willing to endorse and implement the precautionary approach to the prevention of pollution from dumping at sea and the transboundary transport of hazardous wastes. While regional agreements offer greater flexibility in accommodating the economic, ecological, and geopolitical needs of particular seas and adjacent states, Birnie and Boyle conclude:

> at best it can be said of the regional seas programme as a whole that it has exercised some influence on the problem of land-based pollution in some of the areas which it covers. * * * [However,] the main consequence of this regionalization of the problem has been legitimization of weak standards and weak supervisory institutions. States have simply not addressed the regional problems with the seriousness merited by scientific reports.

Birnie and Boyle, *op. cit.* at 301, 303, 309

2. Regional efforts to protect seas from land-based pollution continue. Consider the Black Sea, where the environmental situation is dire. Michael Griffin, *Browning the Black Sea*, EuroBusiness, June, 1993.

The Black Sea is dying from a fatal cocktail of pollutants, overfishing and tropical predators.

The six countries bordering the Black Sea are on the verge of signing a landmark agreement that could be the first step towards rescuing eastern Europe's only warm water sea from ecological extinction. But the initiative comes too late to save Turkey's Black Sea fishery, where catches fell from 650,000 to 15,000 tons in the space of three years. And Turkey's new partners—Russia, Ukraine, Georgia, Bulgaria and Romania—may be too weakened by upheavals at home to implement a conservation programme that could require billions of dollars and decades to yield results.

The Bucharest Convention, the fruit of ten years' hard negotiation, will be the first Black Sea accord to include Turkey, a former Cold War enemy of the other participants. The signatories will immediately benefit from a $9.3 million grant from the World Bank and the United Nations Development Programme from Global Environment Facility funds (GEF) aimed at producing the sea's first environmental management plan.

The raising of the Iron Curtain revealed the Black Sea to be the most degraded regional waterway in the world. Pollution from agricultural and industrial sources stretching from Munich to Kiev has induced what look like irreversible changes in the marine food chain. Algae and exotic predators now flourish at the expense of commercial species on which 2 million fishermen once depended.

"In a matter of 25 to 30 years," says Dr Laurence Mee of the Marine Environmental Studies Laboratory in Monaco, "the north-western Black Sea has been converted from a diverse ecosystem to a eutrophic plankton culture unsuitable for most higher organisms. The sea is now green or brown and beaches tend to stink of decaying matter." * * *

... "The Danube alone currently produces 60,000 tons of phosphorous per year," says Laurence Mee, who is also an advisor to the UN Environmental Programme's Regional Seas Programme. "That is equivalent to the total river output of phosphorous to the North Sea and four times that into the Baltic." Loads of inorganic nitrogen, chiefly run off from east European farms, account for a further 340,000 tons a year. The immediate result of increased inflows of nitrogen and phosphorous is a rapid stimulation of the marine population. Fish love nutrients. But so, unfortunately, do algae, whose long-term effect on the marine environment is devastating. In tidal waters, the blooms and decaying matter can be broken up and disturbed. But in enclosed seas, like the Black and Adriatic—where phytoplankton blooms disrupted tourism in 1991—they gobble up the oxygen, displace marine creatures and fall to the seabed in a layer of vegetal lava.

Coming to grips with such a highly complex interplay of little-understood phenomena will prove no easy matter. A priority of any plan of action must be to revive co-operation among the region's scientific establishments, estimated at 8,000 specialists in nearly 50 institutions. The exchange of information will enable them to begin systematically monitoring key factors in the sea's degradation and to devise common responses and controls.

Politically, the road ahead could be a long one. It took ten years and a fundamental shift in world power to produce the Bucharest Convention, which led to the creation of a Black Sea Commission responsible for pollution control.

But despite the momentum gained from the end of the Cold War, the convention will not address the thorny issue of exclusive economic zones within the Black Sea.

Based on what you have read in this section, what approaches would you recommend the States bordering the Black Sea consider to address the LBMP issue? Consider too, the model of the International Joint Commission used for the Great Lakes between the U.S. and Canada (Chapter 11, p. 809).

3. How many LBMP sources should a legal agreement or program of action attempt to cover? Sources such as agricultural run-off and sewage discharge constitute important LBMP sources. What about airborne pollutants from incineration? What about the character of the solid wastes that are sent to the incinerator? At a certain level, if LBMP comes to include "everything" that enters the sea from the land, then legal strategies to combat LBMP risk becoming vacuous, little more than edicts saying, "reduce pollution." Do you agree with this critique? How would you characterize the most effective role for international law in addressing LBMP?

4. The international community has expressed a growing sense of frustration at the slow implementation of the Global Programme of Action (GPA). The GPA is supposed to serve as a clearing-house to help mobilize technical, financial and scientific efforts at the local, national and regional levels. UNEP's governing council said the implementation of GPA must be urgently expedited. To facilitate this goal, UNEP is conducting a review in 2001 to monitor the implementation process. Report of the Secretary–General, UN A/55/61, March 2000.

SECTION V. MARINE POLLUTION FROM DEEP SEABED MINING

[U]nder no circumstances, we believe, must we ever allow the prospects of rich harvest and mineral wealth to create a new form of colonial competition among the maritime nations. We must be careful to avoid a race to grab and to hold the lands under the high seas. We must ensure that the deep seas and the ocean bottoms are, and remain, the legacy of all human beings.

President Lyndon Johnson, 1966

Problem Exercise

Skirting the coasts of most countries, the continental shelf covers about 8% of the ocean's breadth, spreading out below the sea and providing a fertile grounds for fisheries. The continental shelves soon drop off steeply into an area known as the deep seabed. Often more than 3,000 meters below sea level, the deep seabed is shaped by vast plains and occasionally broken by enormous ridges. Remarkably little is known of the biology of the deep seabed but its role in the larger ocean ecology is important. As nutrients drift down through the ocean's depths, they are gradually decomposed and reduced to basic nutrients. These nutrients are swept along the ocean floor by currents and eventually carried to the surface again by upwellings at the juncture of other currents and continental shelves. These upwellings provide a remarkably nutrient-rich basis for plankton, fish and seabird communities. In time their organic debris, too, drift down to the deep seabed again and the cycle is repeated. MYERS, GAIA: AN ATLAS OF PLANET MANAGEMENT 64–73 (1993).

The deep seabed contains rich mineral resources in the form of metallic muds and polymetallic nodules. Metallic muds are, as the name suggests, sediments rich in silver, copper and zinc. Polymetallic nodules, better known as manganese nodules, are potato-shaped rocks found scattered throughout the floors of the world's oceans. The nodules are formed very slowly through crystallization of sea water's minerals and salts. The nodules contain significant amounts of economically valuable minerals such as manganese, cobalt, copper and nickel. It has been estimated that 15 billion tons of high quality ore could be extracted from nodules in the northeast Pacific alone, exceeding many times over the estimated land-based reserves. Shao Ning, *Oceans conceal mineral riches*, CHINA DAILY, Aug. 14, 1993. Indeed, the estimated value of the ocean floor's mineral store has been estimated at $3 trillion. Viewed eagerly by mining interests as the earth's greatest untouched resource, the deep seabed's potential wealth has focused commercial and legal interest.

Most of the deep seabed lies beyond nations' 200 mile EEZ. The potentially richest area to mine manganese nodules lies in a band running from Baja California down to Hawaii. To date there have been no deep sea commercial-scale mining operations but hundreds of millions of dollars have been spent in research and exploration. The current nodule-gathering technology is closer to dredging than mining. A giant sieve or vacuum hose collects the nodules off the ocean floor and transports them up to the surface where the nodules are separated from the mud and dirty water and shipped to port for land-based processing.

Until the late 1960s, international law took little notice of the deep seabed because mining its minerals appeared as remote and technically difficult as mining on the moon. Article 24 of the 1958 Geneva Convention on the High Seas had required nations to prevent pollution of the seas from exploration and exploitation of the seabed, but issues of jurisdiction were never explicitly addressed. Through the 1960s and early 1970s, as mining technology advanced and the potential wealth of undersea riches became known, a number of prominent mining companies formed consortia to develop deep sea mining operations as an alternative to land-based resources. A number of the consortia signed agreements with their respective governments laying claims to portions of the ocean bed. This and other concerns over ocean resources led to a general call for further development of international law, championed in part by the Maltan delegate to the UN, Arvid Pardo. Developed countries sponsoring consortia wanted to resolve the problem of overlapping claims; developing countries sought to arrest the parceling out of the ocean floor before they were left out entirely.

To halt this checkerboard land grab, the General Assembly of the United Nations approved by consensus a Declaration of Principles in 1970. Res. 2749 (xxv), 17 Dec. 1970; *reprinted in* 10 I.L.M. 220–23 (1971).

> Declaration of Principles Governing the Seabed and the Ocean Floor, and the Subsoil Thereof, Beyond the Limits of National Jurisdiction
>
> *Affirming* that there is an area of the seabed and ocean floor, and the subsoil thereof, beyond the limits of national jurisdiction, the precise limits of which are yet to be determined,

Recognizing that the existing legal regime of the high seas does not provide substantive rules for regulating the exploration of the aforesaid area and the exploitation of its resources . . .

Solemnly declares that:

1. The sea-bed and ocean floor, and the subsoil thereof, beyond the limits of national jurisdiction, as well as the resources of the area, are the common heritage of mankind.

2. The area shall not be subject to appropriation by any means by States or persons, natural or juridical, and no State shall claim or exercise sovereignty or sovereign rights over any part thereof.

3. No State or person, natural or juridical, shall claim, exercise, or acquire rights with respect to the area or its resources incompatible with the international regime to be established and the principles of this Declaration. * * *

7. The exploration of the area and the exploitation of its resources shall be carried out for the benefit of mankind as a whole, irrespective of the geographical location of States, whether land-locked or coastal, and taking into particular consideration the interests and needs of the developing countries. * * *

The General Assembly resolution defined the deep seabed as the "common heritage of mankind." Yet this legal appellation had never been detailed in a treaty or binding convention. *See generally* Chapter 7, p. 389. The two traditional international legal doctrines of resource ownership are *res nullius* and *res communis*. *Res nullius* means property of no one— property which presently has no legally recognized owner because it has not yet been claimed or has been abandoned. Such property, while belonging to no one, can be claimed and exclusively owned. Claims to the "virgin land" of the American Wild West are an example. Applied to the deep seabed, *res nullius* would open the mineral resources to exploitation and exclusive claims on a first-come, first-serve basis. Such a regime would favor companies who had already prospected the best mining sites and would not involve obligations for revenue-sharing or technology transfer.

The doctrine of *res communis* is more closely linked to the common heritage of mankind. It means things common to all in areas beyond national borders—communal property which can be used by everyone but owned by no one. A classic example is the village common, where everyone can graze sheep but no one can set off a parcel of one's own. In the context of international law, states may not claim sovereignty over *res communis*. Some commentators have suggested that the doctrine of the common heritage of mankind goes beyond *res communis* by promoting substantive equality, i.e., States must not only act in a way that does not adversely affect the use of common resources by other States, but also must share the *benefits* of use. This doctrine would supersede *res communis* because it ensures that the benefits derived from the use of resources beyond the limits of national jurisdiction are equitably shared by all States. LI, TRANSFER OF TECHNOLOGY FOR DEEP SEABED MINING 45–46 (1994).

Part XI of UNCLOS established an international regime for the management of deep seabed mining and production of the metals found in seabed nodules—particularly manganese, cobalt, and nickel. The consequences for developing countries with mining industries were significant. If large quantities of these critical industrial metals could be extracted at a lower price than land-based minerals, then land-based mineral prices would drop, reducing foreign currency earnings. Conversely, mining deep seabed mineral resources had strategic importance for developed countries because it would lessen their dependence on importing land-based minerals from developing countries. The deal struck in Part XI softened the blow to developing countries.

Part XI created two new international bodies. A UN agency called the International Seabed Authority directed activities in the seabed: approving claims for seabed mining, setting production quotas, and managing technology transfer and revenue-sharing. The "operating arm," a quasi-private body called The Enterprise, has an entrepreneurial role: creating mining joint ventures with developing countries. Part XI also gave substance to the deep seabed's designation as the common heritage of mankind. If resources belong to all nations, it follows that some part of the benefits should flow to all nations, as well. As a result, Part XI required profit sharing and technology transfer. Article 140(2), 144(2)(a).

Subject to numerous compromises during the decade of its negotiation, UNCLOS had been negotiated by diplomats of the successive Nixon, Ford and Carter administrations. Following the election of President Reagan, however, in 1981 the U.S. government withdrew its support for Part XI and, because UNCLOS approval was "all-or-nothing," its support for the entire Convention. Criticizing Part XI as hostile to the free market, the Reagan Administration claimed the interests of American companies that had pioneered the exploration and development of seabed mining were not adequately protected. Seeking to protect long-term investments, the Administration officials charged that Part XI's supranational governance structure, revenue-sharing obligations, and mandatory technology transfer provisions were unacceptably burdensome. Statement of James Malone, Asst. Sec'y of State Designate for the Bureau of Oceans and Intl. Env. and Scientific Affairs, *Hearings Before the Subcomm. on Oceanography of the House Comm. on Merchant Marine,* 97th Cong., 1st sess., 636–37, Apr. 28, 1981.

The Reagan Administration's opposition to Part XI, renouncing the compromise arrangements negotiated by previous administrations, was extremely unpopular with other nations though perfectly legal. Until an agreement is signed and ratified it has no binding force, and the Reagan Administration viewed Part XI as antithetical to its free market policies.

Following the U.S. refusal to accept UNCLOS Part XI, the Reagan State Department faced a dilemma. The 1970 General Assembly Declaration and Principles on deep seabed mining, approved by the U.S., had identified the deep seabed as the "common heritage of mankind." UNCLOS Part XI had similarly declared the deep seabed to be the common heritage of mankind. The precise meaning of this phrase, however, had never been detailed in a treaty nor, prior to UNCLOS, had there been any legally binding agreement delineating jurisdiction over the seabed.

The U.S. had voted in favor of the 1970 General Assembly Declaration stating that the deep seabed is the common heritage of mankind. The current government position promoted deep seabed mining *without* international supervision or sharing of benefits, however, and might be seen in conflict with the Declaration. In reconciling the two positions, the State Department argued instead that deep seabed mining is a "freedom of the high seas." As the U.S. Ambassador to UNCLOS testified to the House of Representatives Committee on Merchant Marine and Fisheries in 1981:

> We agree with, and indeed participated in, the 1970 UN resolution declaring the resources of the deep seabed to be the common heritage of mankind.... It is our judgment, however, that the working premise of the meaning in a juridical sense of "the common heritage of mankind" as applied to the deep seabed, is that essentially of the regime of the freedom of the high seas, that is, that we would be in a position to explore and to exploit deep ocean resources under existing law.

Thus, the State Department contended that as with ocean fisheries, customary international law supports the unrestricted right of companies and nations to mine the resources of the deep seabed. Developing countries strongly opposed this interpretation.

As explained in Section I of this chapter, the doctrine of freedom of the high seas is the accepted basis of oceans law, permitting all nations to fish and navigate on the open ocean. Over time, the high seas freedoms have been expanded to other activities. The 1958 Geneva Convention on the High Seas, Article 2, states:

> The high seas being open to all nations, no State may validly purport to subject any part of them to its sovereignty. Freedom of the high seas is exercised under the conditions laid down by these articles and by the other rules of international law. It comprises, *inter alia*, both for coastal and non-coastal States:
>
> (1) Freedom of navigation;
>
> (2) Freedom of fishing;
>
> (3) Freedom to lay submarine cables and pipelines;
>
> (4) Freedom to fly over the high seas.

In defending its interpretation, the State Department argued that freedom of deep seabed mining was among the *"inter alia"* freedoms mentioned in the headnote of Article 2. To support this position, they pointed to Commentaries prepared by the International Law Commission. Similar to legislative histories prepared for U.S. legislation, the Commentaries are written by international law experts based on the negotiations leading to a treaty. Since they are not voted on by countries, they have no binding legal status but may be used to interpret the context and meaning of ambiguous treaty text. In reference to Article 2, the First Commentary stated in 1955:

> The list of freedoms of the high seas contained in this article is not restrictive; the Commission has merely specified four of the main freedoms. It is aware that there are other freedoms, such as freedom to explore or exploit the subsoil of the high seas and freedom to engage in scientific research therein. * * *

One year later, the Second Commentary on UNCLOS appeared to qualify its previous position, stating:

> The Commission has not made specific mention of the freedom to explore or exploit the subsoil of the high seas. It considered that apart from the case of the exploitation or exploration of the soil or subsoil of a continental shelf ... such

exploitation has not yet assumed sufficient practical importance to justify special regulation.

Article 1 of the 1958 Geneva Convention on the High Seas defines the term, "high seas," as "all parts of the sea that are not included in the territorial sea or in the internal waters of a State."

Assume you are a lawyer in the State Department's Office of Legal Advisor. Write a memo detailing arguments in favor of the United States position, taking into account the 1958 Geneva Convention on the High Seas, the 1970 General Assembly resolution, the freedom of the high seas doctrine, the UNCLOS provisions presented thus far, and the deep seabed's status as the common heritage of mankind. Detail the counter-arguments against your interpretation. Explain why this position may have important consequences for the development of international environmental law. *See* Jon Van Dyke & Christopher Yuen, *"Common Heritage" v. "Freedom of the High Seas,"* 19 San Diego L.Rev. 493, 497 (1982).

Postscript Despite the U.S. refusal to become a party to UNCLOS, diplomats continued to meet after 1984 to negotiate an acceptable regime for deep seabed mining. In 1994, the UN General Assembly adopted by consensus their compromise, the Agreement Relating to the Implementation of Part XI of the United Nations Convention on the Law of the Sea of 10 December 1982. A/RES/48/263, *reprinted in* 33 ILM 1309. The Agreement amends Part XI, keeping intact the basic organizational structure but removing most of the financial and technology transfer obligations.

While the institutional structure of the International Seabed Authority and the Enterprise changed little between 1982 and 1994, the 1994 Agreement fundamentally changed the financial arrangements. In contrast with the original requirements of Part XI, there are no longer any production limits on deep seabed mining, States are under no obligation to fund the joint ventures of the Enterprise, and technology transfer is not mandatory. Rather, the Enterprise and developing States are directed to obtain deep seabed mining technology on the open market or through joint ventures. If they cannot obtain the technology they seek, the International Seabed Authority may request contractors and sponsoring States to facilitate their acquisition of technology on fair and reasonable commercial terms, consistent with effective protection of intellectual property rights. As in the 1982 proposal, financial aid will be provided by an economic assistance fund to "developing land-based States whose economies have been determined to be seriously affected by the production of minerals from the deep seabed." How much and when the assistance will be granted is decided on a case-by-case basis.

As of October, 2001, the Convention remains in the Senate Foreign Relations Committee and awaits hearing. In the meantime, the work of the International Seabed Authority threatens U.S. mining rights as grants are continually distributed. In 1998, for example, an Australian mining company was granted a claim to exploit minerals in an area off the Coast of New Guinea. *Mining Company Finds New Quarry at Sea,* Sustainability Review, Feb. 1998, at 8. Ironically, the United States objected to becoming a party out of fear of international interests trumping national control but, as a result, U.S. mining companies stand to lose any claims to the long-term mining licenses that France, Russia and Japan are expected to receive. Shruti Ravikumar, *Adrift at Sea,* 22 HARV. INT'L REV. 2, July 1, 2000.

QUESTIONS AND DISCUSSION

1. During the 1980s, a number of scholars held out the common heritage of mankind principle, and its application in Part XI, as providing the basis for a new form of international environmental law in the global commons. Consider the following excerpt from Philip Allott.

> At least until the 1982 Convention, the law of the sea has contained nothing other than the international aggregate of aggregated national interests. At least until very recently, there has been no possibility of forming international social objectives in relation to the use of the world's sea space, other than as by-products of international-national aggregation. And hence there has been no question of forming international law as the realization of genuinely international social objectives formed by humanity as a whole from the consideration of the world sea space as a whole.
>
> It has taken time, and it will take an intellectual effort, to make a change of perspective in relation to the social organization of the world. It involves transferring the notional center of gravity of international society from the level of the state systems to the level of the totality of humanity, from the level of the separate national territories to the level of the whole earth.

Philip Allott, *Mare Nostrum: A New International Law of the Sea*, in FREEDOM OF THE HIGH SEAS, *op. cit.* at 58.

After the 1994 Agreement, where the cost-sharing requirements of Part XI were dropped as a result of U.S. pressure, what is left of the common heritage of mankind principle? The Framework Convention on Climate Change and the Biodiversity Agreement use the phrase, "common concern of humanity," instead of the common heritage of mankind principle. Does this mean the common heritage of mankind principle is dead? See Chapter 7 for a more detailed discussion of these issues.

2. Viewed in isolation, the diplomatic activity surrounding deep seabed mining over the last two decades has not had much practical relevance. The first proposal for commercial-scale mining on the deep sea floor was announced in late 1997. Nautilus Minerals Corp., a Papua New Guinea company run by Australians announced their intentions for a major mining operation off the coast of Papua New Guinea in Papuan waters from 3900 to 5600 feet deep. Interest in deep seabed mining is still strong in other regions, as well; for example, both Japan and China continue to dedicate significant resources in prospecting and extraction technology. Indeed the Japanese Agency of Industrial Science and Technology has established a full-scale experimental mining operation in the waters south of Tokyo. The Agency predicts that practical technologies for mining manganese nodules will be employed by 2010 and that exploitation of deep sea hydrothermal deposits and their cobalt-rich crusts will follow soon after. NIKKEI WEEKLY, April 29, 1996.

Viewed in the context of UNCLOS, despite its lack of current economic significance, deep seabed mining proved to be the deal-breaker. Indeed U.S. reservations over deep seabed mining provisions delayed its signing of UNCLOS for 12 years. Comparing the financial obligations on mining companies in the original Part XI of UNCLOS with the 1994 Agreement provides a clear illustration of the dramatic change in prevailing government economic policies since the 1980s, mirroring the shift from support of strong international agencies and mandatory donor programs to an emphasis on free market policies and weaker international institutions.

3. Clearly, scouring the seabed with a giant vacuum or sieve will have significant impacts on the ocean floor, burying and crushing many organisms and harming the ocean floor habitat. This practice has been compared to forest clear-cutting and would be particularly harmful to slow-reproducing organisms. Depending on the scale of the mining operations, the surface discharge of waste water containing particulate matter and trace metals could create "sediment plumes," blocking light penetration and reducing photosynthetic activity in the surface layers and limiting phytoplankton production, the base of the ocean surface food chain. The impact of these plumes on photosynthesis would also reduce oxygen generation, potentially affecting fish populations. The most promising mining areas lie beneath large commercial fisheries, and the impact could be economically important since it may take years for the discharged sediment to settle downward. FRANK, DEEPSEA MINING AND THE ENVIRONMENT 11, 15 (1976). Since deep seabed mining is not yet practiced on a commercial scale, the gravity of these environmental harms remains hypothetical. Part XI makes specific provisions for environmental protection.

UNCLOS, Article 145

Protection of the Marine Environment

Necessary measures shall be taken in accordance with this Convention with respect to activities in the Area to ensure effective protection for the marine environment from harmful effects which may arise from such activities. To this end the Authority shall adopt appropriate rules, regulations and procedures for inter alia:

(a) the prevention, reduction and control of pollution and other hazards to the marine environment, including the coastline, and of interference with the ecological balance of the marine environment, particular attention being paid to the need for protection from harmful effects of such activities as drilling, dredging, excavation, disposal of waste, construction and operation or maintenance of installations, pipelines and other devices related to such activities;

(b) the protection and conservation of the natural resources of the Area and the prevention of damage to the flora and fauna of the marine environment.

The International Seabed Authority holds the power "to issue emergency orders, which may include orders for the suspension or adjustment of operations, to prevent serious harm to the marine environment arising out of activities in the Area," and to "disapprove areas for exploitation by contractors or the Enterprise in cases where substantial evidence indicates the risk of serious harm to the marine environment." Article 162, 2(w), 2(x). The 1994 Agreement adds an explicit requirement for environmental impact assessments.

An application for approval of a plan of work shall be accompanied by an assessment of the potential environmental impacts of the proposed activities and by a description of a programme for oceanographic and baseline environmental studies in accordance with the rules, regulations and procedures adopted by the Authority.

Section 1, Article 7. No environmental regulations and procedures have yet been promulgated. Since so little is known of deep seabed biology, accurately assessing environmental impacts will be difficult.

4. Do you think seabed mining operations should be required to share revenues and technologies with developing countries because the deep seabed is part of the global commons and developing country export markets might be harmed? Does resource extraction of a "common heritage of mankind" status impose any practical obligations? Should there be revenue and technology sharing in the following cases?

- a drug company manufactures a very popular sunscreen cream whose active ingredient is derived from the "waffle fish," a flounder that lives on the floor of the deep seabed in the middle of the Pacific Ocean;

- same as above, only the sale of waffle fish sunscreen will likely reduce manufacturers' need for aloe X, the main export crop of several developing countries.

If you have already studied the biodiversity arguments for revenue sharing in Chapter 13, do you think the argument for revenue sharing of deep seabed resources is stronger or weaker? Does it depend on whether the resources are fish or minerals?

5. The ultimate scale of deep seabed mining will depend on technological development and, more important, the related cost of land-based mineral resources. Only when deep seabed minerals are comparable in price will sea mining operations become profitable. As a result of recent developments in land-based mineral extraction technologies, mining low-grade resources has become even cheaper, pushing further in the future high resource prices needed to make deep seabed mining commercially viable. Indeed, over the last century commodity prices have steadily dropped in real terms as extraction and distribution technologies have become increasingly efficient. Predictions for when deep seabed mining will become commercially viable range from the year 2005 to beyond the year 2080. Statement of Sally Ann Lentz, Co–Director of Ocean Advocates, Before the Subcomm. on Oceanography, Gulf of Mexico and Outer Continental Shelf of the Merchant Marine and Fisheries Comm, Concerning the UN Law of the Sea Treaty and Reauthorization of the Deep Seabed Hard Minerals Act., Apr. 26, 1994.

6. A special court for UNCLOS, the International Tribunal for the Law of the Sea, was established in Hamburg, Germany. Parties engaged in maritime disputes may take their cases to the Tribunal for binding decision. Part XI provided for the creation of the Sea–Bed Chamber, a special panel within the International Tribunal for deep seabed mining disputes.

————

Suggested Further Reading and Web Sites

Colin Woodard, OCEAN'S END

Carl Safina, SONG FOR THE BLUE OCEAN

Two beautifully written, carefully researched books on threats to marine fisheries. If you only read one book on the subject it should one of these.

J.R. McGoodwin, CRISIS IN THE WORLD'S FISHERIES: PEOPLE, PROBLEMS AND POLICIES (1990)

Good treatment of the causes and consequences of overfishing.

R.I. Friedheim, NEGOTIATING THE NEW OCEAN REGIME (1993)

R.R. Churchill and A.V. Lowe, THE LAW OF THE SEA (1988)

One of the classic treatments of UNCLOS.

Elizabeth Mann Borghese and Norton Ginsburg, eds., OCEAN YEARBOOK

A comprehensive review of ocean law and policy published annually.

Jon Van Dyke et al., eds., Freedom for the Seas in the 21st Century (1993)

A comprehensive and readable treatment of the whole range of environmental issues confronting oceans law and governance.

Ocean Development and International Law

This journal often carries very good articles on marine environmental issues.

http://www.un.org/Depts/los/index.htm

Homepage of the UNCLOS Secretariat. Contains useful official information and documents.

http://www.oceanlaw.org/index.html

Homepage of the Council on Ocean Law. Contains useful background information on UNCLOS and commentaries.

http://aloha.net/lsi/seaweb.htm

Homepage of the Law of the Sea Institute, particularly useful for its large number of hypertext links to other relevant oceans Web sites.

CHAPTER ELEVEN

FRESHWATER RESOURCES

SECTION I.   INTRODUCTION

The resolution of competing uses over scarce fresh water supplies promises to be one of the major challenges for the next century. Water, like other natural resources, not only has a commercial value, but also an environmental and social value not readily determined by or reflected in market prices. Access to water is a basic necessity for all people, both for direct consumption and as an integral part of agricultural production. As water becomes more scarce and as the price of water increases, the poor may find their access to water more limited. Environmental uses of water (for example, as habitat for fish or as recreation) may also suffer.

International law has long addressed issues relating to freshwater resources, primarily in the transnational context. Over 200 river basins in the world are shared by more than one country. Many major rivers, such as the Amazon, Nile, Rhine and Mekong involve five or more countries. These shared watercourses can give rise to significant bilateral or multilateral disputes, particularly in a time of scarcity. Such disputes have given rise to a relatively rich body of customary law as well as numerous treaties and other instruments.

In recent years, international policymakers have expanded their concern from transboundary issues to the general adequacy and conditions of the planet's freshwater resources. According to the 1997 *UN Freshwater Assessment,* humans are currently using about "half the 12,500 cubic kilometers of water that is readily available." Yet, population is expected to double in the next 50 years and water consumption has increased in the 1900s at twice the rate of population. If this pattern of water use continues, little water will be left for "instream uses," such as maintaining healthy ecosystems, facilitating navigation or recreation, and generating hydroelectric power.

As bleak as the global picture may be, the situation is even more critical in certain countries and regions. Water is allocated unequally across the planet, and many countries with a significant portion of the world's population do not have secure access to adequate supplies of freshwater. The *UN Freshwater Assessment* found that 460 million people, more than 8 per cent of the world's population, live in countries facing serious water shortages. A further one-quarter of the world's population live in countries where water shortages are likely to become serious in the future. Access to freshwater is in fact one of the most pressing environmental, economic and health issues facing many developing countries.

A.   THE STATE OF THE PLANET'S FRESH WATER RESOURCES

As Sandra Postel has observed, freshwater has four basic attributes that make its management fundamentally different than that for other natural resources. Perhaps most obvious, freshwater is essential to life. Moreover, unlike other important natural resources such as copper or oil, water is not substitutable for most uses (try watering crops without water...). Third, while water is a renewable resource because of the hydrological cycle, it is finite at any given time; indeed the supply of water per capita has more than halved since 1950. Finally, water is not evenly distributed in time or place. Over 90% of freshwater is locked in the polar regions as ice, and much of the remaining renewable water runs off the land in floods and cannot be used. As part of the recent attention on global water resources, the Commission on Sustainable Development requested a comprehensive assessment of global freshwater resources. The following excerpt from that assessment summarizes their global status.

Comprehensive Assessment of the Freshwater Resources of the World, E/CN.17/1997/9, at 4–6 (Feb. 4, 1997) [hereinafter UN Freshwater Assessment]

1.   The assessment presented in the present report shows that in many countries, both developing and developed, current pathways for water use are often not sustainable. There is clear and convincing evidence that the world faces a worsening series of local and regional water quantity and quality problems, largely as a result of poor water allocation, wasteful use of the resource, and lack of adequate management action. Water resource constraints and water degradation are weakening one of the resource bases on which human society is built.

2.   Water use has been growing at more than twice the rate of the population increase during this century, and already a number of regions are chronically water-short. About one-third of the world's population lives in countries that are experiencing moderate to high water stress partly resulting from increasing demands from a growing population and human activities. By

the year 2025, as much as two-thirds of the world population could be under stress conditions.

3. Water shortages and pollution are causing widespread public health problems, limiting economic and agricultural development, and harming a wide range of ecosystems. They may put global food supplies in jeopardy, and lead to economic stagnation in many areas of the world. The result could be a series of local and regional water crises with global implications. * * *

5. There is a steady increase in the number of regions of the world where human demands are outstripping local water supplies, and the resulting water stress is limiting development, especially of poor societies. Owing largely to poverty, at least one fifth of all people do not have access to safe drinking water, and more than one half of humanity lacks adequate sanitation. At any given time, an estimated one half of the people in developing countries suffer from water-and food-related diseases caused either directly by infection, or indirectly by disease-carrying organisms that breed in water and food.

6. Water demands are so high that a number of large rivers decrease in volume as they flow downstream, with the result that downstream users face shortages, and ecosystems suffer, both in the rivers and in adjacent coastal areas. [Five of Asia's great rivers now run dry and in 2001, for the first time, the Rio Grande went dry.] Many underground water resources, known collectively as groundwater, are being drained faster than nature can replenish them.

7. A growing number of the world's rivers, lakes and groundwater aquifers are being severely contaminated by human, industrial and agricultural wastes. Not only does the pollution affect freshwater quality, but much of it flows into the world's oceans, threatening marine life. The future health of the oceans depend heavily on how the freshwater systems are managed.

8. High withdrawals of water, and heavy pollution loads have already caused widespread harm to a number of ecosystems. This has resulted in a wide range of health effects, in which humans have been harmed by eating food from contaminated ecosystems. Reproductive failures and death in various wildlife species, particularly at higher levels in the food chain, are being reported in various regions of the world. In addition, rising human demands will put increasing pressure on ecosystems. As more water is withdrawn for human uses, there is an increasing need to make certain that an adequate water supply to wetlands, lakes, rivers and coastal areas is maintained to ensure the healthy functioning of ecosystems. * * *

12. There are driving forces of change that could make water problems worse, unless actions are taken. Those forces include a world population that is now at 5.7 billion, and is heading towards a figure of 8.3 billion by the year 2025. Much of this increase will be in the rapidly growing urban areas of developing countries, many of which are already experiencing serious water stress.

13. Another driving force will be increasing consumption of food and industrial goods produced using water. Irrigation [for agriculture] already accounts for 70 per cent of the water taken from lakes, rivers and underground sources, and there will be pressure to use more water to produce food for the increasing population. An increasing number of water-short countries will have to make choices about the amount of water they allocate for food production as compared with other uses. They may find that limited water resources are more profitably invested in producing goods that can be exported to buy food, rather than in trying to grow all their food at home Countries will also face increasing demands for water supplies for industrial development, hydroelectric genera-

tion, navigation, recreation and domestic use. Unless development stays within the limits of water supplies, shortages could hamper economic development.

***

Agenda 21 also included a chapter on freshwater resources that explores these issues in greater detail.

Report of the United Nations Conference on Environment and Development, A/CONF.151/26 (Vol. II), ch. 18 (Aug. 13, 1992), (*Protection of the Quality and Supply of Freshwater Resources*)

A.   Integrated Water Resources Development and Management

Basis for action

18.6.   The extent to which water resources development contributes to economic productivity and social well-being is not usually appreciated, although all social and economic activities rely heavily on the supply and quality of freshwater. * * * The holistic management of freshwater as a finite and vulnerable resource, and the integration of sectoral water plans and programmes within the framework of national economic and social policy, are of paramount importance for action in the 1990s and beyond. The fragmentation of responsibilities for water resources development among sectoral agencies is proving, however, to be an even greater impediment to promoting integrated water management than had been anticipated. Effective implementation and coordination mechanisms are required. * * *

B.   Water Resources Assessment

18.23.   Water resources assessment, including the identification of potential sources of freshwater supply, comprises the continuing determination of sources, extent, dependability and quality of water resources and of the human activities that affect those resources. Such assessment constitutes the practical basis for their sustainable management and a prerequisite for evaluation of the possibilities for their development. There is, however, growing concern that at a time when more precise and reliable information is needed about water resources, hydrologic services and related bodies are less able than before to provide this information, especially information on groundwater and water quality. Major impediments are the lack of financial resources for water resources assessment, the fragmented nature of hydrologic services and the insufficient numbers of qualified staff. At the same time, the advancing technology for data capture and management is increasingly difficult to access for developing countries. Establishment of national databases is, however, vital to water resources assessment and to mitigation of the effects of floods, droughts, desertification and pollution. * * *

C.   Protection of Water Resources, Water Quality and Aquatic Ecosystems

18.35.   Freshwater is a unitary resource. Long-term development of global freshwater requires holistic management of resources and a recognition of the interconnectedness of the elements related to freshwater and freshwater quality. There are few regions of the world that are still exempt from problems of loss of potential sources of freshwater supply, degraded water quality and pollution of surface and groundwater sources. Major problems affecting the water quality of rivers and lakes arise, in variable order of importance according to different situations, from inadequately treated domestic sewage, inadequate controls on the discharges of industrial waste waters, loss and destruction of catchment areas, ill-considered siting of industrial plants, deforestation, uncontrolled shifting cultivation and poor agricultural practices. This gives rise to the leaching of nutrients and pesticides. Aquatic ecosystems are disturbed and living freshwater resources are threatened. Under certain circumstances, aquatic ecosystems are also affected by agricultural water resource development projects such as dams, river diversions, water installations and irrigation schemes. Erosion, sedimentation, deforestation and desertification have led to increased land degradation, and the creation of reservoirs has, in some cases, resulted in adverse effects on ecosystems. Many of these problems have arisen from a development model that is environmentally destructive and from a lack of public awareness and education about surface and groundwater resource protection. Ecological and human health effects are the measurable consequences, although the means to monitor them are inadequate or non-existent in many countries. There is a widespread lack of perception of the linkages between the development, management, use and treatment of water resources and aquatic ecosystems. A preventive approach, where appropriate, is crucial to the avoiding of costly subsequent measures to rehabilitate, treat and develop new water supplies.* * *

D. Drinking-water Supply and Sanitation

18.47. Safe water-supplies and environmental sanitation are vital for protecting the environment, improving health and alleviating poverty. Safe water is also crucial to many traditional and cultural activities. An estimated 80 per cent of all diseases and over one third of deaths in developing countries are caused by the consumption of contaminated water, and on average as much as one tenth of each person's productive time is sacrificed to water-related diseases. Concerted efforts during the 1980s brought water and sanitation services to hundreds of millions of the world's poorest people. One in three people in the developing world still lacks these two most basic requirements for health and dignity. It is also recognized that human excreta and sewage are important causes of the deterioration of water-quality in developing countries, and the introduction of available technologies, including appropriate technologies, and the construction of sewage treatment facilities could bring significant improvement. * * *

E. Water and Sustainable Urban Development

18.56. Early in the next century, more than half of the world's population will be living in urban areas. By the year 2025, that proportion will have risen to 60 per cent, comprising some 5 billion people. Rapid urban population growth and industrialization are putting severe strains on the water resources and environmental protection capabilities of many cities. Special attention needs to be given to the growing effects of urbanization on water demands and usage and to the critical role played by local and municipal authorities in managing the supply, use and overall treatment of water, particularly in developing countries for which special support is needed. Scarcity of freshwater resources and the escalating costs of developing new resources have a considerable impact on national industrial, agricultural and human settlement development and economic growth. Better management of urban water resources, including the elimination of unsustainable consumption patterns, can make a substantial contribution to the alleviation of poverty and improvement of the health and quality of life of the urban and rural poor. A high proportion of large urban agglomerations are located around estuaries and in coastal zones. Such an arrangement leads to pollution from municipal and industrial discharges combined with overexploitation of available water resources and threatens the marine environment and the supply of freshwater resources. * * *

F.   Water for Sustainable Food Production and Rural Development

18.65.   Sustainability of food production increasingly depends on sound and efficient water use and conservation practices consisting primarily of irrigation development and management, including water management with respect to rain-fed areas, livestock water-supply, inland fisheries and agro-forestry. Achieving food security is a high priority in many countries, and agriculture must not only provide food for rising populations, but also save water for other uses. The challenge is to develop and apply water-saving technology and management methods and, through capacity-building, enable communities to introduce institutions and incentives for the rural population to adopt new approaches, for both rain-fed and irrigated agriculture. The rural population must also have better access to a potable water-supply and to sanitation services. It is an immense task but not an impossible one, provided appropriate policies and programmes are adopted at all levels—local, national and international. While significant expansion of the area under rain-fed agriculture has been achieved during the past decade, the productivity response and sustainability of irrigation systems have been constrained by problems of waterlogging and salinization. Financial and market constraints are also a common problem. Soil erosion, mismanagement and overexploitation of natural resources and acute competition for water have all influenced the extent of poverty, hunger and famine in the developing countries. Soil erosion caused by overgrazing of livestock is also often responsible for the siltation of lakes. Most often, the development of irrigation schemes is supported neither by environmental impact assessments identifying hydrologic consequences within watersheds of interbasin transfers, nor by the assessment of social impacts on peoples in river valleys.

Section II.   The Law of International Watercourses

Despite the growing focus on the total availability of freshwater and the need to ensure access to freshwater, most international law with respect to freshwater relates to transboundary or shared watercourses. Not surprisingly, transboundary rivers and lakes have long been a focus of international law.

The potential for conflict is enormous. Globally, 47 per cent of all land falls within international river basins, and nearly 50 countries on four continents have more than three-quarters of their total land in international river basins. Two hundred and fourteen basins are multinational, including 57 in Africa and 48 in Europe.

In human terms, this means that almost 40 per cent of the world's population lives in international river basins. These two billion people are dependent on the cooperation of all the countries sharing the basin for a guaranteed water supply of consistent quality, and for their environmental stability.

Thirteen river basins are shared by five or more countries. Ten are shared mostly by developing countries, and have few or no treaties to regulate water use; and a number are in areas where water is otherwise scarce. It is not surprising that many [shared rivers] have a history of international tension, particularly the Jordan and Euphrates in the Near and Middle East; the Ganges in Asia; the Nile in Africa; and the Colorado and Rio Grande in North America.

In developed countries, many international agreements have been drawn up to regulate shared basin areas and, as a result, use of shared water supplies is more rarely a source of international dispute. Europe, for instance, has four river basins shared by four or more countries, but these are regulated by no less than 175 treaties.

An absence of regulation on shared water resources is common in developing countries. Africa, in comparison to Europe, has a vast and complex system of river basins: 12 are shared by four or more nations, but only 34 treaties regulate their use. In Asia, only 31 treaties have been drawn up to regulate the five basins shared by four or more countries.

R. Clarke, WATER: THE INTERNATIONAL CRISIS, 91–92 (1993).

In addition to the number of river-basin treaties mentioned in the excerpt above, a relatively rich body of customary law, as well as several treaties of more general applicability currently address the law of international watercourses. This law of international watercourses is often viewed as a separate field from international environmental law. It is concerned with the development and optimal use of the watercourse as much as, or perhaps even more than, the protection of the environment. In particular, the international law of watercourses is concerned with two broad issues: (1) how should uses of the water in a transboundary lake or river be allocated between the two or more States of the watershed; and (2) what procedural rights and responsibilities accrue to States sharing a watershed. In more recent years, concern over the environment has begun to add another dimension to the international law of watercourses. What are the responsibilities to other States and perhaps to the international community generally to protect the environment of transboundary watersheds? Some argue that these environmental obligations are simply a subset of the general issue of what uses are allowed in a shared watercourse, while others believe that environmental obligations coming from the field of international environmental law may be in addition to any obligations between the riparian States.

The history of international cooperation in water issues dates back to the sixteenth century. *See* James L. Westcoat Jr., *Main Currents in Early Multilateral Water Treaties: A Historical–Geographic Perspective, 1648– 1948,* 7 COLO. J. ENVTL. L. & POL'Y 39 (1996). Throughout much of this time, water was viewed solely as an economic resource and the goals of international cooperation were to ensure free navigation and allow the shared use of the waters for fishing, agriculture or industry.

Difficulty in allocating economic uses between States led to several important international decisions that shaped the development of the international law of watercourses. These have included, most notably, the 1957 Lac Lanoux Arbitration (Spain v. France), 12 R. Int'l Arb. Awards 281 (1956) November 16, 1957, *reprinted in* 24 I.L.R. 101 (1957), which is described below, and the 1969 Gut Dam Claims (Canada v. United States), *reprinted in* 8 I.L.M. 114 (1969).

A.   CUSTOMARY LAW OF INTERNATIONAL WATERCOURSES

1.   LAC LANOUX ARBITRATION

The Lac Lanoux Arbitration involved a conflict over use of the waters of Lac Lanoux, lying near the border between France and Spain. The following facts are taken from the Arbitral Proceedings:

Lac Lanoux Arbitration (Spain v. France), **12 R.**
Int'l Arb. Awards 281 (1956), November 16,
1957, *reprinted in* **24 I.L.R. 101 (1957)**

This arbitration concerned the use of the waters of Lake Lanoux, in the Pyrenees. Briefly the French Government proposed to carry out certain works for the utilization for the waters of the lake and the Spanish Government feared that these works would adversely affect Spanish rights and interests, contrary to the Treaty of Bayonne of May 26, 1866, between France and Spain and the Additional Act of the same date. In any event, it was claimed that, under the Treaty, such works could not be undertaken without the previous agreement of both parties.

Lake Lanoux lies on the southern slopes of the Pyrenees, on French territory. It is fed by streams which have their source in French territory and which run entirely through French territory only. Its waters emerge only by the Font–Vive stream, which forms one of the headwaters of the River Carol. That river, after flowing approximately 25 kilometres from Lake Lanoux through French territory crosses the Spanish frontier at Puigcerda and continues to flow through Spain for about 6 kilometres before joining the river Segre, which ultimately flows into the Ebro. Before entering Spanish territory, the waters of the Carol feed the Canal of Puigcerda which is the private property of that town. * * *

The French development scheme for Lake Lanoux comprised, in essence, the following features: Without modifying the springs and the system of streams feeding the lake, the latter would be transformed, in particular by the formation of a dam, so as to enable it to accumulate a quantity of water which would increase its capacity form 17 to 70 million cubic metres. The waters of the lake, which run naturally by a tributary stream of the Carol and thence flow towards Spain, would normally cease to follow that course. They could be used to produce electric energy by a diversion which would lead them towards the Ariege, a tributary of the Garonne. Those waters would then go on to lose themselves in the Atlantic Ocean and not, as previously, in the Mediterranean. In order to compensate for this prior abstraction of the waters feeding the Carol, an underground replacement tunnel would lead a part of the waters of the Ariege to the Carol, to which those waters would be restored in French territory upstream from the intake of the Canal of Puigcerda.

This scheme, then, envisaged the construction of a large reservoir at the very favourable site of Lake Lanoux, to utilize the waters accumulated there after falling a considerable distance and to restore to the Carol, by drawing it from the Ariege, a quantity of water equal to that which was brought to Lake Lanoux by springs and the natural system of streams.

[Thus, the French system promised to deliver exactly the same amount of water to Spain. Moreover, Spain did not argue that the quality of the water would somehow be different. As a result, the tribunal did not find any injury to the quality or quantity of waters delivered to Spain. The Tribunal described Spain's arguments in the following way: "Actually it seems that the Spanish argument is twofold and relates, on the one hand, to the prohibition, in the absence of the consent of the other Party, of compensation between two basins, despite the equivalence of what is diverted and what is restored, and, on the other hand, the prohibition, without the consent of the other Party, of all acts which may create by a *de facto* inequality the physical possibility of a violation of rights."

Both of these arguments were rejected by the tribunal. With respect to Spain's argument that the existing treaties and international common law required the river basin to be treated as one unit and that water could not be exported out of the basin to be replaced by water from another basin, the tribunal found:]

The Tribunal does not overlook the reality, from the point of view of physical geography, of each river basin, which constitutes, as the Spanish Memorial ... maintains, "a unit". But this observation does not authorize the absolute consequences that the Spanish argument would draw from it. The unity of a basin is sanctioned at the juridical level only to the extent that it corresponds to human realities. The water which by nature constitutes a fungible item may be the object of a restitution which does not change its qualities in regard to human needs. A diversion with restitution, such as that envisaged by the French project, does not change a state of affairs organized for the working of the requirements of a social life.

[Spain's second argument, as described by the tribunal, was essentially that France's control over the rivers threatened Spain's national security. Today, we might consider this an issue of environmental security, see chapter 18. In any event, the Tribunal found that nothing prohibited France from pursuing its own interests in ways that might give it the physical and technical ability to harm Spain later.

Spain argued that upstream users did not have the right to alter the natural flows of the water delivered to downstream users. According to Spain:]

The restoration of the equivalent of the abstracted water, as it is projected in the Electricite de France scheme, implies that the water would no longer flow naturally in its own course, the physical cause of its present flowing being supplanted and replace by the will of one country only as much in the abstraction of the waters of Lake Lanoux as in the restoration of an eventual equivalent previously taken from the Ariege. This unilateral modification of the physical cause of the present flow of the Carol and the substitution for its hydraulic substance of another, of differing provenance, would transform the waters of the river basin which are common by nature into waters for the predominant use of one country, thus establishing a physical predominance which does not today exist, as is shown by the fact that the water flows today according to physical [natural] laws, whereas after the scheme has been completed its eventual equivalent will be restored solely by the work of the human will which abstracted it.

[Thus, Spain was concerned about the "physical predominance" gained by France over the resource. In short, the artificial delivery of water, controlled by another State, threatened the national integrity of Spain, because France could turn off the water at any time. The tribunal found the following:]

Elsewhere, the Spanish Government has contested the legitimacy of the works carried out on the territory of one of the signatory States of the Treaty and of the Additional Act, if the works are of such a nature as to permit that State, albeit in violation of its international pledges, to bring pressure to bear on the other signatory. This rule would derive from the fact that the Treaties concerned confirm the principle of equality between States. Concretely, Spain considers that France has not the right to bring about, by works of public utility, the physical possibility of cutting off the flow of the waters of the Lanoux or the restitution of an equivalent quantity of water. It is not the task of this Tribunal to pronounce judgment on the motives or the experiences which may have led the Spanish Government to voice certain misgivings. But it is not alleged that the works in question have as their object, apart from satisfying French interests, the creation of a means of injuring, at least contingently, Spanish interest; that would be all the more improbable since France could only partially dry up the resources that constitute the flow of the Carol, since she would affect also all the French lands that are irrigated by the Carol and since she would expose herself along the entire boundary to formidable reprisals. * * *

In any case, we do not find ... in international common law, any rule that forbids one State, acting to safeguard its legitimate interests, to put itself in a situation which would in fact permit it, in violation of its international pledges, seriously to injure a neighbouring State.

[Finally, the Tribunal rejected Spain's argument that France was required to receive Spain's prior consent before undertaking the project. In rejecting the necessity of reaching a prior agreement, however, the Tribunal did endorse the concept that States must notify neighboring affected states and negotiate in good faith:]

Before proceeding to an examination of the Spanish argument, the Tribunal believes it will be useful to make some very general observations on the nature of the obligations involved against the French Government. To admit that jurisdiction in a certain field can no longer be exercised except on the condition of, or by way of, an agreement between two States, is to place an essential restriction on the sovereignty of a State, and such restriction could only be admitted if there were clear and convincing evidence. Without doubt, international practice does reveal some special cases in which this hypothesis has become reality; thus, sometimes two States exercise conjointly jurisdiction over certain territories; likewise, in certain international arrangements, the representatives of States exercise conjointly a certain jurisdiction in the name of those States or in the name of organizations. But these cases are exceptional, and international judicial decisions are slow to recognize their existence, especially when they impair the territorial sovereignty of a State, as would be the case in the present matter.

In effect, in order to appreciate in its essence the necessity for prior agreement, one must envisage the hypothesis in which the interested States cannot reach agreement. In such case, it must be admitted that the State which is normally competent has lost its right to act alone as a result of the unconditional and arbitrary opposition of another State. This amounts to admitting a "right of assent," a "right of veto," which at the discretion of one State paralyses the exercise of the territorial jurisdiction of another.

That is why international practice prefers to resort to less extreme solutions by confining itself to obliging the States to seek, by preliminary negotiations, terms for an agreement, without subordinating the exercise of their competencies to the conclusion of such an agreement. Thus, one speaks, although often inaccurately, of the "obligation of negotiating an agreement." In reality, the engagements thus undertaken by States take very diverse forms and have a scope which varies according to the manner in which they are defined and according to the procedures intended for their execution; but the reality of the obligations thus undertaken is incontestable and sanctions can be applied in the event, for example, of an unjustified breaking off of the discussions, abnormal delays, disregard of the agreed procedures, systematic refusals to take into consideration adverse proposals or interests, and, more generally, in cases of violation of the rules of good faith. . . .

[The Tribunal found find that France had met its obligation to provide notice to Spain of the potential impacts of the project. It also found that France was under an obligation to take into account the interests of Spain in designing and implementing the project. The Tribunal found:]

France is entitled to exercise her rights; she cannot ignore Spanish interests.

Spain is entitled to demand that her rights be respected and that her interests be taken into consideration.

As a matter of form, the upstream State has, procedurally, a right of initiative; it is not obliged to associate the downstream State in the elaboration of its schemes. If, in the course of discussions, the downstream State submits schemes to it, the upstream State must examine them, but it has the right to give preference to the solution contained in its own scheme provided that it takes into consideration in a reasonable manner the interests of the downstream State.

In this regard, the Lac Lanoux Tribunal upheld France's claims to assert dominion over waters within its jurisdiction, without reaching any formal agreement with downstream users. The Tribunal appeared to uphold general obligations to notify downstream users and to take their interests into account through good faith negotiations. These obligations are discussed further in Chapter 7, pages 430–432, and again below with respect to the 1997 UN Convention on Nonnavigational Uses of Transboundary Watercourses.

QUESTIONS AND DISCUSSION

1. Although the Lac Lanoux arbitration seemed to grant broad rights to the upstream States in using an international river, the case had an unusual set of facts. Because France fully replaced the diverted waters, Spain failed to allege any actual injury due to reduced flows or changes in water quality. Moreover, because France had made significant changes in the scheme to ensure that an equal amount of water would be delivered to Spain, the Tribunal believed France adequately took Spanish interests fully into account. Consider these issues as you review the more recent dispute between Hungary and Slovakia over the Gabcikovo dam and the 1997 UN Convention on Nonnavigational Uses of Transboundary Watercourses, below.

2. In part, the Lac Lanoux holding depended on a view of water as a totally fungible resource. Today, given our increased knowledge and concern with the ecological role of water, would the tribunal find that bringing water from another basin was equivalent and caused no harm? Would we expect a brief on the part of Spain to contain more thorough analyses regarding the quality of water and the introduction of alien species? How would the emerging practice at least in the western United States to prohibit interbasin transfers of water aid Spain's arguments? *See, e.g., Or. Rev. Stat. 537.810* (1989).

---

2. THE GABCIKOVO–NAGYMOROS DECISION

The construction of the Gabcikovo and Nagymoros dams on the Danube River sparked one of the most controversial transboundary environmental disputes in Europe, and the case presented the International Court of Justice with an opportunity to issue a broader decision on international environmental law and international water law.

Hungary and then-Czechoslovakia agreed in 1977 to build a series of dams on the Danube River. *See* Czechoslovakia–Hungary Treaty Concerning the Construction and Operation of the Gabcikovo Nagymaros System of Locks, 1109 U.N.T.S. 235, Treaty No. 17134, done at Budapest, September 16, 1977, *reprinted in* 32 I.L.M. 1247 (1993). During the political transformation from communism in 1989, Hungary suspended construction of the downstream dam (called Nagymaros), which was totally located in Hungarian territory. In 1992, Hungary unilaterally terminated the agreement. Slovakia rejected Hungary's efforts at terminating the treaty and continued the Gabcikovo project, after changing the original design so the dam could be built entirely on Slovak territory. Slovakia's version of the Gabcikovo project was dubbed "Variant C" and was completed in 1992. As part of Variant C, Slovakia unilaterally diverted a substantial part of the Danube River's flow away from the Hungarian–Slovak border.

Hungary and Slovakia ultimately agreed to bring their dispute to the ICJ, resulting in the following decision by the Court.

Case Concerning the Gabcikovo–Nagymoros Project (Hungary–Slovakia), 25 Sept. 1997

16.   The Danube is the second longest river in Europe, flowing along or across the borders of nine countries in its 2,860–kilometre course from the Black Forest eastwards to the Black Sea. For 142 kilometres, it forms the boundary between Slovakia and Hungary. The sector with which this case is concerned is a stretch of approximately 200 kilometres, between Bratislava in Slovakia and Budapest in Hungary. Below Bratislava, the river gradient decreases markedly, creating an alluvial plain of gravel and sand sediment. This plain is delimited to the north-east, in Slovak territory, by the Malý Danube and to the south-west, in Hungarian territory, by the Mosoni Danube. The boundary between the two States is constituted, in the major part of that region, by the main channel of the river. The area lying between the Malý Danube and that channel, in Slovak territory, constitutes the itný Ostrov; the area between the main channel and the Mosoni Danube, in Hungarian territory, constitutes the Szigetköz. Cunovo and, further downstream, Gabcíkovo, are situated in this sector of the river on Slovak territory, Cunovo on the right bank and Gabcíkovo on the left. Further downstream, after the confluence of the various branches, the river enters Hungarian territory and the topography becomes hillier.

Nagymaros lies in a narrow valley at a bend in the Danube just before it turns south, enclosing the large river island of Szentendre before reaching Budapest....

17. The Danube has always played a vital part in the commercial and economic development of its riparian States, and has underlined and reinforced their interdependence, making international co-operation essential. Improvements to the navigation channel have enabled the Danube, now linked by canal to the Main and thence to the Rhine, to become an important navigational artery connecting the North Sea to the Black Sea. In the stretch of river to which the case relates, flood protection measures have been constructed over the centuries, farming and forestry practised, and, more recently, there has been an increase in population and industrial activity in the area. The cumulative effects on the river and on the environment of various human activities over the years have not all been favourable, particularly for the water régime.

Only by international co-operation could action be taken to alleviate these problems. Water management projects along the Danube have frequently sought to combine navigational improvements and flood protection with the production of electricity through hydroelectric power plants. The potential of the Danube for the production of hydroelectric power has been extensively exploited by some riparian States. The history of attempts to harness the potential of the particular stretch of the river at issue in these proceedings extends over a 25–year period culminating in the signature of the 1977 Treaty.

18. Article 1, paragraph 1, of the 1977 Treaty describes the principal works to be constructed in pursuance of the Project. It provided for the building of two series of locks, one at Gabcíkovo (in Czechoslovak territory) and the other at Nagymaros (in Hungarian territory), to constitute "a single and indivisible operational system of works".... The Court will subsequently have occasion to revert in more detail to those works, which were to comprise, inter alia, a reservoir upstream of Dunakiliti, in Hungarian and Czechoslovak territory; a dam at Dunakiliti, in Hungarian territory; a bypass canal, in Czechoslovak territory, on which was to be constructed the Gabcíkovo System of Locks (together with a hydroelectric power plant with an installed capacity of 720 megawatts (MW)); the deepening of the bed of the Danube downstream of the place at which the bypass canal was to rejoin the old bed of the river; a reinforcement of flood-control works along the Danube upstream of Nagymaros; the Nagymaros System of Locks, in Hungarian territory (with a hydroelectric power plant of a capacity of 158 MW); and the deepening of the bed of the Danube downstream.

Article 1, paragraph 4, of the Treaty further provided that the technical specifications concerning the system would be included in the "Joint Contractual Plan" which was to be drawn up in accordance with the Agreement signed by the two Governments for this purpose on 6 May 1976; Article 4, paragraph 1, for its part, specified that "the joint investment [would] be carried out in conformity with the joint contractual plan". * * *

Article 15 specified that the contracting parties "shall ensure, by the means specified in the joint contractual plan, that the quality of the water in the Danube is not impaired as a result of the construction and operation of the System of Locks".

It was stipulated in Article 19 that: "The Contracting Parties shall ... ensure compliance with the obligations for protection of nature arising in connection with the construction and operation of the System of Locks."

Article 20 provided for the contracting parties to take appropriate measures, within the framework of their national investments, for the protection of fishing interests in conformity with the Convention concerning Fishing in the Waters of the Danube, signed at Bucharest on 29 January 1958. * * *

20.   Thus, the Project was to have taken the form of an integrated joint project with the two contracting parties on an equal footing in respect of the financing, construction and operation of the works. Its single and indivisible nature was to have been realized through the Joint Contractual Plan which complemented the Treaty. In particular, Hungary would have had control of the sluices at Dunakiliti and the works at Nagymaros, whereas Czechoslovakia would have had control of the works at Gabcíkovo. * * *

[As a result of intense criticism of the Project, the Hungarian Government decided in 1989 to abandon the works at Nagymaros and suspend the works at Dunakiliti. Czechoslovakia also started investigating "Variant C", which entailed a unilateral diversion of the Danube at Cunovo some 10 kilometres upstream of Dunakiliti and entirely in Czechoslovak territory. Work on Variant C began in November 1991. Discussions continued between the two parties but to no avail, and, in May 1992, the Hungarian Government terminated the 1977 Treaty. Czechoslovakia, on 23 October, proceeded to dam the river. After several unsuccessful efforts to resolve the dispute, the case was submitted to the ICJ. The ICJ turned first to the question of whether in 1989 Hungary was entitled to suspend and subsequently abandon the project.]

40.   Throughout the proceedings, Hungary contended that, although it did suspend or abandon certain works, on the contrary, it never suspended the application of the 1977 Treaty itself. To justify its conduct, it relied essentially on a "state of ecological necessity."

Hungary contended that the various installations in the Gabcíkovo-Nagymaros System of Locks had been designed to enable the Gabcíkovo power plant to operate in peak mode. Water would only have come through the plant twice each day, at times of peak power demand. Operation in peak mode required the vast expanse (60 km2) of the planned reservoir at Dunakiliti, as well as the Nagymaros dam, which was to alleviate the tidal effects and reduce the variation in the water level downstream of Gabcíkovo. Such a system, considered to be more economically profitable than using run-of-the-river plants, carried ecological risks which it found unacceptable.

According to Hungary, the principal ecological dangers which would have been caused by this system were as follows. At Gabcíkovo/Dunakiliti, under the original Project, as specified in the Joint Contractual Plan, the residual discharge into the old bed of the Danube was limited to 50 m3/s, in addition to the water provided to the system of side-arms. That volume could be increased to 200 m3/s during the growing season. Additional discharges, and in particular a number of artificial floods, could also be effected, at an unspecified rate. In these circumstances, the groundwater level would have fallen in most of the Szigetköz. Furthermore, the groundwater would then no longer have been supplied by the Danube—which, on the contrary, would have acted as a drain—but by the reservoir of stagnant water at Dunakiliti and the side-arms which would have become silted up. In the long term, the quality of water would have been seriously impaired. As for the surface water, risks of eutrophication would have arisen, particularly in the reservoir; instead of the old Danube there would have been a river choked with sand, where only a relative trickle of water would have flowed. The network of arms would have been for the most part cut off from the principal bed. The fluvial fauna and flora, like those in the alluvial plains, would have been condemned to extinction.

As for Nagymaros, Hungary argued that, if that dam had been built, the bed of the Danube upstream would have silted up and, consequently, the quality of the water collected in the bank-filtered wells would have deteriorated in this sector. What is more, the operation of the Gabcíkovo power plant in peak mode would have occasioned significant daily variations in the water level in the reservoir upstream, which would have constituted a threat to aquatic habitats in particular. Furthermore, the construction and operation of the Nagymaros dam would have caused the erosion of the riverbed downstream, along Szentendre Island. The water level of the river would therefore have fallen in this section and the yield of the bank-filtered wells providing two-thirds of the water supply of the city of Budapest would have appreciably diminished. The filter layer would also have shrunk or perhaps even disappeared, and fine sediments would have been deposited in certain pockets in the river. For this twofold reason, the quality of the infiltrating water would have been severely jeopardized.

From all these predictions, in support of which it quoted a variety of scientific studies, Hungary concluded that a "state of ecological necessity" did indeed exist in 1989.

41. In its written pleadings, Hungary also accused Czechoslovakia of having violated various provisions of the 1977 Treaty from before 1989—in refusing to take account of the now evident ecological dangers and insisting that the works be continued, notably at Nagymaros. In this context Hungary contended that, in accordance with the terms of Article 3, paragraph 2, of the Agreement of 6 May 1976 concerning the Joint Contractual Plan, Czechoslovakia bore responsibility for research into the Project's impact on the environment; Hungary stressed that the research carried out by Czechoslovakia had not been conducted adequately, the potential effects of the Project on the environment of the construction having been assessed by Czechoslovakia only from September 1990. * * *

44. In the course of the proceedings, Slovakia argued at length that the state of necessity upon which Hungary relied did not constitute a reason for the suspension of a treaty obligation recognized by the law of treaties. At the same time, it cast doubt upon whether "ecological necessity" or "ecological risk" could, in relation to the law of State responsibility, constitute a circumstance precluding the wrongfulness of an act.

In any event, Slovakia denied that there had been any kind of "ecological state of necessity" in this case either in 1989 or subsequently. It invoked the authority of various scientific studies when it claimed that Hungary had given an exaggeratedly pessimistic description of the situation. Slovakia did not, of course, deny that ecological problems could have arisen. However, it asserted that they could to a large extent have been remedied. It accordingly stressed that no agreement had been reached with respect to the modalities of operation of the Gabcíkovo power plant in peak mode, and claimed that the apprehensions of Hungary related only to operating conditions of an extreme kind. In the same way, it contended that the original Project had undergone various modifications since 1977 and that it would have been possible to modify it even further, for example with respect to the discharge of water reserved for the old bed of the Danube, or the supply of water to the side-arms by means of underwater weirs.

45. Slovakia moreover denied that it in any way breached the 1977 Treaty—particularly its Articles 15 and 19—and maintained, inter alia, that according to the terms of Article 3, paragraph 2, of the Agreement of 6 May 1976 relating to the Joint Contractual Plan—research into the impact of the Project on the environment was not the exclusive responsibility of Czechoslovakia but of either one of the parties, depending on the location of the works.

[The Court noted that neither party had ratified the 1969 Vienna Convention on the Law of Treaties at the time of signing the 1977 Agreement, but that nonetheless, the Vienna Convention was potentially relevant to the dispute as a codification of existing customary law. The Court explained the difference between the law of treaties and the law of state responsibility. "A determination of whether a convention is or is not in force, and whether it has or has not been properly suspended or denounced, is to be made pursuant to the law of treaties." On the other hand, an evaluation of the extent to which the suspension or denunciation of a convention, seen as incompatible with the law of treaties, involves the responsibility of the State which proceeded to it, is to be made under the law of State responsibility.

The Court then considered whether there was, in 1989, a state of necessity that would have permitted Hungary, without incurring international responsibility, to suspend and abandon works that it was committed to perform in accordance with the 1977 Treaty and related instruments.]

50. In the present case, the Parties are in agreement in considering that the existence of a state of necessity must be evaluated in the light of the criteria laid down by the International Law Commission in Article 33 of the Draft Articles on the International Responsibility of States that it adopted on first reading. That provision is worded as follows:

Article 33. State of necessity

1. A state of necessity may not be invoked by a State as a ground for precluding the wrongfulness of an act of that State not in conformity with an international obligation of the State unless:

> (a) the act was the only means of safeguarding an essential interest of the State against a grave and imminent peril; and

> (b) the act did not seriously impair an essential interest of the State towards which the obligation existed.

2. In any case, a state of necessity may not be invoked by a State as a ground for precluding wrongfulness:

> (a) "if the international obligation with which the act of the State is not in conformity arises out of a peremptory norm of general international law; or (b) if the international obligation with which the act of the State is not in conformity is laid down by a treaty which, explicitly or implicitly, excludes the possibility of invoking the state of necessity with respect to that obligation; or (c) if the State in question has contributed to the occurrence of the state of necessity." (Yearbook of the International Law Commission, 1980, Vol. II, Part 2, p. 34.)

In its Commentary, the Commission defined the "state of necessity" as being

> "the situation of a State whose sole means of safeguarding an essential interest threatened by a grave and imminent peril is to adopt conduct not in conformity with what is required of it by an international obligation to another State" (ibid., para. 1).

It concluded that "the notion of state of necessity is ... deeply rooted in general legal thinking" (ibid., p. 49, para. 31).

51. The Court considers, first of all, that the state of necessity is a ground recognized by customary international law for precluding the wrongfulness of an act not in conformity with an international obligation. It observes moreover that such ground for precluding wrongfulness can only be accepted on an exceptional basis. The International Law Commission was of the same opinion when it explained that it had opted for a negative form of words in Article 33 of its Draft

> "in order to show, by this formal means also, that the case of invocation of a state of necessity as a justification must be considered as really constituting an

exception—and one even more rarely admissible than is the case with the other circumstances precluding wrongfulness . . . " (ibid., p. 51, para. 40).

Thus, according to the Commission, the state of necessity can only be invoked under certain strictly defined conditions which must be cumulatively satisfied; and the State concerned is not the sole judge of whether those conditions have been met.

52. In the present case, the following basic conditions set forth in Draft Article 33 are relevant: it must have been occasioned by an "essential interest" of the State which is the author of the act conflicting with one of its international obligations; that interest must have been threatened by a "grave and imminent peril"; the act being challenged must have been the "only means" of safeguarding that interest; that act must not have "seriously impair[ed] an essential interest" of the State towards which the obligation existed; and the State which is the author of that act must not have "contributed to the occurrence of the state of necessity". Those conditions reflect customary international law.

The Court will now endeavour to ascertain whether those conditions had been met at the time of the suspension and abandonment, by Hungary, of the works that it was to carry out in accordance with the 1977 Treaty.

53. The Court has no difficulty in acknowledging that the concerns expressed by Hungary for its natural environment in the region affected by the Gabcíkovo-Nagymaros Project related to an "essential interest" of that State, within the meaning given to that expression in Article 33 of the Draft of the International Law Commission.

The Commission, in its Commentary, indicated that one should not, in that context, reduce an "essential interest" to a matter only of the "existence" of the State, and that the whole question was, ultimately, to be judged in the light of the particular case (see Yearbook of the International Law Commission, 1980, Vol. II, Part 2, p. 49, para. 32); at the same time, it included among the situations that could occasion a state of necessity, "a grave danger to . . . the ecological preservation of all or some of [the] territory [of a State]" (ibid., p. 35, para. 3); and specified, with reference to State practice, that "It is primarily in the last two decades that safeguarding the ecological balance has come to be considered an 'essential interest' of all States." (Ibid., p. 39, para. 14.) The Court recalls that it has recently had occasion to stress, in the following terms, the great significance that it attaches to respect for the environment, not only for States but also for the whole of mankind:

> "the environment is not an abstraction but represents the living space, the quality of life and the very health of human beings, including generations unborn. The existence of the general obligation of States to ensure that activities within their jurisdiction and control respect the environment of other States or of areas beyond national control is now part of the corpus of international law relating to the environment." (Legality of the Threat or Use of Nuclear Weapons, Advisory Opinion, I.C.J. Reports 1996, pp. 241–242, para. 29.)

54. The verification of the existence, in 1989, of the "peril" invoked by Hungary, of its "grave and imminent" nature, as well as of the absence of any "means" to respond to it, other than the measures taken by Hungary to suspend and abandon the works, are all complex processes.

As the Court has already indicated (see paragraphs 33 et seq. above), Hungary on several occasions expressed, in 1989, its "uncertainties" as to the ecological impact of putting in place the Gabcíkovo-Nagymaros barrage system, which is why it asked insistently for new scientific studies to be carried out.

The Court considers, however, that, serious though these uncertainties might have been they could not, alone, establish the objective existence of a "peril" in the sense of a component element of a state of necessity. The word "peril" certainly evokes the idea of "risk"; that is precisely what distinguishes "peril" from material damage. But a state of necessity could not exist without a "peril" duly established at the relevant point in time; the mere apprehension of a possible "peril" could not suffice in that respect. It could moreover hardly be otherwise, when the "peril" constituting the state of necessity has at the same time to be "grave" and "imminent". "Imminence" is synonymous with "immediacy" or "proximity" and goes far beyond the concept of "possibility". As the International Law Commission emphasized in its commentary, the "extremely grave and imminent" peril must "have been a threat to the interest at the actual time" (Yearbook of the International Law Commission, 1980, Vol. II, Part 2, p. 49, para. 33). That does not exclude, in the view of the Court, that a "peril" appearing in the long term might be held to be "imminent" as soon as it is established, at the relevant point in time, that the realization of that peril, however far off it might be, is not thereby any less certain and inevitable.

The Hungarian argument on the state of necessity could not convince the Court unless it was at least proven that a real, "grave" and "imminent" "peril" existed in 1989 and that the measures taken by Hungary were the only possible response to it.

Both Parties have placed on record an impressive amount of scientific material aimed at reinforcing their respective arguments. The Court has given most careful attention to this material, in which the Parties have developed their opposing views as to the ecological consequences of the Project. It concludes, however, that, as will be shown below, it is not necessary in order to respond to the questions put to it in the Special Agreement for it to determine which of those points of view is scientifically better founded.

55.   The Court will begin by considering the situation at Nagymaros. As has already been mentioned (see paragraph 40 above), Hungary maintained that, if the works at Nagymaros had been carried out as planned, the environment—and in particular the drinking water resources—in the area would have been exposed to serious dangers on account of problems linked to the upstream reservoir on the one hand and, on the other, the risks of erosion of the riverbed downstream.

The Court notes that the dangers ascribed to the upstream reservoir were mostly of a long-term nature and, above all, that they remained uncertain. Even though the Joint Contractual Plan envisaged that the Gabcíkovo power plant would "mainly operate in peak-load time and continuously during high water", the final rules of operation had not yet been determined ... ; however, any dangers associated with the putting into service of the Nagymaros portion of the Project would have been closely linked to the extent to which it was operated in peak mode and to the modalities of such operation. It follows that, even if it could have been established—which, in the Court's appreciation of the evidence before it, was not the case—that the reservoir would ultimately have constituted a "grave peril" for the environment in the area, one would be bound to conclude that the peril was not "imminent" at the time at which Hungary suspended and then abandoned the works relating to the dam.

With regard to the lowering of the riverbed downstream of the Nagymaros dam, the danger could have appeared at once more serious and more pressing, in so far as it was the supply of drinking water to the city of Budapest which would have been affected. The Court would however point out that the bed of the Danube in the vicinity of Szentendre had already been deepened prior to 1980 in order to extract building materials, and that the river had from that time attained, in that sector, the depth required by the 1977 Treaty. The peril invoked by Hungary had thus already materialized to a large extent for a number of years, so that it could not, in 1989, represent a peril arising entirely out of the project. The Court would stress, however, that, even supposing, as Hungary maintained, that the construction and operation of the dam would have created serious risks, Hungary had means available to it, other than the suspension and abandonment of the works, of responding to that situation. It could for example have proceeded regularly to discharge gravel into the river downstream of the dam. It could likewise, if necessary, have supplied Budapest with drinking water by processing the river water in an appropriate manner. The two Parties expressly recognized that that possibility remained open even though—and this is not determinative of the state of necessity—the purification of the river water, like the other measures envisaged, clearly would have been a more costly technique.

56. The Court now comes to the Gabcíkovo sector. It will recall that Hungary's concerns in this sector related on the one hand to the quality of the surface water in the Dunakiliti reservoir, with its effects on the quality of the groundwater in the region, and on the other hand, more generally, to the level, movement and quality of both the surface water and the groundwater in the whole of the Szigetköz, with their effects on the fauna and flora in the alluvial plain of the Danube (see paragraph 40 above).

Whether in relation to the Dunakiliti site or to the whole of the Szigetköz, the Court finds here again, that the peril claimed by Hungary was to be considered in the long term, and, more importantly, remained uncertain. As Hungary itself acknowledges, the damage that it apprehended had primarily to be the result of some relatively slow natural processes, the effects of which could not easily be assessed.

Even if the works were more advanced in this sector than at Nagymaros, they had not been completed in July 1989 and, as the Court explained in paragraph 34 above, Hungary expressly undertook to carry on with them, early in June 1989. The report dated 23 June 1989 by the ad hoc Committee of the Hungarian Academy of Sciences, which was also referred to in paragraph 35 of the present Judgment, does not express any awareness of an authenticated peril—even in the form of a definite peril, whose realization would have been inevitable in the long term—when it states that:

> "The measuring results of an at least five-year monitoring period following the completion of the Gabcíkovo construction are indispensable to the trustworthy prognosis of the ecological impacts of the barrage system. There is undoubtedly a need for the establishment and regular operation of a comprehensive monitoring system, which must be more developed than at present. The examination of biological indicator objects that can sensitively indicate the changes happening in the environment, neglected till today, have to be included."

The report concludes as follows:

> "It can be stated, that the environmental, ecological and water quality impacts were not taken into account properly during the design and construction period until today. Because of the complexity of the ecological processes and lack of the measured data and the relevant calculations the environmental impacts cannot be evaluated.

The data of the monitoring system newly operating on a very limited area are not enough to forecast the impacts probably occurring over a longer term. In order to widen and to make the data more frequent a further multi-year examination is necessary to decrease the further degradation of the water quality playing a dominant role in this question. The expected water quality influences equally the aquatic ecosystems, the soils and the recreational and tourist land-use.''

The Court also notes that, in these proceedings, Hungary acknowledged that, as a general rule, the quality of the Danube waters had improved over the past 20 years, even if those waters remained subject to hypertrophic conditions.

However "grave" it might have been, it would accordingly have been difficult, in the light of what is said above, to see the alleged peril as sufficiently certain and therefore "imminent" in 1989.

The Court moreover considers that Hungary could, in this context also, have resorted to other means in order to respond to the dangers that it apprehended. In particular, within the framework of the original Project, Hungary seemed to be in a position to control at least partially the distribution of the water between the bypass canal, the old bed of the Danube and the side-arms. It should not be overlooked that the Dunakiliti dam was located in Hungarian territory and that Hungary could construct the works needed to regulate flows along the old bed of the Danube and the side-arms. Moreover, it should be borne in mind that Article 14 of the 1977 Treaty provided for the possibility that each of the parties might withdraw quantities of water exceeding those specified in the Joint Contractual Plan, while making it clear that, in such an event, "the share of electric power of the Contracting Party benefitting from the excess withdrawal shall be correspondingly reduced".

57. The Court concludes from the foregoing that, with respect to both Nagymaros and Gabcíkovo, the perils invoked by Hungary, without prejudging their possible gravity, were not sufficiently established in 1989, nor were they "imminent"; and that Hungary had available to it at that time means of responding to these perceived perils other than the suspension and abandonment of works with which it had been entrusted. What is more, negotiations were under way which might have led to a review of the Project and the extension of some of its time-limits, without there being need to abandon it. The Court infers from this that the respect by Hungary, in 1989, of its obligations under the terms of the 1977 Treaty would not have resulted in a situation "characterized so aptly by the maxim summum jus summa injuria" (Yearbook of the International Law Commission, 1980, Vol. II, Part 2, p. 49, para. 31).

Moreover, the Court notes that Hungary decided to conclude the 1977 Treaty, a Treaty which—whatever the political circumstances prevailing at the time of its conclusion—was treated by Hungary as valid and in force until the date declared for its termination in May 1992. As can be seen from the material before the Court, a great many studies of a scientific and technical nature had been conducted at an earlier time, both by Hungary and by Czechoslovakia. Hungary was, then, presumably aware of the situation as then known, when it assumed its obligations under the Treaty. Hungary contended before the Court that those studies had been inadequate and that the state of knowledge at that time was not such as to make possible a complete evaluation of the ecological implications of the Gabcíkovo-Nagymaros Project. It is nonetheless the case that although the principal object of the 1977 Treaty was the construction of a System of Locks for the production of electricity, improvement of navigation on the Danube and protection against flooding, the need to ensure the protection of the environment had not escaped the parties, as can be seen from Articles 15, 19 and 20 of the Treaty.

What is more, the Court cannot fail to note the positions taken by Hungary after the entry into force of the 1977 Treaty. In 1983, Hungary asked that the works under the Treaty should go forward more slowly, for reasons that were essentially economic but also, subsidiarily, related to ecological concerns. In 1989, when, according to Hungary itself, the state of scientific knowledge had undergone a significant development, it asked for the works to be speeded up, and then decided, three months later, to suspend them and subsequently to abandon them. The Court is not however unaware that profound changes were taking place in Hungary in 1989, and that, during that transitory phase, it might have been more than usually difficult to co-ordinate the different points of view prevailing from time to time.

[The Court also found that even if there was a state of necessity, Hungary would not have been permitted to rely upon that state of necessity in order to justify its failure to comply with its treaty obligations, as it had helped, by act or omission to bring it about.] * * *

The Court thus concluded that Hungary was not entitled to suspend and subsequently abandon the works on the Project.

[The Court then turned to the question of whether in November 1991 Slovakia (at that time the Czech and Slovak Federal Republic) was entitled to construct Variant C and unilaterally divert the waters of the Danube. Slovakia argued that Hungary's suspension of the project had made it impossible to continue to carry out the 1977 Agreement and invoked what it called the "principle of approximate application" to justify the construction and operation of Variant C. Slovakia also argued that it had a duty to mitigate damages from Hungary's breach of the agreement, or alternatively that Variant C, even if found to be illegal, was justified as a countermeasure to Hungary's breach of the Agreement. In addition to arguing against all of the above arguments, Hungary also argued that Variant C was unlawful as the unilateral diversion of the Danube violated Hungary's sovereignty and territorial integrity. The Court's opinion relied heavily on the doctrine of equitable use in rejecting Slovakia's and Hungary's arguments.]

78. Moreover, in practice, the operation of Variant C led Czechoslovakia to appropriate, essentially for its use and benefit, between 80 and 90 per cent of the waters of the Danube before returning them to the main bed of the river, despite the fact that the Danube is not only a shared international watercourse but also an international boundary river.

Czechoslovakia submitted that Variant C was essentially no more than what Hungary had already agreed to and that the only modifications made were those which had become necessary by virtue of Hungary's decision not to implement its treaty obligations. It is true that Hungary, in concluding the 1977 Treaty, had agreed to the damming of the Danube and the diversion of its waters into the bypass canal. But it was only in the context of a joint operation and a sharing of its benefits that Hungary had given its consent. The suspension and withdrawal of that consent constituted a violation of Hungary's legal obligations, demonstrating, as it did, the refusal by Hungary of joint operation; but that cannot mean that Hungary forfeited its basic right to an equitable and reasonable sharing of the resources of an international watercourse.

The Court accordingly concludes that Czechoslovakia, in putting Variant C into operation, was not applying the 1977 Treaty but, on the contrary, violated certain of its express provisions, and, in so doing, committed an internationally wrongful act. * * *

[Because the construction of Variant C was unlawful, Slovakia could not justify it as mitigation of damages. The court did investigate whether the unlawful construction of Variant C was a justifiable countermeasure in response to Hungary's breach of the 1977 Agreement.] * * *

85. In the view of the Court, an important consideration is that the effects of a countermeasure must be commensurate with the injury suffered, taking account of the rights in question.

In 1929, the Permanent Court of International Justice, with regard to navigation on the River Oder, stated as follows:

"[the] community of interest in a navigable river becomes the basis of a common legal right, the essential features of which are the perfect equality of all riparian States in the user of the whole course of the river and the exclusion of any preferential privilege of any one riparian State in relation to the others" (Territorial Jurisdiction of the International Commission of the River Oder, Judgment No. 16, 1929, P.C.I.J., Series A, No. 23, p. 27).

Modern development of international law has strengthened this principle for non-navigational uses of international watercourses as well, as evidenced by the adoption of the Convention of 21 May 1997 on the Law of the Non–Navigational Uses of International Watercourses by the United Nations General Assembly.

The Court considers that Czechoslovakia, by unilaterally assuming control of a shared resource, and thereby depriving Hungary of its right to an equitable and reasonable share of the natural resources of the Danube—with the continuing effects of the diversion of these waters on the ecology of the riparian area of the Szigetköz—failed to respect the proportionality which is required by international law. * * *

[The Court thus found that Slovakia's diversion of the Danube violated international law, then turned to the legal effect of the 1992 notice of termination submitted by Hungary to Slovakia. Hungary presented five arguments in support of the lawfulness, and thus the effectiveness, of its notification of termination. These were the existence of a state of necessity; the impossibility of performance of the Treaty; the occurrence of a fundamental change of circumstances; the material breach of the Treaty by Czechoslovakia; and, finally, the development of new norms of international environmental law. The Court rejected each of Hungary's arguments. Notably, the Court did suggest that the unilateral diversion of the Danube by Slovakia violated the 1977 Agreement, but that diversion took place *after* Hungary's termination of the Agreement; thus, Hungary's termination was "premature." The following excerpts address the argument regarding new norms of international environmental law.]

97. Finally, Hungary argued that subsequently imposed requirements of international law in relation to the protection of the environment precluded performance of the Treaty. The previously existing obligation not to cause substantive damage to the territory of another State had, Hungary claimed, evolved into an erga omnes obligation of prevention of damage pursuant to the "precautionary principle". On this basis, Hungary argued, its termination was "forced by the other party's refusal to suspend work on Variant C".

Slovakia argued, in reply, that none of the intervening developments in environmental law gave rise to norms of jus cogens that would override the Treaty. Further, it contended that the claim by Hungary to be entitled to take action could not in any event serve as legal justification for termination of the

Treaty under the law of treaties, but belonged rather "to the language of self-help or reprisals". * * *

111. Finally, the Court will address Hungary's claim that it was entitled to terminate the 1977 Treaty because new requirements of international law for the protection of the environment precluded performance of the Treaty.

112. Neither of the Parties contended that new peremptory norms of environmental law had emerged since the conclusion of the 1977 Treaty, and the Court will consequently not be required to examine the scope of Article 64 of the Vienna Convention on the Law of Treaties. On the other hand, the Court wishes to point out that newly developed norms of environmental law are relevant for the implementation of the Treaty and that the parties could, by agreement, incorporate them through the application of Articles 15, 19 and 20 of the Treaty. These articles do not contain specific obligations of performance but require the parties, in carrying out their obligations to ensure that the quality of water in the Danube is not impaired and that nature is protected, to take new environmental norms into consideration when agreeing upon the means to be specified in the Joint Contractual Plan.

By inserting these evolving provisions in the Treaty, the parties recognized the potential necessity to adapt the Project. Consequently, the Treaty is not static, and is open to adapt to emerging norms of international law. By means of Articles 15 and 19, new environmental norms can be incorporated in the Joint Contractual Plan.

The responsibility to do this was a joint responsibility. The obligations contained in Articles 15, 19 and 20 are, by definition, general and have to be transformed into specific obligations of performance through a process of consultation and negotiation. Their implementation thus requires a mutual willingness to discuss in good faith actual and potential environmental risks.

It is all the more important to do this because as the Court recalled in its Advisory Opinion on the Legality of the Threat or Use of Nuclear Weapons, "the environment is not an abstraction but represents the living space, the quality of life and the very health of human beings, including generations unborn" (I.C.J. Reports 1996, para. 29; see also paragraph 53 above).

The awareness of the vulnerability of the environment and the recognition that environmental risks have to be assessed on a continuous basis have become much stronger in the years since the Treaty's conclusion. These new concerns have enhanced the relevance of Articles 15, 19 and 20.

113. The Court recognizes that both Parties agree on the need to take environmental concerns seriously and to take the required precautionary measures, but they fundamentally disagree on the consequences this has for the joint Project. In such a case, third-party involvement may be helpful and instrumental in finding a solution, provided each of the Parties is flexible in its position.

[The Court then turned to the legal consequences arising from its decisions thus far in the case.]

140. It is clear that the Project's impact upon, and its implications for, the environment are of necessity a key issue. The numerous scientific reports which have been presented to the Court by the Parties—even if their conclusions are often contradictory—provide abundant evidence that this impact and these implications are considerable.

In order to evaluate the environmental risks, current standards must be taken into consideration. This is not only allowed by the wording of Articles 15 and 19, but even prescribed, to the extent that these articles impose a continuing—and thus necessarily evolving—obligation on the parties to maintain the quality of the water of the Danube and to protect nature.

The Court is mindful that, in the field of environmental protection, vigilance and prevention are required on account of the often irreversible character of damage to the environment and of the limitations inherent in the very mechanism of reparation of this type of damage.

Throughout the ages, mankind has, for economic and other reasons, constantly interfered with nature. In the past, this was often done without consideration of the effects upon the environment. Owing to new scientific insights and to a growing awareness of the risks for mankind—for present and future generations—of pursuit of such interventions at an unconsidered and unabated pace, new norms and standards have been developed, set forth in a great number of instruments during the last two decades. Such new norms have to be taken into consideration, and such new standards given proper weight, not only when States contemplate new activities but also when continuing with activities begun in the past. This need to reconcile economic development with protection of the environment is aptly expressed in the concept of sustainable development.

For the purposes of the present case, this means that the Parties together should look afresh at the effects on the environment of the operation of the Gabcíkovo power plant. In particular they must find a satisfactory solution for the volume of water to be released into the old bed of the Danube and into the side-arms on both sides of the river.

141.   It is not for the Court to determine what shall be the final result of these negotiations to be conducted by the Parties. It is for the Parties themselves to find an agreed solution that takes account of the objectives of the Treaty, which must be pursued in a joint and integrated way, as well as the norms of international environmental law and the principles of the law of international watercourses. The Court will recall in this context that, as it said in the North Sea Continental Shelf cases:

> "[the Parties] are under an obligation so to conduct themselves that the negotiations are meaningful, which will not be the case when either of them insists upon its own position without contemplating any modification of it." (I.C.J. Reports 1969, p. 47, para. 85).

142.   What is required in the present case by the rule pacta sunt servanda, as reflected in Article 26 of the Vienna Convention of 1969 on the Law of Treaties, is that the Parties find an agreed solution within the co-operative context of the Treaty.

Article 26 combines two elements, which are of equal importance. It provides that "Every treaty in force is binding upon the parties to it and must be performed by them in good faith". This latter element, in the Court's view, implies that, in this case, it is the purpose of the Treaty, and the intentions of the parties in concluding it, which should prevail over its literal application. The principle of good faith obliges the Parties to apply it in a reasonable way and in such a manner that its purpose can be realized.

[Ultimately, the Court decided that the 1977 Agreement, not having been terminated, was still in force and ordered the parties to recreate a joint regime, suggesting strongly that they operate the diversion at Cunovo and the Gabcikovo dam together for their joint benefit. The Court seemed to be imposing an obligation of equitable utilization.] * * *

147. Re-establishment of the joint régime will also reflect in an optimal way the concept of common utilization of shared water resources for the achievement of the several objectives mentioned in the Treaty, in concordance with Article 5, paragraph 2, of the Convention on the Law of the Non–Navigational Uses of International Watercourses, according to which:

"Watercourse States shall participate in the use, development and protection of an international watercourse in an equitable and reasonable manner. Such participation includes both the right to utilize the watercourse and the duty to cooperate in the protection and development thereof, as provided in the present Convention." (General Assembly Doc. A/51/869 of 11 April 1997.) * * *

[The Court then turned to find damages with respect to the unlawful acts committed by both Parties, concluding that:]

It is a well-established rule of international law that an injured State is entitled to obtain compensation from the State which has committed an internationally wrongful act for the damage caused by it. In the present Judgment, the Court has concluded that both Parties committed internationally wrongful acts, and it has noted that those acts gave rise to the damage sustained by the Parties; consequently, Hungary and Slovakia are both under an obligation to pay compensation and are both entitled to obtain compensation. * * *

153. Given the fact, however, that there have been intersecting wrongs by both Parties, the Court wishes to observe that the issue of compensation could satisfactorily be resolved in the framework of an overall settlement if each of the Parties were to renounce or cancel all financial claims and counter-claims.

QUESTIONS AND DISCUSSION

1. Both sides in the Gabcikovo Dam Case announced victory. To what extent did both sides win? One group that did not proclaim victory were the environmentalists, who not only hoped that the Court would provide some protection of the Danube ecosystem, but also hoped the Court would further the development of international environmental law. Why were the environmentalists disappointed? To what extent did the Court further international environmental law? What does the Court's opinion imply for the legal status of the principles of environmental impact assessment, sustainable development or the precautionary principle?

2. Some observers did not view the Gabcikovo case as an international environmental law case. They believed it was a case of treaty interpretation or alternatively a case raising issues of the law of international watercourses. To what extent did the Gabcikovo decision emphasize the international law of watercourses over international environmental law? Does this suggest that environmental concerns will play less of a role in future conflicts between watercourse States?

3. Why do you think Hungary sought to void the Treaty on environmental grounds in 1992? Was it because environmental issues became of national concern after the fall of the Berlin Wall? Is it possible Hungary wanted to be released from its treaty obligations for other reasons and simply used the environment as a handy excuse?

4. If the Court's opinion left environmentalists disheartened, they could find hope in the separate opinion of Judge Weeramantry, who used the occasion of this case to write a thoughtful exposition on sustainable development, excerpted in Chapter 6, page 338.

For discussions of the Gabcikovo Dam conflict prior to the decision, see Paul R. Williams, *International Environmental Dispute Resolution: The Dispute Between Slovakia and Hungary Concerning Construction of the Gabcikovo and Nagymaros Dams,* 19 COLUM. J. ENVTL L. 1 (1994), at 13; Gabriel Eckstein, *Application of International Water Law to Transboundary Groundwater Resources and the Slovak–Hungarian Dispute over Gabcikovo–Nagymaros,* 19 SUFFOLK TRANSNATIONAL L.REV. 67 (1995), at 75.

B.   CODIFICATION AND THE 1997 UN CONVENTION ON NONNAVIGATIONAL USES OF WATERCOURSES

In recent years, the ecological services provided by water and the resulting importance of conserving and protecting water quality, have become important concerns of international policy making. Beginning in the 1960s with the International Law Association's Helsinki Rules on the Uses of International Rivers, adopted Aug. 20, 1966, *reprinted in* 52 I.L.M. 484 (1967) [hereinafter referred to as the 1966 ILA Helsinki Rules], efforts to codify the law of international watercourses have begun to include conservation concerns.

Codification efforts received a boost in 1970 when the Sixth Committee of the UN General Assembly requested the International Law Commission (ILC) to address the progressive development of the international law of watercourses. For more information on the role of the ILC as a law-making institution, see Chapter 5, pages 248–49. The ILC finally issued a set of draft articles for non-navigational uses of international watercourses in 1990. After receiving comments from governments, the draft articles were revised in 1994 and submitted to the UN General Assembly for further consideration as the basis of a global framework convention. Over the next three years a U.N.G.A.-authorized Working Group negotiated a convention text, and on May 21, 1997, the U.N.G.A. approved the draft convention and opened it for signature. *See* U.N. Convention on the Law of the Non–Navigational Uses of International Watercourses, May 21, 1997, *reprinted in* 36 I.L.M. 700 (1997).

The 1997 UN Convention is not yet in force, and some observers believe it may never obtain the necessary 35 ratifications. As of June 2001, sixteen countries had signed the convention and 8 had ratified it. Several reasons exist for the slow progress in gaining ratification. Foremost among them is probably the concerns of both downstream and upstream States, who are uncertain about how the Convention's provisions may be interpreted vis-à-vis current conceptions of customary law. In addition, regional approaches to transboundary water issues have grown in recent years, including for example the UNECE Convention and the Southern Africa Development Coordination compact.

Regardless of when or even whether the UN Convention comes into force, the Convention is widely thought to provide a strong codification of customary law in many respects. It thus may act, as the Law of the Sea

Convention has, to further promote the development and clarification of customary law.

The Convention thus also provides a valuable framework for the following discussion of major issues arising with respect to the international law of watercourses. The Convention is divided into six parts, as were the 1994 ILC Draft Articles. The first part (the introduction) sets forth the definition of watercourses and explains that the Convention establishes a framework for the negotiation of agreements applying to specific watercourses. Such watercourse agreements may be required to modify the general provisions in the framework convention to the specific conditions of the watercourse. Part II sets forth general principles governing the allocation and use of watercourses, including the standard of equitable or reasonable utilization, the obligation not to cause significant harm, and general obligations to cooperate and exchange information. Part II was developed after a thorough review of existing treaties and state practice and is considered among many observers to reflect customary international law. Part III sets forth a system of notification and consultation for planned activities affecting an international watercourse. Part III is widely viewed as adding specific detail to obligations of notification and consultation that are well founded in international law. Part IV addresses the protection, preservation and management of watercourse ecosystems. Because this section addresses the relatively new concern of environmental protection and conservation, most observers believe it does not reflect customary law. Experience with State practice in the protection of freshwater ecosystems is not as great as in the issue of water allocation and use. Nonetheless, the approach in Part IV parallels somewhat the approach to pollution and conservation issues in the Convention on the Law of the Sea. Part V addresses harmful conditions and emergency situations, and Part VI includes a set of miscellaneous provisions, including a specific dispute settlement procedure.

---

1. DEFINITION AND SCOPE OF INTERNATIONAL WATERCOURSES

Determining exactly what should be considered the scope of the law on international watercourses has been more difficult than one might at first expect. Traditionally, international watercourses were considered only those parts of rivers or lakes that straddled or crossed borders. This seemed appropriate when the primary concern for international law was to ensure free navigation and transportation along international rivers and lakes.

More recently, environmental concerns have grown and the hydrologic relationships between groundwater and surface rivers and lakes have become better understood. Similarly, the importance of riparian zones to the quality and quantity of water flows is now recognized. This growing understanding of ecology has broadened our view of what should be protected or addressed in international laws and policies to one that encompasses connected groundwater systems, tributaries, headwaters, riparian zones, and other parts of a water basin.

An international law that focused only on the surface water that straddles a border now seems too narrow, and commentators have begun to discuss a broader scope for international law. In this regard, the 1966 ILA Helsinki Rules perhaps represent the "high water mark" for the scope of international law. Those rules applied to international drainage basins, defined broadly to cover "a geographical area extending over two or more states determined by the watershed limits of the system of waters, including surface and underground waters, flowing into a common terminus." Helsinki Rules, Art. II, ILA, 52nd Rep., at 485 (1966).

At the same time, extending international law to entire water basins would subject much larger areas of national territory to international oversight. Many States resisted the resulting loss of sovereignty, particularly as it might be applied to land areas. The 1997 Convention would ultimately drop the use of the term drainage basin, but use a similarly broad definition of watercourse: "a system of surface waters and groundwaters constituting by virtue of their physical relationship a unitary whole and normally flowing into a common terminus." Article 2(a).

―――――

QUESTIONS AND DISCUSSION

1. Compare the definition in the 1997 Convention to that used in the ILA Helsinki Rules noted above. What seems to be the difference if any? Also compare the Convention's definition to that used in Article 1 of the UNECE Convention on Transboundary Watercourses: "Transboundary waters means any surface or ground waters which mark, cross or are located on boundaries between two or more State; wherever transboundary waters flow directly into the sea, these transboundary waters end at a straight line across their respective mouths between points on the low-water line of their banks." Is there any substantive difference between the scope of the two conventions?

2. Among other things, the 1997 Convention did not address "confined groundwater", or that water that is not attached to surface water in any way. Nor did the Convention affect any of the several hundred agreements already existing with respect to transboundary water courses, thus leaving undecided questions about the relationship between this framework convention and preceding regional or bilateral agreements.

―――――

2. ALLOCATION OF INTERNATIONAL RESOURCES

The central focus of most early efforts to address the international law of watercourses was on the issue of how to allocate the waters among competing riparian states and uses. To what extent did downstream states have a right to a certain amount or quality of water left in the river for their use? What basis or standard should be used in resolving disputes between downstream and upstream states?

Four competing theories have dominated discussions over how to allocate water between riparian States, as well as the concept of equitable use: territorial sovereignty, territorial integrity, equitable utilization, and common management. Both territorial sovereignty and territorial integrity have been largely abandoned as rules of decision, although both remain very important for shaping international negotiations with respect to specific disputes. Note, for example, how both concepts were used in the Gabcikovo case, described above. The concept of equitable use is the concept adopted by most efforts at codification, including the 1997 U.N. Convention. The movement towards common or joint management, although encouraged in the 1997 U.N. Convention is not so much a legal requirement at this time as it is a trend in which transboundary water management is moving. *See* P. BIRNIE & A. BOYLE, INTERNATIONAL LAW & THE ENVIRONMENT 218–22 (1992)

Territorial Sovereignty. Under the doctrine of territorial sovereignty, States retain total control over all water in or flowing through their territory. Thus, upstream States are free to use the water anyway they want, without regard to the interests of downstream States. The doctrine is a specific application of the general concept of State sovereignty, discussed in Chapter 7, pages 326–30.

The doctrine is also known as the Harmon Doctrine, named after the U.S. Attorney General who issued the following opinion in a dispute with Mexico over diversions of the Rio Grande River. The Rio Grande flows from the San Juan Mountains in Colorado 1885 miles into the Gulf of Mexico. For most of this length, the river forms the border between the United States and Mexico. The Rio Grande flows through some of the most arid land in the country, and even though it is not by many measures a large river, it is the most significant source of water for that portion of the U.S.-Mexico border. In October 1894, Mexico complained to the United States that diversions of Rio Grande water for irrigation threatened the water supply of several important Mexican cities. The U.S. Secretary of State asked the Attorney General for a legal opinion regarding U.S. rights and responsibilities. The following is an excerpt from Attorney General Harmon's opinion regarding the law of international rivers.

Attorney General Opinion, 21 U.S. Op. Atty. Gen. 274, 280–83; 1895 WL 391 (U.S.A.G.)

The fundamental principle of international law is the absolute sovereignty of every nation, as against all others, within its own territory. Of the nature and scope of sovereignty with respect to judicial jurisdiction, which is one of its elements, Chief Justice Marshall said (Schooner Exchange v. McFaddon, 7 Cranch, p. 136):

"The jurisdiction of the nation within its own territory is necessarily exclusive and absolute. It is susceptible of no limitation not imposed by itself. Any restriction upon it, deriving validity from an external source, would imply a diminution of its sovereignty to the extent of the restriction, and an investment of that sovereignty to the same extent in that power which could impose such restriction. 'All exceptions', therefore, to the full and complete power of a nation within its own territories must be traced up to the consent of the nation itself. They can flow from no other legitimate source." * * *

The immediate as well as the possible consequences of the right asserted by Mexico show that its recognition is entirely inconsistent with the sovereignty of the United States over its national domain. Apart from the sum demanded by way of indemnity for the past, the claim involves not only the arrest of further settlement and development of large regions of country, but the abandonment, in great measure at least, of what has already been accomplished.

It is well known that the clearing and settlement of a wooded country affects the flow of streams, making it not only generally less, but also subjecting it to more sudden fluctuations between greater extremes, thereby exposing inhabitants on their banks to increase of the doubt danger of drought and flood. The principle now asserted might lead to consequences in other cases which need only be suggested.

It will be remembered that a large part of the territory in question was public domain of Mexico and was ceded as such to the United States, so that their proprietary as well as their sovereign rights are involved.

It is not suggested that the injuries complained of are or have been in any measure due to wantonness or wastefulness in the use of water or to any design or intention to injure. The water is simply insufficient to supply to needs of the great stretch of arid country through which the river, never large in the dry season, flows, giving much and receiving little.

The case presented is a novel one. Whether the circumstances make it possible or proper to take any action from considerations of comity is a question which does not pertain to this Department; but that question should be decided as one of policy only, because, in my opinion, the rules, principles, and precedents of international law impose no liability or obligation upon the United States.

The Harmon Doctrine has been largely, although not completely, discredited since the time of this opinion among most international lawyers, and little State practice supports the argument that it is customary law. Even the United States has failed to follow the doctrine, both in its subsequent dealings with Mexico and with Canada where the United States was the downstream user. Rather, the United States seemed to adopt the Harmon opinion as a negotiating strategy, to strengthen its position while it reached an agreement with Mexico over the relative rights and responsibilities regarding allocation of the Rio Grande. On the one hand, the United States continued to deny that it owed Mexico any legal obligation to deliver water in the Rio Grande, but at the same time it went to considerable lengths to keep the negotiations of a treaty open. Ultimately, this resulted in the negotiation of the 1906 *Convention between the United States of America and Mexico concerning the Equitable Distribution of the Waters of the Rio Grande for Irrigation Purposes*, 34 Stat. 2953 (1906). For a thoughtful discussion of the legal status of the Harmon Doctrine, *see* Stephen McCaffrey, *The Harmon Docrine One Hundred Years later: Buried, Not Praised*, 36 Natural Res. J. 549 (1996). Although the doctrine of territorial sovereignty is probably not customary law with respect to shared watercourses, it nonetheless is still an important argument frequently raised by upstream states in international disputes.

Territorial Integrity. The doctrine of territorial integrity is the opposite of the doctrine of territorial sovereignty. Under this theory, upstream States are not allowed to interfere with the "territorial integrity" of a downstream State. Thus, downstream States have a right to receive the full natural quantity and quality of water, and would have an implicit "veto power" over activities in upstream States. To some extent this was the position taken by Spain (and rejected) in the Lac Lanoux case, although as noted above there was no allegation of harm in that case.

Among the few states that have invoked this doctrine is, ironically, the United States. In a memorandum prepared for the United States Agent in the Trail Smelter arbitration, a case involving transfrontier air pollution rather than use of an international watercourse, the Legal Adviser of the U.S. Department of State declared:

It is a fundamental principle of the law of nations that a sovereign state is supreme within its own territorial domain and that it and its nationals are entitled to use and enjoy their territory and property without interference from an outside source.

Interestingly, among the authorities the Legal Adviser cited in support of this proposition was the very U.S. Supreme Court case relied upon by Attorney General Harmon in support of the absolute territorial sovereignty doctrine, The Schooner Exchange v. McFaddon. The Legal Adviser opined that an international wrong had been committed in the Trail Smelter case, consisting of "acts which deprive us of the free and untrammeled use of our territory in a manner which we as a sovereign state have an inherent and incontestable right to use it." While Trail Smelter involved transfrontier air pollution, emanating from a smelter at Trail, British Columbia, Canada, and causing harm in the U.S. state of Washington, the Legal Adviser's memorandum drew no distinction between harm caused by putting something into another state, on the one hand, and withholding something, on the other. Indeed, both change the natural status quo and interfere with a state's ability to dispose of its territory as it sees fit. If and to the extent that the former is prohibited, the latter should be as well. Otherwise, not only wholesale diversions of international watercourses, but also such activities as weather modification to the detriment of another state would be legitimized—a result that promotes neither the reasonable sharing of common natural resources nor friendly relations between states.

Stephen McCaffrey, *op. cit.* Although in its absolute form, the doctrine of territorial integrity has never enjoyed significant State practice and cannot be viewed as customary law, it nonetheless is closely related to the concept that one State should not cause environmental harm to another State. *See* Principle 21 of the *Stockholm Declaration,* and the principle not to cause environmental harm discussed in Chapter 7, pages 419–422.

Equitable Utilization. Both the territorial sovereignty and territorial integrity doctrines emanate directly from the concept of State sovereignty, and both would seem to be equally important for maintaining a State's sovereignty. With territorial integrity, the upstream State's ability to use the water is potentially held hostage to the downstream State's consent, and with territorial sovereignty the downstream State's rights to receive natural flows of water are subject to the development decisions of the upstream State. The need for a compromise is obvious, as a means to settle transboundary disputes peacefully.

The compromise adopted by most analysts in international water law is the concept of equitable utilization, which endorses a balanced approach to allocating among uses of shared watercourses. The doctrine of equitable utilization does not mean that each State receives equal rights, but rather that all States in a watercourse share sovereignty over the resource, and their interests must be reasonably balanced according to a range of factors. The doctrine of equitable utilization is endorsed by most efforts to codify the law of shared watercourses and natural resources, including the 1997 U.N. Convention.

UN Convention on the Law of the Non–Navigational Uses of International Watercourses, May 21, 1997, *reprinted in* 36 I.L.M. 700 (1997)

Article 5

Equitable and reasonable utilization and participation

1. Watercourse States shall in their respective territories utilize an international watercourse in an equitable and reasonable manner. In particular, an international watercourse shall be used and developed by watercourse States with a view to attaining optimal and sustainable utilization thereof and benefits therefrom, taking into account the interests of the watercourse States concerned, consistent with adequate protection of the watercourse.

2. Watercourse States shall participate in the use, development and protection of an international watercourse in an equitable and reasonable manner. Such participation includes both the right to utilize the watercourse and the duty to cooperate in the protection and development thereof, as provided in the present Convention.

Article 6

Factors relevant to equitable and reasonable utilization

1. Utilization of an international watercourse in an equitable and reasonable manner within the meaning of article 5 requires taking into account all relevant factors and circumstances, including:

(a) Geographic, hydrographic, hydrological, climatic, ecological and other factors of a natural character;

(b) The social and economic needs of the watercourse States concerned;

(c) The population dependent on the watercourse in each watercourse State;

(d) The effects of the use or uses of the watercourses in one watercourse State on other watercourse States;

(e) Existing and potential uses of the watercourse;

(f) Conservation, protection, development and economy of use of the water resources of the watercourse and the costs of measures taken to that effect;

(g) The availability of alternatives, of comparable value, to a particular planned or existing use.

2. In the application of article 5 or paragraph 1 of this article, watercourse States concerned shall, when the need arises, enter into consultations in a spirit of cooperation.

3. The weight to be given to each factor is to be determined by its importance in comparison with that of other relevant factors. In determining what is a reasonable and equitable use, all relevant factors are to be considered together and a conclusion reached on the basis of the whole.

Article 7

Obligation not to cause significant harm

1. Watercourse States shall, in utilizing an international watercourse in their territories, take all appropriate measures to prevent the causing of significant harm to other watercourse States.

2. Where significant harm nevertheless is caused to another watercourse State, the States whose use causes such harm shall, in the absence of agreement to such use, take all appropriate measures, having due regard for the provisions of articles 5 and 6, in consultation with the affected State, to eliminate or mitigate such harm and, where appropriate, to discuss the question of compensation. * * *

Article 10

Relationship between different kinds of uses

1. In the absence of agreement or custom to the contrary, no use of an international watercourse enjoys inherent priority over other uses.

2. In the event of a conflict between uses of an international watercourse, it shall be resolved with reference to articles 5 to 7, with special regard being given to the requirements of vital human needs.

QUESTIONS AND DISCUSSION

1. The doctrine of equitable utilization is often considered the cornerstone of the international law of watercourses. It is primarily concerned with the allocation of shared water resources among riparian states. Upstream States obviously prefer equitable utilization to any standard of territorial sovereignty or of one country 'doing no harm'. Is the UN Convention an equitable utilization convention or a do no appreciable harm convention?

Equitable utilization was not developed with broader considerations of environmental protection in mind, and it may be poorly suited for addressing environmental harms that do not conflict with another riparian party's use of the river. For example, marine or estuarine states may not have any clear rights under a doctrine of equitable utilization if they are not riparian states as well. Nor are instream environmental uses of rivers necessarily included in the types of uses that might be protected under the doctrine. Consider in this regard, the following excerpt from Patricia Birnie & Alan Boyle, International Law & The Environment, 250 (1992):

> The importance of viewing an international watercourse not merely as a shared natural resource to be exploited, but as a complete ecosystem whose development has diverse effects of an international character also emphasizes the limited utility of the principle of equitable utilization. Although correctly seen as the main principle of international watercourse law, this principle cannot sustain more than a modest role in allocating riparian rights. It affords an insufficient basis for measures of more comprehensive environmental protection.

Birnie and Boyle argue that equitable utilization may be most acceptable if viewed as a transition toward common management of watercourses aimed at comprehensive environmental and development goals. Do you agree?

2. Article 7 of the Convention presents the obligation not to cause significant harm to other watercourse states. How does this compare with Principle 21 of the

Stockholm Declaration? Does Article 7 provide any protection to the environment or does it apply to interference with the use of the water by watercourse states?

3. The standard of care required to avoid harm has been difficult to determine in many different contexts. Article 7 requires that States "take all reasonable measures" to prevent causing significant harm, which essentially requires the exercise of "due diligence". In choosing to use due diligence, both the ILC and the Convention negotiators rejected efforts to use a stricter standard. As Birnie and Boyle state:

> One ILC rapporteur, [Professor Stephen] McCaffrey has dealt with the choice between a standard of due diligence and more stringent obligations of pollution prevention in international watercourses. Although the latter interpretation is implicit in the view of some member of the Commission who have continued to favour a regime of strict liability for watercourse pollution, the rapporteur could find little or no evidence of state practice recognizing strict liability for damage which was non-accidental or did not result from a dangerous activity. In his view, this indicated that the standard required of the state was generally one of due diligence, implicit in the *Trail Smelter* arbitration and supported by state practice. This standard afforded the appropriate flexibility and allowed for adaption to different situations, including the level of development of the state concerned. Moreover, to minimize any problems of proof, the rapporteur believed that due diligence should be treated as a defence to be established by the source state, which would presumptively be liable.

Birnie and Boyle, International Law and the Environment, at 231–32. As you read Articles 21–23 of the Convention (regarding pollution, invasive species, and protection of the marine environment) consider whether the standard of due diligence applies to them as well—or is a stricter standard implicated? What about Slovakia's diversion of the Danube in the Gabcikovo controversy?

4. Would applying the standard of equitable utilization based on the factors mentioned in the Convention change the outcome of the Lac Lanoux Arbitration. How would you argue that France's unilateral diversion of the water from the Lac Lanoux basin met the requirements of equitable utilization under the Articles? What arguments on behalf of Spain would you make?

5. What other rules of decision might you consider for allocating water among competing users? For example, in the Western United States, water is allocated according to the prior appropriation doctrine, which is based on the concept of "first in time, first in right." Under prior appropriation, no subsequent user in time can use water that interferes with prior rights and uses of water. Could such a concept be used to allocate water across State boundaries? Should prior investments be rewarded in this way? We might also consider a water market that transcended political boundaries, where the rights to divert and use water are traded in an open market. Would the market be an appropriate mechanism for allocating among different users? In this regard, how should either of these approaches be adopted to reflect the concept of ecological uses of water or of "vital human needs" as mentioned in Article 10 of the Convention?

6. During the 1990s, many regional approaches, including for example those involving the Danube, the Mekong, the Ganges and the Rhine, reflected a trend away from a preoccupation with allocating water to a focus on allocating benefits among countries. Thus, countries may develop a river basin more efficiently and equitably, if the focus is less on the gallons used by each country and more on the potential or real economic benefits that can be derived from joint management.

3. NOTIFICATION AND CONSULTATION AMONG WATERCOURSE STATES

Another major recurring issue in the law of international watercourses has been the establishment of procedural rules to guide cooperation among watercourse States. These procedural requirements typically have included information exchange, notification and consultation procedures and can be viewed as a specific application of the principles of transboundary cooperation described in Chapter 7. Articles 9 and 11 of the 1997 UN Convention address general requirements to exchange information and Articles 12 through 19 provide for the procedural requirements placed on a watercourse State when it plans a development that could affect the rights or interests of other watercourse states.

Article 9

Regular exchange of data and information

1. Pursuant to article 8, watercourse States shall on a regular basis exchange readily available data and information on the condition of the watercourse, in particular that of a hydrological, meteorological, hydrogeological and ecological nature and related to the water quality as well as related forecasts.

2. If a watercourse State is requested by another watercourse State to provide data or information that is not readily available, it shall employ its best efforts to comply with the request but may condition its compliance upon payment by the requesting State of the reasonable costs of collecting and, where appropriate, processing such data or information.

3. Watercourse States shall employ their best efforts to collect and, where appropriate, to process data and information in a manner which facilitates its utilization by the other watercourse States to which it is communicated. * * *

Article 11

Information concerning planned measures

Watercourse States shall exchange information and consult each other and, if necessary, negotiate on the possible effects of planned measures on the condition of an international watercourse.

Article 12

Notification concerning planned measures with possible adverse effects

Before a watercourse State implements or permits the implementation of planned measures which may have a significant adverse effect upon other watercourse States, it shall provide those States with timely notification thereof. Such notification shall be accompanied by available technical data and information, including the results of any environmental impact assessment, in order to enable the notified States to evaluate the possible effects of the planned measures. * * *

Article 15

Reply to notification

The notified States shall communicate their findings to the notifying State as early as possible within the period applicable pursuant to article 13. If a notified State finds that implementation of the planned measures would be inconsistent with the provisions of articles 5 or 7 [excerpted, *supra*, at pages

835–36], it shall attach to its finding a documented explanation setting forth the reasons for the finding.

Article 16

Absence of reply to notification

1. If, within the period applicable pursuant to article 13 [a six-month period for reply to notification], the notifying State receives no communication under article 15, it may, subject to its obligations under articles 5 and 7, proceed with the implementation of the planned measures, in accordance with the notification and any other data and information provided to the notified States.

2. Any claim to compensation by a notified State which has failed to reply within the period applicable pursuant to article 13 may be offset by the costs incurred by the notifying State for action undertaken after the expiration of the time for a reply which would not have been undertaken if the notified State had objected within that period.

Article 17

Consultations and negotiations concerning planned measures

1. If a communication is made under article 15 that implementation of the planned measures would be inconsistent with the provisions of articles 5 or 7, the notifying State and the State making the communication shall enter into consultations and, if necessary, negotiations with a view to arriving at an equitable resolution of the situation.

2. The consultations and negotiations shall be conducted on the basis that each State must in good faith pay reasonable regard to the rights and legitimate interests of the other State.

3. During the course of the consultations and negotiations, the notifying State shall, if so requested by the notified State at the time it makes the communication, refrain from implementing or permitting the implementation of the planned measures for a period of six months unless otherwise agreed.

Article 18

Procedures in the absence of notification

1. If a watercourse State has reasonable grounds to believe that another watercourse State is planning measures that may have a significant adverse effect upon it, the former State may request the latter to apply the provisions of article 12. The request shall be accompanied by a documented explanation setting forth its grounds.

2. In the event that the State planning the measures nevertheless finds that it is not under an obligation to provide a notification under article 12, it shall so inform the other State, providing a documented explanation setting forth the reasons for such finding. If this finding does not satisfy the other State, the two States shall, at the request of that other State, promptly enter into consultations and negotiations in the manner indicated in paragraphs 1 and 2 of article 17.

3. During the course of the consultations and negotiations, the State planning the measures shall, if so requested by the other State at the time it requests the initiation of consultations and negotiations, refrain from implementing or permitting the implementation of those measures for a period of six months unless otherwise agreed.

————

QUESTION AND DISCUSSION

1. To what extent do the Convention's provisions on notification and consultation go beyond what was deemed to be required in the Lac Lanoux Arbitration? Will compliance with these provisions be sufficient always to meet the standard of "good faith" negotiations? How do these provisions help to inform the general principles of notice and consultation described in Chapter 7.

2. Article 19 of the Convention allows a State to avoid the detailed procedures where immediate implementation is of the "utmost urgency in order to protect public health, public safety or other equally important interests." What types of projects would you think this should include? Would France's planned development in Lac Lanoux qualify?

3. Compare the notification and consultation requirements here with those in the UN ECE Convention on Environmental Impact Assessment in a Transboundary Context, reprinted in the *Treaty Supplement*.

————

4. PROTECTION OF THE RESOURCE

Environmental concerns and the needs to protect the ecological integrity of water systems raise relatively new issues for the law of international watercourses. It is still unclear how obligations not to harm the environment of a shared watercourse are different than the general rules of equitable utilization. The 1997 UN Convention addresses the environmental protection separately, but the relationship between these provisions and the doctrine of equitable utilization remains somewhat unclear.

Article 20

Protection and preservation of ecosystems

Watercourse States shall, individually and, where appropriate, jointly, protect and preserve the ecosystems of international watercourses.

Article 21

Prevention, reduction and control of pollution

1. For the purpose of this article, "pollution of an international watercourse" means any detrimental alteration in the composition or quality of the waters of an international watercourse which results directly or indirectly from human conduct.

2. Watercourse States shall, individually and, where appropriate, jointly, prevent, reduce and control the pollution of an international watercourse that may cause significant harm to other watercourse States or to their environment, including harm to human health or safety, to the use of the waters for any beneficial purpose or to the living resources of the watercourse. Watercourse States shall take steps to harmonize their policies in this connection.

3. Watercourse States shall, at the request of any of them, consult with a view to arriving at mutually agreeable measures and methods to prevent, reduce and control pollution of an international watercourse, such as:

(a) Setting joint water quality objectives and criteria;

(b) Establishing techniques and practices to address pollution from point and non-point sources;

(c) Establishing lists of substances the introduction of which into the waters of an international watercourse is to be prohibited, limited, investigated or monitored.

Article 22
Introduction of alien or new species

Watercourse States shall take all measures necessary to prevent the introduction of species, alien or new, into an international watercourse which may have effects detrimental to the ecosystem of the watercourse resulting in significant harm to other watercourse States.

Article 23
Protection and preservation of the marine environment

Watercourse States shall, individually and, where appropriate, in cooperation with other States, take all measures with respect to an international watercourse that are necessary to protect and preserve the marine environment, including estuaries, taking into account generally accepted international rules and standards.

Article 24
Management

1. Watercourse States shall, at the request of any of them, enter into consultations concerning the management of an international watercourse, which may include the establishment of a joint management mechanism.

2. For the purposes of this article, "management" refers, in particular, to:

(a) Planning the sustainable development of an international watercourse and providing for the implementation of any plans adopted; and

(b) Otherwise promoting the rational and optimal utilization, protection and control of the watercourse.

QUESTIONS AND DISCUSSION

1. *An Ecosystem Approach.* Article 20 of the 1997 UN Convention requires states to protect the "ecosystems" of international watercourses. Consider the following excerpt from VED NANDA, INTERNATIONAL ENVIRONMENTAL LAW AND POLICY, 274–75 (1994).

> In the context of international agreements, there have been an increasing number of calls for ecosystem management of international watercourses; yet it is only in the last decade that the concept has begun to appear in the language of international documents and resolutions. The United Nations Environment Program in its ten-year review recognized this need, noting that the period from 1972–1982 had seen "increasing recognition of the need for better management of water resources by treating river basins as unitary systems."

However, the concept was slow to be incorporated into actual international agreements. As noted by the ILC, the term "ecosystem" was used in the 1978 Agreement between Canada and the United States on Great Lakes Water Quality, where reference is made to "the Great Lakes Basin Ecosystem." Explicit use of the "ecosystem" also appears in a few documents such as the Convention on the Conservation of Antarctic Marine Living Resources, the World Charter for Nature, and a few regional agreements.

As is apparent from these examples, the use of the term "ecosystem" has generally been limited to those agreements which addressed wildlife resources and biodiversity issues, and not specifically the use of international watercourses.

The increasing usage of the ecosystem concept, as evidenced by these international agreements, as well as the draft articles themselves, is indicative of the trend towards more regional-based management efforts. Article 20 [of the 1997 Convention] is fully consistent with this trend. The ILC recognizes this broadening of focus, noting that the emphasis on protection and preservation of ecosystems intended by this article is part of a larger recognition by states of the necessity to protect ecological processes, rather than just individual species or discrete attributes of the environment. As noted by Professor Odum, "the concept of the ecosystem is and should be a broad one, its main function in ecological thought being to emphasize obligatory relationships, interdependence and causal relationships." Under such a broad definition, the emphasis on flood control, apportionment, or hydropower generation that has dominated previous international agreements concerning international watercourses would no longer be the only concerns of such agreements. This increased breadth encompassed by the ecosystem concept means both increased applicability and increased complexity in application.

Early ILC drafts used the word "environment" instead of "ecosystem". Is environment more or less precise as a legal term than ecosystem? Can both a puddle and the Rhine River be considered an ecosystem? Which term do you prefer? How does the requirement to protect ecosystems relate to the provisions on equitable use and to the general obligation not to cause harm? Is the use of "ecosystem" consistent with the definition of "watercourse"? Does the focus on ecosystems in Article 20 make you less concerned over the choice to address watercourses rather than drainage basins in the Convention?

2. *Threshold of Significant Harm.* Not all harm to the environment or to other users is prohibited under the 1997 UN Convention. In Articles 3, 7, and 21, the Convention requires that harm be "significant." In submitting the Draft Convention to the UNGA, the Working Group noted that the term "significant" is not used in the Convention to mean "substantial." Significant adverse effects "must be capable of being established by objective evidence and not be trivial in nature, it need not rise to the level of being substantial."

As we have seen in other contexts, the threshold for what level of harm is required is frequently a focus of debate. In general three choices for a threshold on the level of harm have been advanced in international environmental policy: "substantial harm," "significant harm" and "appreciable harm." Although precise definitions of these different thresholds are elusive, does "significant harm" imply more or less harm than "appreciable harm"? Than "substantial harm"? What factors would you use in trying to convince the ICJ that a harm to an international watercourse was or was not "significant"? Would it matter that the 1990 draft articles used a standard based on "appreciable harm"?

3. Article 21 also requires prevention, reduction or control of pollution that "may" cause significant harm to other watercourse States. Does this language suggest that the Convention has adopted a precautionary approach to pollution control? How does the Convention articles compare with other instruments in addressing potential harm? Is there a conflict between the threshold of "significant harm" in Article 21 and the requirement to preserve and protect the ecosystems of watercourses in Article 20? Could a State that meets Article 21 still violate Article 20?

4.   Note that the Commentary to the Convention advises that Articles 21, 22 and 23 impose a due diligence standard on watercourse States. In what other areas of international environmental law have we seen requirements for due diligence. What does it mean to act with due diligence?

5.   *Equitable Utilization v. Prevention of Significant Environmental Harm.* Another difficult issue is the relationship of the doctrine of equitable utilization with the provisions relating to environmental harm. Article 7 of the 1997 Convention suggests that the general obligation to prevent harm to another State should be mitigated "having due regard to" the concept of equitable utilization. Yet, the provisions that address pollution do not seem to clarify the relationship between equitable utilization and pollution that may cause "significant harm". Is the obligation not to cause significant harm by pollution a limitation on the rights of equitable utilization of a watercourse, or does it work the other way? For example, does the right to equitable use of a watercourse ever entitle an upstream State to pollute beyond a level that might cause significant harm to other watercourse States? Must one balance the factors suggested by the concept of equitable use or is the determination that significant harm has occurred from pollution sufficient under Article 21 to stop an activity? If the latter, why should harm from pollution be treated more preferentially than other types of harm (which under Article 7 seem subject to equitable utilization)?

To some extent, this may not be settled in customary international law—but the commentary accompanying the ILC Draft Articles clearly showed their intention that equitable utilization should be subservient to the prohibitions against significant harm. Thus, equitable utilization would only be relevant in the pollution context primarily in determining whether pollution that fell below the "significant" harm threshold was permissible. Do you agree with this approach, or do you prefer the approach taken in the ILA Helsinki Rules and suggested by Article 7 of the 1997 Convention that conditions the obligation to prevent pollution on consistency with the principle of "equitable utilization?"

6.   *Joint Management.* The concept of joint or common management is a natural extension of the doctrine of equitable utilization. If every riparian State has an equal right (at least qualitatively), then the States must necessarily share in the management of the resource. Common management reflects the need in light of the doctrine of equitable utilization to manage the development of a watercourse with the active participation of all interested States. Establishing permanent institutions or rules for joint management allow the States to manage the watercourse as an integrated whole, which better reflects the ecological reality and provides greater opportunity for joint development and international regulation. Common management is not yet a requirement of international law, but Article 24 of the 1997 Convention requires all watercourse States to enter into consultations over joint mechanisms if one State requests it.

7.   The 1997 Convention also addresses certain procedural rights for non-State activities, in ensuring at least some equal access to courts. Article 32 of the Convention prohibits discriminating against neighboring states' citizens in judicial proceedings: "Unless the watercourse States concerned have agreed otherwise for the protection of the interests of persons, natural or juridical, who have suffered or are under a serious threat of suffering significant transboundary harm as a result of activities related to an international watercourse, a watercourse State shall not discriminate on the basis of nationality or residence or place where the injury occurred, in granting to such persons, in accordance with its legal system, access to judicial or other procedures, or a right to claim compensation or other relief in respect of significant harm caused by such activities carried on in its territory."

8. As noted above, the 1997 UN Convention is intended as a framework convention, not necessarily in that there will be protocols signed to the convention, but that watercourse States will sign more specific agreements with respect to regions or watersheds, using the UN Convention as a broad framework. What issues would you expect to be addressed in specific watercourse agreements? What direction does this framework convention provide to negotiators of specific watercourse agreements? What differentiates the approach taken in the 1997 Convention from other framework Conventions, such as the 1985 Vienna Convention on the Protection of the Ozone Layer or the 1992 Framework Convention on Climate Change? Although it predates the UN Convention by five years, the 1992 Convention on the Protection and Use of Transboundary Watercourses and Lakes negotiated under the auspices of the UN Economic Commission for Europe (UNECE) can be considered an example of what a regional agreement might look like. Although the UNECE Convention reflects much of the ILC's work up to its 1990 Draft Articles, the Convention is more detailed and probably more protective of the environment than either the ILC Draft Articles or the 1997 UN Convention.

SECTION III.   CROSS-CUTTING THEMES AND CURRENT ISSUES

A.   THE GREAT LAKES AND THE INTERNATIONAL JOINT COMMISSION

One of the most widely respected efforts at joint management is the U.S.–Canada effort to manage the Great Lakes and other boundary waters between the two countries. The Great Lakes, alone, constitute one-fifth of the world's freshwater. Under the 1909 Boundary Waters Treaty, Canada and the United States created the International Joint Commission (IJC), an independent bilateral agency to manage their shared water resources (later the IJC would also address transboundary air pollution). *See* Treaty Relating to Boundary Waters and Questions Arising Between the United States and Canada, (Jan. 11, 1909), U.S.–Britain, 36 Stat. 2448, T.S. No. 548 (1909) [hereinafter Boundary Waters Treaty].

The IJC is composed of six members, three from each country. Its main mission is to provide for the equitable use of the waters, but it also addresses navigation, power generation and pollution issues. The IJC also serves as a conciliatory body, which makes non-binding recommendations to the parties in case of conflict. Paul Marshall Parker, *High Ross Dam: The IJC Takes a Hard Look at the Environmental Consequences of Hydroelectric Power Generation—1982 Supplementary Order*, 58 Wash. L. Rev. 443 (1983). The Commission has administrative, judicial, consultative and arbitral functions, and the parties often consult the Commission before engaging in negotiations.

The Commission began addressing environmental issues in 1945, but water quality became a central focus with adoption of the 1972 Great Lakes Water Quality Agreements, *see* Great Lakes Water Quality Agreement, U.S.–Canada, 23 U.S.T.S. 301, T.I.A.S. No. 7312 (April 15, 1972); 1978

Agreement Between the United States and Canada on Great Lakes Water Quality, U.S.–Canada, 30 U.S.T. 1383, T.I.A.S. No. 9257 (Nov. 22, 1978). These agreements take an ecosystem approach to water quality.

The IJC is advised by a Water Quality Board and a Science Advisory Board. The former is comprised of high-level managers from federal, state and provincial agencies selected equally from both countries. It is supposed to help coordinate policies among the different jurisdictions having responsibility for pollution into the Great Lakes. The Science Advisory Board consists primarily of government and academic experts charged with providing scientific advice and knowledge to the IJC. The following excerpt from the Great Lakes Water Quality Atlas describes the pollution control regime under the Great Lakes Water Quality Treaties.

Environment Canada & U.S. Environmental Protection Agency, Joint Management of the Great Lakes, in The Great Lakes: Environmental Atlas and Resource Book 39–42, (3d ed. 1995).

The Boundary Waters Treaty of 1909

In 1905 the International Waterways Commission was created to advise the governments of both countries about levels and flows in the Great Lakes, especially in relation to the generation of electricity by hydropower. Its limited advisory powers proved inadequate for problems related to pollution and environmental damage. One of its first recommendations was for a stronger institution with the authority for study of broader boundary water issues and the power to make binding decisions.

The Boundary Waters Treaty was signed in 1909 and provided for the creation of the International Joint Commission (IJC). The IJC has the authority to resolve disputes over the use of water resources that cross the international boundary. Most of its efforts for the Great Lakes have been devoted to carrying out studies requested by the governments and advising the governments about problems.

In 1912, water pollution was one of the first problems referred to the IJC for study. In 1919, after several years of study, the IJC concluded that serious water quality problems required a new treaty to control pollution. However, no agreement was reached.

Additional studies in the 1940s led to new concerns by the IJC. The Commission recommended that water quality objectives be established for the Great Lakes and that technical advisory boards be created to provide continuous monitoring and surveillance of water quality.

Public and scientific concern about pollution of the lakes grew as accelerated eutrophication became more obvious through the 1950s. In 1964, the IJC began a new reference study on pollution in the lower Great Lakes. The report on this study in 1970 placed the principal blame for eutrophication on excessive phosphorus.

The study proposed basin-wide efforts to reduce phosphorus loadings from all sources. It was recognized that reduction of phosphorus depended on control of local sources. Uniform effluent limits were urged for all industries and municipal sewage treatment systems in the basin. Research suggested that land runoff could also be an important source of nutrients and other pollutants into the lakes. The result of the reference study was the signing of the first Great Lakes Water Quality Agreement in 1972. * * *

The International Joint Commission

The IJC has three responsibilities for the Great Lakes under the original treaty. The first is the limited authority to approve applications for the use, obstruction or diversion of boundary waters on either side of the border that would affect the natural level or flow on either side.

Under this authority, it is the IJC that determines how the control works on the St. Marys River and the St. Lawrence River will be operated to control releases of water from Lakes Superior and Ontario. It also regulates flows into Lake Superior from Long Lake and Lake Ogoki.

The second responsibility is to conduct studies of specific problems under references, or requests, from the governments. The implementation of the recommendations resulting from IJC reference studies is at the discretion of the two governments. When a reference is made to the IJC, the practice has been to commission a board of experts to supervise the study and to conduct the necessary research. A number of such studies have been undertaken in the history of the IJC.

The third responsibility is to arbitrate specific disputes that may arise between the two governments in relation to boundary waters. The governments may refer any matters of difference to the Commission for a final decision. This procedure requires the approval of both governments and has never been invoked.

In addition to these specific powers under the 1909 Treaty, the IJC provides a procedure for monitoring and evaluating progress under the Water Quality Agreement. For this purpose, two standing advisory boards are called for in the Agreement. * * *

The IJC relies on work done by the various levels of the two governments and the academic community. It maintains an office in each of the national capitals and a Great Lakes Regional Office in Windsor, Ontario. The Great Lakes Office provides administrative support and technical assistance to the boards and a public information service for the programs of the Commission. * * *

The Great Lakes Water Quality Agreement—1972

The Great Lakes Water Quality Agreement established common water quality objectives to be achieved in both countries and three processes that would be carried out binationally. The first is control of pollution, which each country agreed to accomplish under its own laws. The chief objective was reduction of phosphorus levels to no more than 1 ppm (mg per litre) in discharges from large sewage treatment plants into Lakes Erie and Ontario together with new limits on industry. Other objectives included elimination of oil, visible solid wastes and other nuisance conditions.

The second process was research on Great Lakes problems to be carried out separately in each country as well as cooperatively. Both countries established new Great Lakes research programs. Major cooperative research was carried out on pollution problems of the upper Great Lakes and on pollution from land use and other sources.

The third process was surveillance and monitoring to identify problems and to measure progress in solving problems. Initially, water chemistry was emphasized and levels of pollutants were reported. Now, the surveillance plan is designed to assess the health of the Great Lakes ecosystem and increasingly depends on monitoring effects of pollution on living organisms.

The Agreement provided for a review of the objectives after 5 years and negotiation of a new agreement with different objectives if necessary. Tangible results had been achieved when the review was carried out in 1977. The total discharge of nutrients into the lakes had been noticeably reduced. Cultural, or human-made eutrophication, bacterial contamination and the more obvious nuisance conditions in rivers and nearshore waters had declined. However, new problems involving toxic chemicals had been revealed by research and the surveillance and monitoring program.

Public health warnings had been issued for consumption of certain species of fish in many locations. Sale of certain fish was prohibited due to unsafe levels of PCBs, mercury and, later, mirex and other chemicals. In 1975, discovery of high levels of PCBs in lake trout on Isle Royale in Lake Superior demonstrated that the lakes were receiving toxic chemicals by long-range atmospheric transport. These developments and the results of studies that were carried out after the 1972 Agreement set the stage for the next major step in Great Lakes management.

The Upper Lakes Study concluded that phosphorus objectives should be set for Lakes Huron, Michigan and Superior. This development was significant because it recognized the Great Lakes as a single system and called for joint management objectives for Lake Michigan and its tributaries that had not previously been considered boundary waters.

The study on pollution from land use and other nonpoint sources was known as PLUARG (Pollution from Land Use Activities Reference Group). The study demonstrated that runoff from agriculture and urban areas was affecting water quality in the Great Lakes. This significant development confirmed that control of direct discharge of pollution from point sources alone into the Great Lakes and tributaries would not be enough to achieve the water quality objectives. It also called for control of nonpoint pollution into the Great Lakes from land runoff and the atmosphere.

The experience under the 1972 Agreement demonstrated that despite complex jurisdictional problems, binational joint management by Canada and the United States could protect the Great Lakes better than either country could alone. In 1978, a new Great Lakes Water Quality Agreement was signed that preserved the basic features of the first Agreement and built on the previous results by setting up a new stage in joint management.

The Great Lakes Water Quality Agreement—1978

As part of improved pollution control, the 1978 Agreement called for setting target loadings for phosphorus for each lake and for virtual elimination of discharges of toxic chemicals. The target loadings were a step toward a new management goal that has come to be called "an ecosystem approach."

In contrast to the earlier Agreement that called for protection of waters of the Great Lakes, the 1978 Agreement calls for restoring and maintaining "the chemical, physical and biological integrity of the waters of the Great Lakes Basin Ecosystem." The ecosystem is defined as "the interacting components of air, land and water and living organisms including man within the drainage basin of the St. Lawrence River." * * *

The Great Lakes Water Quality Agreement—1987

In 1987, the Agreement was revised to strengthen management provisions, call for development of ecosystem objectives and indicators, and address non-point sources of pollution, contaminated sediment airborne toxic substances and pollution from contaminated groundwater. New management approaches included development of Remedial Action Plans (RAPs) for geographic Areas of Concern and Lakewide Management Plans (LAMPs) for Critical Pollutants.

The ecosystem approach was strengthened by calling for development of ecosystem objectives and indicators, and by focusing RAPs and LAMPs on elimination of impairments of beneficial uses. The uses include various aspects of human and aquatic community health and specifically include habitat. By clearly focusing management activities on endpoints in the living system, additional meaning is given to the goal of restoring and maintaining the integrity of the Great Lakes basin ecosystem. The agreement to prepare Lakewide Management Plans includes a commitment to develop a schedule of reductions in loads of critical pollutants entering the lakes in order to meet water quality objectives and restore beneficial uses.

QUESTIONS AND DISCUSSION

1. *The Gut Dam Arbitration.* Canada built the Gut Dam across the St. Lawrence River with the consent of the United States. As a result of other activities conducted by both the United States and Canada, the water level of Lake Ontario was higher between 1947 and 1952 than it ever was before. The high water levels flooded property along the southern shore of the lake and on some islands in the St. Lawrence. The property owners' efforts to sue Canada in the United States failed, but the United States and Canada agreed to establish an international arbitral tribunal, much as was done with respect to the *Trail Smelter Arbitration, see* Chapter 10, pages 512–19. The Lake Ontario Claims Tribunal was established pursuant to the agreement with Canada concerning the Establishment of an International Arbitral Tribunal to Dispose of United States Claims Relating to Gut Dam, signed March 25, 1965, 17 U.S.T. 1566, T.I.A.S. No. 6114. The case turned on an interpretation of an agreement between the two countries, in which Canada agreed to compensate at least some property owners in the United States for damage caused by their construction and operation of the dam. The dispute centered on whether this provision covered all of the claimants. Ultimately, Canada agreed to pay to the United States $350,000 in full settlement of all claims. The tribunal recorded the settlement and terminated the proceedings. *See* 8 Int'l Leg. Mat. 118, 133–42 (1969); 7 Can. Y.B.Int'l L. 316–18 (1969).

2. The use of river commissions and joint management, like that illustrated by the IJC, has clearly been most effective in developed countries, but several important efforts in developing countries have improved the management of shared rivers through complex regimes of cooperation.

The earliest and in some ways still the most ambitious was the Zambezi River Management Plan. The Zambezi River flows approximately 3,000 kilometers through eight African countries. The river basin drains an area of 1.3 million kilometers and is home to over 20 million people. See J. Teede & A. Teede; The Zambezi, River of the Goods, at 11 (1990). The Zambezi River Action Plan (ZACPLAN) was initiated by the riparian states with the assistance of UNEP, to "promote the development, and implementation of environmentally sound water resources management in the whole river system. It [was intended to] contribute to the incorporation by the river basin States of environmental considerations in water resources management while increasing long-term sustainable development." Para. 15. The Plan is one of the most ambitious efforts to adopt "integrated water basin management" in developing countries. *See* Botswana–Mozambique–Tanzania–Zambia–Zimbabwe: Agreement on the Plan for the Environmentally Sound Management of the Common Zambezi River System, done at Harare, Zimbabwe on May 28, 1987,

Reprinted in 27 ILM 1112 (1988). *See generally* on the implementation of the Zambezi plan, *Effective Management of the ZACPLAN,* Southern African Development Coordination Conference Report (1990)

The Zambezi plan takes an integrated approach to river basin planning and emphasizes environmental protection efforts in a way that is still rare. Most joint management regimes in developing countries emphasize development over environmental considerations. *See, e.g.,* Treaty Between His Majesty's Government of Nepal and The Government of India Concerning the Integrated Development of the Mahakali River including the Sarada Barrage, Tanakpur Barrage and Pacheshwar Project, Feb. 12, 1996, *reprinted in* 36 I.L.M. 540 (May, 1997); Treaty Between the Government of the Republic of India and the Government of the People's Republic of Bangladesh on Sharing of the Ganga/Ganges Waters at Farakka, Dec. 12, 1996, *reprinted in 36* I.L.M. 523 (May, 1997). Both treaties allocated specific amounts of water between the countries and established joint river commissions, but neither made any reference to environmental protection. What principles would you recommend that watercourse States include in any water management plan?

————

B.   INTERNATIONAL TRADE AND THE COMMODIFICATION OF WATER

Many observers believe that a major cause of water misuse and declining water supplies is the provision of water at very low or no cost. At least theoretically, improving price signals so that water users pay a price reflecting the full environmental and social costs of water could significantly improve water-use efficiency and release the pressure on water supplies. Privatizing the distribution systems could also improve the efficiency of water delivery when compared to the performance of large government-run utilities. Potential efficiency gains provide the conceptual justification for promoting privatization of water supplies as a primary response to water shortages.

In practice, however, privatization of water supplies has frequently led to monopoly control of water resources (with their own problems of inefficiency and inequity), as well as to reduced services for the poor and lower ecosystem protection. In short, privatizing water resources can improve efficiency, but, unless significantly regulated and shaped, privatization can also undermine environmental and equity values. The underlying concession agreements (that transfer rights to water to private companies) should adequately lay out specific conditions ensuring environmental protection and access to the poor. Full-cost pricing initiatives should enlist targeted water subsidies for the poor as well as earmark funds for the protection of ecosystems and the extension of water and sanitation services. The long-term impact of these privatization programs on environmental protection and social equity needs to be thoroughly analyzed, particularly in developing countries.

The commodification of water also has implications for international trade policy. Trade in bulk water supplies is becoming more economically viable and is seen as a growing threat in Canada and other relatively water-rich countries. Free trade agreements like the North American Free Trade Agreement include water as a commercial good subject to the disciplines of international trade. NAFTA and other trade agreements thus might prevent countries from putting export controls on water supplies, thereby limiting their ability to ensure water benefits to local populations.

Just such a concern has arisen in the Great Lakes in recent years. Alarmed by a 1998 proposal from a Canadian company to export 158 million gallons from Lake Superior by tankers to Asia, environmental groups and elected officials have scrambled to ensure that the already depleted Great Lakes are not drained further for the benefit of distant populations. Most notably, in June of 2001 the state governors and the Canadian Provincial premiers bordering the Great Lakes agreed to negotiate within three years a legally binding water compact or other instrument to set forth clear standards for reviewing proposals to withdraw water from the Great Lakes. The 2001 agreement set forth specific principles for designing the review system under the future agreement:

> The new set of binding agreement(s) will establish a decision making standard that the States and Provinces will utilize to review new proposals to withdraw water from the Great Lakes Basin as well as proposals to increase existing water withdrawals or existing water withdrawal capacity.

> The new standard shall be based upon the following principles:

> • Preventing or minimizing Basin water loss through return flow and implementation of environmentally sound and economically feasible water conservation measures; and

> • No significant adverse individual or cumulative impacts to the quantity or quality of the Waters and Water–Dependent Natural Resources of the Great Lakes Basin; and

> • An Improvement to the Waters and Water–Dependent Natural Resources of the Great Lakes Basin; and

> • Compliance with the applicable state, provincial, federal, and international laws and treaties.

The Great Lakes Charter Annex: A Supplementary Agreement to the Great Lakes Charter, Directive No. 3 (June 18, 2001) (available at <www.glu.org>). In the meantime, the governors of the eight states agreed that they would use these same principles to review (and presumably reject) any major water withdrawal proposal. *See* William Claiborne, *Governors Curb Use of Great Lakes Water*, THE WASHINGTON POST, A2 (June 19, 2002). The governors would probably have banned such diversions from the Great Lakes altogether, but they were afraid of violating international trade rules that arguably prohibit disparate treatment of proposals to divert water for domestic use versus for export. As you read Chapter 15 on trade and environment, consider how international trade rules will affect the efforts of state and Provincial leaders to protect the Great Lakes.

―――――

C.   ENVIRONMENTAL SECURITY AND FRESHWATER

In recent years, the importance of environmental issues to the overall security of a State has helped to give rise to the concept of environmental security. See Chapter 17. Water scarcity is among the environmental issues most commonly cited as threatening national security. Access to water is an integral component of maintaining food production and a nation's food security. Water scarcity can also be a source of direct hostility between countries. In some instances, most notably in the Gulf War, cutting off access to water has been discussed as a potential weapon of war.

It is in fact in the Middle East where the scarcity of water seems most likely to disrupt regional security. The Middle East already rife with conflict encompasses a range of shared watercourses, any one of which could ignite the region.

ROBIN CLARKE, WATER: THE INTERNATIONAL CRISIS 100–05 (1991)

Existing tensions in the Middle East add an extra dimension to the difficult problem of sharing limited water resources. Populations are increasing, and water is becoming scarce throughout the region. A 1988 study by the Center for Strategic and International Studies ... concluded that the situation is likely to become so acute that, in the near future, water—not oil—will be the dominant resource of the Middle East. Water scarcity severely curtails agricultural and economic development, and increasing shortages will bring desperate competition for water, heighten existing tensions between countries and increase the potential for armed conflict in the region.

In 1965, a dispute arose about Israel's use of water originating in Arab states. Israel wanted to divert water for its own use, and the failure to reach an agreement with neighbouring countries on the details of the plan led to Israel carrying out the diversion unilaterally. In response, the Arab states in which the water originated planned to divert their rivers into other Arab states, thus depriving Israel of some of its water supply. Regarding this as a serious threat to its security, Israel launched a preemptive strike on Syrian construction sites with military aircraft.

Israel's water-supply problems are exacerbated through over-pumping of the Sea of Galilee which has created salinity problems in the nation's main water source. To avoid the potential water crisis, Israel has developed plans to build a canal and pump water from the Mediterranean to the Dead Sea, and to construct reservoirs above the Jordan valley. This, however, has led to conflict with Jordan, which fears that pumping water into the Dead Sea will waterlog areas of irrigated agriculture in the East Ghor Canal region.

Israel has recently made a water-transfer agreement with Egypt, which originally, under President Sadat, offered Israel 400 million cubic metres per year of fresh water in exchange for a Palestinian solution. Up to a quarter of Israel's water resources is available in the aquifer shared with the West Bank, and any action in this region is likely to increase the divisions and tensions that already exist. Increased water pumping by Israel in the Jordan Valley and along the occupied West Bank is said by Palestinians and Jordanians to have lowered the water table throughout the valley. This deprives Arab farmers of water in the Jordanian East Bank and in the occupied West Bank and, in effect, constrains the economic development of the region and limits the number of Palestinians who can settle there.

Even without the problems arising from long-standing Arab–Israeli differences, many other countries of the Middle East are in dispute over water. Many upstream countries have plans to use the waters of shared rivers and aquifers to fill reservoirs and irrigation systems in order to increase agricultural production. Syria is planning to divert water from the Yarmuk River, Turkey from the upper Euphrates and Tigris, Libya from its shared aquifer and Ethiopia from the Blue Nile.

Jordan's water supply is under threat from Syria, which plans to divert 40 per cent of the flow of the Yarmuk River into its irrigation system. This would seriously reduce Jordan's water supply—also used largely for irrigation—and lead to an increase in the salinity of water in the Lower Yarmuk and Lower Jordan. Jordan has therefore signed an agreement with Iraq to transfer water from the Euphrates over the mountains into Jordan.

In turn, both Syria and Iraq are outraged by the action of upstream Turkey, with whom they share the Euphrates–Tigris basin. Turkey reduced the flow of this major river system in January 1990 to allow a huge reservoir behind the newly constructed Ataturk Dam to be filled. The Euphrates is the biggest single source of water for Syria and Iraq, and their supplies are likely to be interrupted for five to eight years. * * *

Competition for the waters of the Nile is severe, as all countries sharing the basin are experiencing water scarcity. The Nile basin covers one-tenth of the African continent, and forms part of nine African countries including downstream countries such as Egypt and the Sudan, and upstream countries such as Tanzania, Kenya and Ethiopia.

Egypt's increasing water supply problems are due to the country's almost total dependence on the Nile for water. As water needs increased in line with its growing population, Egypt negotiated an arrangement under which the Sudan agreed to provide Egypt with its excess water from the Nile. Because the population of the Sudan is now also increasing, the country is developing large-scale irrigation projects to match the demand for food, and has itself reached the limit of its available water supply. Both countries are therefore turning to upstream countries such as Ethiopia to answer their water needs.

However, Ethiopia is not bound by any agreement with Egypt over water supply, and Ethiopia stated at the 1977 UN Water Conference in Argentina that it was "the sovereign right of any riparian state, in the absence of an international agreement, to proceed unilaterally with the development of water resources within its territory." Ethiopia is presently contemplating diverting as much as 4 billion cubic metres of the Blue Nile into its own irrigation projects, despite opposition from Egypt and the Sudan whose water supply would be severely reduced as a result. * * *

Egypt's water resources are now under severe stress and its water needs will increase for the foreseeable future. Failure of co-riparian states to appreciate the gravity of the situation and cooperate in water-sharing schemes could tempt Egypt to take a more active interest in the internal affairs of neighbouring countries and threaten the stability of the entire region.

———

The Middle East is not the only region where water disputes can turn into potential political disputes. As Norman Myers has observed: "Tensions and violence over water-use rights and river-diversion projects have already erupted in the river basins of the Mekong, which is shared by Laos, Thailand, Cambodia, and Vietnam; the Parana, which is shared by Brazil and Argentina; the Lauca, which is shared by Bolivia and Chile; and the Medjerda, which is shared by Tunisia and Libya." Norman Myers, *Environment and Security,* FOREIGN POLICY 23, 29 (1989).

———

QUESTIONS AND DISCUSSION

1. One suggestion for lowering tensions over Mid–East water has been to create a regional water market in the Mid–East for allocating among the different users. Would privatizing water resources in this way help to alleviate inter-State conflict in the region?

2. Consider the Lac Lanoux controversy in light of the concept of environmental security. Does this explain why Spain might have been concerned with France developing a hydroelectric system that did not as planned alter the quantity or quality of the water delivered to Spain? Given current views of environmental security, would we expect Spain's claim to succeed today?

3. Many observers believe that declining quantities of freshwater will inevitably lead to violent conflict and war between States that share water resources. Consider, however, the following discussion:

> In fact, considerable evidence suggests that cooperative solutions to water scarcity problems are more likely than prolonged conflict. The widespread and frequent disputes over water have generally exhibited a rather remarkable feature, at least in the twentieth century, captured in the observation of Samir Saliba that "[s]o far, no international dispute about apportionment of water rights has ever led to war." One need not go that far to notice that no matter how violent conflict between states sharing a common water source might become, and especially when water itself has played a central role in the conflict water facilities have remained off limits to combat, cooperative water arrangements have been negotiated, and pre-existing arrangements have remained intact. One of the best examples is found in the relations of India and Pakistan. Those two states have engaged in three full-scale, albeit limited, wars since 1948, all for reasons largely unrelated to their shared water resources. During this same period, the two states negotiated and implemented a complex treaty on sharing the waters of the Indus River system and during actual periods of hostility they did not target water facilities nor interfere in the cooperative water management arrangements. Historian Robert Collins has cautiously summarized this same reality in a comment on the rivalries in the Nile basin: "Perhaps the weight of history lies too heavy in the silt of the Nile valley, but man will always need water; and in the end this may drive him to drink with his enemies." ... Or, as Munther Haddadin, a Jordanian delegate to the Middle East Peace Talks at Madrid, said, "Water seems to be leading the Peace Talks."

Joseph W. Dellapenna, *The Customary International Law of Internationally Shared Fresh Waters,* in SHARED WATER SYSTEMS AND TRANSBOUNDARY ISSUES WITH SPECIAL EMPHASIS ON THE IBERIAN PENINSULA, 81–82 (2000). What measures or steps would you recommend to two countries sharing a common river basin to decrease the likelihood that there will be a violent conflict over the shared resources?

4. Viewing water as a component of environmental security will undoubtedly raise the visibility and importance of water in national policy-making. But does it necessarily further environmental and equity interests? Reducing conflict over water resources is an important goal in its own right, and even speaking of water in terms of national security tends to 'lift' concerns of water above the interests of environmental protection and access for the poor. Environmental security concerns thus may be both too powerful and too narrow a concept to form the basis for promoting environmental or equity goals.

5. *Water and Food Security.* According to the *UN Freshwater Assessment,* irrigated agriculture takes about 70 percent of water withdrawals, and more than 90 percent in the dry tropics. Agriculture is by far the biggest consumptive use of water by humans, representing 87 percent of the total. At the same time irrigated agriculture contributes nearly 40 percent of the world food production from just 17 percent of cultivated land. Currently, the world produces sufficient food for everyone, although problems with distribution mean that an estimated 840 million people do not receive sufficient food for nourishment.

The amount of land under irrigation per capita worldwide has been dropping. In part, this is due to increased waterlogging and salinization that occurs in some heavily irrigated regions. Salinization, for example, reduces crop output on an estimated 20 per cent of the world's 250 million hectares of irrigated land. Nearly 2 million hectares of land are actually withdrawn from agriculture each year due to waterlogging and salinization. These trends, along with increases in population suggest that world food needs can only be met in the future through increased water use efficiency in agriculture. *See UN Freshwater Assessment, at paras 44, 67; G. Gardner, Irrigated Area Up Slightly, in* L. BROWN, ET AT., VITAL SIGNS: at 42–43 (1997). For thorough and readable treatments of the environmental and social consequences of large irrigation projects, *see* MARC REISNER, CADILLAC DESERT (1986); DONALD WORSTER, RIVERS OF EMPIRE (1985); *see also* discussion of food security in Chapter 1, pages 13–17.

D. WORLD COMMISSION ON DAMS

Over the past few decades, few proposed projects have created as more controversy than various large dams. We now know that the many benefits of dams, including energy production, flood control, and irrigation supply, also come with substantial social and environmental costs. As social protests around dams have escalated, institutions like the World Bank have been stuck in a series of controversial projects that have severely tarnished their reputation. In 1997, the World Bank along with the World Conservation Union (IUCN) and several other institutions organized a meeting among disparate stakeholders to determine if a consensus could be reached regarding criteria for when large dams should be built. The participants in that meeting called for the establishment of an international commission to make recommendations regarding the future of large dams.

Established in February 1998, the World Commission on Dams brought together an international panel of experts representing all major stakeholders in issues relating to dams, including representatives of the dam-building industry, grassroots opponents of dams, and public-sector financiers of dams. Under the chairmanship of Professor Kader Asmal, then South Africas Minister of Water Affairs and Forestry, the Commission set forth two primary objectives: (1) to review the development effectiveness of large dams and (2) to develop internationally acceptable criteria, guidelines and standards for the design, construction, operation, and decommissioning of dams. The Commission undertook eight detailed case studies of large dams and reviewed the country-wide experience of India and China. It also collected and reviewed a briefing paper for Russia and the Newly Independent States, a cross-check survey of 125 existing dams, 17 thematic papers, as well as the results of more than 900 public submissions. The following excerpt is from the Commission's final report.

Executive Summary, Report of
The World Commission on Dams, xxix–xxxv (2000)

During the 20th century, large dams emerged as one of the most significant and visible tools for the management of water resources. The more than 45 000 large dams around the world have played an important role in helping communities and economies harness water resources for food production, energy generation, flood control and domestic use. Current estimates suggest that some 30–40% of irrigated land worldwide now relies on dams and that dams generate 19% of world electricity.

From the 1930s to the 1970s, the construction of large dams became–in the eyes of many–synonymous with development and economic progress. Viewed as symbols of modernisation and humanity's ability to harness nature, dam construction accelerated dramatically. This trend peaked in the 1970s, when on average two or three large dams were commissioned each day somewhere in the world.

While the immediate benefits were widely believed sufficient to justify the enormous investments made–total investment in large dams worldwide is estimated at more than $2 trillion–secondary and tertiary benefits were also often cited. These included food security considerations, local employment and skills development, rural electrification and the expansion of physical and social infrastructure such as roads and schools. The benefits were regarded as self-evident, while the construction and operational costs tended to be limited to economic and financial considerations that justified dams as a highly competitive option.

As experience accumulated and better information on the performance and consequences of dams became available, the full cost of large dams began to emerge as a serious public concern. Driven by information on the impacts of dams on people, river basins and ecosystems, as well as their economic performance, opposition began to grow. Debate and controversy initially focused on specific dams and their local impacts. Gradually these locally driven conflicts evolved into a global debate about the costs and benefits of dams. Global estimates of the magnitude of impacts include some 40–80 million people displaced by dams while 60% of the worlds rivers have been affected by dams and diversions. The nature and magnitude of the impacts of dams on affected communities and on the environment have now become established as key issues in the debate. * * *

In assessing the large dams reviewed by the Commission we found that:

- Large dams display a high degree of variability in delivering predicted water and electricity services–and related social benefits–with a considerable portion falling short of physical and economic targets, while others continue generating benefits after 30 to 40 years.

- Large dams have demonstrated a marked tendency towards schedule delays and significant cost overruns.

- Large dams designed to deliver irrigation services have typically fallen short of physical targets, did not recover their costs and have been less profitable in economic terms than expected.

- Large hydropower dams tend to perform closer to, but still below, targets for power generation, generally meet their financial targets but demonstrate variable economic performance relative to targets, with a number of notable under- and over-performers.

- Large dams generally have a range of extensive impacts on rivers, watersheds and aquatic ecosystems–these impacts are more negative than positive and, in many cases, have led to irreversible loss of species and ecosystems.

- Efforts to date to counter the ecosystem impacts of large dams have met with limited success owing to the lack of attention to anticipating and avoiding impacts, the poor quality and uncertainty of predictions, the difficulty of coping with all impacts, and the only partial implementation and success of mitigation measures.

- Pervasive and systematic failure to assess the range of potential negative impacts and implement adequate mitigation, resettlement and development programmes for the displaced, and the failure to account for the consequences of large dams for downstream livelihoods have led to the impoverishment and suffering of millions, giving rise to growing opposition to dams by affected communities worldwide.

- Since the environmental and social costs of large dams have been poorly accounted for in economic terms, the true profitability of these schemes remains elusive.

Perhaps of most significance is the fact that social groups bearing the social and environmental costs and risks of large dams, especially the poor, vulnerable and future generations, are often not the same groups that receive the water and electricity services, nor the social and economic benefits from these. Applying a 'balance-sheet' approach to assess the costs and benefits of large dams, where large inequities exist in the distribution of these costs and benefits, is seen as unacceptable given existing commitments to human rights and sustainable development. * * *

The decision to build a dam is influenced by many variables beyond immediate technical considerations. As a development choice, the selection of large dams often served as a focal point for the interests and aspirations of politicians, centralised government agencies, international aid donors and the dam-building industry, and did not provide for a comprehensive evaluation of available alternatives. Involvement from civil society varied with the degree of debate and openness to political discourse in a country. However, the WCD Global Review documents a frequent failure to recognize affected people and empower them to participate in the process. In some cases, the opportunity for corruption provided by dams as large-scale infrastructure projects further distorted decision-making.

Once a proposed dam project passed preliminary technical and economic feasibility tests and attracted interest from financing agencies and political interests, the momentum behind the project often prevailed over other considerations. Project planning and appraisal for large dams was confined primarily to technical parameters and the narrow application of economic cost-benefit analyses. Historically, social and environmental impacts were left outside the assessment framework and the role of impact assessments in project selection remained marginal, even into the 1990s.

Conflicts over dams have heightened in the last two decades due largely to the social and environmental impacts of dams that were either disregarded in the planning process or unanticipated. However, it also stems from the failure by dam proponents and financing agencies to fulfil commitments made, observe statutory regulations and abide by internal guidelines. Whereas far-reaching improvements in policies, legal requirements and assessment procedures have occurred in particular countries and institutions, in the 1990s it appears that business-as-usual too often prevailed. Further, past shortcomings and inequities remain unresolved, and experience with appeals, dispute resolution and recourse mechanisms has been poor. * * *

As the Global Review of dams makes clear, improving development outcomes in the future requires a substantially expanded basis for deciding on proposed water and energy development projects–a basis that reflects a full knowledge and understanding of the benefits, impacts and risks of large dam projects to all parties. It also requires introducing new voices, perspectives and criteria into decision-making, as well as processes that will build consensus around the decisions reached. This will fundamentally alter the way in which decisions are made and, we are convinced, improve the development effectiveness of future decisions. * * *

The debate about dams is a debate about the very meaning, purpose and pathways for achieving development. This suggests that decision-making on water and energy management will align itself with the emerging global commitment to sustainable human development and on the equitable distribution of costs and benefits. The emergence of a globally accepted framework of norms rests on the adoption of the Universal Declaration of Human Rights in 1948 and related covenants and conventions thereafter. These later resolutions include the Declaration on the Right to Development adopted by the UN General Assembly in 1986, and the Rio Principles agreed to at the UN Conference on Environment and Development in 1992. The core values that inform the Commissions shared understanding are aligned with this consensus and rest on the fundamental human rights accorded to all people by virtue of their humanity. * * *

Reconciling competing needs and entitlements is the single most important factor in understanding the conflicts associated with development projects and programmes–particularly large-scale interventions such as dams. The approach developed by the Commission of recognising rights and assessing risks (particularly rights at risk) in the planning and project cycles offers a means to apply these core values to decision-making about water and energy resource management. Clarifying the rights context for a proposed project is an essential step in identifying those legitimate claims and entitlements that may be affected by the project or its alternatives. It is also a pre-condition for effective identification of legitimate stakeholder groups that are entitled to a formal role in the consultative process, and eventually in negotiating project-specific agreements relating, for example, to benefit sharing, resettlement and compensation.

The assessment of risk adds an important dimension to understanding how, and to what extent, a project may impact on people's rights. In the past, many groups have not had an opportunity to participate in decisions that imply major risks for their lives and livelihoods, thus denying them a stake in the development decision-making process commensurate with their exposure to risk. Indeed, many have had risks imposed on them involuntarily. Risks must be identified and addressed explicitly. This will require the notion of risk to be extended beyond governments or developers to include both those affected by a project and the environment as a public good. Involuntary risk bearers must be engaged by risk takers in a transparent process to negotiate equitable outcomes.

An approach based on the recognition of rights and assessment of risks can lay the basis for greatly improved and significantly more legitimate decision-making on water and energy resource development. It offers an effective way to determine who has a legitimate place at the negotiation table and what issues need to be included on the agenda. Only decision-making processes based on the pursuit of negotiated outcomes, conducted in an open and transparent manner and inclusive of all legitimate actors involved in the issue are likely to resolve the complex issues surrounding water, dams and development. * * *

Researching and analysing the history of water resources management, the emergence of large dams, their impacts and performance, and the resultant dams debate led the Commission to view the controversy surrounding dams within a broader normative framework. This framework, within which the dams debate clearly resides, builds upon international recognition of human rights, the right to development and the right to a healthy environment.

Within this framework the Commission has developed seven strategic priorities and related policy principles. It has translated these priorities and principles into a set of corresponding criteria and guidelines for key decision points in the planning and project cycles.

Together, they provide guidance on translating this framework into practice. They help us move from a traditional, top-down, technology-focused approach to advocate significant innovations in assessing options, managing existing dams–including processes for assessing reparations and environmental restoration, gaining public acceptance and negotiating and sharing benefits.

The seven strategic priorities each supported by a set of policy principles, provide a principled and practical way forward for decision-making. Presented here as expressions of an achieved outcome, they summarise key principles and actions that the Commission proposes all actors should adopt and implement.

1. Gaining Public Acceptance

Public acceptance of key decisions is essential for equitable and sustainable water and energy resources development. Acceptance emerges from recognising rights, addressing risks, and safeguarding the entitlements of all groups of affected people, particularly indigenous and tribal peoples, women and other vulnerable groups. Decision making processes and mechanisms are used that enable informed participation by all groups of people, and result in the demonstrable acceptance of key decisions. Where projects affect indigenous and tribal peoples, such processes are guided by their free, prior and informed consent.

2. Comprehensive Options Assessment

Alternatives to dams do often exist. To explore these alternatives, needs for water, food and energy are assessed and objectives clearly defined. The appropriate development response is identified from a range of possible options. The selection is based on a comprehensive and participatory assessment of the full range of policy, institutional and technical options. In the assessment process social and environmental aspects have the same significance as economic and financial factors. The options assessment process continues through all stages of planning, project development and operations.

3. Addressing Existing Dams

Opportunities exist to optimise benefits from many existing dams, address outstanding social issues and strengthen environmental mitigation and restoration measures. Dams and the context in which they operate are not seen as static over time. Benefits and impacts may be transformed by changes in water use priorities, physical and land use changes in the river basin, technological developments, and changes in public policy expressed in environment, safety, economic and technical regulations. Management and operation practices must adapt continuously to changing circumstances over the project's life and must address outstanding social issues.

4. Sustaining Rivers and Livelihoods

Rivers, watersheds and aquatic ecosystems are the biological engines of the planet. They are the basis for life and the livelihoods of local communities. Dams transform landscapes and create risks of irreversible impacts. Understanding, protecting and restoring ecosystems at river basin level is essential to foster equitable human development and the welfare of all species. Options assessment and decision-making around river development prioritises the avoidance of impacts, followed by the minimisation and mitigation of harm to the health and integrity of the river system. Avoiding impacts through good site selection and project design is a priority. Releasing tailor-made environmental flows can help maintain downstream ecosystems and the communities that depend on them.

5. Recognising Entitlements and Sharing Benefits

Joint negotiations with adversely affected people result in mutually agreed and legally enforceable mitigation and development provisions. These recognise entitlements that improve livelihoods and quality of life, and affected people are beneficiaries of the project. Successful mitigation, resettlement and development are fundamental commitments and responsibilities of the State and the developer. They bear the onus to satisfy all affected people that moving from their current context and resources will improve their livelihoods. Accountability of responsible parties to agreed mitigation, resettlement and development provisions is ensured through legal means, such as contracts, and through accessible legal recourse at the national and international level.

6. Ensuring Compliance

Ensuring public trust and confidence requires that the governments, developers, regulators and operators meet all commitments made for the planning, implementation and operation of dams. Compliance with applicable regulations, criteria and guidelines, and project-specific negotiated agreements is secured at all critical stages in project planning and implementation. A set of mutually reinforcing incentives and mechanisms is required for social, environmental and technical measures. These should involve an appropriate mix of regulatory and non-regulatory measures, incorporating incentives and sanctions. Regulatory and compliance frameworks use incentives and sanctions to ensure effectiveness where flexibility is needed to accommodate changing circumstances.

7. Sharing Rivers for Peace, Development and Security

Storage and diversion of water on transboundary rivers has been a source of considerable tension between countries and within countries. As specific interventions for diverting water, dams require constructive co-operation. Consequently, the use and management of resources increasingly becomes the subject of agreement between States to promote mutual self-interest for regional co-operation and peaceful collaboration. This leads to a shift in focus from the narrow approach of allocating a finite resource to the sharing of rivers and their associated benefits in which States are innovative in defining the scope of issues for discussion. External financing agencies support the principles of good faith negotiations between riparian States.

If we are to achieve equitable and sustainable outcomes, free of the divisive conflicts of the past, future decision-making about water and energy resource projects will need to reflect and integrate these strategic priorities and their associated policy principles in the planning and project cycles.

For a critique of large dams, *see* PATRICK MCCULLY, SILENCED RIVERS (1997) (discussing the environmental and social impacts of large dams); see also ARUNDHATI ROY, THE GREATER COMMON GOOD (2000) (eloquently and passionately critiquing India's practice of resettling thousands of peasants for the 'common good' of building large hydroelectric dams).

————

QUESTIONS AND DISCUSSION

1. The WCD represents a new approach to looking globally across a specific technology or industry sector to arrive at new standards or approaches consistent with the goals of sustainable development. The World Bank Group, for example, is currently undergoing a similar review of the oil, gas and mining sectors because of repeated concerns that these projects are not contributing effectively to sustainable development goals. Other such reviews sponsored by different institutions have focused on forests and fisheries, for example. To what extent do you think such an approach is useful in moving toward sustainable development? Given that the recommendations of the WCD are not binding on any institution, what steps would you recommend for ensuring that the WCD recommendations make a difference on the ground?

2. The WCD adopted a rights-based approach, relying for basic principles and rights on three international instruments: the 1948 Universal Declaration of Human rights, the 1986 Declaration on the Right to Development, and the 1992 Rio Declaration. The WCD Report uses these documents to define the rights and core values that should be taken into account in making decisions, including to identify those stakeholders that should be given a participatory seat at the table (For example, those residents in river valleys who may have to be resettled). What do you think of applying such a rights-based approach? Do those instruments provide an adequate basis?

3. At the same time that the WCD was undertaking its review of the world's dams, the United States was arguably entering a new era in the history of dams—the decommissioning and removal of dams to return rivers to their natural state. Over 75,000 dams over six feet high have been built in the United States (on average, one a day since the American Revolution). Many of these dams continue to provide important benefits, but many others have outlived their usefulness. In all, an estimated 400 dams have been removed from US rivers, most of which received little or no public notice. That changed, when the Edwards Dam on Maine's Kennebec River was removed in 1999. Not only was the 150–year old Edwards Dam a major structure, but it was also the first dam removal ordered by the Federal government over the dam owners' objection. Edwards Dam marked the entry of dam removal into the mainstream, with Secretary of Interior Bruce Babbitt and most major media heralding the event. There were 17 dam removals in 1999 (including Edwards), and there are 57 scheduled for 2001 (a 300% increase). A drop in the bucket, perhaps, but the trend seems clear. What obligations do you think dam owners and beneficiaries should have for the ultimate removal of their dam? Should the costs of decommissioning be factored in as part of the decision to build a dam? See generally <www.americanrivers.org>.

————

E.   A HUMAN RIGHT TO AFFORDABLE AND SAFE WATER

Access to safe and affordable water for basic needs is increasingly being viewed as a human right. A recent UN subcommittee report on human rights and the environment, for example recommended that all people have the "right to safe and healthy food and water adequate to their well-being." Several domestic constitutions also include access to uncontaminated water within their constitutional guarantees of a human right to a healthy environment. Such a human right to safe water, arguably obligates States to provide—or at least not to restrict—access to clean water to their citizens. Such obligations are hard to enforce, but serve to highlight the importance of water to the poor and establish the use of water for direct human consumption and for food production as highest priority uses. A rights-based approach to water also elevates the concerns of individuals and local communities in national and international policy debates. For further discussion of human rights and the environment, see Chapter 16.

QUESTIONS AND DISCUSSION

1. Because of its absolute protection for the interests of subsistence users of water, the rights-based approach sets an effective floor for water policy. Can it, however, provide meaningful guidance for achieving the types of complex compromises and balances necessary for integrated water management in most water basins? How would elevating access to freshwater as a human right impact on efforts to protect the ecological role of water in a particular watershed? Given that freshwater biodiversity is by most estimates the most endangered category of biodiversity in the world, would you still agree that promoting a human right to water is appropriate?

2. The Commentary to Article 10 of the UN Convention advises that "in determining 'vital human needs', special attention is to be paid to providing sufficient water to sustain human life, including both drinking water and water required for production of food in order to prevent starvation." How do you reconcile the two parts of Article 10? Could you link "vital human needs" to any internationally recognized human rights?

3. Does treating water as a human right suggest any difficulty with allocating water through water rights or through market pricing? Does it have any significance for how water should be treated between nations? Does this human rights dimension, for example, require States to provide water or water-conserving technologies to water scarce States? *See* E. Benevisti, *Collective Action in the Utilization of Shared Freshwater: The Challenges of International Water Resources Law,* 90 AM. J. INT'L L. 384, 384 (1996). For further discussion of human rights, see Chapter 17.

4. The focus on access to safe drinking water is not only about quantities of water, but also about quality of drinking water. Water-borne diseases continue to be among the leading causes of death in many developing countries. This has led to greater concern in recent years with the relationship between public health and the environmental protection of rivers and lakes. The UN Economic Commission for Europe has addressed this issue in the 1999 Protocol on Water and Health to the 1992 Convention on the Protection and use of Transboundary Watercourses and International Lakes. That Protocol reads as follows:

Mindful that water is essential to sustain life and that the availability of water in quantities, and of a quality sufficient to meet basic human needs is a prerequisite both for improved health and for sustainable development. * * *

Article 4: General Provisions

1. The Parties shall take all appropriate measures to prevent, control and reduce water-related disease within a framework of integrated water-management systems aimed at sustainable use of water resources, ambient water quality which does not endanger human health, and protection of water ecosystems.

2. The Parties shall, in particular, take all appropriate measures for the purpose of ensuring:

    (a) Adequate supplies of wholesome drinking water which is free from any micro-organisms, parasites and substances which, owing to their numbers or concentration, constitute a potential danger to human health. This shall include the protection of water resources which are used as sources of drinking water, treatment of water and the establishment, improvement and maintenance of collective systems;

    (b) Adequate sanitation of a standard which sufficiently protects human health and the environment. This shall in particular be done through the establishment, improvement and maintenance of collective systems;

    (c) Effective protection of water resources used as sources of drinking water, and their related water ecosystems from pollution from other causes, including agriculture, industry and other discharges and emissions of hazardous substances. This shall aim at the effective reduction and elimination of discharges and emissions of substances judged to be hazardous to human health and water ecosystems;

    (d) Sufficient safeguards for human health against water-related disease arising from the use of water for recreational purposes, from the use of water for aquaculture, from the water in which shellfish are produced or from which they are harvested, from the use of waste water for irrigation ro from the use of sewage sludge in agriculture or aquaculture;

    (e) Effective systems for monitoring situations likely to result in outbreaks or incidents of water-related disease and for responding to such outbreaks and incidents and to the risk of them.

What value do you think an international agreement on providing safe drinking water would have? Doesn't it seem that all countries would be motivated to provide safe water regardless of the existence of such an agreement?

E. WORLD WATER COMMISSIONS, COUNCILS, FORUMS AND VISIONS

The international community has long been aware of an emerging water crisis. Initiatives such as the International Drinking and Water Supply and Sanitation Decade (1981–90), for example, have aimed at increasing accessibility to affordable drinking water and sanitation. During the 1990s, most international institutions including the World Bank, the Global Environment Facility, and the United Nations Development Program developed water strategies. In addition, a global policy dialogue regarding water issues has emerged over the past few years, catalyzed primarily by the World Water Council, an 'international water think tank' created in 1996. The Council with other institutions has organized two World Water Forums (in 1997 and 2000) with a third planned for 2003. The goal of these forums and the parallel ministerial conferences is to build a global constituency and policy momentum for coordinated efforts at resolving global water scarcity issues.

The Council also convened a World Commission on Water for the 21st Century, which in turn developed a World Water Vision released in 2000. The World Water Vision is a roadmap for the sustainable use of water in the 21st century, developed through an impressive global, multi-stakeholder consultation process, involving a reported 15,000 people. Based on the concept of integrated water resource management (IWRM), the WWV relies on the empowerment of local and community level stakeholders as those most appropriate to ensuring effective water management in the future. The WWV emphasizes water efficiency through both full-cost pricing and targeted subsidies for the poor and traditional communities. It also calls for prioritizing household uses of water in developing countries (which are at relatively low levels) over other uses such as irrigated agricultural, industrial uses or enhanced consumption in developed country households.

This increased international attention on water will clearly lead to an even larger and more impressive Third World Water Forum in Japan in 2003. What is less clear is whether any of this dialogue will be translated into specific actions on the ground to curb future water scarcity.

QUESTIONS AND DISCUSSION

1. The United Nations through its "Millenium Report," called on governments to reduce by half between now and 2015 the proportion of people (currently 20%) who "lack sustainable access to adequate sources of affordable and safe water". United Nations, We the Peoples: The Role of the United Nations in the 21st Century, para. 281 (2000). What concrete steps would you recommend that governments and international institutions take to meet that goal? How can we hold governments accountable for an aspirational goal such as the one set forth in the Millenium Report? Does international law have a potential role to play in meeting such a goal?

Suggested Further Reading

Salman Salman & Laurence Boisson de Chazournes, eds, INTERNATIONAL WATERCOURSES: ENHANCING COOPERATION AND MANAGING CONFLICT: PROCEEDINGS OF A WORLD BANK SEMINAR, World Bank Technical Paper No. 414 (1998).

Stephen McCaffrey, *Current Development: The International Law Commission Adopts Draft Articles on International Watercourses*, 89 AM. J. INT'L L. 395 (1995).

Sandra Postel, *Forging a Sustainable Water Strategy*, in STATE OF THE WORLD 1996 (1996).

SANDRA POSTEL, PILLAR OF SAND: CAN THE IRRIGATION MIRACLE LAST? (1999).

MARC REISNER, CADILLAC DESERT : THE AMERICAN WEST AND ITS DISAPPEARING WATER (1993).

James L. Wescoat Jr., *Main Currents in Early Multilateral Water Treaties: A Historical–Geographic Perspective, 1648–1948*, 7 COLO. J. INT'L ENVTL. L. & POL'Y 39 (1996).

CHAPTER TWELVE

Hazardous Wastes and Materials

The development of synthetic chemicals following World War II has in many ways been miraculous. From the untold uses of plastics to high-tech materials and pharmaceuticals, modern chemistry has provided us with standards of living that past kings could only have dreamt of. As Paul Ehrlich notes in the Preface to this book, however, these benefits have come at a cost. This chapter explores the role of international law and policy in both assessing and reducing the environmental costs associated with chemicals and hazardous waste.

The generation of hazardous waste around the globe has increased more than sixty-fold since World War II. Until recently, the disposal of some of this waste in developing countries to avoid the high fees of local disposal was common practice. Section I discusses the hazardous waste trade and and the international response through the Basel Convention and regional agreements. A pressing issue, still evolving, is how to distinguish the legitimate international trade in waste materials intended for recovery and recycling from that intended for final disposal.

Section II addresses the challenges posed by the over 75,000 synthetic chemicals now in commercial use. While some of these chemicals have been tested in the laboratory for their toxicity and cancer-causing (carcinogenic) properties, very little is known of their potential to mimic hormones (endocrine disruption) or weaken the immune system (immunosuppression), their impacts over long periods of low exposure, and their synergistic effects (i.e. combined impact from the interaction of multiple compounds). These are not merely academic concerns. Up to 500 synthetic chemicals are present in the body fat of every person. What is the impact of these chemicals on us and on our children? What role should international law play in addressing this issue?

Section III turns to nuclear activities. Spurred by the Chernobyl disaster in 1986, international law now addresses numerous aspects of nuclear energy, including the operation of facilities, transport of waste, and assistance in the case of a meltdown. Despite the end of the Cold War, thousands of nuclear weapons remain stockpiled. The last part of Section III describes international efforts to address the threats posed by nuclear weapons and the important International Court of Justice decisions concerning nuclear testing and the legality of nuclear weapons.

SECTION I.   TRANSBOUNDARY MOVEMENT OF HAZARDOUS WASTES

A.   HISTORY AND BACKGROUND

1.   THE NATURE OF THE HAZARDOUS WASTE TRADE

Every population must manage the disposal of its wastes or suffer the health consequences. This is as true for a culture of bacteria in a petri dish as for the inhabitants of New York City. In modern industrial society, this basic ecological fact becomes more challenging as our generation of waste grows in volume, persistence and toxicity. The environmental and human health risks posed by the global movement of hazardous wastes, particularly to countries or facilities that may not be capable of managing wastes in an environmentally sound manner, has led the international community to develop a comprehensive legal regime governing the transboundary movement of hazardous and other wastes.

The universe of waste that is legally considered "hazardous waste" varies from country to country. Accordingly, statistics about the volume of waste generated and transported across international borders are not readily comparable. Nonetheless, the volume of waste generated in both developing and less developing countries has increased significantly in recent decades. Worldwide generation of hazardous waste is estimated to have increased from approximately 5 million metric tons in 1945 to 300 million in 1988–an increase of 60-fold since the end of World War II. Hackett, *An Assessment of the Basel Convention on the Control of Transboundary Movements of Hazardous Wastes and Their Disposal*, 5 AM U. J. INT'L L. & POL'Y 291, 294 (1990). UNEP estimates that more than 400 million tons of hazardous waste is generated annually world wide, representing about 16% of total industrial waste. UNEP, THE WORLD ENVIRONMENT, 1972–1992, at 264 (1997); <http://www.unep.ch/basel/index.html>. This waste presents a risk to human health and the environment if not properly managed regardless of whether its ultimate disposal is within the generating country or another State.

In relative terms, the volume of hazardous waste that crosses international borders is quite limited. For example, only about 4% of hazardous wastes generated by OECD countries are shipped across an international border. Maureen Walsh, *The Global Trade in Hazardous Wastes: Domestic and International Attempts to Cope With a Growing Crisis in Waste Management*, 42 CATH. U. L. REV. 103, 111 (1992); OECD, PRACTICAL INFORMATION FOR THE IMPLEMENTATION OF THE OECD CONTROL SYSTEM: TRANSFRONTIER MOVEMENTS OF WASTES DESTINED FOR RECOVERY OPERATIONS (1997). This waste trade includes a range of materials, from chemical and radioactive wastes to municipal solid waste, asbestos, incinerator ash and old tires. Of the waste generated in developed countries and shipped internationally, less than half is shipped for final disposal (42%) with the remainder shipped for recovery (58%). Nevertheless, while the percentage of waste moving across international borders may be small, the overall volume remains significant. Indeed, numerous environmental disasters associated with the illegal or improper shipment of hazardous wastes from developed to less developed countries have been documented by governments and environmental NGOs in recent years.

A significant factor leading to increased trade in hazardous wastes has been the increased trade in recyclable materials–wastes that contain valuable precious metals or other residues that can be reprocessed to generate raw materials. Exports of secondary materials from developed to less developed countries is valued in the billions of dollars. Environmentally sound recycling can provide substantial environmental benefits by reducing the need to exploit natural resources that might otherwise be mined in the absence of recycled materials.

Another major factor spurring the transboundary shipments of waste is the disparity in disposal costs between developed and developing nations. Disposal of hazardous waste may cost as much as $2,000 per ton in a developed nation, versus $40 per ton in Africa. The high cost of waste disposal in many developed countries is due in part to compliance costs with strict regulation and in part to effective local opposition to siting landfills (often called NIMBY–Not In My Back Yard). By contrast, many developing countries have neither stringent regulatory requirements for waste imports and disposal nor adequate enforcement efforts to ensure compliance. Kirby, *The Basel Convention and the Need for United States Implementation*, 24 GA. J. INT'L & COMP. L. 281, 285 (1994); Kitt, *Waste Exports to the Developing World: a Global Response*, 7 GEO. INT'L ENVT'L L. REV. 485, 488 (1995).

> The importation of toxic wastes by LDCs [developing countries] creates the potential for serious health and environmental problems for those countries. The natural environment and climate of many LDCs make toxic wastes more dangerous than in the developed world. For example, heavy rainfall in sub-Saharan Africa causes landfilled waste to leach into the groundwater supply quickly. This is dangerous because most people in LDCs drink untreated water and are therefore susceptible to even low levels of contaminants. Human contact with dump sites is also more likely in LDCs than in the industrialized world. Landfills are often located near the poorest people, many of whom search landfills for possible items to use or sell.

> In addition, many LDCs do not have the administrative or political infrastructure to regulate hazardous waste disposal properly. Many do not even have adequate disposal facilities for their own municipal garbage. For example, the city of Accra, Ghana collected only ten percent of its municipal garbage in 1989. Eighty-one percent of collected waste was landfilled and nine percent was burned. Researchers found 100 official, communal refuse dumps and 100 unauthorized dumps, many along water courses. Without proper control and enforcement mechanisms, wastes imported from the industrialized world will simply be dumped as well. Even if an LDC imposes a ban on the import of foreign waste, this lack of infrastructure means that enforcement will be weak or nonexistent. To combat this problem, some countries have gone so far as to impose the death penalty for dumping. However, without strict enforcement of environmental laws, the developing world will remain susceptible to illegal dumping.

> Another potential problem is that LDCs often lack the technical capabilities for disposing of hazardous waste. Wealthy countries have technology and expertise to control certain dangers. Lower workforce expertise and limited financial resources in LDCs may increase the risk of accidents. The developing world does not create many industrial wastes; thus, it has had little opportunity to develop proper disposal techniques. Lack of experience with the industrial world's products may result in safety risks. For example, Greenpeace witnessed factory workers pulling batteries apart with their bare hands in a Philippine lead recovery facility. This practice stands in dramatic contrast to the U.S. practice, where law requires workers in lead recycling facilities to wear full-body protection and to shield themselves from the hazardous fumes.

> Finally, the export of hazardous wastes from developed to developing countries creates potential problems at the international level. In effect, when industrial waste is exported to LDCs, poor countries bear the cost of industrialization without receiving the benefits of production. Understandably, many LDCs

immediately blame the country of export, even when a private actor exported the waste.

Kitt, *op. cit.* at 491–92

Despite the potential dangers, developing nations have strong and immediate economic incentives to accept hazardous waste from other nations. Biggs, *Latin America & The Basel Convention on Hazardous Wastes*, 5 COLO. J. INT'L L. & POL'Y 333, 337 (1994). Poverty creates an imperative of economic development. In addition, many developing countries urgently need foreign hard currency to service large foreign debts accumulated during the 1970's and 1980's. The combination of the need for rapid economic growth with the urgency of obtaining hard currency for debt service payments has proven a strong enticement to accept hazardous waste in return for relatively large sums of foreign currency. In one case, the African nation of Guinea Bissau was offered a contract worth four times its GNP and twice the value of its national debt to accept shipments of toxic waste. Kitt, *op. cit.* at 490.

The dangers posed by poorly regulated transboundary shipment of hazardous waste have been the subject of frequent media attention, whether in the form of wandering waste-laden ships or people killed as a result of improper waste disposal. In 1986, for example, the city of Philadelphia, unable to dispose of its incinerator ash in America, loaded 15,000 tons of the hazardous ash on board the ship, the *Khian Sea*, headed for the Bahamas. Denied permission by Bahamian authorities to dump its ash the ship sailed to Haiti. There, the ship's captain informed Haitian authorities that the shipment was "fertilizer ash" and dumped 3,000 tons of incinerator ash on the shore before the ruse was discovered. Julienne I. Adler, *Comment, United States Waste Export Control Program: Burying Our Neighbors in Garbage*, 40 AM. U. L. REV. 885, 886 (1991). After being forced to leave Haiti with the rest of the ash on board, the ship changed its name to the *Felicia* and then to the *Pelicano* while wandering the high seas for 18 months looking for a port to accept the waste. Eventually the *Khian Sea* reached Singapore with its hold empty, claiming to have found a nation to receive the waste. Subsequently, the ship's operators were indicted by a U.S. grand jury for perjury; it is believed that the ship dumped its waste in the Indian Ocean. *After Two Years, Ships Dumps Toxic Ash*, N.Y. TIMES, Nov. 27, 1988, at A22; *Freighter Sinkings Prompt Dutch Look at Hazardous Cargo, Shipping Regulations*, 10 INT'L ENVTL. REP. [BNA] Oct. 14, 1987, at 504.

Most notorious are shipments whose toxic nature is fraudulently concealed to developing countries. The infamous Koko case in 1988 came to represent one of the worst examples of the international hazardous waste trade, though not unique. In return for paying $100 monthly rent to a Nigerian national for use of his farmland, five ships transported 8,000 barrels of Italian hazardous waste to the small river town of Koko, Nigeria. Some waste leached from the barrels, causing chemical burns and a number of deaths. Italy was eventually forced, under the spotlight of international media attention and pressure from Nigeria (after the Nigerian seizure of an unrelated Italian ship), to repackage the waste and send it back to Italy for appropriate disposal. On its return trip to Italy, the ship bearing the waste was refused port in Spain, Denmark, the Netherlands and the United States. As a result of this and similar scandals, Nigeria and Cameroon banned the importation of hazardous waste and instituted the death penalty for anyone found to be violating the ban. Wallace, *Asia Tires of Being the Toxic Waste Dumping Ground for the Rest of the World*, L.A. TIMES, Mar. 23, 1994, at A16; Ovink, *op. cit.* at 294. More recently, waste shipments have been sent to Eastern Europe labeled as humanitarian aid. Poland intercepted over 1,300 deceptively labeled waste shipments from Germany. In 1999, Cambodian villagers found sacks of cement-like material dumped in a field and used the sack materials for tents, mats, and food bags. Only later, after an outbreak of illnesses, was it determined that the waste had been dumped by a Taiwanese company. Seth Mydans, *Cambodia Town's 'Luck' Leaves Illness in Its Wake*, NEW YORK TIMES, Jan. 4, 1999, at A3. Perhaps with reason, developing countries have denounced such practices as "Toxic Colonialism."

2. THE BEGINNINGS OF AN INTERNATIONAL RESPONSE

National and international attention to the hazards associated with the management and international shipment of wastes gained momentum during the 1980s. In the early 1980s, both UNEP and the OECD expanded work on the management of hazardous wastes.

The OECD promulgated the first international agreement regarding the international trade in hazardous waste in 1984 with its Decision and Recommendation on Transfrontier Movements of Hazardous Waste, mandating OECD Member States (the most developed countries, now numbering 29) to ensure that competent authorities of countries affected by the shipment of hazardous waste are provided "adequate and timely" information on its movement. OECD Doc. C(83) 180 (Feb. 13, 1984), *reprinted* in 23 I.L.M. 214 (1984). The OECD also adopted a series of far-reaching, though non-binding, recommendations. These included the principle that prior consent from the importing and any transit States should be obtained for intra-OECD shipments of waste; that the exporter should provide detailed information to the importing country regarding the origin, nature, composition and quantity of the waste to be shipped as well as environmental risks involved in transport; and that if an importer cannot safely dispose of the waste then the generator must assume responsibility for the waste.

In 1986, these same guidelines were extended to transboundary shipments of waste involving OECD Members and non-Member States. Council Decision–Recommendation on Exports of Hazardous Wastes from the OECD Area, OECD Doc. C(86) 64 (June 5, 1986), reprinted in 25 I.L.M. 1010 (1986). The 1986 OECD Decision, among other things, prohibited both the export of hazardous waste to non-OECD countries without prior consent from the receiving country or notice to transit nations, and the export of hazardous waste to non-OECD States that lack the proper disposal facilities. *See also* 1988 OECD Council Decision (revising the definition of hazardous waste), Council Decision on Transfrontier Movements of Hazardous Wastes, OECD Doc. C(88) 90 (May 27, 1988), *reprinted in* 28 I.L.M. 257 (1989). Despite these impressive initiatives, numerous problems accompanied the implementation of this regulatory regime.

Spurred in part by high-profile international incidents involving the shipment of hazardous wastes to developing countries, in 1987 UNEP's Governing Council adopted the "Cairo Guidelines." The Cairo Guidelines were a non-binding agreement on environmentally sound management of hazardous waste. UNEP's Governing Council also agreed to commence international negotiations on a binding legal instrument governing the transboundary movements of hazardous waste. This draft was eventually negotiated into the Basel Convention, signed by 103 nations on March 30, 1989. Carol Annette Petsonk, *Recent Developments in International Organizations: The Role of the United Nations Environment Programme in the Development of International Environmental Law*, 5 Am. U.J. Int'l L. & Pol'y 351, 373 (1990). It is important to note the role of the OECD's earlier decision and recommendations in influencing UNEP action. These agreements served as a template for the Basel Convention negotiations and provide a useful example of how legal developments in one international governmental organization can provide both the impetus and foundation for more far-reaching agreements in another forum. What role do you think the OECD's restricted membership (at the time, of 24 industrialized nations) had on the content and shape of the restrictions on transfrontier trade? Similarly, UNEP's development of the Cairo Guidelines serves as an example of the influence of "soft law" on the creation of subsequent legally binding instruments.

3. WASTE TRADE LEGISLATION IN THE UNITED STATES AND EUROPE

While UNEP and the OECD were taking steps to address international trade in hazardous waste, the United States and the European Community were expanding legal controls on the transboundary shipment of hazardous wastes. Action at the national and regional level reinforced international efforts to address the risks posed by the international hazardous waste trade. United States domestic law did not comprehensively regulate hazardous waste until 1976 with the passage of the Resource Conservation and Recovery Act (RCRA). 42 U.S.C. 6901–6992k. RCRA established standards for the treatment, storage and disposal of hazardous waste. RCRA's export provisions were strengthened in 1984 and the resulting framework provided strong controls on exports, requiring prior informed consent of the importing country and a manifest system tracking the waste's shipment. Such provisions should have created a strong assurance that the international trade in hazardous wastes would be properly controlled and monitored.

Unfortunately, EPA's oversight of waste exports has in the past been poor and was described as being in "shambles" by the Agency's own Inspector General in 1988. Anderson, *Global Poison Trade*, Newsweek, Nov. 7, 1988, at 66–68. Further, even though RCRA contains an expansive definition of hazardous waste, there are significant exceptions for municipal waste and other wastes such as scrap metal that may in some instances contain hazardous constituents. Finally, U.S. law failed to prevent shipments in instances where EPA believed the waste could not be properly managed in its country of destination.

The situation in Western Europe was little different prior to the Basel Convention. While the European Commission promulgated Directives in 1975 and 1978 regulating the transport, treatment, and disposal of certain hazardous wastes to avoid harm to human health or the environment, it was left to each Member State to define "hazardous waste" and to develop its own extensive set of regulations.

A 1984 Directive had established procedures for prior notification, the use of uniform consignment notes, and packaging and labeling requirements. Directive 84/631 On The Supervision and Control Within the European Community of the Transfrontier Shipment of Hazardous Waste, 1984 O.J. (L 326) 31 (Dec. 13, 1984). The Directive, however, was poorly implemented by Member States. Different national definitions of "hazardous waste" led to general regulatory disarray that, in turn, provided a justification for other Member States for their failure to implement the Directive. Hackett, *op. cit.*, 304–305 (1991).

B. THE BASEL CONVENTION

After two years of negotiations involving 116 countries, a conference convened under the auspices of UNEP adopted the Basel Convention on the Control of Transboundary Movements of Hazardous Wastes and their Disposal ("Basel Convention") in 1989. Entered into force May 5, 1992, 28 I.L.M. 649 (1989).

The Basel Convention establishes a global notification and consent system for the transboundary shipments of hazardous and other wastes among Parties, providing the impetus for many nations to revise or enact for the first time laws governing the import and export of hazardous wastes. It also prohibits Parties from trading in covered wastes with non-Parties. As of August, 2001, 148 countries were party to the Basel Convention. In 1995, the Parties agreed to amend the Convention to ban the shipment of wastes destined for disposal or recovery from developed to less developed countries. The "Basel Ban" amendment has proven controversial and is not yet in force. The various provisions of the Basel Convention are dealt with separately in the sections that follow.

1. DEFINITIONS–HAZARDOUS AND OTHER WASTES

The Basel Convention governs all movements of "hazardous wastes" and "other wastes" between Parties. Article 1. In Article 2, the Convention defines "wastes" as "substances or objects which are disposed of or are intended to be disposed of or are required to be disposed of by the provisions of national law." "Disposal" is defined as any operation listed in Annex IV and includes disposal operations *as well as* recovery and recycling operations. A waste may qualify as "hazardous" under the Convention in one of two ways: 1) the waste is within a category of wastes contained in Annex I of the Convention (waste streams from particular manufacturing processes and hazardous constituents of wastes such as copper compounds, lead, and organic solvents), unless it does not exhibit one of the hazardous characteristics contained in Annex III (e.g., explosive, flammable, toxic, corrosive); or 2) the waste is defined or considered hazardous under the domestic legislation of the country of export, import or transit.

This broad definition of hazardous waste includes many recyclable materials. Indeed, so long as a material is listed in Annex I and exhibits hazardous characteristics set out in Annex III, or is considered hazardous under the domestic laws of an exporting, importing or transit country, it is covered by Basel, regardless of whether it is intended for recycling or final disposal. The Convention also covers certain "other wastes" that are identified in Annex II and include household wastes and residues from the incineration of household wastes. Radioactive wastes subject to other international controls (e.g., under the International Atomic Energy Agency) and wastes derived from the normal operations of ships covered by other international instruments (e.g., MARPOL 73/78) are excluded from the Basel Convention's coverage.

Preamble

Fully recognizing that any State has the sovereign right to ban the entry or disposal of foreign hazardous wastes and other wastes in its territory,

Recognizing also the increasing desire for the prohibition of transboundary movements of hazardous wastes and their disposal in other States, especially developing countries,

Convinced that hazardous wastes and other wastes should, as far as is compatible with environmentally sound and efficient management, be disposed of in the State where they were generated, * * *

Concerned about the problem of illegal transboundary traffic in hazardous wastes and other wastes,

Taking into account also the limited capabilities of the developing countries to manage hazardous wastes and other wastes * * *

HAVE AGREED AS FOLLOWS:

Article 1

Scope of the Convention

1. The following wastes that are subject to transboundary movement shall be "hazardous wastes" for the purposes of this Convention:

(a) Wastes that belong to any category contained in Annex I, unless they do not possess any of the characteristics contained in Annex III; and

(b) Wastes that are not covered under paragraph (a) but are defined as, or are considered to be, hazardous wastes by the domestic legislation of the Party of export, import or transit.

2. Wastes that belong to any category contained in Annex II that are subject to transboundary movement shall be "other wastes" for the purposes of this Convention.

3. Wastes which, as a result of being radioactive, are subject to other international control systems, including international instruments, applying specifically to radioactive materials, are excluded from the scope of this Convention.

4. Wastes which derive from the normal operations of a ship, the discharge of which is covered by another international instrument, are excluded from the scope of this Convention.

Article 2
Definitions

For the purposes of this Convention:

1. "Wastes" are substances or objects which are disposed of or are intended to be disposed of or are required to be disposed of by the provisions of national law;* * *

4. "Disposal" means any operation specified in Annex IV to this Convention;* * *

Annex I CATEGORIES OF WASTES TO BE CONTROLLED

Waste Streams

> Y1 Clinical wastes from medical care in hospitals, medical centers and clinics
>
> Y2 Wastes from the production and preparation of pharmaceutical products
>
> Y3 Waste pharmaceuticals, drugs and medicines* * *
>
> Y17 Wastes resulting from surface treatment of metals and plastics
>
> Y18 Residues arising from industrial waste disposal operations

Wastes having as constituents:

> Y19 Metal carbonyls
>
> Y20 Beryllium; beryllium compounds
>
> Y21 Hexavalent chromium compounds
>
> Y22 Copper compounds* * *

Annex II CATEGORIES OF WASTES REQUIRING SPECIAL CONSIDERATION

Y46 Wastes collected from households

Y47 Residues arising from the incineration of household wastes

Annex III LIST OF HAZARDOUS CHARACTERISTICS

H1 Explosive

> An explosive substance or waste is a solid or liquid substance or waste (or mixture of substances or wastes) which is in itself capable by chemical reaction of producing gas at such a temperature and pressure and at such a speed as to cause damage to the surroundings.

H3 Flammable liquids* * *

H11 Toxic (Delayed or chronic)

> Substances or wastes which, if they are inhaled or ingested or if they penetrate the skin, may involve delayed or chronic effects, including carcinogenicity.

H12 Ecotoxic

> Substances or wastes which if released present or may present immediate or delayed adverse impacts to the environment by means of bioaccumulation and/or toxic effects upon biotic systems.

H13

> Capable, by any means, after disposal, of yielding another material, e.g., leachate, which possesses any of the characteristics listed above.

Annex IV DISPOSAL OPERATIONS

A.   OPERATIONS WHICH DO NOT LEAD TO THE POSSIBILITY OF RE-SOURCE RECOVERY, RECYCLING, RECLAMATION, DIRECT RE–USE OR ALTERNATIVE USES

D1 Deposit into or onto land, (e.g., landfill, etc.)

D2 Land treatment, (e.g., biodegradation of liquid or sludgy discards in soils, etc.)

D3 Deep injection, (e.g., injection of pumpable discards into wells, salt domes or naturally occurring repositories, etc.)* * *

D10 Incineration on land

D11 Incineration at sea

D12 Permanent storage (e.g., emplacement of containers in a mine, etc.)

D13 Blending or mixing prior to submission to any of the operations in Section A

D14 Repackaging prior to submission to any of the operations in Section A

D15 Storage pending any of the operations in Section A

B.   OPERATIONS WHICH MAY LEAD TO RESOURCE RECOVERY, RECY-CLING, RECLAMATION, DIRECT RE–USE OR ALTERNATIVE USES

R1 Use as a fuel (other than in direct incineration) or other means to generate energy

R2 Solvent reclamation/regeneration

R3 Recycling/reclamation of organic substances which are not used as solvents

R4 Recycling/reclamation of metals and metal compounds* * *

---

2.   BASIC OBLIGATIONS

Parties are generally prohibited from exporting covered wastes to, or importing covered wastes from, non-Parties to the Convention. Article 4, para. 5. As will be discussed, *infra*, the United States is a non-Party and, as a result, many countries that are parties to the Convention are prohibited from exporting wastes to or importing wastes from the United States. The Convention also commits Parties to honor import bans adopted by other Parties and many governments have gone beyond the requirements of the Basel Convention to ban the import of certain hazardous wastes into their national territory.

The Convention places conditions on the export and import of covered wastes as well as strict notice, consent and tracking requirements for the transboundary movement of wastes. Parties are prohibited from exporting or importing hazardous or other wastes if the exporting or importing country has reason to believe that the wastes would not be managed in an "environmentally sound manner." Basel Convention, Art. 4. Parties are also required to take measures to ensure that transboundary movements are only allowed where: a) the exporting country does not have the technical capacity or facilities to dispose of the wastes in an environmentally sound manner; or b) the wastes being exported are required as a raw material for recycling or recovery in the state of import.

Basel establishes a global written notice and consent regime for the transboundary movement of hazardous and other wastes. Parties may not initiate the export of such wastes without written confirmation that the notifier has received: 1) the written consent of the importing country; 2) the written consent of any transit countries; and 3) confirmation of a written contract between the exporter and the disposer specifying the environmentally sound management of the waste. The notification must contain specific information identified in Annex V(A) of the Convention, including information on the exporter, generator(s), and disposer of the material, competent authorities, means of transport, relevant insurance, and content of the material. The waste shipments must be accompanied by a movement document (a manifest) from the point at which the movement commences until the point of disposal and must comply with applicable international packaging and labeling requirements. Parties are also obligated to re-import wastes under certain circumstances where the wastes cannot be managed in an environmentally sound manner in a receiving country and in instances of illegal traffic.

Article 4
General Obligations

1. (a) Parties exercising their right to prohibit the import of hazardous wastes or other wastes for disposal shall inform the other Parties of their decision pursuant to Article 13 [setting out the requirements for transmission of relevant information under the Convention].

(b) Parties shall prohibit or shall not permit the export of hazardous wastes and other wastes to the Parties which have prohibited the import of such wastes, when notified pursuant to subparagraph (a) above.

(c) Parties shall prohibit or shall not permit the export of hazardous wastes and other wastes if the State of import does not consent in writing to the specific import, in the case where that State of import has not prohibited the import of such wastes* * *

2. Each Party shall take the appropriate measures to:* * *

(e) Not allow the export of hazardous wastes or other wastes to a State or group of States belonging to an economic and/or political integration organization that are Parties, particularly developing countries, which have prohibited by their legislation all imports, or if it has reason to believe that the wastes in question will not be managed in an environmentally sound manner, according to criteria to be decided on by the Parties at their first meeting.

(f) Require that information about a proposed transboundary movement of hazardous wastes and other wastes be provided to the States concerned, according to Annex V(A), to state clearly the effects of the proposed movement on human health and the environment;

(g) Prevent the import of hazardous wastes and other wastes if it has reason to believe that the wastes in question will not be managed in an environmentally sound manner;* * *

5. A Party shall not permit hazardous wastes or other wastes to be exported to a non-Party or to be imported from a non-Party. * * *

7.   Furthermore, each Party shall:

(a) Prohibit all persons under its national jurisdiction from transporting or disposing of hazardous wastes or other wastes unless such persons are authorized or allowed to perform such types of operations;

(b) Require that hazardous wastes and other wastes that are to be the subject of a transboundary movement be packaged, labelled, and transported in conformity with generally accepted and recognized international rules and standards in the field of packaging, labelling, and transport, and that due account is taken of relevant internationally recognized practices;

(c) Require that hazardous wastes and other wastes be accompanied by a movement document from the point at which a transboundary movement commences to the point of disposal.

8.   Each Party shall require that hazardous wastes or other wastes, to be exported, are managed in an environmentally sound manner in the State of import or elsewhere. Technical guidelines for the environmentally sound management of wastes subject to this Convention shall be decided by the Parties at their first meeting.

9.   Parties shall take the appropriate measures to ensure that the transboundary movement of hazardous wastes and other wastes only be allowed if:

(a) The State of export does not have the technical capacity and the necessary facilities, capacity or suitable disposal sites in order to dispose of the wastes in question in an environmentally sound and efficient manner; or

(b) The wastes in question are required as a raw material for recycling or recovery industries in the State of import; or

(c) The transboundary movement in question is in accordance with other criteria to be decided by the Parties, provided those criteria do not differ from the objectives of this Convention* * *

11.   Nothing in this Convention shall prevent a Party from imposing additional requirements that are consistent with the provisions of this Convention, and are in accordance with the rules of international law, in order better to protect human health and the environment* * *

Article 6
Transboundary Movement Between Parties

1.   The State of export shall notify, or shall require the generator or exporter to notify, in writing, through the channel of the competent authority of the State of export, the competent authority of the States concerned of any proposed transboundary movement of hazardous wastes or other wastes. Such notification shall contain the declarations and information specified in Annex V(A), written in a language acceptable to the State of import. Only one notification needs to be sent to each State concerned.

2.   The State of import shall respond to the notifier in writing, consenting to the movement with or without conditions, denying permission for the movement, or requesting additional information. A copy of the final response of the State of import shall be sent to the competent authorities of the States concerned which are Parties.

3.   The State of export shall not allow the generator or exporter to commence the transboundary movement until it has received written confirmation that:

(a) The notifier has received the written consent of the State of import; and

(b) The notifier has received from the State of import confirmation of the existence of a contract between the exporter and the disposer specifying environmentally sound management of the wastes in question.

4.   Each State of transit which is a Party shall promptly acknowledge to the notifier receipt of the notification. It may subsequently respond to the notifier in writing, within 60 days, consenting to the movement with or without conditions, denying permission for the movement, or requesting additional information. The State of export shall not allow the transboundary movement to commence until it has received the written consent of the State of transit* * *

9.   The Parties shall require that each person who takes charge of a transboundary movement of hazardous wastes or other wastes sign the movement document either upon delivery or receipt of the wastes in question. They shall also require that the disposer inform both the exporter and the competent authority of the State of export of receipt by the disposer of the wastes in question and, in due course, of the completion of disposal as specified in the notification. If no such information is received within the State of export, the competent authority of the State of export or the exporter shall so notify the State of import* * *

Article 8
Duty to Re-import

When a transboundary movement of hazardous wastes or other wastes to which the consent of the States concerned has been given, subject to the provisions of this Convention, cannot be completed in accordance with the terms of the contract, the State of export shall ensure that the wastes in question are taken back into the State of export, by the exporter, if alternative arrangements cannot be made for their disposal in an environmentally sound manner, within 90 days from the time that the importing State informed the State of export and the Secretariat, or such other period of time as the States concerned agree. To this end, the State of export and any Party of transit shall not oppose, hinder or prevent the return of those wastes to the State of export.

-----

3.   PARTY TO NON–PARTY BAN

While the Basel Convention generally prohibits Parties from exporting covered wastes to, or importing covered wastes from, non-Parties to the Convention, there is an important exception. The Convention allows imports and exports of covered wastes between Parties and Non–Parties where the transboundary movements are subject to *another* appropriate bilateral, multilateral or regional agreement. Article 11. The United States has entered into a number of such agreements that, in most circumstances, allow the shipment of hazardous waste to or from Basel Parties. With respect to international agreements that pre-date the Basel Convention, trade between Parties and Non–Parties may proceed provided that the agreement is "compatible" with the environmentally sound management of hazardous and other wastes as set forth in the Convention. If the agreement is concluded after the Basel Convention entered into force, the agreement must meet a higher standard–waste shipments may only proceed if the agreement does not "derogate" from the environmentally sound management of hazardous and other wastes as required under the Convention.

Thus although a non-Party, the United States has concluded several important bilateral accords (two of which preceded Basel). *See* the Bilateral Agreement Between the United States and Canada Concerning the Transboundary Movement of Hazardous Waste (1986); the Bilateral Agreement of Cooperation Between the United States of America and the United Mexican States Regarding the Transboundary Shipments of Hazardous Wastes and Hazardous Substances (1986). This includes "import only" bilaterals with Malaysia and Costa Rica, allowing wastes to be shipped *to* the United States but not exports. Some governments, such as Brazil, have refused to enter into bilateral waste agreements with the United States because of the U.S. position allowing imports but not exports. Why do you think the United States only enters into import agreements?

The most commercially significant Article 11 agreement is the Organization for Economic Cooperation and Development (OECD) Council Decision Concerning the Control of Transfrontier Movements of Wastes Destined for Recovery Operations (1992 and subsequent amendments). The Decision establishes a notice and consent system among OECD countries for the transboundary shipment of wastes destined for recovery that supercedes the Basel requirements.

Article 11
Bilateral, Multilateral and Regional Agreements

1. Notwithstanding the provisions of Article 4 paragraph 5, Parties may enter into bilateral, multilateral, or regional agreements or arrangements regarding transboundary movement of hazardous wastes or other wastes with Parties or non-Parties provided that such agreements or arrangements do not derogate from the environmentally sound management of hazardous wastes and other wastes as required by this Convention. These agreements or arrangements shall stipulate provisions which are not less environmentally sound than those provided for by this Convention in particular taking into account the interests of developing countries.

2. Parties shall notify the Secretariat of any bilateral, multilateral or regional agreements or arrangements referred to in paragraph 1 and those which they have entered into prior to the entry into force of this Convention for them, for the purpose of controlling transboundary movements of hazardous wastes and other wastes which take place entirely among the Parties to such agreements. The provisions of this Convention shall not affect transboundary movements which take place pursuant to such agreements provided that such agreements are compatible with the environmentally sound management of hazardous wastes and other wastes as required by this Convention.

––––––

4. WASTE MINIMIZATION AND WASTE MANAGEMENT

Reducing the trade in hazardous wastes can be achieved both through more stringent export controls and through overall *reduction* of waste volumes. An important goal of Basel's restrictions on trade in hazardous wastes is to force countries to keep their wastes at home. There, NIMBY pressures will drive up costs of waste disposal and, it follows, increase the economic incentives for pollution prevention and reduced waste generation. Article 4 contains a pledge by all parties to minimize the generation of hazardous waste. In addition, the parties agree to ensure that adequate disposal facilities are available within their borders, so as to guarantee the environmentally sound management of waste. Finally, parties agree to prevent pollution from hazardous waste and to minimize the transboundary shipment of hazardous waste.

Article 4
General Obligations

... 2. Each Party shall take the appropriate measures to:

(a) Ensure that the generation of hazardous wastes and other wastes within it is reduced to a minimum, taking into account social, technological and economic aspects;

(b) Ensure the availability of adequate disposal facilities, for the environmentally sound management of hazardous wastes and other wastes, that shall be located, to the extent possible, within it, whatever the place of their disposal;

(c) Ensure that persons involved in the management of hazardous wastes or other wastes within it take such steps as are necessary to prevent pollution due to hazardous wastes and other wastes arising from such management and, if such pollution occurs, to minimize the consequences thereof for human health and the environment;

(d) Ensure that the transboundary movement of hazardous wastes and other wastes is reduced to the minimum consistent with the environmentally sound and efficient management of such wastes, and is conducted in a manner which will protect human health and the environment against the adverse effects which may result from such movement;

---

5. VIOLATIONS

The Convention states that illegal traffic in hazardous wastes or other wastes is a criminal offense. Art. 4(2). Article 9 contains an extensive definition of illegal waste trade, including a violation of informed consent provisions, consent obtained through falsification, misrepresentation or fraud, or deliberate disposal in violation of the terms of the Convention. If the exporter or generator of the waste is responsible for the illegal trade, the State of export must within 30 days ensure the wastes are taken back for proper disposal by the generator or, if necessary, by the State itself. If the importer or disposal facility is responsible for the illegal traffic, then the importing State must similarly guarantee environmentally sound disposal. If responsibility for the illegal trade is undetermined, the parties are directed to work cooperatively to ensure the environmentally sound disposal of the waste.

The Convention does not contain any enforcement provisions. Parties are required to take appropriate domestic legal, administrative and other measures to enforce the Convention. In addressing damage from the waste trade, Article 12 directs Parties to prepare a protocol establishing appropriate rules and procedures for compensation for damage resulting from the trade in hazardous wastes. The Protocol on Liability was signed in 1999 at the fifth Conference of the Parties and is described at page 854.

QUESTIONS AND DISCUSSION

1. *Working the treaty*
   - If a party passes a more stringent restriction on the imports of certain wastes must the other Parties comply with these domestic regulations?
   - What written confirmations must exporting Parties receive before exporting hazardous wastes?
   - What provisions, if any, allow Parties to export hazardous wastes to non-Parties?
   - Assume a nation has violated the convention, what penalties exist and who is charged with enforcing these violations?
   - Brazil is a party to Basel. Would a U.S. bilateral treaty with Brazil covering imports and exports violate the treaty?

2. The amounts of money involved in the hazardous waste trade are staggering. As mentioned above, the African nation of Guinea–Bissau was offered $600 million to accept large shipments of hazardous wastes for five years. This figure was double the country's foreign debt and over 35 times greater than its total annual exports. The US businessman who unsuccessfully tried to arrange this deal would have earned up to $400 million in just one year. The contract's detailed environmental protections for disposal were woefully inadequate, stating that "Separation by layers of earth will isolate the products so there is no contact between them. As soon as the dump is full, it will be covered so as to protect the environment and avoid pollution. Another work site will then be opened, and so on." As one environmentalist tracking the issue described, international merchants of hazardous waste can earn "fabulous profits without the risk of drug smuggling or running guns." Harry Anderson, *The Global Poison Trade*, NEWSWEEK, Nov. 7, 1988, at 66.

3. Annex IV(B) of Basel defines "disposal" to include activities that may lead to resource recovery, recycling, reclamation, direct re-use or alternative uses. Yet the acknowledged waste management hierarchy is to reduce, re-use, and recycle waste before landfill or incineration. Why would the negotiators of the Basel Convention require the same prior consent for recycling and reclamation as it does for landfilling and incineration? Would it not make more sense to make the requirements for recycling less burdensome, thus encouraging an environmentally preferable alternative to final disposal?

4. Trade measures such as the Party to non-Party ban serve as important incentives encouraging countries to participate in global environmental agreements such as the Basel Convention. Such measures, however, may impose both economic and environmental burdens. For example, many U.S. companies operating in less developed countries have been barred from exporting hazardous wastes generated by their facilities back to the United States for disposal because the United States remains outside of the Basel Convention. These companies in many instances must decide whether to store the waste on-site, incur the costs of shipping the waste to another developed country that may be able to accept the waste, or use local hazardous waste management facilities that may not provide for safe management and disposal of hazardous wastes. Can Basel be viewed as a success if the world's

wealthiest country, with a highly regulated waste disposal and recycling infrastructure, is off-limits to waste imports from most of the developing world?

5. Although Article 8 requires an exporting State to take back waste from an importing State unable to manage the waste in an environmentally sound manner, that provision does not specify who is to pay for the subsequent re-importation and treatment or disposal. If the importing country had already consented to import the waste based on the informed consent required by Article 8, why should the exporting State have to pay for a mistake by the importing State? *See* Hackett, *op. cit.* at 321–322 (1991).

The Basel Convention text fails, for example, to answer the question of whom among the persons involved with the notorious *Khian Sea* should be liable for dumping incinerator ash onto the Haitian beaches. If you were drafting a liability regime, would you make all actors (generator, exporter, receiver) liable? Should liability be fault-based or based on strict liability? If generators of wastes are strictly, jointly and severally liable for environmental damage, what incentives would such a regime create for the responsible management of wastes by those in operational control of the wastes once they are exported? Keep these questions in mind as you read, *infra*, the Liability Protocol parties finally adopted.

6. Article 11 of the Basel Convention essentially allows the Convention's requirements to be superseded by other bilateral, regional or multilateral agreements. The provision has allowed the OECD to implement its own arrangement for the movement of commodity-like wastes that would otherwise be subject to the Basel Convention's control regime and trade prohibitions. Is this provision an acceptable means of allowing governments to adopt other approaches to managing environmental concerns and trade interests or can it be viewed as a loophole that undermines the fundamental principles of the Convention?

7. Like many environmental issues, the implementation of a global notification and consent regime governing the transboundary movement of hazardous wastes was driven in part by extensive media attention to the problem of illegal and improper waste shipments. Environmental NGOs such as Greenpeace and the Basel Action Network have played a key role in the research and campaigns to create this media attention. Has the attention, however, been focused on the proper issues? Knowing that most hazardous waste does not cross an international border, would it not have been more effective for the international community to focus on expanding the capacity of all countries to safely manage and dispose of hazardous wastes regardless of where the wastes were generated? How effective do you think the requirements of Article 4(2), page 845, are in minimizing waste generation? What might be a more effective approach to address pollution prevention?

8. Nations' use of common definitions for hazardous waste is essential to coherent regulation of international trade and proved a formidable barrier to effective control prior to the Basel Convention. Beyond the definition of hazardous waste, industrialized states also differ in their approach to the classification of mixed wastes and the threshold levels needed to be considered hazardous. On one end of the spectrum, under the U.S. hazardous waste statute, RCRA, any solid waste that is mixed with a listed hazardous waste is itself considered hazardous. 40 C.F.R. 261.3(c)(2)(i). This result provides a perverse version of the King Midas fable, where everything a listed waste comes into contact with turns into hazardous waste.

Within the European Community, however, mixed wastes have sometimes been treated less strictly. In one incident, the German company Weber lawfully mixed woodchips with hazardous waste. The result was a hazardous waste legally transformed through mixing into burnable material exempt from regulation as a hazardous substance. Thereafter, the mixed waste was exported to a Turkish cement plant which accepted 1,500 tons of waste for $70 per ton. The waste sat on site for nearly half a year while its high concentration of PCBs leached into the ground. It would have cost roughly $560 per ton to dispose of the waste in Germany. Harry Anderson, *The Global Poison Trade*, Newsweek, Nov. 7, 1988, at 67. Does this example suggest problems inherent in the strategy of granting countries the right to make their own decisions with respect to the universe of waste deemed "hazardous"?

9. In April, 1993, a United States federal jury convicted two men of criminal violations under RCRA for knowingly exporting hazardous waste from the United States to Pakistan without the required consent of the importing State and without notifying EPA prior to shipment. The cost of legally disposing of the wastes in question would have been $80,000 in the United States but a mere $1,800 in Pakistan. Their waste shipment was intercepted in Dubai and returned to the United States for disposal. This was the *first* such criminal prosecution under RCRA (passed in 1980) for illegal exportation of hazardous waste from the United States. Does the lack of prosecutions suggest that illegal exportation of hazardous waste from the United States without the required prior informed consent rarely occurs or that such illegal acts remain undetected? Henry Weinstein, *2 Found Guilty of Exporting Toxic Waste*, Los Angeles Times, April 16, 1993. It should be noted, however, that criminal prosecutions for illegal waste shipments have since increased.

10. Over 145 countries are party to the Basel Convention. The United States is one of only three countries that has signed but not ratified the Basel Convention. Although the U.S. Senate has given its advice and consent to ratification, amendments to the U.S. hazardous waste law are necessary before the United States could fulfill its obligations. The benefits of ratification are clear. While U.S. government officials and some industry representatives are very active and influential in the technical working groups, they would clearly have more voice if the United States were a party and could participate in the plenary sessions. U.S. industries would no longer have to press the U.S. government to initiate lengthy bilateral agreements with individual countries to allow waste trade. U.S. companies trading in recyclables would see more business in imports and exports, as well. As of August, 2001, however, the U.S. Congress had not passed needed implementing legislation. Pat Phibbs, *Bliley 'Disappointed' as Administration Fails to Respond To Inquiry on Basel Convention*, BNA INT'L ENV'T DAILY (Feb. 7, 2000).

C.   IMPLEMENTATION AND AMENDMENTS

Basel Convention opened for signature	*March 22, 1989*
Lome IV Convention	*March 22, 1990*
Bamako Convention	*January 29, 1991*
OECD Council Decision	*March 30, 1992*
Basel Convention enters into force	*May 5, 1992*
EU Regulation 259/935	*February 3, 1993*
Basel Ban Amendment	*March 25, 1994*
Basel Protocol on Liability and Compensation	*December 10, 1999*

1.   TRADE AMONG OECD NATIONS

In response to the concern that the Basel Convention's entry into force would disrupt existing trade among industrialized nations in recyclable wastes such as scrap precious metals, non-ferrous metals, glass, paper, and batteries, the OECD Council adopted a decision establishing a control system for the transfrontier movements among OECD member countries of wastes destined for recovery operations. Decision of the Council Concerning the Control of Transfrontier Movements of Wastes Destined for Recovery Operations, OECD Doc. C(92)39/FINAL (Mar. 30, 1992)(as amended). The OECD Decision establishes a notice and consent regime governing the transboundary movement of wastes for recovery *among* OECD Member States and qualifies as a compatible multilateral agreement under Article 11 of the Basel Convention. This allows OECD Member States that are Parties to the Basel Convention to continue trading in wastes covered by the OECD Decision with OECD Members who have *not* ratified the Basel Convention (notably the United States). The OECD Decision applies only to wastes destined for recovery and creates three lists of wastes and three corresponding levels of control: Green List (minimal controls); Amber List (tacit consent procedures); Red List (prior written consent procedures). *See also* EU Council Regulation No. 259/93 on February 1, 1993, implementing the requirements of the Basel Convention, the OECD Decision, and the 1989 fourth Lomé Convention (concerning certain developing countries); Council Regulation 259/93 on the supervision and control of shipments of waste within, into and out of the European Community, 1993 O.J. (L 30) 1 (Feb. 1, 1993).

In an effort to harmonize regulation of the waste trade, in June, 2001, OECD governments agreed to amend the 1992 Council Decision by repealing the Green, Amber and Red Waste Lists and, in their place, adopting Basel's List A and List B described below (with some exceptions).

2.   THE BASEL BAN

Restricting trade between OECD and non-OECD Parties was an issue hotly debated during the original negotiations for a convention. In the three initial Conferences of the Parties (CoPs), developing countries and environmental NGOs worked toward the goal of a complete ban between OECD and non-OECD Parties. The first Basel CoP, held in Uruguay in 1992, adopted a Decision that "requests the industrialized countries to prohibit transboundary movements of hazardous wastes and other wastes for disposal to developing countries" and "further requests developing countries to prohibit the import of hazardous wastes from industrialized countries." The next CoP in Geneva in 1994 adopted a Decision banning the export of hazardous wastes intended for final disposal from OECD to non-OECD countries and, by the end of 1997, the export of wastes intended for recovery and recycling. This political declaration was given legal meaning and adopted as an amendment to the Convention at the next CoP in 1995 (Decision III/1). Rather than relying explicitly on the OECD/non-OECD Party distinction, the amendment bans the export of hazardous wastes for final disposal and recycling from countries listed in Annex VII of the Convention (Lichtenstein, EU and OECD member States) to non-Annex VII countries. The amendment is known as the "Basel Ban." *See* David Wirth, *Trade Implications of the Basel Convention Amendment*

Banning North–South Trade in Hazardous Wastes, International Environment Reporter at 976, Sept. 4, 1996.

Thus, when ratified, the Basel Ban amendment will prohibit hazardous
waste shipments from Parties that are OECD or EU countries to *non-*
OECD/EU countries. The new Article 4A provides that:

> 1) each Party listed in Annex VII must prohibit all transboundary movements
> of hazardous wastes that are destined for disposal operations in countries not
> listed in Annex VII; and

> 2) each Party listed in Annex VII must phase out by December 31, 1997, and
> prohibit as of that date, all transboundary movements of hazardous wastes
> under Article 1(1)(a) of the Convention which are destined for recovery/recy-
> cling operations in countries not listed in Annex VII.

Decision III/1 Amendment to the Basel Convention, Third Meeting of the
Conference of the Parties to the Basel Convention on the Control of
Transboundary Shipments of Hazardous Wastes and Their Disposal, U.N.
Doc. UNEP/CHW3/35 (Nov. 28, 1995). Exports from developed to develop-
ing countries would not be permitted, regardless of local environmental
conditions and disposal capacity.

The amendment has been controversial, particularly in the context of
materials destined for recycling, with industry and some developed and
developing countries arguing it will act as a disincentive for recycling.
Moreover, since the ban only covers exports originating from Annex VII
countries, it fails to address South–South trade in wastes. As of August,
2001, 26 countries had ratified the amendment. Sixty-two are required for
it to enter into force.

Following adoption of the Basel Ban amendment, Parties adopted two
new waste lists to clarify the universe of wastes that would be covered by
the Convention and the pending ban. Annex VIII (known as "List A") lists
those wastes deemed hazardous under Article 1(1)(a) and therefore covered
by the ban. Annex IX includes a "List B" of wastes that are not generally
considered hazardous and which are not subject to control under the
Convention.

Since the United States is not currently a Party to the Convention, it is
not bound by the prohibition of Article 4A nor, because Decision III/1 is an
amendment to the Convention, is it binding on those countries refusing to
ratify the Decision. Thus, for example, if Canada does not deposit its
instrument of ratification, it is not bound to the new obligation. Although
not yet in force as a matter of international law, the European Union has
implemented the Basel Ban under EU law.

QUESTIONS AND DISCUSSION

1. *Problem Exercise.* The general counsel of a British Company known as Alpha
Enterprises walks into your office and informs you that Alpha intends to ship its
waste for recycling to a processor, Beta Industries, in the Philippines. The ship
carrying the waste will stop in India to unload other cargo. Alpha wants to know its
obligations under the Basel Convention. The United Kingdom, the Philippines, and
India have all ratified the Basel Convention. What facts will you need to know to
provide legal counsel? Once the OECD to non-OECD ban enters into force, will it

matter that the facility in the Philippines makes use of state-of-the-art recycling operations that are among the most advanced in the world? In addition to the provisions of the Basel Convention, what other sources of law must be consulted?

Assume that Alpha Enterprises is shipping scrap computers and barrels of degreasing wastes to Beta for recycling. Explain in concrete steps what Alpha must do to comply with the requirements of the Basel Convention. What information must British authorities provide to Beta Industries and the Philippine and Indian authorities? What information must the Philippine authorities provide to British authorities? List the possible ways the shipment could be prohibited or regulated.

How would the situation differ if Alpha intended to ship the wastes to Gamma, Inc., located in Taiwan, which has not ratified Basel and has not signed any bilateral or multilateral waste trade treaties?

2. The Basel Ban only applies to trade between Parties in Annex VII and other countries. During the Fourth Conference of the Parties in 1998, Israel and Monaco attempted to gain formal recognition as Annex VII countries. Israel stated that it could meet and fulfill the technical, professional, and legal standards set forth in the Basel Convention as well as any country listed in Annex VII. Monaco argued that it regularly exported medical waste to France and imported French municipal solid waste. Classification as an Annex VII country would greatly simplify this trade. While acknowledging that Monaco presents a unique case, Greenpeace has opposed inclusion of countries into Annex VII as an attempt to undermine the ban. Noting that the Basel Ban had not yet entered into force, the Basel parties postponed consideration of adding Annex VII countries, but requested that the Secretariat undertake a study of issues relating to accession to the Annex and creation of objective criteria. What should such criteria require? Should the distinction rest on whether the country is an OECD member, as Greenpeace has argued, or on the country's capacity to manage hazardous waste in an environmentally sound manner? If the waste is likely to be managed in an environmentally sound manner, why should the Basel Ban apply? At CoP–5, in 1999, Israel withdrew its request to be considered an Annex VII country.

3. The Basel Convention has been harshly criticized by some developing countries, charging that Basel does not prohibit international trade in hazardous waste but, instead, merely provides a detailed tracking mechanism. Do you agree with this assessment or the comments below? Does the Basel Ban resolve these concerns?

> The Basel Convention reflects most industrial nations' strategy to checkmate developing nations into accepting hazardous waste exports. Under such terms as "prior informed consent," "environmentally sound manner," and "adequate disposal activities," the Basel Convention has legitimized the international toxic waste game and proclaimed industrial nations the winners.

> Supporters of the Convention maintain that developing countries benefit from the jobs, income, business activity, and technological education associated with the transboundary waste business. The potential benefits of education and employment, however, are mere short term gains and apply only to the limited market of waste importation. More importantly, those who seek to protect these benefits are not challenging the fundamental bipolar economic inequities that force Third World nations to accept shipments of toxic waste. Developing countries acquiesce to the importation of hazardous wastes because they are poor and have unequal bargaining power. Consequently, the toxic waste trade between industrialized nations and the Third World resembles economic blackmail. Only the Third World's complete ban of toxic waste imports will challenge industrialized nations to confront the uncontrolled generation of hazardous waste. Therefore, the true aim regarding hazardous waste management is to minimize waste generation and develop new recycling methods.

M. Cusack, *International Law and the Transboundary Shipment of Hazardous Waste to the Third World: Will the Basel Convention Make a Difference?* 5 Am. U. J. Int'l & Pol'y, 393, 420–422 (1990).

---

3.   THE BAMAKO CONVENTION

The Bamako Convention on the Ban of Import Into Africa and the Control of Transboundary Movement and Management of Hazardous Wastes Within Africa was signed by all 51 members of the Organization for African Unity (OAU) on January, 1991 in Bamako, Mali. 30 I.L.M. 775 (1991). The Convention, which came into force April 22, 1998, essentially bans the import of hazardous waste generated outside of Africa. The legacy of toxic colonialism, of developing countries' exploitation as cheap disposal sites, was the dominant concern leading up to the Basel Convention.

While 39 African States had attended the negotiating sessions leading up to the Basel Convention, they initially refused to sign, complaining it was not stringent enough. Thirty-two African nations have since ratified the Convention. The members of the OAU favored a complete ban on the export of hazardous waste to developing countries. The OAU States also argued that Basel had failed to address adequately three important problems: 1) how to control shipments of mixed waste; 2) how to address instances where an importing State fails to dispose adequately of the waste; and 3) how to prevent forgery and bribery from circumventing Basel's notice and consent provisions. John Ovink, *Transboundary Movement of Hazardous Waste, the Basel and Bamako Conventions: Do Third World Countries Have a Choice?,* 13 DICK. J. INT'L L. 281, 285 (1995); *see also Corrupt Officials Are Targets for Exporters Trying to Unload Their Toxic Wares,* 135 CONG. REC. at E1949–50, May 31, 1989.

Despite refusing to sign the Basel Convention, African countries could still receive waste from Basel parties through Basel's Article 11 exception for exports by a Party to a non-Party pursuant to a separate bilateral or multilateral agreement. To eliminate this possibility, the OAU made use of Basel's Article 4 provision forbidding a Party from shipping waste to a State that has banned all hazardous waste imports, or that belongs to an economic integration organization that has done so. Art. 4(2)(e). Thus in January 1991, all the nations of Africa (except South Africa which was not a member of the OAU at the time) came together to ban hazardous waste imports by signing the Bamako Convention. Despite this political consensus, the capacity of governments to implement the obligations contained in the Bamako Convention are quite limited.

Bamako requires all Parties to prohibit under their own domestic law the importation of hazardous waste from outside Africa. Article 4(1) of Bamako states that:

> All parties shall take appropriate legal, administrative and other measures within the area under their jurisdiction to prohibit the import of all hazardous wastes, for any reason, into Africa from non-Contracting Parties. Such import shall be deemed illegal and a criminal act.

The Convention requires Parties to adopt laws prohibiting the dumping of hazardous waste at sea or in the territorial water, exclusive economic zone (EEZ), and continental shelf of each party. This provision also declares any dumping of hazardous wastes at sea, including incineration, to be illegal. Bamako Art. 4(2)(a). It exceeds the restrictions of Basel and could outlaw the kind of ocean dumping practiced as a last resort in the *Khian Sea* incident, where a ship loaded with hazardous incinerator ash allegedly dumped its cargo at sea after being refused docking rights by several nations. Bamako's definition of waste is also broader than Basel's. In addition to the Basel wastes, Bamako defines as hazardous waste substances which are radioactive or have been banned, canceled, refused registration by government regulatory action, or voluntarily withdrawn from registration in the country of manufacture for human health and environmental reasons. Bamako Art. 2(1)(d).

Bamako's enforcement provisions provide that: (1) each party must create its own national body to act as a watchdog or "Dumpwatch" as it is labeled by the Convention; and (2) violators of the ban on extra-continental imports of waste are subject to criminal penalties, as are their accomplices including any person who plans, carries, out or assists illegal imports. Bamako Art. 9(2). As noted above, prior to the Bamako Convention the countries of Nigeria and Cameroon had already imposed the death penalty for imports of hazardous waste. Despite its ban on the import of hazardous waste from outside Africa, Bamako does not ban the importation into one African state of waste generated in another African state. Article 4 of Bamako mandates that each generating state shall pass domestic laws requiring generators to report their waste generation and shipments to the Secretariat and subjects generators to strict joint and several liability for the release of hazardous waste. Bamako Art. 4(3)(b). This is in striking contrast to Basel's treatment of liability, which postponed the issue for later negotiations.

4. LOMÉ IV CONVENTION

The Lomé IV Convention ("Lomé IV"), signed in 1990, is a trade agreement that prohibits the exports of hazardous waste from the European Community to the African, Caribbean and Pacific (ACP) states. The Fourth African, Caribbean, and Pacific States European Economic Community Convention of Lomé opened for signature March 22, 1990, 29 I.L.M. 783 (1990). The ACP group represents most of the nations in the geographic regions that comprise its name and includes the former colonies of the Western European powers. As of 1997, 68 nations had ratified Lomé IV.

Sharing the concerns of African nations over the Basel Convention's failure to ban the hazardous waste trade, many developing nations sought the protection of an additional multilateral treaty prohibiting the import of waste within their territories. Lomé IV, therefore, banned the direct and indirect export of any hazardous or radioactive waste from European Community states to ACP states. Lomé IV, Art. 39. In return, the ACP states agreed not to accept waste imports from any other states outside the European Community. This sweeping provision effectively halted developed country waste shipments to ACP states and ensured that European nations had not placed themselves at a competitive disadvantage by unilaterally excluding a destination for its wastes. David J. Abrams, Note, *Regulating the International Hazardous Waste Trade: A Proposed Global Solution*, 28 COLUM. J. TRANSNAT'L L. 801, 840 (1990); Hugh J. Marbury, *Hazardous Waste Exportation: The Global Manifestation of Environmental Racism*, 28 VAND. J. TRANSNAT'L L. 251 (1995).

QUESTIONS AND DISCUSSION

1. One failing that Bamako, Basel and Lomé IV share is the lack of a definition for what management or disposal of hazardous waste in "an environmentally sound manner" means. Working groups for these treaties have met to define this term but, to date, have failed to reach agreement. One proposal in the U.S. Congress would have defined environmentally sound management as "no less strict" than RCRA. However, under this standard, even waste shipments from the U.S. to Canada were at risk of being banned. Should countries be authorized to judge the waste management practices of another country and bar waste shipments on this basis?

2. An important difference between Basel and Lomé IV, on the one hand, and Bamako, on the other, is Bamako's blanket prohibition of hazardous waste imports. Both Basel and Lomé IV, subject to prior informed consent, provide for trade in certain materials intended for recycling. Concerned that much of this recycling trade is simply a sham, however, Bamako bans the importation of waste into Africa for any reason. While establishing a simple enforcement regime of closed walls, this strategy arguably denies African countries the opportunity for economic growth by developing an environmentally sound recycling industry for hazardous waste. Such technological advances may also be important in allowing Africa to safely manage its own wastes. Ovink, *supra*, at 293–94.

3. Basel, Bamako and Lomé IV all implicitly assume that Parties have the institutional capacity to implement their provisions. In practice, this requires an effective customs authority to monitor and seize imports and exports, administrative capacity to handle the requests for consent to shipments, and adequate enforcement authority to ensure the threat of sanction for noncompliance. Do you think this is the case for all Bamako, Basel, and Lomé IV parties? If not, how would you determine which countries lack adequate capacity and the most effective manner to remedy this situation?

4. One of the underlying assumptions of the Basel Ban, the Bamako Convention, and Lomé IV is that developing countries cannot safely manage hazardous wastes. But surely this is an oversimplification. Should the standards that apply to sub-Saharan Africa apply equally to industrializing nations such as Brazil, Chile or Malaysia? How might you argue Basel already takes this into account?

————

5. PROTOCOL ON LIABILITY

As mentioned above, Article 12 of the Basel Convention directed parties to prepare a protocol establishing appropriate liability rules and procedures for damage resulting from the hazardous waste trade. Following ten years of negotiation, the Fifth Conference of Parties adopted the Protocol on Liability in 1999. As of August, 2001, 13 Parties had ratified the Protocol. It will become effective once 20 parties have ratified.

The Protocol applies to transboundary shipments of hazardous wastes, including illegal traffic, from the point the wastes are loaded for transport in the country of export to the point they are accepted by the disposal agent. Liability does not extend to damage that results after disposal (such as that caused by leaking storage tanks or other forms of improper disposal). Strict liability applies in two cases–when both importing and exporting nations are parties, and when trading with a non-Party for damages caused while the waste is in possession of a Party. The Protocol also establishes a fault-based liability regime in the event that a party disregards Convention requirements or acts in a wrongful intentional, reckless, or negligent manner.

Annex B to the Protocol establishes a liability floor for responsible parties, though the level of the floor depends on whether the party is a notifier or disposer and on the quantity of hazardous waste in the shipment. For any single incident, a notifying party will be liable for not less than 1 million Special Drawing Rights (SDR, equal to $1.38 million), and a disposing party for not less than 2 million SDR. The financial limits for strict liability are determined by domestic law. These limits proved extremely contentious and the parties agreed to adopt the liability scheme crafted by the Legal Working Group subject to the understanding that COP–6 may, before the Protocol enters into force, amend the sliding scale of the financial limits. If the liability is fault-based, there is no financial limit to the compensation for injured parties. Sejal Choksi, *The Basel Convention on the Control of Transboundary Movements of Hazardous Wastes and Their Disposal: 1999 Protocol on Liability and Compensation*, 28 Ecology L.Q. 509 (2001).

Legal instruments that impose meaningful liability for international environmental harms are rare indeed in international law, with the notable exceptions of conventions for oil spills (see page 731) and nuclear reactor accidents (see page 897). Thus UNEP has called the Protocol "a major breakthrough."

The Protocol, however, has been roundly criticized by environmental groups for its omissions. They have charged that because liability attaches only to the notifying party for damage resulting from transport, the generator of the hazardous waste can avoid liability by hiring exporters to act as notifying and controlling entities. Choksi, *op. cit.,* at 524. Nor does the Protocol assign liability for management of the waste following disposal. The industry perspective on the negotiations is presented in the Questions and Discussion section at page 862.

While the Protocol requires notifiers, exporters and importers to purchase bonds and insurance as indemnification against liability, it is not clear that the export brokers and waste transporters who are liable will have sufficient funds to compensate injured parties for any incidents in the course of waste movement. To address this concern, developing countries argued that a global fund should be established to provide compensation for incidents where the responsible party was either unknown or insolvent. Developed countries countered that the need for such a fund had not yet been established. The compromise agreement called for increasing the

Convention's Trust Fund with voluntary contributions that could be earmarked for specific purposes (such as damage compensation).

The Protocol also contains a number of significant exceptions. It does not apply to Article 11 bilateral agreements under the Basel Convention, provided that: the damage occurs within the national jurisdiction of one of the bilateral agreement parties; the agreement includes a liability provision that fully meets or exceeds that of the Protocol; the country in which the damage occurs has previously given notice that the Protocol does not apply to the relevant damage; and the agreement parties have not declared that the Protocol applies. As a result, the Protocol does not apply to OECD countries trading with one another. Thus, if the Basel Ban enters into force, the Protocol will primarily address liability for harm arising from the waste trade among developing countries. The Protocol also exempts shipments of hazardous wastes that appear on national lists but are not specifically listed under the Convention. Finally, the Protocol will not effect bilateral, multilateral, or regional agreements concerning liability and compensation in existence prior to the Protocol's adoption.

It is not clear whether the United States will ratify the Protocol (assuming it ratifies Basel). The State Department has criticized the compensation floors as too high, arguing that the liability regime includes recyclable wastes with low-level hazardous characteristics. It is feared this would unnecessarily harm the trade in recyclables. Daniel Pruzin, *Agreement on Liability Protocol Reached at Basel Conference of Parties*, BNA— INT'L ENV'T DAILY, Dec. 13, 1999.

D.   CROSS-CUTTING THEMES

1.   DOMESTIC IMPLEMENTATION

As described previously, in the United States the Resource Conservation and Recovery Act (RCRA) controls the treatment, storage and disposal of hazardous waste. 42 U.S.C. §§ 6901–6992k, as amended by the Hazardous and Solid Waste Amendments of 1984. Section 3017 of RCRA requires the prior informed consent of the importing country before a waste export may proceed. RCRA export and import requirements apply only to wastes that qualify as "hazardous wastes" under RCRA. A waste is only considered hazardous under RCRA if it meets a complex regulatory definition of both a "hazardous waste" and a "solid waste." Section 3017 of RCRA prohibits the export of hazardous wastes unless:

- The exporter has provided EPA with a proper notification of intent to export;

- The United States requests and receives the consent of the importing country;

- Proof of the importing country's consent is attached to the manifest accompanying the shipment; and

- The shipment conforms to the terms of the consent given by the receiving country or to the terms of an agreement entered into by the United States and the importing country governing transboundary waste shipments. 42 U.S.C. § 6938.

Written notice of intent to export must be submitted to EPA 60 days before the waste is to be shipped off-site. 40 C.F.R. § 262.53. EPA regulations are directed to the "primary exporter," defined as the person who is required to originate the manifest for shipment of hazardous waste. 40 C.F.R. § 262.51.

The notification must be signed by the primary exporter and include information concerning the exporter, ultimate receiving facility, type and quantity of waste and means of shipment. Within 30 days of receiving a completed notification, EPA, in conjunction with the Department of State, will transmit the notification to the government of the importing country and any transit countries. EPA will also:

- Advise the government(s) that United States law prohibits the export of hazardous waste without the consent of the importing country;

- Request written notification of consent or objection; and

- Forward a description of federal regulations for the treatment, storage, and disposal of hazardous waste in the United States. 42 U.S.C. 6938(d).

EPA will forward the consent, objection or other communication received from the importing country to the primary exporter within 30 days of the State Department's receipt of the importing country's written response. 42 U.S.C. § 6938(e). EPA will also forward any responses received from transit countries, although transit country consent is not required for the shipment to proceed under RCRA. These notification requirements are augmented by extensive tracking, document reporting, and record keeping requirements.

The United States has signed the Basel Convention and the Senate has provided its advice and consent, but the necessary implementing legislation has not been adopted. Thus the United States is not a Party to the Convention. In particular, RCRA must be amended to create authority for the government to stop transboundary shipments of hazardous waste when it believes the waste will not be managed in an environmentally sound manner, to require re-importation of wastes that cannot be disposed of in accordance with the export contract, to control transboundary movement of household wastes and ash residue from their incineration, and to define the term, "environmentally sound manner." On their face, these amendments are not particularly momentous. Given that the United States was among the first countries to require prior written notice and consent procedures for waste exports, why do you think Congress has not yet adopted the necessary implementing legislation to ratify the Convention?

2. INTERNATIONAL TRADE LAW

Similar to CITES and the Montreal Protocol, the Basel Convention relies on trade-related measures to encourage States to become Parties and enforce its provisions. Thus Article 4 of the Basel Convention states that Parties may not trade in hazardous waste with non-Parties and Article 11 provides an exception for bilateral or multilateral agreements *so long as* the provisions are not less environmentally sound than those provided for by the Basel Convention. In this manner, Basel creates a floor for environmental safeguards in the hazardous waste trade. These provisions do, however, raise potential conflicts with international trade law. While no international environmental agreement has been found in violation of the GATT or WTO agreements by dispute panels, individual laws or regulations of several states have been held inconsistent with GATT.

As discussed in detail in Chapter 15, GATT's coverage is based on three core provisions. GATT Article I requires "most favored nation" treatment (MFN principle)–imports from other GATT parties are not discriminated against on the basis of national origin. Article III guarantees "national treatment"–imports from other parties are treated no less favorably, once border duties are paid, than like domestic products. Article XI prohibits quantitative restrictions such as quotas, bans or licenses on GATT party imports.

The Basel Convention contains several provisions that may be subject to attack under the GATT. Chief among these is its ban on trade in hazardous waste between Basel Parties and non-Parties, except pursuant to a bilateral or multilateral agreement. Basel Article 11 provides that any such agreement, if reached before Basel entered into force, must be "compatible with the environmentally sound management of hazardous wastes." If the agreement is reached after Basel's entry into force (May 5, 1994) then it must not "derogate from the environmentally sound management of hazardous wastes." The purpose behind this restriction is two-fold. It puts pressure on non-Parties to ratify Basel and it ensures that Basel's protections will extend to trade in hazardous wastes if it does occur between Parties and non-Parties. Consider the following:

> Assume country A is a GATT/WTO contracting party but is not a party to the Basel Convention; country B is both a GATT/WTO contracting party and a party to the Basel Convention; country C is, like B, both a GATT/WTO contracting party and a party to the Basel Convention. Under the Basel Convention, country B is obligated to adopt laws that prohibit the export of waste to or the import of waste from country A. Thus, in fulfilling its Basel Convention obligations, country B necessarily violates the MFN principle of article I of GATT/WTO by not affording country A the same trading privileges that it extends to other Basel Convention parties, such as country C. Similarly, country B's prohibition on imports of waste from country A, as well as exports of waste to country A, arguably contravenes article XI's prohibition on quantitative restrictions.

P. Hagen & R. Housman, *The Basel Convention,* in THE USE OF TRADE MEASURES IN SELECT MULTILATERAL ENVIRONMENTAL AGREEMENTS (UNEP 1995).

These apparent GATT violations might be protected through the exceptions provided in GATT Article XX. So long as measures are not applied in an arbitrary manner or amount to unjustifiable discrimination among GATT parties, a violation of the GATT Articles can be justified if the measure is "necessary to protect human, animal, or plant life, or health" GATT Art. XX (b); or to conserve exhaustible natural resources, provided that the measures are "made effective in conjunction with restrictions on domestic production or consumption." GATT Art. XX(g).

The relevance of Article XX(g)'s exception for conservation of exhaustible natural resources is not obvious. One would presumably need to argue that landfill space or hazardous waste treatment facilities qualify as an exhaustible natural resource. This specific issue has never been addressed by a dispute panel, but one must question whether landfills and treatment facilities are natural at all or, rather, an artificial creation.

Article XX(b)'s exception seems more relevant. The Basel Convention's primary purpose in regulating transboundary commerce in hazardous waste is to reduce the threat to human life and health, as well as to animal and plant life and health, posed by improper waste disposal. The key question, however, is not whether the Basel Convention is necessary to protect health and life but whether the *trade restriction* between Parties and non-Parties is "necessary," as that term is used in Article XX(b). If the primary purpose of the trade restriction is to pressure non-Parties to ratify the Convention, is this "necessary to protect human" health? If the primary purpose is to provide safeguards for hazardous waste trade between Parties and non-Parties, is that "necessary"?

Article XX's preamble states that measures exempted under Articles XX(b) and XX(g) must not be applied in a manner which would constitute a means of arbitrary or unjustifiable discrimination between countries where the same conditions prevail, or a disguised restriction on international trade. The ban clearly is not a disguised restriction on trade, so the fundamental issue becomes whether there exists a rational basis for differential treatment between Basel Parties and non-Parties, i.e., do the same conditions prevail in both Parties? How would you decide this issue? The pending OECD to non-OECD party ban raises similar questions about the Convention's overall consistency with GATT/WTO rules.

3. TECHNOLOGY TRANSFER

Both the Basel and Bamako Conventions call for developed nations to transfer hazardous waste processing technology to developing nations. Article 14 in both Conventions addresses financing of technology transfers in virtually identical language.

> 1. The Parties agree that, according to the specific needs of different regions and subregions, regional or sub-regional centres for training and technology transfers regarding the management of hazardous wastes and other wastes and the minimization of their generation should be established. The Parties shall decide on the establishment of appropriate funding mechanisms of a voluntary nature.

Basel Convention, Article 14. Whether voluntary funding for beneficial technology transfers will be made available remains an open question. Of far greater concern to environmental groups is "bad" technology transfer for the disposal of hazardous waste. Greenpeace, in particular, has denounced the transfer of incinerator technology to highly populated developing countries as the transfer of a hazardous technology. Greenpeace argues that incineration of waste only worsens the hazardous waste problem both because hazardous substances such as dioxin are inevitably produced by incineration and the resulting ash is likely hazardous and must be disposed of safely. *See* discussion of technology transfer in Chapter 8, p. 473.

4. ROLE OF NGOs

NGOs have played a prominent role in raising the public's awareness of the pervasive and harmful effects of the hazardous waste trade. Following the negotiation of the Basel Convention, NGOs continued to push for a total ban on the hazardous waste trade, urging nations to enact individual or regional bans on waste imports recognized under Basel Article 11. Greenpeace has taken the highest profile in exposing dangerous hazardous waste shipments all over the world. Greenpeace's success has been due to investigative research, its skillful use of the media to publicize its findings, alliances with local environmental and political groups, and its reputation for humbling large companies.

A representative example of Greenpeace's investigative techniques occurred in South Africa. Working with the South African environmental group, Earthlife Africa, Greenpeace discovered that the Thor Chemical facility in Natal, South Africa, had been importing mercury waste for several years. Mercury, a highly toxic metal, had allegedly been destined for recycling. Earthlife Africa and Greenpeace tracked the movements of mercury waste into the plant and linked it with local mercury contamination problems arising from slipshod recycling. Acting on information from local union members, Earthlife alerted Greenpeace to an impending shipment of mercury waste from the United States to South Africa. The American mercury was reportedly from Borden Chemicals of Geismar, Louisiana, and was headed to the Thor facility. Borden Chemicals is owned by the large international company, Borden Inc.

Greenpeace informed top Borden executives of the impending shipment and Thor's reputation as a dirty company. Borden agreed two days later to recall its ship, which contained 150 barrels of mercury waste. Greenpeace's publicity of the problem prompted an investigation led by the African National Congress which found that at least 10,000 barrels of mercury waste were stored on site. This in turn led Borden officials to tour the site, prompting their discovery that virtually all the barrels they had shipped to Thor in the 3 previous years were still unopened and stored on site. Besides Borden, barrels bearing the names of American Cyanamid and Calgon, two other U.S. companies, were also discovered. Greenpeace Press Release, Jan. 22, 1999.

Case Study: Impact of Trade Restrictions on Indian Secondary Zinc Imports

While NGOs have indisputably played a key role in the development of the Basel Convention and the Basel Ban, its activities are not entirely supported by the developing countries they seek to aid. As with many of the issues discussed in this book, conflicts can arise between environmental protection and economic development. Consider the two excerpts below. The first comes from a Greenpeace news release on its website, <http://www.greenpeace.org/ctox.html>.

REGRESSIVE GOVERNMENTS URGED: BAN TOXIC WASTE TRADE NOW
NEW DELHI, INDIA, 17 APRIL 1997

Environmentalists from more than ten countries today protested against the international trade in toxic waste by holding a peaceful solidarity demonstration outside the Indian Ministry of Environment and Forests.

Greenpeace campaigners from around the world and activists from local Indian groups deployed a large banner "BAN TOXIC WASTE TRADE" in English and Hindi. A statement signed by international groups from 18 countries was delivered [to] the Indian Ministry of Environment, US, Australian, Brazilian and Singapore Embassies demand[ing] that they ban the movement of hazardous wastes from industrialized to developing countries by ratifying and implementing the Basel Ban.

With less that eight months to go before the Basel Ban comes into force in January 1998 hazardous waste trade continues unabated. Pressured by a powerful waste trader lobby, represented by the International Chamber of Commerce, some Governments are vacillating in their support of the Ban

"We want countries like the US and Australia to know that we will not tolerate their attempts to continue using developing countries as a dustbin for their toxic waste" said Malini Morzaria of Greenpeace International. "Countries like India and Brazil are selling the health and future of their people and environment to international waste traffickers. The only solution is to ban this poisonous trade."

In a ten month period from April 1996 to January 1997, over 15,000 metric tonnes of lead and battery waste was exported to India–67% of that came from OECD countries. In the same period almost 12,000 metric tonnes of zinc waste came into India.

Greenpeace research over the years in India and South East Asia has documented that the facilities which recover materials from toxic waste trade are highly polluting and hazardous to people and the environment. Such operations would not be tolerated in rich OECD countries.

Do you agree with Greenpeace's calls to shut down the trade of battery waste to developing countries? Now read the excerpt below and see if it changes your opinion. It comes from a recycling trade association publication concerning the battery recycling sector in India. *Impact of the Basel Convention and Trade Ban on the Supply of Secondary Raw Materials*, BUREAU OF INTERNATIONAL RECYCLING, May 1997.

The zinc industry in India comprises over 300 small to medium-scale operations. The majority of these process secondary zinc materials to retrieve zinc as metal and zinc compounds. The secondary zinc industries in turn support a thriving galvanizing industry (which uses about 70 percent of all zinc consumed in India) and the fertilizer industry (providing zinc sulphate, a micronutrient vital to agriculture).

Current supplies of secondary materials are no longer available as a result of the combined effects of:

- premature implementation of parts of this incomplete Convention;
- uncertain legal status of the lists;
- inconsistent descriptions of materials on the lists; and
- local restrictions on some B list materials.

The uncertainty on the Basel position on zinc wastes has been responsible for the Delhi High Court ruling against their import and has been the major stumbling block to sourcing these materials for more than a year. There has been severe impact on both the recycling and downstream industries. The immediate effect has been closure and unemployment, with 30,000 to 50,000 jobs estimated at risk.

In the longer term, options open to developing countries such as India will be either to import zinc alloys and chemicals, or to alter current processes to suit primary raw materials. Those countries endowed with natural resources can invest in primary production, though this is a long term option, requiring more energy and creating more pollution per tonne of pure zinc produced than recycling.

QUESTIONS AND DISCUSSION

1. India has ratified the Basel Convention. In light of the two excerpts above, would you advise the Indian government to sign a bilateral agreement with the United States to allow waste trade between India (a Party) and the United States (a non-Party)?

2. Environmental NGOs have been criticized by industry groups on at least three counts. First, it is claimed that NGOs have done little to expand the capacity of less developed countries to safely manage hazardous wastes generated within their own borders. Second, Greenpeace has encouraged governments to expand the definition of hazardous waste to include things like computers and other electronic equipment, though industry claims these materials do not typically exhibit hazardous characteristics. Such actions risk disrupting industry "Product Stewardship" efforts where end-of-life products are collected and recycled rather than disposed of in landfills. Finally, industry groups have argued that the Basel restrictions have adverse economic impacts in less developed countries. The example of recycling lead batteries excerpted above would likely be one example.

Do you find these criticisms persuasive? Do you think the efforts of Greenpeace and other NGOs to shut down the trade in hazardous substances has, on balance, helped or harmed the environment? Do you favor a regime that allows trade in hazardous wastes where they can be managed "in an environmentally sound manner" or a regime that entirely prohibits waste trade?

3. Many industry participants in the Liability Protocol negotiations argued that a liability regime was not needed because national laws already imposed liability for harm arising from the transboundary movement of hazardous wastes. Indeed, according to one active participant, neither governments nor environmental NGOs cited any examples where existing national liability mechanisms were unable to redress environmental damage caused by a transboundary waste shipment. Yet millions of dollars were spent by governments and the Basel secretariat, in addition to each Party's costs in preparing for and conducting the negotiations over many years. Given that many observers predict that the Protocol will not enter into force for many years, if ever, would these resources have been better used to address other environmental problems? If the Protocol never enters into force, should we conclude that this was a poor use of resources? If so, whose fault is it?

4. The import of waste PCBs into the United States is banned under the Toxic Substances Control Act (TSCA). The Department of Defense has sought an amendment to TSCA (as part of the Basel implementing legislation) that would permit the military to return PCBs and PCB-containing substances from overseas military installations for disposal in the United States. Some environmental groups have strongly opposed this effort. Do you think the U.S. military has a responsibility to take back PCBs that are currently stored at overseas bases where they may present risks to the local populations? Why do you think NGOs oppose this amendment?

5. For more recent cases of NGOs campaigning to halt shipments of waste, visit the website of The Basel Action Network (BAN) at <http://www.ban.org/>. Working in collaboration with NGOs and government officials around the world, BAN has organized campaigns to block waste shipments, drafted model legislation to help developing countries ban hazardous waste importation, and provide coverage of breaking news. Its press releases (in the Toxic Trade News part of the website) provide extensive coverage from an NGO perspective.

6. Some commentators have suggested that in order to strengthen enforcement of domestic laws and multilateral environmental agreements, UNEP could serve as the super-enforcement agency for the Basel Treaty, Bamako Convention, OECD Decisions, and other agreements. One might think of such an agency as a "super-EPA" or global EPA. Consider the discussion in Chapter 8. Is this a viable suggestion? Catherine Tinker, *Environmental Planet Management by the United Nations, An Idea Whose Time Has Not Yet Come?*, 22 NYU J. INT'L L. & POL. 793 (1991).

7. UNEP serves as the Basel Secretariat, overseeing implementation of the Convention. The Secretariat's Web site is at, <http://www.unep.ch/basel/>.

———

5. PROBLEM EXERCISE: THE SHIPBREAKERS[1]

A. Following World War II and through the Cold War era, the United States steadily increased both the size and capability of its naval fleet, significantly so during the Reagan Administration's military expansion in the 1980s. By the early 1990s, however, with the end of the Cold War and the Defense Department in the midst of an extensive downsizing program, the Navy announced plans to decommission more than one hundred ships from its fleet.

Traditionally, the Navy had sold these ships to domestic "scrapping" companies. These companies bought the ships from the Navy, breaking them down, salvaging metals (particularly steel and copper) and equipment, and selling them on the scrap market. As a result of the huge military expansion in the 1980s, ship decommissioning had virtually halted, driving most of the domestic shipbreaking industry into bankruptcy. Those that were still in operation had high operating expenses. Naval ships contain a variety of hazardous substances (including PCBs, asbestos and fuels) and, as a result, compliance with the relevant safety and environmental regulations during scrapping is expensive.

In 1997, the Navy assessed its options. The domestic shipbreaking industry could not handle 100 or more decommissioned ships. "Mothballing" this fleet (i.e., storing it indefinitely) would cost $58 million over six years. There was, however, another option. The shipbreaking industry was booming in developing countries such as India, Pakistan, and Bangladesh. And these businesses would pay the Navy $100 per ton for the ships rather than the $10 per ton from domestic shipbreakers, resulting in a $54 million increase in revenue by selling overseas. This seemingly effective and

---

1. This problem is based on articles by Jeffrey Paul Luster, *The Domestic and International Legal Implications of Exporting Hazardous Waste: Exporting Naval Vessels* *for Scrapping*, 7 ENVTL. LAW. 75, 84 (2000); and William Langewieche, *The Shipbreakers*, THE ATLANTIC MONTHLY, Aug. 2000, at 31.

profitable solution was complicated, though, by EPA "pre-export remediation" regulations. These required the Navy to remove hazardous materials from each ship before exporting it overseas for scrapping. The Department of Defense estimated that compliance with these regulations for its 111 ships would cost $140 million. Consider, as well, that the Navy expects to double its ship scrapping activities over the next decade.

Following lengthy negotiations, the Navy and EPA reached an agreement the emphasized the principle of prior informed consent. The Navy would be required to extract all *easily accessible* PCBs (e.g., from transformers, capacitators, hydraulic fluids) and disclose the existence of remaining hazardous wastes (in particular, PCBs, asbestos and lead) to EPA's Office of Compliance no later than 45 days prior to export. EPA would be required to notify all countries importing Navy ships of the presence of hazardous materials. The notification for PCBs is excerpted below.

> The United States allows the export for scrapping of vessels formerly owned by the U.S. Government. Like the vessels of other vessel-exporting nations, these vessels may contain [PCBs] in some solid materials, added as plasticizers or fire retardants during the manufacturing process. The types of materials in which such PCBs may be found include paints, rubber products, felt gaskets and machinery mounts, adhesives, and electrical cable insulation. The United States no longer allows the manufacture of products to which PCBs have been intentionally added. Unlike the practices of most other countries that export vessels, the United States has required the removal of transformers and large high and low voltage capacitors that contain dielectric fluid with PCBs in quantifiable concentrations and all hydraulic and heat transfer fluids containing PCBs before these vessels are exported for scrapping.

This agreement dramatically reduced the costs for pre-export remediation and the Navy promulgated the policy for its ship decommissioning.

You are working at the Department of Defense. The Secretary of Defense informs you that the Navy intends to sell 111 of its ships to Indian and Bangladeshi shipbreakers for scrapping. The Secretary seeks your advice in determining:

(1) whether the U.S., though not a party to Basel, is still bound by its obligations under Article 18 of the Vienna Convention (page 303).

(2) If so, do the Navy's sales to Indian or Bangladeshi shipbreakers violate the Convention?

(3) Do they violate the Basel Ban amendment?

(4) Even if these might constitute violations of Basel, does the GATT have any relevance?

This will likely be a high-profile decision, since Greenpeace and the Basel Action Network will almost certainly start a campaign against this action, so the Secretary wants you to explore fully both sides of the argument for each of these questions.

———

B. You work for the international NGO, Natural Development, promoting sustainable development initiatives in developing countries. You learn that the Navy has decided to sell its fleet to shipbreakers in Alang, India for scrapping. At Alang, businesses take advantage of the thirty foot difference between high and low tides by driving the ships hard onshore at high tide, anchoring them down, and relying on local labor with oxacetalyne torches and winches to literally break the ship apart by hand. The reports you read of India's working conditions for the 40,000 workers in the shipbreaking industry are horrifying.

> These men are largely migrant workers, not registered by name; they are difficult to identify. They work in shifts, in highly cramped conditions and mostly without adequate safety equipment. An extremely high casualty rate is annually reported from Alang alone, the world's biggest ship graveyard. The causes of death are explosions, fire, suffocation and injuries from falling steel beams and plates. We have seen people picking asbestos-containing insulation material from ships with their bare hands. We have seen dozens of workers torch-cutting ship steel into small piece, inhaling the toxic fumes of lead paints with no protection at all. We have seen women carrying asbestos waste on their heads to dump directly into the sea. Throughout the shipyards we visited the workers were given no information regarding the hazardous materials they are handling or the safety measures working in such an environment requires.

Greenpeace, *Shipbreaking: A Global Environmental, Health and Labour Challenge*, December, 1999.

Beginning in 1997, when the Baltimore Sun first ran a Pulitzer-prize winning expose on the working conditions of ship breakers, Alang has been flooded with media and environmentalists appalled by the conditions. Activist campaigns, like the one launched by Greenpeace, have come to threaten the survival of the Alang shipbreaking industry. The owners of the companies in Alang that you talk with have a curt response. "The question I want to ask the environmentalists is if you should want to die first of starvation or pollution?" As one of the shipbreakers explains, "The fact remains that workers at Alang are better paid and are probably safer than their counterparts back in the poor provinces of Orissa, Bihar, and Uttar Pradesh. To provide housing and better living conditions is financially impractical for a developing country like India, where forty-five percent of the population is living below the poverty line." Drive up the costs of shipbreaking in Alang by mandating environmental and health protections, the shipbreakers warn, and the activity will simply move to Bangladesh and other countries that pay even lower wages and have even less worker protection. Indeed, it seems this has already happened with the industry moving from the United States to Korea and Taiwan, and then to India in search of the lowest costs.

You are asked to develop a campaign for Natural Development that will make the shipbreaking industry in developing countries more environmentally and socially sustainable. What are the various strategies you should consider? Calls for a ban on exports to Alang? For regulation? High-profile actions? What are their respective pros and cons? What should the goal of the campaign be—to stop the trade, to improve conditions, to raise awareness? Who benefits from each strategy—environmentalists in developed countries, the shipbreakers in Alang, environmental protection in Alang, shipreakers in Bangladesh, or shipbreakers in Baltimore?

SECTION II. CHEMICAL MANUFACTURE AND EXPORTS

When historians look back at the latter half of the twentieth century, the growth of the chemical industry will surely merit special mention. Nobody knows how many different chemicals we currently use. Worldwatch estimates that at least 75,000 different chemicals are used in pesticides, pharmaceuticals, plastics, and other products. Lester Brown et al., VITAL SIGNS 130 (2000). On June 15, 1998, an otherwise obscure date, chemists apparently identified "the 18 millionth synthetic chemical substance known to science." World Resources Institute, STATE OF THE WORLD 80 (2000). All of these compounds have the potential to move across national boundaries. Section II explores how they are regulated by international law and whether the protections in place are adequate.

A. PESTICIDES

1. HISTORY AND BACKGROUND

Modern industry and agriculture rely heavily on the production and use of synthetic chemical pesticides and fertilizers. Since 1945, for example, international pesticide sales have doubled every decade to sales over $18 billion. Incidents of pesticide poisonings have doubled at roughly the same rate. Although pesticide use has been greatest in the industrialized countries of Europe, Japan and the United States, the fastest growing market for pesticides is now in developing countries. World Health Organization, PUBLIC HEALTH IMPACT OF PESTICIDES USED IN AGRICULTURE 28–29, 32 (1990).

Although some pesticides pose significant health and environmental threats they may also offer significant benefits, particularly to developing countries. Pesticides are used to reduce the incidence of insect-borne human diseases and increase crop production through killing plant-eating insects and molds. Although banned in many countries, DDT is still used to battle vector-borne diseases in a number of developing countries such as malaria, yellow fever, river blindness and sleeping sickness. According to the World Health Organization (WHO), malaria "infects up to 500 million people a year and kills as many as 2.7 million." Donovan Webster, *Malaria kills one child every 30 seconds*, SMITHSONIAN, September 1, 2000, at 32–33. In the case of DDT, a debate has developed between Mexico—which still uses DDT to battle malaria—and Canada and the United States—who have banned DDT but still find significant levels as far north as the Great Lakes. The United States and Canada have pointed out that alternative mosquito insecticides are available, but Mexico contends that these are up to five-times more expensive than DDT and are acutely toxic, requiring extreme precaution in their application.

As the use of chemicals and pesticides has intensified, developed countries have become increasingly aware of the potential health and environmental problems and, in response, adopted advanced chemical management systems and regulatory structures to ban or severely restrict the use of certain chemicals within their countries. Although many pesticides and other hazardous chemicals may be banned for use in one country, they may still be exported to other countries. The legal trade of such chemicals presents several international concerns. While every country that imports pesticides has a registration program, generally requiring information on the pesticide's proposed use and efficacy, these programs are largely ineffective in those developing countries that lack the institutional capacity to make an informed decision on pesticide imports or on the proper management techniques after import. Not surprisingly, developing countries experience a high incidence of pesticide misuse, creating public health concerns as well as environmental harms to non-target species such as animals, birds and insects. *Biopesticides Development Consortium Set Up for Developing Countries,* CHEMICAL BUS. NEWSBASE 46, May 19, 2000. Insecticides' benefits and costs are elaborated in the excerpts below.

Bartlett P. Miller, *The Effect of the GATT and the NAFTA on Pesticide Regulation: Hard Look at Harmonization,* 6 COLO. J. INT'L ENVT'L. L. & POL'Y 201, 203–205 (1995)

Pesticides help humans by both preventing the spread of insect-borne diseases and by increasing agricultural productivity. In a program lasting from 1955 to 1970, the World Health Organization (WHO) used pesticides to eradicate malaria and saved as many as 15 million lives. As long as nonchemical means to combat mosquito populations that carry malaria, yellow fever, elephantiasis, and sleeping sickness remain unavailable, pesticides will continue to play an invaluable role in this area.

Pesticides also mitigate crop damage by disease and pests. In 1941 the Mexican government and the Rockefeller Foundation began an agricultural research project to develop a new generation of seeds that would produce much higher yields on a given parcel of land. The success of this new productive yield spawned the Green Revolution and promised to feed the world's growing population. However, the new seeds' genetic design required large amounts of water, fertilizer, and chemical pesticides.

Along with its benefits, pesticide use has many drawbacks. It poses a danger during its manufacture, during application to crops and pests, and through the residue it leaves on food. Pesticides are made from toxic chemicals manufactured in high concentrations to save money during distribution. The dangers of pesticide production often pass unnoticed for years, until a catastrophe like the one in Bhopal, India, underscores the lethal nature of the chemicals involved.

Applying pesticides to crops poses danger to non-target plant and animal species, ground water, and workers. Workers are susceptible to poisoning through ingestion, inhalation, and absorption of pesticides through the skin. The increasing number of workers and handlers affected is staggering. In 1972 the WHO estimated that 500,000 people were poisoned by pesticides and that 9,000 were killed. By 1982 the figures rose to 750,000 poisonings and 13,000 deaths.... Developing countries suffer a disproportionate amount of harm; although eighty percent of all agrichemicals are used in developed countries, ninety-nine percent of pesticide deaths occur in developing countries.

Paul and Anne Ehrlich, Betrayal of Science and Reason 163–65 (1996)

[M]odern agriculture is based on large-scale monocultures, which are especially vulnerable to pest attack. So it has become heavily dependent on the use of synthetic chemicals to control pests, whose populations could otherwise build up to very destructive levels.

Humanity now uses about 2.5 million tons of synthetic pesticides worldwide each year, and pesticide production is a multibillion dollar industry. [*see graph below*, Lester Brown et al., Vital Signs 49 (2000)].Yet despite both natural and human controls, pests and spoilage still destroy about 25 to 50 percent of crops before and after harvest. That proportion is, if anything, *higher* than average crop losses before synthetic pesticides were widely introduced after World War II. The strategy of large-scale broadcast spraying of pesticides has proven a poor one—except from the standpoint of petrochemical company profits.

An important reason for this lack of success is the rapidity with which pest populations evolve resistance to the pesticides. Almost as soon as a new pesticide is deployed, resistance appears in the targeted population. Aided by short generation times and large populations, the bugs, rats, weeds, fungi, and plant diseases are generally winning this co-evolutionary race. More than 500 species of insects and mites have become resistant to insecticides and miticides, and resistance to herbicides has been noted in more that 100 species of weeds. In addition, about 150 species of plant pathogens show resistance to the chemicals used to attack them. [*see graph on next page*, Lester Brown et al., Vital Signs 1994 at 93 (1994)].

Unquestionably, much too great a tonnage of pesticides is used for the results achieved. Only a very small proportion of the pesticides applied to fields ever actually reaches the target pest. For instance, of those delivered by aerial crop dusters, some 50 to 75 percent miss the target area and less than 0.1 percent may actually reach the pest. The remainder by definition is an environmental contaminant that can injure people and non-target species and in some cases can migrate to the far reaches of the globe.

DDT is probably the best known of the persistent pesticides in the latter category. Residues of DDT and its more toxic breakdown products have been found literally everywhere on the planet. Since DDT was banned in the United States and most industrialized nations in the early 1970s, populations of some severely affected wildlife species such as eagles and falcons have partially recovered. DDT concentrations in human tissues also have fallen significantly (but haven't disappeared) in most developed countries. Yet DDT is still manufactured and exported to many developing countries, where it continues to be widely applied. [China, India and Mexico are the leading producers and exporters of DDT.] Although it is less directly dangerous to human health than originally feared, DDT now is a suspect in a new category of hormone-mimicking compounds. And because its effects on wildlife, especially birds, can be serious, DDT remains a threat to non-target organisms in many countries.

The banning of DDT and some other persistent organochlorine compounds led to increased use of shorter-lived pesticides instead, especially organophosphates such as parathion. Many of these are acutely toxic and dangerous to farm workers and non-target organisms, including predators of the pests. In developing countries, pesticides often don't bear labels in the local language. Since many farmers and farm workers are illiterate and untrained in the proper handling of these materials, pesticide poisonings are a common occurrence, and abuse of the chemicals is widespread.

Yet in most cases, pests can be effectively controlled without heavy application of pesticides by using more biologically based methods. Known as integrated pest management (IPM), this approach involves various strategies such as encouraging natural enemies of pests, developing and planting pest-resistant strains of crops, fallowing, mixed cropping, destroying crop wastes where pests shelter, and so on. IPM is generally vastly superior to chemical-based pest-control methods from both economic and environmental perspectives; and it is gradually spreading despite a variety of socio-economic and political problems impeding its progress.

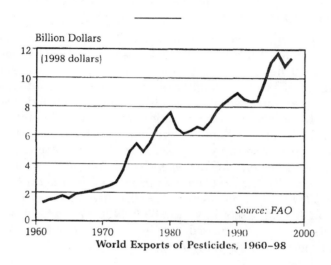

World Exports of Pesticides, 1960–98

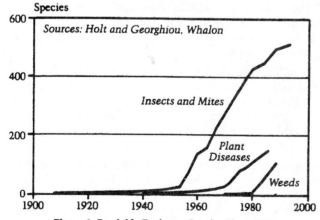

Figure 1: Pesticide-Resistant Species Since 1908

2.   CIRCLE OF POISON

As described above, many pesticides whose use is banned in the industrialized world are legally exported to developing countries. This process can lead to what has been labeled, "the circle of poison." The phrase refers to a pattern where hazardous pesticides are manufactured within a country where their use is either banned or severely restricted. As a result, the chemicals are exported for sale abroad. The foreign countries importing the pesticides use them on food crops that are then exported *back* into the country of manufacture and, in turn, end up on the dinner table and in school lunches. Hence the pesticides come "full circle," creating the circle of poison. Mark Dowie, *The Boomerang Crime*, MOTHER JONES, November, 1979. The U.S. law regulating pesticides, for example, permits exports of pesticides so long as "prior to export, the foreign purchaser has signed a statement acknowledging that the purchaser understands that such pesticide is not registered in the United States and cannot be sold in the United States. . . ." 7 U.S.C. 1360(a).

This trade is substantial. From 1992–1994, the United States shipped over 114,600 tons of banned pesticides. A study by the General Accounting Office in 1989 determined that the circle of poison warranted concern because of the EPA's poor monitoring of the content, quantity, and destination of exported, unregistered pesticides. The GAO concluded that the EPA "does not know whether export notices are being submitted, as required under FIFRA" and that "notices were not sent for three pesticides (out of four) that were voluntarily canceled [by the manufacturer] because of concern about toxic effects." *As quoted in* Jefferson D. Reynolds, *International Pesticide Trade: Is There Any Hope for the International Pesticide Trade: Is There Any Hope for the Effective Regulation of Controlled Substances?*, 13 J. LAND USE & ENVT'L L. 69 (1997). The excerpt below presents the results of a study carried out by an environmental NGO of U.S. pesticide exports in 1995 and 1996.

Banned and never registered pesticides

In 1995 and 1996, at least 21,026,794 pounds of pesticides which are forbidden to be used in the United States were exported from U.S. ports. This total, which includes banned as well as never-registered products, represents an average rate of more than 14 tons shipped per day.

Nearly 9.4 million pounds of "never-registered" pesticides were exported in the years 1995 and 1996—a 40% increase over the 4.6 tons per day noted in the three-year period from 1992 through 1994. These products, produced for export only, are not evaluated by EPA for health or environmental risk. Moreover, FAO has confirmed a general lack of testing of pesticide products in the developing world. * * *

Monocrotophos shipments in 1995 and 1996 totaled 1,008,911 pounds, a 600% increase over the total of 156,326 pounds for the previous three years. The majority (shipped under the trade name Azodrin) went to Mexico. This compound is highly toxic to humans; ingestion of 120 mg of monocrotophos can be fatal. By this standard, one ounce of the chemical would contain more than 250 lethal doses.

Monocrotophos is also highly toxic to birds. In 1996, reports emerged from Argentina of a massive kill of the migrating Swainson's hawk, the result of poisoning by monocrotophos. Losses were conservatively placed at 20,000 birds, about 5% of the world's Swainson's hawk population.

Severely restricted pesticides

Severely restricted pesticides are products "for which virtually all registered uses have been prohibited by final U.S. government regulatory action, but for which certain specific registered use or uses remain authorized." From 1995 through 1996, 11.7 million pounds of severely restricted pesticides left U.S. ports, an average rate of eight tons per day.

The pesticide carbofuran accounted for the great majority of the 1995 and 1996 totals. The U.S. EPA's Worker Protection Standard requires that workers applying the chemical be provided with the following protective equipment: long-sleeved-shirt and long pants; chemical-resistant gloves; shoes plus socks; protective eye wear and an approved respirator. Such equipment is rarely available in the developing world.

Carl Smith, *Exporting Risk: Pesticide Exports from U.S. Ports*, GLOBAL PESTICIDE CAMPAIGNER, Vol. 8, No. 2, June 1998. <http://www.igc.org/panna/resources/_pestis/PESTIS980622.3.html >

The circle of poison presents a paradox. Why do developed countries allow banned pesticides to be exported if they may return on vegetables and fruit, and why do importing countries knowingly import banned pesticides? The answer is two-fold. First, each country's cost-benefit analysis is unique. A developing country may determine its overall interests are served best by using relatively more dangerous chemicals because, it believes, the cost of environmental harms or increased injury among farm workers is outweighed by the benefit in reducing insect-borne disease or increasing crop production (though, as the Ehrlich excerpt noted, over the medium-term pesticide use may be less effective than integrated pest management in increasing crop yields). A developed country may rationally ban the same chemical if it has no malaria to control or other significant benefit to be gained from the chemical's use. If a developing country wishes to import a banned pesticide, it follows, it would be paternalistic for a developed country to forbid such transactions.

The second explanation for the export of banned chemicals is information or, more precisely, lack of information. The cost-benefit analysis described above is only possible if you assume countries have (1) accurate data available on which to base their policy decisions concerning harmful effects of the imported chemicals and (2) adequate institutional infrastructure to control imports, use and disposal of pesticides. If, however, importing countries are not adequately informed of the potential harms of the chemicals, then their cost-benefit analysis will be inaccurately skewed in favor of importation. The key issues, then, are provision of accurate information and institutional capacity to act on it.

---

3.   FAO INTERNATIONAL CODE OF CONDUCT ON THE DISTRIBUTION AND USE OF PESTICIDES

In 1985 the United Nations Food and Agricultural Organization (FAO) adopted the first International Code of Conduct on the Distribution and Use of Pesticides to reduce the hazards associated with the international use of pesticides. U.N. Doc. M/R8130, E/8.86/1/5000 (1986). The Code established voluntary standards to aid countries without existing pesticide regulation. It was designed to provide interim protection until national regulations on the use of pesticides were implemented. Though only voluntary, the Code provided the first global standard for the sale and use of pesticides.

In general language, voluntary responsibilities are allocated among government, industry, and the public. Article 3, for example, states "Governments have the overall responsibility and should take the specific powers to regulate the distribution and use of pesticides in their countries." Manufacturers and distributors of pesticides are called on to follow Code provisions regarding the manufacture, distribution, labeling and advertising of pesticides, especially in countries without legislation or regulation, and to take special care to ensure safe and effective use of the product worldwide. To assess compliance with the Code, the FAO issued a questionaire in 1988. The results were disturbing. Of the 115 responding countries (mostly developing countries), "half did not have legislation to control pesticides, and 84% were unable to control potentially hazardous pesticides according to international standards." James Colopy, *Poisoning the Developing World: The Exportation of Unregistered and Severely Restricted Pesticides from the United States,* 13 UCLA J. ENVTL. L. & PoL'y 167, 173 (1995).

One of the issues left unresolved by adoption of the Code in 1985 was the issue of "prior informed consent" (known as PIC). The principle of prior informed consent would allow importing countries the opportunity to refuse shipments of pesticides banned or severely restricted in exporting countries. Early drafts of the Code had provided for prior informed consent for each and every shipment, but pressure from industry and a number of producing countries resulted in its deletion. Developing countries ultimately consented to the 1985 Code, although not without voicing their disappointment regarding the lack of PIC procedures. In response to these concerns, the FAO in November 1987 adopted a resolution that prior informed consent should be incorporated into the Code within two years. In November 1989, the FAO amended the Code to adopt the principle of prior informed consent.

> Pesticides that are banned or severely restricted for reasons of health or the environment are subject to the Prior Informed Consent procedure. No pesticide in these categories should be exported to an importing country participating in the PIC procedure contrary to that country's decision made in accordance with the FAO operational procedures for PIC.

Article 9.7 on prior informed consent.

FAO's operational procedures for PIC and the guidelines accompanying the amendments to the Code provide an eight-step process in which the FAO plays a central organizational role. According to these steps, exporting nations are expected to participate in the PIC process and importing states are invited to participate. A designated national authority is then required to report pesticide bans, refused registration or severe restrictions for health and environmental reasons to the FAO. In response, the FAO issues a "PIC Decision Guidance Document" for every pesticide recommended by the FAO expert panel or for which notice has been received from national authorities. The PIC Decision Document includes information on the chemical and physical composition of the pesticide as well as its uses, possible source of exposure and information summarizing its toxicity and regulatory status in other countries. The document is then sent to participating countries, which have ninety days to decide whether to ban imports of the pesticide. The status quo is maintained if the importing country does not respond within 90 days. A database is then maintained from which countries can monitor the import status of chemicals in each country.

While an improvement upon the previous international void in pesticide regulation, the FAO Code of Conduct was criticized by developing countries who argued that the Code was too weak—non-binding and voluntary, with no enforcement mechanisms, and no provisions for technical assistance to developing countries for monitoring or enforcement. Its PIC procedure only applies to pesticides that have been banned or severely restricted in five or more countries, so many potentially toxic chemicals were not reviewed. Many developing countries reported that they neither had adequate resources to control pesticides nor the legislative mechanisms to meet the Code's requirements. It should be noted, though, that both industry and many signatories to the Code regarded it only as a first step, and the next development, the London Guidelines, explicitly sought to address these shortcomings.

B. INDUSTRIAL CHEMICALS

1. LONDON GUIDELINES

As concern mounted over pesticide exports during the 1970's and 1980's, similar unease over the growth of international trade in hazardous chemicals led in 1987 to the UNEP Governing Council's adoption of the London Guidelines for the Exchange of Information on Chemicals in International Trade. U.N. Doc. UNEP/GC, 14/17, Annex IV (1987). While not involving the identical State parties, development of the FAO Code and the Guidelines moved in tandem. Thus the London Guidelines should be viewed as complementary to the FAO Code, expanding the scope of coverage to include hazardous chemicals not covered in the Code. Put simply, the FAO Code focuses on pesticides; the London Guidelines on industrial chemicals.

The purpose of the Guidelines was to allow countries access to information on hazardous chemicals in order to facilitate informed choices regarding their importation, handling and use. The Guidelines apply to hazardous chemicals, including pesticides. The Guidelines specifically exempt from coverage pharmaceuticals, radioactive materials, small quantities for research and personal use, and food additives. The Guidelines are non-binding, merely establishing a minimum set of standards that countries should attempt to achieve. The London Guidelines call on States of export and import to work with UNEP and FAO in creating a formal mechanism of information exchange on chemicals involved in international trade. The Guideline's voluntary PIC procedure was added in 1989 to control the imports of chemicals that have been banned or severely restricted. A chemical that is banned or severely restricted in an exporting country because of its threat to human health or the environment should not be shipped to an importing country over that country's objection. Like the FAO Code of Conduct, the PIC procedure reinforces State sovereignty in that it provides relevant information for each country to determine its own analysis of the risks and benefits associated with chemicals it chooses to allow into the country. As of 2000, 155 countries had implemented the PIC procedure.

The International Register of Potentially Toxic Chemicals (now known as UNEP–Chemicals) administers the PIC procedure and was established by UNEP in 1976 in response to a recommendation of the Stockholm Conference. It was the first institution to collect and process information on hazardous chemicals and now operates a global network for the exchange of information on chemicals between countries, regions and international organizations. The network consists of 138 members from 129 countries located on five continents. Its purpose is to make it easier for countries to obtain existing information on the production, distribution, release, disposal and adverse effects of chemicals.

The PIC procedures under the Guidelines are essentially the same as under the FAO Code of Conduct described above. A country seeking to participate in the PIC procedure notifies UNEP and FAO of the import restrictions it wishes to place on a specific chemical. Once UNEP, through its UNEP–Chemicals group, identifies the chemical as one that meets the definition of "banned" or "severely restricted" under the FAO Code of Conduct and the amended London Guidelines, a "decision guidance document" is circulated to other participating countries, who may then notify UNEP–Chemicals and FAO of their decisions concerning the import of the chemical. The country's decisions are then compiled and disseminated to all participating governments. Importantly, the PIC procedure does not operate on a shipment-by-shipment basis.

UNEP–Chemicals also maintains chemical data profiles on nearly 10,000 chemicals selected based on their effects on human health and the environment. *See* <http://irptc.unep.ch/>. The data profiles contain information on a particular chemical's production and consumption, environmental and toxicological aspects as well as risk management information. In addition, a legal file contains information on chemical control and risk management measures from different countries and international organizations.

———

2.   THE ROTTERDAM CONVENTION

While the FAO Code and London Guidelines provide detailed requirements for prior informed consent procedures, they are, as noted above, entirely voluntary. Responding to calls for a binding legal instrument, in September, 1998, the Convention for the Application of Prior Informed Consent Procedure for Certain Hazardous Chemicals and Pesticides in International Trade, also known as the Rotterdam Convention, was adopted. The Rotterdam Convention builds on the earlier non-binding PIC procedures described above, providing more complete information to importing countries on the health and environmental risks associated with pesticide use. As of June 2001, 73 countries (including the United States) had signed the Convention and 15 had ratified. The Convention enters into force once 50 countries have ratified. The Convention website is at <http://www.pic.int/>.

Generally speaking, the Convention bans the export of any chemicals listed on Annex III, unless the importing country has given its prior consent. Chemicals are listed on Annex III when they have been "banned" or "severely restricted" in the exporting country. Whereas the FAO Code had limited banned chemicals to those that have been the subject of affirmative government action, the Convention uses a broader definition, including pesticides voluntarily withdrawn from the market. Banned chemicals include those that have been refused approval for first-time use or "withdrawn by industry either from the domestic market or from further consideration in the domestic approval process where there is clear evidence that such action has been taken in order to protect human health or the environment." Art. 2(b). Similarly, the definition of "severely restricted" has been expanded to include chemicals with clear evidence of a human health or environmental concern.

To add a banned or severely restricted chemical to Annex III, the Secretariat must receive at least one notification from two of the seven designated PIC regions. Upon receipt of a country's notification of banning or restriction, the Secretariat refers the pesticide to the Chemical Review Committee. The Chemical Review Committee then decides whether to propose that the Conference of Parties add the chemical to Annex III based on the following four criteria (in Annex II(c)).

- Whether the final regulatory action led, or would be expected to lead, to a significant decrease in the quantity of the chemical used or the number of its uses;
- Whether the final regulatory action led to an actual reduction of risk or would be expected to result in a significant reduction of risk for human health or the environment of the Party that submitted the notification;
- Whether the considerations that led to the final regulatory action being taken are applicable only in a limited geographical area or in other limited circumstances;
- Whether there is evidence of ongoing international trade in the chemical.

The Convention also allows developing countries to short-cut the Annex III listing process for "severely hazardous pesticide formulations." These are pesticides that produce severe environmental or health effects within a short period from time of exposure. Art. 6.

For severely hazardous pesticide formulations, developing countries must submit information regarding the chemical's active ingredients, descriptions of incidents relating to the chemical and the responses to these incidents. Annex IV, pt. 1. The Secretariat then looks into whether other countries have applicator or handling restrictions and whether any incidents have been reported in other countries. Annex IV, pt. 2. The Secretariat subsequently forwards this information to the Chemical Review Committee, which then decides whether to recommend that the Conference of the Parties include the chemical in Annex III. Annex III initially included the

22 pesticides and 5 chemicals listed in the voluntary PIC framework, but allows for additions.

The Chemical Review Committee's decisions regarding both banned/severely restricted chemicals and severely hazardous chemical formulations must be approved by a consensus of the Conference of Parties. Thus, essentially each country has the power to veto the inclusion of a particular chemical. This is a different listing standard than the FAO code, which required the regulatory action of five or more countries and an Expert Group recommendation.

Once a chemical is listed in Annex III, importing countries are notified and have nine months to review the listing and decide whether to import, exclude, or restrict future importation of the substance. Such decisions must respect the trade principles of most-favored nation (i.e. ban imports of the chemical from all States) and national treatment (a party choosing to exclude imports from another party may not produce the chemical or pesticide domestically). Art. 10.9. Once the importing party makes its decision and notifies the treaty secretariat (directed jointly by UNEP and FAO), exporting parties must then take measures to ensure that exporters within its jurisdiction do not ship listed substances to parties that have chosen to exclude them. Art. 11. Such measures might include encouraging the promotion of chemical safety in industry and creating national registers and databases to document chemical safety. Art. 15.

Importantly, if the importing country has not responded after the nine-month review period, the exporting country must assume the importing country does *not* consent unless the chemical is registered in that country or has been previously used in that country. Art. 11. Exporting countries are also responsible for complying with technical assistance requirements. Article 16 of the Convention requires that Parties "cooperate in promoting technical assistance for the development of the infrastructure and the capacity necessary to manage chemicals to enable implementation of this Convention." This provision has been criticized as too weak, because without adequate financial and technical assistance it is unlikely developing countries will have the resources to evaluate chemical risks, even with the PIC information.

The Convention also applies to unlisted chemicals for which there have been domestic regulatory actions. If a party bans or severely restricts an unlisted chemical, it must notify the Secretariat of these actions prior to the first export following the ban or restriction. Articles 5, 12(2). If the importing country does not acknowledge receipt of this notification, the exporting country is required to send repeat notices. Art. 12(4). While these notification provisions are mandatory, the Convention includes no compliance mechanisms to enforce this provision. This will be addressed at subsequent Conferences of the Parties.

QUESTIONS AND DISCUSSION

1. *Problem Exercise.* Assume Acme Industries in Country A produces a chemical called Dimethyl Terrible. There is a growing market overseas, particularly in Country B. Recent research has linked use of Dimethyl Terrible with a rare form of cancer. Country A decides to ban the use of Dimethyl Terrible within its borders. Both Country A and Country B adhere to the London Guidelines and the FAO Code of Conduct, and recently ratified the Rotterdam Convention. Explain in detail what is required of each country. If Country A is a developed country and Country B is a developing country would this alter their respective obligations?

May Acme continue to export Dimethyl Terrible if Country B does not reply to the notice of Country A's ban? Would it make a difference if Country A or B were not a party to the Rotterdam Convention? Do you think the chemical industry in Country B would encourage its government to adhere to the FAO Code of Conduct, the London Guidelines and the Rotterdam Convention? Would your answer depend on whether Country B were a developed or developing country?

2. *Problem Exercise* Who, if anyone, should be liable for harm caused as a result of the legal use of chemicals and pesticides? Consider the following three examples (See also Chapter 19, page 1462):

a) Plaintiff is a farm worker in Costa Rica employed by Fruit Company. He suffers medical injury, including sterility, as a result of exposure to DBP, a pesticide manufactured by Chemical Company and Oil Company. He sues the two companies in Texas, their U.S. state of incorporation. What are the jurisdictional, choice of law, and tort issues raised by the suit? *See* Dow Chemical Company v. Alfaro, 786 S.W.2d 674 (Tex.1990), *cert. denied*, 111 S.Ct. 671 (1991).

b) Same situation as above, but the suit is brought by Farmer. A citizen of Costa Rica, Farmer is a neighboring landowner whose crops were destroyed by Fruit Company's use of DBP.

c) A class of elementary school students in Michigan are all struck by a mysterious ailment which causes dizziness and nausea. Careful research shows that the medical problems were caused by apples the students ate at school that contained residues of DBP. DBP is banned in the United States because it poses a threat to human health. It is legally sold, however, in a number of countries which export apples to the United States. Only a U.S. company, Chemical Company, produces DBP. The school students bring a class action suit against Chemical Company in federal district court. What are the legal issues Chemical Company will raise as a defense to the suit? What are the policy issues for and against allowing damages against Chemical Company?

3. It is important to keep in mind that in addition to international controls on the transfrontier movement of chemicals many countries have domestic laws controlling the import and export of chemicals. In the United States, for example, the Toxic Substances Control Act (TSCA) contains provisions governing the export and import of chemicals. 15 U.S.C. 2601 *et seq*. If a chemical requires testing under the Act (i.e. if it may present an unreasonable risk of injury to health or the environment), exporters of the chemical "shall notify the Administrator [of the EPA] of such exportation or intent to export and the Administrator shall furnish to the government of such country notice of the availability of the data submitted to the Administrator ..." 15 U.S.C. 2611. Similarly, the government may ban the import of chemicals if it is determined that its manufacture, processing, distribution in commerce, use or disposal presents or may present an unreasonable risk of injury to health or the environment. 15 U.S.C. 2612. Does U.S ratification of the Rotterdam Convention alter TSCA requirements?

4. The FAO Code and London Guidelines preceded and served as early models for the international adoption of PIC procedures. In this regard, the process for developing the Rotterdam Convention serves as a good example of the development of international law—national laws leading to international codes of conduct, non-binding international guidelines, and finally to a binding international treaty. How closely was this model followed in the regulation of transfrontier movements of hazardous waste? What other legal responses to international environmental problems have followed this model?

5. Has the focus on development of PIC procedures put the cart before the horse? As should be clear from the readings, simply providing information to some developing countries may not be sufficient to ensure an informed response. Institutional capacity to assess the data is necessary, as well. Given the non-binding obligation of the Rotterdam Convention that developed countries *should* provide technical assistance, what else should the international community do to address this institutional capacity? Should companies bear some responsibility to help build institutional capacity in countries where they operate?

The Rotterdam Convention has no sanctioning mechanisms. Is that appropriate in this type of information-generating treaty? If not, what types of actions do you think should be sanctioned, and with what types of penalties?

6. Pesticide trade also raises significant issues of gender equity. Consider the report excerpted below by the NGO grassroots coalition, The U.S. Network for Global Economic Justice. <http://www.50years.org/factsheets/pesticide.html>

> Under policy guidance from the World Bank and IMF, and with support through agricultural projects and structural adjustment lending, developing countries are increasingly emphasizing the production of non-traditional agricultural export (NTAE) crops over staple foods. Extensive documentation indicates that the use of all pesticides (insecticides, herbicides, fungicides, nematocides) is much higher in most NTAE crops than in traditional crops.

> Women make up a large proportion of NTAE workers and due to labor patterns in the production and processing of these crops, they are disproportionately exposed to pesticides. A 1991–1995 survey of 2,500 farmers and agricultural workers (mostly women) from Indonesia, Malaysia, Korea, India, Sri Lanka, Pakistan, and the Philippines, by the Pesticide Action Network Asia & the Pacific Regional Center recorded women's frequent, direct exposure to pesticides during application and again when entering fields to hoe, weed, thin plants and harvest. In addition, women are exposed when mixing pesticides, washing spray tanks, washing pesticide-soaked clothes, and disposing of pesticide containers.

> Other gender specific inequities in education, literacy, and access to information and health care compound the risk to women, since most rural women farmers have limited ability to read or understand the written warning labels on pesticide containers, let alone the instructions for use and disposal of unused pesticides. Furthermore, as noted in Senegal, rural women are rarely—if ever—encouraged by their communities to identify and discuss the pesticide-related illnesses which they experience on a virtually on-going basis.

> Despite these facts, government-sponsored, often internationally-financed training programs which teach men about the hazards of pesticides rarely reach women (not only in Asia, but throughout Africa as well). Such programs mistakenly assume that only men need this information, or that men will pass their new knowledge on to the women who are applying pesticides, using the equipment or preparing and storing food in old pesticide containers.

7. Prior informed consent is one form of right-to-know laws. The excerpt below describes the broad classes of right-to-know legislation. Gary Rischitelli, *Developing a Global Right to Know*, 2 ILSA J. Int'l. & Comp. L. 99, 100–110 (1995).

> Right-to-know is a generic term that has been applied to a variety of laws and policies addressing the disclosure of chemical hazard information to populations

at risk. These laws differ in their approach to hazard communication and reflect the objectives and biases of the relevant political and legal authorities. The right-to-know schemes can be roughly divided into those which release information to local authorities and surrounding populations on an "as needed" basis versus those which mandate broad dissemination of information on an "as wanted" basis. The first type reflects a decision to delegate the protection of public health and safety to authorities, without specifically recognizing the value of community involvement or approval. The right-to-know yields to a more pragmatic need-to-know where the ultimate goal of public protection is predominant. This concept will be referred to as the public policy approach.

The other approach is to make information freely accessible, thereby allowing citizens or communities to access the information on demand. This approach appears to recognize more explicitly some underlying or pre-existing need-to-know without inquiring into the need or purpose for disclosure, while implicitly recognizing the individual's and community's right to autonomy and self-determination. The ultimate effect of this expanded access to information transcends emergency planning and may act to marshal public support for toxic use reduction, pollution prevention, and environmental remediation. Due to the implicit support of local involvement and public access to information, this approach will be described as the public opinion approach. Not surprisingly, the choice of approaches is dependent on the historical and political traditions of the continents where they were adopted. The United States with its long tradition of emphasis on individual rights has adopted a public opinion approach, while Europe, with a stronger socialist and majoritarian tradition, has adopted the public policy approach.

Which approach to right-to-know does the Rotterdam Convention adopt? A public opinion approach or a public policy approach? Could it adopt both? *See also* Agenda 21, para. 19.50.

A right-to-know instrument that is becoming widely adopted is known as a "pollutant release and transfer registry." The registry provides a record of industrial releases or transfers to air, water, and soil (including wastes transported to disposal or recycling sites). The registry in the United States is called the Toxic Release Inventory and has been remarkably effective in reducing industrial emissions. *See* 42 U.S.C. 11023. EPA has listed over 650 chemicals that facilities with ten or more employees (and generating in excess of certain threshold amounts) must report annually. In 1993, manufacturers reported releases of 2.8 billion pounds of listed chemicals. Almost half of the releases came from the chemical industry. Glenn Hess, *Toxic Releases*, CHEMICAL MARKETING REPORTER, June 26, 1995. Since the advent of TRI, chemical manufacturers have reduced their TRI emissions by 68%. For details of emissions, *see* <http://www.epa.gov/triexplorer/>.

The Toxic Release Inventory program is generally credited with substantial reductions in emissions for two reasons. First, companies are eager to avoid bad publicity from being seen as a "big polluter." The Inventory data is publicly available and has been used by NGOs and community groups. Second, the Inventory has provided data on waste generation for the very first time to many companies. Companies are now tracking progress in reducing waste, calling to mind two management truisms: "what gets measured gets done," and "waste is just profits down the drain." At least seven countries have passed right-to-know legislation, including Canada and Australia. Some NGOs have taken the data and placed it onto maps on the web, so people can see the local pollution sources around where they work and live. If you live in America, type your zip code into the "Scorecard" website maintained by the NGO, Environmental Defense, at <www.score-card.org/>. Were you surprised by what you found?

————

C. PERSISTENT ORGANIC POLLUTANTS

1. THE DIRTY DOZEN

In recent years, policy makers in different fora have begun to look seriously at a group of synthetic organic chemicals that persist in the environment, known as persistent organic pollutants (POPs). POPs include a wide range of chemicals—pesticides, pharmaceuticals, plastics, industrial chemicals, and the by-products of industrial processes. Most policy debate regarding POPs has been directed at twelve specific chemicals, known euphemistically as the "dirty dozen." These fall under the following categories:

pesticides		industrial chemicals	by-products
aldrin	DDT	PCBs	dioxins
dieldrin	endrin	hexachlorobenzene	furans
chlordane	mirex		PCBs
toxaphene	heptachlor		hexachlorobenzene
			toxaphene

PCBs, hexachlorobenzene, dioxins, furans and toxaphene are produced as by-products from the incineration of chlorine-containing products, including some plastics as well as natural chlorine-containing substances. Dioxins and furans include more than 200 compounds, a number of which are by-products of the manufacture, use and disposal of chlorine and chlorine-containing chemicals, such as the chlorine bleaching of wood pulp and manufacture of PVC plastics.

Although POPs as a general category includes a wide range of chemicals, all of the dirty dozen are in a category of POPs containing chlorine, known as organochlorines. Since World War II, the use of organochlorines has grown dramatically. Indeed, chlorinated compounds form the backbone for much of the industrial sector. Over 10,000 organochlorines are currently in commerce (the vast majority of which, such as chloroform, are not POPs). Chlorine compounds are used to make plastics, refine petroleum, bleach pulp and paper, and to treat wastewater; produce solvents, disinfectants, flame retardants, paints, refrigerants, and insulation; and for dry cleaning. The Chlorine Chemistry Council claims that chlorine underpins 40% of the U.S. economy—212 industries are direct users of chlorine and account for almost 45 million of the 115 million jobs in the U.S. economy, generating more than $1.6 trillion of the total U.S. national income of $4.5 trillion. <http://c3.org/chlorine_what_is_it/chlorine_story2.html>. On the other hand, some environmental organizations, most notably Greenpeace, have called for the eventual elimination of chlorine from the economy.

————

2.   IMPACTS AND POTENTIAL IMPACTS

By definition, all POPs are persistent in the natural environment—some lasting more than 100 years. POPs are fat-soluble, bio-accumulating in the fatty tissue of humans and animals. POPs found in prey are transferred to the fatty tissue of the predator, with the highest concentrations found in animals at the top of the food chain. All of us now have about 500 anthropogenic chemicals in our bodies that did not exist before 1920. Many of these are POPs, with PCBs and DDE—a highly persistent breakdown product of DDT. World Resources Institute, STATE OF THE WORLD 80 (2000). Most POPs are also typically semi-volatile, meaning they change relatively easily from a liquid or solid to a gas, and back again. As gases, POPs are transported long distances through the atmosphere. Given the world's prevailing air currents, POPs tend to concentrate close to the polar regions, where the cold air finally condenses them and they precipitate. For this reason, although most POPs are produced and consumed at lower latitudes, they are highly concentrated in the Arctic and Antarctic regions. Thus large northern carnivores, such as polar bears and beluga whales, have been found to have particularly high concentrations of POPs.

Similarly, although they live far from any industrial centers, the Inuit people in the Canadian Arctic carry higher concentrations of PCBs in their body than any other human population. Levels of PCBs in the breast milk of Inuit women are at least five times higher than women in urban Canada. Their milk also contains high levels of chlordane and toxaphene. It has been reported that some young mothers resort to feeding their babies non-dairy coffee creamer mixed with water to avoid passing on the POPs in their breast milk. Fred Pearce, *Northern Exposure,* NEW SCIENTIST, May 31, 1997, at 25; Linda Hogan, *Silencing Tribal Grandmothers—Traditions, Old Values at Heart of Makah's Clash over Whaling,* THE SEATTLE TIMES, December 15, 1996, at B9. The following figure on the next page, *reprinted from* Theo Colborn et al., OUR STOLEN FUTURE 27 (1996), graphically presents the mechanism of bio-accumulation of PCBs. Showing how PCBs can be magnified up to 25 million times.

The toxicity of some POPs is relatively well understood. The effects of DDT, for example, spurred the writing of Rachel Carson's enormously influential 1963 book, *Silent Spring.* Less well known but still reasonably well understood are the links between some of the POPs and cancers. But some impacts—particularly those relating to endocrine disruption—are at the cutting edge of scientific knowledge. In particular, under some circumstances certain POPs have been found to mimic hormones, thus potentially disrupting endocrine systems in both wildlife and humans. The endocrine system controls the production and release of hormones in our bodies. Hormones are the chemical signals that regulate critical aspects of our development and behavior, particularly crucial to the development of the fetus and the young child. In certain respects hormones are as important as genes in determining physical and psychological characteristics. About fifty POPs have thus far been shown to have the capacity to act as endocrine disruptors under certain circumstances.

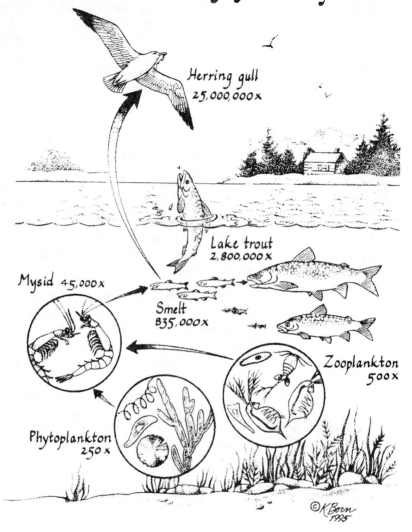

Lake Ontario Biomagnification of PCBs

Herring gull
25,000,000×

Lake trout
2,800,000×

Mysid 45,000×

Smelt
835,000×

Zooplankton
500×

Phytoplankton
250×

©K.Born
1995

Some studies suggest POPs can harm the reproductive and immune systems, and perhaps even change the behavior, of certain wildlife species, by disrupting their endocrine systems. In the Great Lakes, for example, certain species of fish as well as eagles, gulls and cormorants are all showing increased birth defects and other harm that some scientists have linked with the high level of PCBs, dioxins and other POPs in the ecosystem. The decline in beluga whales in the St. Lawrence seaway seems likely related to the high levels of POPs found in their bloodstream. One beluga whale had levels of PCBs in its body ten times higher than the level necessary to qualify as a hazardous waste under Canadian law. Albatross living on remote Midway Island in the center of the North Pacific also carry heavy loads of DDT, PCBs and dioxin-like compounds, and display symptoms consistent with POPs exposure, including egg shell thinning, deformed embryos and a drop in nest productivity. These birds are believed to be contaminated by DDT coming from the coast of southeast Asia, where it is still widely used for mosquito control and crop pests. Alligators exposed to a pesticide (dicofol) in Florida's Lake Apopka—a 12,500 km freshwater lake—have suffered severe damage to both male and female reproductive organs. In many cases the linkage to specific POPs is still debated. For cites supporting these findings, *see* the suggested reading at page 908.

One of the greatest concerns surrounding POPs is that of synergies. Evidence suggests that the combined or "synergistic" effects of one or more chemicals on the endocrine system can be far greater than the sum of the individual effects. If so, then chemical testing of individual pesticides could underestimate their ability to affect the endocrine system. One study found "that four pesticides—endosulfan, dieldrin, toxaphene, and chlordane—are unlikely alone to produce adverse human health effects that disrupt the hormone system." A mixture of endosulfan and dieldrin, however, was "160 times to 1,600 times more potent as an endocrine disruptor than the individual chemicals." When the scientists combined three pesticides—dieldrin, endosulfan, and toxaphene—they were "200 times more potent than when tested individually." *See* J. MacLachlin, *Synergistic Activation of Estrogen Receptor with Combinations of Environmental Chemicals,* SCIENCE, June 17, 1996; D.O. Carpenter et al., *Human health and chemical mixtures: an overview,* 106 Envt'l Health Perspectives, Supplement 6:1263–1270 (1998).

A well-known example of endocrine disruption causing intergenerational effects on humans (and often studied in first year Torts classes) is the case of diethystilbestrol or DES. DES is a synthetic estrogen widely prescribed for pregnant women during the 1950s and 1960s as a means of preventing miscarriage. Although the women who took DES suffered no immediate ill effects from the drug, their children were not so lucky. The plight of "DES daughters" has been widely publicized. These women suffer from increased risk of vaginal and uterine cancer, reproductive organ abnormalities, and reduced fertility. Although less well-documented, the evidence suggests that "DES sons" also suffer from reproductive abnormalities and reduced fertility. *See* Our Stolen Future, *op. cit.*, at 57–61, 267–269; *see, e.g.,* Castrignano v. E.R. Squibb & Sons, Inc., 900 F.2d 455, 457–58 (1st Cir.1990) (upholding a jury verdict finding the manufacturer of DES liable for producing an unreasonably unsafe drug).

It would be inaccurate to state that there is a scientific consensus on the causal link between POPs and human endocrine disruption or increasing cancers outside the laboratory. A consensus is emerging, however, that the potential impacts of POPs, particularly given our ignorance concerning their synergistic effects, require action. For a regularly updated source of current research on POPs, check out the website for Our Stolen Future at <http://www.ourstolenfuture.org/>.

---

3. LEGAL CONTROLS

For the most part, our policy responses to chemical contamination have been designed first to address acute toxicity and then later to address carcinogenicity. In the case of pesticides, for example, the first pesticides that came into use early in this century were arsenic-based and acutely toxic. When new pesticides such as DDT were developed in the post-war "chemical revolution" they were hailed as safe because they did not have the acutely toxic effects of the earlier arsenic-based pesticides. Animals and humans could be exposed to large doses of DDT without dying immediately or becoming ill. In the 1960s, we came to realize that the harms of DDT were more insidious and took place over long periods of time. DDT has since been banned in almost all OECD countries, although it is still manufactured and used in many tropical countries, especially for malaria control.

In the 1960s, a new standard for reviewing and regulating chemicals emerged—one based on a chemical's carcinogenicity (cancer-causing qualities). It was generally assumed that setting levels based on cancer risk would protect humans as well as fish and wildlife from all other hazards as well. Over the past two decades, pesticide manufacturers and federal regulators searched mainly for cancer and other obvious hazards such as lethal toxicity and gross birth defects in screening chemicals for safety. Cancer has also dominated the scientific research programs that explore the effects of chemical contaminants in the environment on humans.

In light of emerging concerns over immune suppression and endocrine disruption, new paradigms may need to be developed. Unlike toxicity, the degree of harm caused by endocrine disruption does not appear directly linked to the dose in a linear fashion. The timing of the exposure may be more significant than the amount. Because the functioning of the hormone system is crucial to the development of the fetus and small child, doses that would be relatively harmless if given to an adult can have profound effects if delivered during pregnancy or to an infant. Moreover, some of the effects on reproduction initially take place in the womb or during early development but do not manifest themselves until the victim is trying to have children of her own.

Below is a short list of actions that international bodies have taken to regulate POPs in recent years.

U.N. Economic Commission for Europe. In February, 1996, signatories to the Long Range Transport of Air Pollutants Treaty (LRTAP) opened negotiations on a protocol for POPs and heavy metals. *See* page 513, discussing the LRTAP Convention.

North Sea Convention. In June 1995, eight European Nations (not including the United Kingdom) agreed to eliminate waste discharges and emissions in the North Sea and its tributaries by 2020 and to phase out discharges of synthetic substances that are persistent, toxic and liable to bioaccumulate.

Mediterranean Sea. The Protocol for Protection of the Mediterranean Sea from Land-based Pollution provides for gradual elimination of discharges into the sea and its tributaries of twelve POPs. It was signed March 7, 1996, by 30 countries.

International Joint Commission. The IJC typically address US–Canada border issues, but called for a global ban on five organochlorine pesticides and industrial chemicals, global capture and destruction of PCBs and a phase out of chlorine and chlorine compounds as industrial feed stocks in 1992.

Commission on Environmental Cooperation. The Commission, created by the NAFTA side agreement, passed a resolution calling for the sound management of chemicals. Specifically aimed at POPs, the resolution calls for the development of regional action plans for the management of mercury, chlordane, PCBs, and DDT—the four POPs chemicals of greatest regional concern.

––––––––

4. UNEP ACTIVITIES

In May 1995, the UNEP Governing Council adopted decision 18/32, targeting the "dirty dozen" priority POPs and setting in motion a process for evaluating the threat of these substances. The Decision called for an experts group to consolidate existing information of POPs impacts on human, plant, and animal health, analyze the relevant transport pathways on a global scale, examine the sources, benefits, risks and other considerations relevant to production and use as well as the costs and benefits of substitutes, and assess realistic response strategies, policies and mechanisms. UNEP Governing Council Resolution 18/32, UNEP/GC.18/40, at 90–91 (May 25, 1995).

The experts convened by UNEP agreed that sufficient evidence existed on the chemistry and toxicology of the dirty dozen as well as the relevant exposure pathways, transport, and deposition of the substances globally, to warrant international action. Their report effectively changed the debate from *whether* there should be international efforts to control these substances to *how* to control these substances. These recommendations were accepted by the UNEP Governing Council and the World Health Organization. Together, UNEP and WHO convened an international negotiating committee with a mandate to prepare by the year 2000 an international legally binding instrument for controlling the twelve priority POPs.

The challenges of the negotiation were clear. The instrument needed to be global in nature, with broad participation and implementation. With many of the pesticides on the dirty dozen list already banned in the United States and other industrialized countries, the total ban of at least some of the dirty dozen was likely. Yet some of the pesticides, such as DDT were still viewed as critical in developing countries for the control of insect-borne diseases such as malaria. With the impacts of POPs contamination primarily evident in the northern countries, the South was understandably reluctant to give up such important chemicals without some confidence that cost-effective alternatives would be available.

––––––––

5. STOCKHOLM CONVENTION ON CERTAIN PERSISTENT ORGANIC POLLUTANTS

In December, 2000, 122 States convened to finalize a new treaty aimed at reducing and eliminating POPs. The treaty opened for signature in May

2001. The treaty reflects a precautionary approach to POPs, expressing its objective as: "Mindful of the precautionary approach as set forth in Principle 15 of the Rio Declaration on Environment and Development, the objective of this Convention is to protect human health and the environment from persistent organic pollutants." Stockholm Convention on Persistent Organic Pollutants, Article 1 (2001).

While disputes between North and South were significant, the treaty language represents just as great a compromise *among* developed countries, themselves. The European Union and Norway, for example, were committed to eliminating POPs; the United States was opposed to such a broad ban; countries such as Canada and Russia supported elimination only if it were both financially and technically feasible. The treatment of dioxins and furans was also the subject of much debate. Some countries believed the goal of elimination was impossible because everyday activities, such as burning wood, driving automobiles, and incinerating waste also release dioxins. The futility of such a commitment prompted some countries to push for elimination "where feasible," but many countries found this language too weak.

In the end, the treaty addresses POPs in three categories: pesticides, industrial chemicals (intentional by-products), and unintended by-products (or wastes). The treaty calls for an immediate ban on eight of the dirty dozen chemicals—aldrin, chlordane, dieldrin, endrin, heptachlor, mirex, hexachlorobenzane, and toxaphene. It bans the production and use of intentionally produced POPs and unintentionally produced POPs, where feasible. Negotiators compromised over the treatment of DDT and agreed to severely restrict its use while maintaining a health-based exemption for countries using the chemical to combat malaria. The treaty permits the use of PCBs in power-generating equipment with some restrictions, but requires governments to find PCB-free alternatives by the year 2025. Parties to the treaty are expected to take steps to reduce the use of, and ultimately eliminate, dioxins and furans. The Convention also calls for the use of environmentally sound management techniques in the disposal and management of POPs through the use of best available POPs replacement techniques and prevention mechanisms for the production of new POPs. As of September, 2001, 97 States had signed the Convention and 2 had ratified. Fifty must ratify for the Convention to enter into force. <http://irptc.unep.ch/pops/>.

Because most of the dirty dozen were already banned or heavily regulated in most countries, some of the most contentious discussions centered around how *additional* chemicals would be added to those already covered by the convention. Following the model of the Montreal Protocol's reliance on Conferences of the Parties to adjust restrictions in light of new scientific findings, the treaty creates a POPs Review Committee. This body will determine whether new chemicals should be added to the list and listed chemicals subject to heightened restrictions. The "POPs Criteria" from which the Review Committee will make its decision will also be useful to pesticide makers in screening promising new products. The listing process and criteria are presented in Article 8 and Annexes D, E, and F of the Convention.

Stockholm Convention on Persistent Organic Pollutants

Article 8

Listing of chemicals in Annexes A, B and C

1. A Party may submit a proposal to the Secretariat for listing a chemical in Annexes A, B and/or C. The proposal shall contain the information specified in Annex D. In developing a proposal, a Party may be assisted by other Parties and/or by the Secretariat.

2. The Secretariat shall verify whether the proposal contains the information specified in Annex D. If the Secretariat is satisfied that the proposal contains the information so specified, it shall forward the proposal to the Persistent Organic Pollutants Review Committee.

3. The Committee shall examine the proposal and apply the screening criteria specified in Annex D in a flexible and transparent way, taking all information provided into account in an integrative and balanced manner.

4. If the Committee decides that:

(a) It is satisfied that the screening criteria have been fulfilled, it shall, through the Secretariat, make the proposal and the evaluation of the Committee available to all Parties and observers and invite them to submit the information specified in Annex E; or

(b) It is not satisfied that the screening criteria have been fulfilled, it shall, through the Secretariat, inform all Parties and observers and make the proposal and the evaluation of the Committee available to all Parties and the proposal shall be set aside. * * *

6. Where the Committee has decided that the screening criteria have been fulfilled, or the Conference of the Parties has decided that the proposal should proceed, the Committee shall further review the proposal, taking into account any relevant additional information received, and shall prepare a draft risk profile in accordance with Annex E. It shall, through the Secretariat, make that draft available to all Parties and observers, collect technical comments from them and, taking those comments into account, complete the risk profile.

7. If, on the basis of the risk profile conducted in accordance with Annex E, the Committee decides:

(a) That the chemical is likely as a result of its long-range environmental transport to lead to significant adverse human health and/or environmental effects such that global action is warranted, the proposal shall proceed. Lack of full scientific certainty shall not prevent the proposal from proceeding. The Committee shall, through the Secretariat, invite information from all Parties and observers relating to the considerations specified in Annex F. It shall then prepare a risk management evaluation that includes an analysis of possible control measures for the chemical in accordance with that Annex; or

(b) That the proposal should not proceed, it shall, through the Secretariat, make the risk profile available to all Parties and observers and set the proposal aside.

8. For any proposal set aside pursuant to paragraph 7 (b), a Party may request the Conference of the Parties to consider instructing the Committee to invite additional information from the proposing Party and other Parties during a period not to exceed one year. After that period and on the basis of any information received, the Committee shall reconsider the proposal pursuant to paragraph 6 with a priority to be decided by the Conference of the Parties. If, following this procedure, the Committee again sets the proposal

aside, the Party may challenge the decision of the Committee and the Conference of the Parties shall consider the matter at its next session. The Conference of the Parties may decide, based on the risk profile prepared in accordance with Annex E and taking into account the evaluation of the Committee and any additional information provided by any Party or observer, that the proposal should proceed. If the Conference of the Parties decides that the proposal shall proceed, the Committee shall then prepare the risk management evaluation.

9.   The Committee shall, based on the risk profile referred to in paragraph 6 and the risk management evaluation referred to in paragraph 7 (a) or paragraph 8, recommend whether the chemical should be considered by the Conference of the Parties for listing in Annexes A, B and/or C. The Conference of the Parties, taking due account of the recommendations of the

Committee, including any scientific uncertainty, shall decide, in a precautionary manner, whether to list the chemical, and specify its related control measures, in Annexes A, B and/or C. * * *

Annex D of the Convention sets forth the information requirements and screening criteria. Parties that are submitting a proposal to list a chemical for regulation under the convention must provide evidence regarding its persistence, bio-accumulation, potential for long-range transport, and adverse impact on human health or the environment. Once the initial screening criteria are met, the Review Committee under the Convention will prepare a risk profile, to guide the parties in determining whether "the chemical is likely, as a result of its long-range environmental transport, to lead to significant adverse human health and/or environmental effects, such that global action is warranted." Annex E. The risk profile includes the following information:

(a) Sources, including as appropriate:

(i) Production data, including quantity and location;

(ii) Uses; and

(iii) Releases, such as discharges, losses and emissions;

(b) Hazard assessment for the endpoint or endpoints of concern, including a consideration of toxicological interactions involving multiple chemicals;

(c) Environmental fate, including data and information on the chemical and physical properties of a chemical as well as its persistence and how they are linked to its environmental transport, transfer within and between environmental compartments, degradation and transformation to other chemicals. A determination of the bio-concentration factor or bio-accumulation factor, based on measured values, shall be available, except when monitoring data are judged to meet this need;

(d) Monitoring data;

(e) Exposure in local areas and, in particular, as a result of long-range environmental transport, and including information regarding bio-availability;

(f) National and international risk evaluations, assessments or profiles and labelling information and hazard classifications, as available; and

(g) Status of the chemical under international conventions.

Some countries called for exports to be subject to the prior approval of importers. The United States, however, argued that such a provision was redundant because notification is already required under the recently ratified Rotterdam Convention (discussed *supra*). The countries decided to add language to the POPs treaty stating it is complementary to the Rotterdam Convention, rather then setting up identical regimes. *Global Treaty to Reduce, Eliminate Persistent Organic Pollutants Finalized*, BNA IED, Dec. 22, 2000.

QUESTIONS AND DISCUSSION

1. The POPs Convention operates at the edge of scientific discovery with respect to the impact of certain chemicals on human health and the environment. To what extent will the listing process and criteria allow the Convention to reflect developments in science? How many chemicals do you think the Convention will eventually cover? Does the listing process reflect a fair and effective process for evaluating potential targets of regulation? What is the substantive standard that will be used in evaluating a chemical for future listing?

2. The precautionary principle was the subject of considerable debate during the POPs negotiations. Because so much is unknown about the health and ecological effects of specific chemicals, the European Union and many environmentalists wanted the precautionary principle to have a predominant role in the shaping and design of the convention, particularly with respect to the listing of additional chemicals for future regulation. The United States and the chemical industry sought to limit use of the principle to the preamble. Ultimately, the precautionary principle was included in the preamble, the objective of the convention and Article 8 setting out the process and criteria for listing new chemicals. To what extent does the convention help to clarify the relationship of the precautionary principle to risk assessments?

3. At least for now, both environmentalists and the chemical industry seem pleased with the treaty. From industry's perspective, most OECD countries had already phased out most of the dirty dozen chemicals. The most notable exceptions to this are dioxins and furans, which are not produced as products but as by-products of burning plastics and other wastes with chlorine in them. Industry fought hard, and will continue to do so, to ensure the convention treats dioxins and furans differently. Because elimination of dioxins and furans appeared to the negotiators to be infeasible, the Convention promotes the best available management techniques for controlling and minimizing their emissions. See Annex C. Greenpeace and the World Wildlife Fund, by contrast, view the convention as simply the first step toward a future without organochlorines. *Officials Say POPs Treaty Precedent–Setting, See New Era in Chemical, Pesticide Controls*, BNA–IED, Dec. 12, 2000, at d5.

4. Even more passionate was the debate over DDT. Malaria affects millions of people around the world. Some developing countries and public health officials were adamant that DDT could not be eliminated until cost-effective and proven alternatives for malaria control were available. The resulting compromise, embodied in Part II of Annex B reproduced below, exempted DDT use in some countries from the ban on production and use of DDT.

1.   The production and use of DDT shall be eliminated except for Parties that have notified the Secretariat of their intention to produce and/or use it. A DDT Register is hereby established and shall be available to the public. The Secretariat shall maintain the DDT Register.

2. Each Party that produces and/or uses DDT shall restrict such production and/or use for disease vector control in accordance with the World Health Organization recommendations and guidelines on the use of DDT and when locally safe, effective and affordable alternatives are not available to the Party in question.

3. In the event that a Party not listed in the DDT Register determines that it requires DDT for disease vector control, it shall notify the Secretariat as soon as possible in order to have its name added forthwith to the DDT Register. It shall at the same time notify the World Health Organization.

4. Every three years, each Party that uses DDT shall provide to the Secretariat and the World Health Organization information on the amount used, the conditions of such use and its relevance to that Party's disease management strategy, in a format to be decided by the Conference of the Parties in consultation with the World Health Organization.

5. With the goal of reducing and ultimately eliminating the use of DDT, the Conference of the Parties shall encourage:

(a) Each Party using DDT to develop and implement an action plan as part of the implementation plan specified in Article 7. That action plan shall include:

(i) Development of regulatory and other mechanisms to ensure that DDT use is restricted to disease vector control;

(ii) Implementation of suitable alternative products, methods and strategies, including resistance management strategies to ensure the continuing effectiveness of these alternatives;

(iii) Measures to strengthen health care and to reduce the incidence of the disease.

(b) The Parties, within their capabilities, to promote research and development of safe alternative chemical and non-chemical products, methods and strategies for Parties using DDT, relevant to the conditions of those countries and with the goal of decreasing the human and economic burden of disease. Factors to be promoted when considering alternatives or combinations of alternatives shall include the human health risks and environmental implications of such alternatives. Viable alternatives to DDT shall pose less risk to human health and the environment, be suitable for disease control based on conditions in the Parties in question and be supported with monitoring data.

6. Commencing at its first meeting, and at least every three years thereafter, the Conference of the Parties shall, in consultation with the World Health Organization, evaluate the continued need for DDT for disease vector control on the basis of available scientific, technical, environmental and economic information, including:

(a) The production and use of DDT and the conditions set out in paragraph 2;

(b) The availability, suitability and implementation of the alternatives to DDT; and

(c) Progress in strengthening the capacity of countries to transfer safely to reliance on such alternatives.

7. A Party may, at any time, withdraw its name from the DDT Registry upon written notification to the Secretariat. The withdrawal shall take effect on the date specified in the notification.

Does the treatment of DDT seem like a reasonable compromise? In evaluating the compromise, recall the statistics about growing resistance to DDT among insects.

Are there sufficient incentives both in this annex and throughout the rest of the convention to move countries away from dependence on DDT?

4. The relationship of international trade rules and the potential controls on the export and import of POPs was a contested issue for much of the negotiations. Two issues were at stake: (1) would the convention invoke trade measures to help enforce the environmental standards placed in the convention; and (2) would the POPs Convention include a "WTO supremacy clause" whereby the WTO and international trade rules would be granted superiority over the standards in the POPs convention if any conflict should subsequently occur. The Convention ultimately rejected the US bid to include a supremacy clause, stating instead that: "this Convention and other international agreements in the field of trade and the environment are mutually supportive?." *See* Claudia Saladin et al., The POPs Convention and International Trade Rules (Center for International Environmental Law, 1999).

5. The financing mechanism of the Convention was the subject of debate throughout the negotiations. Developing countries had sought an independent source of funds to ensure adequate compliance. Developed countries, such as the EU, pushed for funding from the Global Environment Facility (GEF). The GEF is the temporary funding mechanism for the treaty, but negotiators expect the Conference of the Parties to reach a more permanent solution. The treaty also calls for countries to provide financial support for treaty implementation, another possible source of funding for developing countries.

The Convention also continued a trend seen in the Kyoto Protocol and the Cartagena Protocol of explicitly tying developing country substantive obligations (i.e. to eliminate POPs) with the developed countries obligations to provide funding:

> The extent to which the developing country Parties will effectively implement their commitments under this Convention will depend on the effective implementation by developed country Parties of their commitments under this Convention relating to financial resources, technical assistance and technology transfer. The fact that sustainable economic and social development and eradication of poverty are the first and overriding priorities of the developing country Parties will be taken fully into account, giving due consideration to the need for the protection of human health and the environment.

POPs Convention, op cit., at Article 13.4.

Financial considerations even plagued the negotiations as the perpetually under-funded UNEP attempted creative ways of gaining financial support for the negotiations. UNEP, for example, created a "POPs Club" to support the costs of running the negotiations. The POPs Club initially asked governments, intergovernmental actors, and non-governmental organizations to provide financial and in-kind contributions to augment the UN budget for the negotiation, in order to provide greater support to the negotiators and to enhance participation from developing countries. Does this raise any concerns of conflicts of interest? Subsequently, in February 2001, the UNEP Governing Council sought additional contributions to the POPs Club to fund the Convention until it enters into force. To date, donations and pledges have totaled $5.15 million. Some of the primary donors include the United States, the European Commission, Sweden, Belgium, and Canada.

6. The POPs Convention followed shortly after the Cartagena Protocol on BioSafety, discussed *infra* in Chapter 13. These two agreements reflected many of the same tensions regarding such issues as the precautionary principle, liability and the relationship with international trade policy. The Conventions also took similar and new approaches to these and related issues. Read over both conventions. How did they resolve these issues? Do you think the similarities reflect an emerging new consensus on these longstanding issues?

Section III.   International Regulation of Nuclear Activities

A.   History and Background

The world was at war when the first controlled nuclear fission took place in 1942 in a laboratory beneath the football stadium bleachers at the University of Chicago. The objective of the top secret research, known as the Manhattan Project, was the atom bomb. From this bellicose origin, nuclear technology has since been widely applied to peaceful uses such as generating electricity, powering ships and submarines, and medical treatment.

After World War II and the Iron Curtain sealing off Eastern Europe, the United States and the USSR, who had been allies during the war, became competitors in a race to establish military superiority through nuclear weapons. During the Cold War era, from the late 1940s to the early 1990s, both countries stockpiled nuclear weapons to reduce the risk of another world war through a strategy known as Mutually Assured Destruction (MAD). Over 2,000 nuclear test explosions have taken place in the atmosphere, underwater and underground. As a result of the dissolution of the USSR in the early 1990s, the fall of communist governments throughout Eastern Europe, and the 1996 Test Ban Treaty, the threats of nuclear war and nuclear testing have receded. The nuclear weapons, however, remain as do serious environmental and health concerns from their decommissioning and the transportation of nuclear weapon grade radioactive materials.

Nuclear accidents at Three Mile Island in the United States and Chernobyl in the Ukraine have shown that non-military uses of nuclear energy also pose serious environmental and human health threats. In the case of Chernobyl, the transboundary effects of the fallout were severe, as well. Following the nuclear reactor's meltdown, a number of Northern European countries in the radiation's downwind path placed restrictions on the consumption of water, milk, meats and vegetables. In Swedish Lapland, entire herds of reindeer were slaughtered because they were unfit for human consumption due to the radiation contamination of lichen, the reindeers' primary food source. Norwegian and Swedish officials ordered the slaughter of more than one-third of all reindeer in Scandinavia over the five years following the accident. In Austria, traces of radiation were found in both cow and human breast milk following the nuclear accident. *The Arctic Waste Bin*, The Independent (London), July 13, 1997, at 40; *In the Dead Zone: Aftermath of the Apocalypse*, The Nation, April 29, 1996, at 16; *Raising reindeer with Geiger counters*, United Press International, April 17, 1996.

Nuclear weapons production and proliferation, the transport and disposal of nuclear materials, and nuclear reactor operation all pose different management challenges and potential environmental threats. Separate international efforts have mobilized to develop legal safeguards that ensure prudent nuclear management practices. This section surveys the many international agreements regulating the use, transport, and disposal of radioactive materials as well as procedures to notify and assist in the event of a future nuclear accident.

B. NUCLEAR ENERGY

Nuclear power stations, using the heat produced by nuclear fission to boil water and drive steam turbines, provide approximately 23.8% of the world's electric power. The 1999 Brown Book, an annual report on nuclear energy, suggests that this number will drop to 21.6% by 2010. As of 1999, 345 reactors were generating this power in 27 countries. There were eleven reactors under construction in the Czech Republic, France, Japan, and Korea. *Nuclear Power: Sector To Grow Through 2010, But Market Share to Fall, Report Says*, BNA ENV. REP., May 26, 1999.

The most important international organization concerned with nuclear energy is the International Atomic Energy Agency (IAEA). 276 U.N.T.S. 3. The IAEA is a specialized and independent agency within the United Nations that serves as the world's inter-governmental forum for scientific and technical cooperation in the nuclear energy field. The IAEA was created in 1957 as a result of President Dwight D. Eisenhower's historic "Atoms for Peace" speech before the United Nations General Assembly, where he proposed the creation of an international agency to promote the peaceful development and use of nuclear power. The IAEA develops policies for the peaceful development and use of nuclear energy in order to promote international cooperation, international security, economic and social development, and environmental protection. The agency has issued voluntary guidelines, standards and codes of practice for virtually all aspects of operational safety as well as providing extensive safety-related advisory, training, and assessment programs to improve the operation of nuclear power stations. As of June, 2001, 132 countries were Member States of the IAEA. Detailed descriptions of its activities may be found at its homepage, <http://www.iaea.org/worldatom/>.

1. NUCLEAR ACCIDENTS: SAFETY AND RESPONSE

While there had been widespread concern over the threats posed by nuclear energy since at least the 1970s, the 1986 accident at Chernobyl in the Ukraine focused unprecedented international attention on the adequacy of international legal safeguards that might prevent an accident or, once an accident occurred, ensure rapid communication and effective response. The Chernobyl installation is north of the city of Kiev. If the winds had blown south on the day of the accident, the damage would have been far worse. In the excerpt below, Philippe Sands describes the immediate consequences of the Chernobyl accident.

PHILIPPE SANDS, CHERNOBYL: LAW AND COMMUNICATION 1–2 (1988)

On 27 April 1986 Sweden, and then Denmark, Finland and Poland, detected significant increases in radioactivity levels. Immediate steps were taken to discover the source. Within a few hours it became clear that this was somewhere in the USSR. Faced with a pointing finger the Soviet government at first denied that any leak had occurred and then maintained a steadfast silence. As significantly increased levels of radioactivity were detected all over Europe and beyond, the gravity of the situation became apparent.

It was only during the evening of 28 April 1986, some 72 hours after the accident had occurred, that the Soviet Representative to the International Atomic Energy Agency (IAEA) informed the Director General of the IAEA, Dr. Hans Blix, that an accident had occurred at 1:23 a.m. on 26 April 1986 during the testing of a turbo-generator in the fourth unit of the Chernobyl Nuclear Power Plant. The scale of the disaster became clearer when the world learnt that in the 36 hours after the accident more than 100,000 people had been evacuated from a radius of some 20 miles around the reactor.

The full effects of the accident on people, property and the environment are still difficult to assess. In the USSR 31 people died as a direct result within a few weeks and a further three during 1987 as a result of on-site exposure. The United Kingdom National Radiation Protection Board has estimated that in the EEC [European Economic Community] countries 1,000 people will die and 3,000 will contract non-fatal cancers because of the accident.* * *

It came as a considerable shock to the world that an accident in a nuclear power plant could have significant effects thousands of miles away. The accident exposed, in the most serious manner possible, the way in which traditional notions of sovereignty and national frontiers have been transformed by the modern technological and industrial world. Modern technology permitted such an accident to occur. But it also penetrated the sovereignty of the USSR, via satellite, to identify the source of the accident. Faced with the irrefutable evidence picked up by satellites, the USSR was forced to provide its own information to the world.

The Chernobyl Report acknowledges that the accident gave rise to significant international consequences, recognizing the international character of the dangers of the development of the world's nuclear power resources, including the risk of transfers of radioactivity across borders, especially in large scale radiation accidents. These international effects have raised a number of international legal issues of considerable complexity relating to the prevention of nuclear accidents, the provision of information should they occur, assistance in connection with them and liability. Does international law impose upon States any obligation:

(1) to prevent the transboundary release of radioactive material;

(2) to repair any damage resulting from such a release;

(3) to inform other States of an actual or potential transborder release of radioactive material;

(4) to provide assistance to States affected by such a release?

As one consequence of the Chernobyl accident these four issues are now recognized by international society, both public and private, as the core of any arrangement for the establishment of an international safety regime.* * *

There is no single multilateral treaty which establishes comprehensive rules covering all these issues. To ascertain what the present law is one must have general recourse to the traditional sources of international legal obligation set out in Article 38 of the Statute of the International Court of Justice, i.e., multilateral and bilateral treaties, custom, general principles of law recognized by civilian nations, judicial decisions and the teachings of publicists.

[A]ll these sources are defective. The rules existing at the time of the accident were neither comprehensive nor well developed, a demonstration of the difficulties of applying traditional rules of international law to a problem related to the use of new technologies. It is for this reason that States and the IAEA acted with such speed to identify and address the problems.

———

As of April 1999, there were 84 parties, including the United States, and 70 signatories to the Convention. The Convention does not cover nuclear accidents from military operations or sites, though the five traditional nuclear-weapon States (China, France, Russia, the United Kingdom, and United States) have all stated their intent to report accidents involving nuclear weapons or nuclear weapons tests. *See* Elena Molodstova, *Nuclear Energy and Environmental Protection: Responses of International Law,* 12 PACE ENVTL. L. REV. 185 (1994).

The *Convention on Assistance in the Case of Nuclear Accident or Radiological Emergency* creates an international framework for the cooperation of States to facilitate prompt assistance and support in the event of nuclear accidents or radiological emergencies. IAEA INFCIRC 336, *reprinted in* 25 I.L.M. 1377 (1986). The Convention requires State parties to notify the IAEA of the availability of any experts, equipment, and other materials for providing assistance. In the event of an accident, the IAEA serves as the focal point for information among national parties to ensure a coordinated response. The Convention provides legal immunity for claims against parties providing assistance. As of April 1999, there were 74 State parties, including the United States, and 68 signatories to the Convention.

The Convention on Nuclear Safety was adopted in Vienna in June 1994. IAEA INFCIRC 449, *reprinted in* 33 I.L.M. 1514 (1994). Its purpose is to provide incentives for the national adoption of basic standards for the safe operation of land-based nuclear power plants. Parties are encouraged to promulgate appropriate national standards to ensure safe operation, siting, design, and construction of nuclear plants. The Convention also calls on parties to establish a regulatory agency to verify safety, quality assurance, and emergency preparedness. If existing reactors cannot be operated safely, they should be shut down on a timetable taking into account the social, economic and environmental impacts.

The Convention is an incentive instrument. Hence it is based not on sanctions but, rather, on the Parties' common interest to achieve higher levels of safety through information exchange and regular meetings of the Parties. Entirely driven at the national level, the treaty contains no provisions for enforcement or dispute resolution. The Convention requires parties to submit reports describing the implementation of each Party's obligations for "peer review" at IAEA Meetings of the Parties. As of January 2000, there were 53 Parties and 65 signatories to the Convention.

The *Joint Convention on the Safety of Spent Fuel Management and on the Safety of Radioactive Waste Management* was adopted September 5, 1997 but is not yet legally in force. The Convention addresses the management and disposal of spent fuel and radioactive waste from civilian and military nuclear reactors and applications. It will enter into force once 25 states enter their ratification with the IAEA. In October 1999, there were 40 signatories and 13 parties.

————

2. SHIPMENT AND DISPOSAL OF RADIOACTIVE WASTE

A unique problem created by nuclear activities is the disposal of radioactive wastes that may remain dangerous for thousands of years. In most situations, States dispose of the waste within their own borders. Several international conventions address the issue of international shipment and disposal of radioactive waste. The most important treaty regarding ocean disposal is the *London Convention on the Prevention of Pollution by Dumping of Wastes and Other Matter* (London Convention, 1972). The London Convention currently prohibits the disposal of both low-level and high-level radioactive wastes and other radioactive matter. The moratorium on dumping of low-level radioactive materials will be reviewed 25 years after its commencement in light of the current scientific knowledge. This Convention is discussed in detail in Chapter 10 (p. 731), where this issue is presented as a Problem Exercise.

Even though dumping of radioactive waste into the sea has been banned, Russia has admitted dumping large amounts of high-level radioactive wastes, including entire nuclear reactors, into the sea regularly since the 1950's. *Nuclear Material Dumped Off Japan*, N.Y.TIMES, Oct. 19, 1993, at A1. In the United States, radioactive fuel rods are currently stored temporarily in deep water pools or concrete casks to await construction of a final disposal site, expected to be completed in 2010. The United States, Japan, Great Britain and France accept and reprocess foreign spent nuclear fuel and stockpile the uranium for use in their nuclear reactors. Clearly, the international shipment of nuclear wastes for disposal or processing raises serious concerns in the case of accident and requires cooperation among countries to minimize risks.

Potential radiation leaks from aging Russian nuclear technologies has become another area of concern. Russia's dilapidated nuclear submarines and as many as 21,000 spent fuel elements, equal to about 90 reactor cores, are stored in the Andreeva Bay and are corroding. In 1998, Russia and Norway signed the Agreement on Environmental Cooperation with the Dismantling of Russian Nuclear–Powered Submarines Withdrawn from the Navy's Service in the Northern Region, and the Enhancement of Nuclear and Radiation Safety. This is known as the 1998 Agreement on Environmental Cooperation, under which Norway agreed to provide Russia with at least $60 million to assist in the cleanup of its military nuclear facilities. The Bay is about 45 kilometers from the Norwegian border. The agreement also covers safety issues at the Kola nuclear power plant, where relatively old reactors are still operating. *See* Thomas Nilsen, *Nuclear Waste Cleanup to Start in Russian Arctic*, June 6, 1998, at http://www.bellona.no; *See also* (*See* Lakshman D. Guruswamy and Jason B. Aamodt, *Nuclear Arms*

Control: The Environmental Dimension, 10 COLO. J. INT'L ENVTL. L. & POL'Y 267, 301 (1999)).

In 1995, the United States, Japan, the Republic of Korea and the governments of the European Union created a consortium called the Korean Energy Peninsula Development Organization (KEDO), through which North Korea would be provided with nuclear power technology and assistance if North Korea promised to freeze its production of its weapons-grade plutonium. The estimated cost of this project is $4 billion. *U.S., North Korea To Ease Trade Barriers As Part Of Nuclear Agreement*, BNA–IAD, October 26, 1994, at 1. Two of the stations are being built on the east coast of North Korea near the city of Kumho, with funding for construction and commissioning provided by KEDO. Concerns have arisen, however, that North Korea is not complying with the agreement, with allegations that the country's weapons program has grown in the past five years. In May 2000, the House of Representatives passed new legislation in response to this fear, prohibiting the transfer of any United States nuclear technology or equipment to North Korea without the approval of both the House and the Senate. Jim Abrams, *House Wants Say on N. Korea Nukes*, AP Online, May 15, 2000.

In September 1990, the General Conference of the IAEA adopted the *Code of Practice on the International Transboundary Movement of Radioactive Waste*. General Conference Resolution of 21 September 1990 on Code of Practice on the International Transboundary Movement of Radioactive Waste, 30 I.L.M. 557 (1991). This fills a gap that had been created by the exemption of radioactive waste shipments from coverage under the Basel Convention. The Code of Protection, which is advisory, provides guidelines for States concerning the international transboundary shipment of radioactive waste, providing that "[e]very State should take the appropriate steps necessary to ensure that radioactive waste within its territory, or under its jurisdiction or control is safely managed and disposed of, to ensure the protection of human health and the environment." Sec III. The Code also recognizes every State's sovereign right to prohibit the movement of radioactive waste into, from, or through its territory. *See* problem exercise in Chapter 10, p. 671.

---

3. LIABILITY

The international provisions establishing liability for nuclear damage are found in four agreements: the *Vienna Convention on Civil Liability for Nuclear Damage of 1963, the Paris Convention on Third Party Liability in the Field of Nuclear Energy of 1960* (supplemented by the *1963 Brussels Convention*), and the *Joint Protocol of 1988*. 1063 U.N.T.S. 265 (1963); 956 U.N.T.S. 264 (1960); 2 I.L.M. 685; 42 NUCLEAR LAW BULL. 56 (Sept. 21, 1988). These Conventions are based on the principles of strict liability for the operators of nuclear facilities. Liability is limited in both amount and time. The Paris Convention was the first international agreement to provide a liability regime for the peaceful uses of nuclear energy. A regional agreement, it provides a uniform civil liability regime for nuclear harms in Western Europe.

Philippe Sands, *op. cit.*, 51–52, 96

The purpose of the Paris Convention is to harmonize national legislation with regard to third party liability and insurance against atomic risks and to establish a regime for liability and compensation in the event of a "nuclear incident" as defined in Article (1)(a). The Convention generally applies only to nuclear incidents occurring, and damage suffered, in the territory of Contracting States (Article 2).

By Article 3 the operator of a nuclear installation is liable for personal injury or damage to property as a result of a nuclear incident. That operator may be a private entity or the State itself. This applies not only to incidents occurring in the operator's installation but also to incidents involving nuclear substances in the course of carriage to or from that installation. The operator's liability may be established simply by proving the causal connection between the loss and the nuclear incident; proof of fault on the part of the operator is not required (Article 3). Certain limited exceptions to liability are provided for in Articles 4 and 9. Liability for general environmental harm, and the regulation of inter-State actions, lie outside the Convention.

Unless a longer period is provided by national legislation, claims must be brought within 10 years from the date of the nuclear incident (Article 8). The general rule is that jurisdiction over actions lies only with the Courts of the Contracting State in whose territory the nuclear incident occurred (Article 13(a)). If an action is brought against a State itself, it may not, except in respect of measures of execution, invoke any jurisdictional immunities (Article 13(e)). Judgments are enforceable in the territory of any of the Contracting States (Article 13(d)) and the Convention is to be applied without discrimination as to nationality, domicile or residence (Article 14). * * *

The Vienna Convention [1963] was negotiated under the auspices of the IAEA. Its provisions are generally to the same effect as those of the earlier Paris Convention, with the important difference that the Vienna Convention is potentially of worldwide geographical application. Its purpose is to establish minimum standards to provide protection under national law against damage resulting from certain peaceful uses of nuclear energy. Pursuant to Article II, the operator of a nuclear installation is liable for "nuclear damage" (as defined in Article I(1)(k)) upon proof that such damage was caused by a nuclear incident in the installation or, with certain limitations, in the course of carriage to or from the installation. The liability of the operator is absolute although, as is the case under the Paris Convention, provision is made for certain defences and exceptions to liability (Article IV). * * *

Following the Chernobyl accident, the IAEA and Nuclear Energy Agency proposed revising the liability provisions of both the Vienna Convention and the Paris Convention. In its place they established a more comprehensive liability regime in the Joint Protocol Relating to the Application of the Vienna Convention and the Paris Convention. 42 Nuclear Law Bull. 56 (NEA ed. 1988). Essentially the Joint Protocol combines the two Conventions and expands the liability. Parties to the Joint Protocol are treated as if they were Parties to both Conventions; however, a choice of law rule is provided if an incident requires one Convention to apply to the other's exclusion. As of March 2000, there were 32 Parties and 14 signatories to the Vienna Convention and 21 Parties and 22 signatories to the Joint Protocol.

> The Conventions apply in cases that involve, *inter alia,* transportation and disposal of radioactive wastes. Nuclear damage under the Conventions comprises loss of life, personal injury, and damage to property. It does not include economic loss and loss of future earning unless the courts of the competent states so provide. The Brussels Convention prescribes a compensation scheme for damages caused by an incident at a nuclear installation whose operator is liable under the Paris Convention: a portion is provided by the operator's insurance, another by the installation state, and the balance by contracting states, according to a special formula based upon the GNP and the nuclear power of the installation state. Victims can bring claims under the Conventions only in the courts of a state where the incident that caused nuclear damage occurred. However, under the general rules of private international law, any state that suffers damage because of a nuclear incident has jurisdiction over such claims, and plaintiffs can engage in forum shopping.

> The nuclear liability regime does not address nuclear accidents as comprehensively as the oil pollution regime does with oil spills. The liability prescribed is limited, and the liability ceilings are ridiculously low in light of a disaster such as Chernobyl. In addition, the Conventions do not provide mechanisms to update liability limits and to compensate for preventive measures and economic loss as does the 1984 Liability Convention on Ocean Pollution. Moreover, the ten year time frame within which the plaintiff can bring an action does not take into account that the effects of exposure to radiation may not appear for decades. Also there is no international fund to provide for immediate or residual relief after a nuclear disaster. In other words, the particular nature of nuclear accidents makes the nuclear liability regime appear disconnected from reality. Only lately have there been efforts to update the conventions and specify their liability limits. The revision process requires close cooperation between OECD and IAEA.

Elli Louka, *Bringing Polluters Before Transnational Courts: Why Industry Should Demand Strict and Unlimited Liability for the Transnational Movements of Hazardous and Radioactive Waste,* 22 DENV. J. INT'L L. & POL'Y 63, 78–81 (1993).

By channeling liability to the operator of a nuclear reactor, the Conventions avoided the administrative and insurance costs resulting from a wider web of liability extending to other actors such as suppliers and transporters. The Conventions also required operators of nuclear facilities to carry insurance, while the details of the amount, type, and provisions of the insurance are left to each national government's discretion. In September 1997, the *Protocol to Amend the 1963 Vienna Convention on Civil Liability for Nuclear Damage* and the *Convention on Supplementary Compensation for Nuclear Damage* were adopted. The Protocol limited an operator's liability to not less than 300 Special Drawing Rights (about $400 million). In addition, the Protocol extended the geographical scope of the Vienna Convention and provided for a longer period during which a claim could be brought for loss of life or personal injury. The Convention on Supplementary Compensation allowed for additional compensation to be provided by Parties' contributions, based on installed nuclear capacity and UN rate of assessment. Overall, these two agreements increase the amount of compensation possible for those harmed by a nuclear accident. <http://www.iaea.org/worldatom/Documents/Legal/liability.shtml>.

QUESTIONS AND DISCUSSION

1. In light of the international agreements just described, you may be surprised to learn that no claims for damages were ever filed by a country against the Soviet Union as a result of the Chernobyl accident. Why do you think no country tried to make use of international treaty law to gain compensation? Since the precedent of the *Trail Smelter* case would seem to support a claim, why do you think no country filed a case based on customary international law?

Certainly one reason no international claims were filed was that the USSR was not a party to either the Vienna Convention, the Paris Convention, or any other international convention providing third party liability for nuclear damage. Germany, the United Kingdom and Sweden paid out large amounts of compensation to claims from within their countries. These countries reserved their right to make a future claim against the USSR after the full extent of damage is determined, but with the dissolution of the Soviet Union and Ukraine's weak economic condition such claims seem unlikely.

Two civil claims were brought in the German courts by private citizens against the USSR. The first was brought by a German gardener who sought compensation for damages suffered as a result of the Chernobyl nuclear fallout. His claim was rejected because he did not name the proper defendant and, in any case, the Soviet Ambassador to the Federal Republic of Germany would have been entitled to diplomatic immunity. The second claim was brought against the USSR's Industrial Union for Atomic Energy and was forwarded by the German Embassy to the Union's Ministry of Energy and Electrification of the USSR in Moscow. Sands, *op. cit.* 22–28.

In 1979, Canada successfully brought a claim against the USSR seeking damages for harms caused by the disintegration of a Soviet nuclear-powered satellite over Canadian territory. Basing its claims on customary international law and treaty law, the 1972 Convention on International Liability for Damage Caused by Space Objects, Canada received $3 million in compensation from the USSR. The final agreement providing compensation did not, however, state a legal basis for the payment of compensation.

2. Chernobyl is often cited as an example of the *Polluted* Pays Principle, where the threat of transboundary pollution forces the potentially injured parties to pay the likely offending party. Following negotiations, the G–7 countries, the European Commission and Ukraine signed a memorandum of understanding in 1995 ensuring the closure of the Chernobyl facility as well as a package of loans to complete other nuclear and energy projects in the Ukraine to provide the lost energy from Chernobyl. The amounts being considered from foreign donors and lending institutions in 1995 included:

- $43 million in grants to the power sector for restructuring activities;
- $102 million in grants and $1.809 billion in loans for energy investments;
- $349 million in grants for nuclear safety and decommissioning;
- $4 million to aid in lessening the social impacts of these actions.

Lafayette, *op. cit.*, at 262–3.

With international funding, by 2005 the damaged reactor should be permanently encased in a new cement shell that will better contain the radiation. Chernobyl's fourth and final operating reactor was completely shut down on December 15, 2000. Although it supplied about 10% of Ukraine's electricity, the plant was considered too serious a safety concern to the international community. *See* William Drozdiak, *Funding Is Set for Chernobyl Shutdown*, THE WASHINGTON POST, July 6, 2000, p. A14; *The Chernobyl Nuclear Power Plant*, THE NEW YORK TIMES, June 5, 2000, p. 1.

3. Perhaps surprisingly, industry has been a very strong supporter of liability treaties. Why do you think this is so?

One reason is that the lack of an adequate nuclear liability framework has been a serious obstacle to private companies from the West supplying technologies to nuclear plants in Eastern Europe. Currently in Central and Eastern Europe, only Bulgaria, Latvia, and Lithuania have legislation "channeling" liability to the operator of a nuclear plant. As a result, in other countries there is uncertainty over the liability of related business parties. Not surprisingly, this serves as strong disincentive to foreign suppliers. In 1995, Russia signed a Memorandum of Understanding on the Implementation of Technical Assistance Programmes in the Field of Nuclear Safety. This bilateral agreement provides indemnification for the European Union and its contractors working with nuclear power in Russian Federation. This followed closely a similar bilateral agreement negotiated with the U.S. in 1993.

4. Nuclear power plant operation has long been a concern of environmental NGOs, and not just in the United States or Western Europe. Consider the case study described below by the Regional Environmental Center for Central and Eastern Europe, an NGO established with funding by the United States and the Commission of the European Communities. The case study provides an NGO perspective on efforts to oppose funding by the European Bank for Reconstruction and Development (EBRD) for construction of a Soviet-designed nuclear power plant in Slovakia.

> The construction of a nuclear power plant was initiated by the Slovak government in Mohovce in 1994. The future operation of the plant may pose an extremely serious threat to human health and the environment across Europe since it is based on obsolete Soviet technology. The planned construction directly affects the local population, and several surrounding countries, including Hungary, Poland, Czech Republic, Austria and Ukraine.

> The problem became known when the Slovak government decided to build the nuclear plant in Mohovce and applied to the EBRD for funding. The internal Environmental Guidelines of the EBRD require an environmental impact assessment in cases where projects may have a potential transboundary impact. . . .

> As a result of the EIA Procedure initiated by the EBRD in October 1994, the Slovak government advertised the project in Poland and inquired about the possibilities of obtaining EIA documentation.

> Since the Polish government was unwilling to take any position on this issue, the Polish Ecological Club (PKE) decided to become involved and made an independent survey of the project. PKE managed to receive funding from the UNDP Umbrella Program and commissioned a group of independent experts to review the EIA documentation. The critical review was presented in a series of press conferences and events. The Espoo Convention on Transboundary Environmental Impact Assessment could have been applied, but, unfortunately, it is not yet in force.

> Due to the public involvement and NGO activity, MPs from the Environmental Committee of Parliament became aware of the case and were asked to request an official response from the government. As a result of the huge pressure by the public and parliament, the Polish government—despite its initial reluctance and opposition—officially forwarded the reservations concerning the project to the Slovak government. The critical review by Polish independent experts was translated into English and presented to the EBRD. Although the NGO representatives were not allowed to participate in the EBRD meetings concerning the project, their reviews played an important role in the EBRD's decision not to support the project. The Polish, Austrian and German NGOs lobbied the

EBRD regarding the project.... One NGO representative from each country went to London and together submitted their reservations and criticisms to the EBRD. Due to public protests in Poland, Slovakia and other countries and the lobbying activity of NGOs, the EBRD decided not to support the project.

As a result of NGO action, the Polish government was forced to take an official position and formally address the Slovak Government regarding its reservations. The public involvement and concentrated action of the NGOs contributed to the EBRD's refusal of the application for financial support, which has prevented the project from being carried out for the time being.

<http://www.rec.org/REC/Publications/BndBound/Poland.html>

Why do you think the EBRD refused financing for the nuclear plant? Whom did the NGOs represent? Do you think increased burning of high sulfur coal or new hydropower plants to meet Slovakia's energy needs is a preferable alternative to a modern nuclear plant (*see* the Gabcikovo–Nagymaros Dam dispute, p. 780)? Austria argued that Mohovce was an infringement of Austrian national security. What difference does it make to characterize this as a national security issue?

C. NUCLEAR WEAPONS

1. NUCLEAR WEAPONS REDUCTION TREATIES

In Moscow on August 5, 1963, the governments of the United States, United Kingdom, and the USSR signed a general treaty prohibiting nuclear weapons tests in the atmosphere, in outer space, and underwater, including territorial waters or the high seas. Treaty Banning Nuclear Weapon Tests in the Atmosphere, in Outer Space, and Underwater, 4 I.L.M. 393 (1965). The purpose of the treaty was to achieve complete nuclear disarmament. The treaty entered into force on October 10, 1963, and was signed by all the nuclear powers except France and China. This treaty was followed by a number of international agreements reducing levels of nuclear weapons and the testing, development and use of nuclear weapons. These include the Treaty Banning Nuclear Weapons Tests in the Atmosphere, in Outer Space and Under Water, 480 U.N.T.S. 43 (1963), the USSR–US Treaty on the Elimination of Their Intermediate–Range and Shorter–Range Missiles, 27 I.L.M. 84 (1987), and the Treaty on Principles Governing the Activities of States in the Exploration and Use of Outer Space, Including the Moon and other Celestial Bodies, 6 I.L.M. 386 (1967). In 1968 the Treaty on the Non–Proliferation of Nuclear Weapons (NPT) was signed. Of particular significance, it required Member States "to pursue negotiations in good faith on effective measures relating to cessation of the nuclear arms race at an early date and to nuclear disarmament, and on a treaty on general and complete disarmament under strict and effective international control." 7 I.L.M. 809, Article VI. The treaty was extended indefinitely in 1995 with support of more than 170 countries. Final Document on Extension of the Treaty on the Non–Proliferation of Nuclear Weapons, 34 I.L.M. 959 (1995). In July 2000, NPT had 187 signatories. Only four countries have not signed: India, Pakistan, Israel and Cuba.

Between January 1994 and August 1996, the Comprehensive Test Ban Treaty (CTBT) was negotiated. The CTBT bans all nuclear explosions, including test explosions, in an attempt to achieve complete international nuclear disarmament. The CTBT is open to all States and was signed by, at the time, all five declared nuclear powers (U.S., France, U.K., Russia, China) as well as by over 100 countries. Traditionally, atmospheric or underground nuclear tests have been viewed as essential for developing and maintaining a reliable nuclear weapons arsenal. Developments in super-computers have caused governments to reassess this rationale. In signing the CTBT, both the United States and France cited the potential of using powerful supercomputers to design and "test" new nuclear weapons. But whether the treaty will lead to disarmament is unclear.

At its core, the CTBT has operated as a *quid pro quo*, in which non-nuclear states vow to remain as such and, in return, the five acknowledged nuclear weapons states agree (1) to assist non-nuclear states in the development of peaceful nuclear technology, (2) to complete a Comprehensive Test Ban, and (3) to move toward disarmament. As of July 2000, it had been signed by 155 countries and ratified by 60. The five original nuclear powers of the NPT have signed it, but, of those, only the United Kingdom and France have ratified. Article XIV of the CTBT provides that it will not come into effect until forty-four specific states ratify it. Of those necessary states, 16 have not yet ratified, including the United States, Russia, China, North Korea, India, Pakistan and Israel.

Some critics allege that the success of the NPT and CTBT has been minimal. In May of 1998, India conducted underground nuclear weapons tests and was followed by Pakistan less than a month later. In addition to instability in the South Asian region, Iran, Iraq, Syria and Libya are all attempting to build nuclear arsenals and Israel, which is not a member of the NPT, has nuclear capabilities. Iran has conducted medium-range missile tests and has announced that it may be the next declared nuclear power. In addition, the United States is considering building a missile defense system, which has fueled concern in the international community because it appears to reflect a lack of trust in the current treaty regime. Indeed, in 1999 the United States Senate voted to reject ratification of the CTBT. *See* Jon Kyl, *Maintaining "Peace Through Strength": A Rejection of the Comprehensive Test Ban Treaty*, 37 Harv. J. on Legis 325 (2000); Jack Mendelsohn, *History and Evaluation of the Role of Nuclear Weapons in the Cold War*, 31 Case W. Res. J. Int'l L. 609, 616 (1999).

Others contend, however, that the NPT and CTBT have had a significant effect on establishing an international norm against nuclear testing that is being observed by many states who have not yet ratified. In addition, the parties of the CTBT have initiated the development of an International Monitoring System (IMS) as well as an International Data Centre (IDC), which will create a "verification" system that will consist of a network of hundreds of ground and sea-based sensors that will be linked to monitor nuclear testing. See *CTBT Three Years On—Significance, Achievements, The Way Forward*, April 4, 2000, <http://www.clw.org/pub/clw/coalition/ctbto040400.htm>; Vejay Lalla, *The Effectiveness of the Comprehensive Test Ban Treaty on Nuclear Weapons Proliferation: A Review of Nuclear Non–Proliferation Treaties and the Impact of the Indian and Pakistani Nuclear Tests on the Non–Proliferation Regime*, 8 CARDOZO J. INT'L & COMP. L. 103, 106 (2000).

The mixed success of the nuclear weapons treaties is not surprising, given the inevitable tension between (and among) nuclear and non-nuclear parties. Article VI of the NPT requires the nuclear-weapon states to negotiate in good faith both for a cessation of the nuclear arms race at an early date and to complete nuclear disarmament under strict and effective international control. Effective disarmament obviously requires cooperation, but this necessary collaboration must take place in an environment of competition (if not distrust) in the complicated United States–China and United States–Russia relationships (and made even more complicated by the debate over the proposed U.S. missile defense system). *See* George Bunn, *Can the NPT Survive Such Threats as Yugoslavia's Bombing, Russia's Plans for New Nuclear Weapons, U.S. Plans for Missile Defense Systems, and the Duma–Senate Stalemate on Nuclear Treaties?*, CENTER FOR NON-PROLIFERATION STUDIES (1999). Moreover, the five original nuclear-weapon states and many other technologically-advanced countries such as Australia, Belgium, Canada, Germany, Japan and South Africa provide a significant amount of nuclear technology and rocket materials for purportedly peaceful uses that may end up being used in a non-peaceful manner. And finally, as the recent conflict in Kosovo demonstrated (discussed in the Questions and Discussion), low-grade nuclear materials have been, and may increasingly be, used in conventional weapons. Yet the NPT and CTBT do not explicitly address this issue.

---

2. NUCLEAR WEAPON–FREE REGIONS

Five regional conventions have turned much of the world into a nuclear weapons-free zone. The Antarctic Treaty was signed in Washington, D.C. in December 1959 and came into force in June 1961 after ratification by the twelve countries then active in Antarctic exploration. The Antarctic Treaty, December 1, 1959, 402 U.N.T.S. 71 (1959). The treaty explicitly prohibits the disposal of nuclear waste, nuclear explosions, and military activities in the Antarctic region, defined as the region beyond 60 degrees south latitude. The treaty also provides Parties the right to conduct inspections in all areas of Antarctica, including stations, installations, equipment, ships and aircraft. At the tenth inspection that occurred in February of 1995, no prohibited nuclear activity was observed and all observed scientific activities were in compliance with the treaty. *See* Chapter 15, p. 1088.

The Treaty of Tlatelolco for the Prohibition of Nuclear Weapons in Latin America prohibits the use of nuclear weapons by member States. 6 I.L.M. 152 (1968). More recent regional treaties in Africa, the South Pacific, and South–East Asia prohibit the manufacture, acquisition or possession of nuclear weapons. African Nuclear–Weapon–Free Zone Treaty, 35 I.L.M. 698 (1996); South Pacific Nuclear Free Zone Treaty, 24 I.L.M. 1440 (1985); South–East Asia Nuclear Free Zone Treaty, 35 I.L.M. 635 (1996). The scope of the most recent treaty, the South–East Asian Treaty, is comprehensive and has been signed by all ten countries in the region. The treaty only prohibits the disposal of radioactive waste and the possession of nuclear weapons. It does not ban the use of nuclear power for energy.

------

3. NUCLEAR TEST CASES

In the Nuclear Tests Cases of 1973–74, Australia and New Zealand separately asked the International Court of Justice (ICJ) to enjoin France from conducting atmospheric nuclear tests in the Pacific Ocean. Australia v. France, 1974 I.C.J. 253; New Zealand v. France, 1974 I.C.J. 457. France had carried out a series of atmospheric nuclear tests over the Mururoa Atoll in French Polynesia. The location of the tests was thousands of miles from Australia and New Zealand.

Australia's claim rested primarily on the argument that France's tests were illegal under international law because they would pollute Australia's land, atmosphere, and territorial seas without its consent as well as infringe the freedom of the high seas. Australia v. France, 1973 I.C.J. 99, 103. New Zealand's claims were broader, arguing in addition that France's tests resulted in radioactive fall-out that violated the rights of all members of the international community. New Zealand v. France, 1974 I.C.J. 457, 512. Prior to the full hearing, the ICJ granted a preliminary injunction ordering France to "avoid nuclear tests causing the deposit of radioactive fall-out" over Australia and New Zealand. Id., 1973 I.C.J. 106, 142. Prior to the commencement of the full hearings, France agreed to come under the Court's jurisdiction and unilaterally declared it would cease atmospheric nuclear tests in favor of underground testing. Following these actions, the ICJ did not address the issue of the legality of nuclear test explosions and dismissed Australia's and New Zealand's cases as moot. The ICJ did state, however, that "if the basis of this judgment were to be affected, the Applicant could request an examination of the situation" by the ICJ. *Id.* 1974 I.C.J. 271, 477; *see* Don MacKay, *Nuclear Testing: New Zealand and France in the International Court of Justice,* 19 FORDHAM INT'L L.J. 1857, 1863–66 (1996).

Twenty-one years later, on August 21, 1995, New Zealand attempted to re-open its 1974 nuclear test case against France, this time seeking a declaratory judgment that France's proposed underground nuclear weapons testing on the Mururoa and Fangatuafa Atolls of French Polynesia violated international law; and furthermore that such testing was unlawful unless an environmental impact assessment was performed and accepted under international standards.

Why did New Zealand try to re-open the 1974 case rather than file a new suit? France had withdrawn from the ICJ's jurisdiction following the dismissal of Australia's and New Zealand's original complaints. While this did not affect the 1974 case, it barred any new actions against France before the ICJ without its consent. Thus the only way to bring France before the ICJ was to return to the 1974 pleadings and hope the ICJ would re-open the case by arguing that "the basis" of its judgment had been affected by France's renewal of testing. New Zealand claimed that France's tests, although underground, raised basic issues of international environmental law developed since 1974 such as the duty not to cause transboundary harm, the principle of intergenerational equity, and the precautionary principle. In a vote of 12–3, the ICJ dismissed New Zealand's claim on purely procedural grounds, declaring that it could not re-open the 1974 case since that case had involved atmospheric nuclear tests and the current situation concerned underground nuclear tests.

In a more recent case, the ICJ has addressed the status under international law of using or threatening to use nuclear weapons. In the Legality of Nuclear Weapons Case, The World Health Organization and the United Nations General Assembly asked the court for an advisory opinion on whether international law permits the threat or use of nuclear weapons in any circumstances. Twenty-four countries made oral arguments before the Court, with Australia and New Zealand leading the call to outlaw nuclear weapons. The United States, France and Russia (all nuclear powers) argued that the Court should decline to address the issue and that, in any case, the use or threat to use nuclear weapons was legal because they were necessary for global security.

By a slim 8–7 vote, the ICJ ruled that "the threat or use of nuclear weapons would generally be contrary to the rules of international law applicable in armed conflict." The Court did not decide whether the use of nuclear weapons in the case of self-defense when the very survival of the State was at stake would be lawful or unlawful. The ICJ also declared that nations had a legal obligation to enter into agreements with the goal of achieving nuclear disarmament, reinforcing the Nuclear Proliferation Treaty's requirement to make efforts toward nuclear disarmament. *See* Chapter 17 for a fuller discussion of the case, page 1386.

QUESTIONS AND DISCUSSION

1. Why do you think the WHO and UN General Assembly brought the nuclear weapons case? If the ICJ had ruled that the threat or use of nuclear weapons was contrary to the rules of international law in *all* circumstances, what might have been the possible results? Would the nuclear powers have voluntarily disarmed their nuclear arsenals to comply with the ICJ opinion? Recall that the president of the ICJ wrote, "there exists an obligation to pursue in good faith and bring to a conclusion negotiations leading to nuclear disarmament in all its aspects under strict and effective international control."

2. NGOs played a key role in representing some of the parties to the ICJ case on the legality of nuclear weapons. The Foundation for International Environmental Law and Development (FIELD), for example, represented the Solomon Islands, Samoa, and the Marshall Islands in oral arguments before the Court.

3. If France could have shown convincing scientific evidence that the radiation from its nuclear tests would not migrate, i.e. there would be no transboundary effects, could New Zealand and Australia still have challenged its tests? What aspect of the testing would you argue still violates international law?

4. During its operations in the Balkans and Gulf Wars, NATO used Depleted Uranium (DU) ammunition to attack tanks. Because of its high density and melting point, DU munitions are very effective conventional weapons. Upon contact with a tank, the DU ammunition explodes and releases dust that can take up to two hours to settle. Thus soldiers in the tanks and nearby civilians and soldiers are highly susceptible to inhaling or ingesting DU radioactive particles. DU ammunition poses further risks because it can seep into soil and groundwater. *U.N. Team Finds Slightly Elevated Levels of Radiation at Kosovo Sites Hit by NATO*, BNA IED, Jan. 29, 2001.

There has been some speculation that the "Gulf War Syndrome" is linked to DU exposure, but no causal relationship has been established. Serbian doctors have claimed a sharp rise in cancers, as high as 200% in areas directly targeted by the NATO air raids. *Cancer Blinds Kosovo Veterans*, 2001 WL 10130094, Jan. 22, 2001. Others have refuted these findings. According to the International Atomic Energy Agency, the DU in munitions is comprised almost entirely from U–238 isotopes and is about 60% as radioactive as natural uranium. The IAEA's website states that:

Up to now, no adverse health effects have been established in the limited epidemiological studies of internal exposure to radiation through ingestion and inhalation of DU particles or through skin lesions and wounds contaminated by DU or in studies of uranium workers exposed to natural or enriched uranium.

<http://www.who.int/inf-fs/en/fact257.html>. NATO has also consistently denied the claims.

The credibility of NATO's position, however, was drawn into question when a document leaked alleging British army officials knew of DU's possible health risks as early as 1997. This report allegedly warned high level army officials that soldiers working inside vehicles damaged by DU faced uranium exposure eight times acceptable safety levels. *UK Army Aware of Depleted Uranium Risks 4–Yrs Ago*, DOW JONES INT'L NEWS, Jan. 11, 2001. The Balkans Task Force, a team of scientists charged with assessing environmental damage in Yugoslavia, was unable to investigate these allegations due, in part, to the U.S. State Department's refusal to disclose classified documents revealing possible site locations. *Environmental Harm in Balkans Conflict Requires Urgent Steps, U.N. Adviser Says*, DAILY ENVT. REP., Oct. 19, 1999. NATO has denied requests to temporarily ban DU munitions pending investigation and continues to take the position that DU poses no significant health risks.

Did NATO's conduct violate the law of war? A report by the Environmental Committee of the 41–nation Council of Europe concluded that NATO States flagrantly violated the Additional Protocol 1 to the 1949 Geneva Convention obligation to limit environmental damage in armed conflict. NATO justifies most of its actions under the dual-use exemption of Protocol 1. *"Serious Environmental Impact" of Airstrikes on Yugoslavia Cited by Council of Europe*, BNA IED, Jan. 11, 2001, at D3. These issues are further explored in the Problem Exercise in Chapter 17, page 1395.

Suggested Further Reading and Web Sites

Haralambos Athanasopulos, NUCLEAR DISARMAMENT IN INTERNATIONAL LAW (2000)

Comprehensive look at the history and future of nuclear weapons in international law.

http://cns.miis.edu/index.htm

Homepage of the Center for Non–Proliferation Studies

Ramesh Thakur, NUCLEAR WEAPONS–FREE ZONES (1998)

Karen McMillan, *Strengthening the international legal framework for nuclear energy*, 13 GEO. INT'L ENVTL. L. REV. 983–1012 (2001)

Christoph Hilz, The International Toxic Waste Trade (1992)

Useful examination of the scale and impacts of trade in hazardous substances.

Theo Colburn, Dianne Dumanoski, John Peterson Myers, Our Stolen Future (1996)

The controversial book that placed POPs in the public's eye. With a foreword by former Vice–President Al Gore, the book makes the case against POPs.

Rachel Carson, Silent Spring (1962)

The book that first pointed out the dangers of pesticides to the general public. Still makes great reading over 35 years later.

Philippe Sands, Chernobyl: Law and Communication (1988)

Very informative treatment of environmental law and nuclear energy.

R. Repetto and S. Baliga, Pesticides and the Immune System: the Public Health Risks (1996).

http://www.unep.ch/basel/

Homepage of the Basel Secretariat.

http://www.ourstolenfuture.org/

Homepage of the book, *Our Stolen Future*. Contains details of the debate over the book's findings and useful hypertext links, with references for further research on the environmental and health impacts of POPs.

http://c3.org/index.html

Homepage of the Chlorine Chemistry Council.

http://irptc.unep.ch/pops/

UNEP operates a persistent organic pollutants homepage with reports on POPs activites of UNEP and other international organizations.

http://www.iaea.or.at/

Homepage of the IAEA.

CHAPTER THIRTEEN

WILDLIFE AND BIODIVERSITY

SECTION I. HISTORY AND BACKGROUND

Every form of life is unique, warranting respect regardless of its worth to man, and, to accord other organisms such recognition, man must be guided by a moral code of conduct.

—Preamble, World Charter for Nature (1982)

A.   INTRODUCTION

The use and protection of wildlife has historically been considered a matter of domestic law, reflecting every State's claim to permanent sovereignty over its natural resources, including living natural resources. Despite the State's paramount interest, however, wildlife has also long been a subject of international cooperation. Wildlife is not always found, nor does it always stay, within political borders. Conservation of migratory species such as birds, which travel between many States, clearly presents a need for international cooperation. Similarly non-migratory species that have habitats straddling more than one country or that are found in the global commons beyond the borders of any country require international cooperation for their conservation. For example, in 1911 the United States joined with Japan, Russia and the United Kingdom in a treaty to protect the northern pacific fur seal. In a classic tragedy of the commons, hunters from each of the three countries were harvesting as many fur seals as they could—hoping to benefit from the high price paid for seal fur. As one might expect, the fur seal population plummeted. By allocating the rights to exploit the fur seal through negotiations, the countries hoped to reach a sustainable harvest level. Indeed, wildlife treaties like the fur seal treaty were the first to reflect elements of sustainable development—namely through the concept of maximum sustainable yield.

International cooperation has also proven necessary to respond to international economic activities—most notably the growing international trade in wildlife and plants. The Convention on International Trade and Endangered Species (CITES) was adopted in 1973, and has evolved into a detailed and complex regulatory regime covering thousands of plant and animal species. CITES is discussed in Section IV of this Chapter. Similarly a major part of the Biodiversity Convention addresses the international trade in biotechnology and biodiversity resources. *See* Section II of this Chapter.

Despite the efforts under CITES to control the international wildlife trade and numerous other treaties aimed at migratory species conservation, wildlife populations are still plummeting in many regions, sometimes from commercial exploitation but just as often from habitat destruction or other causes. Efforts to identify and protect the most important wildlife habitats, particularly for migratory species, have led to some protection through the Convention on Migratory Species, the Ramsar Convention on Wetlands of International Importance and the UNESCO World Cultural and Natural Heritage Convention. Through increased international interest and attention, these treaties help to provide resources and build political will for the conservation of particularly important habitats. *See* Chapter 15.

For some environmentalists, international controls limiting State sovereignty over wildlife and biodiversity are justified on spiritual, ethical or moral grounds. In arguments analogous to that of human rights, animal rights activists argue that humans are responsible for protecting certain minimum rights of animals and nature. Animal rights activists argue that all life should be treated with respect and animals should not be exploited, except perhaps for the most basic of human needs. The calls for prohibitions on commercial exploitation of wildlife have been the loudest with respect to certain large or beautiful species—so-called "charismatic megafauna." Whales are one example. The International Whaling Commission (IWC) started out as an organization to allocate whale harvesting, but has slowly been transformed into an organization that polices a ban on commercial whaling. The IWC is addressed in Section III of this Chapter.

At least until recently, international wildlife law suffered from a lack of a broad strategy or policy. Wildlife treaties were developed through the 1970s in mostly ad hoc ways to address specific species or varieties of mostly commercially valuable wildlife. Beginning in the late 1970's, it became apparent that the ad hoc approach to wildlife conservation was insufficient for protecting the planet's biodiversity. Moreover, conservation biologists became concerned that an emphasis on charismatic megafauna was resulting in policymakers overlooking the vast rate of decline in other forms of plants and animals. These concerns led to calls for a broad framework convention that would cover all the threats to the diversity of life on the planet. Initially this manifested itself in soft law instruments such as the 1980 World Conservation Strategy and the 1982 World Charter for Nature (see *Treaty Supplement*). Although these documents were nonbinding, both were important milestones in the development of international approaches to conservation. Eventually, the broader approach reflected in the World Charter for Nature would be embraced in the 1992 Convention on Biological Diversity. This Convention falls short of offering specific standards or requirements on the conservation of biodiversity. Nor does it offer the broad framework for all of wildlife and biodiversity law that was originally envisaged. Nonetheless, the Biodiversity Convention does address the full breadth of life on the planet and establishes important guidelines for national conservation efforts. The Convention's Biosafety Protocol addresses the emerging trade in biotechnology. The Biodiversity Convention and its Biosafety Protocol are discussed in Section II of this Chapter.

The following parts of this Introduction introduce the concept of biodiversity, as well as the basic tension underlying wildlife conservation efforts—namely the extent to which wildlife can be exploited sustainably. The remainder of the Chapter addresses major wildlife treaties, including the Biodiversity Convention, CITES, and the Convention on Migratory Species. It also addresses several regimes and action plans aimed at protecting specific species or groups of species, including for example whales. The next Chapter addresses major efforts in the international arena that can help in protecting wildlife habitat, including the two major conventions involved in habitat conservation (the Ramsar Convention and the UNESCO Cultural Heritage Convention) as well as the status of international cooperation with respect to forests.

B. WHAT IS BIODIVERSITY?

Until recently conservation efforts were aimed at something called "wildlife." Beginning in the late 1970s, however, many biologists became concerned that the focus on wildlife was too narrow, that concern over the fate of cute or ferocious mammals or beautiful birds missed the larger issue of a loss in the overall richness of life on the planet. To them, biological diversity (shortened to biodiversity) was a better object of conservation, because it covered all forms of life.

Biodiversity is defined very broadly in the Biodiversity Convention as: "the variability among living organisms from all sources including, *inter alia*, terrestrial, marine and other aquatic ecosystems and the ecological complexes of which they are part; this includes diversity within species, between species and of ecosystems." Biodiversity thus encompasses all of the variability among the building blocks of life (i.e., genetic diversity), different life forms (species diversity) and the interrelationships of life (ecosystem diversity). The concept of biodiversity does not discriminate between wild and domesticated animals and plants.

Biodiversity as a concept allows us to recognize and value the great diversity and variability of life. By focusing on biodiversity, scientists hoped to build political will for conserving all life. The concept of biodiversity demands equal concern for both ant and anteater, rhinoceros beetle and rhinoceros.

Understanding the different components of the definition of biodiversity is important because conservation strategies and efforts will differ depending on which component you are trying to conserve. For example, genetic variability may eventually be so well known or "mapped" that it could be "conserved" in databanks, at least for some specific purposes. Species diversity may be maintained through zoos or exhibits, though population diversity will not be. And focusing on the conservation of population diversity as well as ecosystem diversity would require steps to protect larger areas of the natural world.

An emphasis on biodiversity may also lead to different priorities in conservation. For example, some populations of species may have greater internal genetic variability than other populations. Some species may be more important to maintaining the stability of an ecosystem (so-called "keystone species"). Others are umbrella species, such as large carnivores or the Spotted Owl, the protection of which ensures adequate amounts of habitat for other species; still others are 'sentinel species', which are particularly sensitive to environmental change and thus are important as indicators of the health of an ecosystem. Frogs and other amphibians are frequently viewed as sentinel species. A focus on one or more of these categories of species or on maintaining the basic ecological processes of an area can lead to different strategies for conservation. In this regard, consider the following technical definitions of each component of biodiversity:

Katrina Brown, et al, Economics and the Conservation of Global Biological Diversities 3–5 (1993)

Genetic diversity

Genetic diversity is the sum of genetic information contained in the genes of individual plants, animals and micro-organisms. Each species is the repository of an immense amount of genetic information. The number of genes ranges from about 1,000 in bacteria to more than 400,000 in many flowering plants. Each species consists of many organisms, and virtually no two members of the same species are genetically identical. Thus, even if an endangered species is saved from extinction, it probably has lost much of its internal diversity. Consequently, when populations expand again, they become more genetically uniform than their ancestors. For example, the bison herds of today do not have the same genetic diversity as the bison herds of the early eighteenth century.

Population geneticists have developed mathematical formulas to express a genetically effective population size. These explain the genetic effects on populations that have passed through the bottleneck of a small population size, such as the North American bison or African cheetah. Subsequent inbreeding may result in reduced fertility, increased susceptibility to disease, and other negative effects that are termed "inbreeding depression." These effects depend on the breeding system of the species and the duration of the bottleneck. If the bottleneck lasts for many generations, or population recovery is extremely slow, much variation can be lost. [This is known as the bottleneck effect.] Conversely, "outbreeding depression" occurs when species become genetically differentiated across their range, and individuals from different parts of the range breed. Genetic differentiation within species occurs as a result of either sexual reproduction, in which genetic differences from individuals may be combined in their offspring to produce new combinations of genes, or from mutations, which cause changes in the deoxyribonucleic acid (DNA).

The significance of genetic diversity is often highlighted with reference to global agriculture and food security. This stresses the dependence of the majority of the world's human population on a few staple food species. These staple species have been improved by tapping genes from their wild relatives to foster new characteristics, for example, to improve resistance to pests and disease. [Many varieties of important crops exist only in the wild or in relatively small numbers of traditional farming communities.]

Species diversity

Species are populations within which gene flows occur under natural conditions. Within a species, all normal individuals are capable of breeding with other individuals of the opposite sex, or at least of being genetically linked with them through chains of other breeding individuals. By definition, members of one species do not breed freely with members of another species. * * *

The exact number of species on earth is not known, not even to the nearest order of magnitude. [Well-known biologist] E.O. Wilson estimates that the absolute number of species falls between 5 million to 30 million, although some scientists have put forward estimates of up to 50 million. At present, approximately 1.4 million living species have been described. The best catalogued groups are vertebrates and flowering plants. Such groups as lichens, bacteria, fungi, and round-worms are relatively under-researched. Likewise, some habitats are better researched than others. Coral reefs, the ocean floor, and tropical soils are not well studied.

The most obvious pattern in the global distribution of species is that overall species richness increases with decreasing latitude. Not only does this apply as a general rule, it also holds within the great majority of higher taxa, at order level or higher. However, this overall pattern masks several minor trends. Species richness in particular taxonomic groups, or in particular habitats, may show no significant latitudinal variation, or may actually decrease with decreasing latitudes. In addition, in terrestrial ecosystems, diversity generally decreases with increasing altitude. This phenomenon is most apparent at extremes of altitude, with the highest regions at all latitudes having extremely low species diversity. However, these areas also tend to be relatively small, which may be a factor that results in lower species numbers. In marine systems, depth is the analogue of altitude in terrestrial systems, and biodiversity tends to be negatively correlated with depth. Gradients and changes in species richness are also noticeably correlated to precipitation, nutrient levels, and salinity, as well as other climatic variations and available energy.

Ecosystem diversity

Ecosystem diversity relates to the variety of habitats, biotic communities, and ecological processes in the biosphere, as well as to the diversity within ecosystems. Diversity can be described at a number of different levels and scales. Functional diversity is the relative abundance of functionally different kinds of organisms. Community diversity comprises the size, number, and spatial distribution of communities, and is sometimes referred to as patchiness. Landscape diversity is the diversity of scales of patchiness.

No simple relationship exists between the diversity of an ecosystem and such ecological processes as productivity, hydrology, and soil generation. Nor does diversity neatly correlate with ecosystem stability, its resistance to disturbance, or its speed of .recovery. There is also no simple relationship within any ecosystem between a change in its diversity and the resulting change in its component processes. On the one hand, the loss of a species from a particular area or region (local extinction or extirpation) may have little or no effect on net primary productivity if competitors take its place in the community. On the other hand, there can be cases where the converse is true. For example, if zebra and wildebeest are removed from the African savannah, net primary productivity of the ecosystem would decrease.

———

QUESTIONS AND DISCUSSION

1. Based on the above discussion, you can see why scientists might prefer the concept of biodiversity conservation over, for example, wildlife conservation. Biodiversity offers a vehicle for discussing the importance of conserving all forms of life. Biodiversity also includes the concept of variability as an economic resource. The variation among and within species has great value in agriculture, medicine and the new biotechnology industries. By focusing attention on the economic value of the variability of life, conservationists hoped they would be able to build broader support for overall conservation efforts—in addition to the broad support for conserving the last few rhinos or tigers.

Yet the concept of biological diversity is also a technical one, and one that may not elicit the same kind of broad public support and understanding as wildlife. In this respect, do you think it might be harder to rally public support behind the implementation of a Convention on "Biodiversity" than a Convention on "Endangered Species of Wildlife?"

2. Often when we think of biodiversity, we tend to focus on terrestrial or land-based biodiversity. Yet, much of the world's biodiversity is found either in marine or freshwater ecosystems. These ecosystems are often under serious threat, and our efforts to conserve them are crippled by a lack of available information. The following excerpt from the *Global Biodiversity Strategy* describes some of the richness and threats to freshwater biodiversity.

Freshwaters are also home to a tremendous diversity of fish, amphibians, aquatic plants, invertebrates, and microorganisms. The Amazon River alone contains an estimated 3000 species of fish—only 25 percent less than the total number of mammals worldwide. And freshwater biodiversity is among the most poorly known on Earth. Scientists believe that Thailand may have as many as 1000 species of freshwater fish, but only some 475 have actually been recorded.

Freshwater biodiversity is seriously threatened today—a telling indicator of the status of the world's freshwater ecosystems. All native fish in the Valley of Mexico are extinct. A recent survey in Malaysia found fewer than half of the 266 fish species previously known from the country. On the island of Singapore 18 out of 53 species of freshwater fish collected in 1934 could not be located in exhaustive searches only 30 years later. In the southeastern United States, 40 to 50 percent of freshwater snail species are now extinct or endangered due to the impoundment and channelization of rivers. Even on a continental scale, species loss can be very high. In North America, one-third of the native freshwater fish species are extinct or endangered to some degree.

Biodiversity in freshwater systems is distributed in a fundamentally different pattern from that in marine or terrestrial systems. Organisms on land or in the sea live in media that are more or less continuous over extensive regions, and species adjust their ranges to some degree as climate or ecological conditions change. But freshwater habitats are relatively discontinuous, and many freshwater species do not disperse easily across the land barriers that separate river drainages into discrete units. This has three important consequences: a) freshwater species must survive climatic and ecological changes in place; b) freshwater biodiversity is usually highly localized, and even small lake or stream systems often harbor unique, locally evolved forms of life; and c) freshwater species diversity is high even in regions where the number of species at any given site is low, since species differ between one site and the next.

Freshwater lakes are classical examples of "habitat islands" (in this case, bodies of water surrounded by expanses of land). Like islands in general, the larger, more ancient lakes tend to have high levels of endemism, and in the rift lakes of Africa or Lake Baikal of Central Asia, species diversity can be spectacular. With hundreds of species each—90 percent of them in some cases found nowhere else—the East African lakes harbor some of the world's greatest concentrations of locally endemic species.

Unfortunately, lakes are like islands in another way too: they suffer high rates of extinction when habitat modification begins or when exotic species are introduced. The introduction of non-native species—regrettably still often sanctioned or promoted by governments—is associated with the depletion of biodiversity and the collapse of major fisheries in such lakes as Lake Chapala of Mexico, Lake Gatun of Panama, and the Great Lakes of North America.

Other factors contributing to the decline of freshwater ecosystems and their native biota are chemical and thermal pollution, over-harvesting, and habitat modifications (such as dam construction). These factors have affected biodiversity to different degrees in both industrialized and developing regions. In Europe and North America, pollution, acidification, and the physical modification of streams have had the greatest impact. In much of South America and Africa, over-harvesting and introduction of non-native species are relatively more important as agents of biodiversity loss.

Programs to protect freshwater biodiversity in industrialized countries have lagged far behind the programs for saving terrestrial biota. Many protected areas include lakes or small portions of watersheds, but rivers and streams are often too linear to incorporate adequately into protected areas. Moreover, rivers and streams frequently pass through more than one political jurisdiction or may themselves constitute political boundaries. (The Danube crosses or borders upon seven European nations.) Consequently, effective management of riverine biodiversity is often a casualty of politics.

The primary method of protecting fresh-water biodiversity has been to designate particular species as threatened or endangered, making them subject to national recovery programs or international protection. Unfortunately, this approach is failing. In the United States, for example, no aquatic species has ever graduated from the government's endangered species list, but 10 species of fish have been removed due to extinction.

WORLD RESOURCES INSTITUTE, GLOBAL BIODIVERSITY STRATEGY, Box 3, at 10–11 (1992). Marine biodiversity is similarly rich and relatively unknown. *See* discussion in Section III below.

C.   THE VALUE OF BIODIVERSITY

What is the value of biodiversity? As noted above, scientists and environmentalists emphasized the concept of biodiversity in part because they believe that it connotes a resource of greater economic value than simply "wildlife" or even "ecosystems." Indeed, the definition of biodiversity is broad enough to encompass all the values of both wildlife and ecosystems.

Traditional uses of wildlife are well known, including for example food, pets, ornament, tourist attractions, or recreational purposes such as bird-watching. These are significant motivations for the conservation and use of biodiversity and of particular wildlife species. As Section IV discusses, a conservative estimate places international trade in wildlife at over $10 billion a year. Up to one-third of the trade is likely illegal.

Ecosystems are also now widely recognized to provide substantial economic benefits to humanity. Recent estimates in fact place the value of ecosystem services to be more than the total value of the world's economy. These estimates take into account inter alia the value of freshwater purification, pollination, clean air, flood control, soil stability and climate regulation provided by ecosystems.

Created by the interactions of living organisms with their environment, ecosystem services provide both the conditions and processes that sustain human life. Despite their obvious importance to our well-being, recognition of ecosystem services and the roles they play rarely enter policy debates or public discussion. The primary reason that ecosystem services are taken for granted is that they are free. We explicitly value and place dollar figures on "ecosystem goods" such as timber and fish. Yet the services underpinning these goods almost without exception have no market value—not because they are worthless but, rather, because there is no market to capture and express their value directly. *See* James Salzman, *Valuing Ecosystem Services,* 24 ECOLOGY L.Q. 887 (1997); Gretchen Daily, ed., NATURE'S SERVICES: SOCIETAL DEPENDENCE ON NATURAL ECOSYSTEMS (1997); Robert Costanza et al., *The Value of the World's Ecosystem Services and Natural Capital,* 387 NATURE 253 (1997).

Agriculture and Food Security. Although 30,000 species of plants are edible, only about 5,000 are consumed by humans. Of those, 20 species provide 90 percent of the world's food. Wheat, maize, and rice together provide more than half. The genetic diversity of wild relatives and the numerous traditional varieties of food crops act as a reservoir of potential value for adopting plants to different conditions or for increasing the productivity of domestic strains. U.S. agricultural output is increased by an estimated $1 billion a year due to plant breeding programs that depend heavily on wild strains. However, in recent decades the trend in industrialized agriculture has been to plant ever more extensive fields of ever fewer varieties of these crops. Not only does the expansion of "monocultures" displace traditional varieties, but the lack of diversity makes crops highly susceptible to insects and diseases. For example, in 1970–71 the United States lost 15 percent of its corn crop due to corn blight.

Drugs and Medicines. The development of pharmaceutical drugs and medicines may also depend on derivatives from wild species of plants, microorganisms, fungi, and even animals. As of 1997, 118 of the top 150 prescription drugs used in the United States were based on natural sources: 74% of those on plants, 18% on fungi, 5% on bacteria, and 3% on one vertebrate (snake) species. Nine of the top ten drugs in this list are based on natural plant products. Globally, approximately 80% of the human population relies on traditional medical systems, and about 85% of traditional medicine involves the use of plant extracts. F. GRIFO & J. ROSENTHAL, EDS., BIODIVERSITY AND HUMAN HEALTH (1997); Farnsworth et al., *Medicinal Plants in Therapy*, BULLETIN OF THE WORLD HEALTH ORGANIZATION, 63: 965–81 (1985); P. Principe, *The economic significance of plants and their constituents as drugs*, in H. WAGNER, ET AL., ECONOMIC AND MEDICINAL PLANT RESEARCH, Vol. 3, pages 1–17 (1989). Examples of important drugs derived from wild plants and animals include two alkaloids derived from the rosy periwinkle, a plant found in Madagascar, which are now marketed as cures for Hodgkin's disease and acute lymphocytic leukemia, two deadly cancers. Taxol, a derivative from the bark of the pacific yew tree, is now used as a treatment for ovarian cancer. Even the lowly and unpopular leech produces an anticoagulant called himdin, which now is used to treat rheumatism, hemorrhoids, and other conditions. Future discoveries of similar derivatives are considered quite likely as only 1100 of the 365,000 known species of plants have been examined for medicinal properties.

Intrinsic and Existence Values. To some, speaking of the economic value of wildlife misses the most important reasons for protecting them—that they are living organisms that have an equal right to inhabit, evolve and "develop" on the planet. Animal rights activists argue forcefully that humans should be stewards of wildlife for ethical and moral reasons, that wildlife has an intrinsic value independent of its economic value for humanity. Regardless of whether we accept the concept of animal rights or even intrinsic values, few would dispute that the existence of wildlife adds to the richness of our own life on the planet. These "existence" values may be impossible to quantify precisely but should not be ignored in efforts to protect wildlife and biodiversity.

QUESTIONS AND DISCUSSION

1. To many analysts the most important underlying cause of the loss of biodiversity is the failure to recognize the benefits that wildlife and biodiversity provide or, to put it another way, the costs or loss of benefits that result from the loss of biodiversity. This has led to a growing effort among ecological economists to develop methods for valuing environmental benefits generally, and benefits from wildlife and biodiversity specifically. Monetizing wildlife and biodiversity benefits can enable conservationists to meet economic arguments for exploitation head on with economic arguments for conservation.

Dana Clark & David Downes, What Price Biodiversity?, 5–6 (CIEL, 1995)

Biodiversity has value to humans for a variety of reasons. These include use values (direct use, indirect use, and option values) and non-use values. Direct use values include food, fibers, forest products, pharmaceuticals and other chemicals, and opportunities for education and recreation. Indirect use values include the services provided by biodiversity and the natural ecosystems upon which we depend: water purification and flood control, climate control, regulation of air quality, photosynthesis, pollination, pest control, soil maintenance, decomposition, and disposal of wastes. Option value is the discounted present value of the potential of biodiversity to lead to the development of new goods, such as pharmaceuticals.

Non-use values include aesthetic, intrinsic, ethical, spiritual, existence, and bequest values. Existence value is the satisfaction some individuals derive from knowing that certain species or ecosystems exist even though they may never actually spend money to visit them. Bequest value captures the desire to leave a natural legacy for future generations.

Significant economic value associated with biodiversity can be estimated by tracking revenues from products, such as foods and medicines, extracted from habitats rich in biodiversity. Direct valuation can be used to measure the value of recreational and tourist uses of habitats. Indirect valuation methods, such as surrogate markets, may also be used to measure ecosystem services, such as flood control and water purification.

Existing techniques of economic valuation are, however, incapable of fully evaluating the contributions of biodiversity to human and non-human society. These techniques reflect only economic values of biodiversity, and do not include other values. In addition, economic valuation generally does not capture the important "life support" functions of ecological systems. The shortcomings of purely economic or monetary valuation of biodiversity are illustrated by E.O. Wilson in *The Diversity of Life:*

What then is biodiversity worth? The traditional econometric approach, weighing market price and tourist dollars, will always underestimate the true value of wild species. None has been totally assayed for all of the commercial profit, scientific knowledge, and aesthetic pleasure it can yield. Furthermore, none exists in the wild all by itself. Every species is part of an ecosystem, an expert specialist of its kind, tested relentlessly as it spreads its influence through the food web. To remove it is to entrain changes in other species, raising the populations of some, reducing or even extinguishing others, risking a downward spiral of the larger assemblage.

Although economic valuation of biodiversity is fraught with difficulty and uncertainty, many analysts believe that assigning economic value can help to ensure biodiversity conservation is factored into relevant policy decisions. Initial efforts to evaluate the costs and benefits associated with conservation suggest that maintaining biodiversity and healthy ecosystems is more economically beneficial over the long term than is short-term, destructive exploitation. For example, Robert Costanza, an ecological economist at the University of Maryland, has attempted to determine the economic value of services provided by coastal wetlands in Louisiana. Costanza analyzed the value provided by wetlands in relation to commercial fisheries, fur trapping, recreation, and storm protection. The study concluded that "each acre of coastal wetlands in Louisiana has a present value to society of roughly $2500–$17000 per acre" and that current wetlands management fails to impose true social costs for damage or destruction of wetlands on parties causing the damage. As a result, "the narrow, short-term incentives of those damaging the wetlands are inconsistent with the long-term good of the system."

––––––––––

For more discussion of the difficulty in valuing the environment, *see* Chapter 3. Does the fact that we cannot fully value wildlife and biodiversity suggest that we should not try to value it at all? Do environmentalists gain or lose by trying to engage in discussions of benefits and costs?

2. A thought experiment created by John Holdren illustrates well both the importance of, and the inherent difficulty in, conserving ecosystem services. As ecologist Gretchen Daily explains:

One way to appreciate the nature and value of ecosystem services is to imagine trying to set up a happy, day-to-day life on the moon. Assume for the sake of argument that the moon miraculously already had some of the basic conditions for supporting human life, such as an atmosphere and climate similar to those on earth. After inviting your best friends and packing your prized possessions, a BBQ grill, some do-it-yourself books, the big question would be, Which of the earth's millions of species do you need to take with you?

Tackling the problem systematically, you could first choose from among all the species exploited directly for food, drink, spice, fiber and timber, pharmaceuticals, industrial products (such as waxes, rubber, and oils), and so on. Even being selective, this list could amount to hundreds or even several thousand species. The space ship would be filling up before you'd even begun adding the species crucial to *supporting* those at the top of your list. Which are these unsung heroes? No one knows which—nor even approximately how many— species are required to sustain human life. This means that rather than listing species directly, you would have to list instead the life-support functions required by your lunar colony; then you could guess at the types and numbers of species required to perform each. At a bare minimum, the spaceship would have to carry species capable of supplying a whole suite of ecosystem services that earthlings take for granted. These services include:

- purification of air and water
- mitigation of floods and droughts
- detoxification and decomposition of wastes
- generation and renewal of soil and soil fertility
- pollination of crops and natural vegetation
- control of the vast majority of potential agricultural pests
- dispersal of seeds and translocation of nutrients

- maintenance of biodiversity, from which humanity has derived key elements of its agricultural, medicinal, and industrial enterprise
- protection from the sun's harmful ultraviolet rays
- partial stabilization of climate
- moderation of temperature extremes and the force of winds and waves
- support of diverse human cultures
- providing of aesthetic beauty and intellectual stimulation that lift the human spirit

Armed with this preliminary list of services, you could begin to determine which types and numbers of species are required to perform each. This is no simple task! Let's take the soil fertility case as an example. Soil organisms play important and often unique roles in the circulation of matter in every ecosystem on earth; they are crucial to the chemical conversion and physical transfer of essential nutrients to higher plants, and all larger organisms, including humans, depend on them. The abundance of soil organisms is absolutely staggering: under a square yard of pasture in Denmark, for instance, the soil was found to be inhabited by roughly 50,000 small earthworms and their relatives, 50,000 insects and mites, and nearly 12 million roundworms. And that is not all. A single gram (a pinch) of soil has yielded an estimated 30,000 protozoa, 50,000 algae, 400,000 fungi, and billions of individual bacteria. Which to bring to the moon? Most of these species have never been subjected to even cursory inspection. Yet the sobering fact of the matter is, as Ed Wilson put it: they don't need us, but we need them.

Gretchen Daily, *Introduction: What Are Ecosystem Services?*, in G. DAILY, ED., NATURE'S SERVICES: SOCIETAL DEPENDENCE ON NATURAL ECOSYSTEMS 3–4 (1997).

3. According to the Biodiversity Convention's preamble, Parties signed the Convention "conscious of the importance of biological diversity for evolution...." How is the concept of biodiversity, with its emphasis on variability, related to the process of natural selection and evolution? Do humans have a specific obligation to maintain, or at least a common concern in maintaining, "natural" evolutionary processes? Does the answer depend on whether you view humans (and our impacts) as part of nature or as separate from it? Should we have an interest in providing dolphins— or jellyfish, for that matter—an opportunity to continue evolving?

D. WILDLIFE AND BIODIVERSITY LOSS

We are on the verge of the sixth great wave of extinctions in geologic history. Unlike all the previous mass extinctions, however, this one lies in humankind's control. Evolutionary biologists estimate that the current rate of extinction is 1,000 times the natural rate. Illustrative examples abound: at least two out of every three bird species are in decline worldwide; out of almost 4,400 mammal species, about 11 percent are already "endangered" or "critically endangered," with another 14 percent vulnerable to extinction (including nearly half of all primate species); twenty percent of surveyed reptiles and twenty-five percent of surveyed amphibians currently rank as endangered or vulnerable; one of every eight plant species are threatened or endangered; and studies of fish populations suggest that they may be the worst off—one-third of the world's fish species are already threatened with extinction. A Worldwatch Institute report in State of the World 1998 summarizes these problems.

Table 13.1: Conservation Status of Selected Animal Groups Surveyed

Status	Birds (percent)	Mammals (percent)	Rep/Amph (percent)	Fish (percent)
Not Currently Threatened	80	61	74	70
Nearing Threatened Status	9	14	6	5
Threatened—Vulnerable to Extinction	7	14	12	15
Threatened—In Immediate Danger of Extinction	4	11	8	10

J. Tuxill & C. Bright, *Losing Strands in the Web of Life,* Pages 43–51, in LESTER R. BROWN, ET AL, EDS., STATE OF THE WORLD 1998 (Worldwatch Institute, 1998).

The primary causes of biodiversity loss are described in the following excerpt from the *Global Biodiversity Strategy*:

World Resources Institute et al., GLOBAL BIODIVERSITY STRATEGY, Box 5, at 14–15 (1992)

Habitat Loss and Fragmentation

Relatively undisturbed ecosystems have shrunk dramatically in area over past decades as the human population and resource consumption have grown. Ninety-eight percent of the tropical dry forest along Central America's Pacific coast has disappeared. Thailand lost 22 percent of its mangroves between 1961 and 1985, and virtually none of the remainder is undisturbed. In freshwater ecosystems, dams have destroyed large sections of river and stream habitat. In marine ecosystems, coastal development has wiped out reef and near-shore communities. In tropical forests, a major cause of forest loss is the expansion of marginal agriculture, though in specific regions commercial timber harvest may pose an even greater problem.

Introduced species

Introduced species are responsible for many recorded species extinctions, especially on islands. In these isolated ecosystems, a new predator, competitor, or pathogen can rapidly imperil species that did not co-evolve with the newcomer. In Hawaii, some 86 introduced plant species seriously threaten native biodiversity; one introduced tree species has now displaced more than 30,000 acres of native forest.

Over–exploitation of plant and animal species

Numerous forest, fisheries, and wildlife resources have been over-exploited, sometimes to the point of extinction. Historically, both the great auk and the passenger pigeon succumbed to such pressure, and the Lebanon cedar that once blanketed 500,000 hectares now is found in only a few scattered remnants of forest. Over-exploitation of the Peruvian anchovy between 1958 and 1970 dramatically reduced the population size and the catch. Today, the Sumatran and Javan rhinos have been hunted to the verge of extinction, along with numerous other vertebrates. Many extinctions attend the human harvest of food, but the search for precious commodities—notably, ivory—and for pets, curiosities, and collector's items has also impinged on some populations and obliterated others.

Pollution of soil, water, and atmosphere

Pollutants strain ecosystems and may reduce or eliminate populations of sensitive species. Contamination may reverberate along the food chain: barn owl populations in the United Kingdom have fallen by 10 percent since new rodenticides were introduced, and illegal pesticides used to control crayfish along the boundaries of Spain's Cora Donana National Park in 1985 killed 30,000 birds. Some 43 species have been lost in Poland's Ojcow National Park, due in part to severe air pollution. Soil microbes have also suffered from pollution as industry sheds heavy metals and irrigated agriculture brings on salinization. Acid rain has made thousands of Scandinavian and North American lakes and pools virtually lifeless, and, in combination with other kinds of air pollution, has damaged forests throughout Europe. Marine pollution, particularly from non-point sources, has defiled the Mediterranean and many estuaries and coastal seas throughout the world.

Global climate change

In coming decades, a massive "side-effect" of air pollution—global warming—could play havoc with the world's living organisms. Human-caused increases in "greenhouse gases" in the atmosphere are likely to commit the planet to a global temperature rise of some 1 to 3 degrees Celsius (2 to 5 degrees F) during the next century, with an associated rise in sea level of 1 to 2 meters. Each 1 degree Celsius rise in temperature will displace the limits of tolerance of land species some 125 km towards the poles, or 150 m vertically on the mountains. Many species will not be able to redistribute themselves fast enough to keep up with the projected changes, and considerable alterations in ecosystem structure and function are likely. In the United States rising seas in the next century will cover the entire habitat of at least 80 species already at risk of extinction. Many of the world's islands would be completely submerged by the ocean. And protected areas themselves will be placed under stress as environmental conditions deteriorate and suitable habitat for their species cannot be found in the disturbed land surrounding them. [See Chapter 10, pages 609–74, discussing climate change. Ozone depletion, too, may be having substantial impact on biodiversity, particularly on amphibians. See Chapter 10, 544–608, discussing ozone depletion.]

Industrial Agriculture and Forestry

Until this century, farmers and pastoralists bred and maintained a tremendous diversity of crop and livestock varieties around the world. But on-farm biodiversity is shrinking fast thanks to modern plant-breeding programs and the resulting productivity gains achieved by planting comparatively fewer varieties of crops that respond better to water, fertilizers, and pesticides. Similar trends are transforming diverse forest ecosystems into high-yielding monocultural tree plantations—some of which now resemble a field of maize as much as a natural forest—and even fewer tree genes than crop genes have been preserved off-site as an insurance policy against disease and pests.

Often many factors can come into play at the same time to threaten biodiversity. The overall effect of these factors can lead to general and steep declines in whole categories of biodiversity. Consider the global decline of frogs.

When was the last time you saw a frog? Frogs, toads and salamanders were once abundant. Now they have all but disappeared from many areas. Scientists have documented a worldwide decline in amphibians—unrelated populations subject to different pressures around the globe are experiencing staggering losses. The reasons for the decline of frogs and other amphibians parallel the causes of biodiversity decline generally. Destruction of wetlands results in a loss of breeding pools and other essential riparian habitats; habitat fragmentation disrupts migration and introduces threats (such as roads); and habitat impairment through chemical contamination threatens both amphibians and the aquatic ecosystems on which they depend. Wild frogs are also overharvested for consumption (frog legs) and for sale in pet shops. They are being destroyed by the introduction of alien species such as brook trout in mountain lakes. They are also susceptible to ecological forces such as climate change, ozone depletion, acid rain, and chemical contamination generally of the environment. In December 1997, for example, a scientific study confirmed that increases in UV–B radiation due to ozone depletion is probably a significant cause of the decline of frog populations in the Pacific Northwest. Frogs first evolved approximately 200 million years ago. They have weathered several ecological transitions and have survived the two most recent extinction crises (the last extinction crisis, which occurred 66 million years ago, killed the dinosaurs). Frogs are so-called "sentinel species" warning of what the future decline in environmental quality may mean for all life on Earth. As Emily Yoffe wrote: "Frogs are living environmental assayers, moving over their life cycles from water to land, from plant-eater to insect-eater, covered only by a permeable skin that offers little shield from the outside world." In short, frogs are the amphibian equivalent of a canary in a coal mine, warning of impending ecological disaster.

Adapted from Dana Clark & David Downes, *What Value Biodiversity*; *see also* LESTER BROWN, ET AL., VITAL SIGNS 1995, at 120–21 (1995); KATHRYN PHILLIPS, TRACKING THE VANISHING FROGS 28 (1994); Emily Yoffe, *Silence of the Frogs*, N.Y. TIMES MAGAZINE, Dec. 13, 1992, at 36.

E.   SUSTAINABLE USE V. PRESERVATION

One of the most long-standing and important controversies relating to wildlife conservation, at both the international and national levels, is the extent to which we should exploit wildlife for human consumption rather than preserve it. How do we strike the appropriate balance between exploitation and conservation? This tension underlies virtually every international wildlife or biodiversity regime. The continuing debate over the ban on international trade in elephant ivory under CITES, for example, is in many respects a debate over whether elephants should ever be killed for something as unnecessary as ivory. But the debate is also over what would be the best strategy for the long-term conservation of stable elephant populations in Africa. By providing economic benefit to local communities through controlled ivory sales, some environmentalists believe that the elephant is more likely to be protected over the long-term. Other environmentalists believe that the ban on international trade in ivory was the primary reason for recent increases in elephant populations and should be continued.

Early treaties only rarely addressed wildlife conservation, emphasizing instead the allocation of wildlife resources between different interested States. As environmental concerns grew, many wildlife treaties blended their interest in allocating rights of exploitation between States to attempting to achieve a sustainable level of exploitation, known as "sustainable yield." In many instances, however, the effort to achieve a sustainable yield of wildlife has not been successful. Sometimes, the international treaties have come too late to stabilize populations at a level that could allow a sustainable yield. In others, scientific understanding has not been sufficient to allow an accurate estimate of a sustainable level of harvesting. In addition, even when scientists may have succeeded in setting a reasonable limit, political pressures to exploit have caused policymakers to set yields at unsustainable levels. Given the resulting decline in population levels, environmentalists now call for total bans on the commercial exploitation of many endangered species.

Complicating the debate even further is the fervent belief of animal rights activists and others that wildlife should be respected equally as human life, and that no exploitation of wildlife should be allowed. Although an important position within the environmental movement, it has rarely found expression in international wildlife law. Occasionally, however—for example with respect to whales or elephants—ethical or moral arguments have superceded the search for scientific consensus regarding what levels of exploitation could be allowed without threatening the future survival of the species.

In most cases, however, science plays a key role in international wildlife agreements. Much uncertainty remains regarding sustainable levels of exploitation. In this regard, the question is not so much *whether* to harvest or exploit wildlife but *how* to ensure that such use is sustainable over the long-term. For many decades, "maximum sustainable yield" has been the standard used in guiding international and national wildlife laws, particularly for marine species and fisheries. Inherent in the concept of maximum sustainable yield, however, is a tension between maintaining the long-term viability of the stock while simultaneously allowing for maximum possible annual harvest or "offtake." This approach assumes that we can pinpoint with some confidence the exact level above which harvesting would not be sustainable. As the following excerpt suggests, in practice the maximum sustained yield approach has not successfully protected most wildlife populations. As a result, there is widespread skepticism about our ability to manage the exploitation of wildlife sustainably.

C. Freese, Harvesting Wild Species: Implications for Biodiversity Conservation, 1–36 (1997)

The commercial, consumptive use of wild species is a focal point for much of the current debate regarding the link between sustainable development and biodiversity conservation. More specifically, it is at the center of two often conflicting points of view regarding the best strategy for future conservation efforts. One embraces the "use it or lose it" dictum and the other sees the for-profit motive leading inevitably to overexploitation and biotic impoverishment.

At stake in this debate is how society will manage what is still a major portion of the Earth's land and water surface which is not yet fully converted to urbanization and domestic forms of production or which is securely in protected areas. One view is that more progress will be made toward maintaining biodiversity on this remaining portion by pushing to include a major part of it in fully protected area status. This view is largely based on the premise that commercial use of wild species in wildlands (the term as used here includes natural aquatic ecosystems) has not yet been broadly demonstrated as a sustainable land-use option that maintains biodiversity and other wildland values such as "wilderness," but rather that it has generally led to biotic impoverishment. Thus we must depend on fully protected areas and other forms of non-consumptive use as the principal means for maintaining biodiversity and wildland values.

The "use it or lose it" view advocates that, compared to developing more protected areas, more wildlands and biodiversity will be conserved by making use of the living resources in those wildlands that are not strictly protected. A major part of such use has traditionally been consumptive use, wherein the organism or its parts are harvested (killed or removed from the population). The logic behind this proposition is that revenues generated by the commercial, consumptive use of wild species will provide economic incentives for sound management of the harvested population(s). This in turn implies that the target population's habitat will be protected, thereby benefitting the broader goals of biodiversity conservation. . . . Advocates of this approach do not necessarily believe that the national parks approach has failed, but rather that significant additional conservation gains using that approach are not possible in much of the world.

The above may unfairly suggest a highly polarized set of views in the conservation community. Most conservationists would probably contend that the best strategy is a mixture of these two approaches, with one or the other to be favored depending on the circumstances. Regardless of what conservationists think, much of the world depends on wild species for an array of products, whether for food, fiber, or medicine. Thus, in may cases, the question is not whether to use wild species, but rather how to move from a system of use that is clearly not sustainable toward one that is better.* * *

The Sustainability of Commercial, Consumptive Use: Overview

Skepticism about the "use it or lose it" strategy is understandable. During the last two hundred years, as the human population has continued to grow exponentially and technology for harvesting wild species and their products has advanced at an even faster rate, the majority of wild species resources for which any significant market exists have been overexploited and their ecosystems highly altered and generally simplified. While the perverse effects of economic forces on exploitation of species and habitats are widely evident, well-documented examples of a positive linkage between commercial use and biodiversity conservation have been limited. Moreover, concerns have been raised about the tradeoffs that consumptive use implies for biodiversity, even if the offtake [i.e., the amount harvested] is sustainable.

Nothing illustrates this trend better than timber harvesting, beginning two hundred years ago with the overexploitation of temperate forests, and more recently tropical forests, particularly in Southeast Asia. Marine fisheries have fared no better, as stocks of one species after another have been depleted throughout the world, with attendant large losses and alterations of biodiversity and ecosystem structure in many coastal marine waters. Similar problems caused by commercial use can be cited for other groups of organisms, from parrots and river turtles to palm heart and rattan.

Perhaps no form of consumptive use, however, has had more widespread impoverishing effects on native biota than overgrazing by domestic livestock of native grasslands. The United Nations Environment Program estimates that 73 percent of the world's 3.3 billion hectares (ha) of dry rangeland are at least moderately desertified, largely due to overgrazing.

Despite this dismal record, there are examples of consumptive use where at least the offtake has been sustainable. One of the most sustainable forms during this century, under varying degrees of commercialization, has been sport hunting of large game, particularly cervids [i.e. large herbivores such as deer and antelope], in North America and Europe. Populations of all cervids except the caribou have increased since 1900, and caribou numbers are now increasing also. Similarly, offtake from sport hunting and commercial culling of large game in some regions of southern Africa also appears to be sustainable. While hunting or culling large herbivores may occasionally be a useful biodiversity management tool, offtake and management resulting from the big game hunting market may also have negative consequences for biodiversity.

Uncertainty, Variability and Scale

Natural systems are much less stable than is generally believed over both the short term (measured in years or decades) and long term (measured in centuries or millennia), and we are not yet very good at predicting when, why, how, and at what rate changes in populations and ecosystems occur. The result is that one year's abundant and highly harvestable population may, without warning, drop to low and unharvestable levels a year or two hence. A wide array of economically important wild species resources show such boom-and-bust cycles, from seed production of tropical trees to marine fish stocks. Further, what we perceive to be a static "natural" diversity and ecosystem structure is often, in fact, one stage in a long transition or cycling from one ecosystem configuration to another due to both anthropogenic and nonanthropogenic forces.

Uncertainty emerges both from inherent stochasticity [i.e., random fluctuations] in ecosystems and from our incomplete knowledge of how they work and how they respond to human intervention. Our recognition that ecosystem and population fluctuations are greater and less deterministic than we once thought raises several management issues and suggests that a virtually universal problem with management of most wild species is the assumption by biologists and managers that "given enough research, exact numbers can be determined for population size, components of population dynamics, and the responses of populations to given harvest levels." However, they note, "because of the effects of environmental uncertainty, exact or correct numbers are rarely if ever possible to obtain, and the result is (1) wrong numbers and harvest levels are recommended, or (2) biologists and managers delay recommendations until they have 'more information.' The latter case leads decision makers to set their own limits, based on economic or political considerations instead of scientific ones. This almost always leads to . . . degradation of the resource." * * *

Species Life Histories and Risks of Overexploitation

Management must be sensitive to those life history characteristics of individual species that make them susceptible to overharvest and population decline, as well as to the broader ecosystem effects of management programs. This requires a more precautionary approach to the management of many species. Long-lived, slow-reproducing species, such as whales, sharks, elephants, and primates, may be particularly vulnerable to overharvesting. In some cases, whole communities of organisms, such as those found in deep-sea habitats, may be characterized by low reproductive capacities and thus may be particularly vulnerable to overharvesting. The large population declines caused by hunting of such species, compared to species with higher reproductive rates, are well demonstrated in both African and neotropical forest wildlife. However, to the extent that slow-reproducing species exhibit density-dependent reproductive strategies, managers should be better able to predict population responses to offtake and thus harvest protocols should be easier to design than for species that are more density independent. The difficulty lies in the implementation— the maintenance of very low harvest levels. An examination of fisheries, [for example] suggests that longer-lived species "retain a resilience to catastrophes that is not available to the short-lived species." They caution, however, that though short-lived species are capable of producing high sustainable yields, they "can be particularly vulnerable to a combination of high exploitation and occasional environmental events that devastate the spawning stock."

The determination of sustainable harvest levels is perhaps least understood where some part of the organism, rather than the organism itself, is harvested. Because the effects on survivorship and reproduction in the population are less direct, changes are difficult to monitor and detect. Nontimber forest products, such as fruits and latex, are most prominent in this category. [For example,] the collection of commercial quantities of fruits and seeds can cause changes in the structure and dynamics of a tree population and, if uncontrolled, can result in its gradual extinction. * * *

Effects of Biodiversity on Ecosystem Function

Closely linked to our understanding of uncertainty and variability are questions regarding the link between biodiversity and ecosystem functions. How much ecological redundancy is there among species in a given ecosystem? More precisely, what components of biodiversity must be maintained in the process of optimizing production of economically important species? At what point does directing management toward production and offtake of these species begin to compromise key ecological functions? * * *

Not all species are created equal when it comes to ecological processes. The keystone species concept suggests that some species are particularly important for maintaining certain ecological processes or the species composition of a community. Keystone species, from elephants to nitrogen-fixing fungi, should receive special attention when managing an ecosystem for the consumption use of select species. * * *

Biodiversity may be particularly important in conferring stability and resilience to perturbations in some ecosystems, and ecosystems that lack their full complement of species may be subject to invasion and disruption by other species. Indeed, the most important argument for maintaining species diversity when managing for wild species commodities may be to maintain ecosystem resilience and adaptability to infrequent but large perturbations and long-term environmental change. * * *

Biodiversity Standards and Monitoring

An overarching question regarding specialization and biodiversity is what trade-offs, if any, does sustainable offtake (as opposed to obvious overexploitation) imply for biodiversity? More broadly, if the goal of ecosystem management is to meet a diversity of "environmental, economic, and social benefits," how can we ensure that consumptive use does not degrade ecosystem components that provide these diverse benefits? These questions have received little attention, even in some of the most common and best-studied wild species uses, such as salmon management, waterfowl management, and temperate forest management.

Perhaps the most problematic part of this question from the perspective of biodiversity conservation is the search for standards of "naturalness," including natural fluctuations and change, against which to measure human-induced change, whether at the ecosystem or genetic level. In ecosystem management this elusive goal has been referred to as "native ecosystem integrity." Conservationists have done little to define such standards or benchmarks, and few efforts have been undertaken to monitor such change. The task is not easy. The more we learn about both intrinsic change in ecosystems and historic human impacts on previously labeled "pristine" ecosystems, the more difficult it is to define such standards in terms of biodiversity conservation objectives. Most terrestrial ecosystems have long been altered by human influence. In reviewing marine systems, [one analyst concluded] ... that "all efforts to evaluate bycatch and environmental effects of heavy fishing on natural systems are too late because most sensitive species have long been impacted, leaving no concept of natural relationships or patterns." * * *

The Paradox of Consumptive Use in Biodiversity Conservation

Commercial, consumptive use presents the proverbial double-edged sword for conservationists. If well managed, it can be a tool for nature conservation; if poorly managed, it can readily lead to overexploitation and biotic impoverishment. Even if relatively well managed, however, it is unwise to expect consumptive use to shoulder the full burden for biodiversity conservation. First, overreliance on consumptive use values alone, while ignoring other biodiversity-based values, may fail to offset the opportunity costs of alternative uses of the land. Second, even if consumptive use revenues do offset such opportunity costs, specialization in consumptive use products may entail substantial trade-offs in biodiversity in the wildland under management. * * *

We will fail to stem the tide of biotic degradation if the consumptive use values of biodiversity are not complemented by nonconsumptive values in decision making. To do so, we must identify the array of stakeholders who now enjoy a free ride, often on the back of consumptive uses that currently provide the justification for maintaining wild species and wildlands. We are quick to point the finger at those who are most visible—the illegal poacher or fisher—among the free riders. However, the individual who opts to buy the less-expensive tropical hardwood chair that came from a mined forest rather than pay the premimum for one from a well-managed forest is as much a free rider as the clandestine logger. So is the individual who enjoys nature programs on television, who benefits from medicines derived from wild species, or who through ecological research seeks advancement in academia, but who contributes little or nothing (whether in money, votes, or other means of influence) toward conserving biodiversity and wildlands. Greater attention should be given to identifying and educating these more subtle free riders about their stakeholder interests and responsibilities.

In many cases, however, stakeholders may legitimately view the so-called free ride as more a "right" for which they should not have to pay. Clean air and water may be the most universal examples, but others may place biodiversity in this same category. Where the benefits from biodiversity and wildland are broadly perceived as a public right, and where transfer payments between those who value biodiversity and those who bear the cost of maintaining it are not possible, then governments or other higher authorities must play a strong role in representing and protecting societal interests. Yet governments are apt to exercise this role only when society demands it, and thus the responsibility falls back on those who value biodiversity and recognize its societal benefits to pay their dues via votes, influence, education, and other means. For some members of society, however, particularly for the rural poor that depend on wildland resources but are marginalized from the political process, neither monetary nor nonmonetary avenues for giving voice to their interests are readily available.

Given that areas of great biodiversity value are often used and inhabited by the rural poor, incorporating their interests within a broader framework of biodiversity conservation is crucial.

Thus we must rely on greater responsibility by a broad spectrum of stake holders to help bear the costs of biodiversity conservation. Ecologically sustainable resource use is but one important mechanism among many for bearing those costs. But where market mechanisms fall short, as they often will, we must look to public authorities to play a strong role in protecting societal interests if biodiversity is not to be lost to economic specialization, resource homogenization, and alternative land uses.

―――――――

As discussed above, even where we decide to manage sustainable use of wildlife, our success is severely limited by difficulties in identifying the appropriate level of harvest to achieve sustainability. As part of the effort to improve the sustainable management of wildlife species, much research has gone into developing guidelines and indicators for sustainable use. The International Union for the Conservation of Nature (IUCN), which is an international organization comprised of over 800 governmental wildlife agencies and nongovernmental organizations, established a set of *Guidelines for the Ecological Sustainability of Nonconsumptive and Consumptive Uses of Wild Species*. These *Guidelines* reflect a comprehensive effort to operationalize the concept of sustainable use.

Note by the Director General on Guidelines for the Ecological Sustainability of Nonconsumptive and Consumptive Uses of Wild Species, **Annex 1, IUCN Gen. Ass. Paper, G.A./19/94/3 (1994)**

7. [Our] ... understanding of sustainability has changed over the past 30 years; and "sustainable use" has been interpreted in a number of ways. In these guidelines, "sustainable use" means use that does not reduce the future use potential, or impair the long-term viability, of either the species being used or other species; and is compatible with maintenance of the long-term viability of supporting and dependent ecosystems. "Sustainability" may involve ecological, economic, and social factors, but in this document refers only to ecological sustainability.

8. The purpose of these guidelines is to provide a working definition of sustainable use, and guidance on how to increase the probability that a particular use is sustainable. The matter of probability must be stressed. It is much more difficult to demonstrate that a use is sustainable than it is to show that it does not endanger the species' survival. The intention is neither to condemn nor encourage uses of wild species, but to help ensure that any uses are likely to be sustainable. If wild species are used, then these guidelines should apply. * * *

9. Respect for nature is fundamental to the concepts of sustainable use. It is recognized that ethical perceptions of uses and types of use vary among countries and cultures. Therefore, in certain cases ecologically sustainable uses may be precluded on ethical and other grounds.

10. It is recognized that nature does not exist exclusively for human use but that it has its own intrinsic value. Also, not all species should be regarded as

being available for human use. Therefore, these guidelines are based on the ethical context outlined below:

(a) People should conduct their activities with respect for the viability of wild species and the integrity of natural systems.

(b) There should be recognition of individual and collective responsibility for the commons of nature.

(c) People should seek an equity of benefits among the present generation and between the present and future generations.

(d) People have a right to the resources needed for a decent standard of living, which may include deriving economic, scientific, aesthetic or other benefits from some wild species, provided they do so sustainably.

(e) People have the responsibility to ensure that their uses of wild species are sustainable and non-wasteful.

(f) People should protect wild animals from cruelty and avoidable suffering. * * *

12.   The guidelines provide Criteria and Requirements. The Criteria define conditions to be met if a use of a wild species is to be ecologically sustainable. A use that does not meet the Criteria is unlikely to be sustainable over the long term. The Requirements set out basic operational conditions necessary to fulfill the Criteria.

13.   Together, the Criteria and Requirements are intended to guide policies, laws and administrative procedures aimed at ensuring that any uses of wild species are sustainable and that the affected species and their supporting ecosystems are conserved. They are intended to be. used by governments, resource users, communities, businesses, conservation organizations, research institutions, development banks, aid agencies and others that share this aim.

Criteria for Sustainable Use

19.   A use of a wild species is likely to be sustainable if:

(a) It does not reduce the future use potential of the target population or impair its long-term viability;

(b) it is compatible with maintenance of the long-term viability of supporting and dependent ecosystems;

(c) it does not reduce the future use potential or impair the long-term viability of other species.

* * *

Requirements for Fulfilling the Criteria

29.   These Requirements do not apply to uses whose impacts are obviously inconsequential.

30.   The Requirements for making uses sustainable are:

(a) Information on the target population and its associated ecosystems, on current and proposed uses, and on social and economic factors affecting them.

(b) A management system that can respond rapidly to changing conditions or better information.

(c) A supportive and effective legal framework.

(d) Social or economic incentives for the people living with the target population or its supporting ecosystems to conserve them.

(e) Acceptance of the precautionary principle and safeguards to ensure the survival of wild species, populations and supporting ecosystems. * * *

QUESTIONS AND DISCUSSION

1. In light of the concerns expressed in the excerpt from *Harvesting Wildlife,* do you think we can achieve sustainable management of wildlife harvesting? Do the *IUCN Guidelines* provide a useful model or are they too vague?

2. The *IUCN Guidelines* do recognize that ethical and moral issues may be central to questions about how we treat wildlife and biodiversity. Would the approach in paragraphs 9–10 of the Guidelines be acceptable to the animal rights groups?

3. Much uncertainty surrounds wildlife conservation efforts. As discussed in Chapter 7, page 405, the precautionary principle is a general concept in international environmental law that provides guidance for making decisions in the face of scientific uncertainty. Article 11(b) of the 1982 *World Charter for Nature,* endorsed in a U.N. General Assembly Resolution by most countries (though opposed by the United States), applied the precautionary principle to the conservation of nature: "Activities which are likely to pose a significant risk to nature shall be preceded by an exhaustive examination; their proponents shall demonstrate that expected benefits outweigh potential damage to nature, and where potential adverse effects are not fully understood, the activities should not proceed." Similarly, the Biodiversity Convention's preamble notes that: "where there is a threat of significant reduction or loss of biological diversity, lack of full scientific certainty should not be used as a reason for postponing measures to avoid or minimize such a threat." Applying the precautionary principle in specific circumstances, however, still remains a critical challenge for international wildlife and biodiversity law. The IUCN Guidelines endorse the precautionary principle for informing decisions regarding sustainable use:

> 50. The precautionary principle requires approaching questions of sustainability of use with the commitment to act in the way least likely to impair the viability of the species or ecosystem. This may result in decisions not to use. This precautionary principle is especially important when estimating sustainable use levels. Use levels should always be cautious and well within the calculated capacity of the target population and its supporting ecosystems. Target populations and supporting ecosystems may need to be safeguarded by management regimes that include the designation of protected areas.

> 51. In applying the precautionary principle, it is important to consider those elements of the ecosystem affected by the use that are most vulnerable to long-term or irreversible damage. In some instances, it may be the target population. In others—for example, the harvesting of animals in drought prone areas—it may be the animals' habitat. In the former case, the precautionary principle may be satisfied by a low rate of harvest. In the latter case, it may be satisfied by a higher rate of harvest that protects the habitat from being degraded (for example, by overgrazing).

> 52. Methods of estimating sustainable use levels, and their likely range of error, should be thoroughly investigated and documented in the management plan. Use levels should be set with sufficient room to:

>> a. Accommodate Potential Negative Effects Of Miscalculation, Unforeseen Factors Or Unpredictable Events (Such As Disease, Natural Disasters, Drought).

b.   Allow For Uncertainty And Lack Of Information About The Target Population And Its Supporting Ecosystems, And The Impact Of The Use On Associated Species And Ecosystems.

53.   For example, in the case of consumptive uses, a recommended general rule is that the harvest rate should usually be half or less than half of the intrinsic rate of increase of the population.

Do the IUCN Guidelines implement the precautionary principle adequately? As you read the various conventions in this Chapter, consider whether and how the precautionary principle is reflected in specific efforts to conserve biodiversity.

SECTION II.   THE BIODIVERSITY CONVENTION

A.   THE NEGOTIATING PROCESS

As described in Section I of this Chapter, by the early 1980's independent organizations and scientists had begun to promote the idea of a global convention to conserve biodiversity. An initial effort led by the IUCN and Zaire resulted in the 1982 passage by the U.N. General Assembly of the World Charter on Nature, partly in honor of the ten-year anniversary of the Stockholm Conference. The World Charter remains one of the most progressive and innovative international statements of humanity's obligations to the natural world. Despite its mandatory language, however, the World Charter is a soft law instrument with no independent binding force. Although the World Charter did help to shape future negotiations much of its vision has not carried through to more recent instruments.

IUCN launched a second initiative from 1984 to 1989 when it developed and revised a set of draft articles to be included in a proposed biodiversity treaty. The IUCN draft articles concentrated on global action needed to conserve biodiversity, including a focus on *in situ* conservation, as well as detailed recommendations for a financial mechanism. Ultimately the governments rejected the IUCN draft as a basis for negotiating a biodiversity treaty, but the IUCN effort was still important for building support for biodiversity conservation.

Beginning in 1987, UNEP established a working group to consider "the desirability and possible form of an umbrella convention to rationalize current activities in this field and to address other areas which might fall under such a convention." UNEP G.C. Res. 14/26 (1987). The original purpose of such an "umbrella" convention was to provide a coherent framework for the various international wildlife and habitat conventions. Consolidating the existing treaties was soon considered to be politically too difficult, but the working group did support the need for a new treaty on biodiversity conservation that reflected existing conventions.

It also became apparent during the working group that many States, particularly in the South, were not going to accept a convention that focused only on biodiversity conservation. Rather, the convention would have to be broad enough to address issues of the sustainable use of biodiversity and biotechnology. In fact, the convention's scope would broaden steadily until it addressed virtually all aspects of biodiversity.

The formal negotiations began in 1991 when the UNEP working group was reconstituted as the Intergovernmental Negotiating Committee for a Convention on Biological Diversity. Ultimately the negotiations were folded into the preparations for UNCED, with the hope that the Convention could be opened for signature at Rio in June, 1992. The pressure to reach agreement before Rio had two effects. On the one hand, it led countries to make compromises and forced an agreement sooner than otherwise would have been the case. On the other hand, negotiations were rushed, resulting in a final text that is sometimes contradictory and often unclear. The final text was essentially completed on the last day at the last preparatory committee (PrepCom) meeting on May 22, 1992, and opened for signature two weeks later at UNCED. The Convention was signed by almost every country at UNCED, and entered into force just eighteen months later on December 29, 1993. *See* Convention on Biological Diversity, June 2, 1992, U.N. Doc. DPI/130/7 (1992), *reprinted in* 31 I.L.M. 818 (1992).

The major hold-out regarding the Biodiversity Convention has been the United States. Even though the United States had registered no complaints with the text as reported out of the May, 1992 PrepCom meeting, EPA Administrator Reilly announced on arriving at UNCED that the United States would not sign the agreement. Initially Reilly identified ongoing disagreement over the financial mechanism as the reason for U.S. opposition, but later the United States also objected to the Convention's treatment of intellectual property rights, the requirements to share benefits and technology gained from biological resources, and even the Convention's limited requirements for domestic conservation. The United States would be the only industrialized country not to sign the Biodiversity Convention at Rio. See Chapter 4, page 186, discussing the Earth Summit. President Clinton signed the Convention soon after entering office in 1992, but as of 2001 the Senate has refused to give its advice and consent to ratification, in spite of the support of most pharmaceutical and biotechnology companies as well as environmental organizations.

B. OVERVIEW OF THE CONVENTION

Unlike previous wildlife treaties, the Biodiversity Convention was not aimed specifically at migratory wildlife nor was it aimed at the international trade of wildlife. Biodiversity certainly includes migratory species but it also includes trees, ants, snails and other animals that do not migrate beyond the boundaries of one country. These resources had historically been considered wholly within a State's sovereignty and not subject to international policymaking. Among the most difficult issues facing the drafters was the international status of biodiversity—that is, the justification for taking international action with respect to biodiversity conservation.

As negotiations began over the Biodiversity Convention, some parties sought to have biodiversity deemed a "common heritage of humankind." Some precedent existed for use of the common heritage principle; the 1983 FAO International Undertaking on Plant Genetic Resources stated that "plant genetic resources are a heritage of mankind to be preserved, and to be freely available for use, for the benefit of present and future generations." Report of the Conference of the FAO, U.N. Food and Agriculture Organization, 22d Sess., U.N. Doc. No. C 83/Rep. (1983) (Rome, 5–23 Nov. 1983). This was generally supported by industrialized countries, who wanted to ensure open and free access to the gene banks and other biological resources taken from the South. In the biodiversity negotiations, however, both the North and South were troubled by application of the common heritage principle. Developing countries did not want common heritage applied to all biodiversity, because the concept implies a requirement to allow all States free access to the resource. For their part, industrialized countries voiced concern that the common heritage principle if applied too far might require benefit sharing or open transfers of technology derived from biodiversity. *See* Chapter 7, p. 389.

Given the ambivalence towards the concept of common heritage, the negotiators needed to come up with a different conceptual justification for international restrictions of State sovereignty with respect to biodiversity conservation. Ultimately, the negotiators agreed that conservation of *biological diversity* was a "common concern of humankind," which although lacking somewhat in clarity almost certainly implied less international infringement on sovereignty than did common heritage. Moreover, *biological resources* (i.e. the economically valuable components of biodiversity) were affirmed as being subject to a State's sovereignty. In this way, an uneasy compromise was reached between the North's interests in conservation and the South's interest in benefiting from the biological resources within their borders.

This balance is memorialized in the Preamble to the Convention. Although not legally binding, the Preamble nonetheless sets forth the broad concerns and motivations of the Parties. It is thus important for defining and interpreting the entire Convention.

In reading the following excerpt from the Preamble, consider how the negotiations emphasized many of the principles identified in Chapter 6 as important for sustainable development, including the precautionary principle, international equity and sustainable use. The emphasis on sustainable use was particularly controversial as it reflected the Convention's heavy emphasis on the value of biodiversity to humans. Indeed, only in one paragraph does the Preamble recognize that biodiversity may have some "intrinsic" value.

Convention on Biological Diversity, U.N. Doc. DPI/130/7, June 2, 1992, *reprinted in* 31 I.L.M. 818 (1992)

Preamble

The Parties to the Convention:

Conscious of the intrinsic value of biological diversity and of the ecological, genetic, social, economic, scientific, educational, cultural, recreational and aesthetic values of biological diversity and its components,

Conscious also of the importance of biological diversity for evolution and for maintaining life sustaining systems of the biosphere,

Affirming that the conservation of biological diversity is a common concern of humankind,

Reaffirming that States have sovereign rights over their own biological resources,

Reaffirming also that States are responsible for conserving their biological diversity and for using their biological resources in a sustainable manner, * * *

Noting that it is vital to anticipate, prevent and attack the causes of significant. reduction or loss of biological diversity at source,

Noting also that where there is a threat of significant reduction or loss of biological diversity, lack of full scientific certainty should not be used as a reason for postponing measures to avoid or minimize such a threat, * * *

Determined to conserve and sustainably use biological diversity for the benefit of present and future generations,

Aware that conservation and sustainable use of biological diversity is of critical importance for meeting the food, health and other needs of the growing world population, for which purpose access to and sharing of both genetic resources and technologies are essential,

Desiring to enhance and complement existing international arrangements for the conservation of biological diversity and sustainable use of its components, and

Have agreed as follows:

Article 1

The objectives of this Convention, to be pursued in accordance with its relevant provisions, are the conservation of biological diversity, the sustainable use of its components and the fair and equitable sharing of the benefits arising out of the utilization of genetic resources, including by appropriate access to genetic resources and by appropriate transfer of relevant technologies, taking into account all rights over those resources and to technologies, and by appropriate funding.

The Convention's objectives found in Article 1 clearly reflect a balance between the North and South, providing something for everyone. The North received their objective of biodiversity conservation, but this objective is balanced with the South's emphasis on the sustainable use of biological resources, benefit-sharing with respect to biotechnologies, and new financial support. Article 1 affirms that these are co-equal and integrated goals. To meet these goals, the Convention adopts three broad strategies: promoting biodiversity conservation and sustainable use through national law and policy, creating an international institutional structure to support implementation and achievement of the Convention's three objectives; and establishing a set of principles for the international exchange of genetic resources and the biotechnologies derived from them.

QUESTIONS AND DISCUSSION

1. Before reading on, familiarize yourself with the entire Biodiversity Convention, reprinted in the *Treaty Supplement*. What subject matters are addressed by the

Convention? What principles identified in Chapter 7 can be found throughout the Convention? What role do these principles play?

2.   The Convention's preamble affirms that the conservation of *biodiversity* is a common concern and two clauses later reaffirms that States have sovereignty over their *biological resources*. Is the inherent tension between the concepts of common concern and state sovereignty heightened or reduced by the Convention's respective definitions of biodiversity and biological resources?

> "Biological diversity" means the variability among living organisms from all sources including, inter alia, terrestrial, marine and other aquatic ecosystems and the ecological complexes of which they are part; this includes diversity within species, between species and of ecosystems.

> "Biological resources" includes genetic resources, organisms or parts thereof, populations, or any other biotic component of ecosystems with actual or potential use or value for humanity.

What is the purpose in distinguishing between biodiversity and those components of biodiversity that have "actual or potential use or value for humanity." Isn't part of the justification for saving all biodiversity that it all has value or at least potential value? If that is the case, does the distinction have any real meaning? What parts of biological diversity should not be treated as "biological resources" in the Convention?

The same distinction based on the economic value of the resources separates "genetic material" from "genetic resources." Under Article 2 of the Convention:

> "Genetic material" means any material of plant, animal, microbial or other origin containing functional units of heredity.

> "Genetic resources" means genetic material of actual or potential value.

Again, what distinction is being drawn by focusing on "actual or potential value"? Doesn't all genetic material have actual or potential value to humanity? Doesn't the Convention preamble's reference to the intrinsic value of biodiversity as well as the process of evolution suggest that all biodiversity has value? In reading the substantive provisions of the Convention, be careful to understand which category is being addressed. Biodiversity and biological resources, for example, are not treated the same in the Convention.

C.   ENCOURAGING NATIONAL CONSERVATION OF BIODIVERSITY

Although the conservation of biodiversity is recognized as a common concern of international society in the Convention, the primary rights and responsibilities regarding biodiversity conservation remain at the national level. The Biodiversity Convention's provisions regarding national implementation and compliance are relatively straight-forward and not particularly inspiring. The substantive provisions of the Convention, at least with respect to conservation of biodiversity, are mostly conditioned with language that gives countries significant leeway in applying the Convention. Thus, for example, a Party is only required to meet the various standards "in accordance with its particular conditions and capacity" or "as far as possible and as appropriate." On the other hand, this conditional language is what has allowed so many countries to adopt the Convention so quickly.

Perhaps the most practical aspect of the Convention is its requirement to create a national strategy, plan or program for conserving biodiversity and to integrate biodiversity conservation into economic planning. Article 6. The use of biodiversity strategies and plans is intended to encourage countries to gather accurate and comprehensive information about the opportunities for, and threats to, biodiversity conservation. Article 7. Armed with this information, countries must develop a national biodiversity plan, which is designed to set clear objectives and priorities for biodiversity conservation in the country. While creating the plan, countries are supposed to evaluate their existing policy and institutional framework to ensure that biodiversity conservation is given sufficient priority.

National biodiversity plans have been developed by dozens of countries since passage of the Biodiversity Convention. Many, although not all, of these plans have been developed with widespread participation among various stakeholders. They have been effective to some extent in their goal of increasing the visibility of and political will for biodiversity conservation, as well as facilitating the coordination of international assistance and of interagency activities within a country.

The plans are supposed to reflect the conservation measures identified in the Convention. *See, e.g.,* Articles 8 to 10. The Convention's list of measures provides at least some general guidance regarding national conservation efforts. For example, the negotiators faced the important question of whether conservation of biodiversity in zoos, gene banks or other *ex situ* collections should be considered equal to conservation efforts that retained biodiversity components in their natural habitats (i.e. *in situ* conservation). Ultimately the chapeau to Article 9, which promotes *ex situ* conservation, would emphasize that such measures should be thought of as "complementary to" *in situ* conservation efforts, thus suggesting that priority should be given to conservation in nature.

Among the list of measures that should be taken for *in situ* conservation, the Convention includes some relatively clear requirements—for example, that each Party: establish a protected area system (e.g., a system of national parks), establish means for managing living modified organisms, and take steps to prevent or control alien species. In what was the first environmental convention to recognize the importance of indigenous peoples, Article 8(j) and 10(c) recognized the importance of protecting and maintaining indigenous and traditional lifestyles and knowledge with respect to biodiversity conservation. This latter aspect is described further *infra*, at 986–92.

Biodiversity Convention, op. cit.

Article 6. General Measures for Conservation and Sustainable Use

Each Contracting Party shall, in accordance with its particular conditions and capabilities:

(a) Develop national strategies, plans or programmes for the conservation and sustainable use of biological diversity or adapt for this purpose existing strategies, plans or programmes which shall reflect, inter alia, the measures set out in this Convention relevant to the Contracting Party concerned; and

(b) Integrate, as far as possible and as appropriate, the conservation and sustainable use of biological diversity into relevant sectoral or cross-sectoral plans, programmes and policies.

Article 7. Identification and Monitoring

Each Contracting Party shall, as far as possible and as appropriate, in particular for the purposes of Articles 8 to 10:

(a) Identify components of biological diversity important for its conservation and sustainable use having regard to the indicative list of categories set down in Annex I;

(b) Monitor, through sampling and other techniques, the components of biological diversity identified pursuant to subparagraph (a) above, paying particular attention to those requiring urgent conservation measures and those which offer the greatest potential for sustainable use;

(c) Identify processes and categories of activities which have or are likely to have significant adverse impacts on the conservation and sustainable use of biological diversity, and monitor their effects through sampling and other techniques; and

(d) Maintain and organize, by any mechanism data, derived from identification and monitoring activities pursuant to subparagraphs (a), (b) and (c) above.

Article 8. In-situ Conservation

Each Contracting Party shall, as far as possible and as appropriate:

(a) Establish a system of protected areas or areas where special measures need to be taken to conserve biological diversity;

(b) Develop, where necessary, guidelines for the selection, establishment and management of protected areas or areas where special measures need to be taken to conserve biological diversity;

(c) Regulate or manage biological resources important for the conservation of biological diversity whether within or outside protected areas, with a view to ensuring their conservation and sustainable use;

(d) Promote the protection of ecosystems, natural habitats and the maintenance of viable populations of species in natural surroundings;

(e) Promote environmentally sound and sustainable development in areas adjacent to protected areas with a view to furthering protection of these areas;

(f) Rehabilitate and restore degraded ecosystems and promote the recovery of threatened species, *inter alia*, through the development and implementation of plans or other management strategies;

(g) Establish or maintain means to regulate, manage or control the risks associated with the use and release of living modified organisms resulting from biotechnology which are likely to have adverse environmental impacts that could affect the conservation and sustainable use of biological diversity, taking also into account the risks to human health;

(h) Prevent the introduction of, control or eradicate those alien species which threaten ecosystems, habitats or species;

(i) Endeavor to provide the conditions needed for compatibility between present uses and the conservation of biological diversity and the sustainable use of its components;

(j) Subject to its national legislation, respect, preserve and maintain knowledge, innovations and practices of indigenous and local communities embodying traditional lifestyles relevant for the conservation and sustainable use of biological diversity and promote their wider application with the approval and involvement of the holders of such knowledge, innovations and practices and encourage the equitable sharing of the benefits arising from the utilization of such knowledge, innovations and practices;

(k) Develop or maintain necessary legislation and/or other regulatory provisions for the protection of threatened species and populations;

(l) Where a significant adverse effect on biological diversity has been determined pursuant to Article 7, regulate or manage the relevant processes and categories of activities; and

(m) Cooperate in providing financial and other support for *in-situ* conservation outlined in subparagraphs (a) to (l) above, particularly to developing countries.

Article 9. Ex-situ Conservation

Each contracting Party shall, as far as possible and as appropriate, and predominantly for the purpose of complementing *in-situ* measures:

(a) Adopt measures for the *ex-situ* conservation of components of biological diversity, preferably in the country of origin of such components;

(b) Establish and maintain facilities for *ex-situ* conservation of and research on plants, animals and micro-organisms, preferably in the country of origin of genetic resources;

(c) Adopt measures for the recovery and rehabilitation of threatened species and for their reintroduction into their natural habitats under appropriate conditions;

(d) Regulate and manage collection of biological resources from natural habitats for *ex-situ* conservation purposes so as not to threaten ecosystems and *in-situ* populations of species, except where special temporary *ex-situ* measures are required under subparagraph (c) above; and

(e) Cooperate in providing financial and other support for *ex-situ* conservation outlined in subparagraphs (a) to (d) above and in the establishment and maintenance of *ex-situ* conservation facilities in developing countries.

Article 10. Sustainable Use of Components of Biological Diversity

Each Contracting Party shall, as far as possible and as appropriate:

(a) Integrate consideration of the conservation and sustainable use of biological resources into national decision-making;

(b) Adopt measures relating to the use of biological resources to avoid or minimize adverse impacts on biological diversity;

(c) Protect and encourage customary use of biological resources in accordance with traditional cultural practices that are compatible with conservation or sustainable use requirements;

(d) Support local populations to develop and implement remedial action in degraded areas where biological diversity has been reduced; and

(e) Encourage cooperation between its governmental authorities and its private sector in developing methods for sustainable use of biological resources.
* * *

Article 14. Impact Assessment and Minimizing Adverse Impacts

1.   Each Contracting Party, as far as possible and as appropriate, shall:

(a) Introduce appropriate procedures requiring environmental impact assessment of its proposed projects that are likely to have significant adverse effects on biological diversity with a view to avoiding or minimizing such effects and, where appropriate, allow for public participation in such procedures;

(b) Introduce appropriate arrangements to ensure that the environmental consequences of its programmes and policies that are likely to have significant adverse impacts on biological diversity are duly taken into account;

(c) Promote, on the basis of reciprocity, notification, exchange of information and consultation on activities under their jurisdiction or control which are likely to significantly affect adversely the biological diversity of other States or areas beyond the limits of national jurisdiction, by encouraging the conclusion of bilateral, regional or multilateral arrangements, as appropriate;

(d) In the case of imminent or grave danger or damage, originating under its jurisdiction or control, to biological diversity within the area under jurisdiction of other States or in areas beyond the limits of national jurisdiction, notify immediately the potentially affected States of such danger or damage, as well as initiate action to prevent or minimize such danger or damage; and

(e) Promote national arrangements for emergency responses to activities or events, whether caused naturally or otherwise, which present a grave and imminent danger to biological diversity and encourage international cooperation to supplement such national efforts and, where appropriate and agreed by the States or regional economic integration organizations concerned, to establish joint contingency plans.

2.   The Conference of the Parties shall examine, on the basis of studies to be carried out, the issue of liability and redress, including restoration and compensation, for damage to biological diversity, except where such liability is a purely internal matter. * * *

QUESTIONS AND DISCUSSION

1.   What specific steps must Parties to the Convention take to protect biodiversity? What enforcement measures are there, if any, for failure to comply with the Convention?

2.   The Convention's objectives and strategies promote the sustainable use of biological resources. Sustainable use is defined as "the use of components of biological diversity in ways and at a rate that does not lead to the long-term decline of biological diversity, thereby maintaining its potential to meet the needs and aspirations of present and future generations." Article 2. Note how the definition of "sustainable use" is closely tied to the most common definition of sustainable development as well as to the concept of intergenerational equity. Are this definition and the provisions of Article 6 consistent with the criteria and recommendations regarding sustainable use promoted by the *IUCN Guidelines on Sustainable Use*? Do the IUCN criteria provide a good place to begin for the clarification of what is meant by sustainable use under the Convention? Would you recommend that the Parties to the Biodiversity Convention negotiate a protocol on sustainable use?

3.   To what extent does the United States already meet the conservation requirements of the Biodiversity Convention? The Clinton Administration told the U.S.

Senate that ratifying the Convention would not require the passage of any new legislation, although the memo suggested the Administration might have to develop new regulatory programs. Do you agree? Has the United States developed a biodiversity assessment and national strategy as required by Article 6? Do you think the United States is in compliance with Article 8(j), relating to indigenous peoples?

4. Walt Reid of the World Resources Institute has recommended that the United States establish a National Commission on Biodiversity in part to develop a National Biodiversity Policy.

Walt Reid, *The United States Needs a National Biodiversity Policy,* WRI Issues and Ideas (Feb. 1992)

To frame an integrated National Biodiversity Policy, Congress should establish a National Commission on Biodiversity comprised of high-level representatives from government, academia, non-governmental organizations, and industry. More than 29 federal laws now govern the conservation and use of biological resources in the United States. This federal legislation and corresponding state laws are not adequate to the task of biodiversity conservation and are not meeting the important needs of rural communities facing the transition to sustainable patterns of resource use. The Commission's mandate should be to redefine the role of biological resources in national development for the 1990s and to underscore the nation's commitment to conserving its biotic wealth. Indeed, establishing the Commission will make the United States' commitment to conserving its biotic wealth clear to the world.

More specifically, the Commission should develop recommendations for an integrated national strategy to be implemented at the local, state, and federal level to preserve America's great variety of genetic diversity, species, habitats, and ecosystems for posterity. * * *

The Commission should receive public input through hearings held across the country and set up working groups to examine technical issues. The Commission should provide a final report to Congress and the President within two years that details proposals for action needed to ensure the long-term maintenance of the nation's biotic wealth, the free and open dissemination of information on biodiversity's cultural, economic, and ecological values, and the sustainable use of biological resources.

An integrated National Policy on Biodiversity could enable legislation focused on endangered species protection and wetlands conservation to achieve its goals, minimize conflicts between conservation and short-term development needs, increase national benefits from biological resources, and provide both predictability and new opportunities in the pharmaceutical and biotechnology industries.

Do you think a national biodiversity commission is a good idea? What practical impact would you expect it to have? What questions or issues should it address? How many federal agencies or departments would be implicated by the Commission's recommendations? If the United States ratified the Biodiversity Convention, would it be required to create a Biodiversity Commission and adopt a National Policy?

D.   BIO-PROSPECTING, BENEFIT-SHARING AND INTELLECTUAL PROPERTY

In addition to its conservation measures, the Biodiversity Convention is also an economic treaty—developing and regulating the ongoing exchange of genetic resources and the emerging trade in biotechnology, in particular. The biotechnology trade dominated much of the debate during the convention negotiations, often to the detriment of other issues more directly related to biodiversity conservation. Deep differences existed between the technologically rich North and the biodiversity rich South. The following excerpt introduces the breadth of the biotechnology industry and explores the economic relationship between the mostly northern companies and researchers who invent new uses of biodiversity and the mostly southern communities and citizens who protect biodiversity or maintain knowledge about its uses.

Walt Reid, et. al., *A New Lease on Life,* 6–7, 12–18, in BIODIVERSITY PROSPECTING: USING GENETIC RESOURCES FOR SUSTAINABLE DEVELOPMENT (W. Reid, et. al., eds., 1993)

The driving forces behind the evolution of new biodiversity-prospecting institutions has been the growing demand for new genes and chemicals and a growing awareness that an abundant and virtually untapped supply of these resources exists in wildland biodiversity. While genetic and biochemical resources have long been important raw materials in agriculture and medicine, biotechnology is opening a new frontier. Furthermore, democratization and economic development in many developing countries has fanned interest in the local development of in-country resources.

In the pharmaceutical industry, after a hiatus in natural products research in the 1970s, interest has intensified over the past decade. As a source of novel chemical compounds, natural products research is an important complement to "rational drug design"—the chemical synthesis of new drugs. Natural products research has been revived by the development of efficient automated receptor-based screening techniques that have increased a hundred-fold the speed with which chemicals can be tested. Although only one in about 10,000 chemicals yields a potentially valuable "lead", these new techniques have made large natural products screening programs affordable. Researchers are thus returning to such natural sources of biologically active chemicals as plants, insects, marine invertebrates, fungi, and bacteria.

Another and quite different stimulus to natural products research has come from decades-old ethnopharmacology the study of medicines used by traditional communities. Leads based on the use of plants or animals in traditional medicine can greatly increase the probability of finding a commercially valuable drug. For small pharmaceutical companies, drug exploration based on this indigenous knowledge may be more cost-effective than attempting to compete in expensive random screening ventures. * * *

In the United States, some 25 percent of prescriptions are filled with drugs whose active ingredients are extracted or derived from plants. Sales of these plant-based drugs amounted to some $4.5 billion in 1980 and an estimated $15.5 billion in 1990. In Europe, Japan, Australia, Canada, and the U.S., the market value for both prescription and over-the-counter drugs based on plants in 1985 was estimated to be $43 billion.

Biotechnology has also opened the door to greater use of biodiversity in agriculture. Genetic diversity has always been a key raw material in agricultural research, accounting for roughly one-half of the gains in U.S. agricultural yields from 1930 to 1980. But whereas previously only close relatives of crops could be used in breeding programs, now the genes from the entire world's biota are within reach.

Traditional crop and livestock breeding methods will still comprise most crop-breeding activity for years to come. But genetic engineering is an important new addition to breeders' toolboxes. For example, a gene responsible for a sulfur-rich protein found in the Brazil nut has been isolated, cloned, and transferred into tomatoes, tobacco, and yeast. And pest-resistant genes from the bacterium Bacillus thuringiensis (Bt) have been transferred to tobacco, tomatoes, potatoes, and cotton. All told, more than 40 species of food and fiber crops have been "transformed" through genetic engineering and, as evidence of likely rapid growth in the commercial importance of genetic engineering, almost 600 field tests of genetically engineered crops have now been undertaken in more than 20 countries. * * *

Apart from new chemical leads for pharmaceuticals and new genes for agriculture, other new uses of biodiversity abound. A Brazilian fungus discovered in 1986 has been patented by a University of Florida researcher as a natural fire ant control. Chemicals extracted from the neem tree have been patented as a natural insecticide. Scientists have now genetically engineered plants to produce biodegradable plastic. Naturally occurring micro-organisms can be used in various environmental applications, including oil spill clean-up. And genetically modified organisms are proving valuable in such applications as mining, wastewater treatment, carbon-dioxide scrubbing, chemical detoxification, and bioremediation.

Growth in this "biotechnology industry" foretells increasing demands for novel genetic and biochemical resources. Between 1985 and 1990, the number of biotechnology patent applications filed in the United States grew by 15 percent annually—by 9,385 in 1990 alone. Total product sales for the U.S. biotechnology industry in 1991 totaled approximately $4 billion—a 38 percent increase over 1990—and by the year 2000 sales are expected to have grown more than 10–fold to some $50 billion.

All else being equal, the growing demand for genetic and biochemical resources should increase the potential market value of the raw material. But, given the high revenues generated from the final products developed in the agricultural and pharmaceutical industries, it is easy to misjudge how much money might actually be involved.

Many of the industries using genetic and biochemical resources produce high-value commodities and thus enjoy substantial gross earnings from the commercial product. Two drugs derived from the rosy periwinkle—vincristine and vinblastine—alone earned $100 million annually for Eli Lilly—a figure that is sometimes erroneously cited as the "value" of the rosy periwinkle. But sales of a product provide little indication of the potential market value of the unimproved genetic material in the source country. Most of the industries using these resources are capital-intensive ventures that invest substantial time and money in the production of a commercial product, and most are far removed from the original source of the genetic or biochemical material

In the U.S. pharmaceutical industry, a commercially marketable drug requires an estimated $231 million and 12 years on average to develop. These costs cover the process of screening candidate compounds, isolating active compounds, testing for possible toxicity, and undertaking clinical trials, as well as failed attempts to discover and produce a new drug. Developing agricultural products through genetic engineering also entails substantial costs. For example, the successful introduction of Bt genes into plants took several years and cost some $1.5 million to $3 million.

In any given trial, the likelihood of discovering a valuable compound for the pharmaceutical industry is quite low. By most estimates, only about one in

10,000 chemicals yields a promising lead, and less than one fourth of the chemicals reaching clinical trials will ever be approved as a new drug. For example, of 50,000 extracts put through an HIV screen in the natural products research program of the National Cancer Institute, only 3 are likely to wind up in clinical trials, and of 33,000 extracts screened for cancer only 5 are receiving further study.

Given the high value added in both the pharmaceutical industry and agriculture, the abundance of unimproved genetic and biochemical resources, and the low probability that any specific sample will have commercial value, the holders of unimproved material are likely to receive a relatively low payment for access to the resource, current heightened demand notwithstanding. In agriculture, [according to some] estimates, the total revenue that might be gained if developing countries sought royalties for unimproved genetic material could amount to less than $100 million annually. * * *

In sum, while biodiversity prospecting can return profits to source countries, institutions, and communities, the amounts involved are likely to be small relative to the market value of the final products, a decade or more may pass before significant revenues materialize, a good chance exists that no commercial drugs will be produced, and late-comers may find a market already saturated with suppliers. On the other hand, given the scale of revenues generated in the pharmaceutical industry, even a relatively small share of net profits may amount to extremely large revenues for a developing country. And, if nations add value to genetic resources domestically and build technical capacity for improving the resource themselves, biodiversity prospecting could become an important component of a nation's economic development strategy.

Through the Biodiversity Convention's negotiations, the South wanted to affirm that biodiversity was a resource that fell within their national sovereignty to regulate and manage. In particular, they wanted to retain the right to control the access of northern industries to "prospect" for biodiversity in their countries. In return for allowing such "bioprospecting," the South demanded more of the benefits from the biotechnology developed as a result. In this regard, they saw intellectual property rights (IPR) regimes, which protected the patents of biotechnology firms, as a major obstacle to benefit-sharing and ultimately to biodiversity conservation. To the South, the monopoly rights and profits granted patent holders under most IPR systems made it very difficult to transfer biotechnology to the developing countries, at least on any preferred basis. Moreover, the South thought it particularly unfair that IPR provided strong protection to biotechnology inventions while declining any similar property rights protection for the genetic resources found in the South or for the traditional knowledge that assists in the "discovery" of some biotechnology inventions.

In contrast, the North wanted to ensure free and open access to biodiversity so that pharmaceutical and agricultural research firms could expand their efforts to identify potentially valuable plants and animals. The North wanted to ensure that any technology transfer requirements would honor the intellectual property rights of northern industry—rights established to reward industries that invest in research and product development. In their view IPR provides a fair reward and important incentive to encounter innovation. By increasing the profits available from marketing biotechnology derived from genetic resources, the North argued, IPR actually encourages further conservation of biodiversity.

To the extent that environmentalists engaged in the biotechnology trade debate, they saw biotechnology trade as a potentially profitable and sustainable use of biodiversity that might provide local incentives for conservation. They supported the South's desire for profit sharing with local and indigenous communities both out of a sense of fairness and as a local incentive for conservation. Ultimately these issues were resolved sufficiently for most countries to support the Convention.

David Downes, *New Diplomacy for the Biodiversity Trade: Biodiversity, Biotechnology, and Intellectual Property in the Convention on Biological Diversity*, 4 TOURO J. TRANSNT'L L. 1, 8–14 (1993)

The final text of the Convention that resulted from this debate is muddled, vague, and inconsistent, even by the relaxed standards of international agreements. In many instances, it merely memorializes rather than resolves the deadlocks that characterized the negotiating process. Nevertheless, it establishes, in general terms, several important principles regarding these interrelationships.

1. Genetic Resources Access and Benefit Sharing

First, countries must "endeavour to create conditions to facilitate access to genetic resources for environmentally sound uses by other Contracting Parties and not to impose restrictions that run counter to the objectives of this Convention." Second, countries obtaining genetic resources from other countries must do so on "mutually agreed terms," obtaining "prior informed consent." Third, buyers and source countries must arrange for "fair sharing" of the benefits derived from genetic resources—i.e., compensation for their use.

In these provisions, the Convention rejects the "common heritage" doctrine that has traditionally been applied to genetic resources. This new approach to control of a previously common resource paves the way for commercial trade that could, in theory at least, provide incentives to preserve biodiversity-rich ecosystems in hopes of realizing economic returns from exploitation of the genetic resources that they contain.

On the other hand, the Convention does not treat genetic resources as a type of property like any other natural resource. The control of a sovereign nation over resources within its own jurisdiction is limited by the obligation under Article 15(2) to facilitate access by other countries to genetic resources. In this respect, the developed countries prevailed against the biodiversity-rich countries' desire to assert complete control over their genetic resources.

The North won another battle over treatment of samples of crop varieties already collected and stored in "seed banks" or "gene banks," many of which are situated in the North and all of which traditionally give free access to their collections. Crop genetic variety is one of the types of biodiversity with the greatest proven commercial value. Under the Convention, genetic resources already collected and stored in these banks are excepted from the rule that users of genetic resources must obtain the informed consent of the country where those genetic resources originated and pay benefits to that country. Thus, agribusiness and public sector researchers in the industrialized world will be able to continue to use these collections with no obligation to the country of origin. * * *

3. Technology Transfer

Finally, the Convention requires treaty parties to "provide and/or facilitate" transfer to other parties of biotechnology derived from genetic resources. The Convention also requires transfer of biodiversity-protection technology, but the greater emphasis by far is on genetic resource-derived biotechnology because in the developing country's view transfer of such technology is the principal benefit derived from genetic resources to be shared under the Convention.

Transfer to developing country parties must be "under fair and most favourable terms," while providing for "adequate and effective protection of intellectual property rights." A summarization of the convoluted language of Articles 15(7), 16, and 19, with a simplicity the negotiators probably did not intend, is:

1. Parties to the Convention must arrange for transfer of genetic resource-based biotechnology to other parties (as well as biodiversity-conservation technology).

2. Transfer to developing countries technology must be on "fair and most favourable" terms—including "concessional and preferential terms where mutually agreed."

3. Parties must take measures "with the aim that" the private sector, as well as the public sector, facilitates transfer of both proprietary and non-proprietary technologies (referred to in (1) above) to the private and public sectors of developing countries.

4. Transfer of proprietary technology must "recognize and [be] consistent with the adequate and effective protection of intellectual property rights." On the other hand, parties, "recognizing that patents and other intellectual property rights may have an influence on the implementation of this Convention," shall cooperate in this regard subject to national legislation and international law in order to ensure that such rights are supportive of and do not run counter to its objectives.

4. Definition and Scope

The range of activities subject to the provisions concerning the biodiversity trade is potentially very wide. Genetic resources are defined in the Convention to mean "genetic material of actual or potential value." "Genetic material" is defined broadly in turn as "any material of plant, animal, microbial or other origin containing functional units of heredity." Biotechnology is defined as "any technological application that uses biological systems, living organisms, or derivatives thereof, to make or modify products or processes for specific use." Arguably, these terms cover everything from the application of the latest genetic engineering techniques to genetic material from the Brazilian rainforest in a multinational corporation's agricultural research labs to the planting of a new maize variety by an African peasant using traditional farming methods. On the other hand, a strict reading of the term "genetic resources" might exclude transactions involving the transfer of goods—such as biochemical extracts which are unlikely to contain "functional units of heredity"—from Article 15's access requirements.

The following are the Biodiversity Convention's articles addressing access to genetic resources and technology transfer—i.e. the biotechnology trade.

The Biodiversity Convention, *op. cit.*

Article 15. Access to Genetic Resources

1. Recognizing the sovereign rights of States over their natural resources, the authority to determine access to genetic resources rests with the national governments and is subject to national legislation.

2. Each Contracting Party shall endeavour to create conditions to facilitate access to genetic resources for environmentally sound uses by other Contracting Parties and not to impose restrictions that run counter to the objectives of this Convention.

3. For the purpose of this Convention, the genetic resources being provided by a Contracting Party, as referred to in this Article and Articles 16 and 19, are only those that are provided by Contracting Parties that are countries of origin of such resources or by the Parties that have acquired the genetic resources in accordance with this Convention.

4. Access, where granted, shall be on mutually agreed terms and subject to the provisions of this Article.

5. Access to genetic resources shall be subject to prior informed consent of the Contracting Party providing such resources, unless otherwise determined by that Party.

6. Each Contracting Party shall endeavour to develop and carry out scientific research based on genetic resources provided by other Contracting Parties with the full participation of, and where possible in, such Contracting Parties.

7. Each Contracting Party shall take legislative, administrative or policy measures, as appropriate, and in accordance with Articles 16 and 19 and, where necessary, through the financial mechanism established by Articles 20 and 21 with the aim of sharing in a fair and equitable way the results of research and development and the benefits arising from the commercial and other utilization of genetic resources with the Contracting Party providing such resources. Such sharing shall be upon mutually agreed terms.

Article 16. Access to and Transfer of Technology

1. Each Contracting Party, recognizing that technology includes biotechnology, and that both access to and transfer of technology among Contracting Parties are essential elements for the attainment of the objectives of this Convention, undertakes subject to the provisions of this Article to provide and/or facilitate access for and transfer to other Contracting Parties of technologies that are relevant to the conservation and sustainable use of biological diversity or make use of genetic resources and do not cause significant damage to the environment.

2. Access to and transfer of technology referred to in paragraph 1 above to developing countries shall be provided and/or facilitated under fair and most favorable terms, including on concessional and preferential terms where mutually agreed, and, where necessary, in accordance with the financial mechanism established by Articles 20 and 21. In the case of technology subject to patents and other intellectual property rights, such access and transfer shall be provided on terms which recognize and are consistent with the adequate and effective

protection of intellectual property rights. The application of this paragraph shall be consistent with paragraphs 3, 4 and 5 below.

3. Each Contracting Party shall take legislative, administrative or policy measures, as appropriate, with the aim that Contracting Parties, in particular those that are developing countries, which provide genetic resources are provided access to and transfer of technology which makes us of those resources, on mutually agreed terms, including technology protected by patents and other intellectual property rights, where necessary, through the provisions of Articles 20 and 21 and in accordance with international law and consistent with paragraphs 4 and 5 below.

4. Each Contracting Party shall take legislative, administrative or policy measures, as appropriate, with the aim that the private sector facilitates access to, joint development and transfer of technology referred to in paragraph 1 above for the benefit of both governmental institutions and the private sector of developing countries and in this regard shall abide by the obligations included in paragraphs 1, 2 and 3 above.

5. The Contracting Parties, recognizing that patents and other intellectual property rights may have an influence on the implementation of this Convention, shall cooperate in this regard subject to national legislation and international law in order to ensure that such rights are supportive of and do not run counter to its objectives.

Article 17. Exchange of Information

1. The Contracting Parties shall facilitate the exchange of information, from all publicly available sources, relevant to the conservation and sustainable use of biological diversity, taking into account the special needs of developing countries.

2. Such exchange of information shall include exchange of results of technical, scientific and socio-economic research, as well as information on training and surveying programmes, specialized knowledge, indigenous and traditional knowledge as such and in combination with the technologies referred to in Article 16, paragraph 1. It shall also, where feasible, include repatriation of information. * * *

Article 19. Handling of Biotechnology and Distribution of its Benefits

1. Each Contracting Party shall take legislative, administrative or policy measures, as appropriate, to provide for the effective participation in biotechnological research activities by those Contracting Parties, especially developing countries, which provide tee genetic resources for such research, and where feasible in such Contracting Parties.

2. Each Contracting Party shall take all practicable measures to promote and advance priority access on a fair and equitable basis by Contracting Parties, especially developing countries, to the results and benefits arising from biotechnologies based upon genetic resources provided by those Contracting Parties. Such access shall be on mutually agreed terms.

3. The Parties shall consider the need for and modalities of a protocol setting out appropriate procedures, including, in particular, advance informed agreement, in the field of the safe transfer, handling and use of any living modified organism resulting from biotechnology that may have adverse effect on the conservation and sustainable use of biological diversity.

4. Each Contracting Party shall, directly or by requiring any natural or legal person under its jurisdiction providing the organisms referred to in paragraph 3 above, provide any available information about the use and safety

regulations required by that Contracting Party in handling such organisms, as well as any available information on the potential adverse impact of the specific organisms concerned to the Contracting Party into which those organisms are to be introduced.

QUESTIONS AND DISCUSSION

1. *Problem Exercise.* In light of the above provisions regarding the trade in biotechnology, outline a statute or set of regulations that a biodiversity-rich country might consider enacting to implement the Convention. Include in this exercise provisions for recouping some of the economic benefits that foreign companies might reap from bioprospecting in ther country.

2. According to David Downes of the Center for International Environmental Law, Southern demands for a share in biotechnology profits and environmentalists' hopes that such profits can provide an incentive for conservation are predicated on four plausible, but unproven, assumptions: (1) the economic value of biotechnology will grow rapidly to a very high level; (2) biodiversity will be a valuable "raw material" for biotechnology; (3) source countries of biodiversity will be able to capture a significant proportion of the total value of biotechnology through benefit-sharing or as compensation for the contribution of biodiversity to the final product; and (4) compensation or a share of the benefits will flow back to source countries so as to promote conservation of biodiversity.

Do you think these assumptions are correct? Consider the facts surrounding the discovery and use of taxol in the pacific yew tree. In 1962, the U.S. Department of Agriculture collected bark from the Pacific yew tree. Subsequently, taxol a substance derived from the bark showed anticancer properties. In the 1990s, Bristol–Myers Squibb began marketing taxol for treatment of ovarian cancer. In the meantime, however, populations of the Pacific yew had declined as a result of widespread clearcutting and other logging operations in the Pacific northwest. To loggers, the yew tree was a scrub with little value. Logging in the Pacific Northwest became quite controversial in part because the old-growth forests were the last home of the Northern Spotted Owl. Discovery of the commercial importance of taxol was seen as another reason for slowing timber cutting in the region. Bristol–Myers Squibb even funded studies on the impact of timber harvesting on the pacific yew tree, perhaps because the only way to produce taxol thus far is through extraction from the yew bark. If taxol could be created in a laboratory, would the motivation for Bristol–Myers to support conservation disappear? Does this suggest that the effort to reproduce genetic variability in the laboratory will ultimately undermine efforts to use biodiversity's potential value to biotechnology as a primary reason for biodiversity conservation? See K. Day & G. Frisvold, *Medical Research and Genetic Resources Management: The Case of Taxol,* 11 CONTEMPORARY POL'Y ISSUES 1 (1993); *see also* D. CLARK & D. DOWNES, WHAT PRICE BIODIVERSITY, at Box 3 (CIEL: 1996).

3. Some observers see the exploitation of the South's biological resources as a modern example of Northern colonialism. Under this view, intellectual property rights are simply a vehicle for legalizing the theft of knowledge or resources from the South. In this regard, consider the following critique of the Convention from Ashish Kothari of India:

Ashish Kothari, *Beyond the Biodiversity Convention: A View From India,* 67–72, in Biodiplomacy: Genetic Resources and International Relations (V. Sanchez & C. Juma, eds., 1994)

It is widely recognized that the majority of the world's biological wealth is contained in the tropical regions, under the jurisdiction of southern countries.

Yet in recent history, access to this wealth has been cornered by the industrial nations of the North, by processes of colonization, and by other weapons of economic and military dominance. To add insult to injury, the benefits accruing to the northern countries and companies from the use of biological resources, including those from biotechnology, have not been accessible to the South. In addition, the decision-making elites in the South have been more than eager to follow in the footsteps of their northern counterparts, forcing their countries down paths of development that are fundamentally unsustainable and inequitable. * * *

It is the contention here that the Convention does not explicitly address the global and national roots of biodiversity destruction, and pays mostly lip-service to the genuine needs of disprivileged people everywhere. Yet, even with its weak and inadequate terminology, it provides some basis for action, some possibilities of reversing many historical inequities between and within countries. For this possibility to become manifest, however, a considerable effort at re-interpreting and looking beyond the Convention is necessary. * * *

While elements of the Convention can be used for integrating biodiversity concerns into national planning, there is in the Convention no mention whatsoever of global consumption patterns, terms of trade or other international roots of the biodiversity crisis. A clause in an earlier draft which committed countries to 'take into account the effect of . . . international trade policies' was dropped in the last round of negotiations. * * *

A victim of the North–South conflict during the run-up to the signing of the Convention at the Earth Summit was the ethically superior position of biodiversity as a global heritage. Throughout history, biological species and varieties, technologies and knowledge related to them have been openly exchanged between societies and individuals, resulting in all-round enrichment. This was also the spirit within which the International Undertaking on Plant Genetic Resources was formulated under the aegis of the Food and Agriculture Organization (FAO). However, in an unequal world, a common heritage has every chance of being misused. Thus, the last two centuries have seen the countries of the North, themselves poor in biodiversity, literally looting the resources of the biologically-rich nations of the South while creating protectionist systems to monopolize the technologies and benefits arising out of these resources. A common heritage has been turned into a colony for the North. No wonder that in the negotiations for the Convention, countries of the South fought for the deletion of the terms common heritage and for the acceptance of the principle of national sovereignty over biological resources. Apart from the supreme arrogance of imposing political boundaries on nature, this is a sad diluting of the morally stronger position of common heritage but one which seems inescapable in a politically and economically unequal world. It has been argued by some that the concept of biodiversity as a global commons must not be abandoned, even if it has been compromised in the Convention. Common heritage should include not just genetic resources but also biodiversity-related knowledge and biotechnologies.

In this respect, the Convention has been disappointingly silent on the question of access to international genebanks. It is well-known that a considerable part of the South's genetic variability is present in genebanks in the North, including species and varieties that are now impossible or very difficult to find at their original locations. The Convention must be amended, or a protocol developed under it, to make open access to these genebanks mandatory, and to encourage the repatriation of not just the resources but also the benefits derived from them. It is interesting, in this respect, that Indian

951

citizens have open access to the active genebank collections (such as the National Bureau of Plant Genetic Resources—NBPGR) maintained by the Indian government.

Unfortunately, recent developments within India appear to be going further down the one-way street of open access to the South's biodiversity without concomitant access to the North's breeder lines or biotechnologies. The United States Agency for International Development (USAID) has agreed to provide a sum of US$13 million to India for setting up a genebank and related facilities. The NBPGR is to maintain these facilities, such that by 1995 a comprehensive inventory will have been completed of almost 120 germplasm collection units so that a computerized database management system and plant germplasm will be readily available for research purposes to scientists in the public and the private sector in India and worldwide. However, no concomitant commitment has been made by the USA to provide access to genetic materials or other benefits derived from the germplasm collected within India. In future, American scientists or companies might patent such genetic material and withhold it from Indians or others.

Is Ashish Kothari's critique persuasive? Is a unified effort by the South to gain concessions in the relationship between intellectual property rights and biotechnology likely? Could the South, for example, impose an effective cartel on the raw materials for biotechnology? Or could a relatively few Southern countries saturate the ability of the North to do research on biotechnology? *See also* Vandana Shiva, *Biodiversity, Biotechnology and Profits*, in VANDANA SHIVA, ET AL, BIODIVERSITY: SOCIAL & ECOLOGICAL PERSPECTIVES (1991).

4. Some environmentalists have called for the Convention's Conference of the Parties to establish minimum standards to serve as the basis for national regulation of the biodiversity trade. What standards would you recommend?

5. As noted above, much of the discussion regarding the exchange of genetic resources and the biodiversity trade was over how to ensure that at least some of the economic benefits would revert to the Southern States and communities that are maintaining biodiversity. Ultimately, the Convention promotes such benefit sharing, but does it provide any enforceable mechanism for requiring profits to be shared?

Outside the Convention, there has been some experimentation with the use of contracts between pharmaceutical and other companies from developed countries, and local providers of biological resources. Initially, these contracts simply involved the payment of a fee to collect samples of potentially promising plants or animals so that the companies could conduct their research. These fees did not cover all of the expenses faced in the biodiverse-rich communities, for example the costs of maintaining areas rich in diversity, such as national parks. Developing country leaders wanted these costs to be "internationalized" as well, and included in the fees paid by bioprospecting companies. In addition, as mentioned above some mechanism for benefit sharing was also warranted to reward those with traditional knowledge or those that had husbanded traditional seeds.

Merck Pharmaceutical Company pioneered a novel effort to include more such considerations in a contract to assist in bioprospecting with the Costa Rican National Institute for Biodiversity (INBio), a government-chartered, private non-profit organization. Although InBio is a private organization, it is closely tied to the government: most of the members of INBio are government officials, and much of its work is carried out under an agreement with the Ministry of Natural Resources,

Energy and Mines (MIRENEM). INBio's agreement with MIRENEM covers their joint inventory of the biodiversity in the system of protected wild areas. That agreement reportedly provides that 10 percent of any budget for a research project, and 50 percent of any financial benefits INBio receives, will be donated to the National Parks Fund of MIRENEM.

Merck and INBio originally signed the agreement in 1991 and then renewed it in 1994. Under the original agreement, INBio provides Merck with genetic resources from national conservation areas in Costa Rica. The objective of the agreement is to develop new drugs from chemicals found in wild plants, insects and micro-organisms. INBio reportedly received over $1,000,000 for two years of research and sampling and is entitled to a percentage of the royalties in the event a discovery leads to a new commercial product (this percentage has not been disclosed). Merck will own the rights of any patented material. As part of the agreement, Merck also agreed to provide equipment and training to INBio. Costa Rica's hope is that eventually such transfers of technology and knowledge will lead to the development of a domestic pharmaceutical industry.

The contract approach is heavily criticized from some advocates of traditional communities. First, any contract with one community or institution may benefit that particular community but it pays them for knowledge that many communities may have and that has historically been viewed as common heritage to be passed on freely between communities. Secondly, contracts probably will not be widely used nor provide benefits to more than a relatively few number of communities.

The latter consideration is suggested by the following evaluation of the effectiveness of the use of contracts for protecting the rights of local communities or indigenous peoples. S. Brush, *Whose Knowledge, Whose Genes, Whose Rights?*, 16–17 in S. Brush & D. Stabinsky, Valuing Local Knowledge: Indigenous People and Intellectual Property Rights (1996).

> Contracts between producers of biological resources and private users are a way to avoid the monopoly-related problems associated with intellectual property. Contracts differ from intellectual property in that they do not establish or imply a monopoly over a specific invention. In theory, they are the easiest means to create a market for biological resources because they have fewer transaction costs than intellectual property. Contracts between producers and users of genetic resources might take different forms: e.g., licensing or restrictive-use provisions.

> Contracts are in fact being written by public agencies and private firms for access to biological resources related to plants with potential medicinal properties. The U.S. National Cancer Institute, Merck Pharmaceutical, and Shaman Pharmaceuticals have negotiated contracts with indigenous groups or national institutes for biological prospecting rights.

> The success of using contracts to conserve biological resources depends on the ability of a local group or nation to control and limit the collection and shipment of genetic resources. Also, the group or nation providing biological resources must be able to attract users willing to pay a fee for the right to collect. That fee might either be flat or proportional to commercialization of products derived from the biological resource. The long lag time between collection and use may limit profit sharing for funding immediate conservation programs, but up-front payments can overcome this difficulty to a certain extent. The large number of individuals who maintain crop genetic resources greatly reduces the possibility that a single community could control sufficient resources to attract contracts. A cartel among resource-producing communities is possible but dependent on government willingness to enforce limits on

collection. Governments, in turn, are likely to expect a share of proceeds from the contract.

The role played by public agencies in maintaining and distributing crop germplasm weakens a market for genetic resources operating through contracts. Users of crop genetic resources usually acquire germplasm from secondary public sources, and most of the users are themselves in the public sector. Disease control and quarantine require public agencies to be part of the genetic-resource supply chain. Efficiencies in storage and screening complement these reasons for the role of public agencies. Because most of the costs of new-product development using genetic resources are borne in the laboratory, collectors and users of genetic resources are apt to be more interested in contracts if they guarantee some kind of exclusive exploration rights. Public agencies, however, are unlikely to act as brokers for, or grant exclusive exploration rights to, one company for a particular region or crop species. The proportion of crop germplasm that has been collected from the total pool of germplasm in landraces is estimated to be high for most crops with large commercial seed markets. These estimates can be expected to depress the willingness of seed companies or breeders to underwrite costly contracts that permit access to germplasm in regions of crop diversity.

6. Several fundamental critiques of the commercialization of biodiversity also emerged during the debate over the Biodiversity Convention. For example, should we ever allow ownership through intellectual property rights of any living species? Some argue that biotechnological manipulation of genetic resources and patenting of the results constitutes a commodification of life, and that genetic modification is an immoral tampering with the handiwork of nature or God. Are these arguments for strict control over biotechnological research? Or do they argue for outright prohibition of certain types of genetic engineering and biotechnology trade? Does the Convention reflect either a spiritual or ethical responsibility toward biotechnology?

7. For a further history and overview of the Convention, *see also* L. Glowka, et al., *A Guide to the Convention on Biological Diversity* (IUCN Envtl. Pol'y and L. Paper No. 30, 1994); Secretariat to the Convention on Biological Diversity, HANDBOOK OF THE CONVENTION ON BIOLOGICAL DIVERSITY (Earthscan, 2001); <http://www.biodiv.org/> (Biodiversity Convention Secretariat).

E. THE BIOSAFETY PROTOCOL

Among the most controversial issues under the Biodiversity Convention is the extent to which biotechnologies involving the release of genetically modified organisms (GMOs) pose a threat to the environment. Little is known about potential impacts, even those arising from the commercial introduction of modified agricultural crops—by far the most well studied of GMOs. Indeed there has been little evidence of major environmental damage occurring from the release of GMOs. Yet, some scientists remain concerned that genetically altered plants could transfer a modified gene to weeds or become weeds themselves if the genetic alteration allowed them a competitive advantage that in turn allowed them to disrupt local ecosystems. Some plants are being encoded with viral sequences as a way to protect the plant against certain viruses. The behavior of these viral sequences in the wild is not well known; they could for example combine with natural viruses to create more harmful strains. More generally, the introduction of new genetic information could have an impact on the ecosystem as the migration of DNA through an ecosystem (for example from a plant to soil bacteria) is possible but not well studied.

Perhaps most well known are the potential effects of genetically modified corn on the monarch butterfly. Although scientific studies continue to conflict, it now appears that under some circumstances corn genetically modified to include the protein Bacillus thuringiensis (Bt), which is a toxin that repels certain pests, also harms monarch butterflies. *See Monarch Larvae Killed by Bt–Dusted Leaves, Iowa State University Researchers Report,* BNA Int'l Env't Rep, August 30, 2000, at 682. Bt has also been widely engineered into soybeans and cotton. The apparent harm to untargetted butterflies is an example of what environmentalists fear will happen as GMOs are released broadly.

And GMOs are already used throughout the environment. Genetically altered corn and soybean seeds for example were planted by many farmers in 1999 and 2000. Some estimates identify more than 20 million acres of biotech crops in the United States alone. Until relatively recently, biotech crops were approved without any conditions and with minimal oversight. That has begun to change, due both to pressure from European markets, which do not want Biotech crops, and US environmentalists, who among other things filed suit (later withdrawn) to highlight the weak assessments being undertaken by EPA. More than the threat from the lawsuit, however, has been the market pressure placed on biotech crops internationally. Many grocers in Europe refused to sell products that were not labeled free of GMOs and the resulting furor led to a major and sudden shift in the demand for GMO agricultural products. The US agricultural industry found that it faced declining demand if it could not demonstrate its products were GMO-free, and at the same time the infrastructure for separating biotech crops from biotech-free crops did not exist. Farmers who had been sold the more expensive GMO seed from companies like Monsanto were finding that their crops were valued less than GMO-free crops. Some farmers have even filed a class action suit against Monsanto for their marketing and distribution strategies. See Amended Complaint, *Higginbotham, et al v. Monsanto Company,* Civ. No. 1:99cv03337 (D.C. Dist. 1999).

To make matters worse for the GMO industry Friends of the Earth and several other organizations discovered in 2001 that GMO corn had found its way into taco shells sold in US grocery stores. The particular strain of GMO corn had not been approved for human consumption, and the taco shells had to be recalled. More startling was the realization that GMOs were so widely used in feedstocks and elsewhere that they probably could no longer be prevented from entering the food supply at least in trace amounts.

For some environmentalists, this list of concerns grows as the commercial exploitation of biotechnology increases. Even with minimal scientific knowledge about harmful effects, environmentalists relying on the precautionary principle called for clear and strict testing, labeling and monitoring standards. Because many GMOs are being released in developing countries without any national standards, environmentalists particularly in the Global South argued for an international agreement to establish minimum standards based on a precautionary approach to the regulation and control of natural releases of GMOs. *See, e.g.,* H. Kendall, et. al. *Bioengineering of Crops: Report of the World Bank Panel on Transgenic Crops* (World Bank, 1997); J. Rissler & M. Mellon, *Perils Amidst the Promise: Ecological Risks of Transgenic Crops in a Global Market* (Union of Concerned Scientists: 1993).

Not surprisingly, some scientists have dismissed these concerns as overstated, since plant hybridization, such as developing new strains of roses and tulips, is a form of biotechnology that has been safely practiced for centuries. Given the scientific uncertainty surrounding the potential threats and considering the enormous potential benefits from bioengineering, support for a biosafety protocol was not universal. The United States and other industrialized countries either actively opposed or simply downplayed the idea. Nonetheless, concern over the potential environmental and public health risks of introducing GMO's into the environment is growing internationally. Indeed as early as 1990 UNEP's Working Group on Biodiversity had concluded that any international legal instrument on biodiversity should address biotechnology.

The Biodiversity Convention also called upon Parties to: "consider the need for and modalities of a protocol setting out appropriate procedures, including, in particular, advance informed agreement, in the field of the safe transfer, handling and use of any living modified organism resulting from biotechnology that may have adverse effect on the conservation and sustainable use of biological diversity." The Convention obligates Parties to "provide any available information about the use and safety regulations required by that contracting party in handling such organisms, as well as any available information on the potential adverse impact of the specific organisms concerned to the Contracting Party into which those organisms are introduced." Article 19.

In 1995, the parties to the Convention authorized an Ad hoc Working Group to begin negotiations on a biosafety protocol with an aim of completing the protocol in 1998. See Biodiversity Convention Conference of the Parties, *Annex to Decision II/5* (1995). Negotiations over the Biosafety Protocol proved to be quite contentious. Developing countries were the principal supporters of a protocol, fearing that industrialized country companies were using developing countries as unwitting laboratories for the release of GMOs into the environment without proper testing, notification or impact assessment. Even though there was limited information regarding actual environmental impacts of GMOs, developing countries and most environmentalists sought to invoke the precautionary principle in managing the transfer, disposal, use and handling of GMOs. Among the issues developing countries wanted to address were systems for: ensuring prior informed consent before GMOs can be released in or transferred to another country; liability and compensation for damage from releases; and environmental impact and risk assessment. Not surprisingly, most industrialized countries opposed any system of liability and compensation and they repeatedly sought to restrict the scope of the protocol, e.g., to cover only intentional releases of GMOs.

The Biosafety Protocol was completed in January, 2000. It ultimately differentiated between living modified organisms (LMOs) destined for release in the environment (for example, seeds or live fish) and bulk commodities intended for consumption (for example food and animal feed). This distinction was viewed as critical by the United States and the biotechnology industry, because US farmers and others often commingle agricultural products containing LMOs with those free from LMOs. The Protocol establishes an elaborate notification and prior informed consent procedure for LMOs intended to be released into the environment, but only requires labeling of the bulk commodities. The Protocol also established a BioSafety Information Clearinghouse intended to facilitate transfer of and access to scientific, health and technical information regarding biotechnology. Industry heralded this as an important step in the widespread acceptance of biotechnology.

Cartagena Protocol on Biosafety to the Convention on Biological Diversity, *adopted* Jan. 29, 2000, *reprinted in* 31 I.L.M. 1257 (2000)

The Parties to this Protocol,

Being Parties to the Convention on Biological Diversity, hereinafter referred to as "the Convention", * * *

Recognizing that trade and environment agreements should be mutually supportive with a view to achieving sustainable development,

Emphasizing that this Protocol shall not be interpreted as implying a change in the rights and obligations of a Party under any existing international agreements,

Understanding that the above recital is not intended to subordinate this Protocol to other international agreements,

Have agreed as follows:

Article 1
OBJECTIVE

In accordance with the precautionary approach contained in Principle 15 of the Rio Declaration on Environment and Development, the objective of this Protocol is to contribute to ensuring an adequate level of protection in the field of the safe transfer, handling and use of living modified organisms resulting from modern biotechnology that may have adverse effects on the conservation and sustainable use of biological diversity, taking also into account risks to human health, and specifically focusing on transboundary movements.

Article 2
GENERAL PRINCIPLES

1. Each Party shall take necessary and appropriate legal, administrative and other measures to implement its obligations under this Protocol.

2. The Parties shall ensure that the development, handling, transport, use, transfer and release of any living modified organisms are undertaken in a manner that prevents or reduces the risks to biological diversity, taking also into account risks to human health. * * *

Article 3
USE OF TERMS

For the purposes of this Protocol: * * *

(b) "Contained use" means any operation, undertaken within a facility, installation or other physical structure, which involves living modified organisms that are controlled by specific measures that effectively limit their contact with, and their impact on, the external environment; * * *

(g) "Living modified organism" means any living organism that possesses a novel combination of genetic material obtained through the use of modern biotechnology;

(h) "Living organism" means any biological entity capable of transferring or replicating genetic material, including sterile organisms, viruses and viroids;

(i) "Modern biotechnology" means the application of:

a. In Vitro Nucleic Acid Techniques, Including Recombinant Deoxyribonucleic Acid (Dna) And Direct Injection Of Nucleic Acid Into Cells Or Organelles, or

b. Fusion Of Cells Beyond The Taxonomic Family,

that overcome natural physiological reproductive or recombination barriers and that are not techniques used in traditional breeding and selection; * * *

Article 4
SCOPE

This Protocol shall apply to the transboundary movement, transit, handling and use of all living modified organisms that may have adverse effects on the conservation and sustainable use of biological diversity, taking also into account risks to human health.

Article 7
APPLICATION OF THE ADVANCE INFORMED
AGREEMENT PROCEDURE

1. Subject to Articles 5 and 6, the advance informed agreement procedure in Articles 8 to 10 and 12 shall apply prior to the first intentional transboundary movement of living modified organisms for intentional introduction into the environment of the Party of import.

2. "Intentional introduction into the environment" in paragraph 1 above, does not refer to living modified organisms intended for direct use as food or feed, or for processing.

3. Article 11 shall apply prior to the first transboundary movement of living modified organisms intended for direct use as food or feed, or for processing.

4. The advance informed agreement procedure shall not apply to the intentional transboundary movement of living modified organisms identified in a decision of the Conference of the Parties serving as the meeting of the Parties to this Protocol as being not likely to have adverse effects on the conservation and sustainable use of biological diversity, taking also into account risks to human health.

Article 8
NOTIFICATION

1. The Party of export shall notify, or require the exporter to ensure notification to, in writing, the competent national authority of the Party of import

prior to the intentional transboundary movement of a living modified organism that falls within the scope of Article 7, paragraph 1. The notification shall contain, at a minimum, the information specified in Annex I.

2.   The Party of export shall ensure that there is a legal requirement for the accuracy of information provided by the exporter.

Article 9
ACKNOWLEDGEMENT OF RECEIPT OF NOTIFICATION

1.   The Party of import shall acknowledge receipt of the notification, in writing, to the notifier within ninety days of its receipt.

2.   The acknowledgement shall state:

(a) The date of receipt of the notification;

(b) Whether the notification, prima facie, contains the information referred to in Article 8;

(c) Whether to proceed according to the domestic regulatory framework of the Party of import or according to the procedure specified in Article 10.

3.   The domestic regulatory framework referred to in paragraph 2 (c) above, shall be consistent with this Protocol.

4.   A failure by the Party of import to acknowledge receipt of a notification shall not imply its consent to an intentional transboundary movement.

Article 10
DECISION PROCEDURE

1.   Decisions taken by the Party of import shall be in accordance with Article 15.

2.   The Party of import shall, within the period of time referred to in Article 9, inform the notifier, in writing, whether the intentional transboundary movement may proceed:

(a) Only after the Party of import has given its written consent; or

(b) After no less than ninety days without a subsequent written consent.

3.   Within two hundred and seventy days of the date of receipt of notification, the Party of import shall communicate, in writing, to the notifier and to the Biosafety Clearing-House the decision referred to in paragraph 2 (a) above:

(a) Approving the import, with or without conditions, including how the decision will apply to subsequent imports of the same living modified organism;

(b) Prohibiting the import;

(c) Requesting additional relevant information in accordance with its domestic regulatory framework or Annex I; in calculating the time within which the Party of import is to respond, the number of days it has to wait for additional relevant information shall not be taken into account; or

(d) Informing the notifier that the period specified in this paragraph is extended by a defined period of time.

4.   Except in a case in which consent is unconditional, a decision under paragraph 3 above, shall set out the reasons on which it is based.

5.   A failure by the Party of import to communicate its decision within two hundred and seventy days of the date of receipt of the notification shall not imply its consent to an intentional transboundary movement.

6.   Lack of scientific certainty due to insufficient relevant scientific information and knowledge regarding the extent of the potential adverse effects of a living modified organism on the conservation and sustainable use of biological diversity in the Party of import, taking also into account risks to human health, shall not prevent that Party from taking a decision, as appropriate, with regard to the import of the living modified organism in question as referred to in paragraph 3 above, in order to avoid or minimize such potential adverse effects.

7.   The Conference of the Parties serving as the meeting of the Parties shall, at its first meeting, decide upon appropriate procedures and mechanisms to facilitate decision-making by Parties of import.

Article 11
PROCEDURE FOR LIVING MODIFIED ORGANISMS INTENDED FOR DIRECT USE AS FOOD OR FEED, OR FOR PROCESSING

1.   A Party that makes a final decision regarding domestic use, including placing on the market, of a living modified organism that may be subject to transboundary movement for direct use as food or feed, or for processing shall, within fifteen days of making that decision, inform the Parties through the Biosafety Clearing–House. This information shall contain, at a minimum, the information specified in Annex II. The Party shall provide a copy of the information, in writing, to the national focal point of each Party that informs the Secretariat in advance that it does not have access to the Biosafety Clearing–House. This provision shall not apply to decisions regarding field trials.

2.   The Party making a decision under paragraph 1 above shall ensure that there is a legal requirement for the accuracy of information provided by the applicant.

3.   Any Party may request additional information from the authority identified in paragraph (b) of Annex

4.   A Party may take a decision on the import of living modified organisms intended for direct use as food or feed, or for processing, under its domestic regulatory framework that is consistent with the objective of this Protocol.

5.   Each Party shall make available to the Biosafety Clearing–House copies of any national laws, regulations and guidelines applicable to the import of living modified organisms intended for direct use as food or feed, or for processing, if available.

6.   A developing country Party or a Party with an economy in transition may, in the absence of the domestic regulatory framework referred to in paragraph 4 above, and in exercise of its domestic jurisdiction, declare through the Biosafety Clearing–House that its decision prior to the first import of a living modified organism intended for direct use as food or feed, or for processing, on which information has been provided under paragraph 1 above, will be taken according to the following:

(a) A risk assessment undertaken in accordance with Annex III; and

(b) A decision made within a predictable timeframe, not exceeding two hundred and seventy days.

7.   Failure by a Party to communicate its decision according to paragraph 6 above, shall not imply its consent or refusal to the import of a living modified organism intended for direct use as food or feed, or for processing, unless otherwise specified by the Party.

8. Lack of scientific certainty due to insufficient relevant scientific information and knowledge regarding the extent of the potential adverse effects of a living modified organism on the conservation and sustainable use of biological diversity in the Party of import, taking also into account risks to human health, shall not prevent that Party from taking a decision, as appropriate, with regard to the import of that living modified organism intended for direct use as food or feed, or for processing, in order to avoid or minimize such potential adverse effects.

9. A Party may indicate its needs for financial and technical assistance and capacity-building with respect to living modified organisms intended for direct use as food or feed, or for processing. Parties shall cooperate to meet these needs in accordance with Articles 22 and 28.

Article 12
REVIEW OF DECISIONS

1. A Party of import may, at any time, in light of new scientific information on potential adverse effects on the conservation and sustainable use of biological diversity, taking also into account the risks to human health, review and change a decision regarding an intentional transboundary movement. In such case, the Party shall, within thirty days, inform any notifier that has previously notified movements of the living modified organism referred to in such decision, as well as the Biosafety Clearing-House, and shall set out the reasons for its decision.

2. A Party of export or a notifier may request the Party of import to review a decision it has made in respect of it under Article 10 where the Party of export or the notifier considers that:

(a) A change in circumstances has occurred that may influence the outcome of the risk assessment upon which the decision was based; or

(b) Additional relevant scientific or technical information has become available.

3. The Party of import shall respond in writing to such a request within ninety days and set out the reasons for its decision.

4. The Party of import may, at its discretion, require a risk assessment for subsequent imports. * * *

Article 15
RISK ASSESSMENT

1. Risk assessments undertaken pursuant to this Protocol shall be carried out in a scientifically sound manner, in accordance with Annex III and taking into account recognized risk assessment techniques. Such risk assessments shall be based, at a minimum, on information provided in accordance with Article 8 and other available scientific evidence in order to identify and evaluate the possible adverse effects of living modified organisms on the conservation and sustainable use of biological diversity, taking also into account risks to human health.

2. The Party of import shall ensure that risk assessments are carried out for decisions taken under Article 10. It may require the exporter to carry out the risk assessment.

3. The cost of risk assessment shall be borne by the notifier if the Party of import so requires.

Article 16
RISK MANAGEMENT

1. The Parties shall, taking into account Article 8 (g) of the Convention, establish and maintain appropriate mechanisms, measures and strategies to regulate, manage and control risks identified in the risk assessment provisions of this Protocol associated with the use, handling and transboundary movement of living modified organisms.

2. Measures based on risk assessment shall be imposed to the extent necessary to prevent adverse effects of the living modified organism on the conservation and sustainable use of biological diversity, taking also into account risks to human health, within the territory of the Party of import.

3. Each Party shall take appropriate measures to prevent unintentional transboundary movements of living modified organisms, including such measures as requiring a risk assessment to be carried out prior to the first release of a living modified organism.

4. Without prejudice to paragraph 2 above, each Party shall endeavour to ensure that any living modified organism, whether imported or locally developed, has undergone an appropriate period of observation that is commensurate with its life-cycle or generation time before it is put to its intended use.

5. Parties shall cooperate with a view to:

(a) Identifying living modified organisms or specific traits of living modified organisms that may have adverse effects on the conservation and sustainable use of biological diversity, taking also into account risks to human health; and

(b) Taking appropriate measures regarding the treatment of such living modified organisms or specific traits. * * *

Article 18
HANDLING, TRANSPORT, PACKAGING AND IDENTIFICATION

1. In order to avoid adverse effects on the conservation and sustainable use of biological diversity, taking also into account risks to human health, each Party shall take necessary measures to require that living modified organisms that are subject to intentional transboundary movement within the scope of this Protocol are handled, packaged and transported under conditions of safety, taking into consideration relevant international rules and standards.

2. Each Party shall take measures to require that documentation accompanying:

(a) Living modified organisms that are intended for direct use as food or feed, or for processing, clearly identifies that they "may contain" living modified organisms and are not intended for intentional introduction into the environment, as well as a contact point for further information. The Conference of the Parties serving as the meeting of the Parties to this Protocol shall take a decision on the detailed requirements for this purpose, including specification of their identity and any unique identification, no later than two years after the date of entry into force of this Protocol;

(b) Living modified organisms that are destined for contained use clearly identifies them as living modified organisms; and specifies any requirements for the safe handling, storage, transport and use, the contact point for further information, including the name and address of the individual and institution to whom the living modified organisms are consigned; and

(c) Living modified organisms that are intended for intentional introduction into the environment of the Party of import and any other living modified organisms within the scope of the Protocol, clearly identifies them as living modified organisms; specifies the identity and relevant traits and/or characteristics, any requirements for the safe handling, storage, transport and use, the contact point for further information and, as appropriate, the name and address of the importer and exporter; and contains a declaration that the movement is in conformity with the requirements of this Protocol applicable to the exporter.

3.   The Conference of the Parties serving as the meeting of the Parties to this Protocol shall consider the need for and modalities of developing standards with regard to identification, handling, packaging and transport practices, in consultation with other relevant international bodies. * * *

Article 25
ILLEGAL TRANSBOUNDARY MOVEMENTS

1.   Each Party shall adopt appropriate domestic measures aimed at preventing and, if appropriate, penalizing transboundary movements of living modified organisms carried out in contravention of its domestic measures to implement this Protocol. Such movements shall be deemed illegal transboundary movements.

2.   In the case of an illegal transboundary movement, the affected Party may request the Party of origin to dispose, at its own expense, of the living modified organism in question by repatriation or destruction, as appropriate.

3.   Each Party shall make available to the Biosafety Clearing–House information concerning cases of illegal transboundary movements pertaining to it. * * *

Article 27
LIABILITY AND REDRESS

The Conference of the Parties serving as the meeting of the Parties to this Protocol shall, at its first meeting, adopt a process with respect to the appropriate elaboration of international rules and procedures in the field of liability and redress for damage resulting from transboundary movements of living modified organisms, analysing and taking due account of the ongoing processes in international law on these matters, and shall endeavour to complete this process within four years.

———

QUESTION AND DISCUSSIONS

1.   *Working the Treaty.* Read the BioSafety Protocol to answer the following questions:

    a.   What is a living modified organism? Does the protocol apply to all living modified organisms?

    b.   How does the protocol address human health concerns, given that it is a protocol to the biodiversity convention?

    c.   What labeling requirements does the convention require?

2.   Biotechnology and particularly the use and introduction of LMOs into the environment and into food present many new challenges for regulators. The industry is developing quickly and many countries have yet to develop an adequate approach to regulating it. LMOs present threats much like traditional chemicals (and in fact some LMOs are used as pesticides), but unlike chemicals the mechanisms and pathways by which LMOs may or may not harm human health or the environment are not well understood. The potential benefits from LMOs are also tremendous, placing pressure on regulators not to suffocate what could be very beneficial new technologies. As part of the effort to strike the balance, the Biosafety Protocol reflects both the precautionary approach and the use of risk assessment. Do you see how these two approaches co-exist in the Convention?

This tension between risk assessment and precaution reflected the split between the United States and Europe, who sought to protect their decisions to regulate LMOs even in light of little or no evidence of harm. The debate between risk assessment and precaution also resulted in a debate over the relationship between the Biosafety Protocol and international trade policy set through the WTO. Trade agreements appear to require that regulatory decisions be based on sufficient scientific evidence, but such evidence may not be available for new biotechnologies. The precautionary approach would allow countries to regulate in the face of uncertainty. Thus, whether trade rules would supercede the Biosafety Protocol or, the other way around, made a potentially huge difference over the extent to which developing countries and others would be able to regulate the importation and release of LMOs. The Protocol ultimately put both agreements on the same level, requiring that the Protocol and international trade rules be 'mutually supportive'. Does this approach end the debate? How in practice will the conflicts and tension between precaution and risk assessment be resolved?

3. The Biosafety Protocol was negotiated for six years leading up to its conclusion in January, 2000. It took so long in part because of strong opposition from the United States and also because the tension of how to regulate an emerging new industry required new approaches to precaution, consent, liability and information sharing. The Protocol set an important precedent on many of these issues for the subsequent negotiation of the Convention on Persistent Organic Pollutants, discussed supra in Chapter 12, page 885. Much of the structure, language and approach of the POPs Convention, completed in 2001 after only two years of negotiation, is clearly derived from the Biosafety Protocol. Does it appear that these conventions may mark the beginning of new principles in international environmental law or at least the clarification of some of the principles that were identified at UNCED in 1992?

4. Because so little is known about threats from LMOs, the Protocol emphasized the need to collect and make available information regarding the science, impacts and regulatory approaches relating to LMOs. Article 20 of the Protocol established a BioSafety Clearinghouse that is intended to facilitate the transfer of information to developing countries and the public. Under Article 20.3 of the Protocol,

> [E]ach Party shall make available to the Biosafety Clearing–House any information required to be made available to the Biosafety Clearing–House under this Protocol, and:

> (a) Any existing laws, regulations and guidelines for implementation of the Protocol, as well as information required by the Parties for the advance informed agreement procedure;

> (b) Any bilateral, regional and multilateral agreements and arrangements;

> (c) Summaries of its risk assessments or environmental reviews of living modified organisms generated by its regulatory process, and carried out in accordance with Article 15, including, where appropriate, relevant information regarding products thereof, namely, processed materials that are of living modified organism origin, containing detectable novel combinations of replicable genetic material obtained through the use of modern biotechnology;

(d) Its final decisions regarding the importation or release of living modified organisms; and

(e) Reports submitted by it pursuant to Article 33, including those on implementation of the advance informed agreement procedure.

Thus, for example, all decisions to deny the importation of LMOs must be posted to the Clearinghouse along with the supporting risk assessments. Industry believes this will increase the transparency surrounding regulation and allow for a more complete debate over the potential impacts of specific LMOs. Given the current climate of suspicion that shrouds the use of LMOs, industry views the Clearinghouse as an important mechanism for winning support for biotech. The Protocol's concern with transparency in regulation also led it to address confidentiality of information (Article 21) and public participation (Article 22). Article 22.2 requires that countries "consult the public in decision-making process regarding living modified organisms and shall make the results of such decisions available to the public...." Does this seem to significantly advance Principle 10 of the Rio Declaration?

5. Even as the Biosafety Protocol waits for ratification, the number of incidents where LMOs are unknowingly imported or where they are appearing in the food supply has increased. In May of 2000, during the time that the Conference of the Parties were meeting to sign the Protocol, a Canadian seed company named Advanta announced that it had sold rapeseed contaminated with genetically modified material to European farmers. What steps does the Protocol provide that would be relevant to such a situation?

6. *Problem Exercise.* You are the general counsel for a multinational biotechnology company. Your CEO has asked you for a detailed description of what the company must do to ensure that it is in compliance with the Biosafety Protocol. You plan to export many LMOs both to be released into the environment and to be consumed, and you operate in many countries that are Parties and have implemented the Biosafety Protocol.

7. For discussion of the regulation of biotechnology, see John Kunich, *Mother Frankenstein, Doctor Nature, and the Environmental Law of Genetic Engineering,* 74 So.Cal. L.Rev. 807 (March, 2001); Sean Murphy, *Biotechnology and International Law,* 42 Harv. Int'l L. J. 47 (Winter, 2001).

F.   Cross–Cutting Issues

1.   TRADITIONAL KNOWLEDGE, THE BIODIVERSITY CONVENTION AND THE TRIPS AGREEMENT

Throughout the world, indigenous peoples have lived close to nature, and many of them make use of generations of knowledge regarding the qualities and uses of the plants and animals living around them. This traditional knowledge has proven to be a potentially valuable reservoir of information regarding the medicinal and agricultural uses of plants. Tapping into this knowledge can help focus the bioprospecting activities of pharmaceutical and other companies looking for potentially valuable substances. Companies follow the leads suggested by the traditional knowledge, extract the active ingredients in the plant and animal, and then patent the extract or a synthetic equivalent. The companies can make substantial profits and their product will be protected by intellectual property rights laws. The traditional knowledge, on the other hand, has historically been treated as common heritage open and available to all in the community. This traditional knowledge has not enjoyed any protection under most IPR regimes. Consider the following story of India's neem tree:

In India, the neem tree is known as the "curer of all ailments." For centuries, Indians have used neem tree bark to clean their teeth; neem-leaf juice to prevent psoriasis and other skin disorders and to control parasitic infections; and neem tree seeds as a spermicide and an insecticide. Alerted to the useful properties of the neem tree seeds by Indian farmers, researchers have identified azadirachtin as one of the seed's active substances. Azadirachtin is a powerful insecticide that is not harmful to humans. In June 1992, the United States patent Office issued Patent No. 5,281,618 to W.R. Grace & Co. (Grace), an agricultural chemical company based in Boca Raton, Florida. The Grace patent covers both a method of stabilizing azadirachtin in solution and the stabilized azadirachtin solution itself. While naturally-occurring neem extract has a shelf-life of only a few weeks, storage-stable azadirachtin retains its potency for several years, thereby making it both more valuable to the pesticide industry and more useful to farmers. In March 1994, the EPA registered Neemix, Grace's stabilized azadirachtin solution, for use on food crops. Neemix is the first product derived from the neem tree approved for such use in the United States.

While the Grace story is one of successful Western improvement and commercialization of traditional biocultural knowledge, it is a horror story of inequity in the eyes of some traditional peoples. In response to the issuance of the Grace patent, a coalition of 200 organizations from 35 different nations filed a petition with the U.S. Patent Office seeking to invalidate the patent.

The petitioner's sentiments reflect the growing anger of lesser developed countries (LDCs) toward Westerners who take plants used by traditional cultures, or who learn uses of these plants, invest in improving the traditional technologies, and profit from their commercial development without compensating the traditional people who provided key insights or essential materials. Moreover, developed countries do not protect or even recognize any intellectual property rights in traditional knowledge or traditional plant varieties. The LDCs' complaints have grown more strident as the United States and other developed countries pressure LDCs to adopt and enforce Western-style intellectual property laws. Western researchers' acquisition of traditional knowledge and traditional plants has been particularly criticized since the passage of the Convention on Biological Diversity, which recognizes nations' sovereign rights over natural resources in their respective countries. LDCs and indigenous groups have also attempted to thwart Western research by urging traditional people to refuse to cooperate with biotechnology research until the appropriate mechanisms are in place to protect their rights.

C. Jacoby & C. Weiss, Recognizing Property Rights In Traditional Biocultural Contribution, 16 STAN. ENVTL. L. J. 74–77 (1997). The U.S. Patent Office subsequently dismissed the challenge to the neem tree patent, but the petition helped to highlight the importance of these issues. Jacoby & Weiss cited other instances that give rise to the same concerns manifested in the neem tree controversy.

There are numerous instances of Westerners profiting from improvements upon traditional knowledge and traditional plant varieties without compensating traditional peoples. For example, Indians are calling for the revocation of a U.S. patent directed to use of turmeric in wound-healing on the grounds that medicinal application of turmeric has been known in India for centuries. The classic anti-malarial drug quinine is derived from the bark of South American Cinchona trees, the extract from which was first used to treat fever by the indigenous peoples of Peru in the eighteenth century. The interests of a British company in the medicinal properties of the venom of a Sri Lankan spider, and the company's attempts to obtain patent protection for the venom, have raised concerns among activists and traditional peoples alike. The Grace story has been repeated in Ethiopia with the issuance of a U.S. patent directed to the molluscicide activities of the African Soapberry. The patents, of course, only cover improvement upon the traditional knowledge, not the traditional knowledge itself.

In addition, under current practice, traditional foodcrop seeds are freely exchanged among research centers worldwide. Most of the resulting improved varieties are sold at or below cost to farmers in LDCs; however, some are developed by agri-business companies and sold for profit. LDCs argue that traditional seeds, which represent hundreds of years of careful selection by farmers, should not simply be given away.

Id. at 78. Do you think traditional knowledge should be protected? What mechanisms would you suggest for sharing the benefits with local communities when traditional knowledge assists in the development of a commercially valuable product?

In part because of the difficulty of addressing traditional knowledge, the relationship between the objectives of the Biodiversity Convention, intellectual property rights (IPRs), and the WTO's TRIPS Agreement remains a subject of continuing debate.

Some WTO Members argue that the intellectual property rights required by the TRIPS Agreement help to conserve biodiversity by providing a vehicle for rewarding those who maintain and use biological resources. Others, including many developing countries, have argued that the TRIPS Agreement should be amended to bring it into line with the provisions of the CBD. In the following excerpt, Brazil argues for an amendment to the TRIPS Agreement to ensure that the benefits arising out of the use of genetic resources are shared fairly and to protect traditional knowledge. As you read it, identify the main areas of overlap between the TRIPS Agreement and the CBD, and the ways Brazil seeks to resolve areas of potential conflict.

> 21.   Brazil considers that TRIPs and the CBD should be mutually supportive and promote the sustainable use of resources. At the implementation level, however, conflicts could arise, for instance, in the case of patents claimed over naturally-occurring genetic resources, which are protected by the CBD. Some examples are already well known to the general public: in its paper on "Protection of Biodiversity and Traditional Knowledge" (IP/C/W/198), for instance, India reports its experience with cases of patents claimed over turmeric, karela, basmati and the neem tree; another example is the case of the ayahuasca vine (a native plant of the Amazonian rainforest used by thousands of indigenous peoples of the Amazon for sacred religious and healing ceremonies). Broad patents over microorganisms, plants and animals may result in monopoly rights for the exploitation of the patent's subject matter, thus restricting exploitation of such resources. Additionally, patents over a Member's genetic resource, but granted outside its territory raises the issue of potential conflict with the principle of the sovereignty of the Contracting

Parties of the CBD over their own genetic resources. Such patents claimed over genetic resources are generally obtained without the prior informed consent of the government or of the traditional community that holds the knowledge on that material. Moreover, no fair and equitable benefit sharing from the exploitation of the subject matter is established by the right holder of the patent.

22.   In the absence of clear standards defining the scope of patentability of microorganism (as discussed above) and a framework in TRIPs that clarifies the relationship of that Agreement with Members' obligations under the CBD, implementation of the TRIPs Agreement may result in conflicts with the Convention. With a view to avoiding conflicts in the implementation of both instruments and what is more, to ensure a mutually supportive relationship Brazil considers that amending Article 27.3(b) of TRIPs to accommodate principles of the CBD will be a necessary outcome of the review of that Article. Failure to clarify this relationship may turn out to be detrimental to both instruments.

23.   In order to explore a mutually beneficial relationship, one important step would be to ensure that patenting of genetic resources plants, animals or microorganisms does not run counter to the basic principles of the CBD. Some of those principles are the sovereignty of the Contracting Parties of the CBD over their genetic resources; the principle of benefit sharing; and the principle of prior informed consent. The CBD also has the objective of ensuring protection, at the national level, of traditional knowledge. Today, several countries have to tackle the problem of unauthorized bioprospecting and patenting of genetic resources over which, according to Article 15.1 of the CBD, they have sovereign rights. Several countries today are putting in place legislation to regulate access to genetic resources, many of which may contain intellectual property-related provisions, in line with Article 16 of that Convention. In Brazil, for instance, in June 2000, legislation entered in force to regulate the access to genetic resources, protection and access to associated traditional knowledge, sharing of benefits and access to and transfer of technology for its conservation and use, among other provisions.

24.   We fully agree with the arguments expressed by India in its paper (IP/C/W/198) that it would be less cost-effective to establish an internationally accepted solution to prevent biopiracy than to divert national resources to expensive judicial processes for the revocation of patents that include illegal genetic resources. Developing countries do not have the resources to follow each and every patent issued outside their territories on the use of their resources.

25.   In this connection, Brazil considers that Article 27.3(b) should be amended in order to include the possibility of Members requiring, whenever appropriate, as a condition to patentability: (a) the identification of the source of the genetic material; (b) the related traditional knowledge used to obtain that material; (c) evidence of fair and equitable benefit sharing; and (d) evidence of prior informed consent from the Government or the traditional community for the exploitation of the subject matter of the patent. An interpretative note to Article 27.3(b) should also be made in order to clarify that discoveries or naturally occurring material shall be excluded from patentability.

26.   For the sake of legal consistency, such amendments would be necessary to ensure compatibility between the TRIPs Agreement and the Convention on Biological Diversity. Several countries already establish the abovementioned requirements in their national legislation as a means of implementing the CBD.

27.   Concerning similar suggestions made in other fora, the United States has mentioned in its document that requirements to identify the source of the genetic resource in the patent application would be "a legal and administrative

nightmare''. We are of the view that such concern is exaggerated and unjustified. Fulfilling such requirements, besides addressing a crucial problem of coherence between two binding international agreements, would not be any more burdensome than any other regular requirement in the already existing patent application procedures. Furthermore, evidence of the legitimacy of the access to biological resources and/or to associated traditional knowledge should be imposed only where the Administration has reasonable grounds to suspect that national legislation on the protection of biodiversity has been violated by the patent applicant. This element would restrict the application of the requirement to a few patent applications and would represent a mechanism of biodiversity law enforcement. The burden, therefore, would not normally be imposed on law-compliant companies and individuals. The US also questions whether such a system would actually ensure benefit sharing from the exploitation of any product or process that might be developed from the resource or knowledge. In this respect, Brazil is of the view that once Article 27.3(b) is amended as proposed in paragraph 25, the TRIPs Agreement itself would provide the adequate enforcement of such requirements through its dispute settlement mechanism.

28.   The proposed amendment would have the clear benefit of providing a predictable environment for Governments, investors, traditional communities and researchers. As a consequence, research and development in biotechnology in developing countries would be encouraged, which would be in line with the objectives of the TRIPs Agreement to promote technological innovation and the transfer and dissemination of technology.

QUESTIONS AND DISCUSSION

1.   What are some possible alternative approaches to that proposed by Brazil? Do you think the amendment proposed by Brazil would address the problems they identified? How could cooperation between the Biodiversity Convention and the WTO help to address these issues? The CBD's conference of parties has, on a number of occasions, called for greater cooperation. It has, for example: called for cooperation with the WTO on intellectual property-related issues (decision III/15); noted the need for further work to develop a common appreciation of the relationship between intellectual property rights and the relevant provisions of the TRIPS Agreement and CBD (decision III/17); and stressed "the need to ensure consistency in implementing the Convention on Biological Diversity and the WTO agreements, including the Agreement on Trade–Related Aspects of Intellectual Property Rights" (decision IV/15).... What kind of formal arrangements may be required between the CBD and the WTO to explore these important relationships? How could cooperation between national policy-makers contribute to addressing actual and perceived tensions between the agreements?

2.   A patent was granted by the US Patents and Trademarks Office to a US citizen over a variety of the Ayahuasca vine, which has been used for generations by indigenous people in the Amazon for ceremonial and healing purposes. On behalf of indigenous people from the Amazon Basin, the Center for International Environmental Law challenged the patent in 1999 for lacking novelty. Although their challenge was initially successful, the patent was subsequently reinstated, with no opportunity for appeal. How, in your view, should the patent system strike a balance between the interest of indigenous people and the goal of providing incentives for research? Should indigenous people be required to challenge patents in foreign countries courts on a case-by-case basis, or should some other system at the national, regional or international level—be established? What are the pro's and con's of the status quo?

3. How does the Biodiversity Convention address the rights and needs of indigenous communities and other traditional knowledge holders? Does the Convention hold some promise for greater benefit sharing and respect for traditional knowledge in the future? In this regard, re-read Articles 8(j) and 10(c). What steps could governments take to implement these provisions in ways that protect traditional knowledge?

------

2. INTERNATIONAL TRADE AND THE BIODIVERSITY CONVENTION

Many of the Biodiversity Convention's provisions regarding access to biological resources, benefit sharing and other aspects of the biodiversity trade could in theory place significant conditions on international trade in genetic resources and biotechnology. How does the Convention approach international trade, generally? Do you agree with the following analysis that the Convention presents a challenge to the neoclassical model of international trade?

David Downes, *Global Trade, Local Economies and the Biodiversity Convention*, 202, 206–07 in W. SNAPE, ED., BIODIVERSITY AND THE LAW (1996)

The Biodiversity Convention is innovative in that it is simultaneously a conservation agreement and a trade agreement. Conventional trade agreements treat the environment or conservation as marginal concerns when they mention them at all. They tend to view international trade in isolation from other human activities and detached from its environmental consequences. They show almost no regard for other considerations, such as environment, conservation, labor rights, human rights, public health, or worker safety Indeed, trade agreements are drafted as if trade were not just the optimal means but the sole means of improving human welfare. Compounding the problem, the international legal system lacks mechanisms for linking trade agreements with instruments that cover these other issues.

A number of previous multilateral environmental agreements do link environment and trade, generally by restricting certain categories of trade to accomplish environmental or conservation goals. The Convention on International Trade in Endangered Species (CITES), for instance, provides for special treatment of certain products on environmental grounds. It sets up a system in which parties to the treaty agree to ban substantially all trade in products made from species that are listed as being in danger of extinction because of that trade. Consistent with this, CITES parties have banned the ivory trade because it led to huge declines in populations of African elephants. CITES and other multilateral environmental agreements demonstrate broad-based international understanding that trade must be controlled in certain circumstances to ensure that it does not damage the environment or natural resources. In sum, then, trade agreements treat environmental concerns as marginal and view them with suspicion, as potential obstacles to the overarching goal of free trade, whereas multilateral environmental agreements like CITES tend to place limits on trade that menaces environmental goals such as preservation of endangered species.

The Biodiversity Convention takes a different approach to trade and environment. In contrast to the neoclassical economic view of past trade agreements, the convention recognizes the principle of ecological economics that "the ecosystem contains the economy." Thus the convention places trade squarely within its ecological context. While affirming the value of the genetic resources trade, the convention insists that trade be sustainable within the context of a sustainable process of production. Genetic resources are the raw material for "a process of production that extends from rainforests and coral reefs to drugstores, factories, and supermarkets." The Biodiversity Convention establishes basic rules for each stage of that process, rather than banning it altogether.

The first stage of commercial use consists of "prospecting" for useful genetic resources in the wild or in farmers' fields. This stage is covered by Article 10(b), which requires parties to take measures, "as far as possible and as appropriate," to avoid or minimize harm to biodiversity from "the use of biological resources." Biological resources under the convention include genetic resources and any other living component of ecosystems that is valuable for humanity, such as fish or timber. As we shall see, Article 8(j) also requires prospectors to involve local and indigenous communities.

In later stages in the process, a company or government in one country gains access to the genetic resources in another country and then uses them in research and development. Under Article 15(2), a convention party must take steps to facilitate access to its genetic resources, but only for "environmentally sound uses." In other words, the intended end use—in biotechnology, pharmaceuticals, or crop breeding—must not harm the environment, a key tenet of sustainability. As the power of biotechnology to create radically new organisms increases, this tenet will grow in importance. It is becoming easier and easier to transfer genes among widely different organisms that would never interbreed in nature. Corporations are now developing tomatoes that include genes and traits from flounders, for example. While the range of resulting products has tremendous productive potential, they also pose unprecedented environmental risks. To deal with these risks, parties must comply with the convention's requirement that uses of genetic resources be environmentally sound.

---

3. GENDER ISSUES AND BIODIVERSITY

At least since UNCED, international policymakers have become more aware of the special and critical role that women play in development and environment issues. This is particularly true with respect to biodiversity conservation in developing countries, where women are often primarily responsible for obtaining food and medicines, gathering water and firewood, or making clothing or shelter. These activities take women into the fields and forests, making them often more knowledgeable about the potential value of plants and animals. Yet, women have frequently been underrepresented in policymaking institutions, and their stories are just now being told in ways that can improve our conservation of biodiversity. Consider the questions raised in the following excerpt:

> What does maintaining biodiversity have to do with women in particular, rather than with humanity in general? Environmental degradation is often both a cause and an effect of the lifelong hardship that is commonly the lot of rural women in the developing world. As primary resource users. these women do much of the hard work needed to maintain or restore the surrounding

environment often in the face of great odds against success. But many of them are also the agents of environmental degradation simply because they shoulder the heavy workload needed to keep their families fed, housed, and clothed. Only through sustainable development can this downward spiral of poverty and habitat destruction be reversed.

In most of the developing world, women bear primary responsibility for growing and collecting food, medicines, fuel, and housing materials and for providing cash income for schooling, health care, and other family needs. When development plans fail to take these duties and contributions into account, they lead not only to biotic impoverishment, but also to human impoverishment. It is becoming increasingly clear that unless governments and development planners explicitly address poverty, equity and gender issues, efforts to maintain the earth's biotic wealth will be in vain. The statement that "without women there is no development" should be expanded, for without women there can be no conservation either. * * *

Several questions seem paramount. How do women interact with their natural surroundings? What unique knowledge about local species and ecosystems do they gain from these interactions? And how can this knowledge be tapped to better effect? What structures and policies restrict and undervalue women, and how can these be changed so that sustainable development efforts will have a better chance of succeeding? How do these realities alter the way in which conservation and sustainable development should be pursued?

Janet N. Abramovitz & Roberta Nichols, *Women and Biodiversity: Ancient Reality, Modern Imperative; see also* Rio Declaration, Principle 20; Agenda 21, Chapter 24.

———

4. INVASIVE SPECIES

One of the most significant threats to biodiversity is the introduction, either intentionally or accidentally, into an ecosystem of species that do not belong there. This practice has escalated in recent years due to increased international trade and travel. Larger and faster ships, for example, have increased the likelihood that organisms trapped in the ship's ballast water will survive the trip to the ship's destination and this in turn increases the risk that the organism will be dumped live into the destination waters and possibly survive.

Invasive or alien species are those plants, animals, and microbes not native to a region that, when introduced either accidentally or intentionally, out-compete native species for available resources, reproduce prolifically, and dominate regions and ecosystems. Because they often arrive in new areas unaccompanied by their native predators, invasive species can be difficult to control. Left unchecked, many invasives have the potential to transform entire ecosystems, as native species and those that depend on them for food, shelter, and habitat, disappear.

Many specific examples of invasive species illustrate the varied threats and extensive damage they can cause. Consider the following:

- The **zebra mussel** was transported to the Great Lakes system in the ballast water of tankers from the Caspian or Black Sea in Russia. The zebra mussels found the ecosystem perfect for reproducing and because their natural predators, fish with strong jaws that can crush their shells, are not found in the Great Lakes the zebra mussels reproduced unchecked. These small mussels cover just about anything that is sedentary including the intake tunnels for the water supply industry. The cost of cleaning and maintaining open intake tunnels in the face of the zebra mussel has cost companies in the United States and Canada more than $100 million dollars in the last five years alone.

- The **Brown Tree Snake** was observed leaving a cargo plane on an airforce base in Hawaii. This species of snake has already extirpated 10 of 13 native bird species, 6 of 12 native lizard species, and 2 of 3 bat species on Guam. Anyone caught with any snake, in Hawaii, faces as much as a year in jail and a maximum fine of $25,000. The U.S. federal government has appropriated $1.8 million for brown tree snake eradication on Guam and is researching ways to prevent its spread to Hawaii. Hawaiian farmers also spend an estimated $450 million a year trying to eradicate two introduced species— fruit flies and Formosan ground termites.

- In Brooklyn and Amityville, New York, in the spring of 1997 nearly 1,200 trees were chopped down, chipped and burned to eradicate the **Asian horned beetle** costing New York taxpayers $700,000. It will cost nearly $2 million to replant the trees once the threat is over. Scientists surmise that the beetle was a stowaway on a shipment of milled lumber brought in from China.

- The Everglades are also under threat from a variety of non-native species, including for example the **Mallaluca** tree, which has spread like wildfire throughout southern Florida. More recently, Florida officials have intentionally introduced a non-native beetle in the hopes it will help to control the Mallaluca tree.

- **Purple loosestrife**, a highly aggressive plant invader of wetlands, can produce up to 2.7 million seeds per plant yearly, and spreads across approximately 480,000 additional hectares of wetlands each year. It is now a highly visible (even beautiful) presence throughout the country.

- The **glassy-winged sharpshooter**, an invasive insect recently arrived in California, carries with it the plant bacterium Xylella fastidiosa, a disease that has caused nearly $40 million in losses of California grapes. The disease poses a major threat to grape, raisin, and wine industries.

- The **West Nile Virus**, commonly founding Africa, West Asia, and the Middle East, is an invasive virus now present throughout the east and mid-west. Birds are the natural hosts, but mosquitoes transmit the virus from birds to humans and other animals. Several deaths have already been recorded throughout the east due to this virus.

In the aggregate, each of these different case studies adds up to substantial damage to the country's environmental legacy. Federal officials estimate that the total costs of invasive species in the United States are about $137 billion each year, which is double the annual economic damage caused by all natural disasters in the United States, combined! Nearly half of the species listed as threatened or endangered under the Endangered Species Act are at risk due to competition with or predation by non-native species. The US Department of Agriculture spends $556 million a year just to combat invasive species.

The problem presented by alien invasive species is worldwide. Recent studies have shown that more than 50 non-native species are thriving in

British waters. A toxic underwater plant called, *Caulerpa taxifolia*, is spreading like wildfire on the bottom of the Mediterranean Sea smothering native vegetation and poisoning fish. In the Mediterranean the greatest cause of introduction of alien species is the Suez Canal. Nearly 300 species have invaded from the east. In the Black Sea, the catch of native fish has plummeted nearly 90 percent since the introduction of the American comb jellyfish. Even the most remote places have been impacted by alien species. Antarctica for example now hosts cockroaches, earthworms and a variety of grass species that previously were not present. See generally, *Invasive Alien Species: Status, Impacts and Trends of Alien Species that Threaten Ecosystems, Habitats and Species,* UNEP/CBD/SBSTTA/6/INF/11 (Feb. 26, 2001).

Several international organizations have some authority to address invasive species. For example, the International Maritime Organization has developed guidelines to try to combat the transport of marine alien species by ship's ballast water. The guidelines, which are not universally enforced, require that ships not take on ballast water in shallow waters or where algae blooms are present. Ships should exchange ballast water at sea rather than in port as is done now. Any sediments in the ballast should only be disposed of in approved areas in the port. By dumping the ballast at sea it is hoped that any organism transported from other parts of the world would not survive. *See* Chapter 10, page 707.

The Convention on Biodiversity potentially provides the framework for the broadest and most comprehensive efforts to control invasive species. The Convention calls on governments to "control or eradicate those alien species which threaten ecosystems, habitats or species." In the past few years, the Parties to the Biodiversity Convention have begun to address the issue, first by adopting interim guidelines, which the Parties expect to finalize in April, 2002.

Interim Guiding Principles for the Prevention, Introduction, and Mitigation of Impacts of Alien Species, UNEP/CBD/SBSTTA/5/5, Annex I, 22 October 1999

Guiding principle 1: Precautionary approach

Given the unpredictability of the impacts on biological diversity of alien species, efforts to identify and prevent unintentional introductions as well as decisions concerning intentional introductions should be based on the precautionary approach. Lack of scientific certainty about the environmental, social and economic risk posed by a potentially invasive alien species or by a potential pathway should not be used as a reason for not taking preventative action against the introduction of potentially invasive alien species. Likewise, lack of certainty about the long-term implication of an invasion should not be used as a reason for postponing eradication, containment or control measures.

Guiding principle 2: Three-stage hierarchical approach

Prevention is generally far more cost effective and environmentally desirable than measures taken following introduction of an alien invasive species. Priority should be given to prevention of entry of alien invasive species (both between and within States). If entry has already taken place, actions should be undertaken to prevent the establishment and spread of alien species. The preferred response would be eradication at the earliest possible stage (Principle 13). In the event that eradication is not feasible or is not cost-effective, containment (Principle 14) and long-term control measures should be considered (Principle 15). Any examination of benefits and costs (both environmental and economical) should be done on a long-term basis.

Guiding principle 3: Ecosystem approach

All measures to deal with alien invasive species should be based on the ecosystem approach, 3/ in line with the relevant provisions of the Convention and the decisions of the Conference of the Parties.

Guiding principle 4: State responsibility

States should recognize the risk that they may pose to other States as a potential source of alien invasive species, and should take appropriate actions to minimize that risk. In accordance with Article 3 of the Convention on Biological Diversity, and principle 2 of the 1992 Rio Declaration on Environment and Development, States have the responsibility to ensure that activities within their jurisdiction or control do not cause damage to the environment, of other States or of areas beyond the limits of national jurisdiction. In the context of alien invasive species, activities that could be a risk for another State include:

a. The intentional or unintentional transfer of an alien invasive species to another State (even if it is harmless in the State of origin), and

b. The intentional or unintentional introduction of an alien species into their own state if there is a risk of that species subsequently spreading (with or without a human vector) into another state and becoming invasive. * * *

A. Prevention

Guiding principle 7: Border control and quarantine measures

1. States should implement border control and quarantine measures to ensure that:

    1. Intentional introductions are subject to appropriate authorization (Principle 10):

    2. Unintentional or unauthorized introductions of alien species are minimized.

2. These measures should be based on an assessment of the risks posed by alien species and their potential pathways of entry. Existing appropriate governmental agencies or authorities should be strengthened and broadened as necessary, and staff should be properly trained to implement these measures. Early detection systems and regional coordination may be useful. * * *

B. Introduction of species

Guiding principle 10: Intentional introduction

No intentional introduction should take place without proper authorization from the relevant national authority or agency. A risk assessment, including environmental impact assessment, should be carried out as part of the evaluation process before coming to a decision on whether or not to authorize a proposed introduction. States should authorize the introduction of only those alien species that, based on this prior assessment, are unlikely to cause unacceptable harm to ecosystems, habitats or species, both within that State and in neighbouring States. The burden of proof that a proposed introduction is unlikely to cause such harm should be with the proposer of the introduction.

Further, the anticipated benefits of such an introduction should strongly outweigh any actual and potential adverse effects and related costs. Authorization of an introduction may, where appropriate, be accompanied by conditions (e.g., preparation of a mitigation plan, monitoring procedures, or containment requirements). The precautionary approach should be applied throughout all the above-mentioned measures.

Guiding principle 11: Unintentional introductions

1. All States should have in place provisions to address unintentional introductions, (or intentional introductions that have established and become invasive). These include statutory and regulatory measures, institutions and agencies with appropriate responsibilities and with the operational resources required for rapid and effective action.

2. Common pathways leading to unintentional introductions need to be identified and appropriate provisions to minimize such introductions should be in place. Sectoral activities, such as fisheries, agriculture, forestry, horticulture, shipping (including the discharge of ballast waters), ground and air transportation, construction projects, landscaping, ornamental aquaculture, tourism and game-farming, are often pathways for unintentional introductions. Legislation requiring environmental impact assessment of such activities should also require an assessment of the risks associated with unintentional introductions of alien invasive species.

C. Mitigation of impacts
Guiding principle 12: Mitigation of impacts

Once the establishment of an alien invasive species has been detected, States should take steps such as eradication, containment and control, to mitigate the adverse effects. Techniques used for eradication, containment or control should be cost-effective, safe to the environment, humans and agriculture, as well as socially, culturally and ethically acceptable. Mitigation measures should take place in the earliest possible stage of invasion, on the basis of the precautionary approach. Hence, early detection of new introductions of potentially invasive or invasive species is important, and needs to be combined with the capacity to take rapid follow-up action.

Guiding principle 13: Eradication

Where it is feasible and cost-effective, eradication should be given priority over other measures to deal with established alien invasive species. The best opportunity for eradicating alien invasive species is in the early stages of the invasion, when populations are small and localized, hence early detection systems focused on high-risk entry points can be critically useful. Community support, built through comprehensive consultation, should be an integral part of eradication projects.

Guiding principle 14: Containment

When eradication is not appropriate, limitation of spread (containment) is an appropriate strategy only where the range of the invasive species is limited and containment within defined boundaries is possible. Regular monitoring outside the control boundaries is essential, with quick action to eradicate any new outbreaks.

Guiding principle 15: Control

Control measures should focus on reducing the damage caused rather than on merely reducing the numbers of the alien invasive species. Effective control will often rely on a range of integrated techniques. Most control measures will need to be regularly applied, resulting in a recurrent operating budget and the need for long-term commitment to achieve and maintain results. In some instances biological control may give long-term suppression of an alien invasive species without recurrent costs, but should always be implemented in line with existing national regulations, international codes and Principle 10 above.

QUESTIONS AND DISCUSSION

1. In February 1999, President Clinton issued Executive Order 13112, which created the National Invasive Species Council, now comprising ten federal agencies. The Council is intended to provide national leadership and coordination in federal invasive species activities. In January 2001, the Council issued the National Invasive Species Management Plan, complete with 57 different recommendations aimed at the prevention, detection, control and response to invasive species. See National Invasive Species Management Plan.

2. *Problem Exercise.* Using the guiding principles as a starting point, outline the broad components of a possible protocol to the Biodiversity Convention to address the threat posed by invasive alien species. The protocol should cover at least the following elements and reflect the following considerations.

- The Protocol should have a clear objective.

- It should be consistent with the Biodiversity Convention; the protocol should explain why the issue is being addressed under the biodiversity convention.

- The protocol should address all categories of alien species, including those that are released intentionally and those released accidentally.

- It should include binding requirements that have a plausible chance of being adopted and meeting the objective.

- The Protocol should reflect the principles set forth in the biodiversity convention to the extent appropriate, and reflect the approach taken in the Cartagena Biosafety Protocol.

Do you think an Invasive Species Protocol is worthwhile? What would a binding agreement achieve that cannot be achieve through the guiding principles?

SECTION III.   WILDLIFE CONSERVATION

A.   INTRODUCTION

Wildlife treaties are among the oldest examples of international environmental law and fall into three broad categories–protection of specific species, protection of groups of species, and regional protection of species. *Species-specific treaties* date from the early 1900s and have protected wildlife ranging from polar bears and fur seals to vicuna. Treaties protecting *broad groups of species* include, for example, protections for whales and migratory birds. An important example is the 1979 Convention on the Conservation of Migratory Species of Wild Animals, also known as the

Bonn Convention. It seeks to conserve those species of wild animals that migrate across or outside national boundaries. 19 I.L.M. 15 (1980); <http://www.wcmc.org.uk/cms/>. Its most important provisions call for the development and implementation of cooperative agreements, the prohibition of taking endangered species, and habitat conservation. The Convention is open to membership to all States and has global application. As of October, 2000, the Convention had 49 Parties and had led to the negotiation of separate treaties, including for the protection of small cetaceans in the Baltic and North Seas and seals in the Wadden Sea. The most important example of *regional wildlife protection* is likely the Convention on the Conservation of European Wildlife and Natural Habitats, also known as the Berne Convention. UKTS 56 (1982). The Berne Convention requires parties to take measures to maintain populations of wild flora and fauna (identified in separate appendices) as well as conserve their natural habitats. There are similar regional conventions protecting wildlife in the Americas, Africa, and the South Pacific. *See, e.g.,* The Convention on Nature and Wild Life Preservation in the Western Hemisphere, Oct. 12, 1940, 56 Stat. 1354, 161 U.N.T.S. 193. For an in-depth treatment of international wildlife agreements, *see*, S. LYSTER, INTERNATIONAL WILDLIFE LAW: AN ANALYSIS OF INTERNATIONAL TREATIES CONCERNED WITH THE CONSERVATION OF WILDLIFE (1993).

Rather than providing cursory descriptions of the many wildlife treaties, we focus instead in this section on the efforts to protect whales and dolphins. A section discussing sea turtle conservation may be found on the casebook web site at the Teaching Materials page. The successes and setbacks in protecting these species illustrate well the challenges faced by international wildlife conservation in general.

B. WHALES

Suddenly bubbles seemed bursting beneath my closed eyes; like vices my hands grasped the shrouds; some invisible, gracious agency preserved me; with a shock I came back to life. And lo! close under our lee, not forty fathoms off, a gigantic Sperm Whale lay rolling in the water like the capsized hull of a frigate, his broad, glossy back, of an Ethiopian hue, glistening in the sun's rays like a mirror. But lazily undulating in the trough of the sea, and ever and anon tranquilly spouting his vapory jet, the whale looked like a portly burgher smoking his pipe of a warm afternoon. But that pipe, poor whale, was thy last. As if struck by some enchanter's wand, the sleepy ship and every sleeper in it all at once started into wakefulness; and more than a score of voices from all parts of the vessel, simultaneously with the three notes from aloft, shouted forth the accustomed cry, as the great fish slowly and regularly spouted the sparkling brine into the air.

HERMAN MELVILLE, MOBY DICK (1851).

1. HISTORY

Approximately 100 million years ago, the mammalian ancestors of today's whales left the dry land and returned to the sea. The descendants of this intrepid sea-dweller evolved into cetaceans, an order of marine mammals comprising 78 species and divided into two families. Toothed whales, including dolphins, porpoises and killer whales, are the more ancient and varied of the two families. With the exception of the sperm whale, which grows up to 60 feet long, toothed whales are relatively small. The other family of cetaceans, baleen whales, comprise only eleven species. Over 18 million years ago, these whales' teeth developed into a series of plates hanging from the mouth that function as sieves to capture small organisms strained through sea water taken in the mouth. Baleen whales include some of the largest animals that have ever lived, such as Grey, Sei, Right, and Humpback whales. The enormous Blue Whale grows to a leviathan 115 feet and can weigh 200 tons. No one disputes that whales are intelligent. Though we cannot understand their communication, whales speak with one another through complicated clicking noises and long complex songs that travel great distances. As the table from the International Whaling Commission below shows, while most baleen whales were at the brink of extinction several decades ago, only a few species still face the immediate threat of extinction.

<http://ourworld.compuserve.com/homepages/iwcoffice/Estimate.htm>

Population	Year(s) of survey	Size	95% confidence limits
Minke Whales			
-Southern Hemisphere	1982–1989	761,000	510,000–1,140,000
-North Atlantic	1987–1995	~149,000	120,000–182,000
-Northwest Pacific	1989–1990	25,000	12,800–48,600
Fin Whales			
-North Atlantic	1969–1989	47,300	27,700–82,000
Gray Whales			
-Eastern North Pacific	1997/98	26,000	21,900–32,400
Bowhead Whales			
-Bering, Beaufort Seas	1988	7,500	6,400–9,200
Humpback Whales			
-Western North Atlantic	1979–1986	5,500	2,890–8,120
Blue Whales			
-Southern Hemisphere	1980–2000		400–1,400
Pilot Whales			
-Central and Eastern North Atlantic	1989	780,000	440,000–1,370,000

Whales have been hunted through much of human history as a source of food, oil, building and artistic materials. A strong whaling industry was present throughout much of the 18th and 19th centuries, but the threats to whale populations increased by an order of magnitude as technology improved through the development of steam ships and the invention of the harpoon gun by a Norwegian, Sven Foyn, in 1868. Under the doctrine of freedom of the seas there was no regulation of whaling. As stocks of one species became depleted, whalers turned to others. Five species of large whales were hunted, four to the brink of extinction. Only when a glut in the market for whale oil developed due to overproduction at the turn of the twentieth century did the major whaling companies enter into inter-company agreements to regulate whaling. These agreements were based on the Blue Whale Unit (bwu), which allocated unit values to the three major whales taken: blue, humpback and sei. Under the formula, two-and-a-half humpbacks or six sei whales were equivalent to one blue whale. This early approach to manage the whale fishery largely failed and in 1902 governments became involved, creating the International Council for the Exploration of the Sea (ICES). Patricia Birnie, *International Legal Issues in the Management and Protection of the Whale: A Review of Four Decades of Experience*, 29 Nat. Resources J. 903, 905–906 (1989).

ICES established a central bureau to collect statistics from the whaling industry in an attempt to establish a scientific basis for management. It also sought, with little success, to establish uniformity in the application of national laws. Even so, most whaling took place on the high seas beyond national jurisdictions. In 1931 the League of Nations adopted the Convention for the Regulation of Whaling to strengthen the ICES efforts. 49 Stat. 3079, 155 LNTS 349 (Sept. 24, 1931). In an important advance in international environmental law, the convention's provisions were universal, applying to "all the waters of the world." State parties agreed to license their vessels and take appropriate measures to protect whales in their national jurisdictions. The Convention's protections, however, were quite limited, extending only to calves, immature whales, female whales accompanied by calves, and all right whales. It did not prohibit the taking of any other whale species or provide for any enforcement measures. Anthony D'Amato and Sudhir K. Chopra, *Whales: Their Emerging Right to Life,* 85 Am.J.Int'l 21, 30 (1991). The convention did improve the collection of statistical information which, over time, illustrated clearly the need for increased protection. Subsequent ad hoc protocols to the convention introduced new protection measures, but the protocols were signed by different parties and many never came into force.

Under this weak system, whale populations continued to decline and it became evident to whaling States that, to avoid the increasingly likely extinction of whales, an effective international system must be created with both the means to collect data and the authority to enforce whaling controls. Birnie, *op. cit.* at 905–907. This need was met in 1946 with passage of the International Convention on the Regulation of Whaling (ICRW), 161 U.N.T.S. 72.

———

2. INTERNATIONAL CONVENTION FOR THE REGULATION OF WHALING

The ICRW has been, and remains, the dominant international agreement regulating whaling. Its influence has been dramatic. In just 35 years, its mandate transformed from regulation of the whaling fishery to a ban. How did such a remarkable reversal occur?

To regard the story of whaling as simply management of a specific resource misses the real story. The conflict over management of whales has been one of whaling versus whale conservation, of concerns over fishery management versus concerns over animal rights. Some communities, such as the Inuits, view whaling as an important part of their culture. Since the 1970s, increasing numbers of people from all walks of life have expressed strong ethical beliefs that whales should not be hunted at all, regardless of their population numbers. Indeed whale-watching is now a multi-billion dollar business, far exceeding the income from whaling. The dispute between traditional fisheries management and rights-based conservation has led to international conflict among traditional environmental allies and a challenge for international environmental law. Indeed, as you read this section, consider the limitations of the "sustainable development" paradigm. Why does it not fit easily in the context of whaling?

As with the 1931 League of Nations Convention, the ICRW applies to all waters in which whaling occurs, thus protecting whales throughout their migration. At the time of its creation in 1946, the ICRW was intended to ensure the viability of commercial whaling—relying on scientific expertise in order to manage whale fishery stocks at a sustainable level for commercial fishing. Indeed if parties to the ICRW had intended to protect individual whales based on their inherent right to exist, they would have created a very different legal regime. *See* David D. Caron, *The International Whaling Commission and the North Atlantic Marine Mammal Commission: The Institutional Risk of Coercion in Consensual Structures*, 89 Am.J.Int'l L. 154 (1995). While scholars generally agree that conservation of whales for ethical reasons was not the intention of the ICRW's drafters, the language of the Preamble has given rise to much debate over the purpose of the Convention. In particular, the Preamble calls for potentially contradictory goals, stating that the parties "decided to conclude a convention to provide for the proper conservation of whale stocks and thus make possible the orderly development of the whaling industry." Is the purpose of the ICRW conservation of whales *for* the promotion of whaling? In what instances would these be conflicting goals?

The ICRW's most important innovation was the creation of a new institution known as the International Whaling Commission (IWC). The IWC is composed of one member from each Contracting Government. Each member has one vote. The Commission may encourage, recommend or organize studies and investigations of whale populations and whaling as well as disseminate information concerning methods of maintaining and increasing the populations of whale stocks. All whales taken must be reported to the IWC, which uses the data to determine whether populations of species are threatened and require special protections from whaling.

Importantly, the IWC has no enforcement authority. Prosecution for infractions or contraventions of the ICRW are explicitly the responsibility of relevant national authorities in member States of vessels flying their flag. A reporting requirement mandates each Contracting Government to transmit to the IWC full details of each infraction of the Convention, measures taken for dealing with the infraction, and penalties imposed. It took 18 years after Norway's first proposal in 1972, however, to adopt an international observer program to ensure accurate reporting. In addition, there is no provision for dispute settlement.

The ICRW also created a "Schedule" of regulations. The Schedules list the particular species covered by the ICRW and whaling controls. Decision-making under the Commission structure takes place through amendments to the Schedule and resolutions. Amendments to the Schedule are binding and require a three-fourths majority vote. Resolutions, while easier to pass in that they require only a simple majority, are non-binding. To date, the Schedule has only included large cetaceans because the countries supporting protection of dolphins and smaller cetaceans have never attained the requisite three-quarters majority necessary for amendment. The Schedules may be amended by the IWC in light of scientific "findings." It is these Schedule amendments (i.e. "regulations") that have been the battleground for the conservation versus fisheries management debates. In fact Article V, covering the Schedule amendment process and the objection procedures for newly passed regulations, has been the single most controversial provision of the ICRW.

Under Article V, the IWC may amend the Schedule by adopting regulations with respect to the conservation and utilization of whale resources, including open and closed seasons, designation of sanctuary areas, and gear specifications. Any such amendments must be necessary to carry out the objectives and purposes of the Convention and provide for the conservation, development, and optimum use of whales. Regulations must be based on scientific findings and not restrict the number of factory ships or land stations. Furthermore, regulations must take into consideration the interests of the consumers of whale products and the whaling industry. Pro-whaling States, as will be discussed below, have contended that these requirements have been ignored by the pro-conservation States. If a Contracting Government formally objects to a regulation, the regulation is not binding with regard to that Government and does not become binding until and unless the objection is withdrawn.

Article VIII establishes a Scientific Permit exception to the IWC. Any Contracting Government may grant to any of its nationals a special permit authorizing the killing of whales for purposes of scientific research subject to restrictions that the Contracting Government thinks fit. The exception allows contracting governments to issue whaling permits for the purposes of scientific research, notwithstanding stock status and any IWC quotas that may be in place. Following the imposition of a moratorium on whaling in the early 1980s, several contracting States (particularly Japan) have been accused of misusing this exception to continue commercial whaling. As a consequence, subsequent regulations have granted the IWC Scientific Committee some influence over the issuance of such permits. For example, there is now an IWC comment period on requested permits. Each Contracting Government is required to report to the IWC all scientific research authorizations it has granted. Nonetheless, the abuse of scientific permits risks rendering useless any IWC controls on commercial whaling.

INTERNATIONAL CONVENTION FOR THE REGULATION OF WHALING, 1946

RECOGNIZING the interest of the nations of the world in safeguarding for future generations the great natural resources represented by the whale stocks;* * *

HAVING decided to conclude a convention to provide for the proper conservation of whale stocks and thus make possible the orderly development of the whaling industry;

HAVE AGREED as follows:

Article I

1. This Convention includes the Schedule attached thereto which forms an integral part thereof. All references to "Convention" shall be understood as including the said Schedule either in its present terms or as amended in accordance with the provisions of Article V.

2. This Convention applies to factory ships, land stations, and whale catchers under the jurisdiction of the Contracting Governments, and to all waters in which whaling is prosecuted by such factory ships, land stations, and whale catchers.* * *

Article III

1. The Contracting Governments agree to establish an International Whaling Commission, hereinafter referred to as the Commission, to be composed of one member from each Contracting Government. Each member shall have one vote and may be accompanied by one or more experts and advisers.

2. The Commission shall elect from its own members a Chairman and Vice–Chairman and shall determine its own Rules of Procedure. Decisions of the Commission shall be taken by a simple majority of those members voting except that a three-fourths majority of those members voting shall be required for action in pursuance of Article V. The Rules of Procedure may provide for decisions otherwise than at meetings of the Commission.* * *

Article IV

1. The Commission may either in collaboration with or through independent agencies of the Contracting Governments or other public or private agencies, establishments, or organizations, or independently

a) encourage, recommend, or if necessary, organize studies and investigations relating to whales and whaling;

b) collect and analyze statistical information concerning the current condition and trend of the whale stocks and the effects of whaling activities thereon;

c) study, appraise, and disseminate information concerning methods of maintaining and increasing the populations of whale stocks.* * *

Article V

1. The Commission may amend from time to time the provisions of the Schedule by adopting regulations with respect to the conservation and utilization of whale resources, fixing (a) protected and unprotected species; (b) open and closed seasons; (c) open and closed waters, including the designation of sanctuary areas; (d) size limits for each species; (e) time, methods, and intensity of whaling (including the maximum catch of whales to be taken in any one season); (f) types and specifications of gear and apparatus and appliances which may be used; (g) methods of measurement; and (h) catch returns and other statistical and biological records.

2. These amendments of the Schedule (a) shall be such as are necessary to carry out the objectives and purposes of this Convention and to provide for the conservation, development, and optimum utilization of the whale resources; (b)

shall be based on scientific findings; (c) shall not involve restrictions on the number or nationality of factory ships or land stations, nor allocate specific quotas to any factory ship or land station or to any group of factory ships or land stations; and (d) shall take into consideration the interests of the consumers of whale products and the whaling industry.

3. Each of such amendments shall become effective with respect to the Contracting Governments ninety days following notification of the amendment by the Commission to each of the Contracting Governments, except that (a) if any Government presents to the Commission objection to any amendment prior to the expiration of this ninety-day period, the amendment shall not become effective with respect to any of the Governments for an additional ninety days; (b) thereupon, any other Contracting Government may present objection to the amendment at any time prior to the expiration of the additional ninety-day period, or before the expiration of thirty days from the date of receipt of the last objection received during such additional ninety-day period, whichever date shall be the later; and (c) thereafter, the amendment shall become effective with respect to all Contracting Governments which have not presented objection but shall not become effective with respect to any Government which has so objected until such date as the objection is withdrawn. The Commission shall notify each Contracting Government immediately upon receipt of each objection and withdrawal and each Contracting Government shall acknowledge receipt of all notifications of amendments, objections, and withdrawals.* * *

Article VIII

1. Notwithstanding anything contained in this Convention, any Contracting Government may grant to any of its nationals a special permit authorizing that national to kill, take, and treat whales for purposes of scientific research subject to such restrictions as to number and subject to such other conditions as the Contracting Government thinks fit, and the killing, taking, and treating of whales in accordance with the provisions of this Article shall be exempt from the operation of this Convention. Each Contracting Government shall report at once to the Commission all such authorizations which it has granted. Each Contracting Government may at any time revoke any such special permit which it has granted.

2. Any whales taken under these special permits shall so far as practicable be processed and the proceeds shall be dealt with in accordance with directions issued by the Government by which the permit was granted.

3. Each Contracting Government shall transmit to such body as may be designated by the Commission, in so far as practicable, and at intervals of not more than one year, scientific information available to that Government with respect to whales and whaling, including the results of research conducted pursuant to paragraph 1 of this Article and to Article IV.

4. Recognizing that continuous collection and analysis of biological data in connection with the operations of factory ships and land stations are indispensable to sound and constructive management of the whale fisheries, the Contracting Governments will take all practicable measures to obtain such data.

Article IX

1. Each Contracting Government shall take appropriate measures to ensure the application of the provisions of this Convention and the punishment of infractions against the said provisions in operations carried out by persons or by vessels under its jurisdiction.* * *

4. Each Contracting Government shall transmit to the Commission full details of each infraction of the provisions of this Convention by persons or vessels under the jurisdiction of that Government as reported by its inspectors. This information shall include a statement of measures taken for dealing with the infraction and of penalties imposed.* * *

Article XI

Any Contracting Government may withdraw from this Convention on June thirtieth of any year by giving notice on or before January first of the same year to the depositary Government, which upon receipt of such a notice shall at once communicate it to the other Contracting Governments.* * *

---

3. THE MORATORIUM AND RESPONSES

The most significant amendment to the ICRW Schedule has been the moratorium on commercial whaling adopted in 1982 (in force from 1986). The seeds for this action had been sown ten years earlier at the Stockholm Conference on the Human Environment, which called for a 10–year moratorium on the catching of whales for commercial purposes. The IWC did not ban whaling but, rather, approved a "cessation" of all commercial whaling for an interim period. This moratorium would be kept under review based upon the best scientific advice and, by 1990 at the latest, the IWC would undertake a comprehensive assessment of the effects of this decision on whale stocks and consider modification of this provision and the establishment of other catch limits. The moratorium passed by a 25–to–7 vote with 5 abstentions. Four States (Japan, Norway, Peru, USSR) lodged formal objections to the moratorium; Peru later withdrew its objection. While the moratorium's provision for regular scientific review left open the possibility for resumption of whaling once whale populations recovered, the moratorium was extended following review in 1990. This decision reflected the success of NGOs (particularly Greenpeace and EarthTrust) to shift the debate from sustainable use to species conservation.

In 1994, the IWC adopted the Revised Management Procedure (RMP), developed by its Scientific Committee over an eight-year period. This procedure is based on a catch limit algorithm that calculates allowable catches based on population data and uncertainties. Described by the IWC as "the most rigorously tested management procedure for a natural resource yet developed," the RMP's catch limits would be set for five years. Despite the RMP's adoption, however, the moratorium has remained in place. As the IWC website explains, the RMP's "actual implementation in whale management (at least for those stocks for which it has been tested), is of course a political decision. The Commission will not set catch limits for commercial whaling until it has agreed and adopted a complete Revised Management Scheme (RMS). Any RMS will not only include the scientific aspects such as the RMP, but a number of non-scientific issues, including inspection and enforcement, perhaps to humaneness of killing techniques." <http://ourworld.compuserve.com/homepages/iwcoffice/Estimate.htm>. The requirement of an RMS, which has not yet been established, has been condemned by pro-whaling nations as a delaying tactic to keep the moratorium in place.

Following the IWC's extension of the moratorium, Iceland officially withdrew from the IWC in 1992. At the same time Japan and Norway threatened to leave the Commission, and Norway announced that it would resume commercial whaling in 1993. Norway's actions did not violate the ICRW because it had formally objected to the moratorium. Norway's role as an anti-conservationist pariah is strange because it was a founding member of the IWC and has been in the vanguard of whale conservation efforts throughout much of the IWC's history. Nonetheless, Norway, Japan and Iceland believe that the objectives and requirements of the ICRW have been flagrantly disregarded. The IWC is supposed to be an instrument for the sound management of whales, they contend, not for the complete ban on whaling. And, since the adoption of the moratorium most non-whaling States have shifted their stance in favor of outlawing whaling altogether.

This conflict has played out most clearly in the case of the minke whale. The IWC Scientific Committee estimates over 900,000 minke whales worldwide. Iceland, Japan and Norway argue that small numbers of minke whales can now be taken without risk to the population's viability. Yet the IWC continues to ban *all* commercial whaling, despite the opinion of the IWC Scientific Committee that minke whale stocks may be harvested. In a fascinating response to the IWC's refusal to permit limited harvesting of minke whales, Norway, Iceland, Greenland and the Faeroe Islands have challenged the very legitimacy of the IWC, creating a new international whaling institution, the North Atlantic Marine Mammal Commission (NAMMCO). Agreement on Cooperation in Research, Conservation and Management of Marine Mammals in the North Atlantic, April 9, 1992. The following excerpt describes the debate and origins of NAMMCO in more detail.

David D. Caron, *The International Whaling Commission and the North Atlantic Marine Mammal Commission: The Institutional Risks of Coercion in Consensual Structures, 89 Am.J.Int'l L. 154*

Shortly before Norway took its first whale in 1993 for commercial purposes, its Ambassador to the United States, Kjeld Vibe, said the IWC should be "analyzed anew," and that Norway's actions should serve as "a warning to the anti-all-whaling majority" that the IWC is supposed to be "an instrument for the sound management of whale stocks," not an "instrument for a complete ban on all whaling, regardless of whether we are talking about a threatened or endangered species." This "warning" to the IWC in 1993 leads us to consider the related challenge implicit in the 1992 creation of the North Atlantic Marine Mammal Commission.

Beginning in 1988, meetings sponsored by Norway, Iceland and others were held that brought "together countries which wish to emphasize a rational approach to marine mammal management, in contrast, for example, to the approach taken in recent years with respect to whales in the International Whaling Commission." At the fifth such conference, held in Nuuk, Greenland, on April 9, 1992, representatives of the Faroe Islands, Greenland, Iceland and Norway signed the Agreement on Cooperation in Research, Conservation and

Management of Marine Mammals in the North Atlantic. The Agreement established a regional organization, NAMMCO, for the scientific study, conservation and management of marine mammals in the North Atlantic region. The document clearly responded to what the drafters regarded as inappropriate whale protectionist tendencies of the IWC. As Gudmundur Eiriksson of Iceland stated at NAMMCO's inaugural meeting in 1992, the organization was born out of dissatisfaction with the IWC's zero-catch quota, lack of IWC competence to deal with small cetaceans, and the need for an organization to deal with other marine mammals such as seals.

Under the Agreement, NAMMCO consists of four organs: (1) a plenary Council; (2) management committees; (3) a single Scientific Committee; and (4) a secretariat. The Council is to provide a forum for exchange of information by the parties regarding North Atlantic marine mammals; to form, direct and coordinate appropriate management committees; to coordinate requests for scientific advice; and to negotiate and oversee working cooperation arrangements both with "other appropriate organizations" and with states not party to the Agreement. In defining the role of management committees, Article 5 implies that each committee will have jurisdiction over some subset of marine mammal issues. The management committees are to "propose to their members measures for conservation and management measures." They also will make recommendations to the Council concerning needed scientific research. The Scientific Committee is to consist of experts appointed by the parties, and may additionally (with the Council's approval) invite other experts to participate in its work. The Scientific Committee is to "provide scientific advice in response to requests from the Council, utilizing, to the extent possible, existing scientific information." The secretariat, to be established by the Council, will "perform such functions as the Council may determine."

Looking at these organs as a whole, it is apparently intended that the management committees, to be created by the Council, will propose conservation and management measures to members, and that, in attempting to formulate such proposals, the committees will present requests for scientific research to the Council. In considering those requests, the Council may generate its own additional scientific questions. Upon the request of the Council, the Scientific Committee will provide information and conduct additional research if necessary.

The decision-making process within NAMMCO is highly protective of the interests of individual members. Since the management committees may only "propose" measures to members, the legal authority of NAMMCO over its members is merely recommendatory. Decisions of the Council and the management committees are to be made "by the unanimous vote of those members present and casting an affirmative vote." The Agreement does not provide mechanisms for implementing proposals, monitoring compliance with proposals, or obtaining definitive interpretation of the terms of either the Agreement or proposed conservation measures recommended thereunder. * * *

NAMMCO poses an interesting challenge to the IWC even though, strictly speaking, the organization does not conflict with the IWC. Indeed, the actions of NAMMCO's members need not necessarily conflict with their obligations under the IWC. Norway, for example, is a member of the IWC and, because of its earlier objection, is not legally bound by the moratorium. Yet, although NAMMCO and Norway have not yet acted in a manner legally in conflict with the IWC, the very existence of NAMMCO and the actions of Norway challenge the legitimacy of some of the IWC's decisions. In relying on the RMP of the IWC Scientific Committee in a way that appears appropriate but that the IWC itself has not yet done, NAMMCO and Norway are challenging the integrity of the political process of the IWC. In developing its own data base of marine mammal populations in the North Atlantic, NAMMCO will challenge the legitimacy of the IWC's decision making by contradicting the science and expertise that is the foundation of such legitimacy.

All the while, of course, NAMMCO also becomes an option for those in the North Atlantic region that decide to withdraw from the IWC or, more likely, to opt out of particular IWC obligations. Subsistence Inuit harvesters, for example, appear to view NAMMCO as a desirable complement, perhaps alternative, to the IWC. In July 1992, the Inuit Circumpolar Conference expressed its frustration that "the IWC's operations are influenced by animal protection interests which have caused the demise of fur-trapping and sealing," and that "this anti-whaling trend is increasing within the IWC." The conference introduced a resolution providing that it initiate operation of its own previously established Whaling Commission, and "promote discussions among interested parties within the circumpolar world including a consideration of international cooperation with regional whaling organizations such as the Canada/Greenland Joint Commission and the recently inaugurated North Atlantic Marine Mammal Commission."

The reactions to the challenge to the IWC presented by the creation of NAMMCO and the resumption of commercial whaling by Norway can be divided into three parts: First, several states have threatened to impose sanctions on Norway for its decision to resume commercial whaling. This raises the question of whether the members of the IWC, particularly the United States, are willing to employ their power to support continuation of the moratorium on minke whaling as strongly as they supported the moratorium in the 1980s. Second, several ocean policy scholars have called on the IWC to moderate its position, particularly as regards "artisanal whaling," that is, local small-scale whaling, where profit is almost incidental. This raises the question of whether the IWC, dominated as it is by antiwhaling interests, is capable of such a change. Third, the antiwhaling nations and groups involved in the IWC process have attempted to transform their side of the debate back into one of management expertise and utility by articulating why estimates of whale populations are not sufficient to justify a return to whaling. This raises the question of how persuasive these efforts are.

In response to its 1993 decision to resume commercial whaling, Norway was threatened with economic boycotts, blockage of its bid to join the European Community, and boycotts of the 1994 winter Olympics to be held in Lillehammer. Nonetheless, stating that it was "on solid ground with respect to the law," Norway resumed whaling and took all 160 minke whales apportioned for commercial harvest.

Norway has increased its minke whale quota every season, from 226 whales in 1993 to 753 in 1999. *Whales in Danger Information Service*; <http://whales.magna.com.au>. Despite the mandates of the Pelly and Packwood–Magnuson Amendments (described in the Questions and Discussion section that follows), while the U.S. Commerce Department has expressed "regret" that Norway has resumed whaling, the United States has not certified or imposed sanctions on Norway for its whaling activities.

NAMMCO has since developed into an active international organization strikingly similar to the IWC. Its eighth meeting, for example, was held in 1998. Much as at IWC meetings, NAMMCO's Scientific Committee presented its research findings on minke whales, harp seals and hooded seals in the North Atlantic. Its Management Committee determined that the minke whale population could sustain catches of 292 animals per year, and it implemented an International Observation Scheme. This program monitors sealing and whaling activities in Norway and Greenland and pilot whaling in the Faroes. The international observers are not allowed to intervene in hunting activities, instead reporting violations of NAMMCO or national regulations to the NAMMCO Secretariat for an annual review that forms the basis for possible enforcement actions by the respective national control authority.

Japan has taken a different approach to continue whaling, relying on the Scientific Permit exception. Throughout the 1990s, Japan authorized the taking of minke whales (965 minke whales, for example, in 1996). This whaling has been managed by the Institute of Cetaceous Research, which in 1996 received over $35 million for the sale of whale meat. Meat sales apparently account for 60% of its annual budget. Nick Smith, *University DNA testing exposes whale of a lie,* THE SUNDAY NEWS (AUCKLAND), August 24, 1997, at 11. The excerpt below sets out the Japanese Whaling Association's justification for this activity. <http://www.jp-whaling-assn.com/index_eng.htm>.

> The Japanese whale research program has obtained valuable information on whales by using non-lethal and lethal research. It has also enabled us to calculate the amount of fish consumed by whales—which is approximately between 280 million tonnes and 500 million tonnes per year. In contrast, humans harvest around 90 million tonnes of fish each year... A large range of information is needed for the management and conservation of whales, such as population, age structure, growth rates, age of maturity, reproductive rates, feeding, nutrition and levels of contaminants. This type of important information cannot be obtained through small DNA samples or analysis of organochlorine, but only through lethal research.
>
> In the research program, the vessels are run on a predesigned track formulated by scientists, and conduct surveys and collects specimens such as earplug and ovaries. After scientific examination and removal of tissue and organ samples, the remains of the whales are frozen and marketed in compliance with the provisions of the Convention, which forbid any part of the carcass to be wasted. However, as the cost of research is expensive, the proceeds from sales of whale meat and parts alone cannot cover the costs. The Government of Japan pays the remainder of the costs.

In what has become a ritual, every IWC meeting adopts a resolution condemning this practice, but it has continued unabated. In the Summer of 2000, following its failure to gain IWC approval to hunt bryde's and sperm whales, Japan announced it would expand its scientific whaling to hunt 50 bryde's whales and 10 sperm whales, species that had not been hunted since 1987. Japan's Fisheries Agency said the populations had recovered to sustain an annual harvest and therefore the hunt was needed to gather data on the habitat, diet and migration patterns of the whales.

---

4. BREAKING THE STALEMATE

At the annual meeting of the IWC in 2000, its Secretary over the last 24 years, Dr. Ray Gambell, retired. In leaving the organization he had overseen both before and after the moratorium, Gambell issued a stark warning.

> Whaling is going on at a commercial level. It's outside IWC control. I would think it much better that it was brought within international regulations and oversight. I think the commission will need to move forward on measures which would allow controlled whaling, otherwise it will lose credibility. If the commission cannot set its house in order, people will start to ask: "Why do we need it at all?"

Whaling ban set to end (June 11, 2000) <http://news.bbc.co.uk>.

Iceland's departure from the IWC, Norway's reservation to the moratorium, Japan's vigorous use of the scientific whaling exception, and NAMMCO's creation all call into question the effectiveness, indeed the relevance, of the IWC. The current situation clearly leaves much to be desired, but do the antagonists' fundamentally different visions of the problem–animal rights versus fisheries management–leave space for meaningful compromise? In 1997, Ireland and Australia called for establishment of a global whale sanctuary, and if this could not be achieved, a 50–year moratorium on commercial whaling. Realizing these proposals had little chance of success, and acknowledging the gap between the extremes of zero whaling and full scale commercial whaling, Ireland later proposed the following compromise at the 1997 IWC meeting:

> 1) The Revised Management Scheme should be completed and adopted. The scheme must be conservative and provide in particular for inspection and observation procedures that will engender public confidence.
>
> 2) Where quotas are justified under the RMS, these should be restricted to coastal areas only and to nations who are now whaling. This would result in a de facto sanctuary over the oceans of the world.
>
> 3) Quotas should be issued for local consumption only. This would avoid the pressure on whaling which would arise from international trade.
>
> 4) Lethal scientific whaling should be phased out over a period.
>
> 5) Regulations for whale-watching should be prepared to minimize the impacts of disturbance on whale populations.

Opening Statement of the Government of Ireland, International Whaling Commission, 1997 (IWC/49/OS Ireland).

In 1998, a revised proposal would have allowed countries the right to hunt whales in their own coastal waters up to 200 miles offshore but ban it elsewhere, turning the high seas in effect into a giant whale sanctuary. Neither of these proposals has been adopted, but countries have continued to search for compromises that will resolve the whaling stalemate. In a surprise move, the Worldwide Fund for Nature (WWF) now supports the Irish proposal. As a WWF official explained its change from anti-whaling to support of limited coastal whaling,

> If the IWC can't stop whaling, it has to control it. But it's not controlling it— the IWC is completely insane, almost dysfunctional. There is no willingness by either whalers or conservationists to understand each other. It's totally polar-

ised—you can predict almost every vote before it's cast. This year the commission missed a chance to write into its schedule—effectively its constitution—a highly precautionary management system which would have set all catch quotas at zero while retaining the moratorium on commercial whaling enforced in 1985. It would have been a safety net for any whaling that may happen in the future... Without a proper management regime in place at the IWC, CITES may downlist the minkes at its 2002 meeting. That would mean a free-for-all, with non-IWC members launching a completely uncontrolled hunt on the minkes to supply the Japanese market.

http://news.bbc.co.uk/hi/english/sci/tech/newsid_1458000/1458234.stm

Despite these difficulties, it should be remembered that the IWC has achieved a great deal since its founding. While the humpback whale and, in particular, blue whale populations are at very low numbers, most large whales are still not commercially hunted. In addition to the basic conflict over hunting minke, bryde's and sperm whales, the issues that will confront the IWC in the next few years include: how to address the creation of a rival international institution based on its own legal procedures, the protection of small cetaceans, regulation of whale-watching and non-consumptive uses, and the treatment of aboriginal or other local whaling. Birnie, *op. cit.*, at 933–34.

QUESTIONS AND DISCUSSION

1. Is the seemingly permanent moratorium on whaling contrary to the ICRW's objectives? Do you agree with Norway's argument that the IWC has been subverted from its original purpose of managing a commercial fishery to protection of animal rights by simply banning all whaling? If not, how do you justify the decision to ban hunting of minke whales despite the contrary advice of the Scientific Committee? Conversely, is there any reason the ICRW's purpose cannot change over time?

2. At the CITES conference of the parties in 1997, Japan and Norway proposed transferring bryde's, gray and minke whales from Appendix I to II, thus permitting renewed trade. While Norway did not gain the two-thirds majority necessary for adoption, it did receive strong international support with 57 countries voting in favor and 51 against. This marked the first time there had ever been a CITES vote in favor of this issue. Japan's proposal that CITES establish its own policies on whaling in place of the IWC was defeated 51–27. In a suggestive example of deal-making among parties to international environmental agreements, it had been reported that Norway would support southern African countries' proposal to renew trade in elephant ivory if they supported transferring the whales from Appendix I to Appendix II. Similar proposals by Norway and Japan at the the CITES conference of the parties in 2000 were also defeated. Walter Gibbs, *Whalers Say the Wind Is Turning in Their Favor*, N.Y. Times, July 23, 1997 at A4; Stephen Kass, *Environmental Law*, THE NAT'L L.J. Aug. 11, 1997, at B4; Greenwire, May 21, 1997.

Charges of vote-buying have also surfaced at the IWC. Following a vote that fell six short of establishing a South Pacific whaling sanctuary, Patrick Ramage, of the International Fund for Animal Welfare, charged,

This wasn't a vote, it was an auction, and Japan was the winning bidder. Japan has for several years pursued an international vote consolidation strategy, using development assistance and economic leverage to secure the votes of small developing countries in the IWC and other international conventions. In recent years, the Caribbean countries have been key targets of this effort. Each of the six Caribbean nation delegations to the Adelaide meeting today—

Antigua, Dominica, Grenada, St. Kitts, St. Lucia, and St. Vincent—vocally supported the Japanese effort to sink the sanctuary proposal.

Andrew Darby, *South Pacific Whale Sanctuary Voted Down* (July 4, 2000) <http://ens.lycos.com>. Resorting to the same alleged tactics, a number of NGOs are now actively encouraging Pacific island nations to join the IWC and form a stronger anti-whaling bloc.

3. Addressing the *trade* in whale products is not, technically, within the IWC's mandate. The IWC Infractions Subcommittee has, nonetheless, addressed the issue in order to increase public attention and national embarrassment. At the 1994 IWC meeting, for example, it was reported that a shipment of 232 tons of bryde's whale meat had been discovered in Vladivostock, Russia. The meat had been transported from Taiwan by a Honduran-flagged ship for eventual sale in Japan. Discovering such illegal shipments, however, is rare. *See* Peter Stoett, THE INTERNATIONAL POLITICS OF WHALING 140?41 (1997).

DNA testing is providing a new enforcement mechanism to combat illegal whaling. Over a three year period, researchers from the University of Auckland in New Zealand collected samples of whale meat sold in fish markets in Japan. Of thirty samples tested using DNA analysis, six samples were found to be from whale species protected by the IWC—one came from killer whale, one from humpback whale, and four from finback whale. An official at the Japanese Fisheries Agency claimed that these were likely from whale meat imported legally prior to 1991 and subsequently frozen for later sale. Natalie Angier, *DNA Tests Find Meat of Endangered Whales for Sale in Japan*, N.Y. TIMES, Sept. 13, 1994, at C4.

Perhaps they should test for more than DNA. In early 2001, five Japanese consumer groups opposed any trade of whale meat with Norway on health grounds. The groups cited a 1999 study showing that over half of the whale meat on the market in Japan exceeded national or international standards for at least one toxic chemical. As a wire service reported,

> The study of samples collected from Japanese shops and restaurants revealed that the blubber from 58% of North Pacific minke whales contained levels of at least one contaminant in excess of national or international standards. In a subsequent study, 80% of samples of Antarctic minke whale bacon or blubber and 100% of North Pacific minke whale bacon or blubber tested exceeded advisory limits set in Japan for ingestion of the dioxin group of chemicals. * * *
>
> Japanese law prohibits the sale and import of food that contains toxic substances or is suspected to contain toxic substances. However, the Japanese government remained cautious about the issue, saying that the country has yet to discuss possible whale meat imports with Norway.

Japanese Citizens Groups Oppose Imports of "Contaminated" Whalemeat, AGENCE FRANCE PRESSE ENGLISH, January 19, 2001

4. A number of indigenous cultures depend on the hunting of whales for physical, cultural and spiritual sustenance. In the case of the Alaskan Eskimo, the bowhead whale (more commonly referred to as the right whale because it is a slow swimmer and easy to hunt, making it the "right" whale for hunting) is the focus of concerns about permitting continued aboriginal whaling. The Schedule in 2000 provided for six separate aboriginal subsistence whaling exceptions (e.g., up to 19 West Greenland fin whales may be taken annually by Greenlanders from 1998–2002).

An aboriginal exception has been included in the Schedule as far back as the 1931 League of Nations Convention for specific stocks such as Alaskan bowhead whales. The ICRW Schedule does not define the term, "aborigine," and the IWC still has not defined the term despite the establishment of a working group. This issue is significant because a number of anti-whaling States do support limited exceptions for coastal communities that depend on whaling for their livelihood.

This is the case for the uncomfortable dual role played by the United States, as both an openly anti-whaling nation and staunch defender of the rights of its aboriginal citizens for subsistence whaling. Indeed in 1977 the United States was embarrassed by the Alaskan Eskimos' defiance of the IWC Scientific Committee's advice that a moratorium should be implemented for bowhead whales. The growing prosperity of Eskimos had increased their whaling activities since they could use more sophisticated equipment than traditional means. In response, the IWC removed the aboriginal exception on bowheads, placing the United States in a conflict between upholding the Eskimos' cultural rights while promoting the IWC. The United States challenged the legality of the IWC action, arguing that the moratorium only applied to commercial whaling. As the substantive articles of the ICRW makes no reference to aboriginal exceptions and therefore does not guarantee them, a compromise was reached and the United States undertook research of the bowhead population. As a result of this investigation and lobbying efforts of the Eskimos at subsequent IWC meetings, a small quota has been regularly allowed for the Eskimos. Patricia Birnie, *International Legal Issues in the Management and Protection of the Whale: A Review of Four Decades of Experience*, 29 Nat. Resources J. 903, 929?30 (1989).

This conflict has continued to play out in the whale hunt conducted by the Makah tribe in Northwest Washington state. Based on treaty rights, the United States (but not the IWC) has permitted the Makah to kill up to five gray whales per year. The hunt has been challenged in court and led to violent confrontations on the waters, where the Coast Guard has enforced a 500 yard exclusion zone around the hunters. One of the opposing NGOs, the Sea Shepherd, has offered a reward of $2,000 for information on the Makah tribe's planned hunts at least three hours prior to the launch of whaling boats. The Makah have refused to call off the hunt, citing their treaty rights and the hunt's cultural significance.

Japan, on the other hand, has sought to profit from the aboriginal exception by arguing that the exception ought to apply to its coastal villages with whaling traditions because of their "shared characteristics." What might these shared characteristics be? To date the IWC has rejected this argument because of the commercial aspects of such whaling, e.g., the fact that it is not entirely for local consumption. Michael L. Chiropolos, *Inupiat Subsistence and the Bowhead Whale: Can Indigenous Hunting Cultures Coexist With Endangered Animal Species*, 5 Colo. J. Int'l Envtl. L. & Pol'y 213, 231 (1994).

5.   The effectiveness of the IWC has been due in great measure to the threat of unilateral sanctions by the United States against countries that frustrate the IWC's efforts. The Pelly Amendment to the Fishermen's Protective Act of 1967 grants authority to the executive branch to impose sanctions on nations that violate the policies and objectives of the ICRW's conservation program. The Packwood–Magnuson Amendment allows the President to impose sanctions under the Pelly Amendment when foreign fisheries diminish the effectiveness of U.S. environmental laws. If a country is certified as acting contrary to the aims of the ICRW, the United States may put in place trade sanctions against any products from the certified country. Gene S. Martin Jr., and James W. Brennan, *Enforcing the International Convention for the Regulation of Whaling: The Pelly and Packwood–Magnuson Amendments*, 17 Denv. J. Int'l L. & Pol'y 293, 294 (1989).

While foreign countries have been certified a number of times under these laws for diminishing the effectiveness of the ICRW, until the Japanese hunting of sperm and bryde's whales in 2000 no Pelly Amendment sanctions had ever been imposed and only a few Packwood–Magnuson sanctions had ever been imposed. Nonetheless, the threat of trade sanctions and loss of fishery access are serious and a number of countries, most notably Peru, have modified their behavior to comply with the IWC as a result. In December, 1996, Canada was certified under the Pelly Amendment for conducting whaling activities that diminish the effectiveness of a conservation program of the IWC but no sanctions followed.

Japan has been certified by the Pelly Amendment three times for conducting fishing operations that diminish the effectiveness of an international fishery conservation program. This most recent certification was the result of an expansion of Japan's North Pacific Program, which requested scientific permission to take 10 sperm whales and 50 Bryde's whales, and which the Secretary said had "dubious scientific validity." Japan was also certified under the Packwood–Magnuson Amendment for its activities, which could potentially deprive it of future opportunities to fish in the U.S. exclusive economic zone. <http://www.noaa.gov/whales/minetaletter.htm>.

In addition to the Pelly and Packwood–Magnuson Amendments, the U.S. Marine Mammal Protection Act and the Australian Whale Protection Act provide more direct species-specific protections. The U.S. law, for example, prohibits nationals from taking marine mammals from U.S. waters *or* the high seas. The New Zealand Marine Mammal Protection Act goes even farther, prohibiting its nationals from taking marine mammals within waters subject to the jurisdiction of another State. *See* Birnie, *op. cit.* at 929.

These laws are reinforced by UNCLOS Article 65, which provides that other UNCLOS provisions shall not restrict the right of a coastal State or international organization to prohibit, limit or regulate the exploitation of marine mammals more strictly than provided for in UNCLOS. Moreover, parties must cooperate in conserving marine mammals and "in the case of cetaceans shall in particular work through appropriate international organizations for their conservation, management and study." The IWC, as an international organization, clearly is covered by this provision.

6. Despite Japanese and Norwegian charges that the anti-whaling environmental groups are driven by concern over animal rights rather than science, Greenpeace justifies the moratorium on a scientific basis. It argues that whaling cannot be managed as a traditional fishery because the whale's rate of reproduction is so slow. Instead of releasing enormous numbers of eggs into the water for fertilization by the male, as fish do, whales are mammals and give live birth to a single calf no more than once every year or two. Moreover, the calf needs a year of maternal care before it can survive on its own and many years before it reaches sexual maturity.

Greenpeace also criticizes the science underpinning IWC management, contending that neither the actual whale populations nor their growth rates are known well. Population estimates are extrapolated from sightings of a small fraction of the population. Read again the IWC chart on whale populations at the beginning of this section. The "95% confidence limits" column means that 95% of the time the actual population number will fall within the range between the two numbers. For example, there is a 95% probability that the actual population of blue whales lies between 210 and 1,000 individuals. Greenpeace argues that this supposed confidence is unfounded. As a powerful example, it points to evidence of illegal whaling that has brought into question the accuracy of the Scientific Committee's projections.

In 1994 it was revealed by a former Soviet Fisheries Ministry official that the Soviet Union had deliberately, and egregiously, misled the IWC over the number of whales it was killing. From 1948 to 1973, the Soviet Union officially reported killing 2,710 humpback whales while, in fact, it killed over 48,000. This new information throws in doubt the extrapolations of recovery rates made by scientists over literally the last forty years. The IWC now admits that its estimates of whale harvests could be in error by two orders of magnitude. The sheer size of this deception, Greenpeace and others contend, clearly demonstrates the inability to estimate accurately whale populations and, as a consequence, allowable harvest quotas. Greenpeace's full defense of the moratorium is at its Web site, <http://www.greenpeace.org/cbio.html>; Sander Thoenes, *Soviets Lied On Whales, Adviser Says,* THE MOSCOW TIMES, May 25, 1994.

How should the precautionary principle apply to whaling? For which species does it suggest a total ban on whaling or quotas?

7.   The moratorium has been in place since 1982 and its supporters include both developing and developed countries. As described above, the ICRW applies "to all waters in which whaling is prosecuted." Article 1. Yet some non-member States have argued that this language and scope is limited by the UNCLOS, widely regarded as customary international law. In particular, UNCLOS Articles 56 and 57 grant coastal States sovereign rights for the purpose of exploiting and managing living and non-living natural resources up to 200 miles from their baseline (generally the coast). Under the Vienna Convention's rules for treaty interpretation, since the Law of the Sea Convention is more recent than the ICRW, the Law of the Sea Convention provisions of sovereignty trump the "all waters" provision of the ICRW.

Opponents of this legal position point to UNCLOS Article 192, however, which obligates all States to protect and preserve the marine environment, and Article 61, which declares that coastal States shall ensure through proper conservation and management measures that living resources in their sovereign waters are "not endangered by over-exploitation." Moreover, Article 65 provides that "States shall co-operate with a view to the conservation of marine mammals and in the case of cetaceans shall in particular work through the appropriate international organizations for the conservation, management and study."

Consider the case where a country knows that its commercial vessels are killing humpback whales. Does the State have a legal obligation to prohibit this activity if it is a party to UNCLOS but not the ICRW? What if it is neither a party to UNCLOS nor the ICRW (i.e., should the moratorium on whaling be considered customary international law)? Does your answer change if the vessels are killing minke whales instead of humpbacks? *See,* Howard Scott Schiffman, *The Protection of Whales in International Law: A Perspective for the Next Century,* 22 BROOKLYN J. INT'L L. 303, 331 (1996).

8.   Article 5 of the ICRW provides for establishment of whale sanctuaries. At the 44th meeting of the IWC in 1992, France proposed a Southern Ocean Whaling Sanctuary. This proposal coincided with international efforts to establish a ban on mining and commercial operations in the Antarctic (see p. 1059). In 1994 the IWC approved the creation of the sanctuary around the Antarctic, banning commercial whalers from the Antarctic Ocean south of 40 degrees south latitude and in some areas below the 60th parallel. Japan strongly opposed creation of the Sanctuary, claiming there was no scientific basis for its creation. Since the Sanctuary's creation, Japan has taken minke whales there through its scientific whaling program. *Japan to increase minke whale catch over wider area,* JAPAN ECONOMIC NEWSWIRE, May 20, 1995.

9.   For further reading and web sites, *see* FARLEY MOWAT, A WHALE FOR THE KILLING 31–34 (1972); PETER STOETT, THE INTERNATIONAL POLITICS OF WHALING 140–141 (1997); Judith Berger–Eforo, Note, *Sanctuary for the Whales: Will this be the demise of the International Whaling Commission or a viable strategy for the twenty-first century?,* 8 PACE INT'L L. REV. 439 (1996).

<http://ourworld.compuserve.com/homepages/iwcoffice/> (Homepage of the IWC with useful details on whale populations, aboriginal exceptions, meeting details, and current initiatives)

< http://www.jp-whaling-assn.com/index_eng.htm > (Homepage of the Japan Whaling Association, presents perspective of Japanese whalers and challenges the basis of the IWC moratorium)

<http://www.nammco.no/Default.htm> (homepage of NAMMCO)

< http://whales.greenpeace.org/> (Greenpeace's homepage of its whaling campaign)

<http://www.wdcs.org/> (homepage of the Whale and Dolphin Conservation Society)

C. DOLPHINS

The legal protection of dolphins in the eastern tropical Pacific Ocean (ETP) provides a powerful example of how extraterritorial application of U.S. law can drive the creation of binding international law. Despite complaints that the U.S. actions violated the General Agreement on Tariffs and Trade (GATT) and illegitimately restricted activities by sovereign nations, today dolphin mortality from the tuna fishery in the ETP has been reduced to 1% of its previous levels. In reading the history of the tuna/dolphin conflict, consider the legal/policy interplay between national action and international reaction. In the end the U.S. actions proved effective, but at what cost?

---

1. THE TUNA FISHERY AND DOLPHIN MORTALITY

No one knows exactly why, but yellowfin tuna tend to swim beneath certain species of dolphin in the ETP. Fisherman are well aware of this association and since the 1950's have taken advantage of it to catch large yellowfin tuna by surrounding schools of dolphin with purse seine nets. Purse seine nets can be up to a mile long and 600–800 feet deep. Once a school of dolphins is spotted, motorboats commence a high speed chase to herd the dolphins into a small enough circle so they can be surrounded by the purse seine net. Most chases last about 20 minutes though they can take up to an hour. Once the dolphins are surrounded by the net the bottom is pulled together by cables (like a drawstring purse) to prevent escape beneath the net. Because dolphins must breathe at the surface, dolphins tangled in the net drown. Traditional purse seine net hauls have killed hundreds of dolphins at a time. Since the dolphins have no commercial value, they are simply discarded overboard as bycatch. Betsy Carpenter, *What price dolphin? Scientists are reckoning the true cost of sparing an endearing mammal*, U.S. NEWS & WORLD REP., June 13, 1994.

The U.S. National Marine Fisheries Service estimated in 1992 that more than six million dolphins had been killed in the course of purse seine fishing operations by the United States and foreign fleets in the ETP since 1959. 57 FED. REG. 27010 (1992). During the 1960s and early 1970s, the U.S.

fleet dominated the tuna fishery in the ETP and was responsible for more than 80% of dolphin deaths. MARINE MAMMAL COMMISSION, 1995 ANNUAL REPORT TO CONGRESS 99 (1996). This was a period of expansion for the ETP tuna fishery to satisfy the growing popularity of tuna in the United States, which accounted for more than one-quarter of all fish Americans consumed in 1974. Roughly 30% of the world's yellowfin tuna comes from the ETP. Eugene Buck, DOLPHIN PROTECTION AND TUNA SEINING, CONG. RES. SERV. ISSUE BRIEF (1997). The U.S. tuna fleet reached its peak in the ETP in 1979, with 140 purse seine boats actively fishing. The main target of purse seiners were spotted dolphins, accounting for about 88% of dolphin encirclements. While their numbers have sharply declined as a result of the tuna fishery in the ETP, spotted dolphins have not been listed as threatened or endangered by the U.S. Endangered Species Act, though they are listed as "depleted" under the Marine Mammal Protection Act.

----

2.   U.S. LEGISLATIVE RESPONSE

The incidental take of dolphin in the ETP purse seine tuna fishery was one of the factors leading to passage of the Marine Mammal Protection Act (MMPA) in the United States in 1972. The MMPA, enacted to protect marine mammals from the adverse effects of human activities, states that marine mammal species should be "protected and encouraged to develop to the greatest extent feasible commensurate with sound policies of resource management." 16 U.S.C. 1361(6) (1995). The MMPA's restrictions on fishing established as a legislative goal that "the incidental kill or incidental serious injury of marine mammals permitted in the course of commercial fishing operations be reduced to insignificant levels approaching a zero mortality and serious injury rate." 16 U.S.C. 1371(a)(2).

Implementation took the form of a "general permit" that set limits for the taking of dolphins. In the years following enactment of the MMPA, tuna vessels continued to reach, and often exceed, the take limits set under the general permit. In 1976, dolphin mortality reached 108,000 animals, exceeding the incidental take limit of 78,000. That same year, the National Marine Fisheries Service issued a three-year general permit with annual limits set on a sliding scale, decreasing from 51,945 in 1978, to 31,150 in 1980. In addition, new restrictions on fishing gear and methods were implemented that would better ensure live release of dolphins from the net. To ensure compliance, National Marine Fisheries Service observers were placed on fishing vessels to oversee accurate reporting. Largely due to the institution of these new requirements, by 1980 dolphin mortality had reached a new low of 15,305. While a significant improvement over past levels, it still was far distant from the zero mortality goal mandated by the MMPA. Congress amended the MMPA in 1981 in an attempt to address this issue, by defining zero mortality as a best available technology standard rather than a concrete goal. The relevant MMPA amendment stated that the goal of approaching zero mortality "shall be satisfied in the case of the incidental taking of marine mammals in the course of purse seine fishing for yellowfin tuna by a continuation of the application of the best marine mammal safety techniques and equipment that are ecologically and technologically practicable." 16 U.S.C. 1371(a)(2).

As the decade passed, however, dolphin mortality from the U.S. fleet actually increased slightly, to 18,400 animals in 1988. During this same period, while the U.S. fleet in the ETP fishery declined the number of foreign vessels participating in the fishery grew. In 1960, the tuna catch by U.S. vessels had comprised 90% of the ETP tuna fishery. But by 1991, this percentage had dropped to 11%. Over the same period, the catch by Latin American vessels had increased from 10% in 1960 to 57% in 1991. This shift in fleet composition was due in part to the growth of cannery industries in Asia and to re-flagging by U.S. vessels to foreign registries. As a result, the contribution of foreign tuna vessels began to weigh heavily on dolphin mortality in the ETP, killing roughly 100,000 dolphins in 1986. Seeking a level-playing field in the ETP, animal rights groups and U.S. fishermen requested that Congress take steps to limit dolphin mortality caused by foreign vessels. H.R. Rep. No. 758, 98th Cong., 2d Sess. 6 (1984). This request for extraterritorial application of U.S. law, coupled with growing public concern over the protection of dolphins, led to Congressional amendment of the MMPA in 1984 and 1988.

To address the issue of dolphin mortality in the ETP from foreign vessels, the 1984 MMPA amendments imposed trade restrictions banning the import of tuna into the United States unless each nation exporting tuna adopted a dolphin protection program comparable to that of the United States and that the average rate of incidental take by its fleet was comparable to that of the U.S. fleet. Pub. L. No. 98–364, 98 Stat. 440 (July 17, 1984). The 1988 MMPA amendments detailed the necessary documentation to certify comparability of programs. 16 U.S.C. 1371(a)(2). In addition, the 1988 amendments imposed trade restrictions on *intermediary* nations exporting tuna to the United States, requiring them to provide proof that their shipments did not contain tuna from those nations prohibited from exporting tuna directly to the United States. In practice, these requirements effectively forbade the use of purse seine nets.

Despite this legislation, environmental groups kept the issue in the public's eye and consumers continued to pressure for further action to save dolphins. In 1990, Congress responded to public outcry by proposing the Dolphin Protection Consumer Information Act of 1990 (DPCIA). 16 U.S.C. 1385. The DPCIA required that all tuna caught in the ETP and labeled "dolphin safe" (1) must have been caught by a vessel too small to deploy its nets on dolphins, or (2) must be accompanied by a certification from a qualified observer that no dolphin purse seine sets were made for the entire trip on which the tuna was caught, or (3) cannot have been harvested using a large-scale driftnet. Regulations were implemented in 1991 establishing a tracking and verification system enabling the government to track tuna labeled "dolphin safe" back to the harvesting vessel in order to verify whether the product was properly labeled. Absent that certification, tuna imported into the U.S. could not be marketed as dolphin-safe on US supermarket shelves. In practice, this measure was more effective and less interventionist than the MMPA ban because canners simply would not buy tuna that was not "dolphin-safe."

Anticipating the labeling requirement proposed by the DPCIA and faced with threatened consumer boycotts, the major American tuna canning companies took steps to preempt any adverse market impacts of the legislation. Starkist Seafood Company, a division of H.J. Heinz Company, was the first to announce that it would no longer purchase any tuna caught in association with dolphins and began labeling cans of Starkist tuna with "dolphin safe" symbols bearing the message: "No Harm to Dolphins." Within hours of Starkist's announcement, the other major canning companies announced that they would adopt the same purchasing practice and begin labeling their tuna as "dolphin safe." In a matter of months 84% of tuna sold in the United States was labeled "dolphin safe." 56 FED. REG. 47,418, 47,419 (1991).

As a consequence of these actions, most of the remaining U.S. purse seine fleet shifted to overseas operations in the western tropical Pacific where tuna and dolphins do not associate together as they do in the ETP.

---

3. INTERNATIONAL RESPONSE TO U.S. SANCTIONS

By the end of the 1980s, environmental groups realized that, with the exodus of U.S. vessels from the ETP fishery, the practices of foreign boats were increasingly important yet the Department of Commerce had not imposed *any* of the trade bans required by the MMPA, presumably to avoid international disputes. As a result, environmental groups filed lawsuits in U.S. courts forcing the government to order embargoes against tuna harvesting nations that did not have dolphin protection programs comparable to the US or had average dolphin mortality rates that were in excess of those prescribed under the MMPA. Earth Island Institute v. Mosbacher, 746 F.Supp. 964 (N.D.Cal.1990).

In October, 1990, because its domestic standard for regulating tuna harvesting techniques did not satisfy the MMPA's requirements, a number of countries' tuna exports, including Mexico's, were prohibited from import into the United States. In response, Mexico initiated a challenge under the GATT dispute resolution process against the embargo provisions of the MMPA amendments and the tuna labeling provisions of the DPCIA. In its decision in Tuna/Dolphin I, the GATT Dispute Panel found that the MMPA import ban constituted both a quantitative restriction and illegitimately regulated the method by which the tuna was caught. General Agreement on Tariffs and Trade: Dispute Settlement Panel Report on United States Restrictions on Imports of Tuna, 30 I.L.M. 1594 (1991). The labeling provisions were upheld, however, because they applied equally to all nations fishing for tuna and did not restrict the sale of tuna products. A separate GATT challenge to the embargoes associated with intermediary nations was filed in July, 1992, by the European Union and the Netherlands, claiming that the secondary embargo on intermediary markets constituted an unfair trade practice. In February 1993, a different GATT Dispute Panel held that the MMPA's secondary embargo provisions also violated the GATT. General Agreement on Tariffs and Trade: Dispute Settlement Panel Report on United States Restrictions on Imports of Tuna,

33 I.L.M. 839 (1994). Deeply involved in negotiating the North American Free Trade Agreement with the United States, Mexico did not submit the dispute panel report for adoption by the Contracting Parties to the GATT nor did the European Union or the Netherlands. Thus neither dispute panel decision has been adopted by the GATT Parties. As a result, there was no Congressional action to amend the MMPA. Chapter 15 discusses these dispute panel decisions in detail, *see* page 1160.

The Inter–American Tropical Tuna Commission (IATTC) is the international body charged with oversight of the tuna fishery in the ETP. Established as a bilateral organization with Costa Rica in 1949, the original charge of the IATTC was to study tuna and other species affected by tuna vessels in the region and to recommend management measures designed to maintain fish stocks at levels capable of producing maximum sustainable yields. Convention for the Establishment of an Inter–American Tropical Tuna Commission, May 31, 1949, US–Costa Rica, 1 U.S.T. 230. The IATTC's membership includes the United States, Mexico, France, Japan, Venezuela, Panama, Costa Rica and Vanuatu. Mexico is not a member but attends IATTC meetings as an observer. In an early response to the tuna/dolphin issue in 1976, IATTC members resolved that the Commission should strive (1) to maintain a high level of tuna production, (2) to maintain dolphin stocks at or above levels that assure their survival in perpetuity, (3) with every reasonable effort being made to avoid needless or careless killing of porpoise. In 1979 the IATTC began its international observer program, placing observers on both foreign and domestic vessels. This observer program was perhaps the most significant conservation action since dolphin mortality was significantly higher on vessels not carrying observers than on vessels where observers were present. LouAnna Perkins, *International Dolphin Conservation Under U.S. Law: Does Might Make Right?*, 1 OCEAN & COASTAL L.J. 213, 233 (1995); 55 Fed. Reg. 42,235 (1990).

In response to U.S. legislation and the tuna embargo, in June 1992 the IATTC adopted the La Jolla Agreement–a non-binding multilateral program designed to reduce dolphin mortalities in the ETP over a seven-year period to "levels approaching zero," while maintaining the present maximum tuna yield. Agreement to Reduce Dolphin Mortality in the Eastern Tropical Pacific Fishery, 33 I.L.M. 936 (1992). The Agreement was ratified by all but two IATTC member nations and four non-member nations that fish in the ETP (Mexico, Colombia, Ecuador and Spain. Under the Agreement, dolphin mortality limits for the ETP tuna fishery were set according to a schedule providing for 19,500 mortalities in 1993, reduced to under 5,000 annual mortalities by 1999. A system known as Dolphin Mortality Limit (DML) was used to allocate incidental takings to vessels and any vessel that reached its DML was required to cease further fishing associated with dolphins in the ETP for that season. The La Jolla Agreement also established an international research program and scientific advisory board to coordinate, facilitate, and guide research directed at reducing dolphin mortalities. It required that observers accompany all purse seine vessels with a carrying capacity of 400 short tons or more and established an international review panel to monitor compliance by the international fleet with the conservation program and DML.

The international dolphin conservation program established under the La Jolla Agreement and implemented by the IATTC proved extremely effective. In the first year of the program, dolphin mortality in the fishery was reduced to 3,601 animals, almost 12,000 less than the 1992 mortality level, and well below the 1999 target of 5,000 dolphins. MARINE MAMMAL COMMISSION, 1994 ANNUAL REPORT TO CONGRESS 117 (1995). By 1996, dolphin mortality in the fishery had been reduced further to an estimated 2,700 animals. And this was due entirely to foreign vessels. The five remaining U.S. tuna seiners operating in the ETP did not make any sets on dolphins during 1995.

The La Jolla Agreement was voluntary, however, and not legally binding. It had been created as a direct response to U.S. legislative demands and when the American embargo remained in place, despite significantly reduced dolphin mortality in the ETP, a number of nations threatened to reject the La Jolla agreement or even file a WTO challenge against the MMPA. The political durability of the voluntary La Jolla Agreement weakened as major foreign fishing nations questioned why, with no reward for their good faith efforts in meeting the annual goals of the program, they should continue to comply. Indeed U.S. law provided that the encirclement of even one dolphin by a nation's fleet fishing in the ETP was grounds for an embargo, preventing the importation of technically "dolphin-safe" tuna into the U.S. market.

At the same time, a shift in the tuna market was taking place. While in the mid–1970s the United States consumed 85% of the yellowfin tuna caught in the ETP, by the end of 1992, that percentage had declined to less than 10%. Most of the ETP tuna was now sold to Europe and Latin America, with Mexico increasing its tuna consumption five-fold between 1975 and 1992. Because markets were developing outside the United States that did not have the same harvesting restrictions, access to the U.S. markets no longer provided the same incentive it once had for these nations to achieve further dolphin mortality reductions. Tuna/Dolphin Issues: Hearings on the Provisions of the International Dolphin Conservation Act, How it is Affecting Dolphin Mortality, and What Measures Can Be Effected to Keep the Mortality to a Minimum, and on H.R. 2823 before the Subcomm. on Fisheries, Wildlife and Oceans of the House Comm. on Resources, 104th Cong., 1st & 2d Sess. 304 (1995) (statement of Timothy E. Wirth, Under Secretary for Global Affairs, U.S. Dept. of State).

Making this threat explicit, in July 1995 at the Intergovernmental Meeting of the La Jolla Agreement the governments of Colombia, Costa Rica, Ecuador, Mexico, Panama and Venezuela signed the San Jose Declaration. The Declaration stated that these nations wished to

> reiterate their concern that the stability of the La Jolla Agreement is endangered if the United States fails during this session of the U.S. Congress to resolve these U.S. policy inconsistencies by implementing the following three indivisible acts: lifting the primary and secondary embargoes; codifying the La Jolla Agreement; and redefining dolphin safe to include all tuna and tuna products harvested in accord with the regulatory measures embodied within the framework of the La Jolla Agreement.

In addition, many of these countries were considering other international management bodies and mechanisms such as *Organizacion Latinamericana de Desarrolla Pesquero* to replace the La Jolla Agreement. This action bears considerable similarity to the creation of NAMMCO by whaling nations as a legitimate institutional alternative to the International Whaling Commission (discussed in the preceding section).

To salvage the La Jolla Agreement, five American environmental groups met with Mexican officials to explore a multilateral agreement that would strengthen dolphin conservation measures while lifting the U.S. tuna embargo. The result was signed by 12 nations in October 1995–The Declaration of Panama. In order to secure a binding international agreement, the Declaration required the United States to amend the MMPA's existing comparability standards that had served as the basis for the tuna embargo as well as amend the labeling standards for defining "dolphin safe." The Declaration was, at its core, a quid pro quo agreement. Foreign tuna fleets would maintain their dolphin conservation measures if the United States lifted its trade restrictions.

After nearly two years of failed attempts to pass the necessary legislation in Congress, the International Dolphin Conservation Program Act (IDCPA) was passed and signed in the summer of 1997. 16 U.S.C. 1385(g). These 1997 amendments to the MMPA condition trade restrictions on compliance with the international dolphin conservation program outlined in the Panama Declaration, thus basing the embargo on multilateral rather than unilateral standards (a fundamental concern of the GATT Dispute Panels). The amendments improve the tracking and verification procedures by requiring periodic audits, spot checks, and an observer program. They also modify the "dolphin-safe" label by focusing on whether dolphins are killed rather than encircled in catching tuna. Hence the label is based on a "no mortality or serious injury" standard rather than a "no encirclement" standard. The end result allows the use of purse seine nets so long as no dolphins were killed or seriously injured during the set. It is a performance standard rather than an equipment standard. By conditioning the label on dolphin mortality rather than use of a particular fishing method and ensuring compliance with observers, supporters of the legislation have argued, there is more flexibility to achieve a zero mortality goal.

The IDCPA would not enter into effect until (1) the Secretary of Commerce certified intentional encirclement of dolphins with purse seine nets was not having a significant adverse impact on any depleted dolphin stock in the ETP and (2) the Secretary of State certified that an effective treaty was in place. By March, 1999, United States, Panama, Ecuador and Mexico had signed a treaty implementing the International Dolphin Conservation Program and the National Marine Fisheries Service had issued a report concluding that purse seine encirclement were not having a significant impact on depleted dolphin stocks. The treaty has since been ratified by El Salvador, Venezuela, Nicaragua and, significantly, the European Union.

The dolphin story could serve as a model for future international fisheries management agreements. The binding requirements of the International Dolphin Conservation Program has made the ETP the most heavily regulated fishery in the world. This is no small accomplishment for a fishery that is conducted primarily on the high seas, beyond national jurisdictions. Stock-specific mortality has been capped at a 0.2% level of the total population and at or below the 0.1% level by 2001. While the permissible annual mortality level for each dolphins is limited to 5,000 per year, in 1998 mortality was less than 2,000 dolphins. These mortality levels are more than four times lower than those recommended by the U.S. National Research Council and should permit the recovery of dolphin stocks in the fishery to their former abundance.

QUESTIONS AND DISCUSSION

1. What are the lessons of the Tuna/Dolphin history? Is this an example of international cooperation in dealing with a complex conservation issue or a case of a powerful nation exercising unilateral economic coercion to dictate other countries' actions? Looking only at the final result one conclusion seems obvious–unilateral trade restrictions *work*. Closure of the U.S. market forced foreign countries to regulate their fisheries and reduce dolphin mortality. Tuna boats in the ETP now have observers on board, are using better dolphin-safety equipment, and employing other dolphin-friendly procedures. One might argue that this has all happened because the United States used a trade ban.

But if the trade sanctions worked, what was the cost? Beyond WTO issues, what are the consequences of forcing other countries to improve their environmental performance? Could the same results have been achieved through sole reliance on the labeling requirements? If American consumers want to buy only dolphin-friendly tuna, one might argue, that is their right and the market will respond accordingly. Labeling measures, as former GATT Secretary General Arthur Dunkel noted at the time, would have avoided entirely the GATT problems and unpopular threats of the MMPA ban. Would the labeling requirement alone have caused the same level of international discord?

2. While using purse seine nets to catch tuna clearly harms dolphins, the alternative fishing methods have serious drawbacks, as well. The two most common alternative fishing techniques are casting nets around free-swimming tuna and casting nets around floating logs (which tuna tend to congregate under). Purse seine nets catch far fewer immature tuna than the alternative methods, potentially weakening the population's viability over the longer term. Of greater concern to environmentalists is the bycatch problem. One thousand tons of tuna caught using purse seine nets around dolphins produces an average bycatch of 2 sharks, 29 dolphins, 5 billfish and less than 1 sea turtle. The bycatch from setting nets around logs, however, produces a staggeringly different average bycatch–2,950 sharks, 102 billfish, less than 1 dolphin and 8 sea turtles. All of these species reproduce slowly, making their deaths particularly significant to overall population stability. Carpenter, *What price dolphin? Scientists are reckoning the true cost of sparing an endearing mammal*, U.S. NEWS & WORLD REP., June 13, 1994.

As with so many environmental problems, the cure may be, in some respects, worse than the problem. Unfortunately, efforts by scientists to develop ecologically and commercially viable alternatives to existing fishing methods, in particular to purse-seine setting on dolphin, have been unsuccessful. Fishing for yellowfin by encircling dolphins may be the "cleanest" fishing method to avoid bycatch.

An equally significant problem in finding less harmful fishing alternatives are the costs of failure. Government-sponsored research is necessary but can only do so much. The real test of alternative fishing gear is its performance in a commercial fishery. Yet in the early 1990s, vessels using alternative gear to reduce dolphin mortality reported losing up to $100,000 per trip because their gear was more effective at catching small skipjack and yellowfin tuna rather than the commercially valuable large yellowfin tuna. Few skippers are willing to risk the vessel's loan payments and crew's wages on unproven new fishing gear, regardless of the potential reduction in bycatch mortality. What role can government play in addressing this concern?

3. Debate over repeal of the MMPA trade ban deeply split the American environmental community. In simple terms, the division was between animal rights activists and traditional environmental groups. This debate centered on the question of whether the chase and encirclement method produces such levels of stress in dolphins that the recovery of their populations will be inhibited. No specific scientific information is available directly addressing this issue. The National Academy of Sciences concluded in 1993 that no direct evidence of harm had been associated with chase and encirclement, though the subject had not been extensively studied, and implications of any stress on individual animal and dolphin populations had not been determined. Others have claimed, however, that the chase and encirclement of dolphins causes stress of a duration and magnitude that severely impedes dolphin reproduction or even results in dolphin deaths, referred to as "cryptic kill."

During the 1995 and later congressional hearings, Earth Island Institute, Defenders of Wildlife, the Humane Society of the United States, and 13 other environmental and animal rights organizations argued against relaxing the trade ban on dolphin encirclement methods both because it was contrary to achieving the MMPA's mandated goal of zero mortality and because the harassment and stress of encircling dolphin populations would threaten the population's stability. These groups also attacked the objectivity of the IATTC and questioned the organization's science. Concerned that the IATTC was captive to tuna fishery interests, they alleged that IATTC observers were influenced to under-report dolphin mortalities. Indeed, public access to IATTC data is restricted, impeding independent verification of IATTC conclusions. These groups requested Congress to order a General Accounting Office investigation of the IATTC before accepting the IATTC data on the tuna fishery's impacts on dolphins.

Opposing these groups and arguing in favor of amending the MMPA, the World Wildlife Fund, the National Audubon Society, the National Wildlife Federation, Greenpeace, and three other environmental groups sought to eliminate the tuna embargo and adopt the Panama Declaration's conditions, contending that a multilateral international approach was preferable to unilateral action and that stress from encirclement was not a threat to dolphin survival. A number of these groups had been instrumental in the Panama Declaration negotiations and, with support from the Clinton Administration, were successful in lobbying for passage of the International Dolphin Conservation Program Act. It is no exaggeration to say that the efforts of environmental groups were essential to resolving the tuna/dolphin dispute in a manner acceptable to all the countries involved.

4. The IATTC's ability to enforce the fishery restrictions remains an issue of concern. Under the La Jolla Agreement, 53 major violations (such as non-cooperation with an observer) and several hundred minor violations were reported, but few penalties have been imposed. Since the IATTC has no enforcement powers, it must rely on each vessel's flag State to punish violations under domestic law. This system of enforcement is, with some exceptions, similar to that provided by the U.N. Convention on the Law of the Sea (discussed at page 665). In reviewing 17 infractions of non-cooperation with the observer, the IATTC points out that 2 resulted in suspended licenses, 1 in a warning, 3 in sanctions still to be decided, 3 in decisions of no sanctions, and 8 were still in judicial review. Eugene H. Buck, *Dolphin Protection and Tuna Seining*, Cong. Res. Serv. Issue Brief, updated June 11, 1997.

The Program requires observers on board all large tuna purse seine fishers in the ETP. As the Department of Commerce describes in its Frequently Asked Questions brochure, once the tuna are caught and the observer has verified it was a "dolphin safe" set:

> Dolphin-safe tuna will be stored in different storage wells on-board tuna fishing vessels from those in which non-dolphin-safe tuna will be stored. An Inter-American Tropical Tuna Commission (IATTC) observer will keep track of which storage wells contain dolphin-safe tuna and which do not. At the end of the fishing trip the observer and the vessel captain well sign and date the observer's report and the National Marine Fisheries Service will receive a copy of the observer's report for all U.S. vessels' fishing trips. When the tuna is delivered to U.S. canners, the dolphin-safe tuna will continue to be kept separated from the non-dolphin-safe tuna until it is canned. U.S. canners will be required to inform the NMFS as to where and how their frozen tuna supplies are stored, and NMFS will inspect U.S. canneries to verify the information NMFS is receiving. Non-dolphin-safe tuna can labels will not carry the official U.S. government dolphin-safe mark or any other dolphin-safe mark. From time to time, NMFS representatives will purchase cans of dolphin-safe tuna from food markets, and using can-codes stamped on all tuna cans, the contents of the cans will be checked back to their origin to verify that they are "dolphin-safe."

While this reads well, do you think this system will work? What practical problems might it encounter?

5. The tuna-dolphin saga continues. The Department of Commerce has lifted the tuna embargo for Mexico and Ecuador. The major tuna processors (StarKist, Chicken of the Sea, and BumbleBee), however, have stated that they intend to retain their current dolphin-safe labels (i.e. meaning no encirclement) regardless of whether the IDCPA allows them to use a less strict standard. Thus Mexican and Venezuelan tuna may be sold in the United States, but likely not by the major processors that account for roughly 90% of the market.

In April, 1999, the Secretary of Commerce issued a finding that chase and encirclement of dolphin by purse seine fishermen did not have a significant adverse impact on depleted populations. Under the International Dolphin Conservation Program Act, this finding was necessary for the new meaning of "dolphin safe" tuna to go into effect (i.e., purse seine nets allowed so long as no dolphins killed or injured). The Earth Island Institute, Defenders of Wildlife and Humane Society filed a lawsuit in federal district court challenging this finding as abuse of discretion under the Administrative Procedure Act. Reflecting the split among environmental groups, a lawyer for the Justice Department and lawyers for Greenpeace and World Wildlife Fund argued in favor of the finding. In a decision in April, 2000, the court granted plaintiffs summary judgment, ruling that the agency had not adequately taken into account preliminary results from the stress studies on dolphins in the ETP and issuing a preliminary injunction to ban the import of tuna from Mexico. 93 F.Supp.2d 1071 (2000). On appeal, the 9th Circuit upheld the lower court's decision that the Commerce Department had acted arbitrarily and capriciously by not relying on scientific findings to demonstrate that dolphin populations are not adversely impacted by the chasing, netting, injuring, or killing of dolphins to catch tuna.

6. The Earth Island Institute has claimed that about 100 boats (roughly 5% of the world's tuna fleet) still use purse seine nets. Given the domestic and international discord this conflict has engendered, would it not be more efficient simply to pay off these boats and put an end to the dispute?

7. Access to all the primary documents described in the text as well as recent developments may be found at the Department of Commerce website: <www.nmfs.noaa.gov/prot_res/overview/mm.html>. Press releases and lobbying letters from environmental groups may be found at the Earthtrust website: <http://www.earthtrust.org/dolphin_hotline>. A section on conservation of sea turtles, including a discussion of the Inter–American Convention for the Protection and Conservation of Sea Turtles, is on the casebook web site at <http://www.wcl.american.edu/environment/iel/teachmaterial.htm>.

SECTION IV. TRADE IN ENDANGERED SPECIES

[W]ildlife trade is big business. A conservative estimate places the value worldwide at more than $10 billion a year with at least $2–3 billion of that illegal. If uncontrolled, even legal wildlife trade can have devastating effects. Developing countries, which provide most of the wild animals and plants in trade, earn foreign exchange from this trade and local populations earn their living from it. If, however, the level of trade exceeds the natural ability of wildlife populations to replenish themselves, the income from wildlife trade will disappear along with the species.

Ginette Hemley, ed., INTERNATIONAL WILDLIFE TRADE: A CITES SOURCEBOOK vii-viii (1994).

A. INTRODUCTION

No one can doubt the threat trade poses to endangered species. The demand for scarce wildlife products such as elephant ivory, black rhinoceros horns, and tiger bones coupled with the market for live species such as rare cacti, orchids and exotic birds have driven many species to the brink of extinction. Fewer than 5,000 tigers and 11,000 black rhinos, for example, are estimated to remain in the wild. Between 1981 and 1989, elephant populations were reduced by half mainly due to the trade in ivory. Trade is responsible for an estimated 40% of vertebrate species facing extinction. Ironically, market forces exacerbate the threats from illegal trade, for as species become rarer their value on the market increases to reflect this scarcity, increasing the incentive for further poaching. Sarah Fitzgerald, WHOSE BUSINESS IS IT? 3–8 (1989).

The Convention on International Trade in Endangered Species of Wild Flora and Fauna (CITES) regulates the global trade in threatened and endangered species. 27 U.S.T. 1087, T.I.A.S. No. 8249 (1973). CITES enjoys a broad membership, with over 150 parties. In simple terms, CITES acts as a border guard, restricting the flow of rare species and parts of species across national borders. The level of trade restriction for each species varies from strict to lenient depending on the level of the threat of extinction it faces. In all, CITES protections extend to some 34,000 plant and animal species. Because many wildlife species live only within a country's borders, CITES treads very carefully around issues of national sovereignty (*see*

Chapter 7's discussion of sovereignty over natural resources, p. 379). CITES explicitly does *not* regulate the protection of endangered species within a nation's borders (such as habitat conservation) or other non-trade threats to species (such as pollution or development). Only when an endangered species enters the stream of international commerce do CITES restrictions become legally applicable.

B. CITES PROVISIONS

The core of CITES protections lies in its system of Appendices to the Convention. CITES has three appendices, which establish differing levels of permit requirements for the import and export of endangered species (and parts of species derived therefrom). Placement in an appendix determines the level of restrictions placed on trade. In rare instances, listing can be quite specific, protecting geographically separate populations while allowing trade of the species elsewhere. CITES restrictions cover trade in both "species" and "specimens." "Species" is broadly defined to include any species, subspecies, or geographically separate population. "Specimen" is defined as any readily recognizable part or derivative of an animal or plant. This definition would clearly cover elephant tusks and rhino horns, but its application to ground up tiger bones that are sold in Asia for medicinal purposes, for instance, is unclear. Ultimately each nation deals with this issue on an ad hoc basis.

Each State party to CITES is required to designate a Management Authority to issue permits for trade in species listed in the Appendices and a Scientific Authority to provide scientific advice on imports and exports. In the United States, the U.S. Fish and Wildlife Service serves as both the Scientific and Management Authorities. CITES enforcement is often the responsibility of national customs, police or similar agencies. The CITES Secretariat is located in Geneva, Switzerland.

1. APPENDIX I

Appendix I lists species threatened with extinction that are or may be affected by trade. CITES, Article III. Subject to narrow exceptions, Appendix I prohibits international commercial trade of the roughly 830 species listed and readily recognizable species parts or derivatives. Appendix I species include, for example, the Black Rhinoceros, all the sea turtles, all the great apes, cheetahs, tigers, some cacti and orchids, and all whales covered by the International Whaling Commission moratorium (*see* p. 977). Appendix I species may only be traded if *both* the exporting and importing countries issue permits and consent to the international trade. The requirement of an import permit to ship a species in international commerce is, in fact, the key difference between Appendix I and the other appendices.

For trade in Appendix I species, both the importing and exporting nations' Scientific and Management Authorities must give their advice prior to issuance of the import and export permits. In particular, each party's Scientific Authority must confirm that export will not be detrimental to species survival. The exporting party's Management Authority must also confirm that the specimen was not obtained in breach of State laws, that the method of shipment minimizes the risk of injury, damage to health and cruel treatment, and that an import permit has been granted.

The importing party's Management Authority must confirm that the specimen will not be used for "primarily commercial purposes." This is a discretionary judgment that has been subject to much dispute. An American hunter's sporting trophy of an Appendix I species obtained in Africa, for example, is generally not regarded as subject to the Appendix I commercial purpose restrictions because it is presumed the hunter will not sell the trophy upon her return to the United States. The purpose of importing the hunting trophy is not commercial. This judgment becomes more complicated, however, in the case of imports for research purposes that may lead to commercial activities. Is the import of an Appendix I plant by a geneticist "primarily commercial" if she intends to extract a compound to determine its medicinal properties? What if she may patent the compound for specific applications? *See* discussion of Biodiversity Convention at page 941. CITES Parties have declared that "any transaction that is not wholly non-commercial" should be regarded as primarily commercial. Conference of the Parties Resolution 5.10 (1985). Is this a useful standard? How would you apply it to the examples above?

_____

2. APPENDIX II

Appendix II lists those species not yet threatened with extinction but that may become so if trade in them is not strictly controlled and monitored to avoid exploitation incompatible with species survival. CITES, Article IV. Over 25,000 species are listed in Appendix II, including the Narwhal, the American Alligator and the Polar Bear. Trade in Appendix II species requires the issuance of an export permit but *not* of an import permit. As with Appendix I species, the exporting State must receive the advice of its Scientific Authority that the export will not be detrimental to the species survival, and of its Management Authority that the specimen was not obtained in breach of state laws and that the method of shipment minimizes the risk of injury, damage to health and cruel treatment. Appendix II also includes "look-alike" species; species that are not themselves threatened with extinction but resemble Appendix I species. Do you see why these species require CITES protections, as well?

_____

3. APPENDIX III

Appendix III species are listed when a party currently protects the species under its domestic laws and now seeks the further cooperation of CITES parties to control its international trade. Of the three lists of species, Appendix III species are those least threatened by trade. Parties can simply propose native species for listing and no vote at a Conference of Parties is required. Appendix III species include the Canadian Walrus, the Water Buffalo the Small Indian Mongoose, and many birds. The export of an Appendix III species requires the issuance of an export permit but not of an import permit. In granting the export permit, the exporting State must receive the advice of its Management Authority that the specimen was not obtained in breach of the State's laws, and that the method of shipment minimizes the risk of injury, damage to health and cruel treatment (note that the Scientific Authority need not be consulted). CITES, Article V.

While any State can unilaterally list an Appendix III species, this indirectly imposes obligations on *all* non-listing parties. Article V(3) states that the import of an Appendix III species must be accompanied by a certificate of origin. The next clause, which states that an export from a country that listed the species must also include an export permit, makes clear that the certificate of origin applies to *all* exports, not just exports from the country that listed the species on Appendix III. Thus, other exporting countries must issue certificates of origin, as well. While this feature of Article V makes Appendix III valuable for ascertaining trade volumes without imposing rigorous scientific burdens on the countries of export, some countries view it as yet one more administrative burden they must undertake.

	Advice and Consent of Exporting Country's		Advice and Consent of Importing Country's	
	Scientific Authority	Management Authority	Scientific Authority	Management Authority
Appendix I	●	●	●	●
Appendix II	●	●		
Appendix III		●		

4. EXCEPTIONS AND RESERVATIONS

Article VII of CITES lists a number of exceptions to its permitting requirements, including pre-existing stocks, household effects, and commercially bred species. Assume, for example, a trader has a large supply of Rare Bird feathers in her warehouse in 1997. In 1998 the CITES Conference of the Parties lists the Rare Bird on Appendix I. Can the trader sell her feathers to a merchant located in a CITES party? In a clause known as the "pre-existing stocks exception," Article VII(2) provides that a party's Management Authority may issue a certificate that specimens of a listed species were acquired before the CITES provisions restricting trade were adopted. In this case, the trade restrictions do not apply. CITES also creates exceptions to prohibitions against commercial imports of listed species if they have been captively bred, artificially propagated, or ranched. The reasoning is that such activities do not threaten the existence of wild populations and may, in fact, decrease poaching pressures. Finally, national authorities may choose to waive the permit requirements for species used in scientific research or in a travelling zoo, circus, or exhibition.

In addition to the exceptions, a potentially larger loophole is the use of reservations under Article XXIII. Countries have the right to "opt out" of the Convention with respect to any specific listing. Thus, for example, Southern African countries entered a reservation to the Appendix I listing of the elephant and Japan entered a reservation for the listing of the hawksbill sea turtles. Such reservations mean that the States "shall be treated as a State not a Party to the treaty with respect to trade in the particular species."

Convention on International Trade in Endangered Species of Wild Flora and Fauna

Article I

Definitions

For the purpose of the present Convention, unless the context otherwise requires:

a) "Species" means any species, sub-species, or geographically separate population thereof;

b) "Specimen" means:

(i) any animal or plant, whether alive or dead;

(ii) in the case of an animal: for species included in Appendices I and II, any readily recognizable part or derivative thereof; and for species included in Appendix III, any readily recognizable part or derivative thereof specified in Appendix III in relation to the species; and

(iii) in the case of a plant: for species included in Appendix I, any readily recognizable part or derivative thereof; and for species included in Appendices II and III, any readily recognizable part or derivative thereof specified in Appendices II and III in relation to the species. * * *

Article II

Fundamental Principles

1. Appendix I shall include all species threatened with extinction which are or may be affected by trade. Trade in specimens of these species must be subject to particularly strict regulation in order not to endanger further their survival and must only be authorized in exceptional circumstances.

2. Appendix II shall include:

(a) all species which although not necessarily now threatened with extinction may become so unless trade in specimens of such species is subject to strict regulation in order to avoid utilization incompatible with their survival; and

(b) other species which must be subject to regulation in order that trade in specimens of certain species referred to in sub-paragraph (a) of this paragraph may be brought under effective control.

3. Appendix III shall include all species which any Party identifies as being subject to regulation within its jurisdiction for the purpose of preventing or restricting exploitation, and as needing the co-operation of other Parties in the control of trade.

4. The Parties shall not allow trade in specimens of species included in Appendices I, II and III except in accordance with the provisions of the present Convention.

Article III

Regulation of Trade in Specimens of Species Included in Appendix I

1. All trade in specimens of species included in Appendix I shall be in accordance with the provisions of this Article.

2. The export of any specimen of a species included in Appendix I shall require the prior grant and presentation of an export permit. An export permit shall only be granted when the following conditions have been met:

(a) a Scientific Authority of the State of export has advised that such export will not be detrimental to the survival of that species;

(b) a Management Authority of the State of export is satisfied that the specimen was not obtained in contravention of the laws of that State for the protection of fauna and flora;

(c) a Management Authority of the State of export is satisfied that any living specimen will be so prepared and shipped as to minimize the risk of injury, damage to health or cruel treatment; and

(d) a Management Authority of the State of export is satisfied that an import permit has been granted for the specimen.

3. The import of any specimen of a species included in Appendix I shall require the prior grant and presentation of an import permit and either an export permit or a re-export certificate. An import permit shall only be granted when the following conditions have been met:

(a) a Scientific Authority of the State of import has advised that the import will be for purposes which are not detrimental to the survival of the species involved;

(b) a Scientific Authority of the State of import is satisfied that the proposed recipient of a living specimen is suitably equipped to house and care for it; and

(c) a Management Authority of the State of import is satisfied that the specimen is not to be used for primarily commercial purposes.* * *

Article IV

Regulation of Trade in Specimens of Species Included in Appendix II

1. All trade in specimens of species included in Appendix II shall be in accordance with the provisions of this Article.

2. The export of any specimen of a species included in Appendix II shall require the prior grant and presentation of an export permit. An export permit shall only be granted when the following conditions have been met:

(a) a Scientific Authority of the State of export has advised that such export will not be detrimental to the survival of that species;

(b) a Management Authority of the State of export is satisfied that the specimen was not obtained in contravention of the laws of that State for the protection of fauna and flora; and

(c) a Management Authority of the State of export is satisfied that any living specimen will be so prepared and shipped as to minimize the risk of injury, damage to health or cruel treatment.* * *

Article V

Regulation of Trade in Specimens of Species Included in Appendix III

1. All trade in specimens of species included in Appendix III shall be in accordance with the provisions of this Article.

2. The export of any specimen of a species included in Appendix III from any State which has included that species in Appendix III shall require the prior grant and presentation of an export permit. An export permit shall only be granted when the following conditions have been met:

(a) a Management Authority of the State of export is satisfied that the specimen was not obtained in contravention of the laws of that State for the protection of fauna and flora; and

(b) a Management Authority of the State of export is satisfied that any living specimen will be so prepared and shipped as to minimize the risk of injury, damage to health or cruel treatment.

3. The import of any specimen of a species included in Appendix III shall require, except in circumstances to which paragraph 4 of this Article applies [re-export of a species], the prior presentation of a certificate of origin and, where the import is from a State which has included that species in Appendix III, an export permit.* * *

4. In the case of re-export, a certificate granted by the Management Authority of the State of re-export that the specimen was processed in the State or is being re-exported shall be accepted by the State of import as evidence that the provisions of the present Convention have been complied with in respect of the specimen concerned.

Article VII

Exemptions and Other Special Provisions Relating to Trade

1. The provisions of Articles III, IV and V shall not apply to the transit or trans-shipment of specimens through or in the territory of a Party while the specimens remain in Customs control.

2. Where a Management Authority of the State of export or reexport is satisfied that a specimen was acquired before the provisions of the present Convention applied to that specimen, the provisions of Articles III, IV and V shall not apply to that specimen where the Management Authority issues a certificate to that effect.

3. The provisions of Articles III, IV and V shall not apply to specimens that are personal or household effects. This exemption shall not apply where:

a) in the case of specimens of a species included in Appendix I, they were acquired by the owner outside his State of usual residence, and are being imported into that State; or

b) in the case of specimens of species included in Appendix II:

(i) they were acquired by the owner outside his State of usual residence and in a State where removal from the wild occurred;

(ii) they are being imported into the owner's State of usual residence; and

(iii) the State where removal from the wild occurred requires the prior grant of export permits before any export of such specimens;

unless a Management Authority is satisfied that the specimens were acquired before the provisions of the present Convention applied to such specimens.

4.   Specimens of an animal species included in Appendix I bred in captivity for commercial purposes, or of a plant species included in Appendix I artificially propagated for commercial purposes, shall be deemed to be specimens of species included in Appendix II.

5.   Where a Management Authority of the State of export is satisfied that any specimen of an animal species was bred in captivity or any specimen of a plant species was artificially propagated, or is a part of such an animal or plant or was derived therefrom, a certificate by that Management Authority to that effect shall be accepted in lieu of any of the permits or certificates required under the provisions of Articles III, IV or V.

6.   The provisions of Articles III, IV and V shall not apply to the non-commercial loan, donation or exchange between scientists or scientific institutions registered by a Management Authority of their State, of herbarium specimens, other preserved, dried or embedded museum specimens, and live plant material which carry a label Issued or approved by a Management Authority.

7.   A Management Authority of any State may waive the requirements of Articles III, IV and V and allow the movement without permits or certificates of specimens which form part of a travelling zoo, circus, menagerie, plant exhibition or other travelling exhibition provided that:

a) the exporter or importer registers full details of such specimens with that Management Authority;

b) the specimens are in either of the categories specified in paragraphs 2 and 5 of this Article; and

c) the Management Authority is satisfied that any living specimen will be so transported and cared for as to minimize the risk of injury, damage to health or cruel treatment. * * *

Article X

Trade with States not Party to the Convention

Where export or re-export is to, or import is from, a State not a Party to the present Convention, comparable documentation issued by the competent authorities in that State which substantially conforms with the requirements of the present Convention for permits and certificates may be accepted in lieu thereof by any Party.

Article XI

Conference of the Parties

... 7. Any body or agency technically qualified in protection, conservation or management of wild fauna and flora, in the following categories, which has informed the Secretariat of its desire to be represented at meetings of the Conference by observers, shall be admitted unless at least one-third of the Parties present object:

(a) international agencies or bodies, either governmental or non-governmental, and national governmental agencies and bodies; and

(b) national non-governmental agencies or bodies which have been approved for this purpose by the State in which they are located.

Once admitted, these observers shall have the right to participate but not to vote. * * *

Article XIV

Effect on Domestic Legislation and International Conventions

1. The provisions of the present Convention shall in no way affect the right of Parties to adopt:

(a) stricter domestic measures regarding the conditions for trade, taking, possession or transport of specimens of species included in Appendices I, II and III, or the complete prohibition thereof; or

(b) domestic measures restricting or prohibiting trade, taking, possession or transport of species not included in Appendix I, II or III.* * *

Article XV

Amendments to Appendices I and II

1. The following provisions shall apply in relation to amendments to Appendices I and II at meetings of the Conference of the Parties:

(a) Any Party may propose an amendment to Appendix I or II for consideration at the next meeting.* * *

(b) Amendments shall be adopted by a two-thirds majority of Parties present and voting. For these purposes "Parties present and voting" means Parties present and casting an affirmative or negative vote. Parties abstaining from voting shall not be counted among the two-thirds required for adopting an amendment.

(c) Amendments adopted at a meeting shall enter into force 90 days after that meeting for all Parties except those which make a reservation in accordance with paragraph 3 of this Article.* * *

3. During the period of 90 days provided for by sub-paragraph (c) of paragraph 1 or sub-paragraph (*l*) of paragraph 2 of this Article any Party may by notification in writing to the Depositary Government make a reservation with respect to the amendment. Until such reservation is withdrawn the Party shall be treated as a State not a Party to the present Convention with respect to trade in the species concerned.* * *

Article XXIII

Reservations

1. The provisions of the present Convention shall not be subject to general reservations. Specific reservations may be entered in accordance with the provisions of this Article and Articles XV and XVI.

2. Any State may, on depositing its instrument of ratification, acceptance, approval or accession, enter a specific reservation with regard to:

(a) any species included in Appendix I, II or III; or

(b) any parts or derivatives specified in relation to a species included in Appendix III.

3. Until a Party withdraws its reservation entered under the provisions of this Article, it shall be treated as a State not a Party to the present Convention with respect to trade in the particular species or parts or derivatives specified in such reservation.

QUESTIONS AND DISCUSSION

1. *Working the treaty*

   – How can a Party to the Convention trade a listed species with a non-Party?

   – If a Management Authority concludes a specimen of an animal species was bred in captivity, what permits or certificates are required under the provisions of Articles III, IV, or V?

   – Can a Party enact a stricter enforcement regime for the trade, taking, possession or transport of species than that provided under the treaty?

   – If a State wishes to make a general reservation to the Convention, how does it do so?

   – May a State make a specific reservation to any portion of the Convention?

2. Below is a representative sample of species listed in the three appendices. A list may be found in the Code of Federal Regulations at 50 C.F.R. § 23.23.

Appendix I	**Appendix II**	**Appendix III**
African Elephant	American Black Bear	Golden Jackal (India)
Orangutan	Hippopotamus	Whitetail Deer (Guatemala)
Hawksbill Sea Turtle	Gray Wolf	Turtle Dove (Ghana)
Giant Panda	Mexican Bobcat	Walrus (Canada)
Whooping Crane	Flamingos	Mountain Gazelle (Tunisia)
Humpback Whale	Chameleons	Himalayan Marmot (India)
Tiger	King Cobra	Goliath Heron (Ghana)

3. To reinforce the Convention's trade restrictions, CITES requires parties to take "appropriate measures to enforce" the Convention such as imposing penalties and confiscating illegal specimens, but these restrictions are meant as a floor, allowing parties to take stricter measures. Article XIV. The U.S. Endangered Species Act, for example, prohibits the importation of endangered species listed under the Act. To encourage non-parties to join the Convention, trade in listed specimens is prohibited with non-parties unless they can produce documentation comparable to that required of CITES parties. Enforcement in practice, however, has posed significant problems. A thorough study carried out by NGOs–the IUCN Environmental Law Centre and TRAFFIC–under the direction of the CITES secretariat, for example, examined the national legislation of 81 Parties with high levels of trade in CITES-listed species. Fifteen Parties had national legislation that generally met all the requirements for CITES implementation. None of these Parties were developing countries. Thirty-nine Parties had legislation that met some of the CITES requirements. Twenty-seven Parties, one-third of the countries studied, "are believed to have national legislation that generally does not meet any of the requirements for implementation of CITES." Document 9.24; Ninth Meeting of the Conference of the Parties, November 1994; Doc. SC.42.12.1, Forty-second meeting of the Standing Committee, Oct. 1, 1999.

When the CITES secretariat determines that a country's legislation is inadequate to implement CITES, the country is put on notice that, unless it adopts more effective legislation, the Standing Committee will recommend that Parties prohibit imports of CITES-listed wildlife from that country. This recently happened to Senegal, where the Standing Committee instructed the Secretariat to notify Parties that they "should not issue permits and certificates for any import from and export or re-export to Senegal of CITES specimens and should refuse documents issued by Senegal from 30 October 1999 until further notice." *See* Doc. 11.21.2. As of February, 2001, Fiji, Vietnam and Yemen were under consideration for sanctions, as well, unless they strengthened their domestic legislation.

Recalling the discussion in Chapter 8 of compliance facilitation, do you think countries that fail to implement CITES requirements adequately should be sanctioned or treated differently than other parties? Does this raise potential WTO problems?

4. In one of the most embarrassing failures in CITES enforcement, the Washington Post reported in 2001 that "Benny, a 9–year-old with an uncommon talent for playing the harmonica, sneaked into Mexico from Texas with the help of a $4,500 bribe. Sped on his way by a shadowy go-between and corrupt custom agents who made him 'invisible'. . . ." This feat is all the more impressive when one realizes that Benny is a three ton endangered Asian elephant. Apparently a Mexican circus impressario purchased Benny from a Houston circus and applied for permit to take Benny to Mexico. After two months of waiting, Benny was smuggled in a wooden box (a big one) on a flatbed truck. The Mexican customs agents were bribed $4,500 and the U.S. Customs Agents apparently noticed nothing. Benny is now pleasing crowds in Mexico City by playing the harmonica while dancing. Kevin Sullivan, *3–Ton Elephant Tiptoes Into Mexico*, WASH.POST, Jan. 30, 2001, at A12.

Though an amusing story, it does lead one to wonder that, if all it takes to smuggle a 10 foot tall, three ton elephant across a border is a $4,500 bribe and a little ingenuity, then how difficult can it be to smuggle a rare bird or elephant tusks?

5. *Problem exercise* Assume you are a lawyer in Canada (a CITES party). A client who owns a gift shop in Toronto informs you she is going on safari in Africa and hopes to bring back a necklace of hippo teeth, carved elephant ivory figurines, and a stuffed Goliath Heron. She wants to know what she needs to do to avoid being arrested upon her return at the Toronto airport for a CITES violation. What information do you need from her to determine the applicable CITES restrictions? Citing the appropriate Convention text, for each souvenir what advice will you give her to comply?

6. Country X is a CITES Party without a reservation to the Rare Bird listing in Annex II. Country Y is a CITES Party that has entered a reservation to the Rare Bird listing. Country Z is not a CITES Party.

(a) Trader wants to export Rare Bird feathers from Country Y to Country X. What permits will trader need?

(b) Trader wants to export Rare Bird feathers from Country X to Country Z. What permits will trader need?

(c) Trader wants to export Rare Bird feathers from Country Z to Country Y. What permits will trader need?

(d) Trader wants to export Rare Bird feathers from Country Y to Country Z. What permits will trader need?

7. Trader legally buys 1000 Nile crocodile skins in 1973 in Japan. In 1975, the Nile crocodile is listed on Appendix I. Japan and Italy become Parties to CITES in 1981. In 1983, Trader wants to sell the skins to Buyer in Italy for commercial purposes. Can Trader sell them to Buyer without CITES permits?

The problems in Questions 5 and 6 were provided by Chris Wold. Additional questions by John Dernbach may be found on the casebook website at

<http://www.wcl.american.edu/pub/iel/dernbach.htm#cites>.

C. AMENDMENTS TO THE APPENDICES

CITES is a dynamic convention and its parties meet every two years to decide whether to add, remove, or change the listing of species in the Appendices. Any party may propose an amendment to Appendices I and II. Adoption of an amendment requires a two-thirds majority of parties voting. Gaining this super-majority often requires intensive negotiation and horse-trading. At the 11th Conference of the Parties in 2000, for example, of the 64 proposals to add species, change their listing, or amend their listings, roughly half were adopted while 13 were rejected and 18 withdrawn. To give a sense of how decisions are made to list species or change their appendix listing, the sections that follow provide brief descriptions of recent controversies involving elephants, mahogany, and sturgeon.

––––––

1. THE ELEPHANT CONTROVERSY

The listing of elephants in the CITES appendices has been a significant political issue for over a decade. It has also raised difficult economic, cultural and ecological concerns. While habitat loss has contributed to the decline in elephant populations, poaching has taken a far greater toll. Throughout the 1980s, elephant populations drastically fell in Africa, due largely to poaching for elephant ivory. While the numbers are inexact, it is estimated that the population in Africa fell from 1.2 million elephants in 1980 to under 600,000 by 1989. Kenya's elephant populations fell by two-thirds, Zambia's and Tanzania's by three-quarters. These plummeting populations resulted from both legal and illegal trade in elephant ivory, and were exacerbated by a number of factors–unstable economies and the need for new sources of foreign exchange, political corruption in some nations, and greater availability of automatic weapons.

Seeking to arrest this slaughter, the 1985 CITES Conference of the Parties adopted a new system requiring each African country to set quotas for the number of elephants killed annually and for exports of unworked ivory. The 1989 CITES conference of the parties took the further step of placing the African elephant on Appendix I of CITES, effectively banning the commercial trade in elephant ivory. The ban was coupled with in-creased anti-poaching efforts locally to address the illegal trade in ivory. In response to the listing on Appendix I, Japan reserved the right to import raw ivory from African CITES parties. For these countries, Japan an-nounced it would trade with parties that "managed" their herds. *See,* Michael Glennon, *Has International Law Failed the Elephant?*, 84 AMER. J. INT'L L. 1–33 (1990).

In some respects, the listing on Appendix I proved a success. The United States, which accounted for 10%–15% of global ivory imports prior to the ban, forbade ivory imports. Elephant herds in Southern Africa–in South Africa, Zimbabwe, Botswana, Zambia, Malawi and Namibia–report-edly have increased. Their wildlife management efforts have worked well, they argue, and require culling the populations from time to time (selective thinning) to ensure the elephant populations do not overwhelm the carrying capacity of the habitat and degrade the land. As a result of these cullings, African governments were sitting on up to 470 tons of ivory. Yet because of the Appendix I listing, these countries could not sell the ivory, even if they intended to use the proceeds to support anti-poaching efforts, to compensate villagers whose property had been harmed by elephants, or to inject development funds into those areas adjacent to elephant herds. Since 1992, therefore, these countries have led efforts at the CITES conference of the parties to move the African elephant back to Appendix II or for some other relaxation of the ivory trade ban. In place of a flat ban on trading they have sought a managed trade regime.

Allowing these sales is only common sense, Southern African countries have contended, as a reward for their conservation achievements and as a way to make the local people feel that elephant conservation is in their economic self-interest. Indeed the real responsibility for endangered species management generally falls on local communities, not the central government, and the costs of conservation fall on those rural people who would most benefit by exploiting the resources by poaching. Is it not in the interest of conservationists, the Southern African countries have argued, to provide an economic alternative to illegal poaching for poor people who share their lands with protected species?

Opponents to transferring the elephant to Appendix II, including the United States and African countries such as Kenya, have argued that allowing trade in ivory opens the door to poaching because one cannot practically distinguish between poached ivory and ivory from managed herds once it has been worked. Effective control would become impossible and once again lead to slaughter by poachers. To make this point dramatically, President Moi of Kenya burned a pile of 2,500 seized ivory tusks rather than sell them. Some observers have argued that "eco-tourism" and international aid can provide the necessary local economic development to local communities to create a shared sense of value in the local elephant herds. *See* Michael Lemonick, *The Ivory Wars: After a Seven Year Ban, Three African Nations Want to Sell Tusks. Will the Rest of the World Allow It?*, TIME, June 16, 1997.

At the 1997 CITES conference of the parties, Botswana, Zimbabwe and Namibia proposed transferring African elephants from Appendix I to Appendix II in order to recognize the rapidly growing populations and reduced threat of extinction. Zimbabwe, for instance, reported an elephant population of 65,000, double what its wildlife experts believed the available habitat can sustain. This proposal was rejected out of concern over the inability to monitor adequately a resumed ivory trade, but a later compromise was adopted, creating an annotated Appendix II listing for African elephants in Namibia, Zimbabwe and Botswana. All other African elephants remain in Appendix I. Namibia, Zimbabwe and Botswana were permitted an "experimental" consignment totalling 59 tons of ivory for sale to Japan. Do you see why restricting the consignment to only one sale avoids the problems posed by the pre-Convention stocks exception?

The permitted sale was approved subject to a number of conditions. The CITES Standing Committee must be convinced that deficiencies in enforcement and control measures earlier identified by a CITES Experts

Group are corrected, that the consignment does not contain poached ivory and that Namibia, Zimbabwe and Botswana remove their reservations to the Appendix I listing of the African elephant. Moreover, the net revenues from the sales must be directed toward elephant conservation activities. The conference also approved a decision permitting the non-commercial disposal of ivory to generate funds for elephant conservation. Tenth Meeting of the Conference of the Parties, 1997, Decisions 10.1, 10.2. In a related elephant conservation action, addressing the potential uncertainty over whether carved ivory was covered by CITES restrictions, Resolution 9.16 defined worked ivory as "readily recognizable." *See also,* Resolution 10.10 (rev.). In February 1999, the CITES Standing Committee agreed that the conditions for ivory sales had been met and auctions were subsequently held in Namibia, Zimbabwe and Botswana with Japanese buyers. A total of 49,574 kg of ivory (5,446 tusks) was sold for approximately US $5 million.

At the 2000 CITES Conference of the Parties, a motion by Kenya and India to move all African elephants back to Appendix I was defeated and South Africa was allowed to downlist its elephant population from Appendix I to Appendix II. In exchange for this status, all four Southern African countries have agreed to a zero quota of ivory for the next two years, effectively pushing the issue of further sales off until the next Conference of the Parties. Despite the split votes over listing, parties unanimously approved establishment of two monitoring systems–the Monitoring Illegal Killing of Elephants (MIKE) and Elephant Trade Information System (ETIS). It is hoped these systems will settle the statistical battle between Kenya and Zimbabwe, Botswana, Namibia, and South Africa over the extent to which poaching and illegal ivory sales have increased. *Elephant Nations Call a Truce,* NEW SCIENTIST, Apr. 29, 2000. For the first time, the sale of elephant "bushmeat" also entered CITES discussions. A working group charged with examining the bushmeat trade will now address this issue, previously considered a local concern. Adam M. Roberts, *CITES Averts Crisis,* ANIMALS' AGENDA 12, July 1, 2000. *See* TRAFFIC Network Briefing on Bush Meat Utilization—A Critical Issue in East and Southern Africa <http://www.traffic.org/briefings/bushmeat.html>.

> Despite progress in battling the ivory trade, it remains a difficult battle. The backdrop against which elephant poaching takes place needs to be appreciated. Active domestic ivory markets continue in many elephant Range States in Africa, especially Cameroon, Congo, Ethiopia, Ivory Coast, Mozambique, Nigeria and Senegal, and in Asia, particularly Burma, Thailand and Vietnam. Elsewhere, active ivory markets are found in Egypt, Singapore and throughout the Far East. There is little doubt that considerable volumes of ivory annually move through these markets. TRAFFIC has also documented the emergence of Africa-based, Asian-run ivory processing throughout much of the continent during the CITES ban period. These small-scale operations produce quantities of semi-worked and worked ivory products for illicit export to selected Asian markets. Throughout the CITES trade ban period, demand for raw and worked ivory has continued in China, Taiwan, Korea and parts of Southeast Asia, as evidenced by TRAFFIC's seizures data. For the most part, these are not new markets, and their demand for ivory is a phenomenon which functions independently of the situation in Japan, the traditional and now highly-regulated consuming ivory market into which the legal CITES trade from Southern Africa was directed.

<http://www.traffic.org/briefings/elephants–11thmeeting.html>

––––––

2. MAHOGANY

Failure to change the Appendix listing of a species at a CITES conferences is not always a defeat. Thus far, no commercially valuable tree species has been included in CITES, except when listed voluntarily by a country in Appendix III. Nonetheless, in each of the last four conferences of CITES parties, there have been well-supported proposals to list tropical big-leaf mahogany. This mahogany species is a high-priced tropical timber export, which is over-exploited in Central and South America. The first proposal to list mahogany on Appendix II was in 1992. The proposal was sponsored by the United States and Costa Rica and was supported by a majority of the States in which it was found, including Brazil. Brazil had already listed big-leaf mahogany as endangered. The proposal was withdrawn by the United States following protests from industry and Congress. In 1994, the Netherlands proposed listing big-leaf mahogany on Appendix II, but it failed narrowly to gain the two-thirds majority needed to pass. In light of this failure, Costa Rica listed its big-leaf mahogany on Appendix III. What is the practical importance of listing mahogany on Appendix III?

The 1997 conference of the parties also voted down proposals by the U.S. and Bolivia to list big-leaf mahogany in Appendix II, missing by only 8 votes. Though the proposal was narrowly defeated, the debate led to an informal agreement between the U.S., Bolivia and Brazil and a pledge to work with the mahogany producing and importing states to improve and monitor mahogany management and trade. This is especially significant because Brazil supplies the United States 50% of its mahogany. Perhaps most important, Brazil committed itself to list big-leaf mahogany on Appendix III and called on other mahogany states to do the same. Since then, Brazil, Bolivia and Mexico have listed their big-leaf mahogany in Appendix III. CITES has hired two field specialist positions, held training sessions for customs inspectors and trade associations, and published a manual for inspectors specifically on CITES procedures in relation to big-leaf mahogany. At COP11, mahogany was not listed but the parties created a Mahogany Working Group to explore conservation strategies and review trade data, among other things. Despite these actions, however, TRAFFIC has argued that the $56 million American market (60% of the global trade) continues to drive the species toward an endangered status and recommends listing it in Appendix II of CITES. *See* WORLD WILDLIFE FUND, MAHOGANY MATTERS (2000).

––––––

3. STURGEON

Caviar, perhaps the ultimate symbol of luxury and wealth, is the name for the unfertilised eggs of sturgeons. Today almost 90% of the global caviar trade comes from only only three species found in the Caspian Sea, the largest inland body of water in the world. The beluga, also known as

Giant Sturgeon, produces the most prized caviar and can reach a length of 18 feet and live for 150 years. A female can produce up to 12 per cent of her body weight in caviar, but does not reach sexual maturity until late, up to 25 years for Beluga females. This makes the species particularly vulnerable to overfishing.

Together, Iran and Russia account for 80% of sturgeon exports. Prior to the break-up of the Soviet Union, the USSR and Iran closely regulated the sturgeon fishery. The newly-independent states bordering the Caspian Sea (Azerbaijan, Kazakhstan, Russia and Turkmenistan) have been far less successful in restricting the fishery, with the result of virtually unfettered harvesting and trade. Heavy legal trading of caviar (over 220 tons of caviar in 1998), poaching, and loss of spawning grounds have placed the sturgeon in danger of being fished out of existence. <http://www.traffic.org/publications/sturgeon_threat.html>; <http://www.panda.org/resources/publications/species/cites/fs_strgeon.html>. As a recent study reported:

> In 1994 alone, Russian authorities detained 1452 poachers and confiscated more than 110 tonnes of sturgeon and five tonnes of caviar, according to the Russian Ministry of Internal Affairs. During the same year in Astrakhan, the centre of Russia's caviar production, seven illegal caviar processing plants were shut down. The threat to sturgeon is heightened by the indiscriminate methods used by poachers on the Caspian Sea. While fishing for sturgeon females with eggs ripe for caviar (about seven per cent of the catch), poachers kill all fish they catch, including males and juveniles. In addition, the practice of trawling in the Caspian Sea—banned by the USSR in 1959 and still banned by Russia as well as Iran—is in use once again. The trawl nets pick up all sturgeon in their wake, and by being dragged across the bottom of the sea, destroy the benthic ecosystem upon which sturgeon feed.

<http://www.traffic.org/publications/sturgeon_threat.html>

CITES has listed all 27 species of sturgeon and paddlefish. In addition, 5 of the 10 species and subspecies of sturgeon and paddlefish in the United States are protected under the Endangered Species Act. A campaign known as "Caviar Emptor" and organized by three environmental groups–Wildlife Conservation Society, Natural Resources Defense Council, and SeaWeb–has petitioned to list beluga caviar under the Act, as well. <http://www.caviar-emptor.org/>. At the 11th CoP in April 2000, the Parties decided to explore the creation of a universal labelling system for the identification of caviar. Decision 11.162. In December 2000, the CITES Animals Committee reviewed the status of a number of sturgeon species (including beluga). It recommended against a trade ban, arguing that it would not only threaten the Iranian and Russian economies but, also, that a ban on Caviar exportation would merely divert supplies to the new Russian middle class, thus sustaining the illegal market. Instead, efforts are being made to regulate caviar fishing bordering the Caspian Sea. *Caviar Dealers See Threat From Move to save Sturgeon*, CHIC. TRIB., Dec. 31, 2000, at 8.

––––––––

4.   INNOVATIONS

On its face, CITES has a rather unwieldy, perhaps outdated, structure. A species is either listed in Appendix I, II or III. Despite this apparent rigidity, CITES has proven flexible and parties have created a number of mechanisms to supplement listing on the appendices.

The use of annotations is one such strategy to add extra protections for species while not formally amending their appendix listing. In annotation, a species is transferred from Appendix I to Appendix II subject to specific restrictions on the type of trade that can occur. Thus, in 1987 the parties transferred certain populations of vicuna, a South American animal related to the llama, with the annotation that only wool sheared from live animals could be traded. Partly as a result of this action, according to the Peruvian government its vicuna populations have increased to more than 100,000. In 1994, the Parties increased the number of populations listed in Appendix II and permitted trade in raw wool and Peruvian stockpiles of wool. In addition, the parties transferred the highly endangered South African population of white rhinos to Appendix II with an annotation that only live animals and sport hunted trophies can be traded. As mentioned above, the African elephant populations from Zimbabwe, Botswana, and Namibia were also listed in Appendix II subject to an annotation for trade in ivory stockpiles and skins.

Some parties have embraced the annotation as an innovative solution to conserving endangered species. The annotation allows some trade–something more than Appendix I permits–but not all commercial trade–something less than Appendix II.

Others remain concerned, however, because many annotations could create significant enforcement problems. For example, no one knew what criteria must be met to amend or remove the annotation. If the white rhino population in South Africa declined because of the annotation, it was not clear whether a party needed to develop a full Appendix I proposal to eliminate the annotation or whether the conditions for exporting a specimen pursuant to an annotation also applied to re-exports. For example, the annotation for South Africa's white rhino places the specimen in Appendix II but limits the trade to exports of sport hunted trophies and live animals for non-commercial purposes. Under the language of the annotation, a sport hunter could re-export the rhino horn for commercial purposes, because the white rhino is in appendix II and the annotation created no criteria for re-exports, only exports.

After a six year effort by NGOs and a few governments, particularly the U.S. government, in April, 2000, the parties passed Conference Resolution 11.21 to regulate the use of annotations. The resolution calls on parties to specify the conditions for import, export and re-export, which should eliminate the problems described above with the rhino horn trade. It also directs the Secretariat and the Standing Committee to investigate reports of illegal trade of a species that is regulated by an annotation. If so, the Standing Committee can request parties to suspend trade in that species and ask the Depositary Government (Switzerland) to submit a proposal to return the species to Appendix I. Parties have also created working groups on specific topics, e.g., to study trade in freshwater turtles in trade for traditional Chinese medicine and sea horses. Some view the creation of working groups as failures (because they believe the species should be listed), but these may provide the means for obtaining political support in the near future that ultimately will result in listing.

The use of annotations, quotas, working groups (such as the one for mahogany noted above) and other non-treaty based strategies demonstrate the dynamic, flexible nature of CITES. While one of the older international environmental treaties, CITES is arguably among the most modern because it constantly seeks conservation strategies within the framework of CITES *even if* the language of CITES does not explicitly provide for such mechanisms.

D.   CROSS-CUTTING ISSUES

1.   ROLE OF NGOS

NGOs play a central role in the implementation of CITES. Article XI explicitly allows the participation of expert NGOs in the Conferences of the Parties unless one-third of the Parties present object. Thus the IUCN and World Wide Fund for Nature, for example, provide expert advice on conservation issues. A number of NGOs have led campaigns that resulted in CITES actions. For example, ProWildlife, a Swiss group, has led the campaign on freshwater turtles and the Environmental Investigation Agency has focused on musk. NGOs also play a critical role in the area of enforcement. The most important NGO concerned with monitoring the wildlife trade is a joint effort by the World Wide Fund for Nature and the IUCN, called "TRAFFIC." Founded in 1976, TRAFFIC is an international network operating on five continents in nineteen countries. Working closely with the CITES secretariat, TRAFFIC conducts research on the wildlife trade, holds conferences and provides advice regarding national and regional enforcement and regulatory instruments, and works to ensure the relevant international agreements promote the conservation of wild species in trade. As examples of TRAFFIC's activities, consider the two press releases below taken from TRAFFIC's web site, <http://www.traffic.org/>, and the very different aspects of TRAFFIC they reveal.

YEMENI DEMAND FOR RHINO HORN DAGGERS CONTINUES

Yemen continues to play a central role in the illicit international trade in African rhinoceros horn, according to a new report by TRAFFIC (the wildlife trade monitoring programme of WWF) World Wide Fund for Nature and IUCN released today.

From 1994–1996, an annual average of at least 75 kilos of rhino horn have been smuggled into Yemen, where it is highly sought after for the handles of traditional daggers known as jambiyas. This amount could originate from up to 25 rhinoceroses. Since 1970, horn from as many as 22,350 rhinos may have been imported into Yemen.

The findings come only one month before the tenth meeting of the Conference of the Parties to CITES, the Convention on International Trade in Endangered Species of Wild Fauna and Flora. International commercial trade in rhinoceroses and their products has been banned under CITES since 1977, but member countries will once again be examining the perilous status of rhinoceros species and problems of continuing illegal trade. Yemen has yet to join CITES.

"For 15 years, Yemen has been under international pressure to halt this persistent drain on rhinoceros populations in Africa", TRAFFIC International Executive Director Steven Broad said. "Some important steps have been taken by the Yemen government, but our latest investigations show that significant smuggling continues and simply not enough is being done to bring it to a halt."

Today, there are less than 10,000 rhinos remaining in the wild in Africa, compared to 70,000 in 1970. Snared, speared, shot with poisoned arrows and bullets for their horns, rhino numbers in most populations have plummeted. The demand and trade in horn for jambiyas has been a major contributor.

Though the Yemen Government has banned rhino horn imports and domestic trade in raw rhinoceros horn, TRAFFIC observed several craftsmen filing new rhinoceros horn handles during its surveys in late 1996 and investigators were offered both recently made jambiyas with new rhinoceros horn handles and others with handles of older horn. Traders alleged continuing illegal imports, mainly from Eastern Africa. The investigations also revealed a variety of smuggling methods and routes.

TRAFFIC is calling for immediate action by the Yemen government to strengthen national laws and put into action a comprehensive strategy to combat illegal trade, including co-operation with African nations and promotion of substitute materials for dagger handles. In addition, Yemen should join CITES, an action that it has been promising since at least 1992.

"We have been assured by the Yemen Government that it will soon join CITES," said Esmond Bradley–Martin, co-author of the new report. "As soon as it does, the international community should help Yemen to enforce this international Convention and to put greater efforts into stopping the illegal import of rhino horn into the country."

THE FIRST INTERNATIONAL SYMPOSIUM ON ENDANGERED SPECIES USED IN TRADITIONAL EAST ASIAN MEDICINE: SUBSTITUTES FOR TIGER BONE AND MUSK

In December, TRAFFIC hosted an unprecedented international forum in Hong Kong to explore alternatives to Tiger bone and musk in traditional East Asian medicine.

The symposium, co-hosted by the Chinese Medicinal Materials Research Centre of the Chinese University of Hong Kong, aimed to play a vital role in helping to relieve pressure on Tigers and musk deer in the wild due to demand for their body parts in traditional medicine. Tiger bone is predominantly utilised to treat rheumatism, while secretions from musk deer glands are used to treat a variety of ailments such as delirium and amenorrhoea.

The symposium brought together researchers of possible substitutes to present their findings. In addition, there was also discussion of the sociological and marketing aspects of introducing substitutes for time-tested wildlife medicinals ingredients to key consumer groups.

The event was an important follow-up to a resolution on traditional medicines adopted in June 1997 by member countries of the Convention on International Trade in Endangered Species of Wild Fauna and Flora (CITES). The resolution recognises the importance of research into the use of substitutes for endangered species in medicines and calls for governments to investigate the potential of substitutes for threatened wild species used in traditional medicines.

————

2.   SUSTAINABLE USE

The far-reaching decisions at the 1997 and 2000 CITES conferences of the parties signal a new era in elephant conservation and provides an example of a much larger conservation debate–sustainable use versus strict preservation. The traditional conservation approach advocated by major environmental groups has been one of preservation–fencing off threatened species in protected parks and banning trade. The arguments in favor of such an approach are strong. Following the 1989 CITES ban on trade in elephant ivory, the slaughter from poachers significantly dropped. Eco-tourism to many wildlife parks has brought large amounts of foreign currency to developing nations.

The arguments cut both ways, however. The black rhinoceros has been on Appendix I since the 1980s and the listing has done little to halt its rapid decline toward extinction as a result of poaching. More important, a strict preservation approach may do nothing to channel economic rewards to *local* communities. The basic premise underlying sustainable use is that an endangered species providing local economic benefit also provides a motive for local people to work for its conservation. From this perspective, if African wildlife will survive it must pay its own way. David Concar et al., *Conservation and the Ivory Tower*, NEW SCIENTIST, Feb. 29, 1992. In this context, the role of CITES is paradoxical. Trade can certainly drive a species toward extinction but, equally, it may save a species if closely monitored and the monies from the trade are directed toward conservation and enforcement efforts or to local communities. See IUCN note on sustainability, at page 929.

Ensuring adequate monitoring and proper disbursement of funds are, of course, not easy. In fact, the approach favored by some conservation groups today is often a hybrid of strict preservation and sustainable use. The CITES compromise on elephants is an example. The ban on trading remains in place, subject to a number of limited and closely monitored exceptions. And the elephants go back to Appendix I if poaching increases. A goal shared by all conservation organizations today is to re-establish the link between local communities and the benefits of local wildlife resources. Traditionally, the benefits created by local wildlife resources have gone to the State and distant tourism operators.

How has sustainable use management worked in practice? One example is the Zimbabwe program known as the Community Area Management Programme For Indigenous Resources (CAMPFIRE). CAMPFIRE channels some of the money paid by big-game hunters to the rural poor living in elephant habitats. Hunters pay as much as $12,000 or more for the right to shoot an elephant, in addition to the costs of the safari, and this money is given to the communities where the hunt takes place (though critics have charged that corruption siphons off much of the funds intended for the communities). Some attribute the rapid growth of Zimbabwe's elephant population to this program. Botswana and Namibia have instituted similar programs and report initial success. At its core, the CAMPFIRE program and others seek to provide an attractive alternative to the lucrative and dangerous practice of poaching. THE ECONOMIST, June 21, 1997. This approach allows local communities to determine how their aid money will be spent. Is calling the CAMPFIRE fees "aid" inaccurate? How would you describe the fees? The CAMPFIRE program has been criticized by a number of U.S. animal rights groups who have lobbied the U.S. Agency for International Development to halt its funding of the program. Does CITES present an obstacle to programs like CAMPFIRE?

QUESTIONS AND DISCUSSION

1. *Problem exercise* Assume you are an advisor to the president of Country A, a small African country with a number of popular game parks. Your country complies with the CITES listing of the elephant in Appendix I and poaching has decreased in recent years. A number of villages adjacent to the game parks have suffered serious crop and building damage from the growing herds within the park, however, and a number of elephants have been shot and killed by unknown people, likely as a self-help measure since the tusks were not taken. The cabinet is meeting today and you have been asked to present a number of management and fiscal proposals to address the issues of growing elephant herds, the CITES listing, and local discontent. What are your proposals and what are the potential costs and benefits associated with them? Who else would you invite to the meeting and why?

2. Consider the following passage by David Schmidtz. What does this suggest for wildlife that is not charismatic or valuable in a direct economic sense?

> Whether we like it or not, elephants will not survive except by sharing the land with people, which means their long-term survival depends on whether people can afford to share. Realistically, at least in parts of Africa where this kind of conflict is extreme, threatened species will have to contribute to the local economy if they are to have any hope of survival. Thus, according to Brian Child, "wildlife will survive in Africa only where it can compete financially for space. The real threat to wildlife is poverty, not poaching." With equal bluntness, Norman Myers says, "In emergent Africa, you either use wildlife or lose it. If it pays its own way, some of it will survive." Kreuter and Simmons conclude that, because elephants "compete directly with humans for use of fertile land, we believe elephants will continue to be eliminated unless they provide . . . direct personal benefits to the people who incur the cost of co-existing with them."

David Schmidtz, *Natural Enemies,* 22 ENVT'L ETHICS (2000).

3. At the 1997 Conference of the Parties, Namibia unsuccessfully tried to pass a resolution changing the meaning of "primarily commercial." Namibia's proposal would have required the importing country, when making its finding of whether the use of a specimen is for primarily commercial purposes, to consider the transaction's conservation benefits in the exporting country. Thus, if a portion of the funds were diverted to conservation in the exporting country, the transaction would be considered not for primarily commercial purposes. Currently, the decision of whether a transaction is primarily commercial does not consider how the money will be spent after the transaction. After strong opposition from the United States and other parties, on the grounds that this resolution would vitiate the requirements of Article III, Namibia withdrew the resolution prior to a vote. After considering the outcome of the African elephant case, would such a resolution have helped or hindered conservation efforts? How would it have changed the ultimate result?

4. Nongovernmental groups concerned over threats to the sturgeon fishery have proposed very different approaches. A trade group called the International Caviar Importers Association has argued that the five countries now bordering the Caspian should strictly regulate fishing and the caviar trade. In addition, a monopoly would be created for caviar exports to the West, with a licensing system ensuring that only legally harvested roe could be sold. The Caviar Emptor NGO campaign, on the other hand, has called for a ban on trade in beluga caviar. Both groups have called for increased aquaculture as an alternative to wild sturgeon caviar. Which approach do you think will be more effective?

5. Groups like WWF and the IUCN provide important information on the status of wild species through publications like their annual "Red List" (at <www.red-list.org>). On the eve of the 11th meeting of the Conference of the Parties, the World Wide Fund for Nature once again identified the 10 "Most Wanted" species. They are the tiger (Panthera tigris), giant panda (Ailuropoda melanoleuca), hawksbill sea turtle (Eretmochelys imbricata), Sumatran rhino (Dicerorhinus sumatrensis), Tibetan antelope (Pantholops hodgsonii), Asian box turtles (genus Cuora); Javan pangolin (Manis javanica); Asian ginseng (Panax ginseng); horned parakeet (Eunymphicus cornutus); and Whale Shark (Rhincondon typus). The tiger, rhino and hawksbill turtle have remained on the list over the past decade, indicating little progress in stopping the illegal trade threatening their survival.

6. While national legislation is obviously important to combat illegal trade, everyone involved in wildlife conservation recognizes that effective enforcement at the borders is central to CITES' success. Perhaps surprisingly, then, every time a proposal for a working group on enforcement has been proposed to the Conference of the Parties, the proposal has been voted down. Some commentators have suggested that this vote reflects the fact that many countries are concerned that outside observers will criticize their lack of enforcement authority. As with many other international environmental issues, much of effective enforcement comes down to money. To interdict illegal trading CITES requires an extensive, well-trained staff of customs officials. Indeed, many illegal wildlife trading rings are caught through undercover operations. How would you suggest increasing funding for customs operations in developing countries? Are there compelling reasons why developed countries should provide aid specifically for this purpose?

7. In November, 2000, the United States Humane Society filed a petition asking the Interior Department to certify that Japan's actions are diminishing the effectiveness of International Whaling Commissions and CITES programs. Specifically they are seeking trade sanctions against Japan to stop Japan from efforts to promote commercial whaling (*See* p. 992). *Humane Society of Unites States Files Pelly Petition Urging Sanctions Against Japan over Whaling Policies.* NEW SCIENTIST, Nov. 16, 2000. Such an action is not without precedent. In 1993, the U.S. government certified China and Taiwan's trade in rhinoceros horn and tiger products and sanctioned Taiwan. Trade of Rhinoceros and Tiger Parts–Message from the President, S15319, 103d Congress, Nov. 8, 1993. Do you think trade in whale meat is covered by CITES? Why or why not?

9. In an unexpected twist, elephant poaching appears to be driving natural selection within elephant populations. A South African newspaper reports that on the savannah area of West Africa, elephants are being born with small or no tusks. As Richard Barnwell, a WWF conservation officer observed, "All the elephants with genes that produce big tusks have been taken out of the population. Those that remain either have small tusks or none at all." If the ivory trade is driving most of the poaching, is it possible that evolution will play a role in defeating poaching?

Paul Brown, *Elephants Evolve to Defeat the Poachers,* Electronic Mail & Guardian, Sept. 28, 1998 <http://www.mg.co.za/mg/news/98sep2/28sep-poachers.html>.

For suggested further reading and web sites, *see* D.S. Favre, INTERNATIONAL TRADE IN ENDANGERED SPECIES: A GUIDE TO CITES (1990); John Hutton and Barnabas Dickson, ENDANGERED SPECIES, THREATENED CONVENTION: THE PAST, PRESENT AND FUTURE OF CITES, THE CONVENTION ON INTERNATIONAL TRADE IN ENDANGERED SPECIES OF WILD FAUNA AND FLORA (2000); Michael J. Bean, THE EVOLUTION OF NATIONAL WILDLIFE LAW (3d ed. 1997); <http://www.cites.org> (Homepage of the CITES secretariat); <http://iucn.org/themes/ssc/siteindx.htm> (homepage of IUCN's site on species survival); <http://www.traffic.org> (homepage of TRAFFIC).

CHAPTER FOURTEEN

PROTECTION OF HABITAT

SECTION I.   RAMSAR CONVENTION ON WETLANDS

A.   INTRODUCTION

Wetlands are among the most biologically productive habitats in the world and, translated into monetary terms, some of the most valuable. Approximately two-thirds of the commercially important fish and shellfish harvested along the U.S. Atlantic seaboard, for example, depend on estuaries and associated wetlands for food, spawning grounds and nurseries. Wetlands also provide critical ecosystem services such as controlling floods, maintaining water tables for agriculture, filtering toxic pollutants and improving water quality, controlling shoreline erosion, and providing habitat for species biodiversity.

Today, wetlands cover approximately four percent of the planet and are among the most threatened habitats in the world. Despite the critical, irreplaceable ecological and hydrological services wetlands provide, destruction from building development, filling for agricultural land, dredging for aquaculture ponds, and pollution have more than halved the world's wetlands since 1900. Legal protections for wetlands remain extremely controversial. In the United States, the permitting process for the dredging and filling of wetlands has been under constant political assault for more than a decade by those who denounce it as an unwarranted government intrusion on private property rights. Cheryl L. Jamieson, *An Analysis of Municipal Wetlands Law and Their Relationship to the Convention on Wetlands of International Importance Especially as Waterfowl Habitat*, 4 PACE ENVTL. L. REV. 177 (1986); Sara Galley, *Water II. Wetlands*, 1996 COLO. J. INT'L ENVTL. L. & POL'Y 115 (1996); <http://www.wetlands.ca/wetcentre/wetcanada/RAMSAR/booklet/booklet.html>.

The Convention on Wetlands of International Importance Especially as Waterfowl Habitat was signed in 1971 in Ramsar, Iran, and seeks to improve the conservation and management of internationally significant wetlands. T.I.A.S. No. 11084, 996 U.N.T.S. 245 (entered into force Dec. 21, 1975). Popularly known as the Ramsar Convention, this agreement was the first international treaty focused on conservation of a single type of ecosystem. The Convention's adoption was largely driven by concerns in the 1960's over serious declines in the populations of migratory waterfowl and their habitats, brought to light by the international conferences and technical meetings convened by the non-governmental International Waterfowl Resource Bureau (now known as "Wetlands International").

The Ramsar Convention creates an international framework for funding and monitoring wetlands as well as exacting commitments from its Parties for national wetlands management. As of February, 2001, there were 123 Contracting Parties to the Convention and wetland sites (covering 80.6 million hectares). <http://www.ramsar.org/>. NGOs, particularly the IUCN, play an integral role in the operations of the secretariat.

The Convention is intended to protect "wetlands." This term is broadly defined, covering not only the popular view of wetlands but also areas of "marsh, fen, peatland or water, whether natural or artificial, permanent or temporary, with water that is static or flowing, fresh, brackish or salt, including areas of marine water the depth of which at low tide does not exceed six metres." Article 1(1). This definition includes diverse habitats ranging from mangrove swamps, peat bogs and coastal beaches to tidal flats, mountain lakes, tropical river systems and even coral reefs.

Why does an international agreement address conservation of wetlands that presumably lie within national borders? The Convention preamble suggests at least four reasons:

  – the ecosystems affected by wetlands are often international, lying across the borders of two or more states

– waterfowl in their seasonal migrations may cross national borders and are thus an international resource;

– wetlands constitute a resource of great economic, cultural, scientific, and recreational value, the loss of which would be irreparable; (compare with the Convention for the Protection of the World Cultural and Natural Heritage, discussed *infra*, page 1037)

– in coordination with national policies, international action can play an important role in ensuring the conservation of wetlands and their flora and fauna.

B.   THE LIST OF WETLANDS OF INTERNATIONAL IMPORTANCE

The starting point of the Ramsar Convention's protections is the listing of wetlands. Each Ramsar Party is required to designate at least one wetland in the List of Wetlands of International Importance. While the minimum number of designated sites for each Party is only one, many Parties have listed multiple sites. The United Kingdom, for instance, has 161 Ramsar wetland sites within its borders. Canada has 36 Ramsar sites, varying in size from 586 hectares to 6.2 million hectares. Together, Canada's sites account for almost one-sixth of the Ramsar-designated area. <http://ramsar.org/profiles_canada.htm>. The areas designated as Ramsar wetland sites have increased by almost one-third in the last four years.

The Convention's criteria for listing require States to consider the international significance of the wetland's ecology, botany, zoology, limnology, hydrology, and importance to waterfowl. At the seventh Conference of the Parties in 1999, the parties commenced development of the "Strategic Framework and Guidelines for the Future Development of the List of Wetlands of International Importance of the Convention of the Wetlands." The Strategic Framework seeks, in part, to add specificity to the site listing requirements. The original listing requirements were quite general, stating that a wetland should be considered of international importance if it:

(a) regularly supports 10,000 ducks, geese and swans; or 10,000 coots; or 20,000 waders, or;

(b) regularly supports 1% of the individuals in a population of one species or sub-species of waterfowl or;

(c) regularly supports 1% of the breeding pairs in a population of one species or sub-species of waterfowl.

SIMON LYSTER, INTERNATIONAL WILDLIFE LAW 188 (1985). Similar criteria were also established in regard to a wetland's international importance for plants and animals. These criteria would justify, for example, listing of a wetland if it provided nesting beaches for endangered sea turtles or contained rare endemic crustaceans. The revised criteria, briefly described below, are far more detailed.

1) **Group A** of the Critieria: Sites containing representative, rare or unique wetland types.

- "A wetland should be considered internationally important if it contains a representative, rare, or unique example of a natural or near-natural wetland type found within the appropriate biogeographic region."

2) **Group B** of the Criteria: Sites based on species and ecological communities. A wetland should be considered internationally important if it:

I) Criteria based on species and ecological communities.

- Supports vulnerable, endangered, or critically endangered species or threatened ecological communities.

- Supports populations of plant and/or animal species important for maintaining the biological diversity of a particular biogeopgraphic region.

- Supports animal species at a critical stage in their life cycles, or provides refuge during adverse conditions.

II) Specific Criteria Based on Waterbirds

- Regularly supports 20,000 or more waterbirds.

- Regularly supports 1% of the individuals in a population of one species or subspecies of waterbird.

III) Specific Criteria Based on Fish

- Supports a significant proportion of indigenous fish subspecies, species or families, life-history stages, species interactions and/or populations that are representative of wetland benefits and/or values and thereby contributes to global biological diversity.

- Is an important source of food for fishes, spawning ground, nursery and/or migration path on which fish stocks, either within the wetland or elsewhere, depend.

The Convention does not specify whether Parties should only list sites already protected by domestic legislation or if Parties should also list unprotected sites. Some Parties, including the United Kingdom, Chile, the Netherlands and Poland, have argued that only sites already domestically protected should be included in the List because designation under Ramsar heightens the national commitment to conserve a site and provides extra safeguards to its protected status. Other Parties, including Italy, Canada, Greece and Australia, contend that wetlands without legal protections should be listed because formal Ramsar recognition can secure national attention, perhaps providing the necessary stimulus for sites not yet protected. About 10% of Canada's Ramsar sites, for instance, are not located on protected government lands. Lyster, *op. cit.,* at 189.

Within the List of Wetlands of International Importance, the Montreux Record is a register of wetland sites currently under threat. The purpose of the Montreux Record is to identify wetlands requiring urgent national and international conservation attention. The kinds of problems that may prompt a Party to request placing a wetland on the Record would include threats posed to the wetland's water supply, draining or infilling, and industrial or agricultural pollution. In November, 2000, 58 sites were on the Montreux Register, including the Everglades in the United States, Palo Verde in Costa Rica, Lake George in Uganda, and the Donau–March–Auen in Austria. <http://www.ramsar.org/key_montreux_record.htm>.

The Montreux Record has been successful both in providing useful advice to national and local authorities on technical solutions to wetlands threats and in drawing public attention to these threats. When the Ramsar Bureau (located in the offices of the IUCN in Gland, Switzerland) is notified of a wetland under threat, it seeks further information about the wetland, after which the Member State concerned may invite the Bureau to initiate a process known as the "Management Guidance Procedure." Resolution VI.14 of the Brisbane Conference of the Contracting Parties, 1996. In applying the Procedure, one or more visits will take place by Bureau staff, its consultants, and its specialists. A follow-up report will include a detailed analysis of the situation and a recommendation for future action to resolve the problem. If no solution is readily apparent, the issue is considered by separate Ramsar committees: the Scientific and Technical Review Panel and the Standing Committee. The issue is then formally discussed at the next meeting of the Conference of the Contracting Parties.

C. SITE MANAGEMENT AND WISE USE

The Ramsar Convention is short and to the point. Once a Party lists a wetland it is required to promote the conservation and "wise use" of the wetland, but the Convention offers no more specific guidance for what the "wise use of wetlands" means. Later decisions by Conferences of the Parties have significantly enlarged this requirement, giving it substantive meaning. In particular, the 1990 Guidelines for the Implementation of the Wise Use Concept describe actions a Party should take to improve institutional and organizational arrangements, to address legislation and government policies, to review the status of and identify priorities for all wetlands in a national context, and to conduct environmental impact assessment, monitoring, and evaluation of projects that might affect wetlands. As is the case with other international guidelines (such as the Montreal Guidelines for Land–Based Marine Pollution, page 747), the provisions are nonbinding. Beyond discussion of failures at the triennial Conference of the Parties, there are no sanctions if a Party fails to protect listed wetlands.

In addition to managing for the wise use of listed wetlands, the Ramsar Convention also requires Parties to establish nature reserves on wetlands. Article 4. Although initially more than 80% of wetlands listed were wholly or partially within nature reserves or other protected areas, some Parties, including the United Kingdom, Australia, Denmark, and Germany have established new nature reserves or expanded existing ones. The Convention calls for the establishment of strict protection measures for these sites and wetlands reserves of small size or particular sensitivity. Furthermore, Parties agree to exchange information and publications regarding wetlands, as well as manage wetlands for the benefit of waterfowl. Partly as a result of Ramsar requirements, training in wetland research and management has substantially improved. Exchange of information occurs both at Conferences of the Parties and through periodic reports to the Bureau from Parties concerning transfrontier wetlands, shared water systems, shared species, and development aid for wetland reserves.

Convention on Wetlands of International Importance especially as Waterfowl Habitiat

Article 1

1. For the purpose of this Convention wetlands are areas of marsh, fen, peatland or water, whether natural or artificial, permanent or temporary, with

water that is static or flowing, fresh, brackish or salt, including areas of marine water the depth of which at low tide does not exceed six metres.

2. For the purpose of this Convention waterfowl are birds ecologically dependent on wetlands.

Article 2

1. Each Contracting Party shall designate suitable wetlands within its territory for inclusion in a List of Wetlands of International Importance.... The boundaries of each wetland shall be precisely described and also delimited on a map and they may incorporate riparian and coastal zones adjacent to the wetlands, and islands or bodies of marine water deeper than six metres at low tide lying within the wetlands, especially where these have importance as waterfowl habitat.

2. Wetlands should be selected for the List on account of their international significance in terms of ecology, botany, zoology, limnology or hydrology. In the first instance wetlands of international importance to waterfowl at any season should be included.

3. The inclusion of a wetland in the List does not prejudice the exclusive sovereign rights of the Contracting Party in whose territory the wetland is situated.

4. Each Contracting Party shall designate at least one wetland to be included in the List when signing this Convention or when depositing its instrument of ratification or accession, as provided in Article 9.

5. Any Contracting Party shall have the right to add to the List further wetlands situated within its territory, to extend the boundaries of those wetlands already included by it in the List, or, because of its urgent national interests, to delete or restrict the boundaries of wetlands already included by it in the List and shall, at the earliest possible time, inform the organization or government responsible for the continuing bureau duties specified in Article 8 of any such changes. * * *

Article 3

1. The Contracting Parties shall formulate and implement their planning so as to promote the conservation of the wetlands included in the List, and as far as possible the wise use of wetlands in their territory.

2. Each Contracting Party shall arrange to be informed at the earliest possible time if the ecological character of any wetland in its territory and included in the List has changed, is changing or is likely to change as a result of technological developments, pollution or other human interference. Information on such changes shall be passed without delay to the organization or government responsible for the continuing bureau duties specified in Article 8.

Article 4

1. Each Contracting Party shall promote the conservation of wetlands and waterfowl by establishing nature reserves on wetlands, whether they are included in the List or not, and provide adequately for their wardening.

2. Where a Contracting Party in its urgent national interest, deletes or restricts the boundaries of a wetland included in the List, it should as far as possible compensate for any loss of wetland resources, and in particular it should create additional nature reserves for waterfowl and for the protection,

either in the same area or elsewhere, of an adequate portion of the original habitat.

3. The Contracting Parties shall encourage research and the exchange of data and publications regarding wetlands and their flora and fauna.

4. The Contracting Parties shall endeavour through management to increase waterfowl populations on appropriate wetlands.

5. The Contracting Parties shall promote the training of personnel competent in the fields of wetland research, management and wardening. * * *

Article 8

1. The International Union for the Conservation of Nature and Natural Resources shall perform the continuing bureau duties under this Convention until such time as another organization or government is appointed by a majority of two-thirds of all Contracting Parties.

2. The continuing bureau duties shall be, inter alia:

a. To assist in the convening and organizing of Conferences specified in Article 6;

b. to maintain the List of Wetlands of International Importance and to be informed by the Contracting Parties of any additions, extensions, deletions or restrictions concerning wetlands included in the list provided in accordance with paragraph 5 of Article 2;

c. to be informed by the Contracting Parties of any changes in the ecological character of wetlands included in the List provided in accordance with paragraph 2 of Article 3;

d. to forward notification of any alterations to the List, or changes in character of wetlands included therein, to all Contracting Parties and to arrange for these matters to be discussed at the next Conference;

e. to make known to the Contracting Party concerned, the recommendations of the Conferences in respect of such alterations to the List or of changes in the character of wetlands included therein.

Article 10 bis

1. This Convention may be amended at a meeting of the Contracting Parties convened for that purpose in accordance with this article.

2. Proposals for amendment may be made by any Contracting Party. * * *

5. Amendments shall be adopted by a two-thirds majority of the Contracting Parties present and voting [at a meeting of Contracting Parties].

D. ADMINISTRATION

The Conference of the Contracting Parties meets every three years. The Conference of Parties approves resolutions, recommendations and technical guidelines as well as shares information on implementation of the Convention. In addition to the Conferences, to provide more regular oversight, a Standing Committee composed of Regional Representatives from Ramsar's seven regions meets annually. A Scientific and Technical Review

Panel was established and provides guidance on key issues related to the application of the Convention.

The Ramsar Bureau consists of about 15 people. While the Bureau is an independent body answering to the Contracting Parties to the Convention, it works at the IUCN headquarters, and employees are legally considered IUCN personnel. The Bureau collects and disseminates information from Contracting Parties, organizes and convenes Conferences of the Contracting Parties, and maintains the List of Wetlands of International Importance. Ramsar does not require that its Parties submit periodic national reports on their implementation of the Convention, although most Parties do submit reports upon request by the Bureau. Importantly, while Parties have access to the expert assistance and monitoring available under the auspices of UNESCO, the IUCN and Wetlands International, implementation remains the sole responsibility of individual Parties.

E. THE RAMSAR CONVENTION IN PRACTICE

How has RAMSAR worked in practice? As might be expected, results of listing have varied. A few of the success stories are described below. In Pakistan, the World Wildlife Fund–Pakistan and the government worked together to create a wetland management plan, based on the Ramsar guidelines, for the country's 15 proposed Ramsar sites. The plan takes into account all the Ramsar sites within the Ucchali area. In addition to government and environmental group involvement in creating the management plan, a workshop process was established to include the participation of three local villages. This allowed the local population to express its views on the development and conservation issues and integrate them into the management plan. Working with World Wildlife Fund–International, and World Wildlife Fund–Pakistan, the Pakistani government has been seeking foreign funding to put the wetlands plan into effect. How does this approach compare with the "bottom-up" approach central to the Desertification Convention (page 1109)? <http://www.panda.org/resources/publications/water/pakpra/page1.htm>.

The status of the Donau–March–Auen in Austria, as a Montreux Record site, proved instrumental to its designation as a national park. In September 1982, the U.K. Government informed the Bureau that a drainage pump affecting part of Hickling Broad and Horsey Mere, listed Ramsar sites, would be relocated to a site where chemicals would be released downstream rather than upstream of the Ramsar sites. In Chile, construction of a $1 billion pulp plant was put on hold indefinitely due to concerns regarding the effects of hazardous effluents on the environment. The plant was to be located in Valdivia, on a river whose estuary is surrounded by a Ramsar wetland and Chile's only bird sanctuary. Efforts to build a titanium mine in South African wetlands were stopped after six years of battles between developers and environmentalists led the South African Cabinet to vote against the proposal. Despite the mining company's reclamation of a prior mining site, the Government felt that the affected area, designated as a Ramsar site, needed added protections. The Cabinet instead proposed to use the area for nature conservation, agriculture and ecotourism. *See* SIMON LYSTER, INTERNATIONAL WILDLIFE LAW 183 (1985); Sara Galley, *Water, II.*

Wetlands, 1996 COLO. J. ENVTL. L. & POL'Y 115 (1996). Ramsar listing has also played a role in blocking development projects harmful to wetlands at a proposed marina in Ontario, Canada, and development adjacent to the Swale Estuary in the United Kingdom. In response to a proposed development site adjacent to the Akersvika wetlands in Norway, the Ramsar site was increased in size to provide an extended buffer zone to the development impacts. *See* <http://www.iucn.org/themes/ramsar/>. Local conservation efforts have also played a role. In Sydney, Australia, for example, four local farmers joined together to list 1,000 hectares with the Ramsar Convention. Andrew Clennell, *Farmers Become Guardians of the Wetlands*, SYDNEY MORNING HERALD, February 3, 1999 at 5.

QUESTIONS AND DISCUSSION

1. The concept of the "wise use" of wetlands, described in Article 3, pre-dates the Stockholm Conference on the Environment. Its evolution has closely tracked that of sustainable development. The Third Meeting of the Conference of the Parties, in Regina, Canada, 1987, for example, adopted the following definition of "wise use":

> The wise use of wetlands is their sustainable utilization for the benefit of mankind in a way compatible with the maintenance of the natural properties of the ecosystem.

"Sustainable utilization" was defined as:

> Human use of wetland so that it may yield the greatest continuous benefit to present generations while maintaining its potential to meet the needs and aspirations of future generations.

The "natural properties of the ecosystem" were defined as:

> Those physical, chemical and biological components, such as soil, water, plants, animals and nutrients, and the interactions between them.

Does this extended definition of "wise use" differ in any respects from the definition of sustainable development used by the Brundtland Commission (page 179)? Is it stronger or weaker than Principle 1 of the Rio Declaration (page 198)?

2. Why do you think the listing criteria were revised at CoP 7? Is conservation more likely if the listing criteria are general or specific?

3. The funds available to administer the Convention are limited. The 2000 core budget was 3 million Swiss francs (~$1.8 million). Each Contracting Party pays a percentage related to its contribution to the UN budget. Additionally, many countries and other donors make contributions to special Ramsar projects. The Contracting Parties created the Small Grants Fund at the 1990 Montreux Conference of the Parties. Resolution RES. C.4.3. This Fund is used only to provide assistance to developing countries for activities in furtherance of the purposes of the Convention. Any developing country (as defined by OECD criteria) that is a Contracting Party may apply for a grant from the Fund. The types of projects that qualify have been divided into five categories: (1) preparatory assistance; (2) emergency assistance; (3) training; (4) technical assistance; and (5) assistance for raising awareness and catalyzing action. In granting assistance, the Standing Committee in charge of allocating the funds must ensure there is a balance between commitments for assistance related to various categories, and as much as possible, between African, Asian, Neotropical and Oceana regions. Furthermore, priority should be given to emergency measures to safeguard wetlands designated for the List.

The Small Grants Fund has been active since its creation in 1991. In 1997, 83 projects were proposed for consideration. Of these 55 were considered suitable for funding but only 29 (each from a separate country) were actually funded. The total amount disbursed was approximately $750,000. This is a good deal less than the budget of a small law school.

4. In light of the small amount of funds available under Ramsar's grants program, other funding sources have been sought. In 1998, Ramsar's Secretary General signed an agreement to launch the "Evian Project." Funded by the Groupe Danone (which includes the Evian mineral water company) and the French Global Environment Facility, $1.1 million will support Ramsar work. The funds will be used to promote training, twinning of Ramsar sites, and communications outreach. <http://www.ramsar.org/evian_intro.htm>. This private sector agreement raised more than the Small Grants Program. Do you believe the secretariats of international environmental organizations should accept funds from private sources? Does it matter whether it comes from individuals or from businesses? What if the Danone Group uses its sponsorship in its ads? How would you compare this to Ted Turner's pledge to the UN of $1 billion over ten years?

5. Ramsar listing is not permanent. A Party may de-list a wetland or change the boundaries of a listed wetland in the case of an "urgent national interest." An "urgent national interest" is not defined in the Convention, thus leaving it up to the individual Party to justify this situation. If a Party does de-list or restrict the boundaries of a listed wetland, however, it is required to, as far as possible, compensate for any loss of wetland resources and create additional nature reserves for waterfowl and protection of the original habitat. Under what circumstances do you think flooding a wetlands with a hydroelectric dam should be considered an urgent national interest?

6. The Ramsar Convention shares many similarities with the Convention for the Protection of the World Cultural and Natural Heritage. As you read the next section of this chapter, consider the conventions' similarities and differences, which Convention has been more effective, and why.

7. The Ramsar Convention has a superb website, with extensive documentation, meeting reports, current news on Ramsar, and a database on Ramsar wetlands. <http://www.ramsar.org>.

SECTION II.   WORLD CULTURAL AND NATURAL HERITAGE INTRODUCTION

A.   BACKGROUND

The Convention for the Protection of the World Cultural and Natural Heritage, commonly called the "World Heritage Convention," is the most widely-ratified agreement on the preservation of cultural and natural heritage. UNESCO Convention for the Protection of the World Cultural and Natural Heritage, Nov. 16, 1972, 27 U.S.T. 37, 1037 U.N.T.S. 151. Adopted by the United Nations Education, Scientific and Cultural Organization (UNESCO) in Paris in 1972, the Convention was a product of its times. The widespread destruction of historic sites and objects during World War II had provided dramatic proof that irreplaceable, socially important symbols deserved special protection. In 1960, construction of the Aswan High Dam in Egypt threatened to destroy the 22 temples located along the Nile Valley. With the cooperation of Egypt, UNESCO launched an international campaign that disassembled and rebuilt the Temples on safe ground. A few years later, in 1966, in response to flooding in Florence an international effort was mounted to rescue and restore thousands of sculptures, paintings, and manuscripts from churches, museums, and libraries.

These rescue operations received international media coverage and demonstrated that certain national sites have global significance. As the Convention's Preamble explains, "parts of the cultural or natural heritage are of outstanding interest and therefore need to be preserved as part of the world heritage of mankind as a whole." Given this common interest in unique and irreplaceable heritage sites, the Preamble concluded that "it is incumbent on the international community as a whole to participate in the protection of the cultural and natural heritage of outstanding universal value." The World Heritage Convention was adopted both to accept this responsibility and to provide the means for a rapid international response to threats facing internationally significant sites. The Convention is open for ratification or acceptance by all member States of UNESCO and by other States upon invitation. As of January, 2001, 162 countries had ratified the Convention

The Convention joins together the often separate goals of nature conservation and preservation of cultural sites. Its dual missions are to identify the world's heritage, by creating a list of natural and cultural sites whose irreplaceable value should be preserved for future generations, and to ensure the sites' protection through international cooperation. While the Convention recognizes the responsibility of the international community to preserve sites with universal heritage, it also *explicitly* respects national sovereignty. Each party to the agreement is first and foremost responsible for the preservation and protection of the natural and cultural sites located within its territory.

The Convention's protection strategy is three-fold–listing of heritage sites, recognition of sites in danger, and financial support for maintenance and restoration of sites. Thus the Convention establishes the List of World Heritage in Danger and a World Heritage Committee, charged with administering the World Heritage Fund.

B.   THE WORLD HERITAGE LIST AND LIST OF WORLD HERITAGE IN DANGER

The application for a site's addition to the World Heritage List must come from its country. Thus the United States could nominate the Grand Canyon but not Australia's Great Barrier Reef. The application must include a detailed plan of the site's management and legislative protection. For inclusion on the list, sites must satisfy selection criteria set out in Articles I or II. Article I lists criteria for selection as a *cultural* world heritage site, including, for example, sites that represent a masterpiece of human creative genius, exhibit an important interchange of human values, bear a unique or exceptional testimony to a cultural tradition, or demonstrate an outstanding example of a type of building, landscape, or traditional human settlement. Article II's list of criteria, which addresses selection of *natural* world heritage sites, includes outstanding examples representing major stages of earth's history, outstanding examples representing significant on-going ecological and biological processes, areas of exceptional natural beauty and aesthetic importance, or the most significant natural habitats for in-situ conservation of biological diversity.

Once a site is selected, its name and location are placed on the World Heritage List. As of August, 2001, 690 properties were on the World Heritage List, located in 122 countries. Of these sites, 529 were cultural, 138 natural, and 23 mixed cultural and natural sites. Below is a representative list of sites.

Australia's Great Barrier Reef	Auschwitz Concentration Camp
The Great Wall of China	Historic Center of Warsaw, Poland
Old City of Dubrovnik, Croatia	Kremlin and the Red Square in Moscow
Ecuador's Galapagos National Park	Island of Goree, Senegal
Paris, Banks of the Seine	The Tower of London
Palace and Park of Versailles	Tanzania's Kilimanjaro National Park
Lorentz National Park in Indonesia	Yellowstone National Park
Greece's Temple of Apollo Epicurius at Bassae	The Statue of Liberty
The Acropolis, Athens	Hawaii Volcanoes National Park
Vatican City	Great Zimbabwe National Monument
India's Taj Mahal	Archaeological Site of Olympia, Greece
Venice, Italy, and its Lagoon	Historic Centre of Rome, Italy
Historic Monuments of Ancient Kyoto, Japan	Whale Sanctuary of El Vizcaino, Mexico
The Old City of Jerusalem and its Walls	Historic Centre of Lima, Peru
Morocco's Medina of Marrakesh	New Zealand Sub–Antarctic Islands
Kathmandu Valley, Nepal	Spain's Mosque of Cordoba

Sites that require major operations for their preservation are placed on a special List of World Heritage in Danger. Such sites might be threatened by large scale development, changes in land use or ownership, abandonment, armed conflict, or natural disasters. Placement on the list gives these sites priority in funding and, hopefully, encourages urgent international rescue operations and fund-raising. As of August, 2001, 30 sites were on the special list, including Yellowstone National Park in the United States, four national parks in the Democratic Republic of the Congo, Zaire's Virunga National Park, and Manas Wildlife Sanctuary in India.

C.   THE WORLD HERITAGE COMMITTEE

The World Heritage Committee consists of 21 Parties elected for six-year terms. One-third of the seats are elected at each General Assembly meeting. The Committee approves applications for new additions to the World Heritage List, establishes the World Heritage Fund's annual budget for the following calendar year, examines requests for international assistance, and defines policy matters related to the Convention. The Committee is assisted by two international non-governmental organizations, the International Council on Monuments and Sites (ICOMOS) and the World Conservation Union (IUCN), which provide expert evaluations of each application. In addition, the International Center for the Study of the Preservation and Restoration of Cultural Property (ICCROM), an intergovernmental organization, advises the Committee on issues of monument restoration and training.

D.   THE WORLD HERITAGE FUND

The World Heritage Fund provides the means to protect sites on the World Heritage List and the List of World Heritage in Danger. The Fund receives money from the Convention signatories based on a percentage of their annual UNESCO dues, and also accepts voluntary contributions from any other public or private source, including individuals. Payment is required for a country to be elected onto the World Heritage Committee and for receiving technical cooperation or preparatory assistance. Part of this budget is allocated for immediate assistance to Parties, particularly those from the developing world.

The funds collected are used to provide both advice and financing for the preservation of the listed sites. Four types of international assistance to Parties are available upon the request of the Party itself:

1.   *Preparatory assistance* for the preparation of tentative lists of sites that are eligible for the World Heritage List as well as for the preparation of training courses or large-scale technical assistance projects.

2.   *Technical cooperation* for the conservation and management of sites on the World Heritage List, e.g., studies of the sites, staff training, providing supplies, and financing through low-interest loans or, in special circumstances, subsidies.

3.   *Training assistance* for group training of staff and specialists concerning identification, protection, conservation, presentation and rehabilitation of the sites.

4.   *Emergency assistance* for the preparation of urgent nominations or emergency plans, or to provide emergency safeguarding of sites either nominated or adopted on the World Heritage List.

Conservation of heritage sites is a continuous process. Listing a site accomplishes little if it subsequently falls into a state of disrepair or if development projects risk destroying the qualities that made the site suitable for World Heritage status in the first place. Thus, national measures taken to preserve sites, coupled with effective efforts to raise public awareness of the sites' value, are crucial to the Convention's purpose. If a country fails to fulfill its obligations to the Convention, it risks having its site deleted from the World Heritage List.

Convention for the Protection of the World Cultural and Natural Heritage

Noting that the cultural heritage and the natural heritage are increasingly threatened with destruction not only by the traditional causes of decay, but also by changing social and economic conditions which aggravate the situation with even more formidable phenomena of damage or destruction,

Considering that deterioration or disappearance of any item of the cultural or natural heritage constitutes a harmful impoverishment of the heritage of all the nations of the world,

Considering that in view of the magnitude and gravity of the new dangers threatening them, it is incumbent on the international community as a whole to participate in the protection of the cultural and natural heritage of outstanding universal value, by the granting of collective assistance which, although not taking the place of action by the State concerned, will serve as an efficient complement thereto.* * *

Article 1

For the purpose of this Convention, the following shall be considered as "cultural heritage":

> monuments: architectural works, works of monumental sculpture and painting, elements or structures of an archeological nature ... groups of buildings: groups of separate or connected buildings which, because of their architecture, their homogeneity or their place in the landscape, are of outstanding universal value from the point of view of history, art or science ... archaeological sites which are of outstanding universal value from the historical, aesthetic, ethnological or anthropological point of view.

Article 2

For the purposes of this Convention, the following shall be considered as "natural heritage":

> natural features consisting of physical and biological formations or groups of such formations, which are of outstanding universal value from the aesthetic or scientific point of view; geological and physiographical formations and precisely delineated areas which constitute the habitat of threatened species of animals and plants of outstanding universal value from the point of view of science or conservation; natural sites or precisely delineated natural areas of outstanding universal value from the point of view of science, conservation or natural beauty.

Article 3

It is for each State Party to this Convention to identify and delineate the different properties situated on its territory mentioned in Articles 1 and 2 above.

Article 4

Each State Party to this Convention recognizes that the duty of ensuring the identification, protection, conservation, presentation and transmission to future generations of the cultural and natural heritage referred to in Articles 1 and 2 and situated on its territory, belongs primarily to that State.* * *

Article 5

To ensure that effective and active measures are taken for the protection, conservation and presentation of the cultural and natural heritage situated on its territory, each State Party to this Convention shall endeavor, in so far as possible, and as appropriate for each country:

1. To adopt a general policy which aims to give the cultural and natural heritage a function in the life of the community and to integrate the protection of that heritage into comprehensive planning programmes;

2. To set up within its territories, where such services do not exist, one or more services for the protection, conservation and presentation of the cultural and natural heritage with an appropriate staff and possessing the means to discharge their functions. * * *

4. To take the appropriate legal, scientific, technical, administrative and financial measures necessary for the identification, protection, conservation, presentation and rehabilitation of this heritage. * * *

Article 6

1. Whilst fully respecting the sovereignty of the States on whose territory the cultural and natural heritage mentioned in Articles 1 and 2 is situated, and without prejudice to property right provided by national legislation, the States Parties to this Convention recognize that such heritage constitutes a world heritage for whose protection it is the duty of the international community as a whole to co-operate. * * *

3. Each State Party to this Convention undertakes not to take any deliberate measures which might damage directly or indirectly the cultural and natural heritage referred to in Articles 1 and 2 situated on the territory of other States Parties to this Convention. * * *

Article 11

1. Every State Party to this Convention shall, in so far as possible, submit to the World Heritage Committee an inventory of property forming part of the cultural and natural heritage, situated in its territory and suitable for inclusion in the list provided for in paragraph 2 of this Article. This inventory, which shall not be considered exhaustive, shall include documentation about the location of the property in question and its significance.

2. On the basis of the inventories submitted by States in accordance with paragraph 1, the Committee shall establish, keep up to date and publish, under the title of "World Heritage List," a list of properties forming part of the cultural heritage and natural heritage, as defined in Articles 1 and 2 of this Convention, which it considers as having outstanding universal value in terms of such criteria as it shall have established.* * *

3. The inclusion of a property in the World Heritage List requires the consent of the State concerned. The inclusion of a property situated in a territory, sovereignty or jurisdiction over which is claimed by more than one State shall in no way prejudice the rights of the parties to the dispute. * * *

Article 19

Any State Party to this Convention may request international assistance for property forming part of the cultural or natural heritage of outstanding universal value situated within its territory. It shall submit with its request such information and documentation provided for in Article 21 as it has in its possession and as will enable the Committee to come to a decision. * * *

Article 25

As a general rule, only part of the cost of work necessary shall be borne by the international community. The contribution of the State benefiting from international assistance shall constitute a substantial share of the resources devoted to each programme or project, unless its resources do not permit this.

QUESTIONS AND DISCUSSION

1. Because funding requests greatly exceed available resources, the World Heritage Committee prioritizes requests for assistance. In 2000, for example, 15 States were chosen to receive a total of $325,000 in preparatory assistance, 14 States received $654,000 in technical cooperation assistance, 16 States received $45,000 for promotional assistance, 9 States received $416,000 in emergency assistance and a total of $823,000 was distributed for training purposes. The total 2000 budget for the Convention for the Protection of World Cultural and Natural Heritage was only $3.5 million. This is much less than the operating budget of most law schools and an insignificant amount in comparison to the sums needed to protect the sites. If the World Heritage Fund provides little actual financial assistance, why are countries eager to have their sites accepted on the World Heritage List? What other incentives exist to being named a World Heritage Site?

Clearly one reason is national pride. Do a NEXIS or WESTLAW database search of newspapers using the terms, "World Heritage List." How many stories did you find discussing the listing of sites or sites under threat? How many countries are represented by the sites discussed?

2. Article 6(3) of the Convention prohibits states from taking deliberate measures that might damage directly or indirectly listed cultural and natural heritage sites on the territory of other State parties. Are there any enforcement provisions in the Convention? What legal actions would have been appropriate if, during the Gulf War, Iraq had intentionally destroyed a Kuwaiti mosque listed on the World Heritage List?

3. As one of the first conventions to recognize the principle of the common heritage of humankind, the World Heritage Convention foreshadowed the conflicts surrounding the status of the deep seabed in the 1982 Law of the Sea Convention. Inherent in the World Heritage Convention, however, is a fundamental tension: the potential conflict between respect for the natural sovereignty of States on whose territory heritage sites are located versus the international interest in the sites' protection. How does the World Heritage Convention balance these national and international interests?

4. In 1998, the World Heritage Committee removed the Old City of Dubrovnik, Croatia, from the List of World Heritage in Danger. Dubrovnick, filled with Gothic, Renaissance and Baroque buildings, was among the first sites to be included on the World Heritage List in 1979. In 1991, as the Balkans conflict threatened to destroy the city, Dubrovnik was included on the List of World Heritage in Danger. With UNESCO funding of $300,000 and additional assistance, the Croatian government was able to restore and repair the palaces, the facades of the Franciscan and Dominican cloisters, and other repairs.

5. Not all groups view the designation of a site on the World Heritage List as a good thing. Consider the following news story reported in 1996. If testifying before Congress as an expert on the Convention, how would you reply to the Representatives' concerns?

Ken Miller, *A U.N. occupation of American parks?*, GANNETT NEWS SERV., Sept. 12, 1996

Does the United Nations really have designs on our national parks?

A group of House Republicans seems to think so, and on Thursday they skewered the Clinton administration and every president dating back to President Nixon for winking at the United Nations as it bestows honorary titles on America's natural treasures in what some suspect is a plot on American sovereignty. Outraged GOP westerners went so far as to accuse the White House of possibly committing impeachable offenses by allowing the United Nations Educational, Scientific and Cultural Organization to designate such places as Yellowstone National Park and the Statue of Liberty as "World Heritage Sites" in honor of their natural and cultural importance.

UNESCO's World Heritage Committee has put 469 sites on the international World Heritage List, including 20 in the United States. The very first, Yellowstone National Park, also recently was named a World Heritage Site in Danger, due in part to a now-scrapped gold mine proposed just outside its border.

That designation was the final straw for some western lawmakers, who on Thursday accused the United Nations of meddling in U.S. affairs and attaching titles to U.S. property that can limit how land around the sites is managed.

"The president believes the U.N. has more value than the Congress," growled House Resources Committee Chairman Don Young, R–Alaska, during a hearing on his bill to prohibit the administration from nominating future sites for international recognition without congressional approval.

"I'm not picking on the U.N. on this one," Young said. "I'm picking on the administrations" that ever since the Nixon era have sought international "world heritage" designations for such places as Olympic, Redwood, Yosemite, Yellowstone, Grand Canyon, Mesa Verde, Mammoth Cave, Everglades, Hawaiian Volcanoes and Great Smoky Mountain national parks, as well as such sites as the Statue of Liberty, Independence Hall and Thomas Jefferson's Monticello and University of Virginia.

The United States led creation of the World Heritage Convention, now signed by more than 140 nations. Under the agreement, countries submit national treasures for inclusion as heritage sites, and an international panel decides whether to grant the designation.

Most countries seek heritage designations because they confer added cachet to natural and cultural resources and can also attract international tourism dollars. While the accord leaves all decisions on managing the sites or surrounding lands with the host country or local governments, many disbelieving Republicans see something more sinister afoot. "I do not believe that we can wait any longer to address the U.N.'s insatiable appetite to interfere with U.S. land management policy," said Rep. Helen Chenoweth, R–Idaho. "Over 51 million acres in this country have already been designated by the U.N. as either 'World Heritage Sites' or 'Biosphere Reserves' (a related environmental designation) without congressional approval or involvement."

Chenoweth, a leading critic of federal land management policies in the West, said a large "buffer zone" recommended by UNESCO around Yellowstone has the "potential of creating unconstitutional restrictions on private property and interfering with the congressionally established process for managing federal lands."

Like-minded Rep. Wes Cooley, R–Ore., said anyone telling westerners how to use their land "can go to hell" and said he won't sit still as "a bunch of socialists" at UNESCO dictate land-use policies in the United States.

"This is the first real assault we're seeing toward control of America" and private property, Cooley warned. "I don't understand how a foreign entity can designate anything in the continental United States." He also asked if Americans are ready to allow a "one-world order" to push the United States around.

Warming up, he said any president who lets the United Nations, UNESCO or any other international body meddle in domestic affairs "ought to be impeached" for violating the Constitution.* * *

6. The Convention website is at <http://www.unesco.org/whc/nwhc/pages/home/pages/homepage.htm>.

SECTION III.   THE POLAR REGIONS

A.   ANTARCTICA

The Antarctic holds some of the most pristine and biologically unique ecosystems on Earth. The southern ocean is virtually unmatched in ocean productivity; its extraordinary phytoplankton and krill support much of the ocean food chain globally and . . . provides safe harbor to some of the most critically endangered marine mammals. The magnificent blue whale, for example, survives in the southern ocean today in relic numbers, dwindled to only several hundred individuals as a result of years of overexploitation. From a conservation perspective, there is truly much at stake in the Antarctic. During the last 35 years, however, pressures on the Antarctic environment have increased dramatically.

Statement of Kathryn Fuller, President, World Wild Life Fund, in HEARING ON H.R. 3060, THE ANTARCTIC ENVIRONMENTAL PROTECTION ACT OF 1996, U.S. SENATE COMMITTEE ON SCIENCE 22–23, April 18, 1996.

1. THE ICE–LOCKED CONTINENT

Antarctica, the seventh continent, is larger than the United States and Mexico combined, holding in its massive peaks and icebergs 70% of the world's fresh water. Ninety-eight percent of the continent is covered by ice and snow, often more than a mile thick. Subjected to six months of darkness, sub-freezing temperatures and howling winds, Antarctica is the only continent in the world that has not supported significant human habitation. Far from a wasteland, however, the seas of Antarctica support an abundance of wildlife and the continent plays a critical role in regulating the earth's climate and sea levels. In legal terms, Antarctica is an anomaly, its status an odd compromise between unresolved claims of national sovereignty and aspirations toward a global commons. In practice, the international agreements supporting this unusual arrangement have largely protected the Antarctic natural environment. The 1959 Antarctic Treaty declared that "Antarctica shall continue forever to be used exclusively for peaceful purposes and shall not become the scene or object of international discord." With few exceptions, this has largely come to pass.

Why is Antarctica so special? The famed explorer, Jacques–Yves Cousteau, who did much to preserve the continent's special status as a natural reserve, explains.

Jacques–Yves Cousteau & Bertrand Charrier, *The Antarctic: A Challenge to Global Environmental Policy* in, JOE VERHOEVEN ET AL., EDS., THE ANTARCTIC ENVIRONMENT AND INTERNATIONAL LAW 5–6 (1992)

The Antarctic continent is covered by a sheet of ice which extends over 14 million square kilometres. The sheet represents 90% of all terrestrial ice and 70% of the freshwater on the planet. [If all of Antarctica's ice were to melt, the world's oceans would rise between 160 and 200 feet.] The Antarctic extends well beyond its vast land mass, into an ocean of 36 million square kilometers: the southern ocean which surrounds it and extends northwards is a hydrogeological barrier which separates it from the three other great oceans. Without this southern ocean, which provides a unique source of food, no life would be possible on the land. Inextricably linked, the ocean and the land are part of the same ecosystem.

The harsh climatic conditions, and the region's isolation from other oceans, make the Antarctic ecosystem particularly fragile and unique: the continent harbors a number of special areas where plants of a lower rank have been able to establish themselves; only a handful of marine mammals and a small number of birds have been able to adapt. The food-chain is founded upon the krill [a small but plentiful shrimp], upon which all other animals depend for their survival.

The Antarctic is an immense ice desert; life is concentrated in several coastal oases where it comes up against man, also attracted to these privileged areas which are often more accessible, better protected, and sometimes even ice-free in the summer.

The development of all human activity in the Antarctic (scientific bases and logistical support, tourism, sea and air traffic) increases local pollution, causes the degradation of habitats and disruptions for the animal populations.

The ecosystem is remarkably well adapted to the rigours of the Antarctic climate (temperature, wind, light, etc). But the ability of these living organisms to adapt to additional constraints is limited, as is the possibility of colonizing new nesting areas for birds which are being chased. Factors such as pollution and the modification of habitats resulting from human activities can have dramatic and long-term effects. The consequences of the oil spill caused by the sinking of the Argentinean supply ship *Bahia Praiso* in January 1989 will be felt for many years to come.

Additionally, the Antarctic plays a critical role in maintaining the equilibrium of the planet's climate. The Antarctic system—land, ocean, atmosphere—is the natural refrigerant of the earth's temperature system.

The Antarctic ice sheet returns up to 80% of the sun's incidental rays, contributing to the maintenance of low temperatures in the region. This capacity to "refrigerate" at the heart of a dynamic system regulates the average temperature of the Earth.

It is the contrast between the low temperatures in the polar regions and the heat of the equatorial regions which induces atmospheric and marine currents on the planet. Together with the rotation of the earth, it contributes to the patterns of these currents.

The purity of the Antarctic system, as well as its geographic location, creates a unique laboratory for the study of global processes. The air bubbles which are trapped in the ice at the moment of its creation constitutes a precious source of information to determine the concentrations of greenhouse gases and the temperature of the atmosphere hundreds of thousands of years ago. The most recent analyses show that the temperature variations which have occurred since the beginning of the industrial age are half due to the ice cycle and half to the increase of greenhouse gas concentrations in the atmosphere.

---

2.   TERRITORIAL CLAIMS AND THE ANTARCTIC TREATY

It was not until the turn of the century that countries started establishing initial claims of sovereignty in Antarctica. The advent of aircraft and mechanized vehicles in the 1920s greatly expanded scientific exploration. By 1950, no fewer than seven nations had made territorial claims to Antarctica (Argentina, Australia, Chile, France, New Zealand, Norway, and the United Kingdom). All these nations, except Norway, claimed wedge-shaped territories terminating at the South Pole. Their stakes were based on a variety of claims, ranging from exploration and occupation to a 16th century Papal Decree. Disputes over claims between Argentina, Chile and the United Kingdom were vehement, almost leading to armed conflict. In 1948, the United States attempted to settle claims to Antarctica through a trusteeship governed under the UN This effort failed and in 1955 the United Kingdom brought proceedings against Argentina and Chile before the International Court of Justice (ICJ).

Comment, The Balance of Nature and Human Needs in Antarctica: the Legality of Mining, 9 TEMP. INT'L & COMP. L.J. 387 (1995)

Had Chile and Argentina been cooperative with the ICJ, the ICJ might have been able to "throw additional light on the vexed problems of claims to Antarctica." Instead, Chile and Argentina refused to accept the ICJ's jurisdiction, and in March 1956, the Court decided not to proceed with the question. However, the incident may have added momentum to the Treaty which eventually followed.

Despite the political conflicts, there had been international scientific cooperation as early as 1882 and, remarkably, this cooperation lasted despite the Cold War. The first International Polar Year was declared by the international scientific community in 1882 and a second in 1932–33. In this spirit of international scientific cooperation, future parties to the Treaty, recognizing Antarctica's value as an ideal site to study a vast array of natural phenomena relating to the world as a whole, declared 1957–1958 International Geographical Year (IGY). The IGY was "the most complex and comprehensive international scientific activity ever undertaken."

In 1957, scientists from twelve nations staffed approximately fifty stations in the region. By the time the IGY commenced in 1958, over ten thousand scientists and technicians from over sixty-seven participating countries had worked at 2,500 stations. The Soviet Union, which had not taken much interest in Antarctica prior to World War II, was particularly active in the IGY. This increased Soviet activity led the United States to double its original projected number of scientific bases during that period.

The IGY resulted in the signing of the [Antarctic] Treaty in December 1959, as ATCPs [(Antarctic Treaty Consultative Parties)] recognized the need to be able to peaceably continue their scientific studies. The Treaty, which went into force on June 23, 1961, originally reflected the United States' dominance in world affairs; and it is significant to note that it was made at a time when many Third World countries were still colonies or being treated as such. While the preamble to the Treaty states that its purpose is to further "the purposes and principles embodied in the Charter of the United Nations," the Treaty itself is not a United Nations document. As a result, the original signatories acted independently of the United Nations, and the Treaty does not recognize the rights of developing nations in relation to Antarctica.

Under the Treaty, neither the United States nor Russia acknowledge the claims of Argentina, Great Britain, Chile, Norway, France, or Australia, the parties with pre-existing territorial claims at the time of the Treaty's ratification. The United States and Russia, neither of whom asserted territorial claims under the auspices of the Treaty, retain the rights to assert a territorial claim should either leave the Treaty or if the Treaty expires. The Treaty then, in an effort to protect Antarctica and facilitate peace, allows the parties to agree to disagree over territorial, and ultimately, mineral claims. [Article IV]* * *

The immediate purposes of the Treaty were to ensure that only peaceful activities take place in Antarctica and ensure international scientific cooperation. The Treaty forbids the establishment "of military bases and fortifications, the carrying out of military maneuvers, as well as the testing of any weapons." Article V specifically forbids nuclear explosions and the disposal of radioactive waste, making Antarctica the first continent free of nuclear testing. As its immediate purpose was to protect the continent from conflict, thus allowing scientific research to proceed unhindered, the Treaty inevitably left gaps. Preservation and conservation of living resources are explicitly recognized as matters of "common interest pertaining to Antarctica," but the degree and extent of preservation are left to subsequent agreements. The international agreements governing Antarctica, known collectively as the Antarctic Treaty System (ATS), all build upon the 1959 Antarctic Treaty. Thus it warrants a close reading. Its three main principles of regional management, still upheld today, are non-militarization, nuclear-weapon free, and unrestricted scientific cooperation.

The Antarctic Treaty, 1959
19 I.L.M. 860

The Governments of Argentina, Australia Belgium, Chile, the French Republic, Japan, New Zealand, Norway, the Union of South Africa, the Union of Soviet Socialist Republics, the United Kingdom of Great Britain and Northern Ireland and the United States of America,

Recognizing that it is in the interest of all mankind that Antarctica shall continue forever to be used exclusively for peaceful purposes and shall not become the scene or object of international discord; * * *

Have agreed as follows:

Article I

1.　Antarctica shall be used for peaceful purposes only. There shall be prohibited, *inter alia*, any measures of a military nature, such as the establishment of military bases and fortifications, the carrying out of military maneuvers, as well as the testing of any type of weapons.

2.　The present Treaty shall not prevent the use of military personnel or equipment for scientific research or for any other peaceful purpose. * * *

Article IV

1.　Nothing contained in the present Treaty shall be interpreted as:

a) a renunciation by any Contracting Party of previously asserted rights of or claims to territorial sovereignty in Antarctica;

b) a renunciation or diminution by any Contracting Party of any basis of claim to territorial sovereignty in Antarctica which it may have whether as a result of its activities or those of its nationals in Antarctica, or otherwise;

c) prejudicing the position of any Contracting Party as regards its recognition or non-recognition of any other State's right of or claim or basis of claim to territorial sovereignty in Antarctica.

2.　No acts or activities taking place while the present Treaty is in force shall constitute a basis for asserting, supporting or denying a claim to territorial sovereignty in Antarctica or create any rights of sovereignty in Antarctica. No new claim, or enlargement of an existing claim, to territorial sovereignty in Antarctica shall be asserted while the present Treaty is in force.

Article V

1.   Any nuclear explosions in Antarctica and the disposal there of radioactive waste material shall be prohibited.

2.   In the event of the conclusion of international agreements concerning the use of nuclear energy, including nuclear explosions and the disposal of radioactive waste material, to which all of the Contracting Parties whose representatives are entitled to participate in the meetings provided for under Article IX are parties the rules established under such agreements shall apply in Antarctica.

Article VI

The provisions of the present Treaty shall apply to the area south of 60 degrees South Latitude, including all ice shelves, but nothing in the present Treaty shall prejudice or in any way affect the rights, or the exercise of the rights, of any State under international law with regard to the high seas within that area.

Article VII

1.   In order to promote the objectives and ensure the observance of the provisions of the present Treaty, each Contracting Party whose representatives are entitled to participate in the meetings referred to in Article IX of the Treaty shall have the right to designate observers to carry out any inspection provided for by the present Article. Observers shall be nationals of the Contracting Parties which designate them. The names of observers shall be communicated to every other Contracting Party having the right to designate observers, and like notice shall be given of the termination of their appointment.

2.   Each observer designated in accordance with the provisions of paragraph 1 of this Article shall have complete freedom of access at any time to any or all areas of Antarctica.

3.   All areas of Antarctica, including all stations installations and equipment within those areas, and all ships and aircraft at points of discharging or embarking cargoes or personnel in Antarctica, shall be open at all times to inspection by any observers designated in accordance with paragraph 1 of this article.

4.   Aerial observation may be carried out at any time over any or all areas of Antarctica by any of the Contracting Parties having the right to designate observers.* * *

Article VIII

1.   In order to facilitate the exercise of their functions under the present Treaty, and without prejudice to the respective positions of the Contracting Parties relating to jurisdiction over all other persons in Antarctica, observers designated under paragraph 1 of Article VII and scientific personnel exchanged under subparagraph 1 (b) of Article III of the Treaty, and members of the staffs accompanying any such persons, shall be subject only to the jurisdiction of the Contracting Party of which they are nationals in respect of all acts or omissions occurring while they are in Antarctica for the purpose of exercising their Functions.

2. Without prejudice to the provisions of paragraph 1 of this Article, and pending the adoption of measures In pursuance of subparagraph 1 (e) of Article IX, the Contracting Parties concerned in any case of dispute with regard to the exercise of jurisdiction in Antarctica shall immediately consult together with a view to reaching a mutually acceptable solution.

Article IX

1. Representatives of the Contracting Parties named in the preamble to the present Treaty shall meet at the City of Canberra within two months after the date of entry into force of the Treaty, and thereafter at suitable intervals and places, for the purpose of exchanging information, consulting together on matters of common interest pertaining to Antarctica, and formulating and considering, and recommending to their Governments, measures in furtherance of the principles and objectives of the Treaty, including measures regarding:

a) use of Antarctica for peaceful purposes only;

b) facilitation of scientific research in Antarctica;

c) facilitation of international scientific cooperation in Antarctica;

d) facilitation of the exercise of the rights of inspection provided for in Article VII of the Treaty;

e) questions relating to the exercise of jurisdiction in Antarctica;

f) preservation and conservation of living resources in Antarctica.

2. Each Contracting Party which has become a party to the present Treaty by accession under Article XIII shall be entitled to appoint representatives to participate in the meetings referred to in paragraph 1 of the present Article, during such time as that Contracting Party demonstrates its interest in Antarctica by conducting substantial scientific research activity there, such as the establishment of a scientific station or the despatch of a scientific expedition. * * *

Article X

Each of the Contracting Parties undertakes to exert appropriate efforts consistent with the Charter of the United Nations, to the end that no one engages in any activity in Antarctica contrary to the principles or purposes of the present Treaty.

Article XI

1. If any dispute arises between two or more of the Contracting Parties concerning the interpretation or application of the present Treaty, those Contracting Parties shall consult among themselves with a view to having the dispute resolved by negotiation, inquiry, mediation, conciliation, arbitration, judicial settlement or other peaceful means of their own choice.

2. Any dispute of this character not so resolved shall, with the consent, in each case, of all parties to the dispute, be referred to the International Court of Justice for settlement; but failure to reach agreement on reference to the International Court shall not absolve parties to the dispute from the responsibility of continuing to seek to resolve it by any of the various peaceful means referred to in paragraph 1 of this Article.

Article XII

1.   a) The present Treaty may be modified or amended at any time by unanimous agreement of the Contracting Parties whose representatives are entitled to participate in the meetings provided for under Article IX. Any such modification or amendment shall enter into force when the depositary Government has received notice from all such contracting Parties that they have ratified it. * * *

2.   a) If after the expiration of thirty years from the date of entry into force of the present Treaty, any of the Contracting Parties whose representatives are entitled to participate in the meetings provided for under Article IX so requests by a communication addressed to the depositary Government, a Conference of all the Contracting Parties shall be held as soon as practicable to review the operation of the Treaty. * * *

Article XIII

1.   The present Treaty shall be subject to ratification by the signatory States. It shall be open for accession by any State which is a Member of the United Nations, or by any other State which may be invited to accede to the Treaty with the consent of all the Contracting Parties whose representatives are entitled to participate in the meetings provided for under Article IX of the Treaty. * * *

———

QUESTIONS AND DISCUSSION

1.   *Working the Treaty*

For each of the issues listed below, identify the treaty's relevant provisions and decide whether the issue is resolved, postponed, or even addressed:

– national claims of territorial sovereignty over Antarctica

– rights to explore for minerals

– procedures to monitor compliance with the treaty

– procedures to enforce violations of the treaty (violations by governments, by private parties)

– relations with UN bodies

– use of nuclear power

2.   Since it was negotiated at the height of the Cold War, it is perhaps not surprising that environmental protection was a minor issue in the drafting of the Antarctic Treaty. Its only mention is in Article IX, which commits representatives of contracting parties to meet periodically to exchange information, consult, formulate, consider, and recommend to their governments measures in furtherance of the principles and objectives of the treaty, one of which is "preservation and conservation of living resources in Antarctica." Article IX(1)(f). Are there any other provisions in the treaty that provide *indirect* environmental protection?

3.   Article X provides that the Contracting Parties will "exert appropriate efforts" to ensure that "no one engages in any activity in Antarctica contrary to the principles or purposes of the present Treaty." This provision has been criticized as loosely drafted. Indeed, who is "no one"? Does it refer only to nationals under the control of the Contracting Parties or to citizens of non-Party countries? What "appropriate efforts" does the Treaty envisage?

As an example, Canada was not a party to the Antarctic Treaty. Assume in 1962 a state-owned Canadian company commenced mineral exploration in Antarctica and its activities polluted a local bay. What legal recourse does the treaty provide for the parties to stop this activity? How should they respond if Canada states that it is not a party to the treaty and, therefore, not legally bound to its provisions? Since the treaty had been signed only three years earlier, does the argument of customary law have any force? Are there other principles of international law parties could invoke to halt the company's activities?

4. The Antarctic Treaty differs from most other international environmental treaties. There is no secretariat. The UN plays no formal role. As required in Article IX, the parties meet every year but the meeting sites are rotated among signatory States. At these Consultative Meetings, over 160 recommendations have been adopted by parties covering issues ranging from telecommunications and tourism to environmental protection and meteorology. Voting rights and, until recently, the right to attend the meetings have been limited to signatories who have conducted "substantial scientific research activity" in the Antarctic. These signatories are known as Antarctic Treaty Consultative Parties (ATCPs). All decisions require consensus among the members.

Two independent bodies, the Council of Managers of National Antarctic Programs (COMNAP) and the Scientific Committee on Antarctic Research (SCAR) are

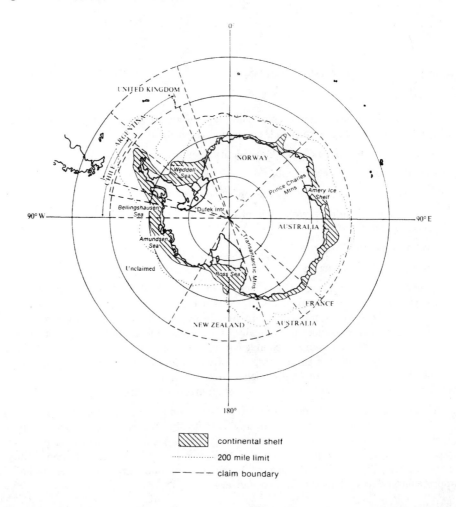

continental shelf

············· 200 mile limit

— — — — claim boundary

influential and attend ATCM meetings regularly, providing their research reports for discussion and recommendation for the development of new policies. Other organizations that are invited to attend the ATCMs include United Nations organizations (IMO, IOC, UNEP and WMO), International Association of Antarctica Tour Operators (IAATO), the World Conservation Union (IUCN), the Pacific Asia Travel Association, the World Tourism Association and the Antarctic and Southern Ocean Coalition (ASOC).

5. The diplomatic master stroke of the Antarctic Treaty is Article IV. By freezing the status quo, disputes over territorial claims were put aside so other issues could be resolved. On the previous page is a map of Antarctica and the current unresolved territorial claims. Note the wedge-shaped sectors of the claims (all passing through the south pole) and the overlapping claims of the United Kingdom, Chile and Argentina. M.J. PETERSON, MANAGING THE FROZEN SOUTH 161 (1988).

3. COMMON HERITAGE OF MANKIND STATUS

The status of the Antarctic Treaty Consultative Parties (ATCPs) proved a matter of concern to those countries left out. Of the 12 signatories of the Treaty, 7 had established territorial claims (left intentionally unresolved) and 5 had carried out scientific research activity on site. Currently there are 43 Antarctic Treaty signatories. Twenty-seven of these have carried out "substantial scientific research activity" in accordance with Article IX(2). They are considered ATCPs and have a voice in the annual treaty meetings. The other 17 nations do not have voting rights and are called Non–Consultative Parties. This two-tier status has generally split along developed/developing country lines, leading to allegations that treaty membership has become a "rich man's club." Indeed, the cost of establishing Germany's research station in 1979 was estimated at $100 million. *Comment*, 9 TEMPLE INT'L AND COMP. L.J. 387, 395 (1995).

Developing countries' concern over lack of influence in the Antarctic was heightened by the discovery of trace gases in Antarctic waters in 1973, suggesting substantial underwater deposits of oil and gas, and preliminary estimates of substantial mineral deposits. Coinciding with the OPEC oil embargo, the potential of Antarctica's mineral wealth mobilized international interest over the continent's governance structure. The Law of the Sea Convention further focused the issues, because the establishment of 200–mile exclusive economic zones forced distant-water fishing nations to seek new waters, and the rich seas around Antarctica seemed particularly promising. Establishing jurisdictional zones off the coast of Antarctica, given the conflicting territorial claims, seemed very likely to increase international tensions (only Chile has formally suggested such zones might exist off Antarctica).

In the 1982 U.N General Assembly, Ghana, Sri Lanka, Tunisia and other developing countries demanded that Antarctica's governance be placed on the agenda. They argued that the Antarctic Treaty was an undemocratic and outdated vestige of colonialism because only the wealthy colonial powers could conduct scientific research there and, when the treaty was signed in 1959, many of the now independent developing nations were still colonies. Some of the non-aligned countries criticized the closed meetings of the treaty parties and the Consultative/Non–Consultative Party structure, and suggested that the treaty served as a clever way to lock up the riches of Antarctica's mineral wealth for a few rich countries.

Using the United Nations as its forum, Malaysia called for a discussion in the General Assembly to "define the problem of these uninhabited lands." General Assembly resolutions were passed in 1983 and 1984 that placed the "Question of Antarctica" on the General Assembly's agenda. G.A.Res. 38/77, UNDoc. A/38/69 (1983); G.A. Res. 39/152, UNDoc. A/39/51 (1984). At the heart of this diplomacy was an effort to revise the Antarctic Treaty's governing structure, introduce UN oversight, and govern Antarctica as the "common heritage of mankind" (CHM). This principle had previously been declared in the Moon Treaty, 18 I.L.M. at 1435, and the Deep Seabed section of the Law of the Sea, 1982. *See* Chapter 7, page 389; Chapter 10, page 759. What are the CHM's implications and why was it favored by the G–77 nations?

[F]ive fundamental qualities would characterize a common heritage regime applied to Antarctica.

(1) The continent would not be subject to appropriation, public or private, national or corporate. Under CHM, Antarctica would be regarded as a land owned by no one, although presumably managed by everyone. Sovereignty as a political/legal quality would be absent. There would be no jurisdictional privileges, rights or obligations fixed by sovereign considerations.

(2) Under a CHM regime, Antarctica would be administered by the international community for the benefit of the international community. All people would be expected to share in managing the Antarctic commons. States or national governments would be precluded from this function, unless they served as the representatives of mankind. Priorities for administrative decisions affecting the region under CHM would be set by universal popular interests, not the interests of individual persons or governments.

(3) If Antarctic natural resources were exploited under CHM, the benefits would be shared internationally. Under a CHM regime, commercial activities would be inappropriate, unless done to enhance common benefits for all mankind. Living resources in the circumpolar Southern Ocean would not qualify as part of Antarctica's common heritage. Legally, these resources remain in the high seas, with free fishing rights there clearly established in international law. Consequently, under an Antarctic CHM regime, benefit sharing would apply only to land-based resources, not to living marine resources.

(4) An Antarctic CHM regime would mandate that the continent be used exclusively for peaceful purposes. No military installations would be permitted, no weapons could be tested, no maneuvers could be conducted and no weapons system could be implanted.

(5) A CHM regime in Antarctica would guarantee opportunities to conduct free and open scientific research. This freedom and access for scientific investigation would be permissible so long as the Antarctic environment was not ecologically threatened or physically impaired. All research results would be made available as quickly as possible to anyone with a genuinely serious interest in them. Under CHM, scientific research in Antarctica would be conducted to benefit everyone, not merely the sponsoring government or scientific organization doing the investigation.* * *

Christopher Joyner, *Book Review: the Evolving Antarctic Legal Regime*, 83 AM. J.INT'L L. 605, 622 (1994).

During the same period, New Zealand and Greenpeace proposed that Antarctica be declared a "World Park," with a ban on natural resource development activities both onshore and offshore. Efforts to establish Antarctica as a CHM or World Park have proven unsuccessful, and the Antarctic Treaty System is still in place. Do you think a CHM or World Park designation would be preferable alternatives to the ATS? Consider the critique of CHM designation below.

Joyner, *op. cit.*, at 624–25.

Noble intentions aside, these CHM corollaries rest on political, legal and economic premises that appear shaky and render attaining a CHM regime for Antarctica unlikely in the foreseeable future.

One premise holds that a CHM regime for Antarctica will resolve the unsettled legal status of the continent; declaration of Antarctica as the common heritage of mankind will *ipso facto* preclude appropriation of the continent. Moreover, an Antarctic CHM regime would resolve existing and potential territorial disputes, and ensure that the continent is forever used exclusively for peaceful purposes. The fundamental query here must be, How? How will declaring Antarctica the CHM accomplish this in real political terms, particularly if the seven claimant states, or the United States and the Soviet Union, refuse to accept the validity of such a declaration?

It is true that Article IV of the Antarctic Treaty does not resolve the claims situation. It only freezes the claims so that cooperation and coexistence may go forward under the Treaty system. Claimant states persist in holding on to asserted titles, and nonclaimants (and the rest of the international community) persist in not recognizing them. The inability to resolve the claims issue remains a serious concern in Antarctic affairs. Claimant states do not take their claims lightly, asserting them to represent integral parts of national territory. It seems simplistic to suppose that a CHM declaration would compel the claims conundrum to vanish. A more likely upshot would find claimant states retreating to irredentism [i.e. territorial claims] and wary nationalism. They would not abandon their assertions of sovereignty on the continent. A move to declare Antarctica part of the CHM might also prompt the United States and the Soviet Union to assert their own claims there, presumably to protect scientific, strategic and economic interests vested in the region. These developments would greatly complicate Antarctic affairs and detract from efforts to keep the region demilitarized. The point is simply this: in view of the intense stakes of certain governments in the Antarctic region, serious consideration must be given by CHM advocates to the negative outcomes likely to result from pushing a CHM declaration—outcomes that probably would arrest treatment of Antarctica as a common heritage regime in fact, though perhaps not formally in name.

A second premise held by CHM proponents is that Antarctica remains the last reservoir on earth of natural resources, both living and nonliving. From this assumption flows the conclusion that these resources as part of the CHM should be exploited and developed for the benefit of all mankind. The problem here is not the aspiration to share Antarctica's wealth, but the actual quality and quantity of the wealth itself. True, traces of several minerals have been discovered in Antarctica, but these are not commercially recoverable deposits. In fact, it is not known how much, if indeed any, mineral wealth exists on, in or around the continent. Geological estimates remain speculative because only 2 percent of Antarctica is ice-free and susceptible to geological exploration. The rest is covered by an ice sheet 2 miles thick, which so far has largely precluded determination of extant minerals or hydrocarbons. As of early 1989, no hydrocarbons have been discovered either in Antarctica or offshore. Only gases such as methane and ethane that are associated with hydrocarbon locations have been detected in a few drilling operations. That does not mean that deposits do not exist, only that at present none are known. As for Antarctica's living marine resources, the circumpolar waters are regarded legally by the international community as high seas and thus may be fished by any person, natural or juridical. The Antarctic seas consequently ought not to be considered part of the Antarctic common heritage and use of their resources should remain available to any and all who might wish to undertake the venture.

A third premise assumes that, given the vast natural wealth of Antarctica, these resources soon will become economically exploitable as advances in science and technology occur. However, geologists are actually pessimistic about the availability of technology permitting large-scale exploitation of Antarctic mineral resources. Antarctic weather conditions are too extreme to support large-scale development operations. The constant subfreezing temperatures, coupled with 100–mile-an-hour winds and blinding blizzard-like conditions, make the human situation there far more of a threatening physical challenge than a lucrative economic opportunity. The logistics of moving people, equipment and raw materials are prohibitively expensive in comparison with the exploitation of more accessible land-based minerals available elsewhere. Current technology for exploiting mineral and hydrocarbon resources in frigid climes, even with the Arctic experience, remains unsuitable for drilling through the Antarctic ice sheet, or surviving the turbulence of iceberg-laden Antarctic seas to get down to the continental shelf. The conclusion reached by experts on mineral development is clear: if mineral wealth does exist in the Antarctic, it will have to be discovered in superabundant quantities to make exploration and exploitation commercially attractive. This prospect appears extremely remote.

––––––––

4. THE CONVENTION ON THE CONSERVATION OF ANTARCTIC MARINE LIVING RESOURCES

In response to overfishing in the 1970s, in 1980 the Convention on the Conservation of Antarctic Marine Living Resources (CCAMLR) was adopted. 19 I.L.M. 837 (1980). CCAMLR (pronounced "camler") protects living marine resources and was the first Antarctic agreement to promote conservation through an ecosystem approach, i.e, focusing not only on the populations of particular species but on the ecological interrelationships between species and their physical environment. By controlling the harvesting of krill, for example, the critical link in the ocean food chain, CCAMLR sought to conserve both the harvested species and their dependent predators. To ensure this ecosystem approach, CCAMLR's coverage extends beyond 60 degrees south latitude to include the southern waters dependent upon the massive upwelling of nutrients and phytoplankton growth. The parties to CCAMLR include Argentina, Australia, Belgium, Brazil, Chile, the European Community, France, Germany, India, Italy, Japan, New Zealand, Norway, Poland, Russian Federation, South Africa, Spain, Sweden, Ukraine, United Kingdom, United States of America, Uruguay and the Republic of Korea. They meet regularly to assess progress and adopt conservation measures as needed. All decisions must be taken by consensus.

The greatest challenge facing CCAMLR (and arguably its greatest failure) has been the conservation of its fisheries. As the Antarctic and Southern Ocean Coalition (ASOC) describes, this is quite an unusual fishery.

> Fish in the Southern Ocean live in waters that would literally freeze most other fish. In order to survive, they have evolved extraordinary adaptations, such as antifreeze in their blood. They also have slower metabolic rates than warm water fish, growing to sexual maturity later in life. Therefore, the Southern Ocean's fish take longer to recover their numbers when they have been overfished.

<http://www.asoc.org/general/fisheries.htm>. When evidence indicates that a fishery has been depleted or fished to the level that predators suffer from a lack of food, CCAMLR's scientific advisory committee and regulatory commission recommend quotas. Quotas require unanimous approval from Parties; thus each may exercise a veto. Despite the establishment of a number of quotas, CCAMLR's effectiveness has been weak. In this regard, consider the current plight of the Patagonian toothfish.

The Patagonian toothfish, better known on restaurant menus as Chilean sea bass, lives primarily off the coasts of South America and the sub-Antarctic islands in the Southern Ocean. The toothfish is very valuable in many foreign markets, especially Japan and the United States, having a landing price of about $5 per kilogram. It can grow up to 2 meters long, has a life span of up to 50 years, and can breed only after 8–10 years. The toothfish fishery developed in the early 1990s as countries' fleets faced depleted fisheries in their national waters. Large fishing vessels first went to waters off the coast of Chile, catching fish such as the Austral Hake and the Golden Kingclip. However, these fisheries collapsed after a few years. The fleets next turned to the coast of Argentina and began catching the Patagonian toothfish; they soon exhausted the resources of those waters and began to move eastward to the Southern Indian Ocean and then to the sub-Antarctic islands belonging to South Africa, France and Australia, where they continue to fish today.

UNEP states that from July 1, 1996 to June 30, 1997, the reported legal catch of Patagonian toothfish was 10,245 tons in the entire fishing region, while the unreported and illegal catch was estimated to be *ten times higher*, around 107,000 to 115,000 tons in just the Indian Ocean sector. <http://www.unep.org/Geo2000/english/0131.htm>. Greenpeace estimates that over half of the Patagonian toothfish catch, worth an estimated $500 million each year, is taken by illegal pirate fishing companies who are based out of countries that are not members of the CCAMLR and, therefore, have not agreed to annual catch limits. At this alarming rate, they predict that the toothfish will be commercially extinct within the next two years. *See* <http://www.greenpeace.org/?oceans/>.

Addressing these concerns, in 1999 the CCAMLR Commission created a Toothfish Catch Documentation Scheme, an Action Plan to persuade other non-member countries to follow the standards set by CCAMLR, and a research program to investigate the impacts of fishing in the region. In addition, as of December 31, 2000, all harvesting vessels were required to carry vessel monitoring systems with them as they fish.

<http://www.asoc.org/currentpress/newdec99.htm>. The Commission did not, however, approve a moratorium, presumably hoping that the new protections would save the fishery. Indeed, the Catch Documentation Scheme does, in principle, ensure that all toothfish sold came from a certified source and had been legally caught. In practice, however, all a captain needs to circumvent the Scheme is to sign a form stating that the fish were caught outside the Convention area. The vessel monitoring system is only effective if the flag State verifies their reported location and, according to Greenpeace, most States do not. In addition, a number of fishing vessels fly flags that are not CCAMLR member States.

Given the difficulty in monitoring where the toothfish were caught, this problem might seem an obvious candidate for listing on the Convention on International Trade of Endangered Species of Wild Fauna and Flora (CITES). Indeed in 1998 the Humane Society of the United States and the International Wildlife Coalition sent nominations to the United States Fish & Wildlife Service for the toothfish to be listed under CITES. Australia apparently planned to propose the toothfish for CITES listing but stopped after the measures taken by CCAMLR Parties in 1999.

QUESTIONS AND DISCUSSION

1.   Consider the challenges facing the Patagonian toothfish fishery in light of the problem of straddling stocks discussed in Chapter 10, p. 694. What measures could CCAMLR adopt that would strengthen its enforcement regime? Does the sheer distance from member States' ports make effective monitoring impractical? Why do you think the United Stated and Australia chose not to propose the toothfish for listing under CITES?

2.   Greenpeace has called for denial of port access to fishing vessels carrying toothfish unless their monitoring systems can prove they were legally fishing. Does this raise trade issues? *See* the Chile–EU conflict over swordfish at p. 679.

3.   In a fascinating use of the web to address illegal fishing, an NGO campaign directed by a group known as "Isofish" reports on the activities of unlicensed longline fishing vessels operating within the fishery area. Check out their website, <http://www.isofish.org.au/boats/index.htm>. You'll notice that it contains available information on all the boats operating in the fishery–their Lloyds number, ownership, flag State, and fishing history. Given that monitoring fishing boat operations on the open sea is notoriously difficult (much less in the Southern Ocean), why do you think Isofish is collecting this type of information? *See* efforts to address illegal fishing in Chapter 10, page 706.

4.   Three major Antarctic environmental treaties (including CCAMLR) have been adopted. The Agreed Measures for the Conservation of Antarctic Fauna and Flora was approved by the ATCPs in 1964 and later amended twice. 17 U.S.T. 992, T.I.A.S. No. 6058 (1964). It requires permits for the killing and capturing of native mammals and birds as well as the import of non-indigenous species, protects Specially Protected Areas from collection and vehicles, and obliges treaty members to minimize water pollution and harmful interference with Antarctic living conditions. The 1972 Convention for the Conservation of Antarctic Seals prohibits the killing and capturing of fur, elephant, and Ross seals and sets annual quotas for crabeater, leopard and Weddell seals in Antarctic waters. Entered into force March 11, 1978, 11 I.L.M. 251 (1972). Unlike the Antarctic Treaty, the Seals Convention controlled activities on the high seas (thus overlapping with Law of the Sea jurisdiction) and was open to all parties. Any nation could accede to the Seals Convention, even if it was not a party to the Antarctic Convention. The International Whaling Commission has also established a sanctuary in the Southern Ocean. Japan, however, has commenced "scientific whaling" in the Southern Ocean and has annually increased the number of whales that it hunts. According to ASOC, Japan expected to catch 440 minke whales during the 2000 season, up from 389 in 1999. *See* Chapter 13, p. 985.

---

5. THE 1991 PROTOCOL ON ENVIRONMENTAL PROTECTION

Despite the fact that Antarctica is not legally regarded as a World Park or as the common heritage of mankind, and notwithstanding the challenges in managing its fisheries, its management has been remarkably benign. It remains demilitarized, nuclear-free, open to all scientific research and, in practice, free of territorial exercise of sovereignty. In the 1980s, however, this rosy picture was far less clear. Indeed, while some argued that Antarctica's unique status made natural resource exploration unthinkable, others contended that the potential riches, and the potential good those riches could do to address the world's miseries, made *not* exploiting the resources unthinkable. This conflict, coupled with the planned 1989 Conference of the Parties required by Article XII of the Antarctic Treaty, led to the creation and failure of one agreement and, in its place, adoption of one of the most protective international environmental agreements the world has seen.

To set the stage, Article XII of the Antarctic Treaty provided for a Conference of the Parties 30 years after its entry into force. With the date of 1989 firmly in sight, the Antarctic Treaty Convention Parties negotiated throughout the 1980s. The result was the signing in 1988 of the Convention on the Regulation of Antarctic Mineral Resource Activities (CRAMRA). 27 I.L.M. 859 (1988). CRAMRA's focus was the regulation of, exploration for, and development of mineral and fuel resources of Antarctica.

CRAMRA attempts to reconcile its two antithetical principles: the preservation of Antarctica for peaceful and scientific purposes and the opportunity for fair and effective participation by all parties in Antarctic mineral resource activities which advance the interest of the international community as a whole.

As mentioned, the [Antarctic] Treaty provisions do not mention mining. The issue of exploitation of mineral resources was so controversial at the time the Treaty was signed that ATCPs realized that making a definitive decision on mining would have precluded the Treaty's ratification. During the 1970s, however, new studies showed the possibility of vast hydrocarbon resources. This coupled with the then current energy crisis increased interest in Antarctica as a source of mineral resources. In an effort to address the unsettled and increasingly popular issue of mining, the ATCPs adopted CRAMRA in June, 1988, after six years of negotiation.

CRAMRA prohibited any activity that had significant adverse effects on air and water quality; caused significant changes in atmospheric, terrestrial or marine environments; caused significant changes in the distribution, abundance or productivity of Antarctic fauna or flora; or resulted in the degradation of areas of special biological, scientific, historic, aesthetic or wilderness significance. In addition, CRAMRA permitted no mineral activity to take place unless it was determined that the activity would not significantly affect global or regional climatic or weather patterns. Finally, CRAMRA ensured that no mineral activities would occur unless technological capacity existed to monitor activities, it could be shown that there would not be an adverse effect, and the capacity existed to respond effectively to environmental accidents.* * *

In the end, CRAMRA was not ratified. France and Australia, both ATCPs and claimant states, were among the first parties to reject CRAMRA. Prior to the 1989 ATCM in Paris, France and Australia circulated a joint proposal calling for a permanent ban on mining and the creation of a world park. Shortly thereafter, four other states submitted draft proposals for comprehensive protection measures. All of the proposals conceded that the framework for protecting the Antarctic environment was inadequate or needed improvement in the form of comprehensive measures. The ATCPs finally decided that they would discuss both the Franco–Australian proposal and the CRAMRA proposal at a special consultative meeting in 1990. This meeting eventually led to the adoption of the Protocol, which would have placed a permanent ban on mining were it not for the United States' insistence on a walkout clause.

The Balance of Nature and Human Needs in Antarctica: the Legality of Mining, 9 TEMP. INT'L & COMP. L.J. 387, 398–99 (1995).

CRAMRA attempted to strike a balance between environmental protection and the prospecting, exploration and extraction of minerals. If inadequate information were available on activities' environmental impact, or there would be significant adverse impact, mining could not take place. These environmental safeguards were stronger than any provisions in previous Antarctic agreements, implementing a precautionary approach. Thus CRAMRA's failure to be adopted was a major diplomatic surprise, particularly since the major critics of CRAMRA had earlier been among its strongest supporters.

Environmental groups played a crucial role in defeating CRAMRA, portraying it as a direct threat to Antarctica's unique conservation status. NGOs predicted the sacrifice of environmental protection in the face of strong national interests in mineral exploitation. Key terms in the treaty such as "significant adverse effects" were undefined. The Antarctic Mineral Resources Commission, which would oversee mining and environmental protection matters that determined these issues, was to be composed of ATCP representatives and "involved parties." Three groups—Greenpeace, the Cousteau Society, and the Antarctic and Southern Ocean Protection group (ASOC)—took the lead in raising public awareness. Greenpeace's description of its activities demonstrates the number of different roles it has played, most importantly its role as on-site inspector.

In 1985 Greenpeace embarked on perhaps its most ambitious campaign to date, a campaign that at its peak would swallow more than half of the organisation's total annual budget. Antarctica has become a unique place in the modern world, the only continent that remains relatively untouched by human interference and therefore arguably the only pristine wilderness left on earth. For Greenpeace it seemed imperative to keep it that way. Some ecologists have even argued that Antarctica could provide important information for future generations seeking to reverse the environmental degradation wrought by humanity in the Twentieth Century.* * *

In the early 80's the threat of commercial exploitation of Antarctica loomed large for a number of reasons: the Antarctic Treaty was reaching its expiration date; the continent although today covered in ice, was thought to be rich in flora and fauna millions of years ago, strong evidence for the existence of oil and mineral deposits under the rock and ice; and technological advances have made it feasible to drill for oil in conditions of extreme cold. It seemed to environmentalists, that the signatories to the Antarctic Treaty were all but lining up to start prospecting.

The idea to plough resources into a campaign to make Antarctica a "World Park" was first mooted by Greenpeace in 1979. At first the plan was modest; some sort of radio station along the lines of "Radio Free Europe" was discussed, but as more research was done it became apparent that the organisation would have to set up a permanent base on the ice if it was to have a voice at the Antarctica Treaty table where the continent's fate would ultimately be decided.

The task was a daunting one. No non-governmental organisation had ever set up a base in Antarctica and there were many practical as well as political obstacles to overcome. Not least because countries that already had bases in the region were unanimously hostile to the idea of being Greenpeace's neighbour on the ice. Officially they made it known that they didn't want to mount rescue missions should something go wrong, but their antagonism also masked their reluctance to encourage outside scrutiny. * * *

Greenpeace had a permanent base in Antarctica for a total of 4 years from 1987 to 1991, the professionalism of its operation gradually earning the respect of other Antarctic Treaty Nations. With each annual re-supply, World Park Base's facilities were gradually improved, better satellite communication was installed and a wind power generator lessened reliance on nonrenewable resources. In 1987 a new ship was purchased, a former icebreaker christened "MV Gondwana" by the campaign, it replaced the MV Greenpeace as the supply vessel.

But the re-supply of World Park Base was only part of the Antarctica campaign. In its annual trips to the ice the MV Gondwana toured bases in the region to monitor how closely they adhered to Antarctic Treaty regulations concerning the environmental impact of such facilities. Many scandals came to light forcing the treaty nations to clean up their act. In the 1987/88 season Greenpeace made headlines around the world when 15 protesters blocked the building site for a French airstrip at Dumont D'Urville. The construction work was controversial because it involved dynamiting the habitats of nesting penguins and even French scientists admitted an airstrip violated the terms of the Antarctica Treaty.

Due in large part to NGOs raising international public awareness, in place of the rejected CRAMRA, the 39 ATCPs signed the 1991 Protocol on Environmental Protection to the Antarctic Treaty, one of the most environmentally protective international agreements ever adopted. 30 I.L.M. 1461 (1991). Rather than focus on mining, the 1991 Protocol states as its objective the "comprehensive protection of the Antarctic environment" and designates the region as a "natural reserve" dedicated to science and peace. Activities in Antarctica have to be planned so they will limit adverse environmental impacts, and any activity with more than minor or transitory impact requires an environmental impact assessment. Most important, all activities relating to mineral resources other than scientific research are prohibited for at least 50 years.

The annexes provided detailed mandatory rules for environmental protection. The environmental impact assessment procedures (Annex I) are the most sophisticated of any international agreement, perhaps stricter than comparable provisions in the U.S. National Environmental Policy Act. The waste management provisions (Annex III) contain guidelines to produce less waste and require most waste to be removed by its producers. The earlier wildlife agreements are reinforced by regulations in Annex II. Annex IV regulates marine pollution. If respected in practice, the 1991 Protocol's provisions and amendments are a powerful protector of Antarctica's natural status.

PROTOCOL ON ENVIRONMENTAL PROTECTION TO THE ANTARCTIC TREATY (1991)

Article 2

Objective and Designation

The Parties commit themselves to the comprehensive protection of the Antarctic environment and dependent and associated ecosystems and hereby designate Antarctica as a natural reserve, devoted to peace and science.

Article 3

Environmental Principles

1. The protection of the Antarctic environment and dependent and associated ecosystems and the intrinsic value of Antarctica, including its wilderness and aesthetic values and its value as an area for the conduct of scientific research, in particular research essential to understanding the global environment, shall be fundamental considerations in the planning and conduct of all activities in the Antarctic Treaty area.

2. To this end:

(a) activities in the Antarctic Treaty area shall be planned and conducted so as to limit adverse impacts on the Antarctic environment and dependent and associated ecosystems;

(b) activities in the Antarctic Treaty area shall be planned and conducted so as to avoid:

(i) adverse effects on climate or weather patterns;

(ii) significant adverse effects on air or water quality;

(iii) significant changes in the atmospheric, terrestrial (including aquatic), glacial or marine environments;

(iv) detrimental changes in the distribution, abundance or productivity of species or populations of species of fauna and flora;

(v) further jeopardy to endangered or threatened species or populations of such species; or

(vi) degradation of, or substantial risk to, areas of biological, scientific, historic, aesthetic or wilderness significance;

(c) activities in the Antarctic Treaty area shall be planned and conducted on the basis of information sufficient to allow prior assessments of, and informed judgments about, their possible impacts on the Antarctic environment and dependent and associated ecosystems and on the value of Antarctica for the conduct of scientific research; such judgments shall take full account of:

(i) the scope of the activity, including its area, duration and intensity;

(ii) the cumulative impacts of the activity, both by itself and in combination with other activities in the Antarctic Treaty area;

(iii) whether the activity will detrimentally affect any other activity in the Antarctic Treaty area;

(iv) whether technology and procedures are available to provide for environmentally safe operations;

(v) whether there exists the capacity to monitor key environmental parameters and ecosystem components so as to identify and provide early warning of any adverse effects of the activity and to provide for such modification of operating procedures as may be necessary in the light of the results of monitoring or increased knowledge of the Antarctic environment and dependent and associated ecosystems; and

(vi) whether there exists the capacity to respond promptly and effectively to accidents, particularly those with potential environmental effects;

(d) regular and effective monitoring shall take place to allow assessment of the impacts of ongoing activities, including the verification of predicted impacts;* * *

Article 7

Prohibition of Mineral Resource Activities

Any activity relating to mineral resources, other than scientific research, shall be prohibited.

Article 8

Environmental Impact Assessment

1. Proposed activities referred to in paragraph 2 below shall be subject to the procedures set out in Annex I for prior assessment of the impacts of those activities on the Antarctic environment or on dependent or associated ecosystems according to whether those activities are identified as having:

(a) less than a minor or transitory impact;

(b) a minor or transitory impact; or

(c) more than a minor or transitory impact.

2. Each Party shall ensure that the assessment procedures set out in Annex I are applied in the planning processes leading to decisions about any activities undertaken in the Antarctic Treaty area pursuant to scientific research programmes, tourism and all other governmental and non-governmental activities in the Antarctic Treaty area for which advance notice is required under Article VII (5) of the Antarctic Treaty, including associated logistic support activities.

3. The assessment procedures set out in Annex I shall apply to any change in an activity whether the change arises from an increase or decrease in the intensity of an existing activity, from the addition of an activity, the decommissioning of a facility, or otherwise.

4. Where activities are planned jointly by more than one Party, the Parties involved shall nominate one of their number to coordinate the implementation of the environmental impact assessment procedures set out in Annex I.* * *

Article 11

Committee for Environmental Protection

1. There is hereby established the Committee for Environmental Protection.

2. Each Party shall be entitled to be a member of the Committee and to appoint a representative who may be accompanied by experts and advisers.

3. Observer status in the Committee shall be open to any Contracting Party to the Antarctic Treaty which is not a Party to this Protocol. * * *

Article 12

Functions of the Committee

1. The functions of the Committee shall be to provide advice and formulate recommendations to the Parties in connection with the implementation of this Protocol, including the operation of its Annexes, for consideration at Antarctic Treaty Consultative Meetings, and to perform such other functions as may be referred to it by the Antarctic Treaty Consultative Meetings. In particular, it shall provide advice on:

    (a) the effectiveness of measures taken pursuant to this Protocol;

    (b) the need to update, strengthen or otherwise improve such measures;

    (c) the need for additional measures, including the need for additional Annexes, where appropriate;

    (d) the application and implementation of the environmental impact assessment procedures set out in Article 8 and Annex I;

    (e) means of minimising or mitigating environmental impacts of activities in the Antarctic Treaty area;

    (f) procedures for situations requiring urgent action, including response action in environmental emergencies;

    (g) the operation and further elaboration of the Antarctic Protected Area system;

    (h) inspection procedures, including formats for inspection reports and checklists for the conduct of inspections;

    (i) the collection, archiving, exchange and evaluation of information related to environmental protection;

    (j) the state of the Antarctic environment; and

    (k) the need for scientific research, including environmental monitoring, related to the implementation of this Protocol. * * *

Article 14

Inspection

1. In order to promote the protection of the Antarctic environment and dependent and associated ecosystems, and to ensure compliance with this Protocol, the Antarctic Treaty Consultative Parties shall arrange, individually or collectively, for inspections by observers to be made in accordance with Article VII of the Antarctic Treaty.* * *

3. Parties shall co-operate fully with observers undertaking inspections, and shall ensure that during inspections, observers are given access to all parts of stations, installations, equipment, ships and aircraft open to inspection under Article VII (3) of the Antarctic Treaty, as well as to all records maintained thereon which are called for pursuant to this Protocol.

4. Reports of inspections shall be sent to the Parties whose stations, installations, equipment, ships or aircraft are covered by the reports. After those Parties have been given the opportunity to comment, the reports and any comments thereon shall be circulated to all the Parties and to the Committee, considered at the next Antarctic Treaty Consultative Meeting, and thereafter made publicly available.

Article 16

Liability

Consistent with the objectives of this Protocol for the comprehensive protection of the Antarctic environment and dependent and associated ecosystems, the Parties undertake to elaborate rules and procedures relating to liability for damage arising from activities taking place in the Antarctic Treaty area and covered by this Protocol. Those rules and procedures shall be included in one or more Annexes to be adopted in accordance with Article 9 (2).* * *

Article 20

Dispute Settlement Procedure

2. The Arbitral Tribunal shall not be competent to decide or rule upon any matter within the scope of Article IV of the Antarctic Treaty [the freezing of territorial claims]. In addition, nothing in this Protocol shall be interpreted as conferring competence or jurisdiction on the International Court of Justice or any other tribunal established for the purpose of settling disputes between Parties to decide or otherwise rule upon any matter within the scope of Article IV of the Antarctic Treaty. * * *

Article 25

Modification or Amendment

1. Without prejudice to the provisions of Article 9 [amendment of annexes], this Protocol may be modified or amended at any time in accordance with the procedures set forth in Article XII (1) (a) and (b) of the Antarctic Treaty.

2. If, after the expiration of 50 years from the date of entry into force of this Protocol, any of the Antarctic Treaty Consultative Parties so requests by a communication addressed to the Depositary, a conference shall be held as soon as practicable to review the operation of this Protocol.

3. A modification or amendment proposed at any Review Conference called pursuant to paragraph 2 above shall be adopted by a majority of the Parties, including 3/4 of the States which are Antarctic Treaty Consultative Parties at the time of adoption of this Protocol.

4. A modification or amendment adopted pursuant to paragraph 3 above shall enter into force upon ratification, acceptance, approval or accession by 3/4 of the Antarctic Treaty Consultative Parties, including ratification, acceptance, approval or accession by all States which are Antarctic Treaty Consultative Parties at the time of adoption of this Protocol.

5. (a) With respect to Article 7, the prohibition on Antarctic mineral resource activities contained therein shall continue unless there is in force a binding legal regime on Antarctic mineral resource activities that includes an agreed means for determining whether, and, if so, under which conditions, any such activities would be acceptable. This regime shall fully safeguard the interests of all States referred to in Article IV of the Antarctic Treaty and apply the principles thereof. Therefore, if a modification or amendment to Article 7 is

proposed at a Review Conference referred to in paragraph 2 above, it shall include such a binding legal regime. * * *

Annex I Environmental Impact Assessment * * *

Annex II Conservation of Antarctic Fauna and Flora * * *

Annex III Waste Disposal and Waste Management * * *

Annex IV Prevention of Marine Pollution * * *

Annex V Area Protection and Management * * *

———

QUESTIONS AND DISCUSSION

1. *Working the Treaty*

– How does a country withdraw from the Protocol?

– Is the Protocol more protective than the Antarctic Treaty? In what ways?

– Reading the text of Article 25, under what circumstances could a party legally commence mineral exploration? How likely is it these circumstances would arise? Could a party extract minerals if it were doing so for "scientific research"?

– Compare the Protocol's provisions with the features of a common heritage of mankind designation discussed earlier. How does the Protocol compare?

– Could the Protocol's provisions be used to transform Antarctica into a World Park?

2. The 50–year moratorium on mining has been hailed as an environmental success. Many environmental groups, however, argued for a permanent ban and continue to do so. Shortly after the defeat of CRAMRA, the United States passed a law making it criminal for U.S. parties to "engage in, finance, or otherwise knowingly provide assistance to any Antarctic mineral resource activity." Antarctic Protection Act of 1990, Pub.L.No. 101–594, 104 Stat. 29750 (1990). Interestingly, however, during negotiations of the 1991 Protocol the United States, likely also speaking for other countries, refused to sign away all future rights to mineral exploration. Is this an unreasonable position? More to the point, how does the precautionary principle apply to this case? Would it suggest a permanent ban or 50–year moratorium on mineral exploration?

3. The dispute resolution procedures under the 1991 Protocol are mandatory if they concern the prohibition of mineral research activities (Article 7), environmental impact assessment (Article 8), emergency response actions (Article 15), the annexes, or compliance (Article 13). Parties must jointly agree to submit their dispute either to the International Court of Justice or the Arbitral Tribunal. If the parties cannot agree amongst themselves, the dispute is heard by the Arbitral Tribunal. Any matters arising under Article IV of the Antarctic Treaty (the agreement to disagree on territorial claims) is expressly excluded from the Tribunal's competence. Created by a Schedule to the Protocol, the Arbitral Tribunal is composed of experts proposed by the ATCPs. In a dispute, each party may select one arbitrator from the list of experts and must jointly agree on the third arbitrator. If they cannot agree on the third arbitrator, the choice is made by the President of the International Court of Justice.

4. There is some concern that the EIA system is not working as well as it should, given the uneven practice in conducting assessments. For example, the United States and Australia account for the creation of 60% of the assessments since 1988.

As of March 1999, twelve of the twenty-seven consultative parties had not written any assessments, only sixty-one Initial Environmental Evaluations had been conducted, and only eight Comprehensive Environmental Evaluations. According to ASOC, this number clearly does not accurately reflect the number of activities that have taken place in the last ten or so years. <http://www.asoc.org/current-press/mar1999nwl.htm>. Does the Protocol anticipate this poor compliance rate? Could this be addressed under the dispute resolution process?

5. One of the renewable resources most under threat globally is fresh water. Antarctica's enormous icebergs present a potential solution to problems of water scarcity. A number of entrepreneurs have already started plans to tow very large icebergs to arid regions and the idea is not as ridiculous as it may seem. One study estimated that an iceberg towed to Saudi Arabia would provide water more cheaply than that generated from de-salinization plants. Its analysis suggested a large iceberg, weighing about 80 million tons, would be worth about $40 million. At the esteemed Scripps Institution of Oceanography in California, scientists calculate that a 10 mile iceberg towed to California from Antarctica could satisfy the fresh water needs of Los Angeles for a month. THE HERALD (GLASGOW), March 22, 1997. Would the 1991 Protocol allow this commercial activity? Why or why not?

Another debate illustrates the scarcity of fresh water resources and the territorial disputes in Antarctica. Lake Vostok is about the size of Lake Ontario but is under 4 kilometers of ice. It is believed to be at least 35 million years old and may have a variety of unknown life forms that scientists hope to study. However, NASA would like to use the lake as a testing ground for its planned mission to Jupiter and Russia would like to continue the drilling of the lake, which was recently halted, and establish a research station to study its life. NASA needed the National Science Foundation's endorsement of the project, which it did not receive. The future of the lake remains undetermined. Many environmental groups would like to see it left untouched. <http://www.asoc.org/currentpress/newdec99.htm>. Before NASA used the lake as a testing ground or Russia started its research program, what would the 1991 Protocol require the parties to do?

6. More and more visitors are coming every year to Antarctica. 43% more tourists were expected to travel to the region in 2000 compared to 1998 and 1999. These cruise ship visits raise concerns over marine pollution, the impacts on nesting areas of seals and penguins, and other flora and fauna. At least two ships have run aground to date. Because of this increased level of disturbance, the Antartic and Southern Ocean Coalition (ASOC) has recommended that the Antarctic Treaty System implement a new program to handle the assessment of tourism and its effects, creating a more stringent environmental impact assessment program and greater enforcement of a passenger limit for all tourist activities. *See* <http://www.asoc.org/campaign/tourpap.htm>. The number of researchers has increased, as well. In 1997, 42 research stations operated in Antarctica, seven of which operated all year round. <http://www.unep.org/Geo2000/english/0214.htm>.

7. The Antarctic Treaty System is now in its fifth decade of existence. Does this constitute the customary law of the Antarctic? Do you agree with the assertions of Professor Charney?

> The record shows that there is substantial support for the following Antarctic norms: non-militarization, non-nuclearization, prohibition of nuclear waste disposal, freedom of scientific research, open access to the entire area, maximum protection of the environment, protection of the flora and fauna of Antarctica, protection of the seals of Antarctica, and protection of the marine living resources of Antarctica. Not only did many states specifically indicate support for these norms, no state opposed them. Some states pronounced that these norms of the Antarctic Treaty system had established rules of interna-

tional law. This consensus added to the state practice appears to provide the necessary elements for the merger of many Antarctic Treaty system norms into customary international law binding on all states

Reprinted in Christopher Joyner, *Book Review: the Evolving Antarctic Legal Regime,* 83 AM.J.INT'L L. 605, 611 (1989).

8. Article 16 of the 1991 Protocol, similar to the London Convention and many other international environmental agreements, calls for the development of a liability regime by the parties. An experts group has been convened to prepare a draft Annex on Environmental Liability and has been circulating a draft which creates a two-tier system. The first tier would impose civil liability on the operator responsible for the damage and, in the event the compensation is inadequate, an Environmental Protection Fund would provide interim relief. There has been no resolution regarding the creation of an annex to the treaty that would cover liability for environmental damage to the region. Some members believe that the annex should comprehensively cover all types of environmental harms. The United Kingdom and United States have argued to exclude from liability damage resulting from impacts which had been judged acceptable according to the provisions of the 1991 Protocol (i.e., from an environmental impact assessment). What are the problems inherent in this proposal? *See* <http://www.asoc.org/currentpress/june98.htm>.

Arguing that any type of activity in the fragile Antarctic region is equivalent to an abnormally dangerous activity, ASOC has argued for a strict liability regime in the region. If this were the case, conducting an environmental impact assessment would not absolve a party from liability. Furthermore, ASOC encourages the establishment of a "Liability Fund" that would serve to clean up environmental damage after insurance funds have been depleted, as well as cover the damage created by non-Treaty parties. *See* <http://www.asoc.org/general /liab.htm>.

9. *Problem Exercise* Refer to the text of the Protocol. What liability law would apply if a tourist were injured by a seal or damaged equipment at a research station? What if tourists injured a seal? *See,* Jonathan Blum, *The Deep Freeze: Torts, Choice of Law, and the Antarctic Treaty Regime,* 8 EMORY INT'L L. REV. 667 (1994). Interestingly, none of the ATS instruments forbid the use of nuclear power. How would liability attach if there were radioactive discharges into the sea from a research station?

10. Antarctica is not on the World Heritage List of the Convention for the Protection of the World Cultural and Natural Heritage. Why not (see the listing requirements set out at page 1038)? Could the United States or the U.K. propose Antarctica for inclusion on the list? What difference might such a listing make for Antarctica's protection?

B.   THE ARCTIC REGION

Like Antarctica, the Arctic is one of the last pristine areas remaining on earth, and one of the most threatened. A fragile environment, the Arctic's low temperatures and short growing season slow the decomposition of wastes while ocean currents and prevailing wind patterns tend to funnel pollutants from heavily industrialized cities in Europe, Russia and Asia to the north, concentrating toxic and radioactive materials. The environmental legacy of industrial and military activities by the former Soviet Union's pipelines, nuclear facilities, military facilities and waste sites in the region pose long-lived threats, as well. A summary of the environmental challenges is provided below.

Acidifying Pollutants. Smelters in Russia and Eastern Europe are major sources of acidifying pollutants carried to the Arctic by long-range air transport. The nickel smelter on the Kola Peninsula of northeastern Russia is one of the largest smelters in the world.

Persistent Organic Pollutants (POPs). Although many circumpolar countries have banned the use of highly toxic pesticides, they still exist in high concentrations in some arctic regions where significant levels of toxic organic compounds such as DDT, dioxin and PCBs have been found in human Arctic communities and high levels of pesticides such as chlordane and dieldrin in whales and seals. Since no local industries produce these chemicals, it is clear they are transported from the south. The Inuit are said to have the highest levels of POPs of any human population on earth–on average 2 to 10 times higher in Arctic adults compared to those living in non-Arctic regions. Part of this is due to the fact that traditional arctic diets consist of animals that have a high fatty tissue content, where many contaminants have bioaccumulated. The health effects of these toxics are serious, including weakened immune response and potential endocrine disruption. See Chapter 12, page 880; UNEP, GLOBAL ENVIRONMENTAL OUTLOOK, THE STATE OF THE ENVIRONMENT: THE ARCTIC, 3 (2000).

Oil Pollution. The waters of the Arctic receive oil through discharges and spills just as other waters on the globe, but the oil degrades much more slowly because of the cold waters. Concern over oil pollution spurred the 1970 Canadian Arctic Waters Pollution Prevention Act (*discussed* in the Questions and Discussion section, below) and has been a central concern of opponents to oil exploration in the U.S. Arctic National Wildlife Refuge. Many fear that discharges and spills will only increase in the future from exploration and aging infrastructure. Between 1991 and 1993, for example, there were 103 major pipeline failures in Russia. With its economic troubles, however, it seems likely that Russia will not repair its pipelines in the near future despite their frequent leaks. *Id.* at 2.

Radioactive Pollution. Lichen, the base of the terrestrial arctic food web, is sensitive to radioactive contaminants and in recent years it has become apparent that the Arctic has long served as a dumping ground for radioactive waste. Contrary to earlier assertions by the Soviet Union, Russia has recently acknowledged that from 1961–1984, the Soviets regularly dumped radioactive waste in the Arctic Ocean, including five nuclear reactors. In addition, Russia has more than 140 retired nuclear submarines that are rusting away at several of its northern naval bases. While the Russian Navy and the Atomic Energy Ministry have acknowledged that there are serious radiation leaks, the country lacks the funding necessary to properly care for and dispose of the submarines' spent fuel elements. Norway entered into an Agreement on Environmental Cooperation with Russia in 1998 to aid with proper disposal (following agreement that parties participating in the clean-up effort will have their liability waived if an accident occurs) but the problems remain significant. See Lakshman D. Guruswamy and Jason B. Aamodt, *Nuclear Arms Control: The Environmental Dimension*, 10 COLO. J. INT'L ENVTL. L. & POL'Y 267, 270 (1999).

Heavy Metals. Marine dumping of industrial waste and runoff significantly contribute to high levels of heavy metal pollutants such as cadmium, mercury and lead in the Arctic. Beluga whales in the St. Lawrence estuary have been called the most polluted animals on earth and birds in northern Norway and the Yukon of Canada have some of the highest levels of cadmium ever noted. Between 1991 and 1994, copper concentrations in the Kola Peninsula (White Sea) and the city of Norilsk (Kara Sea) were 2,500 times the locally-set limits and nickel concentrations up to 130 times the local limits. <http://www.unep.org/Geo2000/english/0122.htm>.

Grazing. Indigenous peoples rely heavily on reindeer husbandry in some regions of the Arctic and, for groups like the Saami in Sweden and Norway, it serves as a traditional focus of their culture. Changes in land practice, however, have led to overgrazing that denudes the vegetative cover and increases erosion. According to a study conducted by the Nordic Council of Ministers in 1996, Norwegian domestic farming tripled in size from 1950 to 1989, reducing access to traditional grazing areas. UNEP, *op. cit.,* at 3.

Tourism. Since the early 1990s, over one million tourists have visited the Arctic each year and the numbers are steadily increasing. Beyond the environmental impact of this activity, there is also concern for respecting indigenous peoples' daily lives and ensuring some of the tourism revenue is shared with Arctic communities.

See generally Richard J. Ansson, Jr., *The North American Agreement on Environmental Protection and the Arctic Council Agreement: Will These Multinational Agreements Adequately Protect the Environment?*, 29 CAL. W. INT'L. L.J. 101, 117 (1998); Gail Osherenko & Oran R. Young, THE AGE OF THE ARCTIC: HOT CONFLICTS AND COLD REALITIES 45 (1989); David Caron, *Toward an Arctic Environmental Regime*, 24 OCEAN DEV. AND INT'L L. 377?385 (1993); Armin Rosencranz & Antony Scott, *Siberia, Environmentalism, and Problems of Environmental Protection*, 14 HASTINGS INT'L COMP. L. REV. 929 (1991).

While the polar regions are both cold climates with vulnerable environments, the jurisdictional and physical challenges to environmental protection in the Arctic differ fundamentally from those of its southern counterpart and have led to very different legal regimes. First, unlike Antarctica, the Arctic is not managed as a global commons area. Despite the fact that ice covers much of the Arctic region, beneath it is mostly water. Hence the governance of the Arctic environment is similar to that of the governance of oceans off a coastal nation. The Arctic environment is almost entirely under the sovereignty of the eight nations' territories that extend into the Arctic Circle. The "Arctic Eight" include the United States, Canada, Russia, and the five Nordic States of Denmark (through Greenland), Iceland, Finland, Norway, and Sweden. *See* map on next page, from Donald R. Rothwell, *The Arctic Environmental Protection Strategy and International Environmental Cooperation in the Far North*, in G. Handl, ed., YEARBOOK OF INTERNATIONAL ENVIRONMENTAL LAW 69 (1996). As a result, environmental protection strategies are implemented on national territory and remain first and foremost domestic decisions. This leaves few opportunities, or leverage, for international governance. Thus cooperative efforts to protect the arctic environment have, with few exceptions, been soft law. There is no arctic equivalent to the Antarctic Treaty System protecting the general environment of the Arctic. The other major difference between the polar regions is that of indigenous inhabitants. While there are no indigenous communities in the Antarctic, the Arctic contains Eskimos, Inuit, Saami and other groups with cultural and subsistence bonds with their environment. Evan T. Bloom, *The Polar Regions and the Development of International Law,* 92 AM. J. INT'L L. 593 (1998).

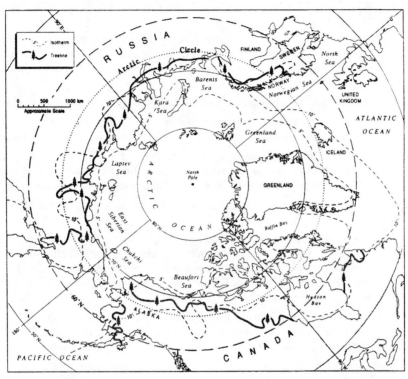

The Arctic Region showing the Arctic Circle, the 5° and 10° Isotherm Line, the Treeline and 60° North.

Growing concern over pollution of the Arctic from distant sources, as well as the increased likelihood of Arctic mineral exploration by new East–West ventures, provided the impetus to bring together the eight Arctic rim nations and adopt a non-binding regional environmental agreement in 1991 30 I.L.M. 624 (1991). The agreement, known as the Arctic Environmental Protection Strategy (AEPS), established broad environmental objectives and, while soft law, represented the first comprehensive effort by Arctic countries to protect the Arctic environment. It called for creation of an "Arctic Monitoring Assessment Program" (AMAP) to monitor air pollutants, persistent organic pollutants, radioactive pollutants and heavy metals and, based on these findings, to develop programs to reduce these threats. Recognizing that no international treaty had focused on wildlife in the Arctic (apart from the 1973 Agreement on Conservation of Polar Bears), the eight Arctic countries pledged to undertake joint research with the input of the indigenous peoples and exchange information to promote the conservation of the Arctic's wildlife. This regional agreement also created an institutional framework for further scientific and political international cooperation in this region. As the Declaration accompanying the Arctic Environmental Protection Strategy explained:

Declaration on the Protection of the Arctic Environment (1991)

We commit ourselves to a joint Action Plan of the Arctic Environmental Protection Strategy which includes:

- Cooperation in scientific research to specify sources, pathways, sinks and effects of pollution, in particular, oil, acidification, persistent organic contaminants, radioactivity, noise and heavy metals as well as sharing of these data;

- Assessment of potential environmental impacts of development activities;

- Full implementation and consideration of further measures to control pollutants and reduce their adverse effects to the Arctic environment.

We intend to assess on a continuing basis the threats to the Arctic environment through the preparation and updating of reports on the state of the Arctic environment, in order to propose further cooperative action.

We also commit ourselves to implement the following measures of the Strategy:

- Arctic Monitoring and Assessment Programme (AMAP) to monitor the levels of, and assess the effects of, anthropogenic pollutants in all components of the Arctic environment. To this end, and Arctic Monitoring and Assessment Task Force will be established. Norway will provide for an AMAP secretariat.

- Protection of the Marine Environment in the Arctic, to take preventive and other measures directly or through competent international organizations regarding marine pollution in the Arctic irrespective of origin;

- Emergency Prevention, Preparedness and Response in the Arctic, to provide a framework for future cooperation in responding to the threat of environmental emergencies;

- Conservation of the Arctic Flora and Fauna, to facilitate the exchange of information and coordination of research on species and habitats of flora and fauna.

We agree to hold regular meetings to assess the progress made and to coordinate actions which will implement and further develop the Arctic Environmental Protection Strategy.

We agree to continue to promote cooperation with the Arctic indigenous peoples and to invite their organizations to future meetings as observers.

———

Five years after the signing of the AEPS, the Arctic Council was established. The Arctic Council Agreement ("Joint Communique and Declaration on the Establishment of the Arctic Council") was signed on September 19, 1996 by the Arctic Eight. A high level intergovernmental forum, the Council has both broader participation and a broader scope than the AEPS, providing a mechanism to address the common concerns and challenges faced by the Arctic governments *and* the people of the Arctic on both environmental *and* community issues. A prime example of sustainable development, the Arctic Council oversees the programs commenced by the AEPS. There is no multilateral fund for the council programs; instead, the countries provide money for particular programs on an ad hoc basis. The Council homepage is at <http://www.arctic-council.org/>.

Declaration on the Establishment of the Arctic Council (1996)

The Arctic Council is established as a high level forum to:

a. provide a means for promoting cooperation, coordination and interaction among the Arctic states, with the involvement of the Arctic indigenous communities and other Arctic inhabitants on common Arctic issues, in particular issues of sustainable development and environmental protection in the Arctic.

b. oversee and coordinate the programs established under the AEPS on the Arctic Monitoring and Assessment Program (AMAP); conservation of Arctic Flora and Fauna (CAFF); Protection of the Arctic Marine Environment (PAME); and Emergency Preparedness and Response (EPPR).

c. adopt terms of reference for and oversee and coordinate a sustainable development program.

d. disseminate information, encourage education and promote interest in arctic-related issues.

As set out in the Declaration *above*, the Arctic Council has five main working groups, four of which existed under the AEPS and a new group on sustainable development, reflecting the broader focus of the Council. The Sustainable Development Working Group's focus includes the improvement of the health of Arctic children, the management of regional fisheries, the assessment of the potential for expanded use of telemedicine throughout the Arctic, and the promotion of cultural and eco-tourism.

In addition to a broader scope of activities, the Arctic Council is much more inclusive than the AEPS. Its category of "Permanent Participants," parties permitted active participation and full consultation, include not only the Arctic Eight governments but also indigenous sub-regional groups such as the Inuit Circumpolar Conference, the Nordic Saami Council, the Aleut International Association, and the Association of Indigenous Peoples of the North, Siberia and the Far East of the Russian Federation. The Arctic Council also recognizes several organizations–non-Arctic states, NGOs, inter-governmental organizations, inter-parliamentary organizations–as "Observers" who can participate in programs. These include Germany, The Netherlands, Poland and the United Kingdom, the International Arctic Science Committee, the Nordic Council, the Northern Forum, the United Nations Economic Commission for Europe, the United Nations Environment Program, the Standing Committee of Parliamentarians of the Arctic Region, and the World Wide Fund for Nature.

More than just a talk shop, the Arctic Council has launched a number of initiatives. Concerned over PCBs in Russia, for example, in February, 2000, the Council agreed to expedite the phase-out of PCBs used and disposed of in Russia as well as encourage Russia to become a party to the

Convention on Long Range Transboundary Air Pollution's Protocol on Persistent Organic Pollutants. Other projects under development include efforts to reduce arctic marine pollution from land-based activities and an "Arctic Climate Impact Assessment," an effort on the part of all Arctic countries to examine the effects of global climate changes and increased UV radiation on the region and its inhabitants.

QUESTIONS AND DISCUSSION

1. Despite the many similarities between the polar regions, the legal regimes are strikingly different. Most significantly, the Antarctic Treaty System is largely composed of hard law while the Arctic relies on soft law. Indeed the Arctic Council describes itself as a "high-level intergovernmental forum," not as a law-making body. Why do you think the legal structures differ so greatly? Is it simply because the Antarctic is a global commons area? What role does hard *domestic* law play in the two regions?

2. The most significant environmental conflict in the Arctic occurred in the Northwest Passage between the United States and Canada. Concerned over the potential harm to the Arctic environment from an oil spill, in 1970 Canada enacted the Arctic Waters Pollution Prevention Act. 9 I.L.M. 543 (1970). The Act created a "special prevention" zone of 100 miles extending around Canada's northern archipelago. Within this zone, Canada mandated certain technical requirements for tankers travelling in its waters such as hull and fuel tank construction, the use of double hulls, certain navigational aids and equipment, maximum quantities of cargo carried, etc. If a foreign nation's vessel did not comply with the law, Canada proclaimed the right to prohibit access to the zone. The United States vigorously opposed Canada's unilateral extension of its national authority to international waters. Citing customary law, the United States argued that the Northwest passage is an international strait subject to the rights of passage and refused to recognize the law. The United States and Canada signed an agreement in 1988 affirming that Arctic navigation and resource development should not adversely affect the unique environment of the region. U.S.-Canada Agreement on the Arctic Cooperation, Jan.11, 1988, T.I.A.S. No. 11565.

3. Despite the lack of strong international protection for the Arctic region, there have been significant conservation measures.

> States have been protecting sites within the Arctic since the beginning of the 20th century. But since 1960 there has been a substantial increase in both the number of sites and total area subject to protection. In 1994, the Conservation of Arctic Flora and Fauna Working Group conducted a report under the Arctic Environmental Protection Strategy that identified 280 areas within the Arctic, with a total coverage of 2.9079 million square kilometers, as protected. The result of this extensive designation of protected areas within the Arctic is that approximately 14% of Arctic land area is subject to some form of protected status. The protected areas range from very large national parks, such as the Greenland National Park, which is approximately 60 million hectares in size, to small bird sanctuaries on Svalbard. All of the identified sites are primarily subject to regulation and control by state authorities; however, some areas have been protected under international agreements of programs.

Donald R. Rothwell, *The Arctic Environmental Protection Strategy and International Environmental Cooperation in the Far North,* in G. HANDL, ED.,YEARBOOK OF INTERNATIONAL ENVIRONMENTAL LAW: 1995, at 69 (1996).

Given the transport of pollutants to the Arctic, though, what do you think are the main benefits of conservation in that region?

Suggested Further Reading

Donald R. Rothwell, THE POLAR REGIONS AND THE DEVELOPMENT OF INTERNATIONAL LAW (1996)

> Analysis of international law in the Arctic and Antarctic.

M.J. Peterson, MANAGING THE FROZEN SOUTH: THE CREATION AND EVOLUTION OF THE ANTARCTIC TREATY SYSTEM (1988)

> History of Antarctic negotiations prior to CRAMRA and the 1991 Protocol.

David Caron, *Toward an Arctic Environmental Regime*, 24 OCEAN DEV. INT'L L. 377–385 (1993)

> Analysis of the Arctic Environmental Protection Strategy.

http://www.arctic-council.org/

> Homepage of the Arctic Council.

http://www.asoc.org/

> Homepage of The Antarctica Project, the only NGO focused exclusively on Antarctica. It also leads the Antarctic and Southern Ocean Coalition (ASOC), comprised of two hundred and forty member groups in fifty countries.

http://www-bprc.mps.ohio-state.edu/

> Homepage for Ohio State University's Byrd Polar Research Center. Excellent site for links and background information.

http://www.antarctica.ac.uk/

> Homepage of the British Antarctic Survey. Useful scientific information on current research.

SECTION IV. INTERNATIONAL PROTECTION OF FORESTS

The forests are the "lungs" of our land, purifying our air and giving fresh strength to our people.

> – Franklin Delano Roosevelt

Start with the rising sun and work toward the setting sun. Take only the mature trees, the sick trees, and the trees that have fallen ... and the trees will last forever.

> – Menominee Oral History

A. INTRODUCTION

The loss of forests, particularly tropical rainforests, has become an increasing focus of international policy. Forests are important ecological systems that provide essential environmental services, including hosting most terrestrial biodiversity, sequestering carbon critical to tempering climate change; maintaining local weather patterns; and protecting water quality. Forests obviously play an integral role in many issues that have warranted significant international attention and would seem an appropriate target for international cooperation, based on humankind's common concern for maintaining the planet's ecological balance.

Forests are also a valuable commercial resource. The annual commercial value of wood and wood products can be measured in the trillions of dollars. A quick glance around the room in which you are now sitting will remind you of how important wood is to our daily lives (and if that doesn't do it, take a look at the textbook you are holding). Annual international trade in wood products is more than $100 billion, most of which comes from developing countries. It is no wonder, then, that the decision of when, how, and how much to develop timber resources is vitally important to many national economies. National authority over timber resources is jealously guarded through the doctrine of State sovereignty over natural resources.

Balancing a State's authority to choose when and how to develop the economic potential of forest resources with the emerging international responsibility toward conservation of forest ecosystem services has proven a virtually insurmountable task for global forestry cooperation. The controversy over whether to impose international standards on national decisions over forests frequently divides along traditional North–South lines. Developing countries of the South see their economic development significantly tied to their ability to exploit domestic timber resources. The North, for its part, is pushing for sustainable management and conservation of forests, particularly tropical forests (which not coincidentally are located primarily in developing countries).

Overcoming the North–South divisions is made even more difficult by the lack of consensus within the scientific and environmental community. A surprising number of gaps exist in our scientific knowledge regarding the current status of forests and even less is known regarding how to exploit forests sustainably over the long-term. Environmental organizations often do not present a unified front, arguing for example whether forest conservation is best achieved through preservation or through the promotion of sustainable forestry.

These factors have effectively crippled the development of international legal standards regarding forest conservation. Despite several different initiatives, the world community has been unable to agree to *negotiate* a global, binding agreement to promote forest conservation. Countries rejected proposals for a forest convention leading up to the 1992 Earth Summit, agreeing instead on a set of non-binding general principles the very title of which indicates the degree of resistance to international standards in this area: the "Non-legally binding authoritative statement of principles for a global consensus on the management, conservation and sustainable development of all types of forests." Subsequently, two UN-sponsored initiatives—the Inter-governmental Panel on Forests (1995–1997) and the Intergovernmental Forum on Forests (1997–2000)—each failed to reach consensus on whether a global legally binding instrument on forests should be negotiated.

With respect to binding international standards, the story of international forest policy is thus really the story of national economic interests triumphing over international environmental issues, of State sovereignty triumphing over "common concern." It is in some ways a case study of the failure and limitations of international cooperation in the field of environmental protection.

Nonetheless, international law and policy do play a role in forest conservation. Most notably, an international consensus now exists that sustainable forest management (SFM) is the appropriate goal for forest policy at the international and national levels. Determining what constitutes SFM has been more problematic, but efforts to identify criteria and indicators for SFM are making substantial progress. Some advances have also been made in regulating the commercial trade of certain forest products. Finally, the cumulative effect of all of the international discussion regarding forest conservation has elevated the importance of forest conservation generally and has sparked some additional assistance to build forest management capacity in developing countries.

The following part provides an introduction to the state of the world's forests, followed by an overview of major international forestry policy initiatives (Part B) and a discussion of current and cross-cutting issues (Part C).

1. STATE OF THE WORLD'S FORESTS

Forests are classified into three basic categories: tropical, temperate, and boreal zones. These categories essentially reflect species composition, climate, and relative latitude. For the most part, international policymakers have targeted deforestation in tropical rainforests, both because in recent years rates of deforestation have been higher in tropical rainforests and because tropical rainforests are the richest terrestrial ecosystems in biological diversity. During the past 50 years, much of the world's tropical forests have been lost. More attention is now also being paid to temperate and boreal zone forests, which comprise half of the world's forest cover. Russia, Canada and the United States hold 70 percent of the world's temperate and boreal forests. According to the FAO, temperate and boreal forests do not appear to be declining significantly; however, these statistics may hide an increase in industrial tree plantations and monocultures, which do not provide habitat for most forest species or provide many other important ecological functions of a natural forest.

Environmentalists also frequently distinguish forests based on whether they have been harvested. *Primary forests*—i.e., forests that have never been cut—are increasingly scarce. Only about one-fifth of global forests are primary. These are mostly located in Siberia, Northern Canada, Papua New Guinea, Amazonia, and the Congo Basin (West and Central Africa). These forests are important because they often harbor the healthiest forest ecosystems, providing important natural habitat for forest species. The remaining four-fifths of today's forests are *secondary* or *replacement forests*. New England's forests, for example, are mostly replacement forests. By the 1850s, more than 70 percent of Vermont's primary forests were gone, and by the end of the century almost all of the forests in Maine had been harvested. Now, Vermont's replacement forests have restored forest coverage so that 75 percent of the state is forested. Although replacement forests are celebrated as environmental success stories, they often do not completely fulfill the roles played by primary forests. Replacement forests are typically smaller and younger, and may be comprised of a different species mix. Many wildlife species that inhabit original forests may not return to replacement forests.

Janet N. Abramovitz, STATE OF THE WORLD 22–24 (1998)

Trends in Forest Area And Quality

Today, forests cover more than one quarter of the world's total land area (excluding Antarctica and Greenland). Slightly more than half of the world's forests are in the tropics; the rest are in temperate and boreal (coniferous northern forest) zones. Seven countries hold more than 60 percent of the world's forest: in order of forest area, they are Russia, Brazil, Canada, the United States, China, Indonesia, and the Democratic Republic of Congo (formerly Zaire).

The world's forest estate has declined significantly in both area and quality in recent decades. [A]lmost half the forests that once blanketed the Earth are gone. Each year another 16 million hectares of forest disappear as land is cleared by timber operations or converted to other uses, such as cattle ranches, plantations, or small farms.

The extent of forest loss and fragmentation was made clear in a recent study by the World Resources Institute that identified what it calls "frontier forests"—areas of "large, ecologically intact, and relatively undisturbed natural forests." The study found that only 22 percent of the world's original forest cover remains in these large expanses, about evenly divided between boreal and tropical forest. More than 75 percent of the frontier forest is in three large areas: the boreal forest of Canada and Alaska, the boreal forest of Russia, and the tropical forest of the northwestern Amazon Basin and the Guyana shield (Guyana, Suriname, French Guiana, northeastern Brazil, Venezuela, and Colombia).

Until recent decades, most forest loss occurred in Europe, North Africa, the Middle East, and temperate North America. By the early part of the twentieth century these regions had been largely stripped of their original cover. Now forest cover in Europe and the United States is stabilizing, as secondary forests and plantation forests fill in. In the last 30–40 years, in contrast, the vast majority of deforestation has occurred in the tropics, where the pace has been accelerating. Indeed, between 1960 and 1990, one fifth of all tropical forest cover was lost. Asia lost one third of its cover, and Africa and Latin America lost about 18 percent each.

Broad regional overviews such as these can mask even more severe forest loss that is taking place in some countries and forest types. Half of the tropical deforestation during the 1980s took place in just six countries: Brazil, Indonesia, the Democratic Republic of Congo, Mexico, Bolivia, and Venezuela. Tropical dry forest types, mangrove forests, and the temperate rainforests of North America have also experienced very high losses.

Deforestation is not the only threat. Serious declines in forest quality are affecting much of the world's forests. Ironically, while many people in northern countries look at tropical forests with concern, they may be unaware that the temperate forests in their own backyards are the most fragmented and disturbed of all forest types. For example, 95–98 percent of forests in the continental United States have been logged at least once since settlement by Europeans. And in Europe, two thirds of the forest cover is gone, while less than 1 percent of old growth remains.

The secondary forest and plantations that are filling in are a very different type than the original. The mix of tree and understory species has changed, and the age is more uniform. The forests are highly manipulated and highly fragmented. Plantations and even-aged stands occupy substantial areas of forestland. In the last 15 years, the area covered by forest plantation has doubled globally. And it is expected to double again in the next 15 years. Worldwide, at least 180 million hectares of forest have been converted to forest plantations. These altered ecosystems usually cannot support the full array of native species and ecological processes that characterize natural forests. Many nonnative species—from tree species to vines to insect and animal pests–have invaded these woodlands.

Atmospheric pollution is also taking a toll on forest quality. Exposure to pollution weakens trees and makes them more vulnerable to the effects of pests, diseases, drought and nutrient deficiencies. This is especially evident in Europe, North America, Asia, and cities throughout the world. More than a quarter of Europe's trees show moderate to severe defoliation from these stresses, according to regular survey by the U.N. Economic Commission for Europe.

As troubling as the statistics on forest loss and declining quality are, the true picture of the global forest situation is undoubtedly much worse. A major obstacle to assessing forests is the quality of the data assembled by U.N. Food and Agriculture Organization (FAO), the most widely used source. FAO relies on self-reporting by governments, and many countries do not have the capacity to carry out systematic forest assessments. Nor is there a system of independent monitoring in place–either by satellite or by ground-truthing. FAO also uses inconsistent and confusing definitions, which in turn can result in some misleading conclusions. "Natural forest" is estimated, and forest quality is not measured at all. Deforestation is defined by FAO as the conversion of forests to other uses such as cropland and shifting cultivation. Forests that have been logged and left to regenerate are not counted as deforested, nor are forests converted to plantation. Thus, some of the land reported by countries as forest actually has no trees on it at all. According to FAO definitions, 80–90 percent of forest cover can be removed by logging without "deforesting" an area. Then when small-scale farmers reduce the remaining forest cover the next few percent they have, according to the official definition, "deforested" the land. This is why "slash-and-burn" farmers are often blamed for deforestation for which they are not responsible.

Rising Pressures on Forests

Widespread reports that poor agriculturalists and fuelwood gatherers are responsible for the rapid loss of the world's forests are greatly exaggerated. Closer examination reveals a different—and more complex—picture. The rising appetite for forest products and trade is a major driving force behind the logging and conversion of many of the world's forests to other uses. Policies and subsidies that encourage conversion (for timber harvest or agriculture and settlements) also drive the process. This holds true in the temperate and boreal forests of Canada, the United States, and northern Siberia as well as in the tropical forests of the Amazon, Central Africa, and Southeast Asia.

Trade in forest products—both legal and illegal—is a strong economic force. Although less than 8 percent of timber and 26 percent of paper production are traded internationally, the legal and recorded trade of $114 billion a year in timber, pulp, and paper makes forest products one of the most valuable sectors in the global marketplace. Tropical timber has received much attention, but nearly 90 percent of the legal and recorded international timber trade comes from temperate and boreal forests.

The demand for forest products has grown rapidly in recent decades. The global production of roundwood—the logs cut for industrial lumber and paper products or used for fuelwood and charcoal—has more than doubled since 1950. Population growth, however, is not the primary cause of rising demand. In fact, most industrial roundwood use takes place in wealthier countries, where population is relatively stable. Over half of the world's timber harvested for industrial use is consumed by the 20 percent of the world who live in Western Europe, the United States, and Japan.

According to FAO statistics, about half of the wood cut worldwide is used for fuelwood and charcoal, mostly in developing countries. In some areas, especially in the dry topics, the portion is even higher, up to 80 percent. But in moist tropical nations such as Malaysia, the vast majority of trees cut are for industrial timber. Most of the live trees that are cut for fuel are used to make charcoal or in other industrial applications, such as brick-making and tobacco-curing, and in cities. This commercial fuelwood collection, especially when concentrated near cities, can cause significant local deforestation. On the other hand, the fuelwood collected by rural households is usually dead wood, which does not contribute to deforestation.

Consumption of paper (including newspaper and paperboard) is increasing faster than any other forest product. The world uses more than five times as much paper today as it did in 1950, and consumption is expected to double again by 2010. About two thirds of the paper produced worldwide is made from virgin logs; only 4 percent is made from non-wood sources such as cotton or rice straw. The rest comes from wastepaper. Soon paper production is expected to account for more than half of the global industrial wood harvest.

Paper consumption is not evenly distributed around the globe. More than 70 percent of the world's paper output is used by the 20 percent of the world living in North America, Western Europe, and Japan. While global per capita use of paper stands at about 46 kilograms a year, the U.S. average is 320 kilograms (the world's highest), Japan's is 232, and Germany's is 200, while in Brazil the figure is 31 kilograms, in China it is just over 24, and in India the average is only 3 kilograms.

QUESTIONS AND DISCUSSION

1. What are the causes of forest loss as identified in the WorldWatch report? What other international environmental regimes have you studied to address these different causes of forest loss? The relative importance of different causes of deforestation varies among countries. For example, commercial logging is the major threat to primary temperate forests, including the world's last extensive temperate rainforests found along the Pacific coast of North America and in Chile. In the tropics, extensive logging has significantly reduced forests in countries such as Malaysia and Papua New Guinea. Logging also has major indirect affects, particularly as logging roads are built to open up previously impenetrable forests, which in turn leads to the conversion of forests to other uses such as agriculture or grazing. This may be the leading direct cause of forest loss worldwide and is certainly the leading threat to dry tropical forests. Forty percent of the Earth's land surface now consists of cropland. In the poorest countries, trees are lost mostly for fuel. For example, in Kenya more than 75% of the energy is generated by fuelwood and charcoal. Growing populations will increase the need for fuelwood into the near future.

Focusing only on direct threats to forests, such as commercial exploitation or conversion to agriculture, can lead one to miss the underlying causes of forest loss— to miss the forest for the trees, so to speak. Underlying causes of forest loss include population growth and migration, poverty, international debt and macroeconomic adjustment policies, national policies that provide subsidies or other incentives for unsustainable consumption, and a failure to recognize or value in the market the public benefits of forests. For further discussion of these underlying causes, *see* Chapter 2, discussing population and consumption; Chapter 3 discussing ecological economics; and Chapter 20, discussing the environmental record of International Financial Institutions.

2. *The Ecological Importance of Forests.* Forests are critical to the global environment. For example, forests are effective carbon reservoirs and sinks, tempering the impacts of industrialization on the planet's climate. Growing forests serve as carbon sinks through the process of photosynthesis where trees and plants convert sunlight to energy using carbon dioxide and emitting oxygen. Forests absorb a net total of 1.5 billion tons of carbon each year, which is one-fourth of the carbon emitted from fossil fuel combustion. Moreover, standing forests serve as carbon reservoirs that hold carbon taken from the atmosphere as long as those trees remain standing. Through deforestation and fires, forests may release much of the carbon that the trees and plants retained during their growth periods. For further discussion of forests' role with respect to climate change, see Chapter 9, page 645 (discussing role of the forests). *See* also R. Houghton, *The Role of the World's Forests in Global Warming,* in K. RAMAKRISHNA & G. WOODWELL, WORLD FORESTS FOR THE FUTURE 21 (1993).

Forests also serve as necessary habitat for a diverse range of species. Forests are home to 50–90 percent of the world's terrestrial species. Consistent forest loss in the tropics, for example, could result in the extinction of 13 percent of the world's species by 2015. Even destroying parts of forests, a process known as fragmentation, can disrupt forest ecosystems. Most species must maintain a minimum undisturbed forest area to carry out activities such as hunting and reproducing. Fragmentation disrupts these areas and thus reduces the number of species living in the particular region. One study of the Amazon basin discovered that the area affected due to fragmentation is on average nearly three times greater than the actual deforested area. Forest fragmentation, both in the tropical wintering grounds and in northern breeding areas, has greatly reduced populations of many North American songbirds, including for example the popular scarlet tanager and the wood thrush. *See* GRETCHEN DAILY, ED., NATURE'S SERVICES 215–36 (1997).

Sometimes the relationship between forests and wildlife is less direct and relates to the overall health of the local ecosystems. Forests prevent soil erosion and retain soil moisture. Forests are critical determinants of local climate and weather conditions. Water quality in many rivers and lakes depends on maintaining forests in the headwaters. For example, deforestation in the Pacific Northwest has been tied to declining salmon populations, because increases in soil erosion after deforestation lead to increases in silt that covers the salmon's gravel spawning habitat.

Perhaps most important—and often ignored altogether by policymakers—is that forests are the homes of many native peoples and cultures. Dozens of cultures are on the verge of being eliminated in part because of the loss of forest lands. How does reconceiving forests as homelands potentially change our policies towards them?

3. The scientific community has long recognized the environmental value of forests. Forest management in industrialized countries, although far from being sustainable, at least now takes into account the ecological role of forests when determining the size, nature and location of timber harvests. This shift from a focus on forests simply as a commercial resource to a critical ecological resource now extends to the global level. Forests' role in harboring biological diversity and in ameliorating the consequences of climate change are now widely understood but just as widely undervalued. Given the role that science has played in identifying potential environmental harms such as ozone depletion and climate change—and in catalyzing the development of international law to respond to these threats—how would you coordinate scientific research today to build support for a forest convention in the future? What questions should be included in any global research agenda?

4. *Valuing forests.* Forests thus provide a range of valuable services and benefits to humankind and to the global environment. Some, like timber and other commercial products, can be measured in dollar terms and traded in the market. Other benefits, particularly those important to the global environment, are not easily valued in dollar terms nor traded in the market place. Forest conservation can be seen as an effort to correct market failures. Consider the following excerpt from a 1996 UN report prepared for the Intergovernmental Panel on Forests.

> Conventional economic approaches to the valuation of forests fail to account for the role played by non-timber forest products and services in decisions about forest management and investment. In many cases, the only product of tropical forests that is considered of economic value is the timber produced, whereas a whole range of non-timber forest products, including fruits, latex and fibres, as well as environmental and ecological services and functions, such as soil protection, water cycling and carbon storage, are not valued. * * *

> Local market failure is the classic economic case of under investment, in which market forces are not able to secure the economically correct balance of land conversion and forest conservation. An underlying assumption, of course is that there is an economically optimum rate of deforestation, which is not zero. local market failure arises because those who convert the land do not have to compensate those who suffer the social and environmental consequences of that conversion, such as increased pollution and sedimentation of waters caused by deforestation. Possible solutions are well known and include such measures as enacting a tax on land conversion, zoning to restrict detrimental land uses and establishing environmental standards.

> The rate of return of forest conservation is distorted by what economists call "missing markets". What this means in the tropical forest context is that systems of habitat and species are serving valuable functions that are not marketed. Effectively, then, no one values such functions because there is no obvious mechanism for capturing their value. Local market failure describes this phenomenon within the context of the country or local area, but there are missing global markets as well, illustrated by the example of the value of carbon storage by forests.

Implementation of Forest–Related Decisions of the United Nations Conference on Environment and Development at the National and International Levels, Including an Examination of Sectoral and Cross–Sectoral Linkages, paras. 46–49 (E/CN.17/IPF/1996/2) (Feb. 13, 1996). *See also, e.g.,* N. Johnson, et al., Developing Markets for Water Services from Forests (Forest Trends, 2001). Related to the issue of whether we value forests adequately is how we account for forest loss when conducting our national economic accounts. When forests are cut into timber, the national economy reflects this as an increase in revenue or in "gross national product." Ignored is the loss of any value of the free-standing forest. Given that the forest provides a revenue stream, environmental economists refer to standing forests as part of a country's long-term wealth or natural capital. Making adjustments to national accounts to reflect the loss in capital when a forest is cut can significantly change how we view the value of cutting trees. For example, a recent World Resources Institute study demonstrated that Indonesia's GNP growth due to timber exports is actually a net loss if natural capital is accounted for. See Chapter 3, page 145. In this regard consider the following excerpt from a UN background paper:

> In national accounts there are several distortions relating to forestry. Apart from the land transfers mentioned above, the value of a number of forest benefits, such as medicinal plants and other non-wood forest products and forest grazing, are not reported at all or are included in the accounts of other sectors. Forest foods, grazing and fodder are often reported under agriculture.

> The total value of forest benefits should be reflected in an integrated manner in the system of national accounts. National Accounts should consider wood products, non-wood forest products and forest influences/intangible benefits as components of an integrated whole. Together with valuation of forest resources stock, these would provide a more realistic and meaningful representation of the value of the forests.

> The total value of the formally recorded production of wood-based forest products in the world in 1993 was $391 billion, of which the share of developing countries was $144 billion. If the value of all forest benefits were included, the value of forest benefits accrued to developing countries would be nearly three times as much, increasing the currently recorded contribution of forestry to gross domestic product (GDP) from 3 to 10 per cent or more. The case of India illustrates the situation: its officially accounted contribution of forestry to national income is only $2.9 billion, against the actual contribution of benefits valued at $43.8 billion.

International Cooperation in Financial Assistance and Technology Transfer for Sustainable Forest Management, E/CN.17/IPF/1996/5, paras. 49–52 (Feb. 20, 1996). How can national or international policy-makers intervene to correct market failures with respect to forest conservation? To what extent does the international trade system reflect these market failures? How can international cooperation be used to improve national accounting? Does this suggest a particular role for international law?

5. Obviously, calculating the dollar value of the ecological benefits provided by a given forest is more difficult than determining the value of timber products from that same forest. As a result, when policy makers look to benefit-cost analyses or other market-based tools for assistance in determining whether to approve timber harvesting, ecological roles of forests are rarely protected. Norman Myers has suggested that we "shift the burden of proof as it concerns forest exploitation . . . [by] requiring an exploiter to demonstrate that his form of forest use will generate economic returns of a sustainable sort exceeding those of any other option." Norman Myers, *The World's Forests: Need for a Policy Appraisal*, Science, vol. 268, at 823 (May 12, 1995). Does this seem an appropriate application of the precautionary principle?

6. Forest issues are among the most controversial environmental issues in the United States. Although northeastern U.S. forests are stabilizing, logging in the forests of Alaska and the Pacific Northwest remain extremely controversial. These old growth forests of the Pacific Northwest are the most productive forests that exist anywhere in the world—at least in terms of biomass and carbon sequestration. Of coniferous forests, they hold the largest bird populations and provide habitat for over 200 species of animals and fish. Among these species is the northern spotted owl (srix occidentalis), which was declared threatened in 1990 and symbolized the fight between the logging industry and environmentalists during the 1990s. The stridency that marked the conflict over primary forests in the Northwest demonstrates the difficult local economic and social issues raised by efforts to slow timber harvesting. As we shall see, these same economic and social issues also constrain international negotiators in adopting norms and standards.

––––––

B. International Negotiations for a Broad Forest Policy

There is still no comprehensive, internationally-binding agreement on forest conservation. Instead, a variety of international soft law instruments and international programs address forest conservation in one way or another. *See* Table 14.2. In addition, several global environmental conventions also cover issues that relate to forest conservation.

Table 14.2: Forestry Instruments and Initiatives

International Tropical Timber Agreement (1985, amended 1994)

A commodity agreement which now includes sustainable management goals for tropical timber

Tropical Forest Action Plan (late 1980s)

FAO, World Bank, UNDP and others coordinate international support of National Forestry Action Plans

Brazilian Pilot Programme (1991)

G–7 funded project to address deforestation in the Amazon

Forest Principles (1992)

Global soft law instrument setting broad principles for forest management

Chapter 11, Agenda 21 (1992)

Global plan of action for achieving sustainable forest management

Biodiversity Convention (1992)

Global convention that addresses forests as part of habitat for biodiversity

Climate Change Convention (1992) and Kyoto Protocol (1997)

Global regime that addresses forests as carbon sinks and reservoirs

Intergovernmental Panel on Forests (1995–1997)

Global forum convened by the CSD to develop a consensus on global forest policy

Intergovernmental Forum on Forests (1997–2000)

Global forum convened to follow up on the Intergovernmental Panel on Forests

UN Forum on Forests (est. 2001)

A permanent institution created to coordinate and promote forest policy within the United Nations

The lack of a binding international agreement on forests is not due to a lack of attention. Beginning in 1990, the G–7 proposed the need for an instrument to "curb deforestation, protect biodiversity, stimulate positive forestry actions and address threats to the world's forests." As countries began to negotiate such an instrument in preparation for UNCED, however, serious divisions between the North and South defeated any chance for consensus on a binding instrument.

1. THE UNCED FOREST PRINCIPLES

Discussions over global forest policy were a major part of the UNCED preparation. The United States and other northern countries hoped to negotiate a global forest convention that would slow the rapid rate of tropical deforestation. Developing countries did not have the same enthusiasm for a global forest convention, however, particularly one that focused only on tropical rainforests. Led by Malaysia, the G–77 saw restrictions on timber production from rainforests as an effort by the North to impose hidden trade barriers in the name of environmental protection. As a counter-proposal, the G–77 insisted that any forest convention address all forests, including the temperate forests of the North. The G–77 also raised issues of financial assistance, the need to curb air pollution to protect forests, and the role of debt and other external forces in exacerbating deforestation. Both Brazil and Malaysia were also interested in linking Southern promises to protect forests as carbon sinks with Northern promises to reduce greenhouse gas emissions, thus ensuring that forest protection would not be used as an excuse to allow continued emissions of greenhouse gases by the industrialized countries. The negotiations over forest issues became among the most controversial at Rio. ANS KOLK, FORESTS IN INTERNATIONAL ENVIRONMENTAL POLITICS: INTERNATIONAL ORGANISATIONS, NGOS AND THE BRAZILIAN AMAZON, at 159–60 (1996).

> Together with financial resources, the forest principles led to an intense North–South conflict. While industrialised countries supported the forest convention, stressing the global importance of forests, the South opposed what was construed as an effort to exert supranational control. A legally binding instrument would impinge on their sovereign rights to use their forest resource and meet development needs. Southern countries perceived the forest convention to be the easiest way for the North to compensate for its own carbon dioxide emissions. Developing countries with substantial forest resources believed that they should be compensated for services to the global community. Moreover, developing countries expected concession on important issues such as trade and debt. When it became clear that UNCED would neither generate considerable funds nor lead to other commitments, the South obstructed the forest principles. Hence the conference did not really deal with trade and debt; it resulted in weak forest principles; and no substantial amounts of money were committed by the industrialized countries.... It has been suggested that since the document on forest principles was the only political document to be discussed extensively at UNCED, all controversies came to the fore in that context....

Ultimately, the G–77 led by Malaysia, India and Brazil effectively blocked adoption of any forest convention at UNCED. Although the resulting "Forest Principles" could claim to reflect the first global consensus on forest management, substantively they also illustrated how far away the world's governments were from mandating strong ecologically-based forest management. Not surprisingly given the rancorous North–South split during the negotiations, the Forest Principles do not set forth many specific standards or break significant new ground. The Principles seem to endorse the goal of sustainable forest management and the need to consider all stakeholders and forest benefits in managing forests. The Principles recognize the vital role that forests play in ecosystem stability; confirm the need to provide financial assistance for sustainable forest management; and acknowledge the role of communities, women and indigenous groups in forest management. On the other hand, the Principles are unmistakably skewed toward the rights of States to exploit their forests as they choose, rejecting any significant international interest in the protection of forests.

Non-Legally Binding Authoritative Statement of Principles for a Global Consensus on the Management, Conservation and Sustainable Development of all Types of Forests, A/CONF.151/26 (Vol. III) 14 Aug. 1992, Report of the United Nations Conference on Environment and Development, Annex III (3–14 June 1992), reprinted in 31 I.L.M. 881

PREAMBLE

(a) The subject of forests is related to the entire range of environmental and development issues and opportunities, including the right to socio-economic development on a sustainable basis.

(b) The guiding objective of these principles is to contribute to the management, conservation and sustainable development of forests and to provide for their multiple and complementary functions and uses.

(c) Forestry issues and opportunities should be examined in a holistic and balanced manner within the overall context of environment and development, taking into consideration the multiple functions and uses of forests, including traditional uses, and the likely economic and social stress when these uses are constrained or restricted, as well as the potential for development that sustainable forest management can offer.

(d) These principles reflect a first global consensus on forests. In committing themselves to the prompt implementation of these principles, countries also decide to keep them under assessment for their adequacy with regard to further international cooperation on forest issues.

(e) These principles should apply to all types of forests, both natural and planted, in all geographic regions and climatic zones, including austral, boreal, subtemperate, temperate, subtropical and tropical.

(f) All types of forests embody complex and unique ecological processes which are the basis for their present and potential capacity to provide resources to satisfy human needs as well as environmental values, and as such their sound management and conservation is of concern to the Governments of the countries to which they belong and are of value to local communities and to the environment as a whole.

(g) Forests are essential to economic development and the maintenance of all forms of life.

(h) Recognizing that the responsibility for forest management, conservation and sustainable development is in many States allocated among federal/national, state/provincial and local levels of government, each State, in accordance with its constitution and/or national legislation, should pursue these principles at the appropriate level of government.

PRINCIPLES/ELEMENTS

1. (a) States have, in accordance with the Charter of the United Nations and the principles of international law, the sovereign right to exploit their own resources pursuant to their own environmental policies and have the responsibility to ensure that activities within their jurisdiction or control do not cause damage to the environment of other States or of areas beyond the limits of national jurisdiction.

(b) The agreed full incremental cost of achieving benefits associated with forest conservation and sustainable development requires increased international cooperation and should be equitably shared by the international community.

2. (a) States have the sovereign and inalienable right to utilize, manage and develop their forests in accordance with their development needs and level of socio-economic development and on the basis of national policies consistent with sustainable development and legislation, including the conversion of such areas for other uses within the overall socio-economic development plan and based on rational land-use policies.

(b) Forest resources and forest lands should be sustainably managed to meet the social, economic, ecological, cultural and spiritual needs of present and future generations. These needs are for forest products and services, such as wood and wood products, water, food, fodder, medicine, fuel, shelter, employment, recreation, habitats for wildlife, landscape diversity, carbon sinks and reservoirs, and for other forest products. Appropriate measures should be taken to protect forests against harmful effects of pollution, including air-borne pollution, fires, pests and diseases, in order to maintain their full multiple value.

(c) The provision of timely, reliable and accurate information on forests and forest ecosystems is essential for public understanding and informed decision-making and should be ensured.

(d) Governments should promote and provide opportunities for the participation of interested parties, including local communities and indigenous people, industries, labour, non-governmental organizations and individuals, forest dwellers and women, in the development, implementation and planning of national forest policies. * * *

4. The vital role of all types of forests in maintaining the ecological processes and balance at the local, national, regional and global levels through, *inter alia,* their role in protecting fragile ecosystems, watersheds and freshwater resources and as rich storehouses of biodiversity and biological resources and sources of genetic material for biotechnology products, as well as photosynthesis, should be recognized.

5. (a) National forest policies should recognize and duly support the identity, culture and the rights of indigenous people, their communities and other communities and forest dwellers. Appropriate conditions should be promoted for these groups to enable them to have an economic stake in forest use, perform economic activities, and achieve and maintain cultural identity and

social organization, as well as adequate levels of livelihood and well-being, through, *inter alia,* those land tenure arrangements which serve as incentives for the sustainable management of forests.

(b) The full participation of women in all aspects of the management, conservation and sustainable development of forests should be actively promoted.

6.   (a) All types of forests play an important role in meeting energy requirements through the provision of a renewable source of bio-energy, particularly in developing countries, and the demands for fuelwood for household and industrial needs should be met through sustainable forest management, afforestation and reforestation. To this end, the potential contribution of plantations of both indigenous and introduced species for the provision of both fuel and industrial wood should be recognized. * * *

7.   (a) Efforts should be made to promote a supportive international economic climate conducive to sustained and environmentally sound development of forests in all countries, which include, *inter alia,* the promotion of sustainable patterns of production and consumption, the eradication of poverty and the promotion of food security.

(b) Specific financial resources should be provided to developing countries with significant forest areas which establish programmes for the conservation of forests including protected natural forest areas. These resources should be directed notably to economic sectors which would stimulate economic and social substitution activities.

8.   * * *(f) National policies and/or legislation aimed at management, conservation and sustainable development of forests should include the protection of ecologically viable representative or unique examples of forests, including primary/old-growth forests, cultural, spiritual, historical, religious and other unique and valued forests of national importance.

(g) Access to biological resources, including genetic material, shall be with due regard to the sovereign rights of the countries where the forests are located and to the sharing on mutually agreed terms of technology and profits from biotechnology products that are derived from these resources.

(h) National policies should ensure that environmental impact assessments should be carried out where actions are likely to have significant adverse impacts on important forest resources, and where such actions are subject to a decision of a competent national authority.

9.   (a) The efforts of developing countries to strengthen the management, conservation and sustainable development of their forest resources should be supported by the international community, taking into account the importance of redressing external indebtedness, particularly where aggravated by the net transfer of resources to developed countries, as well as the problem of achieving at least the replacement value of forests through improved market access for forest products, especially processed products. In this respect, special attention should also be given to the countries undergoing the process of transition to market economies.* * *

10.   New and additional financial resources should be provided to developing countries to enable them to sustainably manage, conserve and develop their forest resources, including through afforestation, reforestation and combating deforestation and forest and land degradation.

11.   In order to enable, in particular, developing countries to enhance their endogenous capacity and to better manage, conserve and develop their forest resources, the access to and transfer of environmentally sound technologies and

corresponding know-how on favourable terms, including on concessional and preferential terms, as mutually agreed, in accordance with the relevant provisions of Agenda 21, should be promoted, facilitated and financed, as appropriate.

12. * * * (d) Appropriate indigenous capacity and local knowledge regarding the conservation and sustainable development of forests should, through institutional and financial support and in collaboration with the people in local communities concerned, be recognized, respected, recorded, developed and, as appropriate, introduced in the implementation of programmes. Benefits arising from the utilization of indigenous knowledge should therefore be equitably shared with such people. * * *

13. (a) Trade in forest products should be based on non-discriminatory and multilaterally agreed rules and procedures consistent with international trade law and practices. In this context, open and free international trade in forest products should be facilitated.

(b) Reduction or removal of tariff barriers and impediments to the provision of better market access and better prices for higher value-added forest products and their local processing should be encouraged to enable producer countries to better conserve and manage their renewable forest resources.

14. Unilateral measures, incompatible with international obligations or agreements, to restrict and/or ban international trade in timber or other forest products should be removed or avoided, in order to attain long-term sustainable forest management.

QUESTIONS AND DISCUSSION

1. Environmental activists were disappointed in the forestry principles, because they viewed the principles as emphasizing a State's sovereign right to exploit the forest resources, with little attention paid to the conservation of environmental values found in forests. Do you agree? Are the principles balanced? Would a binding convention based on these principles add significantly to the global protection of forests?

2. Forests are not traditionally viewed as a resource requiring international cooperation, at least in the sense that they are neither migratory nor found in the global commons. As developing countries emphasized during the UNCED negotiations, forests would seem to be exactly the type of resource covered by the doctrine of state sovereignty over natural resources. The Forest Principles seem to reflect this as they provide some valuable guidance for national policies—but what do the principles say about international cooperation in the field of forest conservation? Do they require any common obligations, or do they simply promote cooperation in the development and conservation of forest resources? In the face of state sovereignty arguments, what legitimacy does international society have in establishing global forestry principles? How is this settled in the principles? More specifically, is the principle of common concern accepted or rejected in the forest principles? In this respect, what is the significance of paragraph (f) of the preamble?

3. Prior to UNCED, several countries were discussing national initiatives to restrict trade in products made from unsustainable forest practices. Principle 14 clearly supports free trade in timber products, with little or no preference given to products resulting from sustainable forest management. It was directly aimed at national efforts to restrict imports of unsustainably harvested forests. Principle 14's reference to attaining long-term sustainable forest management suggests a causal link between expanded trade and sustainable management. Do you think such a link exists?

4. *Problem Exercise.* In light of the discussion and questions raised above, critique the Forest Principles from one or more of the following perspectives.

- northern governments concerned with tropical forest loss;
- an indigenous forest-dweller, who has customary rights to the forests;
- a multi-national forest products company; and
- an international lawyer seeking to strengthen the principles and concepts of international environmental law.

---

2. POST–UNCED DEVELOPMENTS

The international dialogue regarding forests has continued after UNCED. Most significantly, at its third session the UN Commission on Sustainable Development established the "open-ended ad hoc Intergovernmental Panel on Forests" (IPF) to review the fragmented approaches of existing international forest initiatives, improve their coordination and formulate actions for implementing UNCED's forest-related agreements on the domestic and global levels. Some parties, most notably the European Union, hoped that the IPF would take forest policy beyond the UNCED Forest Principles and build consensus for adoption of a legally binding forest convention. The IPF was charged with addressing the following issues:

1) National and international implementation of UNCED decisions related to forests including an examination of sectoral and cross-sectoral linkages;

2) International cooperation in financial assistance and technology transfer;

3) Scientific research, forest assessment and development of criteria and indicators for sustainable forest management;

4) Trade and environment issues relating to forest products and services; and

5) International organizations and multilateral institutions and instruments including appropriate legal mechanisms.

The IPF met four times between 1995 and 1997, and submitted its final report to the Commission on Sustainable Development in May, 1997. The IPF facilitated continuing discussions on such issues as criteria and indicators for sustainable forest management, the need for financial assistance, and the role of international trade, but ultimately the participants could not reach consensus on most of the major issues, including whether to recommend the future negotiation of a binding forestry treaty.

Because the IPF did not reach a consensus, the General Assembly in its 1997 Special Session (to commemorate the Earth Summit's 5th Anniversary) recommended that ECOSOC create an Intergovernmental Forum on Forests. The IFF, which met in four annual meetings, culminated in a consensus statement that once again postponed any commitment to negotiate a legally binding instrument on forests. The compromise language was deliberately ambiguous: the IFF recommended that ECOSOC and the General Assembly make, within five years, an assessment and "consider with a view to recommending the parameters of a mandate for developing a legal framework on all types of forests". The IFF also recommended that a permanent UN Forum on Forests be created to ensure that forest issues would remain high on the political agenda. See J. Herzfeld, *UN Forests Panel Unable To Resolve Issue of Whether to Create Legally Binding Treaty,* Int'l Env't Rep. (BNA, Feb. 16, 2000).

The United States and European Union both originally promoted a legally binding treaty. During both the IPF and IFF, several developing countries including Malaysia and Indonesia surprised observers by stating their support for a treaty as well. They believed that a forest convention at this point would probably not be stronger in environmental terms than the 1992 Forest Principles. Fearing that any treaty would result in a "least common denominator" approach to global sustainable management standards, some environmental organizations still *oppose* negotiations of a treaty, and the United States did not press aggressively for a treaty at either the IPF or IFF. The IFF did clear up one aspect of the debate over a globally binding instrument. The IFF refers to a legal framework for "all types of forests", reflecting that any future instrument will have to cover more than just tropical forests. Its language also ensures that a forest convention must be discussed once again "within five years" (i.e., by 2005).

QUESTIONS AND DISCUSSION

1. The question of whether to begin negotiations on a global forest convention divides both governments and environmental organizations alike. In a "Citizen Declaration" signed by environmental organizations and circulated widely before the final IPF, environmental organizations warned that the "forest convention likely to result from negotiations launched in the near future will fail to safeguard the world's forests, and could actually threaten them." As suggested by Janet Abramovitz, *op. cit.*, at 39:

> Ironically, a forest convention could delay action, as negotiating and ratifying an international treaty can take a decade, plus further years for substantive action to begin once the treaty is "in force." With few exceptions, governments have been unwilling to accept international agreements that have "teeth," so it is likely that a forest convention would formalize weak, non-binding standards. Not coincidentally, many of the nations that now support a forest convention have powerful timber industries. Given the political realities and the urgency of the forest problem, the most effective course of action is to use existing mechanisms and legal instruments, such as the biodiversity and climate change conventions.

What other advantages and disadvantages are there for negotiating a forest convention? Do governments have a different set of reasons than NGOs for opposing the global convention?

2. Forest conservation issues are central to many other environmental conventions and global environmental issues. See, in particular, the discussions regarding the Biodiversity Convention (Chapter 13), and the Climate Change Convention (Chapter 9). Some observers argue that a forest protocol under either the climate change or biodiversity conventions would be an adequate substitute for a forest convention. What are the advantages or disadvantages for developing a protocol under the biodiversity convention rather than an independent forest convention? Under the climate convention?

3. Of course, support or opposition to a proposed global forestry treaty will ultimately depend on what is in the instrument. Environmentalists who currently oppose a forest convention are concerned that it will be predominantly a trade or resource development convention? Do you agree? Consider the following discussion of a forestry convention from a 1995 Note from the Secretariat of the FAO Committee on Forestry, "Assessing the Advantages and Disadvantages of a Legally Binding Instrument on Forests," paras. 21–22:

> The value of a binding instrument on forests should be assessed in relation to requirements specific to forest conservation and development. Any such instrument would need to be resource-based rather than user-oriented (dealing with the forest as a resource rather than merely from the point of view of the impact of forest management on selected elements of the environment); deal with all aspects and interests related to the forest sector and, in particular, provide a mechanism for reconciling the interests of development and conservation; provide a mechanism and channel for substantial resource transfer from developed to developing nations for forest purposes; seek to ensure freedom of trade in forest products; and provide for linkages with the existing forest-related instruments. . . .

> Compared to a "soft law" instrument, a legally binding one may also provide for an institutional framework (a Conference of the Parties) which may have as one of its main functions that of reviewing regularly the implementation of the instrument. It may also provide for a permanent secretariat to assist the Conference of Parties, for financial mechanisms to generate the necessary funding at national, subregional, regional and global levels, in particular to support the efforts of the least favoured countries to implement their obligations, and for procedures to allow for an effective flow of information on the implementation of the instrument, for settlement of disputes between Parties and for the resolution of questions arising in the course of implementation.

4. FAO is formally the lead UN organization for addressing forestry policy, but no fewer than nine different UN organizations have a significant role in forest policy. In addition, a number of other regional institutions address forests. These institutions have different overall objectives and bring different perspectives to forest issues. Not surprisingly, they thus have had different levels of success in making the transition from viewing forests as simply potential commercial resources to resources with important ecological and cultural values. The new permanent UN Forum on Forests is meant to enhance the cooperation and coordination among the different institutions with an interest in forests. Some observers continue to call for a World Forest Organization with even broader authorities. Do you think this is a good idea? What mandate, authorities or responsibilities should a WFO have? What kind of institutional structure? How would it differ from the ITTO or the UN Forum on Forests?

5. Based on the Forest Principles and the other above readings, consider what should be in a global forest agreement, if we ever get one. Consider the different positions of the North and South, and determine what compromises are possible. For example, should the Convention address both tropical and temperate forests? Should their treatment be the same?

C.   CURRENT ISSUES AND CROSS-CUTTING THEMES

1.   SUSTAINABLE FOREST MANAGEMENT

Despite the overall failure to agree on an international forests convention, at least the various international negotiations have helped to shape an emerging consensus that sustainable forest management (SFM) should be the future goal of forest policy. Indeed, the implementation of SFM practices has been promoted as one of the principal means of curbing deforestation and protecting forest ecosystems.

J. Abramovitz, *op cit.*, at 32—33

Sustainable forest management ... recognizes that forests must be managed as complete ecosystems to supply a wide array of goods and services for current and future generations. As Kathryn Kohm and Jerry Franklin of the University of Washington College of Forest Resources put it: "If 20th century forestry was about simplifying systems, producing wood, and managing at the stand level, 21st century forestry will be defined by understanding and managing complexity, providing a wide range of ecological goods and services, and managing across broad landscapes ... managing for wholeness rather than for the efficiency of individual components." In recent years, progress has been made in understanding the complexity of forests, defining SFM, and describing how it can be applied in various forest types and nations. Some of this effort has gone into developing international criteria and indicators to assess conditions in tropical, temperate, boreal, and dry forests....

While the concept of sustainable forest management continues to evolve, some elements are common to most definitions. First is that forests should be managed in ways that meet the social, economic, and ecological needs of current and future generations. These needs include nontimber goods and ecological services. Management should maintain and enhance forest quality, and look beyond the stand to encompass the much larger landscape so that biodiversity and ecological processes are maintained. When trees are cut, the rotation period should follow the longer natural cycle of a forest rather than a short financial cycle.

Sustainable forest management seeks to mirror the conditions in natural forests that are heterogeneous, with many species, ages, and sizes. Natural disturbances are enabled and mimicked. (While industry often claims that its management and harvesting practices mimic natural disturbances, such claims generally cannot be supported.) Sensitive areas like streams and important habitat such as dead tree "snags" are protected. Since forest species are interdependent, species that were once considered "pests," such as fungi and insects, are kept because they are important to ecosystem functioning. Finally, sustaining forests requires the active and meaningful participation of all stakeholders, especially local communities.

So far, governments have been able to agree only on very general definitions of SFM at the international level. *See, e.g.,* Rio Forest Principles, *supra,* at para. 2.b. The ITTO's definition is similarly general, but seems much more focused on continued timber production: "sustainable forest management" is the:

> process of managing permanent forest land to achieve one or more clearly specified objectives of management with regard to the production of a continuous flow of desired forest products and services without undue reduction of its inherent values and future productivity and without undue undesirable effects on the physical and social environment.

International Tropical Timber Organization, *Sustainable forest management,* Decision 6(XI) of the International Tropical Timber Council, December 4, 1991.

Obviously, these definitions offer only the broadest parameters for implementing SFM. The widespread acceptance of SFM as the goal for environmentally sound forest practices has sparked a search for a set of more detailed "criteria and indicators" that can be used to evaluate whether products came from sustainably managed forests. To develop such standards, several international processes, both political and technical, have begun to elaborate SFM "criteria and indicators" that could be put into operation in various regions or types of forest.

Most promising among these has been the development of SFM criteria and indicators for use in eco-labelling and timber certification by the Forest Stewardship Council's (FSC). The FSC is a non-profit independent association established in 1993 and headquartered in Oaxaca, Mexico. The goal of FSC is to promote environmentally responsible, socially beneficial and economically viable management of the world's forests, by establishing a worldwide standard of recognized and respected Principles of Forest Stewardship. The FSC accredits certification organizations in order to guarantee the authenticity of their claims. The FSC now has 500 members from over sixty developed and developing countries, with nearly equal representation from environmental, economic, and social interests. Funding comes from donations, membership dues and fees for accreditation services. *See* the FSC's website at http://www.fscoax.org.

The FSC's principles and criteria serve as broad guidelines for the development of forest management standards. *See* Table 14–3. The FSC Principles and Criteria apply to forest management on the national level, not directly to a forest unit as local forest conditions can differ significantly. Standards for certification of specific forests units are to be developed by multi-stakeholder working groups within the country or region, which are then submitted to the FSC Board of Directors for approval.

Table 14–3: FSC Principles and Criteria:

The FSC applies nine principles and a draft tenth principle addressing plantations as minimum standards for certification:

1. *Compliance with laws and FSC Principles:* Forest management shall respect all applicable laws of the country in which they occur, and international treaties and agreements to which the country is a signatory, and comply with all FSC Principles and Criteria.

2. *Tenure and use rights and responsibilities:* Long-term tenure and use rights to the land and forest resources shall be clearly defined, documented, and legally established.

3. *Indigenous People's Rights*: The legal and customary rights of indigenous peoples to own, use and manage their lands, territories, and resources shall be recognized and respected.

4. *Community Relations and Workers Rights:* Forest management operations shall maintain or enhance the long-term social and economic well being of forests workers and local communities.

5. *Benefits from Forests:* Forest management options shall encourage the efficient use of the forest's multiple products and services to enhance economic viability and a range of environmental and social benefits.

---

6. *Environmental Impact:* Forest management shall conserve biological diversity and its associated values, water resources, soils, and unique and fragile ecosystems and landscapes, and, by so doing, maintain the ecological functions and the integrity of the forest.

7. *Management Plan:* A management plan—appropriate to the scale and intensity of the operations–shall be written, implemented, and kept up to date. The long term objectives of management, and the means of achieving them, shall be clearly stated.

8. *Monitoring and Assessment:* Monitoring shall be conducted—appropriate to the scale and intensity of forest management—to assess the condition of the forest, yields of forest products, chain of custody, management activities and their social and environmental impacts.

9. *Maintenance of High Conservation Value Forests:* Management activities in high conservation value forests shall maintain or enhance the attributes which define such forests. Decisions regarding high conservation value forests shall always be considered in the context of a precautionary approach.

10. *Plantations:* Plantations shall be planned and managed in accordance with Principles and Criteria 1–9, and Principle 10 and its Criteria. While plantations can provide an array of social and economic benefits, and can contribute to satisfying the world's needs for forest products, they should complement the management of, reduce pressures on, and promote the restoration and conservation of natural forests.

Forest Stewardship Council, Document No. 1.2, *Forest Stewardship Council Principles and Criteria,* Oaxaca, Mexico, (Feb. 2000).

FSC is not the only international effort to develop a timber certification system. At the behest of the Canadian timber industry, for example, the Canadian Standards Association (CSA) began in 1994 to develop a voluntary independent certification program as an alternative to the FSC. The CSA is a non-governmental organization founded in 1919 to develop quality, safety, and performance standards of a wide variety of products both in Canada and internationally, as well as provide certification, testing and registration services. CSA standards are all voluntary, but they frequently form the basis for government legislation. The CSA also serves as the Canadian member of ISO, the International Organization for Standardization, and the CSA approach to ecolabelling of forests is intended to be implemented through ISO. *See* Chapter 18, page 1429.

FSC and CSA/ISO present two competing approaches to forest certification. FSC and their accredited certifiers base their certification on performance. In other words, they theoretically at least strive to evaluate production at the forest unit level according to ecological, social, and economic performance indicators. The CSA/ISO approach, by contrast, focuses on the potential of the company's management system to produce sustainably harvested timber and the general condition of the forest reserve. What advantages and disadvantages are presented by each approach? A second, though related, question is on what level should certification occur. The CSA/ISO initiative calls for certification at the national level, rather than the forest-unit level. Although FSC establishes national working groups to develop criteria and indicators particular to that country or region, they expect those criteria and indicators to be applied at and adopted to the forest-unit level. Forest level assessments are necessary to ensure that sustainable management practices are actually implemented. *See*, James Salzman, *The Use and Abuse of Environmental Labels*, J. of Industrial Ecology 11, Spring 1997; Dubois, Robins, and Bass, *Forest Certification, A Report to the European Commission* (IIED, March 1996). For information on these and other certification efforts, *see* the web site for the Forest Stewardship Council at http://www.fscoax.org.

QUESTIONS AND DISCUSSION

1. National governments have also tried to implement unilateral certification plans. Austria was the first country to take unilateral action to reduce imports of tropical timber and promote the use of sustainable management in tropical timber producing countries. In 1992, the Austrian parliament enacted legislation that required all tropical timber to be labeled "made from tropical timber," while simultaneously imposing a 70% tariff increase on the importation of tropical timber, with tariff proceeds predesignated for projects promoting the sustainable management of tropical timber. The law also called for a voluntary eco-label to identify the quality of the wood in terms of sustainable management. In response, tropical timber producing countries, particularly Indonesia and Malaysia, called for a developing-country boycott of all Austrian products and those of any other country that took similar action. The producer countries also questioned whether such a system would be consistent with GATT. In the face of this pressure, Austria backed down, repealing both the import duty and the mandatory labeling scheme. The voluntary eco-labeling requirement remained, but was expanded to include all timber, not just that of tropical origin.

2. Although ecolabelling will remain the primary use for sustainable forest certification, certification may also be used for: (1) tax differentiation, whereby governments institute a reduced sales tax for sustainably produced products or provide favorable tax treatment for investments in sustainable forestry; (2) procurement policies that require the purchase of sustainably harvested timber products for public works projects; and (3) joint implementation, whereby timber certification of sustainable forest management could be one of the elements required for accreditation under the climate change convention. What other potential uses for certification can be developed? What role can the law play in building a market for sustainably managed products?

3. *Timber Ecolabelling and Trade Policy: The Agreement on Technical Barriers to Trade.* A number of trade-related concerns have been raised with respect to timber ecolabelling efforts such as Austria's, described above. These include fears that ecolabelling will be used as a disguised protectionist measure, discriminating against imported products, for example in cases where ecolabelling schemes or proposals in developed country markets focus on tropical timber. Concerns also exist that national or regional criteria may work to the advantage of domestic or regional producers, even absent protectionist motivations, because the criteria were developed on the basis of the specific conditions in that region. For example, European standards that penalize harvesting from old growth forests will tend to work in favor of European producers and against many foreign producers, because Europe has almost no old-growth forest remaining, in contrast to other timber-producing regions. Sustainable forest management and related certification and labeling all impose financial costs and require technical expertise that are less likely to be available to developing country producers as compared to those in developed countries. Similarly, certification and ecolabelling may harm small producers more than larger ones.

Timber labelling schemes to date have primarily been voluntary and non-governmental. Could voluntary ecolabelling systems be found inconsistent with WTO rules relating to Most Favoured Nation (MFN) and National Treatment (NT) Principles? See CIEL, *Current Issues in Timber Ecolabelling and Trade Policy: the WTO Agreement on Technical Barriers to Trade* (1997); James Salzman, *Informing the Green Consumer: The Debate Over the Use and Abuse of Environmental Labels*, JOURNAL OF INDUSTRIAL ECOLOGY (Summer 1997); *see* also Chapter 15, page 1149 (discussing Technical Barriers to Trade).

----

2. INTERNATIONAL TRADE AND THE ITTA

International trade in wood-based products doubled from 1981 to 1992, from US $51 billion to $103 billion. Developed countries account for over 80% of world exports. Trade is dominated by seven countries: Canada, Finland, Germany, Indonesia, Malaysia, Sweden and the United States. Perhaps surprisingly, developed countries account for the vast majority of the forest trade. In some developing countries, logging for export is the largest contributor to deforestation or forest degradation. In the Sarawak state in Malaysia, for example, approximately 80% of logs eventually become exports. Malaysia and Indonesia combine for about 86% of total exports from tropical countries. East Asian countries, led by Japan, Korea, China, Thailand and Japan, are the major importers, accounting for over 75% of world imports. By contrast, European Union countries only represent 13% of world imports. L. BROWN ET AL., VITAL SIGNS 68–69 (1997).

Due to the importance of international trade in forest products for many economies, international cooperation with respect to forests has traditionally concerned market access and other issues relating to trade. Only recently has this international cooperation been extended to issues relating to sustainable forest management. Most notable in this regard is the International Tropical Timber Agreement (ITTA).

Initially conceived as a commodity agreement to provide greater profits to tropical timber-producing countries, the ITTA also embraced the goal of sustainable use and conservation of tropical forests. The ITTA established the International Tropical Timber Organization (ITTO) to administer the Agreement. The ITTO's unique voting structure divides the votes in the International Tropical Timber Council equally between producing and consuming countries. Voting share within each group is determined primarily by the respective countries' share in the timber trade, although voting share for the producing countries also reflects a country's amount of forest cover. Given a voting structure based on each parties' share of the international tropical timber trade, the ITTO is not necessarily well-suited for environmental protection. Afterall, those who benefit most from the international trade and thus have the largest voting power are likely to be the least enthusiastic for environmental conditions that potentially restrict the trade.

Nonetheless, in 1990 ITTO members adopted a non-binding goal that all tropical timber be sustainably managed by the year 2000—the so-called *Target 2000 Initiative*. This Initiative was endorsed again in the revised 1994 ITTA, which is more clearly supportive of sustainable forestry than its predecessor.

Among the objectives of the 1994 ITTA are:

(a) To provide an effective framework for consultation, international cooperation and policy development among all members with regard to all relevant aspects of the world timber economy;

(b) To provide a forum for consultation to promote non-discriminatory timber trade practices;

(c) To contribute to the process of sustainable development;

(d) To enhance the capacity of members to implement a strategy for achieving exports of tropical timber and timber products from sustainably managed sources by the year 2000;

(e) To promote the expansion and diversification of international trade in tropical timber from sustainable sources by improving the structural conditions in international markets, by taking into account, on the one hand, a long-term increase in consumption and continuity of supplies, and on the other, prices which reflect the costs of sustainable forest management and which are remunerative and equitable for members, and the improvement of market access;

(f) To promote and support research and development with a view to improving forest management and efficiency of wood utilization as well as increasing the capacity to conserve and enhance other forest values in timber-producing tropical forests;

(g) To develop and contribute towards mechanisms for the provision of new and additional financial resources and expertise needed to enhance the capacity of producing members to attain the objectives of this Agreement;* * *

(j) To encourage members to support and develop industrial tropical timber reforestation and forest management activities as well as rehabilitation of degraded forest land, with due regard for the interests of local communities dependent on forest resources;

(k) To improve marketing and distribution of tropical timber exports from sustainably managed sources;

(*l*) To encourage members to develop national politics aimed at sustainable utilization and conservation of timber-producing forests and their genetics resources and at maintaining the ecological balance in the regions concerned, in the context of tropical timber trade;

(m) To promote the access to, and transfer of, technologies and technical cooperation to implement the objectives of this Agreement, including on concessional and preferential terms and conditions, as mutually agreed; and

(n) To encourage information-sharing on the international timber market.

ITTA, UNCTAD Doc. No. TD/Timber2/Misc.7/GE.94–50830, Art. 1, *reprinted in* 33 I.L.M. 1014 (1995).

Although seriously criticized for failures in implementation, the ITTA remains a potentially important framework for promoting sustainable production and consumption of tropical timber, and an important precedent for introducing environmental concerns into commodity agreements.

The following excerpt from Nigel Sizer, *Opportunities to Save and Sustainably Use the World's Forests Through International Cooperation,* at 5–6 (World Resources Institute: 1994), summarizes some of the issues raised by the ITTA.

A key issue in the ITTO has been the Year 2000 Objective—the goal of sustainable production of all tropical timbers exported by ITTA's members by the year 2000. The Council adopted the objective during [its] 1990 annual meeting in Bali. The question of whether sustainable management of tropical forests designated for industrial use is widely viable is, however, still being debated by scientists and policy-makers. Some NGOs that initially supported the institution have voiced very strong concerns about ITTO, stating that it is influenced too much by timber trade interests and is politically compromised. Recent evidence of ITTO's reluctance to embrace new initiatives and ideas was their resistance to support studies and efforts to promote timber certification following pressure from various governments. With the wave of attention to certification, ITTO recently reversed its earlier stance.

The 1983 ITTA was due to expire in March 1994. By January 1994, a new agreement had been negotiated, though the old one will remain in force until the new one is ratified. [The 1994 ITTA entered into force in 1997.] Renegotiations encountered several difficulties. It was the first international negotiation of a forest accord since UNCED in 1992, so discussion was colored by the tensions that accompanied that meeting in Rio. Fearing discrimination—past and future—against tropical producers, some key producing countries proposed broadening the agreement to include temperate and boreal timbers As a result, members were asked to commit to no new trade restrictions, and producers called for additional funds to be made available through ITTO to finance projects.

The consumers refused to accept the broadened agreement, would not commit additional financial resources, and could not agree to a statement precluding trade restrictions. Also controversial was the incorporation of the Year 2000 Objective into the text of the agreement. The text presents the Year 2000 Objective as a nonbinding objective, which led some non-governmental organizations (NGOs) to conclude that the new agreement is no better than the old one. On the other hand, others considered the incorporation of "from sustainable sources" in reference to the expansion and diversification of international trade and the inclusion of the statement that timber price should "reflect the costs of sustainable forest management" to be significant improvements upon the previous agreement.

The consumer countries succeeded in keeping the ITTA limited in scope. The "consumer statement" in the new agreement contains a commitment to promote parallel, but separate, efforts for the sustainable management of temperate forests.

The 1994 ITTA thus reaffirmed the Target 2000 goal of ensuring that all exports of tropical timber products be from sustainably managed forests by the year 2000. Consuming countries also committed to meeting the Target 2000 goal for sustainable management of their own forests by the year 2000. The ITTO did not meet its Target 2000 objective, however. An independent assessment initiated found that the producer countries, sometimes with the assistance of the ITTO, had made progress in changing laws and policies to reflect SFM goals in most countries and that some had begun to provide tenure protection for indigenous peoples. The independent review emphasized, however, that new laws and policies were not sufficient to meet the Target 2000 objective. Implementation of SFM in the forests could not be verified in most countries. Indeed, only six countries were deemed to have the capacity to evaluate and monitor sustainable forestry on the ground. The independent assessment also reflected substantial frustration that so few countries made information available and implicitly at least called into question the ITTO's political will to have a meaningful evaluation of the Target 2000 objective. *See* D. Poore & T.H. Chiew, *Review of Progress towards the Year 2000 Objective,* ITTC(XXVIII)/9/Rev.2 (5 November 2000).

QUESTIONS AND DISCUSSION

1. Perhaps the key political limitation on the ITTA is its exclusive focus on the tropical timber trade. During the 1994 ITTA's renegotiations, developing countries pressed for the expansion of the agreement to include all timber, including that from northern temperate and boreal forests. This suggestion was ultimately rejected. It is not clear ecologically or economically why the tropical timber trade, which only amounts to about 20% of all timber trade, should be emphasized so much more than temperate and boreal forests. If the ITTA were expanded to cover all forests, as has been suggested at several of the last meetings, then developing countries might be persuaded to support stronger sustainable management standards under the agreement. To what extent should tropical timber be addressed differently? Does the answer differ depending on whether you're concerned with biodiversity conservation or climate change?

2. The 1994 ITTA was the first major forest policy document negotiated after UNCED, and the developing countries often voiced their reluctance to go beyond the consensus reflected in the UNCED documents, particularly the Forest Principles and Chapter 11 of Agenda 21. To what extent do the ITTA's objectives move the global policy debate forward with respect to sustainable forest management? Compare, for example, ITTA objective 1(d) and (e) to Principle 14 of the Forest Principles.

―――――

3.   INTERNATIONAL FINANCING FOR FOREST CONSERVATION

As with most international environmental concerns, financing for forest conservation is a major issue. The South wants the North to pay the incremental costs of forest conservation—particularly if the primary motivations for protecting southern forests is to provide carbon sinks for northern greenhouse gas emissions or conserve biodiversity resources for northern tourists. See, e.g., Principles 1 (b), 7 (b), 9 (a), and 10. *Agenda 21* estimated the costs for achieving sustainable forest management in all countries at over $31 billion dollars annually between 1993 and 2000. Other estimates have been lower. The ITTO estimated in 1995 that the costs to producer countries would be $2.2 billion annually for taking a few priority actions to achieve SFM by the year 2000, including, for example, improving enforcement of national laws, demarcating and maintaining forest boundaries, and improving logging operations and efficiency.

Overall some 20 donor countries and 13 multilateral agencies are actively involved in providing official development assistance for sustainable forest management. The total amount of assistance however, has not increased significantly since UNCED. Nonetheless, the major challenge may not be the amount of funding available, but the different priorities of the Northern donors and the Southern recipients regarding the goals of forest management. In short, political pressure in the North has driven donor agencies to "do something" about tropical forest loss, but the Southern countries remain more interested in traditional development support—for example to build roads into large, undeveloped forest areas. Moreover, with more than thirty agencies involved in providing official development assistance, coordination between all of the programs has been a major challenge. The most significant efforts to coordinate international donor assistance for sustainable forest management have been the *Pilot Programme for the Brazilian Amazon* and the *Tropical Forest Action Plan*. Both of these efforts pre-dated UNCED, but the difficulties of donor-driven financial assistance programmes demonstrated by them continues today.

The Brazilian Pilot Programme. Beginning in the late 1980's, the Group of Seven (G–7) countries began to address tropical deforestation in their annual meetings. This focus was largely motivated to respond to growing pressure by NGOs in Germany and the United States over World Bank lending and other donor-country activities that were contributing to the destruction of Brazil's Amazonian rainforest. Given the mounting environmental interest leading up to the 1992 UNCED, the G–7 and the Commission of the European Community initiated the Pilot Programme for the Brazilian Amazon.

> The stated objective of the programme was to "maximize the environmental benefits of Brazil's rainforests consistently with Brazil's development goals, through the implementation of a sustainable development approach that will contribute to a continuing reduction of the rate of deforestation".... Achieving this goal would have four other beneficial effects: "(i) demonstrate the feasibility of harmonizing economic and environmental objectives in tropical rain forests; (ii) help preserve the huge genetic resources of the rainforests; (iii) reduce the Amazon's contribution to global carbon emissions; and (iv) provide another example of cooperation between developed and developing countries on global environmental issues."

ANS KOLK, FORESTS IN INTERNATIONAL ENVIRONMENTAL POLITICS: INTERNATIONAL ORGANIZATIONS, NGOS AND THE BRAZILIAN AMAZON, 145–53 (1996). The pilot programme ultimately did not deliver substantial benefits for Brazil's rainforests. The programme could never overcome its donor-driven conception and lack of strong commitment at the local level. The amount of funding ultimately made available was also far less than initially envisioned and the wide range of donors involved in the programme also slowed the process, and political support for the programme in Brazil ultimately weakened.

The Tropical Forest Action Plan. The Tropical Forest Action Plan (TFAP) was initiated at the 1985 World Forestry Congress through a collaboration of the FAO, the World Bank, UNDP, and an NGO, the World Resources Institute. FAO coordinated the implementation of TFAP which was primarily aimed at coordinating international donors in support of the development of National Forestry Action Plans (NFAPs). According to Nigel Sizer of WRI, TFAP "helped stimulate donor coordination and financing, but far less than developing countries hoped. Exact figures are not available, but FAO reported that donor spending dedicated to forests in developing countries had grown from $400 million per year in 1985 to $1.3 billion per year in 1990. The TFAP has also promoted collaboration between the [NFAPs] of several countries at the regional level with particular success in Central America." Nigel Sizer, *Opportunities to Save and Sustainably Use the World's Forests through International Cooperation*, at 4–5 (WRI, 1994).

Despite some initial success, TFAP eventually came under intense criticism from most independent observers as being donor-driven and lacking significant support at the local level. TFAP was one of several international efforts aimed at building national capacity to manage forests sustainably, and it probably did build momentum for national forest planning. According to a 1996 UN background paper prepared for the IPF, 54 developing countries were implementing national forestry programs, and another 26 were engaged in planning processes. These national level programs have been successful in among other things allowing countries to take long-term views toward forest management, integrating forestry issues into national sustainable development plans, increasing the capacity and prestige of national forestry agencies, and strengthening national forest laws. The UN report cited several weaknesses in the planning and implementation of forestry programmes, including the prevalence of top-down planning and implementation, the lack of clearly defined priorities for implementation, and the lack of national capacity. *See* UN CSD, Implementation of Forest–Related Decisions of the United Nations Conference on Environment and Development at the National and International Levels, Including an Examination of Sectoral and Cross–Sectoral Linkages, Programme Element I.1: Progress in National Forest and Land–Use Plans, E/CN.17/IPF/1996/8 (Feb. 9, 1996).

QUESTIONS AND DISCUSSION

1. Both the Pilot Programme for Brazilian Amazon and TFAP suffered from a perception, at least, that they were designed and developed by and for the donor countries, with little "ownership" given to the recipient countries. This, mixed with the developing countries' fierce protection of sovereignty over their own forests, handicapped these programs from the beginning. Unfortunately, these types of problems often befall official development assistance for forest conservation. In this regard, consider the following list of "shortcomings of the ODA system," as recognized in a UN background paper:

(a) There are a large number of donors providing ODA [official development assistance], which have differing policies, priorities, eligibility criteria, modalities and rules. Conflicts of various nature arise because of such differences among providers of ODA within each group (bilateral, multilateral, non-governmental organization), among these groups and between donor groups and recipients;

(b) When donors have the same preference for countries and similar priorities, they often compete among themselves, thus diluting the effectiveness of assistance. Cooperative management and co-financing of projects/programmes does not occur often enough;

(c) Because of the country preferences of bilateral donors, ODA does not get evenly distributed among countries according to their needs;

(d) ODA projects are often decided on an ad hoc basis without any analysis of their linkages and relevance to overall goals of development;

(e) The policies and priorities of donors and recipients often conflict. As a result, some of the high priority needs of developing countries remain unattended and national programmes are patchy rather than comprehensive;

(f) It is very difficult for recipients or anyone else to be well informed on the multiplicity of changing programmes, funds, criteria and procedures that exist. They lack adequate knowledge and capacity to receive access and implement ODA;

(g) Projects are often prepared without sufficient national/local involvement, resulting in the introduction of inappropriate technology and dependence on foreign experts;

(h) There has been a proliferation of frameworks for environmentally sustainable development planning, causing confusion and dissipation of efforts;

(i) The ratio of local funding to ODA funding in projects is small, raising questions about the capacity of recipient countries to maintain investments once external assistance comes to an end;

(j) There is often insufficient national ownership and commitment, resulting in a lack of positive impact and a lack of adequate technical skills and capability to absorb the benefits of assistance.

What steps should be taken to improve this situation? Would an international convention on forests help to improve the effectiveness of ODA? See also Chapter 20, on International Finance.

2. *Prohibition on International Funding of Tropical Forest Harvesting.* Several donor agencies including the World Bank and the U.S. Overseas Private Investment Corporation, also prohibit or disfavor support for projects that harvest primary tropical forests. Yet, these institutions continue to support forest operations in Russia's taiga. What justification, if any, is there not to extend the same protection to primary boreal forests as is extended to tropical forests? Can you see how this disparate treatment of Northern forests versus Southern forests could anger Southern country governments intent on building their domestic economies? The World Bank is currently undergoing a review of its forest policy and is expected to reverse its ban on projects in primary tropical forests, ostensibly so it can support harvesting in sustainable forest management projects. What arguments would you make to support the ban? To eliminate the ban?

3. Given that ODA will never provide sufficient funding to achieve sustainable forest management, other mechanisms for raising revenues for SFM must be found. Debt-for-nature swaps have provided one source of funding for projects that protect forests. *See* Chapter 20, page 1507. The Clean Development Mechanism under the Climate Change regime presents additional opportunities. See Chapter 9, page 640. At the domestic level, the most common form of revenue generation is the use of royalties from the sale or lease of public forest lands. In addition, taxes could be placed directly on forest products and earmarked for specific purposes. Other mechanisms might include requiring other industries to reimburse for the damage they cause to the ecological services provided by forests. For example, Colombia has a law that requires hydropower users to support forest management in the upper watersheds. What other mechanisms or policies might be imposed at the national level to provide public revenues for forest management?

4. *The IMF and National Forest Enforcement.* Timber products are an important export product for many developing countries, and thus an important source of foreign currency. Illegal poaching of timber can rob a country of a major source of foreign currency and taxes. Chronic timber poaching can significantly threaten the macro-economic health of timber-dependent economies. In theory, this could harm a country's ability to participate in the international financial system. Theory met reality in late 1996 when for the first time the IMF withdrew credits from a country because of that country's inability or unwillingness to curb illegal logging. Massive, illegal logging was reportedly occurring on millions of acres in Cambodia, with little revenue being returned to the public finances. The IMF withdrew a $20 million loan to Cambodia until it began effective enforcement of its timber laws. This type of international "enforcement" is rare. The IMF feared that Cambodia was losing one of its primary sources of foreign currencies to timber poachers working in collusion with government officials. Do you think it holds much promise for improving forest management? *See, e.g., IMF Warns Cambodia Logging Threatens Loans,* ASIAN WALL ST. J., Oct. 24, 1996; T. Bardacke, *Cambodia Failing to Curb Illegal Logging,* THE FINANCIAL TIMES, Sept. 16, 1997, at 4.

———

4. INDIGENOUS PEOPLES, COMMUNITY MANAGEMENT AND FORESTS

One of the major challenges facing international and national forest policy is how to respect and protect indigenous peoples' cultural, economic, social and legal relationships with the forests in which they live. Among the challenges are how to ensure fair and open participation in forest planning, how to share the benefits from traditional knowledge and from exploitation of indigenous peoples' forests, and how to protect indigenous rights to forest lands. One of the programme elements of the IPF addressed issues relating to traditional communities.

UN CSD, *Implementation of Forest–Related Decisions of the UNCED at the National and International Levels, Including an Examination of Sectoral and Cross–Sectoral Linkages,* **Programme Element I.3: Traditional Forest-related Knowledge, E/CN.17/IF1996/9, paras 16–19 (Feb. 1, 1996)**

Until the beginning of the 1990s, very few [forest] planning processes promoted the participation of indigenous people in policy programmes and projects formulation. These people felt marginalized and ignored because their political institutions were not recognized, and they suffered from development directed from above. During the last five years, some progress has been observed, in particular due to the creation and action of national and international alliances of indigenous people. * * *

Advances in technological, technical and scientific studies on the nature and substance of indigenous and traditional knowledge and forest management practices underlines the necessity for a broad, coordinated approach. Among the advances already made in this direction is the emergence of scientific evidence to the effect that:

(a) The language, culture and knowledge of indigenous and local communities are disappearing at alarming rates;

(b) Many presumed "natural" ecosystems or "wilderness" areas are in fact "human or cultural landscapes" resulting from millennial interactions with forest-dwellers;

(c) Traditional ecological knowledge is complex, sophisticated and critically relevant to understanding how to conserve forest ecosystems and to utilize them sustainably.

(d) Indigenous and traditional forest management systems are likely to focus on the conservation of non-or semi-domesticated, non-timber species because these provide the majority of food supplies, medicines, oils, essences, dyes, colours, repellents, insecticides, building materials, clothing, etc.;

(e) Most species associated with forests possess existence values for local communities which are often ignored, obscured or even cancelled out by imposed conservation, development and market schemes; [and]

(f) As indigenous and local communities frequently integrate forest and agricultural management system, "foresters" and "farmers" can be seen as forming part of the same continuum. * * *

Recognition of and respect for local values, as well as landscapes modified by human activities, are crucial if the vitality of forest-dwelling societies is to be enhanced rather than undermined. Unfortunately, since the complex links between biological and cultural diversity have not been generally recognized in the past, this has led to the destruction of biological diversity and to the disappearance of languages, cultures and societies.

One way to forge effective links with local communities could be through the development of *sui generis* systems to protect indigenous and local communities and ensure benefit-sharing from the wider use and application of their knowledge about forest use and management—as well as of the biogenetic resources conserved on their lands and territories. Adequate and effective protection and benefit-sharing mechanisms would inevitably require a shift from economic or ecologically determined legal and political frameworks to rights-driven systems. Adopting such a course would, however, enable commitments made by countries under human rights conventions, covenants and agreements to be harmonized at the national level with international commitments on environment, development and trade. It should also enable the provisions of the Convention on Biological Diversity to generate options for stimulating the equitable use and application of the traditional knowledge, innovations and practices of forest-dwellers. * * *

The successful implementation of these mechanisms will depend upon, among other things, effective leadership from among local people based on criteria for carrying out their own inventories, evaluations, monitoring, impact assessments and development progammes for forest use and conservation, drawing upon their cultural aptitudes and based on their traditional knowledge and local criteria. Support from external sources will require the development of more effective tools for intercultural, information exchange, technology training, awareness-raising and education, as well as for interdisciplinary collaboration between the human, natural and social sciences.

Ultimately, supporting forest dwellers will require devolving (or allowing existing) forest management at the community level. This may require recognizing and respecting traditional community rights to forests and related resources. The following case study discusses community-based management in Orissa, India.

O. Lynch, *Community-based Forest Management in Orissa, India,* in N. SIZER, OPPORTUNITIES TO SAVE AND SUSTAINABLY USE THE WORLD'S FORESTS THROUGH INTERNATIONAL COOPERATION (Dec. 1994)

The management of forest resources in India has been one of the most challenging environmental issues in South Asia. Since 1951, degraded lands in India have doubled in size, reaching 174 million hectares by 1990. According to recent estimates, demand for fuelwood and fodder will triple within the next ten years. Large-scale reforestation and watershed-management programs conducted by the Indian government have largely failed. Community-based forest management has proved to be a feasible alternative and as of 1994, fifteen of India's twenty-two states have formally initiated joint forest management (JFM) programs.

Local communities in Orissa now manage 1200 patches of forest, covering a total area of 186,900 hectares, through the efforts of 1,180 "User Group Organizations" (UGO). In the 360–hectare Binjgiri Protected Forest, for instance, environmental protection has been the driving force for improved forest-management practices. Surrounded by rural villages, the forest was almost completely denuded by the late 1960s. Streams dried up, pond sedimentation increased, and fuelwood grew acutely scarce. Following the initiative of a former resident of Kesharpur, a movement to protect the Binjgiri hill was initiated. The villagers of Kesharpur soon realized that the regenerating forest would be endangered if the other villages surrounding Binjgiri were not involved in its protection. This led to the creation of the "Brikshya O'Jeevar Bandhu Parishad" (BOJBP: "Friends of Trees and Living Beings"), a grass-roots organization that provided essential leadership for community involvement in forest conservation.

Thanks to BOJBP's strong cultural links with the villagers of the region and to environmental awareness activities, traditional village councils—the local authority of rural villages in Orissa—established rules for using the Binjgiri forest. Forest cutting and animal rearing were restricted. Families were assigned responsibility for taking turns patrolling the forest. The payoff was the return of streams that had dried out and water flows for months after the rainy season ended. In addition, fish populations grew more abundant as pond water quality improved.

The community-based forest-management systems in Orissa and elsewhere in India vary, depending on the condition and diversity of the local resources. In the Puri district, where the Binjgiri forest is located, the great scarcity of natural resources led to the creation of BJBP. The rules for forest use were well defined and "moral" sanctions, such as requesting the violators to apologize in public, were the rule. In other communities where resources were moderately scarce, as in the Dhenkanal district, the villagers' lack of emotional attachment to the forest made fines and other more formal actions necessary. When resources are less scarce, user groups are often organized more loosely, as happened in the Phulbani district.

Community-based forest-management systems succeed because they rely on the autonomy of villagers: regulatory measures for forest use are based on traditional community directives and norms. Government agencies should act as agile facilitators and legitimators, providing a supportive framework for community organization and supplying technical assistance. The state government in Orissa has realized that decentralization, or sharing of power with the communities, is fundamental to assuring long-term sustainability in the use of forest resources. This realization not only benefits local communities, but also the state and nation.

QUESTIONS AND DISCUSSION

1. Given the historical lack of respect provided to indigenous political and legal institutions and rights, are the initiatives and approaches offered in these excerpts sufficient? How specifically would you empower indigenous peoples and local communities? Consider this in light of the discussions in Chapter 16, page 964, regarding human rights and indigenous peoples or Chapter 13, page 941, regarding the treatment of traditional knowledge under the biodiversity convention. How can international forest policy support community-based forest management like that in Orissa? Does the current international trade system reward such community-based management?

2. Several of the Forest Principles address the role of local communities and indigenous knowledge in forest conservation (e.g., 5(a), 9(b), and 12(d)). Do these principles sufficiently reflect and protect the interest of local communities? Consider this question in the context of Papua New Guinea where much of the land is owned under customary law by indigenous peoples. Where land tenure is disputed, do these forest principles undermine or strengthen claims to forest ownership by indigenous communities?

5. *PROBLEM EXERCISE: NEGOTIATION OF A GLOBAL LEGALLY BINDING FOREST CONVENTION*

It is the year 2005, and after more than fifteen years of frustrating negotiations over forest protection, the time for agreement on a global forest convention has finally arrived. All countries in the world have stated their intention to finalize a binding international instrument for the sustainable management of forests. There is widespread consensus that forests are important both ecologically and economically and that a fair balance must be struck—one that allows the economic value to be gained by developing countries and that protects the ecological values of forests as well.

The negotiations are expected to cover a range of forest issues, including:

(1) Standards for sustainable forest management and certification;

(2) International trade in forest products;

(3) Financial assistance for sustainable forest management;

(4) Protection of forest-dwelling communities;

(5) Institutional arrangements for global forest protection

(6) Provisions for scientific assessment of forests.

The class will be divided into six different groups.

- North American countries, represented by the United States. These countries are large consumers of forest products, are major potential donors to developing countries, have large tracts of primary and secondary temperate forests, and have large environmental lobbying pressure groups.

- Western European countries, represented by Germany. These countries are large consumers of forest products and major potential donors to developing countries. They also have large environmental lobbying groups. They do not have significant forests.

- The economies in economic transition, represented by Russia. They have large tracts of undeveloped northern and temperate forests.

- Large forest-producing and exporting countries from Asia, represented by Indonesia. Forest products are a critical part of their economies and they need the revenue from forest exports to lift their countries' standard of living.

- South American countries, represented by Brazil who have large tracts of undeveloped forests, rich in biological diversity.

- Other developing countries that do not have significant forest resources, represented by South Africa, who is also hosting these negotiations. These countries have varying interests including those of the small island states and Bangladesh that want to ensure forests are used to sequester carbon and very poor African countries that hope to gain financial resources through the negotiations.

Your instructor may divide your class into the groups above to negotiate the convention, or alternatively lead a general discussion of what the resulting consensus on these issues should be. What kinds of compromises do you think will be necessary on the above issues before there can be agreement on a global convention? What other issues do you think will be important to a future global convention?

Suggested Further Reading and Web Sites

Kilaparti Ramakrishna and George M. Woodwell, eds., WORLD FORESTS FOR THE FUTURE (1993).

Charles Little, THE DYING OF THE TREES (1995)

David Humphreys, FOREST POLITICS: THE EVOLUTION OF INTERNATIONAL COOPERATION (1996)

CIEL, *Current Issues in Timber Ecolabelling and Trade Policy: The WTO Agreement on Technical Barriers to Trade* (1997)

Rob Glastra, ed., CUT AND RUN: ILLEGAL LOGGING AND TIMBER TRADE IN THE TROPICS (1999).

http://www.gfpp.net

Homepage of the Global Forestry Policy Project

http://www.rainforest-alliance.org/

Homepage of Rainforest Alliance, a group of NGOs working on rainforest conservation

http://www.ran.org/

Homepage of Rainforest Action Network, an NGO dedicated to conserving the world's temperate and tropical rainforests

http://www.fscoax.org

Homepage of the Forest Stewardship Council

http://www.un.org/esa/sustdev/forests.htm

Homepage of the UN Forum on Forests

Section V.   Desertification

Land degradation is as old as civilisation itself, stretching from the plains of China to the peaks of the Inca empire. The world's first ever written story, a Sumerian epic, tells how a man felled the forests of Mesopotamia, bringing down a curse. The ancient Sumerians failed to heed the parable and went on cutting the trees. As early as 2000 BC their literature carries evocative descriptions of desertification. Their great city state of Uruk, which once contained 50,000 people and produced crop yields comparable to those of North America today, is now just a bump in the sand.

The Centre for Our Common Future, Down to Earth 9 (1995)

A.   The Problem of Desertification

Desertification is a serious environmental and social problem that directly affects over one billion people, fully one-sixth of the world's population, in more than 110 countries. UNEP estimates that desertification currently affects approximately 25% of the world's land surface area and 70% of the world's drylands. These threatened dryland areas are in both developed and developing countries, including parts of Southern Africa and the Middle East, southern Russia, Australia, the United States and Mexico, northeast Brazil, western South America, and even Iceland. Depending on the severity of desertification, it can deepen rural poverty, threatening food production, biodiversity, and even undermine political stability from mass migrations. *See* <http://www.unccd.int/publicinfo/factsheets>.

While some of the dryland areas experiencing desertification border deserts, it is a common misconception that desertification involves sand dunes or the desert actually ''spreading'' into agriculturally productive land. Deserts do naturally expand and contract following wet and dry periods, but desertification can occur in any arid area where prolonged abuse weakens the land's ability to support plant growth. This expresses itself through loss of soil productivity, increased soil deterioration, and loss of biodiversity. Following drought, desertified lands do not recover quickly. Areas surrounding desertified areas are also at risk to downstream flooding.

The process of desertification is not new, and over time local inhabitants have developed cultural and social practices, such as nomadic herding and shifting agriculture, to adapt to the demands of an arid environment. Over the past few decades, however, changes in human settlement, wars and agricultural practices have dramatically increased the rate of desertification in much of the world's arid and semi-arid lands. Too often, local vegetation, wildlife and cultures have not been able to keep up. *Desertification Talks Open Amid Cautious Optimism*, 17 INT'L. ENVTL. REP. 510–11, June 15, 1994; UNEP, *Fact Sheet 3: United Nations Convention to Combat Desertification* (1995); H. Dregne et al., *A New Assessment of the World Status of Desertification*, 20 DESERTIFICATION CONTROL BULL. at 12 (1992).

Dryland regions are not barren expanses of land as many believe but, rather, a critical source of food production accounting for one-fifth of the world's food supply. Desertification thus directly threatens the food-producing capabilities of arid regions. Approximately 80% of the agricultural land in arid regions currently suffers from moderate to severe degrees of desertification. This translates to over 60 million acres of agricultural land directly affected by desertification each year. Africa, with approximately 70% of its land either desert or drylands, is particularly affected by desertification but much of Asia and Latin America's drylands are subject to varying degrees of desertification, as well. Not surprisingly, this results in both direct and indirect economic costs. UNEP estimates that approximately $42 billion dollars of income is foregone each year from lost crops, with the majority of losses occurring in developing countries in Asia and Africa. H. Dregne et al., *A New Assessment of the World Status of Desertification*, 20 DESERTIFICATION CONTROL BULL. 6 (1991). Henry W. Kendall & David Pementel, *Constraints on the Expansion of the Global Food Supply*, 23 AMBIO 198 (1994); UNEP, *Fact Sheet 3: United Nations Convention to Combat Desertification* (1995). R.L. HEATHCOTE, THE ARID LANDS: THEIR USE AND ABUSE 27 (1983); H.E. DREGNE, DESERTIFICATION OF ARID LANDS 11 (1983).

Much uncertainty still surrounds desertification and both the economic and physical estimates cited in the preceding paragraphs are disputed. Neither the geographic distribution nor the severity of desertified lands (usually judged qualitatively) are known with any certainty. Gretchen Daily, *Restoring Value to the World's Degraded Lands*, SCIENCE 350–354, July 21, 1995. The measures to indicate desertification are not straightforward, either. A decline in crop yield might be due to desertification and exhaustion of soil nutrients or, equally, it might be due to poor rainfall, insects, insufficient labor availability, etc. And, to complicate matters further, different studies often use different terms and definitions. A simple fact is clear, though–a single inch of soil can take centuries to build up, but erode and degrade in a matter of a few short years. Despite the debate over which numbers are most accurate, no one doubts the severity and threat of desertification.

In its most dramatic impact, desertification exacerbates famine and creates millions of "environmental refugees," people who are forced to abandon land that can no longer support them. The International Committee of the Red Cross estimates that over half of the global refugee population, more than those fleeing war, are environmental refugees. Not surprisingly, much of Mexico's illegal immigration to the United States, comes from Mexico's driest, most eroded, impoverished areas. <http://ens-news.com/ens/oct2000/2000L-10-20-07.html>. As a tragic example, one-sixth of the population of Niger has been forced to relocate because of desertification. Approximately two to three thousand people each day are displaced. John Madeley, *For Millions Life is a Battle Against the Sand*, MONTREAL GAZETTE, June 26, 1993, at 16; INDEPENDENT COMMISSION ON INTERNATIONAL HUMANITARIAN ISSUES, THE ENCROACHING DESERT 60 (1986). These refugees often migrate to cities to find jobs and social services, adding to the already strong pressures toward urban migration, particularly in developing countries. From 1965 to 1988, the percentage of shepherds in Mauritania plunged from 73% to only 7%. Over the same period, the proportion of the national population living in Nouakchott, the capital city, rose from 9% to 41%. THE CENTRE FOR OUR COMMON FUTURE, DOWN TO EARTH 5 (1995). Such a rapid and uncontrolled urban migration can exacerbate political unrest in crowded and poor cities. Four separate uprisings occurred in the Sahelian urban centers in Northern Nigeria between 1980 and 1985, all triggered by migrants who had been displaced by desertification and drought. UNEP, STATUS OF DESERTIFICATION AND IMPLEMENTATION OF THE UNITED NATIONS PLAN OF ACTION TO COMBAT DESERTIFICATION: REPORT TO THE EXECUTIVE DIRECTOR (1992); E.E. OKPARA & O.A. SALAU, DESERTIFICATION DYNAMICS IN WEST AND NORTH AFRICA (1993).

Desertification also has important environmental consequences. Chief among these is the loss of biodiversity. Crops such as wheat, barley and millet originated in arid and semi-arid lands and many strains grow as indigenous wild plant species. Desertification in these regions may result in the loss of valuable plant species, which translates both into an economic loss and a loss of genetic variability and adaptations that could have been used in the future to supplant crops threatened by disease, pests or climatic changes. These plant species may also supply the critical habitat or be indirectly linked to the survival of other indigenous species. Large-scale desertification can also influence climate change both by reducing the carbon sink (loss of vegetation to fixate carbon dioxide) and increasing the earth's reflectivity (albedo). H. Dregne, *op. cit.*, at 8; *Let Us Not Forget the Reason We Are Here*, ECO, June 13, 1994 at 2; M. Kassas et al., *Desertification and Drought: An Ecological and Economic Analysis*, 20 DESERTIFICATION CONTROL BULL. 19, 22 (1991).

B. THE CAUSES OF DESERTIFICATION

Why has desertification increased so dramatically in recent years? The primary physical factors have been the combination of (1) overcultivation, (2) overgrazing and deforestation, and (3) abandonment and salinization of soil.

Overcultivation occurs when farmers cultivate crops beyond what the land can naturally sustain and deplete the soil of its nutrients. Drylands are particularly susceptible to overcultivation because the amount of water present in the soil is limited and harvested vegetation needs time to recover. As vegetation decreases, topsoil, with fewer roots in the soil, becomes highly vulnerable to wind and water erosion and less able to absorb water. As a result, because the soil is not "anchored" down it is more susceptible to being blown or washed away. Water erosion has important consequences beyond removing valuable topsoil and nutrients, for it may wash away crops, increase sedimentation in reservoirs and rivers, and decrease water quality. Similarly, wind erosion may bury crops, sand-blast plants, and worsen air quality. The subsoil that remains after the topsoil has eroded away is less capable of sustaining vegetation because it has low nutrients and poor water absorption properties. The reduction of available land capable of sustaining vegetation forces the farmers to expand into more marginal lands that are degraded more quickly, thus reinforcing the desertification cycle. ALAN GRAINGER, THE THREATENING DESERT 293 (1990). The UN estimates that, over the past 50 years, the planet has lost an estimated 1.2 billion hectares of topsoil–an area roughly the size of China and India combined. <http://www.un.org/ecosocdev/geninfo/sust-dev/desert.htm>

Similar to overcultivation, *overgrazing* occurs when the number of animals grazed on an area of land exceeds its carrying capacity. The drylands of the world are the site of one-half of the world's cattle, one-third of its sheep, and two-thirds of its goats; these areas are particularly susceptible to overgrazing. Joel Schecter, *New Frontiers in Desert Research,* DESERT DEVELOPMENT 287, 294 (1985). Overgrazing contributes to desertification through loss of vegetation cover from livestock either eating or trampling it. As with overcultivation, the loss of vegetation leads to increased erosion. Furthermore, compaction of the soil by the animals' hooves reduces the soil's ability to absorb water, which also accelerates erosion.

In dryland areas with a shortage of water, poorly planned irrigation projects contribute to desertification. When irrigated land is not properly drained, the salts contained in the irrigation water accumulate in the soil, reducing soil fertility and impairing plant growth. This accumulation of salts in soil, known as *salinization*, is often linked with overcultivation or poor land management.

Underlying these immediate causes are structural and social factors such as population growth, patterns of land ownership, the status of women, international trade flows (e.g. dumping of surplus agricultural produce by developed countries into developing countries), and developing country indebtedness. Disasters such as wars and national emergencies can also add to desertification both directly and indirect from the mass movement of people.

Desertification is self-reinforcing. Those who live in desertified areas are often the very poorest within a country and have little political influence to improve their condition. Poverty at the local level creates pressure on the communities to use inappropriate agricultural techniques or to overexploit the land in order to gain the short-term income and food necessary for survival. Yet these agricultural methods make the land more susceptible to long-term desertification. Increasing population also requires an increase in food production, which may force local communities to exploit land beyond its sustainable level. This is magnified by unequal land distribution, which forces many poor farmers to cultivate fragile areas that are vulnerable to erosion such as steep hillsides and cleared rainforests. Local poverty is thus both a contributor and a result of desertification. PIERS BLAIKIE, THE POLITICAL ECONOMY OF SOIL EROSION IN DEVELOPING COUNTRIES 138 (1985). Michael Renner, *Transforming Security*, in STATE OF THE WORLD 1997, at 119 (1997).

C.   1977 PLAN OF ACTION TO COMBAT DESERTIFICATION

From 1968 to 1974 in the Sahel region in Africa, a six-year drought decreased Lake Chad by one-third its original size resulting in the widespread destruction of vegetation and shrubs. Shallow wells dried up and patches of new desert developed. An estimated 250,000 people in the region died from famine, drought or disease, in addition to millions of domestic animals. As a response to this crisis, the international community turned its attention to the devastating effects of desertification. In December 1974, the United Nations General Assembly adopted a resolution calling for "international action to combat desertification" and a United Nations Conference on Desertification (UNCOD) to achieve this objective.

UNCOD convened in Nairobi, Kenya in September, 1977. Ninety-four countries participated. The conference culminated in the adoption of a non-binding "Plan of Action to Combat Desertification" (PACD), reflecting three fundamental objectives: (1) to prevent and arrest the advance of desertification; (2) to reclaim desertified land for productive use; and (3) to sustain and promote, within ecological limits, the productivity of arid, semi-arid, sub-humid and other areas vulnerable to desertification in order to improve the quality of life of their inhabitants. The PACD called for national and regional actions to combat desertification through an integrated program of land management assessment, the implementation of corrective measures to prevent the degradation of dryland ecosystems, and the strengthening of scientific and technological infrastructures in dryland nations.

William C. Burns, *The International Convention to Combat Desertification: Drawing a Line in the Sand?*, 16 MICH. J. INT'L L. 831, 849–50 (1995).

The original drafters of the Plan of Action to Combat Desertification (PACD) envisioned its complete implementation by the year 2000. The plan called for affected countries to study and monitor desertification, develop national action plans for combating desertification, create insurance funds to compensate people during times of drought, and strengthen scientific and technological research.

The PACD provided a comprehensive list of suggestions but was not legally binding. In addition, the PACD acknowledged the importance of utilizing local knowledge in the preparation of national plans, expanding the role of community organizations, and transferring technologies appropriate for local conditions. This "bottom-up" strategy was innovative for an international agreement but was largely overshadowed by the long list of large-scale technical solutions within the agreement. For example, the PACD recommended that affected areas develop a detailed water management plan with highly technical irrigation schemes.

Overall, the PACD generated some international awareness but was unsuccessful in reversing desertification. Neither affected governments nor donor governments seriously implemented the Plan of Action. Only twenty affected countries ever submitted national action plans and most of those were of poor quality. A. Buanajuti, *External Evaluation of the Plan of Action to Combat Desertification*, 20 DESERTIFICATION CONTROL BULL. 30–31 (1991). In the 1970s, most of the international community appreciated neither the cost nor the complexity of desertification. Most important, the requisite financial support was not provided. At the time the PACD was developed, its proper implementation was estimated to require $4.5 billion annually, of which $2.4 billion was required in the form of aid. Only $600 million was actually provided, and much of this aid was ineffectively applied because the donor countries failed to consult the recipient country's national action plan. Harma A. Diallo, Dealing with Real People, Our Planet: Desertification Issue (1995). Finally, the PACD's focus turned out to be too narrow, focusing on symptoms rather than causes. The PACD provided sound principles to address overcultivation, overgrazing, poor irrigation, and deforestation but failed to address the underlying social and economic factors producing these problems.

By 1992 it was apparent that the PACD had been unable to generate an effective international response to the problem of desertification. Only those countries that had implemented a bottom-up approach were having success in developing effective strategies to combat the effects of desertification. These few successful plans had been implemented with the help of local grass-roots organizations and international NGOs. As a result, the international community's prior strategy of technical solutions was largely replaced by a strategy treating desertification as a local resource management problem that must be addressed locally.

D.   The Convention to Combat Desertification

In preparation for UNCED, many developing countries, led by African countries, insisted that desertification be given priority at the Conference. In response, Chapter 11 of UNCED's blueprint for action, known as *Agenda 21*, set priorities for combating desertification and established both the logistical and financial means for accomplishing these priorities. Agenda 21, U.N. Conference on Environment and Development, U.N. Doc. A/CONF. 151/26 (1992). In addition, participating countries at UNCED agreed to request the UN General Assembly to establish an intergovernmental negotiating committee for a convention on desertification, particularly focusing on the countries of Africa.

On December 22, 1992, the General Assembly established a negotiating committee to develop an international convention to combat desertification. After 13 months of intense negotiations, the *Convention to Combat Desertification in Those Countries Experiencing Serious Drought and/or Desertification, Particularly in Africa*, was adopted on June 17, 1994. 33 I.L.M. 1328 (1994). Known as the "CCD," the Convention became effective December 26, 1996. As of February 2001, 172 countries had ratified the CCD (including the United States).

The CCD differs in a number of important respects from other international environmental agreements. Instead of placing substantive emphasis on State actions, the CCD's focus is on *process* and ensuring popular participation in developing and implementing plans to combat desertification. Hence the dominant feature of the CCD is its reliance on a *"bottom-up"* approach, emphasizing the role of local people and communities. Whereas most international environmental agreements require States to centralize and expand their powers of regulation, the Convention to Combat Desertification requires states to funnel authority and resources *down* to the local land user communities, including local NGOs. The Convention does not create new rules; instead it encourages and creates the mechanisms for the development of new partnerships that link international institutions, States, NGOs, and local communities. KYLE W. DANISH, *International Environmental Law and the "Bottom-up" Approach: a Review of the Desertification Convention*, 3 INDIANA J. OF GLOBAL LEG. STUD. 1 (1995).

The CCD consists of a preamble, forty articles, and four regional implementation annexes (detailing implementation of the treaty in Africa, Asia, Latin America and the Caribbean, and the Northern Mediterranean). The first two principles of the CCD break with tradition. They commit governments to encourage the full participation of local communities in developing and implementing environmental programs, and they reject the one-sided relationship between donor and recipient countries in favor of joint partnership. Articles 3(a), (b). The traditional one-way aid process, often directed from central government institutions onto the local people without adequate consultation, had proven largely ineffective in combating desertification due to misdirected resources, overly-technical or ambitious projects, and lack of commitment at the national level. It was hoped that a collaborative decisionmaking process, involving foreign donors, the affected country, local communities and NGOs, would prove more realistic and effective.

Article 5 details the obligations of affected country parties experiencing desertification. These include, of course, the obligation to give high priority to combating desertification and the effects of drought. Of potentially far greater importance, however, are the commitments to address the underlying socio-economic causes of desertification as well as promoting the participation of women and NGOs in combatting desertification. Article 6 then details the obligations of developed country parties, committing them to provide substantial forms of assistance and technical support to assist the efforts of developing countries and, significantly, "new and additional funding," while giving priority to Africa.

National Action Programs (NAPs) are at the core of the CCD, providing the blueprint to implement the Convention. Unlike the 1977 PACD, which consisted of recommendations for the *content* of action programs, the CCD concentrates on the *process* of developing the programs. Article 9 requires affected country parties to develop and implement NAPs, integrating any existing programs to help ensure success. Article 10 establishes the framework for creating NAPs, relying on "participatory mechanisms." Participants should include representatives of government, local communities and land users and should address the dual goals of combating desertification and eradicating poverty (reflecting the coupling of environment and development at UNCED). NAPs should begin with the development of long-term strategies and priorities for the affected areas. NAPs must also specify the measures to be taken to improve the economic environment of the affected areas. Such measures may include methods to conserve natural resources, drought contingency plans, and improved early warning systems.

Creating comprehensive programs, of course, is not the same thing as implementing them successfully. In order to support the specific actions detailed in the NAPs, Article 19 provides guidance for capacity building. One of the flaws of the 1977 PACD had been its failure to address social factors both driving and ameliorating desertification. Following up on the principle of full participation of local people, Article 19 calls for the explicit promotion of greater participation of women, youth, and NGOs at the local level.

The financing of desertification initiatives is addressed in Articles 20 and 21. The largest source of funds comes from the affected parties themselves. In a concession to developing countries' calls for new and additional funds, the CCD provides that developed country parties will "mobilize substantial financial resources, including grants and concessional loans" as well as "new and additional funding from the Global Environment Facility" to support desertification measures. Article 20(2)(a)-(b). The CCD thus does not establish a new financial mechanism to provide and administer funds. Instead, it emphasizes the need to re-allocate funds from existing sources.

To increase the effectiveness of existing financial sources, the CCD creates a "Global Mechanism" to identify and channel resources to developing country parties. The Mechanism is intended to make desertification funding more effective by coordinating and facilitating disparate aid programs. Activities of the Mechanism include creating an inventory of available multilateral and bilateral aid programs as well as encouraging innovative ways to raise funds and obtain financial assistance. An important challenge for the CCD parties will be to avoid the top-down bloc funding that has characterized most international aid. The CCD recognizes that providing assistance to local people in small packages of grants and loans is preferable to paying for government bureaucracies or consultants, but this requires a different way of doing business. The CCD obliges developing country parties to create National Coordinating Mechanisms to ensure the efficient use and distribution of aid money.

In reading over excerpts of the treaty, below, consider how it differs from hard law, rule-based treaties such as the Basel Convention and framework agreements such as the Vienna Convention on Ozone–Depleting Sustances

United Nations Convention to Combat Desertification in Those Countries Experiencing Serious Drought and/or Desertification, Particularly in Africa (excerpts)

Article 3

Principles

In order to achieve the objective of this Convention and to implement its provisions, the Parties shall be guided, inter alia, by the following:

(a) the Parties should ensure that decisions on the design and implementation of programmes to combat desertification and/or mitigate the effects of drought are taken with the participation of populations and local communities and that an enabling environment is created at higher levels to facilitate action at national and local levels;

(b) the Parties should, in a spirit of international solidarity and partnership, improve cooperation and coordination at subregional, regional and international levels, and better focus financial, human, organizational and technical resources where they are needed;* * *

Article 5

Obligations of affected country Parties

In addition to their obligations pursuant to Article 4 [General obligations], affected country Parties undertake to:

(a) give due priority to combating desertification and mitigating the effects of drought, and allocate adequate resources in accordance with their circumstances and capabilities;

(b) establish strategies and priorities, within the framework of sustainable development plans and/or policies, to combat desertification and mitigate the effects of drought;

(c) address the underlying causes of desertification and pay special attention to the socio-economic factors contributing to desertification processes;

(d) promote awareness and facilitate the participation of local populations, particularly women and youth, with the support of non-governmental organizations, in efforts to combat desertification and mitigate the effects of drought; and

(e) provide an enabling environment by strengthening, as appropriate, relevant existing legislation and, where they do not exist, enacting new laws and establishing long-term policies and action programmes.

Article 6

Obligations of developed country Parties

In addition to their general obligations pursuant to article 4, developed country Parties undertake to:

(a) actively support, as agreed, individually or jointly, the efforts of affected developing country Parties, particularly those in Africa, and the least developed countries, to combat desertification and mitigate the effects of drought;

(b) provide substantial financial resources and other forms of support to assist affected developing country Parties, particularly those in Africa, effectively to develop and implement their own long-term plans and strategies to combat desertification and mitigate the effects of drought;

(c) promote the mobilization of new and additional funding pursuant to article 20, paragraph 2 (b);

(d) encourage the mobilization of funding from the private sector and other non-governmental sources; and

(e) promote and facilitate access by affected country Parties, particularly affected developing country Parties, to appropriate technology, knowledge and know-how.

Article 9

Basic approach

1. In carrying out their obligations pursuant to article 5, affected developing country Parties and any other affected country Party in the framework of its regional implementation annex or, otherwise, that has notified the Permanent Secretariat in writing of its intention to prepare a national action programme, shall, as appropriate, prepare, make public and implement national action programmes, utilizing and building, to the extent possible, on existing relevant successful plans and programmes, and subregional and regional action programmes, as the central element of the strategy to combat desertification and

mitigate the effects of drought. Such programmes shall be updated through a continuing participatory process on the basis of lessons from field action, as well as the results of research. The preparation of national action programmes shall be closely interlinked with other efforts to formulate national policies for sustainable development.* * *

Article 10

National action programmes

1.   The purpose of national action programmes is to identify the factors contributing to desertification and practical measures necessary to combat desertification and mitigate the effects of drought.

2.   National action programmes shall specify the respective roles of government, local communities and land users and the resources available and needed. They shall, inter alia:

(a) incorporate long-term strategies to combat desertification and mitigate the effects of drought, emphasize implementation and be integrated with national policies for sustainable development;

(b) allow for modifications to be made in response to changing circumstances and be sufficiently flexible at the local level to cope with different socio-economic, biological and geo-physical conditions;

(c) give particular attention to the implementation of preventive measures for lands that are not yet degraded or which are only slightly degraded;

(d) enhance national climatological, meteorological and hydrological capabilities and the means to provide for drought early warning;

(e) promote policies and strengthen institutional frameworks which develop cooperation and coordination, in a spirit of partnership, between the donor community, governments at all levels, local populations and community groups, and facilitate access by local populations to appropriate information and technology;

(f) provide for effective participation at the local, national and regional levels of non-governmental organizations and local populations, both women and men, particularly resource users, including farmers and pastoralists and their representative organizations, in policy planning, decision-making, and implementation and review of national action programmes; and

(g) require regular review of, and progress reports on, their implementation. * * *

4.   Taking into account the circumstances and requirements specific to each affected country Party, national action programmes include, as appropriate, inter alia, measures in some or all of the following priority fields as they relate to combating desertification and mitigating the effects of drought in affected areas and to their populations: promotion of alternative livelihoods and improvement of national economic environments with a view to strengthening programmes aimed at the eradication of poverty and at ensuring food security; demographic dynamics; sustainable management of natural resources; sustainable agricultural practices; development and efficient use of various energy sources; institutional and legal frameworks; strengthening of capabilities for assessment and systematic observation, including hydrological and meteorological services, and capacity building, education and public awareness. * * *

Article 19

Capacity building, education and public awareness

1. The Parties recognize the significance of capacity building–that is to say, institution building, training and development of relevant local and national capacities–in efforts to combat desertification and mitigate the effects of drought. They shall promote, as appropriate, capacity-building:

(a) through the full participation at all levels of local people, particularly at the local level, especially women and youth, with the cooperation of non-governmental and local organizations;* * *

Article 20

Financial resources

1. Given the central importance of financing to the achievement of the objective of the Convention, the Parties, taking into account their capabilities, shall make every effort to ensure that adequate financial resources are available for programmes to combat desertification and mitigate the effects of drought.

2. In this connection, developed country Parties, while giving priority to affected African country Parties without neglecting affected developing country Parties in other regions ... undertake to:

(a) mobilize substantial financial resources, including grants and concessional loans, in order to support the implementation of programmes to combat desertification and mitigate the effects of drought;

(b) promote the mobilization of adequate, timely and predictable financial resources, including new and additional funding from the Global Environment Facility of the agreed incremental costs of those activities concerning desertification that relate to its four focal areas, in conformity with the relevant provisions of the Instrument establishing the Global Environment Facility;

(c) facilitate through international cooperation the transfer of technology, knowledge and know-how; and

(d) explore, in cooperation with affected developing country Parties, innovative methods and incentives for mobilizing and channelling resources, including those of foundations, non-governmental organizations and other private sector entities, particularly debt swaps and other innovative means which increase financing by reducing the external debt burden of affected developing country Parties, particularly those in Africa.

3. Affected developing country Parties, taking into account their capabilities, undertake to mobilize adequate financial resources for the implementation of their national action programmes.* * *

Article 21

Financial mechanisms

1. The Conference of the Parties shall promote the availability of financial mechanisms and shall encourage such mechanisms to seek to maximize the availability of funding for affected developing country Parties, particularly those in Africa, to implement the Convention.* * *

3. Affected developing country Parties shall utilize, and where necessary, establish and/or strengthen, national coordinating mechanisms, integrated in national development programmes, that would ensure the efficient use of all available financial resources. They shall also utilize participatory processes

involving non-governmental organizations, local groups and the private sector, in raising funds, in elaborating as well as implementing programmes and in assuring access to funding by groups at the local level. These actions can be enhanced by improved coordination and flexible programming on the part of those providing assistance.

4. In order to increase the effectiveness and efficiency of existing financial mechanisms, a Global Mechanism to promote actions leading to the mobilization and channelling of substantial financial resources, including for the transfer of technology, on a grant basis, and/or on concessional or other terms, to affected developing country Parties, is hereby established. This Global Mechanism shall function under the authority and guidance of the Conference of the Parties and be accountable to it. * * *

QUESTIONS AND DISCUSSION

1. *Working the Treaty*

   - In what ways do the obligations of Parties differ between developed countries and affected countries?

   - What financial requirements are imposed on developed countries? Are these requirements required or merely encouraged?

   - In addition to State parties, what other institutions and individuals does the treaty seek to involve?

   - You have been charged with ensuring your country's compliance with the provisions regarding National Action Programs. Briefly describe your obligations.

2. The most recent comprehensive mapping of global agriculture, carried out by the International Food Policy Research Institute (IFPRI), concluded that nearly 40 percent of the world's agricultural land is seriously degraded. Desertification has already had significant impacts on the productivity of about 16% of the globe's agricultural land, with 75% of crop land in Central America seriously degraded, 20% in Africa, and 11 percent in Asia. PER PINSTRUP-ANDERSEN ET AL., WORLD FOOD PROSPECTS: CRITICAL ISSUES FOR THE EARLY TWENTY-FIRST CENTURY (1999). This is occurring, however, at a time of growing population (with an estimated 1.5 billion more people in 20 years), declining increases in agricultural yields (the levelling off of the green revolution) and a decrease in the addition of new agricultural lands. Put simply, unless we can reverse the impacts of desertification, how will we feed the world?

3. *Role of Women.* An underlying assumption for effective implementation of many of the commitments stemming from the Rio Conference is the importance of involving local women. Both the Rio Declaration and the Convention to Combat Desertification recognize the critical role women play in land management in developing nations. Principle 20 of the Rio Declaration declares: "Women have a vital role in environmental management and development. Their full participation is therefore essential to achieve sustainable development." The Preamble of the Convention to Combat Desertification similarly recognizes: "the important role played by women in regions affected by desertification and/or drought, particularly in rural areas of developing countries, and the importance of ensuring full participation of both men and women at all levels in programmes to combat desertification and mitigate the effects of drought ... " Women play a predominant role as land managers in the production of food crops, producing over ninety percent of the crops in Africa, are responsible for a large portion of animal husbandry, and collect

the vast majority of fuelwood. *See* chart below, WORLD RESOURCES INSTITUTE, WORLD RESOURCES 43, 46 (1994). Nonetheless, many nations do not recognize the valuable role of women in preventing environmental degradation, denying them security of land ownership, access to credit, and education. How does the CCD address this culturally sensitive yet critically important issue?

Gender Labor Division in Africa, Early 1980s

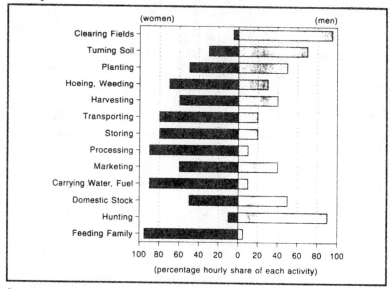

Source: Food and Agriculture Organization of the United Nations and Swedish International Development Authority (FAO/SIDA), *Restoring the Balance: Women and Forest Resource* (FAO/SIDA, Rome, 1988), p. 21.

4. To those countries affected by desertification, the CCD fell short of expectations. Developing countries were disappointed that donor Parties did not commit more clearly to increase technical assistance or to new and additional financing for anti-desertification projects. While any Party may voluntarily provide additional financial resources, the primary source of funding is expected to come from the Global Environment Facility (GEF). As described in Chapter 20, the GEF was established as a pilot program in 1991 under the direction of the UNDP, the World Bank, and UNEP. Its purpose is to grant concessional funding to developing nations to assist them in the implementation of environmental protection programs in four categories: 1) protection of the ozone layer, 2) limitation of greenhouse gas emissions, 3) protection of biodiversity, and 4) protection of international waters. Activities concerning land degradation and deforestation are eligible for funding from the GEF. It remains to be seen whether the GEF will provide adequate funding to implement the CCD in developing countries. As of June 2000, the GEF's portfolio was only roughly $2 billion (including co-financed projects), compared to UNEP estimates of the $10–22 billion needed annually for an effective anti-desertification program. Burns, *op. cit.*, at 831, 865. GEF funding proved an important topic at the Fourth Conference of Parties, in 2001, where nearly 2000 representatives from 172 countries agreed on the need for further study to determine how best to obtain additional GEF funding. Verena Schmitt–Roschmann, *Desertification: COP–4 on Desertification Focuses on Bigger Role for GEF in Funding Programs*, BNA–IED, Jan. 19, 2001.

Analysts estimate that while 18 developed or oil producing countries have sufficient wealth to address their domestic desertification problems, 81 developing countries do not and will need to rely on foreign aid. Indeed the developing countries hardest hit by desertification are also the poorest countries in the world, with weak economies, endemic poverty and growing foreign debts. Attracting private capital to rehabilitate desertified lands has proven difficult because such projects generally do not generate high return on capital.

The CCD requires affected developing countries to allocate adequate resources, given their circumstances and capabilities. Developed countries are to provide substantial financial resources and other forms of support, including grants and concessional loans and new and additional resources from the GEF. Read the text of Article 20 (a)-(d). Do you think developed countries must provide additional funds to desertification projects or can they comply by providing no new additional funds but, rather, re-allocating existing GEF funds so that more goes to desertification projects?

5. The CCD Annexes for Africa, Asia, Latin America and the Caribbean, and the Northern Mediterranean are quite far-reaching in their requirements. Article 8 of the Annex for Africa, for example, requires National Action Programs to consider a wide range of issues, as appropriate, including the following:

(a) measures to improve the economic environment with a view to eradicating poverty:

(i) increasing incomes and employment opportunities, especially for the poorest members of the community, by:

– developing markets for farm and livestock products;

– creating financial instruments suited to local needs;

– encouraging diversification in agriculture and the setting-up of agricultural enterprises; and

– developing economic activities of a para-agricultural or non-agricultural type;

(ii) improving the long-term prospects of rural economies by the creation of:

– incentives for productive investment and access to the means of production; and

– price and tax policies and commercial practices that promote growth;

(iii) defining and applying population and migration policies to reduce population pressure on land; and

(iv) promoting the use of drought resistant crops and the application of integrated dry-land farming systems for food security purposes; * * *

(b) measures to conserve natural resources:

ensuring the development and efficient use of diverse energy sources, the promotion of alternative sources of energy, particularly solar energy, wind energy and bio-gas, and specific arrangements for the transfer, acquisition and adaptation of relevant technology to alleviate the pressure on fragile natural resources;

(c) measures to improve institutional organization:

(i) defining the roles and responsibilities of central government and local authorities within the framework of a land use planning policy;

(ii) encouraging a policy of active decentralization, devolving responsibility for management and decision-making to local authorities, and encouraging initiatives and the assumption of responsibility by local communities and the establishment of local structures; and

(iii) adjusting, as appropriate, the institutional and regulatory framework of natural resource management to provide security of land tenure for local populations;

Do you think this "recipe" for combatting desertification will be effective? Instituting any number of these recommendations will prove politically challenging, particularly the decentralization of central government authority and population policies. These changes will also necessitate up-front costs. What role do donors and non-affected Parties play in implementing these annexes? Do these policy prescriptions pose potential conflicts with the WTO requirement to treat foreign goods and investors equally? That is, can countries build and protect diversified local agriculture, as called for in Article 8, while at the same time modernizing their economy by opening up their agricultural markets to international trade?

6. Many of the parties submitted their National Action Plans in 2000. You can view these (as well as Sub-regional Action Plans) on the web at <http://www.unccd.int/actionprogrammes/menu.php>. Read one of these plans carefully. Does it present a list of actions that can be easily implemented, create a program structure, and/or summarize the state of desertification in the country? Do you think the process in creating the plan involved grassroots consultations? Do you think the report was written locally or by an outside consultant?

7. Desertification is a regional problem affecting many of the world's arid regions. Yet it seems quite different than depletion of the ozone layer or global warming in which *all* countries of the world clearly are affected and have an interest. What incentives do non-affected country Parties have in ensuring that the CCD is implemented? In other words, why is a global convention on desertification a more appropriate international strategy than reliance on solely regional accords? Does this explain the detailed regional annexes? Does protection of fresh water warrant the same type of global framework convention with regional annexes?

8. A major obstacle in addressing the problems of desertification has been the lack of a common definition of the problem. Indeed over 100 definitions of desertification have appeared in the literature with no common understanding of what the process actually involves. Michael Glantz & Nicolai Orlovsky, *Desertification: A Review of the Concept*, DESERTIFICATION CONTROL BULL. No. 9 (1983). For example, the 1977 UNCOD offered the following definition:

Desertification is the diminution or destruction of the biological potential of the land, and can lead ultimately to desert-like conditions. It is an aspect of the widespread deterioration of ecosystems, and has diminished or destroyed the biological potential, i.e. plant and animal production, for multiple use purposes at a time when increased productivity is needed to support growing populations in the quest of development.

The UN's Food and Agricultural Organization revised the definition in 1983:

Desertification is defined as a comprehensive expression of economic and social processes as well as those natural or induced ones which destroy the equilibrium of soil, vegetation, air, and water, in the areas subject to edaphic and/or climatic aridity. Continued deterioration leads to a decrease in, or destruction of, the biological potential of the land, deterioration of living conditions and an increase of desert landscapes.

FAO/UNEP, PROVISIONAL METHODOLOGY FOR ASSESSMENT AND MAPPING OF DESERTIFICATION (1983). In 1991 UNEP adopted the following definition:

> Desertification/land degradation, in the context of assessment, is land degradation in arid, semi-arid and dry sub-humid areas resulting from adverse human impact. Land in this concept includes soil and local water resources, land surface and vegetation and crops. Degradation implies reduction of resource potential by one or a combination of processes acting on the land. These processes include water erosion, wind erosion and sedimentation by those agents, long-term reduction in the amount or diversity of natural vegetation, where relevant, and salinization and sodication.

UNEP, STATUS OF DESERTIFICATION AND IMPLEMENTATION OF THE UNITED NATIONS PLAN OF ACTION TO COMBAT DESERTIFICATION (1991). The final UNCED definition, approved by *Agenda 21* and adopted by the CCD, reads:

> Desertification means land degradation in arid, semi-arid and dry sub-humid areas resulting from various factors, including climatic variations and human activities.

CCD, Article 1(a). Definitions like these from international bodies and in international agreements are the result of careful and lengthy negotiation by diplomats. A skilled negotiator will assess each word combination for its implication not only to the problem at hand but to future situations, as well. In comparing the various definitions, why do you think they changed over time? What were the concerns behind each definition? Why do you think the final definition was so much shorter than its predecessors?

Since the term, "desertification," means so many different things to different audiences, in the technical literature the terms of the debate have started shifting away from "combatting desertification" to more precise language such as "improving natural resource management in dryland regions." This specificity of language focuses attention on the basic point that land and water in dryland regions are, ultimately, resources that must be managed responsibly to avoid problems of desertification. CAMILLA TOULMIN, COMBATTING DESERTIFICATION: SETTING THE AGENDA FOR A GLOBAL CONVENTION 5?6 (1993).

9. The Homepage of the Desertification Convention Secretariat is at <http://www.unccd.ch/>.

III.   International Environmental Law and Other Legal Regimes

CHAPTER FIFTEEN

Environmental Law and International Trade

The 1990s have witnessed an almost blinding pace of international economic activity around the planet. In 1999, world exports of goods and commercial services topped $5.5 trillion and $1.3 trillion, respectively. Capital flows have also seen a spectacular increase. Private capital flows from developed to developing countries–including both foreign direct investment and speculative capital–increased five-fold from $48 billion to $244 billion between 1990 and 1996. This rapid growth has been driven in large part by international efforts to remove barriers to the flow of goods, services, and capital. The growing economic interdependency among nations created by such liberalization has important consequences for the relationship between the global economy and the global environment.

In this chapter we examine the relationship between international trade and investment, on the one hand, and the environment on the other. Section I reviews the "trade and environment debate," examining the arguments for and against international trade, and why the debate is so complex and multifaceted. Section II focuses on the institutional framework governing global trade, particularly the World Trade Organization (WTO) and its General Agreement on Tariffs and Trade (GATT), an institution whose expressed goal is facilitating the unimpeded flow of goods, services, and, to a lesser extent, capital among nations. Section III examines regional trade institutions in the Americas, focusing primarily on the North American Free Trade Agreement (NAFTA). Section IV addresses trade institutions in Europe–the European Union–and in Asia–the Asia Pacific Economic Cooperation (APEC). Section V examines the environmental impact of foreign investment.

SECTION I.   THE TRADE AND ENVIRONMENT DEBATE

In this section we present the main arguments for and against liberalized or "free" trade in the context of sustainable development and some of the reasons why the debate is so complicated. Over the last decade, the influence of trade institutions on the global economy has steadily increased. As you read this section and those that follow, consider whether the regional and international trade systems support sustainable development and, if not, how their rules should evolve to do so.

A.   ARGUMENTS *FOR* LIBERALIZED INTERNATIONAL TRADE

International trade has fueled much of the economic growth in the developed world during this century, particularly following the implementation of global financial and trade reforms after World War II. More recently, trade advocates have argued that liberalized trade (i.e., reducing trade barriers) promotes sustainable development. As discussed below, the arguments supporting this claim fall into four main categories: (1) trade liberalization enhances geopolitical stability by binding nations' economies together and reducing the chance of armed conflict; (2) trade promotes efficient use of the world's scarce resources and allows more to be produced from less; (3) trade promotes wealth maximization and poverty alleviation through economic growth which, in turn, may eventually increase demand and capacity for environmental protection and clean up; and (4) trade enhances communication and sharing of knowledge and technologies.

------

1.   GEOPOLITICAL STABILITY

While most discussions over liberalized trade focus on economic growth and wealth creation, this should not obscure perhaps the key motivating factor behind our most important trade agreements. Liberalized trade serves an important political purpose–countries that are economically interdependent share greater common interests and are less likely to resolve differences through armed conflict. This was a key motivation, for example, behind the creation of the European Community in the aftermath of World War II. Conflict between Germany and France had served as the flashpoint for both World Wars. The founders of the European Community hoped that forging closer economic links between the two countries (at the outset through common steel and coal markets) would make future armed conflict less likely. The same geopolitical motivation underpinned the founding of the GATT, as well. And, if one looks back over the last 50 years, conflicts between former enemies such as France and Germany, the United States and Japan, have been resolved peacefully as these nations have forged ever stronger economic ties.

2.   EFFICIENT USE OF SCARCE RESOURCES

Free trade promotes the efficient use of the world's scarce resources in three ways. First, liberalized trade encourages nations to specialize the production of goods and services, thereby ensuring that goods and services are produced most efficiently. The theoretical underpinnings of this argument, known as the theory of "comparative advantage," derive from the work of the nineteenth century economist David Ricardo who stated:

> Under a system of perfectly free [international] commerce, each country naturally devotes its capital and labor to such employments as are most beneficial to each. This pursuit of individual advantage is admirably connected with the universal good of the whole. By stimulating industry, by rewarding ingenuity, and by using most efficaciously the peculiar powers bestowed by nature, it distributes labor most effectively and most economically: while, by increasing the general mass of productions, it diffuses general benefits. . . .

DAVID RICARDO, THE PRINCIPLES OF POLITICAL ECONOMY AND TAXATION 81 (1817).

The argument underlying Ricardo's theory of comparative advantage is that each nation will specialize in and export those goods which it produces more efficiently relative to other nations. The gains in specialization are realized through trade, which ensures that the strengths of each nation result in maximum productivity for all. The force of Ricardo's theory derives from his theoretical proof that, in a world of two countries and two goods, specialization and trade can benefit both countries even where one country produces *both* goods more efficiently than the other. In simple terms, the argument is that increased global trade is desirable because a rising tide lifts all boats.

Second, the benefits of specialization may be further enhanced by "economies of scale." As the name suggests, "economies of scale" allow goods to be produced more economically when the scale of their production is increased. Economies realized in the acquisition and use of inputs, in production processes, and in waste disposal and recycling may allow more efficient production when goods are produced in larger quantities. By giving producers access to larger markets, international trade allows production to occur at a volume at which economies of scale are maximized.

Third, exposing domestic companies to the discipline of international competition forces them to innovate, to upgrade and to anticipate demand. Global competition provides a powerful catalyst for improvements in efficiency at all levels of production. The resulting efficiencies and cost-savings benefits consumers by providing them with greater choice at lower prices.

3.   WEALTH CREATION

It is also argued that the economic growth and wealth generated by trade, particularly in developing countries, is an essential first step towards generating both the political demand and capacity for environmental protection. If demand for a better environment is "income-elastic" (that is, it increases when income increases) then rising incomes create more wealth for environmental protection, pollution control and remedial clean-up. The WTO Secretariat argues, for example, that:

> Further liberalization of international trade flows, both in goods and services, has a key role to play in advancing economic policy objectives in Member countries. In that respect, WTO Member countries have already made an important contribution to sustainable development and better environmental protection worldwide through the conclusion of the Uruguay Round negotiations. This contribution will steadily increase as the results of the Round move towards full implementation. The UNCED also recognized an open, non-discriminatory trading system to be a prerequisite for effective action to protect the environment and to generate sustainable development. This is based on the perspective that countries, particularly developing countries, are dependent on trade as the main source of continued growth and prosperity.

<http://www.wto.org/wto/environ/tradelib.htm>.

This argument is consistent with the "Kuznets curve" argument, described in Chapter 2 at page 55, and with the "convergence hypothesis," which suggests that increased trade will promote development in poor countries, allowing them to close the income gap with richer countries.

4. DISSEMINATION OF INFORMATION AND TECHNOLOGY

Free trade increases commercial transactions among different nations and cultures, and this should stimulate sharing of experiences, policies, and ideas, which in turn should stimulate more rapid diffusion of technological developments. The most politically repressive regimes have traditionally operated in closed trading blocs. In addition, by removing tariff barriers countries may enhance the inflow of new products and technologies. Put another way, free trade can stimulate the free exchange of ideas such as democracy and environmentalism, and may help provide the tools necessary to convert these ideas into reality. *See, e.g.,* Kevin Gallagher's discussion of NAFTA effects, *infra.*

––––––––

QUESTIONS AND DISCUSSION

1. Recall that in Chapter 3 we discussed a number of definitions of sustainable development and noted that the concept is still not well defined. Now read the WTO Secretariat's statement about the relationship between trade and sustainable development carefully. What assumptions does it make about the relationship between trade, domestic economic policy and sustainable development? What about the role of growth in sustainable development? How do these assumptions compare with those of ecological economists such as Daly and Goodland?

2. While increased trade may promote efficient use of scarce resources and create wealth, increasing per capita income does not automatically lead to environmental improvement across the board. *See* William Harbaugh et al., *Reexamining the Empirical Evidence for an Environmental Kuznets Curve,* NBER WORKING PAPER NO. W7711 (May 2000). Historically, it has led to greater consumption, as evidenced in the United States, Europe, and Japan.

Moreover, while per capita wealth may be increasing, the distribution of the wealth may not be equitable. In countries with a powerful and small elite class, the benefits of trade may flow to the very few. The gap between the richest and poorest nations has been increasing, not decreasing. According to the UN Human Development Report, in 1960 the income gap between the fifth of the world's people living in the poorest countries and the fifth living in the richest countries was 30 to 1. In 1990 the gap had widened to 60 to 1. And by 1998 it was 74 to 1. UN HUMAN DEVELOPMENT REPORT 28 (1999). Note, as well, that this coincides with a steady increase in trade.

3. The WTO secretariat argues that in further liberalizing trade, Member countries have made an important contribution to better environmental protection worldwide. In certain situations, trade may be more beneficial to the environment than self sufficiency or protectionism. The noted international trade scholar Jagdish Bhagwati cites the following two examples of environmental harm caused by protectionism:

> The 1991 GATT Report on *Trade and the Environment* ... shows how agricultural protection shifts agricultural production from efficient producers in low-income countries to inefficient producers in high-income countries. In turn, this is likely to cause more environmental damage because of the greater use of chemical fertilizers and pesticides in the richer countries. * * *

> Another example comes from automobile protection in the rich countries. It is well known that the exports of automobiles from Japan have been restrained during the 1980s by the imposition of voluntary export restraints by the United States and the European Community (EC). Research ... has shown that these restraints shifted the composition of Japanese exports to the United States from small to large cars. The larger cars, in turn, were fuel-inefficient compared to the smaller cars. Thus the net result may well have been that while protection reduced the overall purchases of cars, the shift to larger cars resulted in more carbon dioxide in the air rather than less. Free trade in cars may well have been the better environmental policy.

Jagdish Bhagwati, *Trade and the Environment: The False Conflict?*, in TRADE AND THE ENVIRONMENT: LAW, ECONOMICS AND POLICY 163–164 (Durwood Zaelke, et al., eds 1993). These examples demonstrate two ways in which environmental benefits may accrue from trade. One is by favoring countries with less harmful production methods. The other is by promoting use of products which themselves have lower environmental impacts. The distinction between production methods and products is an important part of the trade/environment debate. This is discussed in more detail below in the section on PPMs (processes and production methods) where we address the concern that international trade may actually favor countries with *more* environmentally harmful production methods. To what extent can we generalize Bhagwati's examples? Can you think of others to show that trade promotes environmental protection? What about counter-examples?

4. Trade may facilitate the sale and transfer of technology to improve efficiency and reduce the environmental effects of economic development. To what extent do you think technological advances can offset the effects of increased consumption promoted by international trade? How might your conclusions relate to the views of technological "optimists" and technological "pessimists" as described in Chapter 2?

5. The premise that liberalized trade promotes efficiency by encouraging international specialization, by realizing economies of scale, and by exposing firms to the disciplines of international competition does not in and of itself ensure sustainability. As Herman Daly describes it: "Optimal *allocation* of a given scale of resource flow within the economy is one thing (a microeconomic problem). Optimal *scale* of the whole economy relative to the ecosystem is an entirely different problem (a macro-economic problem)." Herman E. Daly, *Elements of Environmental Macroeconomics*, Ecological Economics 35 (1991); see also Chapter 1, pages 28–30. How can we ensure that international trade does not promote activity at levels beyond the planet's carrying capacity? Clearly, the poorest developing countries need economic growth to provide them with resources and foreign exchange to fight poverty, disease and the destruction of marginal environmental areas. Is this true of industrialized countries? Should the international trade system differentiate between these groups of countries to ensure that we operate at a sustainable scale? How might the principle of "common but differentiated responsibility" described in Chapter 7 be applied to the international trade system?

6. The traditional understanding of comparative advantage is that a resource-rich country might specialize in resource extraction while a country with rich soil would specialize in agriculture. How might different environmental standards be an example of comparative advantage? Consider the example of emission standards in an island country with strong winds that blow out to sea compared to a mountainous country where an inversion layer traps air in populated valleys.

B. ARGUMENTS *AGAINST* LIBERALIZED TRADE

To some, free trade is a paramount value in international relations. To others it is a threat against competing and equally important values. Despite the wealth maximizing effect of free trade and comparative advantage, there are a number of arguments that suggest unconstrained trade liberalization without appropriate safeguards will not maximize human welfare or approach sustainable development.

A major criticism of traditional trade theory is that it defines what is desirable in purely economic terms. As noted in Chapter 3, human well-being is dependent on more than monetary wealth. After basic physical needs have been met, our well-being is affected by relations of kinship, citizenship and our concrete experiences as a "person in community." These "intangibles" are an integral part of our humanity and cannot easily be valued in the marketplace of economic exchange–sometimes we may wish to opt for local solidarity over the opportunity to purchase cheaper imported products. In the following section we briefly outline three traditional concerns about unconstrained international trade–its effect on the pursuit of social and environmental goals, its impacts on environmental regulation, and its relationship to national sovereignty and defence. Finally we include an article by Herman Daly that examines trade in light of the principles of ecological economics described in Chapter 3.

1. ENVIRONMENTALLY DESTRUCTIVE GROWTH

The simplest criticism against increased trade is from an anti-growth or anti-globalization perspective. Current models of development have proven environmentally destructive, the argument goes, and because free trade will by definition increase commerce and development, increased trade will lead to further environmental degradation. Until we shift from a model of growth to one of development, trade liberalization should be opposed. This argument can take much more sophisticated forms but it is, at its core, a position against current forms of economic development and the institutions that promote such development.

2. THREATS TO DOMESTIC SOCIAL PREFERENCES

Trade is often seen as a threat to a country's ability to choose worthwhile domestic goals—be they high levels of environmental protection, food security or an agrarian lifestyle, or support to certain domestic industries. Attaining these non-economic goals may require a willingness to forgo some of the economic benefits of free trade. A country may choose to levy tariffs on certain agricultural products to promote self-sufficiency in food or to prevent more efficient foreign producers from underselling domestic small family farmers. Alternatively, a society may want to establish a certain industry, but feel that tariff protections are required to ensure that the fledgling industry becomes sufficiently established to compete internationally.

Trade liberalization may affect social, environment and development priorities in a number of ways. It may change the pattern or nature of economic activity. It may increase trade in dangerous products such as hazardous waste or toxic chemicals that may threaten the environment in an importing country. Trade liberalization will also cause structural shifts between sectors as resources flow to the production of those products for which there is a comparative advantage. Naturally, within a given domestic economy, there will be some winners and some losers, but the lesson of comparative advantage is that in the aggregate, the domestic economy will be better off. Nevertheless, a society may be hesitant to allow certain sectors of the domestic economy to suffer severe setbacks even though on balance the economy might gain; the nature, as well as the scale and pace of economic change is important. Protecting the small family farmers, for example, may be a central social goal of the government. This phenomenon has been called the "conservative social welfare function," and it underlies many countries' tendency toward protectionist measures. A related critique of free trade is that the model of comparative advantage assumes limited international capital mobility, and that capital readjusts domestically to the most profitable activity, rather than flowing abroad. Yet this assumption is no longer valid in the modern international economy as capital is highly mobile.

The human rights and labor communities have also expressed concern about the impact of trade liberalization. Recent statements by the UN Sub–Commission on the Promotion and Protection of Human Rights, for example, have urged governments and international economic bodies, including the WTO, to take human rights fully into account. They have also expressed concern about the human rights implications of liberalization of trade in agricultural products, especially the right to food for members of vulnerable communities, and identified the need to clarify certain trade provisions to ensure that they do not contradict States' binding human rights obligations. *See, e.g.* Sub–Commission Resolution 1999/30 (E/CN.4/SUB.2/RES/1999/30). Reports by human rights experts have noted the need to maintain "human rights as the primary objective of international trade, investment and finance policy and practice". Caroline Dommen, *Raising Human Rights Concerns in the World Trade Organisation: Actors, Process-*

es and Possible Strategies, 24 HUMAN RIGHTS Q. No. 1, (forthcoming February 2002).

—————

3. PRESSURE TO LOWER EXISTING ENVIRONMENTAL STANDARDS AND CHILL NEW STANDARDS

Similarly, the citizens of a country may want high levels of environmental protection, and fear that liberalized trade will cause a "race to the bottom" as countries relax or fail to enforce environmental standards in an attempt to gain market share. In response to foreign competition, it is feared, domestic producers will lobby for lower standards to maintain competitiveness in the global market and may even threaten to relocate to countries with lower environmental standards. Richard Revesz describes this phenomenon as "a race from the desirable levels of environmental quality that states would pursue if they did not face competition for industry to the increasingly undesirable levels that they choose in the face of such competition." Richard Revesz, *Rehabilitating Interstate Competition*, 67 N.Y.U. L. REV. 1210, 1210.

There has been a vigorous debate over the extent to which a race-to-the-bottom actually occurs. *See, e.g.,* Kirsten Engel, *State Environmental Standard–Setting: Is There a "Race" and Is It "To the Bottom"?*, 48 HASTINGS L.J. 271, 275 (1997). But even if the race-to-the-bottom does not directly drive down standards, it can still result in "chilling" the development of new environmental law. Governments may be fearful of strengthening environmental standards if doing so harms local industries, i.e., by providing foreign producers with lower environmental standards a cost advantage. Indeed, a standard industry criticism of strict environmental regulation is that it will "give away markets" to foreign firms operating in countries with less stringent environmental laws. Arguing that the cost savings from low foreign environmental standards amount to a de facto subsidy, some commentators assert that countervailing duties should be levied by the importing country to "level the playing field." Perhaps most important, as we shall see in the WTO section, environmentalists fear that international trade bodies may actually strike down national environmental regulations as protectionist trade barriers. *See generally,* Daniel Esty and Damien Geradin, *Market Access, Competitiveness, and Harmonization: Environmental Protection in Regional Trade Agreements*, 21 HARV. ENV. L. REV. 265, 265–73 (1997).

—————

4. PROTECTING NATIONAL DEFENSE AND SOVEREIGNTY

National defense is often advanced as a justification for opposing free trade policies. For example, a country may want to preserve its capacity to build airplanes or ships or to develop certain kinds of domestic infrastructure. A variation on this objection is that unfettered free trade increases reliance on external producers and leads to a loss of sovereignty by placing external powers in a position to influence domestic policy. For instance, nations commonly use economic leverage to try to influence essentially domestic conditions in a particular country–the anti-apartheid boycott of South Africa or the U.S. economic embargo of Cuba, for instance. This cuts both ways, of course, for trade measures can also be used to strengthen the environmental practices of countries. *See* Chapter 19 for a discussion of extraterritorial application of domestic laws.

———

5.   INEQUITABLE DISTRIBUTION OF WEALTH AND UNSUSTAINABLE ECOLOGICAL SCALE

As noted in Chapter 2, continued economic growth is widening the gap between the rich and poor, and the resulting throughput of material resources is unsustainable at the present scale. In the following excerpt Herman Daly examines whether liberalized trade promotes efficient allocation, equitable distribution and sustainable ecological scale. He argues that the goal of economic systems should be qualitative development instead of quantitative growth and that the international political "default" position ought to be domestic production for domestic consumption, with restricted trade as a backup position.

Herman E. Daly, *Problems with Free Trade: Neoclassical and Steady-state Perspectives,* in Zaelke et al., ed., TRADE AND THE ENVIRONMENT: LAW, ECONOMICS AND POLICY 147–152, 155–157 (1993)

No policy prescription commands greater consensus among economists than that of "free trade based on international specialization according to comparative advantage." Free trade has long been the "default position," presumed good unless proven otherwise in specific cases. This presumption should be reversed. The default position should be in favor of domestic production for domestic markets, with balanced (not deregulated) international trade, as a fall back alternative when domestic production is too inconvenient.

Three classes of argument are offered in support of this view. They correspond to the three basic goals of all economic policy: efficient allocation, just distribution, and sustainable scale. The first two are traditional goals of neoclassical economics; the third is newly recognized and is associated with the viewpoint of steady-state economics. Sustainable scale means that the scale (population times resource use per capita, or total resource throughput) of the economy relative to the containing ecosystem must be biophysically sustainable. In other words, the input of raw materials and energy must be within the regenerative capacity, and the output of waste materials and energy must be within the absorptive capacity, of the ecosystem. * * *

A clear conflict exists if a nation follows a domestic policy of internalization of external costs into prices, and, simultaneously, an international policy of free trade with countries that do not internalize their external costs into their prices. The cost-internalizing country should be allowed to employ a tariff to compensate for the higher cost–not to protect an inefficient industry, but to protect an efficient national policy against standards-lowering competition. This does not imply the imposition of one country's environmental preferences or moral judgments on another country. Each country sets the rules of cost internalization in its own market. Whoever sells in another nation's market must play by that nation's rules of cost internalization, or pay a tariff sufficient to remove the competitive advantage of lower standards as a price of admission to that market. * * *

Competition can reduce prices in two ways: by increasing efficiency, or by lowering standards. The lower standards refer to the failure to internalize social and environmental costs. Costs to the firm are reduced by low pollution control standards, low worker safety standards, low wages and standard of living for workers, and, among others, low health care standards. Free trade is not enough to avoid standards-lowering competition. Attaining cheapness by ignoring or externalizing real costs is a sin against efficiency. Even the General Agreement on Tariffs and Trade (GATT) makes an exception for prison labor, recognizing that requiring citizens of one country to compete against foreign prison labor is carrying standards-lowering competition too far. However, no similar exception is made for child labor, uninsured risky labor, or subsistence wage labor. Protection of a truly inefficient industry against competition from a truly more efficient foreign competitor–what is usually meant by "protection"– is very different from protecting an efficient national policy of full cost pricing against standards-lowering competition from nations that, for whatever reason, have lower standards of living for workers, and lower environmental, safety, and health care standards.

Standards-lowering competition exists within, as well as between, nations. Profit-maximizing firms in competition always have an incentive to externalize costs to the degree they can get away with it. Within nations there is a large legal, administrative, and auditing structure designed precisely to keep costs from being externalized, that is, social and environmental standards from being lowered. But there is no analogous body of law and administration internationally. There are only national laws, and they differ widely. If firms are allowed to produce under the most permissive standards and sell their product without penalty in countries with higher standards, they succeed in externalizing costs and bringing pressure to bear on the high-standards country to lower its standards-in effect "imposing" their lower standards.* * *

Only if capital cannot cross national boundaries in pursuit of absolute advantage is there any reason for it to follow the logic of comparative advantage in its allocation within the nation. Once capital is mobile internationally, as it certainly is today, then all the comforting assurances of comparative advantage are irrelevant. Furthermore, the tendency to wage equalization becomes much stronger when freely mobile capital is added to the free flow of goods. When capital flows abroad, there is no longer the same opportunity for new employment domestically as there was when capital remained at home and specialized according to international comparative advantage. Capital now leaves the country, and national labor has fewer employment opportunities. It is worth remembering that the vast majority of citizens are wage earners. Even if free trade and capital mobility raise wages in low-wage countries, and that tendency could be thwarted by overpopulation and rapid population growth in low-wage countries, they do so at the expense of labor and to the benefit of capital in the high-wage countries, thus increasing income inequality in the high-wage countries.* * *

The answer often given to the allocation and distribution problems raised above is that growth will take care of them. The allocation problem of standards-lowering competition will be dealt with by harmonizing all standards upward. The distribution problem of falling wages in high-wage countries will be only temporary. The neoclassical faith is that growth will eventually raise world wages to the former high-wage level and beyond. The third goal, sustainable scale of total resource use, forces us to ask what will happen if the entire population of the earth consumes resources at the rate associated with current real wages in high-wage countries. This question is central to the steady-state paradigm, but remains unasked in the neoclassical view, or is given the facile answer that there are no environmental limits.

Steady-state economics suggests the following answer: the regenerative and assimilative capacities of the biosphere cannot sustainably support even present levels of resource use, much less the many-fold increase required by "upward harmonization" of consumption standards. Still less can the ecosystem afford the upward harmonization of standards for an ever-growing population striving to consume ever more per capita. This heretofore unrecognized limit to development puts a brake on the ability of growth to wash away the problems of allocation and distribution raised by free trade with free capital mobility. In fact, free trade becomes a recipe for standards-lowering competition leading to the downward harmonization of efficient allocation, equal distribution, and ecological sustainability.

In the face of these enormous problems, what is the appeal of ever larger free trade blocs to corporations and governments influenced by corporations? There are, of course, gains in efficiency from greater specialization under free trade, but these are small compared to the losses just discussed. The big attraction is that the larger the free trade area and the larger and more footloose the corporation, the less it will be responsible to any local or even national community. Increasingly, the corporation will be able to buy labor in the low-wage markets and sell its products in the remaining high-wage, high-income markets. The larger the market, the longer corporations will be able to avoid the logic of Henry Ford-that he had to pay his workers enough for them to buy his cars. In a big trading area, you can go on for a long time making cars with cheap labor in one place and selling them to the remaining high-wage earners somewhere else. The larger the free trade bloc, the longer you can get away with depleting resources and absorptive capacities in one area in order to enjoy the benefits produced from these costs in a well-preserved environment somewhere else. The larger the trading area, the more feasible it is to separate costs and benefits spatially, thus avoiding the discipline of cost internalization geographically. That is why transnational corporations like free trade, and why workers and environmentalists do not.

The correct name for "free trade" (who can oppose freedom?) is "deregulated international commerce," which should serve to remind us that deregulation is not always a good policy. Recall recent experience with the deregulation of the savings and loan institutions, the junk bond financed leveraged buyouts, and the current instability in our banking and airline industries. Any profit-making entity has an interest in externalizing costs. Regulation is needed to keep costs internal, so that cost reductions come from true improvements in efficiency, rather than from simply throwing the costs on to others in the form of lowered standards. Again, the point is not to deny that there are gains from international trade. Rather it is to agree with Keynes that there are also gains from national self-sufficiency accompanied by balanced trade in items that are inconvenient to produce nationally: I sympathize, therefore, with those who would minimize, rather than those who would maximize, economic entanglement between nations. Ideas, knowledge, art, hospitality, travel-these are the things which should of their nature be international. But let goods be home spun whenever it is reasonably and conveniently possible; and, above all, let finance be primarily national.

* * *

IMPLICATIONS FOR TRADE POLICY

In the light of the growth versus development distinction, let us return to the issue of trade and consider two questions: What is the likely effect of free trade on growth? What is the likely effect of free trade on development?

Free trade is likely to stimulate throughput growth. Trade offers the possibility of importing environmental carrying capacity in the form of raw materials and waste absorption capacities in exchange for production. It allows a country to exceed its domestic regenerative and absorptive limits by importing these functions from other countries. That tends to increase throughput, other things being equal. But it could be argued that the country exporting carrying capacity might have had to increase throughput even more had it produced the products domestically rather than importing them. Nevertheless, trade does postpone the day when countries must face up to the discipline of living within natural regenerative and absorptive capacities, and by doing that probably serves on balance to increase throughput growth and environmental degradation. Free trade also introduces greater spatial separation between the production benefits and the environmental costs of throughput growth, making it more difficult for the latter to temper the growth of the former. Furthermore, as a result of the increased integration caused by trade, countries will face tightening environmental constraints more simultaneously and less sequentially than they would with less trade and integration. Therefore, there will be less opportunity to learn from other countries' prior experience with controlling throughput. In sum, by making supplies of resources and absorption capacities everywhere available to demands anywhere, free trade will tend to increase throughput growth and with it the rate of environmental degradation.

QUESTIONS AND DISCUSSION

1. The force of the arguments against further trade liberalization has been the catalyst for a broad and growing global coalition of citizens and NGOs from the environmental, human rights, labor, and other social justice movements. Many of these citizens and NGOs came together in the streets of Seattle in 1999 to oppose the launch of the WTO's proposed Millenium Round of global trade negotiations, and their protest played an important role in blocking the Round. Considerable opposition also came from developing countries, who objected to the proposed inclusion of social issues in the negotiating agenda (and to the general arrogance of the U.S. and E.U. negotiators who generally excluded developing countries from the "green room" where the real negotiations took place). Developing countries also feared that proposals to give a larger role to NGOs would move these countries from second place, behind the OECD countries, to third place, behind the NGOs. *See* Zaelke & O'Regan, *U.S. Needs a Special Ambassador for Trade*, JOURNAL OF COMMERCE (January 21, 2000):

> The Seattle Summit failed because the World Trade Organization and the U.S. trade representative didn't think they had to listen to the demands of labor unions, consumer and environmental groups or to the demands of the developing countries, the majority of the WTO membership. Had they listened, they would have known that these disparate interests were unanimous in their opposition to a trade system that wasn't working for them. And they might have understood that the combined forces in Seattle would be too much for the old-style trade negotiations, which saw the few rich countries dictate the terms of any agreement to the rest of the world.

Zaelke and O'Regan also note that building a blocking coalition is easier than building a coalition to guide positive change, and this remains one of the key challenges facing civil society today. *See also* Willian Greider, *After the WTO Protest in Seattle, It's Time to Go on the Offensive. Here's How*, NATION (January 31, 2000).

2. It is important to understand the difference between "development" and "growth," as used by Daly. While growth is premised on the constant addition of new materials, development occurs through a reordering of existing stocks of materials. Daly thus urges a focus on sustainable *development* not sustainable *growth* (an oxymoron). In the absence of free trade, each country would be forced to live within the limits of its own resource base and assimilative capacity. According to Daly, trade postpones these inevitable adjustments. How does this argument compare with the argument that trade promotes efficient use of scarce resources and therefore promotes sustainable development? What are the assumptions underlying each argument? If we were to accept Daly's views about development versus growth, what role is left for international trade? Are excess resources or assimilative capacity "comparative advantages" that should be realized through trade?

3. According to mainstream economics, and to our historical experience, free trade is a powerful engine of wealth maximization. The world, in both economic and environmental terms, is becoming more interrelated and more complex. Wealth maximization might therefore be seen as a component of the broader concept of *welfare* maximization that includes a host of non-economic considerations–including environmental quality. What is the role of wealth maximization in sustainable development? What about welfare maximization? How might the relationship between wealth and welfare change in a steady-state economy as we bump up against our environmental limits? Recall the discussion in Chapter 3 on "redefining progress" to develop a more accurate measure of national wealth and well-being.

4. With half of the world living on $3 a day or less, and the gap between rich and poor widening, the global economic system obviously fails to distribute economic wealth equitably. How much more difficult will it be to achieve equity in a steady state economy, when we must re-allocate the economic pie, by taking from the rich to give to the poor, rather than relying on increasing the size of the pie? How would you address this challenge? Which human rights would assist your effort?

5. Historically, the development of international economic and environmental governance has proceeded on largely separate tracks. If economic integration increases the need for cooperation on environmental matters, then how can these separate tracks be brought together? Should progress on environmental cooperation be linked to, or a prerequisite for, progress in international economic negotiations? This is currently the case with the countries applying for membership in the European Union. These "accession countries", including Hungary and other Central and Eastern European countries, must first improve their environmental protection programs until they "approximate" the high levels of protection within the current member states. *See* discussion of European Union, *infra*.

6. Conflicts between free trade and forms of protection are not solely international. Indeed in any federal system there always exists the tension between free commerce among states and legitimate state protectionist measures that may impede the flow of commerce. This tension is clearly evident in the U.S. Constitution for, in many respects, the early United States was an experiment in creating a large free trade zone among the former colonies. Indeed, the precursor to the Constitutional Convention in Philadelphia was a meeting between Maryland, Virginia and Pennsylvania over trade on the Chesapeake Bay. Disputes between free trade and actions taken by states for internal purposes are controlled by the Constitution's "dormant commerce clause." *See, e.g.*, Pike v. Bruce Church, 90 S.

Ct. 844; Minnesota v. Clover Leaf Creamery, 101 S. Ct. 715 (1981); Chemical Waste Management, Inc. v. Hunt, 504 U.S. 334 (1992) and other "flow control" cases.

————

C.   THE COMPLEXITY OF THE TRADE AND ENVIRONMENT DEBATE

To understand better the difficulty in resolving trade and environment disputes, consider the case of American newsprint. In the late 1980s, over half of the U.S. states either enacted laws or entered into "voluntary agreements" with newspapers to include recycled content in their newsprint, reaching 50% recycled content by the year 2000. This was seen as environmentally a good thing, since it would reduce solid waste going to landfills. The curious thing is that environmental groups were not the key lobbyists for these requirements. It turns out that American pulp and paper producers were behind most of these laws and agreements. It further turns out that it's not cheaper for pulp and paper producers to make recycled paper, and they do not have a larger profit margin. So why did they push for recycled newsprint requirements?

Prior to these laws, most of American newspapers' newsprint was supplied by Canadian companies. As a result of the recycled newsprint requirements, however, the market shifted. Canada's population is too small to provide enough waste paper to raise the level of its virgin pulp to 50% recycled content. As a result, Canadian pulp and paper firms were put in the bizarre position of having to *import* waste paper from the United States and ship it up to its paper plants (near where the forests are, of course) and *ship back* the recycled newsprint to the United States. These added costs shifted market shares, raising U.S. pulp and paper companies from 42% to 49% of the market, all at the expense of Canadian companies. *See* James McCarthy, *The Trade Implications of Recycled Content in Newsprint: The U.S. View*, in OECD, LIFE-CYCLE MANAGEMENT AND TRADE 143 (1994).

It appears that most state and municipal lawmakers were motivated by environmental, not protectionist concerns. But Canadian companies suffered as a result. Is this a law protecting the environment or U.S. companies? What if it's doing both? Who should decide this? How should it be decided? And what are the consequences if the law is found to be protectionist? These questions frame the trade and environment debate.

Unfortunately, for political purposes the trade and environment debate is often polarized by the participants. One side argues that free trade threatens the environment, and the other that environmental protection threatens free trade. They often talk past each other, citing isolated examples to support their views. In reality the relationships are much more complicated. In specific instances, trade may have either a positive or negative effect on the environment, and environmental protection a positive or negative effect on trade. Clearly each has a role to play in achieving sustainable development. We must look for ways to develop those areas where they are mutually supportive, and find principles for mediating between them when they clash.

While the terms "environmentalists" and "free traders" are often used for convenience, the participants in the debate vary widely, adding to its complexity. As well as the more visible participants—the vocal proponents of environmental protection or of free trade—other groups are intimately involved. These include labor and human rights groups, indigenous people, academics, and businesses. Developing and developed country governments also have well developed positions that reflect their differing situations. And a wide spectrum of interests and views exist within each of these groups. For example, Northern environmentalists often focus on large-scale, long-term environmental problems such as ozone depletion and global warming, whereas Southern groups focus on more immediate concerns such as depletion of the soil and water resources that support their communities. Northern groups are thus sometimes criticized for emphasizing the environmental, rather than the developmental, component of sustainable development. Different views also exist within developing countries. Trade policy promoted by a ruling elite may not further the development goals of local people who are often unaware of both the policy and its implications. Yet, it is often local people that are affected most by the use and management of resources.

This debate has been described by Dan Esty and others as a clash of cultures arising as a result of different histories, values and theoretical assumptions. As should be clear from the discussion above, many pro-trade theorists focus on the economics of international trade and its traditional role as the engine of economic growth, prosperity, increased consumer choice, poverty alleviation and development. They believe that "the rising tide will lift all boats" (while many environmentalists believe the tide only lifts the yachts) and that increasing efficiency in production, and increasing wealth creation ultimately will translate to greater environmental protection.

They are deeply concerned that countries may take protectionist measures under the guise of environmental protection, thereby undermining the international trade system. Indeed, in many cases it is difficult to differentiate between valid environmental and protectionist motives. For example, a tax on the import of certain fish may be supported by local fishermen on the basis that it "levels the playing field" and shields them from foreign competition. At the same time, environmentalists may favor the tax's environmental benefit of reducing environmental damage associated with the fishery.

By contrast, many environmentalists believe current international trade rules encourage competitive pressures to weaken environmental standards. Without some protection, stringent local fishing standards may be lowered to reduce cost and ensure local fisheries remain internationally competitive. While environmental compliance costs are generally a small percentage of overall operational costs, insignificant in comparison with labor and material costs, in some sectors (such as the refining and chemical industries) they can be significant. Environmentalists are also concerned that trade rules may override existing environmental law and "chill" development of future efforts towards sustainable development. *See* discussion of NAFTA's investor protection measures, *infra* at page 1202.

From a policy perspective, one might claim that trade rules and trade liberalization have two main kinds of impacts: physical and regulatory. Physical effects arise as trade liberalization may change the pattern or nature of economic activity with resulting impacts on the environment. It may, for example, introduce new products, disseminate new technologies, or increase the scale of impacts on the environment. Regulatory effects, in contrast, arise as trade rules often seek to promote international trade and to reduce protectionism by limiting the kinds of rules regulators may use to protect the environment. The trade system generally pursues a "de-regulatory" strategy, to remove perceived barriers to trade, while sustainable development and environmental protection pursue a "regulatory" strategy to internalize external environmental costs and otherwise keep economic activity within the limits of the biosphere.

Rather than arguing whether trade liberalization, in net terms, harms or benefits the environment, many policy-makers have focused on developing a more sophisticated understanding of the many complex interdependencies between trade liberalization, trade rules, environmental rules, and the environment. Their goal has been to strike a balance between sometimes conflicting, sometimes complementary, objectives, by maximizing areas of synergy between them and making wise compromises where they conflict. In this area, one important developments is the use of "sustainability assessments" of trade liberalization, which allow policy-makers to identify which kinds of trade liberalization may promote their national interests and to design integrated policy packages that allow them to maximize the sustainable development gains from trade. Much work remains to be done in this relatively new field to accommodate the interests of free trade and environmental protection and to ensure that trade rules ultimately promote the over-arching goal of sustainable development.

————

PROBLEM EXERCISES

1. Country "Industry" is an island with a strong industrial economy. Country "Timber", a forested country with a strong timber industry, is located on the continent, 200 miles across the sea from Country Industry. Country Industry burns high sulfur coal in its power plants. This does not pose any problems for Country Industry, for the prevailing winds blow the smoke stack emissions straight out to sea where they eventually fall as acid rain on Country Timber's forests. Country Timber has spent years trying to persuade Country Industry to reduce its sulfur emissions. Assume Country Industry takes one of the two options below:

   1) Country Industry passes legislation banning the burning of high sulfur coal.

   2) Country Industry bans the import of wood harvested in an unsustainable manner by Country Timber.

Which of the above actions would be praised by the international community? Would free traders and environmentalists denounce the same action? Since both actions will protect Country Timber's forests, why should they be treated differently? Explain the reasons why one of the actions is preferable to the other. Present arguments addressing concerns over economics, effectiveness, and equity.

2. Assume you go into a bar in Toronto with a friend and order a beer. You are given a can of beer and your friend a bottle. Reading over the bill you're surprised to find that the can is more expensive than the bottle of beer. Asking the bartender to explain, you learn that the Province of Ontario has levied a tax on all non-refillable containers of alcoholic beverages. The stated purpose of the tax is environmental. Ontario seeks to encourage the use of bottled beer to maintain the high number of bottles necessary for efficient operation of the province's recycling system. Being an environmentalist at heart, you nod approvingly and leave a tip.

A few weeks later, you recount this story to a friend in Milwaukee who works for Suds Beer. She tells you that the tax is not an environmental measure at all, but a protectionist trade measure. She explains that the tax discriminates in favor of Ontario beer producers who ship their beer a short distance in bottles. The tax effectively raises the costs of American beer producers, who now must ship their beer to Canada in bottles instead of cans, adding both to the weight and breakage rate of each shipment. If the tax is environmental, she asks, why does it only apply to cans of beer and not to cans of soda or fruit juice? *See* Crosby, *Green Beer: When is an Environmental Measure a Disguised Restriction on International Trade?*, 7 GEO. INTL. ENVTL. L. REV. 537 (1995).

Assume you were an arbitrator deciding the issue. Is the Ontario tax a legitimate measure to protect the environment, or a protectionist measure hiding in green garb? How would you decide between the two motives? What if it is *both* an environmentalist and a protectionist measure? We next turn to the WTO and GATT to determine how such disputes are resolved at the global level.

---

1.   ENVIRONMENTAL REVIEWS OF TRADE AGREEMENTS

One means to better integrate trade measures and environmental protection is greater reliance on environmental reviews of trade agreements. The United States first carried out reviews of trade agreements as part of the NAFTA negotiations. While its focus was narrower than that of an environmental impact statement required under the National Environmental Policy Act, the NAFTA review identified the real issues of concern early on and assisted in crafting specific negotiating positions to address them. In parallel with the United States, Canada undertook its own reviews of NAFTA and the Uruguay Round. The European Union was active even earlier, publishing studies in 1990 and 1992 on the likely environmental impacts of the Common Market. International organizations have been active as well. Throughout the 1990s, the Commission on Sustainable Development consistently called for development of a framework to facilitate the assessment of the environmental effects of trade. These declarations were complemented by workshops organized by the Organisation for Economic Co-operation and Development to develop a standardized review methodology. In the run-up to the 1999 Seattle Ministerial, President Clinton signed Executive Order 13,141, committing the U.S. government for the first time to conduct environmental reviews of trade agreements. 64 Fed. Reg. 63169 (Nov. 18, 1999).

> Environmental reviews hold the potential to drive two significant developments. The first is integration of environmental considerations into a trade policy process traditionally dominated by commercial concerns. Reviews can characterize, and possibly quantify, the likely environmental impacts of a trade

agreement as well as uncover potential environmental opportunities and vulnerabilities. Thus, reviews heighten the environmental awareness of negotiators. Done well, this analysis can also provide practical, constructive options that mitigate or eliminate negative impacts and, better yet, enhance positive ones (so-called "win-win" solutions). These reviews may persuade governments to modify specific provisions of the draft agreement, propose additional domestic policies or institutions, or create entirely separate agreements. In fact, all three occurred in the North American Free Trade Agreement (NAFTA) negotiations.

The second goal is more daunting—meaningful public involvement in the negotiation process. The environmental community's traditional distrust and opposition to trade and investment liberalization are no secret. However, the formation of negotiating positions largely is. The creation of U.S. trade policy to date has effectively been a closed process, with little opportunity for direct public participation. Formal reviews could possibly temper environmentalists' opposition by opening up the process. Engaging the public in a true dialogue over the environmental consequences of proposed trade rules and their alternatives can allay the fears of hidden deals and policies dictated by powerful economic interests. More important, this constructive partnership creates an alternative to environmentalists' largely binary view of trade–trade as either an unmitigated environmental harm that degrades the environment and promotes the race-to-the-bottom, or trade sanctions as a useful stick to bludgeon undesirable practices of trading partners. Reviews create the space for a third possibility–proactive trade policies that promote environmental protection and increased commerce.

James Salzman, *Seattle's Legal Legacy and Environmental Reviews of Trade Agreements*, 31 ENVT'L. L. 501, 504–5 (2001).

On October 24, 2000 the Free Trade Agreement (FTA) between the United States and the Hashemite Kingdom of Jordan was signed. This is only the fourth free trade agreement the United States has negotiated, after those with Israel, Canada and Mexico (NAFTA), and the first ever with an Arab state. It is also the first U.S. free trade agreement to include both labor and environment obligations in the body of the text. President Bush signed the implementing legislation for this agreement, the United States–Jordan Free Trade Implementation Act passed by Congress. Public Law No: 107–43.

AGREEMENT BETWEEN THE UNITED STATES OF AMERICA AND THE HASHEMITE KINGDOM OF JORDAN ON THE ESTABLISHMENT OF A FREE TRADE AREA
(signed October 24, 2000)

PREAMBLE

The Government of the United States of America ("United States") and the Government of the Hashemite Kingdom of Jordan ("Jordan"),

* * *

Recognizing that Jordan's economy is still in a state of development and faces special challenges;

Recognizing the objective of sustainable development, and seeking both to protect and preserve the environment and to enhance the means for doing so in a manner consistent with their respective needs and concerns at different levels of economic development;

* * *

Wishing to promote effective enforcement of their respective environmental and labor law;

HAVE AGREED AS FOLLOWS:

* * *

ARTICLE 5: ENVIRONMENT

1. The Parties recognize that it is inappropriate to encourage trade by relaxing domestic environmental laws. Accordingly, each Party shall strive to ensure that it does not waive or otherwise derogate from, or offer to waive or otherwise derogate from, such laws as an encouragement for trade with the other Party.

2. Recognizing the right of each Party to establish its own levels of domestic environmental protection and environmental development policies and priorities, and to adopt or modify accordingly its environmental laws, each Party shall strive to ensure that its laws provide for high levels of environmental protection and shall strive to continue to improve those laws.

3. (a) A Party shall not fail to effectively enforce its environmental laws, through a sustained or recurring course of action or inaction, in a manner affecting trade between the Parties, after the date of entry into force of this Agreement.

   (b) The Parties recognize that each Party retains the right to exercise discretion with respect to investigatory, prosecutorial, regulatory, and compliance matters and to make decisions regarding the allocation of resources to enforcement with respect to other environmental matters determined to have higher priorities. Accordingly, the Parties understand that a Party is in compliance with subparagraph (a) where a course of action or inaction reflects a reasonable exercise of such discretion, or results from a *bona fide* decision regarding the allocation of resources.

4. For purposes of this Article, "environmental laws" mean any statutes or regulations of a Party, or provision thereof, the primary purpose of which is the protection of the environment, or the prevention of a danger to human, animal, or plant life or health, through:

   (a) the prevention, abatement or control of the release, discharge, or emission of pollutants or environmental contaminants;

   (b) the control of environmentally hazardous or toxic chemicals, substances, materials and wastes, and the dissemination of information related thereto; or

   (c) the protection or conservation of wild flora or fauna, including endangered species, their habitat, and specially protected natural areas in the Party's territory, but does not include any statutes or regulations, or provision thereof, directly related to worker safety or health.

The Jordanian FTA was the subject of an environmental review pursuant to Executive Order 13141, although the guidelines for implemening it had not yet been issued. 65 FR 79442 (2000). Environmental reviews, under the Executive Order and USTR/CEQ guidelines, are currently underway for the *Multilateral Trade Negotiations on Agriculture and Services in the World Trade Organization,* and the *Free Trade Area of the Americas (FTAA) Agreement.*

QUESTIONS AND DISCUSSION

1. In the end, the Jordanian FTA is a significant breakthrough, even if it is not a strong precedent. Consider the size of the trade between the US and Jordan ($287 million in 1999), Chile ($6 billion) and Singapore ($34.4 billion). Does this make the Jordanian FTA less powerful as a precedent? Will this make it more difficult to include strong environmental and labor provisions in the Chilean FTA? Singapore? How strict do you think Singapore's environmental laws are? Chile's? Jordan's?

2. The environment and labor provisions of the Jordanian FTA can be enforced through the Dispute Settlement procedure in Article 17. These are a bit convoluted, with a dispute first going to the Joint Committee, established under the agreement, then if necessary to a non-binding dispute settlement panel, then back to the Joint Committee for a final determination. The victorious party who survives these procedures is entitled to "take any appropriate and commensurate measures."

3. Compare the language of the Jordanian FTA with the following excerpt from the agreement between the United States and Vietnam:

> ... technical regulations shall not be more trade-restrictive than necessary to fulfil a legitimate objective. ... Such legitimate objectives include national security requirements; the prevention of deceptive practices; protection of human health or safety, animal or plant life or health, *or the environment.* In assessing such risks, relevant elements of consideration include available scientific and technical information, related processing technology or intended end-uses of products (emphasis added).

AGREEMENT BETWEEN THE UNITED STATES OF AMERICA AND THE SOCIALIST REPUBLIC OF VIETNAM ON TRADE RELATIONS, ART. 2(6)(b) (signed July 2000)(H.J.RES, Approving the extension of nondiscriminatory treatment with respect to the products of the Socialist Republic of Vietnam passed by Congress and cleared to White House on 10/03/01). It seems as though environmental considerations were added as an afterthought. Does it matter that this was not a Free Trade Agreement but rather a mutual extension of nondiscriminatory treatment of products between the two nations?

4. Do you think the WTO should require environmental reviews of trade agreements? To date, there has been strong opposition in the WTO's Committee on Trade and Environment to such a requirement. What do you think is the source of this opposition? *See* Salzman, *op. cit.,* at 543.

5. The environmental reviews mandated by Executive Order 13141 are intended to produce trade policies that reflect environmental priorities in a meaningful way. As part of this process, participation both by the public and by agencies with environmental responsibilities and expertise is necessary in the development of proposals for a U.S.-Chile FTA. The environmental review must address the full range of relevant questions, including impacts of a global nature. The following represents a limited and non-exhaustive list of the environmental issues that NGOs believe should be addressed in the environmental review.

Center for International Environmental Law et al., *Comments on Proposed United States–Chile Free Trade Agreement* (2001)

1. As a principal element of its scoping phase, the review should begin by canvassing the areas of commerce that could be or are likely to be affected by the FTA or are otherwise relevant to or affected by the commercial relations between the U.S. and Chile. For each area of commercial activity, a preliminary assessment should be performed of the current environmental dimensions of that commercial activity in both countries. Particular emphasis should be given to identifying areas where substantial improvements are required to raise environmental performance (including husbandry of resources and conservation of biodiversity and ecosystem functions) to achieve sustainable development and/or the application of "best practices" or other measures of environmental excellence. The scoping review should further identify current obstacles to achieving improved environmental performance, with specific attention to market failures and policy failures underlying currently inadequate practices. The potential relevance of trade-related policies and/or complementary policies should be examined.

2. The potential impacts on U.S. and Chilean environmental regulations, statutes, and other binding obligations such as multilateral environmental agreements, and on environmental policy instruments and other commitments.

3. The specific impacts in both Chile and the United States of liberalization of tariff and non-tariff measures on the following sectors:

- forestry;
- mining;
- fisheries;
- shipping transport;
- air transport;
- oil/gas extraction and transport;
- and fruit agriculture.

4. The potential impacts on local and regional air pollution in both Chile and the United States and on global climate change, including changes due to increased energy usage and other effects from export-related production and transport in Chile.

SECTION II.   THE MULTILATERAL TRADING SYSTEM

A.   ORIGINS OF THE GATT AND WTO

Following World War II, the international community established three economic institutions: the World Bank, the International Monetary Fund, and the General Agreement on Tariffs and Trade (GATT). The GATT was originally intended to be a component of a larger agreement establishing an International Trade Organization (ITO). The GATT agreement focused mainly on tariff reduction and the ITO, as initially conceived, would provide a comprehensive code and an institutional framework governing other aspects of international trade.

The GATT negotiations were concluded in 1947 and came provisionally into force in January 1948. 55 U.N.T.S. 194. The ITO negotiations were subsequently abandoned when it became clear that the U.S. Congress would not ratify the agreement, leaving the GATT in the unexpected position of a treaty without an administrative structure. The GATT necessarily evolved as an institution (adding a Council, Secretariat, and Committees) over the next few decades through practice and a series of later agreements. Most of the evolution came through eight successive multilateral negotiating "rounds."

The objective of the GATT is the progressive reduction of trade barriers among members to remove distortions in international markets and to ensure that goods and, more recently, services are not discriminated on the basis of their national origin. To understand the GATT and its progeny, one must recognize its underlying diplomatic objective: that increased trade ties will foster political ties and enhance international security. It was widely believed by the GATT's architects that the spiraling protectionism of the 1930s had directly contributed to the economic instability accompanying the rise of fascism. Just two years after the bloodiest war in human history, protectionist trade barriers represented far more than mere commercial preferences.

The GATT's provisions are almost entirely negative; in order to liberalize trade they prescribe the scope of national regulatory discretion, rather than requiring governments to positively enact regulations. The "Most Favored Nation" (MFN) obligation seeks to prevent nations from discriminating between products from competing importing Member States (e.g., the United States cannot favor products from Uruguay over similar goods from Venezuela). The GATT, through the "National Treatment" obligation, also prevents nations from discriminating against Member States' imports in favor of domestic products (e.g., the United States cannot favor its products over "like" foreign products from Uruguay or Venezuela). It further requires the removal of a variety of restrictions that would limit the quantity of imports permitted. The GATT provides for environmental exceptions to these requirements in Article XX. The core GATT principles and environmental exceptions are discussed in more detail in the sections that follow.

The most recent "Uruguay Round" of trade negotiations was completed in December 1993. It set up a comprehensive legal and institutional structure of the kind envisaged in the original ITO negotiations. Today, as a result of the Uruguay Round negotiations, the World Trade Organization (WTO) forms the legal and institutional framework for the multilateral trading system

Established on January 1, 1995, the WTO provides a forum for implementing the multilateral trading system, negotiating new trade agreements and resolving trade disputes. The Agreement Establishing the World Trade Organization (WTO Agreement) incorporates the original GATT, which continues to apply to issues not covered by the more specific agreements negotiated during the Uruguay Round. 33 I.L.M. 1125 (1994). It also includes specific agreements that cover many trade-related issues including: technical barriers to trade, sanitary and phytosanitary measures, trade-related investment measures, subsidies and countervailing measures, agriculture, intellectual property, and trade in services. The conclusion of the Uruguay Round was celebrated as a great success by businesses and governments. One study estimated the Uruguay Round would generate annual increases in global income of $235 billion and trade of $755 billion by 2000.

QUESTIONS AND DISCUSSION

1. A basic criticism of the original GATT is that its "substantive rules, which predate the emergence of the environment as a critical issue, are too narrowly focused on the commercial benefits of trade facilitation and must be updated to reflect environmental considerations." DANIEL ESTY, GREENING THE GATT 53 (1994). In fact, the word "environment" is not included anywhere in the text of the GATT. At the time the GATT was negotiated, the relationship between environment and trade had not been widely considered, nor were environmental considerations high on the agenda of the public or governments. The primary concern of GATT negotiators was to develop an agreement that would herald in a post-war era of peace, stability and prosperity. To what extent do you think the GATT has succeeded? What are some of the environmental changes that have occurred during this time and what impact do they have on the role and value of international trade as an engine of prosperity?

2. While, unlike the GATT, the WTO Agreement includes a preambular reference to "sustainable development", concerns still arise about its failure to clearly identify the WTO's goal or mission. Mark Halle, of the International Institute for Sustainable Development, notes that "The WTO has increasing difficulty in convincing the public that its approach to economic liberalization responds to a broadly-supported set of economic, social and environmental goals. Part of the problem is that there is no clear statement of the WTO mission, making it nearly impossible for the WTO to respond to its critics." IISD Viewpoint, <www.iisd.org>. How much guidance does the existing preamble to the WTO Agreement give to the organization and its members? If a broader mission statement were developed, what kinds of issues should it address?

B.   THE WORLD TRADE ORGANIZATION AND THE ENVIRONMENT

In this section we examine some of the main issues surrounding the WTO and the environment. We begin with a brief overview of the structure of the WTO, including a discussion of the main WTO Agreements with implications for the environment. We then examine the role of the Dispute Settlement Body and the Committee on Trade and Environment, before turning in the next section to examine key trade and environment issues.

---

1.   STRUCTURE OF THE WTO

As noted above, the WTO forms the multilateral institutional and administrative framework for international trade. Unlike the pre-WTO international trade rules, that consisted of a patchwork of agreements and obligations, the WTO Agreements are structured as an "all or nothing" package to which all members of the WTO must ascribe. This package consists of:

- the GATT 1994, which, in turn, is made up of the GATT 1947, certain legal instruments entered into under the GATT 1947, and certain listed prior "Understandings" regarding the application of various GATT provisions;

- the Uruguay Round Protocol to the GATT 1947;

- the various separate Uruguay Round Agreements, such as the TBT Agreement, the SPS Agreement, and the Subsidies Agreement discussed below; and

- the various annexes to the Uruguay Round's Final Act

The five main WTO agreements with environmental implications are the Agreement on Technical Barriers to Trade (TBT), the Agreement on Sanitary and Phytosanitary Measures (SPS), the Agreement on Subsidies and Countervailing Measures (SCM), the Agreement on Trade–Related Aspects of Intellectual Property (TRIPS), and the General Agreement on Trade in Services (GATS). The first three of these address trade in goods, whereas the last two, respectively, address what are known as the other two "pillars of the trading system": intellectual property and trade in services.

a. *THE AGREEMENT ON TECHNICAL BARRIERS TO TRADE*

The TBT Agreement seeks to prevent countries from using technical regulations on the nature or content of products as disguised measures to protect domestic industries. It also seeks to improve market access by encouraging harmonization of technical regulations and standards to avoid the difficulty of complying with the numerous, often incompatible rules used by different countries. The TBT Agreement covers both technical regulations, which are mandatory, and standards, which are voluntary.

The TBT Agreement requires Members to use international standards "as a basis for their technical regulations" unless the Member can demonstrate that the relevant international standard "would be an ineffective or inappropriate means for the fulfillment of a legitimate objective" (which includes the protection of human, animal or plant life or health). Article 2.4. The TBT Agreement incorporates MFN and National Treatment obligations. Additionally, standards and regulations must not constitute unnecessary obstacles to trade, although if based upon an international standard, it is presumed not to create such an obstacle. In addition, Members must ensure that central governmental standardizing bodies improve transparency and involve interested parties in standard setting; take reasonable measures to ensure that regional standardization bodies of which they are members do the same; and make reasonable efforts to harmonize technical rules at the international level.

The TBT Agreement does *not* contain a comprehensive exception for measures taken to protect the environment. It is currently unclear whether the Article XX environmental exceptions included in the GATT apply to the TBT agreement and to other Uruguay Round agreements.

b. AGREEMENT ON THE APPLICATION OF SANITARY AND PHYTOSANITARY MEASURES

The Sanitary and Phytosanitary (SPS) Agreement governs regulations aimed at protecting human, animal and plant health within a WTO Member's territory from risks due to diseases, pests and disease-causing organisms, as well as from additives, contaminants, toxins or disease-causing organisms in foods, beverages or feedstuffs.

The SPS Agreement requires Members to "ensure that any sanitary and phytosanitary measure is applied only to the extent necessary to protect human, animal or plant life or health, is based on scientific principles ... [and] sufficient scientific evidence." Article 2.2. "In cases where relevant scientific evidence is insufficient, [however,] a Member may provisionally adopt [SPS] measures on the basis of available pertinent information, including that from the relevant international organizations as well as from [SPS] measures applied by other Members." Article 5.7.

Members must ensure that their SPS measures are not "applied in a manner which would constitute a disguised restriction on international trade." Article 2.3. SPS measures "which conform to international standards, guidelines or recommendations shall be ... presumed to be consistent with the relevant provisions of this Agreement and of the GATT 1994." Article 1.

c. THE AGREEMENT ON SUBSIDIES AND COUNTERVAILING MEASURES

The SCM Agreement imposes disciplines both on trade distorting subsidies and on the countervailing measures that may be taken in response to them. It divides subsidies into two categories, prohibited and other subsidies. Other subsidies are in turn divided into those that are actionable by importing countries and those that are non-actionable. Non-actionable subsidies (i.e. those protected from challenge) included certain subsidies to encourage environmental improvement. These, however, were not renewed by WTO Members in 1999 and have therefore expired.

d. THE AGREEMENT ON TRADE–RELATED ASPECTS OF INTELLECTUAL PROPERTY

According to its preamble, the TRIPS Agreement is designed to "promote effective and adequate protection of intellectual property rights" and to "reduce distortions and impediments to international trade" that result from the enforcement of intellectual property rights. The TRIPS Agreement's stated objectives includes "the promotion of technological innovation and to the transfer and dissemination of technology, to the mutual advantage of the producers and users of technological knowledge... (Article 7)."

The TRIPS Agreement establishes uniform, minimum standards for the protection and enforcement of intellectual property rights by all WTO Members. It covers a broad range of intellectual property rights, such as copyright, trademarks, geographical indications, trade secrets, and patents.

Among other things, it requires Members to grant intellectual property protection to nationals of other Members on the same terms as they do their own nationals (the Article 3 'national treatment' provisions), and to extend the same favourable terms they grant to the national of any Member to the nationals of every other Member (the Article 4 'most-favored nation' provision).

The Agreement includes a number of forms of intellectual property rights with implications for environmental protection, including patents and *sui generis* systems for plant variety protection. The main provision of the TRIPS Agreement of relevance to biodiversity protection is Article 27.3(b), which requires WTO Members to offer patents over certain elements of life (e.g. micro-organisms), and to protect plant varieties through either patents or *sui-generis* systems. Its provisions on the transfer of technology may also be relevant to efforts to transfer and disseminate environmental technology.

e. THE GENERAL AGREEMENT ON TRADE IN SERVICES

The GATS establishes binding rules on international trade in services. Services, such as education, health, transport, tourism and the provision of energy, are covered by a series of disciplines and commitments designed to liberalize their "trade". According to the GATS, services are traded through four "modes of delivery": cross-border delivery, consumption abroad, foreign direct investment, and movement of the natural person supplying the service.

As part of the multilateral trading system, the GATS builds on the basic principles of non-discrimination, market access, and transparency. However, unlike the GATT, the GATS adopts a so-called "hybrid approach" to these obligations. For example, the GATS disciplines on national treatment (Article XVII) and market access (Article XVI) only apply in the specific services sub-sectors and modes of supply that a Member agrees to liberalize. The other two of the GATS main disciplines, most favored nation treatment (Article II) and transparency (Article III), by contrast, adopt the traditional GATT approach and apply "horizontally" to all services sectors.

In ongoing GATS negotiations, which are occurring as part of the WTO's "built-in agenda", WTO Members aim to deepen their commitments in individual services sub-sectors and to design new rules, such as disciplines on domestic regulations.

In addition to these agreements, other WTO agreements may have implications for environmental protection, including the Agreement on Agriculture, the Agreement on Government Procurement, and the Agreement on Trade–Related Investment Measures.

QUESTIONS AND DISCUSSION

1. The broad spectrum of areas covered by WTO Agreements gives the WTO preeminence in the international economic order. Some authors have noted with concern that almost any discipline can be brought within the orbit of the WTO just by adding the prefix "trade-related". Dan Esty has suggested the creation of a "Global Environment Organization" to counterbalance the WTO's current institutional pre-eminence. The case for a "GEO" is persuasive for a number of reasons. One is that while the WTO seeks to create a global market, there is currently no institution to address global market failure. Ill-defined property rights over common resources and other imperfect market structures cause international market failure of the kind discussed in Chapter 3 including "tragedy of the commons," cost externalization and free rider problems. Increasingly, environmental problems are international in scope and, like global warming, are the result of an inefficient and unsustainable scale of economic activity. At a domestic level, governments correct market failures by imposing taxes and permit systems on polluters, and by granting incentives for environmentally responsible behavior. At the international level, a forum could be established where governments can agree to harmonize environmental laws, and develop collective, multilateral solutions to international problems. A GEO could also help where environmental harm occurs in the global commons. Further, it could promote economically efficient environmental policies such as the polluter pays principle and administer and encourage compliance with existing multilateral environmental agreements. What arguments can you make for and against a GEO? Is a GEO feasible now or in the future and, if so, how might it be structured? *See* Chapter 5, page 246, for further discussion of this and other proposed new environmental institutions; *see generally* D. Esty, GREENING THE GATT (1994).

2. Government subsidies covered by the SCM Agreement often contribute to environmental damage. As the SCM Agreement requires the removal of many subsidies, some commentators have argued that it could be used to address environmentally harmful subsidies in a way that simultaneously promotes trade and environmental goals. To what extent do government subsidies contribute to the environmental problems such as biodiversity loss and climate change identified in earlier chapters? Do you think that the WTO is the right institution to tackle environmentally harmful subsidies? Which other international organizations might be involved as part of a collective approach to addressing environmentally harmful subsidies?

3. At the WTO, governments are continuing their negotiations to liberalize trade in services. Liberalizing trade in services may have positive impacts on the environment, as it may increase access to environmental technology, and build infrastructure for waste management and other environmental services. At the same time, some environmentalists have noted that the GATS negotiation may raise environmental challenges. How might liberalizing trade in energy, mining, or transportation services increase environmental impacts? If so, what kinds of measures could governments enact to minimize these? What is the role of sustainability assessments in identifying potential effects, and when should they be undertaken?

---

2.   THE DISPUTE SETTLEMENT BODY

The WTO Dispute Settlement Understanding (DSU) establishes one of the most potent dispute settlement systems at the international level. Quick and effective resolution of trade disputes that avoid unilateral retaliation to perceived trade rule violations is central to the smooth operation of the multilateral trading system. The DSU provides for a dispute settlement system designed to provide security, predictability and mutually acceptable solutions to trade disputes. Unlike the dispute-resolution mechanisms of most other international agreements, the WTO system can handle large numbers of disputes with relative efficiency.

Resolution of disputes in the WTO system occurs in a number of stages. Initially, disputing parties are asked to enter consultations to seek a consensus solution. If this fails the WTO Dispute Settlement Body (DSB) establishes a panel to hear the dispute. Terms of reference are composed and the panel convenes a number of meetings with the parties and with interested third parties. After the parties offer submissions on the facts and legal arguments, the panel makes its findings and submits an interim report to the parties for comments. The report is then submitted to the DSB for final adoption. The losing party may appeal to an Appellate Body for review of issues of law.

The current WTO dispute settlement system differs from that previously practiced under GATT, where a party could block adoption of a report. Now, panel and Appellate Body reports are automatically adopted unless the membership decides by consensus against adoption. If a party's measure is found to be inconsistent with its WTO obligations it must lift the measure and compensate the challenging party for the harm caused by the measures, or suffer the effects of proportionate retaliatory measures from the challenging member.

Members of dispute settlement panels operate in their individual capacities and are generally drawn from the trade community. The panelists' trade background has been a cause of concern to many environmentalists who argue that panelists often lack experience in the complexities of the environmental issues implicated in their decisions and consequently often fail to give environmental factors sufficient weight. Environmentalists also believe that the WTO should accept amicus curiae (friend of the court) briefs from public interest non-governmental organizations. In the *Shrimp-Turtle* and *British Steel* decision the Appellate Body has opened the possibility for WTO panels and the Appellate Body to accept amicus briefs. This issue is discussed in further detail below in the context of public participation at the WTO.

Winfried Lang, *WTO Dispute Settlement: What The Future Holds* in ASIAN DRAGONS AND GREEN TRADE 145–53 (1996)

"Dispute settlement procedures assist in making rules effective, adding an essential measure of predictability and effectiveness to the operation of a rule-oriented system in the otherwise relatively weak realm of international norms." This quotation from Croley/Jackson about the new World Trade Organization (WTO) system of dispute settlement reflects in a nutshell the essence of the problem under consideration. Rules, once negotiated, remain frequently vague and require further determination and interpretation by efficient institutions.

The Uruguay Round has added new features to the traditional dispute settlement system of the General Agreement on Tariffs and Trade (GATT). Rulings of the *ad hoc* panels have become quasi-automatically compulsory (unless there would emerge among the contracting parties a negative consensus, which is unlikely to occur). In addition, these rulings may be appealed to a so-called Standing Appellate body. Furthermore, panels, instead of relying almost exclusively on the presentations, arguments and proofs submitted by the parties to a dispute, can broaden their knowledge of the facts. They may proceed with their own investigations. They can have recourse to expert advice or expert commissions.

However, these improvements do not satisfy the environment community, which has adopted a relatively negative position as regards the role of GATT/WTO dispute settlement procedures in respect of so-called "trade and environment" disputes. Some examples may illustrate disputes, real or potential, which put the trade and the environment communities into situations of confrontation:

- A country disagrees with certain production and process methods (harvesting of certain kinds of fish) used in the exporting country and prohibits access to its market for goods produced with such methods.

- A country concerned about air pollution puts importers of oil in a worse position, as regards the quality of oil, than local producers.

- A country concerned about global warming wishes to encourage exporters of tropical timber to manage their forests more carefully, and requests that timber products sold on its market should wear a label which indicates whether that timber stems from a sustainably managed forest.

- A country concerned about the depletion of the ozone layer prohibits the import of ozone-depleting substances from non-members of the ozone-regime. Whereas the importing country belongs to that regime, the exporting country does not, and believes that its GATT/WTO rights of free market access have been impaired.

Numerous cases may be added to the above. The crucial question remains whether the present, already improved, GATT/WTO system of dispute settlement is able to produce outcomes that can be accepted by both trade and environmental communities. Is the present system likely to deliver unbiased, impartial and balanced results?

I shall consider first, different views of the present system—both from the green community and those skeptical of that community. Then, I shall briefly suggest a range of ways to resolve disputes as well as the possibility of avoiding disputes in the first place.

Green View

The environment community is likely to express the following "green views" as regards the fixture of dispute settlement in case of "trade and environment" disputes.

First, this community believes that the present system of WTO, with its strong heritage from the GATT, cannot adequately deal with environmental concerns, because environment was not an issue when the GATT took off in the late forties. This community is also of the view that the recent evolution of the GATT has not internalized environmental concerns as a legitimate policy goal. Even during the Uruguay Round, this position will pretend, environmental concerns were only accepted as exceptions, as derogations to the principles of free trade, and not as objectives of their own. A close analysis of the agreements of the Uruguay Round could at least partially confirm this argument.

Second, members of the environment community argue that the core of the matter—the proportionality of measures (advantage for environment versus damage to trade, or vice versa)—cannot be assessed by trade experts alone. As a consequence of the vagueness of terms used in the GATT ("necessity", "related to", "primarily aimed at"), jurisprudence has been a constant feature of the application of trade rules by means of more rather than less strict interpretations. The object and purpose of this exercise has been clear throughout the history of the GATT in the case of doubt, the more trade-friendly interpretation was preferred. This also explains the shift in respect of certain exceptions (contained in Article XX), namely from "related to," to "primarily aimed at"; the latter formula reduces the scope of that exception concerning natural resources.

Third, it may be argued that, in the trade-environment field, jurisprudence amounts to a balancing test between competing interests, and that an objective, impartial outcome can only be expected if and when the respective body (panel, jury, etc.) is composed in a balanced way, representing both fields of expertise, both areas of law and both interest groups.

Fourth, the "green view" will look with some suspicion to the political position of many developing country governments, which still prefer economic development to environmental protection. As the entire GATT/WTO process, in rule-making, interpretation and the application of rules is heavily lop-sided in favour of governments, countervailing forces such as non-governmental organizations appear to be in demand to achieve a balanced process of decision-making.

Skeptical View

There are others who are skeptical of the "green" perspectives I have considered. This view is quite common among the members of the trade community, be it inside or outside of government. It is also likely to be supported by members of the WTO Secretariat. This view is based on a large body of jurisprudence that clearly prefers free trade, and economic gains resulting from free trade, over any other priority.

First, defenders of this view will argue that it is difficult to define "trade and environment" disputes in the abstract; that it is difficult to identity their specific characteristics. They are of the opinion that there exist only trade disputes, in which one party is more environmentally minded than the other

Second, these skeptics will continue that "trade and environment" disputes really are disputes between contracting parties of WTO, disputes in which one country (or group of countries) believes that the rights it has obtained in the context of the trading system have been impaired by environmentally inspired measures which damage its trade.

Third, defenders of this view will also challenge the correctness of certain environmentally inspired measures. They will entertain the suspicion that most of these measures were taken for some hidden "protectionist" purpose, that environmental arguments were used to shield considerations of competitiveness and economic gain.

Fourth, these proponents would also be afraid that any new mechanism of dispute settlement, which gives room to environmental experts and representatives of the environmental community, would weaken the position of the party which is defending its well acquired rights under the trading system. They would see a new imbalance arising: if environmental exceptions were admitted, this would upset the delicate balance of advantages and concessions which were exchanged between the parties as the very essence of the international trading system. By referring to environmental consideration a party could undermine or even withdraw its earlier concessions; concessions that had not been conditioned by any reference to the protection of the environment.

Options

There are several options starting with the WTO *status quo*. The purpose of the suggested changes would be to improve the consideration of environmental issues arising in the context of a dispute between contracting parties, a dispute in which one of the parties justifies specific measures affecting trade by reference to its environmental policy. Such a policy may be anchored in purely domestic legislation or may be based upon an international environmental agreement.

Option 1 would be a slight improvement of the *status quo*. It would mean that dispute settlement panels would be invited by the Dispute Settlement Body (DSB) which comprises the full membership of WTO to make more frequent use of independent expertise, available either in the WTO context itself or from outside. This right of initiative and self-determination is one of the innovations of the Uruguay Round. Another reform introduced during the Uruguay Round, namely to install an Appellate Body to review panel reports upon request of one party, seems to be of little relevance in our specific context. This is because this review is restricted to "issues of law" covered in the panel report and legal interpretations developed by the panel. In the case of "trade and environment" disputes, the so-called balancing test will most probably amount to questions of fact and rarely to questions of law.

Option 2 would amount to the addition of two environmental experts to the traditional three members of a panel or to the inclusion of an ad hoc environment expert in the Appellate Body, if such a dispute comes before that organ at all. The latter proposal would already require some institutional adjustment.

Option 3 would allow for hearings of non-governmental organizations (NGOs) by the panels, in addition to the sessions with the parties pleading their case. Such hearings would take place after the rebuttals by the parties and would give the panels a chance to broaden their view on the environmental aspects of the case. No formal institutional change would be necessary, but one would have to break with old GATT traditions, which are not friendly towards these NGOs.

Option 4 reflects the idea to install an *"amicus curiae"*, who would give advice to the panel on environmental questions. The crucial point would be whether this person is just another expert consulted by the panel, or whether he or she would be appointed by a representative group of NGOs in order to introduce their views into the proceedings of the panel. Whether institutional changes are necessary depends most probably on the specific nature and mandate of the person concerned.

Option 5 would certainly require some institutional change not only in the WTO but also in the context of the United Nations. This option would mean that a panel which becomes aware of the environmental dimension of the case before it, would ask the International Court of Justice (Chamber for Environmental Affairs) to give an advisory opinion on the environmental aspects and the applicable international environmental law of the case. In the light of the traditional opposition of many WTO members towards too close links between WTO and the United Nations, this option is likely to meet with considerable resistance.

Option 6 continues on the track of institutional innovation and goes much further. It would provide for some kind of "super-appeal" against the decision of the Appellate Body, to the International Court of Justice, if ever a "trade and environment" case would come before the Appellate Body. This would constitute the most radical case of a so-called "overarching jurisdiction". The likelihood of such an innovation seems to be low.* * *

The future of WTO dispute settlement in the field of "trade and environment" remains uncertain. Solutions may not be found by means of a general approach but rather through solutions that are tailor-made for specific categories of disputes. One such solution has been proposed by the European Union for disputes arising out of a conflict between the rules of a multilateral environmental agreement and WTO rules. It has been suggested that panels would not challenge the illegitimacy, and "necessity" of trade measures taken pursuant to such an agreement, provided that this agreement would correspond to the terms of a general "understanding" to be adopted by the Contracting parties. If this, or a similar proposal, could be accepted in the WTO, this would be a major step away from the many dilemmas described in this chapter.

QUESTIONS AND DISCUSSION

1. Ambassador Lang, a highly skilled diplomat, chaired the negotiations of the Montreal Protocol. He suggests that his proposed options 1 and 2 are politically feasible, options 3 and 4 might survive over the longer term, but that his others are politically unlikely. Do you agree with his assessment? Why might countries favor or oppose options 1, 2, 3, and 4?

2. Why do environmental interests deserve special treatment in Lang's proposals? Are they any more deserving than human rights or child labor interests?

3. The WTO's less than enthusiastic approach toward NGOs is less surprising if one realizes that a central goal of the WTO/GATT dispute settlement process is to shield the panels from special interests. It goes without saying that any trade dispute will have potential winners and losers. The problem, according to many observers, is that environmentalists are treated as simply a narrow special interest, in some ways no different than Korean shipbuilding interests. Consider the amicus brief filed by CIEL and other NGOs in the *Shrimp-Turtle* case, discussed below. Whom do these NGOs represent? How would Lang respond to this concern?

3. COMMITTEE ON TRADE AND ENVIRONMENT

The WTO established a Committee on Trade and the Environment to identify the relationships between trade and environmental measures and, if necessary, to make recommendations for modification of the rules of the multilateral trading system. According to the WTO Secretariat:

> Two important parameters have guided the CTE's work. One is that WTO competence for policy coordination in this area is limited to trade and those trade-related aspects of environmental policies which may result in significant trade effects for its Members. In other words, there is no intention that the WTO should become an environmental agency, nor that it should get involved in reviewing national environmental priorities, setting environmental standards or global policies on the environment; that will continue to be the task of national governments and of other intergovernmental organizations better suited to the task. The parameter is that if problems of policy coordination to protect the environment and promote sustainable development are identified through the CTE's work, steps taken to resolve them must uphold and safeguard the principles of the multilateral trading system which governments spent seven years strengthening and improving through the Uruguay Round negotiations.

The CTE's work program includes exploring:

- the relationship between the trade system and the use of trade measures for environmental purposes, including those in multilateral environmental agreements

- the relationship between the trade system, environmental charges and taxes, and environmental standards for packaging, labeling and recycling

- the effect of environmental measures on developing country's market access and the environmental benefits of removing trade restrictions and distortions

- appropriate relations between the WTO and intergovernmental, and non-governmental organisations

The CTE submitted a full report at the December 1997 WTO Ministerial meeting in Singapore. A number of important proposals had been put forward in the months leading up the meeting. The United States had proposed an elaboration of the TBT Agreement's requirements for "transparency" in creating standards. The EU had submitted a proposal to amend Article XX that would explicitly accommodate trade measures in MEAs that satisfied specific criteria of openness, adequate participation, and other factors. The CTE, however, has failed to take substantive action on any of these proposals.

QUESTIONS AND DISCUSSION

1. Many environmental NGO's have been highly critical of the CTE. According to Friends of the Earth International:

> The CTE's current claims to fame include an inability to protect multilateral environmental agreements, such as CITES, the Basel Convention and Montreal Protocol, from the possibility of challenge in the WTO. Negotiators have also failed to clarify whether the WTO's Trade–Related Intellectual Property Rights agreement (TRIPs) conflicts with the Biodiversity Convention; and whether countries would be allowed to use a Border Tax Adjustment to protect domestic businesses paying national product taxes (such as a carbon/energy tax). The CTE has also decided that it will not permit NGOs into CTE meetings.

> One of the CTE's main stumbling blocks seems to have been the fact that it has focused mainly on environmental problems of concern to the rich, industrialized countries in return for looking at increased market access for poor. As a result, environmental issues have wrongly come to be seen as a purely "northern" issue, instead of a common problem.

> It is imperative that the trade and environment debate is taken out of the WTO and broadened to consider a wide range of trade and environment concerns, including international trade in commodities, biopiracy, transport and climate change, technology transfer and the development of sustainable patterns of production and consumption. FoEI believes that this can only be achieved by a balanced, open and accountable intergovernmental panel mandated to promote ecologically sound and socially just development.

Friends of the Earth International press release <http://www.foe.co.uk>.

To what extent do you think the concerns expressed by Friends of the Earth are valid? Is the CTE—a body established by the WTO—likely to be the best forum in which to get balanced recommendations for reform of conflicting trade and environmental regimes? Re-read the Secretariat's statement on the CTE's mandate included at the beginning of this section. What "parameters" guide the CTE's work in the event of "problems of policy coordination"? What other international bodies might be more appropriate fora for resolution of trade and environment issues? How could cooperation among international organizations such as UNEP, the MEAs and the WTO help to identify the way forward?

————

C. KEY TRADE AND ENVIRONMENT ISSUES

1. GATT'S CORE PRINCIPLES AND THE DEBATE OVER "PPMS"

The GATT is founded on three core principles. First, the Most Favored Nation obligation (MFN), found in Article I, prohibits discrimination between the products of different importing member states. It requires any privilege or advantage given to the product of one WTO member to be extended immediately and unconditionally to the "like products" of all other WTO members. This obligation prevents countries playing favorites between their trading partners, ensures equal treatment, and rapid reduction of trade barriers. Article I provides:

> 1. With respect to customs duties and charges of any kind imposed on or in connection with importation or exportation or imposed on the international transfer of payments for imports or exports, and with respect to the method of levying such duties and charges, and with respect to all rules and formalities in connection with importation and exportation, and with respect to all matters referred to in paragraphs 2 and 4 of Article III, any advantage, favour, privilege or immunity granted by any contracting party to any product originating in or destined for any other country shall be accorded immediately and unconditionally to the like product originating in or destined for the territories of all other contracting parties.* * *

Second, the National Treatment obligation, found in Article III, prohibits discrimination between imported and domestically produced goods. It requires foreign products to be treated no less favorably than domestic "like products," and seeks to prevent domestic measures from being used to protect domestic industry. Article III provides:

> 1. The contracting parties recognize that internal taxes and other internal charges, and laws, regulations and requirements affecting the internal sale, offering for sale, purchase, transportation, distribution or use of products, and internal quantitative regulations requiring the mixture, processing or use of products in specified amounts or proportions, should not be applied to imported or domestic products so as to afford protection to domestic production.
>
> 2. The products of the territory of any contracting party imported into the territory of any other contracting party shall not be subject, directly or indirectly, to internal taxes or other internal charges of any kind in excess of those applied, directly or indirectly, to like domestic products. Moreover, no contracting party shall otherwise apply internal taxes or other internal charges to imported or domestic products in a manner contrary to the principles set forth in paragraph 1. * * *
>
> 4. The products of the territory of any contracting party imported into the territory of any other contracting party shall be accorded treatment no less favourable than that accorded to like products of national origin in respect of all laws, regulations and requirements affecting their internal sale, offering for sale, purchase, transportation, distribution or use. The provisions of this paragraph shall not prevent the application of differential internal transporta-

tion charges which are based exclusively on the economic operation of the means of transport and not on the nationality of the product. * * * "

The third core obligation is Article XI's prohibition on quantitative restrictions. It covers restrictions to trade such as bans, quotas, and licenses on exported and imported products.

> 1. No prohibitions or restrictions other than duties, taxes or other charges, whether made effective through quotas, import or export licenses or other measures, shall be instituted or maintained by any contracting party on the importation of any product of the territory of any other contracting party or on the exportation or sale for export of any product destined for the territory of any other contracting party...

The meaning of "like product" is essential to an understanding of both the MFN and National Treatment obligations. If two products are "like products," then a country may not discriminate between them without violating the GATT. Alternatively, if they are not like products, then discrimination is allowed. This distinction is important for environmental regulations often seek to distinguish between similar products on the basis of their environmental impacts. During the last decade, or so, a vocal debate has arisen about the kind of distinctions that the "like product" can and should permit. On one hand, some environmentalists have argued that governments should be entitled to discriminate between products on the basis of how they are produced in the exporting country. On the other hand, the trading community has argued that this has the potential to undermine trade and interfere with the sovereignty of exporting countries.

Previous GATT panels have adopted a fairly restrictive reading of "like products", arguing that likeness should be determined by reference to a products *physical* characteristics, and not by reference to the *process* by which a product is made—in other words, products are "alike" if they are physically similar, even though they are produced using different processes or production methods (PPMs). This was the view adopted in the *Tuna/Dolphin* cases, in which the issue of "like products" initially gained international prominence. The first of these cases, *Tuna/Dolphin I,* involved a challenge by Mexico to U.S. restrictions on imports of tuna that were caught using production methods that harmed dolphins (i.e., using purse seine nets). The history of this case is discussed in more detail in Chapter 13, at page 995. In this case, the panel stated that "regulations governing the taking of dolphins incidental to the taking of tuna could not possibly affect tuna *as a product*" (emphasis added), and consequently the measure discriminated between "like products", and was GATT inconsistent.

This interpretation is generally supported by developing countries whose lower environmental standards may provide them with cost advantages and export market access. For them, improving export performance is an important means of encouraging development and reducing poverty. They also fear that PPMs may be used as pretexts for protectionist measures. The interpretation is, however, criticized by Northern environmental NGOs and, to a lesser extent, Northern governments as being environmentally unsound. Many environmental policies require distinguishing between products according to how they are produced, as part of the effort to internalize the environmental costs of production. From the environmentalist perspective, two cans of tuna that are physically identical are not "alike" if one is produced using a process that kills dolphin and the other is not. In their view, the international trade system currently prevents countries from favoring sustainably produced goods and services and thereby punishes efforts towards sustainable development. The challenge is to find an interpretation of "like products" that ensures developing countries have continued access to export markets whilst allowing industrialized countries to address unsustainable consumption patterns.

Unlike earlier GATT panels, the WTO's Appellate Body has taken a slightly more nuanced approach to the "like products" analysis. Although based on the traditional elements of the "like products" test, their approach seems to provide some room for non-trade concerns, and to move away from a narrow focus on a product's physical characteristics. In the *Asbestos* case the Appellate Body describes its approach to interpreting and applying "like products."

> 101. We turn to consideration of how a treaty interpreter should proceed in determining whether products are "like" under Article III:4. As in Article III:2, in this determination, "[n]o one approach ... will be appropriate for all cases." Rather, an assessment utilizing "an unavoidable element of individual, discretionary judgement" has to be made on a case-by-case basis. The Report of the Working Party on *Border Tax Adjustments* outlined an approach for analyzing "likeness" that has been followed and developed since by several panels and the Appellate Body. This approach has, in the main, consisted of employing four general criteria in analyzing "likeness": (i) the properties, nature and quality of the products; (ii) the end-uses of the products; (iii) consumers' tastes and habits–more comprehensively termed consumers' perceptions and behaviour–in respect of the products; and (iv) the tariff classification of the products* * *

> 102. These general criteria, or groupings of potentially shared characteristics, provide a framework for analyzing the "likeness" of particular products on a case-by-case basis. These criteria are, it is well to bear in mind, simply tools to assist in the task of sorting and examining the relevant evidence. They are neither a treaty-mandated nor a closed list of criteria that will determine the legal characterization of products. More important, the adoption of a particular framework to aid in the examination of evidence does not dissolve the duty or the need to examine, in each case, *all* of the pertinent evidence. In addition, although each criterion addresses, in principle, a different aspect of the products involved, which should be examined separately, the different criteria are interrelated. For instance, the physical properties of a product shape and limit the end-uses to which the products can be devoted. Consumer perceptions may similarly influence–modify or even render obsolete–traditional uses of the products. Tariff classification clearly reflects the physical properties of a product.

> 103. The kind of evidence to be examined in assessing the "likeness" of products will, necessarily, depend upon the particular products and the legal provision at issue. When all the relevant evidence has been examined, panels must determine whether that evidence, as a whole, indicates that the products in question are "like" in terms of the legal provision at issue. We have noted that, under Article III:4 of the GATT 1994, the term "like products" is concerned with competitive relationships between and among products. Accordingly, whether the *Border Tax Adjustments* framework is adopted or not, it is important under Article III:4 to take account of evidence which indicates

whether, and to what extent, the products involved are–or could be–in a competitive relationship in the marketplace.

European Communities–Measures Affecting Asbestos and Asbestos–Related Products, WT/DS135/AB/R, paras. 101–103.

Notably, the *Asbestos* case did not address a PPM-based measure, but rather products that were physically different (i.e. that did, and did not, contain asbestos). Nevertheless, the Appellate Body's approach to the "like product" issue seems to consider non-trade concerns such as a product's environmental impacts. It remains to be seen whether they will explicitly consider process and production methods in the future, at least in so far as they directly affect consumers perceptions of products or the nature and extent of a competitive relationship between and among products.

Despite the development of a more nuanced test for "like products", disputes about PPM-based environmental measures are likely to continue to arise at the WTO. One way to deal with differing production processes is to reduce the difference between nations' environmental laws. Harmonization of domestic environmental standards, through agreed international standards or MEAs, is often suggested as an alternative to trade sanctions for addressing environmentally harmful production processes used by exporting nations. If environmental standards are comparable, then there is less scope for international disputes to arise. To the extent that compatible environmental standards are not developed, disputes may continue to arise about PPM-based measures in the WTO dispute settlement system. Many measures–such as those defended by the United States in the *Shrimp-Turtle* case discussed in the next section–will likely be considered under Article III or under Article XI, and ultimately under the GATT's environmental exceptions embodied in Article XX. See generally, Steve Charnovitz, *Environmental Harmonization and Trade Policy*, in TRADE AND THE ENVIRONMENT: LAW ECONOMICS AND POLICY, *op. cit.*, at 280–82

QUESTIONS AND DISCUSSION

1. Clarifying the PPM issue is one of the most important and difficult challenges in the trade and environment debate. Environmentalists argue that the existing rules fail to provide policy-makers with sufficient clarity about the kinds of measures governments may take to address environmental impacts. Preventing or limiting countries from distinguishing between goods according to the environmental impact of their production gives foreign countries a competitive edge and places downward pressure on domestic environmental standards. It also forces importing countries to import and consume unsustainably produced goods. Trade theorists respond that differing countries may set their own environmental standards and that different preferences for environmental quality are a valid source of "comparative advantage." Allowing countries to distinguish between products on the basis of how they are produced threatens descent down the "slippery slope" to protectionism and would undermine the very foundations of the international trade system. When should trade trump environmental protection? When should environmental concerns trump trade? Does it matter to your answer whether the external environmental effects of lower standards stay within the country that chooses lower standards, or whether they spill over into the global environment? Consider the discussion in Chapter 1. When should trade trump environmental protection?

Sometimes there is a coincidence between economic protectionism and legitimate environmental or other social objectives, as in the *Tuna/Dolphin* and *Asbestos* cases and both interests support trade restrictions. Unless we can further separate these influences, trade panels may continue to treat valid concerns as veiled protectionism and strike them down accordingly. What factors might WTO adjudication bodies consider to distinguish between protectionist and valid measures? How might science be relevant? Should international consensus reflected in international environmental agreements affect their decision? Should countries be allowed to pursue environmental measures in furtherance of the consensus objectives of MEAs, even where there may be a coincidence of economic protectionism? How should the Appellate Body's test described above be applied to strike the right balance?

2. Note that the WTO Agreement Preamble commits the international trade system to promote the "optimal use of the world's resources in accordance with the objective of sustainable development, seeking both to protect and preserve the environment and to enhance the means for doing so.... " Should the overarching goal of sustainable development be invoked as the touchstone against which conflicts between trade and environmental protection are resolved?

3. In addition to harmonizing national environmental standards through MEAs, another strategy, used by the EU, for example, is to require countries that wish to join a trade agreement "approximate" the EU's environmental standards. Could such a strategy be used in the WTO, where the majority of the world's countries are already members?

————

2. THE ENVIRONMENTAL EXCEPTIONS TO GATT—ARTICLE XX

Article XX provides an exception to substantive GATT obligations, including those in Articles I, III and XI described above. Article XX states:

> Subject to the requirement that such measures are not applied in a manner which would constitute a means of arbitrary or unjustifiable discrimination between countries where the same conditions prevail, or a disguised restriction on international trade, nothing in this Agreement shall be construed to prevent the adoption or enforcement by any contracting party of measures: * * *
>
> (b) necessary to protect human, animal or plant life or health; * * *
>
> (g) relating to the conservation of exhaustible natural resources if such measures are made effective in conjunction with restrictions on domestic production or consumption;

These exceptions have been interpreted in a number of WTO panel and Appellate Body decisions, including *Gasoline, Shrimp–Turtle, Korea–Beef* and *Asbestos*.

a. *ARTICLE XX(b)—PROTECTION OF HUMAN, ANIMAL AND PLANT LIFE OR HEALTH*

Article XX(b) allows countries to take trade measures that otherwise conflict with GATT obligations where the measures are "necessary" to protect "human, animal or plant life or health." A number of issues have arisen out of the interpretation and application of Article XX(b) including the meaning of the term "necessary" and whether Article XX can be invoked to save trade measures taken to protect resources—for example, endangered sea turtles threatened by foreign fishing practices—located outside the jurisdiction of the country imposing the trade restriction.

In past GATT decisions, the term "necessary" had been interpreted narrowly to require measures to be least trade restrictive before they could gain the provisional protection afforded by Article XX(b). In the *Tuna/Dolphin I* case, the panel stated that to be necessary, the contracting party invoking Article XX(b) must show that no other GATT-consistent measures were reasonably available. It concluded that the United States had not satisfied this burden.

> If the broad interpretation of Article XX(b) suggested by the United States were accepted, each contracting party could unilaterally determine the life or health protection policies from which other contracting parties could not deviate without jeopardizing their rights under the General Agreement. The General Agreement would then no longer constitute a multilateral framework for trade among all contracting parties but would provide legal security only in respect of trade between a limited number of contracting parties with identical internal regulations.

> The Panel considered that the United States' measures, even if Article XX(b) were interpreted to permit extra-jurisdictional protection of life and health, would not meet the requirement of necessity set out in that provision. The United States had not demonstrated to the Panel—as required of the party involving an Article XX exception—that it had exhausted all options reasonably available to it to pursue its dolphin protection objectives through measures consistent with the General Agreement, in particular through the negotiation of international cooperative arrangements, which would seem to be desirable in view of the fact that dolphins roam the waters of many states and the high seas.

In more recent decisions, under the auspices of the WTO, the Appellate Body seems to have adopted a balancing test in which the "trade restrictiveness" of a measure is weighed along with other factors, as part of a determination whether a WTO-consistent alternative measure which a Member could "reasonably be expected to employ" is available, or whether a less WTO-inconsistent measure is "reasonably available". In *Korea-Beef* (a non-environmental case involving a claim of necessity under Article XX(d)) the Appellate Body stated that:

> 164. In sum, determination of whether a measure ... [may] be "necessary" within the contemplation of Article XX(d), involves in every case a process of weighing and balancing a series of factors which prominently include the contribution made by the compliance measure to the enforcement of the law or regulation at issue, the importance of the common interests or values protected by that law or regulation, and the accompanying impact of the law or regulation on imports or exports. (Korea–Measures Affecting Imports of Fresh, Chilled and Frozen Beef, para. 164, WT/DS169/AB/R)

In the subsequent *Asbestos* decision, the Appellate Body reaffirmed this interpretation, in the context of a case under Article XX(b) involving risks from products containing asbestos to human health, and stated that:

> 172. We indicated in *Korea–Beef* that one aspect of the "weighing and balancing process ... comprehended in the determination of whether a WTO-consistent alternative measure" is reasonably available is the extent to which the alternative measure "contributes to the realization of the end pursued". In

addition, we observed, in that case, that "[t]he more vital or important [the] common interests or values" pursued, the easier it would be to accept as "necessary" measures designed to achieve those ends. In this case, the objective pursued by the measure is the preservation of human life and health through the elimination, or reduction, of the well-known, and life-threatening, health risks posed by asbestos fibres. The value pursued is both vital and important in the highest degree. The remaining question, then, is whether there is an alternative measure that would achieve the same end and that is less restrictive of trade than a prohibition.

So far, the logic embodied in these rulings has not been applied to an environmental case.

QUESTIONS AND DISCUSSION

1.   GATT panels and trade commentators have consistently favored a narrow interpretation of "necessary." What are some of the possible justifications for such an approach? Does a broader reading open the door to the use of environmental measures as veiled protectionism, or as a tool permitting unilateral use of trade power to coerce other nations into changing their law? Consider this issue from the perspective of Northern and Southern governments. Consider it also from the perspective of different non-governmental groups including those promoting environmental protection, business and development. Which groups would support a narrow reading? Which would support a broad reading? If, for environmental reasons, we support a broader reading, how can we address the legitimate concerns over protectionism and unilateralism?

2.   The Appellate Body in *Korea–Beef* identified a number of factors that may help determine whether a measure is necessary. In addition to these, are there any others you would want them to consider? Are each of these factors of similar importance? To what extent do you think a trade adjudication body, such as the Appellate Body, is qualified to undertake such a balancing test, and to make judgments about the "importance" of the common interest or values pursued? How should panels and the Appellate Body compare and value these different factors as part of their "process of weighing and balancing"?

3.   Article 3.2 of the Dispute Settlement Understanding requires WTO panels to interpret GATT "in accordance with customary rules of interpretation of public international law." According to the WTO Appellate Body in *Gasoline* this is an invocation of Article 31 of the Vienna Convention on the Law of Treaties and reflects "recognition that the *General Agreement* is not to be read in clinical isolation from public international law." WTO Appellate Body, *United States— Standards for Reformulated and Conventional Gasoline*, GATT Doc. WT/DS2/AB/R (Apr. 29, 1996), *reprinted in* 35 I.L.M. 603, 621 (1996). What are the implications of this statement? Does it mean only that international rules of treaty interpretation are applicable, or could it be argued that WTO panels should favor interpretations that support broader international law principles? Could one use emerging principles of international law for sustainable development to support a broader reading of "necessary" in Article XX(b)?

4.   Despite the *Tuna/Dolphin* decisions, Article XX does not absolutely prohibit all consideration of PPMs. Article XX(e), for example, provides an exception to GATT rules for "the adoption or enforcement by any contracting party of measures ... relating to the products of prison labour." Thus, the GATT permits countries to discriminate between two physically identical products if one was produced by prison labor. Does this provide any support for PPMs in the environmental context?

---

b.   ARTICLE XX(g)—PROTECTION OF EXHAUSTIBLE NATURAL RESOURCES

Article XX(g) provides protection for measures that "relate to" the protection of "exhaustible natural resources." This latter term has been interpreted to include dolphins, salmon fisheries and clean air. The main issues in applying Article XX(g) is when a measure will "relate to" the protection of an exhaustible natural resource, and whether Article XX(g) may be applied to justify measures by WTO Members to protect resources existing outside their jurisdiction.

Note that the required nexus between the trade measure and the environmental goal differs in Article XX(g) and Article XX(b). In Article XX(b) the measure must be "necessary" to achieve the goal, whereas Article XX(g) includes the less stringent requirement that it merely "relate to" the goal. Despite this difference, GATT panels have consistently applied a similar analysis—one reflecting the more stringent necessity test—to both articles, thereby limiting Article XX(g)'s scope for environmental protection. Recently, however, the WTO's Appellate Body in *Gasoline* rectified this by insisting that the two paragraphs be read according to the ordinary meaning of their texts

Gasoline involved a challenge by Venezuela and Brazil to regulations implementing provisions of the United States Clean Air Act Amendments that seek to reduce emissions of toxic and smog causing agents from motor vehicles. The amendments put in place a clean fuels initiative to address air quality problems plaguing large urban centers of the United States. The program contained two central components: one regulating what is called reformulated gas (RFG), the other regulating conventional gas.

The RFG rules promulgated by the EPA required domestic refiners to establish independent refinery baselines against which the "cleanliness" of fuels could be measured. Baselines were to be derived from actual pollutant levels found in the gas produced in individual refineries in 1990. Domestic refiners were allowed three calculation methods: two methods used formulas to *approximate* the quality of the refiner's 1990 gasoline, the other used the refiner's *actual* 1990 gas quality levels. If a domestic refiner's data were insufficient to allow use of these methods, it was required to use a statutory baseline set at the national performance average for all 1990 U.S. gasoline. Due to difficulties monitoring and enforcing rules abroad, the EPA only permitted importers to use the statutory baseline, not the actual 1990 gas quality.

Venezuela and Brazil challenged the U.S. laws for both conventional and reformulated gasoline, claiming they discriminated against gas from their refineries, that they breached key GATT obligations and that they were not saved by the environmental exceptions included in Article XX. The initial panel decision upheld their claims. The United States responded by appealing to the WTO Appellate Body. While the appeal was unsuccessful on other grounds, the U.S. was successful in arguing their measures satisfied Article XX(g). The Appellate Body's Report clarified the meaning of a number of terms in Article XX including those in Article XX(g). As discussed in the next section, it is also the first report to give detailed consideration of the chapeau to Article XX.

The Appellate Body addressed whether the U.S. measures "related to" the conservation of an exhaustible natural resource. After noting that clean air is an exhaustible natural resource, it stated that the rules were designed to monitor the compliance of foreign refiners, importers and blenders with the "non-degradation" requirements of the legislation, and that without baselines of some kind it would be impossible to exercise this monitoring and that the non-degradation requirements would be substantially frustrated. Given this relationship between the baselines and the goal of maintaining clean air, the Appellate Body held that the measures related to the conservation of an exhaustible natural resource.

The Appellate Body report requires careful consideration as it is the first to consider the Article XX environmental exceptions since the formation of the WTO. The Appellate Body's interpretation of Article XX(g) seeks to balance the competing concerns of trade liberalization and of environmental protection. When reading the following excerpt consider to what extent the Appellate Body was effective in mediating between these concerns, and how the decision could be applied in the future.

Report of the Appellate Body in *United States—Standards For Reformulated and Conventional Gasoline*, May 20, 1996, 35 I.L.M. 603 (1996)

Applying the basic principle of interpretation that the words of a treaty, like the *General Agreement*, are to be given their ordinary meaning, in their context and in the light of the treaty's object and purpose, the Appellate Body observes that the Panel Report failed to take adequate account of the words actually used by Article XX in its several paragraphs. In enumerating the various categories of governmental acts, laws or regulations which WTO Members may carry out or promulgate in pursuit of differing legitimate state policies or interests outside the realm of trade liberalization, Article XX uses different terms in respect of different categories:

> "necessary"—in paragraphs (a), (b) and (d);
>
> "essential"—in paragraph (j);
>
> "relating to"—in paragraphs (c), (e) and (g);
>
> "for the protection of"—in paragraph (f);
>
> "in pursuance of"—in paragraph (h); and
>
> "involving"—in paragraph (I).

It does not seem reasonable to suppose that the WTO Members intended to require, in respect of each and every category, the same kind or degree of connection or relationship between the measure under appraisal and the state interest or policy sought to be promoted or realized.

At the same time, Article XX(g) and its phrase, "relating to the conservation of exhaustible natural resources," need to be read in context and in such a manner as to give effect to the purposes and objects of the *General Agreement*.

The context of Article XX(g) includes the provisions of the rest of the *General Agreement*, including in particular Articles I, III and XI; conversely, the context of Articles I and III and XI includes Article XX. Accordingly, the phrase "relating to the conservation of exhaustible natural resources" may not be read so expansively as seriously to subvert the purpose and object of Article III:4. Nor may Article III:4 be given so broad a reach as effectively to emasculate Article XX(g) and the policies and interests it embodies. The relationship between the affirmative commitments set out in, e.g., Articles I, III and XI, and the policies and interests embodied in the "General Exceptions" listed in Article XX, can be given meaning within the framework of the *General Agreement* and its object and purpose by a treaty interpreter only on a case-to-case basis, by careful scrutiny of the factual and legal context in a given dispute, without disregarding the words actually used by the WTO Members themselves to express their intent and purpose. * * *

Against this background, we turn to the specific question of whether the baseline establishment rules are appropriately regarded as "primarily aimed at" the conservation of natural resources for the purposes of Article XX(g). We consider that this question must be answered in the affirmative.

The baseline establishment rules, taken as a whole (that is, the provisions relating to establishment of baselines for domestic refiners, along with the provisions relating to baselines for blenders and importers of gasoline), need to be related to the "non-degradation" requirements set out elsewhere in the Gasoline Rule. Those provisions can scarcely be understood if scrutinized strictly by themselves, totally divorced from other sections of the Gasoline Rule which certainly constitute part of the context of these provisions. The baseline establishment rules whether individual or statutory, were designed to permit scrutiny and monitoring of the level of compliance of refiners, importers and blenders with the "non-degradation" requirements. Without baselines of some kind, such scrutiny would not be possible and the Gasoline Rule's objective of stabilizing and preventing further deterioration of the level of air pollution prevailing in 1990, would be substantially frustrated. The relationship between the baseline establishment rules and the "non-degradation" requirements of the Gasoline Rule is not negated by the inconsistency, found by the Panel, of the baseline establishment rules with the terms of Article III:4. We consider that, given that substantial relationship, the baseline establishment rules cannot be regarded as merely incidentally or inadvertently aimed at the conservation of clean air in the United States for the purposes of Article XX(g).

The Appellate Body concluded that for a measure to be "related to" the conservation of an exhaustible natural resource, it need not be "necessary." This distinction between the standards for Article XX(b) and Article XX(g) suggests a more environmentally friendly reading for Article XX(g).

This interpretation was confirmed in the subsequent *Shrimp-Turtle* decision, which involved a U.S. ban on imports of shrimp harvested with gear that traps and suffocates endangered sea turtles. A 1989 U.S. amendment to the Endangered Species Act, referred to as Section 609, law requires foreign nations to certify that their shrimp fisheries do not threaten endangered sea turtles as a prerequisite for access to the U.S. market. In practice the law effectively requires foreign fishing fleets to equip their trawling gear with "turtle excluder devices" or "TEDs". TEDs are a simple metal cage with a trapdoor to allow turtles to escape without any significant loss of shrimp. Tests conducted by the U.S. National Marine Fisheries Service showed that TEDs, in addition to protecting turtles, reduced drag and wasteful bycatch of other species.

Concerned about the use of unilateral trade measures by the United States, India, Pakistan, Malaysia and Thailand challenged the U.S. measures, arguing that trade bans taken pursuant to the U.S. legislation were inconsistent with U.S. obligations under the GATT. The Complainants were successful in challenging the measure at the panel level, and the United States responded by appealing the case to the Appellate Body. The Appellate Body ultimately determined that the measure was inconsistent with the "chapeau" provision of Article XX. But before doing so, it considered the measure under Article XX(g). In examining whether the US measure was sufficiently "related to" the goal of protecting sea turtles, the Appellate Body stated:

> 141. In its general design and structure, therefore, Section 609 is not a simple, blanket prohibition of the importation of shrimp imposed without regard to the consequences (or lack thereof) of the mode of harvesting employed upon the incidental capture and mortality of sea turtles. Focusing on the design of the measure here at stake, it appears to us that Section 609, *cum* implementing guidelines, is not disproportionately wide in its scope and reach in relation to the policy objective of protection and conservation of sea turtle species. The means are, in principle, reasonably related to the ends. The means and ends relationship between Section 609 and the legitimate policy of conserving an exhaustible, and, in fact, endangered species, is observably a close and real one, a relationship that is every bit as substantial as that which we found in *United States—Gasoline* between the EPA baseline establishment rules and the conservation of clean air in the United States.

This reading of Article XX(g) is similar to that put forward in an *Amicus Brief* submitted by the Center for International Environmental Law (CIEL) and the Center for Marine Conservation (CMC) from the United States, on behalf of themselves and several developing country NGOs. The *Amicus Brief* was filed with the WTO Appellate Body to help clarify the factual record and to apply the principles of international law and GATT jurisprudence to the dispute, striking an appropriate balance between trade liberalization and species protection.

The *Amicus Brief* advocates a broad reading of Article XX(g), which supports sustainable development and environmental protection. It then examines the facts of the dispute in light of the requirements of Article XX(g) and concludes that the U.S. measures satisfy those requirements. The full text of the brief is available on the CIEL website at <http://www.ciel.org>.

CIEL Amicus Brief to the Panel on United States—Import Prohibition of Certain Shrimp and Shrimp Products

The environmental exception in Article XX (g) should be interpreted broadly in favor of sustainable development and environmental protection.

The environmental exceptions in Article XX (g) should be interpreted broadly in favor of sustainable development and environmental protection. A broad interpretation is compelled by the addition of a commitment to sustainable development in the Preamble to the WTO Agreement, and by the explicit commitment to enhancing the means for protecting and preserving the marine environment.

Under the customary rules of interpretation as expressed in the Vienna Convention, Article XX(g) must be read in light of its context, including the new Preamble with its commitment to sustainable development and to enhancing the means for protecting the environment. Enhancing the means for environmental protection must begin by giving broader protection to a Member State's selection and application of measures to protect global resources such as endangered sea turtles. (It surely cannot mean invalidating such measures when there is no evidence of protectionism, when the measures are designed to protect endangered species from becoming extinct, when the measures flow from and are consistent with explicit multilaterally determined goals and means, and when the measures are narrowly tailored, environmentally safe and cost-effective, and allow shrimping to continue virtually unimpeded.)

The precautionary principle, which supports and is part of sustainable development, also compels a broad interpretation of the environmental exception in Article XX(g). Specifically, the precautionary principle requires that Member States be given broader protection in their selection of measures to prevent serious or irreversible damage, in order not to postpone cost-effective measures while awaiting full scientific certainty.

Finally, the same reasons that compel a broad reading of Article XX(g) also compel a narrow reading of the Chapeau. Measures that are consistent with—indeed here that are virtually identical to—multilaterally agreed measures, and that further multilaterally agreed environmentally goals, must be presumed to be reasoned and justifiable, and not arbitrary or unjustifiable. Such measures also must be presumed not to be protectionist, absent compelling evidence to the contrary.

The U.S. measures satisfy the requirements of Article XX(g).

Sea turtles are an "exhaustible natural resource."

Sea turtles are a natural resource—they are a vital part of the earth's biodiversity; they migrate widely, providing ecosystem services within the environments of each of the parties to this dispute; and they have cultural significance. And sea turtles are exhaustible. All seven species risk extinction, a fact recognized by all Parties as members of CITES, and by their adoption of at least some measures to protect turtles.

The U.S. measures are measures "relating to" the conservation of sea turtles.

The sea turtle conservation measures "relate to" the conservation of sea turtles. The Appellate Body in *Gasoline,* citing previous panel decisions, interpreted "relating to" as meaning "primarily aimed at." In examining the relationship between the measure and its aim—the conservation of sea turtles—it is necessary to examine the measure as a whole, and not merely the trade restrictive aspect of it.

Section 609 seeks to protect sea turtles in two main ways. First, it calls for the negotiation of international agreements for the conservation of sea turtles. Second, recognizing that sea turtles are endangered, that shrimping without TEDs is a major cause of sea turtle mortality, and that the United States is the world's second largest shrimp consumer, the measures require that shrimp imported into the United States must be harvested in a way that does not endanger sea turtles. Breaking the nexus between U.S. shrimp consumption and unsafe fishing methods is necessary to protecting endangered sea turtle populations. Given the fundamental relationship between the measures, and the underlying policy objective of sea turtle conservation, Section 609 "relates to" the conservation of sea turtles.

The test for "relating to" does not require a balancing of the rights and obligations of the parties. The panel in *United States—Restrictions on Imports of Tuna*, erroneously imported such a requirement. The Panel held that measures making market access contingent on another country changing its policies seriously impairs the balance of rights and obligations, particularly the right of market access, and therefore can not "relate to" legitimate conservation goals. But equating "relating to" with a balancing test is both inconsistent with the ordinary meaning of "relating to" and with the purpose of Article XX which provides exceptions to the GATT, qualified only by limits found in the Chapeau.

Balancing the substantive GATT rights and obligations within Article XX(g) or the Chapeau threatens to empty the Article XX of its contents. Further, a balancing test of the kind used in *Tuna II* is inconsistent with basic economics. Efficiency and the optimal use of resources require full cost internalization. Failure to internalize costs reduces efficiency and harms the environment. While countries may decide not to internalize costs domestically, they should not adopt policies which externalize costs to the global commons through, for example, fisheries practices that harm endangered species. Such policies are not a legitimate source of comparative advantage. Rather, they are antithetical to both economic efficiency and environmental protection.

These problems are magnified by the trade system if it compels all importing countries to accept goods produced in a way which harms the *global commons* (as opposed to the exporter's domestic environment) by preventing importing nations from conditioning market access on environmentally sound production and process methods. Where the world community has acknowledged a threat to the environment in numerous international agreements, and the solution is efficient and widely accepted, the trade system should not prevent nations from mitigating the effect of their consumption on the environment through carefully tailored trade measures.* * *

However, assuming *arguendo* a balancing test is required, the sea turtle conservation measures respect the balance. They flow from and are consistent with multilateral obligations to protect migratory marine resources that use the global commons, and that are threatened with extinction. They flow from and are consistent with multilateral obligations to reduce unsustainable consumption patterns, making them consistent with the objective of sustainable development found in the Preamble to the WTO Agreement. Moreover, they minimize the effect on other countries' right of market access by permitting the importation of shrimp caught in a location or manner safe to sea turtles. Further, the measures were accompanied by training in the construction and use of TEDs. Thus, the measures do not seriously impair the right of market access and thereby respect the balance of rights and obligations of the parties. If this conclusion is not accepted, the WTO system is forcing Member States to be unwilling participants in the extinction of species.

In *Shrimp-Turtle*, the Appellate Body also examined the Complainants' argument that the United States was not permitted to use trade measures to protect resources located outside its jurisdiction. The Appellate Body considered this in the context of Article XX(g) and noted:

133. . . . The sea turtle species here at stake, i.e., covered by Section 609, are all ... 's jurisdiction. ... migrate to, or

[Is U.S. sovereignty headed for extinction?]

traverse, at one time or another, waters subject to United States jurisdiction. Neither the appellant nor any of the appellees claims any rights of exclusive ownership over the sea turtles, at least not while they are swimming freely in their natural habitat—the oceans. We do not pass upon the question of whether there is an implied jurisdictional limitation in Article XX(g), and if so, the nature or extent of that limitation. We note only that in the specific circumstances of the case before us, there is a sufficient nexus between the migratory and endangered marine populations involved and the United States for purposes of Article XX(g).

Whereas previous GATT panels had interpreted the Article XX(b) exception as including a jurisdictional limitation which prevented trade related measures from being used to protect resources located outside their jurisdiction, the Appellate Body explicitly declined to rule on this issue in Article XX(g).

QUESTIONS AND DISCUSSION

1. On the previous page is an advertisement widely distributed by the Earth Island Institute (designed by Public Media Center). Since the Panel decision was taken by three trade experts in Geneva, why do you think the NGO paid a great deal of money to place the ad in American newspapers?

2. An important issue not yet resolved is the extent to which countries may use trade barriers to influence other countries' practices. Encouraging other countries to reduce their shrimp fisheries' harm to sea turtles, for example, is the clear goal of the U.S. law.

3. In October 2000, Malaysia challenged the U.S. implementation of the Appellate Body Report. On June 15, 2001, the WTO ruled in favor of the U.S., finding that the U.S. had remedied any unfair discrimination. The panel noted that the State Department's revised shrimp-turtle guidelines provided more due process to exporting nations, and further, that the U.S. had made good faith efforts to negotiate a sea turtle conservation agreement with the Indian Ocean and South–East Asian nations affected by the law, including financial assistance to facilitate attendance by developing country representatives. The U.S. also provided technical assistance to countries adopting fishing methods that avoid incidental killing of sea turtles.

————

C. THE CHAPEAU TO ARTICLE XX

The final requirements for Article XX exceptions are found in the chapeau (introductory paragraphs) to Article XX. The chapeau introduces two qualifications to the otherwise absolute requirement that "nothing in this Agreement" shall prevent the adoption of measures to achieve the policy goals enumerated in Article XX(a) to XX(j). The chapeau requires that measures not be applied in a manner that constitutes either:

- arbitrary or unjustifiable discrimination between countries where the same conditions prevail; or

- a disguised restriction on international trade.

The chapeau has been reviewed in detail by the Appellate Body in both the *Gasoline* and *Shrimp-Turtle* cases. According to these decisions, the purpose of the chapeau is to ensure that the Article XX exceptions are not abused. In other words, countries may use trade measures to promote the objectives listed in Article XX, but must not do so in a way that is arbitrary or unjustifiable, or disguised restrictions on international trade.

In *Gasoline*, the Appellate Body concluded that the U.S. measures did not satisfy the chapeau requirements. They stated that the chapeau should not be read so broadly as to allow the Article XX exceptions to frustrate the other rights and obligations of the agreement. Nor should it be read so restrictively as to gut the exceptions. The essential issue upon review, the Appellate Body asserted, is whether the manner in which the inconsistent measure is applied avoids the abuse or illegitimate use of Article XX's exceptions. It stated that the same kinds of factors relevant to whether "arbitrary or unjustifiable discrimination" was present apply also to a determination of the presence of "a disguised restriction on international trade."

First, the Appellate Body noted that the United States had a number of alternative ways to apply the Clean Air Act Amendments that did not discriminate between foreign and domestic suppliers. Citing two such alternatives, it noted that all foreign and domestic refiners could have been granted the option to calculate an individual baseline or alternatively all refiners, domestic and foreign, could have been assigned a statutory baseline.

The United States had argued that alternative means were not feasible for a number of reasons. They would have been difficult to administer and enforce on foreign soil. As gasoline is a fungible commodity it would have been difficult to trace gasoline to specific refineries to ensure that baselines were complied with. The United States would be unable to issue subpoenas for documents in the event they suspected non-compliance, or to claim against refineries operated by foreign governments because of sovereign immunity.

The Appellate Body dismissed these arguments, relying on the panel's finding that the United States had not demonstrated that data available from foreign refiners was inherently less susceptible to established techniques of checking, verification, assessment and enforcement than data for other trade in goods subject to U.S. regulation. It decided that the United States had not pursued cooperative efforts with the complaining parties that could have addressed the administration and enforcement issues raised by the United States.

In *Shrimp-Turtle*, the Appellate Body elaborated on the role of the chapeau, stating that:

> 159. The task of interpreting and applying the chapeau is, hence, essentially the delicate one of locating and marking out a line of equilibrium between the right of a Member to invoke an exception under Article XX and the rights of the other Members under varying substantive provisions (e.g., Article XI) of the GATT 1994, so that neither of the competing rights will cancel out the other and thereby distort and nullify or impair the balance of rights and obligations constructed by the Members themselves in that Agreement. The location of the line of equilibrium, as expressed in the chapeau, is not fixed and unchanging; the line moves as the kind and the shape of the measures at stake vary and as the facts making up specific cases differ.

In its view, the United States had failed to satisfy the chapeau requirements. Among other reasons, the Appellate Body expressed concern over the coercive effect of the US measure on the policies of other governments:

> 161.   We scrutinize first whether Section 609 has been applied in a manner constituting "unjustifiable discrimination between countries where the same conditions prevail". Perhaps the most conspicuous flaw in this measure's application relates to its intended and actual coercive effect on the specific policy decisions made by foreign governments, Members of the WTO. Section 609, in its application, is, in effect, an economic embargo which requires *all other exporting Members*, if they wish to exercise their GATT rights, to adopt *essentially the same* policy (together with an approved enforcement program) as that applied to, and enforced on, United States domestic shrimp trawlers. As enacted by the Congress of the United States, the *statutory* provisions of Section 609(b)(2)(A) and (B) do not, in themselves, *require* that other WTO Members adopt *essentially the same* policies and enforcement practices as the United States. Viewed alone, the statute appears to permit a degree of discretion or flexibility in how the standards for determining comparability might be applied, in practice, to other countries. However, any flexibility that may have been intended by Congress when it enacted the statutory provision has been effectively eliminated in the implementation of that policy through the 1996 Guidelines promulgated by the Department of State and through the practice of the administrators in making certification determinations.

It also referred to the failure of the United States to undertake sufficient negotiations with the Complainants as a reason for denying the US measure protection under the Article XX chapeau:

> 172.   Clearly, the United States negotiated seriously with some, but not with other Members (including the appellees), that export shrimp to the United States. The effect is plainly discriminatory and, in our view, unjustifiable. The unjustifiable nature of this discrimination emerges clearly when we consider the cumulative effects of the failure of the United States to pursue negotiations for establishing consensual means of protection and conservation of the living marine resources here involved, notwithstanding the explicit statutory direction in Section 609 itself to initiate negotiations as soon as possible for the development of bilateral and multilateral agreements. . . .

The tendency of GATT/WTO adjudication bodies to rule systematically against unilateral measures has been criticized by some environmentalists as imposing an unreasonable burden on governments seeking to protect the environment. One commentator, Steve Charnovitz, considers that the viable threat of trade sanctions may complement other positive approaches to developing environmental standards, as part of a package of "carrots and sticks".

Steve Charnovitz, *Environmental Harmonization and Trade Policy*, in TRADE AND THE ENVIRONMENT: LAW ECONOMICS AND POLICY, *op. cit.*, at 281–82

CARROTS, STICKS, AND STANDARDS

Conducting international negotiations is one thing. Attaining a consensus is another. How can an agreement on minimum standards be achieved among a hundred countries with different values and resources? One approach is to devise a clever mix of carrots and sticks from a diverse enough issue garden to allow a cross-fertilization of concerns. The goal is not only to obtain an agreement, but also to maintain its stability.

The carrots are the basic tool. Because countries face different economic trade-offs (for example, some countries may benefit from global warming), an assistance mechanism can be developed to enable gainers to compensate losers and rich nations to "bribe" poor ones. This assistance could be in the form of financial aid or technology transfer, as provided under the Montreal Protocol on Substances that Deplete the Ozone Layer (Montreal Protocol), or it could be trade concessions.

But carrots alone may not be sufficient. Uncooperative countries might attempt to extract more assistance or concessions than the global community is willing to provide. During the past decade, for example, American diplomats attempting to negotiate a dolphin-safe fishing agreement were frustrated by the unwillingness of countries like Mexico to undertake any responsibility for marine mammals. In such cases, sticks like trade sanctions may be needed to force free-riding countries to enter multilateral agreements.

In between carrots and sticks are environmental product and process standards applied equally to both domestic production and imports. Such standards are not carrots because they provide no additional benefit to foreign countries. Yet they are not sticks either so long as such standards are applied to all countries in an evenhanded manner. The characterization of such process standards as "sanctions" is an all too common misnomer.

By taking their own product and process standards to the bargaining table, countries will be better able to strike mutually beneficial deals. If the Tuna–Dolphin panel has its way in defenestrating national standard setting, all that remains are power-based combinations of carrots and sticks. But because the stick of a trade sanction is likely to be GATT-illegal, that leaves only carrots legitimately on the table. While it may be possible to achieve international agreements with carrots alone, it is hard to imagine any such agreement remaining stable as the appetite for carrots increases. * * *

Despite concerns about the potential use of environmental measures as veiled protectionism, some trade theorists are beginning to agree that something must be done about the PPM issue. Where, for example, differing preferences for environmental quality result in environmental harm to areas outside the exporting country's jurisdiction—either transboundary harm or harm to the global commons—then international trade may exacerbate the problem to the detriment of both the importing and the exporting country. In these cases, it has been argued that limited trade measures should be allowed. Trade scholar Ernst Ulrich Petersmann writes:

> The introductory paragraph of GATT Article XX—"that such measures are not applied in a manner which would constitute a means of arbitrary or unjustifiable discrimination between countries where the same conditions prevail"— confirms that Article XX might justify, if "necessary," measures for the protection of life, health or environment of domestic citizens which differentiate according to the sources and degree of foreign transboundary pollution (e.g. resulting from foreign PPMs in countries causing hazardous exports).

Ernst–Ulrich Petersmann, *International Trade Law and International Environmental Law*, 27 JOURNAL OF WORLD TRADE LAW 43, 78 (1993).

––––––––

QUESTIONS AND DISCUSSION

1. Undoubtedly, multilateral solutions to shared environmental problems are preferable to unilateral ones. What criteria should be used by panels and the Appellate Body when determining what kinds of unilateral measures should be permitted under the Article XX chapeau? For example, what lengths should a country go to negotiate with other countries before trade measures become "justifiable" discrimination? Are there situations in which it may not be reasonable to require an importing country to negotiate a bilateral or multilateral agreement before imposing a trade ban? When is extra-jurisdictional unilateralism justified? Consider the fragile nature of MEA negotiations, and the need for a "first mover" to overcome the natural inertia of most countries. Because MEAs are based on consent and require consensus, there is strong pressure to accept the lowest common denominator. A strong "first mover" is often required to overcome this, as was demonstrated with the ozone treaty regime. Recall the discussion in Chapter 6 on lawmaking.

2. The *Shrimp-Turtle* case involved a PPM-based measure (i.e. the use or non-use of turtle excluder devices relates to the process and production methods by which shrimp are caught, and not to their physical characteristics). It seems clear from the Appellate Body's decision that PPM-based measures may be justified under Article XX(g). To what extent do you think the decision will allow future PPM-based measures under the chapeau? Will all PPM-based measures always have a "coercive effect" on the policy of other governments? Is this necessarily fatal to a measure under the Chapeau? What is the basis of "performance-based" rather than "technology-based" regulations, which would leave foreign governments with flexibility as how they achieve the result of protecting a shared environmental resource?

––––––––

3. THE RELATIONSHIP BETWEEN THE WTO AND MULTILATERAL ENVIRONMENTAL AGREEMENTS

A number of multilateral environmental agreements (MEAs) rely on trade measures to protect the environment, sanction noncompliance by parties, or encourage nonparties to join. For example, the Montreal Protocol prohibits trade of listed ozone-depleting substances between parties and non-parties. *See* Chapter 9, page 575. If a party and non-party are both GATT Member States, this could violate GATT's Most Favored Nation requirement. The following excerpt describes the potential conflict between the WTO and MEAs that include trade measures, and suggests ways the relationship may be clarified.

Goldberg, Housman, Van Dyke, and Zaelke, Eds., The Use of Trade Measures in Select Multilateral Environmental Agreements 3, 17–23 (UNEP 1995)

The Substance of Potential Conflicts

Because trade rules and the rules of these multilateral environmental agreements have developed on separate tracks, in many cases their provisions do not fit neatly together. For example, the multilateral environmental agreements often focus on the environmental impacts of a product's production, use and disposal, and may not be concerned with, nor affect, the actual product at issue. From an environmental standpoint this makes perfect sense. However, trade rules have been interpreted to require that regulations effect [sic] the product as opposed to production or disposal of the product. Similarly, as discussed above, these multilateral environmental agreements by their nature can only be effective if they change behavior in both parties and non-parties. Some panels, however, have read trade rules to discourage efforts to change behavior outside of one's own jurisdiction.

As there has never been actual conflict between the rules of GATT and the multilateral environmental agreements ... one can only speculate as to how the environmental and trade rules would apply to such conflicts. For example, while the GATT/WTO may find it unacceptable for one nation to attempt unilaterally to change behavior in the territory of another party, it is plausible, if not likely, that the GATT/WTO would distinguish such unilateral measures from the multilateral efforts of these environmental agreements. Whereas one party acting alone may not be able to use trade measures to change the policies and practices of another country, where the nations of the world act in concert to address a compelling environmental threat, they may be able to use trade measures without violating their obligations under the GATT/WTO—even where those measures apply to non-parties. A GATT/WTO panel confronted with such a challenge could look to the broad language provided in the environmental exceptions to find the trade measures of such agreements compatible with the GATT/WTO.

At least three compelling policy arguments support a finding that the obligations of these multilateral environmental agreements are compatible with the GATT/WTO. First, as discussed above, multilateral environmental protections are the most effective way to deal with transboundary and global environmental threats. The parties to these agreements have determined that trade measures are necessary to achieve their desired goals. If GATT/WTO panels were to find against these multilateral environmental agreements, they would substantially reduce the ability of their own parties to address compelling environmental threats.

Second, multilateral environmental agreements serve to harmonize measures for addressing particular threats, preventing a host of disparate national programs from developing. This, in turn, reduces barriers to trade and the potential for protectionism cloaked in environmental garb.

Third, a cooperative, multilateral approach to transboundary and global environmental problems is generally preferable to unilateral efforts because a multilateral solution is more likely to reflect disparate interests. A multilateral approach is also more likely to deal constructively with the particular concerns of developing nations.

Resolving Conflicts

Conflicts can arise because multilateral environmental agreements and the GATT/WTO have developed on separate tracks and do not explicitly address how they should relate to each other. It is not clear what rules would apply in such conflicts. The Vienna Convention on the Law of Treaties provides rules for the interpretation of treaties. The rule governing conflicts between two treaties on the same subject matter, arising between countries that are party to both of the conflicting agreements, provides that the latest treaty will prevail. However, it is unclear whether the GATT/WTO and these multilateral environmental agreements concern the same subject matter. If they do not, the Vienna

Convention's later in time rule would not apply. Of course, the Vienna Convention's priority rules don't apply if a treaty specifies its own relationship to other international agreements as, for example, the Biodiversity Convention does.

Moreover, while a dispute between two countries that are both party to a multilateral environmental agreement and the GATT/WTO might arise (for example, over a party's implementation), such disputes are less likely than a dispute between a GATT/WTO party that is also party to a multilateral environmental agreement, and a GATT/WTO party that is not a party to the environmental agreement. As to party/non-party disputes, the Vienna Convention provides no practical guidance on how the state that is party to both treaties is to reconcile any conflicting legal obligations.

Apart from the Vienna Convention, general principles of international law might prove useful in resolving such conflicts. As to treaties on the same subject, the treaty that is more specific governs matters under its purview, while the more general treaty governs the broader field at issue. In most instances the multilateral environmental agreements ... lay out specific rules that govern a more narrow area of trade and trade restrictions than the general field of trade and trade restrictions governed by the GATT/WTO.

In addition to the lack of substantive rules that apply to a conflict, it is unclear where such a case should be heard. If the case concerns a party/party dispute, the issue presumably could be dealt with in the dispute processes of the multilateral environmental agreement, or within those of the GATT/WTO. The past practice of the parties would argue for handling these disputes first within the environmental agreement's processes. If the dispute were to involve the non-party provisions of a multilateral environmental agreement, however, a party challenging the application of these provisions to their trade could only bring the case before the GATT/WTO. In both party/party and non-party/party disputes, the International Court of Justice (ICJ) offers an alternative forum for handling such disputes. Another alternative that has been suggested would be to have the environmental issues in a dispute (such as whether the measure at issue is authorized by the environmental agreement) decided within the mechanisms established by the environmental agreement, and then to have these findings referred to a GATT/WTO panel for application of the GATT/WTO's rules. * * *

Clarifying the Relationship

A criteria specific approach would involve setting out the relationship between GATT/WTO and qualifying multilateral environmental agreements and then developing a list of criteria for what constitutes a "multilateral environmental agreement" for these purposes. The criteria might include the number of parties to an agreement, the range of interests represented by the parties, the terms of membership, the degree of trade restraint in relation to the goals of the agreement, the centrality of trade to the goals, the linkage of burdens and benefits of the agreement, and the universality of benefits and harms, as well as the seriousness of the environmental threat. It must be emphasized that under a criteria specific approach, no one factor would be determinative. For example, an agreement might have only a handful of parties and still qualify if it generally met the other criteria.

While the criteria approach would avoid the listing process and review problems, it would provide less certainty as to the relationship between particular multilateral environmental agreements and the GATT/WTO, at least until a challenge were brought with respect to each particular environmental agreement—a cumbersome and uncertain process.

Neither of these approaches addresses the issue of how to handle a party's implementation of a multilateral environmental agreement. Some have suggested that a party's implementation of an agreement should only be protected if it exactly mirrors the requirements of the agreement. This approach, however, ignores the fact that some agreements provide only general obligations, while others state specific obligations but permit or invite parties to take more stringent measures to further the agreement's objectives. Such an approach also overlooks the role that front-runner countries can play in advancing international efforts to address a threat.

QUESTIONS AND DISCUSSION

1. Whereas regional trade agreements such as NAFTA include specific provisions accommodating MEAs, the WTO agreements include no such provision. Consequently, trade measures used either to implement or encourage non-party compliance with MEAs such as the Montreal Protocol and the Basel Convention may be subject to WTO jurisdiction in the event of a trade challenge. Is the WTO the appropriate forum in which to answer this question or should some other body, or combination of bodies, decide?

2. In the event of a conflict, which should prevail, the WTO Agreements or an MEA? Under international law on the interpretation of treaties, would the WTO Agreements prevail if they were concluded after affected MEAs, or would the more specific MEAs prevail? What other factors would be relevant to the answer? In the event the WTO Agreements applied, do you think measures taken pursuant to MEAs would comply with current interpretations of "necessary" in Article XX(b)? What clarifications could be made to Article XX to ensure, for example that the highly effective third-party trade measures in the Montreal Protocol are not trumped by WTO disciplines? Can it be argued that a measure is not "arbitrary or unjustifiable" if taken pursuant to an MEA? If so, what then about measures that are not specifically authorized but that are in furtherance of the goals of international environmental law?

3. MEAs are a special case, it is argued, because they represent an international consensus, and the give and take of the negotiations should ferret out any hidden economic protectionism. Yet what membership represents a consensus? Is it simply the number of signatory countries? The number of countries that have ratified? Or does it matter which countries have ratified? As we have discussed throughout the book, certain treaties will not be effective without the participation of a relatively small number of key States (such as India and China in the context of climate change). Do you think an objective standard could be developed to define "consensus participation" in the context of MEAs?

4. The relationship between the objectives of the Convention on Biological Diversity (CBD), intellectual property rights (IPRs), and the TRIPS Agreement remains a subject of continuing debate. Some WTO Members argue that the intellectual property rights required by the TRIPS Agreement help to conserve biodiversity by providing a vehicle for rewarding those who maintain and use biological resources. Others, including many developing countries, have argued that the TRIPS Agreement should be amended to bring it into line with the provisions of the CBD. Brazil, for example, has called for an amendment to the TRIPS Agreement to ensure that the benefits arising out of the use of genetic resources are shared fairly, and to protect traditional knowledge. We discuss these issues in detail in Chapter 13, page 941.

————

4. THE RELATIONSHIP BETWEEN THE PRECAUTIONARY PRINCIPLE AND THE SPS AGREEMENT

The relationship between the precautionary principle and WTO rules has a number of facets, including the relationship between trade rules and national precautionary measures; the relationship between trade rules and measures in MEAs based on the precautionary principle; and whether the precautionary principle can be used to help interpret and apply trade rules. Of these issues, one of the most important is the relationship between the rules of the SPS Agreement, which establishes disciplines on certain national measures designed to protect health and the environment, and measures based on the precautionary principle.

The SPS Agreement defines the kinds of measures governments may take to regulate risks arising from invasive species, genetically modified organisms, and certain other risks to human, animal or plant life or health. It provides that these sanitary and phytosanitary measures may not be maintained "without sufficient scientific evidence". The precautionary principle, by contrast, provides that "where there are threats of serious or irreversible damage, lack of full scientific certainty shall not be used as a reason for postponing cost-effective measures to prevent environmental degradation" (Rio Principle 15). In the former case, scientific evidence must be used to justify a measure, whereas in the latter, its absence should not be used to postpone taking action.

While not fundamentally in contradiction, these approaches do operate in a certain amount of tension with each other. The potential for conflict is mitigated by Article 5.7 of the SPS Agreement, which provides WTO Members with a limited right to adopt measures on a provisional basis, in cases where scientific information is insufficient. Article 5.7 states:

> In cases where relevant scientific evidence is insufficient, a Member may provisionally adopt sanitary or phytosanitary measures on the basis of available pertinent information, including that from the relevant international organizations as well as from sanitary or phytosanitary measures applied by other Members. In such circumstances, Members shall seek to obtain the additional information necessary for a more objective assessment of risk and review the sanitary or phytosanitary measure accordingly within a reasonable period of time.

According to the Appellate Body, the precautionary principle "finds reflection" in Article 5.7 (*Hormones*, WT/DS48/AB/R, at 124). How the Appellate Body interprets and applies terms such as "insufficient" and "reasonable period of time" will effect the kind of measures governments can take to regulate invasive species, GMOs and other potential risks to health and environment. Some WTO Members, notably the European Union, have asked for the relationship between the precautionary principle and WTO agreements to be further clarified through an interpretive note. Other WTO Members, by contrast believe that the relationship is sufficiently clear, and that a clarification may shift the balance inherent in the existing agreements.

***

QUESTIONS AND DISCUSSION

1. If the precautionary principle has reached the status of a principle of customary international law, then how might it be used to interpret WTO agreements? Could it be argued that the provisions of Article 5.7 of the SPS Agreement should be interpreted more broadly? Which other principles of international law might be relevant to interpretation of the SPS Agreement?

2. In the *Shrimp-Turtle* case, the Appellate Body interpreted the term "natural resources" in light of obligations in international environmental law (notably the United Nations Convention on the Law of the Sea, and the Convention on Biological Diversity). It stated that the term was "by definition, evolutionary", and so it is pertinent to note its use in other modern conventions. Could the SPS Agreement also be read in light of other international obligations? How might the provisions of the SPS Agreement be read in light of the more recently concluded Biosafety Protocol, which sets out detailed procedures for the safe transfer, handling and use of living modified organisms?

***

5.   THE RELATIONSHIP BETWEEN ECOLABELING AND THE TBT AGREEMENT

Ranging from the Blue Angel in Germany and the Nordic Swan in Scandinavia to the Eco-mark in Japan, eco-labeling programs can now be found in over 25 countries around the globe. Eco-labels help consumers to exercise preferences for products whose production, use and disposal impose a lighter burden on the environment than competing products. They provide consumers and retailers with information about the impacts of the products, helping them apply their purchasing power to encourage better environmental practices. Environmentally sound producers may benefit through expanded market shares and possible price premiums, and environmentalists hope that this market-based incentive will increase protection and more thoughtful use of natural resources.

Eco-labelling, as well as other labelling and certification schemes, are covered by the TBT Agreement. As noted earlier in this chapter, the TBT Agreement applies both to both technical regulations, which are mandatory, and standards, which are voluntary, and seeks to reduce barriers to market access by harmonizing these to international standards. The Agreement explicitly applies to any "[d]ocument approved by a recognized body, that provides, for common and repeated use, rules, guidelines or characteristics for products or related processes and production methods, with which compliance is not mandatory. It may also include or deal exclusively with terminology, symbols, packaging, marking or labelling requirements as they apply to a product, process or production method (TBT Agreement, Annex 1)."

The relationship between eco-labeling schemes and trade rules has been discussed extensively by the WTO's Committee on Trade and Environment. The CTE's report to the Singapore Ministerial noted that "[w]ell-designed ecolabeling schemes/programmes can be effective instruments of environmental policy to encourage the development of an environmentally-conscious consumer public." It also noted that ecolabeling schemes/programmes "have raised, in certain cases, significant concerns about their possible trade effects." (WTO/CTE 1996, ¶¶ 183–186). Despite the CTE's discussions, a number of unresolved issues exist, particularly in relation to the TBT Agreement.

One is whether the TBT Agreement permits labels that identify how product's process and production methods (PPMs), rather than its physical characteristics. The PPM issue was discussed above in relation to the GATT's core obligations. WTO Members remain divided over whether the TBT Agreement permits, bans or does not cover PPM-based eco-labels. The better argument seems to be that it covers and permits PPM based labels, but requires them to be non-discriminatory, and to avoid creating unnecessary obstacles to international trade. This state of uncertainty is of some concern to some environmentalists who believe that labels, by informing consumers of how a product was produced, provide an important way of encouraging environmentally sound consumption.

A second issue is the extent to which the TBT Agreement can and does regulate the activities of sub-national and private labelling organizations. The TBT Agreement establishes a Code of Good Practice for local government and non-governmental standardizing and labelling bodies. It also provides that WTO Members must take "such reasonable measures as may be available" to ensure that local government and private standardizing bodies comply with the Code (TBT Agreement, Article 4.1). The precise scope of obligations in the Code, as well as the type of "reasonable measures" Members must take to enforce it, remains somewhat unclear.

———

QUESTIONS AND DISCUSSION

1. The environmental community has expressed concern that the TBT Agreement's requirement that countries use international standards "as a basis for their technical regulations" unless they can demonstrate that the standard "would be an ineffective or inappropriate means for the fulfillment of a legitimate objective" may force the downward harmonization of environmental laws. Chapter 18's discussion of ISO, pages 1420–1432, is particularly relevant and discusses this issue in more detail. In what circumstances might the TBT Agreement's MFN and National Treatment obligations be used to challenge domestic environmental law? How might a lack of environmental exceptions in the text of the TBT Agreement affect the ability of countries to defend such a challenge? Many environmental groups have argued that the Article XX environmental exceptions apply to all the agreements consolidated under the WTO including the TBT Agreement. What arguments can you make to support this assertion? How might the TBT Agreement's preambular language on human, animal and plant life and health impact on these arguments? Which of the two main environmental exceptions would be applicable?

2. The TBT Agreement states that both regulations and standards may relate to "terminology, symbols, packaging, marking or labeling requirements as they apply to a product, process or production method." As described above, it is unclear whether criteria that distinguish between products according to *non-product* factors fall within the TBT Agreement. What policy arguments are there either in favor of, or against, applying trade discipline under the TBT to the specific case of ecolabels? *See,* James Salzman, *Informing the Green Consumer: The Debate Over the Use and Abuse of Environmental Labels,* JOURNAL OF INDUSTRIAL ECOLOGY (Summer 1997).

————

6. PUBLIC PARTICIPATION IN THE WTO

Currently the role of civil society organizations in the WTO is circumscribed. For example, non-governmental organizations are not permitted to observe or participate in WTO meetings. Yet broader NGO participation could benefit the WTO, as suggested by Steve Charnovitz in the following excerpt, where he also describes how NGOs might participate.

Charnovitz, *Opening the WTO to Nongovernmental Interests,* 24 FORDHAM INT'L. L. L. 173, 212–16 (2000).

Should the WTO move away from its state-centrism and toward greater respect for the individual? In the author's view, the answer is yes. Economic nationalism and protectionism are deeply rooted, and so providing opportunities for civil society groups to challenge these practices can help the World Trade Organization use trade to achieve a better World.

Consultation and cooperation with NGOs should occur in all three branches of the WTO. Because the legislative, executive, and judicial functions differ, appropriate modalities need to be tailored for each branch. Some suggestions are offered below.

A. Legislative

The key legislative activities of the WTO are the Ministerial Conferences, the General Council, and trade negotiations. The government officials who attend the Ministerial Conference are trade ministers who are sometimes elected to parliament within their country but are usually appointed by elected officials. Currently, the WTO permits NGOs to be silent observers at Ministerial Conferences, and that may be sufficient. If the Seattle experiment of having a parallel inter-parliamentary meeting is repeated in the future, the parliamentarians could hold WTO oversight hearings and invite NGOs to testify.

The WTO needs to provide a channel for NGO input into trade negotiations. During the Uruguay Round, business NGOs and transnational corporations worked through governments to influence the negotiations, but other NGOs did not have equivalent access. This author has not yet seen any good proposals for regularizing the infusion of NGO ideas into a future trade round. Until a method is devised, governments could put some individuals from NGOs on their delegations.

B. Executive

The executive activities of the WTO occur in the various Councils (such as the Council for Trade in Services), Bodies (such as the Textiles Monitoring Body), and Committees (such as the Committee on Agriculture). At present, none of these organs have organized consultations with NGOs. Yet all of them should.

Article V(2) of the WTO Agreement provides authority for holding such consultations. Until the WTO General Council reaches a consensus to do so, the chairs of the various WTO subsidiary organs should meet with interested NGOs on a regular basis pursuant to the authority in the current NGO Guidelines. For instance, the chair of the Committee on Sanitary and Phytosanitary Measures could meet with NGOs interested in promoting food safety.

Ideally, NGO interventions would spring from experience rather than merely ideology. Some NGOs in Geneva will be part of networks that include local grassroots groups, and often this local-level experience can provide valuable insights to policymakers at the center. If well-structured, the competition among NGOs will help distinguish good ideas from bad.

In preparing for NGO input, the WTO can draw lessons from the way that other international organizations involve NGOs. Two useful examples are the Organisation for Economic Co-operation and Development ("OECD") and UNCTAD [U.N. Commission on Trade and Development]. The OECD Trade Committee holds consultations with a broad range of NGOs. So does UNCTAD, and these efforts demonstrate that developing country NGOs can participate effectively. The WTO needs to hear more from Southern NGOs in order to counteract the domination of WTO politics by Northern governments.

The WTO can also take advantage of its proximity to the International Labor Organization ("ILO") in Geneva and the World Conservation Union ("IUCN") in Gland to secure convenient NGO input through those organizations. If the WTO agrees to provide observer status for the ILO, as it has with seven other international organizations, then the ILO attendance will be tripartite with governments, employer NGOs, and worker NGOs. The IUCN is a hybrid organization whose membership comprises seventy-eight States, 112 government agencies, and 735 NGOs. By giving the IUCN observer status on appropriate WTO committees, the WTO could secure advice from environment ministries and NGOs.

The approach of mainstreaming NGOs into the WTO's work is better than setting up an overall NGO advisory committee. Recently, Supachai Panitchpakdi, who will be the next WTO Director–General, gave new support to the idea of an NGO advisory committee. But as the WTO symposia showed, bringing a rainbow of NGOs together in one room frustrates any in-depth discussions on particular issues.

C. Judicial

The WTO should establish procedures to enable NGOs and individuals to submit amicus curiae briefs to panels and to the Appellate Body. The government delegates to the WTO apparently believe this matter should be dealt with by them rather than the Appellate Body, and so the governments should act quickly to promulgate needed procedures. Many close observers of WTO dispute settlement would favor such action. Thomas Cottier, a frequent GATT/WTO panelist, has written that "publicity of hearings of panels and amicus curiae briefs from non-governmental organizations could further enhance the legitimacy, and acceptance, of the WTO dispute settlement process." In 2000, the International Law Association recommended "allowing individual parties, both natural and corporate, an advisory *locus standi* in those dispute settlement procedures where their own rights and interests are affected."

Boosting the transparency of the WTO dispute process will improve public confidence in the adjudications and also facilitate the submission of briefs by civil society groups. To that end, the following steps should be taken. First, WTO rules should be changed so that government briefs to the panels become public documents. (Of course, governments should be able to designate specific information as confidential.) Second, the WTO Secretariat should release the names and brief biographies of panelists. Third, the Secretariat should prepare a toolkit for how to submit an amicus brief. Such a toolkit might also be designed by an NGO such as the International Centre for Trade and Sustainable Development. A toolkit could include contact information for law school clinics in the United States or elsewhere that might be willing to prepare a brief for a developing country NGO.

CONCLUSION

The debate about the appropriate role of NGOs at the WTO will continue in the years ahead. Before he joined the WTO in 1999, Director–General Moore wrote about the "virtue" of civil society in exposing "the corruption and inherent dishonesty of closed minds and closed systems." Inside the WTO, Moore has butted against some closed minds. Certainly, NGOs are not more virtuous than governments. Yet as voluntary groups, NGOs consist of individuals who care enough about an issue to work for or against it. The WTO will stand a better chance of reaching enlightened decisions and implementing them if governments welcome competing views and try to get NGOs to work for a better trading system. Moreover, inviting NGOs into the WTO will keep them off the streets.

See also, D. Esty, *Non-Governmental Organizations at the World Trade Organization: Cooperation, Competition, or Exclusion,* J. INT'L. ECON. LAW 1 (1998) at 123–47 (arguing that NGOs should be welcomed in the international policymaking process as "competitors" to governments).

Indeed, a number of arguments support much greater public participation in the WTO in general, and in its dispute settlement system in particular. First, public participation can enhance the perceived legitimacy of the WTO. NGOs reflect diverse views held by the many stakeholders in the international trade system. Many of these views are not represented by governments, which must present a unified voice. Hearing these views would ensure that the trade community is kept abreast of the evolution in civil society. It would also broaden support for the dispute settlement process by blunting claims from within Member states that the WTO process lacks transparency and impinges on national sovereignty and by encouraging stakeholders in the international trade system to adopt a constructive role.

Second, greater public participation would assist in creating a fair, open trading system which contributes to the goal of sustainable development. Replacing unsustainable practices with sustainable ones requires a sense of common purpose by all members of the international community, including those from the trade and environmental communities. Encouraging public participation fosters the communication, cooperation and coordination necessary to achieve the goal of sustainable development.

Third, enhanced public participation in the WTO dispute settlement process would contribute to improved panel decision-making. Access to full scientific and technical information is essential to sound Panel deliberations. As recognized by the DSU, experts within the NGO community, including business, environmental organizations, and local governments, are well-placed to provide this information. Further, NGO's facilitate creative technical and legal solutions by providing ideas and information unavailable from normal bureaucratic channels, and ensure thorough solutions by subjecting prevailing wisdom to rigorous and ongoing review.

In recent cases, including the *Shrimp-Turtle* and *British Steel* cases, the Appellate Body has acknowledged that both panels and the Appellate Body may accept amicus briefs. In the *Shrimp-Turtle* case the panel had rejected the amicus brief submitted by NGOs on the basis that:

> Accepting non-requested information from non-governmental sources would be, in our opinion, incompatible with the provisions of the DSU as currently applied. We therefore informed the parties that we did not intend to take these documents into consideration. We observed, moreover, that it was usual practice for parties to put forward whatever documents they considered relevant to support their case and that, if any party in the present dispute wanted to put forward these documents, or parts of them, as part of their own submissions to the Panel, they were free to do so. If this were the case, the other parties would have two weeks to respond to the additional material.

The panel's ruling was overturned by the Appellate Body, which confirmed that panels do have the capacity to accept amicus briefs, stating,

> ... authority to *seek* information is not properly equated with a *prohibition* on accepting information which has been submitted without having been requested by a panel. A panel has the discretionary authority either to accept and consider or to reject information and advice submitted to it, whether requested by a panel or not.

During the appeal, the Appellate Body also determined, as part of its procedural ruling, that it was permitted to accept amicus briefs and determined that it would:

> ... accept for consideration, insofar as they may be pertinent, the legal arguments made by the various non-governmental organizations in the three briefs attached as exhibits to the appellant's submission of the United States, as well as the revised version of the brief by the CIEL which was submitted to us on 3 August 1998. (*Shrimp-Turtle*, at para 83)

The legal basis for this was explained in the later *British-Steel* case, in which the Appellate Body cited Article 17.9 of the Dispute Settlement Understanding, which permits it to adopt procedural rules which do not conflict with any rules and procedures in the DSU or the covered agreements. In considering acceptance of an amicus brief it stated: "We are of the opinion that we have the legal authority under the DSU to accept and consider *amicus curiae* briefs in an appeal in which we find it pertinent and useful to do so." (Appellate Body Report, *US–British Steel*, para. 42, WT/DS138/AB/R).

While these statements mark an important development in WTO jurisprudence, it remains to be seen whether panels and the Appellate Body make adequate use of amicus briefs. Some commentators have argued that to clarify the WTO's practice relating to amicus briefs, WTO Members should develop procedural and substantive criteria. Marceau and Stilwell argue that the WTO should take the following steps:

> 1. WTO Members should negotiate and agree to rules regarding the acceptance and consideration of *amicus* briefs by panels and the Appellate Body–not to do so in the circumstances is to maintain the present state of legal uncertainty.

2. Failing this, panels and the Appellate Body will be under pressure to develop rules of procedure regarding the acceptance and consideration of *amicus* briefs. For panels, these should be defined in consultation with the parties at the organization meeting.

3. To ensure that *amicus* briefs do not come too late in proceedings, and do not unduly burden the dispute settlement process, the timetable (or part thereof) should be made public.

4. For panels, specific rules of procedure for *amicus* briefs should be confirmed in consultation with the parties at the organization meeting. At that time the panel may decide to call for *amicus* briefs on specific issues and thus impose criteria, conditions and time limits.

5. *Amici* should always notify their briefs (solicited or non-solicited) directly and simultaneously to parties, third-parties and the panel. The panel should ensure that this due process requirement is complied with.

6. The process for administering *amicus* briefs should include at least two stages: *prima facie* admission of the brief ("first stage"); and substantive consideration of its contents ("second stage").

7. At the *first stage*, panels should examine whether the brief satisfies basic *procedural* criteria, and that it satisfies, on a *prima facie* basis, certain *substantive* criteria, and rule accordingly.

8. *Procedural* criteria should ensure that briefs are: received before the closure of the period for receiving evidence; accompanied by a brief cover page (or motion to submit) describing the *amici* and its main evidence/arguments; and notified to the parties and third parties.

9. *Substantive* criteria should take into account the character of the *amici* (relevant interest in the case, or appropriate expertise); the nature and quality of the brief(s) submitted and their relevance; and the specific needs of the panel in light of the circumstances of the case.

10. In light of the parties' comments, the panels may reject the brief, or recommend that it be attached to a party's submission, ask for further information, or accept the brief, in full or part of it.

11. At the conclusion of the first stage, the panels should issue a preliminary ruling (with reasons) on whether an *amicus* brief is admissible or inadmissible. (Borrowing from the second stage, in light of time constraint the preliminary ruling (of the first stage) may include an indication by the panel of aspects of the briefs that could appear prima facie to be relevant.)

12. At the *second stage*, the panels may decide, or may be requested by the parties, to issue another ruling as to which, or which parts of any, *amicus* briefs are considered particularly relevant. This will require a more in-depth analysis of the briefs submitted.

13. Panels, through specific questions should invite parties to comment on any material arguments or evidence submitted by an *amici* (that are being considered by the panel), but that have not been addressed by the parties.

14. Substantive criteria should also be used by adjudicating bodies when considering the content of the brief, the weight of arguments and evidence, and their implication for the case, while striking a balance between high quality panel reports and avoiding undue delay of the panel process

15. Where an *amicus* brief is "attached" to the submission of a party or a third party, it becomes an integral part of the submissions and should be considered by the panel accordingly.

16.   In its final report, the panel should inform the parties of whether it took into account elements of the *amicus* brief, and offer reasons for its decisions. Such findings are necessary (among other reasons) for the parties and the Appellate Body to identify the origin of factual assessment in light of the rules on the burden of proof.

17.   The *amicus* brief(s) should either be annexed to the panel report or described in the descriptive part of the report.

Marceau & Stilwell, *Practical Suggestions for Amicus Curiae Briefs Before WTO Adjudicating Bodies*, 4 J. INT'L. ECON. L. 155, 185–7 (March 2001).

————

QUESTIONS AND DISCUSSION

1. How could criteria and principles make the acceptance of amicus briefs more palatable to those WTO members that are more skeptical about public participation? What kinds of NGOs should be permitted to submit amicus briefs? What precedents in international environmental law could you invoke to convince the WTO to increase public participation? What other institutions could be used as precedent?

2. Should NGOs be permitted into the WTO's decision-making bodies, such as the General Council and the Dispute Settlement Body? If so, what kinds of NGOs should be permitted access, and under what conditions? What kind of criteria should be applied to these NGOs? Some members of the trading community have also suggested that NGOs should be subjected to a "code of conduct" before gaining access. Do you agree?

3. Closely related to participation by the public is participation by other international organizations. In some cases, requests for formal observer status have been blocked by a few countries for political purposes. For example, a formal request for observer status by the Convention on Biological Diversity to the Council on TRIPS was blocked by a few countries on the basis that it lacked sufficient interest. What are the arguments for and against granting observer status to other international organizations? Do you think, in light of the discussion in Chapter 13 relating to biodiversity conservation and intellectual property, that the CBD has sufficient interest to participate as an observer in the TRIPS Council? What are the counter-arguments?

————

Suggested Further Reading and Web Sites

Daniel Esty, *Bridging the Trade–Environment Divide*, 15 J. of Econ. Perspectives 130 (2001).

David M. Driesen, *What is Free Trade?: The Real Issue Lurking Behind the Trade and Environment Debate*, 41 VA. J. INT'L L. 279 (2001).

Steve Charnovitz, *Opening the WTO To Nongovernmental Interests*, 24 Fordham Int'l L.J. 173 (2000).

James Salzman, *Seattle's Legal Legacy and Environmental Reviews of Trade Agreements*, 31 ENVT'L. L. 501 (2001)

Robert Howse and Elisabeth Tuerk, *The WTO Impact on Internal Regulations: A Case Study of the Canada–EC Asbestos Dispute*, in THE EU AND THE WTO: LEGAL AND CONSTITUTIONAL ISSUES (Hart Publishing 2001).

Jeffrey Dunoff, *From Green to Global: Toward the Transformation of International Environmental Law*, 19 HARV. ENVTL. L. REV. 241 (1995)

Daniel Esty, GREENING THE GATT (1994)
   Excellent treatment of the trade/environment debate. While the cases are now dated, still the most readable and informative background book on the subject.

Bradnee Chambers & Gary Sampson, eds., Trade, Environment and the Millennium (1999)
   Detailed discussion of WTO disciplines.

John H. Jackson, WORLD TRADE AND THE LAW OF GATT (1969)
   The classic treatment of international trade law.

Durwood Zaelke et al., eds., TRADE AND THE ENVIRONMENT: LAW, ECONOMICS AND POLICY (1993)
   Collection of thoughtful essays by various trade and environment experts.

James Cameron et al eds., TRADE AND THE ENVIRONMENT: THE SEARCH FOR BALANCE (1994)
   Collection of probing essays by experts in the field.

<http://www.ictsd.org>
   Bridges Weekly Trade News Digest (available by email and on web page), and *Bridges: Between Trade and Sustainable Development,* International Centre for Trade and Sustainable Development (monthly newsletter)

<http://www.wto.org/>
   Homepage of the WTO.

SECTION III.   TRADE IN THE AMERICAS

A.   INTRODUCTION

In December 1992, the United States, Canada and Mexico concluded the North American Free Trade Agreement (NAFTA), which substantially reduces tariffs and other trade barriers among the three countries. The NAFTA was the first major trade agreement to address the environmental effects of free trade in the agreement itself. It incorporates provisions protecting domestic health and environmental regulations from the downward pressures caused by free trade, giving precedence to the parties' responsibilities under international environmental agreements when those responsibilities conflict with NAFTA, and shifting the burden of proof away from the defending party when environmental or health regulation is attacked as a trade distortion. In addition, the NAFTA parties concluded an "Environmental Side Agreement," the North American Agreement on Environmental Cooperation, Can.–Mex.–U.S., Sept. 14, 1993, *reprinted in* 32 I.L.M. 1480 (1993), to promote environmental cooperation, increase citizen participation in environmental protection, and ensure that each party effectively enforces its environmental laws. NAFTA and its Environmental Side Agreement provide important lessons in reconciling the often conflicting demands of economic integration and environmental protection.

NAFTA is not the first attempt to liberalize trade in the Americas. In addition to many bilateral agreements, several regional and subregional trade agreements have been developed over the past twenty years. In 1968, fifteen Caribbean nations launched the Caribbean Free Trade Area. Renamed the Caribbean Community and Common Market (CARICOM) in 1973, the group continues working to lower trade barriers and increase economic cooperation. The "Andean Pact" among Bolivia, Colombia, Ecuador, Peru and Venezuela was created in 1969, but lay dormant until its "relaunch" in 1988. In December 1991, Argentina, Brazil, Paraguay, and Uruguay concluded a trade agreement which created, in 1994, the Southern Cone Common Market (MERCOSUR). Nor have regional integration efforts stopped with the NAFTA. In October 1993, Costa Rica, El Salvador, Guatemala, Honduras, and Nicaragua revived the Central American Common Market, and in May 1994, Mexico, Venezuela and Colombia created the "Group of 3" partnership. Various other bi-lateral agreements also have been concluded, including a Canada–Chile agreement.

Further integration in the Western Hemisphere is proceeding apace. The original parties designed NAFTA with a view to developing an eventual hemisphere-wide Free Trade Agreement for the Americas (FTAA). Negotiations for the FTAA have been underway since 1998, and are scheduled to conclude by 2004. Meanwhile, NAFTA's southern counterpart, MERCOSUR, is courting new members, with Bolivia and Chile recently becoming associate members.

This section examines the major trade agreements in the Western Hemisphere, their potential impacts on human health and the environment, and the extent to which each agreement addresses these impacts. It then considers how growing awareness of the trade-environment relationship, and increased emphasis on public participation in the negotiation of trade agreements, are shaping the proposed hemisphere-wide FTAA.

B.   NAFTA

The NAFTA, 8 Dec. 1992, Can.–Mex.–U.S., 32 I.L.M. 289, integrates the markets of the United States, Canada and Mexico into a single $8.6 trillion free trade area with 390 million consumers and annual trade flows of more than $600 billion. In this section, we examine NAFTA and the Environmental Side Agreement, with a view to the broader debate about trade liberalization and the environment.

---

1.   THE NAFTA DEBATE

Neither the environmental provisions in the NAFTA text nor the attachment of the Environmental Side Agreement were part of the original NAFTA negotiating text. As originally drafted, NAFTA was similar to the revised GATT that was emerging simultaneously from the Uruguay Round negotiations. The administration of President George Bush Sr., which had negotiated the NAFTA in secrecy and without public participation for the first eighteen months, revised the draft treaty to include minimal environmental protections after early reports of its contents sparked widespread protest among environmentalists, labor groups and others. *See* Walter Russell Mead, *Bushism, Found*, in HARPER'S, Sept. 1992, at 37, 39.

As a general proposition, environmentalists' concerns with NAFTA were based on the five points of trade-environment conflict outlined at the beginning of this chapter. *See* DANIEL ESTY, GREENING THE GATT 2–3 (1997); PIERRE MARC JOHNSON & ANDRÉ BEAULIEU, THE ENVIRONMENT AND NAFTA 8 (1996). In addition, there was concern over the very different levels of protection afforded the environment and human health in the three countries. Over the past quarter century, both the United States and Canada have developed sophisticated and relatively stringent regimes for protecting human health and the environment. Despite legal and institutional advances in the late 1980s and early 1990s, the level of environmental and labor protections in Mexico remains far lower. When NAFTA was being negotiated, Mexico substantially increased its enforcement of environmental and labor laws; nonetheless, enforcement remained seriously inadequate. The consequences of Mexico's inadequate environmental enforcement efforts were most dramatic in the sixty-mile wide free trade zone along the 2000–mile United States–Mexico border, known as the Maquiladora zone.

"Maquiladoras" are factories owned jointly by U.S. and Mexican corporations and operated on the Mexican side of the U.S.–Mexico border. These factories import raw materials or components tariff-free from U.S. suppliers, usually the parent corporation, then produce finished or semi-finished products that are shipped back into the United States for sale, again tariff-free. Since the Maquiladora program was established in 1965, thousands of factories have opened along the border. Before NAFTA, Mexico's government lacked both the resources and the political will to enforce effectively the country's environmental laws. Thus, the Maquiladora facilities on the southern side of the border have gone essentially unregulated for most of their history. Illegal practices, such as the dumping of hazardous wastes onto the ground or directly into waterways, have been common. Transboundary waterways between the United States and Mexico have carried these wastes North across the border, contaminating the entire region and causing serious health effects. *See, e.g.*, Gaynell Terrell, *Tragic Puzzle Grips Families on the Border: Plant Pollution May Cause Brain Not to Develop*, HOUSTON POST, May 17, 1991, at A1.

Fear that NAFTA would prompt a "race to the bottom" among the three parties, spreading Maquiladora conditions throughout North America, fueled environmental and popular opposition to the agreement. *See, e.g.*, Kristin Dawkins & W. Carroll Muffett, *The Free Trade Sellout*, PROGRESSIVE, vol. 57(1), Jan. 1993, at 18–20.

a.   *THE NEGOTIATION OF NAFTA*

Initial efforts to secure environmental protections within the NAFTA met with little success. In the fall of 1990, Presidents Bush and Salinas announced a joint environmental initiative for the U.S.-Mexico border region, but neither side was willing to link this initiative with the proposed trade talks. Environmental and labor groups gained a toe-hold, however, when the Bush administration asked Congress for "fast-track" negotiating authority for NAFTA. Ordinarily, treaties negotiated by the executive branch cannot be ratified until the President presents them to the Senate for advice and consent and, if necessary, Congress passes implementing legislation. These processes can delay ratification for years. It is also possible that the Senate will not consent to the treaty, or Congress will refuse to pass implementing legislation. In addition to rejecting a treaty outright, the Senate can make its consent contingent on the treaty's modification, in which case the treaty must be renegotiated.

In light of the uncertainty engendered by these constitutional requirements, other nations are often reluctant to undertake lengthy and costly treaty negotiations with the United States, particularly on complex and potentially controversial issues such as trade. The "fast-track" scheme was developed in the 1970s to minimize this uncertainty. *See* Trade Act of 1974, 19 U.S.C. §§ 2191–2193. Under "fast-track," Congress statutorily limits its own discretion, agreeing to act on certain specified types of agreements within a specific period, usually sixty days, and approve or reject the agreement as a whole, without amendment or modification. Fast-track authority was scheduled to expire in 1992, prior to completion of the NAFTA negotiations. Canada and Mexico refused to go forward with NAFTA negotiations unless the Bush Administration first secured renewed fast-track approval from Congress. The Bush administration's request for fast-track renewal not only raised the visibility of NAFTA's adverse environmental effects, it also provided NGOs with an opportunity to participate in the legislative process. While the administration could exclude NGOs from the negotiating table, it could not exclude them from the halls of Congress. Thus, the "fast-track" debate provided the first opportunity for environmental NGOs to exercise real influence in the trade talks.

Fast–Track, now called "trade promotion authority," has not been granted by Congress since it last expired in 1994. Despite continuing concerns in Congress, past and current administrations lobby hard for Trade Promotion Authority. President Bush's most recent attempt in the Fall of 2001 to gain this authority has been opposed by House Democrats concerned about environment, labor, human rights and other social issues.

----

b. *PUBLIC PRESSURE*

When the NAFTA negotiations began in earnest in August 1991, the U.S. government formed twenty working groups to address the various trade issues. Of these, only five groups included representatives from the environmental community. NGOs fought to compensate for their exclusion by issuing a number of position papers and statements specifying their concerns with NAFTA, and the conditions for their support of the agreement. Their efforts were directed chiefly at the U.S. negotiating team headed by Trade Representative Carla Hills, but papers were also forwarded to Congress, the media, and anywhere they might make an impact. Although the NGO position was not uniform, an informal consensus emerged around certain critical demands, including:

(1) Guarantees for upward harmonization of environmental standards in the NAFTA area; (2) more transparency and NGO participation in the administration and dispute settlement mechanism of NAFTA; (3) better enforcement of environmental regulations as well as some built-in procedure to make violations of this principle actionable under NAFTA ... ; (4) elaborated protection of environmental laws and regulations against preemption and NAFTA trade discipline challenges; and (5) a major and well-financed effort to clean up the Mexico–U.S. border area.

JOHNSON & BEAULIEU, *op. cit.*, at 28–29.

In response to this public pressure, the administration negotiated minor modifications to the text to ensure some measure of environmental protection. Throughout the 1992 U.S. presidential campaign, environmental and labor groups called on the candidates to revise both the NAFTA and GATT treaties to include greater protection for labor and the environment and on Congress to vote down the treaties unless such revisions were made. Environmentalists and labor unions are traditionally key constituencies of the Democratic Party in the United States. In order to respond to these constituencies, Democratic candidate Bill Clinton made the negotiation of environmental and labor side agreements for NAFTA a key plank in his presidential campaign. *See e.g. Expanding Trade and Creating American Jobs*, Remarks by Governor Bill Clinton, Delivered at North Carolina State University, Raleigh, NC (Oct. 4, 1992)(promising to protect the environment and increase public participation through side agreements while reaffirming his commitment to NAFTA).

Many of the specific suggestions in Clinton's speech were based upon recommendations by the environmental groups. There were, of course, strong corporate interests lobbying, as well, during both the NAFTA and GATT talks.

The overall strategy for the United States in the GATT negotiations was designed by James D. Robinson III, chief executive officer of American Express.... The original U.S. proposal for the GATT agricultural agreement was drafted by Daniel Amstutz, a former senior vice president of Cargill. Cargill has an enormous financial stake in reducing agricultural regulations everywhere. Advisory committees packed with more than 1000 representatives from the business world counsel the official U.S. trade negotiators for both GATT and NAFTA. By contrast, the U.S. trade representative asked only five environmentalists, belatedly, for their suggestions on NAFTA.

Kristin Dawkins & W. Carroll Muffett, *The Free Trade Sellout*, PROGRESSIVE vol. 57(1), January 1993, at 18.

In many ways, the NAFTA talks represent, in microcosm, the evolution from old to new methods of international lawmaking. In the absence of formal public participation, the trade negotiations were disproportionately influenced by a few government economists and private, generally corporate, interests. As public debate moved into the open, however, and included an ever wider array of participants, the new treaty regime came to strike a better balance between the competing interests at stake.

c. THE MEXICAN PERSPECTIVE ON NAFTA

Internal debate on NAFTA was not limited to the United States. Nor was the nature of the debate identical from one country to the next. Each of the three NAFTA parties had particular concerns based on its needs, its resources, and its traditional relationship with the other parties. As you read the following excerpt from the Red Mexicana de Accion Frente al Libre Comercio (Mexican Action Network on Free Trade), compare it with the concerns of the U.S. NGOs summarized above. Which issues are similar? Which are unique to Mexico? What might account for these differences?

Red Mexicana de Accion Frente al Libre Comercio, Ten Reasons for Suspending the Free Trade Agreement Negotiations, Press Release (July 7, 1992)

The Red Mexicana de Accion Frente al Libre Comercio (Mexican Action Network on Free Trade; RMALC) considers that this is a special opportunity for the Mexican Government to take a clear and firm position in face of the recent attitude of George Bush's Administration which has made evident its lack of interest in fulfilling the agreements and treaties to which it subscribes.* * *

Given the lack of conditions for the FTA to favorably incorporate the interests of the people, the RMALC demands that the ongoing negotiations be suspended until a more propitious climate, and different premises for it, can be found. Our demand is based on the following reasons:

1. The negotiations are subject to the political timing of the United States. Contrary to what the ministers of the three nations have declared, that the content would determine the rhythm and timing of the FTA, the reality is that the FTA itself is now hostage to the U.S. domestic political calendar....

In addition, the very dynamics of the negotiation have not permitted a broad and open public debate on its purpose and orientation within the Mexican, American and Canadian societies. The negotiations have been characterized by their secrecy and those proposals that differ from the official position, that show a legitimate preoccupation regarding the evolution of the talks, have not modified the positions of the Mexican negotiating team.* * *

3. Since the beginning of the negotiations (for the FTA), trade disputes (remember cement, textiles, avocados and so forth) between Mexico and the U.S. have increased, not lessened. Such is the case in tuna, steel and, more recently, canned fruit juices. The U.S. has not shown a great willingness to resolve these controversies, the very same ones that would not be easily resolved within the context of a FTA....

4. The Dallas (FTA) draft and the latest information that has been available up until this moment reflects, in worrisome way, that the marked asymmetries among the Mexican, American and Canadian economies are not being fully considered.

Compensatory mechanisms are not under consideration, such as measures regarding real relief from the foreign debt burden on the Mexican economy. Neither have specific dispositions been formulated to soften the social impact of the implementation of a FTA, particularly for the most vulnerable sectors such as small and medium business and the least favorable areas of the nation....

5. According to available information, the Mexican government continues to yield to U.S. government pressures on natural resources and strategic sectors, despite the fact that at the outset of the negotiations the principles of cooperation, reciprocity and complementarity were established as the basis for

the exchange. We insist that energy resources, basic grains, dairy products and forestry must be barred from the negotiations....

6. The Mexican government's interest in offering national treatment to foreign investment without conditions that it be minimally productive, non-polluting or that it offer appropriate technology for the country and that it be directed to areas where national economic needs demand it, has worked in detriment to national investment. In addition, the government's economic policy continues to favor a speculative climate for foreign capital which leaves the financial and productive system as a whole in a fragile situation.

The policy of capturing investment at all cost compromises stability, sovereignty and the possibility of a model for sustainable development.

7. The Mexican government affirmed from the beginning that the FTA would be subjected to the Constitution of Mexico and to our laws. Nevertheless, since the negotiations were initiated 40 regulations have been modified, not always regarding trade and economic globalization, but demonstrating the protectionist nature of big business, as shown by the legislation on intellectual property....

8. Despite the Mexican government's insistence that environmental, labor, immigration and human rights problems would not be included in the negotiation, in practice it has negotiated these issues, through bilateral agendas, without the due judicial weight or the required framework; and furthermore, without taking into account civil society....

Nor is the participation of autonomous social organizations in the supervisory and oversight mechanisms for compliance of bilateral agreements being considered. The Mexican government establishes commitments for the purpose of courting the U.S. congress rather than in response to national interests, compromising our sovereignty, provoking what it wanted to avoid by not sustaining its negotiations based on a consensus of its own society.* * *

10. There continues to be evidence in Mexico of the lack of guarantees for the respect of the popular vote. The evidence from the federal elections of August 1991 and the existing conditions prior to the state elections of 1992 delineate a context in which the modernization of the Mexican political system is limited to a greater sophistication of the means of control that the state uses to deny Mexicans the exercise of our political rights. The democratic process continues to be subordinated to the government's economic program....

Due to all these reasons, we insist that the position of the Mexican government at the upcoming meeting with President Bush should be the SUSPENSION OF THE NORTH AMERICAN FREE TRADE AGREEMENT NEGOTIATIONS, so as to negotiate with dignity and to consider strategies in accordance with the national and popular interest.

This will permit the whole of Mexican society to establish a more solid basis for productive investment and to generate real national consensus as to the kind of country we wish to build.

QUESTIONS AND DISCUSSION

1. Although Mexico has experienced profound economic transformation since the 1980s, political reform has proceeded more slowly. As a consequence, NAFTA and the environmental side agreement were negotiated with little involvement by Mexican civil society. Intent on concluding NAFTA to increase investment flows

into Mexico and spur vital economic growth, the administration of President Carlos Salinas de Gortari orchestrated a massive political and media campaign to sell NAFTA to the Mexican people. The government blocked efforts by citizens groups and even the opposition Partido de la Revolucion Democratica (Party of the Democratic Revolution) to actively participate in the process. Claudio Torres-Nachon, *Participation by Mexican NGOs in the NAFTA Negotiations*, CIEL WORKING PAPER (November 17, 1997). What relationship do you think effective democratic institutions bear to the management of trade negotiations? Are weak democratic systems more or less likely to put effective environmental protections at risk during trade negotiations?

C. NAFTA's ENVIRONMENTAL PROVISIONS

The parties completed negotiations on NAFTA in 1992 and signed the agreement on December 17, 1992. Because of widespread public opposition to the agreement, NAFTA received a hostile reception in the U.S. Congress. Public debate on NAFTA continued within the United States for the next year. NAFTA was ratified by the House of Representatives on November 17, 1993 (by a vote of 234 to 200) and by the Senate on November 20th (61 to 38), following the conclusion of negotiations on the labor and environmental side agreements in September of that year. North American Free Trade Agreement Implementation Act, Pub. L. No. 103-182, 107 Stat. 2057 (1993). All three agreements—NAFTA, the Labor Side Agreement, and the Environmental Side Agreement—were signed by President Bill Clinton on December 8, 1993 and entered into force on January 1, 1994.

---

1. SUMMARY OF ENVIRONMENTAL PROVISIONS

NAFTA has relatively few provisions for environmental protection, included at the last minute to mitigate the more serious environmental effects of free trade rather than promote environmental protection and sustainable development more generally. Nonetheless, environmental provisions were incorporated into the preamble and several chapters of the agreement. Following the addition of these environmental provisions, NAFTA proponents began to characterize the agreement as the "greenest" trade liberalization treaty ever. In view of the environmental hostility of other trade agreements, this assertion was not difficult to justify. As you read the following discussion of these provisions, consider whether they are sufficient to address the problems potentially engendered by NAFTA. In other words, does the NAFTA treaty ensure adequate safeguards against the negative environmental effects of trade to warrant its characterization as a "green" agreement?

Robert Housman, *The North American Free Trade Agreement's Lessons for Reconciling Trade and the Environment*, 30 STANFORD J. INT'L L. 379, 394–410 (1994)

1. Preamble

Coming in the wake of [the Rio Earth Summit in 1992], the NAFTA differs somewhat from previous trade agreements in that it places the goal of trade liberalization in the context of the over-arching goal of sustainable development. To this end the NAFTA's preamble specifically provides that the agreement is intended to:

> Contribute to the harmonious development of world trade ... in a manner consistent with environmental protection and conservation; ... Promote sustainable development ... ; [and] strengthen the development and enforcement of environmental laws and regulations. ...

2. Investment

The NAFTA's approach to environment-driven industrial relocation and investment flight [includes] ... Article 1114.2 [which] ... provides that:

> The Parties recognize that it is inappropriate to encourage investment by relaxing domestic health, safety, or environmental measures. Accordingly, a Party should not waive or otherwise derogate from or offer to waive or other wise derogate from, such measures as an encouragement for the establishment, acquisition, expansion, or retention in its territory of an investment of an investor.

Article 1114.2 applies to a wide range of activities aimed at encouraging investment at the expense of environmental protection. In exchange for its expanded scope, article 1114.2, however, limits an aggrieved party's recourse to consultations and publicity. Article 1114.2's lack of enforcement measures has raised serious questions regarding the provision's ultimate ability to discourage investment flight. ...

The NAFTA investment provision is one of the first instances where a group of nations has determined that the failure of environmental protection is an unacceptable means of encouraging investment and development, and has addressed this objectionable behavior in a trade agreement. Clearly, there are more effective ways to thwart investment flight and industrial relocation than those provided in the NAFTA....

2. International Environmental Agreements

... Throughout the trade and environment debate a great deal of emphasis has been placed on the preference for multilateral solutions to multilateral environmental problems. Thus, it follows that there has been considerable support for protecting the trade provisions of certain widely accepted IEAs [international environmental agreements] from trade challenges.

Article 104 and its annexes ... list three multilateral agreements [the Montreal Protocol, Basel Convention, and CITES] and two bilateral agreements [the 1986 Canada–U.S. Agreement Concerning the Transboundary Movement of Hazardous Wastes, and the 1983 U.S.–Mexico Agreement Concerning Cooperation for the Protection and Improvement of the Environment in the Border Area] for [such] protection ... Article 104 then provides that in the event of an inconsistency between the NAFTA and the trade provisions of these listed IEAs, the obligations of a party under the IEA "shall prevail to the extent of the inconsistency, provided that where a Party has a choice among equally effective and reasonably available means of complying with such obligations, the Party chooses the alternative that is least inconsistent with the other provisions of [the NAFTA]." ...

[T]he parties may add other existing and future IEAs to the protected list through the unanimous consent of the NAFTA parties.... Although the requirement of unanimous consent raises serious concerns, the parties have succeeded in adding at least two bilateral treaties to this list. ...

3.   Standards Provisions

Within the trade and environment debate, many of the most difficult issues revolve around the requirements a party imposes on its domestic products and also on products in international commerce when they enter its market. The difficulty here lies in the tension that exists between the trade community's desire to eliminate unnecessary trade barriers and the environmental community's desire to preserve the rights of each nation to enact and implement needed environmental protections.

The frictions that exist in the area of standards can be divided into three general categories: (1) frictions over the role of the harmonization of standards; (2) frictions over the trade rules that will be used to determine when an environmental standard violates a trade obligation; and (3) frictions over the right or ability of a party to use standards that discriminate between products because of differences in their production process methods. * * *

The NAFTA's standards provisions are set forth in chapters 7 and 9 of the agreement. Chapter 7, section B, establishes sanitary and phytosanitary (SPS) measures. Chapter 9 sets forth rules on all other standards-related measures (SRM).... The standards rules set forth in both chapters 7 and 9(b) are unique in a number of respects important to environmental protection.

a.   Right to Set Appropriate Levels of Protection

... [B]oth the SPS and SRM rules begin with the basic premise that all the NAFTA parties have the right to establish their own "appropriate levels of protection." NAFTA, arts. 712.2, 904.2. If a party determines that the risks from a given product or service are too great, the party can choose to ban that product or service outright—set a zero risk standard—and so long as that ban is implemented in a non-discriminatory fashion, the ban cannot violate the NAFTA. ...

b.   Right to Apply Standards

Despite the NAFTA's gains in recognizing the right of a party to set its own appropriate levels of protection, the NAFTA still leaves environmentalists concerned over restrictions on the manner in which a party may apply its standards once a level of protection has been selected. The NAFTA SPS text requires a party to apply its standards "only to the extent necessary to achieve its appropriate levels of protection, taking into account technical and economic feasibility." [Art. 712.5.] The SRM text similarly requires parties not to create "unnecessary obstacles" to trade in applying their standards. [Art. 904.4.]

c.   Role of Science

... Under NAFTA's SPS rules a party does not need to prove a scientific justification for its measures. It must only show that its standards are "based on scientific principles" and the product of an acceptable risk assessment process. NAFTA, Art. 712.3. Similarly, under chapter 9's SRM rules, a party need not conduct a risk assessment before setting a standard. Nor does the SRM text require a party to advance a scientific rationale for its standard. All a party must do is ensure that the "demonstrable purpose" of its standard is to advance the legitimate goals of, among other things: "safety", "protection of human, animal or plant life or health, the environment, or consumers," or "sustainable development". [Art 904.4 and 915.1.] ... Once a risk has been identified (not proven) by a NAFTA party, that party is free to decide how much of that risk is acceptable (for example, a 1 in 100 risk of cancer versus a 1 in 10 risk). ...

d. Harmonization

The NAFTA also attempts to chart a new path for the harmonization of standards. First, the NAFTA seeks to ensure that the harmonization of standards will not occur in a downward fashion towards a lowest common denominator. To this end, the NAFTA's SPS rules explicitly provides that any harmonization is to occur "without reducing the level of protection of human, animal or plant life or health." [Art. 713.1.]

Thus, while the NAFTA encourages harmonization and the use of international standards it does so with the explicit recognition of each party's right to exceed the protections of such international standards. [Arts. 703.3, 905.3].

e. Precautionary Principle

The standards provisions of the NAFTA also break new ground for the formation of trade policy by explicitly recognizing the precautionary principle of environmental law. Articles 715.4 of the SPS text and 907.3 of the SRM text each allow the NAFTA parties leeway to adopt environmental, health, and safety measures where the scientific evidence is insufficient to determine the actual risk posed by a given product or service. Whereas the other NAFTA standard provisions, discussed above, provide leeway for environmental protections where the science is conflicting, these precautionary provisions provide leeway where the science is incomplete. A party must, however, revisit a precautionary standard once adequate information becomes available and eliminate the standard if no scientific basis can be found for it. * * *

f. Production Process Methods

Negotiations over restrictions based on production process methods ("PPMs") proved more difficult than in other standard areas. The essential issue in the NAFTA and other PPM negotiations is determining when a party may restrict trade in products based upon the PPMs of the products in question. * * *

The NAFTA's SRM text provides that a standard may include rules that apply to "goods or related processes and production methods." [Art. 915.] Although article 915.1 of the SRM text recognizes PPM restrictions as standards, neither article 907 nor article 915 explicitly includes PPM-based restrictions as "legitimate objectives" that are protected from challenge. Thus, it appears that while an environmental PPM-based restriction may be considered a standard, it may not be able to receive the additional protections the SRM text typically provides for other environmental SRMs. The effect of this duality may be to leave PPMs essentially in the same posture as they are under the GATT: at risk in all instances.

The NAFTA's inability to resolve the PPM issue reflects the issue's inherent difficulty. From an environmental perspective, the manner in which a product is produced is an essential element of the product that can not be parceled off in determining how a given product is to be treated at market. This perspective finds support in the fact that the greatest environmental impacts of most products often occur not at the consumer or post-consumer stages, but at the production stage.

The trade perspective, however, views PPMs as the proverbial slippery slope—allowances for regulating environmental PPMs will open the door for restrictions on a vast array of issues related to production (such as labor standards) that will completely disrupt international trade. . . .

4. Dispute Resolution

The NAFTA's dispute resolution provisions also attempt to move the trade and environment debate forward. First, the NAFTA provides that in disputes among the NAFTA parties concerning IEAs or an environmental, health, or safety measure, the challenged party has the right to have the case heard exclusively under the substantive and procedural provisions of the NAFTA. [Articles 2005.3, 2005.4.] This provisions secures the added protections the NAFTA provides to environmental measures by preventing the challenging party from undercutting these protections by bringing the dispute under GATT where no such protections exist.

The NAFTA also explicitly provides that a NAFTA party challenging another NAFTA party's environmental, health, or safety standards bears the burden of proof in the dispute. [Articles 723.6, 914.4]. The degree of protection actually provided by these burden-shifting provisions is, however, unclear because the NAFTA text is silent as to the level of burden imposed on the challenging party (*prima facie* or reasonable doubt).

———

QUESTIONS AND DISCUSSION

1. As a result of the incorporation of environmental protection provisions in the treaty text and President Clinton's commitment to negotiate an environmental side agreement, NAFTA ultimately won the support of several important environmental NGOs. Many other groups remained convinced that NAFTA would be inadequate unless the agreement itself were re-opened and re-negotiated. This difference lead to a split in the environmental community which, ironically, gave the White House and Congress environmental backing, regardless of whether NAFTA were adopted or rejected.

2. The NGOs that refused to accept NAFTA believed that no trade agreement could be truly "green" unless its environmental impacts were taken into consideration throughout the entire process. Do you agree with their assessment? Consider again whether the environmental provisions laid out in the Housman reading seem adequate to address the environmental impacts of free trade? Consider, for example, Article 1114.2, on Investment.

> The Parties recognize that it is inappropriate to encourage investment by relaxing domestic health, safety, or environmental measures. Accordingly a Party should not waive or otherwise derogate from ... such measures as an encouragement for the establishment ... of an investment....

While this language might discourage the parties from waiving environmental standards to encourage investment, what effect does it have on the significant regulatory disparities that already exist between the three countries? Remember that Articles 712.2 and 904.2 reaffirm each party's sovereign right to establish the level of protection "the Party considers appropriate." *See* the discussion of investor-state claims in the next section.

3. As Housman's discussion demonstrates, NAFTA negotiators added new provisions to the chapters on sanitary and phytosanitary standards (chapter 7) and other standards-related measures (chapter 9) to protect each party's right to adopt environmental and safety measures it considers appropriate. In disputes between two parties, NAFTA shifts the burden of proof to the party charging that these measures violate the agreement. Is this adequate to protect each government's freedom to adopt new environmental laws and policies?

----

2.   CHAPTER 11: INVESTOR PROTECTION VS. ENVIRONMENTAL PROTECTION

a.   *INVESTOR–STATE DISPUTES*

NAFTA has been described as "an investment protection agreement" at its core, and the agreement has many provisions for protecting foreign investors. Perhaps must unique is the "investor-state" provision in Chapter 11, which allows a private investor to sue the host State directly for a claim that an investor right has been breached. This is in contrast to the more usual practice for the State of the national whose investment has been expropriated or otherwise injured to press the claim against the host State. The following excerpt gives an overview of Chapter 11 along with a discussion of four obligations that protect investors: national treatment [art. 1102]; most favored nation [art. 1103]; minimum international standards [art. 1105(1)]; and performance requirement prohibitions [art. 1106].

Howard Mann, Private Rights, Public Problems: A Guide to NAFTA's Controversial Chapter on Investor Rights 9–13, 25–30 (2001)

The scope of Chapter 11

Chapter 11 provides rights to foreign investors and their investments. A foreign investor is defined as any person or company who makes an investment into another NAFTA Party. Investments are broadly defined, and include the traditional foreign direct investment, as well as all types of financial investments.... Investors and investments are protected, of course, from certain types of measures taken by governments. But governments are many-layered and take many different types of actions, so the definition of "measures" becomes important. Under Chapter 11 the definition is broad: a measure includes all laws adopted by national, state or provincial legislatures; regulations that implement these laws; local or municipal laws and bylaws; and policies that affect government interaction with businesses. Chapter 11 also applies to laws and regulations that existed prior to its entry into force, unless these are specifically excluded by being listed in a special annex. All provincial and state laws in force before 1994 have been excluded as well.

The rights of investors under Chapter 11

Chapter 11 provides a broad set of investor protection and investment liberalization rights to foreign investors, and obligations for governments ... This list shows the range of issues investment agreements deal with ... such as taking profits out of the host country, nationalities of senior managers and directors, national treatment, and expropriation provisions. Many of these rights have over the years become a standard part of international investment agreements, without provoking any controversy. Chapter 11 contains two dispute settlement processes. The predominant process is the investor-state process which, as its name suggests, is initiated directly by the foreign investor against the host state. The results of the process are binding on both participants, and there are very limited opportunities to appeal or review a decision. One arbitrator is appointed by each participant, and the third one is either jointly agreed upon or is appointed by a neutral third Party. The arbitration takes place with limited public access to the written documents produced for the case, and no public access to the actual proceedings unless all participants agree to open them up (something that has not happened to date). The secrecy surrounding the investor-state process has been a major source of civil society criticism. As of April 2001, there were 17 such cases known to have been initiated. The normal state-to-state dispute settlement process set out in Chapter 20 of NAFTA is also applicable to Chapter 11. Thus far, only one state-to-state case has addressed the investment obligations. * * *

Chapter 11's environmental provisions

Chapter 11 makes only three references to environmental issues. One is a relatively minor reference to the right of dispute panels to hear from environmental experts. Less trivial, but still of limited importance ... , are certain exceptions applicable to NAFTA's prohibition on performance requirements. The environmental language in Chapter 11 that has so far drawn the most public attention is contained in Article 1114, which makes some effort to ensure that NAFTA's investment provisions do not encourage a "race to the bottom" by countries seeking to attract investment through lax environmental laws. Article 1114 has two provisions. The first holds that nothing in Chapter 11 prevents a country from adopting or maintaining an environmental measure that is otherwise consistent with the chapter. This ... simply means that nothing in the chapter prevents you from doing what the chapter does not prohibit you from doing. The second paragraph of Article 1114 is an unprecedented international commitment to avoid relaxing environmental laws as a means of competing for foreign investment. However, the paragraph is couched in partly hortatory language—the core commitment is expressed as a "should" rather than a "shall," but if any Party believes the spirit of commitment is being violated it can require other Parties to enter into consultations. Unlike the investor protection provisions of Chapter 11, there is no mechanism under NAFTA for private Parties to seek enforcement of Article 1114, or for governments to engage in binding dispute settlement with regard to it. Article 2101 of NAFTA covers general exceptions to NAFTA obligations, including exceptions for environmental measures to protect human, plant and animal life and health, and to conserve natural resources. While these exceptions are made applicable to trade in goods and obligations affecting such trade, they are not made applicable to the investment obligations in Chapter 11, despite the more direct and longer-term environmental impacts that investments can have. * * *

*What are the obligations under Chapter 11? * * **

NATIONAL TREATMENT, MOST FAVORED TREATMENT

A key objective of any investment agreement is to avoid discrimination against investors based on their country of origin. Under Chapter 11, a host government must treat foreign investors and their investments "no less favourably" than it treats domestic investors or investors from other countries. This does not always mean identical treatment, but it does mean that any differences cannot disadvantage the foreign investor relative to domestic or foreign competitors. * * *

The key to determining how these principles will work in any agreement is the meaning of the term "in like circumstances," since it is when companies are "in like circumstances" that no less favourable treatment must be granted. As a simple example, is an investor seeking to open a factory next to a protected wilderness area in like circumstances to a city-based investor in the same sector? A range of trade law cases give us the understanding that "like circumstances" does not mean the exact same circumstances, but rather *similar* ones. * * *

MINIMUM STANDARDS

Like most bilateral investment agreements, Chapter 11 contains provisions requiring host countries to treat foreign investors in a way that meets minimum international standards. This requirement is expressed in very general language as "treatment in accordance with international law, including fair and equitable treatment and full protection and security." [Article 1105.1.] Exactly what this means has never been comprehensively spelled out in NAFTA, or in other investment agreements. Still, when investment provisions were used only as a shield this created little controversy; it was understood that the intention was to provide a floor of minimum standards of fair treatment, regardless of whether domestic firms were being treated equally badly. But with the change in the use of the provisions from shield into sword, the lack of precision simply invites new scope for claims under this discipline, often coming from different areas of law.

PERFORMANCE REQUIREMENTS

Prohibitions on performance requirements aim to prevent a host government from imposing conditions on an investor that may limit its ability to achieve economic efficiency and profits. They are, thus, tied to the investment liberalization objectives of the Chapter. Article 1106 prohibits host governments from imposing such requirements as:

- Exporting a given portion of production;
- Using a given level of local inputs or services in business operations, or otherwise showing a preference for domestic goods or services;
- Generating foreign exchange flows based on the firm's levels of imports or exports;
- Using or transferring certain technologies (with some exceptions); or
- Employing specified types or levels of personnel.

It was originally anticipated that this provision would apply only to measures specifically targeted at a foreign investor or its investment. Therefore, even though the provision covered all stages of the investment cycle—from initiating to operating to terminating the investment—it was thought that only a narrow range of measures would be captured. The early cases have shown otherwise. It is now clear that under Chapter 11 even non-discriminatory measures of general application (that is, measures not targeted at a specific investor or sector), both new and pre-existing, can be considered to be performance requirements.

Using this reasoning, it can and has been argued that an import ban on a product used by manufacturers is in effect a requirement to use local substitute products. The result is that foreign investors that might be affected by such a ban are able to bypass the traditional state-to-state process for challenging such trade measures—a process that has been the hallmark of the development of trade law in NAFTA and the WTO—and themselves directly challenge the measure. The expanded use of this provision is worrisome; it may seriously weaken the ability of governments to protect human health and the environment from undesirable imports or exports.

No investor has yet won a Chapter 11 claim based on this obligation, though this was a major plank in the *Ethyl* case that Canada settled by withdrawing the measure in question and paying compensation. It remains a "sleeper" in the Chapter 11 arsenal, but one that has significant potential

———

In addition to these investor protections, NAFTA also provides protection against uncompensated expropriation of investments. Article 1110– which incorporates the minimum standards of Article 1105.1–provides:

1. No Party may directly or indirectly nationalize or expropriate an investment of an investor of another Party in its territory or take a measure tantamount to nationalization or expropriation of such an investment ("expropriation"), except:

(a) for a public purpose;

(b) on a non-discriminatory basis;

(c) in accordance with due process of law and Article 1105(1); and

(d) on payment of compensation.

Mann mentioned that there have been 17 Chapter 11(b) cases, many attacking environmental regulations for "expropriating" private investments. In *Ethyl Corp. v. Canada*, for example, a U.S. firm sued the Canadian government because of its decision to ban the import and interprovincial transport of MMT, a manganese-based gasoline additive that could pose a significant health risk. There also was evidence that MMT damaged pollution control equipment in cars, and increased emissions in general. Because there was inadequate data on the direct health risks of long-term exposure to the emissions, MMT could not be prohibited under Canada's Environmental Protection Act. As a result, the only way to prevent the use of MMT in Canada was to ban the import and interprovincial transport of the substance. Ethyl Corporation, the only manufacturer of MMT, filed a notice of intent to arbitrate in April 1997, claiming violations of national treatment, minimum standards, performance requirements, and expropriation resulting in damages of $251 million. Even though MMT is not produced in Canada, Ethyl claimed that Canada acted in a discriminatory manner by banning the import of MMT without also banning domestic production or use. It argued that this discriminatory action reduced the value of a facility operated by Ethyl in Canada to blend MMT with other petroleum products, and that the ban was "tantamount to expropriation" of that facility. Ethyl's claim also included damages to their "good reputation" because of the ban on its product. The arbitration panel accepted jurisdiction, AWARD OF JURISDICTION (June 24, 1998), and shortly thereafter Canada settled the case, paying Ethyl $13 Million for costs and lost profits. Canada also withdrew the legislation and "gave Ethyl a letter to use as it saw fit saying there was no scientific evidence of any health risk of MMT or any impact on car exhaust systems." Mann, *op. cit.* at 73.

In *S.D. Myers v. Canada*, the Canadian Government imposed a temporary ban on the export of PCB wastes to the United States. S.D. Myers, a U.S. hazardous waste disposal company, claimed that the Canada's ban on exporting PCB wastes to the U.S. was a violation of national treatment, minimum standards, performance requirements, and expropriation. In its defense, Canada cited NAFTA's Article 104, which provides express permission to employ trade restrictions to achieve international environmental goals pursuant to CITES, the Montreal Protocol and the Basel Convention along with any other agreements contained in Annex 104.1. Canada argued that its ban was required under both the *Basel Convention on the Control of Transboundary Movements of Hazardous Wastes and their Disposal*, and the *Agreement between Canada and the US Concerning the Transboundary Movement of Hazardous Wastes* (contained in the annex). The Partial Award found in favor of the company with regard to national treatment and minimum standards but not on performance requirement or expropriation. FINAL AWARD ON THE MERITS (November 13, 2000). The Tribunal noted that "[t]he general body of precedent usually does not treat regulatory action as amounting to expropriation." The Tribunal did not find an expropriation since the measure was temporary. *Id.* at para. 284. A final award, that includes compensation, has not been issued.

Metalclad is the first investor-state claim to work its way through the appellate process. State and local officials in Mexico had blocked the siting of a hazardous waste landfill owned by a U.S. corporation and the company brought an action under Chapter 11. The Arbitral Tribunal found that an expropriation had occurred and granted an Award and Mexico appealed. Chapter 11 makes no specific provision for appeal of panel decisions. The rules for appeal are provided by the international arbitration regime (ICSID or UNCITRAL, discussed *infra*) selected by the parties and domestic law. Thus the standards of appeal can vary from case to case. In *Metalclad*, the appeal took place in British Columbia. As you read the opinion below, pay attention to the court's scope and standard of review.

As you read *Metalclad,* also keep in mind the broader battle between investor protection and environmental protection. On the one hand, private foreign investors need to be accorded the protection warranted under customary international law, which includes "fair and equitable treatment" and "full protection and security" from the host country for their investment, under NAFTA's Article § 1105.1. Indeed, as we will see in Chapter 16, the Human Rights and Environment Chapter, human rights law includes such protections for private property. This is discussed further in the excerpt from the RESTATEMENT, below.

On the other hand, the NAFTA countries—indeed, all countries of the world—must be able to use their police power to regulate private property to protect public health and the environment, as well as to promote sustainable development, and they must be able to regulate without the fear that they will have to pay the polluter for such regulation, except in the most serious cases when there is no reasonable use left of the property, as is the case under the U.S. Fifth Amendment takings jurisprudence. This is a complex issue, however, even in the U.S., and there is much work to be done to find the right balance under NAFTA for resolving these two interests.

The *Metalclad* case is instructive for several points, including the question of who should interpret the environmental law involved in the alleged regulatory taking? The host government? Perhaps with a rebuttable presumption? The Arbitral Tribunal, comprised usually of specialists in investment law? The Tribunal, but relying on independent legal experts they appoint? This issue is related to the question of exhaustion of domestic remedies. Another issue to keep in mind when reading the case is what the appropriate scope and standard of review should be when reviewing an award by an arbitral tribunal? Finally, consider what the legitimate economic expectations of the U.S. investor were, and what economic interest remained after the Ecological Decree (and after the denial of the municipal construction permit).

United Mexican States v. Metalclad Corp., 2001 BCSC 664 (May 5, 2001). Reasons for Judgment of the Honourable Mr. Justice Tysoe

[1] This proceeding involves a challenge by the Petitioner, the United Mexican States, of an arbitration award issued on August 30, 2000 by a tribunal constituted under Chapter 11 of "NAFTA".... In the Award, the Tribunal granted damages in the amount of $16,685,000 (U.S.) against Mexico in favour of the Respondent, Metalclad Corporation , an American corporation.... Mexico seeks to set aside the Award. The matter comes before this Court because the place of the arbitration was designated to be Vancouver, B.C.

UNDERLYING FACTS * * *

[3] The subject matter of the Award is a site in La Pedrera, a valley located within the municipality of Guadalcazar (the "Municipality"), in the State of San Luis Potosi (the "State of SLP"), Mexico. . . .

[4] The Site has been owned at all material times by a company incorporated under the laws of Mexico, "COTERIN".... The Site and COTERIN were initially owned by Mexican nationals who sold COTERIN to a subsidiary of Metalclad in 1993 (at which time ownership of the Site was transferred into COTERIN). To be consistent with the approach utilized in the Award, a reference to Metalclad after 1993 will include COTERIN; although COTERIN may have taken an action in question, Metalclad was the operating mind and decision maker for COTERIN.

[5] COTERIN began operating a hazardous waste transfer station at the Site in 1990 pursuant to an authority granted by the federal government of Mexico. However, 20,000 tons of waste were not transferred from the Site and were deposited on the Site without treatment or separation. The federal government of Mexico ordered the closure of the transfer station on September 26, 1991 and this closure remained in effect until February 1996.

[6] COTERIN applied to the Municipality for a permit to construct a hazardous waste landfill at the Site in 1991. The application was refused at the time and confirmed in 1992.

[7] In 1993, COTERIN received three permits in respect of a hazardous waste landfill at the Site. Two of the permits were environmental impact authorizations issued by the National Institute of Ecology, an agency of Mexico's Secretariat of the Environment, National Resources and Fishing (the "Secretariat of the Environment"), in respect of the construction and operation of the landfill. The third permit was a land use permit issued by the State of SLP.

[8] In April 1993, Metalclad entered into an option agreement to purchase COTERIN. The option agreement (as amended) provided that the payment of the purchase price was subject to, among other things, the condition that either (a) a municipal permit was issued to COTERIN or (b) COTERIN had received a definitive judgment from the Mexican courts that a municipal permit was not

required for the construction of the landfill. Metalclad completed its purchase of COTERIN without either of these conditions being satisfied (although Metalclad alleged in the arbitration, and the Tribunal found, that Mexican federal officials had assured Metalclad that COTERIN had all the authorities required to undertake the landfill project).

[9]   COTERIN commenced construction activities at the Site in the absence of a municipal construction permit. After the construction began, COTERIN received a further construction permit from the federal authorities; it was issued in January 1995 and authorized the construction of the final aspects of the facility.

[10]   On October 26, 1994, the Municipality issued a stop work order due to the absence of a municipal permit. COTERIN made application for a municipal construction permit on November 15, 1994. The Municipality officially denied this application over a year later, on December 5, 1995.

[11]   In the meantime, COTERIN continued with construction of the landfill facility at the Site. It was completed by March 1995. . . . . The landfill facility was not actually opened and it has not subsequently been operated.

[12]   Metalclad [negotiated] . . . an agreement called the *Convenio* . . . . . . on November 25, 1995 with two sub-agencies of the Secretariat of the Environment. The *Covenio* [stated] . . . that Metalclad would be permitted to operate the landfill for an initial period of five years and that it would remediate the previous contamination during the first three years of this period. After the *Convenio,* . . . the federal authorities issued a further permit . . . in February 1996 and increased the annual permitted capacity of the facility from 36,000 tons to 360,000 tons.

[13]   It was shortly after the *Convenio* was entered into that the Municipality formally denied COTERIN's application for a construction permit on December 5, 1995. The considerations taken into account by the municipal council in denying the application were that (i) COTERIN had been denied a construction permit in 1991/2, (ii) COTERIN had commenced construction before applying for the permit and finished the construction while the permit application was pending, (iii) there were environmental concerns and (iv) a great number of the Municipality's inhabitants were opposed to the granting of the permit. * * *

[15]   [When] . . . the Municipality rejected the request in April 1996 [to reconsider the permit,] COTERIN then filed a writ of *amparo* in a Mexican federal court. . . . The proceeding was dismissed . . . on the basis that COTERIN had not exhausted its administrative remedies. COTERIN appealed to the Mexican Supreme Court but subsequently abandoned its appeal as a sign of good faith to the Municipality for the purpose of negotiations.

[16]   Further negotiations were not fruitful and Metalclad . . . commenced the arbitration proceeding by filing a Notice of Claim in January 1997. . . .

[17]   After the arbitration proceeding was underway, but before the hearing in the arbitration was held, the Governor of the State of SLP issued an ecological decree (the "Ecological Decree") on September 20, 1997, which was three days prior to the expiry of the Governor's term. The Ecological Decree declared an area of 188,758 hectares within the Municipality, which included the Site, to be an ecological preserve for the stated purpose of protecting species of cacti.

[18]   A three person tribunal was constituted . . . [and it was agreed] that the . . . arbitration would be [in] Vancouver, B.C. . . . and the Tribunal rendered the Award on August 30, 2000.

NAFTA PROVISIONS

[The court refers to Articles 1116, 1101, and 1114, and quotes 1105 and 1110]

[21] Article 102 sets out the objectives of the NAFTA. Paragraph 1 reads, in part, as follows:

> The objectives of this Agreement, as elaborated more specifically through its principles and rules, including national treatment, most-favored-nation treatment and transparency, are to: . . .
>
> > (c) increase substantially investment opportunities in the territories of the Parties . . .

Paragraph 2 of Article 102 reads as follows:

> The Parties shall interpret and apply the provisions of this Agreement in the light of its objectives set out in paragraph 1 and in accordance with applicable rules of international law.

To similar effect, Article 1131 provides that a tribunal in an arbitration pursuant to Chapter 11 is to decide the issues in dispute in accordance with the NAFTA and applicable rules of international law.

[22] Chapter 18 of the NAFTA contains provisions promoting the concept of transparency. . . . Article 1802 requires each Party to ensure that its laws, regulations, procedures and administrative rulings of general application are published or otherwise made available to enable interested parties to become acquainted with them. . . .

THE AWARD

* * *

(a) Applicable Law

[24] After setting out the general facts and allegations of the parties, making some findings of fact and giving its reasons for considering issues relating to the Ecological Decree (which was enacted after the arbitration proceeding was commenced), the Tribunal set out the law which it considered to apply to the arbitration. It made reference to Article 1131(1) . . . and Article 102(2) (which I have quoted above). It then stated that the objectives referred to in Article 102(2) specifically include transparency and the substantial increase in investment opportunities in the territories of the Parties . . .

(b) Fair and Equitable Treatment

[27] After quoting Article 1105, the Tribunal stated that an underlying objective of the NAFTA is to promote and increase cross-border investment opportunities and ensure the successful implementation of investment initiatives. It referred to "transparency" as being prominent in the statement of the principles and rules which introduce the NAFTA. The Tribunal understood "transparency" to include the idea that all relevant legal requirements for the purpose of initiating, completing and successfully operating investments should be capable of being readily known to all affected investors of a Party and that there should be no room for doubt or uncertainty. . . .

[28] The Tribunal considered that a central point in the case was whether a municipal permit for the construction of a hazardous waste landfill was required. It briefly reviewed the opposing views of the expert opinions presented by Metalclad and Mexico [on the interpretation of Mexican law], and found that if a municipal construction permit was required, the federal authority's jurisdiction was controlling and the authority of the Municipality only extended to appropriate construction considerations (i.e., those related to the physical

construction or defects in the Site). The Tribunal found that Metalclad had been led to believe by federal authorities that the federal and state permits issued to COTERIN allowed for the construction and operation of the landfill, and it made reference to Metalclad's position (which the Tribunal appeared to have implicitly accepted) that it was also told by federal officials that if it submitted an application for a municipal construction permit, the Municipality would have no legal basis for denying the permit. The Tribunal found that the Municipality's denial of the construction permit was improper because it did not have reference to construction aspects or flaws of the physical facility.

[29]   The Tribunal went on to hold that Mexico failed to ensure a transparent and predictable framework for Metalclad's business planning and investment. It said that the totality of the circumstances demonstrated a lack of orderly process and timely disposition in relation to an investor acting in the expectation that it would be treated fairly and justly in accordance with the NAFTA. The Tribunal stated that, moreover, the acts of the State of SLP and the Municipality (which were attributable to Mexico) failed to comply with or adhere to the requirements of Article 1105.

[30]   Accordingly, the Tribunal held that Metalclad had not been treated fairly or equitably under the NAFTA and succeeded on its claim under Article 1105.

(c) Expropriation—Pre Ecological Decree

[31]   The Tribunal defined expropriation under Article 1110 of the NAFTA as the ... [direct] taking of property, as well as covert or incidental interference with the use of property which has the effect of depriving the owner, in whole or in significant part, of the use or reasonably-to-be-expected economic benefit of property even if not necessarily to the obvious benefit of the host State.

[32]   The Tribunal held that Mexico took a measure tantamount to expropriation in violation of Article 1110 by permitting or tolerating the conduct of the Municipality in relation to Metalclad (which the Tribunal had already held was unfair and inequitable treatment) and by thus participating or acquiescing in the denial to Metalclad of the right to operate the landfill.

[33]   The Tribunal made reference to (i) its holding that the exclusive authority for permitting a hazardous waste landfill rested with the Mexican federal government and (ii) its holding that the Municipality acted outside its authority by denying the construction permit without any basis in the physical construction or any defect in the Site. ... The Tribunal held that these measures, together with the representations of the Mexican federal authorities and the absence of a timely, orderly or substantive basis for the denial of the construction permit, amounted to an indirect expropriation.

(d) Expropriation—Post Ecological Decree

[35]   ... [T]he Tribunal went on to hold that the Ecological Decree was a further ground for a finding of expropriation, but stated that it was not strictly necessary for its conclusion.

[36]   The Tribunal found that the Ecological Decree had the effect of barring forever the operation of Metalclad's landfill. It rejected Mexico's representations to the contrary by making reference to provisions of the Decree. The Tribunal stated that it considered that the implementation of the Decree would, in and of itself, constitute an act tantamount to expropriation. * * *

STANDARD OF REVIEW

[50]   The extent to which this Court may interfere with an international commercial arbitral award is limited by the provisions of *International CAA*. ... [U]nless the arbitral award contained decisions beyond the scope of the

submission to arbitration, the court has no jurisdiction to set the award aside
... even if it could be shown that the arbitration tribunal had erred in
interpreting the contract. * * *

ARTICLE 1105—MINIMUM STANDARD

[57] ... This normal type of arbitration provision [of State-to-State] is found
in Chapter 20 of the NAFTA, which is the general section in the NAFTA
dealing with arbitrations of disputes between the NAFTA Parties.

[58] Section B of Chapter 11 establishes a separate arbitration procedure. It
allows investors of a NAFTA Party (who are not themselves a party to the
NAFTA) to make claims against other NAFTA Parties by way of arbitration. If
an investor of a Party feels aggrieved by the actions of another Party in relation
to its obligations under the NAFTA other than the obligations imposed by
Section A of Chapter 11 and the two Articles of Chapter 15, the investor would
have to prevail upon its country to espouse an arbitration on its behalf against
the other Party.

[60] Articles 1102 [national treatment] and 1103 [most favored nation] are
both framed in relative terms by way of a comparison to the way in which the
NAFTA Party treats other investors. On the other hand, Article 1105 is framed
in absolute terms. In considering Article 1105, the way in which the Party
treats other investors is not a relevant factor. Article 1105 is intended to
establish a minimum standard so that a Party may not treat investments of an
investor of another Party worse than this standard irrespective of the manner
in which the Party treats other investors and their investments.

[61] The rationale of Article 1105 was discussed in a partial arbitration award
issued shortly after the Tribunal issued the Award in this case. In *S.D. Myers,
Inc. v. Government of Canada* (13 November 2000), the Tribunal said the
following about Article 1105:

> ... The inclusion of a "minimum standard" provision is necessary to avoid
> what might otherwise be a gap. A government might treat an investor in a
> harsh, injurious and unjust manner, but do so in a way that is no different
> than the treatment inflicted on its own nationals. The "minimum stan-
> dard" is a floor below which treatment of foreign investors must not fall,
> even if a government were not acting in a discriminatory manner. (para.
> 259)

[62] The tribunal in the *Myers* partial award went on to discuss the proper
approach to the interpretation of Article 1105:

> Article 1105(1) expresses an overall concept. The words of the article must
> be read as a whole. The phrases ... *fair and equitable treatment* ... and
> ... *full protection and security* ... cannot be read in isolation. They must
> be read in conjunction with the introductory phrase ... *treatment in
> accordance with international law*. (para. 262)

What the *Myers* tribunal correctly pointed out is that in order to qualify as a
breach of Article 1105, the treatment in question must fail to accord to
international law. Two potential examples are "fair and equitable treatment"
and "full protection and security", but those phrases do not stand on their own.
For instance, treatment may be perceived to be unfair or inequitable but it will
not constitute a breach of Article 1105 unless it is treatment which is not in
accordance with international law. In using the words "international law",
Article 1105 is referring to customary international law which is developed by
common practices of countries. ...

[63]   The *Myers* tribunal also discussed the level of treatment which violates Article 1105:

> The Tribunal considers that a breach of Article 1105 occurs only when it is shown that an investor has been treated in such an unjust or arbitrary manner that the treatment rises to the level that is unacceptable from the international perspective. That determination must be made in the light of the high measure of deference that international law generally extends to the right of domestic authorities to regulate matters within their own borders. The determination must also take into account any specific rules of international law that are applicable to the case. (para. 263)

[64]   After these Reasons for Judgment had been prepared in draft, counsel for Metalclad provided a copy of the arbitral award in *Pope & Talbot Inc. v. Canada* (April 10, 2001), in which the tribunal declined to follow the interpretation of Article 1105 given by the *Myers* tribunal. The *Pope & Talbot* tribunal concluded that "investors under NAFTA are entitled to the international law minimum, *plus* the fairness elements". . . .

[65]   With respect, I am unable to agree with the reasoning of the *Pope & Talbot* tribunal. It has interpreted the word "including" in Article 1105 to mean "plus", which has a virtually opposite meaning. . . .

[66]   Mexico maintains that the Tribunal committed two acts in excess of jurisdiction in connection with Article 1105. First, counsel says that the Tribunal used the NAFTA's transparency provisions as a basis for finding a breach of Article 1105. Second, counsel maintains that the Tribunal went beyond the transparency provisions contained in the NAFTA and created new transparency obligations. Further, counsel submits that these excesses of jurisdiction were compounded by the Tribunal improperly making decisions of Mexican domestic law and mistakenly interpreting Mexico to concede during the arbitration that Metalclad was not required to exhaust its local remedies before commencing the NAFTA arbitration. . . .

[67]   In the framework of the *International CAA*, the issue is whether the Tribunal made decisions on matters beyond the scope of the submission to arbitration by deciding upon matters outside Chapter 11. In my opinion, the Tribunal did. . . .

[68]   On my reading of the Award, the Tribunal did not simply interpret Article 1105 to include a minimum standard of transparency. No authority was cited or evidence introduced to establish that transparency has become part of customary international law.

* * *

[70]   In the present case, however, the Tribunal did not simply interpret the wording of Article 1105. Rather, it misstated the applicable law to include transparency obligations and it then made its decision on the basis of the concept of transparency.

[71]   In addition to specifically quoting from Article 1802 in the section of the Award outlining the applicable law, the Tribunal incorrectly stated that transparency was one of the objectives of the NAFTA. In that regard, the Tribunal was referring to Article 102(1), which sets out the objectives of the NAFTA in clauses (a) through (f). Transparency is mentioned in Article 102(1) but it is listed as one of the principles and rules contained in the NAFTA through which the objectives are elaborated. The other two principles and rules mentioned in Article 102, national treatment and most-favored nation treatment, are contained in Chapter 11. The principle of transparency is implemented through the provisions of Chapter 18, not Chapter 11. Article 102(2) provides that the

NAFTA is to be interpreted and applied in light of the objectives set out in Article 102(1), but it does not require that all of the provisions of the NAFTA are to be interpreted in light of the principles and rules mentioned in Article 102(1).

[72] ... After discussing the facts and concluding that the Municipality's denial of the construction permit was improper, the Tribunal stated its conclusion which formed the basis of its finding of a breach of Article 1105; namely, Mexico had failed to ensure a transparent and predictable framework for Metalclad's business planning and investment. Hence, the Tribunal made its decision on the basis of transparency. This was a matter beyond the scope of the submission to arbitration because there are no transparency obligations contained in Chapter 11. * * *

[76] As I have concluded that the Tribunal decided a matter beyond the scope of the submission to arbitration in connection with its finding that there was a failure of transparency, it is not necessary to decide whether the Tribunal. ... made decisions of Mexican domestic law or whether the Tribunal was incorrect in its understanding that Mexico had conceded that Metalclad was not required to exhaust its local remedies before resorting to the arbitration.

ARTICLE 1110—PRE ECOLOGICAL DECREE

[77] Prior to its consideration of the Ecological Decree, the Tribunal concluded that the actions of Mexico constituted a measure tantamount to expropriation in violation of Article 1110. The Tribunal based this conclusion on its view that Mexico permitted or tolerated the conduct of the Municipality, which amounted to unfair and inequitable treatment breaching Article 1105 .... The Tribunal subsequently made reference to the representations by the Mexican federal authorities and the absence of a timely, orderly or substantive basis for the denial of the construction permit by the Municipality in concluding that there had been indirect expropriation. * * *

[79] The Tribunal based its conclusion that there had been a measure tantamount to expropriation/indirect expropriation, at least in part, on the concept of transparency. In finding a breach of Article 1105 on the basis of a lack of transparency, the Tribunal decided a matter beyond the scope of the submission to arbitration. In relying on the concept of transparency, at least in part, to conclude that there had been an expropriation within the meaning of Article 1110, the Tribunal also decided a matter beyond the scope of the submission to arbitration. * * *

ARTICLE 1110—POST ECOLOGICAL DECREE

[81] Counsel for Mexico submits that the Tribunal improperly considered the Ecological Decree but that, in any event, it did not base its decision on the Decree. With respect, I cannot agree.

[82] It is true that the Tribunal stated that it did not attach controlling importance to the Ecological Decree and that a finding of expropriation on the basis of the Decree was not strictly necessary or essential to its finding of a violation of Article 1110....

[83] Although the Tribunal used an incorrect tense in the Award when it stated that it considered that the implementation of the Ecological Decree *would*, in and of itself, constitute an act tantamount to expropriation, it is clear from another passage of the Award that the Tribunal considered that the implementation of the Decree *did* constitute expropriation. In the second

paragraph preceding the misuse of the future tense, the Tribunal stated that the Decree *had* the effect of barring forever the operation of the landfill.

* * *

(a) Consideration of the Ecological Decree

* * *

[91]   I conclude that no error has been demonstrated in the arbitral procedure as a result of the Tribunal considering the claim based on the Ecological Decree.

(b) Beyond the Scope of the Submission

* * *

[94]   In my opinion, the Tribunal's conclusion with respect to the Ecological Decree stands on its own and is not based on a lack of transparency or on the Tribunal's finding of a breach of Article 1105. The Tribunal considered the Decree in isolation of its other findings of breaches of the NAFTA. It specifically identified the issuance of the Decree as a further ground for a finding of expropriation. * * *

(c) Patently Unreasonable Error

[96]   Counsel for Mexico [argues]...that patently unreasonable error can be seen as one variety of excess of jurisdiction or can be ... an independent ground for setting aside an award on the basis that it conflicts with public policy....

[97]   As I ... do not believe ... that the Tribunal made a patently unreasonable error with respect to the Ecological Decree, I need not decide whether a patently unreasonable decision is a ground for setting aside an arbitral award ...

[98]   Counsel for Mexico identifies 19 areas in respect of which it is asserted that the Tribunal failed to have regard to relevant evidence and thereby made patently unreasonable findings. Only one of these areas relates to the Ecological Decree. I do not propose to deal with the other 18 areas ....

[99]   The Tribunal gave an extremely broad definition of expropriation for the purposes of Article 1110. In addition to the more conventional notion of expropriation involving a taking of property, the Tribunal held that expropriation under the NAFTA includes covert or incidental interference with the use of property which has the effect of depriving the owner, in whole or in significant part, of the use or reasonably-to-be-expected economic benefit of property. This definition is sufficiently broad to include a legitimate rezoning of property by a municipality or other zoning authority. However, the definition of expropriation is a question of law with which this Court is not entitled to interfere under the *International CAA*.

[100]   The Tribunal reviewed the terms of the Ecological Decree and concluded that it had the effect of barring forever the operation of Metalclad's landfill and constituted an act tantamount to expropriation. It made reference to the Ninth Article of the Decree, which requires that all activities in the area are subject to guidelines established by the management plan for ensuring ecological preservation of the cacti reserve. The Tribunal also made reference to the Fourteenth Article of the Decree, which forbids the spillage or discharge of polluting agents on the soil, subsoil or water of the reserve area. In my view, the Tribunal's conclusion that the issuance of the Decree was an act tantamount to expropriation is not patently unreasonable.

[101] Although the Tribunal did not make reference in the Award to the transitional provision of the Ecological Decree stating that all permits... granted before the date of the Decree were legal, it is not at all clear how any such permits... would interact with the Fourteenth Article. It is implicit in the Award that the Tribunal concluded that the Fourteenth Article prevailed over any such permits..., and this conclusion is not patently unreasonable.

* * *

[103] Counsel for Mexico also says that the Tribunal ignored a letter from an official with the Secretariat of the Environment stating that the operation of a hazardous waste landfill was consistent with the Fourteenth Article of the Ecological Decree. While it is true that the Tribunal did not explicitly make reference to this letter, it reviewed the terms of the Decree and came to its own conclusion. The actual terms of the Decree have more probative value than the interpretation given to the Decree by an official of Mexico. The Tribunal considered Mexico's representation that the Decree did not prevent the operation of the landfill and stated that it was not persuaded by the representation.

* * *

(d) Conclusion

[105] There is no ground ... to set aside the Award as it relates to the conclusion of the Tribunal that the issuance of the Ecological Decree amounted to an expropriation of the Site without compensation.

METALCLAD'S IMPROPER ACTS

[The court discusses Mexico's claim that Metalclad's chief witnesses regarding representations made by Mexican federal officials to Metalclad, Humberto Rodarte Ramon, was improperly affiliated with Metalclad. It was alleged that Mr. Rodarte's wife improperly received approximately $150,000 worth of Metalclad stock and two payments of $10,000 each from Metalclad (the two $10,000 payments were part of the expenses which Metalclad was reimbursed by the Award). It also was alleged that Mr Rodarte was owed a commission for his role in arranging the sale of the site to Metalclad. The Court concluded that "The Tribunal implicitly accepted the evidence of Mr. Rodarte and this Court should not interfere with its determination...."]

FAILURE TO ADDRESS ALL QUESTIONS

[132] ... There is a mechanism within the Additional Facility Rules to remedy an alleged failure of the tribunal to answer all questions submitted to it. There should be recourse to that mechanism before going outside of the ICSID Additional Facility Rules and asking a court to set aside the award on the basis of a failure to follow the proper arbitral procedure.

CONCLUSION

[133] In order to have this Court set aside the Award in its entirety, Mexico was required to successfully establish that all three of the Tribunal's findings of breaches of Articles 1105 and 1110 of the NAFTA involved decisions beyond the scope of the submission to arbitration or that the Award should be set aside in view of Metalclad's allegedly improper acts or the Tribunal's alleged failure to answer all questions submitted to it. Although Mexico succeeded in challenging the first two of the Tribunal's findings of breaches of Articles 1105 and 1110, it was not successful on the remaining points. Accordingly, the Award should not be set aside in its entirety [but only in part, to address the error of having the award run from the date the municipality denied the construction permit; the correct date for the interest calculation is the date of the Ecological Decree.] ...

If the parties are unable to agree on the interest re-calculation, the matter is remitted back to the Tribunal.

[136]   . . . If Metalclad wishes to pursue the portion of the interest contained in the Award which I have set aside, by establishing a breach of Article 1105 or Article 1110 prior to the issuance of the Decree without regard to the concept of transparency, the matter is remitted to the Tribunal.

———————

The strong outcry from NGOs to Metalclad and the other Chapter 11 cases led the NAFTA Free Trade Commission to issue an Interpretative Note on July 31, 2001, less than three months after the *Metalclad* appellate decision. The Note clarifies that the standard used in at least some of the Chapter 11 cases should be limited to "the customary international law minimum standard of treatment of aliens" and their property. It is not clear what effect the Note will have on the *Metalclad* case, although the British Columbia Supreme Court stated that "If the parties are unable to agree on the interest re-calculation, the matter is remitted back to the Tribunal." If you were the counsel for Mexico, would you agree to the re-calculation of interest? Or would you prefer to go back to the Tribunal and argue that the Note required a re-hearing?

NAFTA Free Trade Commission, Notes of Interpretation of Certain Chapter 11 Provisions *(July 31, 2001)*

Having reviewed the operation of proceedings conducted under Chapter Eleven of the North American Free Trade Agreement, the Free Trade Commission hereby adopts the following interpretations of Chapter Eleven in order to clarify and reaffirm the meaning of certain of its provisions: * * *

B.   Minimum Standard of Treatment in Accordance with International Law

   1.   Article 1105(1) prescribes the customary international law minimum standard of treatment of aliens as the minimum standard of treatment to be afforded to investments of investors of another Party.

   2.   The concepts of "fair and equitable treatment" and "full protection and security" do not require treatment in addition to or beyond that which is required by the customary international law minimum standard of treatment of aliens.

   3.   A determination that there has been a breach of another provision of the NAFTA, or of a separate international agreement, does not establish that there has been a breach of Article 1105(1).

CLOSING PROVISION

The adoption by the Free Trade Commission of this or any future interpretation shall not be construed as indicating an absence of agreement among the NAFTA Parties about other matters of interpretation of the Agreement.

———————

QUESTIONS AND DISCUSSION

1.   What effect does the Interpretive Note have on the BC Supreme Court in Metalclad? What effect does it have on the interpretation of the expropriation

provision in Article 1110.1? Does it overrule the "extremely broad definition of expropriation" upheld in the Metalclad appeal? *See* para. 99, *op. cit.*

2.   The Interpretative Note uses as the minimum standard the customary law relating to the protection of aliens' property, which is set out in the RESTATEMENT OF THE LAW, THIRD, FOREIGN RELATIONS LAW OF THE UNITED STATES (1987), §§ 711 and 712.

§ 711   State Responsibility for Injury to Nationals of Other States

A state is responsible under international law for injury to a national of another state caused by an official act or omission that violates ...

> (c) a right to property or another economic interest that, under international law, a state is obligated to respect for persons, natural or juridical, of foreign nationality, as provided in § 712.

COMMENTS & ILLUSTRATIONS:

Comment:

a.   Human rights, "denial of justice," and injury. ... As used in this chapter, "injury" means any loss, detriment, or damage to liberty, property, or other interest, of the kind that is generally protected by law under the major legal systems of the world [including] ... loss, detriment, or damage resulting from violation of customary law....

b.   International human rights as minimum standard. ...A state is responsible for injury to foreign nationals resulting from violations of their internationally recognized human rights.... * * *

d.   Right to property as human right. Article 17 of the Universal Declaration of Human Rights declares: 1. Everyone has the right to own property ....2. No one shall be arbitrarily deprived of his property.

There is lack of agreement on the scope of this right and permissible limitations on it.... Customary international law accords additional protection to the...economic interests of foreign nationals, as provided in clause (c) and in § 712. ...

§ 712   State Responsibility for Economic Injury to Nationals of Other States

A state is responsible under international law for injury resulting from:

(1) a taking by the state of the property of a national of another state that

(a) is not for a public purpose, or

(b) is discriminatory, or

(c) is not accompanied by provision for just compensation;

For compensation to be just under this Subsection, it must, in the absence of exceptional circumstances, be in an amount equivalent to the value of the property taken. ...

COMMENTS & ILLUSTRATIONS:

Comment:

a.   *Responsibility under general principles of international law.* ... A state is responsible under this section for injury to property and other economic interests of private persons who are foreign nationals. Injury by a state to property or economic interests of another state or state instrumentality is covered by general principles of state responsibility, § 206, Comment e and

Reporters' Note 1. See also the principles of state responsibility to other states in regard to particular matters, such as economic interests in the sea (Part V) or pollution of the environment (Part VI). * * *

c. *Requirement and standard of compensation.* International law requires that a taking of the property of a foreign national, whether a natural or juridical person, be compensated. . . .

In exceptional circumstances, some deviation from the standard of compensation set forth in Subsection (1) might satisfy the requirement of just compensation. Whether circumstances are so exceptional as to warrant such deviation, and whether in the circumstances the particular deviation satisfies the requirement of just compensation, are questions of international law. An instance of exceptional circumstances that has been specifically suggested and extensively debated, but never authoritatively passed upon by an international tribunal, involves national programs of agricultural land reform. * * *

g. *Expropriation or regulation.* Subsection (1) applies not only to avowed expropriations in which the government formally takes title to property, but also to other actions of the government that have the effect of "taking" the property, in whole or in large part, outright or in stages ("creeping expropriation"). A state is responsible as for an expropriation of property under Subsection (1) when it subjects alien property to taxation, regulation, or other action that is confiscatory, or that prevents, unreasonably interferes with, or unduly delays, effective enjoyment of an alien's property or its removal from the state's territory. . . . A state is not responsible for loss of property or for other economic disadvantage resulting from bona fide general taxation, regulation, forfeiture for crime, or other action of the kind that is commonly accepted as within the police power of states, if it is not discriminatory, Comment f, ... As under United States constitutional law, the line between "taking" and regulation is sometimes uncertain. See Reporters' Note 6. * * *

REPORTERS NOTES:

* * *

2. *Standard of compensation.* . . . Mexico asserted that "appropriate compensation" was satisfied . . . if aliens were compensated to the same extent as nationals. . . . The [U.S. has] held resolutely to the view that international law requires compensation that is "prompt, adequate and effective." . . . United States representatives to international financial institutions are directed to oppose loans to countries that have expropriated property of United States citizens without prompt, adequate, and effective compensation, in the absence of certain exceptional circumstances. See e.g., 22 U.S.C. §§ 283r, 285o, 290g–8. * * *

6. *Taking or regulation.* It is often necessary to determine, in the light of all the circumstances, whether an action by a state constitutes a taking and requires compensation under international law, or is a police power regulation or tax that does not give rise to an obligation to compensate even though a foreign national suffers loss as a consequence. In general, the line in international law is similar to that drawn in United States jurisprudence for purposes of the Fifth and Fourteenth Amendments to the Constitution in determining whether there has been a taking requiring compensation. . . .

One test suggested for determining whether regulation and taxation programs are intended to achieve expropriation is whether they are applied only to alien enterprises. In many instances, however, particularly in developing countries, there may be no comparable locally-owned enterprise. . . . A challenged regulation might be compared with the practice of major legal systems; the fact that a given regulation is supported by guidelines adopted by an international agency to guide the behavior of multinationals may be seen as evidence of its legitimacy. . . .

3. Note the discussion of exhaustion in *Metalclad*. Was there sufficient exhaustion of domestic remedies to give Mexico the opportunity to resolve its own interpretation of the conflict among the various levels of government? To give Mexico the opportunity to decide whether it would accept Metalclad's operation, rather than face an expropriation claim? Was there sufficient exhaustion regarding the interpretation of the Ecological Decree, including whether the Management Plan and Guidelines for activities, together with the grandfather provision, would have allowed Metalclad to operate its facility, or otherwise to use its land for some other economic purpose?

4. What were the legitimate economic expectations of Metalclad? Did the history of permit denials for the previous owner temper Metalclad's legitimate expectations? The options agreement required either a municipal permit or a definite court decision clarifying that such a permit was not needed, as conditions for the purchase of the hazardous waste site. Does this cautious approach show Metalclad's real expectations? What about Metalclad's valuation—for tax purposes—of the site at only $136,339? Was it legitimate for Metalclad to rely on assurances from the federal officials in Mexico? What do you make of the failure of the court (or Tribunal, for that matter) to cite any documents from Mexico's federal officials containing such assurances to Metalclad? Assuming that the assurances were all unwritten, do you think they were an attempt to seek investment by lowering environmental protection? Why didn't Article 1114 figure more prominently in the case? Keep in mind the strength of the Chapter 11 investor protection and mandatory dispute resolution process when you read the protection provided for the environment, and the dispute resolution provisions for environmental issues, discussed later in this chapter.

5. The most recent Chapter 11 case is *Methanex Corporation v. United States*. On March 25, 1999 the Governor of the State of California issued an Executive Order that provided, inter alia, for the removal of MTBE from gasoline at the earliest possible date. MTBE is a gasoline additive that has raised concerns since it moves readily through soil into groundwater. Drinking water tainted with even tiny amounts of MTBE gives off a strongly unpleasant odor, and exposure to MTBE has been linked to tumors and nervous system disorders in mice and rats. The U.S. Environmental Protection Agency has classified it as a possible cancer-causing agent. On March 8, 2001, Methanex Corporation, which manufactures an MTBE component, filed a notice of intent to arbitrate under Chapter 11 citing violations of national treatment, minimum standards and expropriation allegedly causing $970 million in damages.

6. The disenchantment with Chapter 11 is not limited to the environmental community. The Canadian Government has argued that "NAFTA Parties never intended the expropriation and compensation provisions of NAFTA Chapter Eleven to limit the legitimate rights of governments to regulate." Nihal Sherif, *Canadian Memo Identifies Options for Changing NAFTA Investment Rules,* Inside US Trade 1, 20 (Feb 12, 1999). *See also* Charles N. Brower and Lee A. Steven, *NAFTA CHAPTER 11: Who Then Should Judge?: Developing the International Rule of Law under NAFTA Chapter 11* 2 Chi. J. Int'l L. 193, 201–202 (2001) (Judge Brower served as arbitrator in the NAFTA Chapter 11 arbitration in *Ethyl* and as counsel for the investor in the pending NAFTA Chapter 11 arbitration in *Mondev v International Ltd v United States of America*).

7. The Tribunal in Metalclad operated under rules developed by the International Center for Settlement of Investment Disputes (ICSID). ICSID clauses have been included in about twenty investment laws, 900 bilateral investment treaties and four recent multilateral trade and investment treaties. The latter are NAFTA, the Energy Charter Treaty, the Cartagena Free Trade Agreement and the Colonia Investment Protocol of Mercosur. *See <http://www.worldbank.org/icsid>. See also* Ibrahim F.I. Sihata, *Towards a Greater Depoliticization of Investment Disputes: The Roles of ICSID and MIGA*, 1 Foreign Inv. L.J. 4 (1986). Compare the ICSID approach to that of the environmental arbitration rules set out by the Permanent Court of Arbitration (PCA) in the Hague. *See* Optional Arbitration Rules for Arbitrating Disputes Relating to the Environment and/or Natural Resources (2001)< http://www.pca-cpa.org/EDR/ENRrules.htm >. Under the PCA approach the panel of arbitrators must have experience and expertise in environmental or conservation of natural resources law. Id. at art. 8, para. 3.

----

b. *TRANSPARENCY*

There are two perspectives on transparency in the context of Chapter 11: civil society and the investor. In general, most stages of the NAFTA Chapter 11 proceedings have been secret. Civil society has consistently criticized the process for its lack of transparency. Mann comments that "Chapter 11 must be understood as being embedded in a broader NAFTA regime that is itself remarkably short of the kinds of transparent and accessible checks and balances that are common for most bodies having significant impacts on government." Mann, *op cit.*, at 20. In response to these concerns, the NAFTA Free Trade Commission addressed these issues in the following excerpt of the Interpretive Notes discussed *supra*.

Notes of Interpretation, *op cit.*, July 31, 2001

A. Access to documents

    1. Nothing in the NAFTA imposes a general duty of confidentiality on the disputing parties to a Chapter Eleven arbitration, and, subject to the application of Article 1137(4), nothing in the NAFTA precludes the Parties from providing public access to documents submitted to, or issued by, a Chapter Eleven tribunal.

    2. In the application of the foregoing:

        a. In accordance with Article 1120(2), the NAFTA Parties agree that nothing in the relevant arbitral rules imposes a general duty of confidentiality or precludes the Parties from providing public access to documents submitted to, or issued by, Chapter Eleven tribunals, apart from the limited specific exceptions set forth expressly in those rules.

        b. Each Party agrees to make available to the public in a timely manner all documents submitted to, or issued by, a Chapter Eleven tribunal, subject to redaction of:

            i. confidential business information;

            ii. information which is privileged or otherwise protected from disclosure under the Party's domestic law; and

            iii. information which the Party must withhold pursuant to the relevant arbitral rules, as applied.

c. The Parties reaffirm that disputing parties may disclose to other persons in connection with the arbitral proceedings such unredacted documents as they consider necessary for the preparation of their cases, but they shall ensure that those persons protect the confidential information in such documents.

d. The Parties further reaffirm that the Governments of Canada, the United Mexican States and the United States of America may share with officials of their respective federal, state or provincial governments all relevant documents in the course of dispute settlement under Chapter Eleven of NAFTA, including confidential information.

The Parties confirm that nothing in this interpretation shall be construed to require any Party to furnish or allow access to information that it may withhold in accordance with Articles 2102 or 2105. * * *

Investors have a different transparency concern. They want clear rules for investing. This is difficult in the United States let alone a nation with an emerging economy such as Mexico. In *Metalclad*, the Tribunal found that Mexico had violated minimum standards when it "failed to ensure a transparent and predictable framework for Metalclad's business planning and investment." *Metalclad, op cit.* at para. 99. The Tribunal stated that one of the objectives of NAFTA is "to promote and increase cross-border investment opportunities and ensure the successful implementation of investment initiatives." Id. at para 75 (*citing* NAFTA, *Article 102(1)*). They go on to note that the same article identifies "transparency" as an underlying goal of the entire agreement. Id. at para 76. Mann comments that "[t]his extremely broad reading of minimum international standards requirements was groundbreaking in international investment law." Mann *op cit.* at 29. The Supreme Court of British Columbia rejected the Tribunal's analysis, *Metalclad, op cit.* at para 66, as did the Interpretive Note, *op cit.* at B(3). Investors are given no more protection than that afforded to aliens under customary international law. *See* discussion *supra* page 1217.

QUESTIONS AND DISCUSSION

1. In *Methanex* the tribunal agreed to accept *amicus curiae* briefs in Chapter 11 investor-state disputes, in contrast with the WTO, which took two steps forward with amicus briefs in the *Shrimp Turtle* case but then moved back to rejecting all briefs submitted in the *Asbestos* case.

2. The Interpretive Note explicitly states that investors are entitled to the same treatment afforded an alien under customary international law. In a concurring opinion to *S.D.Myers*, Dr. Schwartz notes, in dicta, that "It is far from obvious, in the absence of evidence, that basic GATT norms like transparency and procedural fairness have been accepted by states throughout the world and so have passed into the body of general (or "customary") international law."

c. CRITIQUES

Environmental NGOs were not satisfied with either the content or clarity of the Interpretative Notes. The following excerpt discusses some of these concerns.

International Institute for Sustainable Development, *Note on NAFTA Commission's July 31, 2001, Initiative to Clarify Chapter 11 Investment Provisions* (October 3, 2001)

What does the statement say about transparency?

The statement says that there is nothing in the NAFTA rules (with limited exceptions) that restricts Parties from releasing, or that compels them to keep confidential, any documents submitted to or issued by a Chapter 11 Tribunal. It further says that there is nothing in the rules of arbitration (Chapter 11 disputes are heard under either of two existing international sets of rules: ICSID or UNCITRAL) that imposes such restrictions either, other than certain, very limited specific exceptions. Finally, it pledges that the Parties to a Chapter 11 dispute will "make available to the public in a timely manner all documents submitted to, or issued by, a Chapter Eleven tribunal." This pledge is subject to three possible exceptions, one of which is vitally important: except for "information which the Party must withhold pursuant to the relevant arbitral rules, as applied." The implications of this exception are discussed below.

What does this mean?

The first two statements are simply legal facts. There is indeed nothing in the NAFTA or the arbitral rules that imposes a general confidentiality of documents (beyond the limited exceptions referred to). But they are important statements nonetheless, since they shift the focus to the appropriate place—the additional rules of procedure, such as confidentiality orders, that each Tribunal establishes for the proceedings at the outset. It is within these rules, agreed to in each case by the disputing Parties, that every Tribunal to date has established high levels of secrecy.

The third statement is not a fact, but a positive commitment. It obliges the Parties to make all the case documents available in a timely manner. This level of access, to put it in context, is beyond even what the Methanex Tribunal had agreed to grant IISD in the event that it is successful in its petition to intervene in that case as a friend of the court.

But the exception noted above is critical. In effect, it makes the statement that Parties will release all documents submitted to and issued by the Tribunal, unless the arbitral rules established by the Tribunal prohibit such an action. Given that all tribunals to date have established strong rules of secrecy, does this mean that the statement is completely empty? Not necessarily. We will have to wait to see how this statement interacts with the confidentiality orders issued by the Tribunals. Clearly, the intent of the Ministers is to impose openness on the proceedings, but their statement does not specifically direct Tribunals to adopt open procedures in future (their legal power to do so is unclear in any case). They would be subject to embarrassing criticism if their much-trumpeted statement had no impact on transparency in the end. Consequently, the statement will also impose a duty on government lawyers acting in these cases to support open access to the documents, something that has not always been the case to date. At a minimum, the statement will precipitate debate among the Parties about the drafting of confidentiality orders where previously, secrecy was assumed.

What does the statement say about Article 1105?

Article 1105 says that the NAFTA Parties should treat investors of other Parties "in accordance with international law, including fair and equitable treatment . . ." The statement clarifies an important issue. It states that the obligation for a "minimum standard of treatment" is no more onerous than that granted under customary international law. It further says that a breach of some other NAFTA provision, or of the provisions of some other international agreement, do not necessarily constitute a breach of Article 1105. The three Ministers have the power to issue such interpretations of NAFTA provisions that are then binding on all future Chapter 11 Tribunals—and arguably on existing ones—by virtue of Article 1131 (2).

What does this mean?

With this interpretation, Article 1105's key problem seems to have been repaired. In several Chapter 11 cases the argument has been made that because a government breached rules in other parts of NAFTA, or even in non-NAFTA law such as the WTO's Technical Barriers to Trade Agreement, it has automatically breached its obligations on minimum standards of treatment. This broad interpretation of minimum standards of treatment—essentially giving firms the right to litigate any international law obligation—has not been seen outside of the NAFTA context. The statement puts an end to this. It brings us back to an interpretation of minimum standards of treatment that corresponds to customary international law, which has generally reflected basic rights of fairness and due process. The possibility still remains that individual rulings on this provision will be troubling, but the direction set out here seems clear and should be welcomed.

What still remains to be done?

IISD's public criticisms of Chapter 11 cover the process of arbitration as well as the substance of the provisions as interpreted to date. While the statement is a welcome advance in meeting our concerns, much work remains to be done in both areas. On substance, the statement covered only one of the four problematic Chapter 11 provisions, and not even the foremost among them. The three left to address are:

1. *Article 1110: Expropriation.* In a number of Chapter 11 cases it has been argued successfully that a regulation can be considered tantamount to expropriation, even if it is non-discriminatory and undertaken for a valid public purpose. Again the Chapter 11 Tribunals have broken new ground here, ignoring the traditional exemptions for so-called "police powers"— the rights of governments to regulate in the broad public interest. The final effect is to make governments liable for any significant damages caused to investors by their regulations, an imposition of the "takings" doctrine that is sure to chill new environmental lawmaking. The NAFTA Ministers need to state clearly that non-discriminatory laws serving broad public interests such as environment and public health should enjoy the police powers exemption from Article 1110 obligations.

2. *Article 1106: Performance Requirements.* This obligation normally prevents governments from requiring investors to fulfill certain economic requirements as a condition of entry and operation. These include requirements to purchase local inputs, to export a certain percentage of output, to transfer proprietary technologies and so on. But at least one firm has argued under Chapter 11 that an import or export ban can in fact constitute a performance requirement, specifically, the requirement to source the banned product locally or use only domestic services for further

treatment or development of a product. While there was no ruling on this argument, this provision risks becoming another wide open back door for firms to litigate trade-related obligations in an investment agreement. The Ministers should issue an interpretation to avoid this potentially troubling potential development.

3.   *Article 1102: National Treatment.* This provision obliges the NAFTA Parties to treat investors from other Parties no worse than they treat domestic ones "in like circumstances." The Ministers need to define "like circumstances" and to specify what types of operations will be compared to determine "no worse" treatment. On the latter point there has already been a ruling whose standard was set by comparing quite different operations. On the former point, consider four factories on a stream whose emissions are regulated such that the stream is at capacity for receiving pollution. If the government denied a foreign investor permission to set up a fifth such operation in the same place, would that violate national treatment? The firm would in fact be receiving treatment worse than that accorded the existing firms. This obligation is more complex for investment than it is for trade in goods.

On process, the success of the statement will depend on whether it is reflected in future orders of the arbitral Tribunals. However, even if we assume the best possible result for the statement, there still remain areas for improvement. The statement addresses only the issue of public access to documents after the arbitration is commenced. There is a need to ensure access to documents created before the arbitration even begins, in particular the notices of intent to arbitrate. As well, there is a need to actually override the rules of arbitration that prevent public access to hearings. There is also a need for fair and systematic rules for allowing *amicus curiae* (friend of the court) participation in hearings.

QUESTIONS AND DISCUSSION

1.   Twelve members of Congress criticized Chapter 11 and the Interpretative Note in a letter to President Bush on October 4, 2001:

We appreciate that Ambassador Zoellick recently joined with his ministerial colleagues from Canada and Mexico to issue an interpretation of some Chapter 11 provisions, thereby acknowledging that changes in the Chapter 11 model are needed. However, we do not believe that these interpretations address many of the most fundamental and critical problems with Chapter 11 rules.

Nor do we believe that the interpretations successfully resolve the difficulties they attempt to repair. Most notable, the interpretation limiting the minimum standard of treatment to customary international law does not specify in any fashion what the terms of customary international law are, leaving in place what amounts to an extremely vague and open-ended standard that can be used to challenge efforts to protect the environment and the public interest. Further, the interpretation providing transparency for documents is undercut by the interpretation's acknowledgement that the arbitration rules applied by tribunals in specific cases, which have been used to limit disclosure of document, would not be affected.

The lack of substantial change carried out by the NAFTA ministers' recent actions indicates that a new model for investment rules must be developed. We therefore urge that the U.S. government seek much broader and more fundamental changes to the Chapter 11 model in developing proposals for any future trade agreements. Specifically, we urge that the following revisions be made:

- Ensure that foreign investors will enjoy no greater protection than that afforded to domestic U.S. investors under U.S. constitution;

- Require that all private investors gain approval from their home country government before bringing a case under the investment provisions;

- Limit expropriation to cases in which there is direct expropriation of all economically beneficial use of property; * * *

- Provide a clear exception for the governmental exercise of police powers...;

- Establish a standing appellate mechanism to correct erroneous decisions by tribunals; and

- Ensure that all proceedings, submissions, findings, and decisions are promptly made public and that all hearings are open to the public, and ensure that amicus briefs will be accepted and considered by the tribunals.

How do the Congressional concerns square with the concerns discussed in the IISD excerpt? *See also Understanding Fast Track: Key Environmental Problems with the Thomas Bill*, a fact sheet from American Lands Alliance, CIEL, Defenders of Wildlife, Friends of the Earth, NRDC, Sierra Club, and WWF (undated).

D. ENVIRONMENTAL SIDE AGREEMENT: THE NORTH AMERICAN AGREEMENT ON ENVIRONMENTAL COOPERATION

In addition to inserting a few corrective provisions in the NAFTA treaty itself, the three parties also negotiated two side agreements to address the public's two biggest concerns with the agreement: labor and the environment. The North American Agreement on Environmental Cooperation, 8 September 1993, 32 I.L.M. 1480 [hereinafter "Environmental Side Agreement"] takes important steps to ensure that the NAFTA parties continue to develop and enforce environmental norms. In addition to addressing some of the perceived inadequacies in the NAFTA text itself, the Environmental Side Agreement also represents a comprehensive effort at increased environmental cooperation among the three NAFTA parties. The Environmental Side Agreement is not limited to specific regions, species, media, or types of pollutants, but applies wherever the parties feel environmental protection can be enhanced by cooperative efforts. As a response to popular concerns about trade liberalization and as a mechanism for continent-wide environmental cooperation, the Environmental Side Agreement was considered a landmark treaty.

---

1. OBJECTIVES AND GENERAL COMMITMENTS

NORTH AMERICAN AGREEMENT ON ENVIRONMENTAL COOPERATION

PART ONE

OBJECTIVES

Article 1—Objectives

The objectives of this Agreement are to: (a) foster the protection and improvement of the environment in the territories of the Parties for the well-being of present and future generations; (b) promote sustainable development based on cooperation and mutually supportive environmental and economic policies; (c) increase cooperation between the Parties to better conserve, protect, and enhance the environment, including wild flora and fauna; (d) support the environmental goals and objectives of the NAFTA; (e) avoid creating trade distortions or new trade barriers; (f) strengthen cooperation on the development and improvement of environmental laws, regulations, procedures, policies and practices; (g) enhance compliance with, and enforcement of, environmental laws and regulations; (h) promote transparency and public participation in the development of environmental laws, regulations and policies; (i) promote economically efficient and effective environmental measures; and (j) promote pollution prevention policies and practices.

PART TWO
OBLIGATIONS

Article 2—General Commitments

1. Each Party shall, with respect to its territory: (a) periodically prepare and make publicly available reports on the state of the environment; (b) develop and review environmental emergency preparedness measures; (c) promote education in environmental matters, including environmental law; (d) further scientific research and technology development in respect of environmental matters; (e) assess, as appropriate, environmental impacts; and (f) promote the use of economic instruments for the efficient achievement of environmental goals.

2. Each Party shall consider implementing in its law any recommendation developed by the Council under Article 10(5)(b).

3. Each Party shall consider prohibiting the export to the territories of the other Parties of a pesticide or toxic substance whose use is prohibited within the Party's territory. * * *

Article 3—Levels of Protection

Recognizing the right of each Party to establish its own levels of domestic environmental protection ... and to adopt or modify accordingly its environmental laws and regulations, each Party shall ensure that its laws and regulations provide for high levels of environmental protection and shall strive to continue to improve those laws and regulations.

Article 4—Publication

1. Each Party shall ensure that its laws, regulations, procedures and administrative rulings of general application respecting any matter covered by this Agreement are promptly published or otherwise made available in such a manner as to enable interested persons and Parties to become acquainted with them.

2. To the extent possible, each Party shall: (a) publish in advance any such measure that it proposes to adopt; and (b) provide interested persons and Parties a reasonable opportunity to comment on such proposed measures.

Article 5—Government Enforcement Action

1. With the aim of achieving high levels of environmental protection and compliance with its environmental laws and regulations, each Party shall effectively enforce its environmental laws and regulations through appropriate governmental action ... such as: (a) appointing and training inspectors; (b) monitoring compliance and investigating suspected violations ... ; (c) seeking

assurances of voluntary compliance and compliance agreements; (d) publicly releasing non-compliance information; ... [and] (j) initiating, in a timely manner, judicial, quasi-judicial or administrative proceedings to seek appropriate sanctions or remedies for violations of its environmental laws and regulations....

2. Each Party shall ensure that judicial, quasi-judicial or administrative enforcement proceedings are available under its law to sanction or remedy violations of its environmental laws and regulations. * * *

Article 6—Private Access to Remedies

1. Each Party shall ensure that interested persons may request the Party's competent authorities to investigate alleged violations of its environmental laws and regulations and shall give requests due consideration in accordance with law.

2. Each Party shall ensure that persons with a legally recognized interest under its law in a particular matter have appropriate access to administrative, quasi-judicial or judicial proceedings for the enforcement of the Party's environmental laws and regulations. * * *

Article 7—Procedural Guarantees

1. Each Party shall ensure that ... [such proceedings] are fair, open and equitable, and to this end shall provide that such proceedings: (a) comply with due process of law; (b) are open to the public, except where the administration of justice otherwise requires; ... (d) and are not unnecessarily complicated and do not entail unreasonable charges or time limits or unwarranted delays.* * *

———

QUESTIONS AND DISCUSSION

1. Article 3 mandates that each party "shall" seek high levels of environmental protection, but at the same time recognizes each party's right to choose its own level of environmental protection. What, if any, obligations does Article 3 create for the NAFTA parties to develop new environmental law and increase their levels of environmental protection?

2. For environmentalists, labor unions, and citizens groups, one of the most important purposes of the NAAEC was to "promote transparency and public participation in the development of environmental laws, regulations and policies." Environmental Side Agreement, Art. 1(h). In light of the history of the NAFTA negotiations, particularly in Mexico, can you understand why citizens attributed particular importance to this function? How does the Side Agreement promote public participation and transparency? As you read the materials in the following sections, consider how the institutions and the mechanisms discussed are contributing to increased public participation.

———

2. THE COMMISSION FOR ENVIRONMENTAL COOPERATION (CEC)

To provide a centralized forum for environmental cooperation among the parties, Article 8 of the Environmental Side Agreement creates the North American Commission for Environmental Cooperation, or "CEC". An intergovernmental agency directed and funded equally by the three parties, the CEC is comprised of three organs: the Council, the Secretariat, and the Joint Public Advisory Committee.

The Council is the CEC's political organ and its governing body. It is composed of one cabinet-level representative from each of the three parties: Canada's Minister of the Environment, Mexico's Secretary of Environment, Natural Resources and Fisheries, and the Administrator of the United States Environmental Protection Agency. The Council oversees implementation of the agreement, directs the Secretariat, addresses disputes between the parties, and serves as a general forum for environmental cooperation among the parties.

The Secretariat is the administrative arm of the CEC. It is in charge of implementing the cooperative work programs authorized by the Council. The permanent Secretariat is located in Montreal, Quebec, Canada. It is headed by an Executive Director, who must be a citizen of one of the parties (the first was Victor Lichtinger of Mexico, now Mexico's Secretary of Environment). The Executive Director is appointed for a three-year term—with a two-term limit—and the directorship rotates among nationals of each party.

Each year, in accordance with Council instructions, the Secretariat prepares a report on Environmental Side Agreement activities for distribution to the public. Significantly, the annual report must include a discussion of the actions each party has taken in connection with its obligations under the agreement, including data on each party's environmental enforcement activities. The report may also reflect views and information provided by NGOs and private citizens if the Council deems it appropriate. Environmental Side Agreement, Art. 12.

The Joint Public Advisory Committee (JPAC) serves as a formal mechanism by which NGOs and individuals may influence the decision making process of the CEC. The Agreement defines NGOs broadly to include "any scientific, professional, business, non-profit, or public interest organization or association which is neither affiliated with, nor under the direction of, a government." Environmental Side Agreement, Art. 45(1). Paragraphs four to seven of Article 16 outline the JPAC's duties and its relationship to the other CEC organs. The JPAC is comprised of fifteen members, five appointed by each party.

In addition to the JPAC, each party may convene two additional committees. The National Advisory Committees comprise representatives of non-governmental organizations and other members of the public. The Governmental Committees may include representatives of federal and state or provincial governments. Appointment of these committees is discretionary with each party. Both committees serve to advise each party on the "implementation and further elaboration" of the Environmental Side Agreement, Art. 17.

a.   ARTICLE 13 REPORTS

Article 13 of the Environmental Side Agreement authorizes the Secretariat to prepare a report "on any matter within the scope of the annual program" without Council approval, and on "any other environmental matter related to the cooperative functions of this Agreement" unless the Council objects by a two-thirds vote. Environmental Side Agreement, Art. 13(1). Recall that "the cooperative functions of [the] Agreement" include almost every aspect of environmental law and policy. The one explicit restriction on the scope of Article 13 is that the CEC may not report on "issues related to whether a Party has failed to enforce its environmental laws and regulations." *Id.* The agreement envisions these complaints being handled through the Article 14 and 15 citizen submission process discussed *infra*.

If the Secretariat lacks expertise in the matter being examined, it must obtain the assistance of "independent experts of recognized experience in the matter" in the preparation of the report.

> [T]he Secretariat may [also] draw upon any relevant technical, scientific or other information, including information: (a) that is publicly available; (b) submitted by interested non-governmental organizations and persons; (c) submitted by the Joint Public Advisory Committee; (d) furnished by a Party; (e) gathered through public consultations, such as conferences, seminars and symposia; or (f) developed by the Secretariat, or by independent experts engaged pursuant to paragraph 1.

Id. at Art. 13(2). In 1995, responding to a complaint from United States and Mexican NGOs, the Secretariat prepared a report evaluating the death of 40,000 migratory birds at the Silva Reservoir in Guanajuato, Mexico. With the cooperation of the Mexican government, the Secretariat sent an international team of scientists to investigate. The team determined that the deaths were caused by an outbreak of avian botulism. As a result of this discovery, the CEC began with the Guanajuato government to clean up the Reservoir. A second research team formed to develop a better understanding of the causes and prevention of avian botulism and make recommendations on a course of action. The Secretariat endorsed the conclusions and suggested to the Council of the CEC that:

> the governments of the United States, Canada and Mexico establish a Task Force of officials with responsibilities for migratory birds and aquatic habitat to:
>
> a) work with Mexico in developing a national program for wildlife surveillance and for the investigation of, response to, and reporting of wildlife disease outbreaks;
>
> b) build on existing programs and develop a cooperative North American system for the surveillance, investigation of, response to, and reporting of wildlife disease outbreaks. * * *

CEC SECRETARIAT, REPORT ON THE DEATH OF MIGRATORY BIRDS AT THE SILVA RESERVOIR (1995)

Article 13 also empowers the secretariat to create reports on CEC programs and initiatives. In May 1997, the Secretariat of the CEC launched the Upper San Pedro Initiative to formulate measures to protect migratory species in upper San Pedro River basin. Initially, a technical report was prepared by an interdisciplinary team of experts on the physical and biological conditions required to sustain and enhance the riparian migratory bird habitat of the area. See *Sustaining and Enhancing Riparian Migratory Bird Habitat on the Upper San Pedro River* (Final Draft–March 1999). Over 650 people participated in focus groups and workshops in the region that reviewed the draft. More than 300 written comments were submitted, roughly half of which originated from outside the basin. Finally, an experts panel developed recommendations.

CEC, RIBBON OF LIFE: AN AGENDA FOR PRESERVING TRANSBOUNDARY MIGRATORY BIRD HABITAT ON THE UPPER SAN PEDRO RIVER (1999)

Having considered the issues raised in this report, Council may wish to formulate recommendations to the Parties and/or direct the Secretariat to undertake the following actions:

1) Designate an interagency working group to develop an implementation strategy for selected panel recommendations, including a mechanism for binational consultation and cooperation.

2) Provide direct support for local efforts, such as the Upper San Pedro Partnership and other emerging proposals, as part of the CEC's North American Bird Conservation Initiative. . . .

3) Direct the Secretariat to work with the Parties and others to identify potential funding mechanisms to support the implementation of selected advisory panel recommendations

4) Organize a workshop on lessons learned in transboundary water management, with a particular emphasis on regional, basin-specific management frameworks for transboundary groundwater resources. Workshop attendees would include representatives from relevant local, state and federal government and others. . . .

5) Initiate a pilot project to apply the principles and approaches developed in the CEC's work on Sustainable Tourism in Natural Areas (Project 99.01.05). . . .

---

b.   *CITIZEN SUBMISSIONS UNDER ARTICLES 14 AND 15 OF THE ENVIRONMENTAL SIDE AGREEMENT*

Article 14 of the *North American Agreement on Environmental Cooperation* (NAAEC) creates a mechanism for citizens to file submissions in which they assert that a Party to the NAAEC is failing to effectively enforce its environmental law. The Secretariat of the North American Commission for Environmental Cooperation (the "Secretariat") initially considers these submissions based on criteria contained in Article 14(1) of the NAAEC.

The Secretariat may consider a submission from any non-governmental organization or person asserting that a Party is failing to effectively enforce its environmental law, if the Secretariat finds that the submission:

(a) is in writing in a language designated by that Party in a notification to the Secretariat;

(b) clearly identifies the person or organization making the submission;

(c) provides sufficient information to allow the Secretariat to review the submission, including any documentary evidence on which the submission may be based;

(d) appears to be aimed at promoting enforcement rather than at harassing industry;

(e) indicates that the matter has been communicated in writing to the relevant authorities of the Party and indicates the Party's response, if any; and

(f) is filed by a person or organization residing or established in the territory of a Party.

NORTH AMERICAN AGREEMENT ON ENVIRONMENTAL COOPERATION BETWEEN THE GOVERNMENT OF CANADA, THE GOVERNMENT OF THE UNITED MEXICAN STATES AND THE GOVERNMENT OF THE UNITED STATES OF AMERICA, Art. 14(1), (1993). Once the Secretariat finds that a submission meets these criteria it will determine if a response is warranted from the Party named in the submission.

Where the Secretariat determines that a submission meets the criteria set out in paragraph 1, the Secretariat shall determine whether the submission merits requesting a response from the Party. In deciding whether to request a response, the Secretariat shall be guided by whether:

(a) the submission alleges harm to the person or organization making the submission;

(b) the submission, alone or in combination with other submissions, raises matters whose further study in this process would advance the goals of this Agreement;

(c) private remedies available under the Party's law have been pursued; and

(d) the submission is drawn exclusively from mass media reports.

Id at Art. 14(2). Where the Secretariat makes such a request, it shall forward to the Party a copy of the submission and any supporting information provided with the submission. In light of any response from the Party, the Secretariat may inform the Council that it believes a factual record is warranted. *Id.* at Article 15. The Council may approve preparation of the factual record by simple majority vote. Thus, an investigation cannot be blocked simply because the party complained against refuses to consent. Id. This record must include all information submitted by the party concerned, and may also include "any relevant technical, scientific or other information: (a) that is publicly available; (b) submitted by interested non-governmental organizations or persons; (c) submitted by the Joint Public Advisory Committee; or (d) developed by the Secretariat or by independent experts." *Id.* When the draft record is completed, any Party to the agreement may submit comments that are incorporated in the final factual record must incorporate these comments. Once the final record is completed, the Council may make it available to the public by majority vote; otherwise it remains confidential. *Id.*

The Secretariat recently recommended a factual record in the submission on *Migratory Birds*. Article 15(1) Notification to Council that Development of Factual Record is Warranted, A/14/SEM/99–002/11/ADV (December 15, 2000). In its submission, the Center for International Environmental

Law (CIEL) asserts that the United States Government was "failing to effectively enforce" § 703 of the Migratory Bird Treaty Act (MBTA), 16 U.S.C. § 703, which prohibits the killing or "taking" of migratory birds, including destroying nests, crushing eggs, and killing nestlings and fledglings, "by any means or in any manner," unless the U.S. Fish & Wildlife Service (FWS) issues a valid permit. CIEL argued that the United States "has completely abdicated its enforcement obligations" under the MBTA because of its failure to prosecute logging operations that they claim routinely violate the Act. CIEL, *Submission to the Commission on Environmental Cooperation Pursuant to Article 14 of the North American Agreement on Environmental Cooperation*, A14/SEM–99–002/01/SUB (November 17, 1999). The following excerpt discusses the Secretariat's rational for recommending a factual record.

Article 15(1) Notification to Council that Development of Factual Record is Warranted, A/14/SEM/99–002/11/ADV 8–10, 25–27 (December 15, 2000)

Application of Articles 14 and 15 to Assertions of Wide-ranging Failure to Enforce Environmental Law Effectively

The focus of the submission is on an asserted failure to effectively enforce that is nationwide in scope. While the Submitters identify some specific logging operations that allegedly violated the MBTA, the reference to particular operations is clearly intended to be illustrative. The Submitters' primary concern is with an asserted nationwide failure on the part of the Party to investigate or prosecute logging operations that violate the MBTA by killing birds or destroying bird nests.

Given the Submitters' broad focus on an asserted nationwide failure to effectively enforce, the Secretariat now considers whether the citizen submission process is intended for assertions of this sort. One possible view is that the citizen submission process is reserved for assertions of particularized failures to effectively enforce. Under this view a factual record would be warranted, only when a submitter asserts that a Party is failing to effectively enforce with respect to one or more particular facilities or projects. This view of the Article 14 process, in short, reads the opening sentence of Article 14(1) to confine the citizen submission process to asserted failures to effectively enforce with respect to particular facilities or projects. Under this view, assertions of a wideranging failure to effectively enforce that do not focus on individual facilities or projects would not be subject to review under the citizen submission process.

The text of Article 14 does not appear to support limiting the scope of the citizen submission process in this way. The opening sentence of Article 14 establishes three specific parameters for the citizen submission process. It thereby limits assertions of failures to effectively enforce to those meeting these three elements. First, the assertions must involve an "environmental law." Next, they must involve an asserted failure to "effectively enforce" that law (the assertion may not focus on purported deficiencies in the law itself). Third, assertions must meet the temporal requirement of claiming that there *is* a failure to effectively enforce. The Parties' inclusion of these three limitations on the scope of the Article 14 process reflects that they knew how to confine the scope of the process and that they decided to do so in specific ways. * * *

[T]he text of the opening sentence of Article 14(1) supports the view that a submission may warrant preparation of a factual record, regardless of the scope of the alleged enforcement failure, so long as the submission focuses on an asserted failure to effectively enforce an environmental law. Moreover, in deciding whether to request a response from a Party, Article 14(2) of the NAAEC directs the Secretariat to be guided by whether a submission "raises matters whose further study in this process would advance the goals" of the Agreement. The goals of the NAAEC are ambitious and broad in scope. These goals include, for example, "foster[ing] the protection and improvement of the environment in the territories of the Parties for the well-being of present and future generations," as well as "enhanc[ing] compliance with, and enforcement of, environmental laws and regulations." * * *

In sum, Article 14(1) establishes parameters for the scope of the citizen submission process. These parameters limit the scope of the process in several ways but they do not reflect an intention only to allow "particularized" assertions of a failure to effectively enforce and to exclude assertions such as those made here that there is a widespread failure to effectively enforce. Article 14(2) provides further support for the notion that the citizen submission process may include either type of assertion. Preparing factual records on submissions that take either approach would promote the objects and purposes of the NAAEC. * * *

Preliminary Framework For Analysis Of Articles 45(1) Issues

The submission charges that the United States has failed to effectively enforce the MBTA. As indicated above, Article 45(1) of the NAAEC provides that a Party has not failed to effectively enforce its environmental law if the action or inaction in question by agencies or officials of that Party either "reflects a reasonable exercise of their discretion in respect of investigatory, prosecutorial, regulatory or compliance matters" or "results from *bona fide* decisions to allocate resources to enforcement in respect of other environmental matters determined to have higher priorities." The United States asserts that it has not failed to effectively enforce the MBTA for both of these reasons.

The purpose of the citizen submission process suggests that the Secretariat should dismiss a submission if the relevant Party establishes that there is no failure to effectively enforce. A fundamental purpose of the process is to enhance domestic environmental enforcement by the three Parties. Accordingly, if a Party has made a persuasive case that there is no failure to effectively enforce, there will be little point in going forward.

This is the first Party response in which a Party has made a detailed assertion that Article 45 makes continued review of the submission inappropriate. The nature of the Secretariat's review of the submission in light of the response with respect to these issues will likely be determined on a case-by-case basis. The Secretariat anticipates, however, that the following analysis will generally be relevant. In a particular submission, if a Party has asserted that its enforcement reflects a reasonable exercise of its discretion, the Secretariat should review at least two questions in assessing the extent to which the Party provides support for this assertion. First, to what extent has the Party explained how it has exercised its discretion? Second, to what extent has the Party explained why its exercise of discretion is reasonable under the circumstances? If the Party has provided a persuasive explanation of how it has exercised its discretion, and why its exercise of discretion is reasonable, then under Article 45(1)(a), the Party would not have failed to effectively enforce its environmental law. In such a situation there would seem to be little reason to continue with further study of the matters raised in the submission. If, on the other hand, the Party has not explained how it exercised its discretion or why its exercise of discretion is reasonable, dismissal would not be warranted under

Article 45(1)(a). The Secretariat might nevertheless determine that dismissal is warranted for other reasons.

With respect to the assertion that a Party's enforcement practices result "from *bona fide* decisions to allocate resources to enforcement in respect of other environmental matters determined to have higher priorities," the Secretariat should review the extent to which the Party has explained at least three points: 1) its allocation of resources; 2) its priorities; and 3) the reasons why the Party's allocation of resources constitutes a *bona fide* allocation given the Party's priorities. If a Party has explained its allocation of resources and its priorities, and has provided a persuasive explanation of why its allocation of resources is *bona fide* in light of those priorities, then, again, under Article 45(1)(b), there is not a failure to effectively enforce. As a result, there is little reason to continue with further study of the submission. * * *

[The Secretariat reviewed the submission and the US response]

For the reasons stated above, the Secretariat considers that the submission, in light of the Party's response, warrants development of a factual record. The Submitters assert that logging operations have violated and are continuing to violate the MBTA on a nationwide basis and in particular identified situations. The Submitters further assert that the Party has not brought a single prosecution under the MBTA for such alleged violations. In its response the Party does not challenge the first assertion. The Party acknowledges that no prosecution under the MBTA has been brought against a logging operation. In the Secretariat's view the Party has not adequately supported its claim that its failure to bring a single prosecution against logging operations is the result of a reasonable exercise of its discretion or a bona fide allocation of its resources. The Secretariat is not expressing a view as to the ultimate resolution of these issues. Instead, it has determined that the purposes of the NAAEC would be well served by developing in a factual record additional information of the types referred to above concerning them. In accordance with Article 15(1) of the NAAEC, the Secretariat so informs the Council and in this document provides its reasons.

———

The following excerpt from the Factual Report in the B.C. Hydro case in Canada illustrates the techniques available to the CEC to gather relevant information about a country's performance with respect to enforcement of their environmental laws.

Council for Environmental Cooperation, Factual Record, *BC Aboriginal Fisheries Commission et al.*, SEM–97–001 (June 2000).

A Summary of Other Relevant Information, And Facts Presented by the Secretariat

A. An Overview of the Process Used to Solicit and Develop Information

38. The Submission presents a particularly challenging context in which to obtain information relating to whether a Party is failing to effectively enforce its environmental laws. It involves a substantial number of hydroelectric operations, located in different parts of the Province of British Columbia. ... The Submitters claim that these hydroelectric operations are harming fish habitat, and thereby violating Canadian environmental law, in several different

ways (reduced flows, rapid flow fluctuation, flow diversion, etc.). In reply, Canada has identified a wide array of responses to the operations' alleged violations of the *Fisheries Act.* * * *

40. Because the Submission and Response raise a series of complex, highly technical issues, the Secretariat convened an Expert Group comprised of individuals with expertise in three relevant areas [hydroelectric operations, regulatory and compliance matters, fish habitat-related issues] ...

The Expert Group produced a report containing information it developed. This report is attached to the Factual Record. . . . The Factual Record also incorporates information developed by the Expert Group, as referenced below.

41. The Secretariat identified four key stakeholders in this Factual Record process:

Canada, the Submitters, the Province of British Columbia and BC Hydro (collectively, the "Stakeholders"). The Submitters and Canada have an obvious, particularly strong interest in the Factual Record process in their respective capacities as the parties that launched the process and the Party whose enforcement practices are under review. The Province of British Columbia's role as a partner in many of Canada's initiatives and its independent responsibilities for water resources management, including regulation of BC Hydro operations, gives it a key interest. BC Hydro, the operator of the dams at issue, has a strong interest as well. The Secretariat made several efforts to obtain information from each of these Stakeholders.

42. ... The Secretariat further advised the Stakeholders that it was convening an Expert Group to assist it, and the Secretariat invited each of the four Stakeholders to meet with, and present information to, the Expert Group. * * *

44. * * *

As indicated above, the focus of the Secretariat's information-gathering process is on whether Canada has been effectively enforcing its environmental laws. The following types of information, especially information beyond that already provided to the Secretariat, are particularly relevant:

● Information concerning the nature of the incidents or alleged violations identified in the Submission and Response and their impacts on fish habitat;

● Information relating to the nature of the Canadian responses to these incidents; and

● Information relating to the effectiveness of these responses. Such information may include, among other things, information relating to the strengths and weaknesses of a particular response or responses in: a) preventing harmful impacts from continuing, reducing the severity of continuing impacts, and/or reducing the likelihood of impacts continuing; b) preventing harmful impacts from recurring in the future, reducing the likelihood of recurrence, and/or reducing the impact of any future incidents; or c) repairing or otherwise redressing any adverse impact to fish habitat caused by incidents. * * *

45. On 22 January 1999 a letter was sent to the Stakeholders notifying them that the Factual Record would focus particular attention on a limited subset of six BC Hydro facilities ...

The letter explained the focus as follows:

The experts believe that a focus on these facilities will enable them to develop information concerning the primary types of adverse impacts on fish habitat sometimes caused by hydroelectric operations and the full range of Canada's responses. Further, this focus will enable the experts to develop information concerning the system as a whole and it will capture the major watersheds involved. The experts are interested in developing information concerning the nature of the impacts on fish habitat caused by the BC Hydro operations' alleged non-compliance, the types of actions the government has taken to reduce the impacts, and the extent to which the government's actions and BC Hydro's efforts have been successful in reducing impacts. (22 January 1999 Letter, Appendix 1).

The letter requested that the Stakeholders identify any other facilities that should be selected.

[Paragraphs 46–51 summarized the work of the Expert Group who notified, met with, and discussed the case with the stakeholders; they also attempted to meet with the Canadian government.]

52. Because much of the Factual Record, based on the Council Resolution, concerns the nature of Canadian enforcement efforts and the effectiveness of those efforts, the Secretariat contacted the government of Canada on several occasions in an effort to schedule meetings with knowledgeable government officials in order to make the Factual Record as comprehensive and accurate as possible. Such meetings never occurred and the Secretariat developed as accurate and complete a Factual Record as possible under these circumstances.

The following commentary discusses the potential effectiveness of the CEC as a model of citizen enforcement.

Bella Sewall, *The NAAEC and the Development of Transnational Legal Process for Environmental Law,* CIEL Discussion Paper (April 2001)

The Preamble to the NAAEC explicitly lists objectives ranging from the promotion of sustainable development to the coordination of policies to protect wild flora and fauna, in addition to certain procedural goals such as coordinated development and implementation of environmental laws ... and increasing transparency and public participation in the enforcement of environmental laws. Yet the steps from articulation of these long-term objectives to their actual implementation ... seem increasingly arduous the more one considers the complex mix of economic and political interests at stake in environmental law development and enforcement. The United States, Canada, and the United States have all developed domestic administrative and legal mechanisms in an effort to protect the environment and to balance the economic and environmental needs of constituencies. How do the international institutions established by the NAAEC fit into these domestic programs? More prescriptively, what can the CEC and other NAAEC institutions do in order to play a supportive role in the formulation and enforcement of environmental policy in the Parties?

The NAAEC is ... an international legal instrument of strong rhetorical power but limited enforcement authority. In this sense the NAAEC resembles many of the emerging international treaty regimes addressing international concerns. ... While these treaty regimes are far from perfect in their ability to enforce the norms which they enunciate, they play an important role in the development of both international and domestic law and policy through facilitating what scholars describe as "transnational legal process."

In his essay, *Why Nations Obey International Law*, professor of international law Harold Koh describes transnational legal process as "the complex process of institutional interaction whereby global norms are not just debated and interpreted, but ultimately internalized by domestic legal systems."

Koh emphasizes that international law understood in this sense seeks not to "simply ratify existing practice, but to elevate it." International institutions formed under treaty regimes such as NAAEC aim explicitly to change current national conduct, to actually influence the behavior of domestic agencies within the states party to the regime. The NAAEC works by enabling nongovernmental organizations to attract international attention to pressing environmental situations, opening up a new forum for dialogue and dispute resolution through its citizen submission procedure and in so doing promoting a ground-breaking interpenetration between international and domestic law.

The concept of transnational legal process draws upon the ideas of international lawyers Abram and Antonia Chayes, who studied the mechanisms by which international legal regimes are playing an "active role...in modifying preferences, generating new options, persuading the parties to move toward increasing compliance with regime norms, and guiding the evolution of the normative structure in the direction of the overall objectives of the regime." The Chayeses describe seven stages through which international regimes promote compliance: first, collecting and analyzing data about the situation and parties regulated through the regime in question, second, the identification of behavior that may not comply with the requirements of the regime, third, diagnosing the sources of the apparently deviant behavior, fourth, considering the reasons for the lack of compliance, fifth, the offer of technical assistance to the party to enable it to comply, followed in some cases by a sixth and a seventh stage through which noncompliance results either in the invocation of a dispute-settlement mechanism or else leads to the acceptance that the party is for one reason or another not able to comply with the norm under the current circumstances.

The NAAEC's citizen submission procedure and process for preparing a "factual record" creates a forum for accomplishing the first four of these stages, identifying instances of noncompliance with environmental law as described in the treaty and diagnosing the causes for such noncompliance. Through promoting research into environmental law and policy and allowing parties to ultimately submit disputes for arbitration, the treaty also establishes the ground rules for the final stages: the offering of technical assistance to parties who are not in compliance or the arbitration of disputes when State actors decide to invoke this dispute settlement mechanism. While it may be many years before the NAAEC's goals are actually implemented, the processes established in the NAAEC help to create an international context that rewards compliance and makes noncompliance increasingly costly for state parties.
* * *

At first glance the NAAEC's sweeping goals and comparatively modest enforcement authority do seem incongruous. However, as a mechanism for promoting an ongoing transnational legal process, the NAAEC is on the forefront of a new type of international treaty regime. These treaty regimes seek to provide international reinforcement to domestic movements through research, advocacy, and the creation of new international data collection and dispute resolution fora. By establishing such a forum, articulating international norms of compliance with environmental law, and increasing the number of stakeholders who are able to participate in its transnational legal processes, the NAAEC will play a vital role in developing effective, transparent, and environmentally sound international governance. As the NAFTA trade regime attests, such international governance is more and more necessary for peaceful and effective dispute resolution in an economically and socially interdependent world polity.

———

QUESTIONS AND DISCUSSION

1. By January 1998, 11 submissions had been made under the citizen submission process. Of these, the Secretariat requested a response from the party in five cases and recommended the preparation of a factual record in only one. By June 2001, the total number of submission had risen to 30 with the number growing from two in 1995 to six in 2000. The Secretariat requested fifteen responses and recommended the creation of seven factual records. To date, at least three factual records have been ordered by the Commission. Only one has been completed. What do these statistics say about the process? For a more detailed treatment of the CEC citizen submission process, *see* David L. Markell, *The Commission for Environmental Cooperation's Citizen Submission Process*, 12 Geo. Int'l Envtl. L. Rev. 545 (2000).

2. Article 45(2) limits the number of laws subject to the submission process. Article 45(2)(a) defines "environmental law" as "any statute or regulation, or provision thereof, the *primary purpose* of which is the protection of the environment, or the prevention of a danger to human life or health...." Because this definition focuses on individual provisions, rather than entire laws, this *primary purpose* limitation is not particularly restrictive. Article 45(2) goes on, however, to clarify an important class of laws to which the term does not apply: "[T]he term 'environmental law' does not include any statute or regulation, or provision thereof, the primary purpose of which is managing the commercial harvest or exploitation ... of natural resources." Article 45(2)(b). Although the issue has yet to be tested in a submission, this language appears to exclude laws relating to such vital environmental issues as mining and timber concessions from the purview of both the Article 5 "enforcement" obligation and the Article 14/15 process.

Recall, moreover, that the Secretariat will not prepare a factual record if it determines that the matter about which the submission is made is the subject of a pending judicial or administrative proceeding. Article 14(3)(a). Article 45(3) defines the phrase "judicial or administrative proceeding" to afford it the broadest possible scope.

> Such actions comprise: mediation; arbitration; the process of issuing a license, permit or authorization; seeking an assurance of voluntary compliance or a compliance agreement; seeking sanctions or remedies in an administrative or judicial forum; ... the process of issuing an administrative order; and ... an international dispute resolution proceeding to which the Party is a party.

Article 45(3). If the party complained of has instituted any such proceeding in a timely manner and according to its laws, further consideration by the CEC is foreclosed until the proceeding is final. Article 14(3)(a). *See, e.g.,* Secretariat's Determination Pursuant to Articles 14 & 15, Submission of Mr. Aage Tottrup, SEM–96–002 (28 May 1996). The mechanism created by Chapter 11 of NAFTA for settlement of investment disputes qualifies as an international dispute resolution proceeding. Determination pursuant to Article 14(3) of the North American Agreement on Environmental Cooperation, Submission of Neste Canada, A14/SEM/99–001/06/14(3) (June 30, 2000).

3. The CEC Secretariat may undertake reports under Article 13 largely on its own initiative or citizens may spur it to action. Recall, for example, that the CEC's response to the Silva Reservoir bird die-off under Article 13 was precipitated by a request from a group of environmental NGOs. Thus, Article 13 provides an alternative to the Article 14/15 process for citizens seeking to call international attention to an environmental problem in the territory of a party. A Secretariat's report under Article 13, however, "shall not include issues related to whether a Party has failed to enforce its environmental laws and regulations." Art. 13. In view of this limitation, when is it appropriate to request an Article 13 report rather than asserting a claim under Article 14/15?

4. Compare the submission process under Articles 14 and 15 to the non-compliance procedure under the Montreal Protocol on Substance that Deplete the Ozone Layer discussed *infra* at 565. Can you identify any similarities? The Protocol is widely acclaimed for its level of compliance. What are the main characteristics of the Protocol that contribute to this success? Next look at the World Bank Inspection Panel, page 1488.

The citizen submission process established by Articles 14 and 15 is an important step forward in facilitating public participation in international environmental protection efforts and ensuring that the NAFTA parties maintain high or at least moderate levels of environmental protection. Increasingly, NGOs and private citizens are using the process to bring environmental problems to the attention of both party governments and the public as a whole. Nonetheless, the earliest submissions to the Secretariat have highlighted weaknesses that will need to be remedied if the citizen process is to fulfill its role as a true citizen enforcement mechanism.

Jay Tuchton, *The Citizen Petition Process Under NAFTA's Environmental Side Agreement: It's Easy to Use, But Does it Work?*, 26 ENVTL. L. REP. 10018 (1996)

Procedural Flaws

[In addition to the potential for significant delay,] [t]he second major procedural flaw in the citizen submission process is that once a submission is filed, the submitter has almost no opportunity to participate in the review process. A submitter is not allowed to see, much less reply to, the challenged Party's response. Thus, a citizen has no ability to determine if the response is truthful or accurate. Furthermore, there is no explicit provision allowing a submitter to participate in the development of a draft factual record. More importantly, however, only Parties may offer comments on the draft factual record. The submitter is not allowed to review Party's comments for truth or accuracy. In essence, the submitter loses the ability to "prosecute" the case and is forced to rely on the Secretariat to pursue or "litigate" the claim. This is a dramatic departure from the typical judicial model in which the parties, in this case the submitter and the challenged Party, make their case to a neutral body. The Secretariat should at least allow the citizen submitter to respond to arguments advanced against the submission.

The Substantive Flaw

The glaring substantive flaw in the citizen submission process is the lack of a guaranteed remedy. Even if (1) a submitter successfully survives the hurdles of Articles 14 (1) and 14 (2), (2) the Secretariat determines that the Party's response is inadequate, (3) the Council votes to allow the Secretariat to prepare a factual record, and (4) the Council votes to make the factual record public, nothing necessarily happens. A citizen submitter has no direct ability to force a Party to effectively enforce its environmental laws. Rather, the citizen submitter must hope that another Party chooses to act on the factual record and pursue a claim under the NAAEC dispute resolution and enforcement provisions. Accordingly, even though a citizen submission might prove that a Party is failing to effectively enforce its environmental laws, the violation may never be redressed.

A Troubling First Decision

Regardless of the significance of the procedural and substantive flaws in the submission process, the first citizen enforcement submission filed with the Secretariat has uncovered an even more troubling loophole in the NAAEC's purported requirement that all NAFTA Parties effectively enforce their environmental laws. On July 5, 1995, Earthlaw, a public interest law firm housed at the University of Denver College of Law, filed an Article 14 submission on behalf of one Mexican and four American environmental groups. The submission alleged that the United States was failing to effectively enforce the Endangered Species Act (ESA). The submitters' complaint arose out of enactment of the Emergency Supplemental Appropriations and Rescissions for the Department of Defense to Preserve and Enhance Military Readiness Act of 1995, which was signed into law by President Clinton on April 10, 1995. Buried within this bill is an unrelated amendment, labeled a budgetary rescission, that is commonly known as the ESA Moratorium. The ESA Moratorium suspends enforcement of ESA section 4 for the remainder of the U.S. government's fiscal year.

The Earthlaw submission acknowledged that the NAAEC explicitly recognizes "the right of each Party to establish its own levels of domestic environmental protection and environmental development policies and priorities, and to adopt or modify accordingly its environmental laws and regulations." The submitters argued, however, that based on U.S. case law, the United States had not modified or amended the ESA through the ESA Moratorium; rather Congress had simply suspended the Act's enforcement. In evaluating the submission under Article 14 (2), the Secretariat correctly framed the issue presented by the submission as "whether a 'failure to effectively enforce' under Article 14 may result from the enactment of a law which suspends the implementation of certain provisions of another statute." The Secretariat concluded that "(t)he enactment of legislation which specifically alters the operation of pre-existing environmental law in essence becomes part of the greater body of environmental laws and statutes on the books. ... The Secretariat therefore cannot characterize the application of a new legal regime as a failure to enforce an old one."

While the Secretariat's position can be faulted for ignoring a U.S. district court's determination that the ESA Moratorium did not amend the ESA, the Secretariat's reasoning reveals a more troubling problem. The Secretariat noted that Article 14 (1) allows it to consider submissions regarding a Party's failure to effectively enforce environmental laws. The Secretariat then observed that:

> (o)n its face, there is little to support the notion ... that the word Party (in Article 14(1)) is restricted to include only the executive functions of agencies or departments, or that the term should mean anything other than "government" in a broader sense, including its separate branches. However, Articles 14 and 15 read in conjunction with other provisions of the Agreement strongly suggest that a failure to enforce environmental law

applies (only) to the administrative agencies or officials charged with implementing laws and regulations.

While the Secretariat may yet reverse itself, if this ruling stands, the Secretariat has effectively exempted all legislative actions from the NAAEC's promise of effective enforcement of environmental laws. . . .

This legislative loophole threatens to render the NAAEC citizen submission process useless as an environmental enforcement tool. The NAAEC was intended to require the NAFTA countries, including all the branches of their respective governments—executive, judicial, and legislative—to effectively enforce their environmental laws. If the Secretariat refuses to redress legislative suspensions of environmental enforcement under Article 14, then interests that wish to avoid NAAEC oversight of compliance with these laws will simply lobby the legislature to grant them a suspension. Environmental laws will remain technically on the books, but will not be enforced. The NAAEC's effective enforcement promise will mean nothing.

QUESTIONS AND DISCUSSION

1. How might you respond to Tuchton's complaint that the citizen submission process under Articles 14 and 15 fails to provide an enforcement mechanism—that the preparation of a factual record is a procedural dead end? Is Tuchton right? One response might be that the public pressure associated with the citizen submission process should convince the offending party to come into compliance under most circumstances. Do you agree? How does the Article 14/15 process under NAAEC compare to NAFTA Articles 1110.1 and 1116, discussed *supra,* which allow investors to bring monetary claims against a party for "expropriation" of their investments?

2. Tuchton notes that the Secretariat narrowed the scope of the citizen submission process when it read a "legislative exception" into the NAAEC. This legislative exception emerged in the first two submissions. In the first submission, Submission of the Biodiversity Legal Foundation, SEM–95–001 (30 June 1995), the submitters alleged that the U.S. Congress had failed to effectively enforce the environmental laws of the United States when it passed a Rescissions Act that not only rescinded $1,500,000 that had previously been allocated for making "endangered" and "threatened" species determinations and "critical habitat" determinations under the Endangered Species Act but also forbade the U.S. Fish and Wildlife Service from compensating for the lost funds from other programs. In the second submission, Submission of the Sierra Club, SEM–95–002 (30 August 1995), the submitters complained that the U.S. Congress had failed to effectively enforce environmental law when it passed a "Logging Rider" to the same Rescissions Act, which effectively suspended the enforcement of environmental laws for two logging programs. The Secretariat rejected both submissions on Article 14(1) grounds. It pointed out that upon enactment by Congress and signature by the President, the Rescissions Act itself became law, and thus superseded existing environmental laws to the extent of any inconsistency. *See* Determination Pursuant to Articles 14 & 15, Submission of the Sierra Club, SEM–95–002 (8 December 1995). How does this exception compare to the treatment of investment interests under NAFTA Articles 1110.1 and 1116?

3. The U.S. National Advisory Committee for the CEC in its advice to EPA dated May 21, 1999 states:

Article 5(1) provides an extremely important context for interpreting the phrase "failing to enforce its environmental law," . . . Article 5 (1) states: "With the aim of achieving *high levels of environmental protection* and *compliance with its environmental laws and regulations*, each Party shall effectively enforce its environmental laws and regulations through appropriate government action...." (Emphasis in original.)

Should the CEC investigate whether enforcement is achieving "high levels of environmental protection"?

4. In addition to the submission procedures, the NACEE operates an Enforcement Cooperation Program, though these two functions are not directly connected. What about using the Enforcement Cooperation Program as a follow up mechanism for Article 14/15 cases? *See* John H. Knox, *A New Approach to Compliance with International Environmental Law: The Submission Procedure of the NAFTA Environment Commission*, 28 ECOLOGY L.Q. 1 (2001).

5. In June 2001, Joint Public Advisory Committee submitted a report to the CEC evaluating the submission process.

> The Articles 14 and 15 process does not currently include provisions for enforcement or follow-up of a completed factual record, even when a Party's failure to enforce its environmental laws is indicated by the factual record. While we received a number of comments addressed to this issue, many of the suggestions went beyond the scope of our study or suggested significant amendments to the NAAEC itself. We believe that the present Articles 14 and 15 procedure lends itself to increased oversight, by both the public and the CEC, of the steps that a Party takes (or fails to take) to remedy any enforcement failures that are revealed in a factual record.

> Since the majority of comments by members of the public referred to monitoring subsequent to publication of a factual record, the public monitoring role is applicable after publication, as well as prior to and during the Articles 14 and 15 review process. It is clear that "enforcement" of environmental laws cannot be left to private citizens or NGOs.

> To respond to the concern regarding monitoring, one option would be for the Party involved to report to the CEC within a reasonable period of time (for example, not exceeding 12 months) after the release of a factual record pursuant to Council authorization on the actions, if any, that it has taken to address the matters set forth in that factual record. Such a report should be made public in the next CEC annual report, after an opportunity for JPAC members to review and provide comments, through the draft CEC annual report in accordance with the Article 16(6) of the NAAEC. In this way, the Parties would manifest an ongoing and real commitment of the CEC to make the Articles 14 and 15 process meaningful, transparent and effective.

Joint Public Advisory Committee, *Lessons Learned: Citizen Submissions under Articles 14 and 15 of the North American Agreement on Environmental Cooperation: Final Report to the Council of the Commission for Environmental Cooperation* (6 June 2001)

---

c.   *STATE-TO-STATE CONSULTATIONS AND DISPUTE RESOLUTION*

If a party to the Environmental Side Agreement believes that another party has engaged in a "persistent pattern of failure" to effectively enforce its environmental law, it may request consultations with an eye to resolving the dispute. Environmental Side Agreement, Art. 22(1). In the following excerpt, Steve Charnovitz examines the processes and problems of the NAAEC dispute resolution procedure.

Steve Charnovitz, *The NAFTA Environmental Side Agreement: Implications for Environmental Cooperation, Trade Policy, and American Treatymaking*, 8 Temp. Int'l & Comp. L.J. 257, 266–70 (1994)

Part V, the longest section in the NAAEC, concerns dispute resolution. If one government complains that another is not effectively enforcing the environmental laws, the Council can convene an arbitral panel. Such complaints can only allege non-enforcement of environmental laws as they pertain to goods traded in the North America or produced by export-competing industries. The NAAEC contains no environmental injury test, and the complaining country does not have to show environmental injury to it or to the scofflaw country. . . .

The panel must submit its initial report within 180 days after formation. The report will include "a determination as to whether there has been a persistent pattern of failure by the Party complained against to effectively enforce its environmental law." A "persistent pattern" is defined as a "sustained or recurring course of action or inaction." In addition, the NAAEC states that a determination of ineffective enforcement shall not be made when there is a "reasonable exercise" of investigatory, prosecutorial, or regulatory discretion, or when there have been "bona fide decisions to allocate resources" to enforcement of higher priority environmental matters. There is no commitment in the NAAEC to increase agency enforcement budgets.

The term "environmental law" is also sharply circumscribed. The NAAEC takes a narrow approach to environmentalism by specifically excluding laws whose "primary purpose" is to manage the harvesting of natural resources. Thus, it is unclear whether important environmental issues such as strip mining, soil conservation, energy extraction, coastal fishing, and sustainable timber harvesting are included or excluded. Moreover, environmental laws pertaining to wildlife outside of a party's own territories are excluded from NAAEC's conception of the environment. For example, if Mexico had a law preventing its fishing vessels from harvesting shrimp without turtle excluder devices, this law would not be subject to NAAEC factual records or dispute panels (except possibly when the shrimping occurs in Mexico's territory).

. . . The parties, but not the public, get the opportunity to comment on the initial report. The final report must be issued within 60 days of the initial report. If a party is found to be engaged in a pattern of ineffectively enforcing its environmental law, the panel may propose an action plan. The disputing parties will then attempt to agree upon an action plan to remedy this situation. If no agreement is reached within 60 days, the panel may be reconvened. Within 90 days, the panel will approve or impose an "action plan."

The "action plan" may be significant for several reasons. First, it may provide an objective way for the panel to measure progress toward better enforcement. Second, bureaucratic benefits may develop in having an action plan imposed on a country. For example, an environmental agency might use the plan as justification for a larger budget request for its regulatory staff. Third, the action plan may embarrass a government into mending its ways.

Whenever a complaining party believes that an action plan is not being fully implemented, it may reconvene the panel. If the panel decides that the defendant country is not fully implementing the plan, the panel must impose a "monetary enforcement assessment" within 60 days. For 1994, the penalty is capped at $20 million. The panel has broad discretion in determining the amount of the penalty. In a remarkable departure from enforcement norms, the monetary assessment is paid to the Commission, and then expended by the Council to "improve the environment or environmental law enforcement" in the scofflaw country. It is unclear what theories of deterrence underlie this novel approach to punishment.

Thus, these fines are not penalties in the usual sense of the term. In other words, the "teeth" barely bite. As one Administration official explained, the value of the penalties "would be primarily symbolic." On the other hand, there may be domestic political fallout for a government in being named an environmental scofflaw. The use of fines in international trade or environmental agreements may be unique.

If the plaintiff party remains dissatisfied, it may, reconvene the panel after six months. The panel must then make a determination within 60 days as to whether the defendant party is fully implementing the "action plan." If not, the plaintiff party may increase certain tariffs to collect an amount equal to the monetary assessment. Of course, as with all tariffs, it is the importers and ultimately the consumers in the country imposing the tariffs who pay these costs. These tariffs may only be imposed against the United States or Mexico; Canada chose not to be on the receiving end for trade sanctions. The use of such tariffs to collect arbitral fines may be unprecedented.

Imposing trade sanctions against a country that fails to enforce its environmental laws is a protracted and cumbersome process. At a minimum, it would take 755 days from the initiation of a complaint to the attainment of a trade sanction. . . .

---

d.   CEC PROGRAMS AND THE NORTH AMERICAN FUND FOR ENVIRONMENTAL COOPERATION

In furtherance of its mission to increase environmental cooperation among the parties, the CEC has developed a variety of programs aimed at assessing the state of the environment and natural resources in North America, and taking corrective and preventative measures for environmental preservation. The CEC's efforts are divided among five program areas: environmental conservation; protecting human health and the environment; environment, trade and economy; enforcement cooperation and law; and information and public outreach.

Council on Environmental Cooperation, 2002–2004 PROPOSED PRO-
GRAM PLAN AND BUDGET FOR THE COMMISSION FOR ENVIRONMENTAL COOP-
ERATION OF NORTH AMERICA, **2001C/C.01/01–07/PLAN, September
2001**

APPROACHES

The scale and scope of emerging environmental issues of regional concern call for an unprecedented degree of cooperation between and among Canada, Mexico and the United States. The CEC is mandated to help build consensus and a shared understanding of the nature, scope and magnitude of the environmental challenge in North America, and facilitate actions to address it.

The CEC promotes sustainable solutions to preserve and protect North America's natural systems by working in partnership with a growing number of private and public actors at the local, regional and global level. Through these partnerships, the CEC can maximize the impact of its actions and avoid duplicating the work of others by clearly defining our role and employing our unique attributes to act as convenor, catalyst, and a center for policy, research and information at the North American level. The three-year program plan presents a combination of actions and strategies employing one or more of these functions, depending on the stated objectives of the activity.

ROLE OF THE CEC

The CEC can play a number of roles that can vary depending on the issue being addressed. They include: [Convenor, Catalyst, Research and Policy Analyst, and Information Hub] . . .

PUBLIC PARTICIPATION AND CAPACITY BUILDING

. . . The three-year program plan attempts to integrate capacity building and public participation activities directly into the project descriptions . . .

Similarly, the Parties recognize that lasting environmental protection and conservation strategies can only be sustained by building national capacities to design, implement and maintain the policies and measures that are adopted in the region. Accordingly, the CEC also builds capacity-building mechanisms, such as training, scientific and technical exchange and education, directly into the three-year program plan.

The CEC also provides over $400,000 in funding per year to small, community-based, environmental projects through the North American Fund for Environmental Cooperation (NAFEC) to strengthen the public participation in small, specific environmental projects.

E. THE U.S.–MEXICO BORDER ENVIRONMENT COOPERATION AGREEMENT

As noted in the introduction to the NAFTA section, the U.S.–Mexico border region raises highly sensitive environmental issues. With the number of maquiladoras growing rapidly, and the region's population expected to top 20 million people by 2010, its environment will continue to deteriorate unless significant corrective measures are taken. The estimated cost to deal effectively with environmental issues in the border region in the next decade is in the range of $5.7–8.7 billion.

The border was discussed during the NAFTA negotiations, but was not addressed in NAFTA or the Environmental Side Agreement. Instead, the United States and Mexico adopted a separate, bilateral agreement for the protection of the border region. *See* Agreement Between the Government of the United States of America and the Government of the United Mexican States Concerning the Establishment of a Border Environment Cooperation Commission and a North American Development Bank, Nov. 16, 18, 1993, *reprinted in* 32 I.L.M. at 1545. The Border Environment Cooperation

Agreement (BECA) established two new institutions to work exclusively on the environmental and development needs of the border region: the Border Environment Cooperation Commission (BECC) and the North American Development Bank (NADBank). The purpose of these institutions is to identify and fund environmental infrastructure projects throughout that region.

The BECC's primary function is to certify environmental infrastructure projects in the border region so that state, local, or private investors in the project may seek financial assistance from the NADBank and other funding sources. To be eligible for certification, a project must generally fall within the 100 km limit on either side of the border that defines the border region. The BECC may also certify or provide assistance to an environmental infrastructure project outside the border zone if that project would remedy a transboundary environmental or health problem and both the U.S. EPA and Mexico's Ministry of Environment, Natural Resources, and Fisheries (SEMARNAP) concur. In all cases, preference must be given to projects relating to water pollution, wastewater treatment, municipal solid waste and related matters. BECA ch. I, art. II § 2.

Chapter II of the BECA establishes the NADBank, which was created to provide financing for projects certified by the BECC, to otherwise assist the BECC in fulfilling its development assistance role, and to provide financing endorsed by either the United States or Mexico "for community adjustment and investment" in support of the NAFTA. BECA ch. II, art. I, § 1. In furtherance of these purposes, NADBank's functions are:

> (a) to promote the investment of public and private capital contributing to its purposes;
>
> (b) to encourage private investment in projects, enterprises, and activities contributing to its purposes, and to supplement private investment when private capital is not available on reasonable terms and conditions; and
>
> (c) to provide technical and other assistance for the financing and, in coordination with the [BECC], the implementation of plans and projects.

BECA ch. II, art. I, § 2.

As with the BECC, primary decision-making authority for NADBank is vested in its six member Board. BECA ch. II. art. VI, §§ 2–3.

NADBank was established with an initial authorized capital stock of US $3 billion dollars, with each Party required to subscribe to shares equaling half that amount. BECA ch. II. art. II, § 1. Shares worth US $450 million were paid in immediately, with the remaining $2.55 billion callable by the Board.

There is widespread agreement that the BECC and the NADB have been successful.

> Though the road has not always been smooth, the border region now has more environmental infrastructure projects completed, under construction, or in the planning stage than at any other time in history. Moreover, the BECC and NADB have created a new paradigm for sustainable development in the border region. As this model is beginning to bear fruit, it should be strengthened and supported by the U.S. and Mexico.

National Wildlife Federation, *NGO Statement on the Border Environment Cooperation Commission and the North American Development Bank*, June 8, 2001 <http://www.nwf.org/trade/finalletter.html>.

The BECC and NADB are working with over 100 communities on both sides of the border and, "As of June 2001, the NADB has authorized $294.7 million in loans and/or grant resources for 36 infrastructure projects. These projects will represent a total investment of about $913 million." BECC AND NADB, JOINT STATUS REPORT (2001).

F.   NAFTA'S ENVIRONMENTAL IMPACT

In light of the intense public interest in NAFTA's environmental impact, one might expect that an initial assessment of this impact had been made. Although some assessment of NAFTA's environmental institutions— the CEC, the BECC and NADBank—has been undertaken, neither the party governments nor the treaty bodies have released specific findings on the environmental effects of NAFTA itself.

Article 10(6) of the Environmental Side Agreement requires the CEC Council to cooperate with the NAFTA Free Trade Commission to achieve the environmental goals and objectives of the NAFTA. In furtherance of this mission, Article 10(6)(e) requires the Council to consider "on an ongoing basis the environmental effects of the NAFTA." Since beginning its assessment of NAFTA's environmental effects in 1995, the CEC has produced four reports laying out the major issues and developing a framework for the assessment. The CEC is currently developing a framework for analyzing NAFTA's environmental effects. *See* Council on Environmental Cooperation, *Assessing Environmental Effects of the North American Free Trade Agreement (NAFTA): An Analytic Framework (Phase II) and Issue Studies* (March 1999).

In 1997, the Office of the United States Trade Representative released an extensive report on NAFTA's effects on trade, investment, labor and the environment. OFFICE OF THE UNITED STATES TRADE REPRESENTATIVE, STUDY ON THE OPERATION AND EFFECT OF THE NORTH AMERICAN FREE TRADE AGREEMENT (1997). Although the study includes an extensive chapter on the environment, it expressly avoids discussing "how NAFTA's trade flows may affect the North American environment." *Id.* at 115. In 2000, the Institute for International Economics issued a study of the environmental impacts of NAFTA after seven years.

> In determining whether the NAFTA has improved or damaged the North American Environment, it is critical to define the relevant counterfactual. Some environmentalists believe that tougher environmental clauses could have been built into the agreement. Most negotiators disagree: The side agreements crafted by the Clinton Administration in 1993 stretched the patience not only of Mexico and Canada, but also of Republicans in the US Congress. In our view, the relevant counterfactual was not tougher provisions, but no agreement. Without the NAFTA, the Mexican government would have had less incentive to pass environmental legislation or to improve its enforcement efforts, and the achievements, modest though they are, of the Commission on Environmental

Cooperation, NADB, and BECC would not exist. Despite the positive environmental incentives of the NAFTA and achievements of the environmental institutions created by the side agreements, the NAFTA's environmental record is imperfect and there is ample room for improvement.

Cary C. Hufbauer, Daniel C. Esty, Diana Orejas, Luis Rubio, and Jeffery J. Schott, NAFTA AND THE ENVIRONMENT: SEVEN YEARS LATER 55 (2000).

Several NGO's have stepped forward to identify where there is "room for improvement." For example, Public Citizen argues that NAFTA has increased U.S. food imports from Mexico by more than forty percent, while the number of border inspections for those imports has steadily decreased. Based on its own analysis of FDA data, the group contends that imported produce is more than three times as likely as domestic produce to be contaminated with illegal pesticides. Yet the FDA inspects only one to two percent of imported food shipments. Public Citizen links this influx of uninspected and potentially contaminated food with a dramatic increase in the rates of foodborne illness in the United States over the last decade. PUBLIC CITIZEN, NAFTA'S BROKEN PROMISES: FAST-TRACK TO UNSAFE FOOD (1997). These arguments are buttressed by a recent Government Accounting Office (GAO) report, which concluded that the nation's food and agriculture inspection system has been overwhelmed by the rapid growth in international trade and travel since 1990. GAO further noted that the inspection problems associated with this growth have been exacerbated by policy changes that emphasize facilitating trade, and place pressure on both regulators and inspectors to minimize disruptions to that trade through inspections. U.S. GAO, AGRICULTURAL INSPECTION: IMPROVEMENTS NEEDED TO MINIMIZE THREAT OF FOREIGN PESTS AND DISEASES 1–2 (Letter Report, 05/05/97, GAO/RCED–97–102).

The next excerpt discusses NAFTA's effect on pollution in Mexico.

Kevin Gallagher, *Trade Liberalization and Industrial Pollution in Mexico: Lessons for the FTAA,* GLOBAL DEVELOPMENT AND ENVIRONMENT INSTITUTE WORKING PAPER NO. 00–07 (October 2000).

The study finds that many of the industries deemed the dirtiest in the world economy are actually cleaner in Mexico than in the US, and the industries labeled the cleanest are dirtier in Mexico. To generalize, this exhibits that trade liberalization can have both positive and negative environmental effects in developing economies. Sectors where plant vintage determines pollution levels can benefit from their ability to take advantage of newer technologies after liberalizing trade, as is the case with the Mexican steel industry. However, if pollution is a function of end of pipe technology, as in the paper industry, pollution levels are determined by levels of regulation, enforcement and compliance, which are lower in Mexico. * * *

2. The most interesting of these calculations is the Mexico–U.S. pollution intensity ratio.... Most striking are the ratios for Textiles (which are 137 to 1225 times as dirty in Mexico depending on the pollutant), and Paper (which are 70 to 592 times as dirty). If those two are taken out of the sample then the twelve largest Mexican industries are on average 6.23 times dirtier than U.S. industries. In addition to Textiles and Paper, the Food and Beverage industries range from 2 to 10 times worse than those in the U.S. PT in the Mexican Machinery industry is close to 100 times as dirty as Machinery in the U.S. Electrical Machinery PT CO. * * *

Air emissions in the Paper industry are not determined by core technology, but by pollution control technology. The last significant wave of innovation in basic technologies in paper production occurred from the late eighteenth to the mid-twentieth centuries. Controlling air emissions then, has been left to the development of "end of pipe technologies" which are often imposed by governments or civil society. Thus, in the Mexican case, relatively high pollution intensity in the paper industry could be due to the degree of Mexican legal and institutional commitment toward air pollution in the Paper sector. If there are lax regulations or enforcement in this sector, substitution effects may occur where the Paper industry would spend their money on factors other than pollution control. At Mexico's highest period of plant level inspections, it was only visiting six percent of all establishments in manufacturing.

Perhaps what is most surprising are the industries that are as clean or cleaner than those in the United States. Other Chemicals pharmaceuticals, cosmetics, film, etc.), Iron and Steel, and Non–Ferrous Metals each fall into this category-some of the very industries deemed the dirtiest in the world economy! Mexican plants are relatively newer than in the US, since Mexico's industrial growth is recent. If pollution intensity depends primarily on plant vintage, and is hard to vary after installation, Mexico may benefit from newer, cleaner plants in these sectors. While it is known that significant FDI (Foreign Direct Investment) has flowed to Mexico since NAFTA, sectoral FDI data is difficult to obtain. A recent OECD study however, indicates that most of new FDI has gone into Petrochemicals, Chemicals, Fertilizer, and Steel. It is likely that the new FDI in Chemicals and Steel has been in the form of the cleanest technology. This is the case in the Mexican steel sector, which has experienced diffusion of electric technology. Another possibility, but less plausible, relates to the data. The World Bank reports that 25 of the dirtiest polluters were omitted from the sample because they caused an outlier problem. It is possible that these 25 plants account for a large share of the output in the apparently cleanest sectors. * * *

From 1994 until the present however, total pollution almost doubles. As discussed earlier in the paper, using a fixed coefficient for pollution intensity may underestimate pollution intensity previous to 1997. Further research is needed to determine the spatial distribution of these industries. If total pollution is concentrated in just a few areas in Mexico, critical health thresholds may be in jeopardy. * * *

In the 1990s Mexico began to step up its system of enforcement and created a system of citizen complaints. Mexico's environmental enforcement record has risen sharply since its inception in the late 1980s (although it has dropped off considerably in recent years). In addition, Mexico has established a formal system of citizen complaints. In 1992 1,281 were filed, in 1997 there were 5,644. During the 1990s, it has also been documented that a number of environmental initiatives have been sparked by the private sector. ... As a result of all these efforts, the OECD concludes that large firms now meet environmental standards, but small and medium sized firms do not. * * *

The results from this study have three important implications for the FTAA (Free Trade Agreement of the Americas, discussed infra) process ... The first two implications are related to technology. If specialization occurs in sectors where pollution is in part a function of plant vintage, this study implies that those nations may be able to "leap frog" into cleaner technology in sectors where environmentally sound technological innovation has occurred. The Mexico–US pollution intensity ratio used in this study showed that industrial sectors such as Iron and Steel are "cleaner" in Mexico than their counterparts in the

United States. In this case, Mexico's relatively late industrialization allowed Mexico to deploy newer, cleaner mini-mill technology rather than some of the larger blast furnace technology in the US. If other nations in the Americas will specialize in industries with improved core technology, they may be able to enjoy a lower level of pollution intensity in such industries as well. Conversely, when Latin American nations specialize in industries where pollution intensity is determined by pollution control technologies, not the vintage of core technologies, the pollution intensity of such industries will be determined by the level of environmental stringency in those nations. This has been shown to be the case in the Mexican Paper industry. Paper is one of the most pollution intensive industries in Mexico, especially for air emissions of Sulfur Dioxide. Pollution in the Paper industry is relatively less varied by core technology than by pollution control technology. This is an indication that when specialization occurs in such sectors, and environmental policy is also lax, pollution intensive industry may rise. Perhaps the most significant implication of this study for the FTAA process is the need to stress the importance of reducing the levels of pollution intensity in manufacturing. All nations in an FTAA will be looking to increase economic growth in manufacturing. Such growth is much needed and will be most welcome to help spur the development of Latin American economies. This study has shown that unless increases in output in pollution intensive sectors are drastically accompanied by reductions in pollution intensity, total pollution will rise with such output. In Latin American regions already approaching critical environmental thresholds, such increases in total pollution may jeopardize the benefits of increasing economic activity in those areas.

COMMISSION FOR ENVIRONMENTAL COOPERATION, FREE TRADE AND THE ENVIRONMENT: THE PICTURE GETS CLEARER (2001)

Last year, the Commission for Environmental Cooperation (CEC) invited members of the public to road test the CEC developed methodology for assessing the environmental impact of free trade. . . . Below is a general summary of some of the key considerations emerging from the two-day symposium, followed by an annex summarizing the findings of some of the papers presented at the event.
* * *

Changes in Industrial Pollution

The effects of NAFTA on industrial pollution are mixed. Economic modeling work suggests that changes in industrial air pollution resulting from NAFTA are concentrated in three sectors: petroleum, base metals, and transportation equipment. The main increases in air pollution resulting from NAFTA are carbon monoxide and sulfur dioxide in the United States and sulfur dioxide in Mexico. Modeling work suggests significant reduction may occur in air pollution in the Canadian and Mexican paper sectors and in the Canadian chemicals sector. For particulate matter, carbon monoxide, sulfur dioxide, and nitrogen oxides, the greatest increases occur in the US base metals sector and in the Mexican petroleum sector. The transport equipment sectors of Canada and the US are large sources of volatile organic compounds. * * *

Hazardous Wastes: Another study analyzed changes in the transborder flow of hazardous wastes since NAFTA came into effect, and provides some interesting evidence on the other side of the pollution haven debate. Since NAFTA, approximately a five-fold increase in hazardous waste imports to Canada from the US has occurred. This sharp increase in waste imports has originated mainly from US steel and chemical industries. However, the increase in trade should be seen against an absolute decline in waste generation: since NAFTA, hazardous waste generation has declined in the US. After examining several explanations for the increase, the authors point to the comparatively less stringent environmental standards in Canada compared to the US. In addition, the authors note that during the time of NAFTA implementation, spending in several Canadian jurisdictions on environmental protection decreased dramatically, by as much as 30–40 percent. . . .

NAFTA and Renewable Natural Resources

Fisheries: The effects of NAFTA on the sustainable management of renewable resources appears mixed, and depends on the resource examined. NAFTA has had little impact on the sustainability of North American fisheries at the aggregate level. Most trade in fish and fish products was duty-free prior to NAFTA, and therefore any effects of tariff-related liberalization have been negligible. NAFTA may have relieved pressure on fisheries in Mexico on the margins, by increasing the substitution of imported fish for domestic catches. Non–NAFTA fish trade and, in particular, trade between North America and Asian countries, remains substantial, and international trade may be linked to the chronic over-fishing that plagues much of the world's fish stocks.

The effects of NAFTA on the forestry sector have been marginal, particularly given very low pre-NAFTA tariff rates. Case studies suggest that with NAFTA, foreign direct investment into Mexico's forestry sector has increased competition within the country, placing pressures on the remaining Mexican-owned paper and forest product companies to lower production costs to remain competitive in world markets. Although empirical evidence is scarce, what is available suggests that increased exposure to international competition may increase pressures on wood processing companies to circumvent environmental controls, thereby making sustainable forestry management practices difficult.

Trade liberalization may also indirectly compound environmental and human-health stresses resulting from intensive farming. Among the causes of the drinking water contamination crisis in Ontario has been the increase in intensive animal farming, coupled with a retreat of regulatory authority and provincial downloading of various responsibilities to the municipal level, the privatization of water management, the disruption to the chain of reporting and responsibilities among appropriate authorities, and significant reductions in environmental budgets.

Policy Implications

To date, growth in trade has not been matched by a comparable growth in environmental protection policies. In some instances, evidence to the contrary—that environmental expenditures were being reduced in tandem with trade liberalization—has led to increased environmental stress. This is especially true with the lag between an absolute increase in economic scale, and lagging investments in infrastructure as well as in monitoring and enforcement. A major challenge, therefore, is to find ways to ensure that revenues from increased trade strengthen environmental policies and cooperative management systems.

QUESTIONS AND DISCUSSION

1. There is considerable dispute regarding how to measure NAFTA's effect. The CEC has labored for several years to develop a framework for analyzing NAFTA's environmental impact. Even this attempt to establish a methodology has stirred debate. See REPORT OF INFORMAL WORKSHOP OF EXPERTS AND GOVERNMENT OFFICIALS ON ENVIRONMENT AND TRADE: COMMISSION FOR ENVIRONMENTAL COOPERATION, Montreal, 13 December 1999, <http://www.cec.org/programs_projects/trade_environ_econ/pdfs/13dece.pdf>. Part of the reason is the complicated and interconnected nature of the relationships. Part is due to lack of reliable data. But another reason is lack of political will. Many policy makers across boarders may not want to know what the effects are.

2. If we are still unable to assess NAFTA's environmental impacts eight years after the agreement, how successful do you think we will be preparing environmental assessments for proposed trade agreements? *See supra* at 1142.

––––––––

G.   TOWARD TRADE LIBERALIZATION THROUGHOUT THE AMERICAS

1.   FREE TRADE AGREEMENT OF THE AMERICAS

Negotiations to form a Free Trade of the Americas (FTAA) began in December 1994 in Miami at the Summit of the Americas with the goal of concluding negotiations by 2005. The declaration issued at the summit stated four broad goals relating to the environment: (1) create cooperative partnerships that will strengthen hemispheric capacity to prevent and control pollution, (2) protect ecosystems, (3) use biological resources on a sustainable basis, and (4) encourage clean, efficient, and sustainable energy production and use. SUMMIT OF THE AMERICAS: DECLARATION OF PRINCIPLES AND PLAN OF ACTION, Dec. 11, 1994, 34 I.L.M. 808. Negotiations on specific issues proceed under nine working groups: market access, agriculture, services, investment, government procurement, intellectual property, subsidies/anti-umping/countervailing duties, competition policy, and dispute settlement. Note the absence of the environment, for while the Summit Declaration linked trade and economic integration with environmental protection, at the same time it minimized the role for the environment by establishing distinct negotiation tracks, one for economic integration, another for other social issues including labor and environmental considerations.

As a result of this decision, environmental negotiations have been sidelined, along with a number of other "trade related" issues of public concern, into an ineffective Government Committee on Civil Society. This is made up of government representatives who may solicit views from non-governmental groups, activists, academics, and business representatives but "is not obligated to actually consider the views expressed." Americas-Trade, Final FTAA Declaration Falls Short of at Least Two Key U.S. Demands, Mar. 23, 1998, at 1 (1998). At the San Jose Ministerial, the committee was "given the responsibility to receive inputs from civil society, analyze them and present the range of views to the FTAA Trade Ministers." Committee of Government Representatives on Civil Society <http://www.ftaa-alca.org/SPCOMM/COMMCS_E.ASP> (10/10/01). The Trade Ministers stated: "We recognize and welcome the interests and concerns that different sectors of society have expressed in relation to the FTAA. Business and other sectors of production, labor, environmental and academic groups have been particularly active in this matter. We encourage these and other sectors of civil societies to present their views on trade matters in a constructive manner." *Id*. The Committee met for the first time on October 19–20, 1998, in Miami, where it agreed to a work plan which included extending an "Open Invitation to Civil Society", inviting members of the public to submit their views on the FTAA negotiations. The Committee received seventy-four submissions from a variety of groups, including a number of environmental organizations, which it compiled into a cursory summary of all the points raised in the submissions. The paragraph concerning the environment reads as follows:

> Some of the submissions advocated the inclusion of environmental issues in the FTAA. They raised in particular the environmental impact of the FTAA, not lowering environmental standards to attract investment or to gain competitive advantage, and made procedural recommendations. Some other submissions emphasized concerns that inclusions of environmental issues would delay progress on other trade issues, particularly if trade sanctions were used to enforced environmental standards. Also, some submissions suggested that environmental issues should be handled completely independent of trade discussions. Some of the submissions also noted that the increased prosperity generated by trade liberalization creates the resources necessary to protect the environment.

Committee on Civil Society, Free Trade Area of the Americas (FTAA), Report of the FTAA Committee of Government Representatives on the Participation of Civil Society, para. 29 (1999), <http://www.ftaa-alca.org/spcomm/derdoc/cs3e.doc>. The 6th Ministerial Meeting was held in Buenos Aires, Argentina in April 2001 and again neglected mention of environmental issues except to require that the contributions of civil society, including environmental groups, be presented directly to the FTAA negotiators thereby giving depth to the positions "abridged" by the Committee on Civil Society. In August 2001, the draft FTAA text was released for comment. Most of its provisions are still bracketed (i.e. debated) but one telling sign is the conspicuous absence of any real environmental protections. It states simply that:

> The Parties recognize that it is inappropriate to encourage investment by relaxing domestic environmental laws. Accordingly, each Party shall strive to ensure that it does not waive or otherwise derogate from, or offer to waive or otherwise derogate from, such laws as encouragement for the establishment, acquisition, expansion or retention of an investment of an investor in its territory.

THE FREE TRADE AREA OF THE AMERICAS DRAFT AGREEMENT, Article 19. The official position of the United States on environment and the FTAA has been that:

> The FTAA should expand trade and promote economic and social development while reflecting a strong commitment to achieving high levels of environmental protection; it should support, and not undermine, a country's ability to maintain and enforce its environmental laws, while ensuring against trade protectionist abuse. . . .

> To promote the view of the United States that strong and effective protection of the environment can be fully consistent with international trade liberalization in the FTAA, U.S. negotiators are working . . . to identify and incorporate relevant environmental considerations into the FTAA agreement. In the Investment chapter, for example, the United States seeks a provision similar to that

found in the NAFTA, obligating FTAA countries to strive to ensure that environmental laws are not relaxed to attract an investment. . . .

Another important means by which the United States is taking into account the environmental implications of the FTAA negotiations, both positive and negative, is through an environmental review, as directed by Executive Order 13141. USTR recently initiated a written environmental review of the FTAA and is in the process of obtaining public comment on the scope of that review. See 65 Fed. Reg. 75,763 (Dec. 4, 2000).

OFFICE OF THE UNITED STATES TRADE REPRESENTATIVE, ENVIRONMENT AND THE FTAA: PUBLIC SUMMARY OF U. S. POSITION, <http://www.ustr.gov/regions/whemisphere/envir.html>.

Originally, NAFTA was envisioned to be the springboard for the FTAA, but the lack of fast-track authority has changed the negotiating dynamic as described in the next excerpt.

J.   Steven Jarreau, *Negotiating Trade Liberalization in the Western Hemisphere: The Free Trade Area of the Americas*, 13 TEMP. INT'L & COMP. L.J. 57, 74–82 (1999)

NAFTA is the most significant trade agreement in the hemisphere in terms of economic influence and population. The gross domestic product of the NAFTA countries is approximately $8.6 trillion and their cumulative population is 390 million. NAFTA is not, however, undertaking a commensurate role in hemispheric economic integration. The NAFTA countries as a trade group have only sought a single unsuccessful expansion of the agreement when Chile was invited to seek accession, but the offer was never consummated.

Early in the preparatory phase, the concept of a hub and spoke integration of the region's economies into the FTAA was considered a possibility. The hub and spoke concept called for NAFTA to be the hub and the other nations and subregional trading groups to be the spokes upon accession. It is now unlikely that the FTAA will develop in this manner. The United States' lack of fast track negotiating authority has essentially precluded expansion of NAFTA, allowing MERCORSUR to become a more significant player in the region's economic integration.

NAFTA, once thought to be the sole basis of the FTAA, will likely be the only trading group in which the member countries negotiate individually rather than as a bloc. The NAFTA countries are exhibiting no concerted effort toward the development of the FTAA and have currently taken separate paths in their quest for broadening and deepening their trading relationships.

1.   The United States

The United States, with an economy that accounts for approximately sixty-seven percent of the gross domestic product of the entire hemisphere, is not an active participant in the process of hemispheric integration. While the United States is a strong advocate of the FTAA, it is not providing leadership for its development nor is it engaging in negotiations on a bilateral or subregional level. In a hemisphere with more than thirty trade agreements in effect, the United States is a signatory to only one, NAFTA.

The void of U.S. leadership stems from the inability of the Administration and Congress to reach an agreement on fast track negotiating authority. . . .

Absent fast track, some nations suggest that they do not know with whom to negotiate, the president or Congress.

The lack of substantial integration activity on the part of the United States has provided opportunities for others, most notably Brazil and MERCOSUR.

2. Canada and Mexico

Contrary to the United States, Canada and Mexico have most aggressively pursued broader and deeper trade relations within the hemisphere. Ten years ago, Canada was not a member of the OAS and Latin America did not attract its attention. Today, Canada is a member of the OAS and has forged trade agreements with Mexico, Chile, and the Central American countries. Canadian Prime Minister Jean Chretien has traveled the region with Canadian business and governmental leaders cultivating relations. Canada has sponsored a negotiating workshop for the Central American trade negotiators, and the International Development Research Center, an entity created by the Canadian federal government, maintains a MERCOSUR web site "to contribute to the dispersion of knowledge and information on issues related to MERCOSUR." Canada considers the development of bilateral and subregional trade agreements and the FTAA to be stepping stones in its global trade policy.

Mexico, similar to Canada, has further integrated its economy into the rest of Latin America. Along with Colombia and Venezuela, Mexico negotiated the Group of Three Free Trade Agreement which came into effect in January of 1995. Mexico also signed trade agreements with Costa Rica, Chile, and Nicaragua, and is negotiating with six other Central and South American countries and MERCOSUR. * * *

C. The Andean Community

The Andean Community of Bolivia, Colombia, Ecuador, Peru and Venezuela, is one of the older integration arrangements in the hemisphere. The Community, organized in 1969 with the Cartagena Accord, is striving to become more cohesive. Revitalization efforts began in the early 1990's and culminated in the 1996 Reform Protocol of the Cartagena Agreement.

The Community, formerly known as the Andean Group or Pact, formulated an institutional process "to make ... integration smoother and more dynamic." The institutions of the community designed to facilitate this process are the Council of Presidents, the Council of Ministers of Foreign Affairs, a commission that serves as a regulatory body, a general secretariat, a court of justice, and a community parliament. The aim of the Community is to deepen Andean integration and harmonize economic policies. A common market is sought for 2005, a year after the FTAA negotiations are to conclude.

The Community, as previously mentioned, is negotiating with MERCOSUR. The initial stage of the Andean Community–MERCOSUR negotiations is focusing on tariff preferences. The second stage of the negotiations will address the development of a free trade area.

The Andean Community has also ventured beyond MERCOSUR. Chile and Canada have entered into agreements with the Community and stronger ties are being developed with the countries of Central America and the Caribbean. If the Community expands, Panama is likely to be the next member. * * *

D. The Central American Common Market

The Central American Common Market (CACM), similar to the Andean Community, dates back to the early 1960s. The CACM includes the countries of Costa Rica, Guatemala, El Salvador, Honduras, and Nicaragua. It was founded under the General Treaty of Central American Economic Integration. The treaty sought the establishment of a free trade area between the member countries and a common external tariff as to third countries. Political differences and civil strife in Central America from the 1970s to the 1990s negatively impacted the integration process.

Revitalization of the CACM began in 1990 with the CACM and individual member countries negotiating trade agreements with Mexico, Panama, and the countries of the Andean Community. CACM has also undertaken negotiations with the Dominican Republic. The most ambitious effort of the CACM involves MERCOSUR. The CACM and MERCOSUR initiated discussions directed toward the development of a free trade area between the two trade groups* * *

E. The Caribbean Community and Common Market

The Caribbean Community and Common Market (Caricom) is comprised of thirteen former British territories, Haiti, and Suriname. Caricom was organized in 1973, succeeding a previous free trade association established in 1968. It maintains a common external tariff and seeks the establishment of greater economic integration through the development of a common market, although not all members of the community are members of the common market. The integration of the Caricom nations extends beyond economic matters to include political integration fostered through foreign and social policy. * * *

F. Chile

Chile is unique among the nations of the Western Hemisphere. It is not one of the larger economies, nor is it a full member of any of the region's trade groups. It has, however, embraced economic integration and trade liberalization in a manner unlike any other country. A representative of the Chilean Embassy in Washington, D.C. stated that Chile's unilateral openness originated in the 1970s and 1980s. Chile enacted a foreign investment code in 1974, and its constitution includes a prohibition against import quotas. It was not, however, until the 1990s that the domestic political climate permitted trade liberalization to ensue.

In the mid–1990s, the NAFTA countries invited Chile to become the "fourth amigo." The talks stalled as the result of the United States' lack of fast track negotiating authority. Initially perceived as a loss for Chile, the failure of NAFTA to expand into South America has worked to Chile's benefit. Chile has embarked on an effort to integrate itself into the entire hemisphere and has done so without entering into agreements which preclude the country's accession into other trade agreements. Chile's position of relative trade independence and the trade experience of its negotiators' position it to serve as a moderating influence during the FTAA negotiations. Chile's trade experience in the hemisphere and its willingness to share its expertise will place it in a leadership role.

Chile is intent on preserving its trade independence, even though it is an associate member of MERCOSUR, and it has concluded agreements with Argentina, Bolivia, Ecuador, Colombia, Venezuela, Mexico, and Canada. It will negotiate the FTAA independent of any trade group, but will consult its neighbors, including MERCOSUR.

G. Postscript To Track II

Now that the [FTAA] negotiations are underway, the trading blocs, particularly MERCOSUR, the Andean Community and Caricom, are "speaking with one voice." Representatives of the member-nations of MERCOSUR, the Andean Community, and Caricom position themselves together during meetings of the TNC and in the negotiating groups. Generally, however, only the individual designated as the trading bloc's representative addresses the meetings. The

Central American Common Market has not demonstrated the same level of unity as the other trading blocs and is not approaching the negotiations with a common agenda. The Dominican Republic, Panama, and the NAFTA countries, the United States, Canada, and Mexico, are participating in the FTAA proceedings as individual nations.

---

2. MERCOSUR

As noted, MERCOSUR is an ambitious trade and economic integration effort involving Argentina, Brazil, Paraguay and Uruguay, with Bolivia and Chile as associate members. While it aims to be something similar to the European Union in scope and degree of economic and political integration, at present it remains at best a tentative tariff union, unifying tariffs duties among its members. Its more ambitious objectives include: 1) improving the economies of their countries by making them more efficient and competitive and by enlarging their markets and accelerating their economic development by means of a more efficient use of available resources; 2) preserving the environment; 3) improving communications; 4) coordinating macroeconomic policies; and 5) harmonizing the different sectors of their economies.

Integration efforts leading to MERCOSUR date back to 1985 with the signing of the Foz de Iguazú Declaration, creating the High Level Bilateral Commission for the Integration of Argentina and Brazil. Around the end of 1990, Argentina and Brazil signed, and registered with ALADI, an Agreement on Economic Cooperation (Acuerdo de Complementación Económica) that systematized and strengthened pre-existing bilateral commercial agreements. Subsequently, Uruguay and Paraguay expressed interest and on March 26, 1991 four countries signed the Treaty of Asunción. The Treaty did not create a common market, instead it was intended to make the implementation of the Common Market possible. The Treaty is an economic integration agreement that any ALADI member may join. Under the auspices of the Treaty, the four countries signed an Agreement of Economic Cooperation within the legal framework of ALADI. In December 1994 the Ouro Preto Protocol established the institutional structure of MERCOSUR.

The Preamble to the Treaty of Asuncion declares that integration " . . . must be achieved through the efficient use of the available resources and the preservation of the environment." Despite this passing reference, MERCOSUR has only recently begun to consider the need for environmental and other social legislation. An effort began several years ago to draft an Environmental Protocol, which would set out the environmental framework for the trading block countries. This protocol would have laid out the international environmental agenda and defined the mechanisms by which environmental externalities caused by trade between the member countries could be brought to conflict resolution mechanisms. However, country negotiators preferred to lower what they considered to be environmental trade barriers, to the least common denominator, so as not to harm any country's trade flows due to environmental concerns. What resulted was a watered-down version of the protocol, now called the Environmental Accord, with little teeth.

In 1992, MERCOSUR's Common Market Working Group (CMG) established the Reunion Especializada de Medio Ambiente (REMA) to analyze and, as far as possible, harmonize, the environmental laws of the parties. Recently, REMA was elevated to a subgroup of CMG entitled "The Environment." "The general objective of [the subgroup] consists of formulating and proposing strategies and directives that guarantee the protection and the integrity of the environment in the Member States in a context of free trade and the consolidation of a customs union, assuring at the same time, uniform conditions of competitiveness." *See* Jonathan S. Blum, *The FTAA and the Fast Track to Forgetting the Environment: A Comparison of the NAFTA and the MERCOSUR Environmental Models as Examples for the Hemisphere*, 35 Tex. Int'l L.J. 435, 446–447 (2000).

QUESTIONS AND DISCUSSION

1.   MERCOSUR is likely to negotiate the FTAA as a bloc, seeking to coordinate its efforts with their trading groups in the hemisphere, particularly Bolivia, Chile and the Andean Community. How will this affect efforts to include environmental safeguards into the FTAA? NGOs are the moving force behind US efforts to include environmental safeguards in the FTAA. What role do you think civil society is playing in Latin America on this issue?

2.   The Cartagena Agreement, creating the Andean Community, provides that the members "shall undertake joint policies that enable a better use of their renewable and nonrenewable natural resources and the preservation and improvement of the environment." Art. 146 (1969) <http://www.comunidadandina.org/ingles/treaties/trea/ande_trie1.htm>. On July 3, 2001, the Community approved "Guidelines for Environmental Management and Sustainable Development in the Andean Community." These guidelines consist of measures to be taken over the next five years in four major areas: conservation and sustainable use of the biodiversity, environmental quality, trade and the environment, and international environmental forums. Specifically it calls for the implementation of Decision 391. It states, in part,

> The Member Countries exercise sovereignty over their genetic resources and their by-products and consequently determine the conditions for access to them, pursuant to the provisions of this Decision. The conservation and sustainable use of the genetic resources and their by-products are regulated by each Member Country in keeping with the principles and provisions of the Biological Diversity Agreement and of this Decision.

> The genetic resources and their by-products, which originated in the Member Countries, are goods belonging to or the heritage of the Nation or of the State in each Member Country, as stipulated in their respective national legislation. Those resources are inalienable, not subject to prescription and not subject to seizure or similar measures, without detriment to the property regimes applicable to the biological resources that contain those genetic resources, the land on which they are located or the associated intangible component.

Andean Community, Decision 391: Common Regime on Access to Genetic Resources, Art 5 & 6 (1996) <http://www.comunidadandina.org/ingles/treaties/dec/d391e.htm>.

US trade relations with the Andean Community are regulated under the Andean Trade Preference Act (ATPA), 19 U.S.C. 3201 et seq., authorized the President to designate Bolivia, Colombia, Ecuador and Peru as recipients of preferential trade benefits similar to the benefits granted to beneficiary countries under the Caribbean Basin Economic Recovery Act (CBERA) 19 U.S.C. 2701 et seq. The ATPA provides duty-free access to the U.S. market for all products not excluded by law. The Act is scheduled to expire 10 years after the date of enactment, or December 4, 2001. The benefits of the ATPA are contingent on the Andean's continued cooperation in the "war on drugs."

3. Latin American and Caribbean countries collectively oppose the inclusion of environment and labor issues in trade agreements. The Secretary General of CARICOM typifies the attitude in stating that "there is no link between trade and economic issues and labor and environmental matters." Samuel, Richard, *Region Retreats from Integration Process, INTER PRESS SERVICE, Jan. 19, 2000,* available in 2000 WL 4089492.

4. The EU requires potential members to revise their environmental laws to "approximate" the EU standards before they may join. *See infra,* page 1267. Would it be feasible to adopt a similar process for the FTAA? What environmental standards would you require for approximation? If the US standard were used, what timetable would you employ to provide an adequate transition for Latin America?

5. As we discussed above, the United States' negotiating partners have been reluctant to proceed with trade negotiations or at least to make significant compromises in the absence of fast-track negotiating authority. The fact that environmental protection measures have not been a hallmark of regional trade agreements in the Americas suggests that many countries may resist the introduction of more than hortatory environmental commitments into an FTAA. If the Administration failed to receive fast-track approval but chose to proceed with regional trade negotiations, how might the lack of fast-track authority affect the level of environmental protection afforded by any resulting trade agreements?

6. Do you believe the "side-agreement" formula has been successful in the case of NAFTA? By setting a different negotiating agenda for environmental issues, the FTAA seems to be directed towards inheriting the same "side-agreement" recipe. As the NAFTA case exemplifies, side agreements are relatively easy to negotiate but the compromises are hard to bring to reality, either because of procedural flaws or because of a lack of political will. How would you secure effective environmental provisions in a free-trade agreement involving both developing and industrialized countries? What are the prospects of including environmental provisions in the treaty itself, that is, to "green it from the inside"? In light of the most recent fast-track debate, might circumstances be more favourable to such an approach than in the early 1990s?

7. Johnson and Beaulieu conclude that expanding the Environmental Side Agreement (NAAEC) and building up the CEC could prove the "greatest environmental opportunity" arising from the economic integration process. JOHNSON & BEAULIEU, *op. cit.,* at 275. They offer the following caution, however:

> Because of the focus on environmental issues and the inflation of expectations, Chile and other NAFTA hopefuls like Honduras and Argentina are adopting new far-reaching environmental legislation, creating or designing new environmental agencies, and evaluating their environmental infrastructure. In principle, this new appreciation of environmental issues, even if it is not disinterested, ought to be welcomed. There is, however, a danger that such would-be NAFTA members may be overly ambitious: They are adopting laws for which they may not have the resources to effectively implement. NAAEC, on the other hand, is geared towards maximizing environmental enforcement. Indeed, in the

words of one official, few countries in Latin America and the Caribbean "are at this time likely to be far enough in their reform efforts, or ... environmental policies to meet the NAFTA standard." It must be remembered that the Mexican environmental laws and practices that were so scrutinized during the NAFTA debate are within or above the Latin and South American average.

JOHNSON & BEAULIEU, *op. cit.,* at 273–74.

8. The Canada–Chile Free Trade Agreement (CCFTA) was negotiated as a spring-board for Chilean accession to NAFTA. The agreement was signed on December 5, 1996, and entered into force on July 5, 1997. The CCFTA follows the NAFTA model by addressing environmental issues in an environmental side agreement. Consider Daley's discussion of that agreement in light of the concerns raised by Johnson and Beaulieu.

> **Daniel Daley, *Canada-Chile Free Trade Agreement: Introductory Note,* 36 I.L.M. 1067 (1997)**
>
> In keeping with its objective of providing a bridge to Chile's NAFTA accession, the CCFTA is broadly consistent with the NAFTA in terms of its structure, scope and coverage.... There are, however, significant differences between the CCFTA and the NAFTA. Most notably, the CCFTA does not contain an energy chapter, it does not deal with sanitary and phytosanitary measures affecting agricultural trade, it does not have a general set of provisions with respect to standards-related measures, and it does not contain chapters on government procurement, financial services or intellectual property.* * *
>
> *Canada-Chile Agreement on Environmental Cooperation (CCAEC)*
>
> The CCAEC, [36 I.L.M. 1193 (1997),] which was concluded on February 6, 1997 and entered into force on July 5, 1997, incorporates the principal substantive features of the North American Agreement on Environmental Cooperation. In view of the fact that the CCAEC is intended to be interim in nature, pending Chile's accession to the NAFTA, some departures have been made from the North American model to minimize the institutional requirements. These modifications include creating a small National Secretariat within each government rather than having an independent secretariat, and using the Steering Committee of the existing Canada–Chile Memorandum of Understanding on Environmental Cooperation to manage the implementation of the cooperative work plans developed under the Agreement. ...
>
> Perhaps the most significant difference between the Canada–Chile Agreement on Environmental Cooperation and the NAAEC is that the application of the enforcement provisions of the CCAEC to Chilean laws will be phased in over the two year period ending on June 2, 1999. The CCAEC lists approximately 160 Chilean laws that will be covered immediately. The list includes most of the modern environmental laws in Chile, including all laws that entered into force after March 1994. The CCAEC contains a second list of laws, numbering fourteen, to which the Agreement will apply within six months after its entry into force. As well, Chile will present a schedule, no later than six months after the entry into force of the CCAEC, indicating when the Agreement will apply to its remaining laws.

SECTION IV. TRADE IN THE EUROPEAN UNION

The European Union (EU) is, first and foremost, a regional trade organization. The EU is the direct descendant of the European Community, created after World War II with the express objective of binding Europe's traditional rivals together through strengthened economic and, eventually, political ties arising from a common market. While the early European Community exercised some environmental authority, protection of the environment was not an important objective. In fact, the Treaty of Rome (EEC Treaty), creating the Community, did not include the word, "environment." It soon became apparent that this was a considerable omission, for certain environmental issues clearly had transboundary impacts and, more important, national environmental laws requiring businesses to meet different standards could in some circumstances create considerable barriers to trade. The 1987 Single European Act remedied this omission, providing the EU with specific powers to implement environmental measures. Its environmental protection authority was further strengthened by the Maastricht Treaty of 1992.

The doctrinal issues of trade and environment in the EU closely parallel the conflicts within the GATT discussed earlier in the chapter. That is, GATT trade and environment cases have pitted provisions prohibiting certain barriers to trade, found in Articles I, III, and X, against specific exemptions for environmental protection, found in Article XX. Similarly, the most important EU trade and environment cases have addressed the conflict between Treaty of Rome articles ensuring the free movement of goods and services, embodied in Article 30, and exceptions for environmental protection, in Article 36.

Treaty of Rome, Article 30

Quantitative restrictions on imports and all measures having equivalent effect shall, without prejudice to the following provisions, be prohibited between Member States.

Treaty of Rome, Article 36

The provisions of Articles 30 to 34 shall not preclude prohibitions or restrictions on imports, exports or goods in transit justified on grounds of public morality, public policy or public security; the protection of health and life of humans, animals or plants; the protection of national treasures possessing artistic, historic or archaeological value; or the protection of industrial and commercial property. Such prohibitions or restrictions shall not, however, constitute a means of arbitrary discrimination or a disguised restriction on trade between Member States.

The first significant trade and environment case was *Cassis de Dijon.* 120/78, 1979 E.C.R. 649 (1979). The European Court of Justice's decision in the case established a "rule of reason" to determine when Article 36's environmental exception could legitimately restrict the free movement of goods and services. The case is described below.

West Germany banned the importation of certain low-alcohol beverages, including Cassis de Dijon liquor, on the purported basis of public health. Such drinks, Germany argued, fostered a more permissive attitude toward the consumption of alcohol and were deceptive to consumers accustomed to higher-proof products. Furthermore, the Germans claimed the banned imports were at a comparative advantage over domestic beverages because tax rates for liquors were tied to the percentage of alcohol they possessed. Importers of Cassis de Dijon challenged the ban as an unfair restriction on trade before the European Court of Justice.

The Court had to consider the relationship between Article 30 and Article 36 of the EEC Treaty. Article 30 specifically establishes a prohibition against quantitative restrictions on imports among member states, including measures with an effect equivalent to trade restrictions–nontariff barriers. Article 36 offers exceptions to Article 30 for purposes of public policy, security, or morality; the protection of health and life of humans, plants, and animals; and the protection of national heritage and property. While the environment is not explicitly mentioned and Article 36 is meant to be interpreted strictly, the Court concluded that the relationship between the environment and human, animal, and plant health is sufficient to merit the use of Article 36 exceptions for environmental purposes.

In applying Article 36, the Court developed a "rule of reason" analysis. The Court adopted a balancing test weighing the means and the ends of an environmental measure against its impacts on trade. Applying this proportionality test, the Court struck down the ban, finding that the banned beverages posed no real health threat to consumers, that Germans routinely watered down their alcoholic beverages, and that if the German objective were the protection of public health, less-intrusive measures were available, such as labeling requirements.

The adoption of a balancing test established that disparities in national laws for the sake of protecting public goods were legitimate and to be expected until full harmonization of standards could be accomplished within the common market. While this case specifically addressed health measures, subsequent decisions have extended the *Cassis* precedent to include environmental measures and established the "rule of reason" and proportionality analysis as the basis for adjudication of cases involving environmental regulations with trade effects.

Daniel C. Esty, Greening the Gatt: Trade, Environment, and the Future 262 (1991).

The most important trade and environment case in EU jurisprudence, the *Danish Bottles* case, built upon the *Cassis de Dijon* decision. In 1981, Denmark implemented legislation to strengthen its nationwide collection program for reusable bottles. Seeking to ensure a steady supply of bottles (to support infrastructure investments), the law established design specifications for beer, soda, lemonade and mineral water containers. Specifically, in order to sell drinks containers in Denmark they had to be: (1) collectable and reusable, (2) designs pre-approved by the Danish government. Effectively, this law banned the sale of metal beverage cans since only glass bottles were both collectable and reusable.

Danish manufacturers supported the legislation; their products satisfied the new requirements. Foreign manufacturers however, most notably in Germany and Great Britain, denounced the law as blatant protectionism, arguing that the new requirements would place them at a competitive disadvantage. Since glass is heavier than cans and breakable, they argued, foreign manufacturers' shipping costs would increase compared to the current practice of shipping cans. Moreover, bottling in only pre-approved bottles could require costly modifications in the production lines.

In 1984, in response to these concerns, the Danish government amended the law's design requirements, allowing foreign companies to import into Denmark up to 3,000 hectoliters of liquids in non-approved bottles every year. The European Commission deemed these measures inadequate and filed suit against Denmark. In its case before the European Court of Justice, the Commission claimed that Denmark had implemented the legislation to protect the Danish soft drink and beer industries, imposing an unnecessary restriction on the free flow of goods in violation of Article 30 of the Treaty of Rome.

Re Disposable Beer Cans: EC Commission (U.K. intervening) v. Denmark Court of Justice of the European Communities [1988] ECR 4607, [1989] 1 CMLR 619

The system alleged by the Commission to be incompatible with Community law is characterised by an obligation on producers to market beer and soft drinks only in containers which can be re-used. The containers must be approved by the National Agency for the Protection of the Environment, which may refuse approval for a new type of container, especially if it considers that the container is not technically adapted to a system of return, that the system of return set up by those concerned does not ensure actual re-use of a sufficient proportion of containers, or if a container of equal capacity which is both available and suited to the intended use has already been approved.

The above rules were amended by Order 95 of 16 March 1984 which allowed the use, provided that a deposit-and-return system had been set up, of non-approved containers, but excluding metal containers, within a limit of 3,000 hl per producer per year, and also in connection with operations by foreign manufacturers in order to test the market. * * *

For the purpose of deciding the present case it should be observed that, firstly, in accordance with settled case law (Case 120/78, REWE ([1979] ECR 649, [1979] 3 CMLR 494); Case 261/81, RAU ([1982] ECR 3961, [1983] 2 CMLR 496)), in the absence of common rules relating to the marketing of the products concerned, obstacles to movement within the Community resulting from disparities between the national laws must be accepted in so far as such rules, applicable to domestic and imported products without distinction, may be recognised as being necessary in order to satisfy mandatory requirements of Community law. It is also necessary for such rules to be proportionate to the aim in view. If a member-State has a choice between various measures to attain the same objective, it should choose the means which least restrict the free movement of goods.

In the present case the Danish Government contends that the compulsory system for the return of beer and soft drink containers in force in Denmark is justified by a mandatory requirement for the protection of the environment.

The protection of the environment has already been considered by the Court in Case 240/83, Association de Defense des Bruleurs D'huiles Usagees ([1985] ECR 531), as 'one of the essential objectives of the Community' which may, as such, justify certain restrictions on the principle of the free movement of goods. Furthermore this assessment is confirmed by the Single European Act.

In view of what has been said it must be concluded that protection of the environment is a mandatory requirement which may limit the application of Article 30 of the Treaty.

The Commission argues that the Danish regulations infringe the principle of proportionality because the objective of protecting the environment could be attained by means which are less restrictive of trade within the Community.

On this point it should be borne in mind that, in Case 240/83 cited above, the Court stated that measures adopted to safeguard the environment should not exceed the inevitable restrictions justified by an objective for the general good such as the protection of the environment.

Under these circumstances it is necessary to determine whether all the restrictions which the legislation in question imposes on the free movement of goods are necessary to attain the objectives of these regulations.

Firstly, with regard to the obligation to set up a deposit-and-return system for empty containers, it should be noted that this obligation is an essential element of a system aiming to secure the re-use of containers and therefore appears to be necessary to attain the objectives of the disputed regulations. In view of this finding, the restrictions which they impose on the free movement of goods should not be considered as disproportionate.

Secondly it is necessary to consider the obligation on manufacturers or importers to use only the containers approved by the National Agency for the Protection of the Environment.

During the procedure before the Court the Danish Government indicated that the operation of the present deposit-and-return system would be affected if the number of approved containers were to exceed thirty because retailers who had joined the system would not be prepared to accept too many types of bottles owing to increased handling costs and the greater storage space which this would entail. This is said to be the reason why the Agency has hitherto arranged matters so that new approvals are normally accompanied by the withdrawal of existing approvals.

Even if these are cogent arguments, it must nevertheless be said that the system at present in force in Denmark enables the Danish authorities to refuse approval to a foreign producer even if he is prepared to ensure that returned containers are used again.

In such a situation a foreign producer who nevertheless wishes to sell in Denmark would be compelled to manufacture or purchase containers of a type already approved, which would entail considerable extra cost for him and would therefore make it very difficult to import his products into the country.

To overcome this obstacle, the Danish Government amended the regulations by the above mentioned Order 95 of 16 March 1984 which authorises a producer to market up to 3,000 hl of beer and soft drinks per annum in non-approved containers, provided that he sets up a deposit-and-return system.

The provision of Order 95 limiting to 3,000 hl the quantity of beer and soft drinks which can be marketed by each producer per annum in non-approved containers is disputed by the Commission on the ground that it is not necessary for attaining the objectives of the system.

On this point it should be observed that certainly the existing system of return for approved containers guarantees a maximum percentage of re-use and therefore gives considerable protection to the environment because the empty containers can be returned to any retailer of beverages, whereas non-approved containers can only be returned to the retailer who sold the beverage because of the impossibility of setting up such a complete organisation for such containers also.

However, the system for returning non-approved containers is intended to protect the environment and, so far as imports are concerned, covers only limited quantities of beverages by comparison with the quality consumed in the country because of the restrictive effect of the compulsory return of containers on imports. Under these conditions, limiting the quantity of products which can be marketed by importers is disproportionate to the objective.

Therefore it must be concluded that by restricting, by Order 95 of 16 March 1984, to 3,000 hl per producer per annum the quantity of beer and soft drinks which may be marketed in non-approved containers, the Kingdom of Denmark has failed, in relation to imports of those products from other member-States, to fulfil its obligations under Article 30 EEC.

The remainder of the application should be dismissed. * * *

While *Danish Bottles* remains the preeminent trade and environment case in Community law, and is often held up as an example of the level of environmental protection provided by the Community treaties, the environment does not always come out ahead. In particular, the European Court of Justice has been reluctant to allow the use of trade measures to protect the environment outside the jurisdiction of the nation implementing the measure. In the *Scottish Red Grouse* case, excerpted below, The Netherlands enacted unilateral trade restrictions to protect wild birds in Europe. One of the birds protected by the statute was the Red Grouse, a wild bird found only in Scotland. The EC had already passed a law, Directive 79/409, protecting migratory birds. By the terms of the Directive, the Red Grouse was neither endangered nor migratory.

Re Gourmetterie Van den Burg BV (Case 169/89) European Court of Justice (Sixth Chamber) [1990], I ECR 2143

In 1984 inspectors entrusted with ensuring compliance with the Netherlands Vogelwet [Law on Birds] confiscated a dead red grouse on the premises of Gourmetterie Van den Burg. The trader was subsequently prosecuted and convicted for infringing the provisions of the law in question, which is designed to protect birds occurring in the wild state in Europe. It appealed against that conviction on the ground that the confiscated red grouse had been lawfully killed in the United Kingdom. . . .

The Hoge Raad, [Dutch high court], hearing the case at last instance, found that Article 7 of the Vogelwet precluded the bird in question from being bought or sold on the domestic market and that the application of that Law hindered trade in a British game bird, lawfully shot and freely marketed in the country of origin. The Hoge Raad considered that, in so far as the prohibition laid down in the Vogelwet also extends to the importation and keeping of dead red grouse, it was in the nature of a measure having an effect equivalent to a quantitative restriction within the meaning of Article 30 of the Treaty. In its view, the assessment of the appeal depends on the question whether the prohibition in question may be considered justified under Article 36 of the Treaty on grounds of the protection of health and life of animals.

The Hoge Raad accordingly referred the following question to the Court:

"May the prohibition applicable in the Netherlands by virtue of Article 7 of the Vogelwet [Law on Birds] on the importation and keeping of red grouse, shot and killed in the United Kingdom without any breach of the law applicable in that country, be regarded as a prohibition which is justified under Article 36 of the EEC Treaty on grounds of the protection of health and life of animals, regard being had to the fact that:

in the first place, the exception referred to in Article 6(2) of Directive 79/409/EEC applies to red grouse, which are referred to in Annex III/1 to the directive;

secondly, the purpose of the prohibition laid down in Article 7 of the Vogelwet is the preservation of wild birds and in particular that protection of all species of birds occurring in the wild state in Europe, subject to certain exceptions which do not, however, include the red grouse?'' * * *

In its question, the national court raises in substance a problem concerning the interpretation of Article 36 of the Treaty, according to which the principle of the free movement of goods does not preclude prohibitions or restrictions on imports which are justified on grounds of the protection of health and life of animals.

It is not disputed that the national measure in question constitutes a prohibition on imports and that the red grouse is a species which does not occur within the Netherlands.

With regard to Article 36 of the Treaty, the Court has consistently held (see, most recently, the judgment of 14 June 1988 in Case 29/87, Dansk Denkavit ApS v Danish Ministry of Agriculture, [1988] ECR 2965) that a directive providing for full harmonization of national legislation deprives a Member State of recourse to that article.

As regards the degree of harmonization brought about by Directive 79/409, it should be noted that, although the bird in question may, in accordance with Article 6(2) and (3) of the directive, be hunted within the Member State in which it occurs, the fact remains that Article 14 authorizes the Member States to introduce stricter protective measures than those provided for under the directive. The directive has therefore regulated exhaustively the Member States' powers with regard to the conservation of wild birds.

It is therefore appropriate to define the scope of the powers conferred on the Member States by Article 14 of the directive. In that regard, reference should be made to the principal criteria on which the Community legislature has relied in the matter.

First of all, as the Court emphasized in its judgment of 27 April 1988 in Case 252/85 (Commission v France, [1988] ECR 2243), Directive 79/409 grants special protection to migratory species which constitute, according to the third recital in the preamble to the directive, a common heritage of the Community. Secondly, in the case of the most endangered birds, the directive provides that the species listed in Annex I must be the subject of special conservation measures in order to ensure their survival and reproduction.

It follows from those general objectives laid down by Directive 79/409 for the protection of birds that the Member States are authorized, pursuant to Article 14 of the directive, to introduce stricter measures to ensure that the aforesaid species are protected even more effectively. With regard to the other bird species covered by Directive 79/409, the Member States are required to bring into force the laws, regulations and administrative provisions necessary to comply with the directive, but are not authorized to adopt stricter protective measures than those provided for under the directive, except as regards species occurring within their territory.

Next, it should be noted that the red grouse is neither a migratory species nor a seriously endangered species set out in Annex I to the directive.

Furthermore, Council Regulation (EEC) No 3626/82 of 3 December 1982 on the implementation in the Community of the Convention on international trade in endangered species of wild fauna and flora (Official Journal 1982 No L 384, p 1) does not refer to the red grouse as an endangered animal within the meaning of that Convention.

It follows from the foregoing that Article 14 of the directive does not empower a Member State to afford a given species which is neither migratory nor endangered stricter protection, by means of a prohibition on importation and marketing, than that provided for by the legislation of the Member State on whose territory the bird in question occurs, where such legislation is in conformity with the provisions of Directive 79/409.

The answer to the question submitted for a preliminary ruling must therefore be that Article 36 of the Treaty, read in conjunction with Council Directive 79/409/EEC of 2 April 1979 on the conservation of wild birds, must be interpreted as meaning that a prohibition on importation and marketing cannot be justified in respect of a species of bird which does not occur in the territory of the legislating Member State but is found in another Member State where it may lawfully be hunted under the terms of that directive and under the legislation of that other State, and which is neither migratory nor endangered within the meaning of the directive.

————

QUESTIONS AND DISCUSSION

1. Denmark, Germany and the United Kingdom are also parties to the GATT. Why was the Danish Bottles case brought before the European Court of Justice and argued in terms of the Treaty of Rome instead of before a GATT Dispute Panel? Do you think the result would have been the same under the GATT? Could the Scottish Red Grouse case have been brought under the GATT? The Netherlands is a GATT party.

2. Interestingly, despite the European Court of Justice decision in the Scottish Grouse case, the case likely was not over. Under the EU legal system, a domestic court case involving Community law may be appealed to the European Court of Justice to clarify the law's application in a specific instance. This operates as a sort of interlocutory appeal. The Dutch court trying the case, upon receiving the European Court of Justice's decision, would incorporate the ruling into the case at hand. Assume, though, that the British government, at the urging of Scottish Grouse exporters, challenged the Dutch law before the WTO. How is this case different from the Tuna/Dolphin cases?

3. Perhaps one of the reasons there have been few trade and environment conflicts in the EU is the rigorous process new members must go through to redesign and strengthen their environmental laws before they can join the Union, so their laws "approximate" the EU laws. The following guidance is provided to countries wishing to accede to the EU:

1.1   What is Approximation?

The approximation of law is a unique obligation of membership in the European Union. It means that countries aspiring to join the European Union must align their national laws, rules and procedures in order to give effect to the entire body of EU law contained in the *acquis communautaire*. [This includes the directives, regulations, and decisions adopted on the basis of the various Treaties, which together make up the primary law of the European Union and Communities.]

As the obligation to approximate continues after accession, the pre-accession approximation process becomes an opportunity for countries to organize their institutions and procedures and to train their staff for the daily processes and responsibilities of European Union law making, implementation and enforcement.

There are three key elements:

- First, to adopt or change national laws, rules, and procedures so that the requirements of the relevant EU law are fully incorporated into the national legal order. Although countries have considerable discretion in choosing the most appropriate national mechanism to reflect Union environmental obligations, this discretion is limited in some respects by general principles of Union law. In most cases it will be necessary to adopt national legislation passed by Parliament or in some countries by Presidential or Governmental Decree . . .

- Second, to provide the institutions and budgets necessary to carry out the laws and regulations (known as the "Implementation" or "Practical Application" of the directive).

- Third, to provide the necessary controls and penalties to ensure that the law is being complied with fully and properly (Enforcement).

1.2   What is the Scope of Environmental Approximation?

Following the principles laid down in Agenda 2000, each applicant country will eventually have to adopt the entire acquis communautaire into its national legal order and to adapt its administrative system accordingly. In broad terms, EU environmental legislation covers:

- Products: for example, control of noise from construction equipment, control of emissions from motor vehicles, control of hazardous chemicals in some consumer products, waste movements, control of hazardous chemicals and preparation in general, and trade in endangered species. Many of these requirements are covered in the White Paper.

- Activities or production processes which can have environmental or health impacts: construction, operation of industrial plants, waste disposal, nature protection

- Environmental quality protection: for example controlling dangerous substances in air, water or soil, land development; nature and resource conservation; and biodiversity.

- Procedures and procedural rights such as impact assessment, access to information and public consultation.

EUROPEAN COMMISSION, GUIDE TO APPROXIMATION OF EUROPEAN UNION ENVIRONMENTAL LEGISLATION 2 (1997). The majority of the EU environmental requirements must be met before the country can accede, although certain ones may be phased in over a longer period, e.g., pollution control plans, designation of protect or "sensitive" areas, compliance with emission limits or environmental quality standards. *Id.* at § 2.2.

SECTION V.   FOREIGN INVESTMENT AND THE ENVIRONMENT

A.   INTRODUCTION

While the growth of trade in recent years has been remarkable, the flood of foreign capital to developing countries has perhaps been even more extraordinary. From 1982–1993, flows increased ten-fold and almost twenty-fold by 1996, with a 40% increase in foreign direct investment (FDI) from 1994 to 1995 alone. Total FDI now exceeds the value of goods in trade by more than five-fold yet, remarkably, no comprehensive agreement governing FDI exists at the international level. Despite recent economic downturns, FDI is expected to continue to expand in developing countries over the next decade. LESTER BROWN ET AL., STATE OF THE WORLD 2000, at 194 (2000); Eric Burt, *Developing Countries and the Framework for Negotiations on Foreign Direct Investment in the World Trade Organization*, 12 AM. U. J. INT'L L. & POL'Y 1015, 1019 (1997).

Multinational enterprises engage in FDI for a host of reasons that lower their costs of doing business–avoiding tariffs, reducing transport costs, securing access to natural resources, taking advantage of cheap labor, etc. And the attractive benefits offered by FDI to host developing countries are also undeniable. For the host country, FDI can provide needed capital, spur technology transfer, create jobs, and increase domestic competition and foreign exchange. But, equally, there are potential downsides, including (1) the increasing loss of local control and responsibility over resources; (2) the distribution of potentially environmentally damaging technologies to ill-prepared communities; (3) double-standards that allow companies to operate in developing countries with lower environmental and health safeguards; and (4) the concern that countries will lower their environmental and health standards to attract investment.

From Local to Global Control. Globalization of the market economy, and with it the growth of multinational corporations, presents a conflict, at least conceptually, with the goal of sustainable development, which requires local participation and control over development choices. In the global economy, owners who may benefit from environmentally damaging processes typically do not live in or near the local communities that are affected by the environmental harm. Local concerns may thus not be adequately reflected in corporate decision making. Since the political and economic power is vested in people physically separated from the environmental harm, less environmental protection might be expected. Moreover, when States agree to broad investment agreements such as the proposed Multilateral Agreement on Investment discussed *infra*, they may be ceding some of their sovereign power to assert local control over the environmental and social impacts of foreign investment.

Dangerous and Inappropriate Technologies. Just as important as these global environmental issues are the issues raised by foreign investment at the national level. Environmental disasters, such as the 1984 isocyanate gas leak in Bhopal, India, that killed several thousand people, highlight the problems that occur when foreign investment brings environmentally hazardous technologies to countries with neither the environmental law framework nor the technical infrastructure to address the resulting environmental problems. Consequently, some types of investments perhaps should be restricted until adequate environmental and public health controls can reasonably be expected to be in place.

Double-standards and Fairness. The export of technologies and practices that are prohibited in industrialized countries to developing countries also raises issues of fairness and equity. Many chemical products, for example pesticides like DDT, that are illegal in OECD countries are nonetheless produced by subsidiaries of OECD-country companies in developing countries. Practices in certain other industries, for example oil production and gold mining, have repeatedly involved serious allegations of environmental and human rights abuses. Texaco in Ecuador, Shell Oil in Nigeria, Ok Tedi in Papua New Guinea, and Freeport McMoran in Indonesia, described in Chapter 16, are well known cases. The disparity between how companies operate in developing countries when compared to their industrialized home countries has led to some discussions about controlling the exports of domestically prohibited technologies and goods, or imposing minimum industry operating standards on multinational corporations. Some of these "codes of conduct" or standards are discussed *infra* in Chapter 18 at page 1409.

Competitiveness and the Lowest Common Denominator. Some environmentalists fear that competition for foreign investment could lead developing countries to sacrifice environmental standards and public health in a 'race to the bottom' to lure foreign investments. Environmental standards and performance have little competitiveness impact for most industries because they represent a small percentage of their operating costs, at least in developed countries, but this does not stop developing countries from resisting stronger environmental policies, at least in part to attract investment (as described above, this is known as a "chilling effect"). As sovereign countries, States clearly are free to choose relatively lower environmental standards than other States, but as the examples in Chapter 16 make clear, this can encourage foreign investment that harms local populations, provides little or no local participation in the decision, nor local benefits from jobs or profits. NGOs argue that minimum national environmental standards and laws should be a prerequisite for open trade and investment.

Environmental Opportunities. Of course, foreign investment not only presents challenges, but also opportunities, both for environmental protection and sustainable development. Official development assistance is declining and has never met the levels required for moving developing countries toward sustainable development. Private sector investments will thus have to provide the majority of environmentally sustainable investments in the future. The markets for environmental investments are increasing; for example, investments in energy efficiency projects are expected to reach another $250 billion in the next 20 years. The promise of technology is also discussed further in Chapter 2, *supra*, at page 69.

The scope of foreign investment as well as its environmental challenges are discussed in the following excerpt by Hilary French of the Worldwatch Institute.

Hilary F. French, *Assessing Private Capital Flows to Developing Countries* State of the World 149–65 (WORLDWATCH 1998)

[A] dramatic and unanticipated shift has occurred since Rio that is powerfully influencing prospects for sustainable development: international private investment in and lending to developing countries has exploded, rising from $44 billion at the beginning of this decade to $244 billion in 1996, according to the World Bank. In 1990, less than half the international capital moving into the developing world came from private sources, but by 1996 the private share had risen to 86 percent. * * *

[T]he resulting inflows of foreign capital have helped fuel a record-breaking economic boom in the countries receiving them. This is perhaps the strongest magnet for international money, as investors gamble on achieving higher returns than they can find at home. China, for instance, with far and away the largest overall inflow of funds, expanded its economy at double-digit annual rates during the first half of the 1990s. Indeed economic growth in the developing world as a whole has far outpaced that of industrial countries in recent years, their economies expanded three times as fast in 1996–at 6 percent. Measured in conventional economic terms, the new openness to international investment has thus had generally impressive results. [Note this was written prior to the Asian financial crisis] * * *

A better yardstick of long-term success, however, is whether the large influxes of international capital are contributing to the goals of environmentally sustainable development–meeting human needs today in a manner that does not jeopardize prospects for future generations by damaging the health of the natural resource base. This is a far more difficult question to answer, as the impact of growing private capital movements on the well-being of people and the health of the natural world are at once enormous, complex and somewhat contradictory. * * *

For the environment, perhaps the most worrisome implication of the surging inflows of foreign capital is the fact that they help export western consumerism. Given the profligate rates of resource consumption in industrial countries, this spread of the consumer culture is ominous. The newfound mobility of international capital also allows it to seek out the most hospitable home–which may well be a place with weak or unenforced environmental laws. * * *

Yet on the positive side, international investment often brings with it cutting-edge environmental technologies that may help developing countries leapfrog over the dirtiest and most damaging phases of the development path pioneered by the industrial world. Furthermore, private investors as well as national governments and international organizations have begun to devise a growing array of deliberately "green" international investment strategies. These programs aim to promote the transition to enterprises that nurture rather than decimate the natural world.

Although international capital flows may appear to be beyond the reach of effective regulation, a range of policy tools exist that could help point today's burgeoning private capital flows in a more environmentally sound direction. * * *

During the 1970s, most of the funds came in the form of loans from commercial banks, as the petrodollars piling up in the North allowed these institutions to extend more and more credit to developing-country governments. Much of this money unfortunately was squandered on uneconomical projects, paving the way for the debt crisis of the 1980s and the consequent stagnation in lending. The last few years have seen a resurgence of commercial bank loans, but this time the recipients are more likely to be private enterprises than governments. Often the money is used to help finance large infra-structure projects such a highways or power plants. In 1996, commercial bank lending accounted for 14 percent of total private flows, or $34 billion.* * *

The other traditional route for private capital moving into the developing world is as foreign direct investment (FDI) by transnational corporations setting up local plants, often through joint ventures with local companies. In recent years, FDI inflows into the developing world have expanded rapidly, climbing more than threefold between 1990 and 1996–from $25 billion to $110 billion, accounting for 45 percent of total private flows in 1996. In comparison, gross domestic investment from public and private sources in developing countries added up to $905 billion in 1990 and to $1.2 trillion in 1995. Thus though domestic sources of investment continue to overwhelm foreign ones, the foreign share of total investment is growing. FDI is the international capital flow of greatest significance for development, as it is long-term and it brings with it technology, know-how, and management skill. It has the added advantage of not contributing to a country's debt burden. * * *

The quest for natural resources has traditionally drawn international investors into distant ventures in the developing world. Oil has been a particularly strong pull since the dawn of the petroleum age, with oil-producing countries accounting for fully half of all FDI flows to developing countries between 1979 and 1981. But this picture has changed rapidly in recent decades. First, investment in manufacturing began to climb. Now, the services sector, which includes diverse activities such as construction, electricity distribution, finance, and telecommunications, is poised for takeoff. Oil-producing countries, meanwhile accounted for only one fifth of FDI flows into the developing world in 1995 and 1996. The World Bank estimates that the Services sector now accounts for more than a third of overall FDI flows to these countries, while manufacturing has declined to less than half of the total. The primary sector, which includes agriculture, forestry, and mining, makes up the remainder–roughly 20 percent. * * *

Although primary commodities are receiving a declining share of total international investment in the developing world, these investments continue to increase in absolute terms in many countries. Indeed, international investment in resource extraction is now flowing rapidly into the developing world, with its rich endowments of natural assets, including primary forests, mineral and petroleum reserves, and biological diversity. Among other things, this trend reflects degraded environmental conditions in the countries that are a source of the capital, as well as the greening impact of environmental legislation in these countries aimed at minimizing further destruction.* * *

The flow of funds into natural resources is particularly pronounced within the mining industry. From 1994 to 1997, spending on exploration of nonferrous minerals doubled in Latin America, almost tripled in the Pacific region, and more than tripled in Africa, while leveling off in the traditional mining countries of Australia, Canada, and the United States.* * *

The U.S. mining industry blames environmentalists for the migration. More to the point, perhaps, is the fact that host countries are inviting international investors in with open arms; some 70 countries have rewritten their national mining codes in recent years with the aim of encouraging investment. Yet few are devoting similar energy to strengthening environmental laws and enforcement. And no matter how good the laws are, mining takes a heavy environmental toll. Even in the United States, a country with relatively strong environmental controls, for every kilogram of gold produced, some 3 million kilograms of waste rock are removed from the Earth. The social costs are also high: one out of every five gold prospecting sites over 1995–96 was on land owned or claimed by indigenous peoples. * * *

Multinational oil and gas companies are also continually looking for new horizons, as the most accessible fields in industrial countries have already been tapped. Indeed, more than 90 percent of known gas and oil reserves are now in the developing world.... Uncontrolled logging by international companies poses yet another threat to the world's rapidly dwindling tropical forests and those who inhabit them. * * *

As the pace of natural resource exploitation picks up in many countries, intriguing research is raising questions about whether this is a sound economic strategy–let alone a wise environmental one. Research by Jeffrey Sachs and Andrew Warner of Harvard University demonstrates that countries rich in natural resources have on average actually performed worse economically than resource-poor countries in recent decades. One reason may be that resource extraction often leads to only marginal spin-off benefits when it involves few linkages with other segments of economies. Furthermore, natural resource extraction creates relatively few jobs. The mining and petroleum sectors in Papua New Guinea, for example, employ less than 2 percent of the population, although the sectors' exports provide 25 percent of the country's GDP. A wiser strategy for both the environment and the economy would be to funnel international capital into activities that sustain rather than destroy natural endowments. This is what a number of innovative experiments now under way aim to do.

"Bioprospecting" is one example.... Ecotourism also shows promise as a strategy for channeling international investment capital into the preservation of threatened ecosystems, if it is pursued in an ecologically sensitive way.... Finally, although the vast majority of international investment in forestry continues to support destructive practices, there is nonetheless an opportunity offered by a growing demand for timber that has been independently certified as being sustainably produced. * * *

QUESTIONS AND DISCUSSION

1. The French article describes the various types of foreign investment, including foreign direct investment, which represents the largest percent at 45%, portfolio investment in stocks, both equity at 19% and debt at 19%, and commercial bank loans at 14%. French points out that private efforts are underway to "green" stock market investments, whereby investors can consider environmental factors in their investment strategies. The emerging evidence is that the better environmental performers also may be the better market performers. The growth of "Socially Responsible Investing" (SRI) has led to over $500 billion placed in investment funds that are subject to some social screening. Even the IFC and the GEF have gotten into the act, creating two venture capital funds, one to promote sustainable forestry and agriculture and ecotourism in Latin America, and another to promote energy efficiency and renewable energy worldwide.

2. French discusses the evidence suggesting that foreign investment in natural resource extraction may not be a sound economic strategy, let alone a sound environmental one. In contrast, she reports three examples of economic activity that sustain the environment: bioprospecting, ecotourism, and sustainable forestry. How significant economically do you think these activities are today? How significant could they become tomorrow? What type of foreign investment strategy would you design if you were advising a developing country, Chile for example, where the current economy is based overwhelmingly on natural resource extraction? What environmental facts would you need before giving your advice?

3. French notes that 70 countries have revised their national mining laws in order to encourage investment. What changes do you think they have made to their laws? Is this an example of the "race-to-the-bottom" discussed earlier, or simply an example of comparative advantage? Would this lowering of standards be permissible under NAFTA?

4. Consider the following concerns raised by John Cavanagh and Sarah Anderson:

Ironically, it was the terms of the resolution of the most recent phase in international capital flows that set the stage for this new and very dynamic phase [of foreign investment]. The most recent phase, commonly known as the "Third World Debt Crisis," ran from the late 1960s to the late 1980s. From the late 1960s through 1982, hundreds of billions of dollars were lent by large commercial banks to a wide range of countries in Latin America and Asia. For a variety of reasons Mexico and most other debtor nations began announcing as early as 1982 that much of the debt could not be serviced. With the support of the commercial banks, the IMF and the World Bank stepped in to take on more powerful roles in reshaping developing countries economic policy. The new package of preferred policies, often referred to as "structural adjustment" or "the Washington Consensus" centered on cutting government spending, increasing exports, selling off state enterprises, and liberalizing the climate for foreign investment and other financial flows.

During this period, the World Bank helped many countries with privatization schemes as well as in opening up new stock exchanges to foreign investors. While this entire set of policies is extremely controversial amongst environmentalists and many Third World non-governmental organizations, it created the atmosphere for new forms of financial flows into developing countries.

By 1997, the movement of private capital into developing countries had reached unprecedented levels. The rise in private finance flowing into developing countries jumped $60 billion in 1996 (from $184 billion to $244 billion). A participant in the March 1997 InterAmerican Development Bank annual meeting in Spain described the scene at that meeting: "The halls were filled with representatives of J.P. Morgan–they alone sent 60 people–and other Western financial institutions pressing funds on representatives from Latin America. The pushing of money was reminiscent of the heyday of the large-scale lending of the 1970s". * * *

These flows point dangerously toward a new global economic apartheid, with the 24 rich countries growing slowly, 10–12 rapid emerging markets growing very fast, and the remaining 140 developing countries (particularly Africa) being left behind. In 1996, almost three quarters (72.5 percent) of total private capital flows to the developing countries went to just 10 countries.

John Cavanagh & Sarah Anderson, International Financial Flows: The New Trends in the 1990s and Projections for the Future (Institute for Policy Studies, 1997).

5. French mentions three strategies for making foreign investment sustainable. The first is to strengthen national environmental laws. Consider how this complements the discussion by Haas et al. in Chapter 8 of the need to strengthen national environmental law capacity for implementing international environmental obligations. The second strategy French mentions is to condition *public* investment funds on environmental standards, starting with the World Bank. This is discussed further in Chapter 19 at page 1460. The third is to fashion a multilateral response to integrate environmental standards into the "official ... rules of international commerce." This is discussed next.

B.   INTEGRATING ENVIRONMENTAL STANDARDS INTO INVESTMENT AGREEMENTS

Just as sustainable development ultimately must be fully incorporated into the WTO, sustainable development and associated environmental standards must be integrated into international investment agreements. The use of NAFTA's investment measures to demand compensation for companies that lose market share as a result of governmental health, safety and environmental regulation–the expropriation debate–has become extremely contentious and is discussed *supra* at page 1202. The most important recent attempt to develop international investment standards was the failed attempt to negotiate a Multilateral Agreement on Investment (the MAI) among the 29 member States of the Organization for Economic Cooperation and Development (OECD).

Absent a GATT or other treaty, the international legal framework governing FDI has developed incrementally through a broad network of bilateral investment treaties (BITs), which both establish and clarify the rights of foreign investors. Mirroring the growth of FDI, the number of BITs has dramatically increased as well. From 1989 to 1995, more BITs were negotiated than during the previous three decades. By 1995, over 900 BITs had been signed between more than 150 nations. * * *

Since the late 1970s, governments both within and outside the OECD have reversed their traditional opposition to liberalization of FDI, increasingly warming to the role of inward direct investment and creating legal structures to attract further investment. This has primarily occurred through the gradual removal of legal barriers and restrictions to capital movements, opening up previously restricted sectors to investors, eliminating performance requirements, offering attractive investment incentives, and implementing better protections for foreign investors. Often, these policies have been expressed through BITs.

Most BITs provide the same basic protections—national treatment, most favored nation (MFN) treatment, prohibition of exchange controls, prohibition of uncompensated expropriation, and resolution of disputes by binding arbitration. Importantly, BITs have not addressed linkages with other fields. If the only concerns raised by FDI were expropriation of property and repayment of debts, this lack of linkages would make good sense. In practice, however, FDI can have a direct relation to labor, environmental and other social welfare concerns because the goals of multinational business and host countries may conflict. * * *

During the Uruguay Round, a number of countries had sought to harmonize the patchwork of BITs through an MAI [multilateral agreement on investment]. The United States and others proposed a comprehensive investment agreement but faced concerted opposition from developing countries. The ultimate compromise, the Agreement on Trade–Related Investment Measures (TRIMS), addressed investment restrictions that directly affect trade flows in goods. While it represented the first global agreement specifically directed at FDI since 1947, the TRIMS Agreement focuses narrowly on measures that distort trade, leaving the most important investment measures outside the agreement and, therefore, outside the scope of the WTO dispute settlement process. Described by one commentator as "a useful if somewhat meagre result of five years of tough negotiation," the TRIMS Agreement was not viewed at the time as a significant achievement, in part because it largely restated GATT law...Developing country opposition to a comprehensive investment agreement at the WTO has not weakened since the close of the Uruguay Round. In fact, when development of investment rules was again proposed at the WTO in 1996, opposition by developing countries blocked negotiations, leading to the weak compromise of new working groups on trade and investment and trade and competition policy to examine these areas more deeply.

Against this backdrop of failure, after completing over 70 preparatory studies ... [the OECD] Council decided to move from research of BITs to negotiation of the MAI. The stated goal was to complete the treaty by May 1997. A high-level negotiating group was established outside the directorate structure, serviced by DAFFE (primarily from CIME) secretariat staff. They were given a mandate to create an agreement that would:

> provide a broad multinational framework for international investment with high standard for the liberalisation of investment regimes and investment protection and with effective dispute settlement procedures [and] be a free-standing international treaty open to all OECD Members and the European Communities, and to accession by non-OECD Member countries.

Drafting Groups and Preparatory Groups were established to address specific issues and flesh out areas of agreement before going to the main Negotiating Group in Plenary session. All the Member countries participated and, within two years, eight non-Member countries joined as observers.

From the outset, the OECD Secretariat regarded the MAI negotiations as a technical harmonization exercise. Given the great deal of commonality among the many investment treaties, it was expected that the OECD secretariat would review the range of BIT texts, identify common features, and create a unifying draft that would form the basis of a general agreement. The MAI, it was hoped, would be the first comprehensive international investment treaty and would create uniform rules for FDI protection, liberalization, and dispute settlement. By creating a more level playing field than the bumpy terrain of BITs, the MAI would greatly reduce distortions to investment flows and therefore speed the growth of FDI, significantly promoting the liberalization of investment measures and performance requirements beyond the results of the Uruguay Round agreements.

James Salzman, *Labor Rights, Globalization and Institutions: The Role and Influence of the Organization for Economic Cooperation and Development,* 21 MICHIGAN JOURNAL OF INTERNATIONAL LAW 769, 805, 809–12 (2001).

Following the model of NAFTA, the MAI provided for a binding dispute settlement process, one that arguably gave investors the right to file claims for compensation resulting from regulatory takings. There were concerns over the forum of the negotiations, as well. While non-Member countries were invited to participate, the fact that the OECD, the organization for the wealthy industrialized countries, was the site for the negotiations sent strong messages over whose interests the final agreement would represent. While the OECD made no secret of the MAI negotiations, the secretariat did not release any negotiating drafts. This left them open to the charge, merited or not, that they had something to hide. Finally, the balance of the MAI gave potential cause for concern. The MAI clearly gave new rights to foreign investors. These included not only national treatment and MFN but also binding dispute settlement provisions. The potential benefits for investors were obvious–fewer restrictions on placement (and removal) of their investments. What would nations receive in return for giving up sovereign control over inward investments? One could argue that the quid pro quo would arise in the form of greater flows of FDI, increased economic growth, and improved social welfare from this new wealth. This was a variant on the refrain that "a rising tide lifts all boats," heard so often in trade and development debates. But there was very real concern that the MAI without linkages, that is without explicit social, labor and environmental protections, created investors' rights without balancing them with similar responsibilities. And the only environmental linkage, strongly opposed by some of the countries, was to incorporate the nonbinding OECD Guidelines on Corporate Conduct (discussed in Chapter 18, page 1410).

In retrospect, the MAI negotiations marked a watershed in the globalization movement. During the first year, with the draft MAI text kept secret, the NGO community was largely unaware of the negotiations. This changed dramatically, however, when a copy of the text was leaked and posted on the Internet: NGOs mounted an effective campaign against the MAI almost overnight.

[T]he rapidity and effectiveness of NGO opposition to the MAI was unprecedented. From the end of 1995, a small number of NGOs started to follow the negotiations and oppose both the goals and content of the MAI process. At the start, these were primarily environmental and social rather than labor groups. Labor groups were not far behind, however. The OECD held an informal meeting with interested NGOs in December of 1996. While the OECD was open in terms of announcing the process of the negotiations and their general status, in keeping with OECD procedures the internal documents were restricted. In February 1997, however, the Public Citizen group, founded by Ralph Nader, got hold of the current Chairman's draft (i.e., the consolidated negotiating text up to that point) and posted it on the Internet. This posting provided the catalyst for widespread and hard line opposition of NGOs against the MAI. Just two months later, a more formal meeting for NGOs was hosted by members of the Negotiating Group and secretariat officials. While the OECD's first consultative meeting with interested groups about the MAI had been in an empty room, the October briefing attracted over 70 representatives from 30 groups around the world. In a matter of mere months, through the Internet and e-mail, a global campaign against the MAI had come into being. Drafts and bulletins on the MAI were now regularly posted on a host of NGO websites. By 1998, anti-MAI campaigns were active in more than half of the OECD countries as well as many developing countries. * * *

The impact of a global NGO campaign against the MAI was quickly felt ... Despite earlier protests by some Member countries, text was inserted to prohibit the lowering of social and environmental standards to attract FDI, to ensure that treaty obligations would not prevent governments from maintaining (or heightening) protective social and environmental standards, and to ban claims by foreign investors for compensation for losses caused by non-discriminatory regulatory actions.

These concessions, however, came too late, for the NGO campaign had taken on a life of its own in domestic politics. In early 1998, seeking to resurrect the chances of renewed Fast Track authority from Congress, the Clinton Administration sought NGO support by denouncing the MAI as "fatally flawed" and demanding that it be reconsidered. Domestic opposition also flared up in Paris, where demonstrations in February took aim at the impact of the MAI on France's ability to protect its cultural heritage...Reflecting this course of events, the OECD issued a press release on December 3, 1998 stating that "Negotiations on the MAI are no longer taking place."

James Salzman, *op. cit.*, at 824–5.

QUESTIONS AND DISCUSSION

1. Significant foreign investment now flows from developed to developing countries, where lack of institutional capacity and weak civil society can leave the developing country in an unequal bargaining position. The result often is that investment agreements protect the capital of the investor, first and foremost, with the developing countries held hostage to their real or perceived need for foreign investment. Protections for environment, labor, and human rights are generally omitted. As the IFC advises developing countries:

> Appropriate policies are key to capturing foreign investor interest and to successful instruments. Ingredients for a sound policy framework include few restrictions on foreign ownership, a liberal trade and payment regime, open access to land and labor, low and uniform taxes, limited public sector involvement in the economy, and a minimum of red tape.

<www.worldbank.org/ifc/PUBLICAT/PRESS/DATE/1997/FDI.HTM>.   Speaking specifically of the proposed MAI, Joel Bergsman of the Foreign Investment Advisory Service of the World Bank Group noted:

> On balance MAI standards would be good for Latin American countries to adopt. But they are only a part, and not the greatest part, of the changes that are needed to attract more FDI and to get more out of it. Globalization has made the whole package that constitutes the investment environment more and more important, as MNCs themselves are subject to more competition and can less afford to produce in sub-standard locations.
>
> <www.worldbank.org/ifc/PUBLICAT/FDINEWS/VOL13/MAI.HTM>.

What do you think Bergsman meant by "sub-standard locations"?

2. A surprising participant in the international debate over the MAI was the Western Governors' Association in the United States. Consider its critique of the draft MAI.

> 1. State enterprises would be required to act "solely in accordance with commercial considerations," and could no longer use financial policies to promote social objectives. Arizona, for example, might no longer use its bonding authority to promote investment in pollution-control technology. California could have to give up its moratorium on commercial salmon fishing licenses. In short, states could no longer hold state resources in trust for state residents. To do so might exclude new market entrants, to the disadvantage of foreign investors. At the federal level, the government could not impose sanctions on human rights violators–as with South Africa or Burma, without having such moves challenged as barriers to trade.
>
> 2. A limitation on "Performance Requirements" might make community reinvestment laws and recycled content laws illegal. Some 20 states–including Washington, Iowa, Minnesota and Pennsylvania–allow investors to acquire banking assets only if they reinvest locally. Arizona, New Mexico, Iowa, Ohio and another 16 states deposit state funds only with local banks that invest locally. Under MAI, they could no longer make it a requirement to do so. Similarly, Wisconsin mandates a minimum percentage of recycled content in

glass or plastic containers, but foreign investors could argue this amounts to an investment-distorting performance requirement.

3. If corporations receive tax breaks or free training, they could not be required to give anything in return. When Colorado offers customized job training, it could no longer attach "clawback" provisions requiring companies to certify how many jobs they will create and how much they will pay workers. Enterprise zones, like Oregon's property tax exemption for businesses that locate in economically disadvantaged areas, could become illegal.

4. Laws requiring companies to reclaim stripmined areas could be challenged as "expropriation of assets." Maryland, Virginia, and Pennsylvania use coordinated wetlands laws to protect the Chesapeake Bay–placing restrictions on destruction of plant life and changes to drainage patterns. Such laws could be challenged as "creeping expropriation". American courts say these regulations don't require compensation to owners–but OECD arbitrators might see things differently.

5. The enforcement mechanism of the current MAI gives investors and corporations the right to sue governments, to force a change in the law that "expropriates" their investment, or payment of money for the loss. Governments, however, do not get the right to sue investors for damages they might cause, nor do NGOs.

6. To what extent do multilateral environmental agreements, such as the Montreal Protocol or climate change regimes, impose any direct or indirect standards on foreign investment? To what extent do those regimes encourage or discourage foreign investment?

Do you think the drafters of the MAI considered these local impacts of their proposed text? How often do you think local governments are consulted in international treaty negotiations?

3. The power of the global NGO community to halt the MAI in its tracks was impressive. Much of this was due to the times. Such a loose coalition could not have formed so rapidly without the Internet, and the Asian financial crisis had already slowed the juggernaut of globalization through reduced barriers to trade and investment. While this power is impressive (particularly to those who agree with the NGOs' agenda), it carries concerns, as well. As James Salzman notes in recounting the MAI history,

> it must be added that a number of NGOs made claims with no basis in fact at all. There were assertions that the MAI would establish protectionist standards against developing countries and that if the MAI had been in force Nelson Mandela would still be in prison. It is not news, of course, to observe that the advent of the Internet and e-mail is revolutionizing the techniques and influence of NGOs, permitting the creation of global campaigns remarkably quickly. The experience of the MAI is a case in point that the increased ease and rapidity of information dissemination applies equally to misinformation.

James Salzman, *op. cit.*, at 825

Do you agree with Professor Salzman that the NGO predictions had "no basis in fact"? How would you investigate the accuracy of the NGO predictions? How legitimate is it to predict a "worse case" scenario for something like the MAI, especially when it is negotiated in relative secrecy, and then to use that prediction in the political debate? Where NGO or industry information is inaccurate or misleading, how should countries respond? Can the marketplace of ideas weed out truth from distortions when the negotiations are closed to the public? Would allowing a select number of NGOs to participate as observers address this problem?

CHAPTER SIXTEEN

Human Rights and Environment

Section I.   Introduction

This chapter considers the linkages between human rights and the environment, how such linkages can assist efforts to protect both human rights and the environment, and what further collaboration between these two fields might be pursued. It includes a discussion of specific human rights that implicate the environment and the cases interpreting such rights. It also discusses the use of the U.N. and regional human rights systems, as well as national courts, for enforcing human rights to protect environmental interests. The chapter concludes with a discussion of how human rights may be applied directly to corporations to protect the environment.

————

A.   HUMAN RIGHTS AND ENVIRONMENT LINKAGES

Today, more than ever, it is clear that environmental degradation has an adverse impact on the quality of human life, and more specifically on the full enjoyment of human rights, as well as the achievement of sustainable levels of development respectful of economic, social, and cultural rights. Environmental degradation too often leads to violations of human rights, including the right to life, health, habitation, culture, equality before the law, and the right to property. Many of the human rights already enshrined in existing agreements are extremely sensitive to environmental threats.

Conversely, the failure to protect and promote human rights prevents progress towards environmental protection and sustainable development. This is the case, for example, when there are violations of the rights to information, assembly, press, access to justice, and participation in governance. Violations of these mostly procedural rights prevent groups affected by environmental degradation from working within their political process to secure the level of environmental protection necessary to protect their health and well being. Where human rights are weak, civil society is not able to raise environmental concerns effectively. Indigenous and other vulnerable groups often have limited opportunities to participate in the political process, and can suffer environmental discrimination and a disproportionate burden of environmental degradation as a result.

Thus it is no accident that where the environment has been most devastated from large uncontrolled development projects, human rights abuses are the most severe. Moreover, with enormous wealth at stake in many of these conflicts, environmental and human rights activists are being targeted, sometimes directly by the government or at least with its tacit approval. A well-known example is Ken Saro–Wiwa, who was hung by the Nigerian dictatorship in 1996, along with several other activists, for raising environmental concerns about oil development by Royal Dutch Petroleum in their native Ogoni lands. In Kenya, Wangari Muta Maathai, the internationally recognized founder of one of the most important developing country grassroots movements, the Green Belt Movement, has been teargassed, beaten and arrested. India's Medha Paktar and other activists opposing the Narmada dam have regularly been beaten and arrested for their efforts to protect their homes from being flooded. In Brazil, ranchers with close ties to local government officials murdered Chico Mendes because of his efforts to protect rubber tapping reserves in the Amazon. To fight these and other threats, human rights and environmental organizations around the world are joining forces to create networks dedicated to protecting the human rights of environmental activists. *See* AMNESTY INTERNATIONAL & SIERRA CLUB, ENVIRONMENTALISTS UNDER FIRE: 10 URGENT CASES OF

HUMAN RIGHTS ABUSES, (2000) <www.sierraclub.org/human-rights/>; HUMAN RIGHTS WATCH & NATURAL RESOURCES DEFENSE COUNCIL, DEFENDING THE EARTH: ABUSES OF HUMAN RIGHTS AND THE ENVIRONMENT (1992).

Another recurring pattern of environmental abuse that sparks human rights abuse is one in which outside interests, generally multinational corporations, are exploiting oil, minerals, timber, or other natural resources, in lesser developed countries. Repression of local communities, including indigenous peoples, appears to be the most convenient way to pursue "development" in frontier lands. This is in contrast with what might be expected in developed countries, where the local communities generally have access to the political process to negotiate economic benefits in exchange for the development, as well as guarantees for protecting human rights and the environment. Using examples from gold mining in Irian Jaya and oil development in the Amazon region of Ecuador, Richard Herz of Earth Rights International describes this typical fact pattern in the following excerpt.

RICHARD L. HERZ, LITIGATING ENVIRONMENTAL ABUSES UNDER THE ALIEN TORT CLAIMS ACT: A PRACTICAL ASSESSMENT, 40 VA. J. INT'L L. 545, 547–49 (2000)

All too often, transnational corporations (TNCs) and governments inflict devastating environmental harms on local people in developing countries. Typically, the damage is obvious and preventable, but ignored by those who cause it. Texaco's oil development in the Ecuadorian Amazon and Freeport–McMoRan's copper and gold mine in the highlands of Irian Jaya, Indonesia are noteworthy examples. Texaco drilled oil in the Ecuadorian Amazon for twenty years, ending in 1992. During that time, the company opened over 300 wells and cut 18,000 miles of trail and 300 miles of road in pristine rainforest. Disregarding the established industry practice of pumping wastes back into wells, Texaco dumped massive quantities of toxic byproducts onto roads and into streams and wetlands local people used for drinking, fishing and bathing. Texaco also filled over 600 pits with toxic waste, which often washed out in heavy rain. A farmer, describing the rupture of just one of these pits, stated, "[i]t has been three years, and my wife is still covered with rashes. I have eight children. All of them have been sick with rashes, flus, their stomachs, swollen throats. We did not have that before the spill." The rupture also ruined his farm and water supply. At least 30,000 people have suffered injuries similar to those experienced by that farmer and his family as a result of Texaco's Amazonian operations.

Freeport's practices are equally outrageous. The company has removed the top 400 feet of a mountain sacred to the local Amungme people. It currently dumps 160,000 tons of untreated, toxic mine tailings into the local waterways each day, a figure that will soon rise to 285,000 tons, the equivalent of a ten ton dump truck-full every three seconds. This massive release of sediment has created an artificial floodplain on a local river, destroying the river and inundating surrounding rainforests. The mine has also devastated lakes and polluted ground and surface water with toxins. This damage has threatened the lives and health of the entire Amungme people, through starvation, exposure to toxic chemicals, pollution of their water, and destruction of their lands. [The above facts are based on JOE KANE, SAVAGES 190 (1995) in the case of Texaco's Amazon drilling and the allegations presented by plaintiff's pleadings with respect to Freeport's mine.]

Political, legal and practical barriers to TNCs' entry into Third World economies are rapidly disappearing. Moreover, many nations are unwilling or unable to protect their citizens from the kinds of actions described above through domestic law. Thus, the Texaco and Freeport examples beg the question of whether effective means exist to ensure corporate environmental accountability in an increasingly global economy. Growing awareness of the suffering environmental abuses inflict has led many observers to consider the extent to which such abuses violate human rights norms. The fact that governments and TNCs often commit brutal civil rights violations, such as summary executions and torture, to suppress opposition to ecologically destructive projects strengthens the trend toward viewing environmental degradation itself as a human rights abuse. * * *

Indigenous peoples are particularly vulnerable to environmental threats, as they are often completely dependent on their immediate environment for survival. This relationship is described in an amicus curiae brief filed in the Inter–American Human Rights Commission on behalf of the Wichi and other Lhaka Honhat aboriginal communities from the Chaco region of Argentina. The brief urges the Commission to recognize the symbiotic relationship between indigenous peoples and their land; the Wichi and the other communities depend on their environment for their food, shelter, and culture. The environmental threat comes from a transcontinental highway that will cut through their aboriginal lands as it crosses from the east coast of Brazil to the west coast of Chile to facilitate international trade. The Wichi fear that heavy truck traffic and pollution will affect the environment, culture, and lifestyle of their communities, and will open up their insular populations to AIDS and other diseases. Work already underway in their traditional territory is disrupting their hunting patterns, fishing resources, and natural habitat, putting their culture and, ultimately, their very survival at risk. The amicus brief requests precautionary measures to halt the road until the government of Argentina prepares an environmental impact assessment and consults with the indigenous peoples threatened by the development.

Amicus Curiae Brief, *Association of Lhaha Honhat Aboriginal Communities (Nuestra Tierra/Our Land) v. The State of Argentina*, 3–8, Center for Human Rights and Environment (CEDHA) & Center for International Environmental Law (CIEL), September 19, 2000 <www.cedha.org.ar/docs.htm>

Summary of the Argument

CIEL and CEDHA contend that there is a recurring pattern throughout the world, including South American states, whereby:

- large-scale development projects are undertaken which result in irreparable environmental harm to lands historically used, occupied, and claimed by indigenous peoples;

- such projects are typically undertaken without prior assessment of their environmental impacts;

- such projects are typically undertaken without prior assessment of their social impacts;

- such projects are typically undertaken without providing adequate and timely information to the parties affected;

- such projects are typically undertaken without prior consultation with the affected indigenous peoples;

- such projects inevitably lead to severe violations of the human rights of the affected indigenous people; and

- the absence of precautionary measures in these kinds of large-scale development projects produces irreparable environmental and human rights damage. * * *

While the Commission is considering the merits of the underlying claims in this case, the Lhaka Honhat peoples risk daily incursions into their way of life, as the construction of the road project that is at the heart of this dispute continues apace. In order for the Commission's ultimate decision on the merits to have any meaning, the Lhaka Honhat peoples' lifestyle, culture, and very survival must be guaranteed in the interim. This requires invoking the familiar provisional remedy of precautionary measures in the context of an environmental threat to the human rights of an indigenous people. * * *

The Need for Special Protection of Indigenous Peoples Is Most Acute When Violations of Their Human Rights Will Result From Irreparable Harm to Their Environment

Both this Commission and the Inter–American Court of Human Rights have had repeated occasion to consider the need of indigenous peoples for "special protection" of their human rights resulting from environmental harm to lands traditionally used by indigenous peoples for their physical and cultural survival.

As the following review of the cases previously and presently before the Commission and the Court makes all too plain, when the lands used by indigenous people are subjected to development by others, when participation by the indigenous people in the development decision is not allowed, and when prior study of the environmental impacts of the proposed development is not undertaken, the result is invariably environmental damage to the land, severe injury to the health and way of life of the indigenous people, and wholesale violations of their human rights. [The brief then discusses the Yanomani and Huaoromi cases, discussed *infra*]. * * *

As these case studies demonstrate, there is grave danger to the human rights of indigenous peoples threatened with environmental harm. Such harm by its very nature is as irreversible and ultimately as life-threatening as the threats to the immediate health and safety of individuals that this Commission is so often asked to protect.

B.   ADVANTAGES TO USING A HUMAN RIGHTS APPROACH

Over the past fifteen years, international environmental law scholars and activists have increasingly looked to the law of human rights as a model for the progressive development of international environmental law as well as an independent legal strategy for protecting the environment. Significantly, and in contrast to international environmental law and institutions, the human rights system already provides various courts, commissions, and other bodies where individuals and NGOs can raise human rights and associated environmental issues with the legitimate expectation of securing some relief.

These "supervisory mechanisms" offer models for environmental lawyers not only to use, but also to borrow and incorporate into the international environmental law system. The mechanisms vary. Some are independent commissions that investigate individual assertions of rights, as well as broader investigations into country compliance. Others are specialized courts with compulsory jurisdiction and the power to grant a full range of remedies, including damages and attorneys fees. There are also special rapporteurs to investigate broad thematic areas, such as the UN's Special Rapporteur on Human Rights and the Environment, special fact-finding missions and extensive country reporting requirements.

More fundamentally, the evolutionary path of human rights law, which is anchored more in general, or universal, principles, provides insights that may help environmental lawyers accelerate the development of more robust international environmental law. The focus of human rights on the individual also is both a model and an inspiration for reforming international environmental law, which still resists participation by individuals and NGOs.

Finally, much can be learned from the rights-based approach of human rights law. Environmental law is largely regulatory in its approach, often based on scientific standards, technological feasibility of pollution control, and other technical considerations. While many national law systems have some rights that individuals can enforce, including constitutional provisions, and common law nuisance actions, which were critical to the pre-regulatory success of the U.S. environmental law movement, the systems in the U.S. and Europe lack broad environmental rights that individuals can enforce.

Thus, many environmentalists argue for the recognition of "environmental rights"—based on the fundamental human needs for clean air and water, a stable climate system, the ozone layer's protection from ultraviolet radiation, and more generally an environment conducive to human life and health. The right to a healthy environment does in fact exist in the African and Inter–American human rights systems, as well as in many modern national constitutions in Africa and Latin America, and will be discussed later in the chapter. What are some of the advantages of using a human rights approach to protect the environment, as opposed to a regulatory approach, or an approach based on tort law, or criminal law?

> First, a human rights approach is a strong claim, a claim to an absolute entitlement theoretically immune to the lobbying and trade-offs that characterize bureaucratic decision-making. Its power lies in its ability to trump individual greed and short-term thinking. A second advantage is that the procedural dimensions of an environmental right can provide access to justice in a way that bureaucratic regulation, or tort law, simply cannot. A robust environmental right can mobilize redress where other remedies have failed. * * * Thirdly, a human rights approach may stimulate concomitant political activism on environmental issues. Concerned citizens and NGOs are more likely to rally

around a general statement of right than a highly technical, bureaucratic regulation expressed in legalese. Fourthly, a human rights approach can provide the conceptual link to bring local, national, and international issues within the same frame of legal judgment. At present, environmental damage is unequally distributed at both the national and international level; a non-discriminatory human rights standard could facilitate comparison, and foster political mobilization linking local concerns with more global issues. * * * Fifthly, a general expression of right can be interpreted creatively as issues and contexts change. ... Thus, definitions and trade-offs evolve gradually in the light of experience rather than needing to be defined comprehensively and rigidly in a single piece of regulatory legislation.

Michael R. Anderson, *Human Rights Approaches to Environmental Protection: An Overview* in Alan E. Boyle & Michael R. Anderson, Eds., HUMAN RIGHTS APPROACHES TO ENVIRONMENTAL PROTECTION 1–4, 21–23 (1996)

Regardless of whether one favors a rights-based approach to environmental protection, the field of human rights will remain vital for environmental protection and achieving sustainable development. Environmental law and human rights are necessarily converging, and the many linkages between their legal and institutional systems demonstrate their underlying indivisibility. The threats addressed by each can only be fully redressed by a comprehensive legal approach. Mechanisms that might be considered to promote further collaboration and cooperation range from soft law declarations to guide the interpretation of existing human rights instruments to ensure that the proper environmental dimensions are included, to the possibility of new regional or international instruments that could guide and direct the interpretation of regional and national law, expand existing rights, or create new rights, as appropriate. In addition, filing fact-specific actions in the various human rights bodies provides a critical evolutionary force for the further development of both environmental and human rights law.

QUESTIONS AND DISCUSSION

1. Human rights and environment issues are not restricted to developing countries. Environmental burdens in the United States are disproportionately borne by poor and minority communities that have less political and economic power. Recognition of this has led to the growth of the "environmental justice" movement and efforts to apply civil rights standards to environmental discrimination. *See e.g.,* Luke W. Cole & Sheila R. Foster, FROM THE GROUND UP: ENVIRONMENTAL RACISM AND THE RISE OF THE ENVIRONMENTAL JUSTICE MOVEMENT (2001); B. Goldman & L. Fitton, TOXIC WASTES AND RACE REVISITED (1994); R. Bullard, DUMPING IN DIXIE: RACE, CLASS AND ENVIRONMENTAL QUALITY (1990).

2. Anderson notes that "[o]ften, the real value of a human right is that it is available as a moral trump card precisely when legal arrangements fail." Anderson, *op. cit.,* at 12–13. How can such a moral trump card be used in practice? If you cannot appeal to courts or to international processes for protection of a right, to whom can you appeal? The government itself? The public? By what means? Is the availability of a "moral trump card" an adequate substitute for binding obligations on the State to protect important rights, or should it instead be considered a supplement to such obligations? Do we have equivalent "moral trump" cards in environmental law?

3. In discussing enforcement of environmental rights, Anderson suggests that environmental treaties may be a more appropriate source of protection for environmental rights than human rights treaties because "international law is already replete with rules ... and criteria for ensuring environmental quality, and ... most important environmental treaties already possess sophisticated supervisory institutions, often with more enforcement power than analogous human rights treaties." Anderson, *op. cit.*, at 20. Many international environmental lawyers would disagree that existing environmental treaties provide the supervisory institutions necessary to protect environmental rights. Which environmental treaties provide mechanisms for individuals to enforce the parties' environmental obligations or seek vindication when those obligations are violated? How important is the distinction between a rights-based approach and a regulatory approach to a given environmental problem? In terms of legal strategy? Available remedies? In the U.S. and other common law countries individuals can bring a nuisance action against a polluting activity, or an action for damages under a negligence or strict liability theory. Would these be considered a rights-based approach? The essence of nuisance is balancing the competing interests at stake. Are human rights ever subject to a balancing test?

4. In Chapter 3, we examined the relationship between the human economy and environmental degradation. We argued that environmental quality is not sustainable over the long term if the underlying economic causes of environmental degradation are not addressed. In a similar vein, Anderson states that recognizing environmental rights concerned merely with the symptoms of environmental damage will not prevent the violation of those rights. To be effective, a rights approach must "address the relationships of political economy which underlie much environmental damage ... including technology choice, forms of production, and distribution of the social product." Anderson, *op. cit.* at 22. Is it possible to craft such a right? What might it look like?

5. Anderson also discusses possible disadvantages of a human rights approach. First, a simple rights-based approach may not be appropriate for complex environmental threats, which often involve underlying issues of political economy. The present system of international environmental law—based on inter-state commitments—may be more appropriate for marshaling the resources and political will for long-term environmental management. Second, rights-based approaches may be co-opted to protect elitist environmental interests. Third, rights-based litigation may displace other more suitable remedies. And fourth, "the language of human rights may politicize and draw attention to environmental claims in a way that may attract more opposition from polluters, or even exacerbate government repression." How can these potential disadvantages be overcome?

C. Moral Foundations of Human Rights and the Recognition of General Principles of International Environmental Law

An examination of the separate evolutionary paths of human rights and environmental protection disclose some important affinities. They both witness, and precipitate, the gradual erosion of so-called domestic jurisdiction. The treatment by the State of its own nationals becomes a matter of international concern. Conservation of the environment and control of pollution become likewise a matter of international concern. The *internationalization* of human rights protection reached a watershed immediately following the horrors of World War II, with the 1948 Universal Declaration on Human Rights, although for centuries there has been an ebb and flow between the sphere of domestic jurisdiction and international concern. The internationalization of environmental protection started much later, with widespread recognition by the time of the 1972 Stockholm Declaration on the Human Environment. Both fields of law developed a vast normative corpus of international law mainly in the form of responses to specific challenges leading in many cases to conventions that followed a *sectoral* approach (e.g. torture, disappearance, waters, oceans, wildlife, atmosphere). Finally, concern for human rights can be found in international environmental law and, *vice versa*, concern for the environment can be found in the realm of international human rights law. *See generally,* A.A. Cancado Trindade, The Parallel Evolutions of International Human Rights Protection and of Environmental Protection and the Absence of Restrictions upon the Exercise of Recognized Human Rights, *Revista del Instituto Interamericano de Derechos Humanos,* Nro. 13, at 35–76 (1991).

While World War II was the impetus for much of modern human rights, human rights go back to antiquity. As you read the following excerpt, note the changing role of the individual.

David Weissbrodt, Joan Fitzpatrick, and Frank Newman, International Human Rights: Law, Policy, and Process (3rd ed. 2001), at 2–4.

Concepts of human rights can be traced to antiquity—e.g. the Ten Commandments, the Code of Hammurabi's approach to law as a means of preventing the strong from oppressing the weak, and the Rights of Athenian Citizens. ... Religious, moral, and philosophical origins can be identified not only in biblical and classical history but also in Buddhism, Confucianism, Hinduism, Judaism, Shinto, and other faiths. Rights concepts began to appear in national documents such as the Magna Carta of 1215. Also in the 13rh century, St. Thomas Aquinas used the theory of natural rights to argue that state sovereignty should not be respected when a government is mistreating its subjects. Following the revolution of 1688 in England, Parliament enacted the Declaration of the Rights of Man (1689) to protect citizens from violations by the monarchy. ...

With the rise of nation states in the 17th century, however, classical international law rejected the notion of human rights and favored state sovereignty.... During the 18th and 19th centuries, governments took further measures to recognize inherent rights of the individual under national law. The 1776 American Declaration of Independence proclaimed, "as self evident," the "inalienable rights" of all men to "life, liberty and the pursuit of happiness." Those rights were based on 18th century theories of natural law philosophers like Locke and Rousseau, who argued that fundamental rights were beyond state control and that individuals are autonomous in nature. ...

Belief in such rights produced the French Declaration of the Rights of Man and of the Citizen in 1789 and led federated states to insist on adding the Bill of Rights to the U.S. Constitution between 1789 and 1791. A number of nations followed the French and U.S. examples in their constitutions.... In addition, 19th century efforts to abolish the slave trade and protect workers' rights evidenced a growing international concern for human rights ... [and ultimately] awoke concern for women's rights...].

The parallels between the evolution of international human rights and of international environmental law suggest that we might be able to use the philosophical basis of human rights to devise a process that will help us identify and recognize general principles of international environmental law, in addition to the current regulatory approach. According to Jerome J. Shestack, "...human rights are a set of moral principles and their justification lies in the province of moral philosophy". Shestack, THE PHILOSOPHICAL FOUNDATIONS OF HUMAN RIGHTS (1984), at 32. Thus, if we understand the moral force of human rights, we may be able to use it to reinforce the authority of international environmental law, particularly valuable for an area lacking legal enforcement mechanisms. The moral justification of human rights gives coherency to the set of principles that govern or should govern the ways we treat one another. It is worth considering how we can use this morality to justify general principles of international environmental law that will determine the right mode of individual conduct towards the environment. The following excerpt outlines several of the principal theories of the moral philosophy of human rights.

Jerome J. Shestack, "The Philosophical Foundations of Human Rights," IN HUMAN RIGHTS: CONCEPTS AND STANDARDS (Janusz Symonides, Ed.) (2000), 33–36

Sources of Human Rights

Natural Law: the Autonomous Individual

Philosophers and jurists did not leave human rights solely to theologians. In their search for a law which was higher than positive law, they developed the theory of natural law. Natural law theory has underpinnings in Sophocles and Aristotle, but it was first elaborated by the stoics of the Greek Hellenistic period and later of the Roman period. Natural law, they believed, embodied those elementary principles of justice that constituted right reason—that is, in accordance with nature, unalterable and eternal. ...

According to Grotius, a natural characteristic of human beings is the social impulse to live peacefully and in harmony with others. Whatever conformed to the nature of men and women as rational social beings was right and just; whatever opposed it by disturbing the social harmony was wrong and unjust. Grotius defined natural law as a "dictate of right reason"; that is, an act, according to whether it is or is not in conformity with rational nature, has in it a quality of moral necessity or moral baseness. * * *

Natural law theory led to natural rights theory, the theory most closely associated with modern human rights. The chief exponent of this theory was John Locke, who developed his philosophy within the framework of seventeenth-century humanism and political activity, known as the Age of Enlightenment. Locke imagined the existence of human beings in a state of nature, in which men and women were in a state of freedom, able to determine their actions and also in a state of equality in the sense that no one was subjected to the will or authority of another. However, to end the hazards and inconveniences of the state of nature, men and women entered into a 'social contract' by which they mutually agreed to form a community and set up a body politic. However, in setting up that political authority, individuals retained the natural rights of life, liberty and property, which were their own. Government was obliged to protect the natural rights of its subjects and, if government neglected this obligation, it would forfeit its validity and office.

In practice, natural rights theory was the philosophical impetus for the wave of revolt against absolutism during the late eighteenth century. It is seen in the French Declaration of the Rights of Man, in the United States Declaration of Independence, and later in the constitutions of numerous states created upon liberation from colonialism and, still later, in the principal United Nations human rights documents.

Under Locke's view of human beings in the state of nature, all that was needed was the opportunity to be self-dependent; life, liberty and property were the inherent rights which met this demand. But what of a world unlike the times of Locke, in which there are not ample resources to satisfy human needs? Does natural law theory have the flexibility to satisfy new claims based on contemporary conditions and modern human understanding? * * *

Modern Human Rights Theories

Rights Based on Natural Rights: Core Rights

There exists a large variety of presentations and analyses among scholars addressing theories of moral philosophy. While the new rights do not wear the same metaphysical dress as the early expounders of the Rights of Man, most adopt what may be called a qualified natural law approach, in that they try to identify the values which have an eternal and universal aspect. They agree that only a positive legal system that meets those values can function as an effective legal system. In a larger sense, the object of much of revived natural rights thought can be viewed as attempts to work out the principles which might reconcile the "is" and the "ought" in law.

The common theme merged from a huge family of theories is that a minimum absolute or core postulate of any just and universal system of rights must include some recognition of the value of individual freedom or autonomy. Underlying such foundational or core rights theory is the omnipresence of Immanuel Kant's compelling ethic. Kant's ethic maintains that persons typically have different desires and ends, so any principle derived from them can only be contingent. But the moral law needs a categorical foundation, not a contingent one. The basis for moral law must be prior to all purposes and ends. The basis is the individual as a transcendental subject capable of an autonomous will. Rights then flow from the autonomy of the individual in choosing his or her ends, consistent with a similar freedom for all.

In short Kant's great imperative is that the central focus of morality is "personhood", namely the capacity to take responsibility as a free and rational agent for one's system of ends. A natural corollary of this Kantian thesis is that the highest purpose of human life is to will autonomously. A person must always be treated as an end and the highest purpose of the state is to promote conditions favoring the free and harmonious unfolding of individuality.

In variant forms, modern human rights core theories seem to be settling for concepts of natural necessity, that is, necessity in the sense of prescribing a minimum definition of what it means to be human in a morally tolerable society. In other words, some modes of treatment of human beings are so fundamental to the existence of anything we would be willing to call a society, that it takes better sense to treat an acceptance of them as constitutive of man and woman as social beings, than as artificial conventions. This view does not entail verified propositions, as science requires. Rather, it views human life as encompassing certain freedoms and sensibilities without which the designation 'human' would not make sense. To use a linguistic metaphor, humanity has a grammatical form of which certain basic human rights are a necessary part. This concept of what we take human beings to be is a profound one, even if it is deemed self-evident. * * *

Rights Based on the Value of Utility

Jeremy Bentham, who expounded classical utilitarianism, believed that every human decision was motivated by some calculation of pleasure and pain. He thought that every political decision should be made on the same calculation, that is, to maximize the net produce of pleasure over pain. Hence, both governments and the limits of governments were to be judged not by reference to abstract individual rights but in terms of what tends to promote the greatest happiness of the greatest number of persons.

Under utilitarian doctrine, all count equally at the primary level and any of us may have to accept sacrifices if the benefits they yield to others are large enough to outweigh the personal sacrifice. In short, utilitarianism is a maximizing and collectivizing principle requiring government to maximize the total net sum of the happiness of all of its subjects. This principle is in contrast to natural rights theory, which is a distributive and individualizing principle assigning priority to the specific basic interests of each individual subject.

Rights Based on Justice

Principles of justice, according to Rawls, provide a way of assigning rights and duties in the basic institutions of society. These principles define the appropriate distribution of the benefits and burdens of social cooperation. Rawls's thesis is that each person possesses "an inviolability founded on justice" that even the welfare of society as a whole cannot override. "Justice denies that the loss of freedom for some is made right by a greater good shared by others. Therefore, in a just society the liberties of equal citizenship are settled; the rights secured by justice are not subject to political bargaining or to the calculus of social interests."

Rawls assumes that the principles of justice (morality) are not self-evident to our common sense but that they can be formulated through the tradition of the social contract in moral and political philosophy

[Shestack then describes Rawls's "veil of ignorance" thought experiment, and how it is used to derive universal principles of justice. Rawls is discussed in Chapter 2, at 107.]

QUESTIONS AND DISCUSSION

1. How might we use the philosophical foundation of human rights to formulate a theory that will help us justify the legitimacy of international environmental rights? Do you think that a theological approach could provide the needed philosophical foundation for environmental duties? Revisit the discussion of natural law and general principles in Chapter 6, at pages 325–332.

2. Based on Bentham's theory, can we argue that the protection of the environment promotes the greatest happiness of the greatest number of persons and therefore both governments and the limits of governments are to be judged by reference to their level of environmental protection? Would the WTO agree with this approach? *See* Chapter 15.

3. According to Rawls' argument what do you think are the rights of justice concerning the environment? In other words, what are the principles of "environmental morality" or the foundation of rules that would be agreed upon by all members of a society? *See* earlier discussion of Rawls in Chapters 2 and 6.

SECTION II.   HUMAN RIGHTS THAT BENEFIT ENVIRONMENTAL PROTECTION AND SUSTAINABLE DEVELOPMENT

This section discusses specific human rights that can benefit environmental protection and sustainable development. International human rights bodies are increasingly willing to extend human rights protections to situations of environmental concern. Other applicable rights that have not yet been invoked only await the right case and the right advocate. The section begins with substantive rights, including the right to life and health, the right to a healthy environment, the right to privacy, and the right to culture, expression, and religion. The following section discusses procedural rights, which often parallel existing environmental rights, including the right to information, the right to non-discrimination, and the right to have access to justice and remedies. In focusing on the specific rights, this section looks at a number of rights as they appear in the different international human rights instruments. Each right is accompanied by relevant cases and other interpretive material. In this regard, it should be noted that international commissions and courts of the various systems sometimes refer to the jurisprudence from the other systems to assist with the interpretation of "their" rights. The application of human rights to environmental concerns is a relatively new and evolving area with great potential. Understanding these rights and their interpretation within the international human rights systems will assist lawyers and other practitioners in their efforts to protect the environment.

A.   SUBSTANTIVE RIGHTS

1.   THE RIGHT TO LIFE AND THE RIGHT TO HEALTH AND WELL-BEING

The right to life is the most important of the human rights guaranteed and protected by contemporary international law. It is a universal and obligatory; without it, no other rights would make sense, to use the concept of H.L.A. Hart in Chapter 6. Because our lives depend upon clean air and clean water, as well as adequate food and shelter, the quality of the environment is directly connected to the enjoyment of the right to life. Environmental destruction threatens survival, and can result directly or indirectly in death, especially for indigenous communities and other vulnerable groups. Thus, the right to life requires protection for the human environment under certain circumstances. As Judge Weeremantry states in his separate opinion in the *Gabcikovo-Nagymaros Case*, Chapter 6, at pages 338,

> The protection of the environment is ... a vital part of contemporary human rights doctrine, for it is a *sine qua non* for numerous human rights such as the right to health and the right to life itself. It is scarcely necessary to elaborate on this, as damage to the environment can impair and undermine all the human rights spoken of in the Universal Declaration and other human rights instruments.

All international human rights instruments proclaim the right to life. For example, the Universal Declaration of Human Rights states in Article 3 that "Everyone has the right to life, liberty, and the security of person." UNIVERSAL DECLARATION OF HUMAN RIGHTS, Dec. 10, 1948, G.A. Res. 217A, U.N. GAOR, 3d Sess., art.3, U.N. Doc. A/810 (1948) The meaning and scope of this right is clarified in the International Covenant on Civil and Political Rights, which requires that no person may be arbitrarily deprived of her life. The Inter–American Convention frames the right in a slightly different manner, stating, in Article 4 that "Every person has the right to have his life respected. This right shall be protected by law and, in general, from the moment of conception. No one shall be arbitrarily deprived of his life." AMERICAN CONVENTION ON HUMAN RIGHTS, July, 18 1978, 1144 U.N.T.S. 143, art. 4. The European Convention contains the right under Article 3, pairing it with the right to security. EUROPEAN CONVENTION FOR THE PROTECTION OF HUMAN RIGHTS AND FUNDAMENTAL FREEDOMS, Nov. 4, 1950, art. 3, 312 U.N.T.S. 222, 246. The African Convention contains the right in Article 4. AFRICAN CHARTER ON HUMAN AND PEOPLES' RIGHTS, June 27, 1981, O.A.U. Doc. CAB/LEG/67/3/Rev. 5, 21 I.L.M. 58 (entered into force Oct. 21, 1986). The right to life is a *jus cogens* norm, and no derogation is permitted.

At the time most human rights instruments were drafted, the right to life was aimed at preventing arbitrary killing by the government. Yet,

> Established human rights standards which do not directly touch upon environmental issues may house an implicit relevance capable of juridical development. The right to life, for example, may be deemed to be infringed where a state fails to abate the emission of highly toxic products into supplies of drinking water. If enforcement bodies explicitly recognize such links, then environmental criteria may be incorporated overtly into the monitoring and enforcement of the right to life. This approach has been developed probably most fully by the Indian judiciary, which ... has been active for more than a decade in fashioning environmental rights out of a more conventional catalogue of constitutional rights....

Anderson, *op. cit.* at 40.

The right to life has been evolving in recent years as environmental and human rights advocates present cases to the various human rights bodies, domestic courts, and even the ICJ. A central concern in this evolution is the extent to which the right to life involves a positive obligation on the state to take steps to promote life expectancy.

In addition to protecting the right to life, many human rights instruments separately treat the right to health, as well as the closely related rights to food, adequate living conditions, and safe and healthy working conditions. The right to health in the American Declaration on the Rights and Duties of Man states:

Article XI. Right to the preservation of health and well-being

Every person has the right to the preservation of his health through sanitary and social measures relating to food, clothing, housing and medical care, to the extent permitted by public and community resources.

Similarly, Article 10 of the Additional Protocol to the American Convention on Human Rights states:

1. Everyone shall have the right to health, understood to mean the enjoyment of the highest level of physical, mental, and social well-being.

2. In order to ensure the exercise of the right to health, the States Parties agree to recognize health as a public good and, particularly to adopt ... measures to ensure that right.

a.   THE YANOMANI

In the following report, the Inter–American Human Rights Commission establishes a link between environmental quality and the right to life and health of the Yanomani Indians of Brazil.

REPORT ON THE SITUATION OF HUMAN RIGHTS IN BRAZIL OEA/Ser.L/V/II.97, Doc. 29 rev.1 (1997)

C.   Socioeconomic And Cultural Rights Of Brazil's Indigenous Peoples

22.   [T]he situation of the indigenous communities in regard to health care, food, education and, in particular, land property is extremely serious. Problems of food supply were observed in 198 of the 297 areas examined. ... Almost all of them were experiencing problems of invasion by squatters or intruders; destruction of the environment by such means as pollution from mercury in the waste matter discarded by the "garimpeiros" (prospectors for gold, diamonds, etc.); illegal exploitation of lumber and agriculture; and the inadequate size of their land, which did not suffice for sustenance purposes. * * *

G.   The Yanomami: The Fragility of Their Culture and Conditions for Physical and Cultural Survival

63.   [T]he traditional uses of land have permitted the physical and cultural survival of the Yanomami along with protection of the ecology. That stability is now being threatened by the successive encroachment of outsiders, some of whom—such as the prospectors for gold and other items (*garimpeiros*)—are engaged in unlawful activities that cause damage to the lives and survival of these Indians and their culture and environment.

65.   To understand the delicate situation of the Yanomami's human rights, it is important to recall relatively recent phenomena that have resulted in quantitatively significant loss of lives. The years between 1974 and 1976 saw the start of construction work on the Northern Perimeter Highway built mostly for the hauling of minerals. By the time it had covered a distance of 225 kilometers in Yanomami territory—and because the construction company workers had not been vaccinated (nor had vaccines been provided for the natives there)—the Yanomami population of thirteen villages along the first several kilometers of construction was besieged by epidemics that resulted in the death of one out of every four Indians. At the same time, the incidence of

conflicts between immigrants and indigenous escalated, resulting in untold numbers of deaths. * * *

J.   Conclusions and Recommendations

82.   Based on the foregoing, the Commission concluded that: * * *

b.   The situation of the Indian peoples of Brazil in the areas of health, nutrition, and access to public services is worrying. Indicators demonstrate clearly discriminatory conditions as compared with standards and services for the general population;

c.   Security guarantees that every state should provide for its inhabitants and which, in the case of the Indian peoples of Brazil, require special protective measures, are insufficient in terms of preventing and finding a solution to the ever-continuing usurpation of their possessions and rights. * * *

f.   The Yanomami people have obtained full recognition of their right to ownership of their land. Their integrity as a people and as individuals is under constant attack by both invading prospectors and the environmental pollution they create. State protection against these constant pressures and invasions is irregular and feeble, so that they are constantly in danger and their environment is suffering constant deterioration.

The Commission therefore makes the following recommendations:

b.   To provide FUNAI [the national agency for indigenous affairs] with all types of resources to enable it to carry out its functions as regards completing the demarcation of lands as well as providing advisory services and legal advice to the Indian peoples. * * *

e.   To institute federal protection measures with regard to Indian lands threatened by invaders, with particular attention to those of the Yanomami, and in Amazonia in general, including an increase in controlling, prosecuting and imposing severe punishment on the actual perpetrators and architects of such crimes, as well as the state agents who are active or passive accomplices. * * *

b.   PORT HOPE

In another case addressing the right to life, the United Nations Human Rights Committee indicated a willingness to recognize environmental harm as a violation of the right to life contained in Article 6(1) of the International Covenant on Civil and Political Rights, although the petition was dismissed for failing to exhaust domestic remedies. *See* Port Hope Environmental Group v. Canada, Decision of the Human Rights Committee under the Optional Protocol to the International Covenant on Civil and Political Rights, U.N. Communication CCPR/C/17/D/67/1980.

The right to life in an environmental context has also been addressed by several national courts. *See infra* Section IV.B.

c.   MENS REA REQUIREMENT FOR VIOLATIONS OF THE RIGHT TO LIFE

As the interpretation of the right to life continues to evolve to address environmental threats, it is necessary to consider the mental state the defendant must have to prove a violation of that right. This is discussed in the following excerpt from Herz, who also discusses the possibility of "a consistent pattern" of violations of the right to life, and how such a pattern may enhance the customary status of a norm.

Mens rea is a critical issue [in U.S. courts at least], since plaintiffs will be unlikely to be able to show a TNC purposefully threatened lives through environmental damage, even in cases where it would be relatively easy to prove that the company acted with knowledge or recklessness regarding this effect.
. . .

Neither [Port Hope] . . . nor the Yanomami Case involved allegations that the State acted with the purpose of threatening plaintiffs' lives. Member States of the Council of Europe have agreed to impose criminal sanctions on those who create pollution that causes death or serious injury through negligence, or, if a party expressly declares, gross negligence. Moreover, commentators observe that international legal liability for damaging the environment in ways that pose "grave risks to life . . . should arise irrespective of whether the act or omission in question is deliberate, reckless or negligent." [The requirement] " 'that States adopt positive measures,' such as 'measures to reduce infant mortality and to increase life expectancy . . . [and] eliminate malnutrition and epidemics' " [shows that] international law takes a broad view of the mental state required to violate the right to life, and clearly does not require purpose.
. . .

Under the customary state practice which emerged from international and national military prosecutions involving mistreatment of war prisoners and civilians, "murder" includes the creation of conditions likely to result in death if the creation of such conditions rises to the level of common-law manslaughter. That offense typically involves some degree of negligence additional to that necessary to support ordinary tort liability, although how much more is not entirely clear. The critical point for present purposes is that international law does not require a *mens rea* of purpose or even knowledge to prove murder. Therefore, [a claim that the right has been violated should be sufficient] in cases in which a corporation's environmental degradation displays a sufficient degree of indifference to human life. American jurisprudence supports this conclusion, since courts ordinarily apply an "indifference" standard in right to life cases under substantive due process law. Thus, American practice itself contributes to the international consensus recognizing that standard.

The fact that the above discussion looks in part to the law of "murder" does not mean that right to life claims exist only where a plaintiff has actually died. Under international law, environmental harms presenting grave risks to life also violate the right. For example, in [Port Hope], the Human Rights Committee found that the complainant made out a prima facie case based on the threat to life the waste dump presented. Indeed, Article 3 of the Convention on the Protection of the Environment through Criminal Law mandates that States criminalize negligent or grossly negligent discharge of pollution which creates significant risk of death or serious injury, unless they specifically declare that this provision does not apply. American practice supports the view that actual deaths are unnecessary, since plaintiffs in due process cases can enjoin governmental actions that will violate constitutional rights in the future so long as a "real and immediate" danger right to life claims are proper in appropriate cases. . . .

While customary international law forbids even a single violation of the right to life, an aggregation of right to life claims may give rise to an additional claim. Customary law forbids a state-sponsored consistent pattern of gross violations of internationally recognized human rights. Where a defendant over a period of time degrades the environment or otherwise presents environmental hazards posing grave risks to life, in a manner severe enough to give rise to numerous right to life claims, plaintiffs should alternatively plead those claims as a "consistent pattern." Moreover, according to the Restatement, the "consistent pattern" norm precludes "infringements of recognized human rights that are not violations of customary law when committed singly or sporadically."

Herz, *op. cit.* at 577–80.

————

QUESTIONS AND DISCUSSION

1. The Human Rights Committee considered in its General Comment 6 that the right to life is "the supreme right from which no derogation is permitted even in time of public emergency which threatens the life of the nation.... It is a right which should not be interpreted narrowly ... [and] the protection of this right requires that States adopt positive measures," such as "measures to reduce infant mortality and to increase life expectancy ... to eliminate malnutrition and epidemics." CCPR/C/21/Rev.1, at. 4–5.

2. Do States, or the international community as a whole, have a duty to take measures to prevent and safeguard against environmental hazards? *See* R.G. RAMCHARAN, THE RIGHT TO LIFE, at 310–11 (The Hague, 1983) arguing that:

1. There is a strict duty upon States, as well as upon the international community as a whole, to take effective measures to prevent and safeguard against the occurrence of environmental hazards which threaten the lives of human beings. 2. Every State, as well as the United Nations (UNEP), should establish and operate adequate monitoring and early-warning systems to detect hazards or threats before they actually occur. 3. States which obtain information about the possible emergence of an environmental hazard to life in another State should inform the State at risk or at least alert UNEP on an urgent basis. 4. The right to life, as an imperative norm, takes priority above economic considerations and should, in all circumstances, be accorded priority. 5. States and other responsible entities (corporations or individuals) may be criminally or civilly responsible under international law for causing serious environmental hazards posing grave risks to life. This responsibility is a strict one, and should arise irrespective of whether the act or omission in question is deliberate, reckless or negligent. 6. Adequate avenues of recourse should be provided to individuals and groups at national, regional or international levels, to seek protection against serious environmental hazards to life. The establishment of such avenues of recourse is essential for dealing with such risks before they actually materialize.

3. Given that the right to life is non-derogable, how would you balance environmental protection with other rights, including the right to development?

4. The European Court of Human Rights has been less willing to recognize that environmental pollution may violate an individual's right to life as contained in Article 2 of the European Convention on Human Rights. In the case of *X. v. Austria*, the Court narrowly interpreted Article 2, holding that it primarily protects *physical life* and deprivations of it. *See X. v. Austria*, App. No. 8278/78, 18 Eur. Comm'n H.R. Dec. & Rep. 154 (1980).

5. Food security is inextricably linked to an environment free from degradation and it depends on environmentally and socially sustainable development. *See* Asbjørn Eide, Right to Adequate Food as a Human Right, Study Series No. 1, United Nations publication, Sales No. E.89.XIV.2, 1989. International articulations of the right to an adequate standard of living–including those set forth in the Universal Declaration of Human Rights and the International Covenant on Economic, Social and Cultural Rights–recognize the right to food as an essential component of the right to health. Principle 31 of the Vienna Declaration and Program of Action of the World Conference on Human Rights also proclaims that food shall not be used as a tool for political pressure. In her Final Report to the Sub–Commission on Prevention of Discrimination and Protection of Minorities, the U.N. Special Rapporteur Fatma Ksentini included food security and the issue of food deprivation as a weapon. The Report states:

> Special attention should be devoted to eliminating the use of food as a weapon, whether in times of armed conflict or as a more general tool of oppression. In either case, interference with access to, production of and distribution of food often leads to severe environmental stresses and forces people to sacrifice long-term environmental sustainability in order to meet short-term subsistence needs.

See Ksentini Report, at 190.

––––––––

2. RIGHT TO A HEALTHY ENVIRONMENT

The right to a healthy environment is contained in both the African and Inter–American human rights systems. The African Charter provides that "All peoples shall have the right to a generally satisfactory environment favorable to their development." AFRICAN CHARTER ON HUMAN AND PEOPLES' RIGHTS, June 27, 1981, art. 24, 21 I.L.M. 58, 60. While the Commission has not addressed the right, several national courts have addressed the right as expressed in their national constitutions. These cases are discussed in Section IV.B., *infra.*

The Inter–American system also contains the right to a healthy environment, although it cannot be enforced through an individual petition: "Everyone shall have the right to live in a healthy environment and to have access to basic public services." ADDITIONAL PROTOCOL TO THE AMERICAN CONVENTION ON HUMAN RIGHTS IN THE AREA OF ECONOMIC, SOCIAL AND CULTURAL RIGHTS, art. 11(1), 28 I.L.M. 161 ("Protocol of San Salvador" or "SSP"). While Article 11 cannot be enforced through an individual petition, it is incorporated, through Article 29 of the Declaration on the Rights and Duties of Man, into the existing rights in the Convention and Declaration, which must be interpreted accordingly. The following excerpt from the *Lhaka Honhat* amicus brief relies on Article 29 to support its argument that a trans-continental road cutting through the traditional territory of the Lhaka Honhat violated their right to a healthy environment.

Lhaka Honhat Amici Curiae Brief, *op. cit.* at 14–16

While the right to life and other rights of indigenous peoples have previously been interpreted in a manner that implicitly recognizes a corollary right to a healthy environment, Argentina has gone further and signed the "Protocol of San Salvador"....which gives express recognition to that right [in Article 11].... Argentina has also expressly recognized the right to a healthy environment in Article 41 of its Constitution:

All individuals have the right to a healthy and harmonious environment, conducive to human development and to productive activities that satisfy present needs without compromising future generations; and have the duty to preserve the environment. Environmental damage generates the priority and obligation to repair, according to law. The authorities will provide the protection of this right, the rational utilization of environmental resources, and the preservation of natural and cultural patrimony, biological diversity, and environmental information and education. The Nation will dictate the norms that contain the minimum budget for the protection, and to the provinces the necessary norms to complement these, without altering local jurisdictions. Dangerous, potentially dangerous, or radioactive wastes are prohibited from entering national territory.

By virtue of Article 29 of the American Convention, Argentina is bound to enforce this right.

This express recognition of the right to a healthy environment in the Inter–American system reflects the general trend in human rights and environmental law to recognize the right to a healthy environment. Despite stylistic variations, each articulation of the right to a healthy environment contains the same identifiable core: the right to an environment that supports physical and spiritual well being and development.

[Although Article 11's right to a healthy environment is not enforceable through an individual petition, it nevertheless must be enforced, by virtue of Article 29 of the American Convention, which provides a mechanism for the Court to adapt the Convention to the evolution of international law, as well as new concepts and trends, including the emergence of a right to a healthy environment as articulated in the San Salvador Protocol and the Argentine Constitution. Article 11 reflects the evolution of international law, as well as the trend of modern constitutions to create a right to a healthy environment, and it must be applied through the existing rights in the Convention and Declaration to protect the environment. As Judge Rodolfo E. Piza Escalante of the Inter–American Court of Human Rights instructed, Article 29 requires the Court,

> to interpret and integrate each standard of the Convention by utilizing the adjacent, underlying or overlying principles in other international instruments, in the country's own internal regulations and in the trends in effect in the matter of human rights, all of which are to some degree included in the Convention itself by virtue of the aforementioned Article 29, whose innovative breath is unmatched in any other international document.

Inter-Am.Ct.H.R., Proposed Amendments to the Naturalization Provisions of the Constitution of Costa Rica, Advisory Opinion OC–4/84 of January 19, 1984, (Ser. A.) No. 4 (1984), para.2,3, and 6.

Similarly, in Advisory Opinion No. 5, the Court stated that "if . . . both the American Convention and another international treaty are applicable, the rule most favorable to the individual must prevail."

QUESTIONS AND DISCUSSION

1. Many national constitutions have included the right to a healthy environment, *see infra* Section IV.B. Additionally, a growing number of national judicial decisions have recognized this right. *See* Fatma Zohra Ksentini, *Report on Human Rights and the Environment: Final Report of Special Rapporteur*, Annex III E/CN.4/Sub.2/1994/9, 6 July 1994; G.A. Res. 45/94, U.N. Doc. A/45/94, at 2 (1991)("all individuals are entitled to live in an environment adequate for their health and well-being"); *see also* HAGUE DECLARATION ON THE ENVIRONMENT, Mar. 11, 1989, 28 I.L.M. 1308, 1309 (recognizing "the right to live in dignity in a viable global environment"). The right to a healthy environment is expressed in several other "soft law" instruments, including the 1972 Stockholm Declaration ("Man has the fundamental right to freedom, equality and adequate conditions of life, in an environment of a quality that permits a life of dignity and well-being, and he bears a solemn responsibility to protect and improve the environment for present and future generations") and the 1992 Rio Declaration ("Human beings are at the center of concerns for sustainable development. They are entitled to a healthy and productive life in harmony with nature").

2. The ILO Convention on the Rights of Indigenous and Tribal Peoples states:

Article 4:1 Special measures shall be adopted as appropriate for safeguarding the ... cultures and environment of the peoples concerned. ...

Article 7:4 Governments shall take measures, in co-operation with the peoples concerned, to protect and preserve the environment of the territories they inhabit. ...

Article 15:1 The rights of the peoples concerned to the natural resources pertaining to their lands shall be specially safeguarded. These rights include the right of these peoples to participate in the use, management and conservation of these resources.

CONVENTION CONCERNING INDIGENOUS AND TRIBAL PEOPLES IN INDEPENDENT COUNTRIES, June 27, 1989, arts. 4, 7, 13, 15, 28 I.L.M. 1384, 1385–87. The Proposed American Declaration on the Rights of Indigenous Peoples, approved by the InterAmerican Commission on February 26, 1997, contains a specific "Right to Environmental Protection" in Article XIII, which states:

1. Indigenous peoples have the right to a safe and healthy environment, which is an essential condition for the enjoyment of the right to life and collective well-being.

2. Indigenous peoples have the right to be informed of measures which will affect their environment, including information that ensures their effective participation in actions and policies that might affect it.

3. Indigenous peoples shall have the right to conserve, restore and protect their environment, and the productive capacity of their lands, territories and resources.

4. Indigenous peoples have the right to participate fully in formulating, planning, managing and applying governmental programmes of conservation of their lands, territories and resources.

5. Indigenous peoples have the right to assistance from their states for purposes of environmental protection, and may receive assistance from international organizations.

See also DRAFT UNITED NATIONS DECLARATION ON THE RIGHTS OF INDIGENOUS PEOPLES, Article 28, U.N. Doc. E/CN.4/Sub.2/1994/2/Add.1 (recognizing the right of indigenous peoples to "protection of the total environment ... of their lands ... as well as to assistance for this purpose from States and through international cooperation").

3. The right to a healthy environment and common law nuisance share many similarities and antecedents. A public nuisance is an "act or omission 'which obstructs or causes inconvenience or damage to the public in the exercise of rights common to all' . . . [including] . . . interference with the public health. . . ." *See* W. PAGE KEETON ET. AL., PROSSER AND KEETON ON THE LAW OF TORTS, § 90, at 644 (5th ed. 1984). A successful plaintiff in a nuisance action must prove "substantial and unreasonable interference" with the public. *See* 58 AM. JUR. 2D *Nuisances* § 41–42 (1989). Such an interference may be found when defendant's conduct decreases the environmental quality of the affected property to a level lower than that which the public reasonably expects. In *Georgia v. Tennessee Copper Co.,* a Tennessee copper company was discharging "noxious" gases that crossed over into Georgia causing the destruction of "forests, orchards and crops." 206 U.S. 230, 236 (1907). Justice Holmes, delivering the opinion of the court, stated "we are satisfied by a preponderance of evidence that the sulphurous fumes cause and threaten damage on so considerable a scale to the forests and vegetable life, if not to health, within the plaintiff State as to make out a case" of nuisance. *Id* at 238–239. *See also United States v. Reserve Mining Co.,* 380 F.Supp. 11, 54–55 (D.Minn.1974) ("Defendants are exposing thousands to significant quantities of a known human carcinogen. . . . The sanctity of human life is of too great value to this Court to permit such a thing.")

4. The *Trail Smelter Arbitration*, discussed supra, Chapter 9, at 504, applied the concept *of sic utere ut alienum non laedas* (one should use one's own property in such a manner as not to injure that of another) when it held that "[a] State owes at all times a duty to protect other States against injurious acts by individuals from within its jurisdiction." *Trail Smelter (U.S. v. Can.),* 3 R.I.A.A. 1905, 1963 (1941)(*citing* C. Eagleton, The Responsibility of States in International Law 80 (1928)). *Sic utere* is the equivalent of nuisance in international law but is available only to States, not individuals.

---

3. THE RIGHT TO RESPECT FOR PRIVATE AND FAMILY LIFE AND HOME

The right of privacy in Article 8 of the European Convention on Human Rights has been used successfully to address environmental harm. Article 8 states:

1. Everyone has the right to respect for his private and family life, his home and his correspondence.

2. There shall be no interference by a public authority with the exercise of this right except such as is in accordance with the law and is necessary in a democratic society in the interests of national security, public safety or the economic well-being of the country, for the prevention of disorder or crime, for the protection of health or morals, or for the protection of the rights and freedoms of others.

EUROPEAN CONVENTION FOR THE PROTECTION OF HUMAN RIGHTS AND FUNDAMENTAL FREEDOMS, Nov. 4, 1950, art. 8, 312 U.N.T.S. 222, 246.

The right to privacy and family life are also contained in Article 12 of the Universal Declaration, Article 17 of the American Convention, Article VI of the American Declaration, and Article 18 of the African Charter. The European Human Rights Court discussed the right to privacy in the following case involving a waste treatment facility operating without compliance with environmental standards. Noxious fumes from the facility made the petitioner's daughter sick and forced the family to abandon their home.

Lopez Ostra v. Spain

App. No. 16798/90, 20 Eur. H.R. Rep. 277 (1994) (Eur. Ct. H.R.)

The case was referred to the Court by the European Commission of Human Rights.

Mrs. Gregoria López Ostra, a Spanish national, lives in Lorca (Murcia). At the material time she and her husband and their two daughters had their home in the district of "Diputación del Rio, el Lugarico", a few hundred metres from the town centre.... The town of Lorca has a heavy concentration of leather industries. Several tanneries there, all belonging to a limited company called SACURSA, had a plant for the treatment of liquid and solid waste built with a State subsidy on municipal land twelve meters away from the applicant's home.

The plant began to operate in July 1988 without the license from the municipal authorities required by Regulation 6 of the 1961 regulations on activities classified as causing nuisance and being unhealthy, noxious and dangerous ("the 1961 regulations")....

Owing to a malfunction, its start-up released gas fumes, pestilential smells and contamination, which immediately caused health problems and nuisance to many Lorca people, particularly those living in the applicant's district. The town council evacuated the local residents and rehoused them free of charge in the town center for the months of July, August and September 1988.

On 9 September 1988, following numerous complaints and in the light of reports from the health authorities and the Environment and Nature Agency ... for the Murcia region, the town council ordered cessation of one of the plant's activities—the settling of chemical and organic residues in water tanks—while permitting the treatment of waste water contaminated with chromium to continue.... In October the applicant and her family returned to their flat and lived there until February 1992 ....

2. Complaint of an environmental health offence ...

An initial report of 13 October 1992 by a scientist from the University of Murcia ... stated that hydrogen sulfide (a colorless gas, soluble in water, with a characteristic rotten-egg smell) had been detected on the site in concentrations exceeding the permitted levels....

The investigation file contains several medical certificates and expert opinions concerning the effects on the health of those living near the plant. ... Dr de Ayala Sánchez, a pediatrician, stated that Mrs. López Ostra's daughter, Cristina, presented a clinical picture of nausea, vomiting, allergic reactions, anorexia, etc., which could only be explained by the fact that she was living in a highly polluted area....

In an expert report of 16 April 1993 the Ministry of Justice's Institute of Forensic Medicine in Cartagena indicated that gas concentrations in houses near the plant exceeded the permitted limit. It noted that the applicant's daughter and her nephew, Fernando López Gómez, presented typical symptoms of chronic absorption of the gas in question, periodically manifested in the form of acute bronchopulmonary infections. It considered that there was a relationship of cause and effect between this clinical picture and the levels of gas.

* * *

The applicant alleged that there had been a violation of Articles 8 and 3 (art. 8, art. 3) of the Convention on account of the smells, noise and polluting fumes caused by a plant for the treatment of liquid and solid waste sited a few meters away from her home. She held the Spanish authorities responsible, alleging that they had adopted a passive attitude.

II. ALLEGED VIOLATION OF ARTICLE 8 OF THE CONVENTION

... Mrs. López Ostra maintained that, despite its partial shutdown on 9 September 1988, the plant continued to emit fumes, repetitive noise and strong smells, which made her family's living conditions unbearable and caused both her and them serious health problems. She alleged in this connection that her right to respect for her home had been infringed.

The Government disputed that the situation was really as described and as serious.

Naturally, severe environmental pollution may affect individuals' well-being and prevent them from enjoying their homes in such a way as to affect their private and family life adversely, without, however, seriously endangering their health.

Whether the question is analyzed in terms of a positive duty on the State— to take reasonable and appropriate measures to secure the applicant's rights under paragraph 1 of Article 8 (art. 8–1)-, as the applicant wishes in her case, or in terms of an "interference by a public authority" to be justified in accordance with paragraph 2 (art. 8–2), the applicable principles are broadly similar. In both contexts regard must be had to the fair balance that has to be struck between the competing interests of the individual and of the community as a whole, and in any case the State enjoys a certain margin of appreciation. Furthermore, even in relation to the positive obligations flowing from the first paragraph of Article 8 (art. 8–1), in striking the required balance the aims mentioned in the second paragraph (art. 8–2) may be of a certain relevance.

It appears from the evidence that the waste-treatment plant in issue was built by SACURSA in July 1988 to solve a serious pollution problem in Lorca due to the concentration of tanneries. Yet as soon as it started up, the plant caused nuisance and health problems to many local people

Admittedly, the Spanish authorities, and in particular the Lorca municipality, were theoretically not directly responsible for the emissions in question. However, as the Commission pointed out, the town allowed the plant to be built on its land and the State subsidized the plant's construction ...

The Court notes, however, that the family had to bear the nuisance caused by the plant for over three years before moving house with all the attendant inconveniences. They moved only when it became apparent that the situation could continue indefinitely and when Mrs. López Ostra's daughter's pediatrician recommended that they do so. Under these circumstances, the municipality's offer could not afford complete redress for the nuisance and inconveniences to which they had been subjected.

Having regard to the foregoing, and despite the margin of appreciation left to the respondent State, the Court considers that the State did not succeed in striking a fair balance between the interest of the town's economic well-being— that of having a waste-treatment plant—and the applicant's effective enjoyment of her right to respect for her home and her private and family life.

There has accordingly been a violation of Article 8 (art. 8).

Lopez Ostra was a turning point for environmental considerations in the European system. In addition to being the first time the Court found a breach of the Convention as a consequence of environmental harm, Spain was found to have breached an affirmative duty to ensure the respect of a derivative right not explicitly set forth under the Convention.

QUESTIONS AND DISCUSSION

1. Note that this case was brought by a private individual for harm caused by a privately owned industrial plant. The European Court, like other human rights courts, requires that cases be brought against a government. The case focuses not on the environmental harm itself, but on the duty of the State to protect its citizens from environmental harm. In holding against the State, the Court acknowledged the positive duty of public authorities to take necessary measures to protect the individual's rights.

2. In this case, the Court awarded compensatory damages for the environmental harm. Specifically, it held that, the applicant was entitled to compensation because "she undeniably sustained non-pecuniary damage." These included damage for distress and anxiety at the situation in addition to the nuisance caused by the fumes, noise and smells. The decision marked a departure from the general practice envisaged by the European Convention's drafters, which presumed that determinations of damages would be remanded to the national judicial bodies of the Contracting Parties.

---

4. RIGHT TO SELF–DETERMINATION, CULTURAL EXPRESSION, AND RELIGION

The survival of indigenous peoples depends upon the integrity of their environment. One way in which environmental degradation violates indigenous rights is through direct and indirect harm to the people and the resources that sustain them. Yet destruction of the environment also affects indigenous rights relating to self-determination, the right to cultural expression, and the right to religion.

---

a. SELF–DETERMINATION

The right to self-determination of peoples (Art.
1) CCPR General comment 12 (1984)

1. In accordance with the purposes and principles of the Charter of the United Nations, article 1 of the International Covenant on Civil and Political Rights recognizes that all peoples have the right of self-determination. The right of self-determination is of particular importance because its realization is an essential condition for the effective guarantee and observance of individual human rights and for the promotion and strengthening of those rights. It is for that reason that States set forth the right of self-determination in a provision of positive law in both Covenants and placed this provision as article 1 apart from and before all of the other rights in the two Covenants.

2. Article 1 enshrines an inalienable right of all peoples as described in its paragraphs 1 and 2. By virtue of that right they freely "determine their political status and freely pursue their economic, social and cultural development". The article imposes on all States parties corresponding obligations. This right and the corresponding obligations concerning its implementation are interrelated with other provisions of the Covenant and rules of international law.

3. Although the reporting obligations of all States parties include article 1, only some reports give detailed explanations regarding each of its paragraphs. The Committee has noted that many of them completely ignore article 1, provide inadequate information in regard to it or confine themselves to a reference to election laws. The Committee considers it highly desirable that States parties' reports should contain information on each paragraph of article 1.

4. With regard to paragraph 1 of article 1, States parties should describe the constitutional and political processes which in practice allow the exercise of this right.

5. Paragraph 2 affirms a particular aspect of the economic content of the right of self-determination, namely the right of peoples, for their own ends, freely to "dispose of their natural wealth and resources without prejudice to any obligations arising out of international economic cooperation, based upon the principle of mutual benefit, and international law. In no case may a people be deprived of its own means of subsistence". This right entails corresponding duties for all States and the international community. States should indicate any factors or difficulties which prevent the free disposal of their natural wealth and resources contrary to the provisions of this paragraph and to what extent that affects the enjoyment of other rights set forth in the Covenant.

The following General Comment distinguishes self-determination from the related right to culture and from the right to equal protection and non-discrimination:

HUMAN RIGHTS COMMITTEE, GENERAL COMMENT 23
ARTICLE 27 (Fiftieth session, 1994)

Compilation of General Comments and General Recommendations
Adopted by Human Rights Treaty Bodies, U.N. Doc.
HRI/GEN/1/Rev.1 at 38 (1994).

1. Article 27 of the Covenant provides that, in those States in which ethnic, religious or linguistic minorities exist, persons belonging to these minorities shall not be denied the right, in community with the other members of their group, to enjoy their own culture, to profess and practice their own religion, or to use their own language. The Committee observes that this article establishes and recognizes a right which is conferred on individuals belonging to minority groups and which is distinct from, and additional to, all the other rights which, as individuals in common with everyone else, they are already entitled to enjoy under the Covenant.

2. In some communications submitted to the Committee under the Optional Protocol, the right protected under article 27 has been confused with the right of peoples to self-determination proclaimed in article 1 of the Covenant. Further, in reports submitted by States parties under article 40 of the Covenant, the obligations placed upon States parties under article 27 have sometimes been confused with their duty under article 2.1 to ensure the enjoyment

of the rights guaranteed under the Covenant without discrimination and also with equality before the law and equal protection of the law under article 26.

3.1.   The Covenant draws a distinction between the right to self-determination and the rights protected under article 27. The former is expressed to be a right belonging to peoples and is dealt with in a separate part (Part I) of the Covenant. Self-determination is not a right cognizable under the Optional Protocol. Article 27, on the other hand, relates to rights conferred on individuals as such and is included, ... and is cognizable under the Optional Protocol.

3.2.   The enjoyment of the rights to which article 27 relates does not prejudice the sovereignty and territorial integrity of a State party. At the same time, one or other aspect of the rights of individuals protected under that article—for example, to enjoy a particular culture—may consist in a way of life which is closely associated with territory and use of its resources. This may particularly be true of members of indigenous communities constituting a minority.

4.   The Covenant also distinguishes the rights protected under article 27 from the guarantees under articles 2.1 and 26. The entitlement, under article 2.1, to enjoy the rights under the Covenant without discrimination applies to all individuals within the territory or under the jurisdiction of the State whether or not those persons belong to a minority. In addition, there is a distinct right provided under article 26 for equality before the law, equal protection of the law, and non-discrimination in respect of rights granted and obligations imposed by the States. It governs the exercise of all rights, whether protected under the Covenant or not, which the State party confers by law on individuals within its territory or under its jurisdiction, irrespective of whether they belong to the minorities specified in article 27 or not. Some States parties who claim that they do not discriminate on grounds of ethnicity, language or religion, wrongly contend, on that basis alone, that they have no minorities.

---

b.   CULTURE

Article 27 of the Universal Declaration; Article 13 of the American Declaration; and Articles 15.1 and 15.2 of the ICESCR all contain articulations of the right to culture. In addition, Article 27 of the International Covenant on Civil and Political Rights states:

> In those States in which ethnic, religious or linguistic minorities exist, persons belonging to such minorities shall not be denied the right, in community with the other members of their group, to enjoy their own culture, to profess and practice their own religion, or to use their own language.

International Covenant of Civil and Political Rights, Dec. 16, 1966, art. 27, 999 U.N.T.S. 171.

The next cases consider how environmental impact can affect the right to culture. In the first case, the U.N. Human Rights Committee addresses the level of environmental harm necessary to violate the cultural rights of the Sami–an ethnic group from Finland–who depend upon the integrity of the environment for their cultural survival. The case considers a claim made by the chief of the Lake Lubicon band in Canada, alleging that destruction of the lands that provided the band with subsistence violated their rights. This case illustrates an important distinction between a claim based on the right to self-determination and a claim on the basis of the right to culture. Finally, in the Report on the Situation of Indigenous People in Ecuador, the Inter–American Commission discusses the violation of the cultural rights of the Huaorani Indians due to the construction of a road through their territory.

Landsman v. Finland
U.N. Communication CCPR/C/58/D/671/1995

2.1   The authors are reindeer breeders of Sami ethnic origin; they challenge the plans of the Finnish Central Forestry Board to approve logging and the construction of roads in an area covering about 3,000 hectares of the area of the Muotkatunturi Herdsmen's Committee. The members of the Muotkatunturi Herdsmen's Committee occupy areas in the North of Finland, covering a total of 255,000 hectares, of which one fifth is suitable for winter herding. The 3,000 hectares are situated within these winter herding lands. * * *

2.3   The activities of the Central Forestry Board were initiated in late October 1994, but stopped on 10 November 1994 by an injunction of the Supreme Court of Finland (Korkein oikeus). According to the authors, a representative of the Central Forestry Board has recently stated that the activities will resume before the winter; they express concern that the logging will resume in October or November 1995, since the injunction issued by the Supreme Court lapsed on 22 June 1995. * * *

2.4   The authors affirm that some 40 per cent of the total number of the reindeer owned by the Muotkatunturi Herdsmen's Committee feed on the disputed lands during winter. The authors observe that the area in question consists of old untouched forests, which means that both the ground and the trees are covered with lichen. This is of particular importance due to its suitability as food for young calves and its utility as "emergency food" for elder reindeer during extreme weather conditions. * * *

2.6   The authors observe that logging is not the only activity with adverse consequences for Sami reindeer herding. They concede that the dispute concerns a specific geographic area and the logging and construction of roads in the area. However, they believe that other activities, such as quarrying, that have already taken place, and such logging as has taken place or will take place, as well as any future mining (for which licences have already been granted by the Ministry of Trade and Industry), on the total area traditionally used by the Samis, should be taken into consideration when considering the facts of their new case. In this context, the authors refer to the Central Forestry Board's submission to the Inari Court of First Instance (Inarin kihlakunnanoikeus) of 28 July 1993, where the Board expressed its intention of logging, by the year 2005, a total of 55,000 cubic metres of wood from 1,100 hectares of forests in the Western parts of the winter herding lands of the Muotkatunturi Herdsmen's Committee. The authors observe that logging has already been carried out in other parts of the winter herding lands, in particular in the Paadarskaidi area in the Southeast. * * *

The complaint

3.1   The authors claim that the facts as described violate their rights under article 27, and invoke the Committee's Views on the cases of Ivan Kitok v. Sweden (communication No. 197/1985), Ominayak v. Canada (communication No. 167/1984) and Ilmari Länsman et al. v. Finland (communication No. 511/1992), as well as ILO Convention No. 169 on the rights of indigenous and tribal people in independent countries, the Committee's General Comment No.

23[50] on article 27, and the United Nations Draft Declaration on Indigenous Peoples.

3.2 Finally, the authors, who contend that logging and road construction might resume in October or November 1995 and is therefore imminent, request interim measures of protection under rule 86 of the rules of procedure, so as to prevent irreparable damage. * * *

Examination of the merits

10.1 ... The issue to be determined is whether logging of forests in an area covering approximately 3,000 hectares of the area of the Muotkatunturi Herds-men's Committee (of which the authors are members)—i.e. such logging as has already been carried out and future logging—violates the authors' rights under article 27 of the Covenant.

10.2 It is undisputed that the authors are members of a minority within the meaning of article 27 of the Covenant and as such have the right to enjoy their own culture. It is also undisputed that reindeer husbandry is an essential element of their culture; that some of the authors practice other economic activities in order to gain supplementary income does not change this conclusion. The Committee recalls that economic activities may come within the ambit of article 27, if they are an essential element of the culture of an ethnic community. ...

10.3 Article 27 requires that a member of a minority shall not be denied the right to enjoy his culture. Measures whose impact amounts to a denial of the right are incompatible with the obligations under article 27. As noted by the Committee previously in its Views on case No. 511/1992, however, measures that have a certain limited impact on the way of life and the livelihood of persons belonging to a minority will not necessarily amount to a denial of the rights under article 27.

10.4 The crucial question to be determined in the present case is whether the logging that has already taken place within the area specified in the communication, as well as such logging as has been approved for the future and which will be spread over a number of years, is of such proportions as to deny the authors the right to enjoy their culture in that area. The Committee recalls the terms of paragraph 7 of its General Comment on article 27, according to which minorities or indigenous groups have a right to the protection of traditional activities such as hunting, fishing or reindeer husbandry, and that measures must be taken "to ensure the effective participation of members of minority communities in decisions which affect them". ...

10.5 It transpires that the State party's authorities *did* go through the process of weighing the authors' interests and the general economic interests in the area specified in the complaint when deciding on the most appropriate measures of forestry management, i.e. logging methods, choice of logging areas and construction of roads in these areas. The domestic courts considered specifically whether the proposed activities constituted a denial of article 27 rights. The Committee is not in a position to conclude, on the evidence before it, that the impact of logging plans would be such as to amount to a denial of the authors' rights under article 27 or that the finding of the Court of Appeal affirmed by the Supreme Court, misinterpreted and/or misapplied article 27 of the Covenant in the light of the facts before it.

10.6 As far as future logging activities are concerned, the Committee observes that on the basis of the information available to it, the State party's forestry authorities have approved logging on a scale which, while resulting in additional work and extra expenses for the authors and other reindeer herdsmen, does not appear to threaten the survival of reindeer husbandry. . . . .

10.7   The Committee considers that *if* logging plans were to be approved on a scale larger than that already agreed to for future years in the area in question or if it could be shown that the effects of logging already planned were more serious than can be foreseen at present, then it may have to be considered whether it would constitute a violation of the authors' right to enjoy their own culture within the meaning of article 27. The Committee is aware, on the basis of earlier communications, that other large scale exploitations touching upon the natural environment, such as quarrying, are being planned and implemented in the area where the Sami people live. Even though in the present communication the Committee has reached the conclusion that the facts of the case do not reveal a violation of the rights of the authors, the Committee deems it important to point out that the State party must bear in mind when taking steps affecting the rights under article 27, that though different activities in themselves may not constitute a violation of this article, such activities, taken together, may erode the rights of Sami people to enjoy their own culture.

11.   The Human Rights Committee, acting under article 5, paragraph 4, of the Optional Protocol to the International Covenant on Civil and Political Rights, is of the view that the facts as found by the Committee do not reveal a breach of article 27 of the Covenant.

In the case of *Bernard Ominayak & The Lubicon Lake Band v. Canada*, the applicants alleged that the government of the province of Alberta had deprived the Lake Lubicon Indians of their means of subsistence and their right to self-determination by selling oil and gas concessions on their lands. The right to self determination, however, is conferred upon peoples, and cannot be the basis for an individual petition under Article 1. Nevertheless, the Human Rights Committee found that historical inequities and certain more recent developments, including oil and gas exploration, were threatening the way of life of the Lake Lubicon Band and were thus violating minority rights, relying on Article 27 of the ICCPR protecting the right to culture. U.N. GAOR Human Rights Comm., 45th Sess., Supp. No. 40, Annex IX, Communication No. 167/1984, at 27, U.N. Doc. A/45/40 (1990).

The Inter–American Commission also discusses the right to culture in relation to the Huaorani indians. *See* Report on the Situation of Human Rights in Ecuador, Inter–Am. C.H.R., at 81–83, OEA/ser. L./V./II.96, doc. 10 rev. 1 (1997).

––––––

5.   THE RIGHT TO USE AND ENJOY PROPERTY

Several international human rights instruments affirm the right to the use and enjoyment of property, for example, Protocol 1 of the European Convention and Article 21 of the Inter–American Convention, which states:

1.   Everyone has the right to the use and enjoyment of his property. The law may subordinate such use and enjoyment to the interest of society.

2.   No one shall be deprived of his property except upon payment of just compensation, for reasons of public utility or social interest, and in the cases and according to the forms established by law. . . .

American Convention on Human Rights, July, 18 1978, 1144 U.N.T.S. 143, at art. 21.

The first decision protecting property rights in a case concerning the environment was decided August 31, 2001 by the Inter–American Court of Human Rights. In the case of the *Mayagna (Sumo) Community of Awas Tingni,* the Court affirmed the existence of indigenous peoples' collective rights to their land, resources, and environment and declared that the government of Nicaragua had violated the Community's rights to property and judicial protection when it granted concessions to a foreign company to log on the Community's traditional land without either consulting with the Community or obtaining its consent. Deeming Nicaragua's legal protections for indigenous lands "illusory and ineffective," the Court declared that the government not only discriminated against the Community by denying them equal protection under the laws of the State, but also violated its obligations under international law to conform its domestic laws to give effect to the rights and duties articulated in the American Convention on Human Rights.

Case of The Mayagna (Sumo) Indigenous Community of Awas Tingni, Judgment, August 31, 2001, Inter-Am. Ct. H.R. (Ser. C) (2001)

144. "Property" can be defined as those material goods capable of being acquired, as well as all rights that can be deemed to make up the assets of a person; this concept encompasses all movable and immovable goods, tangible and intangible goods as well as any other intangible object to which a value can be assigned. * * *

146. The terms of an international human rights treaty have autonomous meaning, such that they may not be limited by the meaning attributed to them under domestic law. Also, international human rights treaties are living instruments, the interpretation of which should be adapted to changes over time, and, in particular, to present-day conditions. * * *

149. Given the characteristics of the instant case, it is necessary to understand the concept of property in indigenous communities. Among indigenous communities, there is a communal tradition as demonstrated by their communal form of collective ownership of their lands, in the sense that ownership is not centered in the individual but rather in the group and in the community. By virtue of the fact of their very existence, indigenous communities have the right to live freely on their own territories; the close relationship that the communities have with the land must be recognized and understood as a foundation for their cultures, spiritual life, cultural integrity and economic survival. For indigenous communities, the relationship with the land is not merely one of possession and production, but also a material and spiritual element that they should fully enjoy, as well as a means through which to preserve their cultural heritage and pass it on to future generations.

150. In respect of this, . . . Nicaragua [law] . . . declares in article 36 that:

Communal property is comprised of the land, water, and forest which have traditionally belonged to the Communities of the Atlantic Coast, and they are subject to the following provisions:

1. Communal lands are inalienable; they cannot be gifted, sold, seized, or encumbered, and are imprescriptible.

2.   The Communities' inhabitants have the right to work parcels on the communal property and to the usufructory rights of the resources generated by that work.

151.   The customary law of indigenous peoples should especially be taken into account because of the effects that flow from it. As a product of custom, possession of land should suffice to entitle indigenous communities without title to their land to obtain official recognition and registration of their rights of ownership. * * *

153.   The Court deems that, consistent with the terms of article 5 of the Political Constitution of Nicaragua, the members of the Awas Tingni Community have a communal property right over the lands they currently inhabit, without prejudice to the rights of the neighboring indigenous communities. However, the Court emphasizes that the limits of the territory over which that property right exists have not been effectively delimited and demarcated by the State. This situation has created a climate of permanent uncertainty among the members of the Awas Tingni Community inasmuch as they do not know with certainty the geographic extension of their right of communal property, and consequently they do not know up to what point they may freely use and enjoy the corresponding resources. In this context, the Court considers that the members of the Awas Tingni Community have the right that the State,

a) delimit, demarcate, and title the territory of the Community's property; and

b) cease, until this official delimitation, demarcation and titling is performed, acts which could cause agents of the State, or third parties acting with its acquiescence or tolerance, to affect the existence, value, use, or enjoyment of the resources located in the geographic area in which the Community members live and carry out their activities.

Because of the reasons stated, and keeping in mind the criterion adopted by the Court in its application of article 29(b) of the Convention (*supra* , para. 148), the Court finds that, in light of article 21 of the Convention, the State has violated the right of the members of the Awas Tingni Mayagna Community to the use and enjoyment of their property, by not delimiting and demarcating their communal property, and by authorizing concessions to third parties for the exploitation of the land and natural resources in an area that, wholly or partially, corresponds to the lands that should be delimited, demarcated, and titled in their favor. * * *

155.   For the above reasons, the Court concludes that the State violated article 21 of the American Convention, to the detriment of the members of the Mayagna (Sumo) Community of Awas Tingni, in connection with articles 1(1) and 2 of the Convention.

———

QUESTIONS AND DISCUSSION

1.   The *Awas Tingni* case is the first case before the Inter–American Court that directly addresses the territorial rights of indigenous communities. Human rights for indigenous peoples necessarily include land rights, since indigenous communities' economic, cultural and spiritual traditions depend upon secure access to their ancestral lands. Without demarcation of their lands, the Community of Awas Tingni remains vulnerable to invasion by parties interested in natural resource exploitation. Threats to indigenous lands throughout the Atlantic Coast of Nicaragua have raised the possibility of social unrest and even violence. The Court's decision sets a far reaching precedent affirming indigenous land rights not only for the indigenous communities of the Atlantic Coast, but also for indigenous peoples throughout the hemisphere. *See* Press Release, *Landmark Victory for Indians in International Human Rights Case Against Nicaragua*, Indian Law Resource Center (2001).

2. The *Awas Tingni* case has already attracted significant attention worldwide from indigenous, environmental, and human rights groups, as well as influential media coverage. Significantly, the World Bank has conditioned a financial aid package set for Nicaragua on the development by the government of a specific plan to demarcate the traditional lands of the Miskito and Mayagna communities. This was the first time that the World Bank had placed such a condition on an aid package. *See* World Bank—Ministry of Agriculture and Forestry, Sustainable Forestry Investment Project, PID 52080, (appraisal date July 7, 1998) (Nicaragua).

3. A Report by the Inter–American Commission on the situation of indigenous people in Ecuador also concluded that the state had violated the land rights of an indigenous group in Ecuador. Specifically, in 1990 an indigenous coalition filed a petition on behalf of the Huaorani people, challenging Ecuador's approval of a proposal by Conoco Oil Company to build an access road dividing their territory. *See* the INTER-AMERICAN COMMISSION ON HUMAN RIGHTS REPORT ON THE SITUATION OF HUMAN RIGHTS IN ECUADOR, INTER-AM. C.H.R., AT 81–83, OEA/SER. L./V./II.96, DOC. 10 REV. 1 (1997)

4. Indigenous communities are entitled to special protections under human rights law, and because they depend so immediately on their environment, are particular sensitive to environmental abuses. But we all depend on our environment, and at some level, even those who are not members of vulnerable groups are subject to environmental threats. At what point would an environmental threat in your neighborhood become a human rights violation?

B.   PROCEDURAL RIGHTS

Procedural rights are a critical complement to substantive rights. They are enabling rights in that they make it possible for people to contribute actively to the protection of their environment. Denial of the fundamental rights such as freedom of association, of expression, and of the right to public participation, endangers the protection of substantive human rights, and increases the likelihood of environmental degradation and the chances that such damage will be irreversible.

The rights to receive information about and to participate in decisions that effect the environment, along with the right to an effective remedy, constitute "environmental due process." The Universal Declaration of Human Rights codifies these procedural rights in Article 8 (effective remedy); Article 19 (freedom of opinion and expression); Article 20 (freedom of association); Article 21 (right to take part in government); and Article 26 (right to education). The International Covenant on Civil and Political Rights set forth these same procedural guarantees as fundamental human rights in Articles 2(3), 19, 21, 22, and 25.

Violations of procedural rights were asserted in many of the cases discussed above, including: the right of individuals to information about government activities threatening the environment (*Yanomani* case), and a corresponding duty of the state to inform individuals directly affected

(*Guerra* case); the right of individuals to participate in decision-making which concerns the environment (*Huaorani* case), and a corresponding duty of states to facilitate citizen participation; and the right of individuals to recourse or remedy for environmental harm suffered (*Awas Tingni* case). *See generally,* Laura S. Ziemer, *Application in Tibet of the Principles on Human Rights and the Environment* 14 HARV. HUM. RTS. J. 233, 265 (2001).

———

1. RIGHT TO POPULAR PARTICIPATION

The right of popular participation is found in Article 23 of the Inter–American Convention:

> 1. Every citizen shall enjoy the following rights and opportunities:
>
> a. to take part in the conduct of public affairs, directly or through freely chosen representatives;
>
> b. to vote and to be elected in genuine periodic elections, which shall be by universal and equal suffrage and by secret ballot that guarantees the free expression of the will of the voters; and
>
> c. to have access, under general conditions of equality, to the public service of his country.
>
> 2. The law may regulate the exercise of the rights and opportunities referred to in the preceding paragraph only on the basis of age, nationality, residence, language, education, civil and mental capacity, or sentencing by a competent court in criminal proceedings.

See also Article 13 of the African Charter, Article 21 of the Universal Declaration of Human Rights, and Article 25 of the ICCPR.

In its 1997 Report on Ecuador, the Inter–American Commission found that the Huaorani Indian's rights to participation and to information (delineated in articles 23 & 13 of the American Convention) were violated because the State failed to inform them or consult them about oil development projects undertaken on their lands. In this regard, the Commission found that that:

> [The] State [must] take the measures necessary to ensure the meaningful and effective participation of indigenous representatives in the decision-making processes about development and other issues which affect them and their cultural survival. "Meaningful" in this sense necessarily implies that indigenous representatives have full access to the information which will facilitate their participation.

Inter–American Commission on Human Rights, Report on the Situation of Human Rights in Ecuador, Inter–Am. C.H.R., at 81–83, OEA/SER. L./V./II.96, Doc. 10 Rev. 1 (1997). *See also* Rio Declaration on the Human Environment, Principle 10 (1992), discussed *supra* Chapter 7, page 435; UNECE Convention on Access to Information, Public Participation in Decision-making and Access to Justice in Environmental Matters, 25 June 1998 (Aarhus, Denmark).

———

2.   THE RIGHT TO EQUAL PROTECTION AND TO BE FREE FROM DISCRIMINATION

Equal protection of the law and freedom from discrimination are two additional procedural rights that can impact indigenous communities and affect their ability to protect and enjoy their environment. The following excerpt illustrates these rights in the dispute between the Huaorani and the Government of Ecuador.

The American Convention protects the rights of minorities and prohibits minority discrimination. The American Convention, pursuant to the terms of Article 24, requires that all persons subject to the jurisdiction of a State Party be regarded as equal before the law, and be accorded equal protection of the law. This commitment is reinforced by the obligation set forth in Article 1.1 of the Convention to respect and ensure the guarantees set forth "without any discrimination for reasons of race, color, sex, language, religion, political or other opinion, national or social origin, economic status, birth, or any other social condition." * * *

A frequent complaint concerns the treatment of indigenous inhabitants within the judicial system. Indigenous representatives indicated that legal processes fail to respect or take into account indigenous legal systems and traditions. Representatives complained that processes against indigenous defendants were conducted in Spanish, and that translation was not provided for those who understood only their native language. Article 8 of the American Convention states that "the right of an accused to be assisted without charge by a translator or interpreter, if he does not understand or does not speak the language of the tribunal" is a minimum guarantee. The Commission expects that the recognition accorded to indigenous languages in their areas of use through the recent amendments to the Constitution will ensure that translation between Spanish and the indigenous language of the defendant is available in every case where it is required. * * *

Report on the Situation of Human Rights in Ecuador, op.cit.; *see also* Human Right Committee, General Comment 23, ¶ 4, *supra*.

———

3.   RIGHT TO REMEDY

The rights to judicial recourse and remedy are also key procedural rights that are applicable to environmental circumstances. While not an environmental case, the Inter–American Court's decision in *Velásquez Rodríguez* illustrates the States' obligation to provide a remedy. The case concerns a man who was forcibly disappeared and probably killed by the Honduran army or unknown attackers. In its decision, the Court held that, even if the attackers were private individuals, the total failure of the government authorities to try to find the victim or to give any remedy to the family was itself a violation.

An illegal act which violates human rights and which is initially not directly imputable to a State (for example, because it is the act of a private person ...) can lead to international responsibility of the State, not because of the act itself, but because of the lack of due diligence to prevent the violations or to respond to it as required by the Convention.... (para. 172) Where act of private parties that violate the Convention are not seriously investigated, those parties are aided in a sense by the government, thereby making the State responsible on the international plane (para. 177)

Velásquez Rodríguez case, Judgement of 29 July 1988, Inter–Am. C.H.R. (Ser. C) No. 4 (1988).

The European Court of Human Rights considered the issue of remedy in the case of a 16–year–old mentally handicapped Dutch girl who was sexually abused by the son-in-law of the director of a private nursing home. The Court held that the Dutch government violated the girl's right to privacy by not ensuring such a criminal remedy. The Court said that the positive obligation of the State to ensure respect for private and family life "may involve the adoption of measures designed to secure respect for private life even in the sphere of the relations of individuals between themselves". *X & Y v. Netherlands*, Ser. A, No. 91, 8 Eur. H.R. Rep. 235 (1985).

QUESTIONS AND DISCUSSION

1. Denial of standing denies the applicant the possibility to prevent harm and it also denies the possibility of reparations, compensation or other remedies. The Ksentini Report notes that in cases with environmental concerns, the Inter–American Commission on Human Rights has allowed "interest group" or "interested citizen" to bring actions, while the Council of Europe has required actual victims or relatives of actual victims. The United Nations Human Rights Committee allows collective communications but has implied that each of the individuals of the group must be able to allege essentially the same injury. In the view of the Special Rapporteur, standing must always be broadly granted to foster public participation and to better protect all human rights in an environmental context.

2. ILO Convention No. 169, June 27, 1989, 28 I.L.M. 1382 (entered into force Sept. 5, 1991) provides:

Article 6

1. In applying the provisions of this Convention, governments shall:

(a) consult the peoples concerned, through appropriate procedures and in particular through their representative institutions, whenever consideration is being given to legislative or administrative measures which may affect them directly;

(b) establish means by which these peoples can freely participate, to at least the same extent as other sectors of the population, at all levels of decision-making in elective institutions and administrative and other bodies responsible for policies and programs which concern them;

Article 7

3. Governments shall ensure that, whenever appropriate, studies are carried out, in co-operation with the peoples concerned, to assess the social, spiritual, cultural and environmental impact on them of planned development activities. The results of these studies shall be considered as fundamental criteria for the implementation of these activities.

4. Governments shall take measures, in co-operation with the peoples concerned, to protect and preserve the environment of the territories they inhabit.

Critics argue that the ILO Convention lacks clout because of the limited number of ratifying countries. But among the fourteen ratifying countries are many with large indigenous populations. *See also* Principle 10 of the Rio Declaration, which states:

> Environmental issues are best handled with the participation of all concerned citizens, at the relevant level. At the national level, each individual shall have appropriate access to information concerning the environment that is held by public authorities, including information on hazardous materials and activities in their communities, and the opportunity to participate in decision-making processes. States shall facilitate and encourage public awareness and participation by making information widely available. Effective access to judicial and administrative proceedings, including redress and remedy, shall be provided.

3. For a discussion on public participation in environmental decision-making, *see* Alexandre Kiss, *The Right to the Conservation of the Environment*, in LINKING HUMAN RIGHTS AND ENVIRONMENT, *Picolotti, R. and Taillant, J.D.,* Eds. (Center for Human Rights and Environment, forthcoming).

----

4.   THE RIGHT TO INFORMATION

The right to information is a human right as well as an environmental one. Human rights are implicated because knowledge of environmental risks and information on how to minimize or avoid those risks can directly affect the quality of a person's life. Freedom of information also provides a kind of due process for persons affected by government-sanctioned harm to the environment.

The right to information requires that information be relevant and comprehensible; that it be provided in a timely manner; that the procedures to obtain information, if established, be simple and brief; that the cost to individuals and groups be reasonable; and that it be available across State boundaries. *See* Ksentini Report, *op. cit.* This right includes the right to be informed, even without a specific request, of any matter having a negative or potentially negative impact on the environment, and thus imposes a duty on governments to collect and disseminate information and to provide due notice of significant environmental hazards. *See* article 19 of the Universal Declaration of Human Rights; article 19 of the International Covenant on Civil and Political Rights; European Convention, Article 10(1); and American Convention, Article 13, which provides for freedom of expression, including the right to disseminate information and the right to receive information:

> 1. Everyone has the right to freedom of thought and expression. This right includes freedom to seek, receive, and impart information and ideas of all kinds, regardless of frontiers, either orally, in writing, in print, in the form of art, or through any other medium of one's choice.

The right to information is frequently presented as an individual and group right which constitutes an essential attribute of the democratic processes and the principle of popular participation. Indeed, the concept of democratic government as stated in article 21 of the Universal Declaration of Human Rights is meaningless unless individuals and groups have access to relevant information on which to base the exercise of the vote or otherwise express the will of the people.

The European Convention on Human Rights does not explicitly provide for a right to information; however this right was recently derived from another right encompassed in the Convention. Surprisingly, perhaps, the right was not derived from the right to expression, but from the right to privacy–under which other environmental claims have been successfully considered at the European Court of Human Rights, including *Lopez Ostra v. Spain,* above.

In *Guerra & Others v. Italy,* for example, the European Court of Human Rights held that Italy failed to respect the applicant's right to privacy and family life in breach of the European Convention, by not providing essential information that would have enabled the applicants to assess the environmental risks of living in proximity to a chemical factory. *Guerra & Others v. Italy,* App. No. 14967/89, 26 Eur. H.R. Rep. 357, 383 (1998)(Eur.Ct.H.R.).

QUESTIONS AND DISCUSSION

1. The right to information not only protects individuals and groups, but also Governments themselves. In this light, the Ksentini Report noted that in the context of human rights and the environment, the right to information may also be considered a right of States *vis a vis* other States or of States *vis-à-vis* transnational corporations. In this context a State's access to information would enable it to transmit the information to its residents and to otherwise protect the human rights of those residents. The Ksentini Report also stressed that the States' aspect of the right to information is particularly important regarding the issue of toxic waste disposal, the use of nuclear power and disposal of nuclear wastes, and the production or use of toxic waste because of the human hazards these matters pose.

2. The right to information is implicated also when a court prevents a person or group from disseminating information regarding ecological problems. For example, the use of the *sub judice* rule has been effective in many areas in suppressing vital environmental information. Under the *sub judice* rule once a legal action has been filed, it may not be commented on or reported on in the public media at the risk of being cited for contempt of court. Ksentini Report at 212. The Special Rapporteur also stressed that Governments should only use national security defenses in conformity with the relevant derogation or limitation clauses of international human rights instruments, and that "trade secrets", *sub judice* and other defenses must be reviewable to ensure that the public's right to information is not unduly restricted.

3. For more information on access to environmental information, *see supra* Chapter 7, at page 432; *see also* UNECE Convention on Access to Information, Public Participation in Decision–Making and Access to Justice in Environmental Matters, 25 June 1998(Aarhus, Denmark).

SECTION III. USING HUMAN RIGHTS SYSTEMS TO ENFORCE ENVIRONMENTAL HUMAN RIGHTS

The human rights systems consist of the U.N. system, as well as regional systems for Europe, the Americas, and Africa. The following section describes these systems, and how they are being engaged to enforce environmental human rights. The European and Inter–American systems both have human rights courts, while the African system only has a commission. All three provide opportunities for individuals to bring claims, although the African system is the least robust. The U.N. system also has opportunities for individuals to raise claims, although it does not have its own human rights court (and the ICJ is open only to States and select U.N. organs).

———

A.   THE INTERNATIONAL HUMAN RIGHTS SYSTEMS

After the rise of the nation State in the 17th century, and up to World War II, the only individuals protected under international law were diplomats and soldiers—and their rights were derivative of the rights of States. Offenses against diplomats and soldiers violated international law not because they offended the rights of the individuals themselves, but because they offended the rights of another State in the safety of its subjects. International law was not implicated by a State's actions with respect to its own citizens, no matter how oppressive those actions might be.

International horror over the atrocities committed during World War II, however, compelled the international community to abandon the notion of absolute sovereignty and recognize that certain fundamental rights inhere in individuals, not simply in the States of which they are subjects. Although a proposal to include a list of fundamental human rights in the United Nations Charter failed, the Charter nonetheless included as one of its purposes "promoting and encouraging respect for human rights and for fundamental freedoms for all without distinction as to race, sex, language, or religion." UN Charter, Art. 1(3).

With the U.N.'s adoption of the Universal Declaration of Human Rights in 1948, individuals became subjects of international law in their own albeit limited right. The Universal Declaration was adopted as a UN General Assembly Resolution. U.N.G.A. Res. 217A (III) U.N.Doc. A/810 (Dec. 10, 1948). The Declaration was later followed by two human rights covenants adopted in 1966 and entering into force in 1976: the International Covenant on Civil and Political Rights (ICCPR) and the International Covenant on Economic, Social and Cultural Rights (ICESCR). The International Bill of Rights is comprised of the Universal Declaration and two covenants, along with the First Optional Protocol to the International Covenant on Civil and Political Rights. The body of human rights law now includes twenty universal treaties, more than a dozen regional conventions, and scores of declarations, resolutions and soft law instruments.

The human rights system includes important mechanisms for implementing and enforcing rights. Global bodies such as the UN Human Rights Committee and the UN Sub–Commission on the Prevention of Discrimination and Protection of Minorities receive and review communications from individuals in more than 100 countries. Under Article 62(2) of the Charter, the Economic and Social Council (ECOSOC) is tasked with making "recommendations for the purpose of promoting respect for, and observance of, human rights and fundamental freedoms for all." The UN Commission on Human Rights was subsequently created as a subsidiary body to ECOSOC to develop proposals, recommendations and reports regarding human rights. The Commission consists of forty-three members representing UN member governments. Among other things, the UN Commission took the lead in drafting the various UN instruments on human rights.

The UN Commission did not originally have the power to hear individual petitions regarding human rights violations. In 1967, however, ECOSOC passed Resolution 1235, authorizing its subsidiary bodies to address specific cases revealing a consistent pattern of gross and reliably attested violations of internationally recognized human rights. By petitioning the Commission, NGOs and others can trigger a formal process that can lead to a UN General Assembly Resolution calling on the governments concerned to comply with their Charter obligations concerning the protection of human rights.

Although the environment is not expressly referred to in the U.N. human rights system, the following excerpt describes how that system can be used to advance environmental rights. Specific cases and other "jurisprudence" are discussed in Section II, above.

DOMMEN CAROLINE, *Claiming Environmental Rights: Some Possibilities Offered by the United Nations' Human Rights Mechanisms,* 11 GEO. INT'L ENVTL. L. REV. 1, 1–48 (1998).

Treaty Bodies

Currently, there are six functioning treaty bodies. The mandates of the Committee on the Rights of the Child (CRC), the Committee on the Elimination of Racial Discrimination (CERD), the Human Rights Committee (H.R. Committee), and the Committee on Economic, Social and Cultural Rights (CESCR) are the most relevant to environmental issues. . . .

Many of the structures and functions of these treaty bodies are essentially similar. For example, each treaty body meets for a total of four to nine weeks a year, usually in two or three-week sessions. Treaty body members are experts who serve in their personal capacity rather than as representatives of their governments, although they are elected by states.

Monitoring of states' compliance with human rights treaties is accomplished by examination of the reports states are required to submit periodically (every few years) to the different committees. Usually a state whose report is being examined will send representatives to the committee's session to answer questions committee members have on their state's report. At the end of its examination of a report, the treaty body will draft concluding observations on the situation in that country. These concluding observations summarize the committee's main concerns and contain suggestions and recommendations to the reporting state. The H.R. Committee and CERD can receive and consider communications from one state alleging that another is not fulfilling its obligations under the treaty. The H.R. Committee, Committee Against Torture, and CERD each have competence to receive and consider individual complaints.

All four of these treaty bodies adopt "General Comments," which are in a sense the Committee's jurisprudence, and which provide . . . authoritative interpretations of the general obligations and rights embodied in the different treaties. General Comments are intended to indicate to states how they can promote implementation of human rights norms. General Comments often give substance and clarity to vague or inadequately defined human rights provisions. General Comments can also serve to give substance and clarity to issues that are not specifically covered by, but which arise in the context of, the human rights treaties.

In recent years, the treaty bodies have been improving their capacity and procedures for effective monitoring and implementation of human rights by carrying out fact-finding visits or missions, or by asking states to take follow-up measures to issues that have arisen in the context of examination of the state's report Committees can recommend that technical assistance or advisory services be provided when it seems necessary or appropriate. . . .

The Reporting Procedure

Each of the human rights treaties provides that states parties must submit reports every few years on measures taken to give effect to the rights contained in the treaty and/or on the progress made in the enjoyment of those rights. Each of the treaty bodies has adopted guidelines for states relating to the content of states' initial and periodic reports. Although there are a number of problems with the reporting process, it is more than a formalistic requirement because it can fulfill several important functions. One such function is the fact that the preparation of a report gives a state the opportunity to become aware of the legal and factual situation in its country as regards to the rights contained in each treaty. This in turn provides the state with a basis for elaborating implementation policies and provides the Committee with a basis for evaluating progress toward realization of treaty obligations. . . .

Environmental Issues

The mandate of each treaty body is limited to the rights set out in its governing treaty. The right to a clean environment per se is not recognized by any of the U.N.'s human rights treaties, although a number of other rights such as the right to life or the right to health relate closely to environmental issues. . . .

Environmental Issues in the Context of Periodic Reporting Procedures and Treaty Bodies Mandates

For many years, states have reported on environmental issues in the context of their obligations under the human rights treaties. This is partly in response to the reporting guidelines, but mainly due to the nature of the rights themselves, a number of which are clearly linked to environmental issues. The reporting guidelines of the ICESCR request information on environmental measures in a number of contexts. State parties are asked, for instance, to provide information on access to safe water, measures taken to improve environmental and industrial hygiene, and measures taken to ensure the application of scientific progress for the benefit of everyone, including those measures aimed at promoting a clean and healthy environment. States are asked to indicate how steps taken to improve methods of production, conservation and distribution of food have contributed to or impeded the realization of the right to adequate food. Further, states are asked to describe the impact of these measures on ecological sustainability. Information is also solicited on hunger and/or malnutrition with a particular focus on the situation of vulnerable or disadvantaged groups, such as landless peasants and indigenous peoples. . . .

The reporting guidelines for the Convention on the Rights of the Child ask for information on how the best interests of the child have been given consideration in areas such as planning and development policies, including transport and environmental policies. They also request details on measures taken to combat disease and malnutrition through, inter alia, the provision of adequate food and clean drinking water, taking into account the risks and dangers of environmental degradation and pollution. States are also asked to elaborate on risks from pollution and the measures adopted to prevent and combat it.

The Committee on the Elimination of Racial Discrimination (CERD)

In 1995, CERD asked the Nigerian government what was being done to preserve the identity of ethnic groups affected by the changes in and deterioration of their environment. Earlier in the same year, pursuant to its urgent procedure, CERD expressed concern to the government of Papua New Guinea regarding reports of serious human rights violations in Bougainville, including large-scale mining operations carried out with no regard for the rights of the ethnically distinct population or the adverse effects of environmental degradation.

Committee on the Rights of the Child

The Committee on the Rights of the Child has also considered environmental issues. Bolivia reported to the Committee on its action plan "aimed inter alia, at improving the health situation of women and children by promoting full attention to the economy, housing, environment, and education. "In its examination of the report of Belarus in 1994, the CRC said that it was concerned about the "health status of children, particularly in the aftermath of the Chernobyl nuclear disaster"....

General Comments

Environmental concerns have also been apparent in some of the committees' General Comments. The ICESCR's fourth General Comment on the Right to Housing has recognized that environmental pollution can interfere with a person's enjoyment of his or her right to housing. CERD has recently adopted a General Recommendation on indigenous peoples which touches on indigenous groups' relationship with their land and resources. The Human Rights Committee's General Comments on the right to life and on minority rights, discussed below, also reflect environmental concerns.

Non-Governmental Input into the Reporting Procedure and into the Treaty Bodies' Work

In practice, state reports tend to present their country's human rights situation in a highly favorable light and seek to avoid attracting too much attention to domestic problems or difficulties. Some states associate NGOs with the process of preparation of state reports. This approach has been taken by Chile, Luxembourg, Nepal and Thailand for their reports to the Committee on the Rights of the Child. But most frequently, states fill their reports with extracts of legislative provisions rather than the factual information asked for in the reporting guidelines. For these reasons, Committee members tend to welcome NGO information which augment the state's report and help members get a better sense of the actual human rights situation in the country they are examining. Some Committees have a formal procedure for receiving NGO information. Even in the absence of such a procedure, all treaty bodies now receive and use information from NGOs, and the secretaries of some treaty bodies actively seek such information.

Another activity that can usefully be undertaken by those who would like to see more attention paid to environmental issues by human rights bodies is to seek adoption by treaty bodies of General Comments on environmental issues, or to seek to ensure that environmental concerns are reflected in other General

Comments. General Comments are not necessarily limited to rights specifically set out in the human rights treaties. Some General Comments touch on tangential issues, as did the recent CERD General Recommendation on indigenous peoples.... Infusing environmental issues into a General Comment may seem somewhat removed from activities aimed at protecting the environment. However, the aim of General Comments is to indicate to states parties how they can promote implementation of the rights they are bound to respect. In this sense, working towards a General Comment can contribute to the jurisprudence of a treaty body and is a way to participate in an aspect of international standard-setting. ...

IV.   Individual Complaint Mechanisms

Three treaty bodies—the Human Rights Committee (H.R. Committee), the Committee on the Elimination of Racial Discrimination (CERD) and the Committee Against Torture (CAT)—fulfill a quasi-judicial function by implementing individual complaints procedures.

The complaint procedures of the ICCPR and of the ICERD are particularly interesting in the environmental context, as they allow individuals (and groups, in the case of the ICERD) to complain and seek redress beyond their government when their rights have been affected. The Committee can receive Communications from individuals within the jurisdiction of a state that has recognized the Committees' competence to receive and consider such communications. All domestic remedies must have been exhausted before a Committee is able to consider an individual complaint.

Both CERD and the H.R. Committee can ask states to take "interim measures of protection" to avoid irreparable damage to the alleged victim of the violation. Rule 86 of the Committee's rules of procedure allow the Committee to ask the reporting state to take interim measures before it has even considered the admissibility of the communication, without prejudice to the admissibility or the merits of the application. This injunction-like possibility will be of particular interest to environmentalists, as environmental damage is often impossible to repair once it has occurred. Although requests, by either Committee, that a state take interim measures are not legally binding, they do have moral force and are usually respected.

There are clear indications that the individual complaints procedures of the H.R. Committee and of CERD can provide a useful channel for activists seeking redress for environmental wrongs, although the number of environmental cases submitted to these bodies is limited. The impacts of environmental harm often fall hardest on individuals or groups suffering discrimination, thus a case brought to CERD regarding environmental discrimination would likely succeed. So far, however, none of the ten cases submitted to this Committee relate to environmental issues. The H.R. Committee, on the other hand, has examined a number of environmentally-related cases. ...

The "Non–Treaty" Bodies: The Commission and Sub–Commission

The Commission on Human Rights (Commission) is the global body with comprehensive responsibility for promoting and protecting all human rights—its agenda now covers a wide variety of issues and country situations. The Commission meets for six weeks each year, and although its members are fifty-three states elected by the U.N. Economic and Social Council (ECOSOC), it is usually attended by more than 2,000 representatives of governments, U.N. specialized agencies, NGOs, and a variety of other experts and interested individuals.

The Sub–Commission on Prevention of Discrimination and Protection of Minorities (Sub–Commission) was set up in 1947 by the Commission to undertake studies and make recommendations to the Commission concerning prevention of discrimination of any kind and to perform other functions with which ECOSOC or the Commission entrusts it. The Sub–Commission, which is at the bottom of the U.N.'s human rights hierarchy, is composed of twenty-six "independent" experts.

Environmental Issues

Other agenda items under which environmental issues have been raised include economic, social, and cultural rights; human rights and scientific and technological developments; and the right to development. Environmental issues have also arisen in the Commission and Sub–Commission in the context of specific country situations such as Tibet, Burma, Nigeria, Ecuador, and Peru.

In 1989, at the behest of a number of NGOs, the Sub–Commission launched the process that led to a study of environmental issues and their relation to human rights. Sub–Commission member Fatma Zohra Ksentini carried out this study. In 1991, Ksentini presented her preliminary report to the Sub–Commission, and in 1992 and 1993 she submitted progress reports. Beyond the value of identifying different national and international norms and cases relating to human rights and the environment, and presenting some of the theoretical issues raised by the consideration of a human right to a clean environment, the Special Rapporteur's work had some direct influence. In her 1993 progress report, Ksentini discussed several national court cases involving environmental rights claims, including a Colombian case where the court explicitly relied on materials from the Sub–Commission study on human rights and the environment. More recently, a 1997 Inter–American Commission on Human Rights report on Ecuador, spelled out the strong links between environmental degradation and the violation of basic human rights. It quotes Ksentini's final report on human rights and the environment in support for its view that indigenous peoples maintain special ties with their traditional lands and a close dependence upon their natural resources, and that such respect is essential to their physical and cultural survival.

Ksentini submitted her final report to the Sub–Commission in 1994. This report recommended, *inter alia*, that the U.N. Center for Human Rights establish a coordination center to deal with human rights and the environment, and that the Commission on Human Rights appoint a Special Rapporteur on the subject. The latter recommendation may at first sight seem superfluous to non-human rights specialists, but there is in fact a significant difference between Sub–Commission and Commission Rapporteurs. The former are limited to studying a subject in general, whereas Commission Rapporteurs may investigate allegations of violations, and examine, monitor and publicly report on specific human rights violations. In her final report, Ksentini also expressed her hope that the Draft Declaration of Principles on Human Rights and the Environment—developed by an NGO-organized meeting on the subject and annexed to her final report—would serve as a basis for the United Nations to adopt a set of norms consolidating the right to a satisfactory environment. To date, the Special Rapporteur's recommendations have not been taken up . . . .

In 1995, however, the Commission created the position of Special Rapporteur on the adverse effects of the illicit movement and dumping of toxic and dangerous products and wastes on the enjoyment of human rights, and appointed Ksentini to this post.

The impetus for the creation of this mandate came from African countries, particularly Nigeria, possibly in response to dissatisfaction with the Basel Convention on Transboundary Movements of Hazardous Wastes.

The Special Rapporteur's first three-year mandate allowed her: to investigate and examine the effects of the illicit dumping of toxic and dangerous products on the enjoyment of human rights; to investigate, monitor and examine communications, and gather information on the illicit traffic and dumping of toxic and dangerous products in developing countries; to make recommendations on measures to control and reduce illicit traffic in and transfer of toxic and dangerous products and wastes to developing countries; and to produce annually a list of the countries and transnational corporations engaged in the illicit dumping of toxic and dangerous products and wastes in African and other developing countries including a census of people killed or injured in developing countries through "this heinous act." The Commission renewed her three-year mandate with Resolution 1998/12.

Possible NGO Environmental Action in the Commission and Sub–Commission

There are a number of ways environmental groups can raise questions that are of concern to them: (1) NGOs can bring an issue to public attention by making a speech before the Commission or Sub–Commission or by submitting the information for publication in a Commission or Sub–Commission document; (2) NGOs can lobby for adoption of a resolution by either body, or for insertion of a paragraph in an existing resolution; (3) the Sub–Commission or the Commission can be lobbied to set up machinery to examine the question of human rights and the environment, or to undertake standard-setting on the subject; (4) groups or individuals can submit communications on environmental problems that lead to human rights violations to one of the Commission thematic or country mechanisms; and (5) NGOs can provide information to Sub–Commission Rapporteurs to help ensure that they take environmental issues into account whenever appropriate in the context of their studies.

Country Mechanisms

A number of countries—including Afghanistan, Bougainville, Cambodia, Cuba, Cyprus, East Timor, Nigeria, Rwanda and the Sudan—are subject to scrutiny by a Human Rights Commission Special Rapporteur.

All country Special Rapporteurs or Representatives have fact-finding mandates and report to the Commission publicly each year. In general, country Rapporteurs or Representatives can take into account information from anyone—whether they are an individual, a group or a government. NGO information is usually heavily relied upon in the preparation of country reports....

Environmental issues have been referred to in several country reports, such as those concerning Iraq and Cambodia. ... The Special Representative recommended *inter alia* that the Cambodian Government review its laws and policies, and if necessary adopt new ones in a number of environmental fields, including sustainable use of biological resources and environmental impact assessment.

Thematic Mechanisms

... A number of the existing thematic mandates are of potential relevance to environmental issues. This is the case, for instance, of those on toxic and dangerous products and wastes, contemporary forms of racism, internally displaced persons, and freedom of opinion and expression. ...

The Commission has a number of inter-sessional and pre-sessional Working Groups some of which consider issues of interest to environmental groups—

including the right to development, structural adjustment programs, or economic, social, and cultural rights. Each year the Commission may create or end the mandates of thematic Rapporteurs or working groups. . . .

IV. Overall Conclusions

The above analysis has demonstrated that there is great potential for raising environmental issues within the U.N.'s human rights mechanisms. There are currently few international bodies to which individuals may turn to raise violations of environmental law and those that do exist—such as the Commission for Environmental Cooperation and the World Bank Inspection Panel–are limited in scope. Some of the U.N. human rights procedures may be burdensome to use, but others are very simple and provide a place to testify to the effects of environmental degradation on human rights. They also provide a forum to raise consciousness of environmental issues, mobilize the politics of shame and, sometimes, to stimulate real change. The complaint possibilities offered by the human rights treaties constitute a major distinction from traditional environmental law as practiced at the international level, and stand at the forefront of international law, which is increasingly evolving to give individuals direct access to international procedures that were only open to states until recently.

QUESTIONS AND DISCUSSION

1. Based on the Dommen excerpt, reconsider Anderson's comment in the introduction to this chapter, that environmental treaties may be a more appropriate source of protection for environmental rights than human rights treaties because environmental treaties "often [have] more enforcement power than analogous human rights treaties." Do you agree?

2. In pressing a case for human rights abuse from environmental destruction, such as the oil development in Burma or the gold mining in Irian–Jaya, how would you use the various mechanisms provided by the U.N.? What sequence would you use them? Would it be possible to build a factual record that would be entitled to deference in a court, including a U.S. court, under the Alien Tort Claims Act, for example? Would you be concerned about collateral estoppel? In many environmental cases, the first thing the lawyer must consider is whether it is possible to get an injunction to stop the destruction during the pendency of the action. Is an injunction available under the U.N. system? Consider the relation of these mechanisms to a tort action, as discussed in Section IV. A., *infra*.

3. The International Labour Organization, which was created in the wake of World War I, also addresses the human rights and environment field. Most notably, the ILO Convention on Indigenous and Tribal Peoples states:

Governments shall take measures . . . to protect and preserve the environment of the territories they inhabit. . . . [G]overnments shall respect the special importance for the cultures and spiritual values of the peoples concerned of their relationship with the lands or territories, or both . . . [T]the rights of the peoples concerned to the natural resources pertaining to their lands shall be specially safeguarded. These rights include the right of these peoples to participate in the use, management and conservation of these resources.

ILO INDIGENOUS AND TRIBAL PEOPLES CONVENTION (No. 169), Article 7, 13, 15. The ILO has an elaborate system for supervising and monitoring implementation of its various conventions, which it has used to address the situation in Myanmar (formerly Burma), which has one of the worst human rights and environmental records in the world. This includes the military's use of forced labor on massive construction projects initiated with little consideration for the environment. *See* Earth Rights International, TOTAL DENIAL 2000 <http://www.earthrights. org/pubs/td2000.html> (visited 10/4/01)(catalogue of human rights and environmental abuses associated with the Yadana pipeline project).

The ILO's supervisory bodies have criticized Myanmar's use of forced labor for 30 years. In an unprecedented vote the Conference, by an overwhelming majority, voted to call upon Myanmar to "take concrete action" to implement the recommendations of a 1998 Commission of Inquiry, which found that resort to forced labor in the country was "widespread and systematic". These recommendations call upon the government to amend and enforce existing law and to insure that "no more forced or compulsory labor be imposed by the authorities, in particular the military." International Labor Organization, *Report of the Commission of Inquiry appointed under article 26 of the Constitution of the International Labour Organization to examine the observance by Myanmar of the Forced Labour Convention*, 1930 (No. 29) Geneva, 2 July 1998.

----

1.   THE EUROPEAN HUMAN RIGHTS SYSTEM

The European Convention for the Protection of Human Rights and Fundamental Freedoms, 213 U.N.T.S. 222 (1950), which entered into force in 1953, created both the European Commission and Court of Human Rights. These institutions were charged with guaranteeing the human rights included in the European Convention and Protocols, the 1965 European Social Charter, and the European Convention for the Prevention of Torture and Inhuman or Degrading Treatment or Punishment in force since 1989. In 1998, the European Court and Commission were fused into one body—the "European Court on Human Rights".

The environment is not referred to in the human rights guaranteed by the European Convention. Nonetheless, the European Commission has had a long and involved history with environment-related cases. The Commission and the Court have dealt with environmental questions under Article 8 (Rights to Privacy), Article 6 (Right to Life) and Article 1 (Right to Property) of Protocol I.

The European Convention on Human Rights constitutes the legal basis of the European Human Rights System. Over the years amendments have been made to the Convention in the form of Protocols. While Protocol 11, which merged the Commission and the Court, made some "radical changes" in the structure of the Convention system, it leaves other matters relatively untouched, including for example, the admissibility criteria (i.e. the grounds for dismissing an application). Thus, the practice of the Commission and its case law on admissibility is highly relevant for the new Court.

Iain Cameron, AN INTRODUCTION TO THE EUROPEAN CONVENTION ON HUMAN RIGHTS., at 23–34, 47–51 (3rd Ed.1998)

The Convention as adopted in 1950 created two bodies, the Commission and the Court. Both were independent bodies, working part-time and consisting of prominent lawyers from the contracting states acting in their personal capacity. The individual petition system worked as follows. The Commission received applications from individuals or groups of individuals complaining that a state party had breached their Convention rights. The Commission registered the applications and proceeded to decide whether they were admissible—simply put, whether there was a *prima facie* case against the state. Around 90% of all applications were rejected at the admissibility stage, usually because the Commission considered that the complainant was not a "victim" of a violation of the Convention, or because the acts complained of were not a violation of a Convention rights. Once an application had been declared admissible the Commission proceeded to investigate the facts of the case and the applicable law in detail. At the same time, it tried to secure a friendly settlement between the applicant and the state which the application concerned (the "respondent state"). If it failed to do so it produced a report on the merits of the case which stated its opinion as to whether the Convention was breached or not. The report was then sent to the Committee of Ministers. Within a period of 3 months, the Commission, or a member state could choose to refer the case to the Court. [In 1990, Protocol 9 created a right for individuals at this stage to refer their cases to the Court, but this right was conditional, i.e. a panel of three judges had to give their permission first.] If the case was referred to the Court, the Court's judgment was binding on the respondent state. The Committee of Ministers monitored the respondent state's compliance with the Court's judgment. If the case was not referred to the Court, the Committee of Ministers determined whether a violation of the Convention had taken place and its decision was binding on the respondent state. * * *

Protocol 11 abolished the Commission and Court and replaced them with a single Court. ... Under the new system, the Court is a full-time body and the right of individual application to the Court is made obligatory for both the Convention and the protocols, although states are only bound by the additional protocols they have ratified. The jurisdiction of the Court is also exclusive; i.e. no cases may now be referred to the Committee of Ministers for decision, although the Committee of Ministers will continue to supervise the execution of judgments. * * *

The Court's judgment is binding on the respondent state. The judgment does not as such bind other states, although judgments concerning other states can nonetheless involve a state sooner or later having to make changes in its own law and practice. This means that all states tend to review continuously the implications for their own laws of cases concerning other states. They may even ask to intervene in such cases, in order to inform the Court of their views of what a particular Convention right demands. The institution of the *amicus curiae* brief is recognized in Article 36 which provides for an unqualified right for the state party whose national is involved in the case to submit an *amicus curiae* brief and, with the permission of the President of the Court, the possibility for other states, non-governmental organizations and individuals to submit such briefs. The Court does not, formally speaking, have a doctrine of precedent, i.e. its earlier judgments are not binding upon it. On the other hand, the Court has been very anxious to build up a coherent body of case law interpreting the Convention, and so it is reluctant to overrule or diverge significantly from an earlier judgment. When it does not follow an earlier ruling which covered a similar point, it tends to follows the common law practice of "distinguishing" it, i.e. it states why the two cases differ. The position of the individual was strengthened by Protocol 9 and now that Protocol 11 has entered into force, the individual has full procedural capacity. * * *

Under Article 46(2), the Committee of Ministers supervises the execution of the Court's judgment. This is a necessary function because, when it finds a state's law or practice in violation of the Convention, the Court nonetheless does not specify the measures which a state has to take to bring itself into line with the judgment. [The Directorate of Human Rights of the Council of Europe is the Committee's agency that that follows up on the Court's decisions.] But while the Directorate of Human Rights can express its view to the Committee of Ministers ... it lacks the right, and the capacity, to engage in a detailed follow up investigation to see if the amended law or practice really does satisfy the demands of the Convention as developed by the Court. Even where the Directorate might feel that the respondent state has not done, or is not doing, what is required, the Committee of Ministers, being a political body, is seldom inclined to make difficulties for a [member states].

———

In addition to a large body of human rights case law and a strong record of compliance, the European system has developed a broad range of remedies for victims. The Court now regularly provides for damages, including damages for pecuniary (monetary) losses, non-pecuniary (i.e. moral and emotional) losses, and costs and expenses. Although the Court does not have the formal authority to compel revisions to national laws or other equitable relief, most countries comply with the European Court's decisions. Weissbrodt *op. cit.* at 650, 658.

———

B.   THE INTER-AMERICAN HUMAN RIGHTS SYSTEM

1.   BACKGROUND

The Inter–American Human Rights System uses both a Commission and a Court to protect and promote human rights in the hemisphere. The Commission can hear individual petitions and conduct country studies to investigate wide-spread human rights abuses. The Commission also can refer cases to the court, which has compulsory jurisdiction. In addition to the Charter of the American States, the American Declaration of the Rights and Duties of Man, and the American Convention on Human Rights, the Organization of American States (OAS) has developed various other treaties and protocols, including on economic, social and cultural rights. This section begins with an overview of the system by Jorge Daniel Taillant.

Jorge Daniel Taillant, *Environmental Advocacy and the Inter–American Human Rights System*, The Center for Human Rights and Environment

<www.cedha.org.ar/docs.htm>

The Inter–American Human Rights System (IAHRS) dates to 1948, the year the Organization of American States (OAS) was founded, and the year of the proclamation of the American Declaration of the Rights and Duties of Man. The Inter–American Commission on Human Rights was created before the Court on Human Rights, in 1959, in order to further respect for human rights in the American Hemisphere and is governed by the American Convention on Human Rights which was signed in 1969 and came into force in 1978. The

Statute and the Regulations of the Commission, detailing its faculties and procedures, were approved in 1979 and 1987, respectively.

In 1969, the Inter–American Specialized Conference on Human Rights, drawing upon the American Declaration, the European Convention on Human Rights, and the International Covenant of Civil and Political Rights, approved the American Convention on Human Rights (the Convention). Twenty-five of the thirty-five countries of the hemisphere have ratified the Convention and are legally committed to observing and protecting the rights it contains. The Convention significantly strengthened human rights protection in the hemisphere by standardizing over two dozen rights within the Convention's 82 Articles. The Convention established a two-tiered, treaty-based structure (which includes the Inter–American Court on Human Rights, which sits in San Jose, Costa Rica, alongside the Commission, which sits in Washington, DC) that has characterized the Inter–American system for the protection of human rights ever since.

. . . The American Convention was strongly influenced by the European Convention on Human Rights as well as the American Declaration on Human Rights approved in 1948, and the International Covenant of Civil and Political Rights. However, the American Convention, of all international instruments, covers human rights more extensively. The State parties to the Convention agree to respect and ensure the free exercise of the rights enumerated in the Convention to all persons under their jurisdiction. In this context, governments of State parties have both positive and negative duties. States have the obligation not to violate the rights of persons, while at the same time they must adopt reasonable and necessary measures to guarantee the free exercise of the rights of the individual.

The American Declaration also contains a complete list of the rights that States should observe and protect. Apart from most of those contemplated in the Convention, the American Declaration includes various social and economic rights. The Convention is different in this respect because it only provides that States are committed to adopting measures to achieve the recognition of cultural, social and economic rights. Nevertheless, the Convention establishes individual human rights in greater detail.

While before the Convention, the Commission acted as the primary human rights organ in the Inter–American system, conducting studies from its inception and receiving individual petitions, under the Convention the Inter–American Court can dictate binding decisions on member States. Further, the Convention designates a dependent relationship between the Commission and Court, since a case cannot reach the Court without having first passed through and completed the duties of the Commission with respect to the case.

. . . While the American Declaration is *not* an international treaty, . . . it has been incorporated indirectly via the Charter of the OAS, by means of Article 150. . . .

———

2.   FUNCTIONS OF THE INTER–AMERICAN COMMISSION AND COURT

The following excerpt from the Special Rapporteurs on Indigenous Rights, Claudio Grossman, First Vice–Chairman, and Julio Prado Vallejo, Commissioner, sets out the procedures of the Commission. It also describes the Court, the various protective mechanisms the Commission uses, the individual petition system, and the opportunity to request precautionary or provisional measures.

The Human Rights Situation of the Indigenous Peoples in the Americas, OEA/Ser.L/V/II.108, Doc. 62 (Oct. 20, 2000), reprinted at http://www.oas.org/

The inter-American system of human rights establishes and defines a set of basic rights for all inhabitants, as well as obligatory standards of conduct for the states and their agents to promote, protect and ensure those rights; and possesses organs that promote and defend observance of those rights and standards. The American Convention on Human Rights (Pact of San José) and the American Declaration of the Rights and Duties of Man, the principal normative instruments of the system, provide a series of individual rights that are particularly relevant to the plight of indigenous people of the member countries. The Preamble of the Declaration states that:

All men are born free and equal, in dignity and in rights, and, being endowed by nature with reason and conscience, they should conduct themselves as brothers one to another. Since culture is the highest social and historical expression of [. . .] spiritual development, it is the duty of man to preserve, practice and foster culture by every means within his power.

Other articles of the Declaration and the Convention establish the obligation of the states to respect and ensure respect for life, personal liberty, and humane treatment. . . .

The Commission and the Court may also apply special international instruments as complementary provisions: for instance, ILO Convention No. 169 concerning "Indigenous and Tribal Peoples in Independent Countries."

The Inter–American Commission, the organ of the OAS in charge of promotion of observance and protection of human rights in the Americas, has a special role to play in furthering compliance with international provisions on human rights. In addition to processing petitions on individual cases of alleged violations of rights of persons or groups . . . and, as appropriate, of submitting them to the Court, the Commission also permanently monitors the general situation of human rights in each member state and, when it believes it to be warranted, conducts observation missions. It also prepares special reports, which may encompass the general situation of a member country, or be issue-specific, for instance, on the status of women or prison conditions in the region.

As well as processing petitions on individual cases and monitoring the general situation of human rights in the member states, a third area of work of the Commission is preparation of future inter-American instruments on issues within its sphere of competence, such as, for instance, the Proposed American Declaration on the Rights of Indigenous Peoples, which it adopted and referred to the General Assembly for consideration in 1997 . . . .

The Court exercises compulsory jurisdiction to interpret and apply the provisions contained in the Convention in individual cases submitted to it by the Commission or the states, when the latter have accepted the jurisdiction of the Court. The Commission has referred to the Court several cases dealing with violations of rights of indigenous individuals and communities. The Inter–American Court of Human Rights, established by the American Convention, further exercises advisory jurisdiction to interpret human rights norms in force in the Americas. The advisory opinions of the Court constitute authoritative interpretations of said norms.

B. The Protection Mechanisms of the Inter–American System of Human Rights

As the principal organ of the OAS mandated to promote and protect human rights in the hemisphere, the Inter–American Commission on Human Rights has a unique role to play in assisting the member states in their efforts to respect and ensure the rights of the individuals subject to their jurisdiction. Among its many functions, the Commission is charged with:

- promoting awareness of human rights in the Americas;
- providing member states with advisory services in the field of human rights;
- monitoring the situation of human rights in each member state and carrying out on-site observations;
- acting on individual petitions alleging human rights violations; preparing studies and reports; and
- making recommendations to OAS member states for the adoption of progressive measures in favor of human rights. . . .

C. The individual petition system

Any person or group can file a petition alleging the violation of the American Convention, or of the American Declaration. While it is usually necessary to identify the victim so that the respective state can investigate and respond to the allegations, the identity of the petitioner may be kept in confidence. The petition must be in writing, it must be signed, and it must set forth facts that tend to show the violation of a protected right. * * *

In order for the Commission to admit a case under the American Convention or the American Declaration, for consideration on the merits, it must be satisfied that certain requirements have been met. First, and most importantly, because international and regional human rights systems are designed to be subsidiary to national systems, the party alleging the violation must have exhausted all available remedies under domestic law. Exceptions may be made when the legislation of the state concerned did not provide due process, the party was denied access to those remedies, or when there was unwarranted delay in reaching a final judgment—in other words, if remedies were unavailable as a matter of law or fact.

Second, a petition must be submitted in a timely manner. . . . Third, the Commission will not examine a complaint that essentially duplicates a petition pending or previously settled by itself or by another international governmental organization of a similar nature. Where a case is opened, but the basic requisites such as the foregoing are not shown to have been met, the Commission will declare the case inadmissible. . . .

When a case has not been resolved through friendly settlement, and is ready for decision, the Commission draws up an initial report of its findings referred to in Article 50 of the Convention to send to the State in question. In cases where a violation has been established, the Commission sets forth recommendations to be implemented by the State, generally aimed at securing a full investigation of the facts, the prosecution and punishment of those determined responsible, and action to repair the consequences suffered by the victim. The State has a first confidential opportunity to take action on the recommendations, and is asked to report within a fixed time on the measures taken. The Commission will evaluate any response received and decide between two alternatives. It may adopt a final report, referred to in Article 51 of the Convention, to be sent to both parties, in which it will report on the extent of compliance with its recommendations, and, where necessary, issue recommendations with an additional period for action. After that period has expired, the Commission will decide whether to publish the final report. As an alternative to adopting a final report, if the State in question has accepted the compulsory jurisdiction of the Inter–American Court, the Commission may decide to submit the case for adjudication.

D.   Request to states for precautionary or provisional measures

The Commission and Court also have the capacity to request that a State take protective action on an urgent basis. Pursuant to Article 29 of its Regulations, in "urgent cases, where it becomes necessary to avoid irreparable damage to persons, the Commission may request that precautionary measures be taken to avoid irreparable damage in cases where the denounced facts are true." The Commission may request that the Court order the adoption of provisional measures under similarly grave circumstances in a matter that has not yet been submitted to the Court for consideration.

The Inter–American Human Rights Court has jurisdiction to hear contentious cases submitted by States accepting its jurisdiction. The Court also can render advisory opinions. Individuals do not have access to the Court, except through the individual petitioning process to the Commission. The Court can issue a temporary injunction for cases already pending before the Court and for cases being dealt with by the Commission (but not yet referred to the Court). Beyond submitting to the General Assembly a report specifying which states have not complied with its judgments, the Court has no enforcement mechanism for its judgments. Thomas Buergenthal, *The Inter–American Court of Human Rights,* 76 AM. J. INT'L. L. 231–240 (1982); *The Advisory Practice of the Inter-American Human Rights Court,* 79 Am.J.Int'l L. 1 (1985).

----

3.   THE PROTOCOL OF SAN SALVADOR

J. D. Taillant, *op. cit.*

The Additional Protocol to the American Convention on Human Rights in the area of Economic, Social and Cultural Rights, or more commonly, "the Protocol of San Salvador", was signed in San Salvador in 1988 by 18 member states and came into force only in 1998. The San Salvador Protocol (SSP) contains 22 articles outlining economic, social and cultural rights. To date 12 countries have ratified the protocol.

Article 11 is especially relevant to the environment and to environmental advocates seeking assistance of international law. It reads:

The Right to a Healthy Environment. Everyone shall have the right to live in a healthy environment and to have access to basic public services. The States Parties shall promote the protection, preservation, and improvement of the environment.

Another important environmental right cited in the SSP (with respect to workspace conditions) is Article 7(e) stating that:

State Parties undertake to guarantee in their internal legislation, particularly with respect to: safety and hygiene at work.

The SSP ... is a bold step to reaffirm and regulate economic, social and cultural rights. Due to the difficulty and reluctance of most States to ensure economic, social and cultural rights, these rights have been for the most part ignored by international tribunals.... It is important to understand that the SSP is an addendum to the American Convention. The spirit of the SSP, and the specific language it contains, sets out a series of useful and enforceable obligations and duties, while at the same time, limiting the capacity of the system to achieve some of its objectives. Existing Inter–American human rights institutions *may not* use their full powers with respect to the rights outlined in the SSP. The SSP, for example, limits the Commission to very specific powers:

The Commission (and in certain cases the Court) can receive petitions against States based on violations of the Rights cited (only) in Articles 8A and 13 (Trade Unions and Education) of the SSP; receive Annual Reports of the States on the state of observance and protection of economic, social and cultural rights (as submitted to the Secretary General by the States); and formulate observations and recommendations on the status of Economic, Social and Cultural Rights in all states parties in its annual reports or special reports and present these before the General Assembly. * * *

NGOs can take several concrete steps with respect to the rights, duties, and institutional powers contained in the SSP [such as] including references to Article 11's right to a healthy environment in individual petitions before the Commission through the use of Article 29 of the American Convention.

... In most of the cases that have come before the system, an NGO has been the representative of the petitioner before the Commission, and acted as an advisory to the Commission ... when before the Court. We recall that by charter, the system permits any individual or group to bring a complaint representing oneself, or on behalf of another. In fact, only a handful of NGOs have regularly represented victims of human rights abuses. These NGOs have extensive experience with the OAS and its human rights organs, and are an important source of historical and procedural information, [including the Center for Human Rights and Environment in Argentina, and the Center for Justice and International Law in Washington, DC]. ...

These non-official actors of the system are in fact fundamental facilitators of the system, and ensure that States, Commissioners, and Court judges receive vital information about cases, and help guarantee a transparent and effective process.

———

QUESTIONS AND DISCUSSION

1. Taillant, *op. cit.*, outlines several practical litigation issues to consider in the Inter–American system:

- The system is a forum for individuals to bring suits against States, or for States to bring suits against other States. Unlike national fora, the system *cannot* be used to bring suits against corporations. One way around this limitation is to litigate against the State for not taking the necessary preventive measures to avoid corporate abuse.

- When a given case is still at the Commission level (prior to the Court), the procedure is confidential, and cannot be shared with the press. This may limit alternative campaign strategies. Once the case is at the Court level, the case can be publicized.

- A case can take from one year to four years to run its course in the system.
  . . .

- Unlike most national courts, the Commission and Court have *low* standards of proof. The Court, as a result, has admitted circumstantial evidence as long as it assists the Court in clarifying the facts. The burden of proof of the case is on the State. That is, according to Article 42 (Presumption) of the Commission's Statute, the facts reported in the petition shall be presumed to be true if, during the maximum period set by the Commission, the State has not provided pertinent information to the contrary. . . .

2. *Problem Exercise*: Consider the following set of facts. Government B has provided Company X with a permit to cut down one million hectares of rainforest per year for ten years, part of which is in an indigenous peoples' territory, with the promise that it will provide new housing for any displaced communities of the forested areas in an alternative forest region in another part of the country. The Company also promises to replenish the cut forest with abundant new trees in 25 urban areas undergoing new park works, to compensate for the carbon emissions that contribute to global warming. The indigenous communities have fought for over a year to halt the development project, but have had their case rejected from the highest level of the national judicial system. The cutting will eliminate one-third of the country's forestry resources in ten years, placing at risk the sustainable use of the forestry supply. Along with the trees, over 1,000 plant and animal species will die, and the country's micro-climate will drastically change in that ten-year period. Company X has not done a proper environmental impact assessment, and therefore, it cannot anticipate what the extent of the environmental impact of the cutting will be. Discuss how you would argue this case to the Inter–American Human Rights Court? What rights are violated? *See* J.D. Taillant, *op.cit.*

3. NGOs are increasingly active in the field of human rights and environment, including most prominently the Center for Human Rights and Environment, in Argentina, (<http:www:cedha.org,ar/>), and Earth Rights International, (<http:www.earthrights.org>). Other NGOs with a more traditional focus on human rights also are beginning to incorporate environmental issues in their agenda, including the Center for Justice and International Law (CEJIL) (<www.derecho.org/cejil/>) and the Centro de Estudios Legales y Sociales (CELS) (<www.cels.org.ar>).

C.   THE AFRICAN HUMAN RIGHTS SYSTEM

Africa has the youngest of the regional systems. The African Charter on Human and Peoples Rights, 21 I.L.M. 58 (1982), was adopted by the Organization of African Unity (OAU) and entered into force in 1986. The Charter enumerates the traditional list of civil and political rights, but also includes economic, social and cultural rights and, more controversially, third-generation rights of solidarity. Included in this last category is an explicit right of peoples to "a general satisfactory environment favorable to their development." Article 24, African Charter. The current system consists only of a commission. A court will join it once the Protocol establishing the new African Court of Human and Peoples Rights is ratified by the requisite number of States. The following excerpt discusses strengths and weakness of the African system.

RACHEL MURRAY, THE AFRICAN COMMISSION ON HUMAN AND PEOPLES' RIGHTS AND INTERNATIONAL LAW 10–13 (2000)

The African Charter is seen as a "unique" document among the instruments that exist on human rights because it represented the "African" concept of rights. The aim of the drafters was to create an instrument that was based on African philosophy and responsive to African needs. This uniqueness is illustrated by, for example, the inclusion of civil and political rights, economic, social and cultural rights and peoples' rights in one document treating them as indivisible; and the drafting of provisions relating to the latter and to duties of the individual in considerable detail.

The Charter established an African Commission [but not a court] ... to promote and interpret the rights in the Charter. [The commissioners are elected by the OAU with geographical balance as a goal, but in practice most of the Commissioners are from northern or western Africa.] ... Most of the Commissioners have been lawyers [but] some have also been members of their home governments. This detracts from the status of the Commission as a judicial organ.

* * *

Although the OAU is required under the Charter to finance the Commission ... this has been lacking. As a result there were, for many years, few, or only temporary, staff and the facilities in the secretariat in Banjul were minimal, a fact which, when added to poor telecommunications and electricity supply, rendered work conditions difficult. [As a result the Commission has relied on NGO and Western government assistance including temporary legal interns. This may explain the greater level of NGO participation in the Commission discussed *infra*.]

———

The Charter tasks the Commission with promoting and monitoring human rights in member States. The Commission promotes human rights by researching specific situations, organizing seminars, giving recommendations to States, laying out human rights principles and cooperating with other international organizations. Its power to monitor human rights violations is considerably less:

The Commission monitors states' behavior via two procedures: First, the Charter requires that states submit reports on implementation of human rights to the Commission every two years. The Commission reviews the Report, conducts an oral examination with representatives of the state, and gives its opinions and recommendations to the governments. In practice, the process has not been effective. [Few states have submitted any reports] ... Results of the examinations have not been published ... If the states did comply with the reporting requirement [given the Commissions limited resources] it would likely be overwhelmed.

The Commission also has power to receive and review communications from states and [victims of violations or their representatives]. Most complaints have been filed by NGOs on behalf of African Citizens. ... After receiving a communication, the Commission makes a decision first on admissibility and then on the merits. The decision is communicated to the applicant, the state and the OAU Assembly of Heads of State and Governments. Remedies for violations are limited. When communications reveal a series of serious violations the OAU Assembly may request an in-depth study and a report from the Commission. Other possible but less formal remedies include publicity, fact-finding missions, and the use of special rapporteurs.

Weissbrodt, et al., INTERNATIONAL HUMAN RIGHTS: LAW, POLICY, AND PROCESS (3rd ed.) at 618 (2001).

Weissbrodt points out that the Commission may bring communications to the attention of the OAU, which can request the Commission to undertake an in-depth study of the case, make a factual report, and submit formal findings and recommendations. The report of the Commission is only made public, however, if the OAU Assembly agrees. Consider the following critique.

> [The] [p]receding discussion of the mandate of the African Commission reveals that it does not make binding resolutions, even if, on the merits of a complaint against a State party to the Charter, it finds that a violation of human or peoples' rights has actually occurred. It only makes such recommendations, as it deems useful. No sanction attaches if a State Party fails to abide by any of its recommendation. Also the Commission is unnecessarily tied to . . . the Assembly of Heads of State and Government of the OAU . . . . The state of human rights under the Charter is therefore what the Assembly wants it to be. The Commission is therefore, far from being independent . . .

Edward Kofi Quashigah and Obiora Chinedu Okafor, LEGITIMATE GOVERNANCE IN AFRICA: INTERNATIONAL AND DOMESTIC LEGAL PERSPECTIVES 367 (1999).

In December 1997, the OAU adopted the Protocol to the African Charter on Human and People's Rights on the Establishment of an African Court on Human and Peoples Rights (Addis Protocol), Addis Ababa, OAU/LEG/MIN/AFCHPR/PROT (1) Rev.2. When the Protocol goes into effect, it will create a new Court with the ability to give advisory opinions at the request of OAU States, the OAU or other African organs. It may hold public contentious proceedings. Those who appear before the court will be entitled to free legal council. Significantly, the Court will have the power to order the payment of compensation and to take provisional measures. Questions remain about the relationship between the new Court and the commission, which continues under the Protocol. Article 6 states that the Court shall rule on admissibility of a case but it "may request the opinion of the commission" and "may consider cases or transfer them to the Commission." Article 6. One improvement in the Protocol is that "the Court may entitle relevant NGOs with observer status before the Commission, and individuals to institute cases directly before it." Article 5(3). In these circumstances, the Court will need a declaration accepting jurisdiction from a State before it can proceed. *See* Murray, at 41. Because the Protocol is not yet in force, our discussion turns to the jurisprudence of the Commission.

While Article 24 of the Charter provides "the right to a generally satisfactory environment", the environmental cases submitted to the African system have generally invoked the right to health, protected by Article 16 of the Charter. In *Communications 25/89, 47/90, 56/91 and 100/93 against Zaire*, the Commission held that failure by the Government to provide basic services such as safe drinking water constituted a violation of

Article 16. The Commission currently has pending a communication involving the Ogoni region of Nigeria that presents complex issues of the right to life, health, and environment. *See also* Dinah Shelton, REMEDIES IN INTERNATIONAL HUMAN RIGHTS LAW (1999).

QUESTIONS AND DISCUSSION

1. How would you interpret the failure of the OAU to provide adequate financing for the Commission? What does it say about the political will of African leaders to promote human rights in the region?

2. Reports of the Commission are only made public if the OAU Assembly agrees. In the name of solidarity among State leaders, the OAU apparently never agrees. As noted by Quashigah and Okafor, "The state of human rights under the Charter is . . . what the Assembly wants it to be." Much skepticism exists about the proposed Court as well. If you were the advisor to an African head of State, what advice would you give concerning the Court, which could ultimately hold them accountable for any violations of human rights?

D.   OTHER REGIONAL APPROACHES IN ASIA AND THE MIDDLE EAST

Asia has not created a regional human rights system, although there are several sub-regional efforts where human rights are considered, including the South Asian Association for Regional Cooperation, the Association of Southeast Asian Nations, the South Pacific Forum, and the South Pacific Commission. *See* Jon van Dyke, *Prospects for the Development of Intergovernmental Human Rights Bodies in Asia and the Pacific*, in NEW DIRECTIONS IN HUMAN RIGHTS 51 (Elen Lutz, Hurst Hannum & Kathryn Burke, eds. 1989). A proposal has been made to establish the Pacific Charter on Human Rights, with a commission to oversee compliance. *See* Virginia Leary, *The Asian Region and the International Human Rights Movement, in* ASIAN PERSPECTIVES ON HUMAN RIGHTS, 13 (Claude Welch & Virginia Leary, eds., 1990). *See also*, Vitit Muntarbhorn, *Asia, Human Rights and the New Millennium: Time for a Regional Human Rights Charter?*, 8 TRANSNAT'L L. & CONTEMP. PROBS. 407 (1998).

The League of Arab States established a Human Rights Commission in 1968, and adopted the Arab Charter on Human Rights in 1994, although no State has yet ratified the Charter. The Organization of the Islamic Conference adopted the Cairo Declaration on Human Rights in Islam in 1990. *See* Ann Elizabeth Mayer, *Universal Versus Islamic Human Rights A Clash of Cultures or a Clash with a Construct?* 15 MICH. J. INT'L. L. 307 (1994).

SECTION IV.   USING NATIONAL COURTS TO ENFORCE HUMAN RIGHTS

Domestic courts may be available to enforce human rights, including rights implicating the environment. This section begins by discussing enforcement in U.S. federal courts, focusing on the Alien Tort Claims Act, 28 USC § 1350. It then discusses cases from other national courts, where constitutional rights have been used to protect environmental interests.

A.   U.S. Federal Courts and the Alien Tort Claims Act

Many of the most egregious environmental threats to human rights have arisen from oil development, hard rock mining, commercial forestry operations, and other larger scale development projects undertaken by transnational corporations in developing countries, often in concert with corrupt governments. Under the Alien Tort Claims Act, the victims of such abuses may be able to bring an action for damages in U.S. federal courts. As Richard Herz notes,

> The stakes in such suits are enormous. For the plaintiffs, an ATC action might represent the only means even theoretically available to prevent or receive some compensation for the loss of their livelihoods, cultures, health and even lives. Conversely, because corporations like Freeport and Texaco cause such extensive harm, the costs of a judgment involving damages, remediation and/or the future operation of a project in an environmentally responsible manner would be high. More generally, these suits challenge the impunity with which TNCs have heretofore destroyed the environments of unwilling communities. Indeed, the very existence of ATC suits may cause at least some TNCs to reevaluate the way they do business abroad in order to avoid potential liability [*citing, inter alia* Charles E. Harrell, *et al.*, *Securitization of Oil, Gas, and Other Natural Resource Assets: Emerging Financing Techniques*, 52 Bus. Law. 885, 885 n.2 (1997) (which notes that the case against Freeport–McMoRan's mining operation in Irian Jaya "is indicative of litigation risks that must now be evaluated by international companies which engage in the development and exploitation of natural resources")].

Herz, *op. cit. at* 545, 547–551 (2000).

The ATC was adopted in 1789 as part of the original Judiciary Act, and remained largely dormant for almost two hundred years, with only a few decided cases. *See, e.g. Bolchos v. Darrel*, 1 Bee 74, 3 Fed.Cas. 810 (D.S.C.1795) (finding jurisdiction over a suit to determine title to slaves on board an enemy vessel taken on the high seas).

This trend began to change in the 1980's when a number of human rights claims were filed under the ATC. *See, e.g., Filartiga v. Pena–Irala*, 630 F.2d 876, 880–885 (2d Cir.1980); *Abebe-Jira v. Negewo*, 72 F.3d 844 (11th Cir.1996) (alleging torture of Ethiopian prisoners); *In re Estate of Ferdinand Marcos*, 25 F.3d 1467 (9th Cir.1994) (alleging torture and other abuses by former President of Philippines); *Tel-Oren v. Libyan Arab Republic*, 726 F.2d 774 (D.C.Cir.1984) (alleging claims against Libya based on armed attack upon a civilian bus in Israel). A more recent case attempts to hold U.S. corporations responsible for the actions of their overseas subsidiaries and franchisees. In this case, the International Labor Rights Fund filed a lawsuit, under the ATC, on behalf of a Colombian union alleging that Coca–Cola hired right-wing death squads to terrorize workers at its Colombian bottling plant. In one instance, they allege that the manager of the plant threatened to kill Isidro Segundo Gil, a trade union leader, if he continued his union activities. Later Mr. Gil was found murdered. The case, filed in U.S. District Court in Miami, was still pending at the time of publication. BBC News, *Coke Sued Over Death Squad Claims*, <http://news.bbc.co.uk/hi/english/business.

In addition to the cases using the ATC to redress traditional human rights abuses, environmental lawyers have started bringing cases under the ATC to address human rights abuses that result from large scale development projects that damage the environment. This modern history of litigation under the ATC is a testament to the ingenuity of public interest lawyers who have revitalized a statute that went unused for almost two centuries.

---

1. ANATOMY OF AN ATC CASE

The ATC provides that a U.S. district court shall have subject matter and federal question jurisdiction over "any civil action [1] by an alien [2] for a tort only, [3] committed in violation of the law of nations or a treaty of the United States." 28 U.S.C. § 1350. The seminal ACT case is *Filartiga v. Pena–Irala*, 630 F.2d 876 (2d Cir.1980). In that case, the Second Circuit held that Dr. Joel Filartiga and his daughter, who were citizens of Paraguay, could sue Americo Norberto Pena–Irala, also a citizen of Paraguay, but living in Brooklyn, for the wrongful death of Dr. Filartiga's 17 year old son by deliberate torture carried out by Pena under color of Paraguayan state authority, in violation of universally accepted norms against state torture. Since *Filartiga,* a "majority of courts" have interpreted the ATC to grant "both a federal private cause of action as well as a federal forum in which to assert the claim." *Xuncax v. Gramajo*, 886 F.Supp. 162, 179 (D.Mass.1995).

Definition of an "Alien". A plaintiff in an ATC action must be an alien. 28 USC § 1350. Aliens may be permanent residents anywhere in the world, including the United States, and still sue under the ATC. *See Filartiga v. Pena–Irala*, 630 F.2d 876 (2d Cir.1980)(plaintiffs were citizens of Paraguay, although one was a permanent resident in the United States); *Beanal v. Freeport–McMoRan*, 969 F.Supp. 362 (E.D.La.1997)(plaintiff was a resident of Indonesia). U.S. citizens may not sue under the ATC even if they reside outside of the United States. *Miner v. Begum*, 8 F.Supp.2d 643, 644 (S.D.Tex.1998).

Definition of a "Tort". The plaintiff must allege a tort. A tort is "a civil wrong, other than breach of contract, for which the court will provide a remedy in the form of an action for damages." William Prosser and W. Keaton, PROSSER AND KEETON ON THE LAW OF TORTS 2 (1984). In ATC actions, the plaintiff must allege first, that the "law of nations" or a "treaty of the United States" gives rise to a right; second, that the defendant violated that right; and third, that the plaintiff suffered damages as a result. *Jogi v. Piland, et al.,* 131 F.Supp.2d 1024, 1027 (C.D.Ill.2001)(holding that plaintiff had "alleged a violation of a United States Treaty . . . [but had not] alleged a tort" since he did not "allege how the defendants' failure to abide by the treaty damaged him").

Definition of a "Treaty of the United States". While the ACT does not define what constitutes a treaty under this provision, it appears that even non-self executing treaties would be included. *See* Beth Stephens & Michael Rather, International Human Rights Litigation in U.S. Courts 59 (1996), *cited in* Herz, *op. cit.*, at 553–54, n. 44 (noting that "if ATC does not allow such suits, the treaty provision is entirely unnecessary because self-executing treaties are already actionable under sec. 1331 'arising under' jurisdiction"). Commentators suggest that the meaning of "treaty of the United States" may not be limited to treaties ratified pursuant to Article II, Section 2 of the Constitution. Some courts, however, have interpreted the ATC to mean that a plaintiff "may bring an action under § 1350 only for a tort committed in violation of a United States treaty, not for a violation of [any] treaty." *Jogi v. Piland, et al.*, 131 F.Supp.2d 1024, 1027 (C.D.Ill.2001)(*citing Xuncax v. Gramajo*, 886 F.Supp. 162, 181 (D.Mass. 1995). Such treaties may of course reflect or catalyze custom, even when the U.S. is not a party. *Cf., Filartiga*, where the Court suggested that the Universal Declaration of Human Rights, while not a binding treaty of the United States, may be an authoritative statement of customary international law. 630 F.2d at 884.

Determining the "Law of Nations". The "law of nations" includes customary law, which, according to the *Filartiga* Court, " 'may be ascertained by consulting...the general usage and practice of nations....' *United States v. Smith*, 18 U.S. (5 Wheat.) 153, 160–61...(1820)....'' *Filartiga* F.2d at 880. The Court added, "[m]odern international sources confirm the propriety of this approach," quoting Article 38 of the ICJ Statute, which includes custom, as well as treaties and general principles. *See* Chapter 6 at 291 (providing a discussion on the sources of international law). Proving even a customary norm of international law is a significant challenge for those prosecuting ATC cases, but the dynamic nature of customary law also presents an opportunity for creative lawyering, as pointed out by Herz, *op. cit.*, 558–59,

> Customary international law is based upon state practice, and therefore changes over time. ATCA requires courts to apply current international law, not to apply the international law extant in 1789, the time of ATCA's enactment. To date, courts have recognized the customary international law status of only a limited number of norms, including torture, crimes against humanity, war crimes, genocide, disappearance, summary execution, arbitrary detention, forced labor, and cruel, inhuman and degrading treatment. These however, are not necessarily the only norms actionable under ATCA. Certain long-established customary norms simply have not yet been raised by plaintiffs or recognized by U.S. courts. Moreover, because the content of the "law of nations" evolves over time, the scope of torts actionable under ATCA necessarily changes accordingly. Therefore, new norms can be recognized as actionable under ATCA. The dynamic nature of customary international law presents both a challenge and an opportunity for attorneys seeking redress under ATCA for abuses suffered by their clients. Attorneys must not only be familiar with the *corpus* of norms already held to violate "the law of nations"; they must also recognize when an emerging norm has crystallized into an actionable norm.

Furthermore, they must be able to prove it to a court which is likely to be skeptical of the very idea of customary international law.

QUESTIONS AND DISCUSSION

1. The Ninth Circuit recently confirmed that a customary norm was sufficient under the ATC, rejecting the argument that only violations of *jus cogens* norms are actionable. *Alvarez-Machain v. United States, et al.*, at 7-8 (9th Cir.2001).

> [Defendants'] contention that there must be a jus cogens violation for the ATCA to apply finds no support in the cases. ... This Court has held that a jus cogens violation satisfied the [ATCA]..., *Hilao v. Estate of Marcos*, 103 F.3d 789, 795 (9th Cir.1996), but it has never held that a jus cogens violation is required to meet the standard. In *Martinez*, 141 F.3d [1373], 1383 [(9th Cir.1998)] we stated that arbitrary arrest and detention were actionable under the ATCA, but did not consider whether they constituted jus cogens. We have recognized that the "law of nations," the antecedent to customary international law, and jus cogens are related but distinct concepts. *See Siderman de Blake v. Republic of Argentina*, 965 F.2d 699, 714–716 (9th Cir.1991). Therefore, we reject [defendants'] argument that the ATCA requires a violation of a jus cogens norm and decline to decide whether arbitrary detention and kidnapping reach this heightened standard.

Id. at *7–8.

At least until the *Alvarez-Machain* decision, there has been some confusion whether a violation of jus cogens is the standard under the ATC, rather than the wider liability afforded under violations of customary international law. Judge Bork's concurring opinion in *Tel-Oren v. Libyan Arab Republic* contributed to this when he stated that only actions that violate "definable, universal and obligatory norms ... [fall within] the limits of § 1350 reach." 726 F.2d 774, 781 (D.C.Cir. 1984). Many commentators have criticized the *Tel-Oren* holding, and subsequent courts citing it, for using the word "universal". *See* David Weissbrodt, *et al.*, INTERNATIONAL HUMAN RIGHTS, THIRD EDITION 768 (2001). Weissbrodt states that "Universal conceivably could create confusion if it suggest 'unanimous.' Less ambiguous terms include 'international consensus,' 'internationally recognized,' and 'widely accepted' "). *See also Forti v. Suarez–Mason*, 694 F.Supp. 707 (N.D.Cal. 1988) and Herz, *op. cit.* at 557, note 69. Another case where the same mistake is made is *Doe, et al., v. Unocal*, 110 F.Supp.2d 1294 (C.D.Cal.2000).

2. Is the analysis in *Alvarez-Machain* complete? Consider how customary norms of environmental law might evolve.

---

2. VIOLATIONS OF THE "LAW OF NATIONS" BY STATE AND NON-STATE ACTORS

Oil drilling, mining, timber harvesting and other large scale resource extraction projects in developing countries often are undertaken by transnational corporations through a joint venture with the national government where the resources are located. Because the government partner in these projects may be protected by sovereign immunity from an ATC suit, it may be necessary to establish liability by the private corporation. This is the central issue in many of the cases.

Some norms of customary international law provide for individual liability, and can be violated by non-State actors. *Kadic v. Karadzic,* 70 F.3d 232, 240 (2d Cir.1995), *cert. denied Karadzic v. Kadic,* 518 U.S. 1005 (1996). These include "certain offenses recognized by the community of nations as of universal concern, such as piracy, slave trade, attacks on or hijacking of aircraft, genocide, war crimes, and perhaps certain acts of terrorism, even where [no other basis of jurisdiction] is present." *Id.* (*citing* THE RESTATEMENT (THIRD) OF THE FOREIGN RELATIONS LAW OF THE UNITED STATES § 404 (1986)).

Direct liability of a non-State actor is available under select norms because they are designed to apply to individuals, and historically have been applied to individuals. *See* CONVENTION ON THE PREVENTION AND PUNISHMENT OF THE CRIME OF GENOCIDE, art. IV ("Persons committing genocide or any of the other acts enumerated in article III shall be punished, whether they are constitutionally responsible rulers, public officials or private individuals"); CONVENTION ON THE LAW OF THE SEA, art. 101(a) (defining piracy in part as "any illegal acts of violence or detention, or any act of depredation, committed for private ends by the crew or the passengers of a private ship or a private aircraft"). If the actions of a corporation violate one of these norms, for example by enslaving laborers, they would be liable under the ATC, irrespective of whether they act in conjunction with a State.

A showing of State action is required, however, if the norm of customary international law does not encompass individual liability. *Kadic,* 70 F.3d at 240. The Supreme Court has articulated four different tests for determining when a private actor is liable under "color of law" within the meaning of the Civil Rights Act, 42 USC § 1983. These tests are discussed within the context of the ATC in the following case. *Beanal v. Freeport–McMoran* involved allegations of a US corporation committing human rights and environmental violations while operating a gold and copper mine in Irian Jaya, Indonesia. 969 F.Supp. 362, 373–379 (E.D.La.1997), *aff'd,* 197 F.3d 161 (5th Cir.1999). Beanal, a community leader of the Amungme, an indigenous tribe, alleged that Freeport was destroying their natural habitat and religious symbols forcing his people to relocate. 197 F.3d 161, 163 (5th Cir.1999), and therefore constituted "cultural genocide." *Id.* In addition, he alleged that "Freeport's private security force acted in concert with the Republic to violate international human rights." *Id.* The District court dismissed Beanal's claims because, *inter alia,* he failed to show State action.

Beanal v. Freeport–McMoRan, 969 F.Supp. 362, 373–379 (E.D.La.1997), *aff'd* 197 F.3d 161 (5th Cir.1999)

The Restatement provides that "a state violates international law, if as a matter of state policy, it practices, encourages or condones" certain proscribed conduct. [RESTATEMENT (THIRD) OF THE FOREIGN RELATIONS LAW OF THE UNITED STATES § 702.] To allege state action, the challenged conduct must be attributable to the state, in other words, it must be official conduct. Restatement § 207, comment c. A state is responsible for any violation of its obligations under international law resulting from action or inaction by, "any organ, official, employee, or other agent of a government or of any political subdivision, acting within the scope of authority or under color of such authority." *Id.* The fact that [a corporation] is itself not a "state" does not preclude its liability for violation of the law of nations since state actors, not merely the state itself, can be held liable for such violations. *Id.* at § 207.

The court must determine whether Plaintiff has sufficiently alleged that [a corporation's] alleged conduct constitutes state action. . . . [In making this determination] the court considers the test contained in Restatement section 207 and the "under color of law" jurisprudence of 42 U.S.C. § 1983 ("§ 1983") . . .

> In determining whether an act was within the authority of an official or an official body, or was done under color of such authority, (clause (c)), one must consider all the circumstances, including whether the affected parties reasonably considered the action to be official, whether the action was for public purpose or for private gain, and whether the persons acting wore official uniforms or used official equipment.

RESTATEMENT § 207 . . . Both private individuals and private entities can be state actors and can be held liable under § 1983. . . . Section 1983 does not require that the defendant be an officer of the State. . . . "Private persons jointly engaged with state officials in the challenged action, are acting under color of law for purposes of § 1983 purposes." * * *

The Supreme Court has recognized several circumstances in which a private actor can be held to have acted under color of law within the meaning of § 1983.

> The Court has taken a flexible approach to the state action doctrine, applying a variety of tests to the facts of each case. [1] In some instances, the Court has considered whether there is a sufficiently close nexus between the State and the challenged action of the regulated entity so that the action of the latter may be fairly treated as that of the State itself. [2] The Court has also inquired whether the state has so far insinuated itself into a position of interdependence with the private party, that there is a symbiotic relationship between them. [3] In addition the court has held that if a private party is a willful participant in joint activity with the State or its agents then state action is present. [4] Finally the court has ruled that a private entity that exercises powers traditionally exclusively reserved to the State is engaged in state action. * * *

The Nexus Test

> Under the nexus test, a plaintiff must demonstrate that there is a sufficiently close nexus between the government and the challenged conduct such that the conduct may fairly be treated as that of the State itself. . . . Governmental regulation, subsidy, approval of or acquiescence in the private conduct does not make the State responsible for the conduct. To satisfy the nexus test, the state must be significantly involved in or actually participate in the alleged conduct. * * *

The Symbiotic Relationship Test

State action can be established under the symbiotic relationship test if the state "has so far insinuated itself into a position of interdependence" with a private party that "it must be recognized as a joint participant in the challenged activity. . . . To establish a symbiotic relationship, the state and the private entity need be 'physically and financially integral.' " * * *

The Joint Action Test

State action is present where a private party is a "willful participant in joint action with the State or its agents." . . . [T]he joint action test looks to whether the state officials and private parties acted in concert in effecting a particular deprivation of constitutional rights. . . . The Fifth Circuit appears to require some actual participation or cooperation on behalf of the state and private actor in violating complainant's rights. . . . As with the nexus test, state acquiescence or approval of the challenged conduct does not appear sufficient to satisfy the joint action test. Rather, the presence of government officers must have influenced or been an integral part of the challenged conduct. * * *

The Public Function Test

Finally, state action can exist where a private entity performs a function traditionally the exclusive prerogative of the State. . . . Few public functions have been found to satisfy this test. . . . Among those activities which satisfy the public function test is the operation of a company owned town, i.e. where the "streets, alleys, sewers, stores, residences, and everything else that goes to make a town" are privately owned. . . . The management of a city park is also deemed an exclusive public function

---

3. HUMAN RIGHTS AND ENVIRONMENT CASES UNDER THE ALIEN TORT CLAIMS ACT

In recent years, several cases have been brought under the ATC for human rights violations from environmentally destructive projects. In *Jota v. Texaco Inc.* villagers in Ecuador alleged that over the course of thirty years, Texaco "polluted the rain forests and rivers in Ecuador and Peru." 157 F.3d 153, 155 (2d Cir.1998). Specifically, they alleged that Texaco dumped toxic by-products of the oil drilling process into local rivers and "used other improper means of eliminating toxic substances, such as burning them, dumping them directly into landfills, and spreading them on the local dirt roads." *Id.* The Second Circuit Court of Appeals held that the district court's dismissals based upon forum non conveniens and comity, were erroneous absent a condition requiring Texaco to submit to jurisdiction in Ecuador's courts. *Id.* at 163. Upon remand, the District Court dismissed the case on the basis of forum non conveniens, but required that Texaco submit to jurisdiction in Ecuador. *Aguinda v. Texaco, Inc.*, 142 F.Supp.2d 534 (S.D.N.Y.2001). That dismissal is currently on appeal.

In *Wiwa v. Royal Dutch Petroleum* the company was accused of complicity in the imprisonment, torture and murder of members of the Ogoni tribe in Nigeria. Most notable among those killed was Ken Saro–Wiwa, a prominent environmental activist. 226 F.3d 88, 93 (2d Cir. 2000)(*cert. denied* 121 S.Ct. 1402, 149 L.Ed.2d 345 (2001)(reversing district courts dismissal on forum non conveniens). The case is now back before the district court, which is currently considering Royal Dutch/Shell's assertion that plaintiffs have not alleged any cognizable claims against it. Earth Rights International, *Wiwa v. Royal Dutch Petroleum (Shell)*, <http://www.earthrights.org/shell/>.

Another environment and human rights case under the ATC, currently on appeal to the Ninth Circuit, is *Doe v. Unocal*, 110 F.Supp.2d 1294 (C.D.Cal.2000) (Ninth Circuit docket no. 00–56603 and 00–56628). In *Doe*

Burmese villagers sued the military government of Burma, as well as Total, a French corporation, and Unocal, a U.S. corporation. The corporations were partners with a company owned by the ruling military junta, the State Law and Order Restoration Council (SLORC), in a natural gas pipeline. The project hired SLORC to provide security for the pipeline. The villagers allege that in the course of providing that security, the military committed rape, torture, forced relocation, forced labor, and murder. They further allege that Total and Unocal should be held liable for the violations of customary international law committed by SLORC in the course of fulfilling its security commitments. The District Court held that the government and its corporation were entitled to sovereign immunity, *Doe v. Unocal*, 963 F.Supp. 880 (C.D.Cal.1997). This holding is currently on appeal to the Ninth Circuit. Total was dismissed for lack of personal jurisdiction. *Doe v. Unocal*, 27 F.Supp.2d 1174 (C.D.Cal.1998), *aff'd.* 248 F.3d 915 (9th Cir.2001). Thus the only remaining defendant in the case is Unocal, a corporation that did not actually commit the torture, rape, forced labor, and murder alleged. Nonetheless, the plaintiffs argue that the relationship between SLORC and Unocal makes the corporation liable. Although the District Court found that Unocal knew or should have known that slave labor would be used on the pipeline and that Unocal benefited from the slave labor, the Court dismissed plaintiffs' claims on summary judgment.

Doe v. Unocal, 110 F.Supp.2d 1294, 1310 (C.D. Cal. 2000)

In 1988, Burma's military government suppressed massive pro-democracy demonstrations by jailing and killing thousands of protesters and imposing martial law. At that time, a new military government took control naming itself the State Law and Order Restoration Council ("SLORC") and renaming the country Myanmar. . . .

The international community has closely scrutinized the SLORC's human rights record since it seized power in 1988. Foreign governments, international organizations, and human rights groups have criticized SLORC for committing such human rights abuses as torture, abuse of women, summary and arbitrary executions, forced labor, forced relocation, and arbitrary arrests and detentions.

. . . [A]bout 1991, several international oil companies, including Unocal, began negotiating with SLORC regarding oil and gas exploration in Burma. In May 1992, Control Risk Group, a consulting company hired by Unocal to assess the risks involved in foreign investment, issued a report informing Unocal of Burma's economic and political climate. The report states:

> Throughout Burma the government habitually makes use of forced labour to construct roads. In Karen and Mon states the army is forcing villagers to move to more secure sites (similar to the "strategic hamlets" employed by the US army in Vietnam) in the hope of cutting off their links with the guerrillas. There are credible reports of military attacks on civilians in the regions. In such circumstances UNOCAL and its partners will have little freedom of manoeuvre. The local community is already terrorized: it will regard outsiders apparently backed by the army with extreme suspicion.

[The court continues with a discussion of the various phases of the project, holding companies established, contractual rights and obligations, and controlling interest surrounding the project. The court then turns its attention to Unocal's knowledge of the military's actions related to the pipeline.]

* * *

On March 16, 1995, Joel Robinson of Unocal wrote Unocal President John Imle a letter in which he states that he had received "more of the publications from the 'Karen press' which depicted in more detail than I have seen before the increased encroachment of SLORC activities into the villages of the pipeline area. Our assertion that SLORC has not expanded and amplified its usual methods around the pipeline on our behalf may not withstand much scrutiny." (Richardson Decl., Ex. 158 at 16514.)

* * *

A May 1995 United States State Department cable from the U.S. Embassy in Rangoon, Myanmar, states:

> On the general issue of the close working relationship between Total/Unocal and the Burmese Military, Robinson [of Unocal] had no apologies to make. He stated forthrightly that the companies have hired the Burmese military to provide security for the Project and pay for this through the Myanmar Oil and Gas Enterprise (MOGE). He said three truckloads of soldiers accompany Project officials as they conduct survey work and visit villages. He said Total's security officials meet with military counterparts to inform them of the next day's activities so that soldiers can ensure the area is secure and guard the work perimeter while the survey team goes about its business.

* * *

A U.S. State Department cable summarizes a conversation the U.S. government official had with Unocal's Joel Robinson regarding the Project's relationship to the Myanmar military the State Department official noted:

* * *

> Robinson acknowledged that army units providing security for the pipeline construction do use civilian porters, and Total/Unocal cannot control their recruitment process. . . .

B.   The Alien Tort Claims Act

. . . To state a claim under the ATCA, a plaintiff must allege (1) a claim by an alien, (2) alleging a tort, and (3) a violation of the law of nations (international law). The parties do not dispute that the first two elements are satisfied. The issue is whether the conduct of the Myanmar military violated international law, and if so, whether Unocal is liable for these violations.

Actionable violations of international law must be of a norm that is specific, universal, and obligatory. *Id.* at 1475 (citing *Filartiga v. Pena–Irala*, 630 F.2d 876, 881 (2d Cir.1980)); *Tel-Oren v. Libyan Arab Republic*, 233 U.S. App. D.C. 384, 726 F.2d 774, 781 (D.C.Cir.1984). When ascertaining the content of the law of nations, the Court must interpret international law not as it was in 1789 (the year the ATCA was enacted), but as it has evolved and exists among the nations of the world today. *Kadic v. Karadzic*, 70 F.3d 232, 238 (2d Cir.1995) (citing *Filartiga*, 630 F.2d at 881). * * *

3.   Liability as a State Actor

"The 'color of law' jurisprudence of 42 U.S.C. § 1983 is a relevant guide to whether a defendant has engaged in official action for purposes of jurisdiction under the Alien Tort Claims Act." . . . A private individual acts under "color of law" within the meaning of section 1983 when he acts together with state officials or with significant state a*Id*.

... The Supreme Court has taken a flexible approach to the state action doctrine, ... applying four distinct tests to the facts of each case: public function, state compulsion, nexus, and joint action. ... Under each of these four tests, the unlawful conduct must be fairly attributable to the state. ...

Plaintiffs argue that Unocal's participation in the Joint Venture constitutes state action under the joint action test. Under the joint action test, state action is present if a private party is a "willful participant in joint action with the State or its agents."... "Courts examine whether state officials and private parties have acted in concert in effecting a particular deprivation of constitutional rights." ...

In presenting the joint action test, the Ninth Circuit stated that one way to prove joint action is to demonstrate a conspiracy between the private and state actors. ... The other way is to show that the private party is "a willful participant in joint action with the State or its agents. Private persons, jointly engaged with state officials in the challenged action, are acting 'under color' of law for purposes of [section] 1983 actions." ...

* * *

Here, Plaintiffs present evidence demonstrating that before joining the Project, Unocal knew that the military had a record of committing human rights abuses; that the Project hired the military to provide security for the Project, a military that forced villagers to work and entire villages to relocate for the benefit of the Project; that the military, while forcing villagers to work and relocate, committed numerous acts of violence; and that Unocal knew or should have known that the military did commit, was committing, and would continue to commit these tortious acts. ... Unocal and SLORC shared the goal of a profitable project. However, ... this shared goal does not establish joint action. Plaintiffs present no evidence that Unocal "participated in or influenced" the military's unlawful conduct; nor do Plaintiffs present evidence that Unocal "conspired" with the military to commit the challenged conduct.

4. State Action and Proximate Cause

...In this case, the *government* [emphasis added] committed the challenged acts. In order for a private individual to be liable for a section 1983 violation when the state actor commits the challenged conduct, the plaintiff must establish that the private individual was the proximate cause of the violation. ... In order to establish proximate cause, a plaintiff must prove that the private individuals exercised control over the government official's decision to commit the section 1983 violation. ...

* * *

In this case, Plaintiffs present no evidence Unocal "controlled" the Myanmar military's decision to commit the alleged tortious acts. Accordingly, Plaintiffs' claims that Unocal acted under "color of law" for purposes of the ATCA fail as a matter of law.

* * *

5. Forced Labor

The International Labor Organization ("ILO") ... prohibits the use of forced labor and defines forced labor as "all work or service which is exacted from any person under the menace of any penalty and for which the said person has not offered himself voluntarily. '' ILO CONVENTION No. 29, Article No. 2 (1930). Over the past 40 years, the ILO has repeatedly condemned Burma's record of imposing forced labor on its people contrary to Convention 29. . . .

In international law, the prohibition of recourse to forced labour has its origin in the efforts made by the international community to eradicate slavery, its institutions and similar practices, since forced labour is considered to be one of these slavery-like practices. . . . Although certain instruments, and particularly those adopted at the beginning of the nineteenth century, define slavery in a restrictive manner, *the prohibition of slavery must now be understood as covering all contemporary manifestations of this practice.* [Emphasis added.]

* * *

6. Unocal's Role in the Forced Labor

To prevail on their ATCA claim against Unocal, Plaintiffs must establish that Unocal is legally responsible for the Myanmar military's forced labor practices. Plaintiffs contend that under international law principles of direct and vicarious liability, Unocal is legally responsible for the Myanmar military's forced labor practices. Specifically, Plaintiffs cite three decisions issued by United States Military Tribunals after World War II involving the prosecution of German industrialists for their participation in the Third Reich's slave labor policies. Plaintiffs argue that under these holdings, knowledge and approval of acts is sufficient for a finding of liability.

* * *

In the first of the three industrialist cases, *United States of America v. Friedrich Flick, "The Flick Case,"* 6 Trials of War Criminals Before the Nuremberg Military Tribunals Under Control Council Law No. 10 (1952), Frederick Flick, a dominant figure in the German steel industry, and five of his business associates, were charged with participating in the Third Reich's slave labor program. The Tribunal concluded that four of the six defendants were entitled to the affirmative defense of necessity and were therefore not guilty. In reaching its decision, the Tribunal acknowledged that the German slave labor program was created and supervised by the Nazi government and that it would have been futile and dangerous for these defendants to have objected. *Id.* at 1196–97. Two of the defendants were convicted. The Tribunal found that Bernhard Weiss, with the knowledge and approval of his superior Frederick Flick, sought an increase in the factory's production quota of freight cars and attempted to procure a corresponding increase in his firm's allotment of forced laborers. *Id.* at 1202. These active steps to participate in the Reich's slave labor program, reasoned the Tribunal, deprived these two defendants of the necessity defense. *Id.*

* * *

The Court disagrees with Plaintiffs that these cases hold that an industrialist is liable where he or she has knowledge that someone else would commit abuses. Rather, liability requires participation or cooperation in the forced labor practices. In the *Flick Case*, Weiss took "active steps" with the "knowledge and approval" of his superior to procure forced laborers so that the company could increase its production quota. The Tribunal's guilty verdict rested not on the defendants' knowledge and acceptance of benefits of the forced labor, but on their active participation in the unlawful conduct.

Plaintiffs also argue that *Iwanowa v. Ford Motor Co.*, 67 F.Supp.2d 424 (D.N.J.1999), supports their argument that Unocal is liable for the Myanmar military's forced labor practices. In Iwanowa, the plaintiff alleged that after being abducted by Nazi troops and transported from Rostov, Russia to Germany, Ford Werke, a German subsidiary of Ford Motor Co., purchased her and forced her to perform heavy labor from 1942 until Germany surrendered in 1945. *Id.* at 433–34. The district court denied Ford's motion to dismiss for lack of jurisdiction, finding there to be jurisdiction for the plaintiff's claims of slave labor under the ATCA. The court held that Ford Werke's "use of unpaid, forced labor during World War II violated clearly established norms of customary international law." *Id.* at 440.

In this case, there are no facts suggesting that Unocal sought to employ forced or slave labor. In fact, the Joint Venturers expressed concern that the Myanmar government was utilizing forced labor in connection with the Project. In turn, the military made efforts to conceal its use of forced labor. The evidence does suggest that Unocal knew that forced labor was being utilized and that the Joint Venturers benefited from the practice. However, because such a showing is insufficient to establish liability under international law, Plaintiffs' claim against Unocal for forced labor under the Alien Tort Claims Act fails as a matter of law.

QUESTIONS AND DISCUSSION

1. For Unocal's description of its victory, *see* Unocal, *The Story You Haven't Heard...the Activist's Lawsuits*, <http://www.unocal.com/myanmar/suit.htm>(visited 9/14/01). The villagers appealed and re-filed their pendent state claims in state court. The state claims had been dismissed without prejudice when the federal court dismissed the ATC claims. In August 2001, California Superior Court Judge Victoria Chaney denied Unocal's motion for dismissal. *John Doe I et. al. v. Unocal Corp. et. al.*, BC237980, Superior Court of California, County of Los Angeles, Dept. 311 (August 20, 2001).

2. Did the District Court correctly analyze the state/non-state issue? On appeal, the villagers in *Doe* claim that the Court misconstrued and misapplied the state action test. They present several alternative theories of liability including aiding and abetting, conspiracy, and joint-venture liability. The appellant's reply brief presents the question as "whether Unocal, a California corporation, is liable under the Alien Tort Claims Act, 28 U.S. C. 1350 ('ATCA') when it participates as a partner in a joint venture with one of the world's most repressive military dictatorships knowing that the joint venture will utilize slave labor and other human rights abuses to fulfill its economic mission—the building of a natural gas pipeline across Burma." If you represented the villagers, what arguments would you advance in the brief? Consider both international law and federal common law.

The appellant's view of liability under the ATC was supported by an Amicus Brief submitted by the Center for International Environmental Law on behalf of the Sierra Club, Global Exchange, and the Rainforest Action Network. BRIEF OF AMICI CURIAE IN SUPPORT OF PLAINTIFFS-APPELLANTS URGING REVERSAL,

<http://www.ciel.org/Announce/unocalamicus.html>. The brief addressed issues of liability based on aider and abettor, vicarious liability and respondeat superior.

3. Professor Steinhardt's paper on corporate governance, *infra*, notes that,

In *Filartiga* the court ruled that the United States had an interest in common with all other countries—a mutual, long-term sophisticated self-interest—in punishing certain kinds of behavior wherever the perpetrator can be found. The Court deployed the ancient notion of hostes humanis generis, the enemy of all mankind, and equated the modern-day torturer with the 18th century exemplar of mankind's enemy, namely pirates. The principle of universal jurisdiction expresses this sense that some international wrongs are sufficiently intolerable that every state has a legally-protectable interest in its suppression to apply its own law. From this perspective, the domestic courts are not acting unilaterally. They are acting as agents for the international legal order. And, it must be said, in each of these cases, there was a link in fact: the defendant was physically in the United States and brought the dispute within US territory, triggering the transitory tort doctrine—the ancient idea that committing a tort creates an obligation to make reparation and that obligation follows the defendant wherever he or she goes in the world.

What are the advantages and disadvantages of providing "universal jurisdiction" in the U.S. Federal Courts?

4. One of the best-known cases applying universal jurisdiction is that of Chilean dictator, Augusto Pinochet. The following excerpt summarizes the universal jurisdiction element of the "Pinochet precedent":

> The most striking feature of the Pinochet case was that a Spanish judge had the authority to order Pinochet's arrest for crimes committed mostly in Chile and mostly against Chileans. This authority derives from the rule of "universal jurisdiction": the principle that every state has an interest in bringing to justice the perpetrators of particular crimes of international concern, no matter where the crime was committed, and regardless of the nationality of the perpetrators or their victims ... Normally, jurisdiction over a crime depends on a link, usually territorial, between the prosecuting state and the crime itself. But, as one leading lawyer said, "in the case of crimes against humanity that link may be found in the simple fact that we are all human beings." A principal pragmatic reason why international law provides for universal jurisdiction is to make sure that there is no "safe haven" for those responsible for the most serious crimes.

Human Rights Watch, THE PINOCHET PRECEDENT: HOW VICTIMS CAN PURSUE HUMAN RIGHTS CRIMINALS ABROAD (2000).

5. Professor Steinhardt asks whether ATC cases "impose a uniquely American form of liability that disadvantages U.S. corporations in the global marketplace?" Do you agree? Is this issue addressed in any of the voluntary corporate social responsibility codes discussed in the last section of the chapter?

---

4.   RELATED JURISDICTIONAL ISSUES

The ATC gives federal and subject matter jurisdiction but cases brought under the Act are still vulnerable to other procedural challenges. In *Wiwa v. Royal Dutch Petroleum,* 226 F.3d 88 (2d Cir. 2000)(*cert. denied* 121 S.Ct. 1402, 149 L.Ed.2d 345 (2001), the company was accused of complicity in the killing of Ken Saro–Wiwa, a prominent environmental activist. An important fact in *Wiwa* was that one of the plaintiffs was a U.S. resident. The District Court granted the corporation's motion for dismissal on the basis of forum non conveniens. The court of appeals reversed holding that "the district court failed to give weight to three significant considerations that favor retaining jurisdiction for trial: (1) a

United States resident plaintiff's choice of forum, (2) the interests of the United States in furnishing a forum to litigate claims of violations of the international standards of the law of human rights, and (3) the factors that led the district court to dismiss in favor of a British forum were not particularly compelling." *Id.* at 101. In addition, the court noted that a ruling of forum non conveniens presupposes that that there are "at least two forums in which the defendant is amenable to process." *Id.* (*citing Gulf Oil Corp. v. Gilbert*, 330 U.S 501, 506–07 (1947)). *See also In re Union Carbide Corp. Gas Plant Disaster*, 809 F.2d 195 (2d Cir.1987)(affirming dismissal for forum non conveniens conditioned upon defendant's consent to personal jurisdiction in India). The existence of an alternative forum is also central to a comity analysis

Comity is the recognition which one nation allows within its territory to the legislative, executive or judicial acts of another. Under this principle, courts ordinarily refuse to review acts of foreign governments and defer to proceedings taking place in foreign countries, allowing those acts and proceedings to have extraterritorial effect in the United States. In the next excerpt, the court in *Jota v. Texaco, Inc.*, 157 F.3d 153 (2d Cir.1998) addressed the issue of comity in the context of an ATC case. Indigenous tribes located in the Oriente region of Ecuador sued Texaco for environmental and personal injuries resulting from oil exploration and extraction in the region. The complaint alleges that Texaco polluted the rain forests and rivers by improperly dumping large amounts of toxic by-products into local rivers, burning additional waste, dumping waste directly into landfills, or spreading it on local dirt roads. The trial court dismissed the claim on the grounds of forum non conveniens and comity. After determining that the court abused its discretion concerning forum non conveniens, it turned its attention to the comity ruling.

Jota v. Texaco, Inc., 157 F.3d 153, 161–162 (2d Cir.1998).

In dismissing the complaints in this litigation on the ground of comity, the District Court explicitly adopted the comity considerations articulated by the District Court in *Sequihua* in dismissing a similar case. [*See* Sequihua v. Texaco, Inc., 847 F.Supp. 61, 63 (S.D.Tex.1994).] Applying the factors set forth in Restatement (3d) of Foreign Relations § 403 (1986), the Court in *Sequihua* had concluded that "the challenged activity and the alleged harm occurred entirely in Ecuador"; that the conduct at issue was regulated by the Republic and "exercise of jurisdiction by this Court would interfere with Ecuador's sovereign right to control its own environment and resources"; and that "the Republic of Ecuador has expressed its strenuous objections to the exercise of jurisdiction by this Court." *Id.* When a court dismisses on the ground of comity, it should normally consider whether an adequate forum exists in the objecting nation and whether the defendant sought to be sued in the United States forum is subject to or has consented to the assertion of jurisdiction against it in the foreign forum. That is the approach usually taken with a dismissal on the ground of forum non conveniens, as we noted in Part 1, and it is equally pertinent to dismissal on the ground of comity. Though extreme cases might be imagined where a foreign sovereign's interests were so legitimately affronted by the conduct of litigation in a United States forum that dismissal is warranted without regard to the defendant's amenability to suit in an adequate foreign forum, this case presents no such circumstances.

* * *

Ecuador contends that dismissal on the ground of comity is not warranted because it now supports the litigation of this lawsuit in a United States forum, contrary to its earlier opposition. The extent to which a court should consider the changed position of a sovereign nation in a case in which direct review has not been completed is an issue rarely encountered ... On the one hand, the interests in the orderly conduct of litigation and in the finality of judgments valid when rendered weigh in favor of holding a nation to the litigating position it asserted prior to the entry of judgment. On the other hand, inherent in the concept of comity is the desirability of having the courts of one nation accord deference to the official position of a foreign state, at least when that position is expressed on matters concerning actions of the foreign state taken within or with respect to its own territory. Of course, consideration of a nation's altered litigating stance cannot justify an altered outcome that would unduly prejudice a party that had acted in reliance on a judgment entered in light of the nation's original position or would result in a significant waste of judicial resources by renewing litigation fully tried.

* * *

Upon remand, it will be appropriate for the District Court to give renewed consideration to the comity issue in light of all the then current circumstances, including Ecuador's position with regard to the maintenance of this litigation in a United States forum.

QUESTIONS AND DISCUSSION

1. The doctrine of forum non conveniens is seen as an insult to foreign judges. A U.S. judge "who unilaterally imposes work on a Latin American colleague is acting as if he were hierarchically superior. The foreign [U.S.] judge who imposes, again acting unilaterally, the commission of certain procedural acts in Latin America, establishing conditions, terms, etc. behaves in no less offensive way." *Proposal for an Inter–American Convention on the Effects and Treatment of the Forum Non Conveniens Theory*, prepared by Dr. Gerardo Trejos Salas, Organization of American States, Comité Jurídico Interamericano, OEA/Ser.Q,CJI/doc.29/99 (14 July 1999). The OAS Proposal gives an insightful analysis of the forum non conveniens problematic from the perspective of the foreign judiciary. It concludes,

> [I]f life, health and the environment in foreign countries are considered "cheap", by a law of economics there will be enterprises willing to degrade such values for a bigger profit. Forum non conveniens allows, precisely, the opportunity to dislodge the lawsuit from where liability is "expensive", to a jurisdiction where it is "cheap". Consequently, while forum non conveniens is not eradicated, there will always be enterprises ready to speculate with merchandise and with techniques harmful to life, health and the environment of developing countries. * * *

Forum non conveniens might be a good theory within the boarders of certain countries. However, its internationalization and its export to Latin American countries create serious legal distortions. Forum non conveniens violates several constitutional guarantees and it is injurious to national sovereignty. It also disturbs important rules of procedural law and it poses considerable practical problems. For such reasons, a claim following a forum non conveniens order does not generate jurisdiction.

Id. at 12. The Proposal states that forum non conveniens violates human rights guaranteed in the American Declaration of the Rights and Duties of Man, specifically Articles II, XVII, and XVIII. Do you agree? Explain the argument you would make to support this position?

---

5.   EXPANDING THE REACH OF THE ATC

The courts have limited the reach of the ATC by recognizing only a few norms of customary international law under which States, and those acting in concert with them, may be held accountable. Even fewer norms that bind individuals, or corporations, acting independent of a State action have been identified. But the "law of nations" evolves and so too do the rights and obligations of State and non-State actors alike. *See Filartiga*, 630 F.2d at 881. Creative advocates are constantly developing innovative arguments to extend the scope of ATC claims.

Herz, *op. cit.*, at 565–637

The Scope of Substantive Claims

Courts have thus far recognized the customary international law status of only a limited number of norms. While ATC allows plaintiffs to sue for violations of newly crystallized international human rights norms, the judiciary's general mistrust of international law strongly suggests that plaintiffs cannot successfully assert unrecognized claims indiscriminately. Given that courts have not yet held environmental claims to be actionable, plaintiffs seeking redress for environmental harms should proceed with caution. As detailed below, environmental harms may give rise to various claims for violations of rights already recognized under ATC or whose status as customary international law is not controversial. The theories advanced in this Article directly address or are closely tied to the kinds of core human rights (such as the prohibition of genocide, crimes against humanity and war crimes) whose application should not inspire undue judicial apprehension.

* * *

Perhaps the most obvious question raised in addressing the actionability of environmental damage under ATC is whether customary international law recognizes a definable right to a healthy environment. The district court in *Beanal* specifically rejected the argument that in causing massive environmental devastation, Freeport violated the "law of nations." Beanal, however, based his environmental claims on the Polluter Pays and Precautionary Principles of international environmental law. These arguments are very different from the human rights based approach detailed below.

This Section argues that international law recognizes a right to a healthy environment based on, although independent from, the rights to life, health and security of the person. The right to a healthy environment is universal and obligatory. Moreover, it has a definable core of prohibited behavior. At a minimum, the right affords protections equivalent to the environmental protections afforded by the laws of war and prohibits degradation that deprives a people of its own means of subsistence. As a result, the right to a healthy environment should at least be cognizable under ATC for cases that involve a violation of one of those standards, even if the harms are purely intra-state.

* * *

Rights applicable in war can usually be considered the minimum safeguards international law affords. International law bans extreme environmental abuses, even during the exigencies of war. In particular, the widely ratified [Protocol Additional (I) to the Geneva Conventions of August 12, 1949]'s ban on means of warfare that may be expected to cause widespread, long-term and severe damage [to the natural environment and "thereby to prejudice the health or survival of the population"] strongly suggests that, at a minimum, the right to a healthy environment prohibits peacetime environmental abuses of the same magnitude.

* * *

International Environmental Law Claims

All of the claims discussed above are based upon customary human rights law. Where environmental effects originate in one state but cause harm in another, customary international environmental law also supports an ATC action. Under the *Trail Smelter Arbitration*'s classic formulation of the "state responsibility" doctrine, "no state has the right to use or permit the use of its territory in such a manner as to cause injury . . . in or to the territory of another or the properties or persons therein, when the case is of serious consequence." The "state responsibility" doctrine clearly is customary international law. Moreover, states owe this duty to private individuals in neighboring states as well as to the neighboring states themselves. One court has concluded that the norm has a state action requirement, so plaintiffs should be prepared to demonstrate TNCs are state actors for ATC purposes in order to hold them liable.

The "state responsibility" norm is specific enough for courts to apply. In *Beanal*, the court noted that the state responsibility principle is "sufficiently substantive at this time to be capable of establishing the basis of an international cause of action; that is to say, to give rise to an international customary legal obligation the violation of which would give rise to a legal remedy." Conversely, the court in *Amlon Metals* [Amlon Metals, Inc. v. FMC Corp., 775 F.Supp. 668, 671 (S.D.N.Y.1991)] rejected an ATC state responsibility claim because it found Stockholm Principle 21 to lack specific proscriptions. The *Amlon Metals* court, however, looked to no sources other than the Stockholm Declaration to determine the content of the norm. The *Restatement*'s view of that content in particular suggests that the state responsibility principle is sufficiently "specific" for ATC purposes. Therefore, *Beanal*, which concluded the norm is actionable, is the more persuasive authority. Under *Beanal*, plaintiffs should, at least in some circumstances, have an ATC cause of action for significant cross-border environmental damages.

For example, the complaint in *Jota v. Texaco, Inc.* alleges that Texaco's pollution of rivers in Ecuador has caused environmental and personal injuries to Peruvian plaintiffs living downstream. Because Texaco released toxins directly into rivers which flow to Peru rather than following prevailing industry practice of pumping wastes back into emptied wells, plaintiffs have a strong claim that Texaco failed to take measures, to the extent practicable, to prevent significant injury to the environment of another state.

QUESTIONS AND DISCUSSION

1. In theory, a successful plaintiff in an ATC case has the full range of common law remedies at her disposal. Unfortunately, even successful claims under the ATC often end with an uncollected judgment. Consider the example in *Filartiga*. 630 F.2d 876 (2d Cir.1980). Joelito Filartiga was tortured to death in Paraguay by Pena–Irala, a local police officer. Joelito's family sued the officer in federal court after learning he immigrated to the United States and was living in New York. The Filartigas received a verdict and judgment but the defendant had already fled the U.S. They are still waiting for their award after twenty years. Compare this to the outcome in *In re Estate of Marcos Human Rights Litig.,* 910 F.Supp. 1460 (D.Haw. 1995) where plaintiffs who suffered human rights violations at the hands of the former Philippine dictator were awarded $1.2 billion in compensatory and almost $800 million in punitive damages. How much do you think was collected?

In the case of a state defendant, the foreign nation often does not have assets in the United States, or if it does, they may be protected under other national or international laws such as the VIENNA CONVENTION ON DIPLOMATIC RELATIONS; AND PROTOCOLS (18 Apr 1961) or VIENNA CONVENTION ON CONSULAR RELATIONS; AND PROTOCOLS (24 Apr 1963). In cases involving multinational corporations, the search for a suitable defendant with assets to satisfy a judgment often leads to the large parent corporation whose subsidiary was the operating entity, but is beyond the reach of the court's personal jurisdiction. This raises the issue of whether the plaintiff can pierce the corporate veil (or whether the parent was directly involved in the challenged actions). In addition to the possibility of collecting damages, what other advantages might there be for bringing such cases against the parent corporation?

2. When traditional human rights violations, such as torture, are included with other torts, is there a risk of diminishing the significance of the human rights violations? Many of these cases are brought by not-for-profit organizations. How would they handle their percentage of any contingency award? Could these cases interfere with the developing international criminal law system exemplified by the International Criminal Court? *See* ROME STATUTE OF THE INTERNATIONAL CRIMINAL COURT, <http://www.un.org/law/icc/>(visited on 09/28/01).

3. U.S. courts are often reluctant to hear ATC cases, perhaps because they are less familiar with international law. This can lead to an outcome contrary to purposes of international law and the goals of human rights and environmental protection. Richard Herz has the following advice:

> Claims with two characteristics have the best chance of success. First, when plaintiffs present claims based on egregious facts, courts are less likely to hesitate to apply international law and are instead inclined to focus their attention on those facts. [All other things being equal, a court may be more receptive to an action alleging environmental damage, where plaintiffs also have claims for non-environmental human rights abuses committed in support of the project that caused the environmental harm.] Second, prudent plaintiffs will base their claims on legal principles which only apply to egregious facts, even where a broader, definable customary norm exists. Courts are likely to consider environmental ATC claims with an eye towards future cases. The narrower the scope of plaintiffs' claims, the less a court may be concerned that a ruling for the plaintiffs will allow future claims that the court might consider overly broad.

Herz, *op cit.* at 573.

4. The jurisdictional controversies surrounding the ATC reoccur around the world in international negotiations. The Hague Conference is debating two alternatives for Article 18(3) of the Draft Convention on Jurisdiction and Foreign Judgements in Civil and Commercial Matters:

> Nothing in this Article shall prevent a court in a Contracting State from exercising jurisdiction under national law in an action [seeking relief] [claiming damages] in respect of conduct which constitutes–

Variant One

> [*a)*] genocide, a crime against humanity or a war crime [as defined in the Statute of the International Criminal Court]; or]
>
> [*b)*] a serious crime against a natural person under international law; or]
>
> [*c)*] a grave violation against a natural person of non-derogable fundamental rights established under international law, such as torture, slavery, forced labour and disappeared persons.]

> [Sub-paragraphs [*b)* and] *c)* above apply only if the party seeking relief is exposed to a risk of a denial of justice because proceedings in another State are not possible or cannot reasonably be required.]

Variant Two:

> a serious crime under international law, provided that this State has established its criminal jurisdiction over that crime in accordance with an international treaty to which it is a party and that the claim is for civil compensatory damages for death or serious bodily injury arising from that crime.

DRAFT CONVENTION ON JURISDICTION AND FOREIGN JUDGMENTS IN CIVIL AND COMMERCIAL MATTERS, <http://www.hcch.net/e/conventions/draft36e.html>(visited on 09/20/01). *See* Weissbrodt, *et al., op. cit.* and Beth Van Schaack, *In Defense of Civil Redress: The Domestic Enforcement of Human Rights Norms in the Context of the Proposed Hague Judgments Convention*, 42 Harv. Int'l L.J. 141 (2001). How would these proposals affect the ATC cases?

6. *Doe, Wiwa,* and *Jota* all had similar fact patterns. A multinational corporation enters into a partnership with a repressive government in a lesser-developed country to exploit the natural resources of that nation, and local peoples suffer human rights violations in connection with the project while the local ecosystem is damaged. A major problem with many of these projects is that the company's partner often is an undemocratic, military junta without any regard for the rights of its people, as was the case in Abacha's Nigeria, and in SLORC's Burma. Ecuador, however, is a democracy, and this fact was one of the reasons the case was dismissed (although the oil-rich area of Ecuador's Oriente was heavily militarized at the time). Another key similarity in all of these cases is that the development occurred on the lands of politically marginalized ethnic minorities. The question of course is what blame rests with the corporations? Projects that would go through years of environmental impact studies if carried out by the same company in North America or Europe proceeded with little thought of environmental consequences when they are located in Africa or South America. *See An Examination of the Context and Impacts of Exxon Mobil's Security Arrangements with the Indonesian Armed Forces,* <http://.preventconflict.org/portal/main/research/jereski.htm>.

What is the relationship between the ability of affected local people to participate in the political process and a multinational corporation's efforts to protect human rights and the environment? *See* Richard Herz, *Making Development Accountable to Human Rights and Environmental Protection*, American Society of Int'l Law, Proceedings of the 94th Annual Meeting 216, 217 (2000):

When a country lacks political rights, such as rights to meaningful participation, information, expression, access to judicial remedies and at least some measure of local control, we often see distorted types of "development" ... Repressive regimes are not accountable to their people, particularly minority groups. Accordingly, they are free to impose projects that destroy environments local people depend on for their subsistence, without providing substantial local benefits. Governments understand that such projects will be unpopular, and therefore commit abuses to squelch or even preempt opposition ... Thus, an absence of respect for political rights can directly result in a type of development that is not only destructive to the environment and environmental rights, but that is often accompanied by abuses against those who protest or those who are perceived by the government as likely protestors. The projects in turn give the governments the hard currency they need to stay in power, thus funding further repression. Only meaningful political participation can break this vicious cycle, under which repression, environmental degradation and destructive "development" persist *ad infinitum*.

7. The Foreign Sovereign Immunities Act (FSIA) sets forth the general rule that foreign States are immune from the jurisdiction of both federal and state courts subject to certain exceptions. 28 U.S.C. §§ 1330(a) & 1604. A federal court lacks subject matter jurisdiction over a claim against a foreign state unless the claim falls within one of these exceptions. *Argentine Republic v. Amerada Hess Shipping Corp.*, 488 U.S. 428, 439 (1989)(holding that FSIA is "sole basis for obtaining jurisdiction over a foreign state in federal court"). *Siderman de Blake v. Republic of Argentina*, 965 F.2d 699, 707 (9th Cir.1992); *see also* (finding an implied waiver of sovereign immunity by Argentina when that country's government sought to use US courts to persecute the Sidermans).

The FSIA was enacted in 1976 and codified a strict interpretation of sovereign immunity. With the changing role of nation states and the increasing participation of non-state actors in international law, is sovereign immunity an anachronism? Consider *Doe v. Unocal*, 963 F.Supp. at 887, which dismissed claims against SLORC because it said, that the human rights abuses were "peculiarly sovereign" in nature. The appellants in *Doe* argued in response that private parties are fully capable of committing abuses in support of an oil pipeline, and that therefore the commercial activity exception applies. This dispute is relevant to other cases involving abuses committed on behalf of corporations.

8. Jordan J. Paust argues that "laws...of the United States" as contained in 28 U.S.C. § 1331 includes customary international law. He relies, in part, on the RESTATEMENT which states that "[m]atters arising under customary international law also arise under 'the laws of the United States' since international law is 'part of our law'...and is federal law." Jordan J. Paust, INTERNATIONAL LAW AS LAW OF THE UNITED STATES, 6–7 *cited* in Jordan J. Paust, et al., INTERNATIONAL LAW AND LITIGATION IN THE U.S. 117 (2000). If, as Paust suggests, customary international law is already part of federal law, why do we need the Alien Tort Claims Act? Do you agree with Paust? Does his analysis effectively meld domestic and international law into one body of jurisprudence? What would be the practical effect on the U.S. judicial system of adopting Paust's position?

9. The court in *Filartiga* defines the "law of nations" under the ATC to include customary international law. As Chapter 6 points out, there is another source of international law in addition to custom: "general principles of law recognized by civilized nations." STATUTE OF THE INTERNATIONAL COURT OF JUSTICE, Art. 38(1). *See* Chapter 6, page 291. In the context of ATC litigation, general principles could be used to support alternative theories of liability. An example of this can be found in CIEL's Amici Curiae brief, *supra*, filed in *Doe,* which argues at page 20 that:

"Vicarious liability and respondeat superior are basic legal concepts common to many national laws and enshrined in a variety of international conventions. The principles are thus part of the body of international law by virtue of their status as a general principle of law." Using the discussion of the right to life and health, and the right to a healthy environment in the previous section, what arguments would you make that these reflect custom? General principles?

10. In *Beanal v. Freeport–McMoRan, Inc.*, 969 F.Supp. 362, 374–382 (E.D.La. 1997)(*aff'd* 197 F.3d 161 (5th Cir.1999) Freeport was accused of human rights violations including "cultural genocide." The District Court for the Eastern District of Louisiana concluded:

> Beanal has failed to allege what role, if any, that Indonesian military personnel played in committing the alleged conduct. More importantly, Beanal has failed to allege facts which would convert Freeport's alleged conduct into official action. State action is required to state a claim for violation of the international law of human rights.

This holding is an example of the consequences of poor pleading. On appeal, the 5th Circuit stated that the:

> district court exercised considerable judgment, discretion, and patience below. In light of the gravity and far ranging implications of Beanal's allegations, not only did the court give Beanal several opportunities to amend his complaint to conform with the minimum requisites as set forth in the federal rules, the court also conscientiously provided Beanal with a road-map as to how to amend his complaint to survive a motion to dismiss assuming that Beanal could marshal facts sufficient to comply with the federal rules. Nevertheless, Beanal was unable to put before the court a complaint that met minimum pleading requirements under the federal rules.

Beanal v. Freeport–McMoran, Inc., 197 F.3d 161, 169 (5th Cir.1999). *Beanal* is a reminder to lawyers that they are not just litigating a case, but creating case law that those who follow must contend with.

B. OTHER NATIONAL COURTS

In addition to the ATC litigation in U.S. Federal Courts, many important cases have been decided around the world, including India, the Philippines, Chile, Costa Rica, and Ecuador, using constitutional guarantees to the right to a healthy environment and the right to life.

1. CONSTITUTIONAL RIGHT TO A HEALTHY ENVIRONMENT

The following article provides a comprehensive survey of national courts enforcing constitutional rights to a healthy environment.

Carl Bruch, Wole Coker, & Chris VanArsdale, *Constitutional Environmental Law: Giving Force to Fundamental Principles in Africa*, 26 COLUM. J. ENVTL. L. 131, 133–(2001), at 133–160

A nation's constitution is more than an organic act establishing governmental authorities and competencies: the constitution also guarantees citizens basic fundamental human rights such as the right to life, the right to justice, and increasingly the right to a clean and healthy environment. With heightened environmental awareness in recent decades, the environment has become a higher political priority, and many constitutions now expressly guarantee a "right to a healthy environment," as well as the procedural rights necessary to implement and enforce this right. Similarly, courts around the world have interpreted the near-universal provision of "right to life" to implicate the right to a healthy environment in which to live that life. * * *

Several other countries also view these constitutional principles and objectives as enforceable. In Juan Antonio Oposa v. Factoran, the petitioners claimed that the Philippines' natural forest cover was being destroyed at an alarming rate and asserted their constitutional right to a "balanced and healthful ecology" under Article 16 of the Philippine Constitution. Regarding the fundamental right to a healthful ecology, the Philippine Supreme Court enforced the petitioners' rights stating, "the fact that it was included under the Declaration of Principles and State Policies and not under the Bill of Rights did not make it any less important." The Court reasoned that a basic human right such as the right to a healthy environment need not be written in the constitution, and the fact that it is mentioned explicitly in the fundamental national charter highlights its continuing importance and imposes upon the state a solemn obligation to protect and advance that right. Similarly, in Ecological Network v. Secretary of Environment and Resources, the plaintiffs also relied on Article 16 to bring a taxpayers' suit seeking to cancel existing and future timber licenses. The Supreme Court again held that the plaintiffs had enforceable constitutional rights and declared the timber licenses invalid.

Nepal's Supreme Court has . . . arrived at the same conclusion. In Prakash Mani Sharma v. Ministers of Council, the petitioner, relying on the Directive Principles in the Constitution of Nepal, sought a writ of mandamus from the Supreme Court to prevent a construction project on public lands adjacent to Rani Pokhari ("Queen's Pond"), a pond with historical, cultural, and environmental significance. Despite arguments by the respondent that these principles and policies are not enforceable by any court, the Supreme Court determined that it is the duty of all (including the Executive and Legislature) to abide by these directives and principles, and where they are contravened the Court will make the appropriate order and give these provisions meaningful effect. * * *

Of the many countries that have interpreted constitutional environmental provisions, India has the most experience. The environmental provisions of the Indian Constitution, specifically Articles 48A (protection of the environment) and 51A (fundamental duties), are both principles of state policy. Though the application of these principles has been interwoven with the separate right-to-life provision, the scope of these environmental rights and duties has been interpreted and applied in different circumstances. One application of this right, illustrated by L.K. Koolwal v. State of Rajasthan, is that the constitutional rights to health, sanitation, and environmental preservation could be violated by poor sanitation resulting in a "slow poisoning" of the residents, without any more specific allegations of injury. Furthermore, in Rural Litigation and Entitlement Kendra v. Uttar Pradesh, the right to a "healthy environment" was invoked even though no direct link with human health had been demonstrated in the case at hand. The petitioner alleged that unauthorized mining in the Dehra Dun area adversely affected the ecology and resulted in environmental damage. Without establishing harm to human health, the Supreme Court upheld the right to live in a healthy environment and issued an order to cease mining operations, notwithstanding the significant investments of money and time by the mining company. According to this thread of interpretation, protection of this right may be sought when ongoing behavior is damaging or is likely to damage the environment, regardless of an effect on human health.

Other Indian cases emphasize that the right to a healthy environment relates principally to pollution rather than health. According to this interpretation, the guarantee of "pollution[-]free air and water" referred to by the Indian Supreme Court, does not contemplate an environment completely free from pollution since the judgment directs the state "to take effective steps to protect" the right, rather than placing an absolute duty on the state to ensure air and water that is completely free from pollution.

A third view in India views the right as an entitlement to "ecological balance." Issuing the Order in Rural Litigation and Entitlement Kendra, the Supreme Court stated:

> The consequence of this Order made by us would be that the lessees of lime-stone quarries which have been directed to be closed down permanently under this Order ... would be thrown out of business in which they have invested large sums of money and expended considerable time and effort. This would undoubtedly cause hardship to them, but it is a price that has to be paid for protecting and safeguarding the right of the people to live in healthy environment with minimal disturbance of ecological balance.

Similarly, in T. Damodhar Rao v. Municipal Corp of Hyderabad, the court stated that consideration of physical and biological data is "the legitimate duty of the Courts ... to forbid all action of the State and the citizen from upsetting the environmental balance." In all three approaches, the Indian Supreme Court has found that the right to a healthy environment necessarily includes freedom from air and water pollution.

European courts, primarily civil law, have interpreted and applied the constitutional right to a healthy environment in a range of contexts. * * *

Similarly, a number of civil law countries in Latin America also have given life to their constitutional right to a healthy environment. In the Ecuadorian case of Fundacion Natura contra Petro Ecuador, the Constitutional Court upheld a civil verdict that the defendant's trade in leaded fuel violated a congressional ban on leaded fuel, and thus violated the plaintiffs' constitutionally guaranteed right to a healthy environment. Similarly, in Arco Iris contra Instituto Ecuatoriano de Mineria, Ecuador's Constitutional Court held that "environmental degradation in Podocarpus National Park is a threat to the environmental human right of the inhabitants of the provinces of Loja and Zamora Chinchipe to have an area which ensures the natural and continuous provision of water, air humidity, oxygenation and recreation."

In the Trillium case, Chile's Supreme Court voided a timber license when the government approved an environmental impact assessment without sufficient evidence to support the conclusion that the project was environmentally viable and without incorporating the conditions proposed by different specialized agencies. The Court held that by acting in such an arbitrary and illegal way, the government violated the rights of all Chileans, not just those who would be affected locally, to live in an environment free of contamination.

In Fundacion Fauna Marina contra Ministerio de Produccion de la Provincia de Buenos Aires, an Argentine court voided a permit to capture a number of dolphins and killer whales, stating that it was first necessary to conduct an environmental impact assessment. The judge relied on Article 41 of Argentina's national constitution (recognizing the right to a clean environment and establishing a correlative duty to protect the environment), and Article 28 of the Buenos Aires provincial constitution, which requires authorities to control the environmental impacts of any activity that could damage the environment. . . .

The court held that the way to ensure the general constitutional environmental rights and duties found in these constitutions was by imposing an obligation to execute an environmental impact assessment before issuing a permit. [Cases from Peru and Costa Rica also are discussed.] * * *

Constitutional environmental provisions also impose duties to protect the environment, either through explicitly imposing a duty on the state and other parties or by implicitly granting a right to a healthy environment. Although the legal effect of such constitutionally provided duties is unclear, courts occasionally have relied upon the fundamental duties to interpret ambiguous statutes.

The constitutional duty to protect, or not harm, the environment can be borne by the government and its organs, individuals, legal persons, or some combination of these parties. In some cases, constitutional environmental duties explicitly addressed to citizens have been expanded to apply also to the state. In L.K. Koolwal v. Rajasthan, an Indian court ruled that the fundamental duty to protect the environment in Article 51A(g) extended not only to citizens, but also to instrumentalities of the state. As a result, the court held that by virtue of Article 51A(g)'s duty, citizens have the right to petition the court to enforce the constitutional duty of the state. The application of constitutional environmental rights and duties to the state is fairly straightforward. The more difficult question is whether constitutional environmental duties and rights operate only between governmental bodies and private persons ("vertical" operation), or whether these rights and duties also operate between private legal persons, so that one citizen could invoke the provision against another legal or natural person ("horizontal" operation). * * *

Two Indian cases illustrate this point. In M.C. Mehta v. Union of India (Tanneries), the petitioner sought to halt the pollution of the Ganges River by tanneries and soap factories. The Supreme Court observed that the pollution of the river was a serious public nuisance and the pollution so widespread that the water could not be used for either drinking or bathing. Issuing its order, the court held that:

> Having regard to ... the need for protecting and improving the natural environment which is considered to be one of the fundamental duties under the Constitution ... it is the duty of the Central Government to direct all the educational institutions ... to teach at least for one hour in a week lessons relating to the protection and the improvement of the natural environment including forests, lakes, rivers and wild life in the first ten classes.

Similarly, in M.C. Mehta v. Union of India, the petitioner contended that if citizens were to fulfill their duties to protect the environment as required by Article 51A(g) of the constitution, then the people needed to be better educated about the environment. The application sought to move the Supreme Court to issue directions to cinema halls, radio stations, and schools to disseminate information on the environment and to educate citizens. Granting the petition, the Supreme Court ordered

(a) the State Governments and Union Territories, to make it a prerequisite to licensing for all cinema halls to show slides dealing with environmental issues;

(b) the Ministry of Information and Broadcasting to start producing short films dealing with the environment and pollution;

(c) all radio stations to broadcast interesting programs on the environment; and

(d) the University Grants Commission to require universities to prescribe a course on the environment.

In both of these cases, the Indian Supreme Court found that in order for the constitutional provision imposing a duty upon citizens to achieve real significance, the court needed to interpret the provision as extending correlative duties to the government, media, and educational system. The court opined that imposing a constitutional duty on ordinary citizens to protect the environment is in vain if the citizens are not knowledgeable about the subject matter.

QUESTIONS AND DISCUSSION

1. In several cases in India and other jurisdictions, the courts shut down a business, despite the economic cost involved. If these cases took place in one of the NAFTA countries, would they be vulnerable to an expropriation claim under Chapter 11? What difference does it make under NAFTA that the Supreme Court took this action based on the constitutional right to a healthy environment? See Chapter 15, page 1202.

---

2.   THE RIGHT TO LIFE CASES

As discussed in the following excerpt, a constitutionally based right to life can be used effectively against environmental threats, especially in countries without a constitutional right to a healthy environment, or a strong statutory scheme. Indeed, most of the decisions on the right to life have found an implied right to a healthy environment.

Bruch, et al., *op. cit.* at 145–60.

Courts have found violations of the right to life in a variety of factual contexts. The release of pollutants that directly affect physical health or the failure of governments to regulate the release of such pollutants are the most common scenarios in which courts have found violations of the right to life. Thus, for example, the discharge of toxic substances into agricultural areas and drinking water supplies..., the release of harmful air contaminants near residential areas..., or the dumping of radioactive waste in coastal areas have been found to violate the right to life... In addition, a government's failure to perform regulatory functions that protect health or environment has also been found to violate the right. .... Finally, even actions that may not directly affect physical health, but that "disturb the environmental balance" have been found to violate the right to life broadly interpreted. Thus, for example, a government's failure to protect a recreational area or park from development was found to violate the right....

The remedies available to litigants seeking vindication of a right to life are both injunctive and compensatory in nature: courts have ordered parties to cease polluting activities and to compensate victims for harm done. Courts have also ordered governments to enforce existing regulations, create new regulations, impose penalties on polluters, deny licenses to polluters, and carry out specific tasks to alleviate an ongoing harm.

Cases Interpreting the Right to Life

1. Tanzania

Tanzania appears to be the first African nation in which courts have addressed the scope of constitutional right-to-life provisions in the context of environmental protection. Article 14 of Tanzania's constitution provides that "everyone has the right to exist and to receive from the society protection for his life, in accordance with the law." The decisions in Joseph D. Kessy v. Dar es Salaam City Council and Festo Balegele v. Dar es Salaam City Council illustrate the expansive interpretation of Article 14 by the High Court of Tanzania at Dar es Salaam.

In Kessy, the City Council of Dar es Salaam sought another extension of time to comply with the 1988 court order enjoining the city from dumping garbage in Tabata, a suburb of Dar es Salaam. The citizens of Tabata brought suit against the City Council of Dar es Salaam, seeking to enjoin the city from operating a garbage dump that created severe air pollution in nearby neighborhoods. The foul smells and air pollution had caused respiratory problems in area residents, particularly in children, pregnant women, and the elderly. The citizens won a judgment in 1988 in which the court ordered the City Council to cease using the Tabata area for dumping garbage and to construct a dumping ground where the garbage would pose no threat to the health of nearby residents. The City Council subsequently sought several extensions to comply with the court's order, effectively extending the time for compliance until August 1991. In denying the City Council's petition for an extension, the court noted that the air pollution created by the garbage dump endangered the health and lives of nearby residents, and consequently that the operation of the dump violated Article 14.

2. India

. . . India has generated by far the largest body of jurisprudence regarding the environmental aspects of the constitutional right to life. India's constitution contains provisions protecting both human health (Article 47) and the natural environment (Articles 48 and 51), in addition to extending a fundamental right to life (Article 21). Notwithstanding these other provisions relating to health and environment, India's Article 21 is often invoked to protect environmental resources. Article 21 states, "no person shall be deprived of his life or personal liberty except according to procedure established by law." Procedurally, most of the Article 21 cases protecting the environment are brought in the Supreme Court pursuant to Article 32, which grants citizens standing to sue directly in the Indian Supreme Court for violations of constitutional rights.

Indian courts have interpreted the scope of the constitutional right to life expansively to forbid all actions of both state and citizen that disturb "the environmental balance." The courts have found violations of the right to life in a variety of factual contexts. * * *

In Vellore Citizens Welfare Reform v. Union of India, the Indian Supreme Court found that tanneries in the state of Tamil Nadu violated citizens' right to life by discharging untreated effluents into agricultural areas and local drinking water supplies. The discharges rendered thousands of hectares of agricultural land either partially or totally unfit for cultivation and severely polluted the local drinking water. In granting the petitioners' requested relief, the court relied upon the idea of sustainable development, and the "precautionary" and "polluter-pays" principles and considered them integral to an interpretation of the Article 21 constitutional mandate to protect and improve the environment. The court defined the precautionary principle to mean that (1) the state must anticipate, prevent, and attack the causes of environmental degradation; (2) lack of scientific certainty should not be used as a reason for postponing measures to prevent pollution; and (3) the onus of proof is on the polluter to show that his or her actions are environmentally benign. The polluter-pays principle was defined to mean that

> polluting industries are "absolutely liable to compensate for the harm caused by them to villagers in the affected area, to the soil and to the underground water ..." [and] liability for harm ... extends not only to compensate the victims of pollution but also the cost of restoring the environmental degradation.

Applying these principles to the facts of the case, the court ordered more than nine hundred tanneries operating in Tamil Nadu to "compensate the affected persons ... and also [pay to] restore the damaged environment."

In Indian Council for Enviro–Legal Action v. Union of India, the Supreme Court found that the national government's failure to control an industry's release of toxic chemicals violated the citizens' right to life. The plaintiff-petitioner brought this action to stop and remedy pollution caused by several chemical industrial plants in the village of Bichhri in Rajasthan. The defendant-respondents operated chemical plants producing highly toxic chemicals, such as sulfuric acid, without permits and discharged waste which polluted the soil and aquifers. The defendants had failed to obey several previous court orders directing them to control the discharge of toxic materials. Relying on the constitutional right to life, the court ordered the appropriate governmental regulatory agency to impose controls on the industry, carry out remedial measures, and charge the industry for the cost of cleanup.

3. Pakistan, Bangladesh, and Nepal

Following India, the courts of Pakistan, Bangladesh, and Nepal have also interpreted constitutional right-to-life provisions expansively to include environmental protection. The constitutions of all three countries share nearly identical right-to-life provisions, stating "no person shall be deprived of life or liberty save in accordance with law." In addition, all three countries share liberal rules with regard to standing.

The courts of these three countries have invoked the right to life in a variety of factual contexts. In General Secretary, West Pakistan Salt Miners Labour Union (CBA) Khewral, Jhelum v. Director, Industries and Mineral Development, Punjab, Lahore, the Supreme Court of Pakistan found an imminent violation of the right to life where citizens' water supplies were in danger of being polluted by nearby mining operations. The court held:

> The access to water is scarce, difficult or limited, the right to have water free from pollution and contamination is a right to life itself. This does not mean that persons residing in other parts of the country where water is available in abundance do not have such right. The right to have unpolluted water is the right of every person wherever he lives.

The court ordered the mining companies to take specific measures to prevent polluting the drinking water, including the relocation of their operations. The court also appointed a commission with both powers of inspection to monitor implementation of the court's orders and the ability to order further measures to ensure the area's drinking water remained unpolluted. Finally, the government agencies involved were ordered not to grant any new mining licenses or to renew old ones without leave of the court.

In the case In re: Human Rights Case (Environmental Pollution in Balochistan), the Supreme Court of Pakistan itself initiated a proceeding against industries seeking to dump radioactive waste in a coastal area. The court found that the dumping could "create environmental hazard and pollution" in violation of the constitutional right to life. . . .

In Dr. Mohiuddin Farooque v. Bangladesh, the court held that the petitioner had standing to bring an action against the state for an alleged violation of the constitutional right to life. The petitioner, the Secretary General of the Bangladesh Environmental Lawyers Association, filed suit seeking to halt the implementation of a flood-control program that would adversely affect the region's natural resources and the flora and fauna of the surrounding area. The court noted that citizens have a "right to life as a fundamental right. It encompasses within its ambit, the protection and preservation of the environment, ecological balance free from pollution of air and water, sanitation without which life can hardly be enjoyed."

In LEADERS, Inc. v. Godawari Marble Industries, Nepal's Supreme Court held that a marble mining operation contaminating the water supplies and the soil violated nearby residents' constitutional right to life. The petitioners alleged that Godawari Marble Industries had caused serious environmental degradation of the Godawari forest and its surroundings. They further alleged that the industries' activities contaminated nearby water bodies, soil, and air to the detriment of local inhabitants, members of the petitioner's organization, and laborers in the mining industry. The court noted that "[life] is threatened in [a] polluted environment . . . " and "it is the legitimate right of an individual to be free from [a] polluted environment." The court reasoned that "since [a] clean and healthy environment is an indispensable part of a human life, the right to [a] clean, healthy environment is undoubtedly embedded within the Right to Life." It then ordered the government ministries to "enact necessary legislation for protection of air, water, sound and environment and to take action for protection of the environment of [the] Godawari area." * * *

4. Colombia, Ecuador, and Costa Rica

The civil law jurisdictions of Colombia, Ecuador, and Costa Rica have all recognized a constitutional right to life in the context of environmental protection. In many cases, Latin American litigants use an "amparo," a form of legal action or proceeding used to guarantee constitutional rights other than the right of physical freedom covered by the writ of habeas corpus.

Colombian courts have applied the constitutional right to life in a variety of factual contexts, expansively interpreting it and holding that environmental protection must be understood as an extension of the rights of physical integrity and personal security. In Victor Ramon Castrillon Vega contra Federacion Nacional de Algodoneros y Corporacion Autonoma Regional del Cesar (CORPOCESAR), the Supreme Court of Colombia found that an industry's release of toxic fumes from an open pit endangered the health and life of nearby residents and therefore violated their constitutional rights to health and life. The court ordered the respondent industry to remove the waste and safely dispose of it, to pay for the costs of safely moving and disposing of the waste, and to pay past and future medical expenses of those who fell ill as a result of the illegal waste.

FUNDEPUBLICO, a Colombian NGO, has brought many cases to protect Colombians' constitutional right to health and life. In FUNDEPUBLICO contra SOCOPAV, Ltda., FUNDEPUBLICO filed an action requesting relocation of an asphalt plant located in an urban area. The Constitutional Court granted the petition, holding in part that pollution emanating from the plant threatened the right to life. The court held that the right to live in a healthy environment is a basic human right, and that environmental protection was an extension of the constitutional right to life. In FUNDEPUBLICO contra Compania Maritima de Transporte Croatia Line y Comar S.A., a Colombian court found that the rights to life and health were violated by the respondents' importation of toxic waste into Colombia, and the court ordered the companies to remove 575 drums of toxic industrial waste. In Organizacion Indigena de Antioquia contra Corporacion Nacional de Desarrollo del Choco, the Constitutional Court held that the constitutional rights to life, work, property, and cultural integrity had been infringed upon by an illegal clear-cut, ordering the regional authority to restore the area and to develop a reliable estimate of the economic damages that the indigenous people living in the area had suffered. Other right-to-life cases brought by FUNDEPUBLICO have addressed tannery wastes, unsanitary waste dumps, and a highly polluting asphalt factory.

In the Ecuadorian case Fundacion Natura contra Petro Ecuador, an Ecuadorian environmental law NGO brought suit against both a corporation for illegally cutting trees on indigenous lands and against the government agency for its failure to take care of the lands and protect the indigenous community. The court ordered the agency to assess the damage and to compensate the community, holding that the community could sue the corporation once the assessment was completed. The court also passed a general prohibition making "illegal" any activity that diminishes or harms the area that was the subject of this litigation.

In the Costa Rican case Carlos Roberto Mejia Chacon contra Ministerio de Salud y la Municipalidad de Santa Ana, the Supreme Court held that a waste disposal site in a small canyon threatened the constitutional right to life of the petitioner, ordered the municipality to stop disposing of waste at the site, and closed the illegal dump. Interestingly, the Chacon court relied on the right to life and not the right to a healthy environment recognized by the Costa Rican constitution.

———

QUESTIONS AND DISCUSSION

1. Note the range of remedies in the right to life cases, including damages for liability, injunctions, and various orders. How do these remedies compare with the remedies available in the U.N. human rights system, and the various regional systems? Which would you prefer to use to vindicate the right to life? Consider the requirement for exhaustion. Where national legal systems are corrupt, weak, or otherwise not independent enough to provide justice, the human rights system may be the best place to bring your claim. But where national courts are strong and independent, they may be superior. Consider the Suni reindeer case in Finland.

2. How do the standing requirements compare in the human rights systems and the national courts considered in the previous article? How might human rights law assist a plaintiff in a national court establish standing?

3. How did the Indian Supreme Court utilize the precautionary principle and the polluter pays principle to find a violation of the right to life in the *Vellore* case in India? Is there a human right to an effective tort system? What arguments would you make to support such a right?

4. What degree of environmental harm is necessary before a court will find a violation of the right to life? Are there any circumstances when it is not necessary to show environmental harm? Consider the *West Pakistan Salt Miners Labour Union* case. What kind of a showing by plaintiffs did the Court find acceptable? Is there a right to water in the traditional human rights instruments?

5. When is it appropriate to balance the various interests in cases under the right to life? Recall the discussion of common law nuisance.

————

SECTION V. APPLYING ENVIRONMENTAL HUMAN RIGHTS DIRECTLY TO CORPORATIONS

Human rights are principally directed to governments and are principally the responsibility of governments. Yet private actors have always been within the scope of human rights law, including norms against piracy, slavery, and war crimes As Professor Steinhardt states in the reading below, "there is no doctrinal firebreak that keeps private corporations from being liable for any violation of international law, ever."

This is a critical point, as a great deal of the world's wealth and power is controlled by transnational corporations, of which there were 37,000 in 1994, with over 200,000 affiliates spread around the world, compared to only 7,000 in 1970. Consider that 51 of the world's 100 largest economies are corporations, and only 49 are countries; that the combined sales of the world's top 200 corporations are greater than a quarter of the world's economic activity; and that the top 200 corporations have almost twice the resources of the poorest four-fifths of humanity. *See* Sarah Anderson and John Cavanagh, *The Top 200: The Rise of Global Corporate Power* (1996), at <http://www.corpwatch.org/trac/corner/glob/ips/top200.html>.

As TNCs outdistance the national legal systems that traditionally regulated their activities, efforts to design appropriate international legal responses are gathering momentum. Chapter 18 focuses on international corporate standards for environmental performance. Another approach is to apply human rights directly to corporations—including environmental human rights—and these efforts are advancing on several fronts, as we have seen throughout this chapter, including through virtually all of the human rights bodies, as well as domestic courts.

In the following reading, Professor Steinhardt notes four different regimes for regulating corporate human rights: a market-based regime, a regime of domestic regulation, an emerging regime of international regulation, and a regime of civil liability—"now overarching and perhaps propelling those regulatory and market-based initiatives." He states that "it seem[s] clear that the prospect of litigation may have accelerated the voluntary, marketplace initiatives and that litigation will define the primitive minimum beneath which the market will not operate.... [T]here are times when the market works best because there are clear liability rules...."

Ralph G. Steinhardt, *"Litigating Corporate Responsibility"*, New York, United Nations, 1 June 2001, at 1–12

http://www.globaldimensions.net/articles/cr/steinhardt.html

[There are] four regimes of corporate responsibility, emerging as it were simultaneously in the human rights field and very much inter-related:

First, *a market-based regime*, under which corporations compete for consumers and investors by conforming to international human rights standards. ...

Second, a *regime of domestic regulation*, exemplified by directives and legislation in the United States, which, through human rights conditionality, recruit the transnational corporation as an instrument of foreign policy. Legislation designed to curb the corporate presence in Burma, Libya, and Cuba, preceded in the United States by the Anti-apartheid Act of 1986, exemplifies this approach.

Third, there is *an emerging regime of international regulation* and soft law by intergovernmental organizations [which] have attempted to channel corporate conduct in ways that are thought to be socially responsible. Here the inkblot includes the OECD's principles, the UN's Global Compact, the Human Rights Commission's Proposed Draft Human Rights Code of Conduct for Companies, and the decisions of the international financial institutions, which by historical standards anyway increasingly reflect human rights concerns.

Fourth, now overarching and perhaps propelling those regulatory and market-based initiatives is a regime of civil liability enforced through private lawsuits in domestic courts. Here we start with the truth that various domestic courts in the United States have ruled that corporations may in principle be obliged to pay substantial damage awards for their complicity in abuses by the governments with which they do business.

Consider for example the Holocaust cases, which have generated the most attention in the popular press: these are suits, sometimes authorized by special statutes in particular states, addressing Holocaust claims, brought against Swiss, German, Austrian, and French companies including banks, insurance companies, and manufacturers, to recover looted assets or converted accounts, or seeking damages for wrongful death or slave labor. ...

Of course, not all of these private lawsuits arise out of World War II. Currently pending in the California Supreme Court for example is a suit against Nike under the state statute regulating deceptive advertising and unfair business practices. The complaint is that Nike falsely proclaims a commitment to human rights that is allegedly violated in fact. The theory of liability is that manufacturers cannot lie about the processes by which they make and market their products. A consumer who relies on Nike's human rights commitment in deciding which sneakers to buy has been just as misled–assuming that the commitment is more public relations than reality–as someone who buys a gallon of milk falsely labeled "pasteurized." That case was dismissed in March 2000 on the ground that the particular plaintiff had no standing to complain, but the underlying theory of the case remains to be tested.

Other possible litigation or litigation-like vehicles for the enforcement of corporate human rights standards are the so-called quo warrant to proceedings which seek the cancellation or the forfeiture of a company's corporate charter for abusing the public trust or acting ultra vires. It would of course take more than a failure to live up to best practices to justify such an extraordinary remedy, but again one can imagine the argument that a corporation acting consistently in violation of international law would lose the privilege of the corporate form.

A very different and so far hypothetical alternative arises out of the power of the US Securities and Exchange Commission to issue disclosure regulations as "necessary or appropriate in the public interest or for the protection of investors." In a seminal article in the Harvard Law Review (The SEC and Corporate Social Transparency, 1999), Professor Cynthia Williams has argued that the SEC should expand the requirements for so-called social disclosure, including information on the countries in which a company does business; information on its domestic and global labor practices, and on its domestic and global environmental effects. ... Even more specialized statutory grounds for corporate liability litigation in the U.S. are provided by the Racketeer Influenced and Corrupt Organizations Act (RICO), which has been invoked to advance human rights claims against companies engaged in human rights violations that take criminal form.

It is possible, of course, that special legislation or perhaps some international instrument would attempt to define the requisite relationship more directly, and doubtless as the cases proliferate, the pressure for that kind of legislative instrument will build. But I am not optimistic that legislation will anticipate every nexus issue that is likely to arise in future cases; indeed, if the history of codifying common law causes of action proves anything, it is that the common law process doesn't stop just because there is a statute in the picture. The process of interpretation will continue even if there is a statutory framework
. . . .

... [L]let me conclude that domestic litigation offers one imperfect but legitimate mode for maintaining the general impetus towards corporate responsibility in the human rights field. But I suspect that the proliferation of such cases will justify a global standard that is so grounded in international law as to offer corporations a measure of protection from overly aggressive or idiosyncratic approaches to human rights.

In addition to liability regimes, constitutional guarantees, and traditional human rights litigation, there are other efforts designed to persuade TNCs that it is in their best corporate interest and the interest of their shareholders to respect human rights and the environment. Two business school professors who are at the forefront of this effort as it concerns the environment are Michael Porter at the Harvard Business School, and Stewart Hart at the business school at University of North Carolina, Chapel Hill. Their rigorous research shows that good environmental management leads to higher corporate value.

Similar evidence exists for good human rights practices. For example, the U.N. High Commissioner for Human Rights, indicates that business concern for human rights helps companies:

(1) ensure compliance with local and international laws; (2) satisfy consumer concerns; (3) promote stable legal environments; (4) build corporate community goodwill; (5) aid in the selection of ethical, well-managed, and reliable business partners; (6) aid in producing a predictable, stable, and productive business enterprise; (7) keep markets open; and (8) increase worker productivity and retention. Further, if human rights guidelines for companies become widely accepted, companies will enjoy greater predictability [and] ... a level playing field for business competition. Such predictability is a basic foundation for sustainable development and prosperity.

United Nations High Commissioner for Human Rights, Business and Human Rights, http://www.unhchr.ch/global.htm. *See also Draft Universal Human Rights Guidelines for Companies, Introduction, U.N. Doc.* E/CN.4/Sub.2/2002/WG.2/WP.1 (2001), Introduction, at para. 2.

Partly as a result, companies interested in promoting sustainable development are increasingly described as having a "triple bottom line," profits, social performance, and environmental performance. As Shell Oil describes itself, this means focusing on "people, planet and profits." In the following excerpt, Bennett Freeman argues that the companies that fail to consider their triple bottom line do so at their peril.

[T]here is unprecedented interest in the corporate responsibility world in human rights—and unprecedented interest in the human rights world in corporate responsibility. I think this is the case for three major reasons. First, the corporate responsibility movement has evolved over the last three decades and has now fully embraced human rights. The movement got its greatest initial impetus in the Seventies from environmental issues, picked up steam in the mid-Seventies to the mid-Eighties on South Africa and infant formula marketing as well as nuclear weapons, with social investors and shareowner activists playing a more important supporting role year by year. The child labor and sweatshop issues emerged in the mid-Nineties, together with the whole nexus of human rights issues confronting the extractive sectors. The corporate social responsibility movement now has a comprehensive scope and direct link to the human rights community and agenda around the world as never before.

Second, the human rights movement has evolved beyond political and civil rights, beyond even an abstract interest in cultural and economic rights, and is now beginning to embrace a corporate social responsibility agenda as well. The Universal Declaration may have fostered a dominant focus on the rights of individuals and the responsibilities of states, but its text included a tantalizing reference to the duty of "every organ of society" to promote respect for human rights. That reference, of course, has been the touchstone for human rights lawyers and advocates who have developed and deployed tools and tactics in recent years to hold companies accountable for their conduct in the workplace and for their impact on indigenous communities. Moreover, the human rights community has come to recognize that multinational companies are the most powerful non-state actors in the world, and therefore represent both a problem and an opportunity for human rights activists—sometimes as a target but also a potential constituency.

The third reason why I believe that there is such a convergence of interests and agendas between the corporate responsibility and human rights—and why there should be a powerful new engagement on the part of the corporate community with both—is globalization. Globalization is clearly the greatest revolutionary force of our time, and clearly of greatest benefit thus far to multinational enterprises who with their technology, trade and investment have done so much to drive this juggernaut forward. But just as clearly, the backlash against globalization that has emerged over the past several years is the greatest boost ever for the corporate social responsibility movement—a boost which I believe will sustain the movement's new momentum or at least make its forward direction irreversible. This forward direction is irreversible because, in my view, the backlash against globalization has fundamentally shifted the balance of power in global governance by putting company after company in sector after sector on the defensive as they are targeted, boycotted, sued, or merely scrutinized and criticized on issue after issue. Indeed, corporate social responsibility is now established as one of the three interlocking arenas of the battle over globalization, along with the place of labor and environmental protections in trade and investment agreements, and the accountability of international institutions such as the WTO, the World Bank and the IMF.

At stake are human rights and building a broader future constituency for human rights. At stake is the "social license to operate" of the multinational enterprise, and the quality and sustainability of the business and investment environment it will inhabit. At stake is the future of globalization, or at least a chance to build a consensus for a more balanced, inclusive globalization that will serve civil society's interest in democratic accountability and the business community's interest in expanded trade, sustainable investment and growth. With so much at stake, and with so many apparently clashing but potentially converging interests coming together, we should seek further opportunities to find common ground.

Bennett Freeman, *Converging Corporate Responsibility and Human Rights Agendas: three reasons*, New York, United Nations, 1 June 2001, at 1–7, <http://www.globaldimensions.net/articles/cr/freeman.html>. *See also* Chapter 18, describing the rise of corporate guidelines. The U.N. Sub–Commission on the Promotion and Protection of Human Rights recently established a Working Group to develop a code of conduct for companies based on human rights standards, with participation from business and NGOs. This draft was presented to the Working Group and to the Sub–Commission in August, 2001.

Draft Universal Human Rights Guidelines for Companies, Addendum 1, U.N. Doc. E/CN.4/Sub.2/2001/WG.2/WP.1/Add.1 (2001)

A. General Obligations

1. While governments have the primary obligation to respect, ensure respect for, and promote internationally recognized human rights, companies also have the obligation to respect, ensure respect for, and promote international human rights within their respective spheres of activity and influence.

2. Nothing in these Guidelines shall diminish the human rights obligations of governments.

* * *

C. Right to security of persons

4. Companies shall not engage in nor benefit from war crimes, crimes against humanity, genocide, torture, forced disappearance, hostage-taking, abuses in internal armed conflict, and other international crimes against the human person

5. Security arrangements for companies shall observe the law and professional standards of the country in which they operate in so far as those laws do not conflict with international human rights standards.

D. Rights of Workers

6. Companies shall not use forced or slave labour.

7. Companies shall not use child labour and shall contribute to its abolition.

8. Companies shall provide a safe and healthy working environment

* * *

13. Companies shall respect the rights to health, adequate food, and adequate housing, and refrain from actions that obstruct the realization of those rights. Companies shall also respect other economic, social, and cultural rights, such as the rights to primary education, rest and leisure, and participation in the

cultural life of the community and refrain from actions that obstruct the realization of those rights.

F. Obligations with regard to Consumer Protection

15. Companies shall act in accordance with fair business, marketing, and advertising practices and should take all reasonable steps to ensure the safety and quality of the goods and services they provide.

G. Obligations with regard to Environmental Protection

16. Companies shall carry out their activities in accordance with national laws, regulations, administrative practices, and policies relating to the preservation of the environment of the countries in which they operate and with due regard to relevant international agreements, principles, objectives, and standards with regard to the environment as well as human rights; shall take due account of the need to protect the environment, public health, and safety; and shall generally conduct their activities in a manner contributing to the wider goal of sustainable development.

———

QUESTIONS AND DISCUSSION

1. Other codes and declarations for business practices include OECD Guidelines, ILO's Tripartite Declaration, the U.N.'s Global Compact, and earlier, the U.N.'s Code of Conduct for Transnational Corporations. The UN and OECD codes are described in Chapter 18. The ILO's Tripartite Declaration of Principles concerning Multinational Enterprises was adopted in 1977, with periodic amendments, including in 2000, to incorporate new conventions and recommendations adopted after its original passage. *See* International Labor Organization, Updating of References Annexed to the Tripartite Declaration of Principles concerning Multinational Enterprises and Social Policy, ILO Doc. GB.277/MNE/3 (2000). The U.N.'s Global Compact was proposed in January 1999, U.N. Doc SG/SM/6448 (1999), with nine core principles in categories dealing with general human rights obligations, standards of labor, and standards of environmental protection, whereby businesses should:

> (1) support and respect the protection of internationally proclaimed human rights within their sphere of influence; (2) make sure they are not complicit in human right abuses; (3) uphold the freedom of association and the effective recognition of the right to collective bargaining; (4) eliminate all forms of forced and compulsory labour; (5) abolish child labor; (6) eliminate discrimination in respect of employment and occupation; (7) support a precautionary approach to environmental challenges; (8) undertake initiatives to promote greater environmental responsibility; and (9) encourage the development and diffusion of environmentally friendly technologies.

The Global Compact < http://www.unhchr.ch/global.htm> (last visited on October 7, 2001). The earlier U.N. Commission on Transnational Corporations' draft U.N. Code of Conduct for Transnational Corporations, was never fully adopted by the U.N. Development and International Economic Cooperation: Transnational Corporations, U.N. Doc. E/1990/94 (1990).

2. However human rights and environment are pursued, there remains the difficult problem of measuring progress. A Philippine NGO, for example, is current-

ly developing standards and indicators for economic, social and cultural rights to respond to the needs of victims of human rights violations arising from "development aggression," which it defines to include the following practices:

- demolition;

- land use conversion;

- labor contractualization;

- displacement; and

- environmental destruction.

See Ayesha Dias, *Human Rights, Environment and Development: with Special Emphasis of Corporate Accountability* (UNDP 2000), http://www.undp.org/hdro/Dias2000.html (describing among other things the efforts of the Task Force for Detainees of the Philippines). What indicators would you suggest for measuring progress in the field of human rights and the environment? What do you think of the concept of "development aggression".

3. What is the relationship between the various voluntary codes of conduct and potential liability under the Alien Torts Claims Act, or other theories of damages?

Suggested Further Reading and Web Sites

Lance A. Compa & Stephen F. Diamond (eds.), *Human Rights, Labor Rights, and International Trade*, (1996).

> Arguing that there is a place for the ATC within the fabric of the transnational labor rights regime.

Jed Greer, *Plaintiff Pseudonymity and the Alien Tort Claims Act: Questions and Challenges*, 32 Colum. Human Rights L. Rev. 517 (2001).

> Discusses techniques to maintain confidentiality including the appointment of a "special master" in ATC cases.

Armin Rosencranz and Richard Campbell, *Foreign Environmental and Human Rights Suits Against U.S. Corporations in U.S. Courts*, 18 STANFORD ENV. L.J. 145 (1999).

Richard L. Herz, *Litigating Environmental Abuses Under the Alien Tort Claims Act: A Practical Assessment*, 40 Va. J. Int'l L. 545 (2000)

> Insightful article on ATC litigation from the plaintiff's perspective.

Russell Mokhiber & Robert Weissman, CORPORATE PREDATORS: THE HUNT FOR MEGA-PROFITS AND THE ATTACK ON DEMOCRACY (1999).

> Highlights human rights violations and environmental degradation committed by corporations around the world.

ARMIN ROSENCRANZ, ENVIRONMENTAL LAW AND POLICY IN INDIA (2nd ed., 1991)

> Discussions of right to life and right to a healthy environment.

Romina Picolotti & Jorge Daniel Taillant, Human Rights Accountability of Private Business: A Question of Sustainable, International Council on Human Rights Policy, January 2000; and by the same authors, Human Rights and Corporations: Legal Responsibility of Corporations for Human Rights Abuses in Argentina, International Council on Human Rights Policy, October 2000.

These papers provide a framework for discussion of the human rights obligations of private business in the context of recently developed environmental principles and international standards for corporate activities.

Ralph G. Steinhart & Anthony A. D'Amato, THE ALIEN TORT CLAIMS ACT: AN ANALYTICAL ANTHOLOGY (1999)

Provides an overview of the ATC, jurisdictional questions, and international torts. Includes bibliographical references and index to cases.

Beth Stephens and Michael Ratner, INTERNATIONAL HUMAN RIGHTS LITIGATION IN U. S. COURTS (1996).

http://www.earthrights.org

Homepage of organization serving as co-counsel in both *Doe v. Unocal* and *Wiwa*.

http://www.laborrights.org

Homepage of the organization representing plaintiffs in suits against Coca Cola and Exxon under the ATC. The International Labor Rights Foundation also represents the plaintiffs in *Roe v. Unocal,* a companion case to *Doe v. Unocal* consolidated on appeal.

http://www.unocal.com/myanmar

An example of a corporate defendant's point of view in ATC litigation.

CHAPTER SEVENTEEN

NATIONAL SECURITY, THE LAW OF WAR, AND ENVIRONMENTAL PROTECTION

> *If trees could speak they would cry out that since they are not the cause of war it is wrong for them to bear its penalties.*
>
> HUGO GROTIUS, ON THE LAW OF WAR AND PEACE (1625)

SECTION I.   NATIONAL SECURITY AND ENVIRONMENTAL PROTECTION

Throughout history, environmental degradation has threatened the stability of States. Tensions created by resource degradation, resource scarcity, and forced migration have exacerbated conflict both within and between nations. Traditional visions of national security have focused on military and economic measures of strength, but comparing relative numbers of tanks, planes and submarines, while easy to do, ignores the destabilizing influences of resource scarcity and social inequities.

For years, environmentalists have argued that responsible environmental protection and resource management reduce conflict. NATO and its member governments now agree, and have started directing significant resources to study the relationship between environmental degradation and conflict. The implications of this research are clear–considerations of resource allocation (particularly fresh water), wide-scale pollution, resource management, and land tenure become unavoidable when assessing national and international security. Consider the following threats to national security. Is there a military solution to the problems they pose?

- In the past 50 years, some 10 million Bangladeshis have fled their homeland and immigrated illegally into India, greatly exacerbating ethnic tensions there, occasionally into open conflict. The refugees have fled from traditional lands that, now degraded, can no longer support them. Nick Robins and Charlie Pye–Smith, *The ecology of violence*, NEW SCIENTIST, March 8, 1997, at 12.

- On the isolated Easter Island in the Pacific Ocean, site of the enormous statues made famous by Thor Heyerdahl's research, inhabitants cut down the island's last remaining forests in the 17th century. This soon led to water scarcity and food shortages, since trees no longer held groundwater and no more canoes could be built for fishing. In a matter of years, the society disintegrated into civil war and cannibalism. C. Ponting, A GREEN HISTORY OF THE WORLD: THE ENVIRONMENT AND THE COLLAPSE OF GREAT CIVILIZATIONS (1992).

- Scientists predict that a likely consequence of global warming might be a rise in sea level. Low-lying countries may, quite literally, sink beneath the ocean waves.

- In the early 1990s, Slovakia designed and began construction of a nuclear power plant using Soviet technology and design. The Mohovce Power Station was sited near the Austrian border. Austria complained formally to Slovakia over the siting of an unreliable and potentially dangerous facility so close to its borders.

How do environmental threats rise to the level of national security concerns? The first is through *direct* threats to the territorial integrity of a nation. It is impossible to protect national borders against "spill-over harms" such as acid rain and ozone depletion. While these environmental problems may seem irrelevant to national security, the direct impact on citizens from skin cancers and respiratory ailments can be no less harmful than battlefield injuries. In this regard, efforts to reach meaningful international environmental agreements are of similar importance to arms control agreements. Both reduce the risk of harm to the nation's citizens. It is no surprise that a number of low-lying island nations have formed a negotiating bloc in the climate change negotiations.

The second source of threats to national security is *indirect*, such as environmental degradation in one nation that undermines the stability of another. The most obvious security threat created in this manner is mass migration. People forced to leave their traditional land because it can no longer support them have been described as "environmental refugees," and their numbers are increasing on an unprecedented scale. One estimate places the number of environmental refugees at 25 million people. *See* Lester Brown et al., VITAL SIGNS 83 (1997). These people displaced for environmental causes outnumber the roughly 23 million refugees displaced by civil wars, political oppression, and ethnic and religious persecution. Often environmental refugees are subsistence farmers, impoverished and vulnerable to soil degradation and water scarcity, with little or no political influence. Their number may double by the year 2010 if soil and fresh water degradation continue at current rates. Indeed, should global warming lead to rises in sea level, the number of environmental refugees will grow far higher as low-lying coastal areas are submerged, forcing their current population to move. *See* Norman Myers and Jennifer Kent, ENVIRONMENTAL EXODUS (1995). An example of this in the United States was the thousands of "boat people" from Haiti, fleeing a nation whose ability to feed itself has been washed away as a result of extensive deforestation and soil erosion.

See Jessica Mathews, *Redefining Security*, FOREIGN AFFAIRS, Spring 1989, at 162–177.

Few would argue that environmental problems often are the prima facie source of a conflict, but it is self-evident that they can exacerbate existing tensions that ultimately lead to conflict. Some scholars contend, for example, that deforestation and soil erosion were major contributors to the revolt in the Chiapas region in Mexico and much of the immigration from Mexico to the United States, since more than 60% of Mexico's land is severely degraded. Does this condition make Mexican illegal immigrants to the United States economic migrants or environmental refugees? Should it matter? Researchers at the University of Toronto in Canada have studied over 10 cases of conflict in developing countries. They conclude that three principal factors increase conflict over environmental resources–degradation and depletion of a key resource, population growth that increases resource demands, and disproportionate allocation of the resource within society. Their research, they contend, establishes a causal link between environmental scarcity, poverty, and migration; and all three factors interact to undermine State stability. Nick Robins and Charlie Pye–Smith, *The ecology of violence*, NEW SCIENTIST, March 8, 1997, at 12; T. Homer–Dixon and V. Percival, PAPER OF THE PROJECT ON ENVIRONMENT, POPULATION, AND SECURITY: THE PEACE AND CONFLICT STUDIES PROGRAM 6 (1996).

The Clinton administration reacted to the linkage between national security and environmental protection by creating a high-level position in the State Department, the Under Secretary of State for Global Affairs, focusing on international environmental issues which bear on national security. The State Department also pledged to publish an annual report on environmental diplomacy, assessing diplomatic efforts to address environmental threats to national security. Below is the preface to the first report from Secretary of State, Madeleine Albright, describing the initiative. *See* <http://www.state.gov/www/global/oes/earth.html>.

Madeleine K. Albright, Environmental Diplomacy: The Environment and U.S. Foreign Policy (1997)

Just over one year ago, then-Secretary of State Christopher announced that the State Department would spearhead a government-wide effort to meet the world's environmental challenges. He said, "The United States is providing the leadership to promote global peace and prosperity. We must also lead in safeguarding the global environment upon which that prosperity and peace ultimately depend." This report is an outgrowth of that initiative. It will be released every year on Earth Day. Its purpose is to update global environmental challenges and policy developments and to set our priorities for the coming year.

Not so long ago, many believed that the pursuit of clean air, clean water, and healthy forests was a worthy goal, but not part of our national security. Today environmental issues are part of the mainstream of American foreign policy.

We are building on three basic premises.

First, we know that damage to the global environment, whether it is overfishing of the oceans, the build-up of greenhouse gases in the atmosphere, the release of chemical pollutants, or the destruction of tropical forests, threatens the health of the American people and the future of our economy. We know that rapid population growth exacerbates these problems and has consequences that transcend national borders. And we know that the global environment can be protected most effectively if nations act together. For these reasons, this effort must be a central concern of American foreign policy.

Second, environmental problems are often at the heart of the political and economic challenges we face around the world, In Russia and central Europe, environmental disasters left over from the Soviet era shorten lives and impede reform. In central Africa, rapid population growth combined with the competition for scarce resources fuels conflict and misery. We would not be doing our jobs as peacemakers and as democracy-builders, if we were not also good stewards of the global environment.

Third, we believe, as did President Kennedy, that "problems created by man can be solved by man." The environmental problems we face are not the result of natural forces or the hidden hand of chaos; they are caused by human beings. These problems can be solved if America works in partnership with governments, NGOs and businesses that share our commitment to a cleaner and healthier world.

To meet this challenge, the State Department is changing the way we do business. Four years ago, we appointed an Under Secretary for Global Affairs. Our embassies and bureaus are developing regional environmental policies that advance our larger national interests. To help coordinate these policies, we are opening regional environmental hubs at our embassies in Costa Rica, Uzbekistan, Ethiopia, Nepal, Jordan, and Thailand. We have made environmental cooperation an important part of our relationships with countries like Japan, India, Brazil and China. * * *

Environmental diplomacy is a work in progress.

The depletion of our fisheries, the increase in the level of greenhouse gases, and the destruction of habitats and species did not occur overnight and cannot be reversed overnight. We must work with the Congress and the American people to obtain the resources we need to support our diplomacy in this area, as in all others.

QUESTIONS AND DISCUSSION

1. One important legal issue raised by the sheer number of environmental refugees is the definition of refugee status. In many countries the right of asylum is granted to refugees with a well-founded fear of persecution in their country as a result of their race, religion, ethnicity, or political opinion. Economic hardship and environmental collapse are not recognized as justifications for the right of asylum. Should the legal treatment of asylum seekers be modified to include those fleeing serious environmental degradation (e.g. famine or drought) or would that open a nation's borders too wide? Consider the perspective of Richard Lamm, presented in Chapter 2, page 96.

2. Assume you are a skeptical environmental journalist. What information would you want from the State Department to ensure that its Environmental Diplomacy initiative described by Secretary of State Albright is not simply a public relations exercise?

3. For further analysis of these issues, check out the Global Environmental Change and Human Security (GECHS), an interdisciplinary project seeking:

1) to promote research activities in the area of global environmental change and human security;

2) to promote dialogue and encourage collaboration among scholars from around the world; and

3) to facilitate improved communication (and cooperation) between the policy community, other groups, including NGOs, and the research community.

Its URL is <www.gechs.org>

SECTION II. THE LAW OF WAR AND ENVIRONMENTAL PROTECTION

A. BACKGROUND

The limits of international law have perhaps proven most glaring in times of war. Despite the United Nations Charter's prohibition of the threat or use of force in international relations, war unfortunately remains a hallmark of human society. Art. 2(4) of the Charter of the United Nations, 15 UNCIOD (1945). Though unable to abolish warfare, international law has played a useful role regulating wartime conduct. Over the last 300 years, international law has with some success developed effective rules restricting the means and methods of warfare. Over this period, coverage of the law of war has expanded from protection of objects to protection of people and, most recently, to protection of the environment.

In 1625, Hugo Grotius published ON THE LAW OF WAR AND PEACE, the seminal work defining the international law of war. Grotius identified four basic principles regulating the conduct of warfare:

- it is unnecessary to destroy anything in areas unoccupied by the enemy;
- destruction should not occur if victory is imminent;
- or if the object to be destroyed can be obtained elsewhere;
- or if the object cannot be used to wage war.

Grotius' principles of law were not adopted by any major powers during the Thirty Years' War of 1618–1648 nor during the Napoleonic Wars of 1796–1815. It was not until the American Civil War of 1861–1864 that the law of war moved from principle to practice. During the Civil War, the Union Army adopted a code of conduct known as the Lieber Code of 1863. The Lieber Code imposed rules on the treatment of civilians and prisoners of war as well as restricting the means and methods of warfare to protect property whose destruction was not necessary to the war effort.

The underlying principle of the law of war (also known as the law of armed conflict) is that limits exist on the rights of belligerents to adopt means of injuring the enemy. Derived from this core principle are four generally accepted principles: military necessity (defined by the Lieber Code as "those measures which are indispensable for securing the ends of war, and which are lawful according to the modern law and usages of war"), proportionality (actions should not cause damage which is excessive in relation to the military advantage gained), prevention of unnecessary suffering, and discrimination between civilian and military targets. Francis Lieber, *Instructions for the Government of Armies of the United States in the Field*, promulgated as General Order No. 100 by President Lincoln, April 24, 1863 (Art. 14).

Later conventions created rules for the protection of those wounded in war (1864 Geneva Convention) and banned particular weapons of war that "uselessly aggravate the suffering of disabled men, or render their death inevitable . . . , contrary to the laws of humanity." 1868 St. Petersburg Declaration Renouncing the Use, in Time of War, of Explosive Projectiles Under 400 Grammes Weight.

B.   THE HAGUE CONVENTIONS OF 1899 AND 1907 (HAGUE I–IV)

The Hague series of conventions began in 1899 at the initiative of Tsar Nicholas II of Russia for the purpose of limiting armaments. These were followed by a subsequent Hague Conference in 1907, convened at the initiative of President Theodore Roosevelt. Together, these conferences resulted in a series of Conventions that expanded the law of war's coverage to asphyxiating gases (Hague I), the use of expanding bullets (Hague II), the rights of neutral powers and persons (Hague III), and the laws and customs of war on land (Hague IV). The Hague Law, as these combined conventions are commonly known, based its restrictions on the principle that "the right of belligerents to adopt means of injuring the enemy is not unlimited." Hague Declaration (IV) Respecting the Laws and Customs of War on Land, Article 22 Annex, Sec.2, ch. I.

The Hague Law did not address the environment directly, though the annex to Hague IV provides some indirect environmental protection. Hague IV is concise, consisting of a preamble and nine articles. However, the core of the convention is its annex of fifty-six articles addressing the laws and customs of war on land. Article 23 provides indirect environmental protection:

Article 23

In addition to the prohibitions provided by special Conventions, it is especially forbidden-

(a) To employ poison or poisoned weapons;* * *

(e) To employ arms, projectiles, or material calculated to cause unnecessary suffering;* * *

(g) To destroy or seize the enemy's property, unless such destruction or seizure be imperatively demanded by the necessities of war;* * *

Article 3 of Hague IV provides for sanctions in the form of monetary compensation for all acts committed by persons forming part of its armed forces. The convention, however, does not provide for any criminal liability nor for any mechanism to enforce the civil penalties. No parties have been held liable under Article 3. Many nations now regard Hague IV as customary international law. Indeed the international military tribunal at Nuremberg, following World War II, stated that the rules of land warfare expressed in Hague IV "undoubtedly represented an advance over existing International Law at the time of their adoption . . . but by 1939 these rules

... were recognized by all civilizations and were regarded as being declaratory of the laws and customs of war." U.S. DEPARTMENT OF DEFENSE, CONDUCT OF THE PERSIAN GULF WAR 606 (1992).

C. GENEVA CONVENTIONS OF 1949 (GENEVA CONVENTIONS I–IV)

The Geneva series of conventions began in 1864 with the first Geneva Convention on the wounded of war, followed by subsequent conventions and protocols in 1868, 1906, and 1929. Due in part to these conventions, prisoners of war were no longer put to the sword and hospitals and hospital ships were generally not the subject of intentional attack. Following the horrors of World War II and recognition of the need for more specific provisions to protect victims of war, four additional Geneva Conventions were signed in 1949 by sixty-four nations. These conventions expanded the 1907 Hague Conventions to address the wounded and sick in the field (Geneva I), the wounded and sick at sea (Geneva II), prisoners of war (Geneva III), and civilians (Geneva IV). In contrast to Hague Law that addressed the means and methods of warfare, the "Geneva Law," created by the Geneva Conventions, addressed the protection of victims during wartime. The principles established in both the Hague and Geneva Conventions form the foundation of the modern law of war. Col. James P. Terry, *The Environment and the Laws of War: The Impact of Desert Storm*, 45 NAVAL WAR COLLEGE REV. 62 (Winter 1992).

D. PROTOCOL I ADDITIONAL TO THE GENEVA CONVENTIONS

While early international agreements focused on the protection of objects and individuals and lacked any direct reference to the environment, various agreements did indirectly provide environmental protection. The use of poisonous gas during World War I resulted in the 1925 Geneva Gas Protocol, which prohibits the use in war, though not the possession, of biological and chemical weapons. Protocol for the Prohibition of the Use in War of Asphyxiating, Poisonous or Other Gases, and of Bacteriological Methods of Warfare, June 17, 1925. More recently, the 1972 Bacteriological Convention prohibits the development, production, and stockpiling of chemical and biological weapons, thus protecting flora and fauna from the effects of such toxins. Convention on the Prohibition of the Development, Production and Stockpiling of Bacteriological (Biological) and Toxic Weapons and on their Destruction of 10 April 1972.

Such agreements, however, did not address intentional attacks on the environment during wartime. Environmental manipulation for hostile military purposes has been employed in the past through means such as intentional deforestation or flooding through the destruction of dams. During the Second Sino–Japanese War of 1937–1945, for example, destroyed dams resulted in the drowning of advancing troops as well as the destruction of local farmlands and the loss of over 4000 Chinese villages. Dams were also targets of destruction during World War II and the Korean War. Arthur H. Westing, *Environmental Warfare*, 15 ENVTL. L. 645, 651–52 (1985). In the Vietnam War, large-scale use of 'agent orange' and other chemical herbicides caused major defoliation. Other potential environmental threats include the intentional generation of tsunamis for the military purpose of destroying coastal cities and near-shore facilities, the release of radioactive elements, and most recently, the burning of oil wells.

In 1977, to reduce the threats from chemical warfare, two international agreements directly addressed environmental protection during warfare for the first time. Articles 35 and 55 of *Protocol I Additional to the Geneva Conventions* prohibit attacks on the environment that may cause "widespread, long term, and severe" environmental damage. During the treaty negotiations, parties understood the words, "long term," to mean a period of years, even decades. This clarification was important because obviously most conventional battlefield operations cause environmental damage, but only short term damage. Article 56 addresses the danger to the environment resulting from the destruction of dams, dikes or nuclear electrical generating stations if the result will be severe losses among the civilian population. Article 54 prohibits in certain circumstances the destruction of, *inter alia*, agricultural areas or irrigation works. Article 36 mandates parties to determine whether the acquisition, development or use of a new weapon would be compatible with existing international law. During this assessment rules on the protection of the environment are to be taken into account.

Protocol I provides for both criminal and civil sanctions for violations of "grave breaches" as defined in Article 85 of the Protocol. Article 91 provides that civil liability and the obligation to pay compensation may be imposed upon a State Party or members of its armed forces. Article 86 provides that criminal liability may be imposed upon superiors for failure to prevent "grave breaches" of the Convention under certain circumstances.

Protocol I does not address battlefield damage incidental to warfare. Furthermore, during the negotiations the International Committee of the Red Cross and the United States expressed the position that the new rules of Protocol I do not have any effect on and do not regulate or prohibit the use of nuclear weapons (though other nations do regard Articles 35(3) and 55(1) as placing limitations on nuclear weapons). The United States is not a party to the Protocol. Col. James P. Terry, *The Environment and the Laws of War*, 45 Naval War College Rev. 61, 64 (Winter 1992).

Protocol I came into force in 1978 and was ratified without qualification by 59 countries, and with qualification by another 19 by the end of 1990. Thirty-seven countries, including the United States, have signed Protocol I but not ratified it. G. Plant, Environmental Protection and the Law of War (1992). In reading the excerpts below, pay attention to the cases when environmental damage is permitted in pursuit of a legitimate military objective.

Protocol I Additional to the Geneva Convention of 12 August 1949, and Relating to the Protection of Victims of International Armed Conflicts Dec. 12, 1977, 1125 U.N.T.S., 6 U.S.T. 3516.

Article 35
Basic Rules

1. In any armed conflict, the right of the Parties to the conflict to choose methods or means of warfare is not unlimited.

2. It is prohibited to employ weapons, projectiles and material and methods of warfare of a nature to cause superfluous injury and unnecessary suffering.

3. It is prohibited to employ methods or means of warfare which are intended, or may be expected, to cause widespread, long-term and severe damage to the natural environment.

Article 36

New Weapons

In the study, development, acquisition or adoption of a new weapon, means or method in warfare, a High Contracting Party is under an obligation to determine whether its employment would, in some or all circumstances, be prohibited by this Protocol or by any other rule of international law applicable to the High Contracting Party.

* * *

Article 54

Protection of Objects Indispensable to the Survival of the Civilian Population

1. Starvation of civilians as a method of warfare is prohibited.

2. It is prohibited to attack, destroy, remove or render useless objects indispensable to the survival of the civilian population, such as foodstuffs, agricultural areas for the production of foodstuffs, crops, livestock, drinking water installations and supplies and irrigation works, for the specific purpose of denying them for their sustenance value to the civilian population or to the adverse Party, whatever the motive, whether in order to starve out civilians, to cause them to move away, or for any other motive.

3. The prohibitions in paragraph 2 shall not apply to such of the objects covered by it as are used by an adverse Party:

(a) as sustenance solely for members of its armed forces; or

(b) if not as sustenance, then in direct support of military action, provided, however, that in no event shall actions against these objects be taken which may be expected to leave the civilian population with such inadequate food or water as to cause its starvation or force its movement.

4. These objects shall not be made the objects of reprisals.

5. In recognition of the vital requirements of any Party to the conflict in the defence of its national territory against invasion, derogation from the prohibitions contained in paragraph 2 may be made by a Party to the conflict within such territory under its own control where required by imperative military necessity.

Article 55

Protection of the Natural Environment

1. Care shall be taken in warfare to protect the natural environment against widespread, long-term and severe damage. This protection includes a prohibition of the use of methods or means of warfare which are intended or may be expected to cause such damage to the natural environment and thereby to prejudice the health or survival of the population.

2. Attacks against the natural environment by way of reprisals are prohibited.

Article 56
Protection of Works and Installations Containing Dangerous Forces

1.   Works or installations containing dangerous forces, namely dams, dikes and nuclear electrical generating stations, shall not be made the object of attack, even where these objects are military objectives, if such attack may cause the release of dangerous forces and consequent severe losses among the civilian population. Other military objectives located at or in the vicinity of these works or installations shall not be made the object of attack if such attack may cause the release of dangerous forces from the works or installations and consequent severe losses among the civilian population.

2.   The special protection against attack provided by paragraph 1 shall cease:

(a) for a dam or dyke only if it is used for other than its normal function and in regular, significant and direct support of military operations and if such attack is the only feasible way to terminate such support:

(b) for a nuclear electrical generating station only if it provides electrical power in regular, significant and direct support of military operations and if such attack is the only feasible way to terminate such support.

(c) for other military objectives located at or in the vicinity of these works or installations only if they are used in regular, significant and direct support of military operations and if such attack is the only feasible way to terminate such support.

4.   It is prohibited to make any of the works, installations or military objectives mentioned in paragraph 1 the object of reprisals.

E.   THE ENMOD CONVENTION

The other international law of war agreement specifically directed at environmental protection is the *Convention on the Prohibition of Military or Any Other Hostile Use of Environmental Modification Techniques.* 31 U.S.T. 333, 1108 U.N.T.S. 151 (May 18, 1977). Known as the 1977 ENMOD Convention, it was ratified by 36 countries. A short document, the ENMOD Convention prohibits the use of techniques that modify the environment and cause "widespread, long-lasting or severe" destruction, damage or injury to another party. "An understanding defines the terms 'widespread, long-lasting or severe.' 'Widespread' is defined as 'encompassing an area on the scale of several hundred square kilometers;' 'long-lasting' is defined as 'lasting for a period of months, or approximately a season;' and 'severe' is defined as 'involving serious or significant disruption or harm to human life, natural and economic resources or other assets.' " United States Arms Control and Disarmament Agency, ARMS CONTROL AND DISARMAMENT AGREEMENTS: TEXTS AND HISTORIES OF THE NEGOTIATIONS 211–213 (1990)

Recall that Protocol I prohibits actions that are "widespread, long-lasting *and* severe." Many commentators have argued that the difference between ENMOD's language ("*or* severe") and Protocol I's make ENMOD's coverage broader. Any State Party that has reason to believe another State Party is acting in breach of the Convention's obligations may lodge a complaint with the United Nations Security Council, which will investigate the claim and issue a report. Art. V, Para 2. If the report concludes that a State has been harmed, or will likely be harmed, the complaining State may request assistance from the other Parties. The ENMOD Convention does not provide for any civil or criminal liability.

Environmental Modification Convention (ENMOD), 31 U.S.T. 333, 1108 U.N.T.S. 151 (May 18, 1977)

Article 1

1. Each State Party to this Convention undertakes not to engage in military or any other hostile use of environmental modification techniques having widespread, long-lasting or severe effects as the means of destruction, damage or injury to any other State Party.

Article 2

As used in article 1, the term "environmental modification techniques" refers to any technique for changing–through the deliberate manipulation of natural processes–the dynamics, composition or structure of the Earth, including its biota, lithosphere, hydrosphere and atmosphere, or of outer space.

Article 3

1. The provisions of this Convention shall not hinder the use of environmental modification techniques for peaceful purposes and shall be without prejudice to the generally recognized principles and applicable rules of international law concerning such use.

2. The States Parties to this Convention undertake to facilitate, and have the right to participate in, the fullest possible exchange of scientific and technological information on the use of environmental modification techniques for peaceful purposes. States Parties in a position to do so shall contribute, alone or together with other States or international organizations, to international economic and scientific co-operation in the preservation, improvement, and peaceful utilization of the environment, with due consideration for the needs of the developing areas of the world.

F. 1980 PROTOCOL III TO THE UNITED NATIONS CONVENTIONAL WEAPONS CONVENTION

In 1980, with the use of napalm during the Vietnam War in mind, the international community regulated the use of incendiary weapons or those capable of causing fire. Article 2(4) of Protocol III to the UN Conventional Weapons Convention prohibits making "forests or other kinds of plant cover the object of attack by incendiary weapons except when such natural elements are used to cover, conceal or camouflage combatants or other military objectives, or are themselves military objectives." Convention on the Prohibitions or Restrictions on the use of Certain Conventional Weapons which May be Deemed to be Excessively Injurious or to have Indiscriminate Effects, Oct. 10, 1980, Protocol on Prohibitions or Restrictions on the Use of Incendiary Weapons (Protocol III), *reprinted in* 19 I.L.M. 1523, 1534 (1980).

G. NUCLEAR WEAPONS

In 1991, a General Assembly resolution stated that the use of nuclear weapons would be a violation of the United Nations Charter (which forbids the threat or use of force against the territorial integrity or political independence of any State) and a crime against humanity. U.N.G.A. Res. 46/37 D (1991). Two years later, the UN's General Assembly and the World Health Organization requested the International Court of Justice to issue an advisory opinion on the legality of the use of nuclear weapons. The international community took an active interest in the case and 42 nations filed written comments to the Court. A key question concerning the law of war was whether Protocol I and ENMOD applied to nuclear weapons at all. Recall the language in both agreements restricting methods and means of warfare causing widespread, long-term and/or severe damage to the environment. How did this text relate to the use of nuclear weapons?

On July 8, 1996, the ICJ decided by a margin of one vote that the threat or use of nuclear weapons would generally be contrary to the law of war's rules on armed conflict. However, in view of the current state of international law, the ICJ stated it could not conclude whether the threat or use of nuclear weapons would be lawful or unlawful in the extreme case of self-defense in which the State's very survival were at stake. This decision's treatment of environmental issues provides practical application of the different sources of the modern law of war and makes an important contribution to international environmental law.

Legality of the Threat or Use of Nuclear Weapons General List No. 95, Advisory Opinion of July 8, 1996

27. In both their written and oral statements, some States furthermore argued that any use of nuclear weapons would be unlawful by reference to existing norms relating to the safeguarding and protection of the environment, in view of their essential importance.

Specific references were made to various existing international treaties and instruments. These included Additional Protocol I of 1977 to the Geneva Conventions of 1949, Article 35, paragraph 3, of which prohibits the employment of "methods or means of warfare which are intended, or may be expected, to cause widespread, long-term and severe damage to the natural environment"; and the Convention of 18 May 1977 on the Prohibition of Military or Any Other Hostile Use of Environmental Modification Techniques, which prohibits the use of weapons which have "widespread, long-lasting or severe effects" on the environment (Art. 1). Also cited were Principle 21 of the Stockholm Declaration of 1972 and Principle 2 of the Rio Declaration of 1992 which express the common conviction of the States concerned that they have a duty "to ensure that activities within their jurisdiction or control do not cause damage to the environment of other States or of areas beyond the limits of national jurisdiction." These instruments and other provisions relating to the protection and safeguarding of the environment were said to apply at all times, in war as well as in peace, and it was contended that they would be violated by the use of nuclear weapons whose consequences would be widespread and would have transboundary effects.

28. Other States questioned the binding legal quality of these precepts of environmental law; or, in the context of the Convention on the Prohibition of

Military or Any Other Hostile Use of Environmental Modification Techniques, denied that it was concerned at all with the use of nuclear weapons in hostilities; or, in the case of Additional Protocol I, denied that they were generally bound by its terms, or recalled that they had reserved their position in respect of Article 35, paragraph 3, thereof.

It was also argued by some States that the principal purpose of environmental treaties and norms was the protection of the environment in time of peace. It was said that those treaties made no mention of nuclear weapons. It was also pointed out that warfare in general, and nuclear warfare in particular, were not mentioned in their texts and that it would be destabilizing to the rule of law and to confidence in international negotiations if those treaties were now interpreted in such a way as to prohibit the use of nuclear weapons.

29. The Court recognizes that the environment is under daily threat and that the use of nuclear weapons could constitute a catastrophe for the environment. The Court also recognizes that the environment is not an abstraction but represents the living space, the quality of life and the very health of human beings, including generations unborn. The existence of the general obligation of States to ensure that activities within their jurisdiction and control respect the environment of other States or of areas beyond national control is now part of the corpus of international law relating to the environment.

30. However, the Court is of the view that the issue is not whether the treaties relating to the protection of the environment are or not applicable during an armed conflict, but rather whether the obligations stemming from these treaties were intended to be obligations of total restraint during military conflict.

The Court does not consider that the treaties in question could have intended to deprive a State of the exercise of its right of self-defence under international law because of its obligations to protect the environment. Nonetheless, States must take environmental considerations into account when assessing what is necessary and proportionate in the pursuit of legitimate military objectives. Respect for the environment is one of the elements that go to assessing whether an action is in conformity with the principles of necessity and proportionality.

This approach is supported, indeed, by the terms of Principle 24 of the Rio Declaration, which provides that:

"Warfare is inherently destructive of sustainable development. States shall therefore respect international law providing protection for the environment in times of armed conflict and cooperate in its further development, as necessary."

31. The Court notes furthermore that Articles 35, paragraph 3, and 55 of Additional Protocol I provide additional protection for the environment. Taken together, these provisions embody a general obligation to protect the natural environment against widespread, long-term and severe environmental damage; the prohibition of methods and means of warfare which are intended, or may be expected, to cause such damage; and the prohibition of attacks against the natural environment by way of reprisals.

These are powerful constraints for all the States having subscribed to these provisions.

32. General Assembly resolution 47/37 of 25 November 1992 on the Protection of the Environment in Times of Armed Conflict, is also of interest in this context. It affirms the general view according to which environmental considerations constitute one of the elements to be taken into account in the

implementation of the principles of the law applicable in armed conflict: it states that "destruction of the environment, not justified by military necessity and carried out wantonly, is clearly contrary to existing international law." Addressing the reality that certain instruments are not yet binding on all States, the General Assembly in this resolution "[a]ppeals to all States that have not yet done so to consider becoming parties to the relevant international conventions."

In its recent Order in the Request for an Examination of the Situation in Accordance with Paragraph 63 of the Court's Judgment of 20 December 1974 in the Nuclear Tests (New Zealand v. France) Case, the Court stated that its conclusion was "without prejudice to the obligations of States to respect and protect the natural environment" (Order of 22 September 1995, I.C.J. Reports 1995, p. 306, para. 64). Although that statement was made in the context of nuclear testing, it naturally also applies to the actual use of nuclear weapons in armed conflict.

33. The Court thus finds that while the existing international law relating to the protection and safeguarding of the environment does not specifically prohibit the use of nuclear weapons, it indicates important environmental factors that are properly to be taken into account in the context of the implementation of the principles and rules of the law applicable in armed conflict.

34. In the light of the foregoing the Court concludes that the most directly relevant applicable law governing the question of which it was seised, is that relating to the use of force enshrined in the United Nations Charter and the law applicable in armed conflict which regulates the conduct of hostilities, together with any specific treaties on nuclear weapons that the Court might determine to be relevant.

* * *

53. The Court must therefore now examine whether there is any prohibition of recourse to nuclear weapons as such; it will first ascertain whether there is a conventional prescription to this effect.

54. In this regard, the argument has been advanced that nuclear weapons should be treated in the same way as poisoned weapons. In that case, they would be prohibited under:

(a) the Second Hague Declaration of 29 July 1899, which prohibits "the use of projectiles the object of which is the diffusion of asphyxiating or deleterious gases";

(b) Article 23 (a) of the Regulations respecting the laws and customs of war on land annexed to the Hague Convention IV of 18 October 1907, whereby "it is especially forbidden: ... to employ poison or poisoned weapons"; and

(c) the Geneva Protocol of 17 June 1925 which prohibits "the use in war of asphyxiating, poisonous or other gases, and of all analogous liquids, materials or devices".

55. The Court will observe that the Regulations annexed to the Hague Convention IV do not define what is to be understood by "poison or poisoned weapons" and that different interpretations exist on the issue. Nor does the 1925 Protocol specify the meaning to be given to the term "analogous materials or devices." The terms have been understood, in the practice of States, in their ordinary sense as covering weapons whose prime, or even exclusive, effect is to

poison or asphyxiate. This practice is clear, and the parties to those instruments have not treated them as referring to nuclear weapons.

56.   In view of this, it does not seem to the Court that the use of nuclear weapons can be regarded as specifically prohibited on the basis of the above-mentioned provisions of the Second Hague Declaration of 1899, the Regulations annexed to the Hague Convention IV of 1907 or the 1925 Protocol (see paragraph 54 above).

57.   The pattern until now has been for weapons of mass destruction to be declared illegal by specific instruments. The most recent such instruments are the Convention of 10 April 1972 on the Prohibition of the Development, Production and Stockpiling of Bacteriological (Biological) and Toxin Weapons and on their destruction-which prohibits the possession of bacteriological and toxic weapons and reinforces the prohibition of their use-and the Convention of 13 January 1993 on the Prohibition of the Development, Production, Stockpiling and Use of Chemical Weapons and on Their Destruction-which prohibits all use of chemical weapons and requires the destruction of existing stocks. Each of these instruments has been negotiated and adopted in its own context and for its own reasons. The Court does not find any specific prohibition of recourse to nuclear weapons in treaties expressly prohibiting the use of certain weapons of mass destruction.

58.   In the last two decades, a great many negotiations have been conducted regarding nuclear weapons; they have not resulted in a treaty of general prohibition of the same kind as for bacteriological and chemical weapons. * * *

QUESTIONS AND DISCUSSION

1.   Do you consider that a duty to protect the environment during armed conflict is emerging as a binding customary principle of international law? Which laws of war would you cite in support of this position? What other instruments or actions would you cite? Does the International Court of Justice opinion on nuclear weapons qualify this principle? In practical terms, do you think the ICJ could have decided that the use of nuclear weapons under any circumstances violated international law? For a series of essays by many of the leading international law scholars on the decision and pleadings, *see* LAURANCE BOISSONS DE CHAZOURNES AND PHILIPPE SANDS, INTERNATIONAL LAW, THE INTERNATIONAL COURT OF JUSTICE AND NUCLEAR WEAPONS (1998).

2.   The United States Navy's manual of operations specifically addresses the protection of the environment during armed conflict. In reading its contents, *below,* identify which treaty provisions it refers to.

It is not unlawful to cause collateral damage to the natural environment during an attack upon a legitimate military objective. However, the commander has affirmative obligation to avoid unnecessary damage to the environment to the extent that it is practicable to do so consistent with military accomplishment. To that end, and as far as military requirements permit, methods or means of warfare should be employed with due regard to the protection and preservation of the natural environment. Destruction of the natural environment not necessitated by mission accomplishment and carried out wantonly is prohibited. Therefore, a commander should consider the environmental damage which will result from an attack on a legitimate objective as one of the factors during targeting analysis.

The Commander's Handbook on the Law of Naval Operations, US Navy Doc. NWP1–14M, 1995, para. 8.1.3. *As quoted in* Edward Page, *Theorizing the Link Between Environmental Change and Security,* 9 Review of European Community & International Environmental Law 33 (Issue 1, 2000).

3. The International Committee of the Red Cross (ICRC) has, since its origins, been concerned with the conduct of war. Following the Gulf War, it drafted the Guidelines for Military Manuals and Instructions on the Protection of the Environment in Times of Armed Conflict. ICRC argued that existing protections, if properly implemented and respected, provided sufficient protection. Similar in some ways to restatements in American law, the Guideline's main purpose was to collect the various requirements together in a coherent series of rules. In 1994, the UN Secretary–General attached the guidelines to a report on the UN Decade of International Law and the General Assembly urged all States to disseminate the Guidelines widely. UN Doc. A/49/323, Aug. 19, 1994; A/RES/49/50. Some of the Guidelines are excerpted below.

Specific Rules on the Protection of the Environment

(8) Destruction of the environment not justified by military necessity violates international humanitarian law. Under certain circumstances, such destruction is punishable as a grave breach of international humanitarian law. [followed by specific cites to the various laws of war]

(9) The general prohibition on destroying civilian objects, unless such destruction is justified by military necessity, also protections the environment. [followed by specific cites to the various laws of war]

In particular, States should also take all measures required by international law to avoid:

(a) making forests or other kinds of plant cover the object of attack by incendiary weapons except when such natural elements are used to cover, conceal or camouflage combatants or other military objectives, or are themselves military objectives. [followed by specific cites]

(b) attacks on objects indispensable to the survival of the civilian population, such as foodstuffs, agricultural areas or drinking water installations, if carried out for the purpose of denying such objects to the civilian population. [followed by specific cites]

(c) attacks on works or installations containing dangerous forces, namely dams, dikes and nuclear electrical generating stations, even where they are military objectives, if such attack may cause the release of dangerous forces and consequent severe losses among the civilian population and as long as such works or installations are entitled to special protection under Protocol I additional to the Geneva Conventions. [followed by specific cites]

(d) attacks on historic monuments, works of art or places of worship which constitute the cultural or spiritual heritage of peoples. [followed by specific cites]

(10) The indiscriminate laying of landmines is prohibited. The location of all pre-planned minefields must be recorded. Any unrecorded laying of remotely delivered non-self neutralizing landmines is prohibited. Special rules limit the emplacement and use of naval mines. [followed by specific cites]

See Jean–Marie Henckaerts, *Towards Better Protection for the Environment in Armed Conflict: Recent Developments in International Humanitarian Law,* 9 Review of European Community & International Environmental Law 13 (Issue

1, 2000); Hans–Peter Gasser, *For Better Protection of the Natural Environment in Armed Conflict: A Proposal for Action*, 89 AJIL 637 (1995).

Problem Exercise: 1990 Persian Gulf War

Jessica E. Seacor, *Note, Environmental Terrorism: Lessons from the Oil Fires of Kuwait* 10 AM.U.J.INT'L.L. & POL'Y 481, 484–88 (1994)

On August 2, 1990, Iraqi military forces invaded the neighboring nation of Kuwait. * * *

The United Nations closely monitored the Iraqi occupation of Kuwait. Between the August 2, 1990 invasion and the end of November 1990, the U.N. Security Council drafted a series of resolutions mandating the unconditional withdrawal of Iraqi forces from Kuwait. On December 3, 1990, the U.N. Security Council adopted Resolution 678, authorizing member states to employ the necessary means to uphold the previous resolutions if Iraq continued to disobey them.

The deadline for withdrawal expired on January 15, 1991. The next day, an allied coalition of military forces from thirty-four nations initiated Operation Desert Storm with U.N. authorization to use force against Iraq for its failure to comply with the withdrawal order. Within a week, intense and unprecedented bombing by the coalition forces maimed the massive Iraqi army.

In retaliation, however, the Iraqi forces launched an attack on the environment of the Persian Gulf that some suggest was a foreseeable disaster. Saddam Hussein's apparent motive was to deter an allied invasion of Kuwait by air, land, and water. Iraqi forces bombed one of the largest Kuwaiti oil fields near the Saudi Arabian border, two major mainland refineries, an offshore loading terminal, and anchored tankers.

By late January 1991, Iraq pumped several million barrels of oil into the Persian Gulf from supply lines between the refineries and an offshore terminal, creating a slick at least nine miles long. The spill immediately affected the wildlife of the region, including migratory birds and sea turtles. Moreover, the spill contaminated the fresh water supply of Kuwait and eastern Saudi Arabia provided by desalination facilities. The burning oil facilities and Gulf spill captured worldwide media attention and prompted grave concern for the environmental consequences. Nevertheless, Iraqi troops continued to attack Kuwait's oil fields as the forces retreated, igniting oil wells and facilities at several hundred locations. By the end of February, the troops had surrendered.

Although the war officially ended on March 1, 1991, concluding forty-three days of technologically sophisticated "hyperwar," the retreating Iraqi's final act of igniting hundreds of Kuwaiti oil wells remains the most enduring legacy of the war. As the fires consumed ten percent of the world's daily oil ration each day, environmental concerns heightened. This final act, coupled with the oil spills and earlier fires, galvanized the international community to respond to the deliberate destruction of the Persian Gulf environment.

Major Walter G. Sharp, Sr., *The Effective Deterrence of Environmental Damage During Armed Conflict: A Case Analysis of the Persian Gulf War* 137 MIL. L. REV. 1, 40–41 (1992)

The Iraqi invasion of Kuwait on August 2, 1990, resulted in the "The most momentous and destructive war in modern history ... [and] unprecedented environmental ruin." This environmental damage was caused primarily by the torching of oil wells, the flooding of oil into the Persian Gulf, and the incidental damage caused by military bombing and maneuvers.

During its retreat, the Iraqi Army intentionally dynamited 732 producing oil wells in Kuwait. Over 650 of these oil wells caught fire, causing oil laden clouds as high as 22,000 feet. Some of the blazes reached 200 feet into the air, while the eighty-two dynamited wellheads that did not catch fire continuously poured oil into the countryside. At the peak of destruction, the fires burned about five million barrels of oil daily, generated more than half a million tons of aerial pollutants per day, and consumed more than 100 million dollars of oil daily. * * *

The New York Times reported that these fires were believed to be one of the world's "gravest air pollution disasters," and just two days after the fires began, Iran reported that "black rain" had fallen on its lands.* * *

The last oil well fire was not extinguished until November 1991–eight months after the Iraqi retreat. The intentional flooding of the oil into the Persian Gulf was equally disastrous. Oil spills estimated at four to six million barrels covered some 600 square miles of the sea surface of the Persian Gulf and 300 miles of its coastline. The enormous oil slick created by this flooding irreparably has damaged a unique ecosystem full of marine life. The destruction of this food source will be felt for generations, and the seeping oil could taint the groundwater supply. Thousands of migratory birds have perished, mistaking the oil lakes for water. The toxic metals released by the oil slicks and torched wells that will enter the food chain can cause brain damage and cardiovascular disorders in humans. * * *

Twenty-eight teams from ten countries joined in "history's biggest fire fight." These teams exceeded ten thousand workers from the United States, Canada, Britain, China, Iran, France, Hungary, the Soviet Union, Romania, and Kuwait.

The last oil well fire ceremoniously was sealed on November 6, 1991. The total cost for the operation to put out the fires was estimated to be almost two billion dollars. The next step in the clean-up was to begin to drain the twenty-five to fifty million barrels of oil in the hundreds of lakes that dot the Kuwaiti countryside. Total reconstruction and rehabilitation is estimated to cost twenty-two billion dollars.

While the Gulf War obviously was not the first war resulting in environmental damage, it was the first for which parties actively relied on international law to seek compensation for wartime environmental damage. This reflected both an increasing international concern for the environment and the fact that environmental targets had been deliberately attacked during the Gulf War beyond what military necessity required, carrying, as one commentator later observed, "a scorched earth policy to the extreme." Howard S. Levie, *War Crimes in the Persian Gulf,* 1996 ST. LOUIS-WARSAW TRANSATLANTIC L.J. 153 (1996).

On the same day that the Gulf War began, the United Nations Security Council passed Resolution 660 condemning the Iraqi invasion. A number of resolutions followed, including Resolution 678 which authorized the use of force that eventually resulted in the liberation of Kuwait, and Resolution 687. U.N. Doc. S/RES/687 (1991). Resolution 687 states:

Iraq ... is liable under international law for any direct loss, damage, including environmental damage and the depletion of natural resources, or injury to foreign governments, nationals and corporations, as a result of Iraq's unlawful invasion and occupation of Kuwait.

Following the conflict, in addition to charges of destroying Kuwaiti property and the use of chemical and biological weapons, Iraq was alleged to have violated Article 23(g) of the Annex to the 1907 Hague Convention IV Respecting the Customs of War on Land of 18 October 1907 (forbidding the destruction of "enemy property unless imperatively demanded by the necessities of war;") and Article 147 of the 1949 Geneva Civilians Convention (designating the "extensive destruction ... of property, not justified by military necessity and carried out unlawfully and wantonly" a grave breach). Howard S. Levie, *Id.* In theory, the International Court of Justice may hear claims for compensation from a violating party; however, nations must submit themselves to the jurisdiction of the court. Iraq is not a party to Hague IV, Protocol I Additional to the 1949 Geneva Convention, or the ENMOD Convention. The United States, the U.K. and France are not parties to Protocol I.

Security Council Resolution 687 created a Compensation Commission to administer claims paid from a fund generated by Iraqi oil sales after April 2, 1991. All revenue from these sales would be received by an escrow account with thirty percent allocated to the compensation fund, and seventy percent allocated to Iraq for food, medicine, and other essential needs. As of 2000, about $6.8 billion had been paid out. In the past decade, 2.6 million claimants have come forward asking for over $300 billion in damages. Even if most of these were granted, with the fund receiving about $400 million a month it would take many years to compensate them. Most, if not all, of the compensation awarded has been for property rather than environmental damage, though in June, 2001, the Commission awarded Kuwait $108.9 million for environmental remediation efforts. Colum Lynch, *Kuwaiti War Claim Approved*, WASH. POST, Sept. 28, 2000 at A24; *Kuwait Unveils Plan to Treat Festering Desert Wound*, 293 SCIENCE 1410 (2001).

QUESTIONS AND DISCUSSION

1. What rules of international law, both customary and treaty, did Iraq violate during the Gulf War? Assume Iraq claimed its actions were military in nature–it sought to clog shipping lanes with oil to impede naval operations and set oil well heads on fire to obscure visibility and thereby impede air and ground force activities. Do these claims have any legal significance?

2. Are any enforcement mechanisms provided in the conventions Iraq violated? In practice, what sanctions exist in current international law to punish the "environmental terrorism" demonstrated by Iraq during the Gulf War? Be sure to address both criminal and civil liabilities. Who is authorized to hear these claims? Do you foresee any problems with the current regime in place to deter similar destruction in the future?

As the Gulf War example demonstrates, despite provisions for liability and punishment, most law of war depends upon the self-interest of nations to avoid using weapons and tactics they would consider unjust if used against themselves.

Ultimately, it is the responsibility of each nation to discipline members of its own forces who fail to comply.

3. Interestingly, Iraq was forced to admit liability in accepting the terms of the cease-fire agreement (in a manner, some have suggested, reminiscent of Germany accepting liability in the Treaty of Versailles after World War I). Would the fact that Iraq never had a chance to defend itself against this claim of liability in an international court create any legal problems in enforcing such liability? Is the acceptance of liability by Iraq an example of State practice? In this regard, is the law of war a law at all, or rather a voluntary code of conduct? In this regard, do you agree with the following statement?

> [T]he Gulf War was an atypical conflict from which it is risky to draw definite conclusions about the application of specific prescriptive norms to concrete situations. It is in the more ambiguous case, where a potential defendant nation has not effectively relegated itself international pariah status by its actions, and where no obvious predisposition exists to assess liability on any terms whatsoever, that the true viability of the substantive legal regime must be tested and measured.

Peter Richards and Michael N. Schmitt, *Mars Meets Mother Nature: Protecting the Environment During Armed Conflict*, 28 STETSON L. REV. 1047, 1060 (1999).

4. Iraq's actions in the Gulf War caused physical and economic harm to both civilians and military personnel throughout the Persian Gulf region. The environmental damage that occurred will likely affect future generations in the region. How does the current regime of international environmental law protect against such future damage? For example, does current international law provide a compensation mechanism for any future effects that the Gulf War may have on the wildlife in the area or on the future effects on the local population from the pollution that resulted from the oil spills? *See* Luan Low and David Hodgkinson, *Compensation for Wartime Environmental Damage: Challenges to International Law After the Gulf War,* 35 VA J. INT'L L. 405 (1995).

5. What additional amendments or treaties are necessary to strengthen the law of war? In 1991, Japan proposed that the UNEP Governing Council adopt a declaration of principles ensuring that the kind of environmental destruction that occurred during the Gulf War would never again occur as an act of war. France offered two additional proposals. The first was a prohibition on targeting ecological (non-property) areas during war, and the second called for protection of World Heritage sites during wartime (*see* p. 1037). At their next meeting, the UNEP Governing Council recommended that action be taken to prohibit weapons that "cause particularly serious effects on the environment." UNEP, Governing Council, 16th Session, Resolution 16/11 on Military Conflicts and the Environment (May 31, 1991); James P. Terry, *op. cit.,* at 65.

As a result of that recommendation, the United Nations Conference on Environment and Development (UNCED) included in its 1992 Rio Declaration on Environment and Development the following:

Principle 24

> Warfare is inherently destructive of sustainable development. States shall therefore respect international law providing protection for the environment in times of armed conflict and cooperate in its further development, as necessary.

Despite the extensive debates following the Gulf War over the scope of environmental protection during wartime, the adequacy of current protections remains disputed. The United States has argued that the customary law of war in the Hague and Geneva Conventions provides adequate environmental protection. These conventions do not, however, provide compensation for wartime environmental damage because the obligations only protect the environment indirectly. The International Committee of the Red Cross contends that the provisions of Protocol I and the ENMOD Convention that directly protect the environment are adequate. Only about one-third of all countries have ratified ENMOD, and less than sixty percent have approved Protocol I. S. DYCUS, NATIONAL DEFENSE AND THE ENVIRONMENT (1996). The Red Cross advocates increasing the number of signatories to these conventions so they develop into customary international law. This limited acceptance of the conventions may not provide adequate protection to the environment during wartime.

Greenpeace has urged the creation of a "Fifth" Geneva Convention on the Protection of the Environment in Time of Armed Conflict. The proposed provisions include a statement that the environment cannot be used as a weapon, that weapons aimed at the environment be banned, and that indirect damage to the environment be forbidden. James P. Terry *op. cit.* at 65. Given that Protocol I has not yet been accepted as customary law, however, the acceptance of an additional Geneva Convention seems unlikely. Finally, some commentators advocate that current conventions should be amended to provide more explicit environmental protection during wartime. The ENMOD Convention could be clarified and the terms of Protocol I and ENMOD should be interpreted similarly. As described in the text, ENMOD and Protocol I use very similar terms to describe their scope of coverage. Protocol I requires damage to be "widespread, long-term *and* severe." ENMOD requires the effects of the damage to be "widespread, long-lasting *or* severe." In Protocol I these terms are not defined, thus no threshold exists to determine which types of environmental destruction are prohibited.

Which of these proposals strike you as the most effective? The most practical? Do you think this is primarily a debate over word choice or something more fundamental?

Problem Exercise: The 1999 Kosovo Conflict

In a more recent example of environmental destruction during wartime, the conflict in the Balkans led to disputes not only over proper application of the law of war but the very nature of environmental damage. Following the escalation of violence in Kosovo between the predominantly Albanian population and Yugoslav (primarily Serbian) forces, the Security Council adopted Resolution 1160/98, condemning both the excessive use of force by Serbian Police against civilians in Kosovo and acts of terrorism by the Kosovo Liberation Army. Exercising its Chapter VII powers, the Security Council called for a cease fire to encourage dialogue among the parties. The resolution also stated that if parties failed to act then further measures would be taken to maintain or restore peace and stability in the region.

Ida L. Bostian, *The Environmental Consequences of the Kosovo Conflict and the NATO Bombing of Serbia,* 1999 COLO. J. INT'L ENVTL L. & POL'Y 230 (2000).

On March 19, 1999, a peace agreement aimed at resolving the conflict between FRY [the Federal Republic of Yugoslavia] and the Kosovo Province was negotiated in the French City of Rambouillet, but FRY refused to sign it. On March 24, 1999, NATO initiated an air campaign against FRY known as

"Operation Allied Force." FRY responded by intensifying offensives in Kosovo. The NATO campaign lasted almost three months, with tens of thousands of refugees continuing to flee Kosovo throughout the bombing. * * *

Through Operation Allied Force, NATO bombs hit industrial facilities, factories, oil refineries, and fuel storage facilities in various location throughout the FRY. On April 4, an oil refinery was hit in Pancevo. The next day, an oil refinery was hit in Novi Sad, and a warehouse at the same refinery was hit and destroyed three days later. On April 16 and 19, 1999, NATO launched further attacks on a Serbian petrochemical complex in Pancevo, producing widespread benzopyrene emissions. On April 24–28 and May 2, NATO hit oil refineries in Novi Sad again.

By May, the Worldwide Fund for Nature was receiving reports of dead fish floating in the Danube, and Yugoslav authorities were warning people to avoid eating freshwater fish. Near Novi Sad, a oil slick was reported to be thirty kilometers long, two to three centimeters deep, and moving two to three kilometers a day. On May 15, a fuel storage facility and transformer facility was hit again on May 17 and May 27. On June 7, the oil refinery in Pancevo was again bombed. In the meantime, the total number of Kosovar refugees in countries of asylum rose above one million. * * *

Because the bombing included attacks on chemical facilities in FRY, concerns began to grow in the region that the Danube River was being polluted. Environmentalists in the neighboring state of Romania, which is downstream from the bombed chemical facilities, were told that damage from the bombs to chemical and oil pipelines was causing Serbian factory owners to dump the toxic materials into the Danube out of desperation. Romanian as well as Bulgarian officials and environmental groups expressed concern over the long-term effects of oil spills and toxic chemical dumping on the rich Danube wildlife... Greek authorities feared that dioxins formed by the burning of chemicals at bombed oil refineries, fertilizer complexes, and explosives factories were being carried by the wind toward Greece. The French government warned consumers that asparagus imported from Greece might be contaminated. In addition, NATO had to assure Italian officials that it would retrieve bombs jettisoned from NATO warplanes into the Adriatic Sea...

Other less obvious forms of environmental and health impacts were also felt. Albania and the former Yugoslav republic of Macedonia faced huge numbers of refugees from Kosovo, whom the two countries were unprepared to receive. Sanitation and drinking water services were severely strained in the overcrowded refugee camps. In addition, many people, both within and outside of FRY were afraid of the adverse health consequences from the depleted uranium (DU) weapons fired by NATO. According to Doug Rokke, an environmental scientist and former US army health psychiatrist, DU could poison the land NATO was attempting to protect. Stated Rokke, "[U]nless the uranium is cleaned up, those [in Kosovo who] survive the Serb atrocities and the NATO aerial attacks will have to return to a contaminated environment where they may become ill."

During the bombing campaign, on April 29, 1999, Yugoslavia filed cases before the International Court of Justice (ICJ) against ten NATO member countries. In advance of proceedings on the merits of the cases, Yugoslavia sought provisional measures of protection, calling for the named States to cease the use of force and refrain from engaging in future threats or use of force against Yugoslavia. In its pleadings against the various States, Yugoslavia alleged a number of environmental claims:

> – by taking part in the bombing of oil refineries and chemical plants,[the United States] has acted against the Federal Republic of Yugoslavia in breach of its obligation not to cause considerable environmental damage;

> – by taking part in the use of weapons containing depleted uranium, [the United States] has acted against the Federal Republic of Yugoslavia in breach of its obligation not to use prohibited weapons and not to cause far-reaching health and environmental damage; * * *

> – by taking part in activities listed above, and in particular by causing enormous environmental damage and by using depleted uranium, [the United States] has acted against the Federal Republic of Yugoslavia in breach of its obligation not to deliberately inflict on a national group conditions of life calculated to bring about its physical destruction, in whole or in part;

> – [the United States] is responsible for the violation of the above international obligations;

> – [the United States] is obliged to stop immediately the violation of the above obligations vis-à-vis the Federal Republic of Yugoslavia;

> – [the United States] is obliged to provide compensation for the damage done to the Federal Republic of Yugoslavia and to its citizens and juridical persons. * * *

> 4.1. Continued bombing of the whole territory of the State, pollution of soil, air and water, destroying the economy of the country, contaminating the environment with depleted uranium inflicts conditions of life on the Yugoslav nation calculated to bring about its physical destruction.

Oral Pleadings (CR/99/14) in the case concerning Legality of Use of Force (Yugoslavia v. United States of America) (May 10, 1999)

On June 2, 1999, the Court refused to grant provisional measures of protection, in essence holding that, as an initial matter, it had severe doubts about its jurisdiction over Yugoslavia's claims against Belgium, Canada, France, Germany, Italy, Netherlands, Portugal, and the United Kingdom. Moreover, the Court not only refused to grant provisional measures of protection in the cases against the U.S. and Spain, but entirely dismissed those cases on grounds that the Court manifestly lacked jurisdiction over them. Consequently, the eight NATO states are now seeking a final decision by the Court regarding its jurisdiction over each of those cases and the admissibility of the claims; only if jurisdiction and admissibility are found will a case proceed to the merits. In the excerpt below, Bruch and Austin assess NATO's defenses to charges of environmental destruction, claims that could have been brought, and the balancing test that weighs the military necessity of destroying a target against the resulting environmental and civilian harm

Carl E. Bruch and Jay E. Austin, *The 1999 Kosovo Conflict: Unresolved Issues in Addressing the Environmental Consequences of War,* 30 ENVTL. L. REP. 10069, January 2000

... According to NATO, in addition to making products for civilian consumption, the Pancevo complex supplied gasoline and other essential materials to the

Serb army, and thus was a legitimate military target. In all, NATO bombed more than 80 industrial facilities, with some of the most severe environmental impacts occurring at Pancevo and Novi Sad. Other categories of concern included: pollution of the Danube River resulting from bombing of industrial facilities; impacts of the war on protected natural areas; and use of depleted uranium shells, land mines, and cluster bombs.

In the case of Pancevo, it is not yet known what advance intelligence NATO commanders had, or what environmental damage they projected would result from the strikes, though the plant was built with western assistance and its operations should have been well-known. Initial assessments indicated that the bombing released approximately 1,500 tons of vinyl chloride (a known carcinogen), 15,000 tons of ammonia, 800 tons of hydrochloric acid, 250 tons of liquid chlorine, 100 tons of mercury, and significant quantities of dioxin (a carcinogenic and mutagenic industrial byproduct that is also found in Agent Orange); subsequent estimates have suggested lower, but still significant, releases. According to reports, a massive cloud of poisonous gases doubled the rate of miscarriages over that of the previous year, caused widespread human illness, contaminated food crops and fish stocks, and caused unknown long-term damage to human health and the environment. The impacts were not confined to the immediate area: the facility's location near the Danube River led to contamination downstream, with reports of oil slicks and other war-related contamination coming from as far away as the Danube Delta and the Black Sea port of Odessa, Ukraine.

Following the conflict, an extensive factual assessment was carried out by a Balkans Task Force (BTF), headed by the U.N. Environment Programme (UNEP), which confirmed many of those assertions while revising or downplaying others. But it is unlikely that international politics will permit a similarly objective evaluation of the rationale underlying the decisions to bomb Pancevo or other industrial targets in Yugoslavia. In justifying its decision to bomb the Pancevo complex, NATO asserted that "Pancevo was considered to be a very, very important refinery and strategic target, as important as tactical targets inside Kosovo." This remarkable statement underscores the vagueness and inherent manipulability of the existing law-of-war provisions limiting wartime environmental damage, and the difficulty in trying to make them universally applicable. Simply put, the complex calculations that are supposed to factor into the balancing test cannot and should not be reduced to the number of times the target's alleged importance is prefixed with the word "very."

If NATO's decision violated applicable international law, then the thorny issue arises of how responsibility, and possibly liability, should be determined. Alternatively, the NATO countries might be absolved of responsibility and liability on the theory that they were merely responding to Serbian aggression in Kosovo that violated international law. But if it is determined that NATO conducted its balancing assessment correctly, and the decision to bomb Pancevo and similar targets was in fact legal, then the resulting human and environmental damage raises some grave questions about the adequacy of the existing norms for protection of the environment and human health, as well as the availability of institutions to determine responsibility and liability for violating these norms.

Potential Responsibility of the NATO Countries

... Much of the contamination in Pancevo was focused in the municipal area– Serbian officials estimate that the bombing of Pancevo endangered as many as 70,000 people–but it appears that various toxic materials also may have moved into and down the Danube River. In part, the question presented to the ICJ was whether this contamination is sufficient to trigger the environmental provisions of Protocol I. Since these provisions have yet to be applied in practice, the scope of the terms "widespread" and "severe" remains uncertain; and if, as some commentary suggests, "long-term" is to be "measured in decades," this prong of the test also might not be satisfied (or it could well take decades to determine whether it was)

The ICJ also might have considered Article 56 of the Protocol, which protects "works and installations containing dangerous forces ... even where these objects are military objectives." A refinery, fertilizer, and petrochemical complex contains a variety of dangerous forces, particularly explosive and toxic elements, whose release could and did cause severe health damage to the surrounding civilian population. However, Paragraph 2 of Article 56 provides that this protection ceases if such a facility is used "in regular, significant and direct support of military operations." Thus, the facility's asserted contribution to the Serb military, if proven, would curtail the protections of Article 56. Nonetheless, Article 57 further requires that "those who plan or decide upon attack shall take all feasible precautions in the choice of means and methods of attack with a view to avoiding, and in any event to minimizing, incidental loss of civilian life, injury to civilians and damage to civilian objects." The question remains whether direct bombing of Pancevo was strictly necessary, or whether other equally effective but less destructive options existed, such as cutting off supplies or delivery routes from the facility, particularly given the availability of laser-guided precision missiles.

The ICJ also could have examined the NATO bombing campaign in light of Protocol I's prohibition on indiscriminate attacks. Under Protocol I, these are attacks "which employ a method or means of combat the effects of which cannot be limited as required by this Protocol, and consequently ... are of a nature to strike military objectives and civilians or civilian objects without distinction." Protocol I specifically prohibits as indiscriminate "an attack which may be expected to cause incidental loss of civilian life, injury to civilians, damage to civilian objects, or a combination thereof, which would be excessive in relation to the concrete and direct military advantage anticipated." Again, NATO's assertion that the anticipated "very, very important" military advantage outweighed the incidental human and environmental loss underscores the highly subjective nature of this decision, as well as the lack of meaningful criteria for evaluating it. Such a decision might well have been reviewed by the ICJ or a comparable tribunal, and its rationale called into question.

Ultimately, the United States and NATO rest their decision on the "dual-use" exemption contained in various provisions of Protocol I: although Pancevo may have been a civilian facility, the argument runs, once it started producing gasoline and other products for the Serb military, it became a legitimate target. Article 52 of Protocol I prohibits attacks on civilian objects and "strictly" limits attacks to military objectives, but Paragraph 2 of that Article permits attacks on "those objects which by their nature, location, purpose or use make an effective contribution to military action and whose total or partial destruction, capture or neutralization, in the circumstances ruling at the time, offers a definite military advantage." As discussed above, Article 56 prohibiting attacks on installations containing "dangerous forces" includes a similarly explicit exemption. In addition to justifying the attacks on the Pancevo complex, NATO and the United States invoked the dual-use exemption to justify controversial attacks on other civilian infrastructure, including power plants and sewage treatment facilities, as well as television and other media facilities.

While the dual-use exemption explicitly applies to the traditional humanitarian provisions of the law of war, including the rule of discrimination, again there is no similar exemption for the environmental provisions of Articles 35(3) and 55. Thus, if the environmental damage in Kosovo is not "widespread, long-term, and severe" under international law, resorting to other humanitarian protections would be necessary, but the dual-use exemption may then apply. Given the wide range of civilian facilities that have a potential military purpose, broad application of the dual-use exemption in the Kosovo conflict could effectively eviscerate the law-of-war protections for human health and the environment. In fact, the same dual-use exemption could apply to the various Chechen civilian structures targeted by the Russian military: oil refineries and depots, brickworks, power stations, and railway stations. * * *

Inadequacy of Existing International Institutions

. . . The greatest limitation would be finding a forum that is receptive to such a petition, which is unlikely to be entertained by the ad hoc tribunal. The most natural venue would appear to be the ICJ, but, as discussed, the ICJ has already held that it lacks jurisdiction over the matter.

If the ICJ or another tribunal had found jurisdiction, it remains an open question not only whether it would have found a violation of Protocol I, but also whether it could have–in addition to enjoining the bombing campaign– applied the remedies found in Article 91 of Protocol I, which provides that states party to the Protocol or the Geneva Conventions "shall, if the case demands, be liable to pay compensation."

However, although the United States is party to the Geneva Conventions, it is not party to Protocol I, and other international institutions are politically unlikely to entertain a claim based on it. Thus, once the health and environmental impacts of the Pancevo bombing became known, Serb lawyers also considered the possibility of filing civil damage suits against the United States in national courts

Again, if the United States and other NATO countries appear to be actually responsible for violating the law of war, yet are not held liable, then the existing legal norms become subject to the assertion that they are simply "victor's justice" enshrouded in a cloak of legitimacy. Critics have highlighted the lack of parity in applying comparable law-of-war proscriptions in the Vietnam War and the 1990–1991 Gulf War, depending primarily on whether the country conducting the environmental warfare was the United States or its opponent. While the environmental damage in Kosovo is significantly less than in these previous two wars, a credible examination of NATO actions in Kosovo is necessary to maintain the legitimacy of the law-of-war regime, as well as to clarify the scope of norms at issue, such as what constitutes widespread, long-term, and severe damage, which weapons are "inhumane," and what is the scope of the dual-use exemption.

QUESTIONS AND DISCUSSION

1. Yugoslavia had to file separate complaints against all ten of the countries that actively participated in the NATO bombing. In considering the ICJ litigation, what role should NATO have played? Do you think the ICJ has jurisdiction over NATO as an organization? If not, how do you think liability and responsibility should be determined?

2. In addition to its environmental claims, Yugoslavia also alleged additional violations of international obligations. These included prohibitions against using force against another state, intervening in the affairs of another state, destroying historical monuments and cultural targets, using weapons calculated to cause unnecessary suffering (cluster bombs), and ignoring the obligation to spare civilians and civilian targets). In February 2001, the ICJ extended the deadline for Yugoslavia's filing of written statements regarding the Court's jurisdiction and the admissibility of the claims to April 5, 2002. *See* <http://www.icj-cij.org/icjwww/idecisions.htm> for updated information regarding the remaining eight claims.

3. As mentioned in the Bruch and Austin excerpt, in response to reports of environmental damage UNEP created the Balkans Task Force (BTF) to gather information and guide cleanup efforts. While the BTF identified a number of environmental 'hot spots' (such as Pancevo) requiring immediate action to curb long-term ecological damage, it admitted that some of these problems were mainly the result of decades of environmental neglect and not directly linked to the bombings. The task force's main conclusion was that "Our findings indicate that the Kosovo conflict has not caused an environmental catastrophe affecting the Balkans region as a whole." UNITED NATIONS ENVIRONMENT PROGRAMME AND UNITED NATIONS CENTRE FOR HUMAN SETTLEMENTS, THE KOSOVO CONFLICT: CONSEQUENCES FOR THE ENVIRONMENT AND HUMAN SETTLEMENT 5 (1999), available at <http://www.grid.unep.ch/btf/final/finalreport.pdf>.

4. Whether NATO violated international law is in many respects a question of fact. Investigation is necessary to determine what military advantage resulted from the bombings, what environmental damage occurred, and to some extent how the NATO commanders perceived this balance. Investigating environmental damage is complicated both by scientific disputes regarding the extent of environmental damage and a barrage of visceral images showing refugees fleeing their homes by the thousands, pictures of burning oil refineries, and a flood of toxic chemicals streaming into the River Danube. Serb sources had an obvious interest to exaggerate the extent of environmental damage but so, too, did the NATO forces have incentives to minimize the extent of harm. International observers, in this case the BTF created by the more neutral UNEP, offer one means of assessing the claims of harm and gathering information. But even the BTF report notes that "[p]erhaps the most endangered natural resource in times of war is truth." Are there better ways to determine what really happened? What scientific indicators or methodologies should such reviews employ? Bruch and Austin suggest the collection of baseline environmental data to serve as comparative measurements as a possible way to alleviate these complications. How might this be done?

5. What lessons can be drawn from comparing the Gulf War with the Balkans conflict? Some commentators have suggested that, in practice, the law of war is really the law of victors. How likely is it that the international community would hold *itself* liable for environmental damage inflicted on the defeated country (particularly if it is characterized as the aggressor)? Bruch and Austin assert that,

> [A]s in the Gulf War, while scientific assessments proceed, there is little international support for any serious consideration of legal responsibility for the NATO countries; the BTF's final report explicitly avoids addressing responsibility or liability. Yet, if the law of war is to maintain its legitimacy and universal applicability, and not become something imposed ad hoc by victors, the international community needs to undertake a credible examination not only of the factual circumstances, but also of whether and to what extent NATO's actions comported with the international law of war.

If liability is imposed on the defeated nation (and it's not a member of OPEC), will it likely have the resources necessary to pay environmental reparations? Practically speaking, how would an international tribunal enforce a judgment for civil damages against Yugoslavia?

6. In response to informal requests, the Prosecutor of the International Criminal Tribunal for the former Yugoslavia (ICTY) conducted an investigation pursuant to Article 18 of the Statute of the International Tribunal (authorizing the prosecutor to conduct investigations, pursuant to informal requests, to determine if enough evidence exists to proceed with charges). In its review, the ICTY examined, among other items, the BTF study and documents filed before the ICJ. The ICTY prosecutor determined that there were insufficient grounds to investigate further into the NATO bombing. The final report explains well the difficulty in applying the law of war to environmental damage. In reading the excerpt below, what kind of evidence do you think would have convinced the prosecutor to commence a case? As the prosecutor described them, are the standards to show violations of Articles 35(3) or 55 of Protocol I or the requirement of proportionality too high for any practical enforcement?

Final Report to the Prosecutor by the Committee Established to Review the NATO Bombing Campaign Against the Federal Republic of Yugoslavia (2000)

15.   Neither the USA nor France has ratified Additional Protocol I. Article 55 may, nevertheless, reflect current customary law (see however the 1996 Advisory Opinion on the *Legality of Nuclear Weapons*, where the International Court of Justice appeared to suggest that it does not). In any case, Articles 35(3) and 55 have a very high threshold of application. Their conditions for application are extremely stringent and their scope and contents imprecise. For instance, it is generally assumed that Articles 35(3) and 55 only cover very significant damage. The adjectives 'widespread, long-term, and severe' used in Additional Protocol I are joined by the word 'and', meaning that it is a triple, cumulative standard that needs to be fulfilled. Consequently, it would appear extremely difficult to develop a *prima facie* case upon the basis of these provisions, even assuming they were applicable. For instance, it is thought that the notion of 'long-term' damage in Additional Protocol I would need to be measured in years rather than months, and that as such, ordinary battlefield damage of the kind caused to France in World War I would not be covered.

The great difficulty of assessing whether environmental damage exceeded the threshold of Additional Protocol I has also led to criticism by ecologists. This may partly explain the disagreement as to whether any of the damage caused by the oil spills and fires in the 1990/91 Gulf War technically crossed the threshold of Additional Protocol I.

It is the committee's view that similar difficulties would exist in applying Additional Protocol I to the present facts, even if reliable environmental assessments were to give rise to legitimate concern concerning the impact of the NATO bombing campaign. Accordingly, these effects are best considered from the underlying principles of the law of armed conflict such as necessity and proportionality. * * *

It is the opinion of the committee, on the basis of information currently in its possession, that the environmental damage caused during the NATO bombing campaign does not reach the Additional Protocol I threshold. In addition, the UNEP Report also suggests that much of the environmental contamination which is discernible cannot unambiguously be attributed to the NATO bombing. * * *

19.   It is difficult to assess the relative values to be assigned to the military advantage gained and harm to the natural environment, and the application of

the principle of proportionality is more easily stated than applied in practice. In applying this principle, it is necessary to assess the importance of the target in relation to the incidental damage expected: if the target is sufficiently important, a greater degree of risk to the environment may be justified.

20.   The adverse effect of the coalition air campaign in the Gulf war upon the civilian infrastructure prompted concern on the part of some experts regarding the notion of "military objective." This has prompted some experts to argue that where the presumptive effect of hostilities upon the civilian infrastructure (and consequently the civilian population) is grave, the military advantage conferred by the destruction of the military objective would need to be decisive. Similar considerations would, in the committee's view, be warranted where the grave threat to the civilian infrastructure emanated instead from excessive environmental harm resulting from the hostilities. The critical question is what kind of environmental damage can be considered to be excessive. Unfortunately, the customary rule of proportionality does not include any concrete guidelines to this effect.

21.   The military worth of the target would need to be considered in relation to the circumstances prevailing at the time. If there is a choice of weapons or methods of attack available, a commander should select those which are most likely to avoid, or at least minimize, incidental damage. In doing so, however, he is entitled to take account of factors such as stocks of different weapons and likely future demands, the timeliness of attack and risks to his own forces. Operational reality is recognized in the Statute of the International Criminal Court, an authoritative indicator of evolving customary international law on this point, where Article 8(b)(iv) makes the infliction of incidental environmental damage an offence only if the attack is launched intentionally in the knowledge that it will cause widespread, long-term and severe damage to the natural environment which would be clearly excessive in relation to the concrete and direct overall military advantage anticipated. The use of the word "clearly" ensures that criminal responsibility would be entailed only in cases where the excessiveness of the incidental damage was obvious.

22.   Taken together, this suggests that in order to satisfy the requirement of proportionality, attacks against military targets which are known or can reasonably be assumed to cause grave environmental harm may need to confer a very substantial military advantage in order to be considered legitimate. At a minimum, actions resulting in massive environmental destruction, especially where they do not serve a clear and important military purpose, would be questionable. The targeting by NATO of Serbian petro-chemical industries may well have served a clear and important military purpose.

23.   The above considerations also suggest that the requisite *mens rea* on the part of a commander would be actual or constructive knowledge as to the grave environmental effects of a military attack; a standard which would be difficult to establish for the purposes of prosecution and which may provide an insufficient basis to prosecute military commanders inflicting environmental harm in the (mistaken) belief that such conduct was warranted by military necessity.... In addition, the notion of 'excessive' environmental destruction is imprecise and the actual environmental impact, both present and long term, of the NATO bombing campaign is at present unknown and difficult to measure.

24.   In order to fully evaluate such matters, it would be necessary to know the extent of the knowledge possessed by NATO as to the nature of Serbian military-industrial targets (and thus, the likelihood of environmental damage flowing from their destruction), the extent to which NATO could reasonably have anticipated such environmental damage (for instance, could NATO have

reasonably expected that toxic chemicals of the sort allegedly released into the environment by the bombing campaign would be stored alongside that military target?) and whether NATO could reasonably have resorted to other (and less environmentally damaging) methods for achieving its military objective of disabling the Serbian military-industrial infrastructure.

25.   It is therefore the opinion of the committee, based on information currently available to it, that the OTP should not commence an investigation into the collateral environmental damage caused by the NATO bombing campaign.

———

Suggested Further Reading and Web Sites

Carl Bruch and Jay Austin, Eds. THE ENVIRONMENTAL CONSEQUENCES OF WAR: LEGAL, ECONOMIC AND SCIENTIFIC PERSPECTIVES (2000)

> Papers from the first international conference on environmental damage and the law of war.

Daniel Esty, *Pivotal States and the Environment*, in PAUL KENNEDY, ED., UNITED STATES STRATEGY AND THE PIVOTAL STATES: TESTING AND INTELLECTUAL HYPOTHESIS (1998)

> A useful overview of the relationship between environmental protection and national security at the international level.

Daniel Deudney, Richard Matthew, eds., CONTESTED GROUND (1998)

> A survey of the diverse views concerning the relationship between environmental concerns and national security matters.

Jessica Mathews, *Redefining Security*, FOREIGN AFFAIRS (Spring 1989)

> A thoughtful overview of the environment-security issue.

THE ENVIRONMENTAL CHANGE AND SECURITY PROJECT REPORT

> An annual report published by The Environmental Change and Security Project, based in Princeton University's Woodrow Wilson Center. Articles focus on environment and security issues.

http://ecsp.si.edu/

> Homepage of the Princeton University's Environmental Change and Security Project, a multi-disciplinary effort examining the interrelationships between environment, population and security.

CHAPTER EIGHTEEN

INTERNATIONAL CORPORATE STANDARDS

The business of America is business

Calvin Coolidge

SECTION I.   TRANSNATIONAL CORPORATIONS & THE GLOBAL ECONOMY

Much of international environmental law and policy focuses on interactions among States. The transnational nature of business and immense financial influence of corporations, however, are of fundamental importance to international governance. The annual revenue of General Motors is far larger than the GNP of most countries. Indeed the concentrated economic power exercised by a small number of corporations is enormous. Consider that 100 of the world's largest transnational corporations hold $1.8 trillion in foreign assets and employ six million people. A small percentage of transnational corporations account for an estimated one-quarter of global output and control over half of foreign direct investment. The ten largest companies control over one-quarter of transnational corporations' total assets. Ikrramul Haq, *World Investment Report 2000 Released: Developing States Warned Against Unbridled Cross–Border Mergers, Acquisitions,* BUSINESS RECORDER, Oct. 4, 2000; Robert J. Fowler, *International Environmental Standards for Transnational Corporations,* 25 ENVTL. L. 1 (1995).

Robert J. Fowler, *International Environmental Standards for Transnational Corporations* 25 ENVTL. L. 1 (1995)

By the early 1990s, there were almost 37,000 transnational corporations (TNCs) in the world, and their influence on the global economy is enormous. In 1990, the worldwide outflow of foreign direct investment (FDI), which is a measure of the productive capacity of TNCs, totalled $234 billion. In 1992, the stock of FDI had reached $2 trillion. Parent TNCs have generated some

170,000 foreign affiliates, forty-one percent of which are located in developing countries. Nevertheless, the reins remain firmly held in developed countries, where ninety percent of parent TNCs are headquartered.

The growth in the number, size, and influence of TNCs has been a matter of international concern, particularly to developing countries, for over twenty years. The expansion of TNCs after the Second World War resulted from a number of factors, including spiralling labor costs in developed countries, the increasing importance of economies of scale, improved transportation and communication systems, and rising worldwide consumer demand for new products. By the early 1970s, TNCs had begun to attract considerable interest and concern. Critics of TNCs have argued that their post-war expansion has become increasingly focused on the exploitation of the natural and human resources of developing countries. Ethical issues arising from TNC activities include bribery and corruption, employment and personnel issues, marketing practices, impacts on the economy and development patterns of host countries, environmental and cultural impacts, and political relations with both host and home country governments.

It is also frequently argued that TNCs have grown beyond the control of national governments and operate in a legal and moral vacuum "where individualism has free reign." The notion of corporate nationality may become obsolete in a global economy. The trend towards integrated international production and the resultant reorganization of TNC structures to establish "non-equity" arrangements which allow some control over foreign productive assets contribute to this situation.

Despite the long-held concerns about ethical and other aspects of TNC activity, promotion of FDI has been a recent global political trend. A new international consensus was reached at the seventh United Nations Conference on Trade and Development in 1987 on "structural adjustment," in the form of privatization, deregulation, and liberalization of national economies in return for the easing of the debt burden on developing countries. This has paved the way for a substantial expansion in TNC activities, particularly in the developing world. This expansion has been assisted by recent regional and global free trade agreements, the principal beneficiaries of which may be TNCs.* * *

TNCs are key players in terms of development activity, and the perception that they operate in a vacuum between ineffective national laws and non-existent or unenforceable international laws has heightened concerns about the current reach and effectiveness of environmental regulation, particularly where TNCs are operating in developing countries. A considerable amount of attention has been devoted in recent years by TNCs and others to the notion of self-regulation of environmental, health, and safety matters. This may in part reflect a belief that TNCs are beyond any form of regulatory control and should develop their own rules to meet public expectations. It may also constitute an effort by TNCs to anticipate further regulation, either by forestalling it or by being prepared in advance to comply with it.

Hilary F. French, *Assessing Private Capital Flows to Developing Countries*, in STATE OF THE WORLD 149–65 (1998)

[M]any developing countries are now welcoming foreign capital with open arms–a dramatic reversal of the prevailing development fashion of earlier decades. . . . [T]he resulting inflows of foreign capital have helped fuel a record-breaking economic boom in the countries receiving them.

Companies based in industrial countries–principally France, Germany, Japan, the United Kingdom, and the United States–are the source of most FDI outflows, accounting for some 85 percent of the global total in recent years. Ranked by the size of their foreign assets, the five largest transnationals as of 1995 were Royal Dutch Shell, Ford Motor Company, General Electric, Exxon, and General Motors, with combined foreign assets of $339 billion and overseas work forces of some 553,000 people. Developing countries represent a significant and increasing share of these totals.* * *

Yet transnational corporations are no longer headquartered only in the industrial world. In recent years, several developing countries and their enterprises have become significant sources of capital as well as recipients of it. Companies based in Brazil, Chile, China, Hong Kong, Kuwait, Malaysia, Singapore, South Korea, Taiwan, and Thailand, are all investing abroad, increasingly as far afield as Africa, Europe, and North and South America.* * *

Nearly all the remaining private flows–just under 40 percent of the total–are moving through a category that barely existed less than a decade ago. This is "portfolio" investment, in which developing-country stocks and bonds are purchased abroad–increasingly by large institutional investors, such as insurance companies, mutual funds, or pension plans. * * *

These investments are the most volatile ingredient in the mix of private flows. Investors may withdraw their funds quickly if they lose confidence in a country's economic prospects, as happened in Mexico during the peso crisis of 1994 and in Southeast Asia in 1997.* * *

Studies suggest that industries are generally drawn to the developing world by the low cost of labor, the availability of natural resources, or the strategic access to new markets. In most cases, environmental control costs alone are not high enough to be a determining factor in location decisions. But even if companies move to the developing world for other reasons, they may well take advantage of lax environmental laws and enforcement once there.

In a few cases, moreover, relaxed enforcement does appear to have been a motivating factor in companies' location decisions. * * *

Despite the environmental risks, international investment in manufacturing also offers environmental opportunities for developing countries. One of them is access to cutting-edge production technologies, which are usually cleaner and more efficient in their use of energy and materials than older equipment. A 1992 World Bank study compared the rates at which 60 countries were adopting a cleaner wood pulping process, and concluded that countries open to foreign investment acquired the new technology far more rapidly than did those that were closed to it. Furthermore, privatizing state-owned factories by selling them to domestic or foreign private investors can lead to environmental improvements by eliminating the conflict of interest that can arise when the government is being both a producer and a regulator. Limited evidence also suggests that the pressure to turn a profit can introduce an incentive to adopt manufacturing techniques that reduce energy and materials use and thus pollution.

Foreign investment can also help disseminate new, more environmentally sound products worldwide. For example, efficient compact fluorescent light bulbs, first produced in the United State, are increasingly manufactured in the

developing world. In 1995, China made some 80–100 million of these bulbs–
more than any other country.

———————

Headquartered in one country, the reach of these artificial citizens
extends in some cases to every region in the world. Despite their international character, corporations are creatures of domestic law. In the United
States, corporations are incorporated under and regulated by the laws of
the various states. These laws, however, with rare exception do not address
the environmental impacts of corporations' overseas operations. To some
extent, international environmental treaties seek to address this gap. For
example, the Montreal Protocol regime imposes a clear prohibition on
corporate activities relating to CFCs. Similarly, the Basel Convention is
aimed at corporations in the hazardous waste trade. Viewed in the context
of the enormous foreign direct investment by corporations and their broad
range of activities, however, the scope of such conventions is very narrow
indeed.

Why might corporations be concerned over their social and environmental performance? Consider the excerpt below by Bennett Freeman, who
served as the United States Deputy Assistant Secretary of State for
Democracy, Human Rights and Labor in the Clinton Administration,

Bennett Freeman, *Converging Corporate Responsibility and Hu-man Rights Agendas: Three reasons*, New York, United Nations, 1 June 2001, at 1–7
<http://www.globaldimensions.net/articles/cr/freeman.html>

[T]he backlash against globalization has fundamentally shifted the balance of
power in global governance by putting company after company in sector after
sector on the defensive as they are targeted, boycotted, sued, or merely
scrutinized and criticized on issue after issue. Indeed, corporate social responsibility is now established as one of the three interlocking arenas of the battle
over globalization, along with the place of labor and environmental protections
in trade and investment agreements, and the accountability of international
institutions such as the WTO, the World Bank and the IMF. * * *

[C]creating competitive advantage and strengthening the fundamental social
and political operating environment that business needs to thrive is a more
positive and persuasive case to make, and an easier one for business to accept.

Bottom line-minded business leaders and managers are likelier to embrace
corporate responsibility when they look within their own companies, and to
their closest constituencies. They can recognize that more individual and
especially institutional investors care about social and environmental standards
and performance, as do more customers and consumers. They can also heed
current and prospective employees, who want to identify their values with
those of their companies and want to believe that they are "doing good" as they
are "doing well," or at least that they are "doing no harm." ...

Yet another more subtle but perhaps even more compelling interest that
governments should have in encouraging corporate responsibility is not only
promoting not only sustainable development but also sustainable investment
for their flag companies around the world. Durable and stable business environments that are conducive to secure, profitable long-term investment are best

guaranteed by good governance and the rule of law than by corruption and repression, as a number of extractive sector companies in particular are now recognizing. This convergence of interests should command a constituency of global companies and civil society forces at the global and local levels. At the same time, home country governments should recognize an interest in working with companies, NGOs and host country governments to build such coalitions on a country and issue-specific basis. . . .

. . . At stake are human rights and building a broader future constituency for human rights. At stake is the "social license to operate" of the multinational enterprise, and the quality and sustainability of the business and investment environment it will inhabit. At stake is the future of globalization, or at least a chance to build a consensus for a more balanced, inclusive globalization that will serve civil society's interest in democratic accountability and the business community's interest in expanded trade, sustainable investment and growth. With so much at stake, and with so many apparently clashing but potentially converging interests coming together, we should seek further opportunities to find common ground.

While the environmentalist critique of the 1970s may have been that "industry is the problem," this simplistic labeling is no longer useful. To be sure, the operations of some companies do pose very real threats to environmental protection. But in recent years a number of companies have become leading voices for environmental protection by greatly reducing waste and engaging in consensus-building dialogues with environmental groups and governments. The World Business Council for Sustainable Development, a group of now more than 120 companies originally created to provide industry counsel to the Earth Summit, has adopted the goal of sustainable development and is promoting a business strategy known as, "eco-efficiency." *See* Chapter 2, page 73. An important factor driving such business initiatives has been the increasing recognition by environmental groups and governments that business, although often the primary source of environmental problems, *must also* be part of the long-term solution. The role of corporations in promoting human rights is further discussed in Chapter 16, page 1367.

SECTION II. CORPORATE CODES OF CONDUCT

Given the limited role international law plays in governing transnational corporate activities, perhaps the most promising recent development in corporate behavior has been the adoption of a series of international voluntary corporate standards for environmental management. Voluntary corporate compliance with codes of conduct can be both a signal by companies that they are responsible partners in environmental protection and a recognition that responsible environmental management increases profits. Though no more binding upon signatory companies than soft international law is upon signatory States, voluntary codes of conduct may become a marketplace requirement in certain sectors for companies to remain competitive.

A. THE UN CODE OF CONDUCT AND OECD GUIDELINES

Following revelations in the early 1970s of wide-scale unethical and illegal activities by multinational companies–including the involvement of U.S. companies in the 1973 Chilean coup that overthrew President Salvador Allende–the International Labor Organization, Organization for Economic Cooperation and Development (OECD), United Nations and national governments focused on means to influence TNC behavior. Much of the early activity centered on the UN's attempt to draft a Code of Conduct for Transnational Corporations. The UN's General Assembly adopted a consensus resolution on measures against corrupt transnational practices, but failed to follow up with a stronger legal instrument. One year later, in 1976, the OECD Council of Ministers adopted a recommendation entitled the Declaration on International Investment and Multinational Enterprises. As its name suggests, the overriding purpose of the Declaration was to promote foreign investment, calling for Member countries to respect national treatment (according comparable treatment to foreign-controlled enterprises as accorded to domestic enterprises), minimize conflicting requirements on TNCs by different governments, and make transparent incentives and disincentives to investment. Building on activities at the UN, the Declaration also contained a section setting forth voluntary rules of conduct for TNCs. Known as the OECD Guidelines, it was hoped these would ensure the operation of TNCs was compatible with the expectations of the host country by establishing a baseline of labor rights. In 1991, a new chapter was added on the environment, with further amendment in 2000.

V. Environment

Enterprises should, within the framework of laws, regulations and administrative practices in the countries in which they operate, and in consideration of relevant international agreements, principles, objectives, and standards, take due account of the need to protect the environment, public health and safety, and generally to conduct their activities in a manner contributing to the wider goal of sustainable development. In particular, enterprises should:

1. Establish and maintain a system of environmental management appropriate to the enterprise, including:

   a) collection and evaluation of adequate and timely information regarding the environmental, health, and safety impacts of their activities;

   b) establishment of measurable objectives and, where appropriate, targets for improved environmental performance, including periodically reviewing the continuing relevance of these objectives; and

   c) regular monitoring and verification of progress toward environmental, health, and safety objectives or targets.

2. Taking into account concerns about cost, business confidentiality, and the protection of intellectual property rights:

   a) provide the public and employees with adequate and timely information on the potential environment, health and safety impacts of the activities of the enterprise, which could include reporting on progress in improving environmental performance; and

b) engage in adequate and timely communication and consultation with the communities directly affected by the environmental, health and safety policies of the enterprise and by their implementation.

3. Assess, and address in decision-making, the foreseeable environmental, health, and safety-related impacts associated with the processes, goods and services of the enterprise over their full life cycle. Where these proposed activities may have significant environmental, health, or safety impacts, and where they are subject to a decision of a competent authority, prepare an appropriate environmental impact assessment.

4. Consistent with the scientific and technical understanding of the risks, where there are threats of serious damage to the environment, taking also into account human health and safety, not use the lack of full scientific certainty as a reason for postponing cost-effective measures to prevent or minimise such damage.

5. Maintain contingency plans for preventing, mitigating, and controlling serious environmental and health damage from their operations, including accidents and emergencies; and mechanisms for immediate reporting to the competent authorities.

6. Continually seek to improve corporate environmental performance, by encouraging, where appropriate, such activities as:

a) Adoption of technologies and operating procedures in all parts of the enterprise that reflect standards concerning environmental performance in the best performing part of the enterprise;

b) Development and provision of products or services that have no undue environmental impacts; are safe in their intended use; are efficient in their consumption of energy and natural resources; can be reused, recycled, or disposed of safely;

c) Promoting higher levels of awareness among customers of the environmental implications of using the products and services of the enterprise; and

d) Research on ways of improving the environmental performance of the enterprise over the longer term.

7. Provide adequate education and training to employees in environmental health and safety matters, including the handling of hazardous materials and the prevention of environmental accidents, as well as more general environmental management areas, such as environmental impact assessment procedures, public relations, and environmental technologies.

8. Contribute to the development of environmentally meaningful and economically efficient public policy, for example, by means of partnerships or initiatives that will enhance environmental awareness and protection.

Implementation of the Guidelines commences at the National Contact Points. Often housed within government agencies, the National Contact Points serve as the initial stage of consideration for issues and conflicts arising under the Guidelines. Any party who believes the Guidelines have been violated may request consultations with the Contact Points. If the discussions at this level do not resolve the issue between the parties, it can be passed to the OECD's Committee on International Investment and

Multinational Enterprises (CIME), which is ultimately responsible for adjudication and development of the Guidelines. In response to disputes passed up by the National Contact Points, CIME responds by clarifying or interpreting specific language.

CIME's role under the Guidelines should not be thought of as a traditional judicial model, for its decisions have no retrospective applicability. Indeed since the Guidelines were adopted as recommendations, they cannot be treated as binding standards. CIME's judgments do not "enforce the Guidelines" against either of the parties. Perhaps surprisingly, given the formality of the process, CIME never makes a judgment on the behavior of the companies in question. Instead it uses the case to clarify the *meaning* of how a provision in the Guidelines should be applied in *future* cases. The logic behind this system is similar to that of the common law's clarification of doctrine in specific applications. Unlike the common law analogue, however, CIME's interpretation are never binding once established. In a legislative context, the closest analogy to this practice would be if Congress could continue creating legislative history *after* its passage of a statute. *See* James Salzman, *Labor Rights, Globalization and Institutions:The Role and Influence of the Organization for Economic Cooperation and Development*, 21 MICH. J. INT'L. L. 769 (2000); THE OECD GUIDELINES FOR MULTINATIONAL ENTERPRISES, 2000 REVISIONS <http://www1.oecd.org/daf/investment/guidelines/minbooke.pdf>.

B.   THE CERES PRINCIPLES

Voluntary corporate codes of conduct are important precisely because international law plays such a small role in controlling the environmental impacts of transnational corporations. The first nongovernmental mover in this regard was the Coalition for Environmentally Responsible Economies (CERES). Following the Exxon Valdez oil spill in 1989, a group of concerned consumers, investors and environmentalists formed CERES and developed a set of principles known as the Valdez Principles. Now known as the CERES Principles, they set broad standards for evaluating corporate activity and are intended both to improve the environmental performance of signatory companies and to enable investors to make informed decisions on a company's environmental performance. The CERES Principles are a model code of environmental conduct applicable to all corporations, public or private, regardless of size or industry.

The CERES group of investors include public pension trustees, foundations, labor unions, environmental, religious and public interest groups. Members include the National Audubon Society, National Wildlife Federation, Sierra Club, Natural Resources Defense Council, the Social Investment Forum, the Interfaith Center on Corporate Responsibility, U.S. PIRG, and the AFL–CIO Industrial Union Department. CERES' basic proposition is that sustainable economic activity must be environmentally responsible. Its mission is to encourage companies to endorse and put in practice the CERES Principles.

A company adopting the CERES Principles pledges to monitor and improve the environmental impacts resulting from its use of natural resources, reduce and dispose of wastes, conserve energy, reduce risk, create safe products and services, restore any environmental damage, and improve environmental management through audits, reports, and public communication. Companies that endorse the CERES Principles must also annually publish a CERES Report, providing information related to the company's commitment to the Principles. The report assesses the company's policies and practices related to each specific principle. These reports must be made available to shareholders and to interested members of the public. It is hoped the report will both inform stakeholders and internal management. Unlike the EMAS or ISO 14000 standards (described below), there is no independent third party verification of compliance with the CERES Principles.

The CERES Principles

Introduction

By adopting these Principles, we publicly affirm our belief that corporations have a responsibility for the environment, and must conduct all aspects of their business as responsible stewards of the environment by operating in a manner that protects the Earth. We believe that corporations must not compromise the ability of future generations to sustain themselves.

We will update our practices constantly in light of advances in technology and new understandings in health and environmental science. In collaboration with CERES, we will promote a dynamic process to ensure that the Principles are interpreted in a way that accommodates changing technologies and environmental realities. We intend to make consistent, measurable progress in implementing these Principles and to apply them to all aspects of our operation throughout the world.

Protection of the Biosphere

We will reduce and make continual progress toward eliminating the release of any substance that may cause environmental damage to the air, water, or the earth or its inhabitants. We will safeguard all habitats affected by our operations and will protect open spaces and wilderness, while preserving biodiversity.

Sustainable Use of Natural Resources

We will make sustainable use of renewable natural resources, such as water, soils and forests. We will conserve nonrenewable natural resources through efficient use and careful planning.

Reduction and Disposal of Wastes

We will reduce and where possible eliminate waste through source reduction and recycling. All waste will be handled and disposed of through safe and responsible methods.

Energy Conservation

We will conserve energy and improve the energy efficiency of our internal operations and of the goods and services we sell. We will make every effort to use environmentally safe and sustainable energy sources.

Risk Reduction

We will strive to minimize the environmental, health and safety risks to our employees and the communities in which we operate through safe technologies, facilities and operating procedures, and by being prepared for emergencies.

Safe Products and Services

We will reduce and where possible eliminate the use, manufacture or sale of products and services that cause environmental damage or health or safety hazards. We will inform our customers of the environmental impacts of our products or services and try to correct unsafe use.

Environmental Restoration

We will promptly and responsibly correct conditions we have caused that endanger health, safety or the environment. To the extent feasible, we will redress injuries we have caused to persons or damage we have caused to the environment and will restore the environment.

Informing the Public

We will inform in a timely manner everyone who may be affected by conditions caused by our company that might endanger health, safety or the environment. We will regularly seek advice and counsel through dialogue with persons in communities near our facilities. We will not take any action against employees for reporting dangerous incidents or conditions to management or to appropriate authorities.

Management Commitment

We will implement these Principles and sustain a process that ensures that the Board of Directors and Chief Executive Officer are fully informed about pertinent environmental issues and are fully responsible for environmental policy. In selecting our Board of Directors, we will consider demonstrated environmental commitment as a factor.

Audits and Reports

We will conduct an annual self-evaluation of our progress in implementing these Principles. We will support the timely creation of generally accepted environmental audit procedures. We will annually complete the CERES Report, which will be made available to the public.

Disclaimer

These Principles established an ethic with criteria by which investors and others can assess the environmental performance of companies. Companies that endorse these Principles pledge to go voluntarily beyond the requirements of the law. The terms may and might in Principles one and eight are not meant to encompass every imaginable consequence, no matter how remote. Rather, these Principles obligate endorsers to behave as prudent persons who are not governed by conflicting interests and who possess a strong commitment to environmental excellence and to human health and safety. These Principles are not intended to create new legal liabilities, expand existing rights or obligations, waive legal defenses, or otherwise affect the legal position of any endorsing company, and are not intended to be used against an endorser in any legal proceedings for any purpose.

As of April, 2000, 54 companies had endorsed the CERES Principles. These include influential corporations such as General Motors, Ford Motor

Company, Polaroid, American Airlines and Timberland as well as Ben & Jerry's Ice Cream, The Body Shop International, and Domino's Pizza Distribution Corporation. Although not widely adopted, the CERES Principles have increased international public awareness on corporate environmental accountability and served as a model for future initiatives. As a result of the CERES Principles, ranking of companies' corporate environmental reports by organizations such as Sustainability, and pressure from investors, far more corporate environmental reports have been published in recent years but, absent uniform reporting practices, they have proven difficult to compare.

> Unfortunately, while the quantity of [corporate environmental] information rapidly expands, it is far from clear that the value of information has kept pace. The reasons behind this phenomenon become evident with even a cursory look at a sample of reports. Each firm utilizes its own format, its own indicators, and its own metrics, thereby making comparisons between reports impossible. The result: the substantial resources firms spend on data development and analysis, report production, and report dissemination yield far less value than they could and should. Report users–investors, environmentalists, consumers, employees, and other stakeholders, and other firms–have great difficulty in using reports to inform investment decisions, guide consumer product choices, and benchmark performance against comparable firms. These, and many other valuable purposes remain under-served by the growing quantity of non-standardized information reported in non-uniform formats. http://www.ceres.org/reporting/globalreporting.html.

In part to address this comparability concern and in part to expand the coverage of corporate reporting to broader concerns of sustainable development, the Global Reporting Initiative (GRI) was founded in 1997. It seeks to establish uniform guidelines for corporate reporting on their "triple bottom line"–economic, environmental, and social performance. GRI's mission is "to elevate the comparability and credibility of sustainability reporting practices worldwide."

The GRI consists of two components–a multistakeholder, global consultation process based on the principles of transparency and inclusiveness, and development and dissemination of sustainability reporting guidelines. The basic goal of GRI is to make sustainability reporting as commonplace as financial reporting. By establishing itself as a permanent body, GRI can raise the standard of current reporting, act as a storehouse for reported information, and disseminate and analyze the information received. Major companies have participated in this initiative, including British Airways, Proctor & Gamble, Shell, The Body Shop International, Ford, and General Motors. GRI's broad-based steering committee, which might reflect the make up of its eventual governing body, now includes, among others, CERES, General Motors, UNEP, World Resources Institute, World Business Council for Sustainable Development, Canadian Institute of Chartered Accountants, and Association of Chartered Certified Accountants. In 2002, GRI will become a permanent, independent entity. GRI's website is at <www.globalreporting.org>.

C. INTERNATIONAL CHAMBER OF COMMERCE'S BUSINESS CHARTER FOR SUSTAINABLE DEVELOPMENT

The International Chamber of Commerce (ICC) is a Paris-based non-governmental organization created in 1919. The ICC currently has over 7,000 member companies and business organizations operating in 125 countries. In April 1991, two years after the publication of the CERES Principles and in response to recommendations in the 1987 Brundtland Report, the International Chamber of Commerce developed its own set of voluntary corporate standards known as the Business Charter for Sustainable Development. The Charter contains 16 principles for environmental management that companies should integrate into their daily operations. More than 2300 companies have pledged their support for the Charter since it was issued. <http://www.iccwbo.org/sdcharter/charter/about_charter/about_charter.asp>

The key principles set out in the Charter are: (1) the recognition of environmental management as among the highest corporate priorities, (2) the prior assessment of a new project's environmental impact, and, (3) the development of products and services with no undue environmental impact and safe for their intended use. The objective of the Charter is to assist a wide variety of organizations in improving their environmental performance by implementing management practices in accordance with the Charter's principles, measuring progress, and reporting progress both internally and externally.

The ICC's International Environmental Bureau is responsible for the Charter program and a related project to document case studies of organizations who demonstrate sound environmental management practices advocated by the Charter. The goal is to provide "best practice" examples to serve as guides and incentives for companies implementing the Charter. The ICC has also developed guidelines explicitly directing companies how to implement the charter. *ICC Establishes Industry Council as Advocate on Environmental Issues*, BNA DAILY ENV'T REP., Feb. 2, 1993.

The International Chamber of Commerce Business Charter for Sustainable Development Principles for Environmental Management

1. Corporate priority. To recognize environmental management as amongst the highest corporate priorities and as a key determinant to sustainable development; to establish policies, programs, and practices for conducting operations in an environmentally sound manner.

2. Integrated management. To integrate these policies, programs, and practices fully into each business as an essential element of management in all its functions.

3. Process of Improvement. To continue to improve corporate policies, programs, and environmental performance, taking into account technical developments, scientific understanding, consumer needs, and community expectations, with legal regulations as a starting point; and to apply the same environmental criteria internationally.

4. Employee education. To educate, train, and motivate employees to conduct their activities in an environmentally responsible manner.

5. *Prior assessment.* To assess environmental impacts before starting a new activity or project and before decommissioning a facility or leaving a site.

6. *Products and services.* To develop and provide products or services that have no undue environmental impact and are safe in their intended use; that are efficient in their consumption of energy and natural resources; and that can be recycled, reused, or disposed of safely.

7. *Customer advice.* To advise, and, where relevant, educate, customers, distributors, and the public in the safe use, storage, and disposal of products provided; and to apply similar considerations to the provision of services.

8. *Facilities and operations.* To develop, design, and operate facilities and conduct activities, taking into consideration the efficient use of energy and materials, the sustainable use of renewable resources, the minimization of adverse environmental impact and waste generation, and the safe and responsible disposal of residual wastes.

9. *Research.* To conduct or support research on the environmental impacts of raw materials, products, processes, emissions, and wastes associated with the enterprise and on the means of minimizing such adverse impacts.

10. *Precautionary approach.* To modify the manufacture, marketing, or use of products or services or the conduct of activities, consistent with scientific and technical understanding, to prevent serious or irreversible environmental degradation.

11. *Contractors and suppliers* To promote the adoption of these principles by contractors acting on behalf of the enterprise, encouraging, and, where appropriate, requiring improvements in their practices to make them consistent with those of the enterprise; and to encourage the wider adoption of these principles by suppliers.

12. *Emergency preparedness.* To develop and maintain, where significant hazards exist, emergency preparedness plans in conjunction with emergency services, relevant authorities, and the local community, recognizing potential transboundary impacts.

13. *Transfer of technology.* To contribute to the transfer of environmentally sound technology and management methods throughout the industrial and public sectors.

14. *Contributing to the common effort.* To contribute to the development of public policy and to business, governmental and intergovernmental programs, and education initiatives that will enhance environmental awareness and protection.

15. *Openness to concerns.* To foster openness and dialogue with employees and the public, anticipating and responding to their concerns about the potential hazards and impacts of operations, products, wastes, or services, including those of transboundary or global significance.

16. *Compliance and reporting.* To measure environmental performance; to conduct regular environmental audits and assessments of compliance with company requirements, legal requirements, and these principles; and periodically to provide appropriate information to the Board of Directors, shareholders, employees, the authorities, and the public.

D.   THE GLOBAL COMPACT

Following up on the efforts described above to create corporate codes of conduct, in July, 2000, United Nations Secretary–General Kofi Annan launched the "Global Compact" for TNCs to demonstrate "good global citizenship" in their international operations. Corporations joining the Compact must adopt nine principles derived from the Universal Declaration of Human Rights, the Declaration of the International Labor Organization on fundamental principles and rights, the Copenhagen Summit, and the Rio Declaration of 1992. Members are urged to incorporate these principles into their corporate mission statements and management practices.

Human Rights

1. Business should support and respect the protection of internationally proclaimed human rights within their sphere of influence; and

2. Ensure that they are not complicit in human rights abuses.

Labor

3. Businesses should uphold the freedom of association and the effective recognition of the right to collective bargaining; and

4. The elimination of all forms of forced and compulsory labor; and

5. The effective abolition of child labor; and

6. Eliminate discrimination in respect of employment and occupation.

Environment

7. Businesses should support a precautionary approach to environmental challenges; and

8. Undertake initiatives to promote greater environmental responsibility; and

9. Encourage the development and diffusion of environmentally friendly technologies.

<http://www.un.org/partners/business/fs1.htm>

Critics of the Global Compact have focused on the problems in formally linking the UN with corporations. From the UN's perspective, they argue that its image will suffer by creating alliances with corporations that have questionable human rights, labor, or environmental records (they cite Nike and Shell as examples). Conversely, critics claim that TNC's should not be able to "wrap themselves in the flag of the UN" to improve their public images. Allowing corporations to claim the UN stamp of approval is particularly troubling since the Global Compact provides for no verification or enforcement measures. To highlight these concerns, an alliance of NGOs has launched the "Citizen's Compact" on the UN and TNCs. <http://www.corpwatch.org/trac/globalization/un/gccc.html>.

QUESTIONS AND DISCUSSION

1. The drafters of the OECD Guidelines, CERES Principles and the ICC Business Charter faced a similar problem. They wanted their guidelines to be specific enough to be meaningful, yet flexible enough to be adopted by both small local businesses and huge multinational corporations. Do the standards take the same approach? If you were advising the CEO of a large business, which standard would you recommend adopting and why? If you were an environmentalist on the company's Board of Directors, which standard would you recommend adopting and why?

2. These standards have been criticized as too vague and lacking any compliance mechanism. Given the goals of the standards, is this a fair criticism? Is it accurate? As an environmentally conscious investor, beyond a company's public adherence to these principles, what additional information would you want in order to assess its environmental credentials?

3. What do the ICC Charter, OECD Guidelines, and the CERES Principles require a company to do if it causes environmental damage through its activities?

4. One of the key arguments for business adoption of the CERES Principles, ICC Business Charter or environmental management systems (*infra*) is that companies that do better environmentally do better financially. Evaluating over 70 research studies, The Alliance for Environmental Innovations "found no studies recording a negative association between financial and environmental performances." Rather, the results showed that companies that outperform competitors environmentally also outperform them in the stock market. Harvey Meyer, *The Greening Corporate America*, J. Bus. Strategy, Vol. 21, iss. 1, at 38 (Jan. 2000).

5. The ICC Charter's 10th point is called, "Precautionary approach." Contrast this with the precautionary principle in the Rio Declaration: "In order to protect the environment, the precautionary approach shall be widely applied by States according to their capabilities. Where there are threats of serious or irreversible damage, lack of full scientific certainty shall not be used as a reason for postponing cost-effective measures to prevent environmental degradation." Do the two principles differ and, if so, what are the consequences of these differences in guiding corporate action?

6. Compared to the over 37,000 transnational corporations in operation, the number of CERES and ICC signatories is tiny. The wealth of transnational corporations, however, is highly concentrated. Over half the transnational corporations are based in the United States, Japan, Germany, France and the United Kingdom. Do you think voluntary codes of conduct are an effective means to ensure corporate environmentally responsible behavior?

7. In countries with a vigorous free press and closely regulated securities markets, monitoring companies' environmental performance is occasionally difficult, but usually possible. In many developing countries, however, companies are not required to share information on their environmental impacts with the local community of stakeholders. Even shareholders find monitoring their companies' performance is difficult. A number of NGOs dedicate their efforts to monitoring the social, environmental, and labor aspects of companies' operations. Their information is often shared with the social investment community as well as with the media. Some of the more influential "watchdog" and socially responsible investment NGOs (and their web sites) include the Investor Responsibility Research Center <www.irrc.org>, Business for Social Responsibility <www.bsr.org>, Council for Economic Priorities <www.cepnyc.org>, Transparency International <www.transparency.de>, Students for Responsible Business <www.srb.org>, Human Rights Watch <www.hrw.org>, and the Fair Labor Association (the successor organization to the Apparel Industy Partnership) < http://www.fairlabor.org/>. Visit some of these web sites to learn more about these organizations' activities. Do you recognize any of the companies they examine? How influential do you think such activities are on corporate decisionmaking?

SECTION III.   ENVIRONMENTAL MANAGEMENT SYSTEMS

A.   EMAS

Two common maxims in corporate environmental management are, "what gets measured gets done," and "waste is just profits down the drain." Putting these theories to practice, environmental management systems provide standards for managing the environmental impacts of business operations. To encourage the adoption of these systems, the European Union has adopted the Eco–Management and Audit Scheme (EMAS). 1993 O.J. (L 168/1). Launched in 1993 as a voluntary program for European-based industry, the regulation became effective in 1995 and establishes a series of requirements for certification of an environmental management system. By 1999, 1900 companies were participating in EMAS. Participating EU companies establish an environmental management system for their production site and then are assessed for compliance at periodic intervals by an accredited third party.

The requirements for EMAS certification include a written corporate environmental policy, an inventory of the environmental impacts of a company's (or industrial site's) production processes, a program of environmental measures to track performance, and a management system including procedures to implement periodic audits. Importantly, EMAS also requires continuous improvement in environmental performance. If the system complies with the standard then the company may use an EMAS symbol on its stationary for a certified site to show it complies with the EMAS standard and the statement, "This site has an environmental management system and its environmental performance is reported on to the public in accordance with the Community Eco–Management and Audit Scheme." The EMAS symbol cannot, however, be used to advertise products or appear on product packaging. Companies or sites that violate EMAS are de-registered until the problems have been resolved. *Corporate Environmental Reporting: Embraced or Resisted?*, BNA INT'L ENV'T DAILY, April 20, 1994.

The European Commission has taken steps to enforce EMAS. The Commission filed an application before the Court of Justice charging that Greece and Portugal had failed to take "certain necessary implementing measures to give effect to the EU's eco-management and audit scheme Regulation." *Press Release on Action Against Member States Re EMAS*, SPICERS, January 30, 1999.

B.   ISO 14000

The International Organization for Standardization (ISO), an international organization with members from 110 countries, was established in Geneva in 1946 to standardize industrial and consumer products moving across national borders. ISO promotes worldwide standards in industry to promote international commerce. Its goal is to minimize non-tariff trade barriers. As a simple example, ISO has established standards for the size and thickness of plastic credit cards. Thus you can use your credit card issued in America to withdraw money from cash machines in Japan or to charge goods in Chile. Without such a standard, each country or region might have its own credit card specifications, thus preventing international use of one uniform card. ISO also promotes uniform management systems for industry. ISO's complicated decision-making structure is described below. Rod Hunter, *Standardization and the Environment*, BNA INT'L ENV'T DAILY, March 29, 1993.

> ISO is made up of national standards bodies. To be allowed to participate, a national body must be the "most representative of standardization in its country," there being only one such body accepted for ISO membership per country. More than 70 percent of the ISO member bodies are governmental institutions or organizations incorporated by public law. Many of the remainder have close links with their national public administration.

> ISO's technical work is carried out through technical committees (TC's). The decision to establish a TC is taken by the ISO Council, and its scope is approved by the ISO Technical Board on behalf of the Council.

> Within this scope, the TC determines its own work program. A TC may, in turn, establish subcommittees and working groups to cover different aspects of its work. Any member body interested in a subject for which a TC has been authorized has the right to participate in that committee. [There are over 2,700 Technical Committees in ISO]

> An international standard is the result of agreement between the member bodies of ISO. An international standard may be used as such or may be incorporated in the national standards of the various countries.

> The first important step towards an international standard is the committee draft (CD)–a document circulated for study and comment within the TC or subcommittee. When agreement is finally reached within the TC, the committee draft is sent to the ISO Central Secretariat for registration as "draft international standard" (DIS).

> The DIS is then circulated to all member countries for voting. If 75 percent of the votes are cast in favor of the DIS, it is published as an international standard.

The most successful ISO management standard has been the ISO 9000 series. Reflecting the business strategy of total quality management (TQM), the ISO 9000 Quality Standards Program is a series of five international standards that assures customers throughout the world that registered suppliers have in place a certified management system to ensure quality. As with the standard for credit cards, the ISO quality standard promotes international commerce because it avoids the problem suppliers might face in evaluating quality management systems in countries and industries employing different certification standards. The ISO 9000 standards include the following basic requirements:

1) a description of the quality system in detail;

2) an understanding by each employee of the requirements of the system along with a commitment to comply with them:

3) constant monitoring through auditing by both internal and external auditors; and

4) routine adjustments and updating to reflect changing requirements of customers.

Implementing an ISO 9000 quality management system is a major undertaking for any business, requiring implementation of procedures which measure the quality (and variance) of a business' processes and documentation to ensure the procedures are working. The main impact of ISO 9000 has been in the marketplace. An increasing number of corporate buyers, particularly in Europe, now *require* that their suppliers comply with ISO 9000 as assurance that the products or services provided are kept to a high level through a quality management program. Thus many organizations have obtained ISO 9000 certification simply to meet customer demand in order to remain competitive. Hank Barnette, *Meeting Quality Standards: ISO 9000, 9002, 14000 and QS 9000*, Iron Age New Steel at 112, June 1996.

With ISO 9000 as a model and in response to the growing interest in environmental standards around the world, ISO formed a Strategic Advisory Group on the Environment in 1991 to consider the need for international environmental management standards. In 1992, this group recommended the creation of technical committees to develop a series of environmental standards. Comprised of representatives from industry, government and a few environmental organizations around the world, the committees have been drafting the "ISO 14000 series" of voluntary standards for environmental management systems, environmental audits, environmental performance evaluations, product life cycle assessments, and environmental product labeling. To obtain ISO certification an organization must be inspected by an accredited third party who ensures compliance with the relevant standard.

Like EMAS, support for ISO 14001 has grown in recent years, increasing twenty-fold since its inception in 1996. As of October, 1997, 2,300 companies worldwide had been certified in compliance with ISO 14001. The leader in certifications was the United Kingdom (with 440 companies certified). Germany followed with 320 and the Netherlands with 230 companies. In 1997, just over 50 U.S. companies were certified, but by the year 2000, the number had multiplied to 2000. Ruth Hillary, *Environmental Management System Standards: Environmental Protection the Voluntary Way*, Safety & Health Prac., vol. 18, iss. 4, at 52 (Apr. 1, 2000); *Global uptake of ISO 14001 shows uneven picture*, ENDS Report at 3 (Oct. 1997); *Rockwell Business Unit Headquarters Earns ISO 14001 Certification*, PR Newswire, June 13, 2000. This increased success has also raised the commercial pressure to register. For example, the car manufacturers Rover and Jaguar, located in the UK, have required that more than 1000 of their first-tier suppliers of products either achieve or move towards ISO 14001 certification by 2000. Ruth Hillary, *Environmental Management System Standards: Environmental Protection the Voluntary Way*, Safety & Health Prac., vol. 18:4, at 52 (Apr. 1, 2000). Below are four justifications commonly offered in support of the ISO 14000 initiative and its potential impact in the marketplace. Do you find them persuasive?

Customer Demands: If the series proves as important in the marketplace as the ISO 9000 series, customers will increasingly require ISO 14000 certification as a condition of doing business. Currently, companies are driven to comply with environmental regulations to avoid legal liability. However, in the face of market-driven standards based on consumer demand and competition, a company will seek compliance with an international standard not to avoid liability but, rather, to remain competitive in the market.

Corporate Image: The growing public awareness of environmental performance is a major driving force in implementing ISO 14000. Stating that a company complies with all environmental regulations represents only minimum performance when compared to the many companies who have publicly set waste reduction goals of 50% and more. For a company to develop a positive public image with both its shareholders and customers, it must expand beyond minimum requirements and ISO 14000 provides one possible mark of recognition.

Regulatory Relief: While ISO 14000 certification is unlikely to relieve companies from compliance with environmental regulations, it may provide regulatory relief from demonstrating compliance. That is, regulatory agencies may accept some of the documentation proving compliance with ISO 14000 in place of paperwork to show compliance with the regulations. Thus it is hoped by some in industry that ISO 14000 certification may lead to relief through the consolidation of permitting paperwork or the reduction of inspections.

Cost Savings: A review of an organization's environmental performance will likely uncover opportunities for improved operations and savings as well as responding to new regulatory requirements and the changes more efficiently. The overall result may be improvement in the long-term capital and operating costs of the organization.

To understand better how ISO standards operate in practice, it is instructive to examine the first standard adopted in the ISO 14000 series. ISO 14001 contains the required elements and criteria that an organization must satisfy to receive certification of its environmental management system. In principle, any company whose operations cause an environmental impact can establish an environmental management system, whether it be a car manufacturer, a restaurant, or a law school. The basic requirements of ISO 14001 are a corporate environmental policy statement, compliance with relevant environmental legislation, and a commitment to continual improvement.

The ISO 14001 standard can be described as a five part system, each of which is necessary for a satisfactory environmental management system:

C. Foster Knight, *Comment: Voluntary Environmental Standards vs. Mandatory Environmental Regulations and Enforcement in the NAFTA Market* 12 ARIZ. J. INT'L. & COMP. LAW 619, 623–26 (1995)

ISO 14001 is an auditable standard governing the essential elements of an environmental management system. Its requirements are stated broadly to accommodate any kind of organization, small or large, in different economic, social, cultural, and environmental settings. Yet, it contains specific "hard" provisions that will force important environmental performance improvements in participating industrial and commercial organizations.

Key requirements of the ISO 14001 standard are briefly summarized below.

A. Environmental Policy

A cornerstone of the environmental management system is a written environmental policy aligned with the organization's business or mission which also commits the organization to compliance with applicable laws and regulations, prevention of pollution, and continuous improvement. [This is the only document that must be made available to the public.]

B. Planning Processes

The environmental management system must have a documented planning process that identifies the "environmental aspects" of the organization's activities, products and processes, as well as applicable legal and regulatory requirements. The planning process must result in specific environmental objectives and targets ... must be measurable to the extent feasible, and are critically important to the organization's credibility with its stakeholders in demonstrating continuous improvement. Additionally, the planning process must include documented environmental management programs for achieving the environmental objectives and targets.

C. Implementation And Operation

Organizational structure and responsibilities are the architecture of implementation. There must be defined roles, responsibilities and authorities associated with essential components of the environmental management system, including a direct accountability link to senior management. Environmental management responsibilities cannot be confined to the environmental function, but must extend to operations management and other important functions in the organization.

Training, awareness, and competence in managing the organization's environmental aspects are key components. Training must ultimately be carried out at the individual employee level, connecting the individual employee's job with specific environmental aspects and measures the employee should be taking to protect the environment.

Communication processes are an essential component of implementing the ISO 14001 environmental management system. Communication processes must include internal systems for employees and managers, and external systems for "interested parties" such as customers, suppliers, the community living near operations facilities, shareholders, and regulatory agencies. ISO 14001 does not require the organization to issue a formal environmental report on its activities, but it must maintain a formal process for receiving, documenting, and responding to relevant information and requests from "interested parties."

Operational control procedures are another required component of implementation systems. The organization must identify specific operations and activities associated with significant environmental impacts (e.g. industrial boilers can create significant NOx emissions) and then develop and document operating procedures (e.g. to monitor and control NOx emissions) to ensure each activity causing significant environmental impacts is carried out under specific conditions. Operational control procedures must cover significant environmental aspects of the organization's products and services as well as its manufacturing and other activities. For example, an organization that manufactures electronic products will need a process for minimizing significant environmental effects in or from its products created by hazardous materials in parts and components. This might be done through training and environmental requirements specifications to its parts vendors.

Emergency preparedness and response plans and procedures are another required component of implementation systems. Emergency procedures must include prevention and mitigation procedures such as spill prevention and cleanup measures.

Environmental management system documentation and document control procedures are also required as part of implementation systems.

D. Performance Measurement And Corrective Action

A critical requirement in the ISO 14001 EMS is a system of procedures to monitor and measure the organization's compliance with regulations (e.g. an audit program), its operational environmental performance involving significant environmental impacts (e.g. wastewater monitoring), and its overall performance toward its environmental objectives and targets. An important part of this effort is an environmental management system audit to determine if the systems continue to conform to the requirements of ISO 14001. The organization must also maintain a process for investigating "non-conformance" (e.g. non-compliance or incidents such as spills causing environmental impacts), for taking action to mitigate environmental impacts and for initiating and completing corrective and preventive actions.

E. Management Review

The final component of the ISO 14001 standard requires the organization to have a system for conducting a management-level review of the overall effectiveness of the environmental management system. The management review is not an audit or conformity assessment of the environmental management system but rather more like a traditional management operations review. It includes an evaluation of how successfully environmental management has been integrated with business operations. The management review also serves to redirect the environmental management system. For example, if the organization is close to meeting a specific environmental objective, the management review can initiate setting a new environmental objective, consistent with its environmental policy and commitment to continuous improvement.

To provide a concrete example of what a certification system looks like, below is an excerpt from the ISO 14001 standard concerning "checking and corrective action." This excerpt will also be used in the Problem Exercise at the end of this section.

ISO 14001 Environmental management system– Specification with guidance for use

4.5 Checking and corrective action

4.5.1 Monitoring and measurement

The organization shall establish and maintain documented procedures to monitor and measure, on a regular basis, the key characteristics of its operations and activities that can have significant impact on the environment. This shall include the recording of information to track performance, relevant operational controls and conformance with the organization's environmental objectives and targets.

Monitoring equipment shall be calibrated and maintained and records of this process shall be retained according to the organizations procedures.

The organization shall establish and maintain a documented procedure for periodically evaluating compliance with relevant environmental legislation and regulations.

4.5.2   Nonconformance and corrective and preventive action

The organization shall establish and maintain procedures for defining responsibility and authority for handling and investigating nonconformance, taking action to mitigate any impacts caused and for initiating and completing corrective and preventive action.

Any corrective or preventive action taken to eliminate the causes of actual and potential nonconformances shall be appropriate to the magnitude of problems and commensurate with the environmental impact encountered.

The organization shall implement and record any changes in the documented procedures resulting from corrective and preventive action.

4.5.3   Records

The organization shall establish and maintain procedures for the identification, maintenance and disposition of environmental records. These records shall include training records and the results of audits and reviews.

Environmental records shall be legible, identifiable and traceable to the activity, product or service involved. Environmental records shall be stored or maintained in such a way that they are readily retrievable and protected against damage, deterioration or loss. Their retention times shall be established and recorded.

Records shall be maintained, as appropriate to the system and to the organization, to demonstrate conformance to the requirements of this International Standard.

---

1.   ENVIRONMENTALIST CRITIQUES OF ISO 14000

The ISO 14000 series has not been without its critics. In particular, some environmentalists have denounced the standards' emphasis on conformance rather than performance, the lack of public access to data, and the failure to address international environmental laws. The excerpt below is a well-researched assessment of ISO 14001's text and potential implications. As you read, consider the criticisms in light of the potential benefits of the ISO 14000 series cited earlier.

Harris Gleckman & Riva Krut, *Neither International nor Standard: The Limits of ISO 14001 as an Instrument of Global Corporate Environmental Management*, GLOBAL MANAGEMENT INTERNATIONAL (April 1996)

In the full text of ISO 14001, the language is both precise and confusing. In reading the text, it is important to note that apparently non-technical terms were the subject of intense debate. Several major issues of linguistics and definition were crucial. The first is the emphasis on measuring environmental *conformance* (to an internal set of standards), not environmental *performance*. Related issues are the agreements to drop most references to corporate environmental "impact" in favour of the term environmental "aspects", to select "certifier" over "verifier" as the designation of an ISO 14001 auditor, and to replace the commitment to "pollution prevention" (which has legal consequences, at least in the USA) with commitment to the "prevention of pollution" (which has no legal consequences and includes end-of-pipe solutions). * * *

Companies that are grappling with environmental management must address the very difficult question of what material benefits can come from sound environmental management under existing market conditions. Businesses tend to make environmental investments where there is a short-term bottom line reward, or where there is some other economic benefit: for example in marketing or public relations. At the same time, companies that are interested in this area are undertaking a range of exercises to address the larger question of what the relationship should be between industry and environment. For example, industry leaders have been experimenting with innovative ways to create global environmental performance standards without sacrificing local autonomy or corporate competitiveness. The ISO 14000 series will reverse this trend, and will effectively discourage transnational corporate experimentation because it will grant an "easy A" to companies with ISO 14001, even if they have low environmental performance standards. * * *

Although ISO 14001 claims Agenda 21 as its ideological parent, commitments in ISO 14001 are retrograde in comparison to Agenda 21. The ISO 14000 series does not include any reference to the Montreal Protocol, the Basel Convention, the Convention on Biological Diversity, the OECD Guidelines on Hazardous Technologies, or any other international environmental agreement. The only compliance aspects are to conform to applicable laws and legal regulations and, although it cites Agenda 21 in its Appendix, the principles are not reproduced in the ISO 14000 series.

The implications of this for global environmental management are significant. A trend in international environmental performance standard-setting has been to generalise from existing national and industrial best practice. For example, Agenda 21 recommended that transnational corporations "report annually on routine emissions of toxic chemicals even in the absence of host country requirements," drawing on the model of the US Toxic Release Inventory. In addition, Agenda 21 contained recommendations to transnational corporations to "introduce policies and commitments to adopt equivalent or not less stringent standards of operation as in the country of origin;" and to "be encouraged to establish worldwide corporate policies on sustainable development." Moreover, Agenda 21 recommends that firms adopt standards for public reporting, improved environmental performance and full cost accounting. None of these recommendations are cited in ISO 14001, even though many governments and leading international organisations are working towards full implementation of such programmes. * * *

ISO proponents have argued that registration should be a demonstration of environmental commitment and proof that they are delivering on the promises of the industry–environmental initiatives such as Agenda 21, the ICC Business Charter on Sustainable Development and the chemical industry's Responsible Care Programme. They assert that ISO 14001 will provide demonstrable proof that the company is environmentally sound, and advocate that certification in itself should therefore reduce compliance and liability costs. * * *

While the ISO 14000 series is seeking credibility as the international environmental standard, it fails to advance the goals and legal principles set over the last ten years through international agreements and conventions. ISO 14001 is trying to claim an intellectual and political legitimacy from the international community while it fails to include mandatory requirements for any external references to sound engineering or to sound public policy decisions from the international community, in the required environmental policy (as does the EU's Eco–Management and Audit Scheme [EMAS] requirement). * * *

ISO 14001 is a specification standard for conformance, not performance, and environmental aspects, not environmental impacts. A sound ISO 14001 EMS will give a firm the capacity to measure and monitor the environmental 'aspects' of its operations. In a speech at MIT, Joe Cascio [chairman of the TC207 subcommittee drafting ISO 14001] said that he does not care "how much" waste an ISO-certified firm dumps into a river. What is important is that the company's EMS knows that it has happened.

Environmental performance relates only to the measurable performance of the environmental management system. The environmental management system can be internally defined and system performance results are confidential. The public and public authorities are being asked to depend on the corroboration of the certification bodies that ISO 14001 companies will:

1. Improve their environmental performance in accordance with their environmental policy

2. On discovery of an environmental problem, will correct and remedy the situation

However, one should remember Mr. Cascio's anecdote about the waste in the river. Getting demonstrably and measurably better at the ISO 14001 standards does not necessarily improve the firm's environmental performance. Moreover, reference to environmental impact has been diluted and recast into commitments to examine environmental "aspect". Commitments to environmental performance are commitments simply to comply with "applicable" regulations.

The nature of environmental, health and safety standards. There are no requirements for health and safety standards in the ISO 14000 series as it now stands. All work on health and safety was put aside in the ISO discussions. * * *

The business argument for performance-oriented management systems. * * *Under ISO 14001, environmental information is gathered for purposes of helping track and manage the corporate environmental management system, and is viewed as company-confidential.

This moves against all international environmental agreements and leading voluntary corporate environmental management initiatives which have been moving progressively towards greater disclosure of environmental information in line with public requirements for corporate environmental reporting. Agenda 21 established a public "right to know," and made several specific reporting recommendations. Since then, the OECD has sponsored several workshops for governments, industry and non-governmental organisations, to implement national pollutant release and transfer registers, based on the US Toxic Release Inventory. These will create a public information vehicle that can be used to benchmark corporate and governmental accountability for environmental performance, while stimulating and measuring the shift to cleaner production and products.

Among international firms, levels of disclosure and reporting formats vary enormously, but leading industries and many international firms now routinely produce environmental reports. At minimum, they indicate environmental investments, liabilities and expenditures. Increasingly, they include figures on performance and relative performance in reducing emissions and toxic emissions, decreasing waste, integrating lifecycle analyses into new projects, widening the circle of stake-holders to include local communities, and so on.

A core idea of the EU's EMAS, which does have a disclosure requirement, is that public pressure will motivate companies to improve environmental performance. However, in order for this to work, there needs to be disclosure of corporate environmental performance. Without external audit and public disclosure, self-monitoring is an oxymoron.

––––––––

Another concern regarding the content of the ISO 14000 standards relates to the identity of the drafters who negotiated them. While many governments and non-governmental organizations have the right to participate in the work of the Technical Committees, in practice the majority of the parties involved in developing the standards represent large corporate entities in developed countries. Small businesses and non-governmental organizations are under-represented, as are representatives of developing countries generally. In part this results from the expensive facts that ISO meetings are held all over the world, from South Africa to Canada. This lack of input from developing countries and public interest groups has serious representational implications in the context of trade law, discussed below. Moreover, the possibility of regulatory pre-emption has become a concern. While some environmental agencies, such as the U.S. EPA, have stated clearly that compliance with ISO 14001 does not relieve corporations from compliance with environmental laws, a number of developing countries have discussed compliance with ISO 14001 as a potential substitute for substantive regulatory standards.

––––––––

2.   TRADE LAW AND ISO 14000

As Chapter 15 describes, one of the Uruguay Round agreements is the Technical Barriers to Trade Agreement (TBT). The TBT creates trade rules ("disciplines") for technical regulations, standards, and labels. Its goal is to ensure that such rules do not create unnecessary obstacles to international trade, primarily in the fields of environment, health and safety. Article 2.4 states:

> Where technical regulations are required and relevant international standards exist or their completion is imminent, Members shall use them, or the relevant parts of them, as a basis for their technical regulations except when such international standards or relevant parts would be an ineffective or inappropriate means, for instance, because of fundamental climatic or geographical factors or fundamental technological problems.

The TBT defines "technical standards" as *mandatory* technical requirements. The TBT's provisions also address *voluntary* standards through Annex III, known as the Code of Good Practice. The Code of Good Practice contains an identical requirement to use international standards unless they are inappropriate. TBT, Annex III, Part F. Do you see why this rule effectively raises the voluntary ISO standards to the status of international trade disciplines?

Despite the fact that the ISO 14000 series can be approved with little NGO involvement and virtually no public accountability in the decision-making process, countries are told they "shall" use such standards in promulgation of their own standards unless they can justify their inappropriateness. Countries that cannot justify the inappropriate nature of the ISO standards may face and lose a WTO challenge should they maintain higher standards. If they lose the dispute, they would either have to bring their regulations into conformity with the international standard or face punitive sanctions in the form of countervailing tariffs. In the context of environmental labeling, for example, this would require private programs to comply with the ISO 14020 standard or face possible WTO challenges.

Thus the TBT raises the legal significance of ISO standards, placing them on a level with international agreements negotiated among governments. As a result, the ISO 14000 standards could provide a basis for challenging environmental, health and safety standards as well as voluntary eco-labeling programs before the WTO. Whether programs could justify their noncompliance with ISO standards on the basis of the exceptions listed above is unclear. In any case, it places them on the defensive before a WTO Dispute Panel. *See* James Salzman, *Informing the Green Consumer: The Debate Over the Use and Abuse of Environmental Labels*, J. OF INDUSTRIAL ECOLOGY, at 11, Summer 1997.

QUESTIONS AND DISCUSSION

1. As described in the excerpt by Gleckman and Krut, the environmental management standard in ISO 14001 does not set specific targets for discharges or emissions but, instead, establishes auditing and record-keeping procedures for companies to implement. This was a major source of disagreement between Europeans and Americans in the negotiation of ISO 14001. The United States objected to a fixed set of mandatory improvements and, as published, the ISO 14001 standard "does not establish absolute requirements for environmental performance beyond commitment, in the policy, to compliance with applicable legislation and regulation and to continual improvement." Naomi Roht–Arriaza, *Shifting the Point of Regulation: The International Organization for Standardization and Global Lawmaking on Trade and the Environment*, 22 ECOLOGY L.Q. 479, 505 (1995).

This result has been criticized as the equivalent of requiring "a six inch high jump." That is, ISO 14001 certification attests that an organization has an operating environmental management system in place but says nothing about its progress in reducing its environmental impacts beyond a commitment to "continual improvement." The standard response to this criticism is that the general goal of international standards is to encourage environmental management. Market forces, not voluntary standards, should be relied on to drive environmental performance improvements. What does this response mean by "market forces" and how would you relate it to the experience of the ISO 9000 series? How could the ISO 14000 standard provide a more meaningful requirement for improved environmental performance?

2. Saying that transnational corporations should behave in "an environmentally responsible manner" means different things to different people. To some it means compliance with domestic and international laws, to others it means full disclosure of toxic releases and other environmental impacts to local stakeholders, and to others it means uniform standards of operations throughout the world. It is clear, however, that with the exception of a few activities controlled by international environmental agreements (such as trade in hazardous waste and the production and sale of ozone-depleting substances), international controls on the environmental aspects of transnational corporations are extremely difficult to promulgate and implement. As mentioned in the Gleckman and Krut excerpt, *Agenda 21* calls on corporations to report annually on routine emissions of toxic chemicals, adopt equivalent standards of operation throughout the world, and adopt standards for public reporting, improved environmental performance and full cost accounting. *Agenda 21* is not, however, enforceable law. Indeed, in 1992 the UN formally abandoned its two decade-long effort to gain support for its Code of Conduct for Transnational Corporations. It had been strongly opposed by developed countries and industry who claimed its impact was the equivalent of international regulation.

Research on transnational corporations shows that while a number of TNCs have uniform environmental management systems, very few companies employ a uniform performance standards (e.g. fixed emission and effluent levels) in all countries of operation. Nonetheless, transnational corporations generally have a better record of environmental performance in developing countries than local companies. This is due to greater resources (both financial and technical), higher visibility, and corporate headquarter demands. Research is mixed on whether "dirty industries" flee the stringent regulations of developed countries to operate in developing countries with weaker environmental regulations and lax enforcement (sometimes called "pollution havens"). In most cases, factors such as geographic location, infrastructure, natural resources, and training of workforce are more influential in determining the location of a facility than the stringency of environmental regulation. A number of industries, however, including primary metals processing, asbestos, and some chemical manufacturing industries, including those manufacturing benzidine-based dyes and trichlorophenol, have been shown to leave developed countries in order to escape strict regulations. This has been cited by some as evidence of a "race-to-the-bottom," as discussed in Chapter 15 on Trade and the Environment. Fowler, *op. cit.* at 14, 17; A. Rappaport and M. Flaherty, *Corporate Responses to Environmental Challenges*, 14 INT'L ENV'T REP. 261 (May 8, 1991).

3. What alternatives are there to voluntary international standards in addressing corporate conduct overseas? One possibility would be a domestic law in the United States, for example, requiring companies to maintain regulatory compliance with U.S. standards in their foreign operations. What do you consider the benefits and problems with such a proposal? How would it be enforced? Is it economically efficient? The extraterritorial application of domestic law is addressed in Chapter 19. *See,* Alan Neff, *Not in Their Backyards, Either: A Proposal for a Foreign Practices Act*, 17 ECOLOGY L.Q. 477 (1990).

4. Presently 47% of companies registered to EMAS also hold ISO 14001 accreditation. *EMAS Revisited*, Mod. PAINT & COATING, Vol. 89, Iss. 1, at 22 (Jan. 1999). EMAS has been criticized for its inability to induce small and medium-sized enterprises (SMEs) to participate. Only 18% of EMAS registered sites are SMEs. One UK survey found that 36% of SMEs could not list a single benefit of following positive environmental actions. The study also found that SMEs lack awareness of the environmental regulations that apply to them. Ruth Hillary, *Environmental Management System Standards: Environmental Protection the Voluntary Way*, SAFETY & HEALTH PRAC., vol. 18, iss. 4, at 52 (Apr. 1, 2000).

The geographic distribution of adopted standards has been uneven. The United States and the United Kingdom have displayed a preference for ISO 14001 over EMAS while Sweden and Germany have favored EMAS. To make this more concrete, consider that Germany has just over double the number of registered business sites than in the United Kingdom, but over *31 times* the number of EMAS sites (2,238 versus 71). The reason for the divided preferences is unclear. Perhaps it is to avoid the more stringent EMAS requirement of issuing a public statement of environmental performance, perhaps due to the larger number of American subsidiaries in the U.K. than in Germany or Sweden (and whose parent companies in North America do not value EMAS certification). Ruth Hillary, *Environmental Management System Standards: Environmental Protection the Voluntary Way*, SAFETY & HEALTH PRAC., vol. 18, iss. 4, at 52 (Apr. 1, 2000). Recently, proposals have been put forth suggesting that EMAS be expanded to include organizations with significant environmental impact, both direct and indirect. This would allow financial institutions, public authorities and agriculture to also take part in the scheme.

Problem Exercise

Congratulations! You have just been appointed the chair of the environmental committee of your school. Your committee's first responsibility is to obtain ISO 14001 certification for your school. Refer back to the ISO 14001 excerpt on page 1425. What specific steps would your school need to take to comply with its requirements? Make a list of the environmental impacts caused by your school. Which of these can be addressed by a management system? How would progress be measured?

Suggested Further Reading and Web Sites

Riva Krut and Harris Gleckman, ISO 14001: A MISSED OPPORTUNITY FOR GLOBAL SUSTAINABLE DEVELOPMENT (Earthscan, 1998)

> A critical assessment of the process and content of the ISO 14000 series.

Chris Sheldon, ed., ISO 14001 AND BEYOND: EMSs IN THE REAL WORLD (Greenleaf Publishing, 1997)

> A thoughtful review of environmental management systems.

John Elkington and Tom Burke, THE GREEN CAPITALISTS (1987)

John Elkington, CANNIBALS WITH FORKS (1997)

John Elkington, THE CHRYSALIS ECONOMY (2001)

> Elkington is one the leading thinkers on corporate sustainability (first coining the terms "sustainability" and the "triple bottom line"). These books explore the role of business in environmental protection and sustainable development.

B.R. Allenby And D.J. Richards, Eds., THE GREENING OF INDUSTRIAL ECOSYSTEMS (1994)

Robert U. Ayres and Leslie W. Ayres, INDUSTRIAL ECOLOGY : TOWARDS CLOSING THE MATERIALS CYCLE (1996)

Two books exploring the new field of industrial ecology: the study of economic activity within an ecosystem. Relying on a systems approach to environmental management, industrial ecology focuses on material and flows between companies and the surrounding environment.

http://www.ceres.org/reporting/overview.htm

The CERES Help Guide.

www.globalreporting.org

Homepage of the Global Reporting Initiative.

http://www.iso.ch/iso/en/ISOOnline.frontpage.

The homepage of ISO.

http://www.wbcsd.ch/

The homepage of the World Business Council for Sustainable Development, a coalition of 122 international companies. Interesting and relevant publications on a range of business/environment issues.

http://www.mindspring.com/~benchmark

The homepage of Benchmark Environmental Consulting, one of the most influential critics of the ISO 14000 series.

http://www.sustainability.com/

The homepage of Sustainability, an environmental consulting firm that works with both NGOs and industry.

CHAPTER NINETEEN

EXTRATERRITORIAL APPLICATION OF DOMESTIC ENVIRONMENTAL LAW

> ... *Unilateral actions to deal with environmental challenges outside the jurisdiction of the importing country should be avoided. Environmental measures addressing transboundary or global environmental problems should, as far as possible, be based on international consensus.*
>
> Principle 12 of the Rio Declaration on Environment and Development (1992)

SECTION I.   INTRODUCTION

Often the most effective laws protecting the international environment are not, in fact, international laws. The use of *domestic* laws that regulate conduct beyond a nation's borders, known as "extraterritorial application," has proven powerful in a number of circumstances. Yet, as Principle 12 from the Rio Declaration above suggests, most nations disapprove the use of unilateral actions to protect the global environment.

This chapter focuses on the United States, both because it is the largest economy in the world and because it aggressively extends the reach of its laws to actions outside U.S. territory.

Efforts to extend the protections of U.S. environmental laws beyond the nation's borders reflect both altruistic and self-serving motivations. On the one hand, many in the United States seek to protect environmental conditions in other countries, many of which lack the legal mechanisms and enforcement resources necessary to safeguard their environment from harmful wastes and environmentally unsound practices. On the other hand, environmental degradation is rarely confined to specific geographic areas and can prove costly to all nations, be it in the form of ocean dumping, deforestation, greenhouse gases, or ozone depletion. Traditionally, the global community has relied on multilateral negotiations and agreements such as the Basel Convention to address such international problems. Such agreements, however, take years to complete and often contain only vague and indefinite standards with ineffective enforcement mechanisms. These shortcomings are precisely those that have led to unilateral efforts to protect the global environment.

S. Spracker & E. Naftalin, *Applying Procedural Requirements of U.S. Environmental Laws to Foreign Ventures: A Growing Challenge to Business*, 25 THE INT'L LAWYER 1043, 1051–52 (1991).

Consider the following unilateral efforts by the United States (or U.S. citizens) to control or influence activities occurring outside its borders:

- Seeking to promote the conservation of marine mammals, Congress passes a law prohibiting persons and vessels subject to the jurisdiction of the United States from "taking" (i.e., killing or injuring) marine mammals on the high seas.

- Alarmed over declining numbers of elephants in Asia and Africa, Congress passes a law banning the import of ivory from countries that do not have effective elephant protection programs.

- Concerned over pollution from the New River in Mexico flowing into the United States, the EPA issues subpoenas to American companies demanding information on the use and release of chemicals at companies located in Mexico that are owned or operated by the U.S. parent companies.

- Seeking to protect the fragile environment of Antarctica, an environmental group challenges the government's failure to prepare an environmental impact assessment before constructing an incinerator at its South Pole scientific station.

- Seeking to ensure that public funds are used responsibly, Congress forbids the Overseas Private Investment Corporation from funding foreign projects that pose an unreasonable or major environmental impact.

In these examples and others like them, the U.S. government uses its laws either to regulate or influence activities *beyond* its national borders with the aim of protecting the environment. Such actions are applauded by some as a valuable complement to existing treaties and international agreements since, as a rule, domestic compliance and enforcement mechanisms are more sophisticated and effective than those created by international agreement. Nations can move more quickly and effectively than international institutions and such actions may serve as the basis for developing customary international law or spurring the international community to seek a common agreement to avoid future unilateral actions. Others denounce such actions as infringing other nations' sovereignty, as a form of "eco-imperialism." As you read the chapter, consider whether unilateral extraterritorial application of environmental laws promotes or hinders the development of international law.

Principle 21 of the Stockholm Declaration declares that a State has a duty to ensure that activity within its jurisdiction and control does not cause damage to the environment of another State or the global commons. *See* Chapter 7, page 419. To some extent, extraterritorial application of national environmental laws can be viewed as an extension of the Stockholm Declaration's Principle 21, extending the concept of "jurisdiction and control" to citizen and government activities abroad, affirmatively preventing damage to another State or the global commons.

This chapter first addresses the jurisdictional rules governing the extraterritorial application of domestic laws. These rules, and particularly the "Foley/Aramco doctrine," create a presumption against extraterritorial application. Despite the potential importance of extraterritorial application of U.S. laws, Congress rarely passes laws solely directed at extraterritorial activities. In the environmental field, since 1970 the United States has enacted a wide range of statutes primarily directed at actions within the United States, including controls on the release of pollutants into the environment, protection of endangered species, marine mammals and other wildlife, and environmental impact assessment requirements for major federal actions. These statutes have occasionally given rise to litigation concerning their extraterritorial reach. The next part of the chapter examines this jurisprudence–the extraterritorial application of RCRA, NEPA, the Endangered Species Act, and the Marine Mammal Protection Act. This is followed by the best known, and notorious, extraterritorial application of domestic law–the use of trade sanctions to promote wildlife protection. The chapter ends with a review of recent attempts to use U.S. courts in claims for environmental damages abroad and the role of legal doctrines such as "forum non conveniens" in dismissing these cases.

SECTION II. AUTHORITY TO REGULATE EXTRATERRITORIALLY

Whenever the extraterritorial application of a statute is challenged, one must determine why the United States should become involved at all. In practice, two questions are central to the determination of whether an extraterritorial application of a national law is proper:

1) Does the State have the authority to exercise extraterritorial jurisdiction?

2) Is the exercise of that authority reasonable (weighing the importance of the statute against potential foreign policy conflicts)?

A State must first have the authority to enact and apply its laws over a certain subject or activity. This is called *Jurisdiction to Prescribe*. International law places limits on the authority of a State to prescribe law. Section 402 of the Restatement (Third) of Foreign Relations Law of the United States provides four principles for Jurisdiction to Prescribe. If the conduct or persons sought to be regulated does not fall within one of the principles that serve as a basis for jurisdiction, it is generally recognized that a State could not prescribe a law related to that conduct or person.

The *territorial principle* is the most common basis for the exercise of jurisdiction to prescribe. The principle holds that a State has the power to regulate persons or conduct located *within the territory* of the State. For example, the United States can require any chemical plant in Ohio to comply with the Clean Air Act, regardless of whether it is owned by Americans, Canadians, or British. In American Banana v. United Fruit Co., 213 U.S. 347 (1909), plaintiffs alleged that the actions of the defendant in Central America monopolized trade in bananas and violated U.S. law. The Supreme Court dismissed the claim, with Justice Holmes confirming that "the general and almost universal rule is that the character of an act as lawful or unlawful must be determined wholly by the law of the country where the act is done.... [These] considerations would lead in the case of doubt, to a construction of any statute as intended to be confined in its operation and effect to the territorial limits over which the lawmaker has general or legitimate power."

The *effects principle*, often referred to as the "effects doctrine," provides a basis for States to extend jurisdiction to activities occurring outside the State that have or are intended to have a substantial effect within the State's territory. The scope of the effects doctrine has evolved with the globalization of the world economy. Despite the Supreme Court's early reliance in *American Banana* on the territorial principle, federal courts gradually justified extraterritorial applications based on the effects doctrine, particularly in the antitrust context where the prohibited conduct is intended to, and does, have an effect on economic interests in the United States. *See* United States v. Aluminum Co. of America, 148 F.2d 416 (2d Cir.1945) (ruling that the Sherman Act applied extraterritorially where a prohibited agreement is intended to affect and does affect United States imports or exports); Hartford Fire Ins. Co. v. California, 509 U.S. 764, 796 (1993) (stating that "it is well established by now that the Sherman Act applies to foreign conduct that was meant to produce and did in fact produce some substantial effect in the United States"). No court has yet fully applied the effects principle to foreign activities having environmental impacts in the United States.

The *nationality principle* provides for States to extend jurisdiction based on the nationality of the persons conducting the activity in question. For example, the Marine Mammal Protection Act prohibits "any person subject to the jurisdiction of the United States or any vessel ... subject to the jurisdiction of the United States" from taking protected marine mammals within U.S. territorial waters *or on the high seas.* 16 U.S.C. § 1372. The extension of the Act to conduct outside of U.S. territory is based on the nationality of the vessel. Should corporations operating abroad be subject to U.S. regulations because of the corporation's "nationality"? In this regard, consider how extraterritorial application of U.S. laws could affect other issues, for example the use of marijuana by U.S. citizens in countries where it is legal. Is that situation any different than the case of a corporation releasing massive pollution in a country with weak environmental laws?

The *protective principle* recognizes the right of a State to prescribe law covering conduct outside its territory directed against the national security of a State (e.g., espionage). This basis of jurisdiction has generally not been relied upon by States seeking to extend their environmental laws. Will this change if the concept of "environmental security" is increasingly adopted by policy makers? *See* Chapter 17, page 1377.

Even where a State has the jurisdiction to prescribe law over a specific activity, the exercise of this jurisdiction by a State must be reasonable, taking into account, among other things: the connection between the regulated conduct and the territory of the regulating State; the extent to which another State may have an interest in regulating the activity at issue; and the likelihood of conflict with another State. These limitations are designed to minimize conflicts between States when both desire to regulate the person or conduct at issue. *See* Section 403 of the Restatement (Third) of Foreign Relations Law of the United States (1987).

SECTION III. THE EXTRATERRITORIAL REACH OF U.S. STATUTES

While in certain circumstances Congress has the "jurisdiction to prescribe" or the authority to regulate conduct outside the territorial limits of the United States, whether Congress has actually *exercised* that authority is a matter of statutory interpretation. The seminal case addressing Congressional authority to regulate conduct outside U.S. territory is Foley Bros., Inc. v. Filardo, 336 U.S. 281 (1949). In *Foley,* the Supreme Court reviewed whether the language and legislative history of a federal law concerning an eight hour work day applied to plaintiffs' claim for overtime pay for work performed in Iran and Iraq. Ruling that the law did not apply extraterritorially to plaintiffs, the Court stated that legislation passed by Congress applies only within the territorial jurisdiction of the United States unless there is a clear Congressional intent to apply a particular statute extraterritorially. Referred to as the "Foley Doctrine," this rule of statutory construction creates a presumption *against* the extraterritorial application of U.S. laws–that a statute extends only to the territorial limits of the United States *unless* a contrary Congressional intent appears either in the statute or in relevant legislative history.

In EEOC v. Arabian American Oil Co. (known as "Aramco"), 499 U.S. 244 (1991), the Supreme Court reaffirmed the Foley Doctrine's principle of statutory construction. The Court held that Title VII of the Civil Rights Act of 1964 does not apply to employment practices of U.S. employers who employ U.S. citizens abroad. In reaching this result, the Court summarized the policy reasons underlying the presumption against extraterritoriality as follows. 499 U.S. at 248.

> It is a long-standing principle of American law "that legislation of Congress, unless a contrary intent appears, is meant to apply only within the territorial jurisdiction of the United States." *Foley Bros.,* 336 U.S., at 285, 69 S.Ct., at 577. This "canon of construction . . . is a valid approach whereby unexpressed congressional intent may be ascertained." *Ibid.* It serves to protect against unintended clashes between our laws and those of other nations which could result in international discord. *See McCulloch v. Sociedad Nacional de Marineros de Honduras,* 372 U.S. 10, 20–22, 83 S.Ct. 671, 677–678, 9 L.Ed.2d 547 (1963).

In applying this rule of construction, we look to see whether "language in the [relevant act] gives any indication of a congressional purpose to extend its coverage beyond places over which the United States has sovereignty or has some measure of legislative control." *Foley Bros., supra*, 336 U.S., at 285, 69 S.Ct., at 577. We assume that Congress legislates against the backdrop of the presumption against extraterritoriality. Therefore, unless there is "the affirmative intention of the Congress clearly expressed," *Benz, supra*, 353 U.S., at 147, 77 S.Ct., at 704, we must presume it "is primarily concerned with domestic conditions." *Foley Bros., supra*, 336 U.S., at 285, 69 S.Ct., at 577.

Title VII has subsequently been amended to apply extraterritorially, but Aramco's general proposition still stands. Under the rules for statutory construction set forth in Foley and Aramco, courts are to consider three factors in determining whether Congress intended to apply U.S. law extraterritorially: (1) the express language of the relevant statute; (2) the legislative history; and (3) the overall design of the statutory scheme. With respect to the third factor, courts are to evaluate whether extraterritorial application makes sense in the context of the statutory provisions. For example, are there venue provisions that can accommodate or anticipate extraterritorial application of the statute? Does the statute address overseas enforcement or government investigative authority? Are there provisions (e.g., notice requirements) intended to reduce the risks of conflicts of law? Conversely, would limiting the statute to domestic application undermine its effectiveness, or curtail its scope and usefulness?

Most statutes are unclear regarding their scope of coverage. Nonetheless, in practice courts have generally been more lenient in permitting extraterritorial application of antitrust and securities statutes than environmental statutes. Jonathan Turley, *When in Rome: Multilateral Misconduct and the Presumption Against Extraterritoriality*, 84 Nw. U. L. REV. 598 (1990). One might explain this result as a consequence of the effects doctrine, because the potential impacts of foreign antitrust and securities violations on the U.S. economy are more readily apparent than the impacts of overseas environmental harms. Is this justification defensible in the case of harms to the global commons, particularly in light of our improved understanding of environmental science? Should we expect more extraterritorial application of U.S. statutes as our understanding of global environmental linkages improve?

QUESTIONS AND DISCUSSION

1. Consider the following example. Jerry Mitchell, an American citizen, captures 15 dolphins while working in the Bahamas, where he has legally obtained a permit from local authorities to capture dolphins. The dolphins are captured within three miles of the Bahamian coast and Mitchell ships them to an aquarium in England. He has no intention of importing the animals to the United States. Upon his return to the United States, Mitchell is arrested. At trial, his attorney claims that the Marine Mammal Protection Act cannot control actions outside the United States, i.e., that Mitchell's actions took place outside the court's jurisdiction. How should the Court treat this jurisdictional challenge? How would you apply the rules of statutory construction recited in the Foley and Aramco cases to show that the Marine Mammal Protection Act should be applied extraterritorially? Section 102 of the Act prohibits the unauthorized taking of a marine mammal "on the high seas" by "any person subject to the jurisdiction of the United States." Does the plain language of the statute provide Mitchell with a plausible defense to the charges or seal his fate? We will read his case later in the chapter.

2. In discussing the history of extraterritorial application, Jonathan Turley argues that the present rules of statutory construction no longer make sense. While it may have been reasonable to assume through the 1940s that, when statutory language was unclear, Congress was probably not concerned with extraterritorial interests, in today's world of global markets and communication this assumption is clearly wrong. Jonathan Turley, *"When in Rome":Multinational Misconduct and the Presumption Against Extraterritoriality*, 84 Nw. U.L. REV. 598, 655–60 (1990).

> Both an analysis of the past case law and the original dual rationales behind the presumption against extraterritoriality strongly support a reversal of the rule of construction. Instead of beginning with a presumption that Congress intends all statutes to apply only territorially, it would make more sense to presume that, unless expressly limited, Congress intends statutes to apply extraterritorially. Consequently, in cases like *Boureslan,* courts would presume congressional intent to apply Title VII extraterritorially in their analysis of subject matter jurisdiction. Then they would ask, as they do in market cases, whether the particular case at hand involves adequate effects or conduct to justify prescriptive jurisdiction under international law. This structure, of course, would still allow courts to deny jurisdiction in employment–or environmental–cases that fall short of the necessary territorial effects or conduct. Under this two-step structure of analysis, however, the question of subject matter and prescriptive jurisdiction would be distinct. Courts would also interpret the statutes on a case-by-case basis, as they have in the market cases, instead of limiting entire statutes to domestic applications. Perhaps more importantly, the presumption on extraterritoriality would be reflective of the world as it is at the dawn of the twenty-first, not the twentieth, century.

Consider whether Turley's proposed standard described below would lead to different results in the cases in the next section on extraterritorial application of environmental laws. Would they be better results?

SECTION IV.   APPLICATION OF U.S. ENVIRONMENTAL STATUTES

The courts have addressed the extraterritorial application of U.S. environmental statutes in three contexts: (1) the application of U.S. pollution control laws abroad (RCRA); (2) whether U.S. government actions abroad must be preceded by environmental impact statements (NEPA); and (3) the use of domestic law to influence the behavior of parties outside the United States (ESA, MMPA, and multilateral lending institutions).

A.   RESOURCE CONSERVATION AND RECOVERY ACT (RCRA)

The Resource Conservation and Recovery Act (RCRA) regulates the generation, transportation, treatment, storage, and disposal of hazardous wastes. 42 U.S.C. §§ 6901 et seq. RCRA is the federal statute intended to ensure the "cradle to grave" management of hazardous wastes. In Amlon Metals v. FMC Corp., the Court addressed whether RCRA's "imminent and substantial endangerment" provisions apply to hazardous wastes located overseas. 775 F.Supp. 668 (S.D.N.Y.1991). Amlon Metals, the American agent of a British company, Wath, entered into a contract with a Delaware corporation, FMC Corp., for the reclamation of copper residue from wastes generated by FMC's facility. FMC would ship the wastes across the Atlantic for treatment in England by Wath. All parties agreed that the material would be free from certain hazardous constituents. With respect to the shipments at issue, FMC apparently failed to uphold its part of the agreement and shipped wastes containing high levels of xylene and other contaminants. Unbeknownst to Amlon or to Wath, the drivers who transported the cargo containers in question from FMC to the cargo ship were told to wear respirators to protect themselves from hazards associated with the material. When the containers arrived in England, they gave off strong odors and, upon investigation, were found to contain hazardous residues. After seeking and being denied relief in the British courts, Wath and Amlon brought suit against FMC in U.S. federal court seeking injunctive relief and damages under RCRA's citizen suit provisions, alleging that the material presented imminent and substantial endangerment to human health and the environment in the United Kingdom.

In reading the excerpt below, consider the Court's application of the Foley/Aramco Doctrine and its reliance on both the statutory language and legislative history of RCRA. Given the environmental risks posed to workers and the environment by the hazardous wastes, and RCRA's purported goal of ensuring the "cradle to grave" management of hazardous waste, do you find the Court's arguments persuasive?

Amlon Metal, Inc. v. FMC Corp.

775 F.Supp. 668, 672–676 (S.D.N.Y.1991).

In their complaint, plaintiffs assert as their Second Claim for Relief a cause of action under RCRA's citizen suit provision, 42 U.S.C. § 6972. Specifically, they seek injunctive relief and damages under Section 6972(a)(1)(B), which provides that any person may commence a civil action

> against any person ... including any past or present generator, past or present transporter, or past or present owner or operator of a treatment, storage, or disposal facility, who has contributed or is contributing to the past or present handling, storage, treatment, transportation, or disposal of any solid or hazardous waste which may present an imminent and substantial endangerment to health or to the environment.

Plaintiffs contend that they are entitled to relief under this provision because potentially toxic chemicals may evaporate from or leak out of containers in which they have stored the copper residue, posing an imminent and substantial danger to workers nearby and the community at large if the chemicals pollute the local water supply.

Defendant avers ... plaintiff's claim under section 6972(a)(1)(B) fails to state a claim upon which relief can be granted because RCRA does not extend to waste located within the territory of another sovereign nation. In support of its contention, defendant points to the well-established principle of American law "that legislation of Congress, unless a contrary intent appears, is meant to apply only within the territorial jurisdiction of the United States." *EEOC v. Arabian American Oil Co.*, 111 S.Ct. 1227, 1230 (1991) (quoting *Foley Bros. v.*

Filardo, 336 U.S. 281, 285 (1949)). Defendant notes further that in applying this canon of construction, courts must determine whether "language in the [relevant act] gives any indication of a congressional purpose to extend its coverage beyond places over which the United States has sovereignty or some measure of legislative control." *Id.* (quoting *Foley Bros.*, 336 U.S. at 285). Thus, defendant maintains that courts must assume that Congress legislates against the backdrop of an underlying presumption against extraterritoriality and therefore must presume that the statute applies only within the United States unless it contains "the affirmative intention of Congress clearly expressed" that it applies abroad. *Id.* (quoting *Benz v. Compania Naviera Hidalgo, S.A.*, 353 U.S. 138, 147 (1957)). * * *

a. Legislative History

While conceding that the initial focus of Congress when passing RCRA was entirely domestic, plaintiffs argue that the legislative history to the Hazardous and Solid Waste Amendments of 1984 ("HSWA"), Pub.L. No. 98–616, 98 Stat. 3221 (codified at scattered sections of 42 U.S.C. (Supp. III 1985)), shows the intention of Congress to allow RCRA to apply extraterritorially. Yet the two pieces of evidence relied on by plaintiffs add little to their case. Plaintiffs cite Representative Mikulski's remarks to the effect that "our own country will have safeguards from the ill effects of hazardous waste upon passage of [HSWA]. We should take an equally firm stand on the transportation of hazardous waste bound for export to other countries." *See* 129 Cong. Rec. 27691 (1984). But these remarks were made in reference to HSWA section 3017, 42 U.S.C. § 6938, RCRA's hazardous waste export provision, which requires notification of a shipment of hazardous waste abroad to the EPA administrator and to the government of the receiving country. Representative Mikulski's remarks, seen in context, almost certainly refer to the export provision and do not apply to RCRA's citizen suit provision, notwithstanding plaintiff's efforts to link this provision with the waste export provision.

The distinct nature of these provisions is well illustrated by plaintiff's second piece of evidence. Plaintiffs cite to Senator Mitchell's remarks that "If I were the U.S. Secretary of State, I would want to be sure that no American ally or trading partner is saddled with U.S. wastes it does not want or does not have the capacity to handle in an environmentally sound manner." 130 Cong. Rec. 20816 (1984). Although these remarks were again made in reference to RCRA's waste export provision, plaintiffs attempt to link them to RCRA's remedial provision. But only a few paragraphs earlier in his statements directed explicitly to RCRA's citizen suit provision, Senator Mitchell reveals the domestic focus of his argument over that provision: "Only EPA can sue to abate an imminent hazard.... In light of the thousands of known hazardous wastes sites across *this country*, this simply does not make sense.... Citizen suits to abate imminent hazards can expand *the national effort* to minimize these very real threats to *our* well being." *Id.* at 20815 (emphasis added). * * *

b. Structure and Language of RCRA

Plaintiffs concede that nothing in RCRA suggests that Congress intended for its regulatory provision to apply extraterritorially and that RCRA's "substantive" provisions "clearly do not apply abroad." ... Yet plaintiffs nonetheless contend that the citizen suit provision of RCRA should be applied extraterritorially. In particular, plaintiffs maintain that two aspects of RCRA, its export provision, 42 U.S.C. § 6938, and the use of the term "any person" in its citizen suit provision, 42 U.S.C. § 6972 support their view.* * *

[T]he use of the term "any person" in RCRA's citizen suit provision without more cannot be said to establish RCRA's extraterritorial applicability. This is especially so when, as defendant notes, other portions of the citizen suit provision itself reflect a domestic focus. Thus, for example, the citizen suit venue provision contained in section 6972(a)(1) provides that a citizen suit "shall be brought in the district court for the district in which the alleged endangerment may occur." RCRA contains nothing prescribing a venue for citizen suits concerning waste located in a foreign country. Similarly, section 6972(b)(2) provides that no citizen suit may be commenced until 90 days after the plaintiff has given notice of the endangerment to "the State in which the alleged endangerment may occur" and that a citizen suit cannot be commenced if the "State" has undertaken action to address the alleged endangerment. As with the venue provision, had Congress intended the citizen suit provision of RCRA to apply extraterritorially, it would have spoken to the question of what pre-suit notice would be required for waste located in the territory of another nation and would have addressed the effect on a citizen suit of a suit pending in that nation.

Also damaging plaintiffs' position is defendant's citation of several other provisions of RCRA that tend to show that in adopting the statute, Congress was concerned with hazardous waste problems in the United States, not in foreign countries. For example, defendant notes that the first section of RCRA, setting forth the findings of Congress with respect to the issues that RCRA was passed to address, characterizes the problem of waste disposal as "a matter national in scope and concern." 42 U.S.C. § 6901(a)(4). Among the congressional findings is that "alternatives to existing methods of land disposal must be developed since many of the cities in the United States will be running out of suitable solid disposal sites within five years unless immediate action is taken." 42 U.S.C. § 6901(b)(8).

In addition, defendant notes that RCRA contains a number of provisions designed to limit the statute's encroachment on state sovereignty, but contains no parallel provisions protecting the sovereignty of other nations. For example, before commencing an action to redress "an imminent and substantial endangerment to health or environment," the administrator of the EPA must provide notice to "the affected State." 42 U.S.C. § 6973(a); there is no analogous provision requiring notice to the appropriate authorities in a foreign country.

Having examined the relevant legislative history and the structure and language of RCRA, this Court is unpersuaded by plaintiffs' claims. Since there is little if any evidence to support plaintiffs' contention that Congress desired RCRA to apply extraterritorially, this Court must decline to apply the statute in the instant case.

———

Amlon originally tried to sue FMC in the United Kingdom but the case was dismissed because the contract had been negotiated and signed in the United States. Yet as a result of the U.S. decision above, a wrong has clearly been committed but Amlon is left without a forum to seek redress. What alternatives are left to Amlon? Given that the action stems from a commercial contract, why do you suppose the plaintiffs sought to extend the reach of U.S. environmental law rather than seek redress under the terms of the contract? The United States has not ratified the Basel Convention. How would the outcome of this case have been different if the

United States had been a party to the Basel Convention? Amlon's holding on extraterritorial application has since been cited in cases involving the bankruptcy code and torture victim protection act. *See* Maxwell, 186 B.R. 807 (1995), and Beneal, 969 F Supp. 362 (1997).

B. NATIONAL ENVIRONMENTAL POLICY ACT (NEPA)

The body of case law pertaining to the extraterritorial application of NEPA, 42 U.S.C. §§ 4321 et seq., is extensive and legislation has been periodically introduced in Congress to "clarify" the extraterritorial reach of this important law. NEPA seeks to ensure that government decision-making takes account of the environmental consequences expected to result from government actions and approvals. Section 102 of NEPA mandates an environmental impact statement (EIS) for "major Federal actions significantly affecting the quality of the human environment." 42 U.S.C. § 4332(c). In particular, NEPA § 102(2)(c) states that all agencies of the Federal government shall:

> include in every recommendation or report on proposals for legislation and other major Federal actions significantly affecting the quality of the human environment, a detailed statement by the responsible official on-
>
> (i) the environmental impact of the proposed action,
>
> (ii) any adverse environmental effects which cannot be avoided should the proposal be implemented,
>
> (iii) alternatives to the proposed action,
>
> (iv) the relationship between local short-term uses of man's environment and the maintenance and enhancement of long-term productivity, and
>
> (v) any irreversible and irretrievable commitments of resources which would be involved in the proposed action should it be implemented.

NEPA's EIS process requires Federal agencies to conduct extensive reviews of the proposed action. Information must be presented on the environmental impact of the proposed project, potential mitigation steps, and alternatives to the project. The assessment process is subject to public participation and judicial review. Delays resulting from an incomplete or inadequate EIS can stop a project, and the information uncovered by an EIS can arouse significant public opposition to a project or provide the basis for a separate legal challenge under other environmental laws. Indeed, NEPA has led to the abandonment of many controversial projects and, more significantly, has encouraged government agencies and the private sector to find ways to reduce the environmental impacts associated with various projects.

NEPA contains broad language aimed at encouraging "productive and enjoyable harmony between man and his environment." 42 U.S.C. § 4321. The statute also requires federal agencies to "recognize the worldwide and long-range character of environmental problems." 42 U.S.C. § 4332(F). NEPA's sweeping language has been the focus of extensive litigation over whether the statute evidences an intent by Congress to apply the EIS requirement to government actions occurring outside the territorial United States.

In ruling on challenges to NEPA's extraterritorial application, courts have been presented with three types of situations–environmental impacts exclusively in foreign countries, environmental impacts in the global commons, and environmental impacts both in the United States and in foreign countries.

In Natural Resources Defense Council v. Nuclear Regulatory Commission the D.C. Circuit ruled that NEPA did not apply to the export of nuclear technology where the environmental impacts would occur *exclusively* in a foreign jurisdiction. 647 F.2d 1345 (D.C.Cir.1981). The court stated: "the NEPA jurisprudence indicates that exclusively foreign impacts do not automatically invoke the statute's environmental obligations. I find only that NEPA does not apply to NRC nuclear export licensing decisions and not necessarily that the EIS requirement is inapplicable to some other kind of major federal action abroad." *Id* at 1366. In another case, plaintiffs in Greenpeace USA v. Stone, 748 F.Supp. 749 (D.Haw.1990), alleged that the United States had failed to comply with NEPA in moving munitions from within Germany to the Johnston Atoll in the Pacific. The court ruled that NEPA did not apply to the movement of munitions within Germany by the United States, noting that such an application of NEPA would have grave foreign policy implications and could give rise to possible conflicts between NEPA's requirements and German laws.

Courts have also considered the application of NEPA to projects outside the United States that could lead to adverse impacts in the United States. In Sierra Club v. Adams, 578 F.2d 389 (D.C.Cir.1978), the D.C. Circuit ruled that an EIS prepared by the United States on the environmental impacts arising from the proposed construction of the Darien Gap Highway in Panama and Colombia satisfied the requirements of NEPA. The United States had agreed to provide two-thirds of the funding needed for construction of the last unbuilt part of the Pan American Highway extending from Alaska to Chile. The district court ruled that although the government complied with the procedural requirements of NEPA, it failed to examine: 1) the effect of the highway on the spread of aftosa (foot and mouth disease) into the United States; 2) alternatives to the proposed route; and 3) the impact on local Indians living in the area. In briefs submitted to the court on appeal, the government stated that it "never questioned the applicability of NEPA to the construction of this highway in Panama" but suggested that its position may not apply with regard to purely local concerns (i.e. impacts not affecting the United States). *Id.* at 392 n. 14. Given the government's position, the court assumed, without deciding, that NEPA was fully applicable to the construction in Panama.

In a marked departure from the analytical approach courts have taken in extraterritorial NEPA cases, the United States Court of Appeals for the District of Columbia in Environmental Defense Fund (EDF) v. Massey questioned whether the application of NEPA to federal government activities in Antarctica raises extraterritorial application issues at all. 986 F.2d 528 (D.C.Cir.1993). Massey addresses the application of NEPA to federal actions that have an impact on the global commons but the reasoning behind the decision raises important threshold questions for the application of NEPA to any major federal action involving projects outside the United States. In Massey, the EDF brought a suit to enjoin the National Science Foundation (NSF) from incinerating food wastes at the U.S. scientific base in Antarctica, McMurdo Station. EDF alleged that because the incineration would harm the environment, NSF must prepare an EIS before commencing the incineration. Citing the Foley/Aramco Doctrine, the district court rejected EDF's claim and held that NEPA's language and legislative history did not contain a clear intent of extraterritorial application. On appeal, the Circuit Court reversed, basing its decision both on Antarctica's unique status—a continent without sovereignty and over which the United States exercises great control—and the location of the government decision making process. The Court's reasoning raises important questions about whether NEPA, a statute primarily concerned with the government decision-making process, even raises extraterritorial questions at all.

Environmental Defense Fund (EDF) v. Massey
986 F.2d 528, 531–35 (D.C.Cir.1993)

[The court first summarized the Foley/Aramco doctrine and the conditions supporting the presumption against extraterritoriality.] ... Finally, the presumption against extraterritoriality is not applicable when the conduct regulated by the government occurs within the United States. By definition, an extraterritorial application of a statute involves the regulation of conduct beyond U.S. borders. Even where the significant effects of the regulated conduct are felt outside U.S. borders, the statute itself does not present a problem of extraterritoriality, so long as the conduct which Congress seeks to regulate occurs largely within the United States. *See generally* Laker Airways, 731 F.2d at 921; RESTATEMENT (SECOND) § 38 (rules of U.S. statutory law apply "to conduct occurring within, or having effect within the territory of the United States"); RESTATEMENT (SECOND) § 17 (1965); RESTATEMENT (THIRD) § 492(1)(a), (b) (1987).

Despite these well-established exceptions to the presumption against extraterritoriality, the district court below by-passed the threshold question of whether the application of NEPA to agency actions in Antarctica presents an extraterritoriality problem at all. In particular, the court failed to determine whether the statute seeks to regulate conduct in the United States or in another sovereign country. It also declined to consider whether NEPA would create a potential for "clashes between our laws and those of other nations" if it was applied to the decision making of federal agencies regarding proposed actions in Antarctica. Aramco, 111 S. Ct. at 1230. After a thorough review of these relevant factors, we conclude that this case does not present an issue of extraterritoriality.

B. Regulated Conduct Under NEPA

NEPA is designed to control the decision making process of U.S. federal agencies, not the substance of agency decisions. By enacting NEPA, Congress exercised its statutory authority to determine the factors an agency must consider when exercising its discretion, and created a process whereby American officials, while acting within the United States, can reach enlightened policy decisions by taking into account environmental effects. In our view, such regulation of U.S. federal agencies and their decision making processes is a legitimate exercise of Congress' territoriality-based jurisdiction, and does not raise extraterritoriality concerns. * * *

NEPA, unlike many environmental statutes, does not dictate agency policy or determine the fate of contemplated action. Robertson, 490 U.S. at 350; Strycker's Bay Neighborhood Council, Inc. v. Karlen, 444 U.S. 223, 227–228, 100 S.Ct. 497, 62 L.Ed.2d 433 (1980) (per curiam). NEPA simply mandates a particular process that must be followed by a federal agency before taking action significantly affecting the human environment. After weighing environmental considerations, an agency decisionmaker remains free to subordinate the environmental concerns revealed in the EIS to other policy concerns. Robertson, 490 U.S. at 350. . . . In many respects, NEPA is most closely akin to the myriad laws directing federal decisionmakers to consider particular factors before extending aid or engaging in certain types of trade. See Comment, NEPA's Role in Protecting the World Environment, 131 U. Pa. L. Rev. 353, 371 (1982). For example, the Foreign Assistance Act of 1961 requires the Agency for International Development, before approving developmental assistance, to consider the degree to which programs integrate women into the economy, as well as the possibility of using aid to "support democratic and social political trends in recipient countries." 22 U.S.C. §§ 2151(k), 2218(c) (1976). Similarly, the Nuclear Nonproliferation Act requires the Nuclear Regulatory Commission to consider a nation's willingness to cooperate with American nonproliferation objectives before approving a nuclear export license. 22 U.S.C. §§ 3201–3282 (1976); 42 U.S.C. §§ 2156, 2157 (Supp. III 1979). Just as these statutes fall short of prescribing action in foreign jurisdictions, and are instead directed at the regulation of agency decisionmaking, NEPA also creates no substantive environmental standards and simply prescribes by statute the factors an agency must consider when exercising its discretionary authority.

Moreover, NEPA would never require enforcement in a foreign forum or involve "choice of law" dilemmas. This factor alone is powerful evidence of the statute's domestic nature, and distinguishes NEPA from Title VII as well as the Federal Tort Claims Act–two statutes that have been limited in their effect by the presumption against extraterritoriality. See Aramco, 111 S. Ct. at 1234 (presumption against extraterritoriality applies where Congress failed to provide for overseas enforcement and failed to address the potential conflicts of law issue); Smith v. United States, 932 F.2d 791, 793 (9th Cir.1991) (an "indication that the [statute] was not intended to apply to Antarctica is the choice of law problem"), cert. granted 112 S.Ct. 2963, 119 L.Ed.2d 585(1992).

In sum, since NEPA is designed to regulate conduct occurring within the territory of the United States, and imposes no substantive requirements which could be interpreted to govern conduct abroad, the presumption against extraterritoriality does not apply to this case.

C.   The Unique Status of Antarctica

Antarctica's unique status in the international arena further supports our conclusion that this case does not implicate the presumption against extraterritoriality. The Supreme Court explicitly stated in Aramco that when applying the presumption against extraterritoriality, courts should look to see if there is any indication that Congress intended to extend the statute's coverage "beyond places over which the United States has sovereignty or some measure of legislative control." Aramco, 111 S. Ct. at 1230, (quoting Foley Bros., 336 U.S. at 285). Thus, where the U.S. has some real measure of legislative control over the region at issue, the presumption against extraterritoriality is much weaker. See, e.g., Sierra Club v. Adams, 188 U.S. App. D.C. 147, 578 F.2d 389 (D.C.Cir.1978) (NEPA assumed to be applicable to South American highway construction where the United States had two-thirds of the ongoing financial responsibility and control over the highway construction); People of Enewetak

v. Laird, 353 F.Supp. 811 (D.Hawai'i 1973) (concluding that NEPA applies to the United States trust territories in the Pacific). And where there is no potential for conflict "between our laws and those of other nations," the purpose behind the presumption is eviscerated, and the presumption against extraterritoriality applies with significantly less force. Aramco, 111 S. Ct. at 1230. * * *

[T]he United States has exclusive legislative control over McMurdo Station and the other research installations established there by the United States Antarctica Program. This legislative control, taken together with the status of Antarctica as a sovereignless continent, compels the conclusion that the presumption against extraterritoriality is particularly inappropriate under the circumstances presented in this case. As stated aptly by a State Department official in congressional testimony shortly following the enactment of NEPA, "application of [NEPA] to actions occurring outside the jurisdiction of any State, including the United States, would not conflict with the primary purpose underlying this venerable rule of interpretation–to avoid ill-will and conflict between nations arising out of one nation's encroachments upon another's sovereignty. . . . There are at least three general areas: The high seas, outer space, and Antarctica." * * *

D.   Foreign Policy Considerations

Although NSF concedes that NEPA only seeks to regulate the decision making process of federal agencies, and that this case does not present a conflict between U.S. and foreign sovereign law, NSF still contends that the presumption against extraterritoriality controls this case. In particular, NSF argues that the EIS requirement will interfere with U.S. efforts to work cooperatively with other nations toward solutions to environmental problems in Antarctica. In NSF's view, joint research and cooperative environmental assessment would be "placed at risk of NEPA injunctions, making the U.S. a doubtful partner for future international cooperation in Antarctica." Appellee's Brief at 45.

NSF also argues that the Protocol on Environmental Protection to the Antarctic Treaty [see page 1059], which was adopted and opened for signature on October 4, 1991, would, if adopted by all the proposed signatories, conflict with the procedural requirements adopted by Congress for the decisionmaking of federal agencies under NEPA. . . . According to NSF, since NEPA requires the preparation of an EIS for actions with potentially "significant" impacts, while the Protocol requires an environmental analysis even for actions with "minor or transitory" impacts on the Antarctic environment, the two regulatory schemes are incompatible and will result in international discord.

We find these arguments unpersuasive. First, it should be noted that the Protocol is not in effect in any form and is years away from ratification by the United States and all 26 signatories. Second, we are unable to comprehend the difficulty presented by the two standards of review. It is clear that NSF will have to perform fewer studies under NEPA than under the Protocol, and where an EIS is required under NEPA, it would not strain a researcher's intellect to indicate in a single document how the environmental impact of the proposed action is more than "minor" and also more than "significant."

More importantly, we are not convinced that NSF's ability to cooperate with other nations in Antarctica in accordance with U.S. foreign policy will be hampered by NEPA injunctions. We made clear in Natural Resources Defense Council v. Nuclear Regulatory Commission, 208 U.S. App. D.C. 216, 647 F.2d 1345, 1366 (D.C.Cir.1981) ("NRDC"), that where the EIS requirement proves to be incompatible with Section 102(2)(F), federal agencies will not be subject to injunctions forcing compliance with Section 102(2)(C). Section 102(2)(F) specifically requires all federal agencies to "recognize the worldwide and long-range character of environmental problems and, where consistent with the foreign policy of the United States, lend appropriate support to initiatives, resolutions, and programs designed to maximize international cooperation...." ... In Committee for Nuclear Responsibility v. Seaborg, 149 U.S. App. D.C. 393, 463 F.2d 796 (D.C.Cir.1971), for example, we refused to issue an injunction under NEPA, despite the real potential for significant harm to the environment, because the government made "assertions of harm to national security and foreign policy." Id. at 798. In that case, conservation groups sought to enjoin an underground nuclear test on the grounds that the Atomic Energy Commission failed to comply fully with NEPA. Although there was reason to believe that the petitioners would succeed on the merits of their claim, we denied the requested injunction in light of the foreign policy concerns.

NRDC and Seaborg illustrate that the government may avoid the EIS requirement where U.S. foreign policy interests outweigh the benefits derived from preparing an EIS. Since NEPA imposes no substantive requirements, U.S. foreign policy interests in Antarctica will rarely be threatened, except perhaps where the time required to prepare an EIS would itself threaten international cooperation, see Flint Ridge Development Co. v. Scenic Rivers Association, 426 U.S. 776, 791, 96 S.Ct. 2430, 49 L.Ed.2d 205 (1976) (EIS requirement must yield where a clear conflict in statutory authority is unavoidable, including conflicts which arise out of timetables imposed by statute), or where the foreign policy interests at stake are particularly unique and delicate. See NRDC, 647 F.2d at 1348. Thus, contrary to NSF's assertions, where U.S. foreign policy interests outweigh the benefits of the EIS requirement, NSF's efforts to cooperate with foreign governments regarding environmental practices in Antarctica will not be frustrated by forced compliance with NEPA.

The Massey decision's logic has potentially significant implications. The Court notes that NEPA is a procedural statute imposing requirements on the decision-making process of federal agencies within the United States. Because the decision-making processes affected by NEPA occur almost exclusively in the United States, however, the court concludes that the case did not present an issue of extraterritoriality even where the federal *action* at issue will occur outside the United States. In other words, NEPA's focus is on *where* the NSF makes the decision (the United States), not where the impacts of the decision occur (Antarctica). This principle is known as the "headquarters theory" and would, logically, remove the extraterritorial issue from most federal decisions impacting the environment outside the United States since they are taken in Washington. K. Bourdeau & P. Hagen, *Courts Examine U.S. Environmental Laws' Extraterritorial Reach*, THE NAT'L L. J., Sept. 6, 1993.

In its first extraterritorial NEPA case after *Massey,* however, the Federal District Court narrowed the potential scope of the *Massey* decision. In NEPA Coalition of Japan v. Aspin, 837 F.Supp. 466 (D.D.C.1993), the Federal District Court for the District of Columbia ruled that NEPA did not apply to the actions of the United States at certain military installations in Japan. In *NEPA Coalition of Japan,* plaintiffs argued that NEPA required the Department of Defense to prepare an EIS for military institutions in Japan. The government argued that NEPA's requirements did not apply when treaty relations would clearly be affected. 837 F.Supp. 466, 467–68 (1993).

Plaintiffs contend that under the controlling precedent in this Circuit the Court should apply NEPA overseas. See Environmental Defense Fund, Inc. v. Massey, 300 U.S. App. D.C. 65, 986 F.2d 528, 531 (D.C.Cir.1993) (applying NEPA to a U.S. research station in Antarctica). Massey, however, involved the unique status of Antarctica, which the Court of Appeals noted "is not a foreign country, but rather a continent that is most frequently analogized to outer space." Id. at 533. The Massey court expressly limited its ruling by refusing to decide whether NEPA might apply to actions involving an internationally recognized sovereign power.

The Court determines that the legal status of United States bases in Japan is not analogous to the status of American research stations in Antarctica. [Department of Defense] operations in Japan are governed by complex and long standing treaty arrangements. U.S. bases there, several of which are also utilized by the Japanese Self Defense Forces, are operated pursuant to the Treaty of Mutual Cooperation and Security of 1960, 11 U.S.T. 1633–35, and the Status of Forces Agreement ("SOFA"), 3 U.S.T. 3342–62. Article XXV of the SOFA establishes the Joint Japanese/American Committee ("Joint Committee") with 15 constituent standing subcommittees. Among the subcommittees is the Subcommittee on Environment and Noise Abatement which meets biweekly to examine the types of concerns expressed by plaintiffs. By requiring the DOD to prepare EISs, the Court would risk intruding upon a long standing treaty relationship.[1]

Plaintiffs are unable to show that Congress intended NEPA to apply in situations where there is a substantial likelihood that treaty relations will be affected. See Natural Resources Defense v. Nuclear Regulatory Commission, 208 U.S. App. D.C. 216, 647 F.2d 1345, 1366–67 (D.C.Cir.1981) (noting a lack of evidence that Congress intended NEPA to apply abroad, and finding that Congress intended cooperation, not unilateral action by the United States in its relations overseas). Therefore, we have no difficulty in determining that the presumption against extraterritoriality applies with particular force to the case at bar.

For completeness, the Court notes that even if NEPA did apply in this case, as an initial proposition, no EISs would be required because U.S. foreign policy interests outweigh the benefits from preparing an EIS. Massey, 986 F.2d at 535 (considering whether NEPA, if enforced, would threaten foreign policy); see also Committee for Nuclear Responsibility v. Seaborg, 149 U.S. App. D.C. 393, 463 F.2d 796, 798 (D.C.Cir.1971) (NEPA requirements must give way when government made "assertions of harm to national security and foreign policy"); and Greenpeace v. Stone, 748 F.Supp. 749, 760 (D.Haw.1990). Plausible assertions have been made that EIS preparation would impact upon the foreign policy of the United States. Therefore, NEPA requirements would necessarily yield.

---

1. Such risks suggest the presence of a nonjusticiable political question. At a minimum they raise prudential concerns over the competence of the judiciary to enter an area with no direct effects in the United States. The preparation of EISs would necessarily require the DOD to collect environmental data from the surrounding residential and industrial complexes, thereby intruding on Japanese sovereignty. In addition, the DOD would have to assess the impact of Japanese military activities at these bases. There is no evidence that Congress intended NEPA to encompass the activities of a foreign sovereign within its own territory.

The Court notes the limits of its holding. We determine that the presumption against extraterritoriality not only is applicable, but particularly applies in this case because there are clear foreign policy and treaty concerns involving a security relationship between the United States and a sovereign power. We do not address whether NEPA applies in other factual contexts.

———

Does *NEPA Coalition of Japan* weaken *Massey's* headquarters theory? How significant do you think the strategic foreign policy issues in NEPA Coalition of Japan were? Would the outcome likely have been different if the issue at stake had involved technical assistance for construction of a dam rather than treaty obligations at a military base?

———

1. EXECUTIVE ORDER 12114

President Carter signed Executive Order 12114 in January, 1979. Without determining the extent or limitations of NEPA's extraterritorial reach, the Executive Order set forth the requirements for analysis of environmental impacts abroad from major federal actions.

Exec. Order 12114 (Jan. 1979)

Section 1.

1–1. *Purpose and Scope*: . . . While based on independent authority, this Order furthers the purpose of the National Environmental Policy Act and the Marine Protection Research and Sanctuaries Act and the Deepwater Port Act consistent with the foreign policy and national security policy of the United States, and represents the U.S. government's exclusive and complete determination of the procedural and other actions to be taken by Federal agencies to further the purpose of the National Environmental Policy Act, with respect to the environment outside the United States, its territories and possessions. * * *

2–3. *Actions Included*: * * *

(a) major Federal actions significantly affecting the environment of the global commons outside the jurisdiction of any nation (e.g., the oceans or Antarctica);

(b) major Federal actions significantly affecting the environment of a foreign nation not participating with the United States and not otherwise involved in the action;

(c) major Federal actions significantly affecting the environment of a foreign nation which provide to that nation

(1) a product, or physical project producing a principal product or an emission or effluent, which is prohibited or strictly regulated by Federal law in the United States because its toxic effects on the environment create a serious public health risk; or

(2) a physical project which in the United States is prohibited or strictly regulated by Federal law to protect the environment against radioactive substances.

(d) major Federal actions outside the United States, its territories and possessions which significantly affect natural or ecological resources of global importance designated for protection under this subsection by the President, or, in the case of such a resource protected by international agreement binding on the United States, by the Secretary of State. Recommendations to the President under this subsection shall be accompanied by the views of the Council on Environmental Quality and the Secretary of State.* * *

2–5. *Exemptions and Considerations*:

(a) Notwithstanding Section 2–3, the following actions are exempt from this Order:

    (i) actions not having a significant effect on the environment outside the United States as determined by the agency;

    (ii) actions taken by the president;

    (iii) actions taken by or pursuant to the direction of the President or Cabinet officer when the national security or interest is involved or when the action occurs in the course of an armed conflict;

    (iv) intelligence activities and arms transfers;

    (v) export licenses or permits or export approvals, and actions relating to nuclear activities except actions providing to a foreign nation a nuclear production or utilization facility as defined in the Atomic Energy Act of 1954, as amended, or a nuclear waste management facility;

    (vi) votes and other actions in international conferences and organizations;

    (vii) disaster and emergency relief action.

(b) Agency procedures ... may provide for appropriate modifications in the contents, timing and availability of documents to other affected Federal agencies and affected nations, where necessary to:

    (i) enable the agency to decide and act promptly as and when required;

    (ii) avoid adverse impacts on foreign relations or infringement in fact or appearance of other nations' sovereign responsibilities; or

    (iii) ensure appropriate reflection of:

        1) diplomatic factors;

        2) international commercial, competitive and export promotion factors;

        3) needs for governmental or commercial confidentiality;

        4) national security considerations;

        5) difficulties of obtaining information and agency ability to analyze meaningfully environmental effects of a proposed action; and

        6) the degree to which the agency is involved in or able to affect a decision to be made. * * *

    3–1. *Rights of Action*: This Order is solely for the purpose of establishing internal procedures for Federal agencies to consider the significant effects of their actions on the environment outside the United States, its territories and possessions, and nothing in this Order shall be construed to create a cause of action.

Some commentators have criticized as overbroad the exemptions for actions taken by the president, or actions taken pursuant to the direction of the President or Cabinet officer, when the national security or interest is involved. What potentially environmentally damaging actions might fall under these exceptions? It is also important to note that Section 3–1 of the Executive Order states that its requirements establish *internal* procedures and that the Order does not create a cause of action. Can a Federal agency be challenged in court for actions that violate E.O. 12114? In some cases, courts have viewed an agency's compliance with Executive Order 12114 as a factor in determining whether NEPA should be applied to the government's actions impacting the global commons. *See, e.g.,* Greenpeace USA v. Stone, 748 F. Supp. 749 (D.Haw.1990).

---

2. EXECUTIVE ORDER 13141

Prior to the WTO Ministerial in Seattle, in November, 1999, President Clinton promulgated Executive Order 13141, requiring the Office of the United States Trade Representative (USTR) and the Council on Environmental Quality (a White House office) to carry out environmental reviews of trade negotiations (including multilateral trade rounds, bilateral and plurilateral free trade agreements, and major new trade liberalization agreements in natural resource sectors). The goal is to inform negotiators of environmental opportunities and threats uncovered by increasing trade flows. While the focus of environmental reviews will be impacts in the United States, the Order provides for review of global and transboundary impacts where appropriate and prudent. This Order is examined in more detail in Chapter 15, page 1142.

C. THE ENDANGERED SPECIES ACT (ESA)

Under Section 7 of the Endangered Species Act (ESA), 16 U.S.C. § 1536, federal agencies are required to consult with the Fish and Wildlife Service or the National Marine Fisheries Service when a proposed agency action may adversely affect a listed endangered or threatened species. The government is prohibited from taking actions that will jeopardize the continued existence of an endangered or threatened species or result in the adverse modification of its critical habitat. Depending on the level of impact of the agency action, consultation can range from informal consultation to the preparation of a biological assessment and formal consultation.

In Lujan v. Defenders of Wildlife, 112 S. Ct. 2130 (1992), environmentalists challenged a decision by the Secretary of the Interior that the ESA's consultation requirements do *not* apply when federal agency activities may harm or destroy critical habitat for endangered species *outside* the United States and the high seas (i.e. in other countries). Plaintiffs alleged injury based on affidavits by members stating they had observed and studied listed species outside the United States that were threatened by projects funded by federal agencies. The affidavits also stated that the individuals expected to return to these areas again in the future. The U.S. Court of

Appeals for the Eighth Circuit ruled that plaintiffs had standing to bring the case and that the consultation requirements of the ESA *did* apply to projects funded by federal agencies in foreign countries. Defenders of Wildlife v. Lujan, 911 F.2d 117 (8th Cir.1990). The court found that Congress intended for the consultation obligation of ESA to extend to all agency actions affecting endangered species, whether within the United States or abroad. Congressional intent to apply the statute extraterritorially overcame the Foley/Aramco presumption. Bourdeau and Hagen, *op. cit.* The Supreme Court reversed the decision. While never addressing the extraterritorial issue directly, the Supreme Court ruled that plaintiff environmental groups did not have standing to challenge the regulations promulgated by the Department of the Interior requiring consultation under the ESA.

Because the individuals did not have "concrete plans" to return to the areas mentioned, the Court held that plaintiffs failed to show actual or imminent injury, and thus did not have standing. This case established what is referred to as the "return ticket rule." The rule implies that if the plaintiffs had made concrete plans, or indeed even indicated any specification of when the "someday" was that they might go back, had bought a return ticket for example, the Court might have found the plaintiffs had standing.

Assuming a plaintiff could establish standing, would a court ruling on the question of the extraterritorial application of the ESA in the future look to the Massey decision and question whether the Section 7 consultation requirement of the ESA presents an extraterritorial question at all? Like NEPA's environmental review process, this provision of the ESA imposes a consultation requirement that occurs largely in the territorial United States.

D. MARINE MAMMAL PROTECTION ACT

As discussed earlier, Jerry Mitchell, a U.S. citizen, was arrested for capturing dolphins in Bahamian waters and transporting them to an aquarium in England. Section 102 of the Marine Mammal Protection Act (MMPA), 16 U.S.C. § 1372, prohibits the unauthorized taking of a marine mammal by any person subject to the jurisdiction of the United States. The District Court convicted Mitchell, ruling that Congress intended to extend coverage of the Act to all takings of marine mammals by U.S. citizens under the MMPA *wherever* such offenses occur, and that this moratorium was an absolute prohibition without geographical limitation. In United States v. Mitchell, the Fifth Circuit reversed the conviction of Mitchell. The Circuit Court found that although Congress prohibited the taking of dolphins within the territorial limits of the United States and on the high seas, neither the language of the MMPA nor its legislative history demonstrated a congressional intent to prohibit a citizen of the United States from taking a dolphin while in the territory of another sovereign. 553 F.2d 996, 1003 (5th Cir.1977).

United States v. Mitchell
553 F.2d 996, 1001–04 (5th Cir.1977)

[The court states that two principles of statutory construction must be considered in determining whether Congress intended to apply the criminal prohibitions of the MMPA extraterritorially–(1) whether the nature of the law mandates extraterritorial application; (2) if not, the presumption is against extraterritoriality.] With regard to the first proposition, the nature of the MMPA does not compel its application in foreign territories. The MMPA is a conservation statute, designed to preserve marine mammals. The nature of such a bill is based on the control that a sovereign such as the United States has over the natural resources within its territory. It can exploit them or preserve them or establish a balance between exploitation and preservation. See, e.g., 16 U.S.C. §§ 1131, 1361, 1371(a)(2), 1531, 1539. The nature of such control is not limited to the sovereignty of the United States. Other sovereign states enjoy similar authority. For example, the United Nations resolution on "Permanent Sovereignty over National Resources", G.A.Res. 1803, 17 U.N. GAOR 1193–94 (1962), recognizes the control of sovereigns over the natural resources within their territories, including the ability to nationalize or expropriate such resources from private ownership. Restatement (Second) of the Foreign Relations Law of the United States § 185 (1965) (Reporters' Note 4). In addition, Article 14 of the Convention on the Territorial Sea and the Contiguous Zone, April 29, 1958, states that the passage of foreign fishing vessels shall not be considered innocent if the crews do not observe the laws promulgated by coastal states to prevent such vessels from fishing in territorial seas. Thus each sovereign may regulate the exploitation of natural resources within its territory. Id. at § 45 (Reporters' Note 1).

When Congress considers environmental legislation, it presumably recognizes the authority of other sovereigns to protect and exploit their own resources. Other states may strike balances of interests that differ substantially from those struck by Congress. The traditional method of resolving such differences in the international community is through negotiation and agreement rather than through the imposition of one particular choice by a state imposing its law extraterritorially. With regard to the MMPA, Congress stated in section 1383 that the Act is not intended to contravene "the provisions of any existing international treaty, convention, or agreement, or any statute implementing the same, which may otherwise apply to the taking of marine mammals". Furthermore, section 1378 establishes the United States approach to international protection of marine mammals by directing the Secretary of State to initiate negotiations for both bilateral and multilateral agreements on the subject. The basic purpose of the moratorium, prohibitions, and permit system therefore appears to be the protection of marine mammals only within the territory of the United States and on the high seas. Conservation in other states is left to diplomatic negotiations. Restricting the territorial scope of the Act would not "greatly curtail the scope and usefulness of the statute" nor frustrate its purpose. We cannot then infer from the nature of the MMPA that Congress intended to apply its restrictions to the territories of foreign sovereigns.

With regard to the second proposition of statutory construction, neither the statute nor its legislative history provide a clear expression of congressional intent for application of the Act in foreign territories.

First, section 1371, which announces the moratorium, and section 1362(7), which defines it, do not deal with the geographic scope of the ban on takings and importation. The Government argues that the definition of the moratorium is absolute: " 'moratorium' means a complete cessation of the taking of marine mammals and a complete ban on the importation into the United States of marine mammals...." The Government therefore concludes that the geographic scope of the moratorium should extend world wide. In Foley Bros. v. Filardo, 1949, 336 U.S. 281, 69 S. Ct. 575, 93 L. Ed. 680, however, the statute in question used all-inclusive language:

> Every contract hereafter made to which the United States ... is a party, and every such contract made for or on behalf of the United States ... which may require or involve the employment of laborers or mechanics shall contain a provision that no laborer or mechanic doing any part of the work contemplated by the contract ... shall be required or permitted to work more than eight hours in any one calendar day upon such work....

40 U.S.C. 324 (1946). Nevertheless, the Supreme Court concluded that the statute and its legislative history did not evidence intent specifically for extraterritorial application. The Court held that the Eight Hour Law did not cover American employees working for American contractors in Iraq and Iran. Similarly, with regard to the MMPA all inclusive language that does not expressly address territoriality cannot be held to indicate clear intent for extraterritorial application.

Second, when Congress did define the geographic scope of the prohibitions in section 1372, it did not make conduct in foreign territory unlawful. Takings without permits were prohibited only in United States territory and on the high seas. The omission of the territory of other sovereigns permits the reasonable inference that Congress concluded the prohibitions should not extend extraterritorially.

* * *

It is no small matter when, in effect, this nation countermands a permit of another nation allowing the permittee to work in the territorial waters of the foreign country. We cannot say that the interests of the United States in preserving dolphins outweighs the interest of the Commonwealth of the Bahamas in preserving its character as a tourist attraction by the issuance of a limited number of permits for the capture of dolphins within its narrow band of territorial waters. If the moratorium was meant to extend the reach of the statute to the territorial waters of every country in the world, the sponsors of the amendment would certainly have recognized a duty to explain the need for such an extension on the floors of Congress and in the committee reports.

In summary, then, the Act and its legislative history do not demonstrate the clear intent required ... to overcome the presumption against extraterritorial extension of American statutes. Congress did extend the force of the MMPA to the high seas, but any further extension to regulate the taking of marine mammals in the territory of other sovereign states is not justified by the Act. The legislative scheme requires the State Department to pursue international controls by the usual methods of negotiation, treaty, and convention. Without a clearer expression from Congress to the contrary, we must presume that United States jurisdiction under the Act ceases at the territorial waters and boundaries of other states.

QUESTIONS AND DISCUSSION

1. Are you persuaded by the court's decision? The court acknowledges that in certain circumstances extraterritorial application can be inferred if the presumption against extraterritoriality would unduly restrict the usefulness of the statute. The Court held that restricting the MMPA in scope to U.S. territories and the high seas would neither greatly curtail the scope and usefulness of the statute nor frustrate its purpose. But presumably the goal of Congress in passing the MMPA was to conserve marine mammal populations by shutting down *entirely* the commercial taking and capturing of marine mammals by U.S. citizens and vessels. Does the Court's decision further this legislative goal? Would it make a difference if the United States demonstrated that the dolphin population in Bahamian waters also spent time in U.S. waters?

2. Principle 12 of the Rio Declaration on Environment and Development declares:

> . . . Unilateral actions to deal with environmental challenges outside the jurisdiction of the importing country should be avoided. Environmental measures addressing transboundary or global environmental problems should, as far as possible, be based on international consensus.

Which U.S. laws described in this chapter comply with Principle 12? Which do not? What alternative negotiating text do you think the United States might have proposed?

3. Consider the issues raised in Amlon Metal, Inc. v. FMC Corp. As a matter of environmental protection, is it better to extend RCRA extraterritorially or should national governments be encouraged to expand their own environmental laws and remedies?

4. Issues related to the extraterritorial reach of U.S. law have also arisen in the context of government information gathering. The Toxic Substances Control Act (TSCA) regulates the sale, manufacturing, processing, distribution (including export and import), use and disposal of toxic chemicals. It contains a subpoena provision that grants authority to the EPA to subpoena "information that the Administrator deems necessary" in carrying out the requirements of the statute. 15 U.S.C. § 2601, § 610(c).

> Under TSCA Section 11(c),

> the EPA may by subpoena require the attendance and testimony of witnesses and the production of reports, papers, documents, answers to questions, and other information that the Administrator deems necessary. . . . [I]n the event of failure or refusal of any person to obey such subpoena, any district court in which venue is proper shall have jurisdiction to order compliance; failure to obey such an order is punishable by the court as contempt.

In September, 1994, EPA issued an administrative subpoena pursuant to Section 11 of TSCA to investigate the extent and type of pollutants that may be entering the United States through the New River from sources in Mexico. This was the first use of TSCA's subpoena authority to investigate transborder pollution. The purpose of the subpoena, EPA explained in its accompanying letter, was "to determine whether any of the chemicals exported to your facility in the area of Mexicali, Mexico, or any chemicals manufactured or produced in Mexicali, as a result of, or in connection with, processing or use of the chemicals you export to Mexicali or products you import to the United States are contaminating the New River, and thereby presenting an unreasonable risk of injury to or an imminent hazard to the population or environment of Imperial County, California."

Is the subpoena, which was sent to corporate headquarters in Ohio but which requests information on facilities operating outside U.S. borders in Mexico, an extraterritorial application of TSCA? American parent companies contended that EPA jurisdiction under TSCA did not extend to their manufacturing or processing chemicals outside the United States, calling the subpoena an overly broad interpretation of TSCA. EPA's issuance of the subpoenas to 95 American companies operating maquiladoras in Mexico raised the question—did Congress intend to give EPA authority to subpoena the American parent companies for information that only the subsidiaries *in* Mexico possess?

EPA took the position that Section 11 of TSCA authorized the Agency to seek information from certain United States companies on the use of chemicals at affiliated facilities located in Mexico even if the relevant records are located outside the United States. The language of Section 11 does not specifically authorize EPA to issue subpoenas for information on the use, treatment, disposal and releases of chemicals at facilities located outside the United States. The argument could be made, however, that Congress intended TSCA to apply because the chemicals in the New River were imports, and that Section 13, which covers "entry into customs territory of the United States," grants EPA the authority to examine those chemicals. EPA took the position that because the subpoenas were directed to companies located in the United States, the subpoenas were not an extraterritorial application of TSCA.

The argument against EPA's exercise of subpoena authority hinges on application of the Foley/Aramco Doctrine, and is based on the premise that Congress did not grant EPA the authority to use TSCA as a vehicle to investigate the chemicals polluting a foreign river. Since pollution in a foreign river does not have the same attributes as an import, the statutory language does not support that characterization by the Agency. In addition, international concerns are generally absent in the statute, meaning that the statute was not intended to address transboundary chemical pollution problems. Assume you are the general counsel to a company receiving a subpoena for data on your Mexican affiliate's water discharges. Senior executives would prefer not to release the data out of concerns over confidentiality. What would you advise the company to do? Does the fact that the river flows into California affect your answer?

5. Under the Restatement of the Foreign Relations Law of the United States (Third), States can prescribe law aimed at conduct outside their national territory if there are effects within the country. As mentioned in the text, no court has expressly ruled on whether Congress intended to extend NEPA to actions occurring outside the United States that have adverse impacts within the United States. In Nat'l Organization for Reform of Marijuana Laws (NORML) v. United States, 452 F. Supp. 1226 (D.D.C.1978), the court assumed without deciding that NEPA was fully applicable to United States participation in herbicide spraying of marijuana and poppy plants in Mexico. NORML is an advocacy organization that seeks the legalization of marijuana use. Plaintiffs alleged that the spraying program had significant environmental and health effects in both Mexico and the United States. The court concluded that the willingness of the United States to prepare an "environmental analysis" of the effects in Mexico together with the EIS on the impacts of the program upon the United States, permitted the court to assume, without deciding, that NEPA fully applied to the Mexican herbicide spraying program. Is NORML a judicial precedent for requiring the preparation of an EIS for major federal actions occurring outside the United States that have impacts within the territorial United States? Why do you think the government sought to avoid a court decision on this issue?

6. *Problem Exercise.* As the problem exercise in Chapter 10, page 671, explained, radioactive waste is routinely shipped between France, Britain and Japan for reprocessing. On January 21, 1998, the Pacific Swan, a British registered freighter left Cherbourg, France, and set sail for Japan. Its route through the Panama Canal brought it within 200 miles of the coast of Puerto Rico. Environmental and fishing organizations in Puerto Rico brought suit against the State Department, Department of Energy, and the Coast Guard, charging that the government's failure to prepare an environmental impact statement examining the passage of such shipments through its Exclusive Economic Zone violated NEPA. Reviewing the materials in the preceding section and the discussion of the EEZ in pages 660–662, how do you think the court should rule? *See* Mayaguezanos por la Salud y el Ambiente v. U.S., 38 F.Supp.2d 168 (D.P.R.1999); 198 F.3d 297 (1st Cir.1999).

SECTION V.   TRADE SANCTIONS

The United States sometimes uses trade measures to influence the behavior of other nations (e.g. attempts during the 1990s to link China's human rights record with most-favored-nation trade status). Unless a nation complies with certain standards set in U.S. law, their goods are banned from import into the United States, U.S. exports are banned to their country, or their nationals are restricted access to U.S. resources. This can be an enormously effective, and controversial, exercise of U.S. law. The use of trade measures and other linkages between trade and environment are discussed in greater detail in Chapter 15. Below we discuss one aspect of the trade and environment debate–namely the use of trade measures to improve wildlife conservation.

The entire Tuna/Dolphin debate, which propelled the GATT into environmental disrepute, arose from an amendment to the Marine Mammal Protection Act banning the import of tuna from nations (and intermediary nations) that did not satisfy specific dolphin protection standards in catching tuna. For a detailed discussion of Tuna/Dolphin, *see* Chapter 13, page 995. U.S. law bans the import of shrimp products unless caught using turtle extruding devices (meant to protect turtles that otherwise are trapped in shrimp trawls) while the European Union bans the sale of fur from animals caught with leg-holding traps. Similarly, the United States has used the threat of trade bans to attack commercial whaling, passing two pieces of legislation to promote the efforts of the International Whaling Commission (IWC). The 1971 Pelly Amendment to the Fisherman's Protective Act of 1967, 22 U.S.C. § 1971–1980 (1982), and the 1979 Packwood–Magnuson Amendment to the Fishery Conservation and Management Act of 1976, 16 U.S.C. § 1821(e) (1988), both impose trade measures on countries diminishing the effectiveness of international fisheries conservation (the Pelly Amendment also permits trade restrictions for actions that diminish the effectiveness of international wildlife agreements). David Caron describes below their application in the context of the International Whaling Commission. David Caron, *International Sanctions, Ocean Management, and the Law of the Sea: A Study of Denial of Access to Fisheries*, 16 Ecology L. Q. 311, 317–319 (1989).

> The Pelly Amendment provides that when the Secretary of Commerce determines that the nationals of a foreign country are diminishing the effectiveness of an international fishery conservation program (including the IWC's program), the Secretary shall certify this fact to the President. The President then has the discretion to ban importation of fishing products from the offending country. The Packwood–Magnuson Amendment provides that when the Secretary of Commerce certifies that a country is diminishing the effectiveness of the work of the IWC, the Secretary of State must reduce that country's fishing allocation in U.S. waters by at least 50%.

The United States employed the Packwood–Magnuson Amendment almost immediately after its passage. Threatened certification in 1980 under both the Packwood–Magnuson and Pelly Amendments led the Republic of Korea to agree to follow IWC guidelines restricting the use of cold (i.e. nonexplosive) harpoons. The Republic of China, threatened with certification for its failure to observe IWC restrictions in 1980 and 1980, placed a complete ban on whaling.* * *

In 1982 the IWC adopted a five-year moratorium on commercial whaling to commence in 1986. Of the seven states that voted against the moratorium, Japan, Norway, Peru and the Soviet Union exempted themselves from its application by objecting to the decision in accordance with the International Convention for the Regulation of Whaling. With the threat of the Pelly and Packwood–Magnuson Amendments in the background, the United States began to press almost immediately for withdrawal of these objections. Peru withdrew its objection not long after. The negotiations were more prolonged with the remaining three. [Shortly after the Secretary of Commerce certified Norway in 1986 for its catch of minke whales, Norway announced it would cease commercial whaling in 1987. The USSR's allocation of fish in U.S. waters was halved and then eliminated, leading the USSR to suspend whaling operations in 1987.]

Compare the application of the Pelly and Packwood–Magnuson Amendments with the foreign policy concerns expressed in the *Mitchell* decision, discussed above. How would you distinguish the application of the MMPA to actions in other nations' waters from threatened trade sanctions against nations that hinder international conservation efforts?

QUESTIONS AND DISCUSSION

1. The advertisement on the next page (designed by the Public Media Center) calls on the Clinton Administration to impose trade restrictions against Taiwan for its role in promoting the illegal trade in tiger parts. The Pelly Amendment states that when:

> the Secretary of Commerce or the Secretary of the Interior finds that nationals of a foreign country, directly or indirectly, are engaging in trade or taking which diminishes the effectiveness of any international program for endangered or threatened species, the Secretary making such finding shall certify such fact to the President [who] may direct the Secretary of the Treasury to prohibit the bringing or the importation into the United States of any products from the offending country for any duration as the President determines appropriate and to the extent that such prohibition is sanctioned by the General Agreement on Tariffs and Trade.

22 U.S.C. § 1978(a). The bottom of the ad provides cards for readers to send to President Clinton, President Lee Teng-Hui of Taiwan, and the Earth Island Institute (an environmental group). Do you think this type of media campaign is effective in influencing U.S. or Taiwanese policy? How effective do you think the ad was in raising the profile of Earth Island Institute or increasing contributions to Earth Island Institute?

2. A number of U.S. laws, regulations and agency policies are directed at ensuring that overseas development or export finance supported by the United States is environmentally sound. While these requirements do not explicitly apply U.S. laws extraterritorially, in practice they impose environmental conditions on U.S. support for multilateral bank projects or U.S. financing for exports. Thus they have a strong influence on activities occurring outside the United States.

Pursuant to the so-called "Pelosi Amendment," 22 U.S.C.A. § 262m–7, for the

example, the U.S. Executive Director for each multilateral development bank (including the World Bank) is prohibited from voting in favor of any proposed action by the bank that would have a significant effect on the human environment unless an environmental assessment has been prepared and circulated to the bank and other interested organizations at least 120 days before the date of the vote. Congress has also directed to the U.S. Export–Import Bank (''Ex–Im Bank''), an independent U.S. agency that finances overseas sales of U.S. goods and services, and

the U.S. Overseas Private Investment Corporation ("OPIC") to consider the environmental effects of projects in determining whether to provide insurance, financing, or reinsurance for a development project overseas for American investments in new ventures and expansions of existing enterprises. In 1996, OPIC supported investments resulting in $9.6 billion in U.S. exports. *See* Chapter 20 for a more detailed discussion of these issues.

3. *Problem Exercise.* A U.S. federal government corporation (OPIC) is funding a coal-fired power plant in India. What would be the result if an American NGO sued under NEPA demanding creation of an EIS, arguing that the atmosphere and the global climate system were part of the global commons and relying on Environmental Defense Fund v. Massey as precedent? How strong is the argument that carbon emissions from the plant would add to global warming, which will harm our coastal cities, thus becoming a case of direct effects in the United States?

SECTION VI. FOREIGN CLAIMS IN DOMESTIC COURTS

The above discussion has focused on whether U.S. law should be applied extraterritorially, for example because the U.S. Congress intended to apply a particular statute overseas. When such cases are actually litigated, however, U.S. courts face another set of jurisdictional issues that must be settled before the Courts will decide to hear the particular case. Thus, for example, the Courts must be able to exercise personal jurisdiction over the defendant. The courts must also find that the specific plaintiffs have standing to bring the claims. Even if the Court has the jurisdictional power to hear the case, several common law rules (most notably forum non conveniens) give the Court discretion to refuse to hear cases it decides should more properly be brought in other jurisdictions.

A. IN PERSONAM JURISDICTION

The application of U.S. law domestically and extraterritorially can give rise to difficult questions over whether a court can exercise jurisdiction over a defendant. In the United States, there are both substantive due process considerations and procedural requirements that must be satisfied before a court can exercise in personam jurisdiction over an individual or corporation located outside the United States. *See* Section 421 of the Restatement (Third) of Foreign Relations Law of the United States (1987).

The U.S. Supreme Court has ruled that the exercise of limited personal jurisdiction over a foreign defendant is proper when there is: 1) notice to the defendant; 2) constitutionally sufficient "minimum contacts" between the defendant and the forum so as to satisfy the requirements of the Due Process Clause; and 3) a statutory grant of jurisdiction to the court, i.e., authorization for service of summons either in a specific statute or a state long-arm statute. *See* Omni Capital Int'l Ltd. v. Rudolf Wolff & Co., 484 U.S. 97 (1987) (affirming a circuit court ruling dismissing claims against British defendants in an action under the Commodity Exchange Act because the Act did not provide for nationwide service of process and the requirements of the Louisiana long-arm statute were not met); Asahi Metal

Indus. Co. v. Superior Court of California, Solano County, 480 U.S. 102 (1987); International Shoe Co. v. Washington, 326 U.S. 310 (1945).

In United States v. Ivey, 747 F. Supp. 1235 (E.D.Mich.1990), the U.S. District Court for the Eastern District of Michigan ruled that under Michigan's long-arm statute, the United States had jurisdiction over alien defendants in Canada in a cost recovery action brought under the Comprehensive Environmental Response, Compensation and Liability Act ("CERCLA"), 42 U.S.C. § 9601 et seq. CERCLA authorizes EPA to investigate and clean-up sites that are contaminated with hazardous substances. Responsible parties are jointly and severally liable to the government for cleanup costs and damages to natural resources. In *Ivey,* the United States brought the action to recover costs the government had incurred in cleaning up a Superfund site in Michigan. Both the Canadian individual and the corporation were alleged to have owned and operated the site and were therefore potentially responsible parties under Section 107 of CERCLA. The Canadian defendants admitted to being personally served process in Canada but argued that Section 113(e) of CERCLA (providing for nation-wide service of process) limited the court's jurisdiction to defendants that are found within the territorial limits of the United States.

The court ruled that although CERCLA did not provide for service of process in a foreign country, Rule 4(e) of the Federal Rules of Civil Procedure allows a court to look to the applicable state long-arm statute to determine whether service is proper; the court found that the Canadian defendants had sufficient ties to Michigan to allow the exercise of limited personal jurisdiction. United States v. Ivey, 747 F. Supp. 1235, 1238–40. In 1995, the Ontario Court of Justice enforced a $4.6 million judgment against the Canadian defendants, marking one of the first times the United States has had a foreign court recognize an award for environmental costs. Rule 4 was revised in 1993, making it easier for federal courts to exercise personal jurisdiction over foreign defendants. The revised Rule 4 allows exercise of personal jurisdiction over defendants in federal question cases who have sufficient contacts with the United States to satisfy fifth amendment due process requirements but insufficient contacts with any individual state to support the assertion of personal jurisdiction by that state's courts. *See* FRCP Rule 4(k); Advisory Committee notes on 1993 amendments to Rule 4(k).

B. STANDING

The issue of standing relates to the ability of the plaintiff to bring the type of suit he has filed before a court. Advances in environmental science now are able to link some distant actions with local effects, but courts are generally unwilling to acknowledge these connections.

Justice Scalia, in Lujan v. Defenders of Wildlife, for example, stated that harm to an ecosystem did not, in and of itself, provide sufficient injury to establish standing of plaintiffs who worked in the ecosystem. To establish standing, plaintiffs must:

use the area affected by the challenged activity and not an area roughly "in the vicinity of it".... To say that the Act protects ecosystems is not to say that the Act creates (if it were possible) rights of action in persons who have not been injured in fact, that is, persons who use portions of an ecosystem *not perceptibly affected* by the unlawful action in question. [emphasis added]

504 U.S. 555, 565 (1992). One question, then, is what constitutes an injury in fact, i.e., what threshold injury constitutes being "perceptibly affected?" Should plaintiffs have standing to challenge the government's failure to comply with NEPA in funding a project overseas that would adversely impact an endangered species? Under what circumstances? With respect to the extinction of a species, could it be argued that we are all "perceptively affected"? Does the principle of common concern discussed in Chapter 7, page 396, strengthen the argument for standing? On the other hand, given that much of the world lives in extreme poverty, is there an ethical problem in allowing plaintiffs in the United States, acting on their environmental values, to stop or delay infrastructure projects (dams, roads, etc.) that could improve living standards? Is this a new kind of "colonialism"?

At least one court has ruled that non-U.S. residents located outside the United States have standing to intervene in NEPA suits involving federal actions with possible cross-border environmental impacts. In Wilderness Society v. Morton, 463 F.2d 1261 (D.C.Cir.1972), the D.C. Circuit Court ruled that non-resident Canadian citizens could intervene in an action initiated by various U.S.-based environmental groups that challenged the adequacy of an EIS prepared by the Department of the Interior for the trans-Alaska pipeline. The court concluded that the interests of the Canadian citizen and Canadian environmental group were not adequately protected by the U.S. plaintiffs and that the Canadian intervenors had interests sufficiently antagonistic to the United States government to allow intervention. Is litigation the best approach to weighing whether individuals impacted by a foreign government's decision can participate in the decision-making process and related legal challenges? Can you think of a better approach? Under the North American Agreement on Environmental Cooperation, Canada, the United States and Mexico began formal negotiations in the fall of 1997 on a binding transboundary environmental impact assessment agreement. If you were drafting the agreement, under what circumstances would you allow citizens of one country to challenge another government's approvals or decisions?

C. FORUM NON CONVENIENS

The doctrine of forum non conveniens refers to a court's discretionary power to decline to exercise jurisdiction when it appears that the case may be more appropriately tried elsewhere. *See, e.g.*, Gulf Oil Corp. v. Gilbert, 330 U.S. 501 (1947). The doctrine of forum non conveniens establishes criteria for ascertaining which of two alternative fora is the appropriate forum in which a case should proceed. In Gilbert, the Supreme Court identified the following factors for determining when jurisdiction should be refused on the basis of forum non conveniens. In terms of the private interests of the litigants, the Court cited the following factors: (1) ease of access to sources of proof; (2) availability of compulsory process for attendance of unwilling witnesses; (3) the costs of obtaining the attendance of unwilling witnesses; (4) the possibility of a need for the trier of fact to view the site, if appropriate to the particular cause of action; (5) questions as to the enforceability of a judgment if one is obtained; and (6) all of the other practical problems that make a trial easy, expeditious and inexpensive. In terms of the public interests in the litigation, the Court cited the following factors: (1) administrative difficulties that would result if litigation is focused in congested centers instead of being handled at the origin of the litigation; (2) the burden on jurors from a community that has no relation to the litigation; (3) the local interest in having local controversies decided in local courts; and (4) the appropriateness of avoiding the difficulty of conflict of law problems by having a court familiar with the applicable substantive law be the court that decides the case.

The doctrine of forum non conveniens as specifically made applicable to federal courts in Gilbert was legislatively overruled with the enactment of 28 U.S.C. Sec. 1404(a). The doctrine as applied to foreign plaintiffs has survived, however. In *Piper Aircraft Co. v. Reyno,* 454 U.S. 235 (1981), the Supreme Court addressed the doctrine of forum non conveniens in a case involving damage that occurred outside the United States. In *Piper Aircraft,* several Scottish citizens were killed in an air crash that took place in Scotland. Representatives of the decedents brought suit in U.S. District Court in Pennsylvania. The defendants moved to dismiss the case based on the doctrine of forum non conveniens. The court of appeals held that a dismissal based on the doctrine of forum non conveniens is automatically barred when the substantive law of the alternative forum (in this case, Scotland) is less favorable to the plaintiff than the forum selected by the plaintiff (the United States).

In reversing the court of appeals, the Supreme Court found that an unfavorable difference in applicable law is only one factor among many to consider in analyzing and applying the doctrine of forum non conveniens. According to the Court, the doctrine of forum non conveniens "is designed in part to help courts *avoid* conducting complex exercises in comparative law." (emphasis added) Otherwise, the Court stated, American courts would become more attractive to foreign plaintiffs and, as a result, "[t]he flow of litigation into the United States would increase and further congest already crowded courts." Nonetheless, the Court noted that if a remedy provided by the alternative forum is clearly inadequate, a court could conclude that a dismissal would not be in the interests of justice. The Court also noted that dismissal under the doctrine of forum non conveniens "would not be appropriate where the alternative forum does not permit litigation of the subject matter of the dispute." 454 U.S. at 252.

The doctrine of forum non conveniens has been invoked to dismiss several cases brought by foreign communities or citizens who allege environmental damage from the activities of U.S. corporations in their country. The plaintiffs generally argue that they will not receive a just or fair trial in their home country and look to the U.S. courts for assistance. Thus, for example, indigenous peoples of Ecuador sued Texaco in New York for damage caused by oil development in their Amazonian homelands; indigenous peoples of Irian Jaya sued Freeport McMoran in Louisiana for environmental damage to their homeland caused by gold mining operations, and agricultural workers in Central America have sued Dow Chemical and others in Texas for personal injuries caused by exposure to pesticides. The phenomenon is not limited to U.S. corporations, as similar lawsuits have been filed against Australian and U.K. companies in their respective home countries for operations in developing countries. At least in the United States, however, the corporations have generally been successful in invoking the doctrine of forum non conveniens (as well as the doctrine of comity, described in the Questions and Discussion section below) to argue that the cases should be heard in the country where the activities took place.

----

1. THE BHOPAL CASES

In the early hours of December 3, 1984, a pesticide plant owned by Union Carbide India, released an estimated 40 tons of methyl isocyanate over the city of Bhopal, India, killing about 2,500 people and causing the evacuation of more than 200,000 people. Estimates suggest up to 100,000 people are still suffering side effects, such as blurred vision, disabling lung diseases, intestinal bleeding, and neurological and psychological disorders. It still ranks as one of the worst industrial disasters in history.

Union Carbide India was more than 50% owned by Union Carbide Corp., a U.S. company, with 22% owned by Indian government. After the death of a worker and serious injuries to several others in the Bhopal plant prior to the disaster, the parent U.S. company sent a safety audit team to inspect the plant. The audit team found a number of hazardous conditions and wrote a report, but its major recommendations were never implemented. The leak was likely caused by a series of mechanical and human errors. A portion of the safety equipment at the plant had been non-operational for four months. The plant sounded an alarm an hour after the toxic cloud had escaped but it had little meaning to local residents. Indeed city health officials claimed they had not been informed of the toxicity of the chemicals used at the factory nor did they have any emergency plans or procedures in place.

One hundred and forty-five lawsuits were filed against Union Carbide in the United States seeking over $250 billion in damages and claiming to represent over 400,000 victims. More than 1,200 lawsuits were filed against Union Carbide in Indian courts. All of the U.S. actions were joined together and assigned to the United States District Court for the Southern District of New York. At approximately the same time, the Government of India enacted legislation establishing that it had the exclusive right to represent Indian plaintiffs in courts in India and elsewhere in connection with the Bhopal gas leak. As a result, the Government of India also filed suit in its representative capacity in the Southern District of New York. The company filed a motion to dismiss all of the actions based on the doctrine of foreign non conveniens. *See generally,* Marc Galanter, *Bhopals Past and Present:*

The Changing Legal Response to Mass Disaster, 10 WINDSOR Y.B. OF ACCESS
TO JUSTICE 151 (1990).

The district court analyzed Union Carbide's motion to dismiss by
applying the Gilbert factors, and concluded that all of the private interest
(the plant and overwhelming majority of injured plaintiffs, witnesses and
documents are in India) and public interest (excessive cost to U.S. taxpayer
to support litigation) factors weighed heavily in favor of dismissing the
consolidated cases. 634 F. Supp. 842 (S.D.N.Y.1986), modified 809 F.2d 195
(2d Cir.), cert denied, 484 U.S. 871 (1987). The district court reached its
conclusion even though the Government of India joined the rest of the
plaintiffs in arguing that the Indian courts were not capable of conducting
the Bhopal litigation. In response to this particular argument, the district
court noted that retaining jurisdiction "would be yet another example of
imperialism," and did not want to deprive the Indian judiciary of an
opportunity "to stand tall before the world and to pass judgment on behalf
of its own people." 634 F. Supp. at 867.

The District Court dismissed the consolidated cases subject to the
following conditions: (1) the company must consent to the jurisdiction of
the courts of India, and must continue to waive statute of limitations
defenses; (2) the company must agree to satisfy any final judgment rendered against it by an Indian court that comports with the minimal
requirements of due process; and (3) the company must subject itself to
discovery under the model of the United States Rules of Civil Procedure.

On appeal, the court of appeals upheld the district court's application
of the Gilbert factors and its analysis of the doctrine of forum non
conveniens. However, the Court reversed the second and third conditions
placed by the District Court on its dismissal of the case. With respect to the
second condition concerning the satisfaction of any final judgment rendered
by an Indian court, the court of appeals expressed concern that the
reference to the "minimal" requirements of due process might infer a due
process standard that would be a lesser standard than what would be
otherwise required by, for example, a New York court. As a result, the
court of appeals held that the district court erred in imposing the second
condition. With respect to the third condition concerning the consent to
discovery under the model of the United States Rules of Civil Procedure,
the court of appeals noted that in litigation, basic justice dictates that both
sides be treated equally. The court of appeals did not rule out the possibility that all parties to the litigation could agree to mutual discovery modeled
after the United States Rules of Civil Procedure. 809 F.2d at 202–205.

———

2.   DOW CHEMICAL v. ALFARO

In Dow Chemical Co. v. Alfaro, 33 Tex. Sup. Ct. J. 326, 786 S.W.2d 674
(Tex.1990), Costa Rican residents and employees of the Standard Fruit
Company sued Dow Chemical Company and Shell Oil Company in a Texas
state court alleging that Dow and Shell manufactured a pesticide (DBCP)
that had been furnished to Standard Fruit for use in Costa Rica with

improper labelling despite full knowledge of substantial health consequences

The trial court held that it did have jurisdiction over the case, but dismissed the case based on the doctrine of forum non conveniens. The court of appeals reversed the trial court, holding that Texas courts lacked the authority to dismiss a case based on the doctrine of forum non conveniens because Texas statutorily abolished the doctrine of forum non conveniens in 1913. The Texas Supreme Court affirmed.

In affirming the court of appeals, the Texas Supreme Court noted that Section 71.031 of the Texas Civil Practice and Remedies Code provided, in relevant part:

> (a) An action for damages for the ... personal injury of a citizen ... of a foreign country may be enforced in the courts of this state, although the wrongful act, neglect or default causing the ... injury takes place in a foreign state, if:

> (1) a law of the foreign state or country or of this state gives a right to maintain an action for damages for the ... injury;

> (2) the action is begun in this state within the time provided by the laws of this state for beginning the action; and

> (3) in the case of a citizen of a foreign country, the country has equal treaty rights with the United States on behalf of its citizens.

786 S.W.2d at 675. The Texas Supreme Court decided that this statute "conferred an absolute right to maintain a properly brought suit in Texas courts." The Texas Supreme Court also noted that the United States and Costa Rica entered into the Treaty of Friendship, Commerce and Navigation in 1851, which provided the reciprocity necessary to satisfy the condition of paragraph (a)(3). "The citizens of the high contracting parties ... shall have free and open access to the courts of justice in the said countries respectively, for the prosecution and defense of their just rights."

The concurring opinion, written by Justice Doggett, addressed the dissents' arguments that failure to dismiss such cases would burden the local courts and Texas citizens.

> The abolition of forum non conveniens will further important public policy considerations by providing a check on the conduct of multinational corporations (MNCs).... The misconduct of even a few multinational corporations can affect untold millions around the world.* * *

> The allegations against Shell and Dow, if proven true, would not be unique, since the production of many chemicals banned for domestic use has thereafter continued for foreign marketing.* * *

> Some United States multinational corporations will undoubtedly continue to endanger human life and the environment with such activities until the economic consequences of these actions are such that it becomes unprofitable to operate in this manner. At present, the tort laws of many third world countries are not yet developed.... When a court dismisses a case against a United States multinational corporation, it [eliminates] the most effective restraint on corporate misconduct.

> The doctrine of forum non conveniens is obsolete in a world in which markets are global and in which ecologists have documented the delicate balance of all

life on this planet. The parochial perspective embodied in the doctrine of forum non conveniens enables corporations to evade legal control merely because they are transnational.... In the absence of meaningful tort liability in the United States for their actions, some multinational corporations will continue to operate without adequate regard for the human and environmental costs of their actions. This result cannot be allowed to repeat itself for decades to come.

786 S.W.2d at 688–89. Despite this concurring language, as explained in the Questions and Discussion section, the demise of forum non conveniens doctrine in Texas was short-lived. More important, the doctrine is alive and well in other jurisdictions and has been relied on to dismiss a number of subsequent cases with similar facts (i.e. cases involving foreign plaintiffs trying to use U.S. courts to recover for environmental damage caused by U.S. companies operating abroad). *See, e.g.,* Sequihua v. Texaco, Inc., 847 F. Supp. 61 (S.D.Tex.1994); Delgado v. Shell Oil Co., 890 F. Supp. 1324 (1995) (dismissing on the basis of forum non conveniens a lawsuit brought by thousands of citizens of twelve foreign countries (Burkina Faso, Costa Rica, Dominica, Ecuador, Guatemala, Honduras, Ivory Coast, Nicaragua, Panama, The Philippines, Saint Lucia and Saint Vincent) who sought damages for personal injuries from alleged pesticide exposure).

D.   LAW OF COMITY

The doctrine of comity of nations, similar to forum non conveniens, has also led to the dismissal of a number of cases brought by foreign plaintiffs against U.S. corporate defendants. In *Sequihua v. Texaco, Inc.,* 847 F. Supp. 61 (S.D.Tex.1994), for example, the Court dismissed a suit brought by Ecuadorian residents for damages caused by environmental contamination from Texaco's oil development. In addition to dismissing jurisdiction on grounds of forum non conveniens, the district court also declined jurisdiction under the doctrine of the comity of nations, which provides that under certain circumstances involving the national interests of foreign companies, deference should be given to the laws and interests of a foreign country. In Sequihua, the Court argued deference should be shown to Ecuador's courts because: (1) the alleged harm occurred entirely in Ecuador; (2) the plaintiffs were all residents of Ecuador; (3) none of the defendants were residents of Texas; (4) enforcement of any judgment in Ecuador would be questionable at best; (5) the challenged conduct was regulated by the Republic of Ecuador and an exercise of jurisdiction would interfere with Ecuador's sovereign right to control its own environment and resources; and (6) the Republic of Ecuador had expressed its strenuous objection to the exercise of jurisdiction by the district court. *Id.* at 63.

A subsequent case with similar facts was initially dismissed in federal district court on the grounds of forum non conveniens and the law of comity. Aquinda v. Texaco, Inc., 945 F.Supp. 625 (S.D.N.Y.1996). Plaintiffs, including members of indigenous tribes in Ecuador, sued Texaco for environmental and personal injuries resulting from the company subsidiary's (TexPet) alleged disposal of toxic by-products of the drilling process by dumping them into local rivers, spreading them on roads, and burning them. The plaintiffs' causes of action included nuisance, trespass, and violations actionable under the Alien Tort Claims Act. At trial, the government of Ecuador submitted a letter sent to the State Department expressing its objection to the suit being brought in U.S. court, calling it an affront to national sovereignty. Plaintiffs also offered letters in evidence from representatives of the Ecuadoran Congress (including its president) stating that "only the adjudication of jurisdiction in the claim filed by Ecuadorians . . . in a federal court of N.Y. against the Texaco Company, will bring to those affected the possibility of finding just treatment and a solution to the serious situation that they are going through." *Id.* at 157. Following the holding in the Sequihua case, however, the judge dismissed the case on grounds of forum non conveniens and international comity. Soon after judgment was entered, the government of Ecuador consented to the jurisdiction of the district court (presumably as a result of recent elections). Because the government did not agree to waive its sovereign immunity (it was a large shareholder in TexPet), the judge denied the motion for reconsideration.

On appeal, the Second Circuit reversed and remanded. Dismissal on the basis of forum non conveniens was improper, the court held, because only TexPet, not Texaco, was subject to suit in Ecuadoran courts. And dismissal on the grounds of comity was inappropriate absent a clear finding that an adequate forum exists in the objecting nation, particularly in light of the Ecuadorian government's retraction of its sovereignty objection. 850 F.Supp. 282 (S.D.N.Y.1994). Upon remand, the district court issued a memorandum order citing the State Department's recent conclusion that Ecuador's "most fundamental human rights abuse stems from shortcomings in [its] politicized, inefficient, and corrupt legal and judicial system." While Ecuador's president had been making progress in judicial reforms, the military coup in January, 2000, placed these reforms in jeopardy. As a result, the judge asked parties for additional submissions regarding the independence and impartiality of Ecuadorian courts to hear the claims in question. Memorandum Order, 94 Civ. 9266 (Jan. 31, 2000 S.D.N.Y.).

For further examination of these issues, see Chapter 16, page 1337.

QUESTIONS AND DISCUSSION

1. In light of the *Gilbert* factors, under what circumstances would cases like Dow Chemical v. Alfaro or Aquinda v. Texaco ever be accepted?

2. In its brief to the court, the Indian government argued that "Justice for the Bhopal victims can only be secured in the United States. In India's courts, even routine and simple proceedings turn into such protracted odysseys that it is not unusual for litigation to long survive the litigants themselves." Consider the following description of the Indian legal system. While the numbers may be imprecise, it has been reported that there is a backlog of 10 million cases in the Indian courts and the average civil case is in litigation for many years. Marc Galanter has studied the Indian system and argues that the tort system is underdeveloped. While punitive damages are available in theory, they are almost never awarded. Tort victims are compensated for lost wages, medical expenses and other losses with an average award of $3,440 and almost never higher than $10,000. There is no contingent fee system and, dating back from a law under British rule in

1870, plaintiffs must pay a court fee if they are suing for civil damages. Nor are there civil juries in tort cases. As a result, Galanter notes that, in practice, in case of injury there is often payment on the spot or none at all. Marc Galanter, *Bhopals Past and Present: The Changing Legal Response to Mass Disastor*, 10 WINDSOR Y.B. OF ACCESS TO JUST. 151, 151–70 (1990).

In considering cases such as Aquinda and Bhopal, what deference should a judge give to foreign governments' assertions that they *do not want* the cases litigated in their courts? Should it matter whether the basis for these assertions are concerns over the size of judgment and its deterrent effect or concerns over the inefficiency or corruption of the domestic judiciary?

3. Soon after the Bhopal accident, private attornies reached a settlement with Union Carbide for $350 million. The Indian government denounced the agreement, stating that there could be no settlement without its participation. In 1989, five years after the explosion, the trial was interrupted by the Indian chief justice who recommended that the parties settle with Union Carbide. While the government had initially sought $3.3 billion, it accepted a payment of $470 million in damages. This civil settlement was appealed by activists but reaffirmed in October, 1991. The court also required Union Carbide to pay for the construction and operation of a hospital in Bhopal.

By 1994, however, only about $100 million had been paid out and by 1998 only 60% of claims had been settled. As an Indian NGO stated, "These claims have taken a very long time and the (Indian) claims courts have demanded unreasonable medical records. Some of these victims are poor people who can't afford to see doctors. Indian officials and judges dealing with the compensation awards have also been charged with corruption. These claims have gone badly for the victims." On average, claimants have been paid $870 for personal injuries and $3,000 for exposure related deaths. The government has deducted over $225 from the compensation of each individual against the interim cash relief paid earlier. By one estimate, 20% to 30% of the Carbide money paid out so far has evaporated in the form of bribes to government officials, magistrates, lawyers, doctors, even secretaries and clerks. *See, See* Edward A. Gargan, *Settlement on Bhopal is Accepted*, THE NEW YORK TIMES, October 4, 1991, p.4; *And Still The Survivors Wait; Snarled Compensation In Bhopal Underlines The Problems That Retard India*, L.A. TIMES, November 23, 1994, p. 6; *Bhopal gas tragedy victims' woes*, THE STATESMAN (INDIA), February 25, 1998; Rohit Jaggi, *Disaster still casts shadow*, FINANCIAL TIMES (LONDON), December 23, 1996, p. 3; <http://www.ucaqld.com.au/community/bhopal/injustice.html>.

4. Should the doctrine of forum non conveniens be abolished for environmental damage caused by U.S. companies abroad? In this regard, consider the concurring opinion of Justice Doggett, excerpted above. Does his justification have anything to do with the Gilbert factors? Is he concerned with the convenience and impartiality of Costa Rican courts or is he making a different kind of argument? Could you argue that the United States violates any international environmental principles by continuing to embrace the doctrine?

If forum non conveniens is abolished, is there a danger of increasing the already considerable judicial backlog in many courts? Even if the relatively large size of U.S. tort judgments compared to other jurisdictions will create significant docket congestion, should administrative concerns trump other policy considerations?

5. The "victory" achieved by the plaintiffs in Alfaro was short-lived. In 1993, the Texas legislature overturned the decision in Alfaro by enacting a new Section 71.051 of the Texas Civil Practice and Remedies Code. The new provision was effective for causes of action filed on or after September 1, 1993, and applies to actions for personal injury or wrongful death. The new provision draws a distinction between persons who are legal residents of the United States and persons who are not legal residents of the United States. When the claimant is not a legal resident of the United States, the standard to be applied is whether the action "would be more properly heard in a forum outside the United States." Section 71.051(a). When the claimant is a resident of the United States, the party seeking dismissal has the burden of proving by a preponderance of the evidence that certain conditions are or can be met. These conditions basically parallel the elements of the traditionally applied doctrine of forum non conveniens. It does not take a long or hard read of Section 71.051 to quickly conclude that it is specifically intended to keep foreign plaintiffs, such as the plaintiffs in Alfaro, from seeking redress in the Texas state court system.

6. *The Local Action Rule.* Under the common law "local action rule," any action relating to real property must be brought in the court where the land is located. Thus, where the local action rule is applied strictly, transboundary pollution cases may not be brought in the country where the pollution originates. The recent trend, however, has restricted the local action rule to cases involving conflicts over land titles or possession, and not applied it in cases of pollution.

The local action rule originated as a common law doctrine in England, primarily to address contests over title to land but was extended to actions involving damage to real property, as well. In the United States, the local action rule was integrated into many state venue statutes, thus taking it out of the realm of common law. Virtually all state venue statutes still require actions concerning title to land to be brought in the jurisdiction in which the land is located. The statutes vary, however, in whether they apply the local action rule to claims for trespass or other harm to land located in another jurisdiction.

In general, courts have found ways to avoid imposing the local action rule in cases involving international disputes (but not land title). For example, in Armendiaz v. Stillman, 54 Tex. 623 (1881), in dicta the Texas Supreme Court relied on a 1584 English precedent, *Bulwer's Case,* in which the U.K. Courts rejected the application of the local action rule to cases involving property damage. The Armendiaz court allowed a plaintiff whose land in Mexico was harmed by an action in Texas to bring suit in Texas. Nonetheless, the local action rule still has the potential in several jurisdictions in the United States as well as in Canada to restrict access to the courts. In fact, the local action rule was one reason why the Trail Smelter controversy could not be decided in British Colombia courts, thus forcing the dispute to international arbitration. *See* Chapter 9, page ___, discussing the Trail Smelter Arbitration.

7. The use of the Alien Tort Claims to address in U.S. courts human rights abuses overseas has become a hot area of litigation in recent years. Chapter 15 discusses this in more detail at page 1338. For further reading, *see* Armin Rosencranz, Richard Campbell, *Foreign Environmental and Human Rights Suits Against U.S. Corporations in U.S. Courts*, 18 STAN. ENVTL. L.J. 145 (1999); Joanna E. Arlow, *Note. The utility of ATCA and the "law of nations" in environmental torts litigation: Jota v. Texaco, Inc. and large scale environmental destruction.* 7 WIS. ENVTL. L.J. 93–138 (2000).

8. *International Efforts to Ensure Equal Access to Courts.* Several international fora have addressed the issue of ensuring equal access to justice, particularly in the case of transfrontier environmental harm. Beginning in 1974, for example, the Organization for Economic Cooperation and Development (OECD) adopted a series of non-binding "recommendations" aimed at ensuring equal access and nondiscrimination between countries with respect to transfrontier pollution.

The United States has never officially adopted or implemented the OECD recommendations, however. In light of the relative lack of official action in this regard, the American Bar Association along with its counterpart Canadian Bar Association developed a Draft Treaty on a Regime of Equal Access and Remedy in Cases of Transfrontier Pollution. Article 2 of the Draft Treaty reads as follows:

> 2(a) The Country of origin shall ensure that any natural or legal person resident in the exposed Country, who has suffered transfrontier pollution, shall at least receive equivalent treatment to that afforded in the Country of origin, in cases of domestic pollution or the risk thereof and in comparable circumstances, to persons of equivalent condition or status in the Country of origin.

> (b) From a procedural standpoint, this treatment shall include but shall not be limited to the right to take part, or have resort to all administrative and judicial procedures existing within the Country of origin, in order to prevent domestic pollution, to have it abated, and/or to obtain compensation for the damage caused.

Both Bar Associations recommended to their respective countries that they negotiate such a treaty applicable to national, state and provincial courts.

In a related effort the U.S. National Conference of Commissioners on Uniform State Laws and the Uniform Law Conference of Canada jointly drafted a *Uniform Transboundary Pollution Reciprocal Access Act* that they recommended be enacted by states and provinces in lieu of a treaty. The Uniform Act provides:

> A person who suffers, or is threatened with, injury to his person or property in a reciprocating jurisdiction caused by pollution originating, or that may originate, in this jurisdiction has the same rights to relief with respect to the injury or threatened injury, and may enforce those rights in this jurisdiction as if the injury or threatened injury occurred in this jurisdiction.

The Uniform Statute has been adopted by seven states and three provinces (Manitoba, Ontario and Prince Edward Island). *See, e.g.,* Mich. Comp. Laws secs. 324.1801 to 324.1807; Mont. Code secs. 75–16–101 to 75–16–109; Wisc. Stat. sec. 144.995; Or. Rev'd Stats. Tit. 36 s.468.o76 et seq. What are the advantages of the Uniform Statute over the Draft Treaty, described above? Would such a treaty make a difference in any of the cases addressed in this Chapter? Does it reverse the local action rule?

CHAPTER TWENTY

ENVIRONMENTAL PROTECTION AND INTERNATIONAL FINANCE

SECTION I.   INTRODUCTION

International financial institutions play two major roles in international environmental policy and law. First, through project financing, and sectoral and structural adjustment lending, institutions such as the World Bank and the International Monetary Fund profoundly affect the development paths of developing countries. Still an open question is whether these institutions are willing or able to move from traditional "development" to "sustainable development" models. Second, some financial institutions, most notably the Global Environment Facility, are critical for the successful implementation and acceptance of international environmental instruments, as they are the mechanism for financing the technological and other changes necessary for compliance with specific environmental obligations. Sometimes, one institution fulfills both roles in seemingly contradictory ways: for example, the World Bank is simultaneously the number one international financier of greenhouse gas emissions (through for example widespread support of coal-fired power plants) and the largest international financier of alternative energy technologies necessary for the reduction of greenhouse gas emissions.

The financial mechanisms are critical components of most environmental treaty negotiations, as global environmental politics often boil down to a debate over money. This debate involves two different issues. First, the northern donor countries and the southern borrowing countries are deeply divided over such issues as the level of financial support that should be made available for environmental protection and development; the number of conditions, if any, that should be placed on financial assistance; and the relative control over financial mechanisms that will be granted to the borrowers. The second major issue revolves around the question of effectiveness of foreign assistance, particularly with respect to achieving the goal of sustainable development. To a large extent, this has been driven by the work of environmental NGOs and others who question the top-down approach to, and ultimately the sustainability of, development as typically promoted by the major financial institutions.

The North–South Issues. At a basic level, the North–South debate is simply over how much assistance industrialized countries will provide to developing countries to facilitate the transition to sustainable development. The UNCED Secretariat estimated that from 1993 to 2000 the implementation of *Agenda 21* in the South would require $125 billion annually in grants or concessional funding from the North. Since UNCED took place in 1992, however, official development assistance (ODA) from the OECD countries has actually declined, at least when adjusted for inflation. Total ODA from the OECD countries was $53.1 billion in 2000, down 1.6% from 1999. Only a few countries (the Netherlands, Norway, Denmark, Sweden and Luxembourg) meet or come close to meeting the UN target for ODA of 0.7% of GDP, a voluntary target reaffirmed at UNCED. The United States provided a little over $9 billion in ODA in 2000, which is 0.1% of our GNP (the OECD as a whole gave .22 percent of its GNP, so the United States gives relatively little in percentage terms). We are also no longer the largest ODA provider in real terms; Japan is now the leader in ODA, giving $13 billion in the year 2000. For updated statistics on ODA, see the OECD web site at http//www.oecd.org.

The debate over ODA is not simply about the amount of money, however, but about what type of projects get funded and about who controls the funding. In general, developing countries argue that global environmental issues such as climate change, ozone depletion, and the conservation of biodiversity, are the priorities of industrialized countries. To gain the cooperation of developing countries, the industrialized countries are expected to provide "new and additional" funding to offset the costs of meeting global environmental obligations. Funding must be "additional" to existing levels of development assistance intended to address traditional, social, and economic development (such as assistance to build economic infrastructure, or strengthen education or health care systems).

The South argues that concepts of economic justice and equity should require the wealthy countries to assist in the alleviation of poverty. Some in the South believe that the requirement to provide development assistance should be legally mandated as an element of the right to development. Moreover, with respect to environmental issues, the South believes that the North is responsible for causing many global environmental issues and should be required to assist the South in responding to global environmental threats. In several environmental treaties, the South's agreement to substantive obligations has been conditioned explicitly on the North's delivery of specific levels of financial and other assistance. The wealthy countries on the other hand try to minimize the legal linkage between their agreement to provide additional financial assistance and developing countries' substantive environmental obligations. They contend that development assistance, including environmental assistance, is a voluntary policy decision of the donor government.

In addition, developing countries want to participate more in establishing funding priorities and minimizing any conditionalities placed on assistance. Donor countries have kept control over the decisionmaking of the key international financial institutions, particularly the World Bank and the International Monetary Fund. This donor-country desire to keep control over the financial mechanisms in part led several donors to promote creation of a centralized Global Environment Facility, the largest development assistance agency dedicated solely to global environmental issues.

The Environmental Issues. Since the 1980s, environmental and social NGOs have actively tried to reform development institutions, particularly through a concerted World Bank reform campaign that has lasted for nearly two decades. NGOs have sought, with some success to: increase the participation of locally affected people in development projects; integrate environmental concerns into all development projects through environmental impact assessments; shift the lending portfolios of the larger development institutions toward sustainable technologies and projects; and increase the accountability and transparency of financial institutions. The environmental critique of the financial institutions has expanded to other social concerns, and in recent years the financial institutions have been the targets of mass anti-globalization protests. Although the violence that now regularly accompanies these protests clouds the protesters' message, the anti-globalization movement highlights just how much the basic approach of the World Bank and the other financial institutions fail to garner broad support.

At the same time, existing financial and development institutions see the growing emphasis on environmental protection as both an opportunity and a challenge. On the one hand, environmental investments are some of the fastest growing parts of the portfolios of most of the existing multilateral institutions. The institutions have begun to broaden their concept of "development" to one that takes into account the critical role of environmental protection and some social concerns. On the other hand, environmental investments still make up a relatively small part of the financial institutions' portfolios.

This Chapter highlights the issues facing international financial institutions as they attempt to shift from "development" to "sustainable development." The Chapter focuses on the World Bank Group, the International Monetary Fund and the Global Environment Facility (GEF).

SECTION II. THE WORLD BANK GROUP

The World Bank Group and the International Monetary Fund (IMF) were created at the Bretton Woods meeting in 1944. The two institutions have a close relationship, both in structure and in function. The World

Bank was intended to finance projects, originally for the reconstruction of war-ravaged Europe and Japan. Supplanted significantly by the Marshall Plan for the reconstruction of Europe, the World Bank eventually turned to poverty alleviation in developing countries as its major objective. The IMF, in contrast, is more concerned with financial markets and macroeconomic stability than with poverty alleviation. In practice, however, the two institutions work closely together on economic policy and their structures are closely parallel. We discuss the World Bank Group below and the IMF in Section III.

A. THE WORLD BANK GROUP'S STRUCTURE

The World Bank Group is comprised of four separate, but related, institutions: the International Bank for Reconstruction and Development (IBRD), the International Development Association (IDA), the International Finance Corporation (IFC), and the Multilateral Investment Guarantee Agency (MIGA). IBRD and IDA provide loans to support public-sector projects. Together IBRD and IDA are most frequently referred to as the "World Bank." The primary difference between the IBRD and IDA is that IDA provides concessional or low-cost loans to the poorest countries (those having per capita annual income below $1465 (in 1994 dollars). The IBRD provides loans at a higher rate (although a rate still below market) to other developing countries and to countries in economic transition. The IFC and MIGA provide financial support to private sector projects in all developing countries or countries in economic transition. IFC makes loans and equity investments in private sector projects, whereas MIGA provides insurance against political risks faced by private sector investments in developing countries (i.e. risks from civil unrest or war). This section discusses the public sector arms of the World Bank and the subsequent section addresses the IFC and MIGA.

The Bank is made up of Member Countries who have agreed to the Bank's By–Laws and Articles of Agreement. The Member Countries are represented in broad policymaking by a Board of Governors that meets once a year. Day-to-day policy decisions at the World Bank as well as decisions on specific loans are made by a 24–member Board of Executive Directors that meets several times a week at the Bank's headquarters in Washington, D.C. Voting at the Executive Directors and at the Board of Governors is based on financial shareholding percentages, which are loosely based on a country's share of the global economy. The U.S. has the largest voting share of 17%. The seven largest industrial countries (the G–7) together comprise 45% of the voting shares at the Bank, and all of the donor countries together comprise a solid majority of the vote. Typically, however, decisions are made by consensus. The Board meetings and decisions are not open to the public, nor are the meeting minutes ever made public. Although most countries are grouped together and share an executive director, several larger countries, including the United States, have their own representative on the Board of Executive Directors.

The World Bank has a staff of over ten thousand. The Bank Management is presided over by the World Bank President who also acts as the Chair of the Board of Directors. The Bank President, currently James

Wolfensohn, is traditionally chosen by the United States (and the IMF head is selected by Europe). The Management is responsible for the day-to-day operations of the Bank, subject to the policies and other decisions set forth by the Executive Directors or Member Governments.

The Bank is the largest development organization in the world. Each year the Bank supports approximately $22 billion in projects, including $6 billion to the poorest countries, and leverages an additional $50 billion from other financial institutions. The Bank is also the recognized intellectual leader among development organizations, often setting precedents for other institutions to follow. The Bank's influence is expanded further by coordinating other donors, mobilizing bilateral and increasingly private-sector financing, conducting policy research, and providing technical assistance to countries.

None of the World Bank Group's Articles of Agreement mention the environment. Indeed, for some time, Bank officials argued that they could not even consider environmental issues in making their deliberations. The Articles of Agreement forbid the Bank from taking into account political factors in making lending decisions. As the connection between poverty alleviation and environmental protection grew clearer, however, the Bank's vision of development expanded and it no longer questions the fundamental relevance of environmental issues to its operations. The inherent tensions within the Bank continue, however, particularly with respect to human rights and governance issues where the Bank still feels constrained by its narrow, traditional vision of development and its prohibition against considering political factors.

B. ENVIRONMENTAL CONTROVERSY OVER THE WORLD BANK

Beginning in the 1970's, independent observers began to recognize that the World Bank and other international financial institutions were providing support for some of the most environmentally damaging projects taking place in developing countries. These projects, mostly large infrastructure projects, were often associated with allegations of severe environmental devastation, human rights abuses, and long-term negative effects on the economic well-being of the poor in the project area. Even assuming good intentions, the size and scale of many of the projects simply dwarfed the legal and policy infrastructure of the borrowing country. *See, e.g.,* Robert Goodland, *The Environmental Implications of Major Projects in Third World Development,* 9–16, in MAJOR PROJECTS AND THE ENVIRONMENT (Morris, ed. Oxford 1987). The following excerpt summarizes two large and notorious dams supported by the Bank.

P. Bosshard, et al., eds. *Lending Credibility: New Mandates and Partnerships for the World Bank* 9 (WWF, 1996)

The Big Dam Controversies

Kedung Ombo. Between 1985 and 1993, construction of the Bank-supported Kedung Ombo dam and reservoir on the island of Java, Indonesia, displaced more than 30,000 people. Almost from the beginning, the resettlement process was crippled by unrealistic assumptions, poor planning, and the government's general lack of commitment to fair and full compensation.

Because of Java's high population density, the resettlement plan anticipated that the majority of displaced persons would join the government's transmigration program and be moved to newly opened areas in the outer islands. When this assumption proved to be unfounded, many residents of soon-to-be-inundated villages refused to abandon their homes and accept grossly inadequate compensation for their land, even in the face of official coercion. Opponents to resettlement faced harassment and intimidation, including death threats and false criminal charges.

Although the Bank had acknowledged the importance of resettlement to the success of the project as early as the 1985 Staff Appraisal Report, Bank staff failed to monitor or supervise the Indonesian government's implementation. The Bank did not take any significant steps to address intensifying problems until 1989, after Indonesian NGOs had organized an international campaign to publicize the extensive human rights abuses associated with the project. The Bank's 1994 Project Completion Report concluded that 72 percent of displaced families were worse off than before the resettlement, a particularly troubling statistic in light of the fact that more than half of those families already lived below the poverty line before they were resettled.

Sardar Sarovar. The Sardar Sarovar dam is part of a massive and complex system of dams and canals planned for India's Narmada River. When completed, the system is expected to irrigate 1.8 million hectares and provide drinking water to 40 million people. The World Bank provided $450 million in loans and credits for the Sardar Sarovar dam and has in the past considered $540 million in additional financing for associated projects.

The Sardar Sarovar dam and the accompanying canals involve the resettlement of an estimated 240,000 people. Major environmental issues also exist with respect to the dam and the diversion of over 9.5 million acre-feet of water. The magnitude of the project and the large number of displaced people led to widespread resistance within the Narmada valley, including huge protests, hunger strikes, and lawsuits.

Opposition to the project was also taken up by international environmental and human rights NGOs. Urged on by these NGOs, the U.S. Congress held hearings on Sardar Sarovar, the European Parliament passed a resolution asking the Bank to withdraw, and Parliamentarians form Sweden, Finland, Japan and other countries wrote letters to the Bank.

Under increasing pressure, the Bank took the unprecedented step in June 1991 of inviting an independent review of the Sardar Sarovar project by what came to be known as the Morse Commission after its chairman, Bradford Morse. After nearly a year-long investigation, the Commission released a scathing report detailing the Bank's failure to provide adequate supervision to the project. Among other things, the report concluded that the Bank failed to ensure adequate resettlement for most of the oustees and had not even included plans for the 140,000 people expected to be displaced by the canal system.

In addition, the report faulted the Bank for failing to conduct any meaningful environmental impact study or to secure timely environmental clearances from Indian officials. The report concluded: "[t]he history of environmental aspects of Sardar Sarovar is a history of non-compliance."

Faced with such a compelling litany of problems, the Bank placed a number of substantial conditions on further support to the project. India, unable to meet those conditions, subsequently withdrew its request for Bank support and has continued the project on its own.

————

The Bank's poor record in environmental protection, human rights and even poverty alleviation has been well documented. *See* CATHERINE CAUFELD, MASTERS OF ILLUSION (1997); BRUCE RICH, MORTGAGING THE EARTH (1996); J. Greisgraber & B. Gunter, eds., The World Bank: Lending on a Global Scale (1996); R. MIKESELL & L. WILLIAMS, EDS., INTERNATIONAL BANKS AND THE ENVIRONMENT: FROM GROWTH TO SUSTAINABILITY: AN UNFINISHED AGENDA (1992). For criticism of development institutions more generally, see GRAHAM HANCOCK, LORDS OF POVERTY: THE POWER, PRESTIGE, AND CORRUPTION OF THE INTERNATIONAL AID BUSINESS (1989).

C. THE GREENING OF THE BANK

Criticism from environmental NGOs turned into increased oversight by donor country legislatures, particularly the U.S. Congress, which in turn led the Bank to begin to green itself. The Bank has taken several steps to respond to environmental concerns, including providing technical assistance to countries; developing operational policies and standards relating to the environment; and conditioning specific project loans on environmental mitigation. In addition, the Bank is a major player in the support and administration of the GEF and other environmentally related funds.

Environmental Lending and Technical Assistance. The World Bank currently boasts that it provides more human and financial resources to environmental issues than any other international organization. The Bank employs over 300 senior environmental staff members. By 1998, according to the Bank, it was the largest financier of "targeted" global environmental projects (i.e. through the GEF and otherwise), with an active portfolio of 166 projects with a funding level of $11.6 billion. Between 1994 and 1998, the Bank provided more than $800 million per year in support for environmental projects (not including GEF grants). The figure dropped considerably in 1999 to $539 million, although this may or may not be reflective of a long-term decline in environmental support. Some of the reduction for "environmental projects" may also reflect that environmental considerations are now common conditions on many projects. The World Bank defines an environmental project as one with "primarily environmental objectives." These range from "brown" environmental projects like the $478.1 million Chongqing Industrial Reform and Pollution Control Project, which is aimed to improve pollution control in parts of China, to "green" projects like the $30 million Native Forests and Protected Areas Project in Argentina and the $65 million Forestry Development Project in Kenya, to technical assistance projects like the $5 million Capacity Building for Environmental Management Project in Gambia. Environmentalists question some of the projects' classification as "environmental"; for example some forest development projects have an overall goal of increasing timber harvesting, even though they may include some components for environmental protection.

In addition to bankrolling environmental projects, the Bank provides significant technical and legal environmental assistance to developing countries. Typically, the Bank may oversee the development of environmental framework legislation and/or provide support for sectoral environmental laws (i.e., mining or industrial sector environmental standards), the development and strengthening of environmental institutions, and the implementation of specific treaties. Examples of other environment-related technical assistance in 1999 include an Urban Environment Strategy for Vietnam, a Water Strategy for Paper for Latin America, a Forestry Sector Review in Turkey and an Environment Study of Ethiopia.

The Bank also assists in the development of Country Environmental Strategies, which identify environmental priorities for foreign assistance, and the Bank has pioneered the use of National Environmental Action Plans (NEAPs), which set priority actions for addressing a country's most pressing environmental issues. Over 90 countries have developed NEAPs as a prerequisite for environmental lending. According to *World Bank Operational Directive 4.02,* which outlines World Bank policies and procedures for assisting borrowing countries in preparing and implementing NEAPs:

> The content and format of an EAP are designed by each country. The reports vary according to the country's size, range of environmental problems, economic complexity, and government capacity to respond to environmental issues. The reports also vary according to the actual process of preparing and EAP. Smaller countries may find it more feasible to prepare a comprehensive and formal EAP covering all sectors, while larger countries may find it useful to focus separately on several high-priority sectors. The EAP describes and establishes the priorities among several areas of environmental concern: (a) environmental issues; (b) plans for specific environmental-related policy, legal and institutional changes; and (c) types of environmentally sustaining investments to be undertaken. It also describes the financial and technical assistance the country needs to address priority environmental problems. Each country's EAP is as detailed and action-oriented as feasible and is updated and revised as conditions change.

World Bank, Op. Dir. 4.02, paras. 4–5. In addition to supporting national environmental planning, the Bank has also taken a lead in planning coordinated responses to address several regional environmental problems, for example by facilitating the development of regional action programmes for Central and Eastern Europe, the Black Sea, the Mediterranean, the Danube River, the Caspian Sea, and the Aral Sea.

Mitigating Environmental Harm From Bank Projects. In an effort to integrate environmental concerns into Bank operations, the Bank has begun to develop operational policies and procedures to guide the conduct of Bank staff in preparing and implementing Bank projects. A number of these policies and procedures relate to the environment, beginning with the 1984 adoption of Operational Manual Statement 2.36 on Environmental Aspects of Bank Work. This sets forth the following eight principles, which still are supposed to guide Bank activities with respect to the environment.

> (a) the Bank will endeavor to ensure that each project affecting renewable natural resources does not exceed the regenerative capacities of the environment;

(b) the Bank will not finance projects that cause severe or irreversible environmental deterioration, including species extinction without mitigatory measures acceptable to the Bank;

(c) the Bank will not finance projects that unduly compromise the public's health and safety;

(d) the Bank will not finance projects that displace people or seriously disadvantage certain vulnerable groups without undertaking mitigatory measures acceptable to the Bank;

(e) the Bank will not finance projects that contravene any international environmental agreement to which the member country concerned is a party;

(f) the Bank will not finance projects that could significantly harm the environment of a neighboring country without the consent of that country. The Bank is willing to assist neighboring members to find an appropriate solution in cases where such harm could result;

(g) the Bank will not finance projects which would significantly modify natural areas designated by international conventions as World Heritage sites or biosphere Reserves, or designated by national legislation as national parks, wildlife refuges, or other protected areas; and

(h) the Bank will endeavor to ensure that projects with unavoidable adverse consequences for the environment are sited in areas where the environmental damage is minimized, even at somewhat greater initial costs.

More recently, the Bank has moved toward a system of "Operational Directives" (OD), "Bank Procedures" (BP), and "Good Practices" (GP) to guide its operations. *Operational Directives* and *Bank Procedures* are substantive policy instructions that Bank staff must follow in all Bank operations and projects. *Good Practices* are discretionary. The following summarizes the operational directives on environmental assessment and involuntary resettlement, two of the most important directives for sustainable development.

Operational Directive 4.00 Annex A (1989) and 4.01 (1991) on Environmental Assessment. OD 4.01 on Environmental Assessment standardizes a screening procedure for environmental assessment (EA) that all World Bank-financed projects must undertake. This screening involves classifying projects into three categories depending on the extent of environmental impacts associated with the project. "Category A" projects, which have "significant adverse impacts that may be sensitive, irreversible and diverse," must undergo a full environmental assessment. "Category B" projects have adverse impacts that "are less significant than Category A impacts. Few if any of these impacts are irreversible. The impacts are not as sensitive, numerous, major, or diverse as Category A impacts, remedial measures can be more easily designed. Preparation of a mitigatory plan suffices for many Category B projects." "Category C" projects normally do not require any environmental analysis "because the project is unlikely to have adverse impacts." World Bank, Op. Dir., paras. 5–7, and Annex E. From 1990 to 1999, 186 projects about 12% of the Bank's portfolio (by loan amount) were classified as Category A, and 931 projects (33%, by loan amount) were classified as Category B.

Under *OD 4.01*, the borrowing country is responsible for preparing the EA, and according to paragraph 19:

the Bank expects the borrower to take the views of affected groups and local NGOs fully into account in project design and implementation, and in particular the preparations of EAs. This process is important in order to understand both the nature and extent of any social or environmental impact and the accountability of proposed mitigatory measures, particularly to the affected groups.

These consultations should occur twice, once following the environmental impact screening and the other upon completion of a draft EA. In addition *OD 4.01* requires that an Environmental Advisory Panel, consisting of independent internationally recognized, environmental specialists, be engaged to assist in the preparation and implementation of the EAs for highly risky or contentious projects with serious environmental concerns.

Operational Directive 4.30 on Involuntary Resettlement (June 1990). OD 4.30 sets forth a main policy objective to avoid or minimize involuntary resettlement whenever possible. Should a project require involuntary resettlement, it will be classified as a Category A project under OD 4.01 and the mandatory EA should cover the environmental impacts of the resettlement. *OD 4.30* dictates that the resettlement plan must be coordinated with the assessment and must address all possible environmental consequences. According to Para. 20 of OD 4.30:

> The screening process for an environmental assessment normally classifies projects involving involuntary resettlement as Category A. The EA of the main investment requiring resettlement should thus cover the potential impacts of the resettlement. The resettlement must be developed in coordination with the EA and define the boundaries of the relocation area, and calculate incremental population density per land unit. In agriculture projects, (involving for example, relocation to the catchment surrounding a reservoir, or downstream command area), if the incoming resettled population is large in relation to the host population, such environmental issues as deforestation, overgrazing, soil erosion, sanitation and pollution are likely to become serious and plans should either include appropriate mitigating measures, including training of oustees, or else should allow for alternative sites to be selected. Urban resettlement raises other density-related issues (e.g. transportation systems, health facilities, etc). Constructive environmental management, provided through EA's mitigation plans may provide good opportunities and benefits to resettlers and host populations alike (e.g., project-financed compensatory afforestation not only replaces the forests submerged by reservoirs but also offers gainful employment). If the likely consequences on the environment are unacceptable, alternative and/or additional relocation sites must be found.

As this edition of the textbook is being written, the Bank is revising its resettlement policy. The World Bank has also developed directives and guidelines in other areas related to sustainable development, including: indigenous people, agriculture pest management, water resource management, forestry, hazardous waste, and access to information. These policies include both general recommendations regarding Bank involvement in these sectors as well as specific conditions, procedures or prohibitions on lending.

Conditioning Loans for Environmental Protection. Beginning in the early 1970s, the Bank began to include in IBRD loans or IDA credit agreements specific covenants relating to environmental protection. After environmental impact assessments became mandatory, the inclusion of environmental conditionalities became more common. Sometimes, detailed implementation plans will be attached to a loan, requiring the implementing agencies to achieve certain benchmarks for environmental protection as the project is implemented. The Bank has also required certain environmental or other steps be taken before a loan will be made effective. Thus, for example, the Bank required that Uganda provide the full benefits of civil service status to forest preserve guards, before a Uganda forest sector loan would be disbursed.

The effectiveness of these environmental conditions depends on the extent to which they are enforced. Even by the Bank's own account, supervision of environmental conditions presents serious problems:

> Appropriate covenants in the legal documents do not of course ensure by themselves that the required action will be taken. For this reason, provisions are included in the General Conditions applicable to all loan agreements to give the Bank power to suspend disbursements if the borrower or the project executing agency defaults in carrying out agreed actions. This is a most potent remedy when project implementation is still ongoing. Problems that arise after the completion of the project and the full disbursement of loan proceeds to the borrower are more difficult to handle. However, the Bank may in such a case still enforce the borrower's commitments by declaring that the borrower has defaulted in performing its obligations under the loan agreement. This could lead, if acceptable action is not taken by the borrower within the period indicated by the Bank, to the acceleration of maturity of the loan and the Bank's insistence on immediate repayment of the loan in full. This is obviously a serious path which has been avoided in practice, although such defaults do affect the level and pace of future Bank operations in the country in question.

> While legal provisions may specify clearly the required actions, it is important to note that the Bank does not rely solely on such provisions to ensure compliance. Each project financed by the Bank is subject to supervision which is carried out by Bank staff. This activity, coupled with the ongoing country dialogue, is often more effective from a practical viewpoint, than punitive action in ensuring the proper implementation of Bank-financed projects. Much greater efforts will have to be exerted, however, to ensure that project implementation is consistent with loan conditionality. While fostering an "implementation culture" is called for in the Bank's operations generally, it is of particular importance in this context. Where the environment is concerned, an ex post discovery of poor implementation often results in irreversible harm.

I. Shihata, *The World Bank and the Environment: Legal Instruments for Achieving Environmental Objectives*, in 2 THE WORLD BANK IN A CHANGING WORLD, at 207–08 (1996). Despite the use of these loan conditionalities, the Bank has rarely if ever suspended disbursements due to environmental concerns. Indeed, the threat of such enforcement is no longer considered credible by most observers, and many projects have failed to meet their loan conditions.

QUESTIONS AND DISCUSSION

1. Former World Bank General Counsel Ibrahim Shihata has written the following:

> In today's world, the World Bank is in fact playing the role of a monitor for the protection of the environment with respect to the projects it finances in its

borrowing member countries. Increasingly, it also supports broader efforts to save the environment in these countries and to address the effects of their actions on the global environment. Regrettably, no other international organization plays a similar role for the countries which do not borrow from the Bank, and to whom most of the damage to the world environment has been attributed.

I. Shihata, *op. cit.,* at 236 (1996). Are developing countries in fact being held to a different, higher standard of international oversight than industrialized countries? Is there any justification for this? Consider this again in light of the discussion of the Inspection Panel, infra.

2. Do World Bank Operational Policies and other standards contribute to the development of international law? How? See Chapter 5, page 322, on the role of international institutions in the law-making process.

3. *Domestic Control Over the Banks: The Pelosi Amendment.* National governments do not have direct control over international agencies like the World Bank and other multilateral development banks (MDBs), but they do have the power to influence the MDBs through the votes of their executive directors. The "Pelosi Amendment" is one attempt to improve the environmental performance of MDBs through national legislation, by instructing the respective U.S. executive directors how to vote.

(a) Assessment required before favorable vote on action

(1) In general, [b]eginning 2 years after December 19, 1989, the Secretary of the Treasury shall instruct the United States Executive Director of each multilateral development bank not to vote in favor of any action proposed to be taken by the respective bank which would have a significant effect on the human environment, unless for at least 120 days before the date of the vote: (A) an assessment analyzing the environmental impacts of the proposed action and of alternatives to the proposed action has been completed by the borrowing country or the institution, and been made available to the board of directors of the institution; and (B) except as provided in paragraph (2), such assessment or a comprehensive summary of such assessment has been made available to the multilateral development bank, affected groups, and local nongovernmental organizations. * * *

(c) Consideration of assessment

The Secretary of the Treasury shall—

(1) ensure that an environmental impact assessment or comprehensive summary of such assessment described in subsection (a) of this section accompanies loan proposals through the agency review process; and

(2) take into consideration recommendations from all other interested Federal agencies and interested members of the public.

Assessment of Environmental Impact of Proposed MDB Actions, Section 521 of the U.S. International Development and Finance Act of 1989, 22 U.S.C. sec. 262m–7 (1989). Thus the Pelosi Amendment seeks to ensure that both the public and the Bank's voting officials have access to critical environmental information before irreversible decisions are made.

Since the Pelosi Amendment became effective on December 19, 1991, the respective U.S. Director no longer votes for a project significantly affecting the environment unless he or she has received the necessary environmental information. The World Bank and most of the regional banks have cooperated with the U.S. government by rewriting their operational policies to ensure that environmental assessments are made available at least 120 days in advance. The only exception has been the European Bank for Reconstruction and Development, which because of the predominant position of European countries in the bank, simply refuses to accommodate the United States. As a result, the United States has occasionally had to abstain or vote against projects significantly affecting the environment. More problematic has been the application of the Pelosi Amendment to the IFC and MIGA, which support private sector development. The Department of Treasury has taken the position that these arms of the World Bank are not "multilateral development banks" within the meaning of the Pelosi Amendment. As a result, their environmental policies do not comply with the 120–day requirement, and the U.S. executive director is still not required to vote no or abstain. Do you agree with the Treasury Department's interpretation of "multilateral development bank"? What authority does the U.S. Congress have to regulate the conduct of the U.S. Executive Director to an international institution? Is this an infringement on the Executive Branch's primary authority over foreign affairs? J. Sanford & S. Fletcher, *Environmental Assessment and Information Policies in the Multilateral Development Banks: Impact of the Pelosi Amendment* (Cong. Res. Serv., July 21, 1997).

4. Today, the World Bank is probably the most closely scrutinized of all international organizations, at least by environmental NGOs. Many of the recent environmental reforms at the Bank, including adoption of policies and creation of the Inspection Panel, can be directly attributed to NGO lobbying efforts. The following statement succinctly presents the environmentalist's critique of the World Bank:

> Since [the 1980s], the Bank has taken many small steps toward improving its environmental performance, but shifting its orientation from an overriding emphasis on economic growth to one consistent with environmental sustainability still requires a giant leap.... The Bank as an institution has not yet questioned the fundamental compatibility of environmental sustainability with the prevailing development paradigm, which subordinates other development objectives to economic growth and efficiency. Indeed, the Bank can be criticized for failing to promote with sufficient vigor environmental reforms that are consistent with the current paradigm, such as the removal of subsidies that encourage overexploitation of natural resources. It is fair to characterize most of the progress to date as incremental improvements to "business-as-usual," not yet constituting the paradigm shift to a "sustainability approach" that is needed.... The challenge is not only to "mainstream" environmental concerns into all Bank operations, but also to move "upstream" and include environmental sustainability as an objective of sector-and country-level assistance strategies.

Frances Seymour, *The World Bank and Environmental Sustainability,* in Lending Credibility: New Mandate and Partnerships for the World Bank, 43–44 (WWF, 1996). NGOs are not the only observers who have concluded that the Bank has failed to integrate effectively environmental concerns into its activities. Even the Bank's own internal evaluation found:

> Achievements, however, have lagged behind expectations raised by the Bank policies, formal commitments and published statements. ... Preliminary findings reveal gaps, inconsistencies and ambiguities in the Bank's approach towards promoting environmental sustainability. While the Bank has been able to increase the general awareness of environmental issues in client countries through its EA guidelines, serious issues still linger about compliance with and implementation of its safeguard policies. In promoting environmental objectives, the Bank has attempted to do many things without establishing clear priorities and focusing its efforts on areas of greatest relevance to its overarching mission and country needs. Mainstreaming the environment in country development strategies still remains an elusive goal.

Operations Evaluation Department, *Promoting Environmental Sustainability in Development: An Evaluation of the World Bank's Performance, Phase I Interim Report*, at iii (Sept. 15, 2000). What steps would you take to move environmental objectives and "sustainability" to the center of all Bank operations? Why is reliance on environmental impact assessments, resettlement plans and other mitigation approaches insufficient for the major shift envisioned by sustainable development?

5. As noted above, one response to the NGO campaign has been for the Bank to do more in the field of sustainable development, for example providing technical assistance for the development of non-profit laws or strengthening environmental regulatory systems. Is this an appropriate role for a development bank? Consider the following, again from Frances Seymour:

> Any discussion of the Bank taking a proactive role in achieving social justice, environmental sustainability or strengthening civil society must also consider the potentially debilitating constraints facing Bank management and staff. Not only does the Board of Directors, reflecting the collective interests of the governments, insist on a narrow role for the Bank, but borrowing countries often have little or no enthusiasm for the reforms or project mix that would be implicated by a more proactive approach. Often the political will or institutional capacity simply does not exist to ensure successful implementation of innovative or sustainable projects. For example, Brazil's lack of commitment to institutional reform is one of the main reasons that the Bank-financed effort to promote sustainable development in the Amazon is being widely criticized . . . . These and other constraints, both real and perceived, hinder the extent to which Bank management can lead the Bank into support for non-traditional development goals.

Seymour, op. cit. This leaves environmentalists and other critics of the Bank in a difficult position. Environmentalists welcome the Bank's growing recognition that development includes and depends on more than traditional approaches, but by encouraging the Bank to address issues of environmental protection, human rights or governance issues, the critics also legitimize the Bank's role in these areas. Do you think an institution with the Bank's history, structure and mandate is appropriate for promoting environmental protection, human rights, and good governance?

6. *The Regional Development Banks.* In addition to the World Bank, six multilateral development banks exist to facilitate development in specific regions. These include the InterAmerican Development Bank, Asian Development Bank, North American Development Bank, African Development Bank, European Bank for Reconstruction and Development, and the Mid–East Development Bank.

For the most part, the regional development banks are structured and operate essentially in the same way as the World Bank. Of course some regional differences do shape the politics, priorities and approaches of the Bank. For example, the Asian Development Bank is much more heavily influenced by Japan than the other banks. Similarly, the European Bank for Reconstruction and Development (EBRD) is heavily dominated by the Western European donors, particularly the United Kingdom, Germany and France. Given the industrialized commercial base of much of the region in which the EBRD operates, the environmental challenges and approaches are somewhat different than at the other banks. For example, the EBRD has always focused heavily on privatization and supporting the private sector. The EBRD has also supported the ongoing process of integrating some of the borrowing countries into the European Union (EU) (a uniquely European issue). Among other things, the close relationship to the EU raises difficult questions about whether to require all new projects to meet EU environmental standards. What are the pros and cons of such an approach? Does it matter if a country has the long-term goal of entering the EU or not? What approaches could you use to soften the requirement that a project must meet EU or other clear standards? What enforcement mechanism do you envision for ensuring that projects meet the standard?

The EBRD was also the first MDB to include sustainable development in its mandate. The EBRD's charter states that the Bank is to "promote in the full range of its activities environmentally sound and sustainable development." Agreement Establishing the European Bank for Reconstruction and Development, Art. 2(vii) (May 29, 1990), *reprinted in* 29 I.L.M. 1077, 1984 (1990). Environmental groups heralded this as a major victory, but within a few short years the mandate was all but forgotten. What steps would you recommend to a development bank to operationalize its mandate to promote sustainable development? What difference should such a mandate make compared to the other MDBs that have no such mandate in their charter? *See generally* Chris Wold & Durwood Zaelke, *Promoting Sustainable Development and Democracy in Central and Eastern Europe: The Role of European Bank for Reconstruction and Development*, 7 Am. U.J. Int'l L. & Pol'y 1 (1991); Donald Goldberg & David Hunter, *EBRD's Environmental Promise: A Bounced Check?*, CIEL Brief (Dec. 1994).

7. *Bilateral Aid and Export Credit Agencies (ECAs).* The level of official development assistance going through bilateral channels now substantially exceeds that going through multilateral development banks. With the exception of the United States export credit agencies (i.e. the Overseas Private Investment Corporation and the Export–Import Bank), virtually no other countries' ECAs have any environmental standards at all. This has prompted a multi-year effort led by the same NGOs who had tackled the Bank to focus on ECAs. Despite commitments from G–7 leaders in 1998 and 1999 to ensure at least some minimum standards by the year 2001, those standards have still not been agreed to. For information on the ECA reform effort, visit http//www/eca-watch.org.

D.   The World Bank Inspection Panel

The idea for an Inspection Panel at the World Bank originated as early as 1990 when environmental organizations began advancing specific proposals for an appeals or investigative body to increase the Bank's accountability. In early 1993, the Center for International Environmental Law joined the Environmental Defense Fund in drafting a detailed proposal for an independent appeals board to allow citizen standing to enforce the Bank's compliance with its environmental policies. Policymakers from other countries and even some of the Bank's Executive Directors voiced support for an Inspection Panel. The U.S. Congress identified the creation of an Inspection Panel as a key condition for continued funding of IDA, the Bank's concessional loan fund. Congressional leadership particularly from subcommittees chaired by Representative Barney Frank and Senator Patrick Leahy ensured that the Bank took the calls for reform seriously. *See* Lori Udall & David Hunter, *The World Bank Inspection Panel*, 9 Env't 36, at 2–3 (Nov. 1994).

On September 1, 1994, the World Bank's Inspection Panel began operations. The panel is authorized to receive claims about the Bank's failure to comply with its own policies and procedures, including its failure to enforce related loan conditions. Claims can be filed by any affected party (other than a single individual) in the borrower's territory. The affected party's local representative, the Bank's Board of Executive Directors, or, in some cases, any one Executive Director are also eligible to file claims. In an obvious attempt to limit the role of NGOs, non-local representatives can represent affected parties only in "exceptional cases" where "appropriate representation is not locally available." The following excerpt from the Panel's Operating Procedures explains the Panel's goals and operating procedures (references in these procedures to the "Bank" include the IBRD and IDA).

> The Panel has been established for the purpose of providing people directly and adversely affected by a Bank-financed project with an independent forum through which they can request the Bank to act in accordance with its own policies and procedures. It follows that this forum is available when adversely affected people believe the Bank itself has failed, or has failed to require others, to comply with its policies and procedures, and only after efforts have been made to ask the Bank Management itself to deal with the problem.

> The role of the Panel is to carry out independent investigations. Its function, which will be triggered when it receives a request for inspection, is to inquire and recommend: it will make a preliminary review of a request for inspection and the response of Management, independently assess the information and then recommend to the Board of Executive Directors whether or not the matters complained of should be investigated. If the Board decides that a request shall be investigated, the Panel will collect information and provide its findings, independent assessment and conclusions to the Board. On the basis of the Panel's findings and Management's recommendations, the Executive Directors will consider the actions, if any, to be taken by the Bank.

World Bank Inspection Panel, Operating Procedures, at 3 (Aug. 19, 1994); *see also* IBRD, Resolution No. 93–10; IDA, Resolution No. 93–6 (Sept. 22, 1993); *see also* Dana Clark, A Citizen's Guide to the Inspection Panel, 2d edition (CIEL, 1999).

As of August, 2001, twenty-four claims had been filed with the World Bank Inspection Panel. Three have been dismissed for not meeting the eligibility requirements. One of the earliest claims is described below. Additional information can be found at the Inspection Panel's web page: <www.worldbank.org>.

Adapted from David Hunter, *Amazon Burning and the World Bank: Lessons From the Second World Bank Inspection Panel Claim*, 2 ECO-NOTES: ENVIRONMENTAL LAW & POLICY 1 (SPRING 1996)

The Rondonia Natural Resource Management Project (known by its Portuguese acronym PLANAFLORO) was conceived in 1992 to showcase Brazil's commitment to the environment leading up to UNCED. The project was designed to reverse the environmental devastation wrought in the 1980's by the Bank-financed POLONOROESTE project, an infamous road project that opened much of Brazil's Amazon to slash-and-burn logging and unsustainable agriculture. The burning of the Amazon and the related murder of activist Chico Mendes galvanized international attention on the environmental and social damage occurring in the Amazon. International criticism highlighted the Bank's role, as well. *See, e.g.,* ALEX SHOUMATOFF, THE WORLD IS BURNING: MURDER IN THE RAIN FOREST (1990); ADRIAN COWELL, THE DECADE OF DESTRUCTION: THE

CRUSADE TO SAVE THE AMAZON RAIN FOREST (1990); SUSANNA HECHT & ALEXANDER COCKBURN, THE FATE OF THE FOREST: DEVELOPERS, DESTROYERS AND DEFENDERS OF THE AMAZON (1990).

The PLANAFLORO project contemplated large-scale social and economic zoning, designed to intensify logging and agricultural activities in developed areas that could sustain them and to demarcate and protect other areas, including indigenous territories and ecological reserves. The PLANAFLORO project eventually received widespread support among environmentalists, rubber tappers, and indigenous peoples, who saw the project as a viable step toward sustainable development in the region. After over two years of implementation, none of the benefits intended for the indigenous peoples or the rubber tappers had occurred, and these former supporters of the project were compelled to bring an inspection panel claim in the hopes of putting the project back on track.

At the center of PLANAFLORO's implementation problems was a lack of political commitment in Brazil to make the changes necessary to defend the economic and social zoning plans. From the beginning, institutional reform was a major condition of the loan agreement. The promised reforms involved sweeping changes in policies, regulations, and investment programs, to provide positive incentives for sustainable development.

After signing the loan, however, Brazil and the state of Rondonia's commitment to these institutional reforms dissolved. Money continued to flow into the region, mostly only to fuel unsustainable forestry and agricultural practices. Little action occurred to demarcate or otherwise protect the indigenous lands or ecological reserves. The Bank explained that external factors made it powerless to improve implementation of PLANAFLORO. The most commonly cited of these external factors included: 1) delays in the release of financial resources, especially counterpart funding by the State and Federal government agencies, 2) deficiencies in the institutional capacities of executing agencies, and 3) political instability during election periods. But the real problem was more fundamental: the Bank's "culture of approval," where internal advancement depends on preparing and negotiating loans, is not well-suited to pressuring large, recalcitrant borrowers such as Brazil into making politically unpopular decisions even if they are conditions in loan agreements.

The PLANAFLORO Inspection Panel claim was filed in June, 1995 by twenty-five Brazilian organizations, representing small farmers, rubber tappers, indigenous communities, local rural unions, and environmental and human rights groups affected by the loan. The 80–page claim documented the Bank's failure to supervise implementation of the loan, as well as violations of several bank policies and directives. The claim was not filed to stop the project, but to encourage the Bank to force Brazil to honor the commitments in the loan agreement.

The extra pressure brought by the claim led almost immediately to improvements in implementation. Several new indigenous lands were demarcated, the federal and state land-use agencies signed a critical reform agreement, and the government finally agreed on a contractor to take the necessary satellite pictures of the region. Bank management also increased its oversight of the projects and prepared a new "action plan" for improving implementation of the project.

Because of the action plan, the Board formally denied the Panel authority to investigate the claim and endorsed management's action plan. Most importantly, the Board also committed to review the project again in six to nine months, with the assistance of the Inspection Panel. Although the claimants were disappointed that their claim was denied, the pressure generated by the claim at least initially improved implementation of the project.

QUESTIONS AND DISCUSSION

1. The Inspection Panel is an interesting example of how international law is expanding to make greater room for citizens. In essence, the Panel is a fact-finding mechanism, perhaps most analogous to human rights commissions. By creating the Panel, the Bank became the first international institution (outside of the European Union) to allow citizens a direct role in monitoring the institution's performance against objective standards. For the Bank, the Panel offered the first meaningful mechanism for enforcing compliance with Bank Operational Directives, such as those described above relating to environmental assessment and resettlement.

2. *Representation.* If a request to the Inspection Panel is submitted by a non-affected representative, he or she must provide evidence of representational authority and the names and contact address of the party. Proof of representational authority, for example, the original signed copy of the affected party's explicit instructions and authorization, must be attached. In addition, in the case of non-local representation, the Panel will require clear evidence that adequate or appropriate representation does not exist in the country where the project is located. What evidence should be required for allowing local or foreign representation? What role can a foreign lawyer have in assisting a requester to the panel under the rules? If you were advising a potential claimant, what information would you suggest they include in the request? How could they gather this information?

3. The role of the Bank's General Counsel with respect to the Panel raises significant questions. Paragraph 15 of the Resolution stated that: "the Panel shall seek the advice of the Bank's Legal Department on matters related to the Bank's rights and obligations with respect to the request under consideration." Why might it be important for the credibility of the Panel process to ensure independence from the General Counsel's office? Is there any potential conflict of interest in the General Counsel's role as the Bank's lawyer that should circumscribe the General Counsel's role in advising the Panel? Who should have the power to interpret the Resolution creating the Panel, particularly for example those provisions relating to the eligibility of claimants?

4. The Panel Resolution provided some restrictions on the members of the Panel in an effort to ensure their independence from the Bank. According to the Resolution the Panel shall consist of three members of different nationalities. Members of the Panel shall be selected on the basis of their ability to deal thoroughly and fairly with the requests brought to them, their integrity and their independence from the Bank's Management, and their exposure to developmental issues and to living conditions in developing countries. Knowledge and experience of the Bank's operations is also desirable. What other requirements would you add to ensure the Panel's independence from the Bank?

5. In June, 1994, the Board of Directors for the InterAmerican Development Bank (IDB) created an "independent inspection mechanism" to "further the transparency, accountability and effectiveness of the Bank's performance in its operations." Like the Inspection Panel at the World Bank, the IDB's inspection mechanism is intended to protect affected citizens in borrowing countries. Any "organization, association, society or other grouping of individuals" can request an inspection by offering "reasonable evidence that its rights or interests have been or are likely to be directly and materially affected by an action or omission of the Bank as a result of a failure of the Bank to follow its operational policies or norms." As of July, 1997, the IDB mechanism had been used one time, in the case of the Yacyreta dam on the border of Argentina and Paraguay. *See* InterAmerican Development Bank, Independent Investigation Mechanism (1994). The Asian Development Bank also has an inspection function, which is currently reviewing its first claim. *See* Asian Development Bank, ADB's Inspection Policy: A Guidebook (1996).

6. Because of its unique approach to accountability, the Inspection Panel has been the subject of a substantial number of books and articles. *See, e.g.,* David Hunter, *Amazon Burning and the World Bank: Lessons From the Second World Bank Inspection Panel Claim,* 2 Eco-notes: Envtl. L. & Pol. 1 (Spring 1996); Daniel Bradlow, *International Organizations and Private Complainants: The Case of the World Bank Inspection Panel,* 34 Va. J. Int'l L. 553 (1994). Ibrahim Shihata, The World Bank Inspection Panel (2d ed., 2000); Lori Udall, The World Bank Inspection Panel: A Three Year Review (Bank Information Center, 1997); Gudmundur Alfredsson & Rolf Ring, eds, The Inspection Panel of the World Bank: A Different Complaints Procedure (2001).

E.   The IFC and MIGA

As noted above, the IFC and MIGA are the private sector arms of the World Bank Group. The IFC provides loans to private companies conducting projects in developing countries. For example, IFC provided a loan to Basic Oil Company to develop an oil field in Guatemala. MIGA provides guarantees against civil war or other political risks. For example, MIGA provided co-insurance to US-based Enron Corporation to protect it against the risk that civil unrest would disrupt a power project in Indonesia. Both IFC lending and MIGA risk guarantees can be critical for leveraging additional private sector capital in developing country projects. IFC and MIGA are the fastest growing parts of the World Bank Group.

The IFC and MIGA are separate, independent organizations within the World Bank Group. They share almost identical Boards of Executive Directors, however, and the President of the World Bank chairs each of the World Bank Group organizations.

IFC and MIGA projects, like those of the rest of the World Bank Group, have not escaped controversy. For example, in 1996 the Grupo Accion de Bio Bio (GABB), a Chilean NGO, filed a claim at the World Bank Inspection Panel challenging the continued role of the IFC in financing the construction of the Pangue/Ralco complex of dams on the BioBio River. GABB claimed the project sponsors had failed to assess the downstream impacts sufficiently and had failed to provide adequate resettlement support to the region's indigenous peoples. Because the Inspection Panel does not have explicit authority to review IFC-financed projects, the claim was immediately rejected; however, World Bank President James Wolfensohn agreed to authorize an independent investigation into the allegations of the claim. The final report uncovered significant policy violations by IFC and systemic problems with the Pangue Project. It made specific recommendations on mitigation measures for the project, as well as general recommendations on institutional reforms for the IFC and World Bank. *See* Pangue Audit Team, *Pangue Hydroelectric Project (Chile): An Independent Review of the International Finance Corporation's Compliance with Applicable*

World Bank Group Environmental and Social Requirements (World Bank, 1997).

The Pangue report prompted the IFC and to a lesser extent MIGA to clarify their environmental and social policies. IFC issued specific policies closely tailored or in some cases copied directly from the World Bank's operational policies and directives. Thus, IFC and MIGA now have clear information disclosure, environmental assessment, resettlement and indigenous peoples policies, for example. In addition, the IFC has issued an influential set of pollution prevention standards. These standards are industry-specific pollution standards determined by reviewing international and domestic pollution standards from around the world. The World Bank Group as well as many other lenders often look at these standards as a way of determining whether their project is having an unreasonable impact on the environment. *See* World Bank Group, Pollution Prevention and Abatement Handbook: Toward Cleaner Production (1998).

In part because of the revelations uncovered in the Pangue report, IFC and MIGA also established a new office of the Compliance Advisor and Ombudsman (CAO) in 1999. The CAO is an independent office that answers directly to the President of the World Bank Group. As set forth in its operational guidelines, the CAO has three distinct roles:

[1] Responding to Complaints by persons who are affected by projects and attempting to resolve the issues raised using a flexible, problem solving approach (the Ombudsman role).

[2] Providing a source of independent advice to the President and the management of IFC and MIGA. The CAO will provide advice both in relation to particular projects and in relation to broader environmental and social policies, guidelines, procedures, resources and systems (the Advisory role).

[3] Overseeing audits of IFC's and MIGA's social and environmental performance, both overall and in relation to sensitive projects, to ensure compliance with policies, guidelines, procedures, and systems (the Compliance role).

Compliance Advisor and Ombudsman, Operational Guidelines, at 7 (April, 2000). The ombudsman role is like the World Bank Inspection Panel in that it is driven by the concerns and interests of locally affected communities. The CAO enjoys a more proactive and flexible mandate aimed at solving problems, rather than reporting on what has happened in the past. According to the CAO Guidelines, the "aim is to identify problems, recommend practical remedial action and address systemic issues that have contributed to the problems, rather than to find fault." Within its first eighteen months of operation (up to September, 2001), the CAO had received nine complaints. For more information, see www.ifc.org/cao.

QUESTIONS AND DISCUSSION

1. In recent years, critics of the IFC have begun to question its development impact. Because the IFC receives unsolicited project proposals from the private sector, it is more reactive than the World Bank, which frequently takes the lead in a country's overall development planning. The IFC has yet to articulate criteria for screening proposed projects significantly different than those financial criteria used by private sector lenders. As a result, the IFC has no systematic way for screening investments and loans for their social, environmental and equitable impacts. This leaves the IFC with no clear link between the bulk of its activities and the goals of poverty alleviation and sustainable development, other than the same arguments for the private sector generally.

Beginning in the year 2000, the IFC launched an organization-wide process to identify its mission in terms of sustainable development and to reshape its culture toward sustainable poverty alleviation. How would you advise top IFC management in preparing such a "roadmap to sustainability"? To some extent, the IFC can promote sustainability by supporting or perhaps requiring its borrowers to integrate environmental and social concerns into their businesses. Will this approach alone, be sufficient to shift the IFC's portfolio toward sustainability. What objectives, criteria and indicators would you suggest for the IFC to ensure it is having a sustainable development impact?

2. The IFC will not publicly release any information provided to it by the company, if the company claims the information is confidential. It also will not release the specific social and environmental covenants that may be put in a loan as a condition to its approval. Assume that you are representing a locally affected community, what incentive would you have to engage in a constructive dialogue with the company and IFC if there is no chance you will see any resulting social or environmental conditionalities. If the IFC subsequently chooses not to enforce the conditionalities, for example with respect to environmental harm or resettlement, could the locally affected communities bring a lawsuit for breach of contract? Would IFC's status as an international organization prevent such a lawsuit?

3. Criticisms of IFC have led some to argue for the privatization of the IFC, arguing in essence that the IFC is unnecessary corporate welfare. The same reasons offered for privatizing most government-owned businesses might apply to the IFC. For example, privatizing the IFC would create fiscal space in public international financial affairs. The money saved or the money earned by privatizing the IFC could be used to target microlending, investments and loans in the poorest countries, environmental projects, or other activities that would more clearly provide public benefits, particularly to the poor. What arguments are there for a private sector lending arm of the World Bank? What is the difference between the IFC and a commercial bank? Would you require any benchmarks for the continued operation of the IFC?

SECTION III.   THE INTERNATIONAL MONETARY FUND

As noted above the IMF was created in 1944 at the Bretton Woods conference that created the World Bank. The IMF began operations in 1947 and today has 181 member countries. The top policymaking body at the IMF is the Board of Governors, made up of members from each country. The Board of Governors meets once every three years. Day-to-day operations are managed by the Board of 24 Executive Directors, who meet three times a week at the IMF offices in Washington, D.C.

The International Monetary Fund was the centerpiece of the Bretton Woods system of fixed exchange rates. It was designed as the place where countries with temporary balance-of-payments problems could obtain short-term loans in order to avoid exchange-rate shifts, which were to be permitted only in exceptional circumstances. Its sister institution, the International Bank for Reconstruction and Development (IBRD-better known today as the World

Bank), stood ready to help the war-torn countries of Europe and Asia with the tasks of reconstruction.

* * *

In 1978 the International Monetary Fund's sphere of operation was adjusted to deal with the changes which had been brought about by the transition to flexible exchange rates. It was given an oversight mandate, so that exchange-rate distortions and payments-balance problems could be recognized as early as possible, and suggestions worked out for their resolution. But the IMF really came into its own with the outbreak of the international debt crisis. In the 1980s, as the mediator between debtor nations, banks, and the wealthy creditor countries of the so-called Paris club, the IMF designed "structural adjustment programs" (sometimes even more draconic than the banks themselves were comfortable with) aimed at keeping the channels of credit to the debtor nations open.

In the course of this latest phase, too, there have been subtle position shifts. Initially, debtors complained that the Fund was acting too much as advocate of the creditors (especially the acutely threatened U.S. banks). But after passage of the Brady initiative, the tables were turned and the IMF became the defender of the poor, leaving the banks little alternative but to write off many of their repayment claims.

Daniel Hofmann, The IMF and World Bank in Changing Times, Swiss Rev. of World Affairs, Aug. 1992, at 4. The IMF has described their current operations in the following way:

> First, the IMF continues to urge on its members the unrestricted exchange of their currencies. As of 1992, 70 members had agreed to full convertibility of their national currencies. Second, in place of monitoring members compliance with their obligations in a fixed exchange system, the IMF now plays a major role in supervising economic policies that influence their balance of payments in the presently legalized flexible exchange rate environment. This supervision provides opportunities for an early warning of any exchange rate or balance of payments problem. In this, the IMF's role is principally advisory. It confers at regular intervals (usually once a year) with its members, analyzing their economic positions and apprising them of actual or potential problems arising from their policies, and keeps the entire membership informed of these developments. Third, the IMF continues to provide short-and medium-term financial assistance to member nations that run into temporary balance of payments difficulties. The financial assistance usually involves the provision by the IMF of convertible currencies to augment the afflicted member's dwindling foreign exchange reserves, but only in return for the governments promise to reform the economic policies that caused the balance of payments problem in the first place. The IMF sees its financial role in these cases as easing a country's painful transition to living within its means rather than subsidizing further deficits.

See David Driscoll, *The IMF and the World Bank: How Do They Differ?* (IMF: 1992), at 10; David Driscoll, *What is the International Monetary Fund?* (IMF: 1993).

Like the World Bank, the IMF has drawn the ire of anti-globalization protestors in recent years, who see the IMF as one of the major architects of an unjust, undemocratic and opaque economic system. Some of the critique of the IMF also centers around its environmental impact. Two aspects of the IMF's operations are most important for understanding its impact on the environment: the imposition of structural adjustment policies to force a country to "live within its means" and the failure to use IMF resources to alleviate developing country debt. These are discussed below.

The environmental impacts of structural adjustment are complex and difficult to determine in some cases. In part, this is because of the wide range of policies usually implemented during structural adjustment. For example, the money supply and government spending are reduced. Property rights for agriculture and land-use are often clarified, perhaps to the detriment of traditional community-based land rights. Export crops are often promoted to increase foreign currency exchange. Trade barriers are eliminated. The following two excerpts suggest how these policies can impact the environment.

> The basic aim of adjustment programmes is, of course, economic. Through measures of price liberalisation, trade liberalisation, devaluation, fiscal and financial reform, etc. a more efficient allocation and use of resources will be ensured. The move towards more market-determined prices will lead to prices that reflect scarcities better, including scarcities of natural resources.

> However, although prices may better reflect market scarcities, they will not reflect external environmental effects and they may not adequately reflect the resource depletion that takes place. This becomes clear when we look at some of the major prices that are central to the adjustment efforts, such as agricultural prices and the exchange rate.

> Adjustment measures are likely to lead to higher agricultural output prices (through the reduction of price controls, devaluation, etc.) To the extent that land owners expect these price changes to last, it will increase the implicit value of their land and this may induce them to cultivate the land more carefully and to invest in land improvement. Of course, if they expect the price rise to be only temporary, they may engage in excessive exploitation of land, and they may bring marginal lands under cultivation, in the hope of short-term profits.

> The devaluation of the currency and the removal of trade controls are likely to improve the relative price of export crops with respect to food crops. The environmental effect of any substitution that may arise from this price shift depends on the characteristics of the export crops and the food crops in question. Some export crops may have a good environmental impact, but others not. The shift out of food crops may lead to food shortages that may lead to environmentally damaging behaviour.

> The devaluation and the removal of subsidies will make imported agricultural inputs (fertiliser, pesticides, farm equipment) more expensive. This may be good in itself, as it reduces the use of environmentally damaging inputs and it may lead to shifts back to more sustainable organic manures and pest controls. But when such shifts lead to lower yields, this will, in turn, neutralize some of the effect of higher output prices on sustainable land use, mentioned above.

> Higher import prices and less subsidies for fuel energy will lead to its more economic use, but it may also lead to an increased use of environmentally less desirable energy sources such as coal or fuelwood.

> Trade liberalisation and devaluation will make the importation of 'clean' technology easier, but also dearer. The reduction of import controls may lead to an increase in imports of luxury goods with negative effects on the environment (e.g. cars).

Structural adjustment programmes put pressure on public spending. The need to bring the fiscal deficit down to a manageable size makes it necessary to scrutinize all spending plans. This may put programmes of agricultural research and extension, land improvement, the cleaning-up of pollution, or the introduction of cleaner technology in public enterprises into jeopardy. On the other hand, some public sector programmes may have, unwittingly, contributed to environmental degradation (e.g. rural road programmes or irrigation schemes that can contribute to deforestation), in which case a reduction would be beneficial to the environment.* * *

The list of possible environmental effects of even a few of the structural adjustment measures is long and can easily be made still longer and more detailed. The examples given above do not attempt to provide an exhaustive account of environmental impacts, but are rather intended to show the complexity of the interaction between economic policy changes and their ecological effects. Many of these can go either way and a lot seems to depend on the specific conditions of the country or even of the region with the country.

Karel Jansen, Structural Adjustment and Sustainable Development, International Spectator, vol. 45, No. 11, at 696–701 (Nov. 1991). A World Resources Institute study on the impacts of structural adjustment in the Philippines concluded that the "development pattern was to deplete natural resource assets in order to finance current consumption and the acquisition of relatively unproductive industrial capital." The WRI study offered the following conclusion:

Policies that depress savings and lower the returns to investment shift resource use toward the present. Unmanageable domestic and external indebtedness are widely observable symptoms of this intertemporal reallocation. Less scrutinized but even more serious has been the depletion of natural resource assets. And yet, the analysis of the Philippines experience demonstrates that the rise in external debt and the depletion of natural wealth are both par t of a general deterioration in the national balance sheet. They both arise from short-sighted policies. To promote sustainable development, macroeconomic policies must provide strong incentives to build capital—not just financial and industrial capital, but also natural resource and human capital. The deterioration of a nation's natural resource endowment is at least as serious an obstacle to sustainable development as the deterioration of its international credit standing.

Reallocation of productive resources among sectors to achieve greater efficiency is the essence of structural adjustment programs. Changes in market incentives through reform of trade regimes, domestic price structures, taxes, and subsidies are the policy instruments of reallocation. However, if full environmental and resource costs are not reflected in the incentives resource users face, then efficiency will not be achieved either in the short or the long run. The Philippines study shows that macroeconomic policies without adequate environmental controls have increased emissions, concentrated pollution and congestion, increased pressure on open-access resources, and encouraged overexploitation of depletable resources. Structural adjustment policies have been designed without adequate consideration of such effects and implemented without the safeguards and corrective policies needed to control and reduce adverse environmental impacts. Without these intrinsic environmental components promote sustainable development.

Such safeguards should not be regarded s impediments to structural adjustment policies or burdensome concessions to environmental interest groups.

Indeed, policy and institutional reforms to correct environmental failures are complementary and essential components of a structural adjustment program. Policies can readily be identified that reduce environmental damage and simultaneously promote other economic objectives, such as fiscal balance, poverty alleviation, and economic efficiency. The Philippines study identifies several important examples, such as the taxation of resource rents, energy taxes, and the elimination of industrial incentives.

World Resources Institute, *The Environmental Effects of Stabilization and Structural Adjustment Programs: The Philippines Case* (1992).

QUESTIONS AND DISCUSSION

1. Environmentalists typically criticize the conditionalities that the IMF places on governments as part of its structural adjustment, and indeed the evidence suggests that many of these policies lead to environmental degradation. Yet, in a few recent circumstances environmentalists have actually sought the intervention of the IMF to place environmental conditions on their structural adjustment lending. In 1996, the IMF even withheld a loan to the government of Cambodia in an effort to get Cambodia to crack down on massive poaching of commercial timber. The IMF feared that one of Cambodia's most important resources, timber, would be stolen and traded in the black market, thus denying the State an opportunity to build a tax base and gain foreign currencies—both of which were being relied on to repay the IMF loan.

A. THE MULTILATERAL DEBT CRISIS

Both the World Bank and the IMF are frequently criticized for their contribution to the debt burden of the poorest countries. International debt owed by developing countries is often cited as an underlying cause of short-term overexploitation of natural resources. The need for immediate foreign currency to repay debts pushes developing countries toward unsustainable policies. The Worldwatch Institute provides the following description and analysis of the debt crisis.

David Malin Roodman, Still Waiting for the Jubilee: Pragmatic Solutions for the Third World Debt Crisis, 6–9 Worldwatch Paper No. 155 (April 2001)

Currently to use the World Bank's measuring sticks, some 47 nations are very poor—having a gross national product (GNP) of less than $855 per person—and heavily indebted, with their governments owing foreigners the equivalent of at least 18 months of export earnings. All but 10 of the 47 are in Africa. [The others include: Bolivia, Guyana, Honduras, Nicaragua, Afghanistan, Pakistan, Cambodia, Indonesia, Burma, and Vietnam.] . . . For most people in these nations, life is hard. Civil wars, coups d'etat, corruption, AIDS, famine, illiteracy are all relatively common. And almost no one thinks these countries can repay more than a small fraction of their foreign debts, which now total some $422 billion, or $380 per resident. [Equivalent to only 11 months of Western military spending. Commercial banks held 31 percent of the debt, bilateral creditors 37 percent, and multilaterals 32 percent.] * * *

[O]fficial lenders have run aground in the poorest nations, and in a way that is undermining the worldwide fight for sustainable development. Hundreds of billions of dollars of official loans have disappeared into corruption, capital flight, weapons buying, white elephants, and projects that worked better on paper than in practice. And now the need to service debts has cut into government budgets for roads, environmental protection, primary education, and basic healthcare. Indeed, many low-income debtors spent more servicing debts to the world's richest nations in the late 1990s than giving social services to their own impoverished citizens. Meanwhile, private investors and local entrepreneurs—the proverbial haters of uncertainty—have been discouraged by doubts about what debtor governments, cornered by their creditors, will do next. Will they raise tariffs on exports? Or print money, thereby feeding inflation?

Because debt trouble set in gradually in low-income countries, no one can point to a particular child dying in Mozambique from tetanus or to a particular plot of forest cleared by a poor farmer in Honduras and say with confidence, "Debt caused that." But the experience of middle-income countries, where debt crisis developed with a suddenness that spotlighted the link between cause and effect, offers a vivid picture of its impact. In Mexico, wages halved between 1982 and 1988. In the Philippines, a million or more desperate peasants moved into the hills, where they cleared erodible slopes of protective trees and farmed to survive. And in southeastern Brazil, immunization cutbacks opened the way for a measles epidemic that killed thousands of babies in 1984.

The debt crisis in the poorest nations thus confronts the world with a dilemma. Critics on one side of the issue point to the theft and waste and ask why taxpayers in rich countries should let incompetent or unaccountable governments off the hook. Debt is a promise to pay, and a promise is a moral obligation. But critics on the other side, represented most effectively by the international Jubilee 2000 coalition of churches and nongovernmental organizations (NGOs), decry the "chains of debt" that enslave the world's poorest nations to the richest ones and, they submit, choke off government spending for immunizing poor children or teaching them how to read.

Two things are obvious when looking at third world debt. First, it is inconceivable that many of these poorest countries are ever going to be able to repay their existing debt. Currently, they simply borrow more each year to service the debt from earlier years and earlier regimes. Such a "pyramid scheme" works no better for countries than for individuals, and is a sure way for financial ruin. Secondly, the debt burden of many countries squeezes the public sector's ability to provide basic social services, perpetuating inequity and poverty. The table below illustrates how servicing foreign debt can in some countries exceed inflows from current borrowing and more importantly how it exceeds expenditures on basic social services including health and education, clean water, sanitation, family planning and nutrition (Worldwatch, *op cit.* at 24).

Shares of Government Spending Borrowed from Foreign Creditors, and Devoted to Foreign Debt Service or Basic Social Services, 1996–1997

Country	Share Covered by Foreign Borrowing	Share Devoted to Foreign Debt Service	Share Devoted to Basic Social Services
Belize	8	6	20

Country	Share Covered by Foreign Borrowing	Share Devoted to Foreign Debt Service	Share Devoted to Basic Social Services
Benin	29	11	10
Bolivia	16	10	17
Cameroon	36	36	4
El Salvador	47	27	13
Jamaica	14	31	10
Zambia	13	40	7

As reflected by the statistics for Zambia, many countries in sub-Saharan Africa are in particularly difficult debt situations. According to Oxfam International, for example:

> In Uganda, $3 per person is spent on health compared to $17 on debt repayments, mainly to multilateral creditors. This is despite the fact that one-in-five children in Uganda do not reach their fifth birthday because of diseases, which could be prevented through investment in primary health. Between 1990 and 1993 the government of Zambia spent $37 million on primary school education. Over the same period, it spent $1.3 billion on debt repayments. Repayments to the IMF alone were equivalent to ten times government spending on primary education. This was during a period of deep crisis in the education system caused by chronic under-funding. In Tanzania, spending on external debt is double the level of spending on water provision. Yet more than 14 million people lack access to safe water, exposing them to the threat of water-borne diseases, which are the main cause of premature death and disability.

Oxfam, *Multilateral Debt: The Human Costs,* at 3 (1996).

Given the obvious importance of debt relief to sustainable development, developing countries and environmentalists hoped that debt reduction might be considered during the 1992 UNCED negotiations, but it was never really put on the table. Not until religious and other activists, organized under the name of Jubilee 2000, successfully raised the profile of third world debt did the donor governments begin to act. In the late 1990s, the Jubilee 2000 movement took off and what seemed impossible only a few years before became a reality when the Bank, the IMF and the large donor countries agreed to forgive over 200 billion dollars in debt. According to Worldwatch,

> In 1996, British Christian aid groups launched one of the most successfully organized international movements ever: the Jubilee 2000 campaign. By 2000, more than 100 organizations belonged, ranging from small nongovernmental groups in Uganda to dozens of local, church-based chapters to heavyweights such as Oxfam. They demanded that creditors cancel debt immediately and that debtors use the savings to fight poverty. The campaign gained clout from the 24 million signatures on its petitions, and endorsements from Pope John Paul II, the Dalai Lama, and U2 lead singer Bono. And it drew strength from the Bible's Book of Leviticus, which records God's laws for ancient Israel. Leviticus declared that every 50th year was to be a year of Jubilee, in which creditors forgave debtors and farmers reclaimed land they had sold off to survive a bad year. Such redistribution was intended to prevent extreme inequalities from arising to tear the fabric of Israelite society.

> Jubilee 2000 scored a major victory at the G–7 summit in 1999 when official creditors announced the enhanced Debt Initiative for Heavily Indebted Poor

Countries (HIPCs). The initiative, which is administered by the IMF and the World Bank, represents an artful political compromise among the opponents and proponents of quick cancellation, and multilateral lending agencies as well. The initiative bows to Jubilee's demand by promising that bilateral and multilateral creditors alike will write off substantially more debt than before—up to 45 percent, on average, for 41 qualifying nations. It also requires each debtor to first design a Poverty Reduction Strategy Paper in consultation with civil society groups, such as NGOS and churches, and then to implement the strategy with savings from debt cancellation. But by requiring structural adjustment, the HIPC initiative accommodates those skeptical about writing blank checks to dictators. And it helps the multilaterals by partially reimbursing them (through a HIPC Trust Fund) for canceling debt. Finally, it attempts to head off criticism of official lenders by casting the write-offs more as a one-time act of generosity than an unavoidable consequence of ongoing problems.

Worldwatch, *op cit.*, at 55–56. In addition, Canada, the United Kingdom, the United States and other countries all offered to write off their bilateral debt to poor debtors, which could bring the total reduction to 55 percent of outstanding third world debt. As this textbook goes to press, however, it is not yet clear whether these promises will be kept and whether donor countries will indeed follow through on their promises made in 1999.

SECTION IV.   THE GLOBAL ENVIRONMENT FACILITY

A.   GEF's MANDATE

The Global Environment Facility (GEF) is the largest multilateral source of grant funds available for environmental protection. The GEF is the primary mechanism for providing financial assistance to developing countries to address specific *global* environmental priorities. Its funding is restricted to "new and additional" funding to meet the agreed full "incremental" cost of measures in four focal areas: climate change, conservation of biological diversity, protection of international waters, and ozone depletion. *See Instrument for the Establishment of the Restructured Global Environment Facility,* preamble, para. 2 (1994). In addition, the "agreed incremental costs of activities concerning land degradation, primarily desertification and deforestation, as they relate to the four focal areas shall be eligible for funding." *Id.* at para. 3. Other approved activities under Agenda 21 are also eligible for funding "insofar as they achieve global environmental benefits by protecting the global environment in the four focal areas." *Id.* at para. 4.

The GEF also operates as the interim financial mechanism under the Climate Change Convention, the Biodiversity Convention, and most recently the POPs Convention. In order to gain the participation of developing countries in these agreements, the North promised to provide additional financial resources to aid in implementing the Conventions. The Parties chose the GEF as the mechanism for providing these resources, at least until the respective Conferences of the Parties could decide on the appropriate institutional structure for the long-term. The respective Conferences of the Parties have established eligibility criteria for the GEF to apply in making grants under the framework of the Climate Change and Biodiversity Conventions (the POPs Convention is not yet in force). GEF funds related to the focal areas of biodiversity or climate change, even if made outside the framework of the financial mechanism of the convention, are only available to countries that are *party* to the relevant convention.

As of 1999, GEF's committed grants totaled $2.7 billion, which leveraged co-financing of more than $6 billion. GEF funding was distributed between five areas as follows: 36% for biodiversity conservation, 36% for climate change, 13% for international waters, 13% for ozone depletion, and 5% for land degradation. Thus, for example, the $3.3 million GEF grant to Costa Rica to install wind turbines to generate power that would otherwise have been provided by thermal plants was classified as a climate-change grant, just as the $2.3 million for the work of five NGOs in the Patagonian Coastal Zone Management Plan was classified as an international waters project. For updated information, see the Global Environment Facility's website at http/www.gefweb.org.

B. GOVERNANCE AND STRUCTURE OF THE GEF

In October 1991, the GEF was formally established as a three-year pilot project implemented by UNEP, UNDP, and the World Bank. The GEF's pilot phase became extremely controversial, with environmentalists complaining that the facility was too closely linked to the World Bank and causing more harm than good. Developing countries objected to the undemocratic nature of the institution given that it was generally controlled by donor countries. In 1993, a year earlier than planned, the GEF implementing agencies agreed to an independent evaluation of the GEF's operating record. As a result of that highly critical evaluation, the GEF was restructured in 1994. *See The Report of the Independent Evaluation of the Global Environment Facility* (Nov. 23, 1993); *Instrument for the Establishment of the Restructured Global Environment Facility* (May 24, 1994).

The GEF may have been restructured, but it was not simplified. The restructured GEF is governed by an Assembly, a Council and a Secretariat. The Assembly, consisting of representatives of all 160 countries participating in the GEF, meets once every three years to review and revise the GEF's general policies and operations. The Assembly also decides by consensus on any amendments to the GEF structure recommended by the Council.

The Council consists of thirty-two Members representing constituency groupings; it meets at least semi-annually and has primary authority for developing, adopting and evaluating the operational policies and programs for GEF-financed activities. The Council also reviews, approves and monitors the implementing agencies' work programs, reviews individual projects, and oversees the Secretariat's work. Council Decisions are generally taken by consensus. If no consensus can be reached, a formal Council vote shall be taken by a double-weighted majority—that is, an affirmative vote representing both a 60% majority of the total number of participants and a 60% majority of the total voting shares as weighted by the actual cumulative contributions made to the GEF Trust Fund.

The GEF Secretariat is responsible for implementing the policies and decisions of the Assembly and the Council, primarily through coordinating and monitoring of the "implementing agencies." The Secretariat is supported administratively by the World Bank, but is supposed to operate in a "functionally independent and effective manner." The Secretariat designs and oversees implementation of program activities, ensures implementation of the operational policies adopted by the Council, and coordinates with the Secretariats of other relevant international bodies. The Chief Executive Officer, who heads the Secretariat, is selected for a three-year term by the Council on the recommendation of the implementing agencies.

The World Bank, UNEP and UNDP remain the GEF's "Implementing Agencies" and are accountable to the Council for their GEF-funded activities. Each of the Implementing Agencies has particular roles that are coordinated by the Secretariat. The World Bank, by far the most influential of the implementing agencies, is the trustee of the GEF Trust Fund, to which thirty-four countries initially contributed $2 billion. Contributions were based on the same proportions as those to the Bank's concessional loan window (IDA). The Bank is also the lead agency in ensuring the development and management of all GEF projects, as well as in mobilizing private sector resources for projects consistent with GEF objectives. *See Restructured GEF Instrument,* Annex D. UNDP's primary role is ensuring the development and management of capacity-building programs and technical assistance. UNEP's primary responsibility is to catalyze the development of scientific and technical analysis and promote environmental management in GEF-financed activities. UNEP is also primarily responsible for establishing and supporting the Scientific and Technical Advisory Panel (STAP), an advisory body to the GEF.

QUESTIONS AND DISCUSSION

1. *Choice of Focal Areas and Priorities.* According to the 1993 *Interim Evaluation of the GEF:*

> The rationale for the selection of the four focal areas that have been defined for the Pilot Phase of the GEF is rather obscure in origin and can be traced to the World Bank and to a few developed countries' interests in "internationalizing" certain environmental problems. They represent areas that have been long the subject of environmentalists concern. However, the overarching rationale for the GEF in its distinctive role of protecting the global environment has not been adequately defined and articulated. Also the basis for the choice of focal areas and the guidelines for allocating GEF resources among them are not apparent.
>
> Similarly, the global strategies for addressing the problems in the focal areas that constitute the primary responsibility of the GEF have not been developed. Thus, the criteria for the allocations of GEF resources set forth by the STAP was arbitrary and not sufficiently spelled out to guide the Implementing Agencies. Although it is assumed that the biodiversity and global warming conventions will help fill this gap, the GEF experience during the Pilot Phase should be drawn on to help shape these strategies.

Exec. Summ., at vii. What other focal areas would seem to be appropriate for a "global" environmental facility? What global issues would address developing countries' priorities? Why wouldn't the whole of *Agenda 21* be the guide for what should be fundable under the GEF? Does the focus on these four areas suggest a lack of commitment to *Agenda 21's* promises in other areas?

2. *Incremental Costs of Global Benefits.* The analytical discussion of how to measure the incremental costs (i.e., those costs that are additional to the costs that the country would have incurred if it did not consider global environmental factors) has continued inside and outside the GEF. According to the 1993 *Independent Evaluation of the GEF:*

> On the incremental cost principle, the Evaluators find that, while attractive in concept, it: (i) has not been developed as a useful tool in assessing project eligibility or sizing GEF funding, which in many cases appears arbitrary; guidelines for its application in decisions on GEF funding of its projects have not been developed and few project documents provide incremental cost calculations; (ii) encourages a narrow project approach, when joined with the GEF project taxonomy, that fails to encompass the broader considerations of national policy, program strategies and institutional capacities that are fundamental to achieving global benefits; (iii) diverts attention from the analysis and significance of the global benefits and encourages too sharp a distinction between global and national benefits; and (iv) weakens a sense of mutual responsibility for the protection of the global environment. In general, guidelines that provide a relatively uniform approach to assessing global benefits and an acceptable methodology to quantify the incremental costs are needed.

Exec. Summ., at vii-viii. Although additional technical methodologies are being accepted, the process still largely depends on case-by-case negotiations with the grantee, particularly regarding the amount of additional costs incurred or the amount of benefits being received domestically. Both of these remain important factors in establishing the incremental costs eligible for GEF funding. What other factors might be appropriate for measuring the incremental costs associated with global environmental protection?

3. *Additionality of Resources.* The key to developing countries' support of the climate change and biodiversity conventions, as well as for Agenda 21, was the commitment from donor countries that there would be new and additional financial resources made available for financing the costs of developing country's compliance. The promise of additional financial resources was seen as just as important legally as the substantive commitments made by the developing countries. The donor countries' noncompliance with the financial provisions of the conventions is seen as sufficient reason to justify noncompliance on the part of the developing countries. After considering the issue, the 1993 independent review concluded:

> Additionality as a guiding criterion for the GEF is understandable and appropriate. However, it is an exceedingly difficult principle to evaluate in practical operations. At the country level, only the donor can judge whether its GEF contribution is part of or an addition to planned assistance for the country, especially in the case of cofinancing. How does one tell whether a donor's contribution to the GEF core fund or to cofinancing is additional to its overall budget for international assistance? The Evaluators have not attempted to explore this question with the donors who have contributed to the GEF.

Exec. Summ. at viii-ix. Can you think of any mechanisms for proving that additional funds donated to the GEF were or were not in addition to other development assistance? Where might you look for such evidence? Is it sufficient proof that ODA from most countries has declined since UNCED?

4. During the restructuring of the GEF, the Facility's subservience to the Conference of the Parties (CoP) for each of the conventions was assured. Paragraph 6 of the *Restructured GEF Instrument,* for example, confirms that "the GEF shall function under the guidance of, and be accountable to, the Conferences of the Parties which shall decide on policies, program priorities and eligibility criteria for the purposes of the conventions." Likewise, Paragraph 24 states: "the use of the GEF resources for purposes of such conventions shall be in conformity with the policies, program priorities and eligibility criteria established by the Conference of the Parties of each of those conventions." Ultimately it is up to the Convention Parties to determine whether and on what terms the GEF will continue as the permanent fiscal instrument. If you were the Conference Secretariats, what criteria would you propose for determining the GEF's "effectiveness"?

5. *The Montreal Protocol Fund.* Although funding can be made available under the GEF for activities designed to reduce discharges of ozone destroying substances, the primary multilateral funding mechanism for activities to combat ozone depletion is the Multilateral Fund for the Montreal Protocol. See discussion of the Montreal Protocol Fund in Chapter 9, page 569. What advantages or disadvantages exist between having a separate funding mechanism for each convention versus having a centralized GEF? *See generally* Peter Sand, *Carrots without Sticks? New Financial Mechanisms for Global Environmental Agreements,* MAX PLANCK YEARBOOK OF UNITED NATIONS LAW, vol. 3, at 363 (1999).

6. *The Funding of Agenda 21.* Every chapter of *Agenda 21* originally included the estimated cost of implementation. At the last minute, donor countries prevailed in having the the cost estimates excised from the final version. Thus, for example, implementation of Chapter 12, "Desertification and Drought," was estimated to cost $1.0 billion per year (from 1993–2000) with at least $500 million required from international community grants or concessional funding. In sum, the total estimated costs of implementing *Agenda 21* in developing countries was over $600 billion annually to the year 2000. The estimated contribution of concessional development assistance, like that available from the GEF, was estimated at 25% or $125 billion. *Agenda 21's* estimates are not meant to be precise, but rather to offer a general figure so we can evaluate our progress toward financing sustainable development. Obviously, the GEF's $1.3 billion in current funding is not sufficient to meet these demands. Indeed all ODA, together, totals only $59 billion. Should the North give more? What arguments would you make to build domestic support for greater foreign assistance in the environmental field? How can we ensure that development assistance is used efficiently and promotes sustainable development? To what extent can private sector capital be used to replace ODA in the pursuit of sustainable development?

SECTION V. ALTERNATIVE FUNDING MECHANISMS

Several issues have recurred throughout this chapter. The first is whether development assistance and other forms of public financing are sufficient and targeted at the right types of investments to ensure sustainability. After the end of the Cold War, many observers hoped that a so-called peace dividend would allow the United States and other countries to provide substantial new funding for global environmental concerns. The peace dividend has never appeared and, despite a booming global economy in the years since Rio, development assistance and other aid flows have not increased to the levels promised at Rio. Few donor countries will meet the goal set over twenty years ago and reaffirmed at Rio to achieve a level of development assistance equal to 0.7% of the GNP by the year 2000. In short, public funds, at least from traditional sources, do not appear likely to be sufficient to meet the demands of sustainable development, and efforts have begun to develop new and innovative funding mechanisms. A second and related issue is whether the current structure of finance institutions, like the World Bank, are inherently too unwieldy and too beholden to traditional development models to provide real leadership toward sustainable development. These questions have led observers to seek new and additional sources of financing for protection of the global environment. The following discussion addresses first some alternatives that have already proven to be useful, at least in some circumstances, and then concludes with some unproven proposals, including a Tobin Tax and a Global Commons Trust Fund.

A.   MICRO–CREDIT AND THE GRAMEEN BANK

Perhaps the most important alternative development funding mechanism currently being employed is simply the concept of making smaller loans directly to poorer people. These so-called "micro-credit" programs have gained considerable support in recent years, even from traditional lending institutions such as the World Bank. Micro-credit programs have the advantage of providing money directly where it is needed, rather than assuming that the poor will benefit from the indirect, "trickle-down" effect of large infrastructure projects. Micro-credit also supports small-scale economic development, so it inherently does not raise the kind of environmental and social disruption that large dams, power plants, or other traditional development projects do. Micro-credit operations are now active in many countries throughout the world. The leading example is the Grameen Bank in Bangladesh.

J. Barnes, et al., Bankrolling Successes: A Portfolio of Sustainable Development Projects, at 11–12 (1995)

The Grameen Bank in Bangladesh has been praised as one of the most effective poverty alleviation initiatives in the world. Traditional banks operate on the premise that only people with collateral will pay back their loans. Thus, banks do not lend to very poor people. The Grameen Bank has demonstrated, however, that poor people have both the incentive and the honesty to pay back loans, and the skills to use borrowed funds; it is only the *opportunity* that is denied them.

Based on faith in the integrity of the poor, the Grameen Bank was incorporated in 1983 with the explicit purpose of lending to the very poorest of the poor in a country where poverty is endemic. Bank staff are specially trained, and travel out to the small villages, by foot or bicycle of necessary, to reach rural residents. Loans are made for very small businesses such as food preparation, cloth or basket weaving, and domestic animal raising. Groups of about five borrowers form loan circles, and work together in deciding who will receive each loan, and help each other assure repayment. The bank provides information and instruction in literacy, accounting, sanitation, family health and nutrition, small business management, etc.

Today, the Grameen Bank lends to over 2 million people in 32,000 villages in Bangladesh and the repayment rate is around 97%. The Bank continues to lend to the poorest of the poor, with 61% of the women borrowers belonging to households with less than 0.1 acre of land.

The Grameen Bank operates on the principle that conventional aid, given to people as handouts, does not provide a long-term solution to poverty, in part because it does not increase the self-confidence or the skills of the poor. Instead, it tends to foster dependence upon the donor. The trust that the microlender places in the borrowers creates self-confidence, which helps them to pull themselves out of poverty.

Grameen also rejects the traditional notion that only men can be engaged in "productive" work. Instead its program is based on the assumption that women engage in important economic activity and that they should be given opportunities to balance traditional tasks with this other work. * * *

The astonishing success of the Grameen Bank's methods demonstrate the wisdom of its approach. Rather than relying on traditional aid, or on the creation by outsiders of jobs for wage-employment, the Bank gives loans to encourage microentrepreneurs to create self-employment. Credit provided to people who are considered uncreditworthy by conventional banks creates an environment for the stable improvement of people's lives in many ways. * * *

The program's main goal is to decrease poverty. Its leaders learned that targeting women is a better way to guarantee that the loans are used to increase the standard of living. As the founder, Dr. Mohammed Yunus, explains: "In the families in which the women received the loans, the children were better cared for, the houses were better maintained. I realized women were the real agents of change in rural society."

Ninety-six percent of women in a study of Grameen Bank borrowers reported that they perceived an improvement in their socio-economic status. The percentage of husbands who said they considered their wives to be their equals rose from 43% to 93%.... Other studies report similar success. Data from the Bangladesh Institute for Development Studies indicates that incomes of Grameen borrowers increased as much as 53% in real terms over three years and calorie consumption increased by 9% in Grameen borrower households. In addition, contraceptive use in Grameen Bank villages is higher than in comparison villages, not only among borrowers but in whole communities, by 54% versus 43%.

What are the lessons of the Grameen Bank's experience? Is it simply that smaller lending is more efficient at alleviating poverty, without the environmental and social disruption of larger infrastructure projects? That more development assistance should be funneled to women in rural areas? Or that in designing financial assistance mechanisms, much more attention should be paid to tailoring the institutions to the specific cultural context in which they are operating?

B.   DEBT-FOR-NATURE SWAPS

Debt-for-nature swaps remain one of the more innovative and successful efforts to develop alternative financing for environmental protection. The following excerpt explains how these swaps work:

A typical debt-for-nature swap transaction involves a purchase of commercial bank debt by a foreign nonprofit organization or a foreign government agency acting in conjunction with a local private conservation or environmental organization. The purchase may be made on the secondary market or directly from

the selling bank. After purchasing the debt, the investor presents it to the debtor country's central bank in exchange for ecological bonds or local currency at the prevailing exchange rate or at near face value. The investor then uses the converted funds for the management and the preservation of the environment, usually with the support of the host country government and local environmental group. The debtor country's rules govern the redemption of external debt claims. These rules may be foreign investment laws, exchange control laws, or special regulations promulgated to govern such transactions.
* * *

Bolivia was the first country to implement a debt-for-nature swap program. The transaction was concluded in 1987 and covered some 4 million acres of forest and grassland in the Beni River Region. Under the arrangement Conservation International (a U.S conservation organization) purchased $650,000 of substantially discounted Bolivian debt for about $100,000 and swapped it for the shares of anew company set up to help preserve some 1.6 million hectares of forests and grasslands. The debts used in this transaction were owed to private lenders. Citicorp Investment Bank (a subsidiary of Citibank) brokered the transaction and arranged the debt purchase from undisclosed foreign debt creditors. Financing was provided by the San Francisco-based Frank Weeden Foundation.

The transaction sought to protect land adjoining the Beni Biosphere Reserve. This reserve was created in 1982 as a model for the preservation of flora and fauna, water resources, and the native peoples. Under the agreement, the Bolivian Government undertook to pass legislation to protect the parcels of the land adjoining the 334,000 acre reserve. Part of the area covered by the agreement will be designated exclusively for research while the other part will be open to the nomadic Himane Indians and to agriculture and forestry development. To ensure effective management of the project, an endowment fund of approximately $250,000 in local currency, was created.

Derek Asiedu–Akrofi, *Debt-for-Nature Swaps: Extending the Frontiers of Innovative Financing in Support of the Global Environment*, 25 THE INT'L LAWYER 557, 564–65 (Fall 1991). Debt-for-nature swaps have been used effectively in Ecuador, Costa Rica, the Philippines, Madagascar, and Poland, among others. Although innovative and important in certain specific instances, debt-for-nature swaps will never meet a significant part of the overall demand for sustainable development financing. As of 1996, only about $76 million had been swapped for nature conservation, although the technique has now been adopted for other social and environmental concerns as well. *See also* World Resources Institute, *Debt-for-Nature Swaps*, in Natural Endowments: Financing Resource Conservation for Development (Sept. 1989).

C. NATIONAL ENVIRONMENTAL FUNDS

In recent years, the need for domestic funding to support new environmental agencies, the creation of national parks and other environmental activities has led to the development of national environmental funds (NEFs). Most NEFs are started with outside funding from sources that want to ensure greater environmental effectiveness from their support. The concept is to provide a dedicated source of public financing that is not subject to the political control of a country's regular state budget and that provides a mechanism for local participation in addressing environmental issues. The governance structures usually involve many different stake-holders and ensure greater transparency than many other financial mecha-nisms. The following excerpt explains some of the advantages of NEFs.

> NEFs were created to find a way around the problems that have limited the success of traditional donor support to developing country projects. These problems have included: top-down planning from distant capitals; donor-driven agendas that fail to respond to community needs; projects of unrealistic size, scope, and time frames; burdensome reporting requirements; and minimal local institutional capacity. In contrast, NEFs are structured to afford maximum stakeholder involvement and to be flexible, innovative, and responsible to both constituents and donors. These funds are designed to embody the democratic values of participation, transparency, and accountability. They can offer dis-tinct advantages over traditional approaches to environmental projects:

> NEFs provide for local ownership of environmental programs, thus enhancing prospects for maintaining those programs over the long term.

> NEFs can expedite and catalyze national environmental priorities, especially if linked to national environmental strategies.

> NEFs provide a mechanism to strengthen the capacities and roles of NGOs, which are increasing in number and importance in determining environment and development programs in many countries. NEFs can provide a means for coordination among local NGOs, governments, and donors.

> NEFs can provide sustained financing for environmental programs and thus promote long-term planning.

> NEFs can serve as a means for international donor coordination in the environmental sector in a particular developing country. Through a NEF, even small local and community-based organizations can have access to these inter-national donor resources.

> NEFs provide institutional stability and project security. * * *

> NEFs can be used as a vehicle to invest financial resources generated from sources such as fines for environmental pollution and fees for use of natural resources. These resources can be applied, as a result, directly to environmental purposes.

NEFs now operate in more than twenty countries. Some are quite small and relatively narrow in scope like the $700,000 Jamaica Parks Trust Fund and others like the Phillipine foundation for the environment are larger ($24 million) and more general. Some are controlled by government officials, but increasingly many are controlled by nature conservation groups or other NGOs. *See generally* M. Dillenbeck, *National Environmen-tal Funds: A New Mechanism for Conservation Finance*, Parks, Vol. 14, No. 2, 1994, at 45.

D. PRIVATE PHILANTHROPY

Private philanthropy has always been an important source of funding for environmental and development NGOs. Large U.S. foundations, in particular, have led the way in providing support for global environmental protection. As wealth becomes even more concentrated and the number of billionaires increases, the role of individual donors in influencing international environmental governance could increase. George Soros through his Open Society Foundation, for example, has provided hundreds of millions of dollars over the past decade to support human rights and civil and political freedom in the former Soviet bloc and elsewhere. Even more interesting for international environmental affairs, media mogul Ted Turner announced on September 19, 1997 that he would provide $1 billion to the U.N. for environment and development projects. He subsequently established the UN Foundation, which provides support directly to UN agencies involved in certain environmental issues like climate change. *See, e.g., Ted Turner to Give U.N. $1 Billion,* THE WASHINGTON POST, Sept. 19, 1997, at A1.

Philanthropists like Soros and Turner may have a profound impact on future international environmental governance. Not only will such support undoubtedly continue to be crucial for the future of international civil society to continue to participate and influence international environmental issues, but private individuals may now become significant supporters of the United Nations. The $100 million-a-year Turner gift is a larger donation to the United Nations than the contributions of all but two countries in the same period. And UN agencies are becoming more aggressive in soliciting such non-State support. UNEP created a POPs Club and actively sought funding from companies and NGOs to support financially the negotiations of a POPs Convention. Is there any reason for concern about private funding for international governance? What does such a new role for non-State actors suggest for the future role of the public sector? Governments often place conditions on their provision of funds to the U.N. If you were Ted Turner what conditions would you place on the gift? Recall the readings of Phillip Allot in Chapter 6, in which he calls for an international society that responds to individuals and not just governments. What would Allot think about Ted Turner's gift to the United Nations?

E.   NEW FUNDING MECHANISMS

Given the growing need for additional financing, many observers have called for wholly new and innovative funding sources. The Brundtland Commission, for example, concluded:

> Given the current constraints on major sources and modes of funding, it is necessary to consider new approaches as well as new sources of revenue for financing international action in support of sustainable development. The commission recognizes that such proposals may not appear politically realistic at this point in time. It believes, however, that—given the trends discussed in this report—the need to support sustainable development will become so imperative that political realism will come to require it.

> The search for other, and, especially more automatic, sources and means for financing international action goes almost as far back as the UN itself. It was not until 1977, however, when the Plan of Action to Combat Desertification was approved by the UN General Assembly that governments officially accepted, but never implemented, the principle of automatic transfers. That Plan called for the establishment of a special account that could draw resources not only from traditional sources but also from additional measures of financing, including fiscal measures entailing automaticity.

Since then, a series of studies and reports have identified and examined a growing list of new sources of potential revenue, including :

revenue from the use of international commons (from ocean fishing and transportation, from sea-bed mining, from Antarctic resources, or from parking charges for geostationary communications satellites, for example)

taxes on international trade (such as a general trade tax; taxes on specific traded commodities, on invisible exports, or on surpluses in balance of trade; or a consumption tax on luxury goods)

international financial measures (a link between special drawing rights and development finance, for example, or IMF gold reserves and sales). * * *

[G]iven the compelling nature, pace, and scope of the different transitions affecting our economic and ecological systems as described in this report, we consider that at least some of those proposals for additional and more automatic sources of revenue are fast becoming less futuristic and more necessary. This Commission particularly considers that the proposals regarding revenue from the use of international commons and natural resources now warrant and should receive serious consideration by governments and the General Assembly.

World Commission on Environment and Development, OUR COMMON FUTURE 342–43 (1987).

The following two excerpts develop further some of the above-mentioned ideas for raising international financing for conservation efforts, including in the next excerpt the so-called "Tobin Tax" and in the following excerpt by Professor Christopher Stone, the Global Commons Trust Fund.

Overseas Development Institute, *New Sources of Finance for Development* (Feb. 1, 1996)

The Tobin Tax (sometimes called a Foreign Exchange Transactions Levy) was first put forward by Nobel Laureate Professor James Tobin in 1972 as a way of discouraging speculation in short-term foreign-exchange dealings, and thus minimizing shocks from large currency movements. Although Tobin himself disputes this, many critics argue that the tax would make markets less efficient, and thus inherently less stable, by distorting price signals. It might inhibit certain types of operation and encourage others, which would make the market as a whole shallower. This, in turn, could make it harder for developing countries to raise money on international markets.

More recently, Tobin has suggested that such a tax might also prove a useful revenue earner, with the proceeds devoted to international development. This puts it into the 'piggyback' group of global taxation ideas. To illustrate the potential scale, a tax levied at only 0.01% of turnover, which would add about 20% to the costs of trading in currencies (a significant deterrent), might yield between $12 and $24 billion a year, based on a global turnover in these markets of around $900–1,000 billion a day. If this very tentative figure were really within grasp, it would be a major contribution to development resources: at maximum, it would be as much as half the present level of bilateral aid flows. * * *

The Tobin Tax would certainly be progressive, because there would be a shift of resources from the players in financial markets, mainly situated in industrial countries, towards the developing countries. Bankers and other financial institutions who make their living in the foreign-exchange markets would object; but if there were sufficient political will at international level, this pressure would probably not be sufficient to deter action. However, exemptions would be needed to exclude small personal transactions and, for example, purchases of currency for tourism, etc., or political objections would soon multiply.

At national level, the losers would be the larger industrial countries, especially the G–7. Even if they were to support the proposal because of its currency stabilisation, they would no doubt prefer to hold on to the revenue themselves. For this reason, the developing countries could not enforce such a measure (e.g. through a majority vote in a UN body) against the wishes of the industrial countries. Some small offshore financial centres might also protest. However, there are no obvious international claimants to the proceeds of a tax, apart from the international financial institutions and the UNDP.

Opinions differ about the need for a general agreement. Some critics argue that provided sufficient major trading nations agree, the costs of evasive action are high enough to make universality unnecessary. Others believe that evasion could be made fairly cheap, so that the tax would have to be enforced by all countries. If the latter are right, then a completely new international agreement would probably be required: no manipulation of existing instruments (such as the Articles of the IMF) could deliver the required action, and concerted voluntary action in such a complex area seems impracticable. There would also need to be some standing international mechanism to set and adjust the level of the tax, and oversee its collection from national agencies and its transfer to the receiving institutions. Experience of such international negotiations (e.g. the Law of the Sea Convention described below) suggests that setting up all this would take a long time.

Professor Chris Stone has developed the concept of obtaining money from the use of the global commons into a proposal for a Global Commons Trust Fund:

Christopher Stone, THE GNAT IS OLDER THAN MAN 208–20 (1993)

I would establish a Global Commons Trust Fund (GCTF). Essentially, on the funding side, the idea is to capitalize on revenues from all commons-connected activities, and not only from charges for carbon "storage" in the atmosphere, the most familiar fund-raising scheme; on the expenditure side, the funds so raised would be applied to the conservation and repair of the commons areas rather than to distribute them back to individual nations to let them expend them on developmental projects of their choice, however tenuously connected the projects are to the environment.

Let me expand. The reason we criticize GHG emissions is not only the anticipated damage, but the fact that individual nations are saving themselves money–the costs of pollution abatement—by appropriating, free of charge, a valuable feature of the commons areas: the transport and storage capacity of the atmosphere. But of course there is the same seizure of a common-property right when nations dump waste or overfish the seas. Assuming the commons areas—the atmosphere, oceans, space, and so on—to be the Common Heritage of Humankind, the common property of all nations, one may argue that the users of the commons areas ought to be charged for their use. The charges would curtail the level of abuse and at the same time underwrite the expenses of repairing the damage we have already done.

The revenues, while difficult to estimate, are potentially enormous. Consider some rough projections.

The oceans. Start with the oceans. The world harvests 175 billion pounds of marine fish annually. A tax of only one-half of one percent on the commercial value would raise approximately $250 million for the proposed fund. The same token rate on offshore oil and gas would add perhaps $375 million.

There is another, dirtier use to which the world community puts the oceans: as a dump site for waste. The official figures, almost certainly underreported, amount to 212 million metric tons of sewage sludge, industrial wastes, and dredged materials yearly. A tax of only $1 a ton would raise $200 million more.

The atmosphere. Nations use the atmosphere as they use the oceans—as a cost-free sewer for pollutants. By burning fossil fuels and living forests, humankind thrusts 22 billion metric tons of carbon dioxide into the atmosphere annually. (The equivalent of approximately 8 billion tons of *carbon,* which can alternatively be the basis for a "carbon tax.") A CO_2 tax of only ten cents a ton would raise $2.2 billion each year, thirty times the current budget of UNEP. Taxing other GHGs such as nitrous oxides at a comparably modest (dime-a-ton) rate, indexed to their "blocking" equivalent to CO_2, would bring the total to $3.3 billion. The same ten-cents-a-ton tax could be levied on other (non-GHG) transfrontier pollutants; a sulfur dioxide levy, for example, would produce $16 million.

Space. Commercially tapping the riches of the planets may remain futuristic, but the rights to "park" satellites in the choice slots represent a potential source of enormous wealth right now. Most valued are points along the "geostationary orbit," the volume of space 22,300 miles directly above the earth's equator in which a satellite can remain in a relatively fixed point, relative to the surface below. The number of available points is restricted by minimal distances required between satellites to avoid interference. Rights to spots directly above the earth's equatorial belt are also valued because they are exposed to exceptionally long hours of sunlight and are therefore ideally situated for production of energy from solar radiation, both as a support for special operations such as high-tech, gravity-free manufacturing, and perhaps ultimately for commercial redirecting to earth.

The geostationary orbit being directly above their heads, the equatorial nations, in their Bogota Declaration of 1986 declared the orbital space to be among their natural resources, "an integral part of the territory over which the equatorial States exercise their national sovereignty." While the world community has accepted the coastal states' extending their jurisdictions laterally outward into the sea, it has totally ignored the analogous and inconvenient claim of the equatorial states. (As my international relations colleagues would quip, although the equatorial states' reasoning may be as strong, their armies are feebler.)

As a result, frequencies in space, "the most precious resource of the telecommunications age"—worth to users an estimated $1 trillion globally over the next decade—are now parceled out by the World Administrative Radio Conference (WARC). WARC's assignment is, admittedly, tough, but the approach it has adopted is folly. The slots are simply apportioned by formulas too cryptic for any outsider to follow and handed out free. The tiny island nation of Tonga, after being awarded three to six orbital positions gratis, turned right around and put them up for sale, recently striking a deal with a satellite company for $2 million a year "rental." And it is reportedly seeking more such deals.

Why should the rights to any of these slots and spectrum positions, the legacy and province of all humankind, and worth trillions of dollars to users, be doled out like free lottery tickets, while those who would mend the planet are severely hobbled by a lack of resource?

Biodiversity. I am a little more ambivalent about including biodiversity as part of the Common Heritage of Humankind in the sense of making it a tax base for the fund. While many of the seas' riches lie in commons areas beyond any nation's jurisdiction, when we talk about dividing up biological riches, we mean resources that lie within established national territories. Of course, those who want to tap the biotechnological and pharmaceutical potential are not proposing to appropriate physical matter from a nation's forests. The hope is to copy and exploit *genetic information.* But that makes small difference to the biologically rich nations such as Colombia and Brazil, who regard global demands to share the good luck of their biological wealth about the same way the Saudis would react to arguments that the world should co-own its oil on the grounds that it is the Common Heritage of Humankind, and then having so much of it is pure luck, anyway. The proposal may simply intrude too far into the host nation's sovereign space and prerogatives, which is why the Rio negotiators rejected labeling biodiversity part of the Common Heritage in favor of the limper "common concern."

On the other hand, perhaps a compromise could be worked out whereby the industrial world's pharmaceutical companies, which will presumably manage the exploitation of the potential, pay a modest royalty into the GCTF (or perhaps even into the GCTF earmarked for environmental development in the nations from which the genetic information came). In either event, whether or not we emerge including biological diversity as part of the resource base for purposes of a GCTF tax, projects to protect biodiversity would qualify for support under the GCTF as furthering the protection and repair of the commons.

And even if we do not include biological diversity in the "tax" base, the total thus far is over $6 billion a year. And that is before adding the yield of a surcharge on uneliminated HCFCs and other ozone-depleting agents, on toxic incineration at sea, or on the liquid wastes that empty into the oceans from rivers. Consider also fees on the minerals that someday will be taken from the seabed and, perhaps, depending on the staying power of the conservation movement that is fighting the prospect, the Antarctic.

Legal Charges

Another way to bolster the fund would be to designate it the receptacle for legal charges assessed under existing and envisionable commons-protecting treaties, such as those regulating ocean pollution. Consider, for example, the treatment of oil spills on the high seas. No individual nation can claim to have been damaged, but ocean pollution agreements could easily be amended to provide that "damages" (perhaps according to a schedule, if measurement of actual damages is too conjectural) be paid into the trust fund to be available for general research and repair. There are illustrations of this technique domestically. After the spill of the highly dangerous pesticide Kepone into the James River in the United States, Allied Chemical, which was responsible, established such a fund for the James. More recently, in the wake of the catastrophic incident at the Sandoz factory in Basel, Switzerland, in 1986, Sandoz established a $10 million fund to further the ecological recovery of the Rhine. Part of the fund is being used to establish an interactive data base on the Rhine ecosystem. * * *

Objections on the Expenditures End

In terms of where the money would go, once gathered, the GCTF is distinguishable from its rivals. The proponents of the carbon tax schemes, like the proponents of taxes on national wealth, have typically left the details of payout strategically inexplicit. In general, the Third World is assured that the proceeds would be distributed to them; the environmentalists are encouraged to believe that, once in those countries, the money would be earmarked to meeting the challenges of industrialization in a still hazy "environmentally benign" manner—although, at the same time, Third World spokepersons rejoin that to attach any strings is an affront.

Under the GCTF proposal, funds would be restricted to underwriting only internationally significant efforts, those that most connect to the Common Heritage of Humankind. Thus, the expenditures, all of which originate from a "use" *of* the commons, would return *to* the commons. Funds would be available to improve global monitoring and modeling; to prepare adaptive strategies, such as the development of fast-growing (and carbon-withdrawing) trees; to inaugurate and police improved methods of waste disposal; to inventory, gather, and store genetic material; to underwrite the transfer of environment-benign technology to developing nations; and to promote energy conservation and general antiwaste behavior. The funds could underwrite developing institutional readiness to respond to various sorts of crises with the global equivalent of "firefighters." For example, no single nation can afford to keep on full-time alert a staff trained and equipped to contain oil spills with oil-eating bacteria, etc. No single nation anticipates enough incidents to warrant the expense. But a force with global responsibilities, financed out of the fund, might well be justified. Similarly, to deal with nuclear accidents one might want to have on call at least a crew of administrators with plans and power to assemble an emergency team on short notice. It has been estimated that $150 million a year would underwrite an effective worldwide system to give early detection to viral diseases—so that the next AIDS-type epidemic does not overrun us by surprise. All these ideas have, I believe, intuitive appeal, and some congenial forerunners in the literature.

———

QUESTIONS AND DISCUSSION

1. What do you think of Professor Stone's proposal for a Global Commons Trust Fund? What are the major objections to it?

2. Do we need additional financial mechanisms, or is part of the problem that we have too many that are simply not operated effectively? In this regard, consider again the controversies regarding the governance of the World Bank and GEF. To what extent can environmental assistance be improved simply through better coordination among donors? With so many multilateral and bilateral financial agencies potentially involved in sustainable development activities, coordination and cooperation can be very difficult. For example, some 20 donor countries and 13 multilateral agencies are actively involved in providing development assistance in the forestry sector. A lack of coordination has plagued financing in that sector, as has the fact that much of the assistance is being driven by the North with inadequate buy-in from the South. See discussion in Chapter 14, page 1100, of the Pilot Programme for Brazil's Amazon and the Tropical Forest Action Programme. How would you propose to coordinate and control financial assistance? Do we need another institution for this?

3. Why should environmental protection be the beneficiary of a Tobin Tax or trust fund? What other competing causes would argue that the funds should be directed to their objectives?

Suggested Web Sites

http://www.worldbank.org

> This World Bank homepage provides links to the four arms of the World Bank Group: IBRD, IDA, IFC, and MIGA (plus ICSID). The Inspection Panel is also accessible through this page.

http://www.imf.org/

> Website of the International Monetary Fund

http://www.iadb.org/

> Website of the Inter–American Development Bank

http://www.adb.org/

> Website of the Asian Development Bank

http://www.nadbank.org/

> Website of the North American Development Bank

http://www.ebrd.com/

> Website of the European Bank for Reconstruction and Development

http://www.gefweb.org/

> Website of the Global Environment Facility.

http://www.ciel.org/

> The Center for International Environmental Law (CIEL) is a nongovernmental organization that focuses extensively on International Financial Institutions generally and the World Bank specifically.

http://www.50years.org/

> Website of 50 Years Is Enough, a coalition of over 200 U.S. NGOs "dedicated to the profound transformation of the World Bank and the International Monetary Fund (IMF)."

ANNEX I

RESEARCHING INTERNATIONAL ENVIRONMENTAL LAW

While the casebook citations and *Suggested Reading* sections in each chapter provide a starting point for further research in many areas of international environmental law, their are standard reference sources can also facilitate research. The sources for researching international environmental law may be divided into three separate categories: treaties and documents, judicial decisions, and commentaries. The use of electronic research tools is addressed separately at the end.

Treaties and Documents

In researching a treaty, you may wish to read the authoritative text of the treaty, determine whether it is in force, identify which countries are currently parties to the treaty and whether they have entered reservations, and explore its negotiating history. There are many separate sources for this information.

The starting point in most law libraries for major treaties is the American Society of International Law bi-monthly publication, INTERNATIONAL LEGAL MATERIALS (cited as I.L.M., call #JX27 .I5 v. __). Many international environmental agreements, however, are not included in the I.L.M. series.

If the United States is a party to a treaty, there are a number of other sources to search. The most convenient reference, if you have access to the Internet, may be the State Department's home page on the World Wide Web at <http://www.state.gov>.

When a treaty or an agreement is first published by the United States, it is assigned a number and published in slip form in TREATIES AND OTHER INTERNATIONAL ACTS SERIES (cited as T.I.A.S.). The delay between the proclamation of a treaty and its publication in this form is approximately six to eight years.

The *Department of State Bulletin*, published monthly and found in the periodicals section, is another useful source of U.S. pre-ratification treaty information. Included in this bulletin is information on negotiations, Congressional status, developments between signing and ratification, and final ratifications and proclamations.

For information on treaties in force, one may find U.S. treaties and executive agreements since 1950 published in a chronological series called UNITED STATES TREATIES AND OTHER INTERNATIONAL AGREEMENTS (cited as U.S.T. with call #JX231.A34). The series is published by the State Department and includes treaty texts.

TREATIES IN FORCE is published annually by the State Department. It documents and indexes those treaties in the above series and is the most important current index to U.S. treaties and agreements in force, including citations to all the major treaty publications. Each issue is divided into two parts; the first part lists bilateral treaties alphabetically by country and then, under each country by subject. The second section lists multilateral treaties alphabetically by subject and indicates which nations are parties to the treaty.

As an alternative, the series, TREATIES AND OTHER INTERNATIONAL AGREE-MENTS OF THE UNITED STATES OF AMERICA, 1776?1949 (C.I. Bevans, comp., Department of State, 13 vols., 1968?75) is a definitive historical collection. The first four volumes contain multilateral treaties arranged chronological-ly by date of signature. The next eight volumes include bilateral treaties, arranged alphabetically by country; and volume thirteen contains indexes by country and subject. Volume eight of the *Statutes at Large* contains a compilation of treaties entered into by the U.S. between 1778 and 1845, while volume eighteen is a compilation of the treaties in force as of 1873.

Overall, the most comprehensive source for modern treaties is the UNITED NATIONS TREATY SERIES (cited as U.N.T.S. and call #JX1976 .A45 v.__). This series began in 1946 and consists of over twelve hundred volumes; there is however, approximately a four-year delay between ratifi-cation and appearance of a treaty in the U.N.T.S.

Below are several guides and indexes to international treaties and agreements.

MULTILATERAL TREATIES DEPOSITED WITH THE SECRETARY?GENERAL (United Nations, 1981?date) is an annual publication comparable to the U.S. TREATIES IN FORCE providing information on the status of treaties and references to the location of texts. Call #JX171 .M84 19__

M.J. Bowman & D.J. Harris, MULTILATERAL TREATIES: INDEX AND CURRENT STATUS (Butterworths, 1984, With Annual Supplements). Call #Jx171 .B68

Peter Rohn, WORLD TREATY INDEX, 2d ed. (ABC?Clio, 5 vols., 1983?84) provides access to approximately 44,000 treaties from 1900 to 1980. Call #JX171 .R63 1983 v.__

Many important international environmental law texts, however, are not treaties. The best research aid for UN documents is the official monthly index called UNDOC: CURRENT INDEX which issues annual cumulations in paper and on microfiche (call #JX1977 .A21 U52 19__ v.__). UNDOC does not index the subsidiary bodies of the UN, or the technical agencies.

If none of these sources leads you to the primary document, consider calling the State Department or a specialized treaty secretariat directly. Useful contact numbers and e-mail addresses are provided in the relevant home pages on the World Wide Web.

Judicial Decisions

The decisions of international courts and arbitral bodies provides useful information on the interpretations of treaties and international legal principles. Below are several sources of information on the rulings of the International Court of Justice and other international bodies.

REPORTS OF JUDGMENTS, ADVISORY OPINIONS AND ORDERS provides the decisions of the International Court of Justice. Call #JX1971.6 .A244 19＿ v.＿

INTERNATIONAL LAW REPORTS (London: Butterworths) provides decisions of the International Court of Justice, as well as selected decisions of the Court of Justice of the European Communities, the European Commission and the Court of Human Rights; the administrative tribunals of several international organizations; arbitration claims and conciliation commissions; and national courts adjudicating international issues. Call #KZ199. I58 v.＿

L. Neville Brown & Francis G. Jacobs, THE COURT OF JUSTICE OF THE EUROPEAN COMMUNITIES, 3rd ed. (London: Sweet & Manwell, 1989) provides decisions of the European Court of Justice. Call #KJE924 .B76 1989.

Commentaries

Before turning to primary texts, you may wish to familiarize yourself with prior writings in the field. The law review articles and books cited in the casebook chapters are a good place to begin. In addition to the environmental law reviews that often carry international environmental law articles, such as the ECOLOGY LAW QUARTERLY, ENVIRONMENTAL LAW, and the HARVARD ENVIRONMENTAL LAW REVIEW, at least two U.S. law reviews are dedicated to international environmental law. These are the COLORADO JOURNAL OF INTERNATIONAL ENVIRONMENTAL LAW AND POLICY, and the GEORGETOWN INTERNATIONAL ENVIRONMENTAL LAW REVIEW.

The most useful treatises on international environmental law include:

Patricia W. Birnie & Alan E. Boyle, INTERNATIONAL LAW AND THE ENVIRONMENT (New York: Oxford University Press, 1992) Call #K3585.4 .B57 1992

Gunther Handl, Ed., YEARBOOK OF INTERNATIONAL ENVIRONMENTAL LAW (Boston: Graham & Trotman, 1991) Call #JX21 .Y37

Alexandre C. Kiss & Dinah Shelton, INTERNATIONAL ENVIRONMENTAL LAW (New York: Transnational Publishers, 1991) Call #K3585.4 .K574 1991

Ved Nanda, INTERNATIONAL ENVIRONMENTAL LAW & POLICY (Irvington, NY: Transnational Publishers, 1995) Call #K3585.6 .N36 1995

Computer Resources

In writing this casebook, we have been surprised and impressed by the amount of useful information available on the World Wide Web. The text of virtually every treaty discussed in the casebook is on the Web. In addition, most organizations, both domestic and international, have created home pages on the Web, providing free and easy access to information. Many of the treaty secretariats' home pages, for example, contain documents prepared for Conferences of the Parties, updates, and breaking news that simply were not readily accessible prior to the early 1990s. As a result, research can often be facilitated and supplemented by at least a general search of the Internet. The following are some websites that provide excellent starting points for research of international legal materials.

<http://www.wcl.american.edu/environment/iel>

This is our casebook website, providing additional information on the chapters and hypertext links to useful sites.

http://untreaty.un.org/

The United Nations Treaty Collection web site providing an overview of the UN Treaty Collection and access to that database.

http://www.ext.grida.no/ggynet

Homepage for the Green Globe Yearbook. Excellent site with hypertext links to treaty texts, secretariats, NGOs, and international institutions.

http://www.iisd.ca/linkages/

Linkages is provided by the International Institute for Sustainable Development (IISD). It is an electronic clearing-house for information on past and upcoming international meetings related to environment and development. The site contains documents and updates concerning the Commission on Sustainable Development, the Climate Change, Biodiversity, and Desertification Conventions, global forest policy, trade, sustainable consumption and production, and chemicals.

http://www.asil.org

The American Society of International Law (ASIL) maintains an excellent link page to international law sites. The ASIL page has the advantage of being organized by source type: primary sources, secondary sources, cases, as well as by practice area.

http://www.pace.edu/lawschool/env/vell6.html

The Virtual Environmental Law Library at Pace University; includes a link to a comprehensive index of international environmental law treaties in force and other sites.

http://www.law.du.edu/library/research_links/intl/intl_res.htm

The University of Denver's Westminster Law Library, providing links to many international law sites (not exclusively environmental).

http://www.lawschool.cornell.edu/lawlibrary/International_Resources/default.htm

Excellent database for information and documents from a variety of international organizations, including the United Nations, the World Bank and the World Health Organization.

http://iucn.org/themes/law/index.html

The IUCN's link page to its environmental law information system. The page contains links to about United Nations documents, multilaterial agreements, and other international resources.

http://www.ili.org

Homepage for the International Law Institute, a private, not-for-profit organization whose activities include scholarly research, publishing and legal training and technical assistance on many aspects of international legal and economic policy and practice. The website provides links to the Institute's International Law Database.

The electronic legal databases, WESTLAW and LEXIS, also provide access to treaty texts and newsletters.

On WESTLAW, one may go under "Directories and Reference Materials," then under "Government and Politics" to the "Foreign Relations" library for relevant information. Furthermore, access may be had through the "Topical Materials by Area of Practice," "International & Foreign Law" to information on international agreements and treaties, foreign laws, the WTO and GATT, foreign environmental, health and safety regulations and more. The choice, BNA–IED will bring you to the BNA International Environment Daily, an excellent newsletter of breaking international environmental news.

LEXIS's international law library (INTLAW) provides links to information and documents regarding the NAFTA, GATT, WTO, American Society of International Law, the European Community, the Restatement of Foreign Relations Law, the State Department Bulletin, Mealey Publications and more. More information from the State Department may be found in the library accessed under DSTATE. For access to the BNA International Environmental Law Reporter, enter the BNA library and then access the BNA–IED library on the second page; this will allow you access to the Reporter.

*

INDEX

†